August 17–21, 2015
London, United Kingdom

Association for Computing Machinery

Advancing Computing as a Science & Profession

SIGCOMM'15

Proceedings of the 2015 ACM Conference on Special Interest Group on Data Communication

Sponsored by:

ACM SIGCOMM

Supported by:

NSF, CISCO, ERICSSON, HUAWEI, NetApp, Google, Facebook, Microsoft, COMCAST, HP, LINX, VMWARE, VERISIGN and Akamai

Association for
Computing Machinery

Advancing Computing as a Science & Profession

The Association for Computing Machinery
2 Penn Plaza, Suite 701
New York, New York 10121-0701

Notice to Past Authors of ACM-Published Articles
ACM intends to create a complete electronic archive of all articles and/or other material previously published by ACM. If you have written a work that has been previously published by ACM in any journal or conference proceedings prior to 1978, or any SIG Newsletter at any time, and you do NOT want this work to appear in the ACM Digital Library, please inform permissions@acm.org, stating the title of the work, the author(s), and where and when published.

ISBN: 978-1-4503-3542-3 (Digital)

ISBN: 978-1-4503-4025-0 (Print)

Additional copies may be ordered prepaid from:

ACM Order Department
PO Box 30777
New York, NY 10087-0777, USA

Phone: 1-800-342-6626 (USA and Canada)
+1-212-626-0500 (Global)
Fax: +1-212-944-1318
E-mail: acmhelp@acm.org
Hours of Operation: 8:30 am – 4:30 pm ET

Printed in the USA

Message from the General Chairs

It is our great pleasure to welcome you to London, UK, for SIGCOMM 2015, the flagship conference of the ACM Special Interest Group on Data Communications!

We have put together an inspiring technical program that includes 42 full-length papers that will be presented over three days; a keynote talk by the SIGCOMM Award winner, **Albert Greenberg**; the announcement of the SIGCOMM Test-of-Time Award; four workshops; four tutorials; and three sessions with 29 posters and 19 demos as well as the recently introduced industrial demos session.

We are very excited about introducing some new things at SIGCOMM 2015. The main novelty this year are the "mentoring moments" that provide an opportunity for graduate students to obtain a private meeting with two well-known researchers to get feedback on a research idea. Then, we want to reinforce the importance of posters and demos, which we believe are a huge opportunity to bring ideas to life, spark a lot of discussions and debate. We have therefore ensured that enough time is available for the poster/demo sessions.

The conference venue is strategically located in the centre of London, with multiple landmarks at walking distance, such as the Royal Albert Hall, the Science Museum, the Natural History Museum, and Hyde Park. Our social program is designed to encourage the audience to sample the cultural wealth of London. The reception takes place at the Science Museum located nearby the conference venue, the banquet at the Brewery in East London, and the student dinner at the Marylebone cricket club, Lord's ground.

Organizing a large conference is a substantial undertaking that requires the combined energy of a large number of volunteers, and our heartfelt thanks go to our team which made this event possible. We thank **Brad Karp** and **Jitendra Padhye** for leading a highly accomplished and dedicated program committee. We thank **Hamed Haddadi** and **Paolo Costa** for relentlessly handling a large number of local arrangements. We thank **Renata Teixeira** and **Nick Feamster** for organizing the workshops; **Andrew Moore** and **Miguel Rio** for organizing the tutorials; **Olivier Bonaventure**, **Richard Mortier**, **Cristel Pelsser**, and **Cigdem Sengul** for jointly organizing the posters and demonstrations; and the members of the industrial liaison board for the organization of the industrial demos. Also, we wish to thank **Felix Cuadrado** for timely and thoroughly managing the website; **Georgios Smaragdakis** for managing all publication matters; **Gonca Gursun** for handling registrations; **Vyas Sekar** and **Christian Kreibich** for leading the travel grant committee; **Theophilus Benson**, **Gaogang Xie**, and **Chadi Barakat** for handling publicity; **Matthew Roughan** for adding a touch of realism to our financial optimism; **Jorg Ott** and **Yashar Ganjali** for providing the collective help in all matters; and last but not least the ACM HQ staff with whom working has been a pleasure.

We are particularly appreciative of our supporters for enabling us to provide you with a first-rate experience and making it accessible to a wide range of attendees. Cisco, Ericsson, Huawei, Netapp, Google, Facebook, Microsoft, Comcast, HP, LINX, VMware, Verisign, and Akamai all generously contributed to SIGCOMM 2015, and the NSF and ACM (SIGCOMM) provided additional travel support. Thanks to these funds, we were able to provide a large travel program to help attendees who would otherwise find it difficult to attend. The travel grant committee awarded a total of 34 grants to a diverse group of students, postdocs, researchers and faculty.

Steve Uhlig
SIGCOMM 2015 General Co-Chair
Queen Mary University of London, UK

Olaf Maennel
SIGCOMM 2015 General Co-Chair
Tallinn University of Technology, Estonia

Message from the Program Chairs

Dear Colleagues,

Welcome to the 2015 ACM SIGCOMM Conference, and welcome to London!

This year, a program committee of 49 networking researchers reviewed a total of 242 submissions. Reviewing was double-blind, and review assignment avoided conflicts of interest as defined in the submission instructions posted on the SIGCOMM 2015 web site. The PC's composition represented the breadth of the community: from industry and academia, with expertise across the range of topics within the field of networking. Roughly a third of the PC consisted of members serving for the first time. The PC included members of the EE communications research community whose work overlaps physical-layer topics of interest to SIGCOMM. The PC was augmented by 37 outside domain expert reviewers.

The PC and the domain experts together wrote more than 1100 reviews over three rounds of reviewing. The PC met in person on April 23rd and 24th, 2015, in Redmond, Washington, to select the final program. During the one and a half-day PC meeting, the PC discussed 74 papers, each of which had received between 5 and 8 reviews; the result is this outstanding final program of 40 papers. A PC member shepherded every accepted paper to assist the authors in improving their work for the paper's camera-ready version. We share the PC's strong enthusiasm for the work appearing in the program, and hope that you enjoy reading the papers and hearing the presentations at the conference.

We are particularly excited to introduce a new track, the Experience Track, to SIGCOMM this year. This track, as the CFP stated, is for "experience papers on the design, analysis, and evaluation of techniques in commercial or otherwise widely used deployment." Our aim in creating this track is for SIGCOMM to help extend the community's knowledge of how known techniques fare in realistic settings, and particularly in settings that most in the community cannot duplicate, for reasons of scale or otherwise.

To allow the Best Paper Award to reflect not only the content of the camera-ready papers, but also the reception work receives from the community at the conference—particularly in questions and answers following a presentation—the SIGCOMM 2015 Best Paper Award will be decided at the conference, and will be announced at the start of the conference's third day. Papers with any authors in conflict with either PC chair are excluded from consideration for a Best Paper Award.

Our deepest thanks to the authors of all submissions, for submitting their new insights into networking; to the program committee and external reviewers for their vibrant participation in the selection of the program; and to all the organizers of this year's conference.

Brad Karp
SIGCOMM 2015 Program Co-Chair
University College London, UK

Jitendra Padhye
SIGCOMM 2015 Program Co-Chair
Microsoft, USA

Table of Contents

Session: Experience Track 1

Session Chair: Sujata Banerjee *(HP Labs)*

Session: Experience Track 2

Session Chair: Sujata Banerjee *(HP Labs)*

Session: Middleboxes

Session Chair: Vyas Sekar *(Carnegie Mellon University)*

Session: Wireless

Session Chair: Kyle Jamieson *(University College London)*

Session: CDN and Wide Area Infrastructure

Session Chair: Aditya Akella *(University of Wisconsin - Madison)*

Session: Posters and Demos 2

Session: Wide Area Networks and Traffic

Session Chair: Anja Feldmann *(TU Berlin)*

Session: Posters, Industrial Demos, and Best of CCR

Session Chair: Dean Hildebrand *(IBM Research Almaden)*

Session: Security, Privacy, and Censorship

Session Chair: John Byers *(Boston University)*

ACM SIGCOMM 2015 Conference Organization

General Chairs: Steve Uhlig *(Queen Mary University of London, UK)*
Olaf Maennel *(Tallinn U. of Technology in Estonia, Estonia)*

Program Chairs: Brad Karp *(University College London, UK)*
Jitendra Padhye *(Microsoft, USA)*

Local Arrangement Chairs: Hamed Haddadi *(Queen Mary University of London, UK)*
Paolo Costa *(Microsoft Research, UK)*

Advisory Board: Jon Crowcroft *(University of Cambridge, UK)*
Christophe Diot *(Technicolor, France)*
Luigi Rizzo *(Universita di Pisa, Italy)*

Workshop Chairs: Renata Teixeira *(INRIA Paris-Rocquencourt, France)*
Nick Feamster *(Princeton University, USA)*

Poster Chairs: Olivier Bonaventure *(U. Catolique de Louvaine, Belgium)*
Cristel Pelsser *(IIJ, Japan)*

Demo Chairs: Richard Mortier *(U. of Nottingham, UK)*
Cigdem Sengul *(Oxford-Brookes U., UK)*

Tutorial Chairs: Andrew Moore *(University of Cambridge, UK)*
Miguel Rio *(University College London, UK)*

Publicity Chairs: Theophilus Benson *(Duke University, USA)*
Gaogang Xie *(ICT CAS, China)*
Chadi Barakat *(INRIA Sophia Antipolis, France)*

Publication Chair: Georgios Smaragdakis *(MIT, USA and TU Berlin, Germany)*

Registration Chair: Gonca Gursun *(Ozyegin University, Turkey)*

Travel Grant Chairs: Vyas Sekar *(Carnegie Mellon University, USA)*
Christian Kreibich *(ICSI, UC Berkeley, USA)*

Mentoring Chair: Craig Partridge *(Raytheon BBN, USA)*

Treasurer: Matthew Roughan *(U. of Adelaide, Australia)*

Web Chair: Felix Cuadrado *(Queen Mary University of London, UK)*

Student Research Competition Chairs: Cristel Pelsser *(IIJ, Japan)*
Cigdem Sengul *(Oxford-Brookes U., UK)*

Conference Coordinator: Yashar Ganjali *(U. of Toronto, Canada)*

Program Committee: Aditya Akella *(Univ. of Wisconsin, Madison, USA)*
Mohammad Alizadeh *(MIT and Cisco, USA)*
Katerina Argyraki *(EPFL, Switzerland)*
Aruna Balasubramanian *(Stony Brook University, USA)*
Hitesh Ballani *(Microsoft Research, UK)*
Sujata Banerjee *(HP Labs, USA)*
Keren Bergman *(Columbia University, USA)*
John Byers *(Boston University, USA)*
Jeff Chase *(Duke University, USA)*
Mung Chiang *(Princeton University, USA)*
Jon Crowcroft *(University of Cambridge, UK)*
Bruce Davie *(VMware, USA)*
Nandita Dukkipati *(Google, USA)*
Anja Feldmann *(Technische Univ. Berlin, Germany)*
Bryan Ford *(Yale University, USA)*
Nate Foster *(Cornell University, USA)*
Lixin Gao *(Univ. of Massachusetts Amherst, USA)*
Brighten Godfrey *(UIUC, USA)*
Sharon Goldberg *(Boston University, USA)*
Kyle Jamieson *(University College London, UK)*
Srikanth Kandula *(Microsoft Research, USA)*
Dina Katabi *(MIT, USA)*
Sachin Katti *(Stanford University, USA)*
Ethan Katz-Bassett *(Univ. of Southern California, USA)*
Teemu Koponen *(VMware, USA)*
John C. S. Lui *(Chinese Univ. of Hong Kong, Hong Kong)*
Z. Morley Mao *(Univ. of Michigan, USA)*
Dave Oran *(Cisco, USA)*
George Papen *(UC San Diego ECE, USA)*
KyoungSoo Park *(KAIST, Korea)*
George Porter *(UC San Diego CSE, USA)*
Luigi Rizzo *(Universita di Pisa, Italy)*
Ashutosh Sabharwal *(Rice University, USA)*
Stefan Savage *(UC San Diego CSE, USA)*
Michael Schapira *(Hebrew University, Israel)*
Vyas Sekar *(Carnegie Mellon University, USA)*
Kun Tan *(Microsoft Research, China)*
Pramod Viswanath *(UIUC, USA)*
Geoff Voelker *(UC San Diego CSE, USA)*
Michael Walfish *(NYU, USA)*
Jia Wang *(AT&T Research, USA)*
Philip Watts *(University College London, UK)*
David Wetherall *(Google and Univ. of Washington, USA)*
Walter Willinger *(NIKSUN, USA)*

Program Committee (continued): Keith Winstein *(Stanford University, USA)*
Xiaowei Yang *(Duke University, USA)*
Minlan Yu *(Univ. of Southern California, USA)*
Ming Zhang *(Microsoft Research, USA)*
Lin Zhong *(Rice University, USA)*

Additional reviewers:
Sharad Agarwal *(Microsoft, USA)*
Paul Barford *(UW Madison, USA)*
Nikolaj Bjorner *(Microsoft, USA)*
Bill Bolosky *(Microsoft, USA)*
Dan Boneh *(Stanford, USA)*
Nikita Borisov *(UIUC, USA)*
Stewart Bryant *(CISCO, USA)*
Ranveer Chandra *(Microsoft, USA)*
George Danezis *(UCL, UK)*
Jeff Dean *(Google, USA)*
Prabal Dutta *(U. Michigan, USA)*
Jason Flinn *(U. Michigan, USA)*
Harald Haas *(U. Edinburgh, UK)*
Mark Handley *(UCL, UK)*
Cheng Huang *(Microsoft, USA)*
Te-Yuan Huang *(Netflix, USA)*
Ethan Jackson *(VMware, USA)*
Eddie Kohler *(Harvard, USA)*
He Liu *(UCSD, USA)*
Harsha Madhyastha *(U. Michigan, USA)*
Nick McKeown *(Stanford, USA)*
Frank McSherry *(U. Edinburgh, UK)*
Todd Millstein *(UCLA, USA)*
Jeff Mogul *(Google, USA)*
Robert Morris *(MIT, USA)*
Reza Nejabati *(U. Bristol, UK)*
Rong Pan *(CISCO, USA)*
Michael Piatek *(Google, USA)*
Lenin Ravindranath *(Microsoft, USA)*
Pablo Rodriguez *(Telefonica, Spain)*
Hovav Shacham *(UCSD, USA)*
Scott Shenker *(UC Berkeley, USA)*
Josh Smith *(U. Washington, USA)*
Don Towsley *(UMass, USA)*
George Varghese *(Microsoft, USA)*
Haifeng Yu *(NUS, Singapore)*
Matei Zaharia *(MIT, USA)*

SIGCOMM Conference Technical Steering Committee:
Anja Feldmann *(Technische Univ. Berlin, Germany)*
Yashar Ganjali *(U. of Toronto, Canada)*
Dina Katabi *(MIT, USA), Chair*
Srinivasan Keshav *(University of Waterloo, USA)*
Venkat Padmanabhan *(Microsoft Research, USA)*
Sylvia Ratnasam *(UC Berkeley, USA)*
Srini Seshan *(Carnegie Mellon University, USA)*
David Wetherall *(Google and Univ. of Washington, USA)*

ACM SIGCOMM 2015 Sponsor & Supporters

Sponsor:

Supporters:

BwE: Flexible, Hierarchical Bandwidth Allocation for WAN Distributed Computing

Alok Kumar, Nikhil Kasinadhuni, Björn Carlin, Sushant Jain, Enrique Cauich Zermeno, Mihai Amarandei-Stavila, Stephen Stuart, Uday Naik, C. Stephen Gunn, Mathieu Robin, Amin Vahdat, Anand Raghuraman, Jing Ai, Aspi Siganporia

Google Inc.
bwe-sigcomm@google.com

ABSTRACT

WAN bandwidth remains a constrained resource that is economically infeasible to substantially overprovision. Hence, it is important to allocate capacity according to service priority and based on the incremental value of additional allocation. For example, it may be the highest priority for one service to receive 10Gb/s of bandwidth but upon reaching such an allocation, incremental priority may drop sharply favoring allocation to other services. Motivated by the observation that individual flows with fixed priority may not be the ideal basis for bandwidth allocation, we present the design and implementation of Bandwidth Enforcer (BwE), a global, hierarchical bandwidth allocation infrastructure. BwE supports: i) service-level bandwidth allocation following prioritized bandwidth functions where a service can represent an arbitrary collection of flows, ii) independent allocation and delegation policies according to user-defined hierarchy, all accounting for a global view of bandwidth and failure conditions, iii) multi-path forwarding common in traffic-engineered networks, and iv) a central administrative point to override (perhaps faulty) policy during exceptional conditions. BwE has delivered more service-efficient bandwidth utilization and simpler management in production for multiple years.

CCS Concepts

•**Networks → Network resources allocation;** *Network management;*

SIGCOMM '15 August 17-21, 2015, London, United Kingdom

ACM ISBN 978-1-4503-3542-3/15/08.
DOI: http://dx.doi.org/10.1145/2785956.2787478

Keywords

Bandwidth Allocation; Wide-Area Networks; Software-Defined Network; Max-Min Fair

1. INTRODUCTION

TCP-based bandwidth allocation to individual flows contending for bandwidth on bottleneck links has served the Internet well for decades. However, this model of bandwidth allocation assumes all flows are of equal priority and that all flows benefit equally from any incremental share of available bandwidth. It implicitly assumes a client-server communication model where a TCP flow captures the communication needs of an application communicating across the Internet.

This paper re-examines bandwidth allocation for an important, emerging trend, distributed computing running across dedicated private WANs in support of cloud computing and service providers. Thousands of simultaneous such applications run across multiple global data centers, with thousands of processes in each data center, each potentially maintaining thousands of individual active connections to remote servers. WAN traffic engineering means that site-pair communication follows different network paths, each with different bottlenecks. Individual services have vastly different bandwidth, latency, and loss requirements.

We present a new WAN bandwidth allocation mechanism supporting distributed computing and data transfer. BwE provides work-conserving bandwidth allocation, hierarchical fairness with flexible policy among competing services, and Service Level Objective (SLO) targets that independently account for bandwidth, latency, and loss.

BwE's key insight is that routers are the wrong place to map policy designs about bandwidth allocation onto per-packet behavior. Routers cannot support the scale and complexity of the necessary mappings, often because the semantics of these mappings cannot be captured in individual packets. Instead, following the End-to-End Argument[28], we push all such mapping to the source host machines. Hosts rate limit their outgoing traffic and mark packets using the DSCP field. Routers use the DSCP marking to determine which path to use for a packet and which packets to drop when congested. We use global knowledge of network topology and link utilization as input to a hierarchy of bandwidth enforcers, ranging from a global enforcer down to enforcers on each host. Bandwidth allocations and packet marking policy flows down the hierarchy while measures of demand flow up, starting with end hosts. The architecture allows us to decouple the aggregate bandwidth allocated to a flow from the handling of the flow at the routers.

BwE allocates bandwidth to competing applications based on flexible policy configured by *bandwidth functions* capturing application priority and incremental utility from additional bandwidth in different bandwidth regions. BwE supports hierarchical bandwidth allocation and delegation among services while simultaneously accounting for multipath WAN communication. BwE is the principal bandwidth allocation mechanism for one of the largest private WANs and has run in production for multiple years across hundreds of thousands of end points. The systems contributions of our work include:

- Leveraging concepts from Software Defined Networking, we build a unified, hierarchical control plane for bandwidth management extending to all end hosts. In particular, hosts report per-user and per-task demands to the control plane and rate shape a subset of flows.
- We integrate BwE into existing WAN traffic engineering (TE) [17, 11, 12] mechanisms including MPLS AutoBandwidth [22] and a custom SDN infrastructure. BwE takes WAN pathing decisions made by a TE service and re-allocates the available site-to-site capacity, split across multiple paths, among competing applications. At the same time, we benefit from the reverse integration: using BwE measures of prioritized application demand as input to TE pathing algorithms (Section 5.3.1).
- We implement hierarchical max-min fair bandwidth allocation to flexibly-defined FlowGroups contending for resources across multiple paths and at different levels of network abstraction. The bandwidth allocation mechanism is both work-conserving and flexible enough to implement a range of network sharing policies.

In sum, BwE delivers a number of compelling advantages. First, it provides isolation among competing services, delivering plentiful capacity in the common case while maintaining required capacity under failure and maintenance scenarios. Capacity available to one service is largely independent of the behavior of other services. Second, administrators have a single point for specifying allocation policy. While pathing, RTT, and capacity can shift substantially, BwE continues to allocate bandwidth according to policy. Finally, BwE enables the WAN to run at higher levels of utilization. By tightly integrating loss-insensitive file transfer protocols running at low priority with BwE, we run many of our WAN links at 90% utilization.

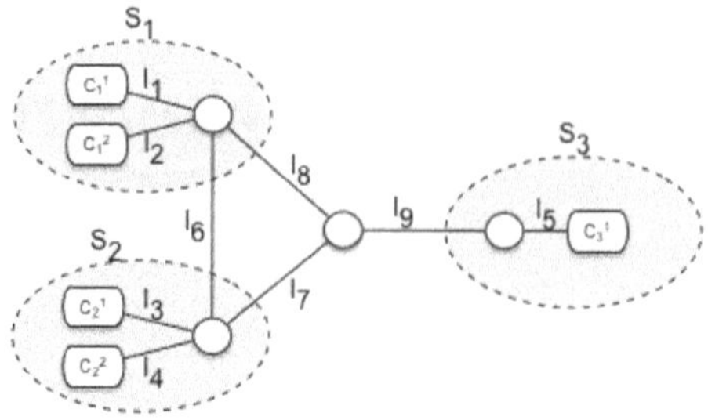

Figure 1: WAN Network Model.

2. BACKGROUND

We begin by describing our WAN environment and highlight the challenges we faced with existing bandwidth allocation mechanisms. Thousands of individual applications and services run across dozens of wide area *sites* each containing multiple *clusters*. Host machines within a cluster share a common LAN. Figure 1 shows an example WAN with sites S_1, S_2 and S_3; C_1^1 and C_1^2 are clusters within site S_1.

We host a combination of interactive web services, e.g. search and web mail, streaming video, batch-style data processing, e.g., MapReduce [13], and large-scale data transfer services, e.g., index copy from one site to another. Cluster management software maps services to hosts independently; we cannot leverage IP address aggregation/prefix to identify a service. However, we can install control software on hosts and leverage a control protocol running outside of routers.

We started with traditional mechanisms for bandwidth allocation such as TCP, QoS and MPLS tunnels. However these proved inadequate for a variety of reasons:

- *Granularity and Scale:* Our network and service capacity planners need to reason with bandwidth allocations at different aggregation levels. For example, a product group may need a specified minimum of site-to-site bandwidth across all services within the product area. In other cases, individual users or services may require a bandwidth guarantee between a specific pair of clusters. We need to scale bandwidth management to thousands of individual services, and product groups across dozens of sites each containing multiple clusters. We need a way to classify and aggregate individual flows into arbitrary groups based on configured policy. TCP fairness is at a 5-tuple flow granularity. On a congested link, an application gets bandwidth proportional to the number of active flows it sends across the links. Our services require guaranteed bandwidth allocation independent of the number of active TCP flows. Router QoS and MPLS tunnels do not scale to the number of service classes we must support and they do not provide sufficient flexibility in allocation policy (see below).
- *Multipath Forwarding:* For efficiency, wide area packet forwarding follows multiple paths through the network, possibly with each path of varying capacity. Routers hash individual service flows to one of the available paths based on packet header content.

Any bandwidth allocation from one site to another must simultaneously account for multiple source/destination paths whereas existing bandwidth allocation mechanisms—TCP, router QoS, MPLS tunnels—focus on different granularity (flows, links, single paths respectively).

- *Flexible and Hierarchical Allocation Policy:* We found simple weighted bandwidth allocation to be inadequate. For example, we may want to give a high priority user a weight of 10.0 until it has been allocated 1 Gb/s, a weight of 1.0 until it is allocated 2 Gb/s and a weight of 0.1 for all bandwidth beyond that. Further, bandwidth allocation should be hierarchical such that bandwidth allocated to a single product group can be subdivided to multiple users, which in turn may be hierarchically allocated to applications, individual hosts and finally flows. Different allocation policies should be available at each level of the hierarchy.

- *Delegation or Attribution:* Applications increasingly leverage computation and communication from a variety of infrastructure services. Consider the case where a service writes data to a storage service, which in turn replicates the content to multiple WAN sites for availability. Since the storage service acts on behalf of thousands of other services, its bandwidth should be charged to the originating user. Bandwidth delegation provides differential treatment across users sharing a service, avoids head of line blocking across traffic for different users, and ensures that the same policies are applied across the network for a user's traffic.

We designed BwE to address the challenges and requirements described above around the principle that bandwidth allocation should be extended all the way to end hosts. While historically we have looked to routers with increasingly sophisticated ASICs and control protocols for WAN bandwidth allocation, we argue that this design point has resulted simply from lack of control over end hosts on the part of network service providers. Assuming such access is available, we find that the following functionality can be supported with a hierarchical control infrastructure extending to end hosts: i) mapping WAN communication back to thousands of flow groups, ii) flexibly sub-dividing aggregate bandwidth allocations back to individual flows, iii) accounting for delegation of resource charging from one service to another, and iv) expressing and enforcing flexible max-min bandwidth sharing policies. On the contrary, existing routers must inherently leverage limited information available only in packet headers to map packets to one of a small number of service classes or tunnels.

Figure 2 shows an instance of very high loss in multiple QoS classes during a capacity reduction on our network. TCP congestion control was not effective and the loss remained high until we turned on admission control on hosts.

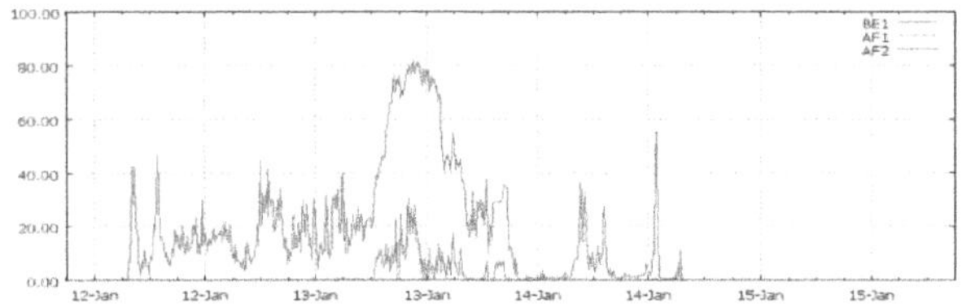

Figure 2: Reduction in TCP packet loss after BwE was deployed. Y-axis denotes packet loss in percentage. Different lines correspond to different QoS classes (BE1 denoting best effort, and AF1/AF2 denoting higher QoS classes.)

3. ABSTRACTIONS AND CONCEPTS

3.1 Traffic Aggregates or FlowGroups

Individual services or users run *jobs* consisting of multiple *tasks*. Each task may contain multiple Linux processes and runs in a Linux container that provides resource accounting, isolation and information about user_name, job_name and task_name. We modified the Linux networking stack to mark the per-packet socket buffer structure to uniquely identify the originating container running the task. This allows BwE to distinguish between traffic from different tasks running on the same host machine.

BwE further classifies task traffic based on destination cluster address. Optionally, tasks use setsockopt() to indicate other classification information, e.g. for *bandwidth delegation*. Delegation allows a task belonging to a shared infrastructure service to attribute its bandwidth to the user whose request caused it to generate traffic. For example, a copy service can delegate bandwidth charges for a specific file transfer to the user requesting the transfer.

For scalability, baseline TCP regulates bandwidth for most application flows. BwE dynamically selects the subset of flows accounting for most of the demand to enforce. Using TCP as the baseline also provides a convenient fallback for bandwidth allocation in the face of a BwE system failure.

BwE allocates bandwidth among *FlowGroups* at various granularities, defined below.

- Task FlowGroup or *task-fg*: <delegating_service, user_name, job_name, task_name, source_cluster, destination_cluster>. This FlowGroup is the finest unit of bandwidth measurement and enforcement.

- Job FlowGroup or *job-fg*: Bandwidth usage across all *task-fg*s belonging to the same job is aggregated into a *job-fg*: <delegating_service, user_name, job_name, source_cluster, destination_cluster>.

- User FlowGroup or *user-fg*: Bandwidth usage across all *job-fg*s belonging to the same user is aggregated into a *user-fg*: <delegating_service, user_name, source_cluster, destination_cluster>.

- Cluster FlowGroup or *cluster-fg*: Bandwidth usage across all *user-fg* belonging to same user_aggregate and belonging to same cluster-pair is combined into a *cluster-fg*: <user_aggregate, source_cluster,

destination_cluster>. The user_aggregate corresponds to an arbitrary grouping of users, typically by business group or product. This mapping is defined in BwE configuration (Section 3.2).

- Site FlowGroup or *site-fg*: Bandwidth usage for *cluster-fgs* belonging to the same site-pair is combined into a *site-fg*: <user_aggregate, source_site, destination_site>.

BwE creates a set of trees of FlowGroups with parent-child relationships starting with *site-fg* at the root to *cluster-fg*, *user-fg*, *job-fg* and eventually *task-fg* at the leaf. We measure bandwidth usage at *task-fg* granularity in the host and aggregate to the *site-fg* level. BwE estimates demand (Section 6.1) for each FlowGroup based on its historical usage. BwE allocates bandwidth to *site-fgs*, which is redistributed down to *task-fgs* and enforced in the host kernel. Beyond rate limiting, the hierarchy can also be used to perform other actions on a flow group such as DSCP remarking. All measurements and rate limiting are done on packet transmit.

BwE policies are defined at *site-fg* and *user-fg* level. Measurement and enforcement happen at *task-fg* level. Other levels are required to scale the system by enabling distributed execution of BwE across multiple machines in Google datacenters.

3.2 Bandwidth Sharing Policies

3.2.1 *Requirements*

Our WAN (Figure 1) is divided in two levels, the inter-site network and the inter-cluster network. The links in the inter-site network (l_7, l_8 and l_9 in the figure) are the most expensive. Aggregated demands on these links are easier to predict. Hence, our WAN is provisioned at the inter-site network. Product groups (user_aggregates) create bandwidth requirements for each site-pair. For a site-pair, depending on the network capacity and its business priority, each user_aggregate gets approved bandwidth at several allocation levels. Allocation levels are in strict priority order, ex, *Guaranteed* allocation level should be fully satisfied before allocating to *Best-Effort* allocation level. Allocated bandwidth of a user_aggregate for a site-pair is further divided to all its member users.

Even though provisioning and sharing of the inter-site network is the most important, several links not in the inter-site network may also get congested and there is a need to share their bandwidth fairly during congestion. We assign weights to the users that are used to subdivide their user_aggregate's allocated bandwidth in the inter-cluster network. To allow more fine grained control, we allow weights to change based on allocated bandwidth as well as to be overridden to a non-default value for some cluster-pairs.

3.2.2 *Configuration*

Network administrators configure BwE sharing policies through centralized configuration. BwE configuration specifies a fixed number of strict priority allocation levels, e.g., there may be two levels corresponding to Guaranteed and Best-Effort traffic.

(a) fg_1

Allocation Level	Weight	Bandwidth (Gbps)
Guaranteed	0	0
Best-Effort	20	10
	5	∞

(b) fg_2

Allocation Level	Weight	Bandwidth (Gbps)
Guaranteed	10	10
Best-Effort	10	∞

Table 1: BwE Configuration Example.

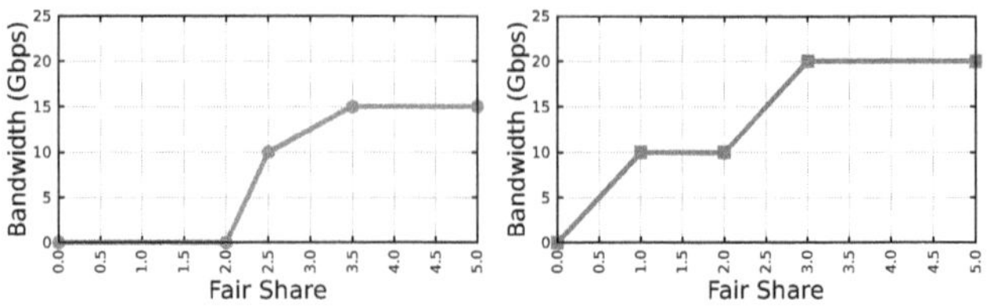

(a) fg_1 (b) fg_2

Figure 3: Example Bandwidth Functions.

The BwE configuration maps users to user_aggregates. Mapping from *user-fg* to *site-fg* can be derived from this. The BwE configuration policies describe how *site-fgs* share the network and also describe how *user-fgs* within a *site-fg* share bandwidth allocated to the *site-fg*. For all FlowGroups in a level of hierarchy, the BwE configuration defines: 1) bandwidth for each allocation level and 2) within each allocation level, weight of the FlowGroup that can change based on allocated bandwidth. An example of a BwE configuration for the relative priority for two FlowGroups, fg_1 and fg_2 is shown in Table 1.

3.2.3 *Bandwidth Functions*

The configured sharing policies are represented inside BwE as *bandwidth functions*[1]. A *bandwidth function* [17] specifies the bandwidth allocation to a FlowGroup as a function of its relative priority on an arbitrary, dimensionless measure of available fair share capacity, which we call *fair share*. *fair share* is an abstract measure and is only used for internal computation by the allocation algorithm. Based on the config, every *site-fg* and *user-fg* is assigned a piece-wise linear monotonic *bandwidth function* (e.g. Figure 3). It is capped at the dynamic estimated demand (Section 6.1) of the FlowGroup. They can also be aggregated to create *bandwidth functions* at the higher levels (Section 3.2.4).

The *fair share* dimension can be partitioned into regions (corresponding to allocation levels in the BwE configuration) of strict priority. Within each region, the slope[2] of a FlowGroup's *bandwidth function* defines its relative priority or weight. Once the bandwidth reaches the maximum approved for the FlowGroup in a region, the *bandwidth function* flattens (0 slope) until the start of the next region. Once the

[1]Bandwidth functions are similar to *utility functions* [8, 6] except that these are derived from static configured policy (Section 3.2) indicating network fair share rather than application-specified utility as a function of allocated bandwidth.

[2]Slope can be a multiple of weight as long as the same multiple is used for all FlowGroups.

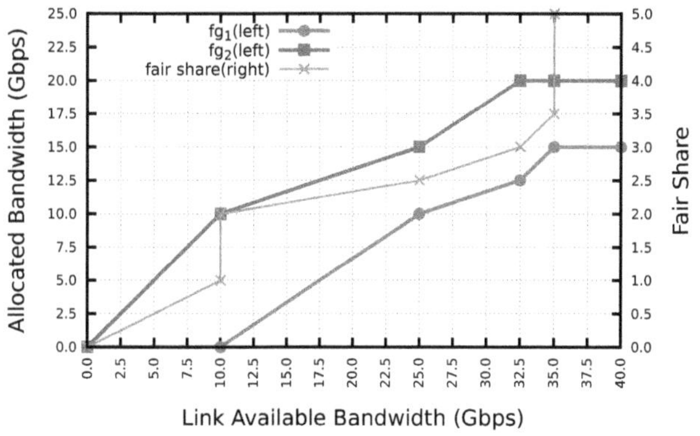

Figure 4: Bandwidth Sharing on a Bottleneck Link.

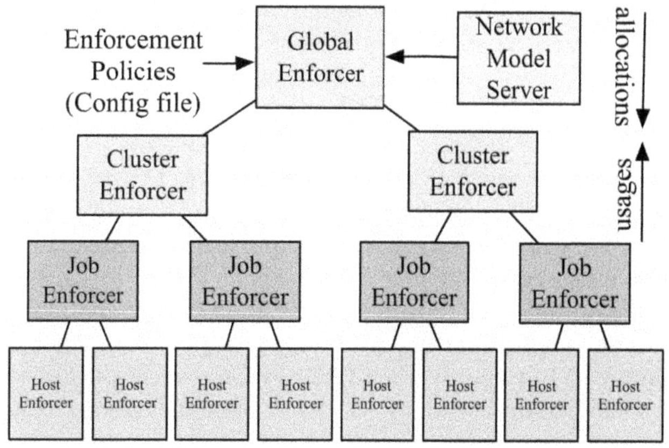

Figure 5: BwE Architecture.

bandwidth function reaches the FlowGroup's estimated demand, it becomes flat from that point for all the following regions.

Figure 3 shows example *bandwidth functions* for two FlowGroups, fg_1 and fg_2, based on BwE configuration as defined in Table 1. There are two regions of *fair share*: Guaranteed (0-2) and Best-Effort (2-∞). The endpoints for each region are system-level constants defined in BwE configuration. BwE's estimated demand of fg_1 is 15Gbps and hence, its *bandwidth function* flattens past that point. Similarly, fg_2's estimated demand is 20Gbps.

We present a scenario where fg_1 and fg_2 are sharing one constrained link in the network. The goal of the BwE algorithm is to allocate the bandwidth of the constrained link such the following constraints are satisfied: 1) fg_1 and fg_2 get maximum possible but equal *fair share*, and 2) sum of their allocated bandwidth corresponding to the allocated *fair share* is less than or equal to the available bandwidth of the link. Figure 4 shows the output of the BwE allocation algorithm (Section 5.3) with varying link's available bandwidth shown on the x-axis. The allocated *fair share* to the FlowGroups is shown on the right y-axis and the corresponding bandwidth allocated to the FlowGroups is shown on the left y-axis. Note that the constraints above are always satisfied at each snapshot of link's available bandwidth. One can verify using this graph that the prioritization as defined by Table 1 is respected.

One of BwE's principal responsibilities is to dynamically determine the level of contention for a particular resource (bandwidth) and to then assign the resource to all competing FlowGroups based on current contention. Higher values of *fair share* indicate lower levels of resource contention and correspondingly higher levels of bandwidth that can potentially be assigned to a FlowGroup. Actual consumption is capped by current FlowGroup estimated demand, making the allocation work-conserving (do not waste any available bandwidth if there is demand).

The objective of BwE is the max-min fair [6] allocation of *fair share* to competing *site-fgs* and then the max-min fair allocation of *fair share* to *user-fgs* within a *site-fg*. For each *user-fg*, maximize the utilization of the allocated bandwidth to the *user-fg* by subdividing it to the lower levels of hierarchy (*job-fgs* and *task-fgs*) equally (no weights) based on their estimated demands.

3.2.4 *Bandwidth Function Aggregation*

Bandwidth Functions can be aggregated from one FlowGroup level to another higher level. We require such aggregation when input configuration defines a *bandwidth function* at a finer granularity, but the BwE algorithm runs over coarser granularity FlowGroups. For example, BwE's input configuration provides *bandwidth function* at *user-fg* level, while BwE (Section 5.1) runs across *cluster-fgs*. In this case, we aggregate *user-fgs bandwidth functions* to create a *cluster-fg bandwidth function*. We create aggregated *bandwidth functions* for a FlowGroup by adding bandwidth value for each value of *fair share* for all its children.

4. SYSTEM DESIGN

BwE consists of a hierarchy of components that aggregate network usage statistics and enforce bandwidth allocations. BwE obtains topology and other network state from a network model server and bandwidth sharing policies from an administrator-specified configuration. Figure 5 shows the functional components in BwE.

4.1 Host Enforcer

At the lowest level of the BwE hierarchy, the Host Enforcer runs as a user space daemon on end hosts. Every five seconds, it reports bandwidth usage of local application's *tasks-fgs* to the Job Enforcer. In response, it receives bandwidth allocations for its *task-fgs* from the Job Enforcer. The Host Enforcer collects measurements and enforces bandwidth allocations using the HTB (Hierarchical Token Bucket) queuing discipline in Linux.

4.2 Job Enforcer

Job Enforcers aggregate usages from *task-fgs* to *job-fgs* and report *job-fgs*' usages every 10 seconds to the Cluster Enforcer. In response, the Job Enforcer receives *job-fgs*' bandwidth allocations from the Cluster Enforcer. The Job Enforcer ensures that for each *job-fg*, bandwidth usage does not exceed its assigned allocation. To do so, it redistributes the assigned *job-fg* allocation among the constituent *task-fgs* using the WaterFill algorithm (Section 5.4).

4.3 Cluster Enforcer

The Cluster Enforcer manages two levels of FlowGroup aggregation - *user-fgs* to *job-fgs* and *cluster-fgs* to *user-fgs*. It aggregates usages from *job-fgs* to *user-fgs* and computes *user-fgs' bandwidth functions* based on input from a configuration file. It aggregates the *user-fgs' bandwidth functions* (capped at their estimated demand) to *cluster-fg* bandwidth functions (Section 3.2.4), reporting them every 15 seconds to the Global Enforcer. In response, the Cluster Enforcer receives *cluster-fgs'* bandwidth allocations, which it redistributes among *user-fgs* and subsequently to *job-fgs* (Section 5.4).

4.4 Network Model Server

The Network Model Server builds the abstract network model for BwE. Network information is collected by standard monitoring mechanisms (such as SNMP). Freshness is critical since paths change dynamically. BwE targets getting an update every 30 seconds. The consistency of the model is verified using independent mechanisms such as traceroute.

4.5 Global Enforcer

The Global Enforcer sits at the top of the Bandwidth Enforcer hierarchy. It divides available bandwidth capacity on the network between different clusters. The Global Enforcer takes the following inputs: i) *bandwidth functions* from the Cluster Enforcers summarizing priority across all users at *cluster-fg* level, ii) global configuration describing the sharing policies at *site-fg* level, and iii) network topology, link capacity, link utilization and drop statistics from the network model server. A small fraction of flows going over a link may not be under BwE control. To handle this, for every link we also compute *dark bandwidth*. This is the amount of traffic going over the link which BwE is unaware of. This may be due to packet header overhead (particularly tunneling in network routers) or various failure conditions where BwE has incomplete information. Dark bandwidth is the smoothed value of (actual link usage - BwE reported link usage), and link allocatable capacity is (link capacity - dark bandwidth). BwE reported link usage is computed by taking the set of flows (and their current usage) reported to the Global Enforcer by Cluster Enforcers, and mapping them to the paths and links for those flows. Given these inputs, the Global Enforcer runs hierarchical *MPFA* (Section 5.3) to compute *cluster-fgs'* bandwidth allocations and sends these allocations to Cluster Enforcers.

5. BWE ALLOCATION ALGORITHM

One of the challenges we faced was defining the optimization objective for bandwidth allocation to individual flows. First, we did not wish to allocate bandwidth among competing 5-tuple flows but rather to competing FlowGroups. Second, services do not compete for bandwidth at a single bottleneck link because services communicate from multiple clusters to multiple other clusters, with each cluster pair utilizing multiple paths. Hence, the bandwidth allocation must simultaneously account for multiple potential bottlenecks.

Here, we present an adaptation of the traditional max-min fairness objective for FlowGroups sharing a bottleneck link to multipath cluster-to-cluster communication. We designed a centralized *MultiPath Fair Allocation (MPFA)* algorithm to determine global max-min fairness. We present a simpler version of the problem with a single layer of FlowGroups (Section 5.2) and then extend it to multiple layers of FlowGroups with different network abstractions in hierarchical *MPFA* (Section 5.5).

5.1 Inputs and Outputs

Inputs to the BwE algorithm are *task-fgs'* demands, *bandwidth functions* of *user-fgs* and *site-fgs* and network paths for *cluster-fgs* and *site-fgs*. We aggregate *task-fgs'* demands all the way up to *site-fgs* and aggregate *user-fgs' bandwidth functions* to *cluster-fgs' bandwidth functions* (Section 3.2.4). We run global hierarchical *MPFA* (Section 5.5) on *site-fgs* and *cluster-fgs* that results in *cluster-fgs'* allocations. Then, we distribute *cluster-fgs'* allocations to *task-fgs* (Section 5.4), which are enforced at the hosts.

5.2 MPFA Problem

Inputs for *MPFA* are:

1. Set of n FlowGroups, $\mathcal{F} = \{f_i, \ \forall i \mid 1 \le i \le n\}$ where FlowGroups are defined in Section 3.1. Each f_i has an associated *bandwidth function* (Section 3.2.3), B_{f_i}. B_{f_i} maps *fair share* to bandwidth for f_i. If f_i is allocated *fair share* of s, then it should be allocated bandwidth equal to $B_{f_i}(s)$.
2. Set of m links, $\mathcal{L} = \{l_k, \ \forall k \mid 1 \le k \le m\}$. Each link l_k has an associated allocatable capacity c_{l_k}.
3. Set of n_{f_i} paths for each f_i. Each path, $p_j^{f_i}$, has an associated weight, $w_j^{f_i}$, where $1 \le j \le n_{f_i}$ and for each f_i, $\sum_{1 \le j \le n_{f_i}} w_j^{f_i} = 1$. Each path, $p_j^{f_i}$, is a set of links, i.e, $p_j^{f_i} \subseteq \mathcal{L}$.

We define the fraction of f_i that traverse l_k as $FR(f_i, l_k)$. This is calculated as the sum of weights, $w_j^{f_i}$, for all paths, $p_j^{f_i}$, for the FlowGroup, f_i, such that $l_k \in p_j^{f_i}$.

$$FR(f_i, l_k) = \sum_{1 \le j \le n_{f_i} \mid l_k \in p_j^{f_i}} w_j^{f_i}$$

The output of *MPFA* is the max-min *fair share* allocation s_{f_i} to each FlowGroup, f_i, such that ascending sorted $(s_{f_1}, s_{f_2}, \ldots, s_{f_n})$ is maximized in lexicographical order. Such maximization is subject to the constraint of satisfying capacity constraints for all links, l_k.

$$\sum_{\forall f_i} FR(f_i, l_k) \times B_{f_i}(s_{f_i}) \le c_{l_k}$$

5.3 MPFA Algorithm

The *MPFA* algorithm (Algorithm 1) can be described in the following high-level steps:

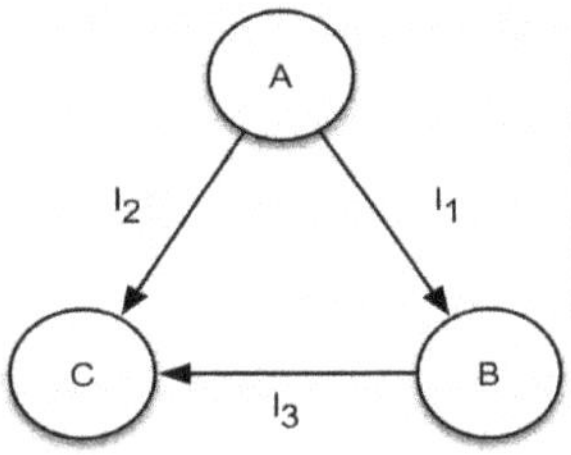

Flow Group	Src	Dst	Paths
f1	A	C	l2: 0.75 l1→l3: 0.25
f2	A	C	l2: 1.00
f3	A	B	l1: 1.00

Figure 6: MPFA Example.

1. For each link, l_k, calculate the link's *bandwidth function*, B_{l_k}, by aggregating *bandwidth functions* of all non-frozen[3] FlowGroups, f_i, in appropriate fractions, $FR(f_i, l_k)$. B_{l_k} maps *fair share*, s, to allocation on the link l_k when all FlowGroups traversing l_k are allocated the *fair share* of s.

2. Find the bottleneck *fair share*, $s^b_{l_k}$, for each remaining (not bottlenecked yet) link, l_k, by finding the *fair share* corresponding to its capacity, c_{l_k} in the link's *bandwidth function*, B_{l_k}. Since *bandwidth function* is a piece-wise linear monotonic function, finding *fair share* for a given capacity can be achieved by a binary search of the interesting points (points where the slope of the function changes).

3. The link, l_b, with the minimum bottleneck *fair share*, s^{min} is the next bottleneck. If the minimum bottleneck *fair share* equals ∞, then terminate.

4. Mark the link, l_b, as a bottleneck link. Freeze all FlowGroups, f_i, with non-zero fraction, $FR(f_i, l_b)$, on l_b. Frozen FlowGroups are not considered to find further bottleneck links. Subtract frozen FlowGroups' *bandwidth functions* beyond the bottleneck *fair share*,s^{min} from all remaining links.

5. If any link is not a bottleneck, continue to step 2.

Figure 6 shows an example of the allocation algorithm with three links, l_1, l_2 and l_3, with capacity 13, 13 and 4 respectively. Assume all bandwidth numbers are in Gbps for this example. There are three FlowGroups: 1) f_1 takes two paths (l_2 and $l_1 \rightarrow l_3$) with weights 0.75 and 0.25 respectively, 2) f_2 takes one path (l_2), and 3) f_3 taking one path (l_1). All FlowGroups have demand of 18. Assume f_1, f_2 and f_3 have weights of 1, 2 and 3 respectively, corresponding *bandwidth functions* of the FlowGroups are: $B_{f_1}(s) = \min(18, s)$, $B_{f_2}(s) = \min(18, 2s)$ and $B_{f_3}(s) = \min(18, 3s)$.

Based on that paths, fraction of FlowGroups(f_i) traversing Links(l_k) are: $FR(f_1, l_1) = 0.25$, $FR(f_1, l_2) = 0.75$, $FR(f_1, l_3) = 0.25$, $FR(f_2, l_2) = 1$ and $FR(f_3, l_1) = 1$.

We calculate *bandwidth function* for links as:

$$B_{l_1}(s) = \begin{pmatrix} 0.25(\min(18, s)) \\ +\min(18, 3s) \end{pmatrix} = \begin{cases} 3.25s & : 0 \le s < 6 \\ 0.25s + 18 & : 6 \le s < 18 \\ 22.5 & : s \ge 18 \end{cases}$$

[3]A frozen FlowGroup is a FlowGroup that is already bottlenecked at a link and does not participate in the *MPFA* algorithm run any further.

Input:
FlowGroups, $\mathcal{F} : \{f_i, \forall i \mid 1 \le i \le n\}$;
Links, $\mathcal{L} : \{l_k, \forall k \mid 1 \le k \le m\}$;
Allocatable capacities for $\forall l_k$: $\{c_{l_k}, \forall k \mid 1 \le k \le m\}$;
bandwidth function for $f_i : B_{f_i}$;
// $\forall f_i, \forall l_k$, Fraction of f_i traversing link, l_k
Function, $FR(f_i, l_k)$: Output is a fraction ≤ 1;

Output:
Allocated fair share for $\forall f_i : \{s_{f_i}, \forall i \mid 1 \le i \le n\}$;

Bottleneck Links , $\mathcal{L}^b \leftarrow \varnothing$;
Frozen FlowGroups, $\mathcal{F}^f \leftarrow \varnothing$;
foreach f_i **do** $s_{f_i} \leftarrow \infty$;
// Calculate *bandwidth function* for each l_k
foreach l_k **do** $\forall s, B_{l_k}(s) \leftarrow \sum_{\forall f_i} FR(f_i, l_k) \times B_{f_i}(s)$;
while $(\exists l_k \mid l_k \notin \mathcal{L}^b) \wedge (\exists f_i \mid f_i \notin \mathcal{F}^f)$ **do**
Bottleneck link, $l_b \leftarrow null$;
Min Bottleneck fair share, $s^{min} \leftarrow \infty$;
foreach $l_k \notin \mathcal{L}^b$ **do**
Find $s^b_{l_k} \mid c_{l_k} = B_{l_k}(s^b_{l_k})$;
if $s^b_{l_k} < s^{min}$ **then** $s^{min} \leftarrow s^b_{l_k}$; $l_b \leftarrow l_k$;
if $l_b \ne null$ **then** Add l_b to $\mathcal{L}^b$;
else break;
// Freeze f_i taking the bottleneck link, l_b
foreach $f_i \mid FR(f_i, l_b) > 0 \wedge f_i \notin \mathcal{F}^f$ **do**
Add f_i to $\mathcal{F}^f$; $s_{f_i} \leftarrow s^{min}$;
// Remove allocated bandwidth from B_{f_i}
$\forall s, B_{f_i}(s) \leftarrow \max(0, B_{f_i}(s) - B_{f_i}(s^{min}))$;
// Subtract B_{f_i} from B_{l_k} for all its links
foreach $l_k \mid FR(f_i, l_k) > 0 \wedge l_k \notin \mathcal{L}^b$ **do**
$\forall s, B_{l_k}(s) \leftarrow B_{l_k}(s) - FR(f_i, l_k) \times B_{f_i}(s)$;

Algorithm 1: MPFA Algorithm

$$B_{l_2}(s) = \begin{pmatrix} 0.75(\min(18, s)) \\ +\min(18, 2s) \end{pmatrix} = \begin{cases} 2.75s & : 0 \le s < 9 \\ 0.75s + 18 & : 9 \le s < 18 \\ 31.5 & : s \ge 18 \end{cases}$$

$$B_{l_3}(s) = 0.25(\min(18, s)) = \begin{cases} 0.25s & : 0 \le s < 18 \\ 4.5 & : s \ge 18 \end{cases}$$

Next, we find bottleneck *fair share*, $s^b_{l_k}$ for each link, l_k, such that $B_{l_k}(s^b_{l_k}) = c_{l_k}$. This results in $s^b_{l_1} = 4$, $s^b_{l_2} \approx 4.72$, $s^b_{l_3} = 16$. This makes l_1 the bottleneck link and freezes both f_1 and f_3 at *fair share* of 4. l_1 will not further participate in *MPFA*. Since f_1 is frozen at *fair share* of 4, B_{l_2} and B_{l_3} need to be updated to not account for B_{f_1} beyond *fair share* of 4. The updated functions are:

$$B_{l_2}(s) = \begin{cases} 2.75s & : 0 \le s < 4 \\ 2s + 3 & : 4 \le s < 9 \\ 21 & : s \ge 9 \end{cases}$$

$$B_{l_3}(s) = \begin{cases} 0.25s & : 0 \le s < 4 \\ 1 & : s \ge 4 \end{cases}$$

We recalculate $s^b_{l_2}$ and $s^b_{l_3}$ based on the new values for B_{l_2} and B_{l_3}. This results in $s^b_{l_2} = 5$ and $s^b_{l_3} = \infty$. l_2 is the next bottleneck with *fair share* of 5. f_2 is now frozen at the *fair share* of

5. Since all FlowGroups are frozen, MPFA terminates. The final allocation to (f_1, f_2, f_3) in *fair share* is (4, 5, 4), translating to (4Gbps, 10Gbps, 12Gbps) using the corresponding *bandwidth functions*. This allocation fills bottleneck links, l_1 and l_2 completely and *fair share* allocation (4, 5, 4) is max-min fair with the given pathing constraints. No FlowGroup's allocation can be increased without penalizing other FlowGroups with lower or equal *fair share*.

5.3.1 Interaction with Traffic Engineering (TE)

The BwE algorithm takes paths and their weights as input. A separate system, TE [17, 11, 12], is responsible for finding optimal pathing that improves BwE allocation. Both BwE and TE are trying to optimize network throughput in a fair way and input flows are known in advance. However, the key difference is that in BwE problem formulation, paths and their weights are input constraints, where-as for TE [17, 11, 12], paths and their weights are output. In our network, we treat TE and BwE as independent problems.

TE has more degrees of freedom and hence can achieve higher fairness. In the above example, the final allocation can be more max-min fair if f_1 only uses the path l_2. In this case, *MPFA* will allocate *fair share* to flow groups ≈ (4.33, 4.33, 4.33) with corresponding bandwidth of (4.33Gbps, 8.66Gbps, 13Gbps). Hence, a good traffic engineering solution results in better (more max-min fair) BwE allocations.

We run TE [17] and BwE independently because they work at different time-scales and different topology granularity. Since TE is more complex, we aggregate topology to site-level where-as for BwE, we are able to run at a more granular cluster-level topology. TE re-optimizes network less often because changing network paths may result in packet re-ordering, transient loss [16] and resulting routing changes may add significant load to network routers. Separation of TE and BwE also gives us operational flexibility. The fact that both systems have the same higher level objective function helps ensure that their decisions are aligned and efficient. Even though in our network we run these independently the possibility of having a single system to do both can not be ruled out in future.

5.4 Allocation Distribution

MPFA allocates bandwidth to the highest level of aggregations, *site-fgs*. This allocation needs to be distributed to lower levels of aggregation. Distribution of allocation from *cluster-fg* to lower levels is simpler since the network abstraction does not change and the set of paths remains the same during de-aggregation. We describe such distributions in this section. The distribution from *site-fg* to *cluster-fg* is more complex since the network abstraction changes from site-level to cluster-level (Figure 1), requiring an extension of *MPFA* to Hierarchical *MPFA* (Section 5.5) to allocate bandwidth directly to *cluster-fgs* while honoring fairness and network abstractions at *site-fg* and *cluster-fg* level.

To distribute allocation from a *cluster-fg* to *user-fgs*, we calculate the aggregated *bandwidth functions* for the *cluster-fgs* (Section 3.2.4) and determine the *fair share*, s^u, corresponding to the *cluster-fg*'s bandwidth allocation. We use s^u to look up the bandwidth allocation for each *user-fg* using its *bandwidth function*.

Bandwidth distribution from a *user-fg* to *job-fgs* and from a *job-fg* to *task-fgs* is simple max-min fair allocation of one resource to several competing FlowGroups using a *WaterFill* as shown in Figure 7. WaterFill calculates the water level corresponding to the maximum allocation to any FlowGroup.

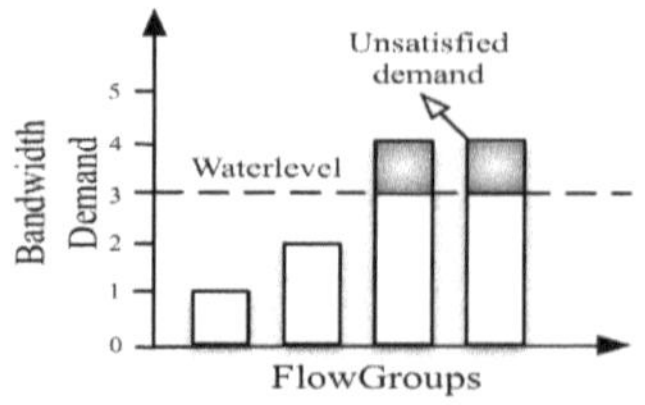

Total Resource = 9 Waterlevel = 3	
Demand	Allocation
1	1
2	2
4	3
4	3

Figure 7: Allocation Using WaterFill.

The allocation to each child FlowGroup is $min(demand, waterlevel)$. If there is excess bandwidth still remaining after running the WaterFill, it is divided among the FlowGroups as bonus bandwidth. Since some (or a majority) of the FlowGroups will not use the bonus assigned to them, the bonus is over-allocated by a configurable scaling factor.

5.5 Hierarchical MPFA

Next, we describe hierarchical *MPFA*, which reconciles the complexity between *site-fg* and *cluster-fg* level allocation. The fairness goal is to allocate max-min *fair share* to *site-fg* respecting bandwidth functions and simultaneously observing inter-site and intra-site topological constraints (Figure 1). Because not all *cluster-fgs* within a *site-fg* share the same WAN paths, individual *cluster-fgs* within a *site-fg* may bottleneck on different intra-site links.

We motivate hierarchical fairness using an example based on Figure 1. All links have 100Gbps capacity, except l_1 (5Gbps) and l_9 (40Gbps). There are two *site-fgs*, sf_1 from S_1 to S_3 and sf_2 from S_2 to S_3. sf_1 consists of *cluster-fgs*: cf_1 from C_1^1 to C_3^1 and cf_2 from C_1^2 to C_3^1. sf_2 consists of a *cluster-fg*: cf_3 from C_2^1 to C_3^1. All *site-fgs* have equal weights and for each *site-fg*, all its member *cluster-fgs* have equal weights. cf_1 and cf_3 have 100Gbps of demand while cf_2 has a 5Gbps demand. If we run *MPFA* naively on *site-fgs*, then sf_1 and sf_2 will be allocated 20Gbps each due to the bottleneck link, l_9. However, when we further subdivide sf_1's 20Gbps among cf_1 and cf_2, cf_1 only receives 5Gbps due to the bottleneck link l_1 while cf_2 only has demand of 5Gbps. cf_3 receives all of sf_2's 20Gbps allocation.

With this naive approach, the final total allocation on l_9 is 30Gbps wasting 10Gbps, where cf_3 could have used the extra 10Gbps. Allocation at the site level must account for independent bottlenecks in the topology one layer down. Hence, we present an efficient hierarchical MPFA to allocate max-min fair bandwidth among *site-fgs* while accounting for cluster-level topology and fairness among *cluster-fgs*.

The goals of hierarchical *MPFA* are:

- Ensure max-min fairness of *fair share* across *site-fg* based on *site-fgs' bandwidth functions*.
- Within a *site-fg*, ensure max-min fairness of *fair share* across *cluster-fgs* using *cluster-fgs' bandwidth functions*.
- The algorithm should be work-conserving.
- The algorithm should not over-allocate any link in the network, hence, should enforce capacity constraints of intra-site and inter-site links.

For hierarchical *MPFA*, we must run *MPFA* on all *cluster-fgs* to ensure that bottleneck links are fully utilized and enforced. To do so, we must create effective *bandwidth functions* for *cluster-fgs* such that the fairness among *site-fgs* and fairness within a *site-fg* are honored.

We enhance *MPFA* in the following way. In addition to *bandwidth function*, B_{cf_i}, for *cluster-fg*, cf_i, we further consider the *bandwidth function*, B_{sf_x} for *site-fg*, sf_x. Using $\forall i, B_{cf_i}$ and $\forall x, B_{sf_x}$, we derive the effective *bandwidth function*, $B^e_{cf_i}$, for cf_i.

We create $B^e_{cf_i}$ by transforming B_{cf_i} along the *fair share* dimension while preserving the relative priorities of cf_i with respect to each other. We call bandwidth values of different cf_i as equivalent if they map to the same *fair share* based on their respective *bandwidth functions*. To preserve relative priorities of $\forall cf_i \in sf_x$, the set of equivalent bandwidth values should be identical before and after the *bandwidth functions* transformation. Any transformation applied in *fair share* should preserve this property as long as the same transformation is applied to all $cf_i \in sf_x$. Allocated bandwidth to each cf_i on a given available capacity (e.g. Figure 4) should be unchanged due to such transformation. In addition, we must find a transformation such that when all $cf_i \in sf_x$ use their effective (transformed) *bandwidth functions*, $B^e_{cf_i}$, they can together exactly replace sf_x. This means that when $B^e_{cf_i}$ are added together, it equals B_{sf_x}. $\forall s, \sum_{\forall i | cf_i \in sf_x} B^e_{cf_i}(s) = B_{sf_x}(s)$.

The steps to create $B^e_{cf_i}$ are:

1. For each *site-fg*, sf_x, create aggregated *bandwidth function*, $B^a_{sf_x}$ (Section 3.2.4):

$$\forall s, B^a_{sf_x}(s) = \sum_{\forall cf_i \in sf_x} B_{cf_i}(s)$$

2. Find a transformation function of *fair share* from $B^a_{sf_x}$ to B_{sf_x}. The transformation function, T_x is defined as:

$$T_x(s) = \bar{s} \mid B^a_{sf_x}(s) = B_{sf_x}(\bar{s})$$

Note that since *bandwidth function* is piece-wise linear monotonic function, just find $T_x(s)$ for values for interesting points (where slope changes in either $B^a_{sf_x}$ or B_{sf_x}).

3. For each $cf_i \in sf_x$, apply T_x on *fair share* dimension of B_{cf_i} to get $B^e_{cf_i}$.

$$B^e_{cf_i}(T_x(s)) = B_{cf_i}(s)$$

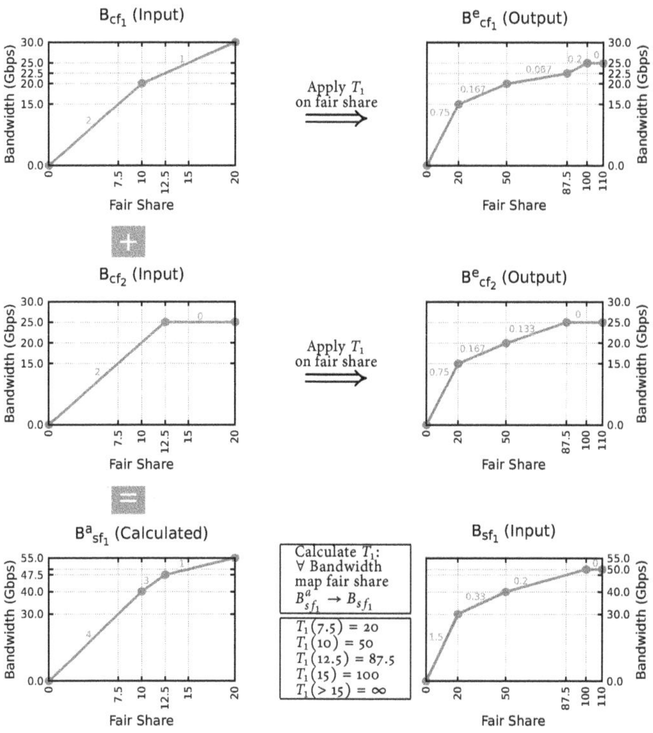

Figure 8: Bandwidth Function Transformation Example

Again, just applying the transformation at the interesting points (points where the slope of the function changes) is sufficient.

An example of creating effective *bandwidth function* is shown in Figure 8. *MPFA* algorithm as described in Section 5.3 is run over *cluster-fgs* as FlowGroups with their effective *bandwidth functions* to achieve hierarchical fairness.

When we run hierarchical *MPFA* in the topology shown in Figure 1, the allocation to cf_3 increases to 30Gbps, fully using bottleneck link l_9. However, if cf_2 has higher demand (say 100Gbps), then it will not receive benefit of cf_1 being bottlenecked early and sf_1 will not receive its full fair share of 20Gbps. To resolve this, we rerun the *bandwidth function* transformation for a *site-fg* when any of its member *cluster-fgs* is frozen due to an intra-site bottleneck link.

6. SYSTEM IMPLEMENTATION

This section describes various insights, design and implementation considerations that made BwE a practical and useful system.

6.1 Demand Estimation

Estimating demand correctly is important for fair allocation and high network utilization. Estimated demand should be greater than current usage to allow each FlowGroup to ramp its bandwidth use. But high estimated demand (compared to usage) of a high priority FlowGroup can waste bandwidth. In our experience, asking users to estimate their demand is untenable because user estimates are wildly inaccurate. Hence, BwE employs actual, near real-time measurements of application usage to estimate demand. BwE estimates FlowGroup demand by maintaining usage history: $Demand = \max(\max_{\Delta t}(usage) \times scale,\ min\_demand)$

We take the peak of a FlowGroup's usage across Δt time interval, multiply it with a factor $scale > 1$ and take the max with min_demand. Without the concept of min_demand, small flows (few Kbps) would ramp to their real demand too slowly. Empirically, we found that $\Delta t = 120s$, $scale = 1.1$ and $min\_demand = 10Mbps$ works well for *user-fg* for our network applications. We use different values of min_demand at different levels of the hierarchy.

6.2 WaterFill Allocation For Bursty Flows

The demands used in our WaterFill algorithm (Section 5.4) are based on peak historical usage and different child FlowGroups can peak at different times. This results in demand over-estimation and subsequently the WaterFill allocations can be too conservative. To account for burstiness and the resulting statistical multiplexing, we estimate a *burstiness factor* (≥ 1) for each FlowGroup based on its demand and sum of its children's demand:

$$burstiness\ factor = \frac{\sum_{\forall children} estimated\ demand}{parent's\ estimated\ demand}$$

Since estimated demand is based on peak historical usage (Section 6.1), the *burstiness factor* of a FlowGroup is a measure of sum of peak usages of children divided by peak of sum of usages of the children. We multiply a FlowGroup's allocation by its *burstiness factor* before running the WaterFill. This allows its children to burst as long as they are not bursting together. If a FlowGroup's children burst at uncoordinated times, then the *burstiness factor* is high, otherwise the value will be close to 1.

6.3 Fair Allocation for Satisfied FlowGroups

A *Satisfied FlowGroup* is one whose demand is less than or equal to its allocation. Initially, we throttled each satisfied FlowGroup strictly to its estimated demand. However we found that latency sensitive applications could not ramp fast enough to their fair share on a congested link. We next eliminated throttling allocations for all satisfied FlowGroups. However, this lead to oscillations in system behavior as a FlowGroup switched between throttled and unthrottled each time its usage increased.

Our current approach is to assign satisfied FlowGroups a stable allocation that reflects the *fair share at infinite demand*. This allocation is a FlowGroup's allocation if its demand grew to infinity while demand for other FlowGroups remained the same. When a high priority satisfied FlowGroup's usage increases, it will ramp almost immediately to its *fair share*. Other low-priority FlowGroups will be throttled at the next iteration of the BwE control loop. This implies that the capacity of a constrained link is oversubscribed and can result in transient loss if a FlowGroup's usage suddenly increases.

The naive approach for implementing *user-fg* allocation involves running our global allocation algorithm multiple times for each FlowGroup, assigning infinite demand to the target *user-fg* without modifying the demand of other *user-fgs*. Because multiple such runs across all FlowGroups does not scale, we run one instance of the global algorithm and pass to Cluster Enforcers the *bandwidth function* for the most constrained link for each FlowGroup. Assuming the most constrained link does not change, the Cluster Enforcer can efficiently calculate allocation for a FlowGroup with ∞ demand in the constrained link, assuming it becomes the bottleneck.

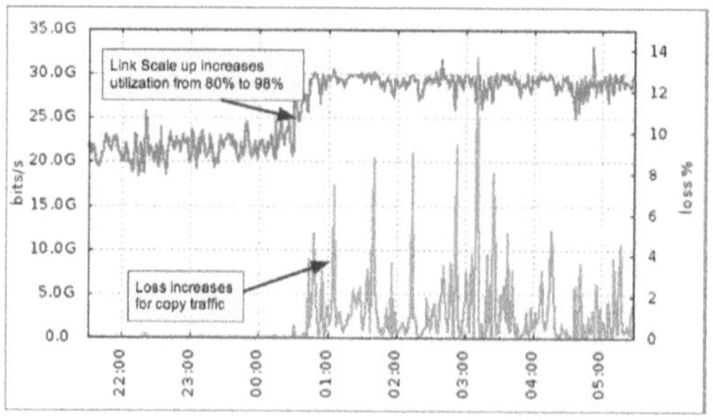

Figure 9: Improving Network Utilization

6.4 Improving Network Utilization

BwE allows network administrators to increase link utilization by deploying high throughput NETBLT [10]-like protocols for copy traffic. BwE is responsible for determining the flow transmission rate for these protocols. We mark packets for such copy flows with low priority DSCP values so that they absorb most of the transient network packet loss. To ensure that the system achieves high utilization (>90%) without affecting latency/loss sensitive flows such as web and video traffic, the BwE Global Enforcer supports two rounds of allocation.

- In the first round, link capacities are set conservatively (for example at 90% of actual capacity). All traffic types are allowed to participate in this round of allocation.
- In the second round, the Global Enforcer allocates only copy traffic, but it scales up the links aggressively, e.g., to 105% of link capacity.
- We also adjust link scaling factors depending on loss on the link. If a link shows loss for higher QoS classes, we reduce the scaling factor. This allows us to better achieve a balance between loss and utilization on a link.

Figure 9 shows link utilization increasing from 80% to 98% as we adjust the link capacity. The corresponding loss for copy traffic also increases to an average 2% loss with no increases in loss for loss-sensitive traffic.

6.5 Redundancy and Failure Handling

For scale and fault tolerance, we run multiple replicas at each level of the BwE hierarchy. There are N live and M cold standby Job Enforcers in each cluster. Hosts report all *task-fgs* belonging to the same *job-fg* to the same Job Enforcer, sharding different *job-fgs* across Job Enforcers by hashing <user name, job name, destination cluster, traffic_type>.

Cluster Enforcers run as master/hot standby pairs. Job Enforcers report all information to both. Both instances independently run the allocation algorithm and return bandwidth allocations to Job Enforcers. The Job Enforcers enforce the bandwidth allocations received from the master. If the master is unreachable Job Enforcers switch to the allocations received from the standby. We employ a similar redundancy approach between Global Enforcers and Cluster Enforcers.

Communication between BwE components is high priority and is not enforced. However, there can be edge scenarios where BwE components are unable to communicate with each other. Some examples are: BwE job failures (e.g. binaries go into a crash loop) causing hosts to stop receiving updated bandwidth allocations, network routing failures preventing Cluster Enforcers from receiving allocation from the Global Enforcers, or the network model becoming stale.

The general strategy for handling these failures is that we continue to use last known state (bandwidth allocations or capacity) for several minutes. For longer/sustained failures, in most cases we eliminate allocations and rely on QoS and TCP congestion management. For some traffic patterns such as copy-traffic we set a low static allocation. We have found this design pattern of defense by falling back to sub-optimal but still operable baseline systems invaluable to building robust network infrastructure.

7. EVALUATION

7.1 Micro-benchmarks on Test Jobs

We begin with some micro-benchmarks of the live BwE system to establish its baseline behavior. Figure 12(a) demonstrates BwE fairness across users running different number of TCP connections. Two users send traffic across a network configured to have 100Mbps of available capacity between the source/destination clusters. User1 has two connections and a weight of one. We vary the number of connections for User2 (shown on the x-axis) and its BwE assigned weight. The graph shows the throughput ratio is equivalent to the users weight ratio independent of the number of competing TCP flows.

Next we show how quickly BwE can enforce bandwidth allocations with and without the infinite demand feature (Section 6.3). In this scenario there are 2 users on a simulated 100 Mbps link. Initially, User1 has weight of 3 and User2 has weight of 1. At 120s, we change the weight of User2 to 12. In Figure 12(b), where the infinite demand feature is disabled, we observe that BwE converges at 580s. In Figure 12(c), where infinite demand feature is enabled, we observe it converges at 160s. This demonstrates BwE can enforce bandwidth allocations and converge in intervals of tens of seconds. This delay is reasonable for our production WAN network since large bandwidth consumers are primarily copy traffic.

7.2 System Scale

A significant challenge for BwE deployment is the system's sheer scale. Apart from organic growth to flows and network scale other reasons that affect system scale were supporting

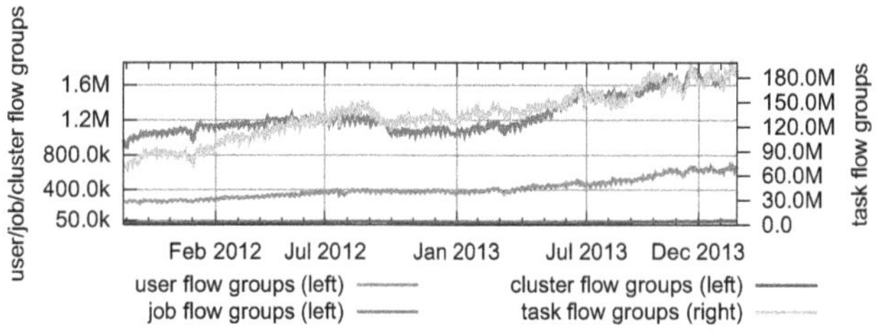

Figure 10: FlowGroup Counts

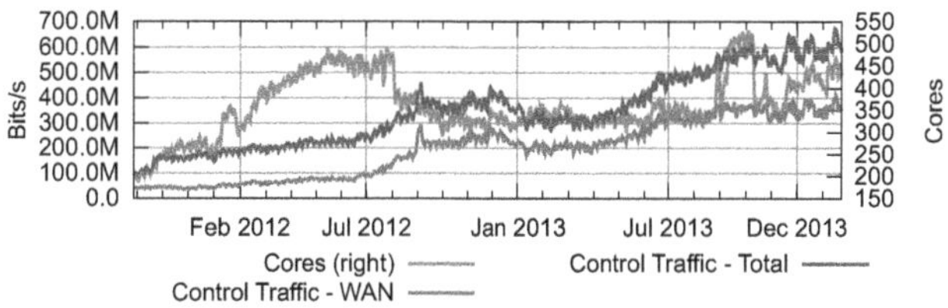

Figure 11: Resource overhead (Control System)

fine-grained bandwidth allocation and decreasing reporting interval for enforcement frequency.

Figure 10 shows growth in FlowGroups over time. As expected, as we go up in the hierarchy the number of FlowGroups drops significantly, allowing us to scale global components. Figure 11 shows the amount of resources used by our distributed deployment (excepting per-host overhead). It also shows the communication overhead of the control plane. We can conclude that the overall cost is very small relative to enforcing traffic generated by hundreds of thousands of cores using terabits/sec of bandwidth capacity.

Table 2 shows the number of FlowGroups on a congested link at one point in time relative to all outgoing flow groups from a major cluster enforcer. It gives an idea of overall scale in terms of the number of competing entities. There are portions of the network with millions of competing FlowGroups. Table 3 shows our algorithm run time at various levels in the hierarchy. We show max and average (across multiple instances) for each level except global. Overall, our goal is to enforce large flows in a few minutes, which we are able to achieve. The table also shows that the frequency of collecting and distributing data is a major contributing factor to reaction time.

	site	cluster	user	job	task
One Congested Link	336	3.0k	40k	400k	12714k
Largest Cluster Enforcer	55	3.5k	63k	165k	15660k
Avg across cluster enforcers	53	1.5k	22k	60k	6496k
Global	1594	47.4k	682k	1825k	194088k

Table 2: Number of *-*fg*s (at various levels in BwE) for a congested link and for a large cluster enforcer.

	Algo Run-time		Algo	Reporting
	Max(s)	Mean(s)	Interval(s)	Interval(s)
Global Enforcer	3	-	10	10
Cluster Enforcer	.16	.15	4	10
Job Enforcer	<0.01	<0.01	4	5

Table 3: Algorithm run time and feedback cycle in seconds. Algorithm interval is how frequently algorithm is invoked and Reporting interval is the duration between two reports from the children in BwE hierarchy.

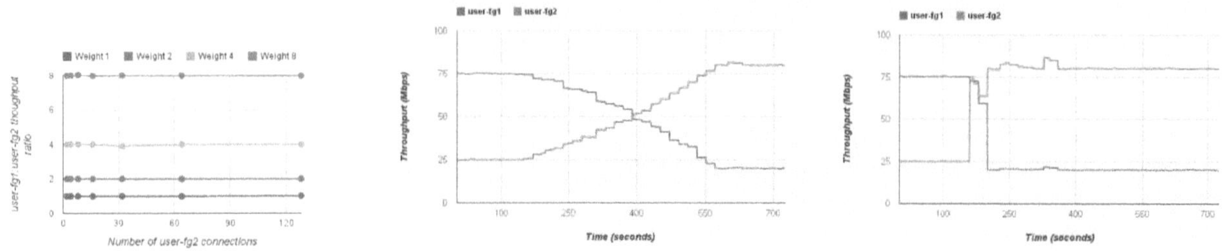

(a) BwE Fairness (b) Allocation Capped at Demand (c) Allocation not Capped at Demand

Figure 12: BwE compliance

	Min	Max	Mean
Number of *user-fg*	3%	11%	7%
Number of *job-fg*	3%	10%	6%
Usage	94%	99%	97%

Table 4: Percentage of FlowGroups enforced.

BwE tracks about 500k *user-fgs* and millions of *job-fgs*, but only enforces a small fraction of these. Processing for unenforced FlowGroups is lightweight at higher levels of the BwE hierarchy allowing the system to scale. Table 4 shows the fraction of enforced flows and the fraction of total usage they represent. BwE only enforces 10% of the flows but these flows account for 94% of the traffic. We also found that for congested links, those with more than 80% utilization, less than 1% of the utilization belonged to unenforced flows. This indicates BwE is able to focus its work on the subset of flows that most contribute to utilization and any congestion.

We introduced a number of system optimizations to address growth along the following dimensions: 1) Flow Groups: Organic growth and increase in specificity (for e.g., delegation). For example, the overall design has been serving us through a growth of 10x from BwE's inception (20M to 200M). 2) Paths: Traffic Engineering introduced new paths in the system. 3) Links: Organic network Growth 4) Reporting frequency: there is a balance between enforcement accuracy and resource overhead. 5) Bottleneck links: The number of bottleneck links affects the overall run time of the algorithm on the Global Enforcer.

8. DISCUSSION AND FUTURE WORK

BwE requires accurate network modeling since it is a key input to the allocation problem. This is challenging in an environment where devices fail often and new technologies are being introduced rapidly. In many cases, we lack standard APIs to expose network topology, routing and pathing information. With Software Defined Networking, we hope to see improvements in this area. Another challenge is that for scalability, we often combine a symmetric full mesh topology into a single abstract link. This assumption however breaks during network failures and handling these edge cases continues to be a challenge.

Our FlowGroup abstraction is limited in that it allows users sending from multiple source/destination cluster pairs over the same bottleneck link to have an advantage. We are exploring abstractions where we can provide fair share to all users across all bottleneck links irrespective of the number and placement of communicating cluster pairs. Other areas of research include improving the reaction time of the control system while scaling to a large number of FlowGroups, providing fairness at longer timescales (hours or days) and including flow deadlines in the objective function for fairness.

8.1 Broader Applicability

Our work is motivated by the observation that per-flow bandwidth allocation is no longer the ideal abstraction for emerging WAN use cases. We have seen substantial benefit of BwE to applications for WAN distributed computing and believe that it is also applicable to a number of emerging application classes in the broader Internet. For example, video streaming services for collaboration or entertainment increasingly dominate WAN communication. These applications have well-understood bandwidth requirements with step functions in additional utility from incremental bandwidth allocation. Consider that a 480P video stream may receive no incremental benefit from an additional 100Kbps of bandwidth; only sufficient additional bandwidth to enable 720P streaming is useful. Finally, homes and businesses are trending toward multiple simultaneous video streams with known relative priority and incremental bandwidth utility, all sharing a single bottleneck with known capacity.

Next, consider the move toward an Internet of Things [29] where hundreds of devices in a home or business may have varying wide-area communication requirements. These applications may range from home automation, to security, health monitoring, to backup. For instance, home security may have moderate bandwidth requirements but be of the highest priority. Remote backup may have substantial, sustained bandwidth requirements. However, the backup does not have a hard deadline and is largely insensitive to packet loss. Investigating BwE-based mechanisms for fair allocation based on an understanding of relative application utility in response to additional bandwidth is an interesting area of future work.

9. RELATED WORK

This paper focuses on allocating bandwidth among users in emerging multi-datacenter WAN environments. Given the generality of the problem, we necessarily build on a rich body of related efforts, including utility functions [8], weighted fair sharing [2, 11, 12, 8] and host-based admission control [9]. We extend existing Utility max-min approaches [8] for multi-path routing and hierarchical fairness.

Weighted queuing is one common bandwidth allocation paradigm. While a good starting point, we find weights are insufficient for delivering user guarantees. Relative to weighted queuing, we focus on rate limiting based on demand estimation. BwE control is centralized and protocol agnostic, i.e., general to TCP and UDP. This is in contrast to DRL [25], which solves the problem via distributed rate control for TCP while not accounting for network capacity explicitly.

Netshare [20] and Seawall [30] also use weighted bandwidth allocation mechanisms. Seawall in particular achieves per-link proportional fairness. We have found max-min fairness to be more practical because it provides better isolation.

Gatekeeper [26] also employs host-based hierarchical token buckets to share bandwidth among data center tenants, emphasizing work-conserving allocation. Gatekeeper however assumes a simplified topology for every tenant. BwE considers complex topologies, multi-path forwarding, centralized bandwidth allocation, and a range of flexible bandwidth allocation mechanisms. Secondnet [15] provides pair-wise bandwidth guarantees but requires accurate user-provided demands and is not work conserving.

Oktopus [4] proposes a datacenter tree topology with specified edge capacity. While suitable for datacenters, it is not a natural fit for the WAN where user demands vary based on source-destination pairs. The BwE abstraction is more fine-grained, with associated implementation and configuration challenges. Oktopus also ties the problem of bandwidth allocation with VM placement. Our work however does not affect computation placement but rather takes the source of demand as fixed. We believe there are opportunities to apply such joint optimization to BwE. Datacenter bandwidth sharing efforts such as ElasticSwitch [24], FairCloud [23] and EyeQ [18] focus on a hose model for tenants. EyeQ uses ECN to detect congestion at the edge and assumes a congestion free core. In contrast, our flow-wise bandwidth sharing model allows aggregation across users and is explicitly focused on a congested core.

Recent efforts such as SWAN [16], and B4 [17] are closely related but focus on the network and routing infrastructure to effectively scale and utilize emerging WAN environments. In particular, they focus on employing Software Defined Networking constructs for controlling and efficiently scaling the network. Our work is complementary and focuses on enforcing policies given an existing multipath routing configuration. Jointly optimizing network routing, and bandwidth allocation is an area for future investigation. TEMPUS [19] focuses on optimizing network utilization by accounting for deadlines for long-lived flows . Our bandwidth sharing model applies to non-long-lived flows as well and does not require deadlines to be known ahead of time. Flow deadlines open up possibility of further optimization (for example, by smoothing bandwidth allocation over a longer period of time) and that remains an area for future work for us.

Work in RSVP, Differentiated Services and Traffic Engineering [14, 27, 7, 22, 21, 1, 5] overlaps in terms of goals. However, these approaches are network centric, assuming that host control is not possible. In some sense, we take the opposite approach, considering an orthogonal hierarchical control infrastructure that leverages host-based demand measurement and enforcement.

Congestion Manager [3] is an inspiration for our work on BwE, enabling a range of flexible bandwidth allocation policies to individual flows based on an understanding of application requirements. However, Congestion Manager still manages bandwidth at the granularity of individual hosts, whereas we focus on the infrastructure and algorithms for bandwidth allocation in a large-scale distributed computing WAN environment.

10. CONCLUSIONS

In this paper, we present Bandwidth Enforcer (BwE), our mechanism for WAN bandwidth allocation. BwE allocates bandwidth to competing applications based on flexible policy configured by *bandwidth functions*. BwE supports hierarchical bandwidth allocation and delegation among services while simultaneously accounting for multi-path WAN communication.

Based on multiple years of production experience, we summarize a number of important benefits to our WAN. First, BwE provides isolation among competing services, delivering plentiful capacity in the common case while maintaining required capacity under failure and maintenance scenarios. Second, we provide a single point for specifying allocation policy to administrators. While pathing, RTT, and capacity can shift substantially, BwE continues to allocate bandwidth according to policy. Finally, BwE enables the WAN to run at higher levels of utilization than before. By tightly integrating new loss-insensitive file transfer protocols running at low priority with BwE, we run many of our WAN links at 90% utilization.

Acknowledgements

Many teams within Google collaborated towards the success of the BwE project. We would like to acknowledge the BwE development, test and operations groups including Aaron Racine, Alex Docauer, Alex Perry, Anand Kanagala, Andrew McGregor, Angus Lees, Deepak Nulu, Dmitri Nikulin, Eric Yan, Jon Zolla, Kai Song, Kirill Mendelev, Mahesh Kallahalla, Matthew Class, Michael Frumkin, Michael O'Reilly, Ming Xu, Mukta Gupta, Nan Hua, Nikhil Panpalia, Phong Chuong, Rajiv Ranjan, Richard Alimi, Sankalp Singh, Subbaiah Venkata, Vijay Chandramohan, Xijie Zeng, Yuanbo Zhu, Aamer Mahmood, Ben Treynor, Bikash Koley and Urs Hölzle for their significant contributions to the project. We would also like to thank our shepherd, Srikanth Kandula, and the anonymous SIGCOMM reviewers for their useful feedback.

11. REFERENCES

[1] Wikipedia: Differentiated services. http://en.wikipedia.org/wiki/Differentiated_services.

[2] Allalouf, M., and Shavitt, Y. Centralized and Distributed Algorithms for Routing and Weighted Max-Min Fair Bandwidth Allocation. *IEEE/ACM Trans. Networking 16*, 5 (2008), 1015–1024.

[3] Balakrishnan, H., Rahul, H. S., and Seshan, S. An integrated congestion management architecture for internet hosts. In *In Proc. ACM SIGCOMM* (1999), pp. 175–187.

[4] Ballani, H., Costa, P., Karagiannis, T., and Rowstron, A. Towards predictable datacenter networks. In *SIGCOMM* (2011).

[5] Blake, S., Black, D., Carlson, M., Davies, E., Wang, Z., and Weiss, W. An Architecture for Differentiated Service. RFC 2475 (Informational), December 1998. Updated by RFC 3260.

[6] Boudec, J.-Y. Rate adaptation, congestion control and fairness: A tutorial, 2000.

[7] Braden, R., Zhang, L., Berson, S., Herzog, S., and Jamin, S. Resource ReSerVation Protocol (RSVP) – Version 1 Functional Specification. RFC 2205 (Proposed Standard), September 1997. Updated by RFCs 2750, 3936, 4495.

[8] Cao, Z., and Zegura, E. W. Utility max-min: An application-oriented bandwidth allocation scheme. In *INFOCOM* (1999).

[9] Choi, B.-K., and Bettati, R. Endpoint admission control: network based approach. In *Distributed Computing Systems, 2001. 21st International Conference on.* (Apr 2001), pp. 227–235.

[10] Clark, D. D., Lambert, M. L., and Zhang, L. Netblt: A high throughput transport protocol. In *Proceedings of the ACM Workshop on Frontiers in Computer Communications Technology* (New York, NY, USA, 1988), SIGCOMM '87, ACM, pp. 353–359.

[11] Danna, E., Hassidim, A., Kaplan, H., Kumar, A., Mansour, Y., Raz, D., and Segalov, M. Upward Max Min Fairness. In *INFOCOM* (2012), pp. 837–845.

[12] Danna, E., Mandal, S., and Singh, A. A Practical Algorithm for Balancing the Max-min Fairness and Throughput Objectives in Traffic Engineering. In *Proc. INFOCOM* (March 2012), pp. 846–854.

[13] Dean, J., and Ghemawat, S. Mapreduce: Simplified data processing on large clusters. *Commun. ACM 51*, 1 (January 2008), 107–113.

[14] Fortz, B., Rexford, J., and Thorup, M. Traffic Engineering with Traditional IP Routing Protocols. *IEEE Communications Magazine 40* (2002), 118–124.

[15] Guo, C., Lu, G., Wang, H. J., Yang, S., Kong, C., Sun, P., Wu, W., and Zhang, Y. SecondNet: A data center network virtualization architecture with bandwidth guarantees. In *CoNEXT* (2010).

[16] Hong, C.-Y., Kandula, S., Mahajan, R., Zhang, M., Gill, V., Nanduri, M., and Wattenhofer, R. Have Your Network and Use It Fully Too: Achieving High Utilization in Inter-Datacenter WANs. In *Proc. SIGCOMM* (August 2013).

[17] Jain, S., Kumar, A., Mandal, S., Ong, J., Poutievski, L., Singh, A., Venkata, S., Wanderer, J., Zhou, J., Zhu, M., Zolla, J., Hölzle, U., Stuart, S., and Vahdat, A. B4: Experience with a Globally-Deployed Software Defined WAN. In *Proceedings of the ACM SIGCOMM 2013* (2013), ACM, pp. 3–14.

[18] Jeyakumar, V., Alizadeh, M., Mazieres, D., Prabhakar, B., Kim, C., and Greenberg, A. Eyeq: Practical network performance isolation at the edge. In *Proc. of NSDI* (2013), USENIX Association, pp. 297–312.

[19] Kandula, S., Menache, I., Schwartz, R., and Babbula, S. R. Calendaring for wide area networks. In *Proc. SIGCOMM* (August 2014).

[20] Lam, T., Radhakrishnan, S., Vahdat, A., and Varghese, G. NetShare: Virtualizing data center networks across services. Tech. rep., 2010.

[21] Minei, I., and Lucek, J. *MPLS-Enabled Applications: Emerging Developments and New Technologies.* Wiley Series on Communications Networking & Distributed Systems. Wiley, 2008.

[22] Osborne, E., and Simha, A. *Traffic Engineering with Mpls (Paperback).* Networking Technology Series. Cisco Press, 2002.

[23] Popa, L., Krishnamurthy, A., Ratnasamy, S., and Stoica, I. Faircloud: Sharing the network in cloud computing. In *Proceedings of the 10th ACM Workshop on Hot Topics in Networks* (New York, NY, USA, 2011), HotNets-X, ACM, pp. 22:1–22:6.

[24] Popa, L., Yalagandula, P., Banerjee, S., Mogul, J. C., Turner, Y., and Santos, J. R. Elasticswitch: Practical work-conserving bandwidth guarantees for cloud computing. In *Proceedings of the ACM SIGCOMM 2013 Conference on SIGCOMM* (New York, NY, USA, 2013), SIGCOMM '13, ACM, pp. 351–362.

[25] Raghavan, B., Vishwanath, K., Ramabhadran, S., Yocum, K., and Snoeren, A. C. Cloud control with distributed rate limiting. In *In SIGCOMM* (2007).

[26] Rodrigues, H., Santos, J., Turner, Y., Soares, P., and Guedes, D. Gatekeeper: Supporting bandwidth guarantees for multi-tenant datacenter networks. In *Workshop on I/O Virtualization* (2011).

[27] Roughan, M., Thorup, M., and Zhang, Y. Traffic Engineering with Estimated Traffic Matrices. In *Proc. IMC* (2003), pp. 248–258.

[28] Saltzer, J. H., Reed, D. P., and Clark, D. D. End-to-end arguments in system design. *ACM Trans. Comput. Syst. 2*, 4 (November 1984), 277–288.

[29] Sarma, S., Brock, D. L., and Ashton, K. The networked physical world–proposals for engineering the next generation of computing, commerce & automatic identification. *White Paper, Auto-ID Center, MIT. Designed b y Foxner. www. foxner. com* (2000).

[30] Shieh, A., Kandula, S., Greenberg, A., Kim, C., and Saha, B. Sharing the data center network. In *NSDI* (2011).

A Declarative and Expressive Approach to Control Forwarding Paths in Carrier-Grade Networks

Renaud Hartert *, Stefano Vissicchio *, Pierre Schaus *, Olivier Bonaventure *,
Clarence Filsfils †, Thomas Telkamp †, Pierre Francois ‡

* Université catholique de Louvain † Cisco Systems, Inc. ‡ IMDEA Networks Institute
* firstname.lastname@uclouvain.be † {cfilsfil,thtelkam}@cisco.com ‡ pierre.francois@imdea.org

ABSTRACT

SDN simplifies network management by relying on declarativity (high-level interface) and expressiveness (network flexibility). We propose a solution to support those features while preserving high robustness and scalability as needed in carrier-grade networks. Our solution is based on (i) a two-layer architecture separating connectivity and optimization tasks; and (ii) a centralized optimizer called DEFO, which translates high-level goals expressed almost in natural language into compliant network configurations. Our evaluation on real and synthetic topologies shows that DEFO improves the state of the art by (i) achieving better trade-offs for classic goals covered by previous works, (ii) supporting a larger set of goals (refined traffic engineering and service chaining), and (iii) optimizing large ISP networks in few seconds. We also quantify the gains of our implementation, running Segment Routing on top of IS-IS, over possible alternatives (RSVP-TE and OpenFlow).

CCS Concepts

•**Networks** → **Network architectures; Traffic engineering algorithms; Network management;** *Routing protocols;* •**Theory of computation** → *Constraint and logic programming;*

Keywords

SDN; traffic engineering; service chaining; segment routing; MPLS; ISP; optimization

*R. Hartert is a research fellow of F.R.S.-FNRS, and S. Vissicchio is a postdoctoral researcher of F.R.S.-FNRS.

SIGCOMM '15, August 17 - 21, 2015, London, United Kingdom
© 2015 ACM. ISBN 978-1-4503-3542-3/15/08...$15.00
DOI: http://dx.doi.org/10.1145/2785956.2787495

1. INTRODUCTION

By promising to overcome major problems of traditional per-device network management (e.g., see [1]), centralized architectures enabled by protocols like OpenFlow [2] and segment routing [3] are attracting huge interest from both researchers and operators. Two features are key to this success: declarativity and expressiveness. The former improves manageability, promoting abstractions and high-level interfaces to configuration. The latter enables flexibility of network behavior, e.g., in terms of packet forwarding and modification.

Unfortunately, prior works on Software Defined Networking (SDN) do not cover carrier-grade networks, i.e., geographically-distributed networks with hundreds of nodes like Internet Service Provider (ISP) ones. Those networks have special needs: Beyond manageability and flexibility, ISP operators also have to guarantee high scalability (e.g., to support all the Internet prefixes at tens of Points of Presence) and preserve network performance upon failures (e.g., to comply with Service Level Agreements). Moreover, the large scale and geographical distribution of those networks exacerbates SDN challenges, like controller reactivity, controller-to-switch communication and equipment upgrade. Consequently, SDN solutions targeting campuses [2], enterprises [4] and data-centers (DCs) [5], cannot be easily ported to carrier-grade networks. Even approaches designed for wide area and inter-DC networks [6, 7, 8] do not fit. Indeed, they assume that (i) the scale of the network (e.g., number of devices and geographical distances) is small, (ii) scalability and robustness play a more limited role (e.g., because of the small number of destinations [6]), and (iii) the SDN controller may apply some control over traffic sources (e.g., [7]).

Nevertheless, carrier-grade networks would also benefit from an SDN-like approach. Currently, network management (i) relies on protocols with practical limitations, either in terms of expressiveness (as for link-state IGPs, constrained by the adopted shortest-path routing model) or of scalability and overhead (like for MPLS RSVP-TE, based on per-path tunnel signaling); and

(ii) requires operators to manually fine-tune those protocols and handle complex interactions between them. This likely leads to erroneous and sub-optimal network configurations, as well as deployment obstacles for new functionalities like service chaining [9].

In this paper, we propose a declarative and expressive approach to program intra-domain forwarding in carrier-grade networks. We make two sets of contributions. First, we propose an effective, easily-deployable centralized architecture, based on a clear separation between connectivity and optimization tasks. In its realization, we rely on the robustness of a link-state Interior Gateway Protocol (IGP) for the former tasks and on the flexibility and scalability of segment routing for the latter ones. Second, we design and implement a network controller called DEFO (Declarative and Expressive Forwarding Optimizer). To support declarativity and expressiveness, DEFO automatically translates high-level goals of operators into network configurations. For efficiency and scalability, DEFO computes optimized paths by smartly combining (i.e., stitching together) paths used for connectivity. Moreover, it systematically takes advantage of opportunities provided by typical carrier-grade networks. Notably, it leverages their high physical redundancy [10, 11] by natively supporting even traffic splitting over multiple (ECMP) paths[1]. As a result, DEFO achieves huge optimizations by spreading the traffic of a small number of flows on multiple (ECMP) paths.

A more detailed list of contributions follows.

Network architecture. We follow the recent trend to separate traffic engineering and connectivity tasks [6, 8, 12]. However, in contrast with previous proposals, our architecture *explicitly* separates two layers. The underlying *connectivity layer* ensures network-wide reachability, robustness and fast failure recovery, by generating and updating *connectivity paths* for each pair of nodes in the network. The overlying *optimization layer* defines optimized paths for specific flows. When defined, optimized paths overwrite connectivity ones. DEFO determines optimized paths, while the connectivity layer is configured by operators. (§2)

High-level controller interface. To support declarativity, DEFO exposes a high-level interface for network configuration, implementing a small Domain Specific Language (DSL). This interface is based on the abstractions of *forwarding functions* and *network goals*, enabling the definition of a wide range of objectives for forwarding paths. Beyond classic traffic engineering, the DEFO API supports the declaration of refined goals, including delay-respectful, multi-objective and service chaining ones. (§3)

Expressive routing model. To overcome limitations of existing models based on shortest-path routing or end-to-end tunneling, we rely on a new model, called Middlepoint Routing (MR). MR abstracts forwarding paths as concatenations of *middlepoints*, i.e., nodes between which paths are pre-defined. By natively encompassing multi-path routing, MR provides a compact representation of sets of paths. Moreover, it supports the definition of optimized paths as combinations of connectivity sub-paths. (§4)

Algorithms for efficient path computation. Computing paths that realize DEFO goals in a carrier-grade network is far from being easy. As an example, a classic traffic engineering goal consists in minimizing the maximally loaded link [13]. Even admitting arbitrary flow splitting on each node (practically impossible to achieve), computing an optimal solution for a 100-node ISP network with the linear program for the corresponding multi-commodity flow problem (MCF) took us more than one night on a powerful server. To achieve scalability and flexibility, DEFO relies on Constraint Programming (CP) [14]. Within CP, we propose efficient data structures and new heuristics that (i) implement MR and leverage it to limit the number of decision variables; (ii) provide building blocks that can be re-used for multiple goals; and (iii) compute, in few seconds, excellent solutions to problems harder than MCF. (§4)

Robust and scalable realization. Our proposed architecture realization leverages existing technologies and can be implemented today. It relies on a link-state IGP like IS-IS at the connectivity layer, and Segment Routing (SR) [3] at the optimization one. SR enables our approach to be expressive and scalable: It indeed enables routers to enrich packets with instructions on intermediate destinations to be traversed, hence providing a perfect match to our MR model. Further, we describe our implementation of DEFO. (§5)

Evaluation on real ISP topologies and traffic matrices. By computing excellent solutions to disparate goals while limiting optimization overhead, DEFO outperforms state-of-the-art traffic engineering techniques like [13, 15]. Intuitively, DEFO's optimization power comes from the adopted routing model (MR), which is less constrained than shortest-path routing and natively supports multi-path routing (contrary to end-to-end tunneling). Given its very limited execution time, DEFO can readily be used both offline (for offline traffic engineering or what-if analyses) and online (for path recomputation upon traffic changes or failures). On the implementation side, our results quantify scalability gains provided by SR (e.g., thanks to its native support for multi-path routing) with respect to alternatives like MPLS and OpenFlow. This also provides the first-of-its-kind assessment of advantages provided by SR in real networks. (§6-8)

We finally discuss possible extensions of our proposal (§9), compare it with related works ((§10), and draw conclusions (§11).

[1]we restrict to even traffic splitting as it is currently supported by all IGP-speaking routers.

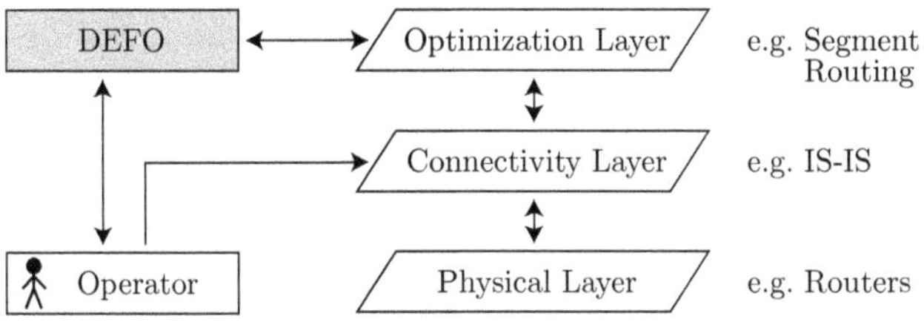

Figure 1: Proposed architecture.

2. ARCHITECTURE

In this section, we detail the role of every component of our architecture, which is illustrated in Fig. 1.

The right part of the figure highlights that two logical layers are installed on top of the physical network topology (routers and links). The underlying connectivity layer is responsible for the default forwarding behavior and for network-wide connectivity. It defines *connectivity paths* between all pairs of routers, hence for any traffic flow possibly traversing the network. In contrast, the optimization layer defines exceptions to this default routing behavior. It implements *optimized paths* used for a subset of the traversing flows (e.g., a subset of router pairs). Optimized paths overwrite connectivity ones: Whenever an optimized path is defined, the corresponding flows always use it. While connectivity and optimization layers represent a logic separation, they can also be implemented by different protocols running on the routers. This provides a cleaner design and comes with a set of advantages. For example, it enables changes in the optimization layer (expected to be frequent) without any impact on the connectivity one. It also simplifies the assessment of the impact of changes in the connectivity layer (e.g., consequently to less frequent events like failures). Finally, it ensures that controller failures do not disrupt forwarding paths.

The connectivity layer is configured (possibly once in the network lifetime) by operators. This choice is motivated by several reasons. First, it maximizes the utility of the operators' domain knowledge (expected traffic matrix, capacity of links, etc.) to provide a good basis for network optimization. Second, it leaves operators with a mean to take back the control of the network, e.g., in the case of major problems on the controller or for maintenance operations that cannot be supported by DEFO (e.g., router physical replacement). Third, it facilitates progressive deployment of our proposal.

DEFO controls the optimization layer to fine-tune forwarding. It receives high-level goals from operators, and automatically translates them into optimized paths, e.g., configurations of the optimization-layer protocol. Since optimized paths are preferred over connectivity ones, DEFO decides the actual forwarding paths used for any traffic flow crossing the network. DEFO can perform this goal-to-path translation for any change of connectivity paths, traffic flows or physical topology, e.g., for online traffic engineering.

function	DSL syntax	semantics
max load	d.`load`	maximum load of any link in $F(d)$
max delay	d.`delay`	maximum delay of source-destination paths in $F(d)$
deviations	d.`deviations`	number of deviations from connectivity paths in $F(d)$
traversal	d `passThrough` S	true if $F(d)$ crosses any node in S, false otherwise
sequencing	d `passThrough` S_1 `then` S_2 ... `then` S_k	true if $F(d)$ sequentially crosses nodes in $S_1 \ldots S_k$
avoid	d `avoid` S	true if no node in S is also in $F(d)$, false otherwise

d, $F(d)$ and $S, S_1, \ldots, S_k$ respectively represent any demand, the forwarding paths for d, and sets of network nodes.

Figure 2: Constructs of the current DEFO DSL.

3. EXPRESSING NETWORK GOALS

DEFO exposes a high-level interface, based on a small Scala DSL [16]. It enables operators to intuitively declare desired characteristics of forwarding paths.

The central abstractions used in the interface are the concepts of demand, forwarding function and goal. A *demand* is an aggregate of flows. In the following, we focus on demands at the granularity of source-destination pairs, for simplicity. A *forwarding function* maps a set of links to the value of a parameter (e.g., maximum load) associated to them. Our DSL includes constructs for pre-defined forwarding functions. It permits forwarding functions to be applied to sets of links, to paths or to demands. In the latter case, a forwarding function maps a demand to the value of a parameter associated to the forwarding paths for that demand. Fig. 2 details the forwarding functions currently supported by DEFO (when applied to demands). A *goal* is defined by forwarding functions applied to demands. Those functions can be composed as (i) constraints that restrict the set of forwarding paths for given demands; and (ii) objective functions specifying parameters to be optimized.

In the following, we show examples of DEFO goal definitions. They illustrate both usage of forwarding functions and practically-meaningful compositions of them. The examples include standard Scala keywords like `val` for value declaration and `<-` for variable assignment in a loop. Variables storing parameters not determined by DEFO, like the network topology (`topology` variable) or sets of traffic demands (`Demands`, `LowDelayDemands` and `SecDemands` variables), are dynamically initialized at runtime, e.g., reading from preconfigured input files provided by operators or routing daemons.

Classic Traffic Engineering Goals. The use of resources often needs to be optimized in carrier-grade networks. For example, the classic *MinMaxLoad* goal consists in minimizing the load of the maximally loaded link, e.g., to avoid performance bottlenecks. It can be declared in DEFO in two lines.

```
var MaxLoad = max(for(l<-topology.links){yield l.load})
val goal = new Goal(topology){ minimize(MaxLoad) }
```

Tactical Traffic Engineering Goals. To limit traffic disruptions, operators are often reluctant to change many forwarding paths, and can prefer sub-optimal configurations to an unbounded number of path changes. DEFO forwarding functions can be combined to express those tactical goals. As an example, the following code instructs DEFO to find the best solution bringing all link utilization under a certain threshold with at most 2 deviations from connectivity paths.

```
val goal = new Goal(topology){
 for(d<-Demands) add(d.deviations <= 2)
 for(l<-topology.links) add(l.load <= 0.9 l.capacity)
 minimize(MaxLoad)}
```

Refined Goals. Operators often have to accommodate specific (e.g., per-customer) needs. In DEFO, goals including arbitrary combinations of the forwarding functions in Fig. 2 are supported by adding constraints and changing the objective function. The following example shows how to define a *delay-respectful goal*, that is, a variant of MinMaxLoad with constraints on the maximum delay experienced by specific demands. In the example, the latency of every network path is assumed to be known by DEFO, e.g., as a result of few active measurements. Our DSL also permits to define other delay-respectful goals, e.g., with delay constraints expressed as a percentage of their current values or delays for given demands in the objective function.

```
val goal = new Goal(topology){
  for(d <- LowDelayDemands) add(d.latency <= 10.ms)
  minimize(MaxLoad)}
```

DEFO also supports *multi-objective goals* [17]. The next snippet shows a goal in which both the maximum link load and the average latency have to be optimized.

```
val goal = new Goal(topology){
  minimize(MaxLoad, AvgLatency)}
```

Support for New Applications. Many operators have lately shown interest for *service chaining*, i.e., the ability to steer packets through a sequence of services. In the example below, each demand in `SecDemands` is forced to pass first through one firewall in `FirewallSet` (whose position is assumed to be known by the operator) and through either `IPS1` or `IPS2` after.

```
val goal = new Goal(topology){
  for(d <- SecDemands){
    add(d passThrough FirewallSet then ('IPS1, 'IPS2))}
  minimize(MaxLoad)}
```

The `avoid` and `passThrough` constructs can also be used to specify *anycast* goals, in which a set of routers must be avoided or forcedly used. This meets the needs of operators that have to comply with political or business rules, like preventing or ensuring that given traffic flows cross a specific country.

Finally, operators can run DEFO to achieve the declared goal, possibly specifying an upper bound for its computation time.

```
DEFOptimizer(goal).solve(30.sec)
```

Note that infeasible goals can be defined in our DSL, e.g., trying to force a demand through an isolated node or requiring a link utilization that cannot be achieved on the given topology and input demands. In our implementation, DEFO discards unsatisfiable constraints, computes a solution satisfying the other ones, and returns a warning to the operator. Similarly, if DEFO does not terminate in the specified time, it returns the best solution found during that time.

4. OPTIMIZED PATH COMPUTATION

In this section, we describe how DEFO computes forwarding paths. Namely, we detail how it tackles the challenges posed by the need for (i) supporting a wide variety of possible input goals (defined by arbitrary combinations of forwarding functions in Fig. 2), and (ii) fast computation of solutions to computationally-hard (translation) problems. First, we present the Middlepoint Routing model, internally used by DEFO for a compact representation of paths (§4.1). Then, we overview DEFO formal representation of input goals in terms of Middlepoint Routing instances (§4.2). Finally, we describe the optimization algorithm that it runs to compute compliant optimized paths (§4.3).

4.1 The Middlepoint Routing Model

DEFO relies on the Middlepoint Routing (MR) model. MR is similar to the pathlet routing model [18, 19] in that it represents paths as concatenations of sub-paths. In contrast to pathlet routing, however, MR is based on forwarding graphs rather than single paths. This generalization enables to incorporate equal-cost multipath in the model, and to provide a compact representation of several distinct paths between any source-destination pair. Moreover, we use MR to represent forwarding paths rather than for routing protocol design.

An MR instance represents acyclic paths from any source s to any destination d as sequences of acyclic graphs $\mathcal{S} = G_1, \dots, G_n$, with $n \geq 1$. In $\mathcal{S}$, any pair of consecutive graphs G_i and G_{i+1} (with $i = 1, \dots, n-1$) share a single common node m_i, which is the sink of G_i and the root of G_{i+1}. We refer to any graph in $\mathcal{S}$ as *partial forwarding graph (PFG)*, and to any shared node between two consecutive PFGs as *middlepoint*. Of course, a PFG can represent a single path. In an MR instance, a source-destination pair is associated to one or more sequences $\mathcal{S}_1, \dots, \mathcal{S}_N$ of PFGs. As an illustration, consider Fig. 3. Circles and arrows respectively represent routers and corresponding forwarding next-hops, while dashed squares identify PFGs. The MR representation of the paths from s to t is then given by sequences $\mathcal{S}_1 = [G_{(s,m)}, G_{(m,t)}]$ and $\mathcal{S}_2 = [G_{(s,t)}]$.

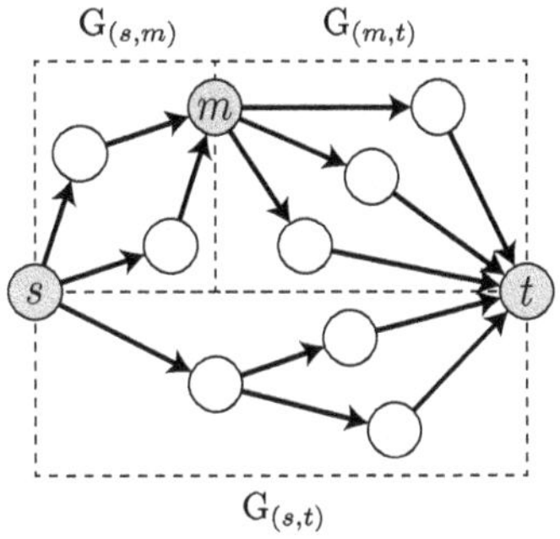

Figure 3: MR representations of $s - t$ paths.

In the specific case of our two-layer architecture, each PFG represents connectivity paths. Since PFGs are defined by the connectivity layer, we can simplify the representation of optimized paths as a set of middlepoint sequences. The right part of Fig. 3 also reports the simplified MR representation of $s - t$ paths, which is $\{[m], []\}$, under the assumption $G_{(s,t)}$ represents the connectivity paths from s to t.

Intuitively, DEFO uses the compact representation of paths provided by MR to limit the number of decision variables in the forwarding optimization. Indeed, it associates decision variables to the sequences of middlepoints to be used for a given traffic flow. In Fig. 3, for instance, DEFO uses 2 variables (for the two middlepoint sequences from s to t) instead of 8 (as needed if variables were associated to single paths) or 23 (as needed to represent traversed links and paths, like in classic linear programming formulations). In the following, we explain how DEFO computes the value for middlepoint sequences.

4.2 Network Goal Formalization

DEFO formalizes an input goal as an (initially empty) MR instance with associated constraints and optimization functions. This formalization is based on the *Constraint Programming (CP)* optimization framework [14]. A CP problem is defined by a set of variables, each having its own finite domain of possible values, and a set of constraints that apply to them. Contrary to linear programming, constraints are implemented by algorithms that preserve consistency between variable domains. For this reason, CP supports high-level, independent and easily composable constraints. An objective function can also be added to a CP problem.

We now describe *novel variables, data structures and constraints* used for goal formalization in DEFO. Consistently with §3, we assume that topology, demands and parameters (like path delays) independent from DEFO computations are provided as an input. More details on our CP formalization are reported in [20].

Middlepoint variables model the MR representation of per-demand forwarding paths. Every input demand is mapped to a middlepoint variable, representing a set of middlepoint sequences. We say that a middlepoint variable is *assigned* to a value when all the represented sequences end with the destination of the corresponding demand. If this condition does not hold, we say that the middlepoint variable is *unassigned*. For example, the forwarding paths for the demand from s to t in Fig. 3 are represented by an assigned middlepoint variable $\{[t], [m, t]\}$. Middlepoint variables represent the *decision variables* of the optimizations performed by DEFO. When forwarding paths need to be optimized, the middlepoint variables are re-initialized to an empty value. Then, they are progressively assigned to values according to the algorithm described in §4.3.

Forwarding function algorithms guarantee the satisfaction of constraints defined on forwarding functions. Every supported forwarding function implemented by a specific algorithm, specialized for that function. For example, the `load` and `delay` forwarding functions are supported by different algorithms. Forwarding function algorithms (i) extract the value of the associated forwarding function (for example, the load of the maximally loaded link for the `load` forwarding function algorithm) from a set of links or from forwarding paths corresponding to the value of a middlepoint variable; (ii) compare the extracted value with a configured threshold, to assess if the represented constraint is satisfied; and (iii) reduce the domain of middlepoint variables by excluding values that violate a constraint on the associated forwarding function. The thresholds checked by those algorithms are initialized by the constraints of the input goal. For example, a constraint `l.link < l.capacity` defined on a link `l` initializes the value to be checked on `l` by the `load` forwarding function algorithm to the link capacity provided by the input topology.

4.3 Middlepoint Selection

We propose an *efficient algorithm* to solve CP problems corresponding to DEFO input goals. By assigning values to middlepoint variables, our algorithms compute which middlepoints to use in the optimized paths of which traffic flow. The same algorithm can also be used to compute backup paths (e.g., to be pre-installed in routers as in well-known fast reroute techniques [21]).

Unfortunately, selecting middlepoints is a hard problem. Indeed, we proved [20] that middlepoint selection problems are NP-hard, even if only link capacity constraints have to be respected. Additional constraint or specific objective function can make the corresponding selection problem even harder. Despite this, our algorithms are required to be efficient and scalable, for the controller to quickly react to events (failures, demand and goal changes, etc.) in large-scale networks.

To quickly compute good solutions, we then propose a *heuristic approach*, mixing a pure CP solution with a local search technique called Large Neighborhood Search (LNS). Intuitively, we use CP to compute the best solution in a given portion of the search space, and we rely

While all the demands have not been optimized:

1. Select a non-optimized demand D which corresponds to the worst value of the objective function (e.g., the most bandwidth-consuming one). Let m_D be the middlepoint variable for D;
2. If m_D cannot be expanded without violating some constraint, backtrack by reconsidering the current value of m_D;
3. Otherwise, expand m_D as follows:
   (a) If the destination of D is a valid expansion candidate, expand m_D to the destination and store the demand as optimized;
   (b) Otherwise, expand m_D to a middlepoint n that locally optimizes the value of the objective function.
4. Update the domain of other variables.

Figure 4: The first-close heuristic that drives the construction step in DEFO.

on LNS to heuristically decide the sequence of subspaces to explore. Starting from a state in which all middlepoint variables are unassigned, DEFO computations keep alternating (i) a *construction step with inference*, used to identify a current best solution; and (ii) a *partial reset step*, which resets a random part of the current best solution. The partial reset step reworks a significant part of the current best solution, hence increasing the likelihood to escape local optima and quickly find solutions close to the optimum. The price for such efficiency consists in losing the proven optimality of a pure CP approach: Indeed, the random-based reset step does not guarantee that the entire search space is explored.

Forwarding Optimization Algorithms. While combining LNS with CP is not completely new [22, 23], we devised *original algorithms* to implement both the construction and the partial reset steps in DEFO.

Construction Step. Starting from an empty or partial solution (with some unassigned variables), this step *expands* all middlepoint variables, assigning values to them. Its output is a complete variable assignment compliant with all input constraints.

In DEFO, the construction step is implemented by a depth-first search combined with branch and bound [24]. This search is driven by the *first-close heuristic* summarized in Fig. 4. Our heuristic iterates over the non-optimized demands, i.e., those with unassigned middlepoint variables. At every iteration, it identifies the demand with the biggest negative contribution to the objective function. Then, it first tries to complete the assignment of the corresponding middlepoint variable by appending the destination to all its internal middlepoint sequences. This attempt is intended to reduce the number of middlepoints in optimized paths, hence the deviations from connectivity paths and the amount of information to be injected in the optimization layer. If

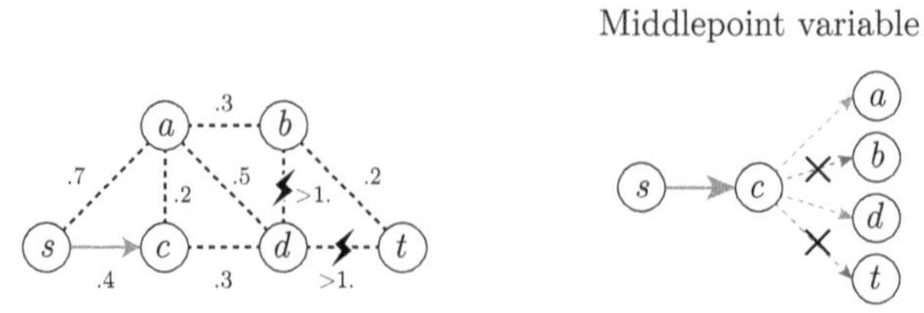

Figure 5: Illustration of a construction-step iteration (with corresponding domain reduction). Numbers aside links represent their utilization.

such an assignment is not feasible, the heuristic expands the middlepoint variable by greedily selecting the middlepoint that locally optimizes the objective function without violating any constraint: This middlepoint is either appended to all internal sequences of the considered middlepoint variable (if possible) or used in a new sequence. The final value of the middlepoint variable is then incrementally built repeating those operations. If no expansion is possible at a given iteration, the algorithm backtracks and replaces the last visited middlepoint with an alternative one.

All those operations are implemented with an inference approach, based on a continuous update of the variable domains. To this end, we run forwarding function algorithms to exclude possible expansions which are not compliant with the input constraints and adjust the domain of every unassigned variable accordingly.

Fig. 5 illustrates an iteration of the construction step algorithm for the middlepoint variable m associated to the demand from s to t. The input goal constrains every link to carry less load than its capacity and aim at minimizing the maximum link load. In the given network, links (d, b) and (d, t) are over-utilized. Assume that connectivity paths are computed as shortest paths and all links have unitary weight. Since connectivity paths from s to t cross (d, t), it is not possible to complete the assignment of m by directly appending the destination t. Hence, our heuristic updates the value of m to $\{[c]\}$, locally minimizing the objective function. Moreover, it runs forwarding function algorithms to update unassigned variable domains. To avoid links (d, b) and (d, t), the `load` forwarding function algorithm excludes b and t from the domain of m, leaving only a and d in it. The first-close heuristic is then re-run until t is reached. Note that values discarded in one iteration may be used in successive iterations. For example, while b is not in the m's domain in the depicted iteration, it re-enters the domain whenever m's value is updated to $\{[c, a]\}$.

Partial Reset Step. The first-close heuristic locally optimizes the expansion of middlepoint variables but does not provide any guarantee on the global optimality of the computed variable assignment. We rely on the partial reset step to statistically ensure the good quality of the returned solution. In this second step, DEFO resets a (large) subset of middlepoint variables of the

1. Let $\mathcal{D}$ be the set of demands with the worst value of the objective function;
2. While fewer than k demands and not all the demands in $\mathcal{D}$ have been selected
   (a) Sort non-extracted demands in $\mathcal{D}$ according to their objective function value (from the worst to the best). Let S be the resulting sorted array;
   (b) Generate a random number $r \in [0, 1[$;
   (c) Extract the $\lfloor r^{\alpha}|S|\rfloor$-th demand from S.
3. Re-initialize the value of all middlepoint variables corresponding to extracted demands.

Figure 6: Partial reset algorithm.

current best solution. This operation identifies a new starting state from which the construction step is re-run, to explore another portion of the search space.

Our proposed partial reset algorithm is summarized in Fig. 6. It randomly selects the middlepoint variables to reset among those associated to demands with the worst value of the objective function, e.g., routed through the most congested link in the MinMaxLoad goal. Let $\mathcal{D}$ be the set of those demands. To allow fine-tuning of the optimization process, the algorithm is parametric: (i) $k \in [1, 15]$ controls the number of variables to reset; and (ii) $\alpha \in [1, 6]$ influences the random choice of which variables are selected. In particular, if $\alpha = 1$, all middlepoint variables corresponding to the demands in $\mathcal{D}$ have the same chance to be selected. In contrast, if $\alpha = \infty$, the k demands in $\mathcal{D}$ with the worst value of the objective function (e.g., highest bandwidth) are deterministically selected. We change the value of k and α during the computation. Namely, depending on whether the previous construction step improved the current best solution or not, we respectively decrease or increase k by 1, hence causing the reset of more or less variables. This is meant to dynamically control the size of the explored parts of the search space during the optimization in order to quickly converge to good solutions and escape local optima. Moreover, to progressively allow more diversification, we decrease α (initially set to 6) with the number of iterations. Values and bounds of the parameters are determined empirically.

5. REALIZATION

In this section, we describe our proposed realization of the architecture depicted in Fig. 1.

A link-state IGP at the connectivity layer. Link-state (LS) IGPs are the routing protocols currently used inside carrier-grade networks. They are well-understood; their implementation is robust to software bugs and optimized for fast convergence [25]. Built-in features also ensure fast reroute in many failure cases [10]. Moreover, LS IGPs natively support (ECMP) multi-path routing through even splitting over multiple shortest paths, a crucial feature to exploit the physical redundancy of carrier-grade networks. Finally, their information flooding mechanism allows DEFO to easily communicate with devices and monitor topological changes. Being based on shortest-path routing, the main limitation of LS IGPs is their relative inflexibility. However, flexibility is not critical for the connectivity layer.

Segment Routing at the optimization layer. Contrary to the connectivity layer, flexibility in the definition of forwarding paths and scalability in the introduced overhead are the main requirements for the optimization layer. We propose to rely on segment routing (SR), in order to avoid both limitations of shortest-path based protocols as well as scalability issues of end-to-end tunneling (e.g., RSVP-TE) and hop-by-hop (OpenFlow) ones. SR is a recently-standardized protocol [3], supported by major router vendors and attracting growing interest from operators. In SR, routers can enrich (MPLS [26] or IPv6 [27]) packet headers with a sequence of *segments*, i.e., instructions forcing packets through specific intermediate nodes or links. The IGP ECMP shortest paths are used to reach those intermediate points. SR provides a perfect match with the MR model used in DEFO. Indeed, any middlepoint used in an MR instance can be mapped to an SR segment, in constant time. Thus, paths computed by DEFO for a given demand can be efficiently translated into sequences of SR segments to be applied by the ingress router for that demand. This has the additional side effect of limiting the optimization overhead to sequences of SR segments (instead of full paths) configured only at ingress routers (with no additional state on internal ones). We evaluate scalability gains of using SR in §8.

Scala implementation of DEFO. We implemented DEFO in about 9,000 lines of Scala code, on top of the OscaR open-source CP solver [28]. Our implementation is provided at [20]. It supports all the constructs defined in Fig. 2, hence all the use cases presented in §3. To gather information on connectivity paths, DEFO can participate in the link-state IGP by maintaining a single adjacency with any IGP router, as in [29, 30]. To configure the optimization layer, it has to push specific SR configurations to routers. The control channel between DEFO and network routers can be implemented in several ways, including OpenFlow [31] and slight modifications of configuration protocols, like Netconf [32] or Flowspec [33]. For compatibility with current routers, we prefer to rely on the PCEP extension for SR [34].

6. EVALUATION SETUP

We evaluated our realization on multiple topologies and demand matrices. We used real and realistic topologies and matrices to assess the results of DEFO in practical cases, and we relied on synthetic data to explore its behavior in corner cases. For example, we experimented with very connected topologies (i.e., with an

Type	ID	# nodes	# links	# demands
Real ISP	R1	600	2150	11,500
Real ISP	R2	400	1200	116,000
Real ISP	R3	200	750	10,000
Real ISP	R4	150	700	24,000
Inferred	I5-9	79-317	296-1,946	6,000-96,000
Synthetic	S10-11	50-100	280-570	2,500-10,000

Table 1: Evaluation dataset summary

average node degree higher than 5) and uniform demand matrices to perform stress tests on DEFO efficiency.

Our dataset is summarized in Table 1. The table provides more detailed information (approximated to preserve anonymity) on real-world ISP topologies. The other topologies in our dataset include inferred ones in the Rocketfuel project [35] and synthetic ones generated with the Delaunay triangulation algorithm in IGen [36]. The table reports aggregated information about those topologies, since they are publicly available at [20].

To run experiments on delay-constrained goals, we enriched each topology with path delays. We relied on direct input from operators for real topologies. In the other cases, we assigned path delays proportionally to the physical distance between the geographical positions of path endpoints.

Our dataset also contains demand matrices (one snapshot per topology). For all real topologies, we used demands provided by operators. In the other cases, we relied on synthetic demand matrices computed with the approach described in [37]. This approach is based on a gravity model fed with independently and identically distributed exponential random variables. It produces highly-skewed demand matrices which are quite realistic, as shown in [37] and as we confirmed by a comparison with real matrices in our dataset. Finally, to consider extreme use cases for worst-cases analyses, we proportionally inflated all the demands until a maximum link usage of at least 120% was reached.

The experiments for our evaluation were run on MacBook Pro laptops, with 2.6 GHz Intel CPU and 16 GB of memory. Unless differently specified in the text, DEFO has been configured with a timeout of 3 minutes for each experiment. Moreover, we set the maximum number of middlepoints per optimized path to 2. Indeed, we experimentally noticed that DEFO solutions with this setting are significantly better than those with at most 1 middlepoint per optimized path, while further increasing the number of middlepoints per path tends to lead to less significant improvements.

7. OPTIMIZED PATH EVALUATION

We now present an experimental evaluation of DEFO. We first compare the forwarding optimization achieved by DEFO on classic goals with solutions provided by Cisco MATE [38], a commercial traffic engineering tool (§7.1-7.2). Namely, we used MATE to simulate IGP weight optimizations (IGP-WO) and RSVP-TE tunnel optimization. The former influences forwarding path computation by tweaking link weights on the topology shared by IGP routers. The latter optimizes paths through explicit RSVP-TE tunnels. We evaluated centralized and distributed RSVP-TE optimizations, which we refer to as cRSVP-TE and dRSVP-TE respectively. In cRSVP-TE a central controller setups the needed tunnels, while a full-mesh of tunnels is individually optimized by single routers (tunnel endpoints) in dRSVP-TE. In the second part of the section, we show results on DEFO support for custom goals (§7.3) and new applications (§7.4), which are largely unsupported by available tools. Those experiments show the effectiveness and time efficiency of DEFO, and the possibility to use it both offline (offline traffic engineering, planning, what-if analyses, etc.) and online (online traffic engineering, reaction to failures, etc.).

Topo ID	Initial Load	Optimum	DEFO ($\leq$ 3mins)	cRSVP-TE	IGP-WO
R1	121%	81%	90%	81%	96%
R2	120%	89%	94%	90%	108%
R3	120%	*NA*	94%	80%	107%
R4	121%	86%	89%	86%	86%
I5	130%	86%	86%	86%	95%
I6	124%	*NA*	76%	77%	77%
I7	142%	72%	82%	76%	80%
I8	120%	66%	72%	69%	78%
I9	195%	*NA*	91%	70%	99%
S10	103%	69%	71%	73%	91%
S11	250%	56%	75%	69%	120%

Table 2: Comparison on maximum link load minimization.

7.1 DEFO Quickly Computes Excellent Solutions for Classic Goals

We start by evaluating DEFO on classic traffic engineering (TE) goals. We take as an example the MinMaxLoad goal that aims at maximizing the spare capacity of the maximally-loaded link (see §3).

Table 2 compares the quality of the solutions (in terms of maximal link load) achieved by the considered optimization techniques with the theoretical optimum. Optimum results are computed by running the standard Linear Program (LP) formalizing the multi-commodity flow problem [39]. This LP assumes the possibility for any node to fractionally split flows with arbitrary proportions. This assumption is not realistic: Even with uneven load balancing, supporting it would require to know in advance the size of all flows and continuously adjust load balancing according to flow sizes. We provided this LP as input to the commercial Gurobi solver. The computation always ran out of memory on the laptop used in our evaluation, except for 3 topologies. We then re-ran the LP solver on a much more powerful server (32 CPU cores and 96 GB of RAM), and reported the results in Table 2. Even on this server, the LP could not be solved in some cases (*NA* values).

DEFO computes excellent solutions. Despite restricting to even load-balancing over IGP paths, DEFO computes forwarding paths that lower the maximum load to a value close to the theoretical optimum. In some cases, this value is even equal to the optimum value, as for $I5$. In all the other cases except one, it is less than 10% worse than the optimum. Moreover, DEFO terminates in 3 minutes (by setting, see §6) on a commodity laptop, while running the LP took us up to many hours (including an entire night for the experiment on $R2$) and sometimes ran out of memory on a much more powerful server.

DEFO optimizes more than IGP-WO. IGP weight tweaking techniques do not have fine-granularity. In particular, they do not allow to modify forwarding paths on a per-demand basis. As a result, contrary to DEFO, IGP-WO could not avoid congestion in some of our experiments. Indeed, the utilization of the maximally-loaded link is above 100% for $R2$, $R3$, $S11$ (i.e., 3 out of our 11 topologies). More generally, IGP-WO results are much less close to the optimum than DEFO ones.

DEFO optimization power is comparable with RSVP-TE. RSVP-TE tunnels allow to enforce arbitrary paths for each demands. Despite this allows fine-grain optimization, results achieved by DEFO tend to be close and sometimes even better than the ones obtained with cRSVP-TE (as for $I6$ and $S10$). Also, DEFO comes with the additional advantage of much higher time efficiency. It indeed always terminated in 3 minutes (by setting, see §6), while cRSVP-TE optimization took hours on our largest topologies.

7.2 DEFO Can Ease Network Operation

Operators often try to limit the number of applied changes. This eases the deployment of the optimized configuration, without the risk of triggering huge traffic shifts and transient disruptions. To evaluate support for those kind of tactical use cases, we experimented with a variant of MinMaxLoad which minimizes the number of optimized paths while ensuring that all links are utilized for at most 90% of their respective capacity.

DEFO is much more effective than incremental IGP-WO. MATE supports an incremental IGP-WO procedure that tries to lower the utilization of the maximally-loaded link with a limited number of IGP weight changes. In our experiments, it did not succeed in lowering the maximally loaded-link under 100% for 3 topologies out of 11. In contrast, DEFO finds a congestion-free solution in all our experiments. Also, observe that the IGP weight changes are more intrusive than those applied in our architecture. For example, IGP weight changes can create forwarding loops [40] and traffic shifts [41] for Internet destinations. In contrast, SR prevents such problems by clearly separating forwarding optimization from IGP-based connectivity.

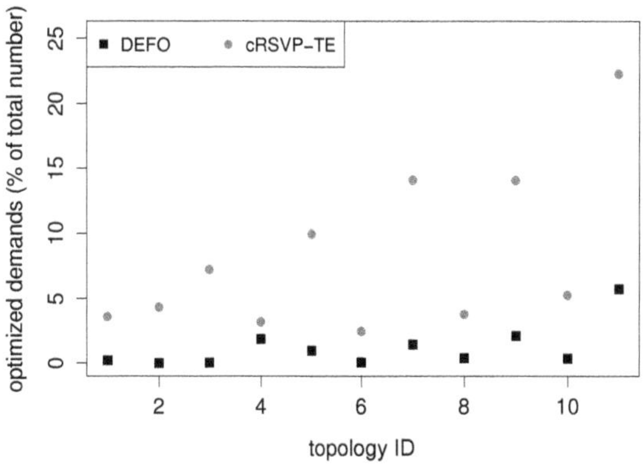

Figure 7: Optimization overhead to bring utilization of the maximally loaded link under 90%.

Load	Min	1st Qu.	Median	3rd Qu.	Max
<98%	0.17s	0.54s	1.38s	3.16s	12.83s
<95%	0.17s	0.59s	1.55s	3.56s	19.78s
<90%	0.22s	0.71s	2.05s	4.33s	46.8s

Table 3: DEFO computation time to lower the maximum link load under a given threshold.

DEFO reduces the overhead of RSVP-TE optimizations. We also let MATE optimize RSVP-TE tunnels according to the considered MinMaxLoad variant. As in Table 2, the resulting maximal load is comparable with DEFO output paths. However, Fig. 7 shows that many more demands have to be optimized with cRSVP-TE. Indeed, cRSVP-TE optimization often affects one order of magnitude more demands than DEFO, that is, typically thousands of demands instead of hundreds. Even worse, dRSVP-TE (omitted in Fig. 7 for readability) requires to optimize 2 to 3 orders of magnitude more demands than DEFO. Hence, both cRSVP-TE and dRSVP-TE optimizations imply a significant increase in (i) routers to be re-configured; (ii) traffic to be shifted from one path to another; and (iii) control-plane overhead. Those three factors contribute to a number of management issues including delay in the application of TE actions and reduced ability for operators to debug post-optimization configurations.

Recent versions of MATE and the commercial WAE controller [42] support a heuristic to compute SR configurations for tactical TE [43]. It achieves optimization overhead reductions very similar to DEFO: Those results are not reported in Fig. 7 for readability.

Another fundamental factor from an operational viewpoint is the computation time. We considered variants of MinMaxLoad with the maximum load constrained to be at most 90%, 95%, or 98%. Consistently with Table 2, DEFO always found a compliant solution except when run on $I9$ with the 90% constraint. In the latter case, it reported the best solution that it found (with 91% maximum link utilization) after the config-

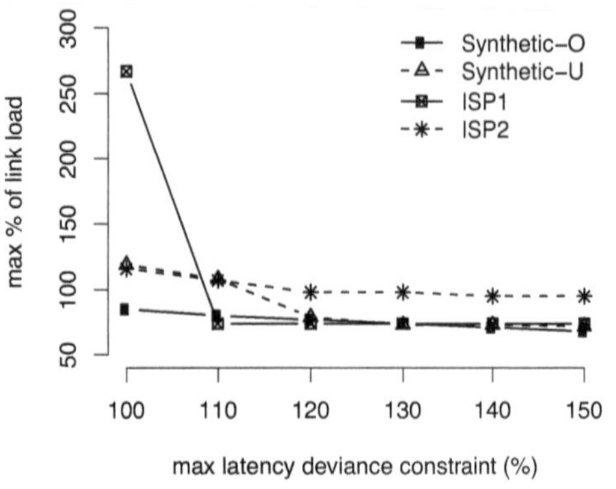

Figure 8: Results of DEFO for the delay-constrained MinMaxLoad goal.

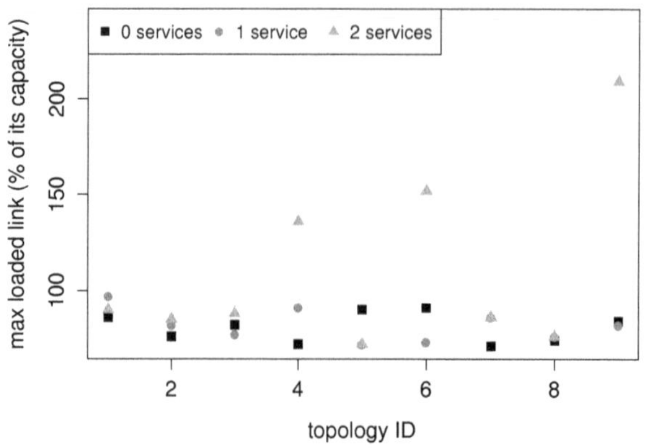

Figure 9: DEFO optimization in different service chaining scenarios.

ured 3-minute timeout. Table 3 reports the time taken by DEFO in all the other experiments. The table shows that DEFO always completed its computation in less than one minute. In the vast majority of the cases, it actually took at most 10 seconds; not rarely, it terminated in a fraction of a second. Those results show that DEFO can readily be used for periodic forwarding optimization, e.g., for online traffic engineering.

7.3 DEFO Supports Refined Goals

We now evaluate DEFO on refined goals, not supported by current IGP-WO and RSVP-TE techniques. We implemented support for some of those goals in a recent SR controller [42].

Delay-respectful TE. We ran experiments on a MinMaxLoad variant with additional constraints forcing the maximum delay of every forwarding path to be lower than a pre-defined threshold. Precisely, for each source-destination pair, we constrained the post-optimization path delay to be lower than a given percentage variation of the initial one. We ran different sets of experiments. In each experiment set, we bound the delay increase to respectively be at most 0% (i.e., no increase admitted), 10%, 20%, 30%, 40% and 50% of the initial delay.

The results obtained on two real topologies ($R1$ and $R2$) and a synthetic one ($S11$) are plotted in Fig. 8. We used two configurations for the synthetic topology, one with uniform link weights (Synthetic-U) and the other with optimized weights (Synthetic-O). The figure correlates the maximum link utilization (y-axis) with increasingly loose constraints on the permitted delay increase (x-axis). Results match the intuition that if a larger delay increase is tolerated, DEFO has more flexibility to distribute traffic on different paths, and can lower the load per link. Interestingly, our experiments also suggest that tolerating 10% or 20% delay increase tends to reduce the maximum link load under 100%, with a maximal link utilization comparable to this obtained with much looser delay constraints (40% or 50%).

Multi-Objective Goals. DEFO accepts input goals with multiple objectives, in which a solution that optimizes all the objectives may not exist. In those cases, *DEFO can build a Pareto front*, i.e., a set of Pareto optimal solutions that cannot be improved in any of the objectives without degrading at least another one. Then, DEFO can either return the Pareto front to the operator or enforce any Pareto optimal solution.

DEFO can also plot the evolution of objective functions over time. This allows operators to use DEFO as a decision support system, e.g., to pick the right tradeoff between optimization time and objectives.

7.4 DEFO Supports Service Chaining

We now evaluate DEFO when used for service chaining applications. We provided DEFO with the goal of minimizing the maximally-loaded link, under the constraint that some demands need to pass through any middlepoint in specified sets. This matches the scenario in which middlepoints in the same set implement the same network service or virtualized function.

In our experience, operators do not deploy service chaining, and are still reluctant to disclose realistic use cases. However, most of them are interested in it. We used DEFO as a what-if analysis tool, to evaluate the degradation of link load optimization in the realistic case in which services are deployed in central network nodes. To provide a benchmark to future approaches, we performed those experiments on inferred and synthetic topologies (adding two new ones to our dataset), and we publicly released them [20].

In each of those experiments, we selected the 5% nodes traversed by the highest number of IGP paths as those deploying services. We then randomly extracted 5% of the demands to pass through those nodes. We performed two groups of experiments. In the first group, the selected demands were forced to pass through any service-enabled node. In the second group, the service-enabled nodes were further split in two service sets, and every selected demand was forced to sequentially pass through any router in the first set and then through any one in the second set.

Services	Min	1st Qu.	Median	3rd Qu.	Max
0	0.24s	9.37s	41.89s	61.06s	140s
1	0.25s	17.21s	41.9s	59.15s	210s
2	0.30s	6.86s	27.09s	59.74s	71.78s

Table 4: DEFO computation time for service chaining goals.

DEFO computed optimized paths always compliant with the input constraints. Unsurprisingly, however, service chaining constraints may prevent DEFO to compute a congestion-free solution. The results on the maximum load after running DEFO are displayed in Fig. 9. In 3 cases (out of 9), no solution can be computed by DEFO when demands needed to pass a sequence of two services. This can be due to both the (i) limited running time, and (ii) the fact that DEFO currently configures acyclic paths. In all the other experiments with one and two services, however, those two factors did not prevent DEFO from optimizing forwarding paths from keeping all link utilization below 100%. In some case, DEFO reduces link loads more in the presence of services than in the absence of them. This is due to the fact that service chaining constraints generally restrict the possible paths to be considered during the optimization; hence, they can increase the likelihood for our optimization heuristics to quickly explore a larger portion of the search space and find a better solution.

Finally, Table 4 shows that service chaining constraints have no statistical effect on DEFO time efficiency.

8. PATH REALIZATION EVALUATION

In this section, we evaluate the effectiveness of our two-layer architecture implementation, both from a scalability (§8.1) and a reactivity (§8.2) point of view.

8.1 Realization Scalability

We first compare different implementations (SR, tunnelling and hop-by-hop ones) of the optimized paths computed by DEFO. For simplicity, we take as reference the MinMaxLoad goal. The entries to be installed on routers for each of the compared implementations are plotted in Fig. 10. For each topology (on the x-axis), the figure reports on y-axis (in logarithmic scale) the ratio between the number of entries needed by a given alternative and those employed by our SR realization.

1.5-10x gain vs end-to-end tunnelling. Provided that a tunnelling technology is supported by all routers, a straightforward implementation of the optimized paths computed by DEFO consists in deploying one (E2E) tunnel per optimized path. Fig. 10 shows that this solution comes with significantly more overhead than SR. This is because end-to-end tunnels scale with the number of paths between each source-destination pair, while SR scales with the number of middlepoints, i.e., factoring all the paths between each middlepoint. Practically, the number of additional entries is between 1.5 to 10

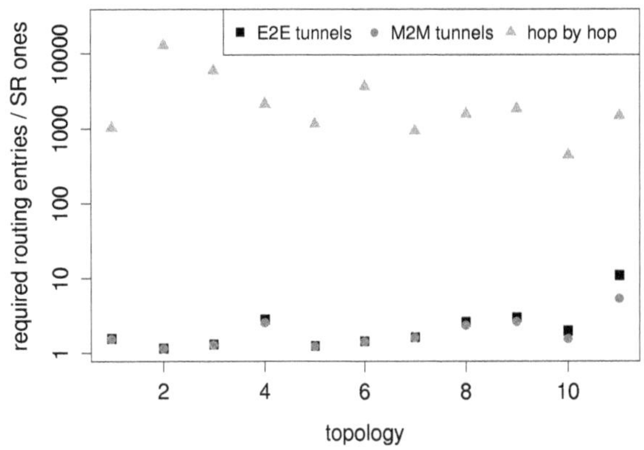

Figure 10: Comparison between different implementations of DEFO optimized paths.

times bigger than those needed by SR. Two topologies ($R2$ and $I5$) make exception, needing about 20% more entries for the E2E tunnels.

1.5-5x gain vs middlepoint to middlepoint tunnelling. A more scalable realization of DEFO paths that can be achieved with tunnelling protocols consists in configuring tunnels between each pair of middlepoints. This way, the total number of tunnels is equal to the sum of the paths between middlepoints in the paths (instead of their combinations). Fig. 10 shows that middlepoint to middlepoint (M2M) tunnels enable to reduce the number of tunnels up to a factor of 2. This, however, means that the entries needed by SR are still between one half and one fifth of M2M tunnel ones.

1,000-10,000x gain vs hop by hop implementation. Finally, optimized path can be implemented with hop-by-hop technologies (e.g., OpenFlow and static routing). In this case, every router must be configured with a forwarding entry for every optimized path crossing it. This leads to an explosion of the number of entries needed to implement DEFO solutions. While this number can be optimized (e.g., by tagging packets), Fig. 10 shows that the gap to fill with respect to the SR (and even with tunnelling solutions) is huge, i.e., among 3 or 4 orders of magnitude in our experiments.

8.2 Reactivity to Network Dynamics

Connectivity needs to be guaranteed and forwarding has to be re-optimized upon a number of events, ranging from network failures (e.g, link failures) to changing demands (e.g., traffic surges). We now describe how components of our architecture react to those changes.

The link-state IGP used at the connectivity layer efficiently re-establishes disrupted paths for all physically-connected node pairs. Indeed, it (i) supports fast local re-routing by relying on per-router decisions [10], and (ii) can recompute new connectivity paths in less than one second even in large networks [25]. Consequently, relying on an IGP mitigates the need for fast reaction to several events. For example, whenever an optimized path includes a set of middlepoints which are still reachable after a failure, traffic can still flow over that path.

Still, forwarding may need to be quickly re-optimized in some cases. Those cases include failures that disrupt the connectivity between middlepoints in some optimized paths, and congestion triggered by new connectivity paths. Fig. 7 and Table 3 show that DEFO can remove forwarding disruptions by very quickly re-optimizing few demands. This enables to use DEFO for (i) online traffic engineering applications in which forwarding is re-optimized periodically, with a period of few minutes [6, 8]; (ii) pre-compute optimized paths for most likely failures; and (iii) react to failures almost in real-time, in many cases. About failure reaction, we also publicly released a simulation (see [20]) of forwarding optimization with DEFO upon single-link failures on our biggest synthetic topology. This reaction took from few milliseconds to a couple of seconds for the vast majority of the cases. As soon as the new optimized paths are computed, they can be directly installed on routers. Since we rely on SR, *only the configuration of the ingress point of the re-optimized demands needs to changed*, which provides additional architectural support for fast forwarding re-optimization.

9. DISCUSSION

We now discuss limitations of our proposal, and how they can be tackled by slightly extending it.

Per-flow forwarding control. For simplicity, we described our approach assuming source-destination granularity. Our evaluation shows that this level of granularity effectively supports practical goals, especially traffic engineering ones. Nevertheless, our proposal can also support finer-grained control, by leveraging capabilities commonly supported by commercial routers. For example, policy-based routing can be configured on most routers, enabling the specification of their routing behavior in terms of rules on additional packet-header fields than only the destination IP. DEFO can also be easily adapted for finer-grained forwarding optimization, since it models traffic with the generic concept of demands (i.e., flow aggregates).

Additional network goals. DEFO currently supports a large but limited set of network goals. However, it can be extended to deal with additional goals. Consider, for example, the case in which some middleboxes add or drop packets, hence modifying en route the size of demands. Within DEFO, we can adjust our algorithms to split any demand D passing through one of those middleboxes m in two demands D_1 and D_2, such that (i) D_1 goes from the source of D to m and carries the same traffic as D, and (ii) D_2 carries the modified amount of traffic from m to the destination of D. More in general, both the concept of demand and the network parameters considered during the optimization can be generalized. To this end, new constructs may be needed in DEFO DSL. Moreover, new forwarding function algorithms may have to be implemented (e.g., to run Step 4 in Fig. 4). Note that those additions would preserve the support for all forwarding functions in Fig. 2, thanks to their implementation as independent CP constraints.

10. RELATED WORK

To the best of our knowledge, DEFO's ability to solve classic, refined and service chaining goals under a common framework, at scale and efficiently, is unmatched by previous research approaches. Moreover, prior techniques typically require major changes in problem formulation and internal algorithms even only to support an additional constraint type (e.g., node avoidance).

Most previous works focused on classic traffic engineering problems in ISP networks [44, 45]. Two main approaches have emerged over the years. The first one consists in tuning IGP weights [13, 46] according to traffic demands. Network operators use commercial tools for basic IGP weight tuning [38, 47]. We compared DEFO against one of these tools [38] in §7. More sophisticated weight optimizations, based on additional routing entries [48] or uneven traffic splitting [49, 50], have also been explored in the literature. However, adding routing entries affects scalability, and arbitrary traffic splitting is hard to enforce in practice. Our experimental results (§7) show that DEFO can achieve huge optimizations with few additional entries and even load splitting. The second approach is to rely on RSVP-TE [51]. It allows to create end-to-end tunnels to forward flows over any network path. RSVP-TE tunnels can be configured in a distributed or centralized mode. In the distributed mode, tunnels are dynamically re-computed by ingress routers to match traffic patterns or topological changes [52]. This mode is prone to operational issues [53] such as routing instability and latency inflation [54]. In the centralized mode, a central component (PCE or the network operator) explicitly specifies the RSVP-TE tunnels to be installed. Algorithms have been proposed to optimize tunnel positioning [15, 55], and some have been implemented in commercial tools [38, 47]. We compared DEFO against distributed and centralized RSVP-TE in §7.

A few contributions looked at refined traffic engineering goals. Notably, FUBAR [56] tackles the problem of maximizing utility of flow aggregates, defined as a specific composition of load and delay metrics. DEFO can solve this problem (see §3) and many more variants of it with arbitrary compositions of delay, load and service chaining constraints and objectives. As partial outcome of this work, we also contributed to support some refined goals in the WAE controller [42] (see §7).

Online traffic engineering has been the target of recent research. Several contributions [6, 8, 57, 58] proposed different techniques to re-optimize forwarding periodically, i.e., every 5-10 minutes. Our results (§7-8) show that DEFO (which computes paths in seconds) and our network realization (quick to converge on a new routing state) can be used for online traffic engineering.

Finally, some SDN works [1, 45] target individual problems that can be solved by DEFO, including service chaining. For example, [59, 60] provide architectures and optimization frameworks to forward traffic through middleboxes. However, previous SDN proposals do not consider stringent robustness and high scalability requirements of carrier-grade networks. Our evaluation shows that both path computation algorithms (e.g., LP- or MILP-based) and network protocols (OpenFlow) used in previous works may not easily match those requirements. In comparison, hybrid SDN architectures, running both IGP and an SDN protocol, have better chances to fit carrier-grade networks. Our proposal can be seen as an integrated hybrid SDN architecture according to the classification in [61]. As such, it enriches previous efforts in the area (e.g., [6, 12, 30, 62]) with an original architecture based on segment routing and a multipurpose declarative controller. Note that DEFO can be used as a translator from abstract goals to forwarding paths in protocols different from SR (see, e.g., §8.1). We plan to compare our SR-based implementation with recent proposals for implementing forwarding paths (like Fibbing [30]) in future work.

11. CONCLUSIONS

This paper presents a proposal to realize appealing promises of SDN, like declarative and expressive management, in carrier-grade networks. To accommodate specific needs of those networks, e.g., robustness and scalability, our proposal is based on a two-layer architecture, separating connectivity and optimization tasks. Our centralized forwarding optimizer, DEFO, exposes a declarative interface enabling operators to naturally define a variety of high-level goals. Given a goal, DEFO automatically computes optimized paths that overwrite the connectivity ones used by default. We proposed and implemented a heuristic which makes this computation effective and efficient (from few hundreds of milliseconds to less than one minute on real ISP networks). Our evaluation also shows that the overhead of DEFO optimizations is very limited (few optimized paths, each implemented with at most two node segments).

We finally compared different realizations of our architecture, providing a quantitative analysis of the tradeoffs achieved by each of them. Among the considered realizations (including MPLS and OpenFlow), the combination of IGP and segment routing currently provides the best results in terms of robustness and scalability.

We contributed to implement some DEFO's capabilities in a commercial controller [42]. In future work, we plan to fully integrate DEFO flexibility in it.

Acknowledgements

We thank SIGCOMM anonymous reviewers and our shepherd, Ming Zhang, for insightful comments. This work has been partially supported by ARC grant 13/18-054 from Communauté française de Belgique. Pierre Francois is fully funded by Cisco Systems.

12. REFERENCES

[1] D. Kreutz *et al.*, "Software-defined networking: A comprehensive survey," *Proceedings of the IEEE*, vol. 103, no. 1, pp. 14–76, 2015.
[2] N. McKeown *et al.*, "OpenFlow: enabling innovation in campus networks," *ACM CCR*, vol. 38, no. 2, pp. 69–74, 2008.
[3] C. Filsfils *et al.*, "Segment Routing Architecture," Internet draft, 2014.
[4] M. Casado *et al.*, "Rethinking enterprise network control," *Trans. Netw.*, vol. 17, no. 4, pp. 1270–1283, 2009.
[5] M. Al-Fares *et al.*, "Hedera: Dynamic Flow Scheduling for Data Center Networks," in *NSDI*, 2010.
[6] S. Jain *et al.*, "B4: Experience with a globally-deployed software defined wan," in *SIGCOMM*, 2013.
[7] S. Kandula *et al.*, "Calendaring for Wide Area Networks," in *SIGCOMM*, 2014.
[8] C.-Y. Hong *et al.*, "Achieving High Utilization with Software-driven WAN," in *SIGCOMM*, 2013.
[9] P. Quinn and T. Nadeau, "Service function chaining problem statement," Internet draft, 2014.
[10] C. Filsfils *et al.*, "Loop-Free Alternate (LFA) Applicability in Service Provider (SP) Networks," RFC 6571, 2012.
[11] R. Krishnan *et al.*, "Mechanisms for Optimizing LAG/ECMP Component Link Utilization in Networks," Internet Draft, 2014.
[12] O. Tilmans and S. Vissicchio, "IGP-as-a-Backup for Robust SDN Networks," in *CNSM*, 2014.
[13] B. Fortz and M. Thorup, "Internet traffic engineering by optimizing OSPF weights," in *INFOCOM*, 2000.
[14] F. Rossi, P. Van Beek, and T. Walsh, *Handbook of constraint programming*. Elsevier, 2006.
[15] A. Elwalid *et al.*, "Mate: Mpls adaptive traffic engineering," in *INFOCOM*, 2001.
[16] D. Ghosh, *DSLs in action*. Manning Publications, 2010.
[17] P. Schaus and R. Hartert, "Multi-objective large neighborhood search," in *CP*, 2013.
[18] P. B. Godfrey, S. Shenker, and I. Stoica, "Pathlet routing," in *HotNets*, 2008.
[19] P. B. Godfrey, I. Ganichev, S. Shenker, and I. Stoica, "Pathlet routing," in *SIGCOMM*, 2009.
[20] R. Hartert, "DEFO Web Site," sites.uclouvain.be/defo.
[21] A. Raj and O. C. Ibe, "A survey of IP and multiprotocol label switching fast reroute

schemes," *Computer Networks*, vol. 51, no. 8, pp. 1882–1907, 2007.

[22] P. Shaw, "Using constraint programming and local search methods to solve vehicle routing problems," in *CP*, 1998.

[23] P. Laborie and D. Godard, "Self-adapting large neighborhood search: Application to single-mode scheduling problems," in *MISTA*, 2007.

[24] A. H. Land and A. G. Doig, "An automatic method of solving discrete programming problems," *Econometrica: Journal of the Econometric Society*, pp. 497–520, 1960.

[25] P. Francois, C. Filsfils, J. Evans, and O. Bonaventure, "Achieving Sub-second IGP Convergence in Large IP Networks," *ACM CCR*, vol. 35, no. 3, 2005.

[26] C. Filsfils *et al.*, "Segment Routing with MPLS data plane," Internet draft, 2014.

[27] S. Previdi *et al.*, "IPv6 Segment Routing Header (SRH)," Internet draft, 2014.

[28] OscaR Team, "OscaR: Scala in OR," 2012, `https://bitbucket.org/oscarlib/oscar`.

[29] A. Shaikh and A. Greenberg, "OSPF Monitoring: Architecture, Design and Deployment Experience," in *NSDI*, 2004.

[30] S. Vissicchio *et al.*, "Central control over distributed routing," in *SIGCOMM*, 2015.

[31] A. Sharafat *et al.*, "MPLS-TE and MPLS VPNS with Openflow," in *SIGCOMM*, 2011.

[32] R. Enns *et al.*, "Network Configuration Protocol (NETCONF)," RFC 6241, 2011.

[33] P. Marques *et al.*, "Dissemination of Flow Specification Rules," RFC 5575, 2009.

[34] S. Sivabalan *et al.*, "PCEP Extensions for Segment Routing," Internet Draft, 2014.

[35] N. Spring *et al.*, "Measuring isp topologies with rocketfuel," *Trans. Netw.*, vol. 12, no. 1, 2004.

[36] B. Quoitin *et al.*, "IGen: Generation of router-level Internet topologies through network design heuristics," in *ITC*, 2009.

[37] M. Roughan, "Simplifying the synthesis of internet traffic matrices," *ACM CCR*, vol. 35, no. 5, pp. 93–96, 2005.

[38] Cisco, "Planning and Designing Networks with the Cisco MATE Portfolio," white paper, 2013.

[39] T. Cormen *et al.*, *Introduction to Algorithms*. McGraw-Hill, 2001.

[40] L. Vanbever *et al.*, "When the cure is worse than the disease: The impact of graceful IGP operations on BGP," in *INFOCOM*, 2013.

[41] R. Teixeira *et al.*, "Network sensitivity to hot-potato disruptions," in *SIGCOMM*, 2004.

[42] Cisco, "Cisco WAN Automation Engine: Greater Traffic and Bandwidth Awareness for Easier Programmability," white paper, 2015.

[43] C. Filsfils, "Segment routing: update and future evolution," MPLS/SDN world congress, 2014.

[44] N. Wang *et al.*, "An overview of routing optimization for internet traffic engineering," *Commun. Surveys Tuts.*, vol. 10, pp. 36–56, 2008.

[45] I. Akyildiz *et al.*, "A roadmap for traffic engineering in SDN-OpenFlow networks," *Computer Networks*, vol. 71, pp. 1–30, 2014.

[46] B. Fortz and M. Thorup, "Optimizing OSPF/IS-IS weights in a changing world," *IEEE J. Sel. Areas Commun.*, vol. 20, no. 4, 2002.

[47] Juniper, "WANDL IP/MPLSView," http://www.juniper.net/assets/us/en/local/pdf/datasheets/1000500-en.pdf.

[48] A. Sridharan *et al.*, "Achieving near-optimal traffic engineering solutions for current OSPF/IS-IS networks," *Trans. Netw.*, vol. 13, no. 2, 2005.

[49] Y. Wang, Z. Wang, and L. Zhang, "Internet traffic engineering without full mesh overlaying," in *INFOCOM*, 2001.

[50] D. Xu, M. Chiang, and J. Rexford, "Link-state routing with hop-by-hop forwarding can achieve optimal traffic engineering," *Trans. Netw.*, vol. 19, no. 6, pp. 1717–1730, 2011.

[51] I. Minei and J. Luceck, *MPLS-Enabled Applications*. Wiley, 2005.

[52] S. Dasgupta *et al.*, "Dynamic traffic engineering for mixed traffic on international networks," *Computer Networks*, vol. 52, no. 11, Aug. 2008.

[53] R. Steenbergen, "Mpls autobandwidth," RIPE 64.

[54] A. Pathak *et al.*, "Latency inflation with MPLS-based traffic engineering," in *IMC*, 2011.

[55] M. Kodialam *et al.*, "Oblivious routing of highly variable traffic in service overlays and IP backbones," *Trans. Netw.*, vol. 17, pp. 459–472, 2009.

[56] N. Gvozdiev, B. Karp, and M. Handley, "FUBAR: Flow Utility Based Routing," in *HotNets*, 2014.

[57] H. Wang *et al.*, "COPE: traffic engineering in dynamic networks," in *SIGCOMM*, 2006.

[58] S. Kandula *et al.*, "Walking the tightrope: responsive yet stable traffic engineering," in *SIGCOMM*, 2005.

[59] D. Joseph *et al.*, "A Policy-aware Switching Layer for Data Centers," in *SIGCOMM*, 2008.

[60] Z. Qazi *et al.*, "SIMPLE-fying Middlebox Policy Enforcement Using SDN," in *SIGCOMM*, 2013.

[61] S. Vissicchio *et al.*, "Opportunities and Research Challenges of Hybrid Software Defined Networks," *ACM CCR*, vol. 44, no. 2, 2014.

[62] S. Agarwal *et al.*, "Traffic Engineering in Software Defined Networks," in *INFOCOM*, 2013.

PGA: Using Graphs to Express and Automatically Reconcile Network Policies

Chaithan Prakash^* Jeongkeun Lee† Yoshio Turner°* Joon-Myung Kang† Aditya Akella^
Sujata Banerjee† Charles Clark‡ Yadi Ma† Puneet Sharma† Ying Zhang†
^University of Wisconsin-Madison, †HP Labs, °Banyan, ‡HP Networking

ABSTRACT

Software Defined Networking (SDN) and cloud automation enable a large number of diverse parties (network operators, application admins, tenants/end-users) and control programs (SDN Apps, network services) to generate network policies independently and dynamically. Yet existing policy abstractions and frameworks do not support natural expression and automatic composition of high-level policies from diverse sources. We tackle the open problem of automatic, correct and fast composition of multiple independently specified network policies. We first develop a high-level Policy Graph Abstraction (PGA) that allows network policies to be expressed simply and independently, and leverage the graph structure to detect and resolve policy conflicts efficiently. Besides supporting ACL policies, PGA also models and composes service chaining policies, i.e., the sequence of middleboxes to be traversed, by merging multiple service chain requirements into conflict-free composed chains. Our system validation using a large enterprise network policy dataset demonstrates practical composition times even for very large inputs, with only sub-millisecond runtime latencies.

CCS Concepts

•**Networks** → **Programming interfaces; Network management;** *Middle boxes / network appliances; Network domains; Network manageability; Programmable networks;* Data center networks;

Keywords

Policy graphs; Software-Defined Networks

*This work was performed while at HP Labs.

SIGCOMM '15, August 17 - 21, 2015, London, United Kingdom

DOI: http://dx.doi.org/10.1145/2785956.2787506

1. INTRODUCTION

Computer networks, be they ISPs, enterprise, datacenter, campus or home networks, are governed by high-level policies derived from network-wide requirements. These network policies primarily relate to connectivity, security and performance, and dictate who can have access to what network resources. Further, policies can be static or dynamic (e.g., triggered). Traditionally, network admins translate high level network policies into low level network configuration commands and implement them on network devices, such as switches, routers and specialized network middleboxes (e.g., firewalls, proxies, etc.). The process is largely manual, often internalized by experienced network admins over time. In large organizations, multiple policy sub-domains exist (e.g., server admins, network engineers, DNS admins, different departments) that set their own policies to be applied to the network components they own or manage. Admins and users who share a network have to manually coordinate with each other and check that the growing set of policies do not conflict and match their individually planned high level policies when deployed together.

Given this current status of distributed network policy management, policy changes take a long time to plan and implement (often days to weeks) as careful semi-manual checking with all the relevant policy sub-domains is essential to maintain correctness and consistency. Even so, problems are typically detected only at runtime when users unexpectedly lose connectivity, security holes are exploited, or applications experience performance degradation.

And the situation can get worse as we progress towards more automated network infrastructures, where the number of entities that generate policies independently and dynamically will increase manyfold. Examples include SDN applications in enterprise networks, tenants/users of virtualized cloud infrastructures, and Network Functions Virtualization (NFV) environments, details in §2.1.

In all of these settings, it would be ideal to eagerly and automatically detect and resolve conflicts between individual policies, and compose them into a coherent conflict-free policy set, well before the policies are deployed on the physical infrastructure. Further, having a high level policy abstraction and decoupling the policy specification from the underlying physical infrastructure would significantly reduce the burden on the admins/users/application developers of the network both in crafting and implementing their policies.

In this paper, we address the open problem of automatic, correct and fast composition of independently generated network policies. Our contributions are:

1. We present a new high-level model called Policy Graph Abstraction (PGA) for expressing network policies. PGA is a simple and intuitive graph-based abstraction for each sub-domain to separately express networking policy on endpoints, independent of underlying network infrastructure. PGA naturally incorporates network middleboxes and enables automatic, eager composition.
2. We develop algorithms to automatically and scalably compose multiple policy graphs. The composition maintains the individually specified invariants from each policy graph. It also systematically determines an appropriate service order when merging service chains.
3. We present the design and implementation of the PGA system. We leverage existing SDN programming languages (e.g., Pyretic) to represent middlebox functionality and analyze service chains. The system can compose over 20K ACL policies from a real policy dataset in under 600s, while incurring sub-millisecond latency for the first packet of a flow when running reactively.

In this paper, we focus on policies related to network endpoints and decouple underlying network state information from the PGA abstraction. PGA treats the underlying network as "one big switch", which in some cases may not reflect all the low level policy requirements: e.g., traffic engineering decisions regarding specific switches/routers/network path [32]. We also do not focus on run-time network state conflicts, which has been recently studied in [33, 39, 13]. Occasionally, there will be a need to consider lower layer network state in making correct overall network-wide policy decisions. We leave this interplay between the PGA abstraction layer and the physical infrastructure state for future work.

2. BACKGROUND

We present three scenarios where the distributed policy specification and composition problem arises, followed by a detailed example that demonstrates technical challenges.

2.1 Target Scenarios

Enterprise networks manage policies using the notion of network compartments, which are defined based on administrative domains (e.g., external access network, geographical site), application/service (e.g., DNS), network protocol (e.g., IPv6) or network technology (e.g., WLAN). There can be hundreds of compartments governed by special policies that are independently specified and managed; the policies generated by multiple compartments may be applied to the same set of network devices.

Cloud infrastructures: tenants want to have their virtual networks with their own policies. These policies at the virtualized network level are created without any knowledge of the underlying physical infrastructure, but must comply with the network operator policies at runtime. A simple change of operator policy may affect and conflict with thousands of existing tenant policies.

NFV service networks aim to virtualize the service functions that are today implemented on specialized hardware middleboxes [10, 11]. A key requirement is to provide service function chaining (SFC) in these environments, with no or minimal knowledge of the network infrastructure and middlebox internals. SFC can be specified as network policies where specific packets/flows have to strictly follow the chain of service functions. Multiple chains devised by different administrative entities may be deployed on the same network infrastructure; the logical chains need to be composed into one coherent service chain.

2.2 Challenges in Policy Composition

We use an example to illustrate the challenges that arise in composing policies in the above scenarios. Consider the two policies depicted graphically in Fig.1(a), inspired by a real enterprise scenario. Suppose a company's marketing department wants to deploy a CRM (Customer Relationship Management) application on some of the company's servers. The CRM admin specifies a network policy, called P1, that allows only marketing employees to send traffic to the CRM servers; the traffic must use TCP port 7000 and must pass through a load balancing service (LB).

Independently, the company-wide network admin specifies another policy, called P2, that restricts company employees to access company servers only through TCP ports 80, 334, and 7000; and the traffic must pass through a firewall service (FW). Note that Marketing employees are a subset of all employees, just as CRM servers are a subset of all the company servers as indicated in Fig. 1(a) by the *subset* symbol $\subset$. These independently specified policies need to be combined into a coherent composed policy that respects the intent of both stakeholders.

Correctly composing P1 and P2 is actually not that simple with currently available tools and languages. First, P1 and P2 contain two different types of policies: access control whitelisting (ACL) and network service chaining (FW, LB). Since the src/dst and port range of P1 are completely encompassed by those in P2, one may naively compose the ACL policies by prioritizing P1 over P2, but this incorrectly allows non-Marketing traffic to reach CRM servers. In addition, assuming the intended order of the service chain is FW followed by LB, the intent needs to be factored in for [Mktg$\rightarrow$CRM] traffic.

Network programming frameworks such as Merlin [38] and GBP [6] are not suitable for independent policy specification. GBP does not support composition and so a single combined program needs to be written manually. Merlin supports distributed but not fully independent policy specification. The network admin needs to explicitly delegate a policy to the CRM admin. The CRM admin is only allowed to modify that delegated policy in restricted ways, and in do-

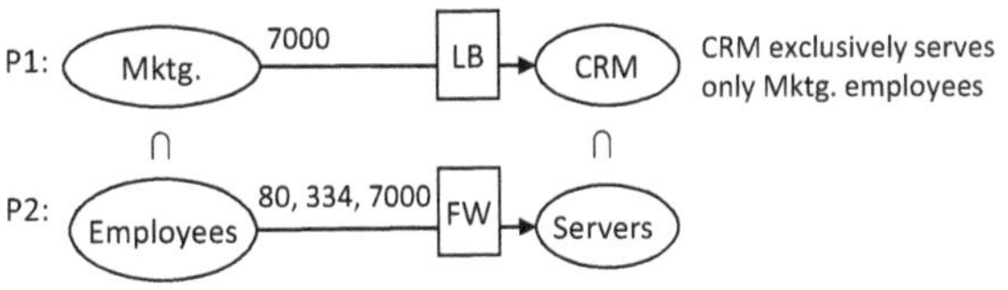

(a) Independently specified policies.

```
if_(match(srcip=Mktg, tcp, dstport=7000, dstip=CRM),
  FW>>LB>>route,
  if_(match(dstip=CRM), drop,
    if_(match(srcip=Empl, tcp, dstport=80|334|7000, dstip=Servers),
      FW>>route, drop)))
```

(b) Pyretic-style composite program.

```
Subject1: CRM-Access
    tcp, dstport =7000 : Permit, FW-LB chain
Subject2: CRM-Block
    * : Deny
Subject3: Server-Access
    tcp, dstport=80|334|7000 : Permit, FW chain
Clauses (Prioritized):
1. Mktg --> CRM : CRM-Access
2. * --> CRM : CRM-Block
3. Employees --> Server : Server-Access
```

(c) composite policy specified in GBP.

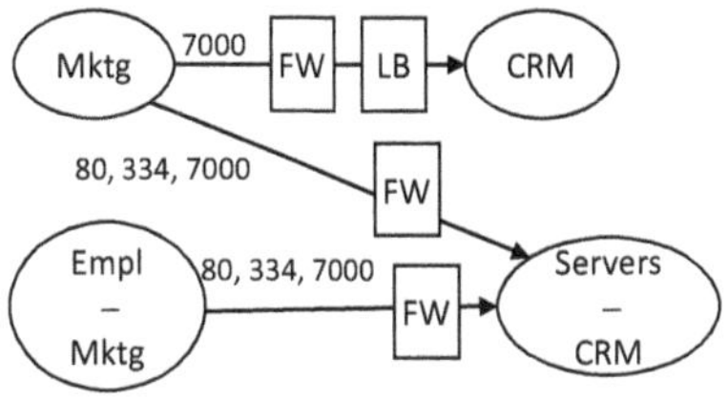

(d) Composed policy in a graph.

Figure 1: Policy composition example.

ing so must be exposed to and take into account the network admin's intent.

Other frameworks such as Frenetic [20] and Pyretic [34] allow users to compose modular policies/programs into a more complex control program. For example, Pyretic users can cause two policies to be sequentially applied to an incoming packet using the $>>$ operator, and this is effective to chain multiple service functions (such as FW>>LB). The sequential operator cannot be used to directly compose P1 and P2: e.g., P1>>P2 composition fails to allow [Empl→ Servers−CRM] traffic since the traffic cannot pass P1's ACL. Pyretic's parallel composition, P1+P2, will apply each policy to a different copy of the same packet and fail to block non-Marketing traffic and to create the FW>>LB chain.

From these failed attempts to combine P1 and P2, we see that a correct composition requires carefully **decomposing** each of P1 and P2 into ACL and service requirements and **re-composing** them into a single program. In particular, Pyretic supports an $if\_(match(), A, B)$ statement for 'if match() do A, else B'. With this, users can write a composite program implementing P1 and P2, as shown in Fig.1(b). However, the user has to carefully consider the flow space relations (P1 $\subset$ P2) and manually compose the FW>>LB chain for [Mktg→CRM], place P1's match() classifier followed by P2, and insert $if\_(match(dstip = CRM), drop, ...)$ in between to implement exclusive access to CRM. A similar manually composed program for GBP is shown in Fig.1(c).

Such manual decomposition and re-composition process is possible when done by a human operator who clearly understands the **joint intent** of P1 and P2. Based on such understanding, the operator can 1) resolve, the ACL conflict between P1 and P2 and 2) decide, the order between FW and LB. P1 and P2 ACL policies do conflict since P1 blocks traffic from non-Mktg employees to CRM while P2 allows the traffic (by allowing its super-set). The joint intent used to resolve this conflict would be *P1's exclusive access policy overrides P2's allow policy*. Similarly, the order of the FW-LB chain is chosen using the operator's internal knowledge of the service functions.

Even if such joint intents are clear to the human operator, it is impractical and error-prone to manually compose thousands of real world policies that have more complex super/sub-set relations and access control requirements: e.g., exclusive access to source/destination, conditional on other attributes such as location and security level.

Thus, automated composition by the system, not by a human, is critical to build a practical and scalable policy framework. The key to enabling automatic composition is to *explicitly capture the internal intents of the individual policy writer in each policy*. Existing policy abstractions [19, 23, 38] do not support this. For instance, they cannot express the intent that an Allow ACL rule MUST allow its specified traffic; thus, the Allow rule can be overridden by a Deny rule from another policy it is combined with. Similarly, existing service chain policy work [38, 31] can only capture the intent that certain service functions should be deployed on the specified path, but they cannot capture the service functions/actions that MUST NOT be applied by other policies. Hence, a human oracle is required to manually combine service function requirements from different policies.

Fig.1(d) shows a correct composition of P1 and P2 in a simple graph. Only Mktg. employees can send to the CRM servers through the FW-LB service chain. The other servers except for CRM, expressed by a primitive set operator *diff* ('−'), accept traffic from all Employee devices including Mktg. An entire policy for any endpoint pair is expressed on the edge between two nodes representing the endpoints, with no need to carefully walk through multiple lines of prioritized rules or if_then statements. We show how to automatically create such composed policies in §4 and §5. We first lay out the required properties for a policy framework.

2.3 Requirements for policy framework

Simple and intuitive: Anecdotally, we found that many network admins and cloud tenants design their policies by drawing diagrams on whiteboards. We believe a policy abstraction must be as simple as drawing diagrams similar to Fig.1(a), yet **expressive** enough to capture their intents for diverse and dynamic SDN, cloud and NFV applications with sophisticated service chain requirements [34, 22, 38].

Independent and Composable: Each policy writer should be able to write policies independently without coordinating with other policy writers; yet ensuring that their intents are being composed and enforced correctly, or receiving notification if there are conflicts or more information is needed.

Eager composition: Composing policies and ensuring that individual policy intents are satisfied prior to deployment, i.e., eagerly, is highly desirable. Eager composition can greatly reduce the number of conflicts/errors that a runtime system has to handle, enable speedy runtime operation, and reduce the chance of system misbehavior compared to lazy composition. However, eager composition without actual endpoints in the system can lead to exponential state explosion because in the worst case, every combination of input policies should be considered. The policy framework design should enable fast composition.

Automated: The policy framework must be highly automated to free network admins from manual and error-prone policy composition. In some cases when the system cannot identify the best policy composition, a human may be required to provide input and pick one composition. However, this is much less burdensome than the existing approach of manual composition.

Well-formed: The composed policy generated from the input policies should be well-formed such that a unique policy can be chosen without ambiguity for any given packet and associated dynamic conditions. This would allow the runtime operation to be deterministic.

Service chain analysis: Handling service chains for correct policy composition is crucial: e.g., a misplaced FW can drop packets that are legitimately allowed by ACL policies. To the extent possible, the policy framework needs to model the behavior of service functions for composition analysis.

Our framework, PGA, provides a simple and intuitive *graphical interface* that is similar to how network admins typically visualize their policies on a whiteboard. In PGA, each user writes policies for arbitrary selection of endpoints based on *logical endpoint properties* that makes sense to them. This gives users the flexibility to write policies independent of each other as well as the underlying physical network infrastructure. PGA achieves automated, eager composition of such policies by capturing the *relationship* between endpoint properties and enabling individual policies to *constrain* each other during composition. Lastly, it provides abstractions to succinctly *model middlebox behavior* that aids in service chain analysis.

3. SYSTEM OVERVIEW

Fig. 2 provides an overview of the PGA system components and their interactions with external components. As mentioned earlier, PGA uses a graph-based abstraction to specify network policies. The users/tenants/admins and SDN applications independently generate their policies as graphs and submit them to the Graph Composer through a PGA User Interface (UI). The UI and composer utilize additional information (e.g., tenant hierarchies, tenant/endpoint locations) from external sources to assist in the policy specification and eager composition. The composer automatically composes input graphs into a combined conflict-free graph, resolving or flagging conflicts/errors and reporting them to users, possibly with suggested fixes.

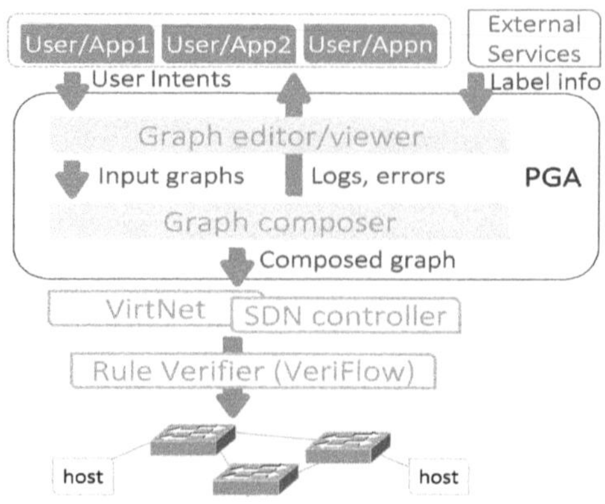

Figure 2: PGA system architecture.

The composed high-level policy can be compiled down to low-level configurations/rules, either proactively or reactively; PGA's eager policy composition is orthogonal to the lower-level compilation methodology. Our prototype supports two different network environments. The first is an SDN environment with OpenFlow enabled network devices, where we use the POX OpenFlow controller to reactively generate OpenFlow rules for pkt-in events based on a composed policy graph. To guard against possible bugs in rule generation, and against the possibility that unrelated SDN modules, e.g., traffic engineering, may generate conflicting rules, we use a rule verification tool (§6) to detect and verify changes in end-to-end communication paths against the ACL policies that PGA has generated for recent pkt-in events.

Our prototype also supports a virtual network abstraction provided by OpenStack Neutron [8]. Our PGA service proactively configures virtual network resources – specifically, Neutron Security Groups and service functions – to implement the polices of a composed graph, and dynamically associates VMs to the best-matching graph nodes at runtime.

Both the SDN and virtual network systems can be extended to support NFV; e.g., PGA's composed graph can be used to generate Network Service Headers (NSH) and Service Classifiers [4] for service function chaining.

For simplicity, our discussion around prototype system will assume the SDN-OpenFlow environment while the graph model and composition algorithm below can be applied to diverse environments.

4. GRAPH MODEL

In PGA, network policies are described using a *graph structure* that represents: 1) allowed communication between network endpoints, and 2) any required service function chain traversal for each communication. PGA is designed so that concise models that contain only a small number of elements are able to express policy for a much larger number of endpoints. PGA achieves this model scalability by describing policies at the granularity of *groups* of endpoints (similar to [6]) that share common properties expressed in terms of primitives called *labels*. Labels can be assigned and changed at runtime as endpoint properties (states) change, enabling a static PGA graph model to capture all the policies that can be dynamically assigned to an endpoint. PGA is a whitelisting model; communication must be explicitly allowed by a PGA model, else it is implicitly denied.

We use the example graph models shown in Fig. 3 to illustrate various features of the PGA model and composition. Model (a) is given by an admin for all Departments of a company and specifies that traffic is allowed from the IT department to the Engineering department using specified protocol port numbers. Model (b) is given by a web application admin. This model allows traffic from any Department to access the Web application using port 80 (`HTTP` protocol) and indicates that the traffic will be load balanced. The model also specifies that traffic is allowed from the Web to DB tiers, and from DB to itself. Model (c) is specified by an SDN application for DNS-based security protection. This model requires that DNS traffic from network endpoints with "Normal" security status must be inspected by a Deep Packet Inspection service when it performs DNS lookups, while network endpoints that are deemed "Quarantined" can only send their traffic (of any type) to a Security Remediation server. Model (d) is actually two models given by the Data Center admin. The first model specifies that traffic coming into the Data Center from the Campus must pass through a Firewall service and a Byte Counter service, while all east-west traffic within the data center also traverses a Byte Counter service. The second model allows monitoring traffic (port 9099) between endpoints within the Data Center.

PGA automatically combines multiple independently specified policy graphs into a coherent composed policy. This requires the novel ability to merge service functions chains in addition to access control policies. The PGA model has three primitives that support composition.

1. The *packet processing behavior* of each network service function in a service function chain is explicitly specified using a variant of the Pyretic network programming language [34] that we developed. Our composition engine (§5) analyzes these descriptions in order to automatically assemble composed service function chains that correctly combine policies from multiple policy graphs.

2. A *label mapping* input is introduced to enable identification of endpoint groups that can have overlapping endpoint membership. This avoids unnecessarily composing endpoint groups that are mutually exclusive, thus greatly reducing computation time and memory requirements. Label mapping is necessary to detect overlapping membership not only between endpoint groups of different graphs but also within a single graph.

3. *Composition constraints* are introduced to give policy writers the flexibility to express invariants that can never be violated under composition. Each policy writer can independently express their intended invariants, and the PGA system will automatically compose these individual policies while respecting the invariants. This avoids imposing rigid universally applied conflict resolution policies (such as static priority), and minimizes the need for human intervention during composition.

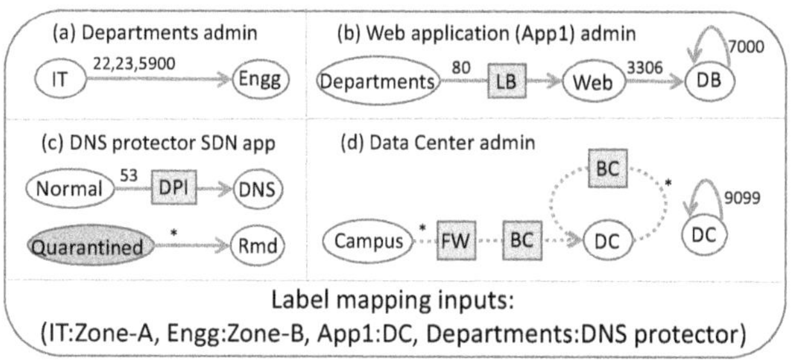

Figure 3: Sample input graphs and label mapping.

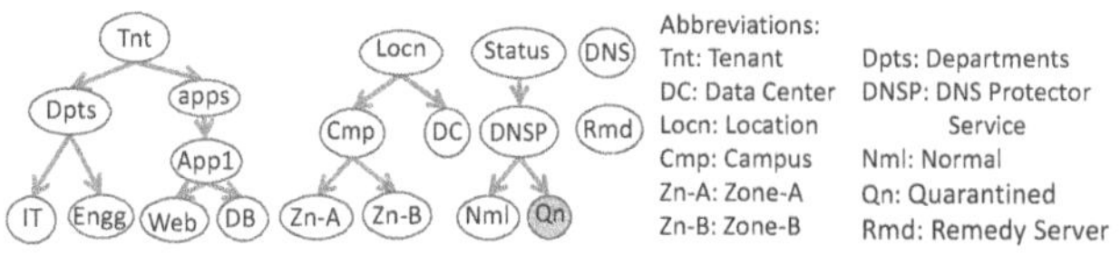

Figure 4: Sample input label namespace hierarchy.

We next describe the basic PGA graph constructs, followed by the primitives that support composition.

4.1 Graph Constructs

Vertices and Labels: Each vertex in a PGA graph model represents an *endpoint group* (EPG) which comprises a set of *endpoints* (EPs). An EP is the smallest unit of abstraction for which a policy is applied, e.g., a server, VM, client device, network, subnet, or end-user. An EPG comprises all EPs that satisfy a *membership predicate* specified for the EPG. In Fig. 3, each membership predicate is given as a *label*, e.g., Web, DC, etc. In general, a membership predicate can be a boolean expression over all labels.

Fig. 4 shows an example set of labels arranged in a hierarchy. The labels at the leaves, e.g., IT, Engg, Web, etc. are the truly basic elements, while each non-leaf label is a composite label that is simply a convenient shorthand for the logical disjunction (boolean OR) of all of its descendant leaf labels, e.g., Dpts is equivalent to IT OR Engg. Though not shown in the figure, composite labels can be defined that do not fit into a hierarchy, and can in general represent shorthand notation for arbitrary expressions over leaf labels. The hierarchy serves another important purpose for PGA composition. As we describe in §5, the composition process translates input graphs into a normalized form in which all EPGs have disjoint membership. PGA therefore needs to know which labels are mutually exclusive, i.e., cannot ever be assigned simultaneously to an EP. For example, in the DNS protector app of model (c), an EP cannot be both Normal and Quarantined. The hierarchy provides this information. Specifically, in any single tree of the hierarchy, any set of labels that do not have an ancestor relationship are mutually exclusive, e.g., {Zn-A, Zn-B}, {Cmp, DC}, and {Dpts, App1}.

The PGA system can restrict the scope of each policy writer to a particular relevant subset of the label space; for example, the admin of the Campus Network might only be allowed to use labels Cmp, Zn-A, and Zn-B for defining EPGs in its policy graphs. Each leaf label represents a collection of boolean variables, one per EP, i.e., leaf label x represents the set of boolean variables $\{e.x|e \in E\}$, where E is the set of all EPs. Assigning a leaf label to an EP sets the value of the corresponding boolean variable to True, otherwise it is False. Labels can be split into three categories: 'tenant' labels identifying end-users or their applications, e.g., IT or Web, 'network location' labels identifying regions of the network topology, e.g., Zn-A or DC, and 'status' labels indicating dynamically changing properties, e.g., Qn for currently quarantined EPs. To illustrate how labels are used, say that server S is an EP that is located in the Data Center and hosts the database of Web Application of Fig. 3. Then, server S would be assigned labels DC and DB, setting its boolean variables $S.DC$ and $S.DB$ to True.

EPs can be assigned labels dynamically at runtime, causing them to move from one EPG to another. For example, a server that was assigned the label Nml (normal) could subsequently be relabeled Qn (quarantined) when a network monitor detects the server issuing a DNS query for a known malicious Internet domain. Thus, a *static* PGA graph model actually describes a set of network policies that are applied *dynamically* to each EP according to the EP's status changes over time (that can be programmed as a finite state machine [28]). Moreover, analysis and composition of policy graphs into a fully composed network policy graph is a procedure that only needs to be invoked when policy graphs are added, modified, or removed. Analysis is not needed when EPs change EPG membership. Instead, the runtime system only needs to perform the lightweight operation of looking up and applying the correct rules for each EP depending on its current EPG membership. As EPs change membership across EPGs, the set of addresses encompassed within an EPG also changes. In general, an EPG can be associated with a variable representing virtual addresses indicating 'some EP' within the EPG – e.g., virtual IPs used for server load-balancing – and policies can be written using the EPG variable as well.

Edges and Service Chains: As stated earlier, PGA is a whitelisting model; by default, no communication is allowed between any EPs. A directed edge between EPGs is required to specify allowed communication in a PGA policy. An edge consists of a classifier, which matches packet header fields to represent the security whitelisting rule. Classifiers may include virtual addresses described above. It also optionally has a service chain consisting of a sequence of one or more *network function boxes*. A network function box may correspond to an SDN controller function or to a network middlebox or a set of middleboxes. A directed edge from endpoint group E to endpoint group E' with Boolean predicate (classifier) B and path expression (service chain) P indicates that a correct implementation will forward traffic from all hosts in E satisfying B along paths that are a prefix of the concatenation of the network function boxes in P and some host in E'. For example, model (c) in Fig. 3 specifies that traffic sent on port 53 is allowed from Normal (Nml) EPs to DNS server EPs and the packets must pass through a DPI network service. The implementation should also take care of forwarding to the right destination EP which might be decided at the source EP or at a network function box (e.g. load balancer). In the degenerate case where E and E' are singletons, B is the trivial predicate that always returns true, and P is the empty path expression, an edge reduces to a specification of point-to-point forwarding.

A model can have multiple directed edges from an EPG, as long as the edge classifiers cover non-overlapping flow spaces. Edge whitelist rules are stateful, such that the reverse traffic on established connections (e.g. TCP) is also allowed. Two types of edges can be specified. A *whitelist edge* is depicted as a solid line and describes an allowed communication, e.g., from IT to Engg in Fig. 3. A *conditional edge* is depicted as a dotted line and specifies a service chain requirement which is instantiated if and only if the edge's match condition overlaps the classifier of a whitelist edge in a *different* policy graph. A conditional edge, by itself, does not allow communication. Fig. 3(d) illustrates the utility of conditional edges. The Data Center admin's intent is not to allow all communication from Campus to DC but to have any communication allowed by any other graph pass through the specified service chain. If no policy graph has a whitelist edge from Campus to DC, then the service chain requirement is not needed in the fully composed policy graph.

4.2 Primitives Supporting Composition

Network Function Box Behavior: To enable automatic composition of service function chains, PGA models need to specify the packet processing behavior of each network function box. For this, PGA uses the open source Pyretic SDN language [34], and extends it to enable programming based on EPGs. This allows a user to specify the full behavior of a network function box as a Pyretic program; we term this *white boxing*. Whiteboxing is not a hard requirement. In cases where middleboxes are used for which the internal logic is not known, we support *gray boxing*. Herein, the corresponding network function box is described by a Pyretic program that captures only the high-level bounding behavior of the middlebox. For example, a commercial L7-aware load balancer can be gray boxed as `match(dstip = Web.virtIP) » modify(dstip = Web.RIPs)`, where `Web.RIPs` is a set of real IP addresses of destination web server EPs and `Web.virtIP` is the exposed virtual address of the web service. While the precise mapping of an input packet to a destination IP address is not known, the model accurately bounds the output header packet space of the middlebox.

We note that whiteboxing and grayboxing may not cover every possible NFV scenario. The current PGA framework does not consider network functions that duplicate and forward packets along different paths; this also implies that a network function box is allowed to modify the destination address to only hosts within the destination EPG of the edge that the box belongs to. Extending PGA to handle those cases is our future work.

Label Mapping: Policy composition combines the EPGs of one graph with EPGs of a second graph, potentially causing exponential growth in the size of the composed graph as the number of graphs to be composed increases. Usually, however, the vast majority of EPG combinations are mutually exclusive, i.e., it is impossible for any EP to belong to both of the original EPGs that are being combined. For example, if all IT dept. EPs are always located in the datacenter and never in the campus network, then a combined EPG that corresponds to EPs that are both in the IT dept. and in the campus network is guaranteed to be the empty set and thus does not need to be generated in the composed policy graph. The *label mapping* input to PGA enables composition to avoid generating such impossible EPG combinations by capturing the relationship between labels across different label trees (e.g. tenant and location label trees). The label mapping is a symmetric relation $F \subseteq L \times L$, where L is the set of all leaf labels. If labels $(x, y) \in F$, then a single EP can be assigned both labels x and y. For example, the label mapping shown in Fig. 3 indicates that an IT EP can also be a Zone-A EP, i.e., the IT dept. is located in the network Zone-A. For simplicity, the syntax used to specify the label mapping can give only one side of the symmetric relation. Also, it can use non-leaf labels as a shorthand for all of the leaf label descendants. The detailed use of label mapping to limit composition complexity is covered in §5.

Composition Constraints: A policy graph can flexibly specify constraints on the policy changes that are allowed when the policy graph is to be composed with any other policy graph. Constraints can be specified for any ordered pair of EPGs in a policy graph. The constraints can limit the addition of new classifiers that would allow additional traffic from source EPG to destination EPG. For example, a policy that strictly allows only port 80 traffic from a source EPG to a destination EPG can use constraints to prohibit additional ports from ever being allowed even if they are allowed for the same EPG pair by whitelists in other policy graphs. Classifier constraints can also limit the removal of allowed traffic as a result of composition.

Regarding service chain composition, the constraints can limit the behavior of function boxes that are added to service chains when the policy graph is composed with another graph. Specifically, the constraints can place limits on the packet header field modifications and packet drop operations that additional function boxes can perform on packets. Since the behavior of function boxes is modeled using our extended Pyretic, composition analysis can check whether adding a specific function box to a given service chain would violate the constraints given by the policy graphs that are being composed together.

	Classifier		Function Box	
Match	Add	Remove	Drop	Modify
port 80	Y	N	N	DSCP=16,18,20
port 88	N			
*	Y			

Table 1: Example composition constraints.

Table 1 shows example composition constraints from a source EPG to a destination EPG. The table indicates that port 80 traffic cannot be disallowed through composition with other graphs, and function boxes that are added cannot drop packets but are allowed to modify the DSCP packet field to a set of specific values. The table also shows that port 88 cannot be allowed through composition, but otherwise all other traffic can be allowed, with no restriction on function boxes. Composition constraints could more generally be specified using a constraint language such as Prolog.

A commonly needed special case for composition constraints occurs when a policy graph specifies that no additional traffic should be allowed to or from a particular EPG. Composition constraints can express that, i.e., in a policy graph, all EPG ordered pairs that contain the EPG have the constraint that composition is prohibited from changing the range of allowed traffic or the service chain. We can more conveniently and concisely represent this set of constraints by marking the EPG as "exclusive". For example, the Qn EPG in Fig. 3 is an exclusive EPG, preventing other policies from thwarting the intention of the policy writer to redirect all traffic from quarantined hosts to a remediation server.

5. GRAPH COMPOSITION

A key goal of PGA is to enable policy writers to specify their policies independently and delegate the composition process to the system. The system should compute the union of all policies from the input graphs, subject to composition constraints, to generate a composed graph. The composed graph should be well-formed (§2), i.e., comprise purely mutually exclusive EPGs to allow the PGA runtime to determine the unique EPG for each EP, and then apply the associated network policies to the EP (or determine that the EP is not in any EPG and so no communication for it is allowed).

Composition in PGA is different from the union (parallel) and sequential composition operators used in NetKAT [12] and Pyretic [34]. Their union (parallel) operator applies each of the constituent policies to a different copy of the input packet and then computes the union of their output packets while the sequential operator applies the output of one policy as input to the other. In PGA, we compute the union of the policies themselves based on set theoretic Venn diagram analysis. A PGA policy in a simplified form is a combination of *match + action*: EPG labels and edge classifiers form the match space while edge types and service chains constitute the action part. Conceptually, PGA composition takes the union of the match spaces of the input graphs: inheriting actions from the input graphs for the non-overlapping match spaces, and combining actions for the overlapping (intersecting) match spaces subject to composition constraints. Note that EPGs can have overlapping EP membership specified as arbitrary Boolean expressions over the label space.

We accomplish this composition in two steps. We first *normalize input graphs* (§5.1) by transforming their EPGs into an equivalent set of disjoint EPGs to easily identify the overlapping space and generate well-formed policies in the composed graph. We then *compute the union of the normalized graphs* (§5.2) by creating directed edges equivalent to the union of the original policies, except where doing so would violate the invariants given by composition constraints. The overlapping policies, identified by a common classifier for the same src-dst EPG pair in the normalized graphs, can require two service chains to be merged in the union. We use composition constraints to select the network function boxes to include in the combined service chain. To select an appropriate service order, PGA detects dependencies between function boxes based on modeling of their packet processing behaviors, and use the dependencies to determine valid orderings. Additionally, we detect possible remaining conflicts that should be flagged to policy writers.

5.1 Normalization of Input Graphs

In normalization, we compute a set of globally disjoint EPGs which represent the equivalence classes of endpoints to which the same set of policies should be applied. We then transform each input graph into an equivalent normalized form where policies are expressed only with respect to the newly computed EPGs.

The first step is to translate input graph EPGs into EPGs with globally disjoint membership. Second, composition constraints from the input graph must be replicated and merged to the normalized graph. Third, edge policies from the input graph must be replicated and merged to the normalized graph, subject to the composition constraints added in the previous step.

The abstractions of label hierarchy and label mapping facilitate the translation of input graph EPGs into globally disjoint EPGs in the normalized graph. As described in §4, label hierarchy captures the sets of mutually exclusive labels. Each EPG in the input graph is first split into locally disjoint EPGs by algebraically rewriting the EPG's membership predicate expression into an equivalent positive disjunctive normal form. Each term in the resulting expression describes a locally disjoint EPG. More specifically, we replace each composite label in the expression with its leaf label equivalents. Then, we expand the expression and remove any negated labels by replacing them with the disjunction of all the other sibling leaf labels in the hierarchy (since they are mutually exclusive). Finally, we convert the expression, which is now using only leaf labels in positive form, into disjunctive normal form, i.e., ORing a collection of terms where each term is the AND of leaf labels. Any conjunctive term that has any mutually exclusive labels must be the empty set, and so we delete these empty terms from the expression. Each remaining conjunctive term defines an EPG that is disjoint within the same input graph.

To obtain globally disjoint EPGs, we may need to further divide each locally disjoint EPG. We take each conjunctive term and check the label mapping to identify all other potentially related labels, i.e., labels that are transitively related to the labels in the term. For example, if the term is $label_1$ AND $label_2$, we check the label mapping starting from each of these labels and add the result to the conjunction. Suppose this adds $label_3$ AND $label_4$ AND $label_5$. If any of the resulting labels are mutually exclusive, e.g., Nml and Qn, we split the terms accordingly. For example, if $label_4$ and $label_5$ are mutually exclusive, we form two terms: 1) $label_1$ AND $label_2$ AND $label_3$ AND $label_4$, and 2) $label_1$ AND $label_2$ AND $label_3$ AND $label_5$. We continue splitting the terms until no term has mutually exclusive labels. This final set of terms corresponds to globally disjoint EPGs.

Once the normalized EPGs are generated, composition constraints from the input graph need to be replicated to the normalized graph. In particular, suppose that EPG S in the original input graph is translated to normalized EPGs S_1, S_2, ..., S_m, and input graph EPG D is normalized to EPGs D_1, D_2, ..., D_n. If the input graph has constraints for source EPG S and destination EPG D, then the constraints must be replicated in the normalized graph for ordered EPG pairs $(S_i, D_j), \forall i = 1..m, \forall j = 1..n$.

Composition constraints may need to be merged in addition to being replicated. If the original graph has constraints for EPGs (G, H), and these EPGs overlap with EPGs (S, D), then any constraint specified for (G, H) must be merged with the constraint for (S, D) in order to construct the constraints for the normalized EPGs that constitute the overlap. Merging composition constraints entails adopting the union of restrictive invariants of two overlapping constraints. However, conflicts may be detected if an invariant from one composition constraint, e.g., never allow port 80 traffic, is opposed by an invariant from another composition constraint, e.g., never deny port 80 traffic. Such conflicts are error conditions flagged to operators.

Finally, normalization replicates and merges edges from the original graph's EPG pairs to the normalized graph's EPG pairs to express equivalent policies. If EPG S has an edge to EPG D in the original graph, then the original edge is replicated to the normalized graph EPGs $(S_i, D_j), \forall i = 1..m, \forall j = 1..n$. Any edges for (G, H) need to be merged with those of (S, D) on the normalized EPG pairs that constitute the overlap. This merging is governed by the (merged) composition constraints.

5.2 Graph Union

In graph union, for each globally disjoint EPG that may be in multiple normalized graphs with different policies, we compute the union of those policies to obtain the final policy that should be applied to its endpoints. This involves merging whitelists and service chains from multiple edges without violating each other's constraints.

In normalized form, EPGs in two different graphs are either disjoint or equal. Partial overlap is not possible. This property enables multiple normalized graphs to be composed together using a simple union operation. The composed graph has the union of all the EPGs of the individual graphs. The union operation also copies and merges composition constraints and directed edges from the individual graphs to the composed graph. Merging composition constraints is performed identically as described in §5.1.

As edges from the individual graphs are added to the composed graph, they are checked against the composition constraints for the source and destination EPGs. This check determines whether an edge's classifier satisfies the constraints or needs to be narrowed to be in compliance with them. If a new edge passes this test with a non-null surviving classifier, then it may be added or merged with existing edges from source to destination EPGs.

The first step in merging the new edge is to find the intersection of its classifier flow space with the existing classifiers. For the non-intersecting classifier space of the new edge, the new edge and its function boxes can be added directly, subject to function box composition constraints. For any intersecting classifier space, merging is needed. We break down the intersecting space into a matching set of subspaces in the existing policies and for the new edge. This allows us to merge, for each subspace, one existing edge with one new edge.

For each pair of edges that need to be merged, if either edge has a service chain for the intersecting space, then service function composition is required that combines function boxes from the service chains of both edges. An important challenge is to determine a proper ordering of the service functions in the composed chain. PGA determines the order by analyzing function box actions on different flow spaces. The analysis identifies input-output dependencies between different function boxes and constructs an ordering that is consistent with the dependencies. In addition, the analysis identifies potential function box conflicts in which two boxes perform apparently incompatible operations on a common packet space. For example, if one function box drops all packets in a packet space for which the other function box has a byte counting action, then there is likely a conflict. Finally, a set of heuristics is used to further improve ordering after satisfying detected dependencies and flagging possible conflicts.

The key to enabling PGA to compose and merge service function chains automatically is that the packet processing behavior of function boxes is explicitly exposed to the PGA system for analysis. PGA models network function *white boxes* and *gray boxes* behavior expressed explicitly in an extended version of Pyretic. The Pyretic compiler can take these descriptions and convert each network function box's behavior into a set of prioritized *match-action* rules. PGA analyzes these rules to characterize the *In Packet Space* and an *Out Packet Space* for each rule of every service function. The In Packet Space of a rule is defined as the flow space that would match and thus be processed by the rule, while the Out Packet Space is the outcome of processing the In Packet Space by the rule.

When merging two service function chains, PGA analyzes every pair of function boxes composed of one function box from each chain to identify a full dependency graph, and possible conflicts between different function boxes. For each function box pair, analysis considers every pair of *match-action* rules across the two service functions to find all dependencies and possible conflicts.

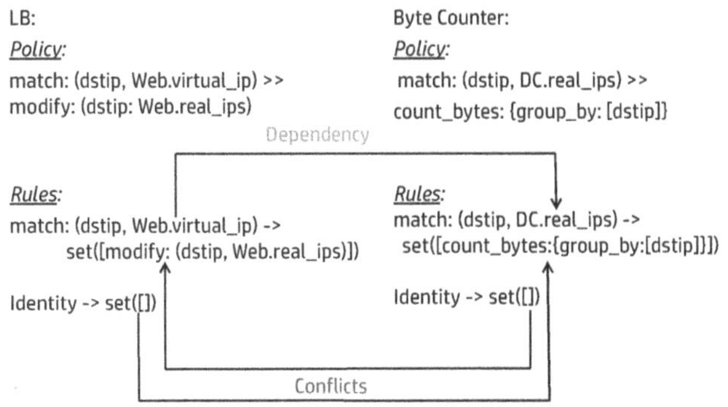

Figure 5: Analysis of service functions to determine order.

A dependency is identified from one rule to another if the first rule actively creates (through modify action) an Out Packet Space that overlaps with the second rule's In Packet Space. In Fig. 5 we show the Pyretic policies for two function boxes, Load Balancer (LB) and Byte Counter. Pyretic's compiler has converted these policies into prioritized match-action rules as shown below each Pyretic policy. In this example, as shown by the Dependency arrow, the In Packet Space of the Byte Counter is dependent on the Out Packet Space of LB, because the action of LB modifies the destination IP address to a real_ip address that is checked by the match portion of the Byte Counter's rule.

Possible conflicts between function boxes may be uncovered by the analysis and avoided through ordering or reported to users as possibly unresolvable conflicts. In Fig. 5, one possible conflict is between the default drop action in the Load Balancer and the byte counting in the Byte Counter, because for the same In Packet Space (destination IP address is not Web.virtual_ip), the two boxes have apparently incompatible actions (drop versus count). Another possible conflict is between the modify destination IP address action of the Load Balancer and the default packet drop action of Byte Counter. For the same In Packet Space (destination IP is Web.virtual_ip) the two actions are modify destination IP address versus drop, which are seemingly incompatible.

The final service order is determined using topological sort over the dependency graph. When there are more than one possible order, we choose an order that satisfies constraints on the input edges, and finally resort to heuristics, such as: a security service function, identified by its policy that actively drops packets based on some criteria, should be placed ahead of other service functions. This is consistent with how networks are typically administered.

For reference, the final composed graph obtained for our example from Fig. 3 is shown in Fig. 6. Note that a single function box from an input graph may be replicated across multiple edges in the composed graph (e.g. DPI). These are logically the same function box.

6. PROTOTYPE

Our prototype implementation contains ≈2.5K SLOC in Python, including the following Pyretic extensions.

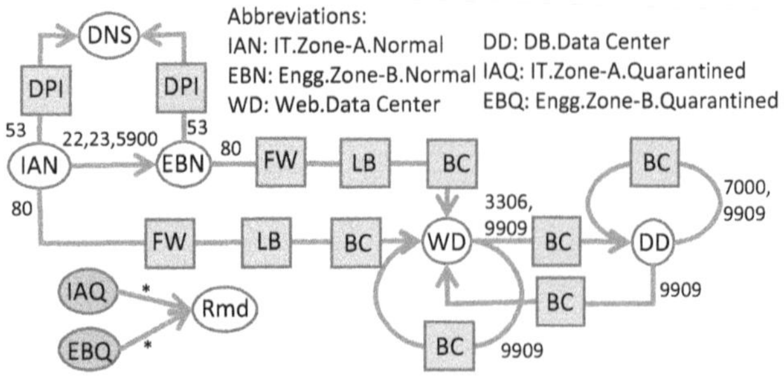

Figure 6: Composed graph for the running example.

6.1 Abstractions

To support policy graph specification, we extend Pyretic with three primitives: EPGs, Function boxes and Whitelists.
EPG. The user may create EPGs and specify membership requirement for endpoints to join the EPG through labels. EPGs also contain member variables indicating the set of L4 ports and endpoint IP addresses, which will be dynamically updated at runtime, and virtual IP addresses (used for load-balancing) of that EPG. The user may reference these variables while writing policies without having to assign values to them.
Function Box. The function boxes in our prototype are expressed in our extended Pyretic programming language. The policies are described in terms of the names of EPG variables, like the set of endpoint IPs and virtual IP, without having to assign values to the variables a priori. Both static and dynamic policies are supported as long as the dynamic policies contain an expression of their bounding behavior as described in §4. This expression is required for analyzing dependencies and conflicts between function boxes to determine their intermixed order when merging edges. The extended Pyretic language provides the necessary constructs to express this behavior.
WhiteList. The user may express Whitelists as arbitrary ranges of values for different flow header fields, e.g. `WhiteList(dstport=[80,>8000],proto=[6])`. Set operations – Union, Intersection and Difference – are supported to express more complex Whitelists.

6.2 System operation

As shown in Fig. 2, a *composer* module takes all the graphs and any auxiliary inputs and generates a composed graph by implementing the algorithm of §5. In our SDN prototype of the runtime system, the composed graph is stored as an in-memory hash table keyed with the source and destination EPGs for fast lookup of policies at runtime.

OpenFlow rule generation: In principle, the eagerly composed PGA policy could be enforced by proactively installing an equivalent set of OpenFlow rules into the network switches, determined using state of the art rule compilers [24, 36]. For simplicity, however, our runtime system implementation takes a fully reactive approach that evaluates the first packet of a new flow ($\approx$ OpenFlow *pkt_in* event) against the composed policy graph and then installs rules to enforce the ACL and service chain policies for the new flow. For this, we modify the Pyretic runtime to query the in-memory graph upon a *pkt_in* event to lookup the ACL and service chain policies, which are then compiled down to OpenFlow v1.0 rules through the Pyretic compiler and POX controller.

The underlying network topology is run on mininet [2]. The prototype system installs flow rules on the edge switches (similar to ref. [29]). The switch/port that each endpoint (EP) is attached to is pulled out from mininet but can be given by external sources such as 802.1X. The path from source EP to destination EP is given by the Pyretic *mac_learner*; more sophisticated waypoint routing algorithms [38, 31, 26] can be used to support middleboxes and include non-edge switches for policy enforcement.

Runtime verification: The presence of service chains in a composed PGA graph complicates runtime policy verification. We leave it to future work; but verify only whether the ACL policies in the composed graph are correctly realized on the network, by using VeriFlow [27] in our prototype, against potential violations due to: 1) the policy-to-rule compiler having a bug in generating flow rules, or 2) there being another control module in charge of other types of policies (e.g., traffic engineering, switch firmware upgrade) that changes flow rules without involving PGA.

VeriFlow runs as a proxy intercepting OpenFlow messages between the controller and switches to detect three event types: reachability setup, blackhole (incomplete routing path) and forwarding loop. We modify VeriFlow to report detected events and affected flows to the PGA runtime, which caches prior pkt_in events and the ACL decisions made for them. PGA compares the reported VeriFlow event with the cached ACL decisions to verify the following: reachability should be set up for allowed flows and no path should be set up for ACL-denied flows. If the allowed path is not set up properly (blackhole, loop, or lack of reachability setup), it is a violation of PGA policy. Similarly, we raise an alarm if a reachability setup event is reported for a pair of EPs for which the composed PGA graph does not allow communication. Note that these VeriFlow verifications may not hold if the service functions in the path drop/add/change packets.

7. PGA IN ACTION

We demonstrate the power of PGA in conflict detection & resolution through two case studies on real world examples.

7.1 Conflict between SDN apps

We consider the following example inspired by a real world anecdote of installing two SDN apps on the same network: one is the QoS app in Fig. 7 and the other is the DNS filtering/protector app (Fig. 3). One way to handle the OpenFlow rules generated from the two apps is to compose them into one prioritized rule table to detect potential conflicts. An exclusive set of non-contiguous priority ranges was manually assigned to each app; e.g., the first and third highest ranges were given to the DNS protector while the second and the fourth highest ranges to the QoS app in one table snapshot. Since there is no global priority coordination across the apps, it is possible for the QoS app's rule that marks QoS bits

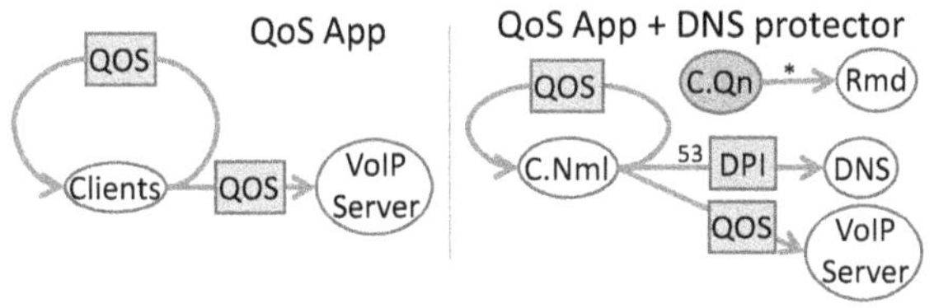

Figure 7: QoS app vs. DNS protector.

of VoIP packets and forwards them to output ports to be assigned a higher priority than one of the DNS protector rules that blocks quarantined IPs, potentially failing to block due to the prioritized QoS rule. This potential conflict between the two SDN apps was not initially detected because the two rules were written for non-overlapping IP addresses in the given snapshot of the rule table, although the two apps can be applied to the same client devices in other settings.

Another potential conflict was detected between the QoS rule and another DNS protector rule that redirects packets from DNS servers to different output ports. However, the detected conflict turned out to be a false positive as DNS servers were not supposed to be VoIP clients, and so the two rules actually don't overlap. These examples demonstrate the limitations of specifying and combining SDN apps at OpenFlow rule level, coupled with prioritization [24] and IP address assignment. PGA's label-based policy specification and graph composition enables eager conflict detection/resolution without requiring prioritized rules and IP addresses.

On the right of Fig. 7 is the composed PGA policy from the two apps. The EPG for quarantined clients (C.Qn) is set to 'exclusive'; this disallows any communication specified by the QoS app graph. And it is clear that DNS servers do not overlap with the client devices as there is no mapping between the two labels (omitted in the figure).

7.2 Large Enterprise ACL

Enterprise dataset: We obtain ACL policies from the policy management system in a large enterprise network. These policies are defined for each compartment, which are EPs that share the same set of ACL rules. The ACLs permit or deny the communications between the EPs within each compartment. Policies are written by network admins or application owners, manually reviewed for correctness and consistency, and then deployed in over 30+ global sites.

By analyzing the policies for the entire 136 compartments, we identified over 20K ACL policies that are written for 4916 EPGs. The sizes of EPGs vary, ranging from one IP address to over 600 non-contiguous subnets (100M IP addresses). We construct label mapping based on the super-sub set relationship between EPGs. Note that one EPG has multiple parents since the EPG may contain non-contiguous address blocks. We aggregate multiple policies for the same EPG pair by listing multiple protocol fields and port ranges for one edge, creating a total of 11,786 edges.

Redundancy and conflict are detected using PGA in this dataset. A rule is redundant if there exists another rule in the same compartment that completely covers the former rule's space with the same action. We have identified that 7% of the aggregated policies are redundant. PGA also detects two types of conflicts: *unmatched outgoing rules*, i.e., an outgoing rule in source compartment without the incoming rule to permit the communication in the destination compartment; and *unmatched incoming rules*, i.e., the incoming rule without the matching outgoing rule. The former is more damaging since it will result in blackholing. The latter means the incoming rules are not used since no traffic will be sent out. In total, we detect that 4.7% of outgoing policies and 4.5% of incoming policies are unmatched.

8. SYSTEM EVALUATION

For our experiments we used three data sets

D1: the synthetic running example from §4 and §5.

D2: the large enterprise dataset as described in §7.2.

D3: D2 with randomly added function boxes.

Our primary results show that due to eager composition, the runtime overhead of PGA is minimal even for very large composed graphs. PGA is practical and scalable, being able to analyze and compose thousands of policies producing nearly a million edges in under 600s when considering only ACLs and 800s in most cases for policy graphs with both ACLs and service chains. As described earlier, the composed graphs are correct by design. Additionally, for D1, we verify the correctness manually and for D2 and D3, we use Veriflow for indirect validation with reachability analysis.

The PGA prototype system is implemented in Python and currently runs as a single threaded program. For our evaluations, PGA is deployed on a server with 2x8 Intel Xeon 2.6 GHz cores with 132 GB memory running Linux kernel 3.13.0. We emulate switches and hosts with mininet 2.1.0 and openvswitch 2.0.2 on the server in order to create a topology and generate packets between hosts in different EPGs. Since the focus here is not to optimally assign flow rules to switches, the results described use simple topologies with one or two switches providing connectivity to the end hosts. We randomly generate packets between hosts to analyze reachability. A POX controller running on the same server uses PGA to look-up the policy to be applied upon receiving a *pkt_in* event. The input graphs are pre-composed by PGA and the composed graph is stored in memory. The composed graph from D1 has 8 EPGs and 11 edges. For D2, the composed graph has nearly 4K unique EPGs and over 76× the number of edges as the input graphs; in this case, high edge multiplication occurred in graph normalization because some input graph EPGs were defined by top-level labels in the label hierarchy.

Runtime Overhead. Fig. 8 shows the additional runtime latency incurred at the controller for the first packet of a flow by relying on PGA for determining the policy from the composed graphs of D1 (Small) D2 (Large). The input samples (pairs of EPGs) were randomly picked for D1. For D2, we picked more samples that had a large number of edges (10-30) between the EPG pair. This is because the prototype evaluates a packet linearly against each edge between the EPG pair until it finds the matching flow space and so

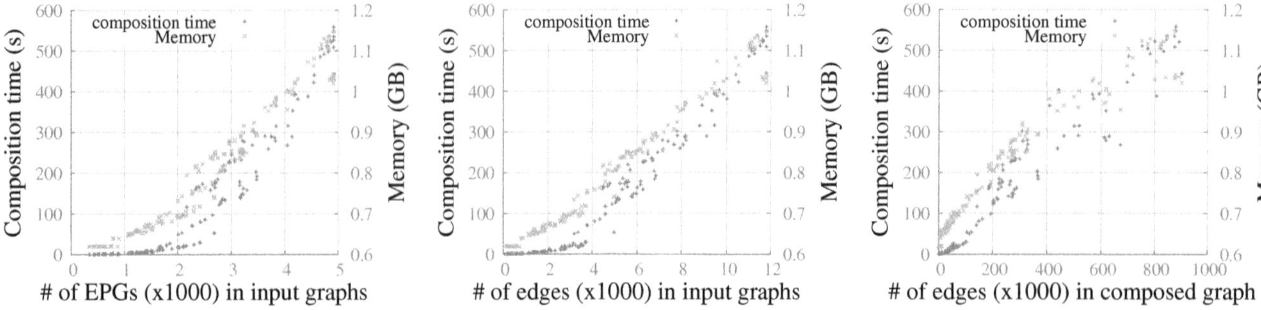

Figure 10: Scalability of PGA with D2.

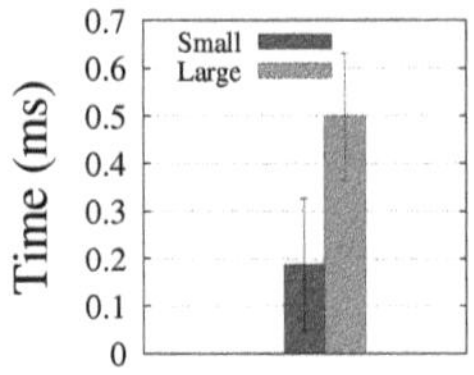

Figure 8: PGA induced additional runtime latency at the controller for D1 (Small), D2 (Large).

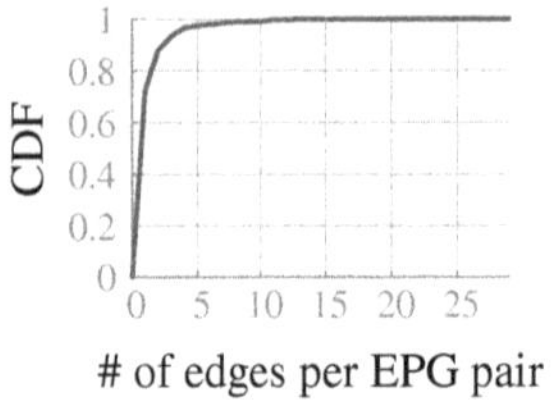

Figure 9: CDF of #edges per EPG pair in composed graph of D2.

incurs additional overhead for every edge; by selecting samples with the highest number of edges, we evaluate the worst case performance of PGA for this dataset.

Overall, the latencies are small for both cases. As expected, D2 results in a higher latency than D1 due to the higher number of edges.[1] Fig. 9 shows the CDF for number of edges per EPG pair in the composed graph of D2. 95% of EPG pairs have less than 4 edges between them and 99% below 11. Even the worst case performance numbers (obtained with >25 edges between EPG pair) have a sub-ms average latency overhead which is still small and practical for real time operation. We thus find that due to eager composition, the runtime overhead of policy lookup is negligible even for very large graphs. Additionally, the lookup time is independent of the network size, number of endpoints or the presence of service chains.

Scalability of PGA. Although PGA composes input graphs eagerly, it still needs to be able to handle very large inputs in a reasonable amount of time and with practical consumption of resources. We exercised PGA by varying the input from D2. We randomly selected different sets of compartments, composed their input graphs and measured the composition time as well as memory consumption. Fig. 10 shows the measures plotted against number of EPGs in input graphs, edges in input graphs, and edges in the composed graph. We omit the measures against number of EPGs in composed graph since it is similar to that for number of EPGs in input graphs. The largest input (entire D2) which produced nearly 1M edges in the composed graph required less than 1.2 GB of memory while completing in under 10 minutes.

If input graphs contain service chains, then the cost of composition is increased because pairwise analysis of function box interactions is required to determine correct function box orderings in the composed graph. Since D2 only contains ACL policies, we simulated a policy dataset with function boxes (D3) by first creating a pool of 16 synthetic function boxes, each having a bounding behavior that compiles to two match-action rules. We then randomly picked input edges from D2 to which we added a randomly chosen function box from the pool; up to 3500 functions boxes were added to D2, larger than 1900 middleboxes observed from very large enterprises (>100K hosts) [37], to yield D3.

Fig. 11 shows the composition time and memory consumption for D3. As expected, composition with service chain analysis is more expensive than composing only ACL policies (Fig. 10). Nevertheless, for most cases the composition time is <800 seconds and memory consumption is <20 GB. These are practical numbers for an engine eagerly composing such large number of policies. Note that the composed graph from D3 can have millions of function boxes, replicated from the 3500 functions boxes randomly placed in the inputs graphs; we cached and reused the results of intermediate chain analysis to prevent redundant computations and to save memory.

We also individually measured the time for each of the two steps of our composition algorithm. The normalization step is quite inexpensive and accounts for only around 1% of the total composition time. Although the graph union operation is expensive, we note that it is done in a progressive manner. We first compute unions for pairs of smaller graphs to get larger graphs and then repeat the procedure on the larger graphs; this algorithm is well suited for a multi-threaded implementation (future work).

9. RELATED WORK

Abstractions. Providing powerful abstractions for programming network policies has received considerable attention recently [20, 34, 41, 35, 12, 21, 19, 38, 6, 23, 14, 28]. However, most of these frameworks ([20, 34, 41, 35, 12, 21, 19, 38]) tie policy expression to low-level specifics such as device IP/MAC addresses or current locations of packets within the network. This keeps their complexity as well as the learning curve for users from lowering, especially when they want to express pure end-to-end communication polices without concerning the topology or other details of the network. It also makes them non-intuitive to express dynamic policies that change based on external events like EP status.

[1]This may be reduced by using packet classification algorithms that run in logarithmic time [16].

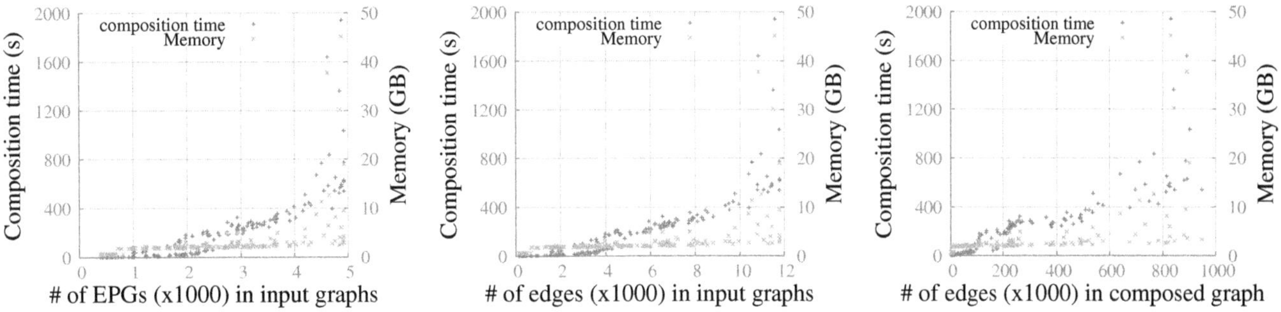

Figure 11: Scalability of PGA with D3 (D2 + function boxes).

Instead, policy intents can be suitably captured using logical labels similar to PGA. Logical labels have been advocated or supported in both networking [6, 23, 14] and non-networking [40, 9, 1] contexts. For example, SELinux [9] assigns arbitrary labels per file in extended attributes and allows users to define access control policies based on the label values. Among network policy frameworks, GBP [6] defines an application-centric policy model that has a notion of EPGs whose membership is determined by logical labels, similar to PGA, although it does not model the relationships between labels or provide a graph model. Flow-based Management Language (FML) [23] is a DATALOG-based query language that specifies access control and forwarding policies on logical entities (e.g., user names queried from external authentication services) and conditions (wireless vs. wired). FML has evolved to Nlog [29] for network virtualization and to OpenStack Congress policy language [7] that expresses policies across multiple cloud services of compute, storage, networking, etc. Despite the expressiveness, it is a generic language, non-trivial to map to graph models which are better suited for networking policies. Further, these abstractions do not model middlebox behavior required for service chain analysis and they do not support automated, eager composition.

Composition. Many frameworks support manual composition of network policies, e.g., [20, 34, 12, 21, 15, 19, 38]. Merlin [38] assumes a hierarchy of users like network admins and tenants and allows tenants to only restrictively refine policies that are explicitly delegated to them by the admin, manually composing both their intents in the process. It is thus not suitable for composing modular policies that can arbitrarily constrain each other where conflict resolution is required. Some frameworks [20, 34, 24, 12, 21] allow network operators to write modular programs and manually compose them into one complex program. These are without conflict resolution support as well. Further, their composition is too coarse-grained and cannot automatically decompose and re-compose complex user policies that often mix different types of intents – ACLs, service chains etc. – in each policy. Others have introduced composition operators to resolve conflicts between independently specified access control policies [15, 19] and bandwidth requirements [19]. They map the set of all input policies onto the leaf nodes of a single hierarchical tree and assign a composition operator to each intermediate node of the tree. Such assignments either require a human oracle [15] or are rigidly pre-determined for each conflict type, making it hard to automatically handle arbitrary conflicts between diverse policy writers.

In GBP [6], users are required to manually write a composite policy connecting multiple EPG pairs. Its users write conditions, prioritized rules etc. such that a unique and correct policy will be chosen for any traffic between endpoints that may have varying statuses (security level, location etc).

In contrast, PGA not only supports automated, eager composition of modular policies, it is also to our knowledge, the first to explore the model of individual policies independently constraining each other for composition.

Extensions. Specifying dynamic temporal behavior of the network as a finite state machine has been studied in [28, 42]. Kinetic [28] can coexist with PGA; different SDN control apps programmed in Kinetic can generate access control and service chain policies in PGA graph model, which the PGA framework can then compose while handling conflicts. I.e., Kinetic controls dynamic label assignments of endpoints while PGA captures and composes the network policy associated with each label (EPG).

Refs. [25, 17, 18] have explored ways to effectively model middleboxes. In comparison, PGA's modeling is more abstract but has been sufficient for the composition scenarios we targeted. Our ongoing work is exploring the utility of the richer modeling capability provided by some of these frameworks for service chain analysis and runtime verification of service chain policies.

Corybantic, Athens and Statesman [33, 13, 39] propose solutions to resolve conflicts on underlying network resources or states between different SDN control modules. NEMO [3] and ONOS [5] provide APIs to model a virtual network topology (of switches and routers) and to specify requirements on the topology links and paths. These systems deal with problems that are orthogonal to PGA which handles end-to-end policies that are agnostic to network specifics. PGA can be extended to incorporate some of these solutions. TAG [30] provides a graph abstraction capturing only bandwidth requirements across application components; extending PGA to incorporate TAG is our future work.

CoVisor [24] composes OpenFlow rule tables, separately compiled from individual SDN controllers, and efficiently updates the composed rule table for a change in an input table. However, composing high-level SDN policies in prioritized OpenFlow rules is inherently inefficient; e.g., adding/removing an SDN app/controller would require re-computation of the entire composed table in [24]. In PGA, incremental update of a composed graph per input graph join/leave/change events is an easy extension. In addition, PGA can use CoVisor to proactively compile OpenFlow rules for the composed graph and to incrementally update the rule table.

10. CONCLUSION

PGA provides an intuitive graph abstraction to express and compose policies. Users (or a policy authoring tool) can simply walk through a composed graph to verify connectivity and service chain requirements. PGA expresses policies and resolves conflicts while minimizing operator interventions. To our knowledge, PGA is the first to model the behavior of closed middleboxes and ensure their correct behavior in a service chain. Automatically combining multiple service chains is another unique feature of PGA. As future work, we plan to enhance PGA in a number of ways: e.g., when a large number of endpoints change their labels at the same time, the PGA runtime should be able to update the network in a scalable, responsive and consistent way. Supporting HW/VM middleboxes, verifying their runtime behaviors and chaining them in more flexible ways (e.g., asymmetric forward/reverse) is additional future work.

11. ACKNOWLEDGEMENTS

We greatly appreciate Nate Foster (our shepherd) and the anonymous reviewers for their insightful feedback. This work is supported in part by National Science Foundation (grants CNS-1302041, CNS-1330308 and CNS-1345249) and the Wisconsin Institute on Software-Defined Datacenters of Madison.

12. REFERENCES

[1] Docker. https://github.com/docker/docker/issues/11187.
[2] Mininet. http://mininet.org/.
[3] NEMO (NEtwork MOdeling) Language. http://www.hickoryhill-consulting.com/nemo/.
[4] Network Service Header. https://tools.ietf.org/html/draft-quinn-sfc-nsh-07.
[5] Open Network Operating System (ONOS) Intent Framework. https://wiki.onosproject.org/display/ONOS/The+Intent+Framework.
[6] OpenDaylight Group Policy. https://wiki.opendaylight.org/view/Group_Policy:Main.
[7] Openstack Congress. https://wiki.openstack.org/wiki/Congress.
[8] Openstack Networking – Neutron. https://wiki.openstack.org/wiki/Neutron.
[9] SELinux. http://selinuxproject.org/page/Main_Page.
[10] Service Function Chaining Architecture. https://tools.ietf.org/html/draft-merged-sfc-architecture-02.
[11] Service Function Chaining General Use Cases. https://tools.ietf.org/html/draft-liu-sfc-use-cases-08.
[12] C. J. Anderson, N. Foster, A. Guha, J.-B. Jeannin, D. Kozen, C. Schlesinger, and D. Walker. NetKAT: Semantic Foundations for Networks. In *POPL*, 2014.
[13] A. AuYoung, Y. Ma, S. Banerjee, J. Lee, P. Sharma, Y. Turner, C. Liang, and J. C. Mogul. Democratic Resolution of Resource Conflicts Between SDN Control Programs. In *CoNEXT*, 2014.
[14] M. Banikazemi et al. Meridian: an SDN platform for cloud network services. *Communications Magazine, IEEE*, 51(2):120–127, February 2013.
[15] P. Bonatti, S. de Capitani di Vimercati, and P. Samarati. A Modular Approach to Composing Access Control Policies. In *CCS*, 2000.
[16] H. Edelsbrunner et al. Optimal Point Location in a Monotone Subdivision. *SIAM J. Comput.*, 15(2):317–340, May 1986.
[17] S. K. Fayaz and V. Sekar. Testing Stateful and Dynamic Data Planes with FlowTest. In *HotSDN*, 2014.
[18] S. K. Fayazbakhsh, L. Chiang, V. Sekar, M. Yu, and J. C. Mogul. Enforcing Network-wide Policies in the Presence of Dynamic Middlebox Actions Using Flowtags. In *NSDI*, 2014.
[19] A. D. Ferguson, A. Guha, C. Liang, R. Fonseca, and S. Krishnamurthi. Participatory Networking: An API for Application Control of SDNs. In *SIGCOMM*, 2013.
[20] N. Foster, R. Harrison, M. J. Freedman, C. Monsanto, J. Rexford, A. Story, and D. Walker. Frenetic: A Network Programming Language. In *ICFP*, 2011.
[21] N. Foster, D. Kozen, M. Milano, A. Silva, and L. Thompson. A Coalgebraic Decision Procedure for NetKAT. In *POPL*, 2015.
[22] A. Gember-Jacobson, R. Viswanathan, C. Prakash, R. Grandl, J. Khalid, S. Das, and A. Akella. OpenNF: Enabling Innovation in Network Function Control. In *SIGCOMM*, 2014.
[23] T. L. Hinrichs, N. S. Gude, M. Casado, J. C. Mitchell, and S. Shenker. Practical Declarative Network Management. In *WREN*, 2009.
[24] X. Jin, J. Gossels, and D. Walker. CoVisor: A Compositional Hypervisor for Software-Defined Networks. In *NSDI*, 2015.
[25] D. Joseph and I. Stoica. Modeling Middleboxes. *Netwrk. Mag. of Global Internetwkg.*, 22(5):20–25, Sept. 2008.
[26] N. Kang, Z. Liu, J. Rexford, and D. Walker. Optimizing the "One Big Switch" Abstraction in Software-defined Networks. In *CoNEXT*, 2013.
[27] A. Khurshid, X. Zou, W. Zhou, M. Caesar, and P. B. Godfrey. VeriFlow: Verifying Network-wide Invariants in Real Time. In *NSDI*, 2013.
[28] H. Kim, J. Reich, A. Gupta, M. Shahbaz, N. Feamster, and R. Clark. Kinetic: Verifiable Dynamic Network Control. In *NSDI*, 2015.
[29] T. Koponen et al. Network Virtualization in Multi-tenant Datacenters. In *NSDI*, 2014.
[30] J. Lee, Y. Turner, M. Lee, L. Popa, S. Banerjee, J.-M. Kang, and P. Sharma. Application-driven Bandwidth Guarantees in Datacenters. In *SIGCOMM*, 2014.
[31] L. Li et al. PACE: Policy-Aware Application Cloud Embedding. In *INFOCOM*, 2013.
[32] H. H. Liu, S. Kandula, R. Mahajan, M. Zhang, and D. Gelernter. Traffic Engineering with Forward Fault Correction. In *SIGCOMM*, 2014.
[33] J. C. Mogul, A. AuYoung, S. Banerjee, L. Popa, J. Lee, J. Mudigonda, P. Sharma, and Y. Turner. Corybantic: Towards the Modular Composition of SDN Control Programs. In *HotNets*, 2013.
[34] C. Monsanto, J. Reich, N. Foster, J. Rexford, and D. Walker. Composing Software Defined Networks. In *NSDI*, 2013.
[35] T. Nelson, A. D. Ferguson, M. J. G. Scheer, and S. Krishnamurthi. Tierless Programming and Reasoning for Software-defined Networks. In *NSDI*, 2014.
[36] C. Schlesinger, M. Greenberg, and D. Walker. Concurrent NetCore: From Policies to Pipelines. In *ICFP*, 2014.
[37] J. Sherry et al. Making Middleboxes Someone else's Problem: Network Processing As a Cloud Service. *SIGCOMM CCR*, 42(4):13–24, Aug. 2012.
[38] R. Soulé, S. Basu, P. J. Marandi, F. Pedone, R. Kleinberg, E. G. Sirer, and N. Foster. Merlin: A Language for Provisioning Network Resources. In *CoNEXT*, 2014.
[39] P. Sun, R. Mahajan, J. Rexford, L. Yuan, M. Zhang, and A. Arefin. A Network-state Management Service. In *SIGCOMM*, 2014.
[40] A. Verma, L. Pedrosa, M. Korupolu, D. Oppenheimer, E. Tune, and J. Wilkes. Large-scale cluster management at Google with Borg. In *EuroSys*, 2015.
[41] A. Voellmy, J. Wang, Y. R. Yang, B. Ford, and P. Hudak. Maple: Simplifying SDN Programming Using Algorithmic Policies. In *SIGCOMM*, 2013.
[42] D. M. Volpano, X. Sun, and G. G. Xie. Towards Systematic Detection and Resolution of Network Control Conflicts. In *HotSDN*, 2014.

Central Control Over Distributed Routing

http://fibbing.net

Stefano Vissicchio*, Olivier Tilmans*, Laurent Vanbever†, Jennifer Rexford‡

* Université catholique de Louvain, † ETH Zurich, ‡ Princeton University

* name.surname@uclouvain.be, †lvanbever@ethz.ch, ‡jrex@cs.princeton.edu

ABSTRACT

Centralizing routing decisions offers tremendous flexibility, but sacrifices the robustness of distributed protocols. In this paper, we present *Fibbing*, an architecture that achieves both flexibility and robustness through central control over distributed routing. Fibbing introduces fake nodes and links into an underlying link-state routing protocol, so that routers compute their own forwarding tables based on the augmented topology. Fibbing is expressive, and readily supports flexible load balancing, traffic engineering, and backup routes. Based on high-level forwarding requirements, the Fibbing controller computes a compact augmented topology and injects the fake components through standard routing-protocol messages. Fibbing works with any unmodified routers speaking OSPF. Our experiments also show that it can scale to large networks with many forwarding requirements, introduces minimal overhead, and quickly reacts to network and controller failures.

CCS Concepts

•**Networks** → **Routing protocols;** *Network architectures; Programmable networks; Network management;*

Keywords

Fibbing; SDN; link-state routing

1. INTRODUCTION

Consider a large IP network with hundreds of devices, including the components shown in Fig. 1a. A set of IP addresses (D_1) see a sudden surge of traffic, from multiple entry points (A, D, and E), that congests a part of the network. As a network operator, you suspect a denial-of-service attack (DoS), but cannot know for sure without inspecting the traffic as it could also be a flash crowd. Your goal is therefore to: (i) isolate the flows destined to these IP addresses, (ii) direct them to a scrubber connected between B and C, in order to "clean" them if needed, and (iii) reduce congestion by load-balancing the traffic on unused links, like (B, E).

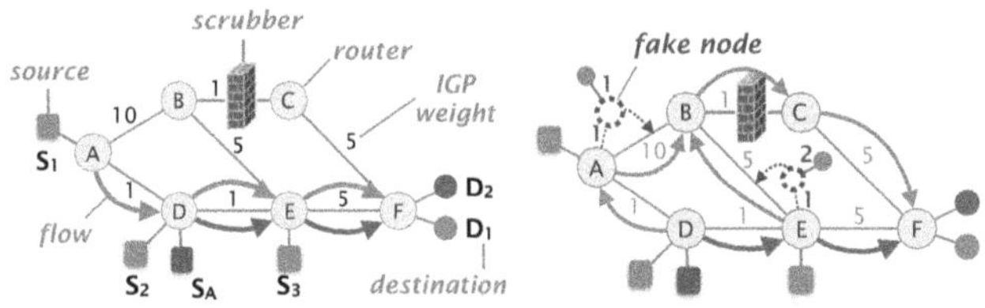

(a) Initial topology (b) Augmented topology

Figure 1: Fibbing can steer the initial forwarding paths (see (a)) for D_1 through a scrubber by adding fake nodes and links (see (b)).

Performing this routine task is very difficult in traditional networks. First, since the middlebox and the destinations are not adjacent to each other, the configuration of multiple devices needs to change. Also, since intra-domain routing is typically based on shortest path algorithms, modifying the routing configuration is likely to impact many other flows not involved in the attack. In Fig. 1a, any attempt to reroute flows to D_1 would also reroute flows to D_2 since they home to the same router. Advertising D_1 from the middlebox would attract the right traffic, but would not necessarily alleviate the congestion, because *all* D_1 traffic would traverse (and congest) path (A, D, E, B), leaving (A, B) unused. Well-known Traffic-Engineering (TE) protocols (*e.g.*, MPLS RSVP-TE [1]) could help. Unfortunately, since D_1 traffic enters the network from multiple points, many tunnels (three, on A, D, and E, in our tiny example) would need to be configured and signaled. This increases both control-plane and data-plane overhead.

Software Defined Networking (SDN) could easily solve the problem as it enables centralized and direct control of the forwarding behavior. However, moving away from distributed routing protocols comes at a cost. In-

*S. Vissicchio is a postdoctoral researcher of F.R.S.-FNRS.

SIGCOMM '15, August 17 - 21, 2015, London, United Kingdom

© 2015 ACM. ISBN 978-1-4503-3542-3/15/08...$15.00

DOI: http://dx.doi.org/10.1145/2785956.2787497

	centralized/SDN OpenFlow [2], PCE [3], SR [4]	*distributed/traditional* IGP [5, 6], RSVP-TE [1]	***hybrid*** **Fibbing**
forwarding paths:			
- *configuration*	simple (declarative & global)	complex (indirect & per-device)	**simple** (declarative & global)
- *manageability*	high (direct control)	low [7, 8] (need for coordination)	**high** (direct control)
- *path installation*	slow (by controller, per-device)	fast (by device, distributed)	**fast** (by device, distributed)
robustness:			
- *network failures*	slow (by controller)	fast (local)	**fast** (local)
- *controller failures*	hard (ad-hoc synch)	native (distributed)	**easy** (synch via IGP)
- *partitions*	hard (uncontrollable devices)	best (distributed)	**best** (fallback on distributed)
routing policies:	highest (any path)	- low for IGP (shortest paths) - highest for RSVP (any path)	**high** (any non-loopy paths)

Table 1: Fibbing combines the advantages of existing control planes, avoiding the main drawbacks.

deed, IGPs like OSPF and IS-IS are scalable (support networks with hundreds of nodes), robust, and quickly react to failures. Building a SDN controller with comparable scalability and reliability is challenging. It must compute and install forwarding rules for all the switches, and respond quickly to topology changes. Even the simple task of updating the switch rule tables can then become a major bottleneck for a central controller managing hundreds of thousands of rules in hundreds of switches. In contrast, distributed routing protocols naturally parallelize this work. For reliability and scalability, a SDN controller should also be replicated and geographically distributed, leading to additional challenges in managing controller state. Finally, the deployment of SDN as a whole is a major hurdle as many networks have a huge installed base of devices, management tools, and human operators that are not familiar with the technology. As a result, existing SDN deployments are limited in scope, *e.g.*, new deployments of private backbones [8, 9] and software deployments at the network edge [10].

This paper introduces *Fibbing*, a technique that offers *direct control* over the routers' forwarding information base (FIB) by manipulating the input of a distributed routing protocol. Fibbing relies on traditional link-state protocols such as OSPF [5] and IS-IS [6], where routers compute shortest paths over a synchronized view of the topology. Fibbing controls routers by carefully *lying* to them, removing the need to configure them. It coaxes the routers into computing the target forwarding entries by presenting them with a carefully constructed augmented topology that includes fake nodes (providing fake announcements of destination address blocks) and fake links (with fake weights). In essence, Fibbing inverts the routing function: given the forwarding entries (*i.e.*, the desired output) and the routing protocol (*i.e.*, the function), Fibbing automatically computes the routing messages to send to the routers (*i.e.*, the input).

Fibbing can solve the problem in Fig. 1a adding two fake nodes (Fig. 1b), connected to A and E with the depicted weights. Both fake nodes advertise that they can reach D_1 directly. Based on the augmented topology, D starts to use A to reach D_1, as the new cost (3) is lower than the original one (6). A and E also select different paths. Since the fake nodes do not really exist, packets forwarded by A or E actually flow through B. Routers B and C do not change their forwarding decisions.

Table 1 gives an overview of how Fibbing improves flexibility and manageability by adopting a SDN-like approach while keeping the advantages of distributed protocols (*e.g.*, robustness and fast FIB modifications).

Fibbing is expressive. Fibbing can steer flows along *any* set of per-destination loop-free paths. In other words, it can exert full control at a per-destination granularity. For this reason, Fibbing readily supports advanced forwarding applications such as: (a) traffic engineering, (b) load balancing, (c) fast failover, and (d) traffic steering through middleboxes. By relying on destination-based routing protocols, Fibbing does not support finer-grained routing and forwarding policies such as matching on port numbers. Though, those policies can easily be supported via middleboxes.

Fibbing scales and is robust to failures. Lying to routers is powerful but challenging. Indeed, Fibbing must be *fast* in computing augmented topologies to avoid loops and blackholes upon network failures. At the same time, Fibbing must compute *small* augmented topologies since routers have limited resources. Finally, Fibbing must be *reliable* and gracefully handle controller failures. We address all three challenges.

Fibbing differs from previous approaches that rely on routing protocols to program routers. Prior approaches like the Routing Control Platform [11] rely on BGP as a "poor man's" SDN protocol to install a forwarding rule for each destination prefix on each router. In contrast, Fibbing leverages the routing-protocol implementation on the routers. Doing so, Fibbing can adapt the forwarding behavior of many routers at once, while allowing them to compute forwarding-table entries and converge on their own. That is, while the controller computes the routing *input* centrally, the routing *output* is still computed in a distributed fashion.

Fibbing works on existing routers. We implemented a fully-functional Fibbing prototype and used it to pro-

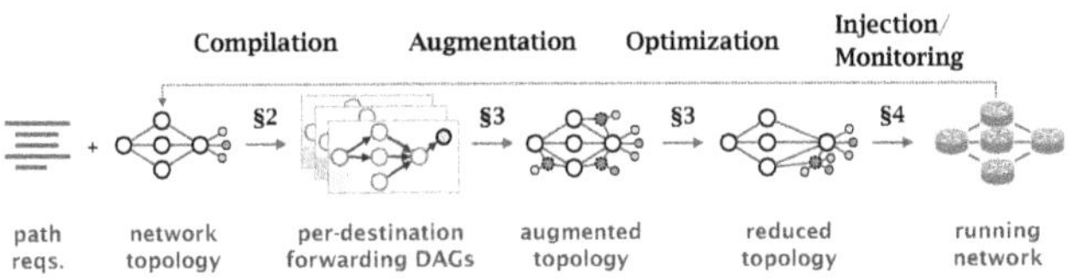

Figure 2: The four-staged Fibbing workflow.

pol	::=	$(s_1; \ldots; s_n)$	Fibbing Policy
s	::=	$p \mid b$	Requirement
r	::=	p_1 and $p_2 \mid p_1$ or $p_2 \mid p$	Path Req.
p	::=	Path(n^+)	Path Expr.
n	::=	$id \mid * \mid n_1$ and $n_2 \mid n_1$ or n_2	Node Expr.
b	::=	r as backupof $((id_1, id_2)^+)$	Backup Req.

Figure 3: Syntax of Fibbing high-level language.

gram real routers (both Cisco and Juniper). Based on an augmented topology, these routers can install hundreds of thousands of forwarding entries with an average installation time of less than 1ms per entry. This offers much greater scale and faster convergence than is possible with state-of-the-art SDN switches [12, 13], without requiring the deployment of new equipment and per-device actions from the controller. This also means that Fibbing can implement recent SDN proposals, like Google's B4 [8] and Microsoft's SWAN [9]—on top of existing networks.

Our earlier work showed that Fibbing can enforce any set of forwarding DAGs [14]. This paper goes further by describing the complete design, implementation, and evaluation of a Fibbing controller managing intra-domain routing. Rather than focusing on specific use cases (like traffic engineering), we describe its support for different higher-level approaches (*e.g.*, [8, 9]). We make the following contributions:

- **Abstraction**: We show how to express and realize high-level forwarding requirements by manipulating a distributed link-state routing protocol (§2).
- **Algorithms**: We propose new, efficient algorithms to compute compact augmented topologies (§3).
- **Implementation**: We describe a complete Fibbing implementation which works with unmodified Cisco and Juniper routers (§4).
- **Evaluation**: We show that our Fibbing controller quickly generates small augmented topologies, inducing minimal load on routers (§5).

2. FLEXIBLE FIBBING

Fibbing workflow proceeds in four consecutive stages based on two inputs: the desired forwarding graphs (one Directed Acyclic Graph, or DAG, per destination) and the IGP topology (Fig. 2). The forwarding DAGs can either be provided directly or expressed indirectly, at a high-level, using a simple path-based language. In the latter case, the **Compilation** (§2) stage starts by compiling the requirements into concrete forwarding DAGs. Then, the **Topology Augmentation** (§3) stage computes an augmented topology that achieves these forwarding DAGs. While computing an augmented topology is fast, the resulting topology can be large. As such, the job of the next **Topology Optimization** (§3) stage is to reduce the augmented topology while preserving the forwarding paths. Finally, the **Injection & Monitoring** (§4) stage turns fake information into actual "lies" that the controller injects into the network.

In this section, we present the high-level language and compilation process (§2.1), and show that Fibbing can express a wide range of forwarding behaviors (§2.2).

2.1 Fibbing high-level language

Fibbing language (Fig. 3) provides operators with a succinct and easy way to specify their forwarding requirements. A Fibbing policy is a collection of *requirements*, naturally expressed as regular expressions on paths. Each requirement is either a *path requirement* which specifies how traffic should flow to a given destination, or a *backup requirement* which specifies how traffic should flow if the IGP topology changes. Each path requirement is recursively defined as a composition of path requirements through logical AND and OR. Operators can express load-balancing requirements using a conjunction of n requirements. Similarly, they can ensure that traffic to a specific destination will take one of n paths (*e.g.*, containing a firewall) using disjunction. Path requirements are composed of a sequence of node requirements. A node requirement is either a node (router) identifier or the wildcard $*$, representing any sequence of nodes. Like path requirements, node requirements can be combined using logical AND and OR. Whenever no path requirement is stated, the original IGP paths should be used. This way, operators do not have to express all the unmodified paths, only deviations from the IGP shortest paths.

The following example illustrates the main features of the language. It states that traffic between E and D_1 should be load-balanced on two paths, traffic between A and D_2 should cross B or C and that traffic from F to D_3 should be rerouted via G if the link (F, H) fails.

```
( (E,C,D1) and (E,G,D1);
  ((A,*,B,*,D2) or (A,*,C,*,D2));
  (F,G,*,D3) as backupof ((F,H))); )
```

Fibbing policies are compiled into per-destination forwarding DAGs by finding convenient network paths (if any). Compilation works in two consecutive stages. First, the compiler expands any requirement with wildcards into paths. This step can be computationally expensive as, in general, a network can have a number of paths exponential in the number of nodes. While this is unlikely, especially for networks designed according to best practices, we bounded the number of paths that can be expanded out of a single requirement. We only expand again if no solution is found with the current set of paths. Once all requirements are expanded, the compiler groups them by destination and computes the Disjunctive Normal Form (DNF) of each requirement. To finally produce a forwarding DAG, the compiler iterates over the disjunction of path requirements and checks whether the resulting graph is loop-free.

2.2 Fibbing expressiveness

Beyond steering traffic along a given path (§1), we now show that Fibbing can also: (i) balance load over multiple paths and; (ii) provision backup paths.

Fibbing can forward any flow on any *set* of paths. Fibbing can load-balance traffic over multiple paths to maximize throughput, minimize response time, or increase reliability. For example, consider the network in Fig. 4a where three sources S_1, S_2, and S_3 send traffic to three corresponding destinations. Demands and link capacities are such that link (F, G) is congested. One way to alleviate congestion is to split traffic destined to D_2 over the top (via (B, C)) and bottom (via (F, G)) paths. Load-balancing traffic coming from E on multiple paths is possible under conventional link-state routing (*e.g.*, by re-weighting links (F, G) to 15. However, this would force the traffic from S_2 *and* S_3 to spread over both paths, creating congestion. More generally, it is impossible to route the traffic destined to D_2 and D_3 on different links under conventional link-state routing.

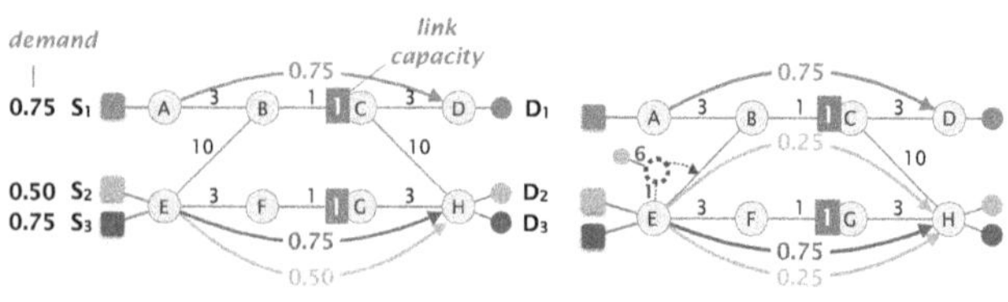

(a) Initial topology (b) Augmented topology

Figure 4: Fibbing supports multi-path forwarding. Here, it avoids the initial congestion (see (a)) by load-balancing traffic for D_2 (see (b)).

This simple requirement can easily be expressed as:

((S2 ,E ,B ,C ,H ,D2) **and** (S2 ,E ,F ,G ,H ,D2))

Fig. 4b shows the augmented topology which realizes this requirement. A fake node announcing D_1 (with a weight of 6) is inserted between E and B. After introducing this node, E has two shortest paths (of cost 7) to reach D_2 and, hence, splits D_2 traffic over B and F. In this example, Fibbing enables maximum network efficiency as each link is used to its full capacity.

Fibbing can provision backup paths for any flow. Fibbing can provision backup paths to prevent congestion or increased delays after link and node failures. As an illustration, consider the network in Figure 5a. The failure of link (E, F) leads to congestion since traffic flows for D_1 and D_2 are both rerouted to the same path via link (A, B). To prevent congestion, traffic destined to D_1 and D_2 should be split over the two remaining disjoint paths but only upon failure on the path (A, D, E, F). This is another example of a requirement that is impossible to achieve with link-state routing, and would require significant control-plane overhead in MPLS. In contrast, it is easily done with Fibbing.

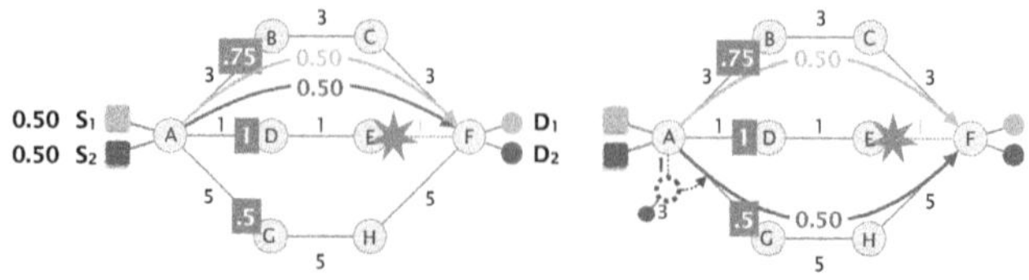

(a) Initial topology (b) Augmented topology

Figure 5: Fibbing can provision backup paths. Here, possible congestion upon a link failure (see (a)) is avoided by adding a fake node (see (b)).

Backup paths can be specified in our language as:

(A ,B ,∗ ,D1) **and** (A ,G ,∗ ,D2)
as backupof((A ,D) **or** (D ,E) **or** (E ,F))

Fig. 5b shows the corresponding augmented topology, which has a single fake node advertising D_2. Weights are set to prevent A from using the fake node to reach D_2 *unless* a failure occurs along the path (A, D, E, F). While successful for this example, Fibbing cannot satisfy all possible requirements for backup paths (§3.3).

3. AUGMENTING TOPOLOGY

In this section, we detail the augmentation problem (§3.1), and we show how the Fibbing controller quickly computes small augmented topologies from a set of forwarding DAGs. We rely on a *divide-and-conquer* approach based on three consecutive steps.

1) Topology initialization (§3.2): We modify the initial weights in the link-state protocol (if necessary), to guarantee that any set of forwarding DAGs can be enforced by Fibbing. If needed, this operation has to be done only once, when Fibbing is first deployed.

2) Per-destination augmentation (§3.3): Starting from an initialized topology, we compute a suitable augmentation, individually for every destination of an input forwarding DAG. We designed two algorithms for this step, achieving different trade-offs between computation time and augmentation size. The fastest one, **Simple**, can compute augmented topologies *within milliseconds*, and works by injecting a dedicated fake node for every router that changes its next-hop. The relatively slower one, **Merger**, reduces the augmentation size by re-using the same fake nodes to program multiple routers. Simple and Merger are suited for different goals. The speed of Simple is useful for quick failure reaction. In contrast, Merger can be run in background to progressively re-optimize the augmented topology. We evaluate the trade-offs achieved by each algorithm in §5.

3) Optimization across destinations (§3.4): We merge the augmentations obtained in the per-destination augmentation step to further reduce the number of fake nodes and edges. Namely, whenever safe, we replace multiple fake nodes announcing different destinations with a single fake node which either announces all the destinations or creates a new path (a shortcut) between routers in the augmented topology.

3.1 The Topology Augmentation Problem

We start the description of the topology augmentation algorithms by precisely defining the basic concepts on which they rely and the problem that they solve.

Fake nodes scoping. A Fibbing controller can generate both *locally-scoped* lies (targeted to a single router) and *globally-scoped* lies (targeted to all routers). Locally-scoped lies are useful as they enable local actions on one router without creating side effects on other routers. Globally-scoped lies affect the entire network. Hence, if carefully computed, they can reduce the size of the augmented topology. All of our previous examples used globally-scoped lies. We detail how to implement both kinds of lies in the current OSPF in §4.

Fake edges to forwarding next-hop mapping function. Fibbing can modify the routing path computed by any IGP router r. In particular, it can augment the IGP topology so that r's shortest path is no longer the one in the original topology but includes some fake sub-paths. Throughout the paper, we assume that a fake edge in the shortest path from any router r to any destination d corresponds to the ability to force the next-hop of r for d to be any of its neighbors. In the example in Fig. 1, for instance, the fake edge between the A and its adjacent fake node translates into A forwarding traffic to B. We discuss in §4 how to achieve this ability in the current OSPF protocol, as well as in future IGPs.

Topology augmentation problem. Since we assume an arbitrary mapping between fake edges and forwarding next-hops, the topology augmentation problem is defined as follows: Given an initial topology G and a set of forwarding DAGs, compute an augmented topology $G' \supset G$ such that for each path $(u, v, \ldots, d)$ in the forwarding DAG for d, the next-hop of u in one of its shortest paths for d in G' is either v or a fake node.

3.2 Topology Initialization

In the topology initialization, we scale the link weights of the original IGP topology G to guarantee arbitrary per-destination control through Fibbing and help reduce the size of topology augmentations. In particular, we proportionally increase link weights (multiplying them by a constant factor) if they are too low in G. Moreover, we set very high announcement cost for any destination, at least equal to the length of the longest path in G times the maximum link weight.

Topology initialization enables full Fibbing expressivity. Indeed, it makes the IGP topology *Fibbing compliant*, which provably avoids cases in which a forwarding DAG cannot be implemented by Fibbing (see [15]). We say that a topology is Fibbing compliant if for every destination d, the cost of the shortest path from every router (including the ones announcing d) to d exceeds 2. In Fibbing compliant topologies, for any router r and destination d the controller can always compute a fake path P such that (i) P is shorter than the original shortest path from r to d; and (ii) P is longer than the original shortest path from any other router $v \neq r$ to d. As proved by the following theorem, this implies the ability of Fibbing to forward flows for the same destination on any set of loop-free paths.

THEOREM 1. *Any set of per-destination forwarding DAGs can always be enforced by augmenting a Fibbing-compliant topology even only with globally-scoped lies.*

PROOF. We prove the statement by showing a simple topology augmentation procedure. Let G be the initial topology. For every forwarding DAG with destination d, we add for each node r in the network a fake node f_r announcing d. This generates a new fake path (r, f_r, d) in the augmented topology. We set the total cost of this newly added fake path to 2. Since G is Fibbing compliant, then the cost of the shortest path from r to d in G is greater than 2. Hence, the shortest path of every node r in the augmented topology will be (r, f_r, d). The forwarding DAG is then implemented by mapping the fake link on the right physical link. □

Note that Theorem 1 applies to destinations in the augmented topology. Those destinations do not need to match the destination prefixes announced in the original IGP. Hence, Fibbing allows to control flows for de-aggregation of the original IGP destinations (up to IP address granularity) or even non-overlapping prefixes.

Topology initialization is non-intrusive. Since it is based on the adaptation of a few configurable parameters, our initialization procedure can be applied to any link-state routing configuration, and *preserves the original forwarding paths.* It can be carried out in a running network, using known lossless reconfiguration techniques [16]. Moreover, it is strictly needed no more than once in the network lifetime. Indeed, since Fibbing compliance does not depend on the routing requirements or the presence of specific links, any topology remains Fibbing compliant independently of new requirements or the failures of nodes or links. Finally, topologies growing in size can be easily kept Fibbing compliant by ensuring that the new destinations are announced with high costs and the new links have weights consistent with pre-existing ones.

3.3 Per-destination augmentation

We now describe Simple and Merger. We use Figure 6 to illustrate the difference of the two algorithms.

3.3.1 Simple

Simple relies solely on locally-scoped lies to avoid having to compute any fake path cost. For every destina-

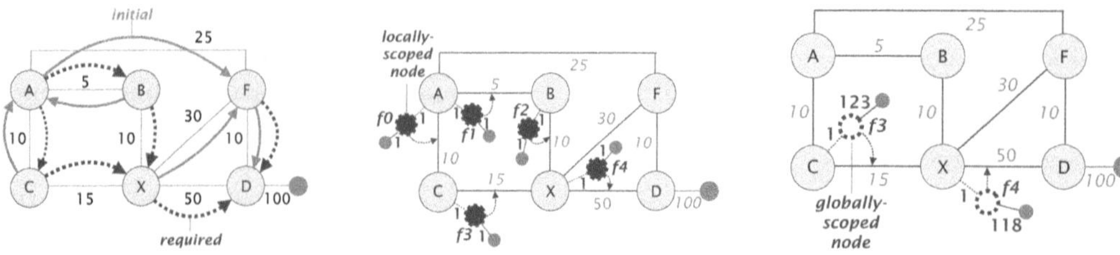

(a) Requirements (b) Simple augmentation (c) Merger augmentation

Figure 6: Outcome of our per-destination augmentation algorithms. Simple produces larger topologies (with locally-scoped lies) in a very short time, while Merger reduces the size of the augmentation by relying on globally-scoped lies and a longer computation.

tion d and corresponding forwarding DAG D, the algorithm adds fake nodes to each router whose next-hops in the original topology differ from those in D. Precisely, for every router r that changes its next-hop for d, Simple adds a fake node $f_{r,d}$ and a fake link $(r, f_{r,d})$. Node $f_{r,d}$ announces d to r with a locally-scoped lie. We set the total cost of path $(r, f_{r,d}, d)$ to 2. Since the topology is Fibbing compliant, r is ensured to change its shortest path. Also, since the lie is locally-scoped, other routers are not affected by it.

Figure 6b shows the output of Simple for the example of Figure 6a. Nodes A, B, C and X are required to change their respective next-hops. Moreover, A needs to load-balance on B and C. Thus, Simple creates five locally-scoped nodes (two connected to A), all providing fake paths to the destination with a cost of 2.

3.3.2 Merger

To reduce the number of fake nodes, Merger relies on globally-scoped lies that can change the forwarding behavior of multiple routers at once. When applied to Figure 6a, Merger creates only two fakes nodes (see Fig. 6c) to change the next-hops of A, B, C and X, instead of the five used by Simple. The added fake nodes create load-balancing on A (cost 134) via B and C, as required.

Merger performs the topology augmentation for any destination d in two phases. First, it adds an excessive number of fake nodes, and computes the lower and upper bounds for their respective cost. Second, it merges fake nodes whenever possible, based on the value of the computed bounds. We now provide an intuitive description of those two phases. Additional details about them and Merger correctness proofs are reported in [15].

Step 1. Fake bounds computation. Merger starts by adding fake nodes to every router r that is required to change the next-hop (according to the input forwarding DAG) for d. In this case, one new fake node $f_{r,d}$ is connected to r for every new r's next-hop in the input forwarding DAGs. However, to enable merging of globally-visible fake nodes, Merger calculates lower and upper bounds for every newly-added fake path $(r, f_{r,d}, d)$. As the initial positioning of fake nodes is as in Simple, we illustrate bound computations referring to Figure 6b.

The *upper bound* $ub(f_{r,d})$ represents the maximum value of the fake path cost that changes r's shortest path to $(r, f_{r,d}, d)$. It is easy to compute by statically considering the non-augmented topology G. Indeed, it is equal to $dist(r, d, G) - 1$, where $dist(u, v, G)$ is the cost of the shortest path from u to v in G.

The *lower bound* $lb(f_{r,d})$ represents the minimal value of the fake path cost that does not change the shortest path of any real node different from r. To compute it, we divide nodes in two sets, depending on whether the input forwarding DAG prescribes to change their respective next-hops or not.

For the next-hop preserving nodes whose shortest path does not traverse r in the input topology, we impose that their original shortest path is not modified by $f_{r,d}$. For example, when computing $lb(f_0)$ in Figure 6b, we ensure that f_0 does not change the shortest path of F, by constraining $lb(f_0) + 25 > dist(F, d, G) = 110$, that is, $lb(f_0) = 86$. More generally, for every fake node $f_{r,d}$ and every next-hop preserving neighbor n of r, we impose that $lb(f_{r,d}) > dist(n, d, G) - dist(n, r, G)$.

For next-hop changing nodes (connected to other fake nodes), the final value of their shortest paths is not known in advance, but is determined by the augmentation itself. That is, the lower bound of any fake node generally depends on the lower bound of other fake nodes. For example, in Figure 6b, $f4$ changes the shortest path of X only if $lb(f4) < dist(X, C, G) + lb(f3)$. To avoid that real nodes pass through fake nodes not directly connected to them, Merger runs a *lower bound propagation procedure.* This procedure takes as input the lower bounds initialized with values from next-hop preserving nodes. It then fixes one lower bound at the time, following a specific order and adjusting the others to be consistent with the fixed one. This order guarantees that each lower bound must be considered only once. Sometimes, lower bounds cannot be made consistent. Indeed, Theorem 1 does not provide guarantees if fake nodes are connected only to next-hop changing nodes. We solve these cases by using locally-visible lie.

Step 2. Fake nodes merging. In this step, Merger tries to merge fake nodes together. More precisely, it iterates over every simple path from a source to d in the input forwarding DAG. For each of those paths, it merges pairs of fake nodes whenever safe.

To assess when it is safe to merge a fake nodes f' into f'', Merger sequentially performs three checks. We illustrate these checks by considering the required path (A, B, X, D) and the merge of f_1 into f_2 in Figure 6b.

First, Merger assesses whether the IGP shortest paths are compliant with the considered source-sink path in the DAG. In our example, it verifies that the shortest path from A and B (*i.e.*, (A, B)) is a sub-path of the required (A, B, X, D). If A had predecessors in the required path not connected to a fake node, this check would have been repeated for those predecessors as well.

Second, Merger checks the possibility to use f'' as part of the shortest path of the real node connected to f' without changing the current next-hops of any node. To this end, the algorithm assess the existence of feasible post-merging bounds for f''. More precisely, it re-computes the modified lower bound of f'' as the minimum value (if any) that forces the new shortest path of the real node connected to f' and its next-hop preserving predecessors in the required path through f'', without affecting nodes previously not crossing f''. In our example, the lower bound of f_2 is modified to exclude the constraint of not changing A's next-hop, hence it is decreased to $lb(f_2) = 81$ (it was greater before, for A's next-hop to be f_1). The upper bound of f'' is also modified to ensure that the real node connected to f' and its next-hop preserving predecessors use the fake path via f''. In our example, $ub(f_2)$ is modified to 129, as the cost of the original shortest path from A to the destination is 135 and those between A and B is 5.

Third, Merger simulates the merge to assess whether all bounds can be consistently adjusted network-wide, given that the merging f' into f'' would change the bounds of f'' and remove one fake node. To this end, we re-run the lower bound propagation procedure, devoting special attention to fake nodes used for load-balancing. In our example, for instance, we constrain the lower bound of f_0 to be equal to the cost of path (A, B, f_2, d), meant to be used by A after the merging.

If all the three checks pass, then Merger actually perform the merge, by removing f' and updating the bounds of all other fake nodes (including f'') according to the values computed during the last check.

3.3.3 *Dealing with backup requirements*

Backup requirements can be specified by providing additional sets of (tagged) forwarding DAGs to our algorithms. Let G' be an augmented topology computed to accommodate primary requirements. To deal with backup ones, slight variants of Simple and Merger can be run after the computation of G'. The main modification of Simple consists in setting the cost of the fake paths added for backup requirements to 3 instead of 2. In contrast, backup requirements are supported in Merger by imposing that lower bounds are always greater than the cost of the shortest path in G'.

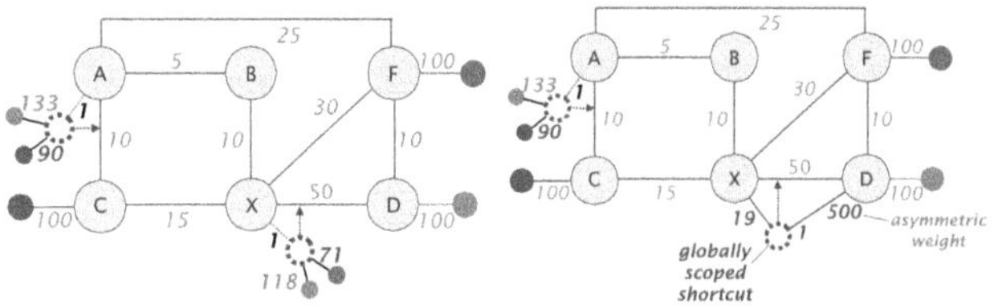

(a) Fake destination merging. (b) Fake shortcuts creation.

Figure 7: Cross-destination optimizations.

Contrary to primary requirements (see Theorem 1), Fibbing may not enforce backup requirements, even in a Fibbing-compliant topology (see [15]). Indeed, if the cost of the original shortest path of a node r is equal to a fake one (used for a primary requirement) in G', then backup paths different from the original shortest path cannot be implemented on r. In those cases, we notify the operator on the impossibility to implement the given backup paths.

3.4 Cross-Destination Optimization

Fake nodes computed on a per-destination basis may be redundant. We reduce such redundancy in two ways, namely, by (i) merging fake nodes connected to the same real node, and (ii) replacing fake destination announcements with fake paths connecting real nodes.

Cross-destination merging. After per-destination augmentations, two fake nodes f_1 and f_2 announcing different destinations d_1 and d_2 can be connected to the same node r and used to force traffic to the same real link (r, n). Those fake nodes can always be merged. Indeed, we can replace f_1 and f_2 with a new fake node f' such that (i) $cost(r, f') = min\{cost(r, f_1), cost(r, f_2)\}$, and (ii) f' announces both d_1 and d_2, with $cost(f', d_i) = cost(r, f_i, d_i) - cost(x, f')$ for $i = 1, 2$. For example, assume that in the network in Figure 6 additional destinations are attached to C and F as in Figure 7a. The result of the cross-destination merging is shown in Figure 7a, where both A and X have a single fake neighbor announcing multiple destinations (rather than multiple fake neighbors each announcing a single destination). This reduces the number of fake nodes from 4 to 2.

Creating shortcuts. One of the most appealing features (unmatched by competitor solutions) of Fibbing is that a single lie can change the paths for multiple destinations. To this end, we need however to replace fake destination announcements with fake paths connecting real nodes together, *i.e.*, *fake shortcuts*.

Currently, we use fake shortcuts only if a real link is never traversed in different directions. Consider, for example, the link between X and D in Figure 7a. It is traversed from X to D for the destinations attached to D and F, and never from D to X. In those cases, we try to transform X's fake neighbor into a fake shortcut, as in Figure 7b. Let u and v be the two real nodes at the endpoints of the shortcut. First, we check if a shortcut cost c exists such that all the shortest paths[1] are kept the same with and without the shortcut. If this condition is met, given a fake node f used to enforce the subpath $(u, \ldots, v)$ in the input forwarding DAGs, all fake destinations announced by f are replaced by a fake shortcut (u, f, v) and the cost of (u, f, v) is set to c. Figure 7b illustrates that we found such a value $c = 20$ for X in our example. Also, we use asymmetric weights to prevent the fake shortcut from being traversed in the opposite direction. To this end, the cost of path (v, f, u) is set to a very high value, *e.g.*, by setting a high weight of the directed link (v, f). In Figure 7b, we indeed set the weight of the link from D to the fake node in the shortcut to 500.

4. IMPLEMENTATION

We built a complete prototype of Fibbing in Python (algorithmic part) and C (interaction with OSPF) by extending Quagga [17]. Fibbing code base spans over 2300 (resp. 400) lines of Python (resp. C) code. It is available at `http://www.fibbing.net`. In this section, we present our prototype (§4.1), describe how Fibbing works with current OSPF routers (§4.2), and propose two small modifications to link-state protocols that would make Fibbing even more efficient (§4.3). Finally, we describe how to ensure controller reliability (§4.4).

4.1 Fibbing Controller

Our prototype consists of three main components:

Fake topology generator applies (i) the compilation algorithms (§2) to turn forwarding requirements into forwarding DAGs and (ii) the augmentation algorithms (§3) to convert the forwarding DAGs into fake nodes and links. The topology generator uses a JSON interface to register for update events produced by the event manager. Upon network updates, the generator automatically recomputes the augmented topology either using Simple to ensure fast convergence, or Merger to reduce the size of the topology. To ensure fast convergence *and* a small augmented topology, the generator also pre-computes augmentations with Merger, *e.g.*, those needed for any single link failure, and stores them in a *deltas database*.

Link-state translator interacts with the routers by establishing routing adjacencies to inject lies and track topology changes. Thanks to the flooding mechanism used by link-state protocols, a single adjacency is sufficient to send and receive all routing messages to/from all routers. Though, maintaining several adjacencies is useful for reliability. In this case, the translator simply injects the lies via all adjacencies. While this slightly increase the flooding load, doing so does *not* impact the routers memory as each message has a unique identifier and routers only maintain one copy per ID in memory.

Event manager maintains an update-to-date view of the network topology by (i) parsing the routing messages collected by the translator and (ii) constructing a network graph for the topology generator. The event manager checks whether each new event (*e.g.*, a node failure or addition) affects any of the forwarding requirements. If so, it first checks the deltas database for a pre-computed lie, and otherwise notifies the topology generator to request a new augmented topology.

4.2 Fibbing with Unmodified OSPF

Our Fibbing prototype works with unmodified OSPF-speaking routers (tested on Cisco and Juniper). To creates lies, our prototype leverages the *Forwarding Address* (FA) [18] field of OSPF messages. Suppose the controller wants routers to think that destination d is directly attached to the router with IP address y. Then, the controller injects the route for d with a forwarding address of y and the desired cost for the fake edge from y to d. Router y ignores the message, and all other routers compute the cost of the route as the sum of their cost to y plus the cost in the message.

Locally-scoped lies in OSPF. To support locally-scoped lies, we reserve a set of IP addresses to be used as FAs. All those addresses are propagated network-wide in OSPF. However, every router is configured not to install routes to all those addresses. Consequently, only the directly-connected router can reach any of those addresses, and accept routes specifying that address as FA. Both allocation and configuration of FA-associated IP addresses can be done just once in the network lifetime.

Globally-scoped lies in OSPF, and limitations. OSPF readily supports globally-scoped lies by simply propagating OSPF messages with the FA set to an IP address announced in OSPF. However, some subtle constraints hold in an unmodified OSPF network due to how FAs are resolved on the router. Prominently, (i) OSPF fake nodes are actually fake routes to the specified FA, hence both their positioning and the path to be used for reaching them are constrained; and (ii) OSPF routers discard any OSPF message whose FA is one of its own IP address and computes its shortest path according to the topology without the fake node. The combination of these two constraints limit the power of globally-scoped lies in OSPF, making them insufficient to implement all possible forwarding DAG. An example of those cases is reported in [15].

Overcoming OSPF limitations. To support the full expressiveness of Fibbing, our prototype controller uses an OSPF-compliant implementation of Merger with a combination of locally and globally-scoped lies. This implementation uses globally-scoped lies whenever possible, and falls back to locally-scoped lies for any requirements that cannot be met that way.

[1]By definition of the shortest path, we only need to check the paths from v and from u neighbors to each destination.

4.3 Proposed Protocol Enhancements

Other link-state protocols, like IS-IS [6], do not support forwarding addresses, and even the OSPF implementation of lies has limitations. However, minor protocol extensions can enable more flexible Fibbing in future routers. Fully-fledged Fibbing needs for the routing protocol to support two functions: (i) the creation of adjacencies (with fake nodes) on the basis of a received message; and (ii) a third-party next-hop mechanism which allows to specify in a route the forwarding next-hop to be used if that route is selected. Support for these functions can be added to protocol specifications (without impacting current functionalities), and can be deployed through router software updates.

Preliminary discussions with router vendors confirm that these changes are reasonable and could be integrated into current protocol implementations. Moreover, backwards compatibility can easily be achieved as legacy routers would simply ignore any Fibbing-specific protocol features. Our algorithms can be modified to account for the fact that the shortest path of a legacy router is never changed by any fake node.

4.4 Controller Replication

As any network component, a Fibbing controller can fail at any time. Reliability can be ensured by running multiple copies the Fibbing controller in parallel and connecting them to different places in the network.

No state needs to be synchronized between the replicas besides the input forwarding requirements (mostly static anyway). Indeed, Fibbing algorithms are deterministic, hence all replicas will always compute exactly the same augmented topology. The only dynamic state maintained by a Fibbing replica is the network graph. This state, however, is implicitly synchronized through the shared topology offered by the underlying IGP: the link-state flooding mechanism keeps the network graph up to date and eventually consistent across all replicas.

The determinism of our algorithms enables all replicas to inject (the same) lies at the same time. However, this would increase the amount of flooded information.

To limit control-plane overhead, our implementation relies on a primary-backup architecture with a single active replica and an inexpensive election process. A pre-defined range of router IDs is reserved for controller replicas. The replica with the lowest router ID across all running ones is the active replica. It is the only one injecting lies, while the others only compute the topology augmentation. When the controller is booted or when an active replica fails, running replicas receive IGP messages on the current network topology. Based on those messages, every replica independently infers the possible presence of other replicas; it also checks whether it is the new active replica by comparing its router ID with the one of the other running replicas.

5. EVALUATION

We now evaluate Fibbing along three axis. First, we show that existing routers are perfectly capable of handling the extra load induced by Fibbing (§5.1). We then demonstrate the efficiency of Fibbing's augmentation algorithms in terms of speed and size of the topology (§5.2). Observe that Fibbing behaves as a plain IGP at the network level. Hence, given its negligible impact on single routers and the efficiency of our controller, current ISP networks can be seen as the best large-scale evaluation for Fibbing. We therefore complete the evaluation by illustrating how Fibbing can be used in a realistic case (§5.3).

5.1 Router measurements

By increasing the size of the link-state routing topology, Fibbing could increase the CPU and memory overhead on the routers, or slow down protocol convergence. Our experiments demonstrate that the impact on load and convergence time is negligible. All our measurements were performed using OSPF on a recent Cisco ASR9K running IOS XR v5.2.2 equipped with 12GB of DRAM assigned to the routing engine, as well as on a (7-year-old) Juniper M120 running JunOS v9.2, equipped with 2GB of DRAM. Both routers are representative of typical edge devices (*i.e.*, aggregation routers) found in commercial networks. We draw the same conclusions on both router platforms, and focus on measurements collected on the Cisco device in the following.

Fibbing induces very little CPU and memory overhead on routers. We first measured the memory increase caused by a growing number of fake nodes (Table 2). Two processes are impacted by the presence of fake nodes: (i) the RIB process, which maintains information about all the routes known to each destination, and (ii) the OSPF process which maintains the entire OSPF topology. Even with a huge number of fake nodes (100,000), the total overhead on both processes was only 154MB—a small fraction of the total memory available. We collected the CPU utilization on the router every minute immediately after we started injecting fake nodes. The utilization was systematically low, at most 4%. This is easily explained as Fibbing relies on OSPF Type-5 LSAs which do not cause the routers to recompute their shortest paths to each other.

# fake nodes	RIB memory (MB)	OSPF memory (MB)
1,000	0.09	0.56
5,000	1.58	5.19
10,000	3.56	10.96
50,000	19.67	56.37
100,000	39.78	113.17

Table 2: Routers easily sustain Fibbing-induced load, even with huge augmented topologies.

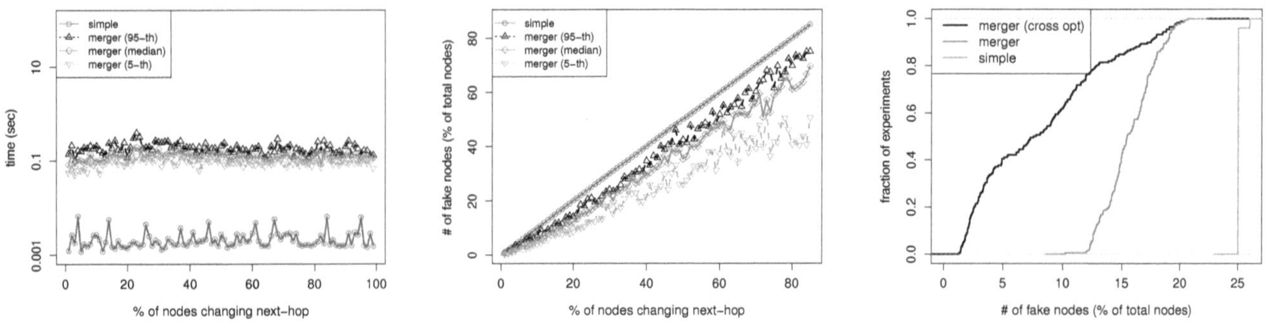

(a) Per-destination time (b) Per-destination augmentation size (c) Cross-destination reduction

Figure 8: Evaluation of our augmentation algorithms.

Fibbing can quickly program forwarding entries. In a second experiment, we measured how long it took for a router to install a growing number of forwarding entries (Table 3). We injected a growing number of fake nodes, one per destination, and measured the total installation time, by tracking the time at which the router updated the last entry in its FIB. The time to process and install one entry was constant (around 900μs), independent of the number of entries. This result is several orders of magnitude better than any OpenFlow switches currently on the market [12, 13]. Since installation of forwarding entries is distributed, routers can install their entries in parallel, meaning *Fibbing can program thousands of network-wide entries within 1 second.*

# fake nodes	installation time (s)	avg time/entry (μs)
1,000	0.89	886.00
5,000	4.46	891.40
10,000	8.96	894.50
50,000	44.74	894.78
100,000	89.50	894.98

Table 3: Programming a forwarding entry in a router with Fibbing is fast, sub 1ms.

Fibbing does not have *any* impact on routing-protocol convergence time. Finally, we compared the total time for routers to converge with and without fake nodes. We failed a link and measured the time for the last FIB entry to be updated considering two cases: (i) no lie was injected and (ii) one lie per destination was injected. Similar to the previous experiments, we repeated the measurements for a growing number of destinations and lies, between 100 and 100,000. In all our experiments, the presence of lies did not have *any* visible impact. The total convergence times with or without lies were systematically within 4ms, with the router being even faster to converge in the presence of lies in some cases.

5.2 Topology Augmentation Evaluation

We now evaluate Simple and Merger (§ 3) according to: (i) the time they take to compute an augmented topology for a given requirement, and (ii) the size of the resulting augmented topology. Results are depicted in Fig. 8. Our evaluation is based on simulation performed on realistic ISP topologies [19], whose sizes range from 80 nodes to over 300. On these topologies, we generated forwarding requirements by randomly changing the next-hop of randomly selected nodes. Destinations of requirement DAGs were also randomly generated.

Fibbing augments network topologies within ms. Fig. 8a shows the time (on the y-axis) taken by Simple and Merger for an increasing number of nodes that must change their next-hop (on the x-axis). The plot refers to simulations we ran on the biggest Rocketfuel topology (AS1239). The time taken by Simple to compute the per-destination augmentation varies in the order of milliseconds, ranging from 0.5 ms to 8 ms. While Merger took more time (as expected), its performance is still one order of magnitude lower than the second. For both algorithms, the computation time does not vary much with the number of nodes changing their next-hops.

Merger and cross-optimization effectively reduce the size of the augmented topology. Fig. 8b plots the fake topology size (on the y-axis) when the number of nodes that have to change their next-hop increases (on the x-axis) for a single destination on all topologies. The plot shows that Merger reduces the number of fake nodes by about 25% in the average case and almost 50% in the best case. Fake topology reduction is further corroborated by our cross-destination optimization procedures (see §3.4). Fig. 8c shows a cumulative distribution function (CDF) of the topology augmentation size computed by Simple, Merger, and Merger with cross-destination optimization. The figure refers to simulations with a number of destinations varying between 1 and 100 with 26% of the nodes changing their nexthop. In more than 90% of our simulations, cross-destination optimization achieves a reduction of the augmented topology. Depending on the experiment, such a reduction is up to about 10% with respect to Merger without cross-destination optimization, and 20% with respect to Simple.

5.3 Case Study

We now show the practicality of Fibbing by improving the performance of a real network consisting of four routers (Cisco 3700 running IOS v12.4(3)) connected in a square with link of 1 Mbps capacity (see Fig. 9a). In this network, we introduce two sources (bottom left) that send traffic to two destinations (bottom right) using `iperf`. The first source is introduced at time $t = 0$, the second one at time $t = 5$. OSPF weights are configured such that all traffic flows along link (C, X).

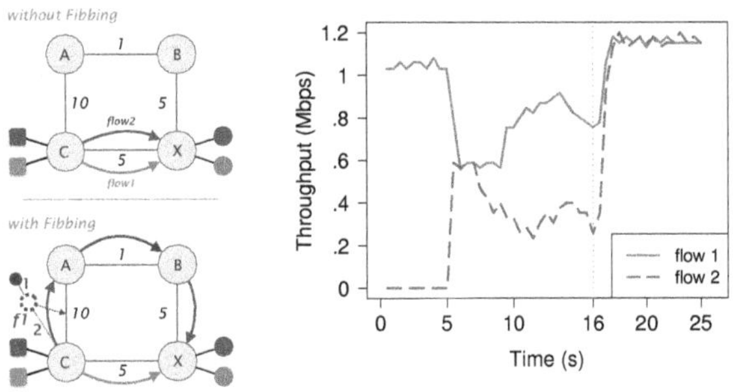

(a) Topology (b) Throughput evolution

Figure 9: Case study on how Fibbing can alleviate congestion. At $t = 16$, a fake node is added to shift one flow to the upper path in the network, increasing the total available bandwidth.

Such a network suffers from two inherent inefficiencies: (i) the upper path is never used and (ii) the two flows systematically traverse the same path, competing for bandwidth, no matter what the link weights are. Fig. 9b plots the throughput of each flow. Immediately after the introduction of the second flow at $t = 5s$, the two flows start competing for the available bandwidth. To improve network efficiency, the Fibbing controller injects a fake node f_1 connected to C and announces one destination at time $t = 16$. A few ms after the injection, we see that the throughput of both flows double as each of them now traverses a different path.

6. REACTION TO FAILURES

We now analyze Fibbing's reaction to different kinds of failures. We distinguish between network (affecting real router or router-to-router links) and controller (shutting down replicas or replica-to-router links) failures. Also, we separately deal with failures inducing network partitions and non-partitioning ones.

Fibbing quickly reacts to non-partitioning failures. Upon network failures, forwarded flows fall in one of the following three cases. First, some flows are not impacted by the failure as their pre-failure forwarding path is not disrupted. Second, flows for which no input requirements have been specified require only the IGP to establish a new path, but no action from the Fibbing controller. Reaction to failures is extremely fast in this case (sub-second even in large networks), thanks to fast convergence [20] and local fast re-route [21] features commonly supported by current IGP implementations. Third, the remaining flows are forwarded on paths modified by the Fibbing controller. They require reaction from the controller, both to remove possible blackholes or loops due to previously injected lies [14], and to avoid requirement violations due to new IGP paths. Theoretically, the total failure reaction time is equal to the sum of the notification time (for the controller to be notified of the failure), the processing time (for the controller to compute the new topology augmentation) and the IGP convergence time (for all routers to install the new lies). Our evaluation (§5) shows that the processing time is negligible, especially for the Simple algorithm. Moreover, the notification time is bounded by the IGP convergence time, as flooding is faster than re-convergence. Thus, in the worst case, the total reaction time is twice the IGP convergence time, that is, still below 2 seconds [20]. Also, in the average case, the notification time is smaller than IGP convergence, because the controller is notified about the failure before all other routers complete convergence; hence, the controller injects new lies *during* the IGP convergence, and the total failure reaction time is slightly higher than IGP convergence without Fibbing.

In addition, if one or more controller replicas fail but others are running, we have no impact on forwarded flows, unless the failed replica is the active one and some of its injected lies expire before the new active replica is elected. Even in the latter case, the new active replica is quickly elected, in a time which is approximately equal to the detection and flooding of the failure event by the IGP. The short election time makes it unlikely that lies expire before the new active replica is elected, and limits the period with possible disruptions.

Fibbing can implement both fail-open and fail-close semantics to deal with partitions. Even if unlikely, catastrophic events like a simultaneous failure of all the controller replicas or network partitions may happen. As for any centralized solution, a major risk in those cases is to leave the network uncontrolled. This happens, for example, if some routers are not reachable by a controller replica after a network partition. With respect to pure SDN solutions, Fibbing has the additional possibility to delegate control to the underlying IGP. This way, Fibbing can implement both the fail-open or fail-close semantics, on a per-destination basis. For non-critical (optimization) requirements like traffic engineering ones, the corresponding destinations can be injected in the IGP, so that connectivity can be preserved as long as the partition leaves at least one source-destination path. For stringent requirements like security ones (*e.g.*, firewall traversal), Fibbing can im-

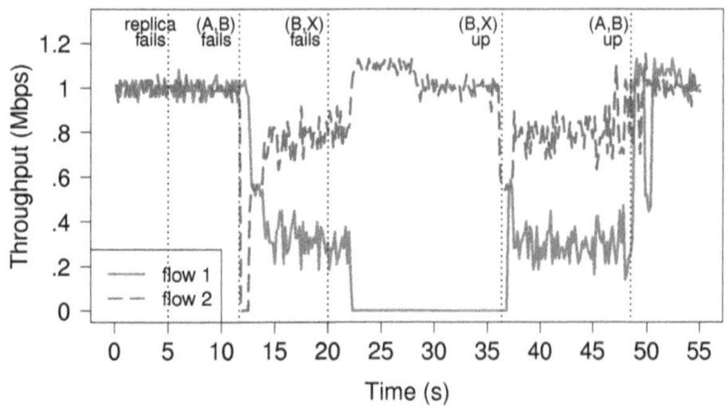

Figure 10: Case study on how Fibbing reacts to failures, and can successfully implement fail-close (flow 1) and fail-open (flow 2) semantics.

plement fail-close semantics by not announcing the corresponding destinations in the IGP. As such, the corresponding flows stop to be forwarded in the absence of the controller. To quickly reach this configuration, we can set a low validity time of the injected lies, making them rapidly expire if not refreshed. This then comes at the cost of additional control-plane overhead.

We confirmed Fibbing resilience. We consider again the topology in Figure 9a, and we connect two controller replicas respectively to routers A and B. The active replica is initially the one connected to A. We assume a strict policy on the red flow forcing it to cross the link (C, X). We then configure a fail-close semantics to it, and a fail-open to the other flow. Starting from a state in which both replicas and all links are up, we successively fail (i) the active replica at time $t = 5$; (ii) link (A, B) at $t = 12$; and (iii) link (B, X) at $t = 20$. Finally, we re-establish both failed links, one at the time (at $t = 36$ and $t = 48$).

The results of this experiment, collected via `iperf`, are reported in Figure 10. Concretely, the *failure of the active replica has no impact* on the forwarded flows. Indeed, the initially passive replica (connected to B) quickly detects the failure of the other replica, and start refreshing the injected lies by the failed controller. When (A, B) fails, the active replica needs to remove the fake node $f1$: Since the physical path (C, A, B, X) is not available anymore, this fake node is creating a loop between C and A for the violet flow. Upon failure detection, the controller then sends the LSA to remove $f1$, re-establishing the connectivity for the disrupted flow in approximately $1s$. Note that this time can be lowered by relying on fast failure detection mechanisms (like BFD). When (B, X) also fails, we create a partition that makes it impossible for the running replica to interact with routers A, C, and X. After about $1s$, the injected lies disappear, because they are not refreshed anymore by any controller. Consistent with the configured failure semantics, the red flow is blackholed (to avoid the IGP routing it over policy-violating paths) while the violet flow keeps using the IGP shortest path. Finally, re-adding the failed links allows the running replica to re-take control of the network: it re-builds a (safe) path for the red flow upon (B, X) restoration, and re-optimizes the distribution of both flow over the available paths when (A, B) is restored.

7. FREQUENTLY ASKED QUESTIONS

We now provide answers to high-level concerns often raised against Fibbing. Since empirical analyses are hardly applicable to those concerns (*e.g.*, debuggability), we describe qualitative considerations.

Is Fibbing a long-term solution? *Yes.* We believe Fibbing is here to stay. In the short run, Fibbing offers programmability and is easy to deploy, at very little cost. A network that ultimately needs even greater flexibility could deploy finer-grained SDN functionality at the edge, and solutions like Fibbing in the core, as advocated by major industry [22] and academic actors [10, 23]. By combining the best of centralized and distributed routing, Fibbing fits the needs of the network core (flexibility, robustness, low overhead) better than current forwarding paradigms.

Does Fibbing make networks harder to debug? *No.* Fibbing relies on "tried and true" protocols. This has several implications. First, Fibbing routing matches the current mental model of operators, a major advantage with respect to other SDN proposals. Moreover, Fibbing is compatible with any existing management, monitoring, and debugging tools. Finally, the Fibbing controller can expose a higher-level interface for debugging, including a mapping between the injected lies and their usage (matched requirements and how).

Does Fibbing sum the complexities of centralized and distributed approaches? *No.* Fibbing uses the underlying IGP in a very simple way. The IGP output is easy to predict and provides the controller with a powerful API to program routers. As a result, the design of the Fibbing controller is significantly simpler than for existing SDN controllers (*e.g.*, [24, 25, 26, 27]) since heavy tasks such as path computation and topology maintenance are offloaded to the routers. Even basic primitives for controller replication and replica consistency are mainly delegated to current distributed routing protocols (see §6).

Does Fibbing impact security? *No.* The lies introduced by the Fibbing controller can easily be authenticated, *e.g.*, using MD5-based authentication [28, 29].

Since Fibbing can only program loop-free paths, can it support middleboxes chaining? *Partially.* Forwarding loops can be encountered when steering traffic through a chain of middleboxes (*e.g.*, [30] and [31]). These requirements *can* be satisfied in Fibbing with local support from routers to break the loops. For instance, a router could match on the input interface in addition to the destination IP address using policy-based routing, a feature widely available on existing routers [32, 33] and provisioned centrally using BGP flowspec [34, 35]. Alternatively, middlebox traffic steering could be implemented through SDN functionality at the network edge, while still using Fibbing in the core.

8. RELATED WORK

Fibbing contributes to the larger debate about centralized and distributed control over routing by identifying a new point in the design space.

Centralized configuration of distributed routing protocols: A centralized management system can perform traffic engineering by optimizing the link weights in link-state routing protocols [36, 37]. Fibbing is more general, since it can implement *any* forwarding paths by injecting fake nodes and links into the link-state routing topology. The extra flexibility enables even better load balancing, as well as a wider range of functionality.

Centralized control using existing routing protocols as a control channel: RCP [11] is a logically-centralized platform that uses BGP to install forwarding entries into routers. RCP must install forwarding entries one-by-one, on each device. In contrast, Fibbing can adapt the forwarding behavior of many routers at once, with little input (*e.g.*, one fake node), and let them compute their own forwarding entries.

Centralized control over the routing/forwarding tables: In SDN, a central controller installs packet-processing rules directly in the switches, possibly reacting to the reception of specific packets. While more flexible (*e.g.*, enabling stateful control logic) than Fibbing, SDN requires updating the switch-level rules one-by-one, and forgoes the scalability and reliability benefits of distributed routing. Recently, the IETF developed I2RS [38] which offers a new management interface for centralized updates the routing information bases (RIBs) in the routers. Still, I2RS must push RIB entries individually to each router.

The Fibbing language for expressing requirements is similar in spirit to Merlin [39], but the mechanism for satisfying the requirements (*i.e.*, fake nodes/links) is entirely different. Our main contributions are the Fibbing techniques and algorithms, not the language.

For the networks which require the extra flexibility provided by OpenFlow, Fibbing helps during the transition by providing access to the FIBs of legacy routers to any SDN controller [40]. This contrasts to techniques like Panopticon [41], where programmability is only available in the SDN-enabled parts of the network.

9. CONCLUSIONS

The advent of SDN makes it clear that network operators want their networks to be more programmable and easier to manage centrally. In this paper, we show how Fibbing can achieve those objectives, by centrally and automatically controlling forwarding without forgoing the benefits of distributed routing protocols. Fibbing is expressive, scalable, and works with existing routers. In future work, we plan to look at extensions of IGP protocols (*e.g.*, for source-destination routing [42] or network service header awareness) to enable finer-grained control via Fibbing. Abstractly, Fibbing shows how centralized and distributed approaches can be profitably combined. We believe that new research can further explore this direction, for example, investigating an alternative division of tasks between centralized and distributed network components.

Acknowledgements

We are grateful to SIGCOMM anonymous reviewers and our shepherd, Teemu Koponen, for insightful comments. We thank Jo Segaert from BELNET and Dave Ward, Clarence Filsfils and Kris Michielsen from Cisco Systems for their support in testing Fibbing on real routers. This work has been partially supported by the EC Seventh Framework Programme (FP7/2007-2013) grant no. 317647 (Leone) and by the ARC grant 13/18-054 from Communauté française de Belgique.

10. REFERENCES

[1] D. Awduche *et al.*, "RSVP-TE: Extensions to RSVP for LSP Tunnels," RFC 3209, 2001.

[2] N. McKeown *et al.*, "OpenFlow: enabling innovation in campus networks," *ACM SIGCOMM CCR*, vol. 38, no. 2, pp. 69–74, 2008.

[3] A. Farrel, J.-P. Vasseur, and J. Ash, "A Path Computation Element (PCE)-Based Architecture," RFC 4655, 2006.

[4] C. Filsfils *et al.*, "Segment Routing Architecture," Internet Draft, 2014.

[5] B. Clouston and B. Moore, "Definitions of Managed Objects for HPR using SMIv2," RFC 2238, 1997.

[6] D. Oran, "OSI IS-IS Intra-domain Routing Protocol," RFC 1142, 1990.

[7] A. Pathak, M. Zhang, Y. C. Hu, R. Mahajan, and D. A. Maltz, "Latency inflation with MPLS-based traffic engineering," in *IMC*, 2011.

[8] S. Jain *et al.*, "B4: Experience with a Globally-Deployed Software Defined WAN," in *SIGCOMM*, 2013.

[9] C.-Y. Hong *et al.*, "Achieving High Utilization with Software-Driven WAN," in *SIGCOMM*, 2013.

[10] M. Casado *et al.*, "Fabric: A retrospective on evolving sdn," in *HotSDN*, 2012.

[11] M. Caesar *et al.*, "Design and implementation of a routing control platform," in *NSDI*, 2005.

[12] X. Jin *et al.*, "Dynamic scheduling of network updates," in *SIGCOMM*, 2014.

[13] C. Rotsos, N. Sarrar, S. Uhlig, R. Sherwood, and A. W. Moore, "OFLOPS: An Open Framework for Openflow Switch Evaluation," in *PAM*, 2012.

[14] S. Vissicchio, L. Vanbever, and J. Rexford, "Sweet little lies: Fake topologies for flexible routing," in *Hotnets*, 2014.

[15] S. Vissicchio, O. Tilmans, L. Vanbever, and J. Rexford, "Central Control over Distributed Routing (Extended Version)," Technical Report, 2015.

[16] L. Vanbever, S. Vissicchio, C. Pelsser, P. Francois, and O. Bonaventure, "Seamless Network-Wide IGP Migrations," in *SIGCOMM*, 2011.

[17] "Quagga routing suite," www.nongnu.org/quagga.

[18] J. Moy, "OSPF Version 2," RFC 2328, Apr. 1998.

[19] N. Spring, R. Mahajan, and D. Wetherall, "Measuring ISP topologies with Rocketfuel," in *SIGCOMM*, 2002.

[20] P. Francois, C. Filsfils, J. Evans, and O. Bonaventure, "Achieving Sub-second IGP Convergence in Large IP Networks," *ACM SIGCOMM CCR*, vol. 35, no. 3, 2005.

[21] C. Filsfils, P. Francois, M. Shand, B. Decraene, J. Uttaro, N. Leymann, and M. Horneffer, "Loop-Free Alternate (LFA) Applicability in Service Provider (SP) Networks," RFC 6571, 2012.

[22] T. Koponen *et al.*, "Network Virtualization in Multi-tenant Datacenters," in *NSDI*, 2014.

[23] "Time for an SDN Sequel? Scott Shenker Preaches SDN Version 2," www.sdxcentral.com/articles/news/scott-shenker-preaches-revised-sdn-sdnv2/2014/10/.

[24] "ONOS: Open Network Operating System," http://onosproject.org/.

[25] T. Koponen *et al.*, "Onix: A distributed control platform for large-scale production networks," in *OSDI*, 2010.

[26] "Project Floodlight," http://www.projectfloodlight.org/floodlight/.

[27] N. Foster *et al.*, "Languages for software-defined networks," *IEEE Comm. Mag.*, 2013.

[28] "Cisco OSPF MD5 Authentication," http://www.cisco.com/c/en/us/support/docs/ip/open-shortest-path-first-ospf/13697-25.html.

[29] "Juniper OSPF MD5 Authentication," http://www.juniper.net/documentation/en_US/junos14.2/topics/topic-map/ospf-authentication.html.

[30] Z. A. Qazi *et al.*, "Simple-fying middlebox policy enforcement using sdn," in *SIGCOMM*, 2013.

[31] S. K. Fayazbakhsh *et al.*, "Enforcing network-wide policies in the presence of dynamic middlebox actions using flowtags," in *NSDI*, 2014.

[32] "Cisco. Configuring Policy-Based Routing," http://www.cisco.com/c/en/us/td/docs/ios/12_2/qos/configuration/guide/fqos_c/qcfpbr.html.

[33] "Juniper. Configuring Filter-Based Forwarding to a Specific Outgoing Interface or Destination IP Address," http://www.juniper.net/techpubs/en_US/junos12.2/topics/topic-map/filter-based-forwarding-policy-based-routing.html.

[34] "Cisco. Implementing BGP Flowspec," http://www.cisco.com/c/en/us/td/docs/routers/asr9000/software/asr9k_r5-2/routing/configuration/guide/b_routing_cg52xasr9k/b_routing_cg52xasr9k_chapter_011.html.

[35] "Juniper. Enabling BGP to Carry Flow-Specification Routes," https://www.juniper.net/documentation/en_US/junos12.3/topics/example/routing-bgp-flow-specification-routes.html.

[36] B. Fortz and M. Thorup, "Internet traffic engineering by optimizing OSPF weights," in *INFOCOM*, 2000.

[37] B. Fortz, J. Rexford, and M. Thorup, "Traffic engineering with traditional IP routing protocols," *IEEE Comm. Mag.*, vol. 40, no. 10, pp. 118–124, 2002.

[38] A. Atlas, J. Halpern, S. Hares, and D. Ward, "An Architecture for the Interface to the Routing System," Internet Draft, 2013.

[39] R. Soulé *et al.*, "Merlin: A language for provisioning network resources," in *CoNEXT*, 2014.

[40] S. Vissicchio, L. Vanbever, and O. Bonaventure, "Opportunities and research challenges of hybrid software defined networks," *ACM SIGCOMM CCR*, vol. 44, no. 2, pp. 70–75, 2014.

[41] D. Levin, M. Canini, S. Schmid, F. Schaffert, and A. Feldmann, "Panopticon: Reaping the Benefits of Incremental SDN Deployment in Enterprise Networks," in *USENIX ATC*, 2014.

[42] F. Baker, "IPv6 Source/Destination Routing using OSPFv3," Internet Draft, 2013.

Poptrie: A Compressed Trie with Population Count for Fast and Scalable Software IP Routing Table Lookup

Hirochika Asai
The University of Tokyo
panda@hongo.wide.ad.jp

Yasuhiro Ohara
NTT Communications Corporation
yasuhiro.ohara@ntt.com

ABSTRACT

Internet of Things leads to routing table explosion. An inexpensive approach for IP routing table lookup is required against ever growing size of the Internet. We contribute by a fast and scalable software routing lookup algorithm based on a multiway trie, called *Poptrie*. Named after our approach to traversing the tree, it leverages the population count instruction on bit-vector indices for the descendant nodes to compress the data structure within the CPU cache. Poptrie outperforms the state-of-the-art technologies, Tree BitMap, DXR and SAIL, in *all* of the evaluations using random and real destination queries on 35 routing tables, including the real global tier-1 ISP's full-route routing table. Poptrie peaks between 174 and over 240 Million lookups per second (Mlps) with a single core and tables with 500–800k routes, consistently 4–578% faster than all competing algorithms in all the tests we ran. We provide the comprehensive performance evaluation, remarkably with the CPU cycle analysis. This paper shows the suitability of Poptrie in the future Internet including IPv6, where a larger route table is expected with longer prefixes.

CCS Concepts

•**Networks** → **Routers;** *Network algorithms;*

Keywords

IP routing table lookup; longest prefix match; trie

SIGCOMM '15, August 17-21, 2015, London, United Kingdom

ACM ISBN 978-1-4503-3542-3/15/08.
DOI: http://dx.doi.org/10.1145/2785956.2787474

1. INTRODUCTION

The fundamental functionality to support high speed communications on the Internet are increasing in importance with the ever-growing traffic size and due to our daily life being highly dependent on the Internet. One of the key technologies is IP routing table lookup: It needs to be extremely fast since the peak traffic size in an Internet core router is multiple hundreds of gigabits per second (Gbps). Ternary Content Addressable Memory (TCAM) performs high speed IP routing table lookup in the Internet core routers. However, departure from a TCAM is an approach worth considering for the two reasons: First, TCAM has issues in power consumption and heat. Second, the advent of Network Functions Virtualization (NFV) [6] may make the use of TCAM impossible, since the virtualized network functions are currently implemented in software without TCAMs. Therefore, it is desired to implement a software high-speed IP router only with general purpose computers; i.e., personal computers (PCs), or commercial off-the-shelf (COTS) devices.

For a long period of time, IP routing table lookup has been the bottleneck [11] in the performance of the software IP forwarding using COTS devices. It is a challenging problem [34, 31] because: 1) the size of the routing table is large and keeps growing (the number of BGP full routes is beyond 500K), 2) it requires a specific compute-intensive processing step called "longest prefix matching," and 3) high-speed communication links require high speed processing (148.8 million lookups per second (Mlps) for wire-rate IP packet forwarding on 100 Gigabit Ethernet (GbE) of minimum-size packets).

Recently, we see a significant improvement in the performance of software routers. There are two approaches; one is expecting the use of specific hardware such as graphics processing unit (GPU). Such hardware inherits, however, similar issues that TCAM has, such as heat and power consumption. The other is a pure software algorithm approach, where we assume the use of the commodity CPUs. A trend of this approach is reducing the memory footprint of the data structure of IP routing table to maximize the benefit of CPU cache [38,

25]. Still, the required performance to accommodate multiple of 100 GbE links has not been achieved.

We propose a novel data structure for fast and scalable IP routing table lookup, called *Poptrie*. It builds on the 64-ary multiway trie, allowing a low number of steps to search in the tree. It implements the descendant node array using a 64-bit vector, leading to the small memory footprint, and enabling a quick check of the descendant nodes. By the use of population count instruction on the bit vector, unnecessary descendant nodes are omitted efficiently, and a quick jump to the corresponding descendant node becomes feasible. Since Poptrie lays the descendant internal and leaf nodes in a contiguous array, the indirect index of smaller size is achieved, greatly reducing the memory footprint of the entire data structure. Poptrie also supports efficient incremental update without blocking the IP routing table lookup process.

We show, by the comprehensive evaluation in this paper, that Poptrie is promising with the friendliness to the larger routing table with longer prefixes of the future Internet, including IPv6. Compared to three state-of-the-art technologies, Poptrie gives superior performance in all evaluations for random and real destination queries on 35 instances of routing tables. It runs in 241 Mlps (1.34 times speed up from the fastest alternative, DXR [38]) even with a single CPU core on a real routing table instance of a global tier-1 ISP's core router, and it can achieve 914 Mlps with four CPU cores. Also, we analyze the consumed CPU cycles per lookup and showed the differences between other lookup technologies and Poptrie. One contribution of Poptrie is the scalability against future routing table growth. We show that Poptrie performs 175 Mlps on a synthetic table with more than 800K routes where DXR slows to 104 Mlps and SAIL [36] does not work.

The rest of this paper is organized as follows. In Section 2 we see related past studies. We describe the poptrie algorithm in Section 3. Section 4 gives the evaluation, where we describe the routing table dataset, how we generate the destination address for queries in the benchmark test, performance comparison, an analysis of the number of CPU cycles, scalability comparison for large routing tables, update performance evaluation, and performance comparison for the IPv6 routing tables. After miscellaneous discussions are given in Section 5, we conclude in Section 6.

2. RELATED WORK

TCAM has been a common technology for routing table lookup for a long time [23, 37, 39]. However, TCAM has problems with its power consumption, heat, monetary cost, and scalability issues [4, 16]. Bando et al. [4] proposed an FPGA-based routing table lookup engine, called FlashTrie, that can provide 200 Mlps per engine. Another approach to achieve fast IP routing table lookup is relying on GPUs [14]. Although GPU-based technologies like GPU-Click [32] and GAMT [21] are as fast as 500 Mlps, they require power-consuming GPUs, and need to process packets in large batch sizes. The large packet batch size is likely to lead to the higher worst case packet forwarding latency, and jitters.

Departing from dedicated hardware, there have been studies to achieve high performance IP routing on COTS devices. Click [19] is a modular software router that enables fast packet I/O (for the era), and RouteBricks [10] advanced the model further. Rizzo focuses on speeding up the packet I/O in Unix systems [26], in virtual machines [28], and in virtual switches [27]. The emergence of NFV [6] makes the fast IP routing lookup more important in producing a software router implementation with these fast packet I/O technologies on COTS devices.

The radix tree [29, 7, 18] and Patricia trie [24, 30] are fundamental data structures for the longest prefix match. In general, they require some tens of memory accesses for each IP routing table lookup, which result in low lookup performance. Waldvogel et al. [34] reduced the memory access both for IPv4 and IPv6 routing table lookup using binary search on prefix length. Gupta et al. [13] focused on the distribution of the prefix length in the routing table that most of the prefixes are no longer than `/24`. They proposed the DIR-24-8-BASIC data structure that extracts each `/24` or shorter prefix into `/24` prefixes to provide the lookup algorithm with O(1) for these entries.

There are studies that utilize bloom filters [9], memory pipelining [5, 15, 20], and bitmaps in the tree [11] to solve these problems, but these technologies fail to provide either a good performance or a reasonable management cost.

The Luleå algorithm [8] was proposed to reduce the memory footprint for the routing table. Srinivasan et al. [31] had taken into account data cache and optimized the data structure to improve the cache efficiency. Tree BitMap [11] provides a succinct data structure of a multiway trie. The prefix and the descendant nodes in a Tree BitMap node are represented by two bitmaps and the pointers to a contiguous array of data. It uses the population count operation in a similar way to Poptrie. In our tests, even in the most favourable situation Tree BitMap only achieved 1/3 of the performance of other modern algorithms. Section 4.5 discusses its perfromance in more detail. Rétvári et al. [25] proposed a compression algorithm of the forwarding information base (FIB) table to maximize the advantage of the data cache. However, a smaller FIB table does not always give a good lookup performance. For example, their algorithm consumes 194 CPU cycles per IPv4 address lookup, thus the lookup rate is only 12.8 Mlps. This is because the depth of their data structure can grow as much as 21. The approach proposed by Zec et al. [38], called DXR, achieved high lookup rate (100 Mlps per CPU core) by taking advantage of cache efficiency. DXR transforms the prefixes in the routing table into an array of address ranges, and searches the range array based on the key address using the binary search. It then introduces a lookup table similar to DIR-24-8-BASIC to optimize the lookup performance for shorter prefixes. The bottleneck of their approach, however, is the binary search for longer prefixes.

Yang et al. have proposed yet another fast IP routing table lookup algorithm called SAIL [36]. Their approach reduces the number of memory access and instructions in the lookup algorithm by splitting the procedure into three levels. Yet, the memory footprint of SAIL exceeds the typical CPU cache size, requiring relatively slow DRAM access in case of cache misses. Therefore, the performance of SAIL relies on the destination IP address locality of the traffic pattern. Moreover, SAIL does not support future growth of the routing table due to its structural limitation as discussed in Section 4.8.

3. POPTRIE

We propose a new data structure called *Poptrie* for fast IP routing table lookup. We assume that Poptrie is only used to look up a FIB index for the purpose of deciding the next hop during the IP forwarding; the routes are preserved in a separate routing table (RIB: Routing Information Base) such as radix or Patricia trie so that we can aggressively compress routes having the same next hop. In this section, we describe how Poptrie works. In general, we can aggregate the routes that are ingested from the RIB to the FIB by removing the redundant prefixes that do not influence the lookup result. This aggregation, called in this paper the "route aggregation", is not our contribution, and is applicable to other lookup technologies as well. The route aggregation performs merger of a set of prefixes with the identical next hop that belong to a subtree without any gap, into the single prefix representing the whole subtree. Unless otherwise noted, the performance results of Poptrie shown in this paper are with the route aggregation option.

Poptrie is extended from the multiway trie (i.e., M-way or M-ary where $M = 2^k$). Each node holds 2^k elements in the descendant array, corresponding to the value of the k-bit chunk in the key IP address. An element in the descendant array points to its next-level child internal node or a leaf node holding an index to the corresponding FIB entry. Although we selected $k = 6$ for our implementation to fit the size of registers of the 64-bit CPU architecture, we illustrate the $k = 2$ case in this section for the sake of brevity. The 2^k-ary multiway trie where $k = 2$ is illustrated in Figure 1. The admirable performance of Poptrie is due to the small memory footprint so that it can be contained completely within the CPU cache, and yet it leverages the effective multiway branching to reduce the total number of steps that is necessary to search down the tree.

We describe the options in Poptrie step by step; the basic mechanism in Section 3.1, the lookup algorithm in Section 3.2, the *leafvec* extension to compress the leaf size in Section 3.3, and the additional options called direct pointing in Section 3.4. The internal node in the basic poptrie contains *vector* (8 bytes), *base0* (4 bytes), and *base1* (4 bytes). Hence the total size of an internal node is only 16 bytes. When we use the *leafvec* extension, it takes 8 bytes additionally, so the internal node size becomes 24 bytes. In our implementation, the contiguous arrays of internal and leaf nodes are managed by the buddy memory allocator [17].

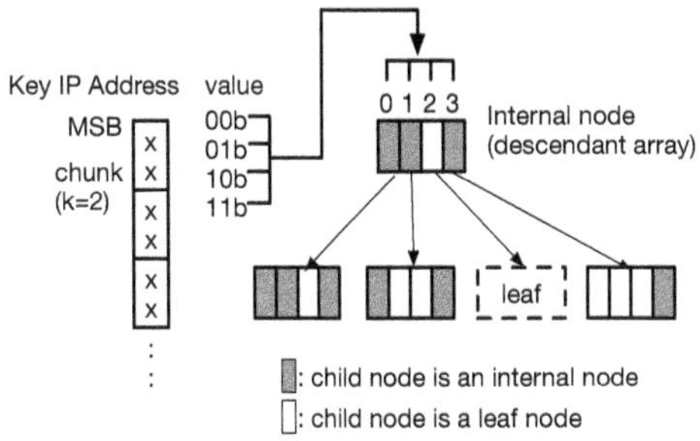

Figure 1: The 2^k-ary multiway trie ($k = 2$).

3.1 Basic Mechanism

First, the descendant array in the multiway trie is changed to a bitwise array (i.e., a bit vector). The *vector* and the *base1* collectively serve as the descendant array. The *vector* is a bit-vector index of the length 2^k bits, for the current k-bit address chunk. The n-th bit in the *vector* corresponds to the child node with the value n in the current k-bit address chunk. Each bit in the *vector* indicates the type of the corresponding child node: the bit is set to 1 if the corresponding child is an internal node, and it is set to 0 if the corresponding child is a leaf node. In other words, the *vector* indicates the existence of the corresponding descendant internal node, and then if there is no descendant internal node, the search will always result in a leaf node at this level of the tree.

The necessary descendant internal or leaf nodes are placed so that they form a contiguous array. The array starts with the descendant node which corresponds to $n = 0$, in the ascending order up to $n = 63$ when $k = 6$. However, unnecessary nodes (i.e., descendant internal or leaf nodes that are not pointed from the node) are skipped; if the node corresponds to $n = 0$ is not necessary, the array can start with $n = 1$, with corresponding bits in *vector* properly set. This way, unnecessary descendant nodes which do not have branches or leaf information are omitted, allowing compact data structure size and efficient use of memory.

The next node in the search within the tree can be obtained as follows: Since the value n of the current k-bit address chunk corresponds to the n-th bit in the *vector*, the number of 1s in the least significant $n+1$ bits of the *vector* can be used as the index of the next node within the current internal node's descendant array. Here, we

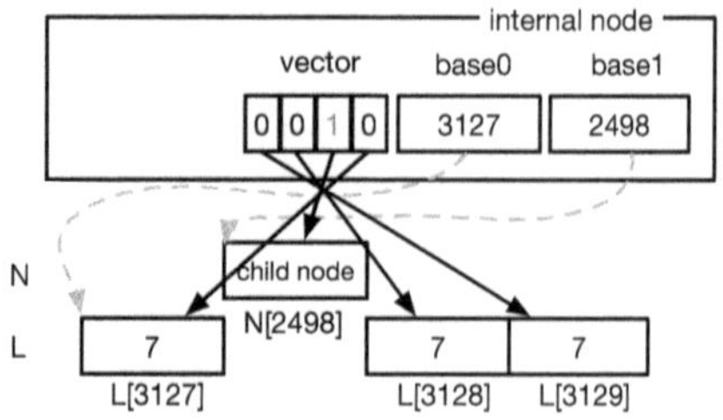

Figure 2: The *vector* in the internal node is configured so that the bit-1 indicates a descendant node, and the bit-0 indicates a leaf node.

can utilize the *popcnt* CPU instruction to accelerate the calculation of the next node in the search procedure, as described later in Section 3.2. Since *vector* bit-vector only provides the indirect address (i.e., index) within the current descendant array, it is necessary to provide the starting point of the descendant array. The *base1* is the base index to the consecutive subsequence of the internal nodes that are the children of this node. Similarly, the indirect index of the leaf node is obtained by counting the 0s in the *vector*. The starting offset for the leaf node is contained in *base0*. Figure 2 illustrates an example of the indirect index of internal and leaf nodes with *vector*, *base1*, and *base0*.

3.2 Lookup Algorithm

The lookup algorithm steps down the tree according to the specified IP address like the normal 2^k-ary multiway trie. At the depth of d, the d-th chunk of the address is used as the index of the *vector* in the internal node. Let the value of the d-th chunk in the key address be n, and then the lookup at the depth of d is executed as follows: If the corresponding bit is one, then the lookup algorithm continues to the next depth. The index of the next internal node in the descendant array is computed by adding to the *base1* the number of 1s in the least significant $n+1$ bits of the *vector* minus 1. If the corresponding bit is zero, then the lookup algorithm finishes the lookup with returning the leaf. The index of the leaf node in the leaf array is computed by adding to the *base0* the number of 0s in the least significant $n+1$ bits of the *vector* minus 1.

The key point in Poptrie is the use of the instruction to count the number of 1s and 0s in a bit string. Those counts are used as the indirect index of the descendant node and the leaf node, respectively. The procedure of counting the number of 1s in a bit string is called "population count", and an instruction executing it, *popcnt*, has been implemented in the x86 processor's instruction set. When the *popcnt* CPU instruction is not available, a fast alternative can be found in the literature [35].

The lookup algorithm with $k = 6$ is shown in Algorithm 1. The algorithm takes the poptrie structure t and the IP address *key* as input, and returns the longest matching leaf. In t, there are the internal node array

Algorithm 1 lookup($t = (N, L)$, *key*); the lookup procedure for the address *key* in the tree t (when $k = 6$). The function extract(*key*, *off*, *len*) extracts bits of length *len*, starting with the offset *off*, from the address *key*. N and L represent arrays of internal nodes and leaves, respectively. ≪ denotes the shift instruction of bits. Numerical literals with the UL and ULL suffixes denote 32-bit and 64-bit unsigned integers, respectively. Vector and base are the variables to hold the contents of the node's fields.

```
1: index = 0;
2: vector = t.N[index].vector;
3: offset = 0;
4: v = extract(key, offset, 6);
5: while (vector & (1ULL ≪ v)) do
6:     base = t.N[index].base1;
7:     bc = popcnt(vector & ((2ULL ≪ v) - 1));
8:     index = base + bc - 1;
9:     vector = t.N[index].vector;
10:    offset += 6;
11:    v = extract(key, offset, 6);
12: end while
13: base = t.N[index].base0;
14: bc = popcnt((~t.N[index].vector) & ((2ULL ≪ v) - 1));
15: return t.L[base + bc - 1];
```

N, and the leaf array L. In Line 1 the index is set to 0 to access the root node. Line 2 accesses to the *vector* of the root node. In Line 4, we obtain the value of the first 6-bit chunk from the offset 0. Lines 5–12 are the main loop that continues as long as there is a corresponding descendant internal node (checked in Line 5). Line 7 gets the population count of set bits in the least significant $v + 1$ bits and store it in **bc**. The next node's index is calculated (Line 8), the next node's *vector* is prepared (Line 9), and the chunk is shifted by 6 bits for the next round (Line 10, 11). Lines 13–15 calculate the indirect index of the corresponding leaf, and returns the content.

3.3 Compression with the Leaf Bit-Vector

The prefix expansion described in the previous subsection yields many duplicate and redundant leaves. In the ordinary 2^k-ary multiway trie, an identical FIB entry corresponding to a shorter prefix may redundantly span to multiple leaves within an internal node, up to $2^k - 1$ leaves. For example when $k = 6$, an internal node can have a next hop of value A and 63 next hops of value B, in its 64-length leaf array. In this way, the redundant leaves (B in this example) can consume significant memory.

In order to avoid them, *leafvec* is introduced in the poptrie internal node. *Leafvec* is a bit vector that indicates the starting points of the identical, contiguous leaf ranges within the leaf array. It is a key technique to keep the memory footprint of Poptrie small, and reduces more than 90% of leaves as we will see in Section 4.3. The *leafvec* and *base0* collectively serve as the base and

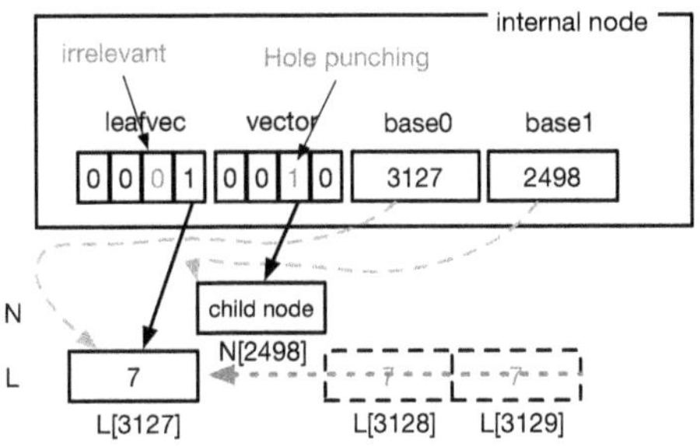

Figure 3: Merging identical leaf nodes with ignoring a hole punching using the *leafvec*

Algorithm 2 The leaf compression algorithm; the differences from the Algorithm 1. Only Line 14 is substituted.

14: bc = popcnt($t.N$[index].leafvec & ((2ULL $\ll v$) - 1));

the indirect index to locate the leaf node, which is similar to the *vector* and *base1* described in the previous section. The indirect index using the *leafvec* and *base0* omits the redundant information as long as the redundant leaf slots are contiguous. For example, if all the 64 leaf slots in an internal node contains the same value, then it can be compressed to just one leaf slot with only the least-significant bit in the *leafvec* being 1. The indirect index for the leaf that corresponds to the value n for the current chunk is calculated as the number of 1s in the least-significant $n + 1$ bits in the *leafvec*. This way, all the indirect indices for any value n fall into the first leaf slot, making the efficient memory compression.

Another benefit of this mechanism lies when *hole punching* occurs. Hole punching is an event such that a longer prefix divides a shorter prefix's address space, necessitating the routing table to deal with the address space as three distinct divisions[1]. Generally hole punching prevents the leaves from being contiguous, disabling the aforementioned efficient leaf compression. However, in Poptrie, the contiguity is recovered by making the leaf slot irrelevant if there is a descendant internal node that corresponds to the leaf slot. The lookup algorithm checks always the existence of the descendant internal node first, and if there is one, the lookup never tracks back from the lower level to the current level. Hence the leaf slot with a corresponding descendant internal node is defined as irrelevant, and is set to 0. Then, we may make the leaf slot contiguous again, ignoring those leaf slots with corresponding descendant internal node, as shown in Figure 3.

The modification in the algorithm is shown in Algorithm 2. Only the Line 14 is changed from Algorithm 1 so that it checks the newly introduced *leafvec* field to compute the corresponding leaf index. An example of the lookup procedure using *leafvec* is illustrated in Figure 4; an 8-bit address `01100111b` is searched as follows: (a) It takes the first two bits (`01b`) from the address, and then picks the bit corresponding to this index (the second bit from the right). (b) It finds the base address of the next subsequence of internal nodes using the *base1* member. (c) It counts the number of 1s in the least significant two bits of the *vector* member minus 1 (= 1), and finds the next internal node. (d) It takes the second two bits from the address (`10b`), and then picks the bit corresponding to this index (the third bit from the right). The bit is 0 in *vector*, so the search switches to find a leaf. (e) It finds the base address for the corresponding leaf nodes from *base0* (128). (f) It counts the number of 1s in the least significant three bits of the *leafvec* minus 1 (= 0), and finally finds the leaf node.

[1]Refer to Freedman et al. [12] for further definition of hole punching.

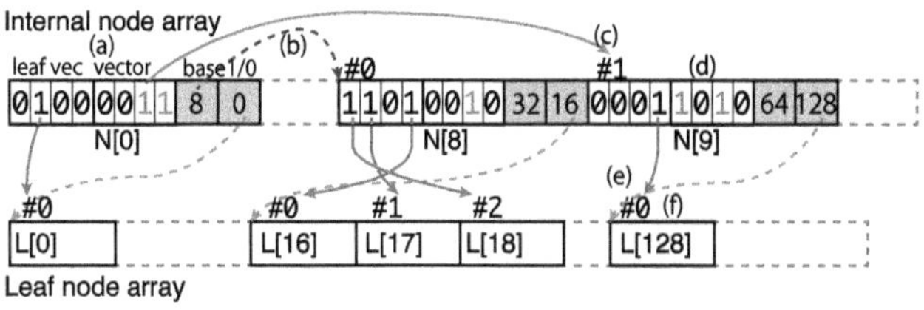

Figure 4: An example of the data structure of Poptrie where $k = 2$, and the lookup procedure for `0110b`.

3.4 Direct Pointing

Although efficient in memory space, the tree structure in general is not sufficient in search speed, especially in our problem. As we will see later in Section 4.1, most prefixes in the real datasets are distributed in the range of prefix length from `/11` through `/24`. This means that, for most IP addresses, the lookup algorithm of any tree structure will *always* need to traverse at least some internal nodes to reach to a leaf node, incurring some expensive memory accesses. This extra process can be omitted and alternatively be finished in $O(1)$ if we employ an additional array as a lookup table, at the expense of more memory consumption. These days, it is common to conduct such an optimization technique; examples can be seen in DIR-24-8-BASIC, DXR and SAIL. In Poptrie, we call this optimization "direct pointing". It is illustrated in Figure 5.

Direct pointing extracts the nodes (either internal or leaf) that corresponds to the most significant s bits to an array of length 2^s. Here, the s variable specifies how many most significant bits should be used as the index of the array. The index is called "direct index", and the value of the most significant s bits of the key address, n, is used as the direct index. It enables us to jump directly to the corresponding FIB entry or internal node, by accessing the n-th element in the top-level array. In our implementation, the most significant bit indicates whether the direct index points to a FIB entry or an internal node; if it is set, the remaining bits constitute

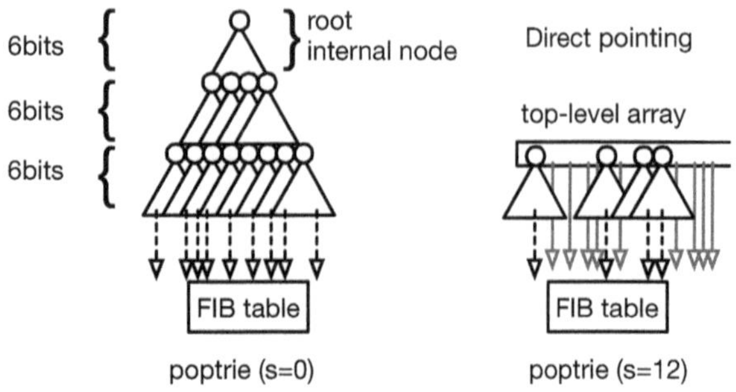

(a) Without Direct Pointing. (b) Direct Pointing.

Figure 5: Direct pointing ($k = 6$, $s = 12$).

Algorithm 3 The direct pointing algorithm; the differences from Algorithm 1. Line 1 and 2 in Algorithm 1 are replaced with the statements below.

```
index = extract(key, 0, t.s);
dindex = t.D[index].direct_index;
if (dindex & (1UL << 31)) then
    return dindex & ((1UL << 31) - 1);
end if
index = dindex;
offset = t.s;
```

an index that points to a FIB entry directly. Otherwise, the direct index points to the internal node and further search is necessary. Since we used the direct index of 4 bytes length, it increases the memory footprint by 4×2^s bytes at maximum. The modifications to Algorithm 1 are shown in Algorithm 3.

3.5 Incremental Update

Although compilation time of Poptrie from scratch, i.e., rebuilding the data structure entirely from the RIB, is short (less than 70 milliseconds as shown later in Table 2), it is generally desired to have a way to quickly update the FIB incrementally. The incremental update of Poptrie is performed by replacing only the updated part of the trie.

Blocking the read access to Poptrie using write lock is not acceptable because it blocks IP forwarding process for a considerable amount of time. Hence, we opt for a lock-free approach for the incremental update in Poptrie. In either way, the data structure must be kept consistent all the time. The strategy here is to let the IP forwarding process keep referring to the current (i.e., older) FIB while the construction of the updated FIB is ongoing. When the update is finished, the current FIB is switched to the new one, by changing the pointer or the index of the FIB using an atomic instruction. Since the FIB lookup is read-only procedure and we assume the single-threaded update operation, the atomic instruction can ensure the consistency.

Poptrie is a data structure to provide the FIB compiled from a RIB. Suppose the RIB is maintained by

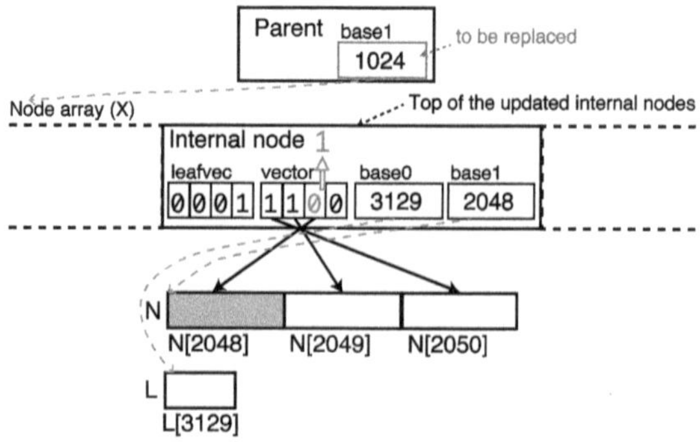

Figure 6: The lock-free update procedure to the internal node.

a binary radix tree. To support the partial update of Poptrie, we add a mark (i.e., a flag) to the radix node indicating that this node needs updating. The internal and leaf nodes of Poptrie corresponding to the marked radix nodes are replaced with new ones. The update procedure of the data structure of Poptrie consists of the following three steps. 1) When a prefix is updated, each radix tree's node of which next hop changes is marked by traversing the subtree. 2) Poptrie constructs the subtree with new descendant internal nodes and leaf nodes from the lowest level of the tree, reusing the internal nodes and leaves corresponding to the non-marked radix nodes. When a Poptrie node consists of only one leaf covering all the range, and it does not hold any descendant node, the node is removed and the leaf is brought to the upper level by clearing the corresponding bit in *vector* of the upper level internal node. The procedure continues until the leaves cannot be brought to the upper level any more. 3) The root of the affected subtree needs to be replaced. When neither of the root's *vector* nor *leafvec* change, then we can replace the root's node array (*base1*) or leaf array (*base0*) to a newly constructed array, with an atomic instruction. Otherwise, when the root's *vector* and/or *leafvec* change, we replace the entire node array that includes the root node (in other words, the node array that is pointed from the parent of the root). This is illustrated in Figure 6. We allocate a new node array for the current array and rebuild it, and finally *base1* of the parent is replaced with an atomic instruction. Note that our buddy memory allocator implementation mitigates the memory fragmentation in allocating a contiguous array.

The update of Poptrie with direct pointing is performed as follows. If the depth of the top marked node in the radix tree equals or is greater than s, the incremental update follows the same way without direct pointing, as described above. If the depth of the top marked node is less than s, the entire top-level array of 2^s entries needs to be replaced.

After the completion of the update procedure, the unused memory space, i.e., the replaced part, is freed after ensuring no lookup procedure is referring to it.

Table 1: RIB Datasets; the name, number of prefixes, and number of distinct next hops.

Name	# of prefixes	# of nhops	Name	# of prefixes	# of nhops	Name	# of prefixes	# of nhops
RV-linx-p46 †	518,231	308	RV-saopaulo-p12 ‡	516,536	510	RV-singapore-p3 †	518,620	136
RV-linx-p50 †	512,476	410	RV-saopaulo-p13 ‡	517,914	504	RV-singapore-p5 †	516,557	129
RV-linx-p52 †	514,590	419	RV-saopaulo-p16 †	521,405	528	RV-sydney-p0 †	520,580	122
RV-linx-p57 †	514,070	142	RV-saopaulo-p18 ‡	521,874	522	RV-sydney-p1 †	515,809	125
RV-linx-p60 †	508,700	70	RV-saopaulo-p2 ‡	523,092	530	RV-sydney-p3 †	517,511	115
RV-linx-p61 †	512,476	149	RV-saopaulo-p20 ‡	523,574	470	RV-sydney-p4 †	519,246	86
RV-nwax-p1 †	519,224	60	RV-saopaulo-p23 ‡	523,013	517	RV-sydney-p9 †	523,400	127
RV-nwax-p2 †	514,627	46	RV-saopaulo-p25 ‡	532,637	523	RV-telxatl-p3 ‡	511,161	56
RV-nwax-p5 †	519,195	49	RV-saopaulo-p26 ‡	516,408	479	RV-telxatl-p6 ‡	519,537	42
RV-paixisc-p12 †	519,142	68	RV-saopaulo-p8 ‡	522,296	477	RV-telxatl-p7 ‡	513,339	49
RV-paixisc-p14 †	524,168	49	RV-saopaulo-p9 ‡	515,639	507			
REAL-Tier1-A *	531,489	13	SYN1-Tier1-A	764,847	45	SYN2-Tier1-A	885,645	87
REAL-Tier1-B *	524,170	9	SYN1-Tier1-B	756,406	19	SYN2-Tier1-B	876,944	33
REAL-RENET ◇	516,100	32						

† Snapshot of 2014-12-17 00:00 UTC, ‡ Snapshot of 2014-12-16 23:00 UTC, * Obtained on Jan. 9, 2015, ◇ Obtained on Jan. 3, 2015.

4. EVALUATION

We evaluate the performance of the proposed lookup algorithm[2] using BGP routing tables (described in Section 4.1). We compare Poptrie with the binary radix tree, Tree BitMap [11], DXR (D16R and D18R) [38] and SAIL (SAIL_L) [36]. We implemented these algorithms ourselves, and validated their correctness by comparing all lookup results of all algorithms for each address of the whole IPv4 space. For fair comparison with Tree BitMap and Poptrie, we use the *popcnt* instruction rather than the lookup table used in the original Tree BitMap implementation.

We use a computer equipped with an Intel(R) Core i7 4770K (3.9 GHz, 8 MiB cache) and 32 GB DDR3-1866 for the experiments. The latencies[3] of L1, L2, L3 cache, and DRAM access are 4-5 cycles, 12 cycles, 36 cycles, and 36 cycles plus Column Address Strobe latency, respectively. The size of L1, L2, and L3 cache are 32 KiB, 256 KiB, and 8MiB, respectively. All evaluations are conducted ten times on the Ubuntu 14.04 server (x86_64) on this computer, except for the CPU cycle analysis in Section 4.6.

4.1 Datasets

Table 1 summarizes the routing table datasets we use in this paper. The dataset name starts with the prefix 'RV' indicates the dataset is obtained from the RouteViews public BGP RIB archives [33]. We omit datasets that do not resemble a core router's RIB by filtering out the datasets with only one next hop, or with routing table size less than 500K. 32 datasets are obtained; the second and the third segments in the dataset name represents the archive name and the peer number, respectively. For example, RV-linx-p46 is the 46th[4] peer in the linx RIB snapshot in the RouteViews archives.

The datasets whose name starts with the prefix 'REAL' are the real routing tables that are obtained from ISP's routers in operation. The key difference between the real and the RouteViews RIB datasets is that the real ones contain routes exchanged via Interior Gateway Protocols (IGPs). These longer prefixes cause the lookup technology to search down to a deeper level of the tree, as we will see later. REAL-Tier1-A is the routing table obtained from a real core backbone router in a global tier-1 ISP. REAL-Tier1-B is obtained from a national backbone router in the same ISP. REAL-RENET is obtained from a router in a research and educational network of WIDE Project [1].

To test the scalability of our technology against future routing table growth, we created two types of synthetic routing tables containing more than 700K entries, by extending REAL-Tier1-A and REAL-Tier1-B. The first type, whose name starts with 'SYN1', is created by the following procedure: Each prefix that is no longer than `/24` and `/16` is split into two and four prefixes, respectively. The second type, whose name starts with 'SYN2', is created by the following procedure: Each prefix that is no longer than `/24`, `/20`, and `/16` is split into two, four, and eight prefixes, respectively. Each split prefix is assigned a different next hop systematically; the i-th split prefix has the next hop $n+i$ where n is the original next hop. Note that the next hop $n+i$ did not overlap any existing next hops in the original datasets. These synthetic datasets are more challenging environments because they have a larger number of route entries, and the aggregation of leaf nodes becomes more difficult due to the distinct next hop values derived from the assignment policies.

It is worth noting that in general, the number of bits checked in the longest prefix matching is larger than the prefix length of individual routes. This is due to the other longer prefixes within the prefix in the address space. We call the number of bits (equivalently, the depth to search in the binary radix tree) that is neces-

[2]The reference implementation of Poptrie is available at https://github.com/pixos/poptrie.

[3]reported at http://www.7-cpu.com/cpu/Haswell.

[4]with zero-based numbering.

Table 2: **The compilation time, the number of nodes, the memory footprint, and the lookup rate for random with direct pointing ($s = 0, 16, 18$).**

Name and options	s	# of inodes	# of leaves	Mem. [MiB]	Compilation (std.) [ms]	Rate (std.) [Mlps]
Radix	–	–	–	30.48	–	8.82 (0.05)
Poptrie (basic) without route aggregation	0	64,009	4,032,568	8.67	31.07 (0.45)	87.71 (1.65)
	16	172,101	10,862,901	23.60	64.18 (0.33)	130.72 (1.72)
	18	61,282	3,911,422	9.40	36.06 (1.14)	170.69 (2.92)
Poptrie (*leafvec*) without route aggregation	0	64,009	280,673	2.00	32.60 (1.25)	89.15 (1.59)
	16	172,101	347,449	4.85	62.97 (0.20)	154.33 (1.53)
	18	61,282	265,320	2.91	33.37 (0.25)	191.95 (1.67)
Poptrie	0	43,191	263,381	1.49	32.84 (0.29)	96.27 (1.84)
	16	86,171	274,145	2.75	65.91 (0.35)	198.28 (5.29)
	18	40,760	245,034	2.40	33.24 (0.24)	240.52 (5.47)

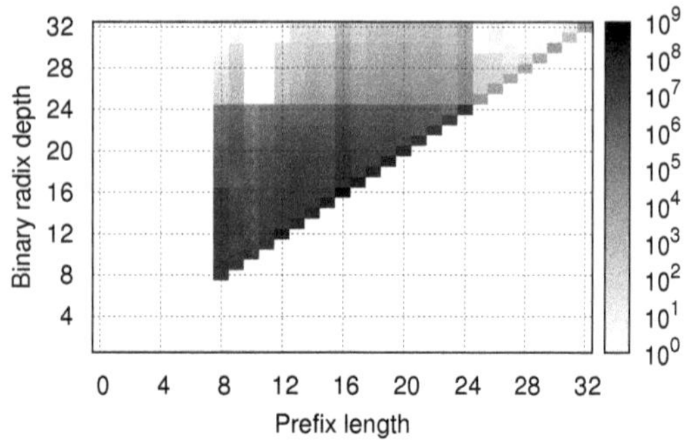

Figure 7: The heat map of the binary radix depth for all 2^{32} IPv4 addresses on REAL-Tier1-A. x-axis is the matched prefix's prefix length. y-axis is the length of checked bits.

sary to decide the resulting longest matching prefix "*binary radix depth*". The binary radix depth is possibly deeper than the prefix length as shown in Figure 7. We see a number of cases where deeper search is required to decide the shorter longest matching prefix. For example, there are many cases where it is necessary to search down to the 24th level to decide that the matching prefix is only /8. This influences the performance of lookup technologies shown in the later sections.

4.2 Traffic Patterns

We take the following traffic patterns into consideration for the lookup performance evaluation: **random**, **sequential**, **repeated**, and **real-trace**. The first three are synthetic ones, and the last one is real traffic.

For **random** traffic pattern, 2^{32} random IP addresses are generated using *xorshift* [22]. If we prepare an array of random numbers on memory in advance, the data structure may be pushed out from the cache. In order to minimize this cache pollution, each random number is generated just before the lookup routine using the xorshift, which allocates only four 32-bit variables. The measured average overhead of the random number generator was 1.22 nanoseconds per generation. Note that we did *not* exclude this overhead from the results. For **sequential**, 2^{32} addresses from `0.0.0.0` to `255.255.255.255` are queried sequentially. **Sequential** represents the traffic with spatial and temporal locality. Technologies tend to show better performance for **sequential** because of the absence of random number generation, and the higher possibility of cache hit in searching down the same part of the tree. **Repeated** is similar to **random** except that each random number address is repeated 16 times (total 16×2^{32} lookups). It represents the traffic with high temporal locality.

Real-trace is a real Internet traffic trace [2], captured on December 16, 2014, for 15 minutes. The trace was captured on a transit link of the same AS border router that produced the REAL-RENET RIB dataset. We excluded an IP address that probes the entire IPv4 address space with a large amount of experimental ICMP packets[5]. The packets accounted for 24.4% of the total IPv4 packets in the trace. The number of IPv4 packets in this trace (after the filtering) is 97,126,495 with 644,790 distinct destination IPv4 addresses. In the evaluation, we load all the destination IP addresses of **real-trace** into an array in memory in advance, and issue the lookup queries one by one in sequence.

4.3 Effect of Extensions in Poptrie

We first evaluate the effectiveness of the extensions and the design options of Poptrie. They are labeled "basic" (Section 3.1), "*leafvec*" (Section 3.3), and "*s*" (the parameter for direct pointing, described in Section 3.4). Using REAL-Tier1-A, we measured the number of internal nodes (labeled "# of inodes"), the number of leaf nodes ("# of leaves"), the memory footprint, the compilation time to construct Poptrie from the binary radix tree, and the average lookup performance. The results are summarized in Table 2. Note that Poptrie without direct pointing is represented as $s = 0$.

The leaf compression by the *leafvec* reduced the memory footprint by 69–79% for $s = 0, 16, 18$, and addition of the route aggregation option reduces the memory footprint by 74–88% compared to Poptrie (basic). They

[5]USC ANT project: http://www.isi.edu/ant/address/

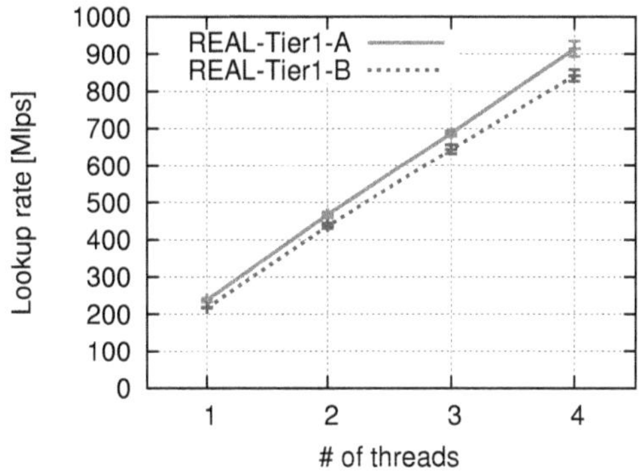

Figure 8: The aggregated lookup rate by the number of threads on the four core CPU.

effectively reduce the memory footprint, leading to the increased lookup rate. Poptrie with $s = 18$ doubles the lookup rate with less than 1 MiB memory increase compared to $s = 0$, without increasing the compilation time. Hereafter, we denote Poptrie with $s = x$ by Poptrie$_x$.

In this paper, we choose 16 or 18 as the value of s to conduct a fair comparison, since SAIL and DXR expand in those bit lengths. Another reason for $s = 18$ is to make the poptrie nodes aligned properly with the prefix length of /24, since the /24 prefixes are the longest and also the largest number of prefixes in the BGP routing domain. $s = 18$ allows Poptrie to require only one internal node traversal (which corresponds to proceeding by 6 bits) for the /24 prefixes, with an acceptable memory footprint increase.

4.4 Expectation in Multi-Core

Modern CPUs commonly implement multiple cores in a single CPU. Therefore, it is still worth evaluating the performance using multiple CPU cores, to indicate how much aggregated performance we can get from a single CPU. Note that the scheduling architecture to distribute packets into multiple CPU cores is beyond the scope of this paper.

Figure 8 presents the aggregated lookup rate of Poptrie$_{18}$ against the number of threads for REAL-Tier1-A and REAL-Tier1-B. Obviously the data structure of Poptrie can be shared among threads, and hence multithreading does not increase memory footprint. Furthermore, the shared cache has enough bandwidth to execute the lookup algorithm in parallel. Therefore, the lookup rate of Poptrie can be linearly scaled up to the number of CPU cores.

4.5 Comparison with Other Algorithms

In this section, we compare the performance of Poptrie with Tree BitMap [11], SAIL [36] and DXR [38], for three synthetic traffic patterns; **random**, **sequential**, and **repeated**, to demonstrate the advantage of Poptrie.

We first compare the performance for the **random** traffic pattern. Figure 9 shows the lookup performance of Radix, Tree BitMap, SAIL, D16R, Poptrie$_{16}$, D18R, and Poptrie$_{18}$ for all of the 35 routing table instances from the RouteViews and the real datasets. The average lookup rate and the standard deviation of ten experiments are shown using the error bars. Poptrie outperforms *all* other lookup algorithms in the average lookup rate for *all* of these 35 RIB datasets; Poptrie$_{18}$ is 24.5–46.1, 3.52–6.78, 1.37–2.62, and 1.04–1.34 times faster than Radix, Tree BitMap, SAIL, and D18R, respectively. There are five RIB datasets where Poptrie$_{16}$ outperforms Poptrie$_{18}$ (e.g., RV-saopaulo-p2). We investigated that, for these RIB datasets, the route aggregation reduced a large number of prefixes that are more specific than /16, and consequently, Poptrie$_{16}$ achieved better performance than Poptrie$_{18}$ through the significant reduction of the memory footprint.

Table 3: The memory footprint and lookup rate for random of each algorithm.

	REAL-Tier1-A		REAL-Tier1-B	
Algorithm	Mem. [MiB]	Rate [Mlps]	Mem. [MiB]	Rate [Mlps]
Radix	30.48	8.82	29.34	8.92
Tree BitMap	2.62	56.24	2.54	62.13
Tree BitMap (64-ary)	3.10	61.61	2.89	68.82
SAIL	44.24	158.22	42.62	159.39
D16R	1.16	116.63	0.93	114.30
D18R	1.91	179.92	1.71	168.80
Poptrie$_0$	1.49	96.27	1.32	92.99
Poptrie$_{16}$	2.75	198.28	1.87	191.83
Poptrie$_{18}$	2.40	240.52	2.25	218.97

Here, we take a close look at the results for REAL-Tier1-A and REAL-Tier1-B, which yielded the worst and second worst lookup rate of Poptrie$_{18}$. Table 3 summarizes the memory footprint and the lookup rate of each algorithm for these two datasets. Poptrie$_{18}$ is 1.52 and 1.37 times faster than SAIL for REAL-Tier1-A and REAL-Tier1-B, respectively. Similarly, Poptrie$_{18}$ is 1.34 and 1.30 times faster than D18R for REAL-Tier1-A and REAL-Tier1-B, respectively. The memory footprint is not the only factor for the performance results; even though the memory footprint of Poptrie$_{16}$ and Poptrie$_{18}$ is larger than DXR (D16R and D18R), they are still within the size of the L3 cache, and therefore, they can still outperform DXR. In contrast, because the memory footprint of SAIL exceeds the L3 cache size, it leads to the cache misses and to the relatively slow DRAM access. Consequently, SAIL exhibited slower performance than Poptrie. Table 3 also presents the performance of Tree BitMap. The use of the *popcnt* instruction instead of a lookup table enables Tree BitMap to increase the order of a multiway trie to reduce the lookup depth, from original 16-ary to 64-ary. However, as shown in Table 3, even the 64-ary Tree BitMap cannot achieve good performance. We suspect that this is because searching a matching prefix within a Tree

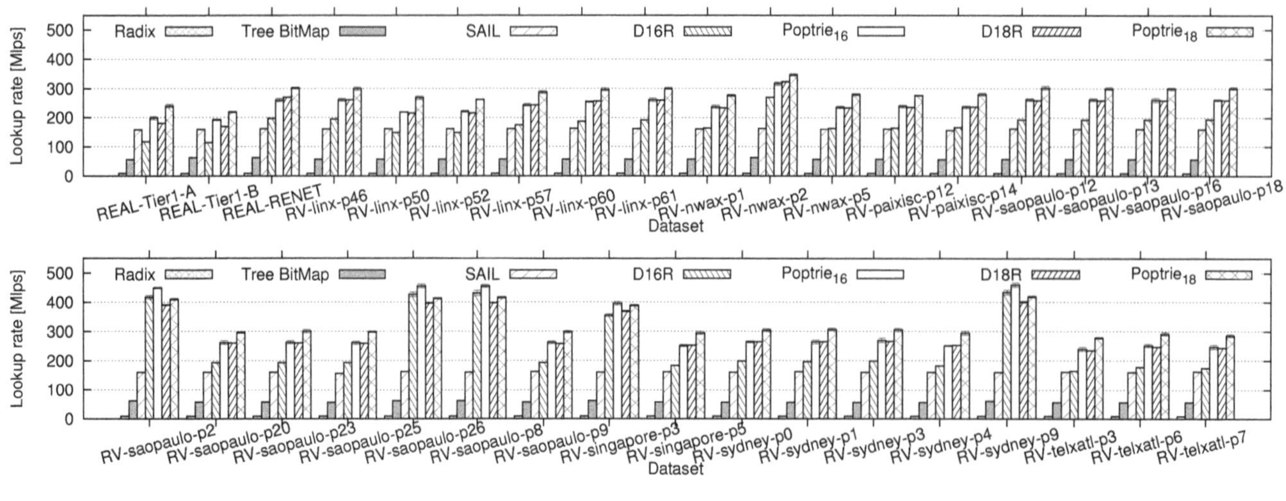

Figure 9: The average lookup rate for random IP addresses on RouteViews' tables.

BitMap node runs in $O(k)$ on a 2^k-ary multiway trie while Poptrie searches a leaf within a node in $O(1)$.

The lookup performance for the high locality traffic patterns is also compared. For **sequential**, all algorithms effectively utilized the CPU cache for the traffic pattern's high locality. For REAL-Tier1-B where Poptrie performed worse, the average lookup rate for **sequential** of SAIL, D16R, D18R, Poptrie_{16}, and Poptrie_{18} were 1264, 628, 911, 955, and 1122 Mlps, respectively. The average lookup rate for **repeated** of SAIL, D16R, D18R, Poptrie_{16}, and Poptrie_{18} on REAL-Tier1-B were 492, 382, 454, 470, and 480 Mlps, respectively. Since SAIL uses the memory access instead of executing some instructions to search down the tree, SAIL achieves high performance when the cache hit rate is high. Poptrie_{16} and Poptrie_{18} are slower than SAIL because our algorithms require bitwise instructions to find the index to the corresponding FIB entry, while SAIL directly accesses to a contiguous array. Moreover, DXR is slower than Poptrie even in the effective utilization of the CPU cache because DXR searches the corresponding FIB entry with the binary search that requires more number of steps.

From the comparison results above, Poptrie_{18} achieves the high lookup rates, independent of the traffic patterns and datasets, while the performance of SAIL depends on the locality of traffic patterns. Furthermore, Poptrie outperforms DXR for any combination of traffic pattern and dataset.

4.6 CPU Cycles per Lookup

In order to conduct the detailed analysis, we investigate the number of CPU cycles it takes for each table lookup. We use REAL-Tier1-A and REAL-Tier1-B for the dataset. We measured the per-lookup CPU cycles with the single task operating system (OS) that we are developing. The single task OS enables us to precisely measure the CPU cycles by eliminating the disturbances of context switches and the cache pollution caused by other tasks. Since the cache behavior cannot be controlled by the OS, we statistically analyze the distribution of the CPU cycles in a large number of lookups.

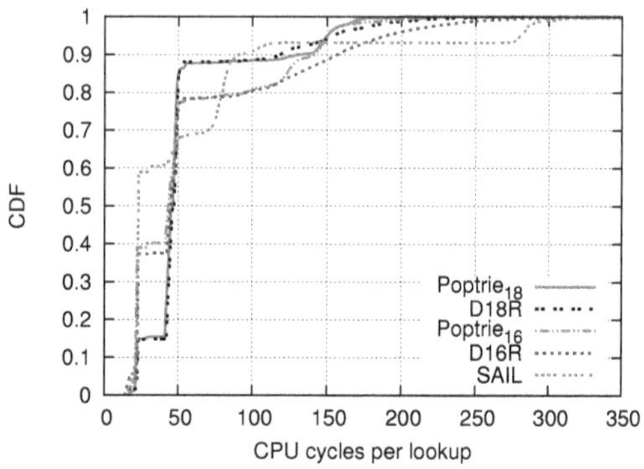

Figure 10: CDF of CPU cycles per lookup.

The CPU cycles are monitored with the performance monitoring counters (PMCs) of the CPU [3]. The overhead to read a PMC is constantly 83 cycles, and is excluded from the results. The CPU cycle measurement was conducted for 2^{24} **random** IP address lookups, for each algorithm. Note that we used the same seed for the random number generator to precisely compare different algorithms.

The CDF of CPU cycles per lookup for the REAL-Tier1-A dataset is shown in Figure 10. We see that D16R and Poptrie_{16}, and D18R and Poptrie_{18} have almost identical distributions where the CPU cycle count is less than 120, except for a small difference around at 22 cycles between D16R and Poptrie_{16}, which will be discussed later. This is because the data structures and lookup algorithms of DXR and Poptrie are almost the same in looking up shorter prefixes. The CPU cycle count of D16R and Poptrie_{16} exhibit the steeper gradients around 21–22 cycles than those of D18R and

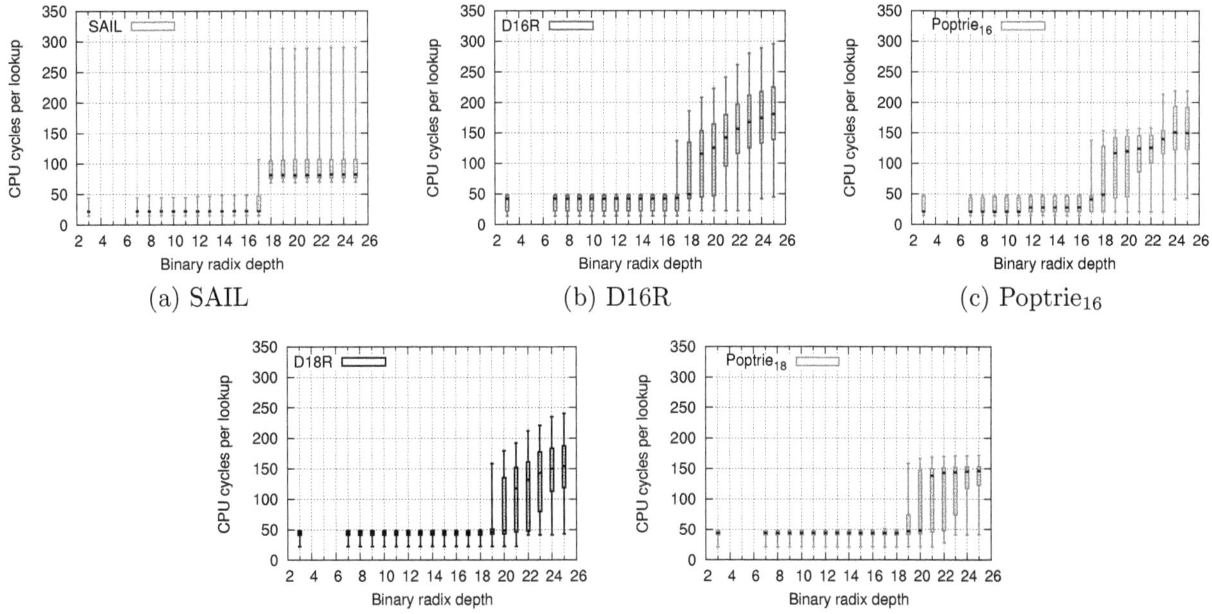

(a) SAIL (b) D16R (c) Poptrie_{16} (d) D18R (e) Poptrie_{18}

Figure 11: The quartiles and 5th/95th percentiles of per-lookup CPU cycles for each binary radix depth on REAL-Tier1-A.

Poptrie_{18}. The reason is that the memory footprints of D16R and Poptrie_{16} for the first memory access are distributed in the range of 256 KiB (4×2^{16}), which can be entirely contained in the L2 cache size, while the memory footprints of D18R and Poptrie_{18} for the first memory access are distributed in the range of 1 MiB (4×2^{18}), which exceeds the L2 cache size and incurs the slower access time. The CPU cycles of SAIL exhibits an even steeper gradient around 21–22 cycles than those of D16R and Poptrie_{16}. This is because the top level part of SAIL is 128 KiB (2×2^{16}), which is half of the L2 cache size. Consequently, it could take advantage of the L2 cache efficiency. However, the tail distribution of SAIL is expanded to the larger CPU cycles because the memory footprint of entire SAIL is larger than the L3 cache size and it leads to the L3 cache misses. Note that the similar characteristics were observed in the CDF of CPU cycles per lookup for the REAL-Tier1-B dataset.

Table 4 summarizes the mean, 50th (median), 75th, 95th, and 99th percentiles of per-lookup CPU cycles for each algorithm on REAL-Tier1-A and REAL-Tier1-B. The n-th percentile value means that n percent of lookups consumed no more CPU cycles than this value. The comparisons of the 95th and 99th percentiles are important because they indicate the worst case guarantees of the lookup performance except for corner cases. For the REAL-Tier1-B, SAIL consumes 124 cycles (74.7%) more than Poptrie_{18} at their 99th percentiles. This can be attributed to the cache misses and slow DRAM access. The 99th percentile of D18R is better than SAIL, but it is 21 cycles (12.7%) larger than that of Poptrie_{18}. This difference is attributed to the binary search stage in DXR.

Table 4: The per-lookup CPU cycles by random traffic on REAL-Tier1-A and REAL-Tier1-B.

Dataset	Algorithm	Mean	50th	75th	95th	99th
REAL -Tier1-A	SAIL	57.43	22	76	279	299
	D16R	60.92	44	49	189	255
	D18R	54.84	46	48	154	207
	Poptrie_{16}	54.58	43	48	150	192
	Poptrie_{18}	53.59	46	48	150	169
REAL -Tier1-B	SAIL	56.34	22	75	279	290
	D16R	61.86	44	50	182	277
	D18R	56.88	47	49	154	187
	Poptrie_{16}	55.53	43	48	141	167
	Poptrie_{18}	55.82	46	48	150	166

Although the first stage (i.e., the direct pointing in Poptrie) is similar in SAIL, DXR, and Poptrie, when the binary radix depth is more than 16 or 18, their behavior should differ, since the second stage of each algorithm is different. Hence, we investigate each case per binary radix depth. Figure 11 shows the CPU cycle distribution for each binary radix depth. The wick of each candlestick represents 5th/95th percentile, the body represents the first and third quartile values, and the internal bar represents the median value. This figure demonstrates a significant difference at greater binary radix depth; for example, the 95th percentiles of Poptrie_{18} are no more than 172 cycles for any binary radix depth while those of SAIL and DXR exceed 234 cycles at the binary radix depth of 24 and 25. Fig-

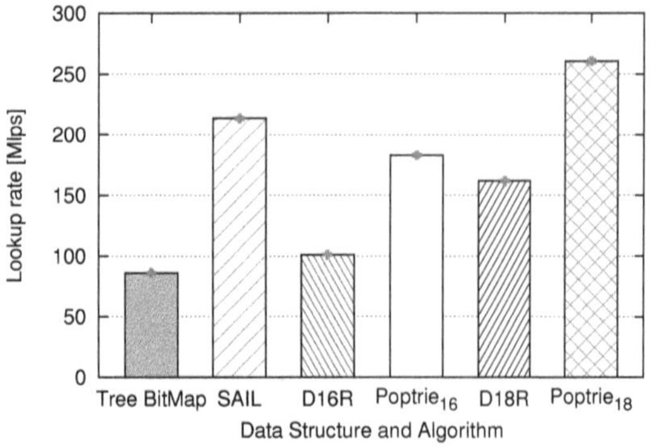

Figure 12: The average lookup rate for real-trace on REAL-RENET.

ure 11 also presents that DXR achieves better performance than Poptrie at some binary radix depths, when you look into the median values of depth of 21 in D18R and $Poptrie_{18}$. This is because the binary search stage of DXR can find the result with a smaller number of steps in cases that the number of prefixes in a range table is small. Overall, Poptrie succeeded in maintaining the lower number of CPU cycles in various cases, gaining superior performance. We found the similar trend also for the dataset REAL-Tier1-B.

When the binary radix depth is smaller than 16, all algorithms kept the CPU cycles consistently small, less than 50. Interestingly, the median of D16R is larger than that of the others. As shown in Figure 10 before, we also see the small difference in the distributions between D16R and $Poptrie_{16}$ around 22 cycles. We suspect that this can be attributed to the DXR's behavior; the binary search for its range table accesses memory many times so that the data structure for smaller binary radix depth are harder to stay in the L2 cache.

4.7 Performance Evaluation with a Real Internet Traffic Trace

Figure 12 shows the average lookup rate for **real-trace** on REAL-RENET. $Poptrie_{18}$ is 3.02, 1.61 and 1.22 times faster than Tree BitMap, D18R and SAIL, respectively. Additionally, we also confirm that $Poptrie_{18}$ outperforms Tree BitMap, DXR (D16R and D18R) and SAIL for **real-trace** on all the other RIB datasets although **real-trace** should be a different pattern from the real traffic on the other RIB datasets.

The lookup rates of Poptrie and DXR for **real-trace** are degraded compared to those for **random**. This is because a larger number of packets goes to IGP routes that are generally more specific than BGP routes in **real-trace**. 32.5% of the packets in **real-trace** on REAL-RENET have the binary radix depth more than 18, while for the whole IPv4 address space only 22.1% have the binary radix depth more than 18. These addresses cannot be looked up in the first stage of the algorithm of $Poptrie_{18}$ and D18R. Moreover, 21.8% of the packets of **real-trace** have binary radix depth more than 24, while only 1.66% of the whole IPv4 address space have binary radix depth more than 24.

SAIL performs better in the lookup rate for **real-trace** than for **random**. This is because SAIL could take advantage of the CPU cache due to the locality of the destination IP addresses, i.e., the sequences of packets with the identical destination IP address.

Table 5: The lookup rates of each algorithm in Mlps for random traffic on synthetic large RIBs. The number of routes are parenthesized.

Algorithm	SYN1 -Tier1-A (764,847)	SYN1 -Tier1-B (756,406)	SYN2 -Tier1-A (885,645)	SYN2 -Tier1-B (876,944)
SAIL	102.86	99.98	N/A	N/A
D18R†	115.45	117.48	102.59	104.22
$Poptrie_{18}$	188.02	187.69	174.42	175.04

† modified

4.8 Scalability

We measure the performance on the synthetic RIBs (i.e., those with 'SYN' prefix) to evaluate the scalability to future routing table growth. SAIL cannot compile SYN2-Tier1-A and SYN2-Tier1-B due to its structural limitation; $C_{16}[i]$ in SAIL is encoded in the 15 bits of $BCN[i]$, but it exceeds 2^{15} for these datasets. The DXR also exceeds its structural limitation of the number of ranges that is supported up to 2^{19}. However, we can extend it to 2^{20} by absorbing one bit for the "short" format flag to the address range index. Thus, we modified DXR and conducted the evaluation. The structural scalability of Poptrie is discussed in Section 5.

The average lookup rates of each algorithm for the **random** traffic pattern on the synthetic RIBs are summarized in Table 5. $Poptrie_{18}$ outperforms SAIL and D18R, and the lookup rate of $Poptrie_{18}$ exceeds the 100 GbE wire-rate, 148.8 Mlps, for these RIBs, while DXR slows down to 102.59 Mlps for SYN2-Tier1-A. Thus, Poptrie is scalable to the routing table growth in lookup performance.

4.9 Update Performance

We also evaluate the performance of updating the $Poptrie_{18}$ data structure. The update is first performed to the radix tree for the RIB maintenance, and then replaces a part of the trie in Poptrie, as described in Section 3.5. We use four 15 minute update archive files (i.e., an hour in total) of RV-linx-p52 to evaluate the update performance. This dataset contains 23,446 route updates (18,141 announced and 5,305 withdrawn) in 7,824 messages. The average number of replacements for the top-level array in direct pointing, the leaf node, and the internal node, per update, are 0.041, 6.05 (12.1 bytes) and 0.48 (11.52 bytes), respectively. This means that an update replaces a small number of objects in the data structure. We also measured the time to complete

Table 6: **Poptrie's size, compilation time, and the performance on 2^{32} random lookups on the IPv6 routing table.**

s	# of inodes	# of leaves	Mem. [KiB]	Compilation (std.) [ms]	Rate (std.) [Mlps]
0	14,925	32,586	414	7.22 (0.00)	138.51 (0.08)
16	16,554	33,047	709	4.77 (0.00)	209.84 (0.12)
18	14,910	32,569	1437	4.73 (0.00)	211.32 (0.09)

the update; 58.90 milliseconds for all 23,446 updates, i.e., only 2.51 microseconds per update.

As another input data for update performance evaluation, we measured the insertion time of the full route in a routing table. Note that the order of the entries is randomized to eliminate any assumptions on the locality of updates. The average insertion time for REAL-Tier1-A and REAL-Tier1-B are 2.71 and 2.40 seconds, respectively, hence the average insertion time per prefix for these datasets are 5.10 and 4.57 microseconds, respectively. All these results demonstrate that the complexity of the update algorithm is practically acceptable.

4.10 Applicability to IPv6

One advantage of Poptrie is that it is general enough to apply to IPv6. For the evaluation, we use the IPv6 routing table from the same router as REAL-Tier1-A. The evaluation on IPv6 routing tables is currently less interesting than IPv4 because the number of prefixes in IPv6 routing table is not large; only 20,440 prefixes are available in the dataset. Table 6 summarizes the performance on this dataset for 2^{32} random addresses within `2000::/8`. The lookup rate of Poptrie with direct pointing (s=16,18) achieves more than the wire-rate of 100 GbE, i.e., 148.8 Mlps. Note that this experiment includes the non-negligible overhead of four xorshift 32-bit random number generation to generate a 128-bit random address. Although direct pointing was originally introduced to optimize the IPv4 lookup performance, Poptrie with direct pointing (s=16,18) achieves the higher performance than that without direct pointing (s=0), by taking advantage of CPU cache while reducing the lookup depth, even in the IPv6 case.

For the comparison, we extend DXR to support IPv6 by disabling the "short" format and extending the *size* by one bit to allow up to 2^{13} entries per chunk. We cannot compare the performance with SAIL because it does not support more specific routes than `/64`. The average lookup rates of D16R and D18R for random traffic with the IPv6 dataset are 163.07 and 169.91 Mlps, respectively; Poptrie$_{18}$ is 1.24 times faster than D18R.

We also evaluate the lookup rate using 13 public RIBs archived at 2014-12-25 00:00 local time by RouteViews that contains more than 20K prefixes and more than one distinct next hops. The worst average lookup rates of Poptrie$_{16}$ and Poptrie$_{18}$ are 209.98 and 211.32 Mlps, respectively, still exceeding the 100 GbE wire-rate. In summary, Poptrie also achieves high lookup rate for IPv6 routing tables.

5. DISCUSSION

Structural scalability: The capacity of routes and next hops are important for real world deployment. In the implementation of Poptrie, the size of a leaf node is 16 bits, hence the number of FIB entries is limited to 2^{16}, though we can simply extend the size at the expense of larger memory footprint. Although we cannot provide the details due to space limitation, we estimate the limitation on the number of internal nodes, leaf nodes, and next hops, and project that Poptrie can support a hundred million and 7 million routes for IPv4 and IPv6, respectively. This is in contrast to DXR and SAIL which already reached at their limitations in our synthetic RIB evaluations.

Evaluation with a different generation of CPU architecture: We confirm that Poptrie is not optimized for one CPU model used in this paper through the performance evaluation with another generation of CPU architecture, Intel(R) Xeon X3430 2.40 GHz with 8 MiB cache. Poptrie outperforms SAIL and DXR for the **random** traffic pattern on all of the 35 routing tables from RouteViews and real network; for example on REAL-Tier1-A, Poptrie$_{18}$ is 1.27 and 1.17 times faster than D18R and SAIL, respectively.

6. CONCLUSION

We proposed Poptrie extended from the 64-ary multiway trie for fast and scalable IP routing table lookup on general purpose computers. Poptrie leverages the population count instruction to give the indirect indices to the descendant nodes in order to keep the small memory footprint within the CPU cache. In this paper, we demonstrated that Poptrie outperformed the existing algorithms for random and real traffic from experiments on three private routing tables of core routers and 32 RouteViews' public BGP routing tables. Poptrie stored a FIB of the tier-1 ISP routing table in small memory footprint, and achieved 241 Mlps lookup performance for random traffic, using just one CPU core. It is suitable for parallel processing, and exhibited as fast as 914 Mlps using four cores of the CPU for random traffic. The CPU cycle analysis revealed the characteristics of each IP routing table lookup algorithm, and demonstrated the advantage of Poptrie for longer prefixes; Poptrie$_{18}$ requires significantly less CPU cycles in the worse case, i.e., the 95th percentile, for longer prefixes than the others. Our evaluations on the future-envisioned larger routing tables also demonstrated the superiority of Poptrie in the structural scalability as well as the lookup performance. Poptrie is efficient and scalable so various applications using longest prefix matching such as software firewall in NFV can be expected.

Acknowledgment

We are grateful to Masafumi Oe and Rodney Van Meter for their continuous and generous support. We also thank the anonymous reviewers, and our shepherd, Luigi Rizzo, for their invaluable comments on our paper.

7. REFERENCES

[1] WIDE Project. http://www.wide.ad.jp/.

[2] WIDE Project MAWI Working Group Traffic Archive. http://mawi.wide.ad.jp/mawi/.

[3] Intel(R) 64 and IA-32 Architectures Software Developer Manuals (version 052), Sept. 2014.

[4] M. Bando, Y.-L. Lin, and H. J. Chao. FlashTrie: Beyond 100-Gb/s IP Route Lookup Using Hash-based Prefix-compressed Trie. *IEEE/ACM Trans. Netw.*, 20(4):1262–1275, 2012.

[5] A. Basu and G. Narlikar. Fast Incremental Updates for Pipelined Forwarding Engines. *IEEE/ACM Trans. Netw.*, 13(3):690–703, June 2005.

[6] M. Chiosi et al. Network Functions Virtualisation – Introductory White Paper. *ETSI*, 2012.

[7] T. H. Cormen, C. Stein, R. L. Rivest, and C. E. Leiserson. *Introduction to Algorithms*. McGraw-Hill Higher Education, 2nd edition, 2001.

[8] M. Degermark, A. Brodnik, S. Carlsson, and S. Pink. Small Forwarding Tables for Fast Routing Lookups. In *ACM SIGCOMM*, pages 3–14, 1997.

[9] S. Dharmapurikar, P. Krishnamurthy, and D. E. Taylor. Longest Prefix Matching Using Bloom Filters. *IEEE/ACM Trans. Netw.*, 14(2):397–409, Apr. 2006.

[10] M. Dobrescu, N. Egi, K. Argyraki, B.-G. Chun, K. Fall, G. Iannaccone, A. Knies, M. Manesh, and S. Ratnasamy. RouteBricks: Exploiting Parallelism to Scale Software Routers. In *ACM SOSP*, pages 15–28, 2009.

[11] W. Eatherton, G. Varghese, and Z. Dittia. Tree Bitmap: Hardware/Software IP Lookups with Incremental Updates. *ACM SIGCOMM Comput. Commun. Rev.*, 34(2):97–122, 2004.

[12] M. J. Freedman, M. Vutukuru, N. Feamster, and H. Balakrishnan. Geographic Locality of IP Prefixes. In *ACM IMC*, pages 13–13, Berkeley, CA, USA, 2005.

[13] P. Gupta, S. Lin, and N. McKeown. Routing Lookups in Hardware at Memory Access Speeds. In *IEEE INFOCOM*, volume 3, pages 1240–1247, 1998.

[14] S. Han, K. Jang, K. Park, and S. Moon. PacketShader: A GPU-accelerated Software Router. In *ACM SIGCOMM*, pages 195–206, 2010.

[15] J. Hasan and T. N. Vijaykumar. Dynamic Pipelining: Making IP-lookup Truly Scalable. In *ACM SIGCOMM*, pages 205–216, 2005.

[16] W. Jiang, Q. Wang, and V. Prasanna. Beyond TCAMs: An SRAM-Based Parallel Multi-Pipeline Architecture for Terabit IP Lookup. In *IEEE INFOCOM*, pages 1786–1794, 2008.

[17] K. C. Knowlton. A Fast Storage Allocator. *Commun. ACM*, 8(10):623–624, Oct. 1965.

[18] D. E. Knuth. *The Art of Computer Programming, Volume 3: Sorting and Searching*. Addison Wesley Longman Publishing Co., Inc., 2nd edition, 1998.

[19] E. Kohler, R. Morris, B. Chen, J. Jannotti, and M. F. Kaashoek. The Click Modular Router. *ACM Trans. Comput. Syst.*, 18(3):263–297, 2000.

[20] S. Kumar, M. Becchi, P. Crowley, and J. Turner. CAMP: Fast and Efficient IP Lookup Architecture. In *ACM/IEEE ANCS*, pages 51–60, 2006.

[21] Y. Li, D. Zhang, A. X. Liu, and J. Zheng. GAMT: A Fast and Scalable IP Lookup Engine for GPU-based Software Routers. In *ACM/IEEE ANCS*, pages 1–12, 2013.

[22] G. Marsaglia. Xorshift RNGs. *Journal of Statistical Software*, 8(14):1–6, 2003.

[23] A. McAuley and P. Francis. Fast Routing Table Lookup using CAMs. In *IEEE INFOCOM*, volume 3, pages 1382–1391, 1993.

[24] D. R. Morrison. PATRICIA—Practical Algorithm To Retrieve Information Coded in Alphanumeric. *J. ACM*, 15(4):514–534, Oct. 1968.

[25] G. Rétvári, J. Tapolcai, A. Kőrösi, A. Majdán, and Z. Heszberger. Compressing IP Forwarding Tables: Towards Entropy Bounds and Beyond. In *ACM SIGCOMM*, pages 111–122, 2013.

[26] L. Rizzo. Netmap: A Novel Framework for Fast Packet I/O. In *USENIX ATC*, pages 9–9, 2012.

[27] L. Rizzo and G. Lettieri. VALE, a Switched Ethernet for Virtual Machines. In *ACM CoNEXT*, pages 61–72, 2012.

[28] L. Rizzo, G. Lettieri, and V. Maffione. Speeding Up Packet I/O in Virtual Machines. In *ACM/IEEE ANCS*, pages 47–58, 2013.

[29] R. Sedgewick. *Algorithms in C, Parts 1-4: Fundamentals, Data Structures, Sorting, Searching*. Addison-Wesley Professional, 3rd edition, 1997.

[30] K. Sklower. A Tree-Based Packet Routing Table for Berkeley Unix. In *USENIX Winter Conference*, pages 93–104, 1991.

[31] V. Srinivasan and G. Varghese. Fast Address Lookups Using Controlled Prefix Expansion. *ACM Trans. Comput. Syst.*, 17(1):1–40, 1999.

[32] W. Sun and R. Ricci. Fast and Flexible: Parallel Packet Processing with GPUs and Click. In *ACM/IEEE ANCS*, pages 25–36, 2013.

[33] University of Oregon. Route Views Project. http://www.routeviews.org/.

[34] M. Waldvogel, G. Varghese, J. Turner, and B. Plattner. Scalable High Speed IP Routing Lookups. In *ACM SIGCOMM*, pages 25–36, 1997.

[35] H. S. Warren. *Hacker's delight*. Pearson Education, 2013.

[36] T. Yang, G. Xie, Y. Li, Q. Fu, A. X. Liu, Q. Li, and L. Mathy. Guarantee IP Lookup Performance with FIB Explosion. In *ACM SIGCOMM*, pages 39–50, 2014.

[37] F. Zane, G. Narlikar, and A. Basu. CoolCAMs: Power-Efficient TCAMs for Forwarding Engines. In *IEEE INFOCOM*, volume 1, pages 42–52, 2003.

[38] M. Zec, L. Rizzo, and M. Mikuc. DXR: Towards a Billion Routing Lookups Per Second in Software. *ACM SIGCOMM Comput. Commun. Rev.*, 42(5):29–36, 2012.

[39] K. Zheng, C. Hu, H. Lu, and B. Liu. A TCAM-based Distributed Parallel IP Lookup Scheme and Performance Analysis. *IEEE/ACM Trans. Netw.*, 14(4):863–875, Aug. 2006.

How to Bid the Cloud

Liang Zheng[*‡] Carlee Joe-Wong[*] Chee Wei Tan[†‡] Mung Chiang[*] Xinyu Wang[‡]
[*]Princeton University [†]National University of Singapore [‡]City University of Hong Kong
{liangz, cjoe, chiangm}@princeton.edu cheetan@alumni.caltech.edu xinywang@cityu.edu.hk

ABSTRACT

Amazon's Elastic Compute Cloud (EC2) uses auction-based spot pricing to sell spare capacity, allowing users to bid for cloud resources at a highly reduced rate. Amazon sets the spot price dynamically and accepts user bids above this price. Jobs with lower bids (including those already running) are interrupted and must wait for a lower spot price before resuming. Spot pricing thus raises two basic questions: how might the provider set the price, and what prices should users bid? Computing users' bidding strategies is particularly challenging: higher bid prices reduce the probability of, and thus extra time to recover from, interruptions, but may increase users' cost. We address these questions in three steps: (1) modeling the cloud provider's setting of the spot price and matching the model to historically offered prices, (2) deriving optimal bidding strategies for different job requirements and interruption overheads, and (3) adapting these strategies to MapReduce jobs with master and slave nodes having different interruption overheads. We run our strategies on EC2 for a variety of job sizes and instance types, showing that spot pricing reduces user cost by 90% with a modest increase in completion time compared to on-demand pricing.

CCS Concepts

•**Networks** → **Network performance evaluation;** *Data center networks;* Cloud computing;

Keywords

Cloud pricing, spot instance, optimization.

1. INTRODUCTION

Cloud providers face an increasingly complicated problem of allocating their resources to different users. These resource allocations must take into account both available capacity within datacenter networks as well as individual jobs' requirements, which are sometimes specified in binding service level agreements. The large number of users submitting different types of jobs to any given cloud further complicates the problem, creating a highly dynamic environment as jobs are submitted and completed at different times [4].

SIGCOMM '15, August 17 - 21, 2015, London, United Kingdom
 ISBN 978-1-4503-3542-3/15/08...$15.00
DOI: http://dx.doi.org/10.1145/2785956.2787473

1.1 Spot Pricing to Shape User Demand

While many works have considered the operational problem of scheduling jobs within a datacenter [8, 14, 22, 33], most have taken user demands as a given input. Yet user demand can be partially controlled by cloud providers' pricing [6]. The majority of today's pricing plans for cloud resources are variants on usage-based pricing, in which users pay a static per-unit price (per workload or per hour) to access cloud resources [21]. Usage-based pricing can affect overall demand levels, but does not even out short-term fluctuations [13]. To manage these fluctuations in demand for a fixed amount of available datacenter capacity, cloud providers could introduce more flexible pricing plans in which resources are priced according to real-time market demand [40]. Amazon's Elastic Compute Cloud (EC2) spot pricing [2] is an example of such a strategy.

Spot pricing creates an auction-based market for available cloud computing resources. Users can submit bids to the market at any time, using the spot price history to help decide how much to bid (i.e., their bid prices). The cloud provider sets the spot price at regular time intervals, e.g., every five minutes, depending on the number of bids received from users (demand) and how many resources are available (supply) at each time slot.[1] In each time slot, users' bids above the spot price are accepted, and those below it rejected. Running spot instances are terminated if their original bid prices fall below the new spot price, and re-launched only when their bids again exceed the spot price. Given that these interruptions may affect user utility, two natural questions then arise: *how might the provider set the spot price*, and *what prices should users bid*?

[1]These available resources include idle resources and those in use by launched spot instances.

We answer these questions in this work. Unlike most works on spot pricing, which consider only the provider's viewpoint [10, 17, 34, 38], we aim to develop both *a reasonable model for how the provider sets the spot prices* and *optimal bidding strategies for the user.* We do not seek to design the auction mechanism used by the provider, only to systematically model and estimate how the provider might set the spot prices before we develop users' optimal bidding strategies. These bidding strategies, in turn, depend not on the specific model of how providers choose the spot prices, but rather on the chosen spot prices themselves. They can thus be applied to other provider pricing models.

1.2 Research Challenges and Contributions

We can gain a basic statistical understanding of Amazon's prevailing spot prices by studying the two-month history made available by Amazon [1, 15]. Though these statistics alone are sufficient for the user to deduce a bid price, they also give us some insights into how the provider sets the spot prices. By developing a model that relates the spot price to users' submitted bids, we can better understand the different factors considered by the provider in setting the spot prices.

Users' job completion times consist of three components: the time to execute the job, idle time while the spot price exceeds the user bid price, and the time to recover from job interruptions. A lower bid price reduces the cost of running the job during its execution time, but can extend the recovery time by inducing more job interruptions. This extra recovery runtime can result in a higher overall job cost, depending on the recovery time from each interruption (i.e., the job's "interruptibility") and the spot prices offered by the provider. Complicating this tradeoff is the fact that user jobs can have long runtimes spanning many changes in the spot price [15]. Users then face two key challenges:

1) Users must predict the spot prices in order to optimize their bids for a given job, not only in the next time slot but also for all future time slots until the job is completed.

2) Different jobs may have different degrees of interruptibility. Even within a single user job that requires many computational nodes, e.g., MapReduce's master/slave node model, different nodes can have different interruptibility requirements.

Figure 1 shows the basic architecture of a user client and its interaction with the cloud provider. The client calculates its bid price based on two inputs: user inputs on job characteristics and the historical distribution of the spot prices offered by the cloud provider. A price monitor keeps the spot price distribution up to date, and a job monitor at the provider tracks whether the job is ever outbid. The monitor also restarts users' jobs when the spot price falls below their bids.

We first give a brief overview of related work in Section 2 and relevant background on Amazon's EC2 in

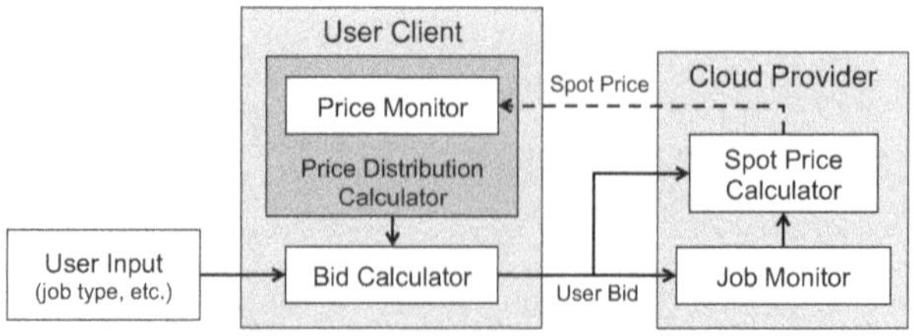

Figure 1: Client and cloud provider interaction.

Section 3 before developing the following results:

A framework for understanding spot prices (Section 4): We develop a model to understand how the provider sets the spot price, using it to bound users' quality of service and testing it against empirical data.

Users' optimal bidding strategies (Section 5): Given a predicted spot price distribution, we derive optimal bidding strategies for different degrees of job interruptibility.

Adaptation to MapReduce jobs (Section 6): We adapt our bidding strategies for the master and slave nodes of MapReduce jobs and implement our bidding strategy for a MapReduce job.

Experiment on Amazon EC2 (Section 7): We run our client on a variety of EC2 instances and job types. The proposed bidding strategies substantially lower users' costs in exchange for modestly higher running times.

Our work considers spot pricing from the point of view of both the cloud provider and users, allowing us to better understand how providers set the spot prices and to develop bidding strategies customized to different user requirements. We discuss some limitations of our work in Section 8 before concluding the paper in Section 9. All proofs can be found in the Appendix.

2. RELATED WORK

Cloud scheduling and pricing. Many works have considered resource allocation in the cloud from a purely operational perspective [8, 14, 22, 33]. Others incorporate pricing considerations, e.g., dynamically allocating cloud resources, so as to maximize the provider's revenue [10, 17, 34] or social welfare [25, 38]. We construct a similar model but relate it to empirical bid prices and use it to develop bidding strategies for users. Joint user-provider interactions for cloud services are considered in [26], but auction-specific works on both provider and user actions are limited to statistical studies of historical spot prices [1, 15].

Game theoretic pricing. Spot pricing is a distributed solution to the problem of allocating cloud resources to users, which can be treated as a game between users. Some works have considered the Nash equilibrium of such a pricing game in cloud scenarios [3, 31, 32], although they do not consider optimal bids in a resource auction. More generally, auctions have been proposed as a solution to generic distributed allocation games over multiple time slots [20]. Users' optimal bidding strategies in such auctions can be quite complex, particularly if multiple users try to optimize their bids at the same time [36]. We assume in this paper that users' bid optimizations do not significantly affect the distribution of the spot prices, and discuss the consequences of relaxing this assumption in Section 8.

Auctions and bidding. User bidding strategies for cloud auctions are much less studied than provider strategies. While some works have shown that users can reduce their costs by using spot rather than on-demand instances [28, 37], they only consider heuristic bidding strategies for single-instance jobs.

In general, auction frameworks assume that users' bids are determined by their valuations of the auctioned resource. Indeed, many works have studied the problem of designing online auctions to ensure truthful user bids [5, 11, 27, 29], including improvements to Amazon's spot pricing [35]. However, *in cloud scenarios, user valuations for the instance in a given time slot depend on (unknown) future spot prices.* While users may know their valuations for completing a job, job interruptions will increase the number of instance-time slots required to complete the job. This dependence differentiates our work from other auctions for computing or utility resources, e.g., auctions for smart grid electricity [9], secondary spectrum access [16], grid computing [19], or Internet data [24].

3. BACKGROUND

3.1 User Jobs and Instance Types

Throughout this work, we consider Infrastructure-as-a-service (IaaS) cloud services, which are essentially remote virtual machines (VMs) with CPU, memory, and storage resources [2]. We follow Amazon's terminology and use the term "instance" to denote the use of a single VM. Instances can be divided into several discrete types, each of which may have different resource capacities; users generally submit resource requests, or bids, separately for different instance types.

The simplest types of user jobs require only one instance and can be served by placing a single bid request for a given instance type. Parallelizable jobs, on the other hand, might require multiple instances running in parallel. The MapReduce framework is a common realization of this job structure. MapReduce divides job functions among a master node and several slave nodes. The master node assigns computational tasks to slave nodes and reschedules the tasks whenever a slave node fails. After all the tasks are finished on the slave nodes, the master node returns a result.

3.2 EC2 Pricing

Amazon offers three types of pricing for instances: reserved, on-demand, and spot instances. Reserved instances guarantee long-term availability (e.g., over a year), and on-demand instances offer shorter-term usage (e.g., one hour on an instance). Both reserved and on-demand instances charge fixed usage-based prices. Spot instances, however, do not guarantee availability; users can use spot instances only if their bids exceed the spot price. Amazon generally updates the spot price every five minutes and encourages users to run interruptible jobs on spot instances.[2]

Spot instances allow two types of bids: one-time and persistent. One-time bids are submitted once and then exit the system once they fall below the current spot price. Thus, submitting a one-time bid runs the risk of having the job interrupted without completing. Persistent bids, however, are resubmitted in each time period until the job finishes or is manually terminated by the user. One-time bids allow for better control over bid completion times (e.g., users may default to on-demand instances if the jobs are not completed), while persistent bids allow the user to submit a bid request and then simply wait until the job finishes.

4. CLOUD PROVIDER MODEL

In this section, we develop an explanatory model for a cloud provider's offered spot prices. Though the model's primary utility for users is in explaining the spot price distribution used in Sections 5 and 6, we also derive some insights into the provider's behavior. In particular, since users' persistent requests are continually reconsidered if not satisfied, the provider might experience unsustainably large numbers of pending bids. We show that the number of pending bids remains bounded under reasonable conditions by formulating a model for a cloud provider to choose the spot prices in Section 4.1 and considering the effects on pending bids in Section 4.2. We validate our model in Section 4.3 by fitting it to two months' history of spot prices offered by Amazon.

Let us consider a series of discrete time slots $t \in \{1, 2, \dots\}$. At time slot t, the demand for a spot instance type is $L(t)$, and we use $\pi(t)$ to denote the spot price at time slot t. We restrict the spot price to not exceed the on-demand price $\bar{\pi}$ of the same instance type. We also impose the constraint $\pi(t) \geq \underline{\pi}$, where $\underline{\pi} \geq 0$ represents the provider's marginal cost of running a spot instance.

4.1 Revenue Maximization

When setting the spot price $\pi(t)$ in each time slot t, the cloud provider wishes to maximize its revenue $\pi(t)N(t)$, where $N(t)$ is the number of accepted bids (i.e., the system workload) and each successful bidder is charged only the spot price $\pi(t)$, regardless of the bid (s)he placed.[3] Other objectives, such as clearing the market, are also possible [10, 38, 39]; in fact, some stud-

[2] Amazon charges users separately for ingress and egress bandwidth to EC2. Since the required bandwidth is determined by the user job rather than the instance on which the job is run, we do not consider these costs.

[3] In practice N is a discrete integer, but for tractable analysis we take N continuous in our model.

ies have suggested that Amazon does not use revenue-maximizing spot prices [1]. Thus, we also include a capacity utilization term $\beta \log(1 + N(t))$, which increases with $N(t)$. This term models the fact that the provider incurs a machine on/off cost for idle spot instances, giving it an incentive to accept more bids. We use a strictly concave function to penalize extremely heavy workloads, which can incur additional capacity costs.

At each time slot t, the provider chooses the spot price $\pi(t)$ so as to maximize the sum of the utilization term and revenue, $\beta \log(1 + N(t)) + \pi(t)N(t)$, subject to the constraint that $\pi(t)$ lie between the minimum and maximum prices ($\underline{\pi} \leq \pi(t) \leq \bar{\pi}$).[4] We denote this optimal price by $\pi^\star(t)$.

We now formulate the provider's optimization problem by using the probability distribution f_p to denote the distribution of bids received by the provider. For instance, if users' bid prices follow a uniform distribution, then $f_p(x) = 1/(\bar{\pi} - \underline{\pi})$. Defining $L(t)$ as the total number of bids submitted, the number of accepted bids is $N(t) = L(t)\frac{\bar{\pi} - \pi(t)}{\bar{\pi} - \underline{\pi}}$, or the fraction of submitted bids that exceed the spot price.[5] The provider then maximizes the sum of its revenue and utilization term:

$$\begin{aligned} \underset{\pi(t)}{\text{maximize}} \quad & \beta \log\left(1 + L(t)\frac{\bar{\pi} - \pi(t)}{\bar{\pi} - \underline{\pi}}\right) \\ & + \pi(t)L(t)\frac{\bar{\pi} - \pi(t)}{\bar{\pi} - \underline{\pi}} \\ \text{subject to} \quad & \underline{\pi} \leq \pi(t) \leq \bar{\pi}. \end{aligned} \tag{1}$$

In the rest of the paper, we use a uniform distribution for f_p, as is often used to model distributions of user valuations for computing services [30].

We solve (1) to find that the optimal spot price $\pi^\star(t)$ satisfies

$$L(t) = \frac{\bar{\pi} - \underline{\pi}}{\bar{\pi} - \pi^\star(t)}\left(\frac{\beta}{\bar{\pi} - 2\pi^\star(t)} - 1\right). \tag{2}$$

We can thus solve for the optimal solution to (1):

$$\begin{aligned} \pi^\star(t) = \max\Bigg\{ & \underline{\pi},\ \frac{3}{4}\bar{\pi} + \frac{1}{2}(\bar{\pi} - \underline{\pi})\frac{1}{L(t)} \\ & -\frac{1}{4}\sqrt{\left(\bar{\pi} + 2(\bar{\pi} - \underline{\pi})\frac{1}{L(t)}\right)^2 + 8\beta(\bar{\pi} - \underline{\pi})\frac{1}{L(t)}}\Bigg\}. \end{aligned} \tag{3}$$

More weight on the utilization term (a higher β) leads to a lower spot price and more accepted bids. Since β will generally be small, we assume that $\beta \leq (L(t) + 1)(\bar{\pi} - 2\underline{\pi})$ and thus that $\pi^\star(t) > \underline{\pi}$ (the optimal spot price is above the minimum) in the rest of the paper.

In the above analysis, we considered user bids in a single time slot. However, bid resubmission may cause the spot price at time t to affect the prices in future time slots. We consider this dependency next.

[4]In practice, we can emphasize the revenue over the utilization term by choosing a small scaling factor β. The provider can keep the number of accepted bids below its available capacity by increasing the minimum spot price $\underline{\pi}$ so that fewer bids are accepted.

[5]A higher spot price may cause more users to choose the more reliable on-demand instead of spot instances, which in turn affects user demand $L(t)$. Since the spot price is generally much lower than the on-demand price (cf. Section 7), we expect this effect to be negligible.

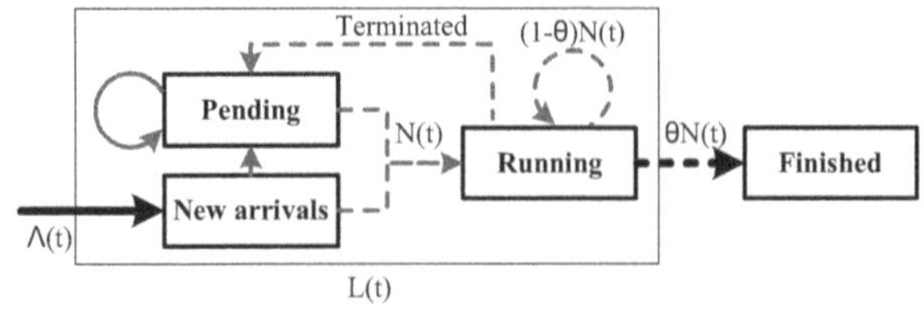

Figure 2: State transitions of spot instances. The solid and dashed arrow lines respectively represent the transitions at the start of the current and next time slots.

4.2 Stable Job Queues

The dynamics of user requests (i.e., bids for an instance) consist of four distinct states: new arrivals, pending, running and finished, as shown in Figure 2.

At the beginning of time slot t, there are $L(t)$ bids for the spot resource remaining in the system, and $\Lambda(t)$ new bid arrivals. After the spot price is determined for this time slot, the $N(t)$ spot requests with the highest bid prices are successfully launched. The new arrivals with lower bid prices are then pended, and some pending requests remain pended until the next time slot.

After time slot t, we assume that a portion $\theta N(t)$ of the running instances are finished (including instances that have completed their jobs and terminated instances with one-time requests), while the other $(1 - \theta)N(t)$ instances are still running and will be considered together along with the pended bids as bids at the next time slot. If terminated, running instances with persistent requests revert to the pending state; hence, the requests in the pending state come from three sources: i) failed new arrivals, ii) failed pending requests, and iii) terminated running instances. The number of requests in the next time slot, $L(t + 1)$, can thus be written in terms of the number of requests $L(t)$ in the previous time slot, along with $\Lambda(t)$ new arrivals and $\theta N(t)$ exiting spot instances: $L(t + 1) = L(t) - \theta N(t) + \Lambda(t)$. Note that $(1-\theta)N(t)$ running instances are included in these $L(t + 1)$ requests. All requests compete with one another via bid prices. After solving (1) with $L(t + 1)$, the cloud provider will terminate the running spot instances whose bid prices are lower than the optimal solution $\pi^\star(t + 1)$, the spot price of the next time slot.

We assume that the $\Lambda(t)$ are independent and identically distributed (i.i.d.), following a distribution f_Λ with expected value λ and variance σ [34]. Writing $N(t)$ in terms of the spot price $\pi^\star(t)$, i.e., $N(t) = L(t)\frac{\bar{\pi} - \pi^\star(t)}{\bar{\pi} - \underline{\pi}}$, the number of submitted bids in each time slot satisfies

$$L(t + 1) = \left(1 - \theta\frac{\bar{\pi} - \pi^\star(t)}{\bar{\pi} - \underline{\pi}}\right)L(t) + \Lambda(t). \tag{4}$$

Note that $0 \leq \theta \leq 1$ and $\underline{\pi} \leq \pi^\star(t) \leq \bar{\pi}$ ensure a positive value of $L(t+1)$. Depending on the value of $\Lambda(t)$, $L(t+1)$ may be larger or smaller than $L(t)$.

If too many user bids are continually re-submitted, the number of submitted bids $L(t)$ might diverge to infinity. To show that such a scenario does not occur, we first define the conditional Lyapunov drift as follows:

$$\Delta(t) \triangleq \frac{1}{2}L^2(t+1) - \frac{1}{2}L^2(t), \tag{5}$$

or the change in the Lyapunov function $\frac{1}{2}L^2(t)$ over one time slot. Taking the conditional expectation, we have an upper bound on the Lyapunov drift (5):

PROPOSITION 1. *Suppose $\Lambda(t)$ follows a distribution with expected value λ and variance σ, and suppose that the spot prices $\pi^\star(t)$ are chosen according to (3). Then the conditional expectation of the Lyapunov drift is upper bounded: $\mathbb{E}(\Delta(t) \mid L(t)) \leq (\bar{\pi} - \underline{\pi})\lambda^2/(2\theta\bar{\pi}) + \sigma/2 - \epsilon L(t)$, where $\epsilon = \frac{\theta\lambda\bar{\pi}}{4(\bar{\pi}-\underline{\pi})}$.*

Proposition 1 implies that when (1) is used to compute the spot price, the queuing system is stable in the sense that the time-averaged queue size at any time t is uniformly bounded [23]. In fact, the number of requests can ultimately reach an equilibrium:

PROPOSITION 2. *The queue sizes of consecutive time slots are in equilibrium, i.e., $L(t+1) = L(t)$, if and only if the optimal spot prices $\pi^\star(t)$ satisfy*

$$\pi^\star(t) = h(\Lambda(t)) = \frac{1}{2}\left(\bar{\pi} - \frac{\beta}{1 + \frac{1}{\theta}\Lambda(t)}\right). \tag{6}$$

We observe from (6) that $\pi^\star(t)$ is only in terms of the request arrivals at that time slot, so $\pi^\star(t)$, like $\Lambda(t)$, is i.i.d. at the equilibrium. Using this result, we can derive the probability density function (PDF) of the spot price in terms of f_Λ, the distribution (i.e., PDF) of $\Lambda(t)$.

PROPOSITION 3. *The probability density function of the spot price is given by:*

$$f_\pi(\pi) \simeq f_\Lambda(h^{-1}(\pi)), \tag{7}$$

where $h^{-1}(\pi) = \theta\left(\frac{\beta}{\bar{\pi}-2\pi} - 1\right)$ is the inverse function of the function given in (6).

We can thus use the distribution of $\Lambda(t)$ at different time slots, f_Λ, to derive the distribution of the spot prices, f_π. Since we do not know the distribution of the bid arrivals, in the next section we instead test different distributions and compare their spot price predictions to the empirically observed spot prices.

4.3 Validation from Historical Spot Prices

We collected the spot price data for four instance types over August 14 – October 13, 2014, in the US Eastern region; we limit ourselves to a two-month dataset since Amazon only provides user access to spot price history for the previous two months. The PDF of these prices is shown by the blue bars in Figure 3. We observe that they approximately follow a power-law or exponential pattern, indicating that the arrival process $\Lambda(t)$ is non-Poisson.[6] Furthermore, the shape of the PDFs across different instance types is consistent, though the spot prices are different, agreeing with [1]'s findings.

We next estimate the spot price PDF with (6) and (7) by assuming Pareto and exponential distributions for $\Lambda(t)$; other distributions could be used in a similar manner. We verify that the spot price distribution does not vary significantly over the day, e.g., due to more jobs submitted during the day, indicating that $\Lambda(t)$ can reasonably be assumed i.i.d. as in Section 4.2. The Kolmogorov-Smirnov test indicates that the distributions of the prices during the daytime and nighttime are similar with p-value > 0.01.

Pareto distribution. The PDF of a Pareto distribution is

$$f_\Lambda(\Lambda) = \frac{\alpha\Lambda_{min}^\alpha}{\Lambda^{\alpha+1}}, \quad \text{for } \Lambda \geq \Lambda_{min},$$

where $\Lambda_{min} = \theta\left(\frac{\beta}{\bar{\pi}-2\underline{\pi}} - 1\right)$ is derived from the monotonic relation between $\pi^\star(t)$ and $\Lambda(t)$ in (6).

Exponential distribution. The PDF of an exponential distribution is

$$f_\Lambda(\Lambda) = \frac{1}{\eta}e^{-\frac{1}{\eta}\Lambda}, \quad \text{for } \Lambda \geq 0.$$

We show the distribution fits in Figure 3; the η, α, β, and θ parameters were chosen to minimize the least-squares divergence between the estimated and empirical PDFs. We use the same β and θ values for each instance type since these parameters do not depend on the distribution of Λ. We observe that the two distributions fit the empirical data well, with a mean-squared error less than 10^{-6}. The small θ values indicate that few instances finish in each time slot due to the long running times of most jobs. For all instance types, the fitted Pareto and exponential distributions have finite mean and variance ($\alpha > 1$, $\eta > 0$). Thus, the conditions in Proposition 1 hold and the system is stable.

5. USER BIDDING STRATEGIES

We now derive users' bidding strategies for jobs running on a single instance, using the spot price PDF from Section 4 to predict future spot prices.[7] Though time series forecasting may be used instead, we note that users' job runtimes generally exceed one time slot, requiring predictions far in advance. Since the spot prices' autocorrelation drops off rapidly with a longer

[6]This observation is consistent with the findings in [18]. Thus, we can expect the cumulative distribution functions to have a knee, as was observed in [1].

[7]As noted in Section 1, the bidding strategies do not explicitly depend on the provider model in Section 4 but rather on the spot price's PDF.

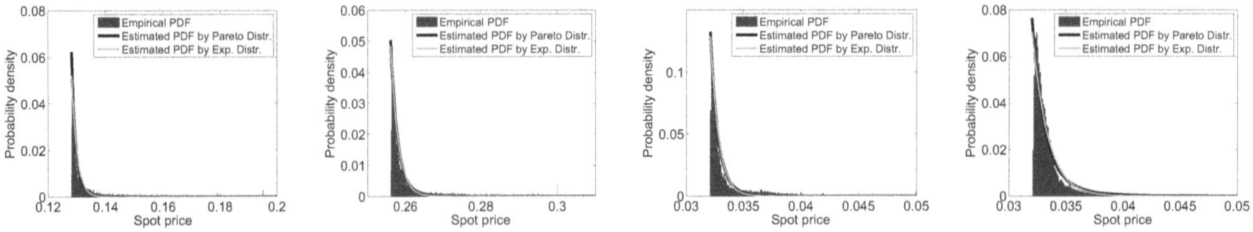

(a) c3.4xlarge. (b) c3.8xlarge. (c) r3.xlarge. (d) m1.xlarge.

Figure 3: Fitting the probability density function of Amazon spot prices in the US Eastern region by assuming Pareto and exponential distributions for $\Lambda(t)$. The fitted parameter values are $(\beta, \theta, \alpha, \eta) = (0.6, 0.02, 5, 0.00013)$, $(1.2, 0.02, 8, 7.1 \times 10^{-5})$, $(0.3, 0.02, 9.5, 0.000108)$, and $(0.3, 0.02, 5.2, 0.000204)$ for (a), (b), (c), and (d) respectively.

Table 1: Key terms and symbols.

Symbol	Definition
p	User bid price
π	Spot price
$\overline{\pi}$	On-demand price
$\underline{\pi}$	Minimum spot price
L	Demand for the spot instance
N	Number of launched spot instances
Λ	New request arrivals
t_k	Length of one time slot
T	Total job completion time
t_s	Job execution time (w/o interruptions)
t_r	Recovery time from an interruption
t_o	Overhead time to run multiple sub-jobs

lag time [1], such predictions are likely to be difficult. We discuss this point further in Section 8.

In this section, we first consider one-time requests (Section 5.1) and then persistent requests (Section 5.2) for a single instance; we consider jobs requiring multiple parallel instances in Section 6. We assume that users wish to minimize the cost of running their jobs. Users thus face a tradeoff between bidding lower prices and experiencing more interruptions, which lead to a longer runtime and potentially higher cost. We obtain the optimal bid prices by minimizing the user's cost subject to job interruptibility constraints (cf. Section 8).[8] As in Section 4, we consider a series of discrete time slots t and suppose the spot prices $\pi(t) = h(\Lambda(t))$, $t = 0, 1, \ldots$ are i.i.d. as in Proposition 2. We use p to denote the user's bid price and F_π to denote the cumulative distribution function of each spot price $\pi(t)$, corresponding to the PDF f_π in (7): $F_\pi(p)$ gives the probability that $p \geq \pi(t)$, i.e., the user's bid is accepted.

We summarize our model's notation in Table 1. Each job is characterized by its execution time t_s, or time required to complete without interruptions. We use T to denote the job's total completion time, i.e., the length of time between its submission and the time it finishes and exits the system. Since jobs with persistent requests may be interrupted, we suppose that persistent jobs are configured to save their data to a separate volume once interrupted and recover it upon resuming. Writing and transferring this data introduces a delay of t_r seconds per interruption. All prices are assumed to be in units of instance/hour, and all times given in units of hours.

[8]Including deadlines on the job completion times does not materially change our model, but we do not explicitly model this constraint. Users with hard job deadlines are more likely to use on-demand instances with guaranteed availability.

5.1 One-time Requests

Since one-time requests are terminated as soon as the bid price falls below the spot price, we assume that users wish to minimize their expected job cost, subject to the constraint that jobs are not interrupted.

Job non-interruptibility. We first find the expected amount of time that a job will continue running without being interrupted:

$$t_k \sum_{i=1}^{\infty} i F_\pi(p)^{i-1} \left(1 - F_\pi(p)\right) = \frac{t_k}{1 - F_\pi(p)}. \quad (8)$$

Here the $F_\pi(p)$ terms represent the probability that $p \geq \pi(t)$, i.e., the request continues to run, and $1 - F_\pi(p)$ the probability that the job will be terminated. We thus find that $t_s \leq t_k / \left(1 - F_\pi(p)\right)$: the expected amount of time that a job will keep running must exceed its execution time.

The optimal price. To find the expected cost of a job with a one-time request, we need to find the expected price that a user must pay to use an instance in each time slot. If a user's bid at price p is accepted, this expected price is simply the expected spot price, or the expected value of all possible spot prices that are less than or equal to p:

$$\mathbb{E}(\pi \mid \pi \leq p) = \frac{\int_{\underline{\pi}}^{p} x f_\pi(x) \mathrm{d}x}{\int_{\underline{\pi}}^{p} f_\pi(x) \mathrm{d}x} = \frac{\int_{\underline{\pi}}^{p} x f_\pi(x) \mathrm{d}x}{F_\pi(p)}, \quad (9)$$

which monotonically increases with p (cf. Proposition 4's proof in the Appendix). Thus, as we would intuitively expect, the user must pay more as his/her bid price increases. The user's expected cost for this job is then the expected spot price, multiplied by the number of time slots it takes for the job to complete. Hence, we have the following cost minimization problem with

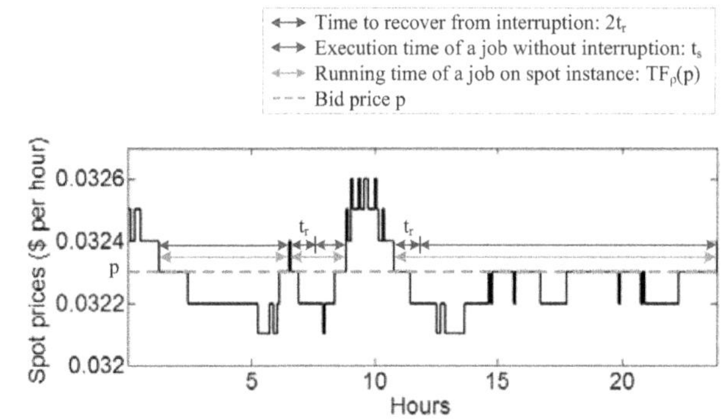

Figure 4: An example of job running times for the spot prices of an r3.xlarge-type instance in the US Eastern region on September 09, 2014.

a completion time constraint:

$$\begin{aligned} \underset{p}{\text{minimize}} \quad & \Phi_{so}(p) = t_s \mathbb{E}(\pi \mid \pi \leq p) = \frac{t_s \int_{\underline{\pi}}^{p} x f_\pi(x) \mathrm{d}x}{F_\pi(p)} \\ \text{subject to} \quad & \Phi_{so}(p) \leq t_s \bar{\pi},\ t_s \leq \frac{t_k}{(1-F_\pi(p))},\ \underline{\pi} \leq p \leq \bar{\pi}. \end{aligned} \tag{10}$$

Since the expected spot price is monotonically increasing in the bid price, the user can minimize his or her expected cost by choosing the lowest possible bid price that satisfies the constraint that the job completes before being terminated:

PROPOSITION 4. *The optimal bid price for a one-time request is*

$$p^\star = \max\left\{\underline{\pi}, F_\pi^{-1}\left(1 - \frac{t_k}{t_s}\right)\right\}. \tag{11}$$

We essentially wish to bid at the appropriate percentile of the spot price distribution F_π. As we would expect, the bid price increases as the number of time slots required to complete the job, t_s/t_k, increases: the job then needs to run for more consecutive time slots, which becomes more likely with a higher bid.

5.2 Persistent Requests

We now consider a job that places a persistent spot instance request. We begin by finding the total time that the job runs on the system, given a bid price, and then briefly discuss the implications of a job's interruptibility before deriving the user's optimal bid price.

Job running time. A job's total completion time T comprises two types of time slots: the running time, in which the job's bid price exceeds the spot price and the job actually runs on the instance, and the idle time. For a bid price p, the job's expected running time is $TF_\pi(p)$ (recall that $F_\pi(p)$ denotes the probability that the bid price $p \geq \pi(t)$, the spot price), and the idle time is then $T(1-F_\pi(p))$. The running time can be further split into the execution time, t_s, and the additional running time required to recover from interruptions. We illustrate the job completion time in Figure 4, in which the bid price of $p = 0.0323$ is represented by an orange dashed line. The grey double-arrowed line represents the total running time. Since the job is interrupted twice, the total recovery time is $2t_r$. Thus, for this example, we have $TF_\pi(0.0323) = 2t_r + t_s$.

To determine the total recovery time, we want to find the expected number of interruptions, i.e., times t in which the job runs on the system but was idle in the previous time slot ($p \geq \pi(t), p < \pi(t-1)$). Note that the number of interruptions equals half of the total number of times the job's state changes between running and idle: each interruption requires both an idle-to-running and running-to-idle transition. We can thus find the expected total number of transitions and divide it by two. To do so, we define $\mathbb{I}_\pi(\pi(t))$ as an indicator function: $\mathbb{I}_\pi(\pi(t)) = 1$ if $p \geq \pi(t)$; otherwise, $\mathbb{I}_\pi(\pi(t)) = 0$. We then consider $\left(\mathbb{I}_\pi(\pi(t)) - \mathbb{I}_\pi(\pi(t+1))\right)^2$, which equals 1 if $\mathbb{I}_\pi(\pi(t)) \neq \mathbb{I}_\pi(\pi(t+1))$ (i.e., a transition happens) and 0 otherwise. The number of idle-to-running transitions in T/t_k time slots is then $\frac{1}{2}\sum_{k=0}^{T/t_k-1}\left(\mathbb{I}_\pi(\pi(t)) - \mathbb{I}_\pi(\pi(t+1))\right)^2$. We take expectation to obtain

$$\begin{aligned} & \mathbb{E}\left(\frac{1}{2}\sum_{k=0}^{T/t_k-1}\left(\mathbb{I}_\pi(\pi(t)) - \mathbb{I}_\pi(\pi(t+1))\right)^2\right) \\ \overset{(a)}{=}\ & \frac{T}{t_k}\left(\mathbb{E}\left(\mathbb{I}_\pi(\pi(t))\right) - \mathbb{E}\left(\mathbb{I}_\pi(\pi(t))\mathbb{I}_\pi(\pi(t+1))\right)\right) \\ =\ & \frac{T}{t_k}F_\pi(p)(1 - F_\pi(p)), \end{aligned} \tag{12}$$

where (a) is due to $\left(\mathbb{I}_\pi(\pi(t))\right)^2 = \mathbb{I}_\pi(\pi(t))$ since the value of $\mathbb{I}_\pi(\pi(t))$ is either 1 or 0.

We now write the expected running time of the job as the sum of the recovery and execution times: $TF_\pi(p) = \left(\frac{T}{t_k}F_\pi(p)(1-F_\pi(p)) - 1\right)t_r + t_s$. Simplifying the terms, the running time becomes

$$TF_\pi(p) = \frac{t_s - t_r}{1 - \frac{t_r}{t_k}(1 - F_\pi(p))}, \tag{13}$$

which decreases with p. As the bid price p increases, the job is less likely to be interrupted and will therefore have a shorter expected running time.

Job interruptibility. We can use the expected running time (13) to observe the effect of the recovery time parameter, t_r, on a job's feasibility for spot instances. Intuitively, spot instances are more effective for more "interruptible" jobs that can quickly recover from interruptions. In fact, a job's running time is finite only if the recovery time is sufficiently small:

$$t_r < \frac{t_k}{1 - F_\pi(p)}. \tag{14}$$

The result in (14) can be obtained by requiring the denominator in (13) to be positive. We note that the upper bound to t_r is exactly the expected running time of a job without interruptions (cf. (8)): intuitively, the time to recover from an interruption should be smaller than the expected time on an instance between job interruptions. We take (14) as a constraint on the bid price: if the job recovery time is high, the user should bid at a higher bid price in order to ensure that the job can complete. However, if the job recovery time is less than one time slot length, $t_r < \min_p \left\{ \frac{t_k}{1-F_\pi(p)} \right\} = t_k$, and a spot instance is feasible at any price.

The optimal bid price. We can now multiply the expected running time (13) with the expected spot price (9) to find that the cost of a job with a persistent request is $\Phi_{sp}(p) = TF_\pi(p)\mathbb{E}(\pi \mid \pi \le p)$. The user's optimal bid price then solves the optimization problem

$$\begin{aligned} \underset{p}{\text{minimize}} \quad & \Phi_{sp}(p) = \frac{t_s - t_r}{1 - \frac{t_r}{t_k}\left(1 - F_\pi(p)\right)} \frac{\int_{\underline{\pi}}^p x f_\pi(x)\mathrm{d}x}{F_\pi(p)} \\ \text{subject to} \quad & \Phi_{sp}(p) \le t_s \bar{\pi},\ t_r < \frac{t_k}{1-F_\pi(p)},\ \underline{\pi} \le p \le \bar{\pi}, \end{aligned} \tag{15}$$

where the first constraint ensures that the cost of running the spot instance is lower than the cost of running the job on an on-demand instance, and the second constraint ensures that the job is sufficiently interruptible. We use $p^\star$ to denote the optimal bid price to (15).

We now observe that the expected running time in (13) decreases with the bid price, while the expected spot price increases with the bid price. We find that the expected cost $\Phi_{sp}(p)$ first decreases and then increases with the bid price p, thus allowing us to solve for the optimal bid price $p^\star$:

PROPOSITION 5. *If the probability density function of the spot price monotonically decreases, i.e., $F_\pi(p)$ is concave, the optimal bid price solving* (15) *is*

$$p^\star = \psi^{-1}\left(\frac{t_k}{t_r} - 1\right), \tag{16}$$

where $\psi^{-1}(\cdot)$ is the inverse function of

$$\psi(p) = F_\pi(p)\left(\frac{\int_{\underline{\pi}}^p x f(x)\mathrm{d}x}{\int_{\underline{\pi}}^p (p-x) f(x)\mathrm{d}x} - 1\right).$$

We can observe from (16) that the optimal bid price does not depend on the execution time t_s: the cost is instead determined by the number of time slots needed for each recovery, t_r/t_k. While the execution time is fixed, a longer recovery time lengthens the total running time and thus the job cost.

6. BIDDING FOR MAPREDUCE JOBS

We now adapt Section 5's bidding strategies for single instances to parallelized MapReduce jobs, in which users bid for multiple instances at the same time. We first consider running only the slave nodes on spot instances and then consider running the full job (i.e., both master and slave nodes) on spot instances.[9] Though the job structure introduces an additional requirement on the master node's running time–the master node should keep running as long as the slave nodes are running–we show that this condition does not change the optimal bid for the master node as long as the job is sufficiently parallelized (i.e., multiple slave nodes run in parallel for a short amount of time).

[9]While master nodes are often run on on-demand instances to guarantee that they will not be interrupted, our experiments in Section 7 show that, with sufficiently high bids, interruptions are rare even on spot instances.

6.1 Bidding for Slave Nodes Only

We first consider running only the slave nodes of a MapReduce job on several spot instances in parallel. We suppose that the job is split into M sub-jobs of equal size, each corresponding to one instance request. We now wish to calculate the optimal (i.e., cost-minimizing) bid prices for these sub-jobs; since we assume that all sub-jobs are bidding for the same type of spot instance, the bid price should be the same for all of them. We again find the total cost by multiplying the expected running time of the job by the expected spot price.

To find a job's expected running time, we denote each sub-job i's total time in the system as T_i. Since splitting a job results in additional overhead, e.g., due to message passing between the sub-jobs, we use t_o to represent a constant additional overhead time from splitting the job.[10] Then the total running time satisfies:

$$\sum_{i=1}^M T_i F_\pi(p) = \sum_{i=1}^M \left(\frac{T_i F_\pi(p)(1 - F_\pi(p))}{t_k} - 1\right) t_r + t_s + t_o,$$

i.e., it is the sum of the recovery, execution, and overhead times. Hence, we can extend the result for a single persistent bid in (13) as

$$\sum_{i=1}^M T_i F_\pi(p) = \frac{t_s + t_o - M t_r}{1 - \frac{t_r}{t_k}\left(1 - F_\pi(p)\right)}. \tag{17}$$

Since all of the sub-jobs run simultaneously, the overall time of the parallelized job execution is $\max_{i=1,\ldots,M} T_i F_\pi(p)$. All of the M sub-jobs are of equal size, so

$$\max_{i=1,\ldots,M} T_i F_\pi(p) = \frac{t_s + t_o - M t_r}{M\left(1 - \frac{t_r}{t_k}\left(1 - F_\pi(p)\right)\right)}. \tag{18}$$

Users can minimize this cost by choosing the optimal number of slave nodes, M. Although the job is split into smaller pieces, the overall running time $\max_{i=1,\ldots,M} T_i F_\pi(p)$ is larger than t_s/M, or the running time without interruptions or overhead. Thus, distributing the job across M instances shortens the completion time as compared to a single instance only if the overhead time is sufficiently small. Comparing the completion times in both cases, we find that using multiple instances shortens the completion time if $t_o < (M-1)t_k/(1 - F_\pi(p))$.

As in Section 5, the expected cost of running a job on M simultaneous instances is the sum of each instance's

[10]This overhead time may depend on M, the (fixed) number of sub-jobs.

expected running time, multiplied by the expected spot price: $\Phi_{mp} = \sum_{i=1}^{M} T_i F_\pi(p)\mathbb{E}(\pi \mid \pi \leq p)$. The user then minimizes this cost by solving the following optimization problem:

$$\begin{aligned} \underset{p}{\text{minimize}} \quad & \Phi_{mp}(p) = \frac{t_s+t_o-Mt_r}{1-\frac{t_r}{t_k}\left(1-F_\pi(p)\right)} \frac{\int_{\underline{\pi}}^{p} x f_\pi(x)\mathrm{d}x}{F_\pi(p)} \\ \text{subject to} \quad & \Phi_{mp}(p) \leq t_s\bar{\pi},\ \underline{\pi} \leq p \leq \bar{\pi}, \end{aligned} \tag{19}$$

where the first constraint ensures that the cost is lower than that of running the job on an on-demand instance. Comparing (19) to bidding for a single persistent request in (15), we see that (19) can be solved similarly to (15) in Proposition 5.

By comparing the costs for multiple bids and for a single bid at the optimal bid prices, we find that when the overhead time is sufficiently small ($t_o < (M-1)t_r$), bidding for multiple spot instances can both lower the cost and shorten the job's overall running time. In contrast, running the job on an on-demand instance will reduce the running time but increase the cost.

6.2 Bidding for Master and Slave Nodes

Running a MapReduce job entirely on spot instances requires us to treat master and slave nodes separately; for instance, we might bid on different instance types for the master and slave nodes, since the slave nodes will likely have higher computing requirements. We thus develop two separate bidding strategies:

1) **Master node:** Since the master node has to be available at all times to manage slave node failures and to periodically check the status of tasks at the slave nodes, we do not allow any interruptions for the master node. We thus place a one-time request for a single spot instance, as in Section 5.1.

2) **Slave nodes:** MapReduce requires many slave nodes to process large jobs, but allows slave nodes to be interrupted. Thus, we place a persistent request for each slave node using the strategy in Section 6.1. The bid prices for the slave nodes must be determined jointly with that of the master node, since the master node's running time should exceed the slave nodes'. We note from Section 6.1 that if many simultaneous bids are submitted, the slave nodes' running time will decrease, shortening the required master node running time.

We can formally describe these strategies in the following optimization problem:

$$\begin{aligned} \underset{p_v,p_m}{\text{minimize}} \quad & \Phi_{so}(p_m) + \Phi_{mp}(p_v) \\ \text{subject to} \quad & \frac{t_k}{1-F_\pi^m(p_m)} \\ & \geq \frac{1}{F_\pi^v(p_v)}\left(\frac{t_s+t_o-Mt_r}{1-\frac{t_r}{t_k}\left(1-F_\pi^v(p_v)\right)} - \frac{(M-1)t_k}{1-F_\pi^v(p_v)}\right), \\ & \underline{\pi} \leq p_v \leq \bar{\pi},\ \underline{\pi} \leq p_m \leq \bar{\pi}, \end{aligned} \tag{20}$$

Table 2: EC2 instance types. Sizes are given as (vCPU, memory in GiB, SSD storage in GB).

	`m3`	`r3`	`c3`
`.xlarge`	4, 15, 1x32	4, 30.5, 1x80	4, 7.5, 2x40
`.2xlarge`	8, 30, 2x80	8, 61, 1x160	8, 15, 2x80
`.4xlarge`	–	16, 122, 1x320	16, 30, 2x160
`.8xlarge`	–	–	32, 60, 2x320

where p_m and p_v denote the bid prices of the master node and slave nodes respectively, and $F_\pi^m(\cdot)$ and $F_\pi^v(\cdot)$ denote the spot prices' cumulative distribution functions for the master and slave node instance types. The first constraint in (20) ensures that the master node runs longer than any of the slave nodes (cf. (8) and (18)), where the righthand side of the inequality represents the worst-case completion time of the M parallel sub-jobs. We use $p_m^\star$ and $p_v^\star$ to denote the optimal bid prices for (20)'s optimization problem.

We can solve (20) by noting that, aside from the first constraint, p_m and p_v are independent variables. Thus, we can set their optimal values $p_m^\star$ and $p_v^\star$ respectively as the optimal bid prices for a one-time single instance request (Proposition 4) and for multiple persistent requests (as in (19)). The first constraint is satisfied if the user submits sufficiently many simultaneous requests for the slave nodes. In practice, this minimum number of nodes, which we denote as $M^\star$, can be as low as 3 or 4, as we show in Section 7's experiments.

7. EXPERIMENTAL RESULTS

In this section, we first examine the optimal bid prices derived in Section 5 on Amazon EC2 spot instances. By comparing the price charged per hour, total job completion time and final cost, we illustrate the tradeoff of using different bidding strategies. We then run a MapReduce example on spot instances to further highlight that our proposed bidding strategy in Section 6 is adaptable to parallelized MapReduce jobs and can substantially lower their costs. Table 2 summarizes the instance types that we use in our experiments. The `m3`, `r3`, and `c3` prefixes denote balanced, memory-optimized, and compute-optimized instances respectively. We test a variety of instance types and sizes and repeat each experiment ten times for each instance type; all performance graphs are shown as averages.[11] We do not include the runtime of the bid price calculations in our measurements since it is much smaller than one minute, and can thus be easily run within one five-minute time slot. For example, the bid price calculations for the `c3.4xlarge` instance with around 1MB of spot price history take 11.305 seconds for a one-time and 4.365 seconds for a persistent bid on a standard laptop.

[11]To ensure accuracy, we use our bills from Amazon to calculate the job costs. Since Amazon does not break the bills into individual jobs, we do not report the cost of each job.

7.1 Single-Instance Bids

Parameter setting: We consider a job that needs one hour (i.e., $t_s = 1h$) to be executed without interruption. The optimal bid prices of five Amazon spot instances (`r3.xlarge`, `r3.2xlarge`, `r3.4xlarge`, `c3.4xlarge` and `c3.8xlarge`) are listed in Table 3 for a one-time request and persistent requests with recovery times $t_r = 10s$ and $t_r = 30s$. We used the spot price history for the two months immediately prior to the experiments to calculate these prices.

Experiment setup: To simulate an exact one hour running time of a spot instance, we created an Amazon Machine Image (AMI), where a shell script was added to `/etc/rc.local` so that a one-hour count-down program will run once the instance is launched using this AMI. In addition, this program writes instance launched time as a sequence of items into Amazon DynamoDB, from which we can obtain the instance status (first run or restarted from interruption) and simulate a recovery time if the instance is interrupted. We then placed all spot requests using this AMI.

Results: We used the optimal bid prices for one-time requests (Table 3) to bid the associated spot instance at random times of the day. None of our experiments were interrupted, verifying that our bidding strategy for one-time requests can ensure reliability. Our bills show that this bidding strategy can reduce user costs by up to 91% compared to running the job on an on-demand instance. Figure 5 compares the cost of one-time requests on spot instances to that of on-demand instances for the instance types in Table 3. We also compare the actual costs (with actual spot price $\hat{\pi}$) to the expected cost from our analytical model; the analytical predictions closely match the experimental results.

We additionally compare against a heuristic called the best offline price in retrospect (shown as $\tilde{p}$ in Table 3 and the grey bars in Figure 5), in which we numerically search the spot price history of the last 10 hours for the minimal price that consistently exceeds the spot prices for one hour. This retrospective price is lower than the actual bid price in some cases, meaning the one-time spot instance would have been terminated if we had bid using this price: 10 hours of history is insufficient to predict the future prices.

We now use the results of the one-time requests for each instance type as a baseline to illustrate that users can further lower their cost in exchange for longer completion times by placing persistent requests. In Figure 6, we plot the percentage difference in performance between the persistent and one-time bids.

Figure 6(a) shows the percentage difference in price between the one-time and persistent requests for the five instance types. The negative values in this figure illustrate a lower optimal bid price for persistent requests: persistent requests can be interrupted. As we would expect from Section 5's analysis, longer recovery times ($t_r = 30$s rather than 10s) yield higher bid prices, since

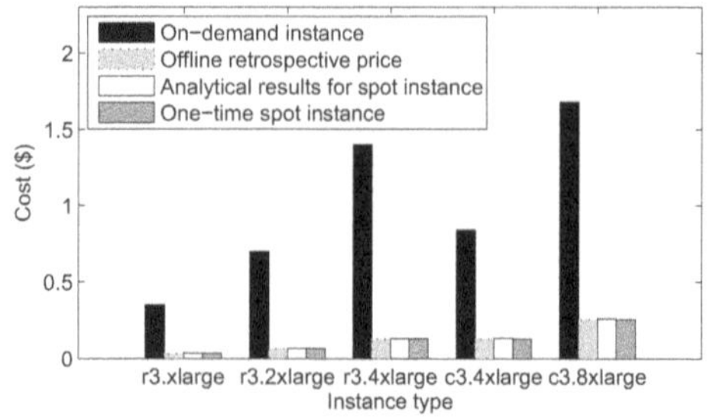

Figure 5: One-time spot instance requests substantially lower user cost compared to on-demand instances (on-demand and bid prices are as in Table 3).

a higher bid price ensures that the job has sufficient time to execute after recovering from interruptions.

Conversely, as shown in Figure 6(b), the completion time of a one-hour job with a persistent request is longer than that of a one-time request. The difference in these completion times includes both the recovery time after the instance is interrupted and the idle time during which the user's bid price is lower than the spot price. Interestingly, the job with longer recovery time t_r has a shorter completion time, though it is still longer than the completion time with a one-time request. We can observe from Table 3 that a longer recovery time leads to a higher optimal bid price, which can consequently increase the likelihood of satisfying the spot price and lead to less idle time.

As shown in Figures 6(a) and 6(b), the price charged per hour is slightly lower, but the completion time is longer for the persistent requests compared to the one-time requests. This makes the final cost underdetermined: Figure 6(c) demonstrates that persistent bids lead to lower overall costs. Smaller recovery times ($t_r =$ 10s versus 30s) have higher completion times but yield lower costs due to their lower bid prices (the higher completion time is mostly due to more idle time, for which the user is not charged, rather than extra time running on the instance). Thus, persistent requests can reduce user cost but lengthen the job completion time.

We also compare against simply bidding the 90th percentile spot price. Compared to our optimal prices, bidding the (larger) 90th percentile price yields a much smaller decrease in cost, despite slightly higher bid prices in Figure 6(a) and lower completion times in Figure 6(b). The jobs running on `r3.4xlarge` with recovery time $t_r = 30s$ instead have a longer completion time and lower bid price, but higher cost, with the 90th percentile spot price. This comparison is consistent with the fact that our bid prices are chosen to minimize users' costs.

7.2 MapReduce Jobs

We implemented our optimal bidding strategy to run Hadoop MapReduce jobs on the Common Crawl Dataset [7] using Amazon Elastic MapReduce (EMR). This dataset, which is hosted on Amazon's Simple Storage Service, maintains an open repository of web crawl data that is accessible to the public for free. In this experiment,

Table 3: Optimal bid prices for a single-instance job on spot instances.

Instance type	$\bar{\pi}$	$\underline{\pi}$	One-time bid				Persistent bid ($t_r = 10s$)		Persistent bid ($t_r = 30s$)	
			$p^\star$	$\mathbb{E}(\pi \mid \pi < p^\star)$	$\tilde{p}$	$\hat{\pi}$	$p^\star$	T	$p^\star$	T
r3.xlarge	\$0.35	\$0.0321	\$0.0374	\$0.0331	\$0.0324	\$0.033	\$0.0332	1.4549h	\$0.0355	1.1903h
r3.2xlarge	\$0.70	\$0.0646	\$0.0795	\$0.0669	\$0.0644	\$0.066	\$0.0661	1.7638h	\$0.0711	1.2558h
r3.4xlarge	\$1.40	\$0.1286	\$0.1430	\$0.1304	\$0.1288	\$0.130	\$0.1327	1.2798h	\$0.1422	1.0976h
c3.4xlarge	\$0.84	\$0.1281	\$0.1669	\$0.1324	\$0.1283	\$0.128	\$0.1322	1.4917h	\$0.1413	1.2180h
c3.8xlarge	\$1.68	\$0.2561	\$0.2903	\$0.2604	\$0.2564	\$0.256	\$0.2648	1.2767h	\$0.2831	1.1209h

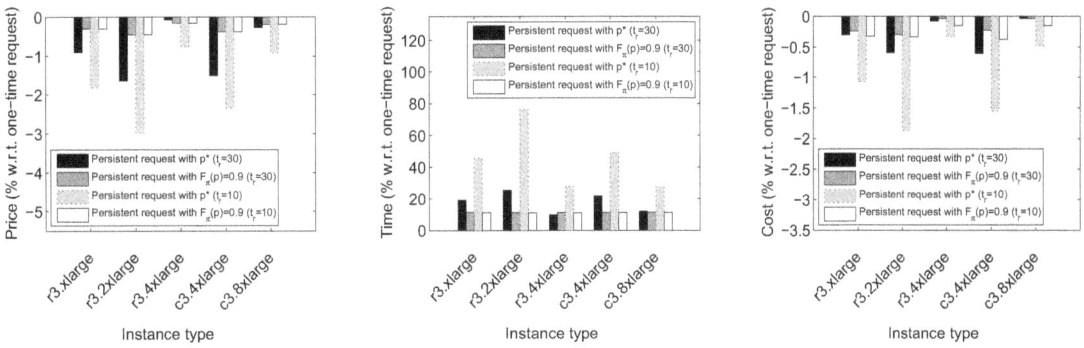

(a) Expected spot price. (b) Job completion time. (c) Total job cost.

Figure 6: Persistent requests yield lower costs but longer completion times compared to one-time requests. The bid prices for each instance type are given in Table 3.

Table 4: Optimal bid prices and actual costs for a MapReduce job.

	Master node			Slave nodes			
Client Setting	Instance type	$p_m^\star$	Actual cost	Instance type	$p_v^\star$	$M^\star$	Actual cost
CS1	c3.xlarge	\$0.133	\$0.10	m3.2xlarge	\$0.070	5	\$0.90
CS2	m3.xlarge	\$0.101	\$0.13	m3.2xlarge	\$0.070	5	\$1.03
CS3	m3.xlarge	\$0.102	\$0.13	r3.2xlarge	\$0.071	3	\$0.51
CS4	r3.xlarge	\$0.042	\$0.13	m3.2xlarge	\$0.070	5	\$0.58
CS5	r3.xlarge	\$0.042	\$0.13	r3.2xlarge	\$0.071	3	\$0.64

we ran the well-known "Common Crawl Word Count" example that counts the frequency of words appearing on the Common Crawl Corpus.

Parameter setting: We consider a word count job with recovery time $t_r = 30s$ and overhead time $t_o = 60s$. Using the bidding strategy proposed in Section 6, we list in Table 4 the optimal bid prices and the number of slave nodes for five client settings with different instance types for the master node and the slave nodes.

Experiment setup: We placed a one-time request for a single spot instance for the master node and persistent requests for multiple spot instances for the slave nodes. Since the master node just distributes the raw data and tracks the status of each task, it does not require a high-performance instance; we therefore bid on instances with better CPU performance for the slave nodes.

Results: We compare the completion time and cost of running MapReduce jobs on on-demand and spot instances for the five client settings. We use the optimal bid prices listed in Table 4 to place the spot instance bids. Using the on-demand instance as a baseline, our bills from Amazon show that the bidding strategy for MapReduce jobs can reduce up to 92.6% of user cost with just a 14.9% increase of completion time.

In Figure 7, we show the completion time and the cost of the five client settings for on-demand and spot instances. Again, our experimental results closely approximate the analytical results from our model. As we would expect, the job completion time is longer on the spot instances than on the on-demand instances (Figure 7(a)), while the costs of the jobs running on the spot instances are much lower than those on the on-demand instances (Figure 7(b)).

In Table 4, we break down the actual costs of the master and slave nodes for each client setting of the MapReduce job. The cost of the master node is 10% to 25% of the slave node cost, indicating that users may wish to pay a higher spot price for the master node: this price does not significantly affect the overall cost, and helps ensure that the master node is not interrupted.

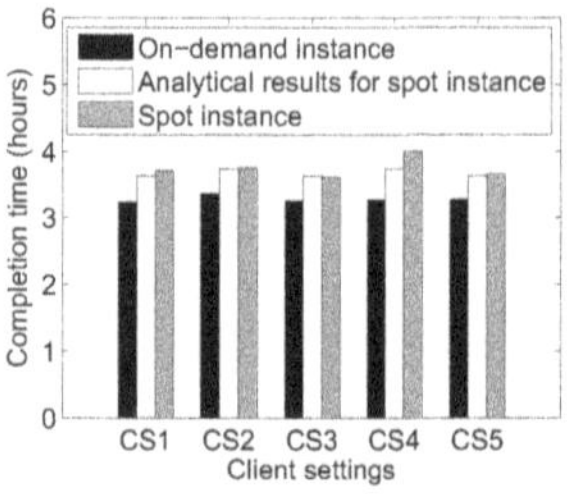

(a) Job completion time.

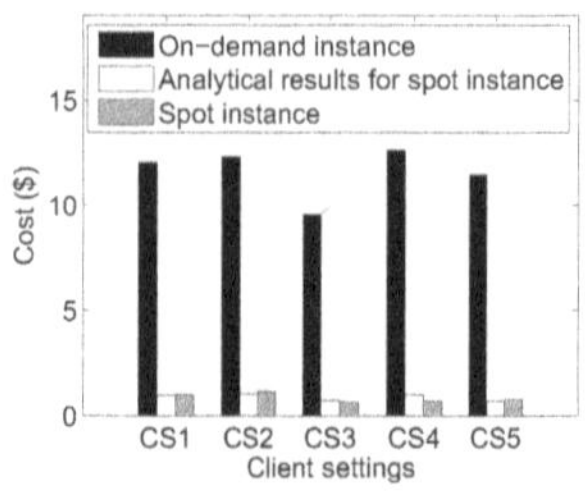

(b) Job cost.

Figure 7: MapReduce jobs can save about 90% of user cost but have a 15% longer completion time on spot compared to on-demand instances.

8. DISCUSSION

Like all work based on analytical models, our work has some limitations. We discuss five important ones here and suggest ways to address them in future work.

Provider objectives. We have assumed that the cloud provider optimizes the sum of a concave utilization term and its revenue, where the concave shape of the utilization term is due to the cost of running large numbers of instances while maintaining users' quality-of-service. We could more explicitly account for user satisfaction by taking the social welfare to be the provider's objective function [25, 38]. While our current formulation matches well with the observed spot prices, including other factors in the provider's spot price optimization problem may shed more light on the provider's behavior. We emphasize, however, that our bidding strategies depend only on the spot prices, not on the provider's objectives or optimization problem.

Temporal correlations. We assume i.i.d. job arrivals that induce i.i.d. spot prices at the equilibrium. However, empirical studies have found temporal correlation in cloud workloads, possibly inducing positive temporal correlation in the spot prices [12]. In fact, a study of the spot prices in 2010 shows the presence of limited autocorrelation for consecutive time slots [1]. Incorporating these correlations into users' spot price predictions may improve their bidding strategies and outcomes: this correlation would likely reduce the degree to which the spot price changes in consecutive time slots. Thus, the user's job would be interrupted less often, leading to lower job running times and costs.

Risk-averseness. We suppose that users choose their bid prices so as to minimize their expected costs, subject to constraints on the expected runtimes. Risk-averse users may also wish to minimize the variance in costs and runtimes, so as to ensure that particularly bad outcomes do not occur. For example, we might choose the bid price so as to minimize the expected cost subject to an upper bound on the cost variance. Other users might allow their jobs' completion time to have a small probability of exceeding a job deadline. Instead of bounding the expected completion time, we could constrain the user's bid price so that the probability of exceeding this deadline is lower than a given small threshold.

Task dependence. Some tasks within a job cannot proceed before other tasks have been completed. While we do not account for such dependent tasks in our model, we can in practice bid on these tasks only after the tasks that they depend on have been completed. Thus, we will not bid on idle tasks that are waiting for other tasks to finish.

Collective user behavior. The bidding strategies that we have developed in Sections 5 and 6 assume that an individual user's bid price will not measurably affect the provider's spot price. While our experiments in Section 7 show that this assumption holds for a single user, it may not hold if multiple users begin to optimize their bidding strategies, which might affect the distribution of the submitted bids. To study this scenario, we can assume that users with a distribution of jobs optimize their bids and use Section 4's model to derive the effect on the provider's offered spot price.

9. CONCLUSION

Spot pricing opens up an auction-based market in which cloud providers can dynamically provision data center resources to meet user demand and users can develop bidding strategies that lower their cloud resource costs. In this work we first consider providers' setting of the spot prices, developing an optimization model for the provider and comparing its results to observed spot prices. We then answer the question of how users should bid for cloud resources. Since spot instances do not guarantee their availability, we consider the tradeoff between bidding higher prices to avoid interruptions (for one-time requests) and bidding lower prices to save money (for persistent requests).

We adapt these bidding strategies to MapReduce jobs with master and slave nodes. Finally, we run our bidding client on Amazon EC2 to verify that our analytical results accurately approximate the real-time experimental results. Our bidding strategies can reduce users' costs by around 90% on a variety of instance types, with modest increases in the job completion times.

Spot pricing has been offered by Amazon for many years, yet the heavy-tailed spot price distributions that we observe suggest that few users bid for spot instances. We thus conjecture that many users are concerned by the possibility of too many job interruptions. Our paper suggests that these concerns might be misplaced: by tailoring their bids to their jobs' interruption constraints, users can save a substantial amount of money with spot instances without excessive job interruption.

Acknowledgments

We thank our shepherd, Michael Schapira, and Sudipta Sengupta for helpful comments. This work was in part supported by the Waterman Award CNS-1347234, the Research Grants Council of Hong Kong Project No. RGC 11212114 and the National Research Foundation Fellowship NRF-NRFF2015-07.

APPENDIX

Proof of Proposition 1.

PROOF. Substituting (4) into (5), the Lyapunov drift can be expressed as $\Delta(t) = \frac{1}{2}\big((1-\theta\frac{\bar{\pi}-\pi^{\star}(t)}{\bar{\pi}-\underline{\pi}})L(t)+\Lambda(t)\big)^2 - \frac{1}{2}L^2(t)$. We now bound the expectation of this quantity by:

$$\begin{aligned}
&\mathbb{E}\big(\Delta(t)\,|\,L(t)\big)\\
&\overset{(a)}{\le} \tfrac{1}{2}\Big(-\tfrac{\theta\bar{\pi}}{\bar{\pi}-\underline{\pi}}+\tfrac{1}{4}\big(\tfrac{\theta\bar{\pi}}{\bar{\pi}-\underline{\pi}}\big)^2\Big)L^2(t)\\
&\quad +\big(1-\tfrac{1}{2}\tfrac{\theta\bar{\pi}}{\bar{\pi}-\underline{\pi}}\big)L(t)\mathbb{E}\big(\Lambda(t)\big)+\tfrac{1}{2}\mathbb{E}\big(\Lambda^2(t)\big)\\
&\overset{(b)}{=} \tfrac{1}{2}\Big(-\tfrac{\theta\bar{\pi}}{\bar{\pi}-\underline{\pi}}+\tfrac{1}{4}\big(\tfrac{\theta\bar{\pi}}{\bar{\pi}-\underline{\pi}}\big)^2\Big)L^2(t)\\
&\quad +\Big(1-\tfrac{1}{2}\tfrac{\theta\bar{\pi}}{\bar{\pi}-\underline{\pi}}\Big)\lambda L(t)+\tfrac{1}{2}(\sigma+\lambda^2)\\
&\le \big(1-\tfrac{1}{4}\tfrac{\theta\bar{\pi}}{\bar{\pi}-\underline{\pi}}\big)\max_{L(t)}\Big\{-\tfrac{1}{2}\tfrac{\theta\bar{\pi}}{\bar{\pi}-\underline{\pi}}L^2(t)+\lambda L(t)\Big\}\\
&\quad -\tfrac{1}{4}\tfrac{\theta\lambda\bar{\pi}}{\bar{\pi}-\underline{\pi}}L(t)+\tfrac{1}{2}(\sigma+\lambda^2)\\
&\overset{(c)}{=} \tfrac{\bar{\pi}-\underline{\pi}}{2\theta\bar{\pi}}\lambda^2+\tfrac{1}{2}\sigma-\tfrac{1}{4}\tfrac{\theta\lambda\bar{\pi}}{\bar{\pi}-\underline{\pi}}L(t),
\end{aligned}$$

where (a) is due to $\pi(t) \le \frac{1}{2}\bar{\pi}$, (b) is due to $\mathbb{E}(\Lambda^2(t)) = \mathrm{Var}(\Lambda(t)) + \big(\mathbb{E}(\Lambda(t))\big)^2$ and the equality in (c) holds when $L(t) = \frac{\bar{\pi}-\underline{\pi}}{\theta\bar{\pi}}\lambda$. □

Proof of Proposition 2.

PROOF. We first prove that (6) is a necessary condition for $L(t+1) = L(t)$. We rewrite (4) as

$$L(t) = \frac{\bar{\pi}-\underline{\pi}}{\theta(\bar{\pi}-\pi^{\star}(t))}\Lambda(t). \tag{21}$$

Solving the system of equations (2) and (21) yields (6).

We then prove that (6) is a sufficient condition for $L(t+1) = L(t)$. From (4), we can derive

$$\begin{aligned}
&L(t+1)-L(t)\\
&\overset{(a)}{=} -\theta\left(\frac{\beta}{\bar{\pi}-2\pi^{\star}(t)}-1\right)+\Lambda(t)\\
&\overset{(b)}{=} \theta\Big(\frac{\beta}{\bar{\pi}-\big(\bar{\pi}-\frac{\beta}{1+\frac{1}{\theta}\Lambda(t)}\big)}-1\Big)+\Lambda(t)=0,
\end{aligned}$$

where (a) and (b) are obtained by respectively substituting (2) and (6). Thus, $L(t+1) = L(t)$. □

Proof of Proposition 4.

PROOF. By taking the first-order derivative of $\Phi_{so}(p)$ in the objective of (10), we have

$$\partial\Phi_{so}(p)/\partial p = \tfrac{t_s}{(F_\pi(p))^2}f_\pi(p)\left(-\textstyle\int_{\underline{\pi}}^{p}xf_\pi(x)\mathrm{d}x+pF_\pi(p)\right).$$

By letting $g(p) = -\int_{\underline{\pi}}^{p}xf_\pi(x)\mathrm{d}x + pF_\pi(p)$, we have $\partial g(p)/\partial p = F_\pi(p) > 0$. So $g(p)$ increases with p. Combining the fact that $g(\underline{\pi}) = -\underline{\pi}f_\pi(\underline{\pi}) + \underline{\pi}F_\pi(\underline{\pi}) = 0$, the nonnegativity and monotonic increasing of $g(p)$ lead to $\partial\Phi_{so}(p)/\partial p > 0$. Therefore, $\Phi_{so}(p)$ also increases with p. Minimizing $\Phi_{so}(p)$ is equivalent to finding the minimum p in its feasible set. From $t_k/\big(1-F_\pi(p)\big)$, we have $p \ge F_\pi^{-1}\big(1-\frac{t_k}{t_s}\big)$ due to the monotonic property of $F_\pi(p)$. Thus, the minimum of the feasible set is the larger one of $\underline{\pi}$ and $F_\pi^{-1}\big(1-\frac{t_k}{t_s}\big)$. □

Proof of Proposition 5.

PROOF. By taking the first-order derivative of $\Phi(p)$ in (15), we have

$$\partial\Phi_{sp}(p)/\partial p = \frac{(t_s-t_r)f_\pi(p)\big((1-\frac{t_r}{t_k})+2\frac{t_r}{t_k}F_\pi(p)\big)}{\Big((1-\frac{t_r}{t_k})F_\pi(p)+\frac{t_r}{t_k}\big(F_\pi(p)\big)^2\Big)^2}g(p),$$

where

$$g(p) = -\int_{\underline{\pi}}^{p}xf_\pi(x)\mathrm{d}x + p\frac{(1-\frac{t_r}{t_k})F_\pi(p)+\frac{t_r}{t_k}\big(F_\pi(p)\big)^2}{(1-\frac{t_r}{t_k})+2\frac{t_r}{t_k}F_\pi(p)}.$$

Note that first three terms before $g(p)$ in $\partial\Phi_{sp}(p)/\partial p$ are positive. To show the positivity of $\partial\Phi_{sp}(p)/\partial p$, we take first-order derivative of $g(p)$ and then have $\partial g(p)/\partial p = \frac{(1-\frac{t_r}{t_k})F_\pi(p)+\frac{t_r}{t_k}\left(F_\pi(p)\right)^2}{\left((1-\frac{t_r}{t_k})+2\frac{t_r}{t_k}F_\pi(p)\right)^2}\Big((1-\frac{t_r}{t_k})+2\frac{t_r}{t_k}\big(F_\pi(p)-pf_\pi(p)\big)\Big)$. Due to the positivity and monotonic decreasing property of $f_\pi(p)$ (cf. Figure 3), $F_\pi(p)$ is concave and $F_\pi(p) - pf_\pi(p) \ge 0$. We then have $\partial g(p)/\partial p \ge 0$. Thus, $g(p)$ monotonically increases with p, so is $\partial\Phi_{sp}(p)/\partial p$. By the fact that $g(\underline{\pi}) < 0$ and $g(\bar{\pi}) > 0$, $\partial\Phi_{sp}(p)/\partial p$ increases monotonically from a negative value to a positive value, i.e., $\Phi_{sp}(p)$ first decreases and then increases with p. Hence, $\Phi_{sp}(p)$ is minimized when $\partial\Phi_{sp}(p)/\partial p = 0$, i.e., $g(p) = 0$. Letting $g(p) = 0$, we thus deduce

$$\begin{aligned}
&\int_{\underline{\pi}}^{p}xf_\pi(x)\mathrm{d}x = p\frac{(1-\frac{t_r}{t_k})F_\pi(p)+\frac{t_r}{t_k}\big(F_\pi(p)\big)^2}{(1-\frac{t_r}{t_k})+2\frac{t_r}{t_k}F_\pi(p)}\\
\Rightarrow\;& \psi(p) = F_\pi(p)\left(\frac{\int_{\underline{\pi}}^{p}xf(x)\mathrm{d}x}{\int_{\underline{\pi}}^{p}(p-x)f(x)\mathrm{d}x}-1\right) = \frac{t_k}{t_r}-1,
\end{aligned}$$

which leads to (16). In addition, $\Phi(p^\star) < \Phi(\bar{\pi}) = (t_s - t_r)\mathbb{E}(\pi\,|\,\pi \le \bar{\pi}) \le t_s\bar{\pi}$ so the constraints in (15) are satisfied at optimality. □

10. REFERENCES

[1] AGMON BEN-YEHUDA, O., BEN-YEHUDA, M., SCHUSTER, A., AND TSAFRIR, D. Deconstructing Amazon EC2 spot instance pricing. *ACM Trans. on Economics and Computation 1*, 3 (2013), 1–16.

[2] AMAZON. EC2 spot instance, 2015. http://aws.amazon.com/ec2/purchasing-options/spot-instances/.

[3] ARDAGNA, D., PANICUCCI, B., AND PASSACANTANDO, M. A game theoretic formulation of the service provisioning problem in cloud systems. In *Proc. of WWW* (2011), ACM, pp. 177–186.

[4] ARMBRUST, M., FOX, A., GRIFFITH, R., JOSEPH, A. D., KATZ, R., KONWINSKI, A., LEE, G., PATTERSON, D., RABKIN, A., STOICA, I., ET AL. A view of cloud computing. *Communications of the ACM 53*, 4 (2010), 50–58.

[5] BLUM, A., SANDHOLM, T., AND ZINKEVICH, M. Online algorithms for market clearing. *Journal of the ACM (JACM) 53*, 5 (2006), 845–879.

[6] BUYYA, R., YEO, C. S., AND VENUGOPAL, S. Market-oriented cloud computing: Vision, hype, and reality for delivering IT services as computing utilities. In *Proc. of IEEE HPCC* (2008), IEEE, pp. 5–13.

[7] Common Crawl. Common Crawl Corpus. *online at: http://commoncrawl.org/* (2015).

[8] Dogar, F. R., Karagiannis, T., Ballani, H., and Rowstron, A. Decentralized task-aware scheduling for data center networks. In *Proc. of ACM SIGCOMM* (2014).

[9] Fang, X., Misra, S., Xue, G., and Yang, D. Smart grid – The new and improved power grid: A survey. *IEEE Communications Surveys & Tutorials 14*, 4 (2012), 944–980.

[10] Feng, G., Garg, S., Buyya, R., and Li, W. Revenue maximization using adaptive resource provisioning in cloud computing environments. In *Proc. of ACM/IEEE Grid* (2012), pp. 192–200.

[11] Friedman, E. J., and Parkes, D. C. Pricing WiFi at Starbucks: Issues in online mechanism design. In *Proc. of ACM EC* (2003), ACM, pp. 240–241.

[12] Guenter, B., Jain, N., and Williams, C. Managing cost, performance, and reliability tradeoffs for energy-aware server provisioning. In *Proc. of IEEE INFOCOM* (2011), IEEE, pp. 1332–1340.

[13] Ha, S., Sen, S., Joe-Wong, C., Im, Y., and Chiang, M. TUBE: time-dependent pricing for mobile data. In *Proc. of ACM SIGCOMM* (2012).

[14] Jain, N., Menache, I., Naor, J. S., and Yaniv, J. Near-optimal scheduling mechanisms for deadline-sensitive jobs in large computing clusters. *ACM Trans. on Parallel Computing 2*, 1 (2015), 3.

[15] Javadi, B., Thulasiram, R. K., and Buyya, R. Statistical modeling of spot instance prices in public cloud environments. In *Proc. of IEEE/ACM UCC* (2011), IEEE/ACM, pp. 219–228.

[16] Jia, J., Zhang, Q., Zhang, Q., and Liu, M. Revenue generation for truthful spectrum auction in dynamic spectrum access. In *Proc. of ACM MobiHoc* (2009), pp. 3–12.

[17] Jin, H., Wang, X., Wu, S., Di, S., and Shi, X. Towards optimized fine-grained pricing of IaaS cloud platform. *IEEE Trans. on Cloud Computing* (2014), to appear.

[18] Juan, D.-C., Li, L., Peng, H.-K., Marculescu, D., and Faloutsos, C. Beyond poisson: Modeling inter-arrival time of requests in a datacenter. In *Advances in Knowledge Discovery and Data Mining*. Springer, 2014, pp. 198–209.

[19] Kang, L., and Parkes, D. C. A decentralized auction framework to promote efficient resource allocation in open computational grids. In *Proc. Joint Workshop on The Economics of Networked Systems and Incentive-Based Computing* (2007).

[20] Kutanoglu, E., and Wu, S. D. On combinatorial auction and Lagrangean relaxation for distributed resource scheduling. *IIE Trans. 31*, 9 (1999), 813–826.

[21] Lampe, U., Hans, R., Seliger, M., and Pauly, M. Pricing in infrastructure clouds–an analytical and empirical examination. In *Association for Information Systems Conference* (2014).

[22] Lee, G., Chun, B.-G., and Katz, R. H. Heterogeneity-aware resource allocation and scheduling in the cloud. *Proc. of HotCloud* (2011), 1–5.

[23] Leonardi, E., Mellia, M., Neri, F., and Ajmone Marsan, M. Bounds on average delays and queue size averages and variances in input-queued cell-based switches. In *Proc. of IEEE INFOCOM* (2001), vol. 2, IEEE, pp. 1095–1103.

[24] MacKie-Mason, J., and Varian, H. Pricing the Internet. In *Public Access to the Internet*, B. Kahin and J. Keller, Eds. Prentice-Hall, Englewood Cliffs, NJ, 1995.

[25] Menache, I., Ozdaglar, A., and Shimkin, N. Socially optimal pricing of cloud computing resources. In *Proc. of VALUETOOLS* (2011), ICST, pp. 322–331.

[26] Nair, J., Subramanian, V. G., and Wierman, A. On competitive provisioning of cloud services. *ACM SIGMETRICS Performance Evaluation Review 42*, 2 (2014), 30–32.

[27] Ng, C., Parkes, D. C., and Seltzer, M. Virtual worlds: Fast and strategyproof auctions for dynamic resource allocation. In *Proc. of ACM EC* (2003), ACM, pp. 238–239.

[28] Poola, D., Ramamohanarao, K., and Buyya, R. Fault-tolerant workflow scheduling using spot instances on clouds. *Procedia Computer Science 29* (2014), 523–533.

[29] Porter, R. Mechanism design for online real-time scheduling. In *Proc. of ACM EC* (2004), ACM, pp. 61–70.

[30] Sen, S., Jin, Y., Guérin, R., and Hosanagar, K. Modeling the dynamics of network technology adoption and the role of converters. *IEEE/ACM Trans. on Networking 18*, 6 (2010), 1793–1805.

[31] Teng, F., and Magoulès, F. A new game theoretical resource allocation algorithm for cloud computing. In *Advances in Grid and Pervasive Computing*. Springer, 2010, pp. 321–330.

[32] Upadhyaya, P., Balazinska, M., and Suciu, D. How to price shared optimizations in the cloud. *Proc. of the VLDB Endowment 5*, 6 (2012), 562–573.

[33] Van den Bossche, R., Vanmechelen, K., and Broeckhove, J. Cost-optimal scheduling in hybrid IaaS clouds for deadline constrained workloads. In *Proc. of IEEE CLOUD* (2010), IEEE, pp. 228–235.

[34] Wang, P., Qi, Y., Hui, D., Rao, L., and Liu, X. Present or future: Optimal pricing for spot instances. In *Proc. of IEEE ICDCS* (2013).

[35] Wang, Q., Ren, K., and Meng, X. When cloud meets eBay: Towards effective pricing for cloud computing. In *Proc. of IEEE INFOCOM* (2012), IEEE, pp. 936–944.

[36] Wellman, M. P., MacKie-Mason, J. K., Reeves, D. M., and Swaminathan, S. Exploring bidding strategies for market-based scheduling. In *Proc. of ACM EC* (2003), ACM, pp. 115–124.

[37] Yi, S., Andrzejak, A., and Kondo, D. Monetary cost-aware checkpointing and migration on Amazon cloud spot instances. *IEEE Trans. on Services Computing 5*, 4 (2012), 512–524.

[38] Zhang, L., Li, Z., and Wu, C. Dynamic resource provisioning in cloud computing: A randomized auction approach. In *Proc. of IEEE INFOCOM* (2014).

[39] Zhang, Q., Zhu, Q., and Boutaba, R. Dynamic resource allocation for spot markets in cloud computing environments. In *Proc. of IEEE/ACM UCC* (2011), IEEE/ACM, pp. 178–185.

[40] Zhou, Y., and Wentzlaff, D. The sharing architecture: sub-core configurability for IaaS clouds. In *Proc. of ACM ASPLOS* (2014), ACM, pp. 559–574.

Coracle: Evaluating Consensus at the Internet Edge

Heidi Howard
University of Cambridge
heidi.howard@cl.cam.ac.uk

Jon Crowcroft
University of Cambridge
jon.crowcroft@cl.cam.ac.uk

ABSTRACT

Distributed consensus is fundamental in distributed systems for achieving fault-tolerance. The Paxos algorithm has long dominated this domain, although it has been recently challenged by algorithms such as Raft and Viewstamped Replication Revisited.

These algorithms rely on Paxos's original assumptions, unfortunately these assumptions are now at odds with the reality of the modern internet. Our insight is that current consensus algorithms have significant availability issues when deployed outside the well defined context of the datacenter.

To illustrate this problem, we developed Coracle, a tool for evaluating distributed consensus algorithms in settings that more accurately represent realistic deployments. We have used Coracle to test two examples of network configurations that contradict the liveness claims of the Raft algorithm. Through the process of exercising these algorithms under more realistic assumptions, we demonstrate wider availability issues faced by consensus algorithms when deployed on real world networks.

CCS Concepts

•**Computer systems organization → Availability;** *Redundancy;*

Keywords

Distributed consensus; Fault-tolerance; Dependable systems

1. INTRODUCTION

Modern distributed systems depend on the centralised cloud rather than deal with the complexity of the internet edge. In the wake of censorship concerns, mass-surveillance and data breaches, users are demanding viable alternatives to third-party centralised systems. Building distributed systems across hosts on the internet edge is one such alternative. Such systems have the potential to provide low latency services and the ability to operate without a full internet connection. Ensuring consensus algorithms are resilient to common failures at the internet edge is vital for building reliable systems.

Paxos [2] has been synonymous with distributed consensus for over a decade. This domain has been recently challenged by algorithms such as Raft [4] and Viewstamped Replication Revisited [3]. These algorithms (like many others) are difficult to use in practice as they are based on Lamport's original model of the internet, which is at odds with the current reality, particularly at the internet edge.

Paxos family consensus algorithms assume homogeneous, static hosts on a fixed, fully-connected network. Deployment of these algorithms requires knowledgeable sysadmins with accurate understanding of network properties and failures are assumed to be rare.

In reality, consensus algorithms are deployed beyond the datacenter. Here, we have heterogeneous hosts with various resource constraints, managed by everyday people. They are on mobile networks with unpredictable link characteristics and poorly understood middleboxes. Networks and hosts change over time and a diverse range of failures are commonplace.

We could try to modify the consensus algorithms to mitigate these issues but these changes may in turn introduce other issues or violate correctness.

Furthermore, consensus algorithms commonly depend on the correct selection of various parameters (such as timeouts for failure detection) to reach a stable state. Choosing such values is challenging enough in a datacenter context, let alone in a dynamic environment such as the internet edge.

2. EXAMPLES

Raft claims that consensus algorithms are fully functional as long as any majority of the hosts are operational and can communicate with each other and with clients.

In the two examples that follow, the majority of hosts are live and able to communicate yet the system is unavailable as the leadership algorithm is non-convergent. Although these issues are common among distributed consensus algorithms, we have chosen Raft to illustrate this point due to its popularity and understandability.

In Raft, each host stores its current mode, either *follower*, *candidate* or *leader*, and its current term, a monotonically increasing value used to order events. Nodes begin as *followers* and receive regular heartbeats from the *leader*. If a *follower* fails to hear a valid *leader's* heartbeat then it will increment its term and become a *candidate*.

SIGCOMM '15 August 17-21, 2015, London, United Kingdom

ACM ISBN 978-1-4503-3542-3/15/08.

DOI: http://dx.doi.org/10.1145/2785956.2790010

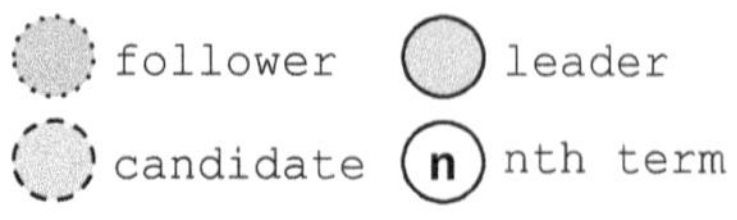

Figure 1: Legend for Figures 2 and 3

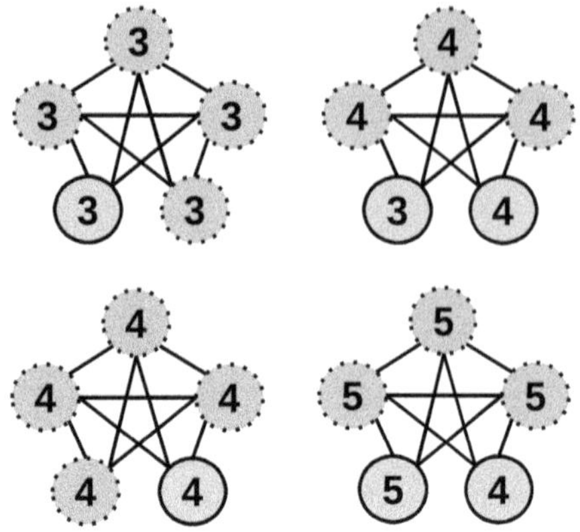

Figure 2: Four snapshots in time of Raft running across five hosts with non-transitive reachability

This host will ask all the other hosts to vote for it, including its current term in that request. A host will vote for the *candidate* if its term is the same or higher than its own and it has not yet voted in that term[1]. If the *candidate* receives votes from a strict majority of hosts, then it becomes *leader* in that term. Otherwise, it increments its term and restarts the election. If a host hears from another host with a higher term, it will step down to a *follower* in that new higher term.

Figure 2 shows the reachability between 5 hosts, all hosts are connected except the two at the bottom. Here we see leadership bouncing between the two disconnected hosts because if one of these hosts is the *leader* then the other is unable to hear the *leader's* heartbeat. This causes the host to timeout, increment its term and start a new election. This host will likely be elected *leader*. The old *leader* will step down to a *follower* when it hears about this from another host. The old *leader* will soon timeout and start a new election as it cannot hear from the new *leader*.

Figure 3 shows the reachability between 4 hosts, one of which is behind a poorly configured NAT, allowing it to transmit messages to all hosts but not hear responses. This host will never be able to hear the *leader's* heartbeats and thus will continually timeout, increment its term and start a new election. When contacting the other hosts, it will remove the current *leader* and continuously force *leader* election, rendering the system unavaliable.

3. APPROACH

We have informally argued that consensus algorithms cannot tolerate many common faults at the internet edge, but it is difficult to systematically study and thus address these issues, given the vast state space and complex experimental setups required.

[1]Raft includes extra conditions of voting, though these details are not included for simplicity.

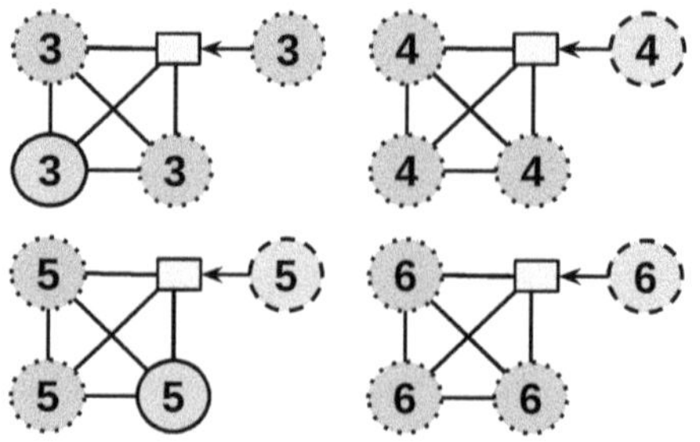

Figure 3: Four snapshots in time of Raft running across four hosts with asymmetric reachability

In response, we developed Coracle, an event-based simulator for distributed consensus algorithms on the internet edge. Building on our earlier work on reproducing Raft [1], we utilize state machine replication [5] as a common intermediate abstraction for consensus protocols like Raft and Viewstamped Replication Revisited. We provide a graphical front-end for selecting from our test suite of network environments (like the examples in Figures 2 & 3) or users can design their own network. In contrast to traditional network simulators, our pure protocol implementations allow Coracle to store a complete trace of all local state and communication. This allows it to rerun traces, run traces though a trace checker to check safety guarantees, and extract performance metrics. Coracle enables users to investigate the best algorithm parameters for a particular deployment. Likewise, users can model modifications to an existing consensus algorithm (or implement a new algorithm altogether) and evaluate it against our test suite of internet edge environments.

Acknowledgements

We appreciate constructive feedback on this abstract from Matthew Huxtable, Matthew Grosvenor, Mindy Preston, Frank McSherry, Richard Mortier and Helen Oliver. Thanks to the generous support from Microsoft.

4. REFERENCES

[1] H. Howard, M. Schwarzkopf, A. Madhavapeddy, and J. Crowcroft. Raft refloated: Do we have consensus? *ACM SIGOPS Operating Systems Review*, 49(1):12–21, 2015.

[2] L. Lamport. The part-time parliament. *ACM Transactions on Computer Systems (TOCS)*, 16(2):133–169, 1998.

[3] B. Liskov and J. Cowling. Viewstamped replication revisited. 2012.

[4] D. Ongaro and J. Ousterhout. In search of an understandable consensus algorithm. In *USENIX Annual Technical Conference.*

[5] F. B. Schneider. Implementing fault-tolerant services using the state machine approach: A tutorial. *ACM Computing Surveys (CSUR)*, 22(4):299–319, 1990.

Challenging Entropy-based Anomaly Detection and Diagnosis in Cellular Networks

P. Fiadino, A. D'Alconzo, M. Schiavone, P. Casas
FTW Vienna
surname@ftw.at

ABSTRACT

In this paper we challenge the applicability of entropy-based approaches for detecting and diagnosis network traffic anomalies, and claim that full statistics (i.e., empirical probability distributions) should be applied to improve the change-detection capabilities. We support our claim by detecting and diagnosing large-scale traffic anomalies in a real cellular network, caused by specific OTT (Over The Top) services and smartphone devices. Our results clearly suggest that anomaly detection and diagnosis based on entropy analysis is prone to errors and misses typical characteristics of traffic anomalies, particularly in the studied scenario. [1]

1. MOTIVATION & METHODOLOGY

The complexity of current Internet, with highly popular and omnipresent services accessed over multiple networks (cellular, WiFi, FTTH, etc.) and distributed through massive CDNs has revamped the relevance of automatically detecting and diagnosing traffic anomalies impacting large numbers of users. A particularly popular approach for detecting anomalies in network traffic is the one represented by entropy-based analysis [1]. In a nutshell, entropy-based anomaly detection consists of detecting abrupt changes in the time series of the empirical entropy of certain traffic features, related to the specific anomaly. The entropy of a feature captures the dispersion of the corresponding probability distribution in a single number, becoming highly appealing for the analysis. However, such a compression necessarily looses relevant information about the distribution of the analyzed feature, masking in many cases the effects of the anomaly.

Although entropy-based approaches have been successfully applied for anomaly detection in the past [1–3], in fixed-line networks and using only transport-layer features such as IPs and ports, their application in the aforementioned context has severe limitations, given the characteristics of current traffic anomalies. In this paper we propose a generic framework to detect and diagnose large-scale network traffic anomalies, and use it to show that entropy-based approaches are not suitable for the analysis of traffic anomalies observed in an operational cellular network. To overcome this limitation, we apply an empirical distribution-based anomaly detection approach we have recently introduced in [4], which analyzes the complete distribution of the monitored features.

Given that the types of anomalies we target are related to large-scale services, the proposed framework is based on the analysis of DNS traffic. From our operational experience, application-specific anomalies are particularly visible in the DNS traffic. Indeed, abrupt changes in the DNS requests count can be considered as a symptom of such anomalies. From DNS transactions we derive two sets of time-series (signals from now on) denoted as *symptomatic* and *diagnostic* signals. All signals are checked for significant changes from their reference of "normality". However, the symptomatic signals are designed such that their changes directly relate to the presence of abnormal and potentially harmful events. On the other hand, changes in the diagnostic signals per-se do not have a negative connotation, but rather ease and guide the interpretation of the anomalous event. In the diagnosis of a detected anomaly, deviations of the symptomatic signals are correlated with the subset of simultaneously changing diagnostic signals to provide a comprehensive event characterization. The features are the following: information about the mobile device (ID, manufacturer, OS), the network settings (APN, RAT, DNS server IP), the host name (FQDN) of the requested service, and the status of the transaction (i.e., successful, time-out, retransmission).

To evidence the limitations of entropy-based anomaly detection, we test and compare an entropy- and a distribution-based approach, applied to both symptomatic and diagnostic signals. The entropy of a random variable X is $H(X) = -\sum_{i=1}^{n} p(x_i) log(p(x_i))$, where $x_1, \dots, x_n$ is the range of values for X, and $p(x_i)$ is the probability that X takes the value x_i. The entropy is normalized to a scaling factor $log(n_0)$, where n_0 is the number of distinct x_i values in a given time bin. Given the time-series of the entropy of a feature, we use any simple adaptive-threshold detector (e.g., Moving Average, EWMA) to spot abrupt changes. The distribution-based detection consists of computing the distance between the empirical distribution of a certain feature and a reference set of anomaly-free distributions previously observed. We rely on a symmetrized and normalized version of the well known Kullback-Leibler divergence to compute such a distance. The complete approach and the heuristics used for the construction of the reference set are described in [4].

The analysis is performed on top of two different example

[1] This work has been done in the framework of the EU-IP project mPlane, funded by the EC under grant 318627.

SIGCOMM '15 August 17-21, 2015, London, United Kingdom

ACM ISBN 978-1-4503-3542-3/15/08.

DOI: http://dx.doi.org/10.1145/2785956.2790011

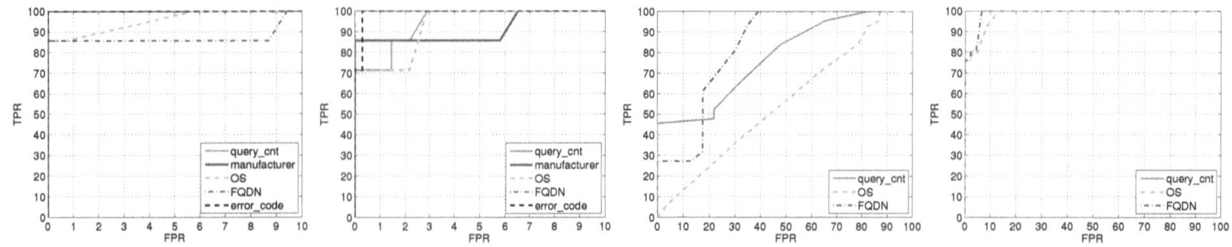

(a) E_1 - Entropy (b) E_1 - Distribution (c) E_2 - Entropy (d) E_2 - Distribution

Figure 1: ROC curves for the detection of abrupt changes in the corresponding symptomatic and diagnostic signals. Entropy-based detection performs properly with anomaly E_1, but completely fails with E_2.

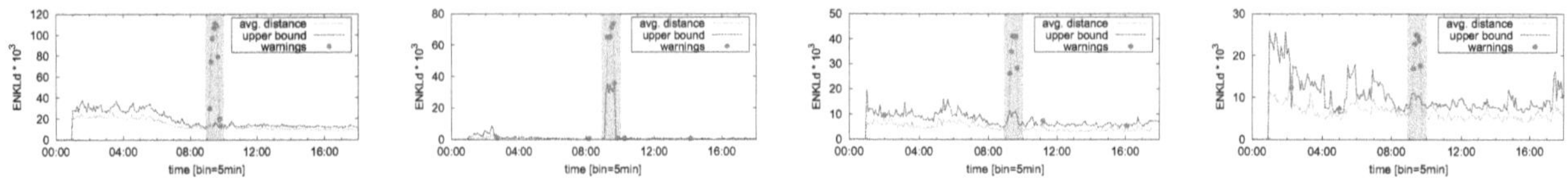

(a) FQDN (b) Error Code (c) Manufacturer (d) OS

Figure 2: Output of the distribution-based detector for the diagnostic signals in E_1. All the signals exhibit distribution changes during the event.

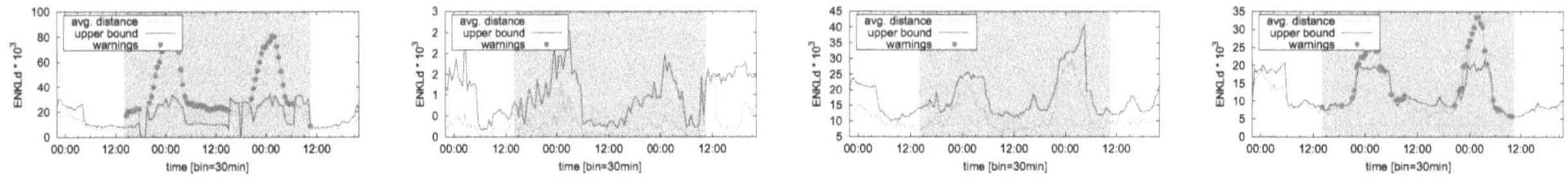

(a) FQDN (b) Error Code (c) Manufacturer (d) OS

Figure 3: Output of the distribution-based analysis for the diagnostic signals in E_2. Distributions of FQDN and OS exhibit changes during the event, while manufacturer and Error Flag are unaffected.

anomalies which we have observed in the cellular network of a national wide ISP in EU; we refer to them as E_1 and E_2. Both anomalies were manually analyzed, thus we have a solid ground truth describing both events. The anomaly E_1 is a short lived (i.e., hours) high intensity anomaly (e.g., about 10% of devices repeating a request every few seconds), where all the involved devices are produced by a single manufacturer and run the same OS. In this case, the number of involved terminals and the overall number of additional queries is such to overload the local DNS servers, increasing the number of time-out codes in the Error Flag field. The anomaly is related to the Apple Push Notification service on iPhone devices (FQDN = `*.push.apple.com`). The event E_2 corresponds to a long lasting (i.e., days) low-intensity anomaly (e.g., about 5% of devices repeating requests every few minutes). Differently from E_1, the involved terminals are produced by multiple manufacturers, even if they share the same OS. In this case, the anomaly is related to Android devices accessing the Google Push service.

2. WHEN ENTROPY FAILS

Fig. 1 depicts the ROC curves obtained in the detection of E_1 and E_2. The curves reflect the True Positive and False Positive Rates (TPR and FPR) obtained when changing the detection thresholds of both approaches. Each anomalous sample corresponds to a 5 minutes time bin, during the entire span of the anomaly (about 1hr for E_1, and about 2 days for E_2). The symptomatic signal is in all the cases the DNS query count per device, using either its entropy or the full distribution. Given the characteristics of E_1, there are four relevant diagnostic signals which show an abrupt change at the time of the anomaly: the manufacturer and OS (same type of devices are impacted), the FQDN (points to the requested, unavailable service) and the error code (the local DNS servers get overloaded and time-outs increase). Figs. 1(a) and 1(b) show that both approaches are capable of detecting the abrupt changes induced by this anomaly, resulting in almost perfect detection for the impacted signals. Fig. 2 depicts the output of the distribution-based detector for the aforementioned diagnostic signals.

Fig. 1(c) shows how the entropy-based approach completely fails to capture the characteristics of the E_2 anomaly, as the FPR becomes too high to be applicable in the practice. In the case of E_2, only the OS and the FQDN diagnostic signals are impacted. Fig. 3 shows how both signals are detected as anomalous by the distribution-based approach during the almost the 2 days that the anomaly lasted. In addition, it shows how the other 2 signals (Error Code and Manufactures) correctly remain un-flagged. Finally, Fig. 1(d) shows very similar performance to the one attained by the distribution-based approach in the previous scenario, reinforcing the evidence of its supremacy.

To sum up, evaluations show that lower intensity anomaly E_2 is not correctly captured by the entropy-based detector, as the entropy results in this case into a too coarse metric, failing to reveal the effects of this type of anomalies. This limitation calls for the adoption of a distribution-based approach, which is perfectly suited for both tested scenarios.

3. REFERENCES

[1] A. Lakhina et al., "Mining Anomalies using Traffic Feature Distributions", in *ACM SIGCOMM*, 2005.
[2] G. Nychis et al., "An Empirical Evaluation of Entropy-based Traffic Anomaly Detection", in *ACM IMC*, 2008.
[3] Y. Kanda et al., "ADMIRE: Anomaly Detection Method using Entropy-based PCA with three-step Sketches", in *Computer Communications*, vol. 36(5), pp. 575-588, 2013.
[4] P. Fiadino et al., "On the Detection of Network Traffic Anomalies in Content Delivery Network Services", in *ITC*, 2014.

Toward Automated Testing of Geo-Distributed Replica Selection Algorithms *

Kirill Bogdanov
KTH Royal Institute of Technology
kirillb@kth.se

Miguel Peón-Quirós
University Complutense of Madrid (UCM)
Spain
mikepeon@gmail.com

Gerald Q. Maguire Jr.
KTH Royal Institute of Technology
maguire@kth.se

Dejan Kostić
KTH Royal Institute of Technology
dmk@kth.se

ABSTRACT

Many geo-distributed systems rely on a replica selection algorithms to communicate with the closest set of replicas. Unfortunately, the bursty nature of the Internet traffic and ever changing network conditions present a problem in identifying the best choices of replicas. Suboptimal replica choices result in increased response latency and reduced system performance. In this work we present GeoPerf, a tool that tries to automate testing of geo-distributed replica selection algorithms. We used GeoPerf to test Cassandra and MongoDB, two popular data stores, and found bugs in each of these systems.

CCS Concepts

•**Software and its engineering** → *Software testing and debugging;* •**Networks** → *Wide area networks;*

Keywords

Symbolic Execution, Replica Selection Algorithms

1. INTRODUCTION

Today, many popular services are deployed in cloud environments such as Amazon EC2[1], Microsoft Azure[3], and Google Cloud[2]. These services are used by hundreds of millions of users who are spread across the globe. For reasons of performance, reliability, and survivability many such services are replicated across geo-distributed datacenters. Ensuring low latency response time in such an environment is both highly important and difficult [8, 7]. To achieve lower response times, clients of these services often use *replica selection algorithms* to choose a replica or set of replicas they will contact.

Unfortunately, Internet traffic is bursty and routing can change. This directly affects end-to-end characteristics of a wide-area network paths such as latency, bandwidth and packet loss rate. Therefore, in order to operate in such conditions, replica selection algorithms need to continuously measure the networks state and use past history in order to anticipate future changes. All of these factors make replica selection very hard.

To better understand the underlying conditions, we performed detailed measurements of application-level round-trip latencies among all the Amazon EC2 regions. Our measurements demonstrate high variability in network conditions over time. Figure 1 shows round-trip measurements over a period of one day from the Ireland EC2 datacenter to datacenters in all other EC2 regions. From the point of view of Ireland, the set of nearest replicas based on the network latency change. Moreover, this demonstrates the need for dynamic adaptation to ever-changing conditions, as despite running over a dedicated infrastructure, any static configuration of replicas would be suboptimal.

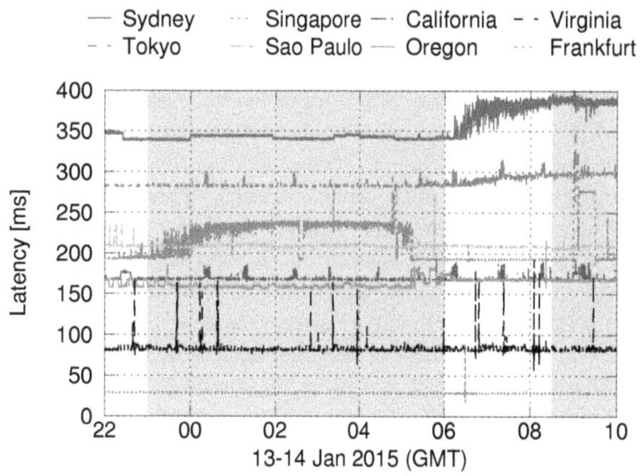

Figure 1: RTT measurement over UDP from the Ireland EC2 datacenter to 8 other EC2 regions (after low pass filter). Red background highlights the time of the day when the order of replicas change (Singapore-São Paulo).

*Work funded by ERC project 259110. Miguel performed his work while working at IMDEA Networks.

SIGCOMM '15 August 17-21, 2015, London, United Kingdom

ACM ISBN 978-1-4503-3542-3/15/08.

DOI: http://dx.doi.org/10.1145/2785956.2790013

It is extremely difficult to identify errors in replica selection algorithms. First, such errors usually do not lead to critical system failures. Second, often it is hard to determine the optimal choices of replicas in the absence of up-to-date full global knowledge. Debugging is difficult due to the number of potential bug causes, such as problems in latency sampling, math calculations, replica selection logic, etc.

All of these factors significantly complicate testing of replica selection algorithms. To perform comprehensive testing would require trying numerous network topologies with variable latency, bandwidth, and loss rate characteristics. Moreover, one would need to predict duration, intensity, and frequency of changes of these network characteristics. Therefore, it is unlikely that simple unit testing would be able to uncover all possible errors. Instead, we need a *systematic testing tool.*

Next, we describe GeoPerf, our tool for automating the process of testing replica selection algorithms. We believe that it is the first such tool.

2. GEOPERF

We choose to apply symbolic execution [6], because it performs systematic code path exploration. It uses an automatic constraint solver to derive concrete input values that will cause a particular code path within a program to be executed. As an input we use network latencies that could be observed by the replica selection algorithm under test, while code paths represent different replica decisions made by the algorithm.

Each replica choice is defined by the set of different code paths that can lead to that choice. Under normal execution a single code path is determined by the system state (i.e., past and current set of network RTTs, time, random numbers) and the implementation of the replica selection algorithm itself. However, by using symbolic execution we can explore alternative code paths that lead to different replica choices given the symbolic state of the system. This allow us to generate latency inputs that could force a replica selection algorithm to choose one or another subset of nodes. However, to reason about correctness of such choices we need to know the ground truth. For this purpose, GeoPerf provides a simplified replica selection mechanism that represents the minimum bound on the achievable latency. This algorithm act as a comparison point to the target algorithm and allows us to evaluate individual replica choices.

First we develop a controlled environment where we can generate, monitor, and replay events deterministically. Second, we isolate target replica selection algorithm from the system under test. Then we use our controlled environment to compare two replica selection algorithms while both algorithms share one view of the network. GeoPerf uses symbolic execution to determine if two algorithms make different choices under identical network conditions.

GeoPerf is based on our own discrete event-based simulator, which contain a set of geo-distributed nodes connected via wide-area network paths with variable latency. We simulate arrival of client requests and use replica selection module, first to monitor the state of network paths and then to periodically choose a set of nodes to serve incoming requests. We use GeoPerf to create two instantiations of the simulator and run them in parallel in the identical environments with synchronized clocks, and deterministic pseudo-random number generators. One simulation is configured to use the reference replica selection algorithm and the other the algorithm under test.

We use the symbolic execution engine to explore possible code paths and to generate latency inputs that define the network conditions among the nodes. The purpose of this exploration is to identify a sequence of latency values that can expose a weakness in the target replica selection algorithm. This is done by demonstrating that the target algorithm repeatedly exhibits inferior performance (i.e., choices) in the simulated environment.

3. EVALUATION

Using GeoPerf we found bugs in replica selection algorithm of two popular geo-distributed data stores, Cassandra[5] and MongoDB[4]. In addition, we quantify the impact of the bugs that GeoPerf found. Specifically, we replay the trace of the latencies we collected across Amazon EC2 using GeoPerf's event simulator, and compute the median time that is wasted due to the bugs. Figure 2 shows the comparison between the buggy and fixed versions of Cassandra's replica selection algorithms, it demonstrates that over 20% of all requests were affected by the bug. The median loss for 10% of all requests is above 50 ms.

A video clip showcasing the work: http://prophet.ssvl.kth.se/wp-content/uploads/2015/05/Kirill-src.mp4

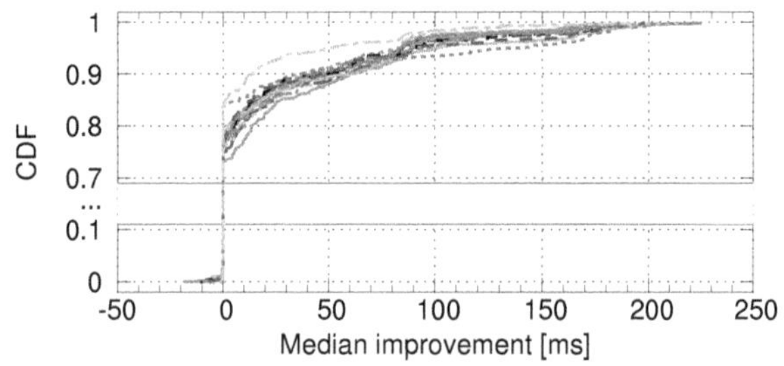

Figure 2: The CDFs of medians of the requests completion time differences between buggy and fixed versions of the Cassandra's replica selection algorithms (EC2 latency trace replay via GeoPerf). The figure contains 14 CDFs, one for each day of the trace of latency samples.

4. REFERENCES

[1] Amazon ec2. http://aws.amazon.com/ec2/.
[2] Google cloud. https://cloud.google.com/.
[3] Microsoft azure. http://azure.microsoft.com/.
[4] Mongodb. http://www.mongodb.org/.
[5] Apache. Cassandra. http://cassandra.apache.org/.
[6] Cadar, C., Dunbar, D., and Engler, D. R. KLEE: Unassisted and Automatic Generation of High-Coverage Tests for Complex Systems Programs. In *OSDI* (2008).
[7] Dean, J., and Barroso, L. A. The tail at scale. *Commun. ACM 56*, 2 (Feb. 2013), 74–80.
[8] Decandia, G., Hastorun, D., Jampani, M., Kakulapati, G., Lakshman, A., Pilchin, A., Sivasubramanian, S., Vosshall, P., and Vogels, W. Dynamo: Amazon's Highly Available Key-value Store. In *SOSP* (2007).

The Internet of Names: A DNS Big Dataset

Actively Measuring 50% of the Entire DNS Name Space, Every Day

Roland van Rijswijk-Deij[1,2], Mattijs Jonker[1], Anna Sperotto[1], Aiko Pras[1]
[1]University of Twente, [2]SURFnet bv
{r.m.vanrijswijk, m.jonker, a.sperotto, a.pras}@utwente.nl

ABSTRACT

The Domain Name System (DNS) is part of the core infrastructure of the Internet. Tracking changes in the DNS over time provides valuable information about the evolution of the Internet's infrastructure. Until now, only one large-scale approach to perform these kinds of measurements existed, passive DNS (pDNS). While pDNS is useful for applications like tracing security incidents, it does not provide sufficient information to reliably track DNS changes over time. We use a complementary approach based on active measurements, which provides a unique, comprehensive dataset on the evolution of DNS over time. Our high-performance infrastructure performs Internet-scale active measurements, currently querying over 50% of the DNS name space on a daily basis. Our infrastructure is designed from the ground up to enable big data analysis approaches on, e.g., a Hadoop cluster. With this novel approach we aim for a quantum leap in DNS-based measurement and analysis of the Internet.

Categories and Subject Descriptors

C.4 [**Performance of Systems**]: Measurement Techniques

Keywords

DNS; active measurements; big data; Internet evolution

1. INTRODUCTION

Next to IP, DNS is arguably the most important infrastructure on the Internet. DNS is pervasive as almost all networked applications and services rely on DNS to map names to IP addresses. Consequently, measuring what is in the DNS can teach us a lot about the state of the Internet. If performed systematically over time, such measurements allow us to observe the evolution of the Internet.

The applications of measuring DNS over time are myriad. An important area of application is network security. Knowledge of what names an IP address mapped to in the past, for example, can be a valuable tool to track malicious activity. There are also many applications in network research. Knowledge of DNS content over time provides empirical data about operational practices and deployment of new protocols. If, for example, we wanted to answer the question how the use of cloud e-mail providers develops over time, knowledge of the DNS is vital (as who handles mail for a domain is configured in DNS through the `MX` record type).

SIGCOMM '15 August 17-21, 2015, London, United Kingdom

ACM ISBN 978-1-4503-3542-3/15/08.
DOI: http://dx.doi.org/10.1145/2785956.2789996

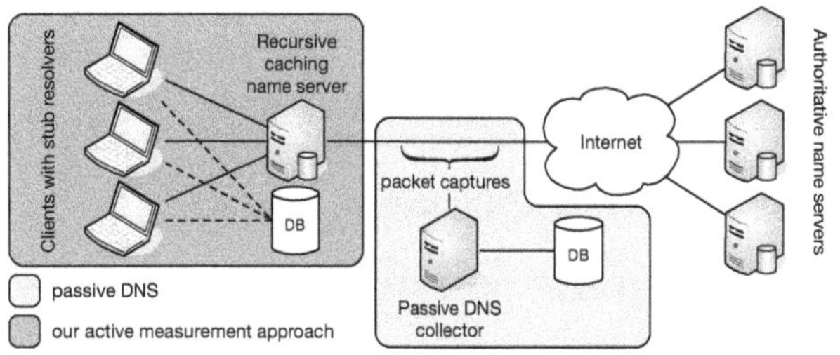

Figure 1: pDNS compared to our approach

Passive DNS

Development of the only existing large-scale approach to DNS measurements, passive DNS (pDNS) [1], was driven by security benefits. Fig. 1 shows an abstract view of the DNS. pDNS typically collects data on the link between recursive caching name servers ("resolvers") and authoritative name servers (light grey area). Data from pDNS setups[1] can, e.g., be used to track names associated with IP addresses that exhibit malicious activity. From a network research perspective, pDNS is also of interest but it suffers from one problem: it does not provide reliable data over time. This is because 1) pDNS will only record data for domains in which clients behind the resolvers where pDNS data is collected are interested and 2) pDNS has no influence over temporal spacing of queries.

Our approach

Driven by a research need for reliable data from the DNS over time, we have developed a complementary approach to pDNS, based on active measurements. Given the DNS zone files from top-level domains (TLDs) as input, we send a fixed selection of queries for each domain in a TLD once per 24 hours. Effectively, if we compare our approach to pDNS, we control the behaviour of the clients performing queries (shown in dark grey in Fig. 1). It is highly challenging to make such an approach scale. For example, the `.com` domain alone (the largest TLD on the Internet), already contains >116M names. In the remainder of this poster abstract, we provide a brief outline of our approach and we highlight the potential of the resulting dataset with a case study.

[1]e.g., DNSDB – https://www.dnsdb.info/

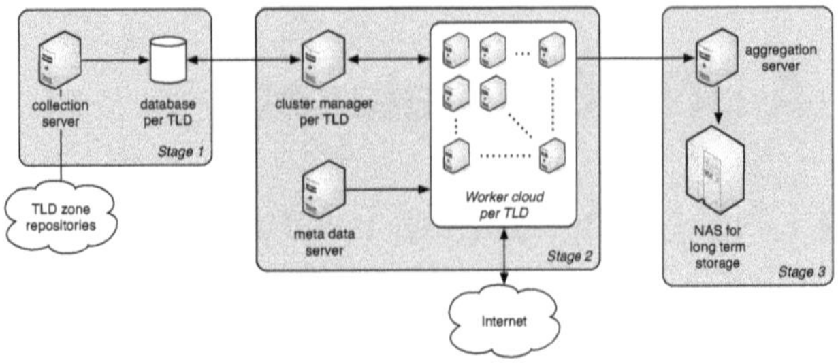

Figure 2: High-level infrastructure overview

TLD	#domains	#workers	avg. time	#queries/day	data/day
.org	10.5 mil.	10	6h45m	127 mil.	2.4GB
.net	15.0 mil.	10	13h30m	181 mil.	3.3GB
.com	116.5 mil.	80	17h30m	1427 mil.	27.2GB
total	142.0 mil.	100	-	1735 mil.	32.9GB

Table 1: Active measurement characteristics

2. INFRASTRUCTURE

2.1 High-level overview

Fig. 2 gives a bird's eye view of our measurement setup. We divide the measurement process into three stages:

- **Stage 1:** input collection – in this stage, we collect the DNS zones for the TLDs to measure. We compute daily deltas and track both the active zone content as well as changes in the zone over time in a database.
- **Stage 2:** main measurement – this is the active measurement stage; we will explain this stage in more detail in Sec. 2.2 below.
- **Stage 3:** aggregate and prepare for analysis – in this final stage we convert the output from the measurement to the Parquet columnar storage format, which is well-suited for processing on a Hadoop cluster.

2.2 Main measurement

Our main active measurement runs on a cloud-based cluster. Every TLD measurement is orchestrated by a cluster management host. This host is responsible for distributing chunks of work, of 100k domains each, to a set of worker nodes. Each worker node runs custom-built software that performs a pre-defined selection of DNS queries for each domain in a chunk of work. Queries are performed against a local DNS resolver instance running on the worker node. Data collected by workers is sent to a central aggregation point for further processing and analysis. Tab. 1 shows an overview of our current setup. It shows the TLDs we measure, the number of worker nodes, the average time to complete a full measurement, the average number of queries per day, and the amount of data collected per day.

2.3 Analysis

As mentioned in Sec. 2.1, we store data such that it is well-suited for processing on a Hadoop cluster. We use such a cluster for analysis, defining map/reduce operations on the data, but also more advanced forms of analysis using, e.g., the Impala massively parallel query engine[2].

[2] http://www.cloudera.com/content/cloudera/en/products-and-services/cdh/impala.html

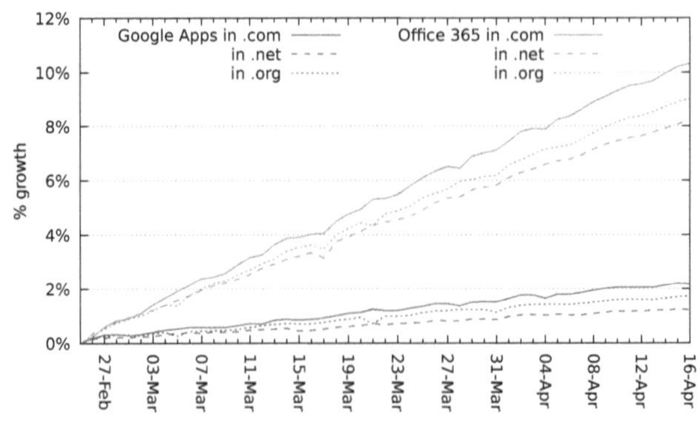

Figure 3: Use of cloud mail platforms over time

3. CASE STUDY

As case study, we have analysed the use of cloud mail platforms over a 50-day period. We focused on two particular platforms, Microsoft's Office 365 and Google Apps. Fig. 3 shows the growth in the fraction of domains per TLD that use either of these platforms. Growth is presented as a percentage relative to the start of the 50-day period. To perform the analysis, our platform processed over 84 billion query results. The full analysis was performed by a single 40-core node in about 7.5 hours. This can easily be improved by running the analysis on a larger Hadoop cluster.

This simple example showcases what can be achieved using our measurement platform and data. The growth in use of, e.g., cloud mail platforms illustrates how the Internet is evolving from every organisation managing its own services to a few large providers offering these services in bulk.

4. CONCLUSIONS AND FUTURE WORK

We created a unique active measurement infrastructure for the DNS. Our infrastructure actively measures over 50% of the total DNS name space on a daily basis. The resulting dataset enables reliable DNS-based analysis of the evolution of the Internet for the first time. And not only do we measure on a large scale, we have also carefully designed for optimal analysis of the collected data through the Hadoop toolchain. The simple case study included in this abstract showcases use of our dataset. It answers the simple question about cloud mail platforms that we provided as an example in the introduction.

The goal of this poster is to invite other researchers to collaborate with us, to analyse this unique new dataset. To provide insight into its potential, we plan to create a web portal with daily statistics. Furthermore, we have already started several research projects that investigate Internet phenomena and that rely on measurement data from this platform.

5. ACKNOWLEDGEMENTS

This work has been supported by the EU-FP7 FLAMINGO Network of Excellence Project (318488) and by SURF, the Netherlands collaborative organisation for higher education and research aimed at breakthrough innovations in ICT.

6. REFERENCES

[1] Florian Weimer. Passive DNS Replication. In *Proc. of the 17th FIRST Conference (FIRST 2005)*, 2005.

BitMiner: Bits Mining in Internet Traffic Classification

Zhenlong Yuan[*‡], Yibo Xue[†‡] and Mihaela van der Schaar[‖]
[*]Department of Automation, Tsinghua University, Beijing, China
[‖]Department of Electrical Engineering, UCLA, Los Angeles, CA, USA
[†]Tsinghua National Lab for Information Science and Technology, Beijing, China
[‡]Research Institute of Information Technology, Tsinghua University, Beijing, China
yuanzl11@mails.tsinghua.edu.cn, yiboxue@tsinghua.edu.cn, mihaela@ee.ucla.edu

ABSTRACT

Traditionally, signatures used for traffic classification are constructed at the byte-level. However, as more and more data-transfer formats of network protocols and applications are encoded at the bit-level, byte-level signatures are losing their effectiveness in traffic classification. In this poster, we creatively construct bit-level signatures by associating the bit-values with their bit-positions in each traffic flow. Furthermore, we present BitMiner, an automated traffic mining tool that can mine application signatures at the most fine-grained bit-level granularity. Our preliminary test on popular peer-to-peer (P2P) applications, e.g. *Skype*, *Google Hangouts*, *PPTV*, *eMule*, *Xunlei* and *QQDownload*, reveals that although they all have no byte-level signatures, there are significant bit-level signatures hidden in their traffic.

CCS Concepts

•**Networks** → **Network management;**

Keywords

Traffic classification, bit-level signatures, bits mining

1. INTRODUCTION

Signature based traffic classification has been playing an important role in a broad range of network operations and security management, such as quality-of-service control and intrusion detection. However, due to the increasing number of network applications and their frequent updates, it is becoming more challenging to keep track of the signatures. To address this challenge, a number of existing solutions have focused on automatically extracting signatures at the byte-level [4, 5], which first divide packet payloads into groups of consecutive bytes and then analyze to get the possible signatures. However, those solutions have two major limitations. Firstly, they are unable to discover signatures at the more fine-grained bit-level granularity. Note that previous work [1, 2] have revealed that bit-level characteristics (group of 4 bits, less than 1 byte) are of great importance in identifying a few P2P applications. Secondly, they confine signatures to groups of consecutive bytes and thus are hard to discover the signatures that consist of inconsecutive bytes (e.g. 1 byte) in packet payloads. In this poster, we propose the novel bit-level signatures, and present an automated traffic mining tool (BitMiner) that can mine signatures at the most fine-grained bit-level granularity.

SIGCOMM '15 August 17-21, 2015, London, United Kingdom

ACM ISBN 978-1-4503-3542-3/15/08.
DOI: http://dx.doi.org/10.1145/2785956.2789997

2. BITMINER

In this poster, we have two observations. The first is that an application signature should be robust enough to support per-flow identification due to the prevalence of asymmetric routing. For this reason, a favorable application signature should be one of the most frequent patterns in captured traffic after running an application for plenty of times. Therefore, our goal can turn into mining the most frequent patterns[1] in the application traffic. The second is that the bit-value of a bit-position in a flow often determines the bit-values of other bit-positions in this flow. Therefore, we are motivated to associate all the bit-values with their bit-positions in a flow for frequent pattern mining.

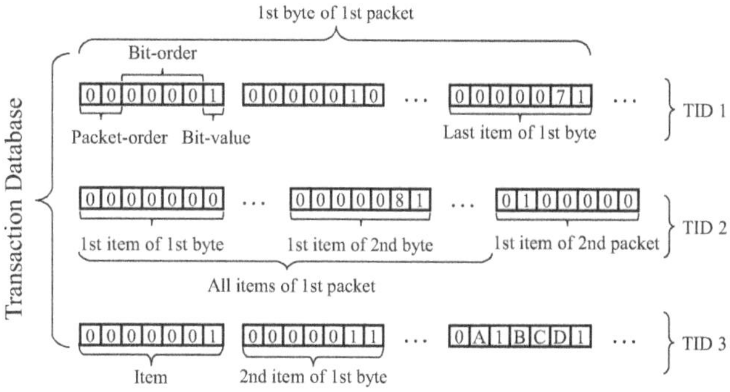

Figure 1: Format Traffic Flows to Transactions

As shown in Figure 1, we can take a bit-value with its position in a flow as an *item* and take all the bit-values with their individual positions in this flow as a *transaction*. Notice that we use only two hexadecimal characters to represent an *item*'s packet-order in a flow because application signatures are generally required to achieve early identification in practical use and the first 256 (0x00~0xFF) packets of a flow are sufficient enough. Similarly, we use four hexadecimal characters to represent one *item*'s bit-order in a

[1]From here, we start using some *terms* in *Data Mining*.

Applications	**Application Signatures**	**Support** (Recall)
Skype	**^(002_0x02)+(002_0_0 & 002_4_1 & 002_5_1 & 002_6_0 & 002_7_1)*$**	100.00%
Xunlei (Thunder)	**^(001_0_0 & 003_0_0 & 003_1_1 & 003_2_0)*$**	100.00%
eMule	**^(000_0_0 & 000_4_0 & 001_0_0 & 001_4_0 & 000_6_0 & 001_1_0 & 001_5_0) | (000_0_0 & 000_4_0 & 001_0_0 & 001_4_0 & 000_6_1 & 001_1_1 & 001_5_1)*$**	100.00%
Google Hangouts	**^(000_0_1 & 000_1_0 & 001_1_1 & 001_3_0)*$**	100.00%
PPTV (PPLive)	**^(007_0_0 & 007_1_0 & 007_2_0 & 007_3_0 & 008_0x00 & 009_0_0 & 009_1_0 & 009_2_0 & 009_3_0 & 009_6_0 & 00A_0_0 & 00A_1_0 & 00A_2_0 & 00A_3_0)*$**	100.00%
QQDownload	**^(000_1_1 & 000_2_1 & 000_5_1 & 000_7_0 & 001_0_0 & 001_1_0 & 002_0_0 & 002_1_0 & 002_7_0 & 003_0_0 & 004_0_0 & 005_0_0 & 007_5_0 & 009_0_0 & 00A_1_0)*$**	100.00%

Table 1: The Generated Bit-level Signatures

packet payload because the MTU of an IP packet over Ethernet networks is 1500-byte where 1 byte has 8 bit-orders.

Transaction Database		
TID	**Original Items**	**Sorted Items**
01	I4, I5, I7, I8	I7, I4, I5, I8
02	I4, I6, I7, I9	I7, I4, I9, I6
03	I1, I2, I3, I5	I1, I2, I3, I5
04	I1, I2, I3, I7	I7, I1, I2, I3
05	I1, I2, I3, I5, I9	I1, I2, I3, I5, I9
06	I4, I5, I7, I8	I7, I4, I5, I8
07	I1, I2, I3, I9	I1, I2, I3, I9
08	I4, I6, I7, I9	I7, I4, I9, I6
09	I1, I2, I3, I6	I1, I2, I3, I6
10	I4, I5, I7, I8	I7, I4, I5, I8

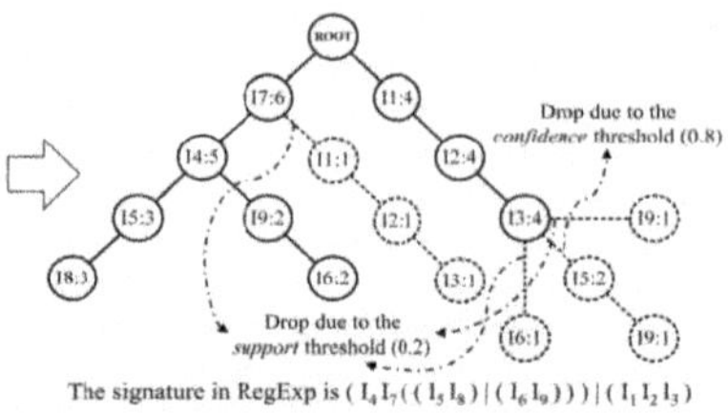

Figure 2: An Example of How *BitMiner* Works

BitMiner consists of two parts: *Bit-table* and *Miner-tree*. Figure 2 shows an example of how BitMiner works. *Bit-table* is a hash table used for hashing and storing all the *items* read from a *transaction database*. In this process, *Bit-table* will read the transaction database twice. For the first time, *Bit-table* will count the *support* of every *item*. For the second time, *Bit-table* will remove the items whose *support* is below the initially set *support threshold* and sort the remaining *items* in every *transaction* by their *supports* (maximum to minimum). After that, all the sorted *transactions* will be entered into *Miner-tree* as a new *transaction database*.

Miner-tree is a prefix tree of the new *transactions*, which takes idea from the FP-tree [3] but is different. Note that there are probably multiple tasks running within an application and thus the signature could be a regular expression. Considering a *transaction* (flow) can only belong to one of the tasks, all the *transactions* are divided into multiple clusters to represent different tasks. Since the *items* in each *transaction* have been sorted by their *supports*, it is extremely fast to construct the *Miner-tree*.

After constructing the *Miner-tree*, there will be a pruning process controlled by two thresholds: *minimum support* and *minimum confidence*. Particularly, the *support* (defined as the proportion of *transactions* in a node from the whole *transaction database*) will be checked for every single node. Moreover, the *confidence* (defined as the proportion of *transactions* in all the child-nodes of a node from the node itself) will be checked for every parent node. In this way, it can be determined whether a branch should be removed or a parent node should stop splitting. Finally, the branches of the pruned *Miner-tree* are the target signature.

3. EVALUATION

BitMiner has been tested on the UDP traffic of six popular applications. As shown in Table 1, every signature is generated by BitMiner within a few seconds. The "(p)" represents a pattern (p) matching within one packet's payload, the "$^\wedge(p)$" represents this matched packet is the first packet of a flow, the "$(p)\$$" represents this matched packet is the last packet of a flow, the "$(p)+$" represents this matched packet appears one or more times in succession within a flow, the "$(p)*$" represents this matched packet appears zero or more times in succession within a flow, the "`002_0x02`" represents the **`third`** byte value of a packet's payload is `0x02`, the "`002_4_1`" represents the **`fifth`** bit value of the **`third`** byte is `1`, the "$p\&p$" represents two patterns matching with one packet's payload simultaneously and the "$(p)|(p)$" represents either one matched packet appears within a flow. For instance, the **`third`** byte values of the first one or more packets of a Skype flow are always `0x02` while **`five`** bit values of the **`third`** bytes of all the other packets are fixed. Specially, we also examine the other bits adjacent to the mined ones, such as the '*second, third* and *fourth*' bits of the **`third`** bytes of Skype flows and the '*fourth, fifth, sixth, seventh* and *eighth*' bits of the **`fourth`** bytes of Thunder flows. The results show that those bit-values are completely random (i.e. uniformly distributed). Also as shown in Table 1, the *support* represents the proportion of flows matched with the mined signature, which is equivalent to the *recall* in traffic classification. In addition, a longer signature generally means a better *precision*. For example, if we check the first 10 packets of a Thunder flow, the signature used for matching is totally 40 bits long, which may be robust enough to get a high precision in real-world situations.

4. ACKNOWLEDGEMENT

This work was supported by the National Key Technology R&D Program of China under Grant No.2012BAH46B04.

5. REFERENCES

[1] D. Bonfiglio, M. Mellia, M. Meo, D. Rossi, and P. Tofanelli. Revealing skype traffic: when randomness plays with you. In *ACM SIGCOMM*, 2007.

[2] A. Finamore, M. Mellia, M. Meo, and D. Rossi. Kiss: stochastic packet inspection classifier for udp traffic. *IEEE/ACM Transactions on Networking*, 2010.

[3] J. Han, J. Pei, and Y. Yin. Mining frequent patterns without candidate generation. In *ACM SIGMOD*, 2000.

[4] J. Ma, K. Levchenko, C. Kreibich, S. Savage, and G. M. Voelker. Unexpected means of protocol inference. In *ACM SIGCOMM IMC*, 2006.

[5] Z. Zhang, Z. Zhang, P. P. Lee, Y. Liu, and G. Xie. Proword: an unsupervised approach to protocol feature word extraction. In *IEEE INFOCOM*, 2014.

Coarse-grained Scheduling with Software-Defined Networking Switches

Myriana Rifai
University Nice Sophia Antipolis, France
mrifai@i3s.unice.fr

Dino Lopez-Pacheco
University Nice Sophia Antipolis, France
dino.lopez@unice.fr

Guillaume Urvoy-Keller
University Nice Sophia Antipolis, France
urvoy@i3s.unice.fr

ABSTRACT

Software-Defined Networking (SDN) enables consolidation of the control plane of a set of network equipments with a fine-grained control of traffic flows inside the network. In this work, we demonstrate that some coarse-grained scheduling mechanisms can be easily offered by SDN switches without requiring any unsupported operation in OpenFlow. We leverage the feedback loop - flow statistics - exposed by SDN switches to the controller, combined with priority queuing mechanisms, usually available in typical switches on their output ports. We illustrate our approach through experimentations with an OpenvSwitch SDN switch controlled by a Beacon controller.

Categories and Subject Descriptors

C.2.3 [**Computer-Communication Networks**]: Network Operations

Keywords

Software-Defined Networking, Size-Based Scheduling

1. INTRODUCTION

Software-Defined Networking (SDN) offers a centralized control of the traffic flowing inside a network. The flexibility of the flow definition enables implementation of advanced functions like virtual networks or firewalls. In contrast, the data plane remains opaque and cannot be directly influenced by the controller. Few works have addressed the extension of SDN to the data-plane with scheduling in mind. A noticeable exception is [6] where the authors first advocate the need to use different scheduling or buffer management solutions in different scenarios as there is no one-fit-all solution.

Our objective in this work is to demonstrate that despite the limited toolbox offered by SDN to directly manipulate the data plane, one can however implement some form of coarse grained scheduling with legacy SDN equipments. Our focus is on size-based scheduling [1, 5], where priority is given to flows in their early stage. This approach is valuable in the current Internet and data centers networks where (i) the bulk of traffic is carried by TCP and (ii) consists of a majority of short flows. Our approach takes advantage of the feedback loop offered in SDN where a switch exposes to the controller per rule statistics. The latter enables us to identify long flows and separate them from short flows using multiple queues per port that serve to implement 802.1p QoS mechanisms. Our objective is to minimize flow completion of the majority of flows.

Related work includes [7] where the authors divert some flows on longer rarely used paths to decrease completion time. In [2], the authors rely on the same capacity of (non SDN) commodity switches to offer several queues with a tagging process performed at the end hosts, complemented with ECN in the network. The authors in [4] propose to improve the performance of TCP in SDN networks, albeit at the cost of modifying the end-hosts protocol stack.

In contrast, we investigate a purely network centric approach, with no modification of the end-hosts for SDN networks.

We demonstrate the feasibility of building an SDN based size-based scheduler using OpenvSwitch with Beacon controller. We further propose a scalable version of our scheduler to avoid continuous monitoring of each active flow by the switch and the controller.

SIGCOMM '15 August 17-21, 2015, London, United Kingdom

ACM ISBN 978-1-4503-3542-3/15/08.

DOI: http://dx.doi.org/10.1145/2785956.2790004

2. DESIGN

We have devised two size-based schedulers, a state-full and a scalable scheduler, and implemented them as applications on top of a Beacon controller. Both solutions require two queues per port (802.1p mandates 8 queues per port) and assume that those queues are managed with a strict priority scheduler where the high priority queue is served as long as it has packets - the other queue is served when the first one is empty. We next detail the two schedulers:

State-full scheduler: The switch monitors all ongoing flows and the controller queries every $T_{\text{monitor}} = 10ms$ flow statistics. Upon arrival of a new flow, the controller installs a new rule for this flow and assigns it the high priority queue of the corresponding port. If a flow has exceeded $T_{\text{threshold\_pkts}} = 100$ packets, then the controller modifies the queue used by this flow and assigns it the lower priority queue.

Scalable scheduler: Continuous monitoring of each active flow is resource consuming, and installing per-flow rules could quickly overload the forwarding table of SDN devices. Also, when the load on the port is low, say lower than 50%, all schedulers typically offer the same performance as queues do not build up. To address these concerns, we propose a second scheduler where the controller initially sets up one default rule for a set of flows. Then, if the throughput for that rule exceeds a threshold $T_{\text{threshold\_utilization}} = 0.1 \times \text{LinkCapacity}$, then the scheduler zooms in the traffic to separate large flows from short flows. To zoom in traffic, the scheduler uninstalls the forwarding rule triggering the mechanism and installs per flow rules on traffic demand. Every $T_{\text{monitor}} = 10ms$ the scheduler will check the flow size, if it is more than $T_{\text{threshold\_pkts}} = 100$ packets it will modify the queue used to the lower priority one. After a few T_{monitor} cycles, large flows are isolated and the grouped forwarding rule is reinstalled with a high priority.

3. PRELIMINARY RESULTS

To illustrate our approach, we consider the experimental set-up described in Figure 1. We have ten clients and one server that acts as a sink for traffic and an OpenvSwitch (OVS) switch connected to a Beacon controller. The traffic workload is generated using impt [1] and consists of bulk TCP transfers. The distribution of flow size follows a bounded Zipf distribution with a flow size between 15 KB (10 packets) and 10 MB. The average flow size is around 100 packets, in line with typical average flow size in the Internet. The Zipf distribution is the discrete equivalent of a Pareto distribution, which is known as a reasonable model of Internet and also data center flow size [3]. The load is controlled by tuning the flow inter-arrival time, which follows a Poisson process.

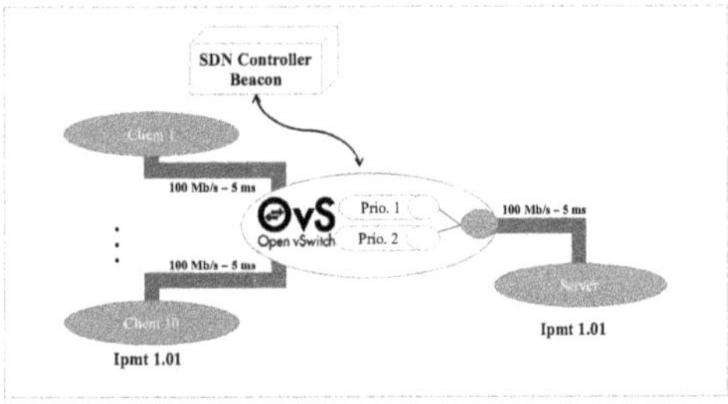

Figure 1: Experimental set-up

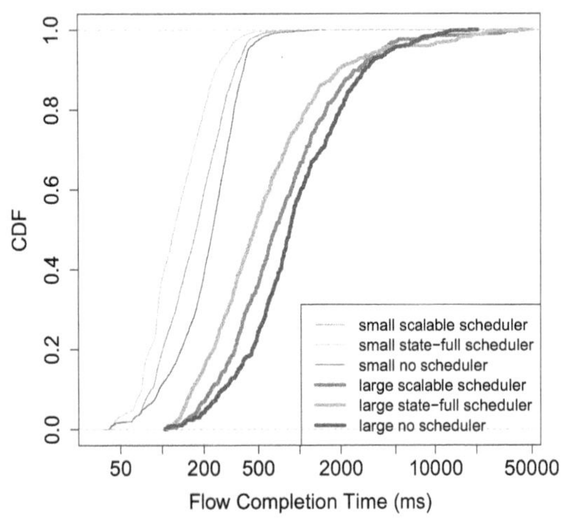

Figure 2: Flow completion time CDF for long and short flows

We present in Figure 2 results obtained out of 10 experiments for a load of about 90%. We distinguish between small flows and large flows, where small flows are defined as flows smaller than the 90-th quantile of the flow size distribution. The 90-th quantile corresponds to about 95 packets (close to $T_{\text{threshold\_pkts}}$). It is important to note that small flows represent about 15% of the load.

We can observe from Figure 2 that the state-full scheduler offers the best response time for small flows and for the majority of large flows as their 100 first packets will take advantage of the scheduling mechanism. Only a minority of the largest flows suffer in the state-full scheduler. As for the scalable scheduler, it offers intermediate results between the state-full scheduler and the absence of scheduler as it needs 10 additional ms ($= T_{\text{monitor}}$) to detect large flows. As we cannot simultaneously obtain better response times for all flows, one can observe the longer tails of response times for the two schedulers as compared to the case with no scheduler.

Though preliminary, those results are encouraging and clearly highlight the validity of our approach.

4. FUTURE WORK

In terms of future direction, we intend to develop an autonomic version of the scheduler that would adjust its parameters dynamically. For instance, $T_{\text{threshold\_pkts}}$ could be set as a quantile of the flow size distribution. Estimating the tail of a highly varying distribution is complex; however, we are interested in separating large flows from short flows only, which does not require a high precision on the computation of quantiles of the distribution. More interestingly, variations in the input distribution or load are easily exposed through the statistics offered by SDN and we expect to be able to take advantage of this feature to build a fully adaptable scheduler.

We also would like to explore the use of size-based scheduling in the data center, where it could be deployed at any switch. Using size-based scheduling at several bottleneck links has never been explored so far, to the best or our knowledge.

Last but not least, SDN enables to enlarge our vision of scheduling as the controller enables us to mix routing and scheduling. This could be useful for specific applications such as VM migration, a crucial operation in modern data centers.

5. REFERENCES

[1] K. Avrachenkov, U. Ayesta, P. Brown, and E. Nyberg. Differentiation between short and long TCP flows: Predictability of the response time. In *Proceedings of IEEE INFOCOM 2004*, 2004.

[2] W. Bai, K. Chen, H. Wang, L. Chen, D. Han, and C. Tian. Information-agnostic flow scheduling for commodity data centers. In *12th USENIX Symposium on Networked Systems Design and Implementation (NSDI 15)*, pages 455–468, Oakland, CA, May 2015. USENIX Association.

[3] T. Benson, A. Anand, A. Akella, and M. Zhang. Understanding data center traffic characteristics. *Computer Communication Review*, 40(1), 2010.

[4] M. Ghobadi, S. H. Yeganeh, and Y. Ganjali. Rethinking end-to-end congestion control in software-defined networks. In *Proceedings of HotNets-XI*, 2012.

[5] I. A. Rai, E. W. Biersack, and G. Urvoy-Keller. Size-based scheduling to improve the performance of short TCP flows. *IEEE Network*, 19(1), 2005.

[6] A. Sivaraman, K. Winstein, S. Subramanian, and H. Balakrishnan. No silver bullet: Extending sdn to the data plane. In *Proceedings of HotNets-XII*, 2013.

[7] F. P. Tso, G. Hamilton, R. Weber, C. S. Perkins, and D. P. Pezaros. Longer is better: Exploiting path diversity in data center networks. In *Proceedings of IEEE ICDCS '13*, 2013.

[1] http://ipmt.forge.imag.fr/

FlyCast: Free-Space Optics Accelerating Multicast Communications in Physical Layer

Jinzhen Bao,Dezun Dong,Baokang Zhao,Zhang Luo,Chunqing Wu,Zhenghu Gong
College of Computer
National University of Defense Technology
Changsha, Hunan,China
{baojinzhen, dong, bkzhao, jiftluo, wuchunqing, gong}@nudt.edu.cn

ABSTRACT

In this paper, we propose FlyCast, an architecture using the physical layer of free-space optics (FSO) to accelerate multicast communication. FlyCast leverages off-the-shelf devices (e.g. switchable mirror, beam splitter) to physically split the FSO beam to multi receivers on demand, which enables to build dynamical multicast trees in physical layer and accelerates multicast communications. We demonstrate the feasibility of FlyCast through our theoretical analysis and the proof-of-concept prototype.

CCS Concepts

•Networks → Hybrid networks; Data center networks;

Keywords

Data Center Network; Free Space Optics; Multicast

1. INTRODUCTION

One-to-many group communication is common in modern data centers running cloud and web-based applications, or high performance computing (HPC) applications. Those examples of cloud computing applications include publish-subscribe services, Hadoop using data replication for higher availability, network virtualization installing OS and application images on a group of virtual machines. High performance and scientific computing applications, often using MPI group communication extensively, have been examined and deployed in existing cloud computing infrastructures.

Multicast, an efficient mechanism for group communications, benefits the network by reducing bandwidth overhead and latency between group members, alleviating in hotspot or network congestion due to huge volume and high fan-out traffics. Traditional multicast solutions in cloud and HPC data center mainly is optimized and implemented on top of network, transport or upper layers [1], which suffer from suboptimal multicast trees and high complexity. Recently, hybrid network architecture that combines wireless (e.g. 60GHz, free-space optics) or optical space switches (OSS) to traditional wired electrical switches has been proposed to dynamically adapt to traffic demand .The physical layer broadcast media of wireless and optics have the nature of one-to-many communication, which are very suitable for group traffic pattern. Yu, et. al., utilizes the narrow-beam of 60GHz to construct a wired and wireless mixed multicast tree [4]. Xia, et. al., uses passive power splitters and OSS to set up a dynamical multicast tree, and the data is optically replicated from source to destinations [3].

Free-Space Optics (FSO) is an emerging technology with the advantage of free wiring and low latency in constructing flexible data center network [2]. Compared with 60GHz, it has the benefits of high bandwidth and low interference. Additionaly, with the switchable mirror (SM), it's more flexible and expandable than OSS. To the best of our knowledge, no existing equivalent work leverages the physical layer of FSO to accelerate multicast communication. In this paper, we propose an architecture named FlyCast, which utilizes commercial off-the-shelf devices (e.g. SM, beam splitter) to split the FSO beam to multi receivers on demand.

SIGCOMM '15 August 17-21, 2015, London, United Kingdom

ACM ISBN 978-1-4503-3542-3/15/08.

DOI: http://dx.doi.org/10.1145/2785956.2790002

2. THE ARCHITECTURE OF FLYCAST

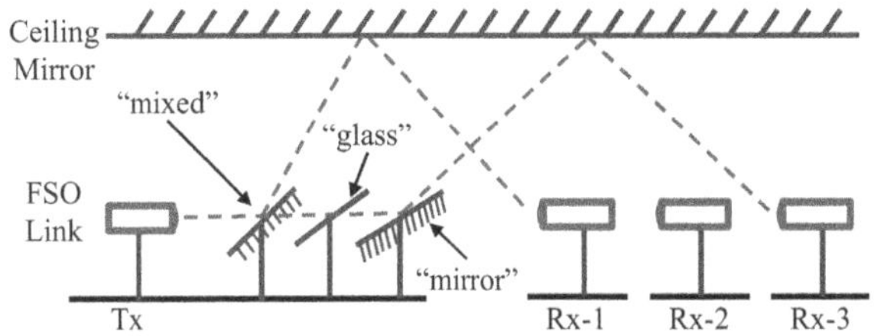

Figure 1: The Architecture of FlyCast

Our work is inspired by the Firefly, which exploits SMs to construct a flexible and fully FSO interconnected network [2]. Each FSO device is equipped with multiple SMs. The SMs are made up of a special liquid crystal material which can be electrically controlled to rapidly switch between pure-reflection (mirror), half-reflection (mixed) and total transparent (glass) states. Firefly dynamically establishes the link by switching one of the SMs to mirror state, while leaving the rest in glass state. The Firefly only supports one-to-one communication. However, FlyCast makes use of the mixed state of SMs to optically duplicate data to multiple receivers, as shown in Fig. 1. The glass state (e.g. 2nd SM) means that the related terminal does not receive the data, meanwhile there exist receivers at behind. On the contrary, the SM with mirror state (e.g. 3rd SM) steers all the received beam to the related receiver. When both the related terminal and followed terminals can receive data, the SM leaves in mixed state (e.g. 1st SM). Hence, the source can simultaneously send data to Rx-1 and Rx-3 at line-rate.

Next, we will use a motivating example to show what kind benefits of FlyCast delivers, as shown in Fig.2. We assume that every Top-of-Rack (ToR) switch has two ports and each port is equipped with two SMs (links with same color mean that the SMs share the common FSO), and the dynamical topology is shown as Fig. 2(a). The runtime topology can be changed between Fig. 2 (b) and (c) by the controller. When ToR A sends the same data to ToR E and C, no matter what routing paths are used or how to change the states of SMs according to Firefly, it needs at least three hops to complete the multicast communication. In this scenario, using the physical layer of FSO, ToR A can simultaneously send data to C and E via one hop, as shown in Fig. 2(d) and (e).

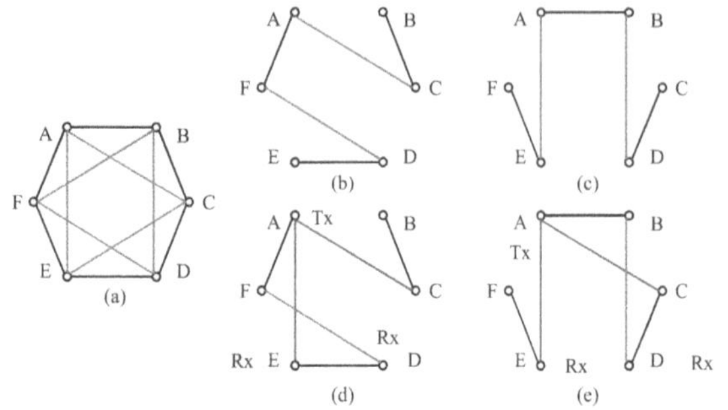

Figure 2: An Example of the Advantage of FlyCast

Traditional distributed multicast routing protocols are difficult to realize in the asymmetric network. The FlyCast performs routing protocol in the control plane of software-defined networking (SDN) architecture. Moreover, the controller manages the joining and leaving of group members through interacting with the applications, and the SDN switches should support multicast rules. Given the group members, network controller runs the control algorithm to compute network topology and adjust the states of SMs. The problem of computing network topology turns into building a directed Steiner tree with additional constraints. Though it is a NP-hard problem, there exist solutions based on approximation algorithms. However, edges sharing the same port are conflicted, we have to modify the existing approaches to construct multicast trees. For the direct edge <a, b> chosen as the subset of the multicast tree, we will prune the other edges connected to b except <b, a>, thus guaranteeing the in-degree of successors at most 1.

3. THE FEASIBILITY OF FLYCAST

The signal of FSO will be degraded when passing through a beam splitter. Let l denote the transmittance (from 0.5 to 0.9) and let S/N denote the signal-noise ratio of the initial FSO. From Eq. 1 we can find out that the degradation of FSO signal is determined by the transmittance.

$$10\lg(l * S/N) = 10\lg(S/N) + 10\lg(l) \quad (1)$$

Only the power of last received signal R_k and R_{k+1} which passes through k beam splitters are greater than the transceivers' receiver sensitivity, all data can be recovered correctly.

$$Max : k, subjectto :$$

$$R_k, R_{k+1} > B \quad (2)$$

$$R_{k+1} = A - n * k \quad (3)$$

$$R_k = A - n * (k-1) - m \quad (4)$$

$$n = -10\lg(l) \quad (5)$$

$$m = -10\lg(1-l) \quad (6)$$

The calculation process is as follows: Let A denote the output power of the transceiver and B denote the receiver sensitivity. Eq. 2 to Eq. 4 guarantee that the reflected and passed signal are stronger than the receiver sensitivity. The degradations of signal under different transmittances are described in Eq. 5 and Eq. 6. The goal is to maximize the number of beam splitters.

The transceiver has a maximum output power of 4dBm and a receiver sensitivity of -15dBm. Fig. 3 illustrates the relationship between the transmittances and number of beam splitters. Note that the initial FSO can be split up to 20 times with the transmittance of 0.9. Though the transmittance of SM in mixed state is about 0.5, the SM can be replaced with continuous switchable glass or MEMS-based mirrors and beam splitters with different transmittances.

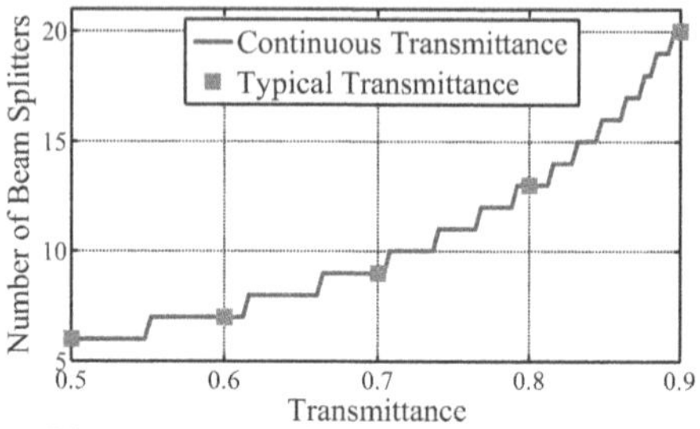

Figure 3: The Number of Beam Splitters under Different Transmittances

Furthermore, we develop a proof-of-concept prototype to validate the result of above theoretical analysis, as shown in Fig. 4. We test the signal loss from one to three beam splitters with the transmittance of 0.5. Considering the misalignment of collimator and the number of beam splitters, the signal loss is consistent with the theoretical value (3dBm), as shown in Tab. 1.

Figure 4: The Prototype of FlyCast

Num	Loss
1	3.22
2	2.76
3	3.17

Table 1: Signal Loss

4. ACKNOWLEDGMENTS

The authors thank Junjie Wu and Huiquan Wang for their support of FSO devices, and the reviewers for their feedback. This work is supported by NSFC grant No.61202488 and No.61272482.

5. REFERENCES

[1] M. Chowdhury, M. Zaharia, J. Ma, M. I. Jordan, and I. Stoica. Managing data transfers in computer clusters with orchestra. *ACM SIGCOMM Computer Communication Review*, 41(4):98–109, 2011.

[2] N. Hamedazimi, Z. Qazi, H. Gupta, V. Sekar, S. R. Das, J. P. Longtin, H. Shah, and A. Tanwer. Firefly: a reconfigurable wireless data center fabric using free-space optics. In *Proceedings of the 2014 ACM conference on SIGCOMM*, pages 319–330. ACM, 2014.

[3] Y. Xia, T. E. Ng, and X. S. Sun. Blast: Accelerating high-performance data analytics applications by optical multicast. 2015.

[4] Y.-J. Yu, C.-C. Chuang, H.-P. Lin, and A.-C. Pang. Efficient multicast delivery for wireless data center networks. In *Local Computer Networks (LCN), 2013 IEEE 38th Conference on*, pages 228–235. IEEE, 2013.

Analysis of Game Bot's Behavioral Characteristics in Social Interaction Networks of MMORPG

Seong Hoon Jeong
Korea University
Seoul, Korea
seonghoon@korea.ac.kr

Ah Reum Kang
Korea University
Seoul, Korea
armk@korea.ac.kr

Huy Kang Kim
Korea University
Seoul, Korea
cenda@korea.ac.kr

ABSTRACT

MMORPG (Massively Multiplayer Online Role-Playing Game) is one of the best platforms to observe human's behaviors. In collaboration with a leading online game company, NCSoft, we can observe all behaviors in a large-scale of commercialized MMORPG. Especially, we analyzed the behavioral differences between game bots and human users. We categorized the five groups, Bot-Bot, Bot-All, Human-Human, Human-All and All-All, and we observe the characteristics of six social interaction networks for each group. As a result, we found that there are significant differences in social behaviors between game bots and human.

CCS Concepts

•Information systems → Massively multiplayer online games;

Keywords

Social network analysis, Game bot, Massively multiplayer online game

1. INTRODUCTION

MMORPG is a huge social network with 15 million subscribers. The interactions in MMORPGs are not too different from how the real-world works. They can interact with other users by doing various actions such as party-play, player-to-player combat, item trading, and chatting in the game. These activities form multi-relational social interaction networks in the game.

However, not all of these activities are taken by human players. In popular MMORPGs, there exist game bots that are automated AI programs executing repetitive tasks. [1] The game bots interfere the gameplay of another human user. Game bots also make honest users feel deprived and annoying. Moreover, they continuously produce in-game items and money to gain illegal benefits, so they raise economic problems. We analyze the social network to present aspects of the game bots in Aion[1], which is the world's third most popular online game serviced by NCSoft. We analyzed the anonymized in-game log data that contained all of the interactions between users for 88 days (from April 9th of 2010 to July 5th of 2010). In order to distinguish the game bot group from the human user group, we use the banned account list provided by NCSoft as a ground-truth. During our observational period, about 96,806 characters played the game, and 14,378 characters were suspected of using game bots.

To find the characteristics of game bot and human user's behaviors, we categorize all in-game interactions as the six distinct interaction networks based on our previous work. [2] Each social interaction record contains a sender and a receiver: (1) Friend: S adds R to S's friend list. (2) Whisper: S sends a private message to R. (3) Party: S joins R's party. (4) Trade: S trades items or game money with R. (5) Mail: S sends a mail to R. (6) Shop: S buys an item from R's shop.

We define five groups to outline the differences between game bots and human users' interactions: (i) Bot-All: A game bot sends an event to anyone, (ii) Bot-Bot: A game bot sends an event to another game bot, (iii) Human-All: A human user sends an event to anyone, (iv) Human-Human: A human user sends an event to another human user, (v) All-All: Anyone sends an event to anyone.

2. RESULTS

Table 1 shows the basic network characteristics for each social interaction network and group. We observed the difference between human users and game bots. First, the Bot-Bot group only has social interactions in Party, Friendship, Trade and Whisper networks while the Human-Human group has social interactions in all networks. Second, the Bot-Bot group has more transactions for trading per party-play than the Human-Human group. The game bot group seems to exchange items frequently, but rarely buys an item via private shops. Third, the number of human users is 5.7 times higher than that of game bots. Nevertheless, the Bot-Bot group sent a mail more than the Human-Human group as shown in Table 1. Fig. 1 indicates the cumulative degree distribution of the in-degrees and the out-degrees in Mail network. The 90% of game bots send one mail and receive four mails, while the 90% of human users send one mail and receive seven mails. We identified that nine game bots respectively sent about 10,000 mails that have no attachment.

Fig. 2 shows the reciprocity of edges in each interaction network. The reciprocity is the fraction of reciprocal node

[1]AION Online, http://www.aiononline.com

SIGCOMM '15 August 17-21, 2015, London, United Kingdom

ACM ISBN 978-1-4503-3542-3/15/08.

DOI: http://dx.doi.org/10.1145/2785956.2790005

Table 1: **Summary of the basic network characteristics.**

	Party		Friendship		Trade		Whisper		Mail		Shop	
	#nodes	#edges	#nodes	#edges	#nodes	#edges	#nodes	#edges	#nodes	#edges	#nodes	#edges
Bot-All	21,511	108,575	12,889	22,906	19,710	42,094	11,970	36,362	42,553	103,442	2	1
Bot-Bot	4,063	14,223	1,717	3,803	7,120	19,137	1,919	5,328	0	0	2	1
H.-All	44,460	962,287	30,266	194,372	41,160	189,433	21,373	290,837	38,934	92,833	7,410	19,283
H.-H.	40,345	864,160	26,829	175,332	35,957	168,047	17,813	252,775	38,934	92,833	6,160	12,656
All-All	46,896	1,070,862	30,917	217,278	46,560	231,527	21,771	327,199	56,663	196,275	7,411	19,284

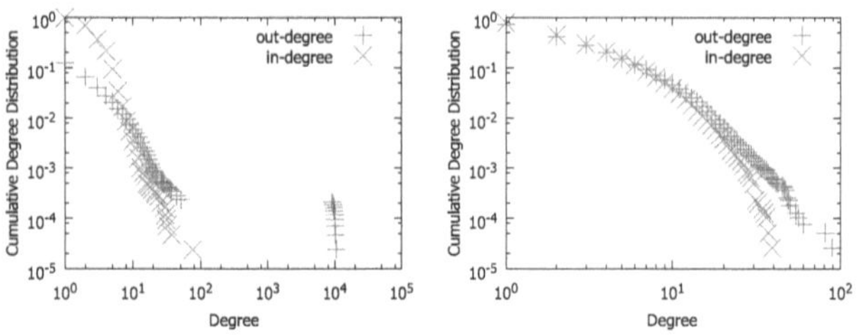

Figure 1: The in- and out-degree distribution of the Bot-All group (left) and the Human-All group (right) in Mail network.

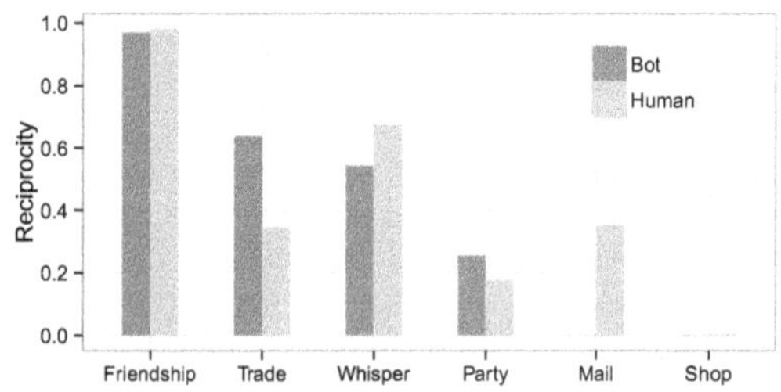

Figure 2: The reciprocity of edges in each interaction network.

pairs out of all connected node pairs. We found that Friendship, Trade, Whisper, and Party networks have the reciprocal property in both the Bot-Bot group and the Human-Human group. Interestingly, the Bot-Bot group is more reciprocal in Trade and Party networks. This fact implies that the main activities of game bots are party-play and trading items. We also confirmed that game bots have the friendship with each other. It seems that users in the same gold-farming group add game bots to their friend list for ease of management. In Whisper network, game bots have reciprocal property. This result explains that game bots share their coordinates with each other. Moreover, game bots have no reciprocal property in Mail network. There are just some game bots that send mails a lot (e.g. item selling spam).

Fig. 3 shows the results for the link overlaps for network pairs. In our study, the similarity about pairwise network overlaps is obtained using Jaccard coefficient. [3] The Bot-Bot group has the link overlaps in six pairwise networks, Party-Friendship, Party-Trade, Party-Whisper, Friendship-Trade, Friendship-Whisper, and Trade-Whisper networks. On the other hand, the Human-Human group has the link overlaps with the other social interactions in all pairwise networks except Shop network. It represents that game bots execute repetitive tasks associated with gold-farming and real-money trading.

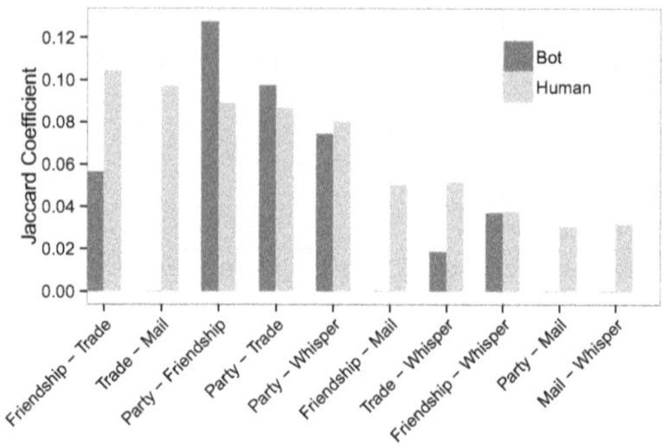

Figure 3: The Jaccard similarity coefficient: pairwise network overlaps indicating the similarity between interactions.

We reported the differences between game bots and human users in the six social interaction networks. Because of the gold-farming and real-money trading, game bots are more active in Friendship, Trade, and Party networks than human users. Besides game bots have no interactions in Mail and Shop network.

In our future study, we will present the triad network motif that shows the interactions visually among three characters in the six distinct networks. Using the Pearson correlation in the pairwise networks, we will investigate that whether a user trades items with many people when the user has a long buddy list or joins the party-play with various users. We believe that this would provide new insight to identify the behavioral pattern of game bots and human users. Finally, we expect to apply the game bot detection through not only the behavior analysis but also the social network analysis.

3. ACKNOWLEDGEMENT

This research was supported by Basic Science Research Program through the National Research Foundation of Korea (NRF) funded by the Ministry of Science, ICT & Future Planning (2014R1A1A1006228).

4. REFERENCES

[1] A. Kang, J. Woo, J. Park, H. Kim. Online Game Bot Detection based on party-play log analysis. *Computers & Mathematics with Application*, 65(9), 2013.

[2] S. Son, A. Kang, H. Kim, T. Kwon, J. Park, H. Kim. Analysis of Context Dependence in Social Interaction Networks of a Massively Multiplayer Online Role-Playing Game. *PLoS ONE*, 7(4), 2012.

[3] J. Onnela, J. Samamaki, J. Hyvonen, G. Szabo, M. Menezes, K. Kaski, A. Barabasi, and J. Kertesz. Analysis of a Large-scale Weighted Network of One-to-one Human Communication. *New Journal of Physics*, 9(6), 2007.

Could End System Caching and Cooperation Replace In-Network Caching in CCN?

Haibo Wu
wuhaibo@cstnet.cn

Jun Li[+]
lijun@cnic.cn

Jiang Zhi
zhijiang@cstnet.cn

Computer Network Information Center, Chinese Academy of Sciences, Beijing, China, 100190

ABSTRACT

CCN has been witnessed as a promising future Internet architecture. In-network caching has been paid much attention, but there is still no consensus on its usage, due to its non-negligible costs. Meanwhile, massive storage and bandwidth resources of end systems still remain underutilized. To this end, we present an **E**nd **S**ystem **C**aching and **C**ooperation scheme in CCN, called ESCC to realize content distribution of CCN, without using costly in-network caching. ESCC enables fast content distribution through clients caching and sharing contents with each other. Experiments show that ESCC can achieve better performance than the universal caching. It is also quite simple, efficient, robust and has low overhead. ESCC could be a candidate substitute for the costly and unnecessary universal caching.

Categories & Subject Descriptors: C.2.1 [Computer-Communication Networks]: Network Architecture and Design

Keywords: CCN, end system, caching, cooperation

1. INTRODUCTION

CCN (Content Centric Networking) [1] has been proposed as a promising alternative to current host-to-host communication paradigm. In-network caching is regarded as its key feature. Overall in-network routers equipped with caches potentially store named contents, which can be used for subsequent requests. In-network caching can reduce bandwidth consumption and content retrieval time by making contents closer to requesters. However, these benefits come at a non-negligible cost. Such universal caching introduces numerous extra operations to routers (e.g., content storage, lookup and replacement) and aggravates routers' overhead. Especially, this poses serious challenges on line-speed forwarding of routers.

So far, there has been no consensus on its feasibility. Current trace-driven studies [2] show that in-network caching is not fundamental necessary. Meanwhile, relevant studies indicate larger and larger contents are being exchanged between nearby end systems [3]. Especially, end systems have spare storages and bandwidth resources, which remain underutilized.

To this end, we propose a simple end system caching and cooperation scheme in CCN, aiming to replace the costly universal in-network caching. Our scheme is named ESCC, and several major advantages are listed as below.

- **Simple**: ESCC is an incrementally deployable scheme. The request processing remains the same as CCN. The only modification is associated with data processing and none of extra components is required.
- **Efficient**: ESCC enables requesters to retrieve contents from nearby neighbors through client cooperation. Data sharing works in a P2P-like fashion.
- **Robust**: ESCC is robust to client failure and unavailable content, because the adaptive forwarding [4] of CCN can detect and correct wrong routes by timeout.
- **Low Overhead**: ESCC does not need to advertise content available information like the literature [5], when routing changes. In essence, the "advertising process" is done through the update of FIB. ESCC has a low overhead.

2. SCHEME DESIGN

The main idea of ESCC is that each client caches contents and shares them with other neighbors. The requester/client equipped with a cache potentially turns into a content provider after a period of time. When data is transmitted back to the requester, some nearby routers record the route trace in their FIBs. Following the route trace, subsequent requests could be redirected to the former requester (now content provider). In this way, ESCC can enable fast access to contents within client's neighborhood.

Specifically, the request message processing remains the same as CCN. The mere modification is related to data processing. When a data message is transmitted back to a requester, some nearby routers record a route trace to the requester in FIB. Following the route trace, subsequent requests from other nearby clients could be redirected to the requester (now content owner). The route trace enables fast access to data within neighborhood.

Now, we give an example. Assume client 1 wants to retrieve a content named "/cinc.cn/ccn.jpg", which is possessed by the server. As shown in Fig. 1, first client 1 issues a request message with a name of "/cinc.cn/ccn.jpg/chunk1". It will traverse a path through A-C-D-E and reach the server. Then the data message returns back in the opposite direction. When the data message travels to a location close to client 1, e.g., router C, a route trace with the name of "/cinc.cn/ccn.jpg/chunk1" toward A will be

---

[+]Jun Li is the corresponding author.

SIGCOMM '15, August 17-21, 2015, London, United Kingdom.
ACM 978-1-4503-3542-3/15/08. http://dx.doi.org/10.1145/2785956.2790006

added into C's FIB. Likewise, router A also adds a route trace toward client 1 in its FIB.

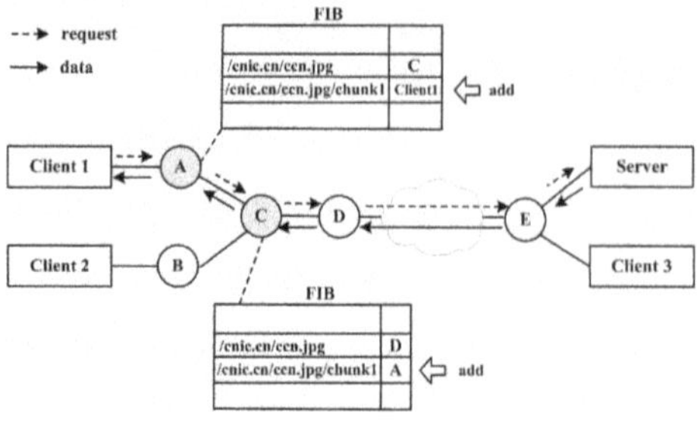

Figure1. Client 1 retrieves content from server

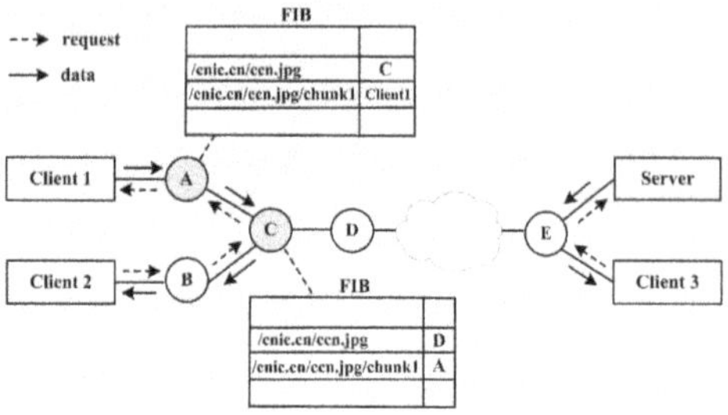

Figure 2. Client 2 retrieves content from client 1

As shown in Fig. 2, when client 2 requests for the same content later, the request will be redirected by router C to client 1 rather than to server. As the longest prefix match is used in FIB, the entry of "/cinc.cn/ccn.jpg/chunk1" has a high priority over the entry of "/cinc.cn/ccn.jpg". Thus, the longest prefix match still fits for ESCC.

Actually, end systems only cooperate with each other in the neighborhood, while FIBs of far routers remain unchanged. Note that FIB of A and C is updated, while E's FIB stays intact. Thus, client 3 can still retrieve content from the nearby server, rather than from the remote client 1.

3. ALGORITHM

The algorithm for data message processing at each router is shown in Table I (request message processing is the same as CCN). If FIB records the route trace for all passing data packets, FIB will expand dramatically. To tackle this issue, first, route trace can be only added to the FIB of routers in short distance away from the requester. Second, route trace can be only generated for popular contents.

TABLE I. ALGORITHM FOR DATA MESSAGE PROCESSING

```
/* r:current router; d:current data; pd:popularity of d;
   hr:hop count from r to client; Tp, Th: popularity/hop threshold */
FOR (each matched PIT entry)
  forward data d via corresponding face to user;
  delete the corresponding PIT entry;
  IF (pd>Tp)   /* Content selection */
     IF (hr<Th)   /* Router selection */
         record the route trace in FIB;
     End IF
  End IF
End FOR
```

4. EVALUATION

To evaluate ESCC, we conduct extensive simulation experiments based on the NDNSim. We utilize the Watts-Strogatz (WS) model [6] to generate the topology, which can capture the characteristics of Internet topology structure. In-network caching and ESCC is compared under the same

TABLE II. PARAMETER SETTING

Parameter	Value	Parameter	Value	Parameter	Value
Warmup time	10s	Cache size	50	Server num	1
Request rate	200req/s	Replacement	LRU	Core router num	66
Content num	50000	Hop threshold	2 hops	Edge router num	33
Parameter α	0.7~1.3	Pop threshold	Top 30%	Client num	33

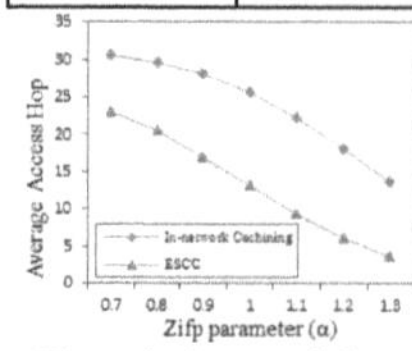

Figure3. Access delay

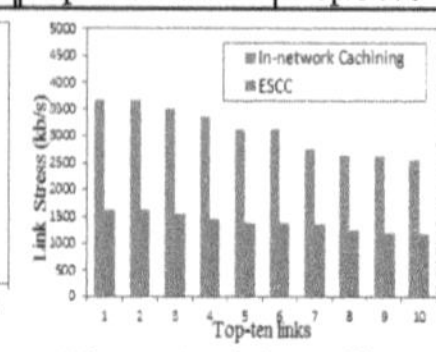

Figure4. Link traffic

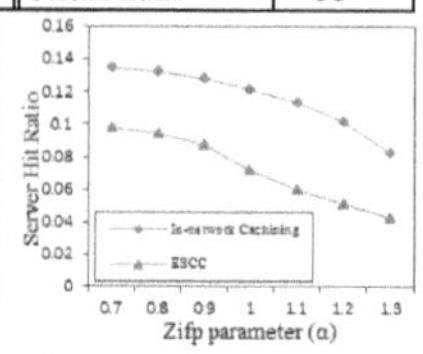

Figure5. Server load

total deployment cost. We assume the storage cost of per MB for in-network caching is 5 times the storage cost for clients, according to literature [7]. Clients' requests follow Zipf distribution with the parameter 0.7<α<1.3.

Experiments show that ESCC (only leave trace in routers two hops from clients), has already achieved better performance than the universal caching, in term of access delay, link traffic and server load reduction (Fig.3-5). Thus, ESCC could be a substitute for the costly universal caching.

5. CONCLUSION

In this paper, we propose a lightweight way to realize content distribution in CCN through client caching and cooperating with each other, without using costly in-network caching. When data is transmitted to a requester, some routers close to the requester leave route traces in their forwarding tables. Following the route traces, the subsequent requests can be redirect to the requester (data owner). Experiments show that ESCC (only leave trace in routers two hops away from clients) has already achieved lighter better performance gain than the universal caching. It is also quite simple, efficient, robust and has low overhead. We argue that ESCC could be a candidate substitute for the costly and unnecessary universal caching.

6. ACKNOWLEDGMENTS

This work was supported by Five Top Priorities of "One-Three-Five" Strategic Planning, CNIC under Grant No. CNIC_PY-1401.

7. REFERENCES

[1] Jacobson V, Smetters D K, Thornton J D, et al. Networking Named Content. In *Proc. CoNEXT*, 2009.

[2] Seyed Kaveh Fayazbakhsh, Yin Lin, Amin Tootoonchian, et al. Less pain, most of the gain: incrementally deployable ICN. In *Proc. SIGCOMM*, 2013.

[3] Haiyong Xie, Yang Y R, Krishnamurthy A, et al. P4P: Provider Portal for Applications. In *Proc. SIGCOMM*, 2008.

[4] Cheng Yi, Alexander Afanasyev, Lan Wang, et al. Adaptive Forwarding in Named Data Networking. *ACM SIGCOMM Computer Communication Review*, 42(3), July, 2012.

[5] Yaogong Wang, Lee K, Venkataraman B, et al. Advertising Cached Contents in the Control Plane: Necessity and Feasibility. In *Proc. INFOCOM Workshop on computer communications*, 2014.

[6] D. J. Watts and S. H. Strogatz. Collective dynamics of smallworld networks. *Nature*, 393(6684), June, 1998.

[7] Perino D, Varvello M. A reality check for content centric networking. In *Proc. SIGCOMM workshop on ICN*, 2011.

Yo-Yo Attack - Vulnerability in auto-scaling mechanism

Mor Sides
Interdisciplinary Center
Herzliya, Israel
mor.sides@idc.ac.il

Anat Bremler-Barr
Interdisciplinary Center
Herzliya, Israel
bremler@idc.ac.il

Elisha Rosensweig
Cloudband, Alcatel-Lucent
elisha.rosensweig@alcatel-lucent.com

CCS Concepts

•Security and privacy → Denial-of-service attacks; *Distributed systems security;* **•Computer systems organization → Cloud computing;** *Reliability;* **•Networks** → *Middle boxes / network appliances;*

1. INTRODUCTION

In the last few years, more and more public and private networks rely on cloud and virtualization to provide the service while meeting their SLA commitments. One attractive property of the cloud is its support for rapid elasticity - the ability to scale the number of machines up and down according to the load on the machine, which can be configured to occur automatically, according to customer-set thresholds.

This auto-scaling mechanism provides an ability to cope with many of the basic Distributed Denial of Service (DDoS) attacks (as describe in [4]), but opens the door to a new type of attack, the Economic Denial of Sustainability attacks (EDoS) [2]. In DDoS, an attacker overwhelms the victim with bogus traffic, blocking the service from legitimate users. With a cloud-based operation, the auto-scaling mechanism ensures that a victim can cope with an attack by providing the victim with more resources to handle the attack. This solution, however, comes with an economic penalty termed EDoS, since the victim needs to pay for the extra not beneficial resources that process the bogus traffic.

In many DoS attacks, the danger of the attack impact is mitigated by the expected cost to the attacker: the more effort required on the side of the attacker, who has to invest in generating large amounts of traffic, the less likely it is to occur. In this work we present the 'Yo-Yo attack', an efficient attack on the auto-scaling mechanism, which results in an Economic Denial of Sustainability attack (EDoS) that is difficult to detect. The attack cycles between two phases repeatedly: In the *on-attack* phase, the attacker sends a short burst of traffic that causes the auto-scaling mechanism to perform a scale up. In the *off-attack* phase, the attacker stops sending the excess traffic. This second phase takes place when the attacker identifies that the scale up has occurred. Once the attacker determines that the scale down occurred, the process is repeated. Clearly, the strength of the attack is partially determined by the ability of the attacker to determine when to switch between the two phases.

We demonstrate the Yo-Yo attack on Amazon cloud service, and show how the attacker can detect the state of the auto-scaling mechanism. The incentive of the attacker is to reduce the cost of the attack, i.e., minimize the attack traffic, and produce maximum damage, i.e., maximize the number of extra VMs used to process the attack. Reducing the attack cost has two impacts: the attacker uses his resources efficiently, and the attack is harder to detect. In our experiments over AWS, the attacker remained in the *off-attack* phase approximately 77% of the time, while the victim is constantly in flux.

The Yo-Yo attack can also be considered a Reduction of Quality (RoQ) attack [3]. RoQ attacks aim to keep an adaptive mechanism oscillating between over-load and under-load conditions. In other areas, it has been shown that load-balancing mechanisms are vulnerable to such attacks. To the best of our knowledge, our work is the first to demonstrate such a vulnerability in the auto-scaling mechanism.

2. AUTO-SCALING MECHANISM

An auto-scaling mechanism is standardly managed by the orchestrator component (also known as service controller). Each cloud solution comes with its own auto-scaling engine: Heat in Openstack, autoscaler in Google Cloud, and auto-scaling in Amazon Elastic Compute Cloud (Amazon EC2) [1]. Basically, in each of these systems the underlying algorithms lets the cloud customer, referred to in our work as the *user*, to define a scaling criteria, and the corresponding thresholds for overload and underload. In Amazon auto-scaling, which is where we conducted our experiment, the possible metrics to use for this criteria are CPU utilization, in/out network traffic in bytes and disk read/write in bytes or operations. In our experiment we choose the CPU utilization criteria, and correspondingly implement a service where each connection requires high CPU consumption.

Each user needs to configure rules for performing scale up and down, as well as the minimum and maximum number of machines allowed. Each scale rule is defined by a threshold and a scale-interval, s.t. if the threshold was exceeded for the duration of the scale-interval, the scaling operation is performed. For example in our experiment, we defined that scale down is performed if the CPU utilization is below 10% for 1 minute. We begin with a single machine, the minimum

SIGCOMM '15 August 17-21, 2015, London, United Kingdom

ACM ISBN 978-1-4503-3542-3/15/08.
DOI: http://dx.doi.org/10.1145/2785956.2790017

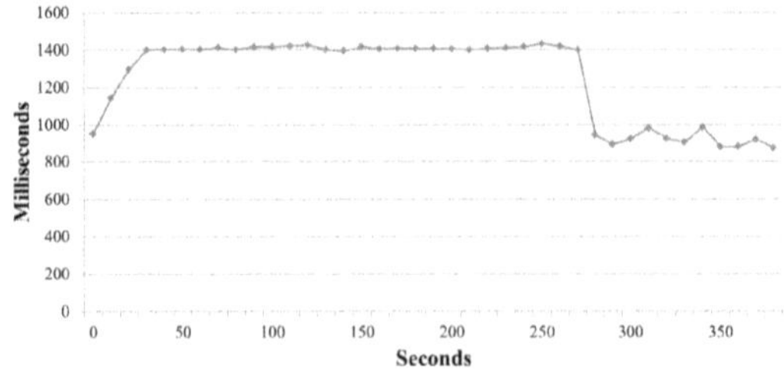

Figure 1: Scale up approximation

amount allowed, and cap it at two machines at maximum. Another important configurable parameter is the cooldown period, i.e., the number of seconds after a scaling activity completes before another can begin (in our experiment this was set to two minutes). We note that according to our experiments the initialization of a new machine takes around 2-2.5 minutes, which includes the time duration between the scale up event starts and a new machine is allocated, until the service is up on the new machine.

The attacker motivation is to maximize the attack potency, which as defined in [3] is equal to k/m, where k is the fraction of time an extra machine is required by user, and m is the fraction of time an attacker must be transmitting traffic. If the internal parameters are known to the attacker, which is not the usual case, the attacker can easily optimize its attack cost. The attack should be in the *on-attack* phase for a duration equal to the scale-up-interval, and then switch to *off-attack* for the duration equal to the initialization of a new machine plus the maximum time between scale-down-interval and the cooldown period. While these parameters are usually unknown to attacker, we find that the attacker can determine a good approximation for them. The key idea is that scale is done usually in order to improve the response time, thus the response time reveals some information on the state of the auto-scaling mechanism. Figure 1 shows the response time (in milliseconds) as a function of the elapsed time (in seconds), where the attack began at $t = 10$ seconds. It is clear that after 280 seconds a new machine is up and running, since the response time is reduced by half.

3. YO-YO ATTACK

We named our attack the *Yo-Yo attack* since the attacker oscillates from the *on-attack* phase to the *off-attack* phase. We demonstrate the Yo-Yo attack on Amazon, using simple attack where the goal of the attacker is to add extra machine and thus performing a EDoS attack. In our work here we simulate the best case attack from the attacker perspective, where we assume the attacker is aware of when scaling occurs relying on diagnosis Fig.1.

Figure 2 shows the number of machines as a function of attack time, where we compares a brute force DDoS attack that sends a constant amount of traffic to a Yo-Yo attack where the factor between *off-attack* to *on-attack* is almost 3.5, i.e., reducing the attack cost in about 77%. In our experiment the damage is the time the user has two machines running, and the cost is the fraction of time during which the *on-attack* phase is active. In a full DDoS attack, the attack is always on and thus the potency is 1, while in our simulated Yo-Yo attack the potency is 0.71/0.23 which is 3.08. Thus the attacker is 3 time more effective.

Figure 3 demonstrates that in Yo-Yo attack, there is addi-

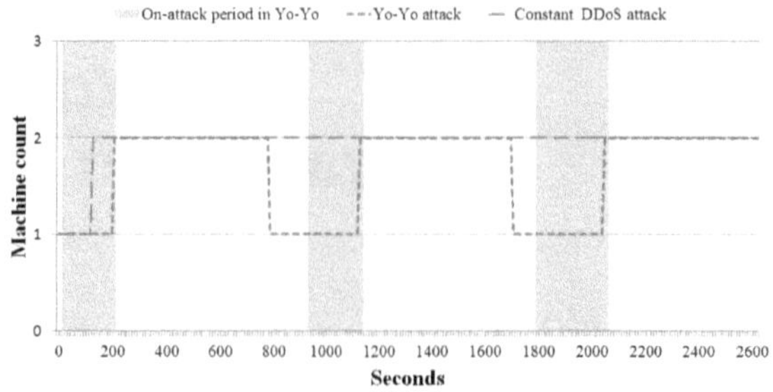

Figure 2: Machine count comparison

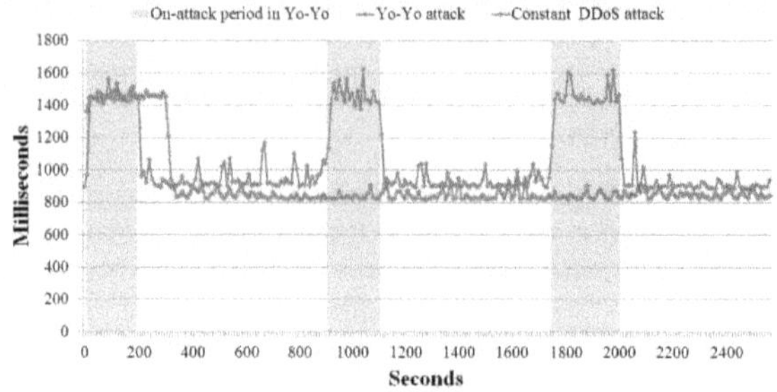

Figure 3: Response time comparison

tional damage in the form of high response time to a regular client. The regular client suffer a high response time while the system is under attack and the scale up is in process. While in constant DDoS attack, it happens only once at the begining, under the Yo-Yo attack it happens every *on-attack* phase. We note that in stateful services the damage can be larger. If the client's state move to another VM in every scale action it will increase the scaling duration. Hence a scheduling mechanism should minimize the number of times a client changes machine. Designing such scheduling mechanism is part of our ongoing research.

4. CONCLUSION

In this work we shed some light on the potential of exploiting the auto-scaling mechanism to perform an efficient attack, that impacts the cost of a service and the response time of standard users. While part of the promise of Network Function Virtualization (NFV) is that network services and middleboxes will enjoy the auto-scaling property, our work shows that special care should be taken to prevent attackers from using this mechanisms to reduce the value of NFV.

5. REFERENCES

[1] Amazon web services, auto scaling. http://aws.amazon.com/autoscaling/.

[2] Z. A. Baig and F. Binbeshr. Controlled virtual resource access to mitigate economic denial of sustainability (edos) attacks against cloud infrastructures. In *Cloud Computing and Big Data (CloudCom-Asia)*, 2013.

[3] M. Guirguis, A. Bestavros, I. Matta, and Y. Zhang. Reduction of quality (RoQ) attacks on dynamic load balancers: Vulnerability assessment and design tradeoffs. In *INFOCOM*, 2007.

[4] S. Rajagopalan, D. Williams, H. Jamjoom, and A. Warfield. Split/merge: System support for elastic execution in virtual middleboxes. In *NSDI*, 2013.

This research was supported by European Research Council (ERC) Starting Grant no. 259085.

Towards the 5G Revolution: A Software Defined Network Architecture Exploiting Network Coding as a Service

Dávid Szabó, Felicián Németh, Balázs Sonkoly*, András Gulyás†
HSN Lab, Budapest Univ. of Technology and Economics
{szabod,nemethf,sonkoly,gulyas}@tmit.bme.hu

Frank H.P. Fitzek
5G Lab Germany, Technische Universität Dresden
frank.fitzek@tu-dresden.de

ABSTRACT

Many networking visioners agree that 5G will be much more than the incremental improvement, in terms of data rate, of 4G. Besides the mobile networks, 5G will fundamentally influence the core infrastructure as well. In our vision the realization of the challenging promises of 5G (e.g. extremely fast, low-overhead, low-delay access of mostly cloudified services and content) will require the massive use of multipathing equipped with low overhead transport solutions tailored to fast, reliable and secure data retrieval from cloud architectures. In this demo we present a prototype architecture supporting such services by making use of automatically configured multipath service chains implementing network coding based transport solutions over off-the-shelf software defined networking (SDN) components.

Categories and Subject Descriptors

C.2.3 [**Computer-Communication Networks**]: Network Operations - Network management

Keywords

SDN; Network Coding; Mininet; NFV

1. INTRODUCTION

Future communication systems will face dramatic changes compared to state of the art systems. With the Internet of Things (IoT) the number of mobile and wireless devices will increase by one or even two orders of magnitude resulting in 500 billion devices by 2020. This will lead to dramatic bandwidth request for the overall communication system. Furthermore 5G is on the horizon introducing the tactile Internet which impose massive requirements on security, safety, resilience, throughput, and delay reduction. The huge demand for dramatic reduction in delay and increased throughput needs a new area of communication systems. Packet switched networks, the core of today's Internet, usually provision a single path between two communication endpoints on which each router performs store and forward operation for each incoming packet. The single path does not only limit the throughput of the network, it is also vulnerable against hackers and outages. With respect to the tactile Internet the current architecture is problematic as the long distance between the cloud service and the mobile device results in too large delays.

In order to achieve high throughputs, resilience, security and low delays a revolutionary change is currently discussed [3], namely the code centric networks. In the latter, suitable routers may perform a different strategy referred to as compute and forward using random linear network coding. This enables efficient multi path communication over possibly lossy channels while providing inherent algebraic security as hackers would need to tap all involved communication systems. The use of network coding is also enabling another important feature which is a dynamic allocation of distributed clouds on top of each router, placing the cloud in close proximity of the user, which enable low latencies for the tactile Internet.

In order to use network coding efficiently, we have to orchestrate the coders, recoders[1] (a new entity introduced by network coding) and decoders to meet the constraints of the physical topology and we have to take care of steering the traffic over them. Good news is that such orchestration and steering is in perfect agreement with the current practice of Internet Service Providers (ISPs) that services are implemented in the form of appropriately concatenated middleboxes, also known as *service chains*. In this respect we seem to have a lower adoption barrier for network coding at ISPs. However, today's service chains are usually built around special purpose networking hardware elements, configuring and operating these chains is a highly non-trivial task which still requires human interaction. SDN and virtualization can be a promising way out of this managerial trap as these technologies may enable flexible and automated deployment of service chains containing also software middleboxes or Virtualized Network Functions (VNF).

In this demonstration we present a system which enables the definition, configuration and automated deployment of service chains implementing code centric operation over off-the-shelf SDN components. Building on the ESCAPE [1]

*MTA-BME Future Internet research group
†MTA-BME Information systems research group

[1]The application of recoders inside the network can significanlty reduce latency and increase goodput with respect to the approaches coding only at endpoints e.g. in case of Fountain codes.

SIGCOMM '15 August 17-21, 2015, London, United Kingdom

ACM ISBN 978-1-4503-3542-3/15/08.
DOI: http://dx.doi.org/10.1145/2785956.2790025

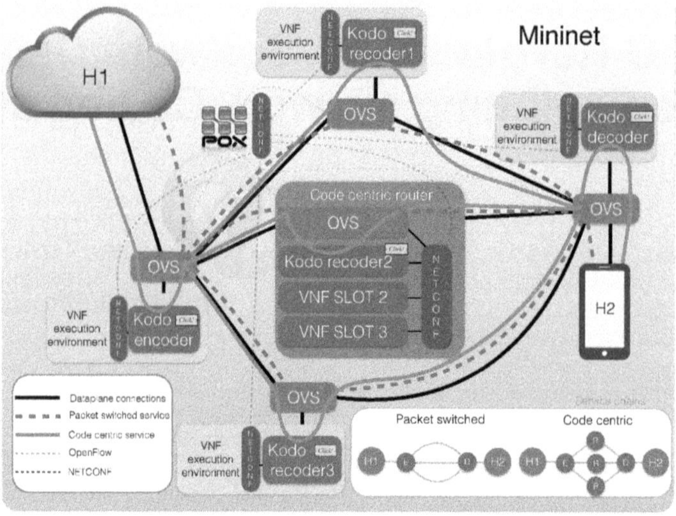

Figure 1: The prototype architecture.

prototyping framework, we combine a Mininet emulated OpenFlow 1.0 network controlled by POX with VNFs implementing network coding in the Click [2] modular router platform using the Kodo [4] network coding software library for prototyping a novel communication infrastructure paving the future of 5G networking.

2. ARCHITECTURE AND DEMO

Fig. 1 presents the architecture of our prototype and an outline of the demo scenario. We build our OpenFlow network in Mininet using Open vSwitch (OVS) instances and hosts (H1/H2) which can represent any sources of traffic e.g. a simple smartphone or a server in a data center. The switches are controlled by a POX controller which contains our steering module handling the flow tables according to the configuration of the running service chains. Besides the switches and hosts we have virtualized network functions implementing encoders, recoders and decoders in the click router platform using the Kodo library. Kodo implements random linear network codes which allows flexible recoding of the packets anywhere in the network. These VNFs can be run in two ways. VNF execution environments (yellow boxes) are advanced Mininet hosts running a NETCONF (OpenYuma) agent. Our NETCONF client implemented as a POX module can connect to these agents and can start a given VNF process on the host. This solution stands for the case when we run VNFs outside the routers e.g. in a near OpenStack data center having built-in NETCONF support. This solution may slightly increase latency but provides the possibility of scaling out in the presence of massive network loads combined with more complex coding schemes (e.g. more efficient random linear codes using larger field size). Alternatively, we have also built a visionary prototype of the code centric router (green box). This router consist of a standard OVS (no modifications in OpenFlow) instance but has the capability to execute VNFs and connect them to virtual ports of the switch through NETCONF. Using code centric routers adds less delay but there is no way to scale out beyond the router's hardware resources. Our POX orchestrator module receives service chains as inputs (can be given by GUI) and configure the switches and start the appropriate VNFs accordingly.

During the course of the demo we define two multipath service chains over our network with 50% loss configured for each link. The first chain (bottom right corner of Fig. 1) uses end-to-end codes (like Reed Solomon or Raptor) and ordinary packet switching as packets follow the dashed brown paths between H1 and H2. Then we start a VLC server/client on H1/H2 respectively configured to send and receive a real-time video stream using UDP. The video has nice quality but at the cost of +115% redundancy at the encoder, which has to flow through the network. At this point we upgrade our service by adding the recoder elements (as shown explicitly in the bottom right corner of Fig. 1). Our system reconfigures the switches and launches the required VNFs thus transiting the service to the code centric area (the green path). Without noticeable interruption in the video stream we witness perfect video quality at H2 but with a 30% less total number of sent packets in the network and reduced latency due to the recoder elements. Our demo[2] presents a plausible way to combine network coding with SDN and realizing code centric services on top of off-the-shelf SDN components. Our framework comprising OpenFlow, Click and Kodo enables experimenting with code centric networks and may promote their transition from a vision to the reality of future 5G networks.

Acknowledgements – The research leading to these results has received funding from the European Union Seventh Framework Programme under grant agreement № 619609.

3. REFERENCES

[1] A. Csoma et al. Escape: extensible service chain prototyping environment using mininet, click, netconf and pox. In *ACM SIGCOMM*. ACM, 2014.

[2] E. Kohler et al. The click modular router. *ACM Trans. Comput. Syst.*, 18(3):263–297, Aug. 2000.

[3] M. Medard et al. Network coding mythbusting: Why it is not about butterflies anymore. 2012.

[4] M. V. Pedersen et al. Kodo: An open and research oriented network coding library. In *NETWORKING 2011 Workshops*, pages 145–152, 2011.

[2] A screencast showing a simplified version of the demo is available at: https://youtu.be/TG3xduqpD_4

RPKI MIRO: Monitoring and Inspection of RPKI Objects

Andreas Reuter
Freie Universität Berlin
andreas.reuter@fu-berlin.de

Matthias Wählisch
Freie Universität Berlin
m.waehlisch@fu-berlin.de

Thomas C. Schmidt
HAW Hamburg
t.schmidt@haw-hamburg.de

ABSTRACT

The Resource Public Key Infrastructure (RPKI) stores attestation objects for Internet resources. In this demo, we present RPKI MIRO, an open source software framework to monitor and inspect these RPKI objects. RPKI MIRO provides resource owners, RPKI operators, researchers, and lecturers with intuitive access to the content of the deployed RPKI repositories. It helps to optimize the repository structure and to identify failures.

Categories and Subject Descriptors

C.2.3 [**Computer-Communication Networks**]: Network Operations; H.5.2 [**Information Interfaces and Presentation**]: User Interfaces

Keywords

PKI monitoring, RPKI measurement, secure inter-domain routing

1. INTRODUCTION

The RPKI [1] is a public key infrastructure for Internet resources. Basically, it consists of three parts: (i) extended X.509 certificates that attest the ownership of IP prefixes and autonomous system (AS) numbers, i.e., the Internet resources, (ii) RPKI signed objects, which do not follow the X.509 data structure but are necessary to implement secure Internet routing (e.g., route origin objects), and (iii) a distributed repository system, which stores and provides all of the signed objects to Internet operators and other users. So-called relying party software fetches RPKI objects via the *rsync* protocol from the Certificate Authorities (CA) and cryptographically verify the data for further processing.

On top of the RPKI, approaches have been developed to improve routing security. A recently deployed example is prefix origin validation, which authorizes an AS to announce an IP prefix. Corresponding route origin authorization objects (short ROAs) have already been created by several operators and service providers such as AT&T, Deutsche Telekom, and Mozilla. As for any PKI, the success of RPKI applications depend on stable and coherent repository data. Surprisingly, almost no high-level monitoring tools are available to inspect (R)PKI content. Available tools mostly focus on gathering statistical measures and meta data about RPKI repositories (e.g., [2]), or only allow limited inspection of RPKI repository contents [3,4].

SIGCOMM '15 August 17-21, 2015, London, United Kingdom

ACM ISBN 978-1-4503-3542-3/15/08.

DOI: http://dx.doi.org/10.1145/2785956.2790026

Why do we need RPKI MIRO?

The core tools for RPKI were primarily built for experts and provide only limited convenience functions. Furthermore, monitoring, in particular distributed measurements, is not easily supported. Several user groups would benefit from an extendable and easy-to-use monitoring framework.

CA Operators There are two options to deploy the RPKI: The *hosted mode*, (i.e., each Regional Internet Registry runs the CA and repositories for the resource owners), and the *delegated mode*, (i.e., each participant becomes their own RPKI and maintains the repository). Currently, the delegated mode is rarely supported by the RIRs. This will change and larger ISPs will switch to this model in the future. Our experience already showed that RPKI MIRO helps to improve the repository structure of RIRs, and we expect additional demand for RPKI MIRO with increasing deployment of the delegated model.

Resource Owners Transparency is crucial for the acceptance of the RPKI. Public RPKI data does not need to be correct [5]. RPKI MIRO aims for easy access on RPKI certificates, revocation lists, ROAs etc. to finally give Internet operators more confidence in their data. RPKI MIRO is modular to add additional views or to integrate components that alarm individual resource owners in case of failures.

Researchers Even though the basic functionality of RPKI has been standardized within the IETF, there are still open research questions, in particular with respect to the ongoing deployment. For example, the mechanism to retrieve RPKI objects from the distributed repositories is still under discussion [6,7]. The modular architecture of RPKI MIRO allows it (a) to plug different fetching strategies in, (b) to perform distributed measurements, (c) to coherently analyse the results.

Lecturers Public Key Infrastructures and thus also the RPKI are complex systems. The interplay of the different (R)PKI objects is usually hard to grasp for students. Real data may help when teaching. However, current tools to inspect these objects are based on command line interfaces. In particular, they do not visualize the link between different object types. RPKI MIRO provides an intuitive graphical browser to visualize object content as well as the relation between the objects, which will help students to better understand the RPKI concepts. It is worth noting that the visualization is tailored to RPKI but can be easily updated for other X.509 extensions.

In the remainder of this abstract, we briefly explain the basic architecture of RPKI MIRO, report about experiences, and discuss future work.

Repository	W/o Prefetching # rsync Calls	Time	W/ Prefetching # rsync Calls	Time
AfriNIC	35 calls	96 s	3 calls	11 s
APNIC	534 calls	1745 s	2 calls	35 s
APNIC AfriNIC	5 calls	16 s		
APNIC ARIN	25 calls	81 s		
APNIC IANA	492 calls	1610 s		
APNIC LACNIC	2 calls	6 s		
APNIC RIPE	10 calls	32 s		
ARIN	1 call	7 s	1 call	7 s
LACNIC	1 call	9 s	1 call	9 s
RIPE	1 call	23 s	1 call	23 s

Table 1: Performance comparison of collecting RPKI data without and with prefetching

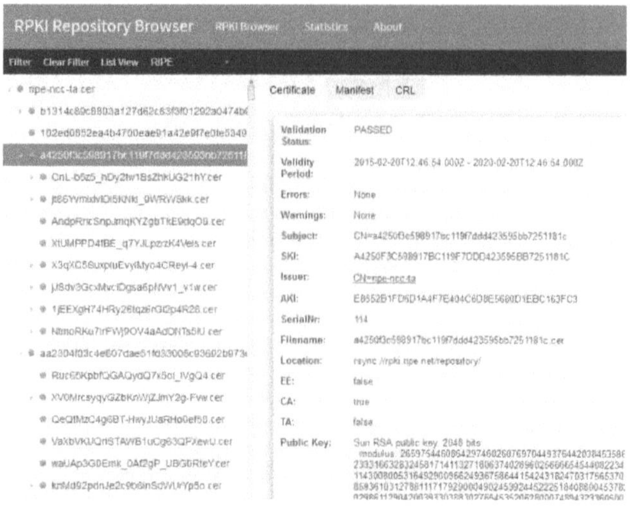

Figure 1: One component of RPKI MIRO: The repository browser showing the content of a certificate of the RIPE CA.

2. ARCHITECTURE OF RPKI MIRO

The source code of RPKI MIRO is publicly available (https://github.com/rpki-miro) and licensed under MIT. RPKI MIRO consists of the following components:

Backend—Validator The validator downloads, parses, and validates RPKI objects. Based on this processing chain, the validator component provides statistics which are relevant for evaluating the functions of a relying party. The data of validated repositories can be exported in multiple formats for further processing.

Efficient fetching of objects is crucial for any relying party. A new rsync call will result in a new TCP connection, which leads to overhead on the server side. However, timing is important for a secure Internet backbone. To minimize the amount of separate calls, we implemented a pre-fetching strategy that derives the longest common prefix of multiple publishing points, which then is used to access the data. Table 1 shows the performance gain in terms of rsync calls and download time thanks to reduced communication overhead.

Backend—Statistics Separate modules calculate statistical measures (e.g., number of valid objects) to evaluate the repository state. Such information is helpful for two reasons: First, it allows an analysis of the coherence of the distributed repository among different vantage points. Second, it allows the comparison of different implementations of the validator. Our work revealed some bugs in existing relying party software.

Frontend—Browser The browser component visualizes the content of RPKI objects and their relationship. It is worth noting that the current tree view per trust anchor is *not* a direct representation of the underlying file system structure—this would overload the presentation. Instead of that, we decided to show only certificates and ROAs within the tree and present their meta data as well as relationships to manifest and CRLs in a separate detail view. Due to the model view controller concept of RPKI MIRO, additional views can be easily added. A public instance of the RPKI browser is available under http://rpki-browser.realmv6.org/.

Frontend—Statistics This component visualizes previously gathered statistics. It allows for an easy comparison of the repository state with other relying parties.

3. EXPERIENCES AND FUTURE WORK

RPKI MIRO is used by the research as well as the operator community. It has already helped to better understand the current state of RPKI deployment. For example, with RPKI MIRO it was easy to identify that the cross-RIR resource space has increased and includes route origin attestation objects. Cross-RIR resources are resources which have been signed by one RIR and are transferred to another RIR. This requires that the provisioning protocol [8] is functional between the Regional Internet Registries—something that lacked attention.

RPKI MIRO has also helped to better understand how the five RIRs have implemented majority-minority address space, i.e., IP address space of which a super prefix is managed by one RIR but some sub-prefixes of this prefix are managed by another RIR. This fragmentation has implications for creating resource certificates.

Part of our ongoing research work will be the analysis of the different protocol proposals to retrieve RPKI objects from the repositories. For this we will leverage the distributed measurement functionality of RPKI MIRO. We will also refine our pre-fetching strategy to automatically adapt to the repository structure.

On the feature side of RPKI MIRO, we will extend the web interface to allow for the uploading of external repository data. We will also enable users to configure monitoring of repository changes and to initiate alarms.

Acknowledgments We thank the SIDR community and the RIR community for discussions and their valuable feedback, special thanks to Rob Austein, Tim Bruijnzeels (RIPE), and Carlos M. Martinez (LACNIC). This work has been supported within the BMBF project Peeroskop.

4. REFERENCES

[1] M. Lepinski and S. Kent, "An Infrastructure to Support Secure Internet Routing," IETF, RFC 6480, February 2012.
[2] J. Kloots, "RPKI Dashboard," http://rpki.surfnet.nl/, 2015.
[3] RIPE NCC, "RPKI Validator," https://github.com/RIPE-NCC/rpki-validator, 2015.
[4] LACNIC, "Origin Validation Looking Glass," http://www.labs.lacnic.net/rpkitools/looking_glass/, 2015.
[5] E. Heilman, D. Cooper, L. Reyzin, and S. Goldberg, "From the consent of the routed: Improving the transparency of the rpki," in *Proc. of ACM SIGCOMM* 2014.
[6] T. Bruijnzeels, O. Muravskiy, B. Weber, R. Austein, and D. Mandelberg, "RPKI Repository Delta Protocol," IETF, Internet-Draft – work in progress 00, February 2015.
[7] E. Osterweil, T. Manderson, R. White, and D. McPherson, "Sizing Estimates for a Fully Deployed RPKI," Verisign Labs, TR 1120005 version 2, December 2012.
[8] G. Huston, R. Loomans, B. Ellacott, and R. Austein, "A Protocol for Provisioning Resource Certificates," RFC 6492.

WiMAC: Rapid Implementation Platform for User Definable MAC Protocols Through Separation

Simon Yau†, Liang Ge†, Ping-Chun Hsieh†, I-Hong Hou†, Shuguang Cui†, P. R. Kumar†, Amal Ekbal*, and Nikhil Kundargi*
†Texas A&M University
†{symoyau, geliang87, lleyfede, ihou, cui, prk}@tamu.edu
*National Instruments
*{amal.ekbal, nikhil.kundargi}@ni.com

ABSTRACT

This demo presents WiMAC, a general-purpose wireless testbed for researchers to quickly prototype a wide variety of real-time MAC protocols for wireless networks. As the interface between the link layer and the physical layer, MAC protocols are often tightly coupled with the underlying physical layer, and need to have extremely small latencies. Implementing a new MAC requires a long time. In fact, very few MACs have ever been implemented, even though dozens of new MAC protocols have been proposed. To enable quick prototyping, we employ the mechanism vs. policy separation to decompose the functionality in the MAC layer and the PHY layer. Built on the separation framework, WiMAC achieves the independence of the software from the hardware, offering a high degree of function reuse and design flexibility. Hence, our platform not only supports easy cross-layer design but also allows protocol changes on the fly. Following the 802.11-like reference design, we demonstrate that deploying a new MAC protocol is quick and simple on the proposed platform through the implementation of the CSMA/CA and CHAIN protocols.

CCS Concepts

•**Networks** → **Network experimentation;**

Keywords

Wireless testbed; MAC; software-defined radio

1. INTRODUCTION

Driven by the emerging applications such as multimedia streaming and VoIP, a wide variety of wireless protocols have been proposed to meet the increasingly stringent requirements for wireless networks, such as quality of service (QoS) and power saving. For example, the IEEE 802.11 standard, which is one of the most widely used wireless protocols, has undergone several major enhancements in each layer over the past decade. Moreover, due to the substantial rate improvement in the physical layer, much effort has been dedicated to design new protocols in the Medium Access Control (MAC) layer to enhance the original CSMA/CA mechanism. Despite the abundance of the theoretical studies on wireless MAC protocols, very few of them make it beyond simulation towards real implementation with transmissions over the air. The main reason is that the MAC layer is often tightly coupled with the PHY layer, with the result that MAC developers are often required to implement not only the MAC functionality but also the features in the physical layer, which lie outside their main expertise. Therefore, new protocols often need to be reconfigured from the very ground up, leading to long development time.

To reduce the prototyping time of new protocols, one promising alternative is to make the MAC layer programmable by adopting the software-defined radio (SDR). Conventionally, SDR implements the time-critical functionality in the programmable hardware domain, either using FPGAs or MCUs, while it handles time-insensitive signal processing on a computer host. Based on this split architecture between software and hardware, various techniques have been presented in [3] to allow flexible MAC customization directly from the host while maintaining the real-time performance. However, the exact criterion for splitting the MAC functions is still not clear. To enable efficient modular design in wireless testbeds, Ansari *et al.* [1] studied the commonality of popular MAC protocols to define a class of elementary MAC blocks. Despite such a flexible framework, the platform is mainly hardware-based and thus the programmability outside the proposed class of elementary blocks might not be guaranteed. Tinnirello *et al.* [4] also present a MAC processor based on the runtime composition of several IEEE 802.11 standards to achieve flexibility in the MAC layer. Nevertheless, the processor is implemented on the target commodity hardware, which offers less freedom than required by a general-purpose MAC implementation.

Different from the prior efforts, WiMAC is the first general-purpose wireless testbed that supports multi-user medium access control with tested real-world implementation of both CSMA and non-CSMA protocols. To provide easy configuration for the wireless MAC protocols, WiMAC is built on the philosophy of *mechanism vs. policy separation* to achieve higher programmability. The "mechanism" refers to the category of low-level operations that handle the real packet transmissions over the network, while the "policy" indicates the high-level schemes for channel contention and packet scheduling. By describing the policies in a high-level language, the mechanisms can be easily adapted to different policies. For example, to avoid possible collisions during transmissions, a random backoff algorithm has been implemented in the CSMA/CA protocol. No matter how the contention window is chosen at each time, a backoff timer is required for any possible backoff algorithms. Therefore, a backoff timer is considered as a mechanism, while determining the size of the contention window is categorized as a policy. Hence, the effort needed to develop new

SIGCOMM '15 August 17-21, 2015, London, United Kingdom

ACM ISBN 978-1-4503-3542-3/15/08.

DOI: http://dx.doi.org/10.1145/2785956.2790031

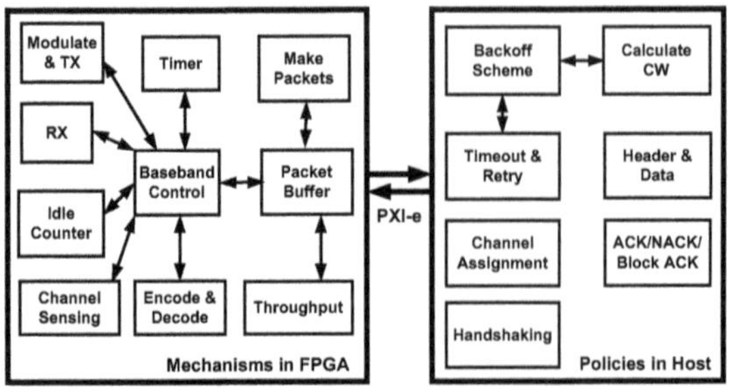

Figure 1: Mechanism vs. policy separation in WiMAC.

MAC protocols is greatly reduced. Figure 1 shows a more detailed illustration of the separation framework.

We now summarize the important features of WiMAC.

- **Independence of software from hardware.** In WiMAC, the software-defined policies are decoupled from the hardware functionality based on the separation framework. Therefore, developers are not required to redesign the hardware from scratch since the functional blocks can be reused. The independence of software from hardware minimizes the deployment overhead for emerging protocols.
- **Enabling protocol changes on-the-fly.** Given the programmability from the computer host, WiMAC provides a user-friendly GUI and allows the users to switch between different MAC protocols while the testbed is in operation.
- **Supporting cross-layer design.** The MAC layer, which serves as an interface between the link layer and the physical layer, is often tightly coupled with the underlying physical layer. Built on a dedicated FPGA, WiMAC provides enough freedom for developers to reconfigure the physical layer, enabling protocol design across layers.
- **Quick prototyping.** Based on the above three features, WiMAC lowers the barrier that currently blocks novel ideas from being implemented, helping researchers implement new MAC protocols with short development time.

To the best of our knowledge, there is no existing wireless testbed that exhibits all the features described above. We believe that WiMAC is a promising platform for the networking research community.

As a design example to illustrate the proposed wireless testbed, we use an 802.11-like reference design to implement the CSMA/CA and the CHAIN [6] protocols. A demo video of WiMAC is available on YouTube[1]. The illustratory implementation is only meant to serve as a starting point to explore the common mechanisms used in most MAC protocols. Based on the current deployment, our short-term goal is to bring a broader class of the real-time protocols, such as the debt-based policies for real-time wireless [2], and the energy-saving protocol SOFA [5], to the implementation stage.

2. WIRELESS MAC IMPLEMENTATION

First, we briefly describe the 802.11-like reference design in the proposed testbed. We mainly employ the platform supported by National Instruments, which includes a PXI Chassis and several USRPs as wireless nodes. Instead of using commercial wireless PHY cards, we build the mechanisms in the FPGAs to enable more flexible protocol deployment since we can thereby make the PHY management also available to users if necessary. The design primarily uses the 2.4GHz ISM band with a channel bandwidth of either 20MHz or 40MHz. In terms of the coding rate, WiMAC supports the options of BPSK, QPSK, 16-QAM, and 64-QAM. In the present design, we use fixed-size packets with the standard ACK for all packets.

2.1 CSMA/CA

As a starting point, we illustrate the separation framework by implementing the popular CSMA/CA protocol. On the software side, the computer host handles the programmable policies, such as ACK control, packet header, and contention window calculation, etc. In the FPGA domain, we have built the core mechanisms that are fundamental to most MAC protocols. We have studied a list of several proposed MAC protocols to determine the common functional blocks. We have thereby identified and implemented a group of features in the FPGA, such as configurable slot times, configurable inter-frame time, configurable congestion window algorithm, backoff timer, and channel sensing, etc. To handle time-critical mechanisms, instead of using a state-diagram structure, we use flags or simply preload values to the FPGA to update information packet by packet. These features serve as the foundation for developing any new MAC protocol in the testbed.

2.2 CHAIN

CHAIN [6] is a MAC protocol for enhancing the uplink efficiency. Consider a wireless network with one AP and several clients. Conventional CSMA uses random exponential backoff to handle contention in medium access. However, as the network becomes more congested, collisions happen so frequently that the network efficiency becomes extremely low. While being compatible with the existing CSMA, CHAIN employs a sequential *piggyback transmission* scheme where a client that has obtained initial access triggers a *chain* of transmissions in a predetermined order when the traffic is heavy. The precedence is assigned and maintained in the AP, and followed by the clients. Based on the CSMA configuration, CHAIN can be implemented by reusing the core mechanisms in the FPGA and adding a few new functional blocks in the FPGA, such as ACK overhearing and a debt system for fairness. The complexity of implementing CHAIN is greatly reduced due to the decomposition strategy.

3. ACKNOWLEDGEMENT

This material is based upon work partially supported by AFOSR Contract FA9550-13-1-0008, NSF under Contract Nos. CNS-1302182, Science Technology Center Grant CCF-0939370, CNS-1343155, ECCS-1305979, CNS-1265227, DoD with grant HDTRA1-13-1-0029, and by grant NSFC-61328102.

4. REFERENCES

[1] J. Ansari, X. Zhang, A. Achtzehn, M. Petrova, and P. Mahonen. Decomposable MAC framework for highly flexible and adaptable MAC realizations. In *Proc. IEEE Symposium on New Frontiers in Dynamic Spectrum*, pages 1–2, 2010.

[2] I.-H. Hou and P. R. Kumar. Utility maximization for delay constrained QoS in wireless. In *Proc. IEEE INFOCOM*, pages 1–9, 2010.

[3] G. Nychis, T. Hottelier, Z. Yang, S. Seshan, and P. Steenkiste. Enabling MAC protocol implementations on software-defined radios. In *Proc. 6th USENIX Symposium on Networked Systems Design and Implementation (NSDI)*, pages 91–105, 2009.

[4] I. Tinnirello, G. Bianchi, P. Gallo, D. Garlisi, F. Giuliano, and F. Gringoli. Wireless MAC processors: Programming MAC protocols on commodity hardware. In *Proc. IEEE INFOCOM*, pages 1269–1277, 2012.

[5] Z. Zeng, Y. Gao, and P. R. Kumar. SOFA: A sleep-optimal fair-attention scheduler for the power-saving mode of WLANs. In *Proc. International Conference on Distributed Computing Systems (ICDCS)*, pages 87–98, 2011.

[6] Z. Zeng, Y. Gao, K. Tan, and P. R. Kumar. CHAIN: Introducing minimum controlled coordination into random access MAC. In *Proc. IEEE INFOCOM*, pages 2669–2677, 2011.

[1] A demo video is available: http://youtu.be/yj7YEWjx1HM

Extreme Web Caching for Faster Web Browsing

Ali Raza, Yasir Zaki
NYU Abu Dhabi, UAE
{ali.raza, yasir.zaki}@nyu.edu

Thomas Pötsch
University of Bremen, Germany
tpoetsch@uni-bremen.de

Jay Chen, Lakshmi Subramanian
NYU and CTED, NYUAD
{jchen,lakshmi}@cs.nyu.edu

ABSTRACT

Modern web pages are very complex; each web page consists of hundreds of objects that are linked from various servers all over the world. While mechanisms such as caching reduce the overall number of end-to-end requests saving bandwidth and loading time, there is still a large portion of content that is re-fetched – despite not having changed. In this demo, we present *Extreme Cache*, a web caching architecture that enhances the web browsing experience through a smart pre-fetching engine. Our extreme cache tries to predict the rate of change of web page objects to bring cacheable content closer to the user.

CCS Concepts

•**Networks** → *Network architectures;*

1. INTRODUCTION

There have been a number of recent projects that explore how caching can effect the performance of web browsing. Xia et. al.[2] found that layout and source code of web pages that block subsequent objects to load are highly cacheable. The authors have also shown that a large amount of content (especially HTML) does not change significantly over the course of days or months.

Motivated by their findings, we analyzed Alexa's top 20 web pages over the course of three months to see how web pages change over time. We periodically (every 10 minutes) downloaded pages and observed that a large portion of the page objects does not change frequently over time (such as CSS, Javascripts, Images, HTML, and etc.). Moreover, even when a certain object changes, we observe that for text-based objects the changes are relatively small. In many cases, the changes are only limited to a few lines of code within the entire object. We also observed that these minor changes are mostly related to advertising or randomly generated (tracking) IDs and are probably not of major importance to the user.

Most existing caching solutions rely on HTTP max-age headers option [1] to identify the freshness of a cached object. To confirm whether the max-age option is actually set correctly by the content provider and if it reflects the correct number (i.e. timestamp) on when an object would change, we compared the max-age option of every object and of every version of our recorded set of Alexa's top 20 web pages. Since there were 10 min between consecutive page requests, we can tell whether an object has changed or not by comparing the MD5 hash of the objects in both versions. We find that the max-age option does not reflect the reality of when objects change. This causes either a large number of unnecessary requests or stale objects in the cache.

In order to cope with the findings mentioned above, we developed a novel caching architecture called *Extreme Cache* that aims to (a) estimate the correct rate of change for every object within a web page and then overwrites the max-age option which was set by the content provider and (b) bring web content closer to the user. Hence, unnecessary web requests can be avoided and content can be served from a closer edge cache.

2. KEY FINDINGS

We looked into how objects change over time within several popular web sites and have discovered that a large number of objects did not change over time. In addition, even though some objects might have changed over time, the ratio of the change to the overall object size is very small and does not require to fetch the entire object again. Moreover, caching policies are not dictated properly by the content owners. The key observations that we have made in our analysis can be summarized as follows:

- Web publishers do not configure the cache-control headers in HTTP correctly/carefully. For the top 20 web pages from Alexa, we found that a large number of objects violate this, i.e. changing either before or after the specified max-age.

SIGCOMM '15 August 17-21, 2015, London, United Kingdom

ACM ISBN 978-1-4503-3542-3/15/08.
DOI: http://dx.doi.org/10.1145/2785956.2790032

- Changes in Javascript, HTML, and CSS objects are not significant and it is not required to fetch the whole object again. Sending only diffs can tremendously speed up page load times.

Figure 1 shows the correlation between the max-age and the change rate of all objects for the recorded top 20 Alexa web sites. The x-axis represents the actual max-age set by the content provider that is communicated through the HTTP headers; the y-axis represents the actual time the object took to change. If the max-age value is a true mean of the object's change rate, then the data should be highly correlated along a 45 degree line. The figure shows that the max-age generally does not correlate with the object's actual rate of change.

For the same dataset, Figure 2 shows the percentage of objects that stays the same after a certain time has elapsed in comparison to the first version of the website. The idea is to show how similar a certain web page stays after a certain time. The x-axis indicates the times at which the similarity is computed and the y-axis represents the similarity index calculated as number of similar objects/total number of objects. It can be seen that for a long period of time, around five hours, the similarity index is above 65%. For certain web pages, the similarity index remains above 90% even after a day.

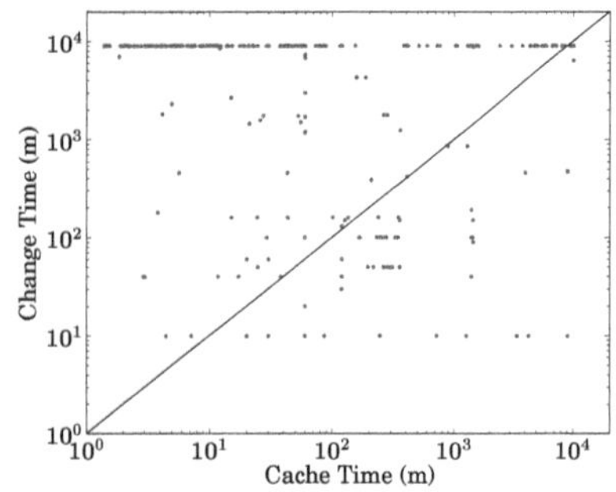

Figure 1: Per object max-age vs. change rate

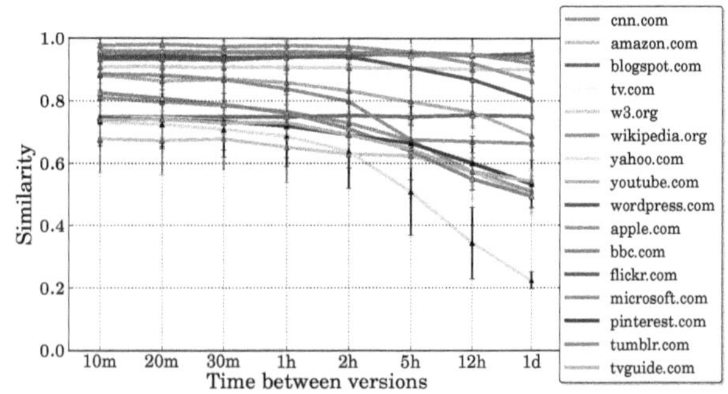

Figure 2: Page similarity over time

3. ARCHITECTURE

Our extreme cache architecture aims at enhancing the hit rate of legacy caching systems and to reduce unnecessary content requests. Our solution is easy to deploy since it neither requires any additional changes to the network nor to the client browsers and web servers.

The extreme cache architecture is implemented at different locations in the network and consists of the following two components: a cloud controller and an edge cache. Figure 3 shows the basic framework of the extreme cache. As can be seen in the figure, the edge cache is close to the client and has a backhaul connection to the Internet so as to accommodate cache misses or non-cacheable content. The cloud controller is connected to both, the Internet (for pre-fetching) and to the edge cache so as to populate, prioritize, and update its cache. The edge cache contains the most recent version of each object even before it is requested by a user. The cloud controller is responsible for pre-fetching the web pages, estimating the objects rate of change, and populating/updating the edge cache.

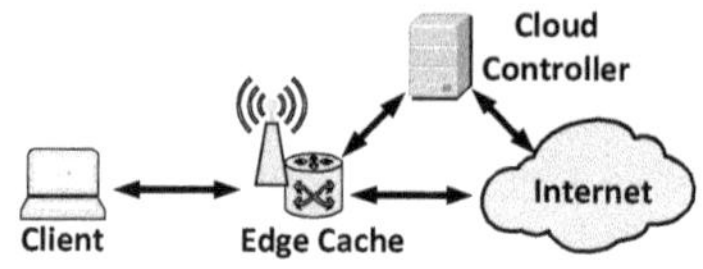

Figure 3: Extreme cache architecture

3.1 Cloud Controller

The functionality of the cloud controller is to periodically request objects of web pages from the Internet and then comparing the objects with the previous (cached) version. This enables the cloud controller to estimate the rate at which the objects change and will help to decide when and how frequently it needs to update the edge cache. If possible, the updates are done in terms of delta updates (i.e. only sending the changes (diffs) instead of the whole object) in order to save bandwidth. Further, it overrides the max-age option with the predicted change rate (one option for the estimated max-age of an object is to use to use the moving average of the object's change rate). The cloud controller can control several edge caches and prioritizes objects based on their expected benefits to the cache hit rate.

3.2 Edge Cache

The edge cache is a regular caching proxy that does not have any additional intelligence. It is responsible for serving the client requests with content stored in its cache. In case of a cache hit, it delivers the cached objects; otherwise it requests the content from the origin. The edge cache also records its client's access patterns and updates the cloud controller to help it prioritize and decide on what to pre-fetch.

4. REFERENCES

[1] R. Fielding, M. Nottingham, and J. Reschke. Hypertext transfer protocol (http/1.1): Caching, June 2014. RFC7234.

[2] X. S. Wang, A. Krishnamurthy, and D. Wetherall. How much can we micro-cache web pages? In *Proceedings of the 2014 Conference on Internet Measurement Conference*, IMC '14, pages 249–256, New York, NY, USA, 2014. ACM.

i-tee: A fully automated Cyber Defense Competition for Students

Margus Ernits
Tallinn University of Technology
Akadeemia tee 15a, Tallinn,
Estonia
margus.ernits@gmail.com

Johannes Tammekänd
Estonian IT College
Raja 4C, Tallinn,
Estonia
johannes.tammekand@gmail.com

Olaf Maennel
Tallinn University of Technology
Akadeemia tee 15a, Tallinn,
Estonia
olaf.maennel@ttu.ee

Abstract

We present an *Intelligent Training Exercise Environment* (*i-tee*[1]), a fully automated Cyber Defense Competition platform. The main features of i-tee are: automated attacks, automated scoring with immediate feedback using a scoreboard, and background traffic generation. The main advantage of the platform is easy integration into existing curricula and suitability for continuous education as well as on-site training at companies. The platform implements a modular approach called *learning spaces* for implementing different competitions and hands-on labs. The platform is highly automated to enable execution with up to 30 teams by one person using a single server.

The platform is publicly available under MIT license[2].

Categories and Subject Descriptors

C.2.4 [**Computer Systems Organization**]: Distributed Systems—*Client/server*

Keywords

Cyber Security Exercises; auto-configuration; Virtual Networks

1. INTRODUCTION

Practical hands-on and problem-based learning is an efficient way to study Information and Communications Technology (ICT) subjects, as it provides a playful and exciting learning experience [1]. Therefore, Cyber Defense Exercises (CDX) are used to give a realistic, intensive learning experience for students [1].

Given the huge and proven benefits of such learning events, one might ask: Why are CDX-s not integrated into every ICT curriculum?

The problem: Although a CDX is an effective learning method it is rarely used because designing a new cyber competition is a complex and time consuming task that contains many design steps such as: Objectives, Approach, Topology, Scenario, Rules, Metrics and Lessons Learned [2].

Creating a new CDX demands a huge amount of effort from the organizer—well beyond that of designing a new course. In addition, one may not have all the competences needed for developing a new CDX.

To the best of our knowledge there are no defense oriented CDX platforms publicly available that are open source, easily integrated into existing curriculum, provide modular learning spaces, and can be executed by one instructor alone.

2. EXAMPLE OF A LEARNING SPACE

Our platform consist of an underlying framework on which several learning spaces can be hosted. We will discuss an example of one learning space, "CyberOlympics 2015". This event was held in Estonia on February 14, 2015[3].

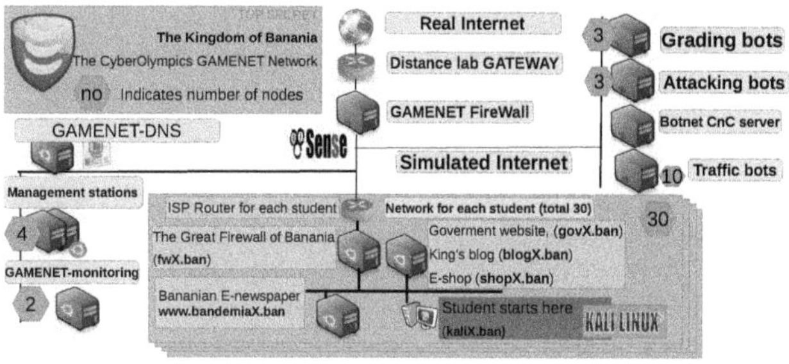

Figure 1: The GameNet

The Scenario brings the participant to a role-play in the *Kingdom of Banania* as intern for system administration of Bananian e-Government[4]. The task is to ensure the availability and functionality of the websites such as: Governmental site govX.ban (where X represents the No of participant/team), King's Blog blogX.ban and e-shop shopX.ban as shown in Figure 1.

Several events emerge, such as: defacement of government's website, threatening video from Hacker group Acronymous #OP Banania followed by intensive attacks.

The full scenario can be found from competition's website[5]. We are using Blue team type CDX [3], where the defending (Blue) teams compete with each other and against automated attacks performed by the system.

[1]**i-tee** — In Estonian "tee" means way/path/street. So i-tee can be understood as "Information-way".

[2]https://github.com/magavdraakon/i-tee

[3]http://www.kmin.ee/en/news/unique-student-cyberwar-games-be-held-estonia

[4]https://www.youtube.com/watch?v=-nzMTk0Nkbw

[5]http://www.kyberolympia.ee/competition

SIGCOMM '15 August 17-21, 2015, London, United Kingdom

ACM ISBN 978-1-4503-3542-3/15/08.

DOI: http://dx.doi.org/10.1145/2785956.2790033

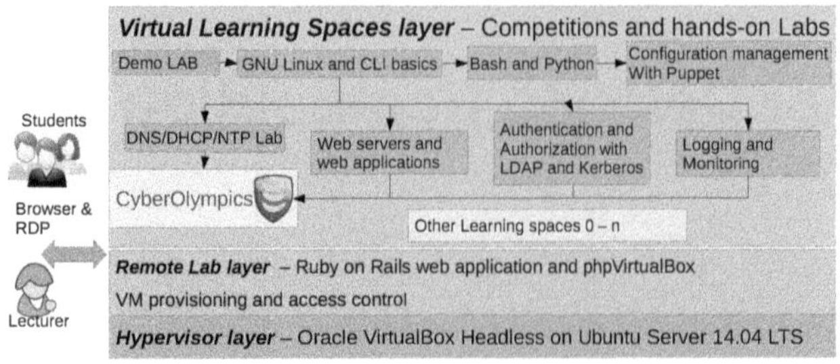

Figure 2: The architecture of the system

The students are in the role of defenders and after completing the tasks they are able to recognize common attacks against web applications, install different application level firewalls such as web application firewalls, SQL firewalls, intrusion detection and prevention systems. For each student the scoring system assesses the availability and functionality of the websites, attack-proofing, and the time to recover. This provides valuable feedback to the learners during and after the execution.

3. ARCHITECTURE OVERVIEW

Our proposed framework is an open source platform that enables an easy creation of a new cyber security competition with up-to-date content and resource-friendly execution. The game environment is accessible over the Internet using a web browser and a Remote Desktop Protocol (RDP) client. Each team or participant operates in the game environment their own isolated network and virtual machines, see Figure 1.

The automation includes the setup of Virtual Machines (VM's) for each participant, configuring private and shared networks and most crucially, performing malicious attacks against each team, providing automated scoring of objectives.

The platform has three layers as seen in Figure 2. First, the **Virtualization Layer** runs the VM's and is driven by upper layers. Second, the **Virtual Lab Layer** provides Remote Access (web, RDP) and Control functions for the VM's (start, stop, pause, console access) and for executions (start, stop, pause, attack, open objective, end). Third, the **Virtual Learning Space Layer** provides the scenario, objectives, automated scoring and automated attacks for objectives. Immediate feedback for competitors shows the progress and score using the scoreboard. The automated traffic generator provides smoke cover for automated attacks and hides scoring traffic as well, therefore making the cyber event more realistic and difficult. Some key functions are:

Automated VM provisioning is template-based and on demand when a new student starts their own learning space or joins the competition. Particular VMs are built using *Puppet* configuration manager, shell and Python scripts to customize the VM and networks based on the VM's role, student and the learning space. In addition, all virtual networks needed for new students are generated on the fly. For example, when a new VM starts, the configuration of network interfaces and networks are automatic based on template name, username and learning space name.

Automated attacks are executed after opening the corresponding objective. Attacks are generated by attack bots residing in simulated Internet subnet as shown in Figure 1. Attacks currently available in *i-tee* include: Distributed Denial of Service DDOS, shellshock, Heartbleed, SQL injections, Command injections, cross site scripting (XSS) and several attacks against security misconfigurations, outdated software and cookie security. More attacks will be added in the future and can also be shared among all contributors. Attack bots have functionality to change the attackers' IP address on the fly, making blocking harder. For example, an attack using SQL injection logs into a web-shop, manipulates with prices and buys items.

Automated scoring is performed for each objective and gives visualized feedback for students using the scoreboard[6]. Scoring is done by scoring-bots which are located in the same IP space as attack-bots (Figure 1). When one particular IP is used by attack bots then the scoring-bot will not reuse this IP and vice versa, because a student can block attackers but is not allowed to block scoring as non malicious traffic.

Noise generation: When students investigate the attacks and try to separate an attacker's traffic from legitimate traffic, such as scoring, the attacks could easily be distinguished without background noise. The platform provides a responsive customizable application level traffic generator that simulates real users and hides the attacks. The traffic generators are controlled by the central control server (CnC) and the amount of traffic is tunable during the execution.

Hardware used to run CDX learning space was: HP ProLiant DL380 G7, 2CPU total 12 core (24 threads). RAID 10 2TB disk, 148GB RAM. Actual resources required for a competition depend on the number of participants and complexity of team networks. In the CyberOlymics each student required about 4GB RAM and less than 20GB HDD.

4. CONCLUSIONS

The main contribution is the open source framework *i-tee* itself, which provides automation for cyber defense exercises and training. It allows running different types of complex exercises with little preparation by the facilitators. The *i-tee* platform was successfully tested during a live CDX and has proven useful during several hands-on classes in the context of a university curriculum. The platform is able to run several learning spaces in parallel and has modular architecture enabling reuse of fragments from different learning spaces. We hope that this platform will be used by the community to develop and share new learning spaces and improve the quality of studies by providing a hands-on playful learning experience.

5. REFERENCES

[1] C. Eagle. Computer security competitions: Expanding educational outcomes. *IEEE Security and Privacy*, 11(4):69–71, 2013.

[2] A. FurtunaÌĘ, V.-V. Patriciu, and I. Bica. A structured approach for implementing cyber security exercises. In *Communications (COMM), 2010 8th International Conference on*, pages 415–418, June 2010.

[3] J. Rursch and D. Jacobson. When a testbed does more than testing: The internet-scale event attack and generation environment (iseage) - providing learning and synthesizing experiences for cyber security students. In *Frontiers in Education Conference, 2013 IEEE*, pages 1267–1272, Oct 2013.

[6]Scoreboard 2015 – http://scoring.kyberolympia.ee/

See How ISPs Care: An RPKI Validation Extension for Web Browsers

Matthias Wählisch
Freie Universität Berlin
m.waehlisch@fu-berlin.de

Thomas C. Schmidt
HAW Hamburg
t.schmidt@haw-hamburg.de

ABSTRACT

The Resource Public Key Infrastructure (RPKI) allows BGP routers to verify the origin AS of an IP prefix. In this demo, we present a software extension which performs prefix origin validation in the web browser of end users. The browser extension shows the RPKI validation outcome of the web server infrastructure for the requested web domain. It follows the common plug-in concepts and does not require special modifications of the browser software. It operates on live data and helps end users as well as operators to gain better insight into the Internet security landscape.

Categories and Subject Descriptors

C.2.2 [**Computer-Communication Networks**]: Network Protocols—*Routing Protocols*

Keywords

BGP, RPKI, secure inter-domain routing, deployment, web

1. INTRODUCTION

The successful hijack of an IP prefix within the Internet backbone—either intended or by misconfiguration—is a severe problem albeit it happens surprisingly often. For end users, the consequences of such incidents have been nicely illustrated when Pakistan Telecom claimed to own the IP prefix of YouTube, and China Telecom maliciously announced more than ≈ 37k IP prefixes. Web sites went offline, which was noticeable by the end users but they could not discover why. Furthermore, it was speculated whether parts of the traffic were intercepted and forwarded to its correct destination. Then an end user who opened a website would not necessarily be able to experience any difference.

Most recently the deployment of basic counter measurements against prefix hijacking started. However, those activities on the BGP layer are hardly visible for the end user. The end user needs to rely on the ISP. Note that SSL/TLS helps on the application layer to reveal packet interception but an attacker may forge certificates.

SIGCOMM '15 August 17-21, 2015, London, United Kingdom

ACM ISBN 978-1-4503-3542-3/15/08.

DOI: http://dx.doi.org/10.1145/2785956.2790034

In this abstract we argue for an open and user-friendly view on the current state of the Internet backbone security. We present a proof-of-concept which checks the IP prefix of the requested domain name within a web browser.

In the following, we briefly present the background of currently deployed security measures in the Internet backbone (§ 2) and describe design principles and implementation details of our application (§ 3).

2. RPKI, RTR, AND ORIGIN VALIDATION

To prevent simple prefix hijacking, i.e., an autonomous system (AS) maliciously claims successfully the ownership of an IP prefix, BGP peers need to verify the origin AS of an IP prefix carried in BGP updates. The **Resource Public Key Infrastructure (RPKI)** is a distributed repository that includes attestation objects to prove the ownership of IP resources (AS numbers, IP prefixes). The so called Route Origin Authorizations (ROAs) objects implement the binding between origin AS number and IP prefix.

RPKI-enabled routers [2] do not store ROAs itself but only the validated content of these authorities. The cryptographic validation of ROAs will be performed by trusted cache servers, which will be deployed at the network operator. The **RPKI/ RTR protocol** [1] defines a standard mechanism to maintain the exchange of the prefix to origin AS mapping between the cache server and routers. In combination with a BGP **prefix origin validation scheme** [4] a router is able to verify received BGP updates without suffering from cryptographic complexity. A BGP update can be valid, invalid, or not found (i.e., no information about this prefix in the RPKI).

The deployment of RPKI repositories and the creation of ROAs started in 2010. Major ISPs such as ATT and DTAG, as well as big companies such as Mozilla added their prefixes to the RPKI, and the quality of ROA data improved [6], [3]. However, the ratio of prefixes that cover web servers is low, in particular popular sites are less secured as preliminary results show [7]. We now describe how the RPKI validation can be performed natively within a browser.

3. RPKI VALIDATION IN WEB BROWSERS

Design The design of our solution is driven by real-time analysis and flexibility. To verify the BGP prefix of the web server a URL resolves to, basically the following steps are necessary: (a) DNS resolution of the web domain, (b) mapping of the IP address to prefix and origin AS visible in BGP, (c) comparison of the prefix/origin AS with ROA data. It is worth noting that the DNS resolution as well as

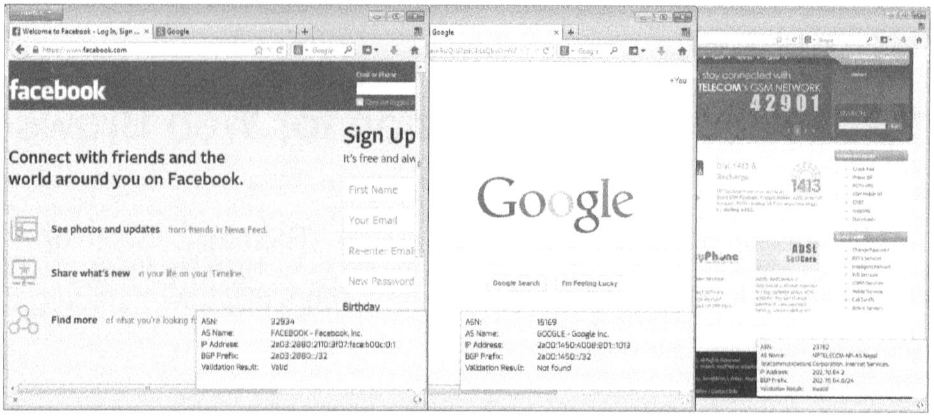

Figure 1: RPKI validation in Mozilla Firefox for the requested websites with different validation outcome

the BGP data depend on the location of the client. However, in contrast to the name to address mapping in the DNS, there is no standard mechanism to request the prefix/AS pair for an IP address with respect to the customer's ISP routing table. An accurate mapping might be a new service provided by ISPs in the future.

There are two options to implement origin validation in web browsers: (a) the browser extension implements the full router part (i.e., receives valid ROAs from cache server and performs origin validation of BGP data), (b) the extension resolves only the IP address of the web domain and a remote back-end performs the origin validation. We decide for the latter as this allows for easy applicability in most browser platforms, which usually provide add-on concepts based on JavaScript. Back-end and front-end communicate via HTTP as this is native in browsers and does not conflict with most firewall settings.

Implementation—Back-end Currently, the back-end uses the Team Cymru community service to resolve the IP prefix of the web server IP address and the corresponding origin AS. We admit that the result does not necessarily comply with the BGP entry of the client's upstream but the vantage points of Team Cymru provide a good coverage. Furthermore, our architecture is flexible enough to consider multiple BGP sources as well as future mappig services.

To fetch ROAs and to validate the BGP information, we deploy the RTRlib [5], an open source implementation of the RPKI/RTR router part. This C library is very efficient with respect to memory and processing resources. Per default, the implementation establishes RTR sessions to two cache servers for fallback reasons. However, end users can configure their own end point for a cache server in the browser extension, and multiple instances of the RTRlib will be started.

Implementation—Front-end The browser extension is implemented as dynamic add-on for Mozilla Firefox and Chrome. Other browsers can be easily supported as the browser extension only needs to support the REST interface to the back-end. The source code is available on Github[1]. The extension visualizes three states: green (the web server prefix is valid in the BGP), orange (the prefix was not found in the RPKI), and red (the prefix is invalid, the website might be suspicious), see Fig. 1. Note that if an attacker blocks plugin traffic, none of the three states apply, indicating that the communication to the trust anchor is broken. Advanced users can request information about the autonomous system/the IP prefix and configure the host address and port of the RPKI cache server, which will be used by the back-end.

[1]https://github.com/rtrlib

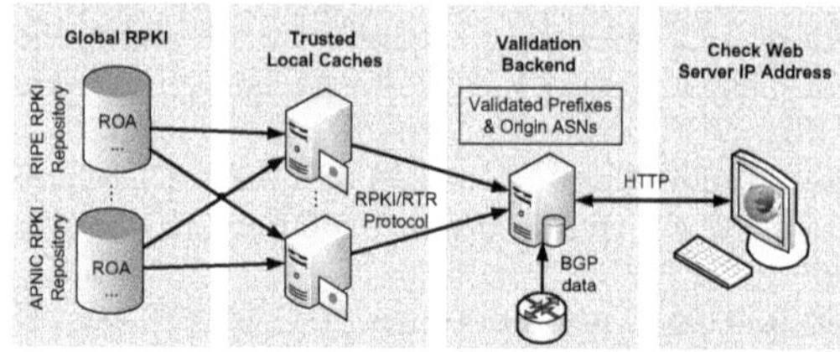

Figure 2: System architecture

Future Challenges Our current solution checks the BGP data for the web server infrastructure of the landing page. Many web pages include embedded content linked via different domains. Analyzing the HTML content fast and combine the different results to a complete picture for the whole web page will be part of our future work.

Acknowledgments We would like to thank Tas Sóti and Sebastian Meiling for helping on the implementation. This work is supported by the German BMBF within the project Peeroskop (http://peeroskop.realmv6.org).

4. REFERENCES

[1] Bush, R., and Austein, R. The Resource Public Key Infrastructure (RPKI) to Router Protocol. RFC 6810, IETF.

[2] Bush, R., Austein, R., Patel, K., Gredler, H., and Waehlisch, M. Resource Public Key Infrastructure (RPKI) Router Implementation Report. RFC 7128, IETF, 2014.

[3] Iamartino, D., Pelsser, C., and Bush, R. Measuring BGP route origin registration validation . In *Proc. of PAM* (Berlin, 2015), LNCS, Springer, pp. 28–40.

[4] Mohapatra, P., Scudder, J., Ward, D., Bush, R., and Austein, R. BGP Prefix Origin Validation. RFC 6811, 2013.

[5] Wählisch, M., Holler, F., Schmidt, T. C., and Schiller, J. H. RTRlib: An Open-Source Library in C for RPKI-based Prefix Origin Validation. In *Proc. of USENIX Security Workshop CSET'13* (Berkeley, 2013), USENIX Assoc.

[6] Wählisch, M., Maennel, O., and Schmidt, T. C. Towards Detecting BGP Route Hijacking using the RPKI. *ACM Computer Communication Review 42*, 4 (2012), 103–104.

[7] Wählisch, M., Schmidt, R., Schmidt, T. C., Maennel, O., and Uhlig, S. When BGP Security Meets Content Deployment: Measuring and Analysing RPKI-Protection of Websites. Technical Report arXiv:1408.0391, Sep. 2014.

Programming the Home and Enterprise WiFi with OpenSDWN

Julius Schulz-Zander
TU Berlin
Berlin, Germany
julius@inet.tu-berlin.de

Carlos Mayer
TU Berlin
Berlin, Germany
carlosnmayer@gmail.com

Bogdan Ciobotaru
TU Berlin
Berlin, Germany
bogdan.ciobotaru1@gmail.com

Stefan Schmid
Deutsche Telekom Innovation Laboratories / TU Berlin
Berlin, Germany
stefan@inet.tu-berlin.de

Anja Feldmann
TU Berlin
Berlin, Germany
anja@inet.tu-berlin.de

Roberto Riggio
CREATE-NET
Trento, Italy
rriggio@create-net.org

ABSTRACT

The quickly growing demand for wireless networks and the numerous application-specific requirements stand in stark contrast to today's inflexible management and operation of WiFi networks. In this paper, we present and evaluate OPENSDWN, a novel WiFi architecture based on an SDN/NFV approach. OPENSDWN exploits datapath programmability to enable service differentiation and fine-grained transmission control, facilitating the prioritization of critical applications. OPENSDWN implements per-client virtual access points and per-client virtual middleboxes, to render network functions more flexible and support mobility and seamless migration. OPENSDWN can also be used to out-source the control over the home network to a participatory interface or to an Internet Service Provider.

Categories and Subject Descriptors

C.2.3 [**Computer Communication Networks**]: Network Operations; C.2.1 [**Computer Communication Networks**]: Network Architecture and Design

Keywords

Network Function Virtualization; Software-Defined Networking; Programmable RAN; Enterprise WLANs; Wi-Fi

1. INTRODUCTION

In this demo, we show the potential and benefits of introducing programmability and virtualization in *wireless networks*. Wireless networks are very different from wired networks—the domain where SDN/NFV has been studied most intensively so far—as communication happens over a shared medium whose characteristics can change quickly over time and in an unpredictable manner, and as users are often mobile and associations dynamic. WiFi networks offer several unique knobs to influence the probability of successful transmissions, such as transmission rate and power, as well as retry chains. This introduces opportunities for a fine-grained and application specific transmission control, e.g., for service differentiation.

Our proposed architecture, OPENSDWN [2], is based on a unified, programmable control plane which allows to manage both the datapath as well as the virtualized middleboxes. Specifically, OPENSDWN implements per-client virtual access points and per-client virtual middleboxes, to render network functions more flexible and support mobility and seamless migration of network processing functions.

This demo presents interesting use cases of OPENSDWN: (1) OPENSDWN enables service differentiation capabilities, and allows administrators or users to specify application and flow priorities. These priorities are implemented using a fine-grained transmission control. (2) Using its per-client virtual access points and virtual middleboxes, OPENSDWN supports seamless user mobility, as well as flexible function allocation (e.g., function collocation at night to save energy). (3) Network functions such as firewalls and NATs can be deployed flexibly, e.g., outside user premises. (4) OPENSDWN also introduces flexibilities in terms of network control: the system exposes a participatory interface à la [1], where users can indicate priorities for their applications. The control can also be outsourced to an Internet Service Provider (ISP), e.g., for troubleshooting.

SIGCOMM '15 August 17-21, 2015, London, United Kingdom

ACM ISBN 978-1-4503-3542-3/15/08.

DOI: http://dx.doi.org/10.1145/2785956.2790037

2. THE OPENSDWN SYSTEM

OPENSDWN is based on an SDN+NFV (a.k.a. *SDNv2*) approach and consists of the following components:

1. **Unified Programmability and Abstractions:** The logically centralized control plane unifies SDN and NFV through programmatic abstractions. That is, OPENSDWN virtualizes both access points and virtualized middleboxes (see Figure 1(b)), which facilitates an easy handling and migration of per-client state, also beyond CPE boundaries. The OPENSDWN abstractions can be seen as an extension of Odin [3] to NFV: Odin's *LVAP* concept abstracts the complexities of the IEEE 802.11 protocol stack (client associations, authentication, and handovers), and enables the unified slicing of both the wired and wireless portions of the network by encapsulating the client's Openflow state. OPENSDWN additionally introduces per-client virtual middleboxes, short

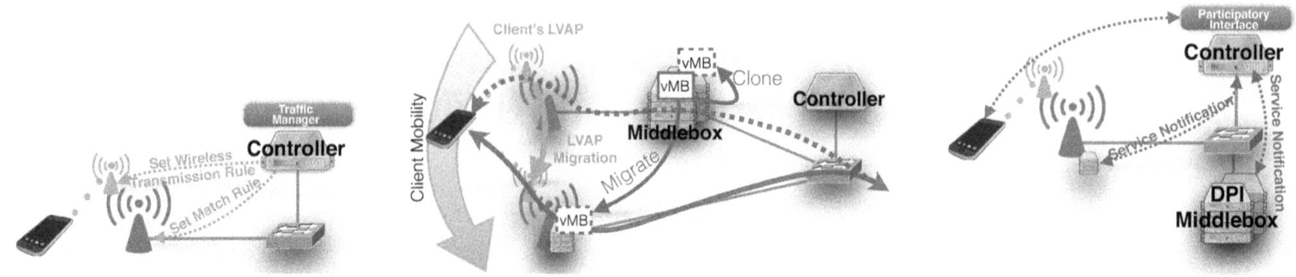

(a) **Transmission control:** The controller sets specific wireless transmission and OpenFlow rules for per-flow wireless transmission control.

(b) **Mobility support:** Virtual middleboxes (e.g., encapsulating firewall connection state) can be migrated in the presence of mobility and cloned for redundancy.

(c) **Participatory interface:** A participatory application provides an interface to the user. Service detection is achieved through DPI.

Figure 1: Three basic operations supported by OPENSDWN.

vMB*s*, which can be transferred seamlessly across the network. Specifically, a *vMB* encapsulates the client's *MB* state as a virtual *MB* object. Thus, OPENSDWN achieves control logic isolation as SDN/NFV applications running on top the controller can only operate on their respective *LVAP*s and *vMB*s.

2. **Programmable Datapath:** The programmable datapath allows us to specify per-flow transmission settings, as shown in Figure 1(a). The settings include transmission power, transmission rate as well as tailored retry chains. It is even possible to differentiate between different packets of the *same flow* (5-tuple): for instance, key frames of a live stream may be given higher priority. This is achieved by using an IDS such as Bro for packet classification and *tagging*: transmission settings are chosen depending on the tag.
3. **Participatory Interface:** OPENSDWN's participatory interface allows us to define flow priorities as well as priorities over customers. The chosen priorities are translated by the controller into meaningful network policies. Priorities can be adjusted anytime. Figure 1(c) depicts the participatory interface.

3. DEMO

User-Defined Service Differentiation

OPENSDWN offers visibility into the network's state and supports a fine-grained transmission control, by allowing administrators and users to set per-flow and per-packet specific transmission settings (such as transmission rate, power, retransmission and RTC/CTS strategy). For instance, as we will demonstrate, OPENSDWN can protect latency-sensitive flows (e.g., live streaming) from competing with background traffic (e.g., a Dropbox synchronization). Especially given today's trend to deploy more and more wireless devices in the user's premises, traffic can significantly interfere, e.g., an unimportant system update for a device can easily interfere with requested *on demand* services such as Spotify or Netflix, resulting in poor performance.

Mobility and migration

By virtualizing not only the per-client access points, but also the middleboxes, OPENSDWN supports both seamless user mobility and a dynamic resource allocation. The more dynamic resource management introduced by OPENSDWN enables the adjustment and migration of resources and functionality with the user, e.g., for flexibly scaling up or down resources depending on the demand. By collocating network functions, e.g., at night, also energy may be saved. The firewall state migration service is a reactive application triggered through external events to move state between MB instances. For example, when Odin [3] detects a client with a higher RSSI at a new AP, a handover event is generated and the client's stateful firewall state migrated to the AP before the handover is executed. The firewall state migration service then decides whether the state associated with the mobile user needs to be migrated and executes the operation. The application keeps a mapping between APs and firewalls. If the client is moving over to an AP that corresponds to a different stateful firewall than the current, a migration of the client's flow state is performed.

Smart Direct Multicast Service

OPENSDWN can also be used in conjunction with group abstractions. Multicast is a standard group communication abstraction, and with the advent of IPv6, the fraction of multicast traffic is likely to grow in the future, e.g., (IPv6 realizes broadcast over multicast and mDNS to broadcast features to neighboring stations.

In IEEE 802.11, multicasts are typically sent at basic rate. However, wireless networks may benefit from a direct multicast service (DMS) which has the potential of reducing the transmission time over regular multicast, by sending 802.11 packets as unicast. Unfortunately, DMS requires a client to signal its DMS capabilities to the AP, which is the reason why DMS is rarely used in 802.11 networks today.

With OPENSDWN, a controller can detect the number of subscriptions for a particular multicast service and control the transmission accordingly. Specifically, a controller can install an OpenFlow rule to switch from multicast to unicast for the transmission. Moreover, OPENSDWN allows to assign *WDTX* group-based transmission rules, e.g., transmit a stream of multicast data at the *maximum common transmission rate*.

Acknowledgments. Research supported by the Federal Ministry of Education and Research (BMBF) Software Campus "SDWN" Project Grant (Reference number 01IS12056).

4. REFERENCES

[1] A. D. Ferguson, A. Guha, C. Liang, R. Fonseca, and S. Krishnamurthi. Participatory networking: An api for application control of sdns. *SIGCOMM Comput. Commun. Rev.*, 43(4):327–338, Aug. 2013.

[2] J. Schulz-Zander, C. Mayer, B. Ciobotaru, S. Schmid, and A. Feldmann. OpenSDWN: Programmatic Control over Home and Enterprise WiFi. In *SOSR '15*.

[3] J. Schulz-Zander, L. Suresh, N. Sarrar, A. Feldmann, T. Hühn, and R. Merz. Programmatic orchestration of wifi networks. In *USENIX ATC '14*.

A Real-time 802.11 Compatible Distributed MIMO System

Ezzeldin Hamed, Hariharan Rahul, Mohammed A. Abdelghany, and Dina Katabi
Massachusetts Institute of Technology
{ezz,rahul,melmotaz,dina}@csail.mit.edu

ABSTRACT

We present a demonstration of a real-time distributed MIMO system, DMIMO. DMIMO synchronizes transmissions from 4 distributed MIMO transmitters in time, frequency and phase, and performs distributed multi-user beamforming to independent clients. DMIMO is built on top of a Zynq hardware platform integrated with an FMCOMMS2 RF front end. The platform implements a custom 802.11n compatible MIMO PHY layer which is augmented with a lightweight distributed synchronization engine. The demonstration shows the received constellation points, channels, and effective data throughput at each client.

CCS CONCEPTS

•Networks → Network protocols; Wireless access points, base stations and infrastructure; •Hardware → Digital signal processing;

1. INTRODUCTION

Recent years have seen the demand for wireless data increase by leaps and bounds, putting tremendous pressure on our limited supply of wireless spectrum. In recent years, distributed multi-user beamforming has been proposed as a solution for this spectrum crunch since it allows wireless througput to scale with the number of transmitters in the network.

Our demonstration builds on recent advances in practical distributed multi-user beamforming. Specifically, MegaMIMO [2] demonstrated an implementation using USRPs that achieved low overhead distributed time, frequency and phase synchronization across transmitters to provide distributed beamforming, and scaled throughput with the number of transmitters. However, these prior systems were not real-time or implemented in hardware.

In contrast, our system, DMIMO, implements a complete 802.11n compatible MIMO physical layer and the synchronization subsystem in hardware. A hardware implementation requires us to address real-time constraints such as integration with carrier sense and response to interference unlike previous systems. Further, we need to ensure that our time, frequency and phase synchronization subsystems are simple enough to meet the timing and resource constraints inherent to hardware, while still achieving the desired accuracy for scaling throughput with the number of transmitters.

SIGCOMM '15 August 17-21, 2015, London, United Kingdom

ACM ISBN 978-1-4503-3542-3/15/08.
DOI: http://dx.doi.org/10.1145/2785956.2790042

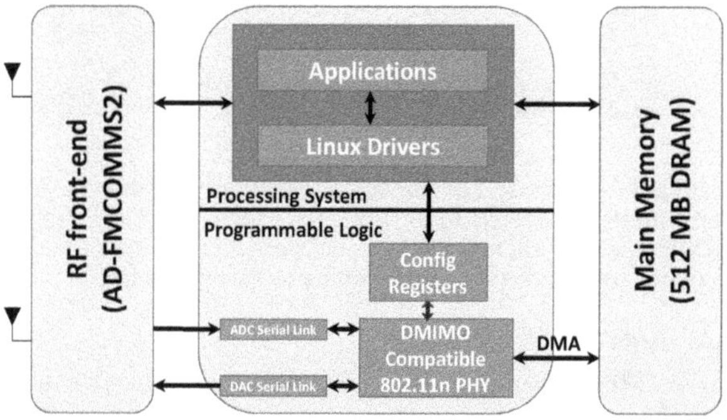

Figure 1—Platform Architecture. The figure shows our software-hardware architecture. The PHY on the FPGA implements an 802.11n MIMO system and the real time synchronization facilities needed for distributed MIMO. The software on the ARM core configures the PHY and manages data transfer to and from the device.

2. SYSTEM ARCHITECTURE

The DMIMO system consists of a hardware access point platform that performs physical layer processing of data and the received signals, and a software controller that coordinates the different transmitters to perform distributed multi-user beamforming.

2.1 Hardware

We implement DMIMO on the Xilinx Zynq platform [3] integrated with the Analog Devices FMCOMMS2/3 RF front end card [1]. The Zynq platform consists of an Artix based FPGA connected by a high speed bus to an ARM dual-core Cortex A9 processor. We implement the PHY layer for our 802.11n compatible MIMO transceiver subsystem using Verilog on the Zynq FPGA. Each MIMO transmitter can precode up to 8 independent streams to 2 antennas. Four such transmitters can therefore coordinate to jointly emulate a single 8x8 MIMO transmitter. We also run Linux on the ARM core with drivers to interact with the PHY layer. The PHY layer exposes read and write registers that enable real time configuration and monitoring by drivers, as well as DMA for bulk data transfer for packet transmission and reception. Fig. 1 shows the hardware architecture of our system.

In addition to the typical transmission and reception functionalities, our PHY has these additional configurable capabilities:

- Reporting the decoded constellation points on all the subcarriers.
- Reporting the estimated channel from the packet headers as well as decoded data.
- Joint transmission with a master transmitter, along with time, frequency, and phase synchronization.

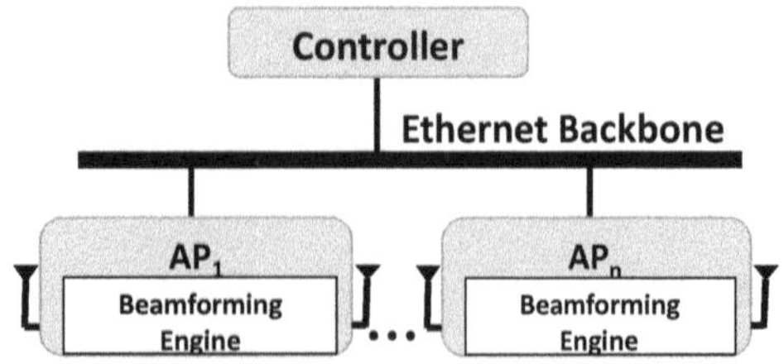

Figure 2—DMIMO Architecture. The controller orchestrates the beamforming engines on the APs.

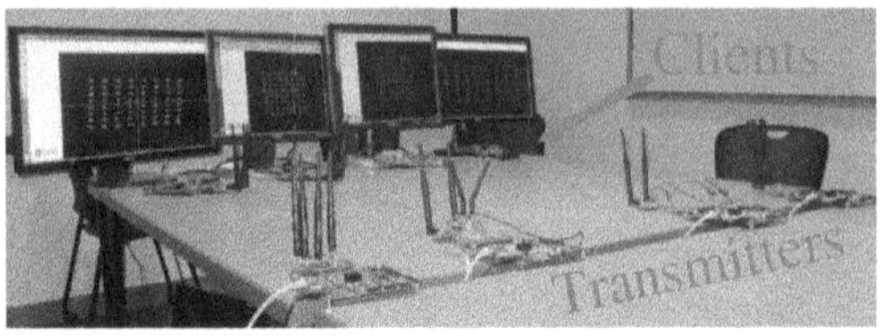

Figure 3—Testbed. The testbed consists of 4 2-antenna MIMO transmitters connected to an Ethernet backhaul, and 4 2-antenna MIMO *wireless* clients. Each client is equipped with a monitor to display parameters associated with its received signal.

2.2 Software Controller

Fig. 2 shows the DMIMO architecture. The software controller coordinates the transmitters in order to measure the channels to clients, as well as to perform distributed multi user beamforming. In particular, it schedules joint channel measurement transmissions from the master and slave transmitters as described in [2]. It then obtains the measured channel information from the clients, and computes a precoding matrix to be used by the transmitters. The controller distributes the appropriate rows of the precoding matrix to each transmitter along with the data for joint transmission, and sets registers to ensure that the master and slave transmissions are synchronized in frequency and phase. The PHY layer then performs the beamforming and synchronized transmission in hardware.

3. DEMONSTRATION

The demonstration consists of four 2-antenna MIMO transmitters capable of distributed MIMO and four 2-antenna MIMO clients as shown in Fig. 3. Each transmitter is capable of participating, along with other transmitters, in an 8 stream distributed MIMO transmission. One of the transmitters is configured as a master, and the others are configured as slaves. The transmitters are connected to an Ethernet backhaul, as can be seen by the yellow ethernet cables to the left of each transmitter device. The clients, on the other hand, are not connected to any wired network and communicate wirelessly with the transmitters. Each client is connected to a monitor, which is used to display various statistics related to the received data, for instance, constellations, channel plots, throughput *etc.*

The transmitters periodically transmit channel measurement packets to the clients. The clients use these measurement packets to estimate the channels from the different transmitters, and then transmit these measured channels back to the transmitters. The software controller, which runs on the master, computes the precoding matrix based on these measured channels and transmits the relevant rows of the precoding matrix to each transmitter. Each transmitter then precodes the 8 streams intended to the clients with its rows of the precoding matrix. Note that the clients themselves are not aware that the transmissions are joint to multiple clients, and each will decode its streams individually.

The system supports 1 and 2 stream 802.11n (*i.e.* 56 subcarriers with 4 pilots) and all the 1 and 2 stream 802.11n modulations and

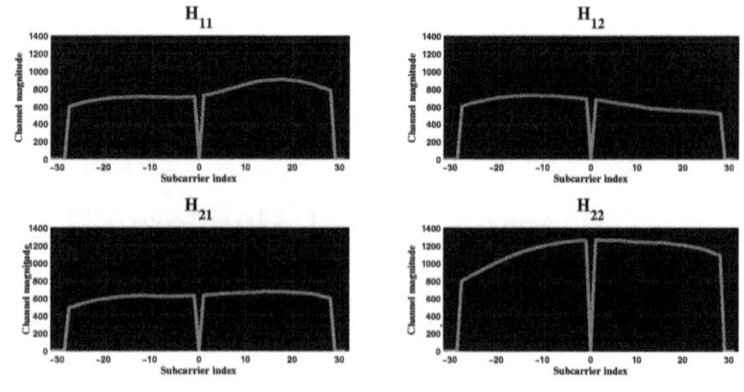

Figure 4—Channel Matrix. The green line shows the 2x2 channel matrix observed at one of the clients.

code rates (BPSK 1/2 rate, 4-QAM 1/2 rate, 4-QAM 3/4 rate, 16-QAM 1/2 rate, 16-QAM 3/4 rate, 64-QAM 2/3 rate, 64-QAM 3/4 rate, and 64-QAM 5/6 rate).

An application on the transmitters chooses the rate for joint transmission to the different clients, as well as the beamforming algorithm to be used (*e.g.* zero forcing beamforming, conjugate beamforming, no beamforming).

The clients demonstrate the following statistics:

(a) Received constellation points: This is as shown on the monitors in Fig. 3 above. The clustering of the constellation points shows the impact of the channel feedback quality and timeliness on the accuracy of beamforming, as well as the performance of the different beamforming algorithms.

(b) Channel at each client: This shows the channel magnitude across all subcarriers for the 2x2 channel matrix at each client. Note that each client receives only a 2 stream packet after the combination of all the transmissions and hence effectively sees only a 2x2 channel. Fig. 4 shows an example channel matrix at a client.

The demonstration shows how this channel matrix will vary as the controller uses different precoding techniques. For instance, when the controller uses a form of zero-forcing that nulls the contribution of all other streams at each antenna, each antenna will effectively see only one stream. As a result, the off-diagonal entries in the effective channel matrix (*i.e.*, H_{12} and H_{21}) will be close to 0.

However, such a restriction is too strict as the interference between two streams destined to the same client need not be nulled relative to each other. Providing this additional degree of freedom to the controller will allow it to compute a channel matrix which can deliver higher throughput than the strict nulling system described above. In such a case, the off-diagonal entries will be non-zero as our demonstration will show.

(c) Throughput as a function of time: The demonstration shows a graph of the effective throughput, *i.e.*, the rate of correctly received and decoded data as a function of time. The graph shows the effect of the transmitted modulation on the received throughput as a function of the quality and timeliness of the channel measurement. Further, it demonstrates the impact of various kinds of interference (single tone and wideband) on the received throughput.

REFERENCES

[1] Analog devices FMCOMMS2. http://www.analog.com/en/design-center/evaluation-hardware-and-software/evaluation-boards-kits/EVAL-AD-FMCOMMS2.html.

[2] H. Rahul, S. Kumar, and D. Katabi. MegaMIMO: Scaling Wireless Capacity with User Demands. In *ACM SIGCOMM 2012*, Helsinki, Finland, August 2012.

[3] Xilinx Zynq. http://www.xilinx.com/products/silicon-devices/soc/zynq-7000.html. Zynq All Programmable SOC.

Sub-Nanosecond Time of Flight on Commercial Wi-Fi Cards

Deepak Vasisht, Swarun Kumar, and Dina Katabi
Massachusetts Institute of Technology
{deepakv,swarun,dk}@mit.edu

1. SYSTEM OVERVIEW

The time-of-flight of a signal captures the time it takes to propagate from a transmitter to a receiver. Time-of-flight is perhaps the most intuitive method for localization using wireless signals. If one can accurately measure the time-of-flight from a transmitter, one can compute the transmitter's distance simply by multiplying the time-of-flight by the speed of light. Today, GPS, the most widely used outdoor localization system, localizes a device using the time-of-flight of radio signals from satellites. However, applying the same concept to indoor localization has proven difficult. Systems for localization in indoor spaces are expected to deliver high accuracy (e.g., a meter or less) using consumer-oriented technologies (e.g., Wi-Fi on one's cellphone). Unfortunately, past work could not measure time-of-flight at such an accuracy on Wi-Fi devices [10, 2]. As a result, over the years, research on accurate indoor positioning has moved towards more complex alternatives such as employing large multi-antenna arrays to compute the angle-of-arrival of the signal [11, 4]. These new techniques have delivered highly accurate indoor localization systems.

Despite these advances, time-of-flight based localization has some of the basic desirable features that state-of-the-art indoor localization systems lack. In particular, measuring time-of-flight does not require more than a single antenna on the receiver. In fact, by measuring time-of-flight of a signal to just two antennas, a receiver can intersect the corresponding distances to locate its source. Thus, a receiver can locate a wireless transmitter with no support from the surrounding infrastructure. This is quite unlike current indoor localization systems, which require multiple access points at known locations, to find the distance between a pair of mobile devices. Furthermore, each of these access points need to have many antennas – far beyond what is supported in commercial Wi-Fi devices.

In this demo, we will present Chronos, a system that combines a set of novel algorithms to measure the time-of-flight to sub-nanosecond accuracy on commercial Wi-Fi cards. In particular, we will measure distance/time-of-flight between two devices equipped with commercial Wi-Fi cards, without any support from the infrastructure or environment fingerprinting.

CCS CONCEPTS

•**Networks** → **Network protocols;** •**Hardware** → *Signal processing systems;*

SIGCOMM '15 August 17-21, 2015, London, United Kingdom

ACM ISBN 978-1-4503-3542-3/15/08.
DOI: http://dx.doi.org/10.1145/2785956.2790043

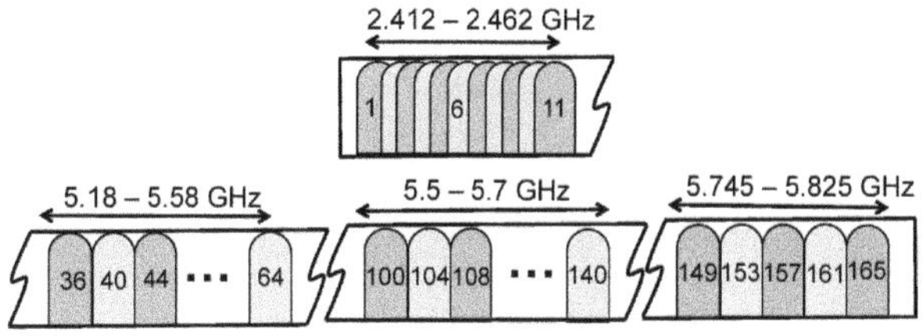

Figure 1: **Wi-Fi Bands:** Wi-Fi bands at 2.4 GHz and 5 GHz.

KEYWORDS

Wireless, RF Localization, Time-of-flight

2. CHALLENGES

Why is it that one cannot accurately measure time-of-flight on commercial Wi-Fi devices? In particular, to achieve state-of-the-art positioning accuracy, one must measure time-of-flight at sub-nanosecond granularity. However, doing so on commercial Wi-Fi cards is fundamentally challenging for the following three reasons.

Limited Time Granularity: First, the straightforward approach to measure time-of-flight is to read off the clock of the Wi-Fi radio when the signal arrives [10]. Unfortunately, the clocks on today's Wi-Fi cards operate at tens of MHz, limiting their resolution in measuring time to tens of nanoseconds [2, 8, 6]. To put this in perspective, a clock running at 20 MHz (the bandwidth of typical Wi-Fi systems), can only tell apart distances separated by 15 m, making it impractical for accurate indoor positioning. Even recent state-of-the-art systems that measure time-of-flight using high-resolution 88 MHz Wi-Fi clocks [5] and super-resolution channel processing techniques [12] suffer a mean localization error of about 2.3 m.

Packet Detection Delay: Second, any measurement of time-of-flight of a packet necessarily includes the delay in detecting its presence. To make matters worse, this packet detection delay is typically orders-of-magnitude higher than time-of-flight for indoor Wi-Fi environments [7]. In fact, in our experiments described later, we observed the median packet detection delay to be $\sim$ 177 ns, with a standard deviation of $\sim$ 25 ns; while the median propagation delay was $\sim$ 22 ns. Today, there is no way to tease apart the time-of-flight from this detection delay.

Multipath: Finally, in indoor environments, signals do not experience a single time-of-flight, but a time-of-flight spread. To see why, observe that wireless signals in indoor environments travel along multiple paths, and bounce off walls and furniture. As a result, the receiver obtains several copies of the signal, each having experienced a different time-of-flight. To perform accurate localization, one must therefore be able to disentangle the time-of-flight of the most direct path from all the remaining paths.

3. OUR SOLUTION

We design algorithms that overcome the above limitations and

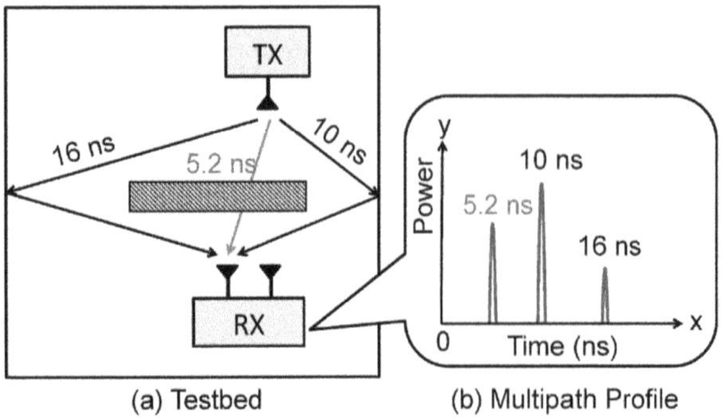

(a) Testbed (b) Multipath Profile

Figure 2: **Combating Multipath:** Consider a signal propagating from a transmitter to a receiver along three paths as shown in (a): an attenuated direct path and two reflected paths of lengths 5.2 ns, 10 ns and 16 ns respectively. The combined signal is processed by Chronos to produce (b). The plot has three peaks corresponding to the propagation delays of the three paths, with peak magnitudes scaled by their relative attenuations.

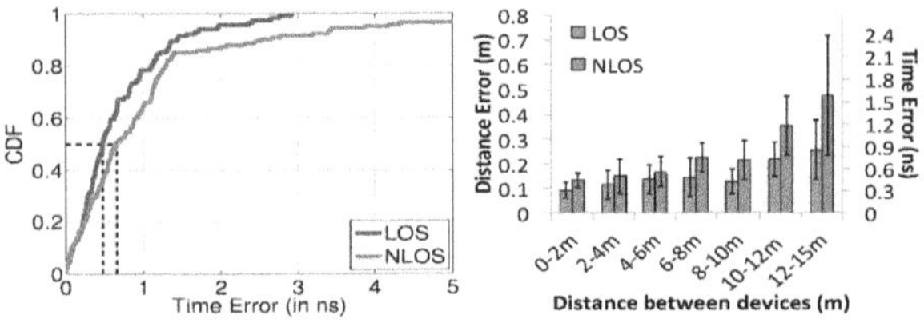

(a) Time of Flight (b) Accuracy with Distance

Figure 3: **Time-of-Flight Accuracy**: (a) measures the CDF of error in time-of-flight between two devices in Line of Sight (LOS) and Non-Line of Sight (NLOS). (b) plots accuracy in time-of-flight between two devices as the distance between them is varied.

measure the time-of-flight at sub-nanosecond accuracy using off-the-shelf Wi-Fi cards. On a high level, our approach is based on the following observation: If one had a very wideband radio (e.g., a few GHz), one could measure time of flight at sub-nanosecond accuracy. While each Wi-Fi frequency band is only tens of Megahertz wide, there are many such bands that together span a very wide bandwidth, as shown in Fig. 1. Our solution therefore collects measurements on multiple Wi-Fi frequency bands and stitches them together to give the illusion of a wide-band radio. Our key contribution is an algorithm that achieves this, despite the fact that Wi-Fi frequency bands are non-contiguous, and in some cases, a few Gigahertz apart. By doing this, we can negate the need for a high bandwidth clock and get accurate time-of-flight measurements.

As discussed before, indoor environments are rich in multipath, causing wireless signals to bounce off objects in the environment like walls and furniture. The received signal is therefore the sum of these multiple signal copies, each having experienced a different propagation delay and attenuation, as shown in Fig. 2. Dealing with multipath effect requires two steps: a) Identifying different signal reflections and, b) Choosing the signal component corresponding to the direct path. To identify different signal reflections, we design an algorithm to leverage the sparsity in signal reflection to tease apart different signal reflections and plot signal profiles (e.g., Fig. 2(b)). Once the different signal reflections have been disentangled, we choose the path with the shortest time-of-flight as the direct path, as any reflected path has travelled a longer distance than the direct path. For lack of space, we refer the reader to [9] for a detailed discussion of these algorithms.

4. EVALUATION

To demonstrate the performance and practicality of our design, we implemented Chronos as a software patch to the iwlwifi driver on Ubuntu Linux running the 3.5.7 kernel. To measure channel-state-information, we leverage the 802.11 CSI Tool [3] for the Intel 5300 Wi-Fi card. We measure wireless channels on both 2.4 GHz and 5 GHz Wi-Fi bands. We evaluated Chronos's performance on pairs of devices equipped with Intel 5300 Wi-Fi cards, including Thinkpad W530 laptops and Asus IEEE PC netbooks. Chronos estimated the distance between a pair of devices, placed at randomly chosen locations in a floor of our office building. The ground truth was measured using a combination of the floor maps and a Bosch GLM50 laser distance measurement tool [1]. We present two representative results here.

As shown in Fig. 3(a), Chronos achieves a median error in time-of-flight of 0.47 ns in line-of-sight and 0.69 ns in non-line-of-sight settings, corresponding to a physical distance accuracy of 14.1 cm and 20.7 cm respectively (95th percentile: 1.96 ns and 4.01 ns). Our results show that Chronos achieves its promise of computing time-of-flight at sub-nanosecond accuracy. To put this in perspective, SourceSync [7], a state-of-the-art system for time synchronization, achieves 95th percentile synchronization error up to 20 ns, using advanced software radios. However, we point out that unlike indoor positioning, tens of nanoseconds of error is sufficient for time-synchronization-the target application for SourceSync. Fig. 3(b) plots the median and standard deviation of error in distance computed between the transmitter and receiver against their true relative distance. We observe that this error is initially around 10 cm and increases to at most 25.6 cm at 12-15 meters. The increase is primarily due to reduced signal-to-noise ratio at further distances.

5. CONCLUSION

In this demo, we will present, Chronos, a system that measures time of flight (and hence, distance) between two devices to sub-nanosecond accuracy, using commercial WiFi cards. To our knowledge, Chronos is the first system that can measure time-of-flight on commercial Wi-Fi cards to this accuracy.

6. REFERENCES

[1] Bosch laser distance measurer glm50. http://www.boschtools.com/Products/Tools/Pages/BoschProductDetail.aspx?pid=GLM\%2050.
[2] T. Bourchas, M. Bednarek, D. Giustiniano, and V. Lenders. Practical limits of wifi time-of-flight echo techniques. In *IPSN*, pages 273–274, April 2014.
[3] D. Halperin, W. Hu, A. Sheth, and D. Wetherall. Tool release: Gathering 802.11n traces with channel state information. *ACM SIGCOMM CCR*, 2011.
[4] K. Joshi, S. Hong, and S. Katti. Pinpoint: Localizing interfering radios. NSDI, 2013.
[5] A. T. Mariakakis, S. Sen, J. Lee, and K.-H. Kim. Sail: Single access point-based indoor localization. MobiSys, 2014.
[6] K. Muthukrishnan, G. Koprinkov, N. Meratnia, and M. Lijding. Using time-of-flight for wlan localization: feasibility study, 2006.
[7] H. Rahul, H. Hassanieh, and D. Katabi. SourceSync: A Distributed Wireless Architecture for Exploiting Sender Diversity. In *ACM SIGCOMM 2010*, August 2010.
[8] L. Schauer, F. Dorfmeister, and M. Maier. Potentials and limitations of wifi-positioning using time-of-flight. In *IPIN*, 2013.
[9] D. Vasisht, S. Kumar, and D. Katabi. Sub-nanosecond time of flight on commercial wi-fi cards. *CoRR*, abs/1505.03446, 2015.
[10] S. B. Wibowo, M. Klepal, and D. Pesch. Time of flight ranging using off-the-self ieee802.11 wifi tags. POCA, 2009.
[11] J. Xiong and K. Jamieson. Arraytrack: A fine-grained indoor location system. NSDI '13, 2013.
[12] J. Xiong, K. Jamieson, and K. Sundaresan. Synchronicity: Pushing the envelope of fine-grained localization with distributed mimo. HotWireless, 2014.

Inside the Social Network's (Datacenter) Network

Arjun Roy, Hongyi Zeng†, Jasmeet Bagga†, George Porter, and Alex C. Snoeren
Department of Computer Science and Engineering
University of California, San Diego

†Facebook, Inc.

ABSTRACT

Large cloud service providers have invested in increasingly larger datacenters to house the computing infrastructure required to support their services. Accordingly, researchers and industry practitioners alike have focused a great deal of effort designing network fabrics to efficiently interconnect and manage the traffic within these datacenters in performant yet efficient fashions. Unfortunately, datacenter operators are generally reticent to share the actual requirements of their applications, making it challenging to evaluate the practicality of any particular design.

Moreover, the limited large-scale workload information available in the literature has, for better or worse, heretofore largely been provided by a single datacenter operator whose use cases may not be widespread. In this work, we report upon the network traffic observed in some of Facebook's datacenters. While Facebook operates a number of traditional datacenter services like Hadoop, its core Web service and supporting cache infrastructure exhibit a number of behaviors that contrast with those reported in the literature. We report on the contrasting locality, stability, and predictability of network traffic in Facebook's datacenters, and comment on their implications for network architecture, traffic engineering, and switch design.

Keywords

Datacenter traffic patterns

CCS Concepts

•**Networks** → **Network measurement; Data center networks;** *Network performance analysis;* Network monitoring; Social media networks;

SIGCOMM '15, August 17–21, 2015, London, United Kingdom

ISBN 978-1-4503-3542-3/15/08...$15.00

DOI: http://dx.doi.org/10.1145/2785956.2787472

1. INTRODUCTION

Datacenters are revolutionizing the way in which we design networks, due in large part to the vastly different engineering constraints that arise when interconnecting a large number of highly interdependent homogeneous nodes in a relatively small physical space, as opposed to loosely coupled heterogeneous end points scattered across the globe. While many aspects of network and protocol design hinge on these physical attributes, many others require a firm understanding of the demand that will be placed on the network by end hosts. Unfortunately, while we understand a great deal about the former (i.e., that modern cloud datacenters connect 10s of thousands of servers using a mix of 10-Gbps Ethernet and increasing quantities of higher-speed fiber interconnects), the latter tend to be not disclosed publicly.

Hence, many recent proposals are motivated by lightly validated assumptions regarding datacenter workloads, or, in some cases, workload traces from a single, large datacenter operator [12, 26]. These traces are dominated by traffic generated as part of a major Web search service, which, while certainly significant, may differ from the demands of other major cloud services. In this paper, we study sample workloads from within Facebook's datacenters. We find that traffic studies in the literature are not entirely representative of Facebook's demands, calling into question the applicability of some of the proposals based upon these prevalent assumptions on datacenter traffic behavior. This situation is particularly acute when considering novel network fabrics, traffic engineering protocols, and switch designs.

As an example, a great deal of effort has gone into identifying effective topologies for datacenter interconnects [4, 19, 21, 36]. The best choice (in terms of cost/benefit tradeoff) depends on the communication pattern between end hosts [33]. Lacking concrete data, researchers often design for the worst case, namely an all-to-all traffic matrix in which each host communicates with every other host with equal frequency and intensity [4]. Such an assumption leads to the goal of delivering maximum bisection bandwidth [4, 23, 36], which may be overkill when demand exhibits significant locality [17].

In practice, production datacenters tend to enforce a certain degree of oversubscription [12, 21], assuming that either the end-host bandwidth far exceeds actual traffic demands,

Finding	Previously published data	Potential impacts
Traffic is neither rack local nor all-to-all; low utilization (§4)	50–80% of traffic is rack local [12, 17]	Datacenter fabrics [4, 36, 21]
Demand is wide-spread, uniform, and stable, with rapidly changing, internally bursty heavy hitters (§5)	Demand is frequently concentrated and bursty [12, 13, 14]	Traffic engineering [5, 14, 25, 39]
Small packets (outside of Hadoop), continuous arrivals; many concurrent flows (§6)	Bimodal ACK/MTU packet size, on/off behavior [12]; <5 concurrent large flows [8]	SDN controllers [1, 22, 28, 32, 34]; Circuit/hybrid switching [7, 20, 30, 39]

Table 1: Each of our major findings differs from previously published characterizations of datacenter traffic. Many systems incorporate one or more of the previously published features as design assumptions.

or that there is significant locality in demand that decreases the need for full connectivity between physically disparate portions of the datacenter. The precise degree of oversubscription varies, but there is general agreement amongst operators that full connectivity is rarely worthwhile [11]. To mitigate potential "hotspots" caused by oversubscription, researchers have suggested designs that temporarily enhance connectivity between portions of the datacenter [5, 25, 40]. The utility of these approaches depends upon the prevalence, size, and dynamics of such hotspots.

In particular, researchers have proposed inherently non-uniform fabrics which provide qualitatively different connectivity to certain portions of the datacenter through various hybrid designs, typically including either optical [30, 39] or wireless links [25, 40]. If demand can be predicted and/or remains stable over reasonable time periods, it may be feasible to provide circuit-like connectivity between portions of the datacenter [20]. Alternatively, network controllers could select among existing paths in an intelligent fashion [14]. Regardless of the technology involved, all of these techniques require traffic to be predictable over non-trivial time scales [14, 20, 25, 30, 39].

Finally, many have observed that the stylized nature of datacenter traffic opens up many avenues for increasing the efficiency of switching hardware itself. In particular, while some have proposed straightforward modifications like decreased buffering, port count, or sophistication [4] in various layers of the switching fabric, others have proposed replacing conventional packet switches either with circuit or hybrid designs that leverage locality, persistence, and predictability of traffic demands [30]. More extreme, host-based solutions advocate connecting end-hosts directly [21, 23]. Obviously, when, where, or if any of these approaches makes economic sense hinges tightly on offered loads [33].

While there have been a number of studies of university [14] and private datacenters [12], many proposals cannot be fully evaluated without significant scale. Almost all of the previous studies of large-scale (10K hosts or larger) datacenters [5, 12, 14, 17, 21, 25, 26] consider Microsoft datacenters. While Facebook's datacenters have some commonality with Microsoft's, such as eschewing virtual machines [14], they support a very different application mix. As a result, we observe a number of critical distinctions that may lead to qualitatively different conclusions; we describe those differences and explain the reasons behind them.

Our study is the first to report on production traffic in a datacenter network connecting hundreds of thousands of 10-Gbps nodes. Using both Facebook-wide monitoring systems and per-host packet-header traces, we examine services that generate the majority of the traffic in Facebook's network. While we find that the traffic patterns exhibited by Facebook's Hadoop deployments comport well with those reported in the literature, significant portions of Facebook's service architecture [10, 15] vary dramatically from the MapReduce-style infrastructures studied previously, leading to vastly different traffic patterns. Findings of our study with significant architectural implications include:

- Traffic is neither rack-local nor all-to-all; locality depends upon the service but is stable across time periods from seconds to days. Efficient fabrics may benefit from variable degrees of oversubscription and less intra-rack bandwidth than typically deployed.
- Many flows are long-lived but not very heavy. Load balancing effectively distributes traffic across hosts; so much so that traffic demands are quite stable over even sub-second intervals. As a result, heavy hitters are not much larger than the median flow, and the set of heavy hitters changes rapidly. Instantaneously heavy hitters are frequently not heavy over longer time periods, likely confounding many approaches to traffic engineering.
- Packets are small (median length for non-Hadoop traffic is less than 200 bytes) and do not exhibit on/off arrival behavior. Servers communicate with 100s of hosts and racks concurrently (i.e., within the same 5-ms interval), but the majority of traffic is often destined to (few) 10s of racks.

While we do not offer these workloads as any more representative than others—indeed, they may change as Facebook's services evolve—they do suggest that the space of cloud datacenter workloads is more rich than the literature may imply. As one way to characterize the significance of our findings, Table 1 shows how our results compare to the literature, and cites exemplar systems that incorporate these assumptions in their design.

The rest of this paper is organized as follows. We begin in Section 2 with a survey of the major findings of previous studies of datacenter traffic. Section 3 provides a high-level description of the organization of Facebook's datacenters, the services they support, and our collection methodologies. We then analyze aspects of the traffic within a number of Facebook's datacenters that impact provisioning (Section 4), traffic engineering (Section 5), and switch design (Section 6), before concluding in Section 7.

2. RELATED WORK

Initial studies of datacenter workloads were conducted via simulation [6] or on testbeds [18]. Subsequently, however, a number of studies of production datacenter traffic have been performed, primarily within Microsoft datacenters.

It is difficult to determine how many distinct Microsoft datacenters are reported on in literature, or how representative that set might be. Kandula *et al.* observe that their results "extend to other *mining* data centers that employ some flavor of map-reduce style workflow computation on top of a distributed block store," but caution that "*web* or *cloud* data centers that primarily deal with generating responses for web requests (e.g., mail, messenger) are likely to have different characteristics." [26]. By that taxonomy, Facebook's datacenters clearly fall in the latter camp. Jalaparti *et al.* [24] examine latency for Microsoft Bing services that are similar in concept to Facebook's service; we note both similarities to our workload (relatively low utilization coupled with a scatter-gather style traffic pattern) and differences (load appears more evenly distributed within Facebook datacenters).

Three major themes are prevalent in prior studies, and summarized in Table 1. First, traffic is found to be heavily rack local, likely as a consequence of the application patterns observed; Benson *et al.* note that for cloud datacenters "a majority of traffic originated by servers (80%) stays within the rack" [12]. Studies by Kandula *et al.* [26], Delimitrou *et al.* [17] and Alizadeh *et al.* [8] observe similarly rack-heavy traffic patterns.

Second, traffic is frequently reported to be bursty and unstable across a variety of timescales—an important observation, since traffic engineering techniques often depend on relatively long-lived, predictable flows. Kapoor *et al.* observe that packets to a given destination often arrive in trains [27]; while Benson *et al.* find a strong on/off pattern where the packet inter-arrival follows a log-normal distribution [13]. Changing the timescale of observation can change the ease of prediction; Delimitrou *et al.* [17] note that while traffic locality varies on a day-to-day basis, it remains consistent at the scale of months. Conversely, Benson *et al.* [14] claim that while traffic is unpredictable at timescales of 150 seconds and longer, it can be relatively stable on the timescale of a few seconds, and discuss traffic engineering mechanisms that might work for such traffic.

Finally, previous studies have consistently reported a bimodal packet size [12], with packets either approaching the MTU or remaining quite small, such as a TCP ACK segment. We find that Facebook's traffic is very different, with a consistently small median packet size despite the 10-Gbps link speed. Researchers have also reported that individual end hosts typically communicate with only a few (e.g., less than 5 [8]) destinations at once. For some Facebook services, an individual host maintains orders of magnitude more concurrent connections.

3. A FACEBOOK DATACENTER

In order to establish context necessary to interpret our findings, this section provides a brief overview of Facebook's datacenter network topology, as well as a description of the application services that it supports; more detail is available elsewhere [2, 9, 10, 15, 19]. We then describe the two distinct collection systems used to assemble the network traces analyzed in the remainder of the paper.

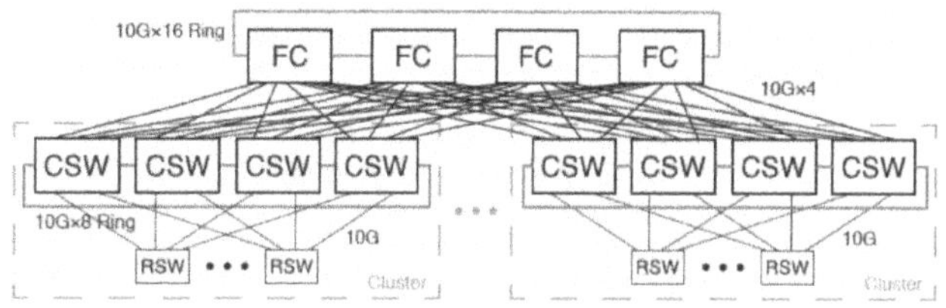

Figure 1: Facebook's 4-post cluster design [19]

3.1 Datacenter topology

Facebook's network consists of multiple datacenter sites (henceforth site) and a backbone connecting these sites. Each datacenter site contains one or more datacenter buildings (henceforth datacenter) where each datacenter contains multiple clusters. A cluster is considered a unit of deployment in Facebook datacenters. Each cluster employs a conventional 3-tier topology depicted in Figure 1, reproduced from a short paper [19].

Machines are organized into racks and connected to a top-of-rack switch (RSW) via 10-Gbps Ethernet links. The number of machines per rack varies from cluster to cluster. Each RSW in turn is connected by 10-Gbps links to four aggregation switches called cluster switches (CSWs). All racks served by a particular set of CSWs are said to be in the same cluster. Clusters may be homogeneous in terms of machines—e.g. Cache clusters—or heterogeneous, e.g. Frontend clusters which contain a mixture of Web servers, load balancers and cache servers. CSWs are connected to each other via another layer of aggregation switches called Fat Cats (FC). As will be seen later in this paper, this design follows directly from the need to support a high amount of intra-cluster traffic. Finally, CSWs also connect to aggregation switches for intra-site (but inter-datacenter) traffic and datacenter routers for inter-site traffic.

The majority of Facebook's current datacenters employ this 4-post Clos design. Work is underway, however, to migrate Facebook's datacenters to a next-generation Fabric architecture [9]. The analyses in this paper are based upon data collected from machines in traditional 4-post clusters, although Facebook-wide statistics (e.g., Table 3) cover hosts in both traditional 4-post clusters and newer Fabric pods.

One distinctive aspect of Facebook's datacenters is that each machine typically has precisely one role: Web servers (Web) serve Web traffic; MySQL servers (DB) store user data; query results are stored temporarily in cache servers (Cache)—including leaders, which handle cache coherency, and followers, which serve most read requests [15]; Hadoop servers (Hadoop) handle offline analysis and data mining; Multifeed servers (MF) assemble news feeds [31]. While there are a number of other roles, these represent the majority, and will be the focus of our study. In addition, a rel-

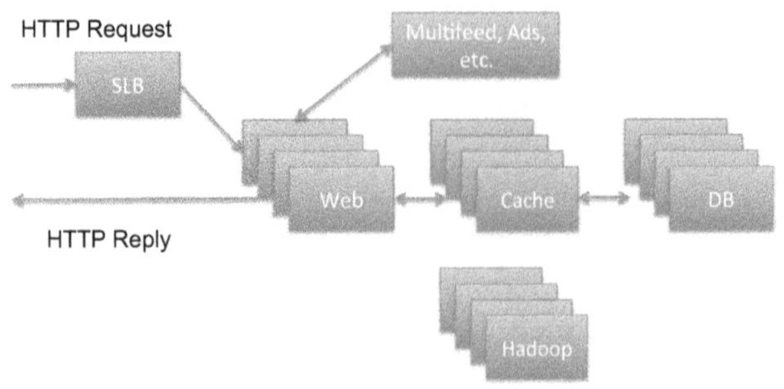

Figure 2: How an HTTP request is served

Type	Web	Cache	MF	SLB	Hadoop	Rest
Web	-	63.1	15.2	5.6	-	16.1
Cache-l	-	86.6	5.9	-	-	7.5
Cache-f	88.7	5.8	-	-	-	5.5
Hadoop	-	-	-	-	99.8	0.2

Table 2: Breakdown of outbound traffic percentages for four different host types

atively small number of machines do not have a fixed role and are dynamically repurposed. Facebook's datacenters do not typically house virtual machines: each service runs on a physical server. Moreover—and in contrast to previously studied datacenters [12]—to ease provisioning and management, racks typically contain only servers of the same role.

3.2 Constituent services

The organization of machines within a cluster—and even a datacenter—is intimately related to the communication patterns between the services they support. We introduce the major services by briefly describing how an HTTP request is served by `http://facebook.com`, shown in Figure 2.

When an HTTP query hits a Facebook datacenter, it arrives at a layer-four software load balancer (SLB) [37]. The query is then redirected to one of the Web servers. Web servers are largely stateless, containing no user data. They fetch data from the cache tier [15]. In case of a cache miss, a cache server will then fetch data from the database tier. At the same time, the Web server may communicate with one or more backend machines to fetch objects such as news stories and ads. Table 2 quantifies the relative traffic intensity between different services by classifying the outbound traffic from four different servers—a Web server, cache leader (cache-l), cache follower (cache-f), and Hadoop—based upon the role of the destination host. (The data is extracted from packet-header traces described in Section 3.3.2.)

In contrast to most service tiers, Hadoop nodes are not involved with serving end-user requests. Instead, Hadoop clusters perform offline analysis such as data mining. HDFS and Hadoop MapReduce are the main applications running on these servers.

3.3 Data collection

Due to the scale of Facebook's datacenters, it is impractical to collect complete network traffic dumps. Instead, we consider two distinct sources of data. The first, Fbflow, constantly samples packet headers across Facebook's entire global network. The second, port mirroring, focuses on a single machine (or rack) at a time, allowing us to collect complete packet-header traces for a brief period of time at particular locations within a single datacenter.

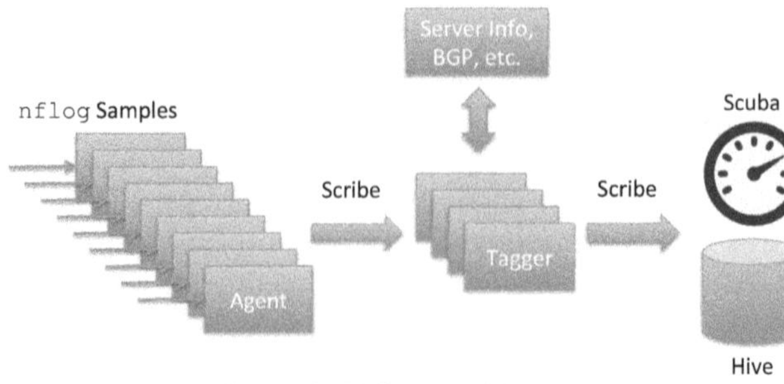

Figure 3: Fbflow architecture

3.3.1 Fbflow

Fbflow is a production monitoring system that samples packet headers from Facebook's entire machine fleet. Its architecture, comprised of two main component types—*agents* and *taggers*—is shown in Figure 3. Fbflow samples packets by inserting a Netfilter `nflog` target into every machine's `iptable` rules. The datasets we consider in this paper are collected with a 1:30,000 sampling rate. A user-level Fbflow agent process on each machine listens to the `nflog` socket and parses the headers, extracting information such as source and destination IP addresses, port numbers, and protocol. These parsed headers—collected across all machines in Facebook's datacenters—along with metadata such as machine name and capture time, are streamed to a small number of taggers using Scribe [2], a log aggregation system.

Taggers, running on a subset of machines, read a portion of the packet-header stream from Scribe, and further annotate it with additional information such as the rack and cluster containing the machine where the trace was collected, its autonomous system number, etc., by querying other data sources. Taggers then convert each annotated packet header into a JSON object and feed it into Scuba [3], a real-time data analytics system. Samples are simultaneously stored into Hive [38] tables for long-term analysis.

3.3.2 Port mirroring

While Fbflow is a powerful tool for network monitoring and management, its sampling-based collection prohibits certain types of data analysis. Specifically, in production use, it aggregates statistics at a per-minute granularity. In order to collect high-fidelity data, we deploy a number of special-purpose trace collection machines within the datacenter that collect packet-header traces over short intervals.

We deploy monitoring hosts in five different racks across Facebook's datacenter network, locating them in clusters that host distinct services. In particular, we monitor a rack of Web servers, a Hadoop node, cache followers and leaders, and a Multifeed node. In all but one (Web) instance, we collect traces by turning on port mirroring on the RSW

(ToR) and mirroring the full, bi-directional traffic for a single server to our collection server. For the hosts we monitor, the RSW is able to mirror the selected ports without loss. In the case of Web servers, utilization is low enough that we are able to mirror traffic from a rack of servers to our collection host. We did not measure database servers that include user data in this study.

Recording the packet traces using a commodity server is not entirely trivial, as `tcpdump` is unable to handle more than approximately 1.5 Gbps of traffic in our configuration. In order to support line-rate traces, we employ a custom kernel module that effectively pins all free RAM on the server and uses it to buffer incoming packets. Our kernel module extracts the packets immediately after the Ethernet driver hands the packets to the kernel to avoid any additional delay or overhead. Once data collection is complete, the data is spooled to remote storage for analysis. Memory restrictions on our collection servers limit the traces we collect in this fashion to a few minutes in length.

4. PROVISIONING

The appropriate design, scale, and even technology of a datacenter interconnect depends heavily on the traffic demands of the services it hosts. In this section, we quantify the traffic intensity, locality, and stability across three different types of clusters inside Facebook datacenters; in particular, we examine clusters supporting Hadoop, Frontend machines serving Web requests, and Cache.

Our study reveals that while Facebook's Hadoop deployments exhibit behavior largely consistent with the literature, the same cannot be said for clusters hosting Facebook's other services. In particular, most traffic is *not* rack-local, yet locality patterns remain stable within and across both long (multiple-day) and short (two-minute) time intervals. We define stable traffic as being close to constant (low deviation from a baseline value) over a time interval, and slowly changing across time intervals. Note that this definition is dependent upon the length of the interval being considered; accordingly, we examine several different timescales.

4.1 Utilization

Given that Facebook has recently transitioned to 10-Gbps Ethernet across all of their hosts, it is not surprising that overall access link (i.e., links between hosts and their RSW) utilization is quite low, with the average 1-minute link utilization less than 1%. This comports with the utilization levels reported for other cloud-scale datacenters [12, 17]. Demand follows typical diurnal and day-of-the-week patterns, although the magnitude of change is on the order of 2× as opposed to the order-of-magnitude variation reported elsewhere [12], Even the most loaded links are lightly loaded over 1-minute time scales: 99% of all links are typically less than 10% loaded. Load varies considerably across clusters, where the average link utilization in the heaviest clusters (Hadoop) is roughly 5× clusters with light load (Frontend).

As in other datacenters with similar structure [12, 13], utilization rises at higher levels of aggregation. Focusing on the links between RSWs and CSWs, median utilization varies between 10–20% across clusters, with the busiest 5% of the links seeing 23–46% utilization. These levels are higher than most previously studied datacenters [12, Fig. 9], likely due to the disproportionate increase in edge-link technology (1→10 Gbps) vs. aggregation links (10→40 Gbps). The variance between clusters decreases, with the heaviest clusters running 3× higher than lightly loaded ones. Utilization is higher still on links between CSWs and FC switches, although the differences between clusters are less apparent because different clusters are provisioned with different numbers of uplinks depending on their demand. We examine link utilization at finer timescales in Section 6.

4.2 Locality and stability

Prior studies have observed heavy rack locality in datacenter traffic. This behaviour seems in line with applications that seek to minimize network utilization by leveraging data locality, allowing for topologies with high levels of oversubscription. We examine the locality of Facebook's traffic from a representative sampling of production systems across various times of the day.

Figure 4 shows the breakdown of outbound traffic by destination for four different classes of servers: a Hadoop server within a Hadoop cluster, a Web server in a Frontend cluster, and both a cache follower and a cache leader from within the same Cache cluster. For each server, each second's traffic is represented as a stacked bar chart, with rack-local traffic in cyan, the cluster-local traffic in blue, the intra-datacenter traffic in red, and inter-datacenter traffic in green.

Among the four server types, Hadoop shows by far the most diversity—both across servers and time: some traces show periods of significant network activity while others do not. While all traces show both rack- and cluster-level locality, the distribution between the two varies greatly. In one ten-minute-long trace captured during a busy period, 99.8% of all traffic sent by the server in Figure 4 is destined to other Hadoop servers: 75.7% of that traffic is destined to servers in the the same rack (with a fairly even spread within the rack); almost all of the remainder is destined to other hosts within the cluster. Only a vanishingly small amount of traffic leaves the cluster.

In terms of dispersion, of the inter-rack (intra-cluster) traffic, the Hadoop server communicates with 1.5% of the other servers in the cluster—spread across 95% of the racks—though only 17% of the racks receive over 80% of the server's traffic. This pattern is consistent with that observed by Kandula *et al.* [26], in which traffic is either rack-local or destined to one of roughly 1–10% of the hosts in the cluster.

Hadoop's variability is a consequence of a combination of job size and the distinct phases that a Hadoop job undergoes—any given data capture might observe a Hadoop node during a busy period of shuffled network traffic, or during a relatively quiet period of computation.

By way of contrast, the traffic patterns for the other server classes are both markedly more stable and dramatically different from the findings of Kandula *et al.* [26]. Notably, only a minimal amount of rack-local traffic is present; even

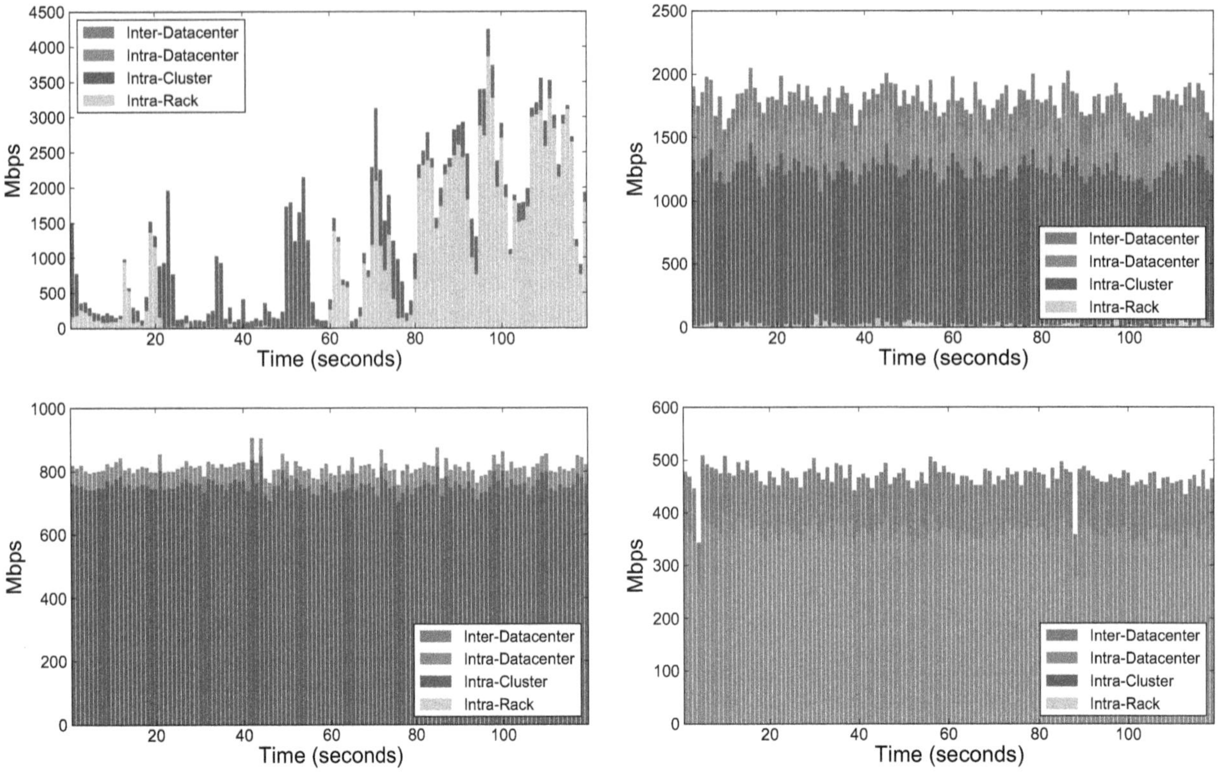

Figure 4: Per-second traffic locality by system type over a two-minute span: Hadoop (top left), Web server (top right), cache follower (bottom left) and leader (bottom right) (Note the differing y axes)

inter-datacenter traffic is present in larger quantities. Frontend cluster traffic, including Web servers and the attendant cache followers, stays largely within the cluster: 68% of Web server traffic during the capture plotted here stays within the cluster, 80% of which is destined to cache systems; the Multifeed systems and the SLB servers get 8% each. While miscellaneous background traffic is present, the volume of such traffic is relatively inconsequential.

Cache systems, depending on type, see markedly different localities, though along with Web servers the intra-rack locality is minimal. Frontend cache followers primarily send traffic in the form of responses to Web servers (88%), and thus see high intra-cluster traffic—mostly servicing cache reads. Due to load balancing (see Section 5.2), this traffic is spread quite widely; during this two-minute interval the cache follower communicates with over 75% of the hosts in the cluster, including over 90% of the Web servers. Cache leaders maintain coherency across clusters and the backing databases, engaging primarily in intra- and inter-datacenter traffic—a necessary consequence of the cache being a "single geographically distributed instance." [15]

The stability of these traffic patterns bears special mention. While Facebook traffic is affected by the diurnal traffic pattern noted by Benson *et al.* [12], the relative proportions of the locality do not change—only the total amount of traffic. Over short enough periods of time, the graph looks essentially flat and unchanging. In order to further investigate the cause and particulars of this stability, we turn our attention to the traffic matrix itself.

Locality	All	Hadoop	FE	Svc.	Cache	DB
Rack	12.9	13.3	2.7	12.1	0.2	0
Cluster	57.5	80.9	81.3	56.3	13.0	30.7
DC	11.9	3.3	7.3	15.7	40.7	34.5
Inter-DC	17.7	2.5	8.6	15.9	16.1	34.8
Percentage		23.7	21.5	18.0	10.2	5.2

Table 3: Different clusters have different localities; last row shows each cluster's contribution to total network traffic

4.3 Traffic matrix

In light of the surprising lack of rack locality and high degree of traffic stability, we examine traffic from the more long-term and zoomed-out perspective provided by Fbflow.

Table 3 shows the locality of traffic generated by all of Facebook's machines during a 24-hour period in January 2015 as reported by Fbflow. Facebook's traffic patterns remain stable day-over-day—unlike the datacenter studied by Delimitrou *et al.* [17]. The clear majority of traffic is intra-cluster but not intra-rack (i.e., the 12.9% of traffic that stays within a rack is not counted in the 57.5% of traffic labeled as intra-cluster). Moreover, more traffic crosses between datacenters than stays within a rack.

Table 3 further breaks down the locality of traffic generated by the top-five cluster types which, together, account for 78.6% of the traffic in Facebook's network. Hadoop clusters generate the most traffic (23.7% of all traffic), and are significantly more rack-local than others, but even its traffic is far from the 40–80% rack-local reported in the literature [12,

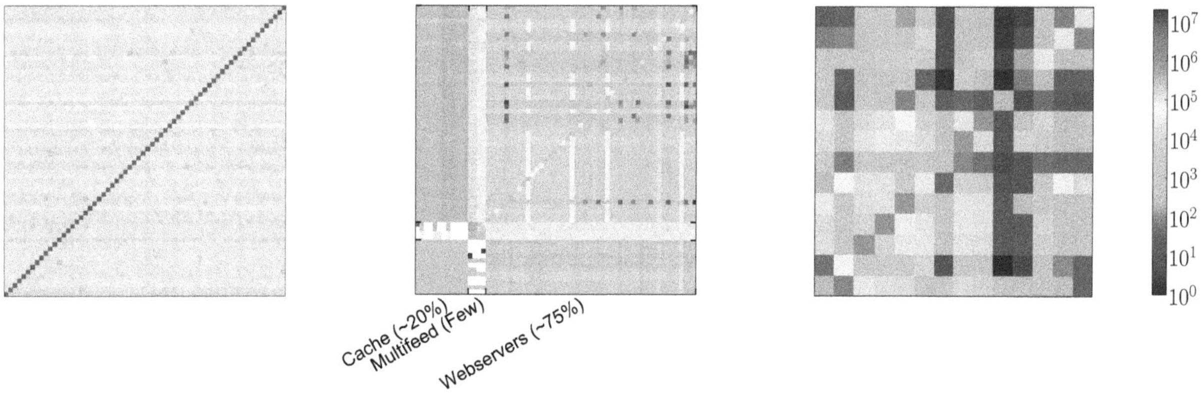

(a) Rack-to-rack, Hadoop cluster (b) Rack-to-rack, Frontend cluster (c) Cluster-to-cluster

Figure 5: Traffic demand by source (x axis) and destination (y axis). The graphs are each normalized to the lowest demand in that graph type (i.e., the Hadoop and Frontend clusters are normalized to the same value, while the cluster-to-cluster graph is normalized independently).

17]. Rather, Hadoop traffic is clearly cluster local. Frontend (FE) traffic is cluster local by design, but not very rack-local, and the locality of a given rack's traffic depends on its constituent servers (e.g., Web server, Multifeed, or cache).

This distinction is clearly visualized in Figure 5, generated in the style of Delimitrou *et al.* [17]. The two left portions of the figure graph the relative traffic demands between 64 racks within clusters of two different types. While we show only a subset of the total set of racks in each cluster, the pattern is representative of the cluster as a whole.

Traffic within the Hadoop cluster (left) is homogenous with a very strong diagonal (i.e., intra-rack locality). The cluster-wide uniformity outside the local rack accounts for intra-cluster traffic representing over 80% of Hadoop traffic—even though traffic to the local rack dominates any given other rack in isolation. Map tasks are placed to maximize read locality, but there are a large number of concurrent jobs which means that it is possible that any given job will not fit entirely within a rack. Thus, some amount of traffic would necessarily need to leave the rack during the shuffle and output phases of a MapReduce job. In addition, the cluster serves data requests from other services which might not strive for as much read locality, which would also contribute to reduced overall rack locality.

The Frontend cluster (center) exhibits three different patterns according to rack type, with none being particularly rack-local. In particular, we see a strong bipartite traffic pattern between the Web servers and the cache followers in Webserver racks that are responsible for most of the traffic, by volume, within the cluster. This pattern is a consequence of placement: Web servers talk primarily to cache servers and vice versa, and servers of different types are deployed in distinct racks, leading to low intra-rack traffic.

This striking difference in Facebook's locality compared to previously studied Internet-facing user-driven applications is a consequence of the realities of serving a densely connected social graph. Cache objects are replicated across clusters; however, each object typically appears once in a cluster (though hot objects are replicated to avoid hotspots, which we discuss in Section 5). Since each Web server needs to be able to handle any request, they might need to access data in a potentially random fashion due to load balancing.

To make this argument more concrete, loading the Facebook news feed draws from a vast array of different objects in the social graph: different people, relationships, and events comprise a large graph interconnected in a complicated fashion. This connectedness means that the working set is unlikely to reduce even if users are partitioned; the net result is a low cache hit rate within the rack, leading to high intra-cluster traffic locality. In addition, partitioning the graph such that users and their data are co-located on racks has the potential to introduce failure modes which disproportionately target subsets of the user base, leading to a suboptimal experience.

The other three cluster types exhibit additional distinctive behaviors (not shown). Traffic in cache leader clusters, for example, has very little intra-rack demand, instead spreading the plurality of its traffic across the datacenter. Traffic in back-end database clusters is the most uniform, divided almost evenly amongst nodes within the cluster, the same datacenter, and worldwide. Service clusters, which host racks supporting a variety of supporting services, exhibit a mixed traffic pattern that lies between these extreme points.

Inter-cluster communication varies considerably by cluster type. Figure 5c plots the traffic demand between 15 clusters within a single datacenter for the a 24-hour period. Hadoop clusters, for example, have a very small proportion of inter-cluster traffic, while cache leader clusters have a large amount of inter-cluster traffic, split between cache followers in other clusters and database clusters. While each cluster may possess the same four-post structure internally, it may make sense to consider heterogenous inter-cluster communication fabrics, as demand varies over more than seven orders of magnitude between cluster pairs.

While the 4-post cluster remains prevalent in Facebook datacenters, Facebook recently announced a new network

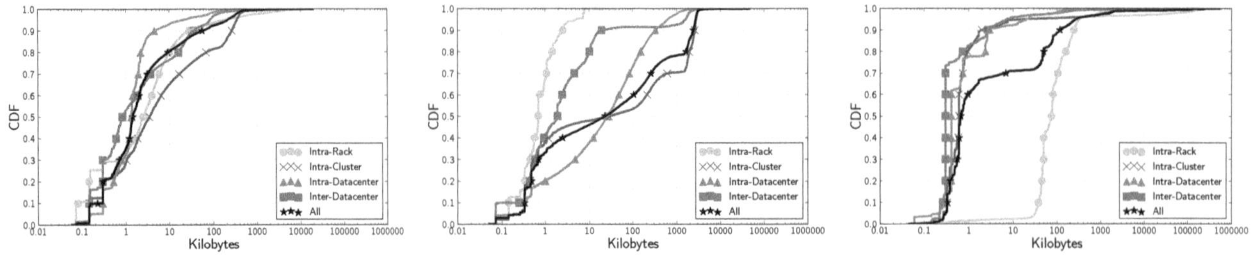

(a) Web servers (b) Cache follower (c) Hadoop

Figure 6: Flow size distribution, broken down by location of destination

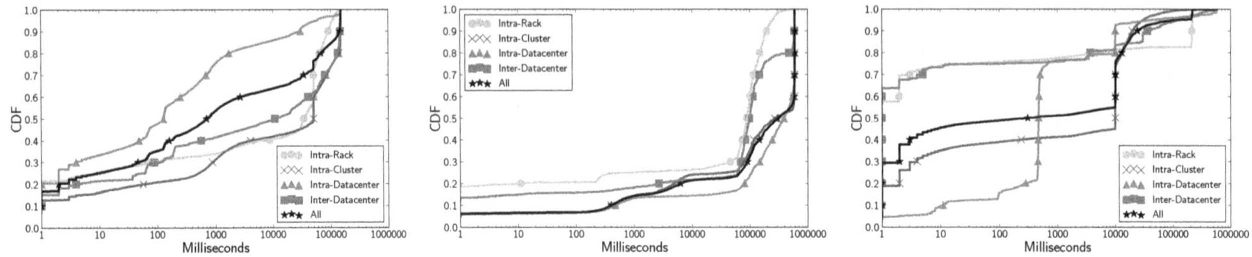

(a) Web servers (b) Cache follower (c) Hadoop

Figure 7: Flow duration distribution, broken down by location of destination

topology that is being implemented in datacenters going forward [9]. While servers are no longer grouped into clusters physically (instead, they comprise pods where all pods in a datacenter have high connectivity), the high-level logical notion of a cluster for server management purposes still exists to ease the transition. Accordingly, the rack-to-rack traffic matrix of a Frontend "cluster" inside one of the new Fabric datacenters over a day-long period (not shown) looks similar that shown in Figure 5.

4.4 Implications for connection fabrics

The low utilization levels found at the edge of the network reinforce common practice of oversubscribing the aggregation and core of the network, although it remains to be seen whether utilization will creep up as the datacenters age. The highly contrasting locality properties of the different clusters imply a single homogenous topology will either be overprovisioned in some regions or congested in others—or both. This reality argues that non-uniform fabric technologies that can deliver higher bandwidth to certain locations than others may find use. Researchers are exploring techniques to ameliorate traffic hotspots. The stability of the traffic patterns we observe, however, suggest that rapid reconfigurability may not be as necessary as some have assumed.

Somewhat surprisingly, the lack of significant levels of intra-rack locality (except in the Hadoop cluster) hints that RSWs (i.e., top-of-rack switches) that deliver something less than full non-blocking line-rate connectivity between all of their ports may be viable. In particular, the bipartite traffic pattern between end hosts and RSW uplinks may afford optimizations in switch design. We return to consider further implications for switch design in Section 6.

5. TRAFFIC ENGINEERING

Prior studies suggest that the stability of datacenter traffic depends on the timescale of observation. In this section, we analyze Facebook's traffic at fine timescales, with an eye towards understanding how applicable various traffic engineering and load balancing approaches might be under such conditions.

5.1 Flow characteristics

Figures 6 and 7 plot the size and duration, respectively, of flows (defined by 5-tuple) collected in 10-minute (2.5-minute for the Web-server rack) packet traces of three different node types: a Web-server rack, a single cache follower (cache leader is similar to follower and not shown due to space constraints), and a Hadoop node. We show the overall distribution (in black) as well as per-destination curves.

Consistent with the literature [26, Fig. 9], we find that most flows in Facebook's Hadoop cluster are short. As discussed previously, the traffic demands of Hadoop vary substantially across nodes and time. We plot the results from tracing one node over a relatively busy 10-minute interval; traces from other nodes or even the same node at different times reveal somewhat different distributions, so we caution against examining the specific distribution too carefully. Even in the graphed interval, however, 70% of flows send less than 10 KB and last less than 10 seconds; the median flow sends less than 1 KB and lasts less than a second. Less than 5% of the flows are larger than 1 MB or last longer than 100 seconds; almost none exceed our 10-minute trace.

Conversely, traces from other service types are much more representative due to load balancing. Moreover, many of Facebook's internal services use some form of connec-

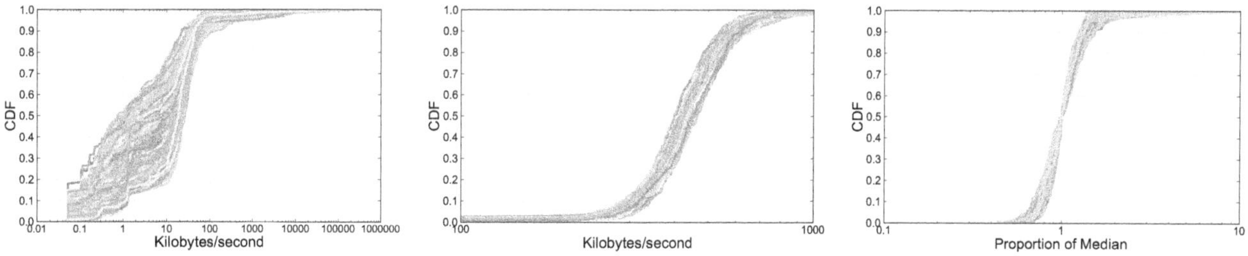

(a) Hadoop (rate, each series is 1 second) (b) Cache (rate, each series is 1 second) (c) Cache (stability, each series is a rack)

Figure 8: Per-destination-rack flow rate distribution (for both Hadoop and cache) and stability (cache).

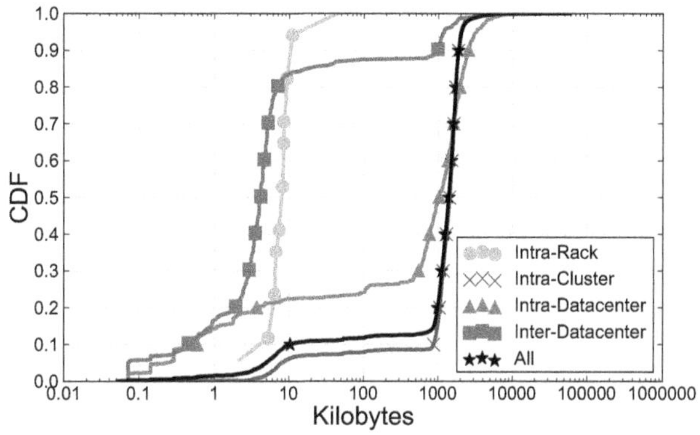

Figure 9: Cache follower per-host flow size

tion pooling [29], leading to long-lived connections with relatively low throughput. Pooling is especially prevalent for cache follower(leader, not shown) nodes, where only 30(40)% of flows are less than 100 seconds in length, with more than 40(25)% of flows exceeding our 10-minute capture period. That said, most flows are active (i.e., actually transmit packets) only during distinct millisecond-scale intervals with large intervening gaps. In other words, regardless of flow size or length, flows tend to be internally bursty. In general cache flows are also significantly larger than Hadoop; Web servers lie somewhere in the middle.

If we consider higher levels of aggregation, i.e., grouping flows by destination host or rack, the distribution of flow sizes simply shifts to the right for Web servers (retaining its basic shape). The behavior is starkly different for cache followers, however: the wide flow-size distribution apparent at a 5-tuple granularity (Figure 6b) disappears at host and rack levels, replaced by a very tight distribution around 1 MB per host (Figure 9). This arises as a consequence of the decision to load balance incoming user requests across all Web servers, combined with the large number of user requests. Since requests and responses are typically small (on the order of a few kilobytes) we do not observe any imbalance created by unequal response sizes.

5.2 Load balancing

Existing traffic engineering efforts seek to leverage variability of traffic; highly regular traffic does not provide much opportunity for improvement. In the previous section, we note that Facebook's approach to load balancing is highly effective on timescales lasting minutes to hours, leaving less room for traffic engineering. We now consider traffic characteristics over the course of a few seconds to determine whether traffic engineering might be effective on short timescales.

We consider how the traffic from a host varies from one second to next. We examine the distribution of flow rates, aggregated by destination rack, per second over a two-minute period and compare each second to the next. Intuitively, the better the load balancing, the closer one second appears to the next.

We first examine the Hadoop cluster by looking at 120 consecutive 1-second intervals. Figure 8a plots a CDF of per-destination-rack flow sizes for each interval (i.e., there are 120 separate curves). While we do not claim this particular server is representative, it does depict widely varying rates (i.e., more than three orders of magnitude) which are common in our observations.

In and of itself, this is unsurprising—Hadoop has periods of varying network traffic, and a production cluster is likely to see a myriad jobs of varying sizes. It is this variability of traffic that existing network traffic engineering schemes seek to leverage. Orchestra [16] relies on temporal and per-job variation to provide lower task completion times for high-priority tasks, while Hedera [5] provides non-interfering route placement for high bandwidth elephant flows that last for several seconds, which are prevalent within Hadoop workloads.

A different story emerges for Frontend traffic, and the cache in particular. Recall from Table 2 that the largest share of cache follower traffic are responses bound for Web servers. Figure 8b shows the distribution of per-second flow rates on a per-rack basis from a single cache follower node to distinct Web server racks during a two minute period. The distributions for each of the 120 seconds are similar, and all are relatively tight, i.e., the CDFs are fairly vertical about the median of $\approx$2 Mbps. Similar patterns (albeit with different scales) can be observed for other services as well.

From the viewpoint of a single host, each second is similar to the next. However, this analysis does not take per-destination variation into consideration. It is conceivable that there could exist consistently high- or low-rate destina-

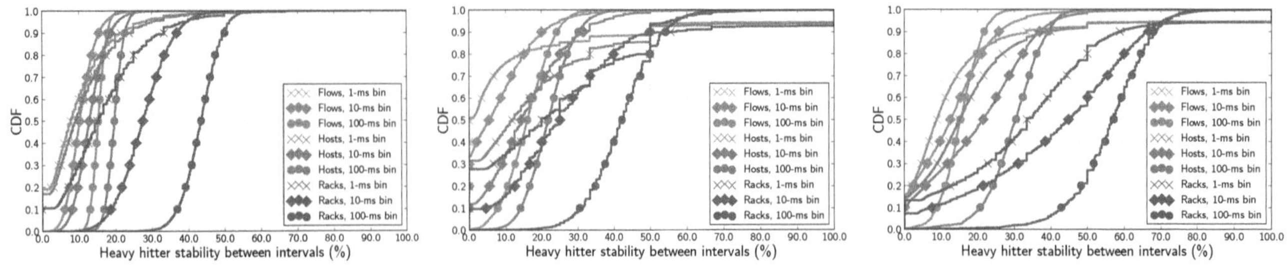

(a) Cache follower (b) Cache leader (c) Web servers

Figure 10: Heavy-hitter stability as a function of aggregation for 1/10/100-ms time windows

tions that potentially could be treated differently by a traffic engineering scheme. For each host, we consider outbound traffic rates per destination rack (normalized to the median rate for that rack), and track the rate over time for each rack. Figure 8c plots these distributions for the outbound traffic for the same cache machine as Figure 8b. Each series represents a single destination; a near vertical series represents a destination rack where the rate does not deviate far from the median rate. We find that per-destination-rack flow sizes are remarkably stable across not only seconds but intervals as long as 10 seconds (not shown) as well. All of the flows are within a factor of two of their median size in approximately 90% of the 1-second intervals—the median flow exhibits "significant change" in only 45% of the 1-second intervals according to the 20% deviation cutoff defined by Benson *et al.* [14]. Contrast this to the traffic leaving a Hadoop node—which is not load balanced—where the middle 90% of flows can vary in size by over six orders of magnitude compared to their median size in the trace (not shown).

Such stability, both over time and by destination, is the result of a combination of workload characteristics and engineering effort. To a cache system, the offered load per second is roughly held constant—large increases in load would indicate the presence of relatively hot objects, which is actively monitored and mitigated. Bursts of requests for an object lead the cache server to instruct the Web server to temporarily cache the hot object; sustained activity for the object leads to replication of the object or the enclosing shard across multiple cache servers to help spread the load. We note further that the request rate distribution for the top-50 most requested objects on a cache server is close across all cache servers, and that the median lifespan for objects within this list is on the order of a few minutes. Per-destination traffic stability is again a consequence of user request multiplexing across all available Web servers, coupled with relatively small request/response pairs.

5.3 Heavy hitters

In this section, we examine the behavior of traffic at sub-second timescales to better understand its stability and whether traffic engineering can apply. In particular, we wish to see if certain flows (aggregated or not) stand out in terms of rate, since such flows would provide the largest opportunity for potential impact on network performance. We define a set of flows that we call *heavy hitters*, representing the minimum set of flows (or hosts, or racks in the aggregated case) that is responsible for 50% of the observed traffic volume (in bytes) over a fixed time period. Intuitively, the presence of heavy hitters can signify an imbalance that can be acted upon—if they are persistent for enough time, and large enough compared other flows that treating them differently makes a difference.

Type		Number			Size (Mbps)		
		p10	p50	p90	p10	p50	p90
Web	f	1	4	15	1.6	3.2	47.3
	h	1	4	14	1.6	3.3	48.1
	r	1	3	9	1.7	4.6	48.9
Cache (f)	f	8	19	35	5.1	9.0	22.5
	h	8	19	33	8.4	9.7	23.6
	r	7	15	23	8.4	14.5	31.0
Cache (l)	f	1	16	48	2.6	3.3	408
	h	1	8	25	3.2	8.1	414
	r	1	7	17	5	12.6	427
Hadoop	f	1	2	3	4.6	12.7	1392
	h	1	2	3	4.6	12.7	1392
	r	1	2	3	4.6	12.7	1392

Table 4: Number and size of heavy hitters in 1-ms intervals for each of flow(f), host(h), and rack(r) levels of aggregation.

Table 4 shows statistics regarding the number and size of the heavy hitters that constitute 50% of the traffic in 1-ms intervals for each of the four server classes. Because we are interested in instantaneously large flows, we measure size in terms of rate instead of number of bytes sent over the lifetime of the flow. Next, we consider the the lifespan of heavy hitters, aggregated by 5-tuple, destination host and rack, and measured across intervals of 1, 10 and 100 milliseconds. Figure 10 shows the fraction of the heavy hitters that remain in subsequent time intervals. We do not show the Hadoop nodes, as our heavy-hitter definition almost always results in the identification of 1–3 heavy hitters at each of flow, host, and rack aggregation levels across all three time intervals.

Heavy hitter persistence is low for individual flows (red): in the median case, no more than roughly 15% of flows persist regardless of the length of period, a consequence of the internal burstiness of flows noted earlier. Host-level aggregation (green) fares little better; with the exception of

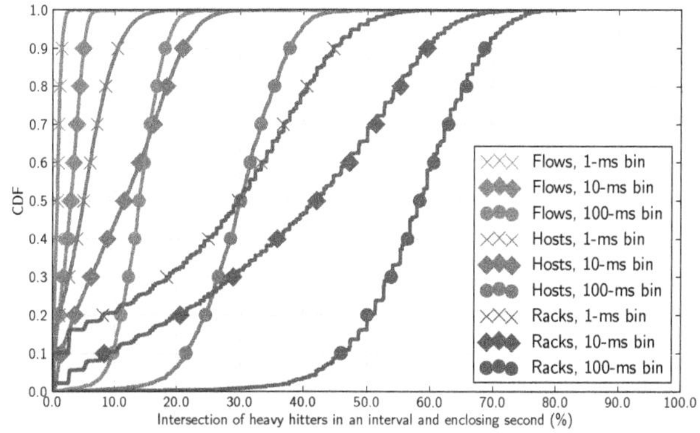

(a) Web server

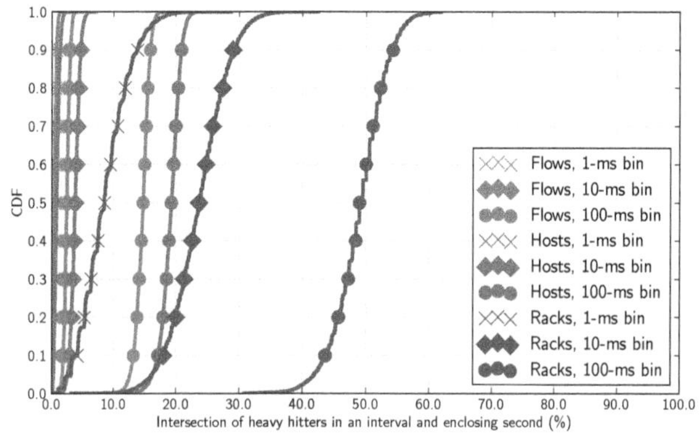

(b) Cache follower

Figure 11: Intersection between heavy hitters in a subinterval with enclosing second

destination-host-level aggregation for Web servers, no more than 20% of heavy hitter hosts in a sub-second interval will persist as a heavy hitter in the next interval. Web servers have a higher rate over 100-millisecond periods since they have a relatively small number of cache servers and load balancers with which they communicate, while cache servers converse with many different Web servers.

It is not until considering rack-level flows (blue) that heavy hitters are particularly stable. In the median case, over 40% of cache heavy hitters persist into the next 100-ms interval, and almost 60% for Web servers. Heavy hitters from Web servers are more stable in general, with 32% of rack-level heavy hitters persisting in the median 1-ms interval case. Even so, heavy hitter persistence is not particularly favorable for traffic engineering. With a close to 50% chance of a given heavy hitter continuing in the next time period, predicting a heavy hitter by observation is not much more effective than randomly guessing.

Even if one could perfectly predict the heavy hitters on a second-by-second timescale, it remains to consider how useful that knowledge would be. We compare the heavy hitters from enclosing one-second intervals to the instantaneous heavy hitters from each of the subintervals within the second to see what fraction of the heavy hitters in a subinterval are heavy hitters across the entire enclosing second. A limited degree of overlap implies three things: First, it establishes an upper bound on the effectiveness of traffic engineering—a significant amount of ephemeral heavy hitter traffic would go unseen and untreated by the TE scheme. Second, it serves as an indicator of the difficulty of prediction in the first place; if a one-second prediction interval is not sufficient, smaller timescales (consuming more resources) may be needed. Finally, this metric is an indicator of burstiness, as it indicates the presence of a large number of ephemeral heavy hitters.

Figure 11 plots a CDF of the fraction of a second's overall heavy hitters that are instantaneously heavy in each 1/10/100-ms interval within the second. We show results for a Web server and cache follower—cache leaders are similar. At 5-tuple granularity, predictive power is quite poor, at less than 10–15%. Rack-level predictions are much more effective, with heavy hitters remaining heavy in the majority of 100-ms intervals in the median case for both services. Host-level predictions are more useful for Web servers than cache nodes, but only the 100-ms case is more than 30% effective.

5.4 Implications for traffic engineering

Facebook's extensive use of connection pooling leads to long-lived flows that seem like potential candidates for traffic engineering. These same services use application-level load balancing to great effect, however, leaving limited room for in-network approaches. Many existing techniques work by identifying heavy hitters and then treating them differently (e.g., provisioning a circuit, moving them to a lightly loaded path, employing alternate buffering strategies, etc.). For any such scheme to work, however, it must be possible to first identify the heavy hitters, and then realize some benefit.

Unfortunately, it appears challenging to identify heavy hitters in a number of Facebook's clusters that persist with any frequency. Moreover, even for the timescales and aggregation levels where it is possible (e.g., rack-level flows over intervals of 100-ms or larger), it is not clear there is a great deal of benefit to be gained, as the heavy hitters are frequently not particularly heavy for the vast majority of the period. Previous work has suggested traffic engineering schemes can be effective if 35% of traffic is predictable [14]; only rack-level heavy hitters reach that level of predictability for either Web or cache servers. This somewhat counter-intuitive situation results from a combination of effective load balancing (which means there is little difference in size between a heavy hitter and the median flow) and the relatively low long-term throughput of most flows, meaning even heavy flows can be quite bursty internally.

6. SWITCHING

Finally, we study aspects of the traffic that bear directly on top-of-rack switch design. In particular, we consider the size and arrival processes of packets, and the number of concurrent destinations for any particular end host. In addition, we examine the impact of burstiness over short timesales and its impact on switch buffering.

6.1 Per-packet features

Figure 12 shows the distribution of packet sizes for each of the four host types. Overall, the median packet size is

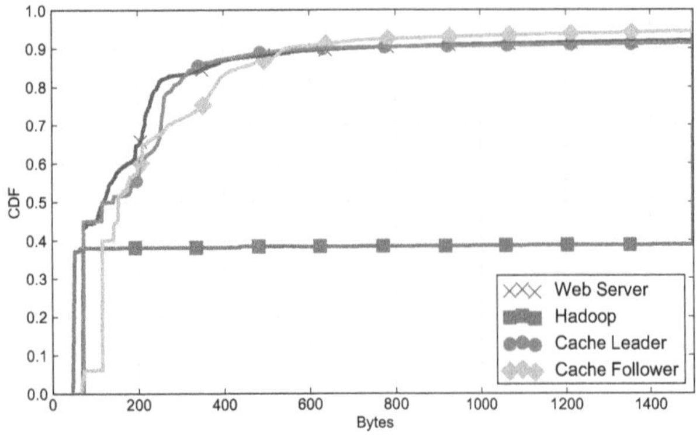

Figure 12: Packet size distribution

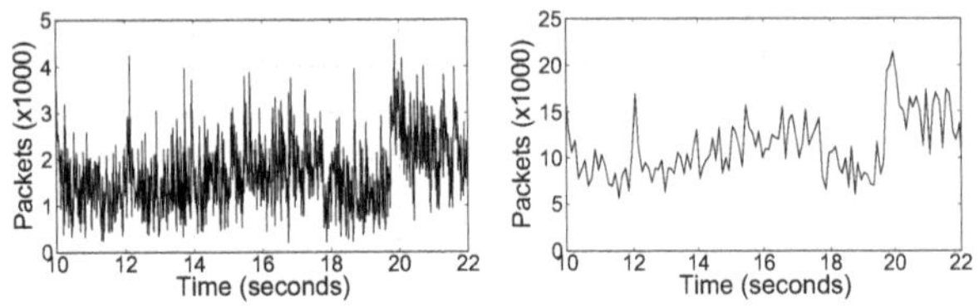

(a) 15 ms

(b) 100 ms

Figure 13: Hadoop traffic is not on/off at 15 nor 100 ms

approximately 250 bytes, but that is significantly skewed by Hadoop traffic. Hadoop traffic is bimodal: almost all packets are either MTU length (1500 bytes for the servers we study) or TCP ACKs. Packets for the other services have a much wider distribution, but the median packet size for all of them is significantly less than 200 bytes, with only 5–10% of the packets fully utilizing the MTU.

Thus, while link utilization is low, the packet rate is still high. For example, a cache server at 10% link utilization with a median packet size of roughly 175 bytes generates 85% of the packet rate of a fully utilized link sending MTU-sized packets. As a result, any per-packet operation (e.g., VLAN encapsulation) may still be stressed in a way that the pure link utilization rate might not suggest at first glance.

6.2 Arrival patterns

Benson *et al.* observe that packet arrivals exhibit an on/off pattern at the end-host level [12, 13]. Hosts in Facebook's datacenter do not exhibit this behavior, even within Hadoop clusters. Figure 13 shows a time series of traffic sent by a Hadoop host (arriving at a RSW port) binned by 15- and 100-ms intervals. (c.f. Benson *et al.*'s analogous graphs [13, Figure 5] and [12, Figure 6]). If one considers traffic on a per-destination host basis, on/off behavior remerges (not shown), suggesting its disappearance may be due to a large number of concurrent destinations.

Figure 14 plots the CDF of inter-arrival times between outgoing TCP flows at each of the four types of servers we study. While a significant amount of traffic is routed over long-lived pooled connections, as is the case for request-response traffic between Web servers and cache followers, ephemeral flows do exist. The inter-arrival periods for flows emanating from all four classes of host are shorter than

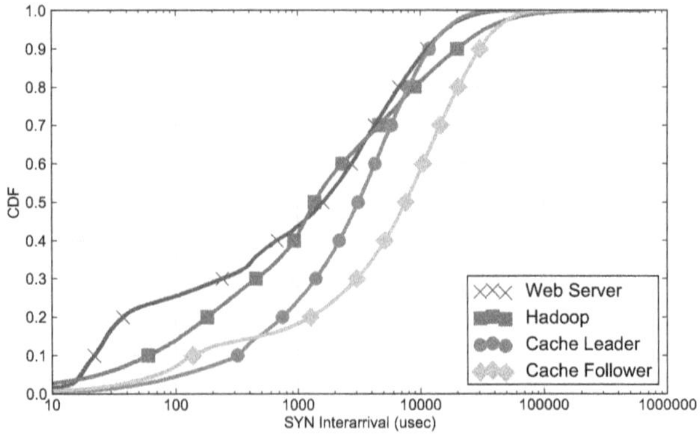

Figure 14: Flow (SYN packet) inter-arrival

those reported in the literature [26, Fig. 11], but to varying degrees. Hadoop nodes and Web servers see an order-of-magnitude increase in flow intensity relative to previous reports—likely due at least in part to the 10× increase in link rate—with median inter-arrival times of approximately 2 ms (i.e., more than 500 flows per second). Perhaps due to connection pooling (which would decouple the arrival of external user requests from the internal flow-arrival rate), the distribution of inter-arrival times for flows at both types of cache node are similar and longer: cache leaders see a slightly higher arrival rate than followers, with median inter-arrival timess of 3 and 8 ms, respectively.

6.3 Buffer utilization

The combination of a lack of on/off traffic, higher flow intensity, and bursty individual flows suggests a potential increase in buffer utilization and overruns. Despite low average link utilization, bursty traffic can still lead to unacceptable loss rates. Recent work at Facebook has led to the development of in-house switching platforms [35], enabling us to gather buffer utilization statistics at fine granularity. In particular, we collect buffer occupancies over a 24-hour period for switches connecting Web servers and cache nodes at a 10-microsecond granularity. Figure 15a plots the median and maximum values per second for the entire period, normalized to the buffer size. In other words, a single point for the median series represents the 50th-percentile buffer occupancy during that second (out of 100,000 samples per second), normalized by the size of the buffer. We also plot the normalized average link utilization (Figure 15b) and egress drop rate (Figure 15c) over the same period, sourced via fbflow and SNMP counters, respectively.

A few trends are apparent from our results. The first is that standing buffer occupancies are non-trivial, and can be quite high in the Web-server case. Even though link utilization is on the order of 1% most of the time, over two-thirds of the available shared buffer is utilized during each 10-μs interval. Diurnal variation exists in buffer occupancies, utilization and drop rate, highlighting the correlation between these metrics over time. Even with the diurnal trafic pattern, however, the maximum buffer occupancy in the Web-server rack approaches the configured limit for roughly three quarters of the 24-hour period. While link utilization is roughly cor-

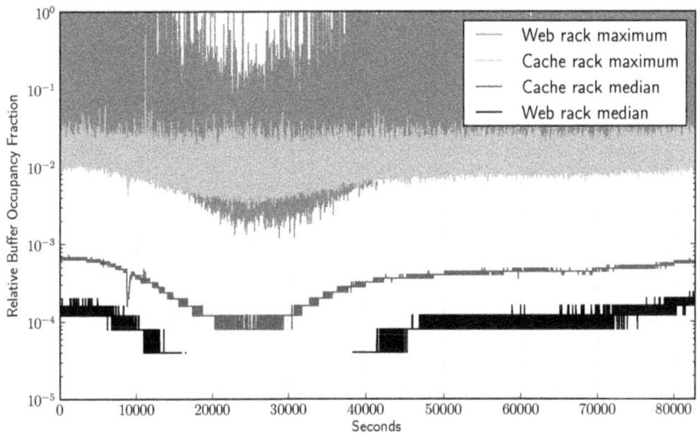

(a) Normalized buffer occupancy, 10-microsecond resolution

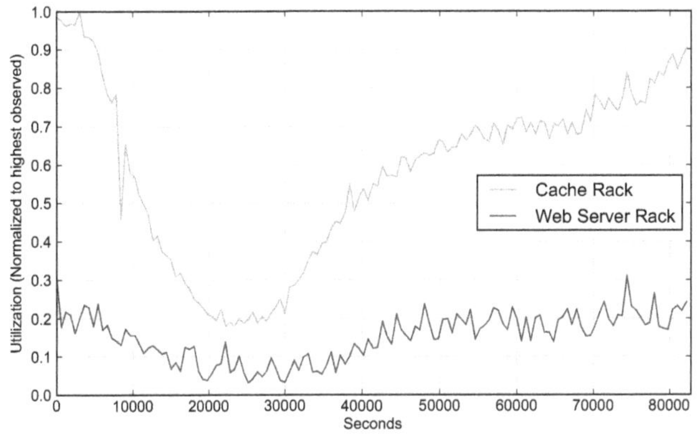

(b) Link utilization, 10-minute average

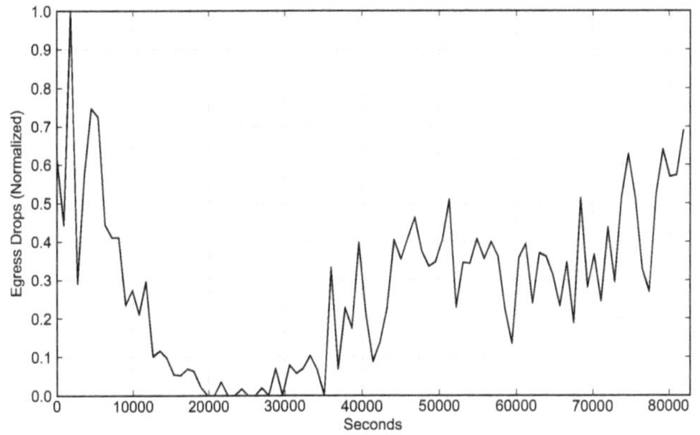

(c) Web rack egress drops, 15-minute average

Figure 15: Correlating buffer occupancy, link utilization and packet drops in Web server and Cache racks

related with buffer occupancy within the Web-server rack, utilization by itself is not a good prediction of buffer requirements across different applications. In particular, the Cache rack has higher link utilization, but much lower buffer utilization and drop rates (not shown).

These buffer utilization levels occur despite relatively small packet sizes (Section 6.1). As utilization increases in the future, it might be through an increase in the number of flows, in the size of packets, or both. Either will have impacts on buffer utilization: larger packets with the same level of burstiness will use up more of the buffer, while a larger number of flows leads to a greater chance of multiple flows sending bursts of packets simultaneously. Thus, careful buffer tuning is likely to be important moving forward.

6.4 Concurrent flows

We consider concurrent to mean existing within the same 5-ms window (c.f. the 50-ms window considered by Alizadeh *et al.* while measuring a datacenter of hosts connected with 1-Gbps Ethernet [8]). We find that Web servers and cache hosts have 100s to 1000s of concurrent connections (at the 5-tuple level), while Hadoop nodes have approximately 25 concurrent connections on average—corresponding quite well with the findings of Alizadeh *et al.* [8, Figure 5]. That said, switches are obviously less concerned with individual connections than destination ports. If we group connections destined to the same host, the numbers reduce only slightly (by at most a factor of two)—and not at all in the case of Hadoop.

Given the general lack of intra-rack traffic, almost all flows will traverse an up-link port. Hence, it is perhaps more interesting to consider flows at the rack level—i.e., considering the number of different racks with which an individual host is communicating. Figure 16 shows the number of concurrent flows sent by a single host over a 5-ms interval to different classes of destination hosts for three different host types: cache follower, cache leader, Web server. Cache followers communicate with 225–300 different racks, while leaders talk to 175–350. In the median interval, both types of cache nodes communicate with approximately 250 other racks—the location of the racks varies dramatically as discussed previously, however. Web servers communicate with 10–125 racks concurrently, 50 in the median interval.

Some proposed switch designs [25, 30] employ different technologies for large flows. Hence, we restrict our focus to the heavy hitter racks, namely those destination racks that constitute the majority of the traffic. The median number of heavy-hitter racks is 6–8 for Web servers and cache leaders with an effective max of 20–30, while the cache follower has 29 heavy hitter racks in the median case and up to 50 in the tail. Due to the differences in locality, Web servers and cache followers have very few rack-level heavy hitters of their cluster, while the cache leader displays the opposite pattern. Even considering only heavy hitter racks, the number of concurrent destinations is still significantly larger than that reported by Alizadeh *et al.* [8]. In addition, the relative impermanence of our heavy hitters suggests that, for Frontend clusters at least, hybrid circuit-based approaches may be challenging to employ.

7. CONCLUSION

Facebook's datacenter network supports a variety of distinct services that exhibit different traffic patterns. We find that several deviate substantially from the services considered in the literature. The different applications, combined

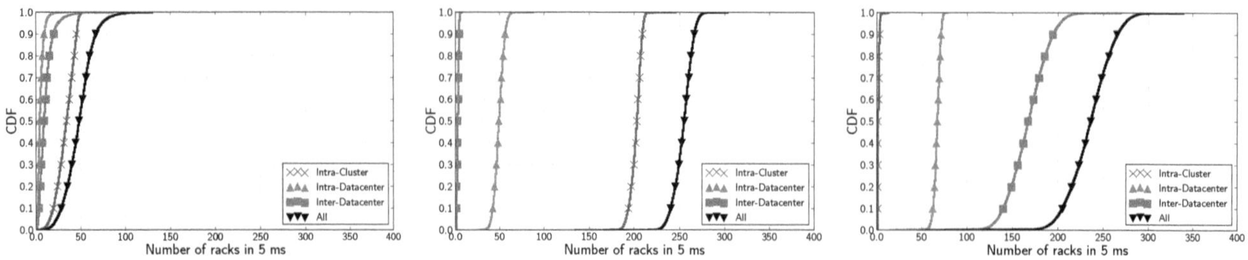

(a) Web server (b) Cache follower (c) Cache leader

Figure 16: Concurrent (5-ms) rack-level flows

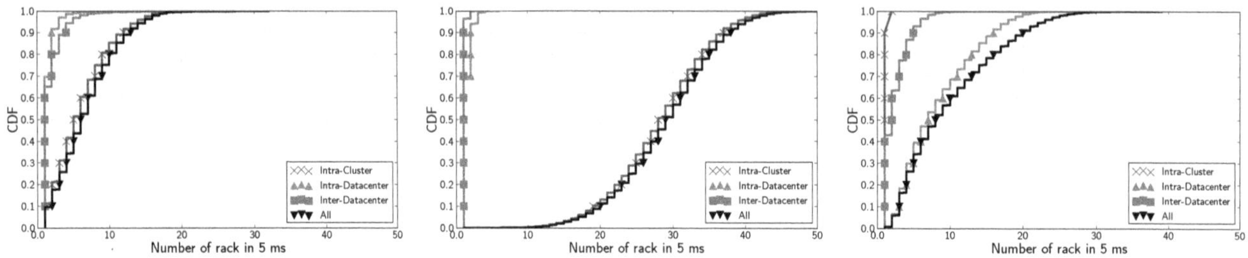

(a) Web server (b) Cache follower (c) Cache leader

Figure 17: Concurrent (5-ms) heavy-hitter racks

with the scale (hundreds of thousands of nodes) and speed (10-Gbps edge links) of Facebook's datacenter network result in workloads that contrast in a number of ways from most previously published datasets. Space constraints prevent us from providing an exhaustive account; we describe features that may have implications for topology, traffic engineering, and top-of-rack switch design.

Our methodology imposes a few limitations on the scope of this study. Using end hosts to capture and timestamp packets introduces scheduler-based variations on timestamp accuracy. In addition, we can only capture traffic from a few hosts at a time without risking drops in packet collection. Together, these constraints prevent us from evaluating effects like incast or microbursts, which are noted as being contributors to poor application performance [24]. Further, per-host packet dumps are necessarily anecdotal and ad hoc, relying on the presence of an unused capture host on the same rack as the target. While Fbflow is deployed datacenter-wide, the sheer amount of measurement data it provides presents another challenge—specifically, one of data processing and retention—which limits the resolution at which it can operate. We thus view effective network monitoring and analysis to be an ongoing and constantly evolving problem.

Acknowledgements

This work is supported in part by the National Science Foundation through grants CNS-1314921 and CSR-1018808. We are indebted to Theo Benson, Nick McKeown, Remzi Arpaci-Dusseau, our shepherd, Srikanth Kandula, and the anonymous reviewers for their comments and suggestions on earlier drafts of this manuscript. Petr Lapukhov, Michal Burger, Sathya Narayanan, Avery Ching and Vincent Liu provided invaluable insight into the inner workings of various Facebook services. Finally, and most significantly, Omar Baldonado catalyzed and faciliated the collaboration that enabled this study.

8. REFERENCES

[1] An open network operating system. http://onosproject.org.

[2] Scribe (archived). https://github.com/facebookarchive/scribe.

[3] L. Abraham, J. Allen, O. Barykin, V. Borkar, B. Chopra, C. Gerea, D. Merl, J. Metzler, D. Reiss, S. Subramanian, J. L. Wiener, and O. Zed. Scuba: Diving into data at Facebook. *Proc. VLDB Endow.*, 6(11):1057–1067, Aug. 2013.

[4] M. Al-Fares, A. Loukissas, and A. Vahdat. A scalable, commodity, data center network architecture. In *Proc. ACM SIGCOMM*, Aug. 2008.

[5] M. Al-Fares, S. Radhakrishnan, B. Raghavan, N. Huang, and A. Vahdat. Hedera: Dynamic flow scheduling for data center networks. In *Proc. USENIX NSDI*, Apr. 2010.

[6] A. Alameldeen, M. Martin, C. Mauer, K. Moore, X. Min, M. Hill, D. Wood, and D. Sorin. Simulating a $2M commercial server on a $2K PC. *IEEE Computer*, 36(2):50–57, Feb. 2003.

[7] M. Alizadeh, T. Edsall, S. Dharmapurikar, R. Vaidyanathan, K. Chu, A. Fingerhut, V. T. Lam, F. Matus, R. Pan, N. Yadav, and G. Varghese. Conga: Distributed congestion-aware load balancing for datacenters. In *Proc. ACM SIGCOMM*, Aug. 2014.

[8] M. Alizadeh, A. Greenberg, D. A. Maltz, J. Padhye, P. Patel, B. Prabhakar, S. Sengupta, and M. Sridharan. Data center TCP (DCTCP). In *Proc. ACM SIGCOMM*, Aug. 2010.

[9] A. Andreyev. Introducing data center fabric, the next-generation Facebook data center network. https://code.facebook.com/posts/360346274145943, 2014.

[10] B. Atikoglu, Y. Xu, E. Frachtenberg, S. Jiang, and M. Paleczny. Workload analysis of a large-scale key-value store. In *Proc. ACM SIGMETRICS/Performance*, June 2012.

[11] L. A. Barroso, J. Clidaras, and U. Hölzle. *The Datacenter as a Computer:An Introduction to the Design of*

Warehouse-Scale Machines. Morgan & Claypool, 2nd edition, 2013.

[12] T. Benson, A. Akella, and D. A. Maltz. Network traffic characteristics of data centers in the wild. In *Proc. ACM IMC*, 2010.

[13] T. Benson, A. Anand, A. Akella, and M. Zhang. Understanding data center traffic charachteristics. In *Proc. ACM SIGCOMM WREN*, Aug. 2009.

[14] T. Benson, A. Anand, A. Akella, and M. Zhang. MicroTE: Fine grained traffic engineering for data centers. In *Proc. ACM CoNEXT*, Dec. 2011.

[15] N. Bronson, Z. Amsden, G. Cabrera, P. Chakka, P. Dimov, H. Ding, J. Ferris, A. Giardullo, S. Kulkarni, H. Li, M. Marchukov, D. Petrov, L. Puzar, Y. J. Song, and V. Venkataramani. TAO: Facebook's distributed data store for the social graph. In *Proc. USENIX ATC*, June 2013.

[16] M. Chowdhury, M. Zaharia, J. Ma, M. I. Jordan, and I. Stoica. Managing data transfers in computer clusters with orchestra. In *Proceedings of the ACM SIGCOMM 2011 Conference*, SIGCOMM '11, pages 98–109, New York, NY, USA, 2011. ACM.

[17] C. Delimitrou, S. Sankar, A. Kansal, and C. Kozyrakis. ECHO: Recreating network traffic maps for datacenters with tens of thousands of servers. In *Proc. IEEE International Symposium on Workload Characterization*, Nov. 2012.

[18] D. Ersoz, M. S. Yousif, and C. R. Das. Characterizing network traffic in a cluster-based, multi-tier data center. In *Proc. IEEE International Conference on Distributed Computing Systems*, June 2007.

[19] N. Farrington and A. Andreyev. Facebook's data center network architecture. In *Proc. IEEE Optical Interconnects*, May 2013.

[20] N. Farrington, G. Porter, S. Radhakrishnan, H. Bazzaz, V. Subramanya, Y. Fainman, G. Papen, and A. Vahdat. Helios: A hybrid electrical/optical switch architecture for modular data centers. In *Proc. ACM SIGCOMM*, Aug. 2010.

[21] A. Greenberg, J. R. Hamilton, N. Jain, S. Kandula, C. Kim, P. Lahiri, D. A. Maltz, P. Patel, and S. Sengupta. VL2: A scalable and flexible data center network. In *Proc. ACM SIGCOMM*, Aug. 2009.

[22] N. Gude, T. Koponen, J. Pettit, B. Pfaff, M. Casado, N. McKeown, and S. Shenker. NOX: Towards an operating system for networks. *SIGCOMM CCR*, 38(3), July 2008.

[23] C. Guo, G. Lu, D. Li, H. Wu, X. Zhang, Y. Shi, C. Tian, Y. Zhang, and S. Lu. BCube: A high performance, server-centric network architecture for modular data centers. In *Proc. ACM SIGCOMM*, Aug. 2009.

[24] V. Jalaparti, P. Bodik, S. Kandula, I. Menache, M. Rybalkin, and C. Yan. Speeding up distributed request-response workflows. In *Proceedings of the ACM SIGCOMM 2013 Conference on SIGCOMM*, SIGCOMM '13, pages 219–230, New York, NY, USA, 2013. ACM.

[25] S. Kandula, J. Padhye, and P. Bahl. Flyways to de-congest data center networks. In *Proc. ACM HotNets*, Oct. 2009.

[26] S. Kandula, S. Sengupta, A. Greenberg, P. Patel, and R. Chaiken. The nature of data center traffic: Measurements & analysiss. In *Proc. ACM IMC*, Nov. 2009.

[27] R. Kapoor, A. C. Snoeren, G. M. Voelker, and G. Porter. Bullet trains: A study of NIC burst behavior at microsecond timescales. In *Proc. ACM CoNEXT*, Dec. 2013.

[28] T. Koponen, M. Casado, N. Gude, J. Stribling, L. Poutievski, M. Zhu, R. Ramanathan, Y. Iwata, H. Inoue, T. Hama, and S. Shenker. Onix: A distributed control platform for large-scale production networks. In *Proc. USENIX OSDI*, 2010.

[29] A. Likhtarov, R. Nishtala, R. McElroy, H. Fugal, A. Grynenko, and V. Venkataramani. Introducing mcrouter: A memcached protocol router for scaling memcached deployments. https://code.facebook.com/posts/296442737213493, Sept. 2014.

[30] H. Liu, F. Lu, A. Forencich, R. Kapoor, M. Tewari, G. M. Voelker, G. Papen, A. C. Snoeren, and G. Porter. Circuit switching under the radar with REACToR. In *Proc. USENIX NSDI*, Apr. 2014.

[31] R. Mack. Building timeline: Scaling up to hold your life story. https://www.facebook.com/note.php?note_id=10150468255628920, Jan. 2012.

[32] B. Pfaff, J. Pettit, T. Koponen, K. Amidon, M. Casado, and S. Shenker. Extending networking into the virtualization layer. In *Proc. ACM HotNets*, 2009.

[33] L. Popa, S. Ratnasamy, G. Iannaccone, A. Krishnamurthy, and I. Stoica. A cost comparison of datacenter network architectures. In *Proc. ACM CoNEXT*, Dec. 2010.

[34] R. Sherwood, G. Gibb, K.-K. Yap, G. Appenzeller, M. Casado, N. McKeown, and G. Parulkar. Can the production network be the testbed? In *Proc. USENIX OSDI*, 2010.

[35] A. Simpkins. Facebook open switching system (fboss) and wedge in the open. https://code.facebook.com/posts/843620439027582/facebook-open-switching-system-fboss-and-wedge-in-the-open/, 2015.

[36] A. Singla, C.-Y. Hong, L. Popa, and P. B. Godfrey. Jellyfish: Networking data centers randomly. In *Proc. USENIX NSDI*, Apr. 2012.

[37] D. Sommermann and A. Frindell. Introducing Proxygen, Facebook's C++ HTTP framework. https://code.facebook.com/posts/1503205539947302, 2014.

[38] A. Thusoo, J. S. Sarma, N. Jain, Z. Shao, P. Chakka, N. Zhang, S. Antony, H. Liu, and R. Murthy. Hive – a petabyte scale data warehouse using Hadoop. In *Proc. IEEE ICDE*, Mar. 2010.

[39] G. Wang, D. G. Andersen, M. Kaminsky, K. Papagiannaki, T. S. E. Ng, M. Kozuch, and M. Ryan. c-Through: Part-time optics in data centers. In *Proc. ACM SIGCOMM*, Aug. 2010.

[40] X. Zhou, Z. Zhang, Y. Zhu, Y. Li, S. Kumar, A. Vahdat, B. Y. Zhao, and H. Zheng. Mirror mirror on the ceiling: Flexible wireless links for data centers. In *Proc. ACM SIGCOMM*, Aug. 2012.

Pingmesh: A Large-Scale System for Data Center Network Latency Measurement and Analysis*

Chuanxiong Guo, Lihua Yuan, Dong Xiang, Yingnong Dang, Ray Huang, Dave Maltz,
Zhaoyi Liu, Vin Wang, Bin Pang, Hua Chen, Zhi-Wei Lin, Varugis Kurien†
Microsoft, †Midfin Systems
{chguo, lyuan, dxiang, yidang, rayhuang, dmaltz, zhaoyil, vinwang, bipang, stchen, linzw}@microsoft.com, vkurien@midfinsystems.com

ABSTRACT

Can we get network latency between any two servers at any time in large-scale data center networks? The collected latency data can then be used to address a series of challenges: telling if an application perceived latency issue is caused by the network or not, defining and tracking network service level agreement (SLA), and automatic network troubleshooting.

We have developed the Pingmesh system for large-scale data center network latency measurement and analysis to answer the above question affirmatively. Pingmesh has been running in Microsoft data centers for more than four years, and it collects tens of terabytes of latency data per day. Pingmesh is widely used by not only network software developers and engineers, but also application and service developers and operators.

CCS Concepts

•**Networks → Network measurement; Cloud computing; Network monitoring;** •**Computer systems organization → Cloud computing;**

Keywords

Data center networking; Network troubleshooting; Silent packet drops

1. INTRODUCTION

In today's data centers there are hundreds of thousands of servers. These servers are connected via network interface cards (NICs), switches and routers, cables and fibers, which form large-scale intra and inter data center networks. The scale of the data center networks (DCNs) is growing even larger due to the rapid development of cloud computing. On top of the physical data center infrastructure, various large-scale, distributed services are built, e.g., Search [5], distributed file systems [17] and storage [7], MapReduce [11].

These distributed services are large and evolving software systems with many components and have complex dependencies. All of these services are distributed and many of their components need to interact via the network either within a data center or across different data centers. In such large systems, software and hardware failures are the norm rather than the exception. As a result, the network team faces several challenges.

The first challenge is to determine if an issue is a network issue or not. Due to the distributed systems nature, many failures show as "network" problems, e.g., some components can only be reached intermittently, or the end-to-end latency shows a sudden increase at the 99th percentile, the network throughput degrades from 20MB/s per server to less than 5MB/s. Our experience showed that about 50% of these "network" problems are not caused by the network. However it is not easy to tell if a "network" problem is indeed caused by network failures or not.

The second challenge is to define and track network service level agreements (SLAs). Many services need the network to provide certain performance guarantees. For example, a Search query may touch thousands of servers and the performance of a Search query is determined by the last response from the slowest server. These services are sensitive to network latency and packet drops and they care about the network SLA. Network SLA needs to be measured and tracked individually for different services since they may use different set of servers and different part of the network. This becomes a challenging task because of the huge number of services and customers in the network.

The third challenge is network troubleshooting. When network SLAs are broken due to various network fail-

*This work was performed when Varugis Kurien was with Microsoft.

SIGCOMM '15, August 17 - 21, 2015, London, United Kingdom
© 2015 ACM. ISBN 978-1-4503-3542-3/15/08...$15.00
DOI: http://dx.doi.org/10.1145/2785956.2787496

ures, "live-site" incidents happen. A live-site incident is any event that results in an impact to the customers, partners or revenue. Live-site incidents need to be detected, mitigated, and resolved as soon as possible. But data center networks have hundreds of thousands to millions of servers, hundreds of thousands of switches, and millions of cables and fibers. Thus detecting where the problem is located is a hard problem.

To address the above challenges, we have designed and implemented Pingmesh, a large-scale system for data center network latency measurement and analysis. Pingmesh leverages all the servers to launch TCP or HTTP pings to provide the maximum latency measurement coverage. Pingmesh forms multiple levels of complete graphs. Within a data center, Pingmesh lets the servers within a rack form a complete graph and also uses the top-of-rack (ToR) switches as virtual nodes and let them form a second complete graph. Across data centers, Pingmesh forms a third complete graph by treating each data center as a virtual node. The calculation of the complete graphs and related ping parameters are controlled by a central Pingmesh Controller.

The measured latency data are collected and stored, aggregated and analyzed by a data storage and analysis pipeline. From the latency data, network SLAs are defined and tracked at both the macro level (i.e., data center level) and the micro level (e.g., per-server and per-rack levels). The network SLAs for all the services and applications are calculated by mapping the services and applications to the servers they use.

Pingmesh has been running in tens of globally distributed data centers of Microsoft for four years. It produces 24 terabytes of data and more than 200 billion probes per day. Because of the universal availability of the Pingmesh data, answering if a live-site incident is because of the network becomes easier: If Pingmesh data does not indicate a network problem, then the live-site incident is not caused by the network.

Pingmesh is heavily used for network troubleshooting to locate where the problem is. By visualization and automatic pattern detection, we are able to answer when and where packet drops and/or latency increases happen, identify silent switch packet drops and black-holes in the network. The results produced by Pingmesh is also used by application developers and service operators for better server selection by considering network latency and packet drop rate.

This paper makes the following contributions: We show the feasibility of building a large-scale network latency measurement and analysis system by designing and implementing Pingmesh. By letting every server participate, we provide latency data for all the servers all the time. We show that Pingmesh helps us better understand data center networks by defining and tracking network SLA at both macro and micro scopes, and that Pingmesh helps reveal and locate switch packet drops including packet black-holes and silent random packet drops, which were less understood previously.

2. BACKGROUND

2.1 Data center networks

Data center networks connect servers with high speed and provide high server-to-server bandwidth. Today's large data center networks are built from commodity Ethernet switches and routers [1, 12, 2].

Figure 1 shows a typical data center network structure. The network has two parts: intra data center (Intra-DC) network and inter data center (Inter-DC) network. The intra-DC network is typically a Clos network of several tiers similar to the network described in [1, 12, 2]. At the first tier, tens of servers (e.g., 40) use 10GbE or 40GbE Ethernet NICs to connect to a top-of-rack (ToR) switch and form a Pod. Tens of ToR switches (e.g., 20) are then connected to a second tier of Leaf switches (e.g., 2-8). These servers and ToR and Leaf switches form a Podset. Multiple Podsets then connect to a third tier of Spine switches (tens to hundreds). Using existing Ethernet switches, an intra-DC network can connect tens of thousands or more servers with high network capacity.

One nice property of the intra-DC network is that multiple Leaf and Spine switches provide a multi-path network with redundancy. ECMP (equal cost multi-path) is used to load-balance traffic across all the paths. ECMP uses the hash value of the TCP/UDP five-tuple for next hop selection. As a result, the exact path of a TCP connection is unknown at the server side even if the five-tuple of the connection is known. For this reason, locating a faulty Spine switch is not easy.

The inter-DC network is to interconnect the intra-DC networks and to connect the inter-DC networks to the Internet. The inter-DC network uses high-speed, long haul fibers to connect data centers networks at different geolocations. Software defined networking (SWAN [13], B4 [16]) are further introduced for better wide area network traffic engineering.

Our data center network is a large, sophisticated distributed systems. It is composed of hundreds of thousands of servers, tens of thousands switches and routers, and millions of cables and fibers. It is managed by Autopilot [20], our home-grown data center management software stack, and the switches and NICs run software and firmware provided by different switch and NIC providers. The applications run on top of the network may introduce complex traffic patterns.

2.2 Network latency and packet drops

In this paper we use the term "network latency" from application's point of view. When an application A at a server sends a message to an application B at a peer server, the network latency is defined as the time interval from the time A sends the message to the time B receives the message. In practice we measure round-trip-time (RTT) since RTT measurement does not need to synchronize the server clocks.

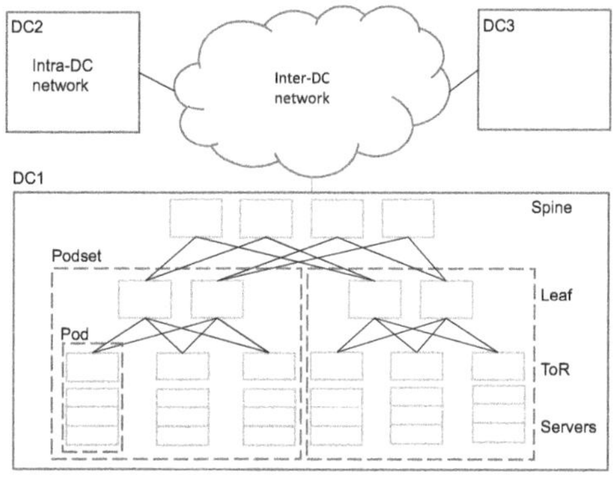

Figure 1: Data center network structure.

RTT is composed of application processing latency, OS kernel TCP/IP stack and driver processing latency, NIC introduced latency (e.g., DMA operations, interrupt modulation) [22], packet transmission delay, propagation delay, and queuing delay introduced by packet buffering at the switches along the path.

One may argue the latencies introduced by applications and kernel stack are not really from the network. In practice, our experiences have taught us that our customers and service developers do not care. Once a latency problem is observed, it is usually called a "network" problem. It is the responsibility of the network team to show if the problem is indeed a network problem, and if it is, mitigate and root-cause the problem.

User perceived latency may increase due to various reasons, e.g., queuing delay due to network congestion, busy server CPU, application bugs, network routing issues, etc. We also note that packet drops increase user perceived latency, since dropped packets need to be retransmitted. Packet drops may happen at different places due to various reasons, e.g., fiber FCS (frame check sequence) errors, switching ASIC defects, switch fabric flaw, switch software bug, NIC configuration issue, network congestions, etc. We have seen all these types of issues in our production networks.

2.3 Data center management and data processing systems

Next we introduce Autopilot [20] and Cosmos and SCOPE [15]. Data centers are managed by centralized data center management systems, e.g., Autopilot [20] or Borg [23]. These management systems provide frameworks on how resources including physical servers are managed, how services are deployed, scheduled, monitored and managed. Pingmesh is built within the framework of Autopilot.

Autopilot is Microsoft's software stack for automatic data center management. Its philosophy is to run software to automate all data center management tasks, including failure recovery, with as minimal human involvement as possible. Using the Autopilot terminology, a cluster, which is a set of servers connected by a local data center network, is managed by an Autopilot environment. An Autopilot environment has a set of Autopilot services including Device Manager (DM), which manages the machine state, Deployment Service (DS) which does service deployment for both Autopilot and various applications, Provisioning Service (PS) which installs Server OS images, Watchdog Service (WS) which monitors and reports the health status of various hardware and software, Repair Service (RS) which performs repair action by taking commands from DM, etc.

Autopilot provides a shared service mode. A shared service is a piece of code that runs on every autopilot managed server. For example, a Service Manager is a shared service that manages the life-cycle and resource usage of other applications, a Perfcounter Collector is a shared service that collects the local perf counters and then uploads the counters to Autopilot. Shared services must be light-weight with low CPU, memory, and bandwidth resource usage, and they need to be reliable without resource leakage and crashes.

Pingmesh uses our home-grown data storage and analysis system, Cosmos/SCOPE, for latency data storage and analysis. Cosmos is Microsoft's BigData system similar to Hadoop [3] which provides a distributed file system like GFS [17] and MapReduce [11]. Files in Cosmos are append-only and a file is split into multiple 'extents' and an extent is stored in multiple servers to provide high reliability. A Cosmos cluster may have tens of thousands of servers or more, and gives users almost 'infinite' storage space.

SCOPE [15] is a declarative and extensible scripting language, which is built on top of Cosmos, to analyze massive data sets. SCOPE is designed to be easy to use. It enables users to focus on their data instead of the underlying storage and network infrastructure. Users only need to write scripts similar to SQL without worrying about parallel execution, data partition, and failure handling. All these complexities are handled by SCOPE and Cosmos.

3. DESIGN AND IMPLEMENTATION

3.1 Design goal

The goal of Pingmesh is to build a network latency measurement and analysis system to address the challenges we have described in Section 1. Pingmesh needs to be always-on and be able to provide network latency data for all the servers. It needs to be always on because we need to track the network status all the time. It needs to produce network latency data for all the servers because the maximum possible network latency data coverage is essential for us to better understand, manage, and troubleshoot our network infrastructure.

From the beginning, we differentiated Pingmesh from various public and proprietary network tools (e.g., traceroute, TcpPing, etc.). We realized that network tools do not work for us because of the following reasons. First, these tools are not always-on and they only produce

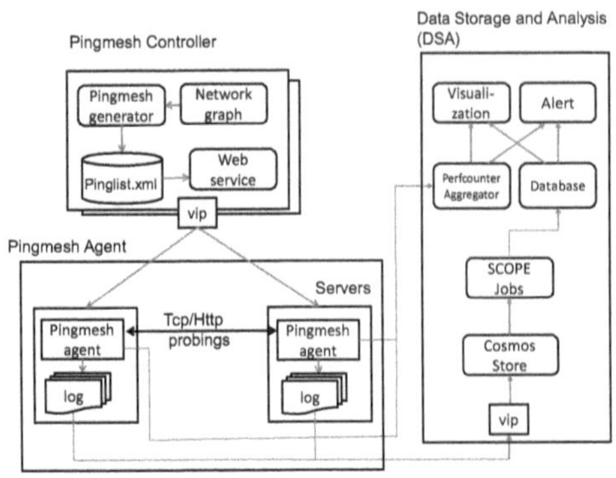

Figure 2: Pingmesh architecture.

data when we run them. Second, the data they produce does not have the needed coverage. Because these tools are not always-on, we cannot count on them to track the network status. These tools are usually used for network troubleshooting when a source-destination pair is known. This, however, does not work well for large-scale data center networks: when a network incident happens, we may not even know the source-destination pair. Furthermore, for transient network issues, the problem may be gone before we run the tools.

3.2 Pingmesh architecture

Based on its design goal, Pingmesh needs to meet the requirements as follows. First, because Pingmesh aims to provide the largest possible coverage and measure network latency from applications' point of view, a Pingmesh Agent is thus needed on every server. This has to be done carefully so that the CPU, memory, and bandwidth overhead introduced by Pingmesh Agent is small and affordable.

Second, the behavior of the Pingmesh Agent should be under control and configurable. A highly reliable control plane is needed to control how the servers should carry out network latency measurement.

Third, the latency data should be aggregated, analyzed, and reported in near real-time and stored and archived for deeper analysis. Based on the requirements, we have designed the architecture of Pingmesh as illustrated in Figure 2. Pingmesh has three components as we describe as follows.

Pingmesh Controller. It is the brain of the whole system, as it decides how servers should probe each other. Within the Pingmesh Controller, a Pingmesh Generator generates a pinglist file for every server. The pinglist file contains the list of peer servers and related parameters. The pinglist files are generated based on the network topology. Servers get their corresponding pinglist via a RESTful Web interface.

Pingmesh Agent. Every server runs a Pingmesh Agent. The Agent downloads the pinglist from the Pingmesh Controller, and then launches TCP/HTTP pings to the peer servers in the pinglist. The Pingmesh Agent stores the ping results in local memory. Once a timer times out or the size of the measurement results exceeds a threshold, the Pingmesh Agent uploads the results to Cosmos for data storage and analysis. The Pingmesh Agent also exposes a set of performance counters which are periodically collected by a Perfcounter Aggregator (PA) service of Autopilot.

Data Storage and Analysis (DSA). The latency data from Pingmesh Agents are stored and processed in a data storage and analysis (DSA) pipeline. Latency data is stored in Cosmos. SCOPE jobs are developed to analyze the data. SCOPE jobs are written in declarative language similar to SQL. The analyzed results are then stored in an SQL database. Visualization, reports and alerts are generated based on the data in this database and the PA counters.

3.3 Pingmesh Controller

3.3.1 *The pinglist generation algorithm*

The core of the Pingmesh Controller is its Pingmesh Generator. The Pingmesh Generator runs an algorithm to decide which server should ping which set of servers. As aforementioned, we would like Pingmesh to have as large coverage as possible. The largest possible coverage is a server-level complete graph, in which every server probes the rest of the servers. A server-level complete graph, however, is not feasible because a server needs to probe $n-1$ servers, where n is the number of servers. In a data center n can be as large as hundreds of thousands. Also a server-level complete graph is not necessary since tens of servers connect to the rest of the world through the same ToR switch.

We then come up with a design of multiple level of complete graphs. Within a Pod, we let all the servers under the same ToR switch form a complete graph. At intra-DC level, we treat each ToR switch as a virtual node, and let the ToR switches form a complete graph. At inter-DC level, each data center acts as a virtual node, and all the data centers form a complete graph.

In our design, only servers do pings. When we say a ToR as a virtual node, it is the servers under the ToR that carry out the pings. Similarly, for a data center as a virtual node, it is the selected servers in the data center that launch the probings.

At the intra-DC level, we once thought that we only need to select a configurable number of servers to participate in Pingmesh. But how to select the servers becomes a problem. Further, the small number of selected servers may not well represent the rest of the servers. We finally come up with the idea of letting *all* the servers participate. The intra-DC algorithm is: for any ToR-pair (ToR_x, ToR_y), let server i in ToR_x ping server i in ToR_y. In Pingmesh, even when two servers are in the pinglists of each other, they measure network latency separately. By doing so, every server can calculate its own packet drop rate and network latency locally and independently.

At the inter-DC level, all the DCs form yet another complete graph. In each DC, we select a number of servers (with several servers selected from each Podset).

Combining the three complete graphs, a server in Pingmesh needs to ping 2000-5000 peer servers depending on the size of the data center. The Pingmesh Controller uses threshold values to limit the total number of probes of a server and the minimal time interval of two successive probes for a source destination server pair.

3.3.2 Pingmesh Controller implementation

The Pingmesh Controller is implemented as an Autopilot service and becomes part of the Autopilot management stack. It generates Pinglist file for every server by running the Pingmesh generation algorithm. The files are then stored in SSD and served to the servers via a Pingmesh Web service. The Pingmesh Controller provides a simple RESTful Web API for the Pingmesh Agents to retrieve their Pinglist files respectively. The Pingmesh Agents need to periodically ask the Controller for Pinglist files and the Pingmesh Controller does not push any data to the Pingmesh Agents. By doing so, Pingmesh Controller becomes stateless and easy to scale.

As the brain of the whole Pingmesh system, the Pingmesh Controller needs to serve hundreds of thousands of Pingmesh Agents. Hence the Pingmesh Controller needs to be fault-tolerant and scalable. We use Software Load-Balancer (SLB) [14] to provide fault-tolerance and scalability for the Pingmesh Controller. See [9, 14] for the details of how SLB works. A Pingmesh Controller has a set of servers behind a single VIP (virtual IP address). SLB distributes the requests from the Pingmesh Agents to the Pingmesh Controller servers. Every Pingmesh Controller server runs the same piece of code and generates the same set of Pinglist files for all the servers and is able to serve requests from any Pingmesh Agent. The Pingmesh Controller can then easily scale out by adding more servers behind the same VIP. Also once a Pingmesh Controller server stops functioning, it is automatically removed from rotation by the SLB. We have setup two Pingmesh Controllers in two different data center clusters to make the controller even more fault tolerant geographically.

3.4 Pingmesh Agent

3.4.1 Pingmesh Agent design considerations

The Pingmesh Agent runs on all the servers. Its task is simple: downloads pinglist from the Pingmesh Controller; pings the servers in the pinglist; then uploads the ping result to DSA.

Based on the requirement that Pingmesh needs to be able to distinguish if a user perceived latency increase is due to network or not, Pingmesh should use the same type of packets generated by the applications. Since almost all the applications in our data centers use TCP and HTTP, Pingmesh uses TCP and HTTP instead of ICMP or UDP for probing.

Because we need to differentiate if a 'network' issue is because of the network or the applications themselves, Pingmesh Agent does not use any network libraries used by the applications. Instead, we have developed our own light-weight network library specifically designed for network latency measurement.

The Pingmesh Agent can be configured to send out and respond to probing packets of different lengths, other than the TCP SYN/SYN-ACK packets. As a result, the Pingmesh Agent needs to act as both client and server. The client part launches pings and the server part responds to the pings.

Every probing needs to be a new connection and uses a new TCP source port. This is to explore the multi-path nature of the network as much as possible, and more importantly, reduce the number of concurrent TCP connections created by Pingmesh.

3.4.2 Pingmesh Agent implementation

Though the task is simple, the Pingmesh Agent is one of the most challenging part to implement. It must meet the safety and performance requirements as follows.

First, the Pingmesh Agent must be fail-closed and not create live-site incidents. Since the Pingmesh Agent runs on every server, it has the potential to bring down all the servers if it malfunctions (e.g., uses large portion of CPU and memory resources, generates large volume of probing traffic, etc.). To avoid bad things from happening, several safety features have been implemented into the Pingmesh Agent:

- The CPU and maximum memory usages of the Pingmesh Agent are confined by the OS. Once the maximum memory usage exceeds the cap, the Pingmesh Agent will be terminated.

- The minimum probe interval between any two servers is limited to 10 seconds, and the probe payload length is limited to 64 kilobytes. These limits are hard coded in the source code. By doing so, we put a hard limit on the worst-case traffic volume that Pingmesh can bring into the network.

- If a Pingmesh Agent cannot connect to its controller for 3 times, or if the controller is up but there is no pinglist file available, the Pingmesh Agent will remove all its existing ping peers and stop all its ping activities. (It will still react to pings though.) Due to this feature, we can stop the Pingmesh Agent from working by simply removing all the pinglist files from the controller.

- If a server cannot upload its latency data, it will retry several times. After that it will stop trying and discard the in-memory data. This is to ensure the Pingmesh Agent uses bounded memory resource. The Pingmesh Agent also writes the latency data to local disk as log files. The size of log files is limited to a configurable size.

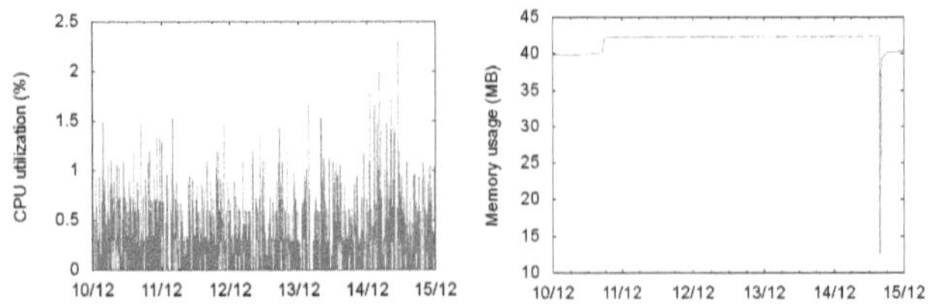

(a) CPU usage (b) Memory usage

Figure 3: CPU and memory usages of Pingmesh Agent.

Second, a Pingmesh Agent needs to launch pings to several thousand of servers by design. But as a shared service, the Pingmesh Agent should minimize its resources (CPU, memory, and disk space) usage. It should use close to zero CPU time and as small memory footprint as possible, so as to minimize its interference with customers' applications.

In order to achieve the performance goal and improve Pingmesh's latency measurement accuracy, we use C++ instead of Java or C# to write Pingmesh Agent. This is to avoid the common language runtime or Java virtual machine overhead. We have developed a network library specifically for Pingmesh. The goal of the library is solely for network latency measurement, and it is designed to be light-weight and to handle a large number of concurrent TCP connections. The library is directly based on the Winsock API, and it uses the Windows IO Completion Port programming model for efficient asynchronous network IO processing. The library acts as both client and server, and it distributes the probing processing load to all the CPU cores evenly.

We have done extensive measurements to understand and optimize Pingmesh Agent's performance. Figure 3 shows the CPU and memory usages of the Pingmesh Agent on a typical server. During the measurement, this Pingmesh Agent was actively probing around 2500 servers. The server has 128GB memory and two Intel Xeon E5-2450 processors, each with 8 cores. The average memory footprint is less than 45MB, and the average CPU usage is 0.26%.

We note that the probing traffic generated by a Pingmesh Agent is small, typically tens of Kb/s. As a comparison, our data center network provides several Gb/s throughput between any two servers in a data center.

3.5 Data Storage and Analysis

For Pingmesh data storage and analysis, we use the well established existing systems, Cosmos/SCOPE and Autopilot's Perfcounter Aggregator (PA) service, instead of reinventing the wheel.

The Pingmesh Agent periodically uploads the aggregated records to Cosmos. Similar to the Pingmesh Controller, the front-end of Cosmos uses load-balancer and VIP to scale out. At the same time, the Pingmesh Agent performs local calculation on the latency data and produces a set of performance counters including the packet drop rate, the network latency at 50th the 99th percentile, etc. All these performance counters are collected and aggregated and stored by the PA service of Autopilot.

Once the results are in Cosmos, we run a set of SCOPE jobs for data processing. We have 10-min, 1-hour, 1-day jobs at different time scales. The 10-min jobs are our near real-time ones. For the 10-min jobs, the time interval from when the latency data is generated to when the data is consumed (e.g., alert fired, dashboard figure generated) is around 20 minutes. The 1-hour and 1-day pipelines are for non real-time tasks including network SLA tracking, network black-hole detection, packet drop detection, etc. All our jobs are automatically and periodically submitted by a Job Manager to SCOPE without user intervention. The results of the SCOPE jobs are stored in a SQL database, from which visualization, reports, and alerts are generated.

In practice, we found this 20-minute delay works fine for system level SLA tracking. In order to further reduce response time, we in parallel use the Autopilot PA pipeline to collect and aggregate a set of Pingmesh counters. The Autopilot PA pipeline is a distributed design with every data center has its own pipeline. The PA counter collection latency is 5 minutes, which is faster than our Cosmos/SCOPE pipeline. The PA pipeline is faster than Cosmos/SCOPE, whereas Cosmos/SCOPE is more expressive than PA for data processing. By using both of them, we provide higher availability for Pingmesh than either of them.

We differentiate Pingmesh as an always-on service from a set of scripts that run periodically. All the components of Pingmesh have watchdogs to watch whether they are running correctly or not, e.g., whether pinglists are generated correctly, whether the CPU and memory usages are within budget, whether pingmesh data are reported and stored, whether DSA reports network SLAs in time, etc. Furthermore, the Pingmesh Agent is designed to probe thousands of peers in a light-weight and safe way.

All the Pingmesh Agents upload 24 terabytes latency measurement results to Cosmos per day. This is more than 2Gb/s upload rate. Though these look like large numbers, they are only a negligible fraction of the total capacity provided by our network and Cosmos.

4. LATENCY DATA ANALYSIS

In this section, we introduce how Pingmesh helps us better understand network latency and packet drops, define and track the network SLA, and determine if a live-site incident is because of network issues or not. All the data centers we describe in this section have similar network architecture as we have introduced in Figure 1, though they may vary in size and may be built at different times.

4.1 Network latency

Figure 4 shows the intra-DC latency distribution of two representative data centers DC1 in US West and DC2 in US Central. DC1 is used by distributed storage and MapReduce and DC2 is by an interactive Search service. Servers in DC1 are throughput intensive and the average server CPU utilization is as high as 90%. Servers in DC1 use the network heavily and transmit and receive several hundreds of Mb/s data on average all the time. DC2 is latency sensitive and servers have high fan-in and fan-out in that a server needs to communicate with a large number of other servers to service a Search query. The average CPU utilization in DC2 is moderate and the average network throughput is low but the traffic is bursty.

The CDFs in Figure 4 are calculated from latency data of one normal working day, when there were no network incidents detected and no live-site incidents because of the network. We track both intra-pod and inter-pod latency distributions, with and without TCP payload. If not specifically mentioned, the latency we use in the paper is the inter-pod TCP SYN/SYN-ACK RTT without payload.

Figure 4(a) shows the overall inter-pod latency distributions and Figure 4(b) shows the inter-pod distribution at high percentile. We once expected that the latency of DC1 should be much larger than DC2 since servers and the network in DC1 are highly loaded. But this turned out not the case for latencies at the 90th or lower percentile.

But DC1 does have much higher latency at the high percentile as shown in Figure 4(b). At P99.9, the inter-pod latencies are 23.35ms and 11.07ms for DC1 and DC2, respectively. At P99.99, the inter-pod latencies become 1397.63ms and 105.84ms. Our measurement result shows it is hard to provide low latency (e.g., sub-milliseconds level) at three or four 9s, even when the servers and network are both light-loaded at macro time scale. This is because the server OS is not a real-time operating system and the traffic in our network is burst. We see 10^-5 packet drop rate for intra-pod communications (Section 4.2) even when average network utilization is low to moderate.

Figure 4(c) compares the intra-pod and inter-pod latency distributions, and Figure 4(d) studies the inter-pod latency with and without payload, all in DC1. For latency measurement with payload, after TCP connection setup, we let the client send a message (typically 800-1200 bytes within one packet). The client measures the payload latency once it receives the echoed back message from the server.

As shown in Figure 4(c), intra-pod latency is always smaller than inter-pod latency as expected. The 50th (P50) and the 99th (P99) intra-pod and inter-pod latencies are (216us, 1.26ms) and (268us, 1.34ms) for DC1. The differences at P50 and P99 are 52us and 80us, respectively. These numbers show that the network does introduce tens of microsecond latency due to queuing delay. But the queuing delay is small. Hence we can infer that the network provides enough network capacity.

Figure 4(d) shows the latency difference with and without payload. With payload, the latency increases from 268us to 326us at P50, and from 1.34ms to 2.43ms at P99, respectively. The increase is mainly because of the increased transmission delay [1] and the user space processing overhead for the receiving servers to echo back the message. In most cases, the latency distributions with and without payload are similar. We introduced payload ping because it can help detect packet drops that are related to packet length (e.g., fiber FCS errors and switch SerDes errors that are related to bit error rate).

Based on the Pingmesh data, we are able to calculate not only the latency distributions of the data centers, but also the latency CDFs for all the applications and services. From these results, we are able to track network latency for all of them all the time.

Data center	Packet drop rate	
	Intra-pod	Inter-pod
DC1 (US West)	1.31×10^{-5}	7.55×10^{-5}
DC2 (US Central)	2.10×10^{-5}	7.63×10^{-5}
DC3 (US East)	9.58×10^{-6}	4.00×10^{-5}
DC4 (Europe)	1.52×10^{-5}	5.32×10^{-5}
DC5 (Asia)	9.82×10^{-6}	1.54×10^{-5}

Table 1: Intra-pod and inter-pod packet drop rates.

4.2 Packet drop rate

Pingmesh does not directly measure packet drop rate. However, we can infer packet drop rate from the TCP connection setup time. When the first SYN packet is dropped, TCP sender will retransmit the packet after an initial timeout. For the rest successive retries, TCP will double the timeout value every time. In our data centers, the initial timeout value is 3 seconds, and the sender will retry SYN two times. Hence if the measured TCP connection RTT is around 3 seconds, there is one packet drop; if the RTT is around 9 seconds, there are two packet drops. We use the following heuristic to estimate packet drop rate:

$$\frac{probes\_with\_3s\_rtt + probes\_with\_9s\_rtt}{total\_successful\_probes}.$$

Note that we only use the total number of successful TCP probes instead of the total probes as the denominator. This is because for failed probes, we cannot differentiate between packet drops and receiving server failure. In the numerator, we only count one packet drop instead of two for every connection with 9 second RTT. This is because successive packet drops within a connection are not independent: the probability the second SYN is dropped is much higher if the first SYN is

[1] We have disabled cut-through switching at the switches in our data centers. This is to stop FCS errors from propagation.

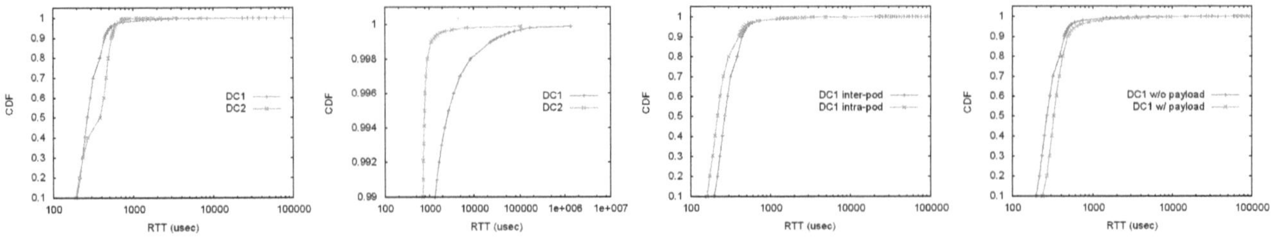

(a) (b) (c) (d)

Figure 4: (a)Inter-pod latency of two data centers. (b) Inter-pod latency at high percentile. (c) Intra-pod and inter-pod latency comparison. (d) Latency comparison with and without payload.

dropped. We have verified the accuracy of the heuristic for a single ToR network by counting the NIC and ToR packet drops.

In our network, SYN packets are treated the same as other packets. Hence the drop rate of SYN packets can be considered representative drop rate of the other data packets in normal condition. This assumption, however, may not be true when packet drop rate is related to packet size, e.g., due to FCS errors. We did see packets of larger size may experience higher drop rate in FCS error related incidents. In what follows, the results we present are when the networks were in normal condition.

Our network does not differentiate packets of different IP protocols (e.g., TCP vs. UDP). Hence, our packet drop calculation holds for non-TCP traffic as well.

Table 1 shows the packet drop rates of five data centers. We show both the intra-pod and inter-pod packet drop rates. For intra-pod packet drops, those are drops at ToR switch, NIC, and end-host network stack. The inter-pod packet drops may come from the Leaf and Spine switches and the corresponding links, in addition to the ToR, NIC, and end-host stack.

From Table 1, several observations can be made. First, the packet drop rates are in the range of $10^{-4} - 10^{-5}$. We track the packet drop rates for all our data centers every day and we find the drop rate is in this range unless network incidents happen. Second, the inter-pod packet drop rate is typically several times higher than that of intra-pod. This indicates most of the packet drops happen in the network instead of the hosts. Third, the intra-pod drop rate is around 10^{-5}, which is larger than we have expected.

Our experience tells us packet drops may occur due to many reasons, e.g., switch buffer overflow, NIC receiving buffer overflow, optical fiber FCS errors, switching ASIC malfunction, etc. Though our measurement results suggest that the packet drop rate at normal condition is around $10^{-4} - 10^{-5}$, we are still at the early phase in understanding why it stays in this range.

Many data center applications, e.g., Search, may use hundreds or even thousands of TCP connections simultaneously. For these applications, high latency tail therefore becomes the norm due to the large number of con-

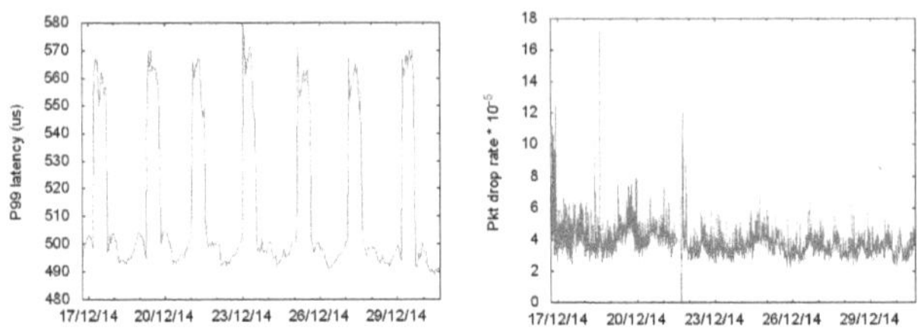

(a) The 99th percentile latency (b) Packet drop rate

Figure 5: The 99th network latency and packet drop rate metrics for a service.

nections used. Applications have introduced several application level tricks to deal with packet drops [10].

From the per server latency data, we can calculate and track network SLAs at server, pod, podset, and data center levels. Similarly, we can calculate and track network SLA for individual services.

4.3 Is it a network issue?

In large distributed data center systems, many parts may go wrong. When a live-site incident happens, it is not easy to identify which part causes the problem. There are occasions that all the components seem fine but the whole system is broken. If the network cannot prove it is innocent, the problem will then be called a "network problem": I did not do anything wrong to my service, it must be the fault of the network.

The network team is then engaged to investigate. A typical procedure is as follows. The network on-call engineer asks the service which is experiencing issues for detailed symptoms and source-destination pairs; he then logs into the source and/or destination servers and runs various network tools to reproduce the issue; he may also look at the switch counters along the possible paths for anomaly; if he cannot reproduce, he may ask for more source-destination pairs. The procedure may need several rounds of iterations.

The above approach does not work well for us, since it is a manual process and does not scale. If the issue turns out not to be caused by the network, the service owners waste their time in engaging with the wrong team. If the issue is indeed because of the network, the manual process causes long time-to-detect (TTD), time-to-mitigate (TTM), and time-to-resolve (TTR).

Pingmesh changed the situation. Because Pingmesh collects latency data from all the servers, we can always pull out Pingmesh data to tell if a specific service has network issue or not. If Pingmesh data does not correlate to the issue perceived by the applications, then it is not a network issue. If Pingmesh data shows it is indeed a network issue, we can further get detailed data from Pingmesh, e.g., the scale of the problem (e.g., how many servers and applications are affected), the source-destination server IP addresses and TCP port numbers, for further investigation.

We define network SLA as a set of metrics including packet drop rate, network latency at the 50th percentile and the 99th percentile. Network SLA can then be tracked at different scopes including per server, per pod/podset, per service, per data center, by using the Pingmesh data. In practice we found two network SLA metrics: packet drop rate and network latency at the 99th percentile are useful for telling if an issue is caused by the network or not. Figure 5 shows these two metrics for a service in one normal week. The packet drop rate is around 4×10^{-5} and the 99th percentile latency in a data center is 500-560us. (The latency shows a periodical pattern. This is because this service performs high throughput data sync periodically which increases the 99th percentile latency.) If these two metrics change significantly, then it is a network issue.

We currently use a simple threshold based approach for network SLA violation detection. If the packet drop rate is greater than 10^{-3} or the 99th percentile latency is larger than 5ms, we will categorize this as a network problem and fire alerts. 10^{-3} and 5ms are much larger than the normal values. We keep Pingmesh historical data for 2 months, and we run various data analysis on top of the Pingmesh data to track the network SLAs for different data centers and customers. There are huge opportunities in using data mining and machine learning to get more value out of the Pingmesh data.

In Section 5, we will study one specific packet drop in detail: switch silent packet drops.

5. SILENT PACKET DROP DETECTION

In this section, we introduce how Pingmesh helps detect switch silent packet drops. When silent packet drops happen, the switches for various reasons do not show information about these packet drops and the switches seem innocent. But applications suffer from increased latency and packet drops. How to quickly identify if an ongoing live-site incident is caused by switch silent packet drops therefore becomes critical.

In the past, we have identified two types of switch silent packet drops: packet black-hole and silent random packet drops. Next, we introduce how we use Pingmesh to detect them.

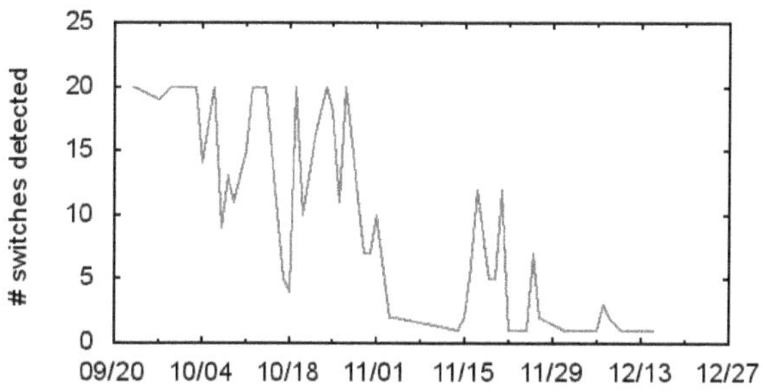

Figure 6: The number of switches with packet black-holes detected.

5.1 Packet black-hole

Packet black-hole is a special type of switch packet drops. For a switch that is experiencing packet black-holes, packets that meet certain 'patterns' are dropped deterministically (i.e., 100%) by the switch. We have identified two types of packet black-holes. In the first type of black-hole, packets with specific source destination IP address pairs get dropped. The symptom is as following: server A cannot talk to server B, but it can talk to servers C and D just fine. All the servers A-D are healthy.

In the second type of black-hole, packets with specific source destination addresses and transport port numbers are dropped. Note that for this type of black-hole, packets with the same source destination address pair but different source destination port numbers are treated differently. For example, Server A can talk to Server B's destination port Y using source port X, but not source port Z.

The first type of black-holes is typically caused by TCAM deficits (e.g., parity error) in the switching ASIC. Some TCAM entries in the TCAM table may get corrupted, and the corruption causes only packets with certain source and destination address patterns been dropped. (Since only destination address is used for next-hop lookup for IP routing, on may wonder why source IP address plays an role. Our guess is that a TCAM entry includes not only destination address but also source address and other meta data.)

We know less about the root causes of the second type of black-hole. We suspect it may be because of errors related to ECMP which uses source and destination IP addresses and port numbers to decide the next forwarding hop.

Based on our experience, these two types of packet black-holes can be fixed by reloading the switch. Hence the question becomes how to detect the switches with black-holes.

We have devised a ToR switch black-hole detection algorithm based on Pingmesh data. The idea of the algorithm is that if many servers under a ToR switch experience the black-hole symptom, then we mark the

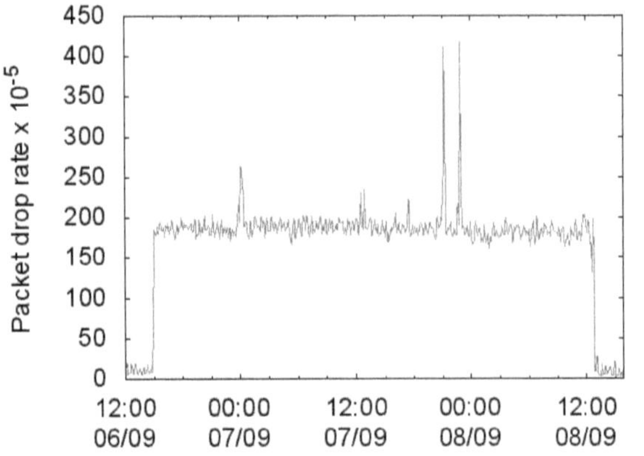

Figure 7: Silent random packet drops of a Spine switch detected by Pingmesh during an incident.

ToR switch as a black-hole candidate and assign it a score which is the ratio of servers with black-hole symptom. We then select the switches with black-hole score larger than a threshold as the candidates. Within a podset, if only part of the ToRs experience the black-hole symptom, then those ToRs are blacking hole packets. We then invoke a network repairing service to safely restart the ToRs. If all the ToRs in a podset experience the black-hole symptom, then the problem may be in the Leaf or Spine layer. Network engineers are notified to do further investigation.

Figure 6 shows the number of ToR switches with black-holes the algorithm detected. As we can see from the figure, the number of the switches with packet black-holes decreases once algorithm began to run. In our algorithm, we limit the algorithm to reload at most 20 switches per day. This is to limit the maximum number of switch reboots. As we can see, after a period of time, the number of switches detected dropped to only several per day.

We would like to note that the TCP source port of the Pingmesh Agent varies for every probing. With the large number of source/destination IP address pairs, Pingmesh scans a big portion of the whole source/destination address and port space. After Pingmesh black-hole detection came online, our customers did not complain about packet black-holes anymore.

5.2 Silent random packet drops

The higher the tier a switch is located in the network, the more severe impact it will have when it begins to drop packets. When a Spine switch drops packets silently, tens of thousands of servers and many services will be impacted and live-site incidents with high severity will be triggered.

Here we introduce how Pingmesh helped locate silent random packet drops of a Spine switch. In one incident, all the users in a data center began to experience increased network latency at the 99th percentile. Using Pingmesh, we could confirm that the packet drops in that data center has increased significantly and the drops were not deterministic. Fig. 7 shows the packet drop rate change of a service. Under normal condition, the percentage of latency should be at around $10^{-4} - 10^{-5}$. But it suddenly jumped up to around 2×10^{-3}.

Using Pingmesh, we could soon figure out that only one data center was affected, and the other data centers were fine. Packet drops at ToR and Leaf layers cannot cause the latency increase for all our customers due to the much smaller number of servers under them. The latency increase pattern shown in Figure 8(d) pointed the problem to the Spine switch layer.

But we could not find any packet drop hint (FCS errors, input/output packet discards, syslog errors, etc.) at those switches. We then suspected that this is likely a case of silent packet drops. The next step was to locate the switches that were dropping packets.

Again, by using Pingmesh, we could figure out several source and destination pairs that experienced around 1%-2% random packet drops. We then launched TCP traceroute against those pairs, and finally pinpointed one Spine switch. The silent random packet drops were gone after we isolated the switch from serving live traffic. The postmortem analysis with the switch provider revealed that the packet drops were due to bit flips of a fabric module of that switch.

The above case is one of the first silent random packet drop cases we met and it took us long time to resolve. After that we ran into more cases and we have improved both Pingmesh data analysis and other tools for better automatic random silent packet drop detection. Our experiences told us that random silent packet drops may be because of different reasons, e.g., switching fabric CRC checksum error, switching ASIC deficit, linecard not well seated, etc. These types of switch silent packet drops cannot be fixed by switch reload and we have to RMA (return merchandise authorization) the faulty switch or components.

Compared to packet drops due to network congestion and link FCS errors, packet black-holes and silent random drops are new and less understood to us. Due to the whole coverage and always-on properties of Pingmesh, we are able to confirm that switch silent packet drops do happen in real-world and categorize different silent packet drop types, and further locate where the silent packet drops happen.

6. EXPERIENCES LEARNED

Pingmesh is designed to be scalable. We understand that not all the networks are of our size. We believe that the lessons we learned from Pingmesh are beneficial to networks of both large and small scales. One of the lessons we learned is the value of trustworthy latency data of full coverage. If the data is not trustworthy, then the results built on top of it cannot be trusted. Our experience told us that not all SNMP data are trustworthy. A switch may drop packets even though its SNMP tells us everything is fine. We trust Pingmesh data because we wrote the code, tested and ran it. When there are bugs, we fixed them. After several iterations, we knew we can trust the data. Because of the full coverage and trustworthy of its latency data, Pingmesh could carry out accurate black-hole and silent packet drop detection. As a comparison, simply using switch SNMP and syslog data does not work since they do not tell us about packet black-holes and silent drops.

In what follows, we introduce several additional lessons we have learned from building and running Pingmesh, which we believe can be applied to networks of different scales as well.

6.1 Pingmesh as an always-on service

From the beginning of the project, we believed that Pingmesh needs to cover all the servers and be always-on. But not everyone agreed. There were arguments that latency data should only be collected on-demand; that we should only let a few selected servers participate in latency measurement, so as to reduce the overhead. We disagree with both of them.

In its essence, the first argument is always-on vs on-demand. One may argue that it is a waste of resource if the always-on latency data is not used, hence we should only collect latency data when it is needed.This argument has two issues. First, we cannot predict when the latency data will be needed since we do not know when a live-site incident will happen. When a live-site incident occurs, having network latency data readily at hands instead of collecting them at that time is a much better choice. Second, when something bad happens, we typically do not know which network devices caused the trouble, hence we do not even have the source destination pairs to launch latency measurement.

Using only a small number of selected servers for latency measurement limits the coverage of Pingmesh data, and poses challenges on which servers should be chosen. As we have demonstrated in the paper, letting all the servers participate gives us the maximum possible coverage, and easily balance the probing activity among all the servers. As we have demonstrated in the paper, the CPU, memory and bandwidth overhead introduced by Pingmesh is affordable.

Having latency data that is always-on brings benefits that we did not recognize in the beginning. After experiencing a few live-site incidents due to packet black-hole and switch silent packet drops, we found that we could use the Pingmesh data to automatically detect these types of switch failures, because of the whole coverage and always-on nature of Pingmesh data (Section 5).

6.2 Loosely coupled components help evolvement

Pingmesh benefits from a loosely coupled system design. Pingmesh Controller and Pingmesh Agent interact only through the pinglist files, which are standard XML files, via standard Web API. Pingmesh Agent provides latency data as both CSV files and standard performance counters.

Due to its loosely coupled design, Pingmesh could be built step by step in three phases. In the first phase, we focused on Pingmesh Agent. We built a simple Pingmesh Controller which statically generates pinglist files using a simplified pinglist generation algorithm. The latency data was simply put into Cosmos without automatic analysis. This phase demonstrated the feasibility of Pingmesh. At the end of this phase, the latency data was already used for network SLA calculation.

In the second phase, we built a full fledged Pingmesh Controller which automatically updates pinglists once network topology is updated or configuration is adjusted. The new version of Pingmesh Controller is also of higher capacity and more fault tolerant by setting up multiple controllers in geo-distributed data centers.

In the third phase, we focused on data analysis and visualization. We built a data processing pipeline which automatically analyzes the collected latency data in every 10 minutes, one hour, one day, respectively. The processed results are then stored in database for visualization, report and alert services.

The major tasks of these three phases were finished in June 2012. After that, many new features were added into Pingmesh:

Inter-DC Pingmesh. Pingmesh originally worked for intra-DC. However, extending it to cover Inter-DC is easy. We extended the Pingmesh Controller's pinglist generation algorithm so as to select a set of servers from every data center and let them carry out Inter-DC ping and the job was done. There is no single line of code or configuration change of the Pingmesh Agent. We did add a new inter-DC data processing pipeline though.

QoS monitoring. After Pingmesh was deployed, network QoS was introduced into our data center which differentiates high priority and low priority packets based on DSCP (differentiated service code point). Again, we extended the Pingmesh Generator to generate pinglists for both high and low priority classes. In this case, we did need a simple configuration change of the Pingmesh Agent to let it listen to an additional TCP port which is configured for low priority traffic.

VIP monitoring. Pingmesh was originally designed to measure network latency of physical networks. In our data centers, load-balancing and IP address virtualization is widely used. Address virtualization exposes a logical Virtual IP address (VIP) to users, and the VIP is mapped to a set of physical servers. The physical IP addresses of these servers are called DIP (destination IP). In our load-balancing system, there is a control plan maintains the VIP to DIP mapping and a data plan that delivers packets that target for a VIP to the DIPs via packet encapsulation. When Pingmesh got deployed, a natural extension is let Pingmesh to monitor the availability of the VIPs. This again is done by extending the Pingmesh Generation algorithm to cover

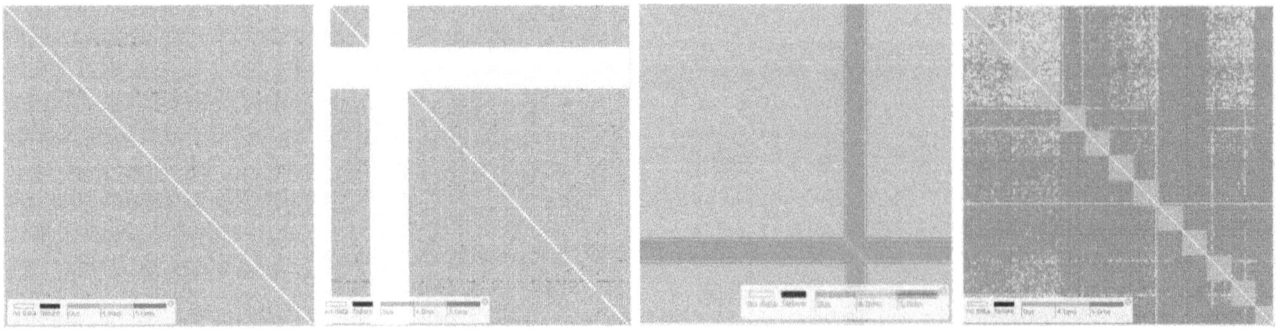

(a) Normal (b) Podset down (c) Podset failure (d) Spine failure

Figure 8: Network latency patterns through visualization.

the VIPs as the target, without touching the rest of the Pingmesh pipeline.

Silent packet drop detection. As we have discussed in Section 5, we have been using Pingmesh for silent packet drop detection. Since the latency data is already there, we only need to figure out the detection algorithm and implement the algorithm in the DSA pipeline without touching other Pingmesh components.

Network metrics for services. Two Pingmesh metrics have been used by service developers to design and implement better services. The Pingmesh Agent exposes two PA counters for every server: the 99th latency and the packet drop rate. Service developers can use the 99th latency to get better understanding of data center network latency at server level. The per-server packet drop rate has been used by several services as one of the metrics for server selection.

For the above extensions, only inter-DC Pingmesh and QoS monitoring were by design, the rest three just happened out of our expectation. Thanks to Pingmesh's loosely coupled design, all these features were added smoothly without adjusting its architecture.

6.3 Visualization for pattern discovery

We have invested heavily in Pingmesh data analysis and visualization. Our happy findings are that data speaks for themselves and that visualization helps us better understand and detect various latency patterns.

Figure 8 shows several typical visualized latency patterns. In the figure, a small green, yellow, or red block or pixel shows the network latency at the 99th percentile between a source-destination pod-pair. Green means the latency is less than 4ms, yellow means the latency is between 4-5ms, and red is for latency larger than 5ms. A white block means there is no latency data available.

Figure 8(a) shows an (almost) all-green pattern, which means the network works fine. Though looks straightforward, this all-green pattern is one of the most widely used feature of Pingmesh. Using this pattern, we can easily tell the global healthy status of the network.

Figure 8(b) shows a pattern of a white-cross. The width of the white-cross corresponds to a Podset, which contains around 20 pods. This pattern shows a Podset-down scenario. Podset-down typically is due to the loss of power of the whole Podset.

Figure 8(c) shows a pattern of a red-cross. The width of the red-cross again corresponds to a Podset. The red-cross shows high network latency from and to the Podset. This pattern shows there is a network issue within the Podset, since the network latency of other Podsets are normal. There may be several causes of the Podset red-cross. If both Leaf and ToR switches are all L3 switches, then at least one of the Leaf switches is dropping packets. If the whole Podset is a L2 domain, then it is possibly caused by broadcast storm, e.g., due to some switches loss their configuration.

Figure 8(d) shows a pattern of red-color with green-squares along the diagonal. Here each small green-square is a Podset. It shows that the network latencies within the Podsets are normal, but cross-Podset latency are all out of network SLA. It shows a network issue at the Spine switch layer.

The success of the visualization is beyond our expectation. It has become a habit for many of us to open the visualization portal regularly to see if the network is fine. The visualization portal has been used not only by network developers and engineers, but also by our customers to learn if there is a network issue or not. We also observed an interesting usage pattern: When the visualization system was first put into use, it was typically used by the network team to 'prove' to our customers that the network was fine. Now our customers usually use the visualization to show that there is indeed an on-going network issue. This is a usage pattern change that we are happy to see.

6.4 Pingmesh limitations

During the period of running Pingmesh, we have uncovered two limitations of Pingmesh. First, though Pingmesh is able to detect which tier a faulty network device is located in, it cannot tell the exact location. In our network, there are tens to hundreds of switches at the Spine layer. Knowing the Spine layer is experiencing some issue is good but not enough. We need methods to locate and isolate the faulty devices as fast as possible. This is a known limitation of Pingmesh from beginning. As described in Section 5.2, we combine Pingmesh and TCP traceroute to address this issue.

The second limitation comes from Pingmesh's current latency measurement. Though the Pingmesh Agent can send and receive probing messages of up to 64 KB, we only use SYN/SYN-ACK and a single packet for single RTT measurement. Single packet RTT is good at detecting network reachability and packet-level latency issues. But it does not cover the case when multiple round trips are needed. We recently experienced a live-site incident caused by TCP parameter tuning. A bug introduced in our TCP parameter configuration software rewrote the TCP parameters to their default value. As a result, for some of our services, the initial congestion window (ICW) reduced from 16 to 4. For long distance TCP sessions, the session finish time increased by several hundreds of milliseconds if the sessions need multiple round trips. Pingmesh did not catch this because it only measures single packet RTT.

7. RELATED WORK

Our experiences running one of the largest data center networks in the world taught us that all the components including applications, OS kernel, NIC, switching ASIC and firmware, and fibers may cause communication failures. See [4] for a summary of various failures that may cause network partition.

[21] and [6] studied traffic and flow characteristics of different types of data centers, by collecting network traces. Pingmesh focuses on network latency and is complementary to these works.

Both Pingmesh and [18] are designed to detect packet drops in the network. Both use active probing packets and are capable of covering the whole network. The approaches, though, are different. [18] uses RSVP-TE base source routing to pinpoint the routing path of a probing packet. It hence needs to create the routing paths and maps in advance. It also means that the probing packets are traversing the network in LSPs (label switched paths) different from those used by the non-probing packets. Second, RSVP-TE is based on MPLS, which, though is widely used for WAN traffic engineering, is not used within the data centers. Pingmesh can be used for both intra-DC and inter-DC networks. Using source routing does provide an advantage: [18] can directly pinpoint the switches or links that drop packets. We have shown in Section 5.2 Pingmesh can localize faulty devices together with traceroute.

Cisco IPSLA [8] also uses active packets for network performance monitoring. IPSLA is configured to run at Cisco switches, and is capable of sending ICMP, IP, UDP, TCP, and HTTP packets. IPSLA collects network latency, jitter, packet loss, server response time, and even voice quality scores. The results are stored locally at the switches and can be retrieved via SNMP or CLI (command-line interface). Pingmesh differs from IPSLA in several ways. First, Pingmesh uses server instead of switches for data collection. By doing so, Pingmesh becomes network device independent whereas IPSLA works only for Cisco devices. Second, Pingmesh focuses on both measurement and latency data analysis. To achieve its goal, Pingmesh has not only Pingmesh Agent for data collection, but also a control plane for centralized control and a data storage and analysis pipeline. IPSLA does not have such a control plane and data storage and analysis pipeline.

NetSight [19] tracks packet history by introducing postcard filters at the switches to generate captured packet events called postcard. Several network troubleshooting services, nprof, netshark, netwatch, ndb, can be built on top of NetSight. Compared with NetSight, Pingmesh is server-based in that it does not need to introduce additional rules into the switches. Further Pingmesh is capable of detecting switch silent packet drops. It is not clear how silent packet drop rules can be written for NetSight, since it is not known in advance which type of packets may be dropped.

ATPG [25] determines a minimal set of probing packets that cover all the network links and forwarding rules. Pingmesh does not try to minimize the number of probings. As long as the overhead is affordable, we prefer to let Pingmesh run all the time. Further it is not clear how ATPG can deal with packet black-holes where the rules for black-holes cannot be determined in advance.

Pingmesh focused on physical network and it uses active probings by installing the Pingmesh Agent in the servers. For third party VMs and virtual networks, however, installing the Pingmesh Agent may not be feasible. In this case passive traffic collection as explored by VND [24] may be used.

8. CONCLUSION

We have presented the design and implementation of Pingmesh for data center network latency measurement and analysis. Pingmesh is always-on and it provides network latency data by all the servers and for all the servers. Pingmesh has been running in Microsoft data centers for more than four years. It helps us answer if a service issue is caused by the network or not, define and track network SLA at both macro and micro levels, and it has become to be an indispensable service for network troubleshooting.

Due to its loosely coupled design, Pingmesh turned out to be easily extensible. Many new features have been added while the architecture of Pingmesh is still the same. By studying the Pingmesh latency data and learning from the latency patterns via visualization and data mining, we are able to continuously improve the quality of our network, e.g., by automatically fixing packet black-holes and detecting switch silent random packet drops.

9. ACKNOWLEDGEMENT

We thank Lijiang Fang, Albert Greenberg, Wilson Lee, Randy Kern, Kelvin Yiu, Dongmei Zhang, Yong-guang Zhang, Feng Zhao, the members of the Wireless and Networking Group of Microsoft Research Asia for their support at various stages of this project. We thank our shepherd Sujata Banerjee and the anonymous SIG-COMM reviewers for their valuable and detailed feed-back and comments.

10. REFERENCES

[1] M. Al-Fares, A. Loukissas, and A. Vahdat. A Scalable, Commodity Data Center Network Architecture. In *Proc. SIGCOMM*, 2008.

[2] Alexey Andreyev. Introducing data center fabric, the next-generation Facebook data center network. https://code.facebook.com/posts/360346274145943/, Nov 2014.

[3] Hadoop. http://hadoop.apache.org/.

[4] Peter Bailis and Kyle Kingsbury. The Network is Reliable: An Informal Survey of Real-World Communications Failures. *ACM Queue*, 2014.

[5] Luiz Barroso, Jeffrey Dean, and Urs Hölzle. Web Search for a Planet: The Google Cluster Architecture. *IEEE Micro*, March-April 2003.

[6] Theophilus Benson, Aditya Akella, and David A. Maltz. Network Traffic Characteristics of Data Centers in the Wild. In *Internet Measurement Conference*, November 2010.

[7] et.al Brad Calder. Windows Azure Storage: A Highly Available Cloud Storage Service with Strong Consistency. In *SOSP*, 2011.

[8] Cisco. IP SLAs Configuration Guide, Cisco IOS Release 12.4T. http://www.cisco.com/c/en/us/td/docs/ios-xml/ios/ipsla/configuration/12-4t/sla-12-4t-book.pdf.

[9] Citrix. What is Load Balancing? http://www.citrix.com/glossary/load-balancing.html.

[10] Jeffrey Dean and Luiz André Barroso. The Tail at Scale. *CACM*, Februry 2013.

[11] Jeffrey Dean and Sanjay Ghemawat. MapReduce: Simplified Data Processing on Large Clusters. In *OSDI*, 2004.

[12] Albert Greenberg et al. VL2: A Scalable and Flexible Data Center Network. In *SIGCOMM*, August 2009.

[13] Chi-Yao Hong et al. Achieving High Utilization with Software-Driven WAN. In *SIGCOMM*, 2013.

[14] Parveen Patel et al. Ananta: Cloud Scale Load Balancing. In *ACM SIGCOMMM*. ACM, 2013.

[15] R. Chaiken et al. SCOPE: Easy and Efficient Parallel Processing of Massive Data Sets. In *VLDB'08*, 2008.

[16] Sushant Jain et al. B4: Experience with a Globally-Deployed Software Defined WAN. In *SIGCOMM*, 2013.

[17] Sanjay Ghemawat, Howard Gobioff, and Shun-Tak Leung. The Google File System. In *ACM SOSP*. ACM, 2003.

[18] Nicolas Guilbaud and Ross Cartlidge. Google Backbone Monitoring, Localizing Packet Loss in a Large Complex Network, Feburary 2013. Nanog57.

[19] Nikhil Handigol, Brandon Heller, Vimalkumar Jeyakumar, David Mazières, and Nick McKeown. I Know What Your Packet Did Last Hop: Using Packet Histories to Troubleshoot Networks. In *NSDI*, 2014.

[20] Michael Isard. Autopilot: Automatic Data Center Management. *ACM SIGOPS Operating Systems Review*, 2007.

[21] Srikanth Kandula, Sudipta Sengupta, Albert Greenberg, Parveen Patel, and Ronnie Chaiken. The nature of data center traffic: Measurements & analysis. In *Proceedings of the 9th ACM SIGCOMM Conference on Internet Measurement Conference*, IMC '09, 2009.

[22] Rishi Kapoor, Alex C. Snoeren, Geoffrey M. Voelker, and George Porter. Bullet Trains: A Study of NIC Burst Behavior at Microsecond Timescales. In *ACM CoNEXT*, 2013.

[23] Cade Metz. Return of the Borg: How Twitter Rebuilt Google's Secret Weapon. http://www.wired.com/2013/03/google-borg-twitter-mesos/all/, March 2013.

[24] Wenfei Wu, Guohui Wang, Aditya Akella, and Anees Shaikh. Virtual Network Diagnosis as a Service. In *SoCC*, 2013.

[25] Hongyi Zeng, Peyman Kazemian, George Varghese, and Nick McKeown. Automatic Test Packet Generation. In *CoNEXT*, 2012.

Large-scale Measurements of Wireless Network Behavior

Sanjit Biswas
biswas@samsara.com

John Bicket
jbicket@samsara.com

Edmund Wong
elwong@meraki.com

Raluca Musaloiu-E
ralucam@meraki.com

Apurv Bhartia
apurv@meraki.com

Dan Aguayo
aguayo@meraki.com

Cisco Meraki
500 Terry Francois Blvd.
San Francisco, CA 94158

ABSTRACT

Meraki is a cloud-based network management system which provides centralized configuration, monitoring, and network troubleshooting tools across hundreds of thousands of sites worldwide. As part of its architecture, the Meraki system has built a database of time-series measurements of wireless link, client, and application behavior for monitoring and debugging purposes. This paper studies an anonymized subset of measurements, containing data from approximately ten thousand radio access points, tens of thousands of links, and 5.6 million clients from one-week periods in January 2014 and January 2015 to provide a deeper understanding of real-world network behavior.

This paper observes the following phenomena: wireless network usage continues to grow quickly, driven most by growth in the number of devices connecting to each network. Intermediate link delivery rates are common indoors across a wide range of deployment environments. Typical access points share spectrum with dozens of nearby networks, but the presence of a network on a channel does not predict channel utilization. Most access points see 2.4 GHz channel utilization of 20% or more, with the top decile seeing greater than 50%, and the majority of the channel use contains decodable 802.11 headers.

CCS Concepts

•Networks → Wireless access points, base stations and infrastructure; Network measurement;

SIGCOMM '15, August 17 - 21, 2015, London, United Kingdom
© 2015 ACM. ISBN 978-1-4503-3542-3/15/08...$15.00
DOI: http://dx.doi.org/10.1145/2785956.2787489

Keywords

802.11, large-scale measurements, network usage data

1. INTRODUCTION

Over the past 20 years, wireless LANs based on 802.11 have become common in office and campus environments. Recent estimates suggest over 10 billion WiFi devices have been sold in total and that over 4.5 billion of those devices are in use today [3]. These devices use the same underlying standards and frequency bands defined in the mid-1990s, resulting in an increasingly crowded wireless environment.

Several papers have studied wireless network behavior, from indoor and outdoor links, to campus-scale user behavior. These papers have helped improve our understanding of how real-world networks behave, resulting in improvements to simulators, debugging tools, and protocols. However, there are few studies that analyze a large cohort of wireless LAN networks or over a long period of time.

The Meraki system provides a unique perspective over a wide range of networks due to its cloud-based management architecture. Each Meraki access point is polled periodically by the Meraki system for a number of statistics about the state of the wireless channels, associated clients, and application traffic statistics for each associated client. This information is written to a database, aggregated, and presented to network administrators through a central web service.

Since its inception in 2006, this database has grown to contain information from millions of network devices, including access points, switches, routers, and client devices such as laptops and smartphones.

This paper contributes a detailed look at network behavior, using an anonymized subset of the data contained in the Meraki system. By filtering for devices based on their type of hardware platform and choosing a large set of devices, we are able to plot trends which are not influenced by factors such as variations between chipsets, changes in customer type, or network policy. Specifically, we look at the the following four sets of data:

	Cisco Meraki MR16	Cisco Meraki MR18
CPU	Qualcomm Atheros AR7161 680MHz	Qualcomm Atheros QCA9557 SoC
Memory	64MB DDR	128MB DDR2
Radio	Qualcomm Atheros AR9223 (2.4 GHz), AR9220 (5 GHz) PCI 2x2 802.11n chipset	On-chip Qualcomm Atheros QCA9557 radio (2.4 GHz) with external power amplifier, AR9592 5 GHz PCI 2x2, AR9592 1x1 PCI scanning radio
Transmit power	23 dBm (2.4 GHz), 24 dBm (5 GHz)	24 dBm (2.4 GHz), 24 dBm (5 GHz)
Antenna	Built-in 3dBi 2.4 GHz, 5dBi 5 GHz	Built-in 3dBi 2.4 GHz, 5dBi 5 GHz

Table 1: Hardware platforms used to measure link delivery and channel utilization in Sections 4 and 5

1. For a set of 20,667 networks which serve over five million unique clients a week, we examine the wireless capabilities of the clients as well as the OSes and applications the clients use. Our data also provides insight into the traffic characteristics of various applications as well as how clients have changed in the past year.

2. For a set of 10,000 Cisco Meraki MR16 802.11n access points, we summarize the link delivery characteristics of over 20,000 wireless link pairs measured by periodic broadcasts sent by the access points.

3. Using the same set of access points, we examine the average channel utilization of the 2.4 GHz and 5 GHz bands over a period of six months.

4. With a set of 10,000 Cisco Meraki MR18 802.11n access points, which contain a third radio capable of capturing spectral data, we examine more detailed short-term channel measurements.

The remainder of the paper is organized as follows: Section 2 outlines the architecture of the Meraki system and details about the hardware platforms used in the study. Section 3 studies client and application usage and provides tables demonstrating changes in usage over several years. Section 4 describes our method for measuring link-level statistics between access points and studies the distribution of link delivery rates. Section 5 looks specifically at wireless channel utilization at a fine-grain level. Section 6 describes some real-world challenges faced by the Meraki system. Finally, Section 7 discusses related work, and Section 8 concludes.

2. SYSTEM ARCHITECTURE

The Meraki system consists of access points, switches, and firewalls at customer sites, and a centrally hosted management system, known as the backend system.

Each network in the Meraki system can contain a combination of these wireless and wired network devices that all report data to the backend system in the same way. The backend system itself is distributed across several data centers; for the purposes of this paper, we treat the backend system as a single data store.

Each piece of Meraki networking equipment maintains persistent encrypted tunnels to two different backend data centers. Using these connections, the backend periodically harvests statistics from each network device using protocols, built with Google Protocol Buffers [21] to minimize reporting overhead.

A typical access point averages around 1 kilobit per second to report to the backend. These tunnels are used only for statistics and configuration; client traffic is routed directly to the local network or the Internet. In the event a device is unable to reach the Meraki backend, normal client routing and accounting continues. The backend polls for queued information when the connection is reestablished.

The Meraki backend system is designed to handle machine upgrades, schema changes and new software revisions without affecting the measurement data. The system operates using a pull mechanism, which helps regulate the flow of updates to the database during times of peak load.

2.1 Hardware platforms

The various Meraki hardware platforms contain a similar system architecture and share a Linux codebase, but each product family contains application-specific chipsets. They consist of a general purpose CPU (single or multi-core) running Linux and the Click Modular Router [14], coupled with multiple 802.11 radios (for wireless access points), multiple Gigabit Ethernet interfaces (for security appliances) or a 24/48 port Gigabit or 10 Gigabit switch fabric (for edge switches). This paper focuses only on data from wireless access points.

Each the platform is designed to forward traffic at line-rate while still being able to track client metadata and detailed application usage statistics about individual TCP flows. The fast data path is handled either in hardware (for switching platforms) or in the device driver and in the Click modular router (for security appliances and wireless access points). Elements within the Click modular router on the fast path handle policy routing decisions, client firewall rules, and track application classification and usage for each MAC address. Other specific types of traffic are processed along the slow path, such as ARP, DHCP, DNS, multicast DNS, TCP SYN/FIN, packets containing HTTP headers, and packets containing SSL handshakes. Traffic along the slow path is filtered in the driver or hardware and handled entirely by the Click modular router to identify specific application traffic. Click contains elements to extract additional in-memory metadata information from these traffic flows, such as hostnames, operating system fingerprints, and application-level usage data. This metadata is used to identify flows and update application usage data counters, similar to [17]. There are about 200 application identification rules that use the metadata to identify TCP flows and applications. The user and application analysis was done on a worldwide set of 20,667 networks containing two Meraki access point models, which are further described in Section 3.

The wireless measurements in Section 4 were taken on set of 10,000 identical Cisco Meraki MR16 access points located in the US to simplify analysis. These access points were deployed in between 2010 and 2014 were in continuous operation measurement period from January 2014 through January 2015. Similarly, in Section 5 we consider a set of 10,000 identical Cisco Meraki MR18 access points, equipped with a dedicated scanning radio. All access points were located in the United States and followed the FCC Part 15 regulatory limits. Table 1 describes the access point hardware used to create the data set.

2.2 Firmware revisions

During the measurement period, there were a total of 2 major firmware revisions applied to the access points. The rough dates of these upgrades are January and December 2014. The lower layers of the driver and HAL were not changed, as the updates included routine package security updates and added higher level features related to management and access control features.

2.3 Data collection

In addition to per-client and flow traffic statistics, each access point measures and records wireless channel statistics. The traffic statistics and additional measurements are periodically polled by the Meraki backend system and recorded in long term storage. For usage statistics such as byte counters and application usage, local statistics are aggregated by MAC address in the backend (to account for roaming).

3. NETWORK USAGE

In this section, we take a look at the clients that connect to our access points. In particular, we examine client radio capabilities, the OSes and applications that are most commonly used by clients, and how usage patterns have changed over the past year.

The data presented here were collected from 20,667 wireless networks operated by 11,788 different administrative organizations. All of these networks have at least two wireless access points and have application traffic profiling enabled. All usage data was collected over the one-week period of January 15-22 in 2014 and 2015. We show the numbers for 2015 and provide the percent increase ("% increase") compared to 2014.

The sampled networks include both urban and rural deployments throughout the world. Table 2 describes the mix of networks in the data set organized by industry type.

To preserve anonymity, all of our data are presented only as an aggregate over all of these networks.

Industry	# networks
Architecture/Engineering	127
Construction	333
Consulting	365
Education	4,075
Finance/Insurance	737
Government/Public Sector	1,112
Healthcare	1,382
Hospitality	493
Industrial/Manufacturing	1,220
Legal	264
Media/Advertising	427
Non-Profit	640
Real Estate	386
Restaurants	296
Retail	2,355
Tech	983
Telecom	442
VAR/System Integrator	2,876
Other	2,154
Total	20,667

Table 2: Network deployment types for the application usage data set. There are a wide range of industrial verticals and the networks are not dominated by one particular industry.

3.1 Client devices and signal strength

Our access points collect information about the 802.11 capabilities advertised by every client that connects to the network. Table 4 summarizes how these capabilities have changed over one year.

In summary, we found that:

- 802.11ac clients became much more common over the year: at the end of the sampling period 18% of clients were 11ac-capable.
- A majority of clients now have 5 GHz capability, but nearly 40% of all clients remain 2.4 GHz only.
- Multi-stream clients, became more common, and now about 25% of clients support multiple spatial streams.

Another item of interest is the strength of clients' connections to the network. Our system does not keep a historical record of client signal strength, but, through our centralized infrastructure, we are able to collect a snapshot of RSSI across all connected clients in real time. Figure 1 shows the distribution of client signal strength among about 309,000 clients that were connected one evening in January 2015.

At the time of the snapshot, about 249,000 (80%) of these clients were connected on the 2.4 GHz band, and 60,000 were connected at 5 GHz. This is interesting given the above data which show that about 65% of clients are 5 GHz capable. The difference is presumably due to greater attenuation at 5 GHz, which makes it harder for clients to associate on the higher band.

OS	TB (% total/% download)	% increase	# clients	% increase	MB / client	% increase
Windows	589 (30%/83%)	43%	822,761	28%	751	12%
Apple iOS	545 (28%/88%)	92%	2,550,379	34%	224	44%
Mac OS X	445 (23%/75%)	44%	313,976	24%	1,487	17%
Android	177 (9.1%/89%)	172%	1,535,859	61%	121	69%
Unknown	78 (4.0%/45%)	-9.2%	228,182	-8.9%	357	-0.36%
Chrome OS	62 (3.2%/91%)	275%	178,095	222%	366	16%
Other	26 (1.3%/78%)	80%	13,969	-33%	1,951	168%
Sony Playstation OS	22 (1.1%/96%)	53%	4,267	-13%	5,319	77%
Linux	5.8 (0.30%/68%)	611%	4,402	165%	1,393	169%
RIM BlackBerry	0.14 (0.0074%/94%)	-62%	13,681	-53%	11	-19%
Mobile Windows OSes	0.12 (0.0064%/91%)	-35%	4,943	-42%	26	13%
All	1,950 (100%/82%)	62%	5,578,126	37%	367	18%

Table 3: Usage by operating system during January 15-22, 2015. "% download" is the percentage of download (vs. total) traffic for a particular OS. "% increase" reflects the year-over-year increase from January 15-22, 2014.

	Jan. 2014	Jan. 2015
802.11g	99.9%	99.9%
802.11n	95.7%	97.7%
5 GHz	48.9%	64.9%
40 MHz channels	23.4%	63.8%
802.11ac	2.5%	18.0%
Two streams	7.7%	19.3%
Three streams	2.4%	3.8%
Four streams	0.7%	1.8%

Table 4: Client capabilities advertised by all clients that connected during the same week in January for two consecutive years.

This last point was corroborated by the signal strengths we observed. Median signal strength among all clients was about 28 dB above the noise floor on both bands but was typically lower on 5 GHz connections, again presumably because of attenuation.

3.2 Usage by operating system

Meraki uses a combination of MAC address prefix, DHCP fingerprints, and HTTP User-Agent inspection to determine device types, similar to methods described in [5]. Table 3 summarizes the breakdown of clients by operating system with their total bandwidth usage during a one-week period between January 15 and 22 in both 2014 and 2015. The unknown OS row represents clients where our heuristics could not classify the device, such as with devices running virtual machines or dual-boot operating systems (which would present multiple DHCP fingerprints from a single MAC address) or with embedded devices running Linux. More common is multiple device types presented by the user agent string, sent by browsers such as Chrome or smartphone applications. The reduction in unknown devices between January 2014 and 2015 is due to improvements in our heuristics.

Overall, we observed the total population of clients grow

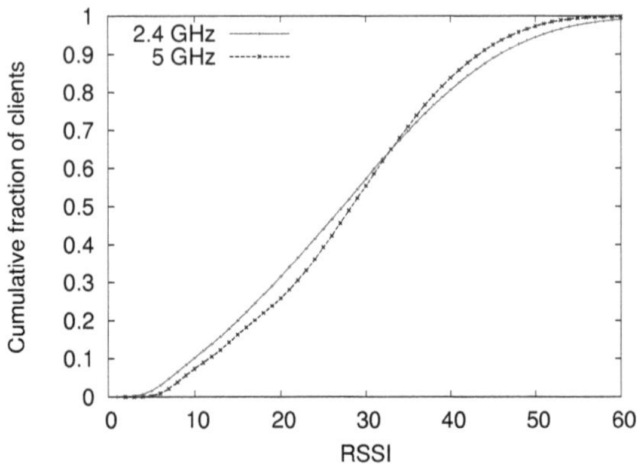

Figure 1: Distributions of received signal strength (RSSI) as measured at the access points, for approximately 309,000 associated clients.

by approximately 37% from 4.07 million to 5.58 million devices year-over-year. Total usage grew by roughly 62%, an increase of 18% per client on average.

Because many OSes are specific to particular devices, Table 3 provides insight into usage by both OS and device type. As mentioned earlier, the classification of device types improved between the two measurement periods, which makes it difficult to compare device type growth in absolute terms. We can, however, compare average usage per client, which shows an steep increase of approximately 69% and 44% for Android and Apple iOS devices, versus a more moderate increase of 12% and 17% for Windows and Mac OS X devices. Even with these increases, mobile devices generally consume at most a few hundred MB of data on average in a week, whereas laptops and desktops running Windows and Mac OS X consume several times more (in particular, Mac OS X devices consumed roughly twice the bandwidth that their Windows counterparts did).

Our data also shows that clients using mobile devices tend to use a larger fraction of their bandwidth consuming content as compared to traditional desktops and laptops. Mobile devices download roughly 9 times more than they upload (in contrast, Mac OS X devices download closer to 3 times more). While mobile platforms have lower average usage, the number of mobile devices greatly outnumber laptops and desktops: we saw three times more Apple iOS devices than Windows devices, making the total usage of Apple iOS comparable to Windows, the most popular OS by usage.

Linux also registered extraordinary growth on our networks, which we attribute to the small number of clients in 2014, improved OS identification heuristics, and the increasing proliferation of Linux-based embedded devices. Finally, we observed significant per-client usage for Sony Playstation and Microsoft Xbox (not shown), most of which is downstream. This usage is not surprising given that game consoles are often used to stream media and play games that use network connectivity for content or functionality.

3.3 Application usage

As described in Section 2.3, Meraki uses several sources of information—including initial DNS lookup, HTTP header inspection, SSL handshake inspection, and port numbers—to determine the application underlying each new network flow. These periodically-updated fingerprints are applied as rule sets within the Click router running on each access point to simplify statistics collection.

Table 5 shows the top 40 applications by bytes transferred (both upstream and downstream) across the same 5.58 million clients as in Section 3.2. The number of clients is displayed along with the usage for a given application. Several of the categories—including miscellaneous web, miscellaneous secure web, miscellaneous video, miscellaneous audio, non-web TCP, and UDP—capture flows from applications not described in the rule set. We also classify each application into a category and show the total usage of various application categories in Table 6. While intuitive, our client usage data enables us to quantify how much traffic various applications and application categories consume in our networks, which applications have grown in the past year, and how individual clients participate in these services. The overhead of data collection was less than 1 kbit/second per access point on average and does not result in enough usage to register in the top 40 applications table.

Video and music applications such as YouTube, Netflix, iTunes, Spotify, and Hulu make up the largest fraction of usage at 34%, with 97% of their usage being download traffic. Looking specifically at Netflix, we found that each client consumed nearly 1.2 GB in a week. These services also recorded significant increases in both the total usage and number of clients that used these services.

File sharing—within a LAN (e.g., Windows file-sharing) and through cloud-based services (e.g., Dropbox)—was the second largest category at 8.4% of total usage with overall growth of approximately 28% year-over-year. Interestingly, we found that content uploaded using file-sharing services is not shared widely on average, as file-sharing services have a very balanced download/upload profile overall. The popularity of file sharing and its balanced downstream/upstream characteristics stand in contrast with web file sharing (services that distribute files via web links, e.g., mediafire.com and hotfile.com). While superficially similar, web file-sharing clients use nearly 45.4 more downstream bandwidth than upstream, implying that content is often uploaded once but downloaded multiple times. Online backup, another similar type of application, is on the other extreme: clients upload 22.8 times more data than they download, as restoring from backup is a relatively rare operation. Overall, our networks generally experience about 4.6 times more downstream traffic than upstream, with VoIP and video conferencing as well as online backup being the rare exceptions of application categories that use more upstream bandwidth than downstream.

One notable data point among the top 40 is Dropcam, a WiFi video-streaming camera and associated cloud backend service for storing and watching the resulting video. Dropcam has the fewest clients (2,940) among the top 40, less than a quarter of the number of clients that the next smallest application has. Yet, each client uses roughly 2.8 GB a week and uploads nearly 19 times more than they download, implying that Dropcam users do not often watch what they record. The extraordinary amount of usage puts Dropcam among the top 30 applications that we observed, above many applications that have far more clients and above several video, P2P, and file-sharing applications, categories that are traditionally heavy hitters.

4. INTERFERENCE LEVELS

As WiFi, Bluetooth, and other unlicensed spectrum devices have gained in popularity, there has been increased interference from nearby devices. In this section, we measure both the number of nearby WiFi access points as well as the amount of time the energy detect mechanism is triggered (a measure of channel utilization), in an effort to understand how busy unlicensed spectrum is in practice.

4.1 Nearby networks

Each Meraki access point is equipped with multiple radios: one dedicated to the 2.4 GHz ban and one dedicated to 5 GHz band (channels selectable based on regulatory region). The newer Meraki MR18 platform also has a third radio that scans both bands simultaneously. The radios are capable of decoding 802.11 a/b/g/n signals in both 20 MHz and 40 MHz formats, making it possible to decode frames from several generations of nearby access points. The radios are not capable of decoding other types of beacons from Bluetooth, Zigbee, or other standards; these beaconds are detected as noise during spectrum analysis.

As with the Meraki radios, many new access points are capable of simultaneous operation in the 2.4 GHz and 5 GHz bands. In most cases, access points send out a Broadcast SSID (BSSID) beacon frame every 102.4 ms (the default BSSID beacon interval) for 0.42 ms in the case of 802.11 a/g/n beacons and 2.592 ms for 802.11b beacons. As the number of nearby SSID broadcasts increase, the beacons and associated data frames may trigger the local AP's car-

Application	Category	TB (% total / % download)	% increase	# clients	% increase	MB / client	% increase
Miscellaneous web	Other	239 (13%/87%)	67%	4,623,630	36%	54	23%
YouTube	Video & music	202 (11%/97%)	93%	1,934,371	53%	110	26%
Netflix	Video & music	188 (9.8%/98%)	76%	161,014	19%	1,224	48%
Non-web TCP	Other	156 (8.2%/64%)	51%	3,656,494	40%	45	8.3%
Miscellaneous secure web	Other	147 (7.7%/70%)	94%	5,115,023	40%	30	38%
iTunes	Video & music	102 (5.4%/98%)	66%	2,230,787	38%	48	20%
Miscellaneous video	Video & music	98 (5.1%/91%)	61%	1,383,386	76%	74	-8.6%
Windows file sharing	File sharing	87 (4.5%/66%)	48%	740,591	31%	123	13%
CDNs	Other	75 (3.9%/72%)	81%	3,157,028	46%	25	24%
UDP	Other	61 (3.2%/61%)	60%	3,705,171	69%	17	-5.6%
Facebook	Social web & photo sharing	53 (2.8%/92%)	127%	3,579,926	35%	16	68%
Google HTTPS	Other	49 (2.6%/85%)	67%	3,953,002	44%	13	16%
Apple file sharing	File sharing	42 (2.2%/44%)	18%	21,951	-1.7%	2,005	21%
apple.com	Other	37 (1.9%/94%)	79%	2,763,663	32%	14	36%
Google	Other	34 (1.8%/85%)	19%	3,804,317	39%	9.5	-14%
Google Drive	Other	24 (1.2%/79%)	374%	1,325,938	138%	19	99%
Dropbox	File sharing	23 (1.2%/60%)	-1.5%	369,068	29%	65	-24%
Software updates	Software & anti-virus updates	18 (0.94%/98%)	36%	689,677	16%	27	18%
Instagram	Social web & photo sharing	17 (0.91%/96%)	45%	831,935	50%	22	-3.3%
BitTorrent	P2P	13 (0.69%/58%)	-8.5%	38,294	15%	360	-21%
Skype	VoIP & video conferencing	13 (0.69%/49%)	48%	392,878	27%	35	16%
Miscellaneous audio	Video & music	13 (0.66%/97%)	54%	460,262	60%	29	-3.7%
Pandora	Video & music	12 (0.64%/97%)	25%	182,753	34%	70	-6.8%
RTMP (Adobe Flash)	Other	12 (0.62%/96%)	10%	141,403	6.2%	88	3.8%
Gmail	Email	12 (0.62%/74%)	26%	1,337,755	42%	9.2	-11%
microsoft.com	Other	11 (0.59%/94%)	15%	861,136	34%	14	-15%
Tumblr	Other	11 (0.57%/97%)	31%	270,482	21%	42	7.9%
Spotify	Video & music	11 (0.56%/98%)	142%	209,219	115%	54	13%
Windows Live Hotmail and Outlook	Email	9.0 (0.47%/64%)	216%	366,272	108%	26	52%
Dropcam	VoIP & video conferencing	8.0 (0.42%/5.0%)	72%	2,940	155%	2,836	-32%
Hulu	Video & music	6.9 (0.36%/98%)	102%	51,667	100%	140	0.90%
Steam	Gaming	6.6 (0.35%/98%)	47%	21,011	45%	332	1.4%
Twitter	Social web & photo sharing	6.4 (0.33%/91%)	67%	1,925,505	34%	3.5	25%
Encrypted P2P	P2P	6.3 (0.33%/97%)	17%	81,673	23%	81	-4.5%
Encrypted TCP (SSL)	Other	6.0 (0.31%/65%)	50%	1,441,775	49%	4.3	0.81%
Remote desktop	Other	5.5 (0.29%/88%)	66%	93,876	13%	61	46%
ESPN	Sports	5.1 (0.27%/98%)	122%	202,971	41%	27	58%
Xfinity TV	Video & music	4.9 (0.26%/98%)	87%	12,802	27%	400	47%
Other web-based email	Email	4.7 (0.25%/49%)	-6.4%	277,919	23%	18	-24%
Microsoft Skydrive	File sharing	4.4 (0.23%/25%)	-10%	269,437	12%	17	-20%

Table 5: Top 40 applications by usage during January 15-22, 2015. See Table 3 for explanations on columns.

Category	TB (% total/% download)	% increase	# clients	% increase	MB / client	% increase
Other	901 (47%/77%)	65%	5,617,395	39%	168	19%
Video & music	648 (34%/97%)	75%	5,047,976	49%	135	17%
File sharing	160 (8.4%/58%)	28%	1,209,821	28%	138	0.12%
Social web & photo sharing	81 (4.2%/93%)	92%	4,691,155	39%	18	38%
Email	32 (1.7%/67%)	41%	2,632,542	38%	13	2.5%
VoIP & video conferencing	24 (1.3%/35%)	55%	483,222	22%	52	27%
Peer-to-peer (P2P)	20 (1.0%/70%)	-1.3%	113,720	22%	184	-19%
Software & anti-virus updates	20 (1.0%/98%)	28%	699,776	15%	29	11%
Gaming	11 (0.57%/96%)	49%	199,804	45%	57	2.8%
Sports	5.3 (0.28%/98%)	117%	225,875	35%	24	60%
News	4.2 (0.22%/95%)	76%	856,913	12%	5.2	57%
Online backup	2.9 (0.15%/4.2%)	10%	7,576	26%	401	-13%
Blogging	0.74 (0.039%/97%)	-34%	487,085	-2.1%	1.6	-32%
Web file sharing	0.32 (0.017%/98%)	-27%	10,822	-22%	31	-6.6%

Table 6: Usage by application categories during January 15-22, 2015. See Table 3 for explanations on columns.

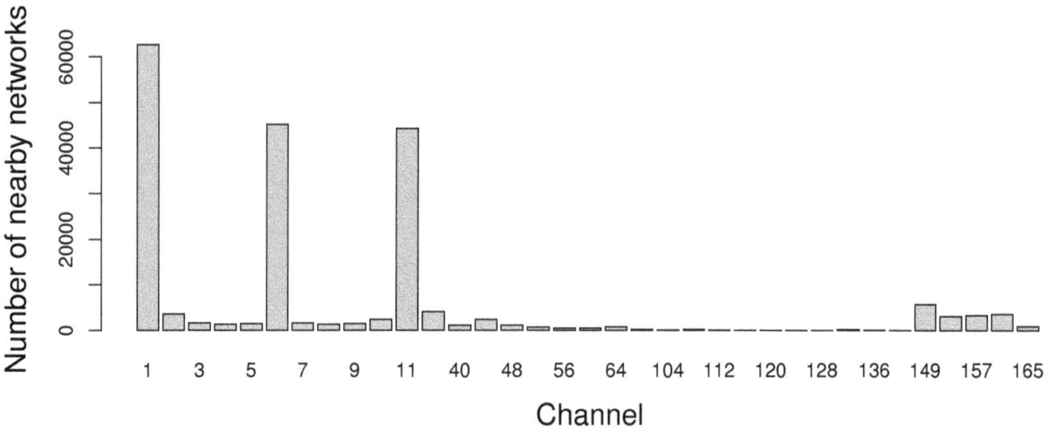

Figure 2: Nearby networks by channel number.

rier sense energy detection, making it more difficult to receive and send packets. Furthermore, some access points are capable of operating as virtual access points, broadcasting multiple SSIDs, which increases channel usage.

Meraki MR16 access points scan for nearby access points whenever clients are not connected and actively transferring data. Figure 2 shows the distribution of detected networks by channel number, demonstrating which channels are most heavily used. This analysis does not include data from any Meraki MR18 access points since they were relatively new during the measurement period and there was not sufficient historical data.

Channels 1-11 reflect the 2.4 GHz spectrum where there are three non-overlapping 20 MHz channels located at channels 1, 6 and 11. Nearby access points are distributed across the non-overlapping channels with channel 1 having around 37% more access points than channels 6 or 11.

In the 5 GHz spectrum, Channels 36 through 48 represent the 5 GHz UNII-1 lower band, channels 52-64 are the UNII-2 middle band, channels 100-140 are the more recently allocated UNII-2 extended band, and channels 149-165 are the UNII-3 upper band. The UNII-2 and UNII-3 bands require the use of a Dynamic Frequency Selection (DFS) protocol where access points first check for the presence of a radar signal and change channels automatically if one exists or is detected during operation. Without DFS bands, there are four non-overlapping 40 MHz channels for 802.11n operation, and with DFS there are ten.

Table 7 compares the average number of nearby networks seen in July 2014 versus January 2015, over the course of a week. In the 2.4 GHz band, the average number of interfering APs (excluding other Meraki devices) is 55, which has grown from 28 six months ago. Given there are only three non-overlapping 2.4 GHz channels, it is likely most Meraki

	Networks	Networks per AP
2.4 GHz (now)	527,087	55.47
2.4 GHz (six months ago)	230,628	28.60
5 GHz (now)	35,010	3.68
5 GHz (six months ago)	19,921	2.47

Table 7: Increase in the number of nearby networks over six months. 9,502 Meraki access points are reporting in January 2015, versus 8,062 access points six months ago. This excludes the SSIDs of nearby Meraki access points.

access point will experience some amount of interference from nearby APs. In the 5 GHz band the average number of non-Meraki access points is 3.68, up from 2.47 six months ago, which suggests it is possible to find a non-overlapping channel, even with 40 MHz channels. We identified that approximately 20% (102,344) of the current nearby networks in the 2.4 GHz band are personal mobile hotspots (Novatel, Pantech, Sierra Wireless, etc.), compared to 56,293 six months ago. In the 5 GHz, only 1.7% of the nearby access networks are mobile hotspots.

4.2 Impact on packet reception

In order to build a table of link metrics for use with mesh routing, each Meraki access point periodically broadcasts a 60-byte packet at 1 megabit/sec on its 2.4 GHz radio and 6 megabits/sec on its 5 GHz radio. These broadcast packets are sent once every 15 seconds and are measured over a sliding window of 300 seconds, and the measurements are recorded by the Meraki backend system.

Figure 3 shows a distribution of link delivery ratios, for 16,583 2.4 GHz links and 5,650 5 GHz links which were reported both six months ago and today. For 2.4 GHz band, the majority of links only receive a fraction of broadcasts, and the overall link delivery ratios have decreased over the past six months. The intermediate links also show variations in delivery rate over time, as demonstrated in Figure 4. In the 5 GHz bands, there are far fewer intermediate links, with over half of the links receiving all of the broadcasts. The 5 GHz links also vary over time as illustrated in Figure 5 but they are more consistent than the 2.4 GHz links.

The data suggests performance as a whole is degrading in the 2.4 GHz band, even for small 60-byte packets. Larger 1,500-byte payloads and frame aggregates will be even more adversely affected, which will have an affect of application performance. Sub-frame error detection and correction techniques such as [16] may be necessary to make effective use of the 2.4 GHz band.

4.3 Impact on packet transmission

As the number of nearby access points grows, each channel is likely to become more heavily utilized, which would reduce the amount of time available for transmissions. Figure 6 shows the fraction of time the carrier sense mechanism was triggered during the last scan interval for each radio, as

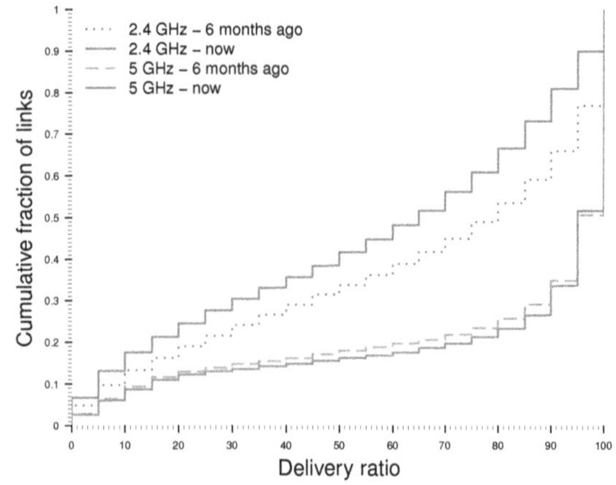

Figure 3: The distribution of the link delivery ratios, six months ago and today. Each data point represents the delivery rate of periodic broadcast packets from one Meraki access point to another where they occupied the same channel.

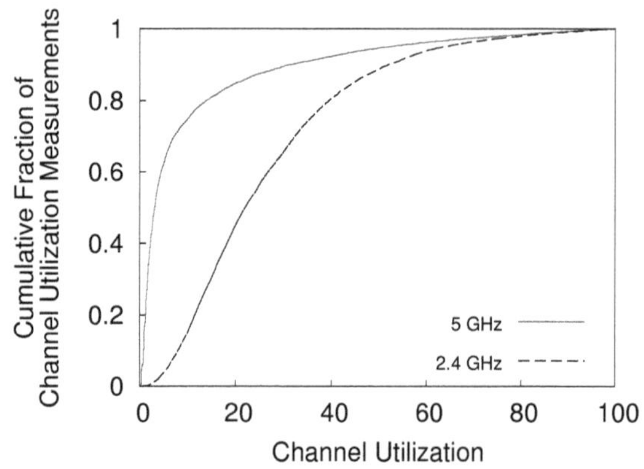

Figure 6: The distribution of channel utilization today in the 2.4 and 5 GHz bands as observed by the Meraki MR16 access points.

measured by the Meraki MR16 access points.

The 2.4 GHz band shows a high level of utilization, with the median access point reporting the energy-detect trigger 25% of the time, and the 90th percentile access point reporting 50%. In the 5 GHz band, channel utilization is lower, with the median access point reporting 5% and the 90th percentile access point reporting 30%. The Meraki MR16 radios can only measure utilization on their current channel, so they do not each provide a view of the complete spectrum. Section 5 examines utilization using the Meraki MR18 radios, which have a dedicated scanning radio that measures utilization across all of the channels.

5. SPECTRUM SCANNING RESULTS

In this section, we take a more complete look at utilization across multiple channels for a given access point. We achieve this through the use of the more recent MR18 access

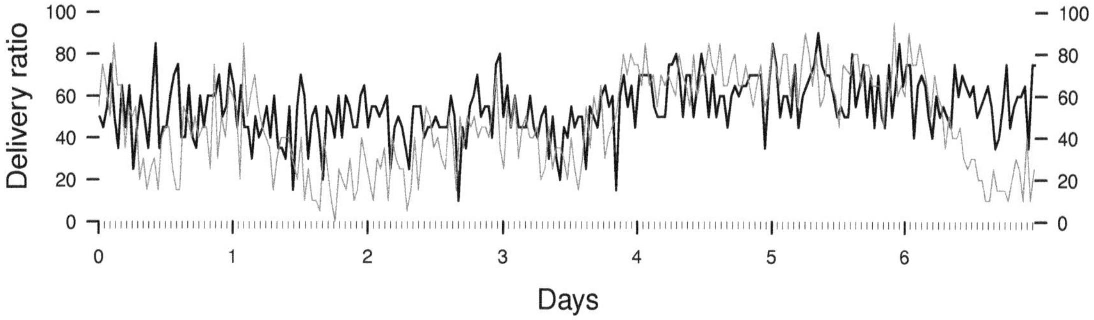

Figure 4: Delivery ratio variation over a week for two randomly chosen 2.4 GHz links.

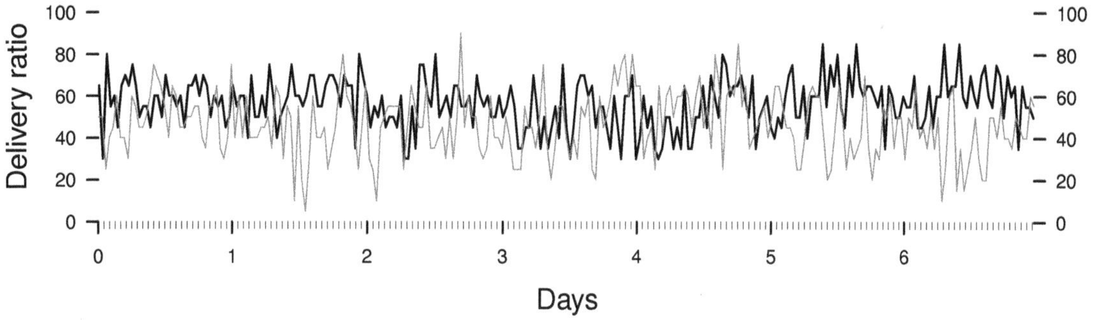

Figure 5: Delivery ratio variation over a week for two randomly chosen 5 GHz links.

point, which includes a third 802.11n radio that is dedicated to scanning the entire 2.4 GHz and 5 GHz spectrum and does not serve clients (unlike the MR16, which only provides utilization on its current channels).

In this section we gather data from 10,000 Meraki MR18 access points, located in the exclusively in the US to simplify complications due to regulatory domains. As it scans, the dedicated radio spends 5 ms on each channel. The backend system collects these results every three minutes, and the results are aggregated over three-minute periods.

5.1 Interfering APs

Figures 7 and 8 plot, for all the access points, the number of access points detected versus the channel utilization for all channels. Because these measurements are taken over three-minute periods (unlike the one-week windows used in Figure 2), these figures provide a more instantaneous view of channel conditions. From the data we do not see a clear correlation between utilization and the number of interferers in either band. This lack of correlation implies that simply using the number of nearby APs is not enough information to accurately select the most available channel and instead it is better to use direct channel utilization measurements.

5.2 Day/night variations

We next examine the relative impact of client usage on channel utilization, by studying variations between day and night. Figure 9 plots CDF of both frequency bands with utilization measurements taken at 10 a.m. and 10 p.m. Pacific time. For the 2.4 GHz band, the median channel (measured at a specific access point), observes around 5% higher utilization during the day versus the night, whereas in 5 GHz the utilization measures are similar.

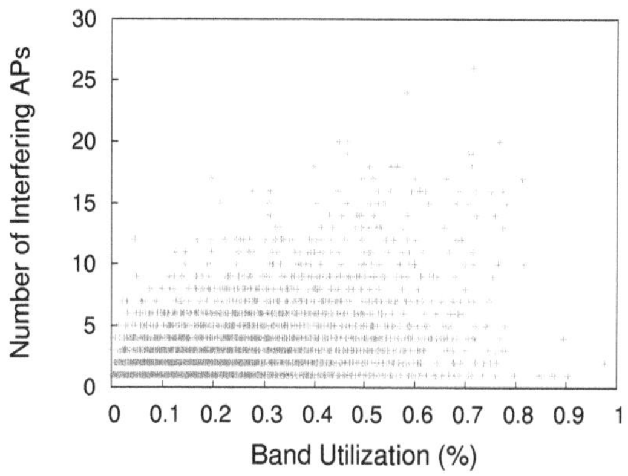

Figure 7: Scatter plot of utilization versus number of nearby APs in the 2.4 GHz band.

These results differ from Figure 6 because the Meraki MR16 is only able to measure utilization on its current channel, versus the Meraki MR18 is able to take measurements from all channels. In the 5 GHz band, the majority of channels are unused as seen in Figure 2, which skews the distri-

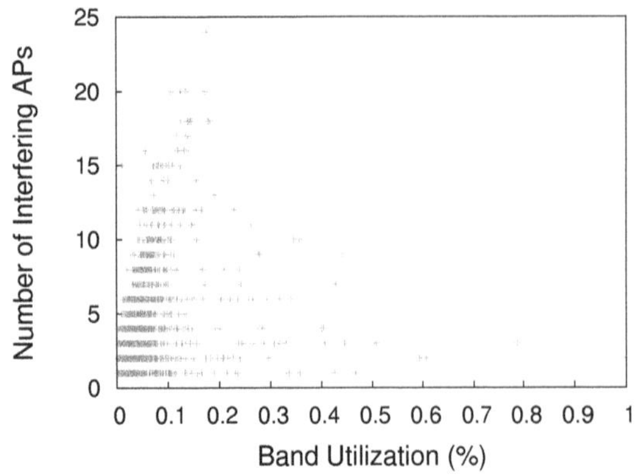

Figure 8: Scatter plot of utilization versus number of nearby APs in the 5 GHz band.

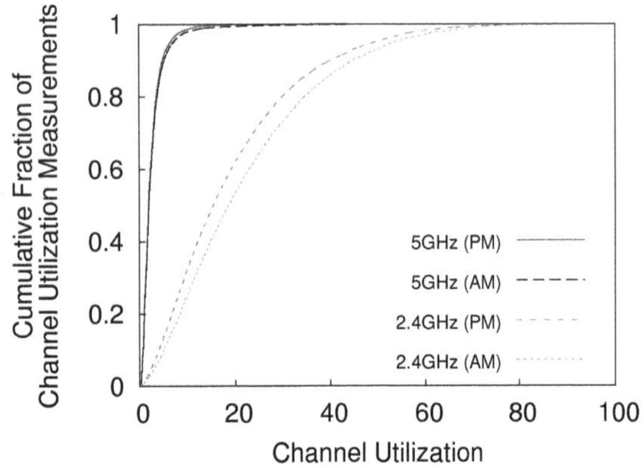

Figure 9: The distribution of channel utilization, during night and day time as observed by the Meraki MR18 access points.

bution towards zero. This also indicates that having a radio dedicated for channel measurement should help in making better channel assignment decisions.

5.3 Presence of Non-802.11 Traffic

For a closer examination of what is using the unlicensed bands, we measure the percentage of utilization that contained decodable 802.11 headers. Similar to the mechanism used to measure the amount of time spent performing energy detection, Atheros chipset exposes a set of microsecond counters which count time receiving 802.11 traffic. These counters look for packets that contain an intact 802.11 PLCP header and preamble (which are sent at a more robust modulation than the data payload) and combine the duration and interframe times to account for 802.11 protocol traffic. These counters do not capture 802.11 frames with corrupt preambles or non-802.11 traffic, which are contained by the overall utilization counter.

Figure 10 shows the majority of the total channel utilization contained decodable 802.11 headers. Furthermore, we inspected the traffic near one access point with a USRP B200 software radio acting as a spectrum analyzer as shown in

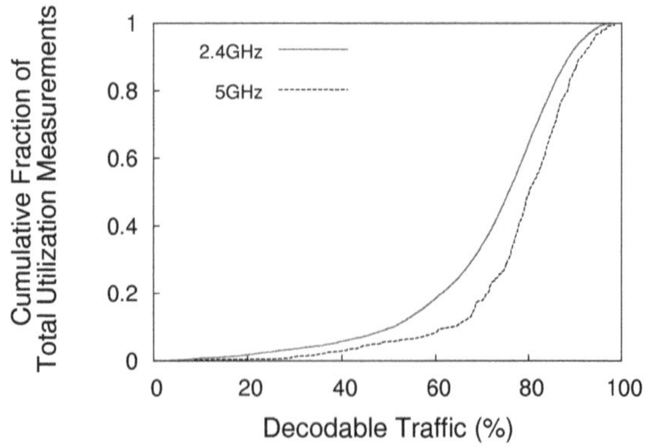

Figure 10: The distribution of decodable traffic (%) in 2.4 and 5 GHz channels.

Figure 11 to examine the structure of the interference. While this view a single instance and is not representative of all access points, we find the 2.4 GHz band to have 22% utilization and includes transmissions from frequency hopping narrow-band interference sources alongside 802.11 frames, similar to observations noted in [11]. The 5 GHz band shows lower average utilization of 2% and is mostly 802.11 transmissions but displays signs of frequency-selective fading as observed in [13].

6. REAL-WORLD EXPERIENCES

The Meraki system was first deployed in 2006, with two models of 802.11b/g radio hardware, for indoor and outdoor environments. Over the next 8 years the system added additional 8 types of wireless access points, ranging from 2x2 and 3x3 802.11n radios, to 802.11ac devices, in both indoor and outdoor variants. The same platform was also used to deploy and manage Ethernet switching equipment and security appliances, which gave the designers a unique understanding of a wide range of network environments.

In this paper, we focused on usage data from two similar indoor radio models to minimize the number of variables that may impact radio link performance measurements. However, building and operating a large-scale system over several years left us with several observations which may be relevant to future work.

6.1 Dealing with bugs in a large system

Debugging large production systems can be complex, particularly in wireless environments where there are a wide range of client devices and physical conditions. The codebase for the `hostapd` portion of the wireless driver, which handles authentication and control traffic for the 802.11 stack is over 350,000 lines of C code.

In addition to the usual practices of using several test harnesses and beta testing, the Meraki system uses a large backend database system to collect information about crashes (firmware and program counter state), along with periodic telemetry about each device's performance, to make it easier to debug problems in the real world.

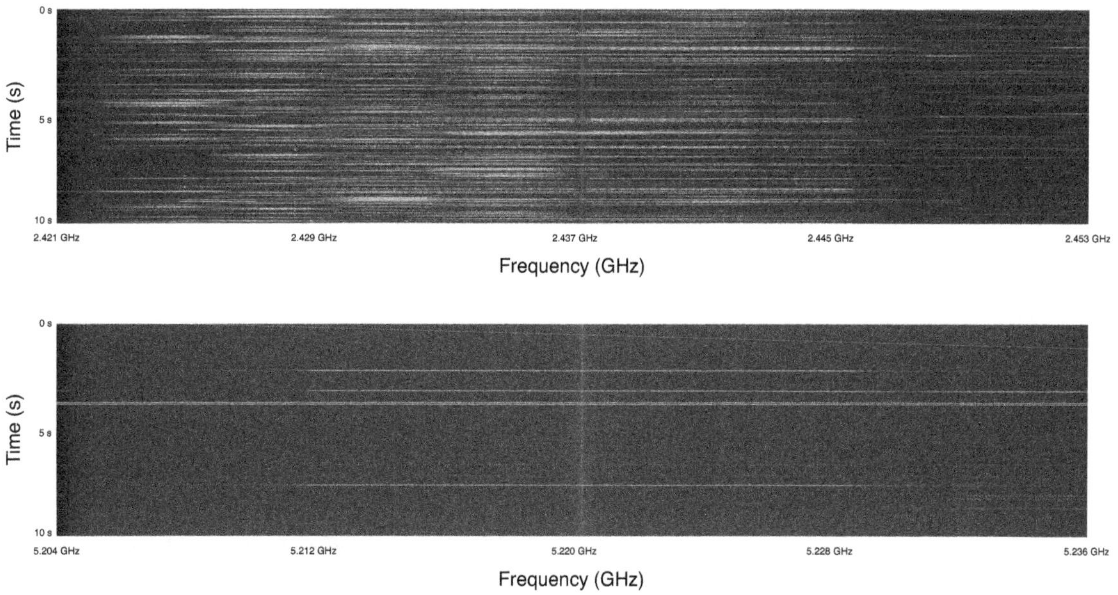

Figure 11: Example spectrum analysis centered at 2.437 GHz and 5.220 GHz, using a 32 MHz wide scan with 4096-point FFT on a USRP B200. The 2.4 GHz scan shows the presence of 20 MHz 802.11 packets, frequency hopping bluetooth with 1 MHz transmissions and other unidentified sources. The 5 GHz scan shows 20 MHz and 40 MHz 802.11 packets and fainter transmissions with frequency selective fading.

As an example of a bug which only surfaced due to the wide range of deployment environments, we received reports of a small number of access points rebooting either minutes or hours after booting on a repeated basis. They all served fewer than a few dozen clients with a typical usage profile. These access points eventually rebooted due to an out-of-memory error (not at the same point in the code). Upon further inspection, we noticed the access points were reporting very large numbers of nearby access points: some of the access points were located in skyscrapers in Manhattan and could decode beacons from miles away, and in another case the access point was on a bus traveling between cities.

Because it is difficult to anticipate such bugs, we found it to be important to measure and instrument the system at large scale and make it possible to examine the system under operation whenever possible.

6.2 Difficulty in predicting user behavior

We also observed client device usage varied over time, which made it difficult for network operators to anticipate usage spikes. In most networks usage between clients was uneven as expected, with a subset of clients driving most of the usage. However, software updates from Apple and Microsoft would drive large downloads across large numbers of clients, sometimes causing sudden increases totaling tens or hundreds of gigabytes.

On a larger timescale, we observed the introduction of smartphones starting around 2006. While we found smartphones consume only around a fifth as much data as laptops, as described in Section 3.2, they exhibit different network connection behavior: roaming across access points, attempting to use cached IP address assignment upon waking from sleep, and implementing aggressive versions of power save poll which increased the data buffered by access points.

Similar to the long-term shift in device types, we observed sustained growth in online video services such as YouTube and Netflix over several years, which increased overall data consumption. While in the past it became common to block heavy bandwidth consuming applications like BitTorrent, we found administrators reluctant to block services such as YouTube given their popularity and wide range of uses.

6.3 Non-wireless problems

Finally, we observed several common problems on networks which resulted in poor performance but were not specific to wireless:

- Overloaded RADIUS/Active Directory servers, resulting in authentication timeouts
- Misconfigured VLANs in campus-scale deployments, either due to numbering or reachability
- Cable problems due to aging building infrastructure, which would result in intermittent connectivity
- MTU configuration and discovery issues
- Upstream bandwidth bottlenecks
- DNS resolution problems
- Protocols like multicast DNS, which work in home environments but cause broadcast issues at campus scale

7. RELATED WORK

Several papers have studied link delivery rates: Aguayo et al. [2] presented data from a 38-node outdoor 802.11b wireless mesh network, and found that the majority of links deliver only a fraction of sent packets and that it is difficult to predict link characteristics from distance or RSSI alone. Reis et al. [18] found similar results with a 15-node indoor 802.11a/b/g testbed. This paper studies a much larger set of approximately 20,000 nodes, with newer 802.11n radios, and finds that even with newer radio technology most links only receive a fraction of packets.

Halperin et. al. [13] studied link delivery in 802.11n and suggested frequency selective fading caused by multipath interference is the primary cause of intermediate links. In their paper, they develop a model for packet delivery based on Channel State Information (CSI) from their Intel radios, which is a better predictor than RSSI alone. The Meraki radios use a different Atheros-based chipset which does not expose CSI in the current driver, but recent work [20, 4] suggests the capability exists for Atheros and Intel radios.

Many papers also indicate non-802.11 sources of interference lead to packet loss. Gummadi et al. [11] showed even weak or narrowband signals from cordless phones, Bluetooth or Zigbee devices can disrupt packet reception or delay transmissions by triggering carrier sense. Gollakota et al. [8] showed similar results with an indoor testbed and studied the physical layer impact of interference at a more granular level before demonstrating software radio-based methods of canceling the interference. In this paper, we quantify the effects of non-802.11 interference on a larger scale but do not employ any active measures for noise cancellation.

Interference alignment and cancellation [10] has also been proposed in different contexts for increasing the throughput of wireless systems. Halperin et al. [12] showed that receivers can recover from colliding packets by employing interference cancellation, and thereby significantly reducing the packet loss rate. Gollakota et al. [9] use interference cancellation to combat hidden terminals, while Lin et al. [15] built a system that enables more nodes to transmit in parallel without harming the ongoing transmissions. Given the observed interference, we expect these mechanisms to improve throughput; however, we currently do not employ any of these techniques in our devices.

There have also been several studies examining usage on 802.11 networks. Rodrig et al. [19] examined usage during a five day technical conference in 2004 and found several link-level phenomena such as bit-rate selection and retransmissions affected overall network capacity.

Ghosh et al. [7] present larger scale data from AT&T's hotspot network, tracing over 243,000 devices over a four-week period. While the data covered several sites, their study was of hotspot users and developed a model of usage distribution in terms of session times and bytes transferred. Their study did not examine specific application usage patterns or present link level measurements.

A 2010 study of Google's WiFi network [1] examined data from 500 outdoor wireless mesh nodes and studied both link-level measurements and usage from 30,000 client devices. Similar to the AT&T study, the Google data primarily focused on outdoor hotspot usage and did not examine the application usage patterns. Both papers also characterized hotspot usage, which differs from campus or office usage.

Gember et al. [6] studied over 32,000 devices connected to the University of Wisconsin's wireless network, with a specific look at application usage inferred from hostname analysis. Similar to this paper, they found web traffic and streaming media to be the largest source of usage, and observed the growing popularity of handheld devices. This paper examines similar types of data but from a much larger set of users and five years later when both applications and devices types have changed.

8. CONCLUSION

Wireless networks using 802.11 have become commonplace, but their performance and link-level characteristics vary because of their use of unlicensed spectrum. In this paper, we conducted a large scale study of several thousand wireless networks, to better understand their behavior.

We surveyed over 20,000 networks and found a wide variety of client devices co-exist, from 2.4 GHz-only 20 MHz mobile devices to three-stream 802.11ac desktop computers supporting 80 MHz channels. Overall client usage grew considerably, driven by bandwidth-intensive applications such as video streaming from YouTube and Netflix and downloading photographs via social media.

We then used measurement data from regular transmissions between access points to study several thousand wireless links over a long period of time. We found that intermediate packet delivery ratios are very common and found in the majority of 2.4 GHz links and many of the 5 GHz links as well. We also noticed the overall delivery ratios of 2.4 GHz links have degraded over the past six months.

Finally, we measured channel utilization using dedicated radio hardware. While most access points share channels with dozens of other access points, but there was no direct relationship between the number of nearby access points and channel utilization. We did, however, observe higher utilization levels during the day, and were able to characterize most of the interference as 802.11, which suggests the 802.11 MAC can avoid interference on the same channel.

These measurements are intended to provide insight into the behavior of unlicensed spectrum for both network and protocol designers. Some practical implications for networks include the importance of (1) traffic shaping at the wireless access point to better serve the growing number of bandwidth hungry clients and applications, and (2) channel planning using a utilization measure to identify the best wireless channel. For protocol designers, the measurements suggest that it is rare to find large blocks of unused unlicensed spectrum and that new protocols will have to co-exist with large amounts of 802.11 traffic.

A copy of the wireless link measurements, nearby networks, and channel utilization data used in this paper is available at http://dl.meraki.net/sigcomm-2015.

9. ACKNOWLEDGEMENTS

We thank our shepherd, Kyle Jamieson, and the anonymous reviewers for their suggestions and feedback. We also thank the engineers who helped build and maintain the Meraki system over the past several years, which made the collection and analysis of this data possible.

10. REFERENCES

[1] M. Afanasyev, T. Chen, G. M. Voelker, and A. C. Snoeren. Usage patterns in an urban wifi network. *Networking, IEEE/ACM Transactions on*, 18(5):1359–1372, 2010.

[2] D. Aguayo, J. Bicket, S. Biswas, G. Judd, and R. Morris. Link-level measurements from an 802.11 b mesh network. In *ACM SIGCOMM Computer Communication Review*, volume 34, pages 121–132. ACM, 2004.

[3] W. Alliance. Total wifi device shipments to surpass ten billion this month, Jan. 2015.

[4] A. Bhartia, Y.-C. Chen, S. Rallapalli, and L. Qiu. Harnessing frequency diversity in wi-fi networks. In *Proceedings of the 17th Annual International Conference on Mobile Computing and Networking*, MobiCom '11, pages 253–264, 2011.

[5] J. Franklin, D. McCoy, P. Tabriz, V. Neagoe, J. V. Randwyk, and D. Sicker. Passive data link layer 802.11 wireless device driver fingerprinting. In *Usenix Security*, 2006.

[6] A. Gember, A. Anand, and A. Akella. A comparative study of handheld and non-handheld traffic in campus wi-fi networks. In *Passive and Active Measurement*, pages 173–183. Springer, 2011.

[7] A. Ghosh, R. Jana, V. Ramaswami, J. Rowland, and N. Shankaranarayanan. Modeling and characterization of large-scale wi-fi traffic in public hot-spots. In *INFOCOM, 2011 Proceedings IEEE*, pages 2921–2929. IEEE, 2011.

[8] S. Gollakota, F. Adib, D. Katabi, and S. Seshan. Clearing the rf smog: making 802.11 n robust to cross-technology interference. In *ACM SIGCOMM Computer Communication Review*, volume 41, pages 170–181. ACM, 2011.

[9] S. Gollakota and D. Katabi. Zigzag decoding: Combating hidden terminals in wireless networks. In *Proceedings of the ACM SIGCOMM 2008 Conference on Data Communication*, SIGCOMM '08, pages 159–170, 2008.

[10] S. Gollakota, S. D. Perli, and D. Katabi. Interference alignment and cancellation. In *Proceedings of the ACM SIGCOMM 2009 Conference on Data Communication*, SIGCOMM '09, pages 159–170, 2009.

[11] R. Gummadi, D. Wetherall, B. Greenstein, and S. Seshan. Understanding and mitigating the impact of rf interference on 802.11 networks. *ACM SIGCOMM Computer Communication Review*, 37(4):385–396, 2007.

[12] D. Halperin, T. Anderson, and D. Wetherall. Taking the sting out of carrier sense: Interference cancellation for wireless lans. In *Proceedings of the 14th ACM International Conference on Mobile Computing and Networking*, MobiCom '08, pages 339–350, 2008.

[13] D. Halperin, W. Hu, A. Sheth, and D. Wetherall. Predictable 802.11 packet delivery from wireless channel measurements. *ACM SIGCOMM Computer Communication Review*, 41(4):159–170, 2011.

[14] E. Kohler, R. Morris, B. Chen, J. Jannotti, and M. F. Kaashoek. The click modular router. *ACM Transactions on Computer Systems (TOCS)*, 18(3):263–297, 2000.

[15] K. C.-J. Lin, S. Gollakota, and D. Katabi. Random access heterogeneous mimo networks. In *Proceedings of the ACM SIGCOMM 2011 Conference*, SIGCOMM '11, pages 146–157, 2011.

[16] A. K. Miu, H. Balakrishnan, and C. E. Koksal. Improving Loss Resilience with Multi-Radio Diversity in Wireless Networks. In *11th ACM MOBICOM Conference*, Cologne, Germany, September 2005.

[17] J. Pang, B. Greenstein, R. Gummadi, S. Seshan, and D. Wetherall. 802.11 user fingerprinting. In *Proceedings of the 13th annual ACM international conference on Mobile computing and networking*, pages 99–110. ACM, 2007.

[18] C. Reis, R. Mahajan, M. Rodrig, D. Wetherall, and J. Zahorjan. Measurement-based models of delivery and interference in static wireless networks. *ACM SIGCOMM Computer Communication Review*, 36(4):51–62, 2006.

[19] M. Rodrig, C. Reis, R. Mahajan, D. Wetherall, and J. Zahorjan. Measurement-based characterization of 802.11 in a hotspot setting. In *Proceedings of the 2005 ACM SIGCOMM workshop on Experimental approaches to wireless network design and analysis*, pages 5–10. ACM, 2005.

[20] S. Sen, B. Radunovic, J. Lee, and K.-H. Kim. Cspy: finding the best quality channel without probing. In *Proceedings of the 19th annual international conference on Mobile computing & networking*, pages 267–278. ACM, 2013.

[21] K. Varda. Protocol buffers: Google data interchange format, 2008.

End-User Mapping: Next Generation Request Routing for Content Delivery

Fangfei Chen
Akamai Technologies
150 Broadway
Cambridge, MA
fachen@akamai.com

Ramesh K. Sitaraman
University of Massachusetts, Amherst
& Akamai Technologies
ramesh@cs.umass.edu

Marcelo Torres
Akamai Technologies
150 Broadway
Cambridge, MA
mtorres@akamai.com

ABSTRACT

Content Delivery Networks (CDNs) deliver much of the world's web, video, and application content on the Internet today. A key component of a CDN is the mapping system that uses the DNS protocol to route each client's request to a "proximal" server that serves the requested content. While traditional mapping systems identify a client using the IP of its name server, we describe our experience in building and rolling-out a novel system called end-user mapping that identifies the client directly by using a prefix of the client's IP address. Using measurements from Akamai's production network during the roll-out, we show that end-user mapping provides significant performance benefits for clients who use public resolvers, including an eight-fold decrease in mapping distance, a two-fold decrease in RTT and content download time, and a 30% improvement in the time-to-first-byte. We also quantify the scaling challenges in implementing end-user mapping such as the 8-fold increase in DNS queries. Finally, we show that a CDN with a larger number of deployment locations is likely to benefit more from end-user mapping than a CDN with a smaller number of deployments.

1. INTRODUCTION

Content Delivery Networks (CDNs) deliver much of the world's web sites, video portals, e-commerce applications, social networks, and file downloads. As an example, Akamai's CDN currently serves 15-30% of all web traffic from a large distributed platform of over 170,000 servers deployed in over 102 countries and 1300 ISPs around the world [2]. The CDN hosts and delivers content on behalf of thousands of enterprises and organizations that represent a microcosm of the Internet as a whole, including business services, financial services, travel, manufacturing, automotive, media, entertainment, e-commerce, software, gaming, and the public sector. The clients[1] who access content on Akamai's CDN are a representative sample of Internet users from nearly every country, every major ISP, and use every major device.

SIGCOMM '15, August 17 - 21, 2015, London, United Kingdom

ISBN 978-1-4503-3542-3/15/08...$15.00

DOI: http://dx.doi.org/10.1145/2785956.2787500

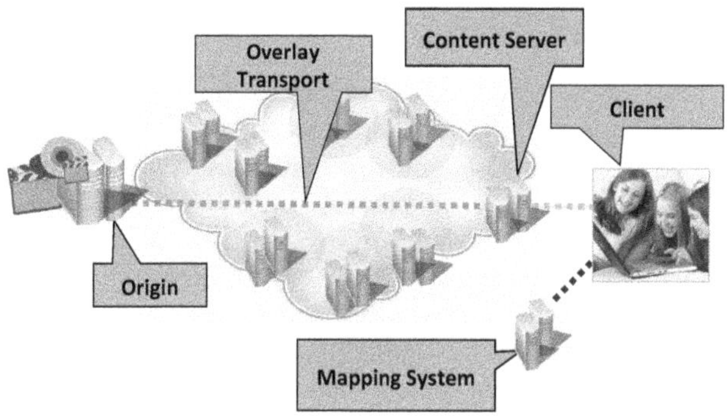

Figure 1: A Content Delivery Network

The goal of a CDN is to host and deliver content and applications to clients around the world with high availability, performance, and scalability [13, 21]. Akamai's CDN achieves its goal by deploying a large number of servers in hundreds of data centers around the world, so as to be "proximal" in a network sense to clients. To understand the overall architecture of the CDN, we enumerate the steps involved when a client accesses content hosted on the CDN. As shown in Figure 1, when the client accesses a Web page, the domain name of the Web page is translated to the IP address (shortened to "IP" in this paper) of a server that is live, has sufficient capacity, and is proximal to the client. The domain name translation is provided by the CDN's mapping system that we study in this paper. The client requests content from the server assigned to it by the mapping system. If the server has the content in cache, it serves the content to the client. Otherwise, the server requests the content from the origin servers that are operated by the content provider

[1] In this paper, we use the term "client" to denote the end-user or his/her device such as a cell phone, desktop or laptop that is connected to the Internet and is running software such as a browser capable of accessing Web pages.

and and serves it to the client. For a more detailed discussion of CDN evolution and architecture, we refer to [21].

A central component of Akamai's CDN is its *mapping system*. The goal of the mapping system is to maximize the performance experienced by the client by ensuring quicker downloads of the accessed content. To speedup the downloads, the mapping system routes each client request to a "proximal" server that can be reached by the client with low latency and loss. Further, the mapping system ensures that the chosen server is live, not overloaded, and is likely to contain the requested content. The last consideration reduces the probability of a cache miss at the server that would result in the content being fetched from origin with longer response times. Conceptually, the mapping system can be viewed as computing the following complex time-varying function:

$$\mathrm{MAP_t} : \Sigma_{\mathrm{Internet}} \times \Sigma_{\mathrm{Akam}} \times \mathrm{Domain} \times \mathrm{LDNS} \rightarrow \mathrm{IPs}. \quad (1)$$

At each time t, $\mathrm{MAP_t}$ takes as input the current state of the global Internet $\Sigma_{\mathrm{Internet}}$, including detailed real-time knowledge of connectivity, liveness, latency, loss, and throughput information; the current state of Akamai's CDN Σ_{Akam}, including real-time knowledge of liveness, load, and other information about servers and routers of the CDN; the domain name of the content that is being accessed by the client; and, the local recursive domain name server (LDNS) that makes the request for domain name resolution on behalf of the client. The mapping system returns two or more IPs[2] of the CDN's servers that can serve the requested content.

Akamai's mapping system routes trillions of client requests per day, controlling tens of terabits per second of content traffic served to clients world-wide. On a typical day, there are 6.4 million LDNS servers located in 240 countries making 1.6 million DNS queries per second (cf. Figure 2), representing 30 million client requests per second around the globe. Ever since the first CDNs were built at Akamai nearly sixteen years ago [13], the mapping system has been the subject of much research to improve its responsiveness and accuracy. However, as represented in Equation 1, traditional mapping systems at CDNs make request routing decisions based on the identity of the client's LDNS rather than that of the client itself. We call this *NS-based mapping* and can be inaccurate in cases when the LDNS is not in a "similar" location as the client, i.e., when the network characteristics of the LDNS is not a good proxy for that of the client. This fundamental limitation arises from the use of the domain name system (DNS) protocol that allows the mapping system to learn the identity of the LDNS but not the client on whose behalf the domain name translation request is made.

To rectify the limitations of the DNS protocol, Google, Akamai and others industry players have recently proposed an extension to the DNS protocol that allows a recursive name server to specify a prefix of the client's IP (usually a /24 prefix) when requesting domain name translations on behalf of a client [11]. For the first time, this mechanism allows the novel possibility of building a mapping system that has *direct* knowledge about the client and uses it to provide more accurate mappings. We call such a system *end-user mapping*. The insights gained from building and rolling-out Akamai's end-user (EU) mapping system is our focus.

[2]While the mapping system checks liveness before returning the IP of a server, more than one server is returned as a additional precaution against transient failures.

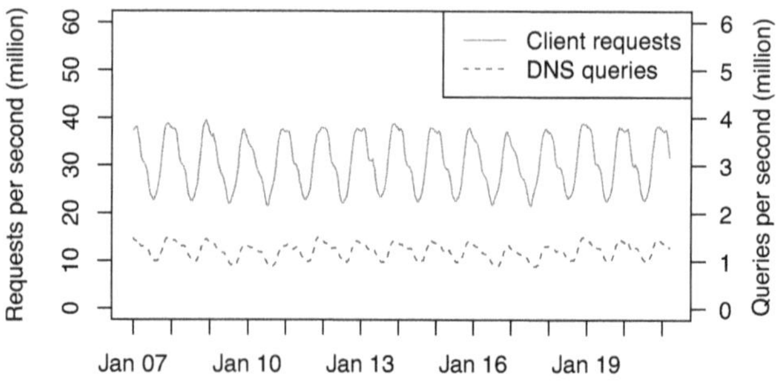

Figure 2: Client requests served (left axis) and DNS queries resolved (right axis) by the mapping system. When the mapping system resolves a DNS query from a LDNS, multiple content requests from clients that use that LDNS may follow.

Our contributions. We list key contributions below.

1. The limitations of NS-based mapping caused by discrepancies in the locations of clients and LDNSes have been known for over a decade [24]. However, we provide the first public analysis of clients and their LDNSes at a global scale across the entire Internet using data from 584 thousand name servers and 3.76 million /24 client IP blocks across 37294 AS'es and 238 countries across the world.

2. Our work presents the architecture and real-world roll-out of Akamai's end-user mapping, a major conceptual advance in mapping technology. We capture the performance impact of the roll-out on actual clients around the world. Web performance is a complex phenomena that is influenced by the global state of the Internet, the connectivity of the client, properties of Web sites and their hosting infrastructure, and a multitude of other factors. Our work captures the impact of the new mapping paradigm in a real-world setting providing insights that are hard to obtain in a controlled experimental setting.

3. End-user mapping requires both measurements and analysis to be performed at a much larger scale, as mapping decisions are made at a much finer granularity. Using extensive data from clients and their LDNS architectures in the global Internet and measurements taken during the end-user mapping roll-out, we provide insights into the scaling considerations in using the EDNS0 client-subnet extension of the DNS protocol.

4. Using latency measurements from over 2500+ server deployment locations around the world to 8K representative client IP blocks that generate the most traffic on the Internet, we study the important question of how deployments impact the performance of traditional NS-based and end-user mapping. We show that end-user mapping provides more incremental benefits for a CDN with servers in a large number of deployed locations than a CDN deployed in fewer locations. Further, we expose an inherent limitation of NS-based mapping in reducing latencies for the worst 1% of clients.

Roadmap. In Section 2, we describe the architecture of a traditional NS-based mapping system and how end-user mapping can be incorporated into this architecture using the EDNS0 client-subnet extension. In Section 3, we analyze the relative locations of clients and their LDNSes in the global Internet with the view of understanding the benefits that we are likely to see from rolling-out end-user mapping. In Sections 4 and 5, we analyze the performance and scalability impact of our roll-out of end-user mapping system to clients who use public resolvers. In Section 6, we study the role of server deployments in end-user mapping. In Section 7 we present related work and conclude in Section 8.

2. THE MAPPING SYSTEM

A Web site hosted on Akamai typically delegates authority for its domain names to authoritative name servers that are part of the mapping system. Further, each client uses a "local" domain name server[3] (LDNS) that works in a recursive fashion to provide domain name translations for the client. The LDNS that provides domain name service for the client is typically hosted by the Internet Service Provider (ISP) who provides Internet connectivity to the client. Alternately, the LDNS could be an *public resolver* that is a name server deployed by a third-party provider that can be used by the client. The location of the LDNS with respect to the client depends on the DNS architecture of the name service provider, whether it be an ISP or a public resolver provider such as Google DNS [5] or OpenDNS [7].

To better illustrate Akamai's mapping system, we trace through the steps of how a client interacts with the system to obtain a domain name resolution (see Figure 3).

(1) Suppose that the client wants to access content at some Web site that is hosted on Akamai. The client requests its LDNS to resolve the domain name of the Web site.

(2) LDNS works in a *recursive* mode as follows. If the LDNS has a valid name resolution for the requested domain in its cache, it responds to the client with the relevant IPs. Otherwise, the LDNS forwards the request to an authoritative name server for the requested domain.

(3) The authoritative name server responds with a valid resolution to the LDNS. LDNS caches the response and in turn forwards the response to the client.

Note that a DNS response from an authoritative name server is associated with a TTL (time-to-live) that dictates how long the response is valid. TTL's are tracked and enforced as the response is forwarded and cached downstream by name servers and resolvers, including the LDNS and the client's resolver. When the TTL expires, the cached entry is made invalid, requiring a new DNS resolution.

NS-based versus end-user mapping. In a traditional NS-based mapping system, the LDNS does not forward any information about the client when it contacts the authoritative name servers in step (2) above. Hence, the mapping system does not know the IP of the client that requested the name resolution and assigns edge servers entirely based on the IP of its LDNS. However, in end-user mapping, the LDNS forwards a prefix of the client's IP to the authoritative name servers in step (2) above using the newly-proposed EDNS0 client-subnet extension. This enables the end-user mapping to use additional client information in providing domain name translations as we describe next.

[3]Despite its name, a LDNS may not be very "local" to the client, the key rationale for end-user mapping.

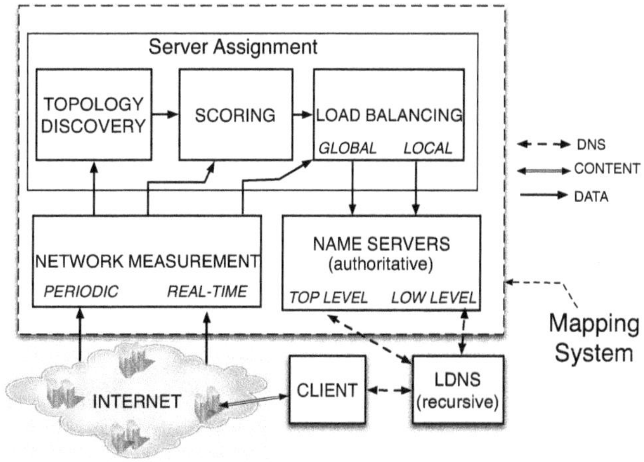

Figure 3: The architecture of the mapping system

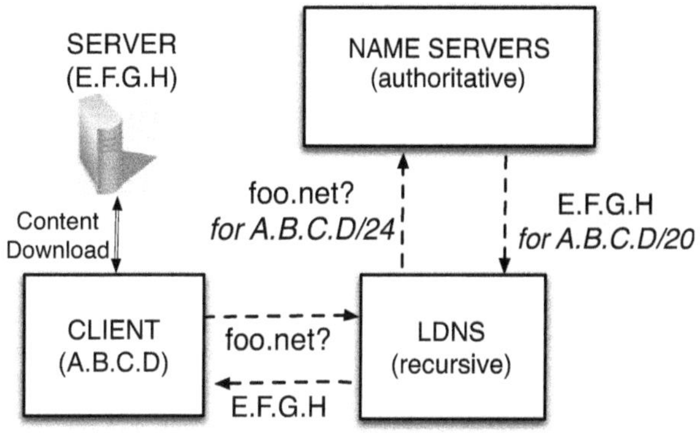

Figure 4: Example of interaction between the client, LDNS, and Akamai's name servers with the EDNS0 extension.

2.1 End-User Mapping

End-user mapping deployed recently at Akamai uses the identity of the client rather than its LDNS. Conceptually, end-user mapping (EUMAP) computes the following time varying function.

$$\text{EUMAP}_t : \Sigma_{\text{Internet}} \times \Sigma_{\text{Akam}} \times \text{Domain} \times \text{Client} \rightarrow \text{IPs}. \quad (2)$$

Compared to NS-based mapping (see Equation 1), end-user mapping uses the client information to make more accurate mapping decisions, even in cases where the LDNS and the client are not proximal to each other. A key enabler for our end-user mapping design is a recent Internet draft to extend the DNS protocol called the EDNS0 client-subnet extension that allows recursive name servers to forward information about the client as a part of their DNS request [11]. Figure 4 shows the interaction between the client, recursive, and authoritative name servers for an example domain `foo.net` when the name servers support the EDNS0 protocol extension. The client with IP `A.B.C.D` contacts its LDNS to resolve `foo.net`. With extension support, when the LDNS forwards the request for `foo.net` to an authoritative name server it can append a /x prefix of the IP of the client who initiated the request, where the prefix[4] used is generally /24. (By /x prefix we mean the first x bits of the IP.) The authoritative name servers, which in the case of a domain hosted on Akamai is part of the mapping system, responds with server IPs appropriate for a /y prefix of the client's IP where $y \leq x$, i.e., the name server can return a resolution that is valid for a superset of the client's /x IP block. (By client's /x IP block, we mean the set of IPs that have same first x bits as the client's IP.) The DNS resolution provided by the authoritative name server can be cached for the duration of the TTL by downstream recursive name servers such as the LDNS. However, the cached resolution is only valid for the IP block for which it was provided and not for any client IPs that do not belong to the block.

2.2 Mapping System Architecture

The mapping system consists of three major functional components as shown in Figure 3 that we describe in turn. We also use data collected from the network measurement component below for our analysis.

1) Network Measurement. Both the global Internet and Akamai's CDN are monitored and measured. The data that needs to be collected on both counts is enormous and varied. The Internet is a large "patchwork" of 71K autonomous systems (AS's) that interconnect with each other in complex and ever-changing ways. The server and network components of Akamai's CDN are deployed in clusters in more than a thousand networks around the globe. A few major sources of data collected include:

(i) AS-level information is collected by Akamai's BGP collectors installed around the Internet that initiate BGP sessions with ISP's and periodically records the BGP session state. This information is used to understand which IPs belong to which AS, how AS'es connect with each other, etc.

(ii) Geographic information such as the city, state, country, and continent is deduced for IPs around the world using various data sources and geolocation methods [1].

(iii) Name server information is collected using the DNS request logs for Akamai-hosted domains from name servers (i.e., LDNSes) around the world.

(iv) Network-level measurements include path information, latency, loss, and throughput between different points on the Internet.

(v) Liveness and load. Liveness and load information of all components of Akamai's CDN is collected in real-time, including servers and routers.

2) Server Assignment. The server assignment component uses network measurement data to create a real-time topological map of the Internet that captures how well the different parts of the Internet connect with each other, a process called *topology discovery*. The topological map is then used to evaluate what performance clients of each LDNS is likely to see if they are assigned to each Akamai server cluster, a process called *scoring*. Different scoring functions that incorporate bandwidth, latency, packet loss, etc can be used for different traffic classes (web, video, applications, etc). The *load balancing* module assigns servers to each client request in two hierarchical steps: first it assigns a server cluster for each client, a process called *global load balancing*. Next, it assigns server(s) within the chosen cluster, a process called *local load balancing*. To perform these tasks, the load balancer uses the output of scoring to evaluate candidate server choices that yield the highest performance for each client request and combines that information with liveness, capacity, and other real-time information about the CDN. The load balancing algorithms are described in greater detail in [19].

3) Name Servers. Akamai has a large distributed system of name servers around the world that act as authorities for Akamai-hosted domain names. For example, a content provider hosted on Akamai can CNAME their domain to an Akamai domain, for example, `www.whitehouse.gov` could be CNAME'd to the Akamai domain of e2561.b.akamaiedge.net. The authority for the latter domain is in turn delegated to an Akamai name server that is typically located in an Akamai cluster that is close to the client's LDNS. This delegation step implements the global load balancer choice of cluster for the client's LDNS, so different clients could receive different name server delegations. Finally, the delegated name server returns "A" records for two or more server IPs to be used by the client for the download, implementing the choices made by the local load balancer.

3. UNDERSTANDING CLIENTS AND THEIR NAME SERVERS

To motivate the need for end-user mapping, we start by analyzing the locations of clients relative to their recursive name servers (i.e., LDNS) in the global Internet. To obtain an accurate picture we need to match a large characteristic set of clients around the world with their respective LDNSes. The matched client-LDNS pairs can then be located using our geo-location database [1] to provide the geographic location and network information needed for the analysis.

3.1 Collecting Client-LDNS pairs

Associating a client with its LDNS has some intrinsic difficulties. Both the LDNS's request for a domain name resolution and the client's subsequent request for an URL on that domain are logged at Akamai's authoritative name servers and content servers respectively. One potential approach is to match these requests to obtain client-LDNS pairings. However, matching the requests is tricky and inexact since the two requests can be spaced within a time window equal to the TTL of the domain name. Further, when the client receives a cached response from its LDNS, the LDNS makes no corresponding downstream request to Akamai's authoritative name servers. While there are heuristic ways of obtaining a smaller sample of client-LDNS pairs [24], our chal-

[4]A prefix longer than /24 is discouraged to retain client's privacy.

lenge is to obtain a large characteristic and definitive set of pairs that have good coverage of the clients who generate traffic on the global Internet.

To obtain a large set of pairs, we use Akamai's download manager called NetSession [3]. NetSession is installed on client devices and is used to perform downloads in a faster and more reliable fashion. Software and media publishers opt-in to use Netsession features to improve http delivery performance for their content. Once they opt-in, clients use Netsession to download that content. Thus, Netsession has a large, representative installed base of clients around the world, making it an ideal measurement platform for our analysis. More than 30 million unique NetSession clients perform transactions every month.

NetSession was instrumented to collect LDNS information as follows. Each NetSession client maintains a persistent connection with a NetSession control plane. Even if the client is behind a NAT, it can reliably learn its external client IP from this persistent connection. NetSession clients also found their LDNS server performing a "dig" command on a special Akamai name `whoami.akamai.net`. The client-LDNS association was then sent to Akamai's cloud storage for processing. The LDNS information for clients around the world were then aggregated in the cloud to the granularity of /24 client IP blocks. Specifically, for each /24 client IP block, the process generates the set of IPs corresponding to the LDNSes used by the clients in that address block. For each LDNS in the set, the relative frequency with which that LDNS appeared was computed.

Using the above process, we collected LDNS data from March 24 to April 7, 2014. On average, about 14.8 million records were processed per day during the course of our data collection. Client-LDNS association data for a total of 3.76 million /24 client IP blocks was computed in aggregate. While the clients that use NetSession are generally a fraction of the total active clients in any given /24 client IP block, our coverage of /24 client IP blocks is representative and significant of the overall Internet. *In particular, the /24 client IP blocks in our dataset account for about 84.6% of the total global client demand[5] served by Akamai.* The number of distinct LDNSes in our data set was just over 584,000. Thus, our data set is a large representative cross-section of clients and LDNSes in the global Internet.

To derive client-LDNS distance estimates, we use Akamai's Edgescape [1] geo-location database that uses registry data and network data distilled from transactions handled by over 170,000 Akamai servers in 102 countries and over a thousand ISP deployments around the world to establish geographical location and network information for IPs around the world. Edgescape can provide the latitude, longitude, country and autonomous system (AS) for an IP. For IPs in mobile networks, the mobile gateway location is used as the reference location. To derive the distance between a client-LDNS pair we use the latitude and longitude information to compute the great circle distance between the two locations.

[5]Client demand is a measure of the amount of content traffic downloaded by a client (or by clients in an IP block).

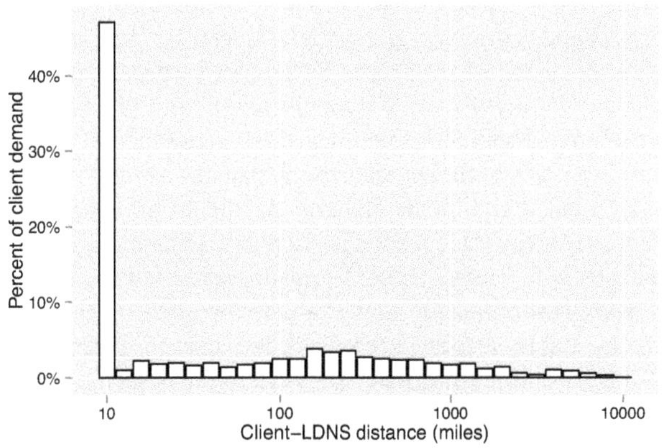

Figure 5: Histogram of client-LDNS distance for clients across the global Internet.

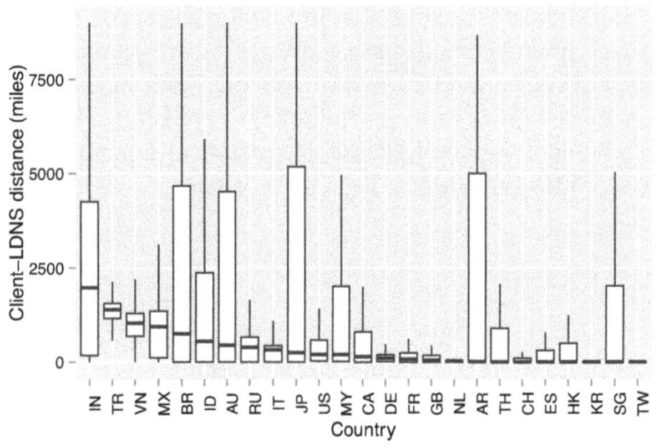

Figure 6: Client-LDNS distances by country.

3.2 How far are clients from their LDNSes

Figure 5 shows the overall global distribution of client LDNS distances. Nearly half of the client population is located very close to its LDNS. The most typical distance lies in a range that is no greater than the diameter of a metropolitan area. At around 200-300 miles, there is a noteworthy increase in the marginal distribution. At around 5000 miles, there is another increase that can be attributed to the small number of clients that use LDNS that are either across the Atlantic or Pacific oceans.

Breakdown by country. Breaking these distances down by country, Figure 6 is a box-plot[6] representing the 5th, 25th, median, 75th, and 95th quantiles of the per-country distributions. We list data for the top 25 countries as measured by aggregate client demand. Overall, most countries have a median distance that is fairly small, though India, Turkey, Vietnam and Mexico have median distances over 1000 miles. India, Brazil, Australia, and Argentina have significant populations whose LDNSes are very far away as over a quarter of the population is served by LDNSes whose distance is over

[6]All box plots in this paper show 5th, 25th, 50th, 75th and 95th percentiles.

4500 miles. Western Europe sees low distances appearing in a small band. However, Korea and Taiwan are significant in having the smallest distances. This is not surprising considering the well-developed Internet infrastructure and the concentration of populations within a small geographical area in the major cities in these countries. Japan has a small median distance but a significant fraction of clients have LDNSes that are far away. One reason is clients at multi-national corporations with centralized LDNSes deployed outside Japan.

Public resolvers. We now evaluate the client-LDNS distance for public resolvers where a client uses an LDNS provided by a public third-party provider such as Google Public DNS or OpenDNS. Such providers have a distributed name server infrastructure and use IP anycast [14] to route clients to the "closest" LDNS deployment. However, the public resolvers use their unicast addresses when communicating with Akamai's authoritative name servers allowing us to geo-locate the public LDNSes. Figure 7 shows client-LDNS distance for clients that use public resolvers. We see that the client-LDNS distances are significantly higher with median distance at 1028 miles, compared to a median distance of 162 miles in the overall client population. This reflects the fact that the LDNS deployments of a public DNS provider may often not be local to the client.

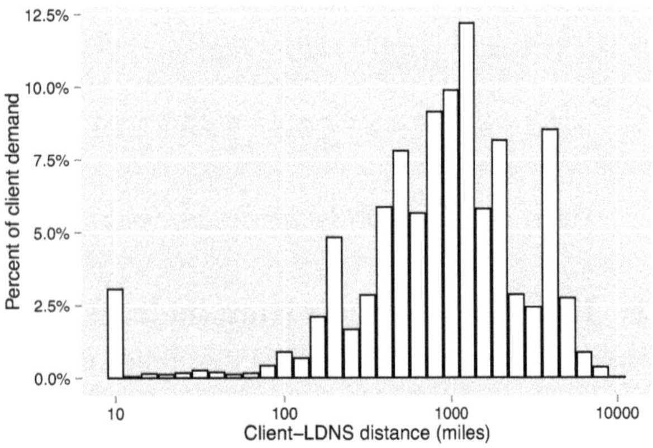

Figure 7: Histogram of the client-LDNS distance for clients who use public resolvers.

The country breakdown in Figure 8 shows disproportionately large distances for clients using public resolvers in some countries in South America, South East Asia and Oceania. The two South American countries of Argentina and Brazil had the largest distances. In this regard, it is notable that the largest public resolver provider, Google Public DNS, does not currently have a presence in many South American countries. Singapore and Malaysia are well served by the public resolvers hosted in Singapore. However, presumably due to peering arrangements, many clients in these countries are routed to more distant public resolvers. Clients who use public resolvers in Western Europe, Hong Kong and Taiwan are relatively close to their LDNS in comparison with other countries, though they are much more distant when compared to clients in those same countries who do not use public resolvers.

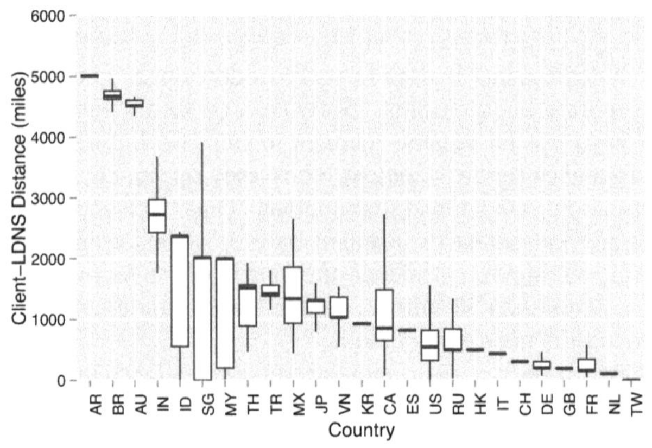

Figure 8: Client-LDNS distance for clients who use public resolvers.

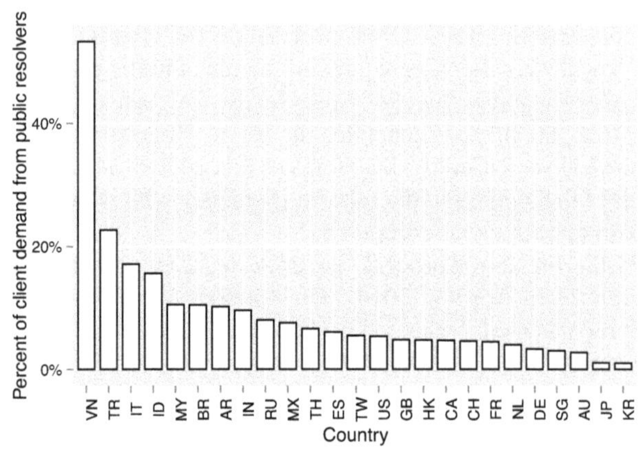

Figure 9: Percent of client demand originating from public resolvers, by country.

The adoption of public resolvers also vary country by country. Figure 9 shows the percentage of client demand originating from public resolvers broken down by country as seen in our NetSession data set. Clients in Vietnam and Turkey are very heavy users of public resolvers. Remarkably, despite the significant client-LDNS distances, a significant fraction of clients in India, Brazil, and Argentina use public resolvers. Overall, percent of client demand from public resolvers approaches 8 percent worldwide.

Breakdown by AS. Figure 10 shows the distribution of the client-LDNS distance as a function of the AS size, where AS size is the client demand originating from that AS as a percentage of the total client demand served by Akamai, i.e., an AS with size 2^{-1} has clients that account for 0.5% of the total client demand served by Akamai. A total of 37,294 ASes with the most demand were analyzed.

As can be seen in the figure, when the AS size is small, the client-LDNS distances are large, especially the higher percentiles of the distance. This may seem counter-intuitive.

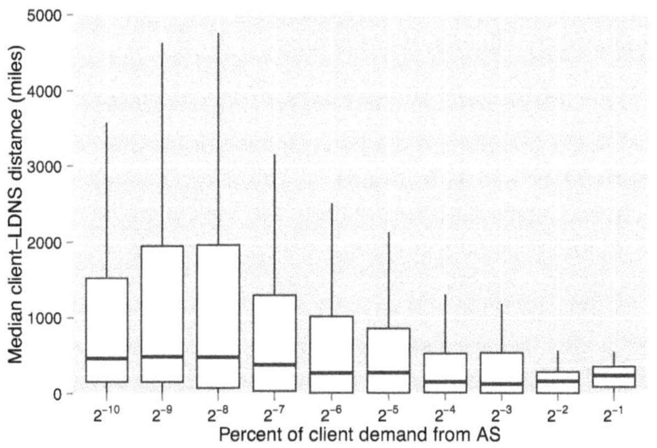

Figure 10: Client-LDNS distance as a function of AS size.

But, the reason is that smaller AS'es include small local ISPs who are more likely to "outsource" their name server infrastructure to other providers. The reason for the outsourcing is economic in nature as the ISP may not want to own and operate a name server infrastructure. So, the ISP may choose the inexpensive option of using a public resolver operated by a provider such as Google Public DNS, OpenDNS, Level 3, UltraDNS, etc. The "outsourcing" of DNS services often causes the LDNSes to be non-local, leading to larger client-LDNS distances. A different category of small AS'es with large client-LDNS distances are enterprises with geographically diverse branch offices who for operational convenience use a centralized name server infrastructure deployed in only one of those offices. Given the large client-LDNS distances, we expect end-user mapping to benefit a large fraction of clients of small AS'es.

Large ISPs typically operate their own name server infrastructures for their clients. Such infrastructure often consists of LDNSes that are deployed in multiple geographically distributed locations. To direct clients to the "nearest" LDNS, the IP anycast [16, 15] mechanism is often used. This explains the smaller values of client-LDNS distance despite the large geographical area covered by these global ISPs. However, IP anycast has many known limitations [23] that can result in a fraction of the clients being routed to far away LDNS locations. Thus, end-user mapping may be beneficial for clients of large ISPs also.

3.3 How far are clients that use the same LDNS from each other?

A *client cluster* is a set of clients that use the same LDNS. The clients on the Internet can be partitioned into client clusters, one cluster for each LDNS. We define the *radius* of a client cluster to be the mean distance of the clients in the cluster to the centroid of the cluster[7]. In traditional NS-based mapping, a client cluster is the unit for making server assignment decisions, i.e., all clients in a client cluster are assigned the same set of server IPs, since they use the same LDNS (cf. Equation 1). If a client cluster of a LDNS has a small radius, i.e., the clients are close together, a more sophisticated form of NS-based mapping could still be effective, *even if the client-LDNS distances are large.* The reason is that the mapping system could discover the client cluster and assign servers that provide good performance for the entire cluster. However, if the client cluster has a large radius, i.e., the clients are far away from each other, there may be no single server assignment for the entire cluster that is optimal for all clients in it. Thus, it is *inherently* difficult for NS-based mapping to perform well when the client cluster has a large radius, even knowing client-LDNS pairings.

Figure 11 reaffirms that on an overall basis a large fraction of clients are close to their LDNSes and the cluster radii are small. However, focusing on the subset of LDNSes that are public resolvers, we see that not only are client-LDNS distances large, but cluster radii are large as well. In fact, 99% of the public resolver demand originates from client clusters with radii between 470 to 3800 miles. The figure also shows that for public resolvers the mean cluster-LDNS distance tends to be larger than the cluster radius. This implies that the LDNS is often not deployed at a "central" location within the client cluster that it serves, i.e., near the centroid that minimize the mean client-LDNS distance. This is in part due to the fact that a public resolver provider does not have fine-grained control over which clients in which locations use their service. e.g., clients from countries where the provider has no deployments often use the service.

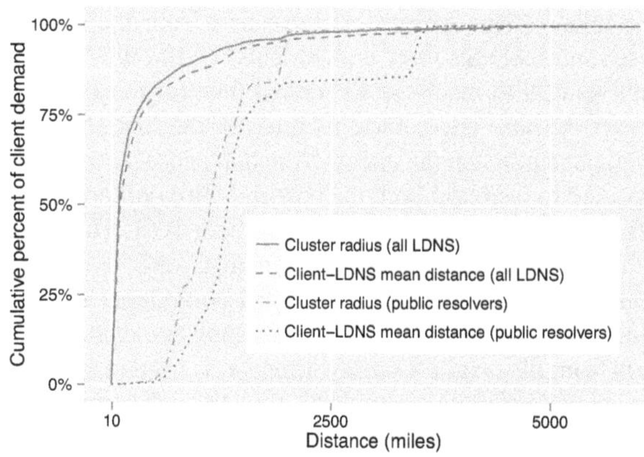

Figure 11: CDFs of mean client-LDNS distance and cluster radius for all LDNSes and for the subset that are public resolvers.

4. PERFORMANCE IMPACT

We present our experience and insights obtained in deploying end-user mapping for clients around the world in the first half of 2014. During this period, Akamai began the roll-out of end-user mapping for clients who use public resolvers such as Google Public DNS and OpenDNS. The reasons for initially targeting clients who use public resolvers were two-fold. Based on our analysis of client-LDNS distances in Section 3, we concluded that clients who use public resolvers

[7]Distances are computed using the latitude and longitude of the clients from our geo-location database. The radius and centroid use client demands as the weights.

are more likely to benefit from end-user mapping, since they tend to be farther away from their LDNSes (cf. Figure 7) and also had large client cluster radii (cf. Figure 11). Further, public resolver providers such as Google Public DNS and OpenDNS support the EDNS0 client-subnet extension that is required for end-user mapping. The end-user mapping roll-out[8] started on March 28th 2014 and completed on April 15th 2014. We present insights based on performance measurements made before, during, and after the roll-out.

4.1 Performance metrics

The performance experienced by clients who download web content can be characterized in many different but complimentary ways. We use the following four metrics measured from real-world clients downloading content from Akamai to evaluate the performance. Each metric sheds light on a different facet of mapping and client-perceived performance. Note that we expect all these metrics to decrease (smaller is better) when end-user mapping is rolled out.

1) Mapping distance is the great circle distance between a client and the server to which it was assigned by the mapping system. This is a purely geographical metric with no network-related component.

2) Round trip time (RTT) between the client and the server to which it was assigned. This is simply the TCP RTT measured from the server's TCP stack. This is purely a network-related metric.

3) Time to first byte (TTFB) is the duration from when the client makes a HTTP request for the base web page to when the first byte of the requested web page was received by the client. This quantity is measured from the client's browser and includes three components: (i) the time for the client's request to reach the server, (ii) time for the server to construct the web page, and (iii) time for the first chunk of the web page to reach the client. Note that end-user mapping is expected to decrease both the first and third component of TTFB above by reducing the server-client RTT. However, since many base web pages are "dynamic" and need to be personalized for the client, the second component of constructing the web page may involve fetching personalized elements from the origin. Overlay transport is used to speedup origin-server communication [26], though such transport is not impacted by the end-user mapping roll-out. Thus, we expect TTFB to show more modest reductions as end-user mapping impacts only some of its time components.

4) Content download time is the duration from the receiving of the first byte of the page to completing the download of the rest of the web page, including the content embedded in the page. This metric is also measured from the client's browser. The embedded content of web pages are typically more static and cacheable and includes CSS, images, and JavaScript that are not personalized to the client. Thus, unlike TTFB, we expect this metric to be significantly impacted by the end-user mapping roll-out as this metric is dominated by client-server latencies.

4.1.1 High and low expectation countries

To better understand the performance impact, we classify the countries into two groups: a "high expectation" group where we expect end-user mapping to have a greater impact and a "low expectation" group where we expect the impact to be lower. Our client-LDNS analysis in Section 3.2 gives us an idea of what benefits to expect in which countries. Specifically, Figure 8 shows the proximity of clients to their LDNS for major countries. Using this analysis, we split the major countries into two halves. We define the high expectation group to be those clients who reside in countries where the median distance to a public resolver is more than 1000 miles and the low expectation group to be those whose median distance is under 1000 miles. We aggregate and present the performance metrics separately for these two groups, as we expect them to show different behaviors.

4.2 Collecting performance information

We collected performance metrics from a large and characteristic set of clients around the world before, during, and after the end-user mapping roll-out. We used Akamai's Real User Measurement (RUM) system [4] for our client-side performance measurements. RUM inserts JavaScript into select web pages delivered by Akamai. That JavaScript runs inside the client's browser when the page is downloaded by the client. The performance measurement is made using the industry-standard navigation timing [6] and resource timing APIs [8]. Using these APIs, the JavaScript running inside the client's browser collects precise timing information when the page download is in progress, including when the DNS lookup started and completed, when the TCP connection was initiated, when the fetch request was sent out, when the first byte of the response was received, and when all the page content was fully downloaded. Using these timing milestones, metrics such as TTFB and content download time can be computed. The timing measurements performed in client browsers around the world was sent to a backend cloud storage system and was subsequently analyzed to produce the aggregate statistics we provide in this section.

We collected RUM measurements from a wide selection of Web sites and clients around the world from Jan 1, 2014 to June 30th, 2014, a period that includes the end-user mapping rollout from March 28th to April 15th. Since the roll-out only impacts clients who use public resolvers, we identified such clients using our client-LDNS pairing data described in Section 3.1 and extracted RUM data from only those qualified clients. Figure 12 shows the total number of qualified RUM measurements collected and used in our analysis from both high and low expectation countries. Our data set has 33 million to 58 million measurements per month, each month from Jan to June 2014, for a total of 273 million measurements. The measurement volume shows an increasing trend on account of more downloads from qualified clients of the pages measured by RUM.

Our goal is to measure performance for a large and char-

[8]We are unaware of any other Akamai software releases or Internet events happening during the roll-out period that could confound our measurements and conclusions.

acteristic cross section of clients, Web sites, devices, and connectivities across the global Internet. To achieve that we measured 6,388 domain names and 2.5 million unique URLs accessed by 149,826 unique clients. Our data set includes all major client platforms such as Windows, FreeBSD, Linux, Android, iOS, and game consoles, and all major browsers including Firefox, Opera, Chrome, and IE. Further, our clients use a variety of ways to access the Internet including cellular, WiFi, 3G, 4G, DSL, cable modem, and fiber.

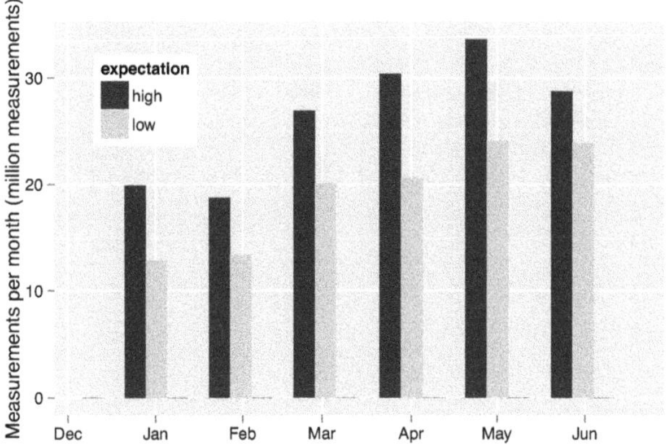

Figure 12: Number of RUM measurements per month.

4.3 Performance Analysis

We analyze the mapping distance, RTT, TTFB, and content download time for clients who use public resolvers before, during, and after the roll-out.

1) Mapping distance. Mapping distance shows a significant improvement during the roll-out period of March 28th to April 15th. Figure 13 shows for the high expectation group, the mean mapping distance dropped from over 2000 miles on average to around 250 miles. Even the low expectation countries experienced shorter mapping distance: the average mapping distance went from 400 miles to 200 miles.

Figure 14 shows the CDF of the mapping distances for both high and low expectation countries both before and after the roll-out is completed. The period after the roll-out is April 15th or later and the period before the roll-out is March 28th or earlier. Note that all percentiles see improvement. But, there is a drastic decrease in the mapping distance around the 90th percentile for high expectation countries from 4573 miles to 936 miles. The decrease is due to improved mapping distance for clients in large countries like India and Brazil who use public resolvers located in Southeast Asia and North America respectively (cf. Figure 8).

2) RTT. Recall that RTT measures the latency between the client and the server assigned to that client. Unlike mapping distance, RTT reflects the state of the network path such as propagation delay, and congestion. As shown in Figure 15, the average RTT for the high expectation group dropped from 200ms to 100ms, a significant 50% decrease. But, the improvement for the low expectation group was modest. Figure 16 shows the CDF of the RTT for both high and low expectation countries before and after the roll-out. All

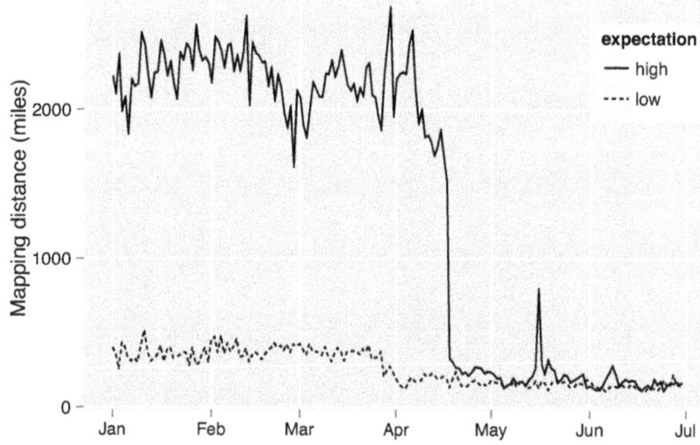

Figure 13: Daily mean of mapping distance.

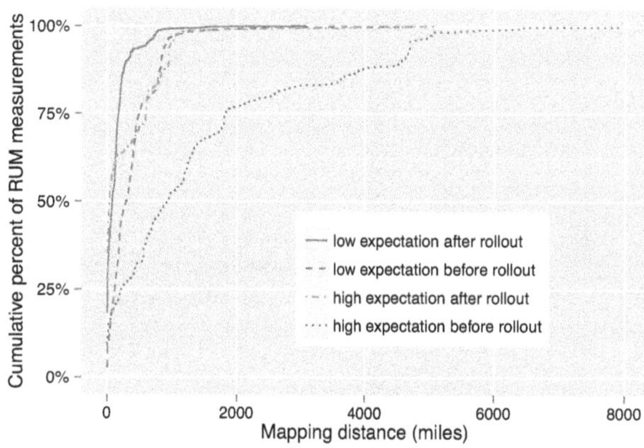

Figure 14: CDFs of mapping distance.

percentiles show improvement. For instance, the 75th percentile of the RTT decreases significantly from 220 ms to 137 ms for the high expectation countries.

3) Time-to-First-Byte. As noted earlier, TTFB includes aspects that are not impacted by better mapping decisions, such as the computation time to generate and transmit a dynamic web page. Consequently, the gains expressed as a percentage are lower but still significant. Figure 17 shows that the mean TTFB of the high expectation countries decreased from around 1000 ms to 700 ms, a 30% improvement. Figure 18 shows the CDF of the TTFB for both high and low expectation countries before and after the roll-out. All percentiles show improvement. For instance, the 75th percentile of the TTFB decreases from 1399 ms to 1072 ms for the high expectation countries and from 830 ms to 667 ms for the low expectation ones.

4) Content Download Time. Figure 19 shows a reduction from 300 ms to 150 ms for the high expectation countries, a 50% reduction. Recall that content download time is dominated by server-client latencies and the decrease is more correlated with corresponding decrease in RTT. The improvement for the low expectation group is small as the download time is already small. Figure 20 shows the CDF of the content download time for high and low expectation countries before and after the roll-out. All percentiles show improvement, e.g., the 75th percentile of the download time reduces

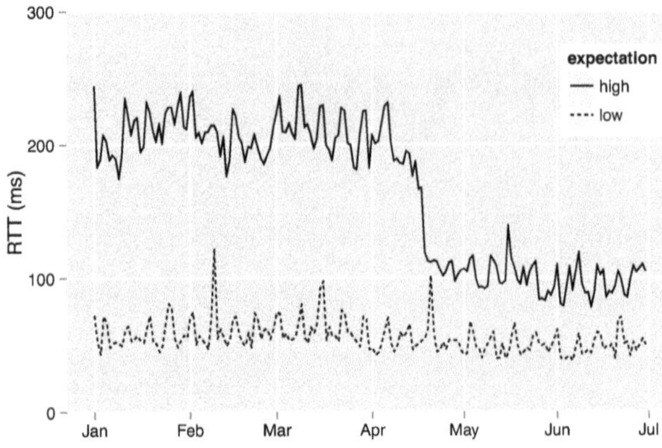

Figure 15: Daily Mean of Round Trip Time (RTT).

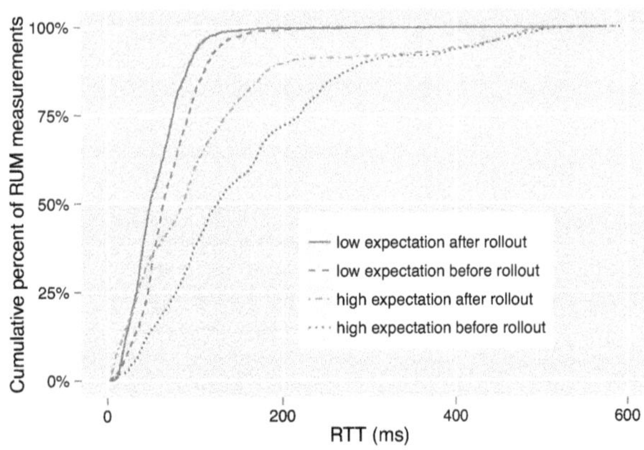

Figure 16: CDFs of Round Trip Time (RTT).

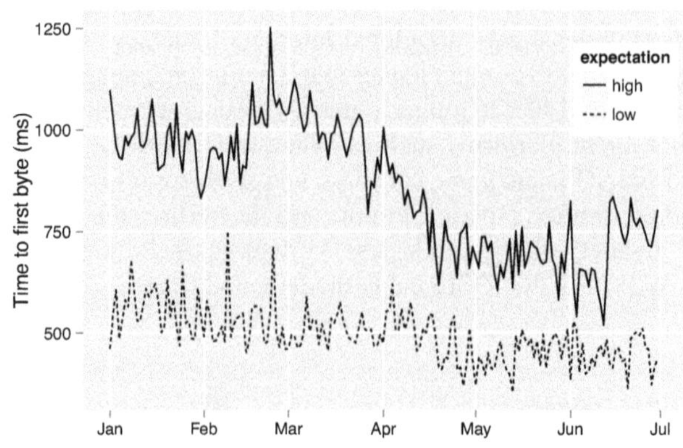

Figure 17: Daily Mean of Time to First Byte (TTFB).

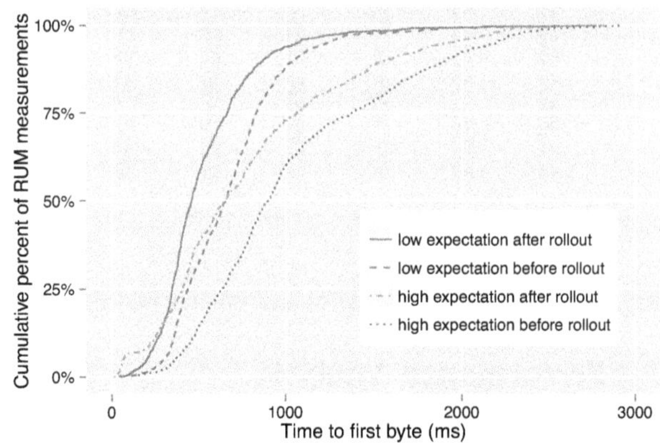

Figure 18: CDFs of Time to First Byte (TTFB).

from 272 ms to 157 ms for the high expectation group and from 192 ms to 102 ms for the low expectation one.

4.4 Why Download Performance Matters

From our results above, we can conclude that end-user mapping provides significant performance benefits to clients who use public resolvers, especially in those countries where client-LDNS distances are high. Faster download times such as those provided by end-user mapping are key to a better Internet experience, resulting in web pages that load more quickly and videos that start playing sooner. Better download performance enhances the client's experience of a content provider's Web site, more satisfied clients in turn favorably impact the business of the content provider, allowing the content provider to invest in even greater performance enhancements, forming a "virtuous cycle" [25]. As an example, an oft-cited recent study by Walmart labs [12] concluded that the download time of Web pages in Walmart's e-commerce site impacts the buying behavior of its users. By correlating RUM performance measurements collected for Walmart.com with back-end business metrics, the study concluded that a 100 ms decrease in web page download time can result in a 1% increase in revenue and a 1 second decrease can result in up to a 2% increase in conversion rates[9]. Numerous other studies show how even a few 100 ms increase in page download times of a Web site can decrease revenues, page views, searches per user, etc [9]. In fact, it is widely held in industry that a Web site that is faster than its competing sites by as little as 250 ms has a significant business advantage to be reckoned with [18]. In addition, search engines rank faster Web sites ahead of slower ones and clients often associate greater brand reputation with faster Web sites. Thus, the "need for speed" is a singular focus for content providers and the CDNs alike and "shaving off" even tens of milliseconds of Web download times for a cross-section of clients is deemed worthy and important. Besides faster download times, the decrease in mapping distance and RTT due to end-user mapping often means that the client-server path crosses fewer AS boundaries, peering points and transnational cable links, hence reducing the likelihood of congestion and failure. Thus, end-user mapping may result in more stable and reliable client-server paths.

4.5 The Benefits of EDNS0 Adoption

To deploy end-user mapping beyond the current set of clients, the client's ISP needs to adopt the EDNS0 exten-

[9]Conversion rate is a key metric for e-commerce sites and is the percentage of visitors to the site who buy a product.

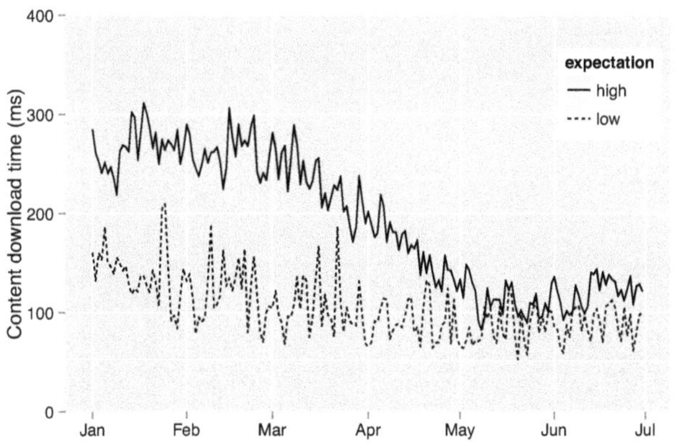

Figure 19: Daily mean of content download time.

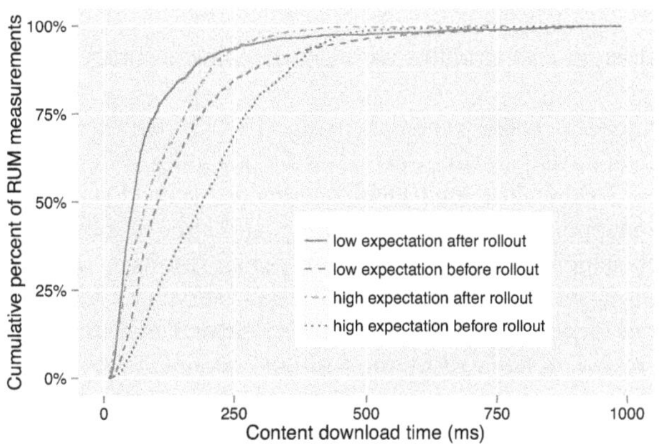

Figure 20: CDFs of content download time.

sion for their DNS services. Our results shed light on the performance benefits such adoption would yield and provides a strong impetus for its adoption. For instance, excluding the public resolvers, we know that 6.2% of the remaining client demand originates from clients whose LDNS are at least 1000 miles away. Extrapolating from our results for similar clients using public resolvers, we could expect a similar 50% reduction in RTT and content download time for these clients. Likewise, excluding the public resolvers, clients with LDNSes between 500 to 1000 miles account for 5.3% of remaining client demand. Extrapolating from similar clients who use public resolvers, we can speculate that these clients will see a 24% decrease in RTTs and content download times. Of course, 54% of the remaining client demand will see no benefit at all from end-user mapping, since they have local LDNSes. However, the fact that at least 11.5% of the remaining client demand will see a significant enough performance improvement is sufficient impetus to EDNS0 adoption.

5. SCALING CHALLENGES

End-user mapping is challenging since it makes mapping decisions at potentially a much finer granularity than traditional NS-based mapping. There are orders of magnitude more clients than there are name servers on the global Internet. An end-user mapping system must perform more fine-grain network measurements and provide resolutions at a finer scale across the global Internet than a NS-based mapping, leading to scaling considerations discussed below.

5.1 Tradeoffs in choosing the mapping units

A mapping unit is the finest-grain set of client IPs for which server assignment decisions are made by the mapping system. A traditional NS-based mapping system uses a LDNS as the mapping unit, i.e., all clients in the client cluster that use a LDNS are mapped together as a unit. An end-user mapping system could use /x client IP blocks that partition the client IP space, where $x \leq 24$. A natural first choice is /24 client IP blocks since LDNSes that support the EDNS0 extension currently use /24 IP blocks in their queries.

To understand the scaling issues in switching from NS-based to end-user mapping, let us first examine the number of relevant /24 client IP blocks on the Internet in comparison to the number of relevant LDNSes. We use our NetSession data to first compute the demand generated by clients in each /24 client IP block. We also computed the demand generated by each LDNS, where the LDNS demand is simply the demand generated by clients who use that LDNS. We then sorted all the /24 client IP blocks (resp., LDNSes) in decreasing order of demand and plotted a CDF of the demand in Figure 21. In the data set, the total number of /24 client IP blocks with non-zero demand is 3.76 million, while 584 thousand LDNSes have non-zero demand. Suppose the mapping system is required to measure and provide mapping decisions for 95% of the total client demand on the Internet. As the figure shows, an NS-based mapping system need only measure and analyze the top 25,000 LDNSes with the most demand, whereas an end-user mapping system must measure and analyze the top 2.2 million /24 client IP blocks, which is several magnitudes higher. Likewise, to cover 50% of the total client demand, the top 1800 LDNSes with the most demand suffice, whereas nearly 430,000 of the /24 client IP blocks with the most demand are needed.

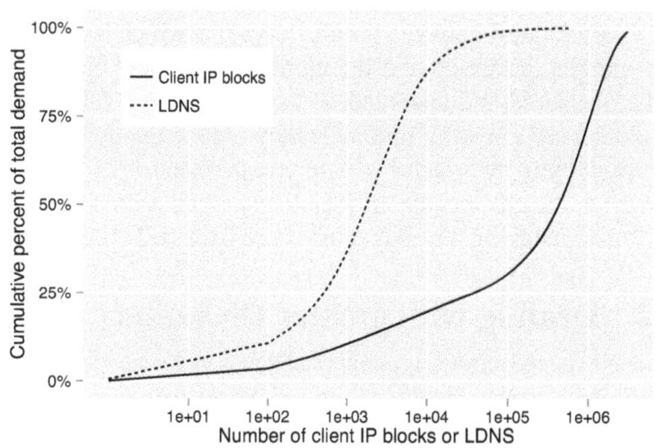

Figure 21: Number of /24 client IP blocks or LDNSes that produce a given percent of total global demand.

One heuristic approach to reducing the number of map-

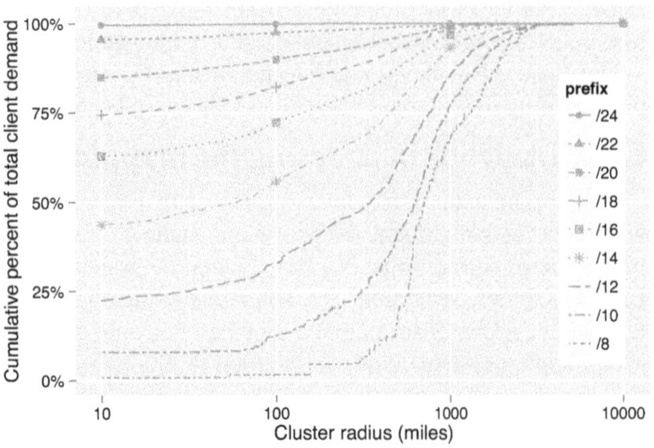

(a) Histogram of the cluster radius for /x client IP blocks.

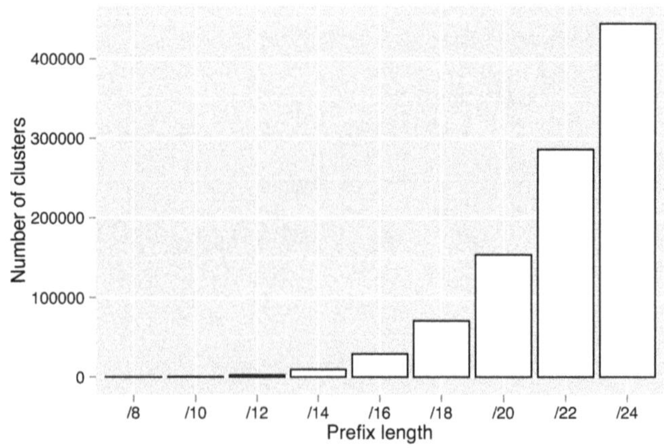

(b) Number of /x client IP blocks with non-zero demand.

Figure 22: A smaller value of x yields fewer mapping units but larger cluster radius with less mapping accuracy.

ping units for end-user mapping is to use the IP blocks (i.e., CIDRs) in BGP feeds that are the units for routing in the Internet. In particular, if a set of /24 IP blocks belong within the same BGP CIDR, these blocks can be combined since they are likely proximal in the network sense. We extracted 517K unique CIDRs with non-zero traffic from BGP feeds across the Internet from the network measurement component of the mapping system. By combining /24 IP blocks whenever they belong to the same BGP CIDR, we reduce the number of mapping units from 3.76 million to 444K. Note that the same technique may be applied to reduce the number of mapping units for /x IP blocks, for any value of x.

After applying the BGP CIDRs to reduce the number of mapping units, there is still the tradeoff of what /x client IP blocks to choose as the mapping unit. One could reduce the number of mapping units by using coarser /x client IP blocks, i.e., by choosing a smaller value of x. However, when coarser IP blocks are used, the set of clients in a given block is larger and span a larger geographical area. This reduces mapping accuracy as the client clusters that are the units of mapping have a larger radius. Figure 22 provides the exact tradeoff between the cluster radius which is a proxy for mapping accuracy and the number of clusters that need to be measured and analyzed. It can be seen that /20 client IP blocks are a worthy option as they reduce the number of mapping units by a factor of 3 in comparison to /24 blocks. However, the clusters are still relatively small with 87.3% of the clusters having a radius of no more than 100 miles.

5.2 Dealing with greater DNS query rates

In NS-based mapping, each LDNS stores one resolution per domain name. However, with end-user mapping, different client IP blocks within the *same client cluster* may get different resolutions for the same domain name. Thus, an LDNS that serves multiple client IP blocks may store multiple entries for the same domain name. Therefore, an LDNS may make multiple requests to an authoritative name server for the domain name, one for each client IP block. This can lead to a sharp increase in the LDNS queries seen by the authoritative name servers of the mapping system. Figure 23 shows the total DNS queries per second served by the mapping system before, during, and after enabling end-user mapping for clients who use public resolvers. Prior to the roll-out, the total queries per second served by Akamai's name servers was 870K queries per second of which public resolvers targeted by the roll-out accounted for roughly 33.5K queries per second. But after the rollout, the total queries per second on the Akamai network was 1.17 million queries per second of which public resolvers accounted for 270K queries per second. Thus, the queries from public resolvers increased by a factor of 270K/33.5K = 8, an increase largely attributable to the roll-out[10]. The gradual increase in query rate seen outside of the roll-out window is simply due to the normal increase in Internet traffic over time.

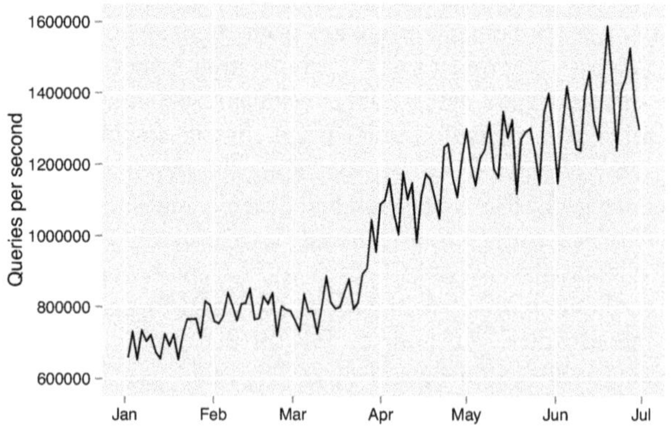

Figure 23: DNS queries received by Akamai's name servers from LDNSes showed a significant increase during the end-user mapping rollout.

[10]DNS queries increase when public resolvers turn on the EDNS0 extension. But, the performance improvements in Section 4.3 occur when Akamai gradually turned on end-user mapping for these public resolvers.

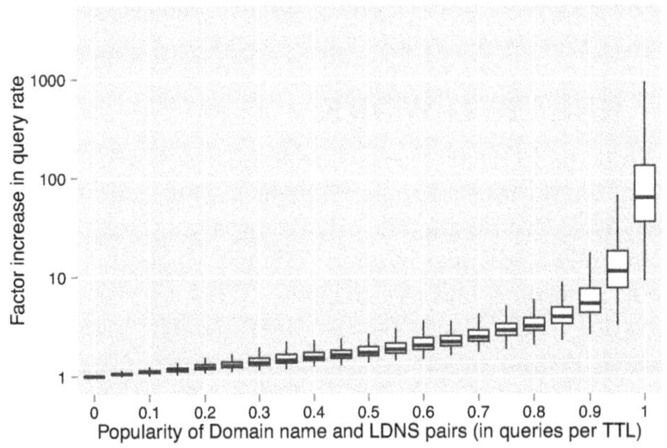

Figure 24: More popular domain name and LDNS pairs show a greater increase in query rate after the roll-out.

The popularity of a domain name among the clients of an LDNS influences the factor increase in DNS queries for that domain name when EDNS0 and end-user mapping are turned on. Prior to the end-user mapping roll-out, the query rate for a domain name from a particular LDNS is at most one query per TTL, since the LDNS can cache the translation for the time of the TTL. We bucket each domain name and LDNS pair according to the number of queries received per TTL *prior* to the roll-out. Figure 24 shows the factor increase in query rate for domain name and LDNS pairs that fall into each bucket. Note that the more popular domain name and LDNS pairs that have pre-roll-out query rates close to 1 query per TTL saw the largest increase in query rate when end-user mapping was rolled out, while less popular domains saw little or no increase. The reason is that a more popular domain name is more likely to be accessed by clients in multiple client IP blocks of the LDNS's client cluster, each IP block requiring a separate domain name resolution when EDNS0 is used. Fortunately, the domain name and LDNS pairs in the highest popularity bucket in Figure 24 accounted for only 11% of total pre-roll-out queries.

6. ROLE OF SERVER DEPLOYMENTS

Server deployments play an important role in determining client performance. More server deployment locations mean better performance for clients, since the mapping system has more options to choose a proximal server for each client. But, what role do deployments play in determining the additional performance benefits provided by end-user mapping over NS-based mapping? Should a CDN with a small number of deployment locations adopt end-user mapping? For a CDN with a given set of deployment locations, what is more beneficial: adding more deployment locations or incorporating end-user mapping? How much can NS-based mapping be improved by making it client-aware?

To provide intuition on these key what-if questions, consider a simplified model. Let a CDN have N deployment locations. The deployments partition the IP address space of the global Internet into sets $E_i, 1 \leq i \leq N$, such that E_i is the set of IPs for whom the ith deployment location is the most proximal among all deployments. Observe that for any client c, if c and its LDNS are *both* in some set E_i, both end-user mapping and traditional NS-based mapping will pick a server in the ith deployment location for client c, i.e., there is no additional benefit for client c from using end-user mapping. Thus, if a CDN has fewer deployments, each set E_i is likely larger and is hence more likely to contain both the client and its LDNS. Thus, we would expect a *a CDN with fewer deployments to benefit less from end-user mapping than a CDN with more deployments.* We quantify answers to this and other key questions using simulations.

Simulation Methodology. We create a universe U of possible deployment locations by using 2642 different locations around the globe with Akamai servers. These deployments are spread over 100 countries and were chosen to provide good coverage of the global Internet. Next, we choose around 20K /24 IP blocks that account for most of the load on the Internet and further cluster them into 8K "ping targets", so as to cover all major geographical areas and networks around the world. We then perform latency measurements using `pings` from each deployment U to each of the 8K ping targets. For any client or LDNS, we find the closest of the 8K ping targets and use that as a proxy for latency measurements, i.e., the latency measurements to the ping target are assumed to be the latency measurements to the client or LDNS. Using the ping latency measurements described above, we simulate three mapping schemes, each with a varying number of deployment locations.

(1) NS-based mapping (NS): Map client to the deployment location that has the least latency to the LDNS of that client.

(2) End-user mapping (EU): Map client to the deployment location that has the least latency to the client's /24 IP block.

(3) Client-Aware NS-based Mapping (CANS): For each client, find the cluster of clients that shares its LDNS. Map client to the deployment location that minimizes the traffic-weighted average of the latencies from the deployment to its cluster of clients.

Note that CANS mapping is an enhancement of pure NS mapping by using the latency measurements to the clients of the LDNS, rather than just the latency measurement to the LDNS. In situations where LDNS is far away from its clients, but its clients are themselves relatively close together, CANS mapping could provide low latency mappings. CANs requires tracking client-LDNS associations on an ongoing basis on the global Internet, an additional complexity in comparison with NS mapping. However, CANS can be viewed as a hybrid between NS and EU that uses client measurements but requires no specific knowledge about the client's IP, i.e., it does not require the EDNS0 protocol extension.

We simulated the three mapping schemes above for a varying number of deployment locations N chosen from the universe U. We performed 100 random runs of our simulation, where we do the following in each run. We randomly order the deployments in U. Then, for each N, we simulate all three mapping schemes assuming the first N deployments in the random ordering. The simulation computes the traffic-weighted mean, 95th, and 99th percentile latencies achieved by the three schemes. Finally, for each value of N, we averaged the metrics obtained across the 100 simulation runs and those values are reported in Figure 25.

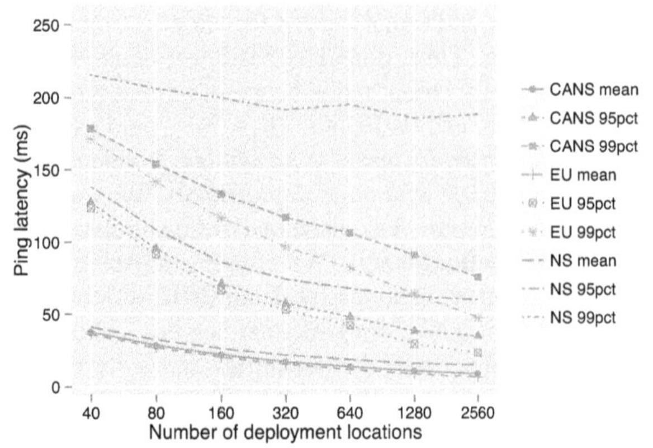

Figure 25: Latencies achieved by EU, CANS, and NS mapping as a function of CDN deployment locations.

An important caveat in interpreting Figure 25 is that the *ping latencies shown are an underestimate of the actual latency or RTT from the server to the client*, since only a ping target (typically a router) enroute to the client is "pinged". So, while the absolute values of the ping latencies are less meaningful except as a lower bound on the actual latencies, the relative values are still meaningful. As shown in the figure, all mapping schemes provide smaller ping latencies with a larger deployment. Further, mean ping latency is nearly identical for all three mapping schemes, reflecting the fact that in many cases a client and its LDNS are proximal to each other and LDNS is a good proxy for the client. Even so, EU performed the best of the three with mean ping latency dropping from 35 ms for a small deployment to under 10 ms as the deployments increase.

However, *mean* latency across all clients on the globe is less interesting than latency of the *worst-performing* clients. In fact, both CDNs and content providers are focused on improving the performance of the worst-performing client. Thus, we computed the 95th and 99th percentiles of the latencies, i.e, latencies for 1-5% of the worst clients. It is clear that EU provides a large benefit over the other schemes for higher percentiles of ping latency. In particular, NS-based mapping provides diminishing benefits beyond 160 deployment locations for the 99th percentile latency, and is in particular unable to reduce it below 186 ms even with 1280 deployment locations. The reason is that NS-based mapping does not work well for clients whose LDNSes are not proximal who are likely among the worst-performing clients. However, EU continues to reduce the latencies with increasing deployments, even beyond 1280 deployments. It can also be seen in the figure that a CDN with larger deployment locations sees a proportionally larger reduction in higher percentiles of ping latency by switching to EU from NS than a CDN with smaller deployments. CAN mapping provides an intermediate point between the extremes of NS and EUM. In particular, the knowledge of latencies to clients behind a given LDNS provides sufficient knowledge to improve NS-based mapping for higher percentiles for latency.

7. RELATED WORK

While the EDSN0 extension provides a systematic mechanism for end-user mapping implementation, other mechanisms have been explored in limited ways in industry. A video CDN at Akamai in circa 2000 used metafile redirection to implement end-user mapping. When a client starts a video, the media player fetches a metafile that contains the server's IP from which to download the video. The server IP embedded in the metafile is dynamically generated by the mapping system using the client's IP derived from the metafile download. However, such a mechanism is hard to extend to the Web and other traffic that do not use metafiles.

Analogous to metafile redirection, systems that use http redirection have also been built where the client is first assigned a server using NS-based mapping. The first server uses its knowledge of the client's IP to redirect the client to a "better" second server if appropriate. The second server then serves the content to the client. However, this process incurs a redirection penalty that is acceptable only for larger downloads such as media files and software downloads.

Tools for discovering client-LDNS pairings have also existed in industry for the past 15 years. In principle, such pairings can be used to create a client-aware NS-based mapping system (cf. Section 6), though it will not be effective for LDNSes with large client clusters (cf. Section 3.3).

We think that the EDNS0 extension is key to building large-scale end-user mapping that overcomes the short comings of prior implementations. The EDNS0 extension removes the overhead of explicit client-LDNS discovery, avoids a redirection performance penalty, and is effective even for LDNSes with large geo-distributed client clusters.

From a research perspective, client-LDNS distances and their potential impact on server selection has been studied in [24], and subsequently in [20, 17]. The prior literature observed larger client-LDNS distances and poorer performance for clients using public resolvers that are increasingly in use [22]. Our measurement study of client-LDNS distances in Section 3 is based on a much wider global cross-section of clients and LDNSes than prior work and largely confirm prior conclusions on public resolvers. However, we go a step further by describing an end-user mapping system to remedy the issue. The EDNS0 extension has also been studied as tool for figuring out deployments of CDN providers who support the extension such as Google [10, 27]. Extensions other than EDSN0 for overcoming client-LDNS mismatch have also been proposed [16].

8. CONCLUSION

In this paper, we described our experience in rolling-out a new mapping system called end-user mapping. By analyzing clients and LDNSes from around the world, we showed that a significant fraction of clients have LDNSes that are not in their proximity and could benefit from end-user mapping. We confirmed the performance benefits by measuring mapping distance, RTT, Time-To-First-Byte (TTFB), and content download time during the roll-out. We showed that for "high-expectation" countries, clients using public resolvers saw an eight-fold decrease in mean mapping distance, a two-fold decrease in RTT and content download time, and a 30% improvement in the TTFB. We also quantified the scaling challenges in implementing end-user mapping such as the 8-fold increase in DNS queries and the greater number of mapping units that need to be measured and analyzed. Finally, we shed light on the role of deployments and showed that a CDN with a larger number of deployment locations is likely to benefit more from end-user mapping than a CDN with a smaller number. While we only describe the roll-out of end-user mapping to clients who are using public resolvers, our analysis shows that a broad roll-out of this technology across the entire Internet population will be quite beneficial. For such a roll-out to occur, more ISPs would need to support the EDNS0 extension. We expect our work that quantifies the real-world benefits of end-user mapping to provide impetus to a broader adoption of the EDNS0 extension.

9. ACKNOWLEDGEMENTS

First and foremost, we thank the many engineers at Akamai who designed, implemented and rolled-out end-user mapping, making it possible for us to evaluate its impact. Special thanks to Mike Conlen who helped collect DNS query data, to Pablo Alvarez who made key contributions to end-user mapping scoring, and to Jason Moreau who made major contributions to name server design. We thank our anonymous referees for copious reviews that helped improve the paper. A special thanks to our shepherd Ethan Katz-Bassett who provided lots of great feedback that strengthened the paper.

10. REFERENCES

[1] Akamai Edgescape. http://goo.gl/P68U6q.

[2] Akamai Facts & Figures. http://goo.gl/Megx1b.

[3] Akamai NetSession Interface. http://goo.gl/FOtjlz.

[4] Akamai Real User Monitoring. http://goo.gl/8oiQyC.

[5] Google Public DNS. https://goo.gl/p8cfJm.

[6] Navigation Timing. http://goo.gl/ePcQrG.

[7] OpenDNS. https://www.opendns.com/.

[8] Resource Timing. http://goo.gl/5eYQtL.

[9] Velocity and the bottom line. http://goo.gl/KTlcYR.

[10] M. Calder, X. Fan, Z. Hu, E. Katz-Bassett, J. Heidemann, and R. Govindan. Mapping the expansion of Google's serving infrastructure. In *Proceedings of the ACM Internet Measurement Conference*, pages 313–326, 2013.

[11] C. Contavalli, W. van der Gaast, D. Lawrence, and W. Kumari. Client subnet in DNS requests. *IETF Internet Draft*, Nov. 2014.

[12] C. Crocker, A. Kulick, and B. Ram. Real user monitoring at walmart.com: A story in three parts. In *San Francisco and Silicon Valley Web Performance Group*, Feb 2012. http://minus.com/msM8y8nyh.

[13] J. Dilley, B. M. Maggs, J. Parikh, H. Prokop, R. K. Sitaraman, and W. E. Weihl. Globally distributed content delivery. *IEEE Internet Computing*, 6(5):50–58, 2002.

[14] X. Fan, J. Heidemann, and R. Govindan. Evaluating anycast in the domain name system. In *Proceedings of the IEEE INFOCOM*, pages 1681–1689, 2013.

[15] T. Hardie. Distributing authoritative name servers via shared unicast addresses. *RFC 3258*, Apr. 2002.

[16] C. Huang, I. Batanov, and J. Li. A practical solution to the client-LDNS mismatch problem. *SIGCOMM Comput. Commun. Rev.*, 42(2):35–41, Mar. 2012.

[17] C. Huang, D. A. Maltz, J. Li, and A. Greenberg. Public DNS system and global traffic management. In *Proceedings of the IEEE INFOCOM*, pages 2615–2623, 2011.

[18] S. Lohr. For impatient web users, an eye blink is just too long to wait. *New York Times*, Feb 2012. http://goo.gl/y70JgH.

[19] B. M. Maggs and R. K. Sitaraman. Algorithmic nuggets in content delivery. *SIGCOMM Comput. Commun. Rev.*, July 2015.

[20] Z. M. Mao, C. D. Cranor, F. Douglis, M. Rabinovich, O. Spatscheck, and J. Wang. A precise and efficient evaluation of the proximity between Web clients and their local DNS servers. In *USENIX Annual Technical Conference, General Track*, pages 229–242, 2002.

[21] E. Nygren, R. Sitaraman, and J. Sun. The Akamai Network: A platform for high-performance Internet applications. *ACM SIGOPS Operating Systems Review*, 44(3):2–19, 2010.

[22] J. S. Otto, M. A. Sánchez, J. P. Rula, and F. E. Bustamante. Content delivery and the natural evolution of DNS: remote DNS trends, performance issues and alternative solutions. In *Proceedings of the ACM Internet Measurement Conference*, pages 523–536, 2012.

[23] S. Sarat, V. Pappas, and A. Terzis. On the use of anycast in DNS. In *Proceedings of the IEEE ICCCN*, pages 71–78, 2006.

[24] A. Shaikh, R. Tewari, and M. Agrawal. On the effectiveness of DNS-based server selection. In *Proceedings of the IEEE INFOCOM*, volume 3, pages 1801–1810, 2001.

[25] R. K. Sitaraman. Network performance: Does it really matter to users and by how much? In *Fifth International Conference on Communication Systems and Networks (COMSNETS)*, pages 1–10. IEEE, 2013.

[26] R. K. Sitaraman, M. Kasbekar, W. Lichtenstein, and M. Jain. Overlay networks: An Akamai perspective. In *Advanced Content Delivery, Streaming, and Cloud Services*. John Wiley & Sons, 2014.

[27] F. Streibelt, J. Böttger, N. Chatzis, G. Smaragdakis, and A. Feldmann. Exploring EDNS-client-subnet adopters in your free time. In *Proceedings of the ACM Internet Measurement Conference*, 2013.

Jupiter Rising: A Decade of Clos Topologies and Centralized Control in Google's Datacenter Network

Arjun Singh, Joon Ong, Amit Agarwal, Glen Anderson, Ashby Armistead, Roy Bannon, Seb Boving, Gaurav Desai, Bob Felderman, Paulie Germano, Anand Kanagala, Jeff Provost, Jason Simmons, Eiichi Tanda, Jim Wanderer, Urs Hölzle, Stephen Stuart, and Amin Vahdat
Google, Inc.
jupiter-sigcomm@google.com

ABSTRACT

We present our approach for overcoming the cost, operational complexity, and limited scale endemic to datacenter networks a decade ago. Three themes unify the five generations of datacenter networks detailed in this paper. First, multi-stage Clos topologies built from commodity switch silicon can support cost-effective deployment of building-scale networks. Second, much of the general, but complex, decentralized network routing and management protocols supporting arbitrary deployment scenarios were overkill for single-operator, pre-planned datacenter networks. We built a centralized control mechanism based on a global configuration pushed to all datacenter switches. Third, modular hardware design coupled with simple, robust software allowed our design to also support inter-cluster and wide-area networks. Our datacenter networks run at dozens of sites across the planet, scaling in capacity by 100x over ten years to more than 1Pbps of bisection bandwidth.

CCS Concepts

•**Networks** → **Data center networks;**

Keywords

Datacenter Networks; Clos topology; Merchant Silicon; Centralized control and management

1. INTRODUCTION

Datacenter networks are critical to delivering web services, modern storage infrastructure, and are a key enabler for cloud computing. Bandwidth demands in the datacenter are doubling every 12-15 months (Figure 1), even faster than the wide area Internet. A number of recent trends drive this growth. Dataset sizes are continuing to explode with more photo/video content, logs, and the proliferation of Internet-connected sensors. As a result, network-intensive data processing pipelines must operate over ever-larger datasets. Next, Web services can deliver higher quality results by accessing more data on the critical path of individual requests. Finally, constellations of co-resident applications often share substantial data with one another in the same cluster; consider index generation, web search, and serving ads.

Ten years ago, we found the cost and operational complexity associated with traditional datacenter network architectures to be prohibitive. Maximum network scale was limited by the cost and capacity of the highest end switches available at any point in time [24]. These switches were engineering marvels, typically recycled from products targeting wide area deployments. WAN switches were differentiated with hardware support/offload for a range of protocols (e.g., IP multicast) or by pushing the envelope of chip memory (e.g., Internet-scale routing tables, off chip DRAM for deep buffers, etc.). Network control and management protocols targeted autonomous individual switches rather than pre-configured and largely static datacenter fabrics. Most of these features were not useful for datacenters, increased cost, complexity, delayed time to market, and made network management more difficult.

Datacenter switches were also built as complex chassis targeting the highest levels of availability. In a WAN Internet deployment, losing a single switch/router can have substantial impact on applications. Because WAN links are so expensive, it makes sense to invest in high availability. However, more plentiful and cheaper datacenter bandwidth makes it prudent to trade cost for somewhat reduced intermittent capacity. Finally, switches operating in a multi-vendor WAN environment with arbitrary end hosts require support for many protocols to ensure interoperability. In single-operator dat-

SIGCOMM '15 August 17-21, 2015, London, United Kingdom

ACM ISBN 978-1-4503-3542-3/15/08.
DOI: http://dx.doi.org/10.1145/2785956.2787508

acenter deployments, the number of required protocols can be substantially reduced.

Inspired by the community's ability to scale out computing with parallel arrays of commodity servers, we sought a similar approach for networking. This paper describes our experience with building five generations of custom data center network hardware and software leveraging commodity hardware components, while addressing the control and management requirements introduced by our approach. We used the following principles in constructing our networks:

Clos topologies: To support graceful fault tolerance, increase the scale/bisection of our datacenter networks, and accommodate lower radix switches, we adopted Clos topologies [2, 9, 15] for our datacenters. Clos topologies can scale to nearly arbitrary size by adding stages to the topology, principally limited by failure domain considerations and control plane scalability. They also have substantial in-built path diversity and redundancy, so the failure of any individual element can result in relatively small capacity reduction. However, they introduce substantial challenges as well, including managing the fiber fanout and more complex routing across multiple equal-cost paths.

Merchant silicon: Rather than use commercial switches targeting small-volume, large feature sets, and high reliability, we targeted general-purpose merchant switch silicon, commodity priced, off the shelf, switching components. To keep pace with server bandwidth demands which scale with cores per server and Moore's Law, we emphasized bandwidth density and frequent refresh cycles. Regularly upgrading network fabrics with the latest generation of commodity switch silicon allows us to deliver exponential growth in bandwidth capacity in a cost-effective manner.

Centralized control protocols: Control and management becomes substantially more complex with Clos topologies because we dramatically increase the number of discrete switching elements. Existing routing and management protocols were not well-suited to such an environment. To control this complexity, we observed that individual datacenter switches played a predetermined forwarding role based on the cluster plan. We took this observation to one extreme by collecting and distributing dynamically changing link state information from a central, dynamically-elected, point in the network. Individual switches could then calculate forwarding tables based on current link state relative to a statically configured topology.

Overall, our software architecture more closely resembles control in large-scale storage and compute platforms than traditional networking protocols. Network protocols typically use soft state based on pair-wise message exchange, emphasizing local autonomy. We were able to use the distinguishing characteristics and needs of our datacenter deployments to simplify control and management protocols, anticipating many of the tenets of modern Software Defined Networking deployments [13]. The datacenter networks described in this paper represent some of the largest in the world, are in deployment at dozens of sites across the planet, and support thousands of internal and external services, including external use through Google Cloud Platform. Our cluster network architecture found substantial reuse for inter-cluster networking in the same campus and even WAN deployments [19] at Google.

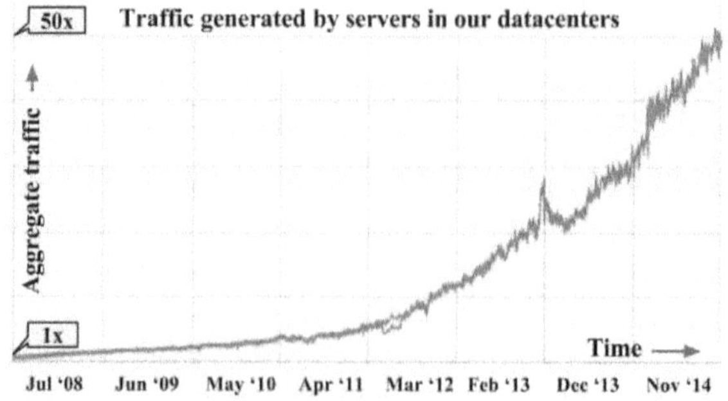

Figure 1: Aggregate server traffic in our datacenter fleet.

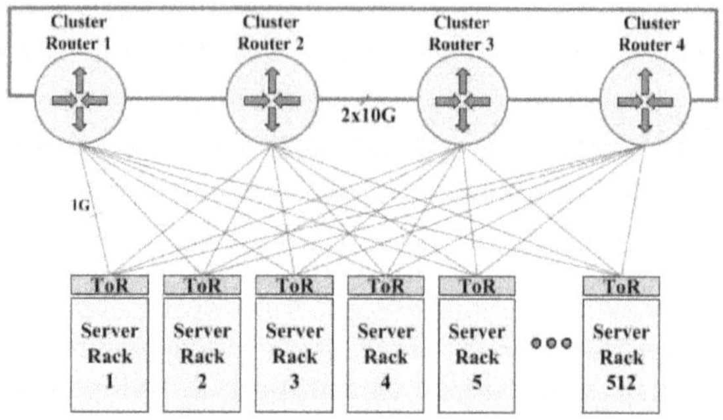

Figure 2: A traditional 2Tbps four-post cluster (2004). Top of Rack (ToR) switches serving 40 1G-connected servers were connected via 1G links to four 512 1G port Cluster Routers (CRs) connected with 10G sidelinks.

2. BACKGROUND AND RELATED WORK

The tremendous growth rate of our infrastructure served as key motivation for our work in datacenter networking. Figure 1 shows aggregate server communication rates since 2008. Traffic has increased 50x in this time period, roughly doubling every year. A combination of remote storage access [7, 14], large-scale data processing [10, 18], and interactive web services [4] drive our bandwidth demands.

In 2004, we deployed traditional cluster networks similar to [5]. Figure 2 depicts this "four-post" cluster architecture. We employed the highest density Ethernet switches available, 512 ports of 1GE, to build the spine of the network (CRs or cluster routers). Each Top of Rack (ToR) switch connected to all four of the cluster routers for both scale and fault tolerance.

With up to 40 servers per ToR, this approach supported 20k servers per cluster. However, high band-

Job Category	B/w (%)
Storage	49.3
Search Serving	26.2
Mail	7.4
Ad Stats	3.8
Rest of traffic	13.3

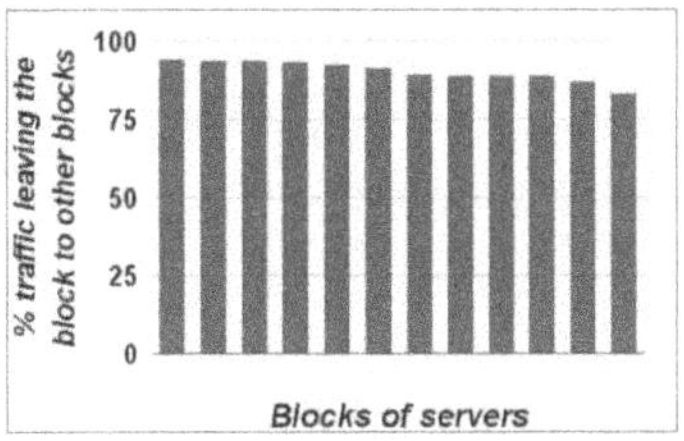

Figure 3: Mix of jobs in an example cluster with 12 blocks of servers (left). Fraction of traffic in each block destined for remote blocks (right).

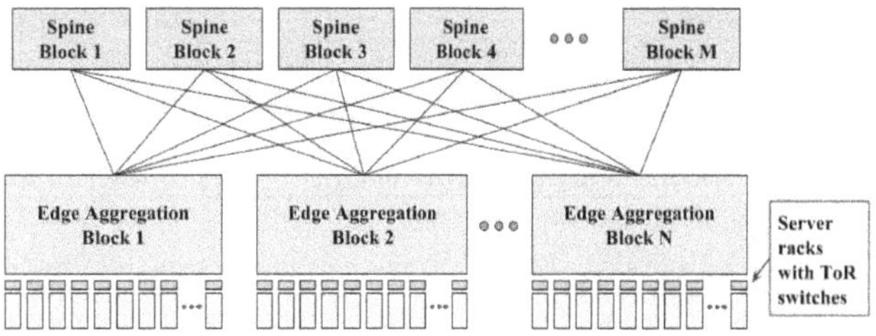

Figure 4: A generic 3 tier Clos architecture with edge switches (ToRs), aggregation blocks and spine blocks. All generations of Clos fabrics deployed in our datacenters follow variants of this architecture.

width applications had to fit under a single ToR to avoid the heavily oversubscribed ToR uplinks. Deploying large clusters was important to our services because there were many affiliated applications that benefited from high bandwidth communication. Consider large-scale data processing to produce and continuously refresh a search index, web search, and serving ads as affiliated applications. Larger clusters also substantially improve bin-packing efficiency for job scheduling by reducing stranding from cases where a job cannot be scheduled in any one cluster despite the aggregate availability of sufficient resources across multiple small clusters.

Maximum cluster scale is important for a more subtle reason. Power is distributed hierarchically at the granularity of the building, multi-Megawatt power generators, and physical datacenter rows. Each level of hierarchy represents a unit of failure and maintenance. For availability, cluster scheduling purposely spreads jobs across multiple rows. Similarly, the required redundancy in storage systems is in part determined by the fraction of a cluster that may simultaneously fail as a result of a power event. Hence, larger clusters lead to lower storage overhead and more efficient job scheduling while meeting diversity requirements.

Running storage across a cluster requires both rack and power diversity to avoid correlated failures. Hence, cluster data should be spread across the cluster's failure domains for resilience. However, such spreading naturally eliminates locality and drives the need for uniform bandwidth across the cluster. Consequently, storage placement and job scheduling have little locality in our cluster traffic, as shown in Figure 3. For a representative cluster with 12 blocks (groups of racks) of servers, we show the fraction of traffic destined for remote blocks. If traffic were spread uniformly across the cluster, we would expect 11/12 of the traffic (92%) to be destined for other blocks. Figure 3 shows approximately this distribution for the median block, with only moderate deviation.

While our traditional cluster network architecture largely met our scale needs, it fell short in terms of overall performance and cost. Bandwidth per host was severely limited to an average of 100Mbps. Packet drops associated with incast [8] and outcast [21] were severe pain points. Increasing bandwidth per server would have substantially increased cost per server and reduced cluster scale.

We realized that existing commercial solutions could not meet our scale, management, and cost requirements. Hence, we decided to build our own custom data center network hardware and software. We started with the key insight that we could scale cluster fabrics to near arbitrary size by leveraging Clos topologies (Figure 4) and the then-emerging (ca. 2003) merchant switching silicon industry [12]. Table 1 summarizes a number of the top-level challenges we faced in constructing and managing building-scale network fabrics. The following sections explain these challenges and the rationale for our approach in detail.

For brevity, we omit detailed discussion of related work in this paper. However, our topological approach, reliance on merchant silicon, and load balancing across multipath are substantially similar to contemporaneous research [2,15]. In addition to outlining the evolution of our network, we further describe inter cluster networking, network management issues, and detail our control protocols. Our centralized control protocols running on switch embedded processors are also related to subsequent substantial efforts in Software Defined Networking (SDN) [13]. Based on our experience in the datacenter, we later applied SDN to our Wide Area Network [19]. For the WAN, more CPU intensive traffic engineering and BGP routing protocols led us to move control protocols onto external servers with more plentiful CPU from the embedded CPU controllers we were able to utilize for our initial datacenter deployments.

Recent work on alternate network topologies such as HyperX [1], Dcell [17], BCube [16] and Jellyfish [22] deliver more efficient bandwidth for uniform random communication patterns. However, to date, we have found that the benefits of these topologies do not make up for the cabling, management, and routing challenges and complexity.

3. NETWORK EVOLUTION

3.1 Firehose 1.0

Table 2 summarizes the multiple generations of our

Challenge	Our Approach (Section Discussed in)
Introducing the network to production	Initially deploy as bag-on-the-side with a fail-safe big-red button (3.2)
High availability from cheaper components	Redundancy in fabric, diversity in deployment, robust software, necessary protocols only, reliable out of band control plane (3.2, 3.3, 5.1)
High fiber count for deployment	Cable bundling to optimize and expedite deployment (3.3)
Individual racks can leverage full uplink capacity to external clusters	Introduce Cluster Border Routers to aggregate external bandwidth shared by all server racks (4.1)
Incremental deployment	Depopulate switches and optics (3.3)
Routing scalability	Scalable in-house IGP, centralized topology view and route control (5.2)
Interoperate with external vendor gear	Use standard BGP between Cluster Border Routers and vendor gear (5.2.5)
Small on-chip buffers	Congestion window bounding on servers, ECN, dynamic buffer sharing of chip buffers, QoS (6.1)
Routing with massive multipath	Granular control over ECMP tables with proprietary IGP (5.1)
Operating at scale	Leverage existing server installation, monitoring software; tools build and operate fabric as a whole; move beyond individual chassis-centric network view; single cluster-wide configuration (5.3)
Inter cluster networking	Portable software, modular hardware in other applications in the network hierarchy (4.2)

Table 1: High-level summary of challenges we faced and our approach to address them.

Datacenter Generation	First Deployed	Merchant Silicon	ToR Config	Aggregation Block Config	Spine Block Config	Fabric Speed	Host Speed	Bisection BW
Four-Post CRs	2004	vendor	48x1G	-	-	10G	1G	2T
Firehose 1.0	2005	8x10G 4x10G (ToR)	2x10G up 24x1G down	2x32x10G (B)	32x10G (NB)	10G	1G	10T
Firehose 1.1	2006	8x10G	4x10G up 48x1G down	64x10G (B)	32x10G (NB)	10G	1G	10T
Watchtower	2008	16x10G	4x10G up 48x1G down	4x128x10G (NB)	128x10G (NB)	10G	nx1G	82T
Saturn	2009	24x10G	24x10G	4x288x10G (NB)	288x10G (NB)	10G	nx10G	207T
Jupiter	2012	16x40G	16x40G	8x128x40G (B)	128x40G (NB)	10/40G	nx10G/ nx40G	1.3P

Table 2: Multiple generations of datacenter networks. (B) indicates blocking, (NB) indicates Nonblocking.

cluster network. With our initial approach, Firehose 1.0 (or FH1.0), our nominal goal was to deliver 1Gbps of nonblocking bisection bandwidth to each of 10K servers. Figure 5 details the FH1.0 topology. Our starting point was 8x10G switches for the fabric and 4x10G switches for ToRs. The fabric switch was deployed with 4x10G ports facing up and 4x10G facing down in all stages but the topmost stage, which had all 8x10G ports facing down. The ToR switch delivered 2x10GE ports to the fabric and 24x1GE south-facing ports of which 20x1GE were connected to servers. Each aggregation block hosted 16 ToRs (320 machines) and exposed 32x10G ports towards 32 spine blocks. Each spine block had 32x10G towards 32 aggregation blocks resulting in a fabric that scaled to 10K machines at 1G average bandwidth to any machine in the fabric.

A key drawback of the topology was the low radix of the ToR switch, which caused issues when links failed. If the left uplink of a source ToR and the right uplink of a destination ToR failed within a MTTR window, machines on these ToRs could not communicate with each other even though they could communicate with other machines - an intransitive disconnect not handled well by applications.

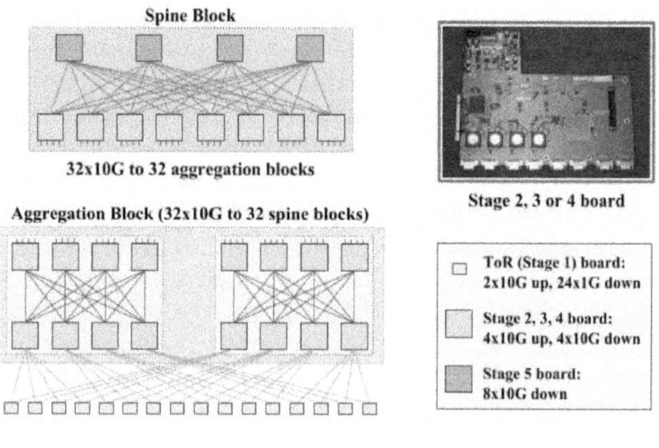

Figure 5: Firehose 1.0 topology. Top right shows a sample 8x10G port fabric board in Firehose 1.0, which formed Stages 2, 3 or 4 of the topology.

Since we did not have any experience building switches but we did have experience building servers, we attempted to integrate the switching fabric into the servers via a PCI board. See top right inset in Figure 5. However, the uptime of servers was less than ideal. Servers crashed and were upgraded more fre-

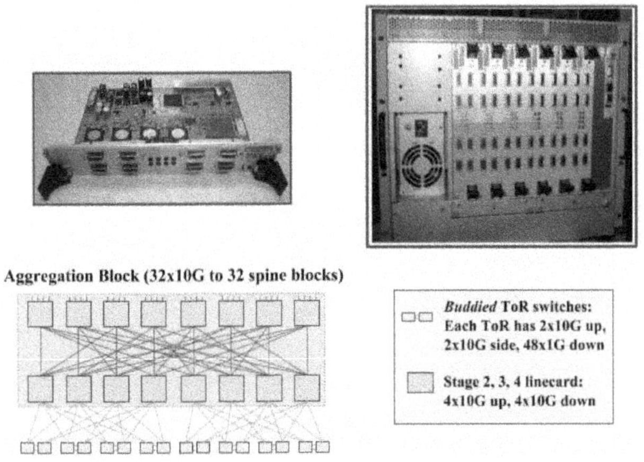

Figure 6: Firehose 1.1 packaging and topology. The top left picture shows a linecard version of the board from Figure 5. The top right picture shows a Firehose 1.1 chassis housing 6 such linecards. The bottom figure shows the aggregation block in Firehose 1.1, which was different from Firehose 1.0.

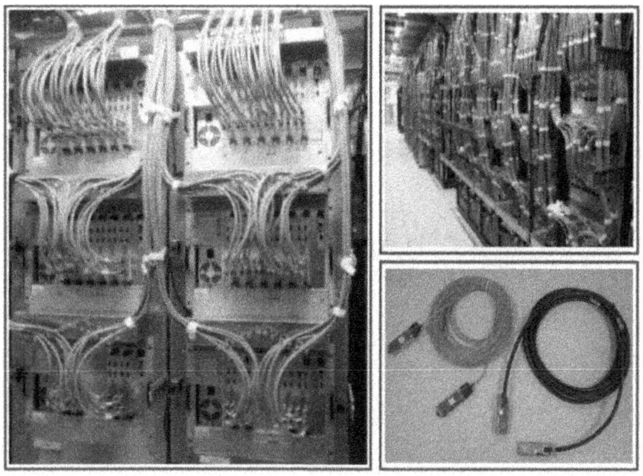

Figure 7: Two Firehose racks (left), each with 3 chassis with bulky CX4 cables from remote racks. The top right figure shows an aisle of cabled racks.

quently than desired with long reboot times. Network disruptions from server failure were especially problematic for servers housing ToRs connecting multiple other servers to the first stage of the topology.

The resulting wiring complexity for server to server connectivity, electrical reliability issues, availability and general issues associated with our first foray into switching doomed the effort to never seeing production traffic. At the same time, we consider FH1.0 to be a landmark effort internally. Without it and the associated learning, the efforts that followed would not have been possible.

3.2 Firehose 1.1: First Production Clos

Our first production deployment of a custom datacenter cluster fabric was called Firehose 1.1 (or FH1.1), a variation of the FH1.0 architecture. We had learned from FH1.0 to not use regular servers to house switch chips. Thus, we built custom enclosures that standardized around the Compact PCI chassis each with 6 independent linecards and a dedicated Single-Board Computer (SBC) to control the linecards using PCI. See insets in Figure 6. The fabric chassis did not contain any backplane to interconnect the switch chips. All ports connected to external copper cables that were wired on the datacenter floor. The linecards were a different form factor of the same boards used in FH1.0 for stages 2-5. We built a separate out-of-band Control Plane Network (CPN) to configure and manage the SBCs of the fabric.

The FH1.1 topology was a variant of the one used in FH1.0. While the spine block was identical to FH1.0, the edge aggregation block illustrated in Figure 6 had a few differences. We used two 4x10G+24x1G switch chips side connected on the board with 2x10G links for ToRs. The resulting configuration was a ToR switch with 4x10G uplinks and 48x1G links to servers. ToRs were developed as separate 1RU switches each with its own CPU controller. To scale to 20k machines with at most 2:1 oversubscription, we decided to *buddy* two ToR switches together. Of the 4x10G uplinks in each ToR, two were connected to the fabric while two were connected sideways to the paired ToR. Traffic from machines under a ToR could use all four uplinks to burst to the fabric, though bandwidth under contention would be lower. The stage 2 and 3 switches within an aggregation block were cabled in a single block (vs. 2 disjoint blocks in FH1.0) in a configuration similar to a Flat Neighborhood Network [11]. With up to 40 machines under each ToR, the FH1.1 aggregation block could scale to 640 machines at 2:1 oversubscription. The changes in the aggregation block allowed Firehose 1.1 to scale to 2x the number of machines while being much more robust to link failures compared to FH1.0.

The copper interconnect for FH1.1 was a significant challenge. Figure 7 shows the chassis in production deployment. Building, testing, and deploying the network was labor intensive and error prone. The 14m length restrictions of our CX4 cables required careful placement of each component of the multistage topology. The longest distances were typically between our ToRs and the next stage of the Firehose switching infrastructure. To improve deployability, we worked on a solution to run fiber only for this stage of the network topology. We collaborated with vendors to develop custom Electrical/Optical/Electrical (EOE) cables for this interconnect. The orange cable in the bottom right of Figure 7 is an EOE cable capable of spanning 100m compared to the bulkier 14m CX4 cable to its right.

A major concern with FH1.1 in production was deploying an unproven new network technology for our mission critical applications. To mitigate risk, we deployed Firehose 1.1 in conjunction with our legacy four-post cluster fabrics as shown in Figure 8. We maintained a simple configuration; the ToR would forward default traffic to the four-post cluster (e.g., for connectivity to external clusters/data centers) while more spe-

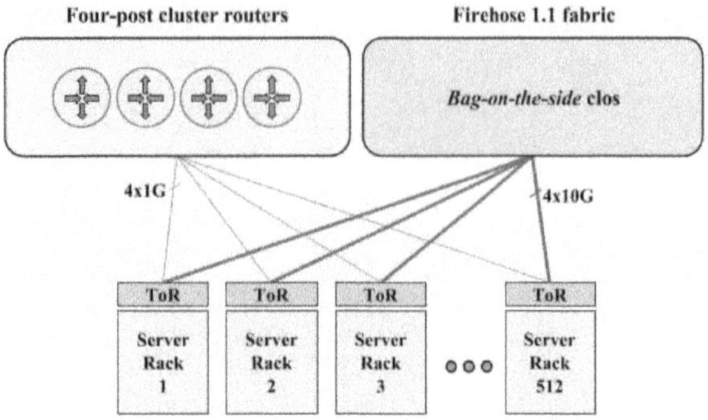

Figure 8: Firehose 1.1 deployed as a *bag-on-the-side Clos* fabric.

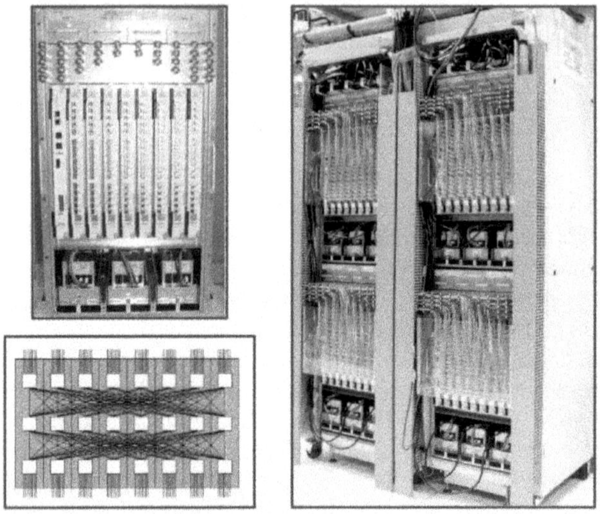

Figure 9: A 128x10G port Watchtower chassis (top left). The internal non-blocking topology over eight linecards (bottom left). Four chassis housed in two racks cabled with fiber (right).

cific intra-cluster traffic would use the uplinks to Firehose 1.1. Since our four-post cluster employed 1G links, we only needed to reserve four 1GE ToR ports. We built a *Big Red Button* fail-safe to configure the ToRs to avoid Firehose uplinks in case of catastrophic failure.

3.3 Watchtower: Global Deployment

Our deployment experience with Firehose 1.1 was largely positive. We showed that services could enjoy substantially more bandwidth than with traditional architectures, all with lower cost per unit bandwidth. Firehose 1.1 went into production with a handful of clusters and remained operational until recently. The main drawback to Firehose 1.1 was the deployment challenges with the external copper cabling.

We used these experiences to design Watchtower, our third-generation cluster fabric. The key idea was to leverage the next-generation merchant silicon switch chips, 16x10G, to build a traditional switch chassis with a backplane. Figure 9 shows the half rack Watchtower chassis along with its internal topology and cabling. Watchtower consists of eight line cards, each with three switch chips. Two chips on each linecard have half their ports externally facing, for a total of 16x10GE SFP+ ports. All three chips also connect to a backplane for port to port connectivity. Watchtower deployment, as seen in Figure 9 was substantially easier than the earlier Firehose deployments. The larger bandwidth density of the switching silicon also allowed us to build larger fabrics with more bandwidth to individual servers, a necessity as servers were employing an ever-increasing number of cores.

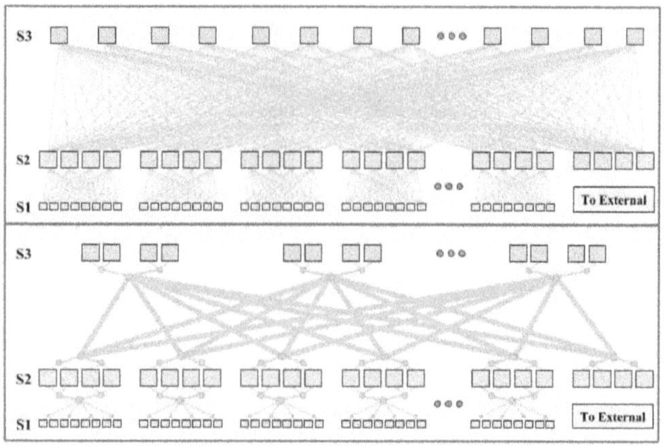

Figure 10: Reducing deployment complexity by bundling cables. Stages 1, 2 and 3 in the fabric are labeled S1, S2 and S3, respectively.

# Individual cables	15872
# S2-S3 bundles (16-way)	512
Normalized cost of fiber/m in 16-way bundle	55%
# S2-ToR bundles (8-way)	960
Normalized cost of fiber/m in 8-way bundle	60%
# Total cable bundles	1472
Normalized cost of fiber/m with bundling (capex + opex)	57%

Table 3: Benefits of cable bundling in Watchtower.

Fiber bundling further reduced the cabling complexity of Watchtower clusters. Figure 10 shows a Watchtower fabric deployment without any cable bundling. Individual fibers of varying length need to be pulled from each chassis location, leading to significant deployment overhead. The bottom figure shows how bundling can substantially reduce complexity. We deploy two chassis in each rack and co-locate two racks. We can then pull cable bundles to the midpoint of the co-located racks, where each bundle is split to each rack and then further to each chassis.

Finally, manufacturing fiber in bundles is more cost effective than individual strands. Cable bundling helped reduce fiber cost (capex + opex) by nearly 40% and expedited bringup of Watchtower fabric by multiple weeks. Table 3 summarizes the bundling and cost savings.

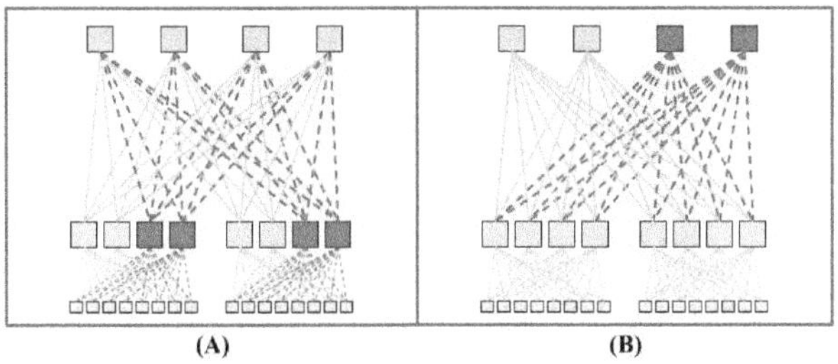

Figure 11: Two ways to depopulate the fabric for 50% capacity.

Figure 10 also depicts how we started connecting our cluster fabric to the external inter cluster networking. We defer detailed discussion to Section 4.

While Watchtower cluster fabrics were substantially cheaper and of greater scale than anything available for purchase, the absolute cost remained substantial. We used two observations to drive additional cost optimizations. First, there is natural variation in the bandwidth demands of individual clusters. Second, the dominant cost of our fabrics was in the optics and the associated fiber.

Hence, we enabled Watchtower fabrics to support depopulated deployment, where we initially deployed only 50% of the maximum bisection bandwidth. Importantly, as the bandwidth demands of a depop cluster grew, we could fully populate it to 100% bisection in place. Figure 11 shows two high-level options, (A) and (B), to depopulate switches, optics, and fiber, shown in red. (A) achieves 50% capacity by depopulating half of the S2 switches and all fiber and optics touching any depopulated S2 switch. (B) instead depopulates half S3 switches and associated fiber and optics. (A) shows 2x more depopulated elements vs. (B) for the same fabric capacity.

(A) requires all spine S3 chassis to be deployed up front even though edge aggregation blocks may be deployed slowly leading to higher initial cost. (B) has a more gradual upfront cost as all spine chassis are not deployed initially. Another advantage of (B) over (A) is that each ToR has twice the burst bandwidth.

In Watchtower and Saturn (Section 3.4) fabrics, we chose option (A) because it maximized cost savings. For Jupiter fabrics (Section 3.5), we moved to option (B) because the upfront cost of deploying the entire spine increased as we moved toward building-size fabrics and the benefits of higher ToR bandwidth became more evident.

3.4 Saturn: Fabric Scaling and 10G Servers

Saturn was the next iteration of our cluster architecture. The principal goals were to respond to continued increases in server bandwidth demands and to further increase maximum cluster scale. Saturn was built from 24x10G merchant silicon building blocks. A

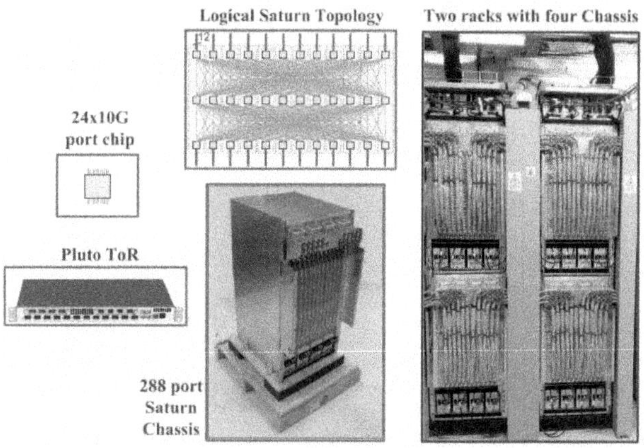

Figure 12: Components of a Saturn fabric. A 24x10G Pluto ToR Switch and a 12-linecard 288x10G Saturn chassis (including logical topology) built from the same switch chip. Four Saturn chassis housed in two racks cabled with fiber (right).

Saturn chassis supports 12-linecards to provide a 288 port non-blocking switch. These chassis are coupled with new Pluto single-chip ToR switches; see Figure 12. In the default configuration, Pluto supports 20 servers with 4x10G provisioned to the cluster fabric for an average bandwidth of 2 Gbps for each server. For more bandwidth-hungry servers, we could configure the Pluto ToR with 8x10G uplinks and 16x10G to servers providing 5 Gbps to each server. Importantly, servers could burst at 10Gbps across the fabric for the first time.

3.5 Jupiter: A 40G Datacenter-scale Fabric

As bandwidth requirements per server continued to grow, so did the need for uniform bandwidth across all clusters in the datacenter. With the advent of dense 40G capable merchant silicon, we could consider expanding our Clos fabric across the entire datacenter subsuming the inter-cluster networking layer. This would potentially enable an unprecedented pool of compute and storage for application scheduling. Critically, the unit of maintenance could be kept small enough relative to the size of the fabric that most applications could now be agnostic to network maintenance windows unlike previous generations of the network.

Jupiter, our next generation datacenter fabric, needed to scale more than 6x the size of our largest existing fabric. Unlike previous iterations, we set a requirement for incremental deployment of new network technology because the cost in resource stranding and downtime was too high. Upgrading networks by simply forklifting existing clusters stranded hosts already in production. With Jupiter, new technology would need to be introduced into the network *in situ*. Hence, the fabric must support heterogeneous hardware and speeds. Because of the sheer scale, events in the network (both planned and unplanned) were expected to

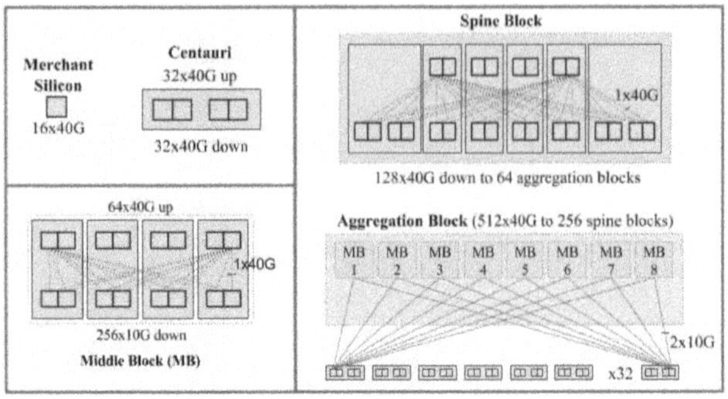

Figure 13: Building blocks used in the Jupiter topology.

be more frequent, requiring Jupiter to react robustly and gracefully to such events.

At Jupiter scale, we had to design the fabric through individual building blocks. However, the size of the building block was a key point of discussion. At one extreme was the Firehose approach, where each switch chip was cabled to others on the datacenter floor. On the other extreme, we could go the way of Watchtower and Saturn fabrics - i.e., build the largest non-blocking, two-stage chassis possible with the current merchant silicon, employing the chassis in various roles within the fabric.

For the first generation of Jupiter (Figure 13), we chose a middle path regarding building block size. Our unit of deployment was a Centauri chassis, a 4RU chassis housing two linecards, each with two switch chips with 16x40G ports controlled by a separate CPU linecard. Each port could be configured in 4x10G or 40G mode. There were no backplane data connections between these chips; all ports were accessible on the front panel of the chassis.

We employed the Centauri switch as a ToR switch with each of the 4 chips serving a subnet of machines. In one ToR configuration, we configured each chip with 48x10G to servers and 16x10G to the fabric. Servers could be configured with 40G burst bandwidth for the first time in production (see Table 2). Four Centauris made up a Middle Block (MB) for use in the aggregation block. The logical topology of an MB was a 2-stage blocking network, with 256x10G links available for ToR connectivity and 64x40G available for connectivity to the rest of the fabric through the spine.

Each ToR chip connects to eight such MBs with dual redundant 10G links. The dual redundancy aids fast reconvergence for the common case of single link failure or maintenance. Each aggregation block exposes 512x40G (full pop) or 256x40G (depop) links towards the spine blocks. Jupiter employs six Centauris in a spine block exposing 128x40G ports towards the aggregation blocks. We limited the size of Jupiter to 64 aggregation blocks for dual redundant links between each spine block and aggregation block pair at the largest scale, once again for local reconvergence on single link failure.

Figure 14: Jupiter Middle blocks housed in racks.

We deploy four MBs in a single networking rack as depicted in Figure 14. Similarly, a spine networking rack houses two pre-wired spine blocks. Cabling on the datacenter floor involves connecting fiber cable bundles between these networking racks and also to ToR switches atop server racks. In its largest configuration, Jupiter supports 1.3 Pbps bisection bandwidth among servers.

4. EXTERNAL CONNECTIVITY

4.1 WCC: Decommissioning Cluster Routers

In this section, we describe how we employed existing cluster networking building blocks to improve the performance and robustness of our inter cluster networking fabrics. Chronologically, this work took place between Watchtower and Saturn.

Through the first few Watchtower deployments, all cluster fabrics were deployed as *bag-on-the-side* networks coexisting with legacy networks (Figure 8). Time and experience ameliorated safety concerns, tipping the balance in favor of reducing the operational complexity, cost, and performance limitations of deploying two parallel networks. Limiting ToR burst bandwidth out of the cluster was particularly restrictive when migrating services or copying large search indexes across clusters.

Hence, our next goal was to decommission the Cluster Routers (CRs) by connecting the fabric directly to the inter-cluster networking layer with Cluster Border Routers (CBRs). This effort was internally called WCC. Figure 15 shows various choices for external connectivity: i) reserve some links from each ToR, ii) reserve ports in each aggregation block, iii) reserve ports in each spine block, iv) build a separate aggregation block for external connectivity. Note that i) was similar to our approach in Firehose 1.1. Further, both options i) and ii) could not improve external burst bandwidth assuming shortest path routing.

However, options iii) and iv) provide the entire pool of external bandwidth to each aggregation block. We

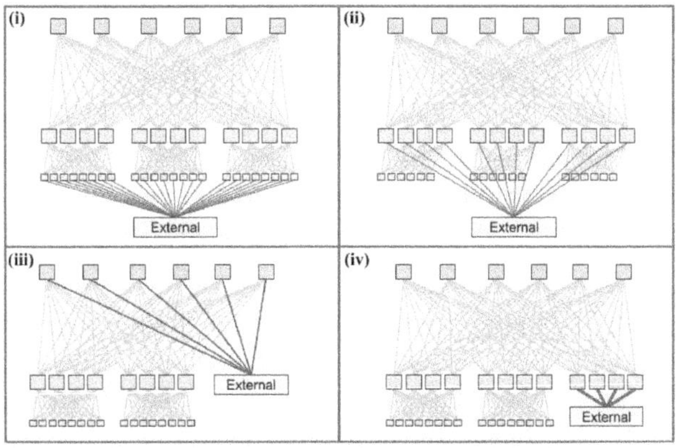

Figure 15: Four options to connect to the external network layer.

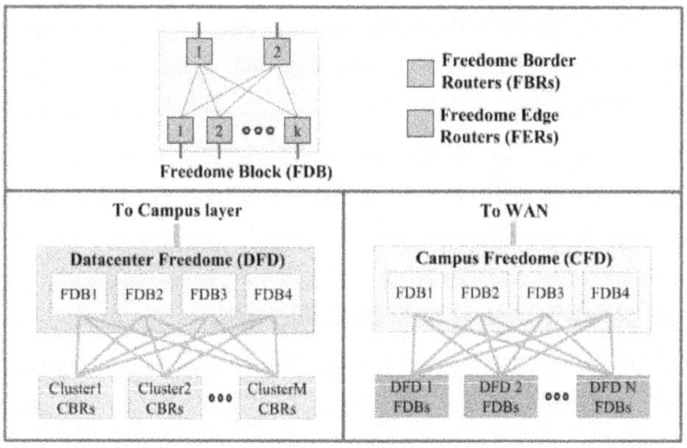

Figure 16: Two-stage fabrics used for inter-cluster and intra-campus connectivity.

chose option iv) because we wanted an isolated layer of switches to peer with external routers rather than spreading peering functionality across the entire set of spine switches. We deemed this approach safer because we wanted to limit the blast radius from an external facing configuration change and because it limited the places where we would have to integrate our in-house IGP (Section 5.2) with external routing protocols.

As a rule of thumb, we allocated 10% of aggregate intra-cluster bandwidth for external connectivity using one to three aggregation blocks. These aggregation blocks were physically and topologically identical to those used for ToR connectivity. However, we reallocated the ports normally employed for ToR connectivity to connect to external fabrics.

We configured parallel links between each CBR switch in these blocks and an external switch as Link Aggregation Groups (LAGs) or trunks. We used standard external BGP (eBGP) routing between the CBRs and the inter-cluster networking switches. CBR switches learned the default route via BGP from the external peers and redistributed the route through Firepath, our intra-cluster IGP protocol (Section 5.2).

WCC enabled the cluster fabric to be truly standalone and unlocked high throughput bulk data transfer between clusters. Moreover, the modular hardware and software of the CBR switch would find application in diverse use cases in our networking hierarchy.

4.2 Inter-Cluster Networking

We deploy multiple clusters within the same building and multiple buildings on the same campus. Given the relationship between physical distance and network cost, our job scheduling and resource allocation infrastructure leverages campus-level and building-level locality to co-locate loosely affiliated services as close to one another as possible. The CBRs developed for WCC enabled clusters to connect to inter cluster networks with massive bandwidth. Each aggregation block supported 2.56Tbps of external connectivity in Watchtower fabrics and 5.76Tbps in Saturn fabrics. However, our external networking layers were still based on expensive and port-constrained vendor gear. The third step in the evolution of our network fabrics involved replacing vendor-based inter cluster switching. Our approach, Freedome, targets massive inter-cluster bandwidth within buildings and the campus at lower cost than existing solutions.

We employed the BGP capability we developed in our cluster routers (Section 5.2.5) to build two-stage fabrics that could speak BGP at both the inter cluster and intra campus connectivity layers. See Figure 16. We configure a collection of routers in blocks called Freedome Blocks as shown in the top figure. Each block exposes 8x more south-facing ports (cluster facing) than north-facing ports (next-level in the hierarchy). Each block has two types of switch roles; the Freedome Edge Routers delivered south-facing ports while the Freedome Border Routers delivered the north-facing ports. The Freedome Block employs eBGP to connect to both north and south facing peers. We use iBGP internal to each block with the Border Routers configured as route reflectors [6].

A Datacenter Freedome typically comprises 4 independent blocks to connect multiple clusters in the same datacenter building. Inter-cluster traffic local to the same building would travel from the source cluster's CBR layer to the Datacenter Freedome, typically staying local to the Edge Router layer, and finally to the CBR layer of the destination cluster. We connect the Freedome Border Router ports to the campus connectivity layer to the north. The bottom left figure in Figure 16 depicts a Datacenter Freedome. We provision 8x more bandwidth for traffic within a building than for traffic between buildings in the same campus.

Recursively, a Campus Freedome also typically comprises 4 independent Freedome Blocks to connect multiple Datacenter Freedomes in a campus on the south and the WAN connectivity layer on the north-facing side. The bottom right figure in Figure 16 depicts a Campus Freedome.

Deploying independent blocks is crucial for maintaining performance on Freedomes since each block can be independently removed from service, or *drained*, and upgraded with an aggregate capacity degradation of 25%. Once we had rolled out the Freedomes for campus networking, the BGP router would also find application in our WAN deployment [19].

5. SOFTWARE CONTROL

5.1 Discussion

As we set out to build the control plane for our network hardware, we faced the following high level trade-off: deploy traditional decentralized routing protocols such as OSPF/IS-IS/BGP to manage our fabrics or build a custom control plane to leverage some of the unique characteristics and homogeneity of our cluster network. Traditional routing protocols had the advantage of being proven and robust.

We chose to build our own control plane for a number of reasons. First, and most important, existing routing protocols did not at the time have good support for multipath, equal-cost forwarding. Second, there were no high quality open source routing stacks a decade ago. Further, it was a substantial amount of work to modify our hardware switch stack to tunnel control-protocol packets running inline between hardware line cards to protocol processes. Third, we were concerned about the protocol overhead of running broadcast-based routing protocols across fabrics of the scale we were targeting with hundreds or even thousands of switching elements. Scaling techniques like OSPF Areas [20] appeared hard to configure and to reason about [23]. Fourth, network manageability was a key concern and maintaining hundreds of independent switch stacks and, e.g., BGP configurations seemed daunting.

Our approach was driven by the need to route across a largely static topology with massive multipath. Each switch had a predefined role according to its location in the fabric and could be configured as such. A centralized solution where a route controller collected dynamic link state information and redistributed this link state to all switches over a reliable out-of-band Control Plane Network (CPN) appeared to be substantially simpler and more efficient from a computation and communication perspective. The switches could then calculate forwarding tables based on current link state as deltas relative to the underlying, known static topology that was pushed to all switches.

Overall, we treated the datacenter network as a single fabric with tens of thousands of ports rather than a collection of hundreds of autonomous switches that had to dynamically discover information about the fabric. We were, at this time, inspired by the success of large-scale distributed storage systems with a centralized manager [14]. Our design informed the control architecture for both Jupiter datacenter networks and Google's B4 WAN [19]. Details of Jupiter's control architecture are beyond the scope of this paper.

5.2 Routing

We now present the key components of Firepath, our routing architecture for Firehose, Watchtower, and Saturn fabrics. A number of these components anticipate some of the principles of modern Software Defined Networking, especially in using logically centralized state and control. First, all switches are configured with the baseline or intended topology. The switches learn actual configuration and link state through pair-wise neighbor discovery. Next, routing proceeds with each switch exchanging its local view of connectivity with a centralized Firepath master, which redistributes global link state to all switches. Switches locally calculate forwarding tables based on this current view of network topology. To maintain robustness, we implement a Firepath master election protocol. Finally, we leverage standard BGP only for route exchange at the edge of our fabric, redistributing BGP-learned routes through Firepath.

5.2.1 Neighbor Discovery to Verify Connectivity

Building a fabric with thousands of cables invariably leads to multiple cabling errors. Moreover, correctly cabled links may be re-connected incorrectly after maintenance such as linecard replacement. Allowing traffic to use a miscabled link can lead to forwarding loops. Links that fail unidirectionally or develop high packet error rates should also be avoided and scheduled for replacement. To address these issues, we developed *Neighbor Discovery* (ND), an online liveness and peer correctness checking protocol.

Neighbor Discovery (ND) uses the configured view of cluster topology together with a switch's local ID to determine the expected peer IDs of its local ports. It regularly exchanges its local port ID, expected peer port ID, discovered peer port ID, and link error signal. Doing so allows ND on both ends of a link to verify correct cabling.

The Interface Manager (IFM) module on each switch's embedded stack continuously monitors the ND state of each port, declaring a port up to the routing process only if it is both PHY UP and ND UP. Linecard LEDs display the ND status of each port to assist physical debugging in the field. Our monitoring infrastructure also collects and displays all link status on various dashboards. ND also serves as a keepalive protocol to ensure peers are alive and functional. If the remote software has crashed or shut down, peer ND instances will eventually report the failure to the interface manager, which in turn will declare the interface down to the routing process.

5.2.2 Firepath

We support Layer 3 routing all the way to the ToRs via a custom Interior Gateway Protocol (IGP), Firepath. Each ToR implements a Layer 2 subnet, i.e.,

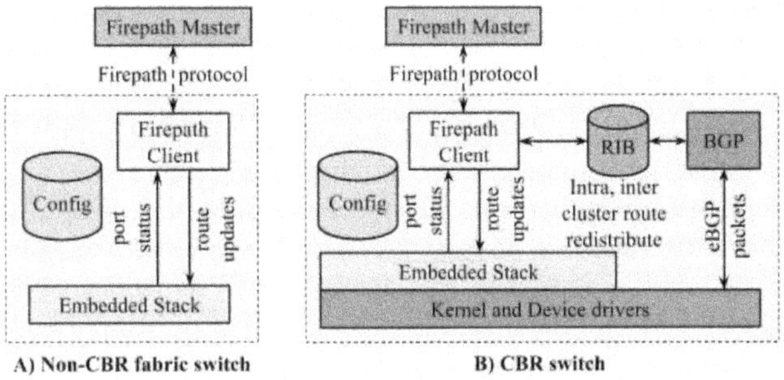

Figure 17: Firepath component interactions.

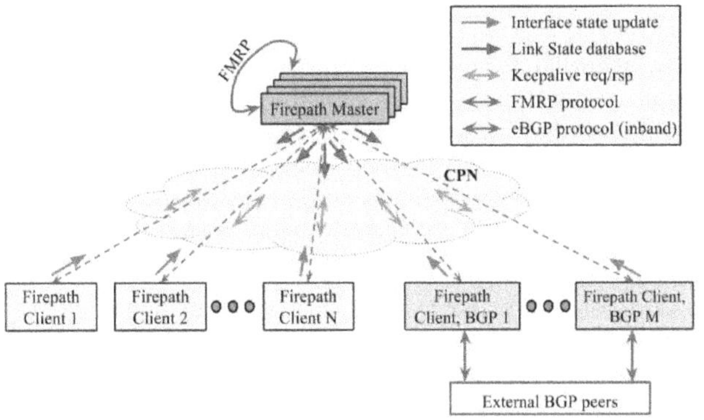

Figure 18: Protocol messages between Firepath client and Firepath master, between Firepath masters and between CBR and external BGP speakers.

all machines under one ToR are part of a broadcast domain. The L3 subnets assigned to ToRs are aligned to aid aggregation in limited forwarding tables in merchant silicon.

Firepath implements centralized topology state distribution, but distributed forwarding table computation with two main components. A Firepath client runs on each fabric switch, and a set of redundant Firepath masters run on a selected subset of spine switches. Clients communicate with the elected master over the Control Plane Network (CPN). Figure 17 shows the interaction between the Firepath client and the rest of the switch stack. Figure 18 illustrates the protocol message exchange between various routing components.

At startup, each client is loaded with the static topology of the entire fabric called the cluster config. Each client collects the state of its local interfaces from the embedded stack's interface manager and transmits this state to the master. The master constructs a Link State Database (LSD) with a monotonically increasing version number and distributes it to all clients via UDP/IP multicast over the CPN. After the initial full update, a subsequent LSD contains only the diffs from the previous state. The entire network's LSD fits within a 64KB payload. On receiving an LSD update, each client computes shortest path forwarding with Equal-Cost Multi-Path (ECMP) and programs the hardware forwarding tables local to its switch. To prevent overwhelming the clients, the master throttles the number of LSD changes it sends to clients.

Failure Event	**Recovery time (ms)**	**Convergence type**
S2-S3 link	125	Local; affected S2, S3 chassis route around failed link
S3 chassis	325	Local; adjacent S2s route around failed S3
ToR-S2 link	4000	Non-local; all S3s avoid one S2 for impacted ToR
S2 chassis	325	Local; adjacent S3s, ToRs route around failed S2

Table 4: Summary of convergence times in a Saturn cluster.

The master also maintains a keepalive protocol with the clients. It sends periodic heartbeat messages with its master ID and the current LSD version number. If a client loses synchronization with the master, e.g., by missing an LSD message, it requests a full LSD update.

5.2.3 Path Diversity and Convergence on Failures

For rapid convergence on interface state change, each client computes the new routing solution and updates the forwarding tables independently upon receiving an LSD update. Since clients do not coordinate during convergence, the network can experience small transient loss while the network transitions from the old to the new state. However, assuming churn is transient, all switches eventually act on a globally consistent view of network state.

Table 4 shows the reaction time to route around component failures. Due to high path diversity, most failures require only local convergence, i.e., elements adjacent to the failure typically have multiple other viable next hops to the eventual destination. The switch's embedded stack can quickly prune the failed link/next hop from an ECMP group containing the impacted link. The ToR-S2 link failure requires non-local convergence and hence takes longer. In this case, all S3 chassis must avoid one particular S2 chassis for the IP prefix of the impacted ToR switch. Even this case can be optimized if ToRs have multiple links to an S2 switch.

Firepath LSD updates contain routing changes due to planned and unplanned network events. The frequency of such events in a typical cluster (from Figure 3) is approximately 2,000 times/month, 70 times/day, or 3 times/hour.

5.2.4 Firepath Master Redundancy Protocol

The centralized Firepath master is a critical component in the Firepath system. It collects and distributes interface states and synchronizes the Firepath clients via a keepalive protocol. For availability, we run redundant master instances on pre-selected spine switches. Switches know the candidate masters via their static configuration.

The Firepath Master Redundancy Protocol (FMRP) handles master election and bookkeeping between the active and backup masters. The active master maintains a keepalive with the backup masters and ensures that the current LSD is in sync with the backup masters on a CPN FMRP multicast group. On startup, a master enters an *Init* state where it invalidates its LSD and waits to hear from an existing master. If it hears a keepalive from an existing master, it enters a *backup* state. Otherwise, it enters the *electing* state where it broadcasts an election request to other master candidates. Typically, the winner of the election is the master with the latest LSD version. Alternately, a preemption mode elects the master based strictly on a priority such as highest IP address. Newly elected masters enter a *master* state.

FMRP has been robust in production over multiple years and many clusters. Since master election is *sticky*, a misbehaving master candidate does not cause changes in mastership and churn in the network. In the rare case of a CPN partition, a multi-master situation may result, which immediately alerts network operators for manual intervention.

5.2.5 Cluster Border Router

Our cluster fabrics peer with external networks via BGP. To this end, we integrated a BGP stack on the CBR with Firepath. This integration has two key aspects: i) enabling the BGP stack on the CBRs to communicate inband with external BGP speakers, and ii) supporting route exchange between the BGP stack and Firepath. Figure 17B shows the interaction between the BGP stack, Firepath, and the switch kernel and embedded stack.

For i) we created a Linux network device (netdev) for each external trunk interface running eBGP. As shown in Figure 18, BGP protocol packets flow across inband links; we use the embedded stack's packet I/O engine to vector these control packets via the netdevs to the BGP stack running on the embedded stack.

For ii) a proxy process on the CBR exchanges routes between BGP and Firepath. This process exports intra-cluster routes from Firepath into the BGP RIB and picks up inter-cluster routes from the BGP RIB, redistributing them into Firepath. We made a simplifying assumption by summarizing routes to the cluster-prefix for external BGP advertisement and the /0 default route to Firepath. In this way, Firepath manages only a single route for all outbound traffic, assuming all CBRs are viable for traffic leaving the cluster. Conversely, we assume all CBRs are viable to reach any part of the cluster from an external network. The rich path diversity inherent to Clos fabrics enables both these simplifying assumptions.

5.3 Configuration and Management

Next, we describe our approach to cluster network configuration and management prior to Jupiter. Our primary goal was to manufacture compute clusters and network fabrics as fast as possible throughout the entire fleet. Thus, we favored simplicity and reproducibility over flexibility. We supported only a limited number of fabric parameters, used to generate all the information needed by various groups to deploy the network, and built simple tools and processes to operate the network. As a result, the system was easily adopted by a wide set of technical and non-technical support personnel responsible for building data centers.

5.3.1 Configuration Generation Approach

Our key strategy was to view the entire cluster network top-down as a single static fabric composed of switches with pre-assigned roles, rather than bottom-up as a collection of switches individually configured and assembled into a fabric. We also limited the number of choices at the cluster-level, essentially providing a simple menu of fabric sizes and options, based on the projected maximum size of a cluster as well as the chassis type available.

The configuration system is a pipeline that accepts a specification of basic cluster-level parameters such as the size of the spine, base IP prefix of the cluster and the list of ToRs and their rack indexes. It then generates a set of output files for various operations groups: i) a simplified bill of materials for supply chain operations; ii) rack layout details, cable bundling and port mapping for datacenter operations; iii) CPN design and switch addressing details (e.g., DNS) for network operations; iv) updates to network and monitoring databases and systems; v) a common fabric configuration file for the switches; and vi) summary data to feed graphical views to audit the logical topology and cluster specifications.

We distribute a single monolithic cluster configuration to all switches (chassis and ToRs) in the cluster. Each switch simply extracts its relevant portion. Doing so simplifies configuration generation but every switch has to be updated with the new config each time the cluster configuration changes. Since cluster configurations do not change frequently, this additional overhead is not significant and often necessary since Firepath requires global topology state.

5.3.2 Switch Management Approach

We designed a simple management system on the switches. We did not require most of the standard network management protocols. Instead, we focused on protocols to integrate with our existing server management infrastructure. We benefited from not drawing arbitrary lines between server and network infrastructure; in fact, we set out to make switches essentially look like regular machines to the rest of fleet. Examples include the image management and installation, large scale monitoring, syslog collection, and global alerting.

The embedded stack exports a single Common Management Access Layer (CMAL) interface for external systems to manage the device. We limit administra-

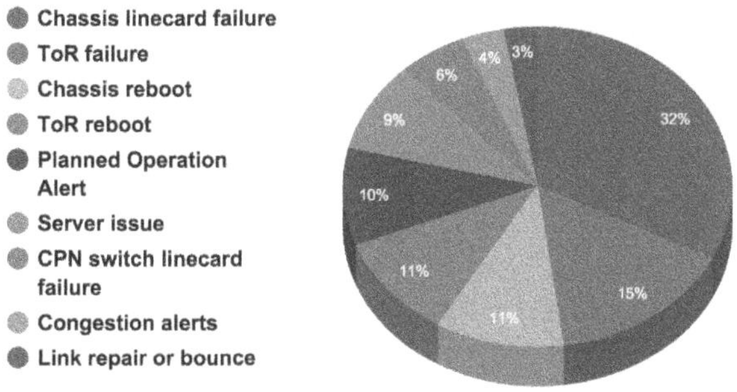

Figure 19: Alerts in Firehose/Watchtower fabrics over 9 months in '08-'09.

tive updates to draining or disabling specific ports. Since there are multiple software components running on each switch, they must all simultaneously accept a new switch configuration. Hence, we employ a standard two-phase verify-commit protocol for components on the switch orchestrated by CMAL to deploy new switch configurations.

Management clients retrieve switch status through a simple API. Important services include a local CLI for an operator to read switch status for debugging, a minimal SNMP agent to support legacy SNMP monitors, and a specific monitoring agent that exports data to the network and machine monitoring system. This last client allows us to reuse all the scalable monitoring, alerting, time-series databases (TSDB) systems built to manage our server machine fleet, saving a huge amount of work. Figure 19 presents a sample breakdown of the type of monitoring/alerts observed in our clusters for a period of 9 months in 2008-2009. The high incidence of chassis linecard failures was due to memory errors on a particular version of merchant silicon and is not reflective of a trend in linecard failure rates.

5.3.3 Fabric Operation and Management

For fabric operation and management, we continued with the theme of leveraging the existing scalable infrastructure built to manage and operate the server fleet. We built additional tools that were aware of the network fabric as a whole, thus hiding complexity in our management software. As a result, we could focus on developing only a few tools that were truly specific to our large scale network deployments, including link/switch qualification, fabric expansion/upgrade, and network troubleshooting at scale. Also important was collaborating closely with the network operations team at Google to provide training before introducing each major network fabric generation, expediting the ramp of each technology across the fleet.

Figure 20 summarizes our approach to fabric software upgrades. Rather than support in-service firmware upgrade on our switches, we exploit fabric redundancy for upgrades. We would like the degradation in fabric capacity not to exceed 25%. The figure shows two ways to upgrade the fabric chassis in multiple steps in the Clos topology. The left figure divides all chassis into four sets. When upgrading the red set, links in dashed red are disabled. However, the figure illustrates that the fabric capacity degrades to 56.25% (75%*75%). The right figure shows a more graceful but more time consuming upgrade process involving eight sets. Upgrading one switch at a time would take too long.

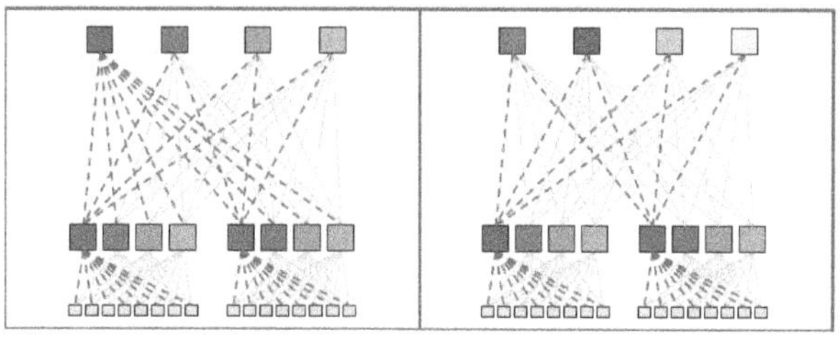

Figure 20: Multi-color fabric chassis upgrade.

Troubleshooting misbehaving traffic flows in a network with such high path diversity is daunting for operators. Therefore, we extended debugging utilities such as traceroute and ICMP to be aware of the fabric topology. This helped with triangulating switches in the network that were potentially blackholing flows. We proactively detect such anomalies by running probes across servers randomly distributed in the cluster. On probe failures, these servers automatically run traceroutes and identify suspect failures in the network.

6. EXPERIENCE

6.1 Fabric Congestion

Despite the capacity in our fabrics, our networks experienced high congestion drops as utilization approached 25%. We found several factors contributed to congestion: i) inherent burstiness of flows led to inadmissible traffic in short time intervals typically seen as incast [8] or outcast [21]; ii) our commodity switches possessed limited buffering, which was sub optimal for our server TCP stack; iii) certain parts of the network were intentionally kept oversubscribed to save cost, e.g., the uplinks of a ToR; and iv) imperfect flow hashing especially during failures and in presence of variation in flow volume.

We used several techniques to alleviate the congestion in our fabrics. First, we configured our switch hardware schedulers to drop packets based on QoS. Thus, on congestion we would discard lower priority traffic. Second, we tuned the hosts to bound their TCP congestion window for intra-cluster traffic to not overrun the small buffers in our switch chips. Third, for our early fabrics, we employed link-level pause at ToRs to keep servers from over-running oversubscribed uplinks. Fourth, we enabled Explicit Congestion Notification (ECN) on our switches and optimized the host stack response to ECN signals [3]. Fifth, we monitored application bandwidth requirements in the face of oversubscription ratios and could provision bandwidth by deploying Pluto ToRs

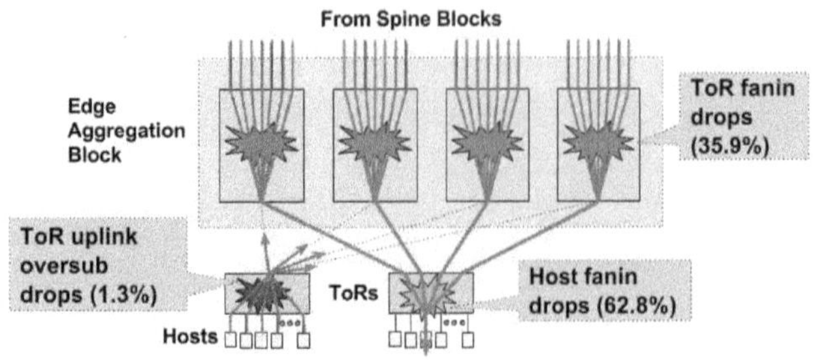

Figure 21: Congestion hotspots in a Saturn fabric.

with four or eight uplinks as required. Similarly, we could repopulate links to the spine if the depop mode of a fabric was causing congestion. Sixth, the merchant silicon had shared memory buffers used by all ports, and we tuned the buffer sharing scheme on these chips so as to dynamically allocate a disproportionate fraction of total chip buffer space to absorb temporary traffic bursts. Finally, we carefully configured switch hashing functionality to support good ECMP load balancing across multiple fabric paths.

Our congestion mitigation techniques delivered substantial improvements. We reduced the packet discard rate in a typical Clos fabric at 25% average utilization from 1% to < 0.01%. Figure 21 shows the breakdown among the three principal sources of congestion in a representative Saturn cluster with 10G hosts. The largest source of loss comes from *host fanin* - traffic fanning in from the ToRs to certain hosts. The next biggest source is *ToR fanin*, which may be caused by imperfect hashing and incast communication to specific ToRs. Finally, a relatively small fraction of discards is due to oversubscription of ToR uplinks towards the fabric. Further improving fabric congestion response remains an ongoing effort.

6.2 Outages

While the overall availability of our datacenter fabrics has been satisfactory, our outages fall into three categories representing the most common failures in production: i) control software problems at scale; ii) aging hardware exposing previously unhandled failure modes; and iii) misconfigurations of certain components.

6.2.1 Control software problems at large scale

In the first example, a datacenter power event caused the entire fabric to restart simultaneously. However, the control software did not converge without manual intervention. The instability took place because our liveness protocol (ND) and route computation contended for limited CPU resources on embedded switch CPUs. On entire fabric reboot, routing experienced huge churn, which in turn led ND not to respond to heartbeat messages quickly enough. This in turn led to a snowball effect for routing where link state would spuriously go from up to down and back to up again. We stabilized the network by manually bringing up a few blocks at a time.

Going forward, we included the worst case fabric reboot in our test plans. Since the largest scale datacenter could never be built in a hardware test lab, we launched efforts to stress test our control software at scale in virtualized environments. We also heavily scrutinized any timer values in liveness protocols, tuning them for the worst case while balancing slower reaction time in the common case. Finally, we reduced the priority of non-critical processes that shared the same CPU.

6.2.2 Aging hardware exposes unhandled failure modes

Over years of deployment, our inbuilt fabric redundancy degraded as a result of aging hardware. For example, our software was vulnerable to internal/backplane link failures, leading to rare traffic blackholing. Another example centered around failures of the Control Plane Network (CPN). Each fabric chassis had dual redundant links to the CPN in active-standby mode. We initially did not actively monitor the health of both the active and standby links. With age, the vendor gear suffered from unidirectional failures of some CPN links exposing unhandled corner cases in our routing protocols. Both these problems would have been easier to mitigate had the proper monitoring and alerting been in place for fabric backplane and CPN links.

6.2.3 Component Misconfiguration

A prominent misconfiguration outage was on a Freedome fabric. Recall that a Freedome chassis runs the same codebase as the CBR with its integrated BGP stack. A CLI interface to the CBR BGP stack supported configuration. We did not implement locking to prevent simultaneous read/write access to the BGP configuration. During a planned BGP reconfiguration of a Freedome block, a separate monitoring system coincidentally used the same interface to read the running config while a change was underway. Unfortunately, the resulting partial configuration led to undesirable behavior between Freedome and its BGP peers.

We mitigated this error by quickly reverting to the previous configuration. However, it taught us to harden our operational tools further. It was not enough for tools to configure the fabric as a whole; they needed to do so in a safe, secure and consistent way.

7. CONCLUSION

This paper presents a retrospective on ten years and five generations of production datacenter networks. We employed complementary techniques to deliver more bandwidth to larger clusters than would otherwise be possible at any cost. We built multi-stage Clos topologies from bandwidth-dense but feature-limited merchant switch silicon. Existing routing protocols were not easily adapted to Clos topologies. We departed from conventional wisdom to build a centralized route controller that leveraged global configuration of a predefined cluster plan pushed to every datacenter switch. This centralized control extended to our management infrastructure, enabling us to eschew complex protocols in favor of best practices from managing the server fleet. Our approach has enabled us to deliver substantial bisection bandwidth for building-scale fabrics, all with significant application benefit.

8. ACKNOWLEDGEMENTS

Many teams contributed to the success of the datacenter network within Google. In particular, we would like to acknowledge the Platforms Networking (PlaNet) Hardware and Software Development, Platforms Software Quality Assurance (SQA), Mechanical Engineering, Cluster Engineering (CE), Network Architecture and Operations (NetOps), Global Infrastructure Group (GIG), and Site Reliability Engineering (SRE) teams, to name a few. We would also like to thank our shepherd Ming Zhang as well as the anonymous SIGCOMM reviewers for their useful feedback.

9. REFERENCES

[1] Ahn, J. H., Binkert, N., Davis, A., McLaren, M., and Schreiber, R. S. HyperX: topology, routing, and packaging of efficient large-scale networks. In *Proc. High Performance Computing Networking, Storage and Analysis* (2009), ACM, p. 41.

[2] Al-Fares, M., Loukissas, A., and Vahdat, A. A scalable, commodity data center network architecture. In *ACM SIGCOMM Computer Communication Review* (2008), vol. 38, ACM, pp. 63–74.

[3] Alizadeh, M., Greenberg, A., Maltz, D. A., Padhye, J., Patel, P., Prabhakar, B., Sengupta, S., and Sridharan, M. Data center TCP (DCTCP). *ACM SIGCOMM computer communication review 41*, 4 (2011), 63–74.

[4] Barroso, L. A., Dean, J., and Holzle, U. Web search for a planet: The Google cluster architecture. *Micro, Ieee 23*, 2 (2003), 22–28.

[5] Barroso, L. A., and Hölzle, U. The datacenter as a computer: An introduction to the design of warehouse-scale machines. *Synthesis lectures on computer architecture 4*, 1 (2009), 1–108.

[6] Bates, T., Chen, E., and Chandra, R. Bgp route reflection: An alternative to full mesh internal bgp (ibgp). RFC 4456, RFC Editor, April 2006. http://www.rfc-editor.org/rfc/rfc4456.txt.

[7] Calder, B., Wang, J., Ogus, A., Nilakantan, N., Skjolsvold, A., McKelvie, S., Xu, Y., Srivastav, S., Wu, J., Simitci, H., et al. Windows Azure Storage: a highly available cloud storage service with strong consistency. In *Proceedings of the Twenty-Third ACM Symposium on Operating Systems Principles* (2011), ACM, pp. 143–157.

[8] Chen, Y., Griffith, R., Liu, J., Katz, R. H., and Joseph, A. D. Understanding TCP incast throughput collapse in datacenter networks. In *Proceedings of the 1st ACM workshop on Research on enterprise networking* (2009), ACM, pp. 73–82.

[9] Clos, C. A Study of Non-Blocking Switching Networks. *Bell System Technical Journal 32*, 2 (1953), 406–424.

[10] Dean, J., and Ghemawat, S. MapReduce: simplified data processing on large clusters. *Communications of the ACM 51*, 1 (2008), 107–113.

[11] Dietz, H. G., and Mattox, T. I. KLAT2's flat neighborhood network. *Proceedings of the Extreme Linux track in the 4th Annual Linux Showcase, Atlanta, GA* (2000).

[12] Farrington, N., Rubow, E., and Vahdat, A. Data center switch architecture in the age of merchant silicon. In *Proc. HOT Interconnects, 2009. 17th IEEE Symposium on* (2009), pp. 93–102.

[13] Feamster, N., Rexford, J., and Zegura, E. The Road to SDN: An Intellectual History of Programmable Networks. *ACM Queue 11*, 12 (December 2013).

[14] Ghemawat, S., Gobioff, H., and Leung, S.-T. The Google file system. In *ACM SIGOPS Operating Systems Review* (2003), vol. 37, ACM, pp. 29–43.

[15] Greenberg, A., Hamilton, J. R., Jain, N., Kandula, S., Kim, C., Lahiri, P., Maltz, D. A., Patel, P., and Sengupta, S. VL2: a scalable and flexible data center network. In *Proc. ACM SIGCOMM Computer Communication Review* (2009), pp. 51–62.

[16] Guo, C., Lu, G., Li, D., Wu, H., Zhang, X., Shi, Y., Tian, C., Zhang, Y., and Lu, S. BCube: A high performance, server-centric network architecture for modular data centers. In *Proc. ACM SIGCOMM* (2009), pp. 63–74.

[17] Guo, C., Wu, H., Tan, K., Shi, L., Zhang, Y., and Lu, S. Dcell: a scalable and fault-tolerant network structure for data centers. *ACM SIGCOMM Computer Communication Review 38*, 4 (2008), 75–86.

[18] Isard, M., Budiu, M., Yu, Y., Birrell, A., and Fetterly, D. Dryad: distributed data-parallel programs from sequential building blocks. In *Proc. ACM SIGOPS Operating Systems Review* (2007), pp. 59–72.

[19] Jain, S., Kumar, A., Mandal, S., Ong, J., Poutievski, L., Singh, A., Venkata, S., Wanderer, J., Zhou, J., Zhu, M., Zolla, J., Hölzle, U., Stuart, S., and Vahdat, A. B4: Experience with a globally-deployed software defined WAN. In *Proc. ACM SIGCOMM* (2013), pp. 3–14.

[20] Moy, J. OSPF Version 2. STD 54, RFC Editor, April 1998. http://www.rfc-editor.org/rfc/rfc2328.txt.

[21] Prakash, P., Dixit, A. A., Hu, Y. C., and Kompella, R. R. The TCP Outcast Problem: Exposing Unfairness in Data Center Networks. In *Proc. NSDI* (2012), pp. 413–426.

[22] Singla, A., Hong, C.-Y., Popa, L., and Godfrey, P. B. Jellyfish: Networking Data Centers Randomly. In *NSDI* (2012), vol. 12, pp. 17–17.

[23] Thorup, M. OSPF Areas Considered Harmful. IETF Internet Draft 00, individual, April 2003. http://tools.ietf.org/html/draft-thorup-ospf-harmful-00.

[24] Vahdat, A., Al-Fares, M., Farrington, N., Mysore, R. N., Porter, G., and Radhakrishnan, S. Scale-Out Networking in the Data Center. *IEEE MICRO*, 4 (August 2010), 29–41.

Multi-Context TLS (mcTLS): Enabling Secure In-Network Functionality in TLS

David Naylor*, Kyle Schomp†, Matteo Varvello‡, Ilias Leontiadis‡, Jeremy Blackburn‡, Diego Lopez‡, Konstantina Papagiannaki‡, Pablo Rodriguez Rodriguez‡, and Peter Steenkiste*

*Carnegie Mellon University †Case Western Reserve University ‡Telefónica Research

ABSTRACT

A significant fraction of Internet traffic is now encrypted and HTTPS will likely be the default in HTTP/2. However, Transport Layer Security (TLS), the standard protocol for encryption in the Internet, assumes that all functionality resides at the endpoints, making it impossible to use in-network services that optimize network resource usage, improve user experience, and protect clients and servers from security threats. Re-introducing in-network functionality into TLS sessions today is done through hacks, often weakening overall security.

In this paper we introduce multi-context TLS (mcTLS), which extends TLS to support middleboxes. mcTLS breaks the current "all-or-nothing" security model by allowing endpoints and content providers to explicitly introduce middleboxes in secure end-to-end sessions while controlling which parts of the data they can read or write.

We evaluate a prototype mcTLS implementation in both controlled and "live" experiments, showing that its benefits come at the cost of minimal overhead. More importantly, we show that mcTLS can be incrementally deployed and requires only small changes to client, server, and middlebox software.

CCS Concepts

•Security and privacy → Security protocols; •Networks → Middle boxes / network appliances; *Session protocols;*

Keywords

TLS; SSL; HTTPS

SIGCOMM '15, August 17 - 21, 2015, London, United Kingdom

© 2015 ACM. ISBN 978-1-4503-3542-3/15/08...$15.00

DOI: http://dx.doi.org/10.1145/2785956.2787482

1. INTRODUCTION

The increased personalization of Internet services and rising concern over users' privacy on the Internet has led to a number of services (e.g., Facebook, Twitter, and Google) offering access solely over HTTPS. HTTPS currently accounts for a significant portion of all Internet traffic (40% in [26], and estimated to grow at 40% every 6 months [27]). Transport Layer Security (TLS), which underlies HTTPS, has become the standard for end-to-end encryption on the web because it ensures (i) entity authentication, (ii) data secrecy, and (iii) data integrity and authentication. Moreover, it will likely be the default transport protocol for HTTP/2.

This is good news for privacy. However, TLS makes a fundamental assumption: all functionality must reside at the endpoints. In reality, Internet sessions are augmented by functional units along the path, providing services like intrusion detection, caching, parental filtering, content optimization (e.g., compression, transcoding), or compliance to corporate practices in enterprise environments. These functional units, often referred to as *middleboxes*, offer many benefits to users, content providers, and network operators, as evidenced by their widespread deployment in today's Internet.

While there are arguments that these services could (and should) be implemented on endpoints, we argue that this is often not optimal or even possible. First, although an in-network implementation might not be *required*, it might be *inherently more effective* than an endpoint-based one (e.g., thousands of users sharing an ISP cache). Second, there might be practical reasons why such a solution needs to reside in-network (e.g., virus scanners can always be up-to-date and immediately protect all clients). Third, certain features (e.g., intrusion detection or content-based routing decisions) simply cannot be implemented without network-wide visibility. Finally, in-network services can lead to increased competition, innovation, and choice for end users.

Recently, industrial efforts—one by Ericsson and AT&T [20] and one by Google [28]—have tried to provide a solution for combining encryption with the richness of today's in-network services. However, as we will discuss, a good solution is still lacking and the topic is still active within the GSMA *ENCRY* and the IETF *httpbis*.

In this paper we present mcTLS, a protocol that builds on top of TLS to allow endpoints to explicitly and securely include in-network functionality with complete visibility and control. mcTLS: (i) provides endpoints explicit knowledge and control over *which* functional elements are part of the session, (ii) allows users and content providers to *dynamically* choose which portions of content are exposed to in-network services (e.g., HTTP headers vs. content), (iii) protects the authenticity and integrity of data while still enabling modifications by selected in-network services by separating read and write permissions, and (iv) is incrementally deployable.

We implemented mcTLS as a simple extension to the OpenSSL library. Our evaluation shows that mcTLS has negligible impact on page load time or data overhead for loading the top 500 Alexa sites and incorporating mcTLS into applications is relatively easy in many cases.

Our contributions are as follows: (i) a practical extension to TLS that explicitly introduces trusted in-network elements into secure sessions with the minimum level of access they need, (ii) a prototype implementation of mcTLS tested in controlled and live environments (our implementation is available online [1]), (iii) an efficient fine-grained access control mechanism which we show comes at very low cost, and (iv) strategies for using mcTLS to address concrete, relevant use cases, many of which can immediately benefit applications with little effort using mcTLS's most basic configuration.

2. MIDDLEBOXES AND ENCRYPTION

It is clear that there is both a growing interest in user privacy and a widespread use of in-network processing in the Internet. In this section, we describe middleboxes and why it is beneficial to keep them around as the Internet moves toward ubiquitous encryption. We then explain why it is difficult to do so with TLS.

2.1 Middleboxes

Middleboxes are services that run "inside" the network, sitting logically between the endpoints of communication sessions. A *client* (e.g., web browser) can connect to a *server* (e.g., web server) via one or more middleboxes that add value beyond basic data transport. Clients and servers are *endpoints*; *users* own/manage clients and *content providers* own/manage servers. The entire communication, across all parties, is a *session*; *connections* link individual hops in the session (e.g., a TCP connection between the client and a middlebox).

Our focus is on application level middleboxes, also called *proxies* or *in-path services*, which we loosely define as middleboxes that access application data, like intrusion detection systems (IDSes), content filters, and caching/compression proxies (see Table 1).

	Request		**Response**	
	Headers	*Body*	*Headers*	*Body*
Cache	○		•	•
Compression			•	•
Load Balancer	○			
IDS	○	○	○	○
Parental Filter	○			
Tracker Blocker	•		•	
Packet Pacer			○	
WAN Optimizer	○	○	○	○

(• = read/write; ○ = read-only)

Table 1: Examples of app-layer middleboxes and the permissions they need for HTTP. No middlebox needs read/write access to all of the data.

Middleboxes are sometimes viewed as undesirable. One reason is privacy concerns, which we address later. Another is that they violate the original Internet architecture, which places all functionality (transport and up) at the endpoints, a design motivated by the end-to-end principle [31]. However, the Internet has changed dramatically: both connectivity and content services are commercially supported, security is a major concern, performance expectations are much higher, the technology is more complex, and users are typically not in a position to manage it. As a result, the decision of where to place functionality depends on more than just technical concerns and, increasingly, "inside the network" is a good solution.

Middleboxes are useful: Providing processing and storage in the network has proven to be an effective way to help users, content providers, and network operators alike. For example, techniques such as caching, compression, prefetching, packet pacing, and reformatting improve load times for users [38, 18], reduce data usage for operators and users [3, 26, 13, 37, 29], and reduce energy consumption on the client [26, 12, 29, 14]. Middleboxes can also add functionality not provided by the endpoints, such as virus scanners in enterprises or content filters for children.

In-network may be better: First, functions such as caching and packet pacing are inherently more effective in the network [13, 12, 14]. Second, client implementations may be problematic because the client may be untrusted or its software, URL blacklists, virus signatures, etc. may be out-of-date (e.g., only a third of Android users run the latest version of the OS and over half are more than two years out of date [2]). Finally, users may trust a middlebox more than the application; for example, apps can unexpectedly leak personal information to a server [36], so users may want a middlebox to act as a watchdog.

They are widely used: In a 2012 survey of network operators, networks of all sizes reported having roughly as many middleboxes as L3 routers [33]. For web proxies in particular, 14% of Netalyzer sessions show evidence of a proxy [35] and all four major U.S. mobile carriers use proxies—connections to the top 100 Alexa sites are all proxied, with the exception of YouTube on T-Mobile [38]. In addition, all actors in the Internet use middleboxes. They are widely deployed in client networks (e.g., enterprise firewalls, cellular networks), and of the three IETF RFCs on using middleboxes with TLS, two are led by operators [20, 18] and one by a content provider [28]. Given this investment, middleboxes are unlikely to go away, so we need a clean, secure way to include them in encrypted sessions.

The Internet is a market-driven ecosystem: The Internet is not a centrally managed monopoly but is a market-driven ecosystem with many actors making independent decisions. For example, while servers can compress data, many only do so selectively [29]. Similarly, content providers may decide not to support device-specific content formatting but instead rely on third party providers, which can be selected by the client or content provider. For functions such as content filtering, clients may decide to pay for the convenience of having a single middlebox provider of their choice, instead of relying on individual content providers. Enterprise networks may similarly decide to outsource functionality [33]. Fundamentally, middleboxes give actors more choices, which leads to competition and innovation.

The bottom line is simple: just like end-to-end encryption, middleboxes are an integral, useful part of the Internet and they are here to stay.

2.2 Middleboxes *and* TLS

Given these trends, it is natural to want the best of both worlds. Before discussing how middleboxes and encryption can be used together today, let us take a closer look at Transport Layer Security (TLS) [11], the standard protocol for secure network communications.

What does TLS give us? TLS comprises two protocols, a *handshake protocol* for session establishment and a *record protocol* for data exchange, which together realize three security properties:

(1) Entity Authentication: During the handshake, the client authenticates the server by verifying that a valid certificate links the server's domain name and public key. Clients can also authenticate themselves to the server with certificates, but this is rarely used; client authentication typically happens in the application layer, e.g., using a password.

(2) Data Secrecy: The endpoints establish a symmetric *session key* during the handshake, which is used by the record protocol to encrypt/decrypt *records* (blocks of application data).

(3) Data Integrity & Authentication: The session key is also used to generate a message authentication code (MAC) for each record; a valid MAC indicates that (1) the data originated from the other endpoint (authenticity) and (2) the data was not changed in flight (integrity).

How do you add a middlebox to a TLS session? In short: you do not. By design, TLS supports secure communication between exactly two parties. Despite this, middleboxes are frequently inserted in TLS sessions, but this has to be done transparently to TLS. Consider an enterprise network that wants to insert a virus scanner in all employee sessions. A common solution is to install a custom root certificate on the client. The middlebox can then create a certificate for itself purported to be from the intended server and sign it with the custom root certificate. After the client connects to the middlebox, the middlebox connects to the server and passes the data from one connection to the other. We refer to this as *Split TLS*) and it gives rise to several problems:

(i) There is no mechanism for authenticating the middlebox. Even worse, the middlebox is completely transparent to the server, and while users can inspect the certificate chain to check who signed the certificate, very few do that or understand the difference. Moreover, even if they do, they have no information about what functions the middlebox performs.

(ii) The client has no guarantees beyond the first hop. While the connection to the middlebox is encrypted, the client cannot verify that TLS is being used from the middlebox to the server, whether additional middleboxes are present, or (depending on what application-level authentication is used) whether the endpoint of the session is even the intended server. The user needs to completely trust the middlebox, which he did not select and may not even know exists.

(iii) Middleboxes get full read/write access to the data stream. Middleboxes can read and modify any data transmitted and received over TLS sessions despite the fact that many middleboxes only need selective access to the data stream (Table 1).

Given these problems, it should not be a surprise that users are concerned about (transparent) middleboxes. One could even argue that using TLS with a middlebox is worse than not using TLS at all [7], since clients and servers are under the illusion that they have a secure session, while some of the expected security properties do not actually hold. In the next section, we propose a protocol based on TLS that explicitly supports middleboxes and addresses the above problems.

3. MULTI-CONTEXT TLS (mcTLS)

This section presents the design of multi-context TLS (mcTLS), which augments TLS with the ability to securely introduce trusted middleboxes. Middleboxes are trusted in the sense that they have to be inserted explicitly by either the client or the server, at both endpoints' consent. We first summarize our design requirements, then introduce the key ideas, and finally describe the key components of the protocol. A more detailed description of mcTLS is available online [1].

3.1 Protocol Requirements

First, we require mcTLS to maintain the properties provided by TLS (extended to apply to middleboxes):

R1: Entity Authentication Endpoints should be able to authenticate each other and all middleboxes. Similar to TLS usage today, we expect that clients will authenticate all entities in the session, but servers may prefer not to (e.g., to reduce overhead).

R2: Data Secrecy Only the endpoints and trusted middleboxes can read or write the data.

R3: Data Integrity & Authentication All members of the session must be able to detect in-flight modifications by unauthorized third parties, and endpoints must be able to check whether the data was originated by the other endpoint (vs. having been modified by a trusted middlebox).

Second, the introduction of middleboxes brings with it two entirely new requirements:

R4: Explicit Control & Visibility The protocol must ensure that trusted middleboxes are added to the session at the consent of both endpoints. Endpoints must always be able to see all trusted middleboxes in the session.

R5: Least Privilege In keeping with the principle of least privilege [32], middleboxes should be given the minimum level of access required to do their jobs [24, 19]. Middleboxes should have access only to the portion of the data stream relevant to their function; if that function does not require modifying the data, access should be read-only.

Finally, our protocol should meet all five requirements without substantial overhead, e.g., in terms of latency, data usage, computation, connection state, burden on users or administrators, etc.

3.2 Threat Model

A successfully negotiated mcTLS session meets the above requirements in the face of computationally bounded network attackers that can intercept, alter, drop, or insert packets during any phase of the session. Like TLS, mcTLS does not prevent denial of service.

We assume that all participants in an mcTLS session execute the protocol correctly and do not share information out-of-band. For example, the client could share keys with a middlebox not approved by the server, or middleboxes could collude to escalate their permissions. We do not consider such attacks because no protocol (including TLS) can prevent a party from sharing session keys out-of-band. Furthermore, such attacks are unlikely since at least two colluding parties would need to run a malicious mcTLS implementation. Major browsers and Web servers (especially open source ones) are unlikely to do this, since they would almost surely be caught. Mobile apps using HTTP would need to implement HTTP themselves instead of using the platform's (honest) HTTP library, which is unlikely. If it is essential to know that parties have not shared keys with unauthorized parties, some sort of remote attestation is the most promising solution.

Finally, even when all parties are honest, adding more entities to a session necessarily increases the attack surface: a bug or misconfiguration on any one could compromise the session. This risk is inherent in the problem, not any particular solution.

3.3 Design Overview

To satisfy the five design requirements, we add two key features to TLS:

(1) Encryption Contexts *(R2, R3, R5)* In TLS, there are only two parties, so it makes no sense to restrict one party's access to part of the data. With trusted middleboxes, however, the endpoints may wish to limit a middlebox's access to only a portion of the data or grant it read-only access. To make this possible, mcTLS introduces the notion of *encryption contexts*, or *contexts*, to TLS. An encryption context is simply a set of symmetric encryption and message authentication code (MAC) keys for controlling who can read and write the data sent in that context (§3.4). Applications can associate each context with a purpose (opaque to mcTLS itself) and access permissions for each middlebox. For instance, web browsers/servers could use one context for HTTP headers and another for content. We describe several strategies for using contexts in §4.2.

(2) Contributory Context Keys *(R1, R4)* The client and server each perform a key exchange with each middlebox after verifying the middleboxes' certificates if they choose to (R1). Next, the endpoints each generate half of every context key and send to each middlebox the half-keys for the contexts to which it has access, encrypted with the symmetric keys derived above. The middlebox only gains access to a context if it receives both halves of the key, ensuring that the client and server are both aware of each middlebox and agree on its access permissions (R4). The server may relinquish this control to avoid extra computation if it wishes (§3.6).

3.4 The mcTLS Record Protocol

The TLS record protocol takes data from higher layers (e.g., the application), breaks it into "manageable" blocks, optionally compresses, encrypts, and then MAC-protects each block, and finally transmits the blocks. mcTLS works much the same way, though each mcTLS record contains only data associated with a single context; we add a one byte context ID to the TLS record format. Record sequence numbers are global across contexts to ensure the correct ordering of all application data at the client and server and to prevent an adversary from deleting an entire record undetected. Any of the standard encryption and MAC algorithms supported by TLS can be used to protect records in mcTLS. (So, details like the order of encryption and MAC depend on the cipher suite; mcTLS makes no changes here.)

Building on [24, 25], mcTLS manages access to each context by controlling which middleboxes are given which context keys. For each context, there are four relevant parties, listed in decreasing order of privilege: *endpoints* (client and server), *writers* (middleboxes with write access to the context), *readers* (middleboxes with read-only access to the context), and *third parties* (blanket term for middleboxes with no access to the context, attackers, and bit flips during transmission). Changes by writers are *legal modifications* and changes by readers and third parties are *illegal modifications*. mcTLS achieves the following three access control properties:

(1) Endpoints can limit read access to a context to writers and readers only.
(2) Endpoints can detect legal and illegal modifications.
(3) Writers can detect illegal modifications.

Controlling Read Access Each context has its own encryption key (called $K_{readers}$, described below). Possession of this key constitutes read access, so mcTLS can prevent a middlebox from reading a context by withholding that context's key.

Controlling Write Access Write access is controlled by limiting who can generate a valid MAC. mcTLS takes the following "endpoint-writer-reader" approach to MACs. Each mcTLS record carries three keyed MACs, generated with keys $K_{endpoints}$ (shared by endpoints), $K_{writers}$ (shared by endpoints and writers), and $K_{readers}$ (shared by endpoints, writers, and readers). Each context has its own $K_{writers}$ and $K_{readers}$ but there is only one $K_{endpoints}$ for the session since the endpoints have access to all contexts.

Generating MACs

- When an **endpoint** assembles a record, it includes three MACs, one with each key.
- When a **writer** modifies a record, it generates new MACs with $K_{writers}$ and $K_{readers}$ and simply forwards the original $K_{endpoints}$ MAC.
- When a **reader** forwards a record, it leaves all three MACs unmodified.

Checking MACs

- When an **endpoint** receives a record, it checks the $K_{writers}$ MAC to confirm that no illegal modifications were made and it checks the $K_{endpoints}$ MAC to find out if any legal modifications were made (if the application cares).
- When a **writer** receives a record, it checks the $K_{writers}$ MAC to verify that no illegal modifications have been made.
- When a **reader** receives a record, it uses the $K_{readers}$ MAC to check if any *third party modifications* have been made.

Note that with the endpoint-writer-reader MAC scheme, *readers cannot detect illegal changes made by other readers*. The problem is that a shared key cannot be used by an entity to police other entities at the same privilege level. Because all readers share $K_{readers}$ (so that they can detect third party modifications), all readers are also capable of generating valid $K_{readers}$ MACs. This is only an issue when there are two or more readers for a context and, in general, readers not detecting reader modifications should not be a problem (reader modifications are still detectable at the next writer or endpoint). However, if needed, there are two options for fixing this: (a) readers and writers/endpoints share pairwise symmetric keys; writers/endpoints compute and append a MAC for *each* reader, or (b) endpoints and writers append digital signatures rather than MACs; unlike $K_{writers}$ MACs, readers can verify these signatures. The benefits seem insufficient to justify the additional overhead of (a) or (b), but they could be implemented as optional modes negotiated during the handshake.

3.5 The mcTLS Handshake Protocol

The mcTLS handshake is very similar to the TLS handshake. We make two simplifications here for ease of exposition: first, although the principles of the mcTLS handshake apply to many of the cipher suites available in TLS, we describe the handshake using ephemeral Diffie-Hellman with RSA signing keys because it is straightforward to illustrate and common in practice. Second, we describe the handshake with a single middlebox, but extending it to multiple middleboxes is straightforward. Table 2 defines the notation we use in this paper.

The purpose of the handshake is to:

- Allow the endpoints to agree on a cipher suite, a set of encryption contexts, a list of middleboxes, and permissions for those middleboxes.
- Allow the endpoints to authenticate each other and all of the middleboxes (if they choose to).
- Establish a shared symmetric key $K_{endpoints}$ between the endpoints.

Notation	Meaning
DH_E^+, DH_E^-	Entity E's ephemeral Diffie-Hellman public/private key pair
$DHCombine(\cdot,\cdot)$	Combine Diffie-Hellman public and private keys to produce a shared secret
PK_E^+, PK_E^-	Entity E's long-term signing public/private key pair (e.g., RSA)
$Sign_{PK_E^-}(\cdot)$	Signature using E's private key
S_E	Secret known only to entity E
$PS_{E_1\text{-}E_2}$	Pre-secret shared by entities E_1 & E_2
$S_{E_1\text{-}E_2}$	Secret shared between entities E_1 & E_2
$PRF_S(\cdot)$	Pseudorandom function keyed with secret S as defined in the TLS RFC [11]
$K_{E_1\text{-}E_2}$	Symmetric key shared by E_1 and E_2
K^E	Key material generated by entity E
$Enc_K(\cdot)$	Symmetric encryption using key K
$MAC_K(\cdot)$	Message authentication code with key K
$AuthEnc_K(\cdot)$	Authenticated encryption with key K
$H(\cdot)$	Cryptographic hash
$\|\|$	Concatenation

Table 2: Notation used in this paper.

- Establish a shared symmetric key $K_{writers}$ for each context among all writers and a shared symmetric key $K_{readers}$[1] for each context among all readers.

Handshake Below we explain the steps of a mcTLS handshake (shown in Figure 1), highlighting the differences from TLS. Note that it has the same 2-RTT "shape" as TLS.

❶ **Setup:** Each party generates a (public) random value and an ephemeral Diffie-Hellman key pair (the middlebox generates two key pairs, one for the client and one for the server). The endpoints also each generate a secret value.

❷ **Client Hello:** Like TLS, an mcTLS session begins with a `ClientHello` message containing a random value. In mcTLS, the `ClientHello` carries a `MiddleboxListExtension`, which contains (1) a list of the middleboxes to include in the session—we discuss building this list in the first place in §6.1—and (2) a list of encryption contexts, their purposes (strings meaningful to the application), and middlebox access permissions for every context. The client opens a TCP connection with the middlebox and sends the `ClientHello`; the middlebox opens a TCP connection with the server and forwards the `ClientHello`.

❸ **Certificate & Public Key Exchange:** As in TLS, the server responds with a series of messages containing a random value, its certificate, and an ephemeral public key signed by the key in the certificate. The middlebox does the same: it sends its random value, certificate, and ephemeral public key to both the client and the server. The client sends an ephemeral public key, which the middlebox saves and forwards to the server. The middlebox piggy-backs its messages on the `ServerKeyExchange` and `ClientKeyExchange` messages (indicated by dashed arrows). The ephemeral keys provide forward secrecy; the middlebox uses different key pairs for the client and the server to prevent small subgroup attacks [22].

[1]Though we describe each as one key for simplicity, $K_{readers}$ and $K_{endpoints}$ are really four keys each (just like the "session key" in TLS): an encryption key for data in each direction and a MAC key for data in each direction. Likewise, $K_{writers}$ is really one MAC key for each direction.

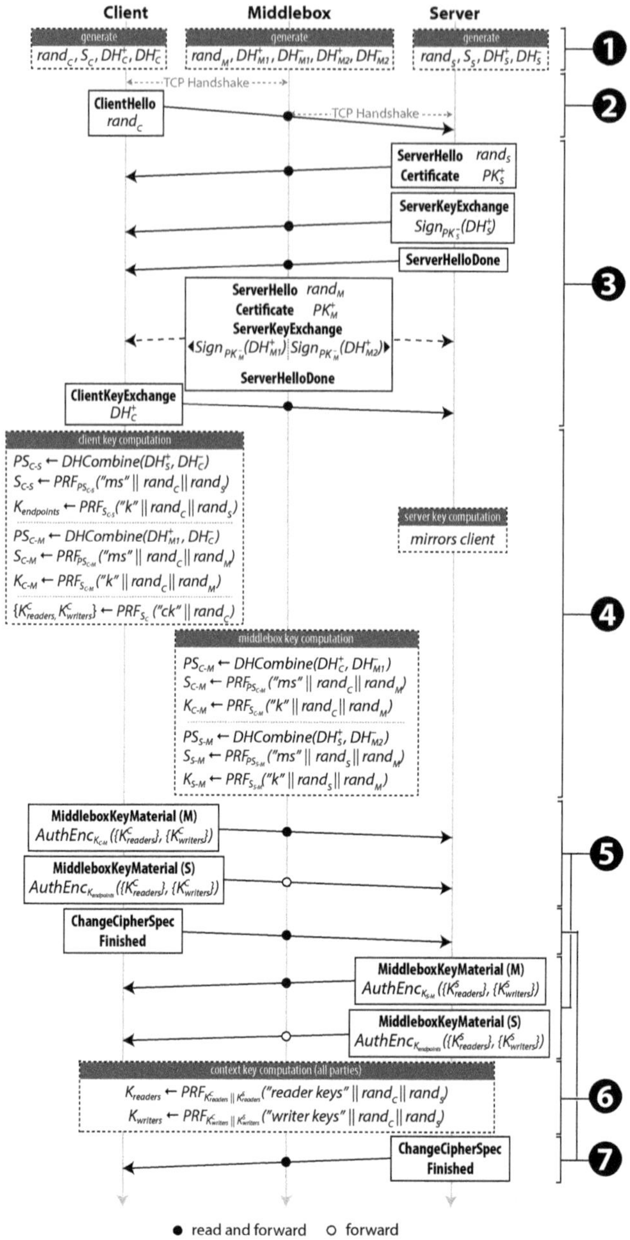

Figure 1: The mcTLS handshake.

	mcTLS			mcTLS (Client Key Dist.)			Split TLS		
	Client	*Middlebox*	*Server*	*Client*	*Middlebox*	*Server*	*Client*	*Middlebox*	*Server*
Hash	$12+6N$	0	$12+6N$	$10+5N$	0	$10+5N$	10	20	10
Secret Comp.	$N+1$	2	$N+1$	$N+1$	1	1	1	2	1
Key Gen.	$4K+N+1$	$(k \leq 2K)+2$	$4K+N+1$	$2K+N+1$	1	1	1	2	1
Asym Verify	$N+1$	$n \leq 1$	$n \leq N$	$N+1$	$n \leq 1$	0	1	1	0
Sym Encrypt	$N+2$	0	$N+2$	$N+2$	0	1	1	2	1
Sym Decrypt	2	2	2	1	1	2	1	2	1

(N = number of middleboxes; K = number of contexts)

Table 3: Cryptographic operations performed by the client, middlebox, and server during the handshake. Assumes no TLS extensions, a DHE-RSA cipher suite, and the client is not authenticated with a certificate.

❹ **Shared Key Computation:** The **client** computes two secrets ($S_{C\text{-}M}$ and $S_{C\text{-}S}$) using the contributions from the server and middlebox, which it uses to generate a symmetric key shared with the middlebox ($K_{C\text{-}M}$) and the server ($K_{endpoints}$). The client also generates "partial keys," $K^C_{writers}$ and $K^C_{readers}$, for each context, using a secret known only to itself.
The **server** follows the same procedure as the client, resulting in $K_{endpoints}$, $K_{S\text{-}M}$, $K^S_{writers}$, and $K^S_{readers}$. The server may choose to avoid this overhead by asking the client to generate and distribute complete context keys (§3.6).
When the **middlebox** receives the `ClientKeyExchange`, it computes $K_{C\text{-}M}$ and $K_{S\text{-}M}$ using the client's and server's ephemeral public keys, respectively; it will use these keys later to decrypt context key material from the client and server.

❺ **Context Key Exchange:** Next, for each context, the endpoints send the partial context keys to the middlebox ($K^C_{readers}$ and $K^S_{readers}$ if it has read access and $K^C_{writers}$ and $K^S_{writers}$ if it has write access). These messages are sent encrypted and authenticated under $K_{C\text{-}M}$ and $K_{S\text{-}M}$, ensuring the secrecy and integrity of the partial context keys. The middlebox forwards each message on to the opposite endpoint so it can be included in the hash of the handshake messages that is verified at the end of the handshake. The endpoints also send all of the partial context keys to the opposite endpoint encrypted under $K_{endpoints}$. The middlebox forwards this message (but cannot read it).

❻ **Context Key Computation:** The client indicates that the cipher negotiated in the handshake should be used by sending a `ChangeCipherSpec` message. Receipt of the `ChangeCipherSpec` message prompts all parties to generate context keys using $PRF(\cdot)$ keyed with the concatenation of the partial context keys. This "partial key" approach serves two purposes: (1) it provides contributory key agreement (both endpoints contribute randomness) and (2) it ensures that a middlebox only gains access to a context if the client and server both agree.

❼ **Finished:** The mcTLS handshake concludes with the exchange of `Finished` messages. As in TLS, the `Finished` message contains a hash of the concatenation of all handshake messages (including those directed to the middlebox): $PRF_{S_{C\text{-}S}}(finished\_label, H(messages))$. Verifying this message ensures that both endpoints observe the same sequence of identical handshake messages, i.e., no messages were modified in flight.

Details There are a few subtle differences between the mcTLS and TLS handshakes. We briefly highlight the changes here and argue why they are safe; for a more detailed security analysis, see [1].

- For simplicity, the middlebox cannot negotiate session parameters (e.g., cipher suite or number of contexts). A more complex negotiation protocol could be considered in future work if needed.
- The server's context key material is not included in the client's `Finished` message, since this would require an extra RTT. However, this key material is sent encrypted and MAC-protected, so an adversary cannot learn or modify it.
- The client cannot decrypt the context key material the server sends the middlebox and vice versa. This would require establishing a three-way symmetric key between both endpoints and each middlebox. Because the middlebox needs key material from *both* endpoints, one rogue endpoint cannot unilaterally increase a middlebox's permissions.
- The middlebox cannot verify the handshake hash in the `Finished` message because it does not know $K_{endpoints}$. We do not include per-middlebox `Finished` messages to avoid overhead. This means it is possible for the middlebox to observe an incorrect sequence of handshake messages. However, this is at most a denial of service attack. For instance, even though the middlebox cannot detect a cipher suite downgrade attack, the endpoints would detect it and terminate the session. Furthermore, context key material is sent encrypted and MAC-protected under keys each endpoint shares with the middlebox, so as long as at least one endpoint verifies the middlebox's certificate, an adversary cannot learn or modify the context keys.

3.6 Reducing Server Overhead

One concern (albeit a diminishing one [17, 4]) about deploying TLS is that the handshake is computationally demanding, limiting the number of new connections per second servers can process. We do not want to make this problem worse in mcTLS, and one way we avoid this is by making certain features optional. For example, similar to TLS, authentication of the entities in the session is optional—in some cases, the server may not care who the middleboxes are. Another burden for servers in mcTLS is generating and encrypting the partial context keys for distribution to middleboxes. Rather than splitting this work between the client and server, it can optionally be moved to the client: context keys are generated from the master secret shared by the endpoints and the client encrypts and distributes them to middleboxes ("client key distribution mode"). This reduces the server load, but it has the disadvantage that agreement about middlebox permissions is not enforced. (Note that this does not sacrifice contributory key agreement in the sense that both endpoints contribute randomness. The client generates the context keys from the secret it shares with the server; if client/server key exchange was contributory, the context keys inherit this benefit.) Choosing a handshake mode is left to content providers, who can individually decide how to make this control-performance tradeoff; servers indicate their choice to clients in the `ServerHello`.

Table 3 compares the number of cryptographic operations performed by mcTLS and the split TLS approach described in Section 2.2. We show numbers for mcTLS both without and with client context key distribution. If we consider a simple example with a single middlebox ($N = 1$), the additional server load using client key distribution mode is limited to a small number of lightweight operations (Hash and Sym Decrypt).

4. USING mcTLS

4.1 Using Contexts

Just as the architects of HTTP had to define how it would operate over TLS [30], protocol designers need to standardize how their applications will use mcTLS. From an application developer's perspective, the biggest change mcTLS brings is contexts: the application needs to decide how many contexts to use and for what. First we give the topic a general treatment and then follow up with some concrete use cases below.

There are two ways to think about contexts: as sections of the data stream or as configurations of middlebox permissions. For example, suppose an application wants to transfer a document consisting of three pieces, A, B, and C, via two middleboxes, M_1 and M_2. M_1 should have read access to the entire document and M_2 should read A, write B, and have no access to C. The application could allocate one context for each piece and assign the appropriate permissions (Figure 2 left), or it could create one context for each combination of permissions and use the appropriate context when sending each piece of the document (Figure 2 right).

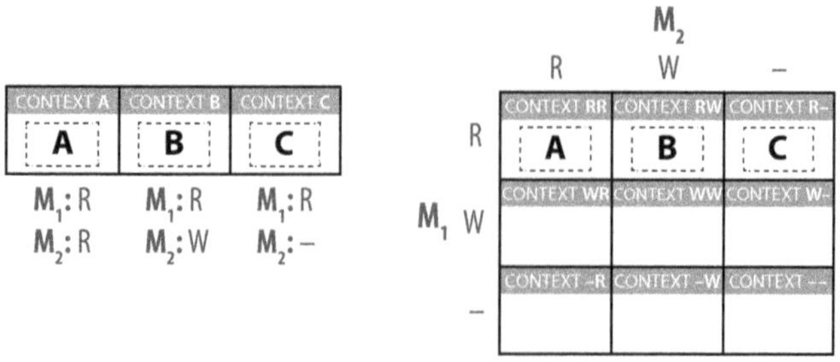

Figure 2: Strategies for using encryption contexts: context-per-section (left) and context-as-permissions (right).

Which model is appropriate depends on the use case: in the context-per-section model, n sections means n contexts. In the contexts-as-permissions model, m middleboxes means 3^m contexts. In practice, we expect at least one of these numbers to be small, since data in a session often is not of wildly varying levels of sensitivity and since most middleboxes need similar permissions (Table 1). For instance, in the case of HTTP, we imagine four contexts will be sufficient: request headers, request body, response headers, and response body. (Though you could imagine extreme cases in which each HTTP header has its own access control settings.)

Finally, the example above uses a static context assignment, but contexts can also be selected dynamically. An application could make two contexts, one which a middlebox can read and one it cannot, and switch between them to enable or disable middlebox access on-the-fly (for instance, to enable compression in response to particular user-agents).

4.2 Use Cases

Data Compression Proxy Many users—particularly on mobile devices—use proxies like Chrome's Data Compression Proxy [3], which re-scale/re-encode images, to reduce their data usage. However, Google's proxy currently ignores HTTPS flows. With mcTLS, users can instruct their browsers to give the compression proxy write access to HTTP responses. One step further, the browser and web server could coordinate to use two contexts for responses: one for images, which the proxy can access, and the other for HTML, CSS, and scripts, which the proxy cannot access. Context assignments can even change dynamically: if a mobile user connects to Wi-Fi mid-page-load, images might also be transferred over the no-access context since compression is no longer required.

Parental Filtering Libraries and schools—and sometimes even entire countries [8]—often employ filters to block age-inappropriate content. Such filters often depend on seeing the full URL being accessed (only 5% of the entries on the Internet Watch Foundation's blacklist are entire (sub-)domains [26]). With mcTLS, IT staff could configure their machines to allow their filter read-only access to HTTP request headers, and user-owned devices connecting to the network could be configured to do the same dynamically via DHCP. The filter drops non-compliant connections.

Corporate Firewall Most companies funnel all network traffic through intrusion detection systems (IDS)/ firewalls/virus scanners. Currently, these devices either ignore encrypted traffic or install root certificates on employees' devices, transparently giving themselves access to all "secure" sessions. With mcTLS, administrators can configure devices to give the IDS—which users can now see—read-only access. Security appliances no longer need to impersonate end servers and users no longer grow accustomed to installing root certificates.

Online Banking Though we designed mcTLS to give users control over their sessions, there are cases in which the content provider really does know better than the user and should be able to say "no" to middleboxes. A prime example is online banking: banks have a responsibility to protect careless or nontechnical users from sharing their financial information with third parties. The server can easily prevent this by simply not giving middleboxes its half of the context keys, regardless of what level of access the client assigns.

HTTP/2 Streams One of the features of HTTP/2 is multiplexing multiple streams over a single transport connection. mcTLS allows browsers to easily set different access controls for each stream.

5. EVALUATION

mcTLS' fine-grained access control requires generating and distributing extra keys, computing extra MACs, and, possibly, sending a larger number of smaller records than TLS. In this section we evaluate this overhead.

Experimental Setup We built a prototype of mcTLS by modifying the OpenSSL[2] implementation of TLSv1.2. The prototype supports all the features of mcTLS's default mode, described in §3.4 and §3.5. We use the DHE-RSA-AES128-SHA256 cipher suite, though nothing prevents mcTLS from working with any standard key exchange, encryption, or MAC algorithm. In addition, though the `MiddleboxKeyMaterial` message should be encrypted using a key generated from the DHE key exchange between the endpoints and the middlebox, we use RSA public key cryptography for simplicity in our implementation. As a result, *forward secrecy* is not currently supported by our implementation. mcTLS requires some additions to the API, e.g., defining contexts and their read/write permissions, but these are similar to the current OpenSSL API.

[2]OpenSSL v1.0.1j from October 2014

Next we wrote a simple HTTP client, server, and proxy and support four modes of operation:

(1) `mcTLS`: Data transferred using mcTLS.
(2) `SplitTLS`: Split TLS connections between hops; middleboxes decrypt and re-encrypt data.
(3) `E2E-TLS`: A single end-to-end TLS connection; middleboxes blindly forward encrypted data.
(4) `NoEncrypt`: No encryption; data transferred and forwarded in the clear over TCP.

We instrumented the mcTLS library and our applications to measure handshake duration, file transfer time, data volume overhead, and connections per second.

We test in two environments. (1) *Controlled*: Client, middleboxes, and server all run on a single machine. We control bandwidth (10 Mbps unless otherwise noted, chosen from the median of SpeedTest.net samples) and latency with `tc`. (2) *Wide Area*: We run the client, middlebox, and server on EC2 instances in Spain, Ireland, and California, respectively. The client connects either over fiber or 3G. Unless otherwise specified, experiments in either environment consist of 50 runs for which we report the mean; error bars indicate one standard deviation. Middleboxes are given full read/write access to each context since this is the worst case for mcTLS performance.

5.1 Time Overhead

Handshake Time Figure 3 (left) shows the time to first byte as the number of contexts increases. There is one middlebox and each link has a 20 ms delay (80 ms total RTT). `NoEncrypt` serves as a baseline, with a time to first byte of 160 ms, or 2 RTT. Up to 9 contexts, `mcTLS`, `E2E-TLS`, and `SplitTLS` each take 4 RTTs. At 10 contexts, `mcTLS` jumps to 5 RTT and at 14 to 7.

The culprit was TCP's Nagle algorithm, which delays the transmission of data until a full MSS is ready to be sent. At 10 contexts, the handshake messages from the proxy to the server exceed 1 MSS and Nagle holds the extra bytes until the first MSS is ACKed. At 14 contexts the same thing happens to the middlebox key material from the client (+1 RTT) and the server (+1 RTT). Disabling the Nagle algorithm (not uncommon in practice [23]) solved the problem. We tried `E2E-TLS`, `SplitTLS`, and `NoEncrypt` without Nagle as well, but their performance did not improve since their messages never exceed 1 MSS.

Time to first byte scales linearly with the number of middleboxes, since in our experiments adding a middlebox also adds a 20 ms link (Figure 3 right). The latency increase and the extra key material to distribute exacerbate the problems caused by Nagle; disabling it once again brings `mcTLS` performance in line with `E2E-TLS` and `SplitTLS`. Finally, if middleboxes lie directly on the data path (which often happens), then the only additional overhead is processing time, which is minimal.

***Takeaway:** mcTLS's handshake is not discernibly longer than `SplitTLS`'s or `E2E-TLS`'s.*

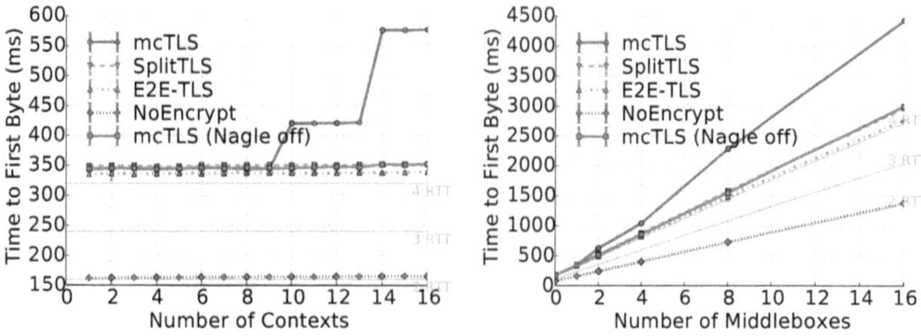

Figure 3: Time to first byte vs. # contexts (left) and # middleboxes (right).

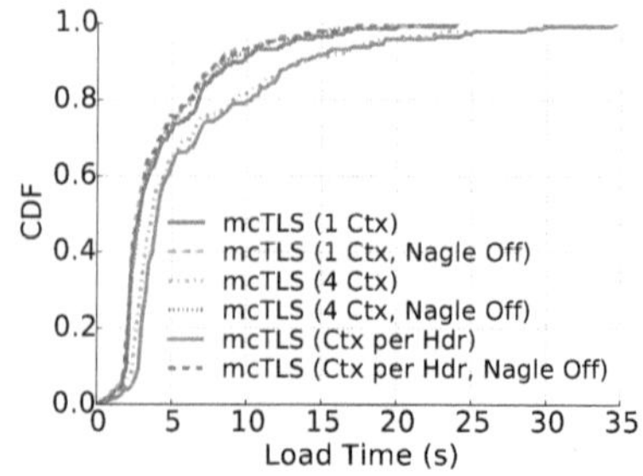

Figure 4: Page load time for different numbers of mcTLS contexts.

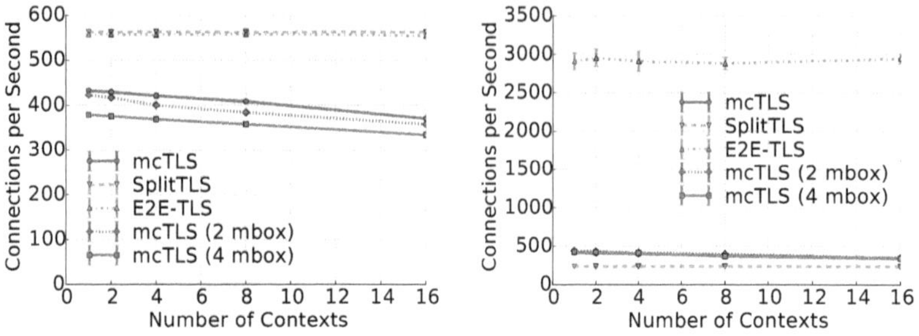

Figure 5: Load sustainable at the server (left) and middlebox (right).

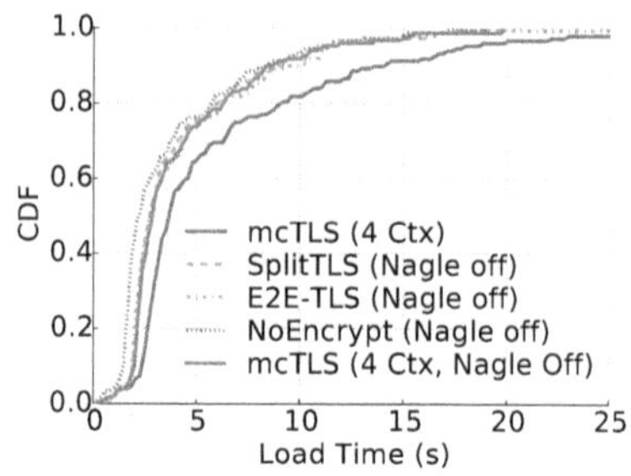

Figure 6: Page load time.

File Transfer Time Next we explore the timing behavior of each full protocol by transferring files through a single middlebox. To choose realistic file sizes, we loaded the top 500 Alexa pages and picked the 10th, 50th, and 99th percentile object sizes (0.5 kB, 4.9 kB, and 185 kB, respectively). We also consider large (10MB) downloads (e.g., larger zip files or video chunks).

The first four bar groups in Figure 7 show the download time for increasing file sizes at 1 Mbps; each bar represents 10 repetitions. As expected, the handshake overhead dominates for smaller files (<5 kB); all protocols that use encryption require an additional ~17 ms compared to `NoEncrypt`. mcTLS is comparable to `E2E-TLS` and `SplitTLS`. We see the same behavior when downloading files at different link rates or in the wide area (last four bar groups). Handshake and data transfer dominate download time; protocol-specific processing makes little difference.

Takeaway: *mcTLS transfer times are not substantially higher than* ***SplitTLS*** *or* ***E2E-TLS*** *irrespective of link type, bandwidth, or file size.*

Page Load Time To understand how the microbenchmarks above translate to real-world performance, we examine web page load time. Though we have not yet ported a full-blown web browser to mcTLS, we approximate a full page load in our simple client as follows. First, we load all of the Alexa top 500 pages that support HTTPS in Chrome. For each page, we extract a list of the objects loaded, their sizes, and whether or not an existing connection was re-used to fetch each one (we cannot tell *which* connection was used, so we assign the object to an existing one chosen at random). Next, our client "plays back" the page load by requesting dummy objects of the appropriate sizes from the server. We make the simplifying assumption that each object depends only on the previous object loaded in the same connection (this might introduce false dependencies and ignore true ones).

First, we compare three mcTLS strategies: 1-Context (all data in one context), 4-Context (request headers, request body, response headers, response body), and ContextPerHeader (one context for each HTTP header, one for request body, and one for response body). Figure 4 shows the CDF of page load times for each strategy. The plot shows similar performance for each strategy, indicating that mcTLS is not overly sensitive to the way data is placed into contexts.

Next we compare `mcTLS` to `SplitTLS`, `E2E-TLS`, and `NoEncrypt` (Figure 6). We use the 4-Context strategy for `mcTLS`, since we imagine it will be the most common. `SplitTLS`, `E2E-TLS`, and `NoEncrypt` perform the same, while mcTLS adds a half second or more. Once again, Nagle is to blame: sending data in multiple contexts causes back-to-back `send()` calls to TCP. The first record is sent immediately, but the subsequent records are held because they are smaller than an MSS and there is unacknowledged data in flight. Repeating the experiment with Nagle turned off closed the gap.

Takeaway: *mcTLS has* no *impact on real world Web page load times.*

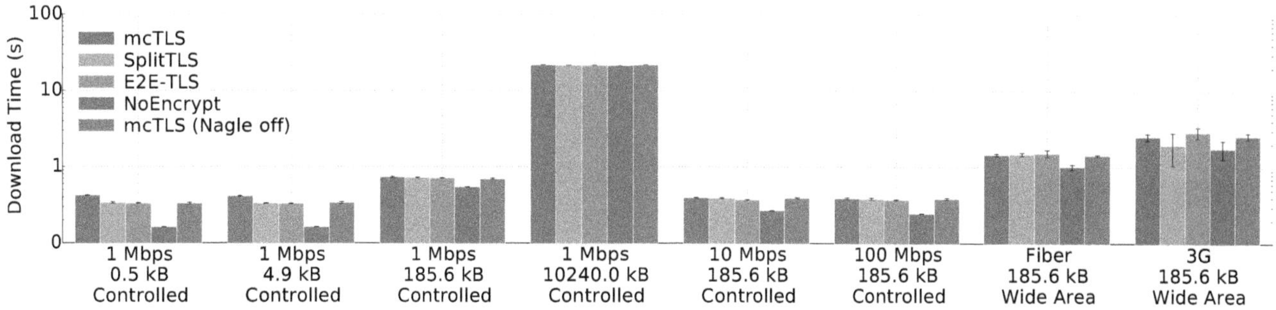

Figure 7: File download time for various configurations of link speed and file size.

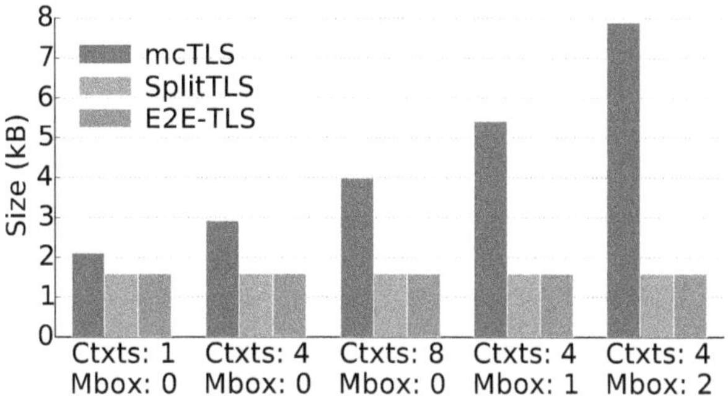

Figure 8: Handshake sizes.

5.2 Data Volume Overhead

Most of mcTLS' data overhead comes from the handshake, and it increases with the number of middleboxes and contexts (due to certificates and context key distribution). Figure 8 shows the total size of the handshake for different numbers of contexts and middleboxes. For a base configuration with one context and no middleboxes, the `mcTLS` handshake is 2.1 kB compared to 1.6 kB for `SplitTLS` and `E2E-TLS`. Note that the handshake size is independent of the file size.

Next, each record carries MACs (three in mcTLS, one in TLS). Their impact depends on the application's sending pattern—smaller records mean larger overhead. For the web browsing experiments in §5.1, the median MAC overhead for `SplitTLS` compared to `NoEncrypt` was 0.6%; as expected, `mcTLS` triples that to 2.4%.

Finally, padding and header overhead are negligible.

Takeaway: *Apart from the initial handshake overhead, which is negligible for all but short connections, mcTLS introduces less than 2% additional overhead for web browsing compared to* `SplitTLS` *or* `E2E-TLS`*.*

5.3 CPU Overhead

Figure 5 (left) shows the number of connections (only handshakes) per second the server can sustain. We see that the extra asymmetric encryption for distributing middlebox key material takes a toll. The `mcTLS` server handles 23% fewer connections than `SplitTLS` or `E2E-TLS`; that number drops to 35% fewer as the number of contexts, and therefore the number of partial context keys the server must encrypt, increases. We note two things: (1) key distribution optimizations, which we intend to pursue in future work, can shrink this gap, and (2) the server can reclaim this lost performance if the client handles key generation/distribution (§3.6).

The results for the middlebox are more interesting (Figure 5 right). First, `E2E-TLS` significantly outperforms `mcTLS` and `SplitTLS` (note the change in Y scale) because it does not participate in a TLS handshake. Second, `mcTLS` performs *better* than `SplitTLS` because in `SplitTLS` the proxy has to participate in *two* TLS handshakes. These results show it is not only feasible, but practical to use middleboxes in the core network.

Takeaway: `mcTLS` *servers can serve 23%–35% fewer connections per second than* `SplitTLS`*, but* `mcTLS` *middleboxes can serve 45%–75% more.*

5.4 Deployment

To begin understanding deployability, we built an extension to the Ruby SSL library that adds support for mcTLS with less than 250 lines of C code. Using the extension, we then built a 17 line Ruby web client with the same functionality as our C/OpenSSL-based evaluation client. While a bit more work is needed to make the extension more Ruby-like, the potential to easily write mcTLS-enabled mobile apps with developer-friendly tools like RubyMotion[3] is promising.

We also modified the OpenSSL `s_time` benchmarking tool to support mcTLS. Again, minimal changes were required: less than 30 new lines of C code were added, and about 10 lines were slightly changed. This means that relatively minor developer effort is required to gain the full benefits of mcTLS.

While supporting fine-grained access control requires the minimal effort of assigning data to a context and setting middlebox permissions for those contexts, many of the benefits of mcTLS are immediately available with just support from the HTTP client library and server. For example, HTTP libraries could use the 4-Context strategy by default, requiring no additional program-

[3]http://www.rubymotion.com/

ming or effort from application developers. Finally, we note that clients and servers can easily fall back to regular TLS if an mcTLS connection cannot be negotiated.

Takeaway: *Upgrading an application or library to mcTLS appears to be straightforward and easy.*

6. DISCUSSION

6.1 Middlebox Discovery

mcTLS assumes that the client has a list of middleboxes prior to initiating a handshake, which it includes in the `ClientHello`. Building this list is largely orthogonal to mcTLS itself; many existing mechanisms could be used, depending on *who* is trying to add a middlebox to the session. For example:

- **Users** or **system administrators** might configure the client (application or OS) directly (e.g., the user might point his browser toward Google's SPDY proxy). If users express interest in, e.g., a "nearby" data compression proxy, rather than a particular one, clients could discover available proxies using mDNS [10] or DNS-SD [9].
- **Content providers** could specify middleboxes to be used in any connection to its servers using DNS.
- **Network operators** can use DHCP or PDP/PDN to inform clients of any required middleboxes (e.g., virus scanners).

If a priori mechanisms like these are not flexible enough, the handshake could be extended to allow, e.g., on-path middleboxes to insert themselves (subject to subsequent approval by the endpoints, of course) during session setup. The costs and benefits of this are not immediately clear; we leave working out the details of more complex session negotiation for future work.

6.2 User Interface

The technical solution for adding middleboxes to secure communication sessions means little without suitable interfaces through which users can control it. The primary challenges for such an interface are:

- *Indicating to the user that the session is "secure."* Re-using the well-known lock icon is misleading, since the semantics of TLS and mcTLS differ.
- *Communicating to the user who can do what.* Which middleboxes can read the user's data? Which can modify it? What modifications do they make? Who owns the middleboxes? Who added them to the session and why?
- *Allowing users to set access controls.* Which sessions can a middlebox see? Within those sessions, which fields can it read or write? The difficulty is making such controls simple and scalable. For instance, asking users to set middlebox permissions for each domain they visit is not practical.

Designing a satisfactory interface atop mcTLS is a project in and of itself, one we cannot begin to do justice here.

	R1	**R2**	**R3**	**R4**	**R5**
mcTLS	•	•	•	•	•
(1) Custom Certificate					
(2) Proxy Certificate Flag	○			○	
(3) Session Key Out-of-Band	•	•		○	
(4) Custom Browser					
(5) Proxy Server Extension	○	○	○	○	

(• = full compliance; ○ = partial compliance)

Table 4: Design principle compliance for mcTLS and competing proposals.

7. RELATED WORK

There has been a lot of recent interest, particularly in industry, for including intermediaries in encrypted sessions. First we describe five previous proposals for doing so in the context of TLS; as shown in Table 4, none of them meets all five of our requirements. Then we discuss alternatives that replace TLS altogether.

(1) Custom Root Certificate Section 2.2 describes a common technique in which network administrators install a custom root certificate on the client.

Discussion: This technique does not meet any of our requirements. First, the server, and in many cases the client, is not aware of the existence of the middlebox (R4) so it clearly cannot authenticate it (R1). Second, the middlebox has full read and write access to all data in the session (R5). Finally, since the client has no control after the first hop, there is no guarantee about the secrecy, integrity, or authenticity of the data (R2, R3) or the identity of the server (R1).

(2) "I'm a proxy" Certificate Flag A 2014 IETF draft from Ericsson and AT&T proposes using the X.509 Extended Key Usage extension to indicate that a certificate belongs to a proxy [20]. Upon receiving such a certificate during a TLS handshake, the user agent would omit the domain name check (presumably with user permission) and establish a TLS session with the proxy, which would in turn open a connection with the server. Based on user preferences, the user agent might only accept proxy certificates for certain sessions.

Discussion: In this case, the client is made explicitly aware of the presence of the middlebox, so it can authenticate it (R1) and can control its use on a per connection basis (R4). The client still cannot authenticate the server and the server is unaware of the middlebox. R2, R3, and R5 remain unaddressed.

(3) Pass Session Key Out-of-Band Another IETF draft, this one from Google, assumes that the client maintains a persistent TLS connection with the proxy and multiplexes multiple sessions over that connection (much how Google's data compression proxy operates). After establishing an end-to-end TLS connection with the server (which the proxy blindly forwards), the client passes the session key to the proxy before transmitting data on the new connection [28]. Again, the user agent can selectively grant the proxy access on a per-connection basis based on user preference.

Discussion: Compared with (1), this solution has the additional benefit that the client authenticates both the middlebox and the server (R1) and knows that the session is encrypted end-to-end (R2). R3, R4, and R5 are still partially or completely unaddressed.

(4) Ship a Custom Browser A fourth option is to modify the browser itself to accept certificates from certain trusted proxies. This is the approach Viasat is taking for its Exede satellite Internet customers [18], arguing that caching and prefetching are critical on high-latency links.

Discussion: This solution is essentially the same as (1), so it also fails all requirements. In addition, it has the drawback that a custom browser may not be updated quickly, is expensive to develop and maintain, and may be inconvenient to users.

(5) Proxy Server Extension The most promising approach so far is Cisco's TLS Proxy Server Extension [21]. The proxy receives a ClientHello from the client, establishes a TLS connection with the server, and includes the server's certificate and information about the ciphersuite negotiated for the proxy-server connection in a ProxyInfoExtension appended to the ServerHello it returns to the client. The client can then check both the proxy's and the server's certificate.

Discussion: The client must *completely* trust the middlebox to provide honest information about the server certificate and ciphersuite, so this solution only partially fulfills R1, R2, and R3. The proxy is not necessarily visible to the server, so only partial R4. Finally, the proxy has read/write access to all data (R5).

Other Approaches An alternative to TLS-based techniques is an extension to IPsec that allows portions of the payload to be encrypted/authenticated between the two end-points of a security association and leaves the remainder in the clear [16]. The authors target this architecture for securely enabling intermediary-based services for wireless mobile users. This solution leaves data for middleboxes completely unencrypted (R2); R1 and R3 are also violated. Furthermore, this approach does not allow explicit control of the data flow to different entities (R4).

Tcpcrypt [6, 5] is an alternative proposal for establishing end-to-end encrypted sessions. Compared with TLS, it reduces the overhead on the server, leaves authentication to the application, can be embedded in the TCP handshake, and uses a session ID to unambiguously identify the endpoints of a session. Similar to TLS, tcpcrypt supports communication between two endpoints only, but we believe that the concepts of encryption contexts and contributory context keys could be applied to it as well. However, because of mcTLS's increased handshake size, it may no longer be possible to embed the entire handshake in the TCP handshake.

An alternative to a transport-layer protocol, like TLS or mcTLS, is supporting trusted intermediaries at the network layer. The Delegation-Oriented Architecture (DOA) [34] and Named Data Networking (NDN) [15] do this with their own security mechanisms and properties. We chose to modify TLS due to its widespread use, making it the perfect vehicle for immediate experimentation and incremental deployment.

8. CONCLUSION

The increasing use of TLS by Internet services provides privacy and security, but also leads to the loss of capabilities that are typically provided by an invisible army of middleboxes offering security, compression, caching, or content/network resource optimization. Finding an incrementally deployable solution that can bring back these benefits while maintaining the security expectations of clients, content providers, and network operators is not easy. mcTLS does this by extending TLS, which already carries a significant portion of HTTP traffic. mcTLS focuses on transparency and control: (1) trusted middleboxes are introduced at the consent of both client and server, (2) on a per session basis, (3) with clear access rights (read/write), and (4) to specific parts of the data stream.

We show that building such a protocol is not only feasible but also introduces limited overhead in terms of latency, load time, and data overhead. More importantly, mcTLS can be incrementally deployed and requires only minor modifications to client and server software to support the majority of expected use cases. By using mcTLS, secure communication sessions can regain lost efficiencies with explicit consent from users and content providers.

Acknowledgments

Many thanks to the reviewers for their comments and to our shepherd, Sharon Goldberg, for going above and beyond. This research was funded in part by NSF under award number CNS-1345305, by DoD, Air Force Office of Scientific Research, National Defense Science and Engineering Graduate (NDSEG) Fellowship 32 CFR 168a, and by the European Union under the FP7 Grant Agreement n. 318627 (Integrated Project "mPlane").

9. REFERENCES

[1] http://mctls.org.

[2] Dashboards—android developers. https://developer.android.com/about/dashboards/index.html. Accessed: Dec. 2014.

[3] V. Agababov, M. Buettner, V. Chudnovsky, et al. Flywheel: Google's data compression proxy for the mobile web. NSDI '15, pages 367–380, Oakland, CA, May 2015. USENIX Association.

[4] D. Beaver. HTTP2 Expression of Interest. http://lists.w3.org/Archives/Public/ietf-http-wg/2012JulSep/0251.html, 7 2012.

[5] A. Bittau, D. Boneh, M. Hamburg, et al. Cryptographic protection of tcp streams (tcpcrypt), Feb. 2014.

[6] A. Bittau, M. Hamburg, M. Handley, D. Mazières, and D. Boneh. The case for ubiquitous transport-level encryption. USENIX Security'10, Berkeley, CA, USA, 2010. USENIX Association.

[7] I. Brown. End-to-end security in active networks. In *University College London PhD Thesis*, 2001.

[8] D. Cameron. The internet and pornography: Prime minister calls for action. https://www.gov.uk/government/speeches/the-internet-and-pornography-prime-minister-calls-for-action. Accessed: Jan. 2015.

[9] S. Cheshire and M. Krochmal. DNS-Based Service Discovery. RFC 6763 (Proposed Standard), Feb. 2013.

[10] S. Cheshire and M. Krochmal. Multicast DNS. RFC 6762 (Proposed Standard), Feb. 2013.

[11] T. Dierks and E. Rescorla. The Transport Layer Security (TLS) Protocol Version 1.2. RFC 5246 (Proposed Standard), Aug. 2008. Updated by RFCs 5746, 5878, 6176.

[12] F. R. Dogar, P. Steenkiste, and K. Papagiannaki. Catnap: exploiting high bandwidth wireless interfaces to save energy for mobile devices. MobiSys '10, New York, NY, USA, 2010. ACM.

[13] J. Erman, A. Gerber, M. Hajiaghayi, et al. To cache or not to cache: The 3g case. *Internet Computing, IEEE*, 15(2):27–34, March 2011.

[14] M. Hoque, M. Siekkinen, and J. K. Nurminen. On the energy efficiency of proxy-based traffic shaping for mobile audio streaming. CCNC, pages 891–895. IEEE, 2011.

[15] V. Jacobson, D. K. Smetters, J. D. Thornton, et al. Networking named content. CoNEXT '09, pages 1–12, New York, NY, USA, 2009. ACM.

[16] S. Kasera, S. Mizikovsky, G. S. Sundaram, and T. Y. C. Woo. On securely enabling intermediary-based services and performance enhancements for wireless mobile users. In *Workshop on Wireless Security, 2003*, 2003.

[17] A. Langley, N. Modadugu, and W.-T. Chang. Overclocking SSL. https://www.imperialviolet.org/2010/06/25/overclocking-ssl.html, 6 2010.

[18] P. Lepeska. Trusted proxy and the cost of bits. http://www.ietf.org/proceedings/90/slides/slides-90-httpbis-6.pdf, 7 2014.

[19] V. Liu, S. Han, A. Krishnamurthy, and T. Anderson. An Internet Architecture Based on the Principle of Least Privilege. Technical Report UW-CSE-12-09-05, University of Washington, Sept. 2012.

[20] S. Loreto, J. Mattsson, R. Skog, et al. Explicit Trusted Proxy in HTTP/2.0. Internet-Draft draft-loreto-httpbis-trusted-proxy20-01, IETF Secretariat, Feb. 2014.

[21] D. McGrew, D. Wing, Y. Nir, and P. Gladstone. TLS Proxy Server Extension. Internet-Draft draft-mcgrew-tls-proxy-server-01, IETF Secretariat, July 2012.

[22] A. Menezes and B. Ustaoglu. On reusing ephemeral keys in diffie-hellman key agreement protocols. *International Journal of Applied Cryptography*, 2(2):154–158, 2010.

[23] J. C. Mogul and G. Minshall. Rethinking the tcp nagle algorithm. *SIGCOMM CCR*, Jan. 2001.

[24] C. Muthukrishnan, V. Paxson, M. Allman, and A. Akella. Using strongly typed networking to architect for tussle. Hotnets-IX, pages 9:1–9:6, New York, NY, USA, 2010. ACM.

[25] D. Naor, A. Shenhav, and A. Wool. Toward securing untrusted storage without public-key operations. StorageSS '05, pages 51–56, New York, NY, USA, 2005. ACM.

[26] D. Naylor, A. Finamore, I. Leontiadis, et al. The Cost of the "S" in HTTPS. CoNEXT '14, pages 133–140, New York, NY, USA, 2014. ACM.

[27] C. Nikolouzakis. Encrypted traffic grows 40% post edward snowden nsa leak. http://www.sinefa.com/blog/encrypted-traffic-grows-post-edward-snowden-nsa-leak. Accessed: Jan. 2015.

[28] R. Peon. Explicit Proxies for HTTP/2.0. Internet-Draft draft-rpeon-httpbis-exproxy-00, IETF Secretariat, June 2012.

[29] F. Qian, S. Sen, and O. Spatscheck. Characterizing resource usage for mobile web browsing. MobiSys '14, pages 218–231, New York, NY, USA, 2014. ACM.

[30] E. Rescorla. HTTP Over TLS. RFC 2818 (Informational), May 2000.

[31] J. H. Saltzer, D. P. Reed, and D. D. Clark. End-to-end arguments in system design. *ACM Trans. Comput. Syst.*, 2(4):277–288, Nov. 1984.

[32] J. H. Saltzer and M. D. Schroeder. The protection of information in computer systems. *Proceedings of the IEEE*, 63(9):1278–1308, 1975.

[33] J. Sherry, S. Hasan, C. Scott, et al. Making middleboxes someone else's problem: Network processing as a cloud service. SIGCOMM '12, pages 13–24, New York, NY, USA, 2012. ACM.

[34] M. Walfish, J. Stribling, M. Krohn, et al. Middleboxes no longer considered harmful. OSDI'04, Berkeley, CA, USA, 2004. USENIX Association.

[35] N. Weaver, C. Kreibich, M. Dam, and V. Paxson. Here be web proxies. In *Passive and Active Measurement*, pages 183–192. Springer, 2014.

[36] C. Wisniewski. Path and hipster iphone apps leak sensitive data without notification. https://nakedsecurity.sophos.com/2012/02/08/apple-mobile-apps-path-and-hipster-and-leak-sensitive-c Accessed: May 2015.

[37] S. Woo, E. Jeong, S. Park, et al. Comparison of caching strategies in modern cellular backhaul networks. MobiSys '13, pages 319–332, New York, NY, USA, 2013. ACM.

[38] X. Xu, Y. Jiang, T. Flach, et al. Investigating transparent web proxies in cellular networks. PAM '15.

BlindBox: Deep Packet Inspection over Encrypted Traffic

Justine Sherry
UC Berkeley

Chang Lan
UC Berkeley

Raluca Ada Popa
ETH Zürich and UC Berkeley

Sylvia Ratnasamy
UC Berkeley

ABSTRACT

Many network middleboxes perform *deep packet inspection* (DPI), a set of useful tasks which examine packet payloads. These tasks include intrusion detection (IDS), exfiltration detection, and parental filtering. However, a long-standing issue is that once packets are sent over HTTPS, middleboxes can no longer accomplish their tasks because the payloads are encrypted. Hence, one is faced with the choice of *only one* of two desirable properties: the functionality of middleboxes and the privacy of encryption.

We propose *BlindBox*, the first system that simultaneously provides *both* of these properties. The approach of BlindBox is to perform the deep-packet inspection *directly on the encrypted traffic*. BlindBox realizes this approach through a new protocol and new encryption schemes. We demonstrate that BlindBox enables applications such as IDS, exfiltration detection and parental filtering, and supports real rulesets from both open-source and industrial DPI systems. We implemented BlindBox and showed that it is practical for settings with long-lived HTTPS connections. Moreover, its core encryption scheme is 3-6 orders of magnitude faster than existing relevant cryptographic schemes.

CCS Concepts

• Security and privacy → Cryptography; Security protocols; • Networks → Middleboxes / network appliances;

Keywords

middlebox privacy; network privacy; searchable encryption

1. INTRODUCTION

Many network middleboxes perform *deep packet inspection* (DPI) to provide a wide range of services which can benefit both end users and network operators. For example, Network Intrusion Detection/Prevention (IDS/IPS) systems (e.g., Snort [9] or Bro [36]) detect if packets from a compromised sender contain an attack. Exfiltration prevention devices block accidental leakage of private data in enterprises by searching for document confidentiality watermarks in the data transferred out of an enterprise network [45]. Parental filtering devices prevent children from accessing adult material in schools, libraries, and homes [13]. These devices and many others [6, 8, 7] all share the common feature that they inspect packet payloads; the market for such DPI devices is expected to grow to over $2B by 2018 [44].

At the same time, HTTPS and other encryption protocols have seen dramatic growth in usage in recent years [35]; encryption protects users' private data from eavesdroppers anywhere in the network, including at a middlebox. Unfortunately, HTTPS poses a long-standing challenge for DPI devices. Since packet payloads are encrypted, network middleboxes can no longer inspect payloads [35] and accomplish their tasks. To enable middlebox processing, some currently deployed middlebox systems support HTTPS in an *insecure* way: they mount a man-in-the-middle attack on SSL and decrypt the traffic at the middlebox [28, 27]. This approach violates the end-to-end security guarantees of SSL and thus causes an unfortunate set of issues as surveyed in [28]. Moreover, users and clients have criticized this approach [51, 31, 41, 48], some expressing worry that the private data logged at the middlebox is given to marketers.

Therefore, one is faced with an unfortunate choice of *only one* of two desirable properties: the functionality of the middleboxes and the privacy given by encryption. At a first glance, it may appear that these two properties are fundamentally at odds with each other: how can a network appliance make decisions based on connection contents when it cannot see these contents?

In this paper, we demonstrate that it is possible to build a system that satisfies both of these seemingly conflicting properties. We present *BlindBox*, the first system that provides both the benefits of encryption and functionality at a DPI middlebox. The name "BlindBox" denotes that the middlebox cannot see the private content of traffic.

Our approach is to perform *the inspection directly on the encrypted payload*, without decrypting the payload at the middlebox. Building a practical such system is challenging: networks operate at very high rates requiring cryptographic operations on the critical path to run in micro or even nano seconds; further, some middleboxes require support for rich operations, such as matching regular expressions. A potential candidate is expressive cryptographic schemes such as fully homomorphic or functional encryption [24, 23, 26],

SIGCOMM '15, August 17 - 21, 2015, London, United Kingdom

 ISBN 978-1-4503-3542-3/15/08...$15.00

DOI: http://dx.doi.org/10.1145/2785956.2787502

but these are prohibitively slow, decreasing network rates by many orders of magnitude.

To overcome these challenges, BlindBox explores and specializes on the network setting. BlindBox enables two classes of DPI computation each having its own privacy guarantees: *exact match privacy* and *probable cause privacy*. Both of BlindBox's privacy models are much stronger than the state-of-the-art "man in the middle" approach deployed today. In both of these models, BlindBox protects the data with strong randomized encryption schemes providing similar security guarantees to the well-studied notion of searchable encryption [46, 29]. Depending on the class of computation, BlindBox allows the middlebox to learn a small amount of information about the traffic to detect rules efficiently.

The first class of computation consists of DPI applications that rely only on exact string matching, such as watermarking, parental filtering, and a limited IDS. Under the associated privacy model, exact match privacy, the middlebox learns at which positions in a flow attack keywords occur; for substrings of the flow that do not match an attack keyword, the middlebox learns virtually nothing.

The second class of computation can support all DPI applications, including those which perform regular expressions or scripting. The privacy model here, probable cause privacy, is a new network privacy model: the middlebox gains the ability to see a (decrypted) individual packet or flow *only if the flow is suspicious*; namely, the flow contains a string that matches a known attack keyword. If the stream is not suspicious, the middlebox cannot see the (decrypted) stream. Hence, privacy is affected *only with a cause*. In practice, most traffic remains encrypted. BlindBox allows users to select which privacy model they are most comfortable with.

To implement these two models, we developed the following techniques:

- **DPIEnc** and **BlindBox Detect** are a new searchable encryption scheme [46] and an associated fast detection protocol, which can be used to inspect encrypted traffic for certain keywords efficiently. As we explain in §3, existing searchable encryption schemes [46, 29, 15] are either deterministic (which can enable fast protocols, but provide weak security) or randomized (which have stronger security, but are slow in our setting). DPIEnc with BlindBox Detect achieve both the speed of deterministic encryption and the security of randomized encryption; detection on encrypted traffic runs as fast as on unencrypted traffic.
- **Obfuscated Rule Encryption** is a technique to allow the middlebox to obtain encrypted rules based on the rules from the middlebox and the private key of the endpoints, without the endpoints learning the rules or the middlebox learning the private key. This technique builds on Yao's garbled circuits [50] and oblivious transfer [34, 39, 22].
- **Probable Cause Decryption** is a mechanism to allow flow decryption when a suspicious keyword is observed in the flow; this is the mechanism that allows us to implement our probable cause privacy model.

We implemented BlindBox as well as a new secure transport protocol for HTTP, which we call BlindBox HTTPS. We evaluated BlindBox HTTPS using several real DPI applications: data watermarking [45], parental filtering, and intrusion detection. We used attack signatures from the open-source community (Snort [9]) and industrial IDSes (McAfee Stonesoft and Lastline).

We show that BlindBox's performance is practical for many settings. For example, the rate at which the middlebox can inspect packets is as high as 186Mbps per core in our experiments. Given that standard IDS implementations, such as Snort [9], peak at under 100Mbps, this performance is competitive with existing deployments. We achieve this performance due to DPIEnc and BlindBox Detect. When compared to two strawmen consisting of a popular searchable encryption scheme [46] and a functional encryption scheme [30], DPIEnc with BlindBox Detect are 3-6 orders of magnitude faster. Nevertheless, a component of BlindBox is not yet as fast as desirable: the setup of an HTTPS connection. This setup performs obfuscated rule encryption and it takes time proportional to the number of attack rules. For rulesets with tens of keywords, this setup completes in under a second; however, for large IDS installations with thousands of rules, the setup can take up to 1.5 minutes to complete. Hence, BlindBox is most fit for settings using long or persistent connections through SPDY-like protocols or tunneling, and not yet practical for short, independent flows with many rules.

We see BlindBox as a first step towards a general protocol that will allow middleboxes and end-to-end encryption to coexist, without sacrificing the benefits of either. BlindBox shows that this coexistence is possible for the class of middleboxes performing deep packet inspection. A future, general protocol will devise mechanisms to address the full range of middleboxes including those that process packet headers, modify packet payloads (such as transcoders and WAN optimizers), or terminate sessions (such as Web or SIP proxies). Consequently, the subject of our current and future work focuses on achieving this end goal: a general protocol to allow all middleboxes to coexist with encryption.

2. OVERVIEW

Fig. 1 presents the system architecture. There are four parties: sender (S), receiver (R), middlebox (MB), and rule generator (RG) – these reflect standard middlebox deployments today. RG generates attack rules (also called signatures) to be used by MB in detecting attacks. Each rule attempts to describe an attack and it contains fields such as: one or more keywords to be matched in the traffic, offset information for each keyword, and sometimes regular expressions. The RG role is performed today by organizations like Emerging Threats [3], McAfee [4], or Symantec [11]. S and R send traffic through MB. MB allows S and R to communicate unless MB observes an attack rule in their traffic.

Network administrators today deploy in-network middleboxes in this way because it gives them a central point of control to enforce security policies in their network (since they often do not control the endpoints). Moreover, having a single in-network device is also easy to manage and

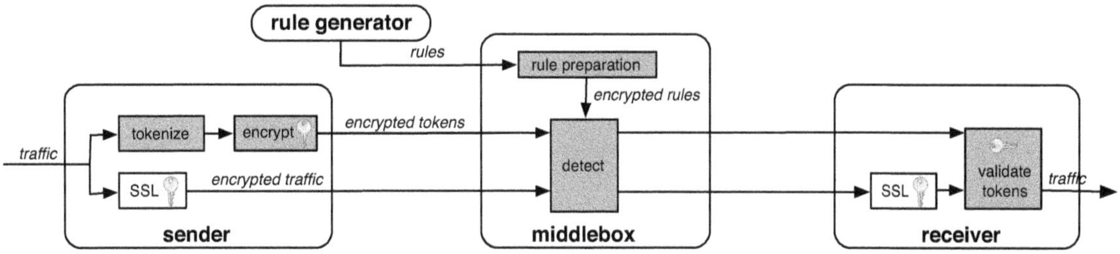

Figure 1: System architecture. Shaded boxes indicate algorithms added by BlindBox.

upgrade. Some research [21] considered alternative (edge) deployments in which endpoints perform all middlebox processing on their own traffic and rules are distributed to the endpoints. BlindBox instead aims to make changes compatible with the network approach in widespread use today. Further, this edge-based model is not compatible with the requirement of keeping rules hidden from endpoints, which we discuss in §2.2.1.

In today's deployments, MB can read any traffic sent between S and R. With BlindBox, MB should be able to detect if attack rules generated by RG match the traffic between R and S, but should not learn the contents of the traffic that does not match RG's attack rules.

2.1 Usage Scenarios

Before formalizing our threat model, we illustrate our usage scenario with three examples. For each individual in these examples, we indicate the party in our model (R, S, MB, or RG) that they correspond to.

Example #1: University Network. Alice (R or S) is a student at the University of SIGCOMM and brings her own laptop to her dorm room. However, university policy requires that all student traffic be monitored for botnet signatures and illegal activity by a middlebox (MB) running an IDS. Alice is worried about her computer being infected with botnet software, so she also desires this policy applied to her traffic. McAfee (RG) is the service that provides attack rules to the middlebox and Alice trusts it. However, she is uncomfortable with the idea of someone she doesn't know (who has access to the middlebox) potentially being able to read her private Facebook messages and emails. Alice installs BlindBox HTTPS with McAfee's public key, allowing the IDS to scan her traffic for McAfee's signatures, but not read her private messages.

Example #2: ISP Service. Bob has two young children (S or R) at home, and registers for parental filtering with his ISP so that all traffic is filtered for adult content. However, Bob has read stories in the news of ISPs selling user browsing data to marketers [48] and wants to prevent his ISP (MB) from using his data in this way. Bob trusts the Electronic Filtering Foundation (RG), a non-profit which generates rulesets for filtering and pledges not to sell user data. Bob installs BlindBox HTTPS on his home computer with the Electronic Filtering Foundation's public key, allowing his traffic to be scanned for EFF rules, but no other data.

In the above examples, Alice and Bob want to have a middlebox in their network check *for the attack rules the corresponding trusted parties permit*, but the middlebox should not learn anything else about the content of the traffic. A key requirement is that there exists an RG which Alice, Bob and the MB trust with rule generation; if this is not the case, the parties cannot use BlindBox.

Anti-Example #1: Political Dissident. Charlie (R or S) is a political dissident who frequently browses sensitive websites, and is concerned about government monitoring. If the government coerces one of MB or RG, Charlie remains protected. However, BlindBox should not be used in a setting in which *both* MB and RG can be controlled by an attacker: in this case, RG can produce signatures for sensitive terms and MB will use these to match the traffic. Hence, if the government can coerce both MB and RG together, Charlie should not use BlindBox. Similarly, if the government can coerce root certificate generators, Charlie should not use vanilla HTTPS either because it may allow man-in-the-middle attacks on his traffic.

2.2 Security and Threat Model

The goal of our work is to protect the privacy of user traffic from MB. Any solution must satisfy a set of systems requirements we discuss in §2.2.1. We then discuss the threat model in §2.2.2 and the privacy guarantees BlindBox provides in §2.2.3.

2.2.1 System Requirements

BlindBox retains key system goals of traditional IDS deployments today: (1) BlindBox must maintain MB's ability to enforce its policies (i.e., detect rules and drop/alert accordingly), and (2) endpoints must not gain access to the IDS rules. The rationale behind the second requirement is twofold. First, in order to make IDS evasion more difficult for an attacker at the user, the rules should be hidden from the endpoints [36]. Second, most vendors (e.g., Lastline and McAfee Stonesoft) rely on the secrecy of their rulesets in their business model, as their value added against competitors often includes more comprehensive, more efficient, or harder to evade rules.

BlindBox maintains these two requirements, and adds an additional one: (3) that the middlebox cannot read the user's traffic, except the portions of the traffic which are considered *suspicious* based on the attack rules.

2.2.2 Threat Model

There are two types of attackers in our setup.

The original attacker considered by IDS. This is the same attacker that traditional (unencrypted) IDS consider and we do not change the threat model here. Our goal is to detect such an attacker over *encrypted* traffic. As in traditional IDS, one endpoint can behave maliciously, but at least one endpoint must be honest. This is a fundamental requirement of any IDS [36] because otherwise two malicious endpoints can agree on a secret key and encrypt their traffic under that key with a strong encryption scheme, making prevention impossible by the security properties of the encryption scheme. Similarly, the assumption that one endpoint is honest is also the default for exfiltration detection and parental filtering today. Parental filters can assume one endpoint is innocent under the expectation that 8-year-olds are unlikely replace their network protocol stack or install tunneling software. Commercial exfiltration detection devices primarily target *accidental* exfiltration (e.g., where an otherwise innocent employee attaches the wrong file to an email), recognizing that deliberate exfiltration requires control of the end host.

The attacker at the middlebox. This is the new attacker in our setting. This attacker tries to subvert our scheme by attempting to extract private data from the encrypted traffic passing through the middlebox. We assume that the middlebox MB performs the detection honestly, but that it tries to learn private data from the traffic and violate the privacy of the endpoints. In particular, we assume that an attacker at MB reads *all* the data accessible to the middlebox, including traffic logs and other state. Given this threat model, BlindBox's goal is to hide the content of the traffic from MB, while allowing MB to do DPI. We do not seek to hide the attack rules from the MB itself; many times these rules are hardcoded in the MB.

2.2.3 Privacy Models

We now describe our privacy models.

Exact Match Privacy gives the following guarantee: the middlebox will be able to discover only those substrings of the traffic that are exact matches for known attack keywords. For example, if there exists a rule for the word "ATTACK", the middlebox will learn at which offset in the flow the word "ATTACK" appears (if it appears), but does not learn what the other parts of the traffic are. Traffic which does not match a suspicious keyword remains unreadable to the middlebox.

Probable Cause Privacy gives a different guarantee: that the middlebox will be able to *decrypt a flow* only if a substring of the flow is an exact match for a known attack keyword. Probable cause privacy is useful for IDS tasks which require regular expressions or scripting to complete their analysis. This model is inspired from two ideas. First, it is inspired from the notion of probable cause from United States' criminal law: one should give up privacy *only* if there is a reason for suspicion. Second, most rules in Snort that contain regular expressions first attempt to find a suspicious keyword in the packet – this keyword is selective so only a small fraction of the traffic matches this string and is passed through the regexp. Indeed, the Snort user manual [47] urges the presence of such selective keywords because otherwise, detection would be too slow. Since rules are structured this way, it becomes easier to implement our probable cause privacy model by decrypting the stream if there is a match to the suspicious keyword.

Exact match privacy provides security guarantees as in searchable encryption [46], which are well-studied. Probable cause privacy is a new privacy model, and we believe it may be useful in other network domains beyond middleboxes (e.g. network forensics or search warrants), although we leave such investigation to future work. We formalize and prove the security guarantees of BlindBox using standard indistinguishability-based definitions in our extended paper [43]. Both models are stronger than the "man in the middle" approach in deployment today, where all traffic is decrypted regardless of suspicion. A user who prefers exact match privacy over probable cause privacy can indicate so within BlindBox HTTPS.

2.3 System Architecture

We now return to Fig. 1 to explain each module and how BlindBox functions from a high level; we delve into the protocol and implementation details in the following sections.

Prior to any connection, RG generates a set of *rules* which contain a list of suspicious keywords known to formulate parts of attacks; RG signs these rules with its private key and shares them with MB, its customer. S and R, who trust RG, install a BlindBox HTTPS configuration which includes RG's public key. Beyond this initial setup, RG is never directly involved in the protocol. We now discuss the interactions between R, S, and MB when R and S open a connection in a network monitored by MB.

Connection setup. First, the sender and receiver run the regular SSL handshake which permits them to agree on a key k_0. The sender and receiver use k_0 to derive three keys (e.g., using a pseudorandom generator):

- k_{SSL}: the regular SSL key, used to encrypt the traffic as in the SSL protocol,
- k: used in our detection protocol, and
- k_{rand}: used as a seed for randomness. Since both endpoints have the same seed, they will generate the same randomness.

At the same time, MB performs its own connection setup to be able to perform detection over S and R's traffic. In an exchange with S and R, MB obtains each rule from RG deterministically encrypted with key k – this will later enable MB to perform the detection. However, this exchange occurs in such a way that MB *does not learn the value of k* and in such a way that R and S *do not learn what the rules are*. We call this exchange *obfuscated rule encryption* and we describe how it is implemented in the following section.

Unlike the above handshake between S and R, which bootstraps off the existing SSL handshake, obfuscated rule encryption is a new exchange. In existing deployments, clients typically do not communicate directly with DPI middleboxes (although for other kinds of middleboxes, such as explicit proxies [17] or NAT hole-punching [20], they may do so). Even though this step removes the complete "transparency" of the DPI appliance, it is an incremental change that we consider an acceptable tradeoff for the benefits of BlindBox.

Sending traffic. To transmit, the sender: (1) encrypts the traffic with SSL as in a non-BlindBox system; (2) tokenizes the traffic by splitting it in substrings taken from various offsets (as discussed in §3); and (3) encrypts the resulting tokens using our DPIEnc encryption scheme.

Detection. The middlebox receives the SSL-encrypted traffic and the encrypted tokens. The detect module will search for matchings between the encrypted rules and the encrypted tokens using BlindBox Detect (Sec. 3.2). If there is a match, one can choose the same actions as in a regular (unencrypted IDS) such as drop the packet, stop the connection, or notify an administrator. After completing detection, MB forwards the SSL traffic and the encrypted tokens to the sender.

Receiving traffic. Two actions happen at the receiver. First, the receiver decrypts and authenticates the traffic using regular SSL. Second, the receiver checks that the encrypted tokens were encrypted properly by the sender. Recall that, in our threat model, one endpoint may be malicious – this endpoint could try to cheat by not encrypting the tokens correctly or by encrypting only a subset of the tokens to eschew detection at the middlebox. Since we assume that at least one endpoint is honest, such verification will prevent this attack.

Because BlindBox only supports attack rules at the HTTP application layer, this check is sufficient to prevent evasion. Almost all the rules in our datasets were in this category. Nonetheless, it is worth noting that, if an IDS were to support rules that detected attacks on the client driver or NIC – before verification –, an attacker *could* evade detection by not tokenizing.

2.4 Protocols

BlindBox provides three protocols. In Protocol I, a rule consists of one keyword. MB must be able to detect if the keyword appears at any offset in the traffic based on equality match. This protocol suffices for document watermarking [45] and parental filtering [13] applications, but can support only a few IDS rules. In Protocol II, a rule consists of multiple keywords as well as position information of these keywords. This protocol supports a wider class of IDS rules than Protocol I, as we elaborate in §7. Protocol I and II provide Exact Match Privacy, as discussed in §2.2.3. Protocol III additionally supports regular expressions and scripts, thus enabling a full IDS. Protocol III provides Probable Cause Privacy, as discussed in §2.2.3.

3. PROTOCOL I: BASIC DETECTION

Protocol I enables matching a suspicious keyword against the encrypted traffic. An attack rule in this protocol consists of one keyword. Even though this protocol is the simplest of our protocols, it introduces the majority of our techniques. The other protocols extend Protocol I.

To detect a keyword match on encrypted text, one naturally considers searchable encryption [46, 29]. However, existing searchable encryption schemes do not fit our setting for two reasons. First, the setup of searchable encryption requires the entity who has the secret key to encrypt the rules; this implies, in our setting, that the endpoints see the rules (which is not allowed as discussed in §2.2.2). Our obfuscated rule encryption addresses this problem.

Second, none of the existing schemes meet both of our security and network performance requirements. There are at least two kinds of searchable encryption schemes: deterministic and randomized. Deterministic schemes [15] leak whether two words in the traffic are equal to each other (even if they do not match a rule). This provides weak privacy because it allows an attacker to perform frequency analysis. At the same time, these schemes are fast because they enable MB to build fast indexes that can process each token (e.g. word) in a packet in time logarithmic in the number of rules. On the other hand, randomized schemes [46, 29] provide stronger security guarantees because they prevent frequency analysis by salting ciphertexts. However, the usage of the salt in these schemes requires combining each token with each rule, resulting in a processing time linear in the number of rules for each token; as we show in §7, this is too slow for packet processing. In comparison, our encryption scheme DPIEnc and detection protocol BlindBox Detect achieve the best of both worlds: the detection speed of deterministic encryption and the security of randomized encryption.

Let us now describe how each BlindBox module in Fig. 1 works in turn. Recall that S and R are the sender and receiver, MB the middlebox and RG the rule generator.

Tokenization. The first step in the protocol is to tokenize the input traffic. We start with a basic tokenization scheme, which we refer to as "window-based" tokenization because it follows a simple sliding window algorithm. For every offset in the bytestream, the sender creates a token of a fixed length: we used 8 bytes per token in our implementation. For example, if the packet stream is "alice apple", the sender generates the tokens "alice ap", "lice app", "ice appl", and so on. Using this tokenization scheme, MB will be able to detect rule keywords of length 8 bytes or greater. For a keyword longer than 8 bytes, MB splits it in substrings of 8 bytes, some of which may overlap. For example, if a keyword is "maliciously", MB can search for "maliciou" and "iciously". Since each encrypted token is 5 bytes long and the endpoint generates one encrypted token per byte of traffic, the bandwidth overhead of this approach is of $5\times$.

We can reduce this bandwidth overhead by introducing some optimizations. First, for an HTTP-only IDS (which does not analyze arbitrary binaries), we can have senders ignore tokenization for images and videos which the IDS does not need to analyze. Second, we can tailor our tokenization further to the HTTP realm by observing how the keywords from attack rules for these protocols are structured. The keywords matched in rules start and end before or after a delimiter. Delimiters are punctuation, spacing, and special symbols. For example, for the payload "login.php?user=alice", possible keywords in rules are typically "login", "login.php", "?user=", "user=alice", but not "logi" or "logi.ph". Hence, the sender needs to generate only those tokens that could match keywords that start and end on delimiter-based offsets; this allows us to ignore redundant tokens in the window. We refer to this tokenization as "delimiter-based" tokenization. In §7, we compare the overheads and coverage of these two tokenization protocols.

3.1 The DPIEnc Encryption Scheme

In this subsection, we present our new DPIEnc encryption scheme, which is used by the Encrypt module in Fig. 1. The sender encrypts each token t obtained from the tokenization with our encryption scheme. The encryption of a token t in DPIEnc is:

$$\mathsf{salt},\ \mathsf{AES}_{\mathsf{AES}_k(t)}(\mathsf{salt}) \bmod \mathsf{RS}, \quad (1)$$

where salt is a randomly-chosen value and RS is explained below.

Let us explain the rationale behind DPIEnc. For this purpose, assume that MB is being handed, for each rule r, the pair $(r, \mathsf{AES}_k(r))$, but not the key k. We explain in §3.3 how MB actually obtains $\mathsf{AES}_k(r)$.

Let's start by considering a simple deterministic encryption scheme instead of DPIEnc: the encryption of t is $\mathsf{AES}_k(t)$. Then, to check if t equals a keyword r, MB can simply check if $\mathsf{AES}_k(t) \stackrel{?}{=} \mathsf{AES}_k(r)$. Unfortunately, the resulting security is weak because every occurrence of t will have the same ciphertext. To address this problem, we need to randomize the encryption.

Hence, we use a "random function" H together with a random salt, and the ciphertext becomes: $\mathsf{salt}, H(\mathsf{salt}, \mathsf{AES}_k(t))$. Intuitively, H must be pseudorandom and not invertible. To perform a match, MB can then compute $H(\mathsf{salt}, \mathsf{AES}_k(r))$ based on $\mathsf{AES}_k(r)$ and salt, and again perform an equality check. The typical instantiation of H is SHA-1, but SHA-1 is not as fast as AES (because AES is implemented in hardware on modern processors) and can reduce BlindBox's network throughput. Instead, we implement H with AES, but this must be done carefully because these primitives have different security properties. To achieve the properties of H, AES must be keyed with a value that MB does not know when there is no match to an attack rule – hence, this value is $\mathsf{AES}_k(t)$. Our algorithm is now entirely implemented in AES, which makes it fast.

Finally, RS simply reduces the size of the ciphertext to reduce the bandwidth overhead, but it does not affect security. In our implementation, RS is 2^{40}, yielding a ciphertext length of 5 bytes. As a result, the ciphertext is no longer decryptable; this is not a problem because BlindBox always decrypts the traffic from the primary SSL stream.

Now, to detect a match between a keyword r and an encryption of a token t, MB computes $\mathsf{AES}_{\mathsf{AES}_k(r)}(\mathsf{salt}) \bmod \mathsf{RS}$ using salt and its knowledge of $\mathsf{AES}_k(r)$, and then tests for equality with $\mathsf{AES}_{\mathsf{AES}_k(t)}(\mathsf{salt}) \bmod \mathsf{RS}$.

Hence, naïvely, MB performs a match test for every token t and rule r, which results in a performance per token linear in the number of rules; this is too slow. To address this slowdown, our detection algorithm below makes this cost logarithmic in the number of rules, the same as for vanilla inspection of unencrypted traffic. This results in a significant performance improvement: for example, for a ruleset with 10000 keywords to match, a logarithmic lookup is four orders of magnitude faster than a linear scan.

3.2 BlindBox Detect Protocol

We now discuss how our detection algorithm achieves logarithmic lookup times, resolving the tension between security and performance. For simplicity of notation, denote $\mathsf{Enc}_k(\mathsf{salt}, t) = \mathsf{AES}_{\mathsf{AES}_k(t)}(\mathsf{salt})$.

The first idea is to precompute the values $\mathsf{Enc}_k(\mathsf{salt}, r)$ for every rule r and for every possible salt. Recall that MB can compute $\mathsf{Enc}_k(\mathsf{salt}, r)$ based only on salt and its knowledge of $\mathsf{AES}_k(r)$, and MB does not need to know k. Then, MB can arrange these values in a search tree. Next, for each encrypted token t in the traffic stream, MB simply looks up $\mathsf{Enc}_k(\mathsf{salt}, t)$ in the tree and checks if an equal value exists. However, the problem is that enumerating all possible salts for each keyword r is infeasible. Hence, it would be desirable to use only a few salts, but this strategy affects security: an attacker at MB can see which token in the traffic equals which other token in the traffic whenever the salt is reused for the same token. To maintain the desired security, every encryption of a token t must contain a different salt (although the salts can repeat across different tokens).

To use only a few salts and maintain security at the same time, the idea is for the sender to *generate salts based on the token value* and *no longer send the salt in the clear along with every encrypted token.* Concretely, the sender keeps a *counter table* mapping each token encrypted so far to how many times it appeared in the stream so far. Before sending encrypted tokens, the sender sends one initial salt, salt_0, and MB records it. Then, the sender no longer sends salts; concretely, for each token t, the sender sends $\mathsf{Enc}_k(\mathsf{salt}, t)$ but not salt. When encrypting a token t, the sender checks the number of times it was encrypted so far in the counter table, say ct_t, which could be zero. It then encrypts this token with the salt $(\mathsf{salt}_0 + \mathsf{ct}_t)$ by computing $\mathsf{Enc}_k(\mathsf{salt}_0 + \mathsf{ct}_t, t)$. Note that this provides the desired security because no two equal tokens will have the same salt.

For example, consider the sender needs to encrypt the tokens A, B, A. The sender computes and transmits: salt_0, $\mathsf{Enc}_k(\mathsf{salt}_0, A)$, $\mathsf{Enc}_k(\mathsf{salt}_0, B)$, and $\mathsf{Enc}_k(\mathsf{salt}_0 + 1, A)$. Not sending a salt for each ciphertext both reduces bandwidth and is required for security: if the sender had sent salts, MB could tell that the first and second tokens have the same salt, hence they are not equal.

To prevent the counter table from growing too large, the sender resets it every P bytes sent. When the sender resets this table, the sender sets $\mathsf{salt}_0 \leftarrow \mathsf{salt}_0 + \max_t \mathsf{ct}_t + 1$ and announces the new salt_0 to MB.

For detection, MB creates a table mapping each keyword r to a counter ct_r^* indicating the number of times this keyword r appeared so far in the traffic stream. MB also creates a search tree containing the encryption of each rule r with a salt computed from ct_r^*: $\mathsf{Enc}_k(\mathsf{salt}_0 + \mathsf{ct}_r^*, r)$. Whenever there is a match to r, MB increments ct_r^*, computes and inserts the new encryption $\mathsf{Enc}_k(\mathsf{salt}_0 + \mathsf{ct}_r^*, r)$ into the tree, and deletes the old value. We now summarize the detection algorithm.

BlindBox Detect: The state at MB consists of the counters ct_r^* for each rule r and a fast search tree made of $\mathsf{Enc}_k(\mathsf{salt}_0 + \mathsf{ct}_r^*, r)$ for each rule r.

1: For each encrypted token $\mathsf{Enc}_k(\mathsf{salt}, t)$ in a packet:

   1.1: If $\mathsf{Enc}_k(\mathsf{salt}, t)$ is in the search tree:

      1.1.1: There is a match, so take the corresponding action for this match.

      1.1.2: Delete the node in tree corresponding to r and insert $\mathsf{Enc}_k(\mathsf{salt}_0 + \mathsf{ct}_r^* + 1, t)$

      1.1.3: Set $\mathsf{ct}_r^* \leftarrow \mathsf{ct}_r^* + 1$

With this strategy, for every token t, MB performs a simple tree lookup, which is logarithmic in the number of rules. Other tree operations, such as deletion and insertion, happen rarely: when a malicious keyword matches in the traffic. These operations are also logarithmic in the number of rules.

3.3 Rule Preparation

The detection protocol above assumes that MB obtains $\mathsf{AES}_k(r)$ for every keyword r, every time a new connection (having a new key k) is setup. But how can MB obtain these values? The challenge here is that no party, MB or S/R, seems fit to compute $\mathsf{AES}_k(r)$: MB knows r, but it is not allowed to learn k; S and R know k, but are not allowed to learn the rule r (as discussed in §2.2.2).

Intuition. We provide a technique, called *obfuscated rule encryption*, to address this problem. The idea is that the sender provides to the middlebox an "obfuscation" of the function AES with the key k hardcoded in it. This obfuscation hides the key k. The middlebox runs this obfuscation on the rule r and obtains $\mathsf{AES}_k(r)$, without learning k. We denote this obfuscated function by ObfAES_k.

Since practical obfuscation does not exist, we implement it with Yao garbled circuits [50, 33], on which we elaborate below. With garbled circuits, MB cannot directly plug in r as input to $\mathsf{ObfAES}_k()$; instead, it must obtain from the endpoints an encoding of r that works with ObfAES_k. For this task, the sender uses a protocol called oblivious transfer [34, 14], which does not reveal r to the endpoints. Moreover, MB needs to obtain a fresh, re-encrypted garbled circuit $\mathsf{ObfAES}_k()$ for every keyword r; the reason is that the security of garbled circuits does not hold if MB receives more than one encoding for the same garbled circuit.

A problem is that MB might attempt to run the obfuscated encryption function on rules of its choice, as opposed to rules from RG. To prevent this attack, rules from RG must be signed by RG and the obfuscated (garbled) function must check that there is a valid signature on the input rule before encrypting it. If the signature is not valid, it outputs null.

Let us now present the building blocks and our protocol in more detail.

Yao garbling scheme [50, 33]. At a high level, a garbled circuit scheme, first introduced by Yao, consists of two algorithms Garble and Eval. Garble takes as input a function F with n bits of input and outputs a garbled function ObfF and

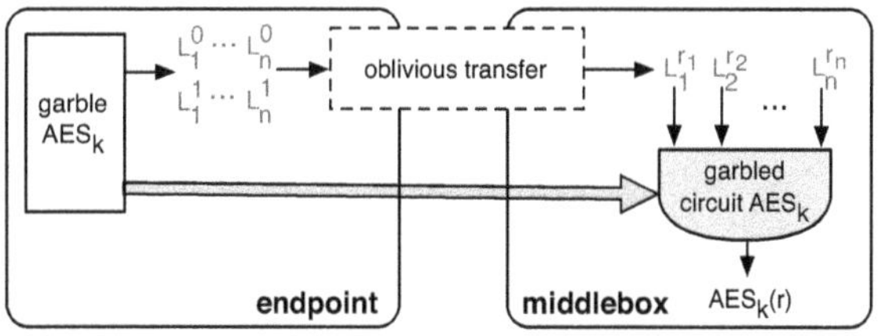

Figure 2: Rule preparation. The endpoint has a key k and the middlebox has a keyword r.

n pairs of labels $(L_1^0, L_1^1), \dots, (L_n^0, L_n^1)$, one pair for every input bit of F. Consider any input x of n bits with x_i being its i-th bit. ObfF has the property that $\mathsf{ObfF}(L_1^{x_1}, \dots, L_n^{x_n}) = F(x)$. Basically, ObfF produces the same output as F if given the labels corresponding to each bit of x. Regarding security, ObfF and $L_1^{x_1}, \dots, L_n^{x_n}$ do not leak anything about F and x beyond $F(x)$, as long as an adversary receives labels for only one input x.

1-out-of-2 oblivious transfer (OT) [34, 14]. Consider that a party A has two values, L^0 and L^1, and party B has a bit b. Consider that B wants to obtain the b-th label from A, L^b, but B does not want to tell b to A. Also, A does not want B to learn the other label L^{1-b}. Hence, B cannot send b to A and A cannot send both labels to B. Oblivious transfer (OT) enables exactly this: B can obtain L^b without learning L^{1-b} and A does not learn b.

Rule preparation. Fig. 2 illustrates the rule preparation process for one keyword r. One endpoint could be malicious and attempt to perform garbling incorrectly to eschew detection. To prevent such an attack, both endpoints have to prepare the garbled circuit and send it to MB to check that they produced the same result. If the garbled circuits and labels match, MB is assured that they are correct because at least one endpoint is honest (as discussed in Sec. 2.2.2). To enable this check, the endpoints must use the same randomness obtained from a pseudorandom generator seeded with k_{rand} (discussed in Sec. 2.3).

Rule preparation:

1: MB tells S and R the number of rules N it has.

2: For each rule $1, \dots, N$, do:

   2.1: S and R: Garble the following function F.

   F on input $[x, \mathsf{sig}(x)]$ checks if $\mathsf{sig}(x)$ is a valid signature on x using RG's public key. If yes, it encrypts x with AES_k and outputs $\mathsf{AES}_k(x)$; else, it outputs $\perp$.

   In the garbling process, use randomness based on k_{rand}. Send the resulting garbled circuit and labels to MB.

   2.2: MB: Verify that the garbled circuits from S and R are the same, and let ObfAES_k be this garbled circuit. Let r and $\mathsf{sig}(r)$ be the current rule and its signature. Run oblivious transfer with each of S and R to obtain the labels for r and $\mathsf{sig}(r)$. Verify that the labels from S and R are the same, and denote them $L_1^{r_1}, \dots, L_n^{r_n}$.

2.3: MB: Evaluate ObfAES_k on the labels $L_1^{r_1}, \dots, L_n^{r_n}$ to obtain $\mathsf{AES}_k(r)$.

Rule preparation is the main performance overhead of BlindBox HTTPS. This overhead comes from the oblivious transfer and from the generation, transmission and evaluation of the garbled circuit, all of which are executed once for every rule. We evaluate this overhead in §7.

3.4 Validate Tokens

As shown in Fig. 1, the validate tokens procedure runs at the receiver. This procedure takes the decrypted traffic from SSL and runs the same tokenize and encrypt modules as the sender executes on the traffic. The result is a set of encrypted tokens and it checks that these are the same as the encrypted tokens forwarded by MB. If not, there is a chance that the other endpoint is malicious and flags the misbehavior.

3.5 Security Guarantees

We proved our protocol secure with respect to our exact match privacy model; the proofs can be found in our extended paper [43]. We formalized the property that DPIEnc hides the traffic content from MB using an indistinguishability-based security definition. Informally, MB is given encryptions of a sequence of tokens $t'_1, \dots, t'_n$ and keywords r_1, $\dots, r_m$. Then, MB can choose two tokens t_0 and t_1 which do not match any of the keywords. Next, MB is given a ciphertext $c = \mathsf{Enc}_k(\mathsf{salt}, t_b)$ for some bit b and salt generated according to the BlindBox Detect protocol. The security property says that no polynomial-time attacker at MB can guess the value of b with chance better than half. In other words, MB cannot tell if t_0 or t_1 is encrypted in c. We can see why this property holds intuitively: if MB does not have $\mathsf{AES}_k(t_b)$, this value is indistinguishable from a random value by the pseudorandom permutation property of AES. Hence, $\mathsf{Enc}_k(\cdot, t_b)$ maps each salt to a random value, and there are no repetitions among these random values due to the choice of salt in BlindBox Detect. Thus, the distributions of ciphertexts for each value of b are essentially the same, and thus indistinguishable.

As part of our privacy model, BlindBox reveals a small amount of information to make detection faster: BlindBox does not hide the number of tokens in a packet. Also, if a suspicious keyword matches at an offset in the traffic stream, MB learns this offset. Hence, BlindBox necessarily weakens the privacy guarantees of SSL to allow efficient detection. (Note that BlindBox preserves the authenticity property of SSL.)

4. PROTOCOL II: LIMITED IDS

This protocol supports a limited form of an IDS. Namely, it allows a rule to contain: (1) multiple keywords to be matched in the traffic, and (2) absolute and relative offset information within the packet. In our industrial dataset, the average *rule* contained three *keywords*; a rule is "matched" if all keywords are found within a flow.

This protocol supports most of the functionality in the rule language of Snort [47]. A few functional commands are not supported, the most notable being *pcre*, which allows arbitrary regular expressions to be run over the payload. This command is supported by Protocol III.

For example, consider rule number 2003296 from the Snort Emerging Threats ruleset:

```
alert tcp $EXTERNAL_NET $HTTP_PORTS
                        -> $HOME_NET 1025:5000 (
  flow: established,from_server;
  content: "Server|3a| nginx/0.";
  offset: 17; depth: 19;
  content: "Content-Type|3a| text/html";
  content: "|3a|80|3b|255.255.255.255"; )
```

This rule is triggered if the flow is from the server, it contains the keyword "Server|3a| nginx/0." at an offset between 17 and 19, and it also contains the keyword "Content-Type|3a| text/html" and "|3a|80|3b|255.255.255.255". The symbol "|" denotes binary data.

Protocol II builds on Protocol I in a straightforward way. The sender processes the stream the same as in Protocol I (including the encryption) with one exception: if the delimiter-based tokenization is used, the sender attaches to each encrypted token the offset in the stream where it appeared. In the window-based tokenization, the offset information need not be attached to each encrypted token because a token is generated at each offset and hence the offset can be deduced.

Detection happens similarly to before. For each encrypted token, MB checks if it appears in the rule tree. If so, it checks whether the offset of this encrypted token satisfies any range that might have been specified in the relevant rule. If all the fields of the relevant rule are satisfied, MB takes the action indicated by the rule.

Security Guarantee. The security guarantee is the same as in Protocol I: for each rule keyword, the middlebox learns if the keyword appears in the traffic and at what offset, but it learns nothing else about the parts of the traffic that do not match keywords. Note that the security guarantee is defined per keyword and not per rule: MB learns when a keyword matches even if the entire rule does not match.

5. PROTOCOL III: FULL IDS WITH PROBABLE CAUSE PRIVACY

This section enables full IDS functionality, including regexp and scripts, based on our probable cause privacy model. If a keyword from a rule (a suspicious keyword) matches a stream of traffic, MB should be able to decrypt the traffic. This enables the middlebox to then run regexp (e.g., the "pcre" field in Snort) or scripts from Bro [36] on the decrypted data. However, if such a suspicious keyword does not match the packet stream, the middlebox cannot decrypt the traffic (due to cryptographic guarantees), and the security guarantee is the same as in Protocol II.

Protocol insight. The idea is to somehow embed the SSL key k_{SSL} into the encrypted tokens, such that, if MB has a rule keyword r that matches a token t in the traffic, MB should be able to compute k_{SSL}. To achieve this goal, we replace the encrypted token $\mathsf{Enc}_k(\mathsf{salt}, t)$ with $\mathsf{Enc}_k(\mathsf{salt}, t) \oplus k_{\mathsf{SSL}}$, where $\oplus$ is bitwise XOR. If $r = t$, MB has $\mathsf{AES}_k(t)$ and can construct $\mathsf{Enc}_k(\mathsf{salt}, t)$, and then obtain k_{SSL} through a XOR operation. The problem is that this slows down detection to a linear scan of the rules because the need to compute the XOR no longer allows a simple tree lookup of an encrypted token into the rule tree (described in Sec. 3.2).

Protocol. To maintain the efficiency of the detection, we retain the same encrypted token as in DPIEnc and use it for detection, but additionally create an encrypted token that has the key embedded in as above. Now, the encryption of a token t becomes a pair $[c_1 = \mathsf{Enc}_k(\mathsf{salt}, t), c_2 = \mathsf{Enc}^*_k(\mathsf{salt}, t) \oplus k_{\mathsf{SSL}}]$, where $\mathsf{Enc}^*_k(\mathsf{salt}, t) = \mathsf{AES}_{\mathsf{AES}_k(t)}(\mathsf{salt} + 1)$ and the salt is generated as in BlindBox Detect (§3.2). Note that it is crucial that the salt in Enc^*_k differs from the salt in any c_1 encryption of t because otherwise an attacker can compute $c_1 \oplus c_2$ and obtain k_{SSL}. To enforce this requirement across different occurrences of the same token in BlindBox Detect, the sender now *increments the salt by two*: it uses an even salt for c_1 (and so does MB for the rules in the tree), while it uses an odd salt for c_2. MB uses c_1 to perform the detection as before. If MB detects a match with rule r using BlindBox Detect, MB computes $\mathsf{Enc}^*_k(\mathsf{salt}, r)$ using $\mathsf{AES}_k(r)$, and computes $\mathsf{Enc}^*_k(\mathsf{salt}, r) \oplus c_2$, which yields k_{SSL}. We prove the security of this protocol in our extended paper [43].

6. SYSTEM IMPLEMENTATION

We implemented two separate libraries for BlindBox: a client/server library for transmission called BlindBox HTTPS, and a Click-based [32] middlebox.

BlindBox library. The BlindBox HTTPS protocol is implemented in a C library. When a client opens a connection, our protocol actually opens three separate sockets: one over normal SSL, one to transmit the "searchable" encrypted tokens, and one to listen if a middlebox on path requests garbled circuits. The normal SSL channel runs on top of a modified GnuTLS [12] library which allows us to extract the session key under Protocol III. On send, the endpoint first sends the encrypted tokens, and then sends the traffic over normal HTTPS. If there is a middlebox on the path, the endpoints generate garbled circuits using JustGarble [16] in combination with the OT Extension library [5].

The middlebox. We implemented the middlebox in multi-threaded Click [32] over DPDK [2]; in our implementation, half of the threads perform detection over the data stream ("detection" threads), and half perform obfuscated rule encryption exchanges with clients ("garble" threads). When a new connection opens, a detection thread signals to a garble thread and the garble thread opens an obfuscated rule encryption channel with the endpoints. Once the garble thread has evaluated all circuits received from the clients and obtained the encrypted rules, it constructs the search tree. The detection thread then runs the detection based on the search tree, and allows data packets in the SSL channel to proceed if no attack has been detected.

When a detection thread matches a rule, under Protocols I and II, the middlebox blocks the connection. Under Protocol III, it computes the decryption key (which is possible due to a match), and it forwards the encrypted traffic and the key to a decryption element. This element is implemented as a wrapper around the open-source ssldump [10] tool. The decrypted traffic can then be forwarded to any other system (Snort, Bro, etc.) for more complex processing. We modeled this after SSL termination devices [18], which today man-in-the-middle traffic before passing it on to some other monitoring or DPI device.

7. EVALUATION

When evaluating BlindBox, we aimed to answer two questions. First, can BlindBox support the functionality of our target applications – data exfiltration (document watermarking), parental filtering, and HTTP intrusion detection? Second, what are the performance overheads of BlindBox at both the endpoints and the middlebox?

7.1 Functionality Evaluation

To evaluate the functionality supported by BlindBox, we answer a set of sub-questions.

Can BlindBox implement the functionality required for each target system? Table 1 shows what fraction of "rules" BlindBox can implement using each of Protocols I, II, and III. We evaluate this fraction using public datasets for document watermarking [45], parental filtering [13], and IDS rules (from the Snort community [9] and Emerging Threats [3]). In addition, we evaluate on two industrial datasets from Lastline and McAfee Stonesoft to which we had (partial) access.

Document watermarking and parental filtering can be completely supported using Protocol I because each system relies only on the detection of a single keyword to trigger an alarm. However, Protocol I can support only between 1.6-5% of the policies required by the more general HTTP IDS applications (the two public Snort datasets, as well as the datasets from McAfee Stonesoft and Lastline). This limitation is due to the fact that most IDS policies require detection of multiple keywords or regular expressions.

Protocol II, by supporting multiple exact match keywords, extends support to 29-67% of policies for the HTTP IDS applications. Protocol III supports all applications including regular expressions and scripting, by enabling decryption when there is a probable cause to do so.

Does BlindBox fail to detect any attacks/policy violations that these standard implementations would detect? The answer depends on which tokenization technique one uses out of the two techniques we described in §3: window-based and delimiter-based tokenization. The window-based tokenization does not affect the detection accuracy of the rules because it creates a token at every offset. The delimiter-based tokenization relies on the assumption that, in IDSes, most rules occur on the boundary of non-alphanumeric characters, and thus does not transmit all possible tokens – only those required to detect rules which occur between such "delimiters". To test if this tokenization misses attacks, we ran

Dataset	I.	II.	III.
Document watermarking [45]	100%	100%	100%
Parental filtering [13]	100%	100%	100%
Snort Community (HTTP)	3%	67%	100%
Snort Emerging Threats (HTTP)	1.6%	42%	100%
McAfee Stonesoft IDS	5%	40%	100%
Lastline	0%	29.1%	100%

Table 1: Fraction of attack rules in public and industrial rule sets addressable with Protocols I, II, and III.

BlindBox over the ICTF2010 [49] network trace, and used as rules the Snort Emerging Threats ruleset from which we removed the rules with regular expressions. The ICTF trace was generated during a college "capture the flag" contest during which students attempted to hack different servers to win the competition, so it contains a large number of attacks. We detected 97.1% of the attack keywords and 99% of the attack rules that would have been detected with Snort. (Recall that an attack rule may consist of multiple keywords.)

7.2 Performance Evaluation

We now investigate BlindBox's performance overheads at both the client and the network. For all experiments, the client software uses Protocol II, which has higher overhead than Protocol I. We do not evaluate Protocol III directly; the differences we would expect from Protocol III relative to II would include a secondary middlebox to perform regular expression processing, and an increase in bandwidth due to the key being embedded in each encrypted token.

Our prototype of the client software runs on two servers with 2.60 GHz processors connected by a 10GbE link. The machines are multicore, but we used only one thread per client. The CPU supports AES-NI instructions and thus the encryption times for both SSL and BlindBox reflect this hardware support. Since typical clients are not running in the same rack over a 10GbE links, in some experiments we reduced throughput to 20Mbps (typical of a broadband home link) and increased latency to 10ms RTT. Our prototype middlebox runs with four 2.6GHz Xeon E5-2650 cores and 128 GB RAM; the network hardware is a single 10GbE Intel 82599 compatible network card. All of our experiments were performed on this testbed. For microbenchmarks (as in Table 2), we measured time to complete a loop of 10,000 iterations and took an average. For flow completion benchmarks we took an average of five runs.

To summarize our performance results, BlindBox is practical for long-lived connections: the throughput of encryption and detection are competitive with rates of current (unencrypted) deployments. Additionally, BlindBox is 3 to 6 orders of magnitude faster than relevant implementations using existing cryptography; these solutions, by themselves, are incomplete in addition to being slow. The primary overhead of BlindBox is setting up a connection, due to the obfuscated rule encryption. This cost is small for small rulesets, but can take as long as 1.5 minutes for rulesets with thousands of rules; hence, BlindBox is not yet practical for systems with thousands of rules and short-lived connections that need to run setup frequently. We now elaborate on all these points.

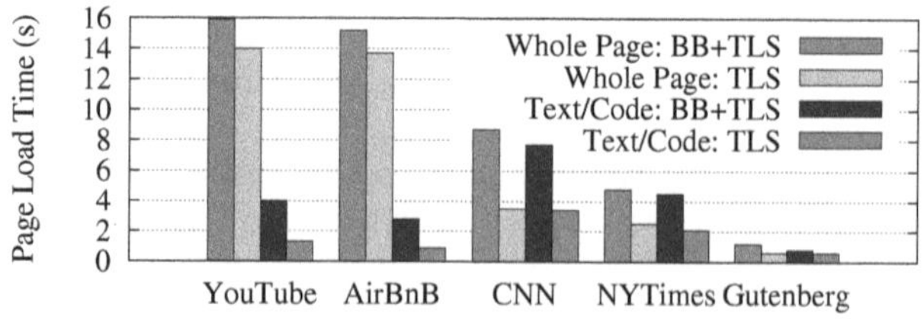

Figure 3: Download time for TLS and BlindBox (BB) + TLS at 20Mbps$\times$10ms.

7.2.1 *Strawmen*

BlindBox is the only system we know of to enable DPI over encrypted data. Nevertheless, to understand its performance, we compare it to standard SSL as well as two strawmen, which we now describe.

A searchable encryption scheme due to Song et al. [46]: This scheme does not enable obfuscated rule encryption or probable cause decryption, but can implement encryption and detection as in Protocols I and II (but not Protocol III). We used the implementation of Song et al. from [37], but replaced the use of SHA512 with the AES-NI instruction in a secure way, to speed up this scheme.

Generic functional encryption (FE) [23, 26]: Such schemes, if enhanced with our obfuscated rule encryption technique, can in theory perform Protocols I, II, and III. However, such encryption schemes are prohibitively expensive to be run and evaluated. For example, one such scheme [26] nests fully homomorphic encryption twice, resulting in an overhead of at least 10 orders of magnitude. Instead, we chose and implemented a simple and specialized functional encryption scheme due to Katz et al. [30]. The performance of this scheme is a generous lower bound on the performance of the generic protocols (the Katz et al. scheme does not support Protocol III because it can compute only inner product).

7.2.2 *Client Performance*

How long does it take to encrypt a token? Table 2 provides micro-benchmarks for encryption, detection, and setup using BlindBox, HTTPS, and our strawmen. With HTTPS (using GnuTLS), encryption of one 128-bit block took on average 13ns, and 3μs per 1400 byte packet. BlindBox increases these values to 69ns and 90μs respectively. These figures include the time to perform HTTPS transmission in the primary channel, as well as the overheads from BlindBox: the tokenization process itself (deciding which substrings to tokenize) as well as the encryption process (encrypting and then hashing each token with AES). The searchable strawman performs encryption of a single token on average 2.7μs and 257μs for an entire packet; the primary overhead relative to BlindBox here is multiple calls to `/dev/urandom` because the scheme requires random salts for every token. With fixed or pre-chosen salts, we would expect the searchable strawman to have comparable encryption times to BlindBox. As we discuss, the detection times for this strawman are slower. The FE strawman takes six orders of magnitude longer than BlindBox and is even further impractical: a client using this scheme could transmit at most one packet every 15 seconds.

		Vanilla HTTPS	FE Strawman	Searchable Strawman	BlindBox HTTPS
Client	*Encrypt* (128 bits)	13ns	70ms	2.7μs	69ns
	Encrypt (1500 bytes)	3μs	15s	257μs	90μs
	Setup (1 Keyword)	73ms	N/A	N/A	588 ms
	Setup (3K Rules)	73ms	N/A	N/A	97 s
MB	*Detection:*				
	1 Rule, 1 Token	NP	170ms	1.9μs	20ns
	1 Rule, 1 Packet	NP	36s	52μs	5μs
	3K Rules, 1 Token	NP	8.3 minutes	5.6ms	137ns
	3K Rules, 1 Packet	NP	5.7 days	157ms	33μs

Table 2: Connection and detection micro-benchmarks comparing Vanilla HTTPS, the functional encryption (FE) strawman, the searchable strawman, and BlindBox HTTPS. NP stands for not possible. The average rule includes three keywords.

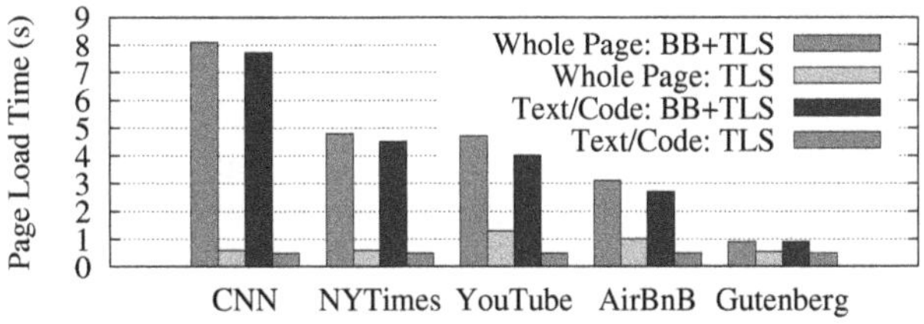

Figure 4: Download time time for TLS and BlindBox (BB) + TLS at 1Gbps×10ms.

How long does the initial handshake take with the middlebox? The initial handshake to perform obfuscated rule encryption runs in time proportional to the number of rules. In the datasets we worked with, the average Protocol II rule had slightly more than 3 keywords; a typical 3000 rule IDS rule set contains between 9-10k keywords. The total client-side time required for 10k keywords was 97 seconds; for 1000 keywords, setup time was 9.5s. In a smaller ruleset of 10 or 100 keywords (which is typical in a watermark detection exfiltration device), setup ran in 650ms and 1.6 seconds, respectively. These values are dependent on the clock speed of the CPU (to generate the garbled circuits) and the network bandwidth and latency (to transmit the circuits from client to sender). Our servers have 2.6GHz cores; we assumed a middlebox on a local area network near the client with a 100μs RTT between the two and a 1Gbps connection. Garbling a circuit took 1042μs per circuit; each garbled circuit transmission is 599KB.

Neither strawman has an appropriate setup phase that meets the requirement of not making the rules visible to the endpoints. However, one can extend these strawmen with BlindBox's obfuscated rule encryption technique, and encrypt the rules using garbled circuits. In this case, for the scheme of Song et al., the setup cost would be similar to the one of BlindBox because their scheme also encrypts the rule keywords with AES. For the scheme of Katz et al., the setup would be much slower because one needs garbled circuits for modular exponentiation, which are huge. Based on the size of such circuits reported in the literature [16], we can compute a generous lower bound on the size of the garbled circuits and on the setup cost for this strawman: it is at least $1.8 \cdot 10^3$ times larger/slower than the setup in BlindBox.

How long are page downloads with BlindBox, excluding the setup (handshake) cost? Figure 3 shows page download times using our "typical end user" testbed with 20Mbps links. In this figure, we show five popular websites: YouTube, AirBnB, CNN, The New York Times, and Project Gutenberg. The data shown represents the post-handshake (persistent connection) page download time. YouTube and AirBnB load video, and hence have a large amount of binary data which is not tokenized. CNN and The New York Times have a mixture of data, and Project Gutenberg is almost entirely text. We show results for both the amount of time to download the page including all video and image content, as well as the amount of time to load only the Text/Code of the page. The overheads when downloading the whole page are at most 2×; for pages with large amount of binary data like YouTube and AirBnB, the overhead was only 10-13%. Load times for Text/Code only – which are required to actually begin rendering the page for the user – are impacted more strongly, with penalties as high as 3× and a worst case of about 2×.

What is the computational overhead of BlindBox encryption, and how does this overhead impact page load times? While the encryption costs are not noticeable in the page download times observed over the "typical client" network configuration, we immediately see the cost of encryption overhead when the available link capacity increases to 1Gbps in Figure 4 – at this point, we see a performance overhead of as much as 16× relative to the baseline SSL download time. For both runs (Figs. 3 and 4), we observed that the CPU was almost continuously fully utilized to transfer data during data transmission. At 20Mbps, the encryption cost is not noticeable as the CPU can continue producing data at around the link rate; at 1Gbps, transmission with BlindBox stalls relative to SSL, as the BlindBox sender cannot encrypt fast enough to keep up with the line rate. This result is unsurprising given the results in Table 2, showing that BlindBox takes 30× longer to encrypt a packet than standard HTTPS. This overhead can be mitigated with extra cores; while we ran with only one core per connection, tokenization can easily be parallelized.

What is the bandwidth overhead of transmitting encrypted tokens for a typical web page? Minimizing bandwidth overhead is key to client performance: less data transmitted means less cost, faster transfer times, and faster detection times. The bandwidth overhead in BlindBox depends on the number of tokens produced. The number of encrypted tokens varies widely depending on three parameters of the page being loaded: what fraction of bytes are text/code which must

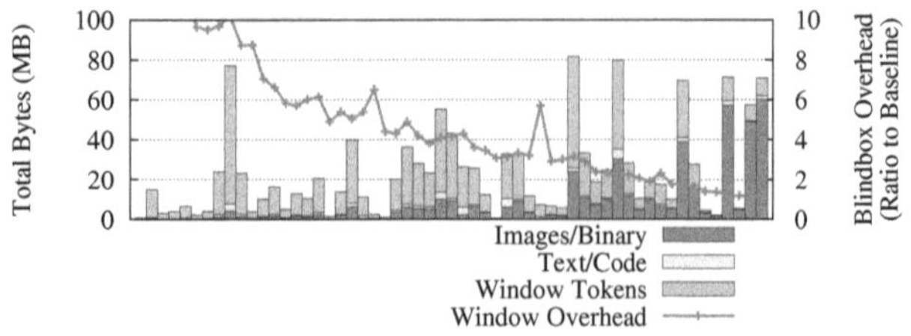

(a) Window-Based Tokenization

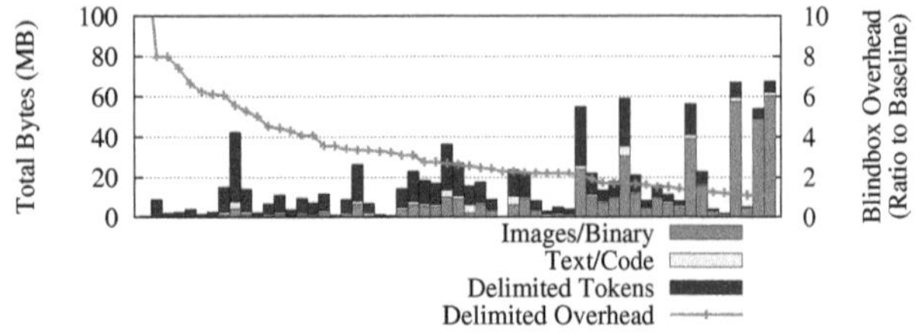

(b) Delimiter-Based Tokenization

Figure 5: Bandwidth overhead over top-50 web dataset.

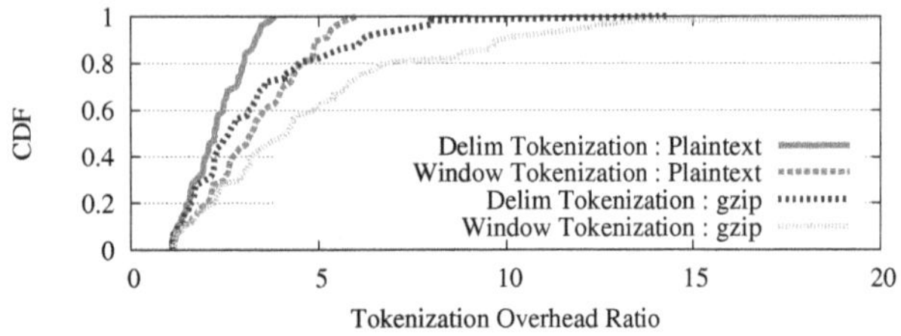

Figure 6: Ratio: transmitted bytes with BlindBox to transmitted bytes with SSL.

be tokenized, how "dense" the text/code is in number of delimiters, and whether or not the web server and client support compression.

Figures 5 (a) and (b) break down transmitted data into the number of text-bytes, binary-bytes, and tokenize-bytes using the window-based and delimiter-based tokenization algorithms (as discussed in §3); the right hand axis shows the overhead of adding tokens over transmitting just the original page data. We measured this by downloading the Alexa top-50 websites [1] and running BlindBox over all page content (including secondary resources loaded through AJAX, callbacks, etc.) The median page with delimited tokens sees a 2.5× increase in the number of bytes transmitted. In the best case, some pages see only a 1.1× increase, and in the worst case, a page sees a 14× overhead. The median page with window tokens sees a 4× increase in the number of bytes transmitted; the worst page sees a 24× overhead. The first observable factor affecting this overhead, as seen in these figures, is simply what fraction of bytes in the original page load required tokenization. Pages consisting mostly of video suffered lower penalties than pages with large amounts of text, HTML, and Javascript because we do not tokenize video.

7.2.3 *Middlebox Performance*

We investigate performance at the middlebox using both micro-benchmarks and overall throughput.

What throughput can BlindBox sustain and how does this compare to standard IDS? When running our BlindBox implementation over synthetic traffic, we measured a throughput of 166Mbps; when running Snort over the same traffic, we measured a throughput of 85Mbps. Hence, BlindBox performed detection twice as fast as Snort, which inspects *unencrypted* traffic. The reason behind this situation is twofold. First, BlindBox reduces all detection to exact matching, pushing all regular expression parsing to a secondary middlebox, invoked rarely. Second, our implementation is built over DPDK-click, a faster packet-capture library than what Snort uses by default. Hence, it is unsurprising that BlindBox performs detection more quickly. Nevertheless, the point of this experiment is not to show that BlindBox is faster than Snort, but instead to demonstrate that BlindBox provides competitive performance to today's deployments.

How does BlindBox compare in detection time against other strawmen approaches? While we did not implement a version of BlindBox which relied on our strawmen, we can compare against it using a smaller benchmark. Once again, in Table 2, the FE strawman is seen to be prohibitively impractical: detection over a single packet against a 3000 ruleset takes more than a day.

The searchable strawman is also prohibitively slow: it performs detection over a 1500 byte packet in 157 ms, which is equivalent to no more than 6-7 packets per second. This performance is three orders of magnitude slower than the performance of BlindBox's middlebox. This overhead results from the fact that the searchable strawman must perform an encryption operation over every keyword to perform a comparison against a client token, resulting in a task linear in the number of keywords. In contrast, BlindBox's DPIEnc scheme encrypts the data in such a way that the middlebox can use a fast, pre-computed search tree (which gives a logarithmic search) to match encrypted tokens to rules.

8. RELATED WORK

Related work falls into two categories: insecure proposals, and work on computing on encrypted data.

8.1 Insecure Proposals

Some existing systems mount a man-in-the-middle attack on SSL [28, 27] by installing fake certificates at the middlebox [31, 41]. This enables the middlebox to break the security of SSL and decrypt the traffic so it can run DPI. This breaks the end-to-end security of SSL, and results in a host of issues, as surveyed by Jarmoc [28].

Some proposals allow users to tunnel their traffic to a third party middlebox provider, e.g. Meddle [40], Beyond the Radio [48], and APLOMB [42]. These approaches allow the middlebox owner to inspect/read all traffic. The situation is preferable to the status queue (from the client's perspective) in that the inspector is one with whom the client has a formal/contractual relationship – but, unlike BlindBox, the client still must grant *someone* access to the plaintext traffic. Further, this approach is not preferable to service providers, who may wish to enforce policy on users in the network, e.g., that no hosts within the network are infected with botnet malware.

8.2 Computing on Encrypted Data

Fully homomorphic encryption (FHE) [24] and general functional encryption [23, 26] are encryption schemes that can compute any function over encrypted data; hence, they can in principle support the complexity of deep packet inspection tasks. However, they do not address all the desired security properties in our threat model, and more importantly, they are prohibitively slow, currently at least 8 orders of magnitude slower than unencrypted computation [25].

Some recent systems such as CryptDB [37] and Mylar [38] showed how to support some specialized computation efficiently on encrypted data. However, these systems perform different tasks than is needed for middleboxes and do not meet our threat model.

There has been a large amount of work on searchable encryption [46, 29, 19, 15]. No searchable encryption scheme provides a strategy for encrypting the rules securely and for supporting arbitrary regexps, both of which BlindBox provides. Moreover, existing schemes cannot provide the performance required for packet processing. For example, BlindBox is three orders of magnitude faster than a system using the symmetric-key searchable scheme of Song et al. [46]. Public-key searchable encryption schemes, such as [19], are even slower because they perform a cryptographic pairing (which takes hundreds of microseconds per pairing), for every pair of token to rule content (a linear, rather than logarithmic task in the number of rules).

9. DISCUSSION

Before concluding, we discuss future directions and implications of BlindBox.

New Security Models. In our extended paper [43], we provide cryptographic proofs that the BlindBox system respects the exact match and probable cause privacy models. We believe our new privacy models are useful. Both approaches raise the bar substantially from the current "man-in-the- middle" model, which de-facto breaks any trust in SSL altogether. Nevertheless, BlindBox allows the middlebox to know when a keyword from an attack rule matches the traffic even though the entire rule (with all its keywords contents) does not match. In our experiments, almost all keyword detections that *didn't* result in the detection of a complete rule were for generic substrings (e.g. onmouseover), which most likely do not leak a user's personal data.

ISP Adoption. In enterprises and private networks, BlindBox provides a good trade-off between the desires of users (who want privacy, and may want processing) and the network administrator (who wants to deploy processing primarily, and is willing to respect privacy if able to do so). Hence, deploying BlindBox is aligned with both parties' interests. However, in ISPs, sales of user data to marketing and analytics firms are a source of revenue – hence, an ISP has an incentive *not* to deploy BlindBox. Consequently, deployment in ISPs is likely to take place either under legislative requirement through privacy laws, or through a change in incentives. The growing trend of middlebox processing being offered as a "service" – which users opt in to and pay for – may offer an incentive for an ISP to deploy BlindBox with the promise of a new revenue stream directly from the user.

Client Adoption. BlindBox proposes a new end-to-end encryption protocol to replace HTTPS altogether. A truly ideal solution would require no changes at the endpoints – indeed, the success of middlebox deployments is partly due to the fact that middleboxes can be simply "dropped in" to the network. Unfortunately, existing HTTPS encryption algorithms use strong encryption schemes, which do not support *any* functional operations and cannot be used for our task; hence one must change HTTPS. Nonetheless, we believe that, in the long run, a change to HTTPS to allow inspection of encrypted traffic can be generic enough to support a wide array of middlebox applications, and not just the class of middleboxes in BlindBox. We believe these benefits will merit widespread "default" adoption in end host software suites.

10. CONCLUSION

In this paper, we presented BlindBox, a system that resolves the tension between security and DPI middlebox functionality in networks. To the best of our knowledge, BlindBox is the first system to enable Deep Packet Inspection over encrypted traffic without requiring decryption of the underlying traffic. BlindBox supports real DPI applications such as IDS, exfiltration detection, and parental filtering. BlindBox performs best over long-running, persistent connections using SPDY-like or tunneled protocols. Using BlindBox Detect, a middlebox running BlindBox can perform detection on a single core at 186Mbps – competitive with many deployed IDS implementations.

We envisage that BlindBox is the first step towards a *general protocol* to resolve the tension between encryption and all categories of middleboxes. BlindBox currently supports middleboxes for DPI filtering only, however, we believe that the general blueprint BlindBox provides – computation over encrypted traffic – can be extended to implement other middlebox capabilities, including caches, protocol accelerators, compression engines.

11. ACKNOWLEDGMENTS

We thank the anonymous reviewers of the SIGCOMM PC for their valuable comments on this work. We especially thank our shepherd Mike Walfish for his detailed and helpful feedback. Vern Paxson coined the term "probable cause" for one of our privacy models. Kay Ousterhout gave many comments on early revisions of this work. McAfee Stonesoft, Lastline, and Palo Alto networks met with us to discuss state-of-the-art IDS today, and Stonesoft and Lastline provided us with metadata about their commercial rulesets. This material is based upon work supported by the National Science Foundation Graduate Research Fellowship under Grant No. DGE-1106400. We also thank Intel Research for their generous funding and technical feedback on this work.

12. REFERENCES

[1] Alexa Top Sites. http://www.alexa.com/topsites.

[2] DPDK: Data Plane Development Kit. http://dpdk.org/.

[3] Emerging Threats: Open Source Signatures. https://rules.emergingthreats.net/open/snort-2.9.0/rules/.

[4] McAfee Network Security Platform. http://www.mcafee.com/us/products/network-security-platform.aspx.

[5] OT Extension library. https://github.com/encryptogroup/OTExtension.

[6] Palo Alto Networks. https://www.paloaltonetworks.com/.

[7] Qosmos Deep Packet Inspection and Metadata Engine. http://www.qosmos.com/products/deep-packet-inspection-engine/.

[8] Radisys R220 Network Appliance. http://www.radisys.com/products/network-appliance/.

[9] Snort. https://www.snort.org/.

[10] ssldump. http://www.rtfm.com/ssldump/.

[11] Symantec | Enterprise. http://www.symantec.com/index.jsp.

[12] The GnuTLS Transport Layer Security Library. http://www.gnutls.org/.

[13] University of Toulouse Internet Blacklists. http://dsi.ut-capitole.fr/blacklists/.

[14] G. Asharov, Y. Lindell, T. Schneider, and M. Zohner. More Efficient Oblivious Transfer and Extensions for Faster Secure Computation. In *Proc. ACM CCS*, 2013.

[15] M. Bellare, A. Boldyreva, and A. O'Neill. Deterministic and Efficiently Searchable Encryption. In *Proc. IACR CRYPTO*, 2007.

[16] M. Bellare, V. T. Hoang, S. Keelveedhi, and P. Rogaway. Efficient Garbling from a Fixed-Key Blockcipher. In *Proc. IEEE S&P*, 2013.

[17] BlueCoat. Comparing Explicit and Transparent PRoxies. https://bto.bluecoat.com/webguides/proxysg/security_first_steps/Content/Solutions/SharedTopics/Explicit_Transparent_Proxy_Comparison.htm.

[18] BlueCoat. SSL Encrypted Traffic Visibility and Management. https://www.bluecoat.com/products/ssl-encrypted-traffic-visibility\-and-management.

[19] D. Boneh, G. D. Crescenzo, R. Ostrovsky, and G. Persiano. Public key encryption with keyword search. In *Proc. IACR EUROCRYPT*, 2004.

[20] S. Cheshire and M. Krochmal. NAT Port Mapping Protocol (NAT-PMP). RFC 6886, Apr. 2013.

[21] C. Dixon, H. Uppal, V. Brajkovic, D. Brandon, T. Anderson, and A. Krishnamurthy. ETTM: A Scalable Fault Tolerant Network Manager. In *Proc. USENIX NSDI*, 2011.

[22] S. Even, O. Goldreich, and A. Lempel. A Randomized Protocol for Signing Contracts. *Commun. ACM*, 28(6):637–647, June 1985.

[23] S. Garg, C. Gentry, S. Halevi, M. Raykova, A. Sahai, and B. Waters. Candidate indistinguishability obfuscation and functional encryption for all circuits. In *Proc. IEEE FOCS*, 2013.

[24] C. Gentry. Fully Homomorphic Encryption using Ideal Lattices. In *Proc. ACM STOC*, 2009.

[25] C. Gentry, S. Halevi, and N. P. Smart. Homomorphic Evaluation of the AES Circuit. In *Proc. IACR CRYPTO*, 2012.

[26] S. Goldwasser, Y. Kalai, R. A. Popa, V. Vaikuntanathan, and N. Zeldovich. Reusable Garbled Circuits and Succinct Functional Encryption. In *Proc. ACM STOC*, 2013.

[27] L.-S. Huang, A. Rice, E. Ellingsen, and C. Jackson. Analyzing Forged SSL Certificates in the Wild. In *Proc. IEEE S&P*, 2014.

[28] J. Jarmoc. SSL/TLS Interception Proxies and Transitive Trust. *Presentation at Black Hat Europe*, 2012.

[29] S. Kamara, C. Papamanthou, and T. Roeder. Dynamic Searchable Symmetric Encryption. In *Proc. ACM CCS*, 2012.

[30] J. Katz, A. Sahai, and B. Waters. Predicate Encryption Supporting Disjunctions, Polynomial Equations, and Inner Products. In *Proc. IACR EUROCRYPT*, 2008.

[31] A. Kingsley-Hughes. Gogo in-flight Wi-Fi serving spoofed SSL certificates. *ZDNet*, 2015.

[32] E. Kohler, R. Morris, B. Chen, J. Jannotti, and M. F. Kaashoek. The Click Modular Router. *ACM Trans. Comput. Syst.*, 18(3):263–297, Aug. 2000.

[33] Y. Lindell and B. Pinkas. A Proof of Security of Yao's Protocol for Two-Party Computation. *J. Cryptol.*, 22:161–188, April 2009.

[34] M. Naor and B. Pinkas. Oblivious Transfer with Adaptive Queries. In *Proc. IACR CRYPTO*, 1999.

[35] D. Naylor, A. Finamore, I. Leontiadis, Y. Grunenberger, M. Mellia, M. Munafò, K. Papagiannaki, and P. Steenkiste. The Cost of the "S" in HTTPS. In *Proc. ACM CoNeXT*, 2014.

[36] V. Paxson. Bro: A System for Detecting Network Intruders in Real-time. *Comput. Netw.*, 31(23-24):2435–2463, Dec. 1999.

[37] R. A. Popa, C. M. S. Redfield, N. Zeldovich, and H. Balakrishnan. CryptDB: Protecting Confidentiality with Encrypted Query Processing. In *Proc. ACM SOSP*, 2013.

[38] R. A. Popa, E. Stark, S. Valdez, J. Helfer, N. Zeldovich, M. F. Kaashoek, and H. Balakrishnan. Building Web Applications on Top of Encrypted Data using Mylar. In *Proc. USENIX NSDI*, 2014.

[39] M. O. Rabin. How to Exchange Secrets with Oblivious Transfer. TR-81, Aiken Computation Lab, Harvard University http://eprint.iacr.org/2005/187.pdf, 1981.

[40] A. Rao, J. Sherry, A. Legout, W. Dabbout, A. Krishnamurthy, and D. Choffnes. Meddle: Middleboxes for Increased Transparency and Control of Mobile Traffic. In *Proc. CoNEXT Student Workshop*, 2012.

[41] Runa. Security vulnerability found in Cyberoam DPI devices (CVE-2012-3372). *Tor Project Blog*, 2012.

[42] J. Sherry, S. Hasan, C. Scott, A. Krishnamurthy, S. Ratnasamy, and V. Sekar. Making Middleboxes Someone Else's Problem: Network Processing As a Cloud Service. In *Proc. ACM SIGCOMM*, 2012.

[43] J. Sherry, C. Lan, R. A. Popa, and S. Ratnasamy. Blindbox: Deep packet inspection over encrypted traffic. Cryptology ePrint Archive, Report 2015/264, 2015. http://eprint.iacr.org/.

[44] Shira Levine. Operators look to embed deep packet inspection (DPI) in apps; Market growing to $2B by 2018. Infonetics Research. http://www.infonetics.com/pr/2014/2H13-Service-Provider-DPI-Products-Market-Highlights.asp.

[45] G. J. Silowash, T. Lewellen, J. W. Burns, and D. L. Costa. Detecting and Preventing Data Exfiltration Through Encrypted Web Sessions via Traffic Inspection. Technical Report CMU/SEI-2013-TN-012.

[46] D. X. Song, D. Wagner, and A. Perrig. Practical Techniques for Searches on Encrypted Data. In *Proc. IEEE S&P*, 2000.

[47] The Snort Project. Snort users manual, 2014. Version 2.9.7.

[48] N. Vallina-Rodriguez, S. Sundaresan, C. Kreibich, N. Weaver, and V. Paxson. Beyond the Radio: Illuminating the Higher Layers of Mobile Networks. In *Proc. ACM MobiSys*, 2015.

[49] G. Vigna. ICTF Data. https://ictf.cs.ucsb.edu/#/.

[50] A. C. Yao. How to Generate and Exchange Secrets. In *Proc. IEEE FOCS*, 1986.

[51] K. Zetter. The Feds Cut a Deal With In-Flight Wi-Fi Providers, and Privacy Groups Are Worried. *Wired Magazine*, 2014.

Rollback-Recovery for Middleboxes

Justine Sherry∗ Peter Xiang Gao∗ Soumya Basu∗ Aurojit Panda∗
Arvind Krishnamurthy• Christian Maciocco† Maziar Manesh† João Martins◁
Sylvia Ratnasamy∗ Luigi Rizzo‡ Scott Shenker◦∗

∗ UC Berkeley • University of Washington † Intel Research ◁ NEC Labs ‡ University of Pisa ◦ ICSI

ABSTRACT

Network middleboxes must offer high availability, with automatic failover when a device fails. Achieving high availability is challenging because failover must correctly restore lost state (e.g., activity logs, port mappings) but must do so quickly (e.g., in less than typical transport timeout values to minimize disruption to applications) and with little overhead to failure-free operation (e.g., additional per-packet latencies of 10-100s of μs). No existing middlebox design provides failover that is correct, fast to recover, and imposes little increased latency on failure-free operations.

We present a new design for fault-tolerance in middleboxes that achieves these three goals. Our system, FTMB (for Fault-Tolerant MiddleBox), adopts the classical approach of "rollback recovery" in which a system uses information logged during normal operation to correctly reconstruct state after a failure. However, traditional rollback recovery cannot maintain high throughput given the frequent output rate of middleboxes. Hence, we design a novel solution to record middlebox state which relies on two mechanisms: (1) 'ordered logging', which provides lightweight logging of the information needed after recovery, and (2) a 'parallel release' algorithm which, when coupled with ordered logging, ensures that recovery is always correct. We implement ordered logging and parallel release in Click and show that for our test applications our design adds only 30μs of latency to median per packet latencies. Our system introduces moderate throughput overheads (5-30%) and can reconstruct lost state in 40-275ms for practical systems.

CCS Concepts

• Networks → Middleboxes / network appliances; • Computer systems organization → Availability;

Keywords

middlebox reliability; parallel fault-tolerance

SIGCOMM '15, August 17 - 21, 2015, London, United Kingdom

 ISBN 978-1-4503-3542-3/15/08...$15.00

DOI: http://dx.doi.org/10.1145/2785956.2787501

1. INTRODUCTION

Middleboxes play a crucial role in the modern Internet infrastructure – they offer an easy way to deploy new dataplane functions and are often as numerous as routers and switches [35,59,62]. Yet, because middleboxes typically involve proprietary monolithic software running on dedicated hardware, they can be expensive to deploy and manage.

To rectify this situation, network operators are moving towards Network Function Virtualization (NFV), in which middlebox functionality is moved out of dedicated physical boxes into virtual appliances that can be run on commodity processors [32]. While the NFV vision solves the dedicated hardware problem, it presents some technical challenges of its own. Two of the most commonly cited challenges have been performance [38, 45, 52, 55, 58] and management [33, 35, 49] with multiple efforts in both industry and academia now exploring these questions. We argue that an equally important challenge – one that has received far less attention – is that of *fault-tolerance*.

Today, the common approach to fault tolerance in middleboxes is a combination of careful engineering to avoid faults, and deploying a backup appliance to rapidly restart when faults occur. Unfortunately, neither of these approaches – alone or in combination – are ideal, and the migration to NFV will only exacerbate their problematic aspects.

With traditional middleboxes, each "box" is developed by a single vendor and dedicated to a single application. This allows vendors greater control in limiting the introduction of faults by, for example, running on hardware designed and tested for reliability (ECC, proper cooling, redundant power supply, *etc.*). This approach will not apply to NFV, where developers have little control over the environment in which their applications run and vendor diversity in hardware and applications will explode the test space. And while one might contemplate (re)introducing constraints on NFV platforms, doing so would be counter to NFV's goal of greater openness and agility in middlebox infrastructure.

The second part to how operators handle middlebox failure is also imperfect. With current middleboxes, operators often maintain a dedicated per-appliance backup. This is inefficient and offers only a weak form of recovery for the many middlebox applications that are stateful – *e.g.*, Network Address Translators (NATs), WAN Optimizers, and Intrusion Prevention Systems all maintain dynamic state about flows, users, and network conditions. With no mechanism to recover state, the backup may be unable to correctly process packets after failure, leading to service disruption. (We discuss this further in §3.2 and quantify disruption in §6.)

Our goal in this paper is to design middleboxes that guarantee correct recovery from failures. This solution must be low-latency (*e.g.*, the additional per-packet latency under failure-free conditions must be well under 1ms) and recovery must be fast (*e.g.*, in less than typical transport timeout values). To the best of our knowledge, no existing middlebox design satisfies these goals. In addition, we would prefer a solution that is general (*i.e.*, can be applied across applications rather than having to be designed on a case-by-case basis for each individual middlebox) and passive (*i.e.*, does not require one dedicated backup per middlebox).

Our solution – FTMB– introduces new algorithms and techniques that tailor the classic approach of rollback recovery to the middlebox domain and achieves correct recovery in a general and passive manner. Our prototype implementation introduces low additional latency on failure-free operation (adding only 30μs to median per-packet latencies, an improvement of 2-3 orders of magnitude over existing fault tolerance mechanisms) and achieves rapid recovery (reconstructing lost state in between 40-275ms for practical system configurations).

The remainder of this paper is organized as follows: we discuss our assumptions and the challenges in building a fault-tolerant middlebox in §2, followed by our goals and an examination of the design space in §3. We present the design, implementation and evaluation of FTMB in §4, §5, and §6 respectively. We discuss related work in §7 and conclude with future directions in §8.

2. PROBLEM SPACE

We present our system and failure model (§2.1 and §2.2) and the challenges in building fault-tolerant middleboxes (§2.3).

2.1 System Model

Parallel implementations: We assume middlebox applications are multi-threaded and run on a multicore CPU (Figure 1). The middlebox runs with a fixed number of threads. We assume 'multi-queue' NICs that offer multiple transmit and receive queues that are partitioned across threads. Each thread reads from its own receive queue(s) and writes to its own transmit queue(s). The NIC partitions packets across threads by hashing a packet's flow identifier (*i.e.*, 5-tuple including source and destination port and address) to a queue; hence all packets from a flow are processed by the same thread and a packet is processed entirely by one thread. The above are standard approaches to parallelizing traffic processing in multicore systems [27, 37, 47, 58].

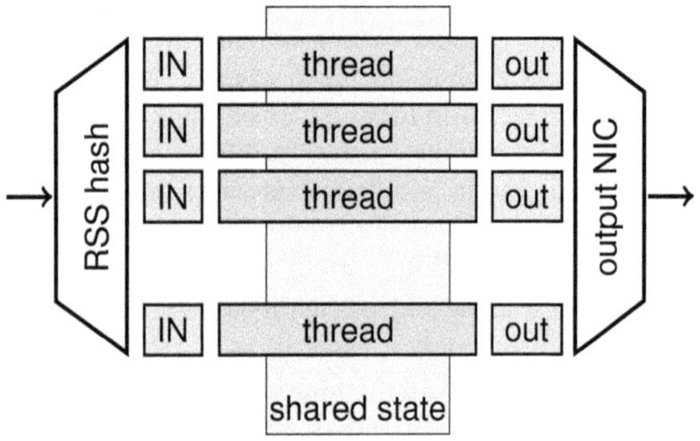

Figure 1: Our model of a middlebox application

Shared state: By shared state we mean state that is accessed across threads. In our parallelization approach, all packets from a flow are processed by a single thread so per-flow state is local to a single thread and is not shared state. However, other state may be relevant to multiple flows, and accesses to such state may incur cross-thread synchronization overheads. Common forms of shared state include aggregate counters, IDS state machines, rate limiters, packet caches for WAN optimizers, *etc.*

Virtualization: Finally, we assume the middlebox code is running in a virtualized mode. The virtualization need not be a VM per se; we could use containers [5], lightweight VMs [44], or some other form of compartmentalization that provides isolation and supports low-overhead snapshots of its content.

2.2 Failure Model

We focus on recovery from "fail-stop" (rather than Byzantine) errors, where under failure 'the component changes to a state that permits other components to detect that a failure has occurred and then stops' [57]. This is the standard failure model assumed by virtual machine fault tolerance approaches like Remus [23], Colo [28], and vSphere [11].

Our current implementation targets failures at the virtualization layer and below, down to the hardware.[1] Our solutions – and many of the systems we compare against – thus cope with failures in the system hardware, drivers, or host operating system. According to a recent study (see Figure 13 in [48]), hardware failures are quite common (80% of firewall failures, 66% of IDS failures, 74% of Load Balancer failures, and 16% of VPN failures required some form of hardware replacement), so this failure model is quite relevant to operational systems.

2.3 Challenges

Middlebox applications exhibit three characteristics that, in combination, make fault-tolerance a challenge: statefulness, very frequent non-determinism, and low packet-processing latencies.

As mentioned earlier, many middlebox applications are *stateful* and the loss of this state can degrade performance and disrupt service. Thus, we want a failover mechanism that correctly restores state such that future packets are processed as if this state were never lost (we define correctness rigorously in §3.1). One might think that this could be achieved via 'active:active' operation, in which a 'master' and a 'replica' execute on all inputs but only the mas-

[1] In §8, we discuss how emerging 'container' technologies would allow us to extend our failure model to recover from failures in the guest OS. With such extensions in place, the only errors that we would be unable to recover from are those within the middlebox application software itself.

ter's output is released to users. However, this approach fails when system execution is *non-deterministic*, because the master and replica might diverge in their internal state and produce an incorrect recovery.[2]

Non-determinism is a common problem in parallel programs when threads 'race' to access shared state: the order in which these accesses occur depends on hard-to-control effects (such as the scheduling order of threads, their rate of progress, *etc.*) and are thus hard to predict. Unfortunately, as mentioned earlier, shared state is common in middlebox applications, and shared state such as counters, caches or address pools may be accessed on a per-packet or per-flow basis leading to frequent nondeterminism.[3] In addition, nondeterminism can also arise because of access to hardware devices, including clocks and random number generators, whose return values cannot be predicted. FTMB must cope with all of these sources of nondeterminism.

As we elaborate on shortly, the common approach to accommodating non-determinism is to intercept and/or record the outcome of all potentially non-deterministic operations. However, such interception slows down normal operation and is thus at odds with the other two characteristics of middlebox applications, namely *very* frequent accesses to shared state and low packet processing latencies. Specifically, a piece of shared state may be accessed 100k-1M times per second (the rate of packet arrivals), and the latency through the middlebox should be in 10-100s of microseconds. Hence mechanisms for fault-tolerance must support high access rates and introduce extra latencies of a similar magnitude.

3. GOALS AND DESIGN RATIONALE

Building on the previous discussion, we now describe our goals for FTMB (§3.1), some context (§3.2), and the rationale for the design approach we adopt (§3.3)

3.1 Goals

A fault-tolerant middlebox design must meet the three requirements that follow.

(1) Correctness. The classic definition of correct recovery comes from Strom and Yemeni [60]: "A system recovers correctly if its internal state after a failure is consistent with the observable behavior of the system before the failure." It is important to note that reconstructed state need not be identical to that before failure. Instead, it is sufficient that the reconstructed state be one that *could* have generated the interactions that the system has already had with the external world. This definition leads to a necessary condition for correctness called "**output commit**", which is stated as follows: no output can be released to the external world until all the information necessary to recreate internal state consistent with that output has been committed to stable storage.

As we discuss shortly, the nature of this necessary information varies widely across different designs for fault-tolerance as does the manner in which the output commit property is enforced. In the context of middleboxes, the output in question is a packet and hence to meet the output commit property we must ensure that, before the middlebox transmits a packet p, it has successfully logged to stable storage all the information needed to recreate internal state consistent with an execution that would have generated p.

(2) Low overhead on failure-free operation. We aim for mechanisms that introduce no more than 10-100s of microseconds of added delay to packet latencies.

(3) Fast Recovery. Finally, recovery from failures must be fast to prevent degradation in the end-to-end protocols and applications. We aim for recovery times that avoid endpoint protocols like TCP entering timeout or reset modes.

In addition, we seek solutions that obey the following two supplemental requirements:

(4) Generality. We prefer an approach that does not require complete rewriting of middlebox applications nor needs to be tailored to each middlebox application. Instead, we propose a single recovery mechanism and assume access to the source code. Our solution requires some annotations and and automated modifications to this code. Thus, we differ from some recent work [50, 51] in not introducing an entirely new programming model, but we cannot use completely untouched legacy code. Given that middlebox vendors are moving their code from their current hardware to NFV-friendly implementations, small code modifications of the sort we require may be a reasonable middle ground.

(5) Passive Operation. We do not want to require dedicated replicas for each middlebox application, so instead we seek solutions that only need a passive replica that can be shared across active master instances.

3.2 Existing Middleboxes

To our knowledge, no middlebox design in research or deployment simultaneously meets the above goals.[4]

In research, Pico [50] was the first to address fault-tolerance for middleboxes. Pico guarantees correct recovery but does so at the cost of introducing non-trivial latency under failure-free operation – adding on the order of 8-9ms of delay per packet. We describe Pico and compare against it experimentally in §6.

There is little public information about what commercial middleboxes do and therefore we engaged in discussions with two different middlebox vendors. From our discussions, it seems that vendors do rely heavily on simply engineering the boxes to not fail (which is also the only approach one can take without asking customers to purchase a separate backup box). For example, one vendor uses only a single line of network interface cards and dedicates an entire engineering team to testing new NIC driver releases.

Both vendors confirmed that shared state commonly occurs in their systems. One vendor estimated that with their IDS implementation, a packet touches 10s of shared variables per packet, and that even their simplest devices incur at least one shared variable access per packet.

[2] Similarly, such non-determinism prevents replicated state machine techniques from providing recovery in this context.

[3] We evaluate the effects of such non-determinism in §6.

[4] Traditional approaches to reliability for routers and switches do little to address statefulness as there is no need to do so, and thus we do not discuss such solutions here.

Somewhat to our surprise, both vendors strongly rejected the idea of simply resetting all active connections after failure, citing concerns over the potential for user-visible disruption to applications (we evaluate cases of such disruption in §6). Both vendors do attempt stateful recovery but their mechanisms for this are ad-hoc and complex, and offer no correctness guarantee. For example, one vendor partially addresses statefulness by checkpointing select data structures to stable storage; since checkpoints may be both stale and incomplete (*i.e.*, not all state is checkpointed) they cannot guarantee correct recovery. After recovery, if an incoming packet is found to have no associated flow state, the packet is dropped and the corresponding connection reset; they reported using a variety of application-specific optimizations to lower the likelihood of such resets. Another vendor offers an 'active:active' deployment option but they do not address non-determinism and offer no correctness guarantees; to avoid resetting connections their IDS system 'fails open' – *i.e.*, flows that were active when the IDS failed bypass some security inspections after failure.

Both vendors expressed great interest in general mechanisms that guarantee correctness, saying this would both improve the quality of their products and reduce the time their developers spend reasoning through the possible outcomes of new packets interacting with incorrectly restored state.

However, both vendors were emphatic that correctness could not come at the cost of added latency under failure-free operation and independently cited 1ms as an upper bound on the latency overhead under failure-free operation.[5] One vendor related an incident where a trial product that added 1-2ms of delay per-packet triggered almost 100 alarms and complaints within the hour of its deployment.

Finally, both vendors emphasized avoiding the need for 1:1 redundancy due to cost. One vendor estimated a price of $250K for one of their higher-grade appliances; the authors of [58] report that a large enterprise they surveyed deployed 166 firewalls and over 600 middleboxes in total, which would lead to multi million dollar overheads if the dedicated backup approach were applied broadly.

3.3 Design Options

Our goal is to provide stateful recovery that is correct in the face of nondeterminism, yet introduces low delay under both failure-free and post-failure operation. While less explored in networking contexts, stateful recovery has been extensively explored in the general systems literature. It is thus natural to ask what we might borrow from this literature. In this section, we discuss this prior work in broad terms, focusing on general approaches rather than specific solutions, and explain how these lead us to the approach we pursued with FTMB. We discuss specific solutions and experimentally compare against them in §6.

At the highest level approaches to stateful recovery can be classified based on whether lost state is reconstructed by *replaying* execution on past inputs. As the name suggests, solutions based on 'replay' maintain a log of inputs to the system and, in the event of a failure, they recreate lost state by replaying the inputs from the log; in contrast, 'no-replay' solutions do not log inputs and never replay past execution.

As we will discuss in this section, we reject no-replay solutions because they introduce high latencies on per-packet forwarding – on the order of many milliseconds. However, replay-based approaches have their own challenges in sustaining high throughput given the output frequency of middleboxes. FTMB follows the blueprint of rollback-recovery, but introduces new algorithms for logging and output commit that can sustain high throughput.

3.4 No-Replay Designs

No-replay approaches are based on the use of system checkpoints: processes take periodic "snapshots" of the necessary system state and, upon a failure, a replica loads the most recent snapshot. However, just restoring state to the last snapshot does not provide correct recovery since all execution beyond the last snapshot is lost – *i.e.*, the output commit property would be violated for all output generated after the last snapshot. Hence, to enforce the output commit property, such systems buffer all output for the duration between two consecutive snapshots [23]. In our context, this means packets leaving the middlebox are buffered and not released to the external world until a checkpoint of the system up to the creation of the last buffered packet has been logged to stable storage.

Checkpoint-based solutions are simple but delay outputs even under failure-free operation; the extent of this delay depends on the overhead of (and hence frequency between) snapshots. Several efforts aim to improve the efficiency of snapshots – *e.g.*, by reducing their memory footprint [50], or avoiding snapshots unless necessary for correctness [28]. Despite these optimizations, the latency overhead that these systems add – in the order of many milliseconds – remains problematically high for networking contexts. We thus reject no-replay solutions.

3.5 Replay-Based Designs

In replay-based designs, the inputs to the system are logged along with any additional information (called 'determinants') needed for correct replay in the face of nondeterminism. On failure, the system simply replays execution from the log. To reduce replay time and storage requirements these solutions also use periodic snapshots as an optimization: on failure, replay begins from the last snapshot rather than from the beginning of time. Log-based replay systems can release output without waiting for the next checkpoint so long as all the inputs and events on which that output depends have been successfully logged to stable storage. This reduces the latency sensitive impact on failure-free operation making replay-based solutions better suited for FTMB.

Replay-based approaches to system *recovery* should not be confused with replay-based approaches to *debugging*. The latter has been widely explored in recent work for debugging multicore systems [16, 41, 61]. However, debug-

[5] This is also consistent with carrier requirements from the Broadband Forum which cite 1ms as the upper bound on forwarding delay (through BGN appliances) for VoIP and other latency-sensitive traffic [14].

ging systems do not provide mechanisms for output commit, the central property needed for correct recovery – they do not need to, since their aim is not to resume operation after failure. Consequently, these systems cannot be used to implement high availability. [6]

Instead, the most relevant work to our goals comes from the classic distributed systems literature from the 80s and 90s, targeting rollback-recovery for multi-process distributed systems (see [31] for an excellent survey). Unfortunately, because of our new context (a single multi-threaded server, rather than independent processes over a shared network) and performance constraints (output is released every few microseconds or nanoseconds rather than seconds or milliseconds), existing algorithms from this literature for logging and output commit cannot sustain high throughput.

With all recovery approaches, the system must check that all determinants – often recorded in the form of vector clocks [42] or dependency trees [30] – needed for a given message to be replayed have been logged before the message may be released. This check enforces the output commit property. In systems which follow an *optimistic logging* approach, this output commit 'check' requires *coordination* between all active process/threads every time output is released. This coordination limits parallelism when output needs to be released frequently. For example, in §5 we discuss a design we implemented following the optimistic approach which could sustain a maximum throughput of only 600Mbps (where many middleboxes process traffic on the order of Gbps) due to frequent cross-core coordination. Other systems, which follow a *causal logging* approach, achieve coordination-free output commit and better parallelism, but do so by permitting heavy redundancy in what they log: following the approach of one such causal system [30], we estimated that the amount of logged determinants would reach between 500Gbps-300Tbps just for a 10Gbps of packets processed on the dataplane. Under such loads, the system would have to devote far more resources to recording the logs themselves than processing traffic on the dataplane, once again limiting throughput.

Hence, instead of following a standard approach, we instead designed a new logging and output commit approach called *ordered logging with parallel release*. In the following section, we describe how our system works and why ordered logging with parallel release overcome the issues presented by previous approaches.

4. DESIGN

FTMB is a new solution for rollback recovery, tailored to the middlebox problem domain through two new solutions:

1. 'ordered logging': an efficient mechanism for representing and logging the information required for correct replay; ordered logging represents information in such a way that it is easy to verify the output commit property.
2. 'parallel release': an output commit algorithm that is simple and efficient to implement on multicore machines.

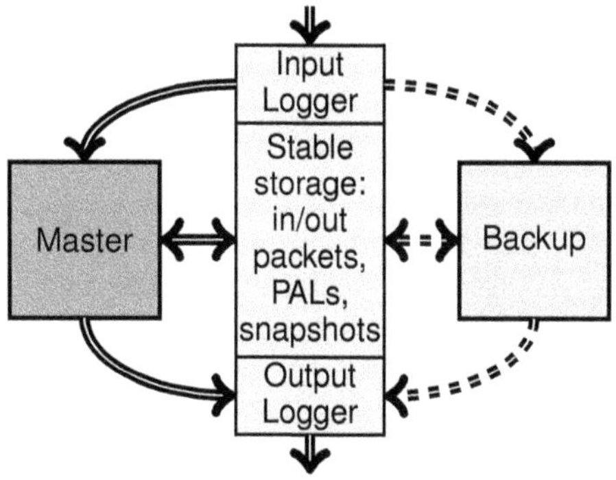

Figure 2: Architecture for FTMB.

The architecture of FTMB is shown in Figure 2. A *master* VM runs the middlebox application(s), with two *loggers* that record its input and output traffic. Periodic system snapshots are sent from the master to stable storage, and used to start a *backup* in case the master crashes. In our prototype, the master and backup are two identical servers; the input and output loggers are software switches upstream and downstream from the master node; and the stable storage is volatile memory at the downstream switch – the storage is 'stable' in that it will survive a failure at the master, even though it would not survive failure of the switch it resides on. [7]

As explained in earlier sections, the crux of ensuring correct recovery is enforcing the output commit property which, for our context, can be stated as: *do not release a packet until all information needed to replay the packet's transmission has been logged to stable storage.* Enforcing this property entails answering the following questions:

- What information must we log to resolve potential nondeterminism during replay? In the language of rollback recovery protocols this defines what the literature calls *determinants*.
- How do we log this information efficiently? This specifies how we *log* determinants.
- What subset of the information that we log is a given packet dependent on for replay? This defines an output's *dependencies*.
- How do we efficiently check when an individual packet's dependencies have been logged to stable storage? This specifies how we check whether the *output commit* requirements for an output have been met.

[6] A second question is whether or not we can adopt logging and instrumentation techniques from these systems to detect determinants. However, as we discuss experimentally in §6, most debugging approaches rely on heavyweight instrumentation (*e.g.*, using memory protection to intercept access to shared data) and often logging data that is unnecessary for our use cases (*e.g.*, all calls to malloc) – this leads to unnecessarily high overheads.

[7] There is some flexibility on the physical placement of the functions; our system can withstand the failure of either the middlebox (Master/Backup) or the node holding the saved state but not both simultaneously. We envisage the use of "bypass" NICs that fail open on detecting failure, to survive failures at the loggers [4].

We now address each question in turn and present the architecture and implementation of the resultant system in §5.

4.1 Defining Determinants

Determinants are the information we must record in order to correctly replay operations that are vulnerable to nondeterminism. As discussed previously, nondeterminism in our system stems from two root causes: races between threads accessing shared variables, and access to hardware whose return values cannot be predicted, such as clocks and random number generators. We discuss each of them below.

Shared State Variables. Shared variables introduce the possibility of nondeterministic execution because we cannot control the order in which threads access them.[8] We thus simply record the order in which shared variables are accessed, and by whom.

Each shared variable v_j is associated with its own lock and counter. The lock protects accesses to the variable, and the counter indicates the order of access. When a thread processing packet p_i accesses a shared variable v_j, it creates a tuple called Packet Access Log (PAL) that contains $(p_i, n_{ij}, v_j, s_{ij})$ where n_{ij} is the number of shared variables accessed so far when processing p_i, and s_{ij} is the number of accesses received so far by v_j.

As an example, figure 3 shows the PALs generated by the four threads (horizontal lines) processing packets A, B, C, D. For packet B, the thread first accesses variable X (which has previously been accessed by the thread processing packet A), and then variable Y (which has previously been accessed by the thread processing packet C).

Note that PALs are created independently by each thread, while holding the variable's lock, and using information (the counters) that is either private to the thread or protected by the lock itself.

Shared pseudorandom number generators are treated in the same way as shared variables, since their behavior is deterministic based on the function's seed (which is initialized in the same way during a replay) and the access order recorded in the PALs.

Clocks and other hardware. Special treatment is needed for hardware resources whose return values cannot be predicted, such as `gettimeofday()` and `/dev/random`. For these, we use the same PAL approach, but replacing the variable name and access order with the hardware accessed and the value returned. Producing these PALs does not require any additional locking because they only use information local to the thread. Upon replay, the PALs allow us to return the exact value as during the original access.

4.2 How to Log Determinants

The key requirement for logging is that PALs need to be on stable storage (on the Output Logger) before we release the packets that depend on them. While there are many options for doing so, we pursue a design that allows for fine-grained and correct handling of dependencies.

[8]Recent research [22, 25] has explored ways to reduce the performance impact of enforcing deterministic execution but their overheads remain impractically high for applications with frequent nondeterminism.

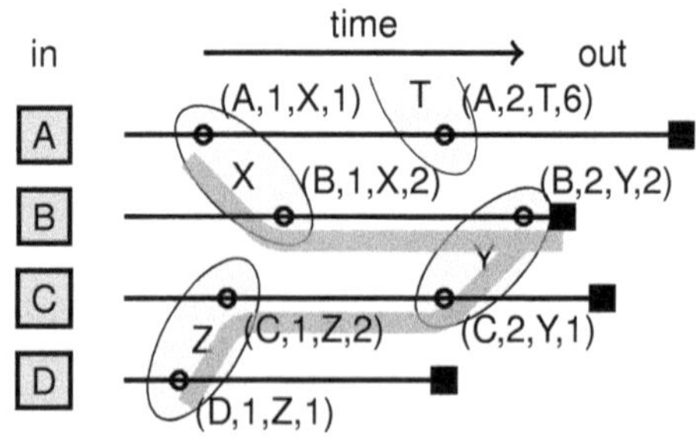

Figure 3: Four threads (black lines) process packets A, B, C, D. As time goes (left to right), they access (circles) shared variables X, Y, Z, T generating the PALs in parentheses. The red tree indicates the dependencies for packet B.

We make two important design decisions for how logging is implemented. The first is that PALs are *decoupled* from their associated data packet and communicated separately to the output logger. This is essential to avoid introducing unnecessary dependencies between packets. As an example, packet B in the figure depends on PAL $(A, 1, X, 1)$, but it need not be delayed until the completion of packet A, (which occurs much later) – it should only be delayed until $(A, 1, X, 1)$ has been logged.

The second decision has to do with *when* PALs are placed in their outgoing PAL queue. **We require that PALs be placed in the output queue before releasing the lock associated to the shared variable they refer to.** This gives two guarantees: i) when p_i is queued, all of its PALs are already queued; and ii) when a PAL for v_j is queued, all previous PALs for the same variable are already in the output queues for this or other threads. We explain the significance of these properties when we present the output commit algorithm in §4.4.

4.3 Defining a Packet's Dependencies

During the replay, the replica must evolve in the same way as the master. For a shared variable v_j accessed while processing p_i, this can happen only if i) the variable has gone through the same sequence of accesses, and ii) the thread has the same internal state. These conditions can be expressed recursively in terms of the PALs: each PAL (p_i, n, v_j, m) in turn has up to two dependencies: one **per-packet** $(p_i, n-1, v_k, s_{ik})$, *i.e.*, on its predecessor PAL for p_i, and one **per-variable** $(p_{i'}, n', v_j, m-1)$, *i.e.*, on its predecessor PAL for v_j, generated by packet $p_{i'}$. A packet depends on its last PAL, and from that we can generate the tree of dependencies; as an example, the red path in the figure represents the dependencies for packet B.

We should note that the recursive dependency is essential for correctness. If, for instance, packet B in the figure were released without waiting for the PAL $(D, 1, Z, 1)$, and the thread generating that PAL crashed, during the replay we could not adequately reconstruct the state of the shared variables used while processing packet B.

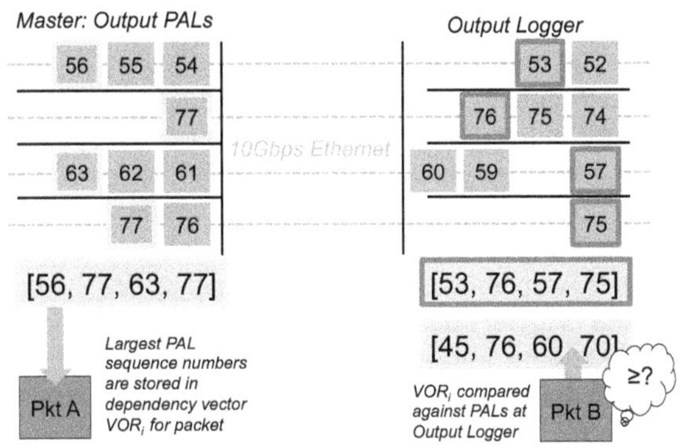

Figure 4: Parallel release. Each PAL is assigned a sequence number identifying *when it was generated* **within that thread; a packet is released from the output logger if all PALs that were queued before it (on any thread) have been logged.**

4.4 Output Commit

We now develop an algorithm that ensures we do not release p_i until all PALs corresponding to p_i's dependencies have arrived at the output logger. This output commit decision is implemented at the output logger. The challenge in this arises from the parallel nature of our system. Like the master, our output logger is multi-threaded and each thread has an independent queue. As a result, the PALs corresponding to p_i's dependencies may be distributed across multiple per-thread queues. We must thus be careful to minimize cache misses and avoid the use of additional synchronization operations.

Rejected Design: Fine-grained Tracking

The straightforward approach would be to explicitly track individual packet and PAL arrivals at the output logger and then release a packet p_i after all of its PAL dependencies have been logged. Our first attempt implemented a 'scoreboard' algorithm that did exactly this at the output logger. We used two matrices to record PAL arrivals: (i) SEQ$[i, j]$ which stores the sequence number of p_i at v_j and (ii) PKT$[j, k]$, the identifier of the packet that accessed v_j at sequence number s_k. These data structures contain all the information needed to check whether a packet can be released. We designed a lock-free multi-threaded algorithm that provably released data packets immediately as their dependencies arrived at the middlebox; however, the overhead of cache contention in reading and updating the scoreboard resulted in poor throughput. Given the two matrices described above, we can expect O(nc) cache misses per packet release, where n is the number of shared variables and c the number of cores (we omit details due to space considerations). Despite optimizations, we find that explicitly tracking dependencies in the above fashion will result in the scoreboard becoming the bottleneck for simple applications.

Parallel release of PALs

We now present a solution that is slightly more coarse-grained, but is amenable to a parallel implementation with very limited overhead. Our key observation here is that the rules chosen to queue PALs and packets *guarantee* that both the **per-packet** and **per-variable** dependencies for a given packet are already queued for release on some thread before the packet arrives at the output queue on its own thread. This follows from the fact that the PAL for a given lock access is always queued *before* the lock is released. Hence, we only need to transfer PALs and packets to the output logger in a way that preserves the ordering between PALs and data packets.

This is achieved with a simple algorithm run between the Master and the Output Logger, illustrated in Fig. 4. Each thread on the Master maps 'one to one' to an ingress queue on the Output Logger. PALs in each queue are transferred as a sequential stream (similar to TCP), with each PAL associated to an per-queue sequence number. This replaces the second entry in the PAL, which then does not need to be stored. Each thread at the Master keeps track of MAX, the maximum sequence number that has been assigned to any PAL it has generated.

On the Master: Before sending a data packet from its queue to the output logger, each thread on the master *reads* the current MAX value at all other threads and creates a vector clock VOR which is associated with the packet. It then reliably transfers the pending PALs in its queue, followed by the data packets and associated vector clocks.

On the Output Logger: Each thread continuously receives PALs and data packets, requesting retransmissions in the case of dropped PALs. When it receives a PAL, a thread updates the value MAX representing the highest sequence number such that it has received all PALs prior to MAX. On receiving a data packet, each thread *reads* the value MAX over all other threads, comparing each with the vector clock VOR. Once all values MAX$_i$ $\geq$ VOR$_i$, the packet can be released.

Performance

Our parallel release algorithm is efficient because i) threads on the master and the output logger can run in parallel; ii) there are no write-write conflicts on the access to other queues, so memory performance does not suffer much; iii) the check to release a packet requires a very small constant time operation; iv) when batching is enabled, all packets released by the master in the same batch can use the same vector clock, resulting in very small overhead on the link between the master and the output logger and amortizing the cost of the 'check' operation.

5. SYSTEM IMPLEMENTATION

We present key aspects of our implementation of FTMB. For each, we highlight the performance implications of adding FTMB to a regular middlebox through qualitative discussion and approximate back-of-the-envelope estimates; we present experimental results with our prototype in §6.

The logical components of the architecture are shown in Figure 2. Packets flow from the Input Logger (IL), to the Master (M), to the Output Logger (OL). FTMB also needs a Stable Storage (SS) subsystem with enough capacity to store the state of the entire VM, plus the packets and PALs accumulated in the IL and OL between two snapshots. In our implementation the IL, OL and SS are on the same physical machine, which is expected to survive when M crashes.

To estimate the amount of storage needed we can assume a snapshot interval in the 50–200 ms range (§6), and input and output traffic limited by the link's speed (10–40 Gbit/s). We expect to cope with a large, but not overwhelming PAL generation rate; *e.g.*, in the order of 5 M PALs/s (assuming an input rate of 1.25M packets/second and 5 shared state accesses per packet).

5.1 Input Logger

The main role of the IL is to record input traffic since the previous snapshot, so that packets can be presented in the same order to the replica in case of a replay.

The input NIC on the IL can use standard mechanisms (such as 5-tuple hashing on multiqueue NICs) to split traffic onto multiple queues, and threads can run the IL tasks independently on each queue. Specifically, on each input queue, the IL receives incoming packets, assigns them sequence numbers, saves them into stable storage, and then passes them reliably to the Master.

Performance implications: The IL is not especially CPU intensive, and the bandwidth to communicate with the master or the storage is practically equal to the input bandwidth: the small overhead for reliably transferring packets to the Master is easily offset by aggregating small frames into MTU-sized segments.

It follows that the only effect of the IL on performance is the additional (one way) latency for the extra hop the traffic takes, which we can expect to be in the 5–10μs range [34].

5.2 Master

The master runs a version of the Middlebox code with the following modifications:

- the input must read packets from the reliable stream coming from the IL instead of individual packets coming from a NIC;
- the output must transfer packets to the output queue instead of a NIC.
- access to shared variables is protected by locks, and includes calls to generate and queue PALs;
- access to special hardware functions (timers, etc.) also generates PALs as above.

A shim layer takes care of the first two modifications; for a middlebox written using Click, this is as simple as replacing the `FromDevice` and `ToDevice` elements. We require that developers annotate shared variables at the point of their declaration. Given these annotations, we automate the insertion of the code required to generate PALs using a custom tool inspired by generic systems for data race detection [56].

Our tool uses LLVM's [43] analysis framework (also used in several static analysis tools including the Clang Static Analyzer [3] and KLEE [19]) to generate the call graph for the middlebox. We use this call graph to record the set of locks held while accessing each shared variable in the middlebox. If all accesses to the shared variable are protected by a common lock, we know that there are no contended accesses to the variable and we just insert code to record and update the PAL. Otherwise we generate a "protecting" lock and insert code that acquires the lock before any accesses, in addition to the code for updating the PALs. Note that because the new locks never wrap another lock (either another new lock or a lock in the original source code), it is not possible for this instrumentation to introduce deadlocks [17, 21]. Since we rely on static analysis, our tool is conservative, *i.e.* it might insert a protecting lock even when none is required.

FTMB is often compatible with lock-free optimizations. For example, we implemented FTMB to support seqlocks [13], which are used in multi-reader/single-writer contexts. seqlocks use a counter to track what 'version' of a variable a reader accessed; this version number replaces s_{ij} in the PAL.

Performance implications: the main effect of FTMB on the performance of the Master is the cost of PAL generation, which is normally negligible unless we are forced to introduce additional locking in the middlebox.

5.3 Output Logger

The Output Logger cooperates with the Master to transfer PALs and data packets and to enforce output commit. The algorithm is described in §4.4. Each thread at M transports packets with a unique header such that NIC hashing at OL maintains the same affinity, enforcing a one-to-one mapping between an eggress queue on M to an ingress queue on OL.

The traffic between M and OL includes data packets, plus additional information for PALs and vector clocks. As a very coarse estimate, even for a busy middlebox with a total of 5 M PALs and vector clocks per second, assuming 16 bytes per PAL, 16 bytes per vector clock, the total bandwidth overhead is about 10% of the link's capacity for a 10 Gbit/s link.

Performance implications: once again the impact of FTMB on the OL is more on latency than on throughput. The minimum latency to inform the OL that PALs are in stable storage is the one-way latency for the communication. On top of this, there is an additional latency component because our output commit check requires *all queued PALs* to reach the OL before the OL releases a packet. In the worst case a packet may find a full PAL queue when computing its vector clock, and so its release may be delayed by the amount of time required to transmit a full queue of PALs. Fortunately, the PAL queue can be kept short *e.g.*, 128 slots each, without any adverse effect on the system (PALs can be sent to the OL right away; the only reason to queue them is to exploit batching). For 16-byte PALs, it takes less than 2μs of link time to drain one full queue, so the total latency introduced by the OL and the output commit check is in the 10-30μs range.

5.4 Periodic snapshots

FTMB takes periodic snapshots of the state of the Master, to be used as a starting point during replay, and avoid unbounded growth of the replay time and input and output logs size. Checkpointing algorithms normally freeze the VM completely while taking a snapshot of its state.

Performance implications: The duration of the freeze, hence the impact on latency, has a component proportional to the number of memory pages modified between snapshots, and inversely proportional to bandwidth to the storage server. This amounts to about 5μs for each 4 Kbyte page. on a 10 Gbit/s link, and quickly dominates the fixed cost (1-2ms) for taking the snapshot. However, a worst case analysis is hard as values depend on the (wildly variable) number of pages modified between snapshots. Hence it is more meaningful to gauge the additional latency from the experimental values in §6 and the literature in general [23].

5.5 Replay

Finally, we describe our implementation of replay, when a Replica VM starts from the last available snapshot to take over a failed Master. The Replica is started in "replay mode", meaning that the input is fed (by the IL) from the saved trace, and threads use the PALs to drive nondeterministic choices.

On input, the threads on the Replica start processing packets, discarding possible duplicates at the beginning of the stream. When acquiring the lock that protects a shared variable, the thread uses the recorded PALs to check whether it can access the lock, or it has to block waiting for some other thread that came earlier in the original execution. The information in the PALs is also used to replay hardware related non deterministic calls (clocks, etc.). Of course, PALs are not generated during the replay.

On output, packets are passed to the OL, which discards them if a previous instance had been already released, or pass it out otherwise (*e.g.*, copies of packets still in the Master when it crashed, even though all of their dependencies had made it to the OL). A thread exits replay mode when it finds that there are no more PALs for a given shared variable. When this happens, it starts behaving as the master, i.e. generate PALs, compute output dependencies, *etc.*

Performance implications: other than having to re-run the Middlebox since the last snapshot, operation speed in replay mode is comparable to that in the original execution. §6.2 presents some experimental results. Of course, the duration of service unavailability after a failure also depends on the latency of the failure detector, whose discussion is beyond the scope of this paper.

6. EVALUATION

We added FTMB support into 7 middlebox applications implemented in Click: one configuration comes from industry, five are research prototypes, and one is a simple 'blind forwarding' configuration which performs no middlebox processing; we list these examples in Table 1.

Our experimental setup is as follows. FTMB uses Xen 4.2 at the master middlebox with Click running in an OpenSUSE VM, chosen for its support of fast VM snapshotting [6]. We use the standard Xen bridged networking backend; this backend is known to have low throughput and substantial recent work aims to improve throughput and latency to virtual machines, *e.g.*, through netmap+xennet [45, 52] or dpdk+virtio [38, 55]. However, neither of these latter systems yet supports seamless VM migration. We thus built two prototypes: one based on the Xen bridged networking backend which runs at lower rates (100Mbps) but is complete with support for fast VM snapshots and migration, and a second prototype that uses netmap+xennet and scales to high rates (10Gbps) but lacks snapshotting and replay. We primarily report results from our complete prototype; results for relevant experiments with the high speed prototype were qualitatively similar.

Middlebox	LOC	SVs	Elts	Source
Mazu-NAT	5728	3	46	Mazu Networks [7]
WAN Opt.	5052	2	40	Aggarwal et al. [15]
BW Monitor	4623	251	41	Custom
SimpleNAT	4964	2	42	Custom
Adaptive LB	5058	1	42	Custom
QoS Priority	5462	3	56	Custom
BlindFwding	1914	0	24	Custom

Table 1: Click configurations used in our experiments, including Lines of Code (LOC), Shared Variables (SVs), number of Elements (Elts), and the author/origin of the configuration.

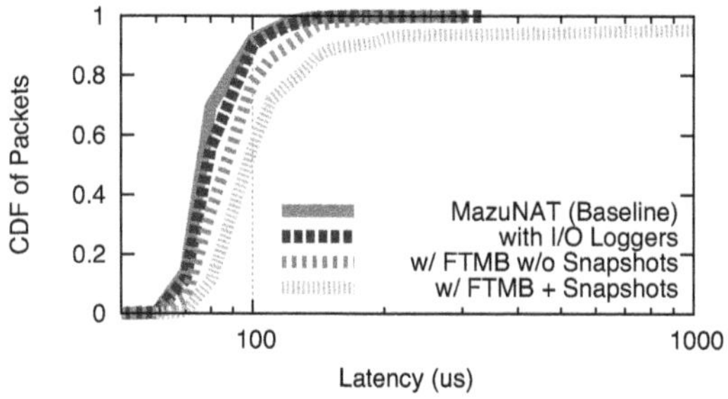

Figure 5: Local RTT with and without components of FTMB enabled.

We ran our tests on a local network of servers with 16-core Intel Xeon EB-2650 processors at 2.6Ghz, 20MB cache size, and 128GB memory divided across two NUMA nodes. For all experiments shown, we used a standard enterprise trace as our input packet stream [26]; results are representative of tests we ran on other traces.

We first evaluate the FTMB's latency and bandwidth overheads under failure-free operation (§6.1). We then evaluate recovery from failure (§6.2).

6.1 Overhead on Failure-free Operation

How does FTMB impact packet latency under failure-free operation? In Figure 5, we present the per-packet latency through a middlebox over the local network. A packet source sends traffic (over a logging switch) to a VM running a MazuNAT (a combination firewall-NAT released by Mazu Networks [7]), which loops the traffic back to the packet generator. We measure this RTT. To test FTMB, we first show the base latency with (a) just the MazuNAT, (b) the MazuNAT with I/O logging performed at the upstream/-downstream switch, (c) the MazuNAT with logging, PAL-

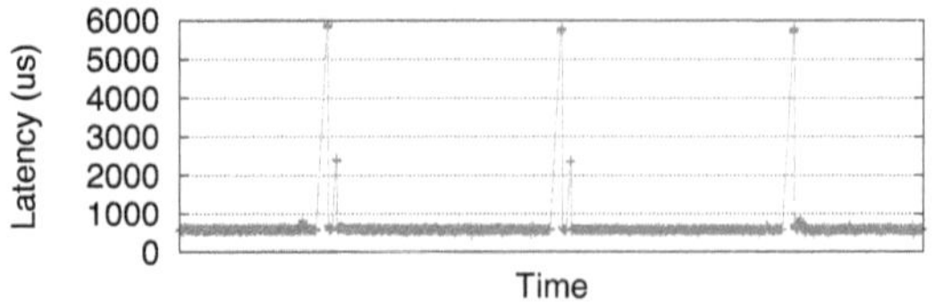

Figure 6: Testbed RTT over time.

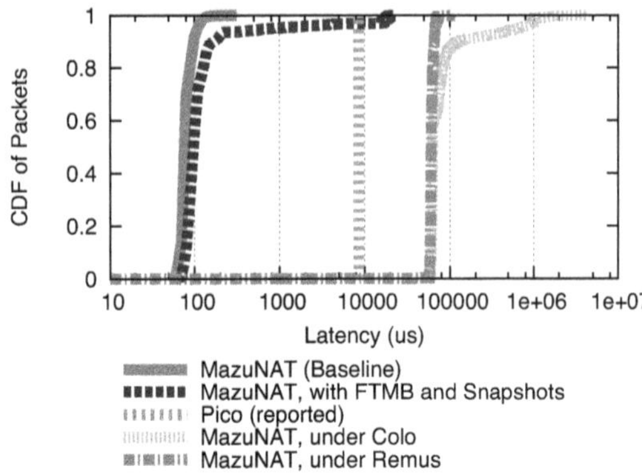

Figure 7: Local RTT with FTMB and other FT systems.

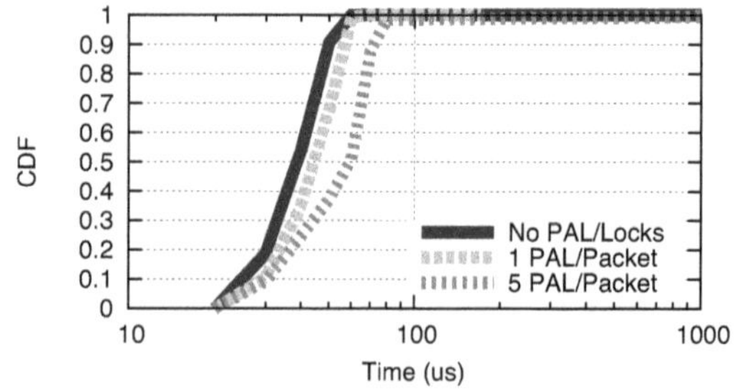

Figure 8: Testbed RTT with increasing PALs/packet.

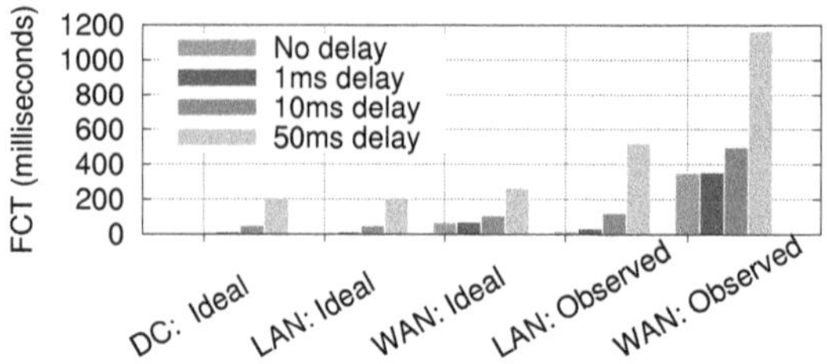

Figure 9: Ideal [46] and observed page load times when latency is artificially introduced in the network.

instrumented locks, parallel release for the output commit condition and (d) running the MazuNAT with all our fault tolerance mechanisms, including VM checkpointing every 200ms. Adding PAL instrumentation to the middlebox locks in the MazuNAT has a negligible impact on latency, increasing 30μs over the baseline at the median, leading to a 50th percentile latency of 100μs.[9] However, adding VM checkpointing does increase latency, especially at the tail: the 95th %-ile is 810μs, and the 99th %-ile s 18ms.

To understand the cause of this tail latency, we measured latency against time using the Blind Forwarding configuration. Figure 6 shows the results of this experiment: we see that the latency spikes are periodic with the checkpoint interval. Every time we take a VM snapshot, the virtual machine suspends temporarily, leading to a brief interval where packets are buffered as they cannot be processed. As new hardware-assisted virtualization techniques improve [1, 20] we expect this penalty to decrease with time; we discuss these opportunities further in §8.

How does the latency introduced by FTMB compare to existing fault-tolerance solutions? In Figure 7, we compare FTMB against three proposals from the research community: Pico [50], Colo [28], and Xen Remus [23]. Remus and Colo are general no-replay solutions which can provide fault tolerance for any VM-based system running a standard operating system under x86. Remus operates by checkpointing and buffering output until the next checkpoint completes; this results in a median latency increase for the MazuNAT by over 50ms. for general applications Colo can offer much lower latency overhead than Remus: Colo allows two copies of a virtual machine to run side-by-side in "lock step". If their output remains the same, the two virtual machines are considered identical; if the two outputs differ, the system forces a checkpoint like Remus. Because multi-threaded middleboxes introduce substantial nondeterminism, though, Colo cannot offer us any benefits over Remus: when we ran the MazuNAT under Colo, it checkpointed just as frequently as Remus would have, leading to an equal median latency penalty.

Pico is a no-replay system similar to Remus but tailored to the middlebox domain by offering a custom library for flow state which checkpoints packet processing state only, but *not* operating system, memory state, *etc.*, allowing for much lighter-weight and therefore faster checkpoint. The authors of Pico report a latency penalty of 8-9ms in their work which is a substantial improvement over Colo and Remus, but still a noticeable penalty due to the reliance on packet buffering until checkpoint completion.

How does inserting PALs increase latency? To measure the impact of PALs over per-packet latency, we used a toy middlebox with a simple pipeline of 0, 1, or 5 locks and ran measurements with 500-byte packets at 1Gbps with four threads dedicated to processing in our DPDK testbed. Figure 8 shows the latency distributions for our experiments, relative to a baseline of the same pipeline with no locks. At 5 PALS/Locks per packet, latency increases to 60μs with 5 PALS/Locks per packet, relative to a median latency under 40μs in the baseline – an increase of on average 4μs per PAL/Lock per packet. Note that this latency figure includes both the cost of PAL creation and lock insertion; the worst case overhead for FTMB is when locks are not already present in the base implementation.

How much does latency matter to application performance? We measured the impact of inflated latency on Flow Completion Times (FCTs) with both measurements and modeling. In Figure 9, we show flow completion times for a 2MB flow (representative of web page load sizes) given the flow completion time model by Mittal et al. [46] marked

[9] In similar experiments with our netmap-based prototype we observe a median latency increase of 25μs and 40μs over the baseline at forwarding rates of 1Gbps and 5Gbps respectively, both over 4 cores.

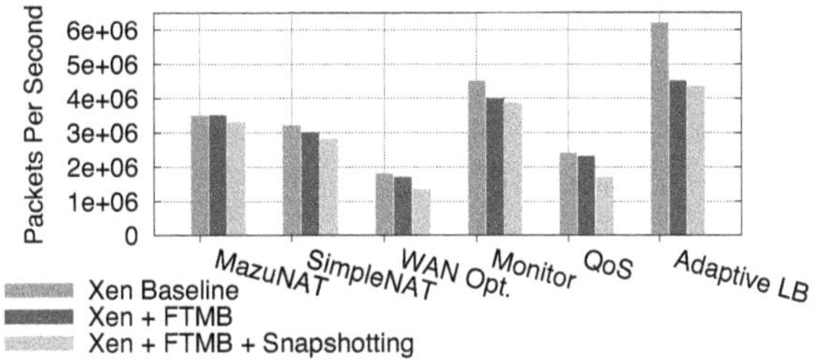

Figure 10: Impact of FTMB on forwarding plane throughput.

as 'Ideal'. Marked as 'Observed', we downloaded the Alexa top-1000 [2] web pages over a LAN and over a WAN and used `tc` to inflate the latency by the same amounts. In both the datacenter and LAN cases, adding 10ms of latency on the forward and reverse path increases flow completion times to 20× the original in the simulated case; in the experimental LAN case it increased FCT to 10×. In the WAN case, page load times increased to 1.5× by adding 10ms of latency from a median of 343ms to 492ms. An experiment by Amazon shows that every 100ms of additional page load time their customers experienced costs them 1% in sales [40].

Given these numbers in context, we can return to Figure 7 and see that solutions based on Colo, Pico, or Remus would *noticeably* harm network users' quality of experience, while FTMB, with introduced latency typically well under 1ms, would have a much weaker impact.

How much does FTMB impact throughput under failure-free operation? Figure 10 shows forwarding plane throughput in a VM, in a VM with PAL instrumentation, and running complete FTMB mode with both PAL instrumentations and periodic VM snapshotting. To emphasize the extra load caused by FTMB, we ran the experiment with locally sourced traffic and dropping the output. Even so, the impact is modest, as expected (see §5.2). For most configurations, the primary throughput penalty comes from snapshotting rather than from PAL insertion. The MazuNAT and SimpleNat saw a total throughput reduction of 5.6% and 12.5% respectively. However, for the Monitor and the Adaptive Load Balancer, PAL insertion was the primary overhead, causing a 22% and 30% drop in throughput respectively. These two experience a heavier penalty since typically they have no contention for access to shared state variables: the tens of nanoseconds required to generate a PAL for these middleboxes is a proportionally higher penalty than it is for middleboxes which spend more time per-packet accessing complex and contended state.

We ran similar experiments with Remus and Colo, where throughput peaked in the low hundreds of *Kpps*. We also ran experiments with Scribe [41], a publicly-available system for record and replay of general applications, which aims to *automatically* detect and record data races using page protection. This costs about 400us per lock access due to the overhead of page faults.[10] Using Scribe, a simple two-threaded Click configuration with a single piece of shared state stalled to a forwarding rate of only 500 packets/second.

[10]Measured using the Scribe demo image in VirtualBox.

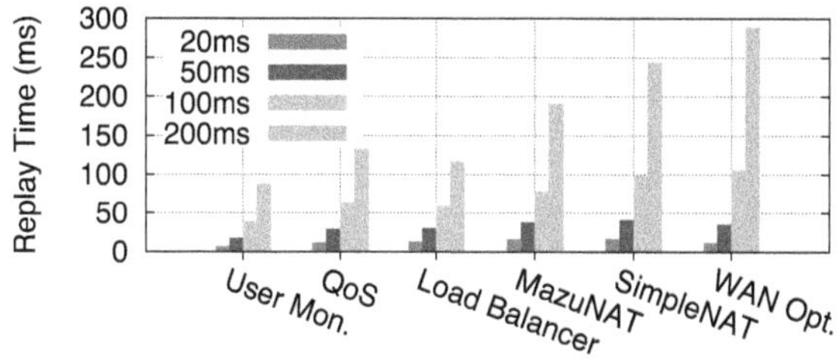

Figure 11: Time to perform replay with varying checkpoint intervals and middlebox configurations.

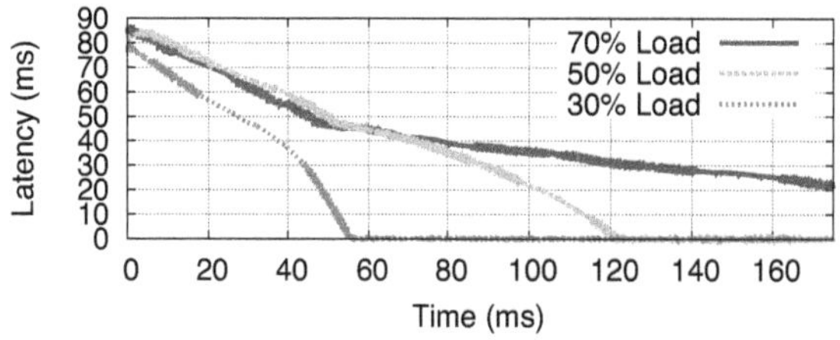

Figure 12: Packet latencies post-replay.

6.2 Recovery

How long does FTMB take to perform replay and how does replay impact packet latencies? Unlike no-replay systems, FTMB adds the cost of replay. We measure the amount of time required for replay in Fig. 11. We ran these experiments at 80% load (about 3.3 Mpps) with periodic checkpoints of 20, 50, 100, and 200ms.

For lower checkpoint rates, we see two effects leading to a replay time that is actually *less* than the original checkpoint interval. First, the logger begins transmitting packets to the replica as soon as replay begins – while the VM is loading. This means that most packets are read pre-loaded to local memory, rather than directly from the NIC. Second, the transmission arrives at almost 100% of the link rate, rather than 80% load as during the checkpoint interval.

However, at 200ms, we see a different trend: some middleboxes that make frequent accesses to shared variable have a *longer* replay time than the original checkpoint interval because of the overhead of replaying lock accesses. Recall that when a thread attempts to access a shared-state variable during replay, it will spin waiting for its 'turn' to access the variable and this leads to slowed execution.

During replay, new packets that arrive must be buffered, leading to a period of increased queueing delays after execution has resumed. In Figure 12, we show per-packet latencies for packets that arrive post-failure for MazuNAT at different load levels and replay times between 80-90ms. At 30%-load, packet latencies return to their normal sub-millisecond values within 60ms of resumed execution. As expected recovery takes longer at higher loads: at 70% load per-packet latency remains over 10ms even at 175ms, and the latencies do not decrease to under a millisecond until past 300ms after execution has resumed.

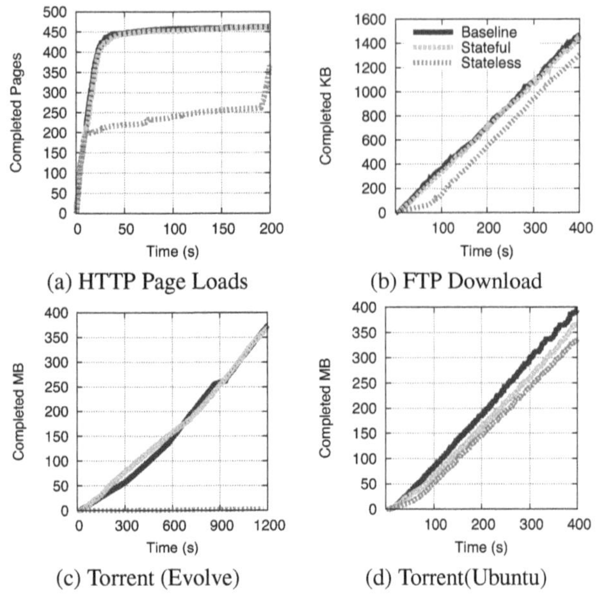

Figure 13: Application performance with and without state restoration after recovery. Key (top right) is same for all figures.

Is stateful failover valuable to applications? Perhaps the simplest approach to recovering from failure is simply to bring up a backup from 'cold start', effectively wiping out all connection state after failure: i.e., recovery is *stateless*. To see the impact of stateless recovery on real applications, we tested several applications over the wide area with a NAT which either (a) did not fail (our baseline), (b) went absent for 300ms,[11] during which time traffic was buffered (this represents stateful recovery), or (c) flushed all state on failure (representing stateless recovery). Figure 13 shows the time to download 500 pages in a 128-thread loop from the Alexa-top US sites, percentage file completion over time for a large FTP download, and percentage file completion for two separate BitTorrent downloads. In all three configurations, stateful recovery performs close to the performance of the baseline. For stateless recovery over the HTTP connections, we see a sharp knee corresponding to the connection reset time: 180 seconds[12]. The only application with little impact under stateless recovery is one of the BitTorrent downloads – however, the other BitTorrent download failed almost entirely and the client had to be restarted! The torrent which failed had only 10 available peers and, when the connections were reset, the client assumed that the peers had gone offline. The other torrent had a large pool of available peers and hence could immediately reconnect to new peers.

Our point in these experiments is not to suggest that applications are fundamentally incapable of rapid recovery in scenarios of stateless recovery, but simply that many existing applications do not.

[11]We picked 300ms as a conservative estimate of recovery time; our results are not sensitive to the precise value.

[12]Firefox, Chrome, and Opera have reset times of 300 seconds, 50 seconds, and 115 seconds respectively.

7. RELATED WORK

We briefly discuss the three lines of work relevant to FTMB, reflecting the taxonomy of related work introduced in §2.

First are no-replay schemes. In §6 we described in detail three recent systems – Remus, Pico and Colo – that adopt this approach and compared FTMB to them experimentally.

The second are solutions for rollback recovery from the distributed systems literature. The literature includes a wide range of protocol proposals (we refer the reader to Elnozahy et al. [31] for an excellent survey); however, to our knowledge, there is no available system implementation that we can put to the test for our application context.[13] More generally, as mentioned earlier, the focus on distributed systems (as opposed to a parallel program on a single machine) changes the nature of the problem in many dimensions, such as: the failure model (partial vs. complete failure), the nature of non-determinism (primarily the arrival and sending order of messages at a given process vs. threads that 'race' to access the same variable), the frequency of output (for us, outputs are generated at a very high rate) and the frequency of nondeterminism (per-packet for us), and where the performance bottlenecks lie (for us, in the logging and output commit decision). These differences led us to design new solutions that are simpler and more lightweight than those found in the literature.

The final class of solutions are the multicore record-and-replay systems used for debugging. These do not implement output commit. We discussed these solutions in broad terms in §2 and evaluated one such system (Scribe) in §6.

In the remainder of this section we briefly review a few additional systems.

Hypervisor-based Fault Tolerance [18] was an early, pioneering system in the 90s to implement fault-tolerance over arbitrary virtual machines; their approach did not address multicore systems, and required synchronization between the master and replica for every nondeterministic operation.

SMP Revirt [29] performs record-and-replay over Xen VMs; unlike FTMB SMPRevirt is hence fully general. As in Scribe, SMP ReVirt uses page protection to track memory accesses. For applications with limited contention, the authors report a 1.2-8x slowdown, but for so-called "racy" applications (like ours) with tens or hundreds of thousands of faults per second we expect results similar to those of Scribe.

Eidetic Systems [24] allow a user to replay any event in the system's history – on the scale of even years. They achieve very low overheads for their target environment: end user desktops. However, the authors explicitly note that their solutions do not scale to racy and high-output systems.

R2 [36] logs a cut in an application's call graph and introduces detailed logging of information flowing across the cut using an R2 runtime to intercept syscalls and underlying libraries; the overhead of their interception makes them poorly suited to our application with frequent nondeterminism.

ODR [16] is a general record-and-replay system that pro-

[13]In their survey paper, Elnozahy et al. state that, in practice, log-based rollback-recovery has seen little adoption due to the complexity of its algorithms.

vides output determinism: to reduce runtime overhead ODR foregoes logging all forms of nondeterminism and instead searches the space of possible executions during replay. This can result in replay times that are several orders of magnitude higher than the original execution (in fact, the search space is NP hard). This long replay time is not acceptable for applications looking to recover from a failure (as opposed to debugging post-failure).

8. DISCUSSION

We presented FTMB, a system for rollback recovery which uses ordered logging and parallel release for low overhead middlebox fault-tolerance. We showed that FTMB imposes only 30μs of latency for median packets through an industry-designed middlebox. FTMB has modest throughput overheads, and can perform replay recovery in 1-2 wide area RTTs. Before closing, we discuss the growing NFV software ecosystem and how FTMB fits into this future.

User-Level Packet Processing Stacks. Significant efforts in industry and research aim to allow for fast packet-processing in user space (*e.g.* netmap [52], DPDK [38]) in and out of virtual machines [39,45,53–55]. At present, none of these new systems support seamless virtual machine migration. This support will be required as NFV stacks become more widely deployed; once these systems do support migration they will be compatible with FTMB.

New Virtualization Techniques and Fast Checkpointing. Linux Containers [5] offer finer-grained virtualization than Xen, offering processes isolation while sharing operating system components. Containers enable cheaper snapshotting, as less memory is copied per snapshot. Several ongoing efforts are exploring hardware and software support for faster snapshotting [1,20] which will improve migration and reliability systems [11,23] thereby improving FTMB's tail latencies introduced by VM suspension.

Varied Operating Systems and Hardware Components. One of the oft-touted benefits of NFV [32] is the potential for a wider range of diversity in system software stacks and hardware; wider at least, than today's closed-down, all-in-one 'appliances'. With this change comes the opportunity to extend the failure model assumed by FTMB and other systems (*e.g.* [23]): by running different drivers, NICs, and operating systems outside of the virtualization layer, one may be able to protect against not only hardware and software failures, but bugs fundamental to the choice of driver, NIC, OS, *etc.*, by failing over to a machine with entirely different components.

Diverse Middlebox Software. The Open Source Community offers software implementations of many middleboxes; *e.g.*, Snort [8], Bro [10], Vyatta [12], and Squid [9], as does the broader industry. While we experimented with Click-based middlebox implementations, we expect our techniques should be equally applicable to these other systems. In addition, vendors of hardware-based appliances are increasingly re-architecting their products as software-only implementations. Hence we expect the potential application of FTMB to only grow in the future.

If the NFV ecosystem continues to gain traction with the above software trends, it will need a practical, low-overhead solution for reliability. We envision FTMB's approach – ordered logging and parallel release – to be that solution.

9. ACKNOWLEDGEMENTS

We thank the anonymous reviewers of the SIGCOMM program committee and our shepherd Jeff Chase for their thoughtful feedback on this paper. We thank the middlebox vendors we spoke with for helpful discussions about FTMB, reliability practices, and state of the art network appliances. Jiawei Chen and Eddie Dong at Intel kindly shared the Colo source code and helped us deploy it in our lab at Berkeley. Kay Ousterhout provided feedback on many iterations of this paper. This material is based upon work supported by the National Science Foundation Graduate Research Fellowship under Grant No. DGE-1106400. This work was in part made possible by generous financial support and technical feedback from Intel Research.

10. REFERENCES

[1] A Peek into Extended Page Tables. https://communities.intel.com/community/itpeernetwork/datastack/blog/2009/06/02/a-peek-into-extended-page-tables.

[2] Alexa: Actionable Analytics for the Web. http://www.alexa.com/.

[3] Clang Static Analyzer. http://clang-analyzer.llvm.org/.

[4] Intel PRO/1000 Quad Port Bypass Server Adapters. http://www.intel.com/content/www/us/en/network-adapters/gigabit-network-adapters/pro-1000-qp.html.

[5] LXC - Linux Containers. https://linuxcontainers.org/.

[6] Remus PV domU Requirements. http://wiki.xen.org/wiki/Remus_PV_domU_requirements.

[7] Riverbed Completes Acquisition of Mazu Networks. http://www.riverbed.com/about/news-articles/press-releases/riverbed-completes-acquisition\-of-mazu-networks.html.

[8] Snort IDS. https://www.snort.org/.

[9] Squid: Optimising Web Delivery. http://www.squid-cache.org/.

[10] The Bro Network Security Monitor. https://www.bro.org/.

[11] VMWare vSphere. https://www.vmware.com/support/vsphere.

[12] Vyatta. http://www.vyatta.com.

[13] Wikipedia:seqlock. http://en.wikipedia.org/wiki/Seqlock.

[14] Multi-Service Architecture and Framework Requirements. http://www.broadband-forum.org/technical/download/TR-058.pdf, 2003.

[15] A. Akella, A. Anand, A. Balachandran, P. Chitnis, C. Muthukrishnan, R. Ramjee, and G. Varghese. EndRE: An End-System Redundancy Elimination Service for Enterprises. In *Proc. USENIX NSDI*, 2010.

[16] G. Altekar and I. Stoica. ODR: Output-Deterministic Replay for Multicore Debugging. In *Proc. ACM SOSP*, 2009.

[17] R. H. Arpaci-Dusseau and A. C. Arpaci-Dusseau. *Operating Systems: Three Easy Pieces*. Arpaci-Dusseau Books, 0.80 edition, May 2014.

[18] T. C. Bressoud and F. B. Schneider. Hypervisor-based Fault Tolerance. In *Proc. ACM SOSP*, 1995.

[19] C. Cadar, D. Dunbar, and D. R. Engler. KLEE: Unassisted and Automatic Generation of High-Coverage Tests for Complex Systems Programs. In *Proc. USENIX OSDI*, 2008.

[20] J. Chung, J. Seo, W. Baek, C. CaoMinh, A. McDonald, C. Kozyrakis, and K. Olukotun. Improving Software Concurrency with Hardware-assisted Memory Snapshot. In *Proc. ACM SPAA*, 2008.

[21] E. G. Coffman, M. Elphick, and A. Shoshani. System Deadlocks. *ACM Comput. Surv.*, 3(2):67–78, June 1971.

[22] H. Cui, J. Simsa, Y.-H. Lin, H. Li, B. Blum, X. Xu, J. Yang, G. A. Gibson, and R. E. Bryant. Parrot: A Practical Runtime for

Deterministic, Stable, and Reliable Threads. In *Proc. ACM SOSP*, 2013.

[23] B. Cully, G. Lefebvre, D. Meyer, M. Feeley, N. Hutchinson, and A. Warfield. Remus: High Availability via Asynchronous Virtual Machine Replication. In *Proc. USENIX NSDI*, 2008.

[24] D. Devecsery, M. Chow, X. Dou, J. Flinn, and P. M. Chen. Eidetic Systems. In *Proc. USENIX OSDI*, 2014.

[25] J. Devietti, B. Lucia, L. Ceze, and M. Oskin. DMP: Deterministic Shared Memory Multiprocessing. In *Proc. ACM ASPLOS*, 2009.

[26] Digital Corpora. 2009-M57-Patents packet trace. http://digitalcorpora.org/corp/nps/scenarios/2009-m57-patents/net/.

[27] M. Dobrescu, N. Egi, K. Argyraki, B.-G. Chun, K. Fall, G. Iannaccone, A. Knies, M. Manesh, and S. Ratnasamy. RouteBricks: Exploiting Parallelism To Scale Software Routers. In *Proc. ACM SOSP*, 2009.

[28] Y. Dong, W. Ye, Y. Jiang, I. Pratt, S. Ma, J. Li, and H. Guan. COLO: COarse-grained LOck-stepping Virtual Machines for Non-stop Service. In *Proc. ACM SoCC*, 2013.

[29] G. W. Dunlap, D. G. Lucchetti, M. A. Fetterman, and P. M. Chen. Execution Replay of Multiprocessor Virtual Machines. In *Proc. ACM SIGPLAN/SIGOPS VEE*, 2008.

[30] E. N. Elnozahy and W. Zwaenepoel. Manetho: Transparent roll back-recovery with low overhead, limited rollback, and fast output commit. *IEEE Trans. Comput.*, 41(5):526–531, May 1992.

[31] E. N. M. Elnozahy, L. Alvisi, Y.-M. Wang, and D. B. Johnson. A Survey of Rollback-Recovery Protocols in Message-passing Systems. *ACM Comput. Surv.*, 34(3):375–408, Sept. 2002.

[32] European Telecommunications Standards Institute. NFV Whitepaper. https://portal.etsi.org/NFV/NFV_White_Paper.pdf.

[33] S. K. Fayazbakhsh, L. Chiang, V. Sekar, M. Yu, and J. C. Mogul. Enforcing Network-wide Policies in the Presence of Dynamic Middlebox Actions Using Flowtags. In *Proc. USENIX NSDI*, 2014.

[34] M. Flajslik and M. Rosenblum. Network Interface Design for Low Latency Request-Response Protocols. In *Proc. USENIX ATC*, 2013.

[35] A. Gember, R. Viswanathan, C. Prakash, R. Grandl, J. Khalid, S. Das, and A. Akella. OpenNF: Enabling Innovation in Network Function Control. In *Proc. ACM SIGCOMM*, 2014.

[36] Z. Guo, X. Wang, J. Tang, X. Liu, Z. Xu, M. Wu, M. F. Kaashoek, and Z. Zhang. R2: An Application-Level Kernel for Record and Replay. In *Proc. USENIX OSDI*, 2008.

[37] S. Han, K. Jang, K. Park, and S. Moon. PacketShader: a GPU-accelerated Software Router. In *Proc. ACM SIGCOMM*, 2010.

[38] Intel. Data Plane Development Kit. http://dpdk.org/.

[39] Intel. PCI-SIG SR-IOV Primer: An Introduction to SR-IOV Technology. http://www.intel.com/content/www/us/en/pci-express/pci-sig-sr-iov-primer-sr-iov-technology-paper.html.

[40] R. Kohavi and R. Longbotham. Online experiments: Lessons learned. *Computer*, 40(9):103–105, 2007.

[41] O. Laadan, N. Viennot, and J. Nieh. Transparent, Lightweight Application Execution Replay on Commodity Multiprocessor Operating Systems. In *Proc. ACM SIGMETRICS*, 2010.

[42] L. Lamport. Time, clocks, and the ordering of events in a distributed system. *Commun. ACM*, 21(7):558–565, July 1978.

[43] C. Lattner and V. Adve. LLVM: A Compilation Framework for Lifelong Program Analysis & Transformation. In *Proc. IEEE CGO*, 2004.

[44] J. R. Lorch, A. Baumann, L. Glendenning, D. Meyer, and A. Warfield. Tardigrade: Leveraging Lightweight Virtual Machines to Easily and Efficiently Construct Fault-Tolerant Services. In *Proc. USENIX NSDI*.

[45] J. Martins, M. Ahmed, C. Raiciu, V. Olteanu, M. Honda, R. Bifulco, and F. Huici. ClickOS and the Art of Network Function Virtualization. In *Proc. USENIX NSDI*, 2014.

[46] R. Mittal, J. Sherry, S. Ratnasamy, and S. Shenker. Recursively Cautious Congestion Control. In *Proc. USENIX NSDI*, 2014.

[47] A. Pesterev, J. Strauss, N. Zeldovich, and R. T. Morris. Improving Network Connection Locality on Multicore Systems. In *Proc. ACM EuroSys*, 2012.

[48] R. Potharaju and N. Jain. Demystifying the Dark Side of the Middle: A Field Study of Middlebox Failures in Datacenters. In *Proc. ACM IMC*, 2013.

[49] Z. A. Qazi, C.-C. Tu, L. Chiang, R. Miao, V. Sekar, and M. Yu. SIMPLE-fying Middlebox Policy Enforcement Using SDN. In *Proc. ACM SIGCOMM*, 2013.

[50] S. Rajagopalan, D. Williams, and H. Jamjoom. Pico Replication: A High Availability Framework for Middleboxes. In *Proc. ACM SoCC*, 2013.

[51] S. Rajagopalan, D. Williams, H. Jamjoom, and A. Warfield. Split/Merge: System Support for Elastic Execution in Virtual Middleboxes. In *Proc. USENIX NSDI*, 2013.

[52] L. Rizzo. netmap: a Novel Framework for Fast Packet I/O. In *Proc. USENIX ATC*, 2012.

[53] L. Rizzo and G. Lettieri. Vale: a Switched Ethernet for Virtual Machines. In *Proc. ACM CoNEXT*, 2012.

[54] L. Rizzo, G. Lettieri, and V. Maffione. Speeding Up Packet I/O in Virtual Machines. In *ACM/IEEE ANCS*, pages 47–58, 2013.

[55] R. Russell. virtio: Towards a De-facto Standard for Virtual I/O Devices. *ACM OSR*, 42(5):95–103, 2008.

[56] S. Savage, M. Burrows, G. Nelson, P. Sobalvarro, and T. Anderson. Eraser: A Dynamic Data Race Detector for Multi-threaded Programs. In *Proc. ACM SOSP*, 1997.

[57] F. B. Schneider. Implementing Fault-tolerant Services Using the State Machine Approach: A Tutorial. *ACM Comput. Surv.*, 22(4):299–319, Dec. 1990.

[58] V. Sekar, N. Egi, S. Ratnasamy, M. K. Reiter, and G. Shi. Design and Implementation of a Consolidated Middlebox Architecture. In *Proc. USENIX NSDI*, 2012.

[59] J. Sherry, S. Hasan, C. Scott, A. Krishnamurthy, S. Ratnasamy, and V. Sekar. Making Middleboxes Someone Else's Problem: Network Processing as a Cloud Service. In *Proc. ACM SIGCOMM*, 2012.

[60] R. Strom and S. Yemini. Optimistic Recovery in Distributed Systems. *ACM Trans. Comput. Syst.*, 3(3):204–226, Aug. 1985.

[61] K. Veeraraghavan, D. Lee, B. Wester, J. Ouyang, P. M. Chen, J. Flinn, and S. Narayanasamy. DoublePlay: Parallelizing Sequential Logging and Replay. In *Proc. ACM ASPLOS*, 2012.

[62] Z. Wang, Z. Qian, Q. Xu, Z. Mao, and M. Zhang. An Untold Story of Middleboxes in Cellular Networks. In *Proc. ACM SIGCOMM*, 2011.

Scaling Up Clustered Network Appliances with ScaleBricks

Dong Zhou, Bin Fan, Hyeontaek Lim, David G. Andersen, Michael Kaminsky†, Michael Mitzenmacher**, Ren Wang†, Ajaypal Singh‡

Carnegie Mellon University, †Intel Labs, **Harvard University, ‡Connectem, Inc.

ABSTRACT

This paper presents ScaleBricks, a new design for building scalable, clustered network appliances that must "pin" flow state to a specific handling node without being able to choose which node that should be. ScaleBricks applies a new, compact lookup structure to route packets directly to the appropriate handling node, without incurring the cost of multiple hops across the internal interconnect. Its lookup structure is many times smaller than the alternative approach of fully replicating a forwarding table onto all nodes. As a result, ScaleBricks is able to improve throughput and latency while simultaneously increasing the total number of flows that can be handled by such a cluster. This architecture is effective in practice: Used to optimize packet forwarding in an existing commercial LTE-to-Internet gateway, it increases the throughput of a four-node cluster by 23%, reduces latency by up to 10%, saves memory, and stores up to 5.7x more entries in the forwarding table.

CCS Concepts

•Networks → Middle boxes / network appliances;

Keywords

network function virtualization; scalability; hashing algorithms

1. INTRODUCTION

Many clustered network appliances require *deterministic* partitioning of a flat key space among a cluster of machines. When a packet enters the cluster, the *ingress* node will direct the packet to its *handling* node. The handling node maintains state that is used to process the packet, such as the packet's destination address or the flow to which it belongs. Examples include carrier-grade NATs, per-flow switching in software-defined networks (SDNs), and, as we will discuss in the next section, the cellular network-to-Internet gateway [1] in the core network of Long-Term Evolution (LTE).

In this paper, we explore a less-examined aspect of scalability for such clustered network appliances: can we create a design in which the forwarding table ("FIB" or Forwarding Information Base) that maps flat keys to their corresponding handling nodes "scales out" alongside throughput and port count as one adds more nodes to the cluster? And, critically, can we do so *without* increasing the amount of traffic that crosses the internal switching fabric? We ask this question because in a typical design, such as RouteBricks [13], adding another node to a cluster does not increase the total number of keys that the cluster can support; it increases only the total throughput and number of ports. In this paper, we explore a design that allows the FIB to continue to scale through 8, 16, or even 32 nodes, increasing the FIB capacity by up to 5.7x.

We focus on three properties of cluster scaling in this work:

Throughput Scaling. The aggregate throughput of the cluster scales with the number of cluster servers;

FIB Scaling. The total size of the forwarding table (the number of supported keys) scales with the number of servers; and

Update Scaling. The maximum update rate of the FIB scales with the number of servers.

In all cases, we do not want to scale at the expense of incurring high latency or higher switching fabric cost. As we discuss further in Section 3, existing designs do not satisfy these goals. For example, the typical approach of duplicating the FIB on all nodes fails to achieve FIB scaling; a distributed hash design such as used in SEATTLE [22] requires multiple hops across the fabric.

The contribution of this paper is two-fold. First, we present the design, implementation, and theoretical underpinning of an architecture called ScaleBricks that achieves these goals (Section 3). The core of ScaleBricks is a new data structure SetSep that represents the mapping from keys to nodes in an extremely compact manner (Section 4). As a result, each *ingress* node is able to forward packets directly to the appropriate *handling* node without needing a full copy of the FIB at all nodes. This small global information table requires only

SIGCOMM'15, August 17-21, 2015, London, United Kingdom
ACM 978-1-4503-3542-3/15/08.
http://dx.doi.org/10.1145/2785956.2787503

$O(\log N)$ bits per key, where N is the number of nodes in the cluster, enabling positive—though sublinear—FIB scaling for realistically-sized clusters. We believe this data structure will prove useful for other applications outside ScaleBricks.

Second, we use ScaleBricks to improve the performance of a commercial cellular LTE-to-Internet gateway, described in more detail in the following section. Our prototype shows that a 4-node ScaleBricks cluster can nearly quadruple the number of keys managed compared with single node solutions, while simultaneously improving packet forwarding throughput by approximately 23% and cutting latency up to 10% (Section 6).

2. DRIVING APPLICATION: CELLULAR NETWORK-TO-INTERNET GATEWAY

To motivate ScaleBricks, we begin by introducing a concrete application that can benefit from ScaleBricks: the Internet gateway used in LTE cellular networks. The central processing component in LTE is termed the "Evolved Packet Core," or EPC [1]; Figure 1a shows a simplified view of the EPC architecture. The following is a high-level description of how it services mobile devices ("mobiles" from here on); more details are described in the Internet draft on Service Function Chaining Use Cases in Mobile Networks [18].

- When an application running on the mobile initiates a connection, the *controller* assigns the new connection a tunnel, called the GTP-U tunnel, and a unique Tunnel End Point Identifier (TEID).[1]
- Upstream traffic (from the mobile to the Internet), sends packets through several middleboxes to the LTE-to-Internet gateway (the red box in the figures). After performing administrative functions such as charging and access control, the gateway decapsulates packets from the GTP-U tunnel, updates the state associated with the flow, and sends them to ISP peering routers, which connect to the Internet.
- Downstream traffic follows a reverse path across the elements. The LTE-to-Internet gateway processes and re-encapsulates packets into the tunnels based on the flow's TEID. The packets reach the correct base station, which transmits them to the mobile.

In this paper, we focus our improvements on a commercially-available software EPC stack from Connectem [10]. This system runs on commodity hardware and aims to provide a cost-advantaged replacement for proprietary hardware implementations of the EPC. It provides throughput scalability by clustering multiple nodes: Figure 1b shows a 4-node EPC cluster. When a new connection is established, the controller assigns a TEID to the flow and assigns that flow to one node in the cluster (its *handling node*). This assignment is based on several LTE-specific constraints, such as geometric proximity (mobile devices from the same region are assigned to the same node), which *prevents* us from modifying it (e.g., forcing hash-based assignment), thereby requiring *deterministic* partitioning. It then inserts a mapping from the 5-tuple flow identifier to the (handling node, TEID) pair into the cluster forwarding table. Upstream packets from this flow are directed to the handling node by the aggregation router. Downstream packets, however, could be received by *any* node in the cluster because of limitations in the hardware routers that are outside of our control. For example, the deployment of an equal-cost multi-path routing (ECMP) strategy may cause the scenario described above because all nodes in the cluster will have the same distance to the destination. Because the cluster maintains the state associated with each flow at its *handling node*, when the ingress node receives a downstream packet, it must look up the handling node and TEID in its forwarding table and forward the packet appropriately. The handling node then processes the packet and sends it back over the tunnel to the mobile.

Our goal in this paper is to demonstrate the effectiveness of ScaleBricks by using it to improve the performance and scalability of this software-based EPC stack. We chose this application both because it is commercially important (hardware EPC implementations can cost hundreds of thousands to millions of dollars), is widely used, and represents an excellent target for scaling using ScaleBricks because of its need to pin flows to a specific handling node combined with the requirement of maintaining as little states at each node as possible (which makes keeping a full per-flow forwarding table at each node a less viable option). ScaleBricks achieves these goals without increasing the inter-cluster latency. Compared with alternative designs, this latency reduction could be important in several scenarios, including communication between mobile devices and content delivery networks, as well as other services deployed at edge servers. In this work, we change only the "Packet Forwarding Engine" of the EPC; this is the component that is responsible for directing packets to their appropriate handling node. We leave unchanged the "Data Plane Engine" that performs the core EPC functions.

3. DESIGN OVERVIEW

In this section, we explain the design choices for ScaleBricks and compare those choices to representative alternative designs to illustrate why we made those choices. We use the following terms to describe the cluster architecture:

- *Ingress Node*: the node where a packet enters the cluster.
- *Handling Node*: the node where a packet is processed within the cluster.
- *Indirect Node*: an intermediate node touched by a packet, not including its ingress and handling node.
- *Lookup Node*: If node X stores the forwarding entry associated with a packet P, X is P's lookup node. A packet may have no lookup nodes if the packet has an

[1]For clarity, we have used common terms for the components of the network. Readers familiar with LTE terminology will recognize that our "mobile device" is a "UE"; the base station is an "eNodeB"; and the tunnel from the UE to the eNodeB is a "GTP-U" tunnel.

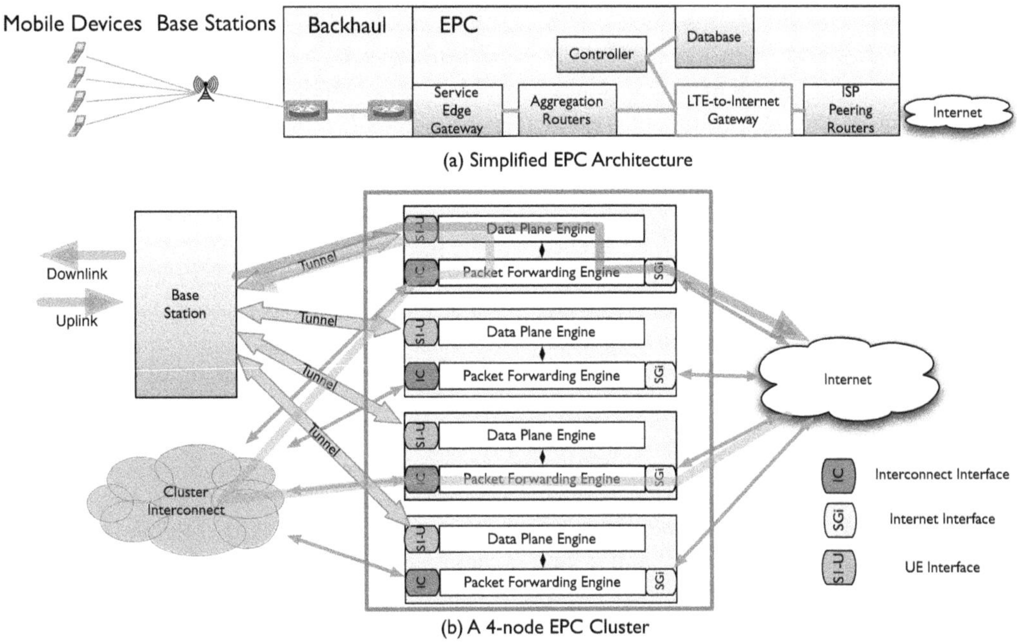

Figure 1: (a) Simplified Evolved Packet Core (EPC) architecture and (b) a 4-node EPC cluster

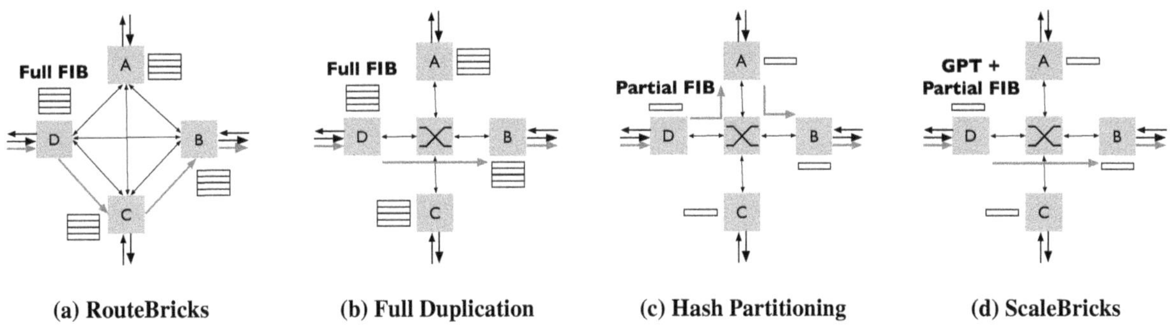

Figure 2: Packet forwarding in different FIB architectures

unknown key, or more than one lookup node if the FIB entry has been replicated to more than one node.

3.1 Cluster Architecture

Two topologies are classically used for building cluster-based network functions. The first connects cluster servers directly to each other, as exemplified by RouteBricks [13]. In such systems, the servers are connected in a full mesh or a butterfly-like topology, as shown in Figure 2a. On top of this topology, load-balancing routing algorithms—e.g., Valiant Load Balancing (VLB) [32]—guarantee 100% throughput and fairness without centralized scheduling.

This solution has the advantage that the total bandwidth of internal links used to construct the full mesh or the butterfly needs to be only 2× the total external bandwidth; furthermore, these links are fully utilized. The disadvantage of VLB, however, is that the ingress node must forward each incoming packet to an intermediate indirect node before it reaches the handling node. This extra step ensures efficient use of the aggregate internal bandwidth. Unfortunately, in most cases, each packet must be processed by three nodes (two hops). This increases packet processing latency, server load, and required internal link capacity.

The second class of topologies uses a hardware switch to connect the cluster nodes (Figures 2b–2d). This topology offers two attractive properties. First, it allows full utilization of internal links without increasing the total internal traffic. To support R Gbps of external bandwidth, a node needs only R Gbps of aggregate internal bandwidth, instead of the $2R$ required by VLB. Second, without an indirect node, packet latency depends on the hardware switch's latency instead of the indirect node. Compared to VLB, a switch-based topology could reduce latency by 33%.

Interestingly, RouteBricks intentionally rejected this design option. The authors argued that the cost of four 10 Gbps switch ports was equal to the cost of one server, and hence a switched cluster was more expensive than a server-based cluster. Today, however, the economics of this argument have changed. New vendors such as Mellanox offer much cheaper hardware switches. For example, a Mellanox 36 port 40 GbE switch costs roughly $13,000, or ~$9 / Gbps. This is 80% lower than the number reported in the RouteBricks paper. More importantly, hardware switches are particularly suitable for building interconnections for the cluster nodes. Their strengths—high bandwidth, low latency, simple and clear topology—are well-suited to our requirements; and their weakness—limited FIB size—is essentially irrelevant with our approach.

ScaleBricks thus connects servers using a switch. This topology reduces the internal bandwidth requirement and provides the opportunity to reduce the packet processing latency. However, this choice also makes the design of a scalable forwarding architecture challenging, as explained next.

3.2 FIB Architecture

Given a switch-based cluster topology, the next question is what forwarding architecture to use. In the simplest design, each node in the cluster stores a full copy of the entire forwarding table (Figure 2b). When a packet arrives at its ingress node, the ingress node performs a FIB lookup to identify the handling node, and then forwards the packet directly to that node. (The ingress node thus also serves as the lookup node.)

This simple architecture requires only one hop, unlike VLB. Unfortunately, the memory required by the globally replicated FIB increases linearly with the number of nodes in the cluster. Furthermore, every update must be applied to all nodes in the cluster, limiting the aggregate FIB update rate to that of a single server.

An alternative is a hash-partitioned design (Figure 2c). For an N-node cluster, each node stores only $1/N$ FIB entries based on the hash of the keys. The ingress node must forward arriving packets to the indirect node that has the relevant portion of the FIB; the indirect node then forwards the packet to the handling node by looking up in its slice of the FIB. This approach is nearly perfectly scalable, but reintroduces the two-hop latency and bandwidth costs of VLB.

In this paper, we present a design that forwards directly from ingress to handling nodes, but uses substantially less memory than a typical fully-replicated FIB (Figure 2d). At a high level, ScaleBricks distributes the entire routing information (mapping from flat keys to their corresponding nodes and other associated values), or "RIB" for short, across the cluster using a hash-partitioned design. From the RIB, it generates two structures. First, an extremely compact global lookup table called the "GPT" or Global Partition Table, that is used to direct packets to the handling node. The GPT is much smaller than a conventional, fully-replicated FIB. Second, the RIB is used to generate FIB entries that are stored only at the relevant handling nodes, *not* globally. In the LTE-to-Internet gateway example, GPT stores the mapping from flow ID to handling node, while FIB stores the mapping from flow ID to TEID.

The GPT relies upon two important attributes of switch-based "middlebox" clusters: First, the total number of nodes is typically modest—likely under 16 or 32. Second, they can handle one-sided errors in packet forwarding. Packets that match a FIB entry must be forwarded to the correct handling node, but it is acceptable to forward packets with no corresponding entry to a "wrong" (or random) handling node, and have the packet be discarded there. This property is true in the switch-based design: The internal bandwidth must be sufficient to handle traffic in which all packets are valid, and so invalid packets can be safely forwarded across the interconnect.

The Full FIB entries that map keys to handling nodes (along with, potentially, some additional information) are partitioned so that each handling node stores the FIB entries that point to it. If the handling node receives, via its internal links, a packet with a key that does not exist in its FIB, the input processing code will report that the key is missing (which can be handled in an application-specific way). The handling node FIB is based upon prior work in space-efficient, high-performance hash tables for read-intensive workloads [34]. We omit in-depth discussion here because we used the prior design nearly unchanged, only extending it to handle configurable-sized values with minimal performance impact.

The Global Partition Table is replicated to every ingress node. This table maps keys to a lookup/handling node. Because the GPT is fully replicated, it must be compact to ensure scalability; otherwise, it would be no better than replicating the FIB to all nodes. For efficiency, the GPT is based upon a new data structure with one-sided error. Observing that the range of possible values (i.e., the number of nodes) in the GPT is small, using a general-purpose lookup table mapping arbitrary keys to arbitrary values is unnecessary. Instead, the GPT's mapping can be more efficiently viewed as *set separation*: dividing a set of keys into a small number of disjoint subsets. In this paper, we extend prior work by Fan et al. [15] to create a fully-functional set separation data structure called SetSep, and use it at the core of the GPT. SetSep maps each key to a small set of output values—the lookup/handling node identifiers—without explicitly storing the keys at all. The tradeoff is that unknown destinations map to incorrect values; in other words, the SetSep cannot return a "not found" answer. This behavior does not harm the correctness of ScaleBricks, because the lookup node will eventually reject the unknown key. The advantage, though, is that lookup is very fast and each entry in the SetSep requires only 2–4 *bits* per entry for 4-16 servers. Section 4 describes the SetSep data structure in detail.

RIB Updates are sent to the appropriate RIB partition node based upon the hash of the key involved. This node generates new or updated FIB and GPT entries. It then sends the updated FIB entry to the appropriate handling node, and sends a delta-update for the GPT to all nodes in the cluster. Because the SetSep data structure used for the GPT groups keys into independently-updatable sub-blocks, the RIB partitioning function depends on how those sub-blocks are partitioned. Section 4.5 provides further details about RIB partitioning.

4. SET SEPARATION

The GPT is stored on every node and is consulted once for each packet that enters the cluster. It must therefore be both space efficient and extremely fast. To achieve these goals, and allow ScaleBricks to scale well as a result, we extended and optimized our previous work on set separation data structures [15] to provide memory-speed lookups on billions of entries, while requiring only a few bits per entry. As discussed in the previous section, the design of SetSep leverages three properties of ScaleBricks:

- The GPT returns integer values between 0 and $N-1$, where N is the number of servers in the cluster.
- The GPT may return an arbitrary answer when queried for the handling node of a packet with an unknown destination key (e.g., an invalid packet). Such packets will be subsequently dropped or dealt with when the handling node performs a full FIB lookup.
- GPT lookups are frequent, but updates much less so. Therefore, a structure with fast lookup but relatively expensive updates is a reasonable tradeoff.

At a high level, the basic idea in SetSep is to use brute force computation to find a function that maps each input key to the correct output (the "set", here the cluster node index). Rather than explicitly storing all keys and their associated values, SetSep stores only indices into families of hash functions that map keys to values, and thereby consumes much less space than conventional lookup tables. Finding a hash function that maps each of a large number of input keys to the correct output value is effectively impossible, so we break the problem down into smaller pieces. First, we build a high-level index structure to divide the entire input set into many small groups. Each group consists of approximately sixteen keys in our implementation. Then, for each small group, we perform a brute force search to find a hash function that produces the correct outputs for each key in the group. The rest of this section carefully presents these two pieces, in reverse order.

4.1 Binary Separation of Small Sets

We start by focusing on a simple set separation problem: *divide a set of n keys into two disjoint subsets when n is small.* We show how to extend this binary separation scheme to handle more subsets in Section 4.3.

Searching for SetSep To separate a set of n key-value pairs (x_j, y_j), where x_j is the key and y_j is either "0" or "1", we find a hash function f that satisfies $f(x_j) = y_j$ for $j \in [0, n)$. Such a hash function is discovered by iterating over a hash function family $\{H_i(x)\}$ parameterized by i, so $H_i(x)$ is the i-th hash function in this family. Starting from $i = 1$, for each key-value pair (x_j, y_j), we verify if $H_i(x_j) = y_j$ is achieved. If any key x_j fails, the current hash function H_i is rejected, and the next hash function H_{i+1} is tested on all n keys again (including these keys that passed H_i). In other words, we use brute force to find a suitable hash function. As shown later, this search can complete very rapidly for small n and an appropriate hash function family.

Once a hash function H_i that works for all n keys is found, its index parameter i is stored. We choose some maximum stopping value I, so that if no hash function succeeds for $i \le I$, a fallback mechanism is triggered to handle this set (e.g., store the keys explicitly in a separate, small hash table).

Storing SetSep For each group, the index i of the successful hash function is stored using a suitable variable-length encoding. As shown in the next paragraph, ideally, the expected space required from this approach is near optimal (1 bit per key). In practice, however, storing a variable length integer adds some overhead, as do various algorithmic optimizations we use to speed construction. Our implementation therefore consumes about 1.5 bits per key.

Why SetSep Saves Space Let us optimistically assume our hash functions produce fully random hash values. The probability a hash function H_i maps one key to the correct binary value is $1/2$, and the probability all n keys are properly mapped is $p = (1/2)^n$. Thus, the number of tested functions (i.e., the index i stored) is a random variable with a Geometric distribution, with entropy

$$\frac{-(1-p)\log_2(1-p) - p\log_2 p}{p} \approx -\log_2 p = n \qquad (1)$$

Eq. (1) indicates that storing a function for binary set separation of n keys requires n bits on average (or 1 bit per key), which is independent of the key size.

Insights: The space required to store SetSep approximately equals the total number of bits used by the values; the keys do not consume space. This is the source of both SetSep's strength (extreme memory efficiency) and its weakness (returning arbitrary results for keys that are not in the set).

Practically Generating the Hash Functions A simple but inefficient approach that creates the hash function family $\{H_i(x)\}$ is to concatenate the bits of i and x as the input to a strong hash function. This approach provides independence across H_i, but requires computing an expensive new hash value for each i during the iteration.

Instead of this expensive approach, we draw inspiration from theoretical results that two hash functions can sufficiently simulate additional hash functions [23]. Therefore, we first compute two approximately independent hash functions of the key, G_1 and G_2, using standard hashing methods. We then compute the remaining hash functions as linear combinations of these two. Thus, our parameterized hash function family to produce random bits is constructed by

$$H_i(x) = G_1(x) + i \cdot G_2(x)$$

where $G_1(x)$ and $G_2(x)$ are both unsigned integers. In practice, only the most significant bit(s) from the summation result are used in the output, because our approach of generating parameterized hash function family will have shorter period if the least significant bits are used instead of the most significant bits.

Both hash computation and searching are fast using this mechanism: H_i can be computed directly using one multiplication and one addition. Furthermore, the hash family can be iterated using only one addition to get the value of $H_{i+1}(x)$ from the previous result of $H_i(x)$.

The hash functions described above are theoretically weak: they lack sufficient independence, and as such are more likely than "random" hash functions to fail to find a suitable mapping. Empirically, however, we observe that this approach fails only once every few billion keys. The fallback mechanism of looking the keys up in a separate, small table handles such failures.

4.2 Trading Space for Faster Construction

One problem with this basic design is the exponential growth of the number of iterations to find a hash function mapping n input items to their correct binary values. We must test and reject 2^n hash functions on average. By trading a small amount of extra space (roughly 5% compared to the achievable lower bound), SetSep optimizes the construction to be an order of magnitude faster.

Instead of generating the possible output value for x using the hash function $H_i(x)$ directly, SetSep adds an array of m bits ($m \geq 2$) and makes $H_i(x)$ map each input x to one of the m bits in the array. In other words, the output value for x is the bit stored in `bitarray[`$H_i(x)$`]` rather than $H_i(x)$. To construct the bit array, at the beginning of the iteration testing hash function $H_i(x)$, all bits in the array are marked "not taken." For each key-value pair (x_j, y_j), if $H_i(x_j)$ points to a bit that is still "not taken," we set the bit to y_j and mark it as "taken." If the bit is marked as "taken," we check if the value of the bit in the array matches y_j. If so, the current hash function is still good and can proceed to the next key. Otherwise, we reject the current hash function, switch to the next hash function H_{i+1}, re-initialize the bit array, and start testing from the first key. Intuitively, with more "buckets" for the keys to fall in, there are fewer collisions, increasing the odds of success. Thus, adding this bit array greatly improves the chance of finding a working hash function.

Space vs. Speed Storing the bit array adds m bits of storage overhead, but it speeds up the search to find a suitable hash function and correspondingly reduces the number of bits needed to store i—since each hash function has a greater probability of success, i will be smaller on average. Figure 3a shows the tradeoff between the space and construction speed for a SetSep of $n = 16$ keys while varying the bit array size (m) from 2 to 30. Increasing the size of the bit array dramatically reduces the number of iterations needed. It requires more than 10,000 hash functions on average when $m = 2$; this improves by 10× when $m = 6$, and when $m \geq 12$, it needs (on average) fewer than 100 trials, i.e., it is 100× faster.

Figure 3b presents analytical results for the total space (i.e., bits required to store the index i plus the m bits of the array) for this SetSep. The total space cost is almost an increasing function of m. The minimum space is 16 bits, but even when $m = 12$, the total space cost is only about 20 bits. (This is less than $16 + 12 = 28$ bits, because of the reduction in the space required to store i.)

Insights: Trading a little space efficiency (e.g., spending 20 bits for every 16 keys rather than 16 bits) improves construction speed by 100×.

Representing the SetSep. In light of the above result, we choose to represent the SetSep using a fixed 24-bit representation per group in our implementation, with up to 16 bits to represent the hash index and $m = 8$. This yields 1.5 bits per key on average. (We show the effect of the choice m later in the paper.) Although we could use less space, this choice provides fast construction while ensuring that fewer than 1 in 1 million groups must be stored in the external table, and provides for fast, well-aligned access to the data.

4.3 Representing Non-Boolean Values

We have described the construction for two disjoint subsets (two possible values). For $V > 2$ different subsets, a trivial extension is to look for *one hash function* that outputs the right value in $\{1, \ldots, V\}$ for each key. However, this approach is not practical because it must try $O(V^n)$ hash functions on average. Even when $n = 16$ and $V = 4$, in the worst case, it could be 65536 times slower than $V = 2$.

We instead search for $\log_2 V$ hash functions, where the j-th hash function is responsible for generating the j-th bit of the final mapping value. As an example, assume we want to construct a mapping to a value in $\{0, 1, 2, 3\}$ from a given set of size 2. If the final mapping is ("foo", 01_2) and ("bar", 10_2), we look for two hash functions so that the first hash function maps "foo" to 0 and "bar" to 1, and the second hash function hashes "foo" to 1 and "bar" to 0. The expected total number of iterations to construct a final mapping is then $\log_2 V \cdot 2^n$, which scales linearly with the number of bits to represent a value. Figure 4 compares the number of iterations needed to build a separation of 4 subsets by searching for one hash function mapping to $\{0,1,2,3\}$ or two hash functions mapping to $\{0,1\}$ respectively. Splitting the value bits is orders of magnitude faster.

4.4 Scaling to Billions of Items

The basic idea of efficiently scaling SetSep to store mappings for millions or billions of keys, as noted above, is to first partition the entire set into many small groups, here of roughly 16 keys each. Then, for each group of keys, we find and store a hash function that generates the correct values using the techniques described above. Therefore, two properties are critical for the scheme that maps a key to a group:

- The mapping must ensure low variance in group size. Although a small load imbalance is acceptable, even slightly larger groups require much longer to find a suit-

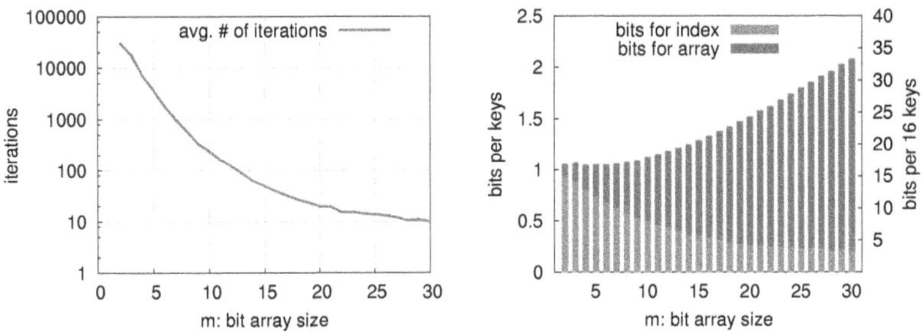

(a) Avg. # of iters. to get one hash func. **(b) Space cost breakdown**

Figure 3: Space vs. time, as the function of bit array size m

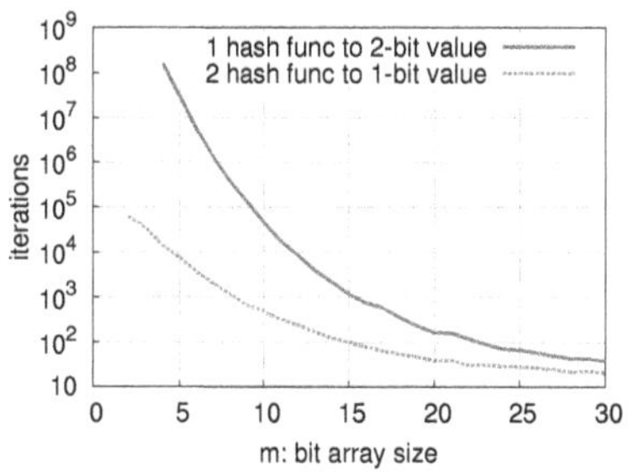

Figure 4: One hash func. vs. multiple hash func.

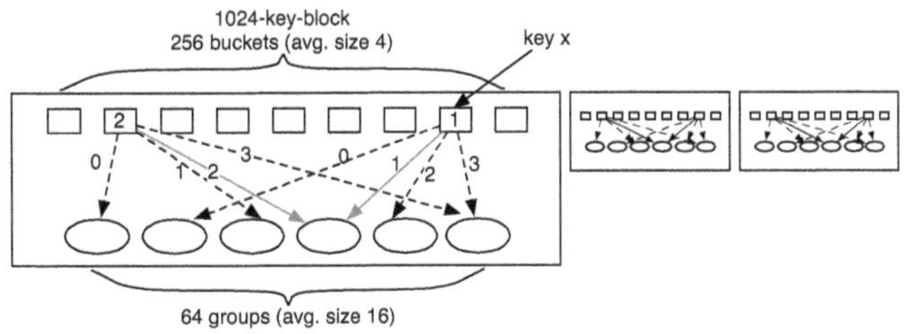

Figure 5: Illustration of two-level hashing

able hash function using brute-force search because the time grows exponentially in the group size.

- The mapping should add little space. The per-group SetSep itself is only a few bits per key, and the partitioning scheme should preserve the overall space efficiency.

Conventional Solutions That Do Not Work Well To calculate the group ID of a given key, one obvious way is to compute a hash of this key modulo the total number of groups. This approach is simple to implement, and does not require storing any additional information; unfortunately, some groups will be significantly more loaded than the average group even with a strong hash function [29]. Our experiments show that when 16 million keys are partitioned into 1 million groups using even a cryptographic hash function, the most loaded group typically contains more than 40 keys vs. the average group size of 16 keys; this matches the corresponding theory. Finding hash functions via brute force for such large groups is impractical.

An alternative solution is to sort all keys and assign every n consecutive keys to one group. This approach ensures that every group has exactly sixteen keys. Unfortunately, it has several serious limitations: (1) it requires storing the full keys, or at least key fragments on the boundary of each group, as an index; (2) it requires a binary search on lookup to locate a given key's group; and (3) update is expensive.

Our Solution: Two-Level Hashing. SetSep uses a novel two-level hashing scheme that nearly uniformly distributes billions of keys across groups, at a constant storage cost of 0.5 bits per key. The first level maps keys to buckets with a small average size—smaller than our target group size of sixteen—using simple direct hashing. These buckets will have the aforementioned huge load variance. To address this problem, at the second level, we assign buckets to groups with the aim of minimizing the maximum load on any group. The storage cost of this scheme, therefore, is the bits required to store the group choice for each bucket.

Figure 5 shows this process. Each first-level bucket has an average size of 4 keys but the variance is high: some buckets could be empty, while some may contain ten or more keys. However, across a longer range of small buckets, the average number of stored keys has less variance. For 256 buckets, there are 1024 keys on average. We therefore take consecutive blocks of 256 buckets and call them a *1024-key-block*. We then map these blocks to 64 groups of average size 16.

Within the block of 256 buckets, each bucket is mapped to one of four different "candidate" groups. We pre-assigned candidate groups for each bucket in a way that each group has the same number of associated buckets. These choices are denoted by the arrow from bucket to groups in Figure 5. All keys in the small bucket will map to one of these four candidate groups. Therefore, the only information that SetSep needs to store is the bucket-to-group mapping (a number in $\{0,1,2,3\}$ indicating which candidate group was chosen).

The effectiveness of this bucket-to-group mapping is important to the performance of SetSep, since as we have explained more balanced groups make it easier to find suitable hash functions for all groups. Ideally, we would like to assign the same number of keys to each group. However, finding such an assignment corresponds to an NP-hard variant of the knapsack problem. Therefore, we use a greedy algorithm to balance keys across groups. We first sort all the buckets in descending order by size. Starting from the largest bucket, we assign each bucket to one of the candidate groups. For each bucket, we pick the candidate group with the fewest keys. If more than one group has the same least number of keys, a random group from this set is picked. We repeat this process until all the buckets have been assigned, yielding a valid assignment. In fact, we run this randomized algorithm several times per block and choose the best assignment among the runs. To lookup a key x, we first calculate the key's bucket ID by hashing. Then, given this bucket ID, we look up the stored choice number to calculate which group this key belongs to. Each bucket has 4 keys on average, and spends 2 bits to encode its choice. So on average, two-level hashing costs 0.5 bits per key, but provides much better load balance than direct hashing. When partitioning 16 million keys into 1 million groups, the most loaded group usually has 21 keys, compared to more than 40 for direct hashing.

4.5 Scalable Update

Allowing lookups without storing keys is the primary reason SetSep is so compact. The original construction and updates, however, require the full key/value pairs to recompute SetSep. In ScaleBricks, this information comprises the RIB, where keys are destination addresses and values are the corresponding handling nodes.

To provide scalability for the RIB size (e.g., the number of flows that the EPC can keep track of) and update rate, ScaleBricks uses a partitioned SetSep construction and update scheme. The RIB entries are partitioned using a hash of the key, so that keys in the same 1024-key-block are stored in the same node. For construction, each node computes only its portion of SetSep, and then exchanges the produced result with all the other nodes. When updating a key k, only the node responsible for k recomputes the group that k belongs to, and then broadcasts the result to other nodes. Because applying a delta-update on the other nodes requires only a memory copy (the delta is usually tens of bits), this approach allows ScaleBricks to scale the update rate with the number of nodes. To allow high-performance reads with safe in-place updates, techniques analogous to those proposed in CuckooSwitch [34] and MemC3 [14] could be applied, although we have not designed such a mechanism yet.

5. IMPLEMENTATION / OPTIMIZATIONS

ScaleBricks is implemented in C. It uses Intel's Data Plane Development Kit (DPDK) for x86 platforms [21] as a fast user-space packet I/O engine.

5.1 Global Partition Table using SetSep

SetSep uses several optimizations to improve performance.

Efficient Use of Memory Bandwidth and CPU Cycles Sequentially issuing memory fetches one at a time cannot saturate the bandwidth between CPU and memory. ScaleBricks instead uses *batched lookups* and *prefetching* [27, 34] (Algorithm 1). Each lookup request is divided into three stages and a subsequent stage accesses a memory location determined by its previous stage. Immediately fetching these memory locations would stall CPU pipelines for many cycles while waiting for the load instruction to complete. Instead, our algorithm first issues a *prefetch* instruction for a set of addresses, which causes the CPU to start loading the data from these addresses into cache. Then, at the beginning of the next stage, it executes normal reads at those prefetched addresses. These loads are then likely to hit in L1/L2 cache and thus complete much faster. Prefetching significantly improves efficiency: Section 6 shows that with appropriate batch sizes, this optimization improves microbenchmark lookup throughput of SetSep by up to 1.8×.

Algorithm 1: Batched SetSep lookup with prefetching

```
BatchedLookup(keys[1..n])
begin
    for i ← 1 to n do
        bucketID[i] ← keys[i]'s bucket ID
        prefetch(bucketIDToGroupID[bucketID[i]])
    for i ← 1 to n do
        groupID[i] ← bucketIDToGroupID[bucketID[i]]
        prefetch(groupInfoArray[groupID[i]])
    for i ← 1 to n do
        groupInfo ← groupInfoArray[groupID[i]]
        values[i] ← LookupSingleKey(groupInfo, keys[i])
    return values[1..n]
```

Hardware Accelerated Construction Constructing SetSep is amenable to parallelization: Each group of keys can be computed independently, and within a group, the computation of the hash function across the sixteen keys can be parallelized using SIMD. In this work, we only explore using multiple hardware threads across groups, which provides sufficiently fast construction for our application. We plan to evaluate the SIMD and GPU-derived speedups in future work.

5.2 Partial FIB using Cuckoo Hashing

Each node in the cluster has a slice of the FIB to provide an exact mapping from keys to application-specific data. In ScaleBricks, this table is implemented using concurrent cuckoo hashing [34], which achieves high occupancy and line-rate lookup performance for read-intensive workloads.

CuckooSwitch [34] used a concurrent cuckoo hash table to build a FIB that maps MAC addresses to output ports. That prior work was optimized to fetch the entire key-value pair in a single cache line read and thus stored values adjacent to their keys. Our target application of ScaleBricks, however, requires storing arbitrarily large application-specific data about each key (instead of a single output port as in CuckooSwitch). We therefore apply the following optimization.

When the table is initialized at run-time, the value size is fixed for all entries based on the application requirements. We assign each slot in the cuckoo hash table a logical "slot number." Instead of storing key/value pairs in an interleaved form, we create a separate *value array* in which the k-th element is the value associated with the k-th slot in the hash table. To lookup the value of a key, we simply index into the value array at the position corresponding to the key's slot number in the hash table. When moving a key from one slot to another during insertion, we need to move the value as well.

The apparent drawback of this approach is an extra memory read during lookup. In practice, however, as we will show in the evaluation, this extra memory read has minimal impact on the lookup throughput.

6. EVALUATION

Our evaluation addresses three questions:

1. How fast can we construct and lookup with SetSep?
2. How does moving to ScaleBricks improve the throughput of the Packet Forwarding Engine of the LTE Evolved Packet Core? What limitations does it add?
3. How does ScaleBricks scale with the number of servers?

We omit the evaluation of the cuckoo hashing-based FIB; prior work has demonstrated that the table is fast enough to serve over 300 million lookups per second [34].

6.1 Micro-Benchmark: SetSep

This section presents micro-benchmark results for SetSep construction and lookup performance on modern hardware.

These micro-benchmarks are conducted on a moderately fast dual-socket server with two Intel Xeon E5-2680 CPUs (HT disabled), each with a 20 MiB L3 cache. The machine has 64 GiB of DDR3 RAM.

6.1.1 Construction

The construction speed of SetSep depends primarily on three parameters:

- The number of bits to store the hash index and to store the bit-array in each group;
- The number of possible values or sets; and
- The number of threads used to parallelize construction.

The first experiments measure the construction rate of SetSep with different parameter combinations. The per-thread construction rate (or throughput) is nearly constant; construction time increases linearly with the number of keys and decreases linearly with the number of concurrent threads. Table 1 shows results for 64 M keys.

The first group of results shows a modest tradeoff between (single-threaded) construction speed and memory efficiency: Using a "16+8" SetSep (where 16 bits are allocated to the hash function index and 8 bits to the bit array) has the slowest construction speed but almost never needs to use the fallback table, which improves both query performance and memory efficiency. "16+16" SetSep also has low fallback ratio, but consumes more space. *We therefore use 16+8 for the remaining experiments in this paper*. Its speed, $\frac{1}{2}$ million keys per second per core, is adequate for the read-intensive workloads we target.

Increasing the value size imposes little construction overhead. The results in practice are even better than linear scaling because we optimized our implementation as follows: as we iterate the hash function, we test the function for each value bit across the different keys in the group before moving on to the next hash function in the hash function family. As a result, we perform less work than searching hash functions for each value bit one at a time. In addition, storing larger values further amortizes the 0.5 bits of overhead added by the first-level key-to-group mapping.

Summary The core SetSep data structure construction speed is fast enough for a variety of important applications in which the read rate is larger than the (already high) update rate that SetSep can handle. ScaleBricks uses SetSep for its global partition tables, which fall into this category.

6.1.2 Lookup

Figure 7 shows the local lookup throughput of SetSep for different numbers of FIB entries (keys). In addition, given a FIB size, this figure also compares SetSep performance with different batch sizes as discussed in Section 5, varying from 1 (no batching) to 32 (the maximum packet batch size provided by DPDK). All lookup experiments use 2-bit values, a "16+8" configuration, and 16 threads.

These lookup micro-benchmarks provide three insights. First, batching generally increases the lookup performance of SetSep. When the batch size is increased to 17, the lookup throughput is ~520 Mops (million operations per second) even with 64 million keys; batch sizes larger than 17 do not further improve performance. Second, as the number of FIB entries increases from 32 million to 64 million, the performance drops dramatically. This occurs because the 64 million entry, 2-bit SetSep exceeds the size of L3 cache, occupying 28 MiB of memory. Third, for small FIBs (e.g., 500 K entries), lookup performance is actually higher *without* batching. This too arises from caching: These small structures fit entirely in L3 or even L2 cache, where the access latency is low enough that large batches are not required, but merely increase register pressure.

Summary ScaleBricks batches for all table sizes to ensure fast-enough lookup performance regardless of the number of entries. Because DPDK receives packets in batches, ScaleBricks handles incoming packets using the *dynamic batching* policy from CuckooSwitch [34]: instead of having a fixed batch size, when a CPU core receives a batch of packets from DPDK, ScaleBricks looks up the entire batch in SetSep. Therefore, the batch size of SetSep adjusts semi-automatically to the offered load.

6.2 Macro-Benchmark: ScaleBricks Cluster

As a concrete application, we optimized the Packet Forwarding Engine of Connectem's EPC stack by migrating it to ScaleBricks. Importantly, the stack already used the Intel DPDK, so structural changes were small. For context, the Packet Forwarding Engine typically runs on three of the cores

Construction setting			Construction throughput	Fallback ratio	Total size	Bits/ key
$x+y$ bits to store a hash function, x-bit hash function index and y-bit array						
16+8	1-bit value	1 thread	0.54 Mkeys/sec	0.00%	16.00 MB	2.00
8+16	1-bit value	1 thread	2.42 Mkeys/sec	1.15%	16.64 MB	2.08
16+16	1-bit value	1 thread	2.47 Mkeys/sec	0.00%	20.00 MB	2.50
increasing the value size						
16+8	**2-bit value**	1 thread	0.24 Mkeys/sec	0.00%	28.00 MB	3.50
16+8	**3-bit value**	1 thread	0.18 Mkeys/sec	0.00%	40.00 MB	5.00
16+8	**4-bit value**	1 thread	0.14 Mkeys/sec	0.00%	52.00 MB	6.50
using multiple threads to generate						
16+8	1-bit value	**2 threads**	0.93 Mkeys/sec	0.00%	16.00 MB	2.00
16+8	1-bit value	**4 threads**	1.56 Mkeys/sec	0.00%	16.00 MB	2.00
16+8	1-bit value	**8 threads**	2.28 Mkeys/sec	0.00%	16.00 MB	2.00
16+8	1-bit value	**16 threads**	2.97 Mkeys/sec	0.00%	16.00 MB	2.00

Table 1: Construction throughput of SetSep for 64 M keys with different settings

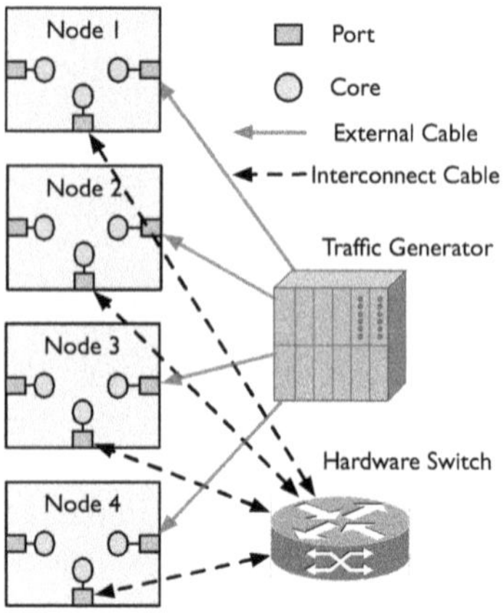

Figure 6: Cluster setup

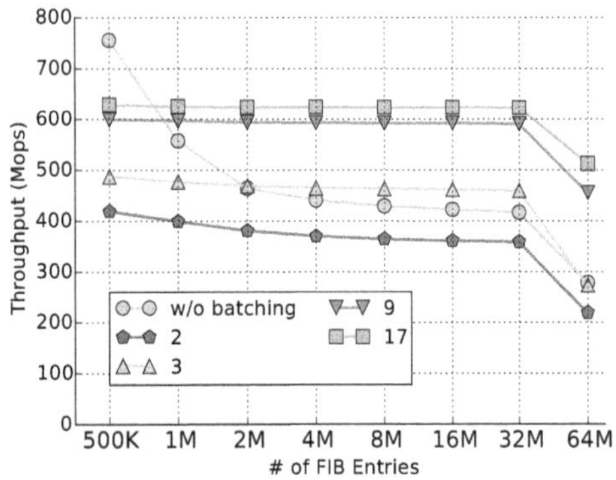

Figure 7: Local lookup throughput of SetSep (GPT)

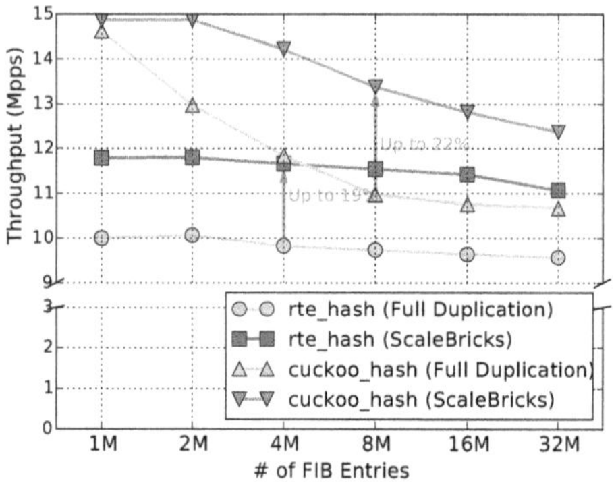

Figure 8: Single node packet forwarding throughput using 30 MiB L3 cache

in each node in the EPC cluster. The initial system was balanced to handle smaller numbers of flows, but the total system throughput drops when the number of flows (and thus the size of the FIB) grows larger. Thus, while we focus here on just the PFE throughput, improvements to the PFE do improve the total system throughput.

We measure PFE performance using 4 dual-socket servers, each with two Intel Xeon E5-2697 v2 CPUs running at 2.70 GHz, each with a 30 MiB L3 cache. Each machine has 128 GiB DDR3 RAM and two dual-port Intel 82599ES 10GbE NICs.

Each server uses three of its four 10Gb ports: one as the interface to the Internet, one as the interface to the base stations, and the other as the interconnect interface. Each port is attached to one core on CPU socket 0, using three cores in total. For all the experiments, we pre-populate the system with a number of static tunnels. As discussed in Section 2, only downstream (Internet to mobile device) packets require inter-cluster forwarding; therefore, the core assigned to handle the interface connected to the base stations is not used in our experiments. We simulate the downstream traffic using a Spirent SPT-N11U Ethernet testing platform [31]. Figure 6 depicts the configuration for the benchmark.

The forwarding engine originally implemented its FIB using a chaining hash table, the performance of which drops dramatically as the number of tunnels increases. To evaluate the benefits of ScaleBricks, we replace the original implementation with two alternative hash table designs—DPDK's `rte_hash` and our extended cuckoo hash table. Figure 8 shows the single node packet forwarding throughput using these hash tables, with and without ScaleBricks. Without ScaleBricks means full duplication, as depicted in Figure 2b.

Both the hash table and use of the SetSep GPT improve throughput measurably for the PFE. Even though our extended cuckoo hash table requires one additional memory read compared to the original design [34], it improves throughput by 50% over the DPDK's `rte_hash`. More key to this work, ScaleBricks improves the single node throughput by up to 20% and 22% within systems using `rte_hash` and extended cuckoo hash table, respectively. Two major factors contribute to this performance improvement. First, reducing the number of entries hosted by each node means smaller hash tables. In this experiment, hash table size is reduced by up to 75%. The smaller table allows many more of the table entries to fit in L3 cache, substantially increasing througput. Second, without ScaleBricks, all the packets coming from the traffic gener-

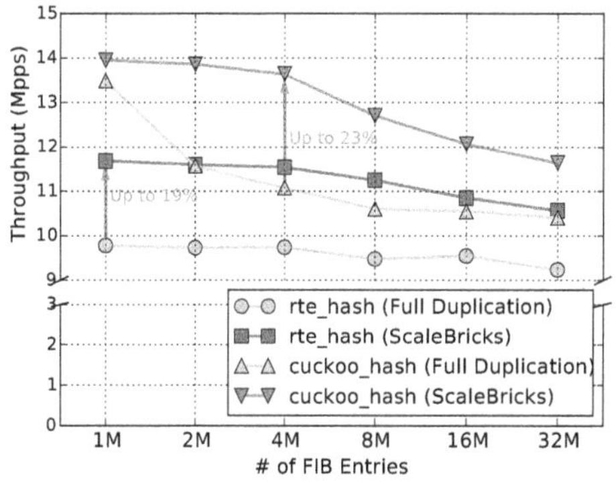

Figure 9: Single node packet forwarding throughput using 15 MiB L3 cache

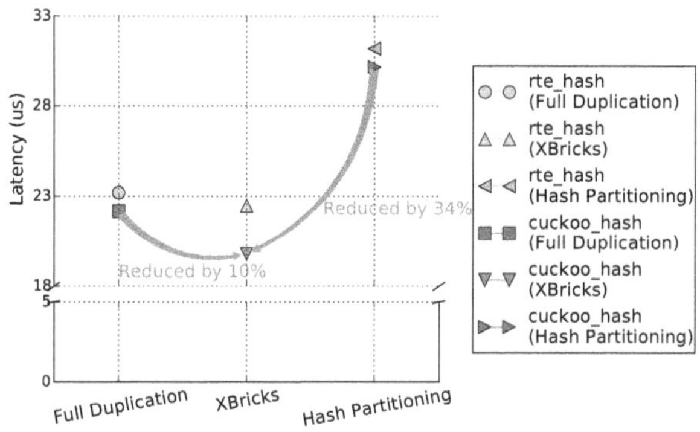

Figure 10: End-to-end latency of different approaches

ator are looked up by the core handling that port. We refer to this core as the "external core." The core processing the traffic received over the internal switch (the "internal core"), however, is mostly idle. In ScaleBricks, the external core on each server performs the global partition table lookup for all the packets, plus the hash table lookup for only those packets belonging to flows that are handled by that same server. The load is therefore more balanced, as the internal cores also perform a hash lookup, but in a smaller table. These two effects combine to improve the throughput and core utilization substantially. Although alternative designs might make better use of the idle cycles by multiplexing packet I/O and hash lookups on the internal cores, such designs—if they exist—are likely complex and introduce non-trivial overhead to switch between internal and external functionality on the internal core.

Throughput with Smaller Cache The EPC forwarding engine shares the CPU cache with other applications. To evaluate the throughput of ScaleBricks under such circumstances, we launch a *bubble* thread on a separate core to consume half of the L3 cache. Figure 9 shows the performance of different hash tables, with and without ScaleBricks, when there is only 15MiB of L3 cache available. Comparing with the results shown in Figure 8, the throughput of all tables drop with the reduced cache, but the relative benefits of ScaleBricks remain.

Latency We measure the end-to-end packet forwarding latency of six different approaches using Spirent SPT-N11U's RFC 2544 [6] benchmark tool. We create 1 M static tunnels for the latency test. Two interesting observations stand out from the average latency results reported in Figure 10. First, compared to the baseline, ScaleBricks reduces the average latency by up to 10%. We believe that ScaleBricks is able to service more of the lookups from cache because of the smaller table size, thereby reducing the memory access latency. Second, compared with the hash partitioning, the latency of ScaleBricks is lower by up to 34%. This matches our expectation. In summary, ScaleBricks improves the end-to-end latency via faster memory access and/or eliminating the extra inter-cluster hop.

Update Rate We measure the update rate of ScaleBricks as follows: a single CPU core can handle 60 K updates/sec. Using a decentralized update protocol allows ScaleBricks to distribute updates to all the nodes in a cluster. In a 4-node ScaleBricks cluster, using one dedicated core on each server provides an aggregated rate of 240 K updates/sec. Because the update is essentially parallelizable, by adding more CPU cores, we can achieve higher update rate if necessary.

6.3 Scalability of ScaleBricks

Compared to naive FIB duplication, ScaleBricks provides a practical leap in scaling by using a compact representation for the information that must be replicated on all nodes. To put its contributions in perspective, it is useful to compare to both FIB duplication and to two-hop FIB partitioning. Recall that FIB duplication and ScaleBricks require only a single hop across the internal switch fabric. Two-hop FIB partitioning, in contrast, incurs higher forwarding cost, but achieves true linear FIB scaling, which ScaleBricks does not.

Although SetSep is compact, its size (i.e., bits per entry) does increase slowly with the number of nodes in the cluster. This creates a scaling tension. At first, ScaleBricks scales almost linearly: for n nodes, each must store only $\frac{F}{n}$ of the F total FIB entries. But those FIB entries are large—perhaps 64 or 128 bits each. In contrast, the GPT must store all F entries on each node, but using only $F \log n$ bits. At first, $\log n$ is very small, and so the GPT is much smaller than the original FIB. But as n increases and more entries are added to the FIB, the GPT size begins to grow, and after 32 nodes, adding more servers actually decreases the total number of FIB entries that can be handled. Analytically, the total number of 64-bit FIB entries that can be stored in an n-node cluster scales as $Mn/(64+(0.5+1.5\log n)n)$, where M is the memory capacity per node. As a result, a ScaleBricks cluster can scale up to handle 5.7 times more FIB entries compared with a cluster using full FIB duplication.

Assuming each server uses 16 MiB of memory, Figure 11 shows analytically the total forwarding entries enabled using full FIB duplication, ScaleBricks, and hash partitioning, for clusters from 1 to 32 servers. ScaleBricks scales better when FIB entries are larger than 64 bits because the total number of FIB entries as well as the size of GPT will decrease.

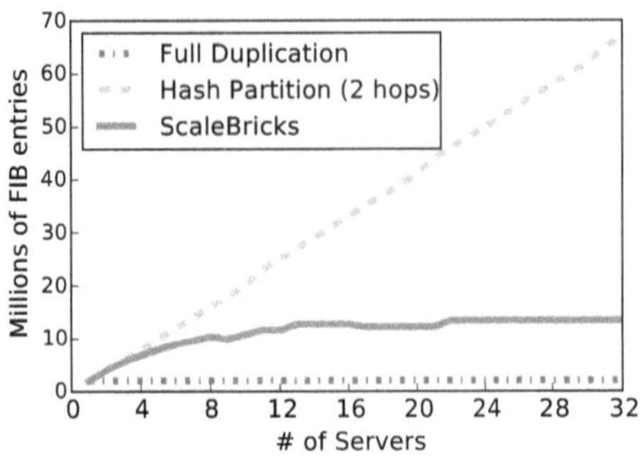

Figure 11: # of FIB entries with different # of servers

As both intuition suggests and the figure shows, traditional FIB duplication does not scale: The ensemble supports only as many FIB entries as a single node does. In contrast, hash partitioning of the FIB scales linearly, but at an extra forwarding cost. In ScaleBricks, the number of FIB entries that can be handled scales nearly linearly for a small number of nodes.

7. DISCUSSION

Skewed Forwarding Table Distribution ScaleBricks assumes the assignment of keys to handling nodes is not under its control; in the case of EPC, a separate controller assigns flows to handling nodes. If the assignment is skewed, some nodes must handle a disproportionately larger number of flows. In such a case, hash partitioning provides linear scalability (at the cost of one more hop) because it evenly distributes the FIB across intermediate lookup/indirect nodes. ScaleBricks, however, uses a combined lookup/handling node, so the FIB partitioning is skewed according to the handling node of each entry. In the ideal case, when each node has the same number of FIB entries, ScaleBricks scales well to up to 8 servers, as we have shown in the evaluation. However, when the distribution of the FIB entries is skewed, ScaleBricks can no longer achieve this scalability. The tradeoff between scalability and latency is fundamental, and ScaleBricks achieves near-optimal scalability with minimal latency (switching hops).

Isolation of Failure In general, ScaleBricks exhibits better failure tolerance properties than hash-partitioned clusters by providing failure isolation—when a server fails, the network communication from/to other servers can continue. This isolation comes from the fate sharing between each server and partial FIB hosted by itself. In a hash-partitioned cluster, however, one failing node could cause forwarding errors for the keys for which the node serves as a lookup node, even if these keys are not handled by the failing node itself.

More Applications ScaleBricks helps improve the performance of stateful, clustered network appliances which assign flows to their specific handling nodes without being able to control the assignment. We demonstrated the usefulness of ScaleBricks by using the LTE-to-Internet gateway as a driving application, and we are currently seeking for more applications that can benefit from ScaleBricks.

8. RELATED WORK

Conventional Solutions for Global Partition Table There is a wealth of related work on building efficient dictionaries mapping keys to values.

Standard **hash tables** cannot provide the space and performance we require. Typically, they store keys or fingerprints of keys to resolve collisions, where multiple keys land in the same hash table bucket. Storing keys is space-prohibitive for our application. To reduce the effect of collisions, hash tables typically allocate more entries than the number of elements they plan to store. Simple hashing schemes such as linear probing start to develop performance issues once highly loaded (70–90%, depending on the implementation). Multiple-choice based hashing schemes such as cuckoo hashing [30] or d-left hashing [28] can achieve occupancies greater than 90%, but must manage collisions and deal with performance issues from using multiple choices.

Perfect Hashing schemes try to find an injective mapping onto a table of m entries for n ($n \leq m$) distinct items from a larger universe. Seminal early work in the area includes [12, 17, 16], Fredman and Komlós [16], and such work refers to set separating families of hash functions. More recent work on attempting to design perfect hash functions for on-chip memory [26] is most similar to ours. Our approach uses both less space and fewer memory accesses.

Perfect hashing data structures can be compressed; for example, both ECT [25], as used in SILT [24], and CHD [3] use fewer than 2.5 bits per key to store the index.[2] However, these schemes must also store the value associated with each key. Nor do these compressed implementations of perfect hashing provide sufficient lookup throughput. ECT is optimized for indexing data in external storage such as SSDs, and its lookup latency is one to seven microseconds per lookup; CHD is faster, but remains several times slower than our solution.

Bloom Filters [4] are a compact probabilistic data structure used to represent a set of elements for set-membership tests, with many applications [7]. They achieve high space efficiency by allowing false positives.

Bloom filters and variants have been proposed for set separation. For example, BUFFALO [33] attempts to scale the forwarding table of a network switch. It does so by looking up the destination address in a sequence of Bloom filters, one per outgoing port. However, this approach to set separation is inefficient. A query may see positive results from multiple Bloom filters, and the system must resolve these false positives. SetSep is also more space efficient. Finally, updating the Bloom filter to change the mapping of an address from port x to port y is expensive, because it must rebuild the filter to delete a single item, or use additional structure

[2] The information theoretical lower bound for minimal perfect hashing is approximately 1.44 bits per key.

(such as counting Bloom filters). Bloomier filters [9] provide an alternative approach; the value associated with a key is the exclusive-or of values set in multiple hash table locations determined by the key. Approximate concurrent state machines [5] similarly provide an alternative structure based on multiple choice hashing for efficiently representing partial functions. Our approach is again more scalable than these approaches.

Fast Software Routers and Switches RouteBricks [13] demonstrated that a commodity server can forward 64-byte IPv4 packets at 19 Mpps by batching packet I/O and parallelizing packet processing on modern multi-core CPUs and multi-queue NICs. PacketShader [20] exploits the parallelism and memory bandwidth of GPUs to provide fast IPv4 and IPv6 forwarding. ScaleBricks similarly exploits modern CPUs by performing batched table lookups that make more efficient use of memory bandwidth and reduce CPU cycles.

Scaling Forwarding Tables Bloom filters [4] have been used to improve memory-efficiency in packet forwarding engines. Dharmapurikar et al. [11] deployed Bloom filters to determine which hash table to use for a packet's next hop. Their scheme often requires additional hash table probes per address lookup on false positives returned by the Bloom filters. BUFFALO has a similar goal, as noted above.

CuckooSwitch [34] scales the forwarding table of a *single node*. ScaleBricks adopts CuckooSwitch's per-node FIB design, but it could use any efficient FIB. The contribution of ScaleBricks is, instead, the use of SetSep to build a global partition table that is divided across switch cluster nodes and helps forward incoming packets to the handling node in a single hop.

Flat Address Routing Flat addresses enable simple network topology and easy manageability of enterprise and datacenter networks (e.g., SEATTLE [22]) as well as straightforward support for wide-area mobility (e.g., ROFL [8], AIP [2], XIA [19]). ScaleBricks provides a new, scalable implementation option for such flat designs.

9. CONCLUSION

ScaleBricks is a new mechanism for helping to "scale up" clustered network applications. Its core contribution is the design and implementation of a new data structure, SetSep, for compactly storing the mapping from keys, such as flow IDs or flat addresses, to values, such as the node ID that should handle that flow. To make this structure practical, ScaleBricks provides efficient mechanisms for partitioning the full forwarding state around a cluster and constructing and updating its SetSep-based global partitioning table. SetSep requires only 3.5 bits/key to store a mapping from arbitrary keys to 2-bit values, and provides extremely fast lookups. ScaleBricks is an effective technique for practical applications, and moving to it improved the packet forwarding throughput of a 4-node LTE-to-packet network gateway by 23% and cut its latency up to 10%.

Acknowledgments

This work was supported in part by NSF grants CNS-1345305, CNS-1314721, IIS-0964473, CNS-1228598, and CCF-1320231, and by the Intel Science and Technology Center for Cloud Computing.

10. REFERENCES

[1] 3GPP. The Evolved Packet Core. http://www.3gpp.org/technologies/keywords-acronyms/100-the-evolved-packet-core.

[2] D. G. Andersen, H. Balakrishnan, N. Feamster, T. Koponen, D. Moon, and S. Shenker. Accountable Internet Protocol (AIP). In *Proc. ACM SIGCOMM*, Seattle, WA, Aug. 2008.

[3] D. Belazzougui, F. Botelho, and M. Dietzfelbinger. Hash, displace, and compress. In *Proceedings of the 17th European Symposium on Algorithms*, ESA '09, pages 682–693, 2009.

[4] B. H. Bloom. Space/time trade-offs in hash coding with allowable errors. *Communications of the ACM*, 13(7): 422–426, 1970.

[5] F. Bonomi, M. Mitzenmacher, and R. Panigrahy. Beyond Bloom filters: From approximate membership checks to approximate state machines. In *Proc. ACM SIGCOMM*, Pisa, Italy, Aug. 2006.

[6] S. Bradner and J. McQuaid. *Benchmarking Methodology for Network Interconnect Devices*. Internet Engineering Task Force, Mar. 1999. RFC 2544.

[7] A. Broder, M. Mitzenmacher, and A. Broder. Network Applications of Bloom Filters: A Survey. In *Internet Mathematics*, volume 1, pages 636–646, 2002.

[8] M. Caesar, T. Condie, J. Kannan, K. Lakshimarayanan, I. Stoica, and S. Shenker. ROFL: Routing on Flat Labels. In *Proc. ACM SIGCOMM*, Pisa, Italy, Aug. 2006.

[9] B. Chazelle, J. Kilian, R. Rubinfeld, A. Tal, and O. Boy. The Bloomier filter: An efficient data structure for static support lookup tables. In *Proceedings of SODA*, pages 30–39, 2004.

[10] Connectem. Connectem Inc. http://www.connectem.net/.

[11] S. Dharmapurikar, P. Krishnamurthy, and D. E. Taylor. Longest prefix matching using Bloom filters. In *Proc. ACM SIGCOMM*, Karlsruhe, Germany, Aug. 2003.

[12] M. Dietzfelbinger, A. Karlin, K. Mehlhorn, F. M. Auf Der Heide, H. Rohnert, and R. E. Tarjan. Dynamic perfect hashing: Upper and lower bounds. *SIAM Journal on Computing*, 23(4):738–761, 1994.

[13] M. Dobrescu, N. Egi, K. Argyraki, B.-G. Chun, K. Fall, G. Iannaccone, A. Knies, M. Manesh, and S. Ratnasamy. RouteBricks: Exploiting parallelism to scale software routers. In *Proc. 22nd ACM Symposium on Operating Systems Principles (SOSP)*, Big Sky, MT, Oct. 2009.

[14] B. Fan, D. G. Andersen, and M. Kaminsky. MemC3: Compact and concurrent memcache with dumber caching and smarter hashing. In *Proc. 10th USENIX NSDI*, Lombard, IL, Apr. 2013.

[15] B. Fan, D. Zhou, H. Lim, M. Kaminsky, and D. G. Andersen. When cycles are cheap, some tables can be huge. In *Proc. HotOS XIV*, Santa Ana Pueblo, NM, May 2013.

[16] M. L. Fredman and J. Komlós. On the size of separating systems and families of perfect hash functions. *SIAM Journal on Algebraic Discrete Methods*, 5(1):61–68, 1984.

[17] M. L. Fredman, J. Komlós, and E. Szemerédi. Storing a sparse table with O(1) worst case access time. *Journal of the ACM (JACM)*, 31(3):538–544, 1984.

[18] W. Haeffner, J. Napper, M. Stiemerling, D. Lopez, and J. Uttaro. *Service Function Chaining Use Cases in Mobile Networks*. Internet Engineering Task Force, Jan. 2015.

[19] D. Han, A. Anand, F. Dogar, B. Li, H. Lim, M. Machado, A. Mukundan, W. Wu, A. Akella, D. G. Andersen, J. W. Byers, S. Seshan, and P. Steenkiste. XIA: Efficient support for evolvable internetworking. In *Proc. 9th USENIX NSDI*, San Jose, CA, Apr. 2012.

[20] S. Han, K. Jang, K. Park, and S. Moon. PacketShader: a GPU-accelerated software router. In *Proc. ACM SIGCOMM*, New Delhi, India, Aug. 2010.

[21] Intel. Intel Data Plane Development Kit (Intel DPDK). http://www.intel.com/go/dpdk, 2013.

[22] C. Kim, M. Caesar, and J. Rexford. Floodless in SEATTLE: A scalable Ethernet architecture for large enterprises. In *Proc. ACM SIGCOMM*, Seattle, WA, Aug. 2008.

[23] A. Kirsch and M. Mitzenmacher. Less hashing, same performance: Building a better Bloom filter. *Random Structures & Algorithms*, 33(2):187–218, 2008.

[24] H. Lim, B. Fan, D. G. Andersen, and M. Kaminsky. SILT: A memory-efficient, high-performance key-value store. In *Proc. 23rd ACM Symposium on Operating Systems Principles (SOSP)*, Cascais, Portugal, Oct. 2011.

[25] H. Lim, D. G. Andersen, and M. Kaminsky. Practical batch-updatable external hashing with sorting. In *Proc. Meeting on Algorithm Engineering and Experiments (ALENEX)*, Jan. 2013.

[26] Y. Lu, B. Prabhakar, and F. Bonomi. Perfect hashing for network applications. In *Information Theory, 2006 IEEE International Symposium on*, pages 2774–2778. IEEE, 2006.

[27] Y. Mao, C. Cutler, and R. Morris. Optimizing ram-latency dominated applications. APSys '13, 2013.

[28] M. Mitzenmacher and B. Vocking. The asymptotics of selecting the shortest of two, improved. In *Proc. the Annual Allerton Conference on Communication Control and Computing*, volume 37, pages 326–327, 1999.

[29] M. Mitzenmacher, A. W. Richa, and R. Sitaraman. The power of two random choices: A survey of techniques and results. In *Handbook of Randomized Computing*, pages 255–312. Kluwer, 2000.

[30] R. Pagh and F. Rodler. Cuckoo hashing. *Journal of Algorithms*, 51(2):122–144, May 2004.

[31] Spirent. Spirent SPT-N11U. http://www.spirent.com/sitecore/content/Home/Ethernet_Testing/Platforms/11U_Chassis.

[32] L. G. Valiant and G. J. Brebner. Universal schemes for parallel communication. In *Proceedings of the Thirteenth Annual ACM Symposium on Theory of Computing*, STOC '81.

[33] M. Yu, A. Fabrikant, and J. Rexford. BUFFALO: Bloom filter forwarding architecture for large organizations. In *Proc. CoNEXT*, Dec. 2009.

[34] D. Zhou, B. Fan, H. Lim, D. G. Andersen, and M. Kaminsky. Scalable, High Performance Ethernet Forwarding with CuckooSwitch. In *Proc. 9th International Conference on emerging Networking EXperiments and Technologies (CoNEXT)*, Dec. 2013.

Laissez-Faire : Fully Asymmetric Backscatter Communication

Pan Hu, Pengyu Zhang, Deepak Ganesan
College of Information and Computer Sciences
University of Massachusetts, Amherst, MA 01003
{panhu, pyzhang, dganesan}@cs.umass.edu

ABSTRACT

Backscatter provides dual-benefits of energy harvesting and low-power communication, making it attractive to a broad class of wireless sensors. But the design of a protocol that enables extremely power-efficient radios for harvesting-based sensors as well as high-rate data transfer for data-rich sensors presents a conundrum. In this paper, we present a new *fully asymmetric* backscatter communication protocol where nodes blindly transmit data as and when they sense. This model enables fully flexible node designs, from extraordinarily power-efficient backscatter radios that consume barely a few micro-watts to high-throughput radios that can stream at hundreds of Kbps while consuming a paltry tens of micro-watts. The challenge, however, lies in decoding concurrent streams at the reader, which we achieve using a novel combination of time-domain separation of interleaved signal edges, and phase-domain separation of colliding transmissions. We provide an implementation of our protocol, LF-Backscatter, and show that it can achieve an order of magnitude or more improvement in throughput, latency and power over state-of-art alternatives.

CCS Concepts

•**Networks** → **Network architectures; Wireless access networks;**

Keywords

Backscatter; Wireless; Architecture

SIGCOMM '15, August 17 - 21, 2015, London, United Kingdom
© 2015 ACM. ISBN 978-1-4503-3542-3/15/08...$15.00
DOI: http://dx.doi.org/10.1145/2785956.2787477

1. INTRODUCTION

As we enter a world where sensors are embedded in walls, wearables, and within bodies, a question that demands attention is what wireless technology is best suited for these devices. Backscatter has emerged as a strong contender for this regime because of its ability to deliver power while simultaneously offering an ultra-low power wireless backhaul.

One of the extraordinary benefits of backscatter is that it can help design wireless sensors that operate at end-to-end power budgets of under a few micro-watts, thereby enabling battery-less operation. For example, a backscatter-based temperature sensor that samples at 1Hz, and operates in a sense-transmit loop with no other overheads (i.e. no receive circuit, no protocol overhead, etc) would barely consume 10 μW of power, which makes it possible for such devices to operate continuously using a small amount of harvested power.

Backscatter is also attractive as a replacement to active radios on battery-powered sensors since it can support hundreds of Kbps while consuming only tens of micro-watts of power [26]. Backscatter achieves this power efficiency by shifting carrier generation to the reader, and only uses power for clocking its RF transistor. High-speed ultra low power radios can enable a paradigm shift in wireless sensing — continuous data offload from a variety of data-rich sensors such as cameras and microphones becomes extremely efficient, thereby enabling sophisticated distributed sensing applications.

While backscatter offers many advantages for wireless sensors, our ability to realize these benefits depends on the design choices made by the protocol. Seemingly innocuous protocol choices have important ramifications. For example, a protocol designed with the expectation that the radio can support bitrates of hundreds of Kbps significantly impacts power efficiency for simple low-rate sensors such as the backscatter-based temperature sensor described above. Despite its low sampling rate and limited communication needs, such a sensor would need to accumulate samples in a buffer, and use a high-speed clock to toggle its RF transistor, which increases power consumption by several tens of μWs over a simpler design that used a slower clock and no packet buffers. This power difference hinders its ability to operate in a battery-less manner. On the other hand, optimizing the protocol for stringently constrained sensors by reducing the transmit and receive bitrate, would clearly hurt overall throughput. Even simple design choices like reader feedback to the tag (e.g. TDMA slot assignment messages [5]) incurs the cost of message decoding at the tag, which adds to the power budget. At its core, the issue is that protocols are often optimized for specific hardware capabilities, and it appears difficult to shoehorn a wide range of hardware scenarios into a protocol without sacrificing efficiency.

While dealing with hardware heterogeneity may appear to be an intractable problem, an examination of the capabilities at the reader presents intriguing possibilities. We have a powerful reader that can sample several orders of magnitude faster than the tags can modulate the signal (even the fastest sensor tags are barely going to exceed 100 Kbps). For example, take the case of a USRP-based EPC Gen 2 reader reading data from backscatter sensors — the reader can sample at 25 Mega samples/second, and even if a tag can transmit at 100 kbps, this means that less than 1% of the time-domain samples contain useful information.

In this paper, we argue that existing backscatter protocols do not take full advantage of its inherent asymmetry. Rather, these protocols make assumptions that often diminish the flexibility to design lower power or higher speed backscatter systems. Our line of attack is the following: we allow nodes to use the least restrictive backscatter protocol, a *laissez-faire* approach that lets nodes blindly transmit data once they see the carrier signal, and focus on the problem of decoding these concurrent streams by leveraging the more powerful reader. Consider the potential benefits of such a fully asymmetric design. One could envisage an extremely low-power tag that is virtually free of any computational logic — it senses and immediately transmits the digitized signal oblivious to any other wireless traffic. Such a design would need no decoding, no MAC, no packet buffers, and no high-speed RF oscillators. The model would benefit faster tags as well — a higher speed backscatter tag would not need to pause and wait for the slow tags to transmit their bits. But despite the intrinsic elegance of the laissez-faire approach, the pragmatics seem daunting. How can the reader cleanly separate the signals from different tags operating at widely different rates?

Our fundamental insight is that the laissez-faire approach is asynchronous, hence it results in temporal interleaving of signal edges caused by toggling of the transmit antenna at different nodes. By leveraging the reader's capability to sample at a much higher rate than the node, this time-domain asynchrony can be exploited to enable concurrent transfers. But temporal separation is insufficient on its own — edge transitions can collide since nodes independently decide when to transmit. To separate such collided signals, we take advantage of phase information about the backscattered signals. The backscatter baseband signal can be represented as comprised of a sine and a cosine wave. This provides us with a phase vector in the in-phase and quadrature dimensions (IQ vector). By leveraging the fact that collisions result in different clusters in the IQ plane, we can separate collided signals without requiring any special mechanism at the tag. The benefit of using time-domain separation followed by IQ-domain separation is important to emphasize — by itself, time-domain separation would not be able to resolve collisions, and IQ-domain separation would only support limited concurrency, but in tandem, they can enable substantial concurrency.

This paper is about the details of designing and implementing such a laissez-faire backscatter protocol. We ask and answer many questions to make the scheme practical — how can we separate signals across tags by leveraging the differences in signals across time, in-phase, and quadrature? what are the minimal restrictions we may want to impose to the laissez-faire model to ensure that the system actually works in practice? what are the performance benefits in terms of throughput, power, and latency? can the scheme support extremely constrained harvesting-based tags and higher rate battery-assisted tags?, and so on. Through this exploration, we hope to convince the reader that we have a system that retains much of the elegance and benefits of the laissez-faire approach, while imposing a few restrictions to make the technique practical.

In summary, our key contributions are:

- We design a novel backscatter system, LF-Backscatter, that is fully asymmetric and enables flexible radio architectures at the tag, while pushing all decoding complexity to the reader. Our decoding algorithm leverages time, in-phase, and quadrature information to enable a high degree of concurrent transmissions from backscatter sensors. Our design has several novel contributions to extract edges robustly from interleaved signals, separate collisions, and correct errors, all without adding complexity at the tag.
- We build a full software and hardware prototype of LF-Backscatter, and evaluate its benefits in a range of scenarios. In a sixteen node experiment, we show that LF-Backscatter's throughput is 7.9× higher than Buzz and 16.4× higher than TDMA, its latency for reading identifiers is 9.5× faster than Buzz and 17× faster than TDMA, and its energy-efficiency is 20× lower than Buzz and two orders of magnitude lower than RFID chips [23].

2. CASE FOR LF-BACKSCATTER

In this section, we look at a variety of methods that have been proposed for supporting backscatter communication from multiple tags. We focus on backscatter

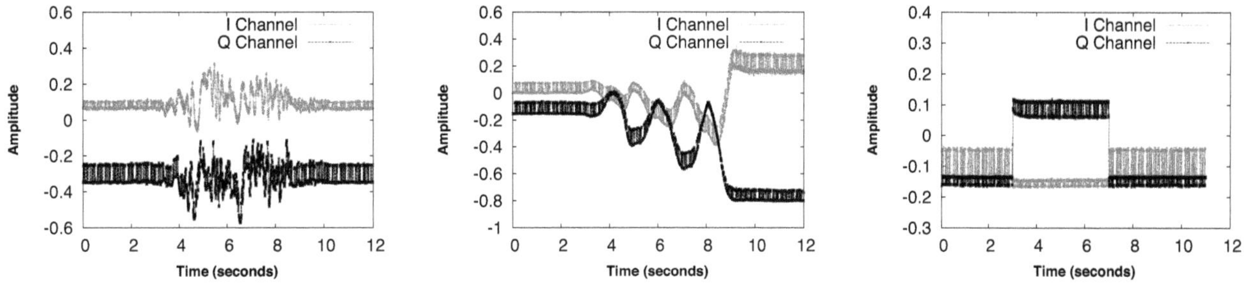

(a) People movement (b) Tag rotation (c) Coupled tags

Figure 1: Dynamics in received signal under different scenarios.

using Amplitude Shift Keying (ASK), which is the dominant backscattering technique since it provides continuous power to tags and enables relatively simple receiver design [8]. We start with sequential access, and work our way through previously proposed concurrent transmission methods, and finally discuss LF-Backscatter.

2.1 TDMA and CDMA-based approaches

Time Division Multiple Access (TDMA) is a natural choice for backscatter because the reader has the resources to co-ordinate transfer by estimating the number of tags, determining how many slots to use, and marking slot boundaries. Most backscatter-based systems are based on TDMA [7, 10, 25, 27], the most well known being EPC Gen 2 [5].

While TDMA is very well understood and easy to deploy, it is not efficient when considering heterogeneous tags with varying capabilities. If TDMA chooses to operate at a rate that is the lowest common denominator of the nodes in the network, then it would be ponderously slow and overall throughput would suffer. If TDMA chooses a faster rate that is high enough to offer better throughput, it forces tags to use more power-hungry components like faster clocks and larger buffers. TDMA is also less than ideal in that the reader issues periodic control messages, and nodes need to expend energy in decoding these messages. Finally, TDMA vastly underutilizes the sampling capability at the reader since it serializes transmissions.

Code Division Multiple Access (CDMA) is another approach for enabling concurrent transmission for backscatter sensors [12, 15, 17]. Here, each sensor exploits an orthogonal code for encoding data where each bit is converted to a long PN sequence (hundreds of bits in length). CDMA is inefficient for backscatter because data transmission takes a much longer time, which hurts throughput, or the tags need to operate higher frequency radios, which increases power consumption by orders of magnitude [22].

2.2 Linear Signal Separation

A recent concurrency-based backscatter protocol, Buzz [22], is based on the idea that backscatter signals combine linearly and therefore can be separated using matrix inversion methods. Buzz lets all nodes transmit in a synchronous bit-by-bit manner, so the received signal can be expressed as:

$$y = \mathbf{d}_{m\times n}\mathbf{h}_{n\times n}\mathbf{b}_{n\times 1} = \begin{pmatrix} d_{11} & \dots & d_{1n} \\ d_{21} & \dots & d_{2n} \\ \vdots & \ddots & \vdots \\ d_{m1} & \dots & d_{mn} \end{pmatrix} \begin{pmatrix} h_1 & 0 & \dots & 0 \\ 0 & h_2 & \dots & 0 \\ \vdots & \vdots & \ddots & \vdots \\ 0 & 0 & \dots & h_n \end{pmatrix} \begin{pmatrix} b_1 \\ b_2 \\ \vdots \\ b_n \end{pmatrix} \quad (1)$$

where y, the received symbol at the reader, is a linear combination of the complex channel coefficient corresponding to node i, h_i, the bit being transmitted by the node, b_i, and a randomization matrix, d_{ij}. Once the randomization matrix and the channel coefficients from each node are known, the function can be inverted to estimate the bits transmitted by each tag.

To implement this method in practice, Buzz first determines the channel coefficients of each node by using compressive sensing-based estimation. Once the channel coefficients are known, nodes transmit their bits in lock-step, re-transmitting each bit multiple times with different random combinations as determined by a pre-defined random matrix $\mathbf{d}_{m\times n}$. This allows the decoder to observe different combinations of the concurrent transmissions, enabling it to decode the stream. Once a combination with low error is determined, nodes move on to transmit the next message.

There are two problems that make this method less than ideal for heterogeneous backscatter sensors. One practical problem is that nodes need to transmit their bits in lock-step. This implies that the clocks on all nodes need to operate at the same rate, which is a reasonable assumption for RFIDs but not for sensors with heterogeneous capabilities and clock speeds. Another problem is that the channel coefficients need to be re-estimated to deal with changing environments and tag positions. Channel coefficients vary for three reasons. The first is when there is mobility of objects in the vicinity of the tag. In Figure 1(a), a tag is stationary in front of a reader while an individual moves around the room, resulting in substantial changes to the channel co-

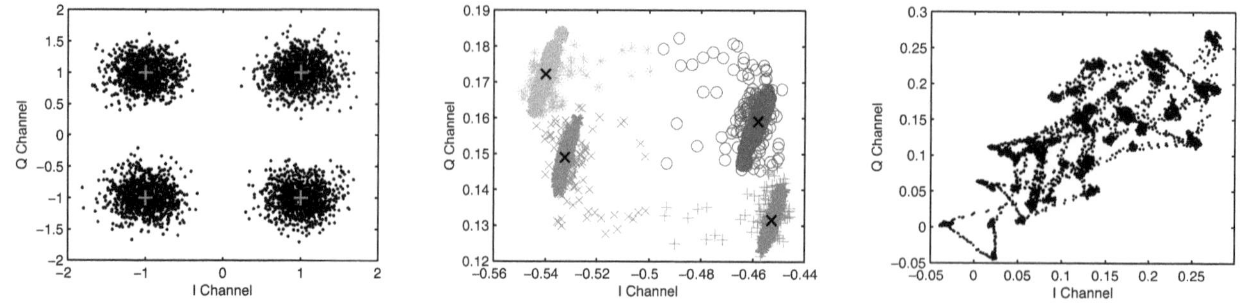

(a) QAM IQ clusters. (b) Clustering of 2 tags (c) IQ clusters of 6 tags

Figure 2: IQ Clusters: (a) shows structured clusters in QAM, (b) and (c) show unstructured clusters. As the number of nodes increases, clusters are harder to separate.

efficients. Second, channel coefficients are also sensitive to movements of the tag. In Figure 1(b), a tag's orientation is varied by rotating it without displacing the tag, again resulting in significant changes to the channel coefficients. Third, channel coefficients also change when there is near-field coupling between the antennas of two or more tags. Figure 1(c) illustrates this case with a simple experiment where two tags were placed far apart, and then brought closer together. As shown, both channel coefficients are unchanged when the tags are about 1m apart, but when tags become closer together (roughly 5cm), there is near-field coupling across the antennas of the tags resulting in variations of channel coefficients. While such variations depend on the dynamics in the environment, adapting to them will incur protocol overhead for channel estimation prior to communication, and associated tag complexity for supporting the protocol functions. Buzz [22] does not explicitly address this problem since it targets one-shot RFID identification.

2.3 Cluster-based Separation of Signals

An alternative approach that has been considered in prior work is separation in the IQ plane [6]. When tags transmit simultaneously, their phase and amplitude information (IQ vector) creates multiple clusters, where each cluster corresponds to a specific combination of values from the tags. This approach could be viewed as the unstructured analogue of methods like Quadrature Amplitude Modulation (QAM) shown in Figure 2(a). While the signals in QAM are structured to be as far apart as possible, the clusters in this case are unstructured and depend on channel coefficients between each node and the reader.

For example, consider that there are two nodes that transmit simultaneously (lets call them 1 and 2) . Define $V(i, s_i)$ as the complex vector corresponding to node i when its antenna state is s_i (s_i is 0 when antenna is detuned and 1 when it is tuned). This vector is composed of the I (in phase) and Q (quadrature) channels, and can be expressed as $V(i, s_i) = I(i, s_i) + Q(i, s_i)$. Thus, the total signal reflected by the two nodes can be one of four options, $V(1, s_1) + V(2, s_2)$, where $s_1, s_2 \in \{0, 1\}$. Besides the signal reflected by the nodes, the reader also receives the signal reflected by the environment. For simplicity, let us assume that the reflection from the environment is a constant, so it won't affect the number of clusters, but will only add an offset to them.

Figure 2(b) shows the empirically obtained IQ constellation of received signal from the 2 nodes. We can see four dense clusters with sparse points between them. The sparse points are imperfect transitions between different states of transmitted signal.

A fundamental issue with this method is that it simply does not scale to a larger number of nodes. In the two nodes example, it is easy to see that simply choosing the closest cluster to a received vector can decode the signal from each node with high probability, but when we try to increase the number of tags, performance using this method degrades rapidly. This is because given N nodes (N $\geq$2), there are 2^N clusters in the IQ plot, resulting in clusters being closer to each other. An example with six nodes is shown in Figure 2(c). The figure has 64 clusters that are very close to each other, and dwell time in each cluster is short. This means that there are more points lie between clusters. In this case, separating the signal by classifying clusters is challenging. This drawback has been noted in prior work, for example, Angerer et al [6] also conclude that the technique does not scale to beyond two nodes.

2.4 Concurrency in Time and IQ

Our laissez-faire approach to backscatter is radically different from the above approaches. The underlying principle for signal separation is to leverage three axes — time, in-phase, and quadrature. When asynchronous ASK signals from tags are combined, two things happen — edges are created whenever there is a transition on any one tag, and the signals combine depending on the state of each tag as well as state of the environment. The underlying intuition in LF-Backscatter is that both the edges and the combined signal are important for separating out the concurrent transmissions. Since the reader can oversample the received signal and edges are temporally localized, there is a lot of room to interleave edges within the time dimension of the combined signal.

As a concrete example, let us see how many UMass Moo tags, each transmitting at 100 Kbps, can be supported by a USRP reader sampling at 25 Mega-samples-per-second. This means that for each bit transmitted by a tag, the reader samples 250 times. An edge is roughly 3 samples wide at the reader's sampling rate, which means that we can stack $\frac{250}{3} = 83$ edges one after the other, so we can support a fairly large number of fast tags.

Of course, perfect interleaving is not achievable in practice, and we need methods to deal with the case where edges from different tags collide. But the fact that edges are finely localized in time means that only a small fraction of the concurrent transmitters are colliding at this edge. We take advantage of the temporal localization of collisions and make tags transmit periodically at multiples of a base-rate, which ensures that colliding nodes repeatedly do so at the same time, thereby giving us more information that can be used to separate the signals. While both linear separation and cluster-based separation are possible candidates given that we have a small number of colliders to separate, we use the latter since it does not require repeated estimation of the channel coefficients to each tag, and is less sensitive to changes in environment and orientation.

At a high level, the above description summarizes the main idea in this paper, but the devil is in the details. We have made several assumptions to narrate the high-level story — we assume that signal edges can be separated in a robust manner, that edges can be finely separated in time to maximize concurrency, that cluster-based separation can identify which bits are being sent by the colliding tags, that we can associate detected bits to the appropriate tag, and so on. We look at these thorny issues in the following section.

3. LF-Backscatter DESIGN

LF-Backscatter is designed to do as much as possible at the reader to ensure minimal complexity at the tag. We describe the sequence of stages involved in recovering data transmitted by the tags, starting with reliable edge detection.

3.1 Reliable edge detection

The first challenge that we face is reliably detecting signal edges, which is central to enabling concurrent laissez-faire transmission. It would seem that we can extract edges by using edge detection techniques on the combined signal received at the reader, but this turns out to be brittle.

Let us understand why this is the case. The backscatter reader sends a carrier wave toward the device, which can be represented as compromise of a sine wave and a cosine wave. These two parts are known as in-phase and quadrature signals. A backscatter device toggles its transistor and reflects this signal back to the reader. The amplitude of the signal is the total power of the received signal. To observe a significant change in amplitude when a node toggles its edge, the change in amplitude must be much higher than the background. However, the background is high when many other nodes are transmitting, and changes continually depending on the state of the tags. As a result, edges are not always clearly visible in this signal.

Our idea is to look at the IQ vector differential caused by the edge. Since the received signal from concurrent transmissions is a linear combination of individual signals (to first approximation), we can express the received backscatter signal at time t from N concurrent transmitters as:

$$S(t) = \sum_{j=1}^{N} S_I^j(t) + iS_Q^j(t) \qquad (2)$$

where I and Q are the in-phase and quadrature channels respectively. To extract a signal edge, we look at the differential between the IQ signal before the edge occurs, and after the edge occurs i.e.

$$\Delta S(t) = S(t_+) - S(t_-) \qquad (3)$$

where $S(t_+)$ and $S(t_-)$ are received signal by the reader at time t_+ after the edge and t_- before the edge. Thus, by subtracting the received signal after and before an edge, we can remove the effect of other background nodes. Since a single instance of t_+ and t_- could result in a noisy edge estimate, we use a set of points between the previous edge to the current edge as candidates for t_+, and a set of points between the current edge and the next edge as t_-, and take the average.

3.2 Separating edges into streams

At this point, we have a sequence of edges, but we do not know which node(s) toggled their transistors to create the edge. Each edge could be a) the result of a single node toggling its transistor, b) a collision resulting from multiple nodes doing so at the same time, or c) a spurious edge as a result of noise. To address this problem, we add some additional structure to the signal. First, the reader chops up time into shorter epochs, where each epoch is initiated by the reader by shutting off and re-starting its carrier wave. At the beginning of an epoch, each node picks a random initial offset, and begins to transmit its bits periodically at a selected rate starting at the offset. The randomization ensures that the collision pattern changes each epoch, so even if edges did collide in an epoch, they are likely to separate the next epoch. Second, we assume that the rate selected by the sensor is not arbitrary, but it is a multiple of a base rate (e.g. in our system, the

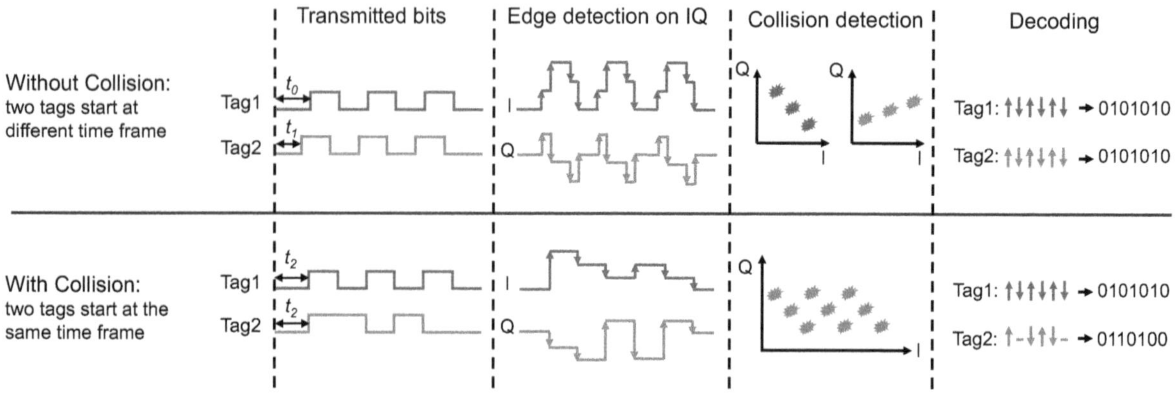

Figure 3: Figure shows processing pipeline of LF-Backscatter — on top, two nodes transmit concurrently but their edges do not collide, and on bottom, their edges collide. Time-domain separation extracts edges followed by cluster-based collision separation. When the nodes do not collide, edge differentials form three clusters in the IQ plane, whereas when edges collide, nine clusters are observed.

base rate is 100 bps, and any multiple of that is a valid data rate). This ensures that when nodes collide as a result of choosing the same offset, they continue to collide periodically throughout the epoch giving us more information to separate the signals. In addition, this assumption helps us detect if an edge is spurious, since such an edge would not have a repeating pattern at one of the valid rates.

Selecting fine-grained offsets One thorny problem that we face is how a node can choose a fine-grained offset when it only has a coarse-grained clock. Ideally, we want edges to be finely separated in time (from the reader's sampling perspective), so that we can support as much concurrency as possible. However, finely separated edges requires a fine-grained clock at the tag that is roughly as fast as the reader's clock, which defeats the very purpose of LF-Backscatter.

In keeping with the laissez-faire spirit, we just let tags start transmission the moment they see that the reader has turned on its carrier wave to signal the beginning of an epoch. Why would this work? To understand, let us look at the receive circuit of a backscatter tag. The energy from the incoming signal charges up a tiny receive capacitor, which in turn triggers a comparator when the voltage reaches a threshold that suggests that the carrier is turned on. There are three sources of randomness that affect exactly when the comparator fires: a) the energy received by the tag from the incoming signal, which depends on placement and orientation of the tag, b) the charging characteristics of the capacitor (typical capacitors have about 20% tolerance), and c) the noise in the charging process, since in practice the charging curve has small oscillations and isn't perfectly smooth as shown in textbook drawings. The end result is that tags exhibit natural variations in when they start their transfer, which gives sufficient temporal separation across edges.

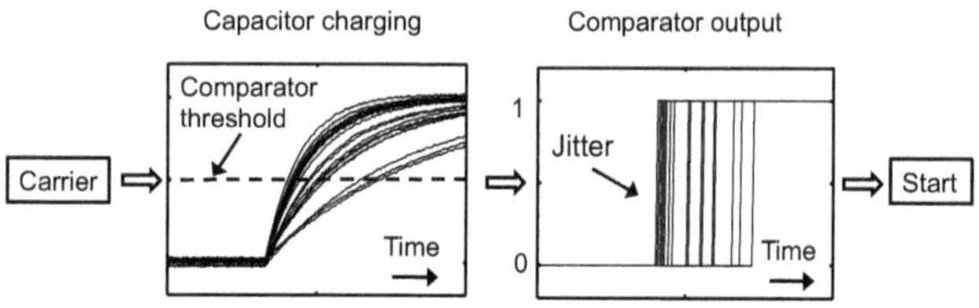

Figure 4: The capacitor charging curve changes depending on incoming energy, which in turn affects the time when the comparator fires to begin transmission.

Decoding edges Another question is how to robustly detect the presence of a stream and filter noise. To address this, the reader leverages the repeated pattern of edges, also referred to as an eye pattern [21]. Here, the analog value of a signal sample $s(t)$ is added to the analog signal sample that is T seconds ahead, $s(t+T)$, where T corresponds to the inverse of the highest bit rate. For example, T is $10\mu s$ for a 100kbps maximum bit rate. The eye pattern is determined for each possible offset, and used to detect the presence of a stream. The benefit of such folding is that it helps smooth out noise. Although each edge might have different strength $S+\sigma$, the noise σ will be averaged as a result of repetitive folding. Therefore, the peaks of eye pattern help explicitly identify edges that belongs to a same stream.

3.3 IQ Cluster-based Collision Detection

Once the streams are identified, the next step is to identify whether it is the result of a collision. To detect collided edges, we use the fact that the possible values of the edge differential vector depends on the number of nodes that are colliding at that position. Lets consider the example in Figure 3, and call the two transmitters as E_1 and E_2. For each node, edge differentials can be in one of three states (rising, falling, and constan-

Table 1: **Single node data recovery. The first bit is the anchor, which helps disambiguate clusters.**

Sent Bits	**1**	0	0	0	0	1	1	0	1	0	⋯
Received Edges		↓	-	-	-	↑	-	↓	↑	↓	⋯
Decoded Bits		1	0	0	0	0	1	1	0	1	0

t). In the top pipeline, time-domain separation unlinks the two streams, so each of them is clustered separately leading to three clusters on the IQ plot. On the bottom, we only have a single combined stream since the edges collide at the same time, so we now have nine states for the overlapped signal edge (each edge has three state, so there are nine combinations). Thus, when there are k nodes colliding, we expect 3^k clusters to be present. Given this intuition, we can detect if collisions are present by performing k-means clustering and determining the best fit in terms of number of clusters. If three clusters is not a good fit, then a collision is likely to have occurred.

We emphasize that it is not important to achieve highly scalable cluster separation since edges are finely localized in time, and a very small number of collisions are expected for a stream. Consider a simple case where nodes transmit at 100 Kbps, which is on the higher end of what we might expect in a real deployment. We use the same parameters as our experimental setup i.e. 16 nodes, 25Msps sampling rate at reader, and 3 sample edges. The probability of two-node collisions is 0.1890, whereas the probability of three node collisions is only 0.0181 making it far less likely. If the bit rate were lower, say 10 Kbps, the probability of three (or higher) node collisions is less than 0.0022 even when 200 nodes transmit concurrently.

3.4 Separating Collided Signals

While the different clusters can be separated using k-means, we need to map from cluster to the bit that each node transmits. Lets consider the case when a single node is transmitting, where an edge can have three states (rising, falling, constant). The cluster for the constant edge is located at the origin, so it is easy to determine. But the clusters for the other two edge states depend on the vector direction, which in turn depend on node placement, orientation, and other factors. The cluster to edge association is even harder when two nodes collide, since there are many more possibilities.

Let us first look at the case when only one node is present. Here, determining the sequence of bits only needs an *anchor* to tell us which cluster is +1. Since every epoch starts with a header from each tag, we embed a single anchor bit at a known location, which helps us disambiguate between the rising vs falling edge clusters. Once the cluster labels are known, the rest of the bits can be easily decoded. The process is shown in Table 1 where the first bit is an anchor with value one.

Lets turn to the case where two nodes collide. After correct classification, we have the centroid of nine clusters $C_1, C_2, ..., C_9$ where each centroid C_i maps to one of the nine pairs of states. Therefore, each centroid can be presented as a linear combination of signal edge vectors and direction coefficients as shown below:

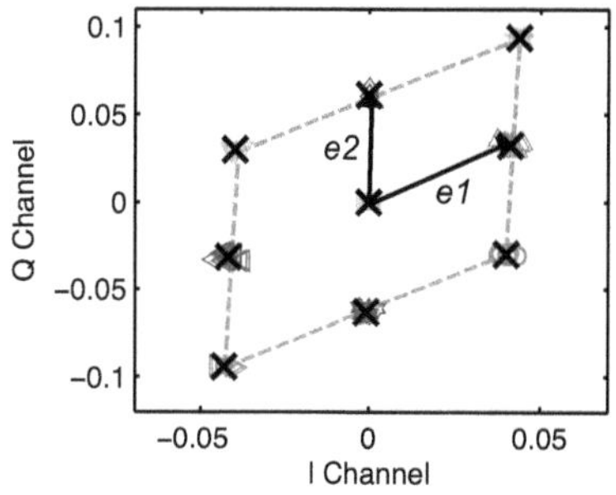

Figure 5: Nine clusters formed by two colliding edges. The clusters are linear combinations of the complex vectors corresponding to the edges.

$$\begin{aligned} a_1e_1 + b_1e_2 &= C_1 \\ a_2e_1 + b_2e_2 &= C_2 \\ &\dots \\ a_9e_1 + b_9e_2 &= C_9 \end{aligned} \tag{4}$$

where a_i and b_i indicate the direction of signal edges generated by these two devices ($a_i, b_i \in \{-1, 0, 1\}$), and e_1 and e_2 are the complex values corresponding to the edge differential. To associate each centroid with corresponding signal edges, we need to solve the above equations and obtain $a_1, a_2, ..., a_9$, $b_1, b_2, ..., b_9$, e_1, and e_2.

This problem is difficult to solve when a large number of nodes collide, but it is easily solved when we just have nine clusters. The cluster centered at the origin is easily decoded as constant from both nodes. From Figure 5, we see that the centroids of the remaining eight clusters form a parallelogram where the clusters in the mod-points of the edges correspond to the cases where only one of the edges is activated and and the other edge is a constant. Thus, if we identify the mid-points, we can find e_1 and e_2, and separate the edges into two streams. To identify the mid-points, we identify which groups of three cluster centroids are co-linear, which tells us which are the edge lines. We then select the mid-points of these co-linear centroids to identify the mid-point clusters, and thereby identify e_1 and e_2.

Note that one major advantage of our method in that it does not require estimation of the channel between the tag and reader. Our only assumption is that that channel coefficients are relatively stable during an epoch, which is reasonable since each epoch is a very short duration.

3.5 Bit Error Correction

The above process assumes that there are no missed edges or erroneously detected edges. If so, this can throw off the subsequent decoding, and cause errors in

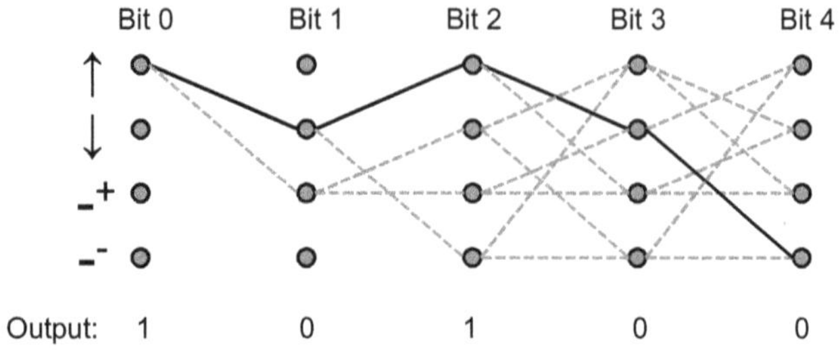

Figure 6: Viterbi decoder that encodes edge constraints. ↑ stands for a positive edge, and ↓ stands for a negative edge. $-^+$ means no edge found but its previous edge is a positive one and $-^-$ means its previous edge is negative

the rest of the sequence. While parity bits and error correction codes are commonly employed for error detection and correction, we would like to avoid having to compute anything at all on the tag-side since that increases complexity.

The fact that we are using signal edges to decode the sequence of ones and zeros transmitted by a tag suggests a possible solution. We simply leverage the fact that certain sequences are just not possible. For example, a rising edge followed by a rising edge is obviously an error. To correct for such errors, we use a Viterbi decoder with four states: ↑ (positive edge), ↓ (negative edge), $-^+$ (no edge found but previous edge is a positive one) and $-^-$ (no edge but previous edge is negative). We learn state transition probabilities, and calculate the emission probability by fitting the IQ values that are empirically observed to a two dimensional normal distribution: $(V_i, V_q) \sim N(\mu_i, \mu_q, \sigma_i, \sigma_q, r)$. We then use a Viterbi decoder to identify the most likely sequence of bits corresponding to the received sequence of edges.

Figure 6 shows an example where the bold line shows the decoded sequence of bits, and the dotted lines show alternate valid sequences. For example, if a node was transmitting a one as the first bit, then the only possibility is to either remain in the same state or see a negative edge (↓) following this state. The decoder leverages the valid state transition constraints together with analog information about the IQ vector length to correct errors that occur in the sequence of edges.

3.6 Tag Complexity

The steps that we have described so far require virtually no tag-side logic. We now describe two additions that could increase the complexity of tag design.

Clock: Since LF-Backscatter is primarily aimed at backscatter-based sensors that use a clock for sampling the sensor values, we can simply use the same clock for communication. LF-Backscatter clocks out bits as and when they are sampled and therefore does not need a separate clock for communication unlike typical wireless sensor platforms. However, since the decoding steps described above require tight timing for the signal edges in-order for the reader to decode the signals, we would need a clock with relatively low drift. If such a clock is not already available on a sensor platform, it can be added at the cost of a small increase to the overall power budget (e.g. the NXP PCF8523 Real Time Clock consumes $1.2\mu W$ [4]).

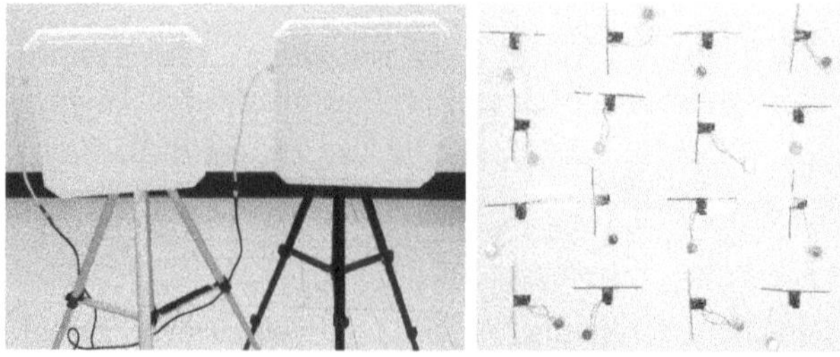

Figure 7: Experimental setup

Reliable data transfer: The design that we have described does not provide link-layer reliability to keep the tags simple. If link-layer reliability is needed, an acknowledgement mechanism can be added at the cost of some complexity at the tag. For example, a simple way to add reliability is for the the reader to send a Broadcast ACK to the entire network asking them to retransmit data for the next epoch. The benefit of this approach is that collision patterns are different across epochs, which can be used to decode messages. Similarly, the reader might broadcast a message to reduce the maximum bit-rate in the network to reduce collisions.

Note that stringently constrained tags can ignore these ACK messages. Since these tags typically transmit at a very slow rate, their transmissions are unlikely to cause collisions, so it is sufficient to slow down the faster nodes to reduce bit errors.

4. IMPLEMENTATION

In this section, we describe key implementation details not covered in earlier sections. We use the USRP N210 software defined radios and UMass Moo backscatter sensors for our instantiation of LF-Backscatter.

4.1 Platforms

The hardware platform is shown in figure 7.

USRP Reader LF-Backscatter is built based on the USRP N210 software radio reader developed by [24] with SBX RF daughterboards and Cushcraft 900 MHz antennas [1]. The SBX daughterboard has two RF interfaces where one (TX/RX) of them can be configured for either transmission or reception and the other (RX2) can only be configured as reception. The sampling rate at the reception antenna is set as 25MHz.

Backscatter node The UMass Moo is a backscatter node that operates in the 902MHz ~ 928MHz band. Our decoding method can tolerate roughly 200ppm of clock drift, so we need to use an external low-drift crystal oscillator rather than the built-in internal DCO on the Moo which has a typical drift of 40,000ppm (4% of the DCO clock speed [2]). The Moo has a low drift 32kHz external oscillator which we can use for decoding, but we replace this with a 8MHz oscillator to be able to experiment with higher speeds [3]. The clock we use has a typical drift of 150ppm.

4.2 Baselines

We compare LF-Backscatter with the following two baseline schemes:

- **TDMA:** We use a stripped down version of EPC Gen 2 where we remove a significant fraction of its protocol overhead (which is often substantial [10]), and keep the essential elements for TDMA operation. Following the EPC Gen 2 standard, we assume that slots are 96 bits long, and the bitrate is 100 kbps.
- **Buzz:** We also compare LF-Backscatter with Buzz [22]. Based on details in the paper, we reproduce the Buzz implementation including the tag-side code on the UMass Moo and reader-side decoding algorithms. The results from our implementation are comparable to numbers shown in [22], so we believe this is a faithful reproduction of their protocol. As with the TDMA scheme, each sensor transmits a 96-bit message each time at a bit rate of 100 kbps.

5. EVALUATION

Our goal in this evaluation is to demonstrate that LF-Backscatter can provide significant improvements in performance across three axes — throughput, latency, and energy.

5.1 Concurrent Transmission Goodput

Our first set of experiments looks at the benefits of LF-Backscatter in terms of throughout. We deploy sixteen backscatter tags at different locations roughly two meters from a backscatter reader, and select subsets of these tags for different experiments.

Aggregate throughput In the first experiment, we fix the bitrate of all the nodes to 100Kbps (since this rate can support most high-rate sensors), and increase the number of nodes from 4 to 16.

Figure 8 compares the aggregate throughput achieved by different schemes — LF-Backscatter achieves very close to the maximum possible throughput in all cases. The aggregate throughput is marginally lower than the maximum for the 12 and 16 node cases, but the difference is small. The throughput benefits are huge — when 16 nodes are present, LF-Backscatter is 16.4× better than TDMA and 7.9× better than Buzz.

Breaking down the benefits Let us now break down aggregate throughput by the different components of our design to see how much each of them matters.

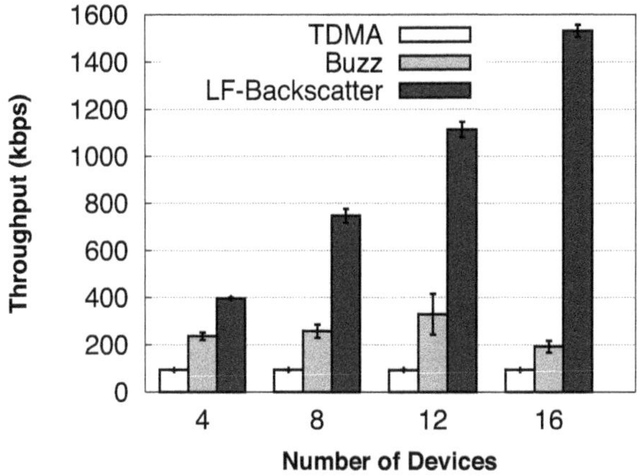

Figure 8: Comparison of throughput achieved by TDMA, Buzz, and LF-Backscatter when the number of nodes increases.

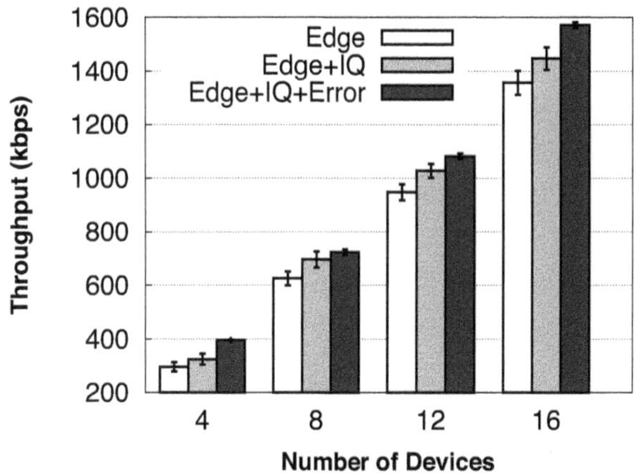

Figure 9: Breakdown of each decoding module's contribution to LF-Backscatter's throughput.

Figure 9 shows the breakdown — we start with an approach that uses only edge-based concurrency, then we add IQ cluster-based collision detection and separation, and finally we add error correction methods. We see that each of these benefits overall throughput — edge-based concurrency does really well by itself, but there's more error as the number of nodes increases.. For example, edge-based concurrency leaves about 15.3% of the throughput on the table for the 16 node case. Collision recovery improves throughput by about 5.6%, and adding error correction improves it by another 7.7%. Thus, all three design components play a crucial role in getting throughput to be close to the maximum.

Varying bitrate We can support sixteen nodes at 100 Kbps, but how far can we push it before we are unable to pack any more edges? Since we're limited in terms of number of available nodes, we instead vary the bit-rate of the sixteen nodes, and plot the aggregate throughput. Figure 10 shows that the aggregate

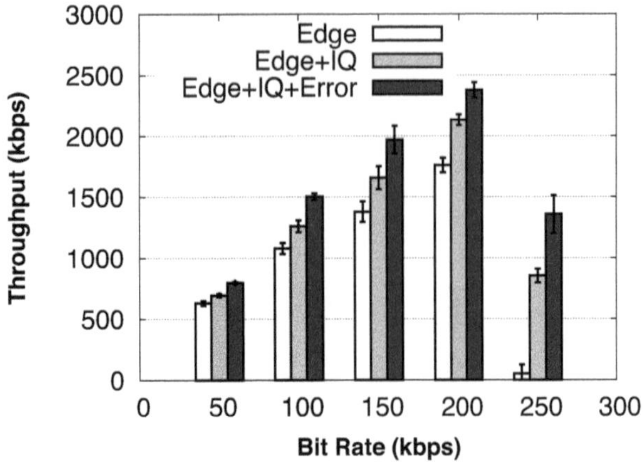

Figure 10: LF-Backscatter throughput when nodes transmit at different bit rates.

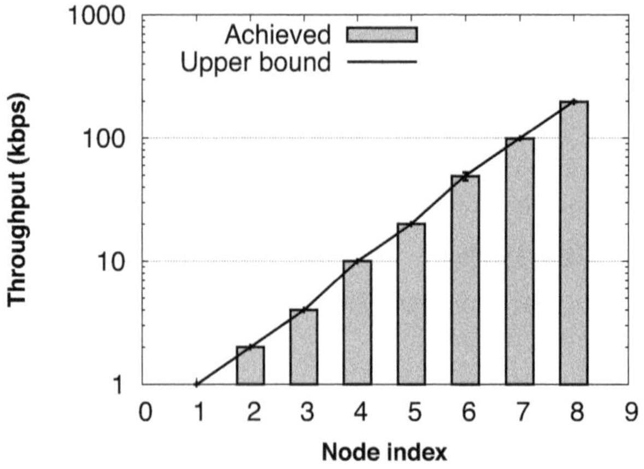

Figure 11: Throughput when a mix of nodes at different bitrates transfer concurrently. (y-axis in logscale)

Table 2: Separating edge collisions with IQ-based classification.

Setting	Accuracy
100 Kbps with background nodes	80.88%
100 Kbps w/o background nodes	86.89%
10 Kbps w/o background nodes	95.40%

throughput crashes after about 200 Kbps, so this gives us an empirical upper bound on the extent of concurrency we can support. The crash is not surprising. Our reader samples at 25 Mega samples/second, and tags transmit at 250 Kbps, so we can pack 33 nodes if their edges were stacked one after the other. Our deployment has 16 nodes, so there is a huge number of edge collisions. It is also interesting to note that the IQ cluster-based recovery and error correction are very useful as the bit-rate increases. Indeed, they pull throughput back to a respectable level at 250 Kbps even though practically all edges are colliding.

The result can be viewed from two lenses. From the perspective of wireless sensors, the result is very positive — concurrent transfer from 16 nodes at 200 Kbps is at least an order of magnitude better than what we can achieve from virtually all low power active radios in the market today, at a fraction of the power consumption. In addition, scalability to a few tens of nodes within a single communication range is often more than sufficient for typical sensor network or IoT deployments that currently rely on technologies like 802.15.4 or Bluetooth Low Energy. From the perspective of RFID deployments that target detection of hundreds or thousands of tags in a pallet, our solution is not ideal since our scalability is limited by our ability to interleave signal edges in the time-domain.

IQ cluster-based separation Let us take a closer look at IQ cluster-based separation, and see under what conditions it works and when it doesn't. Intuitively, our ability to separate depends on the relative distance between IQ vectors of the nodes that collide, which in turn depends on the placement of the nodes. To understand this, we place 16 nodes at different locations in front of a reader, and choose different pairs of nodes to transmit such that *all their edges collide*. We then try three cases: a) the two nodes transmit at 100Kbps, and there are 14 other nodes chattering away in the background, b) the two nodes transmit at 100Kbps, and there are no other tags transmitting in the background, and c) the two nodes transmit at 10Kbps, and there is no background transmissions. The three cases cover the effect of background as well as the effect of averaging noise (since edge decoding is more robust when edges are less frequent as described in §3)

Table 2 shows how well we can separate collided edges in different cases. Our classification accuracy is above 80% in all cases, with the lowest accuracy being in the case when there is a lot of background chatter. This is to be expected, since more nodes in the background increases the noise floor and results in a noisy edge differential, which in turn impacts accuracy. Removing background improves accuracy by 6%. Reducing the bit-rate improves accuracy by another 8.5% because we are able to average the edge differential over more samples (i.e. more samples before the edge and after the edge), so this helps improve SNR.

Co-existence of slow and fast tags So far, we have assumed that all tags are transmitting at the same rate but one of the key benefits of LF-Backscatter is that it can support widely different bitrates, ranging from ultra-low power tags to high-rate tags. To evaluate this benefit, we let two node transmit at each of the following eight sets of bitrates starting from slow to fast — 0.5 Kbps, 1 Kbps, 2 Kbps, 5 Kbps, 10 Kbps, 50 Kbps, and 100 Kbps.

Figure 11 shows the throughput achieved by each node. The results show that the slow nodes are not adversely impacted by the fast nodes, and have a loss rate of zero. This shows that LF-Backscatter supports sufficient concurrency that it can deal with nodes with widely varying data rates that we would typically expect from backscatter-based sensors.

5.2 Node Identification Time

While throughout is important in sensor data transfer scenarios, a canonical application of backscatter is to quickly read RFID identifiers in a shopping cart or warehouse. The performance metric of interest in this case is latency of reads. In general, higher throughout must mean lower latency for reading the identifier of tags, but one additional consideration is that we need to read identifiers in a reliable manner.

The node identification protocol that we build on LF-Backscatter works as follows. Each node transmits its EPC Gen 2 identifier (96 bits + 5 bit CRC) in each epoch with a random offset. Each tag starts at the highest bitrate (100Kbps), and at the end of the epoch, the reader can optionally send a command to use a lower bitrate if it observes too many collisions.

Figure 12 shows the identification time for different number of tags in front of a reader (up to 16). We see that the identification time is 17× lower than TDMA and 9.5× lower than Buzz, which means that RFID identification using our protocol can be considerably faster than existing techniques.

While we do not have hardware to experiment with more than 16 tags, we expect LF-Backscatter to scale quite easily to a larger number of tags. One easy approach is to set bitrate to a lower number, say 10kbps, and allow LF-Backscatter RFIDs to concurrently transmit their ID. In this setting, we can not only support a few hundred tags, we can also enable longer-range operation since the hardware is simpler than passive RFIDs (no decoding overhead, and much less complex circuit). We would also eliminate the achilles heel of TDMA-based RFID identification, which is the estimation of number of tags. It is well known that EPC Gen 2 has enormous overheads due to inexact cardinality estimation. While Buzz does not need cardinality estimation either, it assumes that channel coefficients of nodes are sufficiently distinct to separate, but this assumption may not hold as one scales the number of nodes.

5.3 Energy efficiency and tag complexity

Our third performance metric is energy-efficiency. It is hard to overstate the importance of energy-efficiency for harvesting-based sensors — operating range, throughput, latency, cost, deployability, size, and a variety of other metrics are inexorably connected with energy. The ability to design tags that operate at extremely low power is one of the key reasons to use LF-Backscatter.

To evaluate energy-efficiency, we first construct an FPGA-based implementation of LF-Backscatter so that we can fully understand its hardware complexity and measure power consumption. We implement LF-Backscatter and Buzz [22] in Verilog, and compare the number of transistors used by these protocols against a publicly available EPC Gen 2 implementation in Verilog [23]. All of our implementations currently support only a single bit-rate — while bit-rate adaptation can be added to all implementations, its overhead is similar across the three schemes, and would not affect the conclusions.

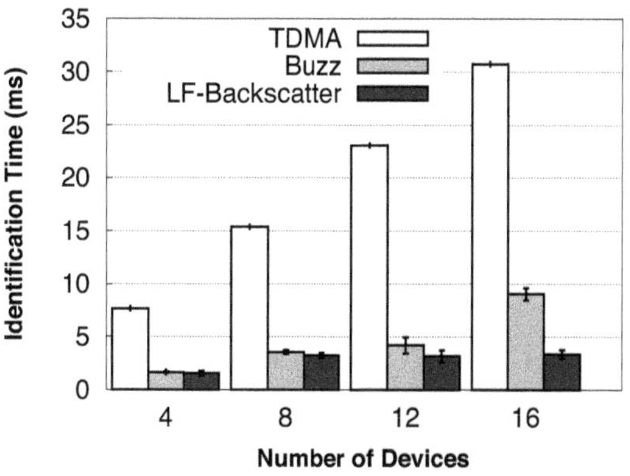

Figure 12: Node identification time when TDMA, Buzz, and LF-Backscatter are used for inventorying RFID tags.

Table 3: Hardware complexity of RFID chip, Buzz, and LF-Backscatter

Num of transistors	w/o FIFO	1k FIFO
RFID chip	22704	34992
Buzz	1792	14080
LF-Backscatter	176	176

Table 3 shows the results. EPC Gen 2 (TDMA) and Buzz need a packet buffer — the former to buffer sensor samples between transmission slots, and the latter to ensure that samples are not lost while bits are retransmitted in lock-step. This increases their complexity, so we provide results with and without the packet buffer. The results show a dramatic difference in hardware complexity — LF-Backscatter requires an order of magnitude fewer transistors than Buzz, and two orders of magnitude fewer transistors than EPC Gen 2, validating our claim that our protocol simplifies hardware design of tags.

Reduced hardware complexity typically implies lower power consumption, so lets look at the communication efficiency of the different protocol + hardware combinations. We obtain power numbers for the different hardware architectures from a SPICE simulation of our Verilog code, and we use throughputs from Figure 8 to calculate communication efficiency. Since the power consumption of EPC Gen 2 and Buzz depend on

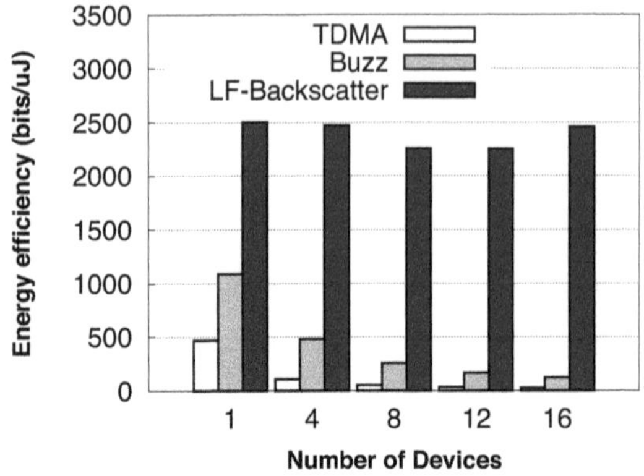

Figure 13: Energy efficiency (bits/μJ) of TDMA, Buzz, and LF-Backscatter.

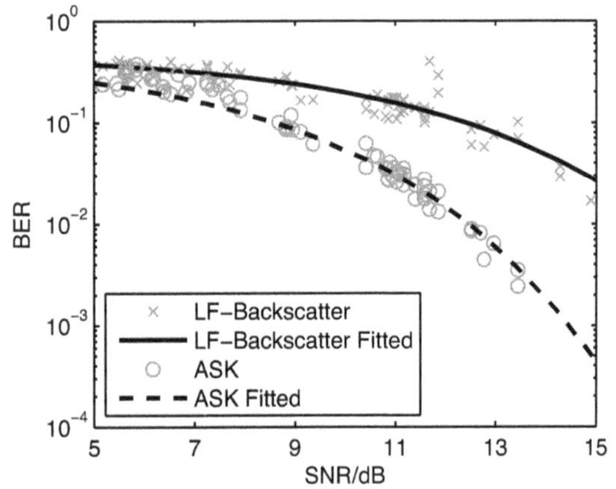

Figure 14: SNR vs BER of LF-Backscatter vs ASK. X-axis is cropped at SNR of 15dB after which BER goes to zero for both schemes.

the number of nodes that are transmitting, we vary the number of nodes from one to 16 and evaluate the power consumption for different approaches.

Figure 13 shows that LF-Backscatter is about 20× higher than Buzz and two orders of magnitude higher than EPC Gen 2 in terms of energy-efficiency. This benefit has huge implications — a 20× reduction in power consumption would mean roughly doubling the range at which the tags get sufficient energy from the reader, or alternately that 20× more data can be transmitted at the same distance. Either way, this is a big win.

5.4 SNR: LF-Backscatter vs ASK

LF-Backscatter has several benefits as described above, but trades off some robustness in the process since it relies on edge detection and requires higher SNR than ASK modulation. To evaluate the tradeoff, we compare the bit-error rates of the two decoding schemes for a single tag transmitting across many distances and reader power levels. We focus on the low SNR regime, which is where we might expect to observe less robustness for LF-Backscatter decoding. Figure 14 shows that there is a difference of approximately 4dB between LF-Backscatter and ASK in terms achieving equivalent bit error rates until the SNR reaches about 15dB, after which the bit error rate drops to zero.

To evaluate the impact of this SNR gap on range, lets consider the classical radar equation [19] used to determine backscatter link budget

$$P_r = P_t G_t^2 (\frac{\lambda}{4\pi d})^4 G_{tag}^2 K$$

where P_r is the received signal strength at the reader, P_t is the power of transmitted signal, G_t is the gain of transmit antenna, λ is the wavelength of received signal, d is the distance between transmit antenna and tag, G_{tag} is the gain of antenna at tag side, and K is the modulation loss of the tag. With this equation, we can calculate that if a tag has a working range of 10ft with ASK, it will have an equivalent range of 8.1ft with LF-Backscatter. Similarity, LF-Backscatter will have a working range of 23.7ft if a tag works 30ft with ASK. Thus, we expect LF-Backscatter to be effective for most of the working range of ASK modulation but at the higher end of the operating range, we need to switch from LF-Backscatter to ASK to improve robustness.

6. RELATED WORK

We discuss related work that we have not touched upon in the previous sections.

Concurrent transfer with active radios Much recent work has explored the problem of concurrent wireless communication with active radios such as WiFi [11, 9], typically using Successive Interference Cancelation (SIC). However, SIC requires significant difference in the SNR level of the collided signals, hence it only applies to limited scenarios [18]. Methods like ZigZag [9] may, however, be useful if we use reliable transfer and nodes repeat the same bits in different epochs.

Alternate modulation schemes While backscatter is predominantly based on ASK modulation which is the basis for our work, other methods like Frequency Shift Keying (FSK) or Quadrature Amplitude Modulation (QAM) are also possible [20]. FSK is less efficient than ASK since it requires multiple edge transitions for each bit, so the energy efficiency and throughput of LF-Backscatter is certainly better. QAM could have similar throughput but it is certain to involve considerably more complex hardware at the tag (consequently more power), as well as more hardware complexity at the reader (consequently more expensive).

Fit with other backscatter systems There have been many exciting new ideas for backscatter-based applications including backscatter of TV or FM signals for credit card transactions [16], gesture recognition using backscatter [14], backscatter with WiFi routers [13], etc. While mileage may vary depending on extent of concurrency that is needed, several of these cases can leverage the ideas in LF-Backscatter to reduce tag complexity, increase throughput, improve energy-efficiency, etc.

EPC Gen 2 Much work on backscatter has focused on addressing issues with EPC Gen 2 (e.g. [10, 24, 25, 27]). While EPC Gen 2 is here to stay, we think it shouldn't limit us from exploring new designs. Indeed, LF-Backscatter allows considerably more efficient tag designs, and lower latencies than EPC Gen 2, so we think there is much to be gained from this exploration.

7. CONCLUSION

In this paper, we introduce LF-Backscatter, a novel asymmetric communication paradigm for backscatter that pushes all the complexity to the reader, and enables tags to communicate virtually without restriction. We think that this is an important design point in backscatter communication, and the laissez-faire approach at the tag has significant ramifications in terms of designing lower power and perhaps lower cost backscatter sensors, while simultaneously being able to support high-speed concurrent backscatter communication. Our experimental results show benefits in many way that backscatter may be used, whether for high-throughput transfer, low-latency reads, or highly energy-efficient tags, typically by an order of magnitude or more over existing schemes.

Acknowledgement

We thank our shepherd Dina Katabi for providing guidance in preparing our final draft and the anonymous reviewers for their insightful comments. This research was partially funded by NSF grants CNS-1218586, CNS-1217606, CNS-1239341, and NIH grant 1U54EB020404.

8. REFERENCES

[1] Laird Technologies. Crushcraft S9028PCRW RFID antenna. http://www.arcadianinc.com/.

[2] MSP430 Mixed Signal Microcontroller. http://www.ti.com/lit/ds/symlink/msp430f2418.pdf.

[3] NX3225GD: 8MHz crystal clock. http://www.ndk.com/images/products/catalog/c_NX3225GD-STD-CRA-3_e.pdf.

[4] PCF8523 real-time clock (RTC) with calendar. http://www.nxp.com/documents/data_sheet/PCF8523.pdf.

[5] Radio-Frequency Identity Protocols Class-1 Generation-2. http://www.gs1.org/gsmp/kc/epcglobal/uhfc1g2.

[6] C. Angerer, R. Langwieser, and M. Rupp. Rfid reader receivers for physical layer collision recovery. *Communications, IEEE Transactions on*, 58(12):3526–3537, 2010.

[7] M. Buettner, B. Greenstein, and D. Wetherall. Dewdrop: An energy-aware runtime for computational rfid. In *NSDI*, 2011.

[8] K. Finkenzeller. Rfid handbook: Fundamentals and applications in contactless smart cards and identification, 2003.

[9] S. Gollakota and D. Katabi. *Zigzag decoding: combating hidden terminals in wireless networks*, volume 38. ACM, 2008.

[10] J. Gummeson, P. Zhang, and D. Ganesan. Flit: a bulk transmission protocol for rfid-scale sensors. In *Proceedings of the 10th international conference on Mobile systems, applications, and services*, pages 71–84. ACM, 2012.

[11] D. Halperin, T. Anderson, and D. Wetherall. Taking the sting out of carrier sense: interference cancellation for wireless lans. In *MobiCom 2008*, pages 339–350. ACM, 2008.

[12] L. Kang, K. Wu, J. Zhang, H. Tan, and L. M. Ni. Ddc: A novel scheme to directly decode the collisions in uhf rfid systems. *Parallel and Distributed Systems, IEEE Transactions on*, 23(2):263–270, 2012.

[13] B. Kellogg, A. Parks, S. Gollakota, J. R. Smith, and D. Wetherall. Wi-fi backscatter: internet connectivity for rf-powered devices. In *Proceedings of the 2014 ACM conference on SIGCOMM*, pages 607–618. ACM, 2014.

[14] B. Kellogg, V. Talla, and S. Gollakota. Bringing gesture recognition to all devices. In *Usenix NSDI*, volume 14, 2014.

[15] L. Kong, L. He, Y. Gu, M.-Y. Wu, and T. He. A parallel identification protocol for rfid systems. *Infocom*, 2014.

[16] V. Liu, A. Parks, V. Talla, S. Gollakota, D. Wetherall, and J. R. Smith. Ambient backscatter: wireless communication out of thin air. In *Proceedings of the ACM SIGCOMM 2013 conference on SIGCOMM*, pages 39–50. ACM, 2013.

[17] A. N. Parks, A. Liu, S. Gollakota, and J. R. Smith. Turbocharging ambient backscatter communication. In *Proceedings of the 2014 ACM conference on SIGCOMM*, pages 619–630. ACM, 2014.

[18] S. Sen, N. Santhapuri, R. R. Choudhury, and S. Nelakuditi. Successive interference cancellation: a back-of-the-envelope perspective. In *Proceedings of the 9th ACM SIGCOMM Workshop on Hot Topics in Networks*, page 17. ACM, 2010.

[19] M. I. Skolnik. Introduction to radar. *Radar Handbook*, 2, 1962.

[20] S. J. Thomas and M. S. Reynolds. A 96 mbit/sec, 15.5 pj/bit 16-qam modulator for uhf backscatter communication. In *RFID 2012*, pages 185–190. IEEE, 2012.

[21] D. Tse and P. Viswanath. *Fundamentals of wireless communication*. Cambridge university press, 2005.

[22] J. Wang, H. Hassanieh, D. Katabi, and P. Indyk. Efficient and reliable low-power backscatter networks. *ACM SIGCOMM*, 42(4):61–72, 2012.

[23] D. Yeager, F. Zhang, A. Zarrasvand, N. T. George, T. Daniel, and B. P. Otis. A 9 a, addressable gen2 sensor tag for biosignal acquisition. *Solid-State Circuits, IEEE Journal of*, 45(10):2198–2209, 2010.

[24] P. Zhang and D. Ganesan. Enabling bit-by-bit backscatter communication in severe energy harvesting environments. In *USENIX NSDI 2014*.

[25] P. Zhang, J. Gummeson, and D. Ganesan. Blink: a high throughput link layer for backscatter communication. In *MobiSys'10*, pages 99–112. ACM, 2012.

[26] P. Zhang, P. Hu, V. Kumar, and D. Ganesan. Ekhonet: High speed ultra low-power backscatter for next generation sensors. In *ACM Mobicom 2014*.

[27] Y. Zheng and M. Li. Read bulk data from computational rfids. *IEEE Infocom*, 2014.

SpotFi: Decimeter Level Localization Using WiFi

Manikanta Kotaru, Kiran Joshi, Dinesh Bharadia, Sachin Katti
Stanford University
Stanford, CA, USA
{mkotaru, krjoshi, dineshb, skatti}@stanford.edu

ABSTRACT

This paper presents the design and implementation of SpotFi, an accurate indoor localization system that can be deployed on commodity WiFi infrastructure. SpotFi only uses information that is already exposed by WiFi chips and does not require any hardware or firmware changes, yet achieves the same accuracy as state-of-the-art localization systems. SpotFi makes two key technical contributions. First, SpotFi incorporates super-resolution algorithms that can accurately compute the angle of arrival (AoA) of multipath components even when the access point (AP) has only three antennas. Second, it incorporates novel filtering and estimation techniques to identify AoA of direct path between the localization target and AP by assigning values for each path depending on how likely the particular path is the direct path. Our experiments in a multipath rich indoor environment show that SpotFi achieves a median accuracy of 40 cm and is robust to indoor hindrances such as obstacles and multipath.

CCS Concepts

•**Information systems** → **Location based services;** *Sensor networks; Global positioning systems;* •**Networks** → **Location based services;**

Keywords

Indoor localization; Wireless; WiFi; OFDM; CSI

1. INTRODUCTION

Indoor localization systems using WiFi infrastructure should ideally satisfy the following three requirements:

- **Deployable**: They should be easily deployable on existing commodity WiFi infrastructure without requiring any hardware or firmware changes at the access points (APs); they should only work with information like RSSI and CSI (Channel State Information) that is already exposed by commodity, deployed APs.

SIGCOMM '15, August 17 - 21, 2015, London, United Kingdom

 ISBN 978-1-4503-3542-3/15/08...$15.00

DOI: http://dx.doi.org/10.1145/2785956.2787487

- **Universal**: They should be able to localize any target device that has a commodity WiFi chip and nothing else. They should not require the target to have any other hardware, be it sensors such as accelerometers, gyroscopes, barometers, cameras, etc., or radios such as UWB, ultrasound, Bluetooth LE, etc.
- **Accurate**: They should be accurate, ideally as accurate as the best known localization systems that use wireless signals (even including those that do not satisfy the above two requirements). To the best of our knowledge, the most accurate such localization systems are ArrayTrack [1] and Ubicarse [2] and these systems achieve an accuracy ranging from 30–50 cm in office environments. Achieving such accuracy would be the target.

If the above three requirements are satisfied, we can imagine indoor localization becoming a ubiquitous service like GPS that can be installed on *already deployed WiFi infrastructure* and made available to any device with a WiFi chip.

However, to the best of our knowledge, no system that satisfies all three requirements exists. RSSI based systems are deployable and universal, but are not accurate; their median accuracy ranges from 2–4 m [3, 4, 5]. Recent techniques that rely on angle of arrival (AoA) estimation such as ArrayTrack and LTEye [6] are accurate and universal but are not deployable as they require hardware modifications. For example, ArrayTrack uses six to eight antennas whereas typical APs have three, and LTEye requires motorized rotating antennas which are not found on deployed APs. Other techniques that combine inputs from multiple sensors such as Ubicarse [2] are accurate and deployable but not universal; they require that the target device has access to other sensing modes such as accelerometers, gyroscopes, etc., which would not be found on many devices (e.g., laptops, Nest thermostats). We refer the reader to Sec. 2 for a more detailed survey of related work and where different systems lie with respect to the above requirements.

The main contribution of this paper is a localization system that satisfies all the three requirements above. We present SpotFi, an indoor localization system that provides a median accuracy of 40 cm using standard, commodity off-the-shelf WiFi radios, which is comparable to the best performing systems such as ArrayTrack [1] and Ubicarse [2]. SpotFi requires no hardware or baseband firmware changes/additions at the APs, nor does it need any calibration or fingerprinting of the environment. SpotFi's localization targets also have minimal requirements, they only require a commodity WiFi chip.

SpotFi incorporates three techniques that enable it to achieve this combination of accuracy and deployment simplicity:

- **Super-resolution AoA Estimation**: The first component of SpotFi is a super-resolution AoA estimation algorithm, i.e., it accurately resolves all the AoAs of the indoor multipath in spite of using just three antennas which is standard in WiFi deployments today. The number of antennas limits the number of multipath components that one can resolve. As prior work has noted [1, 2, 7, 8, 9], the more antennas there are, more multipath AoAs can be resolved more accurately. Our insight is that the multipath not only creates measurable changes in CSI across antennas because of AoA but also affects CSI across subcarriers because of time of flight (ToF, time taken by the signal to reach the AP from the localization target).
Using this fact, instead of just estimating AoA, SpotFi combines CSI values across subcarriers and antennas to jointly estimate AoA and ToF of each path. In the process, SpotFi creates a virtual sensor array with number of elements greater than the number of multipath components, thus overcoming the constraint of limited antennas. Our unique insight here is that these joint AoA and ToF estimation algorithms can be implemented using the CSI information that is already exposed by the commodity WiFi cards. Using the AoA and ToF parameters estimated from CSI, we empirically demonstrate that, in commodity WiFi deployments, although the estimated ToF values are different from the absolute ToFs, the joint estimation procedure provides AoA accuracy that is comparable to systems that require twice as many antennas [8] or non-standard configurations such as rotating antennas used in radar [6, 2].
- **Robust Direct Path Identification**: SpotFi aims to find the AoA of the direct path component in the multipath signal from the target. However among the AoA estimates from the previous algorithm, the one corresponding to the direct path may be erroneous or may not even exist due to several practical reasons such as noisy CSI, obstructed targets, weak signal strength from the target and so on. The second key component of SpotFi is a novel algorithm that assigns values for each path depending on the likelihood that the particular path is the direct path. This metric assignment algorithm enables SpotFi to eliminate AoA estimates that are very likely to be in error and not belonging to the direct path component, thereby avoiding making large errors in localization.
- **Localization**: The final step is a localization algorithm that incorporates both the direct path AoA estimate from the above two steps as well as RSSI information available from each of the APs to calculate the location of the target. Our key contribution here is a framework that appropriately weights the information from different APs to take into account how likely it is that the AoA measurement reported by each AP corresponds to the actual direct path between the target and that AP. This weighting of information enables SpotFi to select information from APs with higher confidence metric and improve accuracy.

We implemented SpotFi using Intel 5300 commodity WiFi cards. We strived to evaluate it under the same environments as the best performing systems ArrayTrack and Ubicarse [1, 2]; we describe the testbed in Sec. 4. Our experiments show that SpotFi achieves a median localization error of 40 cm, and the 80th percentile error is 1.8 m. To put these numbers in context, the best performing prior system achieves a median error of 40 cm using 6 antennas per AP, whereas our APs have only three. We also show that SpotFi works robustly in challenging scenarios; for example, it achieves very good accuracy even when the target has strong direct paths to only a couple of APs. Finally, we also show that SpotFi is lightweight and requires CSI measurements for only ten packets from the target to localize accurately.

2. RELATED WORK

Indoor localization using wireless infrastructure is a well-studied problem. There is a large body of research which, for conciseness, we classify into four types: RSSI based, fingerprinting based, antenna array based, and time based techniques.

RSSI based approaches: This class of systems measures the RSSI from the target at multiple APs, combines them via triangulation along with a propagation model to locate the target [3, 10, 4, 5, 11, 12, 13]. These systems are easy to deploy as RSSI values are easily available in current APs. However the best known systems in this space tend to achieve a median accuracy of around 2–4 m [3, 4], and the 80th percentile error is often as high as 5 m due to insufficient modeling of RSSI which in practice depends not only on the location of the target but also on the changing environment.

Fingerprinting based approaches: The idea of these approaches is that one would collect fingerprints such as the vector of RSSIs from a specific location to all the APs in range, and if in the future a target were at the same location, it would exhibit the same fingerprint, enabling us to localize [14, 15, 16, 17, 18, 19, 20, 21, 22]. The best known such systems provide around 0.6 m of median accuracy [14], and tail accuracy on the order of 1.3 m. However these systems are difficult to deploy since they require an expensive and recurring fingerprinting operation any time there are changes in the environment (e.g., when the furniture is moved).

AoA based approaches: With the proliferation of WiFi APs with multiple antennas to support MIMO communications, antenna array based techniques which use multiple antennas at the AP have gained interest recently. The basic idea of these systems is to calculate the AoAs of the multipath signals received at each AP, find the AoA of the direct path to the target, and then apply triangulation to localize [1, 2, 6, 23, 24, 8, 25]. The best known such systems have demonstrated significant improvements in accuracy with median accuracy on the order of 0.4 m [1, 2]. However these systems are relatively difficult to deploy, since they require hardware changes by introducing as high as 8 antennas [1, 8], or new boxes itself with rotating antennas [6], or require special APs to access IQ samples [1, 24].

There are other recently proposed systems that use sensors such as gyroscopes, accelerometers, etc., along with AoA

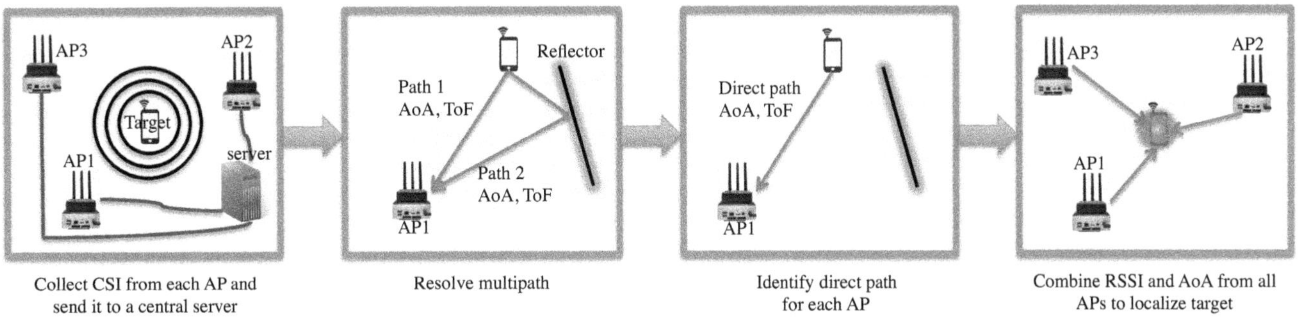

Figure 1: Overall architecture: SpotFi collects CSI and RSSI measurements from all the APs that can hear the packet transmitted by the target. In the first step, SpotFi calculates the ToF and AoA of all the propagation paths from the target to each of the APs. SpotFi then identifies the direct path between the target and the AP that did not undergo any reflections. In the final step, SpotFi estimates the location of the target by using the direct path AoA estimates and RSSI measurements from all the APs.

information [2, 23]. While these sensors are available on some phones, their accuracy varies widely across different phone models. Further there are a large number of devices that may only have a WiFi/Bluetooth chip but none of these other sensors, e.g., wearables or IoT devices such as Nest, wireless cameras, and suitcases [26, 27, 28], that would like to avail of localization capability if possible. Moreover, Ubicarse [2] requires that the human holding the device perform a specific circular motion to enable localization which is not feasible in many scenarios where localization is needed (e.g., locating misplaced or lost objects).

Time based approaches: Systems that use timestamps reported by WiFi cards can obtain time of flight at a granularity of several nanoseconds, resulting in ranging error of few meters [29, 30, 31, 32, 33, 34]. In spite of hardware/firmware modifications to overcome coarse ToF estimates, the best known systems achieve localization error of 2 m [32, 33, 30]. Some systems applied super-resolution algorithms to obtain finer ToF estimates, but require all the APs to be time synchronized [35, 36, 37, 38, 39], which is hard to achieve using commodity WiFi [40]. Algorithms for joint estimation of AoA and ToF, to improve the accuracy of both the parameter estimates, have been developed [41, 42, 43, 44, 45], and tested in simulation [46, 47, 48, 49, 50]. But these algorithms have been implemented in systems where the transmitter and receiver radios are time synchronized [51, 52], which is not possible in commodity WiFi deployments.

Other approaches: For completeness, we refer to localization systems that deploy other modalities like RFIDs [53, 54, 55], ultrawideband [56], ultrasound [57, 58, 59, 60, 61], IR [62, 63, 64], visible light [65, 66] or beacons like the ones Apple recently introduced [67]. However, we believe that none of these are ever likely to be as ubiquitous as commodity WiFi AP infrastructure.

3. DESIGN

SpotFi works in three steps:

1. Estimate the angle of arrival (AoA) and time of flight (ToF) of different multipath components of a target's signal arriving at the AP by using the CSI information that is exposed by commodity WiFi APs.
2. Estimate the likelihood that each AoA and ToF pair is the one corresponding to the direct path between the AP and the target without any reflections.
3. Use the above information to calculate the most likely location of the target that could have produced the observed RSSI and estimated AoA.

Before we describe each step of the design in detail, we briefly discuss SpotFi's architecture. Fig. 1 shows how SpotFi would be deployed. A central server collects CSI measurements for each packet received at the APs. All the major WiFi chip families (Broadcom, Atheros, Intel, and Marvell) expose quantized CSI per subcarrier per antenna [23]. We use Intel 5300 WiFi chips in the current prototype because of the availability of CSI extraction software for these chips [68], but SpotFi can easily be deployed with WiFi APs that use chips from other manufacturers. SpotFi only adds the software required to read the reported CSI values, timestamps, and MAC addresses at the AP and ships it to the central server and nothing else. Hence we believe that SpotFi can be added to any existing, deployed WiFi AP. Also, like many other state-of-the-art localization systems, we assume that we know the locations of the APs themselves from offline, one-time measurements [1, 2, 23].

3.1 SpotFi's super-resolution algorithm for estimating AoA and ToF

A target's signal could reflect off multiple objects and arrive at the AP; typically in an indoor environment there are around 6-8 significant reflectors [69, 30, 70]. So the key question is, how might one be able to disentangle these multipath components and accurately estimate the AoA of each path even when the AP has only three antennas? To gain insight into how SpotFi solves the problem, it is helpful to understand how standard AoA computation with the well known MUSIC algorithm [7] works, which we review next.

3.1.1 Estimating AoA with MUSIC

The basic idea is that different propagation paths have different AoAs, and when the signal from a propagation path is received across an array of antennas, then the AoA will introduce a corresponding phase shift across the antennas in the array. The introduced phase shift is a function of both the distance between antennas and the AoA. To understand how MUSIC takes advantage of this fact to determine AoA,

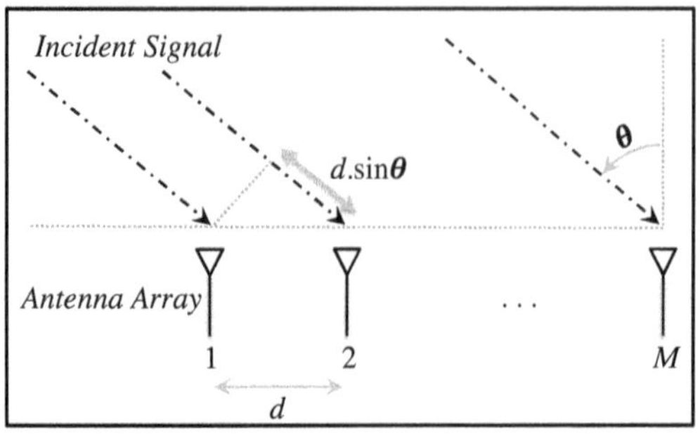

Figure 2: Uniform linear array consisting of M antennas: For AoA of θ, the target's signal travels an additional distance of $d\times \sin(\theta)$ to the second antenna in the array compared to the first antenna. This results in an additional phase of $-2\pi\times d\times \sin(\theta)\times f/c$ at the second antenna.

let's say there are L propagation paths. Let's assume that M antennas are arranged in a uniform linear array, similar to systems like ArrayTrack [1, 23], with equal spacing of d between consecutive antennas. For the kth propagation path, let θ_k denote the angle at which the signal is arriving with respect to the normal of the antenna array of the AP. Let γ_k denote the complex attenuation experienced at the first antenna in the array by the signal traveling along k^{th} propagation path. The attenuation at the second antenna in the array is the same except for an additional phase shift accumulated due to additional distance traveled by the signal, and depends on d and θ_k.

Each propagation path, therefore, has two parameters associated in this model: the attenuation and the AoA. As described in Sec. 2 of ArrayTrack [1] and illustrated in Fig. 2, relative to the first antenna in the array, the phase shift introduced at m^{th} antenna is $-2\times\pi\times d\times(m-1)\times \sin(\theta_k)\times f/c$ where c is the speed of light and f is the frequency of the transmitted signal. For simplicity of representation, let us denote the complex exponential of these introduced phase shifts as a function of the AoA of the propagation path,

$$\Phi(\theta_k) = \mathrm{e}^{-j2\pi\times d\times \sin(\theta_k)\times f/c}. \tag{1}$$

So the AoA can be thought of as introducing a vector of phase shifts at the antenna array (or the sensor array). The resulting vector of received signals due to k^{th} path can be written as $\vec{a}(\theta_k)\gamma_k$, where γ_k is the complex attenuation along the path experienced at the first antenna in the array and

$$\vec{a}(\theta_k) = [1\ \Phi(\theta_k)\ \dots\ \Phi(\theta_k)^{(M-1)}]^\top \tag{2}$$

using the notation introduced in Eq. 1. This vector $\vec{a}(\theta_k)$ is also known as the steering vector. We have as many steering vectors as propagation paths and the overall steering matrix $\mathbf{A}$ is defined as $\mathbf{A} = [\vec{a}(\theta_1),\ \dots,\ \vec{a}(\theta_L)]$, and has dimensions $M \times L$.

The received signal vector $\vec{x}$ at the antenna array is obtained by superposition of signals due to all the paths, i.e.,

$$\vec{x} = \mathbf{A}\vec{\Gamma}, \tag{3}$$

where $\vec{\Gamma} = [\gamma_1\ \dots\ \gamma_L]^\top$ is the vector of complex attenuations along L paths and $\mathbf{A}$ is the steering matrix. In OFDM, data is transmitted over multiple subcarriers each with different frequency. We can write an equation similar to Eq. 3 for each of the subcarriers, and the steering matrix $\mathbf{A}$ does not change because the steering vectors do not change across closely spaced subcarriers [7, 8]. Let us construct measurement matrix $\mathbf{X}$ by using received signal vectors for each of the N subcarriers using Eq. 4 below,

$$\mathbf{X} = [\vec{x}_1\ \dots\ \vec{x}_N] = \mathbf{A}[\vec{\Gamma}_1\ \dots\ \vec{\Gamma}_N] = \mathbf{AF}, \tag{4}$$

where vectors $\vec{x}_1,\ \dots,\ \vec{x}_N$ denote the received signal vectors at each of the subcarriers (correspond to $\vec{x}$ in Eq. 3 obtained for different subcarriers), $\vec{\Gamma}_1,\ \dots,\ \vec{\Gamma}_N$ are the vectors of complex attenuations of the propagation paths at each of the subcarriers (correspond to $\vec{\Gamma}$ in Eq. 3 obtained for different subcarriers), and $\mathbf{F}$ is the matrix of complex attenuations/gains.

The overall attenuation and phase shift introduced by the channel/environment measured at each subcarrier of each antenna is reported by the WiFi card as a CSI value (it's a complex number). For example, Eq. 5 represents a nominal CSI matrix reported by Intel 5300 WiFi card for 3 antennas and 30 subcarriers,

$$\text{CSI matrix} = \begin{bmatrix} \text{csi}_{1,1} & \text{csi}_{1,2} & \dots & \text{csi}_{1,30} \\ \text{csi}_{2,1} & \text{csi}_{2,2} & \dots & \text{csi}_{2,30} \\ \text{csi}_{3,1} & \text{csi}_{3,2} & \dots & \text{csi}_{3,30} \end{bmatrix}, \tag{5}$$

where $\text{csi}_{m,n}$ is the CSI value for m^{th} antenna and n^{th} subcarrier. Thus, the CSI value at each subcarrier is nothing but the received signal due to all the paths. Hence, for the AoA model described above, the received signal vector $\vec{x}$ in Eq. 3 corresponds to one of the columns in the CSI matrix and the measurement matrix $\mathbf{X}$ corresponds to the CSI matrix itself.

The MUSIC algorithm is working with this information and relationship; the WiFi card measurements provide us the matrix $\mathbf{X}$ and the goal is to estimate the matrix $\mathbf{A}$, from which it is easy to deduce the AoAs. The key idea behind the MUSIC algorithm is that *the eigenvectors of* $\mathbf{XX}^{\mathrm{H}}$ *corresponding to the eigenvalue zero, if they exist, are orthogonal to the steering vectors in* $\mathbf{A}$[1]. We omit the mathematical derivation for brevity but refer to the broad literature discussing these ideas [7]. The MUSIC algorithm at a basic level proceeds first by computing the eigenvectors of $\mathbf{XX}^{\mathrm{H}}$ corresponding to the eigenvalue zero, and then computing the steering vectors orthogonal to these vectors. Once the steering vectors are found, the AoAs can be deduced easily.

The key problem however is the assumption that there are eigenvectors of $\mathbf{XX}^{\mathrm{H}}$ that correspond to eigenvalue zero and that they are orthogonal to the steering vectors. Prior work has shown that it's true only if the steering matrix $\mathbf{A}$ is skinny and full rank matrix and the matrix $\mathbf{F}$ is fat and full rank matrix [7]. In other words the number of rows of steering matrix $\mathbf{A}$ should be larger than the number of columns in the matrix. Physically this maps to saying that the number of sensors (in this case antennas) has to be larger than the number of propagation paths. For example, if we have radios with only three antennas and environment where there

[1] $\mathbf{X}^{\mathrm{H}}$ is conjugate transpose of $\mathbf{X}$.

are more than three significant propagation paths (which is quite likely), the above algorithm doesn't work well. This is the reason past works have either used more antennas (eight in ArrayTrack [1]) or used rotating antennas to simulate a larger antenna array (e.g., LTEye [6]). Also, the number of columns of matrix **F** of complex gains should be greater than the number of its rows, i.e., number of measurements at the sensor array should be greater than the number of paths.

3.1.2 Super-Resolution AoA Estimation

How might one increase the resolution of AoA estimation? From the above discussion it's clear that the key factor is the number of sensors from which we can measure properties of the propagation paths and the number of independent measurements we can obtain at the sensor array. SpotFi's insight is that the number of sensors is not limited by the number of antennas, but in fact by leveraging the fact that WiFi has many OFDM subcarriers on each of which we get a CSI measurement, the number of sensors can be expanded to be equal to the product of the number of subcarriers and the number of antennas. For example, for Intel 5300 WiFi cards, number of sensors would be equal to $30 \times 3 = 90$ sensors rather than the 3 antennas with the modeling described in Sec. 3.1.1.

However, if each sensor in this extended sensor array is modeled to measure just AoAs of the paths, then the number of distinct values in our parametric model of sensor measurements is still limited by the number of antennas. This is because AoA of a propagation path does not manifest itself in any measurable way across subcarriers, i.e., AoA does not introduce any phase shift across subcarriers of an antenna. This is easy to see given that the relative phase shift introduced by AoA of the kth path across two subcarriers of the mth antenna is $2\pi(m-1)d(f_i - f_j)\sin(\theta_k)/c$, where f_i and f_j denote the frequencies of the two subcarriers. So, with half-wavelength antenna spacing, for two subcarriers of the second antenna separated by 40 MHz, any AoA introduces a phase shift of at most 0.002 radians which is negligible. Hence, phase shift due to AoA is same across all the subcarriers of an antenna since the speed of light factor in the denominator is much larger than this small frequency difference. So, although there are 90 subcarriers (from all three antennas combined) in Intel 5300 CSI measurements, only 2 distinct phase shifts are introduced due to AoA, since we compute phase shifts relative to the first antenna and there are three antennas.

Obtaining sensor array larger than the number of paths: SpotFi's key insight is counterintuitive. Instead of just estimating AoA per propagation path, SpotFi proposes to also calculate the time of flight (ToF) for each path. By definition each path will likely have a different ToF too. The reason to add ToF as a parameter for each path is that it introduces measurable phase shifts across subcarriers. For example the phase shift across two subcarriers even across the same antenna for the kth path with ToF τ_k is given by $2\pi(f_i - f_j)\tau_k$ which is significant (the reason numerically is the lack of the speed of light factor in the denominator). Here, f_i and f_j denote the frequencies of the two subcarriers as before. For example, for two subcarriers spaced apart by 40 MHz and for ToF of 10 ns, there is significant difference of 2.5 radians in the phase shift introduced at the two subcarriers. Specifically, for equispaced OFDM subcarriers, k^{th} path with ToF τ_k introduces a phase shift of $-2\times\pi\times(n-1)\times f_\delta\times\tau_k$ at the nth subcarrier relative to the first subcarrier of an antenna, where f_δ is the frequency spacing between two consecutive subcarriers. For simplicity of representation, let us denote the complex exponential of the phase shift introduced between two adjacent subcarriers as a function of the ToF,

$$\Omega(\tau_k) = \mathrm{e}^{-j2\times\pi\times f_\delta\times\tau_k}. \tag{6}$$

SpotFi exploits this insight to expand the number of sensors, and specifically design a steering matrix **A** that is skinny and enables the resolution of all the paths.

Specifically, consider the sensor array comprising of all the subcarriers at all the antennas. The measurement matrix **X** is constructed by stacking CSI from all the subcarriers at all the antennas, and hence is a single column matrix. Each propagation path introduces a distinct phase shift at each of the sensors depending both on its ToF and AoA. So, for a path with AoA θ and ToF τ, the steering vector, for the $M \times N$ sensors (M antennas times N subcarriers), is formed by phase shifts introduced at each of the sensors due to both AoA and ToF, and is given by:

$$\vec{a}(\theta,\tau) = [\overbrace{1,\ldots,\Omega_\tau^{N-1}}^{\text{antenna 1}}, \underbrace{\Phi_\theta,\ldots,\Omega_\tau^{N-1}\Phi_\theta}_{\text{antenna 2}},\ldots,\overbrace{\Phi_\theta^{M-1},\ldots,\Omega_\tau^{N-1}\Phi_\theta^{M-1}}^{\text{antenna M}}]^\top, \tag{7}$$

where $\Omega(\tau)$ is written as Ω_τ and $\Phi(\theta)$ as Φ_θ for brevity.

CSI at each sensor is a linear combination of the phase shifts introduced due to all the paths weighted by their attenuations. So, the newly constructed measurement matrix **X** is nothing but a linear combination of the steering vectors in Eq. 7 evaluated for all the paths. Note that phase of complex attenuation in the model described in Eq. 3 has the phase shift due to ToF absorbed into it and is different for different subcarriers, whereas here the phase of attenuation just depends on the objects that the signal interacted with along the path and is same for all the subcarriers of all the antennas. The steering matrix corresponding to this extended sensor array still has number of columns equal to the number of paths. We have thus increased the number of sensors without increasing the number of paths, i.e., we have achieved a skinny steering matrix **A** .

The other fact to note from the previous section's description of MUSIC is that the number of measurements at the sensor array, that can be written as linear combination of the *same steering vectors*, should be greater than the number of paths. However, the measurement matrix obtained by stacking CSI from all the subcarriers at all the antennas is a single column unit rank matrix. We now describe how we obtain a measurement matrix with number of columns greater than number of paths.

CSI smoothing: SpotFi's mathematical trick to obtain a sensor array with multiple independent measurements is best demonstrated through an example. Let's say there are $L = 2$

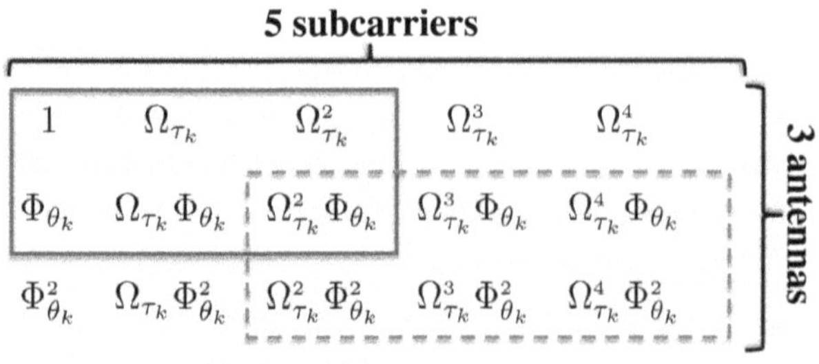

(a) Entries of the steering vector

$$\begin{bmatrix} csi_{1,1} & csi_{2,3} \\ csi_{1,2} & csi_{2,4} \\ csi_{1,3} & csi_{2,5} \\ csi_{2,1} & csi_{3,3} \\ csi_{2,2} & csi_{3,4} \\ csi_{2,3} & csi_{3,5} \end{bmatrix} = \begin{bmatrix} 1 & 1 \\ \Omega_{\tau_1} & \Omega_{\tau_2} \\ \Omega^2_{\tau_1} & \Omega^2_{\tau_2} \\ \Phi_{\theta_1} & \Phi_{\theta_2} \\ \Omega_{\tau_1}\Phi_{\theta_1} & \Omega_{\tau_2}\Phi_{\theta_2} \\ \Omega^2_{\tau_1}\Phi_{\theta_1} & \Omega^2_{\tau_2}\Phi_{\theta_2} \end{bmatrix} \begin{bmatrix} \alpha_1 & \alpha_1\Omega^2_{\tau_1}\Phi_{\theta_1} \\ \alpha_2 & \alpha_2\Omega^2_{\tau_2}\Phi_{\theta_2} \end{bmatrix}$$

CSI values at the two subarrays **Same steering matrix** **Independent vectors of gains**

(b) CSI values at the two sensor subarrays

Figure 3: (a) The elements of the steering vector in Eq. 7 for two subsets of sensors. The elements in the dashed red box (second sensor subarray) are obtained by scaling the corresponding elements in solid blue box (first subarray) by $\Omega^2(\tau_k)\Phi(\theta_k)$. Ω_{τ_k} represents $\Omega(\tau_k)$ and Φ_{θ_k} represents $\Phi(\theta_k)$. (b) $\text{csi}_{m,n}$ represents the CSI obtained at n^{th} subcarrier and m^{th} antenna. So, the two columns on the left hand side of the equation correspond to the CSI values obtained at the two sensor subarrays displayed in (a). CSI measurements obtained for the second sensor subarray are obtained by combining the same steering vectors as the first sensor subarray but with different independent vector of weights. The CSI measurements and the vector of gains corresponding to the first sensor subarray are colored blue and similarly the corresponding values for second sensor subarray are colored red.

paths. Consider the CSI at the subcarriers corresponding to two sensor subarrays displayed in the two columns of the matrix on the left hand side (LHS) of equation in Fig. 3(b). First sensor subarray, corresponding to the first column of Fig. 3(b), is comprised of first three subcarriers at antennas 1 and 2. The second sensor subarray, corresponding to the second column of Fig. 3(b), is comprised of subcarriers 3 to 5 at antennas 2 and 3. We will show in the following paragraphs that the measurements at these two sensor subarrays can be written as linear combination of the same vectors, but with different gains, as illustrated in Fig. 3(b). So, if we can identify L such sensor subarrays whose CSI values can be written as linear combination of same vectors, then the MUSIC algorithm can be applied on the measurement matrix obtained from the CSI measurements at these subarrays.

To gain intuition into why CSI at the two sensor subarrays shown in Fig. 3(b) can be written as linear combination of same vectors, let's look at the entries of steering vector in Eq. 7 evaluated for k^{th} propagation path as illustrated in Fig. 3(a). The phase shifts in the solid blue box correspond to the steering vector entries of the first sensor subarray and the phase shifts in the dashed red box correspond to those in the second sensor subarray. We observe that the phase shift between the corresponding elements of the two sensor subarrays are related through a common scaling factor. For example, phase shift of the top left sensor of second sensor subarray, i.e., subcarrier 3 at antenna 2, is obtained by multiplying phase shift at the top left sensor of the first sensor subarray, i.e., subcarrier 1 at antenna 1, by $\Omega^2(\tau_k)\Phi(\theta_k)$. This scaling factor is infact the phase shift term we would see for this propagation path for a shift of 2 subcarriers and 1 antenna, and is expected since both the sensor subarrays are structurally same except for a shift of 2 subcarriers and 1 antenna. The common scaling factor, $\Omega^2(\tau_k)\Phi(\theta_k)$, depends on the relative shift in antennas and subcarriers of the two sensor subarrays as well as the propagation path parameters, and hence is different for different paths. How can one exploit the above insight?

Let α_1 and α_2 be the complex gains along the two paths. We obtain CSI values at the sensors belonging to first subarray by weighing the corresponding steering vector entries for the two paths by their complex gains α_1 and α_2 (see Fig. 3(b)), and similarly for the second sensor subarray. However, by absorbing common scaling factor $\Omega^2(\tau_k)\Phi(\theta_k)$ into the complex gains at the second subarray, we can write the CSI values at the second sensor subarray by weighing the steering vector entries corresponding to first subarray for the two paths with the modified gains $\Omega^2(\tau_1)\Phi(\theta_1)\alpha_1$ and $\Omega^2(\tau_2)\Phi(\theta_2)\alpha_2$. The same is illustrated in Fig. 3(b). We have thus shown that CSI at these two sensor subarrays can be written as linear combination of the same vectors. Moreover, the vector of complex gains of the second subarray is linearly independent of the vector of the complex gains of first subarray, because attenuations corresponding to different paths are multiplied by different factors to obtain modified gains at the second subarray.

By generalizing these observations, one can prove that the CSI values at different sensor subarrays, that are obtained by shifting a fixed subset of sensors, can be written as linear combination of the same vectors. Infact, the steering vector entries of the fixed subset of sensors for different paths now form the steering matrix **A** and by combining the vectors of this steering matrix with different weights, we obtain CSI values at different sensor subarrays. So, if we construct a measurement matrix **X** using CSI values at different sensor subarrays that are structurally similar but shifted from each other, we can successfully apply MUSIC using this new measurement matrix **X**. Specifically, let's consider CSI measurements from Intel 5300 cards. SpotFi considers CSI values at sensor subarrays that are formed by different shifts of the fixed sensor subarray comprised of the first 15 subcarriers of first two antennas to construct the measurement matrix as illustrated in Fig. 4. We term this new measurement matrix **X** as *smoothed CSI* matrix. In this construction, steering matrix **A** is of dimensions $30 \times L$, where 30 rows is from the fact that each sensor subarray consists of the combinations of 15 subcarriers at 2 antennas and L is the number of propagation paths. The matrix **F**, due to the shifting trick, now has dimensions $L \times 30$, where 30 columns is from the fact that 30 is the maximum number of sensor subarrays we

$$\underset{\mathbf{CSI_{90x1}}}{\begin{bmatrix} \mathrm{csi}_{1,1} \\ \vdots \\ \mathrm{csi}_{1,30} \\ \mathrm{csi}_{2,1} \\ \vdots \\ \mathrm{csi}_{2,30} \\ \mathrm{csi}_{3,1} \\ \vdots \\ \mathrm{csi}_{3,30} \end{bmatrix}} \Rightarrow \underset{\mathbf{Smoothed\ CSI_{30x30}}}{\begin{bmatrix} \mathrm{csi}_{1,1} & \mathrm{csi}_{1,2} & \cdots & \mathrm{csi}_{1,16} & \mathrm{csi}_{2,1} & \cdots & \mathrm{csi}_{2,16} \\ \mathrm{csi}_{1,2} & \mathrm{csi}_{1,3} & \cdots & \mathrm{csi}_{1,17} & \mathrm{csi}_{2,2} & \cdots & \mathrm{csi}_{2,17} \\ \vdots & \vdots & \vdots & \vdots & \vdots & \vdots & \vdots \\ \mathrm{csi}_{1,15} & \mathrm{csi}_{1,16} & \cdots & \mathrm{csi}_{1,30} & \mathrm{csi}_{2,15} & \cdots & \mathrm{csi}_{2,30} \\ \mathrm{csi}_{2,1} & \mathrm{csi}_{2,2} & \cdots & \mathrm{csi}_{2,16} & \mathrm{csi}_{3,1} & \cdots & \mathrm{csi}_{3,16} \\ \mathrm{csi}_{2,2} & \mathrm{csi}_{2,3} & \cdots & \mathrm{csi}_{2,17} & \mathrm{csi}_{3,2} & \cdots & \mathrm{csi}_{3,17} \\ \vdots & \vdots & \vdots & \vdots & \vdots & \vdots & \vdots \\ \mathrm{csi}_{2,15} & \mathrm{csi}_{2,16} & \cdots & \mathrm{csi}_{2,30} & \mathrm{csi}_{3,15} & \cdots & \mathrm{csi}_{3,30} \end{bmatrix}}$$

Figure 4: This figure illustrates construction of smoothed CSI matrix from the input CSI measurements. $\mathrm{csi}_{m,n}$ is the CSI value for m^{th} antenna and n^{th} subcarrier. MUSIC algorithm can be directly applied on the smoothed CSI matrix to obtain the AoA and ToF of all the propagation paths.

can form by trying all possible shifts of 15 subcarriers at 2 antennas in a (30 subcarriers × 3 antennas) system.

At this stage, the standard MUSIC algorithm can be applied on smoothed CSI matrix to find the steering vectors and then the AoA and ToF parameters corresponding to each path. The algorithm now works well because by using the smoothed CSI matrix, SpotFi manages to ensure that the number of sensors is greater than the number of paths as SpotFi now has 30 sensors compared to 3 before.

This method of using shifted subsets of sensors is similar to the spatial smoothing technique [9] applied in localization systems like ArrayTrack [1], where the idea is to use measurements from different antenna subarrays formed by considering different subsets of antennas. In SpotFi, we consider different subsets of the antennas and subcarriers together. Algorithms to jointly estimate AoA and ToF by using different sensor subarrays have been explored in literature [42, 43], and applied in systems where all the WiFi radios are time synchronized [51, 52]. However, SpotFi is the first system that applies these algorithms with commodity WiFi deployments where the APs and the targets are not time synchronized. The idea is that although different WiFi cards are not time synchronized, all the transceiver chains on a single WiFi card share the same sampling clock. As a result, lack of time synchronization introduces the same phase shift in the CSI observed at different antennas of an AP which we describe later in Sec. 3.2.2. This phase shift corrupts the ToF values but the AoA values stay the same as in the case where the radios of the AP and the target are time synchronized. Thus the joint AoA and ToF estimation algorithms are still useful in achieving improved AoA accuracy in spite of having just three antennas at the AP which we empirically demonstrate in Sec. 4.

3.2 Identifying Direct Path AoA

SpotFi's next step is to determine if direct path exists and identify the AoA of the direct path from the target to the AP. As described in section 3.1, SpotFi's super-resolution algorithm provides ToF and AoA for all the paths from the target to an AP. A natural heuristic is to exploit the ToF information. Specifically, at each AP we can identify the path with the lowest ToF and declare that as the direct path. Further, we can use the ToF value along with the speed of light to compute the distance of the target from the AP. In theory, this information at a single AP along with AoA information would be sufficient to localize the target.

The above reasonable technique however does not work in practice because the ToF estimates do not capture the true time taken by the signal to travel from the target to the AP. The reason is that in standard WiFi networks, the sender and the receiver are not time synchronized; so their sampling clocks at the DAC and the ADC are not in sync. Hence the ToF estimate also includes delays from sampling time offset (STO) between the target and AP and is therefore not a true measure of the distance traveled.

However, since the ToFs of all the paths will have the same delay added to them due to STO, we can still use the path with the lowest ToF to identify which path traveled the shortest relative distance. But the path with the smallest estimated ToF may not be the direct path. In many indoor scenarios, the direct path may be too weak or nonexistent due to obstruction by walls, etc. In these scenarios, SpotFi's super-resolution algorithm will not even identify the direct path and all the ToF/AoA estimates will be for indirect paths. In this case assuming that the path with the lowest ToF is the direct path would be a mistake. But in cases where there is a strong direct path, the heuristic works and can be used to calculate the AoA of the direct path. How might one distinguish between these two cases, when using lowest ToF heuristic, without knowing the ground truth?

3.2.1 *Using AoA and ToF from Multiple Packets*

We build on a practical observation that was articulated in earlier localization systems [1, 24]: the AoA (and even ToF) estimates of the direct path over a few consecutive packets will show much smaller variation compared to the estimated AoAs (and ToFs) of indirect paths. We demonstrate this observation in Fig. 5(c) through AoA and ToF estimates calculated from CSI traces collected for one of our experiments. SpotFi leverages this observation to estimate likelihoods for each of the paths to be the direct path between the target and the AP. The idea is to form a measure of the variations of the AoAs and ToFs of paths estimated over consecutive packets, and assign a likelihood metric for each of the paths that is inversely proportional to the amount of variation in the AoA and ToF estimates for that path.

Although measuring variation in the AoA parameter alone is easy, measuring the variation in the ToF parameters is challenging. Apart from sampling time offset, there is also a sampling frequency offset (SFO) between every WiFi sender-receiver pair. SFO changes the sampling time offset from packet to packet for the same sender-receiver pair, which in turn results in additive noise to the ToF estimates across packets. So the variance of ToFs estimated by SpotFi's super-resolution algorithm includes this additional variance introduced due to varying sampling time offset. So for every packet's measurements, we need to remove the effect of the random sampling time offset before estimating variance across packets for AoA and ToF estimates.

3.2.2 *Sanitizing ToF Estimates*

STO adds a constant offset to the ToF estimates of all the paths. This common additional delay manifests itself as a linear in frequency term in the phase response of the channel. Hence, STO of τ_s results in adding $-2\pi f_\delta(n-1)\tau_s$ to the phase of CSI value of the nth subcarrier. The additional phase induced by STO is the same across antennas for a particular subcarrier, as all the receiver chains of the same WiFi card are time synchronized. We will now show that removing the linear fit that is common to the unwrapped phase response of all the antennas before estimating multipath parameters eliminates the varaiance due to changing STO.

Let us consider two consecutive packets transmitted by the target. Let $\psi_i(m,n)$ represent unwrapped phase response of the channel for the ith packet at n^{th} subcarrier of mth antenna, and $\tau_{s,i}$ is the STO for i^{th} packet. By applying ToF sanitization algorithm described in Algorithm 1, say we removed the linear fit of CSI phase response for first packet to obtain modified phase response $\widehat{\psi_1}(m,n)$.

Algorithm 1: SpotFi's ToF sanitization algorithm

Data: Unwrapped CSI phase ψ_i for i^{th} packet

1 Obtain the best linear fit of the unwrapped CSI phase as

$$\widehat{\tau_{s,i}} = \arg\min_{\rho} \sum_{m,n=1}^{M,N} (\psi_i(m,n) + 2\pi f_\delta(n-1)\rho + \beta)^2;$$

2 From the unwrapped CSI phase, subtract the phase that would have been added due to STO $\widehat{\tau_{s,i}}$ to obtain modified CSI phase $\widehat{\psi_i}(m,n)$ as

$$\widehat{\psi_i}(m,n) = \psi_i(m,n) + 2\pi f_\delta(n-1)\widehat{\tau_{s,i}}$$

Phase response of second packet ψ_2 can be written as $\psi_2(m,n) = \psi_1(m,n) - 2\pi f_\delta(n-1)(\tau_{s,2} - \tau_{s,1})$. Using this relationship, one can prove that the modified CSI phase of the second packet is given by $\widehat{\psi_2}(m,n) = \psi_1(m,n) + 2\pi f_\delta(n-1)\widehat{\tau_{s,1}}$, which is same as the modified CSI phase of first packet. The actual and modified CSI phase responses for two packets obtained from CSI traces collected from our experiments are presented in Fig. 5(a) and Fig. 5(b) respectively. The modified CSI phase response, obtained by applying Algorithm 1 for each packet, does not change even if the STO changes, and hence is free from the variations of STO. So, the ToF parameters estimated across packets using modified CSI are free from variance of changing STO. We note that the Algorithm 1 is similar to the data sanitization process in PinLoc [15] and is an extension of the process to multiple antennas. We also note that although we have discussed changes in ToF due to SFO alone, the variance in ToF due to random packet detection delay [40] can also eliminated by following Algorithm 1.

3.2.3 *Estimating Direct Path Likelihoods*

Now we have a collection of AoA and ToF estimates whose variance across packets can be estimated. To assign likelihood estimates for each of the estimated paths to be the direct path between the target and AP, we plot AoA and ToF estimates from multiple measurements in a two- dimensional (one each for AoA and ToF) space and apply a clustering algorithm. The intuition is that AoA and ToF estimates from the same path but different packets will be clustered together, but the diameter of each cluster (i.e., the tightness of each cluster) will be a function of the variations in AoA and ToF values for the corresponding path across packets.

Specifically, we use well-known Gaussian Mean clustering algorithm with five clusters to identify the clusters of the estimated parameters. The number of clusters is chosen as five because typically we see at best five significant paths in an indoor environment [1, 8, 24]. The mean of a cluster is used as an estimate for the actual ToF and AoA of the particular propagation path. The variance in the ToF of a path is estimated by calculating the population variance of the ToF estimates belonging to the cluster of the particular path, and similarly for AoA. Then the likelihood for k^{th} path to be the direct path is calculated as

$$likelihood_k = \exp(w_C \bar{C}_k - w_\theta \bar{\sigma}_{\theta_k} - w_\tau \bar{\sigma}_{\tau_k} - w_s \bar{\tau}_k), \quad (8)$$

where $likelihood_k$ is the likelihood that the kth path is the direct path, $\bar{C}_k$ is the number of points in the cluster corresponding to that path, $\bar{\sigma}_{\theta_k}$ and $\bar{\sigma}_{\tau_k}$ are the population variances of the estimated AoA and ToF respectively for points belonging to that cluster, and $\bar{\tau}_k$ is the mean of ToF for points in that cluster. The weighting factors w_C, w_θ, w_τ, and w_s are constants to account for different scales of the corresponding terms (for example, ToF values are on the order of ns and number of points in the cluster is on the order of 10).

The likelihood estimate incorporates a few other terms apart from the tightness of the cluster. First is the term corresponding to the number of points in the cluster. The insight here is that if a cluster corresponds to a physical propagation path, then it is likely to have more measurements than a cluster which is spurious and doesn't correspond to an underlying physical path. The intuition for the term related to the mean ToF is that the direct path will have the smallest ToF, so a higher ToF term should signify a lower likelihood.

SpotFi declares the path with the highest likelihood metric as the direct path, and stores the AoA and the likelihood value of the corresponding path.

3.3 Localizing the Target

Next, SpotFi attempts to localize the target by combining the direct path AoA estimates and their likelihood values corresponding to different APs. Further, the server also has the access to the RSSI measurements for the packets from the target to each AP that "heard" the target. The server assumes a standard widely used path loss model to relate RSSI to distance as described in prior work [3, 71]. The server then fuses all this information to localize the target.

To localize, SpotFi finds the location that best explains the AoA and RSSI measurements at different APs. We do not use the ToF information to form distance estimates because it still does not capture the true ToF of the signal from the target to the AP. The procedure described in Sec. 3.2.2 to scrub any distortion in the ToF estimates only helps in removing

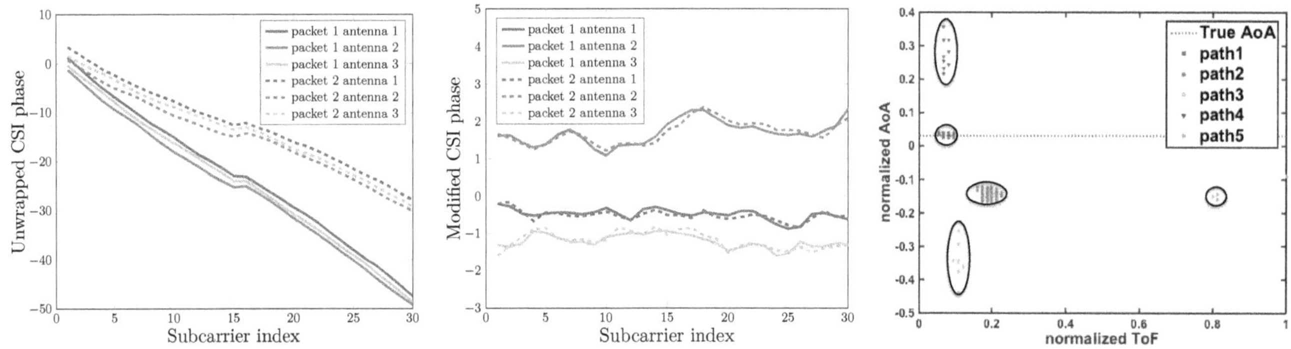

(a) Unwrapped CSI phase (b) Modified CSI phase (c) AoA-ToF parameters for different packets

Figure 5: (a)Unwrapped CSI phase response for two packets. The added phase due to STO is the same for the CSI observed at any of the antennas. (b) Modified CSI phase response obtained after applying Algorithm 1 is same for the two packets in spite of different STOs. (c) ToF-AoA clusters obtained using modified CSI for 170 packets. ToF and AoA values are normalized so that their values lie in the same range. Both path1 and path4 have similar ToF but the reflected path, path4, has a much higher variance in its estimates than the direct path, path1. The estimates of direct path form a tight cluster compared to other paths. SpotFi's direct path likelihood metric rightly chose path1 as direct path as it considers both smallest ToF and tightness of cluster.

the effect of varying STOs and normalize the ToF values across packets to a constant STO, but does not give us the true ToF. To do so, one would need very precise (nanosecond level) synchronization across nodes or across APs. Recent work [40] has shown the feasibility of such synchronization but such mechanisms are not available in current, deployed WiFi infrastructure. Hence, SpotFi uses its ToF estimates only for likelihood estimates but not for determining range.

Specifically, for localization, SpotFi finds the location that minimizes the deviation between AoA and RSSI values that would have been observed at each AP if the target was actually at that location and the corresponding values that were actually observed at each AP. We measure the deviation using standard least squares cost. Mathematically, we find the location that minimizes the following objective function:

$$\sum_{i=1}^{R} l_i[(\bar{p}_i - p_i)^2 + (\bar{\theta}_i - \theta_i)^2], \qquad (9)$$

where there are R APs, i^{th} AP has direct path AoA θ_i and observed RSSI p_i, and $\bar{\theta}_i$ and $\bar{p}_i$ are the AoA and RSSI respectively that would have been observed at the ith AP if the target was transmitting from that location. The weighting factor l_i is the likelihood value of most likely candidate for the direct path from i^{th} AP.

The deviations for different APs have been weighted differently to realize the logical intuition that the APs which have a lower likelihood metric in their estimate of the direct path AoA should be penalized and those with higher likelihood metric should be rewarded. We cannot directly apply convex optimization techniques to find the location that minimizes the objective 9 because the RSSI and AoA observed at an AP are non-convex in terms of the location coordinates. Hence SpotFi applies a well known heuristic known as sequential convex optimization [72] to convexify the objective function piece-wise and obtains the target location that minimizes the objective function 9.

Thus SpotFi accurately determines the location of the target by effectively filtering the reflection paths through likelihood values and then efficiently calculating the target location that best explains the RSSI and estimated direct path AoA observed at the APs. We summarize the complete localization algorithm in Algorithm 2.

Algorithm 2: SpotFi's localization algorithm

Data: CSI and RSSI measurements from target to each of the R APs, and the locations of the APs
Result: Location of the target
for *each AP* $i \in 1, 2, \ldots, R$ **do**
  for *each packet* $p \in 1, 2, \ldots, 10$ **do**
    Remove linear fit in CSI phase response by applying Algorithm 1 ;
    Obtain smoothed CSI matrix **X** as in Fig. 4 ;
    Construct matrix E_N whose columns are eigenvectors of $\mathbf{XX}^{\mathrm{H}}$ corresponding to eigenvalues that are smaller than a threshold;
    Evaluate MUSIC spectrum $P_{MU}(\theta, \tau) = \frac{1}{(\vec{a}^{\mathrm{H}}(\theta,\tau) E_N E_N^{\mathrm{H}} \vec{a}(\theta,\tau))}$;
    Obtain AoA and ToF of multipath components as peaks of MUSIC spectrum ;
  end
  Cluster AoA and ToF from multiple packets ;
  Declare AoA of cluster with highest likelihood value (use Eq. 8) as direct path AoA θ_i ;
end
Minimize objective 9 with optimization variables as target's location and path loss model parameters

4. EXPERIMENTAL EVALUATION

4.1 Implementation

We implemented our system using off-the-shelf Intel 5300 WiFi NICs. We employed Linux CSI tool [68] to obtain the PHY layer CSI information for each packet. The WiFi NICs

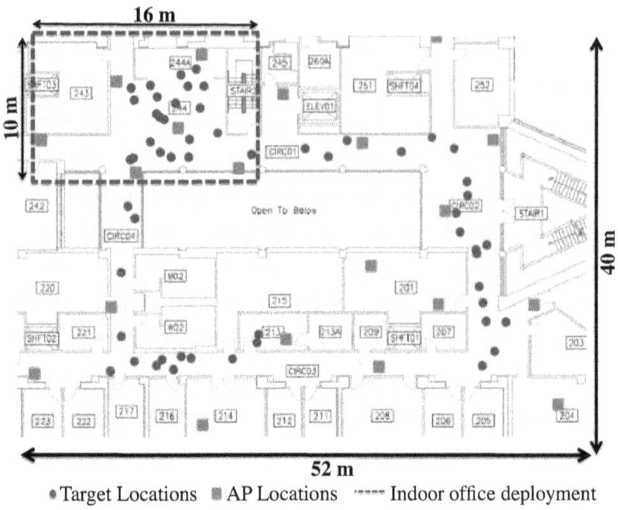

Figure 6: Experiment testbed showing the target locations (blue circles) and the AP locations (red squares). The testbed is designed to evaluate SpotFi in wide variety of deployment scenarios. The region in dashed red box, covering 16 m × 10 m area, represents typical indoor office environment. SpotFi has also been tested when both the APs and the targets are along a corridor. SpotFi has been further stress-tested in locations where the localization targets have atmost two APs in LoS.

operate in 5 GHz WiFi spectrum because of firmware limitations [8]. Note that operating in 5 GHz frequencies is more challenging compared to 2.4 GHz because of higher attenuation. The firmware provides CSI at only 30 of the sub-carriers although the data is sent on 116 subcarriers for 40 MHz bandwidth. Also, the CSI information is quantized, i.e., each of real and imaginary parts of CSI for every subcarrier is represented using 8 bits.

The system consists of multiple computers equipped with WiFi cards which act as access points. One machine which is mobile on a cart acts as the target whose location is of interest. The locations of the access points with respect to a map are measured accurately by using laser range finder and architectural drawings of the building where we deployed SpotFi. The APs operate in monitor mode and obtain the CSI for the packets transmitted by the target. The APs export the CSI, along with a timestamp at which CSI is obtained, to a central server. The server processes and combines the CSI information from multiple access points to determine the location of the target. SpotFi's localization algorithm, that is described in Algorithm 2 and is executed on the server, is implemented using MATLAB in our current prototype and has not been optimized for speed.

Deployments tested: We deployed SpotFi in different locations of our building. Specifically, we deployed SpotFi over almost the entire floor of our building. The building has a variety of spaces, from students labs to a cafeteria to long corridors with smaller offices. Locations of WiFi APs and 55 target locations are depicted in Fig. 6.

Compared Approaches: We compare SpotFi with practical implementation of ArrayTrack based on CSI from a WiFi NIC with three antennas and no further hardware modifications [8]. Throughout this section, ArrayTrack refers to the localization application described in Phaser [8], which is mathematically similar to the method applied in ArrayTrack [1]. We chose ArrayTrack with three antennas as the comparison point because among recently proposed designs it is the best performing system which can be deployed without any hardware or firmware modifications at the APs. Note that we do not use the ArrayTrack implementation described in an earlier paper [1] with WARP boards because it needed 6–8 antennas to be effective. We also do not use a recent proposal [8] from the same group to stitch together two WiFi NICs with additional hardware to create a five antenna AP since once again it requires hardware modifications. Our implementation faithfully reproduces the ArrayTrack algorithm and design but is constrained to use three antennas and the CSI measurements from commodity APs.

Systems such as Ubicarse [2] do not require infrastructure hardware/firmware modifications, but they require that the target has gyroscopes and at least two antennas, and moreover that it should be held by a human and he/she moves it in a particular circular way. SpotFi's requirements do not allow for any such assumptions, localization has to work even if the target has a simple, single antenna commodity WiFi chip and nothing else and is on a completely static target (e.g., locating a phone lost somewhere in a home).

4.2 Overview of Evaluation

We tested a series of hypotheses to understand how well SpotFi performs when deployed in typical indoor environments. Following is a summary of the main results from evaluation.

- SpotFi achieved median localization error of 0.4 m in deployments similar to those used for testing ArrayTrack and Ubicarse.
- Even in challenging conditions where the target has only two APs with a robust direct path, SpotFi still performs well with median localization error of 1.6 m compared to ArrayTrack whose median error is 3.5 m. Similarly in scenarios such as corridors where even though there may be multiple APs the target is not surrounded in all directions by them, SpotFi provides a median error of 1.1 m compared to 4 m for ArrayTrack.
- SpotFi's accuracy stems from two key components. First is its super-resolution AoA estimation algorithm whose median error is less than 5 degrees in LoS conditions and less than 10 degrees in NLoS conditions. The MUSIC algorithm used in practical implementation of ArrayTrack only achieves an estimation error of 7.4 and 15.2 degrees respectively for the same scenarios. Second, SpotFi's likelihood estimation algorithm ensures that among the available estimates, incorrect estimates for the direct path are likely not picked, and even if they are, they will be weighted with low confidence and have a lesser impact on the location estimate.

4.3 SpotFi's Accuracy

In this evaluation, we test the localization accuracy achieved by SpotFi in different deployment scenarios.

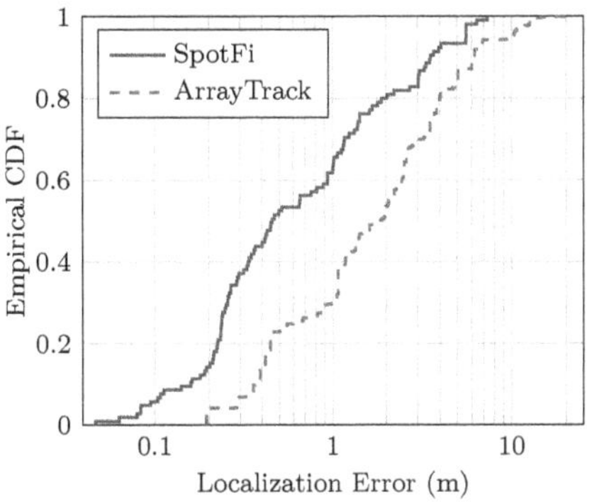

(a) Indoor office deployment

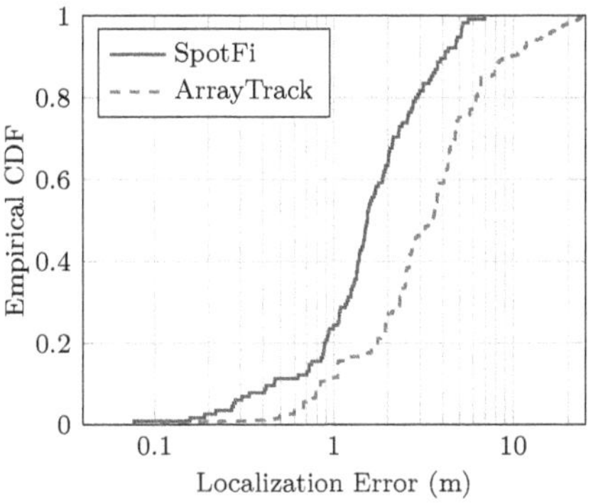

(b) High NLoS deployment

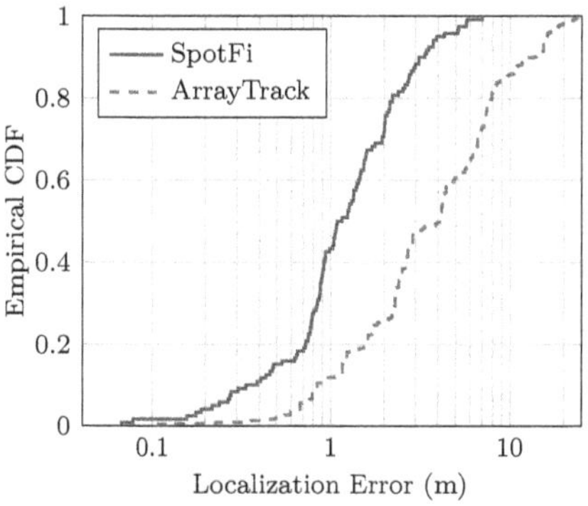

(c) Corridors

Figure 7: Plots CDFs of SpotFi's localization error for different deployments in the testbed in Fig. 6 and compares with the localization error achieved by practical implementation of ArrayTrack with three antennas for the same data.

4.3.1 *Indoor Office Deployments*

Localization accuracy is dependent on the multipath environment, the material used in walls, the presence of metallic objects, the density of WiFi AP deployment and many other factors. Hence we start first by replicating the deployment scenario used in evaluating state-of-the-art systems such as ArrayTrack and Ubicarse. Specifically both these systems used an indoor office environment with an area of roughly 15×10 sq.m and deployed five-six APs to span the area. Target locations are also located within the same area. The environment is very multipath rich and typically has 4–5 APs with a sufficiently strong direct path. Both ArrayTrack (see Sec. 6 and 4 in [1]) and Ubicarse (see Sec. 8 in [2]) use a very similar environment. Our testbed with APs and locations for this experiment are highlighted by a dashed red box in Fig. 6.

Method: All experiments are conducted as follows. First, all APs are set in monitor mode on a channel with 40 MHz bandwidth in the 5GHz band. For every target location shown in the testbed, we place our Intel NUC based WiFi client and configure it to be on the same channel as the APs. First we measure the ground truth location of the client using the lasers as described above. The target then transmits 500 packets with 100 ms interval and six of our AP nodes surrounding the client that can hear the client log the packets as well as the CSI and MAC address associated with that packet. The measured CSI and MAC address traces are sent with timestamps to the central server. The server chops up the CSI traces into groups of forty consecutive CSI measurements at a time on which the localization algorithm 2 is applied. The same data is also used for ArrayTrack as described above. We repeat this experiment for each target location in the testbed. Fig. 7(a) shows the CDF of localization errors for SpotFi and ArrayTrack.

Analysis: We observe from Fig. 7(a), SpotFi achieves a median localization error of 0.4 m compared to 1.8 m for ArrayTrack. The 80th percentile tail errors for SpotFi and ArrayTrack are 1.8 m and 4 m respectively. To put these numbers in context, ArrayTrack with six-eight antennas and Ubicarse/LTEye with rotating antennas achieve between 0.3–0.4 m median accuracy; hence SpotFi achieves the same accuracy as these prior systems while using commodity WiFi cards on both the AP and the client and nothing else. To the best of our knowledge, no other localization system that works only with information that is already exposed by commodity WiFi cards and with no war-driving can achieve even sub-meter accuracy.

4.3.2 *High NLoS Deployments*

Next, we evaluate SpotFi under stressful conditions. First we test SpotFi under conditions where only two or less number of APs have a decent direct path from the client due to blockages. To do this, we use 23 locations in our testbed where this condition holds based on our ground truth estimates. Much prior work [1, 8, 2] does not study such stressful scenarios, so it is hard to comment on how they might perform. However we do compare our system against our ArrayTrack implementation. We repeat the same localization experiments as before and plot the CDF of localization errors in Fig. 7(b).

As expected, localization error is worse in these scenarios. SpotFi achieves a median accuracy of 1.6 m whereas ArrayTrack degrades to 3.5 m. The reason is that the direct path AoA estimation error is higher in such scenarios relative to the indoor office deployment scenario. But SpotFi's super-resolution algorithm still works much better compared to the AoA estimation algorithm which ArrayTrack uses, and the accuracy is still acceptable for many applications. Also, SpotFi's unique direct path likelihood estimates evaluated at each AP result in less weight for measurements from APs which do not have strong direct path to the target thus reducing the inaccuracy in location estimation.

4.3.3 *Corridors*

Another feature of indoor spaces such as offices and malls are corridors, and these are precisely the areas where people desire localization capabilities for indoor navigation. Corridors are challenging, especially narrow ones, because it is unlikely that a particular target location is surrounded by APs such that the target's AoA can be measured from diverse vantage points. Typically APs are deployed just along the side wall of the corridor and many of the AoA measurements at each AP will be very close to each other due to geometry of the corridors. Also, even if the client has more APs in LoS, they are generally farther away than when compared to indoor office deployments. This has an important implication on localization accuracy since it leads to scenarios where many APs have inaccurate and correlated AoA measurements and it becomes harder for some AP to correct the errors of other APs.

We evaluate SpotFi under such a scenario in our testbed. Specifically we look at the target locations in the two corridors that we see in Fig. 6. There are 25 points overall in such locations. We repeat the localization experiments as described above and compute the localization error for both SpotFi and ArrayTrack. Again as seen from Fig. 7(c), the median localization error for SpotFi is around a meter, whereas ArrayTrack's error worsens to 4 m.

Improved localization accuracy of SpotFi is due to two factors. First, SpotFi resolves multipath more accurately with the same number of antennas compared to schemes which use only the relative phase information between the antennas. Second, SpotFi's novel localization algorithm which accurately identifies the direct path between the target and the APs among the estimated multipath components. We now test individually the significance of these factors next.

4.4 Deep Dive into SpotFi

4.4.1 AoA Estimation Accuracy

Method: The goal here is to show that the super-resolution algorithm of SpotFi provides a much more accurate set of AoA estimates for all propagation paths. However, we have ground truth AoA for only the direct path between the target and the AP. So, we measure the accuracy of the AoA estimation algorithm by measuring the difference between ground truth direct path AoA and estimated AoA that is closest to this ground truth. This way, we remove the effect of direct path selection process which identifies the direct path AoA, which we will quantify in the next section separately.

For this evaluation, we classify the data into Line of Sight (LoS) scenarios and Non-Line of Sight (NLoS) scenarios. For AoA estimation error purposes, we define NLoS scenario for an AP as a scenario where there is a strong blocking object like a wall obstructing the line joining the target and the AP and hence the direct path is significantly weaker or non-existent compared to reflected paths. All other scenarios are declared as LoS. We refer to the AoA estimation algorithm used in localization systems like Phaser [8], and described in Sec. 3.1.1, as MUSIC-AoA algorithm.

Analysis: Fig. 8(a) plots the CDFs for AoA estimation error for all the APs. In LoS cases, SpotFi achieves median AoA accuracy of 2.4 degrees better than that achieved by MUSIC-AoA. In NLoS scenarios the accuracy is even better, achieving an improvement of nearly 5.2 degrees in direct path AoA error. The reason is that in LoS scenarios even MUSIC-AoA works reasonably well since the direct path is likely the strongest of all paths. But in NLoS scenarios many reflected paths will have the same or higher power

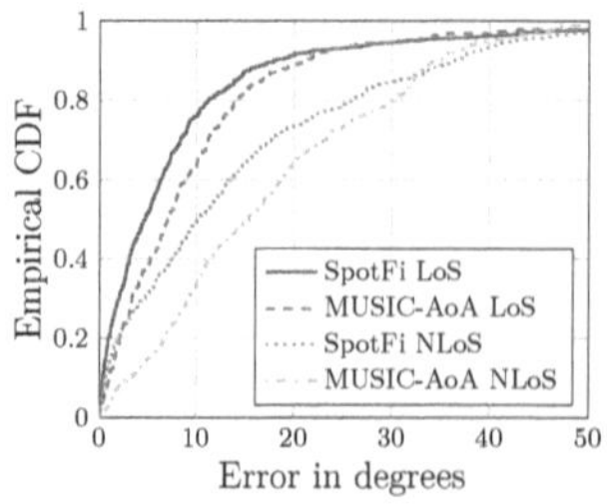

(a) AoA Estimation error

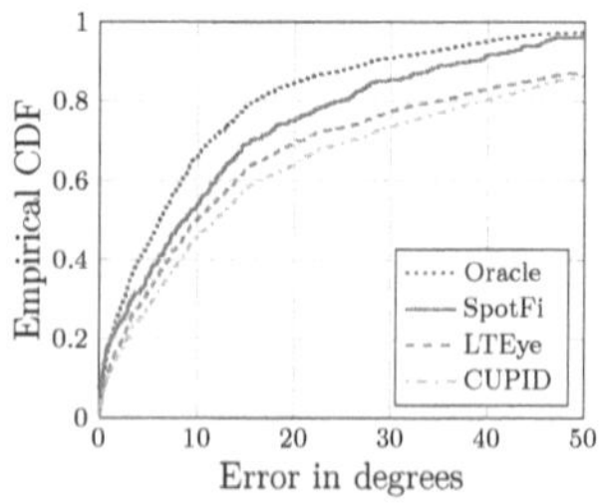

(b) Direct path AoA selection error

Figure 8: Reconstructing the effect of different components of SpotFi in improving the localization accuracy: (a) plots the CDFs of SpotFi's AoA estimation error with respect to the MUSIC-AoA scheme which only models the phase shifts across antennas to estimate AoA. The comparison is made individually for cases where there is a strong obstruction like wall between the target and AP (NLoS) and in cases where there is none (LoS). (b) plots the CDFs of SpotFi's error in selecting the AoA corresponding to direct path AoA and compares with schemes used in CUPID [23] and LTEye [6] systems.

compared to the direct path, and standard AoA-based MUSIC with three antennas does not have sufficient resolution to estimate the direct path's AoA accurately.

4.4.2 Direct Path AoA Selection Accuracy

Method: Next, we compute the efficacy of SpotFi's likelihood based technique to pick out the direct path from a bunch of candidate paths as described in section 3.2. To demonstrate the merit of SpotFi's direct path selection algorithm, we compare it with three other AoA selection algorithms used in prior work [6, 23]:

- LTEye [6] declares the direct path as the one with smallest ToF. However note that, unlike LTEye, we do not have access to the actual ToF between the target and the AP as they are not time synchronized. However, path with smallest estimated ToF also corresponds to the path with smallest actual ToF because lack of synchronization just adds a constant delay to ToFs of all the paths.
- CUPID [23] declares the AoA with the largest value in the MUSIC spectrum as the the direct path AoA.
- Oracle selection algorithm which chooses the AoA closest to the ground truth direct path AoA.

Analysis: We define AoA selection error as the difference between the ground truth direct path AoA and AoA selected by the direct path selection algorithm described in Sec. 3.2. Note that all of these schemes are working with the AoA estimates from SpotFi's super-resolution algorithm, not the standard AoA-based MUSIC. Fig. 8(b) plots the CDF of the error for all the four schemes considering all the deployment scenarios. SpotFi's technique is the best scheme relative to the Oracle, whereas the smallest delay based AoA selection has 80th percentile error 10 degrees worse than SpotFi. Picking the AoA with largest value in MUSIC spectrum, or equivalently direction with largest energy, performs the worst. This is because in a typical indoor environment with objects and humans blocking direct path to the AP, the direct signal can get heavily attenuated compared to signals traveling along reflected paths.

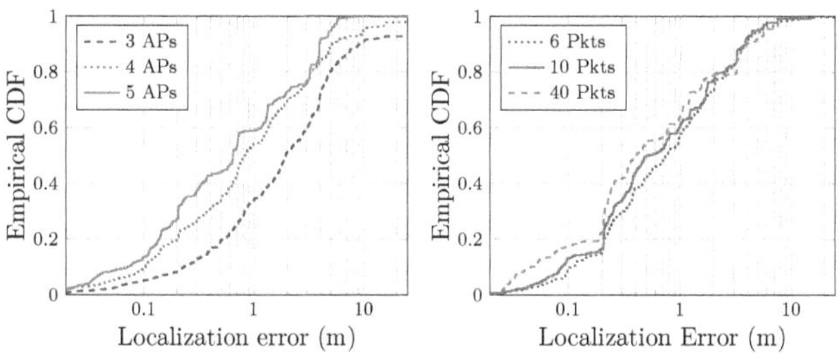

(a) localization error with different AP densities

(b) localization error with different number of packets used for localization

Figure 9: (a) plots CDFs of SpotFi's localization error as we vary the number of APs that can hear the target. This represents deployment scenarios with different densities of WiFi APs. (b) plots the CDFs of SpotFi's localization error as we vary the number of packets used for localizing the target.

4.4.3 Impact of WiFi Deployment Densities

Method: We emulate different WiFi AP densities by localizing using CSI from only random subsets of the APs. We vary the number of APs that can hear the target between three and five to demonstrate the performance of SpotFi with increasing deployment density.

Analysis: Fig. 9(a) plots the localization error for target locations in indoor office deployment. We observe that accuracy improves with increasing number of APs as expected. As we have more APs, it becomes easier to find at least a few APs that have decent direct path signal from the target and thus eliminate spurious estimates. We observe that SpotFi achieves median localization error of 0.6 m, 0.8 m, and 1.9 m with five, four and three APs respectively. So, even with four APs, SpotFi outperforms practical implementation of ArrayTrack with six APs. We observed a big improvement when we increased the number of APs from three to four, and much smaller improvement as we added more APs. The reason for diminishing improvements in accuracy with increasing number of APs is that once we have two strong direct path measurements, additional direct path measurements, if accurate, will only help in improving location accuracy incrementally, and if inaccurate, will effectively not be considered due to SpotFi's robust localization algorithm.

4.4.4 Impact of Number of Packets

Method: Using multiple packets improves SpotFi's accuracy in identifying the direct path among the estimated paths as described in section 3.2. Ideally, we want a localization system to perform well using small number of packets so that localization delay is minimized and the system works robustly even when the target can only send a small amount of traffic. We vary the number of packets SpotFi uses for localization from 6 packets to 40 packets and plot the effect on the localization accuracy for the target locations in indoor office deployment in Fig. 9(b).

Analysis: We observe from Fig. 9(b) that even with 10 packets, SpotFi accurately identifies the direct path and achieves a median localization accuracy of 0.5 m compared to 0.4 m obtained using 40 packets. So, SpotFi works well with just 10 CSI measurements; in other words, SpotFi requires the target to transmit just 10 packets for accurate localization.

5. CONCLUSION

SpotFi provides accurate indoor localization services using commercial off-the-shelf WiFi NICs with three antennas and with an accuracy comparable to state-of-the-art localization systems with large antenna arrays which are not suitable for wide deployments. SpotFi's techniques for AoA estimation and direct path filtering however are more widely applicable for other problems such as device free localization, gesture recognition and motion tracing. Exploring them is future work.

Acknowledgments: This research is partially supported by Thomas and Sarah Kailath Stanford Graduate Fellowship. We thank Aaron Schulman, Rakesh Misra, the reviewers, and our shepherd, Ashutosh Sabharwal for their insightful comments.

6. REFERENCES

[1] J. Xiong and K. Jamieson, "Arraytrack: A fine-grained indoor location system," NSDI '13.

[2] S. Kumar, S. Gil, D. Katabi, and D. Rus, "Accurate indoor localization with zero start-up cost," MobiCom '14.

[3] P. Bahl and V. N. Padmanabhan, "Radar: An in-building rf-based user location and tracking system," INFOCOM 2000.

[4] K. Chintalapudi, A. Padmanabha Iyer, and V. N. Padmanabhan, "Indoor localization without the pain," MobiSys '05.

[5] B. Ferris, D. Fox, and N. Lawrence, "Wifi-slam using gaussian process latent variable models," IJCAI '07.

[6] S. Kumar, E. Hamed, D. Katabi, and L. Erran Li, "Lte radio analytics made easy and accessible," SIGCOMM '14.

[7] R. O. Schmidt, "Multiple emitter location and signal parameter estimation," *IEEE Trans. on Antennas and Propagation 1986.*

[8] J. Gjengset, J. Xiong, G. McPhillips, and K. Jamieson, "Phaser: Enabling phased array signal processing on commodity wifi access points," MobiCom '14.

[9] A. Paulraj, V. Reddy, T. Shan, and T. Kailath, "Performance analysis of the music algorithm with spatial smoothing in the presence of coherent sources," IEEE MILCOM 1986.

[10] K. Wu, J. Xiao, Y. Yi, M. Gao, and L. Ni, "Fila: Fine-grained indoor localization," INFOCOM '12.

[11] H. Lim, L.-C. Kung, J. C. Hou, and H. Luo, "Zero-configuration, robust indoor localization: Theory and experimentation," 2005.

[12] A. Goswami, L. E. Ortiz, and S. R. Das, "Wigem: A learning-based approach for indoor localization," CoNEXT '11.

[13] P. Bahl, V. N. Padmanabhan, and A. Balachandran, "Enhancements to the radar user location and tracking system," tech. rep., 2000.

[14] M. Youssef and A. Agrawala, "The horus wlan location determination system," MobiSys '05.

[15] S. Sen, B. Radunovic, R. R. Choudhury, and T. Minka, "You are facing the mona lisa: Spot localization using phy layer information," MobiSys '12.

[16] R. Nandakumar, K. K. Chintalapudi, and V. N. Padmanabhan, "Centaur: locating devices in an office environment," MobiCom '12.

[17] M. Azizyan, I. Constandache, and R. Roy Choudhury, "Surroundsense: mobile phone localization via ambience fingerprinting," in *MobiCom '09.*

[18] A. Rai, K. K. Chintalapudi, V. N. Padmanabhan, and R. Sen, "Zee: Zero-effort crowdsourcing for indoor localization," Mobicom '12.

[19] Z. Yang, C. Wu, and Y. Liu, "Locating in fingerprint space: Wireless indoor localization with little human intervention," Mobicom '12.

[20] H. Liu, Y. Gan, J. Yang, S. Sidhom, Y. Wang, Y. Chen, and F. Ye, "Push the limit of wifi based localization for smartphones," MobiCom '12.

[21] H. Wang, S. Sen, A. Elgohary, M. Farid, M. Youssef, and R. R. Choudhury, "No need to war-drive: unsupervised indoor localization," MobiSys '12.

[22] M. Youssef and A. Agrawala, "Small-scale compensation for wlan location determination systems," in *IEEE Wireless Communications and Networking, 2003*.

[23] S. Sen, J. Lee, K.-H. Kim, and P. Congdon, "Avoiding multipath to revive inbuilding wifi localization," MobiSys '13.

[24] K. Joshi, S. Hong, and S. Katti, "Pinpoint: localizing interfering radios," NSDI '13.

[25] D. Niculescu and B. Nath, "Vor base stations for indoor 802.11 positioning," MobiCom '04.

[26] L. Atzori, A. Iera, and G. Morabito, "The internet of things: A survey," *Comput. Netw. '10*.

[27] P. Chen, P. Ahammad, C. Boyer, S. i Huang, L. Lin, E. Lobaton, M. Meingast, S. Oh, S. Wang, P. Yan, A. Y. Yang, C. Yeo, L. chung Chang, J. D. Tygar, and S. S. Sastry, "Citric: A low-bandwidth wireless camera network platform," ICDSC '08.

[28] *nest*. https://nest.com/.

[29] M. Youssef, A. Youssef, C. Rieger, U. Shankar, and A. Agrawala, "Pinpoint: An asynchronous time-based location determination system," MobiCom '06.

[30] S. A. Golden and S. S. Bateman, "Sensor measurements for wi-fi location with emphasis on time-of-arrival ranging," *IEEE Trans. on Mobile Computing*, 2007.

[31] A. T. Mariakakis, S. Sen, J. Lee, and K.-H. Kim, "Sail: Single access point-based indoor localization," MobiCom '14.

[32] A. Marcaletti, M. Rea, D. Giustiniano, V. Lenders, and A. Fakhreddine, "Filtering noisy 802.11 time-of-flight ranging measurements," CoNEXT '14.

[33] M. Ciurana, F. Barcelo-Arroyo, and F. Izquierdo, "A ranging system with ieee 802.11 data frames," in *IEEE Radio and Wireless Symposium, 2007*.

[34] S. Lanzisera, D. Zats, and K. S. Pister, "Radio frequency time-of-flight distance measurement for low-cost wireless sensor localization," *IEEE Sensors Journal*, 2011.

[35] J. Xiong, K. Jamieson, and K. Sundaresan, "Synchronicity: Pushing the envelope of fine-grained localization with distributed mimo," HotWireless '14.

[36] F. Zhao, W. Yao, C. C. Logothetis, and Y. Song, "Super-resolution toa estimation in ofdm systems for indoor environments," in *IEEE International Conference on Networking, Sensing and Control, 2007*.

[37] V. Amendolare, D. Cyganski, and R. J. Duckworth, "Transactional array reconciliation tomography for precision indoor location," *IEEE Trans. on Aerospace and Electronic Systems*, 2014.

[38] S. Venkatraman and J. Caffery, "Hybrid toa/aoa techniques for mobile location in non-line-of-sight environments," in *IEEE Wireless Communications and Networking Conference, 2004*.

[39] A. Cavanaugh, M. Lowe, D. Cyganski, and R. Duckworth, "Wpi precision personnel location system: Rapid deployment antenna system and sensor fusion for 3d precision location," in *Institute of Navigation-International Technical Meeting 2010*.

[40] H. Rahul, H. Hassanieh, and D. Katabi, "Sourcesync: a distributed wireless architecture for exploiting sender diversity," *ACM SIGCOMM CCR '11*.

[41] M. Wax and A. Leshem, "Joint estimation of time delays and directions of arrival of multiple reflections of a known signal," IEEE ICASSP 1996.

[42] A.-J. Van Der Veen, M. C. Vanderveen, and A. J. Paulraj, "Joint angle and delay estimation using shift-invariance properties," *IEEE Signal Processing Letters 1997*.

[43] M. C. Vanderveen, A.-J. Van der Veen, and A. Paulraj, "Estimation of multipath parameters in wireless communications," *IEEE Trans. on Signal Processing 1998*.

[44] M. Vanderveen, B. Ng, C. Papadias, and A. Paulraj, "Joint angle and delay estimation (jade) for signals in multipath environments," in *Conference Record of the Thirtieth Asilomar Conference on Signals, Systems and Computers, 1996*.

[45] Y.-Y. Wang, J.-T. Chen, and W.-H. Fang, "Tst-music for joint doa-delay estimation," *IEEE Trans. on Signal Processing*, 2001.

[46] J. Picheral and U. Spagnolini, "Shift invariance algorithms for the angle/delay estimation of multipath space-time channel," in *Vehicular Technology Conference, 2001*.

[47] D. Inserra and A. M. Tonello, "A frequency-domain los angle-of-arrival estimation approach in multipath channels," *IEEE Trans. on Vehicular Technology*, 2013.

[48] J.-T. Chen, J. Kim, and J.-W. Liang, "Multichannel mlse equalizer with parametric fir channel identification," *IEEE Trans. on Vehicular Technology*, 1999.

[49] G. G. Raleigh and T. Boros, "Joint space-time parameter estimation for wireless communication channels," *IEEE Trans. on Signal Processing*, 1998.

[50] J. He, M. Swamy, and M. O. Ahmad, "Joint space-time parameter estimation for underwater communication channels with velocity vector sensor arrays," *IEEE Trans. on Wireless Communications*, '12.

[51] H. Yamada, M. Ohmiya, Y. Ogawa, and K. Itoh, "Superresolution techniques for time-domain measurements with a network analyzer," *IEEE Trans. on Antennas and Propagation*, 1991.

[52] M. Ascione, A. Buonanno, M. D'Urso, L. Angrisani, and R. Schiano Lo Moriello, "A new measurement method based on music algorithm for through-the-wall detection of life signs," *IEEE Trans. on Instrumentation and Measurement*, 2013.

[53] J. Wang, F. Adib, R. Knepper, D. Katabi, and D. Rus, "Rf-compass: robot object manipulation using rfids," MobiCom '13.

[54] J. Wang and D. Katabi, "Dude, where's my card?: Rfid positioning that works with multipath and non-line of sight," in *ACM SIGCOMM CCR '13*.

[55] J. Wang, D. Vasisht, and D. Katabi, "Rf-idraw: Virtual touch screen in the air using rf signals," SIGCOMM '14.

[56] S. Gezici, Z. Tian, G. B. Giannakis, H. Kobayashi, A. F. Molisch, H. V. Poor, and Z. Sahinoglu, "Localization via ultra-wideband radios: a look at positioning aspects for future sensor networks," *IEEE Signal Processing Magazine*, 2005.

[57] A. Ward, A. Jones, and A. Hopper, "A new location technique for the active office," *IEEE Personal Communications*, 1997.

[58] R. K. Harle and A. Hopper, "Deploying and evaluating a location-aware system," MobiSys '05.

[59] N. B. Priyantha, A. Chakraborty, and H. Balakrishnan, "The cricket location-support system," MobiCom 2000.

[60] A. Harter, A. Hopper, P. Steggles, A. Ward, and P. Webster, "The anatomy of a context-aware application," *Wireless Networks*, 2002.

[61] A. Savvides, C.-C. Han, and M. B. Strivastava, "Dynamic fine-grained localization in ad-hoc networks of sensors," MobiCom '01.

[62] R. Want, A. Hopper, V. Falcao, and J. Gibbons, "The active badge location system,"

[63] A. Harter and A. Hopper, "A distributed location system for the active office," *IEEE Network*, 1994.

[64] E. Aitenbichler and M. Muhlhauser, "An ir local positioning system for smart items and devices," in *Distributed Computing Systems Workshops, 2003*.

[65] P. Hu, L. Li, C. Peng, G. Shen, and F. Zhao, "Pharos: Enable physical analytics through visible light based indoor localization," HotNets '13.

[66] Y.-S. Kuo, P. Pannuto, K.-J. Hsiao, and P. Dutta, "Luxapose: Indoor positioning with mobile phones and visible light," MobiCom '14.

[67] *iBeacon*. https://developer.apple.com/ibeacon/.

[68] D. Halperin, W. Hu, A. Sheth, and D. Wetherall, "Tool release: Gathering 802.11n traces with channel state information," *ACM SIGCOMM CCR '11*.

[69] N. Czink, M. Herdin, H. Ozcelik, and E. Bonek, "Number of multipath clusters in indoor mimo propagation environments," *Electronics Letters '04*.

[70] V. Erceg, L. Schumacher, P. Kyritsi, and et al, "Tgn channel models," *Tech. Rep. IEEE P802.11, Wireless LANs, 2004*.

[71] A. Goldsmith, *Wireless communications*. Cambridge university press, 2005.

[72] S. Boyd and L. Vandenberghe, *Convex Optimization*. New York, NY, USA: Cambridge University Press, 2004.

BackFi: High Throughput WiFi Backscatter

Dinesh Bharadia†, Kiran Joshi†, Manikanta Kotaru, Sachin Katti
Stanford University
{dineshb, krjoshi, mkotaru, skatti}@stanford.edu
†co-primary authors

ABSTRACT

We present BackFi, a novel communication system that enables high throughput, long range communication between very low power backscatter IoT sensors and WiFi APs using ambient WiFi transmissions as the excitation signal. Specifically, we show that it is possible to design IoT sensors and WiFi APs such that the WiFi AP in the process of transmitting data to normal WiFi clients can decode backscatter signals which the IoT sensors generate by modulating information on to the ambient WiFi transmission. We show via prototypes and experiments that it is possible to achieve communication rates of up to 5 Mbps at a range of 1 m and 1 Mbps at a range of 5 meters. Such performance is an order to three orders of magnitude better than the best known prior WiFi backscatter system [27, 25]. BackFi design is energy efficient, as it relies on backscattering alone and needs insignificant power, hence the energy consumed per bit is small.

CCS Concepts

•Information systems → **Sensor networks;** **•Hardware** → *Digital signal processing;* Sensors and actuators; Wireless integrated network sensors;

Keywords: Full Duplex Backscatter; Backscatter Communication; Internet of Things (IoT); WiFi Backscatter; Backscatter Decoder; Ambient Backscatter

1. INTRODUCTION

Embedded and connected gadgets - colloquially referred to as the Internet-of-things (IoT) - are increasingly making it possible to continuously monitor our bodies, personal lives and surroundings to improve health, energy usage, security and so on. These gadgets (e.g. wearable, fitness/health trackers, security cameras/microphones, thermostats [35]) integrate with cheaply available sensing technology to continuously measure physical variables such as temperature, heart rate, ambient sounds, etc. and upload them via wireless links to the cloud. Analytics applications then analyze such data to implement useful functionality such as fitness monitoring, intruder detection, regulating HVAC, etc. The future is likely to bring many more such devices helping us instrument more parts of our lives and surroundings, and enable us to measure and analyze almost every aspect of our lives.

We will refer to these IoT gadgets as either IoT sensors, or tags, or simply sensors in the remaining of our paper depending on the context. To widely realize the IoT vision, we believe that the wireless connectivity on these devices needs to satisfy three key requirements:

- **R1: Sufficient throughput & range**: A typical such gadget produces anywhere between a few Kbps (e.g. temperature sensors measuring every 100 ms) to a few Mbps (e.g., security microphones/cameras recording audio/video), and can be placed anywhere in the home or on the body. So the wireless link from the gadget to the wired gateway connected to the Internet should provide at least a *few Mbps of uplink throughput and 1-5 meters of range.*
- **R2: Very low power design**: These gadgets need to be able to operate for a long time without requiring battery replacements, or ideally without batteries at all. Recent work has demonstrated the possibility of powering these devices primarily using power harvesting from ambient RF sources such as TV and cellular signals. A typical RF powered device can harvest upto 100 microwatts of power [51, 44, 29] from TV signals. Hence, ideally the gadget's radio should provide the necessary throughput and range using a *few tens of microwatts of power* to be operable without batteries. If feasible this would eliminate the need for dedicated powering infrastructure such as RFID readers.
- **R3: Reuse ambient signals**: Ideally the IoT sensors should be able to piggyback their data on ambient, widely prevalent communication signals such as WiFi, Bluetooth etc. For example, while a WiFi AP is transmitting a packet to a standard WiFi client, an IoT sensor should be able to modulate its own information on the ambient WiFi signal and communicate its own data back to the AP. However this should not interfere with the normal WiFi communication from the AP to the client. If such a capability is feasible, then one can imagine being able to provide connectivity to IoT sensors using infrastructure that is already being widely deployed for standard wireless communication, thus reducing complexity and cost.

SIGCOMM '15, August 17 - 21, 2015, London, United Kingdom

 ISBN 978-1-4503-3542-3/15/08...$15.00

DOI: http://dx.doi.org/10.1145/2785956.2787490

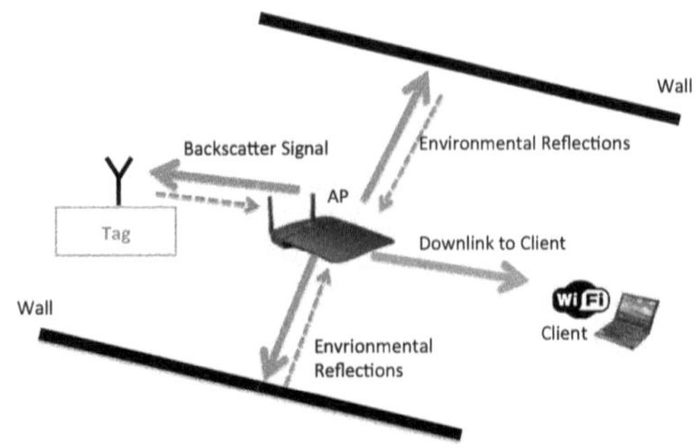

Figure 1: Overview of BackFi backscatter system : The AP transmits packet that is meant for the WiFi client (in blue), the transmitted signal (in red) is also reflected by reflectors in the environments like walls. The IoT sensor also receives these transmissions, and modulates its data on it and backscatters the signal to the AP (in green).

To the best of our knowledge, no current systems satisfies all three requirements. Recent work on WiFi backscatter [27, 25] is the closest, but it does not satisfy **R1**, it only provides around 0.5 Kbps of uplink-throughput and a range of 1 meter which is insufficient for many applications. RFID-based systems satisfy **R1** [55, 19, 49] and some of them satisfy **R2**, but not **R3**. They would require the widespread deployment of dedicated RFID reader infrastructure as well as require their own spectrum band of operation in the unlicensed band. Standard communication radios such as WiFi or Blue-tooth Low Power would satisfy **R1** and **R3**, but clearly cannot satisfy **R2,** they require between $30 - 50$ mW (Bluetooth) to several hundred mW (WiFi) of power to operate.

Our goal is to design a radio uplink for IoT sensors that satisfies all the above requirements. We present BackFi, a novel communication link design between backscatter IoT sensors and WiFi radios. The key contributions are a IoT sensor design for backscattering WiFi signals, and a novel radio circuit and algorithm design at the WiFi AP which doubles up as the (AP) reader decoding the backscatter signals from the IoT sensor. The AP reader operates while it is sending a standard WiFi packet to a standard WiFi client as seen in Fig. 1. The design satisfies the throughput and range requirements described above, it delivers at least 1 Mbps of throughput even at a range of 5m and much higher throughputs upto 6.67 Mbps at shorter ranges of a meter, To put these performance numbers in context, they are between one to three orders of magnitude better than the best known WiFi backscatter system [27, 25].

BackFi's design makes three key technical contributions:

- First, we design a novel low power IoT sensor that can backscatter standard WiFi signals while being able to sustain high data rates of around 5 Mbps. The IoT sensor consists of a low power design for phase modulations ranging from BPSK to 16-PSK as well as mechanism for detecting WiFi transmission on which IoT sensor data can be modulated and backscattered.
- Second, a novel design of the WiFi AP radio such that it can receive the backscatter signals even while it is simultaneously transmitting a WiFi packet to a standard WiFi client. We leverage recent work on self-interference cancelation for full-duplex radios to enable the backscatter signal to be received while the WiFi device is transmitting [17, 20, 43, 12, 8, 11, 9, 8, 26, 16, 39, 10]. Specifically, the backscatter signal is a modulated version of the transmitted signal itself. Hence self-interference cancelation has to be modified to ensure that the backscatter signal itself does not get canceled. We design novel self-interference estimation techniques that protect the backscatter signal from any degradation due to cancelation.
- Third, we invent novel demodulation and decoding algorithms that can estimate fine-grained changes in the backscatter signal to decode the IoT sensor data. Specifically, we show that WiFi backscatter can be modeled as a channel that is linear but time-varying modifying the IoT sensor data. BackFi incorporates novel decoding algorithms that can continuously track the time-varying channel and use standard diversity combining techniques such as Maximal Ratio Combining (MRC) to deliver a reliable, high throughput link [13].

We prototype BackFi and show that it can provide 5 Mbps of throughput at 1 m range and at least 1 Mbps at 5 m range. In comparison the best performing prior WiFi backscatter system [27, 25] provides a throughput of up to 1 Kbps, a range of less than a meter. We also show that BackFi has minimal impact on the operation of the standard WiFi network whose ambient signals it is piggybacking on to backscatter its own data.

We also note that the focus of this paper is on the uplink from the IoT sensor to the BackFi AP. The reason is that the IoT applications that we are designing for are bottle-necked on the uplink. These gadgets (such as fitness trackers, home sensors, wearables, etc) are collecting a lot of sensor data and need to upload them to the cloud and downlink often isn't needed, or if it is, very low throughput of a few Kbps suffice [35, 53]. Hence in the rest of the paper we will focus on the uplink, but note that prior work has already demonstrated WiFi backscatter designs (which can be used with BackFi too) for the downlink that can provide upto 20 Kbps [27]. We further note that although we have chosen WiFi signaling for the description and implementation of BackFi, the system is applicable for other types of communication signals like Bluetooth, Zigbee, etc., as well.

2. RELATED WORK

BackFi is most closely related to recent work on WiFi backscatter [27, 25]. The prior design also uses ambient WiFi transmissions to backscatter data. Specifically, IoT sensors encode data in binary decisions of whether or not to backscatter the received packet transmission which is detected as changes in RSSI/CSI at a nearby helper WiFi device that is also receiving the packet from the AP. The design needs a helper device because the prior design doesn't have self-interference cancellation, hence the transmitting AP cannot detect changes in RSSI/CSI while it is transmitting due to large self-interference. Since information is encoded in binary decisions that span an entire packet, the information rate is only 1 bit per WiFi packet. The range is also low (less than a meter) because the WiFi helper needs the IoT sensors to be close to detect changes in RSSI/CSI. The reason is that the helper device needs to detect the changes in RSSI/CSI while it is receiving the strong WiFi transmission from the AP. This WiFi transmission essentially acts as interference to the detection of weak changes in RSSI/CSI induced by the tag's decision to backscatter or not, and thus limits range.

BackFi on the other hand does not have any of these limitations. Because it modulates information by changing the phase of the received WiFi signal at a much faster rate throughout the WiFi packet, it achieves three orders of magnitude higher throughput. Its range is an order of magnitude higher because self-interference cancellation enables the reader to completely clean out the effect of the ambient WiFi transmission and detect fine-grained changes in the backscatter signal. Finally BackFi provides a framework to analyze energy/bit, which is independent of platform (FPGA, ASIC, discrete) and the technology choice for implementation. However we note that the prior WiFi-backscatter system required no changes to the WiFi AP. BackFi does require the addition of self-interference cancellation hardware. So the trade-off is increased hardware complexity for a much higher throughput and range.

BackFi is related to a large body of work on RFID systems [19, 55, 50, 49, 23, 22, 52, 46, 45, 54, 14, 3], which use dedicated, powered reader infrastructure to supply power as well as receive data from the RFID IoT sensors [30]. The IoT sensors themselves are designed to be low power and may or may not have batteries. However the cost of deploying and maintaining dedicated reader infrastructure has tempered the adoption of these systems. BackFi and other WiFi backscatter systems [27] use ambient WiFi signals for communicating backscatter data, hence deployment is easier.

BackFi is also related to recent work on ambient backscatter communication [28, 34] that enables two RF powered devices to communicate with each other. However these systems do not provide connectivity to the Internet which is BackFi's primary focus. BackFi is also related but complementary to recent work on harvesting power from RF sources such as TV signals [28, 48, 30], cellular transmissions [33] and WiFi [27, 21, 25, 32]. These systems have demonstrated the ability to harvest around $60-100\mu$W from ambient sources such as TV signals [46, 51, 44, 29] which is sufficient power to provide a high throughput battery-less IoT sensor. Hence with BackFi's high throughput, long range, and low power WiFi backscatter connectivity combined with the ability to harvest power from ubiquitous RF sources, we believe we are closer to the vision of RF powered, battery-less IoT sensors ubiquitously deployed and connected to the Internet.

BackFi advances the state-of-the-art in backscatter communication by being able to provide the following:

Improved backscatter decoder: BackFi's decoder presents a first formal framework to decode backscatter on wide-band signals. All the prior backscatter systems use tone as the excitation signals, whereas BackFi uses wideband signals. Further this framework can improve the decoding of the tone based backscatter systems too. The reason is that the silent mode of BackFi eliminates all the backscattered signal by the rest of the environment (including the structural mode of antenna). This allows use of the information on the tone (excitation signal) for decoding, instead of nulling it as in most RFID decoders.

Effective backscatter protocol: BackFi presents a protocol for backscatter devices which allows an efficient decoding for backscatter system. For high order modulation, this design choice becomes imperative to provide good throughput and SNR.

Spectral Efficiency: BackFi presents a high throughput system by piggybacking on the existing data signaling like WiFi or Bluetooth. BackFi capability to reuse existing signaling makes it spectrally efficient and easy to seamlessly deploy. Moreover, since WiFi can be deployed in 900 MHz band too, deploying BackFi is much more effective than deploying RFID readers.

3. OVERVIEW

BackFi's basic mode of operation is shown in Fig. 1. A BackFi capable WiFi AP transmits a WiFi packet to a standard WiFi client. The IoT device with the BackFi tag backscatters the WiFi transmission back to the WiFi AP, and modulates its data on the backscatter signal. The AP decodes the backscatter signal to recover the data from the IoT gadget.

At a high level, the above description also applies to a RFID reader and RFID tag. So why can't we just reuse the RFID design to build WiFi backscatter systems? We argue why but start with a brief primer on standard RFID backscatter first.

3.1 How does traditional RFID work?

In traditional RFID systems, communication happens by the reader first transmitting an excitation signal which is typically a single frequency tone (a sinusoid) in the 900 MHz band. The tag receives this excitation signal and then backscatters (reflects) it after appropriately modifying the phase of the excitation signal. The data that the tag wishes to transmit is modulated on these phase changes. The tag design at a conceptual level is very simple, it is an antenna connected to an array of switches which are turned on and off appropriately to control the phase of the reflected signal from the tag. The array of switches is controlled by logic that reads the information bits, and computes the on-off routine that needs to be implemented on the switch to create the phase difference that encodes the information bits. The backscattered signal is then received by the reader whose goal is then to demodulate the signal by first detecting the phase changes introduced by the tag and then recovering the original data. The design of the tag is fairly standard and is not the focus of this paper, we refer the reader to a large body of literature [49, 30] on the circuit level details of implementing tags.

It is useful to construct a model of the signal that the reader receives after the tag backscatters the signal. If $x(t)$ is the excitation signal transmitted by the reader, it undergoes four distortions before it arrives back at the reader again after reflections and backscatter. First, the signal gets reflected by objects in the environment other than the RFID tag and arrives back at the reader, we model this environmental distortion as h_{env}. The other portion of the signal is the one that first goes to the tag, has its phase changed to modulate data, and then comes back to the reader, i.e, the backscatter signal. We represent the forward channel between the reader and tag as h_f, the phase modulation at the tag is simply a multiplication of the received signal by $e^{j\theta(t)}$ and the backward channel is represented by h_b. The phase $\theta(t)$ is changed at the tag according to the data that is being modulated, for example, if DQPSK is being used, the phase w.r.t. the previous symbols phase is shifted by the appropriate multiple of 90 degrees. Note that $\theta(t)$ is changing at the rate of the symbol period at the tag. So the overall signal received back at the reader is given by:

$$y_{rx}(t) = \underbrace{x(t) * h_{env}(t)}_{environment} + \underbrace{\{(x(t) * h_f(t)).e^{j\theta(t)}\} * h_b(t)}_{backscatter} \quad (1)$$

The goal for the reader of course is to estimate $\theta(t)$ and thus demodulate the tag data. As the above equation shows, there are two challenges in accomplishing that. First is the environmental term; it contains no useful information and therefore acts as interference. This self-interference (because its generated by the reader's own transmission) is likely quite strong relative to the backscatter signal because it consists of direct leakage from the reader's transmitter to the receiver as well as reflections from nearby objects. In many cases, the self-interference and the backscatter signal can be separated by more than the dynamic range of the reader's receiver chain, which would end up completely drowning the backscatter signal. Second, if the environmental interference can be eliminated, the challenge is to estimate h_f and h_b, and then given that we know $x(t)$ it is simple to recover $\theta(t)$ and demodulate the tag data. The above two challenges are true for any backscatter system, we describe how current RFID systems handle them and why we cannot use that design for BackFi next.

3.1.1 Decoding Standard RFID Backscatter

In standard RFID based backscatter, the excitation signal is a sinusoid. So $x(t)$ in the above equation is $e^{j\omega_c t}$, where $\omega_c = 2\pi f_c$ is angular frequency and f_c is the carrier frequency (typically in the 900MHz ISM band). This simple fact ends up making both the interference cancellation and demodulation problem easier.

First, self-interference cancellation is simple because with a tone as the excitation signal, the interference term $x(t) * h_{env}(t)$ is simplified to $H_{env}(\omega_c)e^{j\omega_c t}$, where $H_{env}(\omega_c)$ is the frequency domain channel response corresponding to $h_{env}(t)$ and is evaluated at the tone frequency ω_c. In other words the original excitation signal is modified by a single complex number, essentially a single attenuation value and a phase shift. This is a special property of sinusoidal inputs to LTI channels, convolution simply becomes multiplication with the frequency domain channel response's value at the tone's frequency for tone inputs. This simplification does not apply to wideband signals such as WiFi. Hence to implement interference cancellation, all we need is a tunable phase shifter and attenuator, which is programmed dynamically to emulate $H_{env}(\omega_c)$. The cancellation circuit would get a copy of the transmitted excitation signal as input, pass it through the phase shifter and attenuator which have been tuned to $\angle H_{env}(\omega_c)$ and $|H_{env}(\omega_c)|$ respectively. Finally, the design subtracts it from the received signal at the reader to eliminate the self-interference. Note that this is a well known technique and is implemented in commercial readers today [15, 5].

Similarly, recovering $e^{j\theta(t)}$ becomes easy because $x(t)$ is a simple tone. To see why consider the following mathematical simplification after substituting $x(t)$ with a tone, $e^{j\omega_c t}$:

$$\{(x(t) * h_f(t))e^{j\theta(t)}\} * h_b(t) = H_f(\omega_c)\{e^{j\omega_c t}e^{j\theta(t)}\} * h_b(t)$$

Further simplification happens after down-conversion to baseband at the reader:

$$y_{\text{tag}}(t) = H_f(\omega_c)h_b(t) * e^{j\theta(t)}, \quad (2)$$

which is a standard decoding problem on a linear time invariant system with channel $H_f(\omega_c)h_b(t)$ and input $e^{j\theta(t)}$. Hence standard phase demodulation and decoding techniques [38] can be applied to recover the original phase modulated data.

3.2 Why can't we reuse the above design for BackFi?

The key difference between BackFi and conventional RFID backscatter is that BackFi aims to use standard WiFi signals as the excitation signal. So none of the above simplifications that came about because the excitation signal was a simple tone apply. In fact the self-interference cancellation and demodulation problems become significantly harder as we show below.

First, self-interference cancellation now has to eliminate a relatively wider band signal, not just a tone. The implication is that the self-interference cannot be modeled as a simple attenuation and phase shift applied to the original excitation signal. For WiFi signals that typically span 20-40 MHz or even more wider bandwidths, the frequency domain representation of the distortion introduced by the environment, h_{env} is quite frequency selective. The practical implication is that a simple cancellation circuit that uses a programmable attenuator and phase shifter is not enough to cancel, in fact we need more sophisticated designs that can model the attenuation and phase shifts that happen over the entire bandwidth of the WiFi signal. Hence the traditional reader design for eliminating self-interference doesn't apply.

Second, and more importantly, the decoding problem no longer reduces to a standard demodulation problem at the reader like it did with a tone. To see why, the reader is now trying to recover the phase $\theta(t)$ from the following received signal at the reader after down-conversion:

$$y_{\text{tag}}(t) = (e^{j\omega_c t}x(t) * h_f(t)).e^{j\theta(t)}\} * h_b(t) \quad (3)$$

The above equation represents a **time variant** channel that transports the input $e^{j\theta(t)}$ into the output $y_{\text{tag}}(t)$, and the information that we are trying to decode is buried inside this time variant channel. The reason the channel term is time varying is because the WiFi signal $x(t)$ is also acting as a channel distortion that is modifying $e^{j\theta(t)}$. Consequently standard decoding techniques designed for linear time invariant systems cannot be applied.

The main contributions of this paper are the design of self-interference cancellation and decoding techniques that can work when WiFi signals are used for backscatter. We also describe how BackFi ensures that it does not interfere with standard WiFi communication which the WiFi signal was originally created for.

4. DESIGN

BackFi uses ambient WiFi transmissions that are being sent by a WiFi AP to a standard WiFi client as the excitation signal. The tag receives the WiFi signal, modulates data on the received WiFi signal, and backscatters the signal to the AP. The architectural design of the BackFi tag is shown in Fig. 2. IoT sensor consists of BackFi tag and a sensor populating the data in the tag data memory unit.

4.1 The BackFi Link Layer Protocol

First, we describe how a BackFi AP activates and gets a BackFi tag to backscatter information. The protocol proceeds in two stages as described below.

How is the tag activated?

Whenever a BackFi AP transmits, if it is willing to receive backscatter communication, it follows a special protocol before transmitting the WiFi packet. Specifically, like in prior work [27], it transmits a *CTS_to_SELF* packet to force other WiFi devices to keep silent. Next it transmits a series of short pulses to encode a pseudo-random preamble sequence. If the preamble bit is one, then a pulse is transmitted and if its zero, no pulse is transmitted. The preamble is 16 bits long and each bit period lasts for a 1 μs. The preamble is meant to be the signal to the BackFi tag that the BackFi AP is willing to listen to backscatter transmissions. Note that a preamble can be unique to a particular BackFi tag that is connected to this BackFi AP and can be used to select which BackFi tag gets to backscatter at that instant. In such cases, a tag only backscatters when it detects the preamble meant for it.

A BackFi tag by default is in an energy saving sleep mode if it has no data to transmit. If it has sufficient data to transmit (potentially after a sensor has collected enough data), the tag wakes up and listens for its preamble from the BackFi AP. To listen and detect the preamble, the tag uses an energy efficient detector circuit. To build our preamble detector we leverage a large body of work done in low power wake up radio design [40, 18, 36, 37]. These detectors work at power consumption between $98nW$ [40] to 7.5 μW [18], and can detect input signals with power between -41 dBm and -56 dBm. The design has an envelope detector, a peak finder, a set-threshold circuit and a comparator. The envelope detector removes the 2.4 GHz carrier frequency from the received signal and the peak detector detects and holds the peak amplitude of the received signal after envelope detection. The set-threshold circuit obtains the output of the peak detector and outputs half the amplitude as the threshold. Finally the comparator compares the signal after the output of the envelope detector with the threshold and outputs one bit whenever the received signal is greater than the threshold value and a zero bit otherwise. The comparator outputs a bit decision every microsecond, corresponding to the bit period in the preamble. Finally digital logic on the BackFi tag correlates the detected 16-bit long sequence over sliding windows with the known preamble associated with that tag, and if there is a match it activates the rest of the backscatter circuitry to begin modulation of its data.

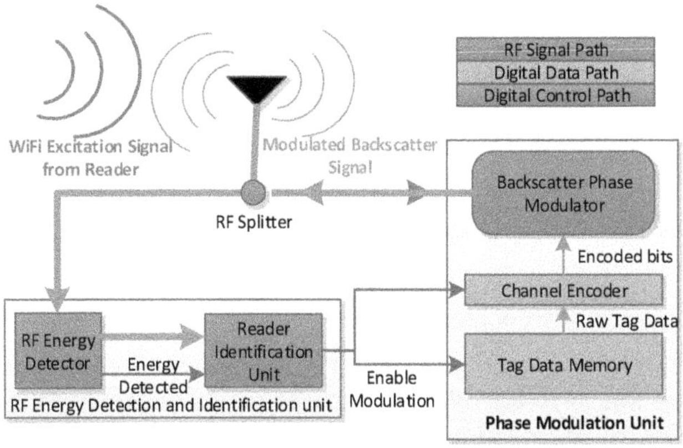

Figure 2: Architecture of the tag used in BackFi: Once the tag senses the WiFi excitation signal from the reader, it wakes up the modulation subsystem. The tag then reads the data to be uploaded and modulates it on the excitation signal by selecting discrete phase using the *Backscatter Phase Modulator*.

How does the tag modulate its data?

Fig. 4 shows the various timing events and packet format used by the BackFi tag. We will describe their functionality in detail later in this section, here we give a brief overview. Once the excitation energy is detected and the reader is identified (which lasts 16 μs), the tag goes into a *silent period* that lasts for another 16 μs. During this time the tag will suppress any backscatter transmission, which allows the reader to estimate the channels needed for self-interference cancellation as described in Sec. 4.2. After that the tag transmits its own *preamble* sequence for 32 μs that is known at the BackFi reader. Using this sequence the reader can estimate the channels it needs for decoding the backscatter data. This sequence is a pseudo random with very high autocorrelation, and is used by the reader to find the symbol timing from the tag.

The tag then sends its data payload by phase modulating the received signal. Specifically, let's say the tag is using QPSK modulation, hence there are four symbols $[e^{j\theta_1}$, $e^{j\theta_2}$, $e^{j\theta_3}$, $e^{j\theta_4}]$ in the constellation map separated by 90 degrees on which two bits of information can be modulated. The tag reads the data that needs to be transmitted, picks out two bits at a time, maps it to the appropriate QPSK symbol and then multiples the received excitation signal from the WiFi transmitter with the corresponding phase signal, $e^{j\theta_i}, i = 1 \ldots 4$ to modulate the data on to the WiFi signal. The specific circuit by which the phase modulation signal $e^{j\theta_i}$ is generated is a well studied problem and has been widely used in RFID

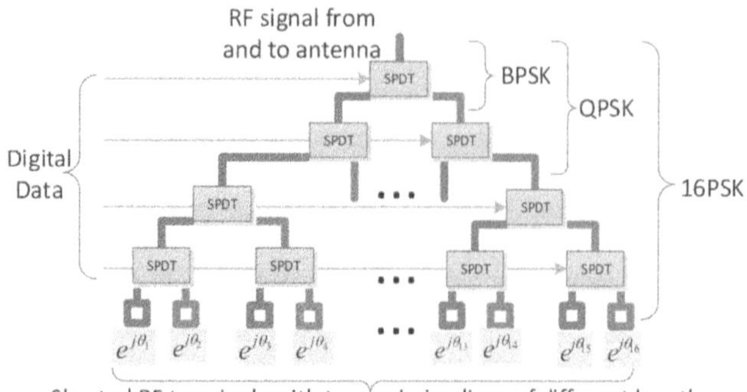

Figure 3: Structure of the backscatter phase modulator used in the tag of BackFi: The four digital signal can be used to select one of the 16 possible phases at the leaf of the tree. The incoming RF signal traverses from the top input port all the way to the selected leaf node and is reflected back from the short circuited terminals to the input RF port.

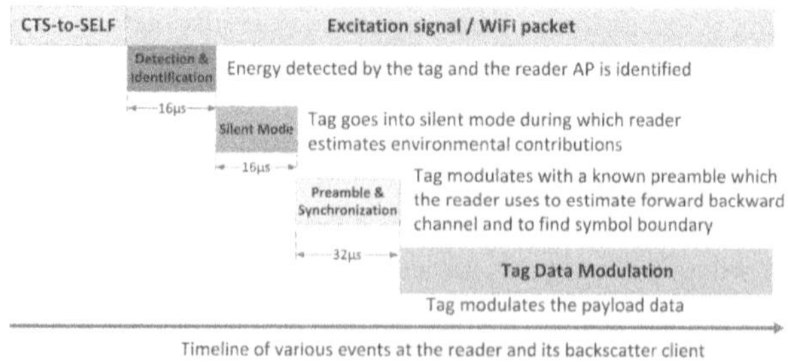

Figure 4: The BackFi AP first sends out the CTS-to-SELF to force other WiFi into silent mode. It then sends out the energy detection and identification data to its backscatter client. Once the WiFi excitation signal is received by the tag, it goes through sequence of operations shown above before modulating its data on the excitation signal. The excitation signal is in fact a WiFi packet meant for a regular WiFi client which receives and decodes the WiFi packet without ever noticing the presence of the backscatter communication that is happening simultaneously.

tags [49]. Fig. 3 shows the detail of the RF phase modulator we use in the BackFi tag.

The phase modulator consists of several RF Single Pole Double Throw (SPDT) switches that are connected in a binary tree structure. These switches can pass incoming RF signal to one of the two ports. These switches can be controlled using digital signals and the tag uses the data to be modulated as the control signal for these switches. At the leaf of the switch tree, different lengths of RF traces are connected. These trace lengths are designed specifically to achieve the discrete phase shift required for the supported constellation. The number of SPDT switches is determined by the number of constellation points that are supported. For example, for BPSK only one switch is needed, for QPSK three switches are needed and for 16-PSK 15 switches are needed. Also, if the tag can support higher modulations, then all the lower modulations can also be supported. For example, the design in Fig. 3 can support 16-PSK, QPSK, and BPSK, by appropriately preventing some of the switches from toggling as shown in the figure.

To improve the performance of the link the tag also employs simple channel encoding using convolutional codes. The convolutional codes are powerful error correcting codes yet their encoders are very easy to implement using few standard digital components which incurs small energy penalty on the tag. For example, a rate $\frac{1}{2}$ convolutional encoders with constraint length of 7, will require 6 shift registers and 8 XOR gates.

Tag Symbol Rate: The BackFi tag also has a choice on the rate at which it will generate the phase modulation symbols by controlling the switching frequencies on the SPDT switches. The trade-off here is that higher frequencies consume more power and energy, hence the actual rate to use is a function of how much energy is available either via batteries or harvesting. In BackFi tags, this is a configurable parameter ranging from 0.01 megasymbols/second (MSPS) to 2.5 MSPS.

Next, the BackFi AP after receiving the phase modulated, backscattered signal proceeds to decode the tag's data. As discussed in the previous section, the two key challenges here are wideband self-interference cancellation and time-varying decoding. We describe how BackFi addresses these challenges next. Note that the channel model of the signal received back at the reader with BackFi is exactly the same as standard RFID backscatter and has been derived in Eq. 3, the only difference of course is that $x(t)$ is the WiFi OFDM signal instead of a tone.

4.2 Self-Interference Cancellation

Like conventional RFID systems, the tag's backscatter signal in BackFi is buried under strong self-interference. This interference stems from two sources: direct leakage from the AP's transmit chain to the receive chain and from reflections of the WiFi transmission by non-tag objects in the environment. But unlike the single tone excitation signal in RFID, BackFi's excitation signal is a wideband WiFi OFDM signal. Because of the wideband nature, scaling the excitation signal by a single attenuation and phase shift is not sufficient to model the self-interference. This is because different frequency components of the WiFi signal add constructively or destructively due to the multi-path effect which results in frequency dependent scaling and phase shifts. However, this problem has been studied extensively in recent years for designing full-duplex radios [12] where self-interference needs to be suppressed to be able to simultaneously listen to weak signals that are being received. The difference in BackFi from those scenarios is that the backscatter signal (which corresponds to the weak signal we want to receive) is a modified version of the transmitted signal, whereas in standard full duplex that is a completely independent signal originating from another sender. So BackFi leverages the recent work on full duplex, but modifies it appropriately to handle the fact that backscatter signals are highly correlated with the self-interference signal.

We briefly review the design of self-interference cancellation systems for completeness, but refer the reader to prior work [12] for a complete description. Self-interference cancellation systems first estimate the channel $h_{env}(t)$ that the leaked and reflected signal have gone through before reaching back at the receiver. This estimated channel distortion

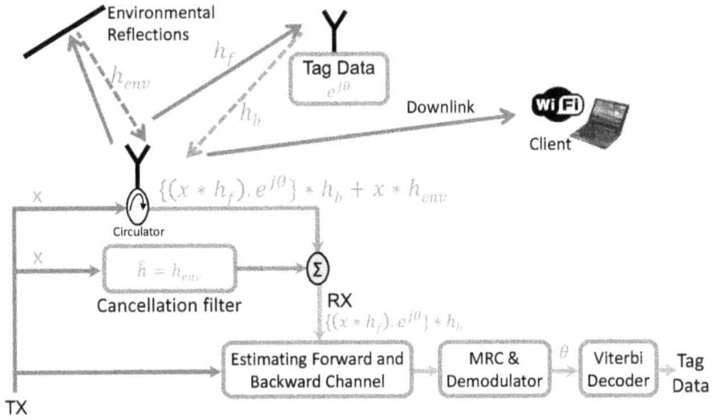

Figure 5: Architecture of the reader used in BackFi: The reader transmits the excitation signal x which is actually a WiFi packet meant for a client. This signal is reflected by the environment, which the reader cancels using *cancellation filter*. The residual signal after cancellation is used to estimate the forward and backward channel from and to the tag. The reader then applies MRC to estimate the tag data $\hat{\theta}$, which is further improved by passing it through Viterbi decoder.

is applied to a copy of the transmitted WiFi signal to recreate the self-interference accurately, and the distorted signal is then subtracted from the received signal to eliminate self-interference. The distortion application and subtraction happens in two stages, analog and digital. Analog cancellation is necessary to ensure that the receiver's ADC is not saturated by self-interference which would drown out the weak backscatter signal before being received in baseband. Analog cancellation is implemented using a combination of RF FIR filters and couplers [12], but cannot completely eliminate self-interference due to the imprecision of analog components. Hence a second digital cancellation stage is employed after the signal is sampled by the receiver's ADC to eliminate the residual self-interference. Digital cancellation is implemented via digital FIR filters. Fig. 5 shows the design.

If we directly apply the prior design, it will end up canceling parts of the backscatter signal too. The reason is that prior design aims to accurately estimate the non-linear transfer function that captures the relationship between the transmitted signal and the received signal [12]. But as we have shown in the previous section, the backscatter signal is actually a non-linear transformation of the transmitted signal. If naively applied, prior designs would end up canceling the backscatter signal too which would reduce the SNR and throughput of tag's transmissions back to the reader.

To tackle this, BackFi's link layer design ensures that during the channel estimation phase of self-interference cancellation, there is no backscatter transmission. Specifically, when a BackFi tag is excited by a WiFi transmission, they do not instantly start backscatter. Instead they employ a *silent period* of 16 μs as shown in Fig. 4, during which they do not backscatter, and only then start modulating their data on to the received signal and performing backscatter. We show experimentally that this small silent period is sufficient for the reader/AP to estimate the self-interference channel and perform cancellation for the rest of the WiFi packet. Since there is no backscatter during the channel estimation phase, self-interference cancellation does not model the backscatter reflections and therefore they are not affected by cancellation.

At this stage, the reader/AP is left with just the non-linear backscatter reflection from the tag, and its goal is to decode the data. We describe this step next.

4.3 Decoder Design of BackFi

As reviewed before, since the WiFi signal $x(t)$ is wideband, the excitation signal received at the tag $z(t) = x(t) * h_f(t)$ cannot be considered as simple scaled and phase shifted version of $x(t)$ as with standard RFIDs. Hence after the removal of the self-interference, the residual signal at the reader after down-conversion to baseband is given by

$$y_{\text{tag}}(t) = \underbrace{\left[(x(t) * h_f(t))e^{j\theta(t)}\right] * h_b(t)}_{\text{tag signal}}. \qquad (4)$$

Here, the signal $x(t)$ is the WiFi transmission that the reader is sending. This signal is wideband and varying but known to the reader. The channels h_f and h_b are the forward and the backward channels. These channels can be considered time invariant for the duration of the tag packet but are unknown. The goal is of course to recover the tag signal $e^{j\theta(t)}$ from the above equation. This is challenging because the tag signal is being modified by a time varying unknown channel, namely $x(t) * h_f(t)$. Contrast this with standard RFID decoding at the reader in Eq. 2, where the tag signal is being modified by a time-invariant channel since both $h_f(t)$ and $h_b(t)$ are time-invariant for the duration of the tag packet. We describe how BackFi tackles this time-varying decoding problem next.

4.3.1 Estimating the forward/backward channels

First, the BackFi AP estimates the forward and backward channels, $h_f(t)$ and $h_b(t)$. We can assume these channels to be time invariant for the duration of the tag packet, hence to estimate them we use a standard communication technique: a preamble. Specifically, after the tag detects that it should backscatter and stays quiet for the *silent period*, it modulates a constant phase $e^{j\theta_{pre}}$ on the backscatter signal for a fixed period of $32\mu S$. Thus during the *preamble interval* the received tag signal at the reader is given by

$$y_{pre}(t) = x(t) * [h_f(t) * h_b(t)].$$

Now since $x(t)$ is known, this becomes a standard channel estimation problem encountered in every communication system. We omit the details of the channel estimation technique and refer the reader to the vast amount of literature on this topic [38]. The channel estimation algorithm thus calculates the value of $h_f(t) * h_b(t)$.

Note that the above procedure only provides an estimate of the combined forward-backward channel, but not the individual channels. Hence the decoding step has to work only with the combined channel estimate.

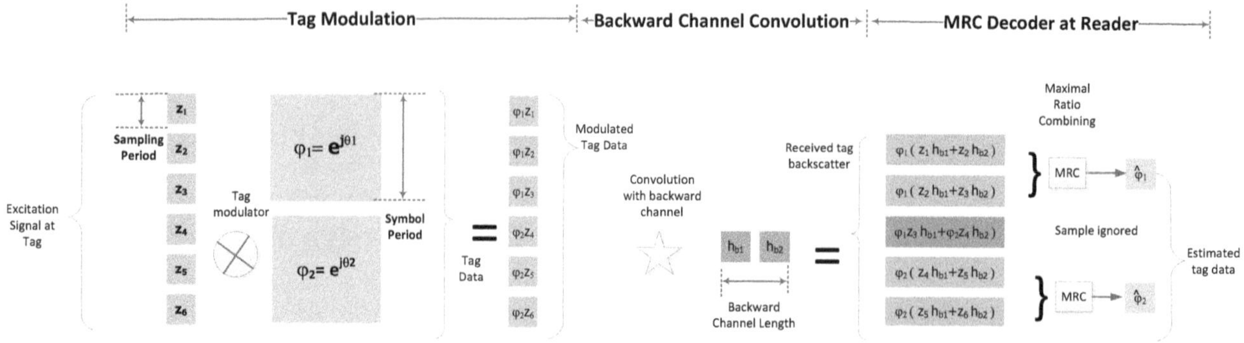

Figure 6: Discrete time representation of the design of BackFi: The samples of the WiFi excitation signal z is multiplied by the data ϕ at the tag.The modulated signal then passes through the backward channel h_b. The sampling period of WiFi is much smaller than the symbol period of the tag. This results in multiple copies of the tag data over several sampling period at the reader. These multiple copes are combined optimally by the MRC to estimate the tag data $\hat{\phi}$.

4.3.2 Decoding the Tag Data

The final step is decoding the tag data itself. BackFi's key insight here is the fact that symbol times for tag data are quite long due to the need to conserve energy at the tag. Specifically the tag modulates data by changing the phase term in $e^{j\theta(t)}$. Changing the phase is implemented by switching a transistor as described in Sec. 4.1. Transistor energy consumption scales linearly with switching frequency, hence tags use low rate switching frequencies. Typical transistor switching frequencies in tags are on the order of $0.5 - 2.5$ MHz in tags, hence the symbol period in a tag is between $500 - 2000$ ns. How can we exploit this insight to decode the data?

Our observation is that the delay spread in a typical channel between the reader and the tag is far smaller than 500 ns. In other words the length of the channel is far smaller. Intuitively this is because typical distances between a reader and a tag are around 10 m, so even accounting for reflections the extra multipath delay spread is small. Hence a channel usually lasts for $50 - 80$ ns. But the symbol period from the tag is much longer at 500 ns, hence for the duration of the channel, we can consider the tag signal to be an unknown constant $e^{j\theta_c}$. BackFi leverages this insight to decode, it looks at the part of the symbol period (with some guard periods at the start and end of the symbol time as shown in Fig. 6 and tries to find the value of the constant phase within that period.

Specifically, with a constant phase from time $t_1 - t_2$, we can rewrite the decoding equation at the reader as:

$$y(t) = (x(t) * [h_f(t) * h_b(t)])e^{j\theta_c} + N; t_1 \leq t < t_2 \quad (5)$$

Note that all the terms except $e^{j\theta_c}$ are known in the above equation. A natural next step might be to divide $y(t)$ by $x(t) * [h_f(t) * h_b(t)]$ but this works poorly because it will also divide the noise term in the above equation and in many scenarios amplify it.

To tackle this, we turn to an old trick in communication theory: maximal ratio combining. To see how this works it helps to write the above equation in the discrete domain (the representations are equivalent assuming sufficient sampling rate) as follows:

$$y_{\text{tag}}[n] = e^{j\theta[n_1]}\mathbf{x}^{\mathbf{T}}_{\mathbf{n,L+M}}\mathbf{h_{fb}} \qquad \forall n \in [n_1, n_2] \quad (6)$$

Here L is the length of the forward channel, and M is the length of the backward channel. The $\mathbf{h_{fb}}$ is the length $L + M$ vector of the combined forward-backward channel and $\mathbf{x_{n,L+M}} = [x_n \dots x_{n+L+M-1}]^T$ is a vector of length $L+M$ constructed using the excitation data $x[n]$, and we have assumed that the tag signal is constant for the period $[n1, n2]$. The above equation is simply a discrete version of Eq. 5 with the discrete convolution operation represented as dot product of vectors $\mathbf{x_{n,L+M}}$ and $\mathbf{h_{fb}}$.

Notice that the tag signal is expressed in terms of the forward-backward channel that we have estimated earlier, and therefore individual estimates of the forward and the backward channel are not needed. Also note that the tag modulation is constant for $n_2 - n_1 + 1$ interval which is larger than $L + M$, this is restating the same insight that length of the forward and backward channels is much smaller than the symbol period of the tag. So we will have $n_1 + n_2 - L_M$ different values of $y_{\text{tag}}[n]$ which contains information of the unknown but constant tag signal $e^{j\theta_c}$. We can leverage this fact to combine all these values to obtain the most likely value of θ_c that could have produced those sequence of observations of $y_{\text{tag}}[n]$ over the period $[n1, n2]$ using maximal ratio combining (essentially the same as temporal diversity combining). Specifically MRC would use the following formula to estimate θ_c,

$$\hat{\theta}_c = \frac{\sum_{n=n_1}^{n_2} \hat{y}_{\text{tag}}[n]^{\mathsf{C}} y_{\text{tag}}[n]}{\sum |\hat{y}_{\text{tag}}[n]|^2}, \quad (7)$$

where $\hat{y}_{\text{tag}}[n]$ is the expected tag backscatter signal without the modulation and can be computed as

$$\hat{y}_{\text{tag}}[n] = \mathbf{x}^{\mathbf{T}}_{\mathbf{n,L+M}}\mathbf{h_{fb}} \qquad \forall n \in [n_1, n_2],$$

and ^{C} is the complex conjugate operator. Essentially the different measurements of y over that interval are weighted appropriately and combined to produce the most likely estimate of θ_c.

At this point, we have a robust estimate of the tag data for that symbol. The algorithm is repeated for all the symbols in the tag packet. There may still be decoding errors of the n-PSK symbols, which we can correct by using a standard channel code on top. In BackFi, we use a convolutional code at the tag to improve the link performance. The coding provides additional robustness and is decoded using a standard Viterbi decoder [38], we omit the details for brevity.

5. IMPLEMENTATION

We build a prototype of both the AP and tag of BackFi system. We describe their implementation details below.

5.1 BackFi AP

The BackFi AP is implemented using WARP software radios. The WARP incorporates a standard 20 MHz WiFi baseband operating in the 2.4 GHz range. We also use the same implementation on a WARP board to work as a WiFi client in our experiments. Further the decoding logic for backscatter signals is also implemented in the WARP FPGA [7]. For self-interference cancellation, we reproduce the recent design on single antenna cancellation [12, 11].

5.2 BackFi Tag

The IoT sensor is designed to operate across the 2.4 GHz WiFi channels. The prototype uses a 2.4 GHz omni-directional antenna that can receive and backscatter WiFi signals and has a gain of 3 dB. In our current prototype, logic implemented on a Kintex Kc705 board [6] supplies the data to be transmitted and configures the backscatter circuitry. This can be replaced with custom ASIC in a full design which would consumes significantly lower energy.

The backscatter circuitry implements two components on the uplink: *the detector*, and *the modulator*. The modulator implements BPSK, QPSK and 16-PSK modulation. The phase modulation is implemented using SP4T switches. We chose phase modulation instead of n-QAM because this will result in the least amount of RF signal degradation during the backscatter modulation.

5.2.1 Energy consumption efficiency metric

In order to compare various implementation choices for IoT sensor, traditionally Energy per Bit (EPB) measured in average joules of energy required to transmit one bit of information has been used as a metric for energy efficiency. However, EPB varies significantly with the implementation platform. For example, the EPB for an IoT sensor implemented using off-the-shelf discrete components can be orders of magnitude larger than the EPB for IoT sensor implemented in a sub-micron ASIC design. Even for the submicron ASIC designs, EPB varies significantly depending on the technology node chosen (say 65-nm CMOS node vs 45-nm CMOS node) and the design choices (low power subthreshold CMOS design vs traditional strong inversion CMOS design). BackFi's contribution is in showing how the EPB of an IoT sensor are related to each other for various communication parameters on a particular implementation platform. For example, if an IoT sensor can choose BPSK or QPSK for communication, an interesting question may be, what is the relationship between the EPB of these two cases. While to the first order the EPB of these two cases should be the same and only the throughput should double going from BPSK to QPSK, a more detailed analysis shows that EPB is not the same for these two cases.

To understand why, let us refer to the architecture of the RF modulator as shown in Fig. 3. While BPSK requires only one SPDT switch, the QPSK requires three SPDT switches with double the throughput, therefore the EPB of the modulator goes up by a factor of $\frac{3}{2}$. Likewise, for 16-PSK we need 15 SPDT switches, but the data rate improvement is only 4 times compared to the BPSK, therefore the relative EPB for modulator increases by a factor of $\frac{15}{4}$. Also, power consumption in IoT sensor has two major components, the first one is dynamic power resulting from the charging and discharging of capacitors in various sub-systems of the IoT sensor as digital logic is computed, and the second is static power which is either due to leakage, or due to constant current required by some of the analog components in the IoT sensor. Because of the static power, the EPB is also effected by the symbol rate of the IoT sensor as the device takes longer time to transmit the same amount of data. For example, an IoT sensor can reduce the symbol rate which results in the improved SNR at the BackFi from MRC, but at the same time the static power consumption of the circuits will increase thereby increasing the overall EPB.

In order to show the energy efficiency trade-offs associated with the various choices offered by BackFi and to decouple them from the energy efficiency gained from actual choice of the implementation platform, we will present the remainder of the results using unit-less Relative Energy per Bit (REPB). We will first describe how energy consumption is modeled for our exemplary IoT sensor as shown in Fig. 2 and then show how we can compute its REPB for different parameter choices.

We have modeled the EPB of the tag by identifying the major power consumption modules of the IoT sensor architecture shown in Fig. 2. The three major contributors for EPB of this design are: *the RF modulator, the channel encoder and the memory*. As discussed earlier, the EPB of RF modulator varies depending on the chosen modulation index because the ratio of bit rate to the number of SPDT switches varies as we change the modulation index. In our current energy model we have computed the static and dynamic EPB of RF modulation unit by appropriately scaling the data provided for an industry standard modulator, the Analog Devices ADG904 [1].

BackFi uses a convolutional encoder to reduce bit error rates (BER). The exact EPB contributed by the encoder circuit is a very small fraction of the total EPB required for communication because convolutional encoders with moderate constraint length (7 in BackFi) require only 6 shift registers and a few XOR gates to encode the IoT sensor data. But the major EPB contribution comes from the coding rate associated with the convolutional encoder. For example, a $\frac{1}{2}$ rate code will essentially double the EPB of the RF modulator because the IoT sensor will transmit twice the actual amount of data on the channel. Likewise, a rate $\frac{2}{3}$ code will bump the RF modulator's EPB by a factor of $\frac{3}{2}$ and so on.

And finally BackFi also models the EPB associated with the memory read of the data in the IoT sensor. Because memory reads are performed for the sole purpose of backscattering the data to the BackFi's reader, we believe it is very important to include the read energy associated with the memory element as part of the overall EPB. In our current energy model we have computed the static and dynamic EPB of the memory read by using data provided for Cypress Semiconductor CY62146EV30 [2].

Using the above energy modeling technique we can now compute the EPB required for a particular choice of communication parameters: *channel code rate, symbol switching rate, modulation index*

$$\mathrm{EPB} = \mathrm{EPB_{mem}} + \mathrm{EPB_{mod}} + \mathrm{EPB_{enc}}. \quad (8)$$

Here $\mathrm{EPB_{mem}}$ is the EPB associated with the memory read inside the IoT sensor. This has two parts, the dynamic EPB that is dependent on the number of read operations per bit of data of IoT sensor, and the static part that is dependent on the symbol switching rate T_s,

$$\mathrm{EPB_{mem}} = \mathrm{EPB_{mem,read}} + \mathrm{P_{mem,static}} \times T_s.$$

Similarly, we can express the EPB associated with the convolutional encoder $\mathrm{EPB_{enc}}$ and the modulator $\mathrm{EPB_{mod}}$ with their constituent dynamic and static EPB.

In order to obtain the unit-less REPB, we use EPB for one set of such communication parameters as a reference and then divide the EPB for all the other choices with this reference EPB. In our current evaluation, we use $\frac{1}{2}$ rate code with BPSK modulation with symbol switching rate of 1 Mbps as reference communication parameters to compute the reference EPB. Based on the datasheets of the referred parts we computed the EPB for this reference case to be 3.15 pJ/bit.

Also, we have excluded the EPB associated with the energy detection logic as we believe their contribution to the overall EPB will be insignificant. The energy detector is based on prior work on wake up radio [40, 31]. The power consumption of this detector is around 100 nW. The energy detection needs to be done once for every backscatter packet and lasts for 16 μs. A typical backscatter packet will have 1000 bits of information in it. Based on these information the EPB contributed by the detection logic is in femtojoules per bits which is practically negligible. The wake up radio can detect input signals as weak as -41 dBm, which provides sufficient range to wake up the tag radio even at a distance of 5 m from the AP. The same detection circuitry can be used to implement the downlink communication to the tag from the AP reader. The protocol for downlink communication has been described in prior work [27]. BackFi reuses this design for the downlink and provides similar throughputs of 20 Kbps. Since our focus in this work is on the uplink design we will evaluate it in detail in the next section by using REPB given by Fig. 8 as one of the metrics.

Symbol switching rate	Metric	BPSK, 1/2 rate	BPSK, 2/3 rate	QPSK, 1/2 rate	QPSK, 2/3 rate	16PSK, 1/2 rate	16PSK, 2/3 rate
10 KHz	REPB	29.2162	28.1984	31.2517	29.7250	40.4117	36.5951
	Thrput (Kbps)	5	6.67	10	13.33	20	26.66
100 KHz	REPB	3.5651	3.3333	4.0287	3.6810	6.1151	5.2458
	Thrput (Kbps)	50	66.7	100	133.3	200	266.6
500 KHz	REPB	1.2850	1.1231	1.6089	1.3660	3.0665	2.4592
	Thrput (Mbps)	.25	.33	.5	.67	1	1.33
1 MHz	REPB	1.0000	0.8468	1.3064	1.0766	2.6855	2.1109
	Thrput (Mbps)	.5	.67	1	1.33	2	2.67
2 MHz	REPB	0.8575	0.7086	1.1552	0.9319	2.4949	1.9367
	Thrput (Mbps)	1	1.33	2	2.67	4	5.33
2.5 MHz	REPB	0.8290	0.6810	1.1250	0.9030	2.4568	1.9019
	Thrput (Mbps)	1.25	1.67	2.5	3.33	5	6.67

Figure 7: Table provides BackFi tag's relative EPB and corresponding data rate for different choices of modulation, coding and tag symbol switching rate.

6. EVALUATION

We evaluate BackFi's design in an indoor environment in our lab with rich multi-path reflections and dense WiFi deployment. Our evaluation reveals the following:

- BackFi provides three orders of magnitude higher throughput, an order of magnitude higher range compared to the best known WiFi backscatter system [27, 25]. Specifically BackFi can provide a throughput of 5 Mbps at 1m range and a throughput of 1 Mbps at 5 m range from the BackFi AP.
- BackFi's throughput and range are comparable to traditional RFID platforms such as Ekhonet [55]. The key benefit of course is that BackFi is a WiFi back-scatter system and does not need dedicated reader infrastructure or frequency spectrum.
- BackFi has negligible (less than 5%) impact on the standard WiFi network's throughput even when the IoT sensor is concurrently backscattering WiFi signals.

6.1 Throughput, Range, and REPB

First, we evaluate the trade-off between throughput, distance, and REPB for BackFi. For any given distance, BackFi can deliver a set of throughputs by picking the appropriate combination of symbol switching rate, modulation, and coding rate. Each choice of symbol switching rate and modulation has a different throughput as well as different REPB as described in Section 5.2.1. Fig. 7 shows the REPB and throughput for every combination of symbol switching rate, modulation, and coding rate. The EPB for each of the these entries can be calculated simply by multiplying REPB and EPB of the reference parameters (BPSK, 1/2 rate with symbol switching rate of 1 MHz).

Note that while throughput monotonically increases from left to right in the table, REPB does not. For example, at an IoT sensor symbol switching rate of 1 MSPS, going from (QPSK, 1/2) to (QPSK, 2/3) results in a decrease in REPB. The reason is that energy needed to switch from 1/2 rate to 2/3 rate is not significant compared to the other energy contributions for this technology node and the increased throughput causes the REPB ratio to decrease. However, if at a certain range if the link SNR is such that both (QPSK, 1/2) and (QPSK, 2/3) encoded backscatter signals can be decoded at

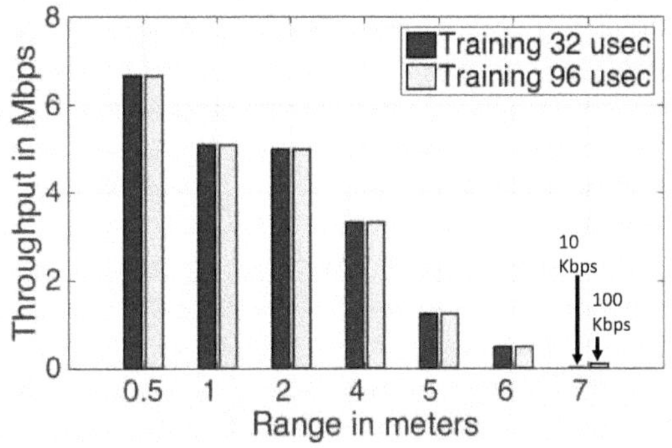

Figure 8: Relationship showing range of BackFi and maximum possible data rate possible for two different training times. At 7 meter, if we increase the preamble duration from 32 μsec to 96 μsec, it provides 10× improvement in the throughput.

the reader, then BackFi would never use (QPSK, 1/2). The rate adaptation algorithm would always pick the modulation, coding rate and symbol switching rate combination with the lowest REPB since the most precious resource here is energy, whether it comes from harvesting or batteries.

Next, we evaluate the throughout and range performance in our testbed. For these experiments we use our WARP based BackFi implementation for the BackFi AP to decode the IoT sensor's backscatter signals. The BackFi AP and the WiFi client are placed such that the maximum WiFi bit rate is 54 Mbps. They are configured to run on WiFi channel-6 in the 2.4 GHz range. The results for other WiFi channels are similar and not presented due to lack of space.

Impact of Range on Throughput: The BackFi's IoT sensor is placed at distances ranging from 0.5 m to 7 m. For each distance, we cycle the IoT sensor through all combinations of symbol switching rates and modulations, and then calculate throughput for combinations that can be decoded at the reader. In each iteration of the experiment, the BackFi's AP reader transmits 1 to 4 ms long packet at 24 Mbps bitrate including the backscatter start sequence as discussed in Sec. 4.1. The IoT sensor backscatters for the entire duration of the packet and stops when its detection logic signals the end of the transmission. We repeat the experiment 20 times at each combination of distance and BackFi throughput. Fig. 8 plots the maximum throughput achieved as a function of range for two different preamble duration of 32 μs and 96 μs.

Results: As we can see, BackFi is able to achieve a maximum throughout of around 6.67 Mbps at a distance of 50 cm. For more practical ranges, BackFi achieves a throughput of 1 Mbps at a distance of 5 m and around 5 Mbps at a distance of 1 m. This performance is three orders of magnitude better in throughput at the same range as compared to the best known WiFi backscatter system [27, 25]. Note, at 7 m the increased preamble duration of 96 μs shows a 10× increase in the throughput. This is due to the fact that a shorter preamble results in an inaccurate estimate of the forward-backward channel which limits the SNR of the backscattered signal. Hence, for 32 μs preamble, the IoT sensor compensates this loss of SNR by increasing the symbol period to 10×, which in turn reduces the throughput.

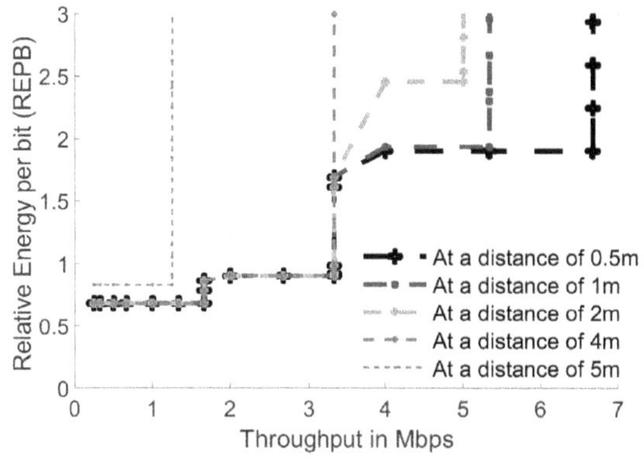

Figure 9: Each plot is BackFi's REPB for corresponding throughput achieved for the range varying between 0.5 m to 5 m. For example, we see that at a distance of 2 m to achieve 4 Mbps throughput we need to spend much more energy per bit than at a distance of 1m. Also, the vertical line indicates the maximum throughput that is achievable at a given distance between the tag and the reader.

To analyze the energy efficiency that BackFi link achieves for different combinations of throughput and range, we plot REPB as a function of throughput achieved for different ranges in Fig. 9. To read this graph, note that for every value of range we studied (0.5 m, 1 m, 2 m, 4 m, 5 m), we have a different curve (with a different color). Now for each particular range, we check what combinations of tag symbol rate, modulation and coding rates employed at the tag can be successfully decoded at the BackFi AP. For each throughput, we look up all combination that achieve it, and their REPB from Table. 7 and choose a minimum REPB and plot a point. All the points for that particular range are now joined by lines to show the feasible points for each range.

Fig. 9 shows that for a given range, throughput increases are obtained by either increasing the symbol switching rate, moving to a denser modulation or higher coding rate or some combination of all three. Each one of these increases energy consumption as expected, which leads to the step increases in REPB. Of course certain throughputs simply cannot be supported at a given range because the link's SNR is not strong enough to decode the data. The vertical line indicates the maximum throughput that can be achieved for a given distance between the tag and the BackFi's reader. Hence we see the curves stopping after a certain throughput for different ranges. Overall REPB lies between 0.5 to 3 for most combinations.

Next, we plot how REPB changes as a function of range assuming we want the same throughput. For this experiment we pick two throughputs, 1.25 Mbps and 5 Mbps, for which we want to optimize the communication link. For each value of range, we pick the combination of tag symbol rate, modulation and coding rate that can achieve those throughputs if there are any. Among the possible combinations we pick the one with the lowest REPB and plot it for that range. Fig. 10 shows the REPB as function of range for these two throughputs.

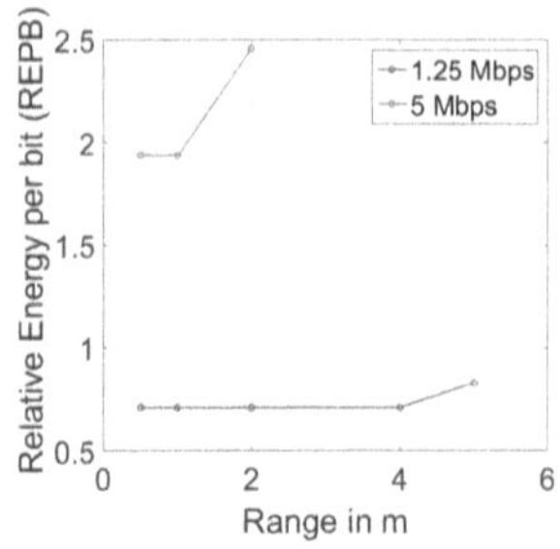

Figure 10: For achieving fixed throughput using BackFi for different distance, the tag needs to spend more energy as it goes far away. For achieving 1.25 Mbps we need to spend 2.5× more than power needed for reference modulation, coding and switching rate.

Here we see expected results. For a fixed throughput, as we go to higher ranges we need to use lower coding rates. In our current design we only support two coding rates: 1/2 and 2/3. Hence for all these experiments we see the REPB change between two levels corresponding to the shift from higher coding rate to lower.

6.2 Reconstructing BackFi's performance

In this section, we aim to understand where do BackFi's benefits come from. As discussed before, BackFi's design has two key components: *self-interference cancellation and the decoding algorithm.* We try to shed light on the impact of each component on BackFi's performance.

Impact of self-interference cancellation: This component helps eliminate the unwanted leakage and environmental reflections from reducing the backscatter signal's SNR. Any uncanceled interference directly acts as noise to the backscatter signal and reduces throughput. To evaluate its impact we measure the SNR for the backscatter link at the reader and compare it to what the SNR would have been if cancellation was perfect. The experiment is conducted by placing the BackFi AP and the IoT sensor at 30 different locations in the testbed. For each location, we do ten runs where during each run we let the BackFi IoT sensor backscatter a known packet and measure the forward and backward channels from the tag using a vector network analyzer. In this scenario the VNA [42] acts as the BackFi AP and is being used so that we can measure the channels accurately for comparison. Next we perform the actual backscatter communication with a BackFi AP and decode the data after self-interference cancellation. We also compute the SNR of the demodulated phase modulated symbols from the tag and compare it to the SNR predicted by the channel measurement from the VNA. We plot these two SNR values for each run and each location as a scatter plot in Fig. 11(a). As we can see cancellation works well, the median degradation in SNR is less than 2.3 dB. This is consistent with earlier self-interference cancellation results from prior work [12, 11] which report a self-interference residue of 1.7 dB after cancellation.

Impact of Symbol Time and MRC: The second component of BackFi's decoder at the BackFi AP is the algorithm for dealing with the time-varying decoding problem. The algorithm has two key components: exploiting the larger symbol times from the tag packet to make an approximation that

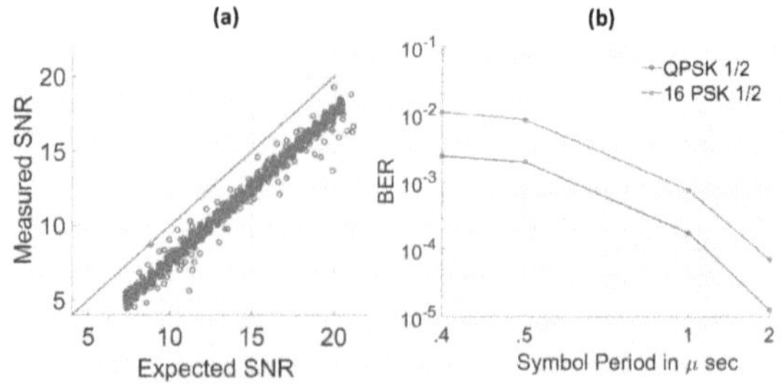

Figure 11: (a) Demonstrates the effect of imperfect cancellation on the degradation of the measured SNR vs the expected SNR at the reader of BackFi. When the cancellation is imperfect the environmental components are no longer completely removed and this acts as interference to the backscatter signal from the tag.**(b)** Demonstrates the diversity gains of MRC : as we increase the symbol time period, we have more samples for averaging, hence it improves the SNR. This increase in SNR results in lower bit error rate (BER) for a given modulation.

the channel can be converted into a simplified time invariant system and then apply MRC to solve it. MRC helps amplify the SNR of the signal by combining signal energy across time appropriately. Hence the key factor here is the tag symbol period which is inversely proportional to the tag symbol rate. To show the impact we plot the BER vs tag symbol rate for two modulations and a fixed coding rate of 1/2. The expectation is that as the tag symbol rate decreases and symbol time increases, the MRC gain will drive the BER down like a waterfall curve. Fig. 11(b) plots the BER as a function of decreasing tag symbol rate. As we can see, for this particular placement of AP and tag, at the highest tag symbol rate the BER is high between $10^{-2} - 10^{-3}$. As tag symbol rate decreases, the time diversity gain from MRC kicks in and BER drops down to between $10^{-4} - 10^{-5}$. This technique essentially points out the trade-off between throughput and range and why it exists.

6.3 Performance in typical WiFi Networks

BackFi tags only backscatter data when the WiFi reader is transmitting and they are activated by the reader with the activation sequence. The best candidate for the WiFi reader device is clearly the AP since it is likely the most dominant transmitter in a typical network. Nevertheless, in a typical network that is fully loaded (i.e. there is always outstanding traffic to transmit from the AP or a client), the AP will be transmitting a fraction of the time which would imply that the BackFi link would also be active for the same fraction. We evaluate the throughput BackFi can provide under such typical network conditions.

To conduct this experiment, we took traces from open source data [24, 47, 41]. The traces are captured for a wide variety of scenarios for heavily loaded networks. If an AP is not loaded and there is a lot of idle channel time, then a BackFi AP can initiate backscatter communication anyway by sending dummy packets just for that purpose. Hence the interesting case is when the network is loaded and backscatter opportunities are limited due to contention.

Next, we filter the traces to only contain AP transmissions and replay the collected trace using our WARP based BackFi AP implementation to simulate the same traffic conditions.

In other words, in our emulated experiment the WARP radio only transmits when the corresponding AP transmitted in the collected trace. We place a BackFi tag at a fixed distance of 2 m from the BackFi AP. We also activate the tag only at the times the AP is transmitting. We repeat this experiment for each AP we captured traces for, a total of 20 different APs. For each replay, we calculate the average throughput obtained by the BackFi link. Fig. 12(a) plots the CDF of these throughputs.

As we can see, in a loaded network, the BackFi link can obtain a median throughput of 4 Mbps. For a range of 2 m, the optimal throughput when the BackFi AP is continuously transmitting an excitation signal is 5 Mbps, hence this amounts 80% of the optimal throughput under realistic WiFi network conditions. The above number can be improved further if more WiFi devices have BackFi functionality. Specifically the above experiment assumed that only the AP has BackFi functionality. However if we can integrate the same into our laptops and smart-phones and turn them into gateways for BackFi links, then the BackFi link can be active for larger fractions of time.

6.4 Impact on the WiFi Network

A natural question is whether BackFi affects the performance of the WiFi network itself when the AP is doubling up as a WiFi backscatter reader. Specifically, one might imagine that the tags backscatter signals could propagate to the actual WiFi client which is the destination of the transmission from the AP and act as interference.

To quantify what impact one might see in a general WiFi network, we place the BackFi AP and ten clients at random locations in the testbed. Next we place the tag at increasing distances from the AP and calculate the WiFi throughput with and without an active BackFi tag. We repeat this experiment for 30 different configurations of the AP and the clients. We plot the throughputs with and without an active BackFi tag for different ranges between the BackFi AP and the tag in Fig. 12(b). The results confirm the previous benchmark, essentially when the tag and the AP reader are extremely close (between $0.25 - 0.5$m), there is a small impact on network throughput of less than 10%. Otherwise the normal WiFi network performance is negligibly affected since the backscatter signals are so weak.

6.5 Micro-benchmark Impact on WiFi

We now evaluate the worst case scenario for the WiFi client. This corresponds to the case where the tag is very close to the AP (at a distance of 0.25m) because in this case the backscatter signals would be the strongest. Next we take a single WiFi client and place it at different distances so that we achieve each of the different rates of WiFi. Now for each WiFi bitrate, we evaluate the PHY layer throughput achieved with and without a BackFi tag being active. Fig. 13.a plots the CDF of WiFi throughputs achieved for this link with and without a BackFi tag active. As we can see, the effect is minimal. The only case where there is a noticeable difference is when the WiFi AP and the client are using the highest bitrate of 54 Mbps where small decreases in SNR (as shown

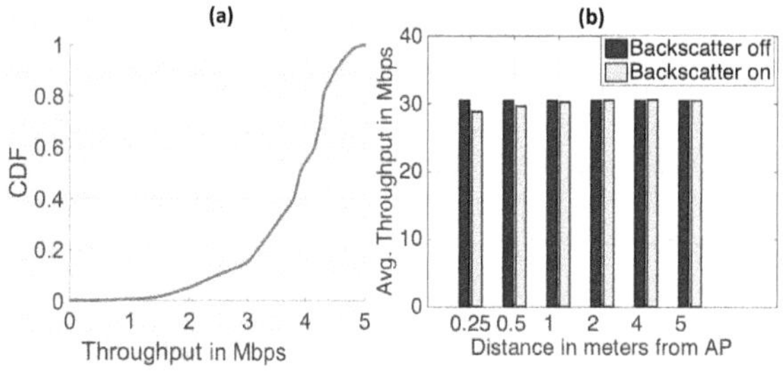

Figure 12: WiFi Deployments: **(a)** Throughput of BackFi's tag at a distance of 1m from the BackFi's reader under normal WiFi deployment. Note that BackFi tag is active only when the BackFi's reader is transmitting. Hence we achieve on an average 4 Mbps throughput vs the maximum throughput of 5Mbps. **(b)** Average throughput for all the clients at different locations as a function of distance of tag from the AP. As the tag moves away from the AP, it receives and radiates a smaller signal which will have smaller effect at the client. Hence, when the tag is at 0.25 m, we see a 10% throughput drop when tag is modulating. As the tag moves away from AP, we see no degradation in the average throughput.

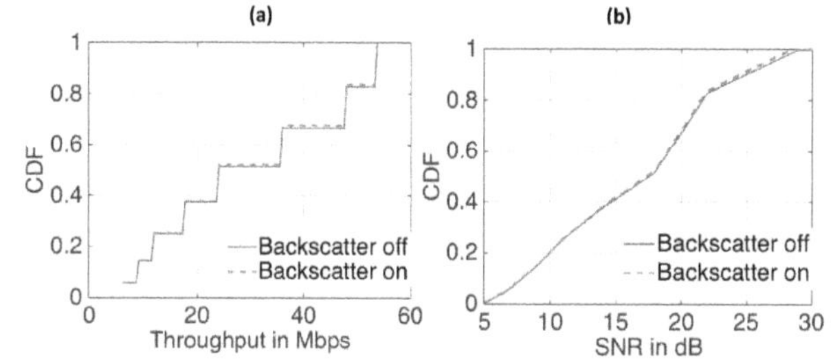

Figure 13: (a) Shows the CDF of the client throughput when the tag is placed at 0.25m from the AP. As seen, there is almost no degradation for lower bit rate of 6 Mbps, as client is farther from AP and the SNR required at the client to decode 6 Mbps is small. However, we observe noticeable difference at 54 Mbps, where both clients are closer to BackFi's AP and need higher SNR to decode data. (b) shows the degradation of SNR for tag on and tag off for each point for the plot on the left.

in Fig. 13.b) can force the WiFi AP to occasionally switch to lower bitrates.

7. CONCLUSION AND FUTURE WORK

BackFi provides a high throughput, sufficient range and a low power backscatter communication link using ambient WiFi signals. BackFi's range and throughput can be enhanced further with the use of multiple antennas at the WiFi APs since multiple antennas at the AP provides additional diversity combining gain. We can incorporate multiple antennas at the AP with minimal changes in BackFi's link layer protocol. Specifically, each transmit antenna would need a silent slot to eliminate the environmental component corresponding to that antenna. We could exploit existing WiFi MIMO packet structure for estimating the environment as it has preamble slots where only one transmit antenna is active. We can then perform MRC combining for the signals received across space from multiple antennas, providing BackFi with better SNR.

We believe, the combination of performance and piggybacking on existing signals demonstrated by BackFi can bring us closer to the vision of ubiquitous RF powered computing and communication gadgets in the physical world. However, much work remains in realizing this vision, including designing protocols to manage a network of BackFi tags connected to an AP and designing techniques to figure out how to balance sensing, computing and communication needs within a constrained energy budget. This continues to be our future work.

Acknowledgments: We would like to thank Kun Tan, the anonymous reviewers, the Stanford Networked Systems Group members, and Pengyu Zhang for their insightful comments.

8. REFERENCES

[1] *Analog Devices ADG904 RF SP4T*. http://www.analog.com/media/en/technical-documentation/data-sheets/ADG904_904R.pdf.

[2] *Cypress Semiconductor CY62146EV30 SRAM*. http://www.cypress.com/?docID=48695.

[3] *EPC Class-1 Gen-2 UHF RFID*. http://www.gs1.org/gsmp/kc/epcglobal/uhfc1g2/uhfc1g2_1_2_0-standard-20080511.pdf.

[4] *Improving whole home coverage and power efficiency*. https://www.qualcomm.com/invention/research/projects/wi-fi-evolution/80211ah.

[5] *ThingMagic. Mercury6e rfid reader module*. http://www.thingmagic.com/embedded-rfid-readers.

[6] *User Guide: KC705 Evaluation Board for the Kintex-7 FPGA*. http://www.xilinx.com/support/documentation/boards_and_kits/kc705/ug810_KC705_Eval_Bd.pdf.

[7] *WARP Project*. http://warpproject.org.

[8] E. Aryafar et. al. Midu: enabling mimo full duplex. In *ACM Mobicom '12*

[9] D. Bharadia, K. R. Joshi, and S. Katti. Full duplex backscatter. In *ACM HotNets'13*

[10] D. Bharadia and S. Katti. Fastforward: Fast and constructive full duplex relays. In *ACM SIGCOMM'14*

[11] D. Bharadia and S. Katti. Full duplex mimo radios. In *NSDI'14*

[12] D. Bharadia, E. McMilin, and S. Katti. Full duplex radios. In *ACM SIGCOMM'13*,

[13] D. Brennan. Linear diversity combining techniques. *IEEE'03*

[14] M. Buettner, B. Greenstein, and D. Wetherall. Dewdrop: An energy-aware runtime for computational rfid. In *NSDI'11*

[15] M. Buettner and D. Wetherall. A software radio-based uhf rfid reader for phy/mac experimentation. In *IEEE RFID'2011*

[16] J. I. Choi et. al. Achieving single channel, full duplex wireless communication. In *MobiCom '10*

[17] M. Duarte, C. Dick, and A. Sabharwal. Experiment-driven characterization of full-duplex wireless systems. *CoRR*, abs/1107.1276, 2011.

[18] M. Durante and S. Mahlknecht. An ultra low power wakeup receiver for wireless sensor nodes. In *SENSORCOMM '09*

[19] J. Ensworth and M. Reynolds. Every smart phone is a backscatter reader: Modulated backscatter compatibility with bluetooth 4.0 low energy (ble) devices. In *RFID IEEE, 2015*

[20] E. Everett, A. Sahai, and A. Sabharwal. Passive self-interference suppression for full-duplex infrastructure nodes. *CoRR*, abs/1302.2185, 2013.

[21] K. Gudan et. al. Feasibility of wireless sensors using ambient 2.4ghz rf energy.

[22] J. Gummeson et. al. On the limits of effective hybrid micro-energy harvesting on mobile crfid sensors. In *ACM MobiSys '10*

[23] J. Gummeson, P. Zhang, and D. Ganesan. Flit: A bulk transmission protocol for rfid-scale sensors. In *ACM MobiSys '12*

[24] A. Gupta, J. Min, and I. Rhee. Wifox: Scaling wifi performance for large audience environments. In *ACM CoNEXT '12*

[25] H. Ishizaki, H. Ikeda, Y. Yoshida, T. Maeda, T. Kuroda, and M. Mizuno. A battery-less wifi-ber modulated data transmitter with ambient radio-wave energy harvesting. In *VLSIC, 2011*

[26] M. Jain, J. I. Choi, T. Kim, D. Bharadia, S. Seth, K. Srinivasan, P. Levis, S. Katti, and P. Sinha. Practical, real-time, full duplex wireless. MobiCom '11

[27] B. Kellogg et. al. Wi-fi backscatter: Internet connectivity for rf-powered devices. In *ACM SIGCOMM '14*

[28] V. Liu, A. Parks, V. Talla, S. Gollakota, D. Wetherall, and J. R. Smith. Ambient backscatter: Wireless communication out of thin air. In *ACM SIGCOMM '13*,

[29] C. Mikeka, H. Arai, A. Georgiadis, and A. Collado. Dtv band micropower rf energy-harvesting circuit architecture and performance analysis. In *RFID-TA IEEE 2011*

[30] P. Nikitin and K. Rao. Theory and measurement of backscattering from rfid tags. *Antennas and Propagation Magazine, IEEE'2006*

[31] S. Oh, N. Roberts, and D. Wentzloff. A 116nw multi-band wake-up receiver with 31-bit correlator and interference rejection. In *CICC, 2013 IEEE*

[32] U. Olgun, C.-C. Chen, and J. Volakis. Design of an efficient ambient wifi energy harvesting system. *IET 2012*.

[33] A. Parks and J. Smith. Sifting through the airwaves: Efficient and scalable multiband rf harvesting. In *IEEE RFID 2014*,

[34] A. N. Parks et. al. Turbocharging ambient backscatter communication. In *ACM SIGCOMM'14*

[35] S. Patel et. al. A review of wearable sensors and systems with application in rehabilitation. *Journal of neuroengineering and rehabilitation, 2012*

[36] N. Pletcher, S. Gambini, and J. Rabaey. A 52 micro w wake-up receiver with - 72 dbm sensitivity using an uncertain-if architecture. *Solid-State Circuits, IEEE 2009*

[37] N. Pletcher and J. M. Rabaey. *Ultra-Low Power Wake-Up Receivers for Wireless Sensor Networks*. PhD thesis, University of California, Berkeley, May 2008.

[38] J. Proakis. *Digital Communications*. McGraw-Hill Series in Electrical and Computer Engineering. Computer Engineering. McGraw-Hill, 2001.

[39] B. Radunovic, D. Gunawardena, P. Key, A. Proutiere, N. Singh, V. Balan, and G. Dejean. Rethinking indoor wireless mesh design: Low power, low frequency, full-duplex. In *WIMESH IEEE 2010*

[40] N. Roberts and D. Wentzloff. A 98nw wake-up radio for wireless body area networks. In *IEEE RFIC 2012*

[41] M. Rodrig, C. Reis, R. Mahajan, D. Wetherall, and J. Zahorjan. Measurement-based characterization of 802.11 in a hotspot setting. In *ACM SIGCOMM Workshop E-WIND '05*

[42] Rohde & Schwarz. *Vector Network Analyzer User Manual*

[43] A. Sahai, G. Patel, C. Dick, and A. Sabharwal. On the impact of phase noise on active cancellation in wireless full-duplex. *CoRR*, abs/1212.5462, 2012.

[44] A. Sample and J. Smith. Experimental results with two wireless power transfer systems. In *IEEE RWS '09*.

[45] A. Sample et. al. Design of a passively-powered, programmable sensing platform for uhf rfid systems. In *IEEE RFID, 2007*

[46] A. P. Sample et. al. Wireless ambient radio power. In *Wirelessly Powered Sensor Networks and Computational RFID*, pages 223–234. Springer, 2013.

[47] A. Schulman, D. Levin, and N. Spring. On the fidelity of 802.11 packet traces. In *PAM'08*

[48] R. Shigeta et. al. Ambient rf energy harvesting sensor device with capacitor-leakage-aware duty cycle control. *IEEE Sensors Journal*

[49] S. Thomas and M. Reynolds. A 96 mbit/sec, 15.5 pj/bit 16-qam modulator for uhf backscatter communication. In *IEEE RFID 2012*

[50] J. Wang et. al. Efficient and reliable low-power backscatter networks. *SIGCOMM Commun. Rev. 2012*

[51] D. Yeager et. al. Wirelessly-charged uhf tags for sensor data collection. In *IEEE RFID 2008*

[52] H. Zhang et. al. Moo: A batteryless computational rfid and sensing platform. 2011.

[53] J. Zhang et. al. Uwb systems for wireless sensor networks. *IEEE 2009*

[54] P. Zhang and D. Ganesan. Enabling bit-by-bit backscatter communication in severe energy harvesting environments. In *NSDI'14*

[55] P. Zhang et. al. Ekhonet: High speed ultra low-power backscatter for next generation sensors. In *ACM MobiCom '14*

Caraoke: An E-Toll Transponder Network for Smart Cities

Omid Abari, Deepak Vasisht, Dina Katabi and Anantha Chandrakasan
Massachusetts Institute of Technology
Cambridge, MA, USA
{abari, deepakv, dk, anantha}@mit.edu

ABSTRACT

Electronic toll collection transponders, e.g., E-ZPass, are a widely-used wireless technology. About 70% to 89% of the cars in US have these devices, and some states plan to make them mandatory. As wireless devices however, they lack a basic function: a MAC protocol that prevents collisions. Hence, today, they can be queried only with directional antennas in isolated spots. However, if one could interact with e-toll transponders anywhere in the city despite collisions, it would enable many smart applications. For example, the city can query the transponders to estimate the vehicle flow at every intersection. It can also localize the cars using their wireless signals, and detect those that run a red-light. The same infrastructure can also deliver smart street-parking, where a user parks anywhere on the street, the city localizes his car, and automatically charges his account.

This paper presents Caraoke, a networked system for delivering smart services using e-toll transponders. Our design operates with existing unmodified transponders, allowing for applications that communicate with, localize, and count transponders, despite wireless collisions. To do so, Caraoke exploits the structure of the transponders' signal and its properties in the frequency domain. We built Caraoke reader into a small PCB that harvests solar energy and can be easily deployed on street lamps. We also evaluated Caraoke on four streets on our campus and demonstrated its capabilities.

CCS CONCEPTS

•**Networks** → **Network protocol design;**

KEYWORDS

Wireless, Smart City, RF Localization, Active RFID, Electronic Toll Collection (ETC)

SIGCOMM '15, August 17 - 21, 2015, London, United Kingdom

ISBN 978-1-4503-3542-3/15/08...$15.00
DOI: http://dx.doi.org/10.1145/2785956.2787504

(a) Bottom view (b) Top view (solar panel)

Figure 1—Caraoke reader. The board is 3 × 4in, and operates by harvesting solar power.

1. INTRODUCTION

Electronic toll collection transponders are simple devices consisting of a battery-powered RFID. They are perhaps among the most-widely used wireless communication technologies. In the US, depending on the state, 70% to 89% of the cars have such transponders [56, 2, 46, 9]. Further, the numbers are growing rapidly. The state of Pennsylvania has announced that E-ZPass will be mandatory on all highways in 2018. The state of California already requires drivers to have the transponder mounted on the windshield per state law in order to drive in the Express-Lanes [55, 9]. Other states are following suit motivated by Congress's decision to have a national electronic toll-collection system by 2016 [4, 9]. Because of this wide-deployment and anticipated growth, multiple businesses are looking into leveraging e-toll transponders to deliver new services. For example, e-toll transponders are currently used to pay for food at some drive-through restaurants [28], and to automate payment at parking garages [5].

More generally, there is a big opportunity for using e-toll transponders to enable smart cities. For example, the city could deploy readers on traffic lights to query the transponders and track the number of cars at every intersection. It can then use the information to adapt the timing of traffic lights to minimize the average wait time for the green light. It can also leverage RF-based localization to localize cars using their transponders' signals, detect cars that run a red-light, and automatically charge their accounts for a ticket. Readers deployed on street-lamps can detect speeding on every street in the city and ticket the offending car, without the need for car-mounted radars and hidden police officers. The same infrastructure can deliver smart street-parking systems, where a user parks anywhere on the street, the city localizes his car, and automatically charges his account.

Unfortunately, today there is a major challenge that hampers the use of e-toll transponders in smart city services, like the ones described above. Specifically, e-toll transponders are designed under the assumption that only one transponder transmits at any point in time, and hence have no MAC protocol to prevent collisions.[1] Collection systems use restricted deployments and highly directional antennas to ensure that only one car responds to the reader's query. Without this physical isolation, all transponders in range would transmit simultaneously, creating collisions. One could think of replacing the current transponders with new transponders that support a MAC protocol. Replacing the large infrastructure of deployed transponders however would take a long time and incur a major cost.[2] In contrast, developing for current transponders allows the cities to obtain immediate benefits even with a small installation on some of the busier streets and intersections. Yet to do that, the system has to deliver its smart services in the presence of wireless collisions.

This paper presents Caraoke, a networked system for delivering smart services using existing e-toll transponders. Caraoke also presents a new reader design that can count, localize, and estimate the speed of the cars on the road using collision signals from their e-toll transponders. The key feature that enables Caraoke to work in the presence of collision is its ability to exploit the carrier frequency offset (CFO) of the transponders. Specifically, since e-toll transponders are active RFIDs, each device has an independent oscillator, and hence it experiences a carrier frequency offset (CFO). Traditional wireless systems view the CFO as a harmful phenomenon that the receiver has to compensate for in order to correctly decode. In contrast, we show that we can leverage the CFO of the transponders to zoom in on individual transponders in the presence of collisions.

In particular, we consider the collision in the frequency domain as opposed to the time domain, and show that each collision exhibits spikes that correspond to the CFOs of the colliding transponders. Further, e-toll transponders have particularly large CFOs that span 1.2MHz [36], creating a significant separation between the spikes. Thus, we can estimate the number of transponders by counting these spikes.

We also show that we can use the differences in CFO to measure the wireless channels to the individual transponders, and hence apply RF-based localization to track cars and measure their speeds. Caraoke can also decode the IDs of the colliding transponders, say to charge a car for parking or speeding. To do this, Caraoke leverages the channels and CFO measurements to combine multiple collisions in a manner that the signals from the target transponder add up coherently, whereas the signals of other colliding transponders combine incoherently. This allows Caraoke to boost the SNR of the target transponder above the others, and enable it to decode the ID of the target transponder.

To demonstrate the practicality of Caraoke, we built Caraoke reader into a custom designed printed circuit board (PCB). Our prototype, shown in Fig. 1, is both small and low-cost, making it amenable to large-scale deployment.[3] Further it is designed as a plug and play device; It connects to the Internet via an LTE modem and harvests its energy from solar power, making it easy to deploy on street-lamps.

We have evaluated Caraoke on four campus streets. We ran multiple experiments with cars that have standard E-ZPass transponders. Our results show the following:

- Caraoke can count transponders accurately despite collisions. The average error in the Caraoke estimator is 2%, and the 90th percentile is less than 5%, which is significantly more accurate than existing camera-based traffic tracking systems [43, 54].
- Caraoke can accurately localize cars into parking spots. Its average location accuracy is 4 degrees. This accuracy is sufficient for detecting occupied/available parking spots between two street lamps.
- Across experiments where we varied the car speed from 10 mile/hour to 40 mile/hour, Caraoke has detected the speed to within 8% (i.e., 1 to 3 mile/hour). The same accuracy was observed in a second set of experiments conducted in an empty lot with a car speed of 50 mile/hour.[4]
- Caraoke successfully decodes transponder ids in the presence of collisions, but the time required to decode increases with the number of colliding transponders. In particular, decoding the ids of a pair of colliding transponders takes 4.2 ms, whereas decoding five colliding ids takes 16.2 ms.
- Measurements of the Caraoke reader show that it consumes only 9mW in average (excluding modem), which is 56× lower than what it can harvest from its solar panel.

2. RELATED WORK

(a) Communication and Localization: Caraoke builds on a rich literature on RFIDs. Past research however has typically focused on EPC RFIDs, like those used in access control and inventory tracking [22, 30]. Such RFIDs *do* support a MAC protocol and hence can communicate without major collisions. In contrast, e-toll transponders use a different protocol that has no MAC support. We note however that past works [58, 34] proposed methods to decode concurrent transmissions from backscatter sensors in time domain. However, such designs are inapplicable to our scenario because they require hardware modification of the RFIDs and do not work with existing e-toll transponders.

Our work is also related to past work on RFID localization and RF-based positioning [60, 29, 59, 63, 26]. While we build on the general area of AoA localization, our approach

[1]This is unlike traditional RFIDs used in access control or retail, which have a MAC protocol.

[2]There were more than 26 million transponders deployed just by E-ZPass as of 2013 [1]. In addition, there are a large number of additional transponders deployed by other agencies such as FasTrak, etc.

[3] The board is about the size of a credit card and cost less than $40 which can be dramatically reduced with mass production.

[4]Almost all states in the US have residential speed limits below 35 mile/hour, and the maximum residential speed limit in any state is 45 mile/hour [8].

differs in that it exploits CFO differences to localize the devices using colliding signals, without even decoding.

There are also commercial RFID readers which are solar powered [7]. However, unlike Caraoke, these readers can not localize, count and identify RFIDs in the presence of wireless collisions.

Finally, a vast majority of past research on issues related to CFO focuses on how to eliminate or estimate the CFO and compensate for it [12, 49, 48, 52]. The closest to our work is [18], which advocates using the CFO of a device as an id for security purposes. None of this work however deals with collisions or the use of CFO for localization or decoding.

(b) Smart Cities: Our work is motivated by the growing interest in smart cities, where urban services are automated to improve efficiency, and reduce waste and pollution [42, 35, 25]. Past work in this area focuses on transportation research [61], software applications [20], and social and economic issues [14]. In contrast, we focus on wireless networking issues such as communication, localization, and counting in the presence of wireless collisions.

There are also a few businesses that market solutions for one of Caraoke's applications. In particular, some apps allow a user to pay for parking using her phone [19]. Those apps however do not address the cost and overhead incurred by the city in checking for parking violations and issuing tickets. Further, they do not automatically detect the occupancy of parking spots. Alternative solutions like Streetline install a sensor in the asphalt pavement of every parking spot [51]. They need to drill the street in every spot incurring a significant cost and causing traffic disturbances. There are also traffic cameras installed in some cities for counting the cars at the corresponding traffic light and providing traffic statistics [38]. These systems are highly sensitive to occlusions, illumination, shadowing, and wind [43]. Finally, traffic radars are typically used to measure car speeds. These devices however cannot tell which speed is associated with which car. A police officer has to be around to identify the speeding car based on the orientation of the device [24]. In contrast to all of the above, Caraoke is a single system that can support all of these applications, and address many of the drawbacks of existing solutions.

(c) VANET: There is a large literature on vehicle networks, or VANET. Research in that area addresses the impact of mobility on ad hoc networks [40]. It focuses on routing [39], quality of service [62], and reliability [64]. It runs on typical communication devices that support a MAC protocol, e.g., WiFi and WiMAX [21, 44].Our work differs from this past work in objectives and techniques. Specifically, our goal is to enable smart cities to leverage the widely-deployed e-toll transponders to deliver new services such as smart-parking and real-time traffic monitoring. Our solutions target a different communication technology, namely e-toll transponders. Such transponders lack a MAC protocol, necessitating new designs that differ from those used in VANET.

3. BACKGROUND

An e-toll transponder is an active RFID, which responds to an inquiry transmitted by the reader. The reader is typically placed in the tollbooth whereas the transponder is attached to the car's windshield. Both transponder and reader work at 915MHz. The query signal is simply a sinewave transmitted at the carrier frequency (i.e. 915MHz) for a short period of time. The transponder responds with its id, which identifies the driver's account. Fig. 2(a) illustrates the timing of the query signal and the transponder's response to it.

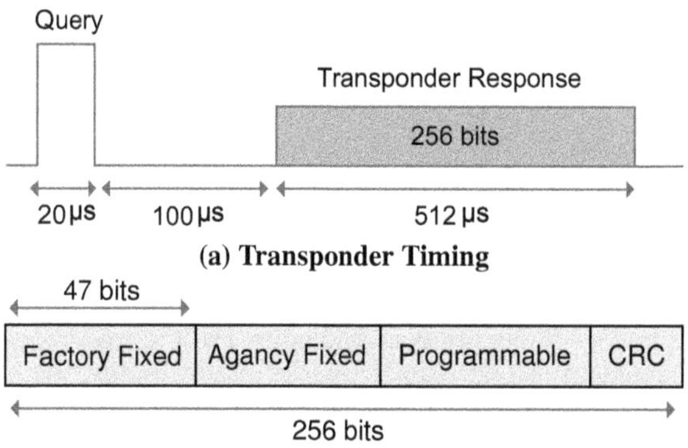

(a) Transponder Timing

(b) Transponder Response

Figure 2—Transponder Transmission. The reader transmits a query signal which is a simple sine-wave at carrier frequency. The transponder responds by transmitting a 256-bit data using OOK Manchester modulation.

A few points are worth noting:

- In contrast to traditional RFIDs (e.g., those used in retail or access control),[5] the active RFIDs used in e-toll transponders lack a medium access protocol (MAC). Thus, once a transponder detects the reader's signal, it immediately transmits its response. Hence, if multiple transponders are in the reader's range, they all respond leading to a collision. Toll systems avoid the need for a MAC by using highly directional antennas, and the fact that cars are separated by a minimum distance.
- E-toll transponders also have a relatively large CFO. Their carrier frequencies vary between 914.3MHz and 915.5 MHz, and hence their CFO can be as high as 1.2MHz [36].
- The simplicity of the transponders results in a cheap and low power device. A transponder can work for 10 years before it runs out of battery, and it operates whether the car is on or off.
- Finally, for the purpose of this paper, it is important to understand the properties of the transponder signal. The transponder transmits its data using on-off keying (OOK) modulation. OOK is a simple modulation, where the radio transmits a "1 bit" by transmitting the carrier frequency, and transmits a "0 bit" by staying silent. This means that the transponder's signal corresponds to the presence and absence of the carrier sinewave. Thus, the transmitted signal can be written as:

$$x(t) = s(t) \cdot e^{j2\pi \cdot f_c \cdot t}, \tag{1}$$

where $s(t)$ is a binary square-wave baseband signal toggling between 0 and 1, and f_c is the carrier frequency. The

[5]Most research targets Electronic Product Code (EPC) RFIDs, which have an Aloha-style MAC protocol [23].

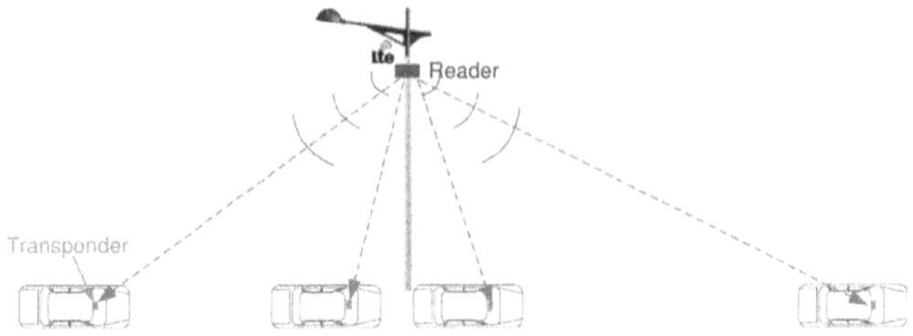

Figure 3—Illustration of Caraoke The Caraoke reader is mounted on a street-lamp. It queries nearby transponders and uses their signals to localize them and estimate their speeds.

received wireless signal can be written as:

$$y(t) = h \cdot s(t) \cdot e^{j2\pi \cdot f_c \cdot t}, \quad (2)$$

where h is the complex channel coefficient. The receiver down-converts the signal to baseband by multiplying it with its own carrier frequency. The received baseband signal $r(t)$ then becomes:

$$\begin{aligned} r(t) &= h \cdot s(t) \cdot e^{j2\pi \cdot \Delta f \cdot t} &(3)\\ &= h \cdot (0.5 + s'(t)) \cdot e^{j2\pi \cdot \Delta f \cdot t}, &(4)\end{aligned}$$

where Δf is the carrier frequency offset between the transmitter and and the receiver, and $s'(t)$ is the same square-wave as $s(t)$ except that it toggles between -0.5 and 0.5 and has zero mean. The frequency representation of the received signal $r(t)$ can be written as:

$$R(f) = \frac{h}{2} \cdot \delta(f - \Delta f) + h \cdot S'(f - \Delta f) \quad (5)$$

where $S'(f)$ is the frequency representation of $s'(t)$ and $\delta(f)$ is the unit impulse function. As it can be seen from the equation, this signal has a peak at the carrier frequency offset, Δf. Further, since $s'(t)$ has a zero mean, $S'(0) = 0$.[6] Thus, the complex value of the peak represents the channel from transmitter to receiver *i.e.*, $R(\Delta f) = \frac{h}{2}$.

4. CARAOKE OVERVIEW

Caraoke is a networked system that enables query-response communication between a Caraoke reader and the e-toll transponders in its range. At the heart of Caraoke is a new device that we call the Caraoke reader; it counts, localizes, and decodes transponders' ids from their signal collisions. It also estimates the speeds of the cars carrying the transponders. The Caraoke reader harnesses its power from solar energy and has an LTE modem to connect to the Internet. Hence, it can be easily deployed without the need for additional infrastructure. As shown in Fig. 3, smart cities can deploy Caraoke readers on street-lamps to support a variety of smart services including: 1) traffic monitoring, 2) speed enforcement, 3) red-light running, 4) smart street-parking, and even 4) allowing a user who forgets where he parked to query the system to locate his parked car.

This paper is focused on the design and implementation of the Caraoke and a small-scale evaluation of the deployment of multiple Caraoke readers on a campus street. Before delving into the details of our design, we note the following two points regarding scope:

- Our objective is to automate smart services, eliminating the personnel cost, and improving the overall accuracy in comparison to the status quo. Note that the current alternatives suffer from significant errors. For example, about 10% to 30% of the speeding tickets based on traffic radars are estimated to be incorrect [6]. The errors are mostly due to the fact that radars cannot associate a speed with a particular car. This task is left to the police officer and hence is prone to human mistakes [6]. Similarly, errors in estimating the number of cars using traffic cameras vary between a few percent to 26%, depending on illumination, wind, occlusions, etc. [43]. Furthermore, the camera lenses have to be manually cleaned every 6 weeks to 6 months [16].
- For a city to use Caraoke to deliver the above services, it needs to connect the system with its own transportation and traffic databases. For example, in order to detect a car that runs a red light, the city needs to combine the output of Caraoke with the timing of the red-light at the corresponding intersection. The process for combining Caraoke's output with the city's transportation and traffic databases is beyond the scope of this paper.

5. COUNTING DESPITE COLLISIONS

Estimating the number of vehicles at major intersections is critical for traffic management and city planning. In this section, we describe how a Caraoke reader counts the transponders in its radio range. Specifically, when a Caraoke reader transmits a query message, transponders in its radio range respond simultaneously with their information. We would like to use the resulting collisions to count the number of transponders.

At a high level, our approach is simple. We exploit the fact that two transponders, typically, do not have the same carrier frequency, and that their carrier frequency offset (CFO) is relatively large. In particular, the specifications of the E-ZPass transponder show that the device's CFO can exceed one MHz [36]. CFO is typically a nuisance for wireless communication systems which have to compensate for CFO before decoding. In Caraoke however, we leverage CFO for our advantage to count the number of colliding transponders. Specifically, we take the FFT of the collision signal. Since different transponders have different carrier frequencies, the Fourier transform shows multiple peaks at different frequencies that corresponds to the various transponders' CFOs. Fig. 4 shows the Fourier transform of a collision signal where five e-toll transponders transmitted at the same time. As can be seen in the figure, there are five peaks, each corresponds to one of five colliding transponders.

This shows that one way for counting the transponders would be to take an FFT of the collision signal and count the peaks in the Fourier domain. To understand the performance of this estimator, we need to tie it to the resolution of the

[6] $s'(t)$ has a zero mean because $s(t)$ is an on-off keying signal with Manchester encoding , and $s'(t)$ is the same as $s(t)$ but shifted by -0.5.

FFT and whether it can distinguish the differences between the CFOs of the transponders. The resolution of the FFT, δf refers to the width of each FFT bin and can be written as:

$$\delta f = \frac{1}{T} \tag{6}$$

where T is the FFT time window. Since the length of the transponder's response is $512\mu s$, the maximum FFT window is $T = 512\mu s$ and hence the resolution of the FFT is $\delta f = 1.95$ kHz. Thus, if two transponders have carrier frequencies that differ by less than 1.95 kHz, their peaks will fall into the same FFT bin and will be counted as one. Given that the CFO range is 1.2 MHz, the peak of a transponder can fall in any of $N = 1.2$ MHz/1.95 kHz $= 615$ FFT bins. If m transponders collide, then the probability of not missing any transponder by counting FFT peaks is:

$$P(\textit{not missing any transponder}) = \frac{\binom{N}{m} \cdot m!}{N^m} \tag{7}$$

Unfortunately this probability decreases quickly as more transponders are in range. The probability of not missing any transponder is 98%, 93% and 73% for $m = 5$, 10 and 20 cars, respectively. The above derivations shows that an estimator that simply counts the number of peaks in the FFT is acceptable at low car density but can easily miss some cars when the number of cars in range is large.

So, how can we improve the quality of our estimate in scenarios of high densities? To overcome this problem, Caraoke distinguishes whether one or more transponders have fallen into the same FFT bin while counting the number of peaks. It does this by leveraging the *phase rotation* property of the Fourier transform, which says that a shift in the time domain translates into phase rotation in the frequency domain:

$$\begin{aligned} \mathcal{F}\{r(t)\} &= R(f) \\ \mathcal{F}\{r(t+\tau)\} &= R(f) \cdot e^{j2\pi \cdot f\tau} \end{aligned} \tag{8}$$

where $r(t)$ is the signal in time domain and $R(f)$ is its frequency representation. Specifically, if the FFT peak contains a single transponder's response, then performing the FFT on the same signal with a time shift τ causes only a phase rotation of the peak value but the magnitude of the peak does not change. In other words, $\|R(f)\| = \|R(f) \cdot e^{j2\pi \cdot f\tau}\|$, where $R(f)$ is the frequency representation of the received signal. In contrast, say the CFOs of two transponders, f and f', fall into the same FFT bin, then the value of the peak in that bin without a time-shift is $R(f) + R(f')$ while its value with a time-shift of τ is $R(f) \cdot e^{j2\pi \cdot f\tau} + R(f') \cdot e^{j2\pi \cdot f'\tau}$. Since the frequencies are slightly different, they rotate by different phases and results in a change in the magnitude of the peak.

The above provides us with a mechanism to determine whether an FFT bin has one or more transponders. To do so, we compare the magnitude of the FFT bin with and without a time-shift. If the two magnitudes are different by more than a noise threshold, then multiple transponders have fallen into that bin. In the following, we explain how this detection significantly improves the probability of getting a correct count.

Probability of getting the correct count: As explained before, Caraoke counts the number of the peaks in the FFT to determine the number of cars in range. However, there is a possibility that two cars have fallen into the same bin. Hence, Caraoke considers the peaks with two or more transponders' signals as two cars when it is counting the peak. Specifically, if an FFT peak includes a single frequency, Caraoke counts it as one car and if it has two or more frequencies, it counts it as two cars. Hence, the result of counting will be incorrect only when there is at least a bin which includes three or more cars. In another word, the probability of not missing any transponder is equal to one minus the probability of having at least one FFT bin which includes three or more transponders' signal. For m colliding transponders and N FFT bins in the 1.2 MHz range, this probability becomes:

$$\begin{aligned} &P(\textit{not missing any transponder}) \\ &= 1 - P(\exists \text{ bin with} \geq 3 \text{ transponders}) \\ &\geq 1 - \sum_{i \in \{1,\ldots,N\}} P(\text{bin } i \text{ with} \geq 3 \text{ transponders}) \\ &\geq 1 - \binom{N}{1}\binom{m}{3}\frac{N^{(m-3)}}{N^m} \end{aligned} \tag{9}$$

Substituting $N = 615$, the probability of not missing any transponder is at least 99.9%, 99.9% and 99.7% for $m = 5$, 10 and 20. Thus, having the capability to detect the peaks that have two or more transponder's signals significantly improves the probability of correctly counting the cars.

Finally, note that for simplicity, our analysis has assumed a uniform distribution for CFO. However, we have also experimentally validated our solution for empirical CFO measurements collected from 155 different transponders.[7] Our empirical results show that the probability of not missing any transponder is 99.9%, 99.5% and 95.3% for $m = 5$, 10 and 20 which are slightly worse than analytical-results.

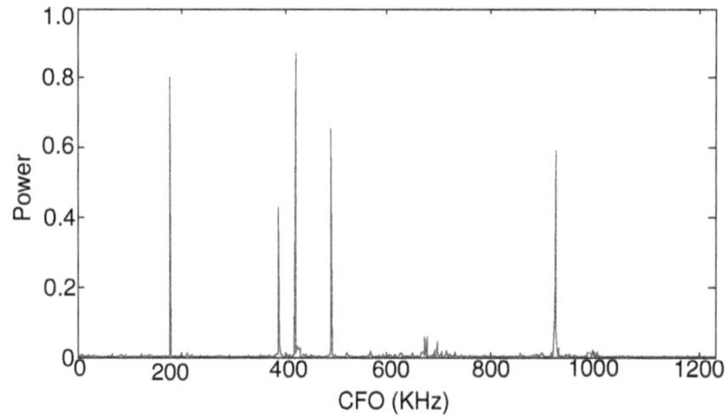

Figure 4—Transponders Response in Frequency Domain. Fourier transform of a collision signal where five e-toll transponders transmitted at the same time. The number of peaks indicates the number of transponders in the area.

6. LOCALIZING E-TOLL TRANSPONDERS

Car localization is an essential function for multiple smart services such as smart parking and detecting red-light runners. The first step in localizing cars is to localize the transponder located on cars' windshield. To do so, Caraoke first calculates the angle at which the signal from

[7]The mean and standard deviation of their carrier frequencies are 914.84 MHz and 0.21 MHz, respectively.

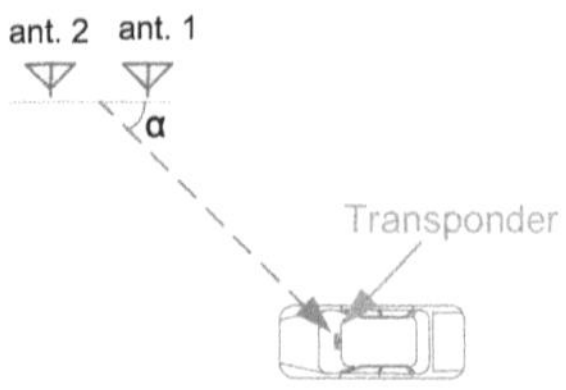

Figure 5—Transponder Localization. Caraoke calculates the spatial angle (α) of transponder by measuring the phase difference in signal received at two antennas.

the transponder arrives at the Caraoke reader. This angle indicates the spatial angle between the transponder and reader, and typically referred to as the angle-of-arrival (AoA).

In order to measure the AoA, a Caraoke reader uses two antennas separated by a distance d. It is widely-known that the angle of arrival can be computed as [60]:

$$\cos\alpha = \frac{\Delta\phi}{2\pi}\frac{\lambda}{d}, \tag{10}$$

where α is the spatial angle between the transponder and the reader, shown in Fig. 5, $\Delta\phi$ is the phase difference between the two antennas (*i.e.* $\Delta\phi = \phi_2 - \phi_1$), and λ is the carrier wavelength [8].

To compute α, we need to substitute the value of the other parameters in Eq. 10. While d and λ are known, $\Delta\phi$ should be measured. In the absence of collisions, $\Delta\phi$ can be measured directly between the signals received by the two antennas on the reader:

$$\Delta\phi = \angle\frac{r_2(t)}{r_1(t)} = \angle\frac{h_2 \cdot s(t) \cdot e^{j2\pi\Delta f \cdot t}}{h_1 \cdot s(t) \cdot e^{j2\pi\Delta f \cdot t}} = \angle\frac{h_2}{h_1},$$

where $r_1(t)$ and $r_2(t)$ are baseband signals received by the first and second antenna, respectively, h_1 and h_2 are the channels to the two antennas, $s(t)$ is the transmitted baseband signal and Δf is the CFO between the transmitter and receiver[9]. However, since in Caraoke reader each antenna receives a collision from multiple transponders, such a direct measurement does not work. This is due to the fact that the received signal is the summation of responses from multiple transponders while each has its own channel. Thus, the received signal at each antenna when m transponders respond can be written as:

$$\begin{aligned} r_1(t) &= r_{11}(t) + r_{12}(t) + \cdots + r_{1m}(t) \\ r_2(t) &= r_{21}(t) + r_{22}(t) + \cdots + r_{2m}(t), \end{aligned} \tag{11}$$

where $r_{1i}(t)$ and $r_{2i}(t)$ are the received signal from the i_{th} transponder to the first and second antenna, respectively. As

[8]Note that since Caraoke reader is placed outdoor on a high pole like a street lamp, it has a strong line-of-sight path to the transponder and the multipath effects which occur in standard indoor environments are significantly weaker. Hence, Caraoke does not require a large antenna array to estimate the angle of arrival. In §12, we empirically show that Caraoke does not suffer from multipath effects.

[9]Note that the received signals on the two antennas experience the same CFO since the antennas are connected to the same oscillator on the Caraoke reader.

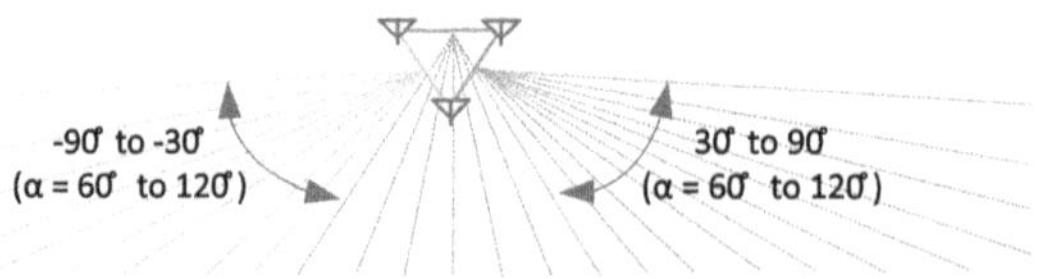

Figure 6—Antenna Re-configuration. Caraoke reader has three antennas arranged in an equilateral triangle to achieve higher accuracy in calculating spatial angle of transponder. In this case the spatial angle, α, is always between 60 to 120 degrees regardless of transponder location

can be seen from the equations, one can not directly compute $\Delta\phi$ for the i_{th} transponder using $\angle\frac{r_2(t)}{r_1(t)}$ since $\angle\frac{r_2(t)}{r_1(t)} \neq \frac{h_2}{h_1}$ for a specific transponder.

Fortunately, however, we can use the same trick we used for counting the transponders. Specifically, we first take the FFT of the collision at each antenna and identify the peaks, where each peak corresponds to the response from one transponder. For each peak in the first antenna's signal, the phase value is compared to the phase value of the same peak in the other antenna's signal. These phase differences are used to calculate the spatial angle α for each transponder. Mathematically, the above approach works because the Fourier transform is linear, i.e.:

$$\mathcal{F}\{ax(t) + by(t)\} = aX(f) + bY(f) \tag{12}$$

Using the above property, the frequency representation of the received signal at the antennas when m transponders respond can be written as:

$$\begin{aligned} R_1(f) &= R_{11}(f) + R_{12}(f) + \cdots + R_{1m}(f) \\ R_2(f) &= R_{21}(f) + R_{22}(f) + \cdots + R_{2m}(f) \end{aligned} \tag{13}$$

where $R_{1i}(f)$ and $R_{2i}(f)$ are frequency representation of the received signals from the i_{th} transponder to the first and second antenna, respectively. As it was explained in §3, the received signal from each transponder has a peak at its CFO where the value of the peak represents the channel coefficient (*i.e.* $R(\Delta f_i) = \frac{h}{2}$). Hence, $R_1(f)$ and $R_2(f)$ signals have multiple peaks where each peak corresponds to the response from only one transponder. Therefore, the $\Delta\phi$ for the transponder i can be calculated as follow:

$$\Delta\phi = \angle\frac{R_2(\Delta f_i)}{R_1(\Delta f_i)} = \angle\frac{h_{2i}}{h_{1i}}$$

where Δf_i is the CFO of transponder i, and $R_2(f)$ and $R_1(f)$ are frequency representation of the received signal at the the first and second antennas. Substituting the measured $\Delta\phi$ in Eq. 10, we can compute the spatial angle between the transponder and reader (*i.e.* AoA).

The above equation allows us to compute the spatial angle from the reader to the transponder. We can however improve the accuracy of our angle estimate with a smart choice of antenna position. Specifically, the accuracy in calculating α is best for angles around 90° and degrades for angles around 0° or 180°. This is due to the fact that $\Delta\phi$ is proportional to $\cos\alpha$, as shown in Eq. 10. Hence, for values close to 0 or 180, α is very sensitive to change in $\Delta\phi$. To reduce this sensitivity, we use three antennas arranged in an equilateral triangle as shown in Fig. 6. At any time, we use a pair of

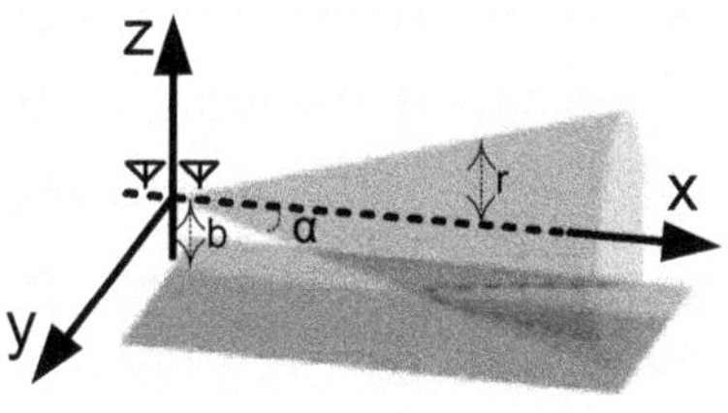

Figure 7—Localizing the Car from AoA: In this figure α is angle of arrival and b is the height of the pole. The car is located on a point on the intersection of the cone and the road plane which is a hyperbola. Hence, By using the information from two poles, one can localize the exact location of the car.

antennas out of the three antennas. We pick the pair using a programmable switch. In this setup, for any transponder position, there exists exactly one pair of antennas for which the spatial angle is always close to 90° (i.e., between 60° and 120°). We compute the angle for all pairs and use the pair whose angle is close to 90° degree to localize the car.

Next we use the spatial angle to locate the transponder. The spatial angle does not correspond to a single point in the space. In fact, as shown in Fig. 7, this angle corresponds to all points on the surface of a cone where its altitude axis is parallel to the road. The cone equation can be written as follow:

$$y^2 + z^2 = r^2 = (\tan(\alpha) \cdot x)^2 \quad (14)$$

where x,y and z are coordinate of the car with respect to the center of measuring antennas, and α is the spatial angle between the car and reader. Cars, however, are always on the road and we can use this as another constraint. The intersection of the cone and the road plane is a hyperbola, as shown in Fig. 7. The equation for this hyperbola is as follow:

$$(\tan(\alpha) \cdot x)^2 - y^2 = b^2 \quad (15)$$

where b is a constant that corresponds to the height of the pole. While a single hyperbola is not enough to localize, we can combine information across two readers to locate the car. Specifically, using a second reader located on the other side of the road provides us another hyperbola equation. Then, by solving these two equations, one can find x and y, and localize the car.[10]

Note, in the case where antennas are tilted by 60° , the process of localizing is the same, except that the cone is tilted by 60°. Hence, the intersection of the cone and road plane is an ellipse instead of a hyperbola. One can simply replace the hyperbola equation with that of an ellipse to find the intersection point.

Finally, in order to intersect location information across two readers, we need this information to be synchronized. We can leverage the readers' connection to the Internet to synchronize them to within tens of ms using the network timing protocol (NTP) [3, 45]. This synchronization level is more than sufficient for localizing parked cars. For moving cars, this introduce some error, which we will discuss in the following section.

[10] The intersection of two hyperbolas may results in more than one point, however, only one of these points is located on the road and the rests are on the sidewalk.

7. Detecting a Car's Speed

As described earlier, Caraoke can also detect the speed of the car. Specifically, Caraoke readers can be deployed on street-lamps and detect speeding on streets in the city. The car speed can be estimated by localizing the car at two different locations and computing the total time the car took to travel between these two locations. Hence, the speed of the car can be written as:

$$v = \frac{x_2 - x_1}{delay}$$

where x_1 and x_2 are first and second locations of the car and *delay* is the amount of time it took to travel from location x_1 to location x_2 which are computed as described §6.

The accuracy of localizing the x_1 and x_2 and estimating the *delay* depends on the time synchronization between the readers. The error in x_1 and x_2 can be upper bounded using the hyperbola equation in the previous section independent of time synchronization. This error depends on reader's height and the number of lanes in the same direction on the street. For example, for a four lane street *i.e.* two lanes in each direction, where the antennas are attached to a street light pole whose height is 13 feet, the maximum error is 8.5 feet. [11] The error in *delay* is the same as the error in timing synchronization. Since the readers are connected to the Internet via LTE modems, they can be synchronized up to tens of ms network timing protocol (NTP) [3, 45].

The accuracy of estimating the speed depends on the accuracy of the above parameters as well as how far x_1 and x_2 are from each other. The farther they are, the more accurate the estimate is. In particular, if x_1 and x_2 are measured at readers that are separated by 4 light poles (*i.e.* a separation of of about 360 feet ($\approx$110 m) [10]), for car speeds of 20 mile/hour and 50 mile/hour, the maximum error is 5.5% and 6.8% respectively. This accuracy can further be improved by taking more measurements along the street from more light poles.

8. Decoding Transponders' Ids

In this section, we explain how Caraoke decodes an individual transponder in the presence of collisions of multiple transponders.

At first glance, it might seem that one can decode a transponder's signal by using a band-pass filter centered around the transponder's CFO peak. This solution however does not work because OOK has a relatively wide spectrum –i.e., the data is spread as opposed to being concentrated around the peak[12].

[11] The exact equation of error is $\frac{\sqrt{b^2} - \sqrt{b^2 + (l \cdot w)^2}}{\tan(\alpha)}$ where b is antenna's height, l is the number of lanes in the same direction on the street and w is the width of the lane (typically 12 feet).

[12] Intuitively this can be seen by recalling that OOK randomly toggles between 0 and 1 and hence it's spectrum resembles white noise.

In contrast, our decoding algorithm is based on combining multiple collisions in a manner that ensures that the signal from the target transponder combines coherently, whereas the signals from other transponders combine incoherently. This allows Caraoke to boost the SNR of the target transponder above others, and hence decode the target transponder.

Specifically, when a Caraoke reader transmits the query signal, multiple transponders respond simultaneously. Without loss of generality, let us assume that we are interested in decoding transponder 1.

$$r(t) = h_1 s_1(t) \cdot e^{j2\pi \cdot \Delta f_1 \cdot t} + \sum_i h_i s_i(t) \cdot e^{j2\pi \cdot \Delta f_i \cdot t}$$

where $s_i(t)$ is the signal transmitted by the i_{th} transponder, Δf_i is its CFO, and the h_i is its channel to the reader. If the reader transmits another query, the received signal will be:

$$r'(t) = h'_1 s_1(t) \cdot e^{j2\pi \cdot \Delta f_1 \cdot t} + \sum_i h'_i s_i(t) \cdot e^{j2\pi \cdot \Delta f_i \cdot t}$$

Note that the channel coefficients have changed from the first received signal to the second one. This is due to the fact that the transponders start with a random initial phase. The channels h_1 and h'_1 as well as the CFO Δf_1 can be estimated from the peak in the frequency domain as described in §3. We can then compensate for the CFO and the channels of transponder 1 and sum up the received signals to obtain the averaged signal $\tilde{s}_1(t)$:

$$\begin{aligned} \tilde{s}_1(t) &= \frac{r(t)}{h_1} \cdot e^{-j2\pi \Delta f_1 t} + \frac{r'(t)}{h'_1} \cdot e^{-j2\pi \Delta f_1 t} \\ &= 2 \cdot s_1(t) + \sum_i \left(\frac{h_i}{h_1} + \frac{h'_i}{h'_1} \right) s_i(t) \cdot e^{j2\pi(\Delta f_i - \Delta f_1)t} \end{aligned}$$

By repeating this process N times we get:

$$\tilde{s}_1(t) = N \cdot s_1(t) + \sum_i \left(\sum_j \frac{h_{ij}}{h_{1j}} \right) s_i(t) \cdot e^{j2\pi(\Delta f_i - \Delta f_1)t}$$

where h_{ij} is the channel from the i-th transponder in the j-th received signal. As can be seen from the above equation, the signals from transponder 1 add coherently, while the other signals add incoherently with random phases and average out. For sufficiently large N, the signal power for transponder 1 will be much more than that for other transponders. In this case, the SNR is enough to be decoded.

Fig. 8 shows an example of this decoding algorithm in which the reader receives a collision of the signals from five transponders. Fig. 8(a) shows the time signal $r(t)$ of the received collisions before any averaging. As can be seen, the signal looks random and undecodable. Fig. 8(b) and (c) show the time signal $\tilde{s}_1(t)$ after averaging 8 and 16 replies respectively. The figures show that after averaging 16 times, the bits of the desired transponder become decodable and the more we average, the better our ability to decode becomes.

9. CARAOKE MULTIPLE READER PROTOCOL

So far, we have assumed that transponders respond to a single reader at any time. However, a transponder on the road might be in the range of two or more Caraoke readers.[13] Therefore, there is a need for a MAC protocol on the readers side to avoid interference from readers. We will start by distinguishing between two interference scenarios:

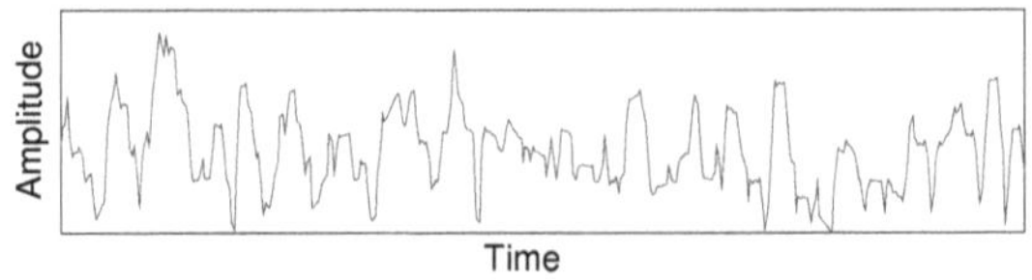

(a) Time signal before averaging

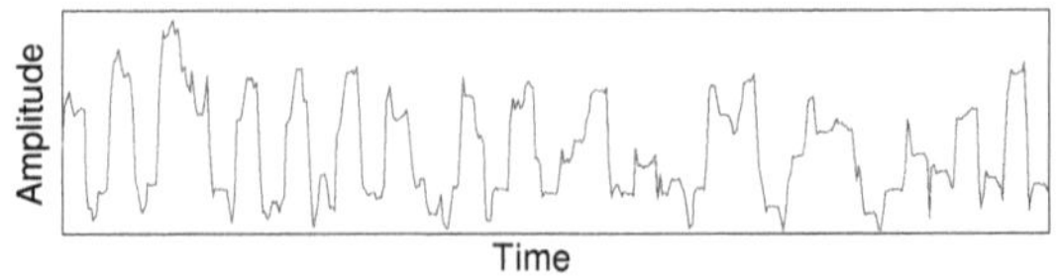

(b) Time signal after averaging 8 times

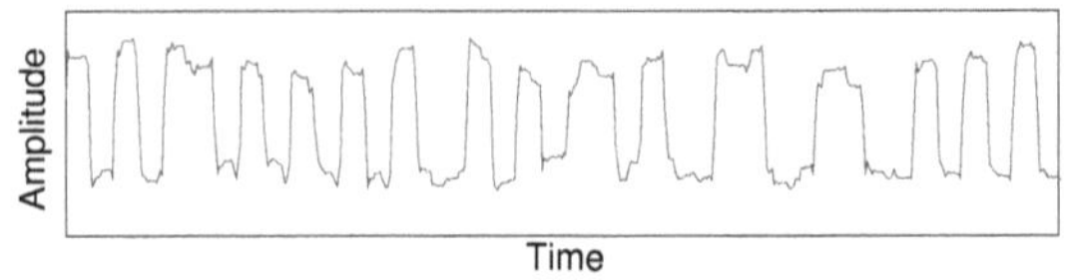

(c) Time signal after averaging 16 times

Figure 8—Decoding a transponder's response: (a) Received signal before averaging, (b) after averaging 8 replies, (c) after averaging 16 replies. Caraoke is able to decode a transponder's response by correcting its channel and then averaging.

1. Collision of Reader Queries: In this case, a query signal from a reader collides with a query signal from another reader. As explained in §3, the query signal transmitted by a reader is simply a sinewave transmitted at carrier frequency. Even if two readers interfere, the combined signal is still a sinewave at the carrier frequency, and hence a valid trigger. Thus, a collision of two queries is not harmful. Our empirical experiments confirm that transponders are still triggered to respond even when queries from different readers collide.

2. Collision of Reader Query with a Transponder Response: In this case, a query signal from a reader collides with the response of a transponder queried by another reader. This collision is harmful and needs to be avoided. To do so, Caraoke uses carrier sense. Specifically, each reader listens to the medium before transmitting a query. If the medium is available, it then transmits its query. *But how long should the reader listen to avoid a collision with a transponder response.* Recall from Fig §2 in §3, that the query signal is only $20\mu s$ and the delay between the query and the transponder response is $100\mu s$. Thus, by listening for more than $120\mu s$, if the reader does not hear any signal it can guarantee that no transponder response will be transmitted after the $120\mu s$ and it can transmit its query.

To summarize, Caraoke uses a MAC protocol for the readers based on CSMA, where each reader listens for an idle medium for $120\mu s$ before it can transmit. The main difference, however, is that there is no need for contention window since collisions between queries are acceptable.

[13]The range of a Caraoke reader is 100 feet.

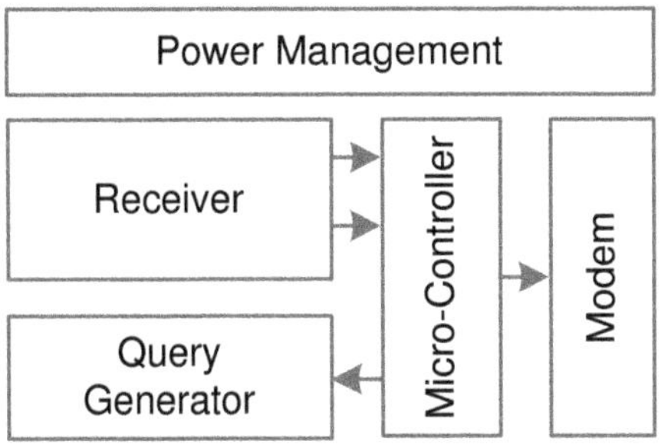

Figure 9—Block diagram of the Caraoke reader

10. CARAOKE READER'S HARDWARE DESIGN

Caraoke is a software-hardware solution. In contrast to the previous sections, which focus on the algorithmic techniques underlying Caraoke, here we describe the hardware design and the optimizations we performed in order to support a low-power low-cost device.

We have developed a custom-design PCB for the Caraoke reader. The device harvests its power from solar energy and connects to the Internet via a wireless modem. Hence, it can be attached to a light pole (or other structures) without the need for external power or wired Internet connectivity.

Fig. 9 illustrates the block diagram of the Caraoke reader. The device has five main block: a query generator, a receiver, a micro-controller, a modem, and a power management unit. The *query-generator* transmits a query signal that invokes a response from nearby transponders, the *receiver* receives the response signal, digitizes it, and provides it to the micro-controller. The *micro-controller* implements the standard receiver processing, i.e., packet detection, phase estimation, etc. It also implements our algorithmic solutions for counting, localization, speed measurement, etc. The processed data is then uploaded to the Internet via an LTE modem. (An alternative approach could use a WiFi modem, and have the readers forming a mesh network to connect to the Internet. However, the mesh network formation is beyond the scope of this paper.) Finally, the *power management* unit includes a small solar panel that attaches on top of the PCB, and a rechargeable battery that stores the harvested energy for operation during night time and on cloudy days. Solar panels can harvest $\sim 10mW/cm^2$ on sunny days [57, 53]. We use a 6cmx7.5cm solar panel, which can provides $500mW$ [47]. In §12, we show that this number is several folds larger than the power consumption of a Caraoke reader.

Finally, the device is equipped with a USB port which is used to program the micro-controller. The same USB port can also be used to power the device and extract the data, during the development phase.

In order to minimize the cost and power consumption of Caraoke reader, we perform multiple optimizations as follows:

- **Eliminating the TX chain:** A Caraoke reader has to transmit a query signal to request a response from the transponders. One approach to generate this query is to use a standard transmitter (TX) chain, which generates the signal in the digital domain. This approach however is inefficient in terms of both power and cost. Specifically, a full TX chain includes a mixer, a frequency synthesizer (PLL), a digital-to-analog-converter (DAC) and some digital logic. These components are necessary to transmit data bits. Yet, the e-toll query signal is just a simple sine-wave and does not carry any data. Such a sine-wave can be generated using a simple frequency synthesizer (i.e., a PLL), and does not need the rest of the components in the standard TX chain. The frequency synthesizer is turned on/off by the micro-controller so that the resulting sine-wave has the proper duration of the e-toll query.
- **Replacing FFT with the Sparse FFT:** As mentioned in §6, Caraoke operates on the response signal in the frequency domain after taking an FFT. At any time, the number of transponders that respond to the query is typically much smaller than the FFT size. In fact in most cases only a handful of transponders respond. Remember that each transponder creates a peak at the output of the FFT. Thus, the output of Fourier transform is sparse. For such sparse signals, one can compute the Fourier transform in sub-linear time [32, 31]. To do so, we use the sFFT algorithm in [33, 11], which is both simple and has low computation complexity. This directly translates into reduction in power consumption and speedup in the computation.
- **Duty Cycling:** Caraoke reader has two operating modes: active mode and sleep mode. In the active mode, the reader transmits queries, receives responses, and processes the signals. In the sleep mode, the query generator and receiver are turned off by the micro-controller by shutting off their power supply. All peripheral blocks are also deactivated. However, the master clock continues to run. A timer (typically called sleep timer) uses this clock to wake the micro-controller up at a specific time. The micro-controller controls the scheduling of the active and sleep modes to satisfy a desired power budget. Since each query takes about 1ms, we expect the average duration of the active mode to last for 10ms, allowing for a maximum of 10 queries. By controlling the duration of the sleep mode, the total power consumption can be dramatically reduced as we show in §12.5.

11. EVALUATION SETUP

Implementation: We implemented Caraoke reader on a printed circuit board (PCB) using off-the-shelf components. For the RF front-ends we use Maxim Integrated MAX2117 [41] and Analog Device AD7356 [15], and the Calliope LTE modem [50]. For the micro-controller, we use an Arduino Due board. The power management circuit includes regulator to regulate the voltage from the solar panel. For the solar panel, we use OSEPP SC10050 [47]. The RF chains share the same clock for accurate synchronization. The antennas are omni-directional and separated by $\frac{\lambda}{2} = 6.5$ *inches*. The ADC resolution is 12 bits. Also, the ADCs have differential inputs, and hence higher robustness to noise and interference. The total cost of the components is less than \$40, making the device amenable to large scale deployment. Further, this cost can be significantly reduced in mass production.

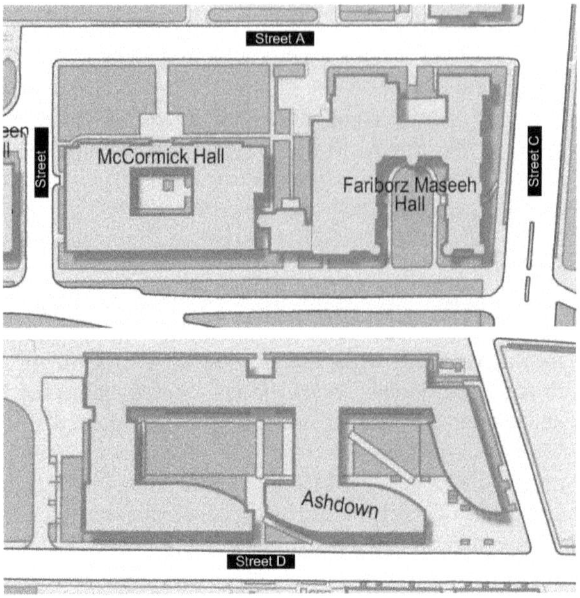

Figure 10—Experimental Setup. We ran our experiments on four streets in our campus, marked as streets A, B and C in the top figure and street D in the bottom figure. All streets have two-way traffic and most have parking spots on one or both sides.

We note that for our setup, we extract the data using the USB port as this does not require an LTE subscription and has no impact on counting, localization, or speed estimation.

Experimental Setup: We conducted our experiments on four campus streets, A, B, C, and D, which are shown in Figs. 10(a) and (b). All streets have 2-way traffic. Streets A, B, and D have street parking one or both sides of the road. Street C is the busiest street on campus, and is a major street in our city. In all of our experiments, the Caraoke reader was placed on a 12.5-feet pole. We used a total of 4 such poles. The poles are portable and hence allow us to experiment with various configurations, as detailed in §12.2.

All experiments were conducted with standard E-ZPass transponders attached to the cars' windshields. We tried to limit our experiments to transponders and cars owned by the authors. However, certain experiments require investigating the distribution of transponder CFOs and its impact on our ability to count vehicles. For that experiment, we collected transponder responses from random cars. We measured only the CFO of the transponders and did not decode the bits. After processing the signals to extract and count the CFOs, we stored only the CFO values with no reference to the ids of the car. We do not believe that the values of the CFOs can be mapped to the owners or used to infer any private information about them. Finally, we note that our transmissions of a sine-wave in the band used by E-ZPass is in accordance with the FCC rules Part 15 [27].

12. EMPIRICAL EVALUATION OF CARAOKE

We evaluate the various functions of Caraoke using outdoor experiments performed with E-ZPass transponders.

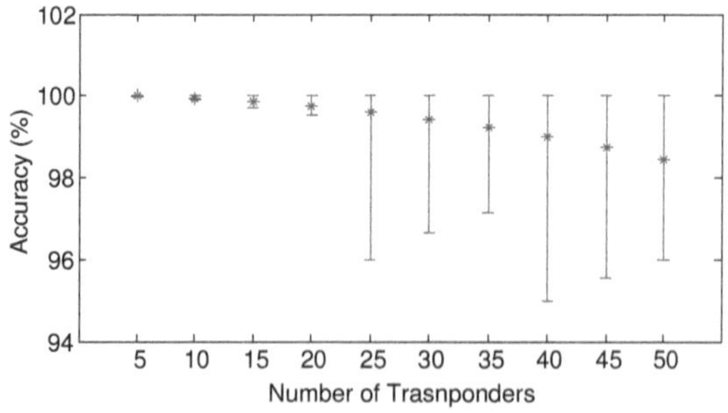

Figure 11—Counting Accuracy: Plot of Caraoke's counting accuracy as the number of colliding transponders increases.

12.1 Counting Accuracy

In the first experiment, we aim to evaluate Caraoke's ability to count transponders based on their CFOs. If we ran this experiment directly on collision signals, we would not know the ground truth. Hence, we needed first to estimate the CFO of each transponder in the absence of collisions. We collected signals from 155 different transponders in one of our campus parking lots. We used a directional antenna to obtain the response of each transponder without collisions. For each transponder, we took the FFT of its signal and noted the FFT bin of its CFO. We then create collisions in post-processing by summing up the time signals from a subset of the transponders. We change the number of transponders in the subset to obtain collisions with different numbers of colliding transponders. Finally, we take an FFT of each collision signal and estimate the number of colliding transponders using the approach described in §5. We have considered collisions of 5, 10, . . . , 50 transponders, and for each case performed 1000 runs.

Fig. 11 plots the average accuracy in counting colliding transponders. The figure shows that when the number of transponders in a collision is relatively small, Caraoke accuracy is very close to optimal. In particular, given the empirical CFO values of e-toll transponders, Caraoke can maintain an accuracy higher than 99% when the colliding transponders are fewer than 40. Note that the overall counting accuracy depends on how often the reader would experience 40-transponder collisions vs. 5-transponder collisions, or other numbers. This depends on the intersection and the amount of traffic. Overall, the results show that Caraoke is effective at counting vehicles using e-toll transponder collisions.

In our second experiment, we deployed Caraoke at the intersection of Street A and Street C in Fig. 10(a), and used it to track the flow of traffic on the two streets. In this experiment, we do not know the ground truth since we do not know which cars have transponders; despite this limitation the results can indicate the ratio of traffic between the two streets and how it relates to the timing of their green-light and red-light.

Fig. 12 plots the number of cars observed by Caraoke as a function of time for both streets. The figure is marked with the green-yellow-red times for the traffic lights on each of the streets. The figure shows how a backlog of cars accumulates during a red-light and clears during a green light. Further,

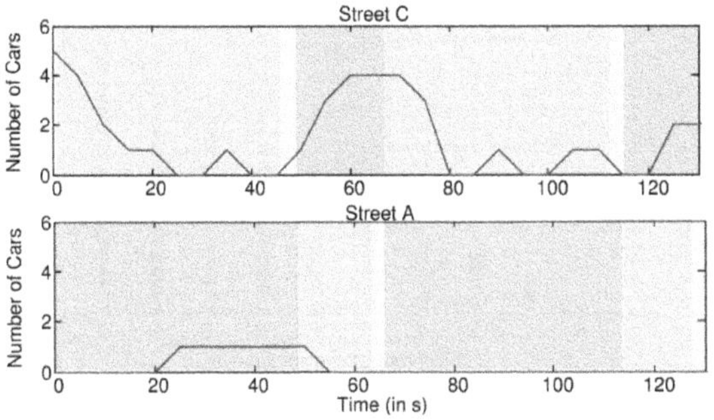

Figure 12—Traffic Monitoring at an Intersection. The figure shows the number of cars counted by Caraoke at an intersection over two periods of green-red lights.

road C is much busier than road A (10 times on average), but its green light is only 3 times longer than that of road A. This shows that Caraoke can help the city understand the relative congestion on various streets, and potentially adapt the timing of the traffic light to reduce car waiting time.

12.2 Localization Accuracy

In this experiment, we focus on localizing cars to parking spots. We ran our experiments on streets A and B, which have parking spots on one or both sides of the road, for a total of 36 spots. We use 4 poles, two deployed on street A and one at the intersection of A and B, and one on street B. We use two cars equipped with E-ZPass transponders, which we move between different parking spots to experiment with different configurations. There are other cars parked on the street, whose transponders collide with our two cars. We ran over 175 localization tests which span 35 configurations for the cars, and 5 runs per configuration which differ by the number and identity of the colliding transponders due to other parked cars and traffic dynamics on the streets. In our processing, we ignore the FFT spikes corresponding to other cars and focus on localizing our transponders using the method described in §6. To measure the ground truth we use a Bosch GLM50 laser distance measurement tool [17], which can measure distances to within a few millimeters. We then measure the ground truth angle using our knowledge of the transponder's distance from the pole, the pole's height, and the transponder's elevation.[14]

Fig. 13 plots the error in the angle of arrival measurement computed by Caraoke. The errors are plotted as a function of the location of the parking spot with respect to the pole carrying the Caraoke reader. The bar graph shows the average and standard deviation of the measurements from all four poles. The figure shows that the average localization error is about 4 degrees. Interestingly the error is the largest at the two ends, i.e., when the car is only 1 spot away or 6 spots

[14]Measuring the ground truth for 3D angles is difficult. However, since the car is parked to the side of the road, the transponder, the pole and the two antennas are approximately in the same plane. Hence, knowing the distances we can measure the ground-truth angle with simple geometry rules. Note that this approximation means that our results are conservative –i.e., Caraoke's actual errors could be slightly smaller.

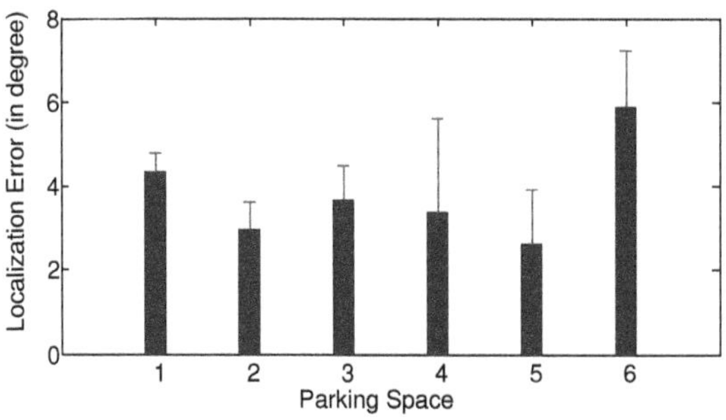

Figure 13—Transponder's Localization Accuracy. Figure shows the accuracy of localization for cars parked in different parking spaces where the spot 1 is closest and spot 6 is the furthest spot to Caraoke pole. Caraoke enables enough accuracy to detect occupied versus available spots

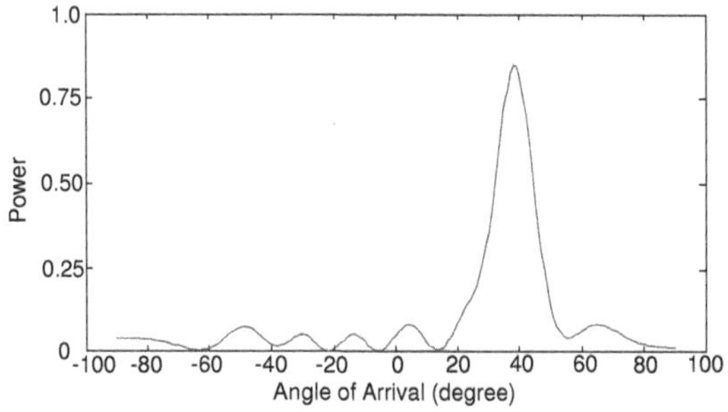

Figure 14—Multipath Profile. Caraoke readers have strong line-of-sight paths to the transponders. Therefore, multipath effects which occur in standard indoor environments are significantly weaker.

away from the pole. This is because the two antennas used for computing the AoA create a 60° angle with the plane of the road. As explained in §6, without this tilt the error in AoA for the farthest spot, i.e., spot 6, would be significantly larger than the closer spots. The results show that our decision of positioning the antennas at 60° angle with the street produces a relatively balanced error across spots.

One may be surprised that Caraoke's AoA accuracy is high despite that it uses a simple two-antenna array. Large antenna arrays are typically needed in multipath scenarios to separate signals that travel along different paths from source to destination. While multipath effect has been a big challenge for indoor localization, it becomes less prominent in Caraoke's design, primarily because Caraoke reader is mounted on a several meter high pole in an outdoor environment, and hence, has a prominent line-of-sight path between transmitter and receiver. To ascertain that this setting indeed has low multipath, we augmented Caraoke with an antenna attached to a rotating arm of radius 70cm. Like past work [37], we use this design to emulate a large antenna array (Synthetic Aperture Radar) and obtain the multipath profile of the signal coming from the car's transponder. As the antenna rotates, we continuously measure the wireless channel of the transponder's signal and then use the measured channels to reconstruct the multipath profile of the transponder's signal using standard phased array processing algorithm and the MUSIC algorithm [60].

A representative multipath profile obtained using this setup is shown in Fig. 14. As expected, the multipath pro-

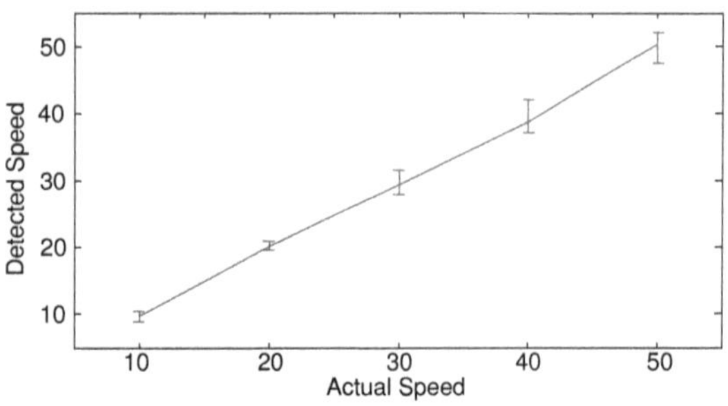

Figure 15—Speed Detection Accuracy. Figure shows the car speed detected by Caraoke versus its actual speed. Caraoke detected the speed to within 8% over a range of different speeds

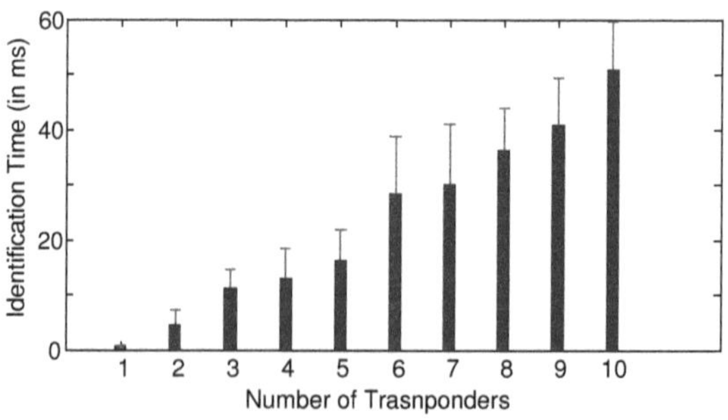

Figure 16—Identification Time versus Number of Transponders. As the number of transponders in Caraoke reader's range increases, Caraoke requires longer sensing time to identify the tags.

file has one dominant peak. To confirm that this is indeed the case across experiments, we repeat the experiment for 100 runs across different times and locations and measure the relative power of the two peaks with the highest amplitude in the multipath profile (i.e., the highest to the second highest peak power). We observe that, on average, the strongest peak has an order of magnitude higher power (specifically, 27 times higher) as compared to the second strongest peak. This confirms our hypothesis, that for line-of-sight outdoor environments, multipath effects are significantly weaker than the line of sight peak and hence, do not interfere with accurate phase based localization.

12.3 Speed Estimation Accuracy

Next, we evaluate Caraoke's ability to estimate car speed. For speeds below 40 mile/hour, we ran our experiments on street A and street D in Figs 10(a) and(b). We used two poles to localize the car and compute the speed as explained in 7. We locate the two poles 200 feet apart. Experiments with speeds higher than 40 mile/hour are performed in an empty lot. We perform 10 experiments at each speed, for a total of 50 experiments. We compare the speed detected by Caraoke with the speed reported by the car. Fig. 15 plots the estimated speed versus the actual speed. The plot shows both the average and the 90th percentile. The figure shows that Caraoke's estimate of the speed is within 8% of the real value –i.e., the error is 1 to 4 mile/hour across the whole range of speeds.

12.4 Decoding Accuracy

We evaluate Caraoke's ability to decode the ids of the transponders in the presence of wireless collisions. We place the Caraoke reader on a pole. The reader receives the colliding responses and decodes the ids of the transponders. Specifically, as described in §8, to decode a particular id, the reader combines the collisions after compensating for the channel and CFO of the desired transponder. The reader keeps combining collisions until the decoded id passes the checksum test. We use a maximum of 10 transponders whose owners agreed to the experiment. We run a total of 100 experiments with a different number of colliding transponders and different distances from the reader.

Fig. 16 shows the time taken to decode a transponder id for different numbers of colliding transponders. Recall that when decoding an id, Caraoke reader sends multiple queries, and combines the resulting collisions to decode. Since the queries are separated by 1ms, the time axis also shows the number of combined collisions in order to decode. As can be seen, the required time increases as the total number of colliding transponders increases. This is because when decoding a transponder, other transponders in the collision act as noise. However, even when there are 10 colliding transponders, Caraoke can still decode the transponder of interest within 50ms, on average.

Note that 50ms is also the time to decode all 10 transponders since one does not need to collect new collisions for individual transponders. One only needs to compensate for the CFO and channel of each of the transponders differently. Since the processing time of each query is negligible in comparison to the time it takes to transmit and receive, decoding all colliding transponders takes as much total time as decoding one transponder.

12.5 Caraoke Reader's Power Consumption

To profile Caraoke reader for power consumption, we removed the solar panel and the battery and used the USB port to power the device. We connected the USB to In-line Voltage and Current Meter [13], which measures the voltage and current drawn by the board. The power measurements reveal that Caraoke reader consumes 900mW in active mode and consumes only 69μW in sleep mode.[15] Since the solar panel delivers 500mW in the sun, Caraoke reader would not be able to run continuously in the active mode. However, as explained in §10, due to duty cycling, the average power consumption of the board is much lower as the duration of the active mode is less than 10ms. Thus, if Caraoke reader takes one measurement every second, it would consume an average power of 9mW, which is $\sim$ 56$\times$ lower than what it can harvest from its solar panel. Hence, the energy harvested from solar during 3 hours can be stored in a rechargeable

[15]These numbers exclude the modem module. LTE and Wi-Fi modems consumes 1-2 W and 100s of mW, respectively, while transmitting at Mbps data rates. A Caraoke reader needs to transmit only a few kbits to convey the results of processing one query (i.e., the channels and CFOs) to a backend. Furthermore, it can batch the results of multiple queries together. Hence, it can use the modem for tens of millisecond then put it to sleep for a minute or so. By duty cycling the modem, one can bring down its average power consumption to mW or hundreds of μW.

battery and run the device for a week regardless of weather condition. Finally, note that this operation time can be further increased by using a larger solar panel or increasing the sleep time.

13. CONCLUSION

This paper presents Caraoke a system that can count, localize, and measure the speed of cars using the RF signal from their e-toll transponders. Caraoke readers are small, low-cost and low-power, and hence can be easily deployed on street lamps to allow cities to deliver smart services, e.g., smart parking, traffic monitoring and speed detection, all using one infrastructure. While we focused mainly on tracking vehicles, once such infrastructure exists, the city may use it for additional services, like locating first responders, tracking the delivery of goods, and enabling people to pay for mobile services.

Acknowledgments: We thank Haitham Hassanieh, Fadel Adib, Hariharan Rahul, the reviewers and our shepherd, Lin Zhong for their insightful comments. This research is supported by NSF. We thank the members of the MIT Center for Wireless Networks and Mobile Computing, including Amazon.com, Cisco, Google, Intel, MediaTek, Microsoft, and Telefonica, for their interest and support.

14. REFERENCES

[1] E-ZPass statistics. http://e-zpassiag.com/about-us/statistics.
[2] E-ZPass taking toll on turnpike collectors. http://www.meadvilletribune.com/news/local_news/article_735f7ca1-82f9-5340-8940-29608aa499d5.html.
[3] NTP org: NTP over cellular. http://support.ntp.org/bin/view/Support/ConfiguringNTP#Section_6.15.
[4] PA turnpike to make E-ZPass mandatory. http://www.bizjournals.com/philadelphia/news/2013/08/29/pa-turnpike-to-make-e-zpass-mandatory.html.
[5] Paying with E-ZPass. http://www.panynj.gov/airports/lga-paying-with-e-zpass.html.
[6] The problems with police radar. http://www.ibiblio.org/rdu/a-btrust.html.
[7] Solar powered RFID system. http://www.gizmag.com/savi-technology-solar-rfid/8373/.
[8] Speed limits in the united states. http://en.wikipedia.org/wiki/Speed_limits_in_the_United_States.
[9] Tunpike tolls to be all-electronic by 2018. http://paindependent.com/2013/08/no-e-zpass-heres-a-bill-electronic-tolling-planned-for-pa-turnpike.
[10] Urban design division/planning and development review department. http://austintexas.gov/sites/default/files/files/Planning/Urban_Design/great_street_site_overview_0512.pdf.
[11] O. Abari, E. Hamed, H. Hassanieh, A. Agarwal, D. Katabi, A. P. Chandrakasan, and V. Stojanovic. A 0.75-million-point fourier-transform chip for frequency-sparse signals. In *IEEE ISSCC*, 2014.
[12] O. Abari, H. Rahul, D. Katabi, and M. Pant. Airshare: Distributed coherent transmission made seamless. In *IEEE INFOCOM*, 2015.
[13] Adafruit. USB Voltage and Current Meter. http://www.adafruit.com/product/1852.
[14] A. Amini, K. Kung, C. Kang, S. Sobolevsky, and C. Ratti. The impact of social segregation on human mobility in developing and industrialized regions. *EPJ Data Science*, 2014.
[15] Analog Device. ADC 7356. http://www.analog.com/static/imported-files/data_sheets/AD7356.pdf.
[16] J. A. Bonneson and M. Abbas. Intersection video detection manual. Technical report, Texas Transportation Institute, Texas A & M University System, 2002.
[17] Bosch Tools. Glm 50 laser distance measurer. http://www.boschtools.com/.
[18] V. Brik, S. Banerjee, M. Gruteser, and S. Oh. Wireless device identification with radiometric signatures. In *ACM MobiCom*, 2008.
[19] CBS Local. New app allows Boston drivers to pay for parking on smartphone. http://boston.cbslocal.com/2015/01/14/new-app-allows-boston-drivers-to-pay-for-parking-on-smartphone/.
[20] W. M. da Silva, A. Alvaro, G. H. R. P. Tomas, R. A. Afonso, K. L. Dias, and V. C. Garcia. Smart cities software architectures: A survey. In *ACM SAC*, 2013.
[21] S. Eichler. Performance evaluation of the ieee 802.11p wave communication standard. In *Vehicular Technology Conference*, 2007.
[22] EPCglobal Inc. Electronic Product Code (EPC): An overview. http://www.gs1.org/docs/epcglobal/an_overview_of_EPC.pdf.
[23] EPCglobal Inc. EPCglobal class 1 generation 2 v. 1.2.0. http://www.gs1.org/gsmp/kc/epcglobal/uhfc1g2.
[24] Escort Radar. The truth about speed enforcement. https://www.escortradar.com/pdf/radar_report.pdf.
[25] European Commission. Smart Cities: Digital agenda for Europe. http://ec.europa.eu/digital-agenda/en/smart-cities.
[26] Z. Farid, R. Nordin, and M. Ismail. Recent advances in wireless indoor localization techniques and systems. *Journal of Computer Networks and Communications*, 2013.
[27] Federal Communications Commission. Title 47, code for federal regulations, part 15.
[28] FOX News. Company lets drive-thru customers pay for fast food with E-Zpass. http://www.foxnews.com/leisure/2013/12/16/fast-food-drive-thrus-get-faster-company-lets-customers-pay-with-e-zpass/.
[29] J. Gjengset, J. Xiong, G. McPhillips, and K. Jamieson. Phaser: enabling phased array signal processing on commodity WiFi access points. In *MobiCom*, 2014.
[30] GS1. Electronic Product Code Implementation. http://www.gs1.org/epcglobal/implementation.
[31] H. Hassanieh, P. Indyk, D. Katabi, and E. Price. Nearly optimal sparse fourier transform. In *STOC*, 2012.
[32] H. Hassanieh, P. Indyk, D. Katabi, and E. Price. Simple and practical algorithm for sparse FFT. In *SODA*, 2012.
[33] H. Hassanieh, L. Shi, O. Abari, E. Hamed, and D. Katabi. Bigband: Ghz-wide sensing and decoding on commodity radios. In *IEEE INFOCOM*, 2014.
[34] P. Hu, P. Zhang, and D. Ganesan. Fully asymmetric backscatter communication. In *ACM SIGCOMM*, 2015.
[35] IEEE. IEEE Smart Cities. http://smartcities.ieee.org/.
[36] Kapsch TrafficCom. Active TDM LMS specifications. http://tdm.kapschtraffic.com//.
[37] S. Kumar, E. Hamed, D. Katabi, and L. Erran Li. LTE radio analytics made easy and accessible. In *ACM SIGCOMM*, 2014.
[38] KY3. Springfield's high tech cameras count cars to ease traffic congestion. http://articles.ky3.com/2012-06-20/springfield-traffic_32340154.
[39] F. Li and Y. Wang. Routing in vehicular ad hoc networks: A survey. *IEEE Vehicular Technology Magazine*, 2007.
[40] Y. Liu, J. Bi, and J. Yang. Research on vehicular ad hoc networks. In *CCDC*, 2009.
[41] Maxim Integrated. MAX2117. http://datasheets.maximintegrated.com/en/ds/MAX2117.pdf.

[42] McKinsey & Company. The smart-city solution. http://www.mckinsey.com/insights/public_sector/the_smart-city_solution.

[43] J. C. Medina, M. Chitturi, R. F. Benekohal, and T. R. Board. Illumination and wind effects on video detection performance at signalized intersections. *Urbana*, 2008.

[44] L. Mojela and M. Booysen. On the use of WiMAX and Wi-Fi to provide in-vehicle connectivity and media distribution. In *ICIT*, 2013.

[45] C. D. Murta, P. R. Torres Jr, and P. Mohapatra. Characterizing quality of time and topology in a time synchronization network. In *GLOBECOM*, 2006.

[46] New Jersey Turnpike Authority. Travel resources: E-ZPass information. http://www.state.nj.us/turnpike/ez-pass.html.

[47] OSEPP. Monocrystalline Solar cell. http://osepp.com/products/solar-cells-arduino-compatible/.

[48] H. Rahul, H. Hassanieh, and D. Katabi. SourceSync: A distributed wireless architecture for exploiting sender diversity. In *ACM SIGCOMM*, 2010.

[49] H. Rahul, S. S. Kumar, and D. Katabi. MegaMIMO: Scaling wireless capacity with user demand. In *ACM SIGCOMM*, 2012.

[50] Sequans Communications. Chipset solution for category 1 LTE devices for the internet of things. http://www.sequans.com/products-solutions/streamlitelte/calliope-lte-platform/.

[51] Streetline. Streetline Inc. http://www.streetline.com/.

[52] K. Tan, J. Fang, Y. Zhang, S. Chen, L. Shi, J. Zhang, and Y. Zhang. Fine grained channel access in wireless LAN. In *SIGCOMM*, 2010.

[53] Texas Instruments. Energy harvesting. http://www.ti.com/corp/docs/landing/cc430/graphics/slyy018_20081031.pdf.

[54] Z. Tian, M. Kyte, and H. Liu. Vehicle tracking and speed measurement at intersections using video detection systems. *ITE Journal*, 2009.

[55] Transportation Corridor Agencies. FasTrak on new I-10 and I-110 ExpressLanes. https://www.thetollroads.com/communications/switchable-transponders-110.php.

[56] Transportation Corridor Agencies. What is FasTrak? how do i use it to pay tolls? https://www.thetollroads.com/ontheroads/commonquestions/fastrak.php.

[57] R. J. Vullers, R. Schaijk, H. J. Visser, J. Penders, and C. V. Hoof. Energy harvesting for autonomous wireless sensor networks. *IEEE Solid-State Circuits Magazine*, 2010.

[58] J. Wang, H. Hassanieh, D. Katabi, and P. Indyk. Efficient and reliable low-power backscatter networks. In *ACM SIGCOMM*, 2012.

[59] J. Wang and D. Katabi. Dude, where's my card?: RFID positioning that works with multipath and non-line of sight. In *ACM SIGCOMM*, 2013.

[60] J. Xiong and K. Jamieson. ArrayTrack: A fine-grained indoor location system. In *NSDI*, 2013.

[61] Z. Xiong, H. Sheng, W. Rong, and D. Cooper. Intelligent transportation systems for smart cities: a progress review. *Science China Information Sciences*, 2012.

[62] S. Xu, P. Guo, B. Xu, and H. Zhou. QoS evaluation of VANET routing protocols. *JNW*, 2013.

[63] L. Yang, Y. Chen, X.-Y. Li, C. Xiao, M. Li, and Y. Liu. Tagoram: Real-time tracking of mobile RFID tags to high precision using COTS devices. In *ACM MobiCom*, 2014.

[64] T. Zinchenko, H. Tchouankem, L. Wolf, and A. Leschke. Reliability analysis of vehicle-to-vehicle applications based on real world measurements. In *VANET*, 2013.

Practical, Real-time Centralized Control for CDN-based Live Video Delivery

Matthew K. Mukerjee* mukerjee@cs.cmu.edu
David Naylor* dnaylor@cs.cmu.edu
Junchen Jiang* junchenj@cs.cmu.edu
Dongsu Han† dongsuh@ee.kaist.ac.kr
Srinivasan Seshan* srini@cs.cmu.edu
Hui Zhang*‡ hzhang@cs.cmu.edu

*Carnegie Mellon University †KAIST ‡Conviva Inc.

Abstract

Live video delivery is expected to reach a peak of 50 Tbps this year [7]. This surging popularity is fundamentally changing the Internet video delivery landscape. CDNs must meet users' demands for fast join times, high bitrates, and low buffering ratios, while minimizing their own cost of delivery and responding to issues in real-time. Wide-area latency, loss, and failures, as well as varied workloads ("mega-events" to long-tail), make meeting these demands challenging.

An analysis of video sessions [32] concluded that a centralized controller could improve user experience, but CDN systems have shied away from such designs due to the difficulty of quickly handling failures [29], a requirement of both operators and users. We introduce VDN, a practical approach to a video delivery network that uses a centralized algorithm for live video optimization. VDN provides CDN operators with real-time, fine-grained control. It does this in spite of challenges resulting from the wide-area (e.g., state inconsistency, partitions, failures) by using a hybrid centralized+distributed control plane, increasing average bitrate by 1.7× and decreasing cost by 2× in different scenarios.

CCS Concepts

•Networks → Traffic engineering algorithms; Overlay and other logical network structures;

Keywords

live video; CDNs; central optimization; hybrid control

SIGCOMM '15, August 17 - 21, 2015, London, United Kingdom

DOI: http://dx.doi.org/10.1145/2785956.2787475

1 Introduction

Demand for live video is increasing by 4–5× every three years and the live video peak streaming rate is expected to reach 50 Tbps this year [7]. This demand spans widely different types of videos (professionally-produced and user-generated) and workloads ("mega-events" to long-tail). The 2014 World Cup, a recent live video mega-event, used traditional CDNs to deliver live streams totaling several terabits per second [38], which is estimated to be 40% of all Internet traffic during that time [37]. At the other extreme, 55 million Twitch users [4] watch more than 150 billion minutes of live video each month, generated by over 1 million users, making it the fourth largest Internet traffic producer in the US [5, 41].

The diversity and volume of live video delivery makes it a complex challenge for modern content delivery infrastructures. However, huge demand isn't the only challenge; users, CDNs, and the network environment impose additional requirements. Users demand high quality, instant start-up (join) times, and low buffering ratios [10]. CDNs want to meet client demands while minimizing their delivery costs and responding to issues in real-time [35]. Finally, operating over the wide-area network environment requires designs that handle common latency variations and communication failures.

The traditional solution to these problems is traffic engineering. However, even state-of-the-art systems [23, 25] work on traffic aggregates at coarse timescales. Users' demands for high per-stream quality and CDNs' demands for fast failure recovery require control over individual streams at fine timescales. Overlay multicast systems [12, 14, 26, 30], while focusing on individual stream optimization, overlook issues that arise with the many concurrent, independent, high-bandwidth streams in today's environment. Internet-scale, video-specific systems like Conviva's C3 [19] use client-side analytics to pick the best CDN for a given client at a given time but ignore the actual data delivery. Although current CDNs provide good video quality, a previous analysis of a large collection of video sessions [32] concluded that

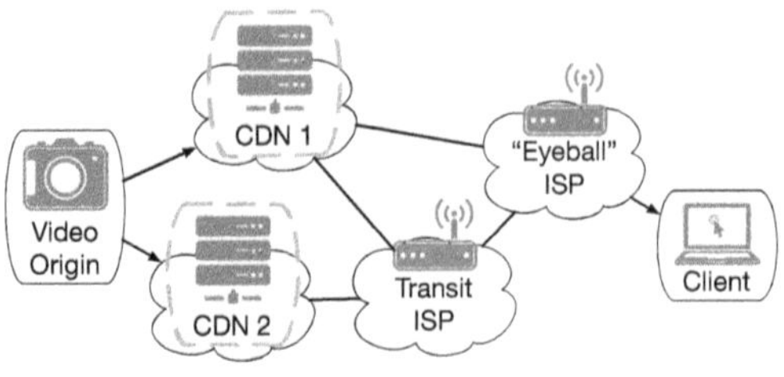

Figure 1: Entities involved in live video distribution. Unlike Conviva's C3 [19], which focuses on clients, we focus on optimizing CDNs.

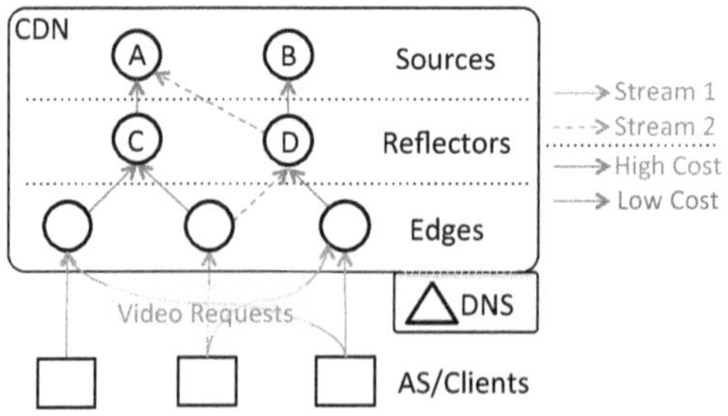

Figure 2: CDN live content distribution [35].

a centralized video controller algorithm could greatly improve end-user experience. Even so, traditional CDNs have shied away from centralized designs due to the difficulty of providing good performance while quickly handling failures in the wide area [29].

Unfortunately, past work on live video delivery does not meet the practical and real-time requirements of both CDNs and users. In summary, we need a live video control plane that: 1) enables proactive control over **cost** and **quality** at fine-grained timescales, 2) **scales** to today's largest CDNs and their workloads, 3) achieves **real-time responsiveness** to minimize join time and respond to failures, and 4) meets these goals despite wide-area network delays and failures.

In order to address these challenges, we propose a new system, called *video delivery network* (VDN), that allows CDN operators to dynamically control both stream placement and restrict bitrates automatically, at a very fine timescale in a WAN environment. Traditionally, clients adapt bitrates independently; VDN gives CDN operators a say, as they have the best view of current resources and delivery costs. At its core, VDN uses a centralized algorithm that performs end-to-end optimization of live stream routing. The centralized algorithm is a piece of the larger VDN framework, which mitigates WAN challenges with a *hybrid* approach that balances the benefits of centralized control with the resilience and responsiveness of distributed control.

We evaluate VDN using traces of real video sessions from multiple live content providers as well as a WAN testbed. We show that, in a variety of scenarios such as heavy-head (e.g., a sports game) and heavy-tail (e.g., user-generated streams), VDN provides a 1.7× improvement in average bitrate and reduces delivery costs by 2× compared to current CDNs. We scale VDN to 10,000 videos and show it can react at a timescale of 200 ms.

In summary, our contributions are:

- A **centralized algorithm** based on integer programming that coordinates delivery to provide high-quality live video streaming at scale while giving control "knobs" to operators to balance cost and quality.
- A responsive **live video delivery framework** that minimizes join time and mitigates WAN challenges using a *hybrid* centralized+distributed control plane.

2 Motivation

2.1 Setting

CDN background: We focus on optimizing CDNs for HTTP-based *live video delivery*. Each entity on the video delivery path (see Figure 1) can be independently optimized (e.g., clients in Conviva's C3 [19]), however the focus of this work is CDN optimization.

Live video: Live video is particularly challenging due to *lack of caching and buffering* within the delivery network. In HTTP-based live streaming, a video is encoded at multiple pre-determined bitrates. At each bitrate, each stream is broken into multiple 2–10 second *chunks*, which clients fetch independently via standard HTTP GETs. Clients typically adapt to network issues by fetching different bitrates [6].

CDN structure: Figure 2 presents the high-level structure of a CDN's video delivery system [29, 35, 40]. Each node represents a cluster of co-located servers. A CDN's internal network consists of three logical pieces: video *sources* that import videos into the system, *reflectors* that forward content internally, and *edge clusters* that directly serve end-users (individual clients or aggregate ASes). Each link has a delivery cost associated with it. These link costs are a result of private business deals, but they tend to be more expensive for source/reflector links (typically long-haul WAN links) and less expensive (some entirely free) for edge/AS links [2]. In Figure 2, the link between A and D is a high cost link.

CDNs and DNS: When clients resolve the name of a video stream, the CDN's DNS-based client mapping service maps them to a nearby edge cluster, based on a number of factors (e.g., load, latency, etc.) [35]. When a client's request for a particular channel arrives at an edge cluster, the edge cluster forwards it to a reflector (found via DNS), which in turn forwards it to a source (found via DNS); the content is returned via the reverse path. When multiple requests for the same content arrive at the same node (e.g., C in the figure), only one request is forwarded upwards. The end result is a *distribution tree* for each video from sources to edge clusters.

This has been the design used by Akamai for live streaming since 2004 [29], externally observed in 2008 [40] and referenced by Akamai in 2010 [35]. We confirm this holds today [2].

Problems with modern CDNs: Using DNS to map requests to the appropriate upstream cluster is very natural as CDN workloads have shifted from web-oriented to live streaming. Mapping clients to edge clusters with DNS makes sense, since most live video content is embedded in websites, which already use DNS. However, using DNS to map internal clusters to upstream clusters causes issues: 1) CDNs can't "push" updates to clusters and must instead wait for clusters to "pull" from DNS after a timeout period (the DNS TTL); and 2) To reduce load on DNS, CDNs group different streams together, reducing granularity [29, 40]. Furthermore, CDNs today update DNS mappings using heuristics [2, 29, 35, 40], impacting performance. We explore these issues in more detail.

DNS TTLs: DNS relies on DNS *clients* (i.e., clusters) to ask for updates when cached DNS results expire (every ~30 seconds) [40], preventing a central controller from sending updates as they are ready. This reduces the efficacy of the controller, thus lowering end-user quality and responsiveness to failures. Furthermore, CDN clusters can spot local network failures long before a TTL-bound DNS update could arrive and thus could react quicker. Lowering the TTL would help approximate a "push"-based system but at the cost of a large increase in the number of DNS queries.

Heuristic-based mapping algorithm: A monitoring system collects performance and load information and, based on this knowledge, updates the DNS system every minute [35]. Generally, CDNs map end-users to edge clusters based on geography, load, whether or not a cluster is already subscribed to the video, and performance relative to the requester [2, 29, 35, 40]. It is implied that the mapping of edge clusters to reflectors is done similarly [35], but the specific algorithm is not publicly known. A measurement study points out that geographically close edge clusters all map to the same reflector for the same groups of videos, providing further evidence [40]. Additionally, an analysis of video traces shows that mapping requests based on a global view of the network [32] could provide major benefits for end-users, implying that there are opportunities to improve this mapping.

Goal: VDN's job is twofold: 1) coordinate the selection of distribution trees for each channel and 2) assign groups of clients within a given geographic region to a good edge server. It must perform these tasks while meeting the goals listed below.

2.2 Design goals

Video-specific quality and low cost (quality/cost tradeoff): CDN operators must satisfy user's expectation for high video quality, while minimizing their delivery cost. Thus, VDN must optimize for video quality directly, while considering its cost.

Internet-scale video delivery (scalability): Many different types of workloads exist for live video: (a) *"mega-events"* (e.g., World Cup) serving 1M+ users [38], (b) *TV-style channels* serving 100K users [3], and (c) *"long tail" user channels* (e.g., Twitch, Ustream) serving 1-10,000 users [11]. (a) tends to be easier as one tree can serve everyone, whereas workload (c) is the toughest, as it requires coordinating across many videos. VDN must support these workloads, out to a target scale of 10,000 channels [40] and 2000 edge clusters [17], beyond the scale of today's largest CDNs. Such scale is challenging as finding the optimal placement is NP-hard.

Fine timescale (responsiveness): VDN must provide fast join time (less than a second) and fast failure recovery, despite challenges in the wide area (e.g., inconsistent state, partitions, loops).

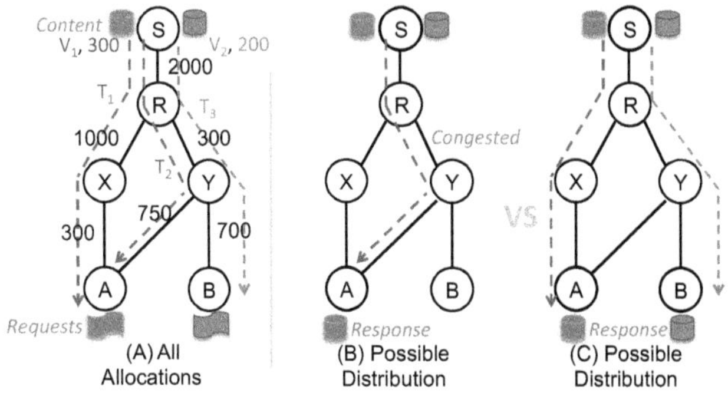

Figure 3: Motivating central coordination.

2.3 Case for centralized optimization

Despite the lack of public information on how the CDN internal mapping is done, prior work has shown that a control plane designed around centralized optimization can provide great benefit [32]. In this section we focus on the reasons for these benefits.

Coordination: Throughout this paper, we use coordination to mean the ability to consider all individual streams simultaneously. As mentioned, modern CDNs have difficulty with this as they aggregate videos and get "locked in" to decisions due to DNS TTLs [40]. Figure 3 illustrates why stream coordination can lead to better resource allocation. Two video channels (V_1 and V_2) originate from a single source, *S*. The goal is to deliver V_1 to AS *A* and V_2 to *B*. Three possible distribution trees exist: T_1, T_2 and T_3 (Figure 3a). We present two feasible distribution strategies in Figure 3b and c. In Figure 3b only client A is served, whereas in Figure 3c both clients are served. The issue is that using distribution tree T_2 would congest the *RY* link. However, knowing this in advance is difficult; it would require not only knowledge of network resources, but also the placement of other streams. A natural solution would be centralization, which affords both a global view of the network and the ability to coordinate streams.

This observation generalizes to large-scale networks. Figure 4 compares a system with a global view that places streams independently without coordination (OM in §7) to one that has a global view *and* coordinates

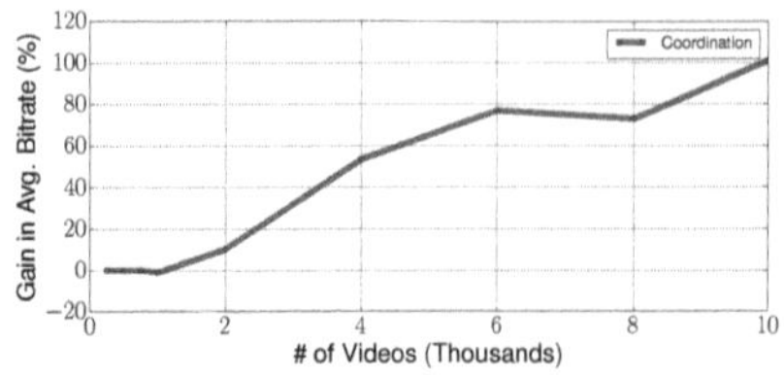

Figure 4: The importance of coordinating streams generalizes to larger systems. This graph shows the gain of our system compared to a multicast-style approach as we'll see in §7.

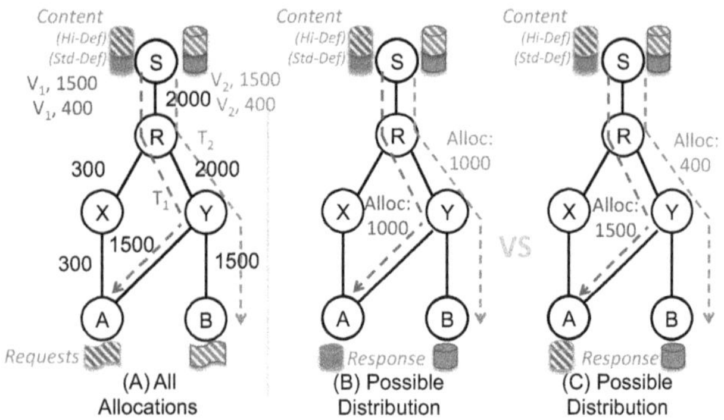

Figure 5: Motivating app-specific optimization.

streams (VDN in §7) for a 100 node topology. With 10K videos, we observe up to a 100% improvement in average bitrate.

Application-specific optimization: Generic traffic engineering at a centralized controller is not enough; we must perform app-specific optimization. For example, in Figure 5, two videos are encoded as low quality (400 Kbps) and high quality (1500 Kbps) versions. Due to bandwidth constraints (Figure 5a), we must deliver both over link RY. We present two ways to allocate bandwidth in Figure 5b and c. Despite fairly allocating bandwidth between the streams, Figure 5b does worse overall, as both clients only receive the low quality stream. Figure 5c is "unfair", but is a better strategy as one client is able to get the higher quality stream. Thus, careful consideration of bitrate at the granularity of streams is needed to provide the best quality.

From the two examples, we conclude that we can improve quality with: 1) a global view of network resources; 2) coordination across streams; and 3) consideration of the streaming bitrates. This argues for a video-specific control plane that is logically centralized.

2.4 Case for hybrid control

Live video-specific, centralized optimization alone is not sufficient. A fully centralized system would require new video requests to reach the controller across WAN latencies before the video could be viewed, yielding terrible join times. Additionally, centralized optimization using an integer program can take quite long (e.g., 10s of seconds), further impacting join time. Yet, a distributed scheme would be highly responsive as clusters could react to requests immediately, yielding low join times and fast failure recovery. However, we argue that a distributed scheme is challenged to provide the high quality demanded by users at reasonable cost, due to the lack of coordination (§2.3).

A combination of the two schemes, with the quality of a centralized system and the responsiveness of a distributed system would be best suited. We refer to this combination as **hybrid control**. We avoid poor interactions between the two schemes by exploiting properties of our highly structured topology (§2.1) and by keeping track of alternate paths with enough capacity for each video channel (§4).

3 VDN system overview

VDN reuses existing CDN internal infrastructure (source clusters, reflector clusters, edge clusters, and DNS) but employs a new control plane based on hybrid control—a centralized controller makes optimal decisions slowly while clusters simultaneously make decisions quickly based on distributed state. VDN treats each cluster as an atomic unit (as in Figure 6) and controls the distribution of live video from sources to clients; traffic management within a cluster is outside the scope of this paper.

When video v is requested at bitrate b by a client in an AS a, a request is sent to VDN's DNS server; the response directs the client to send video chunk requests to a nearby edge cluster. If this edge cluster knows about v (i.e., has a entry for (v, b) in its forwarding table), then it forwards the request upstream accordingly. If not, it runs the *distributed control algorithm* (§4). Reflectors pick source clusters similarly. The video chunk follows this path in reverse. Eventually, centralized control updates the clusters' forwarding tables (§5).

As a control plane, VDN (1) populates application-layer forwarding tables at each cluster with centrally computed entries, (2) creates forwarding table entries on-the-fly when necessary using distributed control, and (3) updates the client to edge server mapping accordingly in the DNS infrastructure.

3.1 Design

Physical view: VDN introduces two physical pieces to the traditional CDN infrastructure: a logically centralized *central controller* and a *local agent* in each server cluster. The central controller and local agents are each decomposed into two pieces: (1) a *control* subsystem that computes path assignments based on network state and (2) a *discovery* subsystem that tracks incoming requests and topology information.

Logical view: VDN's control plane is driven by two control loops, which update clusters' forwarding tables at different timescales. A *central control loop* computes optimal distribution trees (as well as client/server mappings) using the algorithm described in §5. This loop runs continuously and operates on the timescale of tens

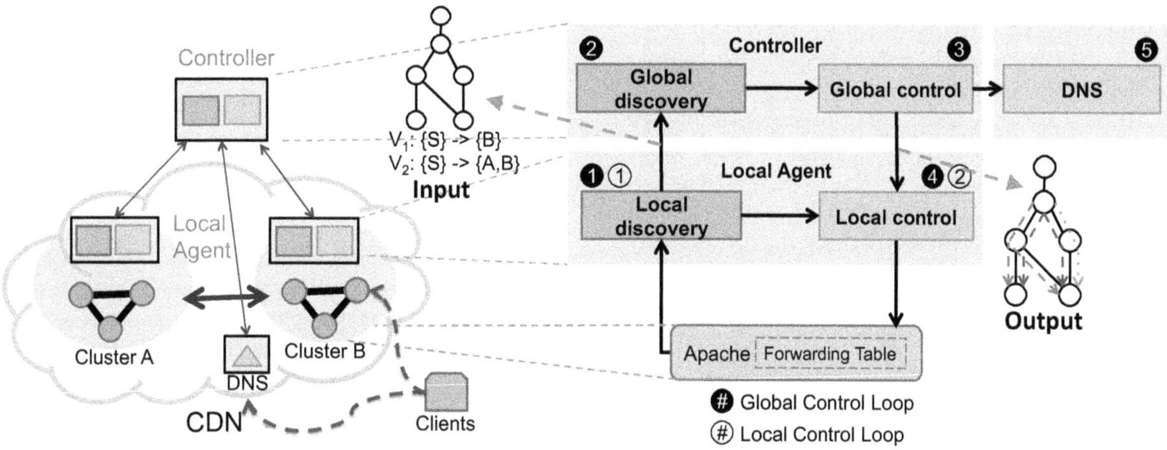

Figure 6: VDN system overview.

Routing Information Base

Central/ Dist.	Channel	Next Hop	Version	Evidence	
				Network Stats	Viewership Stats
C	V_0/800/*	R2	15:20	Link_1: 10Mbps Link_2: 15Mbps	V_0:{800}Kbps, 3000 requests
D	V_0/*/*	R1	15:23	Link_1: 10Mbps Link_2: failed	V_0:{800}Kbps, 3007 requests

Forwarding Information Base

Channel	Version	Next Hop
V_0/*/*	15:23	R1

Figure 7: Sample RIB and FIB entries. The local agent uses network and viewer state as "evidence" to decide when to override potentially stale decisions from the central controller.

of seconds to minutes. Meanwhile, the local agent runs a *distributed control loop* that amends its cluster's forwarding table to quickly (i.e., sub-second) respond to local changes (e.g., link failures) using distributed state.

Central control loop:

❶ Local discovery measures link information and tracks AS- and cluster-level channel viewership.

❷ Global discovery collects measurements from each cluster and builds a global network view.

❸ Global control computes optimal distribution trees.

❹ Local control merges local state with the global decision and updates the forwarding table.

❺ Global control updates DNS.

Distributed control loop:

① Local discovery measures link information and tracks AS- and cluster-level channel viewership.

② Local control merges local state with the global decision and updates the forwarding table.

The two loops have different views of the system, and use their information for different purposes. The central loop sees all clusters, the status of their links, and channel viewership information so that it can assign optimal distribution trees. The distributed loop sees local link conditions and video requests at one cluster as well as a small amount of distributed state. The local agent merges the controller's decision with this information and installs appropriate forwarding rules. Our hybrid control plane strikes a balance between the high quality of a centralized system and the responsiveness of a distributed system.

4 Hybrid control

Running two control loops in tandem can lead to challenges that destroy any benefit that either control loops would have had individually, resulting in a "worst of both worlds" scenario, as hinted in §2.4. When distributed decision-making is used, hybrid control handles this by only considering end-to-end paths that provide enough bandwidth. In this section we examine the interactions of our central and distributed control loops in detail and how we balance them, as well as how hybrid control mitigates issues in the wide-area.

4.1 Central control

Central control takes in a global view of the network (video requests and topology information) as input and uses the algorithm described in §5 to calculate the optimal configuration of distribution trees as output. To avoid having a single point of failure, VDN uses multiple geo-replicated controllers, synchronized with Paxos [31]. After making a decision, VDN's central controller distributes it to individual clusters. To do this, the central controller sends each cluster's local agent a routing information base (RIB) specific to that cluster, as shown in Figure 7. VDN's RIB contains information to support hybrid decision-making in addition to the typical routing information (e.g., a prefix and a next hop). In particular the RIB maintains where the information came from (centralized or distributed control), a version number (timestamp), and a set of "evidence" providing the context when this particular RIB entry was computed (link and viewership information sent by this cluster to the central controller when this decision was computed). Evidence helps distributed control decide if it should override the global decision.

The RIB gets merged with distributed control's own decision to become the *Forwarding Information Base* (FIB), used by the data plane. If distributed control decides nothing is amiss, the global RIB entry's (channel prefix, version number, next hop) tuple is used directly as the FIB entry.

Discovery: In order for central control to generate good distribution trees, it needs to have up-to-date information on the state of the network and requests. Keeping track of new requests is relatively simple at the edge clusters. Estimating changes in link capacity available to applications in overlay networks (e.g., due routing changes, background traffic, or failures) is a well studied topic [33, 36, 39], and is thus considered out of scope in this work.

4.2 Distributed control

Distributed control keeps track of viewership and path information of upstream neighbors to make quick local decisions in response to changes in network performance, viewership, and failures. The objective is to improve responsiveness by avoiding the costly latency of centralized optimization. Thus, distributed control overrides the central decision in response to dramatic changes.

Initial requests (DNS): VDN's DNS takes into account the user's geographic location and AS in order to map them to the proper edge cluster as computed by the central controller. If this particular AS has not previously been assigned to an edge cluster, simple heuristics are used to provide a reasonable starting assignment (e.g., an edge cluster that already is subscribed to this video, an edge cluster that's typically used by this location/AS, etc.). This provides an initial instant mapping of clients to edge clusters.

Distributing state: Clusters distribute video subscription and link information to other nodes via a distance vector-like algorithm to aide in reacting to large changes. Each cluster periodically (e.g., every second) sends all connected clusters at the next lower layer (see Figure 2) its "distance" from each channel+bitrate (v, b), denoted $d(v, b)$, representing how many hops away it is from a cluster that is subscribed to v at bitrate b; if a cluster is already subscribed to v at bitrate b, then $d(v, b)$ at that cluster is 0. Recall that we focus on live video, thus caching is largely unhelpful; clusters only advertise videos they are currently receiving.

When a cluster receives these distance values, it stores them in a table (see Figure 8) along with the available capacity of the bottleneck link on the path to that cluster $c(v, b)$. The cluster propagates the distance to the closest subscribed cluster with enough path capacity for this bitrate downwards, similar to a distance vector protocol.

Distance & Capacity Table

For Node A	Via X	Via Y	Via Z
To v_0,b_1	1, 5000	1, 1500	2, 4500
To v_1,b_1	2, 2000	1, 1500	2, 4000
To v_2,b_1	2, 5000	1, 1500	1, 3000

Figure 8: Example of the distributed state table used in Algorithm 1.

Reacting to large changes: If local discovery has detected significant changes in the local network state or viewership used to calculate the most recent central decision (i.e., the "evidence" in the RIB entry), it concludes that its current central forwarding strategy is out of date. Specifically, a cluster considers a RIB entry stale if one or more of the following conditions are met:

- A link referenced in the evidence changes capacity by some percentage (e.g., 20%) set by the operator.
- A link, node, or controller fails, as detected by a timeout.
- It receives a request it doesn't have a FIB entry for.

Input: request for channel v, bitrate b
Output: next-hop cluster for channel v, bitrate b

```
/* randomly pick a parent that has a
   min-hop path to (v,b) with enough
   capacity to support delivery                */
useful := ∅
for parent in parents do
    if d(v,b)_via_parent == min(d(v,b)) and
      c(v,b)_via_parent > b then
        useful = useful ∪ {parent}
    end
end
return pick_at_random(useful)
```

Algorithm 1: Distributed control algorithm.

If the global "evidence" is deemed invalid, a forwarding strategy is computed by Algorithm 1, using local request and link information as well as the distributed state from upper nodes (Figure 8).

For example, when a cluster receives a request for a video it's not subscribed to, it uses its table to forward the request to the parent "closest" (based on "distance" $d()$ values) to the video that has enough spare path capacity ($c()$). If there are no paths available the request is denied, to be serviced by a different edge cluster. It breaks ties randomly to avoid groups of clusters potentially overloading a high capacity cluster after failure. If the parent is not already subscribed to the video, the process repeats until a subscribed cluster is found. The algorithm produces a forwarding strategy that VDN places in the RIB and FIB of the cluster for future use (Figure 7). Large-scale link variations, link failures, and node failures, can all be handled by treating the existing videos as new requests.

Discussion: The algorithm ensures that video streams that deviate from global control only traverse paths with enough spare capacity to support them. This is critical because it means that (1) if the parent of a cluster is already subscribed to the requested video (and has ample bandwidth to the requesting cluster), requests to this cluster will not propagate past the parent (i.e., 1 hop), (2) more generally, in an n-level CDN (where n is typically 3 today), only $n-1$ clusters are affected by network / viewership changes as clusters only forward to parents on a path with enough capacity, always reaching source nodes after $n-1$ hops, and (3) clusters that are involved in this algorithm will not be forced to degrade the quality of an existing stream, as we know there is enough capacity on the path to support the incoming request. Thus, the distributed algorithm will not interfere with central control's already implemented decisions.

Note, through the use of local/global discovery, the central controller will eventually become aware of new requests and failures. By checking evidence in the RIB, clusters will know when central control has "caught up" to the current network state at which point they make the past local decisions obsolete.

4.3 Issues in the wide area

Handling state transitions: When requests are sent up the distribution tree for a given channel, they are tagged with the version number from the RIB. VDN keeps previous versions of the FIB ("shadow FIBs") to allow clusters to forward requests with old version numbers (e.g., during global state transitions), similar to previous work [20, 28, 34]. When an unknown version is encountered, VDN resorts to using distributed control.

Partitions: Versioning helps with network partitions, where some clusters no longer receive updates from the central controller. Clusters that are partitioned ("invisible" clusters from the controller's perspective) can still interact with "visible" clusters by using these old version numbers. Eventually the partitioned clusters will switch to exclusively distributed control after they detect that they're partitioned (e.g., after a controller timeout). As distributed control and central control interact in beneficial ways, partitions are also not a problem.

Loops: Our system cannot have loops as requests only travel "upwards" towards sources, and responses "downwards" towards ASes in our hierarchy.

5 Centralized optimization

This section describes our optimization algorithm that maximizes the overall service VDN delivers to each video channel while minimizing cost. Our algorithm takes in video requests and topology information and outputs the best way to distribute those videos. While the formulation is relatively straightforward, the easiest way to achieve scalability is to eschew finding the true optimal solution in favor of finding a good approximately optimal solution that can be computed relatively fast.

$$\begin{aligned}
\max\ & w_s * \textstyle\sum_{l\in L_{AS}, o\in O} \text{Priority}_o * \text{Request}_{l,o} * \text{Serves}_{l,o} \\
- \ & w_c * \textstyle\sum_{l\in L, o\in O} \text{Cost}(l) * \text{Bitrate}(o) * \text{Serves}_{l,o} \\
&\textbf{subject to:} \\
\forall l \in L, o \in O &: \text{Serves}_{l,o} \in \{0,1\} \\
\forall l \in L &: \textstyle\sum_o \text{Bitrate}(o) * \text{Serves}_{l,o} \le \text{Capacity}(l) \\
\forall l \in L, o \in O &: \textstyle\sum_{l'\in \text{InLinks}(l)} \text{Serves}_{l',o} \ge \text{Serves}_{l,o}
\end{aligned}$$

Figure 9: Integer program at the controller.

The optimization is called iteratively (around once a minute) allowing parameters (e.g., measured capacities, link costs, new requests) to be modified each iteration.

Input: *Videos:* We denote a set of live video channels as $V = \{v_1, \ldots, v_k\}$. Each video channel v has its own set of bitrate, B_v. Our system treats each item in $V \times B$ as a distinct video object. We denote the set of video objects as $O = \{o_1, \ldots, o_m\}$. Bitrate(o) is the bitrate of the video object o in Kbps. Every video object o has a priority weight associated with it, Priority$_o > 0$, set by operators indicating how important it is to serve o.

Topology: Our network topology (see Figure 10a) is a directed graph made of server clusters (sources, reflectors, and edges as explained in §2) and ASes, connected by links $\{l_1, \ldots, l_n\} \subset L$ in a four-tier topology. We assume each video object is available at each source cluster (not unreasonable [35], but not fundamental). We add additional *dummy* links out of every AS node in the graph [1]. We refer to this set of dummy links as $L_{AS} \subset L$. For some link $l = (s, s')$, InLinks(l) is the set of incoming links to s.

Link capacities: Each link $l \in L$ has a capacity defined by Capacity(l), in Kbps. This capacity is the measured amount of capacity of the overlay link available to video delivery (i.e., the overall path capacity minus background traffic), which is updated by information from local discovery.

Link costs: Additionally, each link $l \in L$ has a cost defined by Cost(l) indicating the relative price for delivering bits over that link. This cost can vary over time (i.e., updated between iterations of the ILP) as updated by management (e.g., after business negotiations a link is perhaps free: $Cost(l) = 0$; perhaps cost varies based on usage, such as "95-percent-rule" billing; or even more complicated policies such as a cap on total externally-bound traffic, etc.).

Requests are associated with a link in L_{AS} (i.e., a requesting AS) and a video object. For some link $l \in L_{AS}$ associated with an AS a, if a request for video o originates from a then Request$_{l,o} = 1$, else Request$_{l,o} = 0$.

Weights: The system operator provides a global weight for cost $w_c \ge 0$ and a global weight for service $w_s \ge 0$ to strike a balance between service and cost.

Formulation: Figure 9 presents our problem formulation. The optimization takes the following as input (and treats them as constants): w_s, w_c, Priority, Request,

[1]This is a common technique in optimization to make the formulation easier.

	Bitrates (Kbps)	Priorities	Requests (at Start)
V_1	[200, 800]	[1, 1]	(A, 800), (B, 800)
V_2	[300, 900]	[1, 100]	None

Service Weight	1000
Cost Weight	0.1

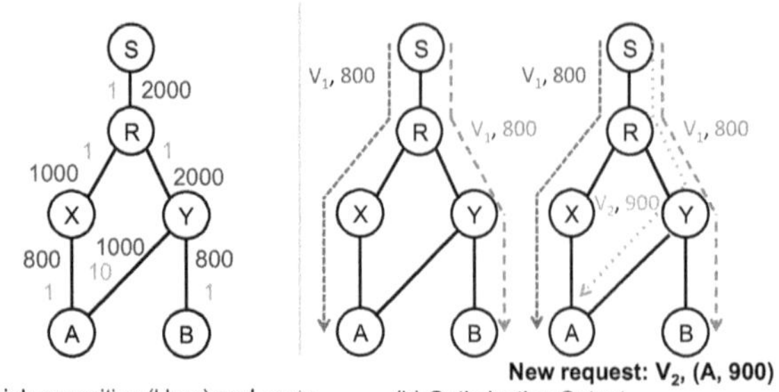

(a) Link capacities (kbps) and costs (b) Optimization Output

Figure 10: Example input and output of the centralized optimization.

Cost, Bitrate, Capacity, and InLinks. It outputs variables $\text{Serves}_{l\in L, o\in O} \in \{0,1\}$, which indicates whether video object o should be distributed over link l.

Our objective function directly maximizes service, while simultaneously minimizing its cost (i.e., max: service − cost). We model service as $\sum_{l\in L_{AS}, o\in O} \text{Priority}_o \cdot \text{Request}_{l,o} \cdot \text{Serves}_{l,o}$. Thus we only serve videos objects to ASes that requested them, with the biggest wins coming from higher priority video objects. Service is only improved if a requested video reaches its destined AS. As for priority, we explore various schemes (exploring the quality/quantity tradeoff) in §7. We model cost as $\sum_{l\in L, o\in O} \text{Cost}(l) \cdot \text{Bitrate}(o) \cdot \text{Serves}_{l,o}$, the amount of data being transferred around (and out of) the CDN times the link costs.

Our constraints encode the following:

1. A link either does or doesn't send a video.
2. Obey the link capacity constraint.
3. Only send videos you've received.

Output: $\text{Serves}_{l,o}$, determines a set of distribution trees for every requested video. This can be easily translated into forwarding tables for incoming requests within the CDN internal network, and DNS records for mapping clients to edge clusters.

Example: Figure 10 gives an example input with two channels V_1 and V_2, with bitrate streams of [200, 800] and [300, 900] kbps respectively. We see that the operator has decided that video object (V_2, 900) has a very high priority (100)—this may be a stream viewers pay to watch (e.g., a pay-per-view sports event). Figure 10a shows the topology, link capacities, and costs. Link YA has a relatively high cost of 10. Figure 10b shows the optimization result in which two requests for V_1 are satisfied. Note, the optimization avoids using the high cost YA link, even though it would have cut down the total number of links used, reducing redundant data transmissions. Once a third request is added (for the high priority stream V_2), we observe that YA is used, as the video's priority outweighs the high link cost.

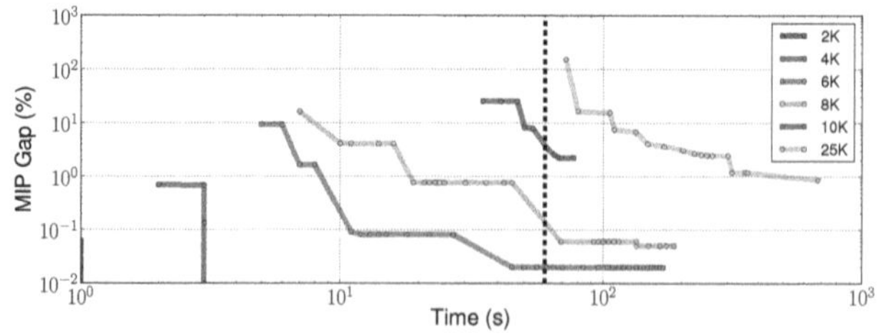

Figure 11: The MIP gap of the centralized optimization shows rapid improvement in a short time-frame, even for large numbers of videos.

Approximating optimality: An integer program can take a very long time to find an optimal solution. We employ two techniques (initial solutions and early termination) for fast approximation.

Often a good initial solution can dramatically reduce the integer program runtime. Although it's tempting to reuse the previous central decision as the initial solution for the next iteration, our formulation changes enough (e.g., new link capacities, video requests, etc.) per iteration that our previous decision may no longer be valid. Thus, we instead we calculate an initial solution greedily.

Another important parameter of integer programs is the termination criteria. Often integer programs will find a feasible solution very quickly that is only slightly worse than optimal, then spend many minutes working towards the optimal solution. This time/quality tradeoff guides our decision to use a timeout to terminate our optimization. In Figure 11 we plot the *MIP gap*[2] as a function of computation time for differing numbers of videos. We see that for all series up to our target scale of 10,000 videos (see §2.2), a 60 second timeout can provide an almost optimal solution (e.g., ~1%)). Although 60 seconds may seem like a long timescale for optimization with respect to view duration, live video viewers watch on average 30 minutes per session [1], making this a reasonable target.

6 Prototype implementation

Control plane: We build a prototype central controller that uses Gurobi [21] to solve the integer program. For trace-driven experiments, we run the controller on an r3.8xlarge EC2 instance [8]. For end-to-end experiments, since our testbed is smaller, we run the controller on a machine with a 2.5GHz quad-core Intel Core i5 processor with 4GB of RAM. For these experiments, our controller communicates with data plane nodes over the public Internet, with ~10ms latency. We believe this to be representative of a real-world deployment.

Data plane: We also build a prototype data plane using Apache [16] running on t2.small EC2 instances. Our data plane uses standard Apache modules: *mod_proxy* configures nodes as reverse HTTP proxies and *mod_cache*

[2]The distance between the current upper and lower bounds expressed as a percentage of the current upper bound

gives us multicast-like semantics. The use of Apache is representative of a real-world deployment as modern live video streaming is HTTP-based. Since these nodes communicate with the controller across the WAN, we see realistic cross-traffic, loss, and delays representative of a real-world deployment.

7 Evaluation

We evaluate VDN in two ways: a trace-driven evaluation of the central optimization focusing on the quality/cost tradeoff and scalability; and an end-to-end wide-area evaluation to test the responsiveness and performance of hybrid control in the presence of variation and failures in real-world environments.

7.1 Trace-driven evaluation

We answer three questions:

1. *Does VDN improve video quality and reduce cost?* VDN improves the average bitrate at clients by 1.7× in heavy-tail scenarios and can reduce cost by 2× in large-event scenarios over traditional CDNs.
2. *How does VDN scale? How sensitive is VDN to the network topology?* We scale VDN's control plane to 10K videos and 2K edge clusters and see it performs well even with low topological connectivity.
3. *How much control do operators have over VDN?* The knobs offered by VDN are sensitive enough for operators to fine-tune the quality/cost tradeoff and distribution of service over bitrates and videos.

Traces: We evaluate the efficacy of our controller with three traces representative of common workloads:

- Average Day: A one-hour trace from a service provider with detailed client-side analytics for a large number of live video providers. It is comprised of 55,000 requests for 4,144 videos from 2,587 cities (18,837 clients) and an average request bitrate of 2725 Kbps. This trace has a long tail: 7% of the videos account for 50% of the requests. This represents an average day for a low-demand live video service.
- Large Event: A partially synthetic trace made by adding four concurrent sports games with 1 million simultaneous viewers each to Average Day. It is comprised of 48M+ requests for 4,148 videos from 2,587 cities (4M clients) and an average request bitrate of 2725 Kbps. This trace has a very heavy head: 99.89% of requests are for one of the sports games. This represents a heavy (but easily coordinated) load. Although the requests are synthesized, the request bitrate and arrival times maintain the same distribution as the raw trace.
- Heavy-Tail: A synthetic trace generated from Average Day imposing a heavy tail distribution with narrower bitrate variety. It is comprised of 240,000 requests for 10,000 videos from 2,587 cities (82,000 clients) and an average request bitrate of 6850 Kbps. This trace has a heavy tail: the lowest 99% of videos (the tail) account for 60% of requests. Bitrates are drawn from the recommended 240p, 480p, 1080p (400, 1000, 4500 Kbps) guidelines from YouTube live [44], with an additional bitrate of 30 Mbps representing future 4K streams. This represents a heavy load that is hard to coordinate, akin to Twitch or Ustream. Although this trace is synthesized, the mapping of clients to cities and the request arrival times maintain the same distributions as the raw trace.

Topology: The traces contain no information about the internal CDN topology, so we generate a three-tiered topology similar to current CDNs [35] consisting of 4 source clusters, 10 reflectors, and 100 edge clusters. Akamai has roughly 1,800 clusters (1,000 networks) located worldwide [17], so this is roughly the right scale for *US-wide* distribution. We push the scale of the topology up to 2,000 clusters in some experiments. We use a "hose model" to determine link capacities in our overlay network. Each source is given 1 Gbps to split between 100 Mbps overlay links to each of the 10 reflectors. Each reflector has 3 Gbps to split into 100 Mbps overlay links to 30 of the 100 edge clusters. Each edge cluster is given 9 Gbps to connect to clients. We chose these capacities based on the high cost of long-haul WAN links (see §2.1).

Our prototype considers requests at the granularity of *client groups*, which we define to be *(city, AS)* pairs; we assume caching and/or multicast with a client group can efficiently distribute videos to individual users. Edge clusters are randomly placed in the 100 largest cities (determined by number of requests from that city) and each client group is connected to the 3 nearest edge clusters with 150 Mbps overlay links. (Cities in our traces are anonymized, so each city ID is randomly assigned a coordinate on a 2D grid to estimate latency.)

In addition, we assign each link a *cost*, loosely modeling a CDN's cost for transferring data on that link. Source-reflector and reflector-edge link costs vary from 10 to 50 units over a normal distribution. Links from edge clusters to client groups are handled differently: half have a cost of 0, since CDNs often strike deals with edge ISPs [2]; the remaining half vary from 1 to 5.

Methodology: We break each trace into one minute windows and compute distribution trees for each window using VDN and three additional strategies:

- Everything Everywhere (EE)—This strawman naively tries to stream all videos to all edge clusters so clients can simply connect to the nearest cluster.
- Overlay Multicast (OM)—This strawman represents an "optimal" overlay multicast-like scheme. Each video channel individually computes the distribution tree with the highest quality (found using our integer program). This is effectively VDN without coordination across channels.
- CDN—We model a DNS-based CDN that extensively monitors links and servers [2, 29, 35, 40]. As there is not public information on the specific algorithm used to produce these DNS mappings, we use the following model (based on measurement studies [32, 40] and

	EE	OM	CDN	VDN
Avg. Bitrate	624	**2,725**	**2,725**	**2,725**
Cost / Sat. Req.	174	1.1	1.54	**1**
Clients at BR	12%	**100%**	**100%**	**100%**

Table 1: **Average Day** trace.

	EE	OM	CDN	VDN
Avg. Bitrate	0.08	**2,725**	**2,725**	**2,725**
Cost / Sat. Req.	167K	1.1	2.0	**1**
Clients at BR	0%	**100%**	**100%**	**100%**

Table 2: **Large Event** trace.

	EE	OM	CDN	VDN
Avg. Bitrate	812	1,641	2068	**3,454**
Cost / Sat. Req.	7.7	4.1	**1.2**	**1**
Clients at BR	25%	34%	54%	**78%**

Table 3: **Heavy-Tail** trace.

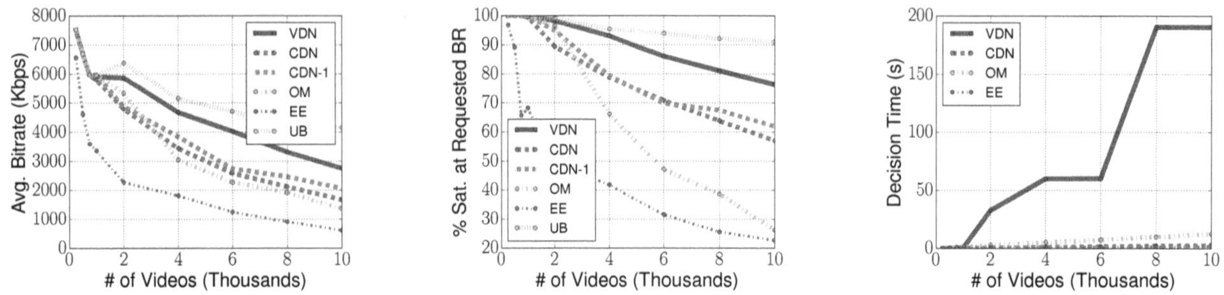

(a) Avg. client bitrate. (b) % at requested bitrate. (c) Processing time.

Figure 12: Scaling load: increasing the number of videos.

a high-level description [2, 35]): upon receiving a request for a new video, a cluster picks the parent with the highest path capacity that is already subscribed to that video. If no parents are subscribed, it picks the parent with the highest path capacity. ASes are mapped to edge clusters that are geographically close (based on their city ID) and lightly loaded. Unlike OM, CDN does *not* focus on optimal end-to-end paths, just individual overlay links. This model is more fine-grained than an actual CDN as it considers each video independently [40]. CDN assumes that server selection is stored in a DNS cache with a TTL of 30 seconds [40]. We also test a variant, CDN-1, with a 1 second TTL. Note that CDN-1 would cause a large number of DNS requests, especially if combined with VDN's per-video control.

Metrics: We use three performance metrics:

- **Average Client Bitrate**—The average bitrate delivered to each client in the trace.
- *Cost / Satisfied Request (***Cost / Sat. Req.***)*—The cost of data transfer per client who receives the bitrate they request, i.e., the sum over all links of (*link cost* × *usage*) / *number of satisfied requests.*
- *% of Clients Satisfied at Requested Bitrate (***Clients at BR***)*—What percentage of the client requests were served at the bitrate they requested? (Clients not served will re-request at lower bitrates.)

7.1.1 Trace results

Tables 1, 2, and 3 summarize the results across our workloads. Each number is the average across one minute time windows in the trace. In Average Day and Large Event, VDN, CDN, and OM serve all videos at their requested quality (thus achieving the best possible average bitrate for the trace). Additionally, VDN reduces the delivery cost by 1.5-2× compared to CDN. As CDN and VDN both satisfy all clients, this decrease in cost must come from VDN finding *lower cost distribution trees* than CDN. The Large Event workload is easy to satisfy as almost all edge clusters should receive the four sports games. OM is as effective as VDN in both workloads.

Heavy-Tail is the toughest workload to coordinate. VDN provides a 1.7× improvement in quality, while serving 24% more clients at their requested bitrate. This is because other schemes react to requests individually; DNS-based schemes like CDN get "locked in" to decisions until DNS records time-out, making it hard to coordinate streams, whereas VDN performs optimization across all requests simultaneously. With OM, the lack of coordination causes a 44% degradation in satisfied requests and a 4× increase in cost.

7.1.2 Exploring the parameter space

Next we use our traces to evaluate the control plane scalability and the topology sensitivity of VDN. Throughout, we compute naive upper bounds (UB) on "average bitrate" and "% satisfied at requested bitrate" by comparing the demand placed on each level in the topology to the aggregate capacity at that level.

Control plane scalability: As we increase the number of videos and the size of the topology, we are interested in (1) the quality of the assignments VDN makes and (2) the time it takes to compute those assignments. *Number of videos:* In Figure 12, we augment Heavy-Tail with increasing numbers of videos and requests, keeping the video/request ratio, topology, and capacity constant. As we stress the system, it becomes more difficult to place videos. Thus, coordination becomes more important with less spare capacity in the network. Since VDN considers all streams simultaneously, unlike CDN and OM, as load increases the gap between them grows in terms of both quality (up to 1.6×; Figure 12a) and the number of clients satisfied at the requested bitrate (Figure 12b). CDN-1 does marginally better

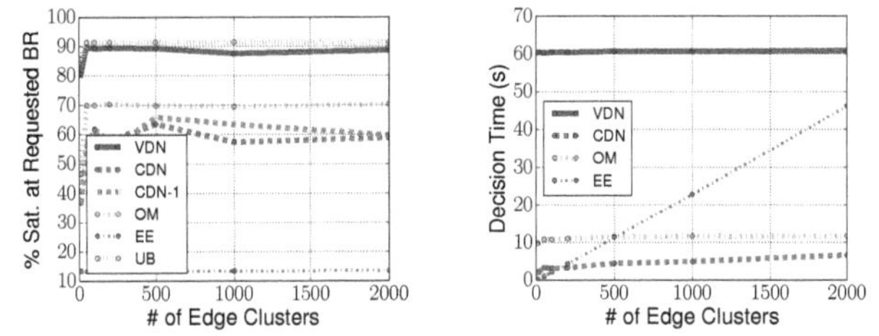

(a) % at requested bitrate. (b) Processing time.

Figure 13: Scaling network size: increasing the number of edge clusters.

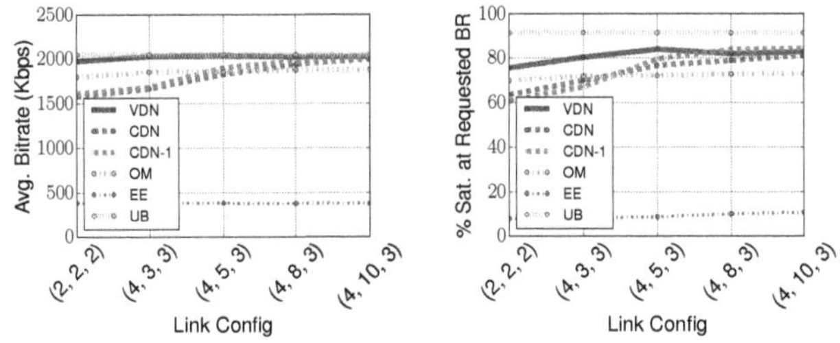

(a) Avg. client bitrate. (b) % at requested bitrate.

Figure 14: Topology sensitivity: (x, y, z) indicates reflectors are connected to x sources, edge clusters to y reflectors, and client groups to z edge clusters.

than CDN, but a system with asynchronous control plane updates (e.g., VDN) does substantially better, as expected. Interestingly, OM satisfies fewer clients than CDN, most likely due to OM grabbing key resources early, starving later clients.

As expected, VDN's improved assignments come at the cost of longer decision times (Figure 12c). However, in this experiment, we intentionally pushed the system outside the bounds of reality; in realistic scenarios for this topology and workload (up to 6,000 videos), decision time remains under 60 seconds (in line with §5). In the real world, if a CDN expects to serve upwards of 6,000 videos in a heavy-tail workload, we imagine the network capacity would be upgraded as well.

Network size: We expand Average Day to 10K videos (to increase demand) and vary the number of edge clusters (Figure 13). We see that VDN maintains the ability to satisfy roughly 90% of clients at their requested bitrate (effectively the naive upper bound) in under 60 seconds for this workload (as opposed to Heavy-Tail, which required 190 seconds; Figure 12c).

Topology sensitivity: Next, we explore the impact of the network topology on VDN, CDN, CDN-1, OM, and EE. We vary two aspects of the topology: (1) the degree of connectivity between tiers of the CDN and (2) the aggregate network capacity between tiers.

Network connectivity: Figure 14 shows the impact of network connectivity. As we increase the number of links between tiers, we decrease their individual capacities

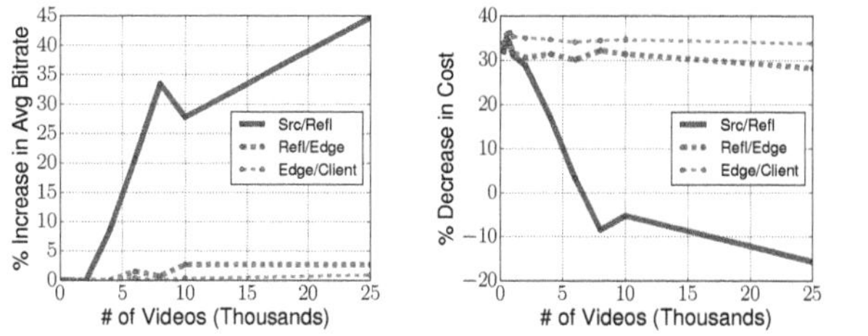

(a) Avg. client bitrate. (b) Cost.

Figure 15: Bottleneck location: improvement over CDN with the bottleneck between source/reflector links, reflector/edge cluster links, and edge cluster/client links.

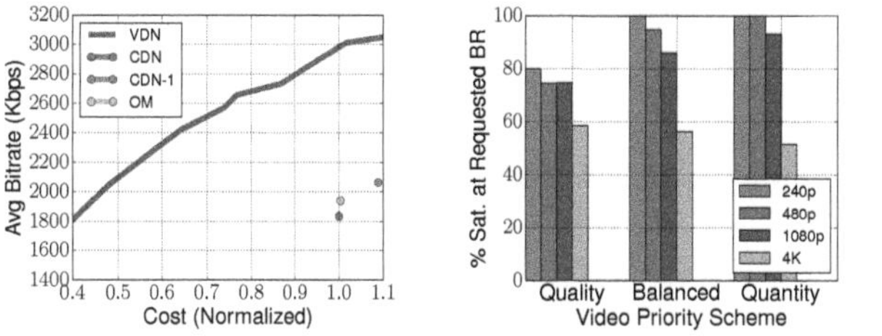

(a) **Quality vs. cost:** the weight of the cost term is varied from 1 to 0. (b) **Quantity vs. quality:** impact of video prioritization strategies.

Figure 16: VDN gives operators fine-grained control.

so the aggregate capacity between those tiers remains constant. In general, a *less* connected topology is going to be *easier* to manage as fewer links potentially means fewer failures. CDN performs better in highly connected topologies, likely because it has more opportunity to find upstream neighbors that already have the video they're looking for. VDN, on the other hand, is not significantly affected; it is able to effectively use a small number of large links. OM does not benefit from more connectivity as it focuses on path quality rather than link quality.

Bottleneck placement: We evaluate the impact of the location of capacity bottleneck. We begin with the topology described in §7.1; the aggregate capacity from sources to reflectors is 4 Gbps, from reflectors to edge clusters is 30 Gbps, and from edge clusters to client groups is 900 Gbps (denoted $(4, 30, 900)$ and named Source Constrained). We now construct two additional topologies: Reflector Constrained $(400, 30, 900)$ and Edge Constrained $(4000, 3000, 900)$.

Figure 15 shows VDN's percentage improvement over CDN as a function of number of videos (generated from Average Day). We see the largest gains in Source Constrained; we expect this scenario to be the most realistic since their long-haul links are more expensive than links at the edges (as pointed to by Akamai [2, 7]). In all three cases, VDN improves average bitrate (Figure 15a). It also reduces cost up through 6,000 videos (Figure 15b), at which point (in Source Constrained) it slightly increases cost in favor of 28%-45% quality improvements—next, we discuss how to explicitly control this tradeoff.

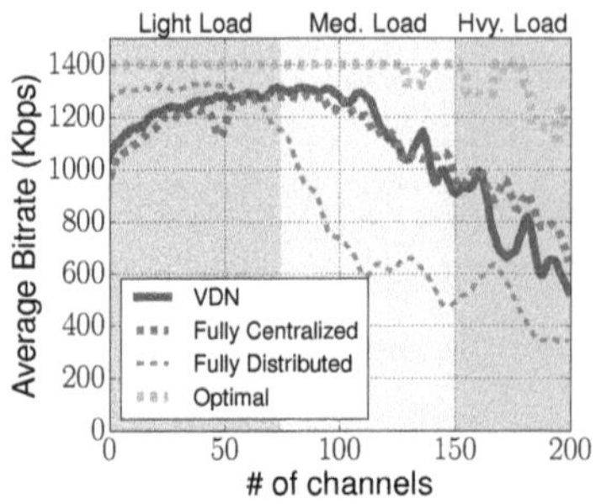

(a) **Avg. client bitrate.**

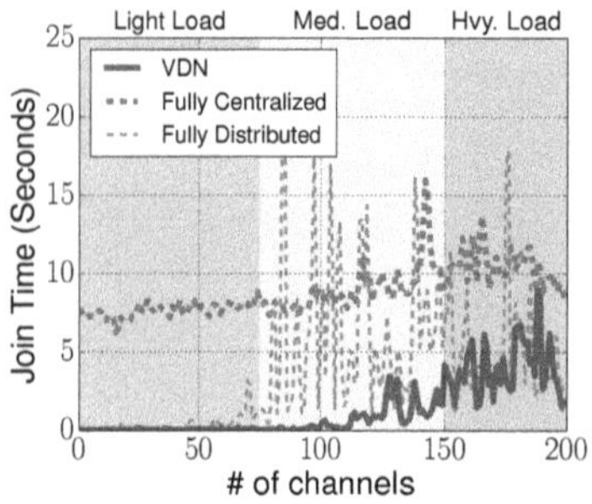

(b) **Join time.**

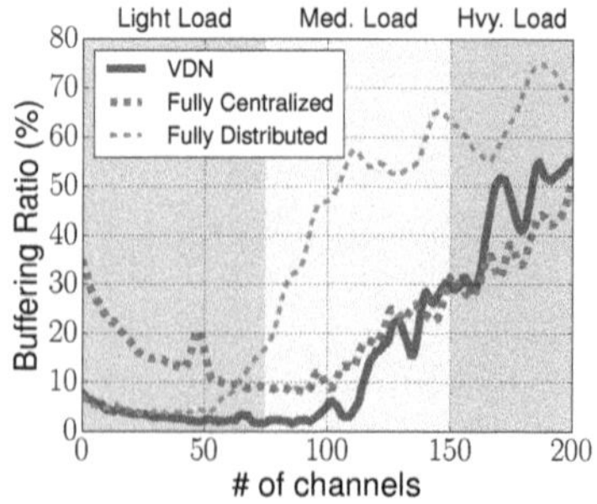

(c) **Buffering ratio.**

Figure 17: Client-side quality in testbed: increasing the number of videos.

7.1.3 Customizing VDN

Quality vs. cost: By adjusting the weight of the global cost term in the objective function, operators can tune the quality/cost tradeoff. Figure 16a shows an ROC-like curve depicting the average bitrate and data transfer cost in Heavy-Tail as the weight of the cost term varies from 1 to 0. For comparison, we plot CDN, CDN-1, and OM's performance on the same trace. VDN achieves about a 1.7× increase in performance over CDN for the same cost (1.5× over OM and CDN-1), or can reduce cost by 60% at similar quality.

Quality vs. quantity: VDN allows operators to assign each $(video, bitrate)$ pair a priority. We test three priority assignment strategies: Quality $(priority = bitrate)$, Balance $(priority = 1)$, and Quantity $(priority = 1/bitrate)$. Quality favors serving high bitrate streams; Quantity favors serving as many streams as possible. Figure 16b shows the percentage of satisfied requests for each strategy broken down per bitrate for Heavy-Tail. Quality favors the 4K streams and Quantity favors sending more streams overall, as expected. This allows operators to not only control how things are delivered, but what is delivered (e.g., ensuring premium customers *always* receive HD streams even when many free customers request SD streams).

7.2 End-to-end experiments

We answer two questions:

1. *Is VDN highly responsive?* VDN reacts to events at a timescale of 200 milliseconds while staying within 17% of the optimal decision.
2. *Does VDN cope well with the issues of a wide-area environment?* Hybrid control allows VDN to function well despite losing controller updates and performs similarly to other schemes during high link fluctuations (traffic dynamics).

Setup and topology: We use 10 co-located nodes on EC2 [8], each representing a cluster, configured in a three-tiered CDN topology (described in §2). Two nodes are sources, another two are reflectors, and the remaining six are edge clusters. Each tier is fully connected to the next one, with measured link capacities of 75 Mbps. The controller is located outside of EC2 in the eastern US, communicating with EC2 via the public Internet.

Methodology and traffic: To demonstrate the benefits of hybrid control, we compare VDN to two other designs. Fully Distributed relies entirely on the distributed control algorithm in §4 and Fully Centralized uses only the centralized controller in §5. For each experiment we generate 200 videos, each requested by one client to a random edge cluster. Each channel has multiple bitrates: 200 Kbps, 600 Kbps, and 1.4 Mbps. We add a new channel to the system once a second. With 10 nodes and 75Mbps links, 100 videos can easily place great load on the system. 100 videos * 1.4Mbps is ~150 Mbps, filling two of the four source/reflector links. 200 videos would fill all four links, overloading the system. The video client is a simple HTTP chunk requester that always fetches a new chunk 2 seconds (the chunk duration) after the previous chunk was received.

7.2.1 Quality of experience

Figure 17a shows the average client bitrate as requests are added. Similar to the trace-driven evaluation, in a system with medium load, VDN gives up to a 2x performance gain over Fully Distributed. As the system becomes more loaded, Fully Distributed sharply drops while VDN and Fully Centralized decay gradually. Even when the system is under medium loaded, VDN stays close to the controller's original decision (Optimal). Once the system reaches heavy load (~150 videos), other problems emerge (e.g., connection establishment overhead, request incast) causing performance to decay.

In Figure 17b, we see that VDN is highly responsive. Although Fully Centralized provides good average bitrate during load, its join time (time from request to first byte of video) suffers (~7 seconds, compared to VDN's ~200 milliseconds). Fully Distributed also provides sub-second join times, but as the system gets loaded, it sees massive spikes in latency as the lack of coordination overloads interior clusters.

Figure 17c shows buffering ratio. Despite having good quality overall, Fully Centralized has a much worse buffering ratio due to its lack of responsiveness.

7.2.2 Coping with network events

Figure 18a shows the effects of link fluctuations. We select 25% of links at random, degrade their capacity by increasing amounts (using `tc`), and measure the perfor-

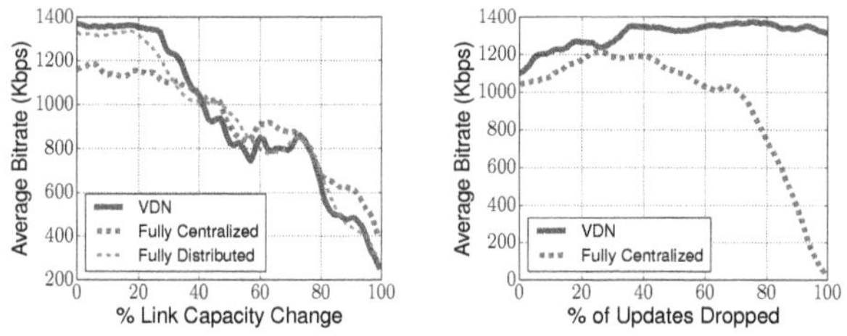

(a) Link fluctuation. **(b) Updates dropped.**

Figure 18: VDN handles network issues without much degradation.

mance 10 seconds after adding 10 channels. We see that all three systems perform similarly.

Figure 18b shows the effects of loss. We drop updates from the controller and measure the performance 10 seconds after adding 10 channels. As expected, Fully Centralized performs much worse as updates are dropped. VDN performs well even when it starts to lose all update messages by falling back to distributed control.

8 Discussion

Complexity versus improvement: Despite the inherent complexity of hybrid control, VDN manages to provide a significant monetary benefit (2×) to CDN operators as well as increased flexibility (see Figure 16a and 16b). Additionally, VDN provides a centralized point of management to adjust link costs and video priorities. Furthermore, as seen in §7, simple tweaks on current CDNs, like shorter TTLs, don't provide these benefits.

Alternate topologies: We assume an n-tiered topology as we feel this is representative of modern CDNs [2, 29, 35, 40]. Additional work would be needed to fit our scheme to arbitrary topologies.

Client-side bitrate adaptation: Although not explicitly included in our system, we assume clients independently do bitrate adaptation through some black-box assessment of delivery quality. Distributed control allows VDN to quickly respond to bitrate switching, but we assume that the rate of switching is fairly low [9].

9 Related work

Content delivery networks: Large- (e.g., [29, 35]) and medium-scale (e.g., [18, 42]) CDN systems have explored various design choices, including peer-to-peer, hybrid [22, 43], centralized, or hierarchical architectures [24] as well as their tradeoffs [45]. None of these papers provides the key combination of global coordination, video-specific optimization, cost-minimization, attention to live-video specific issues, and practical end-to-end system design.

Overlay multicast: Prior work on providing the sustained high-throughput connections needed for live video [12, 14, 26, 30] focuses on how to best organize individual streams. However, they do not perform extensive coordination across video streams. P2P-based approaches [30] can potentially benefit VDN, but may cause additional issues with hybrid control (e.g., loops) as they complicate the topology.

Traffic engineering: Recent work [13, 15, 23, 25] shows the benefits of centralized traffic engineering in ensuring high utilization and fairness in both intra- and inter-datacenter settings. Unlike VDN, they work on flow aggregates at coarse timescales, making it hard for them to provide the fine-grained dynamic control required for live video.

Video optimization: There is much prior work on understanding and improving video delivery, including client-side bitrate adaptation [27], metrics [9, 10], cross-CDN optimization (e.g., [32]), and CDN-selection strategies (e.g., [19]). Our work focuses on end-to-end delivery and provides a practical system design.

10 Conclusion

VDN is a platform for live video delivery that helps balance the concerns of both users and CDN operators by providing real-time control over individual streams from the CDN side. VDN employs centralized quality optimization and hybrid control for responsiveness. We show that centralized optimization can greatly improve video quality while minimizing cost. Our hybrid control plane mitigates WAN challenges, providing quick join times and responsiveness to failures. Using a live video trace, we show that VDN provides a 1.7× improvement in average bitrate and a 2× reduction in delivery cost in different scenarios. Using Amazon EC2, we show that our design is responsive at a timescale of 200 ms.

Acknowledgments

The authors would like to thank Nicolas Feltman for help with the ILP, Eric Anderson and Raja Sambasivan for help with distributed control, JungAh Hong for help with the initial evaluation, Dave Oran for shepherding this paper, and the anonymous reviewers for their feedback. This work is supported in part by the NSF under award #CNS-1345305, NDSEG Fellowship 32 CFR 168a, the National Research Foundation of Korea (NRF-2013R1A1A1076024), and the IITP under grant No. B0126-15-1078 funded by the Korean Government (MSIP).

11 References

[1] Ooyala global video index q3 2013. http://go.ooyala.com/rs/OOYALA/images/Ooyala-Global-Video-Index-Q3-2013.pdf.

[2] Private conversation with Bruce Maggs, vice president, research at Akamai.

[3] Private conversation with Hui Zhang, chief executive officer, at Conviva.

[4] Twitch. http://twitch.tv.

[5] Twitch is 4th in peak us internet traffic. http://blog.twitch.tv/2014/02/twitch-community-4th-in-peak-us-internet-traffic/.

[6] I. Sodagar. The MPEG-DASH Standard for Multimedia Streaming Over the Internet. *IEEE Multimedia* (2011).

[7] Akamai. Akamai investor summit: 2013. http://www.akamai.com/dl/investors/2013_ir_summit_presentation.pdf.

[8] Amazon. Amazon Elastic Compute Cloude (Amazon EC2). `http://aws.amazon.com/ec2/`.

[9] Balachandran, A., Sekar, V., Akella, A., Seshan, S., Stoica, I., and Zhang, H. A quest for an internet video quality-of-experience metric. In *Proceedings of the 11th ACM Workshop on Hot Topics in Networks* (New York, NY, USA, 2012), HotNets-XI, ACM, pp. 97–102.

[10] Balachandran, A., Sekar, V., Akella, A., Seshan, S., Stoica, I., and Zhang, H. Developing a predictive model of quality of experience for internet video. In *Proc. ACM SIGCOMM* (2013), ACM, pp. 339–350.

[11] Bashore, A. Twitch stats. http://stats.twitchapps.com/.

[12] Castro, M., Druschel, P., Kermarrec, A.-M., Nandi, A., Rowstron, A., and Singh, A. Splitstream: high-bandwidth multicast in cooperative environments. In *ACM SIGOPS Operating Systems Review* (2003), vol. 37, ACM, pp. 298–313.

[13] Chowdhury, M., Zaharia, M., Ma, J., Jordan, M. I., and Stoica, I. Managing data transfers in computer clusters with orchestra. *SIGCOMM CCR 41*, 4 (2011), 98.

[14] Chu, Y., Rao, S., Seshan, S., and Zhang, H. Enabling conferencing applications on the internet using an overlay muilticast architecture. *ACM SIGCOMM computer communication review 31*, 4 (2001), 55–67.

[15] Fortz, B., Rexford, J., and Thorup, M. Traffic engineering with traditional ip routing protocols. *Communications Magazine, IEEE 40*, 10 (2002), 118–124.

[16] Foundation, A. Apache HTTP Server Project. `http://httpd.apache.org/`.

[17] Frank, B., Poese, I., Lin, Y., Smaragdakis, G., Feldmann, A., Maggs, B., Rake, J., Uhlig, S., and Weber, R. Pushing cdn-isp collaboration to the limit. *ACM SIGCOMM CCR 43*, 3 (2013).

[18] Freedman, M. J. Experiences with coralcdn: A five-year operational view. In *Proc. USENIX NSDI* (2010).

[19] Ganjam, A., Siddiqui, F., Zhan, J., Liu, X., Stoica, I., Jiang, J., Sekar, V., and Zhang, H. C3: Internet-scale control plane for video quality optimization. In *12th USENIX Symposium on Networked Systems Design and Implementation (NSDI 15)* (Oakland, CA, May 2015), USENIX Association, pp. 131–144.

[20] Ghorbani, S., and Caesar, M. Walk the line: consistent network updates with bandwidth guarantees. In *Proc. HotSDN* (2012), ACM, pp. 67–72.

[21] Gurobi. Gurobi optimization. http://www.gurobi.com/.

[22] Han, D., Andersen, D., Kaminsky, M., Papagiannaki, D., and Seshan, S. Hulu in the neighborhood. In *Proc. COMSNETS* (Jan. 2011), pp. 1 -10.

[23] Hong, C.-Y., Kandula, S., Mahajan, R., Zhang, M., Gill, V., Nanduri, M., and Wattenhofer, R. Achieving high utilization with software-driven wan. In *Proc. ACM SIGCOMM* (2013).

[24] Huang, C., Wang, A., Li, J., and Ross, K. W. Measuring and evaluating large-scale cdns. In *Proc. ACM IMC* (2008).

[25] Jain, S., Kumar, A., Mandal, S., Ong, J., Poutievski, L., Singh, A., Venkata, S., Wanderer, J., Zhou, J., Zhu, M., et al. B4: Experience with a globally-deployed software defined wan. In *Proc. ACM SIGCOMM* (2013).

[26] Jannotti, J., Gifford, D. K., Johnson, K. L., Kaashoek, M. F., et al. Overcast: reliable multicasting with on overlay network. In *Proc. 4th conference on Symposium on Operating System Design & Implementation* (2000).

[27] Jiang, J., Sekar, V., and Zhang, H. Improving fairness, efficiency, and stability in http-based adaptive video streaming with festive. In *Proc. ACM CoNEXT* (2012).

[28] Katta, N. P., Rexford, J., and Walker, D. Incremental consistent updates. In *Proc. HotSDN* (2013), ACM.

[29] Kontothanassis, L., Sitaraman, R., Wein, J., Hong, D., Kleinberg, R., Mancuso, B., Shaw, D., and Stodolsky, D. A transport layer for live streaming in a content delivery network. *Proceedings of the IEEE 92*, 9 (2004), 1408–1419.

[30] Kostić, D., Rodriguez, A., Albrecht, J., and Vahdat, A. Bullet: High bandwidth data dissemination using an overlay mesh. In *ACM SIGOPS Operating Systems Review* (2003), vol. 37, ACM, pp. 282–297.

[31] Lamport, L. The part-time parliament. *ACM Trans. Comput. Syst. 16*, 2 (May 1998), 133–169.

[32] Liu, X., Dobrian, F., Milner, H., Jiang, J., Sekar, V., Stoica, I., and Zhang, H. A case for a coordinated internet video control plane. In *Proc. ACM SIGCOMM* (2012), pp. 359–370.

[33] Liu, Y., Zhang, H., Gong, W., and Towsley, D. On the interaction between overlay routing and underlay routing. In *INFOCOM 2005. 24th Annual Joint Conference of the IEEE Computer and Communications Societies. Proceedings IEEE* (2005), vol. 4, IEEE, pp. 2543–2553.

[34] McGeer, R. A safe, efficient update protocol for openflow networks. In *Proc. HotSDN* (2012), ACM, pp. 61–66.

[35] Nygren, E., Sitaraman, R. K., and Sun, J. The akamai network: a platform for high-performance internet applications. *ACM SIGOPS Operating Systems Review 44*, 3 (2010), 2–19.

[36] Prasad, R., Dovrolis, C., Murray, M., and Claffy, K. Bandwidth estimation: metrics, measurement techniques, and tools. *Network, IEEE 17*, 6 (2003), 27–35.

[37] Sandvine. Global internet phenomena report: 1h 2014. https://www.sandvine.com/downloads/general/global-internet-phenomena/2014/1h-2014-global-internet-phenomena-report.pdf.

[38] Spangler, T. World cup sets new internet-video streaming records for espn, univision, and akamai. http://variety.com/2014/digital/news/world-cup-sets-new-internet-video-streaming-record-1201221997/.

[39] Strauss, J., Katabi, D., and Kaashoek, F. A measurement study of available bandwidth estimation tools. In *Proceedings of the 3rd ACM SIGCOMM Conference on Internet Measurement* (New York, NY, USA, 2003), IMC '03, ACM, pp. 39–44.

[40] Su, A.-J., and Kuzmanovic, A. Thinning akamai. In *Proc. ACM IMC* (2008).

[41] Team, T. How twitch fits in amazon's strategy. http://www.forbes.com/sites/greatspeculations/2014/08/28/how-twitch-fits-in-amazons-strategy/.

[42] Wang, L., Park, K., Pang, R., Pai, V. S., and Peterson, L. L. Reliability and security in the codeen content distribution network. In *Proc. USENIX ATC, General Track* (2004).

[43] Xu, D., Kulkarni, S. S., Rosenberg, C., and keung Chai, H. A cdn-p2p hybrid architecture for cost-effective streaming media distribution. *Computer Networks 44* (2004), 353–382.

[44] YouTube. Live encoder settings, bitrates and resolutions. https://support.google.com/youtube/answer/2853702?hl=en.

[45] Yu, M., Jiang, W., Li, H., and Stoica, I. Tradeoffs in cdn designs for throughput oriented traffic. In *Proc. ACM CoNEXT* (2012), ACM, pp. 145–156.

A Control-Theoretic Approach for Dynamic Adaptive Video Streaming over HTTP

Xiaoqi Yin, Abhishek Jindal, Vyas Sekar, Bruno Sinopoli
Carnegie Mellon University
{yinxiaoqi522, abhishekjindal93}@gmail.com, {vsekar,brunos}@andrew.cmu.edu

ABSTRACT

User-perceived quality-of-experience (QoE) is critical in Internet video applications as it impacts revenues for content providers and delivery systems. Given that there is little support in the network for optimizing such measures, bottlenecks could occur anywhere in the delivery system. Consequently, a robust bitrate adaptation algorithm in client-side players is critical to ensure good user experience. Previous studies have shown key limitations of state-of-art commercial solutions and proposed a range of heuristic fixes. Despite the emergence of several proposals, there is still a distinct lack of consensus on: (1) How best to design this client-side bitrate adaptation logic (e.g., use rate estimates vs. buffer occupancy); (2) How well specific classes of approaches will perform under diverse operating regimes (e.g., high throughput variability); or (3) How do they actually balance different QoE objectives (e.g., startup delay vs. rebuffering). To this end, this paper makes three key technical contributions. First, to bring some rigor to this space, we develop a principled control-theoretic model to reason about a broad spectrum of strategies. Second, we propose a novel *model predictive control* algorithm that can optimally combine throughput and buffer occupancy information to outperform traditional approaches. Third, we present a practical implementation in a reference video player to validate our approach using realistic trace-driven emulations.

CCS Concepts

•Information systems → Multimedia streaming; •Networks → Network protocol design; Application layer protocols;

Keywords

Internet Video; Bitrate Adaptation; DASH; Model Predictive Control

SIGCOMM '15, August 17 - 21, 2015, London, United Kingdom
© 2015 ACM. ISBN 978-1-4503-3542-3/15/08...$15.00
DOI: http://dx.doi.org/10.1145/2785956.2787486

1 Introduction

Many recent studies have highlighted the critical role that user-perceived quality-of-experience (QoE) plays in Internet video applications, as it ultimately affects revenue streams for content providers [24, 35]. Specifically, metrics such as the duration of rebuffering (i.e., the player's playout buffer does not have content to render), startup delay (i.e., the lag between the user clicking vs. the time to begin rendering), the average playback bitrate, and the variability of the bitrate delivered have emerged as key factors.

Given the complex Internet video delivery ecosystem and presence of diverse bottlenecks, the *bitrate adaptation logic* in the client-side video player becomes critical to optimize user experience [16]. In the HTTP-based delivery model that predominates today [44], videos are typically chunked and encoded at different bitrate levels. The goal of an adaptive video player is to choose the bitrate level for future chunks to deliver the highest possible QoE; e.g., maximizing bitrate while minimizing the likelihood of rebuffering and avoiding too many bitrate switches.

Many recent efforts have pointed out key challenges in designing this adaptation logic (e.g., [46, 17, 32, 34]) and several proposals have emerged to try and address these challenges (e.g., [34, 17, 33]). Despite the proliferation of numerous algorithms, however, there appears to be a lack of clarity and consensus across these solutions on several fronts; e.g., some argue for better throughput estimation [47], while others suggest improving chunk scheduling [34]. Some researchers even argue against *rate-based* approaches that rely on throughput estimates from previous chunk downloads and make the case for *buffer-occupancy based* algorithms that make their decisions purely based on buffer occupancy [33].

In order to understand the fundamental tradeoffs between different classes of algorithms (e.g., rate- vs buffer-based) under different operating regimes (e.g., low vs. high throughput variability), we begin by formulating the video bitrate adapdation as a *stochastic optimal control* problem. We formally define the key dynamic variables involved in the video adaptation problem and a concrete objective. This framework allows us to outline the broader design space of control algorithms for this problem. We identify a key shortcoming in existing approaches that rely exclusively on pure rate- or buffer-based strategies, and that might be potentially missing out on strategies that *combine* both signals.

Building on insights from the control-theoretic formulation, we argue that *model predictive control (MPC)* [22] is a suitable class of algorithms that can optimally combine both rate-based and buffer-based feedback signals. At a high level, MPC attempts to predict key environment variables over a moving look-ahead horizon and solve an exact optimization problem based on the prediction. MPC is the technology of choice in a multitude of real world control problems [22]. In addition to its intuitive formulation, it can explicitly handle complex control objectives and constraints, and has a set of well understood tuning parameters such as the prediction horizon. Moreover, MPC has other qualitative advantages as its development time is much shorter compared to advanced control methods and it is easier to maintain, as changing model parameters does not require complete redesign.

In our context, the MPC approach entails predicting the expected throughput for the next few chunks and using this to make optimal bitrate decisions for QoE maximization. Indeed, our simulation results confirm that if we could run an optimal MPC algorithm and the prediction error was low, then the MPC scheme can outperform traditional rate-based and buffer-based strategies.

In practice, however, running a MPC-based algorithm is challenging because it needs to solve a non-trivial discrete optimization problem at each time step. Even ignoring the computational overhead, there are practical difficulties as we might need to bundle this solver logic with every video player or require users to download and install additional software. To address these challenges, we develop a simple-yet-efficient *FastMPC* mechanism. Conceptually, FastMPC essentially follows a table enumeration approach, where we describe the problem state-space, solve the specific instances optimally offline, and store the optimal control decisions for future online use. If implemented naively, however, the size of this table can induce significant memory overhead and startup delays for video players (e.g., additional JavaScript to load). Fortunately, we show that with a simple value binning and compression strategy, we can achieve near-optimal performance with manageable table sizes.

We have prototyped our FastMPC bitrate adaptation algorithm in an open source dynamic adaptive streaming player called `dash.js` [1]. Our choice of platform is a pragmatic one—it is the reference open-source implementation for the MPEG-DASH standard based on the HTML5 specification and is actively supported by leading industry participants [7]. We show that our implementation adds negligible overhead to the baseline `dash.js` player. We also showcase the FastMPC-based player in our demo page [14].

We evaluate our algorithms and prototype implementation using realistic emulation experiments on measured [9, 10] and synthetic throughput variability traces. We also augment these results with simulation-based sensitivity analysis experiments to analyze the effect of key operating parameters on the performance of different classes of algorithms. Our key findings are:

1. Our proposed MPC approach consistently outperforms the state-of-art adaptation algorithms by 15% in broadband (FCC) dataset and 10% in cellular (HSDPA) dataset in terms of median QoE. It also achieves significant improvement (60+% median QoE) compared to the industry reference player `dash.js`;
2. Our fast and low-overhead implementation FastMPC requires similar CPU usage and only 60 kB extra memory usage comparing to other algorithms.

Contributions and roadmap: In summary, this paper makes the following key contributions:[1]

- Development of a formal control-theoretic model of the bitrate adaptation problem (Section 3);
- Design of a MPC approach that subsumes existing rate- and buffer-based strategies (Section 4);
- A practical and fast table enumeration based algorithm FastMPC that near-optimally approximates the performance of an exact MPC approach (Section 5);
- A low-overhead implementation based on the open source reference video player `dash.js` (Section 6);
- A systematic evaluation of different classes of algorithms over a wide range of operating parameters and realistic traces (Section 7)

We begin by discussing background on DASH and related work in the next section.

2 Background and Related Work

We begin with a high-level overview of how HTTP-based adaptive video streaming works, before describing the key shortcomings of today's state-of-art solutions.

Internet video technologies such as Microsoft Smooth-Streaming [13], Apple's HLS [5], and Adobe's HDS [2] rely on *HTTP-based* adaptive streaming. This class of protocols is being standardized under the umbrella of Dynamic Adaptive Streaming over HTTP or DASH [16]. In DASH systems, each video consists of multiple segments or "chunks" (corresponding to a few seconds of play time) and each chunk is encoded at multiple *discrete* bitrates. The chunks from different bitrate streams are aligned so that the video player can switch to a different bitrate if necessary at a chunk boundary. This approach has several pragmatic advantages over custom streaming protocols such as Real-Time Messaging Protocol (RTMP). The use of HTTP enables providers to seamlessly bypass middleboxes. Furthermore, it can use existing commodity CDN servers without requiring custom modifications. Finally, by making the server stateless, one can implement better application-layer resilience using multiple servers and CDNs [41, 40].

Figure 1 shows an abstract model of the adaptive video player. The player uses some inputs (e.g., buffer occupancy or estimates of the network throughput) in its decision logic to choose the bitrate level for the next chunk(s) to be downloaded. In making this decision, there are many potentially conflicting QoE considerations a player must account for: (1) minimizing rebuffering events where the playback buffer

[1] An early workshop version of the paper made the case for a MPC-based approach [50]. However, it did not provide a concrete algorithm, a practical implementation, and evaluation using real throughput traces.

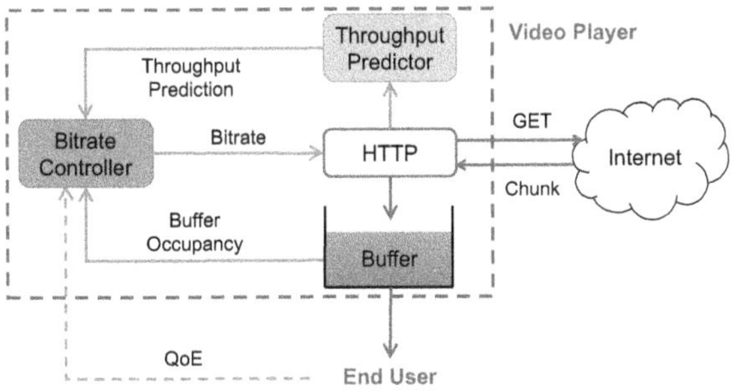

Figure 1: Abstract model of DASH players

is empty and cannot render the video; (2) delivering as high a playback bitrate as possible within the throughput constraints; (3) minimizing startup delay so that the user does not quit while waiting for the video to load; and (4) keeping the playback as smooth as possible by avoiding frequent or large bitrate jumps [24, 35].

To see why these objectives are conflicting, let us consider two extreme solutions. A trivial solution to minimize rebuffering and the startup delay would be to always pick the lowest bitrate, but it conflicts with the goal of delivering high bitrate. Conversely, picking the highest available bitrate may lead to many rebuffering events. Similarly, the goal of maintaining a smooth playback may also conflict if the optimal choice to simultaneously minimize rebuffering and maximizing average bitrate is to switch bitrates for every chunk.

The focus of this paper is on *client-side* adaptation solutions. Other complementary work includes the use of server-side bitrate switching (e.g., [37, 18]), TCP changes to avoid bursts (e.g., [27]), and in-network throughput management and caching (e.g., [31, 45, 42]). We focus on the client-side problem for two key reasons. First, client-side solutions offer the most immediately deployable alternative in contrast to solutions that require in-network support (e.g., [31, 45, 42]), server-side software changes (e.g., [37, 18]), or modifications to lower-layer transport protocols (e.g., [27, 28, 39, 29, 36]). Second, the client is often in the best position to quickly detect performance issues and respond to dynamics. That said, we believe that the formal foundations and algorithms we develop can be equally applied to these other deployment scenarios.

Many measurement studies have shown the poor performance of state-of-art video players with respect to these QoE measures (e.g., [46, 34, 32]). These studies show that most problems are not artifacts of specific players but manifest across all state-of-art players such as SmoothStreaming [13], Netflix [11], Adobe OSMF [3], and Akamai HD [4]. For brevity we do not reproduce these results here but refer interested readers to prior work (e.g., [46, 34, 32]).

To alleviate these problems, there have been several recent proposals in the research literature (e.g., [47, 34, 18, 33, 38]). At a high level, these solutions can be roughly divided into two categories: (1) *rate-based algorithms* and (2) *buffer-based algorithms*. Video players with rate-based methods essentially pick the highest possible bitrate based on the estimated available throughput. However, as shown in prior work throughput estimation on top of HTTP suffers from significant biases [32], which leads to problems with traditional rate-based approaches. Some solutions try to work around these biases by either smoothing out throughput estimates [47] or choosing better scheduling strategies [34]. On the other hand, recent work makes a case for buffer-based algorithms [33]. Rather than using throughput estimates, this class of algorithms uses buffer occupancy as the feedback signal, and designs mechanisms to keep the buffer occupancy at a desired level, essentially discarding any available throughput information.

Despite the broad interest in this topic, what is critically lacking today is a principled understanding of bitrate adaptation algorithms. Each aforementioned solution offers point heuristics that work under specific (and implicit) environmental assumptions. While each approach seen in isolation has been shown to outperform commercial players, there is little effort to systematically compare how different *classes of algorithms* stack up against each other or which of these technical components are *critical*, or how *robust* these algorithms are across different operating regimes (e.g., throughput stability, buffer size, number of bitrate levels). Furthermore, many of these algorithms even fail to formally state what *objective* they seek to optimize making it harder to conduct a meaningful comparison.

Our first-order goal in this work is to bring some clarity to this space. Rather than design yet another point solution, we start by developing a first-principles approach via control theory to develop a general framework to reason about classes of algorithms. In the next section, we use this control-theoretic "lens" to formally define the stochastic optimization that video bitrate adaptation algorithms try to solve.

3 Control-Theoretic Model

In this section, we develop a mathematical model of the HTTP video streaming process and formally define the bitrate adaptation problem. This model gives us a framework to compare and evaluate existing algorithms and serves as the foundation for potential improvements.

3.1 Video Streaming Model

We model a video as a set of consecutive *video segments* or *chunks*, $\mathcal{V} = \{1, 2, \cdots, K\}$, each of which contains L seconds of video. Each chunk is encoded at different bitrates. Let $\mathcal{R}$ be the set of all available bitrate levels. The video player can choose to download chunk k at bitrate $R_k \in \mathcal{R}$. Let $d_k(R_k)$ be the size of chunk k encoded at bitrate R_k. In constant bitrate (CBR) case, $d_k(R_k) = L \times R_k$, while in variable bitrate (VBR) case the $d_k \sim R_k$ relationship can differ across chunks.

The higher bitrate is selected, the higher video quality is perceived by the user. Let $q(\cdot) : \mathcal{R} \rightarrow \mathbb{R}_+$ be a non-decreasing function which maps selected bitrate R_k to video quality perceived by user $q(R_k)$. Note that $q(\cdot)$ may depend on the video-playing device as well as the content of the video. For example, while on HDTV 3Mbps and 1Mbps may lead to significant difference in user experience, the

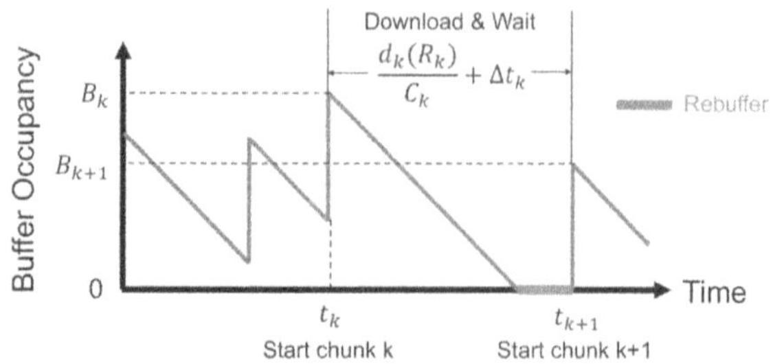

Figure 2: Illustration of buffer dynamics

video quality in 3Mbps and 1Mbps may be similar on a mobile device; Also, improving the bitrate of "dynamic" chunks will result in more QoE gain than improving "static" chunks.

The video segments are downloaded into a *playback buffer*, which contains downloaded but as yet unviewed video. Let $B(t) \in [0, B_{max}]$ be the *buffer occupancy* at time t, i.e., the play time of the video left in the buffer. The *buffer size* B_{max} depends on the policy of the service provider, as well as storage limitations on the player. A typical player buffer may hold few tens of seconds of video segments.

Figure 2 helps illustrate the conceptual operation of the video player. At time t_k, the video player starts to download chunk k. The download time for this chunk will be $d_k(R_k)/C_k$; i.e., it depends on the size of selected chunk with bitrate R_k, as well as average download speed C_k experienced during this download process. Once chunk k is completely downloaded, the video player waits for Δt_k and starts to download the next chunk $k+1$ at time t_{k+1}. We assume that the waiting time Δt_k is small and will not lead to rebuffering events. If we denote by C_t the network throughput at time t, then we have:

$$t_{k+1} = t_k + \frac{d_k(R_k)}{C_k} + \Delta t_k \tag{1}$$

$$C_k = \frac{1}{t_{k+1} - t_k - \Delta t_k} \int_{t_k}^{t_{k+1}-\Delta t_k} C_t \, dt. \tag{2}$$

The buffer occupancy $B(t)$ evolves as the chunks are being downloaded and the video is being played. Specifically, the buffer occupancy increases by L seconds after chunk k is downloaded and decreases as the user watches the video.[2] Let $B_k = B(t_k)$ denote the buffer occupancy when the player starts to download chunk k. The buffer dynamics can then be formulated as:

$$B_{k+1} = \left(\left(B_k - \frac{d_k(R_k)}{C_k} \right)_+ + L - \Delta t_k \right)_+ \tag{3}$$

Here, the notation $(x)_+ = \max\{x, 0\}$ ensures that the term can never be negative. Note that if $B_k < d_k(R_k)/C_k$, the buffer becomes empty while the video player is still downloading chunk k, leading to *rebuffer* events as shown in Figure 2.

[2]The "startup" phase will be slightly different as the player waits for some amount of buffer to build up before draining the buffer.

The determination of waiting time Δt_k, also referred as *chunk scheduling* problem, is an equally interesting and important problem in improving fairness of multi-player video streaming [34]. However, in this paper we assume that the player immediately starts to download chunk $k+1$ as soon as chunk k is downloaded. The one exception is when the buffer is full, the player waits for the buffer to reduce to a level which allows chunk k to be appended. Formally,

$$\Delta t_k = \left(\left(B_k - \frac{d_k(R_k)}{C_k} \right)_+ + L - B_{max} \right)_+ \tag{4}$$

3.2 QoE Maximization Problem

The ultimate goal of bitrate adaptation is to improve the QoE of users in order to achieve higher long-term user engagement [24]. Our goal is to provide a flexible QoE model rather than a fixed notion of QoE as this is an active area of research [19]. While users may differ in their specific QoE functions, we can enumerate the key elements of video QoE as:

1. *Average Video Quality:* The average per-chunk quality over all chunks: $\frac{1}{K}\sum_{k=1}^{K} q(R_k)$;
2. *Average Quality Variations*: This tracks the magnitude of the changes in the quality from one chunk to another: $\frac{1}{K-1}\sum_{k=1}^{K-1} |q(R_{k+1}) - q(R_k)|$;
3. *Rebuffer*: For each chunk k rebuffering occurs if the download time $d_k(R_k)/C_k$ is higher than the playout buffer level when the chunk download started (i.e., B_k). Thus the *total rebuffer time* [3] is $\sum_{k=1}^{K} \left(\frac{d_k(R_k)}{C_k} - B_k \right)_+$.
4. *Startup Delay* T_s, assuming $T_s \ll B_{max}$.

As users may have different preferences on which of the four components is more important, we define the QoE of video segment 1 through K by a weighted sum of the aforementioned components:

$$QoE_1^K = \sum_{k=1}^{K} q(R_k) - \lambda \sum_{k=1}^{K-1} |q(R_{k+1}) - q(R_k)| - \mu \sum_{k=1}^{K} \left(\frac{d_k(R_k)}{C_k} - B_k \right)_+ - \mu_s T_s \tag{5}$$

Here λ, μ, μ_s are non-negative weighting parameters corresponding to video quality variations, rebuffering time and startup delay, respectively. A relatively small λ indicates that the user is not particularly concerned about video quality variability; the large λ is, the more effort is made to achieve smoother changes of video quality. A large μ, relatively to the other parameters, indicates that a user is deeply concerned about rebuffering. In cases where users prefer low startup delay, we employ a large μ_s.

In summary, this definition of QoE is quite general as it allows us to model varying user preferences on different contributing factors.

[3]Alternatively, one can also consider the *number of rebuffering events* formulated as $\sum_{k=1}^{K} \mathbf{1}\left(\frac{d_k(R_k)}{C_k} > B_k \right)$.

$$\max_{R_1,\cdots,R_K,T_s} \quad QoE_1^K \tag{6}$$

$$s.t. \quad t_{k+1} = t_k + \frac{d_k(R_k)}{C_k} + \Delta t_k, \tag{7}$$

$$C_k = \frac{1}{t_{k+1} - t_k - \Delta t_k} \int_{t_k}^{t_{k+1}-\Delta t_k} C_t \, dt, \tag{8}$$

$$B_{k+1} = \left(\left(B_k - \frac{d_k(R_k)}{C_k} \right)_+ + L - \Delta t_k \right)_+, \tag{9}$$

$$B_1 = T_s, \quad B_k \in [0, B_{max}] \tag{10}$$

$$R_k \in \mathcal{R}, \quad \forall k = 1, \cdots, K. \tag{11}$$

Figure 3: Formulation for QoE maximization ($QOE\_MAX_1^K$) subject to buffer and throughput dynamics.

QoE maximization problem: We are now ready to formulate the problem of bitrate adaptation for QoE maximization as in Figure 3, denoted as $QOE\_MAX_1^K$. Given throughput trace $\{C_t, t \in [t_1, t_{K+1}]\}$ as input, the optimization provides the following as output: 1) bitrate decisions $R_1, \cdots, R_K$, and 2) startup time T_s.

Note that the problem $QOE\_MAX_1^K$ is formulated assuming the video playback has not started at the time of this optimization so the start-up delay T_s is a decision variable. However, this QoE maximization can also take place during video playback at time t_{k_0} when the next chunk to download is k_0 and the current buffer occupancy is B_{k_0}. In this case, we can drop the variable T_s and denote the corresponding *steady state* problem as $QOE\_MAX\_STEADY_{k_0}^K$.

3.3 Classes of Algorithms

In this section we characterize problem $QOE\_MAX_1^K$ and describe existing bitrate adaptation algorithms within this framework to understand how they relate to one another.

The problem in Figure 3 is a finite-horizon stochastic optimal control problem. The source of randomness is in the available throughput C_t. At time t_k when the player chooses bitrate R_k, only the past throughput $\{C_t, t \le t_k\}$ is available, while the future values $\{C_t, t > t_k\}$ are not known.

However, a *throughput predictor* can be used to obtain predictions defined as $\{\hat{C}_t, t > t_k\}$. Based on such prediction and on buffer occupancy information (which is instead known precisely), the *bitrate controller* selects bitrate of the next chunk k:

$$R_k = f\left(B_k, \{\hat{C}_t, t > t_k\}, \{R_i, i < k\}\right). \tag{12}$$

The design of effective throughput predictors is an interesting research direction in its own right. In this paper, we focus on bitrate adaptation algorithms only and assume that predictors are given to us and are characterized in terms of their expected prediction errors. Namely, we focus on the design of $f(\cdot)$ and on the effect of the prediction error on the performance of the compared control algorithms. In the following sections, we will systematically evaluate how different algorithms perform with a state-of-art predictor under a variety of variability conditions.

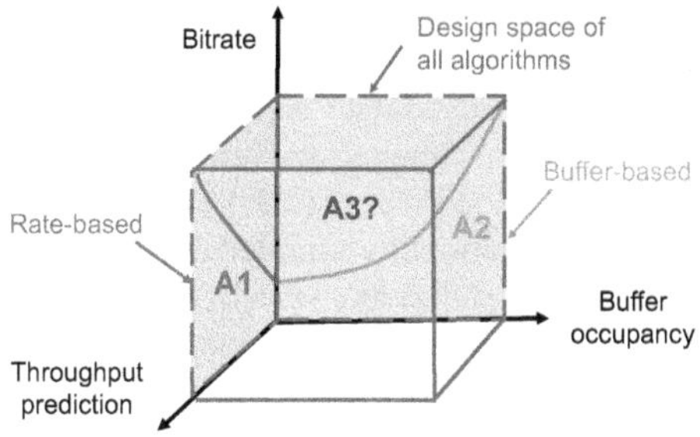

Figure 4: Design space of algorithms for the video adaptation problem: Most current approaches choose the bitrate as a function of only one variable; e.g., A1 is rate-based (RB) while A2 is buffer-based (BB).

Now, different adaptation algorithms essentially adopt different functions $f(\cdot)$. Specifically, two main categories of algorithms appear in the literature: *rate-based (RB)* and *buffer-based (BB)* algorithms. RB strategies essentially choose bitrate only based on throughput prediction, i.e.,

$$R_k = f\left(\{\hat{C}_t, t > t_k\}, \{R_i, i < k\}\right). \tag{13}$$

For example, a typical RB strategy is to choose the maximum possible bitrate below the predicted throughput.

On the other hand, BB strategies advocate decision making based only on buffer occupancy, namely:

$$R_k = f\left(B_k, \{R_i, i < k\}\right), \tag{14}$$

while regarding throughput variations as unmodeled disturbances. For example, Huang et al., illustrate one roadmap for designing BB algorithms [33].

Note, however, that both classes of algorithms are discarding possibly useful information as shown in Figure 4. Consequently, both are in principle suboptimal. Ideally, we want to use both buffer occupancy and throughput prediction, thereby considering a broader design space of bitrate adaptation strategies, as shown in Eq (12) and algorithm A3 depicted in Figure 4.

4 Model Predictive Control Approach for Optimal Bitrate Adaptation

In this section, we make a case for a Model Predictive Control (MPC) approach for bitrate adaptation and describe a concrete MPC-based workflow that can optimally combine throughput prediction and buffer occupancy. We also develop a robust MPC approach that can better handle errors in throughput prediction under highly variable network conditions.

4.1 Why MPC?

First, we provide the intuition behind the choice of MPC in our setting. Note that we cannot claim that MPC is necessary or the optimal choice in the space of all possible control algorithms. Our goal is merely to argue that MPC is a natural fit for the bitrate adaptation problem.

Strawman solutions: As we saw before, bitrate adaptation is essentially a stochastic optimal control problem. In this respect, there are two candidate well-known control algorithms: (1) Proportional-integral-derivative (PID) control [25] and (2) Markov Decision Process (MDP) based control [21]. While PID is computationally simpler compared to MPC, it can only serve to stabilize the system and cannot explicitly optimize our QoE objective. In addition, PID control is designed to work in continuous time and state space and using it in a highly discrete system such as ours may result in performance degradation or instability [25]. Alternatively, with MDP we could consider formulating the throughput and buffer state transition as Markov processes, and find the optimal control policy using standard algorithms such as value iteration or policy iteration [21]. However, this has a strong assumption that throughput dynamics follow Markov processes and it is unclear if this holds in practice. We regard the potential use of MDP and analysis of the throughput dynamics as future work (see Section 8).

Case for MPC: Ideally, given perfect knowledge of future throughput over the entire horizon of a video $[t_1, t_{K+1}]$, the optimal bitrate $R_1, \cdots, R_K$ and startup delay T_s can be calculated in one shot by solving the optimization problem for the entire video $QOE\_MAX_1^K$. In practice, such perfect information is not available, making it difficult to find such optimal solutions using offline optimization.

While perfect information may not be available for the entire future, it is possible that reasonably accurate throughput prediction can be instead obtained for a short horizon to the future $[t_k, t_{k+N}]$. The intuition here is that network conditions are reasonably stable on short timescales and usually do not change drastically during a short horizon (tens of seconds) [51]. Based on this insight, we can run a QoE optimization using the prediction in this horizon, apply the first bitrate R_k, and move the horizon forward to $[t_{k+1}, t_{k+N+1}]$. This scheme is known as model predictive control (MPC) or receding horizon control [22]. MPC algorithms are widely used in different domains, ranging from industrial control to navigation. The general benefits of MPC are in that MPC can utilize predictions to optimize a complex control objective online in a dynamical system under constraints.

4.2 Basic MPC Algorithm

Algorithm 1 shows a high-level overview of the workflow of MPC for bitrate adaptation. In our context, the algorithm essentially chooses bitrate R_k by looking N steps ahead (i.e., the moving horizon), and solves a specific QoE maximization problem (this depends on whether the player is in steady or startup phase) with throughput predictions $\{\hat{C}_t, t \in [t_k, t_{k+N}]\}$, or $\hat{C}_{[t_k, t_{k+N}]}$. The first bitrate R_k is applied by using feedback information and the optimization process is iterated at each step k.

At iteration k, the player maintains a moving horizon from chunk k to $k+N-1$ and carries out the following three key steps, as shown in Algorithm 1.

1. *Predict*: Predict throughput $\hat{C}_{[t_k, t_{k+N}]}$ for the next N chunks using some throughput predictor. Our goal in this paper is not to design a prediction mechanism but to rely on existing approaches. Naturally, improving the accuracy of this prediction will improve the gains achieved via MPC. That said, MPC can be extended to be robust to errors as we discuss below.
2. *Optimize*: This is the core of the MPC algorithm: Given the current buffer occupancy B_k, previous bitrate R_{k-1} and throughput prediction $\hat{C}_{[t_k, t_{k+N}]}$, find optimal bitrate R_k. In *steady state*, $R_k = f_{mpc}\left(R_{k-1}, B_k, \hat{C}_{[t_k, t_{k+N}]}\right)$, implemented by solving $QOE\_MAX\_STEADY_k^{k+N-1}$. In the *start-up phase*, it also optimizes start-up time T_s as $[R_k, T_s] = f_{mpc}^{st}\left(R_{k-1}, B_k, \hat{C}_{[t_k, t_{k+N}]}\right)$, implemented by solving $QOE\_MAX_k^{k+N-1}$. If we ignore practical details about computational overhead, we can simply use off-the-shelf solvers such as `CPLEX` to solve these discrete optimization problems. As we will see in Section 5, we do not need to explicitly solve the optimization problem within the video player in practice.
3. *Apply*: Start to download chunk k with R_k and move the horizon forward. If the player is in *start-up phase*, wait for T_s before starting playback.

Algorithm 1 Video adaptation workflow using MPC

```
Initialize
for k = 1 to K do
    if player is in startup phase then
        Ĉ_[t_k, t_{k+N}] = ThroughputPred(C_[t_1, t_k])
        [R_k, T_s] = f^st_mpc(R_{k-1}, B_k, Ĉ_[t_k, t_{k+N}])
        Start playback after T_s seconds
    else if playback has started then
        Ĉ_[t_k, t_{k+N}] = ThroughputPred(C_[t_1, t_k])
        R_k = f_mpc(R_{k-1}, B_k, Ĉ_[t_k, t_{k+N}])
    end if
    Download chunk k with bitrate R_k, wait till finished
end for
```

This workflow has several qualitative advantages compared with buffer-based (BB), rate-based (RB) as we discuss below. First, this MPC algorithm uses both throughput prediction and buffer information in a principled way. Second, compared to pure RB approaches, MPC smooths out prediction error at each step and is more robust to prediction errors. Specifically, by optimizing several chunks over a moving horizon, large prediction errors for one particular chunk will have lower impact on the performance. Third, MPC directly optimizes a formally defined QoE objective, while in RB and BB the tradeoff between different QoE factors is not clearly defined and therefore can only be addressed in an ad hoc qualitative manner.

4.3 Robust MPC

The basic MPC algorithm assumes the existence of an accurate throughput predictor. However, in certain severe network conditions, e.g., in cellular networks or in prime time when the Internet is congested, such accurate predictors may not be available. For example, if the predictor consistently overestimates the throughput, it may induce high rebuffering. To counteract the prediction error, we develop a *robust MPC* algorithm.

Robust MPC essentially optimizes the worst-case QoE assuming that the actual throughput can take any value in a *range* $[\underline{\hat{C}_t}, \overline{\hat{C}_t}]$ in contrast to a point estimate $\hat{C}_t$. Robust MPC entails solving the following optimization problem at time t_k to get bitrate $R_k = f_{robustmpc}(R_{k-1}, B_k, [\underline{\hat{C}_t}, \overline{\hat{C}_t}])$:

$$\max_{R_k,\cdots,R_{k+N-1}} \min_{C_t \in [\underline{\hat{C}_t}, \overline{\hat{C}_t}]} QoE_k^{k+N-1} \tag{15}$$

$$s.t. \quad \text{Constraints (7) to (11)} \tag{16}$$

In general, it may be non-trivial to solve such a max-min robust optimization problem. In our specific case, however, we can prove that the worst case scenario takes place when the throughput is at its lower bound $C_t = \underline{\hat{C}_t}$. Thus, the implementation of robust MPC is straightforward. Instead of $\hat{C}_t$, we use the lowest possible $\underline{\hat{C}_t}$ as the input to the regular MPC QoE maximization problem. Formally,

THEOREM 1. *The robust MPC controller is equivalent to the regular MPC taking the lower bound of throughput as input, namely,*

$$\begin{aligned} R_k &= f_{robustmpc}(R_{k-1}, B_k, [\underline{\hat{C}_t}, \overline{\hat{C}_t}]) \\ &= f_{mpc}(R_{k-1}, B_k, \underline{\hat{C}_t}) \end{aligned}$$

PROOF SKETCH. Conceptually, QoE function $QoE(R, C)$ can be written as the sum of 3 terms (g_1: total video quality, g_2: total quality change, g_3: rebuffer time), in which only the rebuffer time term depends on throughput C. Thus,

$$\begin{aligned} &\max_R \min_{C \in [\underline{C}, \overline{C}]} QoE(R, C) \\ \equiv &\max_R \left(g_1(R) - \lambda \times g_2(R) - \max_{C \in [\underline{C}, \overline{C}]} \mu \times g_3(R, C) \right) \\ \equiv &\max_R QoE(R, \underline{C}) \end{aligned}$$

As any decrease of throughput C will lead to longer rebuffer time, the minimum QoE is achieved at $C = \underline{C}$. □

The one potential downside is that robust MPC is more conservative than regular MPC by always assuming the lowest throughput. The degree of conservativeness here naturally depends on how loose/tight the lower bound is. In practice, we use maximum prediction error over the past several chunks as bounds in our implementation and find that it works well in practice (discussed in Section 7).

5 Using MPC in Practice — FastMPC

While rate-based and buffer-based algorithms need relatively minor computations, the challenge with MPC is that we need to solve a discrete optimization problem at each time step. There are two practical concerns here:

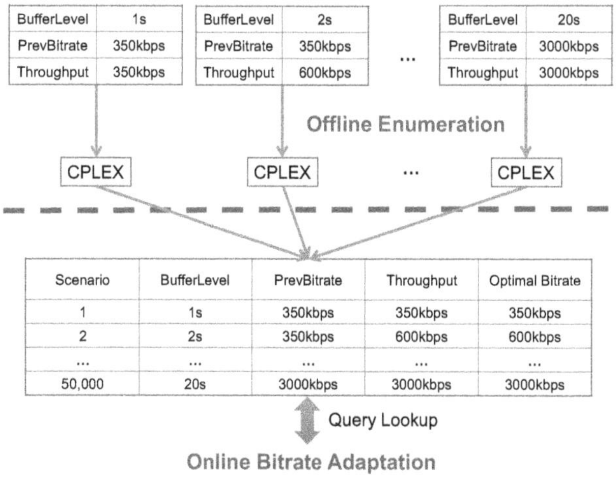

Figure 5: "FastMPC" idea: We enumerate possible scenarios and create a table indexing the optimal decision for each scenario.

- *Computational overhead:* First, the high computational overhead of MPC is especially problematic for low-end mobile devices, which are projected to be the dominant video consumers going forward. Since the bitrate adaptation decision logic is called before the player starts to download each chunk, excessive delay in the bitrate adaptation logic will negatively affect the QoE of the player.
- *Deployment:* Since we do not have a closed-form or combinatorial solution for the QoE maximization problem, we will need to use a solver (e.g., `CPLEX` or `Gurobi`). However, it may not be possible for video players to be bundled with such solver capabilities; e.g., licensing issues may preclude distributing such software or it may require additional plugin or software installations which poses significant barriers to adoption [26].

From the above discussion, it is evident that the solution we develop should be *lightweight* and *combinatorial* (i.e., not solving a LP or ILP online). As such, in this section, we address these two key practical issues by developing a fast and low-overhead FastMPC design that does not require any explicit solver capabilities in the video player [48].

5.1 High-Level Idea of FastMPC

At a high level, FastMPC algorithms essentially follow a table enumeration approach. Here, we do an offline step of enumerating the state-space and solve each specific instance. Then, in the online step we just use these stored optimal control decisions mapped to the current operation conditions. That is, the algorithm will be reduced to a simple table lookup indexed by the key value closest to the current state and the output of the lookup is the optimal solution for the selected configuration.

In our setting (Figure 5), the state-space is determined by the following dimensions: (1) current buffer level, (2) previous bitrates chosen, and (3) the predicted throughput for the next N chunks (i.e., the planning horizon). Thus, FastMPC will entail enumerating potential scenarios capturing different values for each dimension and solving the optimization problems offline.

Unfortunately, directly using this idea will be very inefficient as we have a high dimensional state space. For instance, if we have 100 possible values for the buffer level, 10 possible bitrates, a horizon of size 5, and 1000 possible throughput values, there will be 10^{18} rows in the table![4] There are two obvious consequences of this large state space. First, it may not be practical to explicitly store the full table in the memory. Note that this is not just a hypothetical concern. If we need a practical implementation of this table lookup in the `dash.js` player [1] it will mean very high memory footprint along with large startup delay as the table needs to be downloaded to the player module. Second, it will incur a non-trivial offline computation cost that may need to be rerun as the operating conditions change.

5.2 Optimizing FastMPC Performance

Next, we present two key optimizations to make the table enumeration approach tractable.

Compaction via binning: First, to address the offline exploration cost, our insight is that we may not need very fine-grained values for the buffer and the throughput levels. As a consequence these values may be suitably coarsened into aggregate bins. Moreover, with binning we do not need to explicitly store the row keys as these are directly computed from the bin row indices. The challenge here is to balance the granularity of binning and the loss of optimality in practice. In practice, we find that using 100 bins for buffer level and 100 bins for throughput predictions works well and yields near-optimal performance.

Table compression: Our second insight is that the decision table learned by the offline computation will have significant structure. Specifically, the optimal solutions for several similar scenarios will likely be the same. Thus, we can exploit this structure in conjunction with the binning strategy to explore a simple lossless compression strategy using a run-length encoding to store the decision vector. The optimal decision can then be retrieved online using binary search. In practice, we see that with compression the table occupies less than 60 kB with 100 bins for buffer levels, 100 bins for throughput predictions and 5 bitrate levels.

6 Implementation

In this section, we describe our implementation of the MPC approach in the `dash.js` framework. Our implementation is based on the `dash.js` master branch (v1.2.0 release) as it was the stable version at the time of development. We believe that our implementation can be easily adapted to future versions as we require minimal modifications ($\approx$ 800 lines of JavaScript). For more information on the source code and demo please visit our demo page [14].

Choice of player: Many prior adaptive bitrate players were prototyped using the Adobe OSMF framework [34, 3, 12] and this seemed a natural choice. However, our conversations with industry personnel revealed that almost all content providers are switching to HTML5-based players based on the MPEG-DASH standard [16] and thus OSMF (based on Flash and with decreasing market share) is unlikely to be a platform with real-world impact. Having chosen a DASH player, we qualitatively evaluated several implementations of the DASH standard (e.g., [23, 8, 43]). Unfortunately, these rely either on custom clients or niche video player platforms. Given these considerations, we chose the `dash.js` framework as it is the reference open-source implementation for the MPEG-DASH standard and is actively supported by leading industry participants [7]. We believe our prototype efforts will also inform the evolution of these standardization efforts. For instance, a key requirement for any control algorithms is to know the size (in bytes) of each video chunk, but the standard does not mandate the *manifest* to report chunk sizes, which may be a key shortcoming of the current specification.

`dash.js` **overview:** To understand our implementation and modifications, we begin with some brief background on the architecture of the `dash.js` player. The key components are highlighted in Figure 6.

At a high level, the `dash.js` implementation separates high-level video streaming functionalities from low-level specific DASH standard related components. As we are not particularly interested in standard-specific implementation, we leave the code unmodified and only focus on the adaptive streaming related functions.

The classes and functions that are key to bitrate adaptation and video streaming logic are as follows:

- `BufferController`: This class provides functions to manage buffer levels of the player by requesting new segments and making bitrate change decisions. Specifically, function `validate` is periodically invoked and calls `getPlaybackQuality` function in `AbrController` class to find optimal bitrate. It also maintains a variable `bufferLevel` to record the current buffer occupancy of the player, which can be used for bitrate decisions.
- `AbrController`: This class contains the core bitrate adaptation logic. In the original `dash.js` implementation, a rule-based decision logic is employed to find the bitrate. Specifically, `DownloadRatioRule` selects bitrate based on the "download ratio" (play time of last chunk divided by its download time); On the other hand, `InsufficientBufferRule` chooses bitrate depending on whether the buffer level has reached a lower limit recently to avoid rebuffers. Priorities are assigned to each rule to resolve conflicts and make final bitrate decisions.

Modifications and extensions: We observed two implementation details in `dash.js` that were problematic. First, the code periodically calls the `validate` function to check the status of the buffer and call functions in `AbrController` to decide if the current bitrate should be changed. Note that this implies the bitrate decisions are not always made at chunk boundaries, which may lead to delay of execution of bitrate decisions, or even redownloading previous chunks.

[4]100 buffer levels $\times$ 10 bitrates $\times$ 1000 throughput 1 values $\times \cdots \times$ 1000 throughput 5 values $= 10^{18}$ entries.

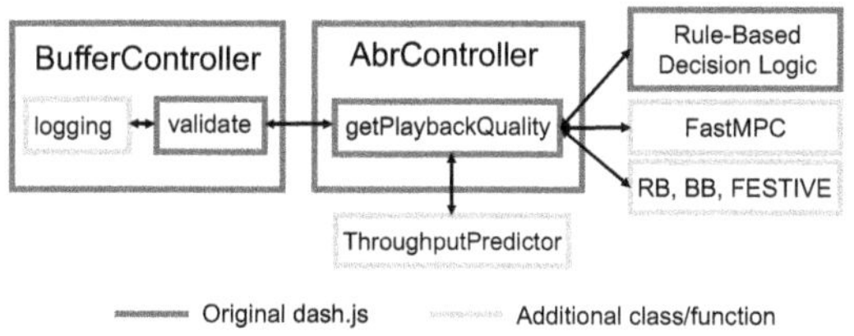

Figure 6: `dash.js` code structure and our modifications

Second, the `dash.js` downloads multiple chunks in parallel even though chunks that are earlier in the video stream should ideally be prioritized.

To address these concerns, we changed the bitrate decision and chunk download process in `dash.js` code by making two key changes to `BufferController` class: 1) bitrate decisions are made at the start of each chunk, 2) chunk download is completely sequential, i.e., no concurrent downloads of multiple chunks are allowed. This allows a basic implementation framework which is consistent with our model and other proposed algorithms.

With these fixes, we implemented different bitrate adaptation algorithms (e.g., FastMPC, BB, RB) by replacing the original rule-based bitrate adaptation logic by our own implementation. The FastMPC implementation has a static table that is used to index control decisions. We also implemented a harmonic mean based throughput prediction scheme based on prior work [34], as well as additional logging functions in the `BufferController` class to record a complete log of the state of the player, including buffer level, bitrates, rebuffer time, predicted/actual throughput.

7 Evaluation

In this section, we compare our approach against existing rate- and buffer-based approaches using a combination of real player and simulation experiments. We also present microbenchmarks on the CPU and memory overhead of our FastMPC implementation.

7.1 Setup

We begin by describing key parameters: (1) throughput variability traces; (2) video-specific parameters; (3) configurations for various adaptation algorithms; and (4) definition of a normalized QoE metric that we use throughout this section.

7.1.1 Input Parameters

Throughput traces: Our goal is to evaluate various bitrate adaptation approaches using realistic network variability conditions. Given the paucity of large-scale sustained throughput measurements over several tens of seconds, however, we use a combination of existing datasets and synthetic models:

1. *Broadband dataset (FCC) [9]:* The FCC dataset consists of more than 1 million sets of throughput measurements, where each set contains six data points each representing average throughput during a 5s interval. We extract throughput traces of the same server and client IP address and concatenate these to match the length of the video. For experiments we randomly pick 1000 of the concatenated traces whose average throughput is between 0 to 3Mbps, to avoid trivial cases where picking the maximum bitrate is always the optimal solution.
2. *Mobile dataset (HSDPA) [10]:* The HSDPA dataset consists of 30min of continuous 1s measurement of video streaming throughput of a moving device in Telenor's 3G/HSDPA mobile wireless network in Norway. We randomly pick 1000 throughput traces from the full dataset.
3. *Synthetic dataset:* Finally we also use a synthetic dataset to supplement the aforementioned datasets. The throughput is based on some hidden state $S_t \in \mathcal{S}$ modeling the number of users sharing a bottleneck link. The actual throughput C_t follows a Gaussian distribution with mean m_s and variance σ_s^2, given the value of hidden state $S_t = s$. We vary both the state transition probability matrix as well as the parameters m_s, σ_s^2 to generate traces.

Figure 7 shows the throughput characteristics of all three datasets. Among three datasets, throughput is the most stable in broadband network and the most variable in mobile network. In other words, the HSPDA dataset is a good stress test for our MPC approach that assumes the throughput is predictable on short timescales.

Video parameters: We use the "Envivio" video from DASH-264 JavaScript reference client test page [6] which is 260s long, consisting of 65 4s chunks. The video is encoded by H.264/MPEG-4 AVC codec in the following bitrate levels: $\mathcal{R} = \{350\text{kbps}, 600\text{kbps}, 1000\text{kbps}, 2000\text{kbps}, 3000\text{kbps}\}$. This is consistent with the requirement for YouTube video bitrate levels for 240p, 360p, 480p, 720p and 1080p respectively [15]. We set the buffer size to $B_{max} = 30s$. We assume $q(\cdot)$ is an identity function. As a default QoE function, we use the weights $\lambda = 1$, $\mu = \mu_s = 3000$, meaning 1-sec rebuffer/start-up time receives the same penalty as reducing the bitrate of a chunk by 3000 kbps. We also run sensitivity experiments that vary the QoE weights.

7.1.2 Algorithms and Metrics

Adaptation algorithms: Determining the optimal algorithm within each class is difficult as it involves optimizing over an infinite-dimensional functional space. To this end, we choose a widely adopted function form for each class of algorithms from prior work, and optimize the free parameters by empirical simulations based on a training dataset containing 100 throughput traces randomly picked across all datasets. We evaluate the following algorithms:

1. *RB:* The bitrate is picked as the maximum available bitrate which is less than $p = 1$ times throughput prediction using harmonic mean of past 5 chunks;
2. *BB:* We employ the function suggested by Huang et al [33], where bitrate R_k is chosen to be the maximum available bitrate which is less than $r_k = f(B_k)$ with reservoir $r = 5s$ and cushion $c = 10s$.
3. *FastMPC:* We use a look-ahead horizon $h = 5$ with throughput predictions using harmonic mean of past 5 chunks; We use 100 bins for throughput prediction and 100 bins for buffer level. We also evaluate the exact MPC with perfect throughput prediction for the next 5 chunks in simulations (denoted as *MPC-OPT*).

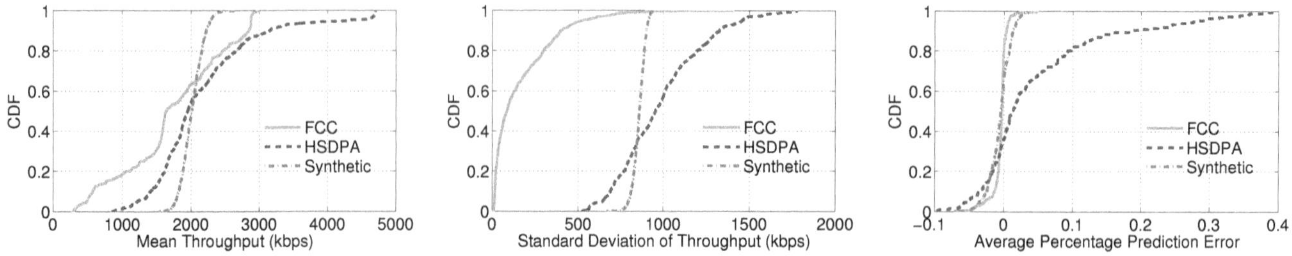

Figure 7: Characteristics of datasets

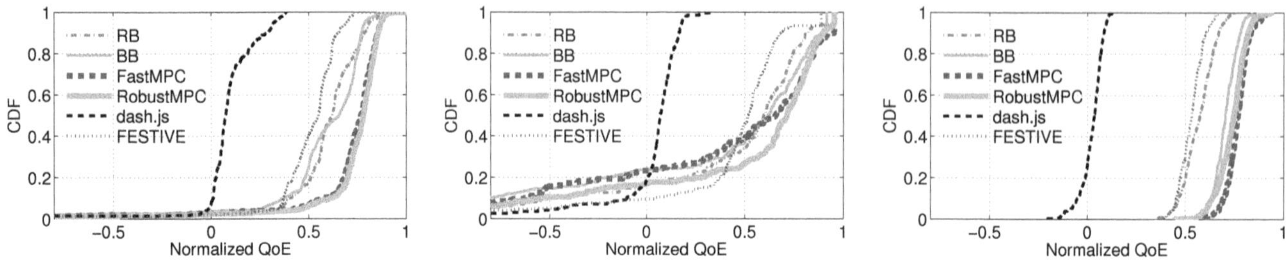

(a) FCC dataset (b) HSDPA dataset (c) Synthetic dataset

Figure 8: Real experiment results with different throughput traces

4. *RobustMPC:* We assume that the throughput lower bound is $\underline{\hat{C}_t} = \hat{C}_t/(1 + err)$, where $\hat{C}_t$ is obtained using harmonic mean of past 5 chunks, while prediction error err is the maximum absolute percentage error of the past 5 chunks.
5. `dash.js`: The original implementation adopts a rule-based bitrate decision logic as shown in Section 6. We keep the original bitrate adaptation logic unmodified, but disable the multi-chunk downloading and allow the bitrate to switch only at chunk boundaries.[5]
6. *FESTIVE [34]:* This rate-based algorithm balances both efficiency and stability, and incorporates fairness across players but that is not a concern in this paper. We assume there is no wait time between consecutive chunk downloads, and implement FESTIVE without the randomized chunk scheduling. Note that this does not negatively impact the player QoE in single player case. Specifically, FESTIVE calculates the efficiency score depending on $p = 1$ times throughput predictions using harmonic mean of past 5 chunks, as well as a stability score as a function of the bitrate switches in the past 5 chunks. The bitrate is chosen to minimize stability score plus $\alpha = 12$ times efficiency score.

Throughput predictor: Note that RB, *-MPC, and FESTIVE need a good throughput predictor. Developing good predictors for different scenarios is outside the scope of the paper. Building on insights from prior work, we use the harmonic mean of the observed throughput of the last 5 chunks because it is robust to outliers in per-chunk estimates [34]. We revisit this issue in Section 8.

[5]This enables a consistent comparison of the algorithms rather than conflate it with other artifacts because of parallel downloads. We also tested the original `dash.js` without any modification, but its performance is worse than our modified version (not shown).

Normalized QoE metric: We define a normalized QoE metric as follows. For a given throughput trace $\{C_t, t \in [t_1, t_{K+1}]\}$, the *offline optimal QoE*, denoted by $QoE(OPT)$, is the maximum QoE that can be achieved with perfect knowledge of future throughputs over the entire horizon. It can be calculated by solving problem $QOE\_MAX_1^K$ [6] and provides a theoretical upper bound of achievable QoE. On the other hand, a real *online* algorithm A selects bitrate R_k based on current throughput predictions $\{\hat{C}_t, t > t_k\}$ without knowing the entire future. We denote the online QoE achieved by algorithm A by $QoE(A)$ and define *normalized QoE of A (n-QoE(A))* for an algorithm A as: $n\text{-}QoE(A) = \frac{QoE(A)}{QoE(OPT)}$.

7.2 Real Player Evaluation

First, we present emulations with the real player setup comparing our FastMPC approach against several prior approaches. Our basic experiment setup consists of two computers (Ubuntu 12.04 LTS) with a 100Mbps direct network connection emulating a video client and server. The video client is a Google-Chrome web browser for linux (version 39) with V8 JavaScript engine while the video server is a simple HTTP server based on `node.js` (version 0.10.32). We use the linux `tc` tool to throttle the throughput of the link between two computers according to the throughput traces employed. We use Emulab [49] to carry out several such experiments in parallel.

Figure 8 show the CDF of normalized QoE over the three sets of throughput traces. First, we see that existing algorithms achieve only 60-70% of optimal QoE confirming that there is still large room to improve video QoE. Second, RobustMPC outperforms non-MPC algorithms in all datasets with an improvement in median normalized QoE of 15%, 10%, and 5% in the FCC, HSDPA, and Synthetic datasets

[6]To make it tractable to compute this offline optimal, we assume it can pick bitrates from a continuous range $[R_{min}, R_{max}]$.

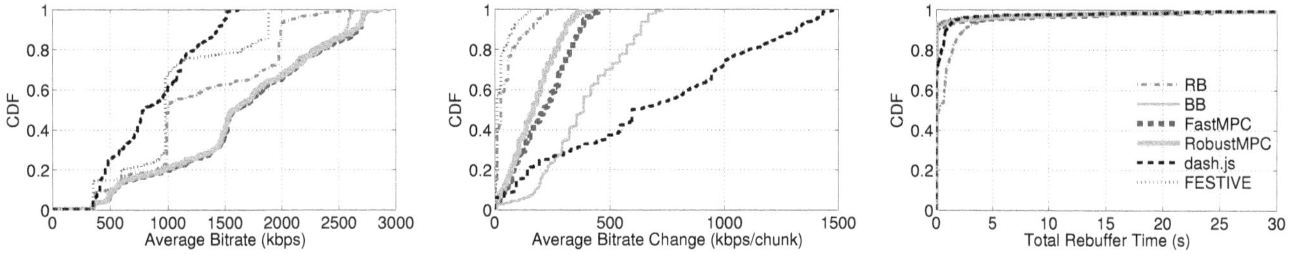

Figure 9: Detailed performance for FCC dataset

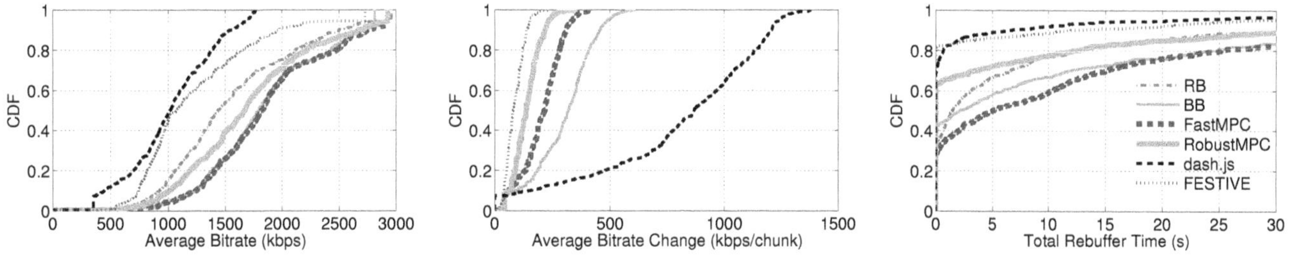

Figure 10: Detailed performance for HSDPA dataset

respectively. Third, we see significant improvement (60+% median normalized QoE) compared with the original `dash.js` player. Finally, we see that the basic FastMPC is more sensitive to prediction errors than RobustMPC. While there is no difference between Fast- and RobustMPC on FCC and Synthetic results, the difference is especially visible in the HSPDA result where regular FastMPC suffers and presents no gains versus RB and BB.

To better understand the impact of prediction error, Figure 7 shows the CDF of per-session average percentage prediction errors for the datasets. In FCC dataset, the average error of our harmonic mean throughput predictor is less than 5%, while in HSPDA dataset, the worst-case prediction error can be as high as 40%. We also observe that the predictor over-estimates the true throughput for more than 20% of the time in HSPDA dataset which leads to significant rebuffering. As such, inaccurate prediction can ruin the decision making of regular FastMPC, while RobustMPC is less affected as it incorporates prediction error to avoid choosing bitrate too aggressively when predictions are inaccurate.

The earlier normalized QoE result shows the aggregate combination of different QoE factors. Next, we zoom in on the individual quality factors to explain the QoE improvements in Figures 9 and 10. In the FCC dataset, all algorithms achieve similarly low rebuffer time as throughput is predictable. The performance difference essentially stems from reducing unnecessary bitrate switches. RobustMPC, FastMPC and BB achieve similar average bitrates, but RobustMPC uses fewer bitrate switches. In the HSPDA result, rebuffer time becomes a more important issue. While FastMPC achieves similar average bitrate and fewer switches comparing to BB, it suffers from large rebuffer time. On the other hand, RobustMPC achieves significant less rebuffer time but at a slightly lower average bitrate: Zero rebuffer in 65% of all cases, versus 40% for BB and FastMPC. As a result, RobustMPC still outperforms other algorithms in overall QoE.

Doing a cross-dataset analysis, we see that the tail distributions of the overall QoE show different characteristics. In the FCC result, only 1% users experience normalized QoE <0 while in HSPDA this occurs in 10% of all cases.[7] Again, the main reason is that the high variability of mobile network induces long rebuffering which affects the overall QoE.

Finally, even though FESTIVE is a rate-based algorithm, it performs slightly worse than regular RB in our datasets because it puts a higher weight on stability and switches up bitrate slowly even when the available throughput is increasing.[8] On the other hand, the `dash.js` heuristic rule-based adaptation achieves low rebuffer time, but incurs many unnecessary switches. Thus, its overall QoE is significantly worse than all algorithms.

7.3 Sensitivity Analysis

For sensitivity analysis we evaluate different algorithms using a custom simulation framework. As before, the simulation takes as input a throughput trace and models the video download/playback process and the buffer dynamics. At time t_k when the bitrate of chunk k is needed, the simulation calls the bitrate controller embedded with different algorithms to get R_k. Using this framework, we study the sensitivity of the approaches to key factors such as: (1) prediction error, (2) choice of QoE function, (3) playout buffer size, (4) number of bitrate levels, and (5) startup delay.

Throughput prediction: Here, we want to study the impact of prediction error of general predictors rather than analyze a particular one (e.g., harmonic mean). To this end, we use the average error level to characterize the performance of a throughput predictor and model the prediction output as being a combination of the true throughput with added random noise according to the average error level. Figure 11a shows

[7]The QoE can be negative when rebuffer time is too long or there are too many switches.

[8]This is not a flaw, but a deliberate choice for achieving multi-player fairness [34].

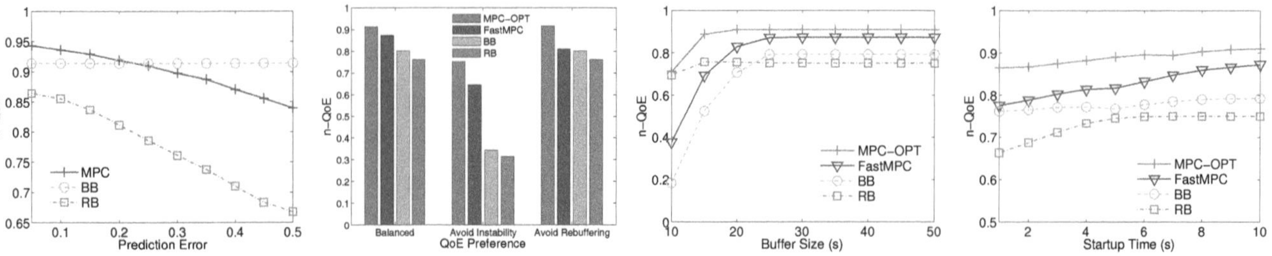

(a) Prediction error (b) QoE preferences (c) Buffer size (d) Startup time

Figure 11: Sensitivity analysis vs. operating conditions

how the throughput prediction errors influence the performance of bitrate adaptation algorithms. As expected, BB is unaffected as it does not use any throughput information. When throughput predictions are accurate, MPC has larger advantage over BB algorithms. As prediction error grows beyond 25%, MPC can be even worse than BB. This suggests that if the actual prediction error is very large, then the video player should drop RB or MPC and use pure BB algorithms. In contrast with regular MPC, robust MPC is less affected by prediction error as it takes into possible error into account and maximizes the worst case QoE.

Users' QoE preferences: We compared the performance of the algorithms under 3 sets of QoE weights, "Balanced" ($\lambda = 1, \mu = \mu_s = 3000$), "Avoid Instability" ($\lambda = 3, \mu = \mu_s = 3000$), "Avoid Rebuffering" ($\lambda = 1, \mu = \mu_s = 6000$). As shown in Figure 11b, as users put more penalty weights to bitrate instability, the MPC algorithms show more advantage over RB and BB. This is because MPC algorithms explicitly model the bitrate vs. bitrate instability tradeoff in the QoE function, while RB and BB do so in ad-hoc ways. However, when rebuffering time is a more important factor, BB algorithms perform similarly with FastMPC algorithms because of two key reasons. First, BB algorithms keep a minimum buffer level so that the player has a better chance surviving low throughput with less/no rebuffering time. Second, while MPC algorithms do a good job with perfect throughput prediction, they can suffer from long rebuffering time since harmonic mean predictor is imperfect. As such, MPC can be improved by maintaining a minimum buffer level and employing a more accurate predictor.

Buffer size and startup delay: Figure 11c analyzes the impact of playout buffer size. First, when buffer size is small (<25s in play time), increasing buffer size improves the performance of all algorithms. A larger buffer protects the player against rebuffering events and also provides more degrees of freedom to optimize performance. As buffer size reaches a certain level (25s of play time), the performances of all algorithms stay constant even buffer size is further increased. Finally, RB is the least affected by buffer size because it does not consider buffer level in its decision logic.

While our approach optimizes startup delay automatically, we analyze how overall QoE (except the startup delay term) is affected if the startup delay is fixed. As shown in Figure 11d, as startup time increases, the performance of all algorithms improves, as the player accumulates more video in the buffer at the start-up phase making it easier to manage rebuffering events.

Bitrate levels: We also study how number of bitrate levels influences the performance (not shown). With BB and MPC, we can achieve better performance using finer-grained set of bitrate levels. With RB, however, the performance of RB first improves as we add more bitrate levels, but decreases when there are too many bitrate levels. The reason is that RB starts changing bitrate more frequently, leading to increased bitrate instability. One caveat with MPC is that finer-grained bitrate levels also require more discretization levels for the FastMPC implementation. Understanding this tradeoff is an interesting direction for future work.

7.4 MPC Configuration and Overhead

Overhead: As discussed earlier, FastMPC might increase player overhead relative to BB and RB style algorithms. We compare the CPU and memory usage of our implementation of FastMPC, BB, and RB algorithm with the default `dash.js` player. We find that FastMPC, BB, and RB all consume similar amount of CPU, while FastMPC uses only 60 kB more memory (not shown).

FastMPC discretization: Recall that the number of discretization levels is an important design parameter for FastMPC. More discretization levels increase FastMPC performance but require more player memory and may also increase startup delay. We study this performance vs. overhead tradeoff in Figure 12a and Table 1. From Figure 12a, we see that more discretization levels imply larger performance gains for FastMPC but the improvement shows diminishing return; e.g., FastMPC achieves 90% of optimal QoE with 100 levels while this drops to 70% if there are only 5 levels. Second, the gain vs. discretization level also has some dependency on the throughput predictor especially with very coarse discretization. Table 1 shows that while the memory overhead

Discretization levels	Extra JavaScript code size	
	Full table	Run length coding
50	25.0 kB	19.1 kB
100	100 kB	56.4 kB
200	400 kB	141 kB
500	2.50 MB	451 kB

Table 1: FastMPC table size

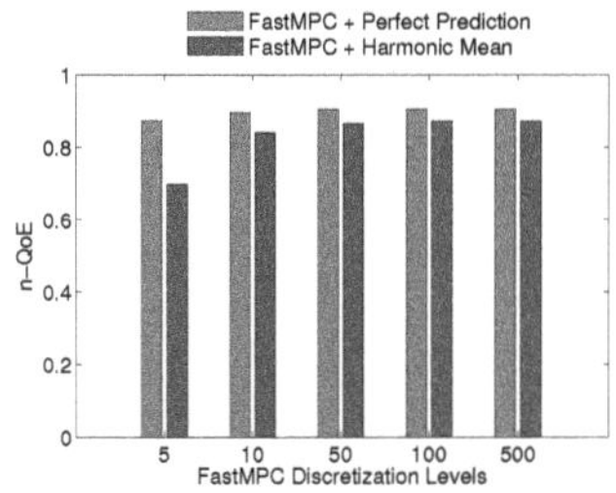

(a) Discretization

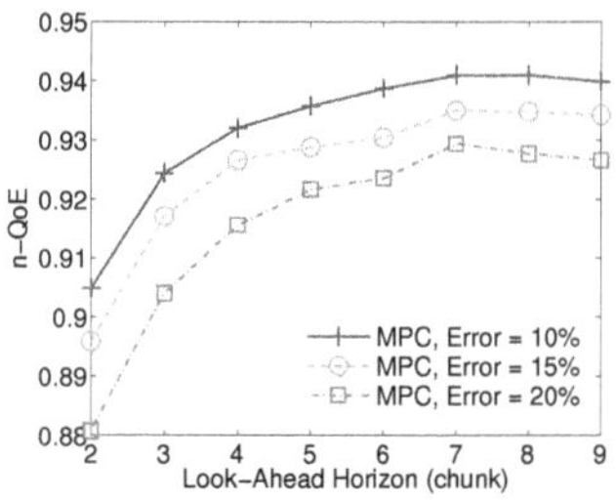

(b) Look-ahead horizon

Figure 12: MPC configuration parameters

increases with more levels, the simple compression scheme we discussed earlier can reduce the memory overhead especially when number of levels is large. For instance, with 100 levels the compression rate is 0.5 while with 500 levels it can reduce the table size by 82%. Even with 500 levels, the table size is quite reasonably low.

Look-ahead horizon: Figure 12b shows how planning horizon impacts the performance of MPC algorithms. As the look-ahead horizon increases, MPC performances grow and stay stable since more information of future throughput is taken into account. However, as we look further into the future, prediction accuracy can reduce. The performance of MPC can even drop if the horizon is too large.

7.5 Summary of Results

Our main findings are summarized as follows:

1. RobustMPC outperforms existing algorithms in both broadband (FCC) and cellular (HSDPA) datasets, while regular FastMPC does not show advantage in cellular network due to high throughput instability;
2. Our implementation of FastMPC algorithm incurs very low overhead: near-zero CPU overhead and 60 kB increase in memory usage compared to original `dash.js`;
3. Sensitivity analysis shows that FastMPC has advantages over BB and RB in wide parameter ranges. However, there is still room for improvement by increasing FastMPC discretization granularity and employing more accurate throughput predictors.

8 Discussion

Before concluding, we revisit two outstanding issues.

Multi-player effects: In this paper, we focused purely on improving the design of a single video player. A natural question is to extend these insights to multiple players and interaction with cross traffic [34, 32]. To fully consider multi-player interaction and fairness, we can extend our control-theoretic model to explicitly consider a fairness term in the QoE function and model the effects of TCP on throughput allocation. For instance, we might be able to reason about fairness from the perspective of game theory or distributed control theory in this context. This is an interesting direction for future research.

Throughput prediction: As observed by other researchers, better throughput prediction can improve video performance in cellular networks [52]. A key limitation of our work is that we do not have accurate algorithms for throughput prediction and the literature is surprisingly scarce and dated [30, 51, 20]. Two interesting directions of future work are in using crowdsourced approaches based on measurements from other clients [41] and developing a better understanding of throughput predictability and stability in the wild.

9 Conclusions

Our paper was motivated by recent debates surrounding the design of dynamic adaptive streaming over HTTP (DASH) algorithms. To bring some rigor to this space, we developed a control-theoretic problem formulation that allowed us to explore the design space systematically and evaluate quantitatively different classes of solutions through well-defined QoE metrics. With the key insights that a broader design space is available compared to existing solutions, we designed and implemented a model predictive control approach to optimally combine buffer occupancy and throughput predictions in order to maximize the user's QoE. We demonstrated a practical implementation of MPC using the `dash.js` reference video player. Our trace-driven emulations using realistic throughput variability traces confirmed the advantages over state of the art solutions in a wide range of operating conditions with negligible increase in computation and memory requirements. As future work, we plan to incorporate more accurate throughput predictions and explicitly capture multi-player interactions.

Acknowledgments

This work was supported in part by the National Science Foundation under awards ECCS-0925964 and CNS-1345305. We thank our shepherd Keith Winstein for helping us improve the final version. We thank Aditya Ganjam and David Oran for useful discussions regarding industry player platforms that informed our implementation.

10 References

[1] Dash-Industry-Forum, dash.js . https://github.com/Dash-Industry-Forum/dash.js/wiki.

[2] Adobe HTTP Dynamic Streaming. www.adobe.com/products/hds-dynamic-streaming.html.

[3] Adobe OSMF player. http://www.osmf.org.

[4] Akamai HD network. www.akamai.com/hdnetwork.

[5] Apple's HTTP Live Streaming. https://developer.apple.com/streaming/.

[6] DASH-264 JavaScript reference client landing page 1.4.0. http://dashif.org/reference/players/javascript/1.4.0/samples/dash-if-reference-player/index.html.

[7] DASH Industry Forum members. http://dashif.org/members/.

[8] DASH VLC plugin. http://www-itec.uni-klu.ac.at/dash/?page_id=10.

[9] FCC dataset. https://www.fcc.gov/measuring-broadband-america. Accessed: 2014-12-01.

[10] HSDPA dataset. http://home.ifi.uio.no/paalh/dataset/hsdpa-tcp-logs. Accessed: 2014-12-01.
[11] Netflix. http://www.netflix.com/.
[12] OSMF 2.0 release code. http: //sourceforge.net/projects/osmf.adobe/files/latest/download.
[13] Smooth Streaming protocol. http://go.microsoft.com/?linkid=9682896.
[14] The demo page for our MPC-based bitrate adaptation. http://users.ece.cmu.edu/~vsekar/mpcdash.html.
[15] YouTube live encoder settings, bitrates and resolutions. https://support.google.com/youtube/answer/2853702?hl=en.
[16] I. Sodagar. The MPEG-DASH Standard for Multimedia Streaming Over the Internet. *IEEE Multimedia*, 2011.
[17] S. Akhshabi, L. Anantakrishnan, C. Dovrolis, and A. C. Begen. What Happens when HTTP Adaptive Streaming Players Compete for Bandwidth? In *Proc. NOSSDAV*, 2012.
[18] S. Akhshabi, L. Ananthakrishnan, A. Begen, and C. Dovrolis. Server-Based Traffic Shaping for Stabilizing Oscillating Adaptive Streaming Players. In *Proc. ACM SIGMM NOSSDAV*, 2013.
[19] A. Balachandran, V. Sekar, A. Akella, S. Seshan, I. Stoica, and H. Zhang. Developing a Predictive Model of Quality of Experience for Internet Video. In *Proc. ACM SIGCOMM*, 2013.
[20] H. Balakrishnan, M. Stemm, S. Seshan, and R. H. Katz. Analyzing Stability in WideArea Network Performance. In *Proc. ACM SIGMETRICS*, 1997.
[21] D. P. Bertsekas, D. P. Bertsekas, D. P. Bertsekas, and D. P. Bertsekas. *Dynamic Programming and Optimal Control*, volume 1. Athena Scientific Belmont, MA, 1995.
[22] E. F. Camacho and C. B. Alba. *Model Predictive Control.* Springer, 2013.
[23] L. D. Cicco, V. Caldaralo, V. Palmisano, and S. Mascolo. TAPAS: a Tool for rApid Prototyping of Adaptive Streaming algorithms. In *Proc. CoNext VideoNext workshop*, 2014.
[24] F. Dobrian, V. Sekar, A. Awan, I. Stoica, D. A. Joseph, A. Ganjam, J. Zhan, and H. Zhang. Understanding the Impact of Video Quality on User Engagement. In *Proc. ACM SIGCOMM*, 2011.
[25] G. F. Franklin, J. D. Powell, and M. L. Workman. *Digital Control of Dynamic Systems*, volume 3. Addison-wesley Menlo Park, 1998.
[26] A. Ganjam, F. Siddiqui, J. Zhan, X. Liu, I. Stoica, J. Jiang, V. Sekar, and H. Zhang. C3: Internet-Scale Control Plane for Video Quality Optimization. In *Proc. NSDI*, 2015.
[27] M. Ghobadi, Y. Cheng, A. Jain, and M. Mathis. Trickle: Rate Limiting YouTube Video Streaming. In *Proc. USENIX ATC*, 2012.
[28] S. Gouache, G. Bichot, A. Bsila, and C. Howson. Distributed and Adaptive HTTP Streaming. In *Proc. ICME*, 2011.
[29] D. Havey, R. Chertov, and K. Almeroth. Receiver Driven Rate Adaptation for Wireless Multimedia Applications. In *Proc. MMSys*, 2012.
[30] Q. He, C. Dovrolis, and M. Ammar. On the Predictability of Large Transfer TCP Throughput. In *Proc. ACM SIGCOMM*, 2005.
[31] R. Houdaille and S. Gouache. Shaping HTTP Adaptive Streams for a Better User Experience. In *Proc. MMSys*, 2012.
[32] T.-Y. Huang, N. Handigol, B. Heller, N. McKeown, and R. Johari. Confused, Timid, and Unstable: Picking a Video Streaming Rate is Hard. In *Proc. IMC*, 2012.
[33] T.-Y. Huang, R. Johari, N. McKeown, M. Trunnell, and M. Watson. A Buffer-Based Approach to Rate Adaptation: Evidence from a Large Video Streaming Service. In *Proc. ACM SIGCOMM*, 2014.
[34] J. Jiang, V. Sekar, and H. Zhang. Improving Fairness, Efficiency, and Stability in HTTP-based Adaptive Video Streaming with FESTIVE. In *Proc. CoNext*, 2012.
[35] S. S. Krishnan and R. K. Sitaraman. Video Stream Quality Impacts Viewer Behavior: Inferring Causality using Quasi-Experimental Designs. In *Proc. IMC*, 2012.
[36] R. Kuschnig, I. Kofler, and H. Hellwagner. Evaluation of HTTP-based Request-Response Streams for Internet Video Streaming. *Multimedia Systems*, pages 245–256, 2011.
[37] L. De Cicco, S. Mascolo, and V. Palmisano. Feedback Control for Adaptive Live Video Streaming. In *Proc. of ACM Multimedia Systems Conference*, 2011.
[38] Z. Li, X. Zhu, J. Gahm, R. Pan, H. Hu, A. Begen, and D. Oran. Probe and Adapt: Rate Adaptation for HTTP Video Streaming at Scale. *Selected Areas in Communications, IEEE Journal on*, 32(4):719–733, 2014.
[39] C. Liu, I. Bouazizi, and M. Gabbouj. Parallel Adaptive HTTP Media Streaming. In *Proc. ICCCN*, 2011.
[40] H. Liu, Y. Wang, Y. R. Yang, A. Tian, and H. Wang. Optimizing Cost and Performance for Content Multihoming. In *Proc. ACM SIGCOMM*, 2012.
[41] X. Liu, F. Dobrian, H. Milner, J. Jiang, V. Sekar, I. Stoica, and H. Zhang. A Case for a Coordinated Internet Video Control Plane. In *Proc. ACM SIGCOMM*, 2012.
[42] R. K. P. Mok, X. Luo, E. W. W. Chan, and R. K. C. Chang. QDASH: A QoE-aware DASH system. In *Proc. MMSys*, 2012.
[43] C. Mueller, S. Lederer, J. Poecher, and C. Timmerer. Libdash - An Open Source Software Library for the MPEG-DASH Standard. In *Proc. ICME*, 2013.
[44] L. Popa, A. Ghodsi, and I. Stoica. HTTP as the Narrow Waist of the Future Internet. In *Proc. HotNets*, 2010.
[45] R. Rejaie and J. Kangasharju. Mocha: A Quality Adaptive Multimedia Proxy Cache for Internet Streaming. In *Proc. NOSSDAV*, 2001.
[46] S. Akhshabi, A. Begen, C. Dovrolis. An Experimental Evaluation of Rate Adaptation Algorithms in Adaptive Streaming over HTTP. In *Proc. MMSys*, 2011.
[47] G. Tian and Y. Li. Towards Agile and Smooth Video Adaption in Dynamic HTTP Streaming . In *Proc. CoNext*, 2012.
[48] Y. Wang and S. Boyd. Fast Model Predictive Control using Online Optimization. *Control Systems Technology, IEEE Transactions on*, 18(2):267–278, 2010.
[49] B. White, J. Lepreau, L. Stoller, R. Ricci, S. Guruprasad, M. Newbold, M. Hibler, C. Barb, and A. Joglekar. An Integrated Experimental Environment for Distributed Systems and Networks. *Proc. OSDI*, 2002.
[50] X. Yin, V. Sekar, and B. Sinopoli. Toward a Principled Framework to Design Dynamic Adaptive Streaming Algorithms over HTTP. In *Proc. ACM SIGCOMM HotNets*, 2014.
[51] Y. Zhang and N. Duffield. On the Constancy of Internet Path Properties. In *IMW*, 2001.
[52] X. K. Zou, J. Erman, V. Gopalakrishnan, E. Halepovic, R. Jana, X. Jin, J. Rexford, and R. K. Sinha. Can Accurate Predictions Improve Video Streaming in Cellular Networks? In *Proc. ACM HotMobile*, 2015.

BitCuts: Towards Fast Packet Classification for Order-Independent Rules

Zhi Liu[1, 2], Xiang Wang[1, 2], Baohua Yang[3] and Jun Li[2, 4]
[1]Department of Automation, Tsinghua University, China
[2]Research Institute of Information Technology, Tsinghua University, China
[3]IBM China Research Lab, Beijing, China
[4]Tsinghua National Lab for Information Science and Technology, China
{zhi-liu12, xiang-wang11}@mails.tsinghua.edu.cn, baohyang@cn.ibm.com, junl@tsinghua.edu.cn

CCS Concepts
• **Networks~Packet classification**

Keywords
Packet Classification; Order-Independent Rules

1. Introduction

Packet classification is required to achieve high throughput while fitting into a commodity memory hierarchy. Therefore, fewer memory accesses and a reasonable memory footprint are the main concerns when designing a packet classification algorithm. Recent work proposed a hybrid packet classification solution incorporating both software and TCAM-based approaches. Specifically, SAX-PAC[1] observed that real-life packet classification rules can be represented by a few groups of *order-independent* rules. In each group, any two rules do not intersect and can possibly be separated on a fraction of fields, reducing the complexity of the classifier. Consequently, it has been suggested that the *order-independent* groups be handled by existing software algorithms, and the rest of the rules (the *order-dependent* part) be handled by TCAM. However, SAX-PAC did not design specific software algorithms for *order-independent* rules. For these rules, existing algorithms are still inefficient in terms of classification speed. Decision-tree algorithms, the state-of-the-art software approach, always traverse tens of tree nodes in order to identify the matching rule. Speed is further decreased when packets need to match multiple *order-independent* groups.

This paper proposes BitCuts, a bit-level decision-tree algorithm targeting a promising classification speed on *order-independent* rules. Our evaluation shows that BitCuts only requires 30%~40% of the number of memory accesses of existing algorithms and still achieves small a memory footprint on large rulesets.

2. Bit-level Separability of Order-Independent Rules

Consider an example of three order-independent rules in Figure 1, each specifying arbitrary ranges on three fields. These rules are "order-independent" since each pair of the rules does not intersect. Also, the first two fields (bits 0-3 and 4-7, as shown in the dashed boxes) can guarantee this property. Figure 1 also illustrates how bits classify order-independent rules efficiently. Field ranges are converted to prefixes for ease of understanding.

SIGCOMM '15, August 17-21, 2015, London, United Kingdom
ACM 978-1-4503-3542-3/15/08.
http://dx.doi.org/10.1145/2785956.2789998

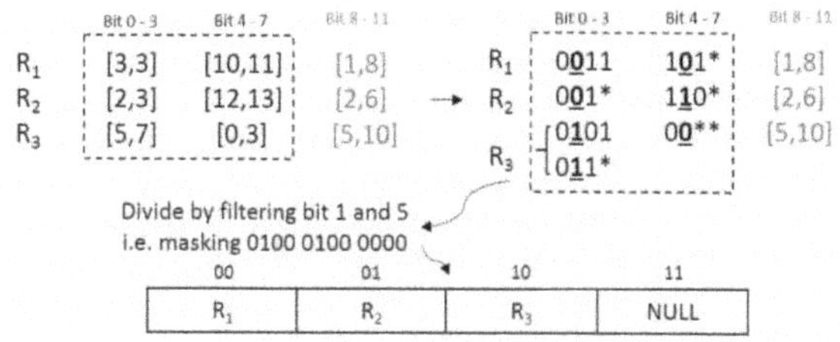

Figure 1. Example ruleset classified by 2 bits

It is shown that a classifier based on bits 1 and 5 is sufficient to separate all of the rules. These bits partition the rules into four subsets. The resulting subsets are stored in an array of buckets, where each bucket is indexed by the concatenated bit values and contains a pointer to the actual rule. It is found that the rules are "fully separated" in these buckets, meaning that each bucket contains at most one rule.

For example, to classify a packet with header {0011, 1101, 1111}, the classification process includes: ***Masking*** the packet header fields with {0100, 0100, 0000} and filtering out the bits at non-zero mask positions, which is "01" in this case; ***Indexing*** to bucket "01" and conducting a "false positive check" with all fields to verify if it matches with rule R_2. In the worst-case, the classification only requires one access to the root bucket, one to the leaf, and a final access to the possible matching rule, dramatically reducing the number of memory accesses.

It can be proved that all of the rules in an order-independent group can be "fully separated" by selecting an appropriate set of bits [2]. To adopt this property for larger rulesets, a naïve solution is to find l bits that "fully separates" the rules and construct the corresponding 2^l buckets, as shown in Figure 1. Table 1 shows the number of required bits l to "fully separate" our evaluated order-independent rulesets, generated with the heuristic proposed in [1]. However, the number of required bits is always prohibitively high, making this solution impractical due to the memory footprint of the 2^l buckets.

3. BitCuts Design

To reduce the number of memory accesses as well as achieve a moderate memory size, we propose the "BitCuts" approach. BitCuts fully utilizes the bit-level separability of order-independent rules and constructs a multi-layer decision-tree to classify incoming packets. An example of resulting data structure and classifying procedure is shown in Figure 2. BitCuts first accesses the root bucket, fetches a bitmask with 10 selected bit positions, and masks the packet header against this bitmask. The concatenated bit values index to another intermediate bucket on the next layer, which contains a bitmask and a bucket array pointer for the next access. This recursion stops until it reaches a leaf bucket, and then a false positive check is conducted to get

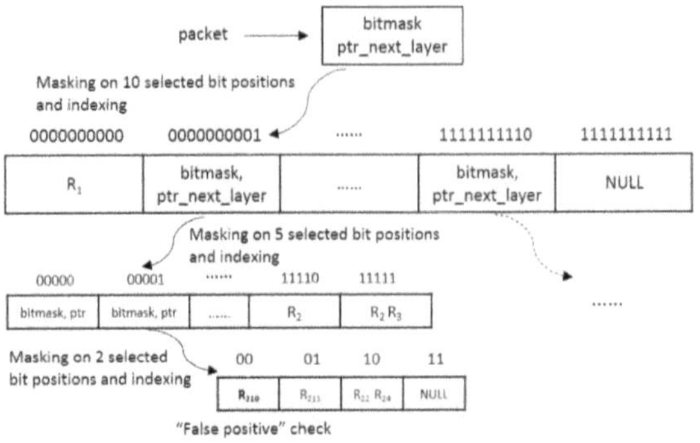

Figure 2. Data structure and packet classification procedure of BitCuts

Algorithm 1 – BitCuts_Tree_Build

```
1  function BitCuts_Tree_Build(ruleset)
2    bitmask = all_zeros()
3    do:
4      bit = bit_select(ruleset, bitmask)
5      bitmask = bitmask.add(bit)
6      subsets = partition(ruleset, bitmask)
7    While(insep_fraction_calculate(subsets) > threshold)
8    L = bitmask.number_selected_bits
9    bucket_array = initialize(pow(2, L))
10   for each i in subsets.indexes:
11     if inseparable(subsets[i]):
12       bucket_array[i].is_leaf = True
13       bucket_array[i].ptr = get_ptr(subsets[i])
14     else:
15       p_next_layer_bucket_array, bitmask =
             BitCuts_tree_build(subsets[i])
16       bucket_array[i].is_leaf = False
17       bucket_array[i].bitmask = bitmask
18       bucket_array[i].ptr = p_next_layer_bucket_array
19   return addr(bucket_array), bitmask
```

the final match. In a nutshell, BitCuts' multi-layer design has the following advantages over the naïve solution:

Better rule separation. On upper layers, each subset in the bucket array always requires a different set of bits in order to be divided further. With the constraint of maintaining a reasonable memory size, BitCuts' multi-layer design is able to select the best bits to divide each subset, thus making use of more bits than naïve solution.

Smaller memory size. The size of each subset varies among different buckets. Some of the subsets are relatively small and might not need additional bits for further dividing, while some might be large and require more bits. Our multi-layer design will prevent the space inflation resulting from unnecessarily dividing very small subsets.

The pseudocode for building BitCuts decision-trees is shown in Algorithm 1. The algorithm iteratively calls *bit_select* and adds the selected bit to the bitmask. Currently, *bit_select* uses a greedy strategy: it tries to add one unused bit to the existing bitmask, splits the ruleset, and gets the maximum size among all the resulting subsets. After a trail with each unused bit, the greedy algorithm selects the bit with the lowest maximum size.

As shown in line 8, the bit selection stops when the fraction of "inseparable" subsets, which will be explained later, exceeds the pre-defined threshold. If L bits are selected at this point, the algorithm checks each of the resulting 2^L subsets. If the subset is "inseparable", the algorithm constructs the corresponding leaf bucket. If not, the subset needs to be divided further by constructing a bitmask and bucket array for the next layer.

The goal of calculating the fraction of "inseparable" subsets (*insep_fraction_calculate*) is to determine when to stop the bit selection on the current layer, which is fundamental to achieve a

Ruleset	*Coverage*	*# of bits*	*BitCuts*			*HyperCuts*			*HyperSplit*		
			Max	Avg	Size (KB)	Max	Avg	Size (KB)	Max	Avg	Size (KB)
acl5k_0	72.45%	70	6	4.2	102	19	9.1	51	16	12.1	65
acl5k_1	18.08%	49	7	3.9	155	35	10.4	20	13	10.2	16
acl10k_0	78.69%	55	7	4.0	278	19	11.0	199	16	13.2	149
acl10k_1	10.49%	30	6	3.9	16	17	9.6	10	12	10.2	19
fw5k_0	68.30%	53	6	4.1	41	18	10.4	88	15	11.9	62
fw5k_1	24.54%	23	5	4.2	16	17	10.4	42	12	10.4	22
fw10k_0	74.61%	12	4	3.7	43	18	11.3	252	14	13.0	135
fw10k_1	24.27%	11	5	4.1	33	17	11.3	97	13	11.3	44
ipc5k_0	52.74%	79	7	4.1	191	19	9.7	184	16	11.7	48
ipc5k_1	24.21%	62	6	4.1	58	21	9.7	29	13	10.6	23
ipc10k_0	53.46%	86	7	3.8	300	21	10.4	307	16	12.7	99
ipc10k_1	26.24%	66	6	4.2	103	24	10.3	71	15	11.7	51

Table 1. Memory access count (worst-case and average-case) and memory size comparison on order-independent groups of ClassBench rulesets

good trade-off between classification speed and memory size. To figure out whether a subset is "inseparable", an obvious criterion is that buckets with no more than 1 rule are naturally "inseparable". On the other hand, adding one additional bit to further divide small subsets is not efficient since it doubles the bucket number on the current layer but provides limited savings in the number of memory accesses. Currently we judge a subset as "inseparable" if its size is no more than 2.

4. Evaluation

We evaluate BitCuts on order-independent groups generated by the algorithm proposed in [1] and compare the performance with two other decision-tree algorithms, HyperCuts [3] and HyperSplit [4]. Table 1 shows the memory access count and the size of the resulting data structure. It's shown that BitCuts greatly reduce the number of memory accesses. In the worst case, the BitCuts memory access count is ~42% that of HyperSplit and ~30% that of HyperCuts. On average, the BitCuts memory access count is only ~35% that of HyperSplit and ~40% that of HyperCuts. When comparing memory size, BitCuts is 2.3x that of HyperSplit and 1.6x that of HyperCuts, on average. For the evaluated 10k rules, the memory size is still reasonable and the data structures could easily fit into the cache. For rulesets that require fewer bits (e.g. order-independent groups 0 and 1 of fw10k), BitCuts achieves the lowest memory size because it requires much fewer intermediate nodes.

5. Conclusion and Future Work

To accelerate software-based classification for order-independent rules, this work proposes BitCuts, a bit-level decision-tree algorithm for fast packet classification. BitCuts is proved promising to achieve much fewer memory accesses compared to existing algorithms while maintaining a reasonable memory footprint. Our future work includes efforts to improve the efficiency of the bit selection algorithm, and further evaluations on real traffic.

6. References

[1] K. Kogan, S. Nikolenko, O. Rottenstreich, W. Culhane, and P. Eugster. SAX-PAC (Scalable And eXpressive PAcket Classification). In ACM SIGCOMM 2014.

[2] B. Yang, J. Fong, W. Jiang, Y. Xue and J. Li. Practical Multituple Packet Classification Using Dynamic Discrete Bit Selection. In IEEE TRANSACTIONS ON COMPUT-ERS, VOL. 63, NO. 2.

[3] S. Singh, F. Baboescu, G. Varghese, and J. Wang. Packet Classification using Multidimensional Cutting. In ACM SIGCOMM 2003.

[4] Y. Qi, L. Xu, B. Yang, Y. Xue and J. Li. Packet Classification Algorithms: From Theory to Practice. In IEEE INFOCOM, 2009.

Supercharge me: Boost Router Convergence with SDN

Michael Alan Chang
Princeton University/ETH Zürich
machang@princeton.edu

Thomas Holterbach
ETH Zürich
thomahol@ethz.ch

Markus Happe
ETH Zürich
markus.happe@tik.ee.ethz.ch

Laurent Vanbever
ETH Zürich
lvanbever@ethz.ch

ABSTRACT

By enabling logically-centralized and direct control of the forwarding behavior of a network, Software-Defined Networking (SDN) holds great promise in terms of improving network management, performance, and costs. Realizing this vision is challenging though as SDN proposals to date require substantial and expensive changes to the existing network architecture before the benefits can be realized. As a result, the number of SDN deployments has been rather limited in scope. To kickstart a wide-scale SDN deployment, there is a need for low-risk, high return solutions that solve a timely problem. As one possible solution, we show how we can significantly improve the performance of legacy IP routers, *i.e.* "supercharge" them, by combining them with SDN-enabled devices. In this abstract, we supercharge one particular aspect of the router performance: its convergence time after a link or a node failure.

CCS Concepts

•**Networks** → *Routers; Network performance analysis;*

1. TODAY'S (SLOW) CONVERGENCE

The convergence time of traditional IP routers is directly linked to the time it takes for the router to update its hardware-based Forwarding Information Base (FIB) after it detects the failure. Each FIB entry maps an IP destination to the L2 Next-Hop address (*i.e.*, MAC address) of the chosen IP NH as well as the output interface. In most routers, the FIB is flat, meaning each FIB entry is mapped to a different (but possibly identical in content) L2 NH entry. This is illustrated by Fig. 1, which depicts a simple network where $R1$ is an edge router connected to the router of two providers, $R2$ and $R3$. Each of these provider routers advertise a full Internet routing table composed of more than 512,000 IPv4 prefixes [1]. As $R2$ is cheaper than $R3$, $R1$ is configured to prefer $R2$ for all destinations. In such a case, each of the 512k FIB entries in $R1$ is associated to a distinct L2 NH entry which all contain the physical MAC address of $R2$. Upon the failure of a $R2$, every single entry of $R1$ FIB has to be updated creating a significant downtime. Our measurements on a recent router (see §3) show that it actually takes *several minutes* for $R1$ to fully converge, during which traffic is lost. With the ever rising cost of downtime [2] and as services increasingly rely on high-availability, convergence of the order of minutes is simply not acceptable.

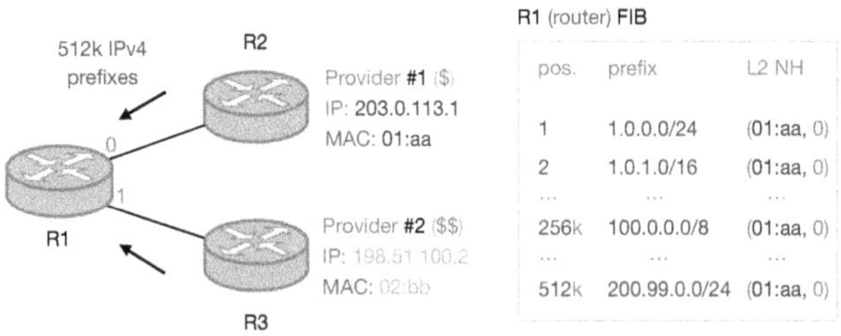

Figure 1: Upon a failure of $R2$, each of the 512k FIB entries have to be updated to restore full connectivity, a time-consuming operation.

2. SUPERCHARGING CONVERGENCE

Equipping routers with a hierarchical FIB [3] is an obvious solution to the convergence problem mentioned above. In a hierarchical FIB, each IP destination is mapped to a pointer that resolves to the actual L2 NH to be used. Upon failure of a L2 NH, only pointer values have to be updated. Since the number of L2 NH is

SIGCOMM '15 August 17-21, 2015, London, United Kingdom

ACM ISBN 978-1-4503-3542-3/15/08.
DOI: http://dx.doi.org/10.1145/2785956.2790007

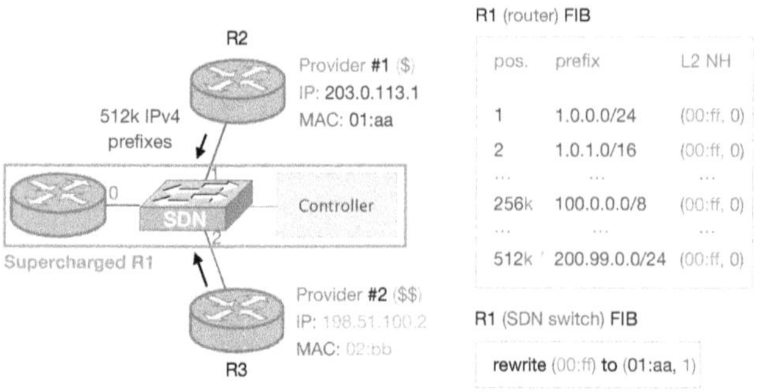

Figure 2: With a supercharged router, upon failure of $R2$, only *one entry*—the pointer value—needs to update to restore full connectivity.

orders of magnitude smaller than the number of FIB entries, convergence is greatly improved. Unfortunately, hierarchical FIB designs also means much more complex hardware, and therefore, more expensive routers.

Fig. 2 illustrates how we can provide *any* router (here $R1$) with a hierarchical FIB, spanning two devices, by combining it with a SDN switch. To provision forwarding entries in this hierarchical FIB, we built a *supercharged controller*. While the controller can rely on (typically) OpenFlow to provision forwarding entries in a SDN switch, dynamically provisioning specific forwarding entries in a router is trickier. Our key insight is that the supercharged controller can use any routing protocol spoken by the router as a provisioning interface. Indeed, FIB entries in a router directs traffic to the L2 NH associated to the L3 NH learned via the routing protocol. To do so, our supercharged controller first interposes itself between the router and its peers (see Fig. 2). Then, it computes primary and backup NH for all IP destinations. Finally, it provisions L2 NH "pointers" by setting the IP NH field to a virtual L3 NH that gets resolved by the router into a L2 NH using ARP. Upon failure of $R2$ in Fig. 2, all the controller has to do to converge is to modify the switch rule to (rewrite(00:ff) to (02:bb,2)) in order to converge *all traffic* to $R3$.

3. EVALUATION

Setup and methodology. Our setup is based on the scenario depicted in Fig. 2. It consists of 3 routers Cisco Nexus 7k C7018 interconnected through a HP E3800 J9575A Openflow-enabled switch. We measured the convergence time of $R1$ with and without supercharging it. To do so, we similarly loaded $R2$ and $R3$ with an increasing number of actual BGP routes collected from the RIPE RIS dataset [4]. In both cases (supercharged and not supercharged), $R1$ was configured to prefer $R2$ for all the destinations. Once all routes were advertised, we started to inject traffic at $R1$ using a FPGA-based generator. We configured $R2$ and $R3$ to send all receiving traffic to another FPGA-based board, acting as sink. We subsequently disconnected $R2$ from the switch, triggering the convergence process at $R1$;

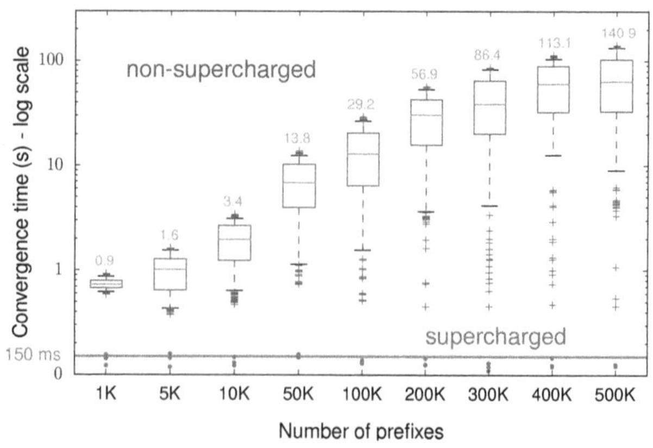

Figure 3: Convergence time with respect to number of advertised prefixes.

subsequently, we measure the time until recovering full connectivity. Results are depicted in Fig. 3.

The non-supercharged R1 takes ~2.5min to converge in the worst case. The convergence time is linearly proportional to the number of prefixes because FIB entries are updated one-by-one. This worst-case highlights undesirability of the non-supercharged approach: as the FIB grows, so does the convergence time.

The supercharged R1 systematically converges *within 150ms*, for all prefixes. Thanks to its hierarchical FIB design, the supercharged R1's convergence time is constant—irrespective of the number of prefixes. This constitutes a 900× improvement factor over the worst case of the non-supercharged solution.

4. CONCLUSION

We boosted the convergence time of legacy routers by combining them with SDN equipment in a novel way, essentially building a hierarchical forwarding table spanning across devices.

We believe this paper opens up many interesting future directions for integrating legacy routing and SDN devices in a more "symbiotic way". By juxtaposing the agility of the SDN with the tried-and-true routers prevalent in the industry, we take the best of both worlds and take the first steps towards electrifying modern day networks through supercharged networking devices.

5. REFERENCES

[1] "CIDR report," http://www.cidr-report.org/as2.0/.
[2] C. Cérin, C. Coti, P. Delort, F. Diaz, M. Gagnaire, Q. Gaumer, N. Guillaume, J. Lous, S. Lubiarz, J. Raffaelli *et al.*, "Downtime statistics of current cloud solutions," *International Working Group on Cloud Computing Resiliency, Tech. Rep*, 2013.
[3] C. Filsfils, P. Mohapatra, J. Bettink, P. Dharwadkar, P. De Vriendt, Y. Tsier, V. Van Den Schrieck, O. Bonaventure, and P. Francois, "BGP Prefix Independent Convergence (PIC)," Cisco, Tech. Rep., 2011.
[4] "RIPE RIS Raw Data," https: //www.ripe.net/data-tools/stats/ris/ris-raw-data.

Towards Scalable SDN Switches: Enabling Faster Flow Table Entries Installation

Roberto Bifulco, Anton Matsiuk
NEC Laboratories Europe, Germany – E-mail: <firstname.lastname>@neclab.eu

CCS Concepts

•**Networks** → **Bridges and switches;** *Network performance analysis;*

Keywords

Software-defined Networking, Reactive Control Plane, OpenFlow

1. INTRODUCTION

SDN applications operate the switching hardware in new ways, uncovering some strict constraints of current switching devices. The large flow table entries installation time is among these constraints, since it limits the applicability of hardware SDN switches, in particular in those applications that require a reactive logic. The source of this performance limitation lays in the technological solutions adopted by current ASICs, which typically rely on Ternary Content Addressable Memory (TCAM) to implement the flow tables. While TCAM can be used to implement very fast and powerful lookups, for instance to search on a range of values, unfortunately their write operations are quite slow. Furthermore, the implementation of flexible lookups may require the writing of more than one entry in the memory, in a precise order, sensibly increasing the installation time.

Inspired by previous work that suggests the combination of software and hardware forwarders [2], and noticing the trend in adding powerful CPUs to commodity *white box* switches[1], we argue that a hybrid software-hardware switch may help in lowering the flow table entries installation time and present ShadowSwitch (sSw), an OpenFlow switch prototype that implements such design. Notice that our work complements the previous work that uses similar hybrid architectures to increase the switch's flow table size [2, 1].

sSw builds on two key observations. First, software tables are very fast to be updated, hence, forwarding tables updates always happen in software first. Eventually, entries are moved to the TCAM-based forwarding tables, to achieve higher overall throughput and offload the software forwarder. However, partially overlapping entries may break the forwarding decision semantic. In fact, an entry in the hardware tables will always have an actual priority which is higher than the priorities of the entries in the software tables, since the lookup in software is performed only in case there are no entries matching a packet in hardware. To re-establish the correct relative priority ordering between overlapping entries, while keeping a small installation time, ShadowSwitch builds on a second observation: deleting entries from TCAM is in most of the cases much faster than adding them. Hence, ShadowSwitch may translate an entry installation in a mix of installation in software tables and deletion from hardware tables.

[1]http://www.opencompute.org/projects/networking/

SIGCOMM '15 August 17-21, 2015, London, United Kingdom

ACM ISBN 978-1-4503-3542-3/15/08.

DOI: http://dx.doi.org/10.1145/2785956.2790008

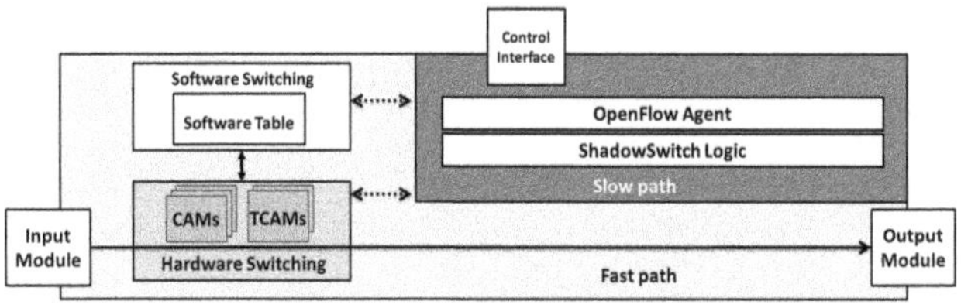

Figure 1: High-level ShadowSwitch's design

2. SHADOWSWITCH

The sSw architecture is shown in Figure 1: a high-performance software switching layer is introduced in the switch's fast path, that is, the part of the switch that performs packet forwarding operations. The software switching layer (SwSw) runs on a general purpose system, generally composed of a CPU with its caches hierarchy, implemented by SRAMs, a slower central memory based on DRAM and a high-speed system bus, which connects the CPU with the central memory and the switching ASIC. The *ShadowSwitch Logic* (sSwLogic), which is located in the sSw's slow path, manages the flow table entries (FTEs) installation.

***flow_mod* handling.** An OpenFlow's *flow_mod* message is used to install, delete or modify a FTE. In sSw the installation of a new FTE is always performed in the SwSw, where the installation time is usually in the sub-millisecond range and constant, being not affected by other entries already installed in the forwarding tables, as it happens when the installation is done in TCAMs. Once the FTE is placed in the SwSw, the *flow_mod* processing terminates and packets start to be forwarded in the fast path. However, since FTEs are eventually moved to the hardware layer (HwSw), additional actions are required if the HwSw contains lower priority FTEs that (partially) overlap the newly installed FTE (which exists only in software). In these cases, together with the FTE installation in the software layer, the sSwLogic performs an additional action that is either the deletion from the HwSw of (all) the FTE(s) that have a dependency on the newly installed one[2] or the installation of the new FTE in the HwSw. The rationale behind this solution is that FTE deletion from a hardware table is, in principle, a faster and simpler operation, while a FTE installation may require a reorganization of the

[2]This may actually need the deletion of the entries which have dependencies also with the ones that have been just deleted.

previously installed FTEs. Nevertheless, deletion of the FTEs from the HwSw is not always possible. In fact, the sSwLogic checks the throughput (in terms of packets and bytes per second) contributed by the FTEs in the HwSw, deleting them only if their aggregated throughput could be afforded by the SwSw. In the other cases, sSw falls back to a direct installation of the new FTE in the HwSw.

When a *flow_mod* contains a FTE deletion request, the sSwLogic deletes the FTE either from the software switching layer or from both layers if the FTE was moved to hardware.

3. PROTOTYPE AND EVALUATION

We implemented a sSw prototype using a commercial hardware OpenFlow switch (HwSw) and an OpenvSwitch (OVS) instance running on a HP DL380G7 server equipped with an Intel Xeon L5640 (6 cores @ 2.26 GHz). The server is connected to the HwSw using both the switch's control port and two 1Gbit data plane ports. The sSwLogic, implemented as a user-level application, works as a proxy between the switches and an OpenFlow controller, which we implemented using POX on the same server. A second server, connected to two switch's ports, works as traffic generator and receiver. In all the tests we compare sSw performance with the performance of a high-end hardware OpenFlow switch.

***flow_mod* performance:** we measured the FTEs installation performance of the hardware switch when different FTEs priority patterns are used. Figure 2 shows the results. It is worth noticing that the FTE installation time increases almost exponentially with the number of already installed entries, when FTEs are installed in ascending priority order, demonstrating that TCAM entries reordering is happening. Instead, when FTEs have same priorities or they are installed in descending priority order, the installation time increases linearly with the number of entries in the forwarding table. Finally, FTE deletion time is much lower than the installation time and does not change in dependence of the FTEs' priorities (thus, we show a single curve for deletion in Fig. 2).

Our sSw prototype has two different performance behaviors. In the best case, it shows a constant FTE installation time, irrespective of the number of already installed FTEs and relative priorities, improving the hardware switch performance by 1 to 3 orders of magnitude. This is the behavior of sSw when the FTE that is going to be installed does not depend on any lower priority FTE in the HwSw. In case of dependencies, sSw deletes the dependent FTEs from HwSw in addition to installing the new FTE in SwSw. Figure 3 shows that the installation time grows linearly with the number of FTEs that have to be deleted. Also, Fig. 3 further shows that the deletion of several FTEs is (almost) always a faster operation than the addition of a single higher priority FTE to the HwSw. If the FTEs deletion is not possible, e.g., it would cause excessive load on the SwSw, sSw falls back to the hardware switch performance.

Reactive flow installation: in a second test we measure the installation delay of 10K network flows handled by a switch's port, using a reactive logic, i.e., a new flow generates an OpenFlow's *packet_in* message that is handled by the POX controller, which in turn installs a new FTE for such flow. We configure our traffic generator to timestamp the moment in which a flow's packet is sent and received. The flow installation delay is the time difference between these two timestamps for the first flow's packet. It is worth noticing that with this definition we include also the delay introduced by the POX controller, i.e., we look at the system as a black box. All the FTEs have same priority and define non-overlapping flows, which are generated at a rate of 1K flows per sec., over a 10 sec. period.

The measured flow installation delays are shown in Figure 4, where each flow is assigned with an id that reflects the generation order, i.e., first generated flow is assigned with id #1, the second

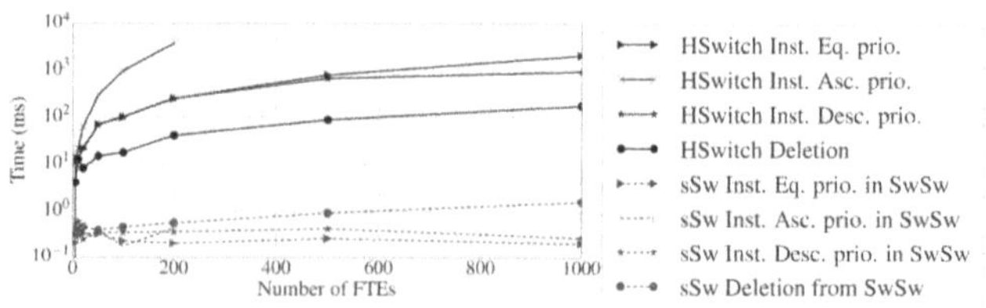

Figure 2: Cumulative execution time for forwarding table updates when installing/deleting a variable number of entries.

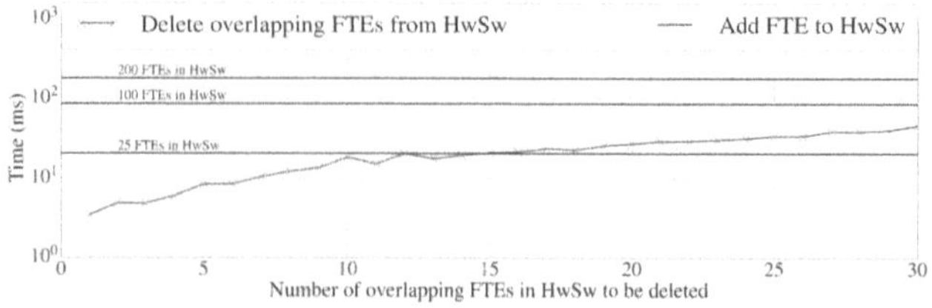

Figure 3: Time to delete a variable number of FTEs compared to the time to install a single FTE.

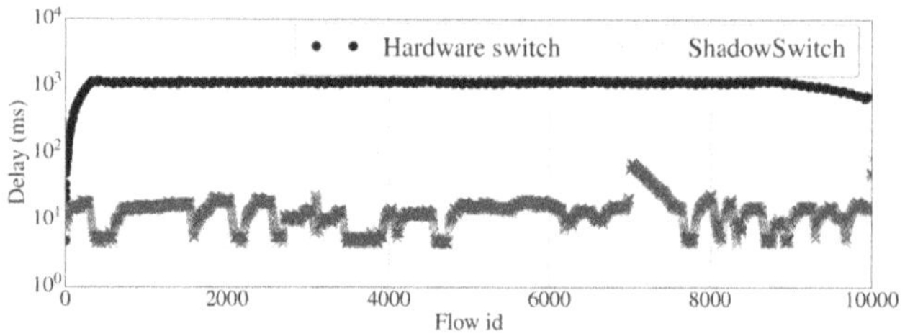

Figure 4: Flow installation delay (in log scale)

has id #2, and so on. The hardware switch drops about the 75% of the 10000 generated flows. The installation delay grows from the 5 ms experienced by flow #1 to about 1.1 s for flows with id bigger than 318. When using sSw no flows are dropped during the test, with an installation delay that is within 22 ms for the 95% of the flows. Figure 4 also shows that, when using sSw (lower line in figure), the flow installation delay experiences variations in the range 5 ms-20 ms. We believe these variations (and the higher delay peak for flows #7000 to #7500) are mainly introduced by our testbed, since we are running the POX controller, OVS and our user-space sSwLogic implementation on the same server.

4. FUTURE WORK

ShadowSwitch demonstrates that a fast software switching layer may help in reducing the flow table's entries installation time, however, the viability of the approach is dependent on the ratio between the software forwarding and hardware forwarding speeds, on the dependencies between flow entries, on the properties of the network flows in terms of packets and bytes per second. Our future work is to evaluate the system behavior when varying these parameters and to design smart algorithms that selects which entries should be moved first to the hardware flow table.

Acknowledgment

This work has been partly funded by the EU in the context of the "BEBA" project (Grant Agreement: 644122).

5. REFERENCES

[1] N. Katta, J. Rexford, and D. Walker. Infinite CacheFlow in software-defined networks. Proceedings of ACM SIGCOMM HotSDN, 2014.

[2] N. Sarrar, S. Uhlig, A. Feldmann, R. Sherwood, and X. Huang. Leveraging zipf's law for traffic offloading. *SIGCOMM Comput. Commun. Rev.*, 2012.

Sampling and Large Flow Detection in SDN

Yehuda Afek*
afek@cs.tau.ac.il

Anat Bremler-Barr†
bremler@idc.ac.il

Shir Landau Feibish*
shirl11@post.tau.ac.il

Liron Schiff*
schiffli@post.tau.ac.il

*Blavatnik School of Computer Science
Tel-Aviv University
Tel-Aviv, Israel

†Computer Science Department
Interdisciplinary Center
Herzliya, Israel

CCS Concepts

•**Networks** → **Programmable networks; Network monitoring;** *Network measurement;*

Keywords

Network monitoring; Software Defined Networks; Heavy Hitters

1. INTRODUCTION

We present techniques for traffic sampling and large flows detection in SDN with Openflow. In many cases, in order to efficiently compute high speed traffic statistics, sampling is needed. While SDN switches are very efficient and considerably simpler to manage than existing routers and switches, they don't offer direct means for sampling and detection of large flows. Both of these capabilities are important for various basic network applications. For example, traffic monitoring is such an application, which is a key ability in providing QoS, capacity planning and efficient traffic engineering. Additional applications which make use of sampling and large flow detection are applications that depend on network visibility, such as security (DDoS and others), anomaly detection, DPI and billing.

Traffic visibility, and specifically measurements and monitoring in IP networks has become a very difficult task due to the overwhelming amounts of traffic and flows. One of the earliest network measurements tools was Cisco Netflow [1], which allowed IP flow level measurement. Netflow provided a variety of monitoring capabilities yet suffered from high processing and collection overheads, which were partially decreased using sampling in the variant *Sampled* Netflow, yet this variant provided reduced accuracy caused by the straightforward use of sampling. In [2] Estan and Varghese significantly improve the accuracy of the sampling process by introducing the *Sample and Hold* algorithm which provides better accuracy while reducing the processing and collection overhead.

In order to increase the availability of monitoring, and following the SDN trend, we explore ways to implement this with the widespread OpenFlow standard for SDN switches. OpenFlow switches provide counters of the number of bytes and packets per flow entry, yet traffic measurement remains a difficult task in SDN for two reasons. The first is the hardware (usually Ternary Content Addressable Memories (TCAMs)) constraints which limit the number of flows which the switch can maintain and follow. The second is the limited number of updates which the switch can process per second, which can therefore limit the amount of updates that the controller will make to the flow table. The algorithms provided herein overcome these limitations by providing efficient building blocks for sampling and large flow detection which can be used by various monitoring applications.

1.1 Our Contribution

First, we present various OpenFlow based methods to sample packets that traverse an SDN switch. These methods are immune to various cyber attacks and are based on Open-Flow 1.3 capabilities. Second, we make use of the sampling mechanisms for the development of an efficient method to detect large flows. The techniques presented are both flow-table size and switch-controller communication efficient.

2. TRAFFIC SAMPLING

2.1 Packet Sampling

In *Packet Sampling* we select each packet in a stream of packets traversing the switch with probability p, $0 \leq p \leq 1$, and send them to a *receiver* that can be the controller or some middlebox (monitoring box). We present three basic approaches for packet sampling, each using different OpenFlow 1.3 optional features which are supported by existing software and hardware switches.

2.2 Pseudo Byte Sampling

In *Pseudo Byte Sampling* we select each byte in a stream of packets traversing the switch with probability p, $0 \leq p \leq 1$, and send the packet containing the sampled byte to a receiver. We present optimized techniques for pseudo-byte sampling, in which we assume that packet size is accessible and can be matched in the OpenFlow pipeline, using the Experimenter extension or any other way. It is expected that with upcoming new OpenFlow and alike SDN archi-

This research was supported by European Research Council (ERC) Starting Grant no. 259085, and the Neptune Consortium, administered by the Office of the Chief Scientist of the Israeli ministry of Industry, Trade, and Labor, and the Ministry of Science and Technology, Israel.

SIGCOMM '15 August 17-21, 2015, London, United Kingdom

ACM ISBN 978-1-4503-3542-3/15/08.

DOI: http://dx.doi.org/10.1145/2785956.2790009

tectures, such as [3] more header fields could be natively matched by the flow tables.

2.3 Evaluation

We evaluate the performance of our sampling schemes by considering the resulting sampled flow size distributions compared to real flow size distribution. Figure 1 shows the three packet sampling methods achieve similar distributions, and closely approximate the real (exact) distribution.

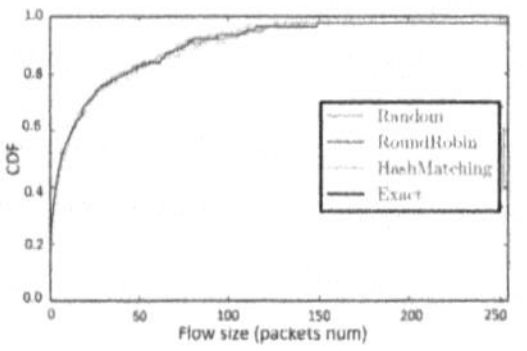

Figure 1: Flow size CDF under three sampling schemes and the exact (not sampled) traffic CDF.

3. HEAVY FLOWS DETECTION

A Heavy flow in a stream of packets S, is a flow which takes up more than T percent of the traffic (i.e., packets) in the stream. Fundamental counter based algorithms for finding Heavy Hitters (or flows) such as that of Metwally et. al. [4], cannot be directly implemented in the SDN framework since in the worst case they would require rule changes for every packet that traverses the switch. A different approach is therefore needed.

First we consider a naive solution which we name Sample&HH, that samples packets in the switch and then sends all sampled packets to the controller. The controller computes the heavy flows using a heavy hitters algorithm. However, as can be seen in Figure 3a (and other works [2]), relying solely on the samples is not accurate enough. Next we consider a solution based on the *Sample&Hold* paradigm of [2] which was devised for identifying elephant flows in traffic of classic IP networks. Sample&Hold achieves very accurate results by using sampling together with accurate in-band counters for sampled flows, yet the high amount of counters and the rate of installing them make Sample&Hold incompatible with SDN switch architecture. Therefore we only consider it as a reference point to evaluate our algorithm.

To deal with the problems of the above solutions, we present our Sample&Pick algorithm. Sample&Pick uses sampling to identify flows that are suspicious of being heavy. For these *suspicious* flows a special rule is placed in the switch flow table providing exact counters for the suspicious flows. The Sample&Pick algorithm considers both the bounded rule space in the switch as well as the time it takes for the controller to install a rule in the switch. Therefore we use two separate thresholds, one for determining which flows are heavy and a second lower threshold for detecting potentially large flows. This lower threshold allows us to install a rule in the switch early enough to get an accurate count of the large flows, yet we do not install rules for too many flows that will remain small.

Our algorithm operates as follows: in the first step we sample the flows going through the switch using one of the sampling techniques mentioned. As can be seen in Fig. 2, these samples are sent to the controller, that feeds them as input to a heavy hitters computation module in order to identify the suspicious heavy flows (steps 2 and 3). Once a flow's counter in the heavy hitters module has passed some predefined threshold t, a rule is inserted in the switch to maintain an exact packet counter for that flow (steps 4 and 5). This counter is polled by the controller at fixed intervals and stored in the controller (steps 6 and 7). Finally the last step increments the counters that are processed by the Heavy Hitters module to maintain correct counters of non-sampled flows.

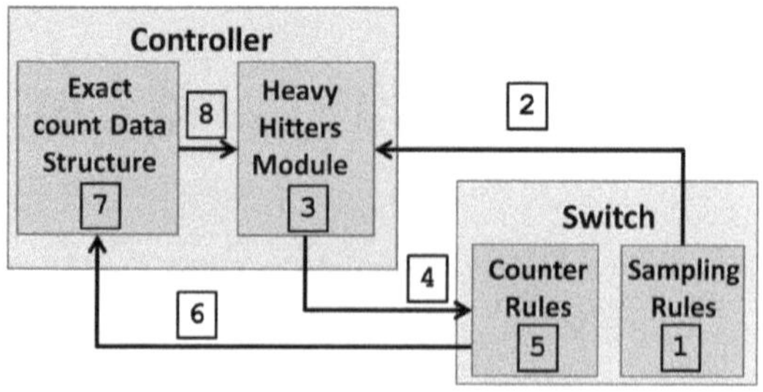

Figure 2: Sample&Pick overview

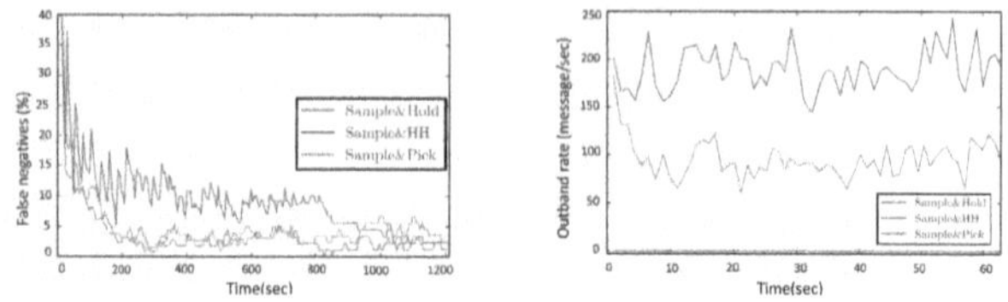

(a) False negative errors, shown by the ratio between the Heavy Hitter (HH) flows missed to the total number of HH flows.

(b) Rate of PacketIn messages (samples) from switch to controller. In Sample&Hold, sampling is switch-contained.

Figure 3: Heavy Flow Detection test results

3.1 Evaluation

We compare our Sample&Pick algorithm to the two additional solutions described above Sample&Hold and Sample&HH.

Testing shows: Considering a line rate of $2 \cdot 10^4$ pps, it takes the scheme about 10^7 packets to stabilize (Figure 3a). Furthermore, the controller in Sample&Pick processes approximately half the samples than in Sample&HH (Figure 3b), due to the fact that Sample&HH has no counters in the switch so all traffic is sampled, whereas Sample&Pick uses switch counters for heavy flows; Parameters used: $T = 10^{-3}$, $p = 0.5 \cdot 10^{-2}$, $t = T/2 = 10^{-3}/2$.

4. CONCLUSIONS AND FUTURE WORK

We have presented techniques for sampling and large flow detection in SDN. Our sampling techniques are unique in that they are simple and remain within the confinements of the OpenFlow standard. Our algorithmdetects large flows with a relatively small error rate while minimizing the computation overhead in the switch and requiring little controller-switch communication.

5. REFERENCES

[1] [Online]. Available: http://www.cisco.com/c/en/us/tech/quality-of-service-qos/netflow/index.html

[2] C. Estan and G. Varghese, "New directions in traffic measurement and accounting: Focusing on the elephants, ignoring the mice," *ACM Trans. Comput. Syst.*, vol. 21, no. 3, pp. 270–313, 2003.

[3] P. Bosshart, D. Daly, G. Gibb, M. Izzard, N. McKeown, J. Rexford, C. Schlesinger, D. Talayco, A. Vahdat, G. Varghese, and D. Walker, "P4: programming protocol-independent packet processors," *Computer Communication Review*, vol. 44, no. 3, pp. 87–95, 2014.

[4] A. Metwally, D. Agrawal, and A. El Abbadi, "Efficient computation of frequent and top-k elements in data streams," in *ICDT*, ser. Lecture Notes in Computer Science, T. Eiter and L. Libkin, Eds., vol. 3363. Springer, 2005, pp. 398–412.

On the Optimization of Request Routing for Content Delivery

Walid Benchaita
Alcatel-Lucent Bell Labs
France
walid.benchaita@alcatel-lucent.com

Samir Ghamri-Doudane
Alcatel-Lucent Bell Labs
France
samir.ghamri-doudane@alcatel-lucent.com

Sébastien Tixeuil
UPMC Sorbonne Universités
& IUF
Sebastien.Tixeuil@lip6.fr

ABSTRACT

We present a flexible scheme and an optimization algorithm for request routing in Content Delivery Networks (CDN). Our online approach, which is based on Lyapunov theory, provides a stable quality of service to clients, while improving content delivery delays. It also reduces data transport costs for operators.

1. INTRODUCTION

The role of content delivery networks (CDN) has been constantly evolving since their first deployment to respond to customer needs (from static web content to media streaming), and expectations are still getting higher. It is hence essential to empower content delivery with effective models and solutions in order to deal with the increasing amount of bandwidth-hungry and demanding applications.

Besides, CDN's performance is sensitive to temporarily high request rates or "flash crowds" [6]. Such (potentially unpredicted) huge amount of traffic overloads the delivery infrastructure and causes congestions that lead to service degradation. Request routing (or redirection), which is at the cornerstone of CDN operation, is one of the main keys to improve performance[1]. It has been the focus of several studies and for various purposes [2, 3].

The challenge is to design a request routing solution that is: *optimized* in order to best use the CDN and transport network resources; *feasible online* in order to adapt quickly to the changing conditions; and *flexible* in order to consider the potential objectives set by the CDN operator. To meet these requirements, we use the Lyapunov optimization theory[4] to design an effective online algorithm for request routing, which is then deployed to offer a flexible redirection scheme. Our solution is evaluated through experiments using both synthetic and real workloads. The results show that our multi-objective algorithm provides a stable quality of service to clients, while improving content delivery delays, especially under flash crowd conditions. Moreover, it helps reducing delivery costs by maximizing cache efficiency.

SIGCOMM'15 August 17-21, 2015, London, United Kingdom

ACM ISBN 978-1-4503-3542-3/15/08.
DOI: http://dx.doi.org/10.1145/2785956.2790016

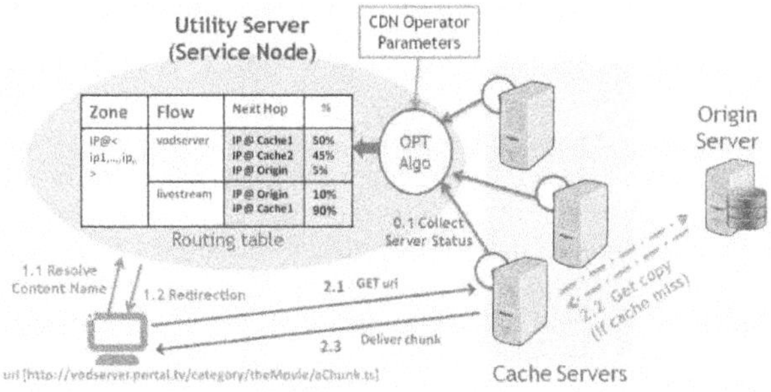

Figure 1: Overview

2. REQUEST ROUTING MODEL AND ALGORITHM

We consider a typical architecture for content delivery as depicted in Figure 1. Initial requests from users are resolved by the CDN service node and a redirection mechanism (DNS-based or HTTP-based, for instance) are used to provide the user host with the relevant cache server to contact. If the content is not available at the cache server, it is retrieved from an upper layer cache or origin server.

In our model, we use a routing table at the CDN service node level to resolve user requests. In our routing table, the clients requests are aggregated according to two criteria: *(i)* user location, and *(ii)* content type. The location plays a key role in reducing the content delivery delay, and is the main parameter used in request routing [5]. The content type characterizes traffic flows, which are classified according to the content provider catalog.

For each input, the routing table provides the most suitable cache servers with specific weights, i.e. the proportion of such requests that each cache server should receive. Our main contribution is the design of an on-line method to update the routing table on runtime (select cache servers and define related weights for each entry). Our multi-objective algorithm, based on Lyapunov optimization theory [4], operates following a slotted time. At the beginning of each time slot, the algorithm uses received inputs in order to compute the new routing table. These inputs are related to both network and cache server status, such as: Average round trip time between clients and cache servers, server loads, hit ratio per flow, etc. Then, the algorithm is composed of two processes.

The first one is a stability process that ensures: *(i)* a continuous service, *(ii)* non-overloaded cache servers, and

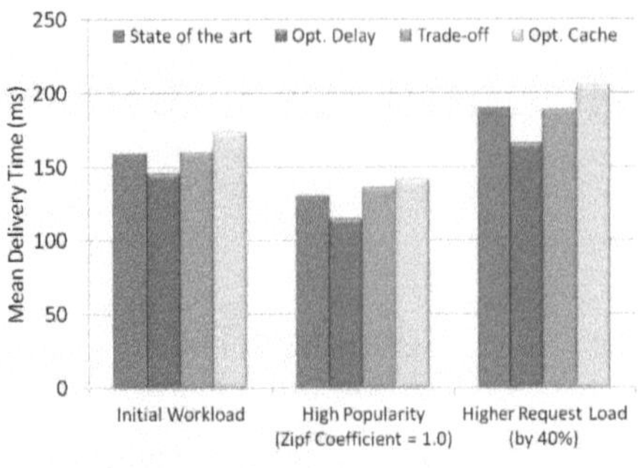

Figure 2: Comparison of average delivery delays using different workloads

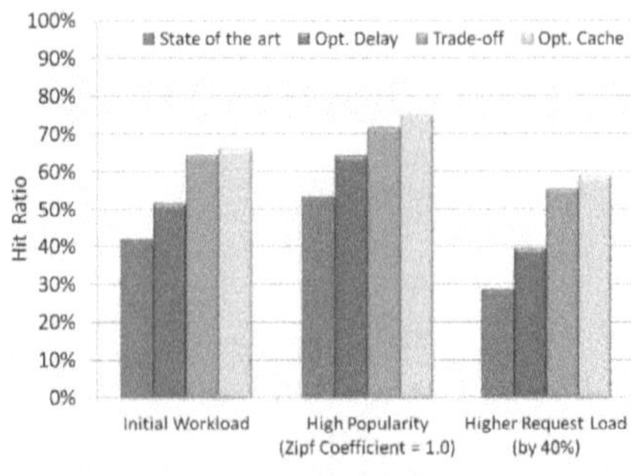

Figure 3: Hit ratio comparison

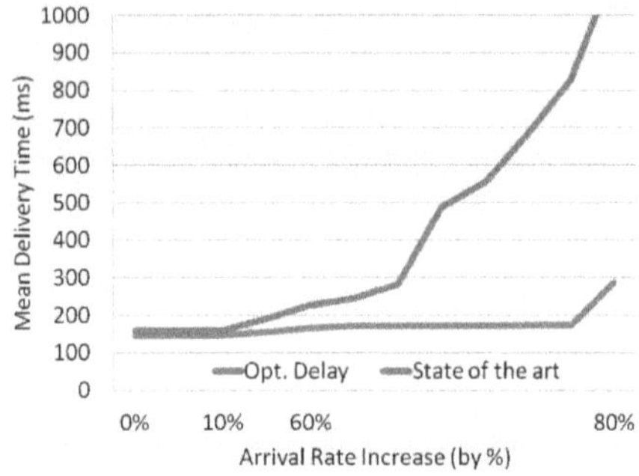

Figure 4: Impact of (increasing) flash crowd rates on delivery delays

(iii) a bounded delivery delay. We use a stochastic model to characterize the system. For every geographical zone i, the clients requests A_i are aggregated according to the type of requested content m into queues: Q_i^m. An allocation to cache servers (the routing table) is noted $U_{i,j}^m$, with j representing each cache. To ensure a continuous service, a relevant allocation will reduce the backlog at all the queues Q. Then, the two other constraints can be represented using virtual queues where, instead of the user requests, the load at each cache server and the average delay of all requests are stabilized. The stability process try to find an opportunistic allocation using the Lyapunov drift minimization techniques[4].

The second process is an optimization one aiming to reduce the delivery costs by increasing the hit ratio at the intermediate cache servers. A high hit ratio (cache efficiency) reduces origin server solicitation and network traffic. The optimization process uses the information related to the hit ratio H_j^m per flow m to direct requests to the cache server j with the highest hit ratio for that flow. The objective function to maximize is: $F = \sum_j \sum_m (H_j^m \times \sum_i (U_{i,j}^m))$

A parameter V is used to characterize the weight (importance) of the optimization process in the allocation scheme. For small values of V, the algorithm privileges the stability process, reducing delivery delays. A high value of V lead to cost optimization, increasing the hit ratio.

3. PERFORMANCE EVALUATION

The performance of our algorithm is evaluated using three targets depicting potential operator objectives: *(i)* optimize delivery delays ($V = 0.15$), *(ii)* optimize cache efficiency ($V = 1.0$), as well as *iii)* a trade-off strategy ($V = 0.55$). A real workload captured from a North American operator CDN was used for evaluations. The network and CDN topologies from this operator are also used. Then, based on the real workload, synthetic ones have been created in order to complete the evaluation by testing alternative conditions. This is done by increasing the content popularity parameter (Zipf's law) and the request load (locally or globally). The obtained results are compared with the best ones from several state of the art solutions that are used in practice.

Figures 2 and 3 assess and compare the delivery efficiency (average delay) and the caching efficiency (hit ratio) for different workloads. The results demonstrate the performance gains brought by our solution, as well as the effectiveness of the multi-objective optimization (performance target).

One of the main advantages of our solution is that it best uses the available resources in order to stabilize the quality of service, even under high request rates. In other terms, it allows reaching the limits of the CDN capacity. Figure 4 demonstrate this by showing the effect of request arrival rate growth on the average delivery delay. Under high pressure, our stability process tends to minimize the miss ratio in order to keep a lower load at all caches and origins. This ensures a good quality of service, while state of the art solutions show very high delivery delays (instability).

4. REFERENCES

[1] A. Barbir, B. Cain, R. Nair, and O. Spatscheck. Known content network (cn) request-routing mechanisms. IETF RFC 3568, 2003.

[2] W. Jiang, S. Ioannidis, L. Massoulié, and F. Picconi. Orchestrating massively distributed cdns. In *ACM International conference on Emerging networking experiments and technologies (CoNEXT)*, 2012.

[3] V. Mathew, R. K. Sitaraman, and P. Shenoy. Energy-aware load balancing in content delivery networks. In *IEEE INFOCOM Conference*, 2012.

[4] M. J. Neely. *Stochastic Network Optimization with Application to Communication and Queueing Systems.* Morgan & Claypool, 2010.

[5] L. Wang, V. Pai, and L. Peterson. The effectiveness of request redirection on cdn robustness. *ACM SIGOPS Operating Systems Review*, 36:345–360, 2002.

[6] P. Wendell and M. J. Freedman. Going viral: flash crowds in an open cdn. In *ACM Internet Measurement Conference (IMC)*, 2011.

Short vs. Long Flows: A Battle That Both Can Win

Morteza Kheirkhah, Ian Wakeman and George Parisis
School of Engineering and Informatics
University of Sussex, UK
{m.kheirkhah, ianw, g.parisis}@sussex.ac.uk

ABSTRACT

In this paper, we introduce MMPTCP, a novel transport protocol which aims at unifying the way data is transported in data centres. MMPTCP runs in two phases; initially, it randomly scatters packets in the network under a single congestion window exploiting all available paths. This is beneficial to latency-sensitive flows. During the second phase, MMPTCP runs in Multi-Path TCP (MPTCP) mode, which has been shown to be very efficient for long flows. Initial evaluation shows that our approach significantly improves short flow completion times while providing high throughput for long flows and high overall network utilisation.

CCS Concepts

•**Networks** → **Data center networks; Transport protocols;** *Network performance analysis;* Network simulations;

Keywords

Data Center; Multi-Path TCP; Packet Scatter; ns-3

1. INTRODUCTION

Modern data centres [1, 3] provide very high aggregate bandwidth and multiple paths among servers. They support a large number of services which produce very diverse intra-data centre traffic matrices. Long flows are bandwidth hungry, while short ones commonly come with strict deadlines regarding their completion time. It has been shown that TCP is ill-suited for both types of traffic in modern data centres, where ECMP [4] is used to exploit the availability of multiple equal-cost paths. Under high load, long flows collide with high probability and, as a result, network utilisation significantly drops and only 10% of the flows achieve their expected throughput [6]. TCP is also inefficient for short flows, especially when competing with long flows. Queue build-ups, buffer pressure and TCP Incast combined with the shared-memory nature of data centre switches results in short TCP flows missing their deadlines mainly due to retransmission timeouts (RTOs) [2].

To cope with these challenges, several transport protocols have been recently proposed. DCTCP [2], D2TCP [7] and D3 [8] aim at minimising flow completion times for latency-sensitive flows. However, they require modifications in the network and/or deadline-awareness at the application layer. Such modifications are problematic because such information may not be known a priori (i.e. at connection time). More importantly, all of these protocols are single-path and thus cannot exploit the multipath potential of data centre networks. Multipath transport protocols, such as Multi-Path TCP [6], transport data using multiple sub-flows and rely on ECMP to achieve higher aggregated throughput over multiple paths. As shown in [6], MPTCP improves the overall network utilisation. However, MPTCP hurts short flows as the number of sub-flows increases. The congestion window of a sub-flow may be very small over the sub-flow lifetime and, as a result, even a single lost packet can force an entire connection to wait for an RTO to be triggered because the lost packet cannot be recovered through fast retransmission. This is clearly illustrated in Figure 1(a)[1], where the mean flow completion time of short flows increases as more sub-flows are used (better shown in the embedded Figure in Figure 1(a)). Note that the number of connections that experience one or more RTOs significantly increases as well, hence the increase in the standard deviation. Even a single RTO may result in flow deadline violation.

Supporting and running multiple transport protocols in a data centre can be problematic. Fairness among different protocols is difficult to achieve; most protocols for latency-sensitive flows are not compatible with TCP or MPTCP [2, 7]. Running multiple transport protocols is also a burden for application developers who would have to decide upon the most suitable transport protocol. Both application requirements and data centre topologies evolve over time and so a transport protocol that performs well over disparate topologies and traffic matrices is a necessity.

In this paper, we introduce MMPTCP, a transport protocol that aims at unifying data transport within data centres. MMPTCP objectives are: (1) high throughput for large flows, (2) low latency for short flows, and (3) tolerance to sudden and high bursts of traffic, all without application-layer information (e.g. flow size and deadline). Co-existence in harmony with TCP and MPTCP flows is also an objective. Data transport takes place in two phases. Initially, packets are randomly scattered in the network under a sin-

[1]All simulations are based on our custom implementation of MPTCP and MMPTCP in ns-3 [5]

SIGCOMM '15 August 17-21, 2015, London, United Kingdom

ACM ISBN 978-1-4503-3542-3/15/08.
DOI: http://dx.doi.org/10.1145/2785956.2790018

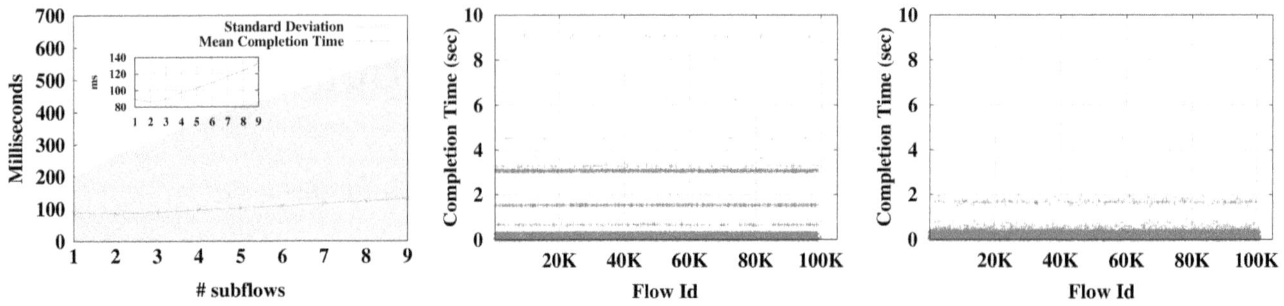

(a) MPTCP (b) MPTCP (8 subflows) (c) MMPTCP (PS and 8 subflows)

Figure 1: Short flow completion times in a simulated 4:1 over-subscribed FatTree topology consisting of 512 servers. One third of the servers run long (background) flows. The rest run short flows (70KBs each) which are scheduled according to a Poisson process). All flows are scheduled based on a permutation traffic matrix.

gle TCP congestion window exploiting all available paths. Most, if not all, short flows are expected to complete before switching to the second phase, during which, MMPTCP runs as standard MPTCP, efficiently handling long flows.

2. MMPTCP DESIGN

Packet Scatter (PS) Phase. The PS protocol applicability to data centre networks has been briefly explored in [6], where it has been shown that it can eliminate network congestion at the network core. In our approach packet scattering is initiated at the end hosts through source port randomisation. Network switches then forward packets to all available paths employing hash-based ECMP. The main challenge here is the graceful handling of out-of-order packets. We are currently exploring the following approaches: (1) Dynamically assigning the duplicate ACK threshold using topology-specific information. For example, FatTree's IP addressing scheme can be exploited to calculate the number of available paths between the sender and receiver. Other data centre topologies, such as VL2, incorporate centralised components which can provide similar information. (2) Alternatively, approaches such as RR-TCP [9] could be used to minimise spurious retransmissions when out-of-order packets are misidentified as lost.

Phase Switching. Switching to MPTCP at the right time is crucial to ensuring that short flows complete very fast (before switching), while long flows are not hurt by running with a single congestion window for long. We are currently investigating two switching strategies. *(1) Data Volume:* Switching occurs when a certain amount of data has been transmitted. Early evaluation suggests that this approach does not exert any negative effects on the throughput of long flows since the opening of multiple sub-flows after switching can wrap up access link capacity in a few RTTs. *(2) Congestion Event:* Switching occurs when congestion is first inferred (i.e. when fast retransmission or an RTO is triggered).

MPTCP Phase. When the switching threshold is reached, MMPTCP initiates a number of sub-flows and data transport is governed by MPTCP's congestion control. No more packets are put in the initial PS flow which is deactivated when its window gets emptied.

3. DISCUSSION AND FUTURE WORK

Figures 1(b) and 1(c) depict the flow completion times for all short flows in a simulated FatTree topology (see Figure 1 caption for details of the simulation setup). It is clear that with MPTCP (1(b)) a lot more short flows experience one or more RTOs leading to very high completion times, compared to MMPTCP (1(c)). During the packet scatter phase, MMPTCP utilises all available paths to distribute packets to receivers, while using a single congestion window, gracefully handling sudden bursts. Note that the majority of short flows completed within 100ms. The average flow completion time and the standard deviation for MMPTCP and MPTCP are 116 milliseconds (standard deviation is 101) and 126 milliseconds (standard deviation is 425), respectively.

Roadmap. Using our custom ns-3 models for MPTCP and MMPTCP, we are currently simulating several data centre topologies, comparing MMPTCP to other transport protocols in a wide range of network scenarios (e.g. effect of hotspots, network loads, traffic matrices and phase switching strategies). We also plan to design multi-homed network topologies as these are well-suited to MMPTCP. The more parallel paths at the access layer, the higher the burst tolerance; hence, potentially, preventing transient congestion.

We expect that MMPTCP will be readily deployable in existing data centres as it can coexist with other transport protocols. In-depth investigation of how MMPTCP shares network resources with TCP and MPTCP is part of our current work. Early results suggest that it could co-exist in harmony with them. MMPTCP requires ECMP, which is deployed in all data centres, and doesn't rely on any changes in the network or any application-layer information.

4. REFERENCES

[1] M. Al-Fares et al. A Scalable, Commodity Data Center Network Architecture. In *Proc. of SIGCOMM 2008*.

[2] M. Alizadeh et al. Data Center TCP (DCTCP). In *Proc. of SIGCOMM 2010*.

[3] A. Greenberg et al. VL2: A Scalable and Flexible Data Center Network. In *Proc. of SIGCOMM 2011*.

[4] C. Hopps. Analysis of an equal-cost multi-path algorithm. RFC 3782, 2004.

[5] M. Kheirkhah et al. Multipath TCP model in ns-3. In WNS3 2014, https://github.com/mkheirkhah/mptcp.

[6] C. Raiciu et al. Improving Datacenter Performance and Robustness with Multipath TCP. In *Proc. of SIGCOMM 2011*.

[7] B. Vamanan et al. Deadline-aware Datacenter TCP (D2TCP). In *Proc. of SIGCOMM 2010*.

[8] C. Wilson et al. Better Never than Late: Meeting Deadlines in Datacenter Networks. In *Proc. of SIGCOMM 2011*.

[9] M. Zhang et al. RR-TCP: A Reordering-Robust TCP with DSACK. In *Proceedings of ICNP 2003*.

Extreme Data-rate Scheduling for the Data Center

Neelakandan Manihatty Bojan, Noa Zilberman, Gianni Antichi, and Andrew W. Moore
Computer Laboratory, University of Cambridge
firstname.lastname@cl.cam.ac.uk

CCS Concepts

•Networks → Bridges and switches; Hybrid networks; Data center networks; •Hardware → Programmable logic elements; Emerging optical and photonic technologies;

Keywords

Data center networks; Optical networks; Switching; Scheduling

1. INTRODUCTION

Designing scalable and cost-effective data center interconnect architectures based on electrical packet switches (EPS) is very challenging [3]. Researchers have tried to explore optics and its advantages (in terms of bandwidth scaling, transmission speed, energy efficiency etc.) to address the challenges in data center environment [2]. This has resulted in various hybrid switching architectures [2, 5] for data centers, wherein an optical circuit switch (OCS) is used alongside an EPS. The OCS is used to serve long bursts of traffic and the EPS is used to serve the remaining traffic and short bursts.

The performance of the hybrid switching architecture depends on its scheduler [4]. The scheduler estimates demand based on the incoming traffic, computes switch configuration and maps the traffic on to either the EPS or OCS in a optimal fashion. Existing software based schedulers [2, 5] lack the speed and flexibility to cope with the faster switching technologies and increasing network demands [3]. Slow schedulers can negatively impact the performance of the data center network due to poor resource utilization. As networking requirements increase, the above problem is going to escalate, motivating the need for faster and scalable schedulers. One approach to do this would be to use a hardware based scheduler. We argue that the first step to achieve a good hybrid-switch scheduler is to have a framework for fast prototyping and evaluation of new hardware-based switch schedulers.

SIGCOMM '15 August 17-21, 2015, London, United Kingdom

ACM ISBN 978-1-4503-3542-3/15/08.

DOI: http://dx.doi.org/10.1145/2785956.2790019

2. MOTIVATION

With increasing data rates and emerging fast optical switching technologies [3][1], software based scheduling can no longer sustain the requirements (i.e., fast demand estimation and efficient schedules computation) of hybrid networks. Software based schedulers used in hybrid switching architectures [2, 5] operate in the order of milliseconds due to their inherent latency (delays during demand estimation, schedule calculation, Input/Output (IO) processing, propagation delay between host and switch). Software based schedulers also requires tight synchronization between the host and switch, which is difficult to achieve at faster switching times and higher transmission rates [3].

The optical switching time is the time taken by the optical device to configure its input and output ports based on the schedule, so that the incoming optical signals (packets) can be routed towards their destination. During the switching time (which can vary from nanoseconds to milliseconds based on its construction), no packets can be sent through the switch and hence need to be buffered.

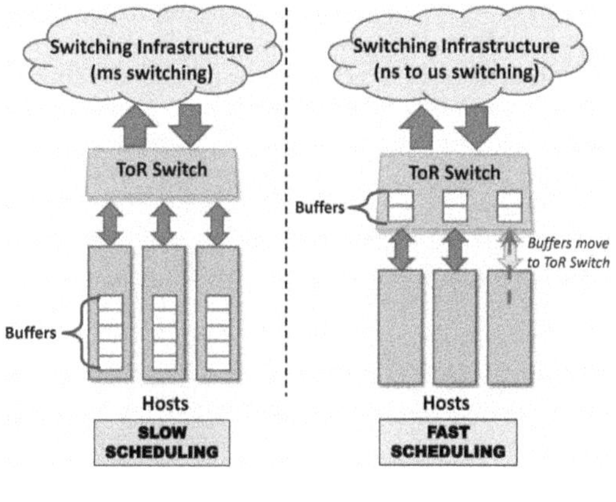

Figure 1: Host buffering vs Switch buffering

As an example, a switching infrastructure containing 64x64 input-queued switch (operating at a rate of 10 Gbps per port) with a millisecond switching time results in approximately gigabytes of buffering memory requirement in order to sustain bursts of traffic without losses. Such an amount of memory was not available in the Top of Rack (ToR) switches, forcing packets to be stored at the hosts (Figure 1, Slow Scheduling). As a result, packets stored in the host can be passed to the switch only at appropriate times, upon a grant from the scheduler. This increases design complexity, end-to-end latency, and forces tight synchronization requirements between hosts and the switch. This can increase the overall traffic latency and jitter of widely used applications (i.e., VOIP, multiuser gaming etc.) and decrease the user quality of experience. As we move towards faster switching times, memory requirements diminish. Under the same configuration, a nanosecond switching time requires only kilobytes of buffering memory. This enables buffering packets directly in the ToR switch (see Figure 1, Fast Scheduling) and would remove issues relating to synchronization between the host and switch, thereby decreasing design complexity.

The scheduler is a key element that determines the performance of the data center network. With the availability of fast optical switches [3, 1] and increasing network demands, rapid scheduling is a necessity and not an option. Compared to its software counterparts, hardware based schedulers can match the speeds of fast optical switches and can be quick in responding to the dynamically varying network demand. This is inherent due to their hardware design: allowing quick demand estimation, fast schedule computation and rapid communication of computed schedules to the switch.

3. PROPOSED DESIGN

In the previous section we motivated the need for hardware based schedulers. Hardware may not be fast by default, but with proper implementation fast, high performance operation can be achieved. To this aim, we argue that the path towards the design and implementation of an optimal hardware scheduler requires a flexible framework for rapid prototyping, exploration and evaluation of novel hybrid schedulers. We aim to prototype the framework using a reconfigurable platform, NetFPGA-SUME [6]. The NetFPGA-SUME platform was designed for data center research, and enables the evaluation of new designs under real traffic workloads and with comparable performance.

We partition our design into processing logic, switching logic and scheduling logic as shown in Figure 2. The processing logic and switching logic are part of the infrastructure that is constant (yet configurable), and the users implement novel design in the scheduling logic module. Incoming packets from hosts H1, H2, .., Hn are sent to the processing logic. There, packets are classified into flows based on configurable look-up rules and places them into their respective Virtual Ouput Queue (VOQ). As the status of a VOQ changes, the subsystem generates scheduling requests and transmits packets upon receiving transmission grants from the scheduling logic. The scheduling logic processes the incoming requests, estimates the demand matrix, and runs the scheduling algorithm, generating corresponding transmission grants. Before providing a grant to the processing logic, the scheduler sends the grant matrix to the switching logic to configure the circuits in the OCS to match the grant matrix. Once the grant message is received by the processing logic, it dequeues packets from the respective VOQ and sends them to the OCS (that has already been configured according to the grant matrix) to be delivered to the respective destination. Based on the scheduling mechanism, residual traffic can be sent through the EPS. The scheme allows for multiple VOQs to be served at once, matching the port dimensions of the switching logic.

The design contains network interfaces, memory interfaces and various logical elements, omitted from the discussion for clarity. Individual partitions can be designed as separate entities and then integrated to realize a setup that emulates or uses commodity network devices. The resulting testbed enables us to explore scheduling architectures for hybrid switching, hybrid topologies for data center networks, synchronization issues, scalability and latency requirements in heterogeneous networks etc. It also allows to detect and analyse transient effects that may not be visible under simulation environments. The proposed architecture has the advantage of supporting both centralized and distributed implementations. A large testbed can be assembled, using tens of processing elements, a centralized scheduling entity and a commercial OCS. This implementation also allows to explore SDN practices over the hybrid network.

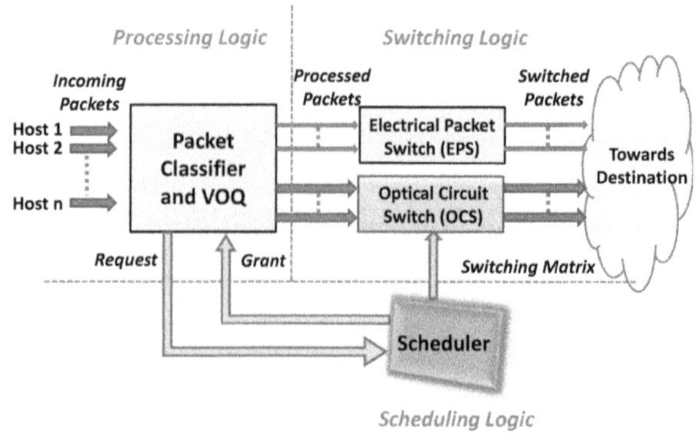

Figure 2: Proposed implementation

4. CONCLUSION

This paper motivates the need for hardware based schedulers in hybrid switches in order to meet emerging data center requirements. We have shown the main drawbacks that arise when using software based schedulers. We argue that the first step to achieve an optimal hybrid switch scheduler is to have a framework for rapid prototyping and assessment of new hardware-based scheduling algorithms. Finally, we show the architecture of the proposed framework, serving as an enabler for new scheduling algorithms.

5. ACKNOWLEDGEMENTS

This project is supported by the EPSRC INTERNET Project EP/H040536/1.

6. REFERENCES

[1] Epiphotonics. Nano-second speed plzt switch. http://www.epiphotonics.com/products3.htm. Accessed: 2015-05-08.

[2] N. Farrington et al. Helios: A hybrid electrical/optical switch architecture for modular data centers. In *SIGCOMM*. ACM, 2010.

[3] H. Liu et al. Circuit switching under the radar with reactor. In *NSDI*. USENIX, 2014.

[4] C. Raffaelli et al. Evaluation of packet scheduling in hybrid optical/electrical switch. *Photonic Network Communications*, 2012.

[5] G. Wang et al. c-through: part-time optics in data centers. *SIGCOMM CCR*, 2010.

[6] N. Zilberman et al. NetFPGA SUME: Toward 100 Gbps as Research Commodity. *Micro*, 2014.

Alternative Trust Sources: Reducing DNSSEC Signature Verification Operations with TLS

Sean Donovan
Georgia Institute of Technology

Nick Feamster
Princeton University

Abstract

DNSSEC has been in development for 20 years. It provides for provable security when retrieving domain names through the use of a public key infrastructure (PKI). Unfortunately, there is also significant overhead involved with DNSSEC: verifying certificate chains of signed DNS messages involves extra computation, queries to remote resolvers, additional transfers, and introduces added latency into the DNS query path. We pose the question: is it possible to achieve practical security without always verifying this certificate chain if we use a different, outside source of trust between resolvers? We believe we can. Namely, by using a long-lived, mutually authenticated TLS connection between pairs of DNS resolvers, we suggest that we can maintain near-equivalent levels of security with very little extra overhead compared to a non-DNSSEC enabled resolver. By using a reputation system or probabilistically verifying a portion of DNSSEC responses would allow for near-equivalent levels of security to be reached, even in the face of compromised resolvers.

1 Introduction

DNSSEC is not a new technology; it has been in development since 1995, with the first RFC published in 1997. [3] Unfortunately, deployment has been slow but incremental due to, among other reasons, significant infrastructure investments needed to handle the overhead costs required to verify DNSSEC responses.

DNSSEC requires verification of a certificate signature chain in order to maintain security. There are fourfold costs. First are calculating the signatures. Fortunately, this cost is getting cheaper due to processor improvements and is not the focus of this paper. Second are the additional DNS query costs. In order to verify signatures, DNS resolvers must request additional signature-related DNS records from various servers on the certificate chain. Third are the additional bandwidth costs. There are additional DNSSEC-specific records contributing, but the extra queries are a bulk of the extra bandwidth needs. In one study, these two costs were estimated such that resolvers would need to be sized to "handle 10 times the query volume ... and a total response traffic volume of 100 times greater." [2] Finally, there are the latency costs for end hosts as the verification activities take non-trivial time.

These costs are significant, especially regarding equipment provisioning. We seek to reduce these costs by relying on an *outside source of trust* in place of signature verification. By using a different way of finding trust between DNSSEC-enabled resolvers, we can cut down on the amount of PKI verifications and further queries that are necessary for traditional DNSSEC.

SIGCOMM '15, August 17-21, 2015, London, United Kingdom
Copyright 2015 ACM 978-1-4503-3542-3/15/08
http://dx.doi.org/10.1145/2785956.2790001

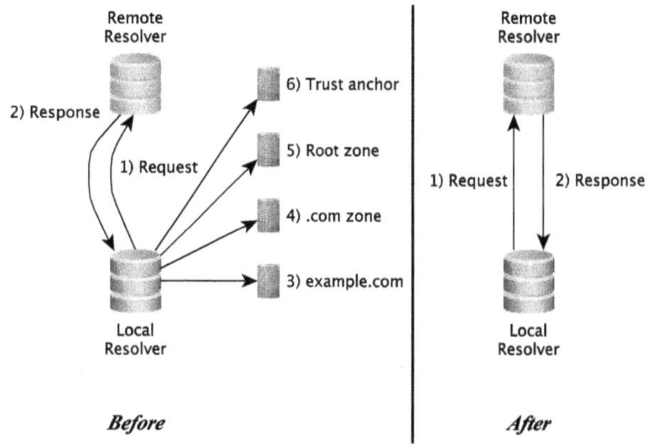

Figure 1: *Before, to verify the certificate chain that DNSSEC relies upon, many further requests for RRSIG and DS resources are necessary to verify signatures. With our proposal, there is a long-lived, mutually authenticated TLS connection between both resolvers that the requests and responses travel across. If the local resolver knows who is at the other end of the connection, and it trusts that the remote resolver has verified signatures, the local resolver should not need to verify the same signatures itself.*

2 Proposal

We want to reduce the overhead of the certificate chain verification in DNSSEC. By reducing the number of signature verifications that are necessary, we reduce the majority of overhead costs — queries, bandwidth, and latency — to near zero. [1]

To do this, we propose using a long-lived, mutually authenticated TLS connection between resolvers. With mutual authentication, both resolvers can provably show that they know who they are talking to. If one resolver trusts what the other resolver says, there should not be a need to re-verify the DNSSEC signature chain. This reduces the overhead to near zero, as there will only be DNSSEC verification if the remote resolver does not use our proposed trust mechanism.

There are two questions that are still left to answer. First, how do we know a DNSSEC resolver is trustworthy? Second, what if the remote resolver has been compromised? These are both variants of the same question: How can we show that the remote resolver is trustworthy? To solve this final problem, we have two solutions. The first solution is entirely internal to the resolver trying to establish trust: verifying a portion of the DNS responses from the remote resolver. If the local resolver verifies, say, 5% of all responses for validity, it probabilistically confirms that the remote resolver is trustworthy. This will reduce the amount of extra work (over

[1] DNS responses will remain larger due to the addition of DNSSEC signature records which are not present in vanilla DNS.

	PKI Ops.	Additional Queries
Traditional DNS	0	0
DNSSEC	N	$\sim 10N$
With Alt. Trust	1	0
5% Verified Alt. Trust	$1+\sim 0.05N$	$\sim 0.5N$

Table 1: *Expected overhead versus traditional DNS.* Alt. Trust *refers to our proposed solution without any additional verification.* 5% Verified Alt. Trust *refers to verifying 5% of "trusted" responses from other DNS resolver. Transfers are estimated as a factor of 10 over traditional DNS. [2]*

traditional DNS) by near 95%. This number can be adjusted up or down, depending on level of trust (or paranoia) that the administrator has in the operator of the remote resolver. One automated method would be to perform DNSSEC certificate chain verification on all responses at the beginning of a session, then slowly tapering down to a much lower level of only a few percent after a while without issue.

The second solution involves using a reputation system, which are typically external to a domain. If a large enough number of resolvers use the probabilistic system described above, a reputation system could be established by aggregating whether or not a particular resolver has "lied" and provided incorrect DNSSEC responses. Other resolvers that use the reputation system could tailor their verification strategy based on reputation of the remote resolver. For instance, one resolver that cares very strongly about security could verify any and all responses from resolvers that it uses, and report on the other resolvers' trustworthiness. A more security lax resolver may verify 50% of responses from resolvers with a "bad" reputation, but only 5% of responses from those with a "good" reputation, just to keep them honest and to report back to the reputation system.

These are two *classes* of solutions. There can be multiple different different versions, each tailored to different behaviors of malicious resolvers. Finding a middle ground to handle different types of behavior well, while reducing DNSSEC signature verification overhead is the main challenge.

There is a certificate chain verification cost when establishing a TLS connection, but it is a one-time cost, rather the constant recurrent cost like DNSSEC signature verifications. The overhead reductions can be seen in Table 1. The overhead reduction is primarily dependent on how much DNSSEC signature verification an administrator wants to use. It is also dependent on how long lived the TLS connections are. Perfect reduction is not possible while still maintaining reasonable security, if only because multiple connections may be needed for different remote resolvers.

3 Conclusion and Future Work

We have proposed using a long-lived, mutually authenticated TLS connection between two DNSSEC-enabled resolvers as an alternative source of trust in order to reduce the overhead of performing DNSSEC signature verification operations. We have shown that, while having potential security issues, we can mitigate compromised machines by probabilistically verifying DNSSEC responses to build trust.

This method is similar to how stub resolvers (*i.e.*, hosts) maintain DNSSEC guarantees. RFC 4033 specifically suggests using IPSEC to maintain security between the stub resolver and the recursive resolver. [1] Using TLS provides similar guarantees. Additionally, this method expands the ongoing work of the DNS privacy working group within the IETF from not only stub-to-recursive resolver connections, but between recursive resolvers. [4]

We have concerns about the use of long-lived connections between resolvers. This may not scale well and may introduce additional overhead. However, one proposed modification to DNS does exactly this: having DNS over a TLS connection between, recursive and authoritative resolvers as well as stub and recursive resolvers. [5] Combined with the DNS privacy working group work, optimistically, this may not be overhead in the near future.

As the security of this proposal hinges on the trustworthiness of the DNS resolver that a TLS connection is established with, our first course of action is to create and simulate our proposed solutions for establishing trust. While some scenarios could be represented by a Bayesian model, others lend themselves to simulation. In particular, as the probabilities for verification change based on previous input, simulation is easier for determining whether a a particular strategy for verification is effective.

These need not involve actual DNS resolution, rather these can be simulated in a much simpler environment. Some scenarios may be modeled using Bayes rules, but only if probabilities are known and consistent. Other scenarios have "moving parts" — such as changes in the probability of verification — where simulation is more appropriate. Finally, different behaviors of a malicious resolver can be more easily simulated, such as a resolver that only 'lies' about one particular domain and provides valid results for all others. Different strategies may be necessary for establishing trust depending on the adversary.

Further, we plan on implementing this scheme on an existing DNSSEC-enabled resolver, such as BIND or Unbound. We will then test this method for both practicality — verifying that there is a processing and network cost savings compared to verifying all DNSSEC messages — and security — by 'compromising' one resolver and seeing the response from the non-compromised resolver, specifically how long it takes to find that the one resolver is "lying".

Further, we see this alternative model of trust could be used in other scenarios. For instance, the various security schemes surrounding BGP (BGPSEC, S-BGP, RPKI, etc.) all rely on PKI verification, much like DNSSEC. This technique could be applied for similar savings with potentially different criteria for verification, such as for any prefixes being announced by autonomous systems (ASes) known to host malware.

This is not a method for absolute security, like DNSSEC is aiming for, rather this is for practical security with low overhead. It can be used to alleviate scalability concerns particularly on a closed network where all DNS resolvers are controlled by the same organization. It is also useful for an organization that has less strict security requirements but wants to benefit from DNSSEC with lower cost.

References

[1] R. Arends, R. Austein, M. Larson, D. Massey, and S. Rose. DNS Security Introduction and Requirements. RFC 4033 (Proposed Standard), Mar. 2005. Updated by RFCs 6014, 6840.

[2] G. Huston. Measuring dnssec performance. `https://labs.apnic.net/?p=341`, 2013. Accessed 2015-04-21.

[3] NLnet Labs. A short history of dnssec. `http://www.nlnetlabs.nl/projects/dnssec/history.html`, 2013. Accessed 2015-04-28.

[4] T. Reddy, D. Wing, and P. Patil. Dns over dtls (dnsod) internet draft. `https://tools.ietf.org/html/draft-ietf-dprive-dnsodtls-01`, 2015. Accessed 2015-06-23.

[5] L. Zhu, Z. Hu, J. Heidemann, D. Wessels, A. Mankin, and N. Somaiya. Connection-oriented dns to improve privacy and security. 2015.

A Case for a Stateful Middlebox Networking Stack

Muhammad Jamshed, Donghwi Kim, YoungGyoun Moon,
Dongsu Han, and KyoungSoo Park
Department of Electrical Engineering, KAIST

1. INTRODUCTION

Statful middleboxes such as intrusion detection systems, application-layer firewalls, and protocol analyzers are increasingly popular as they perform critical operations in modern networks. Such middleboxes typically operate by maintaining flow states of live TCP connections that pass through a network.

Despite its growing demand, developing a stateful middlebox remains a challenging task. The root of complexity stems from a lack of common programming abstraction for middleboxes that clearly separates flow management from custom middlebox logic. As a result, middlebox developers often resort to writing a complex flow management module from scratch, which results in tens of thousands of code lines that are hardly portable [4, 2]. This is in stark contrast to developing networking applications for end nodes, which significantly benefits from a nice network abstraction layer such as Berkeley socket API. The lack of a reusable networking stack for middleboxes makes the code highly dependent on a custom packet library, which greatly reduces readability, modularity, and extensibility.

In this work, we formulate a general-purpose flow management stack that serves the basic requirements of *monitoring* middlebox applications. The flow management stack should satisfy three requirements. First, it should abstract TCP state management such that the developers can focus on the custom middlebox processing instead of dealing with low level detail. Clear separation of flow management and a custom middlebox logic is the key to high code readability and modularity. Second, it should be flexible enough to express any packet or flow-level event that triggers a special middlebox operation. An event can be as simple as TCP state change or packet retransmission. Or one should be able to extend a basic event by evaluating an arbitrary function (e.g., retransmitted packet whose content is different from the original packet). A flexible event-based system enables a developer to write a middlebox application as a set of logical middlebox events and their event handlers. Third, the flow management stack should allow efficient resource management. Depending on the needs of a middlebox, a developer might want to avoid the flow reassembly on the server side while she actively monitors the flow content from the client side. Or one should be able to deallocate all resources for a flow even if the flow has not terminated yet.

SIGCOMM'15, August 17–21, 2015, London, United Kingdom.

ACM ISBN 978-1-4503-3542-3/15/08..

DOI: http://dx.doi.org/10.1145/2785956.2789999

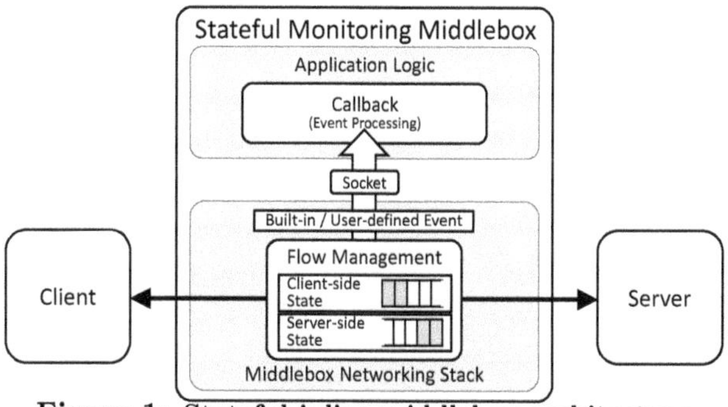

Figure 1: Stateful inline middlebox architecture.

Based on the requirements, we build our networking API for stateful middleboxes based on mTCP [3], a highly-scalable user-level TCP implementation. The mTCP stack serves as the underlying flow management module while we place a number of hooks in flow processing to support basic and extended events. The resulting implementation enables modular middlebox development with high performance.

2. OPERATION MODEL

Figure 1 provides an overview of our middlebox networking stack architecture. The networking stack monitors TCP flows passing through the middlebox, and exposes a socket that abstracts each flow to the application. The application developer defines a set of middlebox events and registers event handlers (or callbacks) that perform custom middlebox logic. When an event handler is called, it is passed a socket for the flow that raised the event, and the application can probe the flow state through our middlebox socket API.

For flow management in the middlebox, each TCP flow context should track both client- and server-side TCP states. This is because a middlebox could act on either the client- or server-side state or both. For example, an IDS could monitor a client-side TCP state transition (e.g., `ESTABLISHED` to `FIN_WAIT_1`) or inspect the data from a server. For efficient resource usage, our stack allows the developer to disable the state management of either side on a per-flow basis.

An event is the critical abstraction in our networking stack, which represents a condition for specific middlebox operation. An event can be either a built-in or a user-defined event (UDE). A built-in event is raised by the flow management module when a certain pre-defined condition is met. For example, a built-in event is generated when a new connection is established or torn down, new data is available in a socket buffer, the TCP state is changed, a new packet arrives, or a packet is retransmitted. A developer can register a handler for a built-in event or can define her own UDE based on a built-in event. That is, a new event can be defined by a built-in event and a custom function that further determines the condition for the event. In short, the user can express a variety of custom events for middlebox processing without dealing with any low level detail.

3. SAMPLE CODE

```
1 static void // callback for SYN retransmission
2 on_syn_rexmit(ctx_t ctx, int sock, int side,
3                event_t e) {
4        static uint64_t syn_retx = 0;
5        syn_retx++;
6 }
7
8 static bool // user-defined SYN filter
9 ft_syn(ctx_t ctx, int sock, int side,
10        event_t e, event_data_t data) {
11       struct pkt_ctx p;
12       // get the current packet context
13       mtcp_cb_getcurpkt(ctx, &p);
14       return (p.tcph->syn && !p.tcph->ack);
15 }
16
...............................................
17
18 // create an UDE for SYN retransmission
19 // it's defined as ON_REXMIT and ft_syn
20 ude_syn = mtcp_define_ude(ON_REXMIT, ft_syn);
21
22 // open a monitoring socket
23 msock = mtcp_socket(ctx, AF_INET,
24                   SOCK_MONITOR_STREAM_PASSIVE, 0);
25
26 // register a callback for ude_syn
27 mtcp_register_callback(ctx, msock, ude_syn,
28                            PRE_TCP, on_syn_rexmit);
```

Listing 1: Sample code that counts # of TCP SYN retransmissions (error checking is omitted)

Listing 1 shows sample code that counts the number of TCP SYN retransmissions for the flows that traverse the middlebox. Due to the space constraint, we explain only the main logic of the code. Line 1 to line 15 show how a callback function and a filter function are defined, which are then used in the later code. In line 20, the code defines a user-defined event (**ude_syn**) that detects retransmitted SYN packets. The UDE is based on a built-in event, **ON_REXMIT**, which is raised by the system when a packet in a TCP flow is retransmitted. **ude_syn** extends the built-in event by a filter function, **ft_syn()**, that determines if the retransmitted packet is a SYN packet. If the filter function returns TRUE registered callback function is invoked to process the event. In line 23, a generic monitoring socket (**msock**) is created. By default, it monitors all TCP flows passing through the middlebox unless the monitoring scope is limited by **mtcp_bind_monitor()**. In line 27, a callback function (**on_syn_rexmit**) is registered for **ude_syn** with the montoring socket. **PRE_TCP** in the function parameter requires that the event should be raised before updating the middlebox TCP state for the flow.

4. PRELIMINARY EVALUATION

We are currently porting popular middlebox applications to our framework. in The preliminary results look promising.

Scalability & Composability: We evaluate the robustness of our system in a testbed that consists of four sets of web client/server machines and an inline network toy web monitor (an Intel Xeon E5-2697 14-core machine with 64 GB RAM) that counts the number of ongoing connections. We test the performance under two scenarios. One monitoring socket is tested without TCP management while the other is used to monitor flows without payload inspection (per-packet processing = without TCP semantics; per-flow processing = TCP sockets without deep payload inspection capability). As the Figure 2 evaluation graph suggests, our toy monitor

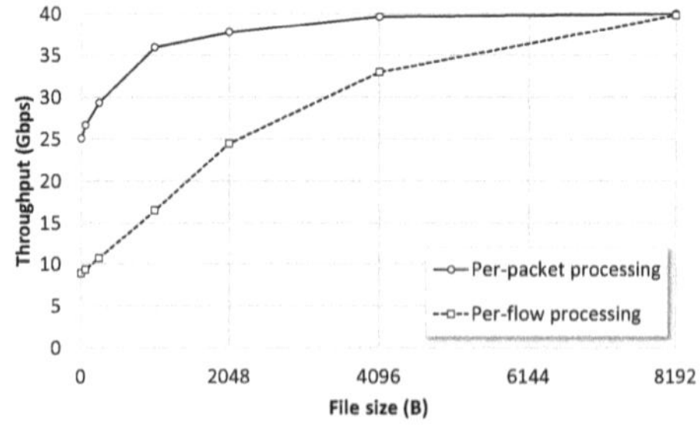

Figure 2: Monitor Performance (HTTP GET 16K reqs/s)

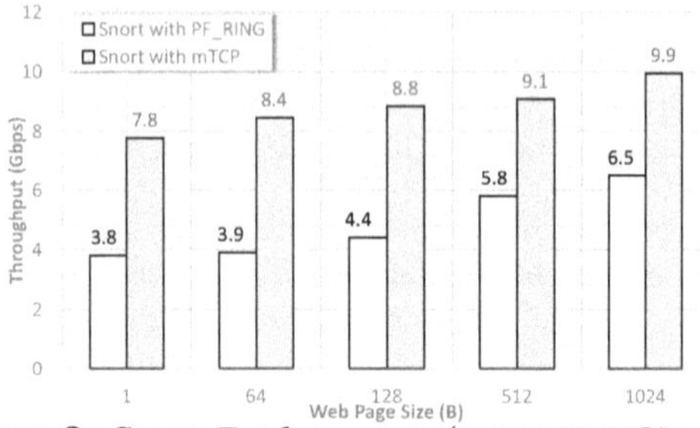

Figure 3: Snort Performance (HTTP GET 16K reqs/s)

can withstand analyzing rates of up to 40 Gbps for 8KB web pages while it can manage flows at a rate of at least 10 Gbps for small file sizes.

Improved abstraction: We have partially ported Snort [4], a popular open-source signature-based network security monitor. We replace around 8,000 lines of source code with only 799 lines to support Snort's default TCP stream management module. At the moment, our version skips some elaborate checks such as segment overlapping and connection anomaly checks (*e.g.* arrival of TCP SYN packet on an already established connection). Our porting process has substantially simplfied the core framework since the new code focuses on pattern matching rather than flow management. We evaluate the performance of our stack by generating innocent client/server web request/response pages for varying file sizes in the same testbed with around 3,000 HTTP Snort attack signatures. For comparison, we also perform the same test with default Snort setup with PF_RING [1] I/O driver. Figure 3 shows that our version outperforms the I/O-optimized Snort by a factor of 1.5 to 2.2.

Enhanced monitoring capabilities: Some security monitors (such as Snort and Suricata) analyze flows against elaborate reassembling routines for examining payload spanning several successive TCP segments. These routines are usually employed to detect attack patterns in malicious flows. Our stack provides user-friendly APIs that make development of such routines much simpler in practice.

5. ACKNOWLEDGEMENT

This work was supported by the ICT R&D program of MSIP/IITP, Republic of Korea [14-911-05-001, Development of an NFV-inspired networked switch and an operating system for multi-middlebox services].

6. REFERENCES

[1] PF_RING I/O Driver. http://www.ntop.org/products/pf_ring/.
[2] Suricata Open Source IDS. http://suricata-ids.org/.
[3] E. Jeong and et al. mTCP: a Highly Scalable User-level TCP Stack for Multicore Systems. In *NSDI*, 2014.
[4] M. Roesch. Snort - Lightweight Intrusion Detection for Networks. In *LISA*, 1999.

FreeSurf: Application-Centric Wireless Access with SDN

Zhen Cao
Leibniz Universität Hannover, Germany
zhen.cao@ikt.uni-hannover.de

Jürgen Fitschen
Leibniz Universität Hannover, Germany
mail@jfitschen.de

Panagiotis Papadimitriou
Leibniz Universität Hannover, Germany
panagiotis.papadimitriou@ikt.uni-hannover.de

CCS Concepts

•**Networks → Network architectures; Wireless access networks;**

Keywords

Wireless Networks; SDN; Authentication; Access Control

1. INTRODUCTION

The increasing need for ubiquitous Internet connectivity has led to the deployment of wireless access infrastructure, including public WiFi networks used for mobile data offloading. Despite the density of public WiFi hotspots especially in residential areas, these networks are severely underutilized, with an average of *ten percent* of active users and an average of *one connection per user per month* [1]. Since the revenue from the public WiFi infrastructure is much lower than the cellular counterpart, the operators seek opportunities to monetize their WiFi networks.

One such opportunity emerges from the intention of mobile application vendors to provide near-ubiquitous Internet access for their clients. In fact, the revenue and any potential business opportunities for mobile application vendors are highly dependent on the users' connection time. Therefore, both network operators and mobile application vendors have incentives to march together towards a ubiquitous WiFi for their clients. However, the traditional wireless architecture hinders any such opportunity, since it requires clients to subscribe and authenticate to the *operator* before establishing Internet access.

To overcome this limitation, we propose *application-centric wireless access*, at which Service Providers (SPs) can authenticate and connect their clients through public WiFi networks, free of charge. Application-centric wireless access requires the delegation of user authentication and access from the operator to the Service Provider (SP) in a secure and auditable manner. In particular, user authentication requests should be redirected to authentication servers deployed by SPs, while access control should be enabled such that only

SIGCOMM '15 August 17-21, 2015, London, United Kingdom

ACM ISBN 978-1-4503-3542-3/15/08.
DOI: http://dx.doi.org/10.1145/2785956.2790000

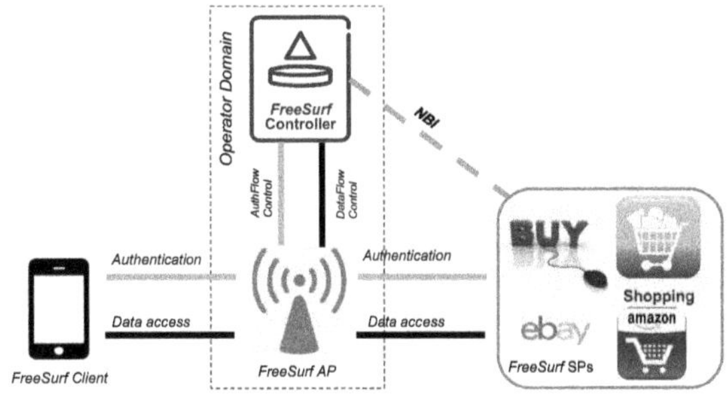

Figure 1: FreeSurf overview.

the traffic associated with the network service should be permitted.

In this paper, we present *FreeSurf*, an architecture that enables an application-centric wireless access service over existing public WiFi networks. FreeSurf leverages on software-defined networking (SDN) to provide open APIs for authentication request routing and access control. This enables SPs to install user authentication and data-flow forwarding policies on access points (APs), so that the SP: (i) can steer user authentication requests to its own authentication servers, bypassing the ones provided by the operator, and (ii) can permit the forwarding only of the authenticated data flows. In this respect, we present *AuthFlow* and a Bloom Filter [2] based lookup method for authentication request routing and policy-based forwarding in the AP, respectively.

2. FREESURF OVERVIEW

The major players involved in FreeSurf include the network operator, the SP, and the user. The network operator controls and manages the access points, their backhaul to the Internet, and the FreeSurf controller. The SP deploys the application and authentication servers. FreeSurf requires the following components:

FreeSurf Controller. The FreeSurf controller is responsible for the installation of authentication flow policies (*AuthFlow Control*, grey line in Fig. 1) and data forwarding policies (*DataFlow Control*, dark line in Fig. 1) on the AP. In addition, the controller provides a northbound interface for the SP to opt in.

FreeSurf Access Point. FreeSurf APs expose APIs to the controller for authentication and access control. The APs are configured to forward authentication requests to the SP's servers and provide Internet access only for the flows that have been authenticated.

FreeSurf Client. The FreeSurf client is authenticated and

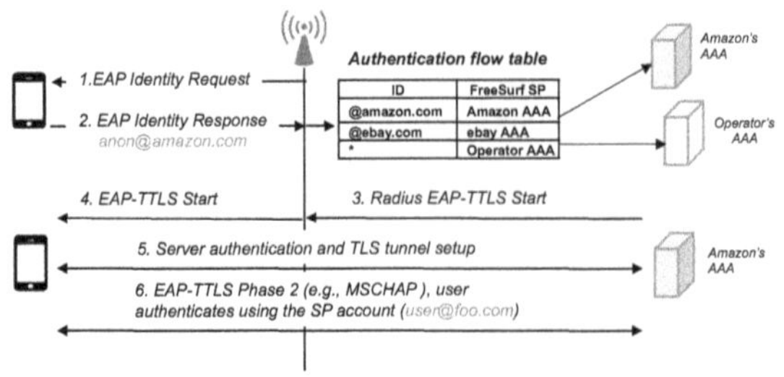

Figure 2: FreeSurf authentication.

establishes Internet access to run the application offered by the SP.

In the following, we discuss the main functions pertaining to application-centric wireless access with FreeSurf.

2.1 Authentication

In order to keep the client unmodified, FreeSurf authentication must be compatible with the EAP standard. Fig. 2 illustrates the authentication steps in FreeSurf. If the client wants to authenticate to a SP (*e.g.*, Amazon), FreeSurf specifies an anonymous id (*e.g.*, *anon@amazon.com*) in `msg` 2. This message is examined by the AP. The realm portion (*@amazon.com*) of this id is used to perform a lookup in the *authentication flow table*. Based on the lookup result, the authentication request is forwarded to the FreeSurf SP's Authentication, Authorization, and Accounting (AAA) server, initiating full authentication (*e.g.*, in Fig. 2 the Amazon AAA initiates an EAP-TTLS authentication (`msg 3-4`)). The server authenticates to the user first with a certificate (`msg 5`), and subsequently the user authenticates to the SP using its associated account name *alice@foo.com* and password (`msg 6`).

Since most applications allow users to choose any valid email address as account names (which cannot be used for the authentication server IP address resolution), FreeSurf authentication requires both an anonymous id and a full SP account name. The use of two authentication identities are supported by EAP-TTLS/PEAP/FAST standards and most mobile devices OSes. Therefore, FreeSurf authentication does not require any client device modifications.

The *authentication flow table* is configured by FreeSurf controllers, such that authentication requests are forwarded to the corresponding AAA server. A low-priority flow entry that matches every request message allows non-FreeSurf users to be authenticated to the Operator's AAA, as shown in Fig. 2.

2.2 Policy-Based Forwarding

After a successful authentication, the SP forwards to the controller the allowed set of destination addresses/ports and the controller, subsequently, installs the required entries to the AP's flow table. This ensures that only authenticated users will be able to access the service.

FreeSurf relies on OpenFlow to enforce SP's access control policy. We leverage on bloom filters (BF) [2] to accelerate the table lookup on the FreeSurf AP. BF brings two significant benefits to FreeSurf APs: (i) flow table compression, since the BF occupies K bits irrespective of the table size, and (ii) lookup performance does not degrade with the increase in the flow table size.

BF raises two issues, *i.e.*, flow entry deletion and false positives. We address them as follows. A flow entry can be removed using the counting BF (CBF), which stores a counter value rather than a bit in each slot. The counter is decreased when a flow is removed. As long as the counter is greater than zero, CBF will report a match. On the other hand, false positives can lead to wrong forwarding decisions. However, false positives do not comprise a serious implication for FreeSurf, since they occasionally allow FreeSurf clients to access other (non-FreeSurf) services.

2.3 Operation

Having discussed the main functional components, we outline the operation of FreeSurf. Initially, the FreeSurf controller installs the authentication flow entries in the AP. The client discovers the FreeSurf AP and starts the EAP authentication, using *e.g.*, *anon@amazon.com* as the user name. The FreeSurf AP forwards the authentication request to the SP's authentication server by performing a lookup in the *AuthFlow* table. Subsequently, the client is authenticated to the SP using his SP account.

After authentication has been completed, the SP forwards its data forwarding policy (*i.e.*, server IP addresses and ports) to the controller. This initiates the accounting session. The controller then installs the required entries to the AP's flow table. When the client initiates a connection with the SP's application servers, the AP performs policy-based forwarding, allowing the client to access the service. In this respect, any client's traffic that is not associated with the FreeSurf service is filtered by the AP.

3. PROTOTYPE AND EVALUATION

We have implemented a FreeSurf prototype using the following components [3]. The FreeSurf AP is built atop a Linux laptop with a USB wireless card. The AuthFlow API is implemented via a Python SSH file I/O. The controller invokes this API to change a local EAP user configuration file of *hostapd* (an open authenticator software) on the AP. This file contains the mapping between FreeSurf SP's realm name and its associated AAA address. On the arrival of client authentication requests, the AP examines the configuration file and forwards the requests to the respective AAA server.

We rely on OpenVSwitch for the OpenFlow data path implementation on the AP, while POX is used as the controller. In this respect, BF is implemented as a POX module. When OpenFlow table lookup does not yield a match, the AP sends a *packet-in* message to POX. Subsequently, POX uses the BF module to examine whether the packet belongs to the access list.

Our experimental results show that FreeSurf incurs a minimal inflation in the delay during authentication compared to non-FreeSurf APs (*i.e.*, 1.7% and 2.4% additional delay with EAP-TTLS and EAP-PEAP, respectively). Furthermore, BF-assisted table lookup reduces RTT by 2%–25% (compared to a non-BF POX module) with flow table size ranging from 1K to 9K entries. As our preliminary evaluation results indicate the feasibility of FreeSurf, future work will be focused on assessing the scalability of the system.

4. REFERENCES

[1] "Public wi-fi survey", http://bit.ly/1bkTAoD, 2013.

[2] A. Broder, et al. "Network applications of bloom filters: A survey", *Internet Mathematics*, Vol. 1, No. 4, 2003.

[3] https://www.github.com/rangzhi/freesurf.

EPOXIDE: A Modular Prototype for SDN Troubleshooting

Tamás Lévai, István Pelle[*], Felicián Németh, András Gulyás[†]
HSN Lab, Budapest University of Technology and Economics
{levait,pelle,nemethf,gulyas}@tmit.bme.hu

ABSTRACT

SDN opens a new chapter in network troubleshooting as besides misconfigurations and firmware/hardware errors, software bugs can occur all over the SDN stack. As an answer to this challenge the networking community developed a wealth of piecemeal SDN troubleshooting tools aiming to track down misconfigurations or bugs of a specific nature (e.g. in a given SDN layer). In this demonstration we present EPOXIDE, an Emacs based modular framework, which can effectively combine existing network and software troubleshooting tools in a single platform and defines a possible way of integrated SDN troubleshooting.

Keywords

SDN, Network troubleshooting; Debugging; Emacs

1. INTRODUCTION

SDN takes away some parts of the forwarding logic from traditional switching devices, but the complexity is now shared among the different layers of a (logically) centralized controller and (virtual) network functions. Finding causes of malfunctions in this heterogeneous distributed system is even more challenging than before. To address this challenge, lots of SDN troubleshooting tools (e.g., OFRewind, NetSight, VeriFlow, NICE, OFTEN, etc.) have been created that are able to investigate one aspect of the SDN architecture for specific errors, failures, misconfigurations, or bugs. Additionally, Heller *et al.* proposed a holistic approach [1] that systematically searches for bugs through different layers of the SDN architecture. Their troubleshooting process narrows down the possible causes by a series of hypothesis testing. In the general case, however, conforming a hypothesis requires an application specific method.

In this paper we present EPOXIDE, an Emacs based modular framework, which can flexibly combine network and software troubleshooting tools in a single platform. EPOXIDE does not try to be a complex troubleshooting software that fully integrates all available tools, but rather a lightweight framework that allows the ad-hoc creation of tailor-made testing methods from predefined building blocks to test troubleshooting hypotheses [2]. In the demonstration, we define automated hypotheses testers as *troubleshooting graphs* (TSG, see Fig. 1b and 1c for an example) by flexible linking of simple wrappers around traditional troubleshooting tools (ping, ipref, ovs-ofctl, etc.), but the framework allows the users to write wrappers to more complex SDN tools listed above. Defining a TSG in the high-level language of EPOXIDE is less error phone than, for example, writing shell scripts for similar tasks. The TSG definition is also useful to share common practice between network engineers. Moreover, EPOXIDE makes convenient to troubleshoot the troubleshooting process itself by allowing to inspect or alter the data flow between wrappers.

*MTA-BME Future Internet Research Group
†MTA-BME Information Systems Research Group

SIGCOMM '15 August 17-21, 2015, London, United Kingdom

ACM ISBN 978-1-4503-3542-3/15/08.
DOI: http://dx.doi.org/10.1145/2785956.2790027

2. ARCHITECTURE

EPOXIDE is an add-on package to the GNU Emacs text editor. Emacs is an ideal prototyping platform because of its many relevant features like efficient remote shell and powerful sub-process handling. Its main concept is the *buffer*, which is a universal data structure to store editable text and general variables. In Emacs everything is a buffer: opened files and interactive shells as well.

TSGs consist of nodes and links that can be defined using our Click-inspired language and stored in .tsg configuration files. Nodes are functional elements either implementing a wrapper for an external tool or written entirely in Emacs Lisp (like the Table-view node discussed later). Links connect nodes by relaying text data between them. The creation, execution and manipulation of TSGs are controlled by the framework that maps nodes and links to buffers and then helps the data distribution among nodes. Node buffers hold node specific attributes and potentially display state information; while link buffers are the inputs and the outputs of the nodes containing human readable text data (e.g., the output buffers of the `iperf` wrapper node contain the intact output of the wrapped tool). The framework with the help of its event scheduler is responsible to call the execution function of a node if one of its input buffers got modified, afterwards it is the responsibility of the execution function to process the input data, and to write into its output buffers.

EPOXIDE offers *easy extensibility*: framework and node functions are implemented in separate Emacs Lisp files and the framework provides a programming interface to node

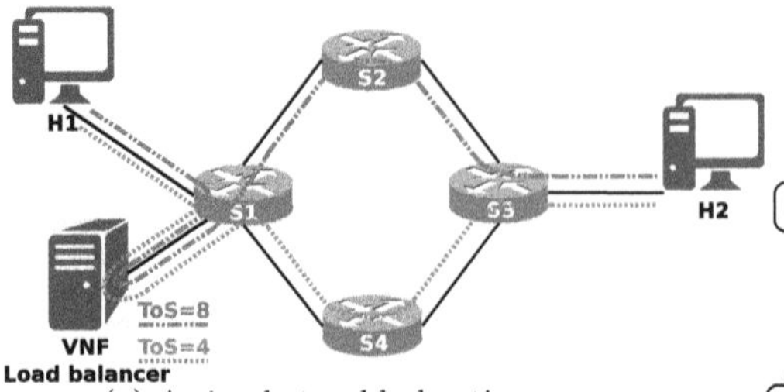

(a) A simple troubleshooting use-case.

```
iperf::Iperf(192.168.123.4, -u -i 1,
             192.168.123.2, -u -i 1
             ) -> view::View();
iperf[1]->[1]view;
clock::Clock()
  ->Flow-stat-ofctl(localhost, s1)
  ->ft::Table-view(packet_count, dpid, nw_tos)
  -->View();
clock->Flow-stat-ofctl(localhost, s2)->[1]ft;
clock->Flow-stat-ofctl(localhost, s4)->[2]ft;
Gdb(192.168.123.3, click);
```

(b) TSG definition in our Click-inspired language.

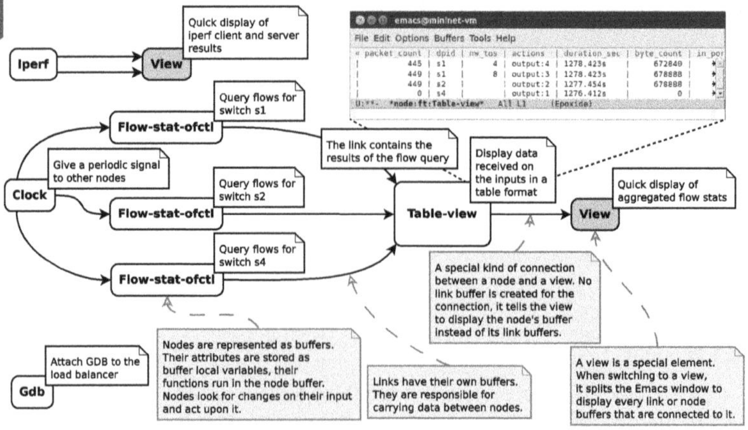

(c) The buffers of EPOXIDE after executing the .tsg config in Fig. 1b.

Figure 1: EPOXIDE through an example.

developers. This allows creating third party node implementations and also external node repositories. Developers only have to write node initialization, execution, and termination functions. Optionally, they can add documentation functions to provide information about node configuration parameters. *Context-aware buffer switching* keeps track of the created buffers and provides support to move among them in an orderly fashion by applying key combinations. When multiple branches of the TSG are available, possible choices are offered as a selectable list, or they can be selected by the same key combination prefixed with the output link's number. Users can also switch to buffers associated with the current EPOXIDE session by selecting from a list of buffer names grouped together based on their types and positions in the TSG. *TSG visualization* offers a graph representation of the interpreted .tsg file, navigation options for graph traversal, and quick access to node and link buffers. *Syntax highlighting and context-aware code completion* is provided for .tsg files. Additional, context-aware help is also shown with the short documentation of the current node, in which the currently typed parameter is highlighted. Intelligent code completion is offered: candidate lists are populated with node classes and phrases from other buffers. *Views* are special TSG elements that can create bundles of link and node buffers to be displayed together by splitting the Emacs window to different sub-windows. In a complex TSG, views provide quick access to a subset of the buffers. Moreover, in case of a long chain of nodes not only the final result is shown but every intermediate partial result is also available for inspection in the corresponding link buffer. *Run-time node creation, reconfiguration and re-linking* provides two possibilities to make modification on a TSG that has already been started. The first one allows reinterpreting a modified .tsg file and then reconfigures the TSG based on file modifications. The second one interactively guides the user to add a new node or reconfigure existing nodes or links between them.

During the course of the demonstration we present EPOXIDE via a simple troubleshooting use-case (Fig. 1a). In this mininet-based scenario we try to implement a load balancer in a VNF which is supposed to mark the packets randomly with ToS values 4 or 8. Flow entries are installed in $s1$ which ensure that the switch will forward the packets marked with ToS 4 and 8 to $s4$ and $s2$ respectively. But there is a software bug in the VNF, hence it marks all packets with ToS 4. A simple way to identify this bug would be (*i*) to run **iperf** between $H1$ and $H2$ (which works but is slow), (*ii*) inspect the flow tables of $s1$, $s2$ and $s4$ with **ovs-ofctl** (which are ok), (*iii*) attach **gdb** to the VNF process and finally identify the bug. Arguably going through this process in the standard way would require many shells (2 for the **iperfs**, 3 for the **ofctls** and 1 for **gdb**) to be opened and managed actively (e.g. ssh to the hosts, keeping in mind in which shell which particular process runs) by the troubleshooting person. EPOXIDE offers another way for doing this by letting the troubleshooter focus more on the troubleshooting process itself and less on the unnecessary details of implementing it. Instead of opening shells, the troubleshooter writes a simple **.tsg** config file incrementally (Fig. 1b). For **iperf** she simply specifies the server, the client and other extra arguments (if any) and redirect both the server and client outputs to an EPOXIDE view. The outputs of the server and client then can be seen together by switching to this view. Using the **ofctl** wrappers and a Table-view node, it is possible to direct the ordered (and possibly filtered) **ofctl** outputs to a shared table and examine them together (see the upper right corner of Fig. 1c). Finally, the **gdb** wrapper of EPOXIDE can connect to remote machines, grep for processes specified in the second argument (in our example this is a click process) and attach **gdb** to the process. The .tsg file then can be saved for future use or shared with another troubleshooter as a footprint of a process for tracking down a specific bug.

The source code is at: http://github.com/nemethf/epoxide.

Acknowledgements – The research leading to these results has received funding from the European Union Seventh Framework Programme under grant agreement № 619609.

3. REFERENCES

[1] B. Heller et al. Leveraging SDN layering to systematically troubleshoot networks. In *ACM SIGCOMM*, HotSDN '13.

[2] I. Pelle et al. One tool to rule them all: A modular troubleshooting framework for SDN (and other) networks. In *ACM SIGCOMM*, SOSR '15, 2015.

nf.io: A File System Abstraction for NFV Orchestration

Md. Faizul Bari, Shihabur Rahman Chowdhury, Reaz Ahmed, Raouf Boutaba
David R. Cheriton School of Computer Science, University of Waterloo
{mfbari, sr2chowdhury, r5ahmed, rboutaba}@uwaterloo.ca

CCS Concepts

•**Networks** → **Network architectures; Network design principles;**

Keywords

Network Function Virtualization; Service Chain Orchestration; File System Abstraction

1. INTRODUCTION

Middleboxes have become an integral part of modern enterprise and data center networks. They are used for realizing various performance and security objectives. Most middlboxes (*e.g.*, firewalls, Intrusion Detection Systems (IDSs), Network Address Translators (NATs), *etc.*) are dedicated hardware appliances. However, recent advancements in cloud and virtualization technologies have fueled the concept of Virtual Middleboxes or Virtual Network Functions (VNFs) along with a new research field known as Network Function Virtualization (NFV). This area of research has gained a lot of traction from both industry and academia. Although much progress has been made in NFV technology, a crucial component for realizing the primary objective of NFV is still missing – a management and orchestration [7] system that conforms to the principles of NFV: open source, open API and standardized software solutions. Without this feature, network operators may end-up with the same situation of vendor lock-in as with proprietary hardware middleboxes. A number of recent proposals like Stratos [8], OpenNF [9], and Split/Merge [10], strive to fulfill the requirements for VNF management and orchestration. However, they propose incompatible northbound APIs. What is really needed is a standardized API that is flexible enough to express a wide range of NFV management and orchestration operations. History shows that standardization efforts usually take a long time and often are futile. Hence, we take a different approach, and propose to use an existing, well known, standardized interface for NFV management and orchestration: the Linux file system interface.

SIGCOMM '15 August 17-21, 2015, London, United Kingdom

ACM ISBN 978-1-4503-3542-3/15/08.
DOI: http://dx.doi.org/10.1145/2785956.2790028

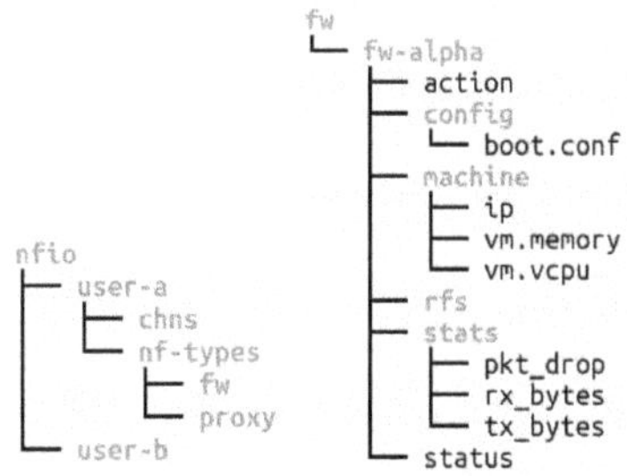

(a) `nf.io` root (b) VNF Instance

Figure 1: `nf.io` File System Abstraction

We call our proposed system `nf.io`. It utilizes the Linux file system as the northbound API for VNF orchestration. It adopts various operating system principles: (i) everything (resource, configuration) is represented as files, (ii) common Linux utility programs (*e.g.*, `mkdir`, `cp`, `mv`, `ln`, *etc.*) are used for state manipulation, (iii) heterogeneous resource pools (*e.g.*, different networking tool-chains like Linux bridge or Open vSwitch [5]) are controlled through a high-level abstraction, and (iv) resource specific drivers are developed similar to device drivers in an OS. Existing NFV management and orchestration systems like Stratos or OpenNF can use the `nf.io` abstraction by developing resource drivers specific to their requirements.

2. SYSTEM DESCRIPTION

2.1 Features

Key features of `nf.io` are as follows:

- **Everything is a file:** States and configurations of a VNF deployment are represented as files organized in a hierarchical directory structure.
- **Centralized control:** A centralized point of control over a distributed VNF deployment.
- **Compatibility:** A rich set of existing file system utilities (*e.g.*, `grep`, `mkdir`, *etc.*) and configuration management tools (*e.g.*, Chef, Puppet, *etc.*) can be used with `nf.io` for VNF management.

2.2 File System Abstraction

`nf.io` uses a simple and intuitive directory hierarchy to store states regarding VNF deployment, configuration and chaining. A high-level view of the `nf.io` directory hierarchy is shown in Figure 1. The root of the file system with two users is shown in Figure 1(a). The `user-a` and `user-b` directories mark the home directory for the users. The VNFs and chains deployed by a user are organized under his home directory. The structure of a directory representing a VNF is shown in Figure 1(b). The **config** and **machine** directories contain configuration parameters. The **action** file is used by the user to perform different VNF operations (*e.g.*, **start**, **pause**, **resume**, **kill**, *etc.*). The **status** file indicated the current status of the VNF (*e.g.*, **running**, **paused**, **error**, *etc.*). The files contained under the **stats** directory are used to collect data like packet drops, transmitted/received bytes, *etc.* The **stats** directory contains one file for each measurement metric. The **rfs** directory mounts the file system of the VNF itself, so that the user can directly change a configuration file and also read different kinds of statistics from the VNF. A VNF chain is deployed by creating a directory under the **chns** directory. A chain directory contains symbolic links to the VNF instances that are part of the chain. It also contains markers to indicate the start and next VNFs in the chain.

2.3 Architecture

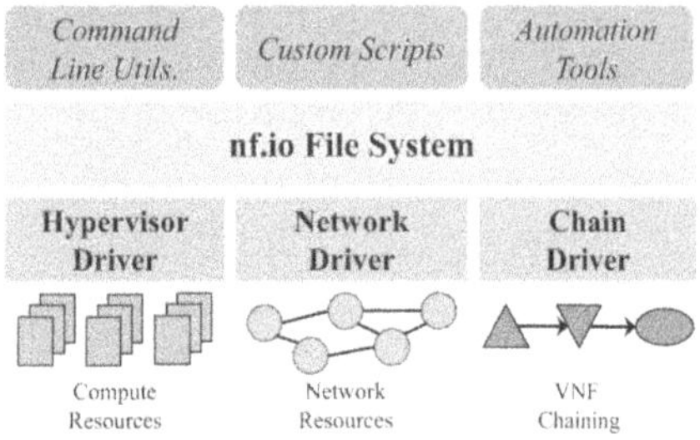

Figure 2: `nf.io` Architecture

A high-level view of the `nf.io` architecture is shown in Figure 2. The `nf.io` File System is a virtual file system that runs on top of the traditional OS file system. VNF operations are triggered when a user writes a operation string in the **action** files. `nf.io` performs these operations by using three resource drivers: (i) Hypervisor Driver, (ii) Network Driver, and (iii) Chain Driver.

2.3.1 *Hypervisor Driver*

In `nf.io`, network functions can be deployed in a number of ways. They can run as processes on a physical machine, VMs on a hypervisor like Xen or KVM, or as light-weigh containers provided by Docker [1] or Linux Container (LXC) [4]. The hypervisor driver abstracts the underlying diversity in these virtualization technologies and provides a uniform interface to `nf.io`.

2.3.2 *Network Driver*

`nf.io` requires support for certain networking functionality from the underlying physical infrastructure. In each physical machine, `nf.io` must have the ability to (i) setup bridges, (ii) create IP links between virtual ethernet (**veth**) pairs, (iii) setup tunnels (*e.g.*, VXLAN or GRE), and (iv) install forwarding rules. Similar to the hypervisor driver, the network driver hides the underlying heterogeneity and provides an abstract network interface to nf.io.

2.3.3 *Chain Driver*

The chain driver interconnects different types of VNFs. It provides a function **chn-cnct(vnf1, vnf2)**, where **vnf1** and **vnf2** are two arbitrary VNFs. For a chain like a → b → c, this function must be called twice: first for a → b, and again for b → c. The task of Interconnecting two VNFs depends primarily on their types, and whether their network interfaces are on the same or different IP subnets.

2.4 Implementation

The `nf.io` prototype is implemented using the python API binding for FUSE [2]. We rewrote a number of file system calls like **mkdir**, **read**, **write**, **symlink**, *etc.* to implement the `nf.io` file system semantics. The Hypervisor Driver currently supports KVM, Xen and Docker. We use libvirt [3] and Docker Remote API to control VMs and containers in KVM/Xen and Docker, respectively. The Network and Chain Drivers currently support two configurations: (i) Linux **iptables** and Linux bridge and (ii) Open vSwitch. In both cases we use GRE tunnels to connect VNFs deployed on different physical machines. Finally, we remotely mount the VNF's file system under the **rfs** directory (Figure 1) using **sshfs** [6]. A demonstration of `nf.io` is available at http://faizulbari.github.io/nf.io/.

3. DEMONSTRATION

We demonstrate the capabilities of `nf.io` by showcasing use cases focused on three primary areas: (i) configuration, (ii) deployment, and (iii) monitoring of VNF instances and chains. First, we will show how to configure different parameters of a single VNF instance. Then we will configure a service chain consisting of multiple VNFs and tweak different chain level parameters. Next, we will deploy the service chain on Docker containers and run a client to generate some test data. Finally, we will demonstrate `nf.io`'s monitoring features by querying data both at the VNF and chain levels.

4. ACKNOWLEDGMENTS

This work was supported by the Natural Science and Engineering Council of Canada (NSERC) under the Smart Applications on Virtual Infrastructure (SAVI) Research Network.

5. REFERENCES

[1] Docker. http://docker.com/.

[2] fusepy. https://github.com/terencehonles/fusepy.

[3] libvirt: The virtualization API. http://libvirt.org/.

[4] LXC: Linux Containers. https://linuxcontainers.org/.

[5] OVS: Open vSwitch. https://linuxcontainers.org/.

[6] sshfs. http://fuse.sourceforge.net/sshfs.html.

[7] Bari, M. F., Chowdhury, S. R., Ahmed, R., and Boutaba, R. On orchestrating virtual network functions in NFV. *CoRR abs/1503.06377* (2015).

[8] Gember, A., Krishnamurthy, A., John, S. S., Grandl, R., Gao, X., Anand, A., Benson, T., Akella, A., and Sekar, V. Stratos: A network-aware orchestration layer for middleboxes in the cloud. Tech. rep., 2013.

[9] Gember-Jacobson, A., Viswanathan, R., Prakash, C., Grandl, R., Khalid, J., Das, S., and Akella, A. OpenNF: Enabling innovation in network function control. In *Proc. of SIGCOMM* (2014), ACM, pp. 163–174.

[10] Rajagopalan, S., Williams, D., Jamjoom, H., and Warfield, A. Split/merge: System support for elastic execution in virtual middleboxes. In *Proc. of USENIX NSDI* (2013), pp. 227–240.

NetFPGA - Rapid Prototyping of Networking Devices in Open Source

Noa Zilberman Yury Audzevich Georgina Kalogeridou
Neelakandan Manihatty Bojan Jingyun Zhang Andrew W. Moore

Computer Laboratory, University of Cambridge
name.surname@cl.cam.ac.uk

ABSTRACT

The demand-led growth of datacenter networks has meant that many constituent technologies are beyond the budget of the wider community. In order to make and validate timely and relevant new contributions, the wider community requires accessible evaluation, experimentation and demonstration environments with specification comparable to the subsystems of the most massive datacenter networks. We demonstrate NetFPGA, an open-source platform for rapid prototyping of networking devices with I/O capabilities up to 100Gbps. NetFPGA offers an integrated environment that enables networking research by users from a wide range of disciplines: from hardware-centric research to formal methods.

CCS Concepts

•**Networks** → **Intermediate nodes;** *Data center networks;*
•**Hardware** → **Reconfigurable logic and FPGAs;**

1. THE NETFPGA PROJECT

The NetFPGA project (www.netfpga.org) provides software, hardware and community as a basic infrastructure to simplify design, simulation and testing, all around an open-source high-speed networking platform. Beyond the hardware and software, the NetFPGA project is backed by community resources that include online forums, tutorials, summer camp events and developer workshops, all supported by the NetFPGA project team. All the projects developed under the NetFPGA project are open-sourced. By reusing building blocks across projects users can compare design utilization and performance. Past experience has shown that both reference and contributed NetFPGA projects are regularly enhanced by community members, redistributed and encourage a virtuous circle.

The most prominent NetFPGA success is OpenFlow, which in turn has reignited the Software Defined Networking movement. NetFPGA enabled OpenFlow by providing a widely available open-source development platform capable of line-rate operation and was, until its commercial uptake, the reference platform for OpenFlow.

The NetFPGA project currently supports three platforms:

- NetFPGA SUME, a new platform with I/O capabilities for 100Gbps operation as a networking device, stand alone computing unit or for test and measurement.
- NetFPGA-10G, a platform with multiple 10Gbps interfaces introduced in 2010, and supporting a large number of open source community projects (e.g. OSNT [1] and BlueSwitch [2])
- NetFPGA-1G-CML, a recent platform replacing the original NetFPGA-1G board, designed for low-bandwidth (e.g. gigabit) applications, and especially suited for network-security applications.

2. NetFPGA SUME

The NetFPGA SUME [3] design aims to create a low-cost, PCIe host adapter card able to support 40Gb/s and 100Gb/s applications. NetFPGA SUME, shown in Figure 1, uses a large FPGA, supporting high-speed serial interfaces of 10Gb/s or more presented both in standard interfaces (SFP+) and in a format that permits easy user-expansion, a large and extensible high-speed DRAM, alongside high-throughput SRAM. All this is constrained by a desire for low cost, enabling access by the wider research and academic communities.

At the core of the NetFPGA SUME board is a Xilinx Virtex-7 690T FPGA device, supporting highly complex reconfigurable designs. There are several peripheral subsystems complementing the FPGA and providing an ideal platform for networking devices prototyping; A high-speed serial interfaces subsystem, composed of 30 serial links running at up to 13.1Gb/s, enables 10Gb/s, 40Gb/s and 100Gb/s applications. Users can use these serial links as standard interfaces (e.g. SFP+, PCI-Express Gen.3) or use proprietary interfaces.

The memory subsystem combines both SRAM (QDRII+, running at 500MHz) and DRAM (DDR3 SoDIMM, running at 1866MT/s) devices. These memory devices can be used for different purposes: from flow tables and off-chip packet buffering to serving as RAM for soft-core processor designs. The Storage subsystem of the design can host both a MicroSD card and external disks through two SATA interfaces,

SIGCOMM '15 August 17-21, 2015, London, United Kingdom

ACM ISBN 978-1-4503-3542-3/15/08.

DOI: http://dx.doi.org/10.1145/2785956.2790029

Figure 1: NetFPGA SUME Board

thus enabling a complete standalone operation of the board. Additional NetFPGA SUME features support debug, extension and synchronization of the board. Special attention was paid to power instrumentation [3]. The board is implemented as a dual-slot, full-size PCIe adapter, that can operate as a standalone unit outside of a PCIe host. It is manufactured by Digilent Inc.(http://www.digilentinc.com).

3. RAPID PROTOTYPING

Networking research attracts interest from a wide range of disciplines. Researchers have different sets of skills and interests and often find it hard to innovate over hardware-based platforms; most platforms require deep understanding of every aspect of the board and an implementation of a complete solution from scratch. This means that a person researching multi-table OpenFlow switch designs is required to know aspects of high-speed serial links, whereas researchers studying power-efficiency in the MAC and physical layers are required to understand aspects of the driver and the DMA engine. Alternately, researchers opt for a partial implementation that is not comparable to real networking devices. A different class of researchers are interested in test and measurement, and do not wish to develop new devices or know implementation details . These researchers often fail to get a hold on commercial devices due to their high cost.

The NetFPGA platform offers a solution to these researchers. First, NetFPGA offers ready-made reference and contributed projects, providing full implementation and an executable application. The user can run these projects, with no further development or modification required. For example, a domain specific language researcher may use the NetFPGA platform for the study of application-level middleboxes.

Second, NetFPGA projects are modular. The hardware and software components are provided as flexible building blocks, that can be modified and replaced without affecting other parts of the design. On one end of the scale, users can opt to modify or develop at the software level alone. For example, an SDN researcher interested in the control plane and lacking any hardware knowledge, can use the BlueSwitch OpenFlow switch project [2] as its data plane, and choose to write a control plane software application to run on top of it. On the other end of the scale, a researcher may choose to explore aspects of hardware-based scheduling, and thus add a new scheduling module to the existing reference router design. A researcher interested in power efficiency can opt to modify only a single interface module in the design, with no need to handle any software aspects or the data path. In all these cases, the users can focus only on research aspects that interest them, with the overheads being handled by the NetFPGA platform.

The NetFPGA development environment provides an integrated solution that enables rapid prototyping. Every NetFPGA release contains several reference projects that are used as basic building blocks for new projects: a reference NIC project, a reference switch project, a reference IPv4 router project and a project that exercises all the I/O interfaces. Each project consists of hardware, software, testing and documentation components. The hardware portion of a project contains the source code for all the modules used in the design, as well as a large set of scripts that generate the platform's configuration file. The software portion contains embedded code (for a soft-core processor), a driver and relevant applications (e.g. router management). The test environment provides unified tests for simulation and hardware test, allowing simple validation of designs. Each project is also well documented, with the documentation covering every element or module used in the project. In addition to the modules used in the reference project, a large library of modules is provided, as well as contributed projects developed by members of the NetFPGA community.

In the demonstration, we provide a development experience over the NetFPGA platform. We introduce the NetFPGA SUME board, and show the various components of the development platform. Visitors are then encouraged to adhoc develop a new project, and experience the meaning of rapid prototyping over the NetFPGA SUME platform. To fully demonstrate the NetFPGA SUME capabilities, we also show a high performance device, and its full implementation, in action.

Acknowledgements

We thank the many people who have contributed to the NetFPGA project. the Xilinx XUP program has been a long-standing supporter of NetFPGA and the NetFPGA SUME project is only possible with their generous support. We thank the people at Digilent Inc. We thank Micron and Cypress Semiconductor for their generous part donations.

This work was jointly supported by EPSRC INTERNET Project EP/H040536/1, National Science Foundation under Grant No. CNS-0855268, and Defense Advanced Research Projects Agency (DARPA) and Air Force Research Laboratory (AFRL), under contract FA8750-11-C-0249. The views, opinions, and/or findings contained in this report are those of the authors and should not be interpreted as representing the official views or policies, either expressed or implied, of the National Science Foundation, Defense Advanced Research Projects Agency or the Department of Defense.

4. REFERENCES

[1] G. Antichi, M. Shahbaz, Y. Geng, N. Zilberman, A. Covington, M. Bruyere, N. Feamster, N. McKeown, B. Felderman, M. Blott, A. Moore, and P. Owezarski. OSNT: Open Source Network Tester. *IEEE Network*, 28(5):6–12, 2014.

[2] J. Han, P. Mundkur, C. Rotsos, G. Antichi, N. Dave, A. Moore, and P. Neumann. Blueswitch: Enabling provably consistent configuration of network switches. In *ANCS*, 2015.

[3] N. Zilberman, Y. Audzevich, G. A. Covington, and A. W. Moore. NetFPGA SUME: Toward 100 Gbps as Research Commodity. *IEEE Micro*, (5):32–41, 2014.

A Mininet-based Virtual Testbed for Distributed SDN Development

Bob Lantz, Brian O'Connor
Open Networking Laboratory, Menlo Park, CA
lantz@onlab.us, bocon@onlab.us

ABSTRACT

The need for fault tolerance and scalability is leading to the development of distributed SDN operating systems and applications. But how can you develop such systems and applications reliably without access to an expensive testbed? We continue to observe SDN development practices using full system virtualization or heavyweight containers, increasing complexity and overhead while decreasing usability. We demonstrate a simpler and more efficient approach: using Mininet's cluster mode to easily deploy a virtual testbed of lightweight containers on a single machine, an ad hoc cluster, or a dedicated hardware testbed. By adding an open source, distributed network operating system such as ONOS, we can create a flexible and scalable open source development platform for distributed SDN system and application software development.

CCS Concepts

•**Networks** → **Network simulations;** •**Computing methodologies** → *Distributed simulation; Interactive simulation; Simulation environments;*

Keywords

Mininet; container based emulation; software defined networking; SDN; network OS; distributed systems

1. INTRODUCTION

The Fat Testbed Problem. Since 2013, we have observed that many users, developers, and testers of distributed SDN controllers and applications have constructed virtual testbeds using full machine virtualization and/or heavyweight containers, often for hosting the network OS or applications. This approach adds complexity and overhead, reducing both the usability and the scalability of the development platform.

In such a fat testbed, an additional (and, we argue, largely unnecessary) orchestration system may be required, such as OpenStack, Vagrant, or Docker. VMs and heavyweight containers consume significant hardware resources and frequently require complicated management. We believe there is a better way: using Mininet [1] to dynamically create virtual testbeds on the fly.

SIGCOMM '15 August 17-21, 2015, London, United Kingdom

ACM ISBN 978-1-4503-3542-3/15/08.

DOI: http://dx.doi.org/10.1145/2785956.2790030

2. A MININET-BASED VIRTUAL TESTBED

Mininet already has the capability of creating containers as well as the network from a single, simple Python API. Using Mininet avoids the need for installing, configuring and administering multiple orchestration systems. Moreover, Mininet hosts do not run unnecessary extra software such as multiple kernels or daemons, and they do not require unwieldy, bulky virtual file system images. To support configurations that exceed the resources of a single server, Mininet's experimental cluster support may be used to easily and seamlessly distribute the virtual testbed across multiple physical (or virtual) servers.

Just Enough Virtualization. By default, Mininet hosts are simply process groups connected to virtual Ethernet interfaces using Linux's network namespace feature. (Since Mininet 2.2, private mount namespaces have also been enabled by default, though this may become optional in the future.)

To make creation of a virtual testbed more convenient, we add a `Server` class which extends Mininet's `Host` class to enable slightly more virtualization on by default, including:

- Copy-on-write directories (e.g. `/var/run`, `/etc`) implemented using `overlayfs`
- A private PID space (PID namespace)
- Private `utmp/wtmp/btmp`
- Optional customized `hostname` (UTS namespace)

In addition, `Servers` can automatically run `sshd` for remote login, and we can run `dnsmasq` to provide DNS service for the virtual cluster if desired.

Most software can be run on unmodified Mininet hosts by simply using custom command line arguments (for example, specifying a local configuration file), but these changes make it easier and more convenient to deploy software onto the virtual testbed using the same scripts and configuration files which are used on a hardware testbed, without adding the computational, storage, and administrative overhead of virtual disk images, unnecessary daemons, or multiple kernels. Copy-on-write directories may either be temporary `tmpfs` file systems or may persist across runs as desired.

Cluster Support. Several distributed Mininet systems have been implemented, the most mature of them being Philip

Wette's Maxinet [2]. Since version 2.2, Mininet has itself included experimental support for simple execution on a cluster, including:

- A single console for control of a distributed experiment
- Support for the existing Mininet API with minimal alteration
- A simple `--cluster` option to create a distributed testbed
- Automatic node placement and tunnel creation
- Pluggable placement algorithms

Figure 1 shows a sample Mininet cluster, and figure 2 shows the code and/or commands which are used to create it.

Mininet's experimental cluster support requires minimal setup and configuration, making it well-suited for ad hoc networks such as a collection of student laptops or a cluster of physical or virtual machines that might only be available for a short time due to sharing or cost constraints.

A Mininet-based virtual testbed can flexibly support a number of use cases and run on a wide range of hardware configurations, anything from a single user's laptop to an ad hoc cluster of machines to a dedicated hardware testbed.

3. DEMONSTRATION

For our demonstration, we will show how an ad hoc cluster of rather ordinary computers (laptops and Raspberry Pi 2s) can be easily transformed into a distributed SDN testbed for development, research, experimentation, demonstration and other purposes. This simple testbed will contain hundreds of nodes running real application, switch, and network OS code – a configuration that is linearly larger in capacity than what Mininet supports on a single system. If time

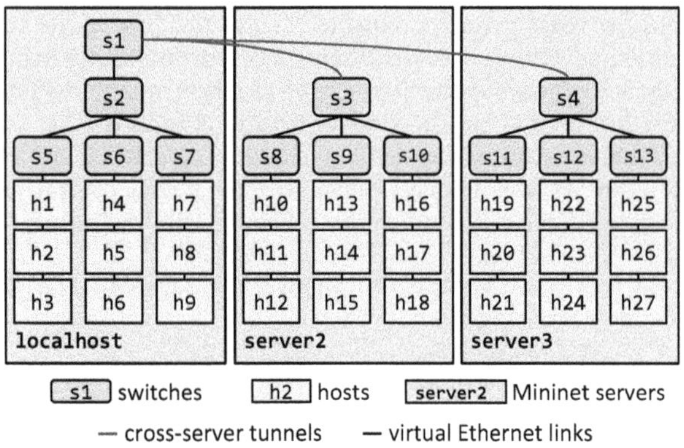

Figure 1: Sample Mininet Cluster

```
topo = Tree(depth=3, fanout=3)
servers = ['localhost','server2','server3']
net = MininetCluster(topo=topo, servers=servers)
net.start()
CLI(net)
net.stop()
```

...or via simple command line options:

```
# mn --topo tree,depth=3,fanout=3
     --cluster localhost,server2,server3
```

Figure 2: Mininet Cluster Python Code & Shell Command

and access permit, we may also add a scale-up demonstration of execution on a cloud or dedicated cluster as well as scale-down creation of a distributed testbed and development platform on a single machine.

We hope to demonstrate the convenience and speed of using Mininet and minimal, lightweight containers as a flexible and scalable platform for distributed SDN development, and to encourage the community to reserve more complicated virtualization for where it is actually required.

4. RELATED WORK

Several systems have been built to extend container based emulation to run on a cluster. Virtual Emulab [3] is a particularly notable example, and CORE [4] also allows cluster-based execution. Mininet has itself been extended to distributed execution in the Maxinet system, the Distributed OpenFlow Testbed [5], and Mininet's own experimental cluster support. Testbeds such as Emulab or DOT can be well-suited to research, teaching, or experimentation, but may introduce issues of contention over shared resources as well as configuration and administration. Maxinet and CORE have simpler installation and cluster configuration, and Mininet avoids configuration files, simplifying ad hoc clustering.

5. DISCUSSION: THE OPEN SOURCE, DISTRIBUTED SDN DEV STACK

By combining free, open source components, we can create a complete distributed SDN system and application software development stack. At the bottom, we have either a native Linux server, or a Linux virtual machine running on a VMM such as VirtualBox or KVM. On top of that, we use Mininet to create a virtual testbed consisting of a network of switches as well as virtual Linux servers for both end-user client/server and network OS applications. For our distributed control plane, we use a set of ONOS [6] instances that cooperate to provide fault tolerance as well as scale-out for capacity. Finally, on top of the ONOS instances, we can run single-instance applications or distributed applications which take advantage of ONOS's abstractions and APIs for managing shared state.

6. ACKNOWLEDGMENTS

Mininet core developers including Vimal Jeyakumar have built virtual testbeds using Mininet. Rich Lane submitted pull requests for mount and UTS namespaces. Brandon Schlinker also implemented mount and PID namespaces to support SDX. [7]

7. REFERENCES

[1] Mininet Project. Mininet. http://mininet.org/.

[2] P. Wette, M. Dräxler, A. Schwabe, F. Wallaschek, M. Zahraee, and H. Karl. MaxiNet: Distributed emulation of software-defined networks. In *IFIP Networking '14*, 2014.

[3] M. Hibler, R. Ricci, L. Stoller, J. Duerig, S. Guruprasad, T. Stack, K. Webb, and J. Lepreau. Large-scale virtualization in the Emulab network testbed. In *USENIX ATC '08*, 2008.

[4] J. Ahrenholz, C. Danilov, T. Henderson, and J. Kim. CORE: A real-time network emulator. In *MILCOM 2008. IEEE*, 2008.

[5] A. R. Roy, M. F. Bari, M. F. Zhani, R. Ahmed, and R. Boutaba. DOT: Distributed openflow testbed. In *SIGCOMM '14*, 2014.

[6] ONOS Project. ONOS. http://onosproject.org/.

[7] A. Gupta, L. Vanbever, M. Shahbaz, S. P. Donovan, B. Schlinker, N. Feamster, J. Rexford, S. Shenker, R. Clark, and E. Katz-Bassett. SDX: A software defined internet exchange. In *SIGCOMM '14*, 2014.

A High-Radix, Low-Latency Optical Switch for Data Centers

Dan Alistarh, Hitesh Ballani, Paolo Costa
Microsoft Research

Adam Funnell, Joshua Benjamin,
Philip Watts, Benn Thomsen
University College London

ABSTRACT

We demonstrate an optical switch design that can scale up to a thousand ports with high per-port bandwidth (25 Gbps+) and low switching latency (40 ns). Our design uses a broadcast and select architecture, based on a passive star coupler and fast tunable transceivers. In addition we employ time division multiplexing to achieve very low switching latency. Our demo shows the feasibility of the switch data plane using a small testbed, comprising two transmitters and a receiver, connected through a star coupler.

CCS Concepts

•**Networks** → **Bridges and switches; Data center networks;**

Keywords

Optical switching; TDMA; WDM;

1. INTRODUCTION

Today's datacenter networks are built using low radix electrical packet switches. They scale by arranging the switches in a multilayer topology (e.g., folded Clos or Fat Tree) [1,3]. However using low radix switches as a building block means that, in large datacenters, a very high number of switches, cables and transceivers are needed. This increases network cost, power and complexity. Lots of cables are particularly problematic as server NICs are upgraded from 10 Gbps to 25 and 100 Gbps — links throughout the network need to be expensive optical cables, and all switches need optoelectronic transceivers to convert optical signals to electronic and back at each hop [5].

These problems can be alleviated through higher radix switches supporting 1000s of ports per switch. In large datacenters, operators already use high-radix chassis switches at higher levels of the hierarchy. Internally, these switches use low radix switching chips connected in a Clos topology. Such chassis switches can economically scale to ~250 ports. However, building a *single* electrical switching chip with a high radix and high per port bandwidth is hard because of limitations on bandwidth at the edge of the chip, mostly because of power constraints [2]. This is not expected to improve in the near future as the ITRS roadmap predicts only a modest increase in the chip pin count and per-pin bandwidth over the next decade [2].

We thus target an all-optical datacenter network built using high-radix optical switches. We will demonstrate a switch design that can scale to a thousand ports with high per-port bandwidth (25 Gbps+) and low switching latency (40 ns, best case). The switching latency here is two to three orders of magnitude less than that of the 2D MEMS-based wavelength selective switches underlying recent hybrid network designs [5,8]. The reduced switching latency means we can switch at the granularity of a few 64 byte packets, and avoids the need for two separate networks.

2. DESIGN

While traditional electrical switches have a switching chip that dynamically connects the input and output ports, we distribute the switching functionality among the nodes connected by the switch. This allows the switch to have a very simple optical core. Overall, our design is based on two key technologies.

First, the switch's core comprises a passive optical device called *star coupler* [4]. A star coupler simply replicates an optical signal on any of its input ports to all output ports. This creates a cost and power-efficient "broadcast and select" network providing one hop connectivity between all nodes connected to it. Second, we use fast tunable transceivers that can tune to a wavelength in 200 ns [6].

The broadcast nature of the star coupler means that, by default, only a single node can transmit across it at any given time. To achieve packet switch like functionality across it, we allow many node pairs to communicate across the coupler simultaneously by combining wavelength and time division multiplexing. This, as we explain below, is achieved through the tunable transceivers.

2.1 Switch components

The switch comprises nodes connected to a star coupler. A "node" can be a server or even a Top-of-Rack switch. Thus the switch can be used as a modular building block in data centers, to connect servers or other switches too. Below we briefly describe the switch design, including the data and control plane setup.

Wavelength multiplexing. A star coupler is colourless, i.e., many wavelengths can be multiplexed through it. An optical fiber can support 160 wavelengths using the C and L-band with 50 GHz spacing between the wavelengths. We equip each node with a wavelength tunable transceiver, and periodically change the wavelength that a transceiver is tuned to. It takes <200 ns to re-tune a transceiver during which period it is not operational. To amortize the tuning latency, the transceivers are tuned at most once every 2 μs, thus imposing a throughput overhead of less than 10%. We call the period after which transceivers are re-tuned an *epoch*.

SIGCOMM '15 August 17-21, 2015, London, United Kingdom

ACM ISBN 978-1-4503-3542-3/15/08.

DOI: http://dx.doi.org/10.1145/2785956.2790035

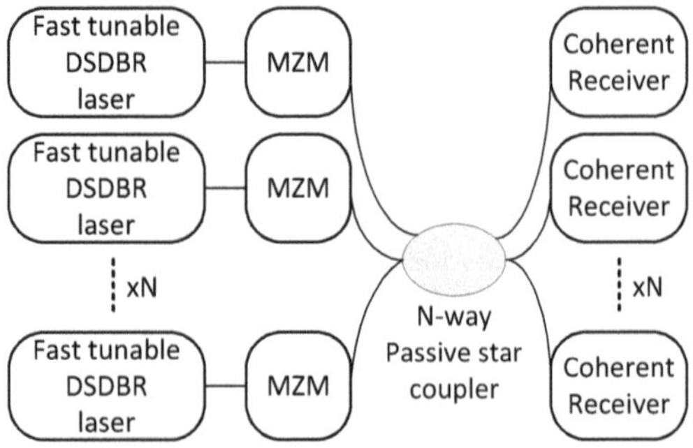

Figure 1: Hardware layout of the switch's data plane, where MZM is Mach-Zehnder modulator and N is the total number of nodes.

Timeslot multiplexing. Since the number of wavelengths across the fiber is significantly less than the number of node pairs, simply relying on dynamic wavelength multiplexing would result in high switching latency. To reduce the switching latency, we use time division multiplexing. Each epoch is divided into many fixed-length *slots*. Multiple node pairs are assigned the same wavelength and thus, can communicate with each other in the same epoch, but never in the same slot. In our prototype, there are 50 slots per epoch, so each slot is 40 ns long. This is the best case switching latency. Such timeslot multiplexing relies on fine-grained time synchronization across the nodes, and the ability of a transceiver to send short bursts of an optical signal at a pre-specified time.

Switch Capacity. To keep transceiver cost low, we use interleaved bipolar line coding at 25 Gbps. Each switch port thus has a bandwidth of 25 Gbps. With 160 wavelengths, the total capacity of the switch is 3.64 Tbps (after accounting for tuning overhead). We can scale up the switch capacity in two ways: *i)* through better modulation which allows each port to have 100 Gbps+ bandwidth, and *ii)* by using more than one star coupler.

Switch Scale. The number of ports supported by a star coupler is dictated by its splitting loss. Specifically, the power lost when transmitting through the coupler is given by $L_{dB} = 3\text{ dB} \times \log_2 N$, where N is the number of ports. We are using a (DSP free) coherent receiver with a sensitivity of -27 dBm. Assuming a transmit power of 6 dBm, and system and coupling losses of 3 dB means that we have a total optical loss budget of 30 dB. Thus, we can support a 1,000 ports — $3\text{ dB} \times \log_2 N \leq 30\text{ dB}$ means that $N \leq 1000$.

2.2 Switch data plane

The switch's data plane is shown in Figure 1. Each node has a transceiver with transmit and receive functionality. The transmitter part contains a fast tunable laser modulated by a Mach-Zehnder Modulator (MZM). We use DS-DBR lasers that have been shown to tune and stabilize within 200 ns [6]. The transmitter is connected to a passive star coupler through an optical fiber. A clock signal using an out of band 1.3 um channel is distributed to all nodes over the same star coupler for synchronisation across the entire network.

The receive part is a DSP-free coherent receiver with a fast tunable local oscillator. This provides full wavelength selectivity. The local oscillator at the receiver is tuned to a single wavelength at the start of each epoch, and can receive all data on that wavelength for the duration of the epoch. Furthermore, this design ensures that the transmitter and receiver are independently tunable.

2.3 Switch control plane

The switch control plane, at the beginning of each epoch, assigns wavelengths to transceivers on all nodes based on the expected traffic demand. We use past traffic statistics and queuing information at the end hosts to estimate the expected traffic for the next epoch. The control plane also determines a timeslot schedule for the epoch, i.e., for each wavelength, determine which pair of nodes that have been tuned to the wavelength is allocated each timeslot.

We are developing an algorithm for this wavelength and timeslot assignment problem with three main design goals: high switch utilization, bounded worst-case performance and freedom from starvation. These goals typically underlie scheduling algorithms even in traditional low radix switches [7]. Beyond this, we want the algorithm to be simple enough to be implemented in hardware.

3. DEMONSTRATION DETAILS

The goal of the demo is to demonstrate the practical feasibility of the switch data plane. In summary, we will show *i)* the ability of our prototype to tune the lasers to a different wavelength within 200 ns and hence, achieve WDM, *ii)* the effectiveness of TDM to achieve low switching latency, and *iii)* the scalability of our approach.

The demonstration comprises two experiments using a small testbed consisting of two transmitter nodes and a single receiver node, all connected to a star coupler. We use an arbitrary waveform generator connected to the transmitter to generate traffic and an oscilloscope connected to the receiver to verify that the signal received matches the modulated input data.

In the first experiment, we tune the lasers of one of the transmitter and the receiver on a common wavelength and we start generating traffic between the two. Then, we re-tune both nodes to a different wavelength λ and show that within 200 ns the receiver can receive traffic again.

In the second experiment, instead, we tune all three nodes on the same wavelength and we configure the transmitters to send back-to-back using alternate 20-ns time slots. This shows the feasibility of TDM at a very fine-grain time scale as required by our design in order to achieve low switching latency.

In both experiments, we artificially introduce the appropriate transmission loss and interfering channels to emulate the conditions of our target scale of 500-1,000 nodes.

4. REFERENCES

[1] M. Al-Fares, A. Loukissas, and A. Vahdat. A Scalable, Commodity Data Center Network Architecture. In *SIGCOMM*, 2008.

[2] N. Binkert, A. Davis, N. P. Jouppi, M. McLaren, N. Muralimanohar, R. Schreiber, and J. H. Ahn. The role of optics in future high radix switch design. In *ISCA*, 2011.

[3] A. Greenberg, J. R. Hamilton, N. Jain, S. Kandula, C. Kim, P. Lahiri, D. A. Maltz, P. Patel, and S. Sengupta. VL2: A Scalable and Flexible Data Center Network. In *SIGCOMM*, 2009.

[4] Q. Li, S. Rumley, M. Glick, J. Chan, H. Wang, K. Bergman, and R. Dutt. Scaling Star-coupler-Based Optical Networks for Avionics Applications. *IEEE/OSA Journal of Optical Communications and Networking*, 5(9), 2013.

[5] H. Liu, F. Lu, A. Forencich, R. Kapoor, M. Tewari, G. M. Voelker, G. Papen, A. C. Snoeren, and G. Porter. Circuit Switching Under the Radar with REACToR. In *NSDI*, 2014.

[6] R. Maher, D. Miller, S. Savory, and B. Thomsen. Fast Wavelength Switching 112 Gb/s Coherent Burst Mode Transceiver for Dynamic Optical Networks. In *ECOC*, 2012.

[7] N. McKeown. The iSLIP Scheduling Algorithm for Input-queued Switches. *IEEE/ACM Trans. Netw.*, 7(2), 1999.

[8] G. Porter, R. Strong, N. Farrington, A. Forencich, P.-C. Sun, T. Rosing, Y. Fainman, G. Papen, and A. Vahdat. Integrating Microsecond Circuit Switching into the Data Center. In *SIGCOMM*, 2013.

Enabling Performance Evaluation Beyond 10 Gbps

Gianni Antichi
University of Cambridge
gianni.antichi@cl.cam.ac.uk

Charalampos Rotsos
Lancaster University
c.rotsos@lancaster.ac.uk

Andrew W. Moore
University of Cambridge
andrew.moore@cl.cam.ac.uk

ABSTRACT

Despite network monitoring and testing being critical for computer networks, current solutions are both extremely expensive and inflexible.

This demo presents OSNT (www.osnt.org), a community-driven, high-performance, open-source traffic generator and capture system built on top of the NetFPGA-10G board which enables flexible network testing. The platform supports full line-rate traffic generation regardless of packet size across the four card ports, packet capture filtering and packet thinning in hardware and sub-μsec time precision in traffic generation and capture, corrected using an external GPS device. Furthermore, it provides a software APIs to test the dataplane performance of multi-10G switches, providing a starting point for a number of different test cases. OSNT flexibility is further demonstrated through the OFLOPS-turbo platform: an integration of OSNT with the OFLOPS OpenFlow switch performance evaluation platform, enabling control and data plane evaluation of 10G switches. This demo showcases the applicability of the OSNT platform to evaluate the performance of legacy and OpenFlow-enabled networking devices, and demonstrates it using commercial switches.

CCS Concepts

•**Networks** → **Network performance analysis;** *Network measurement;* Network performance modeling; Network experimentation; •**Hardware** → *Hardware accelerators;* Networking hardware;

Keywords

Network Testing; OpenFlow; SDN; High-Performance; OSNT; NetFPGA

1. INTRODUCTION

Computer networks are the hallmark of 21st Century society and underpin virtually all infrastructure in the modern world. Consequently, society relies on the correct operation of these networks. To make networks more reliable, enormous resources are poured into all phases of the network-equipment lifecycle. The process starts early in the design phase when simulation is used to verify the correctness of a design, and continues through manufacturing and perhaps months of rigorously trials. With a multitude of Internet RFCs and hundreds of IEEE standards, a typical piece of networking equipment undergoes hundreds of conformance tests before being deployed. Finally, when deployed in a production network, the equipment is tested regularly. Throughout the process, a relentless battery of tests and measurement help ensure the correct operation of the equipment. This has led to a multi-billion dollar industry in network test equipment giving rise to companies such as Ixia, Spirent, Fluke, and Emulex/Endace among others.

Figure 1: NetFPGA: the enabling platform of OSNT

However, such equipment has evolved with a number of undesirable characteristics: commonly closed and proprietary systems with limited flexibility well outside the reach of most universities and research laboratories. Researchers and educators would also like to use test equipment to understand current networks and when prototyping new ideas. We therefore built the Open Source Network Tester (OSNT [1]), primarily for the research and teaching community. The first prototype has been conceived on top of NetFPGA-10G platform [1] – an open source hardware platform supporting full line-rate across the four 10G ethernet ports.

OSNT provides two primary distinct functionalities: traffic generation and monitor. The OSNT *traffic monitor* subsystem provides high–precision inbound timestamping with a loss-limited path that gets (a subset of) captured packets into the host for further processing. The design associates packets with a 64-bit timestamp on receipt by the MAC module, thus minimising queueing noise. The timestamp resolution is 6.25 nsec with clock drift and phase coordination maintained by a GPS input. In addition, the traffic

[1] www.netfpga.org

SIGCOMM '15 August 17-21, 2015, London, United Kingdom

ACM ISBN 978-1-4503-3542-3/15/08.
DOI: http://dx.doi.org/10.1145/2785956.2790036

capture functionality provides wildcard-enabled packet filters and packet cutting and hashing in hardware. The OSNT *traffic generation* subsystem provides a PCAP replay function with a tuneable per–packet inter–departure time. The traffic generator has an accurate timestamping mechanism, located just before the transmit 10GbE MAC. The mechanism, identical to the one used in the traffic monitoring unit, is used for timing-related network measurements, such as latency and jitter. When enabled, the timestamp is embedded within the packet at a preconfigured location and can be extracted at the receiver as required.

The OSNT platform provides a simple and programmer-friendly API to control the traffic generation and monitoring functionality of the OSNT design, enabling the realisation of high precision and throughput measurement tests in software. OFLOPS-turbo is an holistic OpenFlow switch evaluation framework which takes advantage of the OSNT high-precision measurement capabilities. Using OFLOPS-turbo users can develop measurement modules which can access information from multiple measurement channels (data and control plane and SNMP) and measure the impact of the switch OpenFlow implementation in data plane performance with high precision.

OSNT is a highly flexible and function-rich framework, which provides the building blocks for the realisation of a wide range of network test scenarios. By providing an open-source solution we invite everyone from the community to audit (and improve) our implementation as well as adapt it to their needs. We believe that, as an open-source community grows, a low-cost open-source network tester will also prove valuable to the networking industry. We also envisage the enabling of new testing and validation deployments that are simply financially impractical using commercial testers. Such deployments may see the use of hundreds or thousands of testers, offering previously unobtainable insights and understanding.

2. DEMONSTRATION DESCRIPTION

The first part of the demo showcases OSNT and how the original implementation can be used to evaluate the performance of multi-10G legacy switches. The second part of the demo showcases how OSNT can be improved and adapted to different needs. In particular, how the OSNT APIs can be used in order to develop a testing framework to evaluate the performance of multi-10G OpenFlow-enabled switches. Specifically, we present OFLOPS-Turbo [2]: an effort to enhance the measurement capabilities of the OFLOPS [3] switch evaluation framework with support for the emerging protocol requirement.

Part I: Legacy Switch testing.

This part of the demo showcases OSNT main functionalities and how to exploit them to accurately measure the packet-processing latency of a legacy switch under different load conditions. OSNT consists of a software driver supporting command-line and graphic-user interfaces (CLI and GUI), traffic generators and monitors modules. Users can generate traffic at a finely-controllled rate up to 10Gbps per port, and capture high-resolution timestamped packets to evaluate the achievable bandwidth and latency of a network device. Two OSNT ports will be connected to the tested switch. One of the ports will be used to generate traffic at variable rates with the transmission timestamp embedded in each packet, while the other port will be used to capture pakets after they traverse the switch. Packets will be received by a userspace application with transmission and capture timestamps and the application will accurate estimate the switching latency.

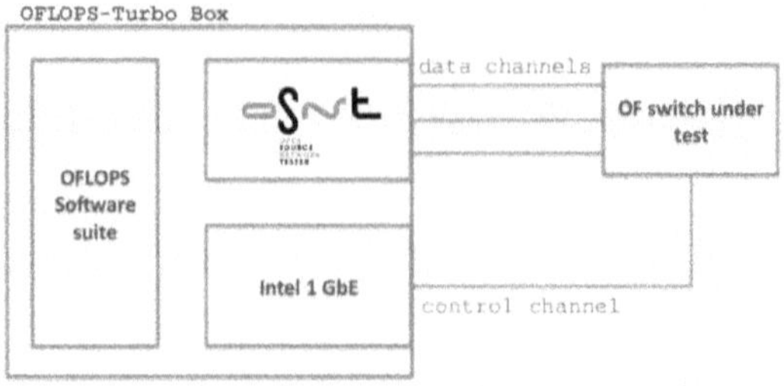

Figure 2: The proposed demo scenario

Part II: OpenFlow Switch testing.

This part of the demo will showcase the ability to leverage the traffic generation and monitoring capabilities of the OSNT platform in software and implement high precision evaluations of a switch control plane functionality. Specifically, we will setup an instance of the OFLOPS-turbo framework on a host and run multiple measurement tests against a production OpenFlow switch. OFLOPS-turbo implements numerous baseline measurement scenarios that target the elementary OpenFlow protocol interactions. During the demo we will focus on a test which measures the latency to modify the entries of the switch flow table through control and data plane measurements, using the topology presented in Figure 2. Through the conducted measurements, we will elaborate on the impact of the control plane implementation on the network performance, as well as on forwarding consistency during large flow table updates.

Acknowledgements

We thank the NetFPGA team and community. This project is jointly supported by the EPSRC INTERNET Project EP/H040536/1, the EPSRC TOUCAN project EP/L020009/1 and by the European Union's Horizon 2020 research and innovation programme under the ENDEAVOUR project (grant agreement 644960).

3. REFERENCES

[1] ANTICHI, G., SHAHBAZ, M., GENG, Y., ZILBERMAN, N., COVINGTON, A., BRUYERE, M., MCKEOWN, N., FEAMSTER, N., FELDERMAN, B., BLOTT, M., MOORE, A., AND OWEZARSKI, P. OSNT: Open Source Network Tester. *IEEE Network Special issue on Open Source for Networking: Tools and Applications* (2014).

[2] ROTSOS, C., ANTICHI, G., BRUYERE, M., OWEZARSKI, P., AND MOORE, A. W. OFLOPS-Turbo: Testing the Next-Generation OpenFlow Switch. In *ICC* (2015), IEEE.

[3] ROTSOS, C., SARRAR, N., UHLIG, S., SHERWOOD, R., AND MOORE, A. OFLOPS: An open framework for OpenFlow switch evaluation. In *PAM* (2012).

Chaos Monkey: Increasing SDN Reliability through Systematic Network Destruction

Michael Alan Chang
Princeton University
machang@princeton.edu

Brendan Tschaen
Duke University
btschaen@cs.duke.edu

Theophilus Benson
Duke University
tbenson@cs.duke.edu

Laurent Vanbever
ETH Zürich
lvanbever@ethz.ch

1. INTRODUCTION

As modern networking applications become increasingly dynamic and high-bandwidth, software defined networking (SDN) has emerged as an agile, cost effective architecture with widespread adoption across industry. In SDN, the control-plane program runs on a logically-centralized controller which directly configures the packet-handling mechanisms in the underlying switches using an open API (e.g., OpenFlow). While the controller makes it exceptionally convenient for a network operator to control and manage a network, the controller requires complex logic and becomes a single point of failure within the network. As a result, configuration errors by the controller could be extremely costly for the network provider.

Several SDN controllers have been developed since the conception of SDN, and network operators have utilized very traditional means of identifying bugs in the controller, such as unit testing and model checking [1]. However, it has become apparent that these methods cannot practically handle the inherent complexity of the controller platform that manages large networks. Ultimately, one major source of this complexity are network failures, as they trigger execution of unexplored portions of code; these network failures are inevitable, costly, and considering all possible interleaving of bugs is simply unfeasible.

To address this problem, we propose "Chaos Monkey" a real-time post-deployment failure injection tool. Inspired by industry practices in the cloud [2], Chaos Monkey is intended to systematically introduce failure (e.g., link failure, network failure) into a network. Chaos Monkey is guided by the following design principles:

- **Realistic:** The distribution of the injected failures should mirror reality.
- **Manageable:** Minimize the changes of completely destroying the network.
- **Coverage:** The injected failures should maximize the amount of controller code executed.

SIGCOMM '15 August 17-21, 2015, London, United Kingdom

ACM ISBN 978-1-4503-3542-3/15/08.
DOI: http://dx.doi.org/10.1145/2785956.2790038

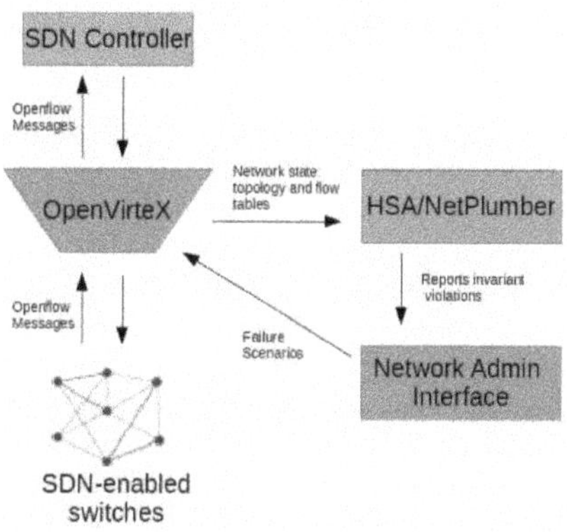

Figure 1: Overview of Chaos Monkey Architecture.

- **Leveraging network redundancies:** The injected failures should not disconnect the graph.
- **Detecting network-wide invariant violations:** The injected failures should aim at uncovering given invariant violations, e.g., reachability guarantees.

The concept of injecting failures into a live production network system is certainly counter-intuitive, but we assert that there is no better way to efficiently simulate actual network usage than within the actual runtime environment. Testbeds cover a limited case and simply do not scale up to production levels; some problems – inherently complex and difficult to reproduce – only manifest at scale.

2. IMPLEMENTATION

There are three major components that are necessary to achieve the ultimate goal of dynamic failure injection and invariant verification. These components and their roles are illustrated in Figure 1.

Chaos Monkey utilizes a OpenVirteX (OVX) [3] as a means of monitoring and affecting the network state. OVX sits between the network and the SDN controller, relaying messages between them. To perform the invariant checking, Chaos Monkey employs NetPlumber [4]. NetPlumber provides a real-time solution to verifying invariants, such as forwarding loops, in the network topology. This module receives updated flow table information from OVX, checks for invariants, and provides the network operator with feedback.

Next, we describe the Chaos Monkey Pipeline and how NetPlumber and OVX fit into it:

Step 1: Define Failure Scenarios The primary purpose of this module is to compute a set of devices to fail under constraints. The anticipated use case of Chaos Monkey is for the network operator to iteratively test and refine the way Chaos Monkey injects failure into the network. Ultimately, the nature of these failures are described by a failure model.

The Failure Scenario constrains the behavior of the Chaos Monkey and the definition of this model is critical in finding a balance where Chaos Monkey realistically injects as many effective failures as possible without totally disrupting the overall functionality of the network. Since there are often several possible sets of failure scenarios, the best models is governed by probabilistic models that can be toggled by the network operator. This allows the network operator to throttle the amount of failures during times of reduced network usage.

Step 2: Inject Failures Up to this point in the process, no failure has actually been injected into the network. The purpose of this module is to schedule and subsequently inject the failures. In the previous step, the network operator has specified which subset of network resources to target; this module determines how frequently Chaos Monkey will fail the nodes. For example, this can allow the network operator to schedule Chaos Monkey by throttling the amount of failures during times of increased network usage. As far as the actual injection of failure, Chaos Monkey has some selection of failure classes to choose from. The failures are injected into the network using OVX's REST API, which has been extended to accommodate additional failure classes. At this point in the research, there exist implementations for network failure scenarios (e.g. switch down, link down) and increasing latency in the OpenFlow channel. There are many failure scenarios to consider beyond these, and we are actively extending our API to encompass more failure scenarios.

Step 3: Check Network Invariants The final module consists of the network invariant checker. Once the failures have been computed and injected into the network, the invariant checker analyzes the latest updates. Upon receiving the new network state, such as a topology change or a new flow table entry, NetPlumber analyzes the information against its invariants. Assuming the network has been properly updated, everything continues to operate with the new failures and the updated policy. If the latest policy violates an invariant, the information is logged for the network operator to analyze, the failure is undone, and the previous policy can be reinstalled in the network.

3. PROOF OF CONCEPT

Our proof of concept consists of creating a scenario in which the controller incorrectly installs a forwarding loop in the network upon the failure of a link.

The figure depicts a route in red from H1 to H2 that is configured by the SDN Controller, while the backup route, in green, is the path that the network should take upon the injection of failure; the backup route is pushed when the S4-S5 link is severed. When OVX reports the updated flows to NetPlumber, there are two outcomes depending on the controller and policies in question. A transient forwarding loop can be created, if the controller pushes flows to the switches in the order: S1, S6, S4, S2, S5. In this case, since the original red route flows have not yet been removed by the controller, there will be a transient forwarding loop circulating between S2, S3, and S4. On the other hand, no network invariants would be violated if the routes are pushed in the order: S5, S2, S4, S6, S1. The Chaos Monkey algorithmically decides on a link to fail and detects the violated network invariant.

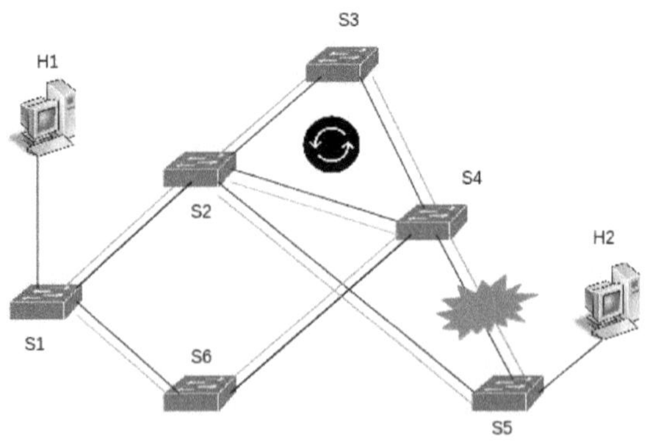

Figure 2: Example topology with a forwarding loop.

4. CONCLUSION

In this paper, we have laid the foundation for post-deployment failure injector for SDN Controllers. While this testing paradigm has been used in various cloud computing applications, this is the first step towards developing a solution for realtime SDN Controller verification. With many classes of network failure, it will be a continued effort to extend the SDN Chaos Monkey such that we can demonstrate coverage across possible failure classes. Developers of the controller platform will be able to use the SDN Chaos Monkey tool to test how the controller responds to any sequence of failures that could reasonably occur in the network. There are truly an endless amount of failures that could appear in the network, and it would be unreasonable for anyone – even Chaos Monkey – to cover them all. However, the Chaos Monkey utility encourages a testing paradigm that leads to continual and constant improvement on a complex piece of software upon which the entire network depends on. As the SDN controller becomes a more reliable and stable software agent, the SDN movement will gain further credibility and continue to disrupt the landscape of networking.

5. REFERENCES

[1] M. Canini, D. Venzano, P. Peresini, D. Kostic, J. Rexford *et al.*, "A nice way to test openflow applications." in *NSDI*, vol. 12, 2012, pp. 127–140.

[2] C. Bennett and A. Tseitlin, "Netflix: Chaos monkey released into the wild. netflix tech blog," 2012.

[3] A. Al-Shabibi, M. De Leenheer, M. Gerola, A. Koshibe, W. Snow, and G. Parulkar, "Openvirtex: A network hypervisor," *Open Networking Summit*, 2014.

[4] P. Kazemian, M. Chan, H. Zeng, G. Varghese, N. McKeown, and S. Whyte, "Real time network policy checking using header space analysis." in *NSDI*, 2013, pp. 99–111.

Network Policy Whiteboarding and Composition

Jeongkeun Lee Joon-Myung Kang Chaithan Prakash°*
Sujata Banerjee Yoshio Turner†* Aditya Akella° Charles Clark‡
Yadi Ma Puneet Sharma Ying Zhang
HP Labs, °University of Wisconsin-Madison, †Banyan, ‡HP Networking

ABSTRACT

We present Policy Graph Abstraction (PGA) that graphically expresses network policies and service chain requirements, just as simple as drawing whiteboard diagrams. Different users independently draw policy graphs that can constrain each other. PGA graph clearly captures user intents and invariants and thus facilitates automatic composition of overlapping policies into a coherent policy.

CCS Concepts

•Networks → Programming interfaces; Network management; *Middle boxes / network appliances; Programmable networks;*

1. INTRODUCTION

Managing network traffic and application workloads based on high-level policy is an important current topic in SDN, cloud and NFV (Network Function Virtualization). Recent policy abstractions and languages proposed in [5, 3, 1, 2] provide high expressiveness for describing policies, but they have steep learning curves and are thus confined mostly to expert users. Moreover, existing work do not yet clearly support modular composition of multiple policies from different stakeholders; SDN and cloud automation enabled a large number of diverse parties (operators, application admins, tenants/end-users) and control programs (SDN-apps, network services) to generate network policies independently and dynamically. Simply running those policies in series/parallel [3], or in a prioritized order often fails to satisfy the intent of stakeholders because 1) each policy can consist of multiple dimensions (security, QoS, middlebox), and 2) their intents can constrain each other in each dimension. And some intents are not clear enough in existing languages to systemically compose them; they need to be manually decomposed and re-composed by a human oracle who has accurate knowledge of the hidden- or joint-intents of different stakeholders.

We proposed Policy Graph Abstraction (PGA) at this year SIGCOMM [4] with two major contributions: 1) intuitive high-level graph model enabling diverse stakeholders to clearly express their portable intents without needing IP/subnet assignment, and 2) eager, automatic composition of independently specified policy graphs, creating one coherent composed policy. In particular, eagerly detecting and composing overlapping policies (on common traffic) prior to system deployment is critical to prevent unexpected runtime behavior caused by incomplete resolution of conflicts between the overlapping policies. Our full paper [4] formally describes and evaluates the model and composition algorithm; this demo prototype shows the full cycle of policy graph specification, composition and deployment in OpenStack cloud platform through our GUI. We will also show how the graph model and its constructs facilitate the eager & automatic composition.

*This work was performed while at HP Labs.

SIGCOMM '15 August 17-21, 2015, London, United Kingdom

ACM ISBN 978-1-4503-3542-3/15/08.
DOI: http://dx.doi.org/10.1145/2785956.2790039

2. POLICY GRAPH

A PGA policy graph takes three forms: input graph, composed graph, and deployed graph. Each policy stakeholder creates one or more *input graphs*, which our graph composer composes together from multiple stakeholders and generates a single system-wide *composed graph* (Fig. 1) with log/error messages. Some input graphs' policies can be rejected or changed during the composition process, e.g., due to global or other policies' constraints. The owners of rejected/changed input graphs can accept the changes or revise their input graphs and resubmit. A composed graph can be approved by an authority (e.g., operators) and becomes ready to deploy. Once deployed down to the underlying network, it is stored as a *deployed graph* and used for runtime policy enforcement.

Graph Model: a PGA user expresses his/her input policy as a directed multi-graph where a vertex represents a group of network endpoints (EPG, endpoint group) sharing common properties expressed in terms of *labels*. A directed edge connecting a pair of EPGs expresses various intents on the communication from the source EPG to the destination EPG. Each edge has a match classifier on L3/L4 header fields, refining the traffic that the edge cares about from the source to the destination. A user can draw multiple edges of different classifiers between the same EPG pair.

EPG Labeling: high-level, portable policy specification must be decoupled from low-level specifics (e.g., IP/MAC addresses). For that, a PGA user can 1) define an EPG (graph vertex) as a boolean expression of logical labels, each representing diverse endpoint attributes such as tenant ownership, network location or security/QoS status, and 2) specify policies for the EPG. In a running system, the policies are applied to a set of endpoints that have labels satisfying the boolean expression specified for the EPG. In a cloud example, an EPG of [Infected&Tenant1&¬AZ2] represents malware-infected VMs of Tenant1 placed in anywhere else than Availability Zone 2.

Decoupling policy specification from address assignment poses a challenge in eagerly identifying the policies that overlap and thus need to be composed together. PGA captures the overlapping or

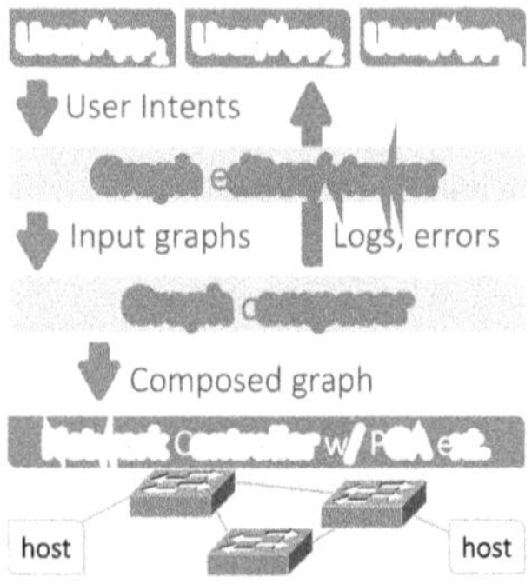

Figure 1: PGA components.

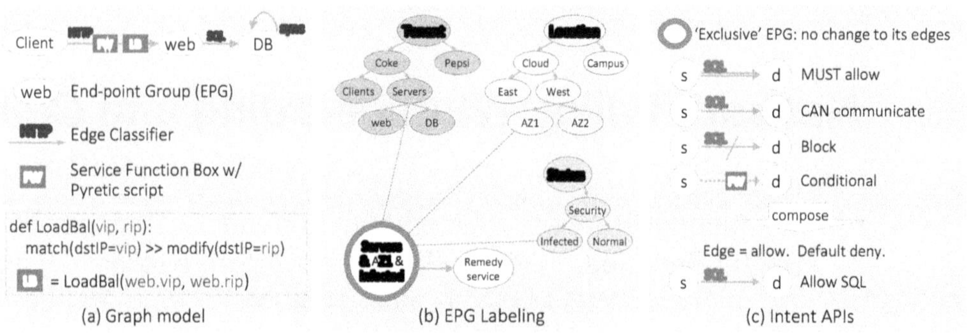

Figure 2: PGA model and APIs.

mutually exclusive relation between labels in *label hierarchy trees* and *label mappings* and uses them to eagerly identify policies to be composed together. A parent label (e.g., 'Servers' label in Fig. 2(b)) is a boolean OR of its children labels (web and DB), thus an EPG defined from the parent label can have overlapping endpoints with EPGs defined from the children labels. Any set of labels in the same tree that do not have an ancestor relationship (e.g., web and DB) are mutually exclusive, thus cannot be assigned on any common endpoint. Two labels from different trees that can be assigned on a common endpoint have a symmetric mapping relation in *label mapping*, e.g., Servers and Infected labels in Fig. 2(b). PGA collects label information from external services (tenant authentication, VM placement, SDN control apps, etc.) and display them in the graph editor to help users easily and correctly create EPGs from the labels.

ACL Intent APIs: Since input policies can be changed during the composition process, PGA provides a few constructs for individual stakeholders to clearly express their intents/invariants in input graphs. A user can choose from four types of edges to express their access control intents: Must Allow, Can Communicate, Block, and Conditional (Fig. 2(c)). These edge types are evolved from the *composition constraint table* construct of [4] that are designed to constrain on the policy changes made by any other policy graph being composed together. We found the edge type representation provides better usability and clarity in GUI than the constraint table form; they achieve the same goal of supporting automatic composition of overlapping ACL policies.

A *Must Allow* edge in an input graph indicates that the communication specified by the edge classifier must be allowed regardless of other policies to be composed with, i.e., an Allow edge must exist for the classifier space in the final composed graph. Management traffic and service-critical communications are examples of this Must Allow type. A *Can Communicate* edge also intends to allow traffic but it can be eventually blocked by other policies. An enterprise IT can use this edge type to 'open' a set of TCP ports for employees to use while allowing them to block some or all the ports per their policies. A *Block* edge type is a constraint that prohibit certain traffic from ever being allowed even if they are allowed by other policy graphs; i.e., the specified traffic must not be allowed in the composed graph. Block edge is useful to implement ACL blacklisting, while using Can type for $\{*\} - BL$ (BL is a set of protocols/ports to block) correctly expresses the weak Allow intent for everything else than BL; using Must Allow for $\{*\} - BL$ might be too strong and might create unnecessary conflicts with Block intents. A *Conditional* edge means there is no need to allow in this graph but it can be allowed in other graphs. By default *no edge* in an input graph is interpreted as Conditional; a policy writer can change the default setting to Block (for whitelisting) or Can (for blacklisting).

With these fine-grained intent APIs, a conflict is clearly detected and resolved: Must/Can edge overrides Conditional while Block wins over Can. A conflict between Must and Block is reported to users or can be resolved based on ranking between policies or stakeholders: e.g., IT admin's Block wins over employee's Must edge. Rejected policies are reported to the policy owners to review, which is possible in PGA's eager policy composition. PGA also provides convenient shorthands such as 'exclusive' EPG that doesn't allow any change or addition of edges of the EPG [4]; e.g, in Fig. 2(b), the EPG of Infected Servers in AZ1 is marked as 'exclusive', preventing other policies from thwarting the intention of the policy writer to redirect all traffic from infected hosts to a remediation server.

Service chaining: An edge of any type except for Block can have a chain of *function boxes*, each representing logical network function (NF) such as firewall, load-balancer or byte-counter. Regardless of its deployment methodology (HW, VM, or SDN programs), each NF can be modeled (by users or vendors) in our variant of Pyretic programming language [3] describing its high-level bounding behavior. This *gray-boxing* approach enables dependency analysis and ordering of NFs in a composed service chains [4]. A service chain on a Conditional edge specifies a pure service chain requirement which is instantiated if and only if the edge's match classifier overlaps the classifier of a Must/Can edge in a different policy graph. E.g, a cloud operator wanting to count bytes of every tenant traffic can use a Conditional edge with a byte-counter function box on it; this edge itself does not allow any traffic, but it counts bytes if any traffic is allowed by tenant policies.

3. COMPOSITION AND DEPLOYMENT

The graph composer computes a union of EPGs of input graphs and merging ACL policies given by edge classifiers and service chain requirements, except when doing so would violate the global invariants and user-given constrains [4]. Our prototype supports two deployment paths: 1) POX OpenFlow controller, reactively generating OpenFlow rules for pkt-in events based on an eagerly composed policy graph, and 2) OpenStack network service, Neutron, for proactively configuring security and service chain rules through Neutron APIs. The demo will show the system running in OpenStack.

4. REFERENCES

[1] OpenDaylight Group Policy. https://wiki.opendaylight.org/view/Group_Policy:Main.

[2] Openstack Congress. https://wiki.openstack.org/wiki/Congress.

[3] C. Monsanto, J. Reich, N. Foster, J. Rexford, and D. Walker. Composing Software Defined Networks. In *NSDI*, 2013.

[4] C. Prakash, J. Lee, Y. Turner, J.-M. Kang, A. Akella, S. Banerjee, C. Clark, Y. Ma, P. Sharma, and Y. Zhang. PGA: Using Graphs to Express and Automatically Reconcile Network Policies. In *SIGCOMM*, 2015.

[5] R. Soulé, S. Basu, P. J. Marandi, F. Pedone, R. Kleinberg, E. G. Sirer, and N. Foster. Merlin: A Language for Provisioning Network Resources. In *CoNEXT*, 2014.

Virtual Network Function Orchestration with Scylla

Roberto Riggio
CREATE-NET
Trento, Italy
rriggio@create-net.org

Julius Schulz–Zander
TU-Berlin
Berlin, Germany
julius@inet.tu-berlin.de

Abbas Bradai
CNRS-LiG
Grenoble, France
bradai@imag.fr

ABSTRACT

Network Function Virtualization promises to reduce the cost to deploy and to operate large networks by migrating various network functions from dedicated hardware appliances to software instances running on general purpose networking and computing platforms. In this paper we demonstrate *Scylla* a *Programmable Network Fabric* architecture for Enterprise WLANs. The framework supports basic Virtual Network Function lifecycle management functionalities such as instantiation, monitoring, and migration. We release the entire platform under a permissive license for academic use.

Categories and Subject Descriptors

C.2.3 [**Computer Communication Networks**]: Network Operations

Keywords

Network Function Virtualization, Enterprise WLANs

1. INTRODUCTION

Network Function Virtualization (NFV) promises to reduce the cost to deploy and to operate large networks by migrating various network functions from dedicated hardware appliances to software instances running on general purpose networking and computing platforms. This in time shall improve the flexibility and the scalability of the network in that the deployment of new features and services can be quicker (software vs hardware life–cycles) and different network functions can share the same computing resources paving the way to further economies of scale.

Nevertheless, current NFV platforms typically only account for (virtualized) computing, storage, and networking resources with each of these resource managed separately. In this demo we want to take a step toward a truly deep programmable network by introducing the concept of *Programmable Network Fabric*. Our architecture leverages on a single platform consisting of general purpose hardware (x86) and operating system (Linux) in order to deliver three kinds of virtualized network resources, namely: basic forwarding nodes (i.e. OpenFlow–enabled Ethernet switches), packet processing nodes, and radio processing nodes (WiFi).

SIGCOMM '15 August 17-21, 2015, London, United Kingdom

ACM ISBN 978-1-4503-3542-3/15/08.
DOI: http://dx.doi.org/10.1145/2785956.2790040

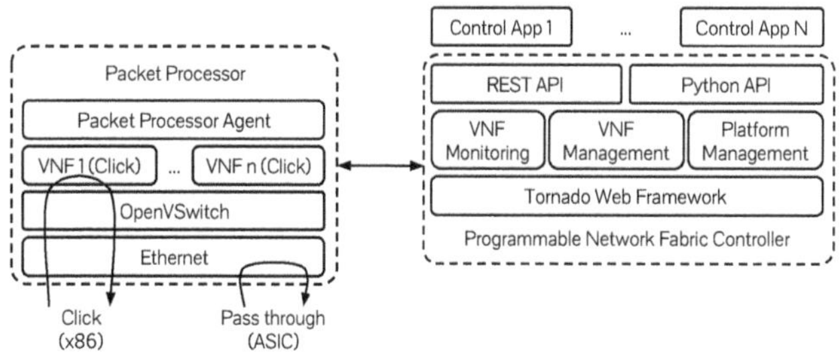

Figure 1: *Programmable Network Fabric Controller.*

During this demo we will show *Scylla* a *Programmable Network Fabric* architecture for Enterprise WLANs. *Scylla* supports basic Virtual Network Function (VNF) lifecycle management functionalities (instantiation, monitoring, and migration). The demo will demonstrate the framework operation using three sample VNFs: a performance enhancing VNF, a security VNF, and a monitoring VNF. Finally we release the code under a permissive license for academic use[1].

2. PROGRAMMABLE NETWORK FABRIC

We name *Programmable Network Fabric* the set of all packet processing nodes. As it can be seen in Fig. 1 each packet processing node includes an OpenVSwitch instance, one or more VNFs, and one Packet Processor Agent. The latter is in charge of monitoring the status of each VNF as well as handling CRUD requests coming from the *Programmable Network Fabric Controller* (*PNFC*). The monitoring features includes: number of packets/bytes transmitted and received as well as the amount of resources (cpu time, memory, and storage) utilized by each VNF.

The *PNFC* acts as an orchestrator deciding whether a particular VNF request can be accepted or if it must be refused [1]. If a request is accepted, then the *PNFC* is in charge of mapping the request onto the substrate network, i.e., network resources must be allocated and configured on the substrate nodes and links and the VNFs must be installed on the selected nodes.

A combination of frameworks is used in our architecture. POX [2] is used in order to configure resources in the switching fabric, while the SD–RAN controller proposed by the authors in [3] is used in the wireless access. Finally, we use Click [4] as a single solution for advanced packet processing. Click allows to build complex VNFs using simple and

[1]http://scylla.create-net.org/

reusable components, called *Elements*. Click includes over 300 elements supporting functions such as packet classification, access control, deep packet inspection. Elements can be composed in order to realize complex VNFs. Finally, Click is easily extensible with custom processing elements making it possible to support features that are not provided by the standard elements.

The *PNFC* is build on top of the Tornado Web Framework [5]. Communication between packet processors and the *PNFC* takes place over a persistent TCP connection. Control applications run on top of the *PNFC* and exploit its programming primitives through either a REST API or a native Python API.

Scylla VNFs are modular and reusable components consisting of a Click instance wrapped inside a Python object exposing lifecycle management functions. A *Manifest* is attached to each VNF specifying the Click configuration, the number of input/output ports as well as a list of events that can be subscribed by control applications. The latter allow programmers to trigger a callback the first time a certain condition is verified. For example the `cpu_util` primitive will trigger a callback the first time the CPU utilization of any Packet Processor in a tenant's network exceeds 70%:

```
cpu_util(relation='GT',
         value=0.7,
         tenant_id='<UUID>',
         callback=cpu_callback)
```

Listing 1: Create an CPU Utilization trigger.

After the trigger has fired the first time and as long as the CPU utilization remains above 70%, the callback method is not called again by the same packet processor however the same callback may be triggered by other packet processors.

Scylla VNFs may also declare a state in their *Manifest* file. A VNF state is defined in the form of Click handlers that must be invoked in order to obtain a snapshot of an active VNF. Such snapshots are atomic and lock the VNF execution for the time required to invoke the handlers. State handlers must support both read and write operations allowing a VNF state to be migrated from one node to another.

3. DEMO

In this demo we show the operation of the *Scylla* framework using three VNFs. This section describes the purpose of each VNF. During the demo a web-based dashboard will be used to both show real-time statistics (traffic, cpu load, memory usage, energy consumption) as well as to deploy and migrate VNFs.

3.1 Uplink/Downlink Decoupling

Wireless, and in particular mobile networks, have been so far designed around the requirements of the downlink. In the recent years, however, we have observed a growth of new uplink-centric applications such as Machine Type Communications and Internet of Things. This calls for a paradigm shift where the traffic originated from a wireless client is opportunistically received by multiple in-range APs. However, if not properly controlled such a feature can lead to an overload in the network core. For example, a wireless client scheduled on N APs in the uplink direction could increase the load on the network core by a factor of N. Moreover, a straightforward implementation of such a mechanism can lead to a significant increase of frames which in turn can trigger an unstable behavior at the transport layer.

In order to address this issue we implemented a VNF which filters out duplicate 802.11 frames based on their sequence number. Traffic originated from clients is received at one or more APs where it is encapsulated (802.11 over Ethernet) and then forwarded to a packet processing node where the frame filtering VNF is deployed. This VNF is also responsible for removing the 802.11 and the LLC headers and for encapsulating the frame into an Ethernet header before forwarding it to its intended destination. The Click script implementing this VNF is reported in the listing below[2].

```
FromHost(vnf0)
 -> in :: Counter
 -> Strip(14)
 -> dupe :: WifiDupeFilter()
 -> decap :: WifiDecap()
 -> out :: Counter
 -> ToHost(vnf0);
```

Listing 2: Duplicate filtering VNF.

3.2 Firewall Migration

Today's enterprise networks often need to deal with BYOD where employees or customers connect their own devices to a corporate network. This, however, raises new requirements on the network access policies. Our second VNF implements a straightforward firewall where rules can be moved from one instance to another depending on the client association state, i.e., rules are migrated when clients perform a handoff from one AP to another. This firewall VNF takes a list of tcpdump-like patterns as input from the controller and applies them to the incoming traffic.

3.3 SLA Monitoring

This VNF aims at implementing a basic SLA monitoring solution. In this scenario a packet sniffing VNF is deployed on radio nodes. This VNF collects all transmissions within decoding range of the radio node. For each link-layer event the following meta-data is tracked: *RSSI* (in dB), *Transmission Rate* (in Mb/s), *Length* (in bytes), and *Duration* (in μsec). The collected meta-data is then forwarded to another VNF which computes aggregate statistics by filtering our duplicate frames. In particular for each active WiFi station the number of packets/bytes transmitted and received as well as the retransmission count are tracked.

4. REFERENCES

[1] R. Riggio, T. Rasheed, and R. Narayanan, "Virtual network functions orchestration in enterprise wlans," in *Proc. of IEEE ManFI*, Ottawa, ON, Canada, 2015.

[2] "POX." [Online]. Available: http://www.noxrepo.org/pox/about-pox/

[3] R. Riggio, M. Marina, J. Schulz-Zander, S. Kuklinski, and T. Rasheed, "Programming abstractions for software-defined wireless networks," *Network and Service Management, IEEE Transactions on*, vol. 12, no. 2, pp. 146–162, June 2015.

[4] E. Kohler, R. Morris, B. Chen, J. Jannotti, and M. F. Kaashoek, "The click modular router," *ACM Trans. Comput. Syst.*, vol. 18, no. 3, pp. 263–297, Aug. 2000.

[5] "Tornado Web Server." [Online]. Available: http://www.tornadoweb.org/

[2] `vnf0` is a virtual interface attached to the OpenVSwitch instance running on the packet processing node.

Multi-Domain Service Orchestration Over Networks and Clouds: A Unified Approach

Balázs Sonkoly[1], János Czentye[1], Robert Szabo[2], Dávid Jocha[2], János Elek[2], Sahel Sahhaf[3], Wouter Tavernier[3], Fulvio Risso[4]
[1]Budapest University of Technology and Economics; [2]Ericsson Research; [3]Ghent University – iMinds; [4]Politecnico di Torino
balazs.sonkoly@tmit.bme.hu

ABSTRACT

End-to-end service delivery often includes transparently inserted Network Functions (NFs) in the path. Flexible service chaining will require dynamic instantiation of both NFs and traffic forwarding overlays. Virtualization techniques in compute and networking, like cloud and Software Defined Networking (SDN), promise such flexibility for service providers. However, patching together existing cloud and network control mechanisms necessarily puts one over the above, e.g., OpenDaylight under an OpenStack controller. We designed and implemented a joint cloud and network resource virtualization and programming API. In this demonstration, we show that our abstraction is capable for flexible service chaining control over any technology domains.

Keywords

NFV; SDN; multi-domain orchestration; SFC control plane

1. INTRODUCTION

On top of cloud platforms, services can be created, managed and scaled on-demand. Efficient virtualization techniques and novel orchestration algorithms enable flexible operation and optimal usage of underlying resources. Besides virtual compute and storage resources, basic networking is also provided in order to connect the virtual machines. In contrast, traditional telecommunication services and carrier networks have a lot of limitations concerning service creation, service deployment or service provisioning due to built-in mechanisms strongly coupled to physical topologies and special purpose hardware appliances. Network Function Virtualization (NFV) opens the door between cloud technologies and carrier networks by providing software-based telecommunication services, which can run in virtualized environments over a wide range of general purpose servers. By these means, recent achievements from cloud researches can be leveraged and adopted in carrier environments.

Flexible service definition and creation may start by abstracting and formalizing the service into the concept of service chain or service graph. It is a generic way to describe high level services and to assemble processing flows for given traffic. Today, remarkable attention is focused on the concept of Service Function Chaining (SFC) and NFV. IETF, ETSI, MEF, Linux Foundation and several research projects address different aspects of SFC. For example, IETF is working on an SFC architecture and data plane elements; ETSI has proposed a management and orchestration framework for NFV; Linux Foundation launched the Open Platform for NFV Project (OPNFV), a carrier-grade open source reference platform.

UNIFY[1] is an EU-funded FP7 project, which aims at unifying cloud and carrier network resources in a common orchestration framework. We designed a novel SFC control plane which is capable of integrating *any* infrastructure domains including different NF execution environments, SDN networks or legacy data centers. Our architecture supports automated, dynamic service creation and multi-domain NFV orchestration. Central to our design is the definition of a joint virtualization and resource programming interface unifying cloud and network resources. In this demonstration, we highlight the power of this approach to control SFC deployments over multi-technology domains.

2. PROOF OF CONCEPT

In UNIFY, we have proposed a *joint, narrow waist SFC control plane* over compute (with storage) and network resources for flexible service creation. Our control plane design enables *recursive orchestration* of several types of resources and supports different even legacy technologies and migration between them. Furthermore, we have introduced a novel infrastructure element called *Universal Node* (UN) which is a COTS hardware based packet processor node with the capability of *i*) high performance forwarding and *ii*) running high complexity NFs in its virtualized environment. Our proof of concept prototype realizing the envisioned architecture is shown in Fig. 1.

Our virtualization is based on the concept of Big Switch with Big Software (BiS-BiS) elements, which is a forwarding element combined with software (compute and storage) resources capable of *i*) running NFs and *ii*) steering traffic transparently among infrastructure and NF ports. The key concept is that BiS-BiS combines cloud resources with forwarding behavior control. The virtualization view may contain arbitrary interconnection of BiS-BiS nodes. SFC pro-

[1]http://www.fp7-unify.eu

SIGCOMM '15 August 17-21, 2015, London, United Kingdom

ACM ISBN 978-1-4503-3542-3/15/08.
DOI: http://dx.doi.org/10.1145/2785956.2790025

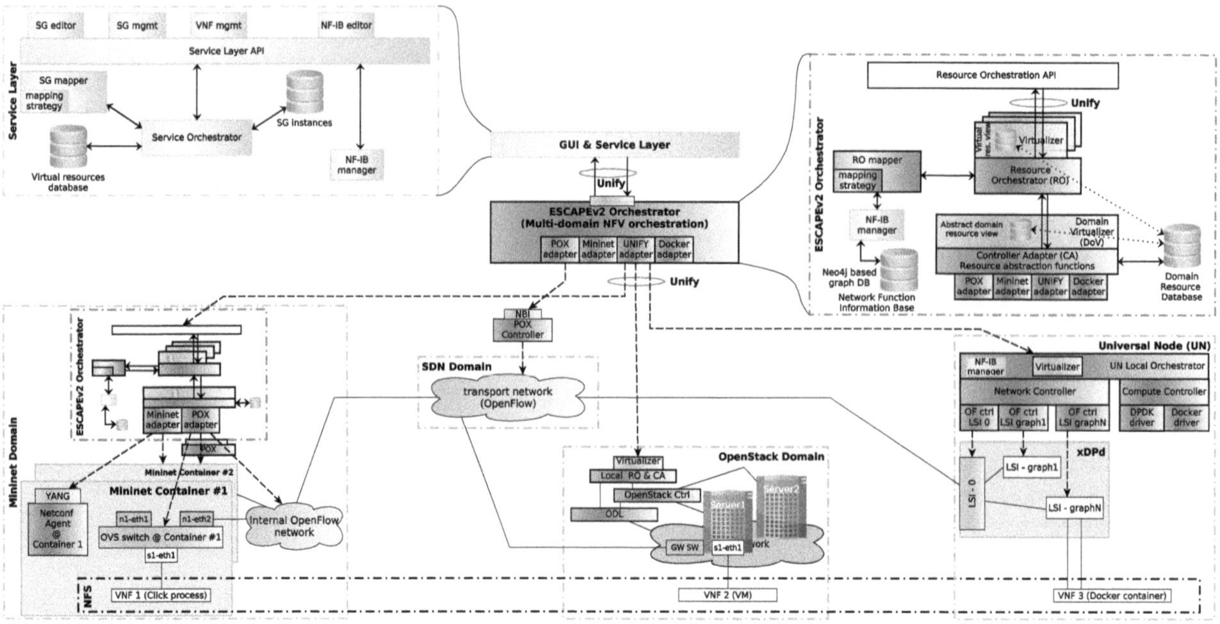

Figure 1: Joint SFC control plane architecture on top of different technological domains.

gramming is realized by *i)* assigning NFs to BiS-BiS nodes and by *ii)* editing the flowrules within BiS-BiS nodes. The task of the resource orchestrator is to map the configurations of different client virtualizations to a configuration at the underlying domain virtualizer. Additionally, we introduced the concept of NF decomposition, i.e., an NF mapped to a BiS-BiS in the client virtualization can be replaced with an interconnection of NFs (components) during the mapping process [2]. The data model of the virtualizer is defined in Yang. In Fig. 1, virtualizers are denoted by green boxes and they provide virtual views (interconnected BiS-BiS nodes) for their managers (clients). Managers are resource orchestrators (shown by red boxes) configuring (controlling) the given view. The manager - virtualizer relationship is recursive, thus Unify domains can be stacked into a multi-level control hierarchy similar to ONF's SDN architecture. The recursive interface is the Unify interface.

The initial version of our open-source NFV orchestration framework was presented in [1]. It has been significantly redesigned in order to meet the design goals and requirements of the joint SFC control plane addressed by UNIFY. Now, ESCAPEv2 framework *i)* enables recursive orchestration by implementing Unify interfaces at north and south; *ii)* operates on our novel joint resource abstraction models; *iii)* supports UNIFY domains directly and several technological domains via adapters; *iv)* can be extended easily with additional plug and play components/algorithms, like NF implementations, network embedding algorithms, NF decomposition models.

On top of ESCAPEv2, we have implemented a simple service layer with GUI (see the upper left part of Fig. 1) where users can define service requests with their requirements, e.g., bandwidth or delay constraints between arbitrary elements in the service graph. The service layer contains a service orchestrator which is responsible for mapping the service request to the virtualizer. If a service orchestrator sees only *a single* BiS-BiS node then its orchestration task is trivial. Such setup allows delegation of all resource management to the lower layer Unify domain which is realized by the resource orchestrator component (see upper right part of Fig. 1). Here, the domain resource view is constructed by our domain virtualizer and controller adapter modules. At the infrastructure level, different technologies are supported and integrated with the framework. We kept our Mininet based domain orchestrated by a dedicated ESCAPEv2 entity via NETCONF and OpenFlow control channels. Here, the NFs are run as isolated Click processes. As a legacy data center solution, we support clouds managed by OpenStack and OpenDaylight. This requires a UNIFY conform local orchestrator to be implemented on top of an OpenStack domain. The control of legacy OpenFlow networks is realized by a POX controller and a corresponding adapter module. And finally, a proof of concept implementation of our Universal Node concept is also provided. UN local orchestrator is responsible for controlling logical switch instances (accelerated by Intel's DPDK) and for managing NFs running as Docker containers.

During the demo, we showcase *i)* how to create joint domain abstraction for networks and clouds; *ii)* how to orchestrate and optimize resource allocation and deploy service chains over these unified resources; *iii)* how we can take advantage of recursive orchestration and NF decomposition[2].

Acknowledgements - This work was conducted within the framework of the FP7 UNIFY project, which is partially funded by the Commission of the European Union.

3. REFERENCES

[1] A. Csoma, B. Sonkoly, L. Csikor, F. Németh, A. Gulyás, W. Tavernier, and S. Sahhaf. ESCAPE: Extensible Service ChAin Prototyping Environment using Mininet, Click, NETCONF and POX. In *Proc. of the ACM SIGCOMM 2014*, 2014.

[2] S. Sahhaf, W. Tavernier, D. Colle, and M. Pickavet. Network service chaining with efficient network function mapping based on service decompositions. In *1st IEEE Conference on Network Softwarization, NetSoft 2015*, 2015.

[2]Further details: http://sb.tmit.bme.hu/UNIFY15

Hopper: Decentralized Speculation-aware Cluster Scheduling at Scale

Xiaoqi Ren[1], Ganesh Ananthanarayanan[2], Adam Wierman[1], Minlan Yu[3]
[1]California Institute of Technology,
[2]Microsoft Research,
[3]University of Southern California,
{xren,adamw}@caltech.edu, ga@microsoft.com, minlanyu@usc.edu

ABSTRACT

As clusters continue to grow in size and complexity, providing *scalable and predictable* performance is an increasingly important challenge. A crucial roadblock to achieving *predictable* performance is stragglers, i.e., tasks that take significantly longer than expected to run. At this point, speculative execution has been widely adopted to mitigate the impact of stragglers. However, speculation mechanisms are designed and operated independently of job scheduling when, in fact, scheduling a speculative copy of a task has a direct impact on the resources available for other jobs. In this work, we present Hopper, a job scheduler that is speculation-aware, i.e., that integrates the tradeoffs associated with speculation into job scheduling decisions. We implement both centralized and decentralized prototypes of the Hopper scheduler and show that 50% (66%) improvements over state-of-the-art centralized (decentralized) schedulers and speculation strategies can be achieved through the *coordination* of scheduling and speculation.

CCS Concepts

•Networks → Cloud computing; •Computer systems organization → Distributed architectures;

Keywords

speculation; decentralized scheduling; straggler; fairness

1. INTRODUCTION

Data analytics frameworks have successfully realized the promise of "scaling out" by automatically composing user-submitted scripts into *jobs* of many parallel *tasks* and executing them on large clusters. However, as clusters increase in size and complexity, providing *scalable* and *predictable* performance is an important ongoing challenge for interactive analytics frameworks [2, 32]. Indeed, production clusters at Google and Microsoft [17, 23] acknowledge this as a prominent goal.

As the scale and complexity of clusters increase, hard-to-model systemic interactions that degrade the performance of tasks become common [12, 23]. Consequently, many tasks become "stragglers", i.e., running slower than expected, leading to significant *unpredictability* (and delay) in job completion times – tasks in Facebook's Hadoop cluster can run up to 8× slower than expected [12]. The most successful and widely deployed straggler mitigation solution is *speculation*, i.e., speculatively running extra copies of tasks that have become stragglers (or likely to), and then picking the earliest copy that finishes, e.g., [12, 14, 15, 24, 50]. Speculation is commonplace in production clusters, e.g., in our analysis of Facebook's Hadoop cluster, speculative tasks account for 25% of all tasks and 21% of resource usage.

Speculation is intrinsically intertwined with job scheduling because spawning a speculative copy of a task has a direct impact on the resources available for *other* jobs. Aggressive speculation can improve the performance of the job at hand but hurt the performance of other jobs. Despite this, speculation policies deployed today are all designed and operated *independently* of job scheduling; schedulers simply allocate slots to speculative copies in a "best-effort" fashion, e.g., [14, 15, 24, 36].

Coordinating speculation and scheduling decisions is an opportunity for significant performance improvement. However, achieving such coordination is challenging, particularly as schedulers themselves *scale* out. Schedulers are increasingly becoming *decentralized* in order to scale to hundreds of thousands of machines with each machine equipped with tens of compute slots for tasks. This helps them make millions of scheduling decisions per second, a requirement about two orders of magnitude beyond the (already highly-optimized) centralized schedulers, e.g., [10, 29, 49]. In decentralized designs

SIGCOMM '15, August 17 - 21, 2015, London, United Kingdom
 ISBN 978-1-4503-3542-3/15/08...$15.00
DOI: http://dx.doi.org/10.1145/2785956.2787481

multiple schedulers operate *autonomously*, with each of them scheduling only a subset of the jobs, e.g., [19, 23, 36]. Thus, the coordination between speculation and scheduling must be achieved without maintaining central information about all the jobs.

Contribution of this paper: In this paper we present the design of the *first speculation-aware job scheduler*, Hopper, which dynamically allocates slots to jobs keeping in mind the speculation requirements necessary for *predictable* performance. Hopper incorporates a variety of factors such as data locality, estimates of task execution times, fairness, dependencies (DAGs) between tasks, etc. Further, Hopper is compatible with all current speculation algorithms and can operate as either a centralized or decentralized scheduler; achieving *scalability* by not requiring any central state.

The key insight behind Hopper is that a scheduler must anticipate the speculation requirements of jobs and dynamically allocate capacity depending on the *marginal* value (in terms of performance) of extra slots which are likely used for speculation. A novel observation that leads to the design of Hopper is that there is a sharp "threshold" in the marginal value of extra slots – an extra slot is always more beneficial for a job below its threshold than it is for any job above its threshold. The identification of such a threshold then allows Hopper to use different resource allocation strategies depending on whether the system capacity is such that all jobs can be allocated more slots than their threshold or not. This leads to a dynamic, adaptive, online scheduler that reacts to the current system load in a manner that appropriately weighs the value of speculation.

Importantly, the core components of Hopper can be *decentralized* effectively. The key challenge to avoiding the need to maintain a central state is the fact that stragglers create heavy-tailed task durations, e.g., see [12, 14, 25]. Hopper handles this by adopting a "power of many choices" viewpoint to approximate the global state, which is fundamentally more suited than the traditional "power of two choices" viewpoint due to the durations and frequency of stragglers.

To demonstrate the potential of Hopper, we have built three demonstration prototypes by augmenting the *centralized* scheduling frameworks Hadoop [3] (for batch jobs) and Spark [49] (for interactive jobs), and the *decentralized* framework Sparrow [36]. Hopper incorporates many practical features of jobs into its scheduling. Among others, it estimates the amount of *intermediate* data produced by the job and accounts for their pipelining between phases, integrates *data locality* requirements of tasks, and provides *fairness* guarantees.

We have evaluated our three prototypes on a 200 node private cluster using workloads derived from Facebook's and Microsoft Bing's production traces. The decentralized and centralized implementations of Hopper reduce the average job completion time by up to 66% and 50% compared to state-of-the-art scheduling and straggler mitigation techniques. The gains are consistent across common speculation algorithms (LATE [50], GRASS [14], and Mantri [15]), DAGs of tasks, and locality constraints, while providing fine-grained control on fairness. Importantly, the gains *do not* result from improving the speculation mechanisms but from improved *coordination* of scheduling and speculation decisions.

2. BACKGROUND & RELATED WORK

We begin by presenting a brief overview of existing cluster schedulers: how they allocate resources across jobs, both centralized and decentralized (§2.1), and how they handle straggling tasks (§2.2). This overview highlights the lack of coordination that currently exists between scheduling and straggler mitigation strategies such as speculation.

2.1 Cluster Schedulers

Job scheduling – allotting compute slots to jobs for their tasks – is a classic topic with a large body of work.

The most widely-used scheduling approach in clusters today is based on *fairness* which, without loss of generality, can be defined as equal sharing (or weighted sharing) of the available resources among jobs (or their users) [4, 26, 30, 45, 47]. Fairness, of course, comes with performance inefficiencies, e.g., [41, 48].

In contrast, the performance-optimal approach for job scheduling is *Shortest Remaining Processing Time (SRPT)*, which assigns slots to jobs in ascending order of their remaining duration (or, for simplicity, the remaining number of tasks). SRPT's optimality in both single [39] and multi-server [37] settings motivates a focus on prioritizing small jobs and has led to many schedulers such as [31, 33, 42].

The schedulers mentioned above are all centralized; however, motivated by scalability, many clusters are beginning to adopt *decentralized* schedulers, e.g., at Google [23], Apollo [17] at Microsoft, and the recently proposed Sparrow [36] scheduler. The scalability of decentralized designs allows schedulers to cope with growing cluster sizes and increasing parallelism of jobs (due to smaller tasks [34]), allowing them to scale to millions of scheduling decisions (for tasks) per second.

Importantly, the literature on cluster scheduling (both centralized and decentralized) ignores an important aspect of clusters: straggler mitigation via speculation. No current schedulers coordinate decisions with speculation mechanisms, while our analysis shows that speculative copies account for a sizeable fraction of all tasks in production clusters, e.g., in Facebook's Hadoop cluster, speculative tasks account for 25% of all tasks and 21% of resource usage.

2.2 Straggler Mitigation via Speculation

Dealing with *straggler* tasks, i.e., tasks that take significantly longer than expected to complete, is an important challenge for cluster schedulers, one that was called out in the original MapReduce paper [24], and a topic of significant subsequent research [12, 14, 15, 50].

Clusters already blacklist *problematic* machines (e.g., faulty disks or memory errors) and avoid scheduling tasks on them. However, despite blacklisting, stragglers occur frequently, often due to intrinsically complex causes such as IO contention, interference by periodic maintenance operations, and hardware behaviors which are hard to model and circumvent [12, 22, 35]. Straggler prevention based on comprehensive root-cause analyses is an open research challenge.

The most effective, and indeed the most widely deployed, technique has been *speculative* execution. Speculation techniques, monitor the progress of running tasks, compare them to the progress of completed tasks of the job, and spawn speculative copies for those progressing much slower, i.e., straggling. It is then a race between the original and speculative copies of the task and on completion of one, the other copies are killed.[1]

There is considerable (statistical and systemic) sophistication in speculation techniques, e.g., ensuring early detection of stragglers [15], predicting duration of new (and running) tasks [16], and picking lightly loaded machines to spawn speculative copies [50]. The techniques also take care to avoid speculation when a new copy is unlikely to benefit, e.g., when the single input source's machine is the cause behind the straggling [46].

Speculation has been highly effective in mitigating stragglers, bringing the ratio of the progress rates of the median task of a job to its slowest down from 8× (and 7×) to 1.08× (and 1.1×) in Facebook's production Hadoop cluster (and Bing's Dryad cluster).

Speculation has, to this point, been done independently of job scheduling. This is despite the fact that when a speculative task is scheduled it takes resources away from other jobs; thus there is an intrinsic tradeoff between scheduling speculative copies and scheduling new jobs. In this paper, we show that integrating these two via speculation-aware job scheduling can speed up jobs by considerably, even on average. Note that these gains are *not* due to improving the speculative execution techniques, but instead come purely from the integration between speculation and job scheduling decisions.

3. MOTIVATION

The previous section highlights that speculation and scheduling are currently designed and operated independently. Here, we illustrate the value of coordinated speculation and scheduling using simple examples.

3.1 Strawman Approaches

We first explore two baselines that characterize how scheduling and speculation interact today. In our examples we assume that stragglers can be detected after a task has run for 2 time units and that, at this point, a speculation is performed if the remaining running time (t_{rem}) is longer than the time to run a new copy (t_{new}). When the fastest copy of a task finishes, other running copies of the same task are killed. Note that while these examples have all jobs arrive at time 0, Hopper is designed to work in an online setting.

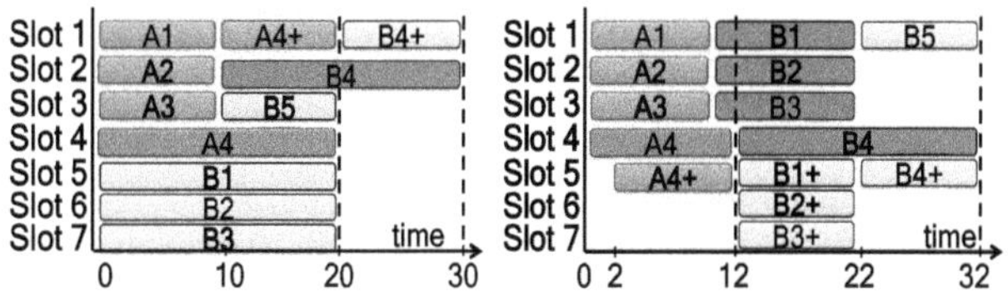

(a) Best-effort Speculation. (b) Budgeted Speculation

Figure 1: **Combining SRPT scheduling and speculation for two jobs A (4 tasks) and B (5 tasks) on a 7-slot cluster. The + suffix indicates speculation. Copies of tasks that are killed are colored red.**

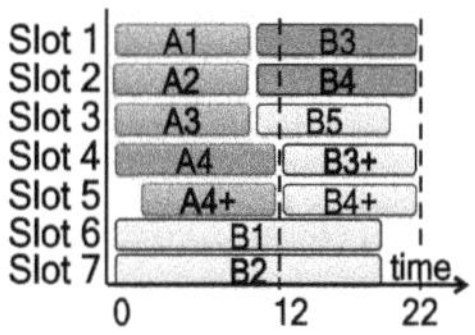

Figure 2: Hopper: **Completion time for jobs A and B are 12 and 22. The + suffix indicates speculation.**

A	A1	A2	A3	A4
t_{orig}	10	10	10	30
t_{new}	10	10	10	10

B	B1	B2	B3	B4	B5
t_{orig}	20	20	20	40	10
t_{new}	10	10	10	10	10

Table 1: t_{orig} **and** t_{new} **are durations of the original and speculative copies of each task.**

Best-Effort Speculation: A simple approach, which is also the most common in practice, is to treat speculative tasks the same as regular tasks. The job scheduler allocates resources for speculative tasks in a "best effort" manner, i.e., *whenever there is an open slot.*

Consider the example in Figure 1a with two jobs A (4 tasks) and B (5 tasks) that are scheduled using the SRPT policy. The scheduler has to wait until time 10 to find an open slot for the speculative copy of A4, despite detecting it was straggling at time 2.[2] Clearly, the scheduler can do better. If it had allocated a slot to A's speculative task at time 2 (instead of letting *B* use it), then job A's completion time would have reduced, without slowing job B (see Table 1 for task durations).

Note that similar inefficiencies occur under Fair scheduling in this example.

Budgeted Speculation: The main problem for best-effort speculation is a lack of available slots for speculation when needed. Thus, an alternative approach is to have the job scheduler *reserve* a fixed "budget" of slots for speculative tasks. Budgeting the right size of the resource pool for speculation, however, is challeng-

[1]Schedulers avoid checkpointing a straggling task's current output and spawning a new copy for just the remaining work due to the overheads and complexity of doing so. In general, even though the speculative copy is spawned on the expectation that it would be faster than the original, it is extremely hard to guarantee that in practice. Thus, both are allowed to run until the first completes.

[2]At time 10, when A1 finishes, the job scheduler allocates the slot to job A because its remaining processing is smaller than job B's. Job A speculates task A4 because A4's $t_{rem} = t_{orig} - \text{currentTime} = 30 - 10 = 20 > t_{new} = 10$ (see Table 1).

ing because of time-varying straggler characteristics and fluctuating cluster utilizations. If the resource pool is too small, it may not be enough to immediately support all the tasks that need speculation. If the pool is too large, resource are left idle.

Figure 1b illustrates budgeted speculation with three slots (slot 5 – 7) being reserved for speculation. This, unfortunately, leads to slots 6 and 7 lying fallow from time 0 to 12. If the wasted slot had been used to run a new task, say B1, then job B's completion time would have been reduced. It is easy to see that similar wastage of slots occurs with the Fair scheduler. Note that reserving one or two instead of three slots will not solve the problem, since three speculative copies are required to run simultaneously at a later time.

3.2 Challenges in Coordination

In contrast to the two baselines discussed above, Figure 2 shows the benefit of coordinated decision making.

At time 0 – 10, we allocate 1 extra slot to job A (for a total of 5 slots), thus allowing it to speculate task A4 promptly. After time 10, we can *dynamically reallocate* the slots to job B. This reduces the average completion time compared to both the budgeted and best-effort strategies. The joint design budgeted slot 5 until time 2 but after task A4 finished, it used all the slots.

Doing such dynamic allocation is already challenging in a centralized environment, and it becomes more so in a decentralized setting. In particular, decentralized speculation-aware scheduling has additional constraints. Since the schedulers are autonomous, there is no central state and thus, no scheduler has complete information about all the jobs in the cluster. Further, every scheduler has information about only a subset of the cluster (the machines it probed). Since decentralization is mainly critical for interactive jobs (sub-second or a few seconds), time-consuming gossiping between schedulers is infeasible. Finally, running *all* the schedulers on one multi-core machine cramps that machine and caps scalability, the original drawback they aim to alleviate.

In the above example, this means making the allocation as in Figure 2 when jobs A and B autonomously schedule their tasks without complete knowledge of utilizations of the slots or even each other's existence.

Thus, the challenges for speculation-aware job scheduling are: (i) *dynamically* allocating/budgeting slots for speculation based on the distribution of stragglers and cluster utilization while being (approximately) *fair* and, in decentralized settings, (ii) using *incomplete information* about the machines and jobs in the cluster.

4. Hopper: SPECULATION-AWARE SCHEDULING

The central question in the design of a speculation-aware job scheduler is how to dynamically (online) balance the slots used by speculative and original copies of tasks across jobs. A given job will complete more

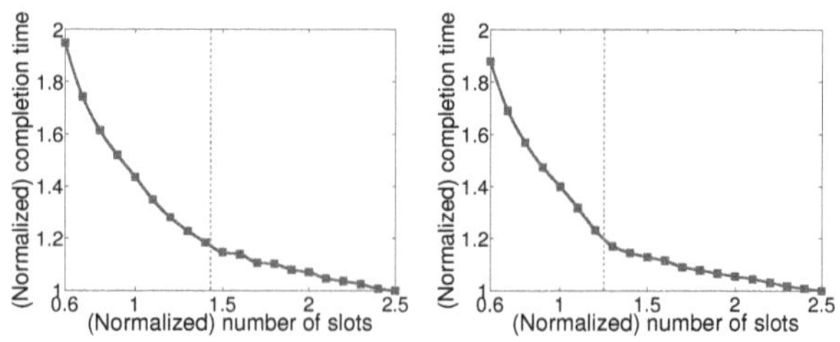

(a) $\beta = 1.4$ (b) $\beta = 1.6$

Figure 3: **The impact of number of slots on single job performance. The number of slots is normalized by job size (number of tasks within the job). β is the Pareto shape parameter for the task size distribution. (In our traces $1 < \beta < 2$.) The red vertical line shows the threshold point.**

quickly if it is allowed to do more speculation, but this comes at the expense of other jobs in the system.

Hopper's design is based on the insight that the balance between speculative and original tasks must dynamically depend on cluster utilization. The design guidelines that come out of this insight are supported by theoretical analysis in a simple model [8]. We omit the analytic support due to space constraints and focus on providing an intuitive justification for the design choices. Pseudocode 1 shows the basic structure.[3]

We begin our discussion of speculation-aware job scheduling by introducing the design features of Hopper in a centralized setting. We focus on single-phased jobs in §4.1, and then generalize the design to incorporate DAGs of tasks (§4.2), data locality (§4.4), and fairness (§4.3). Finally, in §5, we discuss how to adapt the design to a decentralized setting.

4.1 Dynamic Resource Allocation

The examples in §3 illustrate the value of *dynamic* allocation of slots for speculation. Our analysis indicates that this dynamic allocation can be separated into two regimes: whether the cluster is in "high" or "low" load.

The distinction between these two regimes follows from the behavior of the marginal return (in terms of performance) that jobs receive from being allocated slots. It is perhaps natural to expect that the performance of a job will always improve when it is given additional slots (because these can be used for additional speculative copies) and that the value of additional slots has a decreasing marginal return (because an extra slot is more valuable when the job is given few slots than when the job already has many slots). However, surprisingly, a novel observation that leads to the design of Hopper is that the marginal return of an extra slot has a sharp threshold (a.k.a., knee) where, below the threshold, the marginal return is large and (nearly) constant

[3]For ease of exposition, Pseudocode 1 considers the (online) allocation of all slots to jobs present at time t. Of course, in the implementation, slots are allocated as they become available. See Pseudocode 2 and 3 for more details.

```
1: procedure HOPPER(⟨Job⟩ J(t), int S, float β)
      totalVirtualSizes ← 0
2:    for each Job j in J(t) do
          j.V(t) = (2/β) j.T_rem
                        ▷ j.T_rem: remaining number of tasks
                              ▷ j.V(t): virtual job size
      totalVirtualSizes += j.V(t)
3:    SortAscending(J(t), V(t))
4:    if S < totalVirtualSizes then
5:        for each Job j in J(t) do
              j.slots ← ⌊min(S, j.V(t))⌋
              S ← max(S − j.slots, 0)
6:    else
7:        for each Job j in J(t) do
              j.slots ← ⌊(j.V(t)/totalVirtualSizes) × S⌋
```

Pseudocode 1: **Hopper (centralized) allocating S slots to the set of jobs present at time t, $J(t)$, with task distribution parameter β.**

and, above the threshold, the marginal return is small and decreasing.

Figure 3 illustrates this threshold using a simulation of a sample job with 200 tasks (with Pareto sizes, common in production traces) and LATE [50] speculation when assigned various numbers of slots. Crucially, there is a marked change in slope beyond the vertical dashed line, indicating the change in the marginal value of a slot. Note, that such a threshold exists for different job sizes, speculation algorithms, etc. Further, in the context of a simple model, we can prove the existence of a sharp threshold [8].

The most important consequence of the discussion above is that it is desirable to ensure every job is allocated enough slots to reach the threshold (if possible) before giving any job slots beyond this threshold. Thus, we refer to this threshold as the "desired (minimum) allocation" for a job or simply the "virtual job size".

Guideline 1. *It is better to give resources to a job that has not reached the desired (minimum) allocation than a job that has already reached the point.*

This guideline yields the key bifurcation in the Hopper design, as illustrated in line 4 of Pseudocode 1. Additionally, it highlights that there are three important design questions, which we address in the following sections: (i) How can we determine the desired allocation (virtual size) of a job? (ii) How should slots be allocated when there are not enough to give each job its desired allocation, i.e., when the cluster is highly utilized? (iii) How should slots be allocated when there are more than enough to give each job its desired allocation, i.e., when the cluster is lightly utilized?

(i) Determining the virtual size of a job

Determination of the "desired (minimum) allocation", a.k.a., the "virtual" size, of a job is crucial to determining which regime the system is in, and thus how slots should be allocated among jobs. While the virtual job size is learned empirically by Hopper through measurements of the threshold point during operation, it is important to point out that it is also possible to derive a useful static rule of thumb analytically, which can give intuition for the design structure.

In particular, the task durations in production traces (e.g., Facebook and Bing traces described in §7) typically follow a heavy-tailed Pareto distribution, where the Pareto tail parameter β (which is often $1 < \beta < 2$) represents the likelihood of stragglers [12, 13, 14, 25]. Roughly, smaller β means that stragglers are more damaging, i.e., if a task has already run for some time, there is higher likelihood of the task running longer.

Given the assumption of Pareto task durations, we can prove analytically (in a simple model) that the threshold point defining the "desired (minimum) allocation" is $\max(2/\beta, 1)$, which corresponds exactly to the vertical line in Figure 3 (see [8] for details). While we show only two examples here, the estimate this provides is robust across varying number of tasks, β, etc. [4]

Thus, we formally define the "virtual job size" $V_i(t)$ for job i at any time t, as its number of remaining tasks ($T_i(t)$) multiplied by $2/\beta$ (since $\beta < 2$ in our traces), i.e., $V_i(t) = \frac{2}{\beta}T_i(t)$. This virtual job size determines which regime the scheduler should use; see line 2 in Pseudocode 1. In practice, since β may vary over time, it is learned online by Hopper (see §7) making it adaptive to different threshold points as in Figure 3.

(ii) Allocation when the cluster is highly utilized

When there are not enough slots to assign every job its virtual size, we need to decide how to distribute this "deficiency" among the jobs. The scheduler could either spread the deficiency across all jobs, giving them all less opportunity for speculation, or satisfy as many jobs as possible with allocations equaling their virtual sizes.

Hopper does the latter. Specifically, Hopper processes jobs in ascending order of their virtual sizes $V_i(t)$, giving each job its desired (minimum) allocation until all the slots are exhausted (see lines $3-5$ in Pseudocode 1). This choice is in the spirit of SRPT, and is motivated both by the optimality of SRPT and the decreasing marginal return of additional slots, which magnifies the value of SRPT. Additionally, our theoretical analysis (in [8]) shows the optimality of this choice in the context of a simple model.

Guideline 2. *At all points in time, if there are not enough slots for every job to get its desired (minimum) allocation, i.e., a number of slots equal to its virtual size, then slots should be dedicated to the smallest jobs and each should be given a number of slots equal to its virtual size.*

[4] We make the simplifying assumption that task durations of *each job* are also Pareto distributed. A somewhat surprising aspect given the typical values of β ($1 < \beta < 2$) is that even when so many slots are allocated for redundant speculative copies, faster "clearing" of tasks is overall beneficial.

Note that prioritization of small jobs may lead to unfairness for larger jobs, an issue we address shortly in §4.3.

(iii) Allocation when the cluster is lightly utilized

At times when there are more slots in the cluster than the sum of the virtual sizes of jobs, we have slots left over even after allocating every job its virtual size. The scheduler's options for dividing the extra capacity are to either split the slots across jobs, or give all the extra slots to a few jobs in order to complete them quickly.

In contrast to the high utilization setting, in this situation Hopper allocates slots proportionally to the virtual job sizes, i.e., every job i receives $(V_i(t)/\sum_j V_j(t))S$ slots, where S is the number of slots available in the system and $V_i(t)$ is the virtual size; see line 7 in Pseudocode 1. Note that this is, in a sense, the opposite of the prioritization according to SRPT.

The motivation for this design is as follows. Given that all jobs are already receiving their (minimum) desired level of speculation, scheduling is less important than speculation. Thus, prioritization of small jobs is not crucial, and the goal should be to extract the maximum value from speculation. Since stragglers are more likely to occur in larger jobs (stragglers occur in proportion to the number of tasks in a job, on average[5]), the marginal improvement in performance due to an additional slot is proportionally higher for large jobs. Thus, they should get prioritization in proportion to their size when allocating the extra slots. Our analytic work in [8] highlights that this allocation is indeed optimal in a simple model.

Guideline 3. *At all points in time, if there are enough slots to give every job its desired (minimum) allocation, then, the slots should be shared "proportionally" to the virtual sizes of the jobs.*

Since the guidelines specify allocations at the granularity of every job, it is easy to cope with any fluctuations in cluster load (say, from lightly to highly utilized) in an online system.

4.2 Incorporating DAGs of Tasks

The discussion to this point has focused on single-phased jobs. In practice, many jobs are defined by multiple-phased DAGs, where the phases are typically *pipelined*. That is, downstream tasks do not wait for *all* the upstream tasks to finish but read the upstream outputs as the tasks finish, e.g., [6]. Pipelining is beneficial because the upstream tasks are typically bottlenecked on other *non-overlapping* resources (CPU, memory), while the reading downstream takes network resources. The additional complexity DAGs create for our guidelines is the need to balance the gains due to overlapping network utilization with the improvements that come from favoring upstream phases with fewer remaining tasks.

We integrate this tradeoff into Hopper using a weighting factor, α per job, set to be the ratio of remaining work in the downstream phase's network transfer to the remaining work in the upstream phase. Specifically, α favors jobs with higher remaining communication and lower remaining tasks in the current phase. The exact details of estimating α are deferred to §6.3.

Given the weighting factor α, there are two key adjustments that we make to the guidelines discussed so far. First, in Guideline 2, the prioritization of jobs based on the virtual size $V_i(t)$ is replaced by a prioritization based on $\max\{V_i(t), V_i'(t)\}$, where $V_i(t)$ is the virtual remaining number of tasks in the current phase and $V_i'(t)$ is the virtual remaining work in communication in the downstream phase.[6] Second, we redefine the virtual size itself as $V_i(t) = \frac{2}{\beta}T_i(t)\sqrt{\alpha_i}$. This form follows from the analysis in [8] and is similar in spirit to the optimality of square-root proportionality in load balancing across heterogeneous servers [21].

For DAGs that are not strict chains, but are wide and "bushy", we calculate α by summing over all the running and their respective downstream phases.

4.3 Incorporating Fairness

While fairness is an important constraint in clusters, conversations with data center operators reveal that it is not an absolute requirement. Thus, we relax the notion of fairness currently employed by cluster schedulers, e.g., [47], which enforce that if there are $N(t)$ active jobs and S available slots at time t, then each job is assigned $S/N(t)$ slots.

Specifically, to allow some flexibility while still tightly controlling unfairness, we define a notion of *approximate* fairness as follows. We say that a scheduler is ϵ-fair if it guarantees that every job receives at least $(1-\epsilon)S/N(t)$ slots at *all* times t. The fairness knob $\epsilon \to 0$ indicates absolute fairness while $\epsilon \to 1$ focuses on performance.

Hopper can be adjusted to guarantee ϵ-fairness in a very straightforward manner. In particular, if a job receives slots less than its fair share, i.e., fewer than $(1-\epsilon)S/N(t)$ slots, the job's capacity assignment is increased to $(1-\epsilon)S/N(t)$. Next, the remaining slots are allocated to the remaining jobs according to Guidelines 2 or 3, as appropriate. Note that this is a form of projection from the original (unfair) allocation into the feasible set of allocations defined by the fairness constraints.

Our experimental results (§7.3) highlight that even at moderate values of ϵ, *nearly all jobs finish faster than they would have under fair scheduling.* This fact, though initially surprising, is similar to the conclusions

[5]Machines in the cluster are equally likely to cause a straggler [12]; known problematic machines are already blacklisted (see §2).

[6]Results in [31] show that picking the $\max\{T_i(t), T_i'(t)\}$ is 2-speed optimal for completion times when stragglers are not considered.

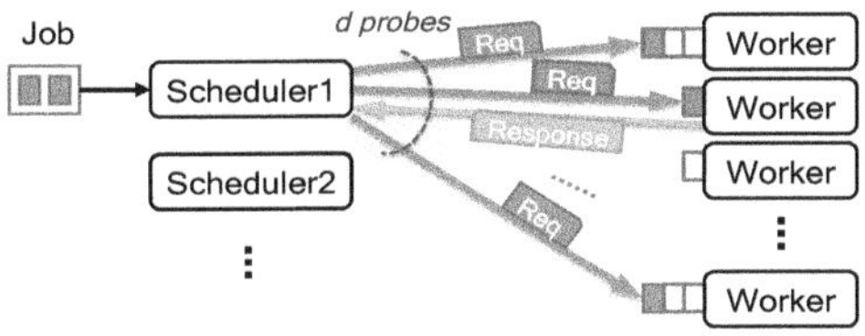

Figure 4: **Decentralized scheduling architecture.**

about SRPT-like policies. Despite being intuitively unfair to large job sizes, it in fact improves the average response time of every job size (when job sizes are heavy-tailed) compared to fair schedulers [28, 43, 44].

4.4 Incorporating Data Locality

As such, the guidelines presented does not consider data locality [11, 48] in the scheduling of tasks. Tasks reading their data from remote machines over the network run slower. In addition, such remote reads also increase contention with other intermediate tasks (like reduce tasks) that are bound to read over the network.

We devise a simple relaxation approach for balancing adherence to our guidelines and locality. Specifically, we adjust the ordering of jobs in Guideline 2 to include information about locality. Instead of allotting slots to the jobs with the smallest virtual sizes, we allow for picking any of the smallest $k\%$ of jobs whose tasks can run with data locality on the available slots. In practice, a small value of k ($\leq 5\%$) suffices due to high churn in task completions and slot availabilities (§7.4).

5. DECENTRALIZED Hopper

In this section, we adapt the guidelines described in §4 to design a decentralized (online) scheduler. Decentralized schedulers are increasingly prominent as cluster sizes grow. As we explain in this section, a key benefit of our guidelines in §4 is that they can be decentralized with little performance loss.

Decentralized schedulers, like the recently proposed Sparrow [36], broadly adopt the following design (see Figure 4). There are multiple independent *schedulers* each of which is responsible for scheduling one or a subset of jobs; for simplicity, a single job never spans across schedulers. Every scheduler assigns the tasks of its jobs to machines in the cluster (referred to as *workers*) that executes the tasks. The architecture allows for an incoming job to be assigned to any of the available schedulers, while also seamlessly allowing new schedulers to be dynamically spawned.

A scheduler first pushes *reservation requests* for its tasks to workers; each request contains the identifier of the scheduler placing the request along with the remaining number of unscheduled tasks in the job. When a worker is vacant, it pulls a task from the corresponding scheduler based on the reservation requests in its waiting queue. In this framework, workers decide which job's task to run and the scheduler for the corresponding job decides which task to run within the chosen job.

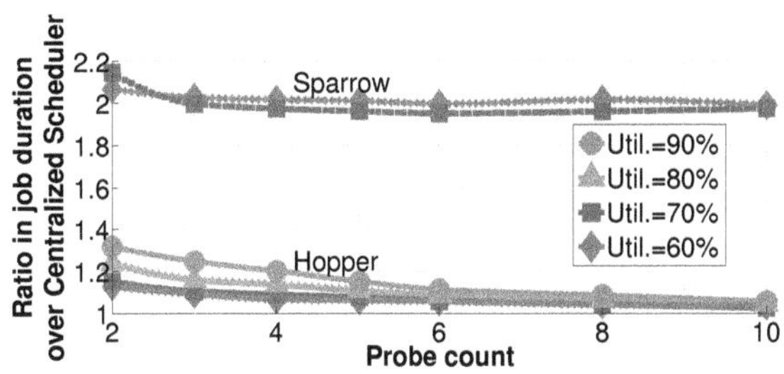

(a) Number of probes, d

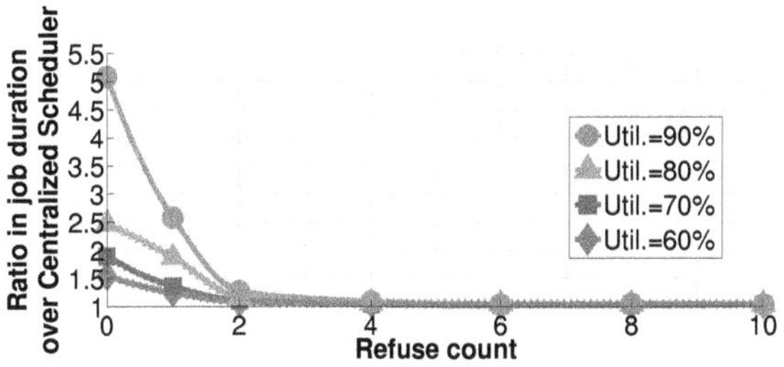

(b) Number of refusals

Figure 5: **The impact of number of probes and number of refusals on Hopper's performance.**

This decoupling naturally facilitates the design of Hopper.

Though we adopt an overall design structure similar to Sparrow for the decentralization of Hopper, it is important to note that Hopper's design is fundamentally different because it integrates straggler mitigation based on the guidelines behind Hopper introduced in §4.

Decentralizing Hopper involves the following steps: approximating worker-wide information at each scheduler (§5.1), deciding if the number of slots are constrained (§5.2), and calculating virtual sizes (§5.3).

5.1 Power of Many Choices

Decentralized schedulers have to *approximate* the global state of the cluster – the states of all the workers – since they are unaware of other jobs in the system. A common way to accomplish this is via the "power of two choices" [38]. This celebrated and widely used result highlights that, in many cases, one nearly matches the performance of a centralized implementation by querying two workers for their queue lengths, and choosing the shorter of the queues. In fact, this intuition underlies the design of Sparrow as well, which combines the idea with a form of "late binding"; schedulers send reservation requests for every task to two workers and then let workers pull a task from the corresponding scheduler when they have a free slot. We adopt "late binding", as used in Sparrow, but replace the "power of two choices" with the "power of many choices".

The reason for this change is that the effectiveness of the "power of two choices" relies on having *light-tailed task size distributions.* The existence of stragglers means that, in practice, task durations are heavy-tailed, e.g., [12, 14, 25]. Recent theoretical results have proven that, when task sizes are heavy-tailed, probing $d > 2$ choices can provide orders-of-magnitude improvements [18]. The value in using $d > 2$ comes from the fact that large tasks, which are more likely under heavy-tailed distributions, can cause considerable backing up of worker queues. Two choices may not be enough to avoid such backed-up queues, given the high frequency of straggling tasks. More specifically, $d > 2$ allows the schedulers to have a view of the jobs that is closer to the global view.

We use simulations in Figure 5a to highlight the benefit of using $d > 2$ probing choices in Hopper and to contrast this benefit with Sparrow, which relies on the power of two choices. Our simulation considers a cluster of 50 schedulers and 10,000 workers and jobs with Pareto distributed ($\beta = 1.5$) task sizes. Job performance with decentralized Hopper is within just 15% of the centralized scheduler; the difference plateaus beyond $d = 4$. Note that Sparrow (which does not coordinate scheduling and speculation) is > 100% off for medium utilizations and even further off for high utilizations (not shown on the figure in order to keep the scale visible). Further, workers in Sparrow pick tasks in their waiting queues in a FCFS fashion. The lack of coordination between scheduling and speculation results in a long waiting time for speculative copies in the queues which diminishes the benefits of multiple probes. Thus parrow cannot extract the same benefit Hopper has from using more than two probes. Of course, these are rough estimates since the simulations do not capture overheads due to increased message processing, which are included in the evaluations in §7.

5.2 Is the system capacity constrained?

In the decentralized setting workers implement our scheduling guidelines. Recall that Guideline 2 or Guideline 3 is applied depending on whether the system is constrained for slots or not. Thus, determining which to follow necessitates comparing the sum of virtual sizes of all the jobs and the number of slots in the cluster, which is trivial in a centralized scheduler but requires communication in an decentralized setting.

To keep overheads low, we avoid costly gossiping protocols among schedulers regarding their states. Instead, we use the following adaptive approach. Workers start with the conservative assumption that the system is capacity constrained (this avoids overloading the system with speculative copies), and thus each worker implements Guideline 2, i.e., enforces an SRPT priority on its queue. Specifically, when a worker is idle, it sends a *refusable* response to the scheduler corresponding to the reservation request of the job it chooses from its queue. However, since the scheduler queues many more reservation requests than tasks, it is possible that its tasks may have all been scheduled (with respect to virtual sizes). A refusable response allows the scheduler to refuse sending any new task for the job if the job's tasks are all already scheduled to the desired speculation level

```
procedure ResponseProcessing(Response response )
    Job j ← response.job
    if response.type = non-refusable then
        Accept()
    else
        if (j.current_occupied < j.virtual_size) Accept ()
        else Refuse()
```

Pseudocode 2: **Scheduler Methods.**

```
procedure Response(⟨Job⟩ J, int refused_count)
        ▷ J: list of jobs in queue of the worker excluding
    already refused jobs
    if refused_count ≥ refusal_threshold then
        j ← J.PickAtRandom()
        SendResponse(j, non-refusable)
    else
        j ← J.min(virtual_size)
        SendResponse(j, refusable)
```

Pseudocode 3: **Worker: choosing the next task to schedule.**

(ResponseProcessing in Pseudocode 2). In its refusal, it sends information about the job with the smallest virtual size in its list which still has unscheduled tasks (if such an "unsatisfied" job exists).

Subsequently, the worker sends a refusable response to the scheduler corresponding to second smallest job in its queue, and so forth till it gets a threshold number of refusals. Note that the worker avoids probing the same scheduler more than once. Several consecutive refusals from schedulers without information about any unsatisfied jobs suggests that the system is not capacity constrained. At that point, it switches to implementing Guideline 3. Once it is following Guideline 3, the worker randomly picks a job from the waiting queue based on the distribution of job virtual sizes. If there are still unsatisfied jobs at the end of the refusals, the worker sends a *non-refusable* response (which cannot be refused) to the scheduler whose unsatisfied job is the smallest. Pseudocode 3 explains the Response method.

The higher the threshold for refusals, the better the view of the schedulers for the worker. Our simulations (with 50 schedulers and 10,000 workers) in Figure 5b show that performance with two or three refusals is within 10% − 15% of the centralized scheduler.

5.3 Updating Virtual Job Sizes

Computing the remaining virtual job size at a scheduler is straightforward. However, since the remaining virtual size of a job changes as tasks complete, virtual sizes need to be updated dynamically. Updating virtual sizes accurately at the workers that have queued reservations for tasks of this job would require frequent message exchanges between workers and schedulers, which would create significant overhead in communication and processing of messages. So, our approach is to piggyback updates for virtual sizes on other communication messages that are anyway necessary between a scheduler and a worker (e.g., schedulers sending reservation requests for new jobs, workers sending responses to probe system state and ask for new tasks). While this introduces a slight error in the virtual remaining sizes, our evaluation shows that the approximation provided by this approach is enough for the gains associated with Hopper.

Crucially, the calculation of virtual sizes is heavily impacted by the job specifics. Job specific properties of the job DAG and the likelihood of stragglers are captured through α and β, respectively, which are learned online. Note that jobs from different applications may have heterogeneous α and β.

6. IMPLEMENTATION OVERVIEW

We now give an overview of the implementation of Hopper in decentralized and centralized settings.

6.1 Decentralized Implementation

Our decentralized implementation uses the Sparrow [36] framework, which consists of many schedulers and workers (one each on every machine) [9]. Arbitrarily many schedulers can operate concurrently; though we use 10 in our experiments. Schedulers allow submissions of jobs using Thrift RPCs [1].

A job is broken into a set of tasks with their dependencies (DAG), binaries and locality preferences. The scheduler places requests at the workers for its tasks; if a task has locality constraints, its requests are only placed on the workers meeting its constraints [13, 40, 49]. The workers talk to the client executor processes (e.g., Spark executor). The executor processes are responsible for executing task binaries and are long-lived to avoid startup overheads (see [36] for a more detailed explanation).

Our implementation modifies the scheduler as well as the worker. The workers implement the core of the guidelines in §4 – determining if the system is slot-constrained and accordingly prioritizing jobs as per their virtual sizes. This required modifying the FIFO queue at the worker in Sparrow to allow for custom ordering of the queued requests. The worker, nonetheless, augments its local view by coordinating with the scheduler. This involved modifying the "late binding" mechanism both at the worker and scheduler. The worker, when it has a free slot, works with the scheduler in picking the next task (using Pseudocode 3). The scheduler deals with a response from the worker as per Pseudocode 2.

Even after *all* the job's tasks have been scheduled (including its virtual size), the job scheduler does not "cancel" its pending requests; there will be additional pending requests with any probe ratio over one. Thus, if the system is not slot-constrained, it would be able to use more slots (as per Guideline 3).

In our decentralized implementation, for tasks in the input phase (e.g., map phase), when the number of probes exceeds the number of data replicas, we queue up the additional requests at randomly chosen machines. Consequently, these tasks *may* run without data locality, and our results in §7 include such loss in locality.

6.2 Centralized Implementation

We implement Hopper inside two centralized frameworks: Hadoop YARN (version 2.3) and Spark (version 0.7.3). Hadoop jobs read data from HDFS [5] while Spark jobs read from in-memory RDDs.

Briefly, these frameworks implement two level scheduling where a central *resource manager* assigns slots to the different *job managers*. When a job is submitted to the resource manager, a job manager is started on one of the machines, that then executes the job's DAG of tasks. The job manager negotiates with the resource manager for resources for its tasks.

We built Hopper as a scheduling plug-in module to the resource manager. This makes the frameworks use our design to allocate slots to the job managers. We also piggybacked on the communication protocol between the job manager and resource manager to communicate the intermediate data produced and read by the phases of the job to vary α accordingly; locality and other preferences are already communicated between them.

6.3 Estimating Intermediate Data Sizes

Recall from §4.2 that our scheduling guidelines recommend scaling every job's allocation by $\sqrt{\alpha}$ in the case of DAGs. The purpose of the scaling is to capture pipelining of the reading of upstream tasks' outputs.

The key to calculating α is estimating the size of the *intermediate* output produced by tasks. Unlike the job's input size, intermediate data sizes are not known upfront. We predict intermediate data sizes based on similar jobs in the past. Clusters typically have many recurring jobs that execute periodically as newer data streams in, and produce intermediate data of similar sizes.

Our simple approach to estimating α works sufficiently well for our evaluations (accuracy of 92%, on average). However, we realize that workloads without many multi-waved or recurring jobs and without tasks whose duration is dictated by their input sizes, need more sophisticated models of task executions.

7. EVALUATION

We evaluate our prototypes of Hopper – with both decentralized and centralized scheduling – on a 200 machine cluster. We focus on the overall gains of the decentralized prototype of Hopper in §7.2 and evaluate the design choices that led to Hopper in §7.3. Then, in §7.4 we evaluate the gains with Hopper in a centralized scheduler in order to highlight the value of coordinating scheduling and speculation. The key highlights are:

1. Hopper's decentralized prototype improves the average job duration by up to 66% compared to an aggressive decentralized baseline that combines Sparrow with SRPT (§7.2).

2. Hopper ensures that only 4% of jobs slow down compared to Fair scheduling, and jobs which do slow down do so by ≤ 5% (§7.3).

3. Centralized Hopper improves job completion times by 50% compared to centralized SRPT (§7.4).

7.1 Setup

Cluster Deployment: We deploy our prototypes on a 200-node private cluster. Each machine has 16 cores, 34GB of memory, 1Gbps network and 4 disks. The machines are connected using a network with no over-subscription.[7]

Workload: Our evaluation runs jobs in traces from Facebook's production Hadoop [3] cluster (3,500 machines) and Microsoft Bing's Dryad cluster (O(1000) machines) from Oct-Dec 2012. The traces consist of a mix of experimental and production jobs. Their tasks have diverse resource demands of CPU, memory and IO, varying by a factor of 24× (refer to [27] for detailed quantification). We retain the inter-arrival times of jobs, their input sizes and number of tasks, resource demands, and job DAGs of tasks. Job sizes follow a heavy-tailed distribution (quantified in detail in [12]). Each experiment is a replay of a representative 6 hour slice from the trace. It is repeated five times and we report the median.

To evaluate our prototype of decentralized Hopper, we use in-memory Spark [49] jobs. These jobs are typical of interactive analytics whose tasks vary from sub-second durations to a few seconds. Since the performance of any decentralized scheduler depends on the cluster utilization, we speed-up the trace appropriately, and evaluate on (average) utilizations between 60% and 90%, consistent with Sparrow [36].

Stragglers: The stragglers in our experiments are those that occur *naturally*, i.e., not injected via any model of a probability distribution or via statistics gathered from the Facebook and Bing clusters. Importantly, the frequency and lengths of stragglers observed in our evaluations are consistent with prior studies, e.g., [14, 15, 50]. While Hopper's focus is not on improving straggler mitigation algorithms, our experiments certainly serve to emphasize the importance of such mitigation.

Baseline: We compare decentralized Hopper to Sparrot-SRPT, an augmented version of Sparrow [36]. Like Sparrow, it performs decentralized scheduling using a "batched" power-of-two choices. In addition, it also includes an SRPT heuristic. In short, when a worker has a slot free, it picks the task of the job that has the least unfinished tasks (instead of the standard FIFO ordering in Sparrow). Finally, we combine Sparrow with LATE [50] using "best effort" speculation (§3); we do not consider "budgeted" speculation due to the difficulty of picking a fixed budget.

The combination of Sparrow-SRPT and LATE performs strictly better than Sparrow, and serves as an aggressive baseline. Our improvements over this aggressive benchmark highlight the importance of coordinating scheduling and speculation.

[7]Results with a 10Gbps network are qualitatively similar.

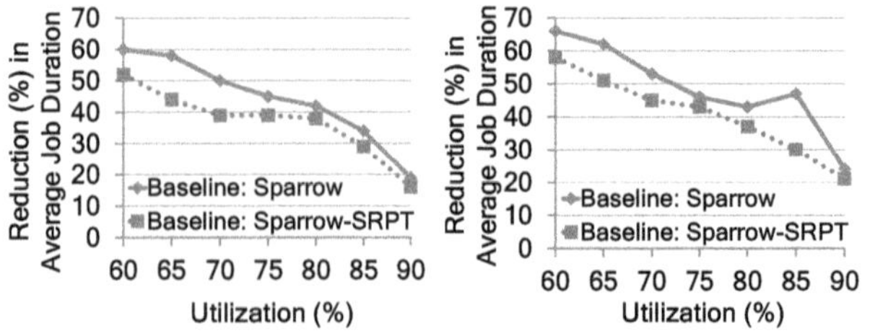

(a) Facebook (b) Bing

Figure 6: Hopper's **gains with cluster utilization.**

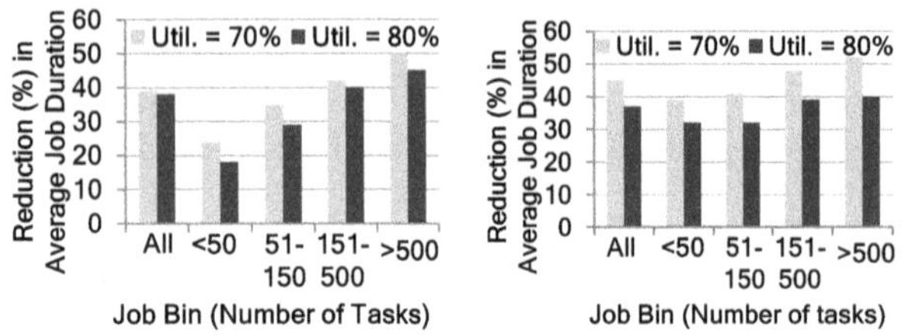

(a) Facebook (b) Bing

Figure 7: Hopper's **gains by job bins over Sparrow-SRPT.**

We compare centralized Hopper to a centralized SRPT scheduler with LATE speculation. Again, this is an aggressive baseline since it sacrifices fairness for performance. Thus, improvements can be interpreted as coming solely from better coordination of scheduling and speculation.

7.2 Decentralized Hopper's Improvements

In our experiments, unless otherwise stated, we set the fairness allowance ϵ as 10%, probe ratio as 4 and speculation algorithm in every job to be LATE [50]. Our estimation of α (§6.3) has an accuracy of 92% on average. As the workload executes, we also continually fit the parameter β of task durations based on the completed tasks (including stragglers); the error in β's estimate falls to ≤ 5% after just 6% of the jobs have executed.

Overall Gains: Figure 6 plots Hopper's gains for varying utilizations, compared to stock Sparrow and Sparrow-SRPT. Jobs, overall, speedup by 50% – 60% at utilization of 60%. The gains compared to Sparrow are marginally better than Sparrow-SRPT. When the utilization goes over 80%, Hopper's gains compared to both are similar. An interesting point is that Hopper's gains with the Bing workload in Figure 6b are a touch higher (difference of 7%), perhaps due to the larger difference in job sizes between small and large jobs, allowing more opportunity for Hopper. Gains fall to < 20% when utilization is high (≥ 80%), naturally because there is not much room for any optimization at that occupancy.

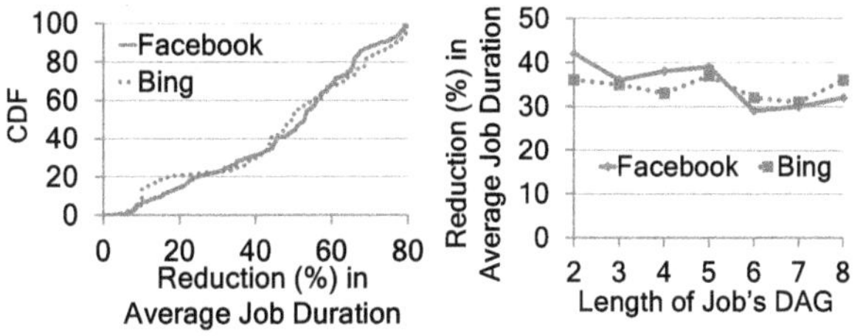

(a) Distribution (b) DAG

Figure 8: **(a) CDF of Hopper's gains, and (b) gains as the length of the job's DAG varies; both at 60% utilization.**

While not plotted, gains at utilizations $\leq$ 30% are no more than 14%. Expectedly, at such low utilizations, there is little requirement for smarter speculation or probing.

Note that the above utilizations are on average and there is considerable variation. At 80% average utilization, Hopper allocates 53% of jobs using Guideline 2 (high utilization) and the remaining 47% of jobs using Guideline 3 (low utilization). This indicates that 53% of jobs in the experimental run arrived such that the cluster did not have enough slots to allocate every job its virtual size.

The results so far highlight that Sparrow-SRPT is a more aggressive baseline than Sparrow, and so we compare only to it for the rest of our evaluation.

Job Bins: Figure 7 dices the gains by job size (number of tasks). Gains for small jobs are less compared to large jobs. This is expected given that our baseline of Sparrow-SRPT already favors the small jobs. Nonetheless, Hopper's smart allocation of speculative slots offers 18% – 32% improvement. Gains for large jobs, in contrast, are over 50%. This not only shows that there is sufficient room for the large jobs despite favoring small jobs (due to the heavy-tailed distribution of job sizes [12, 13]) but also that the value of deciding between speculative tasks and unscheduled tasks of other jobs increases with the number of tasks in the job. With trends of smaller tasks and hence, larger number of tasks per job [34], Hopper's allocation becomes important.

Distribution of Gains: Figure 8a plots the distribution of gains across jobs. While the median gains are just higher than the average, there are > 70% gains at higher percentiles. Encouragingly, gains even at the 10th percentile are 15% and 10%, which shows Hopper's ability to improve even worse case performance.

DAG of Tasks: The scripts in our Facebook (Hive scripts [7]) and Bing (Scope [20]) workloads produce DAGs of tasks which often pipeline data transfers of downstream phases with upstream tasks [6]. The communication patterns in the DAGs are varied (e.g., all-to-all, many-to-one etc.) and thus the results also serve to underscore Hopper's generality. As Figure 8b shows, Hopper's gains hold across DAG lengths.

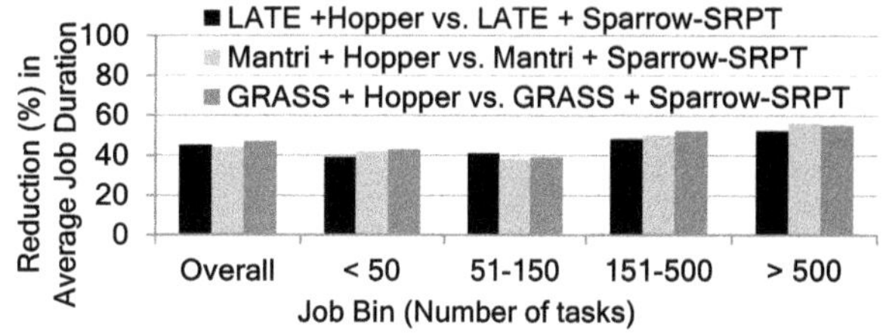

Figure 9: **Hopper's results are independent of the straggler mitigation strategy.**

Speculation Algorithm: We now experimentally evaluate Hopper's performance with different speculation mechanisms. LATE [50] is deployed in Facebook's clusters, Mantri [15] is in operation in Microsoft Bing, and GRASS citegrass is a recently reported straggler mitigation system that was demonstrated to perform near-optimal speculation. Our experiments still use Sparrow-SRPT as the baseline but pair with the different straggler mitigation algorithms. Figure 9 plots the results.

While the earlier results were achieved in conjunction with LATE, a remarkable point about Figure 9 is the similarity in gains even with Mantri and GRASS. This indicates that as long as the straggler mitigation algorithms are aggressive in asking for speculative copies, Hopper will appropriately balance speculation and scheduling. Overall, it emphasizes the aspect that resource allocation *across* jobs (with speculation) has a higher performance value than straggler mitigation *within* jobs.

7.3 Evaluating Hopper's Design Decisions

We now evaluate the sensitivity of decentralized Hopper to our key design decisions: fairness and probe ratio.

Fairness: As we had described in §4.3, the fairness knob ϵ decides the leeway for Hopper to trade-off fairness for performance. Thus far, we had set ϵ to be 10% of the perfectly fair share of a job (ratio of total slots to jobs), now we analyze its sensitivity to Hopper's gains.

Figure 10a plots the increase in gains as we increase ϵ from 0 to 30%. The gains quickly rise for small values of ϵ, and beyond $\epsilon = 15\%$ the increase in gains are flatter with both the Facebook as well as Bing workloads. Conservatively, we set ϵ to 10%.

An important concern, nonetheless, is the amount of *slowdown* of jobs compared to a perfectly fair allocation ($\epsilon = 0$), i.e., when all the jobs are guaranteed their fair share at all times. Any slowdown of jobs is because of receiving fewer slots. Figure 10b measures the number of jobs that slowed down, and for the slowed jobs, Figure 10c plots their average and worst slowdowns. Note that fewer than 4% of jobs slow down with Hopper compared to a fair allocation at $\epsilon = 10\%$. The corresponding number for the Bing workload is 3.8%. In fact, both the average and worst slowdowns are limited at $\epsilon = 10\%$, thus demonstrating that Hopper's focus on performance does *not* unduly slow down jobs.

Probe Ratio: An important component of decentralized scheduling is the probe ratio – the number of re-

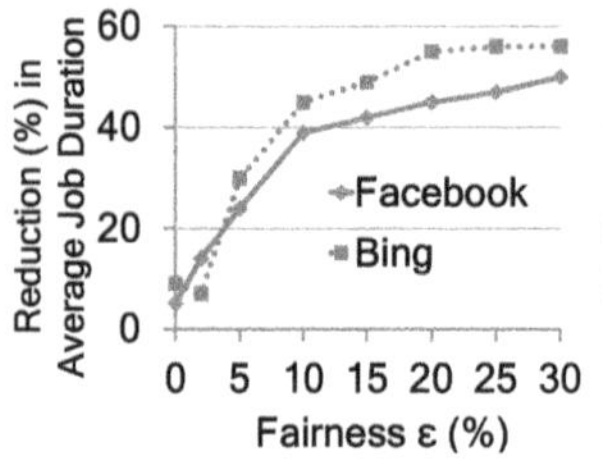

(a) Sensitivity

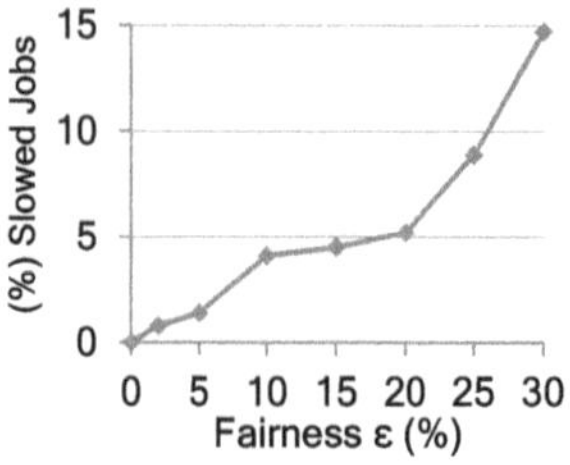

(b) (%) of Jobs Slowed

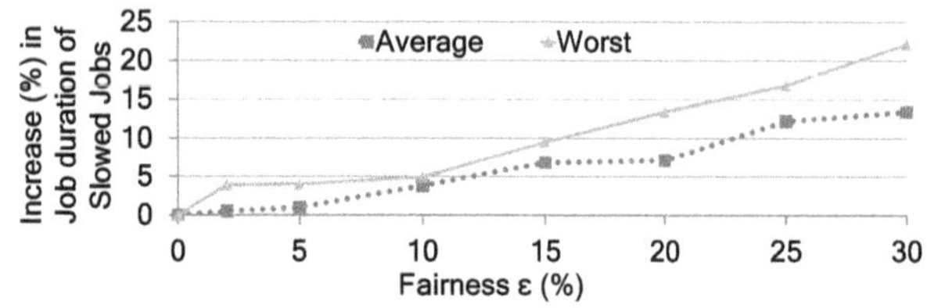

(c) Magnitude (%) of Slowdown

Figure 10: ϵ **Fairness. Figure (a) shows sensitivity of gains to ϵ. Figure (b) shows the fraction of jobs that slowed down compared to a fair allocation, and (c) shows the magnitude of their slowdowns (average and worst).**

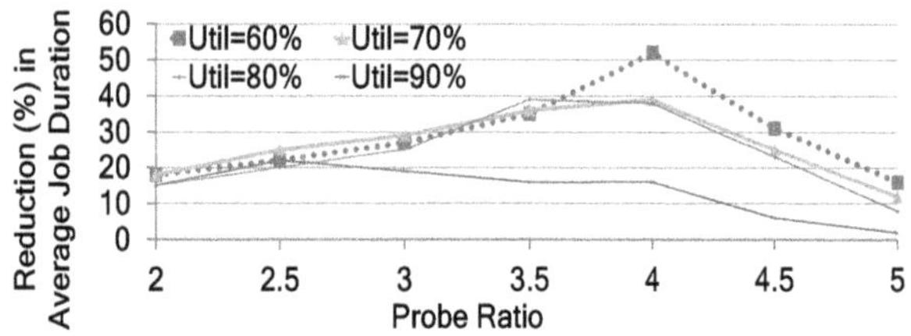

Figure 11: **Power of d choices: Impact of the number of probes on job completion.**

quests queued at workers to number of tasks in the job. A higher probe ratio reduces the chance of a task being stuck in the queue of a busy machine, but also increases messaging overheads. While the power-of-two choices [38] and Sparrow [36] recommend a probe ratio of 2, we adopt a probe ratio of 4 based on our analysis in §5.

Figure 11 confirms that higher probe ratios are indeed beneficial. As the probe ratio increase from 2 onwards, the payoff due to Hopper's scheduling and straggler mitigation results in gains increasing until 4; at utilizations of 70% and 80%, using 3.5 works well too. At 90% utilization, however, gains start slipping even at a probe ratio of 2.5. However, the benefits at such high utilizations are smaller to begin with.

7.4 Centralized Hopper's Improvements

To highlight the fact that Hopper is a unified design, appropriate for both decentralized and centralized systems, we also evaluate Hopper in a centralized setting using Hadoop and Spark prototypes. Figure 12 plots the gains for the two prototypes with Facebook and Bing workloads. We achieve gains of $\sim 50\%$ with the two workloads, with individual job bins improving by up to 80%.

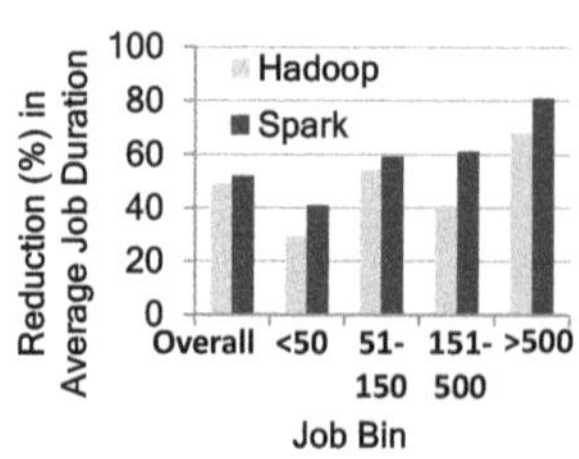

(a) Gains

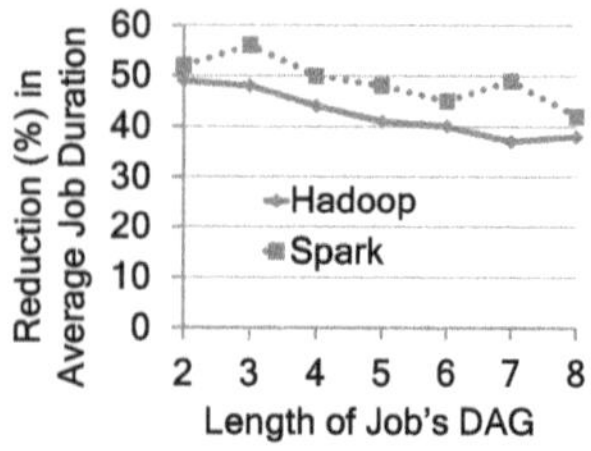

(b) DAG

Figure 12: **Centralized Hopper's gains over SRPT, overall and broken by DAG length (Facebook workloads).**

As with the decentralized setting, gains for small jobs are lower due to the baseline of SRPT already favoring small jobs. Between the two prototypes, gains for Spark are consistently higher (albeit, modestly). Spark's small task durations makes it more sensitive to stragglers and thus it spawns many more speculative copies. This makes Hopper's scheduling more crucial.

DAG of Tasks: Like in the decentralized implementation, Hopper's gains hold consistently over varying DAG lengths, see Figure 12. Note that there is a contrast between Spark jobs and Hadoop jobs. Spark jobs have fast in-memory map phases, thus making intermediate data communication the bottleneck. Hadoop jobs are less bottlenecked on intermediate data transfer, and spend more of their time in the map phase [13]. This difference is captured via α, which is learned as described in §6.3.

Data Locality: Recall from §4.4 that we achieve data locality using a relaxation heuristic to allow any k subsequent jobs (as a % of total jobs).

As Figure 13a shows, a small relaxation of $k = 3\%$, which is what we have used so far, achieves appreciable increase in locality in Spark. Gains are steady for a bit but then start dropping beyond a k value of 7%. This is because the deviation from the theoretical guidelines overshadows any increase in gains from locality. The fraction of data local tasks, naturally, increases with k (Figures 13a). Hadoop results are similar (13b).

Note that even when we enhance a centralized SRPT scheduler to include the above locality heuristic, it gains no more than 20% compared to centralized SRPT (without the locality heuristic). This indicates that Hopper's gains are predominantly due to coordinated speculation and scheduling.

8. CONCLUSIONS

With launching speculative copies of tasks being a common approach for mitigating the impact of stragglers, schedulers face a decision between scheduling speculative copies of some jobs versus original copies of other jobs. While this question is seemingly simple, we find

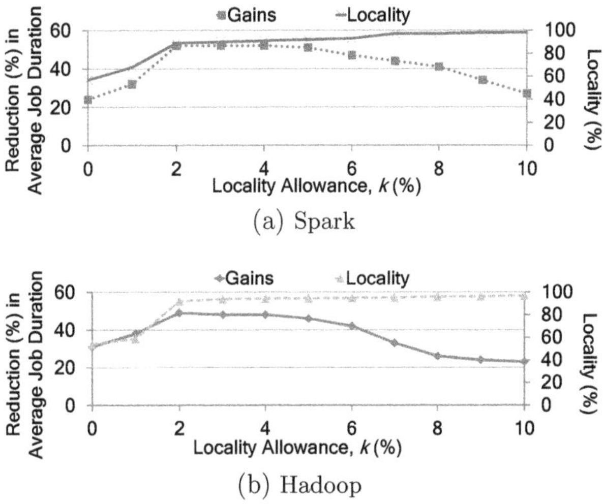

Figure 13: **Centralized Hopper: Impact of Locality Allowance (k) (see §6.2) with Facebook workload.**

that the problem is not only unsolved thus far, but also has significant performance implications.

This paper proposes Hopper, the first speculation-aware job scheduler, and implements both decentralized and centralized prototypes. We deploy our prototypes (built in Sparrow [36], Spark [49] and Hadoop [3]) on a 200 machine cluster, and see job speed ups of 66% in decentralized settings and 50% in centralized settings compared to current state-of-the-art schedulers. In addition to providing performance improvements in both centralized and decentralized settings, Hopper is compatible with all current speculation algorithms and incorporates data locality, fairness, DAGs of tasks, etc.; thus, it represents a unified speculation-aware scheduling framework.

9. ACKNOWLEDGMENT

We would like to thank Michael Chien-Chun Hung, Shivaram Venkataraman, Masoud Moshref, Niangjun Chen, Qiuyu Peng, and Changhong Zhao for their insightful discussions. We would like to thank the anonymous reviewers and our shepherd, Lixin Gao, for their thoughtful suggestions. This work was supported in part by National Science Foundation (NSF) with Grants (CNS-1319820, CNS-1423505).

10. REFERENCES

[1] Apache Thrift. https://thrift.apache.org/.

[2] Cloudera Impala. http://www.cloudera.com/content/cloudera/en/products-and-services/cdh/impala.html.

[3] Hadoop. http://hadoop.apache.org.

[4] Hadoop Capacity Scheduler. http://hadoop.apache.org/docs/r1.2.1/capacity_scheduler.html.

[5] Hadoop Distributed File System. http://hadoop.apache.org/hdfs.

[6] Hadoop Slowstart. https://issues.apache.org/jira/browse/MAPREDUCE-1184/.

[7] Hive. http://wiki.apache.org/hadoop/Hive.

[8] Hopper Technical Report. https://sites.google.com/site/sigcommhoppertechreport/.

[9] Sparrow. https://github.com/radlab/sparrow.

[10] The Next Generation of Apache Hadoop MapReduce. http://developer.yahoo.com/blogs/hadoop/posts/2011/02/mapreduce-nextgen/.

[11] G. Ananthanarayanan, S. Agarwal, S. Kandula, A. Greenberg, I. Stoica, D. Harlan, and E. Harris. Scarlett: Coping with Skewed Popularity Content in MapReduce Clusters. In *EuroSys*, 2011.

[12] G. Ananthanarayanan, A. Ghodsi, S. Shenker, and I. Stoica. Effective Straggler Mitigation: Attack of the Clones. In *USENIX NSDI*, 2013.

[13] G. Ananthanarayanan, A. Ghodsi, A. Wang, D. Borthakur, S. Kandula, S. Shenker, and I. Stoica. PACMan: Coordinated Memory Caching for Parallel Jobs. In *USENIX NSDI*, 2012.

[14] G. Ananthanarayanan, M. Hung, X. Ren, I. Stoica, A. Wierman, and M. Yu. GRASS: Trimming Stragglers in Approximation Analytics. In *USENIX NSDI*, 2014.

[15] G. Ananthanarayanan, S. Kandula, A. Greenberg, I. Stoica, E. Harris, and B. Saha. Reining in the Outliers in Map-Reduce Clusters Using Mantri. In *USENIX OSDI*, 2010.

[16] E. Bortnikov, A. Frank, E. Hillel, and S. Rao. Predicting Execution Bottlenecks in Map-Reduce Clusters. In *USENIX HotCloud*, 2012.

[17] E. Boutin, J. Ekanayake, W. Kin, B. Shi, J. Zhou, Z. Qian, M. Wu, and L. Zhou. Apollo: Scalable and Coordinated Scheduling for Cloud-Scale Computing. In *USENIX OSDI*, 2014.

[18] M. Bramson, Y. Lu, and B. Prabhakar. Randomized load balancing with general service time distributions. In *Proceedings of Sigmetrics*, pages 275–286, 2010.

[19] R. Chaiken, B. Jenkins, P. Larson, B. Ramsey, D. Shakib, S. Weaver, and J. Zhou. SCOPE: Easy and Efficient Parallel Processing of Massive Data Sets. *Proceedings of the VLDB Endowment*, (2), 2008.

[20] R. Chaiken, B. Jenkins, P. Larson, B. Ramsey, D. Shakib, S. Weaver, and J. Zhou. SCOPE: Easy and Efficient Parallel Processing of Massive Datasets. In *VLDB*, 2008.

[21] H. Chen, J. Marden, and A. Wierman. On the Impact of Heterogeneity and Back-end Scheduling in Load Balancing Designs. In *INFOCOM*. IEEE, 2009.

[22] J. Dean. Achieving Rapid Response Times in Large Online Services. In *Berkeley AMPLab Cloud Seminar*, 2012.

[23] J. Dean and L. Barroso. The Tail at Scale. *Communications of the ACM*, (2), 2013.

[24] J. Dean and S. Ghemawat. MapReduce: Simplified Data Processing on Large Clusters. *Communications of the ACM*, 2008.

[25] F. Dogar, T. Karagiannis, H. Ballani, and A. Rowstron. Decentralized Task-aware Scheduling for Data Center Networks. In *ACM SIGCOMM*, 2014.

[26] A. Ghodsi, M. Zaharia, B. Hindman, A. Konwinski, S. Shenker, and I. Stoica. Dominant Resource Fairness: Fair Allocation of Multiple Resource Types. In *USENIX NSDI*, 2011.

[27] R. Grandl, G. Ananthanarayanan, S. Kandula, S. Rao, and A. Akella. Multi-Resource Packing for Cluster Schedulers. In *ACM SIGCOMM*, 2014.

[28] M. Harchol-Balter, B. Schroeder, N. Bansal, and M. Agrawal. Size-based scheduling to improve web performance. *ACM Transactions on Computer Systems (TOCS)*, 21(2):207–233, 2003.

[29] B. Hindman, A. Konwinski, M. Zaharia, A. Ghodsi, A. Joseph, R. Katz, S. Shenker, and I. Stoica. Mesos: A Platform for Fine-Grained Resource Sharing in the Data Center. In *USENIX NSDI*, 2011.

[30] M. Isard, V. Prabhakaran, J. Currey, U. Wieder, K. Talwar, and A. Goldberg. Quincy: Fair Scheduling for Distributed Computing Clusters. In *ACM SOSP*, 2009.

[31] M. Lin, L. Zhang, A. Wierman, and J. Tan. Joint Optimization of Overlapping Phases in MapReduce. *Performance Evaluation*, 2013.

[32] S. Melnik, A. Gubarev, J. J. Long, G. Romer, S. Shivakumar, M. Tolton, and T. Vassilakis. Dremel: Interactive Analysis of Web-Scale Datasets. In *VLDB*, 2010.

[33] B. Moseley, A. Dasgupta, R. Kumar, and T. Sarlós. On Scheduling in Map-reduce and Flow-shops. In *ACM SPAA*, 2011.

[34] K. Ousterhout, A. Panda, J. Rosen, S. Venkataraman, R. Xin, S. Ratnasamy, S. Shenker, and I. Stoica. The Case for Tiny Tasks in Compute Clusters. In *USENIX HotOS*, 2013.

[35] K. Ousterhout, R. Rasti, S. Ratnasamy, S. Shenker, and B. Chun. Making Sense of Performance in Data Analytics Frameworks. In *USENIX NSDI*, 2015.

[36] K. Ousterhout, P. Wendell, M. Zaharia, and I. Stoica. Sparrow: Distributed, Low Latency Scheduling. In *ACM SOSP*, 2013.

[37] K. Pruhs, J. Sgall, and E. Torng. Online scheduling. *Handbook of scheduling: algorithms, models, and performance analysis*, pages 15–1, 2004.

[38] A. Richa, M. Mitzenmacher, and R. Sitaraman. The power of two random choices: A survey of techniques and results. *Combinatorial Optimization*, 2001.

[39] L. Schrage. A proof of the optimality of the shortest remaining processing time discipline. *Operations Research*, 16(3):687–690, 1968.

[40] B. Sharma, V. Chudnovsky, J. L. Hellerstein, R. Rifaat, and C. R. Das. Modeling and Synthesizing Task Placement Constraints in Google Compute Clusters. In *ACM SOCC*, 2011.

[41] J. Tan, X. Meng, and L. Zhang. Delay Tails in MapReduce Scheduling. *ACM SIGMETRICS Performance Evaluation Review*, 2012.

[42] Y. Wang, J. Tan, W. Yu, L. Zhang, and X. Meng. Preemptive ReduceTask Scheduling for Fast and Fair Job Completion. *USENIX ICAC*, 2013.

[43] A. Wierman. Fairness and scheduling in single server queues. *Surveys in Operations Research and Management Science*, 16(1):39–48, 2011.

[44] A. Wierman and M. Harchol-Balter. Classifying scheduling policies with respect to unfairness in an m/gi/1. In *ACM SIGMETRICS Performance Evaluation Review*, volume 31, pages 238–249. ACM, 2003.

[45] J. Wolf, D. Rajan, K. Hildrum, R. Khandekar, V. Kumar, S. Parekh, K. Wu, and A. Balmin. FLEX: a Slot Allocation Scheduling Optimizer for MapReduce Workloads. In *Middleware 2010*. Springer, 2010.

[46] N. Yadwadkar, G. Ananthanarayanan, and R. Katz. Wrangler: Predictable and Faster Jobs using Fewer Resources. In *ACM SoCC*, 2014.

[47] M. Zaharia, D. Borthakur, J. S. Sarma, K. Elmeleegy, S. Shenker, and I. Stoica. Job scheduling for multi-user mapreduce clusters. In *UC Berkeley Technical Report UCB/EECS-2009-55*, 2009.

[48] M. Zaharia, D. Borthakur, J. S. Sarma, K. Elmeleegy, S. Shenker, and I. Stoica. Delay Scheduling: A Simple Technique for Achieving Locality and Fairness in Cluster Scheduling. In *ACM EuroSys*, 2010.

[49] M. Zaharia, M. Chowdhury, T. Das, A. Dave, J. Ma, M. McCauley, M. Franklin, S. Shenker, and I. Stoica. Resilient Distributed Datasets: A Fault-Tolerant Abstraction for In-Memory Cluster Computing. In *USENIX NSDI*, 2012.

[50] M. Zaharia, A. Konwinski, A. D. Joseph, R. Katz, and I. Stoica. Improving MapReduce Performance in Heterogeneous Environments. In *USENIX OSDI*, 2008.

Efficient Coflow Scheduling Without Prior Knowledge

Mosharaf Chowdhury, Ion Stoica
UC Berkeley
{mosharaf, istoica}@cs.berkeley.edu

ABSTRACT

Inter-coflow scheduling improves application-level communication performance in data-parallel clusters. However, existing efficient schedulers require a priori coflow information and ignore cluster dynamics like pipelining, task failures, and speculative executions, which limit their applicability. Schedulers without prior knowledge compromise on performance to avoid head-of-line blocking. In this paper, we present Aalo that strikes a balance and efficiently schedules coflows *without* prior knowledge.

Aalo employs *Discretized Coflow-Aware Least-Attained Service* (D-CLAS) to separate coflows into a small number of priority queues based on how much they have already sent across the cluster. By performing prioritization across queues and by scheduling coflows in the FIFO order within each queue, Aalo's non-clairvoyant scheduler reduces coflow completion times while guaranteeing starvation freedom. EC2 deployments and trace-driven simulations show that communication stages complete $1.93\times$ faster on average and $3.59\times$ faster at the 95th percentile using Aalo in comparison to per-flow mechanisms. Aalo's performance is comparable to that of solutions using prior knowledge, and Aalo outperforms them in presence of cluster dynamics.

CCS Concepts

•**Networks** $\rightarrow$ **Cloud computing;**

Keywords

Coflow; data-intensive applications; datacenter networks

SIGCOMM '15, August 17 - 21, 2015, London, United Kingdom

 ISBN 978-1-4503-3542-3/15/08...$15.00

DOI: http://dx.doi.org/10.1145/2785956.2787480

1 Introduction

Communication is crucial for analytics at scale [19, 8, 12, 20, 25]. Yet, until recently, researchers and practitioners have largely overlooked application-level requirements when improving network-level metrics like flow-level fairness and flow completion time (FCT) [29, 10, 16, 8, 14]. The coflow abstraction [18] bridges this gap by exposing application-level semantics to the network. It builds upon the *all-or-nothing* property observed in many aspects of data-parallel computing like task scheduling [51, 12] and distributed cache allocation [11]; for the network, it means all flows must complete for the completion of a communication stage. Indeed, decreasing a coflow's completion time (CCT) can lead to faster completion of corresponding job [20, 25, 19].

However, inter-coflow scheduling to minimize the average CCT is NP-hard [20]. Existing FIFO-based solutions, e.g., Baraat [25] and Orchestra [19], compromise on performance by multiplexing coflows to avoid head-of-line blocking. Varys [20] improves performance using heuristics like smallest-bottleneck-first and smallest-total-size-first, but it assumes *complete* prior knowledge of coflow characteristics like the number of flows, their sizes, and endpoints.

Unfortunately, in many cases, coflow characteristics are unknown a priori. Multi-stage jobs use pipelining between successive computation stages [30, 22, 46, 3] – i.e., data is transferred as soon as it is generated – making it hard to know the size of each flow. Moreover, a single stage may consist of multiple waves [11],[1] preventing all flows within a coflow from starting together. Finally, task failures and speculation [50, 30, 24] result in redundant flows; meaning, the exact number of flows or their endpoints cannot be determined until a coflow has completed. Consequently, coflow schedulers that rely on prior knowledge remain inapplicable to a large number of use cases.

In this paper, we present a coordinated inter-coflow scheduler – called *Coflow-Aware Least-Attained Service* (CLAS) – to minimize the average CCT *without* any prior knowledge of coflow characteristics. CLAS generalizes the classic least-attained service (LAS) scheduling discipline [45] to coflows. However, instead of independently considering the number of bytes sent by each flow, CLAS takes into account the *total*

[1] A *wave* is defined as the set of parallel *tasks* from the same *stage* of a *job* that have been scheduled together.

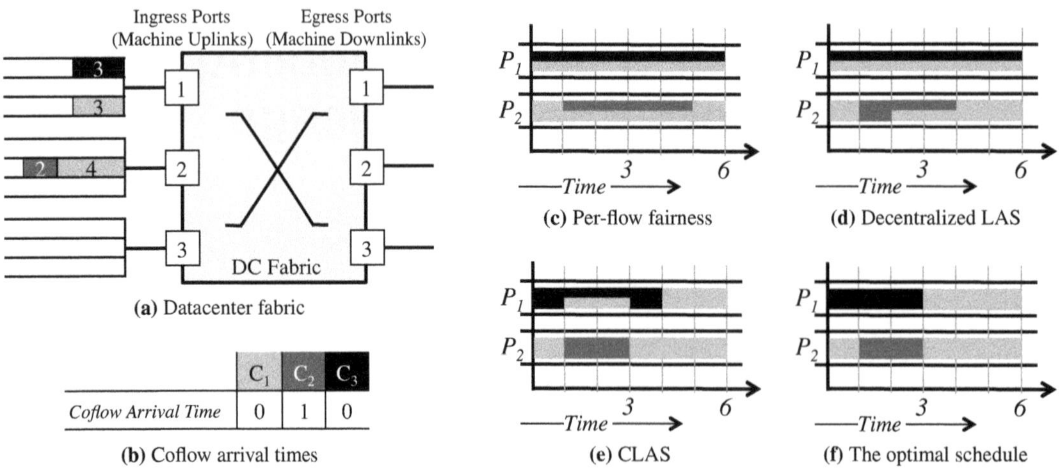

(a) Datacenter fabric

(b) Coflow arrival times

(c) Per-flow fairness

(d) Decentralized LAS

(e) CLAS

(f) The optimal schedule

Figure 1: Online coflow scheduling over a 3×3 datacenter fabric with three ingress/egress ports (a). Flows in ingress ports are organized by destinations and color-coded by coflows – C_1 in orange/light, C_2 in blue/dark, and C_3 in black. Coflows arrive online over time (b). Assuming each port can transfer one unit of data in one time unit, (c)–(f) depict the allocations of *ingress* port capacities (vertical axis) for different mechanisms: The average CCT for (c) per-flow fairness is 5.33 time units; (d) decentralized LAS is 5 time units; (e) CLAS with instant coordination is 4 time units; and (f) the optimal schedule is 3.67 time units.

number of bytes sent by *all* the flows of a coflow. In particular, CLAS *assigns each coflow a priority that is decreasing in the total number of bytes the coflow has already sent.* As a result, smaller coflows have higher priorities than larger ones, which helps in reducing the average CCT. Note that for heavy-tailed distributions of coflow sizes, CLAS approximates the smallest-total-size-first heuristic,[2] which has been shown to work well for realistic workloads [20].

For light-tailed distributions of coflow sizes, however, a straightforward implementation of CLAS can lead to fine-grained sharing,[3] which is known to be suboptimal for minimizing the average CCT [19, 25, 20]. The optimal schedule in such cases is FIFO [25].

We address this dilemma by *discretizing* coflow priorities. Instead of decreasing a coflow's priority based on every byte it sends, we decrease its priority only when the number of bytes it has sent exceeds some predefined thresholds. We call this discipline *Discretized CLAS*, or D-CLAS for short (§4). In particular, we use exponentially-spaced thresholds, where the i-th threshold equals b^i, $(b > 1)$.

We implement D-CLAS using a multi-level scheduler, where each queue maintains all the coflows with the same priority. Within each queue, coflows follow the FIFO order. Across queues, we use weighted fair queuing at the coflow granularity, where weights are based on the queues' priorities. Using weighted sharing, instead of strict priorities, avoids starvation because each queue is guaranteed to receive some non-zero service. By approximating FIFO (as in Baraat [25]) for light-tailed coflows and smallest-coflow-first (as in Varys [20]) for heavy-tailed coflows, the proposed scheduler works well in practice.

We have implemented D-CLAS in Aalo,[4] a system that supports coflow dependencies and pipelines, and works well in presence of cluster dynamics like multi-wave scheduling (§5). Aalo requires *no* prior knowledge of coflow characteristics, e.g., coflow size, number of flows in the coflow, or its endpoints. While Aalo needs to track the total number of bytes sent by a coflow to update its priority,[5] this requires only loose coordination as priority thresholds are coarse. Moreover, coflows whose total sizes are smaller than the first priority threshold require no coordination. Aalo runs *without* any changes to the network or user jobs, and data-parallel applications require minimal changes to use it (§6).

We deployed Aalo on a 100-machine EC2 cluster and evaluated it by replaying production traces from Facebook and with TPC-DS [6] queries (§7). Aalo improved CCTs both on average (up to $2.25\times$) and at high percentiles ($2.93\times$ at the 95th percentile) w.r.t. per-flow fair sharing, which decreased corresponding job completion times. Aalo's average improvements were within 12% of Varys for single-stage, single-wave coflows, and it outperformed Varys for multi-stage, multi-wave coflows by up to $3.7\times$ by removing artificial barriers and through dependency-aware scheduling. In trace-driven simulations, we found Aalo to perform $2.7\times$ better than per-flow fair sharing and up to $16\times$ better than fully decentralized solutions that suffer significantly due to the lack of coordination. Simulations show that Aalo performs well across a wide range of parameter space and coflow distributions.

We discuss current limitations and relevant future research in Section 8 and compare Aalo to related work in Section 9.

[2]Under the heavy-tailed distribution assumption, the number of bytes already sent is a good predictor of the actual coflow size [41].

[3]Consider two identical coflows, C_A and C_B, that start at the same time. As soon as we send data from coflow C_A, its priority will decrease, and we will have to schedule coflow C_B. Thus, both coflows will continuously be interleaved and will finish roughly at the same time – both taking twice as much time as a single coflow in isolation.

[4]In Bangla, Aalo (pronounced \'ä-lō\) means light.

[5]As stated by **Theorem** A.1 in Appendix A, *any* coflow scheduler's performance can drop dramatically in the absence of coordination.

2 Motivation

Before presenting our design, it is important to understand the challenges and opportunities in non-clairvoyant coflow scheduling for data-parallel directed acyclic graphs (DAGs).

2.1 Background

Non-Clairvoyant Coflows A coflow is a collection of parallel flows with distributed endpoints, and it completes after all its flows have completed [18, 20, 19]. Jobs with one coflow finish faster when coflows complete faster [20]. Data-parallel DAGs [30, 50, 46, 2, 3] with multiple stages can be represented by multiple coflows with dependencies between them. However, push-forward pipelining between subsequent computation stages of a DAG [22, 30, 46, 3] removes barriers at the end of coflows, and knowing flow sizes becomes infeasible. Due to multi-wave scheduling [11], all flows of a coflow do not start at the same time either.

Hence, unlike existing work [19, 20, 25], we *do not assume* anything about a coflow's characteristics like the number of flows, endpoints, or waves, the size of each flow, their arrival times, or the presence of barriers.

Non-Blocking Fabric In our analysis, we abstract out the entire datacenter fabric as one non-blocking switch [10, 15, 20, 9, 31, 26] and consider machine uplinks and downlinks as the only sources of contention (Figure 1a). This model is attractive for its simplicity, and recent advances in datacenter fabrics [9, 28, 40] make it practical as well. However, we use this abstraction only to simplify our analysis; we do not require nor enforce this in our evaluation (§7).

2.2 Challenges

An efficient non-clairvoyant [39] coflow scheduler must address two primary challenges:

1. *Scheduling without complete knowledge:* Without a priori knowledge of coflows, heuristics like smallest-bottleneck-first [20] are inapplicable – one cannot schedule coflows based on unknown bottlenecks. Worse, redundant flows from restarted and speculative tasks unpredictably affect a coflow's structure and bottlenecks. While FIFO-based schedulers (e.g., FIFO-LM in Baraat [25]) do not need complete knowledge, they multiplex to avoid head-of-line blocking, losing performance.
2. *Need for coordination:* Coordination is the key to performance in coflow scheduling. We show analytically (**Theorem A.1**) and empirically (§7.2.1, §7.6) that fully decentralized schedulers like Baraat [25] can perform poorly in data-parallel clusters because *local-only* observations are poor indicators of CCTs of large coflows. Fully centralized solutions like Varys [20], on the contrary, introduce high overheads for small coflows.

2.3 Potential Gains

Given the advantages of coflow scheduling and the inability of clairvoyant schedulers to support dynamic coflow modifications and dependencies, a *loosely-coordinated* non-clairvoyant coflow scheduler can strike a balance between performance and flexibility.

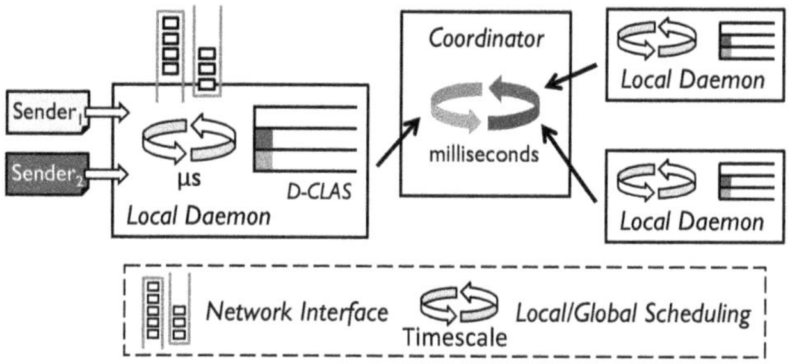

Figure 2: Aalo architecture. Computation frameworks interact with their local Aalo daemons using a client library, and the daemons periodically coordinate to determine the global ordering of coflows.

Consider the example in Figure 1 that compares three non-clairvoyant mechanisms against the optimal clairvoyant schedule. Per-flow fair sharing (Figure 1c) ensures max-min fairness in each link, but it suffers by ignoring coflows [19, 20]. Applying least-attained service (LAS) [42, 45, 14] in a decentralized manner (Figure 1d) does not help, because local observations cannot predict a coflow's actual size – e.g., it shares P_1 equally between C_1 and C_3, being oblivious to C_1's flow in P_2. The FIFO-LM schedule [25] would be at least as bad. Taking the total size of coflows into account through global coordination significantly decreases the average CCT (Figure 1e). The optimal solution (Figure 1f) exploits complete knowledge for the minimum average CCT. The FIFO schedule [19] would have resulted in a lower average CCT (4.67 time units) than decentralized LAS if C_3 was scheduled before C_1, and it would have been the same if C_1 was scheduled before C_3.

This example considers only single-stage coflows without egress contention. Coordinated coflow scheduling can be even more effective in both scenarios (§7).

3 Aalo Overview

Aalo uses a non-clairvoyant coflow scheduler that optimizes the communication performance of data-intensive applications without a priori knowledge, while being resilient to the dynamics of job schedulers and data-parallel clusters. This section briefly overviews Aalo to help the reader follow the analysis and design of its scheduling algorithms (§4), mechanisms to handle dynamic events (§5), and design details (§6) presented in subsequent sections.

3.1 Problem Statement

Our goal is *dynamically prioritizing coflows without prior knowledge of their characteristics while respecting coflow dependencies.* This problem – *non-clairvoyant coflow scheduling with precedence constraints* – is NP-hard, because coflow scheduling with complete knowledge is NP-hard too [20]. In addition to minimizing CCTs, we must guarantee starvation freedom and work conservation.

3.2 Architectural Overview

Aalo uses a loosely-coordinated architecture (Figure 2), because full decentralization can render coflow scheduling pointless (**Theorem A.1**). It implements global and local controls at two time granularities:

• *Long-term global coordination:* Aalo daemons send locally-observed coflow sizes to a central coordinator every $O(10)$ milliseconds. The coordinator determines the global coflow ordering using the D-CLAS framework (§4) and periodically sends out the updated schedule and globally-observed coflow sizes to all the daemons.

• *Short-term local prioritization:* Each daemon schedules coflows using the last-known global information. In between resynchronization, newly-arrived coflows are enqueued in the highest-priority queue. While flows from new and likely to be small[6] coflows receive high priority in the short term, Aalo daemons realign themselves with the global schedule as soon as updated information arrives. A flow that has just completed is replaced with a same-destination flow from the next coflow in the schedule for work conservation.

Frameworks use a client library to interact with the coordinator over the network to define coflows and their dependencies (§6). To send data, they must use the Aalo-provided `OutputStream`. The coordinator has an ID generator that creates unique CoflowIds while taking coflow dependencies into account (§5.1).

We have implemented Aalo in the application layer *without* any changes or support from the underlying network. We have deployed it in the cloud, and it performs well even for sub-second data analytics jobs (§7).

Fault Tolerance Aalo handles three failure scenarios that include its own failures and that of the clients using it. First, failure of a Aalo daemon does not hamper job execution, since the client library automatically falls back to regular TCP fair sharing until the daemon is restarted. Upon restart, the daemon remains in inconsistent state only until the next coordination step. Second, when the coordinator fails, client libraries keep track of locally-observed size until it has been restarted, while periodically trying to reconnect. Finally, in case of task failures and consequent restarts, relevant flows are restarted by corresponding job schedulers. Such flows are treated like a new wave in a coflow, and their additional traffic is added up to the current size of that coflow (§5.2).

Scalability The faster Aalo daemons can coordinate, the better it performs. The number of coordination messages is linear with the number of daemons and *independent* of coflows. It is not a bottleneck for clusters with $O(100)$ machines, and our evaluation suggests that Aalo can scale up to $O(10,000)$ machines with minimal performance loss (§7.6). Most coflows are small and scheduled through local decisions; hence, unlike Varys, Aalo handles tiny coflows well.

4 Scheduling Without Prior Knowledge

In this section, we present an efficient coflow scheduler for minimizing CCTs *without* a priori information. First, we discuss the complexity and requirements of such a scheduler (§4.1). Next, we describe a priority discretization framework (§4.2) that we use to discuss the tradeoffs in designing an efficient, non-clairvoyant scheduler (§4.3). Based on our understanding, we develop discretized Coflow-Aware Least-Attained Service (D-CLAS) – a mechanism to prioritize coflows and a set of policies to schedule them without starvation (§4.4). Finally, we compare our proposal with existing coflow schedulers (§4.5).

For brevity of exposition, we present the mechanisms in the context of single-stage, single-wave coflows. We extend them to handle multi-stage, multi-wave coflows as well as task failures and speculation in Section 5.

4.1 Complexity and Desirable Properties

The offline coflow scheduling problem – i.e., when all coflows arrive together and their characteristics are known a priori – is NP-hard [20]. Consequently, the non-clairvoyant coflow scheduling problem is NP-hard as well.

In the non-clairvoyant setting, smallest-bottleneck-first [20] – the best-performing clairvoyant heuristic – becomes inapplicable. This is because the bottleneck of a coflow is revealed only *after* it has completed. Instead, one must schedule coflows based on an attribute that

1. *can approximate its clairvoyant counterpart* using current observations, and
2. *involves all the flows* to avoid the drawbacks from the lack of coordination (**Theorem** A.1).

Note that a coflow's bottleneck can change over time and due to task failures and restarts, failing the first requirement.

In addition to minimizing the average CCT, the non-clairvoyant scheduler must

1. *guarantee starvation freedom* for bounded CCTs,
2. *ensure work conservation* to increase utilization, and
3. *decrease coordination requirements* for scalability.

Coflow-Aware Least-Attained Service (CLAS) Although the smallest-total-size-first heuristic had been shown to perform marginally worse ($1.14\times$) than smallest-bottleneck-first in the clairvoyant setting [20], it becomes a viable option in the non-clairvoyant case. The *current size* of a coflow – i.e., how much it has already sent throughout the entire cluster – meets both criteria. This is because unlike a coflow's bottleneck, it *monotonically* increases with each flow regardless of start time or endpoints. As a result, setting a coflow's priority that decreases with it's current size can ensure that smaller coflows finish faster, which, in turn, minimizes the average CCT. Furthermore, it is a good indicator of actual size [41], because coflow size typically follows heavy-tailed distribution [20, 11].

We refer to this scheme as Coordinated or Coflow-Aware Least-Attained Service (CLAS). Note that CLAS reduces to the well-known Least-Attained Service (LAS) [42, 45] scheduling discipline in case of a single link.

4.2 Priority Discretization

Unfortunately, using continuous priorities derived from coflow sizes can degenerate into fair sharing (§B), which increases the average CCT [19, 25, 20]. Coordination needed to find global coflow sizes poses an additional challenge. We must be able to preempt at opportune moments to decrease CCT without requiring excessive coordination.

[6]For data-parallel analytics, 60% (85%) coflows are less than 100 MB (1 GB) in total size [20, 25].

In the following, we describe a priority *discretization* framework to eventually design an efficient, non-clairvoyant coflow scheduler. Unlike classic non-clairvoyant schedulers – least-attained service (LAS) in single links [42, 45] and multi-level feedback queues (MLFQ) in operating systems [23, 21, 13] – that perform fair sharing in presence of similar flows/tasks to provide interactivity, our solution improves the average CCT even in presence of identical coflows.

Multi-Level Coflow Scheduling A multi-level coflow scheduler consists of K queues ($Q_1, Q_2, \ldots, Q_K$), with queue priorities decreasing from Q_1 to Q_K. The i-th queue contains coflows of size within $[Q_i^{\text{lo}}, Q_i^{\text{hi}})$. Note that $Q_1^{\text{lo}} = 0$, $Q_K^{\text{hi}} = \infty$, and $Q_{i+1}^{\text{lo}} = Q_i^{\text{hi}}$.

Actions taken during three lifecycle events determine a coflow's priority.

- *Arrival:* New coflows enter the highest priority queue Q_1 when they start.
- *Activity:* A coflow is demoted to Q_{i+1} from Q_i, when its size crosses queue threshold Q_i^{hi}.
- *Completion:* Coflows are removed from their current queues upon completion.

The first two ensure coflow prioritization based on its current size, while the last is for completeness.

4.3 Tradeoffs in Designing Coflow Schedulers

Given the multi-level framework, a coflow scheduler can be characterized by its information source, queue structure, and scheduling disciplines at different granularities. Tradeoffs made while navigating this solution space result in diverse algorithms, ranging from centralized shortest-first to decentralized FIFO [19, 20, 25] and many in between. We elaborate on the key tradeoffs below.

Information Source There are two primary categories of coflow schedulers: *clairvoyant* schedulers use a priori information and *non-clairvoyant* ones do not. Non-clairvoyant schedulers have one more decision to make: whether to use globally-coordinated coflow sizes or to rely on local information. The former is accurate but more time consuming. The latter diverges (**Theorem** A.1) for coflows with large skews, which is common in production clusters [17, 20].

Queue Structure A scheduler must also determine the number of queues it wants to use and their thresholds. On the one hand, FIFO-derived schemes (e.g., Orchestra, Baraat) use exactly one queue.[7] FIFO works well when coflows follow light-tailed distributions [25]. Clairvoyant efficient schedulers (e.g., Varys), on the other hand, can be considered to have as many queues as there are coflows. They perform the best when coflow sizes are *known* and are heavy-tailed [20]. At both extremes, queue thresholds are irrelevant.

For solutions in between, determining an ideal number of queues and corresponding thresholds is difficult; even for tasks on a single machine, no optimal solution exists [13]. Increasing the number of levels/queues is appealing, but

[7]Baraat takes advantage of multiple queues in switches to enable multiplexing, but logically all coflows are in the same queue.

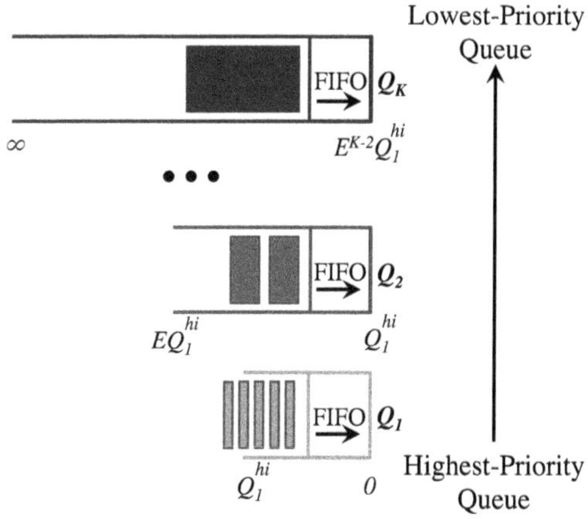

Figure 3: Discretized Coflow-Aware Least-Attained Service. Consecutive queues hold coflows with exponentially larger size.

fine-grained prioritization can collapse to fair sharing when coflow sizes are unknown and hurt CCTs. More queues also generate more "queue-change" events and increase coordination requirements.

Scheduling Disciplines Finally, a coflow scheduler must decide on scheduling disciplines at three different granularities: (i) across queues, (ii) among coflows in each queue, and (iii) among flows within each coflow. The first is relevant when $K > 1$, while the second is necessary when queues have more than one coflow. In the absence of flow size information, size-based rate allocation algorithms like WSS [19] and MADD [20] cannot be used; max-min fairness similar to TCP is the best alternative for scheduling individual flows.

4.4 Discretized Coflow-Aware Least-Attained Service

We propose *Discretized CLAS* or D-CLAS that use more than one priority queues, i.e., $K > 1$, to enable prioritization. The key challenge, however, is finding a suitable K that provides sufficient opportunities for preemption, yet small enough to not require excessive coordination.

To achieve our goals, each queue in D-CLAS contains *exponentially larger* coflows than its immediately higher-priority queue (Figure 3). Formally, $Q_{i+1}^{\text{hi}} = E \times Q_i^{\text{hi}}$, where the factor E determines how much bigger coflows in one queue are from that in another. Consequently, the number of queues remains small and can be expressed as an E-based logarithmic function of the maximum coflow size.

The final component in defining our queue structure is determining Q_1^{hi}. Because global coordination, irrespective of mechanism, has an associated time penalty depending on the scale of the cluster, we want coflows that are too small to be globally coordinated in Q_1. Larger coflows reside in increasingly more stable, lower-priority queues ($Q_2, \ldots, Q_K$).

While we typically use $E = 10$ and $Q_1^{\text{hi}} = 10$ MB in our cluster, simulations show that for $K > 1$, a wide range of K, E, Q_1^{hi} combinations work well (§7.5).

Non-Clairvoyant Efficient Schedulers D-CLAS clusters similar coflows together and allows us to implement different scheduling disciplines among queues and among coflows within each queue (Pseudocode 1). It uses weighted sharing

	Orchestra [19]	Varys [20]	Baraat [25]	Aalo
On-Arrival Knowledge	Clairvoyant	Clairvoyant	Non-clairvoyant	Non-clairvoyant
Coflow Size Information	Global	Global	Local	Global Approx.
Number of Queues (K)	One	Num Coflows	One	$\log_E$(Max Size)
Queue Thresholds	N/A	Exact Size	N/A	$Q_{i+1}^{\text{hi}} = E \times Q_i^{\text{hi}}$
Queue Scheduling	N/A	Strict Priority	N/A	Weighted
Coflow Scheduling in Each Queue	FIFO	N/A	FIFO	FIFO
Flow Scheduling	WSS	MADD	Max-Min	Max-Min
Work Conservation	Next Coflow	Next Queue	Next Coflow	Weighted Among Queues
Starvation Avoidance	N/A	Promote to Q_1	N/A	N/A
HOL Blocking Avoidance	Multiplexing	N/A	Multiplexing	N/A

Table 1: Qualitative comparison of coflow scheduling algorithms. Typically, $E = 10$ for D-CLAS.

Pseudocode 1 D-CLAS Scheduler to Minimize CCT

```
1: procedure RESCHEDULE(Queues Q, ExcessPolicy E(.))
2:   while Fabric is not saturated do                          ▷ Allocate
3:     for all i ∈ [1, K] do
4:       for all Coflow C ∈ Q_i do                   ▷ Sorted by CoflowId
5:         for all Flow f ∈ C do
6:           f.rate = Max-min fair share             ▷ Fair schedule flows
7:           Update Q_i.share based on f.rate
8:       Distribute unused Q_i.share using E(.)         ▷ Work conserv.
9: end procedure

10: procedure D-CLAS
11:   W = ∑ Q_i.weight
12:   for all i ∈ [1, K] do
13:     Q_i.share = Q_i.weight / W      ▷ Weighted sharing b/n queues
14:   reschedule(Q, Max-Min among Q_{j≠i})
15: end procedure
```

among queues, where queue weights decrease with lowered priority; i.e., Q_i.weight $\geq Q_{i+1}$.weight at line 13 in Pseudocode 1. Excess share of any queue is divided among unsaturated queues in proportion to their weights using max-min fairness (line 14).

Within each queue, it uses FIFO scheduling (line 4) so that coflows can proceed until they reach queue threshold or complete. Minimizing interleaving between coflows in the same queue minimizes CCTs, and large coflows are preempted after crossing queue thresholds. Hence, D-CLAS does not suffer from HOL blocking. As mentioned earlier, without prior knowledge, flows within each coflow use max-min fairness (line 6).

Starvation Avoidance Given non-zero weights to each queue, all queues are guaranteed to make progress. Hence, D-CLAS is starvation free. We did not observe any perpetual starvation in our experiments or simulations either.

4.5 Summary

Table 1 summarizes the key characteristics of the schedulers discussed in this section. D-CLAS minimizes the average CCT by prioritizing significantly different coflows across queues and FIFO ordering similar coflows in the same queue. It does so without starvation, and it approximates FIFO schedulers for light-tailed and priority schedulers for heavy-tailed coflow distributions.

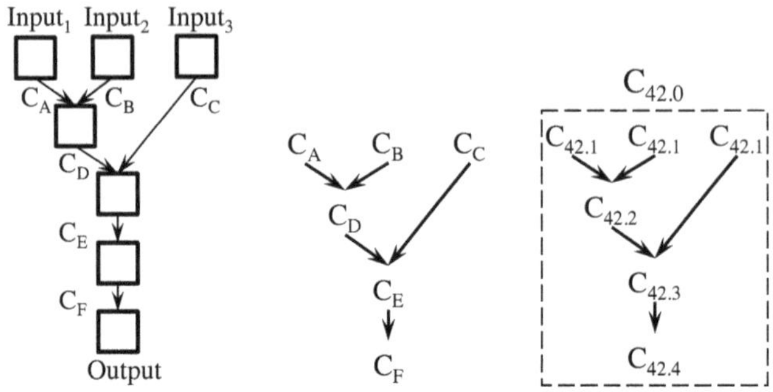

(a) Query Plan **(b)** Dependencies **(c)** CoflowIDs

Figure 4: Coflow dependencies in TPC-DS query-42 [6]: (a) Query plan generated by Shark [48]; boxes and arrows respectively represent computation and communication stages. (b) Finishes-Before relationships between coflows are represented by arrows. (c) CoflowIds assigned by Aalo.

5 Handling Uncertainties

So far we have only considered "ideal" coflows from single-stage, single-wave jobs without task failures or stragglers. In this section, we remove each of these assumptions and extend the proposed schedulers to perform well in realistic settings. We start by considering multi-stage dataflow DAGs (§5.1). Next, we consider dynamic coflow modifications due to job scheduler events like multi-wave scheduling and cluster activities like restarted and speculative tasks (§5.2).

5.1 Multi-Stage Dataflow DAGs

The primary concern in coflow scheduling in the context of multi-stage jobs [30, 50, 3, 2] is the divergence of CCT and job completion time. Minimizing CCTs might not always result in faster jobs – one must carefully handle coflow *dependencies* within the same DAG (Figure 4).

We define a coflow C_F to be dependent on another coflow C_E if the consumer computation stage of C_E is the producer of C_F. Depending on pipelining between successive computation stages, there can be two types of dependencies.

1. *Starts-After* ($C_E \longmapsto C_F$): In presence of explicit barriers [2], C_F cannot start until C_E has finished.
2. *Finishes-Before* ($C_E \longrightarrow C_F$): With pipelining between successive stages [30, 22], C_F can coexist with C_E but it cannot finish until C_E has finished.

Note that coflows in different branches of a DAG can be un-

Pseudocode 2 Coflow ID Generation

NextCoflowID = 0 ▷ Initialization
procedure NEWCOFLOWID(**CoflowId** *pId*, **Coflows** $\mathcal{P}$)
  if *pId* == **Nil then**
    newId = *NextCoflowID++* ▷ Unique external id
    return *newId.0*
  else
    $sId = 1 + \max_{C \in \mathcal{P}} C.sId$ ▷ Ordered internal id
    return *pId.sId*
end procedure

related to each other.

Job schedulers identify coflow dependencies while building query plans (Figure 4a). They can make Aalo aware of these dependencies all at once, or in a coflow-by-coflow basis. *Given coflow dependencies, we want to efficiently schedule them to minimize corresponding job completion times.*

We make two observations about coflow dependencies. First, coflows from the same job should be treated as a single entity. Second, within each entity, dependent coflows must be deprioritized during contention. The former ensures that minimizing CCTs directly affect job completion times, while the latter prevents circular dependencies. For example, all six coflows must complete in Figure 4a, and dependent coflows cannot complete without their parents in Figure 4b.

We simultaneously achieve both objectives by encoding the DAG identifier and internal coflow dependencies in the CoflowId. Specifically, we extend the CoflowId with an *internal* component in addition to its *external* component (Pseudocode 2). While the external part of a CoflowId uniquely identifies the DAG it belongs to, the internal part ensures ordering of coflows within the same DAG (Figure 4c). Our schedulers process coflows in each queue in the FIFO order based on their external components, and they break ties between coflows with the same external component using their internal CoflowIds (line 4 in Pseudocode 1).

Note that optimal DAG scheduling is NP-hard (§9). Our approach is similar to the Critical-Path Method [33] and resolves dependencies in each branch of a DAG, but it does not provide any guarantees for the entire DAG.

5.2 Dynamic Coflow Modifications

A flow can start only after its source and destination tasks have been scheduled. Tasks of large jobs are often scheduled in multiple waves depending on cluster capacity [11]. Hence, flows of such jobs are also created in batches, and waiting for all flows of a stage to start only halts a job. Because the number of tasks in each wave can dynamically change, Aalo must react without a priori knowledge. The same is true for unpredictable cluster events like failures and stragglers. Both result in restart or replication of some tasks and corresponding flows, and Aalo must efficiently handle them as well.

Aalo can handle all three events without any changes to its schedulers. As long as flows use the appropriate CoflowId, how much a coflow has sent *always* increases regardless of multiple waves and tasks being restarted or replicated.

6 Design Details

We have implemented Aalo in about 4,000 lines of Scala code that provides a pipelined coflow API (§6.1) and implements (§6.2) the proposed schedulers.

6.1 Pipelined Coflow API

Aalo provides a simple coflow API that requires just replacing `OutputStreams` with `AaloOutputStream`. Any `InputStream` can be used in conjunction with `AaloOutputStream`. It also provides two additional methods for coflow creation and completion – `register()` and `unregister()`, respectively.

The `InputStream`-`AaloOutputStream` combination is non-blocking. Meaning, there is no artificial barrier after a coflow, and senders (receivers) start sending (receiving) without blocking. As they send (receive) more bytes, Aalo observes their total size, perform efficient coflow scheduling, and throttles when required. Consequently, small coflows proceed in the FIFO order without coordination overhead. The entire process is transparent to applications.

Usage Example *Any* sender can use coflows by wrapping its `OutputStream` with `AaloOutputStream`.

For example, for a shuffle to use Aalo, the driver first registers it to receive a unique CoflowId.

```
val sId = register()
```

Note that the driver does not need to define the number of flows before a coflow starts.

Later, each mapper must use `AaloOutputStream` for sending data. One mapper can create multiple `AaloOutputStream` instances, one for each reducer connection (i.e., socket `sock`), in concurrent threads.

```
val out = new AaloOutputStream(sock, sId)
```

Reducers can use any `InputStream` instances to receive their inputs. They can also overlap subsequent computation with data reception instead of waiting for the entire input. Once all reducers complete, the driver terminates the shuffle.

```
unregister(sId)
```

Defining Dependencies Coflows can specify their parent(s) during registration, and Aalo uses this information to generate CoflowIds (Pseudocode 2). In our running example, if the shuffle (`sId`) depended on an earlier broadcast (`bId`) – common in many Spark [50] jobs – the driver would have defined `bId` as a dependency during registration as follows.

```
val sId = register({bId})
```

`sId` and `bId` will share the same external CoflowId, but `sId` will have lower priority if it contends with `bId`.

6.2 Coflow Scheduling in Aalo

Aalo daemons resynchronize every Δ milliseconds. Each daemon sends the locally-observed coflow sizes to the coordinator every Δ interval. Similarly, the coordinator sends out the globally-coordinated coflow order and corresponding sizes every Δ interval. Furthermore, the coordinator sends out explicit ON/OFF signals for individual flows in order to avoid receiver-side contentions and to expedite sender-receiver rate convergence.

In between updates, daemons make decisions based on current knowledge, which can be off by at most Δ milliseconds from the global information. Because traffic-generating coflows are large, daemons are almost always in sync about their order; only tiny coflows are handled by local decisions to avoid synchronization overheads.

Choice of Δ Aalo daemons are more closely in sync as Δ decreases. We suggest Δ to be $O(10)$ milliseconds, and our evaluation shows that a 100-machine EC2 cluster can resynchronize within 8 milliseconds on average (§7.6).

7 Evaluation

We evaluated Aalo through a series of experiments on 100-machine EC2 [1] clusters using traces from production clusters and an industrial benchmark. For larger-scale evaluations, we used a trace-driven simulator that performs a detailed replay of task logs. The highlights are:

- For communication-dominated jobs, Aalo improves the average (95th percentile) CCT and job completion time by up to 2.25× (2.93×) and 1.57× (1.77×), respectively, over per-flow fairness. Aalo improvements are, on average, within 12% of Varys (§7.2).
- As suggested by our analysis, coordination is the key to performance – independent local decisions (e.g., in [25]) can lead to more than 16× performance loss (§7.2.1).
- Aalo outperforms per-flow fairness and Varys for multi-wave (§7.3) and DAG (§7.4) workloads by up to 3.7×.
- Aalo's improvements are stable over a wide range of parameter combinations for any $K \geq 2$ (§7.5).
- Aalo coordinator can scale to $O(10,000)$ daemons with minimal performance loss (§7.6).

7.1 Methodology

Workload Our workload is based on a Hive/MapReduce trace collected by Chowdhury et al. [20, Figure 4] from a 3000-machine, 150-rack Facebook cluster. The original cluster had a 10 : 1 core-to-rack oversubscription ratio and a total bisection bandwidth of 300 Gbps. We scale down jobs accordingly to match the maximum possible 100 Gbps bisection bandwidth of our deployment while preserving their communication characteristics.

Additionally, we use TPC-DS [6] queries from the Cloudera benchmark [7, 4] to evaluate Aalo on DAG workloads. The query plans were generated using Shark [48].

Job/Coflow Bins We present our results by categorizing jobs based on their time spent in communication (Table 2) and by distinguishing coflows based on their lengths and widths (Table 3). Specifically, we consider a coflow to be *short* if its longest flow is less than 5 MB and *narrow* if it has at most 50 flows. Note that coflow sizes, like jobs, follow heavy-tailed distributions in data-intensive clusters [20].

Shuffle Dur.	$< 25\%$	25–49%	50–74%	$\geq 75\%$
% of Jobs	61%	13%	14%	12%

Table 2: Jobs binned by time spent in communication.

Coflow Bin	**1 (SN)**	**2 (LN)**	**3 (SW)**	**4 (LW)**
% of Coflows	52%	16%	15%	17%
% of Bytes	0.01%	0.67%	0.22%	99.10%

Table 3: Coflows binned by their length (**S**hort and **L**ong) and their width (**N**arrow and **W**ide).

Cluster Our experiments use extra-large high-memory (`m2.4xlarge`) EC2 instances. We observed bandwidths close to 900 Mbps per machine on clusters of 100 machines. We use a compute engine similar to Spark [50] that uses the coflow API (§6.1) and use $\Delta = 10$ milliseconds, $E = K = 10$, and $Q_1^{\text{hi}} = 10$ MB as defaults.

Simulator For larger-scale evaluation, we use a trace-driven flow-level simulator that performs a detailed task-level replay of the Facebook trace. It preserves input-to-output ratios of tasks, locality constraints, and inter-arrival times between jobs and runs at $1s$ decision intervals for faster completion.

Metrics Our primary metric for comparison is the improvement in average completion times of coflows and jobs (when its last task finished) in the workload. We measure it as the completion time of a scheme normalized by Aalo's completion time; i.e.,

$$\text{Normalized Comp. Time} = \frac{\text{Compared Duration}}{\text{Aalo's Duration}}$$

If the normalized completion time of a scheme is greater (smaller) than one, Aalo is faster (slower).

We contrast Aalo with TCP fair sharing and the open-source[8] implementation of Varys that uses a clairvoyant, smallest-bottleneck-first scheduler. Due to the lack of readily-deployable implementations of Baraat [25], we compare against it only in simulation. We present Aalo's results for D-CLAS with Q_i.weight = $K - i + 1$.

7.2 Aalo's Overall Improvements

Figure 5a shows that Aalo reduced the average and 95th percentile completion times of communication-dominated jobs by up to 1.57× and 1.77×, respectively, in EC2 experiments in comparison to TCP-based per-flow fairness. Corresponding improvements in the average CCT (CommTime) were up to 2.25× and 2.93× (Figure 5b). As expected, jobs become increasingly faster as their time spent in communication increase. Across all bins, the average end-to-end completion times improved by 1.18× and the average CCT improved by 1.93×; corresponding 95th percentile improvements were 1.06× and 3.59×.

Varying improvements in the average CCT across bins in Figure 5b are not correlated, as it depends more on coflow characteristics than that of jobs. Figure 6 shows that Aalo improved the average CCT over per-flow fair sharing regardless of coflow width and length distributions. We observe

[8] https://github.com/coflow

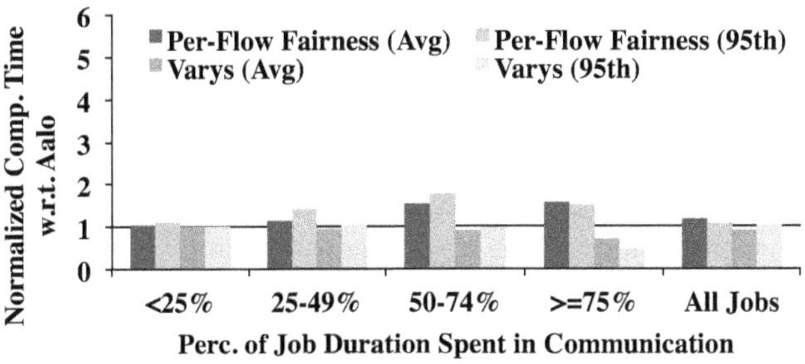

(a) Improvements in job completion times

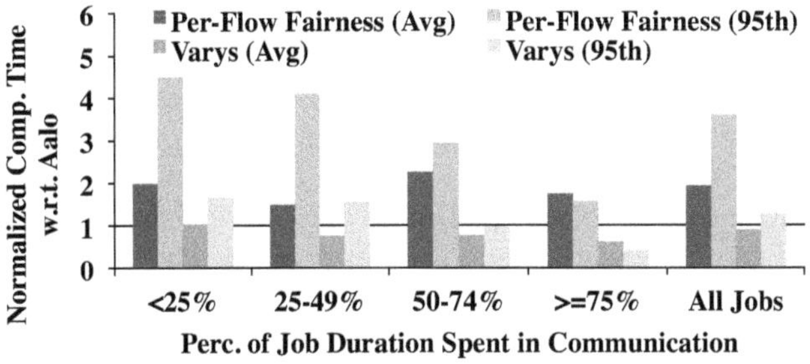

(b) Improvements in time spent in communication

Figure 5: [EC2] Average and 95th percentile improvements in job and communication completion times using Aalo over per-flow fairness and Varys.

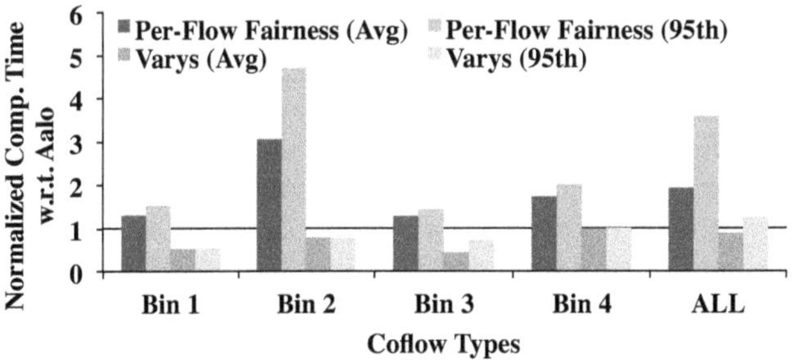

Figure 6: [EC2] Improvements in the average and 95th percentile CCTs using Aalo over per-flow fairness and Varys.

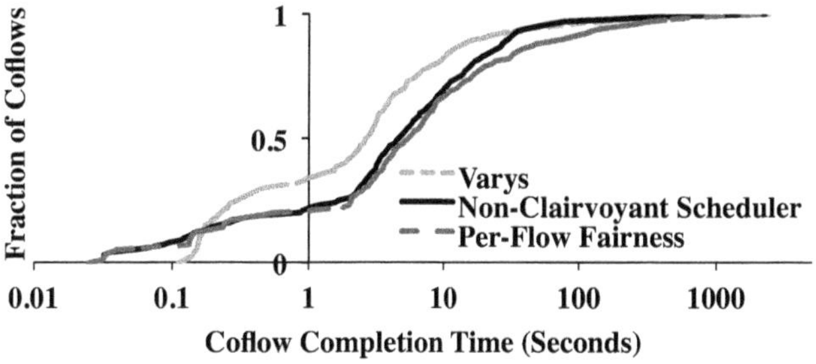

Figure 7: [EC2] CCT distributions for Aalo, Varys, and per-flow fairness mechanism. The X-axis is in log scale.

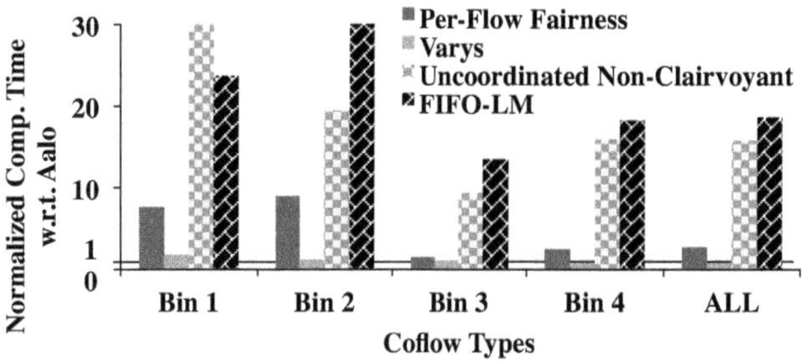

Figure 8: [Simulation] Average improvements in CCTs using Aalo. 95th percentile results are similar.

more improvements in bin-2 and bin-4 over bin-1 and bin-3, respectively, because longer coflows give Aalo more opportunities for better estimation.

Finally, Figure 7 presents comparative CDFs of CCTs for all coflows. Across a wide range of coflow durations – milliseconds to hours – Aalo matches or outperforms TCP fair sharing. As mentioned earlier, Aalo's advantages keep increasing with longer coflows.

What About Clairvoyant Coflow Schedulers? To understand how far we are from clairvoyant solutions, we have compared Aalo against Varys, which uses *complete* knowledge of a coflow's individual flows. Figure 5 shows that across all jobs, the average job and coflow completion times using Aalo stay within 12% of Varys. At worst, Aalo is $1.43\times$ worse than Varys for 12% of the jobs.

Figure 6 presents a clearer picture of where Aalo is performing worse. For the largest coflows in bin-4 – sources of almost all the bytes – Aalo performs the same as Varys; it is only for the smaller coflows, specially the short ones in bin-1 and bin-3, Aalo suffers from its lack of foresight.

However, it still does not explain why Varys performs so much better than Aalo for coflows of durations between 200ms to 30s (Figure 7) given that Δ is only 10ms! Closer examination revealed this to be an isolation issue [43, 36]: Varys delays large coflows in presence of small ones and uses explicit rates for each flow. Because Aalo cannot explicitly control rates without a priori information, interference between coflows with few flows with very large coflows results in performance loss. Reliance on slow-to-react TCP for flow-level scheduling worsens the impact. We confirmed this by performing width-bounded experiments – we reduced the number of flows by $10\times$ while keeping same coflow sizes; this reduced the gap between the two CDFs from $\leq 6\times$ to $\leq 2\times$ in the worst case.

Scheduling Overheads Because coflows smaller than the first priority threshold are scheduled without coordination, Aalo easily outperforms Varys for sub-200ms coflows (Figure 7). For larger coflows, Aalo's average and 99th percentile coordination overheads were 8ms and 19ms, respectively, in our 100-machine cluster – an order of magnitude smaller than Varys due to Aalo' loose coordination requirements. Almost all of it were spent in communicating coordinated decisions. Impact of scheduling overheads on Aalo's performance is minimal, even at much larger scales (§7.6).

7.2.1 Trace-Driven Simulation

We compared Aalo against per-flow fairness, Varys, and non-clairvoyant scheduling *without* coordination in simulations (Figure 8). Similar to EC2 experiments, Aalo outperformed flow-level fairness with average and 95th percentile improvements being $2.7\times$ and $2.18\times$.

Figure 8 shows that Aalo outperforms Varys for smaller coflows in bin-1 to bin-3 in the absence of any coordination overheads. However, Varys performed $1.25\times$ better than Aalo for coflows longer than 10s (not visible in Figure 9).

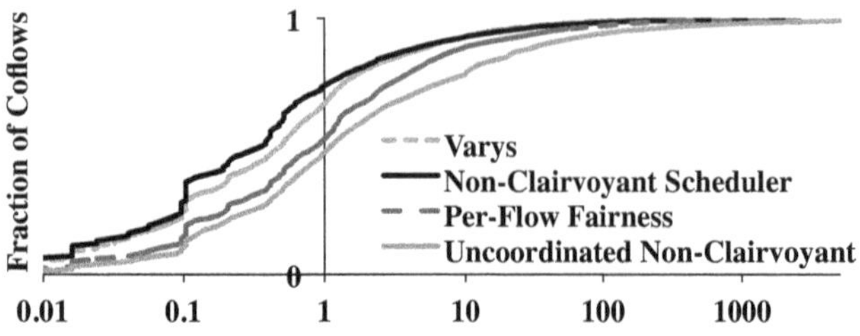

Figure 9: [Simulation] CCT distributions for Aalo, Varys, per-flow fairness, and uncoordinated non-clairvoyant coflow scheduling. X-axis is in log scale.

Number of Waves in Coflow	1	2	3	4
Max Waves = 1	100%			
Max Waves = 2	90%	10%		
Max Waves = 4	81%	9%	4%	6%

Table 4: Coflows binned by the number of waves.

What About Aalo *Without* Coordination? Given that Aalo takes few milliseconds to coordinate, we need to understand the importance of coordination. Simulations show that coflow scheduling without coordination can be significantly worse than even simple TCP fair sharing. On average, Aalo performed 15.8× better than its uncoordinated counterpart, bolstering our worst-case analysis (**Theorem** A.1). Experiments with increasing Δ suggest the same (§7.6).

What About FIFO with Limited Multiplexing in Baraat [25]? We found that FIFO-LM can be significantly worse than Aalo (18.6×) due to its lack of coordination: each switch takes locally-correct, but globally-inconsistent, scheduling decisions. Fair sharing among heavy coflows further worsens it. We had been careful – as the authors in [25] have pointed out – to select the threshold that each switch uses to consider a coflow heavy. Figure 8 shows the results for FIFO-LM's threshold set at the 80-th percentile of the coflow size distribution; results for the threshold set to the 20-th, 40-th, 60-th, 70-th, and 90-th percentiles were worse. Aalo and FIFO-LM performs similar for small coflows following light-tailed distributions (not shown).

How Far are We From the Optimal? Finding the optimal schedule, even in the clairvoyant case, is an open problem [20]. Instead, we tried to find an optimistic estimation of possible improvements by comparing against an *offline* 2-approximation heuristic for coflows *without* coupled resources [37]. For bin-1 to bin-4, corresponding normalized completion times were 0.75×, 0.78×, 1.32×, and 1.15×, respectively. Across all bins, it was 1.19×.

7.3 Impact of Runtime Dynamics

So far we have only considered static coflows, where all flows of a coflow start together. However, operational events like multi-wave scheduling, task failures, and speculative execution can dynamically change a coflow's structure in the runtime (§5.2). Because of their logical similarity – i.e., tasks start in batches and the number of active flows cannot be known a priori – we focus only on the multi-wave case.

The number of waves in a stage depends on the number of

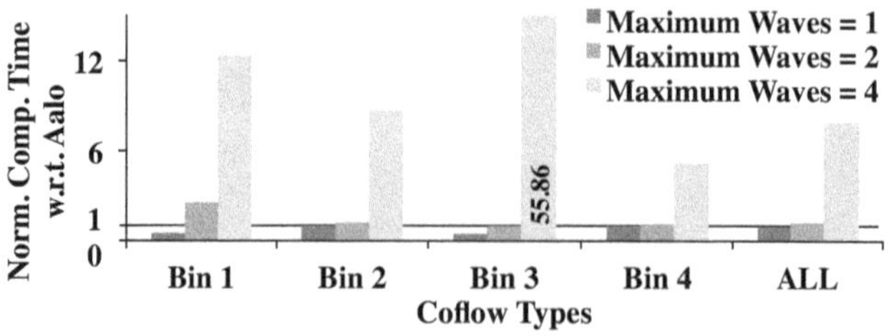

Figure 10: [EC2] Average improvements in CCTs w.r.t. Varys for multi-wave coflows.

senders (e.g., mappers in MapReduce) [11]. In these experiments, we used the same coflow mix as the original trace but varied the maximum number of concurrent senders in each wave while keeping all the receivers active, essentially fixing the maximum number of waves in each coflow. Table 4 shows the fraction of coflows with different number of waves; e.g., all coflows had exactly one wave in Section 7.2.

Figure 10 shows the importance of leveraging coflow relationships across waves. As the number of multi-wave coflows increased, Aalo moved from trailing Varys by 0.94× to outperforming it by 1.21× and 7.91×. Using Varys, one can take two approaches to handle multi-wave coflows – (i) creating separate coflows for each wave as they become available or (ii) introducing barriers to determine the bottleneck of the combined coflow – that both result in performance loss. In the former, Varys can efficiently schedule each wave but increases the stage-level CCT by ignoring the fact that all waves must finish for the stage to finish. The 56× improvement in bin-3 presents an extreme example: one *straggler* coflow was scheduled much later than the rest, increasing the entire stage's runtime. In the latter, artificial barriers decrease parallelism and network utilization. Aalo circumvents the dilemma by creating exactly one coflow per stage for any number of waves and by avoiding barriers.

Aalo's improvements over per-flow fairness (not shown) remained similar to that in Section 7.2.

7.4 Impact on DAG Scheduling

In this section, we evaluate Aalo using multi-stage jobs. Because the Facebook trace consists of only single-coflow jobs, we used the Cloudera industrial benchmark [7, 4] consisting of 20 TPC-DS queries. We ensured that each stage consists of a single wave, but multiple coflows from the same job can still run in parallel (Figure 4c).

Figure 11 shows that Aalo outperforms both per-flow fairness and Varys for DAGs that have more than one levels. Because Aalo does not introduce artificial barriers and can distinguish between coflows from different levels of the critical path, improvements over Varys (3.7× on average) are higher than that over per-flow fairness (1.7× on average).

7.5 Sensitivity Analysis

In this section, we first examine Aalo's sensitivity to the number of queues and their thresholds for heavy-tailed coflow size distributions. Later, we evaluate Aalo's performance for light-tailed distributions.

The Number of Queues (K) Aalo performs increasingly better than per-flow fairness as we increase the number of

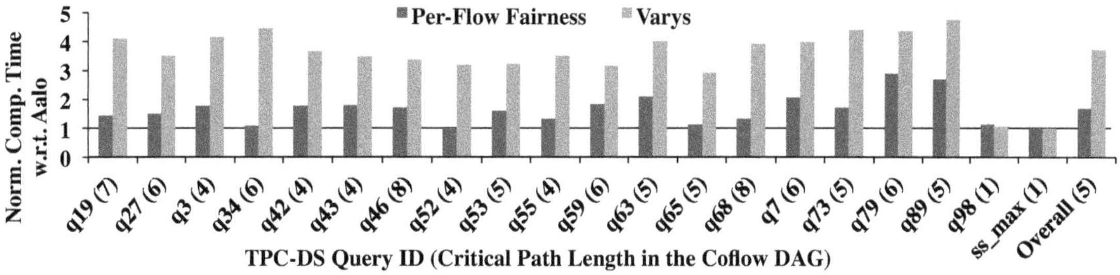

Figure 11: [EC2] Improvements in job-level communication times using Aalo for coflow DAGS in the Cloudera benchmark.

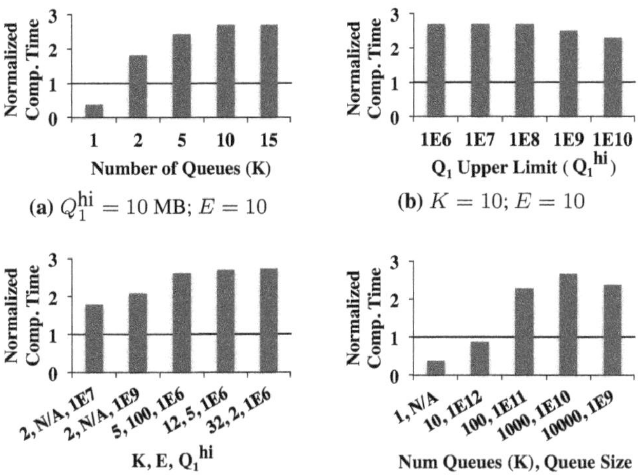

(a) $Q_1^{\text{hi}} = 10$ MB; $E = 10$ (b) $K = 10$; $E = 10$

(c) Exp.-Spaced Queues (d) Equal-Sized Queues

Figure 12: [Simulation] Aalo's sensitivity (measured as improvements over per-flow fairness) to (a) the number of queues, (b) the size of the highest-priority queue, and (c) exponential and (d) linear queue thresholds.

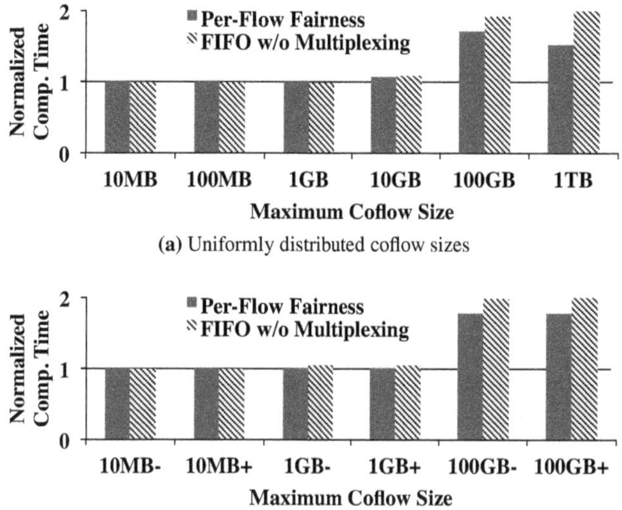

(a) Uniformly distributed coflow sizes

(b) Fixed-size coflows

Figure 13: [Simulation] Improvements in average CCTs using Aalo (a) when coflow sizes are uniformly distributed up to different maximum values and (b) when all coflows have the same size.

queues (Figure 12a). However, we observe the largest jump as soon as Aalo starts avoiding head-of-line blocking for $K = 2$. Beyond that, we observe diminishing returns.

Queue Thresholds For more than one queues, Aalo must carefully determine their thresholds. Because we have defined queue thresholds as a function of the size of the initial queue Q_1^{hi} (§4.4), we focus on its impact on Aalo's performance. Recall that as we increase Q_1^{hi}, more coflows will be scheduled in the FIFO order in the highest-priority Q_1. Figure 12b shows that as we increase Q_1^{hi} up to 100 MB and schedule almost 60% of the coflows [20, Figure 4(e)] in the FIFO order, Aalo's performance remains steady. This is because all these coflows carry a tiny fraction of the total traffic ($\leq$ 0.1%). If we increase Q_1^{hi} further and start including increasingly larger coflows in the FIFO-scheduled Q_1, performance steadily deteriorates. Finally, Figure 12c demonstrates the interactions of E, the multiplicative factor used to determine queue thresholds, with K and Q_1^{hi}. We observe that for $K > 2$, Aalo's performance is steady for a wide range of (K, E, Q_1^{hi}) combinations.

What About Non-Exponential Queue Thresholds? Instead of creating exponentially larger queues, one can create equal-sized queues. Given the maximum coflow size of 10 TB, Figure 12d shows Aalo's performance for varying number of equal-sized queues – it requires orders of magnitude more queues to attain performance similar to exponential spacing. Although creating logical queues is inexpensive at end hosts, more queues generate more "queue-change" events and increase coordination costs.

Impact of Coflow Size Distributions So far we have evaluated Aalo on coflows that follow heavy-tailed distribution. Here, we compare Aalo against per-flow fairness and a non-preemptive FIFO scheduler on coflows with uniformly-distributed and fixed sizes. We present the average results of ten simulated runs for each scenario with 100 coflows, where coflow structures follow the distribution in Table 3.

In Figure 13a, coflow sizes follow uniform distributions $\mathsf{U}(0, x)$, where we vary x. In Figure 13b, all coflows have the same size, and we select sizes slightly smaller and bigger than Aalo's queue thresholds. We observe that in both cases, Aalo matched or outperformed the competition. Aalo emulates the FIFO scheduler when coflow sizes are smaller than Q_1^{hi}(=10 MB). As coflows become larger, Aalo performs better by emulating the efficient Varys scheduler.

7.6 Aalo Scalability

To evaluate Aalo's scalability, we emulated running up to $100,000$ daemons on 100-machine EC2 clusters. Figure 14a

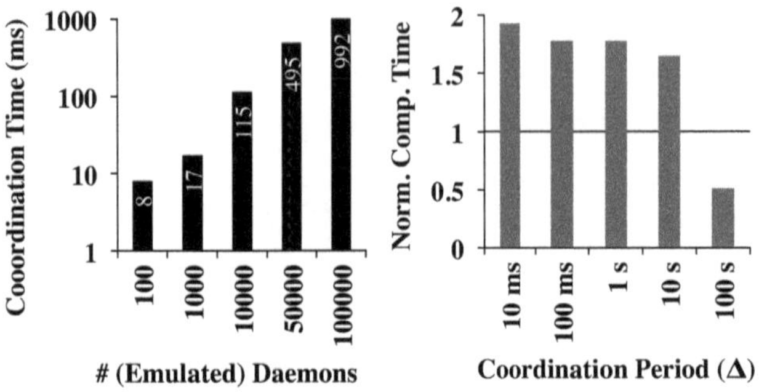

(a) Overheads at Scale (b) Impact of Δ

Figure 14: [EC2] Aalo scalability: (a) more daemons require longer coordination periods (Y-axis is in log scale), and (b) delayed coordination can hurt overall performance (measured as improvements over per-flow fairness).

presents the time to complete a coordination round averaged over 500 rounds for varying number of emulated daemons (e.g., $10,000$ emulated daemons refer to each machine emulating 100 daemons). During each experiment, the coordinator transferred scheduling information for 100 concurrent coflows on average to each of the emulated daemons.

Even though we might be able to coordinate $100,000$ daemons in 992ms, the coordination period (Δ) must be increased. To understand the impact of coordination on performance, we reran the earlier experiments (§7.2) for increasingly higher Δ (Figure 14b). For $\Delta = 1$s, Aalo's improvements over per-flow fairness dropped slightly from $1.93\times$ to $1.78\times$. For $\Delta > 1$s, performance started to drop faster and plummeted at $\Delta > 10$s. These trends hold across coflow bins and reinforce the need for coordination (**Theorem** A.1).

Because Δ must increase for Aalo to scale, sub-Δ coflows can further be improved if Aalo uses explicit switch/network support [27, 25]. However, we note that tiny coflows are still better off using Aalo than per-flow fairness schemes.

8 Discussion

Determining Optimal Queue Thresholds Finding the optimal number of queues and corresponding thresholds remains an open problem. Recent results in determining similar thresholds in the context of flows [14] do not immediately extend to coflows because of cross-flow dependencies. Dynamically changing these parameters based on online learning can be another direction of future work.

Decentralizing Aalo Decentralizing D-CLAS primarily depends on the following two factors.

1. *Decentralized calculation of coflow sizes, and*
2. *Avoiding receiver-side contentions without coordination.*

Approximate aggregation schemes like Push-Sum [34] can be good starting points to develop solutions for the former within reasonable time and accuracy. The latter is perhaps more difficult, because it relies on fast propagation of receiver feedbacks throughout the entire network for quick convergence of sender- and receiver-side rates. Both can improve from in-network support as used in CONGA [9].

Faster Interfaces and In-Network Bottlenecks As 10 GbE NICs become commonplace, a common concern is that scaling non-blocking fabrics might become cost prohibitive.[9] Aalo performs well even if the network is not non-blocking – for example, on the EC2 network used in the evaluation (§7). When bottleneck locations are known, e.g., rack-to-core links, Aalo can be modified to allocate rack-to-core bandwidth instead of NIC bandwidth [17]. For in-network bottlenecks, one can try enforcing coflows inside the network [52]. Nonetheless, designing, deploying, and enforcing distributed, coflow-aware routing and load balancing solutions remain largely unexplored.

9 Related Work

Coflow Schedulers Aalo's improvements over its clairvoyant predecessor Varys [20] are threefold. First, it schedules coflows *without* any prior knowledge, making coflows practical in presence of task failures and straggler mitigation techniques. Second, it supports pipelining and dependencies in multi-stage DAGs and multi-wave stages through a simpler, non-blocking API. Finally, unlike Varys, Aalo performs well even for tiny coflows by avoiding coordination. For larger coflows, however, Varys marginally outperforms Aalo by exploiting complete knowledge.

Aalo outperforms existing non-clairvoyant coflow schedulers, namely Orchestra [19] and Baraat [25], by avoiding head-of-line blocking unlike the former and by using global information unlike the latter. While Baraat's fully decentralized approach is effective for light-tailed coflow distributions, we prove in **Theorem** A.1 that the lack coordination can be arbitrarily bad in the general case.

Qiu et al. have recently provided the first approximation algorithm for the clairvoyant coflow scheduling problem [44]. Similar results do not exist for the non-clairvoyant variation.

Flow Schedulers Coflows generalize traditional point-to-point flows by capturing the multipoint-to-multipoint aspect of data-parallel communication. While traffic managers like Hedera [8] and MicroTE [16] cannot directly be used to optimize coflows, they can be extended to perform coflow-aware throughput maximization and load balancing.

Transport-level mechanisms to minimize FCTs, both clairvoyant (e.g., PDQ [29], pFabric [10], and D^3 [47]) and non-clairvoyant (e.g., PIAS [14]), fall short in minimizing CCTs as well [20].

Non-Clairvoyant Schedulers Scheduling without prior knowledge is known as non-clairvoyant scheduling [39]. To address this problem in time-sharing systems, Corbató et al. proposed the multi-level feedback queue (MLFQ) algorithm [23], which was later analyzed by Coffman and Kleinrock [21]. Many variations of this approach exist in the literature [42, 45], e.g., foreground-background or least-attained service (LAS). In single machine (link), LAS performs almost as good as SRPT for heavy-tailed distributions of task (flow) sizes [45]. We prove that simply applying LAS through-

[9] A recent report from Google [5] suggests that it is indeed possible to build full-bisection bandwidth networks with up to $100,000$ machines, each with 10 GbE NICs, for a total capacity of 1 Pbps.

out the fabric can be ineffective in the context of coflows (**Theorem A.1**). The closest instance of addressing a problem similar to ours is ATLAS [35], which controls concurrent accesses to multiple memory controllers in chip multiprocessor systems using coordinated LAS. However, ATLAS does not discretize LAS to ensure interactivity, and it does not consider coupled resources like the network.

DAG and Workflow Schedulers When the entire DAG and completion times of each stage are known, the Critical Path Method (CPM) [33, 32] is the best known algorithm to minimize end-to-end completion times. Without prior knowledge, several dynamic heuristics have been proposed with varying results [49]. Most data-parallel computation frameworks use breadth-first traversal of DAGs to determine priorities of each stage [50, 2, 3]. Aalo's heuristic enforces the *finishes-before* relationship between dependent coflows, but it cannot differentiate between independent coflows.

10 Conclusion

Aalo makes coflows more practical in data-parallel clusters in presence of multi-wave, multi-stage jobs and dynamic events like failures and speculations. It implements a non-clairvoyant, multi-level coflow scheduler (D-CLAS) that extends the classic LAS scheduling discipline to data-parallel clusters and addresses ensuing challenges through priority discretization. Aalo performs comparable to schedulers like Varys that use complete information. Using loose coordination, it can efficiently schedule tiny coflows and outperforms per-flow mechanisms *across the board* by up to 2.25×. Moreover, for DAGs and multi-wave coflows, Aalo outperforms both per-flow fairness mechanisms and Varys by up to 3.7×. Trace-driven simulations show Aalo to be 2.7× faster than per-flow fairness and 16× better than decentralized coflow schedulers.

Acknowledgments

We thank Yuan Zhong, Ali Ghodsi, Shivaram Venkataraman, CCN members, our shepherd Hitesh Ballani, and the anonymous reviewers of NSDI'15 and SIGCOMM'15 for useful feedback, and Kay Ousterhout for generating Shark query plans for the TPC-DS queries. This research is supported in part by NSF CISE Expeditions Award CCF-1139158, LBNL Award 7076018, and DARPA XData Award FA8750-12-2-0331, and gifts from Amazon Web Services, Google, SAP, The Thomas and Stacey Siebel Foundation, Adatao, Adobe, Apple, Inc., Blue Goji, Bosch, C3Energy, Cisco, Cray, Cloudera, EMC2, Ericsson, Facebook, Guavus, HP, Huawei, Informatica, Intel, Microsoft, NetApp, Pivotal, Samsung, Schlumberger, Splunk, Virdata and VMware.

11 References

[1] Amazon EC2. http://aws.amazon.com/ec2.

[2] Apache Hive. http://hive.apache.org.

[3] Apache Tez. http://tez.apache.org.

[4] Impala performance update: Now reaching DBMS-class speed. http://blog.cloudera.com/blog/2014/01/impala-performance-dbms-class-speed.

[5] A look inside Google's data center networks. http://googlecloudplatform.blogspot.com/2015/06/A-Look-Inside-Googles-Data-Center-Networks.html.

[6] TPC Benchmark DS (TPC-DS). http://www.tpc.org/tpcds.

[7] TPC-DS kit for Impala. https://github.com/cloudera/impala-tpcds-kit.

[8] M. Al-Fares, S. Radhakrishnan, B. Raghavan, N. Huang, and A. Vahdat. Hedera: Dynamic flow scheduling for data center networks. In *NSDI*, 2010.

[9] M. Alizadeh, T. Edsall, S. Dharmapurikar, R. Vaidyanathan, K. Chu, A. Fingerhut, F. Matus, R. Pan, N. Yadav, and G. Varghese. CONGA: Distributed congestion-aware load balancing for datacenters. In *SIGCOMM*, 2014.

[10] M. Alizadeh, S. Yang, M. Sharif, S. Katti, N. Mckeown, B. Prabhakar, and S. Shenker. pFabric: Minimal near-optimal datacenter transport. In *SIGCOMM*, 2013.

[11] G. Ananthanarayanan, A. Ghodsi, A. Wang, D. Borthakur, S. Kandula, S. Shenker, and I. Stoica. PACMan: Coordinated memory caching for parallel jobs. In *NSDI*, 2012.

[12] G. Ananthanarayanan, S. Kandula, A. Greenberg, I. Stoica, Y. Lu, B. Saha, and E. Harris. Reining in the outliers in mapreduce clusters using Mantri. In *OSDI*, 2010.

[13] R. H. Arpaci-Dusseau and A. C. Arpaci-Dusseau. Scheduling: The multi-level feedback queue. In *Operating Systems: Three Easy Pieces*. 2014.

[14] W. Bai, L. Chen, K. Chen, D. Han, C. Tian, and H. Wang. Information-agnostic flow scheduling for commodity data centers. In *NSDI*, 2015.

[15] H. Ballani, P. Costa, T. Karagiannis, and A. Rowstron. Towards predictable datacenter networks. In *SIGCOMM*, 2011.

[16] T. Benson, A. Anand, A. Akella, and M. Zhang. MicroTE: Fine grained traffic engineering for data centers. In *CoNEXT*, 2011.

[17] M. Chowdhury, S. Kandula, and I. Stoica. Leveraging endpoint flexibility in data-intensive clusters. In *SIGCOMM*, 2013.

[18] M. Chowdhury and I. Stoica. Coflow: A networking abstraction for cluster applications. In *HotNets*, 2012.

[19] M. Chowdhury, M. Zaharia, J. Ma, M. I. Jordan, and I. Stoica. Managing data transfers in computer clusters with Orchestra. In *SIGCOMM*, 2011.

[20] M. Chowdhury, Y. Zhong, and I. Stoica. Efficient coflow scheduling with Varys. In *SIGCOMM*, 2014.

[21] E. G. Coffman and L. Kleinrock. Feedback queueing models for time-shared systems. *Journal of the ACM*, 15(4):549–576, 1968.

[22] T. Condie, N. Conway, P. Alvaro, and J. M. Hellerstein. Mapreduce online. In *NSDI*, 2010.

[23] F. J. Corbató, M. Merwin-Daggett, and R. C. Daley. An experimental time-sharing system. In *Spring Joint Computer Conference*, pages 335–344, 1962.

[24] J. Dean and S. Ghemawat. MapReduce: Simplified data processing on large clusters. In *OSDI*, 2004.

[25] F. Dogar, T. Karagiannis, H. Ballani, and A. Rowstron. Decentralized task-aware scheduling for data center networks. In *SIGCOMM*, 2014.

[26] N. G. Duffield, P. Goyal, A. Greenberg, P. Mishra, K. K. Ramakrishnan, and J. E. van der Merive. A flexible model for resource management in virtual private networks. In *SIGCOMM*, 1999.

[27] A. D. Ferguson, A. Guha, C. Liang, R. Fonseca, and S. Krishnamurthi. Participatory networking: An API for application control of SDNs. In *SIGCOMM*, 2013.

[28] A. Greenberg, J. R. Hamilton, N. Jain, S. Kandula, C. Kim,

P. Lahiri, D. A. Maltz, P. Patel, and S. Sengupta. VL2: A scalable and flexible data center network. In *SIGCOMM*, 2009.

[29] C.-Y. Hong, M. Caesar, and P. B. Godfrey. Finishing flows quickly with preemptive scheduling. In *SIGCOMM*, 2012.

[30] M. Isard, M. Budiu, Y. Yu, A. Birrell, and D. Fetterly. Dryad: Distributed data-parallel programs from sequential building blocks. In *EuroSys*, 2007.

[31] N. Kang, Z. Liu, J. Rexford, and D. Walker. Optimizing the "One Big Switch" abstraction in Software-Defined Networks. In *CoNEXT*, 2013.

[32] J. E. Kelley. Critical-path planning and scheduling: Mathematical basis. *Operations Research*, 9(3):296–320, 1961.

[33] J. E. Kelley. The critical-path method: Resources planning and scheduling. *Industrial scheduling*, 13:347–365, 1963.

[34] D. Kempe, A. Dobra, and J. Gehrke. Gossip-based computation of aggregate information. In *FOCS*, 2003.

[35] Y. Kim, D. Han, O. Mutlu, and M. Harchol-Balter. ATLAS: A scalable and high-performance scheduling algorithm for multiple memory controllers. In *HPCA*, 2010.

[36] G. Kumar, M. Chowdhury, S. Ratnasamy, and I. Stoica. A case for performance-centric network allocation. In *HotCloud*, 2012.

[37] M. Mastrolilli, M. Queyranne, A. S. Schulz, O. Svensson, and N. A. Uhan. Minimizing the sum of weighted completion times in a concurrent open shop. *Operations Research Letters*, 38(5):390–395, 2010.

[38] T. Moscibroda and O. Mutlu. Distributed order scheduling and its application to multi-core DRAM controllers. In *PODC*, 2008.

[39] R. Motwani, S. Phillips, and E. Torng. Nonclairvoyant scheduling. *Theoretical Computer Science*, 130(1):17–47, 1994.

[40] R. N. Mysore, A. Pamboris, N. Farrington, N. Huang, P. Miri, S. Radhakrishnan, V. Subramanya, and A. Vahdat. PortLand: A scalable fault-tolerant layer 2 data center network fabric. In *SIGCOMM*, 2009.

[41] J. Nair, A. Wierman, and B. Zwart. The fundamentals of heavy tails: Properties, emergence, and identification. In *SIGMETRICS*, 2013.

[42] M. Nuyens and A. Wierman. The Foreground–Background queue: A survey. *Performance Evaluation*, 65(3):286–307, 2008.

[43] L. Popa, G. Kumar, M. Chowdhury, A. Krishnamurthy, S. Ratnasamy, and I. Stoica. FairCloud: Sharing the network in cloud computing. In *SIGCOMM*, 2012.

[44] Z. Qiu, C. Stein, and Y. Zhong. Minimizing the total weighted completion time of coflows in datacenter networks. In *SPAA*, 2015.

[45] I. A. Rai, G. Urvoy-Keller, and E. W. Biersack. Analysis of LAS scheduling for job size distributions with high variance. *ACM SIGMETRICS Performance Evaluation Review*, 31(1):218–228, 2003.

[46] C. J. Rossbach, Y. Yu, J. Currey, J.-P. Martin, and D. Fetterly. Dandelion: A compiler and runtime for heterogeneous systems. In *SOSP*, 2013.

[47] C. Wilson, H. Ballani, T. Karagiannis, and A. Rowstron. Better never than late: Meeting deadlines in datacenter networks. In *SIGCOMM*, 2011.

[48] R. S. Xin, J. Rosen, M. Zaharia, M. J. Franklin, S. Shenker, and I. Stoica. Shark: SQL and rich analytics at scale. In *SIGMOD*, 2013.

[49] J. Yu, R. Buyya, and K. Ramamohanarao. Workflow scheduling algorithms for grid computing. In *Metaheuristics for Scheduling in Distributed Computing Environments*, pages 173–214. 2008.

[50] M. Zaharia, M. Chowdhury, T. Das, A. Dave, J. Ma, M. McCauley, M. Franklin, S. Shenker, and I. Stoica. Resilient distributed datasets: A fault-tolerant abstraction for in-memory cluster computing. In *NSDI*, 2012.

[51] M. Zaharia, A. Konwinski, A. D. Joseph, R. Katz, and I. Stoica. Improving MapReduce performance in heterogeneous environments. In *OSDI*, 2008.

[52] Y. Zhao, K. Chen, W. Bai, C. Tian, Y. Geng, Y. Zhang, D. Li, and S. Wang. RAPIER: Integrating routing and scheduling for coflow-aware data center networks. In *INFOCOM*, 2015.

APPENDIX

A Coflow Scheduling w/ Local Knowledge

Theorem A.1 *Any coflow scheduling algorithm where schedulers do not coordinate, has a worst-case approximation ratio of $\Omega(\sqrt{n})$ for n concurrent coflows.*

Proof Sketch Consider n coflows $C_1, \ldots, C_n$ and a network fabric with $m \leq n$ input/output ports $P_1, P_2, \ldots, P_m$. Let us define $d^k_{i,j}$ as the amount of data the k-th coflow transfers from the i-th input port to the j-th output port.

For each input and output port, consider one coflow with just one flow that starts from that input port or is destined for that output port; i.e., for all coflows $C_k, k \in [1, m]$, let $d^k_{k,m-k+1} = 1$ and $d^k_{i,j} = 0$ for all $i \neq k$ and $j \neq m-k+1$. Next, consider the rest of the coflows to have exactly k flows that engage all input and output ports of the fabric; i.e., for all coflows $C_k, k \in [m+1, n]$, let $d^k_{i,m-i+1} = 1$ for all $i \in [1, m]$ and $d^k_{l,j} = 0$ for all $l \neq i$ and $j \neq m - i + 1$. We have constructed an instance of *distributed order scheduling*, where n orders must be scheduled on m facilities [38]. The proof follows from [38, Theorem 5.1 on page 3]. ■

B Continuous vs. Discretized Prioritization

We consider the worst-case scenario when N identical coflows of size S arrive together, each taking $f(S)$ time to complete. Using continuous priorities, one would emulate a byte-by-byte round-robin scheduler, and the total CCT (T_{cont}) would approximate $N^2 f(S)$.

Using D-CLAS, all coflows will be in the k-th priority queue, i.e., $Q^{\text{lo}}_k \leq S < Q^{\text{hi}}_k$. Consequently, T_{disc} would be

$$N^2 f(Q^{\text{lo}}_k) + \frac{N(N+1) f(S - Q^{\text{lo}}_k)}{2}$$

where the former term refers to fair sharing until the k-th queue and the latter corresponds to FIFO in the k-th queue.

Even in the worst case, the normalized completion time ($T_{\text{cont}}/T_{\text{disc}}$) would approach $2\times$ from $1\times$ as S increases to Q^{hi}_k starting from Q^{lo}_k.

Note that the above holds only when a coflow's size accurately predicts it's completion time, which might not always be the case [20, §5.3.2]. Deriving a closed-form expression for the general case remains an open problem.

Network-Aware Scheduling for Data-Parallel Jobs: Plan When You Can

Virajith Jalaparti† Peter Bodik‡ Ishai Menache‡
Sriram Rao‡ Konstantin Makarychev‡ Matthew Caesar†
†University of Illinois, Urbana-Champaign ‡Microsoft

Abstract

To reduce the impact of network congestion on big data jobs, cluster management frameworks use various heuristics to schedule compute tasks and/or network flows. Most of these schedulers consider the job input data fixed and greedily schedule the tasks and flows that are ready to run. However, a large fraction of production jobs are *recurring* with predictable characteristics, which allows us to plan ahead for them. Coordinating the placement of data and tasks of these jobs allows for significantly improving their network locality and freeing up bandwidth, which can be used by other jobs running on the cluster. With this intuition, we develop Corral, a scheduling framework that uses characteristics of future workloads to determine an offline schedule which (i) *jointly* places data and compute to achieve better data locality, and (ii) isolates jobs both spatially (by scheduling them in different parts of the cluster) and temporally, improving their performance. We implement Corral on Apache Yarn, and evaluate it on a 210 machine cluster using production workloads. Compared to Yarn's capacity scheduler, Corral reduces the makespan of these workloads up to 33% and the median completion time up to 56%, with 20-90% reduction in data transferred across racks.

CCS Concepts

•Networks → Data center networks; •Computer systems organization → Cloud computing;

Keywords

Data-intensive applications; Cluster schedulers; Joint data and compute placement; Cross-layer optimization

SIGCOMM '15, August 17 - 21, 2015, London, United Kingdom

 ISBN 978-1-4503-3542-3/15/08...$15.00

DOI: http://dx.doi.org/10.1145/2785956.2787488

1 Introduction

Over the past decade, large big data compute clusters running thousands of servers have become increasingly common. Organizations such as Facebook, Google, Microsoft, and Yahoo! have deployed highly scalable data-parallel frameworks like MapReduce [25] and Cosmos [20] to process several petabytes of data every day, running tens of thousands of jobs [5].

These big data jobs are often constrained by the network for several reasons. First, they involve network-intensive stages such as shuffle and join, which transfer large amounts of data across the network. Second, while there is full bisection bandwidth within a rack, modern data intensive computing clusters typically have oversubscription values ranging from 3:1 to 10:1 from the racks to the core [22, 23, 24]. This trend is likely to continue in the future to limit operational costs. Finally, a large fraction of the cross-rack bandwidth (up to 50%) can be used for background data transfers [22], reducing the bandwidth available for these jobs even more.

Existing cluster schedulers try to overcome this problem by optimizing the placement of compute tasks or by scheduling network flows, while assuming that the input data locations are *fixed*. However, different stages in these big data jobs can still run into network bottlenecks. Techniques like delay scheduling [48] and flow-based scheduling [36] try to place individual tasks (e.g., maps) on the machines or racks where most of their input data is located. As this data is spread over the cluster randomly in a distributed file system (such as HDFS [6]), the subsequent job stages (e.g., shuffle) have to read data using cross-rack links, which are often heavily congested [22]. Recently introduced techniques like ShuffleWatcher [16] attempt to localize the shuffle of a job to one or a few racks, but end up using the cross-rack bandwidth to read input data. The benefits from using network flow-level techniques, such as in Varys [24] or Baraat [26], are also limited, as they only schedule network transfers after both the source and destination are fixed. Sinbad [22] schedules flows around network contention but its benefits are limited to file system writes.

However, a large number of business-critical jobs are *recurring*, with pre-defined submission times and predictable resource requirements, allowing us to carefully place job input data to improve network locality. For example, it has been reported that production workloads contain up to 40%

recurring jobs, which are run periodically as new data becomes available [15, 30]. In fact, we show that future job characteristics (e.g., input data size) for such jobs can be predicted with an error as low as 6.5% (Section 2). Using these characteristics, we can plan *ahead* and determine where the input data of a job can be placed in the cluster, e.g., in a particular subset of racks. By coordinating such data placement with job task placement, most *small* jobs can be run entirely within one rack with all their tasks achieving rack-level network locality and no oversubscription. As these small jobs do not use cross-rack links, larger jobs running across multiple racks will also benefit due to more available bandwidth. Further, by running jobs entirely within a subset of racks rather than across the whole cluster, we can achieve better performance isolation across jobs.

With this intuition, we design Corral, a scheduling framework that exploits the predictability of future workloads to *jointly* optimize the placement of data and compute in big data clusters, and improve job performance. Corral includes an *offline planner* which uses the characteristics of jobs (e.g., amount of data read, CPU and memory demands) that will run on the cluster to determine which set of racks should be used to run each job and when the job should start. Job execution is *decoupled* from the planner and only uses the planner's output as *guidelines* for placing data and tasks.

The goal of the offline planner is to optimize job execution while addressing important challenges. First, it needs to determine which racks to assign to a job to maximize network locality while providing sufficient parallelism. Second, it needs to ensure that jobs and their input data are spread across the cluster without overloading any part of it. We formulate this planning problem as a malleable job scheduling problem [19, 27, 45] and develop simple heuristics to solve it efficiently. We show that these heuristics achieve performance close (within 3-15%) to the solution of a Linear Program (LP) relaxation, which serves as a lower-bound to *any* algorithm used for the planning problem (which assigns resources to jobs at the granularity of racks). Using a data imbalance cost (Section 4.5) allows our heuristics to ensure that the input data is balanced across all racks in the cluster.

The offline planner optimizes for both recurring jobs and jobs whose arrival and characteristics are known in advance. Corral executes *ad hoc* jobs, whose characteristics cannot be predicted, using otherwise idle cluster resources. As the jobs planned with Corral finish faster, additional resources will be available for these ad hoc jobs and hence, they will also finish earlier. The techniques in Corral apply to both simple MapReduce jobs as well as complex DAG-structured workloads such as Hive [44] queries.

We note that during job execution, we do *not* exclusively allocate whole racks to a single job. Instead, given the set of racks assigned to a job by the offline planner, one replica of job input data is placed within those racks and all tasks of the job are *restricted* to run within those racks. This forces all job data transfers to stay within those racks. The remaining slots within these racks are used by ad hoc jobs and other planned jobs assigned to the same racks. When a significant fraction of machines in these racks fail (beyond a configured threshold), Corral ignores these constraints and uses any available resources in the cluster to run the planned jobs.

We have implemented Corral as an extension of Yarn [8] and deployed it on a 210 machine cluster. Using four different workloads including traces from Yahoo [21], Microsoft Cosmos (Section 6), and Hive queries derived from TPC-H benchmarks [12], we show that Corral reduces the makespan of a batch of jobs by 10-33% and the median job completion time by 30-56% compared to the Yarn capacity scheduler [7]. Further, using large-scale simulations over a 2000 machine topology, we show that Corral achieves better performance than flow-level techniques (such as those in Varys [24]) and that their gains are orthogonal.

In summary, our contributions are as follows.

(1) We quantify the high predictability of job characteristics in production clusters.

(2) We formulate the joint data and compute placement problem in big data clusters as a malleable job scheduling problem and solve it using efficient heuristics, which lead to significant benefits in practice.

(3) We design, implement and evaluate Corral, a data-driven planning framework which leverages the predictability of future workloads to assign resources to jobs, leading to significant performance improvements.

(4) We show that the benefits of Corral are more than those from just using network flow-level scheduling techniques, and that Corral can work together with such techniques to provide further performance benefits.

2 Motivation

Big data clusters use frameworks like Hadoop [3], Hive [44], or Scope [50] to run simple MapReduce [25] jobs, and more complex, DAG-structured jobs. Each job consists of *stages*, such as map or reduce, linked by data dependencies. Each stage consists of several *tasks*, which process the input data in parallel. When a task has all its inputs ready, it is allocated a *slot* on a machine in the cluster, which gives it a predefined amount of memory and CPU to execute. The input data for these jobs is stored in a distributed file system like HDFS [6]. The data is divided into multiple *chunks*, each of which is typically replicated three times across different machines in the cluster. For fault tolerance, two of the chunks reside on the same rack, while the third one is on a different rack. Each chunk is placed independently of the other chunks. In this section, we present observations about existing cluster frameworks that motivate the design of Corral.

Current schedulers do not jointly optimize over data and compute location. The location of data replicas in the distributed file system is typically determined by the file system itself, irrespective of the computation performed on it (as described above). Thus, the input chunks for a job are spread across the compute nodes uniformly at random.

At the job scheduling level, much effort has been devoted to avoiding and scheduling around network contention, given a fixed location of task input data. For example, Hadoop prefers running map tasks on machines with their input data, instead of loading the data over the network.

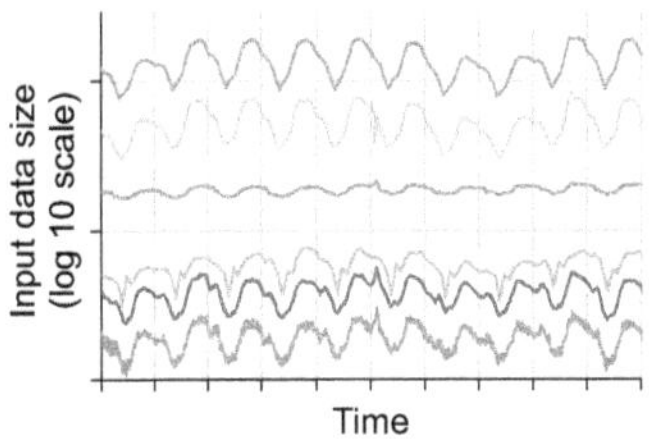

Figure 1: Normalized input data size of six different jobs during a ten-day period. X-axis shows time; each tick is a day. Y-axis shows input size in $\log_{10}$ scale; each tick is a 10x increase.

Figure 2: Cumulative fraction of the number of compute slots requested by jobs across three production clusters. The vertical line represents 240 slots, the size of one rack.

Quincy [36] aims at improving on this greedy heuristic by modeling the tradeoffs between latency and locality[1] preferences of all runnable tasks, and determines their placement using a holistic optimization framework. As the input data is randomly spread across several racks in the cluster, such approaches generally achieve locality for earlier stages of a job (e.g., map in MapReduce, Extract in Scope) but not for the subsequent stages (e.g., shuffle), which typically end up reading data across most of the racks. Given a fixed placement of both input data and tasks, systems such as Orchestra [23], Varys [24], and Baraat [26] schedule network flows to minimize makespan or average job duration. Improper placement of data and tasks can cause flows to utilize congested network links, limiting their potential benefits.

Job input data can be placed in designated locations before job execution. We identify two important scenarios where it is possible to place job input data. First, it is fairly typical in datacenters that data is continuously uploaded from front-end servers into the cluster (e.g., click logs), and data-processing jobs are triggered as new data becomes available [5]. As this data is being uploaded, it is possible to place it at the desired location.

Secondly, in some deployment scenarios (such as running Hadoop in Azure [9] or AWS [2]), the job input data is stored in a separate storage cluster (Azure Storage [10, 13] or Amazon S3 [1]). When a job starts, it processes data by fetching it from the remote storage cluster. By constraining tasks of the job to execute inside a particular subset of racks, we can ensure that the data is placed on those racks.

Job characteristics can often be accurately predicted. Cluster workloads are known to contain a significant number (up to 40%) of *recurring* jobs [15, 30]. A recurring job is one in which the same script runs whenever new data becomes available. Consequently, for every instance of that job, it has a fixed structure and similar characteristics (e.g., amount of data transferred in shuffle, or CPU and memory demands).

We confirm and quantify this intuition by examining twenty business-critical jobs from our production clusters (these jobs are part of the workload W3 described in Section 6). For each job, we compute the input data size of its instances during a recent one-month period. Figure 1 shows the normalized job sizes as a time series for six of those jobs over a 10-day period. Overall, these jobs have input sizes ranging from several gigabytes to tens of terabytes. To predict the input size of a job which is submitted at a particular time (e.g., 2PM), we average the input size of the same job type at the same time during several previous days. In particular, if the current day of the week is a weekday (weekend), we average only over weekday (weekend) instances. Using this, we can estimate the job input data size with a small error of 6.5% on average. We observe similar predictability of the intermediate (or shuffle) data and output data. In turn, this allows us to predict the amount of data transferred during job execution and utilization of network links.

It is possible to run a bulk of jobs within a few racks without losing parallelism. Figure 2 plots the requested number of slots for various jobs across three of our largest production clusters, each of them with more than 10,000 machines. While some jobs require up to 10,000 slots, we find that across these three clusters, 75%, 87%, and 95% of the jobs require less than one rack worth of compute resources (240 slots). Similar observations have been reported earlier [28]. Thus, a large number of jobs can each be run within a single rack without sacrificing their parallelism. This allows these jobs to communicate at full NIC speeds.

In summary, we can achieve better data locality by jointly optimizing the placement of data and compute in big data clusters. The ability to predict the future workload allows us to plan ahead, place job input data in specific racks and subsequently run its tasks in those racks. Thus, we can take advantage of running many small jobs in individual racks, freeing up more core bandwidth for large or ad hoc jobs.

3 Corral design principles

In this section, we describe the architecture of Corral (Section 3.1), design considerations for its offline planning component (Section 3.2), and our approach to formalizing and solving the planning problem (Section 3.3). We leave the details of the planning algorithm to Section 4.

3.1 System architecture

Corral consists of two components – (a) an *offline planner* and (b) a cluster scheduler (Figure 3). The offline planner receives estimates of characteristics of jobs (e.g., arrival time, input data size etc.) that will be submitted to the cluster in future (step 1). It uses these characteristics to estimate job latencies and solve an offline *planning problem* with the goal of minimizing a specified metric (e.g., makespan or average job completion time). The planner creates a schedule which

[1]We use the term locality to refer to the fact that a task has been scheduled on the machine or rack containing most of its input data.

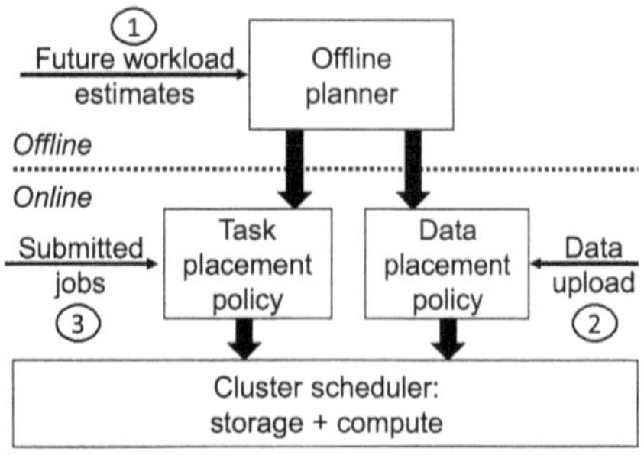

Figure 3: Corral **system architecture.**

consists of a tuple $\{R_j, p_j\}$ for each job j, where R_j is the set of racks on which job j has to run and p_j is its priority.

The cluster scheduler uses the schedule from the offline planner as guidelines to place data and tasks when running jobs on the cluster. As the input data of a job j is uploaded into the cluster (step 2) and stored in a distributed filesystem (such as HDFS), Corral places one replica of each data chunk in a randomly chosen rack from R_j. The remaining replicas are placed on another rack in the cluster, which is randomly chosen from the entire set of racks excluding the one chosen so far. We note that these choices are consistent with the *per-chunk* fault tolerance policy typically used in HDFS.

Finally, when job j is submitted to the cluster (step 3), the cluster scheduler constrains its tasks to be scheduled within the racks in R_j. Whenever a slot becomes empty in any rack, Corral's scheduler examines all jobs which have been assigned that rack and assigns the slot to the job with the highest priority[2]. With such placement of data and tasks in the same set of racks, Corral ensures that not only the initial stage (e.g., map, extract) but also subsequent stages of a job (e.g., reduce, join) achieve data locality. The priority (p_j) of a job ensures that the order in which jobs are scheduled by the cluster scheduler conforms to that assigned by the offline planner.

The offline planner will periodically receive updated estimates of future workload, rerun the planning problem, and update the guidelines to the cluster scheduler. Note that the cluster conditions might change after the guidelines are generated (e.g., racks/machines failing). If the assigned locations are not available for any job, the scheduler will ignore the guidelines for that job and use randomly selected machines in the cluster to hold its data (while ensuring fault tolerance using a policy similar to HDFS) and run its tasks.

The above scheduling approach in Corral applies not only to recurring jobs but also to jobs known a-priori and having predictable characteristics. For ad hoc jobs (whose characteristics are not known in advance), Corral places the input data using regular HDFS policies. The tasks of such jobs are scheduled using existing techniques [48].

3.2 Design considerations

Objective. The goal of the offline planner is to provide guidelines to the cluster scheduler for placing data and compute tasks. The objective is to optimize the network locality of each job and thus, improve the overall performance.

Scenarios. Based on the different cases that arise in practice, we consider two scenarios. In the *batch* scenario, we run a batch of jobs that are all submitted to the cluster at the same time (e.g., a collection of log analysis jobs). Here, our goal is to minimize their *makespan*, i.e., the time to finish the execution of all the jobs in the batch. In the *online* scenario, the jobs arrive over a longer period of time with known arrival times. In this case, our goal is to minimize the average job completion time.

Challenges. Designing the planner raises three important questions. First, at what granularity should the guidelines be provided? For example, one option is to provide a target machine for each task of the job. Second, how to formalize the planning problem to make it tractable at the scale of current big data systems? Finally, as the planner needs to choose among different data and task placement options, how do we estimate the job latency of a particular configuration?

Next, we outline how we address these challenges.

3.3 Solution approach

In order to formulate a tractable offline planning problem, we make several simplifying assumptions, highlighted below. We note that these assumptions apply only to the offline planner, and not to the actual job execution on the cluster.

Planning at the granularity of jobs and racks. The solution to the planning problem can be specified at different granularities. At one extreme, it can prescribe which task of a job should run on which machine in the cluster. However, generating such a solution is non-trivial. This is because while job input sizes can be predicted with small error, the input sizes of individual tasks depend on how the data is partitioned across tasks in a stage and thus, much less predictable. Further, the number of tasks can be several orders of magnitude more than the number of jobs, making the problem practically intractable.

Instead of planning at the level of tasks, one can plan at a stage level, i.e., specify which rack(s) each stage in a job should use. Complex, DAG-structured jobs could potentially benefit from stage-level planning; e.g., two parallel shuffles in a DAG could run in two separate racks, both benefiting from locality. However, after examining a large number of production jobs in our clusters, we found very few DAG jobs where such stage-level planning provides locality benefits.

Therefore, to improve scalability and robustness of the offline plan, we pose the planning problem at the granularity of racks and jobs. Further, most production clusters have full bisection bandwidth within a rack and oversubscribed links from the racks to the core [22, 23, 24]. Planning at the granularity of racks, allows us to assume that all tasks in a rack can communicate at NIC speeds, which in turn simplifies the modeling of job latency.

Planning as malleable job scheduling. We formulate the planning problem as a malleable job scheduling problem [19, 27, 45]. A *malleable* job is a job whose latency depends on the amount of resources allocated to it. While each

[2]To ensure machine-level locality, we use the same techniques as in delay scheduling [48].

job typically has a fixed requirement for the total number of compute slots, the planner's decision on over how many racks the job will execute would affect its latency.

To illustrate the dependency of job latency on the number of racks it uses, consider the shuffle stage in a MapReduce job with a total of S bytes spread over r racks (latency models for an entire job are described in Section 4.3). Suppose each rack has an internal bandwidth of B, and racks are connected with oversubscription ratio V; assume that network is the bottleneck resource affecting latency. When $r = 1$, almost all of S bytes have to be transferred across machines in the rack, with total latency of S/B. For $r > 1$, assuming symmetry for simplicity, each rack sends $(r-1)/r$ fraction of its data to other racks. Hence, the whole shuffle has to transfer $S(r-1)/r$ bytes using aggregate bandwidth of rB/V (from rack to core), resulting in approximate latency of $\frac{(r-1)SV}{r^2B}$ which approaches $\frac{V}{r}\frac{S}{B}$ for large r. Thus, the shuffle latency reduces with r in this example.

Characterizing job latency using simple response functions. With the above intuition, we model job latency using latency response functions $L_j(r)$, where j is the job index and r is the number of racks allocated to j. In particular, we model job latency as depending on the number of racks allocated, and also on fixed job characteristics such as the amount of data transferred between tasks, amount of CPU resources required, and the maximum parallelism of the job. Using these job characteristics, which can be estimated from earlier runs of the job, we derive simple analytical models to compute job latency (Section 4.3).

The actual job latencies can depend on additional runtime factors such as failures, outliers, and other jobs which run simultaneously on the same rack(s). However, as our latency approximation is used only for offline planning (and these factors affect all jobs), we tradeoff accurate (absolute) latency values for simpler and practical planning algorithms. As seen in our evaluation, using approximate latency models suffices for significant latency improvements.

These latency response functions also help us abstract various factors that affect job latency (e.g., number of maps or reducers) and enable us to plan for jobs to minimize the required metric. Such abstraction allows us to account for other factors such as data imbalance across racks (Section 4.5) without modifying our core algorithms.

4 Offline planning in Corral

In this section, we first formally present Corral's planning problem (Section 4.1). We then describe our heuristics to solve it (Section 4.2). Next, we provide details on how to calculate the functions, which are used to estimate job latency (Section 4.3). We then discuss the complexity of our heuristics (Section 4.4), and conclude by describing how we account for potential input data imbalance across racks.

4.1 Problem formulation

Given the design choices in Section 3, Corral's offline planning problem is formulated as follows. A set of jobs $\mathcal{J}$ (of size J) has to be scheduled on a cluster of R racks. Each job j is characterized by a *latency response function* $L_j : [1, R] \rightarrow \Re^+$, which gives the (expected) job completion time as a function of the number of racks assigned to the job. Our model assumes that once a subset of racks is allocated to a job, it is used by the job until completion. That is, we do not allow preemption or a change in the allocation throughout the execution of the job. This assumption simplifies our problem formulation significantly. To ensure work conservation during job execution, Corral's cluster scheduler does not enforce these constraints. Our evaluation results (Section 6) show that even with this deviation from the assumptions, Corral significantly outperforms existing schedulers. In the batch scenario, the goal is to minimize the makespan, *i.e.*, the time it takes to complete all jobs. In the online scenario, each job has its own arrival time. The goal now is to minimize the average completion time, *i.e.*, the average time from the arrival of a job until its completion. Both problems are NP-hard [27, 45]. Hence, we design efficient heuristics that run in low polynomial time.

4.2 Planning heuristics

Solving the planning problem consists of determining (a) the amount of resources (number of racks) to be allocated to a job, and (b) where in the cluster these resources have to be allocated. To address each of these sub-problems and use ideas from existing techniques (e.g., LIST scheduling [31]), we decouple the planning problem into two phases – the *provisioning* phase and the *prioritization* phase. In the provisioning phase, for each job j, we determine r_j, the number of racks allocated to the job. In the prioritization phase, given r_j for all jobs, we determine R_j, the specific subset of racks for j, and T_j, the time when j would start execution. We use T_j to determine the priority ordering of jobs (Section 3.1).

Provisioning phase. Initially, we set $r_j = 1$ for each job. This represents a schedule where each job runs on a single rack. In each iteration of this phase, we find the job j which is allocated less than R racks and has the longest execution time (according to the current r_j allocations), and increase its allocation by one rack. When a job is already allocated R racks it cannot receive additional racks. We proceed iteratively until all jobs reach $r_j = R$.

Intuitively, by spreading the longest job across more racks, we shorten the job that is "sticking out" the most. Note that if the latency of the longest job increases when its allocation is increased by one rack, it will continue to be the longest and thus, its allocation will be increased again in the next iteration. For the latency response curves we observed it practice, we found that the latency of the longest job eventually decreases.

As each job in $\mathcal{J}$ can be allocated any number of racks between 1 and R, a total of R^J different allocations exist for the provisioning phase. The above heuristic is designed to explore a plausible polynomial-size subset of candidate allocations ($J \cdot R$), which can be evaluated within practical time constraints. For each such allocation, we run the prioritization phase described below and pick the allocation (and respective schedule) which yields the lowest value for

Input: Set of jobs $\mathcal{J}$ of size J; $\forall j \in \mathcal{J}$, r_j, the number of racks to be assigned to job j for $L_j(r_j)$ time units and A_j, the arrival time of job j (0 in batch case).
Output: $\forall j \in \mathcal{J}$, R_j, the set of racks allocated to job j and T_j, the start time of job j.
Initialization: *Sort* and re-index jobs according to the scenario (batch or online).
$j := 0$
$F_i := 0$ for all racks $i = 1 \ldots R$
while $j < J$ **do**
  R_j :=set of r_j racks with smallest F_i
  $T_j := \max\{\max_{i \in R_j} F_i, A_j\}$
  for $i \in R_j$, $F_i := T_j + L_j(r_j)$
  $j := j + 1$
end while

Figure 4: Prioritization phase.

the relevant objective (makespan for batch scenario, average completion time for online scenario).

We note that this heuristic is similar to the one used in [19] for scheduling malleable jobs with the objective of makespan minimization. [19] terminates the heuristic when $\sum_{j|r_j>1} r_j = R$, and obtains an approximation ratio of roughly 2 on the makespan, by using LIST scheduling [31] on top of the provisioning heuristic. However, as each iteration is fast, we allow ourselves to run the heuristic for more iterations compared to [19], until reaching $r_j = R$ for every job j. This allows us to explore more options, and to obtain adequate results (including for the objective of average completion time, for which [19] does not provide guarantees).

Prioritization phase. If all jobs are constrained to run on a single rack, the longest processing time first (LPT) algorithm [31] is a well-known scheduling algorithm one could use to minimize makespan. However, jobs can run on multiple racks in Corral. We extend LPT to account for this case (pseudo-code in Figure 4).

In the batch scenario, we first sort jobs in decreasing order of number of racks allocated to them (r_j), i.e., *widest-job first*. Then, to break ties, we sort them in decreasing order of their processing times (similar to LPT). The widest-job first order helps us avoid "holes" in the schedule – for example, a job allocated R racks will not have to wait for a job allocated just one rack to complete, which would result in wasted resources. We then iterate over the jobs in this sorted order, assigning the required number of racks. We keep track of F_i, the time when rack i finishes running previously scheduled jobs. For each job j, we allocate the required set of racks by selecting the first r_j racks that are available (based on F_i). We then update F_i for the selected racks based on the start time of the job and its duration.

For the online scenario, we sort jobs in ascending order of their arrival time; in case of ties, we apply the sorting criteria of the batch case in the same order described above, and then use the algorithm described in Figure 4.

Estimating the quality of our heuristics. Decomposing the planning problem into two phases, as above, can be sub-optimal. However, it turns out that our approach results in near-optimal performance. Our simulations (using workloads described in Section 6) show that the above heuristic for the batch (online) scenario finds a schedule with resulting makespan (average completion time) within 3% (15%) of the solution of an LP-relaxation to the planning problem. The LP-relaxation, which is described in the appendix, serves as a lower-bound to any solution (under the assumptions described in Section 4.1)

4.3 Latency response functions

We now demonstrate how to model the latency response functions for data-parallel jobs, which allow us to approximate the expected latency of a job running on a given number of racks. We borrow the basic modeling principles from Bazaar [37], and adapt them to our setting where racks are the basic allocation units. We would like to emphasize that the models we present here should be viewed as *proxies* for the actual latencies, and need not be highly accurate. More complex models exist in the literature (e.g., Starfish [34], MRPerf [46]), but our goal in designing the response functions is to be able to account for job latency using fast models and simple mathematical expressions.

In what follows, we first present the basic model for MapReduce jobs, and then show how to extend the MapReduce model to the case of general DAGs.

MapReduce model. We can represent any MapReduce job j by the 5-tuple $\langle D_j^I, D_j^S, D_j^O, N_j^M, N_j^R \rangle$, where D_j^I is the input data size, D_j^S is the shuffle data size, D_j^O is the output data size, N_j^M is the number of map tasks and N_j^R is the number of reduce tasks used by the job.

We model the execution of a MapReduce job as consisting of three stages: (a) the map stage, (b) the shuffle stage and (c) the reduce stage. For simplicity we assume here that these stages run sequentially (we note, however, that it is possible to extend the model to account for cases where the map and reduce stage run in parallel). Accordingly, the latency $L_j(r)$ of job j using r racks can be modeled as the sum of latencies of the three stages, i.e., $L_j(r) = l_j^{\text{map}}(r) + l_j^{\text{shuffle}}(r) + l_j^{\text{reduce}}(r)$.

Given r racks and k machines per rack, the map stage runs in $w^{\text{map}}(r) = \lceil \frac{N_j^M}{r \cdot k} \rceil$ waves. Using this, the latency of the map stage is given by $l_j^{\text{map}}(r) = w^{\text{map}}(r) \cdot \frac{D_j^I / N_j^M}{B_M}$, where B_M is the average rate at which a map task processes data (this quantity is estimated from previous runs of the same job). Similarly, the latency of the reduce stage is estimated as $l_j^{\text{reduce}}(r) = w^{\text{reduce}}(r) \cdot \frac{D_r^O / N_j^R}{B_R}$, where B_R is the average data processing rate of a reduce task (estimated from previous runs) and $w^{\text{reduce}}(r) = \lceil \frac{N_j^R}{r \cdot k} \rceil$.

The latency of the shuffle stage is determined by the maximum of two components:

(a) Time to transfer data across the core: This is calculated as $l_j^{\text{core}}(r) = \frac{D_j^{\text{core}}(r)}{B/V}$ where B is the bandwidth per machine, V (> 1) is the oversubscription ratio between the racks and the core, and D_j^{core} is the amount of shuffle data

transferred across the core from a single machine. It is given by $D_j^{\text{core}}(r) = \frac{D_j^S}{r \cdot k} \cdot \frac{r-1}{r}$, if $r > 1$. If $r = 1$, i.e., the job is allocated only one rack, $D_j^{\text{core}}(r) = 0$.
(b) Time to transfer data within a rack: Along with the data transferred across the core, each machine transfers data $D_j^{\text{local}}(r)$ within the rack which is given by $\frac{D_j^S}{r \cdot k} \cdot \frac{1}{r}$. While $\frac{1}{k}^{\text{th}}$ of this data remains on the same machine, the remaining data is transferred to other machines using a bandwidth of $B - B/V$. Thus, the time for transferring data within the rack is given by $l_j^{\text{local}}(r) = \frac{D_j^{\text{local}}(r)}{B - B/V} \cdot \frac{k-1}{k}$.

Thus, the shuffle latency $l_j^{\text{shuffle}}(r)$ is given by $w_{\text{reduce}}(r) \cdot \max\{l_j^{\text{core}}(r), l_j^{\text{local}}(r)\}$, where $w_{\text{reduce}}(r)$ is the number of reduce waves, as defined above.

For ease of presentation, the above model assumes that each machine runs only one task at a time. It can be easily extended to the case where multiple tasks run on a machine by modifying (i) the number of waves of the map and reduce stage, and (ii) the amount of bandwidth available per task during the shuffle stage.

General DAGs. To construct a latency response function for data-parallel DAGs (generated by frameworks such as Hive [44] and Tez [4]), we first model every stage of the DAG as a MapReduce job. Using this abstraction and the MapReduce model developed above, we then determine the latency response function $L_s(r)$ for every stage s in the DAG. Finally, the latency of the DAG is set as the latency of its *critical path* P (i.e., a path from a source stage to a sink stage in the DAG, which takes the longest time to run), namely $L_j(r) = \sum_{s \in P} L_s(r)$.

Assumptions. The above latency models make several assumptions. First, latency of each stage is assumed to be proportional to the amount of data processed by it and similar across all tasks within a particular stage. While this is valid for a wide variety of jobs [37], it may not hold for cases where the computation latency depends on the value of the data read or in the presence of significant data skew across tasks [39]. Second, the resource demands of the map and reduce stages are assumed to be similar to previous runs of the job (on different datasets). We observed this assumption to hold for a variety of workloads we used in our evaluation (Section 6), and has also been shown to hold elsewhere [14, 30]. Finally, we assume that the data (both input and intermediate) and tasks of the various stages in a job are spread uniformly across all the machines in the racks allocated to the job.

While deviations from the above assumptions can lead to errors in predicting the latency of a job, our results (Section 6) show that Corral is robust to such errors.

4.4 Complexity

The complexity of the prioritization phase is $O(JR)$, because for each job we make a pass over all R racks to determine the first r_j racks that become available. The provisioning phase has JR iterations. Hence, the overall complexity of our heuristic is $O(J^2R^2)$. The complexity of calculating the latency response functions is linear in R and thus does not increase the overall complexity[3].

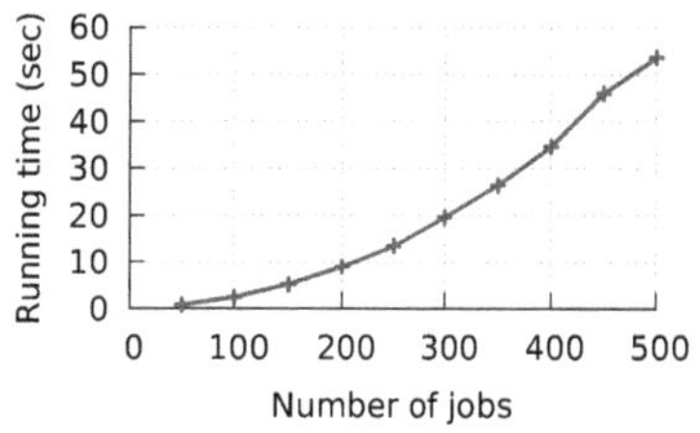

Figure 5: Running time of the offline planner heuristic in Corral for a 4000 machine cluster with varying number of jobs.

In terms of actual running time, our heuristic is highly scalable as shown in Figure 5. Running our heuristic on a single desktop machine with 6 cores and 24GB RAM, we found that it requires around 55 seconds to generate the schedule for 500 jobs on a 4000 node cluster with 100 racks (40 machines per rack). As the planner runs offline, this results in minimal overhead to the cluster scheduler.

4.5 Accounting for data (im)balance.

Using the latency response functions as described above, Corral would directly optimize for latency-related metrics, but would ignore how the input data is spread across different racks. Consequently, it is possible that a large fraction of the input data would be placed in a single rack, leading to high data imbalance and excess delays (e.g., in reading the input data). To address this issue and achieve better data distribution, we add a penalty term to the latency response function, given by $\alpha \cdot D_j^I/r$, where D_j^I/r is the amount of input data of job j in a single rack and α is a tradeoff coefficient. Accordingly, the modified latency response function is given by $L'_j(r) = L_j(r) + \alpha \cdot D_j^I/r$, where $L_j(r)$ is the original response function as described in Section 4.3.

In our experiments (Section 6), we set α to be the inverse of the bandwidth between an individual rack and the core network. The intuition here is to have the penalty term serve as a proxy for the time taken to upload the input data of a job to a rack. Increasing α favors schedules with better data balance. We note that in practice, we supplement this approach by greedily placing the last two data replicas on the least loaded rack. The combination of these approaches leads to a fairly balanced input data distribution (Section 6.2).

5 Implementation

We implemented Corral on top of the Apache Yarn framework (Hadoop 2.4) [8] and HDFS. Corral's offline planner determines the set of racks where (a) the input data of a job has to be stored and (b) its tasks have to be executed. To ensure that these rack preferences are respected (as described in Section 3.1), we made the following changes to the dif-

[3]With DAGs, we find critical path via an efficient shortest path algorithm; using BFS, this adds an $O(V+E)$ to the complexity, where V is the number of stages and E is the number of edges in the DAG. However, because the DAGs are typically small compared to number of racks and jobs, this does not change the complexity of our heuristic.

ferent components in Yarn. The changes involve about 300 lines of Java code.

Data placement policy. We modified HDFS's `create()` API to include a set of ⟨rack, number of replicas⟩ tuples, which allows Corral to specify the racks where different replicas of a file's data chunk are to be placed. These specifications are passed on to the block placement policy in HDFS, which was modified to ensure that at least one replica of the data chunk is placed on a machine which belongs to the rack specified.

Task placement policy. Every job in Yarn uses an Application Manager (AM) to request slots from a centralized Resource Manager (RM). The AM can also specify preferences for locations (e.g., specific machine or rack) where it would like slots to be allocated in the cluster. By default, the MapReduce AM in Yarn specifies location preferences for map tasks only and not for the reducers. For Corral, we modified the Yarn MapReduce AM to specify locality preferences for *all* tasks of a job.

As the subset of racks where a job needs to be scheduled is determined by Corral's offline planner, we pass this to the AM using a new configuration parameter. This is further passed to the RM as a location preference. The RM makes every effort to respect this locality preference while allocating slots to the job. However, in the event that a majority of the machines in the racks preferred by a job are unreachable, the RM will ignore the locality guidelines and allocate slots on the available nodes in the cluster.

6 Evaluation

We evaluate Corral on a 210 machine cluster, using a variety of workloads drawn from production traces. Our main results are as follows.
(a) Compared to Yarn's capacity scheduler, Corral achieves 10-33% reduction in makespan and 26-36% reduction in average job completion time for workloads consisting of MapReduce jobs (Section 6.2). For Hive queries derived from the TPC-H benchmark [12], Corral improves completion times by 21% on average (Section 6.3).
(b) When a workload consists of both recurring and ad hoc jobs, using Corral to schedule the recurring jobs improves the completion times of the recurring and ad hoc jobs by 33% and 20% (respectively), on average (Section 6.4).
(c) Corral's improvements increase by more than 2X when network utilization goes up by 33%, and are robust to errors in predicted job characteristics (Section 6.5).
(d) Using large-scale simulations, we show that the benefits from flow-level schedulers like Varys [24] improve significantly when used in combination with Corral and that Corral's benefits are orthogonal to those of using Varys alone.

6.1 Methodology

Cluster setup. We deployed our implementation of Corral in Yarn/HDFS on a 210 machine cluster, organized into 7 racks with 30 machines per rack. Each machine has 32 cores, 10Gbps NICs, and runs CentOS 6.4. The racks are connected in a folded CLOS topology at 5:1 oversubscription, i.e., each rack has a 60Gbps connection to the core. To match network conditions in production clusters, we emulate background traffic, accounting for up to 50% of the core bandwidth usage [5, 22].

	50%-tile	95%-tile
Number of tasks	180	2,060
Input Data Size (GB)	7.1	162.3
Intermediate data size (GB)	6	71.5

Table 1: Characteristics of workload W3 from Microsoft Cosmos [20]

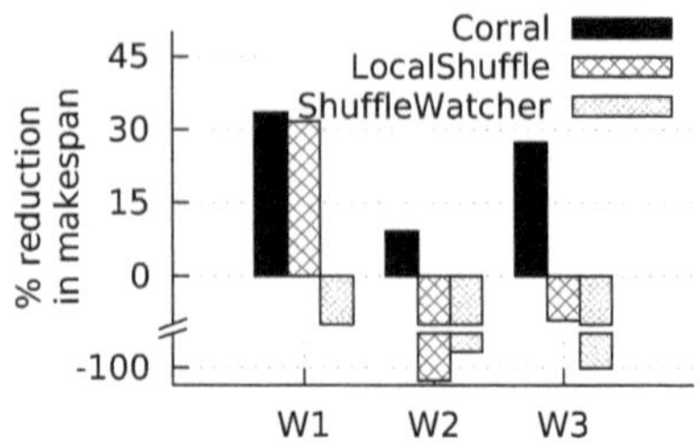

Figure 6: Reduction in makespan for different workloads, compared to Yarn-CS in the batch scenario.

Workloads. We first evaluate Corral using the scenario where all jobs in the workload are assumed to be recurring (or have predictable characteristics). We then consider workloads with both recurring and ad hoc jobs. We use jobs from the following workloads for our evaluation.
(a) W1: Starting from the Quantcast workloads [42], we constructed this workload to incorporate a wider range of job types, by varying the job size, and task selectivities (i.e., input to output size ratio). The job size is chosen from small ($\leq$ 50 tasks), medium ($\leq$ 500 tasks) and large ($\geq$ 1000 tasks). The selectivities are chosen between 4:1 and 1:4.
(b) W2: This workload is derived from the SWIM Yahoo workloads [21] and consists of 400 jobs.
(c) W3: We have chosen 200 jobs, randomly, from a 24 hour trace collected from production big data clusters at Microsoft and constructed this workload. Some characteristics of this workload are given in Table 1.
(d) TPC-H: We run queries from the TPC-H benchmark using Hive [44] to evaluate the performance of Corral for general DAG-structured workloads.

Baselines. We compare Corral against three baselines.
(a) the capacity scheduler in Yarn [7] (referred to as Yarn-CS from now on). The capacity scheduler uses techniques like delay scheduling [48] to achieve locality for map tasks but does not plan for data placement. Comparison with Yarn-CS allows us to show the benefits of achieving better locality for all stages of a job using Corral.
(b) ShuffleWatcher [16], which schedules each job in a subset of racks to reduce the amount of cross-rack data transferred by them. ShuffleWatcher does not place the input data of the job in these racks and as a result, most maps end up reading their input across the core network. It also fails to account for contention between jobs and schedules them

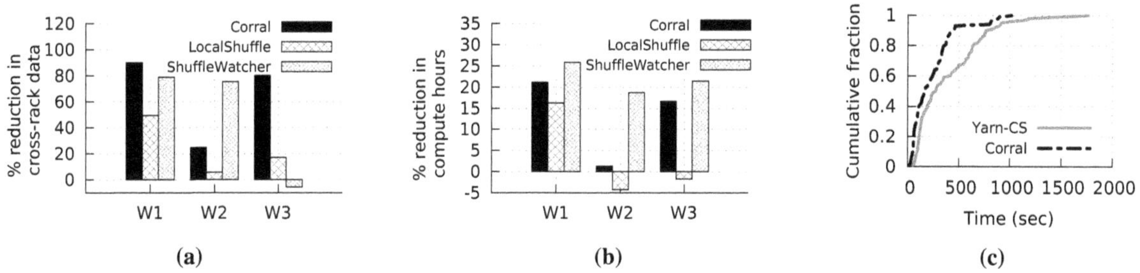

Figure 7: Comparing (a) reduction in cross-rack data transferred and (b) compute hours relative to Yarn-CS, and (c) cumulative fraction of average reduce time, for workload W1 in the batch scenario.

independently from each other. Comparison with ShuffleWatcher allows us to show the benefits of careful planning, and joint data and compute placement in Corral.

(c) LocalShuffle, which uses the task placement of Corral but the data placement policy of HDFS. The comparison of Corral with LocalShuffle allows us to quantify the benefits of proper placement of input data. We note that, unlike ShuffleWatcher, LocalShuffle schedules jobs using the same offline planning phase as Corral.

For all the above baselines, the input data is placed using HDFS's default (random) placement. When using Corral, we run its offline planner taking data balance into account (Section 4.5). Using the generated schedule, the input data of the jobs is placed on the assigned racks while it is uploaded and jobs are run using Corral's task placement policy (as described in Section 3.1).

Metrics. The primary metrics of interest are (a) makespan, in the batch scenario, and (b) average job completion time, in the online scenario.

6.2 MapReduce workloads

In this section, we show the benefits of using Corral to schedule MapReduce jobs in the batch and online scenarios, when all jobs have predictable characteristics.

6.2.1 Batch scenario

Figure 6 shows the improvement in makespan relative to Yarn-CS, for different workloads, when run as a batch – Corral achieves a 10% to 33% reduction. The reduction in makespan for W2 is lower than that for the other workloads because W2 is highly skewed. Almost 90% of the jobs are *tiny* with less than 200MB (75MB) of input (shuffle) data and two (out of the 400) jobs are relatively *large*, reading nearly 5.5TB each. These large jobs determine the makespan of W2 and do not suffer significant contention from the tiny jobs. Out of the 7 racks available, Corral allocates 3 racks each to the two large jobs and packs most of the tiny jobs on the remaining rack. Compared to Yarn-CS, the benefits of Corral stem from running each of the large jobs in isolation, on separate subsets of racks.

Corral's improvements are a consequence of its better locality and reduced contention on the core network. Figure 7a shows that Corral reduces the amount of cross-rack data transferred by 20-90% compared to Yarn-CS. This, in turn, improves task completion times. To quantify this, we use two additional metrics, namely, (a) compute hours, which measures the total time spent by all the tasks in the workload; compared to Yarn-CS, using Corral reduces the compute hours by up to 20% (Figure 7b), and (b) average reduce time, which measures the average execution time of all the reduce tasks in a job. Figure 7c plots the cumulative fraction (over jobs) of this metric for Corral and Yarn-CS, showing that Corral is approximately 40% better at the median, with higher benefits at the tail.

Comparison with other baselines. Corral outperforms LocalShuffle showing that proper input data placement is key for good performance (Figure 6). Even with better shuffle locality, LocalShuffle performs worse than Yarn-CS for W2 and W3 due to its lack of input data locality.

ShuffleWatcher optimizes for each job individually and ends up scheduling several large jobs on the same subset of racks. This leads to increased completion times for all those jobs. In the worst case, it can schedule all jobs on a single rack as it doesn't directly optimize for makespan or job completion time but tries to minimize the cross-rack data transferred. Thus, ShuffleWatcher results in significantly worse makespan compared to Yarn-CS for all workloads (Figure 6). Note that using ShuffleWatcher results in lesser cross rack data for W2 compared to Corral (Figure 7a). This is because the large jobs in W2 have nearly 1.8 times more shuffle data than input data, and Corral spreads them on 3 racks each (as mentioned above, for better makespan) while ShuffleWatcher places them in a single rack.

ShuffleWatcher achieves better compute hours than Corral (Figure 7b) because it loads racks unevenly with some racks running significantly lower number of jobs than others. The tasks of these jobs finish faster, resulting in lower compute hours. However, as shown in Figure 6, ShuffleWatcher is significantly worse than Corral for makespan.

Data balance. Corral optimizes for reducing the imbalance in the data allocated to different racks (Section 4.5). To evaluate this, we measure the coefficient of variation (CoV) of the size of input data stored on each rack. Our results show that Corral has a low CoV of at most 0.004 and performs better than HDFS, which spreads data randomly, resulting in a CoV of at most 0.01[4].

[4]Note that the CoV of a random distribution can be higher than that of uniform distribution, which is 0.

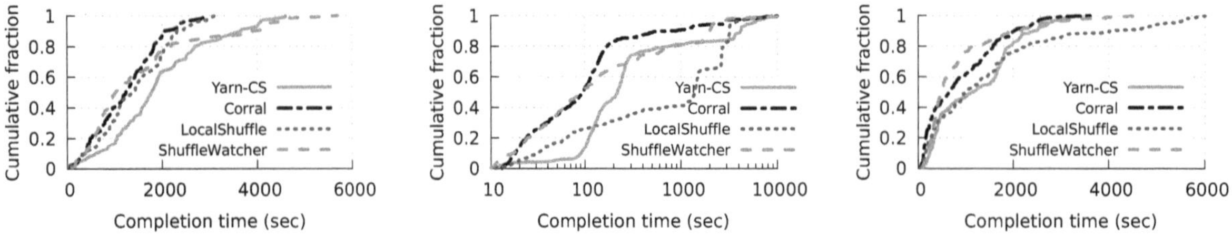

(a) W1 (b) W2 (c) W3

Figure 8: Cumulative fraction of job completion times for different workloads, when jobs arrive online.

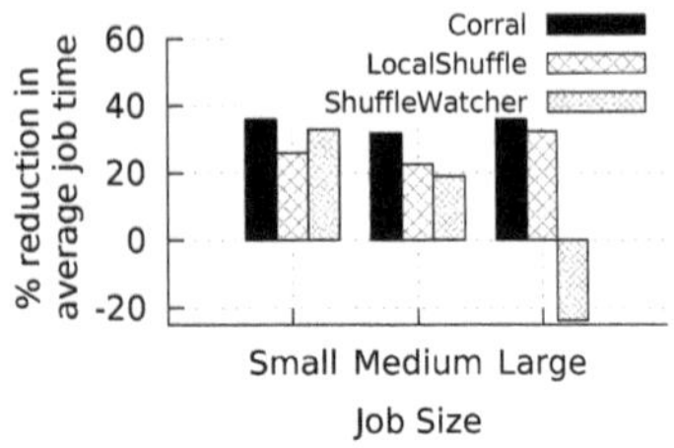

Figure 9: Reduction in average job completion time relative to Yarn-CS, for workload W1 in the online scenario.

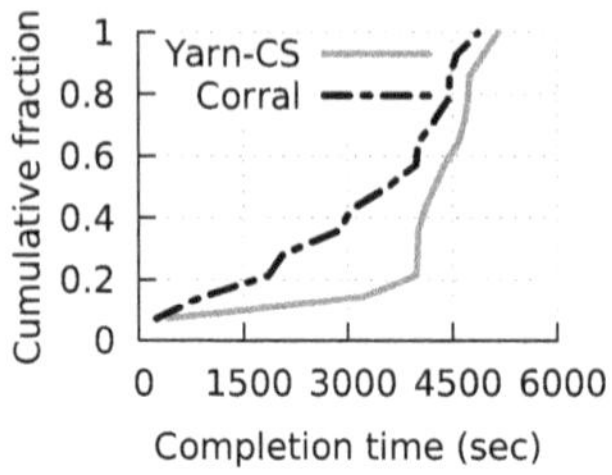

Figure 10: Benefits of running TPC-H queries with Corral**.**

6.2.2 Online scenario

In this scenario, jobs arrive over a period of time instead of as a batch. We pick the arrival times uniformly at random in [0, 60min]. Figure 8 shows the cumulative fraction of job completion times for workloads W1, W2 and W3. Corral outperforms Yarn-CS, with 30%-56% improvement at the median and nearly 26-36% improvement for the average job time (not shown). Further, Corral equally benefits jobs of all sizes. Figure 9 shows the reduction in average job completion time for workload W1, binned by the job size. Corral achieves 30-36% reduction in average job time across the various bins.

Comparison with other baselines. Similar to the batch case, LocalShuffle performs worse than Corral due to the lack of proper input data placement (Figure 8). While ShuffleWatcher is close to Corral at lower percentiles, it is significantly worse at higher percentiles. ShuffleWatcher schedules jobs independently. It ends up placing a large fraction of jobs on a few racks and a smaller fraction of jobs on the remaining racks. Jobs on the lightly loaded racks run faster due to lesser contention and those on the heavily loaded racks slow down. Figure 9 further confirms this, as ShuffleWatcher reduces the completion times of the small/medium jobs relative to Yarn-CS but performs worse for large jobs.

6.3 DAG workloads

To evaluate the benefits of Corral for data-parallel DAGs, we ran 15 queries from the TPC-H benchmark [12], using Hive 0.14.0 [44]. Each query reads from a 200GB database organized in ORC format [11]. These queries are assumed to be recurring, and thus, can be scheduled using Corral. The queries are submitted over a period of 25 minutes, with arrival times chosen uniformly at random. To emulate conditions in a real cluster, along with the queries, we also submit a batch of MapReduce jobs chosen from the workload W1, which are run using Yarn-CS.

Figure 10 plots the cumulative fraction of the query completion times for two cases: (i) the queries are run using Corral (dashed black line) and (ii) the queries are scheduled using Yarn-CS (solid orange line). We see that Corral reduces the median execution time by nearly 18.5% with the average time being reduced by 21%. We found that these queries spend only up to 20% of their time in the shuffle stage, which shows that Corral can also provide benefits for workloads which are mostly CPU or disk bound.

6.4 Scheduling ad hoc jobs

A significant portion of jobs in a production cluster can be ad hoc, e.g., those run for research or testing purposes. Such jobs arrive at arbitrary times and cannot be planned for, in advance. Corral uses the same scheduling policies as Yarn's capacity scheduler (Yarn-CS) for such jobs. To explore the benefits of Corral in this scenario, we run a mix of 50 ad hoc and 100 recurring MapReduce jobs, drawn from W1. The ad hoc jobs are run as a batch with Yarn-CS, while the recurring jobs arrive uniformly over [0, 60min].

Our observations are two-fold. First, even in the presence of ad hoc jobs, using Corral to schedule the recurring jobs is beneficial. Figure 11a shows the cumulative fraction of completion time for recurring jobs in the workload. Corral reduces the average (median) completion times by 33% (27%). Second, using Corral to schedule the recurring jobs leads to faster execution of ad hoc jobs, especially at the tail with a 37% reduction at the 90th percentile compared to using Yarn-CS (Figure 11b). The makespan of the ad hoc jobs reduces by around 28% (not shown). As jobs run with Corral use significantly lower core bandwidth and complete earlier, more network and compute resources are available for the ad hoc jobs, allowing them to also finish faster.

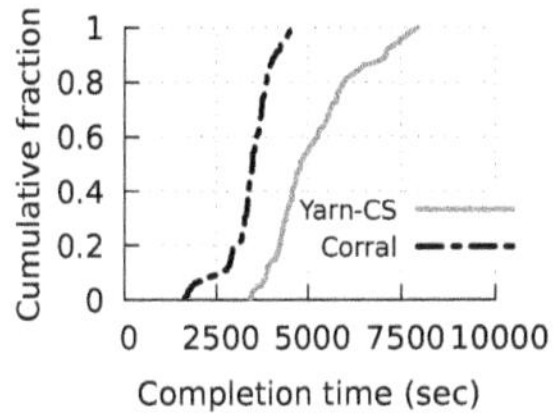

(a) Recurring jobs

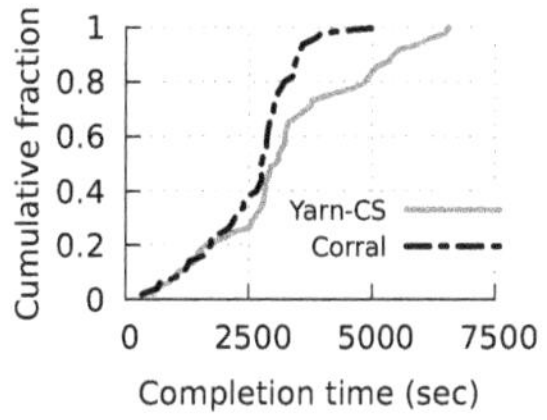

(b) Ad hoc jobs

Figure 11: Using Corral with a mix of jobs.

While it is possible to use (a) techniques such as profiling (e.g., [33]) to estimate the latency of ad hoc jobs, or (b) simple scheduling decisions such as running the next ad hoc job on the least loaded rack, we leave exploration of such *adaptive* techniques to future work.

6.5 Sensitivity analysis

The benefits of Corral depend on (a) the load on the network and (b) the accuracy with which job characteristics can be predicted. Here, we evaluate Corral's robustness to variation in these factors.

Varying network load. Our results indicate that the gains of Corral increase significantly as the network utilization increases. For workload W1, Figure 12 shows that as the per-rack core network usage of background traffic increases from 30Gbps (50%) to 40Gbps (67%), Corral achieves more than 2X higher benefits compared to Yarn-CS in makespan (batch scenario) and average job time (online scenario).

Error in predicted job input data size. Compared to the 6.5% observed in practice (Section 2), we varied the amount of data processed by jobs up to 50% and found that the benefits of Corral relative to Yarn-CS remain between 25-35% (Figure 13a). This shows that Corral's schedule is robust to errors in job sizes seen in practice.

Error in job start times. In practice, the start of a job can vary due to various reasons such as (a) input data upload does not finish in time, or (b) the jobs on which it depends on are delayed. To evaluate the effect of such error in job start times, we choose a fraction f of jobs in a workload and add a random delay between $[-t, t]$, for a fixed t, in their start times. Figure 13b shows the results of running the online scenario for workload W1 with such perturbation in arrival times. We set t at 4 minutes, which is nearly 6.67 times the expected job inter-arrival time and 20% of the average job completion time (and thus, represents a significant error). Varying f from 0% to 50%, we found that the benefits of Corral reduce from 40% to at most 25%.

6.6 Using Corral with flow-level schedulers

Corral schedules the tasks in a job with better locality but does not explicitly schedule the network flows between them. In all experiments above, we use TCP as the transport protocol for Corral. However, several flow-level schedulers proposed in literature (e.g., [24, 26, 35]) have been shown to outperform TCP in datacenter environments. Here, we evaluate how Corral performs when used with such schedulers.

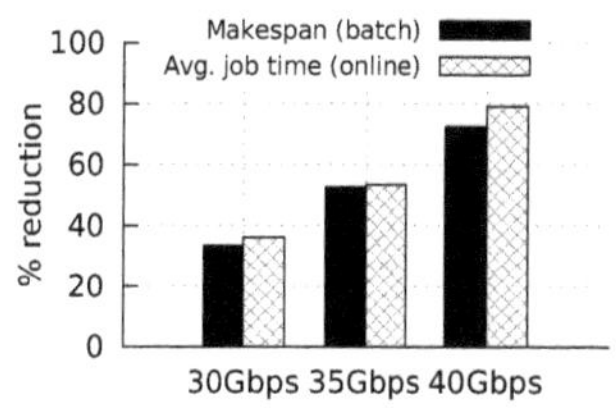

Figure 12: Benefits of using Corral relative to Yarn-CS, as background traffic increases for workload W1.

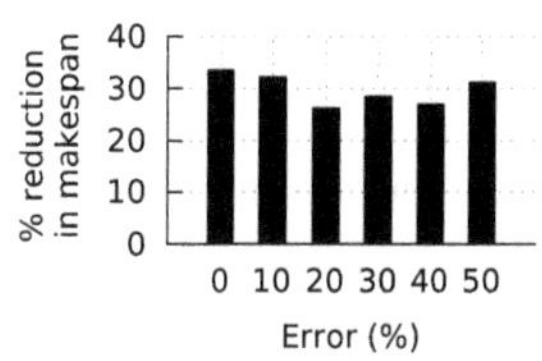

(a) Error in data size

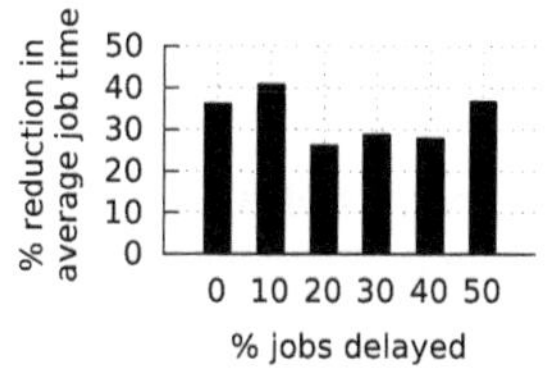

(b) Error in arrival times

Figure 13: Variation in benefits of Corral (relative to Yarn-CS) with error in job characteristics for workload W1.

As our cluster does not support such schedulers, we built a flow-based event simulator for this purpose. The simulator also allows us to evaluate Corral on larger topologies. We use pluggable policies for the job and network schedulers. We have implemented Yarn-CS and Corral to represent job schedulers. For network schedulers, we implemented a max-min fair bandwidth allocation mechanism to emulate TCP, and Varys [24], which uses application communication patterns to better schedule flows.

We simulate a topology of 2000 machines, organized into 50 racks with 40 machines each, connected using the folded CLOS topology with 5:1 oversubscription. Each machine can run up to 20 tasks and has a 1Gbps NIC. We run 200 jobs from W1, arriving uniformly over 15min.

Figure 14 shows the cumulative fraction of the job completion times, when run using all the 4 possible combinations of job and network schedulers. Our main observations are as follows. First, using Varys with Yarn-CS improves the median job completion time by 46% compared to Yarn-CS+TCP. This is consistent with the improvements claimed previously [24]. Second, Corral+TCP outperforms Yarn-CS+Varys across all jobs, with nearly 45% gains at the median. This shows that the benefits of using schedulers like Varys are limited if flow end-points are not placed properly. On the other hand, Corral schedules jobs in their own set of racks, reducing their core bandwidth usage and improving completion times.

Finally, Corral+Varys results in much better job completion times compared to Corral+TCP or Yarn-CS+Varys. Thus, Corral's benefits are orthogonal to those attained with better flow-level scheduling and combining them performs better than using either one of them. Also, Corral is agnostic to the flow-level scheduler used and can potentially perform even better if its decisions take underlying flow-level schedule into account. Such cross-layer optimizations are part of our ongoing work.

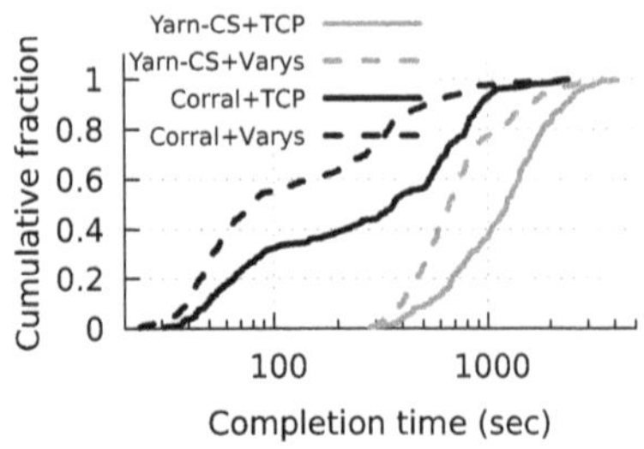

Figure 14: Simulation results: Cumulative fraction of job completion times with different flow-level and job schedulers.

7 Discussion

Dealing with failures. While Corral places one copy of job input data in the racks assigned to it, it spreads the other two copies across the rest of the cluster (similar to HDFS). This ensures that even if the assigned racks fail, the dataset can be recovered. Further, in the event that a majority of the machines (above a threshold) in a rack fail or a whole rack fails, Corral reverts back to using the existing placement policies (e.g., [48]) to run the jobs assigned to that rack, ensuring that they are not slowed down due to insufficient resources.

Data-job dependencies. Corral assumes that each job reads its own dataset. This simplifies the offline planning problem and allows each job to be scheduled independently. However, in general, the relation between datasets and jobs can be a complex bipartite graph. This can be incorporated into Corral by using the schedule of the offline planner and formulating a simple LP with variables representing what fraction of each dataset is allocated to each rack and the cost function capturing the amount of cross-rack data transferred, for any partition of datasets across the racks.

In-memory systems. Systems such as Spark [49] try to use memory to store job input data. While this decreases the dependence on disk I/O, jobs can still be bottlenecked on the network. The benefits of Corral extend to such scenarios as it reduces dependence on the core network and contention across jobs, by scheduling each of them on only a few racks.

Remote storage. As discussed earlier, in a public cloud setting (e.g., Amazon AWS [2]), the storage is separate from the compute cluster. This gives rise to the opportunity to schedule data transfers on the interconnect. One goal here would be to fully utilize both the interconnect and the compute cluster without having to be blocked on either resource. Extending Corral to this scenario is part of our ongoing work.

8 Related work

The techniques in Corral are related to the following areas of research in the context of datacenter applications.

Scheduling techniques for data analytics systems. Improving data-locality in big data clusters has been the focus of several recent works. Techniques like delay scheduling [48] and Quincy [36] try to improve the locality of individual tasks (e.g., maps) by scheduling them close to their input. ShuffleWatcher [16] tries to improve the locality of the shuffle by scheduling both maps and reducers on the same set of racks. Others such as Tetris [32] schedule recurring jobs to ensure better packing of tasks at machines. Corral, on the other hand, couples the placement of data and compute, achieving improved locality for all stages of a job.

Data placement techniques. CoHadoop [29] aims to colocate different datasets processed by a job on the same set of nodes, but does not guarantee locality for subsequent stages (e.g., shuffle). PACMan [18] caches repeatedly accessed data in memory but does not provide locality for intermediate data transfers. Techniques like Scarlett [17] use application access patterns to determine data replication factor or replica placement. None of these techniques coordinate data and compute placement for datacenter applications, which is the main focus in Corral.

Cross-layer scheduling techniques. The idea of placing data and compute together has been explored in systems like CAM [41] and Purlieus [43]. Unlike such systems, Corral exploits the recurring nature of datacenter applications and carefully assigns resources to execute them efficiently. Further, Corral deals with complex DAG-structured jobs which have not been considered previously.

Flow-level scheduling techniques. Several network-level techniques such as D3 [47], PDQ [35], Varys [24] and Baraat [26] have been proposed to finish network flows or groups of network flows faster. The benefits from such techniques are inherently limited as the end-points of the network transfers are fixed. Corral exploits the flexibility in placing input data and the subsequent stages of the jobs, and provides benefits orthogonal to such network-level schedulers (Section 6.6). Sinbad [22] takes advantage of flexibility in the placement of output data in big data clusters, but does not consider other stages in a job.

Malleable job scheduling. The problem of task scheduling across identical servers has been studied for over four decades (e.g., [38]). The basic formulation appears in [31], where tasks have precedence constraints and each task can run on a single server. A different variant of the problem considers malleable tasks, where each task can run on multiple servers [19, 40]. Our offline planning algorithm is inspired by these papers but none of them addresses the issues of (a) malleability in the context of shared networks, and (b) balancing input data required for executing the jobs.

9 Conclusion

In this paper, we argue that current data and compute placement heuristics in big data clusters do not couple the placement of data and compute, and hence, result in increased contention in an already oversubscribed network. Production clusters run a large fraction of recurring jobs with predictable communication patterns. Leveraging this, we propose Corral which considers the future workload and jointly optimizes the location of the job data (during upload) and tasks (during execution). By solving an offline planning problem, Corral improves job performance as it separates large shuffles from each other, reduces network contention in the cluster and runs jobs across fewer racks, improving their data locality. We implemented Corral on top of Yarn.

Running production workloads on a 210 machine cluster, we show that Corral can result in 10-33% reduction in makespan and 30-56% reduction in median job completion time, compared to Yarn's capacity scheduler.

Acknowledgements. We thank Ganesh Ananthanarayan, Hitesh Ballani, Carlo Curino, Chris Douglas, Solom Heddaya, Srikanth Kandula, Subramaniam Krishnan, Rahul Potharaju, Ant Rowstron, Yuan Yu, our shepherd Minlan Yu and the anonymous SIGCOMM'15 reviewers for their useful feedback.

10 References

[1] Amazon S3. https://aws.amazon.com/s3/.

[2] Amazon Web Services. http://aws.amazon.com/.

[3] Apache Hadoop. http://hadoop.apache.org/.

[4] Apache Tez. http://hortonworks.com/hadoop/tez/.

[5] Facebook data grows by over 500 TB daily. http://tinyurl.com/96d8oqj/.

[6] Hadoop Distributed Filesystem. http://hadoop.apache.org/hdfs.

[7] Hadoop MapReduce Next Generation - Capacity Scheduler. http://tinyurl.com/no2evu5.

[8] Hadoop YARN Project. http://tinyurl.com/bnadg9l.

[9] Microsoft Azure. https://azure.microsoft.com/.

[10] Microsoft Azure Storage. https://azure.microsoft.com/en-us/services/storage/.

[11] ORC File Format. http://tinyurl.com/n4pxofh.

[12] TPC Benchmark H. http://www.tpc.org/tpch/.

[13] Windows Azure's Flat Network Storage and 2012 Scalability Targets. http://bit.ly/1A4Hbjt.

[14] S. Agarwal, S. Kandula, N. Bruno, M.-C. Wu, I. Stoica, and J. Zhou. Re-optimizing Data-parallel Computing. In *NSDI 2012*.

[15] S. Agarwal, S. Kandula, N. Bruno, M.-C. Wu, I. Stoica, and J. Zhou. Reoptimizing Data Parallel Computing. In *NSDI'12*, 2012.

[16] F. Ahmad, S. T. Chakradhar, A. Raghunathan, and T. N. Vijaykumar. ShuffleWatcher: Shuffle-aware Scheduling in Multi-tenant MapReduce Clusters. In *USENIX ATC*, 2014.

[17] G. Ananthanarayanan, S. Agarwal, S. Kandula, A. Greenberg, I. Stoica, D. Harlan, and E. Harris. Scarlett: Coping with Skewed Content Popularity in Mapreduce Clusters. In *EuroSys*, 2011.

[18] G. Ananthanarayanan, A. Ghodsi, A. Wang, D. Borthakur, S. Kandula, S. Shenker, and I. Stoica. PACMan: Coordinated Memory Caching for Parallel Jobs. In *NSDI*, 2012.

[19] K. P. Belkhale and P. Banerjee. An approximate algorithm for the partitionable independent task scheduling problem. *Urbana*, 51:61801, 1990.

[20] R. Chaiken, B. Jenkins, P. Larson, B. Ramsey, D. Shakib, S. Weaver, and J. Zhou. SCOPE: Easy and Efficient Parallel Processing of Massive Datasets. In *VLDB*, 2008.

[21] Y. Chen, A. Ganapathi, R. Griffith, and Y. Katz. The Case for Evaluating MapReduce Performance Using Workload Suites. In *MASCOTS*, 2011.

[22] M. Chowdhury, S. Kandula, and I. Stoica. Leveraging Endpoint Flexibility in Data-Intensive Clusters. In *ACM SIGCOMM*, 2013.

[23] M. Chowdhury, M. Zaharia, J. Ma, M. I. Jordan, and I. Stoica. Managing Data Transfers in Computer Clusters with Orchestra. In *ACM SIGCOMM*, 2011.

[24] M. Chowdhury, Y. Zhong, and I. Stoica. Efficient Coflow Scheduling with Varys. In *ACM SIGCOMM*, 2014.

[25] J. Dean and S. Ghemawat. Mapreduce: Simplified data processing on large clusters. In *OSDI*, 2004.

[26] F. R. Dogar, T. Karagiannis, H. Ballani, and A. Rowstron. Decentralized Task-aware Scheduling for Data Center Networks. In *ACM SIGCOMM*, August 2014.

[27] J. Du and J. Y.-T. Leung. Complexity of Scheduling Parallel Task Systems. *SIAM J. Discret. Math.*, 1989.

[28] K. Elmeleegy. Piranha: Optimizing Short Jobs in Hadoop. *Proc. VLDB Endow.*, 2013.

[29] M. Y. Eltabakh, Y. Tian, F. Özcan, R. Gemulla, A. Krettek, and J. McPherson. CoHadoop: Flexible Data Placement and Its Exploitation in Hadoop. *Proc. VLDB Endow.*, 2011.

[30] A. D. Ferguson, P. Bodik, S. Kandula, E. Boutin, and R. Fonseca. Jockey: Guaranteed Job Latency in Data Parallel Clusters. In *EuroSys*, 2012.

[31] R. L. Graham. Bounds on multiprocessing timing anomalies. *SIAM Journal on Applied Mathematics*, 17(2):416–429, 1969.

[32] R. Grandl, G. Ananthanarayanan, S. Kandula, S. Rao, and A. Akella. Multi-resource Packing for Cluster Schedulers. In *SIGCOMM*, 2014.

[33] H. Herodotou, F. Dong, and S. Babu. No One (Cluster) Size Fits All: Automatic Cluster Sizing for Data-intensive Analytics. In *SOCC*, 2011.

[34] H. Herodotou, H. Lim, G. Luo, N. Borisov, L. Dong, F. B. Cetin, and S. Babu. Starfish: A Self-tuning System for Big Data Analytics. In *CIDR*, 2011.

[35] C. Y. Hong, M. Caesar, and P. B. Godfrey. Finishing Flows Quickly with Preemptive Scheduling. In *SIGCOMM*, 2012.

[36] M. Isard, V. Prabhakaran, J. Currey, U. Wieder, K. Talwar, and A. Goldberg. Quincy: Fair Scheduling for Distributed Computing Clusters. In *SOSP*, 2009.

[37] V. Jalaparti, H. Ballani, P. Costa, T. Karagiannis, and A. Rowstron. Bridging the Tenant-provider Gap in Cloud Services. In *SOCC*, 2012.

[38] Y. Kwok and I. Ahmad. Static scheduling algorithms for allocating directed task graphs to multiprocessors. *ACM Computing Surveys (CSUR)*, 1999.

[39] Y. Kwon, M. Balazinska, B. Howe, and J. Rolia. SkewTune: Mitigating Skew in Mapreduce Applications. In *ACM SIGMOD*, 2012.

[40] R. Lepère, D. Trystram, and G. J. Woeginger. Approximation Algorithms for Scheduling Malleable Tasks Under Precedence Constraints. *International Journal of Foundations of Computer Science*, 13(04):613–627, 2002.

[41] M. Li, D. Subhraveti, A. R. Butt, A. Khasymski, and P. Sarkar. CAM: A Topology Aware Minimum Cost Flow Based Resource Manager for MapReduce Applications in the Cloud. In *HPDC*, 2012.

[42] M. Ovsiannikov, S. Rus, D. Reeves, P. Sutter, S. Rao, and J. Kelly. The Quantcast File System. *Proc. VLDB Endow.*

[43] B. Palanisamy, A. Singh, L. Liu, and B. Jain. Purlieus: Locality-aware Resource Allocation for MapReduce in a Cloud. In *SC*, 2011.

[44] A. Thusoo, J. S. Sarma, N. Jain, Z. Shao, P. Chakka, S. Anthony, H. Liu, P. Wyckoff, and R. Murthy. Hive-a warehousing solution over a map-reduce framework. In *VLDB*, 2009.

[45] J. Turek, J. L. Wolf, and P. S. Yu. Approximate Algorithms Scheduling Parallelizable Tasks. In *SPAA*, 1992.

[46] G. Wang, A. Butt, P. Pandey, and K. Gupta. A Simulation Approach to Evaluating Design Decisions in MapReduce Setups. In *MASCOTS*, 2009.

[47] C. Wilson, H. Ballani, T. Karagiannis, and A. Rowtron. Better Never than Late: Meeting Deadlines in Datacenter Networks. In *ACM SIGCOMM*, 2011.

[48] M. Zaharia, D. Borthakur, J. S. Sarma, K. Elmeleegy, S. Shenker, and I. Stoica. Delay scheduling: A Simple Technique for Achieving Locality and Fairness in Cluster Scheduling. In *EuroSys*, 2010.

[49] M. Zaharia, M. Chowdhury, M. J. Franklin, S. Shenker, and I. Stoica. Spark: Cluster computing with working sets. In *HotCloud*, 2010.

[50] J. Zhou, N. Bruno, M.-C. Wu, P.-Å. Larson, R. Chaiken, and D. Shakib. Scope: parallel databases meet mapreduce. *VLDB J.*, 21(5):611–636, 2012.

APPENDIX

A LP Relaxation

To estimate the quality of our heuristics for the planning problem, we formulate a related integer linear program (ILP). The ILP would provide a lower bound on the makespan and the average completion time for *any* algorithm which plans at the granularity of racks and jobs. However, as the ILP is computationally expensive to solve in practice, we relax it to a linear program (LP), whose solution is still a lower bound to our problem. Thus, if the solution from our heuristics is close to that of the LP, it is guaranteed to be close to optimal. We emphasize that the LP relaxation is not used by Corral, but only serves as a benchmark for the solutions we developed in Section 4.2.

We first describe the Integer Linear Program (ILP). Let T be the makespan of the (unknown to us) optimal solution to the planning problem. For every job j and every number of racks $r \in \{1, \ldots, R\}$, we introduce a variable $x_{jr} \in \{0, 1\}$. In the ILP, x_{jr} equals 1 if job j is assigned r racks, and 0 otherwise. Relaxing the integrality constraint, we obtain the following LP.

$$\text{Minimize}_{\{x_{jr}\}} \quad T \qquad (LP - Batch) \tag{1}$$

$$\text{Subject to} \quad \sum_r x_{jr} = 1, \quad \forall j \tag{2}$$

$$T \geq \sum_r x_{jr} L_j(r), \quad \forall j \tag{3}$$

$$TR \geq \sum_{j,r} x_{jr} L_j(r) \cdot r, \tag{4}$$

$$x_{jr} \in [0, 1], \forall j, \forall r \tag{5}$$

The constraint (2) ensures that all jobs are completed. In the integral solution corresponding to a feasible schedule, for each j exactly one x_{jr} equals 1, so the constraint (2) is satisfied. The constraints (3) and (4) give a lower bound on the makespan. Constraint (3) asserts that the makespan is at least as large as the completion time of every job j (since in the integral solution corresponding to a feasible schedule, the right hand side of (3) exactly equals the running time of job j). Constraint (4) is a capacity constraint. It indicates that the capacity used by the LP schedule (the right hand side of inequality) is at most the available capacity (the left hand side).

We emphasize that LP-Batch is a *relaxation* of our original planning problem (Section 4.1) as it does not give an actual schedule (e.g., does not specify the time when a job should start) but only provides the number of racks a job has to be allocated. Still, any feasible schedule (particularly, an optimal schedule) should satisfy the constraints of the LP and thus, the cost (i.e, makespan) returned by the LP is a lower bound on the cost of any schedule.

In the online scenario, we are interested in minimizing the average completion time. Accordingly, we formulate a mixed integer program with the objective function:

$$\text{Minimize}_{\{x_{jr}\},\{d_{jr}\}} \quad \frac{1}{J} \sum_{j,r} x_{jr} L_j(r) + d_{jr} \quad (LP-Online) \tag{6}$$

where $d_{jr} > 0$ is the delay in scheduling job j relative to its arrival. The LP for the online case is more involved and we omit the full description for brevity.

The above bounds are useful for bounding the gap between the performance of our heuristics and the optimal solution to the planning problem (defined in Section 3.3). They should not be viewed as theoretical guarantees for the entire Corral framework, which includes also the (work-conserving) cluster scheduler. Nevertheless, as our experiments indicate, obtaining good solution for the planning problem leads to overall performance enhancements.

Low Latency Geo-distributed Data Analytics

Qifan Pu[1,2], Ganesh Ananthanarayanan[1], Peter Bodik[1]
Srikanth Kandula[1], Aditya Akella[3], Paramvir Bahl[1], Ion Stoica[2]

[1]Microsoft Research [2]University of California at Berkeley
[3]University of Wisconsin at Madison

ABSTRACT

Low latency analytics on geographically distributed datasets (across datacenters, edge clusters) is an upcoming and increasingly important challenge. The dominant approach of aggregating all the data to a single datacenter significantly inflates the timeliness of analytics. At the same time, running queries over geo-distributed inputs using the current intra-DC analytics frameworks also leads to high query response times because these frameworks cannot cope with the relatively low and variable capacity of WAN links.

We present Iridium, a system for low latency geo-distributed analytics. Iridium achieves low query response times by optimizing placement of both data and tasks of the queries. The joint data and task placement optimization, however, is intractable. Therefore, Iridium uses an online heuristic to redistribute datasets among the sites *prior* to queries' arrivals, and places the tasks to reduce network bottlenecks *during* the query's execution. Finally, it also contains a knob to budget WAN usage. Evaluation across eight worldwide EC2 regions using production queries show that Iridium speeds up queries by $3\times - 19\times$ and lowers WAN usage by $15\% - 64\%$ compared to existing baselines.

CCS Concepts

•Computer systems organization → Distributed Architectures; •Networks → Cloud Computing;

Keywords

geo-distributed; low latency; data analytics; network aware; WAN analytics

SIGCOMM '15, August 17 - 21, 2015, London, United Kingdom
© 2015 ACM. ISBN 978-1-4503-3542-3/15/08...$15.00
DOI: http://dx.doi.org/10.1145/2785956.2787481

1. INTRODUCTION

Large scale cloud organizations are deploying datacenters and "edge" clusters globally to provide their users low latency access to their services. For instance, Microsoft and Google have tens of datacenters (DCs) [6, 11], with the latter also operating 1500 edges worldwide [24]. The services deployed on these *geo-distributed sites* continuously produce large volumes of data like user activity and session logs, server monitoring logs, and performance counters [34, 46, 53, 56].

Analyzing the geo-distributed data gathered across these sites is an important workload. Examples of such analyses include querying user logs to make advertisement decisions, querying network logs to detect DoS attacks, and querying system logs to maintain (streaming) dashboards of overall cluster health, perform root-cause diagnosis and build fault prediction models. Because results of these analytics queries are used by data analysts, operators, and real-time decision algorithms, *minimizing their response times* is crucial.

Minimizing query response times in a geo-distributed setting, however, is far from trivial. The widely-used approach is to aggregate *all* the datasets to a central site (a large DC), before executing the queries. However, waiting for such *centralized* aggregation, significantly delays timeliness of the analytics (by as much as $19\times$ in our experiments).[1] Therefore, the natural alternative to this approach is to execute the queries geo-distributedly over the data stored at the sites.

Additionally, regulatory and privacy concerns might also forbid central aggregation [42]. Finally, verbose or less valuable data (e.g., detailed system logs stored only for a few days) are not shipped at all as this is deemed too expensive. Low response time for queries on these datasets, nonetheless, remains a highly desirable goal.

Our work focuses on *minimizing response times* of geo-distributed analytics queries. A potential approach would be to leave data *in-place* and use unmodified, intra-DC analytics framework (such as Hadoop or Spark) across the collection of sites. However, WAN band-

[1]An enhancement could "sample" data locally and send only a small fraction [46]. Designing generic samplers, unfortunately, is hard. Sampling also limits future analyses.

widths can be highly heterogeneous and relatively moderate [43, 47, 48] which is in sharp contrast to intra-DC networks. Because these frameworks are not optimized for such heterogeneity, query execution could be dramatically inefficient. Consider, for example, a simple map-reduce query executing across sites. If we place no (or very few) reduce tasks on a site that has a large amount of *intermediate* data but low uplink bandwidth, all of the data on this site (or a large fraction) would have to be uploaded to other sites over its narrow uplink, significantly affecting query response time.

We build Iridium, a system targeted at geo-distributed data analytics. Iridium views a single logical analytics framework as being deployed across all the sites. To achieve low query response times, it explicitly considers the heterogeneous WAN bandwidths to optimize *data and task placement.* These two placement aspects are central to our system since the source and destination of a network transfer depends on the locations of the data and the tasks, respectively. Intuitively, in the example above, Iridium will either move data out of the site with low uplink bandwidth before the query arrives or place many of the query's reduce tasks in it.

Because durations of intermediate communications (e.g., shuffles) depend on the duration of the site with the *slowest* data transfer, the key intuition in Iridium is to *balance the transfer times among the WAN links*, thereby avoiding outliers. To that end, we formulate the task placement problem as a linear program (LP) by modeling the site bandwidths and query characteristics. The best task placement, however, is still limited by input data locations. Therefore, moving (or replicating) the datasets to different sites can reduce the anticipated congestion during query execution.

The *joint data and task placement*, even for a single map-reduce query, results in a non-convex optimization with no efficient solution. Hence, we devise an efficient and greedy heuristic that iteratively moves small chunks of datasets to "better" sites. To determine *which* datasets to move, we prefer those with high *value-per-byte*; i.e., we greedily maximize the expected reduction in query response time normalized by the amount of data that needs to be moved to achieve this reduction. This heuristic, for example, prefers moving datasets with many queries accessing them and/or datasets with queries that produce large amount of intermediate data.

Our solution is also mindful of the *bytes transferred on the WAN* across sites since WAN usage has important cost implications ($/byte) [53]. Purely minimizing query response time could result in increased WAN usage. Even worse, purely optimizing WAN usage can arbitrarily increase query latency. This is because of the fundamental difference between the two metrics: bandwidth cost savings are obtained by reducing WAN usage on *any* of the links, whereas query speedups are obtained by reducing WAN usage *only* on the bottleneck link. Thus, to ensure fast query responses *and* reasonable bandwidth costs, we incorporate a simple "knob"

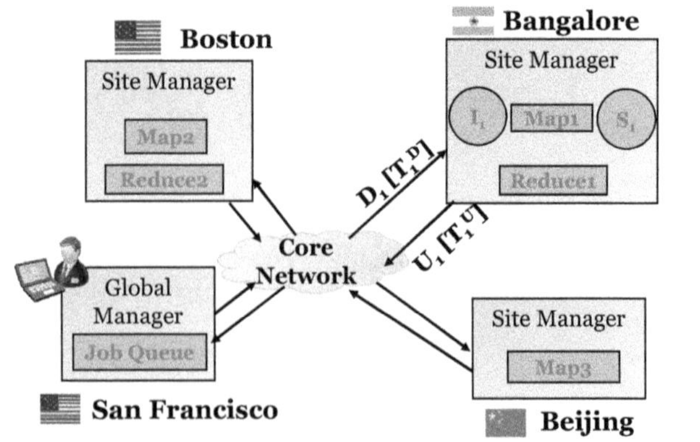

Figure 1: **Geo-distributed map-reduce query. The user submits the query in San Francisco, and the query runs across Boston, Bangalore and Beijing. We also show the notations used in the paper at Bangalore, see Table 1.**

that trades off the WAN usage and latency by limiting the amount of WAN bandwidth used by data moves and task execution. In our experiments, with a budget *equal* to that of a WAN-usage optimal scheme (proposed in [53, 54]), Iridium obtains 2× faster query responses.

Our implementation of Iridium automatically estimates site bandwidths, future query arrivals along with their characteristics (intermediate data), and prioritizes data movement of the earlier-arriving queries. It also supports Apache Spark queries, both streaming [60] as well as interactive/batch queries [59]. [2]

Evaluation across eight worldwide EC2 regions and trace-driven simulations using production queries from Bing Edge, Conviva, Facebook, TPC-DS, and the Big-data benchmark show that Iridium speeds up queries by $3\times - 19\times$ compared to existing baselines that (a) centrally aggregate the data, or (b) leave the data in-place and use unmodified Spark.

2. BACKGROUND AND MOTIVATION

We explain the setup of geo-distributed analytics (§2.1), illustrate the importance of careful scheduling and storage (§2.2), and provide an overview of our solution (§2.3).

2.1 Geo-distributed Analytics

Architecture: We consider the geo-distributed analytics framework to logically span all the sites. We assume that the sites are connected using a network with congestion-free core. The bottlenecks are only between the sites and the core which has infinite bandwidth, valid as per recent measurements [13]. Additionally, there could be significant *heterogeneity* in the uplink and downlink bandwidths due to widely different link capacities and other applications (non-Iridium traffic) sharing the links. Finally, we assume the sites have relatively abundant compute and storage capacity.

Data can be generated on any site and as such, a dataset (such as "user activity log for application X")

[2] https://github.com/Microsoft-MNR/GDA

could be distributed across many sites. Figure 1 shows an example geo-distributed query with a logically centralized *global manager* that converts the user's query script into a DAG of *stages*, each of which consists of many parallel *tasks*. The global manager also coordinates query execution across the many sites, keeps track of data locations across the sites, and maintains durability and consistency of data; durability and consistency, though, are not the focus of our work.

Each of the sites is controlled by a local *site manager* which keeps track of the available local resources and periodically updates the global manager.

Analytics Queries: Input tasks of queries (e.g., map tasks) are executed locally on sites that contain their input data, and they write their outputs (i.e., intermediate data) to their respective local sites. Input stages are extremely quick as a result of data locality [37, 58] and in-memory caching of data [17, 59].

In a geo-distributed setup, the main aspect dictating response time of many queries is efficient transfer of *intermediate* data that necessarily has to go across sites (e.g., all-to-all communication patterns). In Facebook's production analytics cluster, despite local aggregation of the map outputs for associative reduce operations [9, 57], ratio of intermediate to input data sizes is still a high 0.55 for the median query, 24% of queries have this ratio ≥ 1 (more in §6). Intermediate stages are typically data-intensive, i.e., their durations are dominated by communication times [25, 26, 52].

Queries are mostly *recurring* ("batched" streaming [60] or "cron" jobs), e.g., every minute or hour. Because of their recurring nature, we often know the queries that will run on a dataset along with any *lag* between the generation of the dataset and the arrival of its queries. Some *ad hoc* analytics queries are also submitted by system operators or data analysts. Timely completion of queries helps real-time decisions and interactivity.

Objectives: Our techniques for task and data placement work inside the global manager to reduce *query response time*, which is the time from the submission of a query until its completion. At the same time, we are mindful of WAN usage (bytes transferred across the WAN) [53, 54] and balance the two metrics using a simple knob for budgeted WAN usage.

2.2 Illustrative Examples

While Iridium can handle arbitrary DAG queries, in this section, we illustrate the complexity of minimizing the response time of a geo-distributed query using a canonical map-reduce query. As described above, efficient transfer of intermediate data across sites is the key. Transfer duration of "all-to-all" shuffles is dictated by, a) placement of reduce tasks across sites, §2.2.1, and b) placement of the input data, §2.2.2; since map outputs are written locally, distribution of the input data carries over to the distribution of intermediate data. We demonstrate that techniques in intra-DC scheduling and storage can be highly unsuited in the geo-distributed setup. We will also show that techniques to minimize WAN usage can lead to poor query response times.

Symbol	Meaning
I_i	amount of input data on site i
S_i	amount of intermediate (map output) data on site i
α	selectivity of input stage, $S_i = \alpha I_i$
D_i	downlink bandwidth on site i
U_i	uplink bandwidth on site i
r_i	fraction of intermediate (reduce) tasks executed in site i
T_i^U, T_i^D	finish time of intermediate data transfer on up and down link of site i

Table 1: **Notations used in the paper.**

For ease of presentation, we consider the links between the sites and the network core as the only bottlenecks and assume that IO and CPU operations of tasks have zero duration. Table 1 contains the notations. In general, I_i, S_i, D_i, and U_i represent the query input data, intermediate (map output) data, downlink and uplink WAN bandwidths on site i, respectively. The fraction of intermediate (reduce) tasks on a site i is r_i; we use the term *link finish time* to refer to T_i^U and T_i^D which represent the time taken to upload and download intermediate data from and to site i, respectively.

2.2.1 Intermediate Task Placement

Consider a log with the schema ⟨`timestamp`, `user_id`, `latency`⟩ recording latencies of user requests. A user's requests could be distributed across many sites (say, when a user represents a large global customer). Our sample query computes *exact* per-user median latency (`SELECT user_id, median(latency) GROUP BY user_id`). As we execute a user-defined and non-associative function, `median()`, the map tasks output all pairs of ⟨`user_id`, ⟨`latency`⟩⟩, and this intermediate data is shuffled across all sites. Assume the intermediate outputs are half the input size; selectivity $\alpha = 0.5$ (Table 1). Every reduce task collects `latency` values for a subset of `user_id` values and calculates the median per user.

We consider execution of the above query over three sites; see Table 2a for input and intermediate data sizes and bandwidths available at the sites. State-of-the-art approaches to scheduling reduce tasks recommend equal spreading of reduce tasks across sites (or racks and machines) [19, 52]. Such an approach would result in one-third of the tasks on each of the three sites, $r = (0.33, 0.33, 0.33)$, resulting in a query response time of 80s (Figure 2b and 2c). Each of the sites has data traversing its up and down links, whose finish times (T_i^U and T_i^D) depend on their bandwidths. The transfer duration is the maximum of all the link finish times, and we colloquially refer to the slowest site as the *bottleneck*. In this case the bottleneck is site-1 with a slow downlink (1MB/s) which has to download 1/3 of intermediate

	Site-1	Site-2	Site-3
Input Data (MB), *I*	300	240	240
Intermediate Data (MB), *S*	150	120	120
Uplink (MB/s), *U*	10	10	10
Downlink (MB/s), *D*	1	10	10

(a) Setup of three sites.

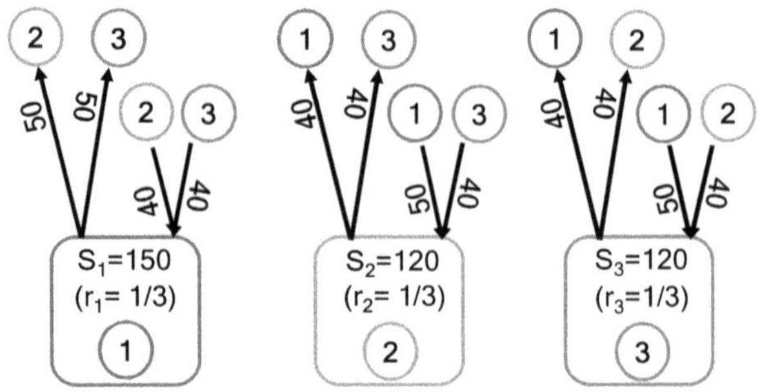

(b) When tasks are *equally spread* across the three sites, $\frac{2}{3}$ of the data (S_i) on each site is sent out (uplink), split equally to the other two sites. The download at each site (downlink) can, thus, be correspondingly summed up.

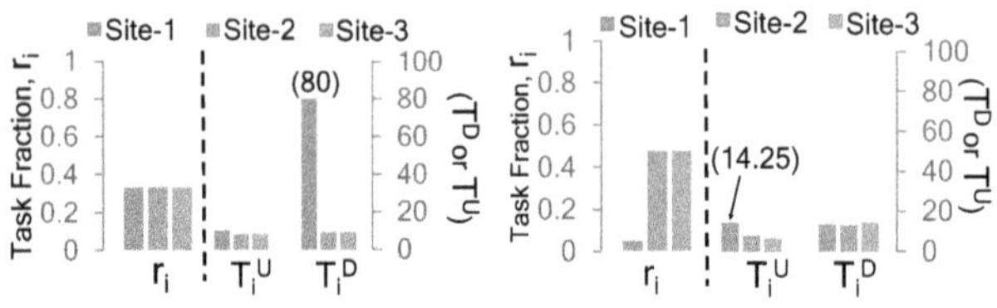

(c) Equal Spread (d) Better Alternative

Figure 2: **Intermediate Task Placement over 3 sites (a), comparing equal spreading of tasks (b, c) and a better alternative (d). Task fractions (r_i) are shown on the left y-axis in ((c) and (d)) while link finish times (T_i^D or T_i^U) are on the right y-axis.**

data from sites 2 and 3, i.e., 120MB/3 + 120MB/3 = 80MB (Figure 2b).

A better alternative, covered in §3, distributes reduce tasks with ratios $r = (0.05, 0.475, 0.475)$ across the three sites, reducing the query response time over five-fold to 14.25s, Figure 2d. The alternative, essentially, identified site-1's downlink to be the bottleneck link in Figure 2c, and hence moved tasks away from it to the other sites. For brevity, we omit the corresponding illustration similar to Figure 2b on calculating link finish times.

We cannot improve the reduce task placement much more, since site-1's up and downlinks have approximately similar link finish times now. Increasing or decreasing r_1 will increase T_1^D or T_1^U, respectively, and thus increase response time. Thus, task placement needs to *carefully balance the up/down link usages* of the sites.

WAN Usage: To minimize WAN usage [53, 54] we need to collect the intermediate data (S_i) from sites-2 and 3 into site-1 since site-1 already contains the most intermediate data. This results in cross-site WAN usage of 240MB, but takes 240s (downlink D_1 = 1MB/s). In contrast, it can be calculated that the alternative task placement we proposed results in 268.5MB of WAN data usage; increase in WAN usage of just 12% reduces query response time 17× (from 240s to 14.25s). Thus, schemes minimizing WAN usage can be highly inefficient for query response time. This is because savings in WAN usage accrue with each link on which we reduce the amount of data transferred, whereas we reduce response time only by optimizing the bottlenecked link.

In fact, task placements of both the policies—equal spreading and minimizing WAN usage—could result in *arbitrarily large* query response times. For example, as S_2 increases, response time of the equal-spread policy increases linearly, while the optimal task placement will place all reduce tasks in site-2 and keep the response time constant. Similarly, as D_1 gets smaller, e.g., when $D_1 = 0.1$MB/s, minimizing WAN usage requires 2400s, while we achieve a response time of 15s by placing no reduce tasks on site-1.

2.2.2 Input Data Placement

In §2.2.1, we assumed that the query inputs stayed on the sites that they were initially generated/stored. Since even the best task placements are limited by the locations of the data, it may be beneficial to move the input data to different sites before starting the query.[3] For example, when input data was generated at time a_0 and query is submitted at time a_1 ($a_1 > a_0$), we can use this *lag* of ($a_1 - a_0$) to rearrange the input data to reduce query response time. Even when $a_0 = a_1$ but intermediate data is larger than input data ($\alpha > 1$, Table 1), moving input data would be more efficient than moving the intermediate data. Recall that since the input tasks write their outputs (intermediate data) to the local site, any change in distribution of input data carries over to the intermediate data.

Rearranging the input data, however, is non-trivial, because as we change S_i's, we have to recompute the optimal r_i's as well. Consider a query with input I = (240, 120, 60)MB across three sites, $\alpha = 1$, and a lag of 24s between data generation and query arrival. As before, we assume that IO and CPU operations of tasks have zero duration and the WAN as the only bottleneck. Figure 3a shows the data and bandwidths at the sites along with query response time when data is left "in place" (Figure 3b). Site-1's uplink is the bottleneck link whose link finish time is 21.6s.

A better input placement will move data out of the bottlenecked site-1 in the available 24s, and Figure 3c shows the benefit of the best movement: from site-1 to site-2. The moving is gated on site-1's uplink (10MB/s) moving 240MB of data in 24s. This new data distribution reduces the response time 4× from 21.6s to 5.4s. The different r_i values between Figures 3b and 3c shows that minimizing query response time indeed requires a *joint optimization over data and task placement.*

[3]While we use the term "move" in describing our solution, we in fact just *replicate*, i.e., create additional copies, §5.

	Site-1	Site-2	Site-3
Input Data (MB), *I*	240	120	60
Intermediate Data (MB), *S*	240	120	60
Uplink (MB/s), *U*	10	10	10
Downlink (MB/s), *D*	1	10	10

(a) Setup of three sites.

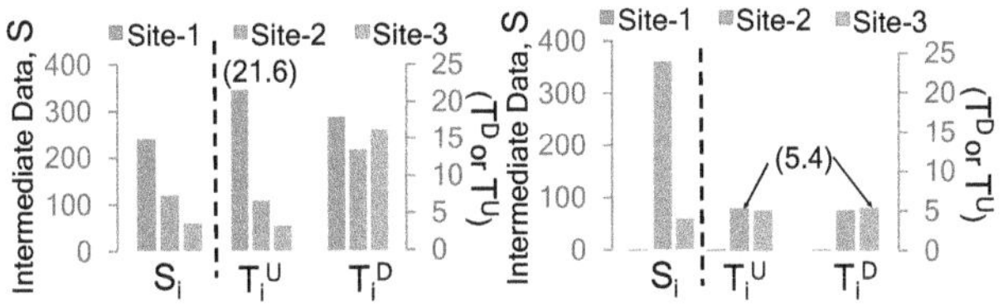

(b) "In-place" Input Placement (c) Better Input Placement

Figure 3: **Input Data Placement for (a). Comparison of transfer durations when data is left *in place* (b) with moving data from site-1 to site-2. The query arrives with a lag of 24s after the data is available. Intermediate data (S_i) is shown on the left y-axis, instead of r_i in Figure 2. Link finish times (T_i^D or T_i^U) are on the right y-axis. The best r_i's for (b) and (c) are** $(0.1, 0.45, 0.45)$ **and** $(0, 0.85, 0.15)$.

In the presence of multiple datasets, an additional challenge is determining *which* datasets to move. For example, it is advantageous to move datasets with *high number of queries* accessing them. As we will show in §6, there is a two orders of magnitude variation in access counts of datasets in Facebook's production cluster.

2.3 Summary and Solution Overview

In summary, we illustrated a setup of WAN-connected sites: a query's dataset is spread across sites (where they were originally generated), each site stores parts of many datasets, and each dataset is accessed by multiple queries. Our goal is to *minimize average query response time* while also being mindful of WAN usage. We achieve this by, a) moving parts of datasets across sites in the *lag* between data generation and query arrival, and b) placing intermediate tasks *during* the query's execution. The intuition is to *identify "bottleneck" sites and balance the number of tasks and/or amount of data on these sites.*

Our solution Iridium is described next.

1. We solve the problem of *task placement* for a single query (given a fixed location of data) using an efficient linear formulation (§3).
2. We devise an efficient heuristic to solve the problem of *data placement* (§4), that internally uses the formulation developed in §3.
3. We incorporate a "knob" for budgeted WAN usage in our data placement (§4.4).

For data and task placement, we ignore the (abundant) CPU and memory resources at the sites.

3. TASK PLACEMENT

In this section, we describe how we *place tasks of a single query to minimize its response time* given a fixed input data distribution. As we described in §2.1, input tasks that load and filter the input data involve no cross-site data movement. For such input tasks, data locality [37, 58] and in-memory caching [17, 59] is sufficient for efficient execution; input tasks write their outputs (intermediate data) locally on the site they run. Other intermediate stages of the query, such as reduce and join, communicate across the different sites and require careful task placement to minimize their duration.

As these tasks are data-intensive, i.e., their durations are dominated by the times spent on communication, our objective is to minimize the duration of the intermediate data transfer. This problem can be solved exactly and efficiently for the most common communication patterns on intermediate data—reduce or join [25]. We explain our solution for these two (§3.1 and §3.2) before extending it to arbitrary DAGs (§3.3).

3.1 Placement of Reduce Tasks

Consider a map-reduce query across sites, where S_i is the intermediate data at site i ($\sum_i S_i = S$). We decide r_i, the fraction of reduce tasks to place on each site i ($\sum_i r_i = 1$) to minimize the longest link finish time.

For formulating the problem, we assume that the reduce tasks are infinitesimally divisible. We also assume that the intermediate data on site i, S_i, is distributed across the other sites proportionally to r_j's.

The main factors involved in the decision of r_i's are the bandwidths of the uplinks (U_i) and downlinks (D_i) along with the size of intermediate data (S_i) at the sites. In the "all-to-all" shuffle communication, given the assumptions above, each site i has to upload $(1 - r_i)$ fraction of its data for a total of $(1 - r_i)S_i$, and download r_i fraction of data from all the other sites for a total of $r_i(S - S_i)$. Therefore, the time to upload data from site i during the intermediate data transfer is $T_i^U(r_i) = (1 - r_i)S_i/U_i$, and time to download the data is $T_i^D(r_i) = r_i(S - S_i)/D_i$. Given our assumption of a congestion-free core, the problem of reduce task placement can, hence, be formulated as a linear program (LP). The LP implicitly avoids bottlenecks; e.g., if a site has a lot of data or links with low bandwidth, the placement avoids sending too much data over the narrow link.

$$\begin{array}{ll} \min & z \\ \text{s.t.} & \forall i : r_i \geq 0 \\ & \sum_i r_i = 1 \\ & \forall i : T_i^U(r_i) \leq z, \quad T_i^D(r_i) \leq z \end{array}$$

The above formulation is highly efficient and invoked (repeatedly) for data placement in §4. Our implementation, described in §5, removes some of the above approximations and uses a more general (but less efficient) MIP for task placement.

3.2 Placement of Join Tasks

The above approach also extends to handle joins, e.g., a join of tables A and B on a common column M. There are two join implementations: *hash* and *broadcast*, automatically chosen by query optimizers [3].

If both tables are large, they are joined using a hash join which is executed as two all-to-all shuffles of both tables (as in §3.1), followed by a pair-wise join operation on data in the same key-range. To reduce the WAN usage of the pair-wise join operation, reduce tasks of the shuffle in both tables that are responsible for the same key-range are scheduled on the same site. Thus, for our purpose, we treat the whole join as a single all-to-all shuffle and use the above LP with S_i as the total amount of data of tables A and B on site i.

If one of the tables is small, broadcast join will send the smaller table to all sites storing any data of the larger table. In the broadcast join, the amount of data sent over WAN is both small and constant (size of the small table). Placement of tasks does not impact join completion time.

3.3 DAGs of Tasks

While task placement for a single intermediate data transfer can be solved using an LP, doing so for general DAGs is a much more challenging problem. For example, placement of tasks for a query with two consecutive intermediate data transfers results in a non-convex optimization (unlike the linear one above).

As a result, Iridium adopts a greedy approach of applying the task placement LP independently in each stage of the query. Starting with the top-level stages, it applies the LP in topological order, which ensures that when placing tasks of a stage, the tasks of their parents have already been placed. While this approach is not optimal, in queries with many stages in sequence, the amount of data processed by each stage typically drops off quickly [14]. The intermediate data transfer at the query's beginning is the most important.

Next, we use the approach described in this section to find the best data placement, i.e., how to adjust I_i's (and S_i's) to minimize query response time.

4. DATA PLACEMENT

In this section, we describe our solution for distributing datasets across the sites to reduce the finishing time on the anticipated bottleneck links (motivated in §2.2.2). Changing the distribution of the input data carries over to the distribution of intermediate data since the input tasks that produce the latter write their outputs locally. Further, as the best task placement (§3) is limited by the distribution of the data (I_i's or S_i's), data placement is *complementary* towards reducing query response time. Again, we use "moving of data" for ease of exposition; our system just replicates additional copies that are tracked by the global manager (§2.1).

	Site-1	Site-2	Site-3
Uplink (MB/s), U	10	10	10
Downlink (MB/s), D	1	10	10

(a) Setup of three sites.

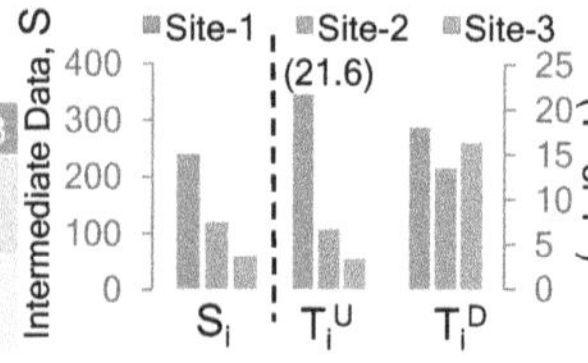

(b) Original Input Placement

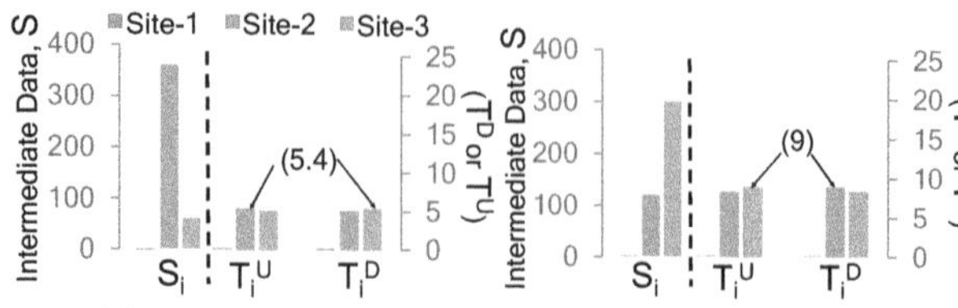

(c) Site-1 → Site-2 (d) Site-1 → Site-3

Figure 4: **Exploring destination options for data movement out of site-1 (same example as Figure 3). In the initial configuration (4b), site-1's uplink is the bottleneck. We evaluate moving 240MB from site-1 to the other two sites, site-2 (4c) and site-3 (4d). Moving to site-2 results in the lowest intermediate data transfer duration of 5.4s, from 21.6s.**

While the task placement problem alone can be solved as an LP, the joint optimization of input *and* task placement contains many local optima (see discussion in §7), making it impossible to formulate it as a linear or a quadratic program, or solve using convex optimization tools. Thus, we proceed to devise an efficient heuristic.

We first provide intuition for a single dataset and query (§4.1), generalize to multiple datasets and queries in §4.2, provide important enhancements in §4.3, and finally describe the knob to budget WAN usage in §4.4.

4.1 Basic Intuition

The LP in §3 provides a useful starting point. It computes the optimal query response time, z, but also identifies the bottleneck link, where link finish time is equal to z. Our heuristic rests on the intuition of moving data *out* of the bottleneck site, thereby reducing this maximum link finish time (and hence the query duration). Two natural questions arise in doing so: (*i*) *where* to move the data? (*ii*) *how much* data to move out? We answer both questions next.

(*i*) Figure 4 illustrates the effect of picking different destinations to move data *to*, using the same example from §2.2.2. Recall that query's input across the three sites was $I = (240, 120, 60)$MB with selectivity $\alpha = 1$, i.e., $S = I$ (see Figure 4a). Figure 4b shows the result of running the query leaving the original data unmoved. Site-1 will be the bottleneck during the intermediate data transfer (r_i's and bottleneck site derived using §3). Options for moving data from site-1 are to the other two sites, 2 and 3. Figure 4c and 4d show the potential effect of both these moves, with r_i's recalculated based on the new S_i's. Moving the data from site-1 to site-2

```
    class Move
        double cost
        ⟨QueryID, double⟩ timeReduction
        Site bottleneck
1: procedure ALLOCATEMOVES(List⟨Dataset⟩ D)
2:     for each Dataset d in D do
3:         Move d.m ← FINDMOVE(d)
4:         lag ← Σ_{q∈d.Queries} q.lag / d.Queries.Count
5:         d.value ← Σ_{q∈d.Queries} d.m.timeReduction[q ] /
   lag
6:         d.score ← d.value / d.m.cost
7:     for each Dataset d in D.SortedByDesc(d.score) do
8:         if d.m.bottleneck.canMove() then
9:             execute d.m
```

Pseudocode 1: Iridium **Solution. The function takes the set of all datasets D and assigns each site to move out part of a dataset. For simplicity, we do not present the calculation of the *destination* site to be moved.**

is the best move as the transfer duration is 5.4s compared to 9s in Figure 4d. While not applicable in this example, we ignore moves to those sites that *increase* the transfer duration.

(*ii*) On the second question of *how much* data to move out of the bottleneck site, the above example ended up moving all the data from site-1 to site-2 because such a move happened to result in the lowest duration for intermediate transfer. In our system, we use a "what-if" calculation to assess moving data out of the bottleneck site in increments of δ (say, 10MB), i.e., move 10MB, 20MB and so forth. We pick the increment of δ that provides the smallest transfer duration.[4]

Iridium's heuristic can be summarized as follows: *iteratively* identify bottlenecked sites and move data out of them to reduce the duration of intermediate data transfer (considering all potential destinations and increments of δ).[5] We extend this simple intuition to a workload of *multiple* competing datasets in §4.2. We then enhance the solution in §4.3 with techniques to predict future query arrivals, minimize contention between data movement and query traffic, etc.

4.2 Prioritizing between Multiple Datasets

In prioritizing between datasets, Iridium seeks to identify and move the high-valued datasets. High-valued datasets are those that are accessed by more queries, and those whose movement results in large improvements in the intermediate data transfer of their queries.

In the example above, the "value" of moving data out of site-1 to site-2 is $(21.6 - 5.4) = 16.2$s. The relative value of moving a dataset also increases if its queries are to arrive sooner, i.e., smaller *lag*. The "cost" of the move is the amount of data that needs to be moved over the WAN to improve the query, 240MB in the example. We select the move that achieves the highest "score", i.e., (value/cost).

Pseudocode 1 lists the two main steps in our heuristic. We defer estimation of future query arrivals to §4.3.

Step a), lines $2-5$, first calls FINDMOVE() that returns the *Move* object that contains the bottlenecked site, data to be moved out, and the reduction in query durations (≥ 0) due to the move. The query durations and bottleneck site are calculated using §3. If there are multiple bottlenecked sites, we arbitrarily pick one.

The value of the move is calculated using the reduction in query durations and query lags (described shortly). The "score" of the proposed move is $\frac{value}{cost}$.

Step b), lines $6-8$, processes datasets in descending order of their score. To prevent new low-value dataset moves from slowing down ongoing high-value moves, we allocate a site's uplink and downlink to *only one* dataset at a time (justified in §6.4). The *canMove* function performs this check.

Query Lag: For two datasets A and B that arrived at 1:00, all else being equal, if dataset A's queries arrive at 1:05 and dataset B's queries at 1:10, we should prefer to move dataset A at 1:00 since we can move B starting at 1:05. This is analogical to the "earliest-deadline-first" scheduling approach.

We adopt this approach by calculating the query *lag* for a dataset, i.e., time between dataset availability and the query's arrival, as the average of the lag of all the queries accessing the dataset. The value for the dataset is then multiplied by $\frac{1}{lag}$. Thus, the smaller the average lag, the higher its value and urgency in moving the dataset. In §6.4, we also evaluate other metrics of arrival lag (e.g., median, earliest, latest) and see that using the average works best.

The ALLOCATEMOVES() function in Pseudocode 1 is invoked every time a new dataset or a query arrives or when a scheduled data movement completes. Arrival of queries aborts any incomplete movements of their data.

4.3 Enhancements

We now present two important enhancements.

Estimating Query Arrivals

For *recurring* workloads ("batch" streams [60] or "cron" jobs), we estimate arrivals based on past executions.

However, this is hard to do for ad hoc queries. For a dataset, we care about the number of queries that will access it and their arrival times, i.e., lag. To that end, we make the following simple assumption that works well in our evaluation (§6.4). We assume the dataset's future query arrivals will repeat as per the query arrivals so far (from the time the dataset was generated). For instance, if the dataset was generated at time t and two queries arrived at times $(t+2)$ and $(t+3)$, we will assume at $(t+3)$ that two more queries would arrive at

[4]This approach brings the transfer duration down to, at least, the second-most bottlenecked link. Thus, this avoids a "loop" of the same data being moved *back* to the site in the next step. In general, fixing δ avoids jointly calculating new values for r_i's and S_i's.

[5]If none of the moves out of the bottleneck site help, we consider analogical moves of data *into* the bottleneck site.

times $(t+3)+2$ and $(t+3)+3$. We use these arrival lags in Pseudocode 1. In general, at the end of n queries, it would assume n *more* queries will arrive.

Such a scheme *under-estimates* the number of accesses initially. But the estimate grows quickly, and it estimates correctly at the "half-way" number of accesses. Beyond this half-way point, it *over-estimates* future accesses, which could lead to unnecessary data movement. In practice however, for even moderate number of accesses, data movements mostly stabilize by the time the over-estimation starts, thus limiting any fallout.

Queries/Data Contention

In an online system, our heuristic makes its data movement decisions even as (tasks of) queries are executing on the sites. This results in contention between the network flows of the tasks and data movement. When we schedule a data movement out of a site, we measure the impact, i.e, increase in duration of the running tasks and the corresponding queries. An increase in task duration need not necessarily increase the query's duration because the latter is bound by its slowest task. In measuring the increase in duration, we assume fair sharing of uplink/downlink bandwidth among all the flows.

We evaluate if the slowdown of the other running queries due to contention is worth the speedup of the queries whose data will be moved. Data is moved *only* if the trade-off is beneficial, otherwise we ignore this dataset and move to the next dataset in the ordered list (not included in Pseudocode 1 for simplicity).

4.4 WAN Usage Budget

WAN usage across sites is an important operational cost ($/byte) for datacenters [53, 54]. Also, third-party services running on AWS or Azure across regions pay based on WAN usage [5]. As described so far, Iridium does not account for WAN usage. If there is enough lag for a query's arrival or if there are not many competing datasets, it will be free to move the datasets *even if* they only marginally improve the response times.

To avoid wasting WAN bandwidths on such movements, we incorporate a *budget* for WAN usage that forces our heuristic to balance between the speedup of queries and WAN costs. The challenge in setting the budget is to ensure it is neither *too low* (and moving very few datasets leading to limited query speedups), nor *too high* (and causing wasted usage of WAN links).

As a baseline for our budget, we start with the WAN consumption, W, of a (data and task placement) scheme that *optimizes* for WAN usage [53, 54]. We set the budget for our heuristic to be $(B \cdot W)$, $B \geq 1$. $B = 1$ implies a strict WAN usage budget, while higher values of B trade it for faster query response.

How do we calculate and keep track of the WAN budget over time? We adopt the following greedy approach. We start with a counter $M = 0$. Every time a new dataset arrives, we compute the W for this dataset and increment $M{+}= W \cdot B$. Every time we execute a data move, we decrement M by amount of data moved. If $M = 0$, we do not execute any new data moves.

Setting the knob B is a matter of policy but our results indeed highlight the presence of a "sweet spot". With $B = 1.3$, Iridium's gains are nearly 90% of the gains with an unconstrained budget. In fact, even with WAN usage equal to a WAN-usage optimal policy, i.e., $B = 1$, its query speedups are 2× more, §6.5.

5. SYSTEM IMPLEMENTATION

Our prototype implementation of Iridium is on top of the Apache Spark [59] framework. The source code is available here: https://github.com/Microsoft-MNR/GDA

To implement our task placement, we override the default scheduler of Spark and plug-in our module that internally uses the Gurobi solver [7]. We would like to note that we solve the task placement problem as a Mixed Integer Problem (in contrast to the simple LP in §3). The MIP uses the exact amount of intermediate data read by every task from each site, thus handles any intermediate communication pattern, and outputs a specific site to place each task. Even though the MIP is less efficient, it is invoked only once per job for task placement. The LP is an efficient approximation and used in the many iterations of data placement decisions.

We incorporate our data placement heuristic inside the Hadoop Distributed File System (HDFS) [8] that Spark uses as its data store. We do not disable the default replication mechanism in HDFS, and all our data movements hence only create *additional* copies of the data, thus leaving data durability unaffected. As storage at the sites is abundant, we believe this to be an acceptable design.

User queries and analytics jobs are submitted through an uniform interface provided by the Spark manager. Because Iridium is built upon Spark, it can leverage two Spark extensions, Spark SQL and Spark Streaming [60], for parsing SQL queries and running streaming jobs.

We use simple techniques to estimate the bandwidths at sites and intermediate data sizes (or α) of queries.

Estimating Bandwidths: Our experiments at the eight EC2 sites (described in §6) indicate that the available bandwidth is relatively stable in the granularity of minutes. Thus, we use a simple test that checks the available bandwidth every few minutes. However, we also get continuous fine-grained measurements by piggybacking measurements on the throughputs of the data movement and task flows. Given our focus on recurring queries, such piggybacking provides a sufficiently rich source of bandwidth values that automatically considers non-Iridium traffic. We plug these in to our heuristics.

Estimating Intermediate Data Sizes: Unlike input sizes of queries, intermediate data sizes are not known upfront. Again, we leverage the recurring nature of our workloads to infer the intermediate data sizes. Repeated queries, even on newer parts of the same dataset, often produce similar filtering of data. We are able to estimate the ratio of intermediate to input data of queries (α) with an accuracy of 92% in our experiments.

6. EVALUATION

We evaluate Iridium using a geo-distributed EC2 deployment as well as trace-driven simulations. The highlights of our evaluation are as follows.

1. Iridium speeds up workloads from Conviva, Bing Edge, TPC-DS [12] and Big-data benchmarks [4] by 64% to 92% (3× to 19×) when deployed across eight EC2 regions in five continents.

2. Iridium saves WAN bandwidth usage by 15% to 64%. Even with usage equal to a WAN-usage optimal policy, its query speedups are 2× more.

6.1 Methodology

We begin by describing our evaluation setup.

EC2 Deployment: We deploy Iridium across eight EC2 regions in Tokyo, Singapore, Sydney, Frankfurt, Ireland, Sao Paulo, Virginia (US) and California (US) [2]. We use c3.4xlarge instances in each region [1] and the WAN connecting them is a more constrained resource than the local CPU/memory/disk. In addition, we also mimic a larger geo-distributed setup of 30 sites within one region.

Workloads: We tested our system using four analytics workloads from Conviva, Bing Edge, TPC-DS and AMPLab Big-data benchmark (§6.2). These workloads consist of a mix of Spark [59] and Hive [49] queries.

Trace-driven Simulator: We evaluate Iridium over longer durations using a trace-driven simulator of production traces (one month, 350K jobs) from Facebook's Hadoop cluster. The simulator is faithful to the trace in its query arrival times (lag), task input/output sizes, and dataset properties of locations, generation times and access patterns. We mimic 150 sites in our simulator; slots within sites are unconstrained.

We predict future query arrivals (lags) using the technique in §4.3, and evaluate its accuracy in §6.4.

Baselines: We compare Iridium to two baselines: (*i*) leave data "in-place" and use stock Spark's scheduling and storage policies, and (*ii*) "centralized" aggregation of data at a main DC whose in-bandwidth is generously and conservatively set to be practically-infinite, i.e., it is rarely the bottleneck during the aggregation. We again use stock Spark's scheduling/storage within the main DC that they are optimized well for.

Metric: Our primary metric is *reduction (%) in average response time* of queries. For a query whose response times with the baseline and Iridium are b and x, we calculate $100 \times \frac{(b-x)}{b}$; maximum is 100%. We also quote b/x, the factor of reduction in response time when appropriate. In §6.5, we measure WAN usage.

We describe our EC2 deployment results in §6.2 and simulation results in §6.3. We assess Iridium's design decisions in §6.4 and the WAN usage knob in §6.5.

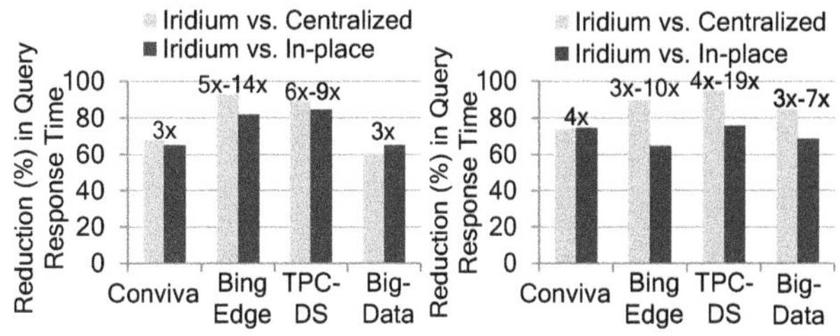

(a) Inter-Region (b) 30 sites

Figure 5: **EC2 Results across eight worldwide regions (a): Tokyo, Singapore, Sydney, Frankfurt, Ireland, Sao Paulo, Virginia (US) and California (US). The figure on the right (b) is on a larger 30-site setup. Iridium is 3× − 19× better compared to the two baselines.**

6.2 EC2 Deployment

We used four workloads to evaluate Iridium on EC2.

(1) Conviva Video Analytics: We use queries from Conviva, a video delivery and monitoring company. Data from clients (e.g., the edge/CDN serving them, their ISP and network characteristics) are analyzed to modify the parameters of video sessions (e.g., codec, buffer sizes) to improve performance (re-buffering ratio [21]). The queries contain a mixture of aggregation ("reduce") and table-joins. Every query has 160GB input.

(2) Microsoft Bing Edge Dashboard: Microsoft's Bing service maintains a running dashboard of its edge servers deployed worldwide. The queries aggregate data from 40,000 raw counters filtered by a range of location (lat/long, city), user-id, etc. values to produce average and 90th percentiles. This is also an example of a *streaming* query that we execute using Spark Streaming's "mini-batch" model [60] in every time period.

(3) TPC-DS Benchmark: The TPC-DS benchmark is a set of decision support queries [12] based on those used by retail product suppliers such as Amazon. These OLAP queries examine large volumes of data (215GB) each, and are characterized by a mixture of compute and disk/network load, the latter of relevance to us.

(4) AMPLab Big-Data: The big-data benchmark [4] is derived from workloads and queries from [45] with identical schema of the data. The suite contain a mix of Hive and Spark queries. The queries contain simple scans, aggregations, joins, and UDF's.

In our inter-region EC2 experiment, we use bandwidths naturally available to the instances on the sites. In our 30-site setup, we vary the bandwidths between 100Mb/s to 2Gb/s (Linux Traffic Control [10]), hoping to mimic the heterogeneous bandwidths across edge clusters and DCs available for analytics frameworks.

Figure 5a plots our average gains for the four workloads across eight-region EC2 regions. Gains compared to the in-place and centralized baselines range from 64% to 92% (3× to 14×). Singapore, Tokyo and Oregon (US) had 2.5× higher bandwidth than Virgina (US) and Frankfurt, and 5× higher bandwidth than Sydney,

	Iridium vs. In-place	Iridium vs. Centralized
Core	26%	32%
Core + Query Lag	41%	46%
Core + Query Lag + Contention	59%	74%
Core + Contention	45%	53%

Table 2: **Progression of Iridium's gains as additional features of considering query lag and contention between query/data movements are added to the basic heuristic. (Facebook workload)**

Sao Paulo and Ireland. Iridium automatically adjusts its data and task placement away from these sites to avoid unduly congesting their links during query execution. Our gains are similar (but a bit higher) with our 30-site setup at $3\times - 19\times$. Note that since the Bing Edge query is a streaming operation executed as a series of "mini-batch" queries, we report the gains per batch.

Gains compared to the centralized baseline is higher than with the in-place baseline for all but the Conviva workload. This is because the intermediate data size is closer to the input size (α) in the Conviva workload, which makes central aggregation less hurtful. In addition, the Conviva and Big-data queries also have a more intensive map stage (during which we do just as good as our baselines via data locality) that relatively brings down the opportunity and gains for Iridium. Finally, the Conviva and Bing Edge queries have lesser skew in their map outputs which limits the value of Iridium's task placement compared to the in-place baseline.

Overheads: Micro-benchmarks show that our data placement iterations are efficient to implement, finishing in under 100ms for up to 200 sites; the LP used (§3.1) calculates fraction of tasks (r_i), thus the number of tasks do not matter in its calculation.

6.3 Trace-driven Simulation

In this section, we present simulation results based on the production trace from Facebook's Hadoop cluster. We use bandwidth values 100Mb/s to 2Gb/s in our simulator, similar to §6.2, but we also present a result when the bandwidths are higher with lower heterogeneity later ($\{10, 50\}$ Gb/s), indicative of only large DCs.

Compared to baselines of leaving data in place and central aggregation, Iridium improves average response time by 59% and 74%, respectively.

Table 2 shows the progression in gains as we start with the basic data placement heuristic, and incrementally add the usage of query lag in the score for datasets, and consideration of contention between query/data traffic. The basic heuristic itself starts with fairly moderate gains, but jumps by a factor of $1.5\times$ when we consider the lag, and a further $1.5\times$ with modeling contentions with query traffic. The final result is also significantly better than adding either one of the features. These results seek to underline the use of query lag in differentiating between datasets, and avoiding contention with running queries.

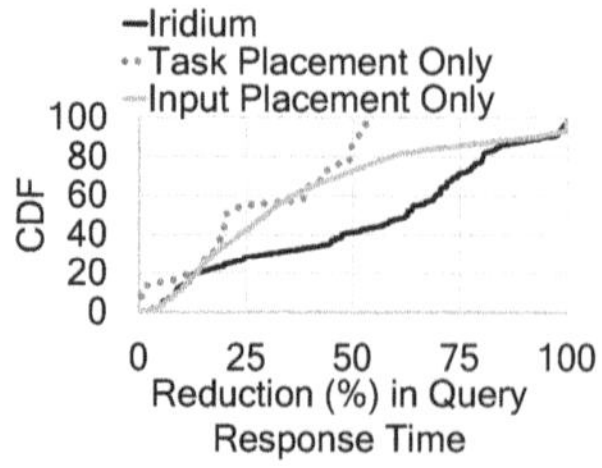

(a) In-place baseline

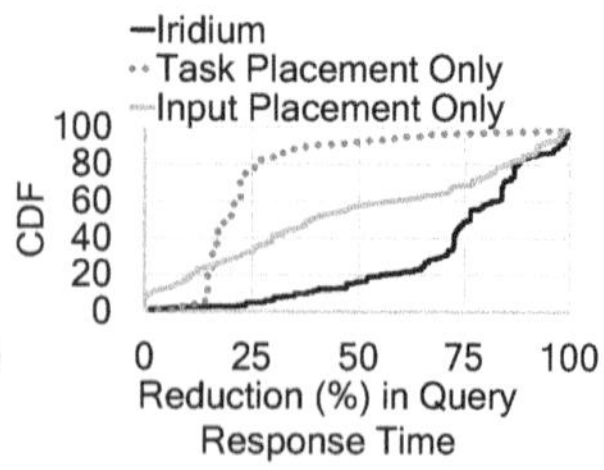

(b) Centralized baseline

Figure 6: **CDF of Iridium's gains with the Facebook workload. We also compare our two techniques—task placement and data placement—standalone.**

Also, keeping data in place is a more stringent baseline than the common approach of central aggregation. This is because reduction in data in intermediate stages ($\alpha < 1$) of many queries results in unnecessary delays using the centralized approach. Iridium automatically makes the right call on placing data and tasks depending on the intermediate data and other factors.

Distribution of Gains: Figure 6 plots the distribution of gains. Gains compared to the in-place baseline are more uniform (and lower) compared to the centralized baseline where the gains are steep overall. The curves converge at the third quartile at $\sim 80\%$. Importantly, Iridium does not make any query worse. This is because its decisions on data and task placements automatically subsume the corresponding decisions by the baselines.

We also compare the effect of our two techniques—task and data placements—*standalone.* With the former, we leave data in-place, and with the latter, we use Spark's stock intermediate task placement. With the in-place baseline, using Iridium's task placement alone moderately outperforms using Iridium's data placement alone (outside of the final quartile); Figure 6a. However, compared to the centralized baseline, it reverses and significantly under-performs. This is roughly intuitive given that smart data movements mainly assuage the problem in moving all the data (centralized baseline) while smart task placement mainly solves the congestion issues due to naive task placement (in-place baseline).

Bucketing the Gains: Given the above variation in gains, *which are the queries that gain more?* Figure 7 buckets queries by different characteristics and plots the average gains in each bucket (along with the fraction of queries). We use the stricter in-place baseline here.

(*i*) *Intermediate/Input Ratio* (α): Among queries with same input size, Iridium's data movement prioritizes those with higher intermediate data as they provide higher value. While Iridium's task placement works for both, queries with higher intermediate data present more opportunity for smart task placement. Consequently, gains are skewed towards queries with high α (Figure 7a). However, even queries with $\alpha < 1$ see significant gains because the times spent on input and intermediate stages is also dictated by the vastly different processing speeds of these stages (in-memory vs. WAN). Thus, optimizing intermediate stages is still valuable.

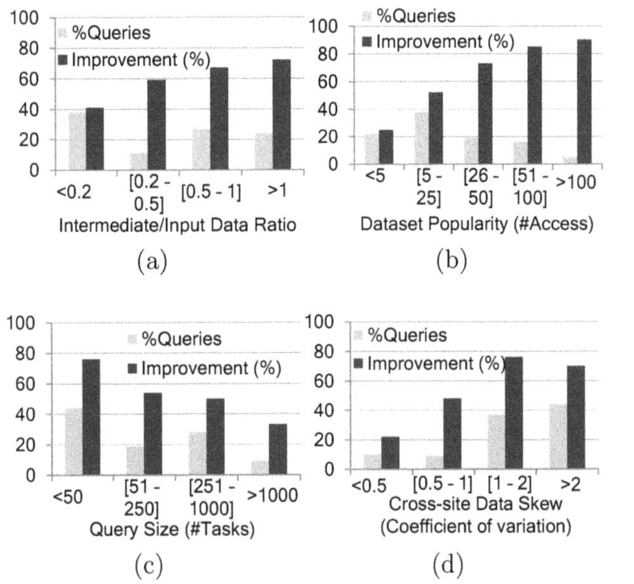

Figure 7: Iridium's **improvements (and % queries), bucketed by various query characteristics: (a) intermediate/input data ratio, (b) dataset access count, (c) query size (# tasks), and (d) cross-site skew in intermediate data.**

(*ii*) *Dataset popularity*: As described in §4.2, Iridium prefers moving datasets that are accessed by many queries because the costs of moving is amortized better; our cost and value in Pseudocode 1 aptly capture this aspect. This is consequently reflected in the gains (Figure 7b). Queries of oft-accessed datasets see 4× the gains compared to queries whose whose input datasets are less popular; the trend is also strictly monotonic.
(*iii*) *Query Size (in number of tasks)*: Somewhat surprisingly, our solution favors smaller queries (Figure 7c). We believe this is due to two reasons. First, their datasets happen to be oft-accessed as these queries are often interactive and exploratory, resulting in repeat accesses. Second, moving their datasets not only has a lower cost but also higher value than those with many tasks. This is due to the property of wave-based gains of parallel jobs [17]. Speeding up a wave of simultaneous parallel tasks, regardless of the *number of* parallel tasks (wave-width), results in the *same gain* in query response time.
(*iv*) *Cross-site skew of intermediate data*: Iridium's task placement, and to a lesser extent, data placement, is most effective when there is substantial skew across sites in the intermediate data of a query. This is a trend we observe in Figure 7d too where we bucket queries by the coefficient-of-variation of their intermediate data sizes across sites; smaller values of COV represent less skew. However, the lower COV buckets have < 20% of queries.
Bandwidth of {10, 50} Gb/s: By making the bandwidths relatively higher and less heterogeneous, there is lesser overlap of flows (flows finish faster due to higher bandwidths), and the baseline task placement is better off. While Iridium's gains continue to be substantial, an interesting aspect is that their values compared to the centralized baseline drops down to 56%, which is also roughly where the gains with the in-place baseline land. Higher and lesser heterogeneous bandwidths *slightly* soften the inefficiencies of the centralized baseline's data aggregation and in-place baseline's task placement, respectively.

Lag Metric	Vs. In-place	Vs. Centralized
Iridium (Avg.)	59%	74%
Iridium (Median)	56%	75%
Iridium (Earliest)	38%	42%
Iridium (Latest)	24%	40%
Oracle	66%	81%

Table 3: **Effectiveness of estimating query lag.** Iridium's **approach of using the average lag outperforms other options and crucially, has gains of ∼ 90% of an oracle that has full knowledge about query arrivals.**

6.4 Iridium's Design Decisions

In this section, we evaluate the design decisions made in Iridium's data placement heuristic in §4.
Query Lag: In calculating the score for datasets to rank them, we use the inverse of *average* lag of the queries accessing them (§4.2). We now compare using alternate metrics of query lag than the average—median, earliest and latest (Table 3). Using the median lag results in nearly similar results indicating that the arrival of queries is not long-tailed, but using the earliest or latest results in substantially poorer performance due to significant under- and over-estimation. They make Iridium either too aggressive and mis-prioritize datasets or too lethargic in its movement of datasets.

An encouraging aspect is the closeness of the gains using the average lag to an "oracle" (∼ 90%) that knows all the query arrivals and uses the exact query lags in its decisions. Our simple predictor that assumes that the arrival of queries henceforth will mimic the query arrivals thus far, in fact, works well in practice.
Dataset at a time: The final design decision we evaluate is to move only one dataset at a time out of a site (step b) in §4.2). We compare it to two alternatives. The first natural alternative is at the other extreme of having no cap. All the data movement flows sharing the link obtain their fair share of bandwidth. The other alternative is to allow many flows but allocate bandwidths between them in proportion to the "value" they are estimated to obtain.

Iridium outperforms both these alternatives whose gains compared to the baselines are 41% and 55% for the first, and 48% and 61% for the second alternative.

6.5 WAN Bandwidth Usage

Finally, we evaluate the functioning of Iridium's knob to budget WAN bandwidth usage (§4.4); our results so far were with the WAN budget knob $B = 1.3$. Figure 8 plots the results as B varies. "MinBW" is the scheme that optimizes for WAN bandwidth usage proposed in [53, 54]. While Iridium's bandwidth gains are lower than those of MinBW, they are still appreciable.

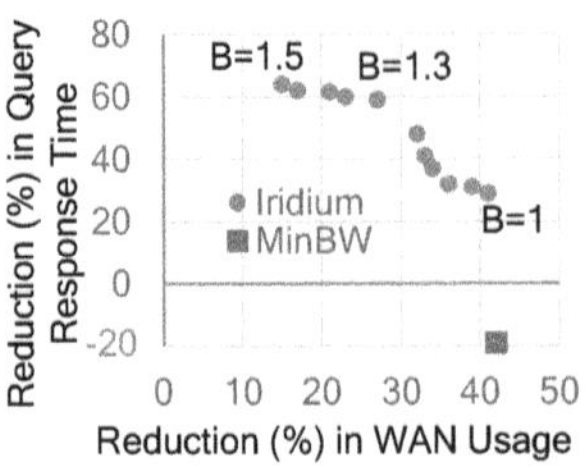

(a) In-place baseline

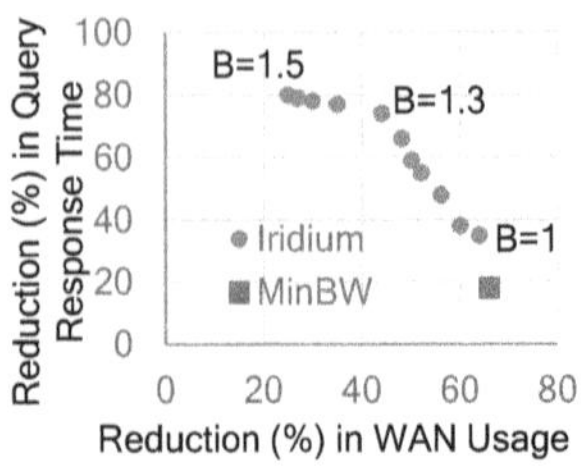

(b) Centralized baseline

Figure 8: **WAN Bandwidth Usage knob, B. MinBW is the scheme that optimizes for WAN bandwidth usage. Even with same WAN usage as MinBW ($B = 1$), Iridium's gains in query response time are significantly higher. MinBW slows down queries against the in-place baseline.**

With just a small value of $B = 1.3$ (i.e., 30% higher WAN usage than MinBW), Iridium's query speedups of 59% and 74% are $\sim$ 90% of those without any WAN usage budget (64% and 80%). This shows that Iridium smartly uses the bandwidth budget to balance gains in bandwidth usage with gains in query response time. This also shows that over long periods, arrival of "high-valued" and "low-valued" datasets overlap sufficiently in the workload. This is an important characteristic for our greedy budgeted scheme to function well.

Even for $B = 1$ (i.e., same WAN bandwidth usage as MinBW), Iridium's gains in query response time are appreciable. Crucially, MinBW results in an *increase* in query response time (negative gains) with the in-place baseline. While MinBW's query gains are positive compared to the centralized baseline, Iridium query gains are handily 2× better *for the same WAN usage.*

7. DISCUSSION AND LIMITATIONS

We now discuss some limitations of our solutions.

Compute and Storage Constraints: Our work did not consider limitations in compute and storage at the sites as we believed that to be reasonable for datacenters. However, as geo-distributed analytics moves to "edge" clusters, it is conceivable that compute and storage are also limitations. Under such a scenario, compute and storage capacity have to be comprehensively considered for task and data placement. A simple approach could do the following. To the task placement formulation in §3, we add the following constraint on every site i: $r_i \cdot D \leq C_i$, where D is the compute required by the stage and C_i is the capacity. In our data placement heuristic, when a site is running out of storage capacity, we will simply not consider moves into that site.

WAN Topologies: How do our heuristics change when the core network connecting the sites is not congestion-free? One could model pair-wise connectivity between sites, say B_{ij} as the available bandwidth from site i to site j. To optimize task placement, we formulate an LP to determine the r_i's, similar to §3.1. Given a distribution of intermediate data S_i, let $T_{ij}(r_j)$ be the time it takes to send data from site i to site j; $T_{ij}(r_j) = S_i r_j / B_{ij}$. The LP to compute z, the minimal shuffle duration, and the corresponding r_i's is as follows: $\min z$, s.t. $\sum_i r_i = 1$ and $\forall i \neq j : T_{ij}(r_j) \leq z$. Redesigning the data placement heuristic, however, is more challenging and requires careful consideration.

Local minima and greedy approach: As we alluded to in §4, the joint problem of data and task placement is non-convex. This means that the greedy approach adopted by our heuristic may get stuck in local minima. Overcoming them requires exploring potential options that could increase query response time temporarily before bringing it down. While our gains are significant even with the greedy solution, depending on the lag and bandwidth available for moving data, one could conceive a larger move with much more significant gain. Extending our heuristic to overcome local minima is part of future work.

8. RELATED WORK

1) Distributed databases: While big-data frameworks currently operate only within a single cluster, work on distributed databases has been a popular topic [22, 27]; see surveys in [40, 44]. Google Spanner [28] is an instance of a distributed database deployed at scale. Our problem is simpler because we do not have to deal with concurrency and deadlocks; data processing systems are typically *append-only.* This gives us more freedom to move data across sites. JetStream [46], a stream processing system for OLAP cubes, uses data aggregation and adaptive filtering to support data analytics. However, unlike Iridium, JetStream does not support arbitrary SQL queries and does not optimize data and task placement. Recent work [53, 54] optimize for WAN bandwidth usage across sites. As we showed, this can lead to poor query response times. In contrast, Iridium optimizes for query response time *and* WAN usage using a budget (§4.4 and §6.5).

2) Reducing data analytics responses: There is a large body of work on improving query response time in data parallel systems [20, 23, 29]. These systems improve data locality of input tasks and fairness [37, 58], and minimize outliers in task execution [16, 19, 61]. While these systems optimize task placement, they do not consider network contentions (which matter less within a DC), and they do not move data around to relieve potential network bottlenecks [33]. Further, Iridium is complementary to approximation techniques [15, 18].

3) Optimizing communication patterns: Flow schedulers like D3 [55], PDQ [35], DeTail [62], and D2TCP [51] aim to improve flow completion times or guarantee deadlines. However, they operate inside a single DC and do not consider complex communication patterns. Orchestra [25], Varys [26], and Baraat [30] are network flow schedulers that optimize for completion time of *coflows,* i.e., collections of flows. However, because the endpoints of the coflows are fixed (e.g., source and destination specified by location of input data and tasks), these cannot schedule around network bottlenecks.

4) Scheduling on the WAN: There has been much work on optimizing WAN transfers including tuning ECMP weights [32] and adapting allocations across pre-established tunnels [31, 39]. Also, both Google [38] and Microsoft [36] recently published details on their production WAN networks. All this work improves the efficiency of the WAN by scheduling network flows *inside the WAN*. Instead, we optimize end-to-end application performance, i.e., reducing response time of big-data jobs, by placing data and tasks to explicitly reduce load on congested WAN links. Other works optimize data placement to improve WAN latencies and utilization [41, 50]. Iridium optimizes much more complex communication patterns, such as shuffles, that require coordination of a large number of flows across many sites. Moreover, most of the above could be used to improve the individual WAN transfers in Iridium.

9. CONCLUSION

Cloud organizations are deploying datacenters and edge clusters worldwide. The services deployed at these sites, first-party and third-party, produce large quantities of data continuously. Results from analyzing these geo-distributed data is used by real-time systems and data analysts. We develop Iridium, a system that focuses on minimizing response times of geo-distributed analytics queries. Our techniques focus on data transfers in these queries that happen across the WAN. By carefully considering the WAN's heterogeneous link bandwidths in the placement of data as well as tasks of queries, we improve query response times in workloads derived from analytics clusters of Bing Edge, Facebook and Conviva by $3\times - 19\times$. However, we would like to point out that our approach is greedy in nature (not optimal) and we offer only a partial solution to optimizing complex DAGs of tasks, both of which we aim to improve.

Acknowledgments

We would like to thank Kaifei Chen, Radhika Mittal and Shivaram Venkataraman for their feedback on the draft. We also appreciate the comments from our shepherd Mohammad Alizadeh and the anonymous reviewers. This work was partially supported by NSF grants CNS-1302041, CNS-1330308 and CNS-1345249.

References

[1] Amazon EC2 Instance Types. http://aws.amazon.com/ec2/instance-types/.

[2] Amazon Web Services. http://aws.amazon.com/about-aws/global-infrastructure/.

[3] Apache Calcite. http://optiq.incubator.apache.org/.

[4] Big Data Benchmark. https://amplab.cs.berkeley.edu/benchmark/.

[5] EC2 Pricing. http://aws.amazon.com/ec2/pricing/.

[6] Google Datacenter Locations. http://www.google.com/about/datacenters/inside/locations/.

[7] Gurobi Optimization. http://www.gurobi.com/.

[8] Hadoop Distributed File System. http://hadoop.apache.org/docs/r1.2.1/hdfs_design.html.

[9] How Map and Reduce operations are actually carried out. http://wiki.apache.org/hadoop/HadoopMapReduce.

[10] Linux Traffic Control. http://lartc.org/manpages/tc.txt.

[11] Microsoft Datacenters. http://www.microsoft.com/en-us/server-cloud/cloud-os/global-datacenters.aspx.

[12] TPC Decision Support Benchmark. http://www.tpc.org/tpcds/.

[13] Measuring Internet Congestion: A preliminary report. https://ipp.mit.edu/sites/default/files/documents/Congestion-handout-final.pdf, 2014.

[14] S. Agarwal, S. Kandula, N. Bruno, M.-C. Wu, I. Stoica, and J. Zhou. Re-optimizing Data-Parallel Computing. In *USENIX NSDI*, 2012.

[15] S. Agarwal, B. Mozafari, A. Panda, M. H., S. Madden, and I. Stoica. BlinkDB: Queries with Bounded Errors and Bounded Response Times on Very Large Data. In *ACM EuroSys*, 2013.

[16] G. Ananthanarayanan, A. Ghodsi, S. Shenker, and I. Stoica. Effective Straggler Mitigation: Attack of the Clones. In *USENIX NSDI*, 2013.

[17] G. Ananthanarayanan, A. Ghodsi, A. Wang, D. Borthakur, S. Kandula, S. Shenker, and I. Stoica. PACMan: Coordinated memory caching for parallel jobs. In *USENIX NSDI*, 2012.

[18] G. Ananthanarayanan, M. C.-C. Hung, X. Ren, I. Stoica, A. Wierman, and M. Yu. GRASS: Trimming Stragglers in Approximation Analytics. USENIX NSDI, 2014.

[19] G. Ananthanarayanan, S. Kandula, A. Greenberg, I. Stoica, Y. Lu, B. Saha, and E. Harris. Reining in the Outliers in Map-Reduce Clusters using Mantri. In *USENIX OSDI*, 2010.

[20] Apache Hadoop NextGen MapReduce (YARN). Retrieved 9/24/2013, URL: http://hadoop.apache.org/docs/current/hadoop-yarn/hadoop-yarn-site/YARN.html.

[21] A. Balachandran, V. Sekar, A. Akella, S. Seshan, I. Stoica, and H. Zhang. Developing a Predictive Model of Quality of Experience for Internet Video. In *ACM SIGCOMM*, 2013.

[22] P. A. Bernstein, N. Goodman, E. Wong, C. L. Reeve, and J. B. Rothnie, Jr. Query Processing in a System for Distributed Databases (SDD-1). *ACM Transactions on Database Systems*, 1981.

[23] E. Boutin, J. Ekanayake, W. Lin, B. Shi, J. Zhou, Z. Qian, M. Wu, and L. Zhou. Apollo: Scalable and Coordinated Scheduling for Cloud-Scale Computing. In *USENIX OSDI*, 2014.

[24] M. Calder, X. Fan, Z. Hu, E. Katz-Bassett, J. Heidemann, and R. Govindan. Mapping the Expansion of Google's Serving Infrastructure. In *ACM IMC*, 2013.

[25] M. Chowdhury, M. Zaharia, J. Ma, M. I. Jordan, and I. Stoica. Managing Data Transfers in Computer Clusters with Orchestra. In *ACM SIGCOMM*, 2011.

[26] M. Chowdhury, Y. Zhong, and I. Stoica. Efficient Coflow Scheduling with Varys. In *ACM SIGCOMM*, 2013.

[27] W. W. Chu and P. Hurley. Optimal Query Processing for Distributed Database Systems. *IEEE Transactions on Computers*, 1982.
[28] J. C. Corbett, J. Dean, M. Epstein, A. Fikes, C. Frost, J. J. Furman, S. Ghemawat, A. Gubarev, C. Heiser, P. Hochschild, W. Hsieh, S. Kanthak, E. Kogan, H. Li, A. Lloyd, S. Melnik, D. Mwaura, D. Nagle, S. Quinlan, R. Rao, L. Rolig, Y. Saito, M. Szymaniak, C. Taylor, R. Wang, and D. Woodford. Spanner: Google's Globally-distributed Database. In *USENIX OSDI*, 2012.
[29] J. Dean and S. Ghemawat. MapReduce: Simplified Data Processing on Large Clusters. *Communications of the ACM*, 2008.
[30] F. R. Dogar, T. Karagiannis, H. Ballani, and A. Rowstron. Decentralized Task-aware Scheduling for Data Center Networks. In *ACM SIGCOMM*, 2014.
[31] A. Elwalid, C. Jin, S. Low, and I. Widjaja. MATE: Multipath Adaptive Traffic Engineering. *Computer Networks*, 2002.
[32] B. Fortz, J. Rexford, and M. Thorup. Traffic Engineering with Traditional IP Routing Protocols. *Communications Magazine, IEEE*, 2002.
[33] R. Grandl, G. Ananthanarayanan, S. Kandula, S. Rao, and A. Akella. Multi-Resource Packing for Cluster Schedulers. In *ACM SIGCOMM*, 2014.
[34] A. a. Gupta *et al.* Mesa: Geo-Replicated, Near Real-Time, Scalable Data Warehousing. In *VLDB*, 2014.
[35] C.-Y. Hong, M. Caesar, and B. Godfrey. Finishing flows quickly with preemptive scheduling. *ACM SIGCOMM*, 2012.
[36] C.-Y. Hong, S. Kandula, R. Mahajan, M. Zhang, V. Gill, M. Nanduri, and R. Wattenhofer. Achieving High Utilization with Software-Driven WAN. In *ACM SIGCOMM*, 2013.
[37] M. Isard, V. Prabhakaran, J. Currey, U. Wieder, K. Talwar, and A. Goldberg. Quincy: Fair Scheduling for Distributed Computing Clusters. In *ACM SOSP*, 2009.
[38] S. Jain, A. Kumar, S. Mandal, J. Ong, L. Poutievski, A. Singh, S. Venkata, J. Wanderer, J. Zhou, M. Zhu, J. Zolla, U. Hölzle, S. Stuart, and A. Vahdat. B4: Experience with a Globally-deployed Software Defined Wan. *ACM SIGCOMM*, 2013.
[39] S. Kandula, D. Katabi, B. Davie, and A. Charny. Walking the Tightrope: Responsive Yet Stable Traffic Engineering. *ACM SIGCOMM*, 2005.
[40] D. Kossmann. The State of the Art in Distributed Query Processing. *ACM Computer Survey*, 2000.
[41] N. Laoutaris, M. Sirivianos, X. Yang, and P. Rodriguez. Inter-datacenter Bulk Transfers with Netstitcher. *ACM SIGCOMM*, 2011.
[42] P. Mohan, A. Thakurta, E. Shi, D. Song, and D. Culler. GUPT: Privacy Preserving Data Analysis Made Easy. In *ACM SIGMOD*, 2012.
[43] E. Nygren, R. Sitaraman, and J. Sun. The Akamai Network: A Platform for High-Performance Internet Applications. In *ACM SIGOPS OSR*, 2010.
[44] M. T. Ozsu and P. Valduriez. *Principles of Distributed Database Systems.* 2011.
[45] A. Pavlo, E. Paulson, A. Rasin, d. Abadi, Daniel an dDeWitt, S. Madden, and M. Stonebraker. A Comparison of Approaches to Large-Scale Data Analysis. In *ACM SIGMOD*, 2009.
[46] A. Rabkin, M. Arye, S. Sen, V. Pai, and M. Freedman. Aggregation and Degradation in JetStream: Streaming Analytics in the Wide Area. In *USENIX NSDI*, 2014.
[47] R. Sitaraman, M. Kasbekar, W. Lichtenstein, and M. Jain. Overlay Networks: An Akamai Perspective. In *Advanced Content Delivery, Streaming, and Cloud Services*, 2014.
[48] S. Sundaresan, W. d. Donato, N. Feamster, R. Teixeira, S. Crawford, and A. Pescape. Broadband Internet Performance: A View From the Gateway. In *ACM SIGCOMM*, 2011.
[49] A. Thusoo, J. Sarma, N. Jain, Z. Shao, P. Chakka, N. Zhang, S. Antony, H. Liu, and R. Murthy. Hive - A Petabyte Scale Data Warehouse using Hadoop. In *ICDE*, 2010.
[50] S. Traverso, K. Huguenin, I. Trestian, V. Erramilli, N. Laoutaris, and K. Papagiannaki. TailGate: Handling Long-tail Content with a Little Help from Friends. In *WWW*, 2012.
[51] B. Vamanan, J. Hasan, and T. N. Vijaykumar. Deadline-Aware Datacenter TCP (D2TCP). In *Proceedings of the ACM SIGCOMM*, 2012.
[52] S. Venkataraman, A. Panda, G. Ananthanarayanan, M. Franklin, and I. Stoica. The Power of Choice in Data-Aware Cluster Scheduling. In *USENIX OSDI*, 2014.
[53] A. Vulimiri, C. Curino, B. Godfrey, T. Jungblut, J. Padhye, and G. Varghese. Global Analytics in the Face of Bandwidth and Regulatory Constraints. In *USENIX NSDI*, 2015.
[54] A. Vulimiri, C. Curino, B. Godfrey, K. Karanasos, and G. Varghese. WANalytics: Analytics for a Geo-distributed Data-intensive World. In *CIDR*, 2015.
[55] C. Wilson, H. Ballani, T. Karagiannis, and A. Rowtron. Better Never Than Late: Meeting Deadlines in Datacenter Networks. *ACM SIGCOMM*, 2011.
[56] Z. Wu, M. Butkiewicz, D. Perkins, E. Katz-Bassett, and H. Madhyastha. SPANStore: Cost-effective Geo-replicated Storage Spanning Multiple Cloud Services. In *ACM SOSP*, 2013.
[57] Y. Yu, P. K. Gunda, and M. Isard. Distributed Aggregation for Data-Parallel Computing: Interfaces and Implementations. In *ACM SOSP*, 2009.
[58] M. Zaharia, D. Borthakur, J. Sen Sarma, K. Elmeleegy, S. Shenker, and I. Stoica. Delay scheduling: a simple technique for achieving locality and fairness in cluster scheduling. In *ACM EuroSys*, 2010.
[59] M. Zaharia, M. Chowdhury, M. Franklin, S. Shenker, and I. Stoica. Spark: Cluster Computing with Working Sets. In *USENIX HotCloud*, 2010.
[60] M. Zaharia, T. Das, H. Li, T. Hunter, S. Shenker, and I. Stoica. Discretized Streams: Fault-Tolerant Streaming Computation at Scale. In *ACM SOSP*, 2013.
[61] M. Zaharia, A. Konwinski, A. Joseph, R. Katz, and I. Stoica. Improving MapReduce performance in heterogeneous environments. In *USENIX OSDI*, 2008.
[62] D. Zats, T. Das, P. Mohan, D. Borthakur, and R. Katz. DeTail: Reducing the Flow Completion Time Tail in Datacenter Networks. *ACM SIGCOMM*, 2012.

Silo: Predictable Message Latency in the Cloud

Keon Jang
Intel Labs
Santa Clara, CA

Justine Sherry*
UC Berkeley
Berkeley, CA

Hitesh Ballani
Microsoft Research
Cambridge, UK

Toby Moncaster*
University of Cambridge
Cambridge, UK

ABSTRACT

Many cloud applications can benefit from guaranteed latency for their network messages, however providing such predictability is hard, especially in multi-tenant datacenters. We identify three key requirements for such predictability: guaranteed network bandwidth, guaranteed packet delay and guaranteed burst allowance. We present Silo, a system that offers these guarantees in multi-tenant datacenters. Silo leverages the tight coupling between bandwidth and delay: controlling tenant bandwidth leads to deterministic bounds on network queuing delay. Silo builds upon network calculus to place tenant VMs with competing requirements such that they can coexist. A novel hypervisor-based policing mechanism achieves packet pacing at sub-microsecond granularity, ensuring tenants do not exceed their allowances. We have implemented a Silo prototype comprising a VM placement manager and a Windows filter driver. Silo does not require any changes to applications, guest OSes or network switches. We show that Silo can ensure predictable message latency for cloud applications while imposing low overhead.

CCS Concepts

•Networks → Data center networks; Cloud computing;

Keywords

Network QoS; Latency SLA; Guaranteed Latency; Traffic Pacing; Network Calculus

1. INTRODUCTION

Many cloud applications are distributed in nature; they comprise services that communicate across the network to generate a response. Often, the slowest service dictates user perceived performance [1,2]. To achieve predictable performance, such applications need guaranteed latency for network messages. However, the consequent network requirements vary with the application. For example, real-time analytics [3,4] and Online Data-Intensive (OLDI) applications like web search and online retail [1,2] generate short messages that are sensitive to *both* packet delay and available network bandwidth. For large message applications like data-parallel jobs [5–7], message latency depends only on network bandwidth.

However, today's public cloud platforms are agnostic to these network demands. Studies of major cloud providers have found that both the bandwidth and packet delay across their network can vary by an order of magnitude [8–12]. As we show in §2.1, this can lead to significant variability in application performance, particularly at the tail. Such performance variability is a key barrier to cloud adoption [13], especially for OLDI applications. For example, moving Netflix to Amazon EC2 required re-architecting their whole system since "AWS networking has more variable latency" [14]. It also complicates application design as programmers are forced to use ad-hoc mitigation techniques [15,16].

We thus try to answer the question: What minimum set of network knobs will allow each tenant to *independently* determine the maximum latency for messages between its virtual machines (VMs)? We identify three key requirements to achieve this, (i) guaranteed bandwidth; (ii) guaranteed packet delay; and (iii) guaranteed burst allowance so that applications can send multi-packet bursts at a higher rate. Of course, some applications may only need some or even none of these guarantees.

These network requirements pose a few challenges. Guaranteeing packet delay is particularly difficult because delay is an additive end-to-end property. We focus on network delay, and argue that in datacenters, queuing is the biggest contributor to it (and its variability). Bounding queuing delay is hard because it requires precise control over how independent flows interact with each other at all network switches along their paths. A further challenge is that guaranteed packet delay is at odds with the guaranteed burst requirement. Allowing some applications to send traffic bursts can increase delay experienced by others; synchronized bursts can even cause packet loss.

*Work done during internship at Microsoft Research

SIGCOMM '15, August 17 - 21, 2015, London, United Kingdom

ISBN 978-1-4503-3542-3/15/08...$15.00
DOI: http://dx.doi.org/10.1145/2785956.2787479

Unfortunately, none of the existing work on cloud network performance meets all three requirements (§7). Guaranteeing tenant bandwidth alone does not cater to bursty applications with small messages [17–21]. Solutions for low network latency [15,22,23] or flow deadlines [24–26] cannot guarantee message latency in multi-tenant settings.

We present Silo, a system that allows datacenter operators to give tenants guaranteed bandwidth, delay and burst allowances for traffic between their VMs. The key insight behind Silo's design is that end-to-end packet delay can be bounded through fine-grained rate control at end hosts. Cruz's pioneering work [27,28] described a calculus for computing delay bounds for multi-hop networks while Parekh and Gallagher [29,30] developed tighter bounds when switches perform weighted fair queuing.

The tight coupling between guaranteed bandwidth and delay also underlies a lot of research on Internet QoS [31]. However, applying it to cloud settings poses new challenges and opportunities. First, unlike Internet QoS, cloud providers have the added flexibility of controlling the placement of traffic sources. Second, instead of guaranteeing per-flow bandwidth, today's cloud pricing model dictates per-tenant guarantees. Finally, the delay bound analysis relies on strict enforcement of burst and bandwidth limits which is hard to achieve at high link rates. For example, enforcing a 9 Gbps rate limit, on a packet-by-packet basis, for a source sending 1.5KB packets on a 10 Gbps link requires an inter-packet spacing of just $133ns$.

Silo's two components, a VM placement manager and a hypervisor-based packet pacer, address these challenges. Overall, this paper makes the following contributions:

- We identify the network guarantees necessary for predictable message latency, and present the design, implementation and evaluation of Silo.
- We present a novel admission control and VM placement algorithm that uses network calculus to efficiently map tenants' multi-dimensional network guarantees to two simple constraints regarding switch queues.
- We design a software packet pacer for fine-grained rate limiting of VM traffic. To achieve sub-microsecond packet spacing while imposing low CPU overhead, the pacer uses a novel technique called Paced IO Batching that couples IO batching with "void" packets—dummy packets that are forwarded by the NIC but dropped by the first hop switch. This allows the pacer to space out actual data packets without NIC support.

An important feature of Silo's design is ease of deployment. It does not require changes to network switches, NICs, tenant applications or guest OSes. Silo can also leverage switch-based prioritization to accommodate best effort tenants that do not need any guarantees. We have implemented a Silo prototype comprising a VM placement manager and a Windows Hyper-V kernel driver for packet pacing. The network driver is able to saturate 10Gbps links with low CPU overhead while achieving a minimum packet spacing of $68ns$. Through testbed experiments, we show that Silo ensures low and predictable message latency for memcached [32] without hurting bandwidth hungry workloads (§6.1). Packet-level simulations show that Silo improves message latency by 22× at the 99th percentile (and 2.5× at the 95th) as compared to DCTCP [15] and HULL [22] (§6.2).

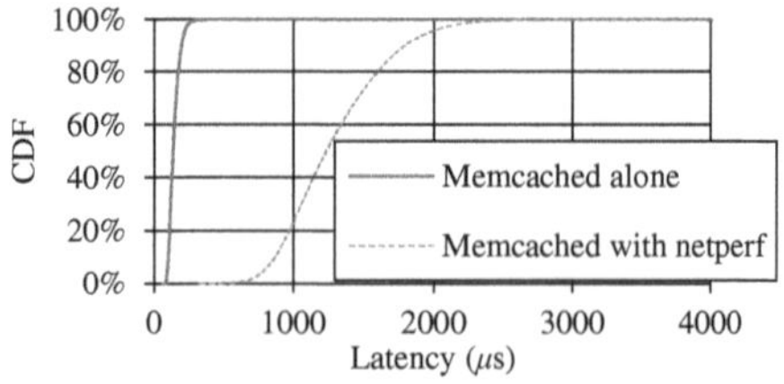

Figure 1: CDF of memcached request latency with and without competing traffic.

A drawback of Silo is its impact on network utilization. Giving delay *and* bandwidth guarantees to tenants can result in up to 11% reduction in network utilization and 4% fewer accepted tenants compared to giving only bandwidth guarantees. Surprisingly, we find that Silo can actually improve both the network and overall cloud utilization than when tenants get no guarantees at all (§6.3).

2. NETWORK REQUIREMENTS

We define a message as a unit of application data, comprising one or more packets, exchanged across the network.[1] Throughout the paper, we use message "latency" as the time to transfer a complete message and "delay" for the packet delay. In this section, we show that network contention can hurt application performance significantly. We also argue why predictable message latency is important for cloud applications and derive the consequent network requirements.

2.1 Motivation

Many recent studies of the internal network in cloud datacenters show that the network bandwidth and packet delay between VMs can vary significantly [8–11]. In recent work, Mogul et al. [12] find that, across two cloud providers, the 99.9^{th} percentile packet delay is typically an order of magnitude more than the median.

To demonstrate the impact of such network-level variability on application performance, we ran a simple experiment with memcached, a popular in-memory key-value store [33]. We use a testbed with five servers, each running six VMs (more details in §6.1). There are two tenants, A and B, each with three VMs per server. Tenant A runs a memcached server on one VM, and clients on all other VMs. Its workload mimics Facebook's ETC workload, and represents general cache usage of multiple cloud applications [33]. Tenant B generates all-to-all TCP traffic using netperf, modeling the shuffle phase of a bandwidth intensive application like MapReduce.

[1]We use the term "message" instead of the more commonly used "flow" since cloud applications often multiplex many messages onto a single flow (i.e. transport connection).

Figure 1 shows the CDF for the latency of Tenant A's memcached requests with and without Tenant B. We find that request latency increases significantly due to network contention; at 99th percentile, it is $270\mu s$ for memcached alone whereas it is $2.3ms$ with interfering traffic. At 99.9^{th} percentile, it suffers from timeouts and latency spikes to $217ms$. Similarly, QJUMP [34] shows that network contention can hurt typical cloud workloads; it is shown to worsen tail performance by 50× for clock synchronization using PTPd and 3× for Naiad, an iterative data-flow application.

2.2 Importance of Predictable Message Latency

For some cloud applications, poor performance directly hurts revenue. More broadly, many cloud applications need to meet service-level latency objectives (SLOs) [12,16]. For example, OLDI applications need to serve end user requests within a time budget, typically 200-300ms [15]. Similarly, users want their data analytics jobs finished in a timely fashion which, given the pay-per-hour cloud pricing model, also ensures predictable job cost [13,35].

To achieve such predictable performance, cloud applications require *predictable message latency*. This is a consequence of two features common to many applications: they rely on distributed execution and messaging latency is a significant fraction of the latency for application tasks. For example, in Facebook's Hadoop cluster [36], 33% of job completion time is due to messaging.

By contrast, to cope with variable network performance in today's cloud platforms, designers resort to ad-hoc techniques like introducing artificial jitter when sending parallel messages [15], replicating request messages and choosing the fastest response [16], etc. Unpredictable network performance even restricts many applications to dedicated clusters. Providing message latency guarantees, apart from helping such applications migrate to the cloud, can obviate the need for band-aid solutions [34]. It can even simplify application logic — if a web-search task that needs to respond in 20ms knows that the response latency is at most 4ms, it can take 16ms to process the query.

2.3 Deconstructing message latency

An open question is the kind of network guarantees that cloud providers can offer and that tenants will benefit from— message latency guarantees, tail latency SLOs, or lower-level guarantees (like bandwidth and packet delay)? We argue that the latter option is most suitable for Infrastructure-as-a-Service (IaaS) cloud providers, and as explained below, can be used by tenants to determine latency bounds for their messages.

The latency for a message comprises the time to transmit its packets into the network and the time for the last packet to propagate to the destination. This simple model excludes end host stack delay. Thus,

$$\text{Msg. Latency} \approx \text{Transmission delay} + \text{In-network delay}$$

$$\approx \frac{\text{Message size}}{\text{Network bandwidth}} + \text{In-network delay} \quad (1)$$

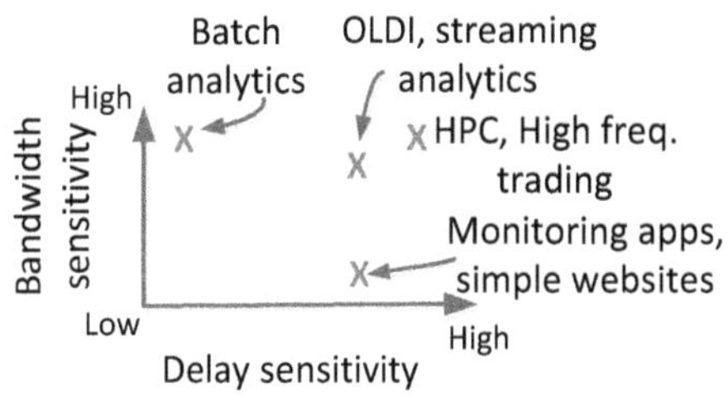

Figure 2: Diverse network demands of cloud apps.

Burst \ Bandwidth	B	$1.4B$	$1.8B$	$2.2B$	$2.6B$	$3B$
M	99	77	55	45	38	33
$3M$	99	22	8	3.6	1.9	1.1
$5M$	99	6.1	0.9	0.2	0.06	0.02
$7M$	99	1.6	0.09	0.01	0	0
$9M$	98	0.4	0.01	0	0	0

Table 1: Percentage of messages whose latency exceeds the guarantee. Messages (size M) have Poisson arrivals and an average bandwidth requirement of B.

For large messages, the latency is dominated by the transmission delay component. This applies to data-parallel applications [5,6] which are thus termed "bandwidth-sensitive". By contrast, applications that send sporadic single packet messages are "delay-sensitive" as the in-network delay component dominates. Examples include monitoring services and simple web services. Between these two extremes are applications that mostly generate small messages but at a high rate. For example, the network traffic for a typical OLDI application like web search is dominated by 1.6–50KB messages [15,24]. For such applications, both components of equation 1 are significant, i.e. the message latency depends *both* on network bandwidth and delay.

Figure 2 summarizes these arguments; some cloud applications are sensitive to available bandwidth, some are sensitive to in-network delay, some to both. Thus, to achieve guaranteed message latency, a general cloud application requires:

R1. *Guaranteed network bandwidth.* This bounds the transmission delay component of message latency.

R2. *Guaranteed packet delay.* This bounds the in-network delay component of message latency.

2.3.1 Burstiness requirement

Requirements R1 and R2, together, are necessary and sufficient to ensure guaranteed message latency. However, this necessitates that an application's bandwidth guarantee match it maximum consumption. This will lead to significant network under-utilization since many cloud applications have bursty workloads, i.e. their maximum bandwidth requirement significantly exceeds the average bandwidth.

To understand the interplay between the amount of guaranteed bandwidth and message latency, we experiment with a synthetic application that generates messages, with Poisson arrivals, between two VMs. Assuming the average bandwidth required is B, the latency for a message of size M

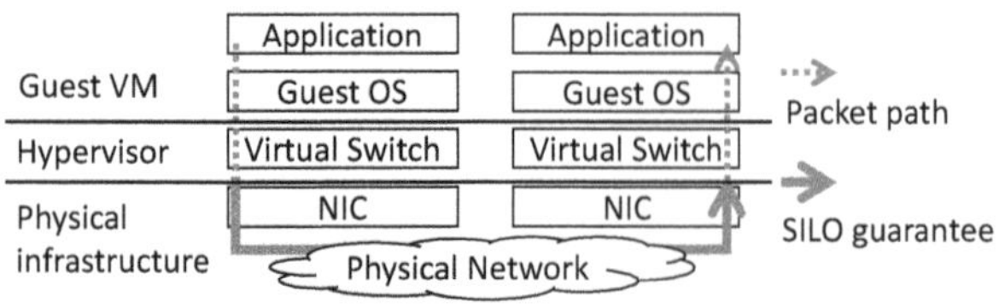

Figure 3: Silo's delay guarantee is from the NIC at the sender to the NIC at the receiver.

should be less than $\frac{M}{B} + d$, where d is the packet delay guarantee (see eq. 1). The first row in Table 1 shows that when the application is guaranteed its average bandwidth requirement, the latency for 99% of messages *exceeds* their guarantee. This is due to exponential inter-arrival times between messages. Increasing the bandwidth guarantee, by itself, is insufficient; even when the guarantee is 3× the average bandwidth, 33% messages are late.

To accommodate such workload burstiness, we propose a burst allowance for VMs. Specifically, a VM that has not been using its guaranteed bandwidth in the past is allowed to send a few messages at a higher rate. Table 1 shows that as we increase both the sending VM's burst allowance and its bandwidth guarantee, the percentage of late messages drops sharply; with a burst of 7 messages and 1.8x the average bandwidth, only 0.09% messages are late. Thus, the third requirement for guaranteed message latency is–

R3. *Guaranteed burst allowance.* Bursty workload applications need to be able to send short traffic bursts.

3. SCOPE AND DESIGN INSIGHTS

Of the three network requirements, guaranteeing packet delay is particularly challenging because all components of the end-to-end path add delay. Below, we define the scope of our delay guarantees and provide intuition regarding the feasibility of guaranteeing packet delay.

Scope. In virtualized datacenters, the end-to-end path of packets comprises many layers. Figure 3 shows this path; at the sender, packets go through the guest OS network stack, the hypervisor and the NIC before being sent onto the wire. Broadly, a packet's total delay comprises two components: end-host delay (shown with dashed line), and network delay (shown with solid line). The latter component includes delay at the NIC and at network switches. Many proposals reduce end-host delay [37,38]. Since we target IaaS cloud settings where tenants can deploy arbitrary OSes, we restrict our focus to the part of the end-to-end path controlled by the cloud provider. Thus, we guarantee network delay, i.e. the delay from the source NIC to the destination NIC.

3.1 Guaranteeing network delay

Network delay comprises the propagation, forwarding and queuing delay across NICs and the network. In datacenters, physical links are short and have high capacity, so the propagation and forwarding delay is negligible, and queuing delay dominates (even for full bisection networks [39,40]).

We build on the observation that *rate limiting the senders in a network ensures a deterministic upper bound for network queuing* [28,30,41]. For example, consider n flows across at a network link. Each flow is guaranteed some bandwidth and is allowed to burst one packet at a time. Assuming the total bandwidth guaranteed across all flows is less than the link capacity, the maximum queue build up at the link is n packets. While Silo shares this insight with Internet QoS architectures like IntServ [31], it further tackles two new challenges posed by cloud settings.

1. Tenant-level guarantees and VM placement. Instead of flow-level guarantees, Silo gives tenants their own private network with tenant-level guarantees. Furthermore, Silo uses the flexibility of VM placement to maximize the number of tenants that can be accommodated. To this end, we extend Cruz's network calculus techniques to derive delay bounds based on tenant-level bandwidth guarantees, and then use them to drive the placement of VMs (§4.2).

2. Fine-grained pacing. Our queuing delay analysis assumes that VM traffic is in strict conformance to its guarantees. Thus, end hosts need to control the rate and burstiness of their traffic at a packet-level timescale. Today's software pacers are typically inaccurate and do not scale with number of flows [42]. The problem is exacerbated by the fact that, to achieve good forwarding performance, network stacks rely on aggressive batching of packets sent to the NIC. This further contravenes the fine-grained pacing requirement.

The obvious solution of pacing at the NIC itself is impractical because NICs only offer small number of rate limited queues, and flows that share the same hardware queue can suffer from head of line blocking. SENIC proposes a hardware and software hybrid approach to achieve scalable and accurate pacing [42]. Instead, we devise a software-only pacing mechanism that uses dummy or "void" packets to precisely control packet gap while retaining I/O batching to handle traffic at 10 Gbps (§4.3.1).

4. DESIGN

Silo couples virtual machines (VMs) with guarantees for network bandwidth, packet delay and burst allowance. It relies on two components: a *VM placement manager* with visibility of the datacenter topology and tenants' guarantees, and a *packet pacer* in the hypervisor at each server. The placement manager admits tenants and places their VMs across the datacenter such that their guarantees can be met (§4.2), and configures the pacers. The pacers coordinate with each other and dynamically determine the rate limit for individual VMs, thus ensuring that VM traffic conforms to their bandwidth and burst allowance (§4.3).

4.1 Silo's network guarantees

With Silo, tenants can imagine their VMs as being connected by a private "virtual" network, as shown in Figure 4. A virtual link of capacity B and propagation delay $\frac{d}{2}$ connects each VM to a virtual switch. Each VM's traffic is shaped by a virtual token bucket with average bandwidth B and size S. The network capabilities of a VM are thus captured using three parameters, $\{B, S, d\}$:

(i). a VM can send and receive traffic at a maximum rate of B Mbps,

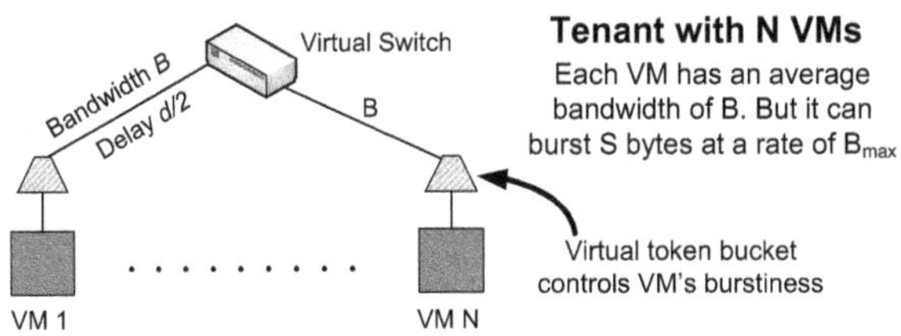

Figure 4: A tenant's virtual network.

(ii). a VM that has under-utilized its bandwidth guarantee is allowed to send a burst of at most S bytes,

(iii). a bandwidth-compliant packet is guaranteed to be delivered, from the sending to receiving NIC, within d μs.

Just as today's cloud providers offer a few classes of VMs (small, medium, etc.), we expect providers will offer a few classes of network guarantees. Tools like Cicada [43] allow tenants to automatically determine their bandwidth guarantees. Inferring delay requirements automatically may be feasible too [12]. Some tenants may only need bandwidth guarantees; for example, a tenant running a data-analytics job. In §4.4, we show that Silo can leverage switch-based prioritization to accommodate tenants without *any* network guarantees and ensure they co-exist with tenants with guarantees.

Guarantee semantics. We have chosen our guarantees to make them useful for tenants yet practical for providers. As with past proposals [18,19,44,45], a VM's bandwidth guarantee follows the *hose model*, i.e. the bandwidth for a flow is limited by the guarantee of *both* the sender and receiver VM. So if a tenant's VMs are guaranteed bandwidth B, and N VMs send traffic to the same destination VM, each sender would achieve a bandwidth of $\frac{B}{N}$ (since the destination VM becomes the bottleneck). By contrast, a VM's burst guarantee is not limited by the destination; all N VMs are allowed to send a simultaneous burst to the same destination. This is motivated by the fact that OLDI-like applications that need to burst often employ a partition aggregate workflow that results in all-to-one traffic pattern [15].

However, allowing VMs to send traffic bursts can result in high and variable packet delay for VMs of other tenants. Synchronized bursts can even overflow switch buffers and cause packet loss. While Silo carefully places tenants VMs to ensure switch buffers can absorb the bursts, we also control the maximum bandwidth (B_{max}) at which a burst is sent. This is a static bandwidth limit that is exposed to the tenant.

Calculating latency guarantee. Silo's network guarantees allow tenants to determine their maximum message latency. Consider a VM, that has not used up its burst allowance sending a message of size M ($\leq S$) bytes. The message is guaranteed to be delivered to its destination in less than $(\frac{M}{B_{max}} + d)$ μs. If $M > S$, message latency is less than $(\frac{S}{B_{max}} + \frac{M-S}{B} + d)$.

4.2 VM Placement

Given a tenant request, Silo's placement manager performs admission control, and places its VMs at servers in the datacenter such their network guarantees can be met. If the guarantees cannot be met, the request is rejected.

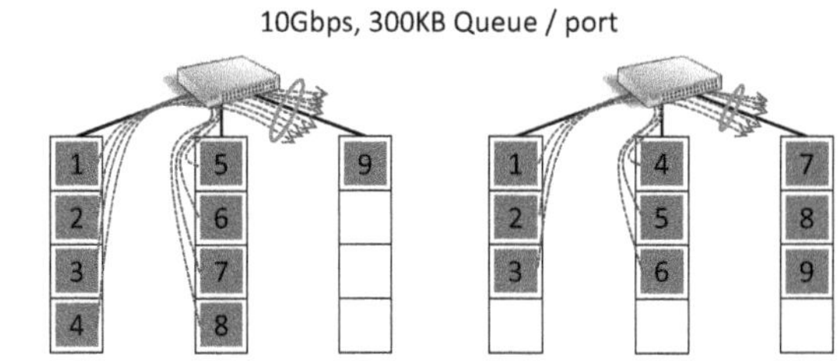

(a) Bandwidth-aware placement; up to 400KB queuing → **overflow** (b) Silo's VM placement limited to 300KB queuing

Figure 5: Example showing bandwidth-aware placement is insufficient. The figure shows two possible VM placements for a tenant requiring nine VMs with 1 Gbps bandwidth, 1 ms delay and 100 KB burst allowance.

4.2.1 Placement overview

Placement of VMs in today's datacenters typically focusses on non-network resources like CPU cores and memory. Recent efforts propose algorithms to place VMs such that their bandwidth guarantees can also be met [17,18,45]. Silo expands VM network guarantees to include packet delay and burst allowance. We begin with a simple example to illustrate the need to explicitly account for these new constraints.

Consider the example in Figure 5 which shows why only accounting for bandwidth guarantees is insufficient. The figure shows a cluster with three servers connected by a 10 Gbps switch with 300 KB buffers per port. A tenant requests nine VMs, each with a guarantee of 1 Gbps, 100 KB burst allowance and 1 ms packet delay. The VMs can burst at 10 Gbps. A bandwidth-aware placement algorithm [18,45] can result in the placement shown in Figure 5(a) which meets the tenant's bandwidth requirement. However, in the worst case, VMs 1–8 can send a simultaneous burst of 100 KB each to VM 9. In this case the switch port connected to the third server receives 800 KB of traffic at 20 Gbps while it is drained at 10 Gbps. So the switch will drop packets—it needs to buffer 400 KB of packets because half of the packets arriving at the port will be queued. By contrast, Silo will place VMs as show in Figure 5(b). In the worst case, when VMs 1–6 send traffic simultaneously to the VMs in the third server, the switch will receive 600 KB of traffic at 20 Gbps, which requires only 300 KB of buffering. Hence, there will be no packet loss and the tenant's delay guarantees will be met.

The main insight behind our approach is that each VM's bandwidth guarantee yields an upper bound for the rate at which it can send traffic. We use this to quantify the **queue bound** for any switch port, i.e. the maximum queuing delay that can occur at the port. Further, we can also determine a port's **queue capacity**, the maximum possible queue delay before packets are dropped. For example, a 10Gbps port with a 100KB buffer has a 80 μs queue capacity. *The key novelty in the placement algorithm is mapping a tenant's multi-dimensional network guarantees to two simple queueing constraints at switches.* To ensure the network has enough capacity to accommodate the bandwidth guarantees of VMs *and* absorb all bursts, we need to ensure that at all switch ports, the queue bound does not exceed queue capacity. This is the first constraint. As we explain later, packet de-

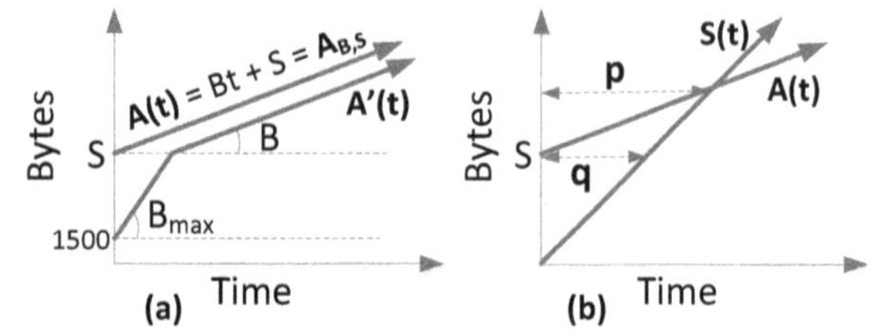

Figure 6: (a) Two arrival curves. (b) An arrival curve, A(t) and a switch's service curve, S(t).

lay guarantees lead to the second queuing constraint. These constraints then dictate VM placement.

In the following sections, we detail our placement algorithm. We assume a multi-rooted tree network topology prevalent in today's datacenters. Such topologies are hierarchical; servers are arranged in racks that are, in turn, grouped into pods. Each server has a few slots where VMs can be placed.

4.2.2 *Queue bounds*

We begin by describing how we use basic network calculus concepts [28,41,46] to determine the queue bounds for network switches. We then take advantage of Silo's tenant-level bandwidth guarantees to tighten the delay bounds, and use this as a building block for our VM placement algorithm.

Source Characterization. Traffic from a VM with bandwidth guarantee B and burst size S is described by a *arrival curve* A(t) = $Bt + S$, which provides an upper bound for traffic generated over a period of time. We will refer to this curve as $A_{B,S}$. This arrival curve is shown in figure 6(a) and assumes that the VM can send a burst of S bytes instantaneously. While we use this simple function for exposition, our implementation uses a more involved arrival curve (labelled A' in the figure) that captures the fact that a VM's burst rate is limited to B_{max}.

Calculating queue bound. Arrival curves can be used to determine queue bounds for network switches. Just as traffic arriving at a switch is characterized by its arrival curve, each switch port is associated with a *service curve* that characterizes the rate at which it can serve traffic. Figure 6(b) illustrates how these two functions can be used to calculate the maximum queuing at the port or its queue bound. Initially the arrival curve A(t) is larger than the service curve S(t) because of initial burst of traffic; so the queue starts to build up. However, as time reaches $t = p$, the aggregate traffic that the switch can serve exceeds the aggregate traffic that can arrive. This means that at some point during the interval $(0, p]$ the queue must have emptied at least once.

The horizontal distance between the curves is the time for which packets are queued. Hence, the maximum queuing delay experienced by a packet at the switch is q, the maximum horizontal distance between the curves (i.e., the largest q such that $S(t) = A(t - q)$). This is the port's queue bound.

The analysis above allows us to calculate the queue bound at a switch directly receiving traffic from a VM. Next we describe how arrival curves can be added (when traffic from VMs merges at a switch) and propagated across switches to determine the queuing across a multi-hop network.

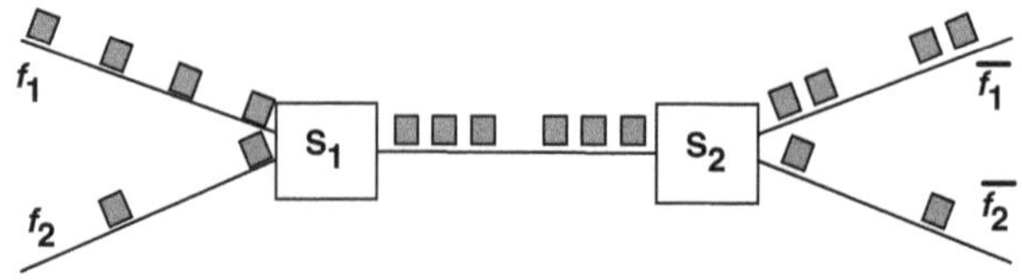

Figure 7: Switch S_1 causes packet bunching for flow f_1.

Adding arrival curves. Arrival curves for VMs can be combined to generate an aggregate arrival curve. For example, adding arrival curves $A_{B1,S1}$ and $A_{B2,S2}$ yields $A_{B1+B2,S1+S2}$. However, as explained below, the semantics of our guarantees allow us to generate a tighter arrival curve when adding curves for VMs belonging to the same tenant.

Consider a tenant with N VMs, each with an average bandwidth B and burst allowance S. The arrival curve for each VM's traffic is $A_{B,S}$. Imagine a network link that connects the tenant's VMs such that m VMs are on the left of the link and the remaining $(N - m)$ are on the right. We want to add the m arrival curves for the VMs on the left to generate an aggregate curve for all traffic traversing the link from left to right. Our choice of bandwidth guarantees using hose-model implies that the total bandwidth guaranteed for the tenant across the link is min(m, $N - m$)*B [18]. By contrast, burst allowances are not destination limited, so the maximum traffic burst across the link from left to right is $m*S$ bytes. Thus, instead of $A_{mB,\ mS}$, we can derive a tighter (i.e. more accurate) aggregate arrival curve: $A_{min(m,N-m)*B,\ mS}$.

Propagating arrival curves. After traffic egresses a switch, it may no longer be shaped according to the properties it arrived at the switch with. For example, consider Figure 7: flow f_1 has a rate of $C/2$ (link capacity is C), and flow f_2 has a rate of $C/4$. Both have a burst size of one packet; so f_1's arrival curve is $A_{\frac{C}{2},1}$ and f_2's is $A_{\frac{C}{4},1}$. However, as shown in the figure, f_1's burst size is doubled as it egresses the switch. Its arrival curve changes to $A_{\frac{C}{2},2}$. Note that a flow's average bandwidth cannot change through a switch, only the burst size is impacted.

To compute the arrival curve for a flow after it egresses a switch, we use Kurose's analysis [41] which shows that the upper-bound on the burst introduced by a switch port depends on its p value—the maximum interval over which its queue must be emptied at least once (see Fig. 6). However, this analysis means that the arrival curve for egress traffic depends on a port's p value which, in turn, depends on other flows using the port. To make the egress arrival curve independent of competing traffic, we use the port's queue capacity c as a looser bound on the egress burst size (to avoid packet loss, $p \leq q$). A port's queue capacity is a static value given by the size of its packet buffer, but can be set to a lower value too. In the worst case, every packet sent by a VM over the interval $[0, c]$ may be forwarded as one burst. Since a VM with arrival curve $A_{B,S}$ can send at most $B.c + S$ bytes in time c, the egress traffic's arrival curve is $A_{B,(B.c+S)}$.

4.2.3 *Placement algorithm*

We have designed a placement algorithm that uses a greedy first-fit heuristic to place VMs on servers. We first describe how we map a new tenant's network guarantees to two simple queuing constraints at switches. These constraints thus characterize a valid VM placement and guide the algorithm.

Valid placement. For the tenant's bandwidth guarantees to be met, we must ensure that network links carrying its traffic have sufficient capacity. Further, VMs can send traffic bursts that may temporarily exceed link capacities. Switch buffers need to absorb this excess traffic, and we must ensure that switch buffers never overflow. In combination, these restrictions imply that for each switch port between the tenant's VMs, the maximum queue buildup (queue bound) should be less than the buffer size (queue capacity). Formally, if V is the set of VMs being placed and $Path(i, j)$ is the set of ports between VMs i and j, the first constraint is

$$\text{Q-bound}_p \leq \text{Q-capacity}_p, \quad \forall p \in Path(i,j),\ i,j \in V$$

For packet delay guarantees, we must ensure that for each pair of VMs belonging to the new tenant, the sum of queue bounds across the path between them should be less than the delay guarantee. However, a port's queue bound changes as tenants are added and removed which complicates the placement. Instead, we use a port's queue capacity, which always exceeds its queue bound, to check delay guarantees. Thus, for a tenant with delay guarantee d, the second constraint is

$$\sum_{p \in Path(i,j)} \text{Q-capacity}_p \leq d, \quad \forall i,j \in V$$

Finding valid placements. A request can have many valid placements. Given the oversubscribed nature of typical datacenter networks, we adopt the following optimization goal: *find the placement that minimizes the "height" of network links that may carry the tenant's traffic*, thus preserving network capacity for future tenants. Servers represent the lowest height of network hierarchy, followed by racks and pods. We place a tenant's VMs while greedily optimizing this goal. First, we attempt to place all requested VMs in the same server. If the number of VMs exceeds the number of VM slots per server, we attempt to place all VMs in the same rack—for each server inside the rack, we use the queuing constraints on the server's uplink switch port to determine the number of VMs that can be placed at the server. If all requested VMs can be accommodated at servers within the rack, the request is accepted. Otherwise we consider the next rack and so on. If the request cannot be placed in a single rack, we attempt to place it in a pod and finally across pods.

Other constraints. An important concern when placing VMs in today's datacenters is fault tolerance. Our placement algorithm can ensure that a tenant's VMs are placed across some number of fault domains. For example, if each server is treated as a fault domain, we will place the VMs across two or more servers. Beyond this, VM placement may need to account for other goals such as ease of maintenance, reducing VM migrations, etc. Commercial placement managers like Microsoft's Virtual Machine Manager model these as constraints and use multi-dimensional bin packing heuristics to place VMs [47]. Our queuing constraints could be added to these systems; we defer an exploration to future work.

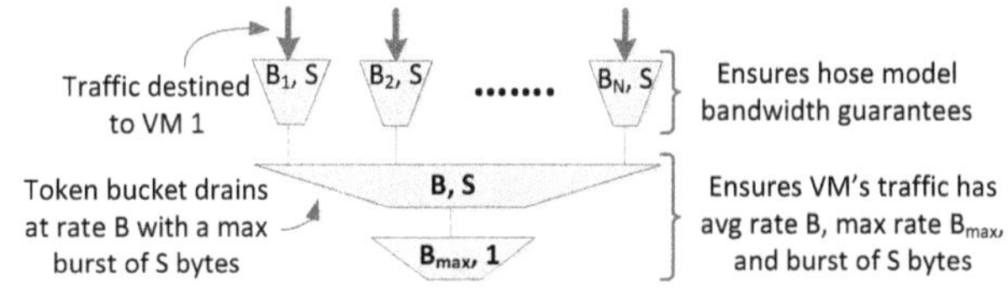

Figure 8: VM traffic is paced using a hierarchy of token buckets to ensure it conforms to network guarantees, i.e. its bandwidth guarantee (B) and burst allowance (S).

4.3 End host pacing

Silo's VM placement relies on tenant traffic conforming to their bandwidth and burstiness specifications. To achieve this, a *pacer* at the end host hypervisor paces traffic sent by each VM. Figure 8 shows the hierarchy of token buckets used by the pacer to enforce traffic conformance. The bottom most token bucket ensures a VM's traffic rate can never exceed B_{max}, even when sending a burst. The middle token bucket ensures the average traffic rate is limited to B and the maximum burst size is S bytes. At the top is a set of token buckets, one each for traffic destined to each of the other VMs belonging to the same tenant. These are needed to enforce the hose model semantics of guaranteed bandwidth; i.e. the actual bandwidth guaranteed for traffic between a pair of VMs is constrained by both the sender and the destination. To enforce the hose model, the pacers at the source and destination hypervisor communicate with each other like EyeQ [20]. This coordination determines the rate B_i for the top token buckets in Figure 8 such that $\sum B_i \leq B$.

4.3.1 Paced IO Batching

The placement of VMs assumes their traffic strictly conforms to their arrival curve. Thus, the token buckets should ideally be serviced at a per-packet granularity with accurate spacing between the packets. For example, if a VM with a 1 Gbps rate limit sends 1.5KB packets on a 10 Gbps link, the packets should be separated by $10.8\mu s$. This precludes the use of I/O batching techniques since today's NICs transmit an entire batch of packets back-to-back [22]. With a typical batch size of 64KB used by offloading techniques like TSO, all packets for our example VM would be sent at line rate. This increases the amount of network queuing and can even result in packet loss. However, disabling IO batching results in high CPU overhead and reduces throughput; in experiments with batching disabled, we cannot even saturate a 10Gbps link. One solution is to implement pacing at the NIC itself [22,42]. However, this requires hardware support. For ease of deployment, we design a software solution.

We propose Paced IO batching, a technique that allows us to reduce the IO overhead while still pacing packets at sub-microsecond timescales. To achieve this, we use "**void packets**" to control the spacing between data packets forwarded by the NIC. A void packet is a packet that will be forwarded by the NIC but discarded by the first switch it encounters. This can be achieved, for example, by setting the packet's destination MAC address the same as the source MAC. Such void packets do not increase the power consumption at the NIC and switch because most of power is

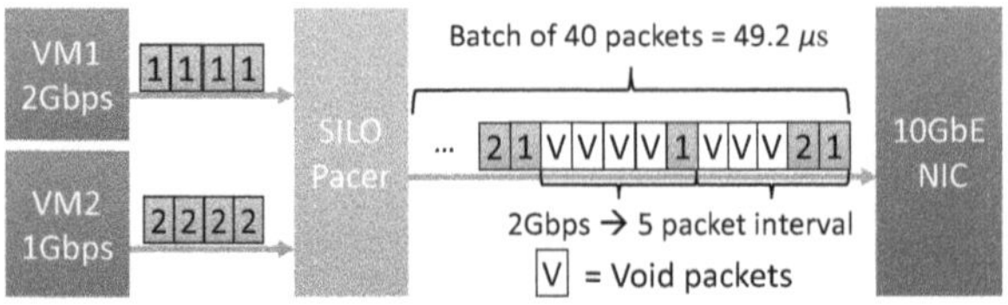

Figure 9: VM1's guarantee is 2Gbps, VM2's is 1Gbps. Use of void packets achieves packet level pacing in the face of NIC burstiness.

consumed for keeping the link active [48]. We note that injecting void packets requires disabling TCP Segmentation Offload (TSO), however VMs can still send large segments to the hypervisor to minimize the overhead for VM-to-hypervisor communication.

Figure 9 illustrates how we use void packets. The link capacity is 10Gbps and VM1 is guaranteed 2Gbps, so every fifth packet sent to the NIC belongs to VM1. In every batch of 40 packets sent to the NIC, twelve are actual data packets, while the rest 28 are void packets. While the NIC forwards the entire batch of packets as is, all void packets are dropped by the first hop switch, thus generating a correctly paced packet stream. The minimum size of a void packet, including the Ethernet frame, is 84 bytes. So, at 10Gbps, we can achieve an inter-packet spacing as low as $68ns$.

4.4 Tenants without guarantees

Silo relies on rate limiting tenants to give packet delay guarantees. However, this can hurt network utilization since tenants cannot use spare network capacity. We evaluate this in §6.3. We note that some cloud applications are indeed not network-limited, so they do not need any network guarantees. Such "best-effort tenants" can be used to improve network utilization. Silo leverages 802.1q priority forwarding in switches to support best-effort tenants. Traffic from such tenants is marked by our pacer as low priority while traffic from tenants with guarantees is higher priority. Thus, such tenants share the residual network capacity. It is also possible for tenant with guarantees to be able to send low priority traffic to achieve higher throughput by using schemes like RC3 [49]. We leave this for future work.

5. IMPLEMENTATION

We have implemented a Silo prototype comprising a VM placement manager and a software pacer implemented as a Windows NDIS filter driver. The pacer driver sits between the virtual switch (vswitch) and the NIC driver, so we do not require any modification to the NIC driver, applications or the guest OS. It implements token buckets and supports token bucket chaining. We use virtual token buckets, i.e. packets are not drained at an absolute time, rather we timestamp when each packet needs to be sent out. This requires an extra eight bytes in each packet's metadata. The overhead is negligible in comparison to the size of the packet buffer structure: 160 bytes in Windows NET BUFFER and 208 bytes in Linux skb [50,51].

At high link rates, I/O batching is essential to keep the CPU overhead low. For accurate rate limiting with I/O batching, we need two key properties. The first is to keep the precise gap between packets within a batch; we achieve this using void packets. The second is to schedule the next batch of packets before the NIC starts to idle. This is essential to guarantee burst allowance but challenging since we want to keep the batch size small so that NIC queuing delay is limited. We borrow the idea of soft-timers [52] and reuse existing interrupts as a timer source. Our pacer does not use a separate timer, but triggers sending the next batch of packets upon receiving a DMA (Direct Memory Access) completion interrupt for transmit packets. We use a batch size of 50 μs when pulling out packets from the token buckets.

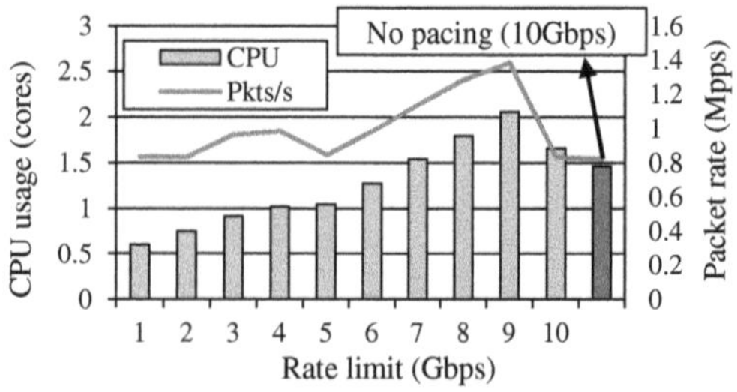

(a) CPU usage

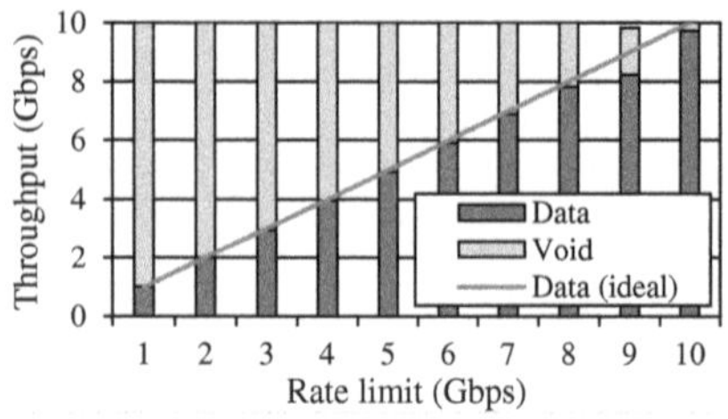

(b) Throughput

Figure 10: Microbenchmarks show Silo's pacer is able to saturate 10Gbps links with low CPU overhead.

Pacer microbenchmarks. We evaluate our pacer implementation in terms of throughput and the CPU overhead. We use physical servers equipped with one Intel X520 10GbE NICs, and two Intel Xeon E5-2665 CPUs (8 cores, 2.4Ghz). Overall, we find that the pacer is able to saturate 10Gbps links with low CPU overhead.

Figure 10(a) shows the CPU usage of the entire system by varying the rate limit imposed by the pacer. The right most bar is CPU usage when the pacer is disabled. LSO is disabled in all cases. The red solid line represents the number of transmitted packets per second, including void packets. The pacer consumes 0.6 cores to generate only void packets at 10 Gbps. As the actual data rate increases, the overall CPU utilization goes up to $\approx$2.1 cores worth of CPU cycles at 9 Gbps. The reason is that at 9 Gbps, the pacer needs to put $1/10^{th}$ of MTU sized packets (150 bytes) between all the data packets, which results in high packet rate. The graph shows that the overall CPU usage is proportional to the packet rate shown in the red line. At full line-rate of 10 Gbps, our pacer incurs less than 0.2 cores worth of extra CPU cycles as compared to no pacing. Since void packets are generated only when there is another packet waiting to be sent, the pacer does not incur any extra CPU overhead when the network is idle.

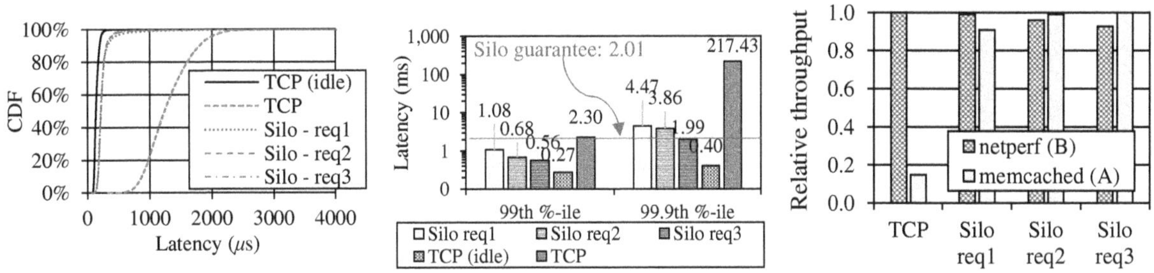

(a) Memcached latency CDF (b) Memcached tail latency (c) Throughput

Figure 11: Testbed experiments involving two tenants, A and B, with 15 VMs each. Silo achieves lower and predictable message latency for memcached, even with a competing bandwidth-hungry workload generated using netperf.

	Req 1		Req 2		Req 3	
Tenant	A	B	A	B	A	B
Bandwidth ($BMbps$)	210	3,123	315	3,018	420	2,913
Burst (S)	1.5KB	1.5KB	1.5KB	1.5KB	1.5KB	1.5KB
Packet Delay (d)	1ms	N/A	1ms	N/A	1ms	N/A
Burst rate (B_{max})	1Gbps	N/A	1Gbps	N/A	1Gbps	N/A

Table 2: Tenant network guarantees for the testbed experiments. We set combined bandwidth at each host ($3 \times (B_A + B_B)$) to be link capacity (10Gbps).

In Figure 10(b), we show the throughput for both void packets and data packets. Except at 9 Gbps, the pacer sustains 100% of the link capacity, and achieves actual data rate at more than 98% of the ideal rate.

Placement microbenchmarks. To evaluate the scalability of the placement manager, we measured the time to place tenants in a simulated datacenter with 100K hosts with an average tenant requesting 49 VMs (as in [18,45]). Over 100K requests, the maximum placement time is 1.15s.

6. EVALUATION

We evaluate Silo across three platforms: a small scale prototype deployment, a medium scale packet-level simulator, and a datacenter scale flow-level simulator. The key findings are as follows:

(i). Through testbed experiments with memcached, we verify that our prototype can offer bandwidth, delay and burst guarantees. This ensures improved and predictable performance for memcached without impacting bandwidth sensitive workloads (who get predictable performance too).

(ii). Through *ns2* simulations, we show that Silo significantly improves tail message latency as compared to state-of-the-art solutions like DCTCP [15], HULL [22], and Oktopus [18]; none of these achieve predictable message latency.

(iii). Through flow-level simulations, we evaluate our VM placement algorithm, and find that it can result in a small reduction in accepted tenants and network utilization as compared to when tenants only get bandwidth guarantees. Surprisingly, as compared to the status quo, Silo can improve both network and overall cloud utilization.

6.1 Testbed experiments

We deployed our prototype across five physical servers connected to a 10GbE switch. Each server is equipped with either two Intel Xeon E5-2630 (6 cores, 2.6Ghz) or two E5-2650 (8 cores, 2.6Ghz) processors, and an Intel X520 10GbE NIC. Our testbed experiments comprise two tenants, A and B, each with 15 VMs. We launch six VMs per server, and assign three to each tenant. Tenant A runs the ETC trace of Facebook workloads [33] using memcached. We generate value sizes and inter arrival times using generalized pareto distribution with parameters from the trace [33]. Tenant B runs netperf to generate TCP traffic emulating the shuffle phase in mapreduce.

Guarantees. To determine Tenant A's network requirements, we measured the bandwidth and packet sizes by running memcached in isolation. The average packet size is around 400 B, and the average value size in our workload is 300 B; the maximum value size is 1 KB. A burst allowance of $1.5KB$ is thus enough to handle a burst of three to four requests on average. The average bandwidth requirement (B_{avg}) is 210 $Mbps$. Since the instantaneous bandwidth required can vary, we experimented with varying bandwidth guarantees for tenant A. This allows us to evaluate the tradeoff between memcached request latency and overall utilization. The tenants' guarantees are shown in Table 2. Requirements 1, 2, and 3 in Table 2 allocate B_{avg}, $1.5 \times B_{avg}$, and $2 \times B_{avg}$ respectively for Tenant A, and the remaining bandwidth for Tenant B.

Memcached latency. We plot the CDF of latency for memcached in Figure 11(a). Figure 11(b) shows the 99th and 99.9^{th} percentile latency. We measure latency for five different scenarios: (a) Tenant A and B running simultaneously with the three different configurations for Silo in Table 2 (Silo req 1–3); (b) Tenant A running memcached in isolation (labelled as "TCP (idle)"); and (c) Tenant A and B running simultaneously without using Silo (labelled as "TCP"). TCP incurs very high latency compared to memcached running in isolation. Figure 11(b) shows it even suffers timeouts at 99.9^{th} percentile resulting in over 200 ms latency.

In these experiments, the message latency guarantee for memcached with Silo is 2.01 ms. Silo stays well within this guarantee even at 99th percentile. At 99.9^{th} percentile, Silo stays within the message latency guarantee when tenant A is guaranteed twice its average bandwidth requirement (req 3). However, it exceeds the guaranteed latency by a little when the bandwidth guarantee is lower (req 1–2). This is due to the bursty nature of the memcached workload. We also experimented with a higher burst allowance of 3 KB, and

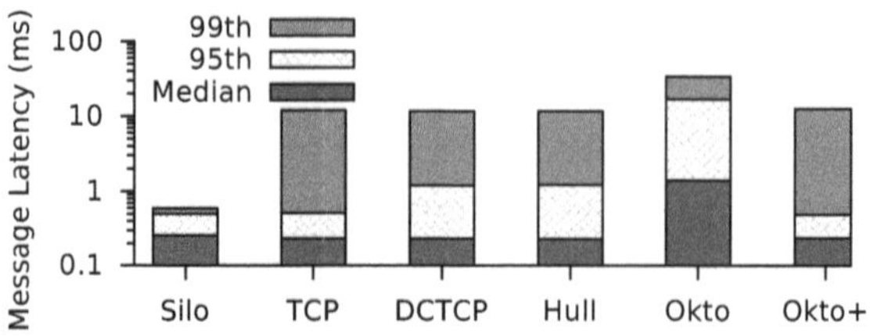

Figure 12: Message latency for class-A tenants.

	Class A	Class B
Communication pattern	All to 1	All to all
Bandwidth (B)	0.25Gbps	2Gbps
Burst length (S)	15KB	1.5KB
Delay guarantee (d)	1000μs	N/A
Burst rate (B_{max})	1Gbps	N/A

Table 3: Tenant classes and their average network requirements.

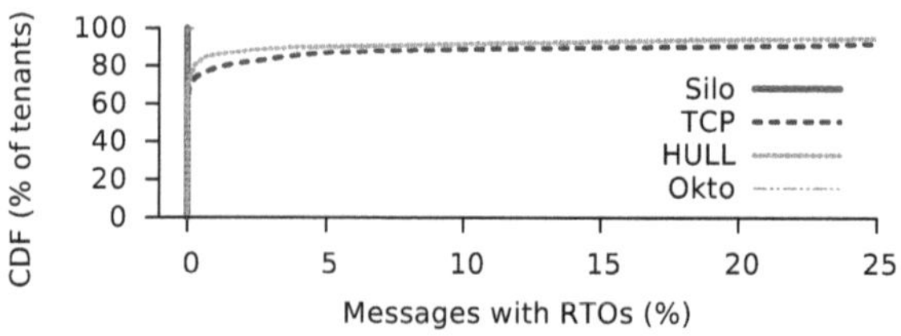

Figure 13: Class-A tenants whose messages incur RTOs.

	Silo	TCP	DCTCP	Hull	Okto	Okto+
Outliers-1x	0	23.1	47.3	46.9	91	20.2
Outliers-2x	0	21.7	17.4	15.6	80.7	19.1
Outliers-8x	0	21.5	14.4	14.4	36.5	19

Table 4: Outlier tenants, i.e. tenants whose 99th percentile message latency exceeds the latency estimate.

found that it lowers memcached's 99.9^{th} percentile latency to 4.3 ms, 2.5 ms, and 1.8 ms for req-1–3 respectively.

Throughput. We measured the throughput of memcached and netperf to evaluate whether Silo's use of strict bandwidth reservation impacts network utilization. In Figure 11(c), we plot the relative throughput of both Silo and TCP against when Tenant A and Tenant B are running alone with standard TCP. For TCP, the netperf traffic gets 94% of the link capacity while memcached transaction rate drops by seven times. This is because memcached does synchronous transactions with limited concurrency, and inflated latency leads to low throughput even when network bandwidth is available. When Silo is used, Tenant A's throughput increases as we increase its reservation, and reaches 100% for req-3. However, at the same time, Tenant B can still use 92% to 99% of bandwidth achieved by TCP alone.

Overall, we find that Silo delivers guarantees for packet delay, burst and bandwidth. This significantly improves the performance of a latency sensitive application like memcached without hurting bandwidth hungry applications. Moreover, both sets of applications get predictable performance.

6.2 Packet level simulations

We use *ns2* to compare Silo against state-of-the-art solutions. Instead of using two specific tenants, we model two classes of tenants. *Class-A* contains delay-sensitive tenants that run a small message application, and require bandwidth, delay and burst guarantees. Each class-A tenant has an all-to-one communication pattern such that all VMs simultaneously send a message to the same receiver. This coarsely models the workload for OLDI applications [15]. *Class-B* tenants only require bandwidth guarantees. Such tenants have an all-to-all communication pattern, as is common for data parallel applications. The bandwidth and burst requirements of tenants are generated from an exponential distribution with the parameters in table 3.

Simulation setup. We model 10 racks, each with 40 servers and 8 VMs per server, resulting in 3200 VMs. We use a multi-rooted tree topology for the cloud network. The capacity of each network link is 10Gbps and the network has an oversubscription of 1:5, as is the norm in datacenters [53]. We model commonly used shallow buffered switches [54] with 312KB buffering per port (queue capacity is 250μs). The number of tenants is such that 90% of VM slots are occupied. For Silo, VMs are placed using its placement algorithm. For Oktopus, we use its bandwidth-aware algorithm [18]. For other solutions, we use a locality-aware algorithm that greedily places VMs close to each other.

Class-A tenants. Figure 12 shows the message latency for class-A tenants across 50 runs. Silo ensures low message latency even at the 99th percentile while all other approaches have high tail latency. With Oktopus, VMs cannot burst, so the message latency is high, both at the median and at the tail. At 99th percentile, message latency is 60× higher with Oktopus as compared to Silo. "Okto+" is an Oktopus extension with burst allowance. Hence, it reduces the median latency but still suffers at the tail. This is because it does not account for VM bursts when placing VMs which can lead to switch buffer overflows (see example in §4.2). We note that TCP is used as the transport protocol for Silo, Okto, and Okto+ on top of their rate enforcement. Using DCTCP with Okto+ still suffers from packet losses and TCP timeouts as the placement of VMs does not ensure switch buffers can actually absorb traffic bursts.

With DCTCP and HULL, message latency is higher by 22x at the 99th percentile (and 2.5x at the 95th). Two factors lead to poor tail latency for these approaches. First, class-A tenants have an all-to-one traffic pattern that leads to contention at the destination. Second, none of these approaches isolate performance across tenants by guaranteeing bandwidth, so class-A small messages compete with large messages from class-B tenants. This leads to high tail latency and losses for small messages. Figure 13 shows that with TCP, for 21% of class-A tenants, more than 1% of messages suffer retransmission timeout events (RTOs). With HULL, this happens for 14% of tenants. Thus, *by itself, neither low queuing (ensured by DCTCP and HULL) nor guaranteed bandwidth (ensured by Oktopus) is sufficient to ensure predictable message latency.*

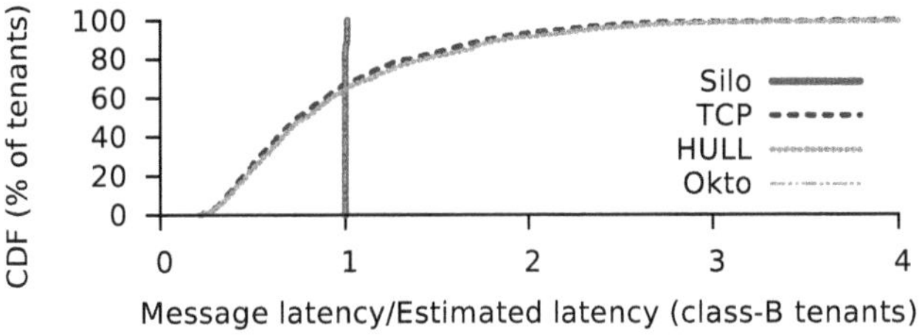

Figure 14: Message latency for class-B tenants.

We also look at *outlier tenants*, i.e. class-A tenants whose 99th percentile message latency is more than the latency estimate. Table 4 shows that Silo results in no outliers. Since we observe outliers with other approaches, we mark the fraction of outliers whose latency exceeds the estimate by 1x, 2x or 8x. With DCTCP and HULL, 14.4% tenants are 8x outliers.

Class-B tenants. Since Silo does not let tenants exceed their bandwidth guarantee, it can impact the performance of class-B tenants with large messages whose completion is dictated by the bandwidth they achieve. Figure 14 shows the average message latency for class-B tenants, normalized to the message latency estimate. For clarity, we omit the DCTCP (similar to HULL) and Okto+ lines. With Silo and Oktopus, tenant bandwidth is guaranteed, so all large messages finish by the estimated time. With TCP and HULL, the message latency varies. 65% of tenants achieve higher bandwidth with HULL as compared to Silo but there is a long tail with many tenants getting very poor network bandwidth. This shows how Silo trades-off best-case performance for predictability.

6.3 Large-scale simulations

We use a flow-level simulator to evaluate Silo's VM placement algorithm and its impact on network utilization at scale.

Simulation setup. We model a public cloud datacenter with 32K servers connected using three tier network topology with 1:5 oversubscription at each level. The arrival of tenant requests is a Poisson process. By varying the average arrival rate, we can control the average datacenter occupancy. Each tenant runs a job that transfers a given amount of data between its VMs. Each job also has a minimum compute time. A job is said to finish when all its flows finish and the compute time has expired. 50% tenants belong to class-A while the rest belong to class-B. We compare Silo's placement against two approaches: *Oktopus* placement that guarantees VM bandwidth only and locality-aware placement (*Locality*) that greedily places a tenant's VM close to each other. For Silo and Oktopus, a tenant's flows are assigned bandwidth based on its guarantee with no bandwidth sharing across tenants, while for greedy placement, we emulate ideal TCP behavior by sharing bandwidth fairly between all flows.

Workload. As before, Class-A tenants have an all-to-one workload. To study the impact of different traffic patterns, Class-B tenants have a "Permutation-x" workload—each VM has flows to x randomly chosen other VMs. By varying x, we control the tenant's traffic pattern. Note that for a tenant with N VMs, Permutation-N is an all-to-all traffic pattern.

Admittance ratio. We first use a Permutation-1 workload for class-B tenants. Figure 15(a) shows the fraction of ten-

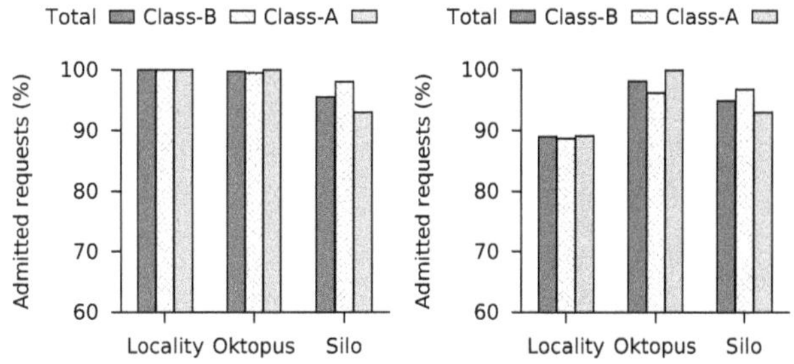

(a) Occupancy = 75% (b) Occupancy = 90%

Figure 15: Admitted requests with Permutation-1 workload for class-B tenants.

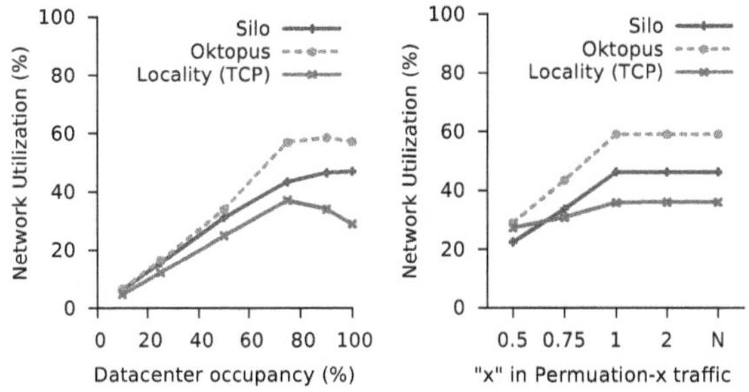

(a) Permutation-1 traffic (b) Occupancy = 90%

Figure 16: Average network utilization with varying datacenter occupancy and varying traffic patterns.

ants admitted with 75% datacenter occupancy. Silo rejects 4.5% of tenants while locality-aware placement accepts all of them and Oktopus rejects 0.3%. This is because Silo ensures that both the delay and bandwidth requirements of tenants are met, and can reject tenants even if there are empty VM slots. With Silo, the rejection ratio is higher for Class-A tenants as their delay requirements are harder to meet.

However, as the datacenter occupancy increases and tenants arrive faster, the admittance ratio of the locality-aware placement drops. Figure 15(b) shows that at 90% occupancy, it rejects 11% of tenants as compared to 5.1% rejects by Silo. This result is counter-intuitive. Locality-aware placement will only reject requests if there are insufficient VM slots. By contrast, Silo can reject a request, even when there are empty VM slots, if the request's network guarantees cannot be met. The root cause is that locality-aware placement does not account for the bandwidth demands of tenants. So it can place VMs of tenants with high bandwidth requirements far apart. Such tenants get poor network performance and their jobs get delayed. These outlier tenants reduce the *overall* cloud throughput, causing subsequent requests to be rejected. With Silo, tenants get guaranteed bandwidth, so no tenant suffers from poor network performance.

Network utilization. With Silo, tenants cannot exceed their bandwidth guarantees which can result in network under-utilization. We study Silo's impact on network utilization with varying occupancy and traffic patterns, and find that, surprisingly, Silo can actually match and even improve utilization as compared to the status quo.

Figure 16(a) shows the average network utilization in our experiments with varying datacenter occupancy. As low oc-

		Unmodified			Guarantee				Cloud support		Work conservation		Fine-grained pacing
		H/W	OS	App	Bandwidth	Packet delay	Burst	Message latency	Placement	Tenant Isolation	Intra tenant	Inter tenant	
	Silo	✓	✓	✓	✓	✓	✓	✓	✓	✓	✓	✗†	✓
Packet delay guarantee	QJUMP [34]	✓	✓	✓	✓	✓	✗	✓	✗	✗	✓	✓	✗
	Fastpass [23]♯	✓	✓	✓	✓	✗	✗	✗	✗	✗	✓	✓	✓
	TDMA Ethernet [55]	✓	✗	✓	✓	✓	✗	✓	✗	✗	✓	✓	✗
Internet QoS	ATM [56]	✗	✗	✗	✓	✓	✓	✓	✗	✓*	✓	✓	✗‡
	IntServ [31]	✗	✗	✗	✓	✓	✓	✓	✗	✓*	✗	✗	✗
	Stop and Go [57]	✗	✗	✗	✓	✓	✓	✓	✗	✓*	✗	✗	✗‡
Bandwidth guarantee	Oktopus [18]	✗	✗	✓	✓	✗	✗	✗	✓	✓	✓	✗	✗
	Hadrian [21]	✗	✗	✓	✓	✗	✗	✗	✓	✓	✓	✓	✗
	EyeQ [20]	✓	✓	✓	✓	✗	✗	✗	✓	✓	✓	✓	✗
Flow deadline	D^3 [24]	✗	✗	✗	✗	✗	✓	✓	✗	✗	✓	✓	✗
	PDQ [26]	✗	✗	✗	✗	✗	✓	✓	✗	✗	✓	✓	✗
	D^2TCP [25]	✓	✗	✗	✗	✗	✓	✓	✗	✗	✓	✓	✗
Low latency	pFabric [58]	✗	✗	✓	✗	✗	✓	✗	✗	✗	✓	✓	✗‡
	DCTCP [15]	✓	✗	✓	✗	✗	✗	✗	✗	✗	✓	✓	✗
	HULL [22]	✗	✗	✓	✗	✗	✗	✗	✗	✗	✓	✓	✓

†Silo's guarantee is not work-conserving across tenants, however Silo can use switch priorities to support tenants without guarantees and achieve work-conservation. ‡These do not require nor benefit from fine-grained pacing at the end host. *Although these systems are not designed for the cloud, their support for traffic classes can achieve tenant isolation. ♯Fastpass's centralized packet scheduling can support any policy in theory. However, it does not provide scheduling mechanisms for guarantees, and its scalability to datacenters is unknown.

Table 5: Comparison of related work in terms of design choices.

cupancy, there is not much difference between the approaches. At an occupancy of 75%, network utilization with Silo is actually 6% higher than with locality-aware placement (which uses an ideal-TCP for bandwidth sharing). This results from two factors. First, locality-aware placement naturally minimizes network traffic by co-locating VMs close to each other while Silo may be forced to place VMs across servers to meet their guarantees. Second, as mentioned above, a small fraction of outlier tenants that get poor network performance with the locality approach also hurt network utilization. As compared to Oktopus, Silo's network utilization is lower by 9-11% at high occupancy. *This is the price we pay for accommodating delay requirements of class-A tenants as it causes Silo to accept fewer requests than Oktopus and reduces network utilization.*

Figure 16(b) shows the utilization with varying traffic patterns for class-B tenants. When such tenants have a sparse traffic matrix (eg., Permutation-0.5 traffic), Silo can result in ~4% drop in utilization. However, as the tenant traffic matrix becomes denser, network utilization with Silo surpasses locality-aware placement.

Other simulation parameters. We repeated these experiments while varying other simulation parameters. We omit the results but highlight a couple of trends. The requests admitted by Silo when datacenter occupancy is lower than 75% are similar to the ones shown in Figure 15(a). As we increase the size of switch buffers or reduce network oversubscription, Silo's ability to accept tenants increases since the network is better provisioned.

7. RELATED WORK

Silo adds to a rich literature on network guarantees and optimization. We briefly discuss the work most relevant to Silo, and summarize the key differences in Table 5.

Many recent efforts look at cloud network sharing. They propose different sharing policies, including fixed guarantees [17,18], minimum bandwidth guarantees [19,20], and per-tenant fairness [59]. However, these proposals focus solely on bandwidth, thus catering to bandwidth-sensitive applications. They do not provide bounded packet delay and the ability to burst.

QJUMP [34] is the closest to Silo among recent works; it uses rate limiting and priorities, and allows different traffic classes at different points of the trade off between network latency and throughput. However, it only provides a latency guarantee for very low bandwidth traffic; higher bandwidth traffic can incur variable message latency. By contrast, Silo provides an intuitive abstraction for tenants described by bandwidth, delay, and burst guarantees. It ensures isolation between tenants, and a tenant can independently determine it message latency. In terms of mechanisms, Silo additionally uses a novel placement algorithm to maximize the number of tenants that can be accommodated.

Numerous solutions achieve low latency in private datacenters by ensuring small network queues [15,22], by accounting for flow deadlines [24–26], through network prioritization [34,58] or centralized rate allocation [23]. Silo targets predictable message latency in multi-tenant datacenters and three key factors differentiate our work. First, these proposals do not isolate performance across tenants; i.e., they do not guarantee a tenant's bandwidth nor control total burstiness on network links. The former hurts the latency of both small and large messages while the latter hurts small messages. In §6.2, we show that DCTCP and HULL can suffer from high and variable message latency, especially when there is competing tenant traffic. Similarly, with D^3 [24], PDQ [26] and D^2TCP [25], there is no guarantee for a message's latency as it depends on the deadlines of messages of other tenants. And a tenant can declare tight deadlines for its messages, thus hurting other tenants.

Second, with public clouds, we cannot rely on tenant cooperation. Tenants can use the transport protocol of their choice and cannot be expected to pass application hints like deadlines. Thus, a hypervisor-only solution is needed. Finally, apart from HULL [22], none of these solutions look at queuing delay at the NIC itself. Overall, while these solutions work well for the class of applications or environment they were designed for, they do not guarantee end-to-end message latency for diverse cloud applications.

The early 1990's saw substantial work on providing network performance guarantees to Internet clients. ATM [56] and its predecessors [60] provided different kinds performance guarantees. Stop and Go [57] is the proposal most similar to Silo in terms of architecture. However, it introduces a new queueing discipline at switches while Silo does not require any switch changes. More broadly, much of the work from this era focuses on novel queueing disciplines at switches [61–63]; Zhang and Keshav [64] provide a comparison of these proposals. We chose to avoid this in favor of better deployability. Silo works with commodity Ethernet. Further, Silo leverages the flexibility of placing VMs, an opportunity unique to datacenters. Finally, Silo pushes to much higher performance in terms pacing traffic; by using void packets, Silo can achieve sub-microsecond granularity pacing with very low CPU overhead. However, Silo can still benefit from using hardware offloading like SENIC [42] which eliminates the overhead of pacing and disabling TSO.

8. CONCLUSION

In this paper we target predictable message latency for cloud applications. We argue that to achieve this, a general cloud application needs guarantees for its network bandwidth, packet delay and burstiness. We show how guaranteed network bandwidth makes it easier to guarantee packet delay. Leveraging this idea, Silo enables these guarantees without any network and application changes, relying only on VM placement and end host packet pacing. Our prototype can achieve fine grained packet pacing with low CPU overhead. Evaluation shows that Silo can ensure predictable message completion time for both small and large messages in multi-tenant datacenters.

Acknowledgements. We thank Richard Black and Austin Donnelly for the suggestion regarding the packet pacing method. We thank the anonymous reviewers and our shepherd Teemu Koponen for their helpful comments. We are grateful to Dongsu Han, Sangjin Han, Thomas Karagiannis, Keunhong Lee, Sue Moon, Aurojit Panda, Greg O'Shea, and Andy Slowey for discussions and help with experiments.

9. REFERENCES

[1] V. Jalaparti, P. Bodik, S. Kandula, I. Menache, M. Rybalkin, and C. Yan. Speeding up Distributed Request-Response Workflows. In *Proc. of ACM SIGCOMM*, 2013.

[2] G. DeCandia, D. Hastorun, M. Jampani, G. Kakulapati, A. Lakshman, A. Pilchin, S. Sivasubramanian, P. Vosshall, and W. Vogels. Dynamo: amazon's highly available key-value store. *ACM SIGOPS*, 41(6), 2007.

[3] C. Engle, A. Lupher, R. Xin, M. Zaharia, M. J. Franklin, S. Shenker, and I. Stoica. Shark: Fast Data Analysis Using Coarse-grained Distributed Memory. In *Proc. of ACM SIGMOD*, 2012.

[4] S. Melnik, A. Gubarev, J. J. Long, G. Romer, S. Shivakumar, M. Tolton, and T. Vassilakis. Dremel: interactive analysis of web-scale datasets. In *Proc. of VLDB*, 2010.

[5] J. Dean and S. Ghemawat. MapReduce: Simplified Data Processing on Large Clusters. In *Proc. USENIX OSDI*, 2004.

[6] M. Isard, M. Budiu, Y. Yu, A. Birrell, and D. Fetterly. Dryad: Distributed Data-Parallel Programs from Sequential Building Blocks. In *Proc. EuroSys*, 2007.

[7] R. Chaiken, B. Jenkins, P.-A. Larson, B. Ramsey, D. Shakib, S. Weaver, and J. Zhou. SCOPE: easy and efficient parallel processing of massive data sets. In *Proc. VLDB*, 2008.

[8] A. Li, X. Yang, S. Kandula, and M. Zhang. CloudCmp: comparing public cloud providers. In *Proc. ACM IMC*, 2010.

[9] J. Schad, J. Dittrich, and J.-A. Quiané-Ruiz. Runtime measurements in the cloud: observing, analyzing, and reducing variance. In *Proc. VLDB*, 2010.

[10] Y. Xu, Z. Musgrave, B. Noble, and M. Bailey. Bobtail: Avoiding Long Tails in the Cloud. In *Proc. of USENIX NSDI*, 2013.

[11] Y. Xu, M. Bailey, B. Noble, and F. Jahanian. Small is Better: Avoiding Latency Traps in Virtualized Data Centers. In *Proc. of SoCC*, 2013.

[12] J. C. Mogul and R. R. Kompella. Inferring the Network Latency Requirements of Cloud Tenants. In *Proc. of USENIX HotOS*, 2015.

[13] Michael Armburst et al. Above the Clouds: A Berkeley View of Cloud Computing. Technical report, University of California, Berkeley, 2009.

[14] 5 Lessons We've Learned Using AWS. http://techblog.netflix.com/2010/12/5-lessons-weve-learned-using-aws.html.

[15] M. Alizadeh, A. G. Greenberg, D. A. Maltz, J. Padhye, P. Patel, B. Prabhakar, S. Sengupta, and M. Sridharan. Data center TCP (DCTCP). In *Proc. ACM SIGCOMM*, 2010.

[16] J. Dean and L. A. Barroso. The tail at scale. *Commun. ACM*, 56(2):74–80, Feb. 2013.

[17] C. Guo, G. Lu, H. J. Wang, S. Yang, C. Kong, P. Sun, W. Wu, and Y. Zhang. SecondNet: A Data Center Network Virtualization Architecture with Bandwidth Guarantees. In *Proc. ACM CoNext'10*.

[18] H. Ballani, P. Costa, T. Karagiannis, and A. Rowstron. Towards Predicable Datacenter Networks. In *Proc. ACM SIGCOMM*, 2011.

[19] L. Popa, G. Kumar, M. Chowdhury, A. Krishnamurthy, S. Ratnasamy, and I. Stoica. FairCloud: Sharing the Network In Cloud Computing. In *Proc. ACM SIGCOMM*, 2012.

[20] V. Jeyakumar, M. Alizadeh, D. MaziÃÍres, B. Prabhakar, and C. Kim. EyeQ: Practical Network Performance Isolation at the Edge. In *Proc. USENIX NSDI*, 2013.

[21] H. Ballani, K. Jang, T. Karagiannis, C. Kim, D. Gunawaradena, and G. O'Shea. Chatty Tenants and the Cloud Network Sharing Problem. In *Proc. USENIX NSDI*, 2013.

[22] M. Alizadeh, A. Kabbani, T. Edsall, B. Prabhakar, A. Vadhat, and M. Yasuda. Less is More: Trading a little Bandwidth for Ultra-Low Latency in the Data Center. In *Proc. USENIX NSDI*, 2012.

[23] J. Perry, A. Ousterhout, H. Balakrishnan, D. Shah, and H. Fugal. Fastpass: A Centralized Zero-Queue Datacenter Network. In *Proc. of ACM SIGCOMM*, 2014.

[24] C. Wilson, H. Ballani, T. Karagiannis, and A. Rowstron. Better Never than Late: Meeting Deadlines in Datacenter Networks. In *Proc. ACM SIGCOMM*, 2011.

[25] B. Vamana, J. Hasan, and T. N. Vijaykumar. Deadline-Aware Datacenter TCP (D^2TCP). In *Proc. ACM SIGCOMM*, 2012.

[26] C.-Y. Hong, M. Caesar, and P. B. Godfrey. Finishing Flows Quickly with Preemptive Scheduling. In *Proc. ACM SIGCOMM*, 2012.

[27] R. Cruz. A Calculus for Network Delay, Part I: Network Elements in Isolation. *IEEE Transactions on Information Theory*, 37(1):114–131, January 1991.

[28] R. Cruz. A Calculus for Network Delay, Part II: Network Analysis. *IEEE Transactions on Information Theory*, 37(1):132–141, 1991.

[29] A. Parekh and R. Gallager. A Generalized Processor Sharing Approach to Flow Control in Integrated Services Networks: The Single-Node Case. *IEEE/ACM Transactions on Networking (ToN)*, 1, June 1993.

[30] A. Parekh and R. Gallager. A Generalized Processor Sharing Approach to Flow Control in Integrated Services Networks: The Multiple -Node Case. *IEEE/ACM Transactions on Networking (ToN)*, 1, April 1994.

[31] D. Clark, S. Shenker, and L. Zhang. Supporting real-time applications in an integrated services packet network: Architecture and mechanism. In *Proc. ACM SIGCOMM*, 1992.

[32] P. Saab. Scaling memcached at Facebook, 2008. http://www.facebook.com/note.php?note_id=39391378919.

[33] B. Atikoglu, Y. Xu, E. Frachtenberg, S. Jiang, and M. Paleczny. Workload Analysis of a Large-scale Key-value Store. In *Proc. ACM SIGMETRICS*, 2012.

[34] M. P. Grosvenor, M. Schwarzkopf, I. Gog, R. N. M. Watson, A. W. Moore, S. Hand, and J. Crowcroft. Queues don't matter when you can JUMP them! In *Proc. USENIX NSDI*, 2015.

[35] H. Herodotou, F. Dong, and S. Babu. No One (Cluster) Size Fits All: Automatic Cluster Sizing for Data-intensive Analytics. In *ACM SOCC*, 2011.

[36] M. Chowdhury, M. Zaharia, J. Ma, M. Jordan, and I. Stoica. Managing data transfers in computer clusters with orchestra. In *Proc. ACM SIGCOMM*, 2011.

[37] B. Lin and P. A. Dinda. Vsched: Mixing batch and interactive virtual machines using periodic real-time scheduling. In *Proc. ACM/IEEE Supercomputing*, 2005.

[38] C. Xu, S. Gamage, P. N. Rao, A. Kangarlou, R. R. Kompella, and D. Xu. vSlicer: latency-aware virtual machine scheduling via differentiated-frequency CPU slicing. In *Proc. HPDC'12*.

[39] A. Greenberg, J. R. Hamilton, N. Jain, S. Kandula, C. Kim, P. Lahiri, D. A. Maltz, P. Patel, and S. Sengupta. VL2: a scalable and flexible data center network. In *Proc. of ACM SIGCOMM*, 2009.

[40] M. Al-Fares, A. Loukissas, and A. Vahdat. A scalable, commodity data center network architecture. In *Proc. of ACM SIGCOMM*, 2008.

[41] J. Kurose. On Computing Per-Session Performance Bounds in High-Speed Multi-Hop Computer Networks. In *Proc. ACM SIGMETRICS*, 1992.

[42] S. Radhakrishnan, Y. Geng, V. Jeyakumar, A. Kabbani, G. Porter, and A. Vahdat. Senic: Scalable nic for end-host rate limiting. In *Proc. USENIX NSDI*, 2014.

[43] K. LaCurts, J. C. Mogul, H. Balakrishnan, and Y. Turner. Cicada: Introducing Predictive Guarantees for Cloud Networks. In *Proc. USENIX HotCloud*, 2014.

[44] N. G. Duffield, P. Goyal, A. Greenberg, P. Mishra, K. K. Ramakrishnan, and J. E. van der Merive. A flexible model for resource management in virtual private networks. In *Proc. ACM SIGCOMM*, 1999.

[45] D. Xie, N. Ding, Y. C. Hu, and R. Kompella. The Only Constant is Change: Incorporating Time-Varying Network Reservations in Data Centers. In *Proc. ACM SIGCOMM*, 2012.

[46] J.-Y. Le Boudec and P. Thiran. *Network Calculus: A Theory of Deterministic Queuing Systems for the Internet*. Lecture Notes in Computer Science. Springer-Verlag, 2001.

[47] S. Lee, R. Panigrahy, V. Prabhakaran, V. Ramasubramanian, K. Talwar, L. Uyeda, and U. Wieder. Validating Heuristics for Virtual Machines Consolidation. Technical Report MSR-TR-2011-9, MSR, 2011.

[48] Energy Efficient Switches , 2009. http://www.cisco.com/c/dam/en/us/products/collateral/switches/catalyst-2960-series-switches/cisco_catalyst_switches_green.pdf.

[49] R. Mittal, J. Sherry, S. Ratnasamy, and S. Shenker. Recursively cautious congestion control. In *Proc. USENIX NSDI*, 2014.

[50] NDIS Filter Driver. http://msdn.microsoft.com/en-us/library/windows/hardware/ff556030(v=vs.85).aspx.

[51] Linux SKB. http://lxr.free-electrons.com/source/include/linux/skbuff.h.

[52] M. Aron and P. Druschel. Soft timers: efficient microsecond software timer support for network processing. *ACM Transactions on Computer Systems (TOCS)*, 18(3):197–228, 2000.

[53] Luiz Andrr Barroso and Urs Holzle. *The Datacenter as a Computer: An Introduction to the Design of Warehouse-Scale Machines*. Morgan & Claypool Publishers, 2009.

[54] 10GE ToR port buffers. http://www.gossamer-threads.com/lists/nanog/users/149189.

[55] B. C. Vattikonda, G. Porter, A. Vahdat, and A. C. Snoeren. Practical tdma for datacenter ethernet. In *Proc. EuroSys*, 2012.

[56] S. Minzer. Broadband isdn and asynchronous transfer mode (atm). *Communications Magazine, IEEE*, 27(9):17–24, 1989.

[57] S. J. Golestani. A Stop-and-Go Queueing Framework for Congestion Management. In *Proc. ACM SIGCOMM*, 1990.

[58] M. Alizadeh, S. Yang, M. Sharif, S. Katti, N. McKeown, B. Prabhakar, and S. Shenker. pFabric: Minimal Near-Optimal Datacenter Transport. In *ACM SIGCOMM*, 2013.

[59] T. Lam, S. Radhakrishnan, A. Vahdat, and G. Varghese. NetShare: Virtualizing Data Center Networks across Services. Technical Report CS2010-0957, University of California, San Diego, May 2010.

[60] G. Finn. RELIABLE ASYNCHRONOUS TRANSFER PROTOCOL (RATP). RFC 916.

[61] D. Ferrari and D. Verma. A Scheme for Real-Time Channel Establishment in Wide-Area Networks. *IEEE Journal on Selected Areas in Communications*, 8(3):368–379, April 1990.

[62] D. Verma, H. Zhang, and D. Ferrari. Guaranteeing Delat Jitter Bounds in Packet Switching Networks. In *Proc. IEEE Conference on Communications Software (TriComm)*, 1991.

[63] C. R. Kalmanek, H. Kanakia, and S. Keshav. Rate Controlled Servers for Very High-Speed Networks. In *Proc. IEEE Global Telecommunications Conference*, 1989.

[64] H. Zhang and S. Keshav. Comparison of Rate-Based Service Disciplines. In *Proc. ACM SIGCOMM*, 1991.

Condor: Better Topologies Through Declarative Design

Brandon Schlinker[1,2], Radhika Niranjan Mysore[1], Sean Smith[1], Jeffrey C. Mogul[1], Amin Vahdat[1], Minlan Yu[2], Ethan Katz-Bassett[2], and Michael Rubin[1]

[1]Google, Inc. — [2]University of Southern California

ABSTRACT

The design space for large, multipath datacenter networks is large and complex, and no one design fits all purposes. Network architects must trade off many criteria to design cost-effective, reliable, and maintainable networks, and typically cannot explore much of the design space. We present Condor, our approach to enabling a rapid, efficient design cycle. Condor allows architects to express their requirements as constraints via a Topology Description Language (TDL), rather than having to directly specify network structures. Condor then uses constraint-based synthesis to rapidly generate candidate topologies, which can be analyzed against multiple criteria. We show that TDL supports concise descriptions of topologies such as fat-trees, BCube, and DCell; that we can generate known and novel variants of fat-trees with simple changes to a TDL file; and that we can synthesize large topologies in tens of seconds. We also show that Condor supports the daunting task of designing multi-phase network expansions that can be carried out on live networks.

CCS Concepts

•**Networks** → **Topology analysis and generation; Physical topologies;** *Data center networks;*

Keywords

Topology design; expandable topologies; SLO compliance

1. INTRODUCTION

During the design of a datacenter topology, a network architect must balance operational goals with technical, physical and economic constraints. An ideal network would be resilient to any failure, fulfill every application's requirements, and remain under budget. Unfortunately, the underlying constraints are fundamentally at odds with one another. No single network topology design is optimal for all use cases [2], due (among other things) to differences in scale and workloads, and changes in the cost and performance of components (such as switch silicon and opto-electronics).

Hence, architects must understand and make tradeoffs between the cost and availability of technologies on the marketplace, the complexity of wiring, limits on physical failure domains, and the fundamental limitations of routing algorithms. Today, balancing these tradeoffs is more art than science. Architects continually go back to the drawing board to adapt and refine existing topologies, or to design new topologies from scratch.

Today, the process of designing topologies is decidedly manual: a network architect must invent a set of candidate topologies, and then try to identify the best. An architect typically begins by evaluating the utility and feasibility of topologies described in literature or already deployed in production. This involves quantifying a topology's bisection bandwidth, resiliency to failure, cost, complexity, scalability, and other metrics. An architect then evaluates minor variations of the topology, including changes to connectivity, infrastructure, and scale. This tedious process of modification and evaluation severely limits the number of topologies that can be explored, leading to heavy reliance on intuition. It is our belief that this has caused architects to overlook superior topologies, such as F10 [25], for many years.

In this paper, we describe *Condor*, a pipeline that facilitates the rapid generation and evaluation of candidate topologies, enabling an architect to aggressively explore the topology design space. In Condor, architects express topology designs through a declarative language, which drives a constraint-based generation system. They can then evaluate the utility of multiple design options for an expected workload, using Condor's analysis framework. This framework facilitates the evaluation and tuning of a topology design.

Condor has several objectives. We want to make it easier for network architects to explore a complex design space,

SIGCOMM '15 August 17-21, 2015, London, United Kingdom

ACM ISBN 978-1-4503-3542-3/15/08.
DOI: http://dx.doi.org/10.1145/2785956.2787476

thus making it easier to discover novel approaches (e.g., the novel "stripings" we describe in §7) or to rapidly try out new intuitions. We also want to make it easier to express, analyze, and refine specific topologies, while understanding the impact of design choices on tradeoffs between metrics such as bandwidth, fault tolerance, and routing convergence. Our approach is especially valuable for designers of large-scale data-center networks, because of the complexity that arises at larger scales, but it should also be useful to many organizations with medium-scale networks.

We make these contributions:

A declarative language for expressing network topology requirements and goals: Instead of asking architects to design topologies by hand or to implement special-purpose topology-generation software, Condor allows an architect to express requirements and goals using a concise, understandable, declarative Topology Description Language (TDL, §5). Architects use TDL to express high-level properties, rather than specifying low-level wiring.

A constraint-based synthesizer for generating candidate topologies: We implemented a topology synthesizer, using an off-the-shelf constraint solver, to generate specific topologies that comply with TDL descriptions (§6).

Support for network expansion: Operators of large networks typically do not deploy an entire network infrastructure at once, but instead expand their networks in increments. Designing networks to be expandable and designing the phases of an expansion are both challenging problems. Condor is designed to help architects navigate these challenges, both through metrics that evaluate the "expandability" of a network and through TDL and synthesizer support for describing expandable networks and planning the expansion phases – including the problem of expanding a "live" network, while it continues to carry traffic (§9).

2. MOTIVATION

Ideally, a network architect would have a tool that converts a set of requirements and a list of available components into the best possible network design.

Such a tool does not exist. Instead, architects must use an iterative process, generating design options based on their experience and intuition, then analyzing these options against a set of metrics, and refining their designs until they are satisfied. The design space, however, is immense, and architects cannot explore much of it in finite time. We therefore seek a way to speed up this iterative process, while avoiding the exploration of unpromising options.

People have developed tools that assist with this exploration. Mudigonda *et al.* [28] designed tools to find good cost vs. bandwidth tradeoffs for HyperX topologies [1] and for Extended Generalized Fat Trees (EGFTs) [29]. However, these tools are not general: they created different algorithms for HyperX and EGFTs; the algorithms required complex heuristics to reduce the search space; and they analyzed a limited set of metrics (cost, bisection bandwidth, and hop-count). Also, their compute time for even a relatively modest network (8K servers) starts to grow rapidly. Solnushkin [34] presents an algorithm for automated design of 2-layer fat-trees, which improves in some ways on Mudigonda *et al.* [28], but is limited to one kind of tree, and has unknown scaling properties.

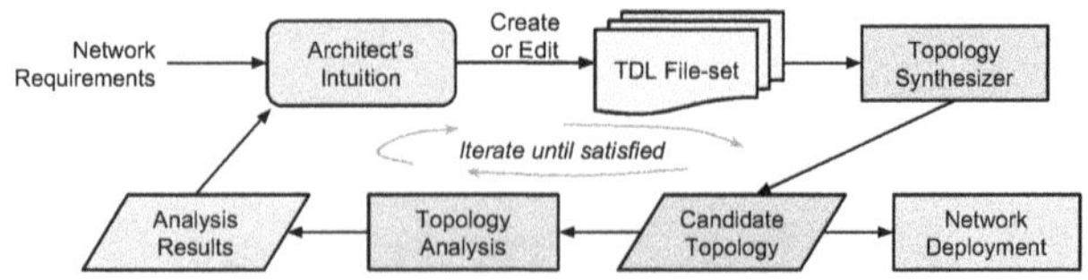

Figure 1: Condor's design iteration loop

Dieter and Dietz [11] described the Cluster Design Rules (CDR) system, which finds an optimal HPC cluster design given a set of requirements. It chooses among a number of network designs (originally not including fat-trees, although this capability was added later [10]), but it does not directly allow specification of network properties, including reliability, and it appears to have hard-coded strategies for network topologies. We could not discover its scalability.

Thus, the current state of the art leads to a relatively long cycle time for iterations that explore novel areas of the design space: someone has to write and debug complex, design-specific, procedural code.

We design the Condor pipeline to *radically decrease the cycle time for this iterative process* and to avoid the need to explore poor tradeoffs. As shown in Figure 1, the architect starts with an intuition about a fabric design, expresses that intuition in a high-level *Topology Description Language* (TDL, §5), invokes a topology synthesizer to generate a set of candidate topologies (§6), and runs these candidates through a suite of topology-analysis functions (§8), to choose the best option.

The architect may have to iterate several times, developing better intuition on each cycle, but Condor does not require anyone to write new topology-specific procedural code, and (as we show in §6.4), Condor's synthesizer runs in minutes or less. Therefore, the architect can iterate rapidly, while optimizing for a combination of many metrics at once.

2.1 The Need for Lifecycle Management

Large datacenter networks often grow to accommodate increasing workloads and evolve to incorporate new technologies. The owner of such a network needs to manage its *lifecycle*, including operations that reconfigure the topology, such as expansions and switch upgrades.

Network operators may need to perform these operations on live networks, without reducing capacity below the network's defined Service Level Objective (SLO) during any operation. It can be difficult to meet this goal, especially given a background rate of component failures [13], the risks inherent in making any changes, and the need to split a major update operation into smaller stages, so as to maintain SLO compliance.

Condor's pipeline addresses two specific aspects of lifecycle management: designing a topology that facilitates future expansions and upgrades, and choosing how to split a network-wide expansion into a set of smaller, SLO-compliant stages. We postpone discussion of these aspects until §9, so as to avoid complicating our initial description of Condor.

3. TERMINOLOGY

We introduce some terms that we will use in this paper:

Topology Description Language (TDL): A human-readable language that enables architects to declaratively express the high-level properties of a topology's design.

Model: A concrete specification of a topology, including physical objects (e.g., switches, links, racks), abstract objects (e.g., link aggregation groups, pods, power domains), and relationships (e.g., "pod P contains switches $S_1, S_2, ..., S_n$" or "switch S_3 contains linecards LC_1 and LC_2"). Condor's **Synthesizer** converts TDL to models, which can then be evaluated and potentially deployed by network operators.

Striping: The pattern of links inter-connecting components in a topology. In a multi-path tree, the striping determines how uplinks from components at layer L_i are spread across switches at layer L_{i+1} [40]. For recursive topologies, the striping determines how links are distributed between groups of components.

Drain: The administrative removal of a link or component from service. Draining a component drains all child components (e.g., draining a rack drains all switches in that rack).

Failure Domain: The set of components that can fail simultaneously. **Power Domain**: The set of components that could fail due to a fault in one power-delivery component.

4. FABRIC DESIGN FACTORS

Prior work has exposed a vast design space, including fat-trees [3], F10 [25], Quasi fat-trees [43], Aspen trees [40], Jellyfish [33], and many others. Ideally, an architect could simply pick a candidate type from this library, based on an understanding of each design's relative strengths and weaknesses, then choose parameters to support a specific use case.

This still leaves architects with many degrees of freedom. First, they may need to modify one of the canonical designs to reduce costs or to meet other requirements – for example, they can create over-subscribed fat-trees.[1] Second,the architect may have to choose a striping out of a large possible space.

In order to choose between the many available options, an architect must consider many constraints and objectives that apply to datacenter networks. In this section, we discuss the most important of these.

Capital, installation, and energy costs: Architects must consider how much it costs to build a network; "bandwidth at any cost" is not a prudent business model. Prior work [11, 28, 31, 34] has covered cost-optimization; we omit further discussion of such costs for reasons of space.

Bandwidth and latency objectives: The efficiency of many applications is dependent on low-loss and low-latency communication with applications and services located on other machines. Architects must ensure that sufficient inter-connection bandwidth is available to minimize the potential for congestion and minimize the path length between machines when possible. However, acceptable bounds on both loss and latency depend heavily on the application workload; two different workloads may vary radically in terms of their tolerance for both loss and latency.

Conceptual complexity: Even if a design is technologically feasible and cost-effective, operators may object to supporting it. For instance, Walraed-Sullivan *et al.* noted [39] that network operators were unwilling to work with random rack-level topologies, such as Jellyfish [33], because it would have been too hard to maintain a human-readable map of the network. Some fat-tree designs also create conceptual complexity for operators and installers; two stripings that are isomorphic may still differ in how easy they are to visualize.

Reliability: While power, cooling, and other critical datacenter infrastructure are often $N + 1$–redundant, it is seldom cost-effective to build $N + 1$–redundant networks. Instead, architects design topologies that gracefully degrade when faced with inevitable component failures. Some prior work has defined reliability in terms of the absence of a partition [8, 9, 39], but an architect may not only want to avoid a partition, but to maintain a given SLO (such as "75% of designed bandwidth") under N component failures.

Some designs, such as F10 [25], are inherently more resilient than others. Alternatively, an architect may choose to add spare capacity to a design, to increase reliability. These choices have costs, so an architect must use a specific failure model, such as MTBF and MTTR for various components, to understand if a design is sufficiently fault-tolerant.

Routing convergence time: Some designs manage routing with distributed routing protocols [4, 7] (e.g., OSPF/BGP); others use centralized SDN controllers [32]. For all such mechanisms, the time for the network to converge to correct routing (loop-free and black-hole-free) depends on the underlying topology. In particular, the topology design determines the number of devices that routing-related information needs to be distributed to, and/or the number of *hops* this information must propagate. We discuss both metrics in §8.

Expandability: As we discussed in §2.1, network owners often need to expand a fabric after installation, sometimes more than once – and may need to do this while the network carries traffic at or near its SLO.

Architects can design fabrics expandable in cost-effective increments [4] that minimize (as much as possible) operational costs while maximizing the chances of maintaining SLOs, even in the face of unplanned component failures during the expansion operation. One may also need to create designs that represent intermediate steps in an expansion, if a single-step expansion would inherently violate an SLO.

Other issues, including physical constraints and compatibility with routing protocols, may also apply; space does not permit us to cover these.

5. TOPOLOGY DESCRIPTION

An architect expresses a network design using Condor's *Topology Description Language* (TDL). TDL is a declarative language that is embedded in an object-oriented language,

[1]Some people reserve the term "fat-tree" for non-blocking fabrics [2]; we use the term in its looser sense.

such as Python or C++, as an Embedded Domain-Specific Language. TDL is "declarative" in the sense that it is not used to procedurally define a concrete network topology. Instead, architects use TDL to express a topology's structural building blocks and the relationships between them (§5.1), along with potential connectivity (§5.2.1), and constraints on connectivity (§5.2.2). Condor's synthesizer (§6) converts TDL into a set of candidate *models* (§3), each of which represents a concrete topology that satisfies the constraints declared in TDL. Thus, Condor allows an architect to focus on defining the characteristics of the desired topology, rather than on writing procedural code to explore the design space.

TDL is most similar to NED [38], a language incorporated into the OMNeT++ [37] network simulation framework. However, an architect uses NED to describe a *concrete* topology, and must procedurally define the connectivity among building blocks.

A given TDL description specifies a (possibly empty) set of candidates, rather than exactly one, because there is no *a priori* reason to assume that exactly one topology satisfies the chosen constraints. We expect an architect will explore the design space by adding and removing constraints, and then applying the analysis suite (§8) to decide which, if any, of the candidates meets their requirements. This iterative process is required because we do not know how to express all of an architect's high-level objectives, such as SLO compliance, as constraints on connectivity. While we expect architects to examine the models (via a visualization tool) to gain insight into the candidates, they never directly edit these models. If they need to make changes, they must modify the building blocks, constraints, and other details in the TDL description, and synthesize new candidates. Separating a topology's description from the procedural code required for generating a model makes it easier to capture and understand an architect's intent, dramatically reducing the potential for errors.

TDL can be spread across multiple files, known as a *TDL file-set*, which in our current system consists of one or more Python modules. The use of multiple files supports modularity and reuse. In addition, TDL makes it easy to re-use common aspects of network designs: not just building blocks, but especially the essential aspects of a "species" of related fabrics. That is, an architect can start with a generic species (e.g, a fat-tree built from 48-port switches) and then include additional constraints to create a concrete "individual" network. We designed the TDL to support a wide range of topology species, including tree [3, 25], Quasi fat-tree [43], recursive [15, 16], some flattened-butterfly topologies [22], Quartz [26], Jellyfish [33], and others.

We show how TDL can be used to express a fat-tree topology [3] in Figure 2. We will refer to this example throughout our discussion of TDL constructs.

5.1 Describing Building Blocks

An architect begins by describing a topology's common *building blocks*, each representing a physical component, such as a switch, patch panel, or rack, or a logical component, such as a "pod" in a fat-tree topology [3]. The architect can also describe parent-child ("contains") relationships between

```
# reusable 10GbE switch building block
class Switch10GbE extends TDLSwitchBlock:
  function Switch10GbE(num_ports, name):
    port = new TDLPortBlock(TENGBPS)
    Contains(port, num_ports)
    ...
# parameterizable FatTree building block
class FatTree extends TDLBuildingBlock:
  function FatTree(num_pods):
    # equations from Alfares et al. 2008
    num_ports = num_pods
    num_spines = pow(num_pods / 2, 2)
    num_sw_per_pod_tier = num_pods / 2

    # spine, agg, & ToR switches
    spine = new Switch10GbE(num_ports, "spine")
    agg = new Switch10GbE(num_ports, "agg")
    tor = new Switch10GbE(num_ports, "tor")

    # a pod contains agg and ToR switches
    pod = new TDLBuildingBlock("pod")
    pod.Contains(agg, num_sw_per_pod_tier)
    pod.Contains(tor, num_sw_per_pod_tier)

    # a fat-tree contains spines and pods
    Contains(spine, num_spines)
    Contains(pod, num_pods)

    # pairs of components eligible for connection
    pod_connector = pod.Connects(agg, tor)
    s_connector = Connects(spine, agg)

    # constraints on the Connector objects
    # in each pod, an agg connects to every ToR
    pod_connector.ConnectPairsWithXLinks(agg, tor, 1)

    # every spine connects to every pod
    s_connector.ConnectPairsWithXLinks(spine, pod, 1)
```

Figure 2: TDL pseudocode describing a fat-tree topology

```
# Base class for all TDL blocks
class TDLBuildingBlock:
  function TDLBuildingBlock(name):
    ...
  function Contains(bb_obj, num_of):
    # Records parent-child relationship
    ...
  function Connects(lhs_bb_obj, rhs_bb_obj):
    # Records and returns new TDLConnector obj
    ...
# Specialized TDL classes
## L2/L3 Device
class TDLSwitchBlock extends TDLBuildingBlock
## L2/L3 Device Port
class TDLPortBlock extends TDLBuildingBlock
```

Figure 3: Pseudocode describing TDL building block classes

building blocks. These blocks and the relationships between them form an abstract tree, with one block designated as the root upon instantiation.

Figure 3 sketches the classes used to describe building blocks in TDL, including specialized classes used to distinguish physical devices (like switches and ports) involved in connectivity. Building blocks can be described by instantiating an instance of one of these classes. In addition, because TDL is embedded in an object-oriented language, architects can generate a library of reusable, parameterizable building block classes by declaring subclasses. These subclasses can be then be reused and shared among topology descriptions.

Building blocks are a natural abstraction for topology description. For instance, a homogeneous fat-tree network constructs spine (called "core" in [3]), pod, aggregation, and top-of-rack (ToR) logical building blocks, all from one physical switch type.

Our corresponding fat-tree example (Figure 2) begins with the declaration of a parameterizable building block class,

Switch10GbE. This building block contains a variable number of ports, and is instantiated to describe spine, aggregation, and ToR switches in the FatTree building block class. During instantiation, a name describes the purpose of each switch block instance.

The parameterizable *FatTree* building block class starts at line 8. An instance of this class serves as the root of the abstract tree, and contains spine and pod building blocks. The pod building block (lines 21 - 23) in turn contains aggregation and ToR switch building blocks (instantiated on lines 17 - 18). Each switch building block object in the FatTree block is instantiated from the Switch10GbE building block class.

This hierarchical model also works for describing recursive topologies, such as DCell [16], a topology that recursively uses two physical building blocks (switches and servers) and a logical building block for each level of aggregation. In a DCell topology, level DCell_0 contains a switch and multiple endhosts, while a $\text{DCell}_{i>0}$ contains multiple DCell_{i-1}s.

In addition to describing hierarchy, the architect can record meta-information, such as the failure properties (Mean Time Between Failures, Mean Time to Recovery) of a physical device (used in §8.4).

5.1.1 *Grouping by Rule*

TDL supports rules to express *groups* of components, in cases where they cannot easily be described with a "Contains" relationship. For instance, after describing a fat-tree's physical and logical network components, an architect can use rules to describe how each physical component is assigned to a rack, to a failure domain, or to an arbitrary group. As with connectivity constraints, architects can quickly modify grouping rules to try different assignment approaches or to handle variations between physical facilities. We use rules to generate groups in §7, when describing F10 with TDL.

5.2 Describing Connectivity

Given a set of building blocks, the architect describes how they should be connected, by defining candidate connections with *connectivity pairs*, and then using *constraints* together with *tiebreakers* to eliminate potential connections.

5.2.1 *Defining Connectivity Pairs*

Connectivity pairs express pairs of components and/or groups that are eligible to be connected. A connectivity pair consists of left-hand and right-hand side (LHS and RHS) building block objects, and is expressed by calling "Connects" on a "scope" building block. The scope building block must "Contain" both of the building blocks in the connectivity pair. During synthesis, for each scope component instantiated from the scope building block, the set of candidate connections is equal to the Cartesian product of the component's successors that were instantiated from the LHS and RHS building blocks, respectively.

For instance, in lines 30 and 31 of our fat-tree example (Figure 2), the architect defines two connectivity pairs, each specifying a pair of building blocks. Abstractly:

1. In every pod, connect aggregation & ToR switches
2. In every fat-tree, connect spine & aggregation switches

```
class TDLConnector:
  ...
  # constraints on connectivity of objects
  # derived from a specified building block
  function ConnectXLinks(bb_obj, x_links)
  function ConnectAtMostXLinks(...)
  ...
  # constraints on pairwise connectivity
  function ConnectPairsWithXLinks(bb_obj_1, bb_obj_2, x_links)
  function ConnectPairsWithAtLeastXLinks(...)
  ...
  # support for custom constraints
  function AddConstraint(constraint_obj)
```

Figure 4: Partial set of TDL constraints

The *In every* part defines the scope of candidate connections. The first connectivity pair, for example, ensures that a ToR switch can only be connected to an aggregation switch in the same pod. Thus, for each pod, the set of candidate connections is the Cartesian product of the pod's aggregation and ToR switches. Similarly, the second connectivity pair permits connections between spine and aggregation switches in the same fat-tree.

For some topologies, such as flattened butterfly [22] and recursive topologies, some connectivity pairs have the same building blocks as the LHS and RHS. For example, for a DCell network, the connectivity pairs are:

1. In every DCell_i where i > 0, connect all DCell_{i-1}s.
2. In every DCell_i where i = 0, connect hosts and switches.

Connectivity pairs can be declared at different *levels* of the hierarchy. In DCell, the pairs could be defined between hosts, instead of between DCell_{i-1}s, which would enable an architect to express constraints at finer granularities. However, it also increases the number of pairings produced by the Cartesian product, expanding the solution space that the synthesizer must navigate. We would need this level of granularity to generate topologies that exactly match those in the DCell paper [16], but not to meet the paper's DCell specification, as discussed in §5.3.

5.2.2 *Constraints and Tiebreakers*

After defining candidate connections, the architect specifies constraints on connectivity. Without such constraints, the synthesizer will simply make arbitrary connections between eligible components until connections are no longer possible (e.g., no more ports, etc.). This, for example, could leave a single ToR switch connected to a single aggregation switch, creating a single point of failure or a disconnected network. Constraints and tiebreakers allow the architect to guide the synthesis process to avoid bad choices.

Constraints: Constraints can be expressed on the building blocks referenced within a connectivity pair or any of their predecessors, and can be specified on individual building blocks, or on pairs or groups of building blocks. Constraints are associated with a TDLConnector object that is returned when a connectivity pair is declared, and constrain the set of candidate connections in the connectivity pair's scope. Figure 4 shows a partial set of TDL constraints.

Constraints applied to an individual building block can set the minimum, maximum, or exact number of connections for every component instantiated from that building block. Every component starts with a default constraint, to ensure that the component never has more connections than available ports. Constraints propagate downwards; e.g., if a switch containing linecards cannot have more than N connections, then the sum of its linecards' connections can not exceed N.

Constraints applied to a pair of building blocks bound the number of connections for every pair of associated components, or between a single component of the LHS descriptor and all components of the RHS descriptor.

An architect's choice of pair-wise constraints is the most important tool for balancing the many tradeoffs in topology design, and hence represents the architect's primary design insights. In particular, an architect can use pair-wise connectivity constraints to achieve fault-tolerance through diversity.

In lines 35 and 38 of our fat-tree example (Figure 2), we use pair-wise constraints to describe a fat-tree's connectivity:

1. Every aggregation switch must connect to every ToR.[2]
2. Every spine switch must connect to every pod.

By default, a solution must satisfy the boolean AND of all per-component and pair-wise constraints. However, TDL supports explicit ORing of constraints (OR operations can be recursive), which is especially useful for pair-wise constraints: e.g., a component pair must have either X connections or 0.

Tiebreakers: Condor's synthesizer (§6) uses a constraint solver to find candidate topologies that meet the constraints in a TDL description. The constraint solver iterates serially through the candidate connections when finding things to connect. Sometimes, but not always, the order of this iteration is key to finding a solution efficiently, or affects a property that matters to the architect, or both (see §9.4).

An architect can include an ordered set of one or more *tiebreakers*, written as callback functions, to control this ordering. (We include a default tiebreaker to maximize human-readability of the generated connectivity.)

Late-bound constraints: An architect may wish to apply constraints whose numeric parameters vary based on decisions made during synthesis. *Late-bound constraints* (LBCs) are pre-defined in TDL as alternatives to architect-written procedures to derive such constraints, and are compiled into min/max pair-wise constraints during synthesis. The only LBC currently defined is "diversity." This LBC spreads connectivity across as many pairs as possible, and ensures the number of connections between pairs is equal ± 1.

5.2.3 Custom and group constraints

Custom constraints: The synthesizer's solver supports more complex constraints than described so far. Since TDL is embedded in an object-oriented language, architects can write custom constraints that interact with the solver by subclassing the *Constraint* class and then defining their constraint. For instance, one could define an *oversubscription ratio* constraint for a tree, bounding the ratio between the number of *incoming* links from a lower stage and the number of *outgoing* links towards an upper stage. We show in §7 how we use custom constraints to express designs such as F10 [25].

Constraints on groups: Connectivity constraints can refer to groups (§5.1.1), so that (e.g.) one can require that every aggregation switch in a fat-tree connects to spine switches in at least two power domains.

As another example, suppose one wants to reserve ports 1–4 on each ToR for connecting to aggregation switches (perhaps to simplify wiring). This could be expressed by adding a new rule to define groups of port objects based on port number, then adding connectivity constraints dictating where these groups can be used.

5.3 Examples of TDL's Concision

We believe (but cannot prove) that TDL's concise descriptions will lead to better designs and fewer errors. To support this, we counted lines of code for TDL descriptions of several networks. As shown in Figure 2, TDL can express all of the fat-tree designs in Al-Fares *et al.* [3] in under 30 non-comment lines. TDL can express BCube networks in 32 lines and Facebook's fabric [4] in 33 lines. To express DCell-like networks,[3] we need only change 2 lines from BCube's description, and add 10 more.

6. NETWORK SYNTHESIS

Condor's synthesizer converts a TDL file-set into a model for a network topology that complies with the TDL specification. A model represents both the parent-child relationships between components (the *hierarchy graph*, §6.1) and the connectivity between components (the *connectivity graph*, §6.2-§6.3). Synthesis of connectivity involves solving three problems: formulating synthesis as a constraint satisfaction problem [36] (§6.2); allowing an architect to influence the results via tiebreakers (§6.2.1); and optimizing the synthesizer's performance to support a rapid design cycle (§6.3).

The synthesizer may fail to generate a model, either because the constraints in the TDL description cannot be satisfied or because finding a suitable result exceeds a timeout. In such cases, the architect may have to try again with different constraints or tiebreakers. If more than one model would satisfy the constraints, the synthesizer generates only one; the architect can generate additional candidate models by adding, removing, or changing the tiebreakers (§6.2.1).

6.1 Synthesizing the Hierarchy Graph

The synthesizer constructs a hierarchy graph, beginning by converting the root building block instance into the graph's root "component," and then recursively converting contained building blocks (expressed with the "Contains" relationship in TDL) into successor components. Each component represents a concrete incarnation of a building block. For instance, in our fat-tree example (Figure 2) the synthesizer generates

[2]Constraints are applied to the set of candidate connections generated during synthesis for each scope; thus, this constraint only requires connections between aggregation and ToR switches in the *same* pod.

[3]It would take more lines of TDL and more solver memory to synthesize the exact striping defined in the DCell paper. The striping we produce meets all of the specifications defined in the paper, and only requires a trivial adjustment to DCell's path lookup algorithm.

a component for the root building block (FatTree). Then, since the root building block contains pod and spine building blocks, the synthesizer instantiates one or more pod and spine components. This recursion continues, resulting in the subsequent instantiation of aggregation, ToR, and port components.

After the synthesizer instantiates a component, it adds a reference from the component back to the building block that it was derived from, and adds a directed edge in the hierarchy graph from the parent component to the child component (i.e., each pod will have a directed edge to each of its ToR switches). Once the synthesizer has instantiated all components, it generates groups based on the grouping rules defined in the TDL (§5.1.1). The synthesizer adds directed edges from each group object to the components it contains.

6.2 Synthesizing Connectivity

Most of the work of synthesis is to find appropriate connectivity between components in the hierarchy graph. The synthesizer generates connectivity by processing the connectivity pairs associated with components in the graph. Components are processed in reverse of the order in which they were instantiated. Thus, connectivity generation begins at the *lowest* non-leaf level or stage in the hierarchy graph (e.g., at the aggregation and ToR components in our fat-tree example).[4]

For each component, the synthesizer identifies the associated building block and determines if the building block references connector objects (generated by the use of the "Connects" construct in TDL). Each connector object is processed independently during synthesis. The synthesizer generates a set of candidate connections and then applies constraints and tiebreakers to choose the connections to add. The chosen connections are then recorded as edges in the connectivity graph, and the process repeats for the next connector and for subsequent components.

Scope: For each component with a connectivity pair, the synthesizer will only consider connections within the component's *scope*, defined as the component's successors in the hierarchy graph. Thus, when processing the connectivity pair associated with a pod in our fat-tree example (Figure 2), the synthesizer will only consider connections between the ToR and aggregation switches within that pod.

Generating candidate connections: For each connector, the synthesizer creates two lists of components in the hierarchy model. Each list contains the in-scope components that correspond to one of the two building blocks referenced in the connector's connectivity pair. The Cartesian product of these two lists (after removing any self-connections) represents all possible *candidate connections* between the components within them. For instance, when the synthesizer processes a pod component in our fat-tree example, it will generate a list of aggregation and ToR switches that are successors of the pod in the hierarchy graph. Every pairing of an aggregation and ToR switch will be considered a candidate connection.

[4]In tree networks, this approach ensures, without the need for additional constraints, that sufficient ports remain available for connectivity at higher levels.

Finding the right connections: Out of the set of candidate connections, it is likely that only a proper subset can be established without violating constraints in the TDL description (although in some cases, constraints may prevent establishment of *any* candidate connections). We treat the problem of determining which connections *should* be made as a constraint satisfaction problem (CSP) [36]. CSPs consist of a set of decision variables, each assigned an integer domain, and a set of constraints on a collection of one or more decision variables. Our implementation uses the open-source *or-tools* constraint solver [14], but other solvers could be used.

Generating decision variables: For every candidate connection, the synthesizer generates an integer variable to represent the number of links that could be established in the current scope for that candidate. This variable has a domain of 0...*MinPairPorts*, where *MinPairPorts* is the minimum, over the two components in the candidate, of the number of successor ports still available for connection, given that some of these components' ports may have already been used.

Following the generation of such an integer variable, the synthesizer stores the variable in a data structure that supports the lookup of candidate connectivity associated with any component, or between any pair of components. This structure also allows retrieval of any variable associated with a component's predecessor, or pair of predecessors.[5] The synthesizer uses this structure to set up constraints.

Constraining decision variables: Next, the synthesizer applies constraints, converting late-bound constraints to numerical constraints based on the model's state.

TDL enables architects to describe constraints on the connectivity of components derived from a building block, or between pairs of components derived from a pair of building blocks. However, these high-level constraints cannot be processed directly by the underlying constraint solver. Instead, the synthesizer must convert these high-level constraints into integer expressions, and then compose constraints from these integer expressions, combined with boolean and relational operators. The synthesizer then provides these constraints to the solver to guide the generation of connectivity.

Custom architect-defined constraint classes (§5.2.3) have a similar workflow. These custom TDL constraints, implemented as callbacks, retrieve the variables associated with one or more components and/or component pairs, then generate and return a set of CSP constraints, which the synthesizer passes to the solver.

6.2.1 *Navigating the Solution Space*

Following the generation of decision variables and the application of constraints, a solution is requested from the constraint solver. The solver operates by choosing a variable from a set of unbound decision variables and assigning it a value within its domain. The solver stops once it has assigned a value to all variables or determines that a solution is infeasible.

[5]This association is important when processing constraints, as a candidate connection between components C_1 and C_2 is also a candidate connection between their predecessors.

Tiebreakers: At the beginning of each decision, the solver must chose a decision variable to operate on next, from a set of unbound variables. By default, the relative rank of these decision variables is equal, and thus unbound variables are processed in the order they were instantiated. The order of this iteration determines which valid solution is returned,[6] and is sometimes key to efficient synthesis (see §9.4).

Architect-defined tiebreakers (§5.2.2), implemented as callbacks, impose a rank ordering on the set of unbound decision variables. When the solver needs to choose the next variable to operate on, it updates the rank of decision variables by serially invoking these callbacks (if any).

6.2.2 *Processing the Solver's Output*

If the solver finds a solution for a scope, it binds each integer variable instantiated for that scope to a single value within its domain, which represents the number of links connecting a pair of components. For each such link, the synthesizer allocates an available successor port[7] from each of the connected components and generates a new link object to represent the connection between these ports. These link objects, taken together, form the connectivity graph. When two components are connected via multiple links, we also add an aggregated logical link to the graph, which simplifies later analysis (§8).

The solver may fail to find a solution for one of several reasons: the constraints are unsatisfiable, or the solver has run longer than a user-specified timeout, or the solver has had to backtrack more than a user-specified number of times. Depending on the reason for failure, the architect might need to change the constraints or improve the tiebreakers in order for the solver to find a solution.

6.3 Efficient Synthesis

Avoiding backtracking during synthesis: Constraint solvers search for a solution by selecting an unbound variable and assigning the variable a value in its domain. Each assignment constrains the solution space and, depending on constraints, may reduce the domains of unbound variables (potentially to the point of forcing an assignment).

Constraint solvers are general purpose tools and are oblivious to our problem domain. Without guidance, a constraint solver may assign values to variables in a manner that constricts the search space to the point that the solver cannot find a valid solution, even when solution is possible. For instance, the *or-tools* constraint solver used by Condor will (by default) assign a variable the minimum value in its domain, thus setting the number of connections between every pair as 0. This naïve approach will almost certainly lead to *backtracking*, a state where the constraint solver detects that a solution is infeasible (given previous assignments) and reverts one or more of its previous decisions. By default, a constraint solver will branch and backtrack until it finds a solution or has explored the entire search space; both backtracking and full search can be costly (see §9.4 for an example where exploring the entire search space is infeasible).

To facilitate a rapid design loop, the synthesizer allows the user to set limits on the number of branching and backtracking operations, and on the maximum time allowed for exploring the solution space. We have also designed heuristics that reduce the potential for backtracking, including (among others, not described due to space constraints):

Greedy connection assignment: We use a "greedy" heuristic to tell the solver to assign as many connections as possible, at each step, to each integer variable; this tends to minimize backtracking. Being greedy also allows the solver to spread connections across a smaller set of components, which is critical when synthesizing expandable topologies (§9).

Efficiently synthesizing recursive topologies: The synthesizer must allocate an integer variable for every candidate connection, so synthesis of large, direct-connect topologies could require millions or even billions of such variables. For instance, synthesizing a DCell_3 [16] network with N=4, described with host-to-host connectivity, would require over half a billion variables. Memory limits often make solving this size of constraint problem infeasible, and, even if sufficient memory is available, solving a CSP with millions of variables can take a long time. Instead, we leverage the recursive nature of these topologies to reduce the number of decision variables required.

For example, in §5.2.1, we defined the connectivity of a DCell topology at the granularity of DCell building blocks ("In every DCell_i where i > 1, connect DCell_{i-1}s"), instead of at the granularity of individual server building blocks. For many recursive topologies, including DCell, it is possible to describe the topology at this level of granularity, as long as links generated between "DCells" are balanced evenly across the end hosts within the group; TDL can express this balance.

6.4 Synthesizer Performance

Table 1 shows synthesizer CPU and memory costs for a variety of networks. We use the NetworkX graph library [17] for storing all graph structures as adjacency lists. NetworkX is written in Python and could probably be replaced with something much faster and more memory-efficient. Our current implementation of the rest of the synthesizer is also in Python, which adds some overhead; we plan to implement a new version in C++. However, the current performance is already fast enough for most purposes, and we see approximately linear CPU and memory scaling (vs. the number of end hosts) within a family of topologies.

7. THE POWER OF TDL: TO F10 AND BEYOND!

In this section, we show that the TDL allows an architect to rapidly discover novel stripings in a fat-tree [3] topology.

The traditional fat-tree striping, shown in Figure 5, can be expressed as: the *Nth* aggregation switch in every pod connects to the same spine switches, and every spine switch

[6] Because an architect expresses connectivity declaratively with pairs and constraints, rather than by procedurally specifying connections between individual components, the constraint solver could return any one of multiple valid solutions.

[7] If a building block has multiple types of successor port (e.g., 10Gb and 40Gb ports), the architect must specify a choice, in TDL, as an attribute of the relevant connectivity pair.

Topology	Switch count	Link count	# of end hosts	CPU secs‡	Mem. (GB)
DCell, n=16,k=2	4641	148512	74256	75	2.59
DCell, n=24,k=2	15025	721200	360600	346	12.5
BCube, n=16,k=3	16384	262144	65536	116	4.0
BCube, n=24,k=3	55296	1327104	331766	597	20.9
FatTree*, 16 pods	320	2048	1024	2	0.069
FatTree, 40 pods	2000	32000	16000	16	0.60
FatTree, 64 pods	5120	131072	65536	61	2.4
FatTree, 80 pods	8000	256000	128000	117	4.8
Facebook Fabric†	5184	36864	221184	57	2.5

*** all fat-trees are 3-stage ‡no trials here needed backtracking**
† assuming this uses 96 pods, 96-port switches, 4 uplinks/ToR

Table 1: Synthesizer performance for various examples

connects to every pod once. Given this striping, if aggregation switch N in pod X fails, none of the Nth aggregation switches in *any* other pod can reach pod X. As discussed in §8.3, such a failure results in packet loss until the network's routing has reconverged.

Describing F10: In F10, Liu *et. al* [25] reduce the impact of an aggregation switch failure on the connectivity between two groups of pods. With F10, pods are connected to spine switches using either of two different stripings (A or B), as shown in Figure 5. The use of two stripings ensures that the Nth aggregation switch in a pod with striping A is able to direct traffic to a destination in a pod with striping B through multiple disjoint (shortest) paths.[8]

Although the F10 authors described the construction of the A and B stripings arithmetically, we use the following constraint to describe their construction: *Where* agg_A *and* agg_B *are aggregation switches in pods with A and B stripings, respectively, every pair of aggregation switches* (agg_A, agg_B) *can connect to each other via at most one spine switch.* This constraint ensures that an aggregation switch in a pod with striping A connects to as many different aggregation switches in a pod with striping B as possible.

Using TDL, we can express a fat-tree with A and B stripings by adding constraints to a traditional fat-tree:

1. We define rules to split pods equally into two groups, A and B (§5.1.1).
2. We define a custom constraint to prohibit any pair of aggregation switches (a, b) (with $a \in A$ and $b \in B$) from from having more than one spine switch in common.

With TDL, we express the difference between fat-trees and F10 in 29 lines (including 18 lines for the custom constraint), much less code than a procedural Python program to model a variable-size AB fat-tree (about 150 lines).

Beyond F10: With TDL, we were able to compartmentalize F10-specific constraints from the basic fat-tree constraints. In this section, we discuss how this modularity led to new insights.

Once we understood how F10's AB stripings could be expressed with TDL, we wondered if we could further reduce the impact of an aggregation switch failure by adding an additional striping. By modifying the TDL grouping rule

[8]The number of disjoint paths increases with topology size.

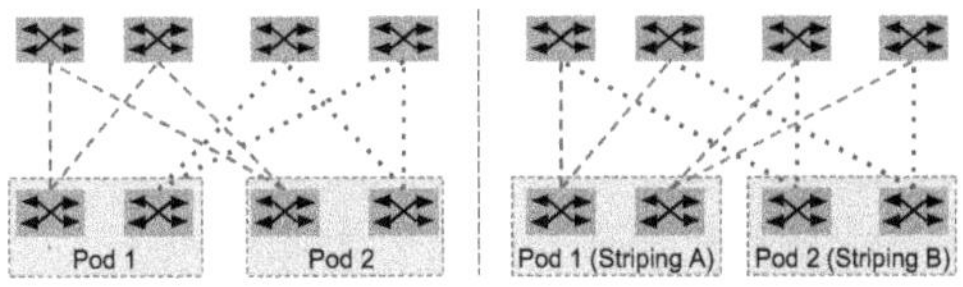

Figure 5: Connectivity with traditional and F10 fat-tree stripings

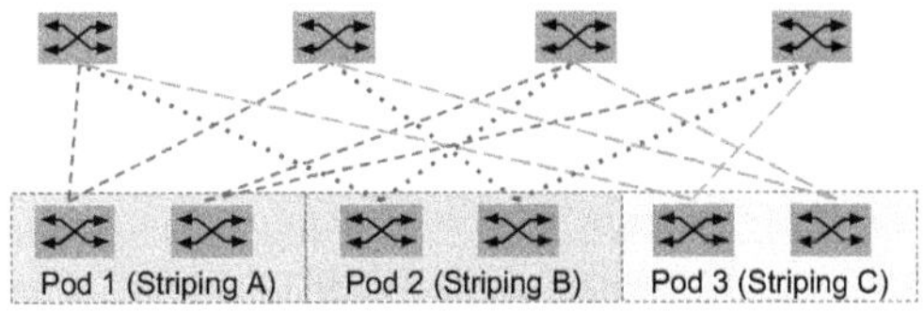

Figure 6: Connectivity with A, B, and C stripings

to split pods into three groups (A, B, C) and applying our F10-inspired constraint to all pairs of groups, we generated the ABC topology shown in Figure 6. Like F10's A and B stripings, every aggregation switch in a pod with striping S has 2+ disjoint paths to a pod with a striping other than S.[8] However, using three stripings increases the probability of any pair of pods having a different striping to 66%.

After generating the ABC stripings, we investigated the bounds on the number of stripings we could create. Using the same TDL, we synthesized larger fat-tree topologies (5+ pods), varying the number of groups that P pods are divided into between 1 and P. Our F10-inspired constraint requires that each group has a distinct striping (e.g., splitting pods into three distinct groups requires three distinct stripings: A, B, and C).

From this experiment, we determined that the number of possible stripings grows sub-linearly with the number of pods. For instance, we can generate up to 4 stripings (A, B, C, and D) for a 6-pod fat-tree, and up to 6 stripings for a 10-pod fat-tree.[9]

We extracted the following intuition from our analysis of the generated stripings and constraints:

- Our constraint specifies that any pair of aggregation switches from pods with different stripings may connect to at most one spine switch in common.
- Let $SpineSet_i$ and $SpineSet_j$ be the sets of spine switches connected to aggregation switches agg_i and agg_j, respectively. From our constraint, for any agg_i and agg_j in pods with different stripings, $SpineSet_i \cap SpineSet_j \leq 1$.
- By construction, *NumUplinksPerAgg* and *NumAggsPerPod* are equal in a fat-tree [3], and their product is equal to *NumSpines*. Thus, for any agg_i and agg_j in different stripings, $SpineSet_i \cap SpineSet_j = 1$.
- Let $AggSet_j$ be a set of aggregation switches from pods with different stripings connected to $spine_j$ ($|AggSet_j|$ = *NumStripings*). Given our constraints, $\forall\ agg_i,\ agg_k \in AggSet_j$, s.t. $i \neq k$, $SpineSet_i \cap SpineSet_k = \{spine_j\}$, meaning each agg_i needs a disjoint $SpineSet_i \setminus \{spine_j\}$. The maximum number of disjoint $SpineSet_i \setminus \{spine_j\}$ (and thus the maximum value of *NumStripings*) is equal to (*Num-*

[9]These stripings are available at http://nsl.cs.usc.edu/condor.

Spines minus $spine_j$) divided by (*NumUplinksPerAgg* minus the uplink to $spine_j$).

From these, we can define an upper bound on the number of stripings possible for a fat-tree of a given size:

$$NumStripings \leq \frac{NumSpines - 1}{NumUplinksPerAgg - 1} \quad (1)$$

Our experimental results coincide with this upper bound (e.g., we were able to generate up to 6 stripings in a 10-pod fat-tree). However, it becomes computationally difficult to synthesize the maximum number of stripings in larger topologies; Condor's synthesizer cannot generate 12 stripings, the upper bound for a 22-pod fat-tree, within 30 minutes. When we investigated how to improve performance, we determined that our F10-inspired constraint generates *Balanced Incomplete Block Designs* [19,42] (BIBDs). Efficient synthesis of BIBDs is a known problem [27], and the exact conditions required for their existence are not known [18].

However, in larger topologies where synthesis is more difficult, we can trade improved synthesizer performance for fault-tolerance. Our F10-inspired constraint provides maximum fault-tolerance, by ensuring that every pair of aggregation switches in pods with different stripings can communicate through the spine layer.[10] Depending on the level of fault-tolerance required, our constraint can be adjusted to allow aggregation switches in different pods to connect to between 1 and *NumUplinksPerAgg* − 1 spine switches in common, which respectively varies fault-tolerance between *NumUplinksPerAgg* and 2 disjoint paths. As the level of fault-tolerance guaranteed by the constraint is reduced, the size of the corresponding solution space is increased, and synthesis performance is dramatically improved.

8. TOPOLOGY ANALYSIS

Once a TDL file-set has been synthesized into a model, an architect can analyze the model against various metrics, such as those described in §4. We would like these analyses to be both accurate (to avoid misleading the designer) and fast (to enable rapid iterations).

Some metrics, such as cost, are easily calculated. However, a topology's utility depends largely on its ability to maintain SLO compliance, determined by how traffic patterns interact with the topology throughout its lifecycle. These interactions can either be calculated precisely through detailed simulation, which is quite hard to scale to large datacenter networks, or through faster but approximate algorithms.

For example, we cannot accurately quantify the "bandwidth" of a topology for a given traffic matrix independent from how routing protocols, transport protocols, switch queueing mechanisms, and traffic engineering interact. The likelihood of failed and "drained" components and links adds more complexity.

Papers about datacenter networks typically fall back on proxy metrics, such as bisection bandwidth and hop-count [8, 15, 16, 28, 31, 33]. These metrics can be relatively easy to compute but do not reflect the full complexity of the problem [20], and they ignore the reality that most networks are never operated under worst-case traffic matrices. Also, "[f]inding the exact value of the bisection width has proven to be challenging for some specific networks" [5]. Network owners learn, through hard-won operational experience, that other proxy metrics are better predictors of SLO compliance.

Yet without a means to quantify a topology's bandwidth, we cannot develop good metrics for concepts such as reliability or expandability, since these are best described as a network's ability to maintain its bandwidth SLO in the face of random link failures or planned drains. (Some prior work has used the probability of a topology becoming partitioned as an indicator of fault-tolerance [8,9,39], but this generally is not sufficient to predict compliance with a minimum-bandwidth SLO.) Therefore, we use an approximate bandwidth metric (§8.1) to illustrate how changes in the TDL for a network (or its expansion plan) affect several metrics of interest.

We do not claim to have solved the problem of quantifying a topology's bandwidth; our metrics have many limitations. We believe that our metrics provide real value to network architects and hope that they motivate further research.

8.1 Approximate Bandwidth Metric

Our approximate bandwidth metric (ABM) evaluates a topology's ability to support an architect-defined traffic matrix. (We do not assume a worst-case traffic matrix, because many networks are unlikely to be operated under such conditions. Architects often maintain spare or protected capacity and employ intelligent scheduling techniques to improve job locality [21,23,30,41].) The ABM can be used to compare an application's predicted throughput against a set of candidate topologies (e.g., tree topologies with varying levels of oversubscription) and to evaluate application throughput when a topology is in a degraded state (§8.2).

An architect uses historical and (projected) future demands to generate one or more pair-wise traffic matrices of offered loads between components (e.g., host-to-host or ToR-to-ToR).[11] For each traffic matrix, the metric estimates the throughput of each flow, assuming fair sharing of overloaded links. We estimate throughput by propagating flow demands through the network and proportionally reducing each flow's demands at each saturated link. We reduce this to an aggregate scalar: the sum of achieved flow rates divided by the sum of offered loads. (Other aggregates are possible.)

In a multipath network, we must split flows as they propagate through each junction point. For the results later in this paper, we treat flows as fluid[12] and split them at each junction between all shortest-path next-hops. By default, flows are split equally among next-hops, but we also support dividing flows based on the number of physical links to each next-hop (comparable to ECMP). We can extend this metric to approximate WCMP [44] or architect-specified routing functions, but we omit these details for space reasons.

[10] E.g. in a 22-pod fat-tree, an aggregation switch with striping *S* has 11 disjoint paths to a pod with a striping other than *S*.

[11] Matrices can be weighted to produce an aggregate score.

[12] We assume flows defined in traffic matrices represent an aggregate of application flows, and thus are fluid and splittable.

Limitations: The ABM only supports tree topologies. In addition, to reduce computation time, we perform two rounds of flow propagation: (1) upwards propagation from ToRs towards higher tiers of the tree and (2) downwards propagation from higher tiers towards ToRs. As a result, our metric only determines a lower bound on the throughput of each flow in the traffic matrix and only works for strict up-down routing. It cannot handle (for example) F10, which uses *ToR bouncing* to route around failures [25].

8.2 Simplified Reliability Metric

Architects need to know the probability that a candidate topology will maintain its bandwidth SLO, given a *failure model* including the Mean Time Between Failures (MTBF) and Mean Time to Repair (MTTR) for each component.

TDL allows specification of MTBF and MTTR for building blocks. We use these values to compute an SLO metric, using Markov Chain Monte Carlo (MCMC) simulation [35]. For each MCMC iteration, we apply the ABM to the topology, treating currently-failed components (and their successors) as missing, and record the bandwidth achieved for each flow.

After a user-specified number of iterations, we compute the fraction of flows that complied with a user-specified SLO. The SLO is stated as a pair of values: a target throughput and a minimum fraction of iterations during which a flow must meet or exceed that target (e.g., "a flow achieves 4Gbps 99.9% of the time").

Limitations: Our simplified reliability metric does not attempt to account for short-term capacity and packet loss that may occur during convergence (§8.3).

8.3 Routing Convergence Metric

When components fail in large networks, it may take some time for the routing system to re-converge. Global re-convergence following a single link or switch failure can require 10s of seconds in a large network, during which time some flows will experience 100% packet loss [40].

Topologies can differ in how rapidly routing can converge. For instance, the stripings described in *Aspen Trees* [40], F10 [25], and §7 can lower or eliminate convergence time in tree topologies after certain failures, by increasing the probability that a switch can handle a failure locally.

We quantify how quickly a topology's routing can converge by calculating two proxy metrics: the number of switching components that routing-related information needs to be distributed to and the number of *hops* this information must propagate. We calculate these metrics in two phases.

In the first phase, for every switching component C, we determine how the failure of any other component affects C's ability to route traffic to destinations (hosts or other networks), subject to the routing algorithm in use (such as strict up-down routing). If C has N paths towards destination D, we compose N sets of "path components," $P_{C,D,1}, \ldots, P_{C,D,N}$, with each set $P_{C,D,i}$ containing all of the components on path i between C and destination D. The intersection of these sets yields a set of components that appears on all N paths. The failure of any component in this set or any of their predecessors will prevent C from routing traffic to destination D. We store this intersection of *Routing Resiliency Limiters* (RRLs) for every (C, D) pair.

In the second phase, we identify which failures a component C can *react* to. For each destination D, component C can react to the failure of any path component F as long as $F \notin RRLs(C, D)$, by making a routing decision. We record each such F as a component whose failure C can react to.

Finally, we compute two metrics: first, the number of components (Cs) that can react when any component F fails; this is useful for SDN networks, as it counts the number of switches needing updates. Second, the maximum distance between C and F over all such pairs; this "routing-info radius" (RIR) can be used to estimate the routing convergence time for distributed routing protocols as it approximates how far F's failure must propagate.

Limitations: Our routing convergence metric does not quantify the amount of *time* required for convergence. Walraed-Sullivan *et al.* [40] used an alternate approach, simulating specific routing protocols to estimate convergence time. However, they found their approach hard to scale, and it is not easily generalized.

8.4 Illustration of Tradeoff Analysis

We illustrate how using Condor's metrics, and rapid specification and synthesis of alternate topologies, allows an architect to explore tradeoffs, in this case between throughput degradation and convergence delay (RIR) following a failure.

For this example, we use a small 3-stage Clos built from 32 x 10 GbE switches, supporting 3072 hosts at 3:1 oversubscription. To reduce wiring complexity, we co-locate spine and aggregation switch nodes as linecards across 4 physical chassis, using backplane wiring to connect linecards.

Each of the ToRs has 2 uplinks to each of the 4 chassis. We compare two options for striping these uplinks:

Diversity-optimized (DO): Each ToR uplink connects to as many chassis linecards as possible (i.e., 2) at each chassis. For (DO), the failure of a single ToR uplink triggers routing table updates across a combined total of 15 ToR and spine switch nodes (RIR=2, because the impact of a link-failure propagates to aggregation and spine switches).

Convergence-time optimized (CO): Connect each ToR's uplinks to just one linecard per chassis. For (CO), assuming ECMP, the failure of a single ToR uplink does not trigger any routing table updates (RIR=0). However, the failure of a single linecard would cause each connected ToR to lose 25% of its uplink bandwidth.

Is (CO)'s faster convergence time worth its lower throughput in the case of a linecard failure? To decide, an architect would need to evaluate the SLO-compliance metric for one or more traffic matrices.[13]

For our evaluation, we use a uniform all-to-all traffic matrix of ToR-to-ToR flows. We set MTBF=150,000hrs and MTTR=24hrs for ToRs, linecards, and physical links. For

[13]The relative weights of SLO compliance and routing convergence is a business judgment outside our scope.

SLO throughput =	100%		99%		95%	
SLO percentile =	99	99.5	99	99.5	99	99.5
Diversity-optimized	**0**	**85.2**	**0**	**85.2**	**0**	85.2
Convergence-optimized	100	100	0.4	94	**0**	**1.7**

Cell values = % of flows experiencing SLO violations (**lower** is better)

Table 2: Comparing options (DO) vs. (CO)

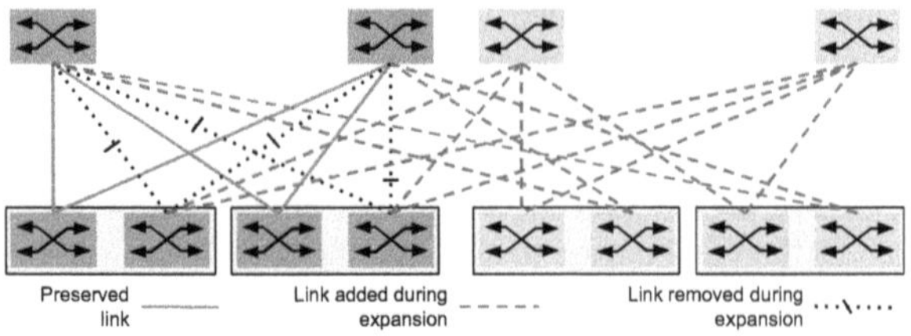

Figure 7: Changes to striping during fat-tree expansion (2 to 4 pods)

simplicity, we assume MTBF=∞ for other components.[14] We ran 10^6 iterations of MCMC for each striping option, which took 45 minutes on 200 non-dedicated cores using non-optimized Python code. It would be much faster in C++. (10^6 iterations is probably enough for high confidence, but we have not yet implemented a confidence metric.) For each option, over all iterations, we count how many flows are SLO compliant. An example SLO could be "achieve 95% of ideal throughput for 99.9% of the samples."

Table 2 shows that, for our simplified example, the fraction of ToR-to-ToR flows experiencing SLO violation varies widely. Option (DO) usually ties or beats (CO) — but not always. Condor thus exposes an architect to complex consequences of relatively simple design choices.

9. ENABLING ONLINE EXPANSIONS

Owners of large datacenters build them to handle years of future growth, initially deploying a small fraction of total server and network capacity because installing all network capacity at once is too expensive. Condor helps architects design topologies that support efficient, incremental expansion, and it also helps plan expansion operations.

While one could perform expansions offline by temporarily removing some or all of the workload, this approach results in costly downtime. We can perform expansions *online* if we can preserve the network's SLO during all phases of an expansion operation. Online expansion is tricky because, for many topologies, including trees and Jellyfish, expansion often requires moving (and thus draining) existing links. For instance, adding a new pod to a tree also requires adding one or more spines (overbuilding spines is too costly), which in turn requires redistributing links so that each pod has the same number of connections to each spine (see Figure 7).

The naïve solution of re-wiring at small increments (e.g., port-by-port) might preserve SLOs but is not cost-effective, leaves the network in a vulnerable state for too long, and increases operational complexity. Instead, architects must decompose an expansion into multiple stages, during which a set of ports is drained, re-wired, and un-drained. These stages must be designed so as to maintain the network's SLO during and after each stage, in the presence of expected failure rates. Condor helps architects design these expansion stages.

[14]The MTBF/MTTR values are illustrative but plausible. They lead to network-wide rates of a link failure/~73hrs and a switch failure/~669hrs, since links outnumber switches by 2048:224.

9.1 Expansions: Practical Considerations

Patch Panels: Architects can use patch panels to reduce the operational complexity of expansions by allowing all re-wiring to happen in one place. For example, one can pre-install cabling from all of a fat-tree's aggregation and spine switches to the back of the patch panels, and then make or modify inter-switch connections via the front of the panels.[15] (Some topologies, e.g., Jellyfish [33], do not support expansion via patch panels.) Condor's TDL and synthesizer can support patch panels and constraints on their wiring (§9.2).

For operational stability (humans working on patch panels can accidentally dislodge or unplug nearby cables), we prefer to design an expansion stage to drain an entire patch panel (or rack of panels), re-wire those ports, test the links, and then un-drain before moving to the next stage.

Constraints on Increments: During the lifetime of a tree topology that evolves by cost-effective expansions, it might be impossible to ensure that each aggregation switch has the same number of links to each spine. For example, in a five-pod tree topology, some pod-spine pairs would have p links, and some would have $p + 1$, for some p. Using ECMP on such unbalanced networks would lead to packet loss at spine switches, which forces operators to drain otherwise-working links to restore balance. An architect must decide, during network design, whether to adopt something other than ECMP (such as WCMP [44]), tolerate these link drains, or accept larger (and costlier) expansion increments. Condor helps architects evaluate the potential impact of unbalanced connectivity, to ensure that expansion increments maintain SLO compliance.

Other constraints besides imbalance apply to choosing expansion increments for other topologies. For instance, DCell [16] and BCube [15] become less fault-tolerant at certain increments. Condor supports ways to identify and avoid these issues, which for space reasons we do not discuss.

9.2 Describing Expansions with TDL

We designed TDL and the synthesizer to ensure that an architect does *not* need to write separate files for each increment of expansion. Instead, an architect describes an incrementally-expandable topology as it would exist following the *final* increment, including building blocks, relationships, connectivity pairs, and constraints. For instance, an architect could design a tree topology with an upper limit of 64 spine switches and 64 pods, with each pod containing 32 aggregation and 32 ToR switches, and then designate the pod as the unit of expansion. The architect can declare, in TDL, the rate at which the topology will expand ("2 pods"). Then, during synthesis of each increment of 2 pods, only

[15]To reduce complexity, an operator may disallow connections between front-side ports on two different panels.

the minimum number of spines required to meet the defined connectivity constraints will be instantiated.

We add a new building block class (*TDLCouplerBlock*) to support descriptions of patch panel ports and other passive connectors. In addition, we extend TDL's connectivity-pairs concept to support describing connectivity via patch panels and other passive devices (which are useful for purposes besides expansion [39]). First, an architect defines connectivity pairs that generate the connectivity from *endpoints* (such as spine and aggregation switches) to patch panels, expressing these pairs using building blocks and associating them with constraints, as in §5. The architect then adds an additional connectivity pair for each set of building blocks to be connected via the patch panels, referring to the patch-panel building block via an extra attribute. By defining constraints on this connectivity pair, the architect can constrain the number of connections between endpoints across *all* intermediary patch panels and/or across each individual patch panel.[16] The architect may also include constraints on the physical patch connections (e.g., that patch panel ports must be wired in pairs, to reduce the number of individual cables).

Late-bound constraints (§5.2.2) enable TDL to capture that the bounds on the number of pair-wise connections between spine and aggregation switches will vary as the network expands.

While we focus here on expanding tree topologies, the TDL and synthesizer can expand other non-random topologies.

9.3 Synthesis for Expansions

Synthesizing connectivity between patch-panel ports presents a challenge, due to the number of candidate connections. Recall (from §6.2) that this number, and thus the number of solver decision variables, is the size of the Cartesian product of the sets of components eligible for connection. If we constrain our use of patch panels to prevent patches that cross between panels, and we divide the ports on any panel equally between two types of components (e.g., aggregation and spine switches), and we use a decision variable for each port-pair, then, for N-port panels, we would need $(N/2)^2$ decision variables. A network using 192 256-port panels needs 3.14×10^6 variables, requiring lots of RAM and CPU.

To avoid this overhead, our synthesizer uses one decision variable for each port connecting to one of the two component types, rather than one per pair of ports, reducing the number per panel from $(N/2)^2$ to $N/2$. Assume we assign decision variables to ports connecting to aggregation switches. The synthesizer then assigns a unique index to each instance of the other component type (spine switches, in this case). It then sets the domain of the decision variables to include the range of this index, as well as 0 (indicating a port not used for patching). (Here, tiebreakers also allow architects to apply a rank-ordering to the set of *values* in each decision variable's domain, as the previously-described "greedy" heuristic (§6.3) no longer applies.) To ensure an injective mapping, the synthesizer adds a constraint: for each panel P and each spine switch S_i, the number of integer variables set to i is no more than the number of links between S_i and P.

[16]Constraints can also be defined on predecessors (racks).

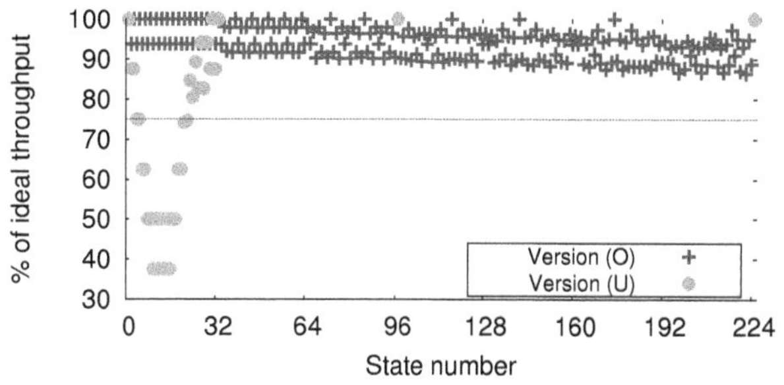

Figure 8: Throughput vs. state number

9.4 Does Condor Help with Expansions?

Does Condor help architects design expandable networks and expansions? We argue that it can, based on experiments with an example topology. We define an expandable network as one that meets its SLOs at all points in its *lifecycle*, including initial and expanded increments, and during expansions.

For this example, we used TDL to model a four-stage fat-tree using 256-port spine switch blocks and 512-port stage-3 aggregation switch blocks (these blocks are composed of smaller switches). Each pod is composed of ToRs, along with stage-2 and stage-3 aggregation switches. We use 256-port patch panels, grouped into racks containing 8 panels each, to support the reconfiguration of the striping between the stage-3 aggregation switches and spine switches during expansions. Our design oversubscribes ToR uplinks by 3:1, and the maximal network supports 49,152 end hosts, in 16 pods of 3072 hosts, connected by 64 spine switch blocks. The smallest possible increment of expansion is two pods.

Using TDL, we defined two versions of this network:

Unoptimized (U): includes constraints that establish balanced, symmetrical connectivity between all components in the maximal configuration. It does not include any constraints that specifically attempt to provide load balance for smaller configurations or during expansion stages.

Optimized for lifecycle throughput (O): Version U, plus a tiebreaker that prefers connecting to spine switches that have fewer connections, a heuristic hypothesized to ease expansion.

We expanded in units of 2 pods. For each expansion (2 to 16 pods), we synthesized a model using both versions. We assumed that operators split each expansion into 16 stages, each re-wiring 1 patch-panel rack. The network can be in $(7 * 16 * 2) + 1 = 225$ states, counting the drained and undrained states for each of the 16 stages for each of the 8 increments.

We evaluated each network, at each state in its lifecycle, using our approximate bandwidth metric (§8.1), and configured it to divide flows at each junction as ECMP would.

We simplified the process of analyzing each stage of expansion by not performing "compensating drains" (draining additional links), a process used to maintain the "equality assumption" that ECMP depends on. (ECMP assumes that all paths to the destination have equal bandwidth capacity [44]). Intermediate phases during an expansion operation can violate this assumption as drained links and rewiring create imbalance. For example, the first aggregation switch in pods 1 and 2 ($agg_{1,p1}$, and $agg_{1,p2}$ respectively) may both connect to spine switches $spine_1$ and $spine_2$. By default, $agg_{1,p1}$ and $agg_{1,p2}$ may both have 20 Gbps capacity to both spines, but during an expansion $agg_{1,p2}$ may only have 10 Gbps of capacity to $spine_2$ because of a drained link. With ECMP, $agg_{1,p1}$ will send traffic to $agg_{1,p2}$ through both spines equally, potentially resulting in packet loss at $spine_2$. To avoid this, operators can drain a link (referred to as a "compensating drain") between $agg_{1,p1}$ and $spine_2$ to equalize the capacity between each aggregation switch and $spine_2$. This simplification in modeling introduces some error, but (we believe) not consistently in one direction.

Figure 8 plots the percent of ideal throughput achieved (using the approximate bandwidth metric) vs. state number. An operator typically wants to maintain a target fraction of ideal throughput, such as the 75% line on the graph. Figure 8 shows that version **O**'s capacity dips during some expansion stages but never below 86%, so **O** is "expandable" with respect to the 75% target. We synthesized all 225 states in about 20 min (and this is easily parallelized). Without Condor, it would be much harder to validate **O**'s expandability.

Figure 8 shows two problems for version **U**. First, between 2 and 4 pods, we cannot perform expansion without dropping to 37.5% of capacity (well below the target). Without Condor's help, this would have been hard to spot.

Second, the missing tiebreaker in **U** caused the solver to backtrack for most other configurations; it cannot efficiently find a solution to the $(p, p+1)$ problem described in §9.1 before our 10-hour timeout. (It did solve the 8-pod and 16-pod states.) We know, from operational experience, that such solutions exist, but we do not know how to construct a tiebreaker that would allow efficient synthesis of **U** (as opposed to simply generating **O**). Existing research discusses heuristics for avoiding backtracking in CSP (e.g., [6, 12]), but we have not yet figured out how best to apply such techniques.

9.5 Prior Work on Expansions

Jellyfish [33] was designed to support incremental expansion, but the authors did not discuss the operational complexity of re-cabling large-scale networks, and it may be hard to design online expansions for large Jellyfish networks.

DCell [16] and BCube [15] support expansions, subject to constraints described in those papers. Condor gives architects a tool to quickly find expansions that meet those constraints.

Curtis *et. al* described algorithms for expanding Clos networks [9] and unstructured topologies [8]. Neither paper discussed how to optimize a design for future expansion or how to support online expansions. Liu *et. al* described zUpdate [24], a technique for coordinating the control and data planes to support non-disruptive online updates, including topology changes, but did not discuss the problem of topology design for expansions. Solnushkin [34], in presenting his algorithm for automated design of 2-layer fat-trees, discusses how to reserve switch ports for future expansion, but does not consider on-line expansion or more general topologies.

10. CONCLUSIONS

Designing a datacenter network requires balancing a range of goals and constraints, but no existing tool allows a network architect to easily explore tradeoffs across candidate topologies. In this paper, we presented Condor, our approach to supporting rapid exploration of the design space. Condor facilitates straightforward specification and exploration of designs with different tradeoffs, compared across a range of metrics. Condor's declarative, constraint-based Topology Description Language enables concise and easily modifiable descriptions of datacenter networks that Condor transforms into constraint-satisfaction problems to support rapid synthesis. We demonstrated that combining the power of TDL with Condor's analysis suite leads to new insights and helps architects navigate complex tradeoffs. Finally, we showed how Condor can support efficient expansions of traffic-carrying networks while preserving Service-Level Objectives. Overall, we believe Condor supports a much faster design cycle.

Acknowledgements

We thank Google colleagues for their insights and feedback, including Abdul Kabbani, Arjun Singh, Blaz Zupan, Chi-Yao Hong, David Zats, Eiichi Tanda, Fabien Viger, Guillermo Maturana, Joon Ong, Junlan Zhou, Leon Poutievski, Moray Mclaren, Google's Operations Research Team, Roy Alcala, Rui Wang, Vijoy Pandey, Wendy Zhao, and, especially, Matt Beaumont-Gay and KK Yap. We also thank Christopher Hodsdon, Tom Anderson and Vincent Liu, our shepherd Aditya Akella, and the SIGCOMM reviewers.

11. REFERENCES

[1] J. H. Ahn, N. Binkert, A. Davis, M. McLaren, and R. S. Schreiber. HyperX: Topology, Routing, and Packaging of Efficient Large-scale Networks. In *SC*, page 41, 2009.

[2] A. Akella, T. Benson, B. Chandrasekaran, C. Huang, B. Maggs, and D. Maltz. A Universal Approach to Data Center Network Design. In *ICDCN*, 2015.

[3] M. Al-Fares, A. Loukissas, and A. Vahdat. A Scalable, Commodity Data Center Network Architecture. In *SIGCOMM*, pages 63–74, 2008.

[4] A. Andreyev. Introducing data center fabric, the next-generation Facebook data center network. http://bit.ly/1zq5nsF, 2014.

[5] J. Arjona Aroca and A. Fernandez Anta. Bisection (Band)Width of Product Networks with Application to Data Centers. *IEEE TPDS*, 25(3):570–580, March 2014.

[6] C. Bessiére, A. Chmeiss, and L. Saïs. Neighborhood-Based Variable Ordering Heuristics for the Constraint Satisfaction Problem. In T. Walsh, editor, *Principles and Practice of Constraint Programming – CP 2001*, volume 2239 of *Lecture Notes in Computer Science*, pages 565–569. Springer Berlin Heidelberg, 2001.

[7] Cisco Systems. Cisco's Massively Scalable Data Center. http://bit.ly/1relWo8.

[8] A. R. Curtis, T. Carpenter, M. Elsheikh, A. López-Ortiz, and S. Keshav. REWIRE: An Optimization-based Framework for Unstructured Data Center Network Design. In *INFOCOM*, pages 1116–1124. IEEE, 2012.

[9] A. R. Curtis, S. Keshav, and A. Lopez-Ortiz. LEGUP: Using Heterogeneity to Reduce the Cost of Data Center Network Upgrades. In *CoNEXT*, pages 14:1–14:12, 2010.

[10] B. Dieter and H. Dietz. A Web-Based Tool for Optimized Cluster Design. http://bit.ly/1fyovAl, 2007.

[11] W. R. Dieter and H. G. Dietz. Automatic Exploration and Characterization of the Cluster Design Space. Tech. Rep. TR-ECE-2005-04-25-01, ECE Dept, U. Kentucky, 2005.

[12] D. Frost and R. Dechter. Look-ahead value ordering for constraint satisfaction problems. In *IJCAI*, pages 572–578, 1995.

[13] P. Gill, N. Jain, and N. Nagappan. Understanding Network Failures in Data Centers: Measurement, Analysis, and Implications. In *SIGCOMM*, pages 350–361, 2011.

[14] Google, Inc. or-tools: the Google Operations Research Suite. https://code.google.com/p/or-tools/.

[15] C. Guo, G. Lu, D. Li, H. Wu, X. Zhang, Y. Shi, C. Tian, Y. Zhang, and S. Lu. BCube: A High Performance, Server-centric Network Architecture for Modular Data Centers. In *SIGCOMM*, pages 63–74, 2009.

[16] C. Guo, H. Wu, K. Tan, L. Shi, Y. Zhang, and S. Lu. DCell: A Scalable and Fault-tolerant Network Structure for Data Centers. In *SIGCOMM*, pages 75–86, 2008.

[17] A. A. Hagberg, D. A. Schult, and P. J. Swart. Exploring Network Structure, Dynamics, and Function using NetworkX. In *SciPy*, pages 11–15, Aug. 2008.

[18] H. Hanani. The existence and construction of balanced incomplete block designs. *The Annals of Mathematical Statistics*, pages 361–386, 1961.

[19] H. Hanani. Balanced incomplete block designs and related designs. *Discrete Mathematics*, 11(3), 1975.

[20] S. A. Jyothi, A. Singla, B. Godfrey, and A. Kolla. Measuring and Understanding Throughput of Network Topologies. *arXiv preprint 1402.2531*, 2014.

[21] S. Kandula, S. Sengupta, A. Greenberg, P. Patel, and R. Chaiken. The Nature of Data Center Traffic: Measurements & Analysis. In *IMC*, pages 202–208, 2009.

[22] J. Kim, W. J. Dally, and D. Abts. Flattened Butterfly: A Cost-efficient Topology for High-radix Networks. In *ISCA*, pages 126–137, 2007.

[23] M. Li, D. Subhraveti, A. R. Butt, A. Khasymski, and P. Sarkar. CAM: A Topology Aware Minimum Cost Flow Based Resource Manager for MapReduce Applications in the Cloud. In *HPDC*, pages 211–222. ACM, 2012.

[24] H. H. Liu, X. Wu, M. Zhang, L. Yuan, R. Wattenhofer, and D. Maltz. zUpdate: Updating Data Center Networks with Zero Loss. In *SIGCOMM*, pages 411–422, 2013.

[25] V. Liu, D. Halperin, A. Krishnamurthy, and T. E. Anderson. F10: A Fault-Tolerant Engineered Network. In *NSDI*, pages 399–412, 2013.

[26] Y. J. Liu, P. X. Gao, B. Wong, and S. Keshav. Quartz: A New Design Element for Low-Latency DCNs. In *SIGCOMM*, pages 283–294, 2014.

[27] B. Mandal. Linear integer programming approach to construction of balanced incomplete block designs. *Communications in Statistics-Simulation and Computation*, 44(6):1405–1411, 2015.

[28] J. Mudigonda, P. Yalagandula, and J. C. Mogul. Taming the Flying Cable Monster: A Topology Design and Optimization Framework for Data-Center Networks. In *USENIX Annual Technical Conference*, 2011.

[29] S. R. Öhring, M. Ibel, S. K. Das, and M. J. Kumar. On Generalized Fat Trees. In *Parallel Processing Symposium*, pages 37–44. IEEE, 1995.

[30] B. Palanisamy, A. Singh, L. Liu, and B. Jain. Purlieus: Locality-aware Resource Allocation for MapReduce in a Cloud. In *SC*, pages 58:1–58:11. ACM, 2011.

[31] L. Popa, S. Ratnasamy, G. Iannaccone, A. Krishnamurthy, and I. Stoica. A Cost Comparison of Datacenter Network Architectures. In *CoNEXT*, pages 16:1–16:12, 2010.

[32] A. Singh, J. Ong, A. Agarwal, G. Anderson, A. Armistead, R. Bannon, S. Boving, G. Desai, B. Felderman, P. Germano, A. Kanagala, J. Provost, J. Simmons, E. Tanda, J. Wanderer, U. Hoelzle, S. Stuart, and A. Vahdat. Jupiter Rising: A Decade of Clos Topologies and Centralized Control in Google's Datacenter Network. In *SIGCOMM*, 2015.

[33] A. Singla, C.-Y. Hong, L. Popa, and P. B. Godfrey. Jellyfish: Networking Data Centers Randomly. In *NSDI*, pages 225–238, 2012.

[34] K. S. Solnushkin. Automated Design of Two-Layer Fat-Tree Networks. *arXiv preprint 1301.6179*, 2013.

[35] Z. Taylor and S. Ranganathan. *Designing High Availability Systems: DFSS and Classical Reliability Techniques with Practical Real Life Examples*. John Wiley & Sons, 2013.

[36] E. Tsang. *Foundations of Constraint Satisfaction*, volume 289. Academic Press, London, 1993.

[37] A. Varga et al. The OMNeT++ discrete event simulation system. In *ESM2001*, 2001.

[38] A. Varga and G. Pongor. Flexible topology description language for simulation programs. In *ESS97*, 1997.

[39] M. Walraed-Sullivan, J. Padhye, and D. A. Maltz. Theia: Simple and Cheap Networking for Ultra-Dense Data Centers. In *HotNets*, page 26. ACM, 2014.

[40] M. Walraed-Sullivan, A. Vahdat, and K. Marzullo. Aspen Trees: Balancing Data Center Fault Tolerance, Scalability and Cost. In *CoNEXT*, pages 85–96, 2013.

[41] X. Wen, K. Chen, Y. Chen, Y. Liu, Y. Xia, and C. Hu. VirtualKnotter: Online Virtual Machine Shuffling for Congestion Resolving in Virtualized Datacenter. In *ICDCS*, pages 12–21. IEEE, June 2012.

[42] F. Yates. Incomplete randomized blocks. *Annals of Eugenics*, 7(2):121–140, 1936.

[43] E. Zahavi, I. Keslassy, and A. Kolodny. Quasi Fat Trees for HPC Clouds and Their Fault-Resilient Closed-Form Routing. In *Hot Interconnects*, pages 41–48. IEEE, 2014.

[44] J. Zhou, M. Tewari, M. Zhu, A. Kabbani, L. Poutievski, A. Singh, and A. Vahdat. WCMP: Weighted Cost Multipathing for Improved Fairness in Data Centers. In *EuroSys*, page 5, 2014.

Presto: Edge-based Load Balancing for Fast Datacenter Networks

Keqiang He[†] Eric Rozner[*] Kanak Agarwal[*]
Wes Felter[*] John Carter[*] Aditya Akella[†]

[†]University of Wisconsin–Madison [*]IBM Research

ABSTRACT

Datacenter networks deal with a variety of workloads, ranging from latency-sensitive small flows to bandwidth-hungry large flows. Load balancing schemes based on flow hashing, *e.g.*, ECMP, cause congestion when hash collisions occur and can perform poorly in asymmetric topologies. Recent proposals to load balance the network require centralized traffic engineering, multipath-aware transport, or expensive specialized hardware. We propose a mechanism that avoids these limitations by (i) pushing load-balancing functionality into the soft network edge (*e.g.*, virtual switches) such that no changes are required in the transport layer, customer VMs, or networking hardware, and (ii) load balancing on fine-grained, near-uniform units of data (flowcells) that fit within end-host segment offload optimizations used to support fast networking speeds. We design and implement such a soft-edge load balancing scheme, called Presto, and evaluate it on a 10 Gbps physical testbed. We demonstrate the computational impact of packet reordering on receivers and propose a mechanism to handle reordering in the TCP receive offload functionality. Presto's performance closely tracks that of a single, non-blocking switch over many workloads and is adaptive to failures and topology asymmetry.

CCS Concepts

•Networks → Network architectures; End nodes; Programmable networks; Data center networks; *Data path algorithms; Network experimentation;*

Keywords

Load Balancing; Software-Defined Networking;

SIGCOMM'15, August 17–21, 2015, London, United Kingdom

 ISBN 978-1-4503-3542-3/15/08... $15.00

DOI: http://dx.doi.org/10.1145/2785956.2787507

1. INTRODUCTION

Datacenter networks must support an increasingly diverse set of workloads. Small latency-sensitive flows to support real-time applications such as search, RPCs, or gaming share the network with large throughput-sensitive flows for video, big data analytics, or VM migration. Load balancing the network is crucial to ensure operational efficiency and suitable application performance. Unfortunately, popular load balancing schemes based on flow hashing, *e.g.*, ECMP, cause congestion when hash collisions occur [3, 17, 19, 22, 53, 54, 63] and perform poorly in asymmetric topologies [4, 65].

A variety of load balancing schemes aim to address the problems of ECMP. Centralized schemes, such as Hedera [3] and Planck [54], collect network state and reroute elephant flows when collisions occur. These approaches are fundamentally reactive to congestion and are very coarse-grained due to the large time constraints of their control loops [3] or require extra network infrastructure [54]. Transport layer solutions such as MPTCP [61] can react faster but require widespread adoption and are difficult to enforce in multi-tenant datacenters where customers often deploy customized VMs. In-network reactive distributed load balancing schemes, *e.g.*, CONGA [4] and Juniper VCF [28], can be effective but require specialized networking hardware.

The shortcomings of the above approaches cause us to re-examine the design space for load balancing in datacenter networks. ECMP, despite its limitations, is a highly practical solution due to its proactive nature and stateless behavior. Conceptually, ECMP's flaws are not internal to its operation but are caused by asymmetry in network topology (or capacities) and variation in flow sizes. *In a symmetric network topology where all flows are "mice", ECMP should provide near optimal load balancing*; indeed, prior work [4, 58] has shown the traffic imbalance ECMP imposes across links goes down with an increase in the number of flows and a reduction in the variance of the flow size distribution.

Can we leverage this insight to design a good proactive load balancing scheme without requiring special purpose hardware or modifications to end-point transport? The system we propose answers this in the affirmative. It relies on the datacenter network's *software edge* to transform arbitrary sized flows into a large number of near uniformly sized small sub-flows and proactively spreads those uniform data units over the network in a balanced fashion. Our scheme is fast (works at 10+ Gbps) and doesn't require network stack configurations that may not be widely supported outside the datacenter (such as increasing MTU sizes). We piggyback on recent trends where several network functions, *e.g.*, firewalls and application-level load balancers, are moving into hypervisors and software virtual switches on end-hosts [10, 36, 51]. Our paper makes a strong case for moving network load balancing functionality out of the datacenter network hardware and into the software-based edge.

Several challenges arise when employing the edge to load balance the network on a sub-flow level. Software is slower than hardware, so operating at 10+ Gbps speeds means algorithms must be simple, light-weight, and take advantage of optimizations in the networking stack and offload features in the NIC. Any sub-flow level load balancing should also be robust against reordering because packets from the same flow can be routed over different network paths which can cause out-of-order delivery. As shown in Section 2, reordering not only impacts TCP's congestion control mechanism, but also imposes significant computational strain on hosts, effectively limiting TCP's achievable bandwidth if not properly controlled. Last, the approach must be resilient to hardware or link failures and be adaptive to network asymmetry.

To this end, we build a proactive load balancing system called Presto. Presto utilizes edge vSwitches to break each flow into discrete units of packets, called *flowcells*, and distributes them evenly to near-optimally load balance the network. Presto uses the maximum TCP Segment Offload (TSO) size (64 KB) as flowcell granularity, allowing for fine-grained load balancing at network speeds of 10+ Gbps. To combat reordering, we modify the Generic Receive Offload (GRO) handler in the hypervisor OS to mitigate the computational burden imposed by reordering and prevent reordered packets from being pushed up the networking stack. Finally, we show Presto can load balance the network in the face of asymmetry and failures.

Our paper makes the following contributions:

1. We design and implement a system, called Presto, that near-optimally load balances links in the network. We show such a system can be built with no changes to the transport layer or network hardware and scales to 10+ Gbps networking speeds. Our approach makes judicious use of middleware already implemented in most hypervisors today: Open vSwitch and the TCP receive offload engine in the OS (Generic Receive Offload, GRO, in the Linux kernel).

2. We uncover the importance of GRO on performance when packets are reordered. At network speeds of 10+ Gbps, current GRO algorithms are unable to sustain line rate under severe reordering due to extreme computational overhead, and hence per-packet load balancing approaches [17, 22] need to be reconsidered. We improve GRO to prevent reordering while ensuring computational overhead is limited. We argue GRO is the most natural place to handle reordering because it can mask reordering in a light-weight manner while simultaneously limiting CPU overhead by having a direct impact on the segment sizes pushed up the networking stack. In addition, our scheme distinguishes loss from reordering and adapts to prevailing network conditions to minimize the time to recover lost packets.

3. Presto achieves near-optimal load balancing in a proactive manner. For that, it leverages symmetry in the network topology to ensure that all paths between a pair of hosts are equally congested. However, asymmetries can arise due to failures. We demonstrate Presto can recover from network failures and adapt to asymmetric network topologies using a combination of fast failover and weighted multipathing at the network edge.

4. Finally, we evaluate Presto on a real 10 Gbps testbed. Our experiments show Presto outperforms existing load balancing schemes (including flowlet switching, ECMP, MPTCP) and is able to track the performance of a single, non-blocking switch (an optimal case) within a few percentage points over a variety of workloads, including trace-driven. Presto improves throughput, latency and fairness in the network and also reduces the flow completion time tail for mice flows.

2. DESIGN DECISIONS AND CHALLENGES

In Presto, we make several design choices to build a highly robust and scalable system that provides near optimal load balancing without requiring changes to the transport layer or switch hardware. We now discuss our design decisions.

2.1 Design Decisions

Load Balancing in the Soft Edge A key design decision in Presto is to implement the functionality in the soft edge (*i.e.*, the vSwitch and hypervisor) of the network. The vSwitch occupies a unique position in the networking stack in that it can easily modify packets without requiring any changes to customer VMs or transport layers. Functionality built into the vSwitch can be made aware of the underlying hardware offload features presented by the NIC and OS, meaning it can be fast. Furthermore, an open, software-based approach prevents extra hardware cost and vendor lock-in, and allows for simplified network management. These criteria are important for providers today [41]. Thanks to projects like Open vSwitch, soft-switching platforms are now fast, mature, open source, adopted widely, remotely configurable, SDN-enabled, and feature-rich [36, 50, 52]. Presto is built on these platforms.

Reactive vs Proactive Load Balancing The second major design decision in Presto is to use a proactive approach to congestion management. Bursty behavior can create transient congestion that must be reacted to before switch buffers overflow to prevent loss (timescales range from 100s of μs to ~4 ms [54]). This requirement renders most of the centralized reactive schemes ineffective as they are often too slow to react to any but the largest network events, *e.g.*, link failures. Furthermore, centralized schemes can hurt performance when rerouting flows using stale information. Distributed reactive schemes like MPTCP [61] and CONGA [4] can respond to congestion at faster timescales, but have a high barrier to deployment. Furthermore, distributed reactive schemes must take great care to avoid oscillations. Presto takes a proactive, correct-by-design approach to congestion management. That is, if small, near-uniform portions of traffic are equally balanced over a symmetric network topology, then the load-balancing can remain agnostic to congestion and leave congestion control to the higher layers of the networking stack. Presto is only reactive to network events such as link failures. Fortunately, the larger timescales of reactive feedback loops are sufficient in these scenarios.

Load Balancing Granularity ECMP has been shown to be ineffective at load balancing the network, and thus many schemes advocate load balancing at a finer granularity than a flow [4, 17, 22, 28]. A key factor impacting the choice of granularity is operating at high speed. Operating at 10+ Gbps incurs great computational overhead, and therefore host-based load balancing schemes must be fast, light-weight and take advantage of optimizations provided in the networking stack. For example, per-packet load balancing techniques [17] cannot be employed at the network edge because TSO does not work on a per-packet basis. TSO, commonly supported in OSes and NICs, allows for large TCP segments (typically 64 KB in size) to be passed down the networking stack to the NIC. The NIC breaks the segments into MTU-sized packets and copies and computes header data, such as sequence numbers and checksums. When TSO is disabled, a host incurs 100% utilization of one CPU core and can only achieve around 5.5 Gbps [34]. Therefore, per-packet schemes are unlikely to scale to fast networks without hardware support. Limiting overhead by increasing the MTU is difficult because VMs, switches, and routers must all be configured appropriately, and traffic leaving the datacenter must use normal 1500 byte packets. Furthermore, per-packet schemes [17, 22] are likely to introduce significant reordering into the network.

Another possibility is to load balance on flowlets [4, 28]. A flow is comprised of a series of bursts, and a flowlet is created when the inter-arrival time between two packets in a flow exceeds a threshold inactivity timer. In practice, inactivity timer values are between 100-500 μs [4]. These values intend to strike a good balance between load balancing on a sub-flow level and acting as a buffer to limit reordering between flowlets. Flowlets are derived from traffic patterns at the sender, and in practice this means the distribution of flowlet sizes is not uniform. To analyze flowlet sizes, a simple experiment is shown in Figure 1. We connect a sender and a receiver to a single switch and start an `scp` transfer designed to emulate an elephant flow. Meanwhile, other senders are hooked up to the same switch and send to the same receiver. We vary the number of these competing flows and show a stacked histogram of the top 10 flowlet sizes for a 1 GB `scp` transfer with a 500 μs inactivity timer.

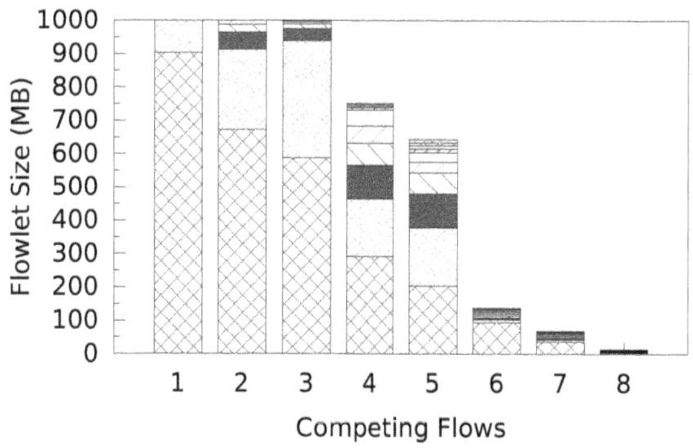

Figure 1: Stacked histogram of flowlet sizes (in MB) for a 1 GB `scp` file transfer. We vary the number of `nuttcp` [44] background flows and denote them as *Competing Flows*. The size of each flowlet is shown within each bar, and flowlets are created whenever there is a 500 μs delay between segments. The top 10 flowlet sizes are shown here. We also analyzed the results of a 1 GB `nuttcp`, `ftp`, and a simple custom client/server transfer and found them to be similar.

The graph shows flowlet sizes can be quite large, with more than half the transfer being attributed to a single flowlet for up to 3 competing flows. Using a smaller inactivity timer, such 100μs, helps (90% of flowlet sizes are 114KB or less), but does not prevent a long tail: 0.1% of flowlets are larger than 1 MB, with the largest ranging from 2.1-20.5 MB. Collisions on large flowlet sizes can lead to congestion. The second problem with flowlets is that small inactivity thresholds, such as 100 μs, can lead to significant reordering. Not only does this impact TCP performance (profiled in Section 5), but it also needlessly breaks small flows into several flowlets. With only one flow in the network, we found a 50 KB mice flow was broken into 4-5 flowlets on average. Small flows typically do not need to be load balanced on a sub-flow level and need not be exposed to reordering.

The shortcomings of the previous approaches lead us to reconsider on what granularity load balancing should occur. Ideally, sub-flow load balancing should be done on near uniform sizes. Also, the unit of load balancing should be small to allow for fine-grained load balancing, but not so small as to break small flows into many pieces or as to be a significant computational burden. As a result, we propose load balancing on 64 KB units of data we call *flowcells*. Flowcells have a number of advantages. First, the maximum segment size supported by TSO is 64 KB, so flowcells provide a natural interface to high speed optimizations provided by the NIC and OS and can scale to fast networking speeds. Second, an overwhelming fraction of mice flows are less than 64 KB in size and thus do not have to worry about reordering [11, 23, 33]. Last, since most bytes in datacenter networks originate from elephant flows [5, 11, 33], this ensures that a significant portion of datacenter traffic is routed on uniform sizes. While promising, this approach must combat reordering to be effective. Essentially we make a tradeoff: the sender avoids congestion by providing fine-grained, near-uniform load balancing, and the receiver handles reordering to maintain line-rate.

Per-Hop vs End-to-End Multipathing The last design consideration is whether multipathing should be done on a local, per-hop level (*e.g.*, ECMP), or on a global, end-to-end level. In Presto, we choose the latter: pre-configured end-to-end paths are allocated in the network and path selection (and thus multipathing) is realized by having the network edge place flowcells onto these paths. Presto can be used to load-balance in an ECMP style per-hop manner, but the choice of end-to-end multipathing provides additional benefits due to greater control of how flowcells are mapped to paths. Per-hop multipathing can be inefficient under asymmetric topologies [65], and load-balancing on a global end-to-end level can allow for weighted scheduling at the vSwitch to rebalance traffic. This is especially important when failure occurs. The second benefit is flowcells can be assigned over multiple paths very evenly by iterating over paths in a round-robin, rather than randomized, fashion.

2.2 Reordering Challenges

Due to the impact of fine-grained, flowcell-based load balancing, Presto must account for reordering. Here, we highlight reordering challenges. The next section shows how Presto deals with these concerns.

Reordering's Impact on TCP The impact of reordering on TCP is well-studied [37, 47]. Duplicate acknowledgments caused by reordering can cause TCP to move to a more conservative sender state and reduce the sender's congestion window. Relying on parameter tuning, such as adjusting the DUP-ACK threshold, is not ideal because increasing the DUP-ACK threshold increases the time to recover from real loss. Other TCP settings such as Forward Acknowledgement (FACK) assume un-acked bytes in the SACK are lost and degrade performance under reordering. A scheme that introduces reordering should not rely on careful configuration of TCP parameters because (i) it is hard to find a single set of parameters that work effectively over multiple scenarios and (ii) datacenter tenants should not be forced to constantly tune their networking stacks. Finally, many reordering-robust variants of TCP have been proposed [14, 15, 64], but as we will show, GRO becomes ineffective under reordering. Therefore, reordering should be handled below the transport layer.

Computational Bottleneck of Reordering Akin to TSO, Generic Receive Offload (GRO) mitigates the computational burden of receiving 1500 byte packets at 10 Gbps. GRO is implemented in the kernel of the hypervisor, and its handler is called directly by the NIC driver. It is responsible for aggregating packets into larger segments that are pushed up to OVS and the TCP/IP stack. GRO is implemented in the Linux kernel and is used even without virtualization. Similar functionality can be found in Windows (RSC [55]) and hardware (LRO [24]).

Because modern CPUs use aggressive prefetching, the cost of receiving TCP data is now dominated by per-packet, rather than per-byte, operations. As shown by Menon [39], the majority of this overhead comes from buffer management and other routines not related to protocol processing, and therefore significant computational overhead can be avoided by aggregating "raw" packets from the NIC into a single `sk_buff`. Essentially, spending a few cycles to aggregate packets within GRO creates less segments for TCP and prevents having to use substantially more cycles at higher layers in the networking stack. Refer to [31, 39] for detailed study and explanation.

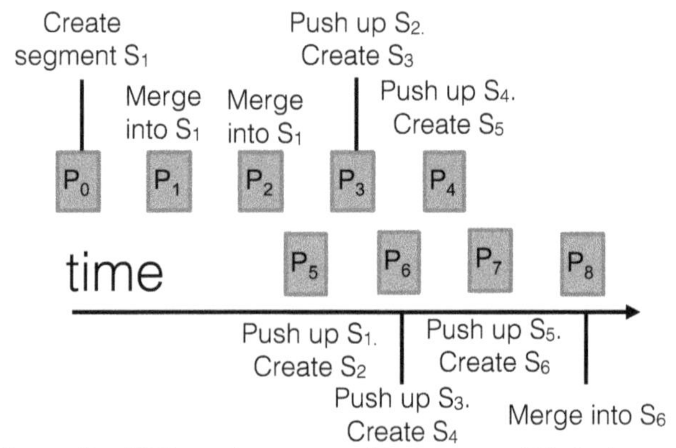

Figure 2: GRO pushes up small segments (S_i) during reordering.

To better understand the problems reordering causes, a brief description of the TCP receive chain in Linux follows. First, interrupt coalescing allows the NIC to create an interrupt for a batch of packets [13, 40], which prompts the driver to poll the packets into an aggregation queue. Next, the driver invokes the GRO handler, located in the kernel, which *merges* the packets into larger segments. The merging continues, possibly across many polling events, until a segment reaches a threshold size, a certain age, or cannot be combined with the incoming packet. Then, the combined, larger segment is *pushed up* to the rest of the TCP/IP networking stack. The GRO process is done on a per-flow level. With GRO disabled, throughput drops to around 5.7-7.1 Gbps and CPU utilization spikes to 100% (Section 5 and [34]). Receive offload algorithms, whether in hardware (LRO) [7, 24] or in software (GRO), are usually *stateless* to make them fast: no state is kept beyond the segment being merged.

We now uncover how GRO breaks down in the face of reordering. Figure 2 shows the impact of reordering on GRO. Reordering does not allow the segment to grow: each reordered packet cannot be merged with the existing segment, and thus the previously created segment must be pushed up. With extreme reordering, GRO is effectively disabled because small MTU-sized segments are constantly pushed up. This causes (i) severe computational overhead and (ii) TCP to be exposed to significant amounts of reordering. We term this the *small segment flooding* problem.

Determining where to combat the reordering problem has not previously taken the small segment flooding problem into account. Using a reordering buffer to deal with reordered packets is a common solution (*e.g.*, works like [17]

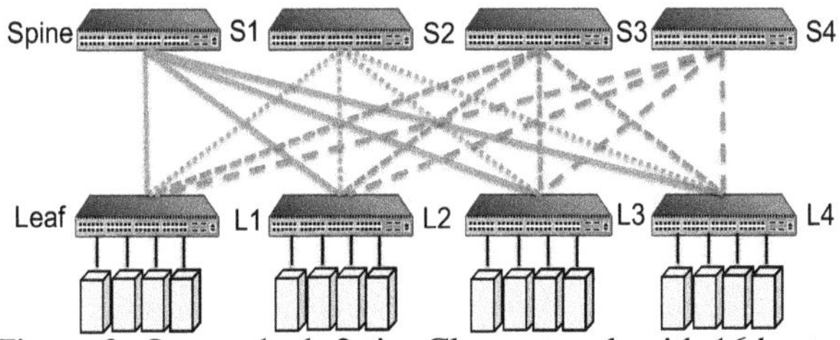

Figure 3: Our testbed: 2-tier Clos network with 16 hosts.

re-sort out-of-order packets in a shim layer below TCP), but a buffer implemented above GRO cannot prevent small segment flooding. Implementing a buffer below GRO means that the NIC must be changed, which is (i) expensive and cumbersome to update and (ii) unlikely to help combat reordering over multiple interrupts.

In our system, the buffer is implemented in the GRO layer itself. We argue this is a natural location because GRO can directly control segment sizes while simultaneously limiting the impact of reordering. Furthermore, GRO can still be applied on packets pushed up from LRO, which means hardware doesn't have to be modified or made complex. Implementing a better GRO algorithm has multiple challenges. The algorithm should be light-weight to scale to fast networking speeds. Furthermore, an ideal scheme should be able to distinguish loss from reordering. When a gap in sequence numbers is detected (*e.g.*, when P_5 is received after P_2 in Figure 2), it is not obvious if this gap is caused from loss or reordering. If the gap is due to reordering, GRO should not push segments up in order to try to wait to receive the missing gap and merge the missing packets into a preestablished segment. If the gap is due to loss, however, then GRO should immediately push up the segments to allow TCP to react to the loss as fast as possible. Ideally, an updated GRO algorithm should ensure TCP does not perform any worse than a scheme with no reordering. Finally, the scheme should adapt to prevailing network conditions, traffic patterns and application demands.

3. DESIGN

This section presents the design of Presto by detailing the sender, the receiver, and how the network adapts in the case of failures and asymmetry.

3.1 Sender

Global Load Balancing at the Network Edge In Presto, a centralized controller is employed to collect the network topology and disseminate corresponding load balancing information to the edge vSwitches. The goal of this design is to ensure the vSwitches, as a whole, can load balance the network in an even fashion, but without requiring an individual vSwitch to have detailed information about the network topology, updated traffic matrices or strict coordination amongst senders. At a high level, the controller partitions the network into a set of multiple spanning trees. Then, the controller assigns each vSwitch a unique forwarding label in each spanning tree. By having the vSwitches partition traffic over these spanning trees in a fine-grained manner, the network can load balance traffic in a near-optimal fashion.

The process of creating spanning trees is made simple by employing multi-stage Clos networks commonly found in datacenters. For example, in a 2-tier Clos network with ν spine switches, the controller can easily allocate ν disjoint spanning trees by having each spanning tree route through a unique spine switch. Figure 3 shows an example with four spine switches and four corresponding disjoint spanning trees. When there are γ links between each spine and leaf switch in a 2-tier Clos network, the controller can allocate γ spanning trees per spine switch. Note that 2-tier Clos networks cover the overwhelming majority of enterprise datacenter deployments and can support tens of thousands of physical servers [4]. The controller ensures links in the network are equally covered by the allocated spanning trees.

Once the spanning trees are created, the controller assigns a unique forwarding label for each vSwitch in every spanning tree and installs the relevant forwarding rules into the network. Forwarding labels can be implemented in a variety of ways using technologies commonly deployed to forward on labels, such as MPLS [18], VXLAN [4, 36], or IP encapsulation [17]. In Presto, label switching is implemented with shadow MACs [1]. Shadow MACs implement label-switching for commodity Ethernet by using the destination MAC address as an opaque forwarding label that can easily be installed in L2 tables. Each vSwitch is assigned one shadow MAC per spanning tree. Note Shadow MACs are extremely scalable on existing chipsets because they utilize the large L2 forwarding table. For example, Trident II-based switches [8, 16, 21] have 288k L2 table entries and thus 8-way multipathing (*i.e.*, each vSwitch has 8 disjoint spanning trees) can scale up to 36,000 physical servers. To increase scalability, shadow MAC tunnels can be implemented from edge switch to edge switch instead of from vSwitch to vSwitch. Switch-to-switch tunneling has been proposed in previous works such as MOOSE [57] and NetLord [43]. Tunneling requires $\mathcal{O}(|\text{switches}| \times |\text{paths}|)$ rules instead of $\mathcal{O}(|\text{vSwitches}| \times |\text{paths}|)$ rules. All shadow MAC labels can route to a destination edge switch that forwards the packet to the correct destination by forwarding on L3 information.

Finally, we note that shadow MACs are also compatible with network virtualization (both L2 and L3 address space virtualization). Tunneling techniques such as VXLAN encapsulate packets in Ethernet frames, which means shadow MACs should still allow path selection in virtualized environments by modifying outer Ethernet headers. VXLAN hardware offload is supported in modern NICs and has little performance overhead [60].

Load Balancing at the Sender After the controller installs the shadow MAC forwarding rules into the network, it creates a mapping from each physical destination MAC address to a list of corresponding shadow MAC addresses. These mappings provide a way to send traffic to a specific destination over different spanning trees. The mappings are pushed from the controller to each vSwitch in the network, either on-demand or preemptively. In Presto, the vSwitch on the

Algorithm 1 Pseudo-code of flowcell creation

```
if bytecount + len(skb) > threshold then
    bytecount ← len(skb)
    current_mac ← (current_mac + 1) % total_macs
    flowcellID ← flowcellID + 1
else
    bytecount ← bytecount + len(skb)
end if
skb ← update(skb, current_mac, flowcellID)
sendToNIC(skb)
```

sender monitors outgoing traffic (*i.e.*, maintains a per-flow counter in the datapath) and rewrites the destination MAC address with one of the corresponding shadow MAC addresses. The vSwitch assigns the same shadow MAC address to all consecutive segments until the 64 KB limit is reached. In order to load balance the network effectively, the vSwitch iterates through destination shadow MAC addresses in a round-robin fashion. This allows the edge vSwitch to load balance over the network in a very fine-grained fashion.

Sending each 64 KB worth of flowcells over a different path in the network can cause reordering and must be carefully addressed. To assist with reordering at the receiver (Presto's mechanisms for combatting reordering are detailed in the next section), the sender also includes a sequentially increasing *flowcell ID* into each segment. In our setup the controller installs forwarding rules solely on the destination MAC address and ARP is handled in a centralized manner. Therefore, the source MAC address can be used to hold the flowcell ID. Other options are possible, *e.g.*, some schemes include load balancing metadata in the reserved bits of the VXLAN header [26] and implementations could also stash flowcell IDs into large IPv6 header fields.[1] Note that since the flowcell ID and the shadow MAC address are modified before a segment is handed to the NIC, the TSO algorithm in the NIC replicates these values to all derived MTU-sized packets. The pseudo-code of flowcell creation is presented in Algorithm 1. Since this code executes in the vSwitch, retransmitted TCP packets run through this code for each retransmission.

3.2 Receiver

The main challenge at the receiver is dealing with reordering that can occur when different flowcells are sent over different paths. The high-level goal of our receiver implementation is to mitigate the effects of the small segment flooding problem by (i) not so aggressively pushing up segments if they cannot be merged with an incoming packet and (ii) ensuring that segments pushed up are delivered in-order.

Mitigating Small Segment Flooding Let's use Figure 2 as a motivating example on how to combat the small segment flooding problem. Say a polling event has occurred, and the driver retrieves 9 packets from the NIC (P_0-P_8). The driver calls the GRO handler, which merges consecutive packets

[1] In our implementation, TCP options hold the flowcell ID for simplicity and ease of debugging.

Algorithm 2 Pseudo-code of Presto GRO `flush` function

```
for each flow f do
    for S ∈ f.segment_list do
        if f.lastFlowcell == getFlowcell(S) then
            f.expSeq ← max(f.expSeq, S.endSeq)
            pushUp(S)
        else if getFlowcell(S) > f.lastFlowcell then
            if f.expSeq == S.startSeq then
                f.lastFlowcell ← getFlowcell(S)
                f.expSeq ← S.endSeq
                pushUp(S)
            else if f.expSeq > S.startSeq then
                f.lastFlowcell ← getFlowcell(S)
                pushUp(S)
            else if timeout(S) then
                f.lastFlowcell ← getFlowcell(S)
                f.expSeq ← S.endSeq
                pushUp(S)
            end if
        else
            pushUp(S)
        end if
    end for
end for
```

into larger segments. The first three packets (P_0-P_2) are merged into a segment, call it S_1 (note: in practice S_1 already contains in-order packets received before P_0). When P_5 arrives, a new segment S_2, containing P_5, should be created. Instead of pushing up S_1 (as is done currently), both segments should be kept. Then, when P_3 is received, it can be merged into S_1. Similarly, P_6 can be merged into S_2. This process can continue until P_4 is merged into S_1. At this point, the gap between the original out-of-order reception (P_2-P_5) has been filled, and S_1 can be pushed up and S_2 can continue to grow. This means the size of the segments being pushed up is increased, and TCP is not exposed to reordering.

The current default GRO algorithm works as follows. An interrupt by the NIC causes the driver to poll (multiple) packets from the NIC's ring buffer. The driver calls the GRO handler on the received batch of packets. GRO keeps a simple doubly linked list, called `gro_list`, that contains segments, with a flow having at most one segment in the list. When packets for a flow are received in-order, each packet can be merged into the flow's preexisting segment. When a packet cannot be merged, such as with reordering, the corresponding segment is pushed up (ejected from the linked list and pushed up the networking stack) and a new segment is created from the packet. This process is continued until all packets in the batch are serviced. At the end of the polling event, a `flush` function is called that pushes up all segments in the `gro_list`.

Our GRO algorithm makes the following changes. First, multiple segments can be kept per flow in a doubly linked list (called `segment_list`). To ensure the merging process is fast, each linked list is kept in a hash table (keyed on flow).

When an incoming packet cannot be merged with any existing segment, the existing segments are kept and a new segment is created from the packet. New segments are added to the head of the linked list so that merging subsequent packets is typically $\mathcal{O}(1)$. When the merging is completed over all packets in the batch, the `flush` function is called. The `flush` function decides whether to push segments up or to keep them. Segments may be kept so reordered packets still in flight have enough time to arrive and can then be placed in-order before being pushed up. Reordering can cause the linked lists to become slightly out-of-order, so at the beginning of `flush` an insertion sort is run to help easily decide if segments are in-order.

The pseudo-code of our `flush` function is presented in Algorithm 2. For each flow, our algorithm keeps track of the next expected in-order sequence number (`f.expSeq`) and the corresponding flowcell ID of the most recently received in-order sequence number (`f.lastFlowcell`). When the merging is completed, the `flush` function iterates over the sorted segments (S), from lowest sequence number to highest sequence number in the `segment_list` (line 2). The rest of the code is presented in the subsections that follow.

How to Differentiate Loss from Reordering? In the case of no loss or reordering, our algorithm keeps pushing up segments and updating state. Lines 3-5 deal with segments from the same flowcell ID, so we just need to update `f.expSeq` each time. Lines 6-10 represent the case when the current flowcell ID is fully received and we start to receive the next flowcell ID. The problem, however, is when there is a gap that appears between the sequence numbers of the segments. When a gap is encountered, it isn't clear if it is caused from reordering or from loss. If the gap is due to reordering, our algorithm should be conservative and try to wait to receive the packets that "fill in the gap" before pushing segments up to TCP. If the gap is due to loss, however, then we should push up the segments immediately so that TCP can react to the loss as quickly as possible.

To solve this problem, we leverage the fact that all packets carrying the same flowcell ID traverse the same path and should be in-order. This means incoming sequence numbers can be monitored to check for gaps. A sequence number gap within the same flowcell ID is assumed to be a loss, and not reordering, so those packets are pushed up immediately (lines 3-5). Note that because a flowcell consists of many packets (a 64 KB flowcell consists of roughly 42 1500 byte packets), when there is a loss it is likely that it occurs within flowcell boundaries. The corner case, when a gap occurs on the flowcell boundary, leads us to the next design question.

How to Handle Gaps at Flowcell Boundaries? When a gap is detected in sequence numbers at flowcell boundaries, it is not clear if the gap is due to loss or reordering. Therefore, the segment should be held long enough to handle reasonable amounts of reordering, but not so long that TCP cannot respond to loss promptly. Previous approaches that deal with reordering typically employ a large static timeout (10ms) [17]. Setting the timeout artificially high can handle reordering, but hinders TCP when the gap is due to loss. Setting a low timeout is difficult because many dynamic factors, such as delays between segments at the sender, network congestion, and traffic patterns (multiple flows received at the same NIC affect inter-arrival time), can cause large variations. As a result, we devise an adaptive timeout scheme, which monitors recent reordering events and sets a dynamic timeout value accordingly. Presto tracks cases when there is reordering, but no loss, on flowcell boundaries and keeps an exponentially-weighted moving average (EWMA) over these times. Presto then applies a timeout of $\alpha * \text{EWMA}$ to a segment when a gap is detected on flowcell boundaries. Here α is an empirical parameter that allows for timeouts to grow. As a further optimization, if a segment has timed out, but a packet has been merged into that segment in the last $\frac{1}{\beta} * \text{EWMA}$ time interval, then the segment is still held in hopes of preventing reordering. We find α and β work over a wide range of parameters and set both of them to 2 in our experiments. A timeout firing is dealt with in lines 14-18.

How to Handle Retransmissions? Retransmitted TCP packets are pushed up immediately in order to allow the TCP stack to react without delay. If the flowcell ID of the retransmission is the same as the expected flowcell ID, then the retransmission will be pushed up immediately because its sequence number will be $\leq$ f.expSeq. If the flowcell ID is larger than the expected flowcell ID (when the first packet of a flowcell is a retransmission), then the packet is pushed up (line 13). If a retransmitted packet has a smaller flowcell ID than the next expected flowcell ID (a stale packet), then it will be pushed up immediately (line 20). Note we ensure overflow is handled properly in all cases.

3.3 Failure Handling and Asymmetry

When failures occur, Presto relies on the controller to update the forwarding behavior of the affected vSwitches. The controller can simply prune the spanning trees that are affected by the failure, or more generally enforce a weighted scheduling algorithm over the spanning trees. Weighting allows for Presto to evenly distribute traffic over an asymmetric topology. Path weights can be implemented in a simple fashion by duplicating shadow MACs used in the vSwitch's round robin scheduling algorithm. For example, assume we have three paths in total (p_1, p_2 and p_3) and their updated weights are 0.25, 0.5 and 0.25 respectively. Then the controller can send the sequence of p_1, p_2, p_3, p_2 to the vSwitch, which can then schedule traffic over this sequence in a round robin fashion to realize the new path weights. This way of approximating path weights in the face of network asymmetry is similar to WCMP [65], but instead of having to change switch firmware and use scarce on-chip SRAM/TCAM entries, we can push the weighted load balancing entirely to the network edge.

As an added optimization, Presto can leverage any fast failover features that the network supports, such as BGP fast external failover, MPLS fast reroute, or OpenFlow failover groups. Fast failover detects port failure and can move corresponding traffic to a predetermined backup port. Hardware failover latency ranges from several to tens of milliseconds [20, 48]. This ensures traffic is moved away from the failure rapidly and the network remains connected when redundant links are available. Moving to backup links causes imbalance in the network, so Presto relies on the controller learning of the network change, computing weighted multipath schedules, and disseminating the schedules to the edge vSwitches.

4. METHODOLOGY

Implementation We implemented Presto in Open vSwitch v2.1.2 [45] and Linux kernel v3.11.0 [38]. In OVS, we modified 5 files and ~600 lines of code. For GRO, we modified 11 files and ~900 lines of code.

Testbed We conducted our experiments on a physical testbed consisting of 16 IBM System x3620 M3 servers with 6-core Intel Xeon 2.53GHz CPUs, 60GB memory, and Mellanox ConnectX-2 EN 10GbE NICs. The servers were connected in a 2-tier Clos network topology with 10 Gbps IBM RackSwitch G8264 switches, as shown in Figure 3.

Experiment Settings We ran the default TCP implementation in the Linux kernel (TCP CUBIC [27]) and set parameters `tcp_sack`, `tcp_fack`, `tcp_low_latency` to 1. Further, we tuned the host Receive Side Scaling (RSS) [56] and IRQ affinity settings and kept them the same in all experiments. We send and receive packets from the hypervisor OS instead of VMs. LRO is not enabled on our NICs.

Workloads We evaluate Presto with a set of synthetic and realistic workloads. Similar to previous works [2, 3, 54], our synthetic workloads include: *Shuffle*: Each server in the testbed sends 1GB data to every other server in the testbed in random order. Each host sends two flows at a time. This workload emulates the shuffle behavior of Hadoop workloads. *Stride(8)*: We index the servers in the testbed from left to right. In stride(8) workload, server[i] sends to server[(i+8) mod 16]. *Random*: Each server sends to a random destination not in the same pod as itself. Multiple senders can send to the same receiver. *Random Bijection*: Each server sends to a random destination not in the same pod as itself. Different from random, each server only receives data from one sender. Finally, we also evaluate Presto with trace-driven workloads from real datacenter traffic [33].

Performance Evaluation We compare Presto to ECMP, MPTCP, and a single non-blocking switch used to represent an optimal scenario. ECMP is implemented by enumerating all possible end-to-end paths and randomly selecting a path for each flow. MPTCP uses ECMP to determine the paths of each of its sub-flows. The MPTCP implementation is still under active development, and we spent significant effort in finding the most stable configuration of MPTCP on our testbed. Ultimately, we found that Mellanox `mlx_en4` driver version 2.2, MPTCP version 0.88 [42], subflow count set to 8, OLIA congestion control algorithm [35], and configured buffer sizes as recommended by [35, 46, 53] gave us the best trade-offs in terms of throughput, latency, loss and stability. Unfortunately, despite our efforts, we still occasionally witness some stability issues with MPTCP that we believe are due to implementation bugs.

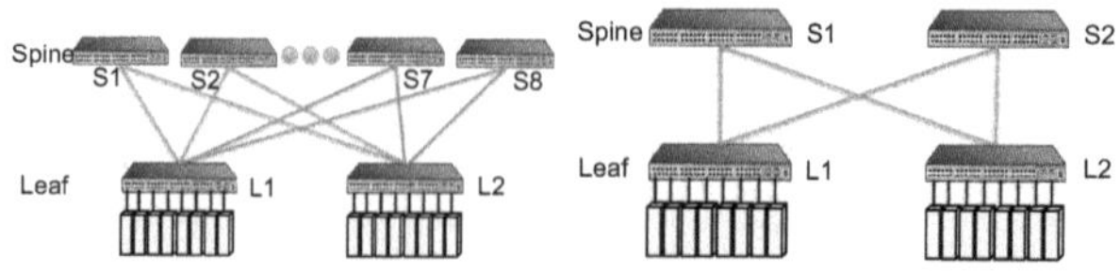

(a) (b)

Figure 4: (a) Scalability benchmark and (b) Oversubscription benchmark topology.

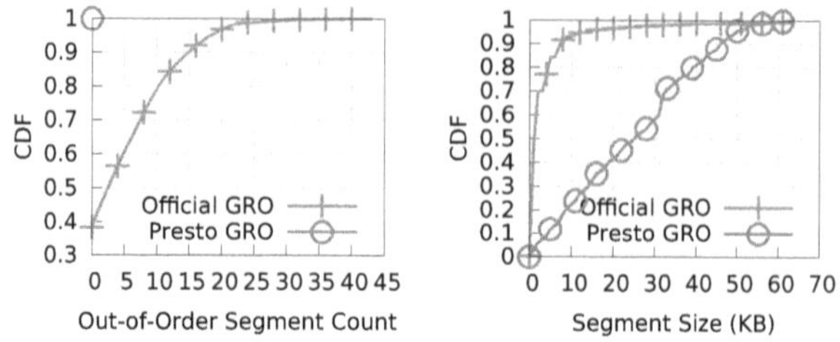

(a) (b)

Figure 5: (a) Illustration of the modified GRO's effectiveness on masking reordering. (b) In case of massive packet reordering, official GRO cannot merge packets effectively such that lots of small packets are processed by TCP which poses great processing overhead for CPU.

We evaluate Presto on various performance metrics, including: throughput (measured by `nuttcp`), round trip time (a single TCP packet, measured by `sockperf` [59]), mice flow completion time (time to send a 50 KB flow and receive an application-layer acknowledgement), packet loss (measured from switch counters), and fairness (Jain's fairness index [30] over flow throughputs). Mice flows are sent every 100 ms and elephant flows last 10 seconds. Each experiment is run for 10 seconds over 20 runs. Error bars on graphs denote the highest and lowest value over all runs.

5. MICROBENCHMARKS

We first evaluate the effectiveness of Presto over a series of microbenchmarks: (i) Presto's effectiveness in preventing the small segment flooding problem and reordering, (ii) Presto's CPU overhead, (iii) Presto's ability to scale to multiple paths, (iv) Presto's ability to handle congestion, (v) comparison to flowlet switching, and (vi) comparison to local, per-hop load balancing.

Presto's GRO Combats Reordering To examine Presto's ability to handle packet reordering, we perform a simple experiment on the topology shown in Figure 4b. Here two servers attached to leaf switch L1 send traffic to their own receivers attached to leaf switch L2 by spreading flowcells over two network paths. This setup can cause reordering for each flow, so we compare Presto's GRO to an unmodified GRO, denoted "Official GRO". The amount of reordering exposed to TCP is presented in Figure 5a. To quantify packet reordering, we show a CDF of the *out-of-order segment count*: *i.e.*, the number of segments from other flow-

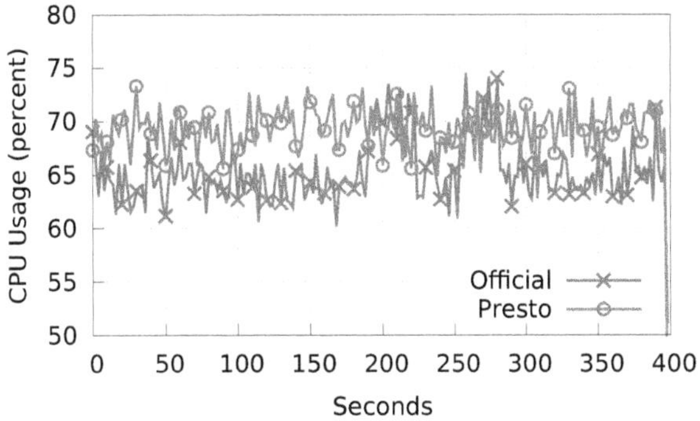

Figure 6: Presto incurs 6% CPU overhead on average.

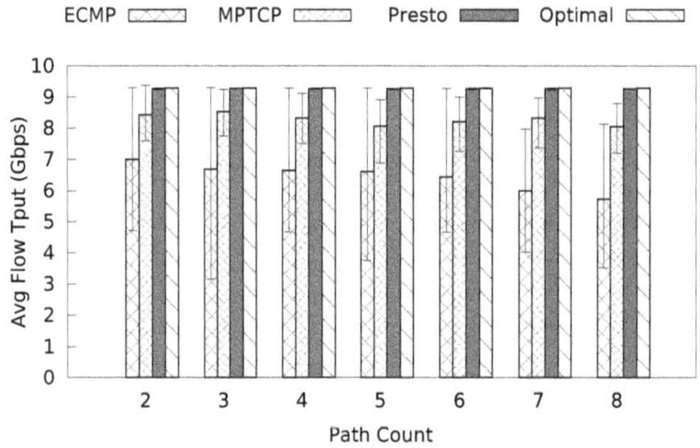

Figure 7: Throughput comparison in scalability benchmark. We denote the non-blocking case as Optimal.

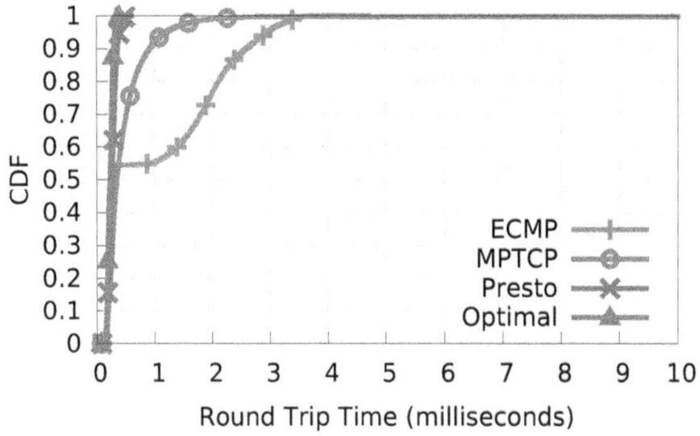

Figure 8: Round trip time comparison in scalability benchmark.

cells between the first packet and last packet of each flowcell. A value of zero means there is no reordering and larger values mean more reordering. The figure shows Presto's GRO can completely mask reordering while official GRO incurs significant reordering. As shown in Section 2, reordering can also cause smaller segments to be pushed up the networking stack, causing significant processing overhead. Figure 5b shows the received TCP segment size distribution. Presto's GRO pushes up large segments, while the official GRO pushes up many small segments. The average TCP throughputs in official GRO and Presto GRO are 4.6 Gbps (with 86% CPU utilization) and 9.3 Gbps (with 69% CPU utilization), respectively. Despite the fact that official GRO only obtains about half the throughput of Presto's GRO, it still incurs more than 24% higher CPU overhead. Therefore, an effective scheme must deal with both reordering and small segment overhead.

Presto Imposes Limited CPU Overhead We investigate Presto's CPU usage by running the stride workload on a 2-tier Clos network as shown in Figure 3. For comparison, official GRO is run with the stride workload using a non-blocking switch (so there is no reordering). Note both official GRO and Presto GRO can achieve 9.3 Gbps. The receiver CPU usage is sampled every 2 seconds over a 400 second interval, and the time-series is shown in Figure 6. On average, Presto GRO only increases CPU usage by 6% compared with the official GRO. The minimal CPU overhead comes from Presto's careful design and implementation. At the sender, Presto needs just two `memcpy` operations (1 for shadow MAC rewriting, 1 for flowcell ID encoding). At the receiver, Presto needs one `memcpy` to rewrite the shadow MAC back to the real MAC and also incurs slight overhead because multiple segments are now kept per flow. The overhead of the latter is reduced because these segments are largely kept in reverse sorted order, which means `merge` on an incoming packet is usually $\mathcal{O}(1)$. The insertion sort is done at the beginning of each `flush` event over a small number of mostly in-order segments, which amortizes overhead because it is called infrequently compared to `merge`.

Presto Scales to Multiple Paths We analyze Presto's ability to scale in the number of paths by setting the number of flows (host pairs) equal to the number of available paths in the topology shown in Figure 4a. The number of paths is varied from 2 to 8, and Presto always load-balances over all available paths. Figure 7 shows Presto's throughput closely tracks Optimal. ECMP (and MPTCP) suffer from lower throughput when flows (or subflows) are hashed to the same path. Hashing on the same path leads to congestion and thus increased latency, as shown in Figure 8. Because this topology is non-blocking and Presto load-balances in a near optimal fashion, Presto's latency is near Optimal. Packet drop rates are presented in Figure 9a and show Presto and Optimal have no loss. MPTCP has higher loss because of its bursty nature [4] and its aggression in the face of loss: when a single loss occurs, only one subflow reduces its rate. The other schemes are more conservative because a single loss reduces the rate of the whole flow. Finally, Figure 9b shows Presto, Optimal and MPTCP achieve almost perfect fairness.

Presto Handles Congestion Gracefully Presto's ability to handle congestion is analyzed by fixing the number of spine and leaf switches to 2 and varying the number of flows (host pairs) from 2 to 8, as shown in Figure 4b. Each flow sends as much as possible, which leads to the network being over-subscribed by a ratio of 1 (two flows) to 4 (eight flows). Figure 10 shows all schemes track Optimal in highly over-subscribed environments. ECMP does poorly under moderate congestion because the limited number of flows can be hashed to the same path. Presto does no worse in terms of latency (Figure 11) and loss (Figure 12a). The long tail latency

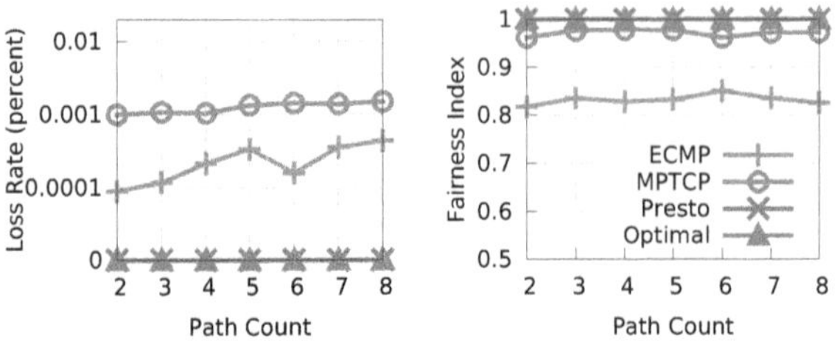

(a) (b)

Figure 9: (a) Loss rate and (b) Fairness index comparison in scalability benchmark.

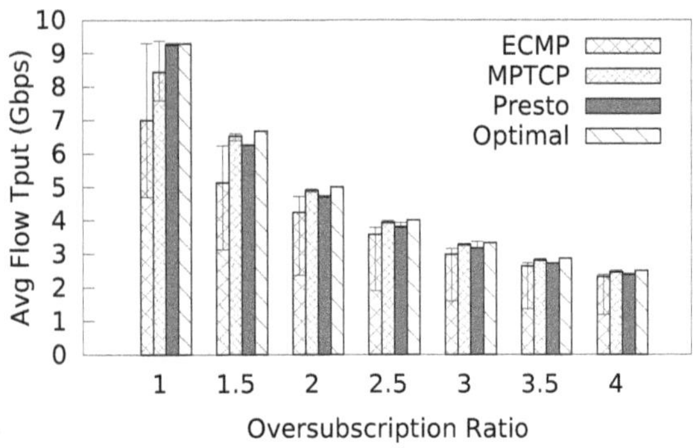

Figure 10: Throughput comparison in oversubscription benchmark.

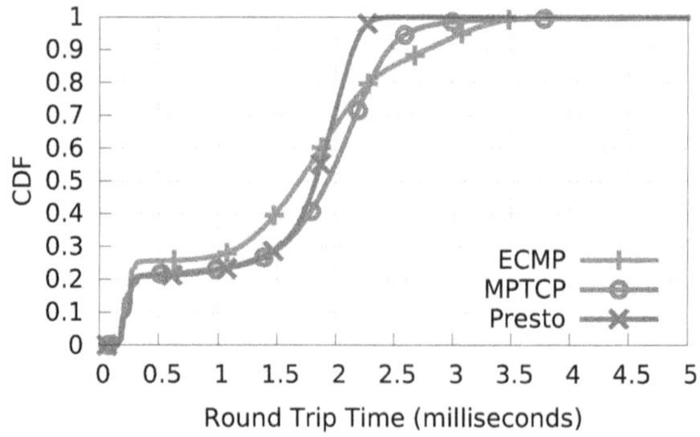

Figure 11: Round trip time comparison in oversubscription benchmark.

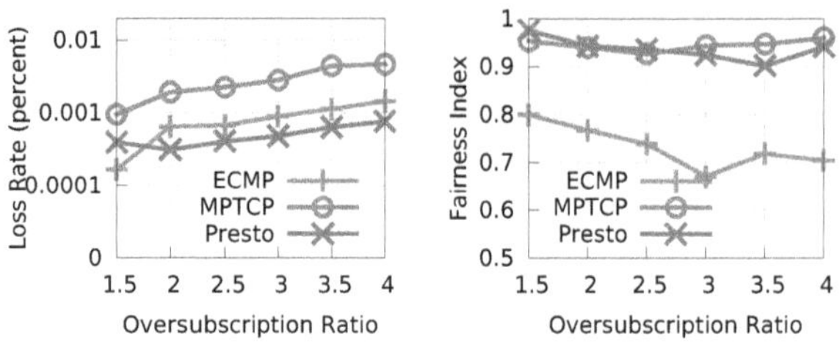

(a) (b)

Figure 12: (a) Loss rate and (b) Fairness index comparison in oversubscription benchmark.

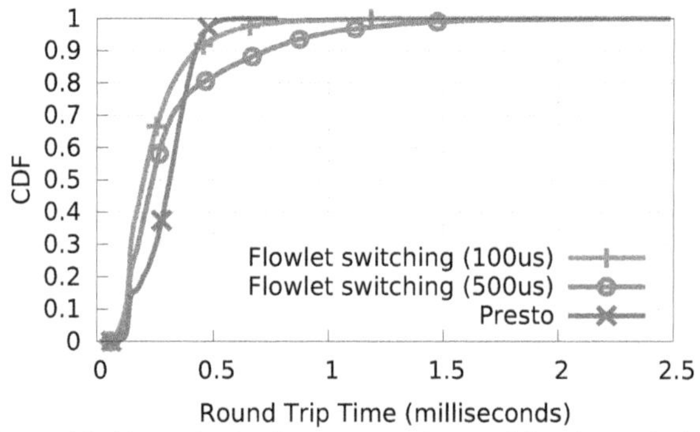

Figure 13: Round trip time comparison of flowlet switching and Presto in Stride workload. The throughputs of Flowlet switching with 100 μs gap, 500 μs gap and Presto are 4.3 Gbps, 7.6 Gbps and 9.3 Gbps respectively.

for MPTCP is caused by its higher loss rates. Both Presto and MPTCP have greatly improved fairness compared with ECMP (Figure 12b).

Comparison to Flowlet Switching We first implemented a flowlet load-balancing scheme in OVS that detects inactivity gaps and then schedules flowlets over disjoint paths in a round robin fashion. The receiver for flowlets uses official GRO. Our flowlet scheme is not a direct reflection of CONGA because (i) it is not congestion-aware and (ii) the flowlets are determined in the software edge instead of the networking hardware. Presto is compared to 500 μs and 100 μs inactivity timers in the stride workload on the 2-tier Clos network (Figure 3). The throughput of the schemes are 9.3 Gbps (Presto), 7.6 Gbps (500 μs), and 4.3 Gbps (100 μs). Analysis of the 100 μs network traces show 13%-29% packets in the connection are reordered, which means 100 μs is not enough time to allow packets to arrive in-order at the destination and thus throughput is severely impacted. Switching flowlets with 500 μs prevents most reordering (only 0.03%-0.5% packets are reordered), but creates very large flowlets (see Figure 1). This means flowlets can still suffer from collisions, which can hurt throughput (note: while not shown here, 500 μs outperforms ECMP by over 40%). Figure 13 shows the latencies. Flowlet 100 μs has low throughput and hence lower latencies. However, since its load balancing isn't perfect, it can still cause increased congestion in the tail. Flowlet 500 μs also has larger tail latencies because of more pronounced flowlet collisions. As compared to the flowlet schemes, Presto decreases 99.9th percentile latency by 2x-3.6x.

Comparison to Local, Per-Hop Load Balancing Presto sends flowcells in a round robin fashion over pre-configured end-to-end paths. An alternative is to have ECMP hash on flowcell ID and thus provide per-hop load balancing. We compare Presto + shadow MAC with Presto + ECMP using a stride workload on our testbed. Presto + shadow MAC's average throughput is 9.3 Gbps while Presto + ECMP's is 8.9 Gbps. The round trip time CDF is shown in Figure 14. Presto + shadow MAC gives better latency performance compared with Presto + ECMP. The performance difference comes from the fact that Presto + shadow MAC provides better fine-

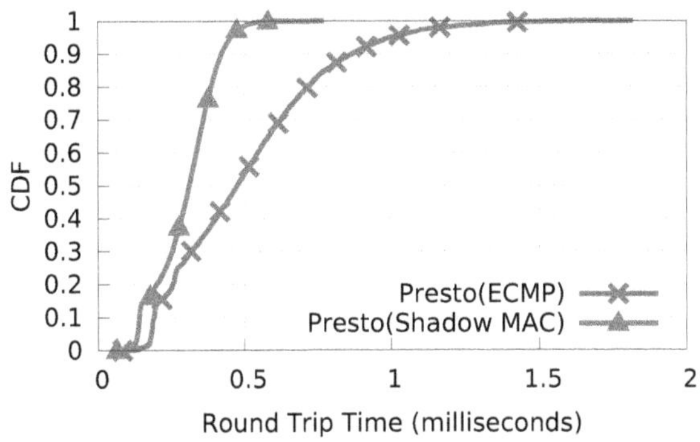

Figure 14: Round trip time comparison between Presto + shadow MAC and Presto + ECMP.

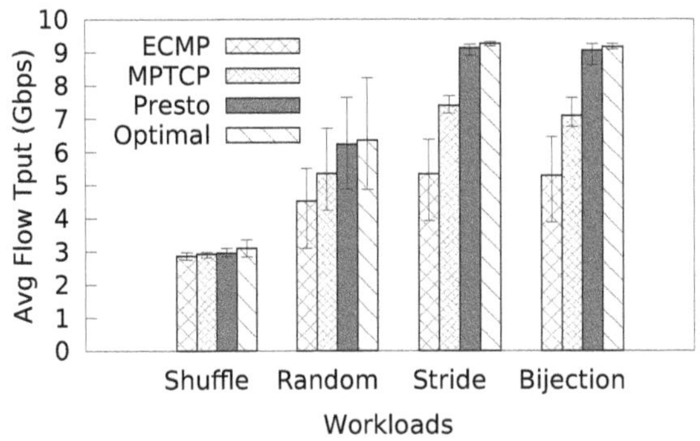

Figure 15: Elephant flow throughput for ECMP, MPTCP, Presto and Optimal in shuffle, random, stride and random bijection workloads.

grained flowcell load balancing because randomization in per-hop multipathing can lead to corner cases where a large fraction of flowcells get sent to the same link over a small timescale by multiple flows. This transient congestion can lead to increased buffer occupancy and higher delays.

6. EVALUATION

In this section, we analyze the performance of Presto for (i) synthetic workloads, (ii) trace-driven workloads, (iii) workloads containing north-south cross traffic, and (iv) failures. All tests are run on the topology in Figure 3.

Synthetic Workloads Figure 15 shows the average throughputs of elephant flows in the shuffle, random, stride and random bijection workloads. Presto's throughput is within 1-4% of Optimal over all workloads. For the shuffle workload, ECMP, MPTCP, Presto and Optimal show similar results because the throughput is mainly bottlenecked at the receiver. In the non-shuffle workloads, Presto improves upon ECMP by 38-72% and improves upon MPTCP by 17-28%.

Figure 16 shows a CDF of the mice flow completion time (FCT) for each workload. The stride and random bijection workloads are non-blocking, and hence the latency of Presto closely tracks Optimal: the 99.9^{th} percentile FCT for Presto is within 350 μs for these workloads. MPTCP and ECMP suffer from congestion, and therefore the tail FCT is much worse than Presto: ECMP's 99.9^{th} percentile FCT is over

Percentile	ECMP	Optimal	Presto
50%	1.0	−12%	−9%
90%	1.0	−34%	−32%
99%	1.0	−63%	−56%
99.9%	1.0	−61%	−60%

Table 1: Mice (<100KB) FCT in trace-driven workload [33]. Negative numbers imply shorter FCT.

7.5x worse (~11ms) and MPTCP experiences timeout (because of higher loss rates and the fact that small sub-flow window sizes from small flows can increase the chances of timeout [53]). We used the Linux default timeout (200 ms) and trimmed graphs for clarity. The difference in the random and shuffle workloads is less pronounced (we omit random due to space constraints). In these workloads elephant flows can collide on the last-hop output port, and therefore mice FCT is mainly determined by queuing latency. In shuffle, the 99.9^{th} percentile FCT for ECMP, Presto and Optimal are all within 10% (MPTCP again experiences TCP timeout) and in random, the 99.9^{th} percentile FCT of Presto is within 25% of Optimal while ECMP's is 32% worse than Presto.

Trace-driven Workload We evaluate Presto using a trace-driven workload based on traffic patterns measured in [33]. Each server establishes a long-lived TCP connection with every other server in the testbed. Then each server continuously samples flow sizes and inter-arrival times and each time sends to a random receiver that is not in the same rack. We scale the flow size distribution by a factor of 10 to emulate a heavier workload. Mice flows are defined as flows that are less than 100 KB in size, and elephant flows are defined as flows that are greater than 1 MB. The mice FCT, normalized to ECMP, is shown in Table 1. Compared with ECMP, Presto has similar performance at the 50th percentile but reduces the 99th and 99.9^{th} percentile FCT by 56% and 60%, respectively. Note MPTCP is omitted because its performance was quite unstable in workloads featuring a large number of small flows. The average elephant throughput (not shown) for Presto tracks Optimal (within 2%), and improves upon ECMP by over 10%.

Percentile	ECMP	Optimal	Presto	MPTCP
50%	1.0	−34%	−20%	−12%
90%	1.0	−83%	−79%	−73%
99%	1.0	−89%	−86%	−73%
99.9%	1.0	−91%	−87%	TIMEOUT

Table 2: FCT comparison (normalized to ECMP) with ECMP load balanced north-south traffic. Optimal means all the hosts are attached to a single switch.

Impact of North-South Cross Traffic Presto load balances on "east-west" traffic in the datacenter, *i.e.*, traffic originating and ending at servers in the datacenter. In a real datacenter environment "north-south" traffic (*i.e.*, traffic with an endpoint outside the datacenter) must also be considered. To study the impact of north-south traffic on Presto, we attach

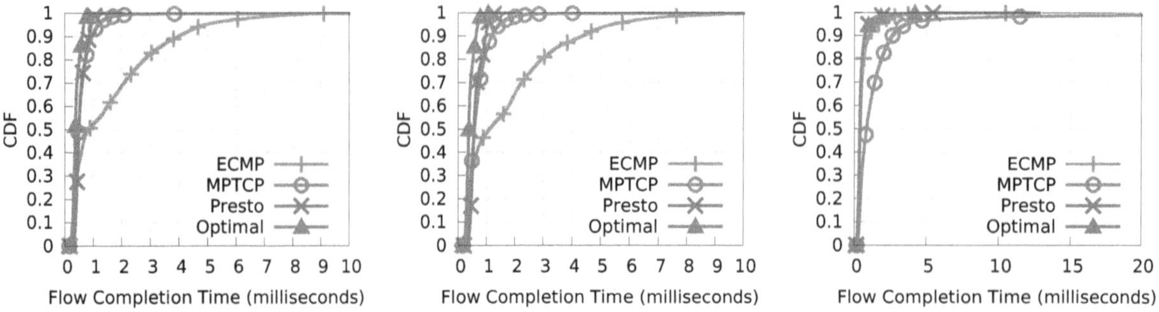

(a) Stride (b) Random Bijection (c) Shuffle

Figure 16: Mice FCT of ECMP, MPTCP, Presto and Optimal in stride, random bijection, and shuffle workloads.

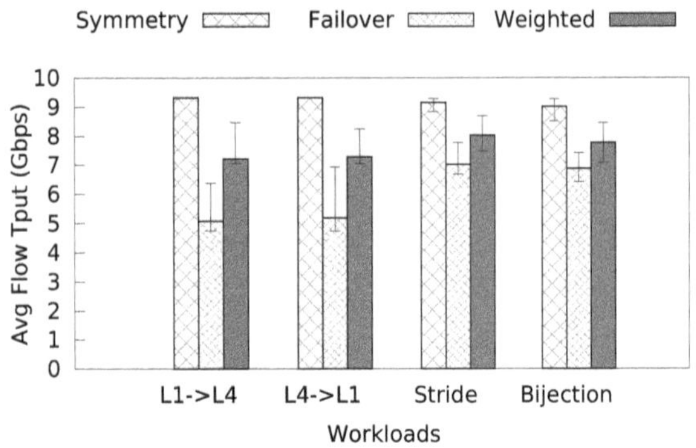

Figure 17: Presto's throughput in symmetry, fast failover and weighted multipathing stages for different workloads.

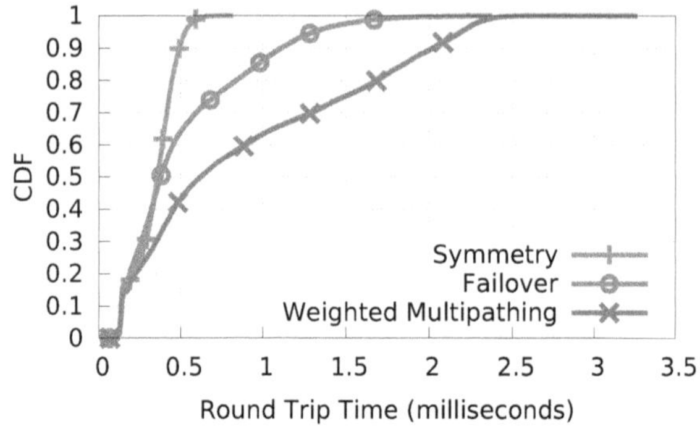

Figure 18: Presto's RTT in symmetry, fast failover and weighted multipathing stages in random bijection workload.

an additional server to each spine switch in our testbed to emulate remote users. The 16 servers establish a long-lived TCP connection with each remote user. Next, each server starts a flow to a random remote user every 1 millisecond. This emulates the behavior of using ECMP to load balance north-south traffic. The flow sizes for north-south traffic are based on the distribution measurement in [29]. The throughput to remote users is limited to 100Mbps to emulate the limitation of an Internet WAN. Along with the north-south flows, a stride workload is started to emulate the east-west traffic. The east-west mice FCT is shown in Table 2 (normalized to ECMP). ECMP, MPTCP, Presto, and Optimal's average throughput is 5.7, 7.4, 8.2, and 8.9Gbps respectively. The experiment shows Presto can gracefully co-exist with north-south cross traffic in the datacenter.

Impact of Link Failure Finally, we study the impact of link failure. Figure 17 compares the throughputs of Presto when the link between spine switch S1 and leaf switch L1 goes down. Three stages are defined: symmetry (the link is up), failover (hardware fast-failover moves traffic from S1 to S2), and weighted (the controller learns of the failure and prunes the tree with the bad link). Workload L1->L4 is when each node connected to L1 sends to one node in L4 (L4->L1 is the opposite). Despite the asymmetry in the topology, Presto still achieves reasonable average throughput at each stage. Figure 18 shows the round trip time of each stage in a random bijection workload. Due to the fact that the network is no longer non-blocking after the link failure, failover and weighted multipathing stages have larger round trip time.

7. RELATED WORK

We summarize the related work into three categories: datacenter traffic load balancing, reducing tail latency and handling packet reordering.

Load Balancing in Datacenters MPTCP [53, 61] is a transport protocol that uses subflows to transmit over multiple paths. CONGA [4] and Juniper VCF [28] both employ congestion-aware flowlet switching [58] on specialized switch chipsets to load balance the network. RPS [22] and DRB [17] evaluate per-packet load balancing on symmetric 1 Gbps networks at the switch and end-host, respectively. The CPU load and feasibility of end-host-based per-packet load balancing for 10+ Gbps networks remains open. Hedera [3], MicroTE [12] and Planck [54] use centralized traffic engineering to reroute traffic based on network conditions. FlowBender [32] reroutes flows when congestion is detected by end-hosts and Fastpass [49] employs a centralized arbiter to schedule path selection for each packet. As compared to these schemes, Presto is the only one that proactively load-balances at line rate for fast networks in a near uniform fashion without requiring additional infrastructure or changes to network hardware or transport layers. Furthermore, to the best of our knowledge, Presto is the first work to explore the interactions of fine-grained load balancing with built-in segment offload capabilities used in fast networks.

Reducing Tail Latency DeTail [63] is a cross-layer network stack designed to reduce the tail of flow completion times. DCTCP [5] is a transport protocol that uses the portion of marked packets by ECN to adaptively adjust sender's TCP's congestion window to reduce switch buffer occupancy. HULL [6] uses Phantom Queues and congestion notifications to cap link utilization and prevent congestion. In contrast, Presto is a load balancing system that naturally improves the tail latencies of mice flows by uniformly spreading traffic in fine-grained units. QJUMP [25] utilizes priority levels to allow latency-sensitive flows to "jump-the-queue" over low priority flows. PIAS [9] uses priority queues to mimic the Shortest Job First principle to reduce FCTs. Last, a blog post by Casado and Pettit [19] summarized four potential ways to deal with elephants and mice, with one advocating to turn elephants into mice at the edge. We share the same motivation and high-level idea and design a complete system that addresses many practical challenges of using such an approach.

Handling Packet Reordering TCP performs poorly in the face of reordering, and thus several studies design a more robust alternative [14, 15, 64]. Presto takes the position that reordering should be handled below TCP in the existing receive offload logic. In the lower portion of the networking stack, SRPIC [62] sorts reordered packets in the driver after each interrupt coalescing event. While this approach can help mitigate the impact of reordering, it does not sort packets across interrupts, have a direct impact on segment sizes, or distinguish between loss and reordering.

8. CONCLUSION

In this paper, we present Presto: a near uniform sub-flow distributed load balancing scheme that can near optimally load balance the network at fast networking speeds. Our scheme makes a few changes to the hypervisor soft-edge (vSwitch and GRO) and does not require any modifications to the transport layer or network hardware, making the bar for deployment lower. Presto is explicitly designed to load balance the network at fine granularities and deal with reordering without imposing much overhead on hosts. Presto is flexible and can also deal with failures and asymmetry. Finally, we show the performance of Presto can closely track that of an optimal non-blocking switch, meaning elephant throughputs remain high while the tail latencies of mice flow completion times do not grow due to congestion.

Acknowledgement

We would like to thank Jon Crowcroft (our shepherd) and the anonymous reviewers for their valuable feedback. This work is supported in part by IBM Corporation, National Science Foundation (grants CNS-1302041, CNS-1330308 and CNS-1345249) and the Wisconsin Institute on Software-Defined Datacenters of Madison.

References

[1] K. Agarwal, C. Dixon, E. Rozner, and J. Carter. Shadow MACs: Scalable Label-switching for Commodity Ethernet. In *HotSDN*, 2014.

[2] M. Al-Fares, A. Loukissas, and A. Vahdat. A Scalable, Commodity Data Center Network Architecture. In *SIGCOMM*, 2008.

[3] M. Al-fares, S. Radhakrishnan, B. Raghavan, N. Huang, and A. Vahdat. Hedera: Dynamic Flow Scheduling for Data Center Networks. In *NSDI*, 2010.

[4] M. Alizadeh, T. Edsall, S. Dharmapurikar, R. Vaidyanathan, K. Chu, A. Fingerhut, F. Matus, R. Pan, N. Yadav, G. Varghese, et al. CONGA: Distributed Congestion-aware Load Balancing for Datacenters. In *SIGCOMM*, 2014.

[5] M. Alizadeh, A. Greenberg, D. A. Maltz, J. Padhye, P. Patel, B. Prabhakar, S. Sengupta, and M. Sridharan. Data Center TCP (DCTCP). In *SIGCOMM*, 2010.

[6] M. Alizadeh, A. Kabbani, T. Edsall, B. Prabhakar, A. Vahdat, and M. Yasuda. Less Is More: Trading a Little Bandwidth for Ultra-Low Latency in the Data Center. In *NSDI*, 2012.

[7] G. Antichi, C. Callegari, and S. Giordano. Implementation of TCP Large Receive Offload on Open Hardware Platform. In *Proceedings of the First Edition Workshop on High Performance and Programmable Networking*, HPPN '13, 2013.

[8] Arista 7250QX Series 10/40G Data Center Switches. http://www.arista.com/assets/data/pdf/Datasheets/7250QX-64_Datasheet.pdf.

[9] W. Bai, L. Chen, K. Chen, D. Han, C. Tian, and H. Wang. Information-Agnostic Flow Scheduling for Commodity Data Centers. In *NSDI*, 2015.

[10] H. Ballani, P. Costa, C. Gkantsidis, M. P. Grosvenor, T. Karagiannis, L. Koromilas, and G. O'Shea. Enabling End Host Network Functions. In *SIGCOMM*, 2015.

[11] T. Benson, A. Akella, and D. A. Maltz. Network Traffic Characteristics of Data Centers in the Wild. In *IMC*, 2010.

[12] T. Benson, A. Anand, A. Akella, and M. Zhang. MicroTE: Fine Grained Traffic Engineering for Data Centers. In *CoNEXT*, 2011.

[13] C. Benvenuti. *Understanding Linux Network Internals.* " O'Reilly Media, Inc.", 2006.

[14] E. Blanton and M. Allman. On Making TCP More Robust to Packet Reordering. *ACM SIGCOMM Computer Communication Review*, 2002.

[15] S. Bohacek, J. P. Hespanha, J. Lee, C. Lim, and K. Obraczka. TCP-PR: TCP for Persistent Packet Reordering. In *ICDCS*, 2003.

[16] Broadcom Extends Leadership with New StrataXGS Trident II Switch Series Optimized for Cloud-Scale Data Center Networks. http://www.broadcom.com/press/release.php?id=s702418, 2012.

[17] J. Cao, R. Xia, P. Yang, C. Guo, G. Lu, L. Yuan, Y. Zheng, H. Wu, Y. Xiong, and D. Maltz. Per-packet Load-balanced, Low-latency Routing for Clos-based Data Center Networks. In *CoNEXT*, 2013.

[18] M. Casado, T. Koponen, S. Shenker, and A. Tootoonchian. Fabric: A Retrospective on Evolving SDN. In *HotSDN*, 2012.

[19] M. Casado and J. Pettit. Of Mice and Elephants. http://networkheresy.com/2013/11/01/of-mice-and-elephants/, November 2013.

[20] W. Chou and M. Luo. Agile Network, Agile World: the SDN Approach. http://huaweiempresas.com/img_eventos/140314/SDN_Workshop_2.pdf.

[21] S. Das. Smart-Table Technology—Enabling Very Large Server, Storage Nodes and Virtual Machines to Scale Using

Flexible Network Infrastructure Topologies. http://www.broadcom.com/collateral/wp/StrataXGS_SmartSwitch-WP101-R.pdf, July 2012.

[22] A. Dixit, P. Prakash, Y. C. Hu, and R. R. Kompella. On the Impact of Packet Spraying in Data Center Networks. In *INFOCOM*, 2013.

[23] A. Greenberg, J. R. Hamilton, N. Jain, S. Kandula, C. Kim, P. Lahiri, D. A. Maltz, P. Patel, and S. Sengupta. VL2: A Scalable and Flexible Data Center Network. In *SIGCOMM*, 2009.

[24] L. Grossman. Large Receive Offload Implementation in Neterion 10GbE Ethernet Driver. In *Linux Symposium*, 2005.

[25] M. P. Grosvenor, M. Schwarzkopf, I. Gog, R. N. Watson, A. W. Moore, S. Hand, and J. Crowcroft. Queues Don't Matter When You Can JUMP Them! In *NSDI*, 2015.

[26] H. Chen and W. Song. Load Balancing without Packet Reordering in NVO3. Internet-Draft. https://tools.ietf.org/html/draft-chen-nvo3-load-banlancing-00, October 2014.

[27] S. Ha, I. Rhee, and L. Xu. CUBIC: A New TCP-friendly High-speed TCP Variant. *SIGOPS Oper. Syst. Rev.*, 2008.

[28] D. R. Hanks. *Juniper QFX5100 Series: A Comprehensive Guide to Building Next-Generation Networks.* " O'Reilly Media, Inc.", 2014.

[29] K. He, A. Fisher, L. Wang, A. Gember, A. Akella, and T. Ristenpart. Next Stop, the Cloud: Understanding Modern Web Service Deployment in EC2 and Azure. In *IMC*, 2013.

[30] R. Jain, D. Chiu, and W. Hawe. A Quantitative Measure Of Fairness And Discrimination For Resource Allocation In Shared Computer Systems. *CoRR*, 1998.

[31] JLS2009: Generic Receive Offload. https://lwn.net/Articles/358910/.

[32] A. Kabbani, B. Vamanan, J. Hasan, and F. Duchene. FlowBender: Flow-level Adaptive Routing for Improved Latency and Throughput in Datacenter Networks. In *CoNEXT*, 2014.

[33] S. Kandula, S. Sengupta, A. Greenberg, P. Patel, and R. Chaiken. The Nature of Data Center Traffic: Measurements & Analysis. In *IMC*, 2009.

[34] R. Kapoor, A. C. Snoeren, G. M. Voelker, and G. Porter. Bullet Trains: A Study of NIC Burst Behavior at Microsecond Timescales. In *CoNEXT*, 2013.

[35] R. Khalili, N. Gast, M. Popovic, U. Upadhyay, and J.-Y. Le Boudec. MPTCP is Not Pareto-optimal: Performance Issues and a Possible Solution. In *CoNEXT*, 2012.

[36] T. Koponen, K. Amidon, P. Balland, M. Casado, A. Chanda, B. Fulton, I. Ganichev, J. Gross, N. Gude, P. Ingram, et al. Network Virtualization in Multi-tenant Datacenters. In *NSDI*, 2014.

[37] K.-C. Leung, V. O. Li, and D. Yang. An Overview of Packet Reordering in Transmission Control Protocol (TCP): Problems, Solutions, and Challenges. *Parallel and Distributed Systems, IEEE Transactions on*, 2007.

[38] Linux Kernel. https://www.kernel.org.

[39] A. Menon and W. Zwaenepoel. Optimizing TCP Receive Performance. In *USENIX Annual Technical Conference*, 2008.

[40] J. C. Mogul and K. Ramakrishnan. Eliminating Receive Livelock in An Interrupt-driven Kernel. *ACM Transactions on Computer Systems*, 1997.

[41] T. P. Morgan. A Rare Peek Into The Massive Scale of AWS. http://www.enterprisetech.com/2014/11/14/rare-peek-massive-scale-aws/, November 2014.

[42] MPTCP Linux Kernel Implementation. http://www.multipath-tcp.org.

[43] J. Mudigonda, P. Yalagandula, J. Mogul, B. Stiekes, and Y. Pouffary. NetLord: A Scalable Multi-tenant Network Architecture for Virtualized Datacenters. In *SIGCOMM*, 2011.

[44] Nuttcp. http://www.nuttcp.net/Welcome%20Page.html.

[45] Open vSwitch. http://openvswitch.org.

[46] C. Paasch, R. Khalili, and O. Bonaventure. On the Benefits of Applying Experimental Design to Improve Multipath TCP. In *CoNEXT*, 2013.

[47] V. Paxson. End-to-end Internet Packet Dynamics. In *ACM SIGCOMM Computer Communication Review*, 1997.

[48] I. Pepelnjak. NEC+IBM: Enterprise OpenFlow You can Actually Touch. http://blog.ipspace.net/2012/02/necibm-enterprise-openflow-you-can.html.

[49] J. Perry, A. Ousterhout, H. Balakrishnan, D. Shah, and H. Fugal. Fastpass: A Centralized "Zero-Queue" Datacenter Network. In *SIGCOMM*, 2014.

[50] J. Pettit. Open vSwitch and the Intelligent Edge. In *OpenStack Summit*, 2014.

[51] B. Pfaff, J. Pettit, K. Amidon, M. Casado, T. Koponen, and S. Shenker. Extending Networking into the Virtualization Layer. In *HotNets*, 2009.

[52] B. Pfaff, J. Pettit, T. Koponen, E. J. Jackson, A. Zhou, J. Rajahalme, J. Gross, A. Wang, J. Stringer, P. Shelar, et al. The Design and Implementation of Open vSwitch. In *NSDI*, 2015.

[53] C. Raiciu, S. Barre, C. Pluntke, A. Greenhalgh, D. Wischik, and M. Handley. Improving Datacenter Performance and Robustness with Multipath TCP. In *SIGCOMM*, 2011.

[54] J. Rasley, B. Stephens, C. Dixon, E. Rozner, W. Felter, K. Agarwal, J. Carter, and R. Fonseca. Planck: Millisecond-scale Monitoring and Control for Commodity Networks. In *SIGCOMM*, 2014.

[55] Receive Segment Coalescing (RSC). http://technet.microsoft.com/en-us/library/hh997024.aspx.

[56] Receive Side Scaling (RSS). https://technet.microsoft.com/en-us/library/hh997036.aspx.

[57] M. Scott, A. Moore, and J. Crowcroft. Addressing the Scalability of Ethernet with MOOSE. In *Proc. DC CAVES Workshop*, 2009.

[58] S. Sinha, S. Kandula, and D. Katabi. Harnessing TCPs Burstiness using Flowlet Switching. In *HotNets*, 2004.

[59] Sockperf: A Network Benchmarking Utility over Socket API. https://code.google.com/p/sockperf/.

[60] VXLAN Performance Evaluation on VMware vSphere 5.1. http://www.vmware.com/files/pdf/techpaper/VMware-vSphere-VXLAN-Perf.pdf.

[61] D. Wischik, C. Raiciu, A. Greenhalgh, and M. Handley. Design, Implementation and Evaluation of Congestion Control for Multipath TCP. In *NSDI*, 2011.

[62] W. Wu, P. Demar, and M. Crawford. Sorting Reordered Packets with Interrupt Coalescing. *Computer Networks*, 2009.

[63] D. Zats, T. Das, P. Mohan, D. Borthakur, and R. Katz. DeTail: Reducing the Flow Completion Time Tail in Datacenter Networks. In *SIGCOMM*, 2012.

[64] M. Zhang, B. Karp, S. Floyd, and L. Peterson. RR-TCP: A Reordering-robust TCP with DSACK. In *ICNP*, 2003.

[65] J. Zhou, M. Tewari, M. Zhu, A. Kabbani, L. Poutievski, A. Singh, and A. Vahdat. WCMP: Weighted Cost Multipathing for Improved Fairness in Data Centers. In *EuroSys*, 2014.

Packet-Level Telemetry in Large Datacenter Networks

Yibo Zhu[1,2] Nanxi Kang[1,3] Jiaxin Cao[1] Albert Greenberg[1] Guohan Lu[1] Ratul Mahajan[1]
Dave Maltz[1] Lihua Yuan[1] Ming Zhang[1] Ben Y. Zhao[2] Haitao Zheng[2]

[1]Microsoft [2]U. C. Santa Barbara [3]Princeton University

ABSTRACT

Debugging faults in complex networks often requires capturing and analyzing traffic at the packet level. In this task, datacenter networks (DCNs) present unique challenges with their scale, traffic volume, and diversity of faults. To troubleshoot faults in a timely manner, DCN administrators must *a)* identify affected packets inside large volume of traffic; *b)* track them across multiple network components; *c)* analyze traffic traces for fault patterns; and *d)* test or confirm potential causes. To our knowledge, no tool today can achieve both the specificity and scale required for this task.

We present Everflow, a packet-level network telemetry system for large DCNs. Everflow traces specific packets by implementing a powerful packet filter on top of "match and mirror" functionality of commodity switches. It shuffles captured packets to multiple analysis servers using load balancers built on switch ASICs, and it sends "guided probes" to test or confirm potential faults. We present experiments that demonstrate Everflow's scalability, and share experiences of troubleshooting network faults gathered from running it for over 6 months in Microsoft's DCNs.

CCS Concepts

•Networks → Network management;

Keywords

Datacenter network; failure detection; probe

1. INTRODUCTION

From online commerce to smartphone apps, datacenter networks (DCNs) are essential to large online services. DCNs typically operate at high utilization levels, and even small performance degradations or fault-induced downtime can lead to millions of lost revenue. These high stakes argue for a proactive model of DCN management, where infrastructure observes, analyzes, and corrects faults in near-real time.

Understanding and debugging faults in DCNs is challenging because faults come in all shapes and sizes. For example:

1. Some packets may experience abnormally high delay between servers A and B, but it may not be clear which of the many links is responsible.
2. Packets destined for a specific set of servers may be dropped, even when the packet-drop counters at switches exhibit no abnormality.
3. TCP connections to a VIP (Virtual IP) may encounter intermittent timeouts, and traceroute probes to debug the issue may be blocked by the load balancers.
4. Load may not be balanced among a group of ECMP (Equal Cost Multi Path) links; the network administrators do not know if this issue is due to flow size differences or a deeper problem (e.g., a poor hash function).

The diagnosis of such DCN faults requires examining network behavior at the granularity of packets. Problems such as faulty interfaces or switch software bugs can produce seemingly random failures that impact specific groups of packets based on any combination of characteristics, such as route taken in the network, packet headers, or timing. As a result of their subtle effects, these failures are often difficult to debug through analyses that rely on flow-level information [7], aggregate counters [5, 36], or sampled traffic [29]. We refer to tracing, collection and analysis of packet-level traffic behavior as *packet-level network telemetry*.

Building a responsive packet-level telemetry system for large DCNs is challenging for at least three reasons. First, today's DCNs carry unprecedented levels of network traffic. A large DCN usually has over 100,000 servers, each with a 10 to 40 Gbps network connection. At high utilization levels, aggregate traffic can easily exceed 100 Tbps. Analyzing even tiny subsets of this data is intractable for today's commodity switches, and moving traces to commodity servers for analysis would congest or even disrupt the network.

Second, DCN faults often occur over multiple hops or switches, and effective diagnosis requires intelligently tracing small subsets of packets over the network, as well as the ability to search the packet traces based on sophisticated query patterns, *e.g.,* protocol headers, sources and destinations, or even devices along the path. This task is not only akin to searching in the proverbial haystack for needles, but for specific needles of arbitrary size, shape and color. Ex-

SIGCOMM '15, August 17–21, 2015, London, United Kingdom

DOI: http://dx.doi.org/10.1145/2785956.2787483

isting systems that rely on packet-level analysis [14, 31] indiscriminately trace packets; they cannot scale to the size of large DCNs or search for packets based on complex patterns.

Finally, passive tracing alone, which captures an instantaneous snapshot of the network, has limited effectiveness. The traces observed in the snapshot may not be enough to identify whether the problem is transient or persistent, and they may not provide enough information to localize the problem. For example, when we see a packet trace stops before reaching its final destination, we may not be able to tell if this is due to a random drop or a blackhole.

We present Everflow, a network telemetry system that provides scalable and flexible access to packet-level information in large DCNs. To consistently trace individual packets across the network, Everflow uses "match and mirror." Commodity switches can apply actions on packets that match on flexible patterns over packet headers or payloads; we use this functionality with mirroring packets to our analysis servers as the action. By installing a small number of well-chosen match-and-mirror rules means we can reap the benefits of packet-level tracing while cutting down the overhead by several orders of magnitude. To quickly search for patterns in large volumes of packet traces, we build a scalable trace collection and analytics pipeline. We leverage switch-based load balancing [12] to distribute tracing and processing across multiple servers while preserving flow-level locality for efficient analysis. Finally, Everflow supports *guided probes*—packets that are specially crafted and injected into the network to follow preset paths. Guided probes help validate the performance and behavior of individual devices or links.

Everflow has been deployed since August 2014 in part of Microsoft's DCN infrastructure, including a cluster of 37 switches and a larger cluster of 440 switches. Both clusters carry a wide range of application traffic. We have also deployed Everflow selectively on-demand to other production clusters to help debug tricky network faults. We capture our deployment experiences by describing several representative debugging cases in §7, including latency problems, packet drops, routing loops, ECMP load imbalance, and protocol-specific issues around RDMA (Remote Direct Memory Access). In each case, we describe the observed symptoms, steps taken, and how a solution was found using Everflow.

We also perform detailed microbenchmarks to quantify the performance of Everflow along key aspects, including packet analysis rate, bandwidth and storage overhead, and overall system scalability. Our evaluations consistently show that all components of Everflow impose low overheads, and scale well to large DCNs with 100 Tbps of traffic.

In developing Everflow, we sought to address a real need for scalable, packet-level telemetry which can debug faults that are hard to tackle via conventional techniques. We prioritized usability and simplicity over functionality or features, *e.g.,* Everflow works on commodity switches and requires no specialized hardware. Our experiences with Everflow demonstrate that it scales well to large DCNs, and provides significant benefits to network administrators.

2. PACKET-LEVEL NETWORK TELEMETRY

Operational DCNs comprise a wide range of hardware and software components, including multiple types of switches, load balancers, and servers dedicated for processing and storage. Faults can and do arise from any single or combination of components, which makes debugging quite challenging in practice. In this section, we describe a number of sample faults that commonly occur in large DCNs, to illustrate why conventional tools are insufficient and why packet-level network telemetry is useful.

Silent packet drops: drops not reported by the culprit switch (*e.g.,* discard counters are zero). This situation may occur due to software bugs or faulty hardware on the switch. Although such drops can be detected on end hosts (*e.g.,* by monitoring TCP retransmissions), it is quite tricky to localize the culprit switch using conventional tools because of the large number of switches in DCNs. With consistent tracing of specific packets across switches, we can immediately locate the last hop switch where the victim packets appear as well as their expected next hop switch(es). We then send guided probes to each next hop switch to confirm the culprit.

Silent blackhole: the type of routing blackhole that does not show up in forwarding tables. Therefore it cannot be detected by tools that examine forwarding table entries [22, 23]. Silent blackhole can happen due to corrupted entries in TCAM tables. Packet-level network tracing will allow us to detect and localize a silent blackhole similar to how we deal with silent packet drops.

Inflated end-to-end latency: high latency for a flow. It is yet another problem that is easy to detect by end hosts, but can be difficult to debug using conventional tools. With packet-level network traces across switches, this problem becomes trivial, since we can obtain hop-by-hop latencies between the two end points.

Loops from buggy middlebox routing: routing problems caused by middleboxes instead of switches (or routers). This may happen when a middlebox incorrectly modifies a packet and its forwarding behavior (see §7.3). Such a problem cannot be found by examining the switch routing or forwarding tables because the tables are all correct. Given the network trace of a packet, we can easily identify such a problem as the trace will violate basic invariants such as loop-freedom.

Load imbalance: the problem of (5-tuple) flows being forwarded unevenly by a group of ECMP links. The naive detection method of comparing load counters at ECMP links can have false positives, since link load differences may actually be caused by differences in flow size (to be expected). Even when load imbalance is confirmed, the counters are too coarse-grained to answer key questions for debugging, such as "is the imbalance caused by flows that match specific patterns?" A packet-level network telemetry system allows us to count the number of specific 5-tuple pattern flows mapped to each link and thus offers a more reliable and direct method of detection and debugging.

Protocol bugs: bugs in the implementation of network protocols such as BGP, PFC (Priority-based Flow Control) and RDMA (Remote Direct Memory Access). When a protocol misbehaves, performance and reliability of the network suffers. Troubleshooting protocol bugs is tricky, because many protocols are implemented by third-party (switch and NIC) vendors and cannot be easily instrumented. Tracing the packets of these protocols offers a reliable yet independent way to identify protocol misbehaviors. Here network telemetry is particularly suitable because host-based tracing may be too expensive (*e.g.,* for RDMA) or unavailable (*e.g.,* for PFC and BGP).

3. OVERVIEW OF EVERFLOW

This section outlines the challenges in designing a scalable packet-level network telemetry system and introduces the key ideas in Everflow to address these challenges.

3.1 Design challenges

Tracing and analysis scalability. The first challenge facing packet-level network telemetry for large DCNs is scalability of trace collection. As mentioned earlier, the traffic in a large DCN (with 100,000+ servers) can easily go beyond 100 Tbps. Tracing packets at this scale will consume a tremendous amount of network and server resources. Consider a typical scenario where the average packet size is 1,000 bytes, each mirrored packet is truncated to 64 bytes (the minimum Ethernet frame size), and the network diameter is 5 hops (in a typical 3-tier Clos topology). If we simply trace every packet at every hop, as proposed in Packet History [14], the tracing traffic will be $\frac{64B}{1000B} \times 5(hops) \times 100(Tbps) = 32(Tbps)$.[1] Such a high rate of tracing traffic may cause congestion and packet drops, especially when network utilization is already high.

A similar same scalability challenge applies to trace analysis. Because commodity switches have limited storage and CPU power, traced packets must be sent to servers for analysis. Even assuming a server can process tracing traffic at line rate (10 Gbps), we will still need $\frac{32(Tbps)}{10(Gbps)} = 3,200$ servers for analysis which is prohibitively expensive.

Done naively, the situation can be worse. For most types of analysis (see §4.1 for details) require the per-hop trace of the same packets to be sent to the same analysis server. This stickiness can be achieved by having switches send traced packets to a set of reshufflers which then reshuffle the packets according to the hash of the packet header. Adding these reshuffling servers will double the total number of servers.

Limitations of passive tracing. In practice, passive tracing alone may not provide enough information for network troubleshooting. Fig 1(a) shows a scenario where a packet p is last seen at switch S_1 but not at the next hop switch S_2. Although this situation indicates that p is dropped at S_2, one cannot determine whether the problem is transient (which could be ignored) or persistent (which requires attention). One possible solution is to correlate multiple traces with dropped packet at S_2. However, there may not be enough traces available for such correlation because: i) the victim flows may have very few packets; ii) only a small fraction of packets are traced due to sampling. Even if we could know it is a persistent drop event, we will still have difficulty in figuring out whether this is a random drop (*e.g.,* due to a faulty cable) or a blackhole that only drops the packets of certain 5-tuples.

Fig 2(a) shows another scenario where a packet p traverses switches S_1 and S_2 and the two traced packets are sent to an analyzer A. To avoid the clock synchronization problem on S_1 and S_2, we try to calculate the latency of link (S_1, S_2) using the timestamps of the two traced packets on A. However, this cannot be done because the path $S_1 \rightarrow A$ can be quite different from the path $S_2 \rightarrow A$.

3.2 Key ideas

Everflow addresses these challenges with four key ideas. The first three tackle the scalability challenge while the last one overcomes the limitations of passive tracing.

Match and mirror on switch. Commodity DCN switches can match based on pre-defined rules and then execute certain actions (*e.g.,* mirror and encapsulate), which do not change original packet forwarding behavior. Everflow leverages this capability to reduce tracing overhead. Specifically, we design three types of matching rules to handle common DCN faults (§2). This rule set is by no means exhaustive and can be expanded to other types of faults.

First, we design matching rules to capture every flow in DCNs. The most straightforward rule is to randomly *trace* 1 out of n packets,[2] which is heavily biased towards large flows. In a DCN where the flow size distribution is highly skewed, this approach will miss many small flows. Yet these small flows are often associated with customer-facing, interactive services with strict performance requirements. To cover small flows, we configure a new set of rules that match based on the TCP SYN, FIN and RST fields in packets. Since DCN traffic is typically dominated by TCP [21], these rules allow us to trace every TCP flow in DCNs.

Second, we configure additional matching rules to enable flexible tracing. Basic TCP matching may not catch every type of fault, *e.g.,* the packet drops in the middle of a TCP flow. In fact, the exact set of traced packets that are needed depends on the nature of the fault. For instance, we may want to trace the packets of a particular application, with a specific port number, or between certain pairs of servers. To support such flexible tracing, we allow the packets to be marked by a special "debug" bit in the header. The marking criteria can be defined in any manner, as long as the total tracing overhead stays below a threshold. In the switches, we install a rule to trace any packet with the "debug" bit

[1]Packet History [14] proposed techniques to reduce the bandwidth overhead. But these techniques require heavy modifications to both switching ASIC and the host networking stack and are thus hard to deploy in current networks.

[2]This differs from the random sampling in sFlow [29] – Everflow ensures the same set of packets will be sampled and traced across all switches while in sFlow different switches may sample a different set of packets. That is one of the reasons why we cannot use sFlow for tracing in our system.

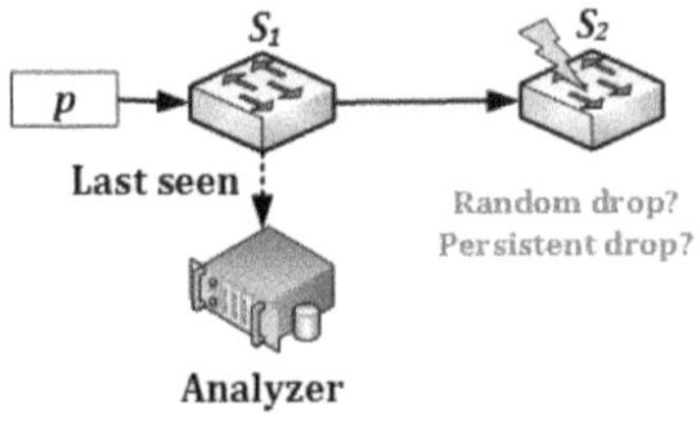

(a) Passive tracing is insufficient

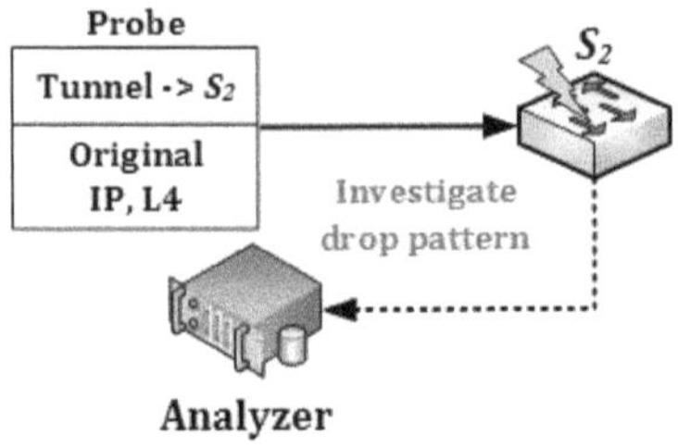

(b) Guided probing confirms the problem

Figure 1: Debugging packet drops

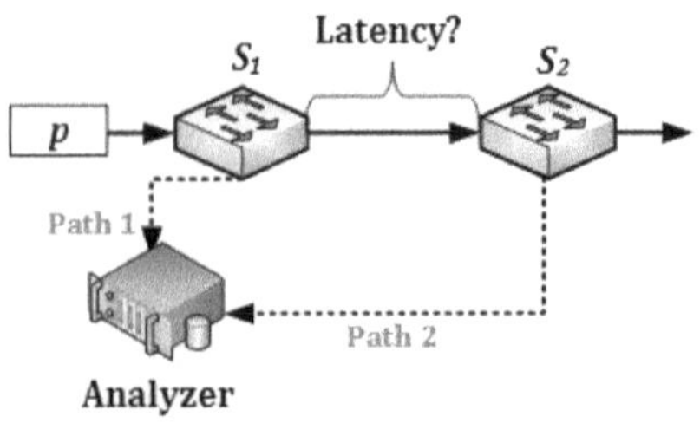

(a) Extracting link latency from passive tracing is hard

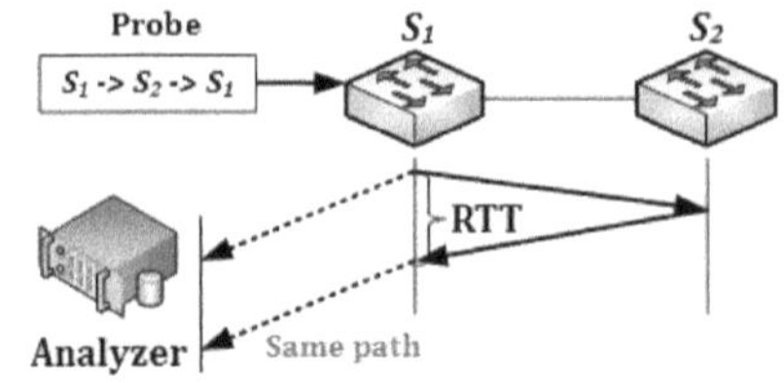

(b) Guided probing can accurately measure link latency

Figure 2: Measuring link latency

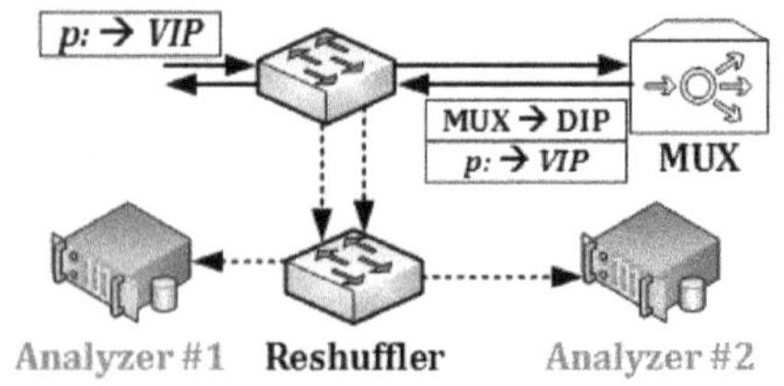

(a) Encapsulation breaks the packet trace

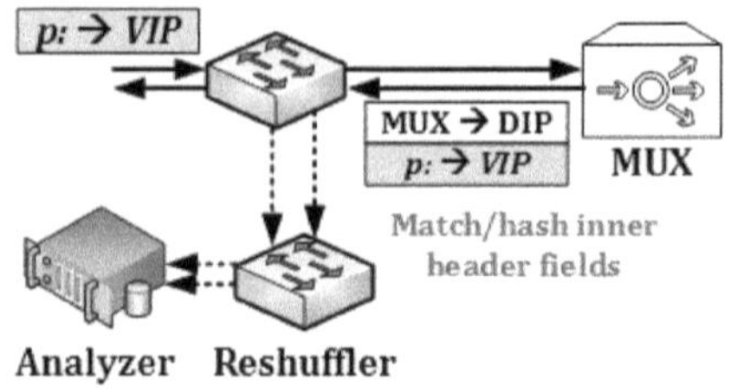

(b) Obtaining the complete packet trace by matching on inner header

Figure 3: Handling packet encapsulation

set, which is similar to how a software developer sets the debug flag during compilation to enable fine-grained tracing in their code. As a result, Everflow can efficiently trace any subset of regular data packets.

Finally, our tracing coverage goes beyond data packets. A DCN has a small amount of traffic associated with network protocols such as BGP, PFC, and RDMA. We call it *protocol traffic* to distinguish from regular data traffic. Although the absolute volume of the protocol traffic is small, it is critical for the overall DCN health and performance. Thus, Everflow has rules to trace all the protocol traffic.

Scalable trace analyzers. Although matching rules limit tracing overhead, the total amount of tracing traffic can still be huge because of the sheer scale of the DCN. To reduce analysis overhead, we observe that at any time only a tiny fraction of the traced packets (<0.01%) will exhibit abnormal behaviors (*e.g.,* loops or drops). This observation motivates us to treat abnormal packet traces differently from normal traces, *e.g.,* keep detailed, per-hop state for the former and aggregate, per-device state for the latter. As we explain in §4.1, this differential treatment helps reduce analysis overhead by three orders of magnitude. If needed, we can selectively recover the lost information in the normal traces via guided probes (described below).

Switch-based reshuffler. As mentioned in §3.1, we need a low-cost way to reshuffle a large volume of tracing traffic. We leverage work on turning a commodity switch into a hardware Mux (HMux) for load balancing [12]. The idea is to first define a VIP (virtual IP) on an HMux, which will map to a set of DIPs (direct IPs) where each DIP corresponds to an analysis server. We then configure all switches to send traced packets to the VIP. When a traced packet p reaches the HMux, the HMux redirects p to a DIP based on the hash of p's 5-tuple. This ensures that the traced packets of the same 5-tuple will be redirected to the same DIP.

An HMux can reshuffle traffic using the full forwarding capacity of a switch (typically > 1 Tbps). This is at least 100 times faster than a server with a 10 Gbps NIC, and dramatically cuts down the cost of reshuffling. We can further increase reshuffling capacity by configuring multiple HMuxes with the same VIP [12].

We need to pay special attention to encapsulated packets. (For now, let us ignore traced packets that are also encapsulated. We explain how to handle them in §6.1.) Packet encapsulation is often used in DCNs for load balancing [28] and network virtualization [24]. Fig 3(a) shows an example of how a SLB (Software Load Balancer) Mux may break the trace analysis. The original destination IP of a packet p is a VIP (Virtual IP). A Mux will encapsulate p with a new DIP (Direct IP) as the destination. Because of this, the traced packets of the original p and the encapsulated p are sent to two different analyzers, and are processed separately. To address this problem, we install a rule that matches on the inner header of an encapsulated packet, and configure HMuxes to hash based on inner header fields. This allows us to trace p's complete path from source to DIP (see Fig 3(b)).

Guided Probing. As mentioned earlier, a packet drop could happen due to multiple reasons. Sometimes, passive tracing alone may be insufficient to disambiguate between these possibilities. This ambiguity leads to the following question: what if we could arbitrarily replay a packet trace? More specifically, what if we could inject any desired packet into any desired switch and trace the behavior of the injected packet (by setting its debug bit)? We call this *guided probing* and will describe it in more detail in §6.2.

One immediate use of guided probing is to recover the lost

tracing information due to trace sampling or aggregation. To recover the trace of any packet p, we simply need to inject p into the first hop switch (with its debug bit set).

Further, guided probing is useful in overcoming the limitations of passive tracing. In the example of Fig 1(b), we can inject multiple copies of p into switch S_2 to see whether p is dropped persistently or not. In addition, we can craft probe packets with different patterns (*e.g.,* 5-tuples) to see if the drops are random or specific to certain 5-tuples. Such probing cannot debug transient faults because they may disappear before probing is initiated. We consider this limitation acceptable because persistent faults usually have a more severe impact than transient ones.

We extend guided probing such that it can not only inject a packet into a desired switch but also cause a packet to traverse a desired sequence of hops (similar to source routing). This extension allows us to measure the roundtrip latency of any link in the network, as illustrated in Fig 2(b). A probe packet p is instructed to traverse $S_1 \to S_2 \to S_1$. Because p traverses S_1 twice, S_1 will generate two traced packets of p at time t_1 and t_2 separately, and $t_2 - t_1$ equals to the roundtrip latency of link (S_1, S_2).

Since many commodity switches today do not provide the timestamping function, we cannot obtain t_1 and t_2 directly. However, observer that the two traced packets of p are close in time (*e.g.,* within 1 ms) and take exactly the same path from S_1 to the analyzer. Thus we can use the difference in their arrival time at the analyzer to approximate $t_2 - t_1$.

4. TRACE COLLECTION AND ANALYSIS

We now present the trace collection and analysis pipeline of Everflow. As shown in Fig 4, it consists of four key components: the *controller*, *analyzer*, *storage* and *reshuffler*. On top of that, there are a variety of *applications* that use the packet-level information provided by Everflow to debug network faults. The controller coordinates the other components and interacts with the applications. During initialization, it configures the rules on switches. Packets that match these rules will be mirrored to the reshufflers and the directed to the analyzers which output the analysis results into storage. The controller also provides APIs which allow Everflow applications to query analysis results, customize counters on the analyzers, inject guided probes, and mark the debug bit on hosts. We describe the analyzer and controller in this section and the reshuffler and storage in §6.

4.1 Analyzers

The analyzers are distributed set of servers, each of which processes a portion of tracing traffic. The reshufflers will balance the loads among the analyzers and ensure that the traced packets of the same 5-tuple are sent to the same analyzer (§3.2). Each analyzer keeps two type of states: packet trace and counter.

Packet trace. The analyzer keeps a table of packet traces where each trace is a chain of the mirrored instances of the same original packet. A trace is uniquely identified by the 5-tuple and the IPID of the original packet. It has one copy

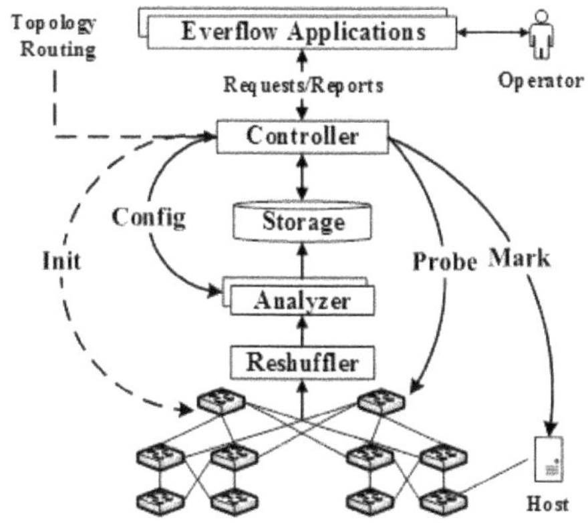

Figure 4: Everflow architecture

of the full packet content and a set of per-hop information, including the IP address of the switch where the packet is mirrored, timestamp, TTL, source MAC address (to identify the previous hop), and DSCP/ECN. A trace is considered complete when no new packet arrives for 1 second (which is much smaller than the end-to-end latency inside a DCN).

For each complete packet trace, the analyzer checks for two types of problems: loop and drop. A loop exhibits as the same device appearing multiple times in the trace. A drop is detected when the last hop of the trace is different from the expected last hop(s) which can be computed using the DCN topology and routing policy. For example, the expected last hop of a packet destined to an internal IP address of the DCN is the ToR switch directly connected to the IP address. The expected last hops of a packet destined to an external IP address are the border switches of the DCN.

To correctly handle packet encapsulation due to SLB (see Fig 3(a)), we merge the traces of an original packet p_o and an encapsulated packet p_e if the 5-tuple and IPID of p_e's inner IP header match those of p_o's IP header.

Despite of the use of match and mirror, the amount of packet traces can still be huge. To further reduce the storage overhead, each analyzer will only write to storage the traces that exhibit abnormal behaviors (*e.g.,* loop or drop), have the debug bit set (*e.g.,* guided probes), or correspond to the protocol traffic (*e.g.,* PFC and BGP). For the other traces (which represent a vast majority of all traces), each analyzer will aggregate them into the types of counters listed below and then periodically (*e.g.,* once every 10 seconds) write these counters into the storage. In the end, the controller combines the counters from individual analyzers into the final ones.

Link load counters. For each link, the analyzer will compute the aggregate load (*e.g.,* number of packets, bytes and flows) from the packet traces. Besides that, it may also compute more fine-grained load counters, *e.g.,* the load generated by certain prefixes or by intra-DC traffic. These fine-grained load counters can be dynamically added or removed by Everflow applications via the controller.

Latency counters. The analyzer will compute the latency of each link from the traces of guided probes (see §6.2). For any packet trace that traverses a SLB Mux, it will also

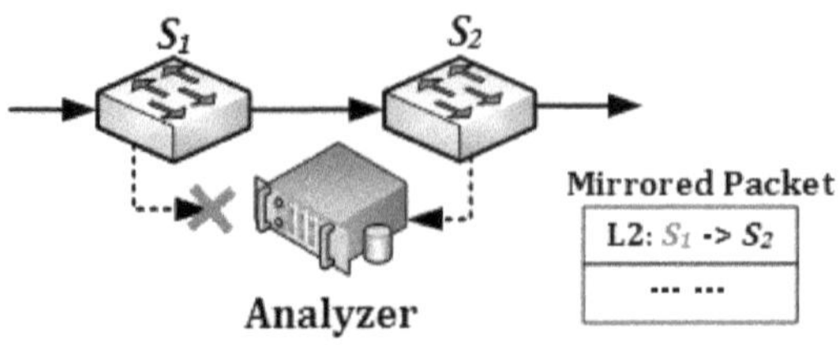

Figure 5: Detecting the drop of mirrored packets

compute the latency of the Mux. This process is shown in Fig 3(b) where a Mux server is connected to a ToR switch that mirrors both the original packet p_o and the encapsulated packet p_e. Because the mirrored instances of p_o and p_e will take the same path from the ToR switch to the same analyzer (as explained in §3.2), we can estimate the Mux latency using the arrival time difference between them at the analyzer. The estimated Mux latency includes the round trip latency of the link between the ToR switch and the Mux, which is negligibly small compared to the Mux latency. To save space, the analyzer will quantize individual latency samples into predefined bins in a latency histogram.

Mirrored packet drop counters. A mirrored packet may be dropped before reaching the analyzer. We can often infer such a drop from the packet trace. Fig 5 shows that a packet p traverses switches S_1 and S_2. However, p's trace contains only S_2 but not S_1, clearly indicating that p's mirrored packet from S_1 is dropped. In our current deployment, we found the drop rate is low (around 0.001%).

Sometimes mirrored packets may be dropped due to congestion near a particular reschuffler or analyzer. To further increase the reliability of our trace collection pipeline, we deploy multiple reshufflers and analyzers in different parts of the DCN and shift mirrored traffic away from any congested reshuffler and/or analyzer that exhibits a high mirrored packet drop rate.

4.2 Controller APIs

Everflow applications interact with the controller via several APIs to debug various network faults. With these APIs, the applications can query packet traces, install fine-grained load counters, trigger guided probes, and selectively trace traffic by marking the debug bit.

GetTrace(Filter, Condition, StartTime, EndTime) is used to get the packet traces between $StartTime$ and $EndTime$. The $Filter$ parameter specifies the types of traced packets to be filtered and is similar to the widely-used display filter in Wireshark. It allows filtering based on the Ethernet, IP, TCP, or UDP headers of the original packets as well as the outer IP header of the mirrored packets (which contains the IP address of the switch that sends the mirrored packets as shown in Fig 6). For example, the $Filter$ "ip.proto == 6 && ip.dst == 192.16.0.0/16 && switch == 10.10.0.10" matches all the TCP packets going to 192.16.0.0/16 and mirrored by switch 10.10.0.10. The $Condition$ parameter specifies the properties of the traces that cannot be extracted from the packet headers. For example, it allows filtering based on whether the traces contain a drop or a loop, or have a SLB Mux latency larger than 1 ms (if the traces traverse a Mux).

GetCounter(Name, StartTime, EndTime) is used to retrieve the counter values between $StartTime$ and $EndTime$. Each counter is identified by a descriptive $Name$, such as "SwitchX_PortY_TCP".

AddCounter(Name, Filter) & RemoveCounter(Name) are used to dynamically add or remove fine-grained load counters. The $Filter$ parameter is the same as above.

Probe(Format, Interval, Count) is used to launch guided probes. The probing results can later be retrieved via $GetTrace()$ and $GetCounter()$. The $Interval$ and $Count$ parameters specify the frequency and total number of probes to send. The $Format$ parameter specifies the format of the probe packets, including the L3 and L4 headers. It is similar to the $Filter$ parameter described above, with a minor change to support packet encapsulation. For example, "ip.src == SIP1,SIP2 && ip.dst == DIP1,DIP2 && ip.proto == 6" defines an IP-in-IP encapsulated TCP probe, whose outer source IP is SIP1, outer destination IP is DIP1, inner source IP is SIP2 and inner destination IP is DIP2.

EnableDbg(Servers, Filter) & DisableDbg(Servers, Filter) are used to mark or unmark packets with the debug bit on certain servers. The $Filter$ parameter is the same as above. The controller accepts the $EnableDbg()$ request if the total amount of traced traffic does not exceed system capacity.

5. EVERFLOW APPLICATIONS

Writing applications using Everflow APIs is straightforward. We now present several example applications to debug the network faults described in §2.

Latency profiler. Many DCN services, *e.g.*, search and distributed memory cache, require low latency. To find out why the latency between any pair of servers is too high, the latency profiler will first mark the debug bit of the TCP SYN packets between the two servers. From the traces of these packets, it knows the network devices on the path and then launches guided probes to measure the per-hop latency. Guided probing measures the roundtrip latency of each link instead of the one-way latency. This degree of localization suffices in practice. With this localization information, the profiler can quickly identify the network devices that cause the problem.

Packet drop debugger. Packet drops can severely degrade application performance, causing low throughput, timeouts or even unreachability. They are notoriously difficulty to debug as they happen due to many different reasons such as congestion, software bugs, or configuration errors. Our packet drop debugger routinely examines the packet traces that show packet drops. Given such a trace of a packet p, the debugger will infer the next hop switch S_n based on the last hop where p is captured. For example, S_n can be inferred either from p's output interface at the last hop switch or from the DCN topology and routing. After that, it will inject guided probes to S_n to determine whether the drops are persistent and, if so, whether the drops are random or have any patterns (*e.g.,* specific 5-tuples).

Loop debugger. Loops are uncommon in DCNs. However, when they do appear, they can cause unnecessary waste of resources or connectivity problems. Our loop debugger watches for packet traces that contain a loop. When a loop is detected, it first injects guided probes to see if the loop is persistent. If so, it reports the list of devices in the loop to the operators who can then break the loop by disabling one of the device interfaces. During this process, the debugger can continue to inject guided probes until the loop disappears.

ECMP profiler. In DCNs, switches often use ECMP to split traffic to the next hops. The load split may be uneven due to poor hash functions or routing problems, causing link congestion. For each switch, our ECMP profiler will monitor the aggregate load of all the links. When an uneven load split is detected, it will drill down through more fine-grained load counters to find out whether the uneven split impacts all traffic or just a subset (*e.g.,* the traffic from/to certain prefixes). The profiling results help the operators quickly detect and localize the problem.

RoCEv2-based RDMA debugger. RoCEv2-based [18] RDMA (Remote Direct Memory Access) is an emerging protocol for achieving high throughput (40 Gbps) and ultra-low latency (several microseconds) with low CPU overhead. By leveraging PFC (Priority-based Flow Control) to enable a drop-free Ethernet fabric, the RDMA protocol implementation can be simplified and offloaded to the NIC. However, in our DCNs, we find that RDMA sometimes cannot attain its ideal performance due to software bugs in the NIC. Debugging these problems is hard because the NICs are built by third-party vendors and we have limited means to instrument the RDMA code on the NICs.

We build a RDMA debugger in Everflow. It traces all the control packets related to RDMA, such as PFC and NACK (Negative Acknowledgement). The control packet traces offer a reliable and yet independent way not only to observe the actual behavior of RDMA flows but also to debug the implementation issues inside the third-party vendor's code.

6. IMPLEMENTATION

The entire Everflow system is implemented in roughly 10K lines of code in C++. The five Everflow applications are written in roughly 700 lines of code in C# in total. Below, we omit the details of the controller (whose implementation is fairly straightforward) and the reshuffler (which is similar to the Mux described in Duet [12]); we focus on other aspects instead.

6.1 Switch configurations

By default, we configure rules in the TCAM table to match on TCP SYN/FIN/RST flags. We use a bit in the DSCP field as the debug bit, and n bits in the IPID field to sample 1 out of 2^n packets. For example, by configuring a rule to match on 10 bits in the IPID field, we will sample 1 out of 1,024 packets. Since every switch has the same rules, the set of sampled packets will be consistent across all switches. For any encapsulated packet, we configure rules to match on its inner TCP/IP headers to ensure that it is sent to the same analyzer as its original packet (§3.2). Finally we configure rules to match on Ethernet type 0x8808 (L2 control packets including PFC), TCP port 179 (BGP packets), and RDMA NACK [17]. The total number of rules is around 20, which consumes only a small fraction of the TCAM table.

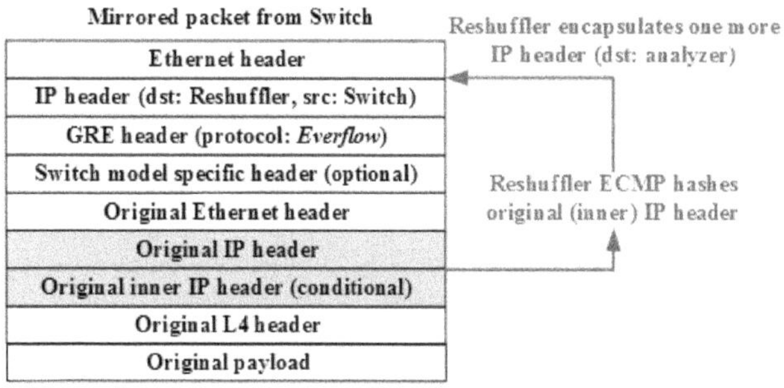

Figure 6: Format of mirrored packet

When a packet matches any rule, the switch will mirror it and encapsulate the mirrored packet using GRE (Generic Routing Encapsulation). Fig. 6 shows the format of the GRE packet, where the source IP is the switch loopback IP, the destination IP is the VIP of the reshufflers, and the payload is the original packet (starting from the L2 header). Inside the GRE header, there is a protocol field which is used to indicate that this is an Everflow mirrored packet. We configure every switch with a blacklist rule to prevent mirroring a mirrored packet.

"Match and mirror" is completely done in a switch's data plane. This implementation leverages the huge packet processing capacity of switching ASIC and incurs zero overhead on a switch's CPU.

6.2 Guided prober

The key function of a prober is to inject any desired packet into any target switch S. It uses the raw socket APIs to craft arbitrary packet fields, *e.g.,* the IP and L4 (TCP, UDP, ICMP, etc.) headers. The crafted packet p has the debug bit set to enable tracing and carries a signature in the payload so that it can be easily identified by the Everflow analyzer. To send p to S, we leverage the decapsulation capability that is widely available on commodity switches. We first create the probe packet p' by encapsulating p with S's loopback IP as the destination, and send p' out. We also configure a rule on S to decapsulate any encapsulated packet destined to S's loopback IP address. Thus upon receiving p', S will decapsulate p' into p and then process p according to the normal forwarding logic.

In fact, we can extend the technique above to instruct p' to follow any desired route by encapsulating p multiple times. This can be used to measure the latency of any link (S_1, S_2) as shown in Fig 2(b). We simply need to craft p with S_1 as the destination, encapsulate it with S_2 as the destination, and encapsulate it again with S_1 as the destination. The resulting p' will follow the route $S_1 \to S_2 \to S_1$ as required in §3.2.

To prevent guided probe packets from interfering with server applications, we deliberately set their TCP or UDP checksum incorrectly so that they will be discarded by servers.

6.3 Analyzer

The analyzers use a custom packet capturing library to capture mirrored packets. The library supports RSS (Receiver Size Scaling) [2] which allows an analyzer to receive packets using multiple CPU cores. The library hashes packets to CPU cores based on source and destination IPs, using inner source and destination IPs if packets are encapsulated. We run multiple analysis threads to maximize throughput.

6.4 Storage

The Everflow storage is built on top of SCOPE [6]—a scalable, distributed data processing system. In SCOPE, data is modeled as tables composed of rows of typed columns. These tables can be processed by SQL-like declarative scripts, which support user-defined operators, such as extractors (parsing and constructing rows from a file), processors (row-wise processing), reducers (group-wise processing), and combiners (combining rows from two inputs).

We store packet traces in a multi-column table, where each row corresponds to a packet trace. The columns contain three parts of information about the packet trace. The first part is the full packet content. The packet header and payload are stored in separate columns to simplify processing. The second part is the per-hop information, *e.g.*, timestamp, TTL, source MAC address and DSCP-ECN. Since the number of hops is variable, we combine all the per-hop information into one column. The last part is the metadata of the trace, including the trace length, whether it is a guided probe, or whether it has a loop or a drop. The traces can be retrieved by the controller based on the $filter$, *condition*, and time range defined in §4.2.

We also store the counters from all the analyzers in a table. Each row in the table represents one snapshot of a counter from an analyzer. Besides the key and value of the counter, a row also contains the analyzer's ID and the timestamp when the snapshot was taken. To respond to a counter query, the controller will sum up the counter values of the rows that match the given counter name and time range.

7. DEPLOYMENT AND EXPERIENCE

We deployed Everflow in two Microsoft DCN clusters in August 2014. The first one is a full deployment in a pre-production cluster (Cluster A) with 37 switches. The second one is a pilot deployment to 440 out of more than 2,500 switches in a production cluster (Cluster B). Both clusters carry traffic for many DC applications. In addition, we also enabled Everflow on certain production switches on demand to debug live incidents. Currently, we are extending Everflow deployment to more switches and clusters. In the following, we will share our experience in using Everflow to debug a variety of common DCN faults (§2).

7.1 Latency problem

A multi-tier search application complained about large latency jitters between a set of servers. The application allocates a strict per-tier latency bound of 1 ms, which includes server processing time. Due to the use of ECMP routing in our DCN (Fig 7(a)), there are hundreds of links that could cause this problem. It was extremely difficult for operators to identify the culprit switch or link.

One possibility was to use traceroute to infer per-link latency. However, traceroute measures the RTT between a probing server and a switch, which is impacted by all the links on the forward and reverse paths. Moreover, because the traceroute probe is processed by the switch CPU, the measured RTT will be inflated by the switch control plane delay which may be highly variable. Thus, the RTT measured by traceroute will be very noisy and even unusable.

Our latency profiler was called for help. It marked the debug bit for the application traffic sent or received on the afflicted servers, and learned the links on the path. It subsequently sent out guided probes to measure all the relevant links in parallel. Fig 7(b) plots a portion of the latency timeseries on a subset of the links. Intermittently, Link A would have a much larger latency variability than the other links, sometimes even approaching 0.8 ms. This left little time for servers to complete their computations. After further investigation, the operators confirmed that this problem was caused by a misconfigured ECN (Explicit Congestion Notification) threshold that allowed excessive queue build up.

Summary. Unusually high latency is one of the most common problems in DCNs and is hard to debug using conventional tools. The fine-grained latency measurements provided by Everflow help operators localize the problem in minutes instead of hours.

7.2 Packet drops

7.2.1 Blackhole

Many clients of an internal web service reported that a fraction of their connection establishment requests were encountering timeouts. However, a few retrials of the connection requests would eventually succeed. This led to the violation of the SLAs (Service Level Agreements) of the web service and raised alerts to the network operator.

The operator suspected that this problem was due to packet drops. However, he had no clue where the drops happened because the web service was behind a VIP (virtual IP) which was hosted on multiple software Muxes. A client's request could be sent to any one of the Muxes and then redirected to any one of the many DIPs (direct IPs). This means the drops could happen anywhere between the clients and the Muxes, on one of the Muxes, or between the Muxes and the DIPs.

He first checked the error counters on the Muxes but found no problem. Then he checked the counters on a number of switches, some of which showed minor drops. But none of the switch counters was significant enough for him to reach a reliable conclusion. At this point, he was stuck and had to elevate the alert.

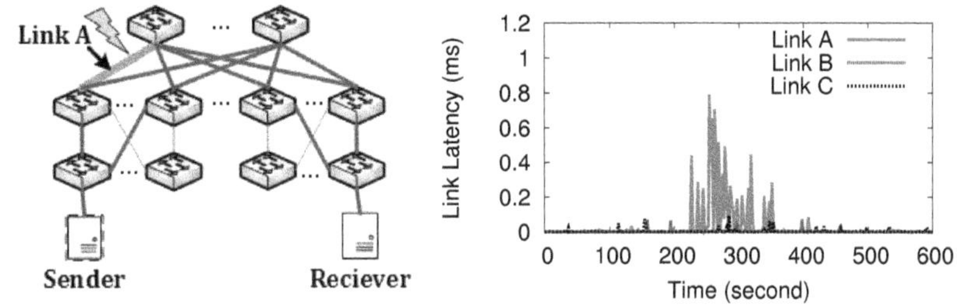

(a) Many links may be responsible for the latency problem

(b) Latency profiling results

Figure 7: Profiling link latency

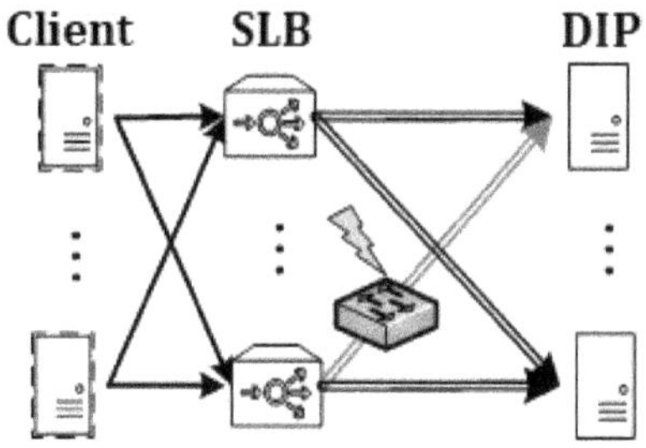

Figure 8: A switch blackholes packets to a DIP behind a SLB Mux

We ran the packet drop debugger to investigate this issue. From the drop debugger, we observed that many SYN packet traces that did not reach the DIPs after traversing the Muxes and that all these abnormal traces stalled one hop before the same switch S. The drop debugger subsequently launched guided probes, with the same 5-tuples as the dropped SYN packets, to S to validate the drops. The results showed that all the SYN packets destined to a specific DIP were dropped by S, suggesting that S was blackholing the packets to the DIP (Fig 8).

Informed by our analysis, the operator analyzed the suspect switch thoroughly and found that one of the forwarding entries in the TCAM table was corrupted. Any packet that hit the corrupted entry would be dropped. Even worse, the switch did not report such drops in any counter. After a reboot, the switch started behaving normally and the timeout problem went away as well.

7.2.2 *Silent packet drop*

Many DC applications in Cluster B detected abnormally high levels of TCP retransmissions. At the same time, the network-wide end-to-end monitoring system also showed that the ping probes between certain server pairs were experiencing around 2% loss rate. This caused severe performance degradation to the applications running in the network.

As was usual, the operator started with the switch counters but did not see anything particularly wrong. Given that the end-to-end probes did show drops, he suspected that this was caused by one switch silently dropping packets. The conventional approach to debug such a problem is to use tomography, *e.g.*, inferring the rough location of the culprit switch by sending many pings and traceroutes to exhaustively explore the paths and links in the network. After narrowing down to a few suspects, the operator would try to pinpoint the culprit by disabling and enabling the suspects one by one. However, since the DCN has nearly 25,000 links, such a brute-force approach will impose significant overhead and can easily take several hours.

Our packet drop debugger simplified the debugging process. From all the packet traces in the storage, it first extracted the ones that encountered drops during the same time period. Based on where the problematic traces stopped, the debugger quickly identified one suspect switch which appeared to be the next hop of most of the problematic traces. It then sent 1,000 guided probes to test each interface on the switch. In the end, the root cause was found to be one faulty interface on the switch that silently dropped a fraction of packets at random. All the application alerts stopped after the faulty interface was disabled.

7.2.3 *Packet drops on servers*

In this incident, one internal application alerted that the throughput between its senders and receivers was 15% lower than normal. The application used UDP as the transport protocol and had many senders and receivers. All the receivers reported roughly equal amount of throughput loss. To isolate the UDP packet drops, the sender's team, receiver's team and network team were involved.

Due to the large number of senders, the sender's team could only sample a few senders and capture packets on those senders. From the captured traces, they confirmed that the packets were indeed sent. The receiver's team did the same thing on several receivers and found that packets were partially received. However, because the loads on the receivers were pretty high, they could not determine whether the missing packets were dropped by the network or by the receivers' NIC. At this stage, neither the network nor the receiver's teams could be released from debugging.

To find out where the packets were dropped, the network team used the Everflow drop debugger to mark the debug bit on a subset of the senders' traffic. From the resulting packet traces, the debugger showed that all the marked UDP packets successfully traversed the network and reached the last hop ToR (Top-of-Rack) switches to which the receivers were connected. Thus, the packet drops were happening at the receivers. After more investigation, the problem was found to be a recent update on the senders that caused some messages to use a new format which were not recognized by the receivers. Without Everflow, the network team would have a hard time proving that the drops were not in the network.

Summary. Packet drop is a common source of performance faults in DCNs. Localizing drops is extremely challenging given the large number of devices involved (servers, switches, Muxes, etc.). Everflow offers an efficient and reliable way to track packets throughout the network and dramatically simplifies the drop debugging process.

7.3 Loop

Under normal circumstances, we do not expect to see any loops in a DCN. Surprisingly, the Everflow loop debugger did catch quite a few loop incidents in Cluster B. All the loop traces showed the same pattern — they involved a packet that kept bouncing back and forth between a SLB Mux and a DIP until its TTL became 0.

Figure 9 shows how a loop forms. Initially a request packet to VIP_0 is sent to a SLB Mux, which then encapsulates and sends the packet to a DIP. When the DIP server receives and decapsulates the packet, it finds that the inner header destination IP (VIP_0) does not match its designated VIP. Instead of discarding the packet, the DIP server throws the packet back to the network. As a result, this packet is sent back to the Mux again, forming a persistent loop.

We call it an *overlay* loop since it results from inconsistent views between two servers (Mux and DIP). Unlike a network-level loop, an overlay loop cannot be detected by examining the forwarding table on switches. In fact, the forwarding tables are all correct. At the same time, an overlay loop can result in unnecessary waste of network and server resources or even unavailability. In these incidents, the loops caused 30x amplification of the affected traffic. The traffic trapped in the loops accounted for roughly 17% of the total traffic received by the problematic DIPs.

Summary. Contrary to conventional wisdom, loops can form in a DCN due to the wide use of server overlays that participate in packet forwarding. Everflow provides an effective way to detect and debug such loops, which allows the loops to be fixed before they trigger severe failures.

7.4 Load imbalance

The SNMP link monitor reported imbalanced loads on the links from four leaf switches to a ToR switch in Cluster A. Fig 10(b) shows the part of the topology that is related to this incident. Because the loads on these links were affected by all the upstream switches of the ToR, the operator had no clue about why this imbalance happened.

The Everflow ECMP profiler was used to debug this problem. It started by requesting fine-grained load counters from the Everflow analyzers and breaking down the load by traffic towards physical server IP prefixes *vs.* traffic towards SLB VIP prefixes. It found that the traffic to physical servers was indeed balanced, but the VIP traffic was doing just the opposite. To understand this phenomenon, the profiler further broke down the traffic by individual VIP prefixes under the ToR. It turned out that only the traffic destined to three VIP prefixes was imbalanced. As shown in Fig 10(a), the load of the three VIP prefixes on link $Leaf_4 \rightarrow ToR$ is 2.6 times that on link $Leaf_3 \rightarrow ToR$.

A follow-up investigation showed that this incident was due to a failure in BGP route advertisement. Specifically, the first three leaf switches failed to advertise the routes for these three VIP prefixes to some of its upstream spine switches (Fig 10(b)). This led to the uneven split of the traffic going to the three VIP prefixes, starting from the spine switches down to the leaf switches.

Summary. Load imbalance can arise due to a variety of reasons. The Everflow ECMP profiler supports flexibly classifying the traffic and providing detailed load information per traffic class. Therefore, it can not only detect load imbalance incidents but also help identify their causes. The latter cannot be easily done based on the aggregate load counters.

7.5 Low RDMA throughput

Our DCN is deploying RoCEv2-based RDMA. However, the RDMA engineering team found that RDMA performed poorly when there were a small amount of packet losses (*e.g.*, due to a switch interface bug or packet corruption). For example, even with 0.01% loss rate, the throughput of a RDMA flow would drop below 10 Gbps (i.e., less than 25% of the optimal throughput of 40 Gbps). Such degradation was far worse than expected.

Initially, the engineers attempted to debug this problem by capturing the RDMA packets on both ends of the servers using a customized tool provided by the RDMA NIC vendor. However, due to the high data rate, the tool would impose significant capturing overhead on the NIC and also miss a fraction of the packets. As a result, when the engineers examined the packet dumps and saw no bad symptom, they could not tell whether this was because the flow behavior had changed (due to the extra capturing overhead) or because there was not enough diagnostic information. Moreover, the tool can capture only L3 packets but not L2 packets like PFC.

We used our RDMA debugger to investigate this problem. The throughput of an RDMA flow is affected by three types of control packets: PFC (Priority-based Flow Control), NACK (Negative Acknowledgment) and CNP (Congestion Notification Packet), all of which are captured by Everflow. From the control packet traces, we saw an unexpected correlation between the PFC and NACK packets. When a receiver generated a NACK in response to a packet loss, it almost always generated another PFC packet with a long PAUSE period. The effect of the PAUSE was propagated hop-by-hop back to the sender,[3] and ultimately slowed the sender.

We reported this problem to the NIC vendor who later found a bug in their NIC driver. This bug caused the NIC to halt the buffer, and subsequently triggered a PFC with a long PAUSE period during the NACK generation.

Summary. Everflow provides a reliable and yet independent way to observe and debug network protocol misbehaviors. This is particularly useful when host-based capturing of protocol packets is too expensive (*e.g.*, for RDMA) or unavailable (*e.g.*, for PFC).

8. SYSTEM EVALUATION

[3] To avoid buffer overflow, a switch uses PFC to force its upstream neighbor (another switch or a server NIC) to PAUSE data transmission.

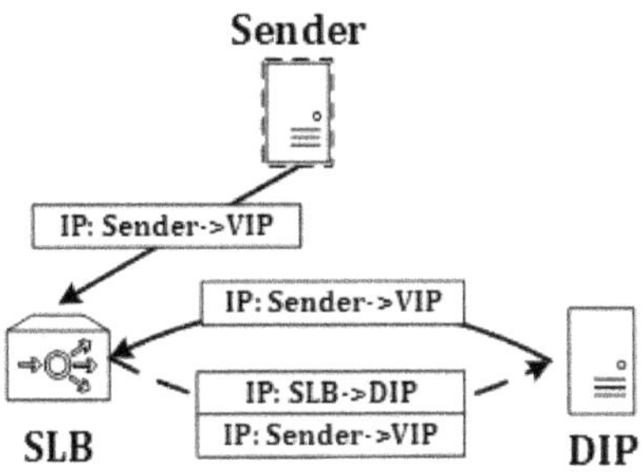

Figure 9: An overlay loop formed between a SLB Mux and a DIP

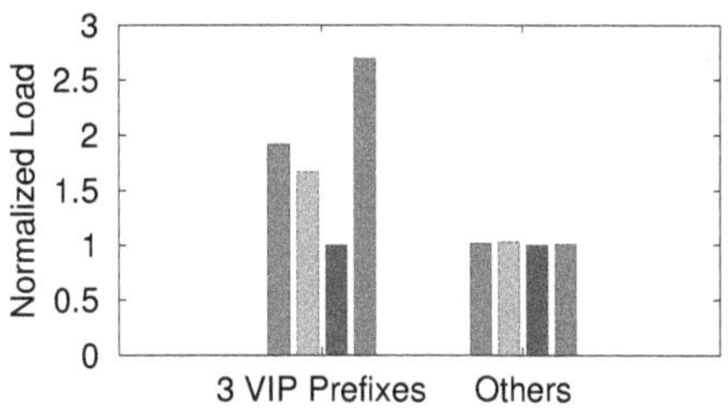

(a) Traffic to 3 VIP prefixes is imbalanced

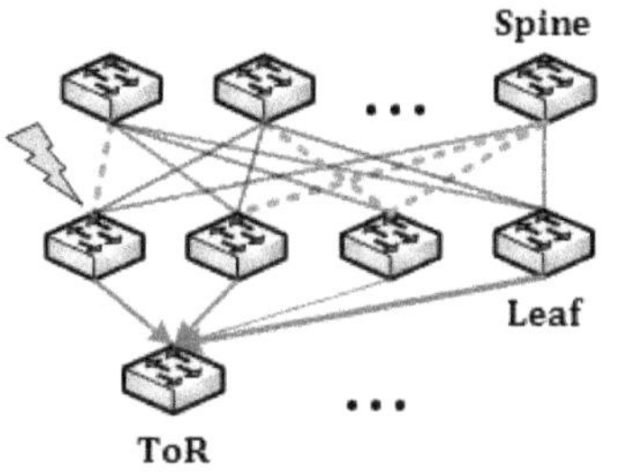

(b) Imbalance due to prefix announcement failure from leaf switches to spine switches

Figure 10: Load imbalance incident

We evaluate Everflow's capacity, overhead and deployment cost and show that it can easily scale to a large DCN with 10K switches, 250K links and 100 Tbps traffic. In the analysis below, we ignore the switch overhead because match-and-mirror is done completely at the switch's data plane and incurs zero overhead on the switch's CPU (§6.1).

8.1 Capacity

Analyzer. We use servers with Xeon 16-core, 2.1 GHz CPU, 128 GB memory and 10 Gbps Ethernet NIC. Depending on the packet size, the bottleneck may be the CPU (capped by number of packets per second, or *pps*) or Ethernet NIC.

For small packets, our packet capturing library achieves around 600K pps per thread. With RSS support, which scales capturing throughput linearly with the number of CPU cores, our library is capable of capturing 4.8M pps using 8 CPU cores.[4] Because our analysis task is light weight, one CPU core can easily analyze more than 600K pps. Thus we run 8 capturing threads and 8 analysis threads, with one thread per core. In total, each server can process ***4.8M pps*** with 16 cores.

For large packets, the NIC becomes the bottleneck. If all packets are 1,500 bytes (standard MTU in DCNs), a server with a 10 Gbps NIC will handle only $10Gbps/8/1500 = 0.83Mpps$. Meanwhile, memory is never a bottleneck. Since the analyzer only buffers packets that arrive in the last second (§4), maximum memory usage is $10Gbps \times 1s = 1.25GB$.

Reshuffler. The reshuffler processes packets at a switch's line rate. Using a switch with $128 \times 10Gbps$ ports, a reshuffler can support 1.28 Tbps or 10 billion pps.

8.2 Overhead

Bandwidth. From our current deployment, the mirrored traffic volume is only ***0.38%*** of the DCN traffic and the average mirrored packet size is 156.4 bytes. Currently we do not truncate packets due to the limitations of commodity switches used in our DCN. Given 100 Tbps of DCN traffic, the mirrored traffic requires ***380 Gbps*** network bandwidth and ***300M pps*** CPU processing power.

Storage. We breakdown the storage overheads into counters and traces. Because the number of links is much larger than the number of switches or Muxes, the link counters dominate all the other counters. For each link, we have 6 load counters (3 in each direction) and 4 latency counters (for latency histogram). Given 250K links, the total number of counters is 2.5M. Since each counter takes 20 bytes and the update interval is 10 seconds, each analyzer consumes only $2.5M \times 20B/10s = 5MB/s$ for uploading all the counters into storage.

In our deployment, analyzers record less than 0.01% of all traces, since most normal traces are aggregated into counters (§4.1). Thus uploading packet traces requires only $380Gbps \times 0.01\%/8 = 4.75MB/s$ in total. Such a data rate can be easily handled by the distributed storage service.

Query delay. The response time of answering a query by an Everflow application mainly depends on the data volume being queried. We benchmark the *GetTrace()* query on 10 GB traces (roughly equal to the amount of traces generated in 30 minutes), and the SCOPE job finishes in one minute. We observe similar query delay for *GetCounter()*. For all the incidents presented in §7, we never need to query more than 10 GB of data.

8.3 Deployment cost

Since most mirrored packets are small, the analyzers are bottlenecked by the CPU. Given a total of 300M pps (or 380 Gbps) mirrored traffic, we need $300Mpps/4.8Mpps = 63$ analyzers. Furthermore, a single switch-based reshuffler is sufficient to handle all the mirrored traffic. We currently use two reshufflers for failure resilience.

9. RELATED WORK

Our work builds on several themes of related work.

Mirroring. Like Everflow, Planck [31] and PacketHistory [14] monitor network through switch mirroring. In Planck, switches mirror traffic at over-subscribed ports to a directly attached server. It focuses on packets at a single device instead of network-wide packet traces. PacketHistory mirrors all packets at switches to remote servers. For large scale

[4]Advanced packet capturing libraries like DPDK [1] NetMap [32] and WireCap [34] can support more than 20Mpps using 8 cores.

DCNs, its approach incurs significant overhead to transmit and process all traffic. It may also cause congestion and hurt ongoing applications. In comparison, to lower overhead, Everflow uses "match" to select the right traffic to mirror.

Sampling. Many recent works [7, 8, 29, 33, 36] focus on sampling network traffic. NetFlow [7] and OpenSketch [36] aggregate information (*e.g.,* number of bytes) at flow level and do not provide fine-grained, packet-level information. sFlow [29] randomly samples packets at switches. It only provides per-device information and cannot track packet paths across multiple devices. Another work [8] proposes sampling packets with a consistent hash function. It does not cover what packets to sample or how to analyze sampled packets. In contrast, Everflow presents a flexible and rule-based end-to-end solution that traces packets of interest across the network and analyzes the traces in real time.

Probing. Per-packet tracing tools such as traceroute, ICMP, and Tulip [25] can track a packet's path in the network. A recent work [27] proposes using IP pre-specific timestamp option to dissect RTT, but is limited to specific portions of the path in the Internet. These works can be classified as out-of-band diagnosis because they use packets that are different from the actual application. In comparison, Everflow focuses on in-band tracing.

OFRewind [35] proposes "record and replay", which is another way of probing. Everflow has a similar capability, but it is more flexible than merely replaying past traffic. For example, Everflow can instrument a probe to bounce between switches for measuring latency.

Further, existing tools cannot trace beyond middleboxes (*e.g.,* load balancers and VNet gateways), which can encapsulate or modify packets. Everflow correlates packets entering and leaving middleboxes to construct full packet traces.

Fault detection. Several works [9, 10, 22, 23] detect network faults by checking routing configuration and policy. They analyze routing rules and validate compliance with network policy (*e.g.,* no forwarding loops). They rely on control plane information and focus on verifying the forwarding tables. As a result, they cannot diagnose packet level problems. Other works monitor virtual switches [26] or use operational data, such as router syslog [3, 11, 15, 30] or AS route dissemination [13], for fault detection. They are complementary to Everflow because they focus on different aspects than Everflow, which targets fine-grained packet-level faults based on data plane tracing.

10. CONCLUSION AND FUTURE WORK

We present Everflow, a scalable packet-level telemetry system for large DCNs. Everflow leverages switch's "match and mirror" capability to capture consistent traces of packets across DCN components and injects guided probes to actively replay packet traces. For fault debugging applications, Everflow provides flexible query interfaces and configurable APIs on top of an efficient and light weight analytics pipeline. Through deployment in Microsoft's DCNs, Everflow demonstrated its utility as an indispensable tool for troubleshooting DCN faults.

In the future, we plan to extend Everflow to make use of the features offered by new programmable switching ASIC [4, 20], including hardware timestamping and packet metadata matching. Switch timestamping will dramatically simplify the measurement of link roundtrip latency, and packet metadata matching (*e.g.,* based on checksum error or parity error) will provide insight into the reason of packet drops. We also plan to extend Everflow to the cloud provider's wide area network [16, 19], where, similar to DCNs, servers and network traffic are under its control.

Acknowledgements

We thank our Microsoft colleagues, especially Paul Wang, Yongqiang Xiong, George Chen, Kamil Cudnik and Ahsan Arefin, for their help in building and deploying Everflow. We also thank the reviewers and our shepherd Geoff Voelker for their constructive feedback. Y. Zhu, H. Zheng and B. Y. Zhao are supported in part by NSF grants IIS-1321083, CNS-1224100, and CNS-1317153.

11. REFERENCES

[1] Data plane development kit. http://www.dpdk.org/.

[2] Receive side scaling. https://msdn.microsoft.com/en-us/library/windows/hardware/ff567236(v=vs.85).aspx.

[3] A. Arefin, A. Khurshid, M. Caesar, and K. Nahrstedt. Scaling data-plane logging in large scale networks. In *MILCOM*, 2011.

[4] P. Bosshart, G. Gibb, H.-S. Kim, G. Varghese, N. McKeown, M. Izzard, F. Mujica, and M. Horowitz. Forwarding metamorphosis: Fast programmable match-action processing in hardware for SDN. In *SIGCOMM*, 2013.

[5] J. Case, M. Fedor, M. Schoffstall, and J. Davin. RFC 1157: Simple network management protocol.

[6] R. Chaiken, B. Jenkins, P.-Å. Larson, B. Ramsey, D. Shakib, S. Weaver, and J. Zhou. Scope: easy and efficient parallel processing of massive data sets. *VLDB*, 2008.

[7] B. Claise. RFC 3954: Cisco systems netflow services export version 9 (2004).

[8] N. G. Duffield and M. Grossglauser. Trajectory sampling for direct traffic observation. *IEEE/ACM Trans. Netw.*, June 2001.

[9] S. K. Fayaz and V. Sekar. Testing stateful and dynamic data planes with flowtest. In *HotSDN*, 2014.

[10] A. Fogel, S. Fung, L. Pedrosa, M. Walraed-Sullivan, R. Govindan, R. Mahajan, and T. Millstein. A general approach to network configuration analysis. In *NSDI*, 2015.

[11] R. Fonseca, G. Porter, R. H. Katz, S. Shenker, and I. Stoica. X-trace: A pervasive network tracing framework. In *NSDI*, 2007.

[12] R. Gandhi, H. H. Liu, Y. C. Hu, G. Lu, J. Padhye, L. Yuan, and M. Zhang. Duet: Cloud scale load balancing with hardware and software. In *SIGCOMM*, 2014.

[13] N. Gvozdiev, B. Karp, and M. Handley. Loup: who's afraid of the big bad loop? In *HotNets*, 2012.

[14] N. Handigol, B. Heller, V. Jeyakumar, D. Mazières, and N. McKeown. I know what your packet did last hop: Using packet histories to troubleshoot networks. In *NSDI*, 2014.

[15] C.-Y. Hong, M. Caesar, N. Duffield, and J. Wang. Tiresias: Online anomaly detection for hierarchical operational network data. In *ICDCS*, 2012.

[16] C.-Y. Hong, S. Kandula, R. Mahajan, M. Zhang, V. Gill, M. Nanduri, and R. Wattenhofer. Achieving high utilization with software-driven WAN. In *SIGCOMM*, 2013.

[17] Infiniband Trade Association. InfiniBand Architecture Volume 1, General Specifications, Release 1.2.1, 2008.

[18] Infiniband Trade Association. Supplement to infiniband architecture specification volume 1 release 1.2.2 annex A17: RoCEv2 (ip routable ROCE), 2014.

[19] S. Jain, A. Kumar, S. Mandal, J. Ong, L. Poutievski, A. Singh, S. Venkata, J. Wanderer, J. Zhou, M. Zhu, J. Zolla, U. Hölzle, S. Stuart, and A. Vahdat. B4: Experience with a globally-deployed software defined WAN. In *SIGCOMM*, 2013.

[20] V. Jeyakumar, M. Alizadeh, Y. Geng, C. Kim, and D. Mazières. Millions of little minions: Using packets for low latency network programming and visibility. In *SIGCOMM*, 2014.

[21] S. Kandula, S. Sengupta, A. Greenberg, P. Patel, and R. Chaiken. The nature of datacenter traffic: measurements & analysis. In *IMC*, 2009.

[22] P. Kazemian, M. Chan, H. Zeng, G. Varghese, N. McKeown, and S. Whyte. Real time network policy checking using header space analysis. In *NSDI*, 2013.

[23] A. Khurshid, X. Zou, W. Zhou, M. Caesar, and P. B. Godfrey. Veriflow: Verifying network-wide invariants in real time. In *NSDI*, 2013.

[24] T. Koponen, K. Amidon, P. Balland, M. Casado, A. Chanda, B. Fulton, I. Ganichev, J. Gross, N. Gude, P. Ingram, E. Jackson, A. Lambeth, R. Lenglet, S.-H. Li, A. Padmanabhan, J. Pettit, B. Pfaff, R. Ramanathan, S. Shenker, A. Shieh, J. Stribling, P. Thakkar, D. Wendlandt, A. Yip, and R. Zhang. Network virtualization in multi-tenant datacenters. In *NSDI*, 2014.

[25] R. Mahajan, N. Spring, D. Wetherall, and T. Anderson. User-level Internet path diagnosis. In *SOSP*, 2003.

[26] V. Mann, A. Vishnoi, and S. Bidkar. Living on the edge: Monitoring network flows at the edge in cloud data centers. In *COMSNETS*, 2013.

[27] P. Marchetta, A. Botta, E. Katz-Bassett, and A. Pescapé. Dissecting round trip time on the slow path with a single packet. In *PAM*, 2014.

[28] P. Patel, D. Bansal, L. Yuan, A. Murthy, A. Greenberg, D. A. Maltz, and R. Kern. Ananta: cloud scale load balancing. In *SIGCOMM*, 2013.

[29] P. Phaal, S. Panchen, and N. McKee. RFC 3176: Inmon corporation's sflow: A method for monitoring traffic in switched and routed networks, 2001.

[30] T. Qiu, Z. Ge, D. Pei, J. Wang, and J. Xu. What happened in my network: mining network events from router syslogs. In *IMC*, 2010.

[31] J. Rasley, B. Stephens, C. Dixon, E. Rozner, W. Felter, K. Agarwal, J. Carter, and R. Fonseca. Planck: Millisecond-scale monitoring and control for commodity networks. In *SIGCOMM*, 2014.

[32] L. Rizzo. netmap: A novel framework for fast packet I/O. In *USENIX ATC*, 2012.

[33] J. Suh, T. Kwon, C. Dixon, W. Felter, and J. Carter. Opensample: A low-latency, sampling-based measurement platform for SDN. In *ICDCS*, 2014.

[34] W. Wu and P. Demar. Wirecap: a novel packet capture engine for commodity NICs in high-speed networks. In *IMC*, 2014.

[35] A. Wundsam, D. Levin, S. Seetharaman, and A. Feldmann. OFRewind: Enabling record and replay troubleshooting for networks. In *ATC*, 2011.

[36] M. Yu, L. Jose, and R. Miao. Software defined traffic measurement with opensketch. In *NSDI*, 2013.

Enabling End-host Network Functions

Hitesh Ballani, Paolo Costa, Christos Gkantsidis, Matthew P. Grosvenor,*
Thomas Karagiannis, Lazaros Koromilas,† and Greg O'Shea
Microsoft Research
Cambridge, UK

ABSTRACT

Many network functions executed in modern datacenters, *e.g.*, load balancing, application-level QoS, and congestion control, exhibit three common properties at the data plane: they need to access and modify state, to perform computations, and to access application semantics — this is critical since many network functions are best expressed in terms of application-level messages. In this paper, we argue that the end hosts are a natural enforcement point for these functions and we present Eden, an architecture for implementing network functions at end hosts with minimal network support.

Eden comprises three components, a centralized controller, an enclave at each end host, and Eden-compliant applications called stages. To implement network functions, the controller configures stages to classify their data into messages and the enclaves to apply action functions based on a packet's class. Our Eden prototype includes enclaves implemented both in the OS kernel and on programmable NICs. Through case studies, we show how application-level classification and the ability to run actual programs on the data-path allows Eden to efficiently support a broad range of network functions at the network's edge.

CCS Concepts

•**Networks → Programmable networks; Network management;** *Data center networks;* Cloud computing;

*Work performed while an intern with Microsoft Research; currently at Cambridge University, UK

†Work performed while an intern with Microsoft Research; currently at University of Crete, Greece

SIGCOMM '15, August 17 - 21, 2015, London, United Kingdom
© 2015 ACM. ISBN 978-1-4503-3542-3/15/08...$15.00
DOI: http://dx.doi.org/10.1145/2785956.2787493

Keywords

Software Defined Networking; SDN; Network Management; Data-plane programming; Network Functions

1 Introduction

Recent years have seen a lot of innovation in functionality deployed across datacenter networks. *Network functions* range from management tasks like load balancing [65, 4, 26, 1, 40] and Quality of Service (QoS) [9, 39, 10, 33, 52, 61, 6, 28] to data-plane tasks like (centralized) congestion control and network scheduling [48, 27, 64, 45, 30] to application-specific tasks like replica selection [17]. Today, such functions are implemented using a mishmash of techniques and at a variety of places—at network switches using SDN and OpenFlow, at physical or virtual middleboxes using NFV, and at end hosts through Open vSwitch or custom implementations.

Despite their differences, three common requirements characterize a large fraction of network functions: i) they maintain state at the data plane, ii) they perform computation at the data plane, and iii) they operate on application semantics. The last feature is particularly important since many network functions are best expressed in terms of application data units or "messages". For example, a load balancing function for memcached, a popular key-value store, may put its messages into two "classes" (GETs and PUTs) and treat them differently. It may even use message-specific details like the key being accessed for load balancing [40].

Traditional network management approaches implement network functions completely decoupled from applications. They infer the application message a packet belongs to using deep packet inspection or through other heuristics. Instead, we propose *messages* and *classes* as first-order abstractions at the network layer. A message refers to an (arbitrary) application data unit while a class is the set of messages (and consequent network packets) to which the same network function should be applied. Applications can provide the class and message information for any traffic they generate.

In this paper, we present Eden, an architecture for implementing network functions at end hosts. End hosts are a natural enforcement point for such functions—

they have plentiful resources that allow for complex computation and large amounts of state to be maintained, and they are ideally placed for fine-grained visibility into application semantics. Finally, in single administrator environments like enterprises and datacenters, some part of end hosts can be trusted. We show that a large number of diverse and interesting network functions can be efficiently realized at the end hosts with minimal support from the network.

Eden comprises three components: a logically centralized *controller*, *stages*, and end host *enclaves*. A stage is any application or library that is Eden-compliant. Stages bridge the gap between network functions expressed in terms of application-level messages and the enclave operating on packets. To achieve this, stages *classify* their network traffic, associating application messages with a class and a message identifier that is carried with it down the host's network stack. The enclave resides along the end host network stack, either in the OS or the NIC. It extends and replaces functionality typically performed by the end host virtual switch. An enclave has a set of match-action tables that, based on a packet's class, determine an *action function* to apply. The action function can modify both the packet and the enclave's global state. Enclaves and stages each expose an API through which they can be programmed. Enclaves and stages, taken together, enable application-aware data plane programmability.

Given a network function, the controller can implement it by programming stages and enclaves across the network. Hence, Eden achieves a careful division of functionality; the controller provides global visibility, stages provide application visibility while enclaves provide a pragmatic enforcement point at the data plane.

A key challenge posed by our design is efficient and safe execution of action functions at enclaves while allowing for the functions to be dynamically updated by the controller without impacting data plane performance. With Eden, action functions are written in a high-level domain specific language using F# code quotations. They are compiled to bytecode which is then interpreted through a stack-based interpreter within the enclave. This approach allows Eden to execute the same computation across multiple platforms and avoids the complexities of dynamically loading code in the OS or the NIC. Indeed, our interpreter can execute the same action function inside the OS or in a programmable NIC.

We have implemented the Eden enclave across two platforms: Hyper-V and Netronome's programmable NICs [46]. We evaluate Eden through case studies across these platforms. These studies highlight how the Eden architecture can implement diverse functions spanning application-aware load-balancing, quality of service and weighted path selection. We show that Eden's interpreter-based data plane computation incurs reasonable overheads with negligible impact on application performance metrics.

Overall, this paper makes the following contributions:

- We highlight that a large class of network functions feature three key requirements: data-plane computation, data-plane state, and operate on application semantics (§2).
- We design and implement Eden, an architecture that enables end host network functions through data plane programmability (§3).
- We present a flexible scheme for application-level classification of network traffic (§3.3).
- We present a language, compiler and runtime for action functions. The compiler decouples state management from the function, thus providing a clean programming abstraction to administrators (§3.4).

The idea of end hosts participating in the implementation of network functions is not new [49, 16, 21, 34, 59, 57]. These state of the art approaches, however, still encourage a low-level, packet-based API for programming the data plane, often a variant of OpenFlow. This ignores end host capabilities and restricts the functions that can be implemented. Instead, Eden adopts a different philosophy by introducing a data plane interface that is wide and rich enough to allow for general, application-informed data-plane computation.

2 Network Functions

This paper is motivated by the observation that three common data-plane requirements underlie many network functions. First, they need to create, access and modify *state*, in many cases on a per-packet basis. This allows for "stateful network functions" where a packet influences the processing of subsequent packets. Second, they require *computation* on the data path.

Finally, they require visibility into *application semantics*. This introduces a mismatch – data-plane elements like the end host network stack and switches operate at the granularity of packets. Instead, each application has its own application data unit or "message". For example, for memcached, a popular key-value store, a message is a GET or a PUT request or response. For a HTTP library, a message is an HTTP request or response. These messages are fragmented into packets before being sent across the network. Many network functions however are best expressed in terms of application messages. Implementing such network functions thus requires a mapping between messages and the consequent network packets.

2.1 Examples

To make the discussion concrete, we now use a few network functions proposed in recent literature as case-studies to highlight the three requirements mentioned above. For each example, we present a pseudo-code sketch for the network function; in Section 5, we show how the functions can be expressed in Eden's language.

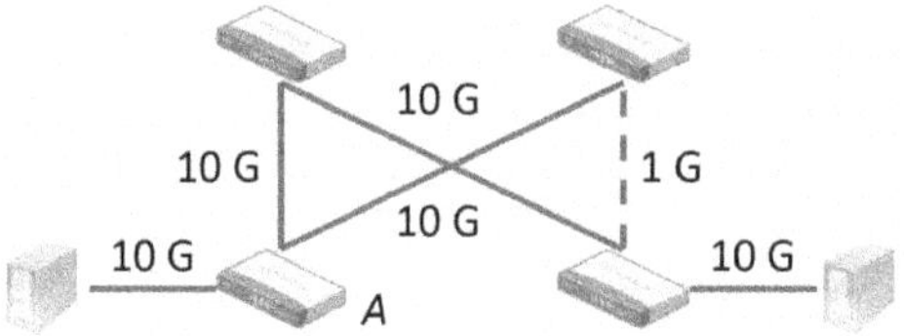

Figure 1: Example of an asymmetric topology.

2.1.1 Load balancing

Many recent proposals focus on load balancing of traffic across network paths and across destinations in datacenters. We begin with a simple path-level load balancing example.

Datacenters today use ECMP to load balance traffic among multiple equal cost paths. However, ECMP assumes that the underlying topology is balanced and regular which is often not true in practice [65]. For example, in Figure 1, ECMP would distribute the traffic at switch A evenly across the two upstream links even though subsequent links along the paths have very different capacities. This can result in unfairness and poor tail performance. Motivated by this, Zhou et al. [65] proposed WCMP, a weighted version of ECMP that balances traffic across links in a weighted fashion. In the example in Figure 1, WCMP can be used to balance traffic across the two upstream links of A in a 10:1 ratio. While the authors present a switch-based implementation of WCMP in [65], we focus on the higher-order network function associated with WCMP and for now, sidestep where this function is implemented.

WCMP requires two main pieces of functionality: (a) for each source-destination pair, computation of paths and weights, and (b) picking a path for packets. The former requires information about the network topology which, in turn, requires a coordination point with global visibility. With SDN-based management approaches, such functionality is typically implemented at a centralized controller, possibly using high-level programming abstractions [25, 62, 24, 54]. Here, we focus on the latter operation that needs to operate at the data path.

The first snippet in Figure 2 implements the `WCMP` data-plane function. It takes a packet as input and chooses its network path based on the weights of the links between the packet's source and destination. These weights are obtained periodically from the controller. Next, we discuss the state maintained by this function and the computation it performs.

State. The function accesses global state—it reads the `pathMatrix` variable that, for each source and destination pair, contains the list of paths between them and their weights. A path's weight is the probability with which it should be used and is a product of the normalized weights of all links along the path.

```
Require: Global program state- pathMatrix, which
    gives the list of paths and their weights for each
    source destination pair.
    pathMatrix:[src, dst] -> {[Path1, Weight1],
    ...}

fun WCMP (packet) {
  Choose a path in a weighted random fashion from
  pathMatrix[p.src, p.dst])

  Send packet
}
```

```
Require: Each packet is tagged with its message iden-
    tifier

fun messageWCMP (packet) {
msg = packet.message
if packet belongs to new message then
    Choose a path in a weighted random fashion from
    pathMatrix[p.src, p.dst]

    cachedPaths[msg] = path

Use cachedPaths[msg] as this packet's path
Send packet
}
```

Figure 2: Network functions implementing weighted load balancing at packet- and message granularity.

Computation. The function performs a simple computation — it chooses the packet's path from the set of possible paths in a weighted random fashion.

Application semantics. The `WCMP` function chooses paths on a packet-by-packet basis. However, as we show in Section 5, this can lead to packet re-ordering across the network which can adversely impact the performance of connection oriented protocols like TCP. Flow-level weighted load balancing [65] can address this problem, at the expense of some load imbalance.

More broadly, datacenter operators can balance the trade-off between application performance and load across network links through *"message-level load balancing"* whereby all packets of the same application message are sent along the same path. For example, for memcached traffic, all packets corresponding to a GET or a PUT operation are sent along the same path. This is implemented by the `messageWCMP` function in Figure 2 which needs to know the message a given packet belongs to.

The previous discussion also applies to other schemes for load balancing in datacenters [4, 26, 1]. For example, Ananta [4] load balances incoming connections across a pool of application servers. This requires a NAT-like functionality along the network path which, in turn, requires both computation and state. Several proposals explicitly use application semantics as

Require: Each packet is tagged with its message, size and tenant information.
Global state: queueMap, a map that returns the rate limited queue for each tenant

```
fun Pulsar (packet) {
msg = packet.message
if msg is a "READ" message then
    Set size to msg.size //if read, policing is based on operation size
else
    Set size to packet.size //policing is based on the packet size
Send packet to queue queueMap[packet.tenant] and charge it size bytes
}
```

Figure 3: Pulsar's rate control function

Require: Each packet is tagged with its message and size information.
Global state: msgTable:[msg] -> bytesSent and priorityThresholds

```
fun PIAS (packet) {
msg = packet.message
if packet belongs to a new message then
    Initialize msgTable[msg] to packet.size
else
    Increment msgTable[msg] by packet.size
Set packet priority according to priorityThresholds
Send packet
}
```

Figure 4: Network function implementing a generalized version of PIAS' dynamic priority logic.

well. For example, Sinbad [17] maximizes performance by choosing endpoints for write operations in HDFS, and Facebook's mcrouter [40] achieves low latency and failover through a distributed middle layer that routes memcached requests based on their key.

2.1.2 Datacenter QoS

Many recent proposals provide quality of service (QoS) guarantees for traffic across the datacenter network. We begin with a recent QoS solution.

Pulsar [6] gives tenant-level end-to-end bandwidth guarantees across multiple resources, such as network and storage. A tenant refers to a collection of virtual machines (VMs) owned by the same user. Enforcing such guarantees at the network layer poses two key challenges. First, it requires determining the tenant a given packet belongs to. Second, since the guarantee spans non-network resources, it requires knowledge of the operation being performed. For example, consider a packet corresponding to a request to a storage server. Network rate limiters pace packets based on their size. However, depending on whether the packet corresponds to a READ or a WRITE request to a storage server, the packet size may not correctly represent its impact on the storage server—read packets are small on the forward path from the client generating the request to the server, but their cost on the server and the reverse network path can be high depending on the read size. Today, information about the type of an operation and its size is not available to network rate limiters at end hosts and at switches.

Figure 3 shows a network function implementing Pulsar's rate control. We describe the state it maintains, the computation it performs and the application semantics it requires.

State. The function accesses global state—it reads from the `queueMap` to determine the rate limited queue a packet should go to.

Computation. The function ensures that the packet is rate limited based on the type of message (*i.e.*, IO operation) that it belongs to. It also queues the packet at the rate limiter corresponding to the tenant generating the packet. This ensures aggregate tenant-level guarantees instead of per-VM guarantees.

Application semantics. For a packet, the function needs to determine its message, the message size, and the tenant it belongs to.

We note that the same features apply to other schemes for datacenter QoS that offer performance guarantees to tenants and applications [9, 39, 10, 33, 52, 61].

2.1.3 Datacenter flow scheduling

Many recent proposals aim to optimize application performance in terms of reduced user-perceived latency by carefully scheduling flows across the network. For example, PIAS [8] minimizes flow completion time without application support by mimicking the shortest flow first scheduling strategy. With PIAS, flows start in the highest priority but are demoted to lower priorities as their size increases.

While PIAS [8] targets flow-level prioritization, the concept can be generalized and applied at a message level. A message could be a flow, a GET/PUT, etc. Figure 4 shows a network function implementing message-level PIAS scheduling.

State. The function uses two pieces of global state. First, `priorityThresholds` provide flow-size thresholds that define the priority for a flow given its current size. These thresholds need to be calculated periodically based on the datacenter's overall traffic load. Second, the function maintains a `msgTable` to track the current size of all active messages.

Computation. When a packet for a new message arrives, the function initializes a `messageTable` entry for it. When a packet for an existing message arrives, the

Function	Example	Data-plane state	Data-plane computation	Application semantics	Network support	Eden (out of the box)
Load Balancing	WCMP [65]	✓	✓		✗	✓
	Message-based WCMP	✓	✓	✓		
	Ananta [47]	✓	✓			
	Conga [1]	✓	✓	✓*	✓	✗
	Duet [26]	✓	✓			
Replica Selection	mcrouter [40]	✓	✓	✓	✗	✓
	SINBAD [17]	✓	✓	✓		
Datacenter QoS	Pulsar [6]	✓	✓	✓	✗	✓
	Storage QoS [61, 58]	✓	✓	✓		
	Network QoS [9, 51, 38, 33]	✓	✓	✓		
Flow scheduling and congestion control	PIAS [8]	✓	✓		✗	✓
	QJump [28]	✓	✓			
	Centralized [48, 27] congestion control	✓	✓	✓*		
	Explicit rate control (D^3 [64], PASE [45], PDQ [30])	✓	✓	✓	✓	✗
Stateful firewall	IDS(*e.g.* [19])	✓	✓		✗	✗
	Port knocking [13]	✓	✓		✗	✓

Table 1: Example network functions, their data-plane requirements and whether they need network support beyond commodity features like network priorities. Eden can support many of these functions out of the box. (✓* refers to functions that would benefit from application semantics. For example, Conga uses flowlets that approximate application messages.)

message's current size is updated. Finally, we use the current message size to determine the packet's priority.

Application semantics. PIAS achieves flow scheduling without application support. However, in closed-environments like datacenters, it is possible to modify applications or the OS to directly provide information about the size of a flow [64, 22, 30]. This would allow for shortest flow first scheduling. In Section 5, we show that this approach, by using application information, can provide increased accuracy compared to PIAS' application-agnostic scheduling.

We note that the same features apply to other schemes for optimizing application performance by reducing flow completion times [30, 45], meeting flow deadlines [64] or similar task-level metrics [18, 22].

2.2 End hosts: A natural enforcement point

Table 1 extends the previous discussion to other categories of common network functions like congestion control and stateful firewalling. The table is certainly not exhaustive; instead, it illustrates how data-plane state, computation and application semantics are common requirements across a large selection of network functions.

Given these requirements, a natural question is where should such functionality be implemented. Traditionally, network functions have been implemented at switches and middleboxes; this however reflects legacy originating from the Internet, where ISPs only control their equipment and end hosts are not trusted. By contrast, in closed settings owned and operated by a single entity, like datacenters and enterprises, end hosts (or some parts of the end hosts) are trusted. Thus, end hosts are well-suited to implement network functions—they have high computational capabilities, significant amounts of memory, can provide fine-grained visibility into application semantics, and by definition, are on the data path.

Placing network functionality at end hosts provides also additional benefits. First, enforcing a function at the source of traffic instead of distributed enforcement along its path makes it easier to achieve consistent behavior even when the function is updated. On the contrary, achieving consistent updates in the network requires complex mechanisms to ensure that all switches along the path make consistent decisions [55]. Second, implementing network functions at end hosts leads to a natural partitioning of both the state and computation overhead of enforcement because hosts are only responsible for a subset of the traffic a switch would need to process. Finally, certain network properties such as flow RTT or loss and network events like flow termination are readily available at the hosts; instead, such properties need to be inferred, typically through heuristics inside the network.

Of course, implementing network functionality at end hosts is not a panacea. As shown in Table 1, some functions do require network support beyond what is offered by commodity equipment. For example, deadline-based congestion control protocols like D^3 [64] and PDQ [30] rely on explicit, fine-grained feedback from the network. In general, network switches have better visibility of instantaneous aggregate network behavior and are needed to implement network functions that rely on such information. Furthermore, despite the resources available at end hosts, some network functions, such as compression or encryption, may be too resource intensive for general purpose processors and may require custom hardware.

In summary, a variety of network functions can indeed be implemented with a modicum of computation and state at the end host data plane. This paper proposes an architecture to enable such functions.

3 Design

This section provides an overview of the Eden architecture. Eden targets environments in which end hosts are owned by a single administrative domain and can therefore be trusted. In this paper, we focus on datacenters, although our approach can also be applied to other scenarios such as enterprises [21, 34].

3.1 Design overview

Eden comprises three components (Figure 5):

1). *Controller.* It provides a logically centralized coordination point where any part of the network function logic requiring global visibility resides (§3.2).

2). *Stage.* Applications are a first-order citizen in Eden. Any application, library or even kernel module in the end-host stack that is Eden-compliant is called a "stage" (§3.3). Stages can *classify* packets based on stage-specific semantics, and this classification is carried through the end host stack to the Eden enclave where it is used to determine the enclave rule(s) to apply. Stages are programmed using the classification API which allows the controller to learn their classification abilities and to configure them with classification rules.

3). *Enclave.* Eden provides a programmable dataplane through an enclave at each end host (§3.4). The enclave may be implemented at the software network stack inside the OS or the hypervisor, or using programmable hardware like FPGAs and programmable NICs. The enclave is programmed by the controller using the enclave API. An enclave program comprises a set of "match-action" rules. However, instead of matching on packet headers, packets are matched based on the *class* associated with each packet. Finally, instead of a pre-defined set of actions, the action part of the match-action rule is an *action function* comprising logic that can access and modify enclave and class state.

3.2 Eden controller

A network function is conceptually a combination of a *control-plane function* residing at the controller and a *data-plane function.* Given a network function, all computation that either needs global network visibility or needs to be invoked at coarse timescales can reside in the control function. By contrast, any computation that needs to be invoked on a per-packet basis or needs to access rapidly changing state should be part of the data function. For our WCMP example (§2.1.1), the control plane function involves (periodically) determining the weight associated with each network link based on the current topology and traffic matrix. These weights are used to compute the `pathMatrix` variable used in the `WCMP` data plane function shown in Figure 2.

Recent work in the SDN literature mostly focuses on controller-based algorithms [24] and languages for expressing control plane functions [25, 62]. Hence, in the rest of this paper, we focus on how data plane functions can be implemented at stages and enclaves, and the APIs that the Eden controller uses to program such functionality.

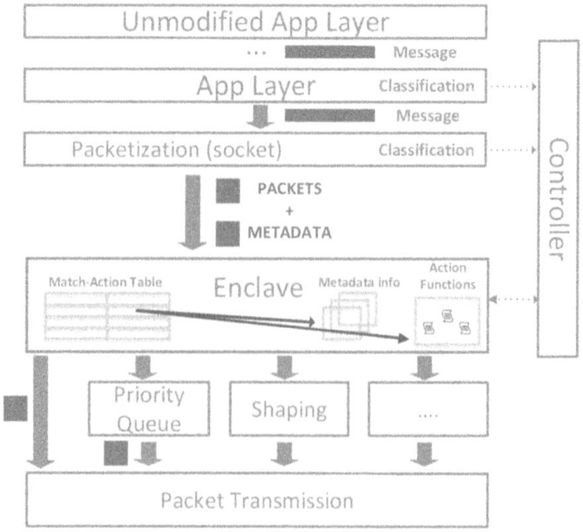

Figure 5: The Eden architecture.

3.3 Eden stages

As shown in Table 1, many network functions require application semantics as they operate at the granularity of application messages. By contrast, the Eden enclave operates at the granularity of packets. Traditional approaches infer the application message a given packet belongs to using deep packet inspection or through other heuristics. Eden adopts a different tack by allowing applications to explicitly share this information.

Applications, libraries (*e.g.*, an HTTP library) and services (*e.g.*, NFS or SMB service) that run either in user space or at the OS can opt to *classify* network traffic generated by them, i.e., identify messages and their class(es). *A* **message** *refers to an (arbitrary) application data unit while a* **class** *refers to the set of packets to which the same action function should be applied.* For example, a memcached-specific load balancing function may pick the destination server based on whether a packet corresponds to a GET or a PUT message. To allow such functions to be implemented at the Eden enclave, the memcached application needs to mark all its traffic as belonging to one of two classes, GETs and PUTs, and to identify each GET/PUT message separately. The class information is carried through the end-host stack to the enclave and is used to determine the action function to apply.

A stage specifies the application-specific fields that can be used for classification, i.e., fields that can categorize messages into classes. It also specifies *meta-data*, i.e., other application-specific data, it can generate. To make the discussion concrete, Table 2 gives examples of the classification and meta-data capabilities of three stages. For instance, an Eden-compliant memcached

Stage	Classifiers	Meta-data
memcache	`<msg_type, key>`	{msg_id, msg_type, key, msg_size}
HTTP library	`<msg_type, url>`	{msg_id, msg_type, url, msg_size}
Eden enclave	`<src_ip,src_port, dst_ip, dst_port, proto >`	{msg_id}

Table 2: Classification capabilities of a few stages.

```
r1 : <GET, - >     → [GET, {msg_id, msg_size}]
r1 : <PUT, - >     → [PUT, {msg_id, msg_size}]
r2 : <*, - >       → [DEFAULT, {msg_id, msg_size}]
r3 : <GET, "a" >   → [GETA, {msg_id, msg_size}]
r3 : <*, "a" >     → [A, {msg_id, msg_size}]
r3 : <*, * >       → [OTHER, {msg_id, msg_size}]
```

Figure 6: Examples of classification rules and rule-sets

client can classify its messages based on whether it is a GET or a PUT (`msg_type`) and the `key` being accessed by the message. Furthermore, the stage can associate the message with meta-data comprising a unique (message) identifier, the message type, the key being accessed, and the message size.

Beyond applications, the Eden enclave itself can also classify traffic. It operates at the granularity of packets, and like Open vSwitch, it can classify packets based on different network headers, including the IP five-tuple. This is shown in the last line of Table 2. Thus, when classification is done at the granularity of TCP flows, each transport connection is a message.

Classification rules. A stage maintains *classification rules*, written as `<classifier>` → [`class_name`, {`meta-data`}]. The `classifier` is an expression that defines the class, while the `meta-data` specifies information, including a message identifier, that should be associated with messages belonging to this class. The message identifier allows the enclave to later recover packets carrying data for the same message. Classification rules are arranged into *rule-sets* such that a message matches at most one rule in each rule-set. Rule-sets are needed since different network functions may require stages to classify their data differently. A given message can be marked as belonging to many classes, one for each rule-set.

Figure 6 lists a few example classification rules for the memcached stage. Rule-set `r1` comprises two rules, the first one matches all GET messages while the second matches PUT messages. The messages are marked as belonging to classes named "GET" and "PUT", and are associated with meta-data including a unique message identifier and the message size. Rule-set `r2` simply puts all messages into the "DEFAULT" class and associates them with a message identifier. Finally, rule-set `r3` classifies any GET requests for the key named "a" into the "GETA" class, any other request for key "a" into the "A" class, and all other requests to the "OTHER" class.

External to a stage, a class is referred to using its fully qualified name: `stage.rule-set.class_name`. Thus, the class named "GET" in rule-set `r1` is referred to as `memcached.r1.GET`. Given the rule-sets above, a PUT request for key "a" would be classified as belonging to three classes, `memcached.r1.PUT`, `memcached.r2.DEFAULT`, and `memcached.r3.A`.

S0	`getStageInfo` () returns the fields that the stage can use to classify data, and the meta-data fields it can output
S1	`createStageRule` (Rule_set s, Classifier c, Class_id i, Meta-data set m) creates classification rule `<c>` → [`i`, {`m`}] in rule_set s returns a unique identifer for the rule
S2	`removeStageRule` (Rule_set s, Rule_id r)

Table 3: Stage API, used by the controller to program data-plane stages.

Stage-Controller interface. The controller can program stages using the stage API shown in Table 3. Through `getStageInfo`, the controller can discover a stage's classification abilities, what fields can be used as classifiers and the meta-data it can generate. The controller can also create and remove classification rules at stages (S1,S2 calls in Table 3).

3.4 Eden enclave

The enclave resides along the end host network stack, and operates on packets being sent and received. The enclave comprises two components:

1). A set of tables with match-action rules that, depending on a packet's class, determine the action function to apply.

2). A runtime that can execute the action functions.

3.4.1 Match-action tables

In allowing data-plane programmability through enclaves, we wanted to achieve flexibility without sacrificing forwarding performance. We chose a match-action model for the enclave for two reasons. First, it is possible to efficiently implement lookup tables using TCAMs when the enclave is implemented in hardware. Secondly, thanks to the popularity of the OpenFlow community, match-action programming is already a familiar model for programmers to express network functions.

As shown in Table 4, each rule matches on class names and produces an action function which is written in a domain specific language. This is in contrast to the predefined set of actions with today's SDN design. Match-

Match	—>	Action
<match on class name>	—>	f (pkt, ...)

Table 4: Match-action table in the enclave

ing on class names allows for two types of functions. First, packet header based classification at the enclave enables functions that simply need to operate at, say, the granularity of a TCP flow. Second, classification by stages means that the enclave can implement functions that operate on a higher-level grouping of packets as defined by applications. Next, we describe the action function language and how enclaves execute the functions.

3.4.2 *Action functions*

Action functions are written in a domain specific language (DSL) built using F# code quotations.[1] The use of a DSL makes it easier to check safety properties of the function. For example, action functions cannot perform pointer arithmetic and they need to rely on limited stack and heap space. We discuss the choice of the specific language in Section 6. As summarized below, the language provides features that allow expressing basic computations including loops, and to manipulate both packets and any state at the enclave.

The action function language is a subset of F#. This subset does not include objects, exceptions, and floating point operations. Such features benefit large code bases; instead, we expect small functions running in the enclave, and hence, the overhead of implementing those features offers little value. Floating point operations are typically not supported in the kernel, and they are also not supported by the programmable NICs we experimented with. The subset of F# that we support includes basic arithmetic operations, assignments, function definitions, and basic control operations.

Action Function example. We use an example to illustrate Eden's action functions. Figure 7 shows how the PIAS function discussed in Section 2 (pseudo code in Figure 4) is written in our action function language. The function takes three parameters, `packet`, `msg` and `_global`. `packet` refers to the actual packet.

It is important to understand message in the context of the program. For an action function, a message refers to packets that should be treated as a unit by it. A message could be a TCP flow, a GET/PUT request, or a HTTP page. As mentioned above, the enclave runtime determines a packet's message identifier. The `msg` parameter thus lets the function access state shared for the processing of all packets of the same message (Section 3.4.4 details how this state is maintained). Finally, the `_global` parameter gives access to state shared by all instances of the action function that may run in parallel.

[1]https://msdn.microsoft.com/en-us/library/dd233212.aspx.

```
1 fun(packet : Packet, msg : Message, _global :
Global) ->
2     let msg_size = msg.Size + packet.Size
3     msg.Size <- msg_size
4
5     let priorities = _global.Priorities
6     let rec search index =
7         if index >= priorities.Length then 0
8         elif msg_size <=
9             priorities.[index].MessageSizeLimit
then
10                priorities.[index].Priority
11        else search (index + 1)
12
13    packet.Priority <-
14        let desired = msg.Priority
15        if desired < 1 then desired
16        else search 0
```

Figure 7: Program for priority selection

For each packet, the program updates the size of the flow (lines 2–3) and then searches in the `_global`.Priorities array to find the priority corresponding to the flow size (using `search`, lines 6–11). Background flows can specify a low priority class (using `flow`.Priority), and the program will respect that (lines 14–15).

An action function can have the following side-effects: (i) It can modify the `packet` variable, thus allowing the function to change header fields, (ii) It can modify the `msg` variable, including the class name and metadata associated with the message. This can be used to control routing decisions for the packet, including dropping it, sending it to a specific queue associated with rate limits, sending it to a specific match-action table or forwarding it to the controller.

We note that while the programmer accesses packet headers, as well as message and global state using the `packet`, `msg`, and `_global` function arguments respectively, this is just a convenient illusion for the programmer. It also helps during development and debugging. As we describe later, Eden's compiler rewrites the use of these function arguments.

3.4.3 *Interpreter-based execution*

A key challenge posed by executing action functions on the data plane is ensuring they can run across platforms and they can be updated dynamically by the controller without affecting forwarding performance. The latter requirement is particularly problematic, especially for today's programmable NIC platforms that do not support dynamic injection of code. Eden sidesteps these issues by using an interpreter to execute action functions. The interpreter uses a stack and heap for keeping action function state.

Additionally, the use of interpreted execution enables monitoring the execution of the action function and guaranteeing that it can read and modify only the state related to that program; *i.e.*, state not associated with the action function is inaccessible to the program. In particular, a faulty action function will result in terminating the execution of that program, but will not affect the rest of the system. Of course, we do rely on correct execution of the interpreter, but we believe that it is easier to guarantee the correct execution of the interpreter than to verify every possible action function.

The use of the interpreter, instead of compiling to native code, hurts performance when executing the action functions. However, as we demonstrate in Section 5, this is a small penalty for the convenience of injecting code at runtime, and for the ability to use the same bytecode across platforms.

3.4.4 Eden compiler

We compile action functions to bytecode which is then interpreted inside the enclave. Given an action function, the most challenging aspect of the compilation process is determining its input dependencies and reflecting any changes made by the function to packet fields and the state maintained by the runtime. For instance, for the PIAS action function in Figure 7, the compiler needs to recover the function's input parameters. This includes packet information like its size, message-specific state (`msg` parameter which is used to determine message size) and global state (`_global` parameter used to determine the priority thresholds). For the output, it needs to determine how to update the packet headers (*e.g.*, 802.1q priority field in the header) or other state (*e.g.*, message size).

This is done using three kinds of *type annotations* for state variables; we expect the programmer to specify these. First, the lifetime of each state variable, *i.e.*, whether it exists for the duration of the message or till the function is being used in the enclave. Figure 8 highlights an example of the lifetime annotations (we omit the rest of the annotations due to space constraints). This lifetime information allows us to decide where to store the state requested. For convenience of state management, the enclave runtime provides the ability to store message-specific state, and makes it available upon function invocation.

Second, the access permissions of a state variable, *i.e.*, whether the function can update its value or whether it is read-only. The access permissions allows us to determine the concurrency level for the function; in Figure 7 the function can update the message size and, hence, we will process at most one packet per message concurrently. This restriction does not apply to the global state which is read-only for the function.

Finally, the mapping to packet header values; for example, the mapping of the packet size field in IPv4 headers to the "size" variable inside the function in Figure 7. Currently, we provide a fixed header parsing scheme, and are investigating more extensible parsing approaches using ideas from P4 [14].

Apart from resolving input and output dependencies, the rest of the compilation process, mainly the translation of the abstract syntax tree to bytecode, is more straightforward. Value types are preferentially placed in the stack and otherwise in the local variables and the heap. More complicated types, such as arrays, are placed in the program heap (when necessary by copying the values from the flow or function state). The layout is then used to generate the bytecode of the program. In the current version, we perform a number of optimizations such as recognizing tail recursion and compiling it as a loop.

```
[<State(lifetime = Granularity.Packet)>]
type Packet () =
  class
    [<AccessControl(Entity.PacketProcessor,
            AccessLevel.ReadOnly)>]
    [<HeaderMap("IPv4", "TotalLength")>]
    [<HeaderMap("IPv6", "PayloadLength")>]
    member val Size = 0L with get, set

    [<AccessControl(Entity.PacketProcessor,
            AccessLevel.ReadWrite)>]
    [<HeaderMap("802.1q", "PriorityCodePoint")>]
    member val Priority = 0 with get, set
  end
```

Figure 8: Example of annotations used by the priority selection policy. The HeaderMap annotations specify the field in the header that corresponds to the property. While the Packet type appears to be a generic class, we expect them to just contain properties of basic types with associated attributes. We also expect the properties to provide default initializers.

Concurrency model. As discussed, the programmer specifies the lifetime and access model of the state used by the action function with type annotations (Figure 8). The authoritative state is maintained in the enclave, and the annotations determine the concurrency model for the action functions. The enclave creates a consistent copy of the state needed by the program in the heap and stack. If the action function requires read-only access to message and global state, the enclave is allowed to schedule multiple invocations of that program in parallel (*i.e.*, the program is allowed to write only to packet state). The state stored by the enclave may change during program execution; however, the program will not see the change.

If the action function requires write-access to the state maintained at the message level, then only one packet from that message can be processed in parallel. Further, if the action function requires write-access to global state, then only one parallel invocation of the action function is allowed. These restrictions are necessary because, after program termination, the enclave must update the authoritative state with the changes, and pass updated values to the next invocation of the same action function. An alternative approach that we have not explored would be to introduce synchronization primitives in the language. This however might lead to a performance penalty while accessing shared state. Overall, the programs should restrict writable state to the finest granularity possible.

3.4.5 *Enclave-Controller interface*

The controller can program enclaves through the enclave API. This allows the controller to create, delete and query both tables and individual match-action rules in an enclave. We omit the API details for brevity.

3.5 Network support

Eden's end-host based approach to network functions requires two features from the network: the ability to specify a packet's priority and its route. For the former, we use 802.1q tags. For the latter, recent proposals have shown how existing technologies like MPLS and VLANs can be used to achieve source routing in datacenters [44, 16]. Here, end hosts specify the path of a network packet as a label in the packet header, *e.g.*, through an MPLS label or VLAN tag, and switches perform label-based forwarding. In our experiments, we use VLAN tagging for route control.

Such source routing requires the controller to configure the label forwarding tables at switches. For MPLS, this can be achieved through a distributed control protocol like LDP [5] while for VLANs, Spain [44] describes a solution involving multiple spanning trees. Hence, label-based forwarding and the corresponding control protocol is the primary functionality Eden requires of the underlying network. Additionally, most existing switches already support statistics gathering capabilities (e.g SNMP) and priority-based queuing.

4 Implementation

We now provide more information about the implementation of the enclave and stages including current limitations. We also describe our evaluation testbed.

4.1 Interpreter and enclave

The Eden interpreter supports relatively small programs that use limited (operand) stack and heap space. The execution is stack based, similar in spirit to the Java Virtual Machine (JVM); we support many of the standard JVM op-codes. Apart from op-codes that specify basic load and store, arithmetic, branches, and conditionals, we have also implemented as op-codes a limited set of basic functions, such as picking random numbers and accessing a high-frequency clock in the system. Unlike general VMs, we do not support many features such as exceptions, objects, and just-in-time compilation. An alternative design would be to base the interpreter on a register machine (as in [41]).

Section 3.4.4 mentioned a number of facilities expected by the enclave that we have implemented: (a) managing flow and function specific state, (b) preparing program inputs and consuming program outputs, and (c) overseeing program invocation. Overall, the enclave, including the interpreter, is about 16K lines of C code.

4.2 Stages

Stages associate class and metadata information with (application) messages; packets generated as a result of those messages will be carrying the extra information and processed by the interpreter accordingly. The implementation of that mechanism in its pure form requires a large number of changes in the current network stack, and application and library code. As a proof of concept, we have extended the socket interface to implement an additional send primitive that accepts class and metadata information (our extension works for sockets using TCP). At the kernel, we record the sequence number of the sender along with the extra information.

At the bottom of the network stack, we intercept packets before they get transmitted. When we detect that they contain data with the appropriate sequence numbers, we update the relevant message state, and schedule the packet for processing inside the enclave.

The mechanism above allows us to associate class and metadata information at a per-packet granularity. We believe that a generic mechanism for associating metadata with events that traverse application and kernel network stacks could be of general use (see also [11]).

4.3 Testbed

Our Eden implementation targets traditional OS network stacks and programmable NICs, and we thus deploy two separate testbeds.

Our *software* testbed comprises five machines, four Intel XEON W3530 (2.8GHz/12GB RAM), and one Intel XEON E7450 (2.4GHz/32GB). All machines use 10GbE Mellanox network cards, and are connected through an Arista 7050QX-32S-R switch. The enclave runs inside a Windows network filter driver. We added a new ioctl that allows the application to communicate metadata to the driver, and used that to implement the (socket-like) message send call.

Our *programmable NIC* testbed consists of four Intel Xeon E5-1620 (3.70GHz/16GB). Each machine is equipped with a dual-port 10GbE Netronome NFE-3240 programmable NIC [46]. These NICs descend from Intel's IXP network processors [31]. The NICs include a 40 core, 8 way multi-threaded CPU (320 threads), and 4GB of memory. We perform CAM operations on main memory (other models of the processor can offload them to a large TCAM). The network switch is a 40x10Gbps Blade RackSwitch.

We have extended the NIC firmware to be able to run the Eden interpreter. Beyond that, we can also execute control programs and keep state in the NIC. Currently, we have limited support for stages in our programmable NIC testbed.

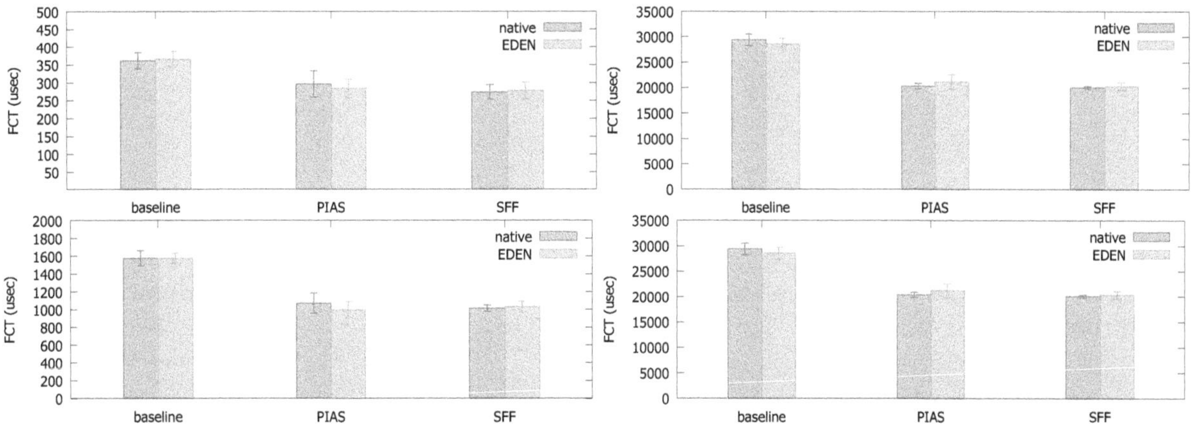

Figure 9: Average flow completion times (FCT) for small (left) and intermediate (right) flows with 95% confidence intervals. The top bars show the average while the bottom the 95th percentile.

5 Evaluation

Our evaluation of Eden spans three axes: i) It highlights Eden's performance while implementing diverse network functions, ii) it covers functions implemented in an OS network stack and in programmable NICs, and iii) it provides micro-benchmarks evaluating Eden's data-plane overheads. We consider the three case studies from Section 2.

5.1 Case Study 1: Flow Scheduling

Our first case study describes how Eden implements network functions that schedule flows so as to reduce flow completion times. We examine two such functions: PIAS, whose logic was discussed in Figure 4 and shortest flow first scheduling (SFF). PIAS requires data-plane computation and state to enable tracking flow sizes and tagging packets with priorities depending on thresholds based on the distribution of flow sizes. SFF, instead, does not track traffic flow sizes but it requires applications to provide the flow size to the Eden enclave, so that the correct priority is enforced.

To assess the impact of Eden on the performance of these functions, we compare Eden with a "native" implementation. The latter implements a hard-coded function within the Eden enclave instead of using the interpreter, similar to a typical implementation through a customised layer in the OS [8]. Figure 7 shows the PIAS action function in our language.

The workload driving the experiments is based on a realistic request-response workload, with responses reflecting the flow size distribution found in search applications [2, 8]. Such applications generate traffic mostly comprising small flows of a few packets with high rate of flows starting and terminating. In our set-up, one worker responds to requests generating load at roughly 70%, while other sources generate background traffic at the same time. Priority thresholds were set up for three classes of flows: small (<10KB), intermediate (10KB-1MB) and background. Small flows have the highest priority, followed by the intermediate ones.

Figure 9 shows the average and the 95th-percentile of the flow completion times for small and intermediate flows when executing the two functions. The figure shows results when running natively in the OS and through the Eden interpreter across ten runs of the experiments. *Baseline* highlights flow completion times without any prioritization. We report two Baseline figures, native and Eden. The latter shows the overhead of running the classification and data-plane functions, but ignoring the interpreter output before packets are transmitted (i.e., the priority marks are not inserted in the packet header). Essentially, the overhead reflects running the Eden enclave over vanilla TCP.

As expected, enabling prioritization significantly reduces the flow completion times; for small flows, flow completion times reduce from $363\mu s$ to $274\mu s$ on the average, and from $1.6ms$ to $1ms$ at the 95th percentile, an overall a reduction of 25%-40%. Similar trends are observed for intermediate flows as well. At the same time, background traffic manages to saturate the rest of the link capacity. SFF, by utilizing application knowledge, typically provides slightly better performance with less variability. In SFF, the mapping of flows to classes occurs when the flow starts, and flows do not change priorities over time.

While similar observations have been reported in previous work, what is important in our context is that the performance of the native implementation of the policy and the interpreted one are similar. In all cases the differences are not statistically significant.

5.2 Case Study 2: Load-balancing

The second case study examines how Eden enables per-packet WCMP on top of our *programmable NIC* testbed. The WCMP function has been discussed in Section 2 (Figure 2). We arranged the topology of our testbed to emulate the topology of Figure 1, with two hosts connected through two paths, one 10Gbps and one 1Gbps.

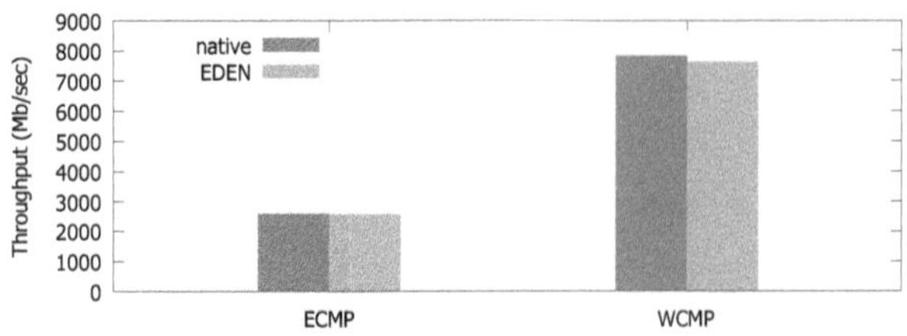

Figure 10: Aggregate throughput for ECMP and WCMP. Confidence intervals are within 2% of the values shown.

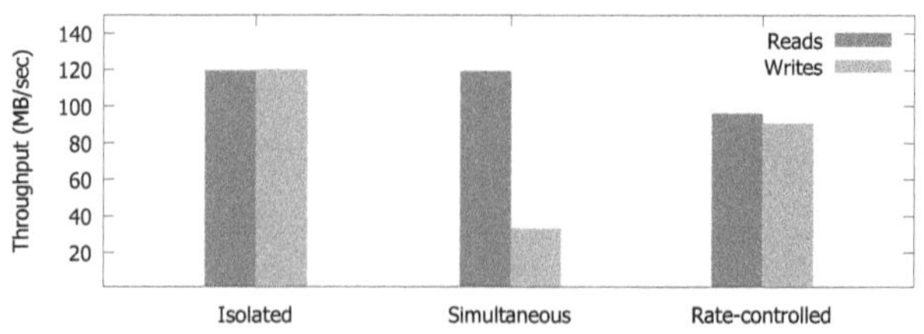

Figure 11: Average READ vs. WRITE throughput when requests run in isolation, simultaneously, and when READ requests are rate-controlled based on the request size. 95% confidence intervals are <0.2% of the mean values.

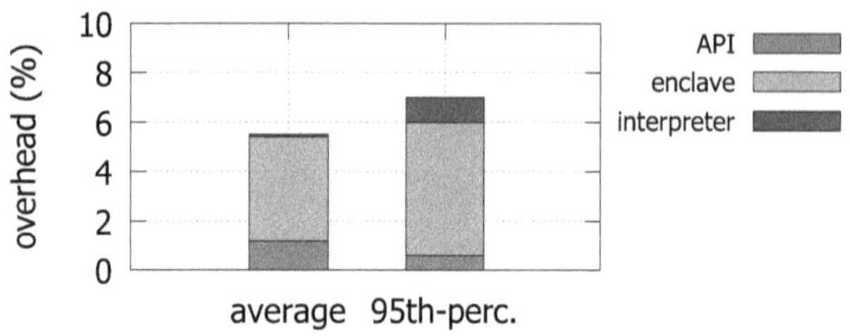

Figure 12: CPU overheads incurred by Eden components compared to running the vanilla TCP stack. API refers to passing metadata information to the enclave.

The programmable NICs run our custom firmware that implements the enclave and the Eden interpreter. The interpreted program controls how packets are source-routed through the two paths. We use per-packet balancing, instead of per-flow balancing to highlight Eden's ability to apply per-packet functions at high rate. In the default case, paths are selected for long-running TCP flows with equal weights, thus implementing ECMP. For WCMP, we enforce a ratio 10:1.

Figure 10 shows the average throughput achieved for the two functions with a native program implemented directly on the programmable NICs and with Eden. For both ECMP and WCMP, Eden's overheads are negligible with the difference between Eden and native not being statistically significant. In ECMP, TCP throughput is dominated by the capacity of the slowest path, and throughput peaks at just over 2Gbps as expected. Instead, with per-packet WCMP, TCP throughput is around 7.8Gbps, 3x better than ECMP. The throughput is lower than the full 11Gbps which is our topology's min cut due to in-network reordering of packets [29]. Modifying TCP's congestion control algorithm can alleviate such issues [53]; however, the goal of this case-study is to highlight how Eden can easily implement network functions such as weighted selection of paths without any impact on performance–in this case with unmodified applications and while running vanilla TCP.

5.3 Case Study 3: Datacenter QoS

We now examine Pulsar's rate control as described in Figure 3. The experiment involves two tenants running our custom application that generates 64K IOs. One of the tenants generates READ requests while the other one WRITEs to a storage server backed by a RAM disk drive. The storage server is connected to our testbed through a 1Gbps link.

The results in Figure 11 show that when WRITE requests compete with READs, their throughput drops by 72%. As previously discussed, this reflects the asymmetry of IO operations; READs are small on the forward path and manage to fill the queues in shared resources. Instead, we account for this mismatch through Pulsar's rate control, by charging READ requests based on the request size and WRITEs on the packet size. This ensures equal throughput between the two operations.

5.4 Overheads

The previous case studies have focused on the overheads incurred by Eden with respect to application metrics. Here, we quantify Eden's CPU overheads and memory footprint of the enclave.

Figure 12 quantifies Eden overheads while running the SFF policy (case study 1). The workload comprises 12 long-running TCP flows in one of our testbed nodes, and Eden can saturate the 10Gbps capacity of its link. The figure shows how the different components of Eden contribute to the CPU load. We consider these overheads reasonable. Note however, that saturating the link capacity assumes that the cycle budget of the interpreted program allows for such speeds. As we discuss in the following section, Eden intentionally avoids posing any restrictions in the cycle budget of data-plane functions.

In the examples discussed in the paper, the (operand) stack and heap space of the interpreter are in the order of 64 and 256 bytes respectively.

6 Discussion

The previous sections discussed Eden's design and demonstrated its expressiveness through case studies. Here, we briefly complement the discussion of our design choices and highlight interesting issues for future research.

Choice of language and environment. Beyond the benefits discussed in Section 3.4 (*i.e.*, expressiveness, portability, safety, dynamically-injected programs), the choice of the DSL and the interpreted environment were further motivated by fast prototyping. In particular, the use of F# code quotations is convenient because it facilitates retrieval of the abstract syntax tree of the program, which is the input to our compiler. Additionally, F# allowed us to experiment with various ways of expressing the action functions, and to run and debug the programs locally (that can even take place with the F# interpreter without invoking the compiler and the enclave interpreter).

Action function composition. In this paper, we assumed a fixed order of network function execution. This is effective when the functions run in isolation, or when their composition can be determined trivially. Network functions, however, can interact in arbitrary ways, hence, it is an open question to define the semantics of function composition. One option is to impose a hierarchy. This can be achieved, for example, by imposing that application specific functions precede flow specific ones or vice versa, or apply priorities to functions which define the execution order.

OS vs NIC program execution. Eden's interpreter can run both in the kernel and in a programmable NIC. When both are available, deciding where functions run is an open question. While it may seem that processing should always be offloaded, the cost of offloading may be prohibitive in some cases. For example, when the associated metadata is large, or when the interaction with the local controller is frequent. Automatically partitioning of a high-level policy across different execution points would thus be very useful.

Cycle budget and memory requirements. Achieving line rates of 10Gbps+ in modern datacenter networks results in a tight cycle budget for data plane computations. Techniques like IO batching and offloading are often employed to reduce the processing overhead. While Eden's action functions express per-packet computation, they can be extended to allow for computation over a batch of packets. If the batch contains packets from multiple messages, the enclave will have to preprocess it and split it into messages.

While the enclave can, in principle, limit the amount or resources (memory and computational cycles) used by an action function, we chose not to restrict the complexity of the computation or the amount of state maintained by them. Instead, we believe that the system administrator should decide whether to run a function or not, irrespective of its overheads. Indeed, deeming such overheads acceptable may depend on exogenous factors such as the expected load in the system.

7 Related work

The idea of a programmable data plane dates back to active networking. Active networks exposed an API that allows control over router and switch resources, enabling processing, storage and packet queue management [60, 56, 63, 12, 3]. However, it has proven difficult to realize a generic programming model implemented by networking devices. Eden avoids this issue by focusing on data plane functions executed by end hosts only. Recently, Jeyakumar et al. proposed the use of tiny programs that can be carried in packets and executed by routers [32]. This provides a flexible mechanism to exchange state information between the network and the end hosts. Eden can benefit from such information, but is agnostic to how it is obtained.

Today, programmable networks are implemented using Software-Defined Networking (SDN) [23, 37]. SDN decouples the control plane from the data plane and requires a way for the control plane to communicate with the data plane programmatically. The most prominent API for such control- and data-plane interaction is OpenFlow [42]. Eden focuses on implementing functionality at the ends with a wider and richer data-plane interface, and goes one step further to take advantage of application knowledge.

P4 [14] proposes a language for programming packet processors, hence, generalizing OpenFlow [42]. P4 targets modern switching chips, *e.g.*, [15], and is tailored to a specific abstract forwarding model comprising parse, match and action. This results in a restricted programming model that limits its expressivity; for example, to policies that can be encoded through exact matches. Using P4 to encode a policy involving comparison operations, like the flow scheduling example used throughout this paper, would be challenging.

The idea of end hosts participating in network functionality has been explored in enterprise and data center networks [49, 16, 21, 34, 59, 57]. For example, Open vSwitch [50] extends the OpenFlow [42] programming model to end hosts. However, even in these proposals, the data-plane interface is narrow—it can be programmed to match (mostly) on packet headers and apply a fixed set of actions. They can thus implement application-agnostic network functions that operate at coarse time-scales. Instead, Eden can accommodate network functions that are dynamic, require application semantics, and operate even at per-packet time-scales.

Network exception handlers [34] was one of the first proposals to incorporate application semantics into management policies. Akin to program exception handlers, end hosts register exception conditions with network controllers, which in turn inform end hosts when exceptions trigger. Corresponding actions at end hosts would then be parameterized with application context. Applications are a first-order citizen in Eden as well; however, Eden goes beyond static actions such as rate limiting, by allowing for functions to be evaluated at end hosts with minimal controller involvement.

Network function virtualization (NFV) targets virtualizing arbitrary network functions, traditionally implemented at specialized physical devices. Eden can be seen as an end host pragmatic and reasoned point in the NFV space.

The Click software router [36] allows the construction of modular data-plane processing pipelines. It emphasizes the flexible chaining of building blocks called elements. Eden also operates in the data-plane, but leverages application information to enables application-level message-oriented policies. The enclaves share similarities with Click's elements. Eden's enclave offers the convenience of a higher-level environment to network policy developers. The elements, however, are more appropriate for performance critical tasks (*e.g.*, rate limiting functionality).

Eden enables rapid prototyping of network functions in the data plane. Other efforts to enable innovation in the data plane include PLUG [20] and SwitchBlade [7]. These efforts focus on implementing full protocols like IPv6 on programmable hardware like FPGAs.

Similarly to packet filters [43, 41], the Eden interpreter processes packets in a constrained execution environment inside the kernel according to user-defined programs. However, the Eden interpreter supports richer packet processing to accommodate more expressive action functions.

The idea of associating metadata with network traffic as it gets processed in the network stack is similar to Mbuf_tags [35]. This work also proposes a user-level mechanism to attach metadata to packets. Eden aims to start the discussion of extending the interface to higher level libraries and applications.

8 Concluding remarks

This paper proposes Eden, an architecture for implementing network functions at end hosts. This involves applications (stages) classifying application data into messages and annotating the messages with meta-data. Enclaves use the message and meta-data information to apply generic stateful actions on network packets.

Network operators express desired actions in a high-level language based on F# code quotations; their programs are compiled to bytecode suitable for execution by an interpreter that operates in the enclave. The enclave compiler and runtime takes care of managing any state in the enclave, freeing the network programmer to focus on the functionality to be achieved. The combination of stages, enclave and the interpreted action language allows expressing a variety of functions in a natural way and with a small performance penalty.

Acknowledgments

We are indebted to our colleague Andy Slowey for providing technical support with our experimental setup. We are also grateful to Rolf Neugebauer, Stuart Wray, and their colleagues at Netronome for their help with the NFP3240 NICs. Finally, we thank Dimitrios Vytiniotis, Z. Morley Mao and the anonymous SIGCOMM reviewers for their feedback.

References

[1] M. Alizadeh, T. Edsall, S. Dharmapurikar, R. Vaidyanathan, K. Chu, A. Fingerhut, V. T. Lam, F. Matus, R. Pan, N. Yadav, and G. Varghese CONGA: Distributed Congestion-aware Load Balancing for Datacenters. In: SIGCOMM. ACM, 2014.

[2] M. Alizadeh, A. Greenberg, D. A. Maltz, J. Padhye, P. Patel, B. Prabhakar, S. Sengupta, and M. Sridharan Data Center TCP (DCTCP). In: SIGCOMM. ACM, 2010.

[3] K. G. Anagnostakis, M. W. Hicks, S. Ioannidis, A. D. Keromytis, and J. M. Smith Scalable Resource Control in Active Networks. In: IWAN. Springer-Verlag, 2000.

[4] G. Ananthanarayanan, S. Kandula, A. Greenberg, I. Stoica, Y. Lu, B. Saha, and E. Harris Reining in the Outliers in Map-reduce Clusters Using Mantri. In: OSDI. USENIX, 2010.

[5] L. Andersson, P. Doolan, N. Feldman, A. Fredette, and B. Thomas *LDP Specification.* RFC 3036. 2001.

[6] S. Angel, H. Ballani, T. Karagiannis, G. O'Shea, and E. Thereska End-to-end Performance Isolation Through Virtual Datacenters. In: OSDI. USENIX, 2014.

[7] M. B. Anwer, M. Motiwala, M. b. Tariq, and N. Feamster SwitchBlade: A Platform for Rapid Deployment of Network Protocols on Programmable Hardware. In: SIGCOMM. ACM, 2010.

[8] W. Bai, K. Chen, H. Wang, L. Chen, D. Han, and C. Tian Information-Agnostic Flow Scheduling for Commodity Data Centers. In: NSDI. USENIX, 2015.

[9] H. Ballani, P. Costa, T. Karagiannis, and A. Rowstron Towards Predictable Datacenter Networks. In: SIGCOMM. ACM, 2011.

[10] H. Ballani, K. Jang, T. Karagiannis, C. Kim, D. Gunawardena, and G. O'Shea Chatty Tenants and the Cloud Network Sharing Problem. In: NSDI. USENIX, 2013.

[11] P. Barham, A. Donnelly, R. Isaacs, and R. Mortier Using Magpie for Request Extraction and Workload Modelling. In: OSDI. USENIX, 2004.

[12] S. Bhattacharjee, K. L. Calvert, and E. W. Zegura An Architecture for Active Networking. In: HPN. Chapman & Hall, Ltd., 1997.

[13] G. Bianchi, M. Bonola, A. Capone, and C. Cascone OpenState: Programming Platform-independent Stateful Openflow Applications Inside the Switch. *SIGCOMM Comput. Commun. Rev.* 44, 2 (2014).

[14] P. Bosshart, D. Daly, G. Gibb, M. Izzard, N. McKeown, J. Rexford, C. Schlesinger, D. Talayco, A. Vahdat, G. Varghese, and D. Walker P4: Programming Protocol-independent Packet Processors. *SIGCOMM Comput. Commun. Rev.* 44, 3 (2014).

[15] P. Bosshart, G. Gibb, H.-S. Kim, G. Varghese, N. McKeown, M. Izzard, F. Mujica, and M. Horowitz Forwarding Metamorphosis: Fast Programmable Match-action Processing in Hardware for SDN. In: SIGCOMM. ACM, 2013.

[16] M. Casado, T. Koponen, S. Shenker, and A. Tootoonchian Fabric: A Retrospective on Evolving SDN. In: HotSDN. ACM, 2012.

[17] M. Chowdhury, S. Kandula, and I. Stoica Leveraging Endpoint Flexibility in Data-intensive Clusters. In: SIGCOMM. ACM, 2013.

[18] M. Chowdhury, Y. Zhong, and I. Stoica Efficient Coflow Scheduling with Varys. In: SIGCOMM. ACM, 2014.

[19] Cisco *Snort.* 2015. url: https://www.snort.org/ (visited on 06/03/2015).

[20] L. De Carli, Y. Pan, A. Kumar, C. Estan, and K. Sankaralingam PLUG: Flexible Lookup Modules for Rapid Deployment of New Protocols in High-speed Routers. In: SIGCOMM. ACM, 2009.

[21] C. Dixon, H. Uppal, V. Brajkovic, D. Brandon, T. Anderson, and A. Krishnamurthy ETTM: A Scalable Fault Tolerant Network Manager. In: NSDI. USENIX, 2011.

[22] F. R. Dogar, T. Karagiannis, H. Ballani, and A. Rowstron Decentralized Task-aware Scheduling for Data Center Networks. In: SIGCOMM. 2014.

[23] N. Feamster, J. Rexford, and E. Zegura The Road to SDN: An Intellectual History of Programmable Networks. *SIGCOMM Comput. Commun. Rev.* 44, 2 (2014).
[24] A. D. Ferguson, A. Guha, C. Liang, R. Fonseca, and S. Krishnamurthi Participatory Networking: An API for Application Control of SDNs. In: SIGCOMM. ACM, 2013.
[25] N. Foster, R. Harrison, M. J. Freedman, C. Monsanto, J. Rexford, A. Story, and D. Walker Frenetic: A Network Programming Language. In: ICFP. ACM, 2011.
[26] R. Gandhi, H. H. Liu, Y. C. Hu, G. Lu, J. Padhye, L. Yuan, and M. Zhang Duet: Cloud Scale Load Balancing with Hardware and Software. In: SIGCOMM. ACM, 2014.
[27] C. Gkantsidis, T. Karagiannis, P. Key, B. Radunovic, E. Raftopoulos, and D. Manjunath Traffic Management and Resource Allocation in Small Wired/Wireless Networks. In: CoNEXT. ACM, 2009.
[28] M. P. Grosvenor, M. Schwarzkopf, I. Gog, R. N. M. Watson, A. W. Moore, S. Hand, and J. Crowcroft Queues Don't Matter When You Can JUMP Them! In: NSDI. USENIX Association, 2015.
[29] H. Han, S. Shakkottai, C. V. Hollot, R. Srikant, and D. Towsley Multi-path TCP: A Joint Congestion Control and Routing Scheme to Exploit Path Diversity in the Internet. *IEEE/ACM Trans. Netw.* 14, 6 (2006).
[30] C.-Y. Hong, M. Caesar, and P. B. Godfrey Finishing Flows Quickly with Preemptive Scheduling. In: SIGCOMM. ACM, 2012.
[31] D. F. Hooper *Using IXP2400/2800 Development Tools. A Hands-on Approach to Network Processor Software Design.* 1st ed. Intel Press, 2005.
[32] V. Jeyakumar, M. Alizadeh, C. Kim, and D. Mazières Tiny Packet Programs for Low-latency Network Control and Monitoring. In: HotNets-XII. ACM, 2013.
[33] V. Jeyakumar, M. Alizadeh, D. Mazières, B. Prabhakar, C. Kim, and A. Greenberg EyeQ: Practical Network Performance Isolation at the Edge. In: NSDI. USENIX, 2013.
[34] T. Karagiannis, R. Mortier, and A. Rowstron Network Exception Handlers: Host-network Control in Enterprise Networks. In: SIGCOMM. ACM, 2008.
[35] A. D. Keromytis Tagging Data in the Network Stack: Mbuf_Tags. In: BSDC'03. USENIX Association, 2003.
[36] E. Kohler, R. Morris, B. Chen, J. Jannotti, and M. F. Kaashoek The Click Modular Router. *ACM Trans. Comput. Syst.* 18, 3 (2000).
[37] D. Kreutz, F. Ramos, P. Esteves Verissimo, C. Esteve Rothenberg, S. Azodolmolky, and S. Uhlig Software-Defined Networking: A Comprehensive Survey. *Proceedings of the IEEE* 103, 1 (2015).
[38] V. T. Lam, S. Radhakrishnan, R. Pan, A. Vahdat, and G. Varghese Netshare and Stochastic Netshare: Predictable Bandwidth Allocation for Data Centers. *SIGCOMM Comput. Commun. Rev.* 42, 3 (2012).
[39] J. Lee, Y. Turner, M. Lee, L. Popa, S. Banerjee, J.-M. Kang, and P. Sharma Application-driven Bandwidth Guarantees in Datacenters. In: SIGCOMM. 2014.
[40] A. Likhtarov, R. Nishtala, R. McElroy, H. Fugal, A. Grynenko, and V. Venkataramani *Introducing mcrouter: A memcached protocol router for scaling memcached deployments.* Facebook. 2014. URL: http://bit.ly/1TpNKo0 (visited on 06/16/2015).
[41] S. McCanne, and V. Jacobson The BSD Packet Filter: A New Architecture for User-level Packet Capture. In: USENIX Winter Conf. USENIX, 1993.
[42] N. McKeown, T. Anderson, H. Balakrishnan, G. Parulkar, L. Peterson, J. Rexford, S. Shenker, and J. Turner OpenFlow: Enabling Innovation in Campus Networks. *SIGCOMM Comput. Commun. Rev.* 38, 2 (2008).
[43] J. Mogul, R. Rashid, and M. Accetta The Packer Filter: An Efficient Mechanism for User-level Network Code. In: SOSP '87. ACM, 1987.
[44] J. Mudigonda, P. Yalagandula, M. Al-Fares, and J. C. Mogul SPAIN: COTS Data-center Ethernet for Multipathing over Arbitrary Topologies. In: NSDI. USENIX, 2010.
[45] A. Munir, G. Baig, S. M. Irteza, I. A. Qazi, A. X. Liu, and F. R. Dogar Friends, Not Foes: Synthesizing Existing Transport Strategies for Data Center Networks. In: SIGCOMM. ACM, 2014.
[46] Netronome *Netronome FlowNICs.* 2015. URL: http://netronome.com/product/flownics/ (visited on 06/03/2015).
[47] P. Patel, D. Bansal, L. Yuan, A. Murthy, A. Greenberg, D. A. Maltz, R. Kern, H. Kumar, M. Zikos, H. Wu, C. Kim, and N. Karri Ananta: Cloud Scale Load Balancing. In: SIGCOMM. ACM, 2013.
[48] J. Perry, A. Ousterhout, H. Balakrishnan, D. Shah, and H. Fugal Fastpass: A Centralized "Zero-queue" Datacenter Network. In: SIGCOMM. ACM, 2014.
[49] B. Pfaff, J. Pettit, T. Koponen, K. Amidon, M. Casado, and S. Shenker Extending Networking into the Virtualization Layer. In: HotNets-VIII. ACM, 2009.
[50] B. Pfaff, J. Pettit, T. Koponen, E. Jackson, A. Zhou, J. Rajahalme, J. Gross, A. Wang, J. Stringer, P. Shelar, K. Amidon, and M. Casado The Design and Implementation of Open vSwitch. In: NSDI. USENIX, 2015.
[51] L. Popa, A. Krishnamurthy, S. Ratnasamy, and I. Stoica FairCloud: Sharing the Network in Cloud Computing. In: HotNets-X. ACM, 2011.
[52] L. Popa, P. Yalagandula, S. Banerjee, J. C. Mogul, Y. Turner, and J. R. Santos ElasticSwitch: Practical Work-conserving Bandwidth Guarantees for Cloud Computing. In: SIGCOMM. ACM, 2013.
[53] C. Raiciu, C. Paasch, S. Barre, A. Ford, M. Honda, F. Duchene, O. Bonaventure, and M. Handley How Hard Can It Be? Designing and Implementing a Deployable Multipath TCP. In: NSDI. USENIX, 2012.
[54] M. Reitblatt, M. Canini, A. Guha, and N. Foster FatTire: Declarative Fault Tolerance for Software-Defined Networks. In: HotSDN. ACM, 2013.
[55] M. Reitblatt, N. Foster, J. Rexford, C. Schlesinger, and D. Walker Abstractions for Network Update. In: SIGCOMM. ACM, 2012.
[56] B. Schwartz, A. W. Jackson, W. T. Strayer, W. Zhou, R. D. Rockwell, and C. Partridge Smart Packets: Applying Active Networks to Network Management. *ACM Trans. Comput. Syst.* 18, 1 (2000).
[57] A. Shieh, S. Kandula, and E. G. Sirer SideCar: Building Programmable Datacenter Networks Without Programmable Switches. In: Hotnets-IX. ACM, 2010.
[58] D. Shue, M. J. Freedman, and A. Shaikh Performance Isolation and Fairness for Multi-tenant Cloud Storage. In: OSDI. USENIX, 2012.
[59] R. Soulé, S. Basu, R. Kleinberg, E. G. Sirer, and N. Foster Managing the Network with Merlin. In: HotNets-XII. ACM, 2013.
[60] D. L. Tennenhouse, and D. J. Wetherall Towards an Active Network Architecture. *SIGCOMM Comput. Commun. Rev.* 26, 2 (1996).
[61] E. Thereska, H. Ballani, G. O'Shea, T. Karagiannis, A. Rowstron, T. Talpey, R. Black, and T. Zhu IOFlow: A Software-defined Storage Architecture. In: SOSP. ACM, 2013.
[62] A. Voellmy, J. Wang, Y. R. Yang, B. Ford, and P. Hudak Maple: Simplifying SDN Programming Using Algorithmic Policies. *SIGCOMM Comput. Commun. Rev.* 43, 4 (2013).
[63] D. Wetherall, J. V. Guttag, and D. Tennenhouse ANTS: a toolkit for building and dynamically deploying network protocols. In: OPENARCH. IEEE, 1998.
[64] C. Wilson, H. Ballani, T. Karagiannis, and A. Rowtron Better Never Than Late: Meeting Deadlines in Datacenter Networks. In: SIGCOMM. ACM, 2011.
[65] J. Zhou, M. Tewari, M. Zhu, A. Kabbani, L. Poutievski, A. Singh, and A. Vahdat WCMP: Weighted Cost Multipathing for Improved Fairness in Data Centers. In: EuroSys. ACM, 2014.

Adaptive Congestion Control for Unpredictable Cellular Networks

Yasir Zaki
NYU Abu Dhabi
Abu Dhabi, UAE
yasir.zaki@nyu.edu

Thomas Pötsch
University of Bremen
Bremen, Germany
tpoetsch@uni-bremen.de

Jay Chen
NYU Abu Dhabi
Abu Dhabi, UAE
jchen@cs.nyu.edu

Lakshminarayanan Subramanian
NYU and CTED
New York, USA
lakshmi@cs.nyu.edu

Carmelita Görg
University of Bremen
Bremen, Germany
cg@comnets.uni-bremen.de

ABSTRACT

Legacy congestion controls including TCP and its variants are known to perform poorly over cellular networks due to highly variable capacities over short time scales, self-inflicted packet delays, and packet losses unrelated to congestion. To cope with these challenges, we present Verus, an end-to-end congestion control protocol that uses delay measurements to react quickly to the capacity changes in cellular networks without explicitly attempting to predict the cellular channel dynamics. The key idea of Verus is to continuously learn a delay profile that captures the relationship between end-to-end packet delay and outstanding window size over short epochs and uses this relationship to increment or decrement the window size based on the observed short-term packet delay variations. While the delay-based control is primarily for congestion avoidance, Verus uses standard TCP features including multiplicative decrease upon packet loss and slow start.

Through a combination of simulations, empirical evaluations using cellular network traces, and real-world evaluations against standard TCP flavors and state of the art protocols like Sprout, we show that Verus outperforms these protocols in cellular channels. In comparison to TCP Cubic, Verus achieves an order of magnitude (> 10x) reduction in delay over 3G and LTE networks while achieving comparable throughput (sometimes marginally higher). In comparison to Sprout, Verus achieves up to 30% higher throughput in rapidly changing cellular networks.

SIGCOMM '15, August 17 - 21, 2015, London, United Kingdom

DOI: http://dx.doi.org/10.1145/2785956.2787498

CCS Concepts

•Networks → Network protocol design; Transport protocols; Network performance analysis;

Keywords

Congestion control, Cellular network, Transport protocol, Delay-based

1. INTRODUCTION

Cellular network channels are highly variable and users often experience fluctuations in their radio link rates over short time scales due to scarce radio resources making these channels hard to predict [26, 20, 7]. TCP and its variants are known to perform poorly over cellular networks due to high capacity variability, self-inflicted queuing delays, stochastic packet losses that are not linked to congestion, and large bandwidth-delay products [15, 32, 33].

Three specific characteristics directly impact the unpredictability of cellular channels. First, the state of a cellular channel between a mobile device and a base station undergoes several complex state transitions that affect channel availability in short time scales [15]; this introduces variability in the underlying channel. Second, the frame scheduling algorithms used in cellular networks cause burstiness in the cellular channel. Based on real-world cellular measurements, we observe that the typical traffic characteristics at a receiver are bursty (even for smooth sending patterns) with variable burst sizes and burst inter-arrival periods. Third, while prior work has considered only self-inflicted queuing delay as a cause for high delays [33], we find that competing traffic does affect end-to-end delay characteristics, especially under high contention or when the cellular channel is near saturation. Finally, device mobility has a substantial impact on channel characteristics that further compounds these challenges. The lack of channel predictability has important implications on the design of new congestion control protocols.

In this paper we present Verus, a delay-based congestion control protocol that is primarily designed for highly variable channel conditions that are hard to predict. Instead of attempting to predict the cellular channel dynamics, Verus uses cues from delay variations to track channel conditions and quickly change its sending window. The key idea of the Verus protocol is to remain in constant exploration mode and continuously learn a *delay profile* that captures the relationship between the sending window size and the perceived end-to-end delay. Using this delay profile and delay variation cues, Verus replaces the conventional Additive Increase (AI) in TCP with a series of increment/decrement steps to quickly adapt to changing channel conditions. While these control steps are primarily for congestion avoidance, Verus retains the loss-based multiplicative decrease step of TCP to quickly respond to congestion.

We implemented and tested Verus across a variety of environments, comparing it against Sprout and variants of TCP including Cubic, NewReno and Vegas. We then evaluated Verus using a combination of simulations, trace-based simulations, and real-world experiments. In these experiments we demonstrate that Verus achieves an interesting trade-off between the throughput and delay characteristics of Sprout and TCP variants in cellular channels. In comparison to TCP Cubic, Verus achieves an order of magnitude (> 10x) reduction in delay over 3G and LTE networks while achieving comparable throughput (sometimes margin-ally higher). In comparison to Sprout, Verus achieves higher throughput under rapidly fluctuating channel conditions while maintaining low delay. Finally, we show that Verus provides good fairness properties when competing with other protocols and that it can rapidly adapt to highly variable channel conditions over short time scales.

2. RELATED WORK

Legacy Congestion Control Protocols

Congestion control is an extensively studied topic with numerous variants of TCP. TCP Reno [5], TCP Tahoe [16] and TCP NewReno [14] were among the early popular variants which are loss-based and TCP Vegas [3] was among the earliest delay-based control protocols. Most current operating systems leverage TCP Cubic [13] or Compound TCP [29]. While TCP Cubic makes specific modifications to the increment function in conventional AIMD-based window control, Compound TCP maintains two congestion windows to adapt its sending window. There are also a number of other TCP flavors such as LEDBAT [27], TCP Nice [30], equation based rate control [9], and Binomial congestion control [2]. None of these legacy congestion control protocols are directly suited for cellular network conditions where the underlying channel changes at short time scales and the basic assumption that a link has a fixed capacity does not hold [31]. In addition, none of these TCP variants can distinguish stochastic losses that are part of the cellular environment from losses caused by congestion. Our work aims to combine ideas from conventional loss-based control with delay-based control drawing inspiration from protocols like TCP Vegas.

Router-feedback-based Protocols

A common approach used in congestion control research to make TCP functional in new network environments (where TCP variants are not well suited) is to use router feedback. Examples of such techniques include Explicit Congestion Notification (ECN) [8], VCP [34], or active queue management like RED [10], BLUE [4], CHOKe [25], AVQ [19], CoDel [22]. The problem with these methods is that they require modifications to intermediate routers which has remained a roadblock for adoption. In our setting, we aim to design an end-to-end congestion control protocol for cellular networks with no middle-box support or router feedback.

Recent Congestion Control Proposals

TCP has remained the gold standard for many years, but there have been several recent publications on new congestion control protocols for various environments. Sprout [33], for example, is a recent protocol specifically designed for the context of cellular networks. Sprout specifically focused on the problem of reducing self-inflicted delay that affects TCP and its variants under varying channel conditions. Sprout shows a significant reduction in the end-to-end delay experienced by flows in cellular networks while maintaining good throughput characteristics. We compare our work against Sprout later in this paper. Remy [32] focuses on the problem of machine generated automated congestion control algorithms where a machine can be trained offline to learn congestion control schemes. The protocol designer specifies the desired targets of the network and Remy uses prior knowledge of the network to parametrize the protocol generation. Sivaraman et. al. [28] looked at the learnability of congestion control under imperfect knowledge of the network through an experimental study leveraging Remy as a design tool.

Another recent congestion control protocol is Data Center TCP (DCTCP) [1] that leverages ECN feedback to address several network impairments of TCP within data center networks. Recursive Cautious Congestion Control (RC3) [21] shows that the initial small window of TCP during slow start often wastes several RTTs until the flow fully utilizes the available link bandwidth. RC3 uses several levels of lower priority services to achieve nearly optimal throughputs. Performance-oriented Congestion Control (PCC) proposes to empirically observe and adopt actions that result in high performance, but PCC's adaptation to "rapidly" changing networks is on the order of seconds and does not consider unpredictable fluctuations on the order of milliseconds that occur in cellular networks [6].

Cellular Performance

Several measurement studies have examined TCP performance problems in cellular networks. Cellular networks tend to over-dimension their buffers by using large buffers at base stations to smooth the overall flow of traffic. As a result, conventional congestion control protocols result in "buffer-bloats" [12] and multi-second delays. Jiang et. al. [18] have shown the severity of bufferbloats through extensive measurements done on 3G and LTE commercial networks. The authors of [23] run long-term measurements to investigate the end-to-end performance of mobile devices within and across a wide range of carriers (i.e., 100), using 11 cellular network access technologies. Their results show that there are significant performance differences across carriers, access technologies, geographic regions and time. Zaki et. al. [35] conclude similar observations on cellular networks in developing regions as well as developed regions. Huang et. al. [15] studied the effect of network protocols on 3G and LTE networks by means of active and passive measurements. They discovered that TCP connections over LTE have various inefficiencies such as slow start. In comparison to 3G networks, LTE shows lower delays while many TCP connections (~52%) under-utilize the available bandwidth of LTE.

3. CHANNEL UNPREDICTABILITY

The physical properties of radio propagation such as path-loss and slow-fading eventually cause changes in link performance despite mitigation techniques. As a result, cellular channels fluctuate rapidly over short time scales (milliseconds) and change more dramatically over slightly longer time scales (seconds). The inherent unpredictability of radio propagation along with the complex interactions between cellular networking components makes it difficult for simple channel prediction models to track channel variations and thus they motivate adaptive exploration protocols like Verus.

We present results from several experiments on commercial 3G/UMTS and LTE networks to highlight these issues. We make three specific observations:

- **Burst scheduling:** Typical traffic characteristics observed at a receiver are highly bursty with variable burst sizes and burst inter-arrival periods. Mobility further amplifies these characteristics.
- **Competing traffic:** When two or more flows contend for radio resources and their sending rates approach network capacity, we observe cross-flow dependencies.
- **Channel unpredictability:** Standard prediction mechanisms even using the most recent samples are far from capturing the bursty behavior of the channel.

We measured cellular network performance under several different conditions, investigating the effects of several factors including: data rates, mobility, competing traffic, and 3G/UMTS or LTE. The measurements were conducted on two commercial cellular networks, Du and Etisalat[1], for both downlink and uplink direction. Our measurement setup consisted of a standard rack server and a client laptop tethered to a Sony Xperia Z1 LTE mobile phone. We implemented a measurement tool that sends/receives UDP packets between the server and client at 0.4 ms sending intervals. We performed clock synchronization, tagged packets with sequence numbers, and included the sender timestamp to calculate the one-way delay at the receiver.

Burst Scheduling

Packet arrivals at receivers exhibit a cellular radio scheduler phenomenon known as "burst scheduling". The radio scheduler serves users at different one millisecond Transmission Time Intervals (TTI) and the amount of data sent during the serving TTI is determined by radio conditions that lead to sending a burst of several packets. Figure 1 illustrates this phenomenon for one of our LTE 10 Mbps downlink measurements.

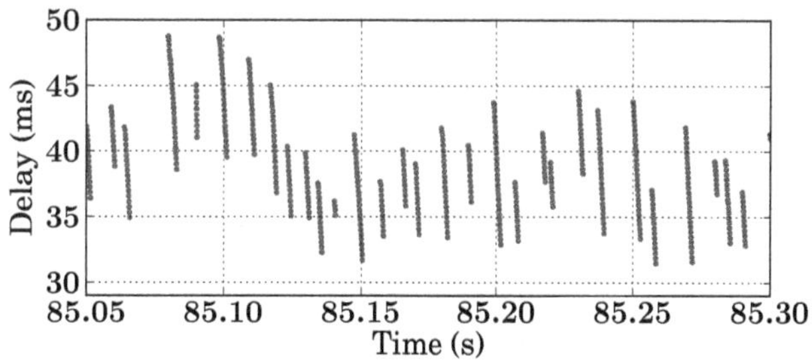

Figure 1: LTE 10 Mbps burst arrival time

Figure 2 summarizes our findings on burst scheduling for the two operators on 3G and LTE. In these downlink measurements our client was stationary and in an urban residential area. We observe that the burst size and inter-burst arrival time are difficult to predict and vary widely over the course of the 5 minute trace despite low contention and mobility. The LTE networks exhibit more frequent smaller bursts. Repeating this experiment while driving in the same area produces qualitatively similar results, but mobility causes both burst size and inter-arrival times to vary more widely. We make similar observations on the uplink.

Competing Traffic

A common assumption made about cellular channels is that since the cellular scheduler maintains separate queues for each user, competing traffic flows may not affect each other. We perform a simple experiment to show that two competing flows especially close to link saturation can affect each other despite queue isolation,

[1]Etisalat and Du are two cellular providers in the United Arab Emirates (UAE) and they provide LTE coverage in most parts of the major cities.

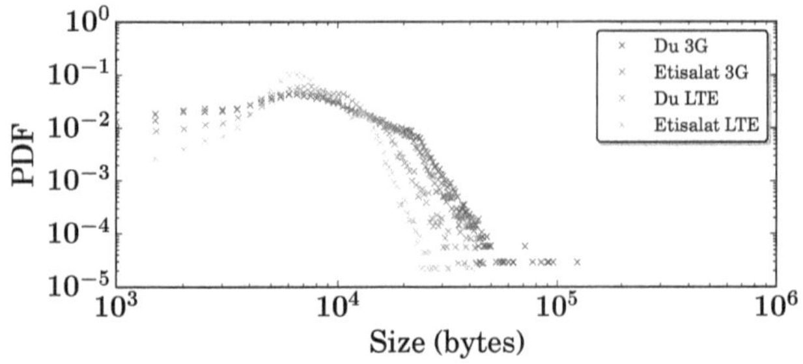

(a) Burst size

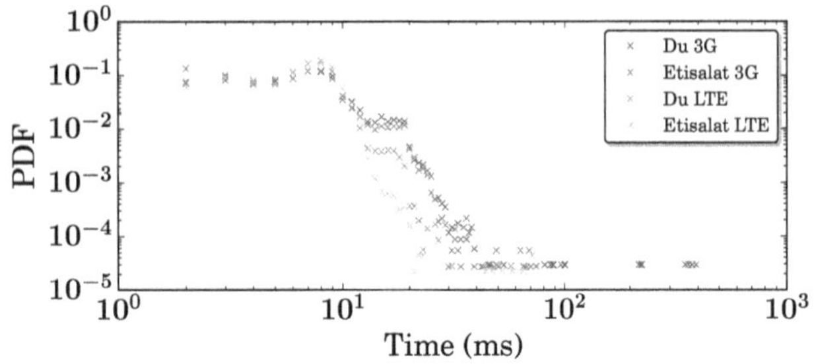

(b) Burst inter-arrival time

Figure 2: Probability distributions 3G/LTE downlink

especially since these flows still compete for the same radio resources. We consider two users competing at the same cellular base station such that when both users are active, their combined data rates are almost equal to the 3G channel capacity. The first user is constantly receiving at a fixed rate (1, 5, 10 Mbps) while the second user is set to operate in ON/OFF periods of one minute intervals receiving at 10 Mbps. Figure 3 shows the packet delays for the first user when the second user is ON/OFF. We observe that during the non-competing periods the average delay is low, but when the second user is ON the average packet delay for the second user increases, especially when the combined data rate approaches the channel capacity.

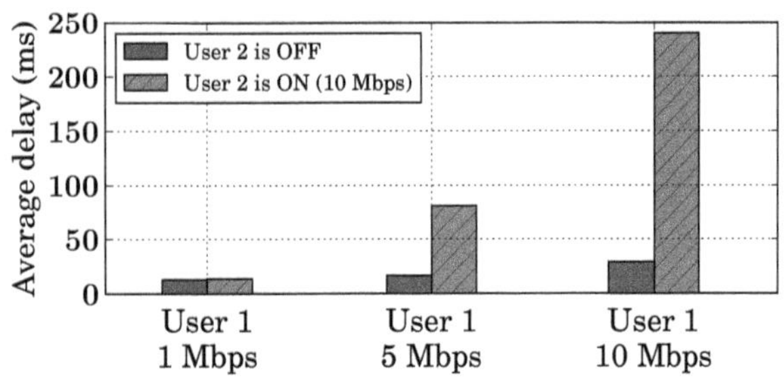

Figure 3: Impact of competing traffic on packet delay over a 3G downlink for User 1 when User 2 is ON/OFF

Channel Unpredictability

To demonstrate that cellular channels are non-trivial to predict, we used simple predictors to compare the measured data with the predicted data on a 3G downlink with one user receiving at 10 Mbps. Figure 4 is one representative trace from our campus parking lot on a 3G stationary downlink. We observe that even at 100 ms windows there are dramatic fluctuations in throughput due to burst scheduling. This variability is persistent and more evident at smaller timescales; if we zoom in to individual packet arrivals we observe the unpredictable variability previously illustrated in Figure 1 and Figure 2. To demonstrate that the channel is non-trivial to predict, we experimented with simple predictors to compare the predicted data with actual transmissions on 3G and LTE downlink. We found that linear predictors and k-step ahead predictors fail to track the high variations of the channel. While one could experiment with a variety of other predictors, the main result is that standard prediction mechanisms are far from capturing the bursty behavior of the channel despite the use of very recent samples.

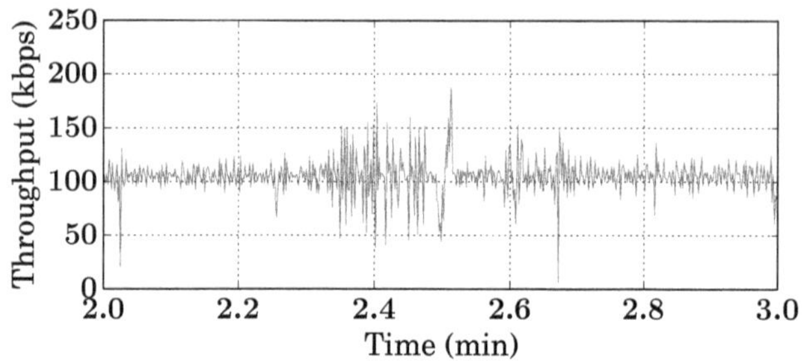

(a) 100 ms windows

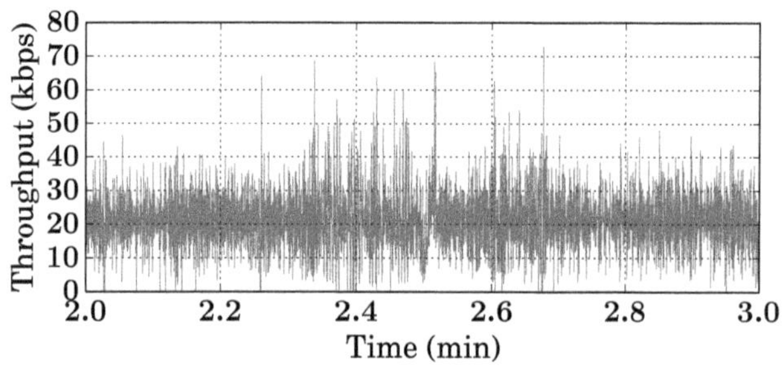

(b) 20 ms windows

Figure 4: Data received on a 3G stationary downlink at 100 ms and 20 ms window sizes

4. THE VERUS PROTOCOL

Verus is an end-to-end congestion control protocol designed for highly variable cellular channels that was heavily inspired by our channel observations. Since cellular channels are highly unpredictable, instead of attempting to predict the cellular channel dynamics, Verus uses delay variations to learn a *delay profile* that reflects the relationship between the network delay and the amount of data that can be sent without causing network congestion. Because contention and competing traffic impact performance, Verus takes into account delay feedback from the network to give an indication of contention and uses delay cues to constantly remain in exploration mode rather than assume that delays are self-inflicted. Finally, because channel fluctuations occur at different time-scales, Verus uses small ε steps to track fast changes and delay profile updates to track slower changes.

Verus borrows a number of features from legacy TCP variants, such as slow start and multiplicative decrease, but changes the way it maintains the sending window. Legacy TCP uses additive increase and increases the congestion window (CWMD) size by 1/CWND, i.e. increasing the congestion window by one packet when it successfully received a full window. This process can be slow. In contrast, Verus increases/decreases the sending window at each ε ms epoch and adapts to the changing cellular channel by rapidly increasing the sending window when the channel conditions allows for more packets. Similarly, Verus seeks to reduce the sending window even before packet losses whereas TCP can only decrease the congestion window through an aggressive multiplicative decrease after a loss.

The main goal of Verus is to avoid congestion by maintaining an appropriate (sliding) sending window W over a period equal to the estimated network Round Trip Time (RTT). Verus does this by replacing the additive increase with a series of small ε steps to adapt quickly to channel fluctuations. Within a sending window, Verus estimates how many packets need to be sent to avoid congestion or packet loss over a smaller ε ms epoch. At each epoch (in the absence of losses) Verus either: increments or decrements W using the delay profile as follows:

$$W(t+1) = f(d(t) + \delta(t)) \tag{1}$$

where, $W(t+1)$ is the next sending window, f is the delay profile function with $d(t)$ being the network delay, and $\delta(t)$ is a delay increment or decrement value.

Verus builds a delay profile using the following four elements:

- **Delay Estimator**: estimates the network RTT using delay measurements reported from the receiver's acknowledgments
- **Delay Profiler**: tracks the relationship between delay and sending window that does not cause network congestion
- **Window Estimator**: estimates the sending window using the estimated delay and delay profile
- **Loss Handler**: handles losses and adjusts the sending window

Delay Estimator

The Delay Estimator is responsible for processing the receiver's acknowledgments and estimating the network delay (estimated network RTT). It calculates the packet round trip delay $D_{p,i}$ for each packet by subtracting the current time (i.e. ACK received time) from the packet sent time; where p represents the packet number and i represents the Verus epoch number.

The Delay Estimator keeps track of all received packet delays within a Verus epoch and stores them in a vector $\vec{D}_i$. This vector contains all received delay values $D_{p,i}$ during that epoch. In order to track the (short-term) channel history and to avoid abrupt changes, the maximum delay $D_{max,i}$ received within that epoch is weighted by an Exponential Weighted Moving Average (EWMA) and calculated as:

$$D_{max,i} = \alpha \cdot D_{max,i-1} + (1-\alpha) \cdot max(\vec{D}_i) \quad \text{with } 0 < \alpha \leq 1 \tag{2}$$

The difference between the averaged maximum delays of the last two epochs is denoted as ΔD_i and represents the increase/decrease of the maximum delay experienced by the network relative to the previous epoch:

$$\Delta D_i = D_{max,i} - D_{max,i-1} \tag{3}$$

ΔD_i is passed to the Window Estimator to estimate how much to send during the next epoch.

Delay Profiler

The creation and maintenance of the delay profile is used to estimate the next upcoming sending window W_{i+1} for epoch $i+1$. The delay profile can be represented as a graph (Figure 5) where the x and y axis correspond to the sending window (W_i) and the packet delay ($D_{p,i}$), respectively. In Verus, each packet p is sent as part of a sending window W_i, i.e. number of packets in flight. Verus keeps track of W_i for each sent packet and thus upon receiving an acknowledgement for packet p, the sender obtains a pair of $D_{p,i}$ and W_i and adds this data point to the delay profile.

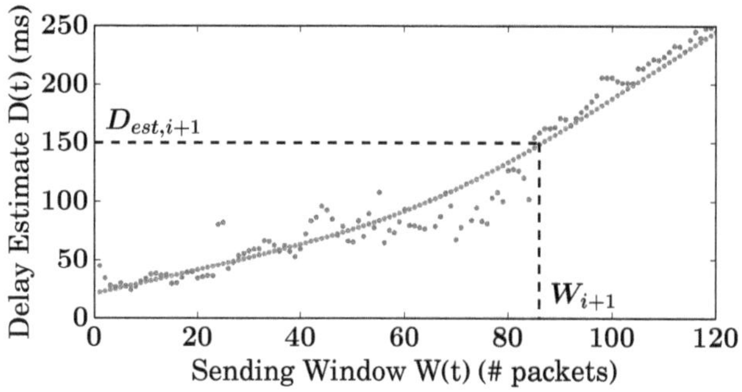

Figure 5: Example of Verus' delay profile. The green dots represent the recorded values and the red line reflects an interpolated delay profile curve.

Window Estimator

Verus uses the current change in the network delay ΔD_i to estimate the sending window W_i that is maintained over the current estimated network RTT. The sending window W_i is divided into smaller epochs with a fixed length to react quickly to channel changes. The next sending window estimate W_{i+1} is maintained over an average of the estimated network RTT. Figure 6 shows the basic time framework of Verus.

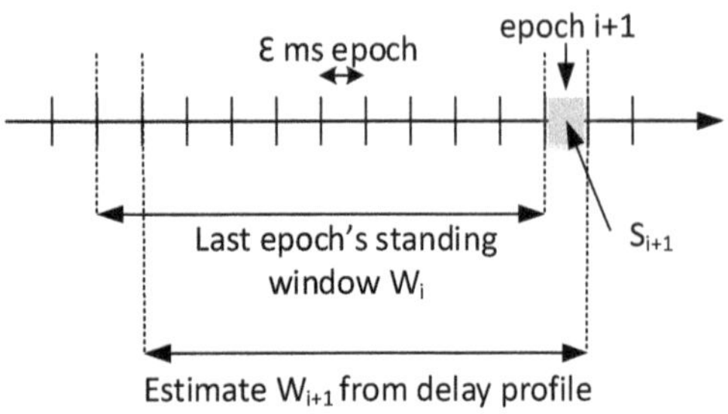

Figure 6: Verus time framework

Based on the sign of ΔD_i, Verus decides whether to increase or decrease the sending window. If ΔD_i is negative, it is an indication that the network/channel conditions are improving and thus more data can be sent to the network. If the ΔD_i is positive, the network/channel conditions may be experiencing congestion or negative changes and thus Verus should reduce the data rate. Verus estimates the delay that the network should have $D_{est,i+1}$ as follows:

$$D_{est,i+1} = \begin{cases} D_{est,i} - \delta_2 & \text{if } \frac{D_{max,i}}{D_{min}} > R \\ max[D_{min}, (D_{est,i} - \delta_1)] & \text{elif } \Delta D_i > 0 \\ D_{est,i} + \delta_2 & \text{otherwise} \end{cases} \tag{4}$$

where D_{min} is the minimum delay experienced by Verus, δ_1 and δ_2 are increment/decrement parameters, and R is the maximum tolerable ratio between D_{max} and D_{min}.[2] Verus then uses the delay estimate $D_{est,i+1}$ to find the corresponding sending window W_{i+1} on the delay profile (see Figure 5).

At the beginning of epoch $i + 1$, Verus calculates the number of packets to send during this epoch. The number of packets to be sent within the next sending window W_{i+1} are calculated as follows:

$$S_{i+1} = max[0, (W_{i+1} + \tfrac{2-n}{n-1} \cdot W_i)] \quad \text{with } n = \lceil \tfrac{RTT}{\varepsilon} \rceil \tag{5}$$

where S_{i+1} is the number of packets to send during the epoch, W_{i+1} is the estimated sending window for the future, W_i is the current sending window at the end of epoch i (i.e. the sending window at the time before making the next epoch decision), and n is the number of epochs per estimated network RTT.

Loss Handler

If Verus detects a packet loss or timeout, the sending window is reduced and the new W_{i+1} is multiplied by a multiplicative reduction factor as:

$$W_{i+1} = M \cdot W_{loss} \tag{6}$$

[2]R is used to tune the protocol trade-off between delay and throughput. We show in the evaluation section the effect of the value of R.

where, W_{loss} is the sending window in which the loss occurred, and M is the multiplicative decrease factor. We choose the sending window of the lost packet W_{loss} because that sending window was responsible for the packet loss.

Once a loss is identified and the sending window is multiplicatively decreased, Verus enters a loss recovery phase. During the loss recovery phase, the delay profile is no longer updated. The loss recovery phase is important because Verus builds its delay profile to reflect what could be sent without incurring network losses. Packets that arrive after a loss would have lower buffer delays and hence are not considered.

During the loss recovery phase and upon receiving an acknowledgement, the sending window W_{i+1} is increased by $1/(W_{i+1})$ (similar to TCP). Verus exits the loss recovery phase once acknowledgments of packets sent after the loss are received, i.e. if the protocol receives an acknowledgement with a sending window that is smaller than or equal to the current sending window. Verus also uses a timeout mechanism similar to TCP in case all packets are lost.

5. VERUS IMPLEMENTATION

Our prototype implementation of Verus consists of sender and receiver applications written in C++. The sender application runs in a multi-threaded environment and uses the real time extension library *librt*. As the underlying transport protocol, UDP is used to transmit the generated packets. A number of implementation details must be addressed in order to realize the Verus protocol in practice. These include delay profile initialization and maintenance, handling of timeouts and retransmissions, and setting of parameters.

5.1 Delay Profile Initialization and Maintenance

Verus relies heavily on the delay profile, which reflects the relationship between the network delay and the sending window without congesting the network. The initial creation of the delay profile is handled during Verus' slow start phase. Verus' slow start is similar to TCP's slow start; where the sender begins by sending a single packet towards the receiver and upon receiving an acknowledgement the sender increments the sending window by one, which leads to exponential growth of the sending window.

Verus maintains a list of sent packets and stores the sending timestamp as well as the sending window with which the packet was sent. The sender uses this information to calculate the packet RTT (i.e. delay) and records a (delay, sending window) tuple. Once one of the exit conditions for Verus slow start are met, the sender will have a number of delay/sending window tuples to build the delay profile. The delay profile is constructed from the stored tuples using the cubic spline interpolation from the *ALGLB* library.

Verus' slow start phase has two exit conditions:

- encountering a packet loss: this can be deduced from acknowledgement sequence numbers
- the RTT delay exceeds the predefined threshold: this threshold is set as N x minimum delay (e.g., N=15)

During the course of operation, the delay profile needs to be updated and maintained over time to capture channel changes. The delay profile is updated as follows: for every received acknowledgement at the sender, the delay value of the point that corresponds to the sending window of the acknowledged packet is updated with the new RTT delay. This update is performed using an Exponentially Weighted Moving Averaging (EWMA) function to allow the delay profile to evolve. Due to the high computational effort of the cubic spline interpolation, this calculation is not performed after every acknowledgement, but instead at certain intervals. In Section 5.3 we discuss reasonable update intervals in more detail.

Figure 7b illustrates how the delay profile may evolve over time. For clarity, only every fifth interpolation is shown and we restricted the channel trace to 200 s. The three curves of each color correspond to the same colored region shown in the throughput graph in Figure 7a. It can be observed that the delay profile curve changes over time with respect to the fluctuations of the channel, i.e. the smaller the available throughput is, the steeper the delay profile becomes.

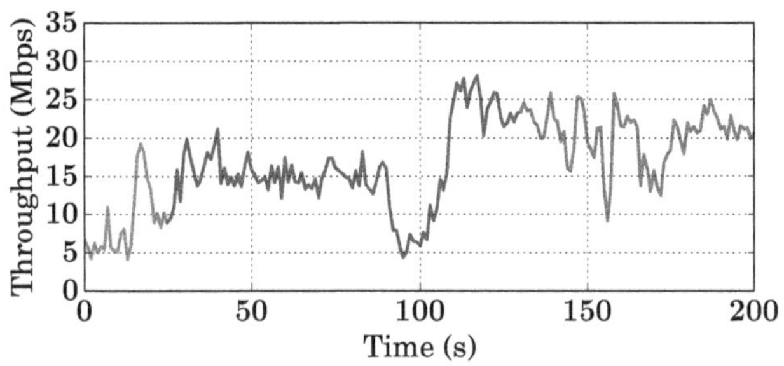

(a) Channel trace for downlink

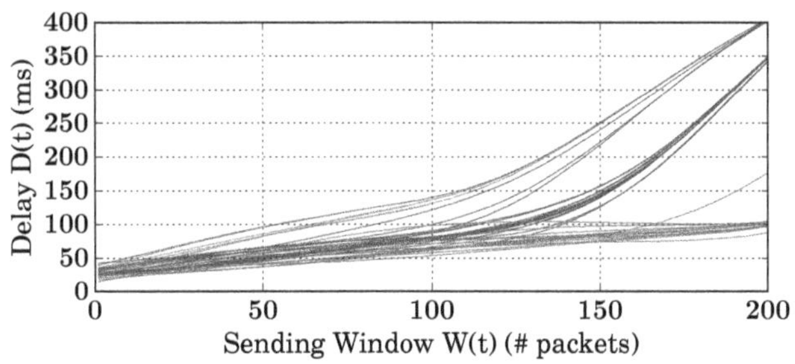

(b) Verus delay profile evolution (excluding slow start)

Figure 7: Channel trace and the corresponding Verus delay profile curve evolution

5.2 Timeouts and Retransmissions

Although Verus is a congestion avoidance protocol designed to handle the fluctuating capacities of a cellular channel, packet losses are sometimes inevitable as an intrinsic property of the cellular medium. Our current implementation of Verus is built on top of UDP. Verus uses sequence numbers to keep track of received packets and their RTTs. These sequence numbers are used to identify packet losses at the sender. To deal with packet reordering, our implementation does the following: for every missing sequence number Verus creates a timeout timer of 3*delay. If the missing packet arrives before the timer expires, no packet loss is identified; otherwise, the sending window is multiplicatively decreased and the missing packet is retransmitted.

5.3 Verus Parameter Settings

Verus makes use of a variety of parameters and the selection of these parameters influences the performance of the protocol or substantially changes the overall protocol behavior. The effects of parameter changes are mainly reflected in throughput, delay, and fairness among flows. In our sensitivity analysis we wanted to identify the specific effects of parameter settings and to understand their relation to common scenarios.

Our sensitivity analysis of Verus parameters were performed using the OPNET network simulator. In order to emulate real cellular network behavior in OPNET, we collected channel traces in uplink and downlink direction from a commercial cellular network provider (Etisalat) and replayed these channel conditions in OPNET to schedule flows under contention.

The setup for collecting the traces consists of four Android smartphones (3x Samsung Galaxy S4 and 1x Sony Xperia Z1) and one server. As the server is connected via a fiber link directly to Etisalat's backbone network so that additional delays and unwanted background traffic are minimized. All smartphones are running a native sender and receiver application to communicate with a server located in our premises. The server runs the same sender and receiver application. Both endpoints, server and smartphones, send UDP packets with an MTU size of 1400 bytes simultaneously with a constant data rate to the other endpoint. The corresponding endpoint acts as a sink and records the timestamp of each packet arrival. We use this bi-directional setup to measure downlink and uplink of the channel.

As the measurement is executed on the 3G HSPA+ cellular network, the data rate for each device is set to 5 Mbps and 2.5 Mbps for downlink and uplink, respectively. These data rates are close to the upper limits of the network, but do not necessarily reflect the maximum capacity of the cellular network. The maximum capacity of the channel is difficult to determine and depends on many factors, e.g. cross-competing traffic, mobility, and interference. We expect that by using these data rates the channel is not over-saturated and packet buffering is minimized under ideal channel conditions.

In total, we ran the measurements for seven different scenarios to capture a variety of conditions with different mobility properties. Each measurement was conducted over five minutes and all devices were started at the same time and in the same location. The seven scenarios are the following: *Campus stationary, Campus pedestrian, City stationary, City driving, Highway driving, Shopping Mall and City waterfront.* The channel traces were generated from the packet arrival timetamps at the receiver and contain inter-arrival times between consecutive packet arrivals. Using these channel traces, our parameter sensitivity analysis in OPNET focused mainly on the following parameters: epoch time (ε), the delay profile update interval, and the delta decrement (δ_1) and delta increment (δ_2).

Epoch ε

In general, cellular channels have three different effects governing the changes, some are short-term (e.g., fast-fading) and others are more long-term (path-loss and slow-fading). The epoch ε determines in which intervals Verus calculates the amount of packets to send S_{i+1}. The smaller the epoch, the faster Verus reacts to fast-fading or other sudden channel changes. Through extensive simulation we found that an epoch of 5 ms is a good value. This value causes Verus to quickly adjust the operating point on the delay profile and adapt to sudden short-term fluctuations. Larger values of ε cause Verus to adjust the sending window too slowly to respond to such fluctuations. Within a 5 ms epoch, the cellular channel does not experience larger long-term channel changes caused by path-loss or slow-fading effects. Instead, these effects are handled by the delay profile update rate as described below.

Delay Profile Updates

Path-loss and slow-fading dramatically change channel conditions, and Verus must adapt the delay profile to match these new conditions. Feedback about channel conditions continuously update the data in the delay profile. Verus re-interpolates the delay profile at fixed time intervals. Our sensitivity analysis indicates that an update interval of 1 s shows reasonable results and is being used in this work. Re-interpolation intervals at higher than 1 s values start causing Verus to miss channel changes and react slowly to slow-fading channel changes. A much smaller update interval than 1 s is too aggressive since path-loss and slow-fading do not occur at such high frequency.

Delta δ_1 and δ_2

The deltas determine how restrictive (δ_1) or aggressive (δ_2) the protocol reacts to delay changes during each epoch. The larger the values, the stronger the effects. We find through simulation that their range should between 1 ms $\leq \delta \leq$ 2 ms with the condition that $\delta_1 \leq \delta_2$. Beyond these guidelines for good Verus performance, these parameters allow Verus behavior to be tuned to the level of desired fairness when competing with other protocols. For the evaluations in this paper we use values of 1 ms for δ_1 and 2 ms for δ_2.

6. VERUS MACRO-EVALUATION

In this section, we evaluate the two main macro-level properties of the performance of the Verus protocol, namely throughput and delay characteristics. We compare Verus against Sprout [33], TCP Cubic, TCP New Reno, and TCP Vegas. We take a two-pronged approach to evaluate Verus against these flavors of TCP and Sprout: real-world and trace-driven evaluation.

In the real-world evaluation, we use mobile devices (Samsung Galaxy S4 and Sony Experia Z1 phones) to run the protocols on 3G and LTE networks. In this evaluation, we are constrained by the number of devices that we are able to simultaneously use; we also restrict the number of flows per device.

In the trace-driven evaluation, we use multiple mobile devices simultaneously connecting to 3G or LTE networks where each device is coupled with traffic generators to generate realistic network traces of the channel under different conditions. Using the procedure described in 5.3, we specifically generate an additional set of traces that capture network contention and mobility scenarios. Then we use the OPNET network simulator to compare Verus with other TCP variants [24].[3]

6.1 Real-world 3G and LTE Networks

We performed this evaluation on the Etisalat network, the largest cellular network operator in the UAE, which provides both 3G and LTE cellular network service. While Verus was running natively on the mobile devices, TCP Verus, TCP Cubic, and Sprout were executed on tethered laptops. We switched the mode of each phone to connect to the appropriate network to test both 3G and LTE. We consider multiple flows between the devices and a server with a public IP address at our university campus with high bandwidth and low network delays. To emulate contention, we simultaneously trigger competing flows between the different devices and the server. To avoid device contention issues, we limit the number of flows per device to three. Specifically, we consider the following scenarios:

1. Three phones each running three Verus flows
2. Three phones each running three Sprout flows
3. Three phones each running three Cubic flows (secure copy (scp) download)
4. Three phones each running three Vegas flows (scp download)

All experiments were performed on Etisalat's 3G and LTE network at fixed locations without mobility and at the same time (late evening in a residential area). The duration of each run was two minutes and each experiment was repeated five times. All tests were done

[3]The Sprout codebase is not compatible with the OPNET simulator, thus we compare against Sprout only in the real-world evaluations. Furthermore, we use the "sendonly" implementation of Sprout to get a fair comparison to Verus and other protocols.

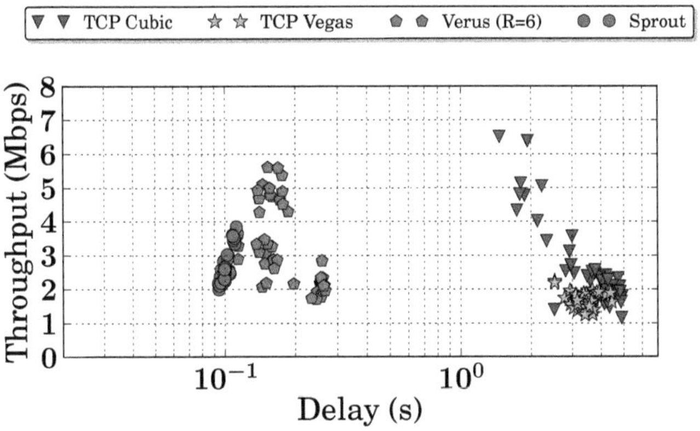

(a) 3G throughput vs. delay

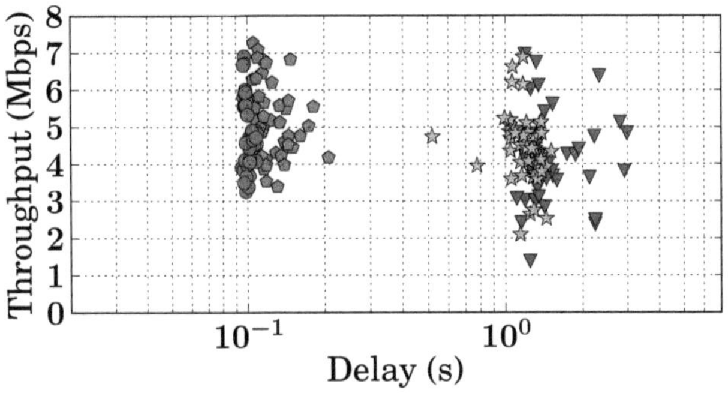

(b) LTE throughput vs. delay

Figure 8: Averaged throughput and delay of Sprout, TCP Cubic, TCP Vegas, and Verus on 3G and LTE

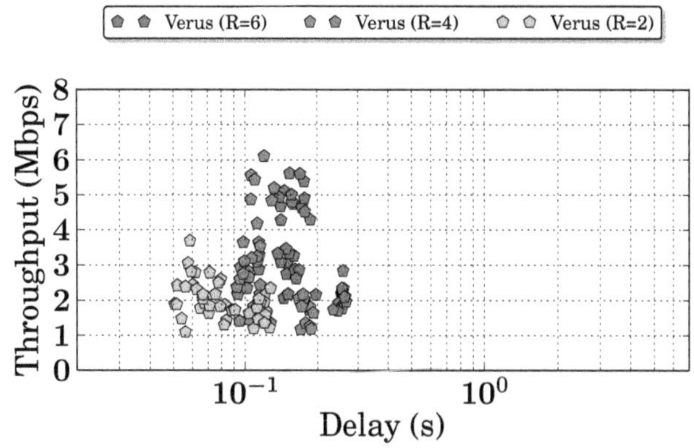

(a) 3G throughput vs. delay

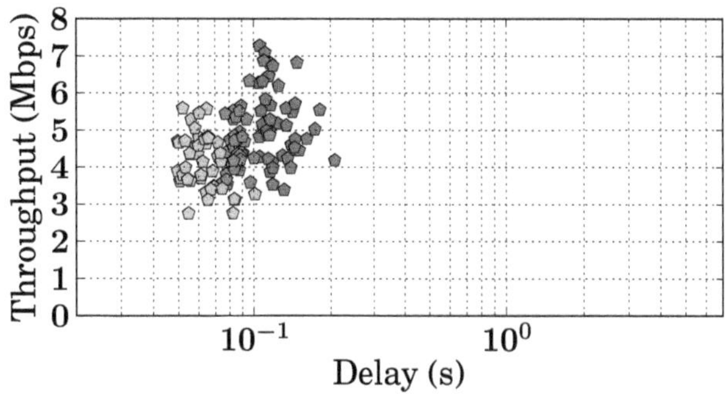

(b) LTE throughput vs. delay

Figure 9: Different values of R in Verus trade-off higher throughput and lower delay

on the downlink and the results from each flow were averaged for each experiment.

Figure 8 shows the average throughput and average delay for each of the flows across all runs on 3G and LTE. We make the following observations: The average delay observed by Verus flows is an order of magnitude lower than the average delay of TCP Cubic and TCP Vegas flows. Comparing 3G and LTE, Verus marginally outperforms TCP Cubic in terms of throughput in 3G network conditions and compares even more favorably in LTE networks. Also, in these scenarios Verus generally performs similar to Sprout with slightly higher throughput and higher delay.

For Verus we repeated the experiments for different values of the ratio R (the maximum tolerable ratio between D_{max} and D_{min}) to show how the value of R tunes Verus to different trade-offs between higher throughput and lower delay. Setting the Verus R parameter to six leads to throughputs higher than Sprout, but with slightly increased delays. Figure 9 shows the impact of the Verus R parameter on the protocol behavior. Depending on the value of R, the Verus protocol can be tuned to achieve a trade-off between a higher throughput or lower delay. By setting R to two, Verus achieves lower delay compared to Sprout with slightly lower throughput.

6.2 Trace-driven Evaluation

Traffic flows over cellular channels are not perfectly isolated and exhibit contention for radio resources. To evaluate Verus in a contention scenario with several competing flows, we rely on the OPNET simulator and use channel traces to emulate real cellular network behavior. Following the procedure in Section 5.3, we collected additional cellular channel traces to perform the evaluations in this section. The channel traces are fed into a traffic shaper and replayed upon packet arrival. In general, the traffic shaper is a modified version of a regular network router (as natively available in OPNET) and also implements a shared queue with Random Early Detection (RED) [11] queue management using the following parameters: minimum queue size 3 MBit, maximum queue size 9 MBit, and drop probability 10%.

We evaluate Verus under high contention within the OPNET network simulator for each of these channel traces to understand how Verus performs under different competing traffic scenarios in terms of throughput and delay. Additionally, our simulations show fairness properties among the flows for the different protocols. We show the results primarily for the downlink direction but the observations are similar for the uplink. Our simulations are configured to run with 2, 5, 10 and 20

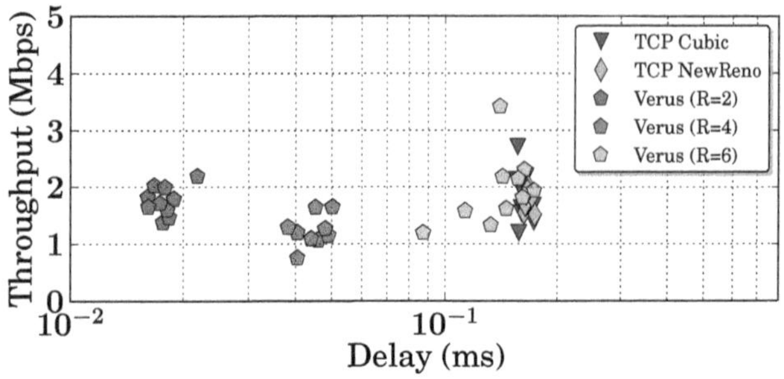

(a) Campus pedestrian

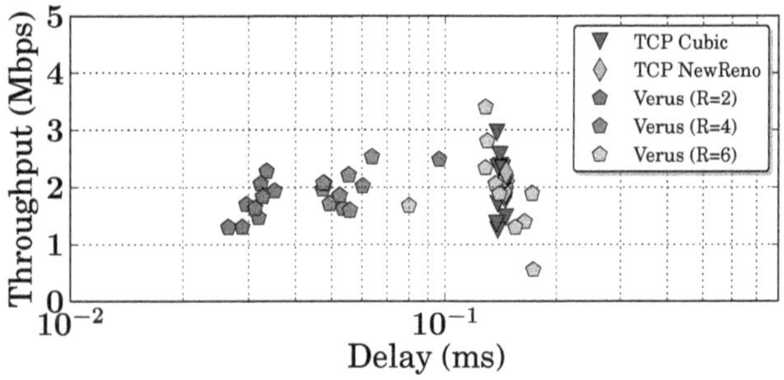

(b) Slow driving within the city with signals

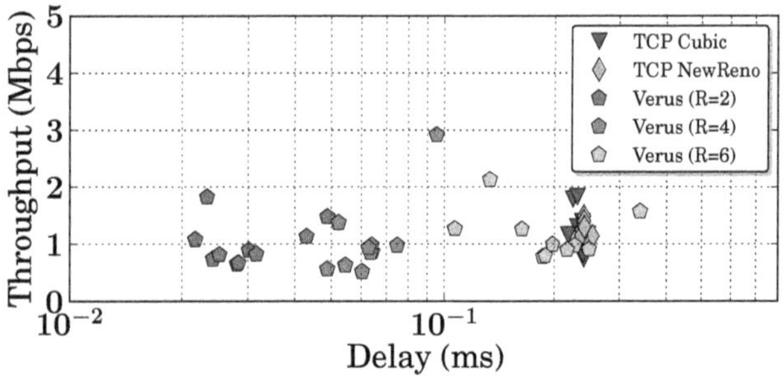

(c) Fast driving on highway

Figure 10: Delay-throughput comparison with 10 flows for different mobility patterns

simultaneous clients for TCP Cubic, TCP NewReno, and Verus. Both TCP scenarios are configured with full buffer FTP traffic and default parameters according to Linux 3.16 (TCP Cubic) and Windows 7 (TCP NewReno) configurations. Verus is configured with the parameters obtained in Section 5.3.

Figure 10a shows a scatter plot of the throughput of all the individual flows of the average delay and average throughput observed by each of the flows in a campus pedestrian environment. Overall, we observe that Verus with lower R ratio experiences an order of magnitude lower delay than TCP Cubic or TCP New Reno while the throughput of Verus is comparable to the throughput of TCP Cubic and TCP New Reno. In all these settings, TCP Cubic and TCP New Reno are slow to adapt to varying channel conditions and therefore incur high buffering delays while Verus quickly adapts to channel variations and experiences much lower buffering delays. Increasing R to six, increases throughput, but also increases delay due to additional buffering.

Mobility

Figures 10b and 10c show the same scatter plot of Verus, TCP Cubic, and TCP New Reno flows under two other mobility patterns. We observe that while the average throughput remains roughly the same, mobility has an impact on the variance of the throughput across competing TCP flows. However, even with high mobility, the variation in throughput across Verus flows is small, which is indicative of Verus being able to quickly adapt and achieves high levels of fairness despite mobility.

Fairness

To better quantify the fairness argument, we consider Jain's fairness index [17] measured as:

$$f(x_1, x_2, ..., x_n) = \frac{(\sum_{i=1}^{n} x_i)^2}{n \cdot \sum_{i=1}^{n} {x_i}^2} \quad (7)$$

where x_i is the normalized throughput of the i-th user and n is the number of clients. The fairness index always ranges from zero to one, where $\frac{1}{n}$ represents the worst case and 1 is perfect fairness. We compute Jain's fairness index over windows of one second and average these one second fairness values for the overall fairness for each protocol for comparison. Here, we vary the number of competing flows for each experiment between 2 to 20 flows. Here and in the following experiments, we set Verus' parameter $R = 2$ unless otherwise stated.

Scenario	TCP Cubic	TCP NewReno	Verus
2 Users	98.1%	89.7%	94.6%
5 Users	93.5%	86.3%	87.6%
10 Users	76.2%	83.8%	90.7%
15 Users	75.2%	83.3%	86.8%
20 Users	70.1%	82.0%	78.6%

Table 1: Jain's fairness index comparison

Table 1 shows Jain's fairness index for all three protocols. We report the average fairness index across all five different scenarios. Our results show that although TCP Cubic achieves high fairness among the scenarios with a small number of users, the fairness drops significantly under high contention (achieving about 70% fairness). In contrast, Verus shows slightly lower fairness compared to TCP Cubic for scenarios with a low number of users, while maintaining reasonable fairness at higher contention. TCP NewReno is almost consistent with the fairness it achieves across all scenarios, but achieves marginally lower fairness compared to Verus for scenarios with low number of users.

7. VERUS MICRO-EVALUATION

While the previous section detailed a macro-evaluation of Verus, in this section we focus on specific micro-evaluations of Verus to describe its fairness and adaptation properties. All the evaluations in this section are performed in a simplified network configuration consisting of a dumbbell topology with three laptops connected to an Ethernet Gigabit switch, which in turn is connected to a server. The server outgoing bandwidth is controlled through the Linux Traffic Control (tc) tool. The tool is also used to emulate delays for each of the clients, this is used to configure the RTT.

Rapidly Changing Networks

We wanted to measure how quickly Verus can adapt to high channel variations. This experiment is configured so that the network condition would change suddenly. Every five seconds the whole network parameters, i.e. link capacity, network RTT, and loss rate, are changed.

We have considered two variations of the experiment: where in the first version the network link capacity varied between 10 Mbps and 100 Mbps. whereas, in the second version, the link capacity varied between 2 Mbps and 20 Mbps. The reason behind the two versions was because the Sprout implementation bandwidth is capped at 18 Mbps. In both scenarios, the RTT was varied between 10 ms and 100 ms, and the loss rate between 0% and 1%.

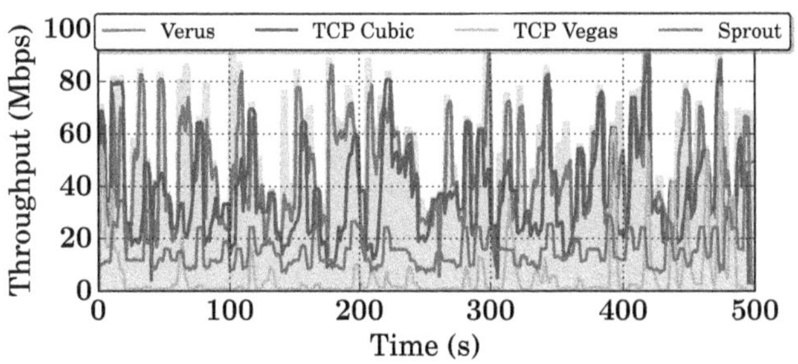

(a) Scenario I

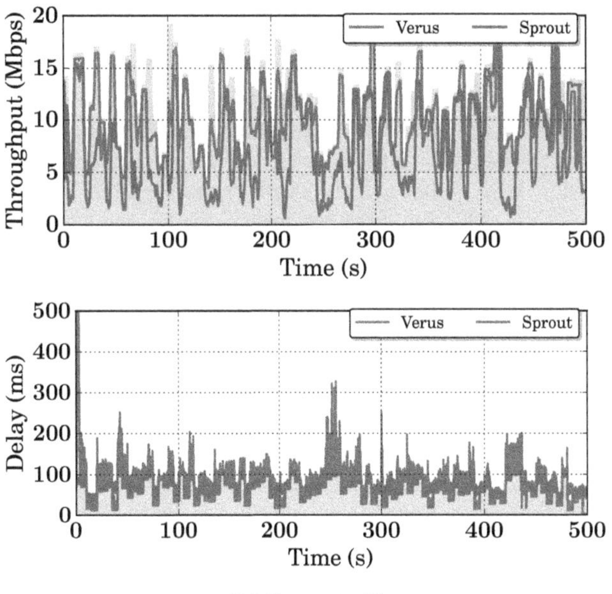

(b) Scenario II

Figure 11: Rapidly changing network evaluations under two different link capacities

Figure 11a shows the throughput over time for the first experiment where the gray shaded area represents the available link capacity. We observe that Verus outperforms the other protocols and manages to adapt very quickly to the rapid network changes. Understandably, Sprout does not perform well because of the bandwidth cap introduced by the Sprout implementation. Figure 11b shows the throughput and delay results of Verus compared to Sprout with a lower link capacity variation up to 20 Mbps. Here, we observe that Sprout performs better than before, but Verus still achieves higher throughput on average than Sprout.

Newly Arriving Flows

To understand the impact of the arrival of new flows, we consider a situation where eight competing Verus flows share a 90 Mbps bottleneck link. The experiment is configured so that every 30 seconds a new Verus flow starts, thus increasing the number of competing flows over time. Figure 12 shows the throughput of seven Verus clients over time. During the first 30 seconds when only one Verus flow is active, the flow is fully utilizing the 90 Mbps link. We observe that Verus quickly adapts to the arrival of new flows and also reaches good fairness across competing Verus flows when new flows arrive and depart.

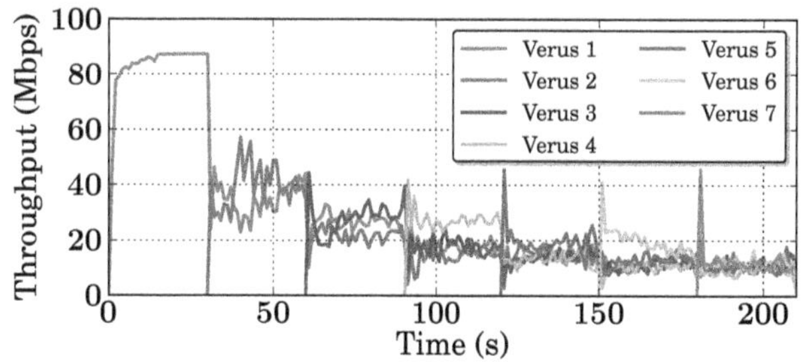

Figure 12: Verus intra-fairness among seven flows

Varying RTTs

To understand the impact of varying RTTs on Verus flows, we consider a simple experiment where three competing Verus flows with three different RTTs of 20 ms, 50 ms and 100 ms share a 60 Mbps bottleneck link. Figure 13 shows the temporal variation in the throughput of the different Verus flows. We observe that the throughput of Verus flows is independent of the RTT of the flows which is indicative that the Verus fairness model is close to Max-Min fairness. Given that delay-based protocols use non-linear control mechanisms, these protocols are harder to model analytically than conventional window-based protocols. We plan to develop a model to more fully characterize the behavior of Verus and other delay-based control protocols in future work.

Verus vs. TCP

One crucial issue when a new congestion control protocol is introduced is fairness to legacy TCP. We investigated how several Verus flows share an Ethernet bottleneck with several other TCP Cubic flows (since TCP

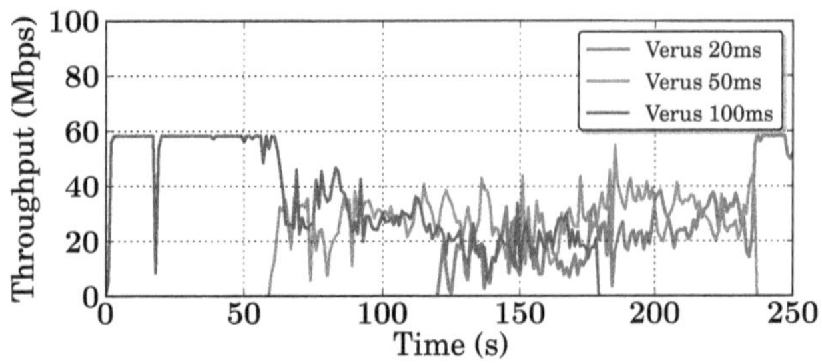

Figure 13: Verus intra-fairness with 3 different RTTs

Cubic is currently used as the standard in most TCP installations). The experiment consisted of three Verus and three TCP Cubic flows sharing a link capacity of 60 Mbps.

At the beginning of the experiment, every 30 seconds one new Verus flow is added to the network. Once all three Verus flows are present, a new TCP Cubic flow is added to the network every 30 seconds (at time 90, 120 and 150 seconds). The throughput comparison over time is shown in Figure 14. Our results show that Verus shares the bottleneck capacity equally with TCP Cubic.

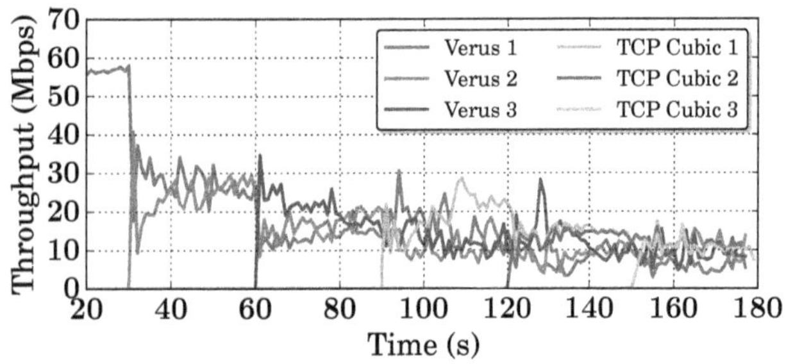

Figure 14: Verus fairness vs. TCP Cubic

Effect of Verus Delay Curve

In order to evaluate the effect of the delay profile curve, we compared two scenarios: one where the delay profile curve would update normally every second, and the second where Verus uses the first curve it generates without updating it. Figure 15 shows the results of this simulation for all of our five different collected traces. The results clearly show that updating the curve has an impact on performance due to the fact that the cellular channel changes and Verus needs to update its operating point on the curve based on these changes.

Short Flows

Short flows are a dominant feature in normal network traffic due to the nature of the commonly retrieved content. Although Verus is not specifically designed to cope with short flows, it is naturally able to handle short connections. When considering a short flow that does not progress beyond slow start, Verus behaves like legacy TCP due to the same slow start mechanism. After slow start, Verus uses the recorded delay profile to adapt quickly as it does with channel changes.

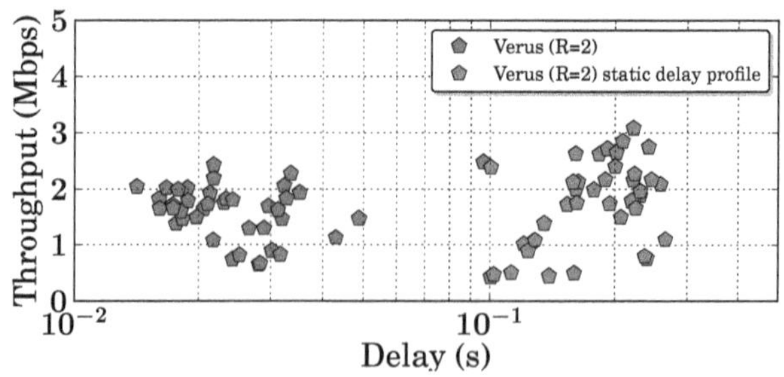

Figure 15: Verus with and without updating delay curve

8. CONCLUSIONS

In this paper, we presented Verus, an adaptive exploration congestion control protocol that is tailored for unpredictable cellular networks. Through continuous exploration using delay measurements and a delay profile, Verus adapts to both rapidly changing cellular conditions and to competing traffic. We tested Verus under a variety of experimental scenarios through simulation and real-world experiments over 3G and LTE networks. We show that in cellular networks Verus achieves higher throughput than TCP Cubic while maintaining a dramatically lower end-to-end delay, particularly over LTE. Verus also outperforms very recent congestion control protocols for cellular networks like Sprout under rapidly changing network conditions. In the future, we plan to experiment with other rapid adaptation mechanisms to theoretically characterize the behavior of Verus and develop a kernel implementation of Verus.

9. ACKNOWLEDGMENTS

We would like to thank Ali Raza for his help running measurements and experiments. We would also like to thank our shepherd Sachin Katti and the anonymous reviewers for their valuable feedback. We also want to extend our gratitude to Keith Winstein for his help with Sprout. Thomas Pötsch has been funded by the International Graduate School for Dynamics in Logistics, University of Bremen, Germany. We thank the the NYU Abu Dhabi Research institute and the Center for Technology and Economic Development (CTED) for supporting Lakshminarayanan Subramanian on this research work.

10. REFERENCES

[1] M. Alizadeh, A. Greenberg, D. A. Maltz, J. Padhye, P. Patel, B. Prabhakar, S. Sengupta, and M. Sridharan. DCTCP: Efficient Packet Transport for the Commoditized Data Center. *ACM SIGCOMM*, January 2010.

[2] D. Bansal and H. Balakrishnan. Binomial congestion control algorithms. In *Proceedings of 20th Conference of the IEEE Computer and Communications Societies. INFOCOM 2001*, Volume 2, 2001.

[3] L. S. Brakmo, S. W. O'Malley, and L. L. Peterson. *TCP Vegas: New techniques for congestion detection and avoidance*, volume 24. ACM, 1994.

[4] W. chang Feng, K. G. Shin, D. D. Kandlur, and D. Saha. The BLUE active queue management algorithms. *IEEE/ACM TRANS. NETWORKING*, pages 513–528, 2002.

[5] D. Cox and L.-R. Dependence. a review. *Statistics: An Appraisal, HA David and HT David (Eds.), The Iowa State University Press, Ames, Iowa*, pages 55–74, 1984.

[6] M. Dong, Q. Li, D. Zarchy, B. Godfrey, and M. Schapira. PCC: Re-architecting congestion control for consistent high performance. *12th USENIX Symposium on Networked Systems Design and Implementation (NSDI)*, 2015.

[7] T. Ekman. *Prediction of Mobile Radio Channels - Modeling and Design.* PhD thesis, Signals and Systems, Uppsala University, Sweden, 2002.

[8] S. Floyd. TCP and Explicit Congestion Notification. *SIGCOMM Comput. Commun. Rev.*, 24(5), Oct. 1994.

[9] S. Floyd, M. Handley, J. Padhye, and J. Widmer. *Equation-based congestion control for unicast applications*, volume 30. ACM, 2000.

[10] S. Floyd and V. Jacobson. Random early detection gateways for congestion avoidance. *IEEE/ACM Transactions on Networking*, 1(4), 1993.

[11] S. Floyd and V. Jacobson. Random early detection gateways for congestion avoidance. *IEEE/ACM Transactions on Networking*, 1(4):397–413, 1993.

[12] J. Gettys. Bufferbloat: Dark Buffers in the Internet. *Internet Computing, IEEE*, 15(3), May 2011.

[13] S. Ha, I. Rhee, and L. Xu. CUBIC: A New TCP-friendly High-speed TCP Variant. *SIGOPS Oper. Syst. Rev.*, 42(5), July 2008.

[14] T. Henderson, S. Floyd, A. Gurtov, and Y. Nishida. The NewReno modification to TCP's fast recovery algorithm, April 2012. RFC6582.

[15] J. Huang, F. Qian, Y. Guo, Y. Zhou, Q. Xu, Z. M. Mao, S. Sen, and O. Spatscheck. An in-depth study of LTE: effect of network protocol and application behavior on performance. In *ACM SIGCOMM 2013 Conference*, Hong Kong, China, August 12-16 2013.

[16] V. Jacobson. Congestion avoidance and control. In *Symposium Proceedings on Communications Architectures and Protocols*, SIGCOMM '88, pages 314–329, New York, NY, USA, 1988. ACM.

[17] R. Jain. *Art of Computer Systems Performance Analysis Techniques for Experimental Design Measurements Simulation and Modeling.* John Wiley & Sons, May 1991.

[18] H. Jiang, Y. Wang, K. Lee, and I. Rhee. Tackling Bufferbloat in 3G/4G Networks. In *Proceedings of the ACM Conference on Internet Measurement Conference (IMC)*, 2012.

[19] S. Kunniyur and R. Srikant. Analysis and Design of an Adaptive Virtual Queue (AVQ) Algorithm for Active Queue Management. In *ACM SIGCOMM*, 2001.

[20] W. Lum Tan, F. Lam, and W. Cheong Lau. An Empirical Study on 3G Network Capacity and Performance. In *Proceedings of the 26th IEEE International Conference on Computer Communications. INFOCOM 2007.*, May 2007.

[21] R. Mittal, J. Sherry, R. Ratnasamy, and S. Shenker. Recursively Cautious Congestion Control. In *11th USENIX Symposium on Networked Systems Design and Implementation (NSDI 14)*, pages 373–385, Seattle, WA, Apr. 2014. USENIX Association.

[22] K. Nichols and V. Jacobson. Controlling Queue Delay. *Queue*, 10(5), May 2012.

[23] A. Nikravesh, D. R. Choffnes, E. Katz-Bassett, Z. M. Mao, and M. Welsh. Mobile Network Performance from User Devices: A Longitudinal, Multidimensional Analysis. In M. Faloutsos and A. Kuzmanovic, editors, *Passive and Active Measurement - 15th International Conference, PAM 2014, Los Angeles, CA, USA, March 10-11, 2014, Proceedings*, pages 12–22. Springer, 2014.

[24] OPNET Modeler. http://www.opnet.com.

[25] P. Rong, B. Prabhakar, and K. Psounis. CHOKe - a stateless active queue management scheme for approximating fair bandwidth allocation. In *Proceedings of 19th Conference of the IEEE Computer and Communications Societies. INFOCOM 2000.*, volume 2, 2000.

[26] R. Schoenen, A. Otyakmaz, and Z. Xu. Resource Allocation and Scheduling in FDD Multihop Cellular Systems. In *ICC Workshops 2009. IEEE International Conference on*, pages 1–6, June 2009.

[27] S. Shalunov. Low extra delay background transport. Internet-draft, Internet Engineering Task Force, 2010.

[28] A. Sivaraman, K. Winstein, P. Thaker, and H. Balakrishnan. An Experimental Study of the Learnability of Congestion Control. In *ACM SIGCOMM 2014*, Chicago, IL, August 2014.

[29] K. Tan, J. Song, Q. Zhang, and M. Sridharan. A compound TCP approach for high-speed and long distance networks. In *Proceedings of 25th Conference of the IEEE Computer and Communications Societies. INFOCOM*, 2006.

[30] A. Venkataramani, R. Kokku, and M. Dahlin. TCP Nice: A mechanism for background transfers. *ACM SIGOPS Operating Systems Review*, 36(SI), 2002.

[31] K. Winstein and H. Balakrishnan. End-to-end Transmission Control by Modeling Uncertainty About the Network State. In *Proceedings of the 10th ACM Workshop on Hot Topics in Networks*, HotNets-X, pages 19:1–19:6, New York, NY, USA, 2011. ACM.

[32] K. Winstein and H. Balakrishnan. TCP Ex Machina: Computer-generated Congestion Control. In *Proceedings of the ACM SIGCOMM 2013 Conference*, 2013.

[33] K. Winstein, A. Sivaraman, and H. Balakrishnan. Stochastic forecasts achieve high throughput and low delay over cellular networks. In *Proceedings of the 10th USENIX conference on Networked Systems Design and Implementation*, 2013.

[34] Y. Xia, L. Subramanian, I. Stoica, and S. Kalyanaraman. One More Bit is Enough. SIGCOMM 2005, 2005.

[35] Y. Zaki, J. Chen, T. Pötsch, T. Ahmad, and L. Subramanian. Dissecting Web Latency in Ghana. In *Proceedings of the ACM Internet Measurement Conference (IMC)*, Vancouver, BC, Canada, 2014.

Congestion Control for Large-Scale RDMA Deployments

Yibo Zhu[1,3] Haggai Eran[2] Daniel Firestone[1] Chuanxiong Guo[1] Marina Lipshteyn[1]
Yehonatan Liron[2] Jitendra Padhye[1] Shachar Raindel[2] Mohamad Haj Yahia[2] Ming Zhang[1]

[1]Microsoft [2]Mellanox [3]U. C. Santa Barbara

ABSTRACT

Modern datacenter applications demand high throughput (40Gbps) and ultra-low latency (< 10 μs per hop) from the network, with low CPU overhead. Standard TCP/IP stacks cannot meet these requirements, but Remote Direct Memory Access (RDMA) can. On IP-routed datacenter networks, RDMA is deployed using RoCEv2 protocol, which relies on Priority-based Flow Control (PFC) to enable a drop-free network. However, PFC can lead to poor application performance due to problems like head-of-line blocking and unfairness. To alleviates these problems, we introduce DCQCN, an end-to-end congestion control scheme for RoCEv2. To optimize DCQCN performance, we build a fluid model, and provide guidelines for tuning switch buffer thresholds, and other protocol parameters. Using a 3-tier Clos network testbed, we show that DCQCN dramatically improves throughput and fairness of RoCEv2 RDMA traffic. DCQCN is implemented in Mellanox NICs, and is being deployed in Microsoft's datacenters.

CCS Concepts

•**Networks** → **Transport protocols;**

Keywords

Datacenter transport; RDMA; PFC; ECN; congestion control

1. INTRODUCTION

Datacenter applications like cloud storage [16] need high bandwidth (40Gbps or more) to meet rising customer demand. Traditional TCP/IP stacks cannot be used at such speeds, since they have very high CPU overhead [29]. The brutal economics of cloud services business dictates that CPU usage that cannot be monetized should be minimized: a core spent on supporting high TCP throughput is a core that cannot be sold as a VM. Other applications such as distributed memory caches [10, 30] and large-scale machine learning demand ultra-low latency (less than 10 μs per hop) message transfers. Traditional TCP/IP stacks have far higher latency [10].

We are deploying Remote Direct Memory Access (RDMA) technology in Microsoft's datacenters to provide ultra-low latency and high throughput to applications, with very low CPU overhead. With RDMA, network interface cards (NICs) transfer data in and out of pre-registered memory buffers at both end hosts. The networking protocol is implemented entirely on the NICs, bypassing the host networking stack. The bypass significantly reduces CPU overhead and overall latency. To simplify design and implementation, the protocol assumes a lossless networking fabric.

While the HPC community has long used RDMA in special-purpose clusters [11, 24, 26, 32, 38], deploying RDMA on a large scale in modern, IP-routed datacenter networks presents a number of challenges. One key challenge is the need for a congestion control protocol that can operate efficiently in a high-speed, lossless environment, and that can be implemented on the NIC.

We have developed a protocol, called Datacenter QCN (DCQCN) for this purpose. DCQCN builds upon the congestion control components defined in the RoCEv2 standard. DCQCN is implemented in Mellanox NICs, and is currently being deployed in Microsoft's datacenters.

To understand the need for DCQCN, it is useful to point out that historically, RDMA was deployed using InfiniBand (IB) [19, 21] technology. IB uses a custom networking stack, and purpose-built hardware. The IB link layer (L2) uses hop-by-hop, credit-based flow control to prevent packet drops due to buffer overflow. The lossless L2 allows the IB transport protocol (L4) to be simple and highly efficient. Much of the IB protocol stack is implemented on the NIC. IB supports RDMA with so-called single-sided operations, in which a server registers a memory buffer with its NIC, and clients read (write) from (to) it, without further involvement of the server's CPU.

However, the IB networking stack cannot be easily de-

SIGCOMM '15, August 17–21, 2015, London, United Kingdom
© 2015 ACM. ISBN 978-1-4503-3542-3/15/08...$15.00
DOI: http://dx.doi.org/10.1145/2785956.2787484

ployed in modern datacenters. Modern datacenters are built with IP and Ethernet technologies, and the IB stack is incompatible with these. DC operators are reluctant to deploy and manage two separate networks within the same datacenter. Thus, to enable RDMA over Ethernet and IP networks, the RDMA over Converged Ethernet (RoCE) [20] standard, and its successor RoCEv2 [22] have been defined. RoCEv2 retains the IB transport layer, but replaces IB networking layer (L3) with IP and UDP encapsulation, and replaces IB L2 with Ethernet. The IP header is needed for routing, while the UDP header is needed for ECMP [15].

To enable efficient operation, like IB, RoCEv2 must also be deployed over a lossless L2. To this end, RoCE is deployed using Priority-based Flow Control (PFC) [18]. PFC allows an Ethernet switch to avoid buffer overflow by forcing the immediate upstream entity (either another switch or a host NIC) to pause data transmission. However, PFC is a coarse-grained mechanism. It operates at port (or, port plus priority) level, and does not distinguish between flows. This can cause congestion-spreading, leading to poor performance [1, 37].

The fundamental solution to PFC's limitations is a flow-level congestion control protocol. In our environment, the protocol must meet the following requirements: (i) function over lossless, L3 routed, datacenter networks, (ii) incur low CPU overhead on end hosts, and (iii) provide hyper-fast start in the common case of no congestion. Current proposals for congestion control in DC networks do not meet all our requirements. For example, QCN [17] does not support L3 networks. DCTCP [2] and iWarp [35] include a slow start phase, which can result in poor performance for bursty storage workloads. DCTCP and TCP-Bolt [37] are implemented in software, and can have high CPU overhead.

Since none of the current proposals meet all our requirements, we have designed DCQCN. DCQCN is an end-to-end congestion control protocol for RoCEv2, to enable deployment of RDMA in large, IP-routed datacenter networks. DCQCN requires only the standard RED [13] and ECN [34] support from the datacenter switches. The rest of the protocol functionality is implemented on the end host NICs. DCQCN provides fast convergence to fairness, achieves high link utilization, ensures low queue buildup, and low queue oscillations.

The paper is organized as follows. In §2 we present evidence to justify the need for DCQCN. The detailed design of DCQCN is presented in §3, along with a brief summary of hardware implementation. In §4 we show how to set the PFC and ECN buffer thresholds to ensure correct operation of DCQCN. In §5 we describe a fluid model of DCQCN, and use it to tune protocol parameters. In §6, we evaluate the performance of DCQCN using a 3-tier testbed and traces from our datacenters. Our evaluation shows that DCQCN dramatically improves throughput and fairness of RoCEv2 RDMA traffic. In some scenarios, it allows us to handle as much as 16x more user traffic. Finally, in §7, we discuss practical issues such as non-congestion packet losses.

2. THE NEED FOR DCQCN

To justify the need for DCQCN, we will show that TCP stacks cannot provide high bandwidth with low CPU overhead and ultra-low latency, while RDMA over RoCEv2 can. Next, we will show that PFC can hurt performance of RoCEv2. Finally, we will argue that existing solutions to cure PFC's ills are not suitable for our needs.

2.1 Conventional TCP stacks perform poorly

We now compare throughput, CPU overhead and latency of RoCEv2 and conventional TCP stacks. These experiments use two machines (Intel Xeon E5-2660 2.2GHz, 16 core, 128GB RAM, 40Gbps NICs, Windows Server 2012R2) connected via a 40Gbps switch.

Throughput and CPU utilization: To measure TCP throughput, we use Iperf [46] customized for our environment. Specifically, we enable LSO [47], RSS [49], and zero-copy operations and use 16 threads. To measure RDMA throughput, we use a custom tool that uses IB READ operation to transfer data. With RDMA, a single thread saturates the link.

Figure 1(a) shows that TCP has high CPU overhead. For example, with 4MB message size, to drive full throughput, TCP consumes, on average, over 20% CPU cycles across all cores. At smaller message sizes, TCP cannot saturate the link as CPU becomes the bottleneck. Marinos et.al. [29] have reported similarly poor TCP performance for Linux and FreeBSD. Even the user-level stack they propose consumes over 20% CPU cycles. In contrast, the CPU utilization of the RDMA client is under 3%, even for small message sizes. The RDMA server, as expected, consumes almost no CPU cycles.

Latency: Latency is the key metric for small transfers. We now compare the average user-level latency of transferring a 2K message, using TCP and RDMA. To minimize TCP latency, the connections were pre-established and warmed, and Nagle was disabled. Latency was measured using a high resolution ($\leq 1\ \mu s$) timer [48]. There was no other traffic on the network.

Figure 1(c) shows that TCP latency (25.4 μs) is significantly higher than RDMA (1.7 μs for Read/Write and 2.8 μs for Send). Similar TCP latency has reported in [10] for Windows, and in [27] for Linux.

2.2 PFC has limitations

RoCEv2 needs PFC to enable a drop-free Ethernet fabric. PFC prevents buffer overflow on Ethernet switches and NICs. The switches and NICs track ingress queues. When the queue exceeds a certain threshold, a PAUSE message is sent to the upstream entity. The uplink entity then stops sending on that link till it gets an RESUME message. PFC specifies upto eight priority classes. PAUSE/RESUME messages specify the priority class they apply to.

The problem is that the PAUSE mechanism operates on a per port (and priority) basis – not on a per-flow basis. This can lead to head-of-line blocking problems; resulting in poor performance for individual flows. We now illustrate

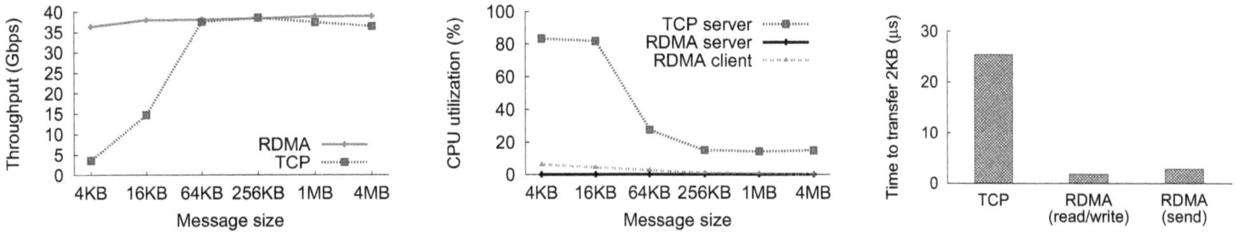

(a) Mean Throughput (b) Mean CPU Utilization (c) Mean Latency

Figure 1: Throughput, CPU consumption and latency of TCP and RDMA

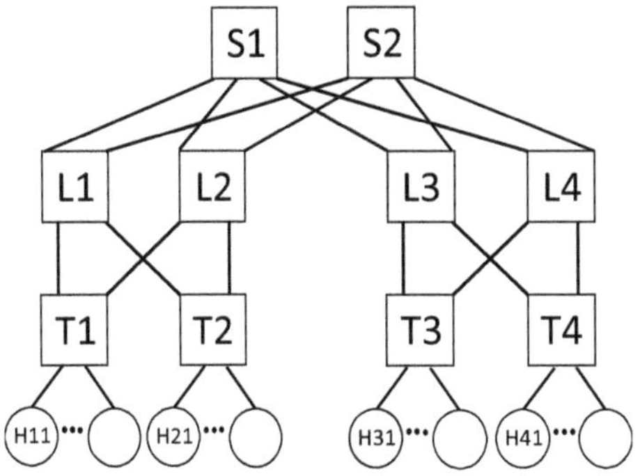

Figure 2: Testbed topology. All links are 40Gbps. All switches are Arista 7050QX32. There are four ToRs (T1-T4), four leaves (L1-L4) and two spines (S1-S2). Each ToR represents a different IP subnet. Routing and ECMP is done via BGP. Servers have multiple cores, large RAMs, and 40Gbps NICs.

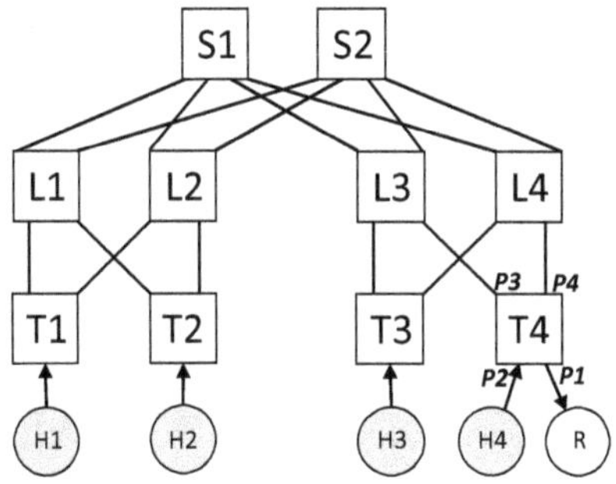

(a) Topology

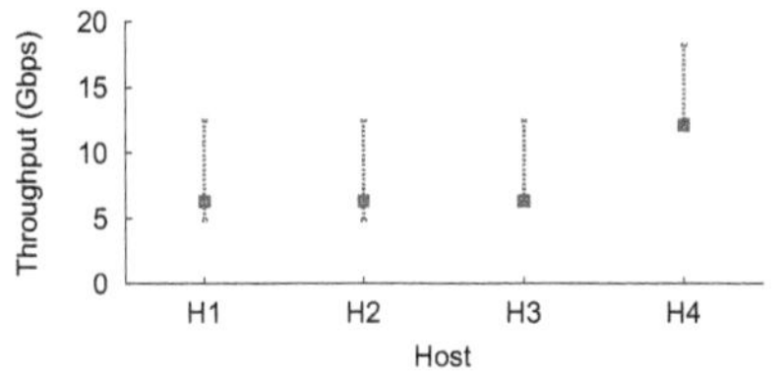

(b) Throughput of individual senders

Figure 3: PFC Unfairness

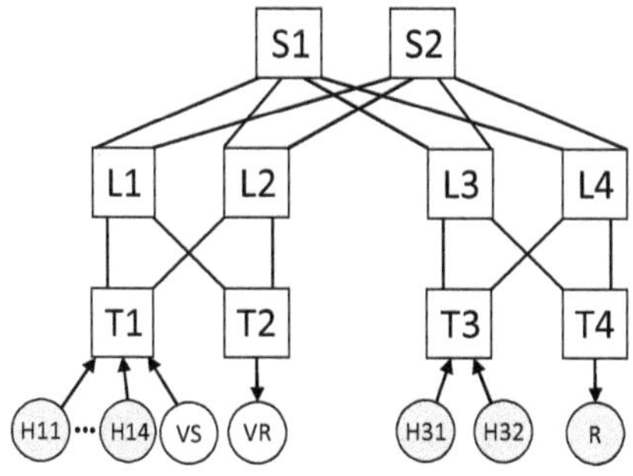

(a) Topology

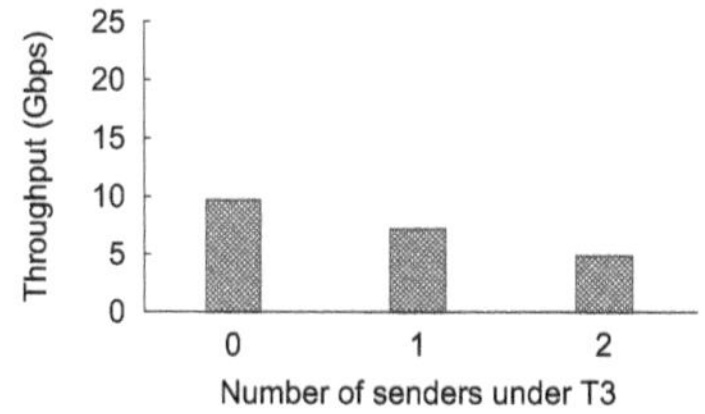

(b) Median throughput of victim flow

Figure 4: Victim flow problem

the problems using a 3-tier testbed (Figure 2) representative of modern datacenter networks.

Unfairness: Consider Figure 3(a). Four senders (H1-H4) send data to the single receiver (R) using RDMA WRITE operation. All senders use the same priority class. Ideally, the four senders should equally share bottleneck link (T4 to R). However, with PFC, there is unfairness. When queue starts building up on T4, it pauses incoming links (ports P2-P4). However, P2 carries just one flow (from H4), while P3 and P4 may carry multiple flows since H1, H2 and H3 must share these two ports, depending on how ECMP maps the flows. Thus, H4 receives higher throughput than H1-H3. This is known as the parking lot problem [14].

This is shown in Figure 3(b), which shows the min, median and max throughput achieved by H1-H4, measured over 1000 4MB data transfers. H4 gets as much as 20Gbps throughput, e.g. when ECMP maps all of H1-H3 to either P3 or P4. H4's minimum throughput is higher than the maximum throughput of H1-H3.

Victim flow: Because PAUSE frames can have a cascading effect, a flow can be hurt by congestion that is not even on its path. Consider Figure 4(a). Four senders (H11-H14), send data to R. In addition, we have a "victim flow" – VS sending to VR. Figure 4(b) shows the median throughput (250 transfers of 250MB each) of the victim flow.

When there are no senders under T3, in the median case (two of H11-H14 map to T1-L1, others to T1-L2. Each of H11-H14 gets 10Gbps throughput. VS maps to one of T1's uplinks), one might expect VS to get 20Gbps throughput. However, we see that it only gets 10Gbps. This is due to cascading PAUSEs. As T4 is the bottleneck of H11-H14 incast, it ends up PAUSEing its incoming links. This in turn leads to L3 and L4 to pause their incoming links, and so forth. Eventually, L1 and L2 end up pausing T1's uplinks to them, and T1 is forced to PAUSE the senders. The flows on T1 that use these uplinks are equally affected by these PAUSEs, regardless of their destinations – this is also known as the head-of-the-line blocking problem.

The problem gets worse as we start senders H31 and H32 that also send to R. We see that the median throughput further falls from 10Gbps to 4.5Gbps, even though no path from H31 and H32 to R has any links in common with the path between VS and VR. This happens because H31 and H32 compete with H11-H14 on L3 and L4, make them PAUSE S1 and S2 longer, and eventually make T1 PAUSE senders longer.

Summary: These experiments show that flows in RoCEv2 deployments may see lower throughput and/or high variability due to PFC's congestion-spreading characteristics.

2.3 Existing proposals are inadequate

A number of proposals have tried to address PFC's limitations. Some have argued that ECMP can mitigate the problem by spreading traffic on multiple links. Experiments in previous section show that this is not always the case. The PFC standard itself includes a notion of priorities to address the head-of-the-line blocking problem. However, the standard supports only 8 priority classes, and both scenarios shown above can be made arbitrarily worse by expanding the topology and adding more senders. Moreover, flows within the same class will still suffer from PFC's limitations.

The fundamental solution to the PFC's problems is to use flow-level congestion control. If appropriate congestion control is applied on a per-flow basis, PFC will be rarely triggered, and thus the problems described earlier in this section will be avoided.

The Quantized Congestion Notification (QCN) [17] standard was defined for this purpose. QCN enables flow-level congestion control within an L2 domain. Flows are defined using source/destination MAC address and a flow id field. A switch computes a congestion metric upon each packet arrival. Its value depends on the difference between the instantaneous queue size and the desired equilibrium queue size, along with other factors. The switch then probabilistically (probability depends on the severity of the congestion) sends the quantized value of the congestion metric as feedback to the source of the arriving packet. The source reduces its sending rate in response to congestion feedback. Since no feedback is sent if there is no congestion, the sender increases its sending rate using internal timers and counters.

QCN cannot be used in IP-routed networks because the definition of a flow is based entirely on L2 addresses. In IP-routed networks the original Ethernet header is not preserved as the packet travels through the network. Thus a congested switch cannot determine the target to send the congestion feedback to.

We considered extending the QCN protocol to IP-routed networks. However, this is not trivial to implement. At minimum, extending QCN to IP-routed networks requires using the IP five-tuple as flow identifier, and adding IP and UDP headers to the congestion notification packet to enable it to reach the right destination. Implementing this requires hardware changes to both the NICs and the switches. Making changes to the switches is especially problematic, as the QCN functionality is deeply integrated into the ASICs. It usually takes months, if not years for ASIC vendors to implement, validate and release a new switch ASIC. Thus, updating the chip design was not an option for us.

In §8 we will discuss why other proposals such as TCP-Bolt [37] and iWarp [35] do not meet our needs. Since the existing proposals are not adequate, for our purpose, we propose DCQCN.

3. THE DCQCN ALGORITHM

DCQCN is a rate-based, end-to-end congestion protocol, that builds upon QCN [17] and DCTCP [2]. Most of the DCQCN functionality is implemented in the NICs.

As mentioned earlier, we had three core requirements for DCQCN: (i) ability to function over lossless, L3 routed, datacenter networks, (ii) low CPU overhead and (iii) hyper-fast start in the common case of no congestion. In addition, we also want DCQCN to provide fast convergence to fair bandwidth allocation, avoid oscillations around the stable point, maintain low queue length, and ensure high link utilization.

There were also some practical concerns: we could not demand any custom functionality from the switches, and since the protocol is implemented in NIC, we had to be mindful of implementation overhead and complexity.

The DCQCN algorithm consists of the sender (reaction point (RP)), the switch (congestion point (CP)), and the receiver, (notification point (NP)).

3.1 Algorithm

CP Algorithm: The CP algorithm is same as DCTCP. At an egress queue, an arriving packet is ECN [34]-marked if the queue length exceeds a threshold. This is accomplished using RED [13] functionality (Figure 5) supported on all modern switches. To mimic DCTCP, we can set $K_{min} = K_{max} = K$, and $P_{max} = 1$. Later, we will see that this is not the optimal setting.

NP Algorithm: ECN-marked packets arriving at NP indicate congestion in the network. NP conveys this information back to the sender. The RoCEv2 standard defines explicit Congestion Notification Packets (CNP) [19] for this purpose. The NP algorithm specifies how and when CNPs should be generated.

The algorithm follows the state machine in Figure 6 for each flow. If a marked packet arrives for a flow, and no CNP has been sent for the flow in last N microseconds, a CNP is sent immediately. Then, the NIC generates at most one CNP packet every N microseconds for the flow, if any packet that arrives within that time window was marked. We use $N = 50\mu s$ in our deployment. Processing a marked packet, and generating the CNP are expensive operations, so we minimize the activity for each marked packet. We discuss the implications in §5.

RP Algorithm: When an RP (i.e. the flow sender) gets a CNP, it reduces its current rate (R_C) and updates the value of the rate reduction factor, α, like DCTCP, and remembers current rate as target rate (R_T) for later recovery. The values are updated as follows:[1]

$$\begin{aligned} R_T &= R_C, \\ R_C &= R_C(1 - \alpha/2), \\ \alpha &= (1 - g)\alpha + g, \end{aligned} \tag{1}$$

The NP generates no feedback if it does not get any marked packets. Thus, if RP gets no feedback for K time units, it

[1]Initial value of α is 1.

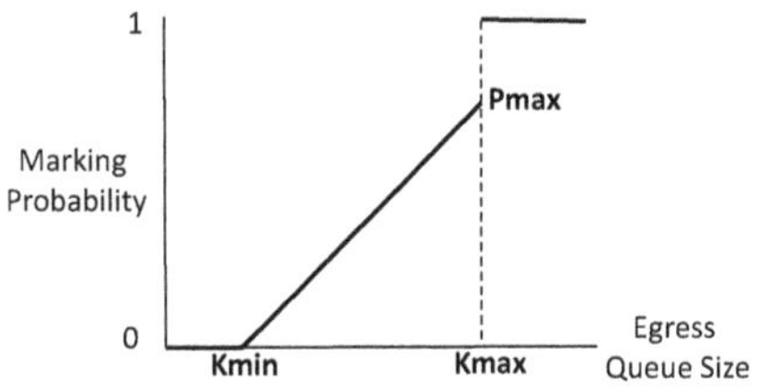

Figure 5: Switch packet marking algorithm

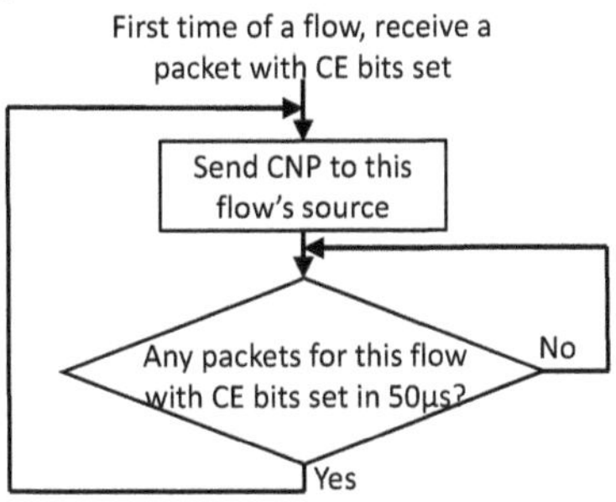

Figure 6: NP state machine

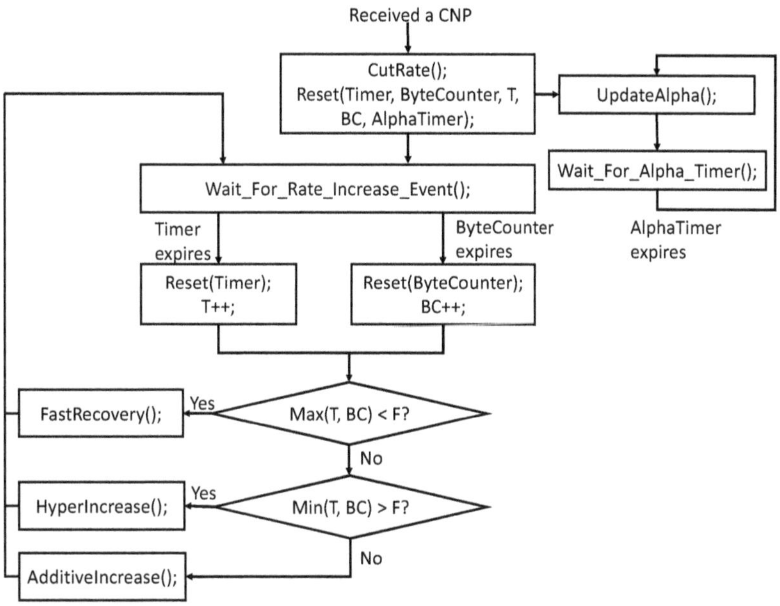

Figure 7: Pseudocode of the RP algorithm

updates α, as shown in Equation (2). Note that K must be larger than the CNP generation timer. Our implementation uses $K = 55\mu s$. See §5 for further discussion.

$$\alpha = \quad (1-g)\alpha, \tag{2}$$

Furthermore, RP increases its sending rate using a timer and a byte counter, in a manner identical to QCN [17]. The byte counter increases rate for every B bytes, while the timer increases rate every T time units. The timer ensures that the flow can recover quickly even when its rate has dropped to a low value. The two parameters can be tuned to achieve the desired aggressiveness. The rate increase has two main phases: fast recovery, where the rate is rapidly increased towards fixed target rate for $F = 5$ successive iterations:

$$R_C = \quad (R_T + R_C)/2, \tag{3}$$

Fast recovery is followed by an additive increase, where the current rate slowly approaches the target rate, and target rate is increased in fixed steps R_{AI}:

$$\begin{aligned} R_T &= \quad R_T + R_{AI}, \\ R_C &= \quad (R_T + R_C)/2, \end{aligned} \tag{4}$$

There is also a hyper increase phase for fast ramp up. Figure 7 shows the state machine. See [17] for more details.

Note that there is no slow start phase. When a flow starts, it sends at full line rate, if there are no other active flows from the host.[2] This design decision optimizes the common case where flows transfer a relatively small amount of data, and the network is not congested [25].

3.2 Benefits

By providing per-flow congestion control, DCQCN alleviates PFC's limitations. To illustrate this, we repeat the experiments in §2.2, with DCQCN enabled (parameters set according to guidelines in §4 and §5.

[2]Otherwise, starting rate is defined by local QoS policies.

Figure 8 shows that DCQCN solves the unfairness problem depicted in Figure 3. All four flows get equal share of the bottleneck bandwidth, and there is little variance. Figure 9 shows that DCQCN solves the victim flow problem depicted in Figure 4. With DCQCN, the throughput of VS-VR flow does not change as we add senders under T3.

3.3 Discussion

CNP generation: DCQCN is not particularly sensitive to congestion on the reverse path, as the send rate does not depend on accurate RTT estimation like TIMELY [31]. Still, we send CNPs with high priority, to avoid missing the CNP deadline, and to enable faster convergence. Note that no CNPs are generated in the common case of no congestion.

Rate based congestion control: DCQCN is a rate-based congestion control scheme. We adopted a rate-based approach because it was simple to implement than the window based approach, and allowed for finer-grained control.

Parameters: DCQCN is based on DCTCP and QCN, but it differs from each in key respects. For example, unlike QCN, there is no quantized feedback, and unlike DCTCP there is no "per-ack" feedback. Thus, the parameter settings recommended for DCTCP and QCN cannot be blindly used with DCQCN. In §5, we use a fluid model of the DCQCN to establish the optimal parameter settings.

The need for PFC: DCQCN does not obviate the need for PFC. With DCQCN, flows start at line rate. Without PFC, this can lead to packet loss and poor performance (§6).

Hardware implementation: The NP and RP state machines are implemented on the NIC. The RP state machine requires keeping one timer and one counter for each flow that is being rate limited, apart from a small amount of other state such as the current value of alpha. This state is maintained on the NIC die. The rate limiting is on a per-packet

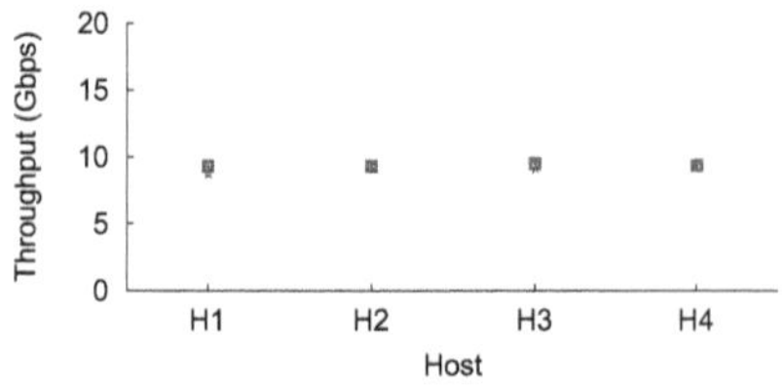

Figure 8: Throughput of individual senders with DCQCN. Compare to Figure 3(b).

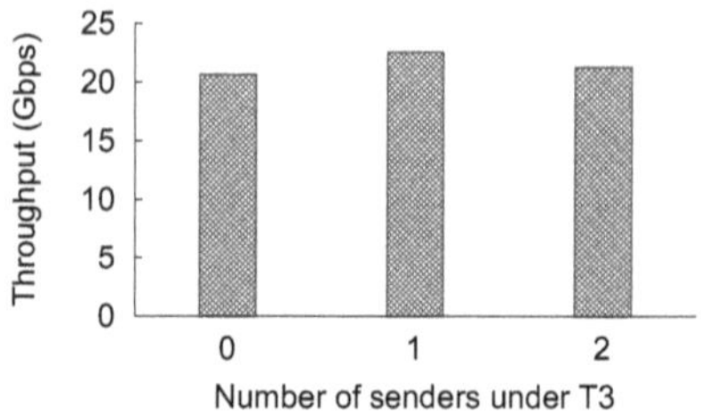

Figure 9: Median throughput of "victim" flow with DCQCN. Compare to Figure 4(b).

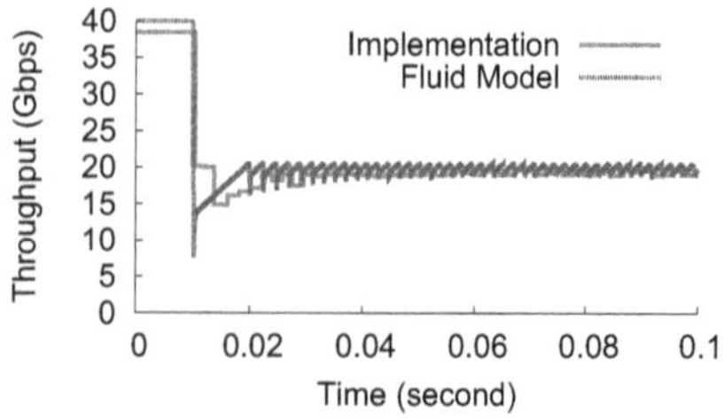

Figure 10: Fluid model closely matches implementation.

granularity. The implementation of NP state machine in ConnectX-3 Pro can generate CNPs at the rate of one per 1-5 microseconds. At link rate of 40Gbps, the receiver can receive about 166 full-sized (1500 byte MTU) packets every 50 microseconds. Thus, the NP can typically support CNP generation at required rate for 10-20 congested flows. The current version(ConnectX-4) can generate CNPs at the required rate for over 200 flows.

4. BUFFER SETTINGS

Correct operation of DCQCN requires balancing two conflicting requirements: (i) PFC is not triggered too early – i.e. before giving ECN a chance to send congestion feedback, and (ii) PFC is not triggered too late – thereby causing packet loss due to buffer overflow.

We now calculate the values of three key switch parameters: t_{flight}, t_{PFC} and t_{ECN}, to ensure that these two requirements are met even in the *worst case*. Note that different switch vendors use different terms for these settings; we use generic names. The discussion is relevant to any shared-buffer switch, but the calculations are specific to switches like Arista 7050QX32, that use the Broadcom Trident II chipset. These switches have 32 full duplex 40Gbps ports, 12MB of shared buffer and support 8 PFC priorities.

Headroom buffer t_{flight}: A PAUSE message sent to an upstream device takes some time to arrive and take effect. To avoid packet drops, the PAUSE sender must reserve enough buffer to process any packets it may receive during this time. This includes packets that were in flight when the PAUSE was sent, and the packets sent by the upstream device while it is processing the PAUSE message. The worst-case calculations must consider several additional factors (e.g., a switch cannot abandon a packet transmission it has begun) [8]. Following guidelines in [8], and assuming a 1500 byte MTU, we get $t_{flight} = 22.4KB$ per port, per priority.

PFC Threshold t_{PFC}: This is the maximum size an ingress queue can grow to, before a PAUSE message is sent to the upstream device. Each PFC priority gets its own queue at each ingress port. Thus, if the total switch buffer is B, and there are n ports, it follows that $t_{PFC} \leq (B - 8nt_{flight})/(8n)$. For our switches, we get $t_{PFC} \leq 24.47KB$. The switch sends RESUME message when the queue falls below t_{PFC} by two MTU.

ECN Threshold t_{ECN}: Once an egress queue exceeds this threshold, the switch starts marking packets on that queue (K_{min} in Figure 5). For DCQCN to be effective, this threshold must be such that PFC threshold is not reached before the switch has a chance to mark packets with ECN.

Note however, that ECN marking is done on *egress* queue while PAUSE messages are sent based on *ingress* queue. Thus, t_{ECN} is an egress queue threshold, while t_{PFC} is an ingress queue threshold.

The worst case scenario is that packets pending on *all* egress queues come from a *single* ingress queue. To *guarantee* that PFC is not triggered on this ingress queue before ECN is triggered on *any* of the egress queues, we need: $t_{PFC} > n * t_{ECN}$ Using the upper bound on the value of t_{PFC}, we get $t_{ECN} < 0.85KB$. This is less than one MTU and hence infeasible.

However, not only we do not have to use the upper bound on t_{PFC}, we do not even have to use a fixed value for t_{PFC}. Since the switch buffer is shared among all ports, t_{PFC} should depend on how much of the shared buffer is free. Intuitively, if the buffer is largely empty, we can afford to wait longer to trigger PAUSE. The Trident II chipset in our switch allows us to configure a parameter β such that: $t_{PFC} = \beta(B - 8nt_{flight} - s)/8$, where s is the amount of buffer that is currently occupied. A higher β triggers PFC less often, while a lower value triggers PFC more aggressively. Note that s is equal to the sum of packets pending on all egress queues. Thus, just before ECN is triggered on any egress port, we have: $s \leq n * t_{ECN}$. Hence, to ensure that ECN is always triggered before PFC, we set: $t_{ECN} < \beta(B - 8nt_{flight})/(8n(\beta + 1))$. Obviously, larger β leaves more room for t_{ECN}. In our testbed, we use $\beta = 8$, which leads to $t_{ECN} < 21.75KB$.

Discussion: The above analysis is conservative, and ensures that PFC is not triggered on our switches before ECN even in the worst case and when all 8 PFC priorities are used. With fewer priorities, or with larger switch buffers, the threshold values will be different.

The analysis *does not* imply that PFC will *never* be triggered. All we ensure is that at any switch, PFC is not triggered *before* ECN. It takes some time for the senders to receive the ECN feedback and reduce their sending rate. During this time, PFC may be triggered. As discussed before, we rely on PFC to allow senders to start at line rate.

Variable	Description
R_c	Current Rate
R_t	Target Rate
α	See Equation (1)
q	Queue Size
t	Time

Table 1: Fluid model variables

Parameter	Description
$K_{min}, K_{max}, P_{max}$	See Figure 5
g	See Equation (1)
N	Number of flows at bottleneck
C	Bandwidth of bottleneck link
F	Fast recovery steps (fixed at 5)
B	Byte counter for rate increase
T	Timer for rate increase
R_{AI}	Rate increase step (fixed at 40Mbps)
$\tau*$	Control loop delay
τ'	Interval of Equation (2)

Table 2: Fluid model parameters

5. ANALYSIS OF DCQCN

We use a fluid model of DCQCN to determine the right parameter settings for good performance.

5.1 Fluid model

Variables and parameters used in the fluid model are listed in Tables 1 and 2, respectively. The model is described in Equations (5)-(9). Like [3, 4], we model N greedy flows at a single bottleneck with capacity C. We assume that DCQCN is triggered well before PFC – and thus ignore PFC in the following analysis.

Equation (5) models the probability of a packet getting marked at the bottleneck. Setting $K_{\text{min}} == K_{\text{max}}$, gives DCTCP-like "cut-off"behavior. We model the more general behavior for reasons discussed later. Equation (6) models the evolution of queue at the bottleneck. We have assumed that all flows have equal rate. We will relax this assumption later. Equation (7) models the evolution of α at the RP.

Equations (8) and (9) model the evolution of current and target sending rate at RP, according to the algorithm shown in Figure 7, and QCN specification [17]. We model the rate decrease, as well as the rate increase due to byte counter and timer, but like [4], ignore the hyper additive increase phase. $\tau*$ models the delay of the control loop. It includes the RTT and NP's CNP generation interval. For simplicity, we use $\tau* = 50\mu s$ (the maximum possible delay of CNP generation).

By setting the LHS of Equations (6)-(9) to zero, we see that the fluid model has an unique fixed point when satisfying Equation (10).

$$R_C(t) = \frac{C}{N} \tag{10}$$

This fixed point represents the state of all flows getting fair bandwidth share C/N. The rest of the fluid model becomes three equations with three variables, R_T, α and p. We solve the equations numerically to determine the ECN marking probability p at the fixed point. The solution of p is unique.

$$p(t) = \begin{cases} 0, & q(t) \le K_{\text{min}} \\ \frac{q(t)-K_{\text{min}}}{K_{\text{max}}-K_{\text{min}}} p_{\text{max}}, & K_{\text{min}} < q(t) \le K_{\text{max}} \\ 1, & q(t) > K_{\text{max}} \end{cases} \tag{5}$$

$$\frac{dq}{dt} = NR_C(t) - C \tag{6}$$

$$\frac{d\alpha}{dt} = \frac{g}{\tau'}\left(\left(1-(1-p(t-\tau*))^{\tau' R_C(t-\tau*)}\right) - \alpha(t)\right) \tag{7}$$

$$\begin{aligned} \frac{dR_T}{dt} = &-\frac{R_T(t)-R_C(t)}{\tau}\left(1-(1-p(t-\tau*))^{\tau R_C(t-\tau*)}\right) \\ &+ R_{AI}R_C(t-\tau*)\frac{(1-p(t-\tau*))^{FB}p(t-\tau*)}{(1-p(t-\tau*))^{-B}-1} \\ &+ R_{AI}R_C(t-\tau*)\frac{(1-p(t-\tau*))^{FTR_C(t-\tau*)}p(t-\tau*)}{(1-p(t-\tau*))^{-TR_C(t-\tau*)}-1} \end{aligned} \tag{8}$$

$$\begin{aligned} \frac{dR_C}{dt} = &-\frac{R_C(t)\alpha(t)}{2\tau}\left(1-(1-p(t-\tau*))^{\tau R_C(t-\tau*)}\right) \\ &+ \frac{R_T(t)-R_C(t)}{2}\frac{R_C(t-\tau*)p(t-\tau*)}{(1-p(t-\tau*))^{-B}-1} \\ &+ \frac{R_T(t)-R_C(t)}{2}\frac{R_C(t-\tau*)p(t-\tau*)}{(1-p(t-\tau*))^{-TR_C(t-\tau*)}-1} \end{aligned} \tag{9}$$

Fluid Model of DCQCN

We omit the proof for brevity. We verified that for reasonable settings, p is less than 1%. According to equation (5), when RED-ECN is enabled, there exists a fixed queue length point close to K_{min} since p is close to 0. The value of g plays an important role in determining the stability of the queue, as we shall later see.

To analyze convergence properties of DCQCN protocol, it is necessary to extend the fluid model to flows with different rates. Take two flows as an example. We model the evolution of each flow's current and target sending rates, as well as their α separately – i.e. we write Equations (7)-(9) for each flow. The flows are coupled by their impact on the queue:

$$\frac{dq}{dt} = R_{C1}(t) + R_{C2}(t) - C \tag{11}$$

We solve this model numerically to understand the impact of various parameters (Table 2) on DCQCN's behavior; particularly convergence and queue buildup.

Experiments show that the fluid model matches the implementation quite well. We show one example in Figure 10. We defer discussion to §6.

5.2 Parameter selection

We focus on a two-flow system, where one flow starts at 40Gbps, and the other starts at 0Gbps. For each parameter setting, we use numerical analysis to solve the first 200 milliseconds. The results are shown in Figure 11. The Z-axis shows difference in throughput of the two flows. For readability, we omit the first 10ms.

We start with recommended parameters from QCN and DCTCP specifications. Specifically, $B = 150KB, T = 1.5ms, K_{\text{min}} = K_{\text{max}} = 40KB, P_{\text{max}} = 1$, and $g = 1/16$.

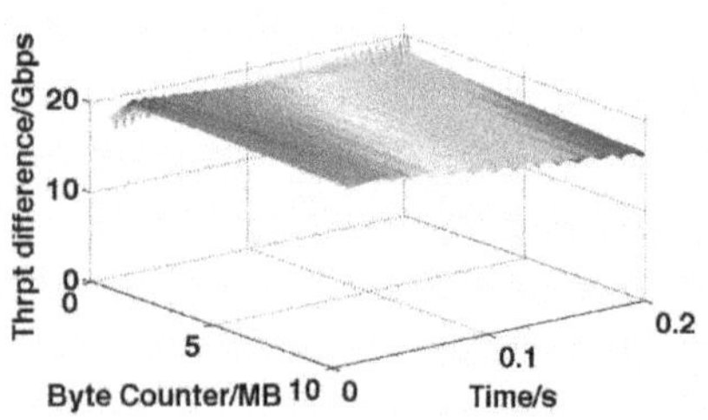

(a) Sweep Byte Counter with strawman parameters

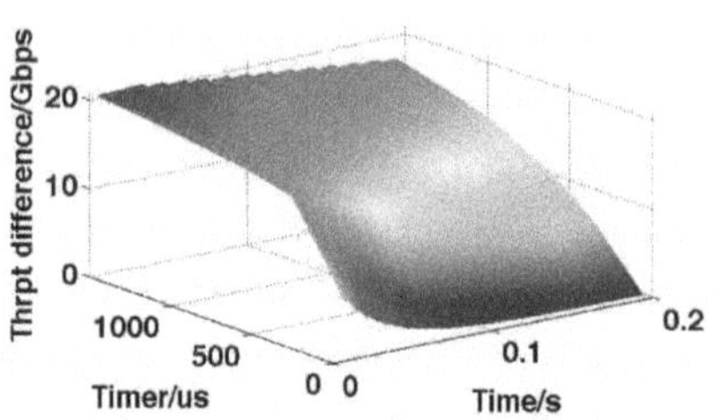

(b) Sweep Timer with 10MB Byte Counter

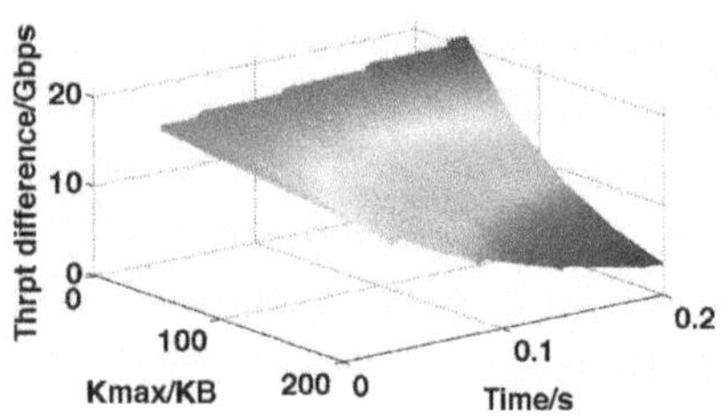

(c) Sweep $K_{\max}$ with strawman parameters

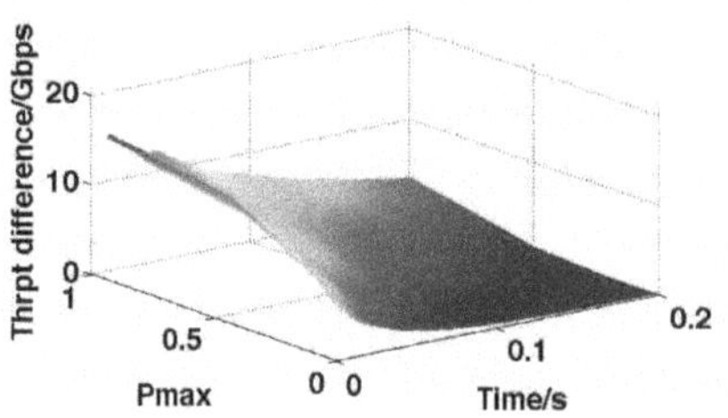

(d) Sweep $P_{\max}$ with $K_{\max} = 200KB$

Figure 11: Parameter sweeping for best convergence. Lower throughput difference (z-axis) means better convergence.

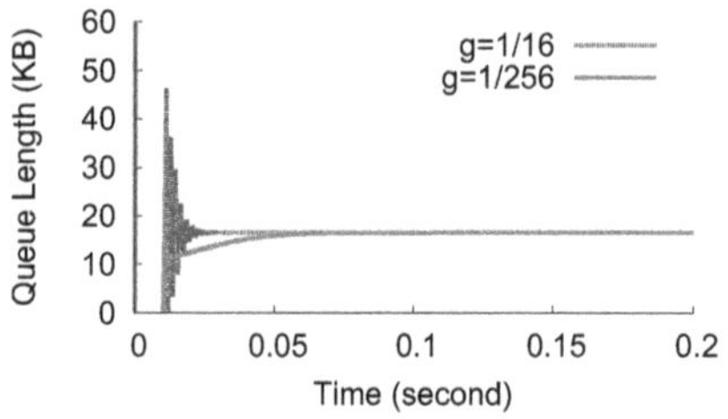

(a) 2:1 Incast

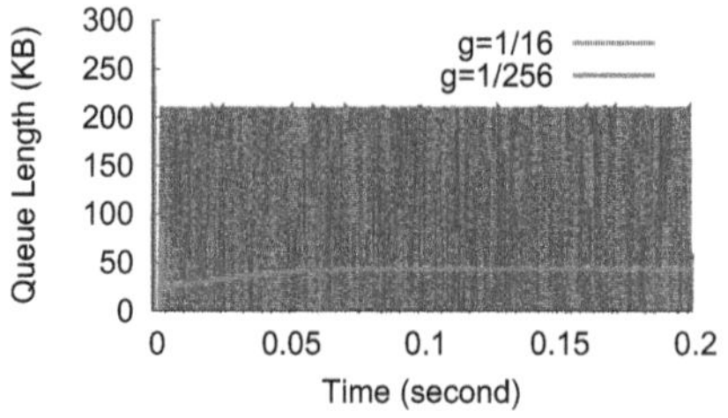

(b) 16:1 Incast

Figure 12: Testing different g for best queue length and queue stability.

Unfortunately we find that with these parameter values, the flows cannot converge (innermost edge of Figure 11(a)). With these settings, QCN byte counter dominates rate increase, and the faster flow grows faster. QCN compensates for this using probabilistic feedback, which DCQCN does not have. Instead, the solution is to either slow down the byte counter, or speed up the rate increase timer. Figure 11(a) shows that slowing down byte counter helps, but it reduces convergence speed. Speeding up the timer (Figure 11(b)) is better. Note that the timer cannot be smaller than 50μs, which is NP's CNP generation interval. As the timer is set aggressively, the byte counter should be set large, *e.g.*, 10MB, to avoid triggering the hyper increase phase too fast, which may harm convergence.

Another solution is to use a RED-like probabilistic packet marking scheme with a small $P_{\max}$, instead of the cut-off (mark all packets once queue length exceeds certain limit) behavior used in DCTCP. The intuition is that DCQCN CNP generation is driven by a timer, and by using RED-like marking scheme with a small $P_{\max}$, we increase the likelihood that the larger flow will get more CNPs, and hence back off faster. Figures 11(c) and 11(d) confirm this intuition.

In conclusion, to achieve fast convergence to fairness, we configure RED-ECN on switches with $K_{\max} = 200KB$ and $P_{\max} = 1\%$. We set $K_{\min} = 5KB$ since we found it sufficient to maintain 100% throughput. Though a 5KB $K_{\min}$ seems shallow, the marking probability around $K_{\min}$ is very little. Fluid model predicts that the stable queue length is usually one order of magnitude larger than 5KB $K_{\min}$. Our deployment experience and experiments (see §6) confirm this. We also set rate increase timer as 55us, and byte counter to 10MB. If the feedback delay is significantly different from the value we assumed (e.g. if RTT is high), parameter values will be different.

The queue length at the bottleneck depends on the value of g. We tested different g from 2:1 incast to 16:1 incast (Figure 12) and found smaller g leads to lower queue length and lower variation. Lower g leads to slightly slower convergence, but it is a price worth paying for lower oscillations.

We now briefly discuss the remaining parameters. Recall that CNP generation interval is fixed at 50μs, due to hardware limitations. We have assumed that feedback delay ($\tau*$) is equal to this value. We have verified that flows converge fast and stably even when an additional 50μs latency is added. We have chosen the α update interval τ' and minimum timer value to be 55μs. These values need to be larger than CNP generation interval to prevent unwarranted rate increases between reception of successive CNPs. We believe that the 5μs margin is sufficient for current hardware. DCQCN is generally insensitive to τ' value: 110μs (twice as default) barely slows down convergence. We also analyzed impact of R_{AI} and F. They both offer trade-off between convergence speed and throughput oscillations. In addition, R_{AI}, working with g, influences DCQCN scalability. For example, in current settings, there is no buffer starvation with 16:1 incast (Figure 12). Halving R_{AI} reduces the convergence speed, but it ensures no buffer starvation with 32:1 incast. The current values are an acceptable compromise.

Discussion The DCQCN model is based on QCN model presented in [4], with two differences. First, the rate reduction in DCQCN is significantly different. Our model also addresses both byte counter and timer mechanisms for rate increase, while [4] only models the byte counter. In future,

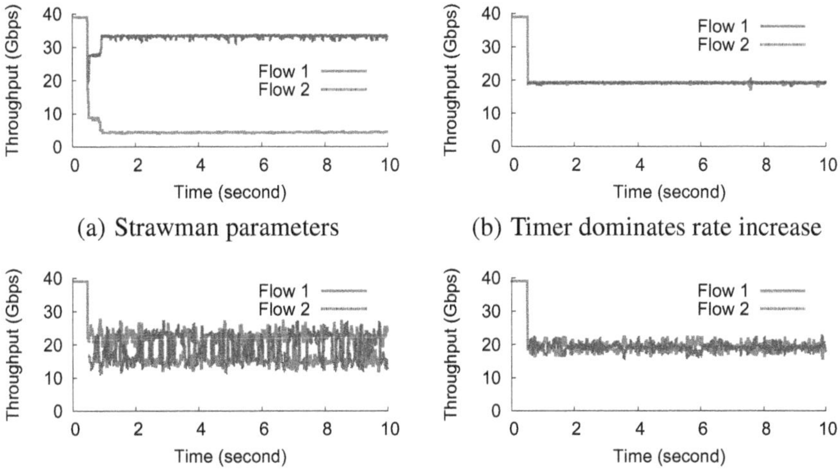

(a) Strawman parameters (b) Timer dominates rate increase (c) Enable RED-ECN (d) RED-ECN plus timer solution

Figure 13: Validating parameter values with testbed microbenchmarks

Parameter	Value
Timer	$55\mu s$
Byte Counter	10MB
$K_{\max}$	200KB
$K_{\min}$	5KB
$P_{\max}$	1%
g	1/256

Figure 14: DCQCN Parameters used in our datacenters

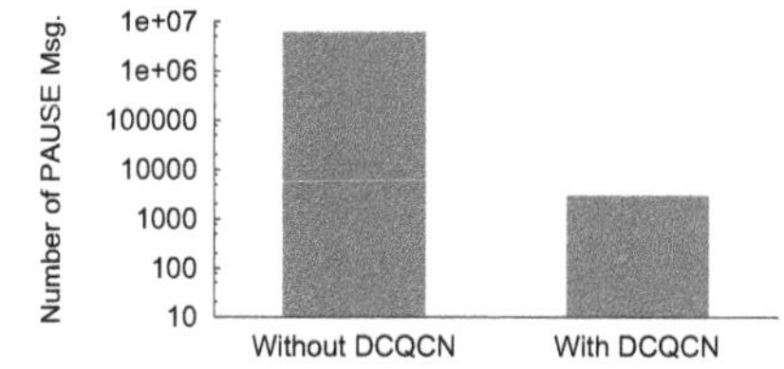

Figure 15: Total number of PAUSE messages received at S1 and S2, with and without DCQCN

we plan to analyze the stability of DCQCN following techniques in [4].

6. RESULTS

We now evaluate the performance of DCQCN in a variety of settings, using Mellanox ConnectX-3 Pro NICs. The results are divided in two parts. First, we validate the findings of the fluid model from §5 using microbenchmarks in a small testbed. This step is essential before we can use the parameter settings derived from the model in actual deployment. Next, we evaluate DCQCN using benchmark traffic derived from traffic traces that roughly model the ongoing DCQCN deployment in our datacenters.

6.1 Microbenchmarks

Validating fluid model: The first step is to show that the fluid model is a good representation of the implementation. We use a simple setup consisting of three machines, connected via an Arista 7050QX32 switch. One of the three machines act as a receiver, while the other two act as greedy senders. The first sender starts at time 0, while the second starts after 10 milliseconds. DCQCN parameters are set according to the discussion in §5, and the switch is configured as per the discussion in §4. Figure 10 shows the evolution of the sending rate of the second sender for the first 100 milliseconds. We see that the model closely matches the firmware implementation.

Validating parameter settings: While we have shown that the fluid model is a good representation of our implementation, we still need to validate the individual parameter values predicted by the model with real hardware. We conduct several tests for this purpose, using the same 3-machine setup as before. In each test, the first sender starts at time 0, and the second sender starts 500 milliseconds later.

We first test the strawman parameter values. Figure 13(a) confirms that as the model predicts, there is unfairness between the two competing flows.

Next we verify that speeding up the rate increase timer alleviates the unfairness. Figure 13(b) shows that this is indeed the case (timer value = $55\mu s$). Note that we used DCTCP-like cut-off ECN for this experiment.

We also test the second solution – i.e. RED-like marking alleviates the unfairness problem, even without changing the timer. To test, we configure the switch with $K_{\min} = 5KB$, $K_{\max} = 200KB$ and $P_{\max} = 1\%$. Figure 13(c) shows that the two flows, on average get similar throughput. However, we see a drawback that isn't shown by fluid model: the throughput is unstable due to the randomness in marking.

These results would imply that in our deployment, we should mark packets like DCTCP, and rely on faster rate increase timer to achieve fairness. However, we have found that in multi-bottleneck scenario (§7), a combination of faster timer and RED-like marking achieves better performance. Figure 13(d) shows the behavior of the combined solution for the simple two-flow scenario.

We have also verified that the value of $g = 1/256$ works well in this scenario, as predicted by the fluid model. Finally, using 20 machines connected via a single switch, we verified that with 55 μs timer, RED-ECN and $g = 1/256$, the total throughput is always more than 39Gbps for K:1 incast, $K = 1 \ldots 19$. The switch counter shows that the queue length never exceeds 100KB (translates to $20\mu s$ at 40Gbps).

In summary, we use the parameters shown in Table 14 in our deployment, and also for the rest of the evaluation.

6.2 Benchmark traffic

One important scenario for large-scale RDMA deployment is the backend network for cloud storage service. In such a network, the traffic consists of user requests, as well as traffic generated by relatively rare events such as disk recovery. The disk recovery traffic has incast-like character-

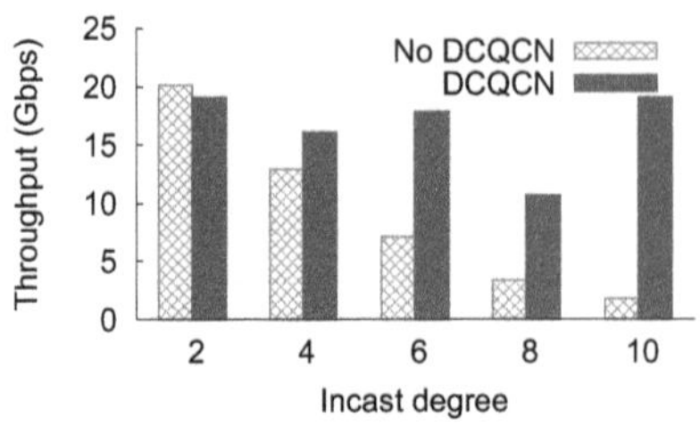

(a) Median throughput of user flows.

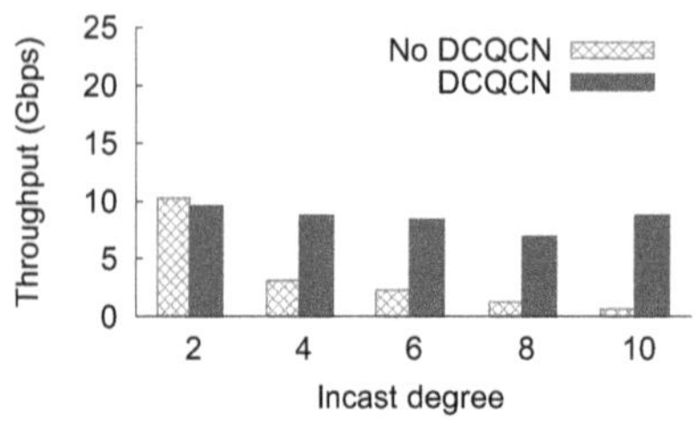

(b) 10th percentile throughput of user flows.

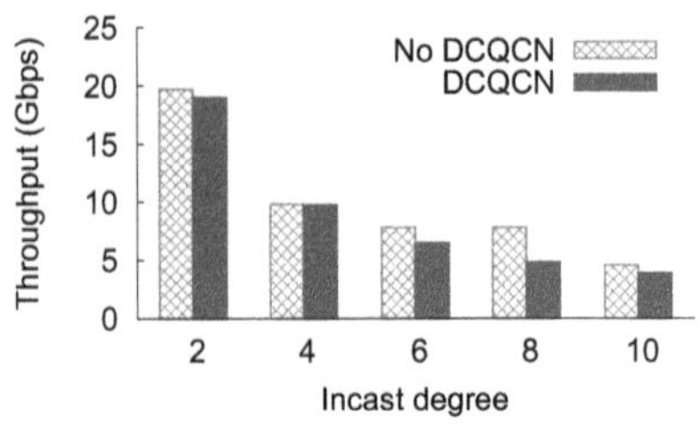

(c) Median throughput of incast flows.

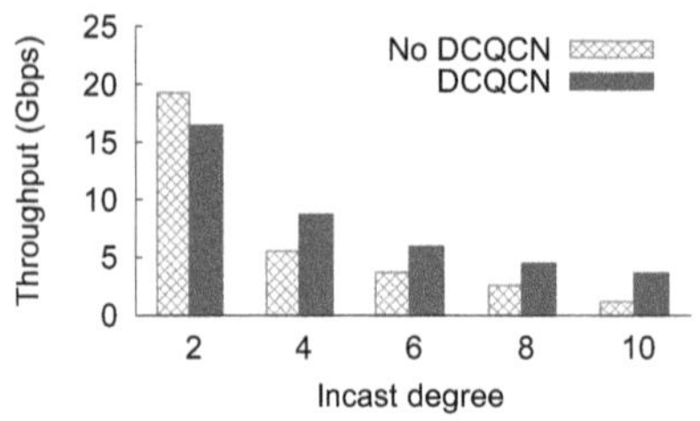

(d) 10th percentile throughput of incast flows.

Figure 16: DCQCN performance with Benchmark Traffic

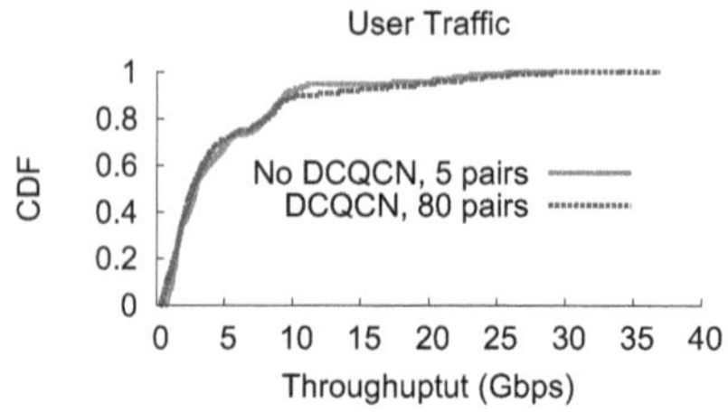

(a) CDF of User traffic

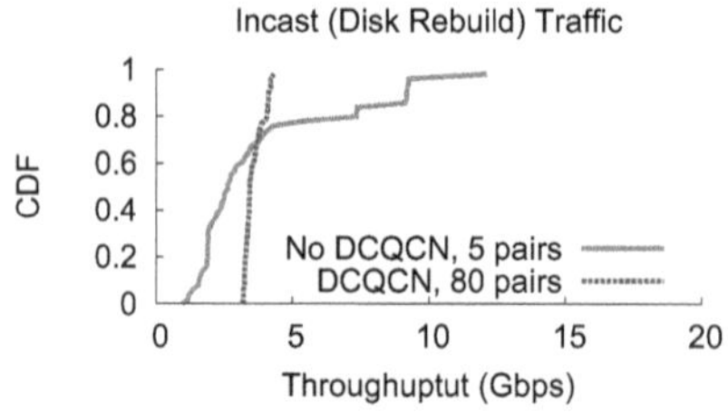

(b) CDF of Incast traffic

Figure 17: DCQCN can handle higher user traffic without hurting performance

istics, as failed disks are repaired by fetching backups from several other servers [16]. We now evaluate the performance of DCQCN in this scenario using the 3-tier testbed shown in Figure 2, with five hosts connected to each ToR.

To mimic user request traffic, we use traces collected from a single cluster in our datacenter. The data was collected for one day on cluster of 480 machines, and includes traffic from over 10 million flows. The trace cannot be directly replayed on our testbed. Instead, like prior work [2, 5, 6], we extract salient characteristics of the trace data, such as flow size distribution and generate synthetic traffic to match these characteristics. We model disk recovery traffic as incast. We don't claim that this benchmark models the real traffic exactly - only that it is a reasonable proxy in a testbed setting.

To simulate user traffic, each host communicates with one or more randomly selected host, and transfers data using distributions derived from traces. The number of communicating pairs is fixed at 20 (we will vary this in a later experiment). The traffic also includes a *single* disk rebuild event (since these are not very frequent). We vary the degree of incast from 2 to 10, to model different erasure coding patterns [16]. We repeat the experiment five times, with and without DCQCN. DCQCN parameters are set according to Table 14. The communicating pairs as well as the hosts participating in the incast are selected randomly for each run. Each run lasts for two minutes.

The metric of interest is the median as well as the tail end (10th percentile) of the throughput[3]. Improved median means better utilization of the network, while improved tail performance leads to more predictable application performance, which in turn leads to better user experience.

The results are shown in Figure 16. Figure 16(a) and 16(b) show that without DCQCN, the throughput of user traffic falls rapidly, as the degree of incast goes up. This result is surprising, because even though the degree of incast goes up, the total traffic generated by incast senders stays the same (because the bottleneck is always at the receiver). The reason is the "damage" caused by PFC. As the degree of incast goes up, more PAUSE messages are generated. As these cascade through the network, they wreak havoc on user traffic. PAUSE messages that affect downlinks from spine switches can cause extensive damage, as many flows pass through these switches. For example, in a single run of the experiment with incast degree 10, the two spine switches together receive over 6 million PAUSE messages. Thus, scenarios like unfairness and victim flow (§2.2) become more likely and affect the throughput of user flows. In contrast, when DCQCN is used, the spine switches see just 3000 PAUSE messages (Figure 15). As a result, the performance of user traffic is much better. Indeed, with DCQCN, as the degree of incast goes up, there is little change in the median and tail throughput of user traffic – exactly as one would hope for.

The disk rebuild traffic also benefits from DCQCN because DCQCN helps divides the bandwidth fairly among competing flows. In the ideal case, the throughput of each incast flow should be equal to 40Gbps divided by degree of incast. Figure 16(d) shows that with DCQCN, the 10th percentile throughput is very close to this value, indicating a high degree of fairness. In contrast, without DCQCN, the 10th percentile throughput is much lower. For example, with incast degree of 10, 10th percentile throughput without DCQCN is less than 1.12Gbps, while with DCQCN it is 3.43Gbps. Note that the median throughput (Figure 16(c)) with DCQCN appears to be lower. This, however, is deceptive: without DCQCN the tail end suffers, and other flows

[3] 90th percentile of response time.

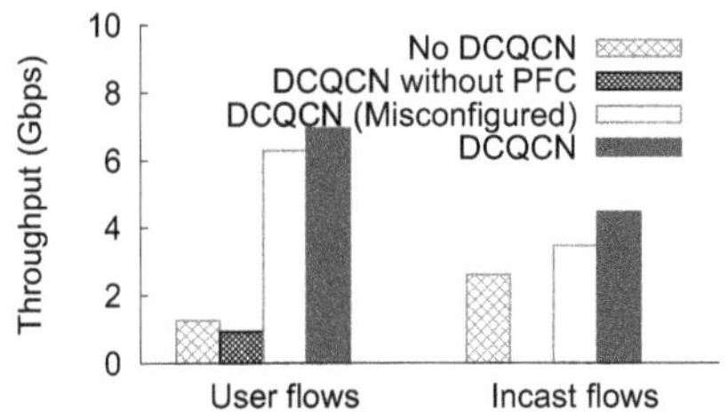

Figure 18: 10th percentile throughput of four configurations for 8:1 incast

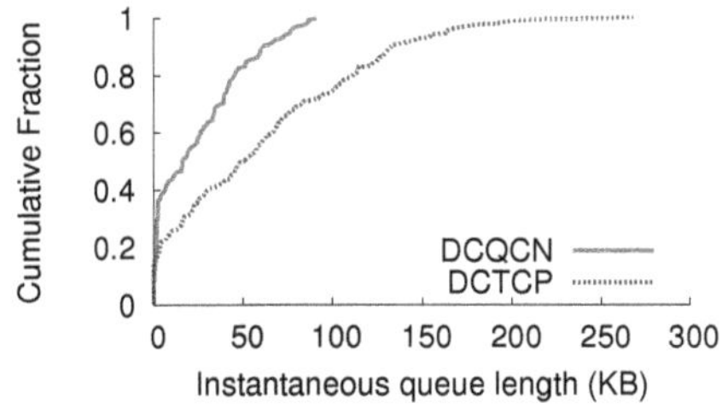

Figure 19: Queue length CDF

grab more than their "fair share". Thus, the median seems higher. With DCQCN, median and 10th percentile values are nearly identical.

Higher user load: In Figure 16, we saw that DCQCN continues to provide good performance to user traffic even as the degree of incast goes up. Now, we hold the degree of incast constant at 10, and vary the amount of use traffic by varying the number of simultaneously communicating pairs from 5 to 80. In Figure 17(a), we see that the performance of user traffic with 5 communicating pairs when no DCQCN is used, matches the performance of user traffic with 80 communicating pairs, with DCQCN. In other words, with DCQCN, we can handle 16x more user traffic, without performance degradation. Figure 17(b) shows that even the performance of disk rebuild traffic is more uniform and fair with DCQCN than without it.

Need for PFC and importance of buffer thresholds: We now demonstrate the need for PFC, and also the need for configuring correct buffer thresholds. To do so, we repeat the experiment of Figure 16 with two other settings. First, we disable PFC entirely, although we do use DCQCN. Second, we enable PFC, but deliberately "misconfigure" the buffer thresholds as follows: instead of using dynamic t_{PFC}, we use the static upper bound – i.e. $t_{PFC} = 24.47KB$ and set $t_{ECN} = 120KB$, i.e. five times this value. With these thresholds, it is no longer guaranteed that ECN will be triggered before PFC.

The results from the experiment are shown in Figure 18 for the 8:1 incast case. In addition to the two configurations discussed above, we also show the DCQCN and No DCQCN (i.e. PFC only) bars, which are copied from Figures 16(b) and 16(d).

Consider the performance when PFC is completely disabled. Recall that DCQCN has no slow start, and hence it relies on PFC to prevent packet loss during congestion. Without PFC, packet losses are common, and this leads to poor performance. In fact, the 10th percentile incast throughput is *zero* – indicating that some of the flows are simply unable to recover from persistent packet losses. This result underscores the need to use DCQCN with PFC.

Next, consider the performance when PFC is enabled, but buffer thresholds are misconfigured. With these thresholds, PFC may be triggered before ECN – thus preventing the full benefit of DCQCN. We see that this is indeed the case. The tail throughput of both user and incast traffic is better than what it would be without DCQCN (i.e. with PFC only), but worse than what it would be with DCQCN. This result underscores the need for correct buffer threshold settings.

6.3 Impact on latency

The above benchmarks use throughput as the primary metric. However, DCQCN can also reduce latency, compared to DCTCP. As a microbenchmark, we looked at the queue length of the egress queue of the congested port during 20:1 incast, with both DCTCP and DCQCN. For DCTCP, we configured 160KB ECN threshold according to the guidelines provided in [2]. DCQCN was configured as described earlier.

With this setup, the queue length with DCQCN is significantly shorter than that with DCTCP (Figure 19). For example, the 95th-percentile queue length is 76.6KB with DCQCN and 162.9KB with DCTCP. These numbers align well with DCQCN fluid model and DCTCP model [2]. DCTCP leads to longer queue, because DCTCP requires a larger ECN threshold to absorb packet bursts, which is a result of the interaction between the OS and the NIC. DCQCN uses hardware rate limiters, and thus can use shallower $K_{\min}$.

7. DISCUSSION

Multi-bottleneck scenario: We mentioned earlier that in a multi-bottleneck scenario combination of faster timer and RED-like marking gives better performance than faster timer alone. We now illustrate this. The multi-bottleneck problem is also known as the parking lot scenario. An example is shown in Figure 20(a). There are three flows: $f1$: H1->R1, $f2$: H2->R2, and $f3$: H3->R2. Consider the case when ECMP maps $f1$ and $f2$ to the same uplink from T1. With this mapping, $f2$ ends up with two bottlenecks (T1 uplink and T4->R2), while $f1$ and $f3$ have only one bottleneck each. Max-min fairness requires each flow should get throughput of 20Gbps. However, with common congestion control protocols like DCTCP, the flow with two bottleneck gets lower throughput because it has higher probability of getting congestion signal. DCQCN, if used with DCTCP-like "cut-off" marking ($K_{\min} = K_{\max}, P_{\max} = 1$, see Figure 5) has the same problem. The problem can be mitigated (but not completely solved) using a less abrupt, RED-like marking scheme (see parameters in Table 14).

The intuition is the same as explained before: CNP generation is driven by a timer, so with RED-like packet marking, we increase the probability that the faster flow will get more CNPs. Figure 20(b) shows the performance of the two marking schemes, and indicates that the intuition is correct. We

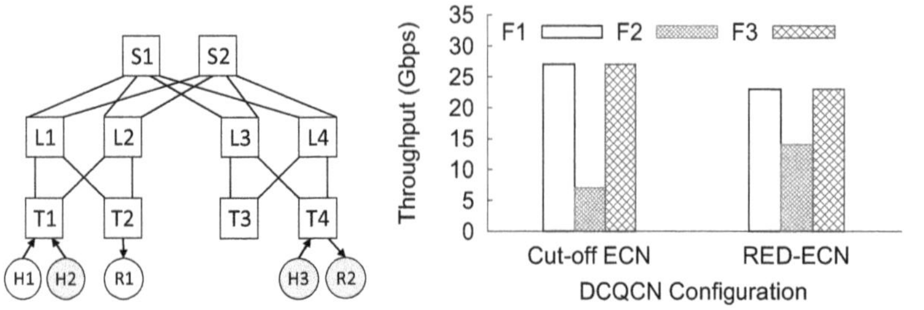

(a) Multi-bottleneck topology (b) Throughput of the three flows. F2 is the long flow (H2->R2)

Figure 20: Multi-bottleneck

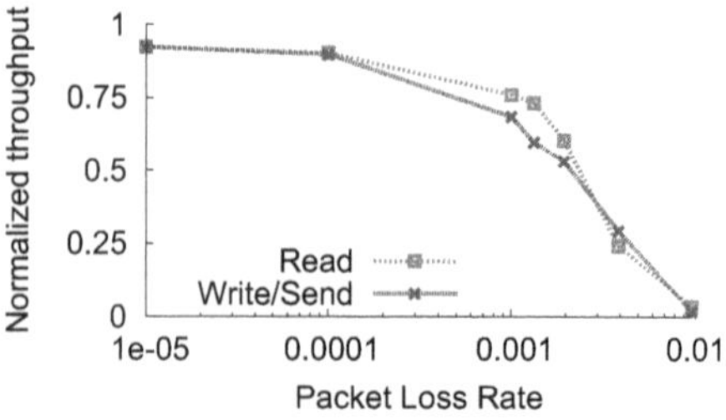

Figure 21: Impact of packet loss rate on throughput

plan to extend the fluid model to gain a better understanding of this scenario and come up with a more concrete solution.

Packet loss: PFC prevents packet loss due to buffer overflow. However, packet corruption, intermittent port failures, or accidental switch or server misconfiguration can induce packet loss in large networks [41]. Unlike TCP, RoCEv2 transport layer assumes that packet losses are rare. For example, when using READ operation [19], the protocol provides no information to the sender of the data about whether packets were correctly received. The receiver can detect packet loss via break in sequence numbers, and must initiate any loss recovery. The ConnectX-3 Pro implements a simple go-back-N loss recovery scheme. This is sufficient for environments where packet loss rate low, as seen in Figure 21. Throughput degrades rapidly once the packet loss rate exceeds 0.1%. With go-back-n loss recovery model, the size of the message matters as well. In our deployment, most message transfers are expected to be less than 4MB in size.

Deadlock: A commonly expressed concern is that use of PAUSE can lead to routing deadlocks [37]. Deadlock formation requires a set of flows that have a cyclic dependency on each other's buffers, as shown in [37]. In a clos-structured network servers are only connected to ToRs, and traffic between a pair of servers never passes through another server, or more than two ToRs. Thus a cyclic buffer dependency cannot arise, without malfunctioning or misconfigured equipment. We omit detailed proof due to lack of space. We are currently studying how to avoid outages that may be caused by a malfunctioning card (e.g. port or a NIC that spews PFCs).

TCP friendliness: TCP-friendliness was not one of the design goals for DCQCN, so we have not attempted to study in the interaction between TCP and DCQCN in this paper. It is easy to isolate TCP and DCQCN traffic from each other at the switch level using 802.3 priority tags, and enforce different transmission priorities, switch buffer utilization limits, and rate limits for each type of traffic.

Incremental deployment: Incremental deployment is not a concern in a datacenter environment.

Large-scale evaluation: We have designed DCQCN for deployment in large datacenter networks. The evaluation in this paper is based on a small, controlled, testbed environment. We have also evaluated DCQCN via large scale simulations (three-tier network of over 800 machines). We omit simulation results due to lack of space, and also because they are qualitatively similar to results from testbed evaluation. A full scale deployment of DCQCN in our datacenters is in progress.

8. RELATED WORK

There is a vast amount of research literature on congestion control, and datacenter networking technologies. Here, we only cover a few closely related ideas that we have not discussed elsewhere in the paper.

Dynamic buffer allocation among output queued switches is discussed in [7]. A number of papers have discussed various aspects of QCN's performance. For example, [9] discusses performance of a QCN in a TCP incast scenario. RECN-IQ [32] is a congestion management proposal for input-queued switches. While related, ideas in these proposals are not directly applicable to our scenario.

The iWarp standard [35] is an alternative to RoCEv2. It implements the full TCP stack on the NIC and builds a reliable connection using TCP's end-to-end loss recovery. RDMA can be enabled atop such a network. Due to end-to-end loss recovery, iWarp cannot offer ultra-low latency like RoCEv2. iWarp is also likely to suffer from well-known TCP problems in a datacenter environment, including poor incast performance [39]. In general, the iWarp technology has lagged behind RoCEv2, because of the complexity involved in implementing the full TCP stack in hardware. While 40Gbps iWarp hardware has only recently become available [43], RoCE2 vendors have started shipping 100Gbps NICs [44].

TCP Bolt [37] is a solution to overcome PFC's limitations. It also relies on flow-level congestion control, enabled by ECN. TCP Bolt is essentially DCTCP [2] without slow start. However, TCP-Bolt is implemented in end host stacks, and thus will have high CPU overhead and high latency. The protocol also does not consider the interplay between PFC and ECN buffer thresholds. Since we did not have access to a TCP-Bolt implementation for Windows, we were unable to compare the performance of DCQCN and TCP-Bolt.

We also note that DCTCP and iWarp have a slow start phase, which can result in poor performance for bursty storage workloads. Furthermore, DCTCP, iWarp and TCP-Bolt are all window-based algorithms. DCQCN is rate-based, and uses hardware rate limiters. Thus, DCQCN offers a more fine-grained control over sending rate, resulting in lower queue lengths, as shown in §6.

TIMELY [31] is a congestion control scheme for datacenter traffic, including RDMA traffic. It uses fine-grained changes in RTT as a congestion signal, instead of ECN marks. Compared to DCTCP, TIMELY can significantly reduce queuing delay. Reducing CPU utilization of end hosts is not a goal for TIMELY. TIMELY was developed at Google in parallel with our work on DCQCN. It would be interesting to compare the performance of DCQCN and TIMELY under various scenarios.

User-level stacks such as Sandstorm [29] are one way to reduce TCP's CPU overhead and latency. While they do have lower CPU overhead than conventional stacks, their overhead is significantly higher than RoCEv2. Some of these stacks also have to be closely integrated with individual applications to be effective. TCP's latency can potentially also be reduced using technologies such as Netmap [28], Intel Data Direct I/O [45] and mTCP [23].

A number of proposals for reducing latency of TCP flows in datacenter and other environments have been put forth. Recent examples include HULL [5], pFabric [6] Detail [42], Fastpass [33] and RCP [12]. These proposals require significant changes to switch architectures, and to our knowledge, are not being deployed on a large scale. Other TCP offloading work optimize TCP performance only for specific scenarios, e.g. for VM [26].

Recent proposals consider the possibility in leveraging machine learning to adapt TCP parameters for better performance [36, 40]. The idea may also apply to DCQCN. We will investigate this in the future.

9. CONCLUSION AND FUTURE WORK

The history of congestion control algorithms is the history of struggle between responsiveness and stability. While we have presented DCQCN as a solution to cure PFC's ills, it also represents a new way to address the tussle between responsiveness and stability, at least in the datacenter environment. DCQCN uses the blunt, but fast PFC flow control to prevent packet losses just in time, and uses a fine-grained and slower end-to-end congestion control to adjust sending rate to avoid triggering PFC persistently. The combination allows DCQCN to be both responsive in short term, and stable over long term. We believe that this design point warrants exploration in a number of different directions. For example, we are exploring the use of DCQCN in other environments, with different RTTs and link bandwidths. More specifically, we are working to model and tune DCQCN and PFC for 100 and 400Gbps networks. We are also planning to investigate the stability of the DCQCN algorithm using the model described in §5.

Acknowledgements

We would like to thank Diego Crupnicoff, Liran Liss, Hillel Chapman, Marcel Apfelbaum, Dvir Aizenman and Alex Shpiner of Mellanox for their help with the design and implementation of DCQCN. We also like to thank the anonymous SIGCOMM reviewers and our shepherd, Nandita Dukkipati for their helpful comments.

10. REFERENCES

[1] M. Alizadeh, B. Atikoglu, A. Kabbani, A. Lakshmikantha, R. Pan, B. Prabhakar, and M. Seaman. Data center transport mechanisms: Congestion control theory and IEEE standardization. In *Allerton*, 2008.

[2] M. Alizadeh, A. Greenberg, D. Maltz, J. Padhye, P. Patel, B. Prabhakar, S. Sengupta, and M. Sridharan. Data Center TCP (DCTCP). In *SIGCOMM*, 2010.

[3] M. Alizadeh, A. Javanmard, and B. Prabhakar. Analysis of DCTCP: Stability, convergence and fairness. In *SIGMETRICS*, 2011.

[4] M. Alizadeh, A. Kabbani, B. Atikoglu, and B. Prabhakar. Stability analysis of QCN: the averaging principle. In *SIGMETRICS*, 2011.

[5] M. Alizadeh, A. Kabbani, T. Edsall, B. Prabhakar, A. Vahdat, and M. Yasuda. Less is more: Trading a little bandwidth for ultra-low latency in the data center. In *NSDI*, 2012.

[6] M. Alizadeh, S. Yang, M. Sharif, S. Katti, N. McKeown, B. Prabhakar, and S. Shenker. pFabric: Minimal near-optimal datacenter transport. In *SIGCOMM*, 2013.

[7] A. K. Choudhury and E. L. Hahne. Dynamic queue length thresholds for shared-memory packet switches. *IEEE/ACM Transactions on Networking*, 6(2), 1998.

[8] Cisco. Priority flow control: Build reliable layer 2 infrastructure. http://www.cisco.com/en/US/prod/collateral/switches/ps9441/ps9670/white_paper_c11-542809_ns783_Networking_Solutions_White_Paper.html.

[9] P. Devkota and A. L. N. Reddy. Performance of quantized congestion notification in TCP incast scenarios of data centers. In *MASCOTS*, 2012.

[10] A. Dragojevic, D. Narayanan, O. Hodson, and M. Castro. FaRM: Fast remote memory. In *NSDI*, 2014.

[11] J. Duetto, I. Johnson, J. Flich, F. Naven, P. Garcia, and T. Nachiondo. A new scalable and cost-effective congestion management strategy for lossless multistage interconnection networks. In *HPCA*, 2005.

[12] N. Dukkipati. Rate control protocol (RCP): Congestion control to make flows complete quickly. In *PhD diss., Stanford University*, 2007.

[13] S. Floyd and V. Jacobson. Random early detection gateways for congestion avoidance. *IEEE/ACM Transactions on Networking*, 1:397–413, 1993.

[14] E. G. Gran, M. Eimot, S.-A. Reinemo, T. Skeie,

O. Lysne, L. P. Huse, and G. Shainer. First experiences with congestion control in infiniband hardware. In *IPDPS*, 2010.

[15] A. Greenberg, J. R. Hamilton, N. Jain, S. Kandula, C. Kim, P. Lahiri, D. A. Maltz, P. Patel, and S. Sengupta. VL2: A scalable and flexible data center network. In *SIGCOMM*, 2009.

[16] C. Huang, H. Simitci, Y. Xu, A. Ogus, B. Calder, P. Gopalan, J. Li, and S. Yekhanin. Erasure coding in Windows Azure storage. In *USENIX ATC*, 2012.

[17] IEEE. 802.11Qau. Congestion notification, 2010.

[18] IEEE. 802.11Qbb. Priority based flow control, 2011.

[19] Infiniband Trade Association. InfiniBand architecture volume 1, general specifications, release 1.2.1, 2008.

[20] Infiniband Trade Association. Supplement to InfiniBand architecture specification volume 1 release 1.2.2 annex A16: RDMA over converged ethernet (RoCE), 2010.

[21] Infiniband Trade Association. InfiniBand architecture volume 2, physical specifications, release 1.3, 2012.

[22] Infiniband Trade Association. Supplement to InfiniBand architecture specification volume 1 release 1.2.2 annex A17: RoCEv2 (IP routable RoCE), 2014.

[23] E. Jeong, S. Woo, A. Jamshed, H. Jeong, S. Ihm, D. Han, and K. Park. mTCP: a highly scalable user-level TCP stack for multicore systems. In *NSDI*, 2014.

[24] S. Kamil, L. Oliker, A. Pinar, and J. Shalf. Communication requirements and interconnect optimization for high-end scientific applications. *IEEE TPDS*, 21:188–202, 2009.

[25] S. Kandula, S. Sengupta, A. Greenberg, P. Patel, and R. Chaiken. The nature of datacenter traffic: Measurements and analysis. In *IMC*, 2009.

[26] A. Kangarlou et al. vSnoop: Improving TCP throughput in virtualized environments via acknowledgement offload. In *SC*, 2010.

[27] S. Larsen, P. Sarangam, and R. Huggahalli. Architectural breakdown of end-to-end latency in a TCP/IP network. In *SBAC-PAD*, 2007.

[28] Luigi Rizzo. netmap: a novel framework for fast packet I/O. In *USENIX ATC*, 2012.

[29] I. Marinos, R. N. Watson, and M. Handley. Network stack specialization for performance. In *SIGCOMM*, 2014.

[30] C. Mitchell, Y. Geng, and J. Li. Using one-sided rdma reads to build a fast, cpu-efficient key-value store. In *USENIX ATC*, 2013.

[31] R. Mitta, E. Blem, N. Dukkipati, T. Lam, A. Vahdat, Y. Wang, H. Wassel, D. Wetherall, D. Zats, and M. Ghobadi. TIMELY: RTT-based congestion control for the datacenter. In *SIGCOMM*, 2015.

[32] G. Mora, P. J. Garcia, J. Flich, and J. Duato. RECN-IQ: A cost-effective input-queued switch architecture with congestion management. In *ICPP*, 2007.

[33] J. Perry, A. Ousterhout, H. Balakrishnan, D. Shah, and H. Fugal. Fastpass: A centralized, zero-queue datacenter network. In *SIGCOMM*, 2014.

[34] K. Ramakrishnan, S. Floyd, and D. Black. The addition of explicit congestion notification (ECN). RFC 3168.

[35] M. Recio, B. Metzler, P. Culley, J. Hilland, and D. Garcia. A remote direct memory access protocol specification. RFC 5040.

[36] A. Sivaraman, K. Winstein, P. Thaker, and H. Balakrishnan. An experimental study of the learnability of congestion control. In *SIGCOMM*, 2014.

[37] B. Stephens, A. Cox, A. Singla, J. Carter, C. Dixon, and W. Felter. Practical DCB for improved data center networks. In *INFOCOMM*, 2014.

[38] H. Subramoni, S. Potluri, K. Kandalla, B. Barth, J. Vienne, J. Keasler, K. Tomko, K. Schulz, A. Moody, and D. Panda. Design of a scalable InfiniBand topology service to enable network-topology-aware placement of processes. In *SC*, 2012.

[39] V. Vasudevan, A. Phanishayee, H. Shah, E. Krevat, D. G. Andersen, G. R. Ganger, G. A. Gibson, and B. Mueller. Safe and effective fine-grained TCP retransmissions for datacenter communication. In *SIGCOMM*, 2009.

[40] K. Winstein and H. Balakrishnan. TCP ex machina: computer-generated congestion control. In *SIGCOMM*, 2013.

[41] X. Wu, D. Turner, G. Chen, D. Maltz, X. Yang, L. Yuan, and M. Zhang. Netpilot: Automating datacenter network failure mitigation. In *SIGCOMM*, 2012.

[42] D. Zats, T. Das, P. Mohan, D. Borthakur, and R. Katz. Detail: Reducing the flow completion time tail in datacenter networks. In *SIGCOMM*, 2012.

[43] Chelsio Terminator 5 ASIC. http://www.chelsio.com/nic/rdma-iwarp/.

[44] ConnectX-4 single/dual-port adapter supporting 100gb/s. http://www.mellanox.com/.

[45] Intel data direct I/O technology. http://www.intel.com/content/www/us/en/io/data-direct-i-o-technology-brief.html.

[46] Iperf - the TCP/UDP bandwidth measurement tool. http://iperf.fr.

[47] Offloading the segmentation of large TCP packets. http://msdn.microsoft.com/en-us/library/windows/hardware/ff568840(v=vs.85).aspx.

[48] QueryPerformanceCounter function. http://msdn.microsoft.com/en-us/library/windows/desktop/ms644904(v=vs.85).aspx.

[49] Receive Side Scaling (RSS). http://technet.microsoft.com/en-us/library/hh997036.aspx.

TIMELY: RTT-based Congestion Control for the Datacenter

Radhika Mittal*(UC Berkeley), Vinh The Lam, Nandita Dukkipati, Emily Blem, Hassan Wassel,
Monia Ghobadi*(Microsoft), Amin Vahdat, Yaogong Wang, David Wetherall, David Zats

Google, Inc.

ABSTRACT

Datacenter transports aim to deliver low latency messaging together with high throughput. We show that simple packet delay, measured as round-trip times at hosts, is an effective congestion signal without the need for switch feedback. First, we show that advances in NIC hardware have made RTT measurement possible with microsecond accuracy, and that these RTTs are sufficient to estimate switch queueing. Then we describe how TIMELY can adjust transmission rates using RTT gradients to keep packet latency low while delivering high bandwidth. We implement our design in host software running over NICs with OS-bypass capabilities. We show using experiments with up to hundreds of machines on a Clos network topology that it provides excellent performance: turning on TIMELY for OS-bypass messaging over a fabric with PFC lowers 99 percentile tail latency by 9X while maintaining near line-rate throughput. Our system also outperforms DCTCP running in an optimized kernel, reducing tail latency by 13X. To the best of our knowledge, TIMELY is the first delay-based congestion control protocol for use in the datacenter, and it achieves its results despite having an order of magnitude fewer RTT signals (due to NIC offload) than earlier delay-based schemes such as Vegas.

CCS Concepts

•**Networks** → **Transport protocols;**

Keywords

datacenter transport; delay-based congestion control; OS-bypass; RDMA

*Work done while at Google

SIGCOMM '15 August 17-21, 2015, London, United Kingdom

ACM ISBN 978-1-4503-3542-3/15/08.

DOI: http://dx.doi.org/10.1145/2785956.2787510

1. INTRODUCTION

Datacenter networks run tightly-coupled computing tasks that must be responsive to users, e.g., thousands of back-end computers may exchange information to serve a user request, and all of the transfers must complete quickly enough to let the complete response to be satisfied within 100 ms [24]. To meet these requirements, datacenter transports must simultaneously deliver high bandwidth (≫Gbps) and utilization at low latency (≪msec), even though these aspects of performance are at odds. Consistently low latency matters because even a small fraction of late operations can cause a ripple effect that degrades application performance [21]. As a result, datacenter transports must strictly bound latency and packet loss.

Since traditional loss-based transports do not meet these strict requirements, new datacenter transports [10, 18, 30, 35, 37, 47], take advantage of network support to signal the onset of congestion (e.g., DCTCP [35] and its successors use ECN), introduce flow abstractions to minimize completion latency, cede scheduling to a central controller, and more. However, in this work we take a step back in search of a simpler, immediately deployable design.

The crux of our search is the congestion signal. An ideal signal would have several properties. It would be fine-grained and timely to quickly inform senders about the extent of congestion. It would be discriminative enough to work in complex environments with multiple traffic classes. And, it would be easy to deploy.

Surprisingly, we find that a well-known signal, properly adapted, can meet all of our goals: delay in the form of RTT measurements. RTT is a fine-grained measure of congestion that comes with every acknowledgment. It effectively supports multiple traffic classes by providing an inflated measure for lower-priority transfers that wait behind higher-priority ones. Further, it requires no support from network switches.

Delay has been explored in the wide-area Internet since at least TCP Vegas [16], and some modern TCP variants use delay estimates [44, 46]. But this use of delay has not been without problems. Delay-based schemes tend to compete poorly with more aggressive, loss-based schemes, and delay

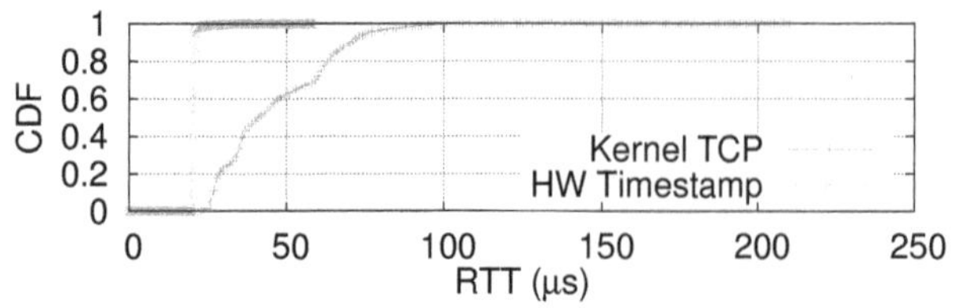

Figure 1: RTTs measured by hardware timestamps have a much smaller random variance than that by kernel TCP stack.

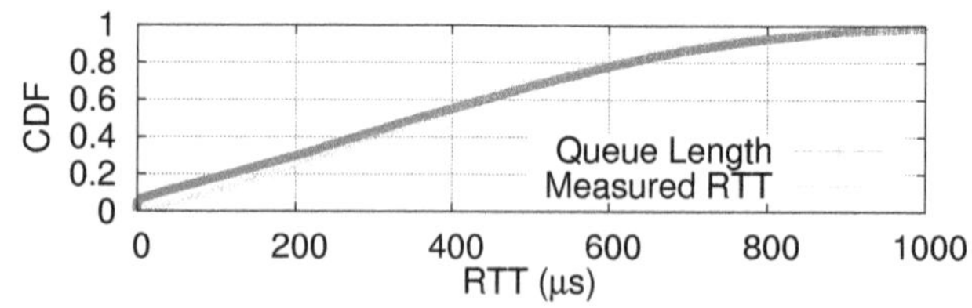

Figure 2: RTTs measured at end-system track closely the queue occupancy at congested link.

estimates may be wildly inaccurate due to host and network issues, e.g., delayed ACKs and different paths. For these reasons, delay is typically used in hybrid schemes with other indicators such as loss.

Moreover, delay has not been used as a congestion signal in the datacenter because datacenter RTTs are difficult to measure at microsecond granularity. This level of precision is easily overwhelmed by host delays such as interrupt processing for acknowledgments. DCTCP eschews a delay-based scheme saying "the accurate measurement of such small increases in queueing delay is a daunting task." [35]

Our insight is that recent NIC advances do allow datacenter RTTs to be measured with sufficient precision, while the wide-area pitfalls of using delay as a congestion signal do not apply. Recent NICs provide hardware support for high-quality timestamping of packet events [1,3,5,8,9], plus hardware-generated ACKs that remove unpredictable host response delays. Meanwhile, datacenter host software can be controlled to avoid competition with other transports, and multiple paths have similar, small propagation delays.

In this paper, we show that delay-based congestion control provides excellent performance in the datacenter. Our key contributions include:

1. We experimentally demonstrate how multi-bit RTT signals measured with NIC hardware are strongly correlated with network queueing.
2. We present *Transport Informed by MEasurement of LatencY* (TIMELY): an RTT-based congestion control scheme. TIMELY uses rate control and is designed to work with NIC offload of multi-packet segments for high performance. Unlike earlier schemes [16,46], we do not build the queue to a fixed RTT threshold. Instead, we use the rate of RTT variation, or the *gradient*, to predict the onset of congestion and hence keep the delays low while delivering high throughput.
3. We evaluate TIMELY with an OS-bypass messaging implementation using hundreds of machines on a Clos network topology. Turning on TIMELY for RDMA transfers on a fabric with PFC (Priority Flow Control) lowers 99 percentile tail latency by $9X$. This tail latency is $13X$ lower than that of DCTCP running in an optimized kernel.

2. THE VALUE OF RTT AS A CONGESTION SIGNAL IN DATACENTERS

Existing datacenter transports use signals from network switches to detect the onset of congestion and run with low levels of latency and loss [15,35,37]. We argue that network queueing delay derived from RTT measurements, without the need for any switch support, is a superior congestion signal.

RTT directly reflects latency. RTTs are valuable because they directly measure the quantity we care about: end-to-end latency inflated by network queueing. Signals derived from queue occupancy such as ECN fail to directly inform this metric. An ECN mark on a packet simply indicates that the queue measure corresponding to the packet exceeds a threshold. Rich use of QoS in the datacenter means it is not possible to convert this threshold into a single corresponding latency. Multiple queues with different priorities share the same output link, but the ECN mark only provides information about those with occupancy exceeding a threshold. Low priority traffic can experience large queueing delays without necessarily building up a large queue. In such circumstances, queueing delay reflects the state of congestion in the network which is not reflected by queue occupancy of low priority traffic. Further, an ECN mark describes behavior at a single switch. In a highly utilized network, congestion occurs at multiple switches, and ECN signals cannot differentiate among them. The RTT accumulates information about the end-to-end path. It includes the NIC, which may also become congested but is ignored by most schemes. Finally, RTTs work even for the lossless network fabrics commonly used to support FCoE [2]. In these fabrics, mere queue occupancy can fail to reflect congestion because of Priority Flow Control mechanisms used to ensure zero packet loss.

RTT can be measured accurately in practice. A key practical hurdle is whether RTTs can be measured accurately in datacenters where they are easily 1000X smaller than wide-area latencies. Many factors have precluded accurate measurement in the past: variability due to kernel scheduling; NIC performance techniques including offload (GSO/TSO, GRO/LRO); and protocol processing such as TCP delayed acknowledgements. This problem is severe in datacenters where each of these factors is large enough to overwhelm propagation and queuing delays.

Fortunately, recent NICs provide hardware support to solve these problems [1,3,5,8,9] and can accurately record the time of packet transmission and reception without being affected by software-incurred delays. These methods must be used with care lest they overly tax the NIC. We describe our use of NIC support later in the paper. These NICs also provide hardware-based acknowledgements for some protocols.

The combination of these features lets us take precise RTT measurements to accurately track end-to-end network

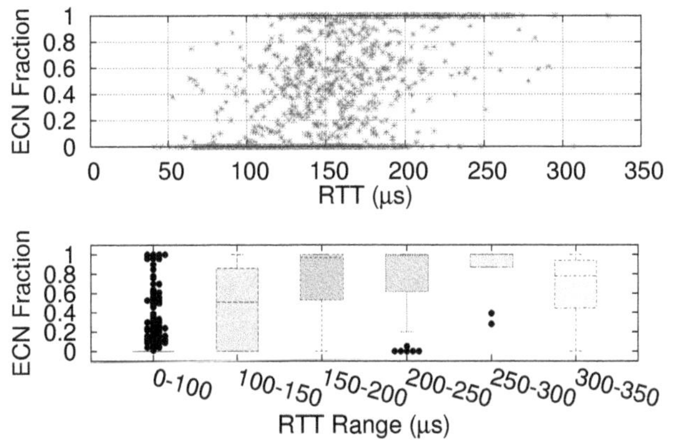

Figure 3: Fraction of packets with ECN marks versus RTTs shown as scatter plot (top) and box plot (bottom).

queues. The following experiment shows this behavior: we connect two hosts to the same network via 10 Gbps links and send 16 KB ping-pong messages without any cross traffic and on a quiescent network. Since there is no congestion, we expect the RTT measurements to be low and stable. Figure 1 compares the CDF of RTTs measured using NIC hardware timestamps and RTTs measured via the OS TCP stack. The CDF for RTTs using NIC timestamps is nearly a straight line, indicating small variance. In contrast, the RTTs measured by kernel TCP are larger and much more variable.

RTT is a rapid, multi-bit signal. Network queueing delay can be calculated by subtracting known propagation and serialization delays from an RTT. Surprisingly, we have found that this method provides richer and faster information about the state of network switches than explicit network switch signals such as ECN marks. As a binary quantity, ECN marks convey a single bit of information, while RTT measurements convey multiple bits and capture the full extent of end to end queueing delay aggregated across multiple switches rather than the presence of queueing exceeding a simple fixed threshold at any one of N switches. Since each packet may carry an ECN mark, it is plausible that the sequence of marks can close this gap and convey multi-bit information about the congestion level, as is done in DCTCP (which in practice is how ECN is used in datacenters). However, modern practices such as 64 KB segmentation offload undermine the independence of marks made closely in time because host sources are bursty. Large bursts at wire speed tend to see most packets either above or below the marking threshold.

Assuming it is accurate, a single high RTT measurement immediately signals the extent of congestion. This RTT measurement works even with packet bursts for a flow sent along a single network path: the RTT of the last packet in the burst tracks the maximum RTT across packets since delays to earlier packets push out later packets. To show how well RTT tracks network queuing delay, we set up an incast experiment with 100 flows on 10 client machines simultaneously transmitting to a single server. To incorporate NIC offload, we send 64 KB messages and collect only a single RTT measurement per message on the client side. The bottleneck link is a 10 Gbps link to the server. We sample the switch queue each microsecond.

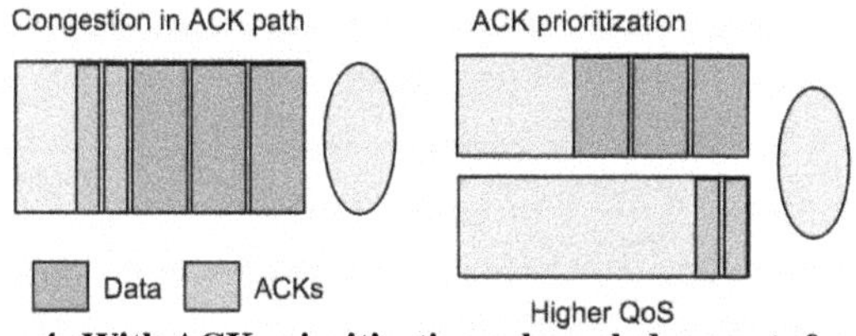

Figure 4: With ACK prioritization acknowledgements from the primary incast are not delayed by the data of the secondary incast.

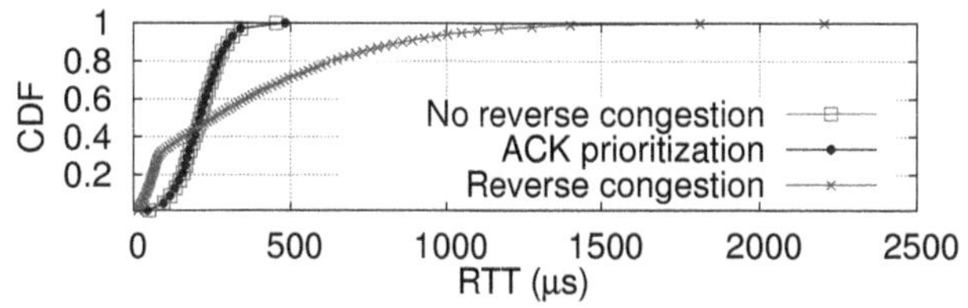

Figure 5: In the presence of reverse congestion, RTT measurements with ACK prioritization are indistinguishable from RTTs that do not experience any reverse path congestion.

Figure 2 shows the CDF of RTTs as measured at the end system compared to the queue occupancy measured directly at the switch and shown in units of time computed for a 10 Gbps link. The two CDFs match extremely well.

In contrast, the ECN signal does not correlate well with RTT and hence with the amount of queuing. We set up a similar incast experiment, except now TCP senders perform long transfers to a single receiver. The bottleneck is the 10 Gbps link to the receiver, with an 80 KB switch ECN marking threshold. We instrument the senders to measure the fraction of packets received with ECN marks in every round-trip time, using the advance of *SND_UNA* [41] to mark the end of an RTT round. We also measure the minimum RTT sample in every round, as prior work has found it to be a robust descriptor untainted by delayed ACKs and send/receive offload schemes. Both the scatter and box plots [1] [4] in Figure 3 show only a weak correlation between the fraction of ECN marks and RTTs.

Limitations of RTTs. While we have found the RTT signal valuable, an effective design must use it carefully. RTT measurements lump queueing in both directions along the network path. This may confuse reverse path congestion experienced by ACKs with forward path congestion experienced by data packets. One simple fix is to send ACKs with higher priority, so that they do not incur significant queuing delay. This method works in the common case of flows that predominantly send data in one direction; we did not need more complicated methods.

We conducted an experiment to verify the efficacy of ACK prioritization: we started two incasts (*primary* and *secondary*) such that the ACKs of the primary incast share the same congested queue as the data segments of the secondary incast, as shown in Figure 4. Figure 5 shows the CDF of

[1]Whiskers extend to the most distant point within $1.2X$ interquartile range. Points outside these limits are drawn individually.

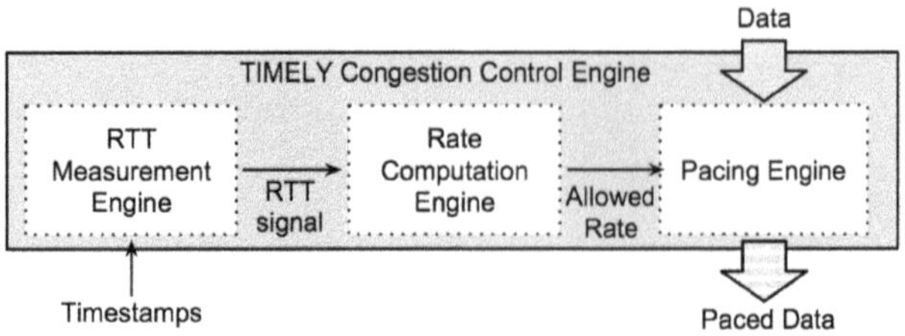

Figure 6: TIMELY overview.

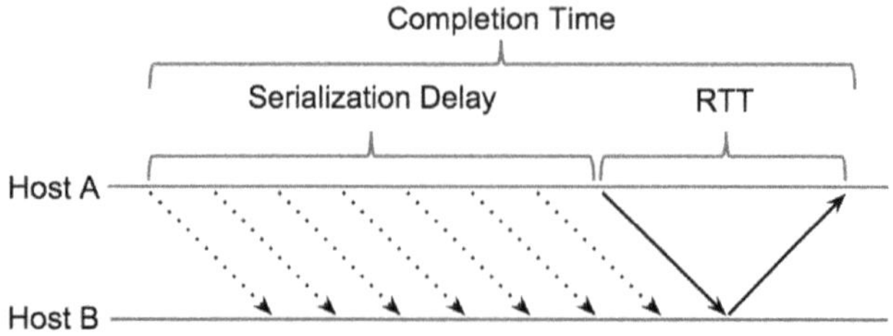

Figure 7: Finding RTT from completion time.

RTTs from the primary incast for the following three cases: 1) no congestion in ACK path (no secondary incast); 2) in the presence of congestion in ACK path; and 3) ACKs from primary incast are prioritized to higher QoS queue in the presence of reverse congestion. We find that the reverse congestion creates noise in RTT measurements of the primary incast and elongates the tail latencies. Throughput of the primary incast is also impacted (and hence the smaller RTTs in the lower percentiles). With ACK prioritization, the RTTs measured in the primary incast are indistinguishable from those measured in the absence of reverse path congestion.

In future work, it would be straightforward to calculate variations in one-way delay between two packets by embedding a timestamp in a packet (e.g., TCP timestamps). The change in queuing delay is then the change in the arrival time minus send time of each packet. This method needs only clocks that run at the same rate, which is a much less stringent requirement than synchronized clocks.

The other classic shortcoming of RTTs is that changing network paths have disparate delays. It is less of a problem in datacenters as all paths have small propagation delays.

3. TIMELY FRAMEWORK

TIMELY provides a framework for rate control that is independent of the transport protocol used for reliability. Figure 6 shows its three components: 1) RTT measurement to monitor the network for congestion; 2) a computation engine that converts RTT signals into target sending rates; and 3) a control engine that inserts delays between segments to achieve the target rate. We implement TIMELY in host software with NIC hardware support, and run an independent instance for each flow.

3.1 RTT Measurement Engine

We assume a traditional transport where the receiver explicitly ACKs new data so that we may extract an RTT. We define the RTT in terms of Figure 7, which shows the timeline of a message: a segment consisting of multiple packets is sent as a single burst and then ACKed as a unit by the receiver. A *completion event* is generated upon receiving an ACK for a segment of data and includes the ACK receive time. The time from when the first packet is sent (t_{send}) until the ACK is received ($t_{completion}$) is defined as the *completion time*. Unlike TCP, there is one RTT for the set of packets rather than one RTT per 1-2 packets. There are several delay components: 1) the serialization delay to transmit all packets in the segment, typically up to 64 KB; 2) the round-trip wire delay for the segment and its ACK to propagate across the datacenter; 3) the turnaround time at the receiver to generate the ACK; and 4) the queuing delay at switches experienced in both directions.

We define the RTT to be the propagation and queueing delay components only. The first component is a deterministic function of the segment size and the line rate of the NIC. We compute and subtract it from the total elapsed time so that the RTTs input to TIMELY's rate computation engine are independent of segment size. The third component is sufficiently close to zero in our setting with NIC-based ACKs that we can ignore it. Of the remaining components, the second is the propagation delay including the packet-based store-and-forward behavior at switches. It is the minimum RTT and fixed for a given flow. Only the last component – the queueing delay – causes variation in the RTT, and it is our focus for detecting congestion. In summary, TIMELY running on Host A (shown in Figure 7) computes RTT as:

$$RTT = t_{completion} - t_{send} - \frac{\text{seg. size}}{\text{NIC line rate}}$$

For context, in a 10 Gbps network, serialization of 64 KB takes 51 μs, propagation may range from 10-100 μs, and 1500 B of queuing takes 1.2 μs. We rely on two forms of NIC support to precisely measure segment RTTs, described next.

ACK Timestamps. We require the NIC to supply the completion timestamp, $t_{completion}$. As shown in §2, OS timestamps suffer from variations such as scheduling and interrupts that can easily obscure the congestion signal. t_{send} is the NIC hardware time that's read by host software just before posting the segment to NIC.

Prompt ACK generation. We require NIC-based ACK generation so that we can ignore the turnaround time at the receiver. An alternative would be to use timestamps to measure the ACK turnaround delay due to host processing delay. We have avoided this option because it would require augmenting transport wire formats to include this difference explicitly.

Fortunately, some modern NICs [1, 3, 5, 8, 9] provide one or both features, and our requirements are met naturally with a messaging implementation that timestamps segment acknowledgement. A specific implementation of TIMELY in the context of RDMA is described in §5. We believe our design is more generally applicable to TCP with some care to work with the batching behavior of the NIC, correctly associate an ACK with the reception of new data, and compensate for ACK turnaround time.

3.2 Rate Computation Engine

This component implements our RTT-based congestion control algorithm as detailed in §4. The interface to the rate computation engine is simple. Upon each completion event, the RTT measurement engine provides the RTT in microseconds to the rate computation engine. While this is the only required input, additional timing information could also be useful, e.g., the delay incurred in the NIC. There is no requirement for packet-level operation; in normal operation we expect a single completion event for a segment of size up to 64 KB due to NIC offload. The rate computation engine runs the congestion control algorithm upon each completion event, and outputs an updated target rate for the flow.

3.3 Rate Control Engine

When a message is ready to be sent, the rate control engine breaks it into segments for transmission, and sends each segment to the scheduler in turn. For runtime efficiency, we implement a single scheduler that handles all flows. The scheduler uses the segment size, flow rate (provided by the rate computation engine), and time of last transmission to compute the send time for the current segment with the appropriate pacing delay. The segment is then placed in a priority queue in the scheduler. Segments with send times in the past are serviced in round-robin fashion; segments with future send times are queued. After the pacing delay has elapsed, the rate control engine passes the segment to the NIC for immediate transmission as a burst of packets. Data is first batched into 64 KB segments, following which the scheduler computes the pacing delay to insert between two such batched segments. Note that 64 KB is the maximum batching size and is not a requirement, e.g., the segment sizes for a flow that only has small messages to exchange at any given time will be smaller than 64 KB. We later present results for segment sizes smaller than 64 KB as well.

TIMELY is rate-based rather than window-based because it gives better control over traffic bursts given the widespread use of NIC offload. The bandwidth-delay product is only a small number of packet bursts in datacenters, e.g., 51 μs at 10 Gbps is one 64 KB message. In this regime, windows do not provide fine-grained control over packet transmissions. It is easier to directly control the gap between bursts by specifying a target rate. As a safeguard, we limit the volume of outstanding data to a static worst-case limit.

4. TIMELY CONGESTION CONTROL

Our congestion control algorithm runs in the rate computation engine. In this section, we describe our environment and key performance metrics, followed by our gradient-based approach and algorithm.

4.1 Metrics and Setting

The datacenter network environment is characterized by many bursty message workloads from tightly-coupled forms of computing over high bandwidth, low-latency paths. It is the opposite of the traditional wide-area Internet in many respects. Bandwidth is plentiful, and it is flow completion time (e.g., for a Remote Procedure Call (RPC)) that is the overriding concern. For short RPCs, the minimum completion time is determined by the propagation and serialization delay. Hence, we attempt to minimize any queueing delay to keep RTTs low. The latency tail matters because application performance degrades when even a small fraction of the packets are late [21]. Consistent low-latency implies low queueing delay and near zero packet loss, since recovery actions may greatly increase message latency. Longer RPCs will have larger completion times because of the time it takes to transmit more data across a shared network. To keep this added time small, we must maintain high aggregate throughput to benefit all flows and maintain approximate fairness so that no one flow is penalized.

Our primary metrics for evaluation are tail (99th percentile) RTT and aggregate throughput, as they determine how quickly we complete short and long RPCs (assuming some fairness). When there is a conflict between throughput and packet RTT, we prefer to keep RTT low at the cost of sacrificing a small amount of bandwidth. This is because bandwidth is plentiful to start with, and increased RTT directly impacts the completion times of short transfers. In effect, we seek to ride the throughput/latency curve to the point where tail latency becomes unacceptable. Secondary metrics are fairness and loss. We report both as a check rather than study them in detail. Finally, we prefer a stable design over higher average, but oscillating rates for the sake of predictable performance.

4.2 Delay Gradient Approach

Delay-based congestion control algorithms such as FAST TCP [46] and Compound TCP [44] are inspired by the seminal work of TCP Vegas [16]. These interpret RTT increase above a baseline as indicative of congestion: they reduce the sending rate if delay is further increased to try and maintain buffer occupancy at the bottleneck queue around some predefined threshold. However, Kelly et al. [33] argue that it is not possible to control the queue size when it is shorter in time than the control loop delay. This is the case in datacenters where the control loop delay of a 64 KB message over a 10 Gbps link is at least 51 μs, and possibly significantly higher due to competing traffic, while one packet of queuing delay lasts 1 μs. The most any algorithm can do in these circumstances is to control the *distribution* of the queue occupancy. Even if controlling the queue size were possible, choosing a threshold for a datacenter network in which multiple queues can be a bottleneck is a notoriously hard tuning problem.

TIMELY's congestion controller achieves low latencies by reacting to the *delay gradient* or derivative of the queuing with respect to time, instead of trying to maintain a standing queue. This is possible because we can accurately measure differences in RTTs that indicate changes in queuing delay. A positive delay gradient due to increasing RTTs indicates a rising queue, while a negative gradient indicates a receding queue. By using the gradient, we can react to queue growth without waiting for a standing queue to form – a strategy that helps us achieve low latencies.

Algorithm 1: TIMELY congestion control.

Data: new_rtt
Result: Enforced rate
new_rtt_diff = new_rtt - prev_rtt ;
prev_rtt = new_rtt ;
rtt_diff = (1 - α) · rtt_diff + α · new_rtt_diff ;
  ▷ α: EWMA weight parameter
normalized_gradient = rtt_diff / minRTT ;
if *new_rtt* < T_{low} **then**
  rate ← rate + δ ;
    ▷ δ: additive increment step
  return;
if *new_rtt* > T_{high} **then**
  rate ← rate · $\left(1 - \beta \cdot \left(1 - \frac{T_{high}}{\text{new\_rtt}}\right)\right)$;
    ▷ β: multiplicative decrement factor
  return;
if *normalized_gradient* ≤ 0 **then**
  rate ← rate + N · δ ;
    ▷ N = 5 if gradient<0 for five completion events (HAI mode); otherwise N = 1
else
  rate ← rate · (1 - β · normalized_gradient)

Delay gradient is a proxy for the rate mismatch at the bottleneck queue. We are inspired by RCP, XCP, PI, and QCN [10, 28, 32, 39] that find explicit feedback on the rate mismatch has better stability and convergence properties than explicit feedback based only on queue sizes; the latter can even cause the queue to be *less* accurately controlled. The key difference is that all of these prior controllers operate at point queues in the network, while TIMELY achieves similar benefits by using the end-to-end delay gradient.

The model we assume is N end hosts all sending data at a total rate $y(t)$ into a bottleneck queue with drain rate C, i.e. the outgoing rate is $\leq C$. We denote the queuing delay through the bottleneck queue by $q(t)$. If $y(t) > C$, the rate at which the queue builds up is $(y(t) - C)$. Since queued data drains at a rate C, the queuing delay gradient is given by $\frac{dq(t)}{dt} = \frac{(y(t)-C)}{C}$. The gradient is dimensionless. It is positive for $y(t) > C$ and signals how quickly the queue is building. The negative gradient when $y(t) < C$, signals how quickly the queue is draining. Hence, the delay gradient measured through RTT signals acts as an indicator for the rate mismatch at the bottleneck. This reasoning holds as long as there is some non-zero queue in the network. When there is zero queueing or queues are not changing in size, the measured gradient is also zero. TIMELY strives to match the aggregate incoming rate $y(t)$ to the drain rate, C, and so adapts its per-connection rate, $R(t)$, in proportion to the measured error of $\frac{(y(t)-C)}{C} = \frac{dq(t)}{dt} = \frac{d(RTT)}{dt}$.

4.3 The Main Algorithm

Algorithm 1 shows pseudo-code for our congestion control algorithm. TIMELY maintains a single rate $R(t)$ for each connection and updates it on every completion event

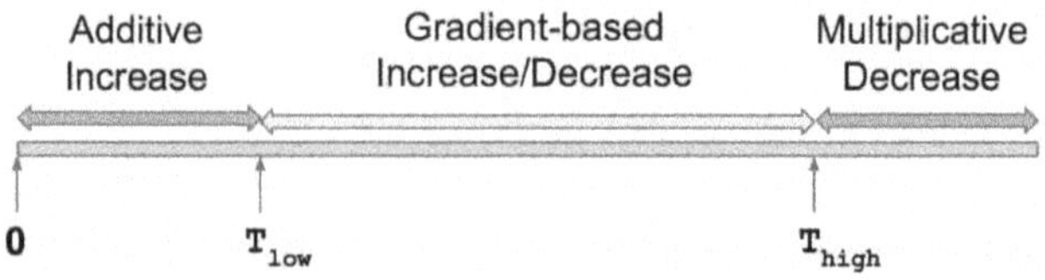

Figure 8: Gradient tracking zone with low and high RTT thresholds.

using RTT samples. It employs gradient tracking, adjusting the rate using a smoothed delay gradient as the error signal to keep throughput close to the available bandwidth. Additionally, we employ thresholds to detect and respond to extreme cases of under utilization or overly high packet latencies. Figure 8 shows the gradient zone along with the two thresholds. When the RTT is in the nominal operating range, the gradient tracking algorithm computes the delay gradient from RTT samples and uses it to adjust the sending rate.

Computing the delay gradient. We rely on accurate RTT measurements using NIC timestamps (§3). To compute the delay gradient, TIMELY computes the difference between two consecutive RTT samples. We normalize this difference by dividing it by the minimum RTT, obtaining a dimensionless quantity. In practice, the exact value of the minimum RTT does not matter since we only need to determine if the queue is growing or receding. We therefore use a fixed value representing the wire propagation delay across the datacenter network, which is known ahead of time. Finally, we pass the result through an EWMA filter. This filter allows us to detect the overall trend in the rise and fall in the queue, while ignoring minor queue fluctuations that are not indicative of congestion.

Computing the sending rate. Next, TIMELY uses the normalized gradient to update the target rate for the connection. If the gradient is negative or equals zero, the network can keep up with the aggregate incoming rate, and therefore there is room for a higher rate. In this case, TIMELY probes for more bandwidth by performing an additive increment for the connection: $R = R + \delta$, where δ is the bandwidth additive increment constant. When the gradient is positive, the total sending rate is greater than network capacity. Hence, TIMELY performs a multiplicative rate decrement β, scaled by the gradient factor:

$$R = R\left(1 - \beta\frac{d(RTT(t))}{dt}\right)$$

The delay gradient signal, which is based on the total incoming and outgoing rates, is common for all connections along the same congested path. The well-known AIMD property ensures that our algorithm achieves fairness across connections [19]. Connections sending at a higher rate observe a stronger decrease in their rate, while the increase in rate remains same for all connections.

While the delay gradient is effective in normal operation, situations with significant under-utilization or high latency require a more aggressive response. Next we discuss how TIMELY detects and responds to these situations.

Need for RTT low threshold T_{low}. The ideal environment for our algorithm is one where packets are perfectly paced.

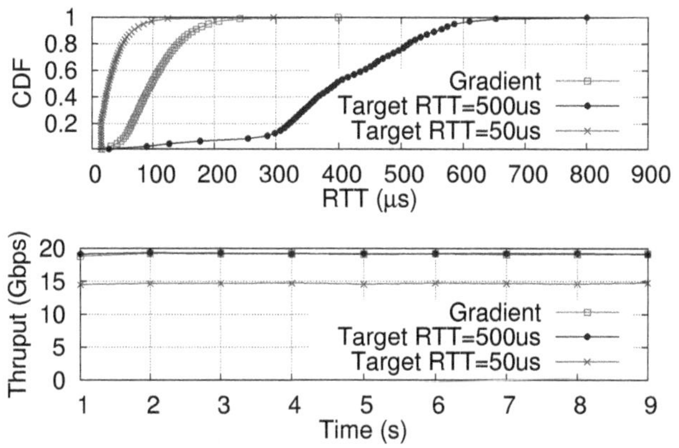

Figure 9: Comparison of gradient (low and high thresholds of 50 μs and 500 μs) with target-based approach (T_{target} of 50 μs and 500 μs).

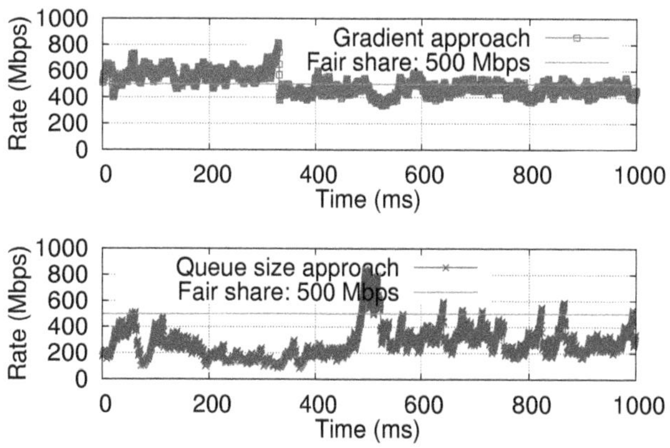

Figure 10: Per-connection rates in the gradient approach are smooth (top) while those in the queue-size based approach (with T_{target} = 50μs) are more oscillatory (bottom).

However, in practical settings, the TIMELY rate is enforced on a segment granularity that can be as large as 64 KB. These large segments lead to packet bursts, which result in transient queues in the network and hence RTT spikes when there is an occasional collision. Without care, the core algorithm would detect a positive gradient due to a sudden RTT spike and unnecessarily infer congestion and back-off. We avoid this behavior by using a low threshold T_{low} to filter RTT spikes; the adjustment based on delay gradient kicks in for RTT samples greater than the threshold. T_{low} is a (nonlinear) increasing function of the segment size used in the network, since larger messages cause more bursty queue occupancy. We explore this effect in our evaluation, as well as show how fine-grained pacing at the hosts can reduce burstiness and hence the need for a low threshold.

Need for RTT high threshold T_{high}. The core gradient algorithm maintains close to the bottleneck link throughput while building very little queue. However, in theory, it is possible for the gradient to stay at zero while the queue remains at a high, fixed level. To remove this concern, T_{high} serves as an upper bound on the tolerable end-to-end network queue delay, i.e., the tail latency. It provides a way to reduce the rate independent of gradient value if the latency grows, a protection that is possible because we operate in a datacenter environment with known characteristics. If the measured RTT is greater than T_{high}, we reduce the rate multiplicatively:

$$R = R\Big(1 - \beta\Big(1 - \frac{T_{high}}{RTT}\Big)\Big)$$

Note that we use the instantaneous rather than smoothed RTT. While this may seem unusual, we can slow down in response to a single overly large RTT because we can be confident that it signals congestion, and our priority is to maintain low packet latencies and avoid loss. We tried responding to average RTT as a congestion indicator, and found that it *hurts* packet latency because of the extra delay in the feedback loop. By the time the average rose, and congestion control reduces the rate, queueing delay has already increased in the network. Our finding is inline with [27] which shows through a control theoretic analysis that the averaged queue length is a failing of RED AQM. We show in §6 how T_{high} lets us ride to the right along the throughput-delay tradeoff curve.

Hyperactive increase (HAI) for faster convergence. Inspired by the *max probing* phase in TCP BIC, CUBIC [42] congestion control, and QCN [10], we include an *HAI* option for faster convergence as follows: if TIMELY does not reach the new fair share after a period of slow growth, i.e., the gradient is negative for several consecutive completion times, then HAI switches to a faster additive increase in which the rate is incremented by $N\delta$ instead of δ. This is useful when the new fair share rate has dramatically increased due to reduced load in the network.

4.4 Gradient versus Queue Size

We highlight through an experiment how the gradient approach differs from a queue size based scheme. If we set the same value for T_{low} and T_{high}, then TIMELY congestion control reduces to a queue size based approach (similar to TCP FAST algorithm; FAST in turn is a scaled, improved version of Vegas). Denote T_{target} as the value of this single RTT threshold, i.e., $T_{target} = T_{low} = T_{high}$. Then the rate is increased additively and decreased multiplicatively with the decrease factor scaled by the queue size above T_{target}.

Figure 9 compares the RTT and throughput for the gradient and queue size based approach for an incast traffic pattern. (See §6 for experimental details.) We use low and high thresholds of 50 μs and 500 μs for gradient, versus T_{target} of 50 μs and 500 μs for the queue-sized approach. We see that the queue size approach can maintain either low latency or high throughput, but finds it hard to do both. By building up a standing queue up to a high T_{target} of 500 μs, throughput is optimized, but at the cost of latency due to queueing. Alternatively, by keeping the standing queue at a low T_{target} of 50 μs, latency is optimized, but throughput suffers as the queue is sometimes empty. By operating on the rising and falling queue, the gradient approach predicts the onset of congestion. This lets it deliver the high throughput of a high queue target while keeping the tail latency close to that of a low target.

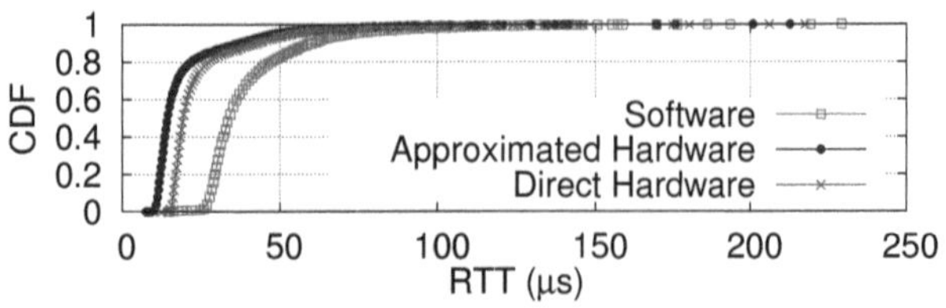

Figure 11: Comparison of the accuracy of NIC and SW timestamps.

Furthermore, as shown in Figure 10, the connection rates oscillate more in the queue-size approach, as it drives the RTT up and down towards the target queue size. The gradient approach maintains a smoother rate around the fair share. Similar results are shown in control theory terms for AQMs using the queue-size approach and gradient approach [28].

The main take-away is that T_{low} and T_{high} thresholds effectively bring the delay within a target range and play a role similar to the target queue occupancy in many AQM schemes. Using the delay gradient improves stability and helps keep the latency within the target range.

5. IMPLEMENTATION

Our implementation is built on 10 Gbps NICs with OS-bypass capabilities. The NICs support multi-packet segments with hardware-based ACKs and timestamps. We implemented TIMELY in the context of RDMA (Remote Direct Memory Access) as a combination of NIC functionality and host software. We use RDMA primitives to invoke NIC services and offload complete memory-to-memory transfers to the NIC. In particular, we mainly use RDMA Write and Read to take a message from local host memory and send it on the network as a burst of packets. On the remote host, the NIC acknowledges receipt of the complete message and places it directly in the remote memory for consumption by the remote application. The local host is notified of the acknowledgement when the transfer is complete. We describe below some of the notable points of the implementation.

Transport Interface. TIMELY is concerned with the congestion control portion of the transport protocol; it is not concerned with reliability or the higher-level interface the transport exposes to applications. This allows the interface to the rest of the transport to be simple: message send and receive. When presented with a message at the sender, TIMELY breaks it into smaller segments if it is large and sends the segments at the target rate. A message is simply an ordered sequence of bytes. The segment is passed to the NIC and then sent over the network as a burst of packets. On the remote host, the NIC acknowledges receipt of the complete segment. At the receiver, when a segment is received it is passed to the rest of the transport for processing. This simple model supports transports ranging from RPCs to bytestreams such as TCP.

Using NIC Completions for RTT Measurement. In practice, using NIC timestamps is challenging. Our NIC only records the absolute timestamp of when the multi-packet operation finishes and therefore our userspace software needs to record a timestamp of when the operation was posted to the NIC. This requires a scheme to map host clock to NIC clock, as well as calibration. We record host (CPU) timestamps when posting work to the NIC and build a calibration mechanism to map NIC timestamps to host timestamps. A simple linear mapping is sufficient. The mechanism works well because the probability of being interrupted between recording the host send timestamp and actually handing the message to the NIC is fairly low. Figure 11 compares RTTs obtained from NIC HW timestamps, the calibration mechanism, and pure software only timestamps. Note that TIMELY does not spin, so interrupts and wakeups are included in the software timestamp numbers. It clearly demonstrates that the calibration mechanism is just as accurate as using only NIC timestamps. Furthermore, the SW timestamps have a large variance, which increases as load on the host increases.

We consider any NIC queuing occurring to be part of the RTT signal. This is important because NIC queuing is also indicative of congestion and is handled by the same rate-based controls as network queueing — even if the NIC were to give us an actual send timestamp, we would want the ability to observe NIC queuing.

RDMA rate control. For RDMA Writes, TIMELY on the sender directly controls the segment pacing rate. For RDMA Reads, the receiver issues read requests, in response to which the remote host performs a DMA of the data segments. In this case, TIMELY cannot directly pace the data segments, but instead achieves the same result by pacing the read requests: when computing the pacing delay between read requests, the rate computation engine takes into account the data segment bytes read from the remote host.

Application limited behavior. Applications do not always have enough data to transmit for their flows to reach the target rate. When this happens, we do not want to inadvertently increase the target rate without bound because the network appears to be uncongested. To prevent this problem, we let the target rate increase only if the application is sending at more than 80% of the target rate, and we also cap the maximum target rate at 10 Gbps. The purpose of allowing some headroom is to let the application increase its rate without an unreasonable delay when it does have enough data to send.

Rate update frequency. TIMELY's rate update equation assumes that there is at most one completion event per RTT interval. The transmission delay of a 64 KB message on a 10 Gbps link is 51 μs; with a minimum RTT of 20 μs, there can be at most one completion event in any given minimum RTT interval. However, for small segment sizes, there can be multiple completion events within a minimum RTT interval. In such a scenario, we want to update the rate based on the most recent information. We do so by updating the rate for every completion event, taking care to scale the updates by the number of completions per minimum RTT interval so that we do not overweigh the new information.

For scheduler efficiency, the rate control engine enforces rate updates lazily. When the previously computed send time for a segment elapses, the scheduler checks the current rate. If the rate has decreased, we recompute the send time, and

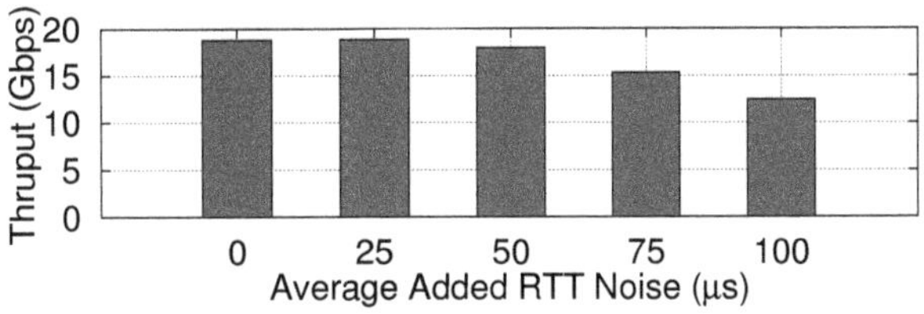

Figure 12: Impact of RTT noise on TIMELY throughput.

re-queue the segment if appropriate. Otherwise, the scheduler proceeds to send the segment to the NIC.

Additional pacing opportunities. By default, thc NIC sends a segment as a burst of packets at the link line rate. We explore another possibility: using NIC rate-limiters to transmit a burst of packets at less than the line rate. The rationale is to supplement the pacing engine that spreads packets of the flow over time with NIC-sized units of work. With hardware rate-limiters [43], it is feasible to offload part of the responsibility for pacing to the NIC. However due to hardware constraints, re-configuring pacing rate every few RTTs is not always feasible. Instead, we use a hybrid approach: software pacing of large segments and hardware pacing at fixed rate below the link rate, e.g. 5 Gbps on a 10 Gbps link. At these high-rates, the purpose of NIC pacing is to insert gaps in the burst so that multiple bursts mix at switches without causing latency spikes. In this case, the rate control engine compensates for the NIC pacing delays by treating it as a lower transmission line rate.

6. EVALUATION

We evaluate a real host-based implementation of TIMELY at two scales. First, we examine the basic properties of the congestion controller such as throughput, fairness, packet latency, and timing accuracy in an incast setting. For these microbenchmarks, we use a small-scale testbed with a rack of equipment. Second, we run TIMELY on a larger scale testbed of a few hundred machines in a classic Clos network topology [12, 34]. Along with running the traffic workload, hosts collect measurements of per-connection throughputs, RPC latencies, and RTTs (we established in §2 that host RTTs correspond well with queueing delays measured at the switches). All links are 10 Gbps unless mentioned otherwise. The OS used in all experiments is Linux.

To place our results in context, we compare TIMELY with two alternatives. First, we use OS-bypass messaging over a fabric with Priority Flow Control (PFC) as commonly used for low loss and latency in FCoE, e.g. DCB [2]. The RDMA transport is in the NIC and sensitive to packet drops, so PFC is necessary because drops hurt performance badly. We add TIMELY to this RDMA setting to observe its benefits; we check that pause message counts are low to verify that there is sufficient switch buffering for TIMELY to work and PFC is not an inadvertent factor in our experimental results. Second, we compare against an optimized kernel stack that implements DCTCP [35] running on the same fabric without the use of PFC. We choose DCTCP as a point of comparison because it is a well-known, modern datacenter transport that has been deployed and proven at scale.

Metric	DCTCP	FAST*			PFC	TIMELY
		10M	50M	100M		
Total Throughput (Gbps)	19.5	7.5	12.5	17.5	19.5	19.4
Avg. RTT (us)	598	19	120	354	658	61
99-percentile RTT (us)	1490	49	280	460	1036	116

Table 1: Overall performance comparison. FAST* is shown with network buffered traffic parameter in Mbps.

Henceforth we refer to: 1) *DCTCP*, for kernel DCTCP over a fabric without PFC; 2) *PFC*, for OS-bypass messaging over a fabric with PFC; 3) *FAST**, for OS-bypass messaging with TCP FAST-like congestion control algorithm; and 4) *TIMELY*, for OS-bypass messaging with TIMELY over a fabric with PFC

Unless mentioned otherwise, we use the following parameters for TIMELY: segment size of 16 KB, T_{low} of 50 μs, T_{high} of 500 μs, additive increment of 10 Mbps, and a multiplicative decrement factor (β) of 0.8.

6.1 Small-Scale Experiments

We use an incast traffic pattern for small-scale experiments (unless otherwise specified) since it is a key congestion scenario for datacenter networks [45]. To create incast, 10 client machines on a single rack send to a single server on the same rack. Each client runs 4 connections, i.e., 40 total concurrent connections. Each connection sends 16 KB segments at a high enough aggregate rate to saturate the server bandwidth of 2x10G link which is the bottleneck for the experiment. This is a demanding workload for testing congestion control: while there are many connections present in the datacenter, the number of connections limited by network capacity is normally small.

Required RTT measurement accuracy. To evaluate the accuracy of RTT samples required by TIMELY, we add noise to the measured RTTs and observe the impact on throughput. We add random noise uniformly distributed in the range of $[0, x]$ μs to each RTT sample, where x is set to 0, 50, 100, 150, 200. Figure 12 shows the total throughput measured on the server at different noise levels. Average noise of 50 μs causes visible throughput degradation, and higher noise leads to more severe performance penalties. A T_{low} value lower than 50 μs lowers the tolerance to RTT noise even further. Note that this level of noise is easily reachable by software timestamping (due to scheduling delays, coalescing, aggregation, etc.). Hence, accurate RTT measurement provided by NIC support is the cornerstone of TIMELY.

Comparison with PFC. Table 1 compares TIMELY with OS-bypass messaging over a fabric with conventional RDMA deployment over PFC. While the throughput is slightly lower with TIMELY, the median and tail RTTs are lower by more than order of magnitude and pauses are not triggered at all. Next, we break out connections to show that TIMELY also delivers excellent performance for individual connections. Figure 13 shows a timeline of the observed RTT and throughput for a sample for four individual connections using TIMELY. Each datapoint represents a single completion event. The fair share for each connection is 500 Mbps. We see that the throughput is close to the

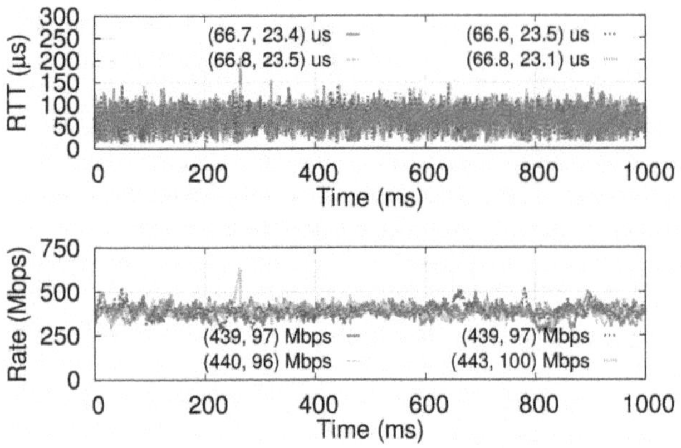

Figure 13: RTTs and sending rates of a sample of connections for TIMELY. The legend gives the mean and standard deviation for each connection.

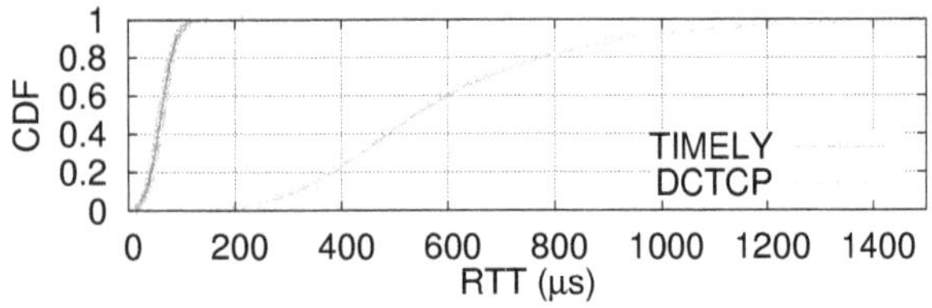

Figure 14: CDF of RTT distribution

fair share and the RTT remains consistently low. To quantify the fairness of bandwidth allocation across connections, we compute a Jain fairness index [31] of 0.953 for TIMELY and 0.909 for PFC. Our design is more fair, and has a high enough index to meet our fairness needs.

Comparison with DCTCP. We compare TIMELY with DCTCP. To review briefly: senders emit ECN capable packets; switches mark each packet queued beyond a fixed threshold; receivers return all ECN marks to the sender; and senders adapt their rate based on the fraction of packets with ECN marks in a window. Note that of necessity our comparison is for two different host software stacks, as DCTCP runs in an optimized kernel without PFC support whereas TIMELY is used with OS-bypass messaging. We did not implement DCTCP in OS-bypass environment due to NIC firmware limitations on processing ECN feedback [48]. We set the switch ECN marking threshold to $K = 80$ KB. This is less than the DCTCP author recommendation of $K = 65$ packets for 10 Gbps operation as we are willing to sacrifice a small amount of throughput to ensure consistently low latency. Table 1 summarizes the results averaged across three runs of ten minutes, with the RTT distribution shown in Figure 14. TIMELY keeps the average end-to-end RTT 10X lower than DCTCP (60 μs vs. 600 μs). More significantly, the tail latency drops by almost 13X (116 μs vs. 1490 μs). No loss nor PFC packets were observed. These latency reductions do not come at the cost of throughput.

Comparison with TCP FAST-like algorithm. We next implement FAST* using TCP FAST congestion control design [46] in place of Algorithm 1. Instead of periodically updating the congestion window, we use the TCP FAST equation to adjust the pacing rate. Note that TCP FAST is tunable

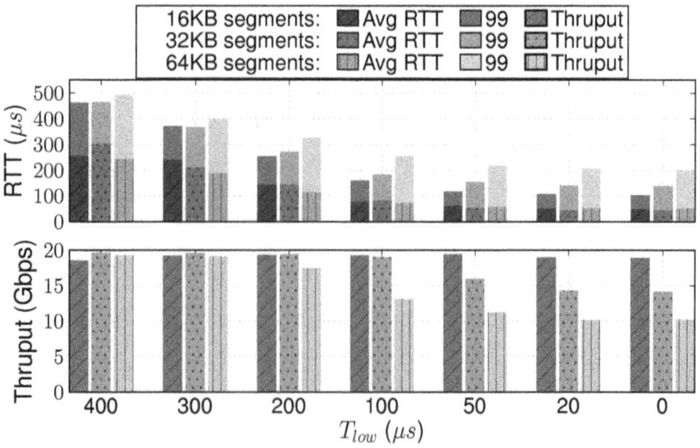

Figure 15: Throughput and RTT varying with T_{low} and segment size

by a protocol parameter α that controls the balance between fairness and the amount of buffered traffic in the network. In [46], α is the number of packets of each flow pending in the network. We convert α to a throughput value since TIMELY is rate-based. Table 1 shows our results with three different values of α. For a small α = 10 Mbps, FAST* can achieve low tail latency 49us albeit at a significant throughput loss – achieving only 7.5 Gbps out of 20 Gbps line rate. At larger values (α = 50 Mbps and 100 Mbps), TIMELY still achieves better throughput and latency trade-offs.

Varying T_{low}. Our performance is influenced by algorithm parameters, which we explore starting with the low threshold. Our purpose is to highlight factors that affect the thresholds, not to tune parameters. By design no more than a default setting is necessary. The low threshold exists to absorb the RTT variation during uncongested network use. The expected variation is related to the maximum segment size, since as segments grow larger the effect on the RTT of occasional segment collisions increases. Figure 15 shows how the bottleneck throughput and RTT times vary with different values of T_{low} for segments of size 16 KB, 32 KB and 64 KB.

We see that decreasing the low threshold reduces the network delay. This is because a lower threshold allows the use of the RTT gradient more often to modulate the rate in response to queue build-ups. But lower thresholds eventually have an adverse effect on throughput. This is best seen with bursty traffic. For 16 KB segment size, when the burstiness is relatively low, a T_{low} of just 50 μs gives us the highest throughput (19.4 Gbps), with the throughput being only slightly lower (18.9 Gbps) without any T_{low}. However, as we increase the segment size and hence the burstiness, the throughput falls quickly when the threshold becomes too small. For 32 KB segments, the tipping point is a T_{low} of 100 μs. For the most demanding workload of 64 KB segments, the transition is between 200–300 μs. Such large bursts make it difficult to obtain both high throughput and low delay. This is unsurprising since each segment is sent as a long series of back-to-back packets at wire speed, e.g., 64 KB is at least 40 packets.

Smoothing Bursts with Fine-Grained Pacers. The Rate Control Engine described in §3.3 introduces a pacing delay

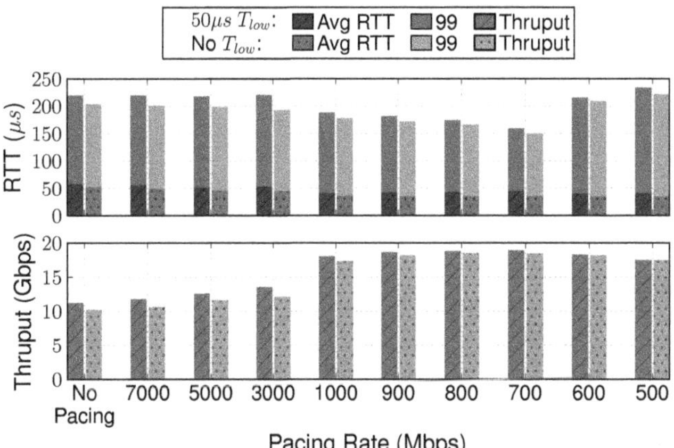

Figure 16: Throughput and RTT varying with pacing rate for 64 KB segments

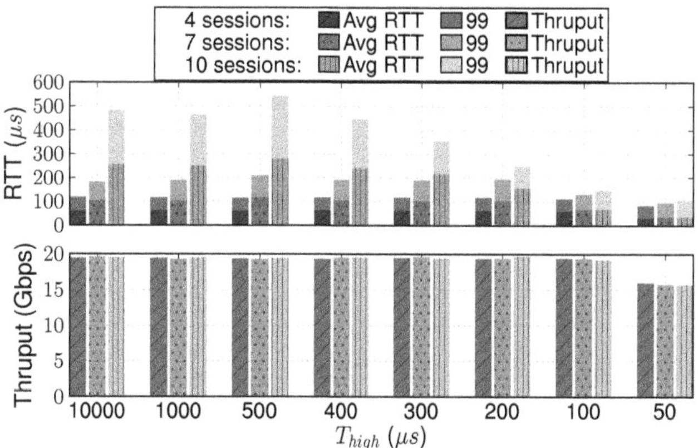

Figure 17: Total throughput and RTT varying with T_{high} for different number of connections. Segment Size = 16 KB, T_{low} = 50 μs

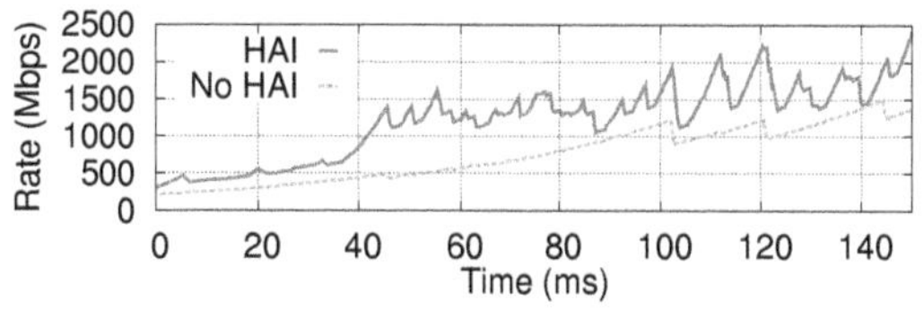

Figure 18: HAI quickly acquires available bandwidth.

between segments. To further mitigate the burstiness with large segments of 64 KB, while still enabling NIC offload, we explore fine-grained pacing. In this model, in addition to the host software pacing segments, the NIC hardware uses pacing to send the packets in each segment at a configurable rate lower than line rate. Pacing allows packets to mix more easily in the network. Programmable NICs such as NetFPGA [6] allow a pacing implementation. Prior work such as HULL [37] has also made use of NIC pacing, and fine-grained pacing queueing disciplines such as FQ/pacing are in Linux kernels [7].

We repeat the incast experiment using 64 KB segments, this time with NIC pacing, with two values of T_{low}: 0 μs and 50 μs. We are not able to implement a dynamic fine-grained pacing rate at this time and so use static rates. When computing RTTs from the completion times, we subtract the serialization delay introduced by NIC pacers to allow for comparison, e.g., pacing a 64 KB message at 1 Gbps introduces a serialization delay of 512 μs. Figure 16 shows the results for different NIC pacing rates. As expected, the reduced burstiness due to pacing leads to increase in throughput and decrease in delay, with larger throughput increases for greater pacing. The most benefit is seen at 700 Mbps: 18.9 Gbps throughput for T_{low} = 50 μs and 18.4 Gbps in the absence of any T_{low} (as opposed to 11.2 Gbps and 10.2 Gbps respectively without any pacing). Note that this also means single flow performance is capped at 700 Mbps, unless the pacing rate is adjusted dynamically. There is a slight dip in the throughput and rise in delay beyond this level, as pacing approaches the fair share and has a throttling effect.

We note that NIC hardware pacing is not an absolute requirement in TIMELY design; but rather helps navigate the tradeoff between lower network tail latency and higher CPU overhead that can be caused by software pacing with smaller segments.

Varying T_{high}. TIMELY employs a high threshold to react quickly to large RTTs. This threshold matters less than the low threshold because it only comes into play for large RTTs, but it becomes useful as the level of connection multiplexing grows and the likelihood of RTT spikes increase.

Figure 17 shows the effect on throughput as the high threshold is reduced for different numbers of competing connections. In our earlier runs with four connections per client, the 99-percentile RTTs are around 100 μs. This means that any $T_{high} > 100\mu s$ has little effect. As the load climbs to 7 connections per client, the 99-percentile RTT settles close to 200 μs. Then there is a drop in RTT as we reduce T_{high} to 100 μs and below. For 10 connections per client, the 99-percentile RTTs remain close to 500 μs for T_{high} of 500 μs or more, and decrease as T_{high} falls. The throughput is quite good for T_{high} down to 100 μs, but is significantly lower at 50 μs for all three connection levels. These results show that a high threshold down to at most 200 μs helps to reduce tail latency without degrading throughput.

Hyper active increment (HAI). HAI helps to acquire available bandwidth more quickly. To show this, we perform an incast with a change in the offered load. The incast starts with 10 clients and 10 connections per client. After an initial period for convergence, every client simultaneously shuts down 9 of its 10 connections, thus increasing the fair share rate of the remaining connection by 10X. Figure 18 shows how HAI ramps up connection throughput from an initial fair rate of 200 Mbps to 1.5 Gbps within 50 ms, and reaches the new fair share of 2 Gbps in 100 ms. In contrast, a fixed additive increment only achieves 1.5 Gbps after 140 ms. We find that a HAI threshold of five successive RTTs strikes a good balance between convergence and stability.

6.2 Large-Scale Experiments

We investigate TIMELY's large-scale behavior with experiments run on a few hundred machines in a classic Clos topology [12, 34]. We show that TIMELY is able to maintain predictable and low latency in large all-to-all and incast network congestion scenarios. The experiment generates RPCs between client server pairs. To stress TIMELY and

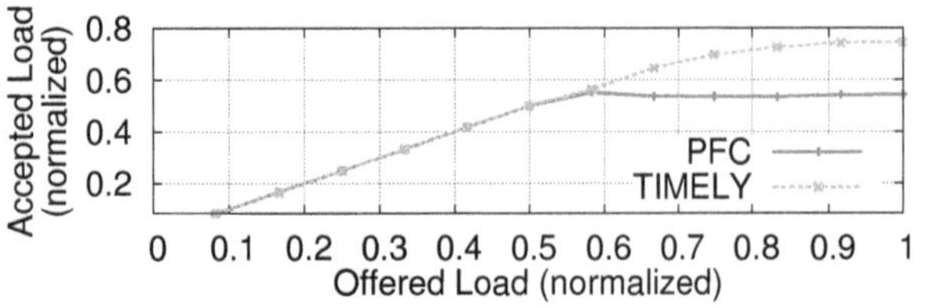

Figure 19: Accepted versus offered load (64 KB messages).

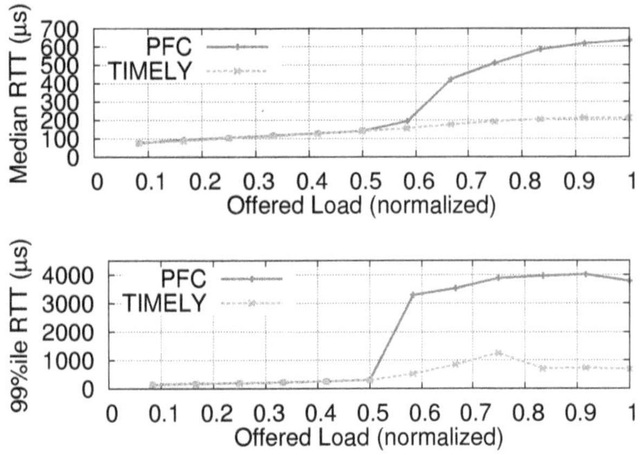

Figure 20: Median and 99-percentile RTTs as measured by pingers under different offered load.

create increased burstiness, we used 64 KB RPCs and segment sizes.

Longest path uniform random. In this traffic pattern, a client picks a server from a set of servers with the longest path through the network. Clients issue 64 KB requests. The server replies with a payload of the same size. The benchmark collects goodput and RPC latency. RPC latency is computed at the client from the time the request is sent to the server, to when it receives a response from the server.

Figure 19 shows normalized throughput (to the maximum offered load used in the experiment) as observed by the application for increasing offered loads on the x-axis. The saturation point of the network (the point at which accepted load is less than the offered load) is higher for TIMELY as it is able to send more traffic by minimizing queueing and thereby also pause frames per second.

Figure 20 shows RTT versus load. TIMELY reduces the median and 99-percentile RTT by $2X$ and $5X$ respectively compared to PFC. This results in a corresponding reduction of RPC median latency of about $2X$ (shown in Figure 21). Without TIMELY, beyond saturation the network queuing increases in an attempt to reach the offered load. With TIMELY, low network queuing is maintained by moving queuing from the shared network to the end-host (where it is included in RPC latency but not in the RTTs). Therefore, the 99-percentile of RPC latency reduction effect diminishes as the offered load increases beyond the saturation point.

Network imbalance (incast). To stress TIMELY's ability to mitigate congestion, we designed an experiment with a background load of longest path uniform random traffic and then added an incast load. We use three levels of background load: low (0.167 of the maximum offered load in Figure 19), medium (0.3) and high (0.5). Figure 22 shows the normalized throughput and 99-percentile RTT for this experiment. We normalize throughput to that of the background load. We know from Figure 19 that TIMELY and PFC throughput are the same for uniform random traffic before network saturation. When we add an incast, without TIMELY, throughput falls by 13% to 54%, depending on the background network load, primarily due to head of line blocking created by PFCs. This observation is confirmed with RTT measurements in Figure 22, which show that TIMELY is able to keep queuing relatively low, preventing congestion spreading [20, 36], by rate limiting only the flows passing along the congested path. The overall throughput for TIMELY remained the same during the incast.

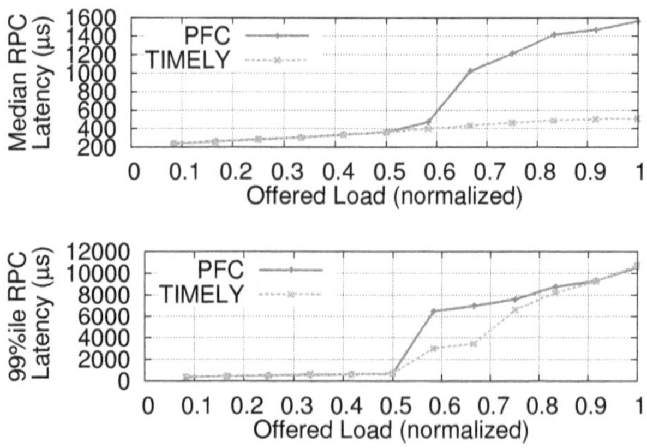

Figure 21: Median and 99-percentile RPC latencies.

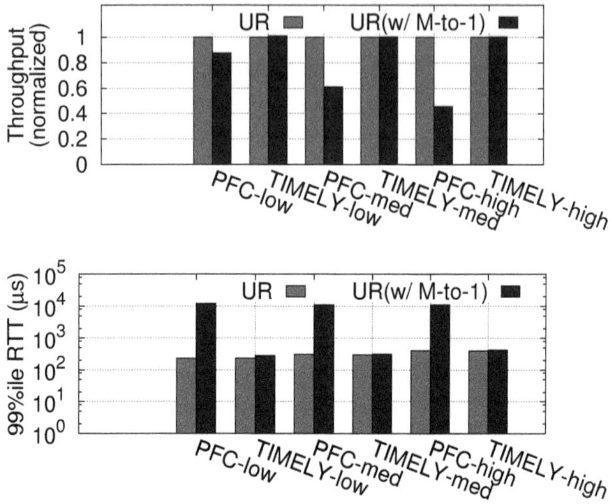

Figure 22: Adding one 40-to-1 pattern to longest path uniform random ((a) Normalized throughput (b) 99-percentile RTT).

Application level benchmark.

Figure 23 shows RPC latency of a datacenter storage benchmark (note that the y-axis is on a log-scale). Without TIMELY, the application is limited in the amount of data it can push through the network while keeping the 99th percentile RTT low enough. With TIMELY, the application is able to push at higher utilization levels without suffering negative latency consequences. Therefore, the drop in application data unit latency (in seconds) is really a reflection of the increased throughput that the application is able to sustain during query execution.

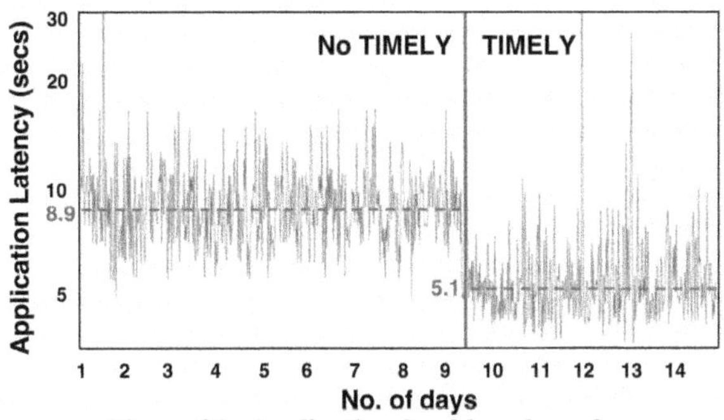

Figure 23: Application-level benchmark.

7. RELATED WORK

Datacenter congestion control is a deeply studied topic [15, 18, 35, 37, 38, 47]. TIMELY focuses on the same problem.

RED [23] and CoDel [40] drop packets early, prompting senders to reduce transmission rates to avoid the large standing queues associated with tail drops. However, loss still drives up latencies for the flows that experience packet drops. To avoid packet drops, many schemes rely on switch-support in the form of ECN, in which packets are marked to indicate congestion [22]. ECN marks are often combined across multiple packets [15, 35, 37] to provide fine-grained congestion information, but our experiments in §2 show that ECN has inherent limitations. There have also been other proposals that rely on switch support to mitigate congestion such as QCN [29] (fine-grained queue occupancy information) and pFabric [38] (fine-grained prioritization).

TIMELY belongs to a different class of algorithms that use delay measurements to detect congestion, which requires no switch-support. We take inspiration from TCP Vegas, FAST, and Compound [16, 44, 46]. These proposals are window-based and maintain a queue close to the minimum RTT. In contrast, TIMELY is a rate-based algorithm that employs a gradient approach and does not rely on measuring the minimum RTT. We show that it works well with NIC support, despite infrequent RTT signals.

A recent scheme, DX [17], independently identified the benefits of using delay as congestion signal for high throughput and low latency datacenter communications. DX implements accurate latency measurements using a DPDK driver for the NIC and the congestion control algorithm is within the Linux TCP stack. DX algorithm is similar to the conventional window-based proposals, with an additive increase and a multiplicative decrease that's proportional to the average queuing delay.

CAIA Delay Gradient [25] (CDG) proposes a delay gradient algorithm for TCP congestion control for wide-area networks. Its key goal is to figure out co-existence with loss based congestion control. Hence the nature of its algorithms are different from those in TIMELY.

Link-layer flow control is used for low-latency messaging in Infiniband and Data Center Bridging (DCB) networks. However, problems with Priority Flow Control (PFC), including head of line blocking and pause propagation or congestion spreading, are documented in literature [20, 36]. Some recent proposals aim to overcome these issues with PFC using ECN markings to maintain low queue occupancy. TCP-Bolt [14] uses modified DCTCP algorithm within the kernel TCP stack. DCQCN [48] uses a combination of ECN markings with a QCN-inspired rate-based congestion control algorithm implemented in the NIC. Evaluations demonstrate that it addresses the HoL blocking and unfairness problems with PFC, thus making RoCE viable for large-scale deployment. TIMELY uses RTT signal, is implemented in host software with support of NIC timestamping, and is applicable to both OS-bypass and OS-based transports. Comparison of TIMELY and DCQCN in terms of both congestion control and CPU utilization is an interesting future work.

Congestion can also be avoided by scheduling transmissions using a distributed approach [18, 47] or even a centralized one [30]. However, such schemes are yet to be proven at scale, and are more complex than a simple delay-based approach.

Finally, load-sensitive routing such as Conga [13] and FlowBender [11] can mitigate congestion hotspots by spreading traffic around the network, thereby increasing throughput. However, host-based congestion control is still required to match offered load to the network capacity.

8. CONCLUSION

Conventional wisdom considers delay to be an untrustworthy congestion signal in datacenters. Our experience with TIMELY shows the opposite – when delay is properly adapted, RTT strongly correlates with queue buildups in the network. We built TIMELY, which takes advantage of modern NIC support for timestamps and fast ACK turnaround to perform congestion control based on precise RTT measurements. We found TIMELY can detect and respond to tens of microseconds of queueing to deliver low packet latency and high throughput, even in the presence of infrequent RTT signals and NIC offload. As datacenter speeds scale up by an order of magnitude, future work should focus on how effective RTTs continue to be for congestion control, alongside rethinking the nature of delay based algorithms.

9. ACKNOWLEDGMENTS

We thank Bob Felderman, Ashish Naik and Philip Wells whose participation and feedback made the work and this submission possible. We thank Mike Marty, Joel Scherpelz, and Dan Gibson for their direct contributions to this work; Sridhar Raman, and Denis Pankratov for their contributions to NIC pacing and hardware timestamps; Mike Ryan for application benchmarks; Varun Gupta and Abdul Kabbani for their insights on various congestion signals; Laurent Chavey and Bill Berryman for their ongoing support of congestion control work. We thank our shepherd, Mohammad Alizadeh, and the anonymous reviewers for providing excellent feedback.

10. REFERENCES

[1] Chelsio T5 Packet Rate Performance Report. http://goo.gl/3jJL6p, Pg 2.

[2] Data Center Bridging Task Group. http://www.ieee802.org/1/pages/dcbridges.html.
[3] Dual Port 10 Gigabit Server Adapter with Precision Time Stamping. http://goo.gl/VtL5oO.
[4] Gnuplot documentation. http://goo.gl/4sgrUU, Pg. 48.
[5] Mellanox for Linux. http://goo.gl/u44Xea.
[6] The NetFPGA Project. http://netfpga.org/.
[7] TSO Sizing and the FQ Scheduler. http://lwn.net/Articles/564978/.
[8] Using Hardware Timestamps with PF RING. http://goo.gl/oJtHCe, 2011.
[9] Who (Really) Needs Sub-microsecond Packet Timestamps? http://goo.gl/TI3r1u, 2013.
[10] A. Kabbani et al. AF-QCN: Approximate Fairness with Quantized Congestion Notification for Multi tenanted Data Centers. In *Hot Interconnects'10.*
[11] A. Kabbani et al. FlowBender: Flow-level Adaptive Routing for Improved Latency and Throughput in Datacenter Networks. In *ACM CoNEXT '14.*
[12] A. Singh et al. Jupiter Rising: A Decade of Clos Topologies and Centralized Control in Google's Datacenter. In *SIGCOMM'15.*
[13] Alizadeh et al. CONGA: Distributed Congestion aware Load Balancing for Datacenters. In *SIGCOMM '14.*
[14] B. Stephens et al. Practical DCB for improved data center networks. In *Infocom 2014.*
[15] B. Vamanan et al. Deadline-aware datacenter TCP (D2TCP). In *SIGCOMM '12.*
[16] Brakmo et al. TCP Vegas: new techniques for congestion detection and avoidance. In *SIGCOMM '94.*
[17] C. Lee et al. Accurate Latency-based Congestion Feedback for Datacenters. In *USENIX ATC 15.*
[18] C.-Y. Hong et al. Finishing Flows Quickly with Preemptive Scheduling. In *SIGCOMM '12.*
[19] D.-M. Chiu and R. Jain. Analysis of the Increase and Decrease Algorithms for Congestion Avoidance in Computer Networks. *Comput. Netw. ISDN Syst.*, 1989.
[20] D. Zats et al. DeTail: Reducing the Flow Completion Time Tail in Datacenter Networks. In *SIGCOMM '12.*
[21] J. Dean and L. A. Barroso. The Tail at Scale. *Communications of the ACM*, 56:74–80, 2013.
[22] S. Floyd. TCP and explicit congestion notification. *ACM SIGCOMM CCR*, 24(5), 1994.
[23] S. Floyd and V. Jacobson. Random early detection gateways for congestion avoidance. *IEEE/ACM Trans. Netw.*, 1, August 1993.
[24] I. Grigorik. Optimizing the Critical Rendering Path. http://goo.gl/DvFfGo, Velocity Conference 2013.
[25] D. A. Hayes and G. Armitage. Revisiting TCP Congestion Control using Delay Gradients. In *Networking IFIP*, 2011.
[26] D. A. Hayes and D. Ros. Delay-based Congestion Control for Low Latency.
[27] C. Hollot, V. Misra, D. Towsley, and W.-B. Gong. A control theoretic analysis of RED. In *IEEE Infocom '01.*
[28] C. Hollot, V. Misra, D. Towsley, and W.-B. Gong. On designing improved controllers for AQM routers supporting TCP flows. In *IEEE Infocom '01.*
[29] IEEE. 802.1Qau - Congestion Notification. http://www.ieee802.org/1/pages/802.1au.html.
[30] J. Perry et al. Fastpass: A Centralized "Zero-Queue" Datacenter Network. In *SIGCOMM '14.*
[31] R. Jain, D. Chiu, and W. Hawe. A Quantitative Measure of Fairness and Discrimination for Resource Allocation in Shared Computer Systems. In *DEC Research Report TR-301*, 1984.
[32] D. Katabi, M. Handley, and C. Rohrs. Internet Congestion Control for Future High Bandwidth-Delay Product Environments. In *SIGCOMM'02.*
[33] F. P. Kelly, G. Raina, and T. Voice. Stability and fairness of explicit congestion control with small buffers. *Computer Communication Review*, 2008.
[34] M. Al-Fares et al. A Scalable, Commodity Data Center Network Architecture. SIGCOMM '08.
[35] M. Alizadeh et al. Data center TCP (DCTCP). In *SIGCOMM '10.*
[36] M. Alizadeh et al. Data Center Transport Mechanisms: Congestion Control Theory and IEEE Standardization. In *Annual Allerton Conference '08.*
[37] M. Alizadeh et al. Less Is More: Trading a Little Bandwidth for Ultra-Low Latency in the Data Center. In *NSDI '12.*
[38] M. Alizadeh et al. Deconstructing datacenter packet transport. In *ACM HotNets*, 2012.
[39] N. Dukkipati et al. Processor Sharing Flows in the Internet. In *IWQoS*, 2005.
[40] K. Nichols and V. Jacobson. Controlling queue delay. *Queue*, 10(5):20:20–20:34, May 2012.
[41] J. Postel. Transmission Control Protocol. RFC 793, 1981. Updated by RFCs 1122, 3168, 6093, 6528.
[42] S. Ha et al. CUBIC: A New TCP-Friendly High-Speed TCP Variant. *SIGOPS Operating System Review '08.*
[43] S. Radhakrishnan et al. SENIC: scalable NIC for end-host rate limiting. In *NSDI 2014.*
[44] K. Tan and J. Song. A compound TCP approach for high-speed and long distance networks. In *IEEE INFOCOM '06.*
[45] V. Vasudevan et al. Safe and effective fine-grained TCP retransmissions for datacenter communication. In *SIGCOMM '09.*
[46] D. X. Wei, C. Jin, S. H. Low, and S. Hegde. FAST TCP: Motivation, Architecture, Algorithms, Performance. *IEEE/ACM Trans. Netw.*, 2006.
[47] C. Wilson, H. Ballani, T. Karagiannis, and A. Rowtron. Better never than late: meeting deadlines in datacenter networks. In *SIGCOMM '11.*
[48] Y. Zhu et al. Congestion Control for Large-Scale RDMA Deployments. In *SIGCOMM 2015.*

R2C2: A Network Stack for Rack-scale Computers

Paolo Costa Hitesh Ballani Kaveh Razavi* Ian Kash

Microsoft Research

ABSTRACT

Rack-scale computers, comprising a large number of microservers connected by a direct-connect topology, are expected to replace servers as the building block in data centers. We focus on the problem of routing and congestion control across the rack's network, and find that high path diversity in rack topologies, in combination with workload diversity across it, means that traditional solutions are inadequate.

We introduce R2C2, a network stack for rack-scale computers that provides flexible and efficient routing and congestion control. R2C2 leverages the fact that the scale of rack topologies allows for low-overhead broadcasting to ensure that all nodes in the rack are aware of all network flows. We thus achieve rate-based congestion control without any probing; each node independently determines the sending rate for its flows while respecting the provider's allocation policies. For routing, nodes dynamically choose the routing protocol for each flow in order to maximize overall utility. Through a prototype deployed across a rack emulation platform and a packet-level simulator, we show that R2C2 achieves very low queuing and high throughput for diverse and bursty workloads, and that routing flexibility can provide significant throughput gains.

CCS Concepts

•**Networks** → **Data center networks;** *Transport protocols; Cloud computing;*

Keywords

Rack-scale Computers; Congestion Control; Route Selection; Rack-scale Network Stack

*Work done during internship at Microsoft Research. Currently, PhD student at VU University Amsterdam.

SIGCOMM '15, August 17 - 21, 2015, London, United Kingdom

ISBN 978-1-4503-3542-3/15/08... $15.00

DOI: http://dx.doi.org/10.1145/2785956.2787492

1. INTRODUCTION

While today's large-scale data centers such as those run by Amazon, Google, and Microsoft are built using commodity off-the-shelf servers, recently there has been an increasing trend towards server customization to reduce costs and improve performance [50, 54, 55, 58]. One such trend is the advent of "rack-scale computing". We use this term to refer to emerging architectures that propose servers or *rack-scale computers* comprising a large number of tightly integrated systems-on-chip, interconnected by a network fabric. This design enables thousands of cores per rack and provides high bandwidth for rack-scale applications. The consequent power, density and performance benefits means that racks are expected to replace individual servers as the basic building block of datacenters. Early examples of rack-scale computers include commercial (HP Moonshot [56], AMD SeaMicro [62], Boston Viridis [51], and Intel RSA [26, 59]) as well as research platforms [7, 9, 19, 34, 38].

A design choice that allows rack-scale computers to achieve high internal bandwidth and high density is to move away from a switched network fabric to a "distributed switch" architecture where each node functions as a small switch and forwards traffic from other nodes. This underlies many existing designs [19, 34, 38, 47, 51, 56, 59, 62], and results in a multi-hop direct-connect topology, with very high path diversity. This is a departure from today's data centers, which mostly use tree-like topologies. While direct-connect topologies have been used in high performance computing (HPC), the use of racks in multi-tenant datacenters means that network traffic is expected to be more diverse and unpredictable than in HPC clusters.

In this paper, we study two fundamental questions for the rack's network fabric: how should traffic be routed and how should the network be shared? The aforementioned peculiarities of rack environments pose challenges on both fronts. For *routing*, a one-size-fits-all approach is undesirable [1]. While there are many existing routing algorithms for direct-connect topologies, no single algorithm can achieve optimal throughput across all workloads (§2.2.1). For network sharing, existing *congestion control* approaches either do not cope with the high path diversity in racks (TCP family), or they are customized to specific workloads (HPC solutions [17, 18, 20]).

We present R2C2,[1] a network stack for rack-scale computers that provides flexible routing and congestion control. R2C2 achieves *global visibility*—each rack node knows all active flows—by broadcasting flow start and finish events across the rack. The scale of rack-scale computers (up to a few thousand nodes) allows for low overhead broadcasting. Given global visibility, each node independently computes the fair sending rates for its flows (§3.3). To account for temporary discrepancies in flow visibility, the rate computation leaves aside a small amount of bandwidth headroom. Such congestion control obviates any network probing or specialized queuing at rack nodes, yet it can accommodate high multi-pathing, and achieves both low network queuing and high utilization. Furthermore, it allows the provider to specify rich rate allocation policies, beyond flow-level policies. For routing, nodes locally determine how flows should be routed to optimize a provider-specified metric like aggregate or even tail rack throughput. Leveraging the global visibility and ensuring that nodes optimize for a global metric instead of selfish optimizations avoids any price of anarchy inefficiency [42] (§3.4).

At the data plane, both the rate allocation and route for a flow are enforced at the sender by rate limiting the flow's traffic (one rate limiter per flow) and encoding its network path into packet headers respectively. Intermediate rack nodes can thus simply forward packets along the path specified in their header, without requiring extra rate limiters or complex queuing mechanisms on path. By placing more functionality at the sender, this design enables a simple forwarding layer that is amenable to on-chip implementation.

Overall, this paper makes the following contributions:

- We describe a novel approach for rate-based congestion control that transforms the distributed network sharing problem into one of local rate computation.
- We describe a routing mechanism that allows for routing protocols to be chosen on a per-flow basis. We also present a greedy heuristic that rack nodes can use to locally determine the routing protocol for each flow in order to maximize a global utility metric.
- We develop a flexible emulation platform that enables accurate emulation of the network fabric in rack-scale computers. We use it to validate R2C2's design.

We implemented R2C2 as a user-space network stack atop our emulation platform. We use platform experiments to benchmark our implementation and cross-validate our packet-level simulator. Our simulation results show that R2C2 can achieve efficient network sharing for diverse network workloads: it achieves high throughput, fairness and low latency, and it imposes low broadcasting overhead. Finally, we show that routing flexibility and the dynamic selection process enables achieving higher performance that what would be possible using a single routing protocol for all flows.

[1]R2C2- Rack Routing and Congestion Control.

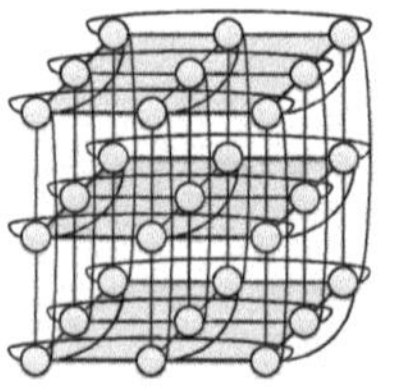

Figure 1: A 27-server (3x3x3) 3D torus. Each server has six neighbors.

2. BACKGROUND AND MOTIVATION

We begin by describing the factors underlying the emergence of rack-scale computers. We then delve into two very basic aspects of the network fabric inside a rack, *routing* and *congestion control*. By highlighting salient features of the network fabric, we argue why traditional solutions are insufficient in the rack environment.

2.1 Rack-scale computing

Rack-scale computers comprise 100s or even 1,000s of micro-servers that are connected by a network fabric. Their emergence is due to two hardware innovations. First, *System-on-chip (SoC)* integration combines cores, caches, and network interfaces in a single die. SoCs enable vendors to build *micro-servers*: extremely small server boards containing computation, memory, network interfaces, and sometimes flash storage. For instance, the Calxeda ECX-1000 SoC [52] hosts four ARM cores, a memory controller, a SATA interface, and a low-radix switch onto a single die.

Second, *fabric integration* means that these micro-servers (or *nodes*) can be connected through a high-bandwidth low-latency network. This is typically done through a "distributed switch" architecture; rather than connecting all nodes to a single ToR switch like in today's racks, each node is connected to a small subset of other nodes via point-to-point links. These links offer high bandwidth (10–100 Gbps) and low per-hop latency (100-500 ns). Any topology that has a small number of links per node can be used; 2D and 3D torus like the one in Figure 1 are popular choices adapted from super-computing architectures. These topologies are often referred to as *multi-hop direct-connect topologies* because packets typically have to travel multiple hops before reaching the destination and nodes are responsible for forwarding packets at intermediate hops (typically using an integrated switching element on the SoC).

Early examples of rack-scale computers have appeared on the market. For example, HP's Moonshot [56] is a 4.3 rack-units chassis with 45 8-core Intel Atom SoCs and 1.4 TB of RAM in a 3D torus topology. The AMD SeaMicro 15000-OP [62] stacks 512 cores and 4 TB of RAM within 10 rack-units using a 3D torus network fabric with a bisection bandwidth of 1.28 Tbps. Intel's proposed Rack-scale Architecture [53, 59] combines SoC and fabric integration with silicon photonics, which support link bandwidths of 100 Gbps and higher. Rack-scale computer designs have also been proposed by the research community such as the Catapult [38], Firebox [7], Pelican [9], and soNUMA [19, 34] platforms.

Workload	Random Packet Spraying	Destination Tag routing	VLB	WLB
Nearest neighbor	4	4	0.5	2.33
Uniform	1	1	0.5	0.76
Bit complement	0.4	0.5	0.5	0.42
Transpose	0.54	0.25	0.5	0.57
Tornado	0.33	0.33	0.5	0.53
Worst-case	0.21	0.25	0.5	0.31

Figure 2: Throughput, as fraction of network bisection capacity, of four routing algorithms on an 8-ary 2-cube on size traffic patterns (table from [20]). No single routing algorithm can achieve optimal throughput across all workloads.

2.2 Rack-scale networking

Rack-scale networking combines the topology of HPC systems with the workloads of traditional datacenters. Like HPC clusters, racks have a multi-hop direct-connect topology with very high path diversity. This is in contrast to tree-like topologies common in datacenters. As for the workload, we expect racks to be used in multi-tenant environments with different applications generating diverse network workloads, unlike the homogeneous and relatively stable workloads typically observed in HPC.

In the following sections, we focus on two fundamental questions for rack-scale networking: how should traffic be routed and how should the network be shared? We describe the shortcomings of existing solutions, and distill design goals for a rack-scale's network stack.

2.2.1 Rack routing

Routing across direct-connect topologies has been extensively studied in the scientific computing and HPC literature [20]. Existing routing algorithms can be broadly classified into two categories. Minimal routing algorithms like randomized packet spraying [22] and destination tag routing [20] route packets only along shortest paths. Non-minimal algorithms like Valiant Load Balancing (VLB) [45] and Weighted Load Balancing (WLB) [44] do not restrict themselves to shortest paths.

High path diversity in direct-connect topologies means that no single routing algorithm can achieve optimal throughput across all workloads. Minimal routing ensures low propagation delay but at the expense of load imbalance across network links which, in turn, results in poor worst-case performance. On the other hand, VLB transforms any input traffic matrix into a uniform random metric by routing packets through randomly chosen waypoints. This ensures guaranteed worst-case throughput across all workloads but hurts average-case throughput, especially for workloads with locality. WLB lies between these extremes; it considers non-minimal paths for load-balancing but biases the path selection in proportion to the path length.

The table in Figure 2 summarizes these arguments by showing the throughput of these routing algorithms for five traffic patterns and their worst-case throughput (the worst-case traffic patterns for each algorithm are different). While VLB has the same performance across all traffic patterns, other algorithms perform better for specific workloads. By contrast, tree-like topologies in today's datacenters have a few orders of magnitude less multi-pathing, so minimal routing algorithms like packet spraying are sufficient [22].

Overall, for multi-tenant datacenters where the network traffic pattern is not known a priori and expected to change over time, a one size fits all approach is undesirable [1]. Thus, our first design goal is:

G1 *Routing flexibility.* The network stack should allow for different routing protocols to be used simultaneously, chosen on a per-application or even on a per-flow basis. Datacenter operators can leverage this knob to optimize metrics like the rack's aggregate throughput.

2.2.2 Rack network sharing

High path diversity, combined with the resource limited nature of micro-servers, also means that congestion control protocols used in today's datacenters are not suited for rack-scale computers. For example, a flow using minimal routing is routed along *all* shortest paths between its source and destination. This means that even in a small 216-node rack with 3D torus topology, an average flow has a 1,680 paths. Furthermore, the number of paths increases exponentially with the topology size. And with non-minimal routing, the path diversity can be nearly unbounded [20].

The TCP family of protocols, including recent proposals targeted towards datacenters [2–4], only uses a single path and imposes high processing overhead [34]. Even multi-path extensions like MPTCP [41] only consider few tens of paths. This is roughly two-three orders of magnitude smaller than the number of paths available here. Furthermore, per-flow fairness, as provided by TCP and its variants, is inadequate for datacenter settings. Instead, operators need to enforce richer policies like deadline-based fairness for user-facing applications [28,48] and per-tenant guarantees [10,11,30].

In recent work, Fastpass [36] shows the feasibility of centralized congestion control in traditional datacenters. While the scale of rack-scale computers is amenable to a centralized design, this would introduce significant communication overhead, as we show in Section 5.2. Further, high path diversity in racks makes computing max-min fair rate allocations much harder than in traditional topologies (§3.3). In RascNet [16], we sketched a preliminary congestion control design for racks that works atop VLB routing. However, this contravenes the routing flexibility requirement. In Section 5.2, we show that taking advantage of routing flexibility provides significant performance gains.

At the other end of the spectrum, HPC platforms and on-chip networks (NoC) systems often use congestion control mechanisms customized to the underlying topology and the expected workload [17, 18, 35]. Such mechanisms do not work for general workloads. We also note that ideal network sharing can be achieved through per-flow queues at each rack node coupled with back-pressure notifications when a node's queues start filling up. Apart from increased forwarding complexity, this massively increases the buffering requirements at rack nodes.

Thus, the design goals for rack network sharing are:

G2 *Accommodate high multi-pathing.* Congestion control

has to cope with high multi-pathing in rack topologies.

G3 *Low network queuing.* While a standard goal for network design, this is particularly important here because micro-servers have limited buffers and the network carries traffic that is very latency sensitive.

G4 *Allocation flexibility.* Datacenter operators should be able to specify different rate allocation policies that encapsulate varying notions of fairness.

3. DESIGN

We present R2C2, a network stack for rack-scale computers. The key insight behind R2C2's design is that while rack topologies pose many challenges, they also present an opportunity—it is possible to efficiently broadcast information across the rack. We use 16-byte broadcast packets (§4.2); with a 512-node rack, each broadcast results in 8 KB of total traffic, aggregated across all rack links. By broadcasting flow start and termination events, we ensure every node knows the rack's global traffic matrix. R2C2's leverages such *global visibility* to implement flexible congestion control and routing.

Determining the rates and routes for flows across a multipath topology can be mapped to the multi-commodity flow (MCF) problem with splittable flows. Several papers propose polynomial time algorithms for this problem with different optimization objectives such as max-min fairness [33] and maximizing total throughput [8]. Many of these algorithms are designed for offline operation; thus they are computationally intensive and have a high running time. Rack nodes, however, have limited compute and buffering, so at least the congestion needs to be controlled at a fine-grained timescale. On the other hand, online MCF algorithms are tightly tied to a specific optimization metric.

R2C2's control plane decouples congestion control and routing, and tackles them at different timescales. For *congestion control*, each node uses global visibility and knowledge of the underlying topology to locally compute the fair sending rate for its traffic (§3.3). This design avoids any network probing and does not require any specialized queuing support at the rack nodes. The rate computation algorithm is fast, ensures low network queuing, and allows for different rate allocation policies. For *routing*, nodes locally determine the routing protocol for each flow that will maximize a provider-chosen global utility metric (§3.4).

At the data-plane, R2C2 uses source routing to enable per-flow routing protocols. This involves three mechanisms: (i). the node sending a flow determines the path for each packet based on the flow's routing protocol and encodes this path in the packet header, (ii). the sender also enforces a flow's rate allocation, (iii). intermediate rack nodes simply forward packets along the path specified in their header.

Overall, our design choices are guided by the expected size of rack-scale computers. Their scale ensures both the network overhead of broadcast traffic and the processing overhead of rate computation is acceptable, even for very bursty workloads. The scale also means that a packet's path can be encoded compactly, allowing for source routing. The data-plane design intentionally places more functionality at the sender that only needs to rate limit its own flows. This can be implemented in software or hardware [39]. Intermediate rack nodes have a simple forwarding layer that is amenable to on-chip implementation; it does not require any additional rate limiting or complex queuing mechanisms.

To give an overview of R2C2's operation, we begin by focusing on the life of a single flow. We then describe R2C2's data- and control-plane mechanisms in detail.

3.1 The life of a flow

When a flow starts, its sender broadcasts information about the new flow, including the routing algorithm the flow is using and its rate allocation parameters (e.g., the flow's weight). Each rack node stores this information to create a local view of the global traffic matrix. Given this traffic matrix and the rack's topology, the sender computes the flow's fair allocation and rate limits it accordingly. To account for temporary discrepancies between the perceived and actual traffic matrix, R2C2 relies on bandwidth headroom; during rate computation, we simply subtract the headroom from each link's capacity.

For every new packet, the source encodes the packet path in its header, and the packets are source routed to their destination. When a broadcast packet (e.g., due to a flow starting or finishing) is received, the sender recomputes the rate for all its *own* flows. When the flow finishes, other rack nodes are informed by broadcasting this event. Nodes also periodically check whether the overall utility would improve if some of the flows were routed using a different protocol. If a significant improvement is possible, their routing protocols are changed and this information is broadcasted.

3.2 Broadcast

R2C2's design builds upon a low overhead broadcast primitive. For broadcasting packets, we create a per-source broadcast tree atop the rack's network topology. This can be done while optimizing various goals; we optimize the broadcast time, i.e., we minimize the maximum number of network hops within which all rack nodes receive a copy of the broadcast packet.

To achieve this goal, we determine the *shortest-path tree* for each rack node. Given a graph representing the rack's topology, a shortest-path tree rooted at source node s is a spanning tree T of the graph such that the length of the path from s to any node in T is the shortest distance from s to the node in the graph.[2] Since all network links inside the rack have the same capacity, finding shortest-path trees for the rack is akin to finding shortest-path trees for an unweighted graph, and can be done through a breadth-first traversal of the graph [14].

For a rack, we enumerate multiple broadcast trees for each source by traversing the rack's topology in a breadth-first fashion. Given this, we construct a broadcast forwarding information base (FIB) for each rack node. A look-up in this FIB is indexed by a two-tuple, `<src-address, tree-`

[2]There can be multiple shortest-path trees for a given source.

id>, comprising the address of the source node and an identifier for the broadcast tree, and yields the set of next-hop nodes the broadcast packet should be forwarded to.

When a node has to send a broadcast packet, it chooses one of its broadcast trees for the packet to be routed along. This selection is done to load balance the broadcasting overhead, and allows the sender to account for link and node failures. The sender inserts its address and the identifier for the chosen broadcast tree into the header of the broadcast packet. The packet is then routed by other nodes by consulting their broadcast FIB.

Broadcast overhead. In Section 4.2, we describe how flow information is encoded into a 16-byte broadcast packet. Each broadcast tree for a rack with n nodes comprises $n-1$ edges. Thus, for a typical rack with 512 nodes, a single broadcast results in a total of $511*16 \approx 8$ KB on the wire. In the worst-case scenario of flows between all pairs of nodes ($\approx$262K flows), the resulting broadcast traffic per link would be 681 KB.

An obvious concern is that in many datacenter workloads, most flows are only a few packets long. For example, in a typical data-mining workload [25], 80% of flows are less then 10KB. The average path length for a flow in a 512-node 3D torus is 6 hops, so a 10 KB flow will, on average, result in 60 KB being transmitted on the wire. Thus, the relative overhead of broadcasting the start and finish events for such small flows is 26.66% (13.33% for each event). Fortunately, small flows only carry a small fraction of the bytes in today's datacenters. For example, traces from a data analytics cluster show that the 95% of all bytes originate from less than 4% of flows [25]. In Section 5.2, we analyze the fraction of network bandwidth used for broadcast traffic as a function of the bytes carried by small flows. When 5% of the bytes are carried by small flows, the fraction of the network capacity used for broadcasting flow information is only 1.3%.

Failures. Broadcast packets can be corrupted across the network, or lost due to drops and failures. To detect corruption, we rely on a packet checksum. To detect drops due to queue overflows at intermediate nodes, the node dropping a broadcast packet informs the sender who can then re-transmit. To detect link and node failures, we rely on a topology discovery mechanism that is required by the routing protocols anyway. Upon detecting a failure, nodes broadcast information about all their ongoing flows. This is reasonable because, given the scale of rack-scale computers, we expect node and link failures to be infrequent. For example, measurements across HPC systems have shown a failure rate of around 0.3 faults per year per CPU [43]. For a 512-node rack with four CPUs per node, this means less than two failures a day.

3.3 Rack congestion control

To ensure the network is not congested and flows achieve rates in accordance to the operator's allocation policy, we require senders to compute the rate allocations for their traffic and enforce them. The basic idea behind our approach is that given knowledge of the allocation policy, the network topology, all active flows, and their current routing protocol,

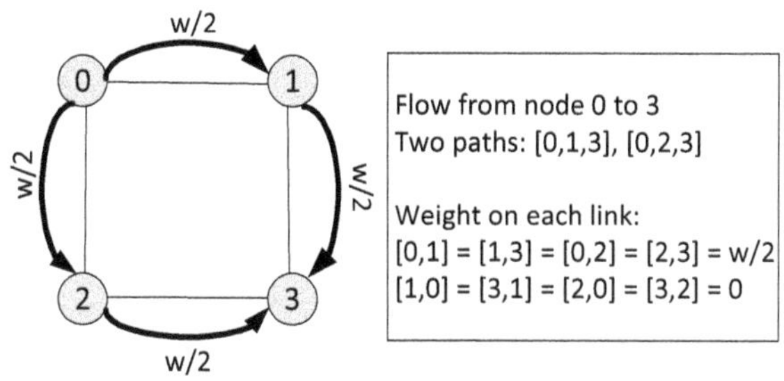

Figure 3: A flow from node 0 to 3, with weight w, being routed using randomized packet spraying.

each node can independently determine the load on each network link and hence, the fair sending rate for its flows. Thus, we transform the distributed congestion control problem into one of local rate calculation. While the rack's topology is relatively static, the set of active flows can change rapidly. We begin with a strawman design which assumes that nodes are aware of the rack's current traffic matrix.

The key challenge in computing rate allocations is accommodating high multi-pathing. Flows are routed across a very high number of paths, thousands or more, which poses a computational burden. For example, consider a provider who wants to allocate the network fairly. Max-min fairness is well studied in the context of single-path routing but is harder to reason about in multi-path settings. Max-min Programming (MP) [40] is a centralized algorithm that uses a linear program to compute max-min fair allocations across general networks. However, using the MP algorithm in our setting would result in a linear program with an exponential complexity solution—each flow takes many paths, each path would be represented by a separate variable.

To make rate computation tractable, we leverage the simple insight that a flow's routing protocol dictates its relative rate across its paths. This holds for the routing protocols we studied. For instance, consider the example in Figure 3, in which a flow from 0 to 3 is routed using random packet spraying [22] across a 2x2 mesh topology. There are two shortest paths between the source and the destination, $0 \to 1 \to 3$ and $0 \to 2 \to 3$, which are chosen randomly on a per-packet basis and hence, are used equally. Therefore, the total rate allocated to the flow should be evenly divided across these two paths.

Overall, the key observation that a flow's routing protocol dictates its relative rate across multiple paths allows us to compute rate allocations at the flow-level, irrespective of the number of paths each flow is routed along.

3.3.1 Congestion control: a strawman design

R2C2's congestion control involves each node independently computing the max-min fair rate for each of its own flows. This comprises two steps. First, we use information about a flow's routing protocol to determine the relative rate of the flow across the paths it is using and, hence, along each network link it is using. We explain this with an example. To achieve per-flow fairness, each flow is assigned the same allocation weight. Given the flow's source, destination and

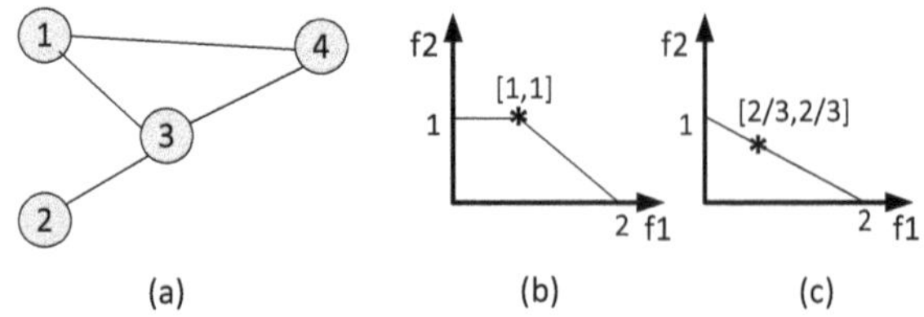

Figure 4: Flow $f1$ from node 1 to 4, and $f2$ from node 2 to 4. Respecting the relative rates dictated by the routing protocol changes the feasible set of rates from (b) to (c). The asterix denotes the max-min fair allocation.

routing protocol, we can determine its weight along any network link. For instance, the flow in Figure 3 is using both minimal paths equally, so its weight on each link that it is using is $\frac{w}{2}$. The flow's weight on each link it is not using (e.g., the link $1 \to 0$ in the figure) is zero. As another example, assume the flow was using WLB routing and using the two paths, $0 \to 1 \to 3$ and $0 \to 2 \to 3$, in the ratio 1:2. Then the flow's weight at links $0 \to 1$ and $1 \to 3$ is $\frac{w}{3}$, and its weight at links $0 \to 2$ and $2 \to 3$ is $\frac{2w}{3}$. We can repeat the above process for all flows to determine per-flow weights at all network links.

Second, given this setup, we compute max-min fair allocations through a weighted version of the water-filling algorithm [12] that we summarize here: the rates for all flows are increased at the same pace, until one or more links become saturated. Note that a flow's rate across a given link is a product of the flow's total rate and its weight across the link. This saturated link(s) is the bottleneck, and its capacity dictates the rates for all flows through it. The rates for these flows are frozen and they marked as allocated. The algorithm continues till all flows have been allocated. The complexity of this algorithm is $O(NL+N^2)$, where N is the number of flows and L is the number of links.

Benefits. This strawman design has a few advantages. First, it avoids the need to probe the network and induce congestion signals like packets drops and queuing to infer a flow's sending rate. High path diversity in rack-scale computers makes the design of an efficient congestion probing mechanism particularly challenging. Second, it obviates the need for any specialized queuing at the intermediate rack nodes.

Drawbacks. The computational tractability of the algorithm comes at the expense of possible network under-utilization. Consider the example scenario in Figure 4(a) (from [40]) with links of capacity one and two flows: flow $f1$ from node 1 to 4, and $f2$ from node 2 to 4. We assume the routes for these flows are given; $f1$ uses two paths ($1 \to 4$ and $1 \to 3 \to 4$) with equal probability while $f2$ uses one path ($2 \to 3 \to 4$). The set of feasible rates for these flows are shown in Figure 4(b), and the ideal max-min fair allocation is $\{1, 1\}$, i.e., each flow sends at a unit rate. This means flow $f1$ only uses the path $1 \to 4$. In contrast, R2C2's congestion control ensures that flow $f1$'s rate across its two paths is equal (as dictated by its routing protocol). The restricted set of feasible rates is shown in Figure 4(c). Our algorithm converges to the max-min fair rate in this set, $\{\frac{2}{3}, \frac{2}{3}\}$.

In summary, respecting the relative rates dictated by the routing protocol can result in network under-utilization. However, as described in Section 3.4, R2C2 also adapts the routing of all long running flows to alleviate this. For our example, flow $f1$'s routing would be changed so it only uses the path $1 \to 4$.

3.3.2 Congestion control extensions

The simple design described above makes several simplifying assumptions. Below we relax these assumptions.

New flows. The strawman design assumes that nodes are aware of the rack's current traffic matrix. While a flow startup event is broadcasted to all other nodes, the sender starts transmitting packets immediately. Thus, there is a small time period when not all nodes are aware of a new flow that has already started. To account for such temporary discrepancy between the actual traffic matrix and what is perceived by rack nodes, we rely on bandwidth headroom. During rate computation, we subtract this headroom from the capacity of network links. Typical datacenter traffic patterns involve many short flows that only contribute a small fraction of the bytes across the network. This indicates that a small spare capacity should absorb such short-lived flows while our congestion control protocol ensures that medium-to-long flows do not congest the network. In our experiments detailed in Section 5, a 5% headroom is sufficient even with bursty traffic patterns.

We note that R2C2 does not need a new data-plane mechanism (like phantom queues at switches [3]) to achieve the bandwidth headroom. Instead, the headroom is incorporated into the rate computation done at the control plane.

Host-limited flows. The strawman design assumes all flows are network limited. In practice, however, flows can be bottlenecked at their end points, e.g., at the application itself or inside the OS. To ensure high network utilization, any bandwidth unused by such host-limited flows should be allocated to flows that can use it. To account for host-limited flows, we estimate flow *demand*—the maximum rate at which it can actually send traffic—at the sender. Given a flow's demand estimate, the rate assigned to it is the minimum between its fair share and its demand. Whenever a flow's demand drops below it current rate allocation, the sender broadcasts this information. This allows all rack nodes to compute allocations in a demand-aware fashion.

Demand estimation is based on the observation that a flow sending at a rate higher than what it is currently allocated will suffer queuing at the sender. The sending node uses this queuing information to estimate the flow's demand. Specifically, flow demand is estimated periodically, and is the sum of the rate it is currently allocated and the amount of queuing it observes. Thus,

$$d[i+1] = r[i] + q[i]/T \qquad (1)$$

where $d[i+1]$ is the estimated demand for the next period, T is the estimation period while $r[i]$ and $q[i]$, respectively, are the rate allocation and queuing observed by the flow in the current period. To smooth out any noisy observations, we use an exponentially weighted moving average of the estimated demand. This estimation applies to open-loop workloads. For closed-loop workloads, demand can similarly be estimated using queuing information [6].

Beyond per-flow fairness. The strawman design provides per-flow fairness. However, R2C2 can accommodate richer allocation policies by allowing the operator to specify a flow's *weight* and *priority*. Many recently proposed high-level fairness policies such as deadline-based [46] or tenant-based [37], can be mapped onto these two primitives, similar to pFabric [4]. A flow's weight and priority are included in the broadcast packet announcing the flow start, so all nodes can use them during the rate computation.

The rate allocation algorithm accounts for flow priorities and weights as follows. Nodes invoke the allocation algorithm over multiple rounds, one for each priority level. At each round, flows belonging to the corresponding priority level are allocated any remaining capacity in a weighted fashion, i.e., instead of using uniform weights (as in Section 3.3.1), each flow is associated with its own weight.

Periodic rate computation. The strawman design recomputes flow rates at every flow event. Even at rack-scale, this will impose too much computation overhead. To amortize the recomputation cost, we opted for a batch-based design in which rates are recomputed periodically. In Section 5, we show that for realistic workloads a recomputation interval in the range of 500 μs-1 ms is sufficient to ensure high utilization and low queuing while introducing a CPU overhead of less than 8% at the 99th percentile (median value is 1.7%).

While this design was motivated by the need to reduce the computation cost, it also naturally filters out very short-lived flows, which would be pointless to rate-limit.

3.4 Selecting routing protocols

For short flows, a minimal routing protocol can improve the flow completion time. Thus, new flows start with minimal routing. As flows age, their routing can be adapted based on the rack's traffic matrix. R2C2 periodically selects the routing protocol for each long flow to maximize a global utility metric specified by the datacenter operator. The adaption is done every few seconds or minutes. Example utility metrics include the rack's aggregate throughput or the tail throughput, as measured across tenants or even across jobs and application tasks [15, 23]. For ease of exposition, here we focus on maximizing the aggregate throughput.

Dynamic selection of routing protocols is challenging because we want to leverage the flexibility of choosing a different routing protocol for *each* flow. This results in a combinatorial number of flow and routing protocol combinations to be evaluated, which makes exhaustive search intractable. Further, the search landscape originating from the utility functions that we considered typically exhibits several local maxima. Therefore, simple greedy heuristics (e.g., hill-climbing) are not effective and more complex global search heuristics must be adopted.

Initially, we considered techniques such as *log linear learning* [5] and *simulated annealing* [13]. However, we found them very sensitive to parameter tuning and workload characteristics. Thus, we opted for *genetic algorithms* [27], a search heuristic that emulates the natural selection and evolution. We found it a good fit for our scenario because it has relatively few tuning parameters and our problem can be naturally encoded as bit strings, where one or more bits are used to identify the routing protocol assigned to a given flow.

The heuristic works as follows. Initially, we generate a population of flow and routing protocol combinations (*genotypes*) that contains the current routing allocation and other randomly-generated ones. For each genotype, we compute the rack's aggregate throughput (*fitness*) using the rate computation mechanism described in Section 3.3 and rank them accordingly. We then generate a new generation that contains the top genotypes of the current population and other genotypes obtained by recombining (*crossover*) and *mutating* existing genotypes. The process is repeated until the time expires or until there has been no improvement over a number of generations. Once the search is over, the server generates broadcast packets containing the new assignment for each flow. Our current implementation uses four bytes for the flow identifier and one byte for the routing protocol per each flow (§4.2). This means that up to 300 {flow, routing protocol} pairs can be advertised using a single 1,500-byte packet. Since this process only applies to long flows, we consider the overhead negligible.

For simplicity, in our prototype, a single node is responsible for periodically performing the routing selection process. In practice, we expect this operation be decentralized with each node in turn executing it. Since nodes optimize a global utility metric, instead of selfishly optimizing for local performance, this design does not suffer from any price of anarchy inefficiency [42]. The next node to run the routing selection heuristic can be chosen randomly using a probability distribution centered around the average adaptation period or using a deterministic token-based scheme whereby nodes are selected serially in a round robin fashion.

3.5 Rack data-plane

R2C2 places most data-plane functionality at the source, resulting in simplified forwarding at intermediate rack nodes. This design is particularly suited to direct-connect topologies as each packet is forwarded through many nodes.

For each packet, its sender uses the corresponding flow's routing protocol to determine the packet's path. The path is then encoded into the packet's header. Further, each flow is associated with a token bucket that rate-limits the flow to its current rate allocation. Intermediate nodes forward packets using source routing. The packet header contains a route index field indicating the index of the next-hop in the packet path. Thus, every intermediate node simply forwards the packet to the indicated next-hop after incrementing the route index in the packet header.

4. IMPLEMENTATION

We have developed a flexible and efficient emulation platform for rack-scale computers, and implemented R2C2 as a user-space network stack atop this platform.

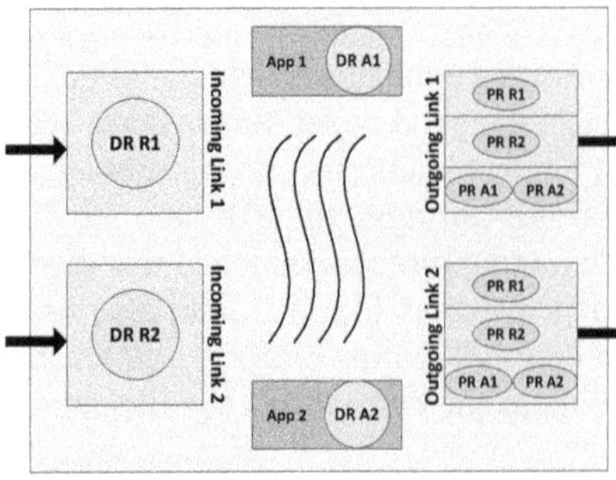

Figure 5: An example of a Maze server emulating a rack node with two incoming and two outgoing links. The emulated node has two applications.

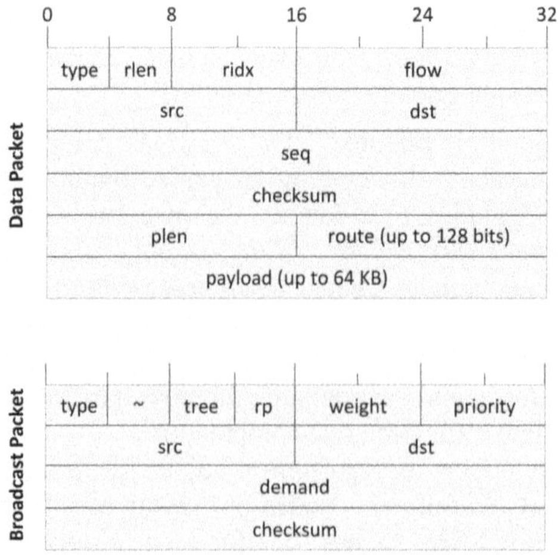

Figure 6: The format of data and broadcast packets.

4.1 Rack emulation platform

Rack-scale computers are currently difficult to acquire. Further, they come pre-configured with static network topologies and routing protocols, making it difficult to ensure that a proposed idea that works on one rack-scale computer will work on another. To address these issues, we implemented *Maze* [60], a cluster-based network emulation platform focusing on rack-scale fabrics. Maze runs on a cluster of servers connected by a high-bandwidth RDMA-based switched network. It emulates a rack's network fabric as a virtual network atop the switched network. Below we describe Maze's key properties and summarize its operation.

Maze provides three key properties: (i) It is *configurable*. It can map any virtual network topology (e.g., tree, mesh, torus, etc.) onto the underlying cluster. It can also support multiple routing strategies and transport protocols. (ii) It offers *high-performance* emulation, with the ability to emulate high capacity network links. Through micro-benchmarks, we find that it can provide up to 38 Gbps on a 40 Gbps link using 8 KB packets, and a latency of 3 μs per hop using small packets. (iii) It achieves *high-fidelity*. Our micro-benchmarks show that Maze can faithfully emulate many virtual links on the same physical network link.

Figure 5 depicts the operation of a Maze server emulating two incoming and two outgoing links. To achieve the properties mentioned above, Maze uses three main techniques: 1) It uses RDMA to transfers packets, 2) uses zero-copy forwarding, and 3) implements flow rate control.

Packet transfer. To provide high-performance yet configurability and ease of experimentation, Maze allows new routing and transport protocols to be implemented in user-space. It uses RDMA writes from the senders to data ring buffers (DR) on receivers' memory (e.g., DR R1 in Figure 5), similar to recent RDMA-based key-value stores [24, 31]. In Maze, incoming links, as well as applications (running emulated nodes), register memory to the RDMA NIC, which is accessed during RDMA writes. Pointer rings (PR) reference the registered memory and they are used in the outgoing links (e.g., PR R1) during RDMA writes.

Forwarding. An outgoing link on a Maze server constitutes a connection to another Maze server (i.e., RDMA queue pair [61]) and a number of pointer rings. To achieve zero-copy forwarding, for each packet, depending on its routing information, we pass the packet pointer that references the incoming ring buffer to the associated pointer ring on the selected outgoing link (e.g., PR R2 on outgoing link 1 sends packets of DR R2 on incoming link 2). Once the packet is sent, we zero the memory of the forwarded packet to make space for new packets in the respective receive ring buffer. We send application packets in the same fashion (e.g., using DR A1 and its respective pointer rings).

Rate control. Maze provides different pointer rings for different flows. This allows for implementation of both back-pressure based and rate-based congestion control approaches. Transport protocols can use Maze's rate limiters to adjust the rate at which data pointers from a flow pointer are inserted on an application's pointer rings belonging to outgoing links.

4.2 R2C2 implementation

We implemented R2C2 as a user-mode network stack in Maze. For routing, we have implemented random packet spraying [22], destination-tag routing [20] and VLB routing [45]. For congestion control, we have implemented our rate-based congestion control protocol. This leverages Maze's rate control functionality. Overall, our complete prototype (including Maze) consists of 9,836 lines of C++ and 967 lines of control scripts.

Rate computation. We implemented an efficient variant of the water-filling algorithm described in Section 3.3.1. A key challenge was how to efficiently compute the link weights for each flow. We solved this by pre-computing on each node the list of link weights for each {routing protocol, destination} pair. Assuming a 512-node rack, the memory footprint per routing protocol is less than 6 MB, i.e., 511 destinations times the number of links ($6 \cdot 512$) times 4 bytes for the weight.

Rate limiters. As explained in Section 3.3.1, the R2C2 congestion control respects the relative rates dictated by the routing protocol. Beside reducing the computation overhead, this also implies that only one rate limiter per flow is needed as opposed to one rate limiter per each of the paths traversed by the flow. Further, flows are only rate-limited at the source and not at the intermediate nodes. Therefore, the number of rate limiters needed by each node is equal to the number of flows that it generates. In our prototype, we rely on software rate limiters, which can achieve very fine-grained rate limiting [29]. Furthermore, we believe that these requirements are well within the reach of today's NICs, which typically support 8-128 hardware rate limiters [39].

Packet formats. Figure 6 shows the format used for data and broadcast packets. Data packets are variable sized, while broadcast packets have a fixed size (16 bytes). The packet type is defined in the *type* field.

The header of a data packet contains length of the route that the packet travels (*rlen*), an index into the packet's route (*ridx*), the flow identifier (*flow*), source (*src*), destination (*dst*), the sequence number (*seq*), the packet checksum (*checksum*), length of the payload (*plen*), the packet's route (*route*), and finally the payload.

The size of endpoints allows for up to 65,536 nodes. Further, the *route* field could be up to 128 bits. We use 3 bits for each hop to select the forwarding link (i.e., we assume at most eight links per node) and increase *ridx* every time we forward a packet. This allows us to store routes with up to 42 hops, which is sufficient for current rack-scale computers and even non-minimal routing strategies.

Apart from source, destination and the packet checksum, broadcast packets include the weight of the flow (*weight*), flow's priority (*priority*), the demand (*demand*) in Kbps between the nodes (up to 4 Tbps), the broadcast spanning tree id (*tree*), and the currently used routing strategy between the two nodes (*rp*).

5. EVALUATION

In our evaluation, we answer the following questions: (i). how effective is R2C2's congestion control mechanism in achieving high throughput and low queuing?, (ii). what is the traffic overhead introduced by broadcast?, (iii). what is the cost of rate computation?, and finally (iv). what are the benefits of supporting per-flow routing selection?

We adopted the following methodology. First, we use R2C2's implementation atop Maze to empirically verify the feasibility and performance of our design, to quantify the computation overhead, and to cross-validate our packet-level simulator. Then, we use the simulator to investigate the performance of R2C2 at scale and under different workloads.

Our results indicate that R2C2 achieves high throughput and fairness while only requiring small queues and the overhead imposed by broadcast is negligible. The computation cost depends on the frequency at which rates are recomputed. However, for realistic workloads, this cost is reasonable. Finally, by enabling individual flows to use different routing protocols and by dynamically selecting among them based on the observed workload, R2C2 achieves higher performance than what would be possible using only a single routing protocol for all flows.

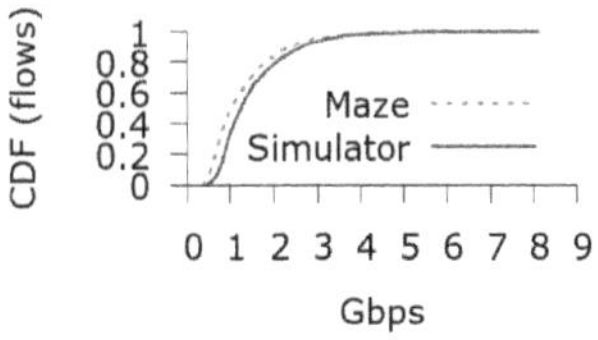

(a) Flow throughput.

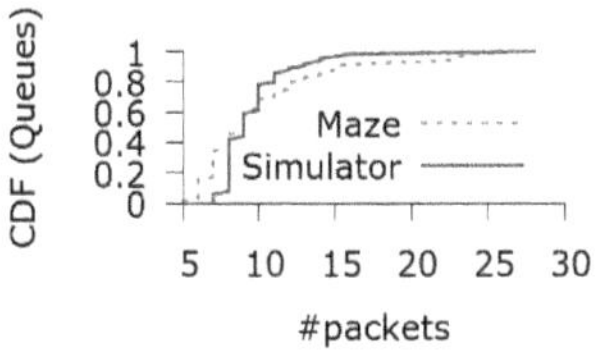

(b) Queue occupancy.

Figure 7: Cross-validation of the flow throughput and maximum queue occupancy between Maze and the simulator using a 4x4 2D torus topology.

5.1 Emulation results

We deploy our Maze platform on a 16-server RDMA cluster. Each server is equipped with two 2.4 GHz Intel Xeon E5-2665 CPUs and 24 GB of memory. The servers are connected using Quad Data Rate (QDR) InfiniBand. We emulated a 4x4 2D torus virtual topology with a bandwidth of 5 Gbps per virtual link.

We generate a synthetic workload, comprising 1,000 flows of 10 MB each. We assume Poisson flow arrivals with a mean inter-arrival time of 1 ms. We use the random packet spraying routing protocol. We measure the throughput and the *maximum* occupancy experienced by each queue throughout the entire experiment. We then repeated the same experiment in the simulator, using the same topology and workload. Results in Figure 7 show that our packet-level simulator exhibits high accuracy, both in terms of flow throughput and queuing occupancy. These cross-validation results improve our confidence in the large-scale simulation experiments presented in Section 5.2.

Computation overhead. Next, we evaluate the computation overhead introduced by R2C2 when recomputing flow rates. To show the behavior at scale, we ran the same workload in the simulator using a 512-node 3D Torus and we recorded the flow arrival and departure events at each node. To account for the increase in scale, we reduce the flow inter-arrival time to 1 us. We then replayed these traces in Maze and measured the execution time of the rate recomputation. We ran this benchmark on two different CPU cores: a 2.4GHz Intel Xeon E5-2665 and a 1.66 GHz Intel Atom D510 [57]. The first one is representative of today's data center servers. The latter, instead, is a first-generation (2009) low-power CPU architecture. This could be used, for instance, as a cheap, dedicated core on each SoC to handle the execution of R2C2.

Figure 8 plots the 99th percentile of the CPU overhead for different values of the recomputation interval ρ. We compute the overhead by dividing the time taken to recompute the rates by the value of ρ. This means that if the overhead is higher than 100% (the horizontal line in the chart), the recomputation would not finish in time and, hence, the interval is not feasible. As discussed in Section 3.3.2, we use a batch-based design in which we only consider the flows that last more than one interval. Therefore, the longer the interval, the lower the number of flows considered, and this explains why high values of ρ exhibit lower overhead. For example, for ρ=500 us, the median overhead on the Intel Xeon is

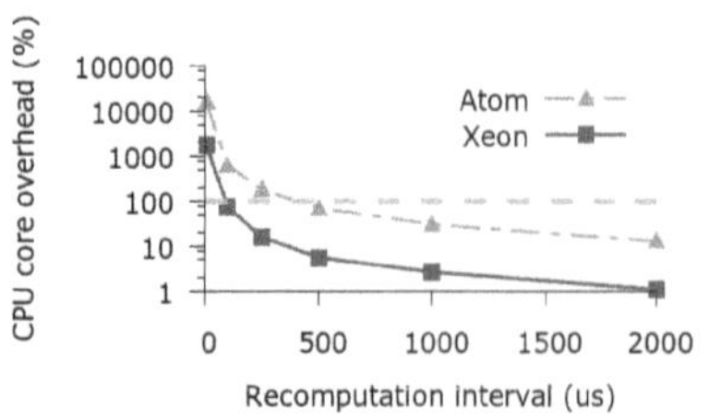

Figure 8: The 99th percentile of the CPU overhead on one 2.4 GHz Intel Xeon E5-2665 core and on a 1.66 GHz Intel Atom D510 core when simulating a 512-node workload with 1 us flow inter-arrival time.

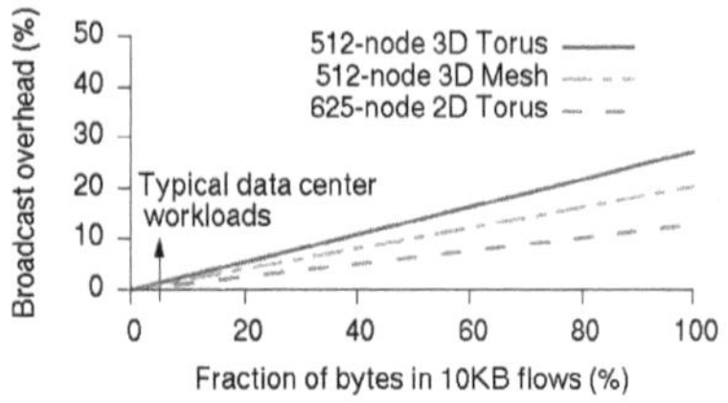

Figure 9: Network capacity used for broadcasting grows linearly with the fraction of bytes carried by small flows. The experiment involves uniform traffic with shortest path routing using 10KB small flows and 35MB long flows.

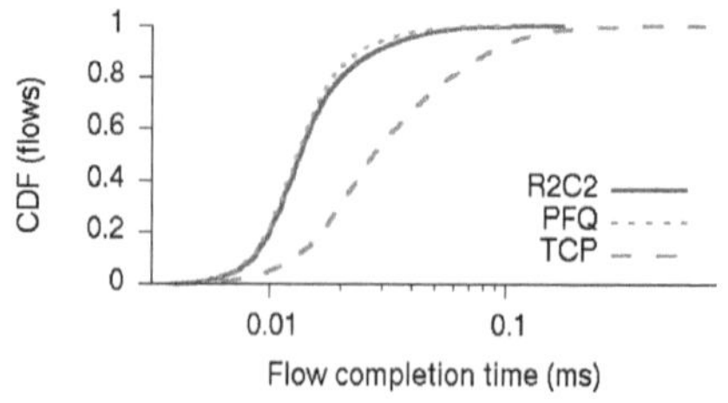

Figure 10: The CDF of FCT for short flows (size < 100 KB) for flow inter-arrival time τ=1us (log scale).

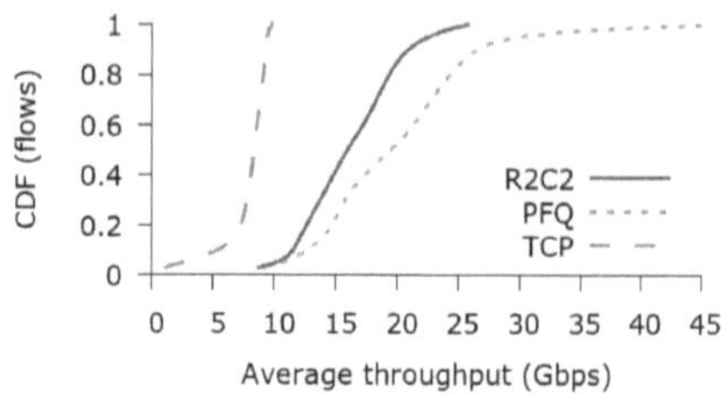

Figure 11: The CDF of average throughput for long flows (size > 1 MB) for flow inter-arrival time τ=1us.

1.7% (99th percentile is 7.9%) and 33.5% on the Intel Atom (99th percentile 71.4%). For low values of ρ, the overhead becomes much higher, e.g., for ρ=100 us the 99th percentile is 73.9% on the Intel Xeon (median is 17.6%) while it is infeasible for the Intel Atom (the normalized CPU usage is higher than 100%). However, as we show in Section 5.2, for the workloads we consider, a value of ρ=500 us is sufficient to achieve good performance.

Broadcast overhead. Finally, we analyzed the overhead of packet broadcasts on flow arrivals and departures. We consider the size of the broadcast and data packets in Maze to analytically project the results for a 512-node 3D torus. Assuming 10 KB flows (§3.2), the average bandwidth overhead is 26.66%. For 10 MB flows, instead, the overhead would just be 0.026%.[3] Thus, the overall broadcasting overhead depends on the fraction of bytes carried by small flows.

Figure 9 shows that the fraction of network capacity used for broadcast traffic grows linearly with the fraction of bytes carried by small flows. In typical datacenter workloads, small flows carry a small fraction of bytes; 95% of all bytes are in the 3.6% flows larger than 35 MB [25]. For such a workload, only 1.3% of the network capacity is used for broadcasting. The figure also shows that for topologies with a greater diameter like a 3D Mesh and a 2D Torus, the broadcast overhead is lower. This is because the average flow traverses more hops, so the relative overhead of broadcasting its arrival and departure is lower.

5.2 Simulation results

In our simulation experiments, we consider a 512-node 3D torus. This is the same size and topology as the AMD SeaMicro 15000-OP. We assume a link bandwidth of 10 Gbps and a per-link latency of 100 ns. We leave 5% headroom and, except where otherwise noted, we use a recomputation interval of 500 us. In our experiments, we use a synthetic workload modeled after traffic patterns observed in production data centers [2, 4, 25]. Flow's source and destination are randomly chosen following a uniform distribution. The flow sizes are generated from a Pareto distribution with shape parameter 1.05 and mean 100 KB [3]. This generates a heavy-tailed workload where 95% of the flows are less than 100 KB, as is commonly observed in data centers. We assume Poisson flow arrivals and we consider flow inter-arrival times varying from 1 us to 100 us. To stress our system, we also consider an extreme flow inter-arrival time of 100 ns, which corresponds to a workload with 10^{10} flows/s with a peak of 2,241 simultaneous flows. This is up to two orders of magnitude lower than the arrival times observed in a recent study on a production cluster [32], which reports a median arrival time of 10 us for a 1,500-server network (i.e., three times bigger than our simulated network).

Flow completion time and queuing. We start our analysis by measuring the flow completion time achieved by R2C2. We compare our approach against TCP and against an idealized baseline, *per-flow queues (PFQ)*, that uses back-pressure and per-flow queues at each node. This baseline is impractical because, apart from forwarding complexity at rack nodes, it results in very high buffering requirements. However, it is useful in our study because it provides the upper bound of the performance achievable by any rate control protocol for minimal and non-minimal routing. For TCP, we use an ECMP-like routing protocol, which selects a single path between source and destination, based on the hash of the flow ID. This ensures that packets belonging to the same flow are routed onto the same path as required by TCP. However, we assign different shortest paths to different flows be-

[3]This assumes uniform traffic and minimal routing. With non-minimal routing, the broadcast overhead is lower.

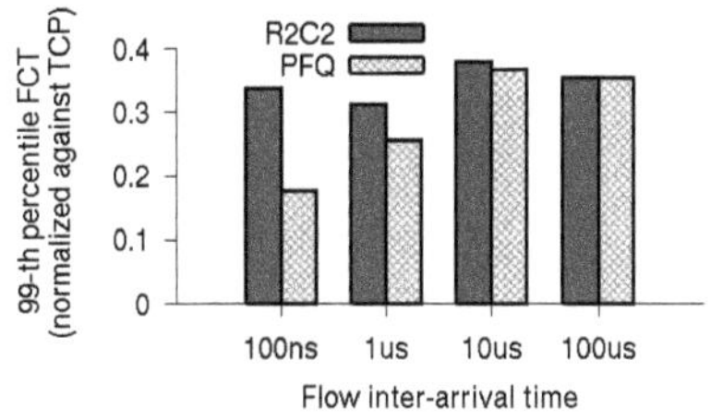

Figure 12: The 99th-percentile of FCT for short flows (size < 100 KB) normalized against TCP for different flow inter-arrival times.

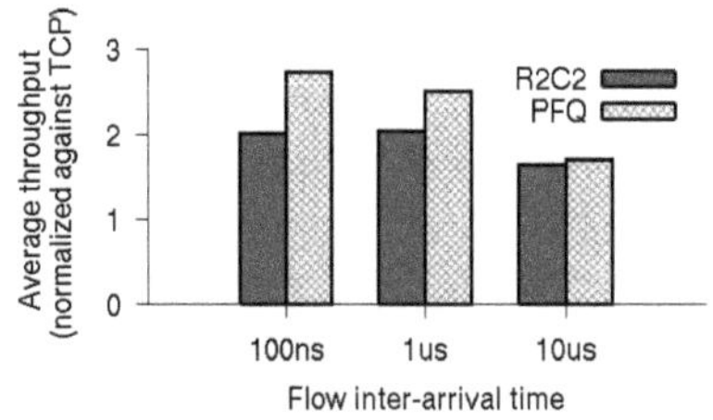

Figure 13: The average throughput for long flows (size > 1 MB) normalized against TCP for different flow inter-arrival times.

tween the same endpoints. For the idealized baseline and R2C2, we use random packet spraying.

Figure 10 and 11 show the CDF of the flow completion time (FCT) for short flows (size < 100 KB) and average throughput for long flows (size > 1 MB) respectively. We do not show the results for intermediate sizes as they are qualitatively similar to the ones for the short flows. As expected, TCP achieves the worst performance both for short and long flows. At the $99th$ percentile, TCP yields a 3.21x higher FCT for short flows and a 2.55x lower average throughput for long flows compared to R2C2. The reason is due to its high queuing occupancy (for short flows) and its dependency on a single-path routing (for long flows). The latter aspect underlines the importance of exploiting path diversity.

The results also show that for short flows R2C2 closely matches the FCT of the PFQ configuration and it does so by only using a single queue per port. This confirms that our protocol is able to achieve fairness among flows without requiring per-flow state at the intermediate nodes. This is particularly important for many data center applications, which are sensitive to load imbalance and long tail latency [21]. For long flows, the gap between R2C2 and PFQ increases. The is due to the fact that a) R2C2 uses a different fairness model that trades off utilization for computation tractability (§3.3.1) and b) it uses headroom to absorb bursts (§3.3.2).

To investigate the performance of R2C2 at different loads, in Figure 12 and 13 we show the 99th percentile of the FCT (short flows) and the average throughput (long flows) normalized against TCP for different inter-arrival times τ. As expected, at very high load (τ=100 ns), the performance of R2C2 deviates from the PFQ's ideal one as the queues start building up due to the inaccuracy introduced by our periodic recomputation. However, as noted, this scenario represents an extreme case; we believe that flow inter-arrival times of the order of (tens of) micro-seconds are more realistic. As the load decreases, R2C2's performance converges to PFQ's.

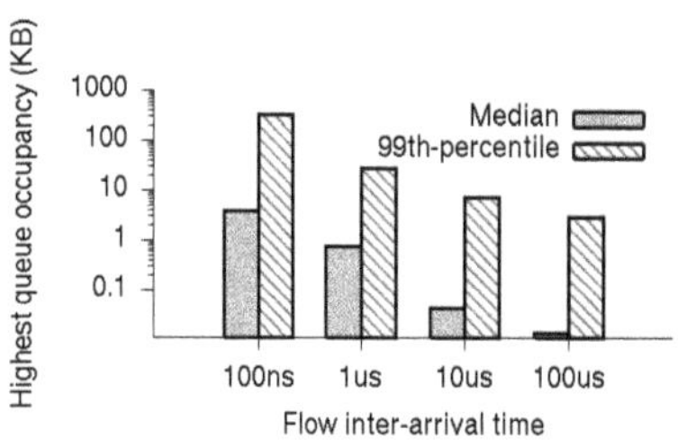

Figure 14: 99th percentile and median of the maximum queue occupancy (log scale).

Figure 14 shows the median and the 99th percentile of the *maximum* queue occupancy observed throughout these experiments across all node queues. For inter-arrival times of 1 us and above, the 99th percentile is lower than 27 KB (median is less than one packet). However, for τ=100 ns, the 99th percentile goes to 330.6 KB (median is 3.8 KB). More frequent recomputation would mitigate this, albeit at the cost of higher recomputation overhead.

Low queue occupancy also reduces the amount of packet reordering caused by multi-path routing. In this experiment, for τ=1us, the 95th percentile of the re-order buffer size was 30 packets with a maximum value of 51 packets.

Impact of the recomputation interval. To understand the impact of the recomputation interval ρ, we measure the *absolute* difference between the average rate assigned to each flow when using different values of ρ and the ideal case of ρ=0. We plot the median and 95th-percentile across *all* flows in Figure 15 using a flow inter-arrival time of τ=1 us (values are normalized against the ideal rates for ρ=0). As expected, lower values of ρ reduce the difference with the ideal rates. Unfortunately, such low values are hard to achieve using a software-only implementation (§5.1). The results in Figure 15 indicate that a value of ρ in the range 500 us-1 ms might be a good compromise between performance and computation overhead. Such a value incurs a modest processing overhead (see Figure 8) and contains the difference w.r.t. ideal rates within 8.2% in the median case (resp. 37.9% at the 95th-percentile). This, however, depends on the workload considered, as shown in Figure 16. At lower load (e.g., τ=100 us), the difference is almost negligible, while at higher load (τ=100 ns) the difference becomes significant and lower recomputation intervals are needed. Hardware offload of the rate computation might be a viable option to enable smaller recomputation intervals but we leave the exploration of this opportunity to future work.

Impact of the headroom. To compensate for the burstiness of the workload and the inaccuracies due to the periodic rate computation, we reserve some headroom when computing the flow rates. The optimal value of headroom depends on the workload. High headroom provides more resilience to bursts but penalizes utilization. While we have not yet designed a mechanism to automatically tune it, in Figure 17 we conduct a sensitivity analysis varying the headroom from zero (i.e., no headroom) up to 20%. The figure shows that

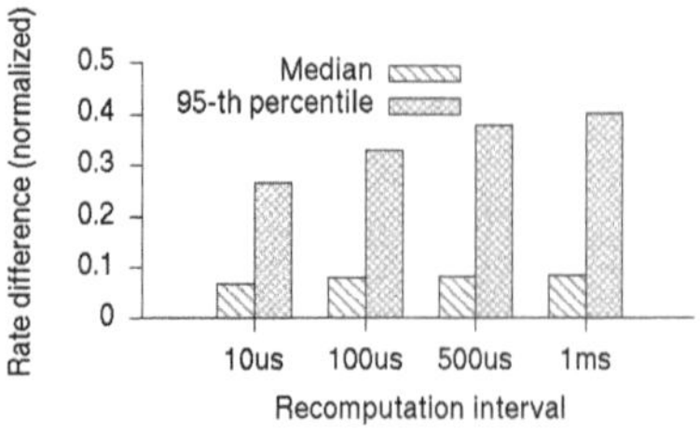

Figure 15: The median and 95th-percentile of the normalized difference between the ideal and computed rates against the recomputation interval (flow inter-arrival time τ=1 us).

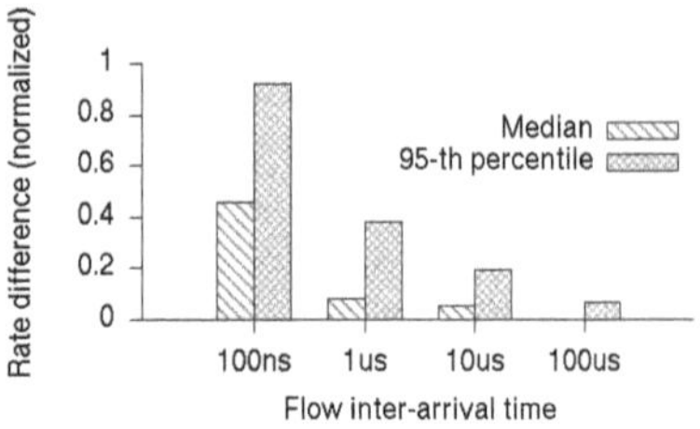

Figure 16: The median and 95th-percentile of the difference between the ideal and computed rates against the flow inter-arrival time (recomputation interval ρ=500 us).

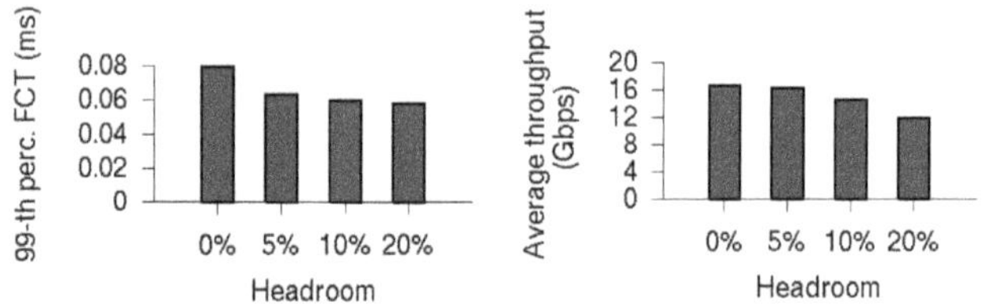

(a) Short flows. (b) Long flows.

Figure 17: The 99th-percentile of FCT (short flows) and average throughput (long flows) against the headroom.

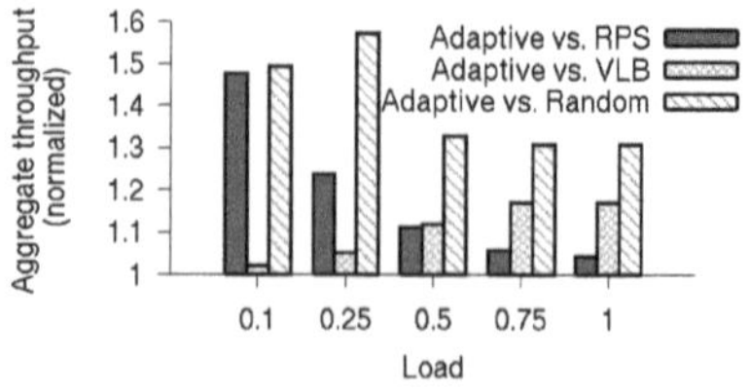

Figure 18: Aggregate throughput achieved by our routing selection heuristic (*Adaptive*) normalized against the three baselines for different load values.

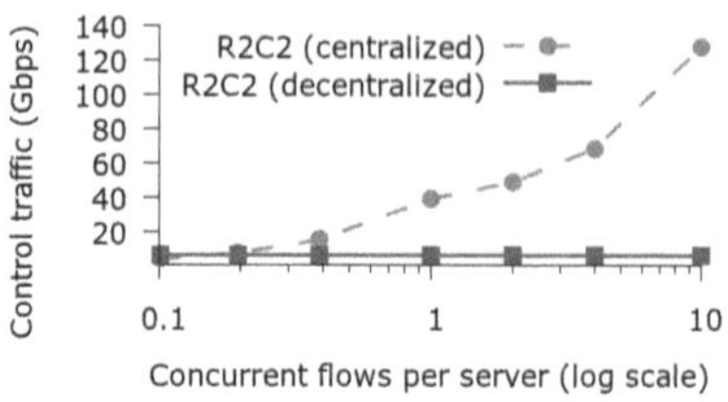

Figure 19: Control traffic with varying number of concurrent long flows per server (flow inter-arrival time τ=1 us).

the performance of R2C2 is not particularly sensitive to the choice of the headroom parameter. Overall, we found that, for our target workloads, a 5% headroom represents a good trade-off. For example, for an inter-arrival time of 1 us, compared to the case in which no headroom is used, a 5% headroom yields a 21.9% reduction in FCT for short flows at the 99th percentile while the reduction in the average throughput for long flows is less than 3%.

Custom routing protocols. Next, we explore the behavior of R2C2's flexible routing stack. In particular, we aim to: i) demonstrate the benefits of having multiple routing protocols running concurrently (as opposed to a single, network-wide, routing) and ii) to evaluate the performance of our adaptive selection of routing protocols. We consider a workload in which a fraction L of nodes generates a long-running flow each to another randomly chosen node such that every node is the source and the destination of at most one flow. We chose this workload for its relative simplicity, which allows for an intuitive analysis. At high load ($L \geq 0.5$), a minimal routing protocol such as RPS achieves the best performance as the hop count is minimized and the utilization is maximized. At low load, instead, a non-minimal routing protocol such as VLB exhibits superior performance as it can exploit the spare network capacity to increase the throughput. We also experimented with other workloads and observed qualitatively similar results.

We use the genetic algorithm-based heuristic described in Section 3.4. For each flow, we consider only two routing protocols, random packet spraying (RPS) and VLB. Each genotype is encoded as a bit string with each bit corresponding to one flow, thus leading to a global search space of up to 2^{512} solutions when $L = 1$. We use a population size of 100 and a mutation probability of 0.01. In Figure 18 we plot the relative performance of our selection heuristic named *Adaptive* against three baselines: one using RPS for all flows (*RPS*), one using VLB for all flows (*VLB*), and one in which each flow randomly chooses either protocol (*Random*). The results show that our selection process is able to *always* achieve the best performance across all load values (the relative performance is always above one). This shows the importance of supporting per-flow routing protocols and the benefits of our dynamic selection.

Comparison against a centralized design. With R2C2, nodes can locally compute a flow's rate and routing protocol. We also considered an alternate design where the computation is done centrally (similar to Fastpass [36]), simply by choosing one of the rack nodes as a centralized controller. Such a design reduces computation overhead at the expense of greater control traffic. We study this trade-off below.

Figure 19 shows the amount of control traffic with a decentralized design and a centralized one when varying the number of concurrent long flows per server. In the decentralized design, a flow arrival (or departure) event is broadcasted to all rack nodes. Instead, with a centralized design, the source sends a unicast message to the controller, which computes the rates and sends to each rack node sourcing a flow a different rate message with all the new rates for its own flows. This is the reason why the control traffic for the centralized design increases with the number of concurrent flows while it remains constant for the decentralized design.

When there are only a few long flows, the centralized design is more efficient because only a few control messages are generated. However, when the number of flows grows, the decentralized becomes more attractive because only the flow events are broadcasted while the rate updates are computed locally. For example, when there is one concurrent flow per server, the centralized design generates 6.2x more traffic than the decentralized one (resp. 19.9x more when the number of concurrent flows per server is equal to 10).

The price paid by the decentralized design is increased computation. Instead of computing rates once at the controller and communicating them to all nodes, the computation is done by each node. However, as shown in Section 5.1, the rate computation overhead is acceptable.

6. DISCUSSION AND FUTURE WORK

R2C2 targets intra-rack communication, and determines how such traffic is routed and how the network fabric is shared. Here we discuss some directions for future work.

Inter-rack networking. A key open question we have not addressed is interconnection of multiple rack-scale computers to form a large cluster. This includes both the physical wiring layout and the network protocols used to bridge between two rack-scale computers.

One simple option for inter-rack networking is to just use traditional switches and tunnel R2C2 packets by encapsulating them inside Ethernet frames. While this would allow for a smooth transition from today's deployments, it has some limitations. First, given the high bandwidth available within a rack, the only way to avoid creating high over-subscription would be to use high-radix switches with large back-plane capacity, in the order of (tens of) Terabits. This, however, would dramatically increase costs and it may even be infeasible if 100+ Gbps links are to be deployed within a rack. Further, the need to bridge between R2C2 and Ethernet would increase the overhead and the end-to-end latency. A more promising (albeit challenging) solution instead is to directly connect multiple rack-scale computers without using any switch, similar to [49]. Theia [47] also proposes such design with multiple parallel connections between racks. Beside saving the cost of the switches, this would also enable a finer-grain control over the inter-rack routing.

Reliability. Even within the context of intra-rack communication, more work is needed. R2C2 does not provide a *complete network transport protocol* — it does not provide end-to-end reliability and flow control. While traditional mechanisms like end-to-end acknowledgements and checksums can be used to achieve these, we believe R2C2's design improves the efficacy of such mechanisms. For example, by decoupling congestion control from reliability, we ensure that acknowledgements are used solely for reliability. This is in contrast with TCP-like protocols that rely on ACK-clocking to determine the fair sending rates of flows. We are currently investigating such extensions.

R2C2 atop switched networks. R2C2's design is motivated by the challenges and opportunities posed by rack-scale computers with direct-connect topologies. However, traditional switched topologies (with silicon photonics or other physical technologies) are also being considered for the intra-rack network [7, 53]. We note that it is the scale of rack-scale computers, not the topology, that makes broadcasting efficient. For example, consider a 512 node rack connected using 32-port switches arranged in a two-level folded Clos topology. A broadcast on this topology results in only 8.7 KB of total traffic. Such a topology does not have multiple paths between nodes, so there is no room for route selection. However, R2C2's congestion control still offers more flexibility over traditional distributed congestion control.

At data center scale, the broadcast overhead is high and distributed control is more appealing. However, even at such a scale, R2C2's design and algorithms could be appropriate if next-generation networks have more efficient means of achieving (approximate) global visibility while providing significant multi-pathing.

7. CONCLUSION

We presented R2C2, a network stack for rack-scale computers comprising a rate-based congestion control protocol and a flexible routing mechanism. By broadcasting flow events, we ensure that rack nodes can locally compute rate allocations and routing decisions. These decisions are enforced at the sources, resulting in simplified packet forwarding. By deploying R2C2 on an emulated rack and a (cross-validated) simulator, we show that R2C2 can achieve good performance across diverse network workloads, and routing flexibility can provide even more gains.

Acknowledgments

We thank Thomas Bigger, Aleksandar Dragojević, Sergey Grant, Sergey Legtchenko, Dushyanth Narayanan, Greg O'Shea, Bozidar Radunović, Michael Schapira, the anonymous SIGCOMM reviewers, and our shepherd George Porter for their feedback and help.

8. REFERENCES

[1] H. Abu-Libdeh, P. Costa, A. Rowstron, G. O'Shea, and A. Donnelly. Symbiotic Routing in Future Data Centers. In *SIGCOMM*, 2010.

[2] M. Alizadeh, A. Greenberg, D. A. Maltz, J. Padhye, P. Patel, B. Prabhakar, S. Sengupta, and M. Sridharan. Data Center TCP (DCTCP). In *SIGCOMM*, 2010.

[3] M. Alizadeh, A. Kabbani, T. Edsall, B. Prabhakar, A. Vahdat, and M. Yasuda. Less Is More: Trading a Little Bandwidth for Ultra-Low Latency in the Data Center. In *NSDI*, 2012.

[4] M. Alizadeh, S. Yang, M. Sharif, S. Katti, N. McKeown, B. Prabhakar, and S. Shenker. pFabric: Minimal Near-optimal Datacenter Transport. In *SIGCOMM*, 2013.

[5] J. M. andJeff Shamma. Revisiting log-linear learning: Asynchrony, completeness and payoff-based implementation. *Games and Economic Behavior*, 2012.

[6] S. Angel, H. Ballani, T. Karagiannis, G. O'Shea, and E. Thereska. End-to-end Performance Isolation through Virtual Datacenters . In *OSDI*, 2014.

[7] K. Asanovic. FireBox: A Hardware Building Block for 2020 Warehouse-Scale Computers. In *FAST*, 2014. Keynote.

[8] B. Awerbuch, R. Khandekar, and S. Rao. Distributed Algorithms for Multicommodity Flow Problems via

Approximate Steepest Descent Framework. *ACM Trans. Algorithms*, 9(1), 2012.

[9] S. Balakrishnan, R. Black, A. Donnelly, P. England, A. Glass, D. Harper, S. Legtchenko, A. Ogus, E. Peterson, and A. Rowstron. Pelican: A Building Block for Exascale Cold Data Storage. In *OSDI*, 2014.

[10] H. Ballani, P. Costa, T. Karagiannis, and A. Rowstron. Towards Predictable Datacenter Networks. In *SIGCOMM*, 2011.

[11] H. Ballani, K. Jang, T. Karagiannis, C. Kim, D. Gunawardena, and G. O'Shea. Chatty Tenants and the Cloud Network Sharing Problem. In *NSDI*, 2013.

[12] D. Bertsekas and R. Gallager. *Data Networks*. Prentice Hall, 1987.

[13] D. Bertsimas and J. Tsitsiklis. Simulated Annealing. *Statistical Science*, 8(1), 1993.

[14] R. S. Cahn. *Wide Area Network Design: Concepts and Tools for Optimization*. Morgan Kaufmann, 1998.

[15] M. Chowdhury and I. Stoica. Coflow: A Networking Abstraction for Cluster Applications. In *HotNets*, 2012.

[16] P. Costa, H. Ballani, and D. Narayanan. Rethinking the Network Stack for Rack-scale Computers. In *HotCloud*, 2014.

[17] Cray Inc. Modifying Your Application to Avoid Aries Network Congestion, 2013.

[18] Cray Inc. Network Resiliency for Cray XC30 Systems, 2013.

[19] A. Daglis, S. Novaković, E. Bugnion, B. Falsafi, and B. Grot. Manycore Network Interfaces for In-memory Rack-scale Computing. In *ISCA*, 2015.

[20] W. Dally and B. Towles. *Principles and Practices of Interconnection Networks*. Morgan Kaufmann, 2003.

[21] J. Dean and L. A. Barroso. The Tail at Scale. *Communications of ACM*, 2013.

[22] A. A. Dixit, P. Prakash, Y. C. Hu, and R. R. Kompella. On the Impact of Packet Spraying in Data Center Networks. In *INFOCOM*, 2013.

[23] F. R. Dogar, T. Karagiannis, H. Ballani, and A. Rowstron. Decentralized Task-aware Scheduling for Data Center Networks. In *SIGCOMM*, 2014.

[24] A. Dragojević, D. Narayanan, O. Hodson, and M. Castro. FaRM: Fast Remote Memory. In *NSDI*, 2014.

[25] A. Greenberg, J. R. Hamilton, N. Jain, S. Kandula, C. Kim, P. Lahiri, D. A. Maltz, P. Patel, and S. Sengupta. VL2: A Scalable and Flexible Data Center Network. In *SIGCOMM*, 2009.

[26] S. Han, N. Egi, A. Panda, S. Ratnasamy, G. Shi, and S. Shenker. Network Support for Resource Disaggregation in Next-generation Datacenters. In *HotNets*, 2013.

[27] J. H. Holland. *Adaptation in Natural and Artificial Systems*. University of Michigan Press, 1975.

[28] C.-Y. Hong, M. Caesar, and P. B. Godfrey. Finishing flows quickly with preemptive scheduling. In *SIGCOMM*, 2012.

[29] K. Jang, J. Sherry, H. Ballani, and T. Moncaster. Silo: Predictable Message Latency in the Cloud. In *SIGCOMM*, 2015.

[30] V. Jeyakumar, M. Alizadeh, D. Mazières, B. Prabhakar, C. Kim, and A. Greenberg. EyeQ: Practical Network Performance Isolation at the Edge. In *NSDI*, 2013.

[31] A. Kalia, M. Kaminsky, and D. G. Andersen. Using RDMA Efficiently for Key-value Services. In *SIGCOMM*, 2014.

[32] S. Kandula, S. Sengupta, A. Greenberg, P. Patel, and R. Chaiken. The nature of data center traffic: measurements & analysis. In *IMC*, 2009.

[33] D. Nace, N.-L. Doan, E. Gourdin, and B. Liau. Computing Optimal Max-min Fair Resource Allocation for Elastic Flows. *IEEE/ACM Trans. Netw.*, 14(6), 2006.

[34] S. Novakovic, A. Daglis, E. Bugnion, B. Falsafi, and B. Grot. Scale-out NUMA. In *ASPLOS*, 2014.

[35] G. P. Nychis, C. Fallin, T. Moscibroda, O. Mutlu, and S. Seshan. On-chip Networks from a Networking Perspective: Congestion and Scalability in Many-core Interconnects. In *SIGCOMM*, 2012.

[36] J. Perry, A. Ousterhout, H. Balakrishnan, D. Shah, and H. Fugal. Fastpass: A Centralized "Zero-queue" Datacenter Network. In *SIGCOMM*, 2014.

[37] L. Popa, G. Kumar, M. Chowdhury, A. Krishnamurthy, S. Ratnasamy, and I. Stoica. FairCloud: Sharing the Network in Cloud Computing. In *SIGCOMM*, 2012.

[38] A. Putnam, A. Caulfield, E. Chung, D. Chiou, K. Constantinides, J. Demme, H. Esmaeilzadeh, J. Fowers, G. P. Gopal, J. Gray, M. Haselman, S. Hauck, S. Heil, A. Hormati, J.-Y. Kim, S. Lanka, J. Larus, E. Peterson, S. Pope, A. Smith, J. Thong, P. Y. Xiao, and D. Burger. A Reconfigurable Fabric for Accelerating Large-Scale Datacenter Services. In *ISCA*, 2014.

[39] S. Radhakrishnan, Y. Geng, V. Jeyakumar, A. Kabbani, G. Porter, and A. Vahdat. SENIC: Scalable NIC for End-Host Rate Limiting. In *NSDI*, 2014.

[40] B. Radunović and J.-Y. L. Boudec. A Unified Framework for Max-min and Min-max Fairness with Applications. *IEEE/ACM Trans. Netw.*, 15(5), 2007.

[41] C. Raiciu, S. Barre, C. Pluntke, A. Greenhalgh, D. Wischik, and M. Handley. Improving Datacenter Performance and Robustness with Multipath TCP. In *SIGCOMM*, 2011.

[42] T. Roughgarden and E. Tardos. How Bad is Selfish Routing? *J. ACM*, 2002.

[43] B. Schroeder and G. A. Gibson. Understanding Failures in Petascale Computers. *Journal of Physics*, 78, 2007.

[44] A. Singh, W. J. Dally, B. Towles, and A. K. Gupta. Locality-preserving Randomized Oblivious Routing on Torus Networks. In *SPAA*, 2002.

[45] L. G. Valiant and G. J. Brebner. Universal Schemes for Parallel Communication. In *STOC*, 1981.

[46] B. Vamanan, J. Hasan, and T. N. Vijaykumar. Deadline-Aware Datacenter TCP (D^2TCP). In *SIGCOMM*, 2012.

[47] M. Walraed-Sullivan, J. Padhye, and D. A. Maltz. Theia: Simple and Cheap Networking for Ultra-Dense Data Centers. In *HotNets*, 2014.

[48] C. Wilson, H. Ballani, T. Karagiannis, and A. Rowtron. Better Never Than Late: Meeting Deadlines in Datacenter Networks. In *SIGCOMM*, 2011.

[49] H. Wu, G. Lu, D. Li, C. Guo, and Y. Zhang. MDCube: A High Performance Network Structure for Modular Data Center Interconnection. In *CoNEXT*, 2009.

[50] Amazon joins other web giants trying to design its own chips. http://bit.ly/1J5t0fE.

[51] Boston Viridis Data Sheet. http://bit.ly/1fBnsQ9.

[52] Calxeda EnergyCore ECX-1000. http://bit.ly/1nCgdHO.

[53] Design Guide for Photonic Architecture. http://bit.ly/NYpT1h.

[54] Google Ramps Up Chip Design. http://ubm.io/1iQooNe.

[55] How Microsoft Designs its Cloud-Scale Servers. http://bit.ly/1HKCy27.

[56] HP Moonshot System. http://bit.ly/1mZD4yJ.

[57] Intel Atom Processor D510. http://intel.ly/1wJmS3D.

[58] Intel, Facebook Collaborate on Future Data Center Rack Technologies. http://intel.ly/MRpOM0.

[59] Intel Rack Scale Architecture. http://ubm.io/1iejjx5.

[60] Maze: A Rack-scale Computer Emulation Platform. http://aka.ms/maze.

[61] RDMA Aware Networks Programming User Manual. http://bit.ly/1ysVa1O.

[62] SeaMicro SM15000 Fabric Compute Systems. http://bit.ly/1hQepIh.

InterTubes: A Study of the US Long-haul Fiber-optic Infrastructure

Ramakrishnan Durairajan†, Paul Barford†*, Joel Sommers+, Walter Willinger‡
{rkrish,pb}@cs.wisc.edu, jsommers@colgate.edu, wwillinger@niksun.com
†University of Wisconsin - Madison *comScore, Inc. +Colgate University ‡NIKSUN, Inc.

ABSTRACT

The complexity and enormous costs of installing new long-haul fiber-optic infrastructure has led to a significant amount of infrastructure sharing in previously installed conduits. In this paper, we study the characteristics and implications of infrastructure sharing by analyzing the long-haul fiber-optic network in the US.

We start by using fiber maps provided by tier-1 ISPs and major cable providers to construct a map of the long-haul US fiber-optic infrastructure. We also rely on previously under-utilized data sources in the form of public records from federal, state, and municipal agencies to improve the fidelity of our map. We quantify the resulting map's[1] connectivity characteristics and confirm a clear correspondence between long-haul fiber-optic, roadway, and railway infrastructures. Next, we examine the prevalence of high-risk links by mapping end-to-end paths resulting from large-scale traceroute campaigns onto our fiber-optic infrastructure map. We show how both risk and latency (*i.e.*, propagation delay) can be reduced by deploying new links along previously unused transportation corridors and rights-of-way. In particular, focusing on a subset of high-risk links is sufficient to improve the overall robustness of the network to failures. Finally, we discuss the implications of our findings on issues related to performance, net neutrality, and policy decision-making.

CCS Concepts

•Networks → Physical links; Physical topologies;

Keywords

Long-haul fiber map; shared risk; risk mitigation

[1]The constructed long-haul map along with datasets are openly available to the community through the U.S. DHS PREDICT portal (www.predict.org).

SIGCOMM '15, August 17–21, 2015, London, United Kingdom
© 2015 ACM. ISBN 978-1-4503-3542-3/15/08...$15.00
DOI: http://dx.doi.org/10.1145/2785956.2787499

1 Introduction

The desire to tackle the many challenges posed by novel designs, technologies and applications such as data centers, cloud services, software-defined networking (SDN), network functions virtualization (NFV), mobile communication and the Internet-of-Things (IoT) has fueled many of the recent research efforts in networking. The excitement surrounding the future envisioned by such new architectural designs, services, and applications is understandable, both from a research and industry perspective. At the same time, it is either taken for granted or implicitly assumed that the physical infrastructure of tomorrow's Internet will have the capacity, performance, and resilience required to develop and support ever more bandwidth-hungry, delay-intolerant, or QoS-sensitive services and applications. In fact, despite some 20 years of research efforts that have focused on understanding aspects of the Internet's infrastructure such as its router-level topology or the graph structure resulting from its inter-connected Autonomous Systems (AS), very little is known about today's *physical* Internet where individual components such as cell towers, routers or switches, and fiber-optic cables are concrete entities with well-defined geographic locations (see, *e.g.*, [2, 36, 83]). This general lack of a basic understanding of the physical Internet is exemplified by the much-ridiculed metaphor used in 2006 by the late U.S. Senator Ted Stevens (R-Alaska) who referred to the Internet as "a series of tubes" [65].[2]

The focus of this paper is the physical Internet. In particular, we are concerned with the physical aspects of the wired Internet, ignoring entirely the wireless access portion of the Internet as well as satellite or any other form of wireless communication. Moreover, we are exclusively interested in the long-haul fiber-optic portion of the wired Internet in the US. The detailed metro-level fiber maps (with corresponding colocation and data center facilities) and international undersea cable maps (with corresponding landing stations) are only accounted for to the extent necessary. In contrast to short-haul fiber routes that are specifically built for short distance use and purpose (*e.g.*, to add or drop off network services in many different places within metro-sized areas),

[2]Ironically, this infamous metaphor turns out to be not all that far-fetched when it comes to describing the portion of the physical Internet considered in this paper.

long-haul fiber routes (including ultra long-haul routes) typically run between major city pairs and allow for minimal use of repeaters.

With the US long-haul fiber-optic network being the main focal point of our work, the first contribution of this paper consists of constructing a reproducible map of this basic component of the physical Internet infrastructure. To that end, we rely on publicly available fiber maps provided by many of the tier-1 ISPs and major cable providers. While some of these maps include the precise geographic locations of all the long-haul routes deployed or used by the corresponding networks, other maps lack such detailed information. For the latter, we make extensive use of previously neglected or under-utilized data sources in the form of public records from federal, state, or municipal agencies or documentation generated by commercial entities (*e.g.*, commercial fiber map providers [34], utility rights-of-way (ROW) information, environmental impact statements, fiber sharing arrangements by the different states' DOTs). When combined, the information available in these records is often sufficient to reverse-engineer the geography of the actual long-haul fiber routes of those networks that have decided against publishing their fiber maps. We study the resulting map's diverse connectivity characteristics and quantify the ways in which the observed long-haul fiber-optic connectivity is consistent with existing transportation (*e.g.*, roadway and railway) infrastructure. We note that our work can be repeated by anyone for every other region of the world assuming similar source materials.

A striking characteristic of the constructed US long-haul fiber-optic network is a significant amount of observed infrastructure sharing. A qualitative assessment of the risk inherent in this observed sharing of the US long-haul fiber-optic infrastructure forms the second contribution of this paper. Such infrastructure sharing is the result of a common practice among many of the existing service providers to deploy their fiber in jointly-used and previously installed conduits and is dictated by simple economics—substantial cost savings as compared to deploying fiber in newly constructed conduits. By considering different metrics for measuring the risks associated with infrastructure sharing, we examine the presence of high-risk links in the existing long-haul infrastructure, both from a connectivity and usage perspective. In the process, we follow prior work [99] and use the popularity of a route on the Internet as an informative proxy for the volume of traffic that route carries. End-to-end paths derived from large-scale traceroute campaigns are overlaid on the actual long-haul fiber-optic routes traversed by the corresponding traceroute probes. The resulting first-of-its-kind map enables the identification of those components of the long-haul fiber-optic infrastructure which experience high levels of infrastructure sharing as well as high volumes of traffic.

The third and final contribution of our work is a detailed analysis of how to improve the existing long-haul fiber-optic infrastructure in the US so as to increase its resilience to failures of individual links or entire shared conduits, or to achieve better performance in terms of reduced propagation delay along deployed fiber routes. By framing the issues as appropriately formulated optimization problems, we show that both robustness and performance can be improved by deploying new fiber routes in just a few strategically-chosen areas along previously unused transportation corridors and ROW, and we quantify the achievable improvements in terms of reduced risk (*i.e.*, less infrastructure sharing) and decreased propagation delay (*i.e.*, faster Internet [100]). As actionable items, these technical solutions often conflict with currently-discussed legislation that favors policies such as "dig once", "joint trenching" or "shadow conduits" due to the substantial savings that result when fiber builds involve multiple prospective providers or are coordinated with other infrastructure projects (*i.e.*, utilities) targeting the same ROW [7]. In particular, we discuss our technical solutions in view of the current net neutrality debate concerning the treatment of broadband Internet providers as telecommunications services under Title II. We argue that the current debate would benefit from a quantitative assessment of the unavoidable trade-offs that have to be made between the substantial cost savings enjoyed by future Title II regulated service providers (due to their ensuing rights to gain access to existing essential infrastructure owned primarily by utilities) and an increasingly vulnerable national long-haul fiber-optic infrastructure (due to legislation that implicitly reduced overall resilience by explicitly enabling increased infrastructure sharing).

2 Mapping Core Long-haul Infrastructure

In this section we describe the process by which we construct a map of the Internet's long-haul fiber infrastructure in the continental United States. While many *dynamic* aspects of the Internet's topology have been examined in prior work, the underlying long-haul fiber paths that make up the Internet are, by definition, *static*[3], and it is this fixed infrastructure which we seek to identify.

Our high-level definition of a long-haul link[4] is one that connects major city-pairs. In order to be consistent when processing existing map data, however, we use the following concrete definition. We define a long-haul link as one that spans at least 30 miles, *or* that connects population centers of at least 100,000 people, *or* that is shared by at least 2 providers. These numbers are not proscriptive, rather they emerged through an iterative process of refining our base map (details below).

The steps we take in the mapping process are as follows: *(1)* we create an initial map by using publicly available fiber maps from tier-1 ISPs and major cable providers which contain explicit geocoded information about long-haul link locations; *(2)* we validate these link locations and infer whether fiber conduits are shared by using a variety of public records

[3]More precisely, installed conduits rarely become defunct, and deploying new conduits takes considerable time.

[4]In the rest of the paper, we will use the terms "link" and "conduit" interchangeably—a "tube" or trench specially built to house the fiber of potentially multiple providers.

documents such as utility right-of-way information; *(3)* we add links from publicly available ISP fiber maps (both tier-1 and major providers) which have geographic information about link *endpoints*, but which do not have explicit information about geographic pathways of fiber links; and *(4)* we again employ a variety of public records to infer the geographic locations of this latter set of links added to the map. Below, we describe this process in detail, providing examples to illustrate how we employ different information sources.

2.1 Step 1: Build an Initial Map

The first step in our fiber map-building process is to leverage maps of ISP fiber infrastructure with explicit geocoding of links from Internet Atlas project [83]. Internet Atlas is a measurement portal created to investigate and unravel the structural complexity of the *physical* Internet. Detailed geography of fiber maps are captured using the procedure described, esp. §3.2, in [83]. We start with these maps because of their potential to provide a significant and reliable portion of the overall map.

Specifically, we used detailed fiber deployment maps[5] from 5 tier-1 and 4 major cable providers: AT&T [6], Comcast [16], Cogent [14], EarthLink [29], Integra [43], Level3 [48], Suddenlink [63], Verizon [72] and Zayo [73]. For example, the map we used for Comcast's network [16] lists all the node information along with the exact geography of long-haul fiber links. Table 1 shows the number of nodes and links we include in the map for each of the 9 providers we considered. These ISPs contributed 267 unique nodes, 1258 links, and a total of 512 conduits to the map. Note that some of these links may follow exactly the same physical pathway (*i.e.*, using the same conduit). We infer such conduit sharing in step 2.

2.2 Step 2: Checking the Initial Map

While the link location data gathered as part of the first step are usually reliable due to the stability and static nature of the underlying fiber infrastructure, the second step in the mapping process is to collect additional information sources to validate these data. We also use these additional information sources to infer whether some links follow the same physical ROW, which indicates that the fiber links either reside in the same fiber bundle, or in an adjacent conduit.

In this step of the process, we use a variety of public records to geolocate and validate link endpoints and conduits. These records tend to be rich with detail, but have been under-utilized in prior work that has sought to identify the physical components that make up the Internet. Our working assumption is that ISPs, government agencies, and other relevant parties often archive documents on public-facing websites, and that these documents can be used to validate and identify link/conduit locations. Specifically, we seek information that can be extracted from government agency filings (*e.g.*, [13, 18, 26]), environmental impact statements (*e.g.*, [71]), documentation released by third-party fiber services (*e.g.*, [3–5, 10]), indefeasible rights of use (IRU) agreements (*e.g.*, [44, 45]), press releases (*e.g.*, [49, 50, 52, 53]), and other related resources (*e.g.*, [8, 11, 23, 27, 28, 59, 67]).

Public records concerning rights-of-way are of particular importance to our work since highly-detailed location and conduit sharing information can be gleaned from these resources. Laws governing rights of way are established on a state-by-state basis (*e.g.*, see [31]), and which local organization has jurisdiction varies state-by-state [1]. As a result, care must be taken when validating or inferring the ROW used for a particular fiber link. Since these state-specific laws are public, however, they establish a number of key parameters to drive a systematic search for government-related public filings.

In addition to public records, the fact that a fiber-optic link's location aligns with a known ROW serves as a type of validation. Moreover, if link locations for multiple service providers align along the same geographic path, we consider those links to be validated.

To continue the example of Comcast's network, we used, in part, the following documents to validate the locations of links and to determine which links run along shared paths with other networks: *(1)* a broadband environment study by the FCC details several conduits shared by Comcast and other providers in Colorado [12], *(2)* a franchise agreement [20,21] made by Cox with Fairfax county, VA suggests the presence of a link running along the ROW with Comcast and Verizon, *(3)* page 4 (utilities section) of a project document [24] to design services for Wekiva Parkway from Lake County to the east of Round Lake Road (Orlando, FL) demonstrates the presence of Comcast's infrastructure along a ROW with other entities like CenturyLink, Progress Energy and TECO/People's Gas, *(4)* an Urbana city council project update [68] shows pictures [69] of Comcast and AT&T's fiber deployed in the Urbana, IL area, and *(5)* documents from the CASF project [70] in Nevada county, CA show that Comcast has deployed fiber along with AT&T and Suddenlink.

2.3 Step 3: Build an Augmented Map

The third step of our long-haul fiber map construction process is to use published maps of tier-1 and large regional ISPs which do not contain explicit geocoded information. We tentatively add the fiber links from these ISPs to the map by aligning the logical links indicated in their published maps along the closest known right-of-way (*e.g.*, road or rail). We validate and/or correct these tentative placements in the next step.

In this step, we used published maps from 7 tier-1 and 4 regional providers: CenturyLink, Cox, Deutsche Telekom, HE, Inteliquent, NTT, Sprint, Tata, TeliaSonera, TWC, XO. Adding these ISPs resulted in an addition of 6 nodes, 41 links, and 30 conduits (196 nodes, 1153 links, and 347 con-

[5] Although some of the maps date back a number of years, due to the static nature of fiber deployments and especially due to the reuse of existing conduits for new fiber deployments [58], these maps remain very valuable and provide detailed information about the physical location of conduits in current use. Also, due to varying accuracy of the sources, some maps required manual annotation, georeferencing [35] and validation/inference (step 2) during the process.

Table 1: Number of nodes and long-haul fiber links included in the initial map for each ISP considered in step 1.

ISP	AT&T	Comcast	Cogent	EarthLink	Integra	Level 3	Suddenlink	Verizon	Zayo
Number of nodes	25	26	69	248	27	240	39	116	98
Number of links	57	71	84	370	36	336	42	151	111

duits without considering the 9 ISPs above). For example, for Sprint's network [60], 102 links were added and for CenturyLink's network [9], 134 links were added.

2.4 Step 4: Validate the Augmented Map

The fourth and last step of the mapping process is nearly identical to step 2. In particular, we use public filings with state and local governments regarding ROW access, environmental impact statements, publicly available IRU agreements and the like to validate locations of links that are inferred in step 3. We also identify which links share the same ROW. Specifically with respect to inferring whether conduits or ROWs are shared, we are helped by the fact that the number of possible rights-of-way between the endpoints of a fiber link are limited. As a result, it may be that we simply need to *rule out* one or more ROWs in order to establish sufficient evidence for the path that a fiber link follows.

Individual Link Illustration: Many ISPs list only POP-level connectivity. For such maps, we leverage the corpus of search terms that we capture in Internet Atlas and search for public evidence. For example, Sprint's network [60] is extracted from the Internet Atlas repository. The map contains detailed node information, but the geography of long-haul links is not provided in detail. To infer the conduit information, for instance, from Los Angeles, CA to San Francisco, CA, we start by searching "los angeles to san francisco fiber iru at&t sprint" to obtain an agency filing [13] which shows that AT&T and Sprint share that particular route, along with other ISPs like CenturyLink, Level 3 and Verizon. The same document also shows conduit sharing between CenturyLink and Verizon at multiple locations like Houston, TX to Dallas, TX; Dallas, TX to Houston, TX; Denver, CO to El Paso, TX; Santa Clara, CA to Salt Lake City, UT; and Wells, NV to Salt Lake City, UT.

As another example, the IP backbone map of Cox's network [22] shows that there is a link between Gainesville, FL and Ocala, FL. But the geography of the fiber deployment is absent (*i.e.*, shown as a simple point with two names in [22]). We start the search using other ISP names (*e.g.*,"level 3 and cox fiber iru ocala") and obtain publicly available evidence (*e.g.*, lease agreement [19]) indicating that Cox uses Level3's fiber optic lines from Ocala, FL to Gainesville, FL. Next, we repeat the search with different combinations for other ISPs (*e.g.*, news article [47] shows that Comcast uses 19,000 miles of fiber from Level3; see map at bottom of that page which highlights the Ocala to Gainesville route, among others) and infer that Comcast is also present in that particular conduit. Given that we know the detailed fiber maps of ISPs (*e.g.*, Level 3) and the inferred conduit information for other ISPs (*e.g.*, Cox), we systematically infer conduit sharing across ISPs.

Resource Illustration: To illustrate some of the resources used to validate the locations of Sprint's network links, publicly available documents reveal that *(1)* Sprint uses Level 3's fiber in Detroit [61] and their settlement details are publicly available [62], *(2)* a whitepaper related to a research network initiative in Virginia identifies link location and sharing details regarding Sprint fiber [27], *(3)* the "coastal route" [13] conduit installation project started by Qwest (now CenturyLink) from Los Angeles, CA to San Francisco, CA shows that, along with Sprint, fiber-optic cables of several other ISPs like AT&T, MCI (now Verizon) and WilTel (now Level 3) were pulled through the portions of the conduit purchased/leased by those ISPs, and *(4)* the fiber-optic settlements website [33] has been established to provide information regarding class action settlements involving land next to or under railroad rights-of-way where ISPs like Sprint, Qwest (now CenturyLink), Level 3 and WilTel (now Level 3) have installed telecommunications facilities, such as fiber-optic cables.

2.5 The US Long-haul Fiber Map

The final map constructed through the process described in this section is shown in Figure 1, and contains 273 nodes/cities, 2411 links, and 542 conduits (with multiple tenants). Prominent features of the map include *(i)* dense deployments (*e.g.*, the northeast and coastal areas), *(ii)* long-haul hubs (*e.g.*, Denver and Salt Lake City) *(iii)* pronounced absence of infrastructure (*e.g.*, the upper plains and four corners regions), *(iv)* parallel deployments (*e.g.*, Kansas City to Denver) and *(v)* spurs (*e.g.*, along northern routes).

While mapping efforts like the one described in this section invariably raise the question of the quality of the constructed map (*i.e.*, completeness), it is safe to state that despite our efforts to sift through hundreds of relevant documents, the constructed map is not complete. At the same time, we are confident that to the extent that the process detailed in this section reveals long-haul infrastructure for the sources considered, the constructed map is of sufficient quality for studying issues that do not require local details typically found in metro-level fiber maps. Moreover, as with other Internet-related mapping efforts (*e.g.*, AS-level maps), we hope this work will spark a community effort aimed at gradually improving the overall fidelity of our basic map by contributing to a growing database of information about geocoded conduits and their tenants.

The methodological blueprint we give in this section shows that constructing such a detailed map of the US's long-haul fiber infrastructure is feasible, and since all data sources we use are publicly available, the effort is reproducible. The fact that our work can be replicated is not only important from a scientific perspective, it suggests that the same effort can be applied more broadly to construct similar maps of the long-haul fiber infrastructure in other countries and on other continents.

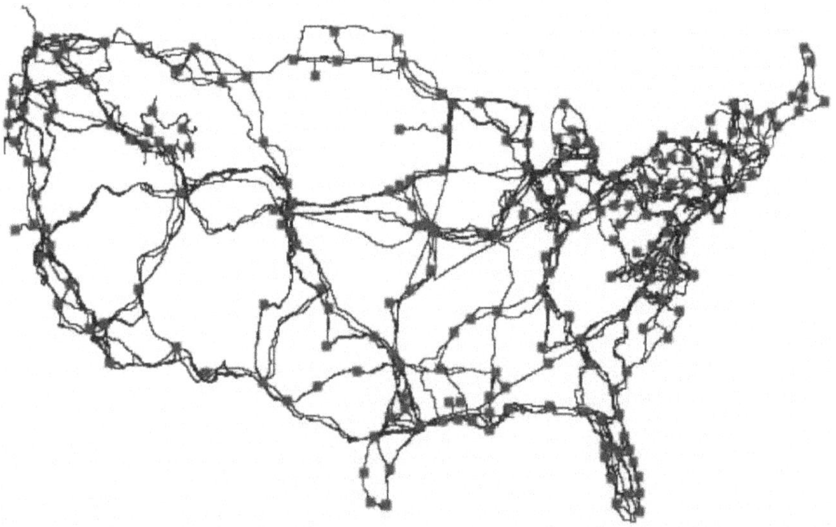

Figure 1: Location of physical conduits for networks considered in the continental United States.

Interestingly, recommendation 6.4 made by the FCC in chapter 6 of the National Broadband Plan [7] states that "the FCC should improve the collection and availability regarding the location and availability of poles, ducts, conduits, and rights-of-way.". It also mentions the example of Germany, where such information is being systematically mapped. Clearly, such data would obviate the need to expend significant effort to search for and identify the relevant public records and other documents.

Lastly, it is also important to note that there are commercial (fee-based) services that supply location information for long-haul and metro fiber segments, *e.g.*, [34]. We investigated these services as part of our study and found that they typically offer maps of some small number (5–7) of national ISPs, and that, similar to the map we create (see map in [41][6]), many of these ISPs have substantial overlap in their locations of fiber deployments. Unfortunately, it is not clear how these services obtain their source information and/or how reliable these data are. Although it is not possible to confirm, in the best case these services offer much of the same information that is available from publicly available records, albeit in a convenient but non-free form.

3 Geography of Fiber Deployments

In this section, we analyze the constructed map of long-haul fiber-optic infrastructure in the US in terms of its alignment with existing transportation networks. In particular, we examine the relationship between the geography of physical Internet links and road and rail infrastructure.

While the conduits through which the long-haul fiber-optic links that form the physical infrastructure of the Internet are widely assumed to follow a combination of transportation infrastructure locations (*i.e.,* railways and roadways) along with public/private right-of-ways, we are aware of very few prior studies that have attempted to confirm or quantify this assumption [36]. Understanding the relationship between the physical links that make up the Internet and the physical pathways that form transportation corridors helps to elucidate the prevalence of conduit sharing by multiple service providers and informs decisions on where future conduits might be deployed.

Our analysis is performed by comparing the physical link locations identified in our constructed map to geocoded information for both roadways and railways from the United States National Atlas website [51]. The geographic layout of our roadway and railway data sets can be seen in Figure 2 and Figure 3, respectively. In comparison, the physical link geographic information for the networks under consideration can be seen in the Figure 1.

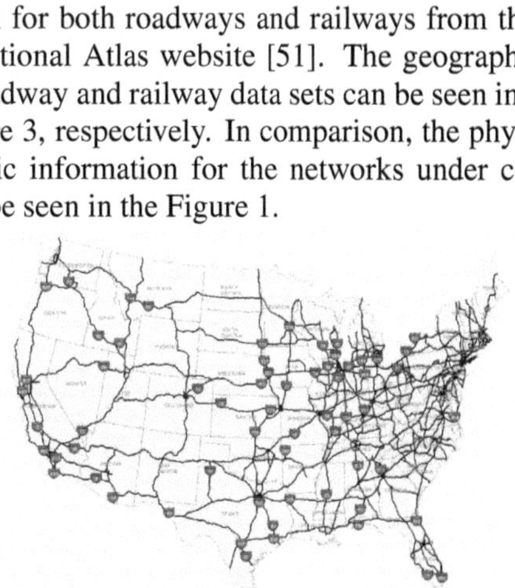

Figure 2: NationalAtlas roadway infrastructure locations.

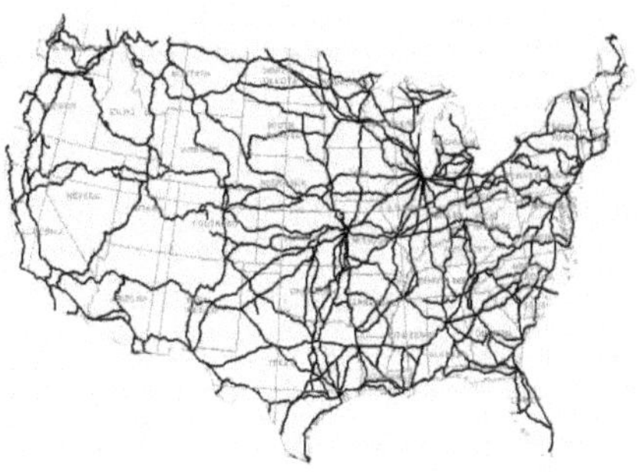

Figure 3: NationalAtlas railway infrastructure locations.

[6]Visually, all the commercially-produced maps agree with our basic map, hinting at the common use of supporting evidence.

We use the *polygon overlap* analysis capability in the ArcGIS [30] to quantify the correspondence between physical links and transportation infrastructure. In Figure 4, aggregating across all networks under consideration, we compare the fraction of each path that is co-located with roadways, railways, or a combination of the two using histogram distributions. These plots show that a significant fraction of all the physical links are co-located with roadway infrastructure. The plots also show that it is more common for fiber conduits to run alongside roadways than railways, and an even higher percentage are co-located with some combination of roadways *and* railway infrastructure. Furthermore, for a vast majority of the paths, we find that physical link paths more often follow roadway infrastructure compared with rail infrastructure.

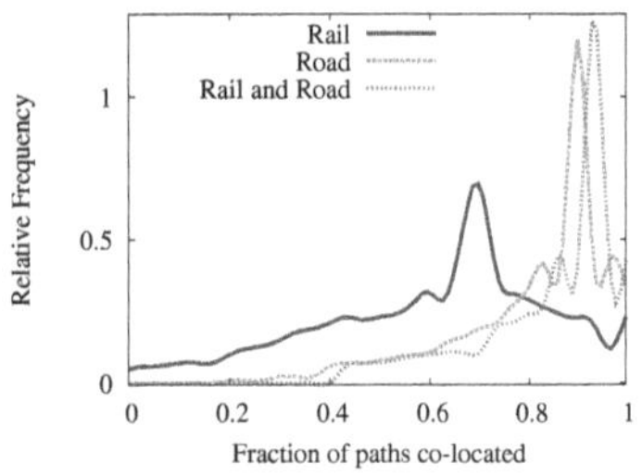

Figure 4: Fraction of physical links co-located with transportation infrastructure.

Despite the results reported above there remain conduits in our infrastructure map that are *not* co-located with transportation ROWs. For example, in the left-hand plot of Figure 5 we show the Level 3-provided physical link locations outside Laurel, MS, and in the right-hand plot we show Google Maps [37] satellite imagery for the same location. These images shows the presence of network links, but no known transportation infrastructure is co-located. In what follows, we list examples by considering other types of rights-of-way, such as natural gas and/or petroleum pipelines, but leave details to future work.

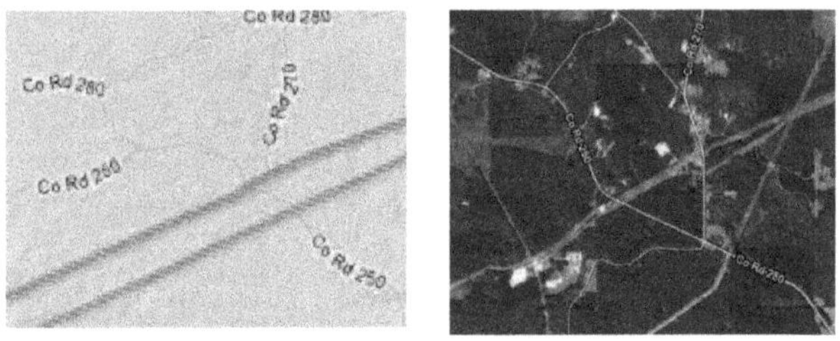

Figure 5: Satellite image validated right-of-way outside of Laurel, MS. (Left) - Level 3 Provided fiber map. (Right) - Google Maps satellite view.

A few examples can be shown in Level3's network [48], where the map shows the existence of link from *(1)* Anaheim, CA to Las Vegas, NV, and *(2)* Houston, TX to Atlanta, GA, but no known transportation infrastructure is co-located. By considering other types of rights-of-way [56], many of these situations could be explained. Visually, we can verify that the link from Anaheim, CA to Las Vegas, NV is co-located with refined-products pipeline. Similarly, the link from Houston, TX to Atlanta, GA is deployed along with NGL pipelines.

4 Assessing Shared Risk

In this section, we describe and analyze two notions of *risk* associated with sharing fiber-optic conduits in the Internet. At a high level, we consider conduits that are shared by many service providers as an inherently risky situation since damage to that conduit will affect several providers. Our choice of such a risk model that considers the degree of link sharing and not the overall physical topology as a means to analyze robustness is based on the fact that our map is highly incomplete compared to the 40K plus ASes and certain metrics (*e.g.*, number of fiber cuts to partition the US long-haul infrastructure) have associated security implications [2]. We intend to analyze different dimensions of network resilience in future work.

4.1 Risk Matrix

Our analysis begins by creating a *risk matrix* based on a simple counting-based approach. The goal of this matrix is to capture the level of infrastructure sharing and establish a measure of shared risk due to lack of diversity in physical connectivity. The risk matrix is populated as follows: we start with a tier-1 ISP that has vast infrastructure in the US and subsequently add other tier-1 and major cable Internet providers to the matrix. The rows are ISPs and columns are physical conduits carrying long-haul fiber-optic links for those ISPs. Integer entries in the matrix refer to the number of ISPs that share a particular conduit. As a result, values in the matrix increase as the level of conduit-sharing increases.

As an illustrative example, we choose Level 3 as a "base" network due to its very rich connectivity in the US. We use our constructed physical network map (*i.e.*, the map we describe in §2) and extract all conduit endpoints across city pairs, such as "SLC-Denver" (c1 below), SLC-Sacramento (c2 below), and Sacramento-Palo Alto (c3 below), etc., and assign 1 for all conduits that are part of Level 3's physical network footprint. A partial matrix is then:

	c1	c2	c3
Level 3	1	1	1

Next, say we include another provider, *e.g.*, Sprint. We add a new row for Sprint to the matrix, then for any conduit used in Sprint's physical network, we increment *all* entries in each corresponding column. For this example, Sprint's network shares the SLC-Denver and SLC-Sacramento conduits with other providers (including Level 3), but not the Sacramento-Palo Alto conduit. Thus, the matrix becomes:

	c1	c2	c3
Level 3	2	2	1
Sprint	2	2	0

We repeat this process for all the twelve tier-1 and eight major Internet service providers, *i.e.*, the same ISPs used as part of constructing our physical map of long-haul fiber-optic infrastructure in the US in §2.

4.2 Risk Metric: Connectivity-only

How many ISPs share a link? Using the risk matrix, we count the number of ISPs sharing a particular conduit. Figure 6 shows the number of conduits (y axis) for which at least k ISPs (x axis) share the conduit. For example, there are 542 distinct conduits in our physical map (Figure 1), thus the bar at x=1 is 542, and 486 conduits are shared by at least 2 ISPs, thus the bar at x=2 is 486. This plot highlights the fact that it is relatively uncommon for conduits *not* to be shared by more than two providers. Overall, we observe that 89.67%, 63.28% and 53.50% of the conduits are shared by at least two, three and four major ISPs, respectively.

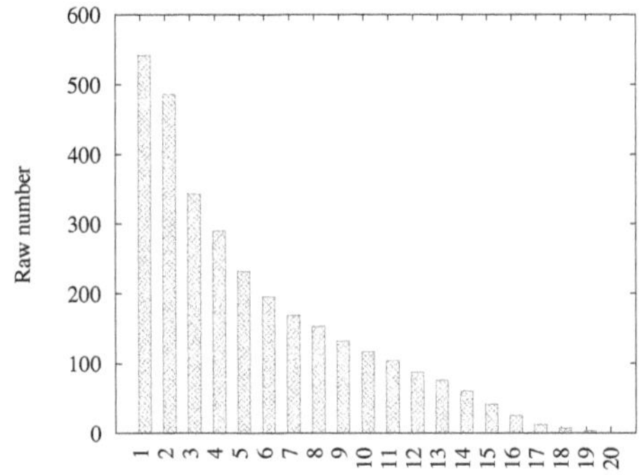

Figure 6: ISP Ranking.

In some of the more extreme cases, we observe that 12 out of 542 conduits are shared by *more than 17 ISPs*. These situations may arise where such conduits run between major population centers, or between cities separated by imposing geographic constraints (*e.g.*, the Rocky Mountains). For example, conduits that are shared by 19 ISPs include *1)* Phoenix, AZ to Tucson, AZ, *(2)* Salt Lake City, UT to Denver, CO, and *(3)* Philadelphia, PA to New York, NY.

Implication: When it comes to physically deployed connectivity, the US long-haul infrastructure lacks much of the diversity that is a hallmark of all the commonly-known models and maps of the more logical Internet topologies (e.g., router- or AS-level graphs [77, 83, 103]).

Which ISPs do the most infrastructure sharing? To better understand the infrastructural sharing risks to which individual ISPs are exposed, we leverage the risk matrix and rank the ISPs based on increasing average shared risk. The average of the values across a row in the risk matrix (*i.e.*, values for an individual ISP) with standard error bars, 25th and 75th percentile are shown in Figure 6. The average values are plotted in a sorted fashion, resulting in an increasing level of infrastructure sharing when reading the plot from left to right.

From this plot we observe that Suddenlink has the smallest average number of ISPs that share the conduits used in its network, which can be explained by its diverse geographical deployments. It is followed by EarthLink and Level 3. Deutsche Telekom, NTT and XO, on the other hand, use conduits that are, on average, shared by a large number of other ISPs.

Implication: Non-US service providers (*e.g.*, Deutsche Telekom, NTT, Tata, etc.) use policies like *dig once* [25] and *open trench* [55], and/or lease dark fibers to expand their presence in the US. Such policies may save deployment

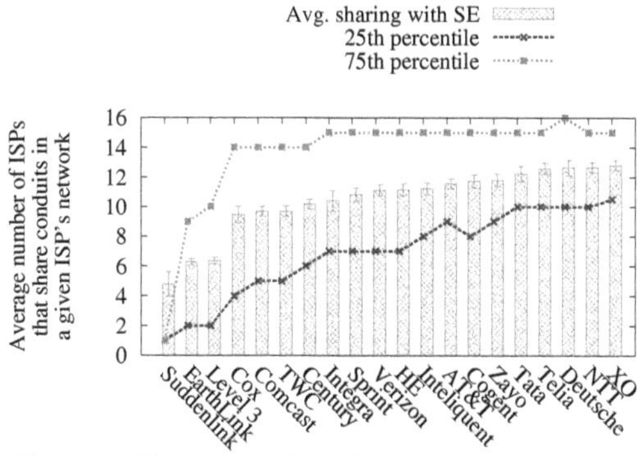

Figure 7: The raw number of shared conduits by ISPs.

costs, but appear to be counter-productive as far as overall network resilience is concerned.

How similar are ISP risk profiles? Using the risk matrix we calculate the Hamming [39] distance similarity metric among ISPs, *i.e.*, by comparing every row in the risk matrix to every other row to assess their similarity. Our intuition for using such a metric is that if two ISPs are physically similar (in terms of fiber deployments and the level of infrastructure sharing), their risk profiles are also similar.

Figure 8 shows a heat map generated by computing the Hamming distance metric for every pair of ISPs considered in the construction of our physical map. For this metric, the smaller the number, the greater the shared risk between the corresponding (two) ISPs. We observe in the plot that EarthLink and Level 3 exhibit fairly low risk profiles among the ISPs we considered, similar to results described above when we consider the average number of ISPs sharing conduits used in these networks. These two ISPs are followed by Cox, Comcast and Time Warner Cable, which likely exhibit lower risk according to the Hamming distance metric due to their rich fiber connectivity in the US.

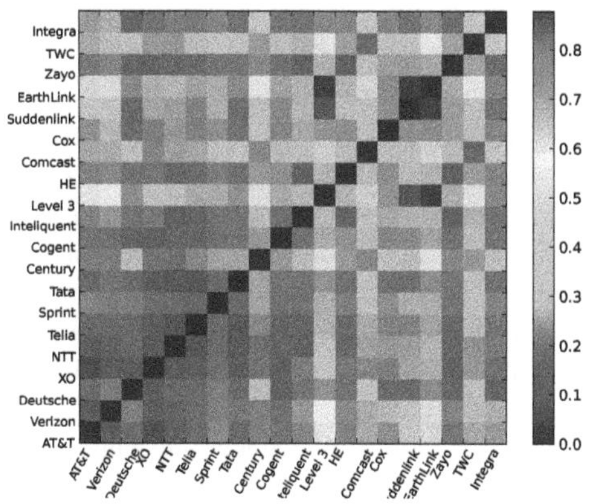

Figure 8: Similarity of risk profiles of ISPs calculated using Hamming distance.

Somewhat surprisingly, although the average number of ISPs that share conduits in Suddenlink's network is, on average, low, the Hamming distance metric suggests that it is exposed to risks due to its geographically diverse deployments. While Level 3 and EarthLink also have geographically diverse deployments, they also have diverse paths that can be used to reach various destinations without using highly-shared conduits. On the other hand, Suddenlink has few alternate physical paths, thus they must depend on certain highly-shared conduits to reach certain locations. TATA, TeliaSonera, Deutsche Telekom, NTT and XO each use conduits that are very highly shared, thus they have similar risk profiles according to the Hamming distance metric.

Implication: Multiple metrics are required to precisely characterize and capture the level of infrastructure sharing by service providers. Geographically diverse deployment may reduce the risk only when the ISP has diverse paths to avoid the critical choke points to reach different destinations.

4.3 Risk Metric: Connectivity + Traffic

In this section, we follow the method of [99] and use the popularity of different routes on the Internet as measured through traceroute probes as a way to infer relative volumes of traffic on those routes. We use traceroute data from the Edgescope [80] project and restrict our analysis to a period of 3 months, from January 1, 2014 to March 31, 2014. These data consisted of 4,908,223 individual traceroutes by clients in diverse locations. By using geolocation information and naming hints in the traceroute data [78, 92], we are able to overlay individual layer 3 links onto our underlying physical map of Internet infrastructure. As a result, we are able to identify those components of the long-haul fiber-optic infrastructure which experience high levels of infrastructure sharing as well as high volumes of traffic.

The prevalent use of MPLS tunnels in the Internet [101] poses one potential pitfall with overlaying observed layer 3 routes onto our physical map. While we certainly do see segments along individual traceroutes that likely pass through MPLS tunnels, we observe the frequency of these segments to be relatively low. Thus, we believe that their impact on the results we describe below is limited.

Ranking by frequency. Table 2 and Table 3 show the top 20 conduits for west-origin east-bound and east-origin west-bound probes[7] ranked based on frequency. Interestingly, for these tables we observe high volumes of traffic flowing through certain cities (*e.g., Dallas, TX, Salt Lake City, UT*) in either direction, and that while many of the conduit endpoints are major population centers, there are a number of endpoint cities that are simply popular waypoints (*e.g.*, Casper, WY and Billings, MT in the East to West direction).

Additional ISPs. Figure 9 compares the CDF of the number of ISPs sharing a conduit with a CDF of conduit frequencies observed through the traceroute data. In the plot, we observe that the conduits identified in our physical map appear on large numbers of paths in the traceroute data, and that when we consider traffic characteristics, the shared risk of certain conduits is *only greater*. Through analysis of naming conventions in the traceroute data, we infer that there are even larger numbers of ISPs that share the conduits identified in our physical map, thus the potential risks due to infrastructure sharing are magnified when considering traffic characteristics. For example, our physical map establishes that the conduit between Portland, OR and Seattle, WA is shared by 18 ISPs. Upon analysis of the traceroute data, we inferred the presence of an additional 13 ISPs that also share that conduit.

[7]Classified based on geolocation information for source/destination hops in the traceroute data.

Table 2: Top 20 base long-haul conduits and their corresponding frequencies of west-origin to east-bound traceroute probes.

Location	Location	# Probes
Trenton, NJ	Edison, NJ	78402
Kalamazoo, MI	Battle Creek, MI	78384
Dallas, TX	Fort Worth, TX	56233
Baltimore, MD	Towson, MD	46336
Baton Rouge, LA	New Orleans, LA	46328
Livonia, MI	Southfield, MI	46287
Topeka, KS	Lincoln, NE	46275
Spokane, WA	Boise, ID	44461
Dallas, TX	Atlanta, GA	41008
Dallas, TX	Bryan, TX	39232
Shreveport, LA	Dallas, TX	39210
Wichita Falls, TX	Dallas, TX	39180
San Luis Obispo, CA	Lompoc, CA	32381
San Francisco, CA	Las Vegas, NV	22986
Wichita, KS	Las Vegas, NV	22169
Las Vegas, NV	Salt Lake City, UT	22094
Battle Creek, MI	Lansing, MI	15027
South Bend, IN	Battle Creek, MI	14795
Philadelphia, PA	Allentown, PA	12905
Philadelphia, PA	Edison, NJ	12901

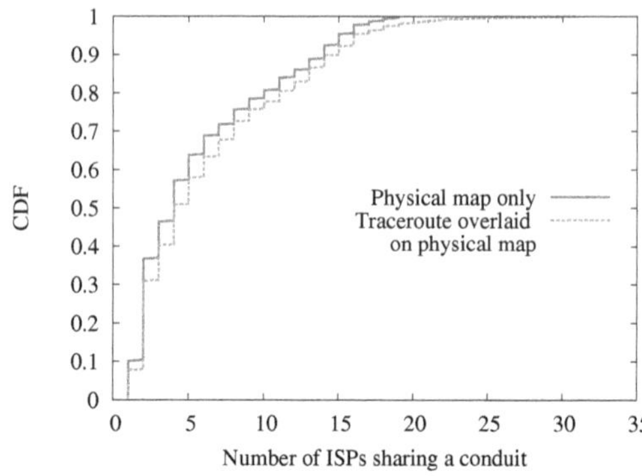

Figure 9: CDF of number of ISPs sharing a conduit before and after considering the traceroute data as a proxy for traffic volumes.

Table 3: Top 20 base long-haul graph conduits and their corresponding frequencies of east-origin to west-bound traceroute probes.

Location	Location	# Probes
West Palm Beach, FL	Boca Raton, FL	155774
Lynchburg, VA	Charlottesville, VA	155079
Sedona, AZ	Camp Verde, AZ	54067
Bozeman, MT	Billings, MT	50879
Billings, MT	Casper, WY	50818
Casper, WY	Cheyenne, WY	50817
White Plains, NY	Stamford, CT	25784
Amarillo, TX	Wichita Falls, TX	16354
Eugene, OR	Chico, CA	12234
Phoenix, AZ	Dallas, TX	9725
Salt Lake City, UT	Provo, UT	9433
Salt Lake City, UT	Los Angeles, CA	8921
Dallas, TX	Oklahoma City, OK	8242
Wichita Falls, TX	Dallas, TX	8150
Seattle, WA	Portland, OR	8094
Eau Claire, WI	Madison, WI	7476
Salt Lake City, UT	Cheyenne, WY	7380
Bakersfield, CA	Los Angeles, CA	6874
Seattle, WA	Hillsboro, OR	6854
Santa Barbara, CA	Los Angeles, CA	6641

Distribution of traffic. We also ranked the ISPs based on the number of conduits used to carry traffic. Table 4 lists the top 10 ISPs in terms of number of conduits observed to carry traceroute traffic. We see that Level 3's infrastructure is the most widely used. Using the traceroute frequencies as a proxy, we also infer that Level 3 carries the most traffic. In fact, it has a significantly higher number of conduits used compared to the next few "top" ISPs. Interestingly, although XO is also considered to be a Tier-1 provider, it carries approximately 25% of the volume that Level 3 carries, at least inferred through these data.

Table 4: Top 10 ISPs in terms of number of conduits carrying probe traffic measured in the traceroute data.

ISP	# conduits
Level 3	62
Comcast	48
AT&T	41
Cogent	37
SoftLayer	30
MFN	21
Verizon	21
Cox	18
CenturyLink	16
XO	15

5 Mitigating Risks

In this section we describe two optimization analyses in which we examine how best to improve the existing physical infrastructure to either increase the robustness of long-haul infrastructure to fiber cuts, or to minimize propagation delay between pairs of cities.

5.1 Increasing Network Robustness (I)

We first examine the possibility of improving the long-haul infrastructure's robustness (*i.e.*, to reduce the impact of fiber cuts by reducing the level of conduit sharing among ISPs[8]) by either *(1)* utilizing existing conduits that are not currently part of that ISPs physical footprint, or *(2)* carefully choosing ISPs to peer with at particular locations such that the addition of the peer adds diversity in terms of physical conduits utilized. In either case, we rely on the existing physical infrastructure and the careful choice of conduits rather than introduce any new links.

We call the optimization framework used in this first analysis a *robustness suggestion*, as it is designed to find a set of links or set of ISPs to peer with at different points in the network such that global shared risk (*i.e.*, shared risk across all ISPs) is minimized. We refer to this set of additional links or peering as the *robust backup infrastructure*. We define the optimized path between two city-level nodes i and j, $OP_{i,j}^{robust}$, as,

$$OP_{i,j}^{robust} = \min_{P_{i,j} \in \mathscr{E}^A} SR\left(\mathbf{P_{i,j}}\right) \quad (1)$$

where $\mathscr{E}^A$ is the set of all possible paths obtained from the risk matrix. The difference between the original set of existing network hops and the hops seen in the optimized paths produced from equation 1 forms the additional peering points. Depending on operational needs and robustness requirements, the framework can used to optimize specific paths or the entire network, thereby improving the robustness of the network at different granularities.

In our analysis of the constructed physical map of the fiber-optic infrastructure in the US, we found that there are 12 out of 542 conduits that are shared by more than 17 out of the 20 ISPs we considered in our study. We begin by analyzing these twelve links and how network robustness could be improved through our robustness suggestion framework. We use two specific metrics to evaluate the effectiveness of the robustness suggestion: *(1)* path inflation (PI) *i.e.*, the difference between the number of hops in the original path and the optimized path, and *(2)* shared risk reduction (SRR), *i.e.*, the difference in the number of ISPs sharing the conduit on the original path versus the optimized path.

[8]When accounting for alternate routes via undersea cables, network partitioning for the US Internet is a very unlikely scenario.

Figure 10 shows the PI and SRR results for optimizing the 12 highly-shared links, for all ISPs considered in our study. Overall, these plots show that, on average, an addition of between one and two conduits that were not previously used by a particular ISP results in a significant reduction in shared risk across all networks. We observe that nearly all the benefit of shared risk reduction is obtained through these modest additions.

Apart from finding optimal paths with minimum shared risk, the robustness suggestion optimization framework can also be used to infer additional peering (hops) that can improve the overall robustness of the network. Table 5 shows the top three beneficial peering additions based on minimizing shared risk in the network for the twelve most highly-shared links. Level 3 is predominantly the best peer that any ISP could add to improve robustness, largely due to their already-robust infrastructure. AT&T and CenturyLink are also prominent peers to add, mainly due to the diversity in geographic paths that border on the 12 highly-shared links.

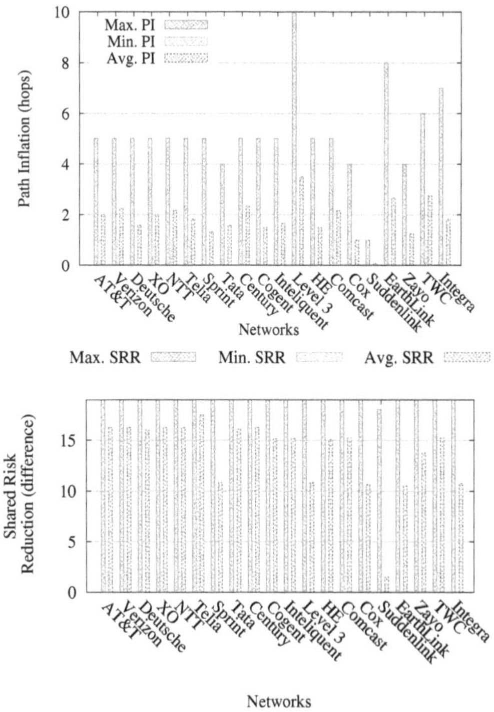

Figure 10: Path Inflation (top) and Shared Risk Reduction (bottom) based on the robustness suggestion framework for the twelve heavily shared links.

Besides focusing on optimizing network robustness by addressing the 12 heavily-shared links, we also considered how to optimize ISP networks considering *all* 542 conduits with lit fiber identified in our map of the physical infrastructure in the US. We do not show detailed results due to space constraints, but what we found in our analysis was that many of the existing paths used by ISPs were already the best paths,

Table 5: Top 3 best peering suggested by the optimization framework for optimizing the twelve shared links.

ISP	Suggested Peering
AT&T	Level 3 | Century | Verizon
Verizon	Level 3 | Century | AT&T
Deutsche	Level 3 | AT&T | Century
XO	Level 3 | AT&T | Century
NTT	Level 3 | AT&T | Century
Telia	Level 3 | Century | AT&T
Sprint	Level 3 | AT&T | Century
Tata	Level 3 | AT&T | Century
Century	Level 3 | AT&T | Verizon
Cogent	Level 3 | AT&T | CenturyLink
Inteliquent	Level 3 | Century | AT&T
Level 3	Century | Integra | EarthLink
HE	Level 3 | AT&T | Century
Comcast	Level 3 | AT&T | Verizon
Cox	AT&T | Level 3 | Century
Suddenlink	Level 3 | AT&T | Sprint
EarthLink	Tata | Integra | AT&T
Zayo	Level 3 | AT&T | Century
TWC	Level 3 | AT&T | Verizon
Integra	Level 3 | Sprint | Century

and that the potential gains were minimal compared to the gains obtained when just considering the 12 conduits.

Overall, these results are encouraging, because they imply that it is sufficient to optimize the network around a targeted set of highly-shared links. They also suggest that modest additions of city-to-city backup links would be enough to get most of the potential robustness gains.

5.2 Increasing Network Robustness (II)

In this section we consider how to improve network robustness by adding up to k new city-to-city fiber conduits. We consider the existing physical map as a graph $G = V, E$ along with the risk matrix A. Our goal is to identify a new set of edges along with E such that the addition *(1)* causes the largest increase in overall robustness, *i.e.*, greatest reduction in shared risk, and *(2)* while imposing the smallest deployment cost (DC), *i.e.*, the cost per fiber conduit mile, compared with alternate shortest paths between two city pairs.

Formally, let $\hat{E} = \{\{u,v\} : u,v \in V \text{ and } \{u,v\} \notin E\}$ be the set of edges not in G and let $\hat{A}$ be the reduced shared risk matrix of network $\hat{G} = (V, E \cup S)$ for some set $S \in \hat{E}$. We want to find $S \in \hat{E}$ of size k such that

$$S = arg\max(\lambda_A - \lambda_{\hat{A}}) \quad (2)$$

where $\lambda = \sum_{i=1,j=1}^{m,n} SRR_{i,j} + \sum_{i=1,j=1}^{m,n} DC_{i,j}$ and $DC_{i,j}$ is the alternate shortest path with reduced cost and physically shortest, different, redundant path between i and j.

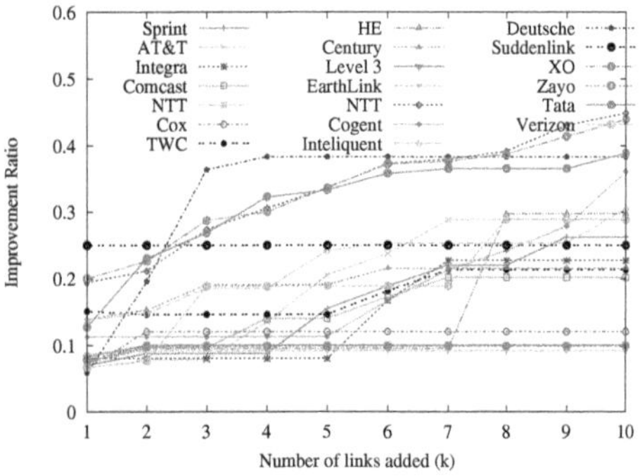

Figure 11: Potential improvements to ISP

Figure 11 shows the *improvement ratio* (avg. shared risk after adding link(s) divided by avg. shared risk before adding link(s)) for the 20 ISPs considered in our study. The objective function is to deploy new fiber at geographically diverse locations such that the deployment cost (*i.e.*, the length of fiber) is minimized and global shared risk is reduced. As expected, we see good improvement for ISPs with smaller infrastructural footprints in the US, *e.g.*, for Telia, Tata, etc. and very little improvement for large US-based ISPs such as Level 3, CenturyLink, and Cogent, since their networks already have fairly rich connectivity. An interesting case is Suddenlink, which shows no improvement even after adding multiple links. We attribute this result to the dependency on the other ISPs to reach destinations because of its geographically diverse conduit paths.

5.3 Reducing Propagation Delay

In this section we examine propagation delays between individual city pairs in our map of the physical fiber infrastructure in the US. Since there may be multiple existing physical conduit paths between two cities, we consider the average delay across all physical paths versus the best (lowest) delay along one of the existing physical paths. We also consider how delay may be reduced by adding new physical conduit paths that follow existing roads or railways (*i.e.*, existing rights-of-way) between a pair of cities. Lastly, we consider the possibility of adding new physical conduit that ignores rights-of-way and simply follows the line-of-sight (LOS). Although following the LOS is in most cases practically infeasible, it represents the minimum achievable delay between two cities and thus provides a lower bound on performance.

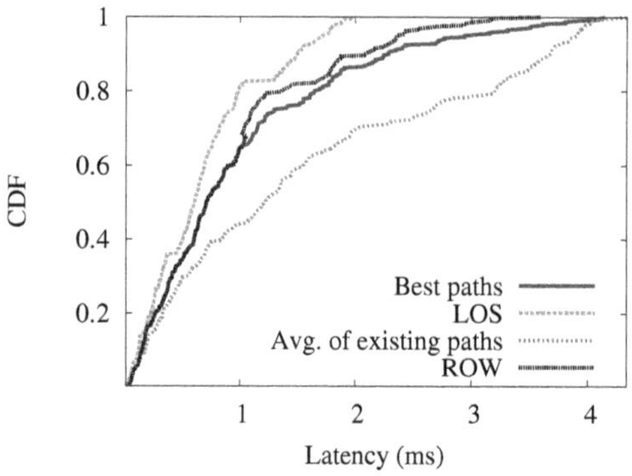

Figure 12: Comparison of best links against avg. latencies of links, ROW links and LOS links.

Figure 12 plots the cumulative distribution function of delays across all city pairs that have existing conduits between them. We first observe in the figure that the average delays of existing links between city pairs are often substantially higher than the best existing link. This result suggests that there are some long-haul fiber links that traverse much longer distances than necessary between two cities, perhaps due to ease of deployment or lower costs in certain conduits. We also observe that even the best existing paths do not follow the shortest rights-of-way between two cities, but that the difference in many cases is fairly small. In particular, about 65% of the best paths are also the best ROW paths. Lastly, we observe that the LOS distance between two cities versus the best ROW path (or best existing path) varies. For 50% of the paths, the difference is under 100 microseconds (*i.e.*, approximately 20 km), but for 25% of the paths the difference is more than 500 microseconds (*i.e.*, more than 100 km), with some differences exceeding 2 milliseconds (*i.e.*, more than 400 km; see [32]). These results indicate that it is important to consider rights-of-way when evaluating possible improvements to propagation delays in the Internet, since line-of-sight distances may differ significantly and may not be practically achievable.

6 Discussion

In this section, we discuss the broader implications of our findings and offer ideas on how the additional infrastructure indicated by our analysis might be practically deployed.

6.1 Implications for Service Providers

Our base map of the US long-haul fiber infrastructure highlights the fiber conduits used to transmit data between large population centers. While infrastructure such as content delivery networks and data centers complicate the details of data flows, this map can support and inform decisions by service providers on provisioning and management of their infrastructures. Beyond performance and robustness analysis, the base map can inform decisions on local/regional broadband deployment, peering, and route selection, as well as provide competitive insights. Further, the fact that there is widespread and sometimes significant conduit sharing complicates the task of identifying and configuring backup paths since these critical details are often opaque to higher layers. Enrichment of this map through the addition of long-haul links in other regions around the world, undersea cable maps for inter-continental connectivity, and metro-level fiber maps will improve our global view of the physical Internet and will provide valuable insights for all involved players (*e.g.*, regional, national, or global-scale providers). Finally, the map also informs regulatory and oversight activities that focus on ensuring a safe and accessible physical communications infrastructure.

While much prior work on aspects of (logical) Internet connectivity at layer 3 and above points to the dynamic nature of the corresponding graph structures as an invariant, it is important to recognize that the (physical) long-haul infrastructure is comparably static by definition (*i.e.*, deploying new fiber takes time). In that sense, the links reflected in our map can also be considered an Internet invariant, and it is instructive to compare the basic structure of our map to the NSFNET backbone circa 1995 [54].

6.2 The FCC and Title II

Over the past several years, there have been many discussions about the topic of network neutrality. The US Communications Act of 1934 [17] is mentioned frequently in those discussions since Title II of that Act enables the FCC to specify communications providers as "common carriers". One implication of the recent FCC decision to reclassify broadband Internet providers as common carriers is that parts of a provider's infrastructure, including utility poles and conduits, will need to be made available to third parties. If this decision is upheld, it will likely lead to third party providers taking advantage of expensive already-existing long-haul infrastructure to facilitate the build out of their own infrastructure at considerably lower cost. Indeed, this is exactly the issue that has been raised by Google in their current fiber deployment efforts [38]. Furthermore, an important consequence of the additional sharing of long-haul infrastructure that will likely take place if the Title II classification is upheld is a significant *increase* in shared risk. We argue that this tradeoff between broader metro-area fiber deployments (*e.g.*, Google) and the increased risks in shared long-haul infrastructure requires more careful consideration in the broader Title II debate.

6.3 Enriching US Long-Haul Infrastructure

On the one hand, our study shows that the addition of a small number of conduits can lead to significant reductions in shared risk and propagation delays. At the same time, our examination of public records also shows that new conduit infrastructure is being deployed at a steady rate. Assuming that the locations for these actual deployments are based on a combination of business-related factors and are not necessarily aligned with the links that our techniques identify, the question that arises is how the conduits identified in our analysis might actually be deployed.

We believe that a version of the Internet exchange point (IXP) model could be adapted for conduits. IXPs largely grew out of efforts by consortia of service providers as means for keeping local traffic local [79]. We argue that the deployment of key long-haul links such as those identified in our study would be compelling for a potentially large number of service providers, especially if the cost for participating providers would be competitive. At the same time, given the implications for shared risk and the critical nature of communications infrastructure, government support may be warranted.[9] In fact, the involvement of some states' DOTs in the build-out and leasing of new conduits can be viewed as an early form of the proposed "link exchange" model [15].

7 Related Work

The Internet's basic design [81] makes it robust against failures of physical components such as routers and links. While IP routing allows the network to dynamically detect and route around failures, events such as natural or technological disasters (*e.g.*, [42,57]), malicious attacks (*e.g.*, [66]) and benign incidents (*e.g.*, [64]) can have localized effects, including the loss of connectivity for varying numbers of Internet users for certain amounts of time. The main reasons for such localized and temporal Internet outages are typically a lack

[9]Similar arguments are being made for hardening the electrical power grid, *e.g.*, http://www.wsj.com/articles/grid-terror-attacks-u-s-government-is-urged-to-takes-steps-for-protection-1404672802.

of geographic diversity in connectivity [2,40] and a tendency for significant physical infrastructure sharing among the affected providers—the very focus of this paper. In particular, this paper is not about the Internet's vulnerability to non-physical cyber attacks (*e.g.*, [46]) that rely on the existence and full functionality of the Internet's physical infrastructure to achieve their goals and do maximal damage [82].

Analyzing the robustness of the physical Internet has been the focus of many prior research efforts. These include studies on its robust yet fragile nature [82, 104], vulnerability [86, 87, 106], survivability [90, 91], resilience analysis [74,84,105], reachability [76,94], security and robustness of components [93], fault detection/localization [85, 95, 98], and the development of resilient routing protocols [75,88,89, 102, 107]. In contrast to these and similar prior efforts, our study is the first to consider the extensive levels of physical infrastructure sharing in today's Internet, use various metrics to quantify the resulting shared risk and offer viable suggestions for improving the overall robustness of the physical Internet to link and/or router failures.

Our study centers around the construction of a high-fidelity map of the long-haul fiber-optic routes in the US Internet and relies critically on a first-of-its-kind analysis of the detailed geography of these routes. On the one hand, there exists prior work on mapping the US long-haul fiber-optic network (see for example [2,36]), but the resulting maps are of uncertain quality, lack important details, and are not reproducible. There have also been prior studies that examine different aspects of the Internet infrastructure and various spatial patterns that have emerged (see for example [97]). On the other hand, the basic map constructed as part of our work is based on rich information from publicly available resources and can be reproduced by anybody who has the time and energy to gather the available but not necessarily easy-to-locate information.

The detailed analysis of our long-haul fiber-optic network map is made possible by using geocoded network maps and the ArcGIS framework [30], and is unprecedented both in terms of accuracy and ability for validation. In contrast to the work by Lakhina *et al.* [96] who use geolocation databases to obtain the approximate link lengths between geolocated routers, our study avoids the issues related to router-level granularity (*e.g.*, errors in geolocating routers, use of line-of-sight for estimating link distances) by exploiting the detailed geography of the long-haul fiber-optic routes between major city pairs and computing their actual lengths. In the process, we compare our long-haul fiber-optic map to existing transportation infrastructure (*e.g.*, railway, roadways) and quantify previously made qualitative observations that place much of the long-haul fiber-optic infrastructure along railways and roadways [36].

8 Summary and Future Work

In this paper we study the Internet's long-haul fiber-optic infrastructure in the US. Our first contribution is in building a first-of-its-kind map of long-haul infrastructure using openly available maps from tier-1 ISPs and cable providers. We validate the map rigorously by appealing to public information sources such as government agency filings, environmental impact statements, press releases, and others. Examination of the map confirms the close correspondence of fiber deployments and road/rail infrastructure and reveals significant link sharing among providers. Our second contribution is to apply different metrics to examine the issue of shared risk in the long-haul map. Our results point to high-risk links where there are significant levels of sharing among service providers. Our final contribution is to identify public ROWs that could be targets for new link conduits that would reduce shared risk and improve path performance. We discuss implications of our findings in general and point out how they expand the current discussion on how Title II and net neutrality. In future work, we plan to appeal to regional and metro fiber maps to improve the coverage of the long-haul map and to continue the process of link validation. We also plan to generate annotated versions of our map, focusing in particular on traffic and propagation delay.

Acknowledgements

We thank our shepherd, David Wetherall, and the anonymous reviewers for their invaluable feedback. This material is based upon work supported by the NSF under grant CNS-1054985, DHS grant BAA 11-01 and AFRL grant FA8750-12-2-0328. Any opinions, findings, and conclusions or recommendations expressed in this material are those of the author and do not necessarily reflect the views of the NSF, DHS or AFRL.

9 References

[1] 50-State survey of rights-of-way statutes. http://www.ntia.doc.gov/legacy/ntiahome/staterow/rowtable.pdf.

[2] A Dissertation So Good It Might Be Classified. http://archive.wired.com/wired/archive/12.01/start.html?pg=10.

[3] American Fiber Services - Response1. http://www.ntia.doc.gov/legacy/broadbandgrants/applications/responses/774PNR.pdf.

[4] American Fiber Services - Response2. http://www.ntia.doc.gov/legacy/broadbandgrants/applications/responses/804PNR.pdf.

[5] American Fiber Services - Zayo Release. http://www.zayo.com/images/uploads/resources/Earnings_Releases/FY2011Q1_10-Q.pdf.

[6] AT&T Network Map. http://www.sura.org/images/programs/att_sura_map_big.gif.

[7] Broadband plan. http://www.broadband.gov/plan/6-infrastructure/.

[8] CapeNet. http://www.muni.ri.net/middletown/documents/technology/RFIresponses/CapeNet.pdf.

[9] CenturyLink Network Map. http://www.centurylink.com/business/asset/network-map/fiber-network-nm090928.pdf.

[10] City of Boulder, CO. http://www.branfiber.net/Conduit%20Lease%20Agreement%20between%20Zayo%20and%20the%20City%20of%20Boulder.pdf.

[11] City of Santa Clara, CA. http://vantagedatacenters.com/wp-content/uploads/2014/06/Vantage-Network-Connectivity-Report.pdf.

[12] Clear Creek and Gilpin Counties Broadband Assessment. http://apps.fcc.gov/ecfs/document/view?id=7521088690.

[13] Coastal Route - SFO. to LA. for several ISPs. http://www.ustaxcourt.gov/InOpHistoric/anschutz.TCM.WPD.pdf.
[14] Cogent Network Map. www.internetatlas.org.
[15] Colorado Department of Tranportation document. http://www.wmxsystems.com/EndUserFiles/44489.pdf.
[16] Comcast Network Map. http://business.comcast.com/about-us/our-network.
[17] Communications Act of 1934. http://transition.fcc.gov/Reports/1934new.pdf.
[18] County document for Zayo and ATT. http://www2.ntia.doc.gov/files/grantees/nt10bix5570098_california_broadband_cooperative_inc_ppr2013_q3.pdf.
[19] Cox and Level3 lease agreement - Ocala, FL. http://ocalafl.iqm2.com/Citizens/FileOpen.aspx?Type=30&ID=2988.
[20] Cox Franchise Agreement in Fairfax county, Virginia. http://www.fairfaxcounty.gov/cable/regulation/franchise/cox/franchise_agreement_cox_fairfax_cty.pdf.
[21] Cox Franchise Agreement in Fairfax county, Virginia. https://www.natoa.org/events/RickEllrod.pdf.
[22] Cox Network Map. http://www.cox.com/wcm/en/business/datasheet/brc-backbone-map-q4-2013.pdf?campcode=brc_un_07_101513.
[23] Dascom Systems Report. http://dascom-systems.com/new/wp-content/uploads/eCare-Overview-of-Nevada-project-for-ICBN-Constituency.pdf.
[24] Design service demonstrating Comcast's presence with other entities along ROW. https://www.cfxway.com/portals/0/procurement_pdf/892ec203-d259-46d7-a6c7-b67b8c01dddd.pdf.
[25] Dig Once ordinance: Muni Networks. http://www.muninetworks.org/tags/tags/dig-once.
[26] Douglas County, CO document for CenturyLink and Level3. http://www.crgov.com/DocumentCenter/Home/View/945.
[27] E-Corridors. http://www.ecorridors.vt.edu/research/papers/stircne/vol02-connecting.pdf.
[28] EAGLENET. https://www.co-eaglenet.net/wp-content/uploads/2013/05/EAGLE-NET-001-Addenda-4-Responses-to-Questions-2013-05-29.pdf.
[29] EarthLink Network Map. http://www.earthlinkbusiness.com/support/network-map.xea.
[30] ESRI ArcGIS. http://www.arcgis.com/features/.
[31] Federal Highway Administration: State by state status report — utility rights of way. http://www.fhwa.dot.gov/real_estate/right-of-way/utility_rights-of-way/utilsr.cfm.
[32] Fiber-optic latency. http://www.m2optics.com/blog/bid/70587/Calculating-Optical-Fiber-Latency.
[33] Fiber Optic Settlement. https://fiberopticsettlements.com.
[34] FiberLocator Online. http://www.fiberlocator.com/product/fiberlocator-online.
[35] Georeferencing in ArcGIS. http://resources.arcgis.com/en/help/main/10.1/index.html#/Fundamentals_of_georeferencing_a_raster_dataset/009t000000mn000000.
[36] GMU Mapping Project.. http://gembinski.com/interactive/GMU/research.html.
[37] Google Maps. http://maps.google.com/.
[38] Google to FCC. http://www.engadget.com/2015/01/01/google-letter-fcc-title-ii/.
[39] Hamming Distance. http://en.wikipedia.org/wiki/Hamming_distance.
[40] How to Destroy the Internet. http://gizmodo.com/5912383/how-to-destroy-the-internet.
[41] Image from Geo-tel. http://www.techrepublic.com/article/the-google-fiber-lottery/.
[42] Impact of the 2003 blackouts on Internet communications (Preliminary report), Nov. 2003. http://research.dyn.com/content/uploads/2013/05/Renesys_BlackoutReport.pdf.
[43] Integra Telecom Network Map. http://www.integratelecom.com/resources/Assets/long-haul-fiber-network-map-integra.pdf.
[44] IRU between Level3 and Comcast. http://investors.level3.com/investor-relations/press-releases/press-release-details/2004/Comcast-Extends-National-Fiber-Infrastructure/default.aspx.
[45] IRU Swaps. http://chogendorn.web.wesleyan.edu/excessive.pdf.
[46] Is Internet backbone vulnerable to cyber attack? http://www.sciencedaily.com/releases/2010/12/101214085539.htm.
[47] Level 3 and Comcast. http://corporate.comcast.com/news-information/news-feed/comcast-extends-national-fiber-infrastructure.
[48] Level3 Network Map. http://maps.level3.com/default/.
[49] Media Advertisement. http://www.wikinvest.com/stock/XO_Holdings_Inc_(XOHO)/Cox_Communications_Las_Vegas_Indefeasible_Right_Iru_Agreement.
[50] Media Advertisement. http://www.wikinvest.com/stock/XO_Holdings_Inc_(XOHO)/Level.
[51] National Atlas. http://www.nationalatlas.gov/.
[52] News article from SMW3. http://www.smw3.com/smw3/signin/download/iru/Standard%20Agreement/AG-IRU-Final%20(Mar03).pdf.
[53] News article from Telecom Ramblings. http://www.telecomramblings.com/2014/09/tw-telecom-pushes-north-new-york/.
[54] NSFNet. http://en.wikipedia.org/wiki/National_Science_Foundation_Network.
[55] Open Trench: Muni Networks. http://muninetworks.org/tags/tags/open-trench.
[56] Pipeline 101. http://www.pipeline101.org/where-are-pipelines-located.
[57] Quake shakes up the net, Dec. 2006. http://www.thestar.com.my/story/?file=%2f2006%2f12%2f28%2fnation%2f16426778&sec=nation.
[58] Reuse of old fiber conduits. https://books.google.co.in/books?id=ynvMx7mMgJAC&pg=PA87&lpg=PA87&dq=reuse+of+old+fiber+conduits&source=bl&ots=_QHokk-JPX&sig=5fIzF6Jc5w6TmsewGS8ITX79VKU&hl=en&sa=X&ei=LTF3VfrDD8Xt8gXd2oGoCg&ved=0CCMQ6AEwAQ#v=onepage&q=reuse%20of%20old%20fiber%20conduits&f=false.
[59] SCAC. http://securities.stanford.edu/filings-documents/1023/GX02/2004322_r01c_02910.pdf.
[60] Sprint Network Map. https://www.sprint.net/images/network_maps/full/NorthAmerica-Global-IP.png.
[61] Sprint using Level3's fiber in Detroit. http://apps.fcc.gov/ecfs/document/view;jsessionid=yzRnRk4NJnlqDtlg0shlW2QDTSd3J2x0nz9Ryg5TJpMyX0rnYXxG!-1694890999!-477673473?id=6516791680.
[62] Sprint using Level3's fiber in Detroit settlement. https://fiberopticsettlements.com/michigan/LinkClick.aspx?fileticket=912Y0QkAV2E%3d&tabid=62&mid=420.
[63] SuddenLink Network Map. http://www.suddenlinkcarrier.com/index.php?page=our-network.

[64] The Backhoe: A Real Cyberthreat. http://archive.wired.com/science/discoveries/news/2006/01/70040?currentPage=all.

[65] The internet is not a big truck. It's a series of tubes. http://en.wikipedia.org/wiki/Series_of_tubes.

[66] The National Research Council of the National Academies, The Internet under crisis conditions: Learning from September 11, 2003. http://www.nap.edu/catalog/10569/the-internet-under-crisis-conditions-learning-from-september-11.

[67] UEN. http://home.chpc.utah.edu/~corbato/montana/montana-friends-25-jul-2013.pdf.

[68] Urbana city council project update. http://media01.atlas.uiuc.edu/gslis/gslis-v-2010-3/Digital_Divide_smeltzer_slidesandnotes.pdf.

[69] Urbana city council project update - pictures. http://urbanaillinois.us/sites/default/files/attachments/uc2b-urbana-council-update-10-25-10s.pdf.

[70] Urbana city council project update - pictures. http://www.tellusventure.com/downloads/casf/feb_2013_round/casf_project_bright_fiber_1feb2013.pdf.

[71] US 36 Corridor Final Environmental Impact Statement: Chapter 4 âAffected Environment and Environmental Consequences. https://www.codot.gov/projects/us36eis/documents/us-36-final-eis-volume-i/section-4-18_utilities.pdf.

[72] Verizon Network Map. https://www22.verizon.com/wholesale/images/networkMap.png.

[73] Zayo Network Map. http://www.zayo.com/network/interactive-map.

[74] P. Agarwal, A. Efrat, S. Ganjugunte, D. Hay, S. Sankararaman, and G. Zussman. The Resilience of WDM Networks to Probabilistic Geographical Failures. In *IEEE INFOCOM*, 2011.

[75] D. Andersen, H. Balakrishnan, F. Kaashoek, and R. Morris. Resilient Overlay Networks. In *ACM SOSP*, 2001.

[76] R. Bush, O. Maennel, M. Roughan, and S. Uhlig. Internet Optometry: Assessing the Broken Glasses in Internet Reachability. In *ACM IMC*, 2009.

[77] K. L. Calvert, M. B. Doar, and E. W. Zegura. Modeling Internet Topology. *IEEE Communications*, 1997.

[78] J. Chabarek and P. Barford. What's in a Name? Decoding Router Interface Names. In *ACM HotPlanet*, 2013.

[79] N. Chatzis, G. Smaragdakis, A. Feldmann, and W. Willinger. There is More to IXPs Than Meets the Eye. *SIGCOMM CCR*, 2013.

[80] D. R. Choffnes and F. E. Bustamante. Taming the Torrent: A Practical Approach to Reducing Cross-ISP Traffic in Peer-to-peer Systems. In *ACM SIGCOMM*, 2008.

[81] D. Clark. The design philosophy of the darpa internet protocols. *SIGCOMM CCR*, 1988.

[82] J. C. Doyle, D. Alderson, L. Li, S. Low, M. Roughan, R. Tanaka, and W. Willinger. The "robust yet fragile" nature of the Internet. In *PNAS*, 2005.

[83] R. Durairajan, S. Ghosh, X. Tang, P. Barford, and B. Eriksson. Internet atlas: A geographic database of the internet. In *ACM HotPlanet*, 2013.

[84] B. Eriksson, R. Durairajan, and P. Barford. RiskRoute: A Framework for Mitigating Network Outage Threats. In *ACM CoNEXT*, 2013.

[85] E. Glatz and X. Dimitropoulos. Classifying Internet One-way Traffic. In *ACM IMC*, 2012.

[86] S. Gorman. *Networks, Security And Complexity: The Role of Public Policy in Critical Infrastructure Protection.* Edward Elgar, 2005.

[87] S. P. Gorman, L. Schintler, R. Kulkarni, and R. Stough. The Revenge of Distance: Vulnerability Analysis of Critical Information Infrastructure. *JCCM*, 2004.

[88] K. P. Gummadi, H. V. Madhyastha, S. D. Gribble, H. M. Levy, and D. Wetherall. Improving the Reliability of Internet Paths with One-hop Source Routing. In *USENIX OSDI*, 2004.

[89] A. F. Hansen, A. Kvalbein, T. Cicic, and S. Gjessing. Resilient Routing Layers for Network Disaster Planning. In *IEEE ICN*, 2005.

[90] P. E. Heegaard and K. S. Trivedi. Network Survivability Modeling. 2009.

[91] P.-H. Ho, J. Tapolcai, and H. Mouftah. On Achieving Optimal Survivable Routing for Shared Protection in Survivable Next-Generation Internet. *IEEE Transactions on Reliability*, 2004.

[92] B. Huffaker, M. Fomenkov, and k. claffy. DRoP:DNS-based Router Positioning. *SIGCOMM CCR*, 2014.

[93] K. Kant and C. Deccio. Security and Robustness in the Internet Infrastructure.

[94] E. Katz-Bassett, H. V. Madhyastha, J. P. John, A. Krishnamurthy, D. Wetherall, and T. Anderson. Studying Black Holes in the Internet with Hubble. In *USENIX NSDI*, 2008.

[95] E. Katz-Bassett, C. Scott, D. R. Choffnes, I. Cunha, V. Valancius, N. Feamster, H. V. Madhyastha, T. E. Anderson, and A. Krishnamurthy. LIFEGUARD: Practical Repair of Persistent Route Failures. In *ACM SIGCOMM*, 2012.

[96] A. Lakhina, J. Byers, M. Crovella, and I. Matta. On the Geographic Location of Internet Resources. In *IEEE JSAC*, 2003.

[97] E. J. Malecki. The economic geography of the internet's infrastructure. *Economic geography*, 2002.

[98] L. Quan, J. Heidemann, and Y. Pradkin. Detecting Internet Outages with Precise Active Probing (extended). In *USC Technical Report*, 2012.

[99] M. A. Sanchez, F. E. Bustamante, B. Krishnamurthy, W. Willinger, G. Smaragdakis, and J. Erman. Inter-domain traffic estimation for the outsider. In *ACM IMC*, 2014.

[100] A. Singla, B. Chandrasekaran, P. B. Godfrey, and B. Maggs. The internet at the speed of light. In *ACM Hotnets*, 2014.

[101] J. Sommers, P. Barford, and B. Eriksson. On the Prevalence and Characteristics of MPLS Deployments in the Open Internet. In *ACM IMC*, 2011.

[102] H. Wang, Y. R. Yang, P. H. Liu, J. Wang, A. Gerber, and A. Greenberg. Reliability as an Interdomain Service. In *ACM SIGCOMM*, 2007.

[103] B. M. Waxman. Routing of multipoint connections. *IEEE JSAC*, 1988.

[104] W. Willinger and J. Doyle. Robustness and the internet: Design and evolution. *Robust-Design: A Repertoire of Biological, Ecological, and Engineering Case Studies*, 2002.

[105] J. Wu, Y. Zhang, Z. M. Mao, and K. G. Shin. Internet Routing Resilience to Failures: Analysis and Implications. In *ACM CoNEXT*, 2007.

[106] L. Zhou. Vulnerability Analysis of the Physical Part of the Internet. In *IJCI*, 2010.

[107] Y. Zhu, A. Bavier, N. Feamster, S. Rangarajan, and J. Rexford. UFO: A Resilient Layered Routing Architecture. *SIGCOMM CCR*, 2008.

Spatiotemporal Traffic Matrix Synthesis

Paul Tune and Matthew Roughan
ARC Centre of Excellence for Mathematical and Statistical Frontiers
School of Mathematical Sciences
University of Adelaide, Australia
{paul.tune,matthew.roughan}@adelaide.edu.au

ABSTRACT

Traffic matrices describe the volume of traffic between a set of sources and destinations within a network. These matrices are used in a variety of tasks in network planning and traffic engineering, such as the design of network topologies. Traffic matrices naturally possess complex spatiotemporal characteristics, but their proprietary nature means that little data about them is available publicly, and this situation is unlikely to change.

Our goal is to develop techniques to synthesize traffic matrices for researchers who wish to test new network applications or protocols. The paucity of available data, and the desire to build a general framework for synthesis that could work in various settings requires a new look at this problem. We show how the principle of maximum entropy can be used to generate a wide variety of traffic matrices constrained by the needs of a particular task, and the available information, but otherwise avoiding hidden assumptions about the data. We demonstrate how the framework encompasses existing models and measurements, and we apply it in a simple case study to illustrate the value.

Categories and Subject Descriptors

C.2.5 [**Computer Communications**]: Local and Wide Area Networks—*Internet*; C.4 [**Performance of Systems**]: Modeling Techniques

Keywords

Maximum entropy; network design; spatiotemporal modeling; traffic engineering; traffic matrix synthesis

SIGCOMM '15, August 17 - 21, 2015, London, United Kingdom

DOI: http://dx.doi.org/10.1145/2785956.2787471

1. INTRODUCTION

A Traffic Matrix (TM) describes the traffic volume between a set of sources and destinations in a network. TMs are used as inputs in a variety of network planning and traffic engineering tasks. For instance, new power aware routing and traffic engineering algorithms [9] need TMs for testing and validation. TMs are also required for network traffic forecasting and planning [32] and topology generation [5]. The lack of public TM data remains an obstacle to researchers in these areas.

The main reason for this lack is the propriety nature of TMs: network operators are reluctant to release such data as they fear it may lead to the erosion of their competitive advantage. Consequently, researchers resort to testing network designs on limited public data, such as from the Abilene [23] or GÉANT [41] networks. These, however, are research and education networks, leading to the possibility that they are not representative of commercial networks. Even the release of a single commercial operator's TM data would not quell the question of representativeness – so we really need many such datasets. Hence, the current deficit is unlikely to be remedied in the foreseeable future.

Researchers also need multiple TMs to test ideas statistically and in order to have ground truth when testing inference techniques. To do this, large ensembles of TMs must be generated, so that confidence intervals on the performance of these techniques be meaningful.

We can solve these issues by synthesizing TMs, but how can we create a good model for synthesis without first having data? The answer is to abandon the typical network modeling approach – measure then model – and think about the problem from first principles.

Additionally, we are not aiming here at the typical target of past TM research: better inference of TMs from limited data [14,22,35,45,48]. When we synthesize a TM, we have different requirements:

- *Control:* A particular network protocol we aim to test will make assumptions. We should be able to generate TMs that match those assumptions to test its performance. For completeness, we also need to generate TMs that violate the assumptions, to test what happens to the protocol in unfriendly situations.

The required assumptions and constraints on TMs will vary from setting to setting. However, in creating TMs that satisfy some set of assumptions, we should not be forced to introduce additional (often hidden) assumptions about the traffic. We want to include the desired constraints on the TMs but no others.

- *Efficiency:* We want to be able to generate potentially large numbers of TMs computationally efficiently to obtain clear statistical measures of performance.
- *Consistency:* We want to make apples to apples comparisons: two studies using the same model should reach the same conclusions (regardless of specific random values), so we need to be able to draw instances from a well-defined, consistent ensemble of TMs.
- *Simplicity:* A model should be "as simple as it can be – but not simpler" [7]. Simplicity has many virtues: it improves our intuitive understanding, reduces the complexity of parameter estimation, and prevents over fitting. Part of simplicity is *parsimony* of parameters, and part is having *meaningful* parameters.

Finally, we might like our TMs to be "realistic", but that might vary tremendously from setting to setting: for instance it seems likely that Wide Area Network (WAN) TMs are nothing like data center TMs. So realism is context dependent, and our goal here is to create a framework that can encompass and be adapted easily to any such setting. Indeed, if some data is available to populate a model in a particular context, we would like our framework to be able to include that data.

Our approach is based on the *principle of maximum entropy (MaxEnt)* [15]. Information theory and its darling *entropy* have been applied to inferring TMs in the past with success [31, 45, 46], but there are some subtle differences between creating models for inference and synthesis. Most notably, we don't necessarily have *any* data, though if we do, we would like to incorporate it.

The resulting MaxEnt framework encompasses and extends most of the existing models for TMs, *e.g.*, [31, 36]. The models it produces are conservative in the sense that they do not assume anything about the TMs beyond the given constraints. The framework also links the constraints and assumptions directly to models, so that we can learn from an existing model exactly what minimal set of assumptions led to it.

A list of our contributions are as follows:

- a systematic methodology for generating *controlled synthetic TMs with prescribed properties*, achieved via the principle of maximum entropy,
- *closed-forms* of example models that would be useful in testing various network algorithms (*e.g.*, routing protocols) and network designs,
- *fast generation* of ensembles of TMs with spatiotemporal properties, and
- a *unification* of previous TM models under the family of maximum entropy models.

We examine the utility of our approach through its use in topology generation [5]. Here, the topology is designed around a set of TMs as input. Our case study's two chief findings are 1. although TMs have an impact on the topology design, the impact of some TM features is small, consistent with the findings of [5], and 2. optimizing a network around the peak TM is almost as good an approach as optimizing with respect to a whole-of-week pattern, supporting the common practice of basing designs around a peak traffic measure such as a *busy hour*.

Our code is at https://github.com/ptuls/MaxEntTM

2. BACKGROUND

2.1 The principle of maximum entropy

The principle of insufficient reason, often credited to Pierre Simon Laplace in the late 18th century, states that given an observation one should remain undecided about all the potential events explaining the observation. In other words, one assigns equal probability to each event. Laplace and Jacob Bernoulli considered the concept to be intuitively obvious, seeing little need to formalize it [37].

The principle of maximum entropy formally defines and generalizes the principle of indifference. Proposed by Jaynes [15] in the context of statistical mechanics the principle advocates that, given data, we should choose the distribution providing a plausible explanation of the observations while making the fewest assumptions. Jaynes showed that several models in statistical mechanics arise as a natural consequence.

The principle is defined in terms of Shannon *information entropy* [10]. If X is a discrete random variable taking values in set $\mathcal{X}$ with probability mass function $p(x)$, then Shannon's entropy is defined as [10]

$$H(X) = -\sum_{x\in\mathcal{X}} p(x)\log p(x), \tag{1}$$

with the convention $0\log 0 = 0$. Entropy measures the average uncertainty of a random source, for instance, if X is completely deterministic, $H(X) = 0$. Shannon's entropy is used because it is the only measure that nicely separates independent components in a joint distribution, and has a natural axiomatic derivation as a measure of uncertainty [34].

The principle of indifference now arises as a special case: when the only constraint is that $p(x)$ be a probability distribution, the entropy is maximized by the uniform distribution. Thus, maximizing entropy is consistent with the intuitive notion of being least committed to any one outcome, *i.e.*, indifference.

If additional observations exist, we describe them as constraints on the data. MaxEnt states that the best strategy is to choose a distribution that maximizes entropy subject to these constraints. The solution is one that conforms to known observations about the data and no more than that.

Jaynes [15] used the Shannon entropy to construct the MaxEnt framework. Since we consider continuous Random Variables (RVs) as an approximation of the traffic volumes, we use the *differential entropy* [10],

$$h(f) = -\int_{-\infty}^{\infty} \cdots \int_{-\infty}^{\infty} f(\boldsymbol{\mathcal{X}}) \log f(\boldsymbol{\mathcal{X}}) \, d\boldsymbol{\mathcal{X}}, \quad (2)$$

of a random TM process $\boldsymbol{\mathcal{X}}$ with distribution $f(\boldsymbol{\mathcal{X}})$.

Suppose by experimental observation, there are $L+1$ constraints on the data $\mathbb{E}[\phi_\ell(\boldsymbol{\mathcal{X}})] = b_\ell$ (where $\phi_\ell(\cdot)$ is a convex function and b_ℓ is a scalar value setting the constraint) are known. The constraint $\mathbb{E}[\phi_0(\boldsymbol{\mathcal{X}})] = 1$ is the normalization constraint (that applies to all probability distributions). The MaxEnt optimization problem is

$$\max_{f(\boldsymbol{\mathcal{X}})} h(f), \text{ s.t. } \{\mathbb{E}[\phi_\ell(\boldsymbol{\mathcal{X}})] = b_\ell\}_{\ell=0}^{L}, \text{ and } \boldsymbol{\mathcal{X}} \succeq \mathbf{0}, \quad (3)$$

where $\boldsymbol{\mathcal{X}} \succeq \mathbf{0}$ denotes non-negativity, a constraint we enforce on all TM models.

In the cases we primarily consider, the problem is convex so any local maximum is the global maximum, the solution being the *maximum entropy model*. Non-convex functions are possible, but more effort is required to search for the globally maximum model.

Boltzmann's theorem [15] states that the optimal solution takes the form of distributions from the exponential family, generically given by

$$f(\boldsymbol{\mathcal{X}}) = \frac{1}{Z} \exp\left(-\sum_{\ell=1}^{L} \lambda_\ell \phi_\ell(\boldsymbol{\mathcal{X}})\right), \quad (4)$$

where the $\{\lambda_\ell\}_{\ell=1}^{L}$ are the Lagrange multipliers obtained via the Calculus of Variations applied to (3), and Z is the normalization factor which incorporates the normalization constraint.

2.2 Entropy and TM models

A general introduction to modeling TMs can be found in [38]. We examine some of these models in detail here so that we can discuss how they relate to our framework.

Zhang *et al.* [45, 46] used a technique referred to as maximizing *relative* entropy to develop TM inference methods. However, this is different from maximum entropy modeling. Zhang *et al.*s' approach was aimed at finding a particular TM that matched data and was close to a prior model (in their case the generalized gravity model). Here we aim to create a model, not estimate a particular TM. The output of our approach is a distribution, not a TM. The part of that work closer to our own is in their prior model: we shall discuss gravity models and their ilk at length here.

Roughan [31] proposed using a random gravity model as a spatial model for TM synthesis, and Oikonomou [25] noted that it is a MaxEnt model for traffic under a certain set of assumptions. In fact, if one examines the transportation literature, that insight is even older [28]. This is a single case of the framework presented here.

The work listed above considered spatial TMs only. The only work of which we are aware specifically on spatiotemporal synthesis was that of Nucci *et al.* [24], who developed static, dynamic stationary and dynamic cyclo-stationary models of TMs. Their spatial model was simple: a log-normally distributed Independent and Identically Distributed (IID) set of TM elements were generated. However, their models' raw outputs might not conform to pre-specified constraints, such as link capacities, necessitating adjustments to make them admissible TMs. We show here how this IID model fits into the MaxEnt framework, and how the framework allows us to avoid this *ad hoc* mapping step.

Most other works proposing spatiotemporal TM models do so with the aim of improving inference accuracy, rather than addressing the synthesis problem (though occasionally, passing reference has been made to potential alternative uses of their models). Soule *et al.* [36] proposed two models of Origin-Destination (OD) flows, one stationary and the other cyclo-stationary. Roughan *et al.* [33] developed a simple purely temporal model of OD flows traversing backbone routers comprising of a growth trend component, a seasonal component and a component for sudden spikes in traffic due to anomalies. Zhang *et al.* [48], exploiting new developments in signal processing, developed a model under the assumption of spatiotemporal low rankedness, enabling accurate TM inference via convex programming [8, 30].

Another work addressing the synthesis problem is [40], but its focus is entirely different. Our conceptual model in that paper was to help a network operator understand the effect of errors in predictions of TMs. In that context, the idea was to generate an ensemble of TMs centered around the prediction, whereas here, we do not require prior data about the TM, only constraints on its general properties. Interestingly, as the errors become large in that model, the results approach a maximum entropy distribution, which is exactly what we propose here: when little is known about the TM, MaxEnt provides a natural path towards modeling.

Notation: The column vector of N ones is denoted by $\mathbf{1}_N$. Some common statistical distributions are used here:

- An exponentially distributed RV X with mean $1/\lambda$ is denoted $X \sim \text{Exp}(\lambda)$.
- The continuous uniform distribution in the interval $[a, b]$ is denoted by $\text{U}(a, b)$.
- $X \sim \mathcal{N}(\boldsymbol{\mu}, \boldsymbol{\Sigma})$ means that X is distributed as a normal distribution with mean $\boldsymbol{\mu}$ and covariance $\boldsymbol{\Sigma}$.
- $X \sim \text{TNorm}(\boldsymbol{\mu}, \boldsymbol{\Sigma})$ means that X is distributed according to a truncated normal distribution with support $\mathcal{I} := [0, \infty)^N$. Note that $\boldsymbol{\mu}$ and $\boldsymbol{\Sigma}$ are the mean and covariance *after* truncation.

We define all other notation when needed.

3. SPATIOTEMPORAL TM SYNTHESIS

Network traffic information is contained in the TM $\boldsymbol{X}(t)$, which measures traffic between locations in a network. Traffic is typically measured in discrete time intervals, with 5 to 15 minutes. So a "traffic matrix" is actually a series of matrices:

$$\boldsymbol{X}(t_k),\ k = 0, 1, \cdots, M-1, \quad (5)$$

where $X_{i,j}(t_k)$ denotes the average volume of traffic entering node i and exiting node j in a measurement interval $[t_k, t_{k+1})$.

Let $\boldsymbol{\mathcal{X}} := \{\boldsymbol{X}(t_k)\}_{k=0}^{M-1}$ denote the TM process. We are concerned here with the distribution governing the generation of $\boldsymbol{\mathcal{X}}$, denoted by $f(\boldsymbol{\mathcal{X}})$. In general, multivariate stochastic processes are all governed by such a distribution, which here define an ensemble of TMs. However, all successful models simplify this high dimensional construct in some (usually dramatic) way.

Although network traffic is discrete in nature (measured in bytes or packets), we model the TM entries as continuous RVs. This assumption is reasonable where we consider high volumes of traffic.

Spatial properties of the TMs refer to the statistical properties between the TM entries either at a fixed t, *i.e.*, a *snapshot* $\boldsymbol{X}(t_k)$, or over time, *e.g.*, the average TM $\frac{1}{M}\sum_{k=0}^{M-1}\boldsymbol{X}(t_k)$. We consider a network with N locations, so each snapshot is an $N \times N$ matrix.

Temporal properties refer to the statistical properties only varying with t, either with fixed spatial indices, *i.e.*, the process $X_{i,j}(t_k)$, or some summary such as the total traffic $S(t_k) = \sum_{i,j} X_{i,j}(t_k)$ at each time point t_k.

3.1 Maximum entropy models

In the introduction we discussed the qualities that make a good synthesis model. In this section our primary foci are simplicity and controllability.

Testing does not (necessarily) require realistic input, since the goal is to understand the effect a specific input has on an algorithm. For instance, inputs could be extreme cases, such as a TM with its total traffic spread uniformly over all entries (called a *uniform load model* [6,38]). What we do need is the ability to control the input of an algorithm to perform systematic tests.

Chiefly, we need to incorporate what we believe about the network. Different types of networks have different properties and constraints. For instance, data centers have entirely different traffic mixes from WANs [1, 16] so there exists different constraints on their respective TMs. The constraints we primarily consider here are in the form of constraints on statistics of the TM: for instance, a constraint on the average or expected value $\mathbb{E}[\cdot]$ of some aspect of the TM. Deterministic constraints can also be added, but are rather simpler to analyze, so we focus on the more difficult case.

Though we primarily focus on WANs, the general methodology provides tools for researchers to develop synthesis models for alternative networks. Part of the goal here is to provide a modeling framework for researchers even *before* a new technology is deployed, to understand its properties under various hypotheses.

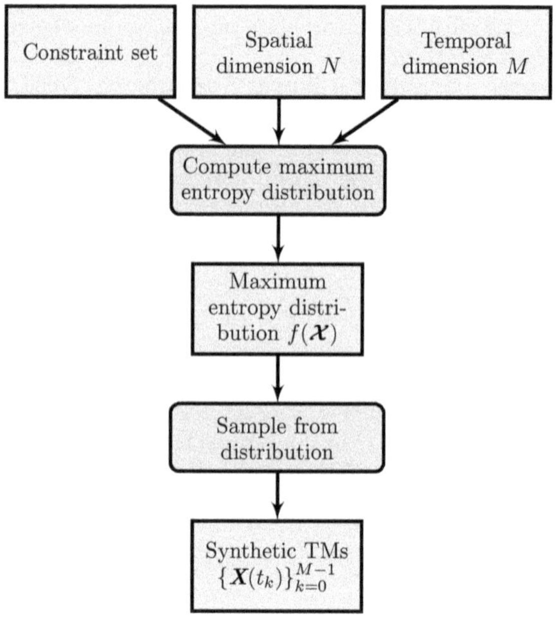

Figure 1: *Methodology of the spatiotemporal synthesis of the maximum entropy TMs. The rectangles denote the inputs and outputs at each stage, while the rounded rectangles denote the stages of the process. The steps generate one run of M matrices.*

Figure 1 presents an overview of our methodology. The inputs are the set of constraints, and the spatial and temporal dimensions N and M respectively. Solving (3) gives the MaxEnt distribution $f(\boldsymbol{\mathcal{X}})$, which entails computing the Lagrange multipliers $\{\lambda_\ell\}_{\ell=1}^{L}$. Generally, these can be computed using the Newton-Raphson method (see [43]), but it is more instructive where we can derive closed forms for the distributions, and so we spend some effort here to derive a number of such models in a manner that is explanatory and extensible.

Finally, $f(\boldsymbol{\mathcal{X}})$ is sampled to generate the synthetic TM process $\boldsymbol{\mathcal{X}}$. Again, this can be achieved numerically, say via Markov Chain Monte Carlo (MCMC) techniques, but we demonstrate several models for which sampling can be performed much more efficiently. Constraints that often arise in TM research lead to closed forms, which in turn provide fast sampling methods.

For all models, let $\boldsymbol{R}(t_k) = \boldsymbol{X}(t_k)\mathbf{1}_N$ and $\boldsymbol{C}(t_k) = \boldsymbol{X}(t_k)^{\mathrm{T}}\mathbf{1}_N$, *i.e.*, the row and column sum processes (total ingress and egress traffic), and $S(t_k)$ denotes the total traffic in each interval t_k.

Model derivations involve (sometimes) lengthy, but standard derivations, and so in the interests of space we omit the details. However, there are some simple facts which should make the results somewhat intuitive:

1. Given the constraints of non-negativity and mean, the MaxEnt distribution is the exponential [27].

2. With both a mean and variance constraint, the MaxEnt distribution is the Normal distribution, and if we add to this the requirement of non-negativity, then the MaxEnt distribution is the truncated normal distribution [39].
3. Many other distributions arise from other moment-based or otherwise constraints on the RVs [27].
4. If we have two (or more) RVs, the MaxEnt model is that the RVs are independent (unless there is a joint constraint on the RVs) [10].

3.2 Purely spatial models

We divide our models into three classes: *purely spatial*, *purely temporal*, and *spatiotemporal models*. First generation TM models such as the gravity model [45] and the discrete choices model [22] are spatial, so we start there, noting that if we have no temporal information, the TM snapshots will be independent (Property 4), so we need only focus on a single interval and thus we drop t_k from our notation.

Independent entries model: In the absence of constraints on the joint distribution of TM entries $X_{i,j}$, by Property 4, these will be independent. If we also have homogenous constraints, *i.e.*, they don't favor any group of entries, then the entries will be IID.

There are many subcases of this type. For instance if the mean or expected value of each entry is fixed, *i.e.*, $\mathbb{E}[X_{i,j}] = \bar{X}$, then the MaxEnt model has entries $X_{i,j} \sim \text{Exp}\left(\bar{X}^{-1}\right)$. If we further impose control on each entry's variance by setting the variance to σ^2 then the MaxEnt model has entries $X_{i,j} \sim \text{TNorm}\left(\bar{X}, \sigma^2\right)$. If instead we only set bounds $[D_L, D_U]$ on each TM entry, the MaxEnt model has IID entries $X_{i,j} \sim \text{U}(D_L, D_U)$.

These models are perhaps oversimplified, but they have been used! For instance, the Poisson model of Vardi [42] and the log-normal model of Nucci *et al.* [24].

In the latter case we can derive an interesting insight. The log-normal distribution is the result of constraints on the average and variance of the *log* of entries [27]. The natural conclusion is that TM entries might be better modeled in the log-domain.

However, the key takeaway message is not the log-normal distribution, but rather that MaxEnt leads to a link between the model and its hidden assumptions, and these can provide potential insights into the data and/or the validity of the model. Perhaps another model provides a slightly less tight fit to the data, but is simpler and more intuitive when considered in this way, and therefore has more explanatory power?

Outer product models: IID models are clearly limited. Real TMs have correlations. Two attempts to build such correlations are the Random Gravity Model (RGM) [31] and the mapping phase of [24].

Let us consider here a simple yet powerful method of creating structure, which is to impose constraints on the row and column sums of the matrix, an idea that recurs through much of the TM literature[1] (*e.g.*, [14, 22, 31, 35, 45, 46]), and even into the realms of oblivious design where TMs are assumed to be unknowable [49] except for these constraints.

If we impose row and column constraints (only), then the MaxEnt model is formed via an outer product: for instance given non-negativity and the constraints

$$\mathbb{E}[\boldsymbol{R}] = \frac{T}{N}\mathbf{1}_N, \; \mathbb{E}[\boldsymbol{C}] = \frac{T}{N}\mathbf{1}_N, \; \mathbb{E}[S] = T,$$

the MaxEnt model is given by the *outer product*

$$\boldsymbol{X} = \frac{T}{N^2}\boldsymbol{U}\boldsymbol{V}^{\mathrm{T}}, \qquad (6)$$

where $U_i, V_j \sim \text{Exp}\,(1)$. This case is in fact the RGM of [31], and that illustrates how we can find new information about minimal assumptions of a model. The RGM was derived from data, but now we can understand the hidden assumptions of the model.

More generally, given constraints $\mathbb{E}[\boldsymbol{R}] = \mathbf{r}$ and $\mathbb{E}[\boldsymbol{C}] = \mathbf{c}$, MaxEnt implies a model that has *outer-product* form

$$\mathbb{E}[\boldsymbol{X}] = \frac{1}{T}\mathbf{r}\mathbf{c}^T, \qquad (7)$$

and from this and the simple distributional arguments above we can derive a set of *rank-1* matrix models.

Much more can be said about outer-product models. There are many generalizations, many appearing in older works in the transportation literature, for instance MaxEnt models that include a distance *friction* term that reduces traffic between distant locations. Such terms have not had a clear justification in most Internet studies, but can be included via a distance-cost constraint within the framework if needed [28].

One point, however, which we must make again is that this type of approach applies to any matrix for which we know row and column properties, and we will reuse this idea in a moment.

3.3 Purely temporal models

An example of a purely temporal traffic model is that proposed in [33], which focused on the long-term trends and cyclical patterns in traffic. There are countless other examples of such models, applied either to single TM entries, link traffic or traffic totals. Our goal here is not to describe the panoply of possible models, but to present how these models fit within the MaxEnt framework.

In the past, temporal models have chiefly been used for traffic prediction[2]. Predictions generally estimate a mean, and sometimes a variance around that mean.

---

[1] Row and column sums are really the ingress and egress traffic volumes, hence their importance.

[2] It may appear that applications such as anomaly detection are otherwise, but a closer look shows that most such techniques revolve around predicting "typical" traffic, and detecting outliers from these predictions.

As before, if only the mean of a set of (non-negative) random variables is given, then the RVs will be independent and exponentially distributed (Property 1). If variance is also fixed, then the RVs will be independent truncated normals (Property 2). More sophisticated models are also possible, for instance, if the autocovariances are also known [27], but these are rarely reported in Internet studies so we won't discuss these models further except to note that they can be added to the MaxEnt framework.

Thus, to derive a MaxEnt temporal model we might choose a mean and variance as function of time and then simulate from the truncated normal distribution. The choice of mean and variance varies with the desired network properties. Commonly, they would not be constants but may include diurnal and weekly cycles.

It should be obvious that the above provides almost too much flexibility. We can accommodate almost any temporal model, so the question is how should it be restricted to a reasonable set of models in practice. A very simple case could arise from modeling cyclical behavior using Fourier analysis, which is designed specifically for that purpose. In this case we do so by choosing constraints on the Fourier coefficients of the traffic:

$$\mathcal{F}\left(\{\mathbb{E}[S(t_k)-T]\}_{k=0}^{M-1}\right)=\mathbf{a}. \tag{8}$$

The coefficients $\mathbf{a}$ would be chosen to reflect the cyclical nature of the traffic. Then the MaxEnt model is an exponential model where the means at each time step are given by $\mathbb{E}[S(t_k)]=\bar{s}(t_k)=T+w(t_k)$, $\{w(t_k)\}_{k=0}^{M-1}=\mathcal{F}^{-1}(\mathbf{a})$ and $\mathcal{F}^{-1}$ denotes the inverse discrete Fourier transform. Notice that now the model generates values that are only conditionally independent, not IID.

As in other cases, we could also control variances and then would arrive at a truncated normal model.

Once again, note that the goal of this paper is to show how knowledge can be exploited to construct a temporal model, not to suggest that the above is the only sensible approach. This approach, however, does have the advantage that both Fourier transforms and expectation are linear operators.

3.4 Spatiotemporal models

Now that we have both spatial and temporal models, we can combine ideas in those models to form spatiotemporal models as follows.

Time modulated traffic: In most situations, we perhaps know or can assume information about the spatial and/or the temporal behavior. Many studies have examined details of these two facets of network traffic [19, 20]. Many more will no doubt follow, but also remember that we wish to consider potential hypothetical future traffic sources, *e.g.,* traffic in hosting centers. It is often possible to reason about the temporal and spatial properties of such hypothetical cases.

Importantly though, we rarely have information correlating spatial to temporal behavior (though we will note an important exception resulting from timezones in the following model).

We proceed in this case using a common trick in TM modeling (*e.g.,* see [44, 48]). We *stack* the columns of a single TM snapshot and then construct a new matrix from the columns at each time interval, that is,

$$\boldsymbol{Y}=\begin{bmatrix}\boldsymbol{X}_{*,1}(t_0) & \boldsymbol{X}_{*,1}(t_1) & \cdots & \boldsymbol{X}_{*,1}(t_{M-1})\\ \boldsymbol{X}_{*,2}(t_0) & \boldsymbol{X}_{*,2}(t_1) & \cdots & \boldsymbol{X}_{*,2}(t_{M-1})\\ \vdots & \vdots & \ddots & \vdots\\ \boldsymbol{X}_{*,N}(t_0) & \boldsymbol{X}_{*,N}(t_1) & \cdots & \boldsymbol{X}_{*,N}(t_{M-1})\end{bmatrix} \tag{9}$$

The new matrix $\boldsymbol{Y}$ is also sometimes called the traffic matrix, but now it is a $N^2\times M$ spatiotemporal matrix.

We are then in the same situation as in generating spatial models: we want to generate a matrix about which we only have row and column constraints. A natural building block towards more complex spatiotemporal models is to consider a model with separate independent spatial and temporal components. Not surprisingly, this has been studied by statisticians, and is called a *separable spatiotemporal model* [11].

In our context, for instance, column-sum constraints correspond to a model for the total traffic $S(t_k)$ at each time t_k, and row-sum constraints correspond to constraints on the average traffic per source/destination $\bar{X}_{i,j}$. The logical construction then is to use the same outer-product MaxEnt suggested for spatial models, *i.e.,*

$$\mathbb{E}[X_{i,j}(t_k)]=\bar{X}_{i,j}\bar{s}(t_k)/T, \tag{10}$$

where T is the time average of $\bar{s}(\cdot)$. When seen as a matrix operation, this is just an outer-product of the stacked vector version of $\bar{X}_{i,j}$ and $\bar{s}(t_k)$.

The MaxEnt model then takes the form $X_{i,j}(t_k)=G_{i,j}P(t_k)$, with $\mathbb{E}[G_{i,j}]=\bar{X}_{i,j}$ and $\mathbb{E}[P(t_k)]=\bar{s}(t_k)/T$, *i.e.,* separate spatial and temporal components. The exact form of $X_{i,j}(t_k)$ depends on the constraints, again with a constraint on means resulting in an exponential distribution, and constraints on mean and variance resulting in a truncated normal. The decomposable nature of the MaxEnt model allows mixing the two, using one for space and the other for time.

We can also include detailed spatial structure. For instance, we could have a model we refer to as the *Modulated Gravity Model (MGM)* where spatially we constrain the traffic by gravity-model-like constraints

$$\frac{1}{M}\sum_{k=0}^{M-1}\mathbb{E}[\boldsymbol{R}(t_k)]=\bar{\mathbf{r}},\ \frac{1}{M}\sum_{k=0}^{M-1}\mathbb{E}[\boldsymbol{C}(t_k)]=\bar{\mathbf{c}}, \tag{11}$$

and temporally we require (8). The MaxEnt model is

$$\boldsymbol{X}(t_k)=T\boldsymbol{U}\boldsymbol{V}^{\mathrm{T}}P(t_k), \tag{12}$$

$$U_i\sim\operatorname{Exp}\left(\frac{T}{\bar{r}_i}\right), V_j\sim\operatorname{Exp}\left(\frac{T}{\bar{c}_j}\right), P(t_k)\sim\operatorname{Exp}\left(\frac{T}{\bar{s}(t_k)}\right),$$

where as before $\bar{s}(t_k) := T + w(t_k)$. Once again, if we aim to control the variances, the relevant components U_i, V_j and/or $P(\cdot)$ would follow appropriate truncated normal distributions. The simplest choice is to set $\mathbf{\Sigma_r} = \mathbf{\Sigma_c} = \sigma^2 \mathbf{I}_N$. Likewise, we can also control $P(\cdot)$ by introducing a single variance parameter σ_p.

Note that these choices result in *simple* models, with minimal parameters, and meaningful parameters that can be directly related to network properties.

The model's name comes from the fact that its conditional mean is the RGM modulated by $\bar{s}(t_k)/T$, *i.e.*,

$$\mathbb{E}[\boldsymbol{X}(t_k)] = \frac{\bar{\mathbf{r}}\bar{\mathbf{c}}^{\mathrm{T}}}{T} \frac{\bar{s}(t_k)}{T}. \tag{13}$$

Non-stationary conditionally independent model (NCIM): Suppose the mean total traffic $\bar{s}(t_k)$ is known, but no temporal correlation information is available. The MaxEnt model is *non-stationary and conditionally independent*, with $\boldsymbol{X}(t_k)$ independent $\forall k$, and

$$X_{i,j}(t_k) \sim \mathrm{Exp}\left(\frac{N^2}{\bar{s}(t_k)}\right), \ \forall i, j, k. \tag{14}$$

This model assumes no information on the row and column sums in each interval. If we also knew the mean row and column sums, *i.e.*, $\mathbf{r}(t_k)$ and $\mathbf{c}(t_k)$, $\forall k$ then,

$$\boldsymbol{X}(t_k) = \bar{s}(t_k)\, \boldsymbol{U}(t_k)\, \boldsymbol{V}(t_k)^{\mathrm{T}}, \tag{15}$$

with $U_i(t_k) \sim \mathrm{Exp}\left(\frac{\bar{s}(t_k)}{r_i(t_k)}\right)$ and $V_j(t_k) \sim \mathrm{Exp}\left(\frac{\bar{s}(t_k)}{c_j(t_k)}\right)$. Including covariance information of $\mathbf{r}(t_k)$ and $\mathbf{c}(t_k)$ leads once again to the equivalent truncated normal forms.

One interesting use of this model is for TMs of networks large enough that differing timezones distort traffic patterns. Traffic cycles are determined by user behavior, which is in turn determined by timezones. In a globe-spanning network, for example, users the side of the world experiencing daytime might be transmitting traffic, while users on the other side might not.

For instance, the Abilene network [23] spans North America, with Points-of-Presence (PoPs) concentrated on the East and West Coast of the United States. A simple way to model the 3 hour difference in the traffic cycle between the coasts is to set $r_i(t_k)$ as a delayed, or phase shifted, version of a base constraint $\tilde{r}(t_k)$ (and similarly for $c_j(t_k)$). Once $r_i(t_k)$ and $c_j(t_k)$ have been generated, we generate the NCIM using (15).

In §5, we study the spatiotemporal characteristics of the above two models using Principle Component Analysis (PCA), which allows us to isolate traffic components. We will find that the models emulate some characteristics of real traffic, despite their simplicity.

In particular, these models are low rank, a property shared by real TMs [3, 19, 20, 48]. The MGM actually has a very good rank-1 approximation, and is in fact a rank-1 (three dimensional) tensor [18]. The NCIM model is hardly more complex, but the simple timezone shift described above increases its rank. However, the rank remains low.

Neither of these models can capture the spikes also seen in real traffic, leading us to the next model.

Spike model: Anomalies occur in networks due to worm propagation, distributed Denial-of-Service attacks, or flash crowds, causing a sudden spike in demand of a specific resource in the network [38]. These spikes have been demonstrated to be a feature of actual traffic in various studies [20,33]. Here, we present a simple model for anomalies.

Under the constraint $\|\boldsymbol{\mathcal{X}}\|_0 = K$ (and non-negativity), *i.e.*, exactly K entries of $\boldsymbol{\mathcal{X}}$ are non-zero and all others are zero, and setting the mean magnitude of the non-zero entries to A, the MaxEnt model is

$$X_{i,j}(t_k) \sim \begin{cases} \mathrm{Exp}\left(A^{-1}\right), & \text{if } (i,j,k) \in \mathcal{S}, \\ 0, & \text{otherwise}, \end{cases} \tag{16}$$

where $\mathcal{S}$ is the support of non-zero entries of size K sampled uniformly without replacement from the set $\{1, 2, \cdots, N\} \times \{1, 2, \cdots, N\} \times \{0, 1, \cdots, M-1\}$. When $K = 1$, the model is an example of the *peak load* model [6] which is used to test network designs.

Traffic class constraints: Network traffic can often be decomposed into several classes. For instance, different network services or applications possess different characteristics, so naturally, there are separate information about each. Assuming no dependencies, the prior information on each of them are to be accounted for separately by MaxEnt.

Several works provide strong evidence of distinct traffic behaviors. Both [20, 33] showed that OD flows can be divided into three groups: large flows with a strong diurnal cycle, spike-like flows corresponding to anomalies, and small, IID white noise-like flows. Suppose we know that the TM process $\boldsymbol{\mathcal{X}} = \boldsymbol{\mathcal{X}}_D + \boldsymbol{\mathcal{X}}_S + \boldsymbol{\mathcal{X}}_N$, where $\boldsymbol{\mathcal{X}}_D$ comprises of large traffic flows with a distinct diurnal cycle, while $\boldsymbol{\mathcal{X}}_S$ and $\boldsymbol{\mathcal{X}}_N$ accounts for anomalies (spikes) and small noise-like flows respectively. With no correlation information between these components, MaxEnt suggests that the processes $\boldsymbol{\mathcal{X}}_D$, $\boldsymbol{\mathcal{X}}_S$ and $\boldsymbol{\mathcal{X}}_N$ are independent. This means that we are free to solve for the MaxEnt distributions of these processes separately. To model large flows, we take $\boldsymbol{\mathcal{X}}_D$ to be the MGM. The spiky traffic process $\boldsymbol{\mathcal{X}}_S$ is modeled by the spike model and IID white noise process $\boldsymbol{\mathcal{X}}_N$ by the independent entries model.

Traffic classes also apply to traffic traversing peering or access links in a network. For instance, let the total traffic $T(t_k)$ be known for all k. Denote the access and peer node sets as $\mathcal{A}$ and $\mathcal{P}$ respectively. Now there are 4 classes of traffic: access-to-access $(\mathcal{A}, \mathcal{A})$, access-to-peer $(\mathcal{A}, \mathcal{P})$, peer-to-access $(\mathcal{P}, \mathcal{A})$ and peer-to-peer $(\mathcal{P}, \mathcal{P})$. Given the average total traffic constraints $T_{\mathcal{A},\mathcal{A}}(t_k)$, $T_{\mathcal{A},\mathcal{A}}(t_k)$, $T_{\mathcal{A},\mathcal{A}}(t_k)$ and $T_{\mathcal{P},\mathcal{P}}(t_k)$, with

$\sum_{m,n\in\{\mathcal{A},\mathcal{P}\}} T_{m,n}(t_k) = T(t_k)$ [47], the model is

$$\boldsymbol{X}(t_k) = T(t_k) \sum_{m,n\in\{\mathcal{A},\mathcal{P}\}} q_{m,n}(t_k)\, \boldsymbol{U}_m(t_k)\, \boldsymbol{V}_n(t_k)^{\mathrm{T}}, \tag{17}$$

such that $\sum_{m,n\in\{\mathcal{A},\mathcal{P}\}} q_{m,n}(t_k) = 1$.

Here, source and destination nodes are independent only within their traffic class. $\boldsymbol{U}_{\mathcal{A}}(t_k)$ and $\boldsymbol{U}_{\mathcal{P}}(t_k)$ are equivalent to source independence stratified according to access and peering nodes. There is independence in the destination nodes through $\boldsymbol{V}_{\mathcal{A}}(t_k)$ and $\boldsymbol{V}_{\mathcal{P}}(t_k)$. This form is equivalent to the generalized gravity model [46,47], a successor to the gravity model [45], where independence is only assumed within each class of traffic, leading to the notion of *conditional independence.*

Providing information on traffic classes is a natural method to include additional data, and increase the rank of the matrices if such is seen to be too low in some problems.

General constraints: The constraints we have considered only scratch the surface of all possible constraints on TMs, for instance, nonlinear constraints. In the examples above, it is assumed that the information is given without error. If one wasn't confident about the mean information of the TM, say, a mean squared error (Frobenius norm) constraint could be used, *i.e.,*

$$\mathbb{E}\|\boldsymbol{X}(t_k) - \bar{\mathbf{X}}\|_F \leq \epsilon,\ \forall k, \tag{18}$$

where $\epsilon > 0$ is a scalar value. Essentially, this expands the set of constraints from just linear to the more general set of convex constraints.

Convex constraints guarantee that (3) has a unique solution. Non-convex constraints may possibly arise in certain applications. In this case, admissible solutions have to be tested to find the global maximum of (3).

In practice, non-convex constraints are unlikely for WANs. In fact, *a priori* information from measurements can often be expressed as simple linear constraints, since linear network measurements are easier to implement (*e.g.,* internal router byte counts or SNMP measurements). Linear constraints, besides guaranteeing the existence of the MaxEnt model, typically result in simple models with closed forms, so generating these models are easy despite the high dimensionality of $\boldsymbol{\mathcal{X}}$. However, in data centers, non-convex constraints might arise due to entry sparsity and clustering constraints of the server-to-server TMs [1,2,16].

Nonlinear constraints are unlikely to lead to analytically tractable closed forms of the distribution, but numerical optimization methods can be used to compute the Lagrange multipliers of (4) instead.

4. PROPERTIES

4.1 Model properties

We briefly remark about the models' connection to the axioms of MaxEnt. The seminal work of Shore and Johnson [34] viewed MaxEnt as a natural consequence of four (desirable) inference axioms:

A1 *uniqueness*: the solution of the inference problem must be unique,

A2 *consistent*: either the optimal solution from a finer set of constraints must also be an admissible solution in a coarser set of constraints, or there is no solution at all in the finer set,

A3 *system independence*: information on several independent systems can be accounted either jointly, or considered for each system separately, and

A4 *subset independence*: information of independent subsystems (*i.e.,* in a system) can be accounted either jointly over the whole system, or separately for each subsystem.

These axioms explicitly define the assumptions our synthesis models satisfy. Generally, modeling relies heavily on two principles: *parsimony* of parameters and *independence* between components. Both are inherent in MaxEnt: parsimony is achieved by eliminating extraneous assumptions, and information of components (and subcomponents) are considered separately, in the absence of evidence that proves otherwise.

Thus, given convex constraints, **Axiom A1** guarantees a unique model. Models only get more refined as new information is given, by **Axiom A2**. The independence between the spatial and temporal processes arise due to **Axiom A3**, since no correlation information between the spatial and temporal processes are known.

As an example, consider model (17). By **Axiom A3**, each traffic class is an independent system. Since the ingress and egress traffic of each traffic class is known, by **Axiom A4**, the source and destination in each traffic class are separated into subsystems. We then have the notion of a hierarchical independence in the model: independence between traffic classes (independent systems) and conditional independence within a class (independent subsystems).

4.2 Computational issues

Generating ensembles of TMs could be surprisingly computationally expensive. For instance, given an arbitrary correlation structure, generating even simple normally distributed RVs would require specification of an N^4M^2 covariance matrix, which might then need to be inverted (depending on the method of generation).

Decomposing the correlation structure, and recomposing via simple matrix and vector products leads to efficient methods for building the complete spatiotemporal correlation structure without ever having to represent this in memory.

Moreover, in our models, the distributions follow that of (4), *i.e.,* the exponential family of distributions. With simple constraints, we need only generate classical distributions such as the exponential distribution, which can be simply generated via von Neumann's inverse method [12], with a very low computational cost.

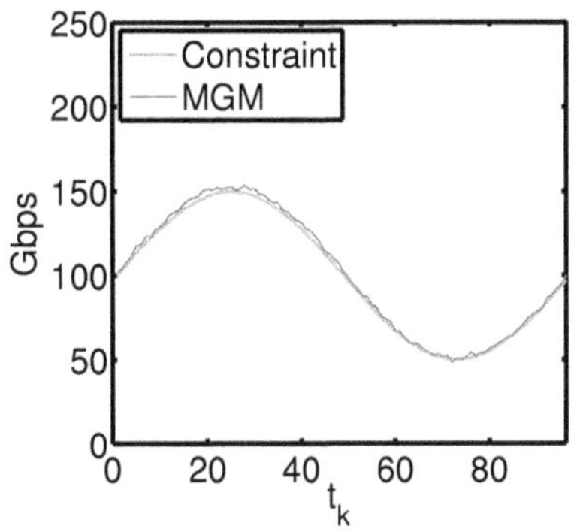

(a) PM: 1.5, $\sigma^2 = 1$, $\sigma_p^2 = 1$

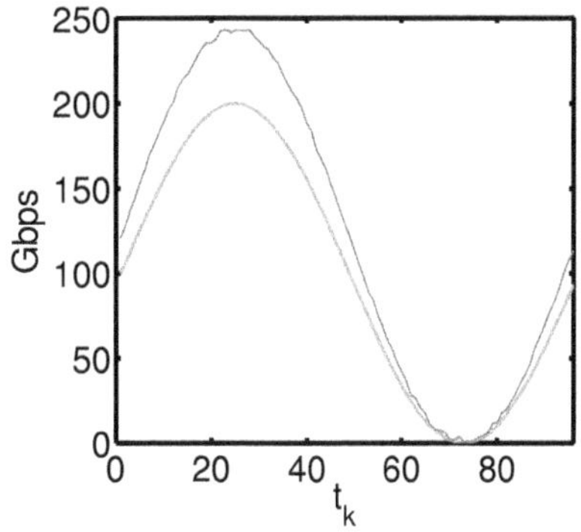

(b) PM: 2, $\sigma^2 = 10$, $\sigma_p^2 = 1$

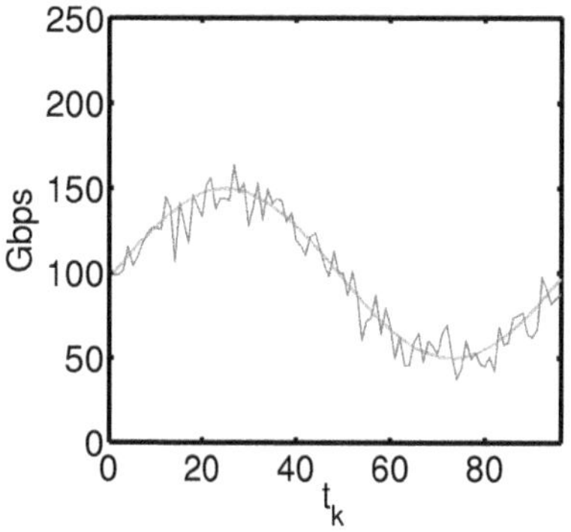

(c) PM: 1.5, $\sigma^2 = 1$, $\sigma_p^2 = 100$

Figure 2: *Total traffic for one day of the MGM with $\sigma^2 = \{1, 10\}$, $\sigma_p^2 = \{1, 100\}$, and PM ratios 1.5 and 2.*

For more complicated distributions, we advocate the use of the Hamiltonian Monte Carlo (HMC) [29], as the method has the closest relationship to the exponential family (4). For instance, the multivariate truncated normal distribution is more efficiently generated via HMC [26] compared to the standard Metropolis-Hastings technique (further supported by our numerical experiments). HMC also avoids random walks, so sampling from the distribution is far more efficient than other canonical MCMC methods.

In addition, the independence property (**Axioms A3** and **A4**), enables parallelization: independent model components can be generated separately. For instance, each independent traffic class can be synthesized in parallel, then combined to form the model.

4.3 An Example

Here, we demonstrate the synthesis of a series of TMs from the MGM. To generate MGM, recall that we need three components: the average incoming and outgoing PoP traffic $\mathbf{c}$ and $\mathbf{r}$ respectively and the total traffic $T(t_k)$ for times $k = 0, 1, \cdots, M-1$. We set $N = 20$ and $M = 672$, which corresponds to 7 days with one hour intervals.

The constraint for the temporal component is a simple one: a sinusoid with the frequency corresponding to a daily cycle. This is a rough approximation of actual traffic, where peak traffic occur around mid-day and troughs at night. The component has two parameters: the *mean traffic* over the synthesis interval and the *peak-to-mean (PM) ratio, i.e.,* how high is the sinusoid's peak relative to the mean traffic. While simple, this approach has been used to test protocols for power-aware routers [9].

The constraints $\bar{\mathbf{r}}$ and $\bar{\mathbf{c}}$ are set as proportions of the mean traffic $\bar{T} = \frac{1}{M}\sum_{k=0}^{M-1} T(t_k)$, *i.e.,* $\bar{r}_i = f_i\bar{T}$ and $\bar{c}_j = f_j\bar{T}$. The fractions f_i are non-negative and $\sum_{i=1}^{N} f_i = 1$, and they are generated randomly. We use the truncated normal distribution for the spatial and temporal components so as to allow control of their variations. Independence between the components allows them to be generated separately by the HMC.

Figure 2 presents the total traffic cycle for a day. Note that the total traffic of the synthetic TMs vary around the shape of the sinusoid. In Figure 2(b), increasing the PM ratio from 1.5 to 2 results in a much larger total traffic, as expected. The larger spatial variation ($\sigma^2 = 10$) will cause large "swings" in traffic due to a larger variation in the starting point *i.e.,* the random gravity model, for each run. As we vary σ_p^2 from 1 to 100, the generated traffic becomes "noisier", so the total traffic has more variations (Figure 2(c)). Note that the constraints will be satisfied over whole ensembles of the generated TMs, not necessarily in a single run.

Here, and in the examples to follow the TMs were generated on a machine with a 3.06 GHz processor and 4 GB of RAM with both models coded in `Matlab`. Generating the TMs for this example took on average less than a second. At $M = 2,016$ in the next section, both MGM and NCIM took about a second.

4.4 Model Analysis

Here, we want to know if our models replicate real traffic properties, such as low-rank behavior. The models we test are the MGM and the NCIM with timezone information (see §3.1).

We isolate the traffic components of the generated TMs via PCA. PCA was used to analyze traffic in [19, 20] to show that there are three types of components of OD flows, described in §3.4.

MGM: To construct constraint (8), we extracted the 23 largest Fourier coefficients from Abilene's total traffic [23], over a week starting 1st March 2003, measured in 5-minute intervals, *i.e.,* $M = 2,016$. Besides the coefficients, all other inputs, such as the mean row sums, of the model were computed from the Abilene data.

NCIM: Base constraints $\tilde{r}(t_k)$ and $\tilde{c}(t_k)$ $\forall k$ (time averages $\tilde{r}$ and $\tilde{c}$) follow cycles derived from 23 Fourier coefficients from the traffic of a PoP belonging to the Abilene network located in New York (NY) over the

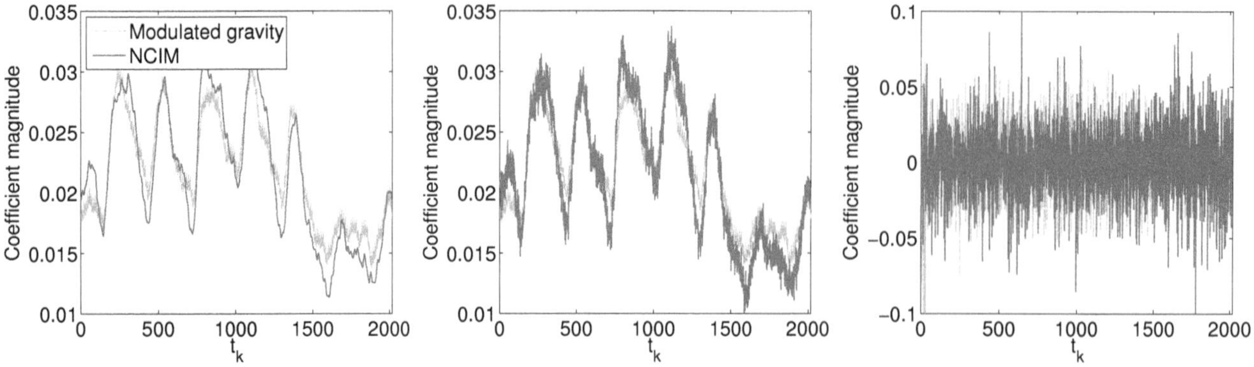

(a) Largest component, $\sigma^2 = 10^{-5}$ (b) Largest component, $\sigma^2 = 10$ (c) Smallest component, $\sigma^2 = 10^{-5}$

Figure 3: *Largest and smallest PCA components of the MGM and NCIM where 23 Fourier coefficients were extracted from Abilene's traffic. Both models were generated from multivariate truncated normal distributions with covariance matrix* $\mathbf{\Sigma_r} = \mathbf{\Sigma_c} = \sigma^2 \mathbf{I}_N$*, and* $\sigma_p^2 = \sigma^2$*. Control of the spatial and temporal variations is achieved by tuning* σ^2*. Here, two examples are shown with* $\sigma^2 = \{10^{-5}, 10\}$*.*

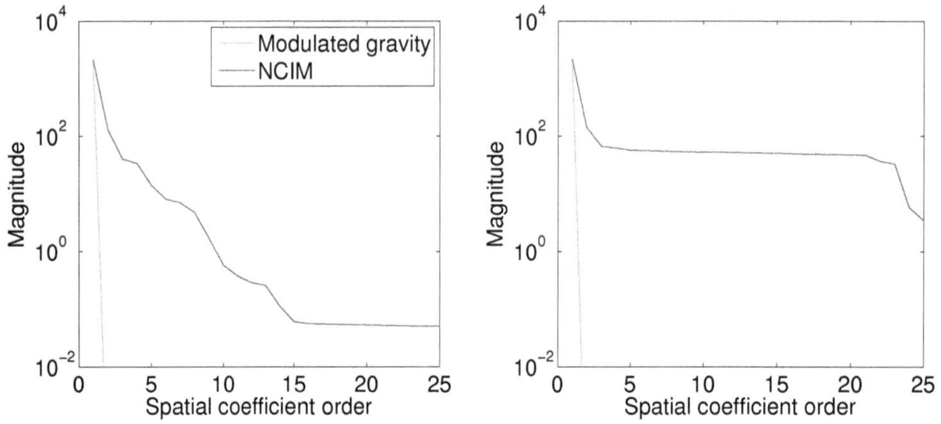

(a) $\sigma^2 = 10^{-5}$ (b) $\sigma^2 = 10$

Figure 4: *Spatial PCA coefficients (25 out of* $N^2 = 144$*) of the MGM and NCIM with variation control provided by* $\sigma^2 = \{10^{-5}, 10\}$*. Only coefficient values above* 10^{-2} *are shown for clarity. Note the log scale of the y-axis. The MGM is single rank, while the NCIM is almost full rank, with a handful of coefficients possessing large magnitudes.*

same duration as before. All other constraints are delayed relative to the NY PoP. For instance, the traffic of the Los Angeles (LA) PoP, is delayed by 3 hours, since LA time is 3 hours behind NY time. The row and column sums are scaled by $r_i/\tilde{r}$ and $c_j/\tilde{c}$, $\forall i, j$, since time averages r_i and c_j are known. Conservation of traffic implies $\bar{s}(t_k) = \sum_i r_i(t_k) = \sum_j c_j(t_k)$.

Both models' spatial and temporal variations are controlled through σ^2, by setting $\mathbf{\Sigma_r} = \mathbf{\Sigma_c} = \sigma^2 \mathbf{I}_N$ and $\sigma_p^2 = \sigma^2$.

Intuitively, we expect the MGM to be rank-1, so it would be too simple to replicate the properties of real traffic. The NCIM would then be a better choice since it would still be low-rank, but with enough variations to approximate a real TM process, since real TMs are unlikely to be rank-1.

Figure 3 shows the coefficients of the PCA components of the MGM and the NCIM with $\sigma^2 = \{10^{-5}, 10\}$. For the MGM, we find that only the first component (with the largest score) has a strong cyclic behavior. Though not shown here, the cyclic behavior persisted to more than one component for the NCIM, which is closer to real traffic (such as Abilene's) compared to the MGM. Smaller components of both models behave similar to white noise, *e.g.,* the smallest component in Figure 3(c).

In Figure 3(b), once $\sigma^2 = 10$, we now find larger variation in the coefficient magnitudes of both models, though the diurnal cycles are still identifiable. Smaller components are also much noisier. Clearly, the models' components have parallels to the cyclic and noise-like components of OD flows [19, 20].

Figure 4 plots the spatial PCA coefficients of models. The contrast between both models is evident: the MGM is rank-1, as expected, while the NCIM has a larger rank. Incidentally, the largest coefficient of both models coincide with the contribution from the average gravity component $\bar{\mathbf{r}}\bar{\mathbf{c}}^{\mathrm{T}}/T$. The NCIM's rank increases as σ^2 increases because σ^2 increases the variety of generated TMs. We omitted showing the temporal PCA coefficients as they match the spatial coefficients [3].

What's interesting here is that just *differences in phase* between the row and column sums lead to a larger rank, rather than the addition of new traffic classes. This may explain the low-rank (but not single rank) behavior of real TMs observed by [19, 20, 48]. This relatively simple model reproduces complex properties such as cycles, noise-like components and low-rank behavior.

Overall, the NCIM's properties are closer to that of real TMs than the MGM, but clearly require more detailed information, *i.e.*, the PoP locations.

5. CASE STUDY

In our case study, we apply our TM synthesis methodology to PoP-level network topology generation.

Real world PoP-level topologies are far from random, as these topologies are *designed* depending on various factors [21] such as demographic and geographical constraints, traffic demand, the designer's experience, and financial costs. Real designs have large variability, with some as simple as a hub-and-spoke network, to more complex and meshy ones [17]. They generally do not reflect the properties of random graphs, such as the Erdös-Rényi [13] model, so a realistic topology generator must account for the above-mentioned factors.

Topology design requires the TM as an input as it determines the capacity of the links of a network. A popular choice is the gravity model [45], with several works employing a single instance of it [5, 21, 49].

First, we ask if using a series of TMs can help improve a network's robustness. "Robustness" here refers to *robustness to TM variation*, not network survival under node removals. Second, a key result of [5] was that topology design is largely unaffected by certain facets of TMs. However, their algorithm, Combined Optimized Layered Design (COLD), used the random gravity model [31]. We extend their work by using a wider range of TMs.

We modified COLD to accept a series of TMs by defining a new optimization scheme, though this new scheme is general enough to be applied elsewhere. As far as we are aware, there is no other work on designing topologies using a series of TMs with prescribed spatiotemporal properties.

Topology generation involves combinatorial optimization, so COLD applies a genetic algorithm as a heuristic to solve for the topology with the minimum cost, based on a function with four cost parameters:

- k_0-*cost*: cost for the existence of a link,
- k_1-*cost*: cost for the physical length of a link,
- k_2-*cost*: the bandwidth cost over the length of the link, factoring in operating expenses, initial expenditures on equipment *etc.*, and
- k_3-*cost*: complexity cost of a PoP with more than one link, called a non-leaf or *core* PoP.

Let $\mathcal{G}(N, E)$ be the set of all undirected graphs with N nodes and E links with sufficient capacity to carry the traffic. Let $\mathcal{N}_C$ be the set of non-leaf nodes *i.e.*, degree > 1 and $\mathbf{w} := \{w_i \,|\, i \in E\}$ be the bandwidth of the links in E. We test the *minimax scheme*, *i.e.*,

$$\min_{\mathcal{G}(N,E)} \max_{\mathbf{w} \in \mathcal{W}(\boldsymbol{\mathcal{X}})} \sum_{i \in E} \left(k_0 + k_1 \ell_i + k_2 \ell_i w_i \right) + k_3 |\mathcal{N}_C|,$$

where $\mathcal{W}(\boldsymbol{\mathcal{X}})$ is the space of all possible link loads computed over $\boldsymbol{\mathcal{X}}$, via OSPF (Open Shortest Path First) routing. The minimax scheme seems like an improvement as it factors in a range of TMs. We test this below.

5.1 Experiments and results

We first fix the locations of the PoPs in a 10 unit by 10 unit square with $N = 12$ PoPs, so randomness only enters via the input TMs. We then generated a week's worth of 5 minute interval TMs ($M = 2,016$) via the MGM (see §4.3) as input for COLD with the recommended settings [4].

We also tested minimax with the Independent Entries Model (IEM) with the constraint $\mathbb{E}[X_{i,j}(t_k)] = \alpha \bar{X}$ to control the size of each entry. Note that we tested the model with $\alpha = 1, 2, 4$, but all results were similar, so results from $\alpha = 1$ were omitted.

The NCIM discussed in §4.3 was tested too, but we obtained similar results to the MGM, so its results were omitted. We explain the reasons for this below.

We defined the *single peak* scheme, where only the TM with the largest total traffic out of the M TMs is chosen as input in the topology design process, to compete against the minimax scheme.

We measured the Global Clustering Coefficient (GCC) of the topologies generated by the schemes. The GCC is a metric on how well-connected (clustered) a PoP is to its neighbors. The more well-connected, the more choices OSPF has in routing traffic flows. The network would then be more robust to variations in the TM.

Figure 5 show the GCC for the minimax and single peak schemes under the MGM with $\sigma^2 = 10^{-5}$, and the minimax scheme via the IEM with $\alpha = 2$. Cost $k_0 = 5$ and $k_1 = 1$, while $k_3 = \{0.1, 1, 10\}$. Each data point on $k_2 = \{0, 0.1, 1, 10, 10^2, 10^3\}$ is an average of 20 trials.

The GCCs of minimax and the single peak schemes (under the MGM) almost match. As k_2 increases, the difference between minimax and the single peak almost vanishes as both topologies become clique-like. The GCC for the IEM is lower with larger variance, especially at low k_2. Even when $\sigma^2 = 10$ and $\alpha = 4$ in Figure 6, results were similar. We also computed other statistics such as the *average shortest paths* which decreases for all schemes and models as k_2 increases. How-

[3]Spatial and temporal PCA are singular value decompositions performed on $\boldsymbol{Y}\boldsymbol{Y}^{\mathrm{T}}$ and $\boldsymbol{Y}^{\mathrm{T}}\boldsymbol{Y}$ respectively.

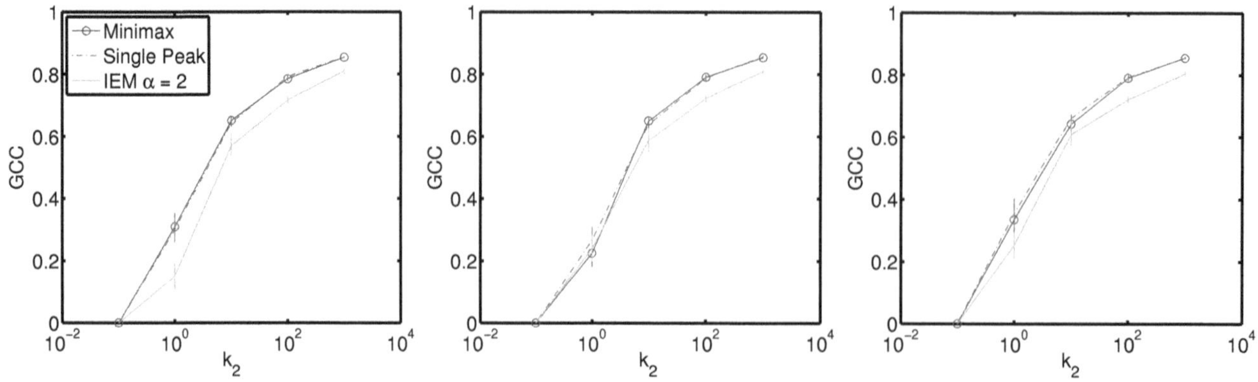

(a) $k_3 = 0.1$ (b) $k_3 = 1$ (c) $k_3 = 10$

Figure 5: *GCC for the topologies generated by the minimax and single peak schemes via the MGM and minimax with IEM, under three values of k_3. The MGM has $\sigma^2 = 10^{-5}$, and the IEM has $\alpha = 2$. Each data point is the average of 20 trials. The 95% confidence intervals appear as vertical bars. Confidence intervals for minimax under MGM are very small that they appear unnoticeable. For all models, GCC is 0 at $k_2 = 0$.*

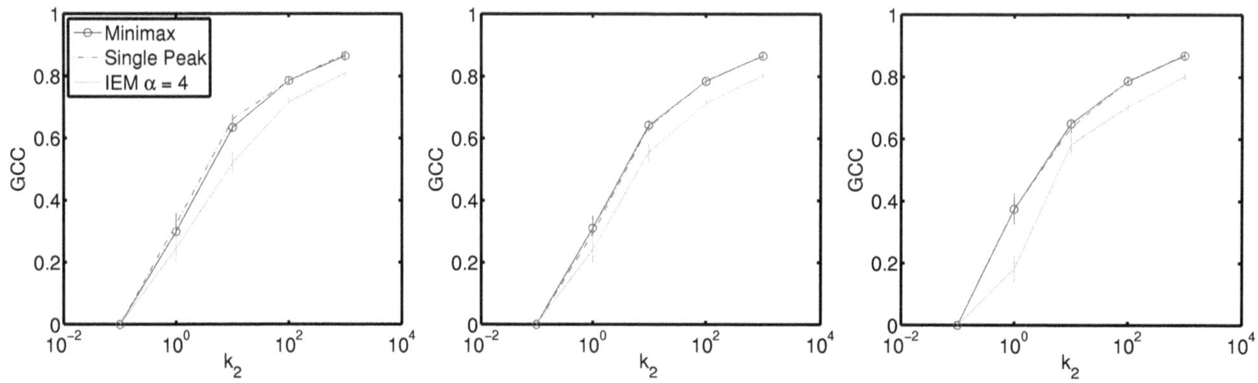

(a) $k_3 = 0.1$ (b) $k_3 = 1$ (c) $k_3 = 10$

Figure 6: *GCC for the topologies generated by the minimax and single peak schemes via the MGM and minimax with IEM, under three values of k_3. Both models have increased variance, i.e., the MGM has $\sigma^2 = 10$, and the IEM has $\alpha = 4$. Each data point is the average of 20 trials. The 95% confidence intervals appear as vertical bars. Confidence intervals for minimax under MGM are very small that they appear unnoticeable. For all models, GCC is 0 at $k_2 = 0$.*

ever, topologies under the MGM consistently have lower average shortest paths than the IEM topologies, suggesting better robustness for the former.

The implication here is that peak TMs dominate the overall topology design. The contrast between the MGM and the IEM topologies is due to the larger peak TMs generated by the MGM. Another highlight is that the minimax topologies show very little variation (unnoticeable 95% confidence intervals) compared to the single peak. Interestingly, COLD is using a distribution of peak TMs to converge on a design that is robust to a much wider range of TMs.

We summarize two key lessons. First, PoP-level topology design is largely unaffected by TMs, in line with the result in [5]. TMs have an effect through k_2 but k_2 has relatively minor impact. This is seen through the little variation in the results even though variance in the models were increased by increasing σ^2 and α. More extreme TMs with entries sampled from the Pareto distribution (which has heavy tails), studied by [5], also had little impact on topology generation.

Second, only peak TMs matter in improving the robustness of a network. This is by no means surprising, as it is standard practice to design networks using peak TMs. As the single peak scheme was competitive with the minimax scheme, average case TMs are not required. Instead, it would be better to use several worse case TMs as input into the design. Models with little variation such as the IEM are not useful here, in contrast to the MGM (and similarly, NCIM) which do generate peak TMs.

6. CONCLUSION

Synthesis of TMs with prescribed spatiotemporal properties is a challenging problem. A big obstacle is the lack of publicly available data for researchers. Another important issue is controllability, as researchers require a way to generate ensembles of TMs with constraints to test network algorithms and protocols.

Our approach goes back to first principles to avoid the measure-then-model paradigm by applying the principle of maximum entropy. MaxEnt allows for control of the TM properties by setting appropriate constraints on them, while avoiding extraneous assumptions. Our models are controllable and satisfy several desirable characteristics, namely consistency and independence between model components. Despite their simplicity, they were able to replicate characteristics of real TMs such as low rank behavior.

We evaluated our models on an application: PoP-level network topology generation. We modified COLD, a topology generator, to accept a series of TMs with prescribed spatiotemporal characteristics. PoP-level topology generation turns out to be largely unaffected by TMs. We also found that only peak TMs are useful in designing networks that are robust to TM variations. Thus, the common practice of using busy period TMs to design topologies is an excellent strategy.

Future work will focus on developing an algorithm for sampling maximum entropy distributions handling general constraints *e.g.,* correlation constraints and cyclostationarity, and studying the TMs of data centers.

Acknowledgments

The work was supported by the Australian Research Council (ARC) grant DP110103505. We thank our shepherd, Anja Feldmann and the anonymous reviewers for their feedback, eResearch South Australia (eRSA) for providing computational resources used in the experiments, and Rhys Bowden for help with COLD.

7. REFERENCES

[1] T. Benson, A. Akella, and D. A. Maltz. Network traffic characteristics of data centers in the wild. In *Proc. ACM SIGCOMM Internet Measurement Conference (IMC)*, pages 267–280, November 2010.

[2] T. Benson, A. Anand, A. Akella, and M. Zhang. MicroTE: Fine grained traffic engineering for data centers. In *Proc. ACM SIGCOMM CoNEXT*, pages 1–12, December 2011.

[3] V. Bharti, P. Kankar, L. Setia, G. Gürsun, A. Lakhina, and M. Crovella. Inferring invisible traffic. In *Proc. ACM SIGCOMM CoNEXT*, pages 22:1–22:12, 2010.

[4] R. Bowden. COLD: PoP-level topology generator. https://github.com/rhysbowden/COLD/, 2014.

[5] R. Bowden, M. Roughan, and N. Bean. COLD: PoP-level topology synthesis. In *Proc. ACM SIGCOMM CoNEXT*, pages 173–184, December 2014.

[6] R. S. Cahn. *Wide Area Network Design*. Morgan Kaufmann, 1998.

[7] A. Calaprice. *The Ultimate Quotable Einstein*. Princeton University Press, 2010.

[8] E. Candes and B. Recht. Exact matrix completion via convex optimization. *Found. of Comput. Math.*, 9:717–772, 2008.

[9] J. Chabarek, J. Sommers, P. Barford, C. Estan, D. Tsiang, and S. Wright. Power awareness in network design and routing. In *Proc. IEEE INFOCOM*, April 2008.

[10] T. M. Cover and J. A. Thomas. *Elements of Information Theory*. John Wiley and Sons, Inc., 2nd edition, 2006.

[11] N. Cressie and C. K. Wikle. *Statistics for Spatiotemporal Data*. Wiley, 2011.

[12] L. Devroye. *Non-Uniform Random Variate Generation*. Springer, 1986.

[13] P. Erdös and A. Rényi. On random graphs. *Publicationes Mathematicae*, 6:290–297, 1959.

[14] V. Erramilli, M. Crovella, and N. Taft. An independent-connection model for traffic matrices. In *Proc. ACM SIGCOMM Internet Measurement Conference (IMC)*, pages 251–256, October 2006.

[15] E. T. Jaynes. Information theory and statistical mechanics. *Phys. Rev.*, 106:620–630, May 1957.

[16] S. Kandula, S. Sengupta, A. Greenberg, P. Patel, and R. Chalken. The nature of datacenter traffic: Measurements and analysis. In *Proc. ACM SIGCOMM Internet Measurement Conference (IMC)*, pages 202–208, November 2009.

[17] S. Knight, H. Nguyen, N. Falkner, R. Bowden, and M. Roughan. The Internet Topology Zoo. *IEEE J. Select. Areas Commun.*, 29(9):1765–1775, October 2011.

[18] T. G. Kolda and B. W. Bader. Tensor decompositions and applications. *SIAM Review*, 51(3):455–500, September 2009.

[19] A. Lakhina, M. Crovella, and C. Diot. Diagnosing network-wide traffic anomalies. In *Proc. ACM SIGCOMM*, pages 219–230, September 2004.

[20] A. Lakhina, K. Papagiannaki, M. Crovella, C. Diot, E. D. Kolaczyk, and N. Taft. Structural analysis of network traffic flows. *SIGMETRICS Perform. Eval. Rev.*, 32(1):61–72, June 2004.

[21] L. Li, D. Alderson, W. Willinger, and J. Doyle. A first-principles approach to understanding the Internet's router-level topology. In *Proc. ACM SIGCOMM*, pages 3–14, August 2004.

[22] A. Medina, N. Taft, K. Salmatian, S. Bhattacharyya, and C. Diot. Traffic matrix estimation: Existing techniques and new directions. In *Proc. ACM SIGCOMM*, 2002.

[23] NLANR. Abilene Trace Data. http://pma.nlanr.net/Special/ipls3.html.

[24] A. Nucci, A. Sridharan, and N. Taft. The problem of synthetically generating IP traffic matrices:

Initial recommendations. *ACM Comput. Commun. Rev.*, 35:19–32, July 2005.

[25] K. N. Oikonomou. Analytic forms for most likely matrices derived from incomplete information. *Int. J. Systems Science*, 43(3):443–458, September 2010.

[26] A. Pakman and L. Paninski. Exact Hamiltonian Monte Carlo for truncated multivariate Gaussians. *J. Comput. Graph. Stat.*, 23(2):518–542, April 2014.

[27] S. Y. Park and A. K. Bera. Maximum entropy autoregressive conditional heteroskedasticity model. *J. Econometrics*, 150:219–230, 2009.

[28] R. B. Potts and R. M. Oliver. *Flows in Transportation Networks*. Academic Press, 1972.

[29] N. M. Radford. MCMC using Hamiltonian dynamics. In S. Brooks, A. Gelman, G. L. Jones, and X.-L. Meng, editors, *Handbook of Markov Chain Monte Carlo*, volume 31-32, pages 113–162. CRC Press, 2010.

[30] B. Recht, M. Fazel, and P. A. Parrilo. Guaranteed minimum–rank solutions of linear matrix equations via nuclear norm minimization. *SIAM Review*, 52(3):471–501, 2010.

[31] M. Roughan. Simplifying the synthesis of Internet traffic matrices. *ACM Comput. Commun. Rev.*, 35(5):93–96, 2005.

[32] M. Roughan. Robust network planning. In C. R. Kalmanek, S. Misra, and R. Yang, editors, *The Guide to Reliable Internet Services and Applications*, chapter 5, pages 137–177. Springer, 2010.

[33] M. Roughan, A. Greenberg, C. Kalmanek, M. Rumsewicz, J. Yates, and Y. Zhang. Experience in measuring backbone traffic variability: Models, metrics, measurements and meaning. In *Proc. ACM SIGCOMM Internet Measurement Conference (IMC)*, 2002.

[34] J. E. Shore and R. W. Johnson. Axiomatic derivation of the principle maximum entropy and the principle of minimum cross-entropy. *IEEE Trans. Info. Theory*, 26(1):26–37, January 1980.

[35] A. Soule, A. Lakhina, N. Taft, K. Papagiannaki, K. Salmatian, A. Nucci, M. Crovella, and C. Diot. Traffic matrix: Balancing measurements, inference and modeling. In *Proc. ACM SIGMETRICS*, pages 362–373, June 2005.

[36] A. Soule, A. Nucci, R. Cruz, E. Leonardi, and N. Taft. How to identify and estimate the largest traffic matrix elements in a dynamic environment. *SIGMETRICS Perform. Eval. Rev.*, 32(1):73–84, June 2004.

[37] S. M. Stigler. *The history of statistics: The measurement of uncertainty before 1900.* Belknap Press of Harvard University Press, 1986.

[38] P. Tune and M. Roughan. Internet traffic matrices: A primer. In H. Haddadi and O. Bonaventure, editors, *Recent Advances in Networking, Vol. 1.* ACM SIGCOMM, August 2013.

[39] P. Tune and M. Roughan. Maximum entropy traffic matrix synthesis. In *ACM SIGCOMM MAMA*, June 2014. http://tinyurl.com/kk7757k.

[40] P. Tune and M. Roughan. Network design sensitivity analysis. In *Proc. ACM SIGMETRICS*, pages 449–461, June 2014.

[41] S. Uhlig, B. Quoitin, J. Lepropre, and S. Balon. Providing public intradomain traffic matrices to the research community. *ACM Comput. Commun. Rev.*, 36(1):83–86, January 2006.

[42] Y. Vardi. Network Tomography: Estimating source-destination traffic intensities from link data. *J. Am. Statist. Assoc.*, 91:365–377, 1996.

[43] A. Zellner and R. A. Highfield. Calculation of maximum entropy distributions and approximation of marginal posterior distributions. *J. Econom.*, 37:195–209, 1988.

[44] Y. Zhang, Z. Ge, A. Greenberg, and M. Roughan. Network anomography. In *Proc. ACM SIGCOMM Internet Measurement Conference (IMC)*, Berkeley, California, USA, October 2005.

[45] Y. Zhang, M. Roughan, N. Duffield, and A. Greenberg. Fast accurate computation of large-scale IP traffic matrices from link loads. In *Proc. ACM SIGMETRICS*, pages 206–217, 2003.

[46] Y. Zhang, M. Roughan, C. Lund, and D. Donoho. An information-theoretic approach to traffic matrix estimation. In *Proc. ACM SIGCOMM*, pages 301–312, 2003.

[47] Y. Zhang, M. Roughan, C. Lund, and D. Donoho. Estimating Point-to-Point and Point-to-Multipoint traffic matrices: An information-theoretic approach. *IEEE/ACM Trans. Netw.*, 13(5):947–960, October 2005.

[48] Y. Zhang, M. Roughan, W. Willinger, and L. Qiu. Spatio-Temporal compressive sensing and Internet traffic matrices. In *Proc. ACM SIGCOMM*, pages 267–278, August 2009.

[49] R. Zhang-Shen and M. McKeown. Designing a predictable Internet backbone with Valiant load-balancing. In *Proceedings of the 13th International Conference on Quality of Service (IWQoS)*, pages 178–192, 2005.

Extractocol: Automatic Extraction of Application-level Protocol Behaviors for Android Applications

Hyunwoo Choi†*, Jeongmin Kim†*, Hyunwook Hong†, Yongdae Kim†
Jonghyup Lee‡, and Dongsu Han†
KAIST†, Gachon University‡

CCS Concepts

•Networks → Application layer protocols; •Security and privacy → *Software reverse engineering;*

Keywords

Android; protocol behaviors; static analysis

1. INTRODUCTION

Android app is an important class of today's Internet applications that generate roughly 40-50% of mobile Web and app traffic. More than 1.4 million Android apps are offered through Google's open market, and tens of thousands of new apps are added every month. However, very little information is known about their application protocol behaviors because they predominantly use proprietary protocols on top of HTTP [3, 6]. The problem is further exacerbated by the popular use of common data representation, such as JSON and XML, due to the popularity of REST-ful web services [5]. As a result, application protocols appear similar to each other, and analyzing them requires an in-depth characterization of each individual application. Despite this, the state of the art remains that even the problem of finger-printing the traffic they generate is extremely challenging [3, 6], let alone a full protocol analysis.

Our vision is to be able to automatically reconstruct the client's protocol state machine and the message format from the program binary. Being able to analyze network protocols provides not only intrinsic values, but also enables many new applications, such as protocol testing [4], flow classification, protocol normalization, and automatic proxying. To this end, we design a system, called Extractocol, that takes only the application binary as input and uses static program analysis. We specifically focus on automatically extracting the request-response formats and signatures for apps that use the popular HTTP protocol as transport. It extracts parts of application code (i.e., program slices) that either generate HTTP(S) requests or parse response messages and

*These authors contributed equally to this work.

SIGCOMM '15 August 17-21, 2015, London, United Kingdom

ACM ISBN 978-1-4503-3542-3/15/08.
DOI: http://dx.doi.org/10.1145/2785956.2790003

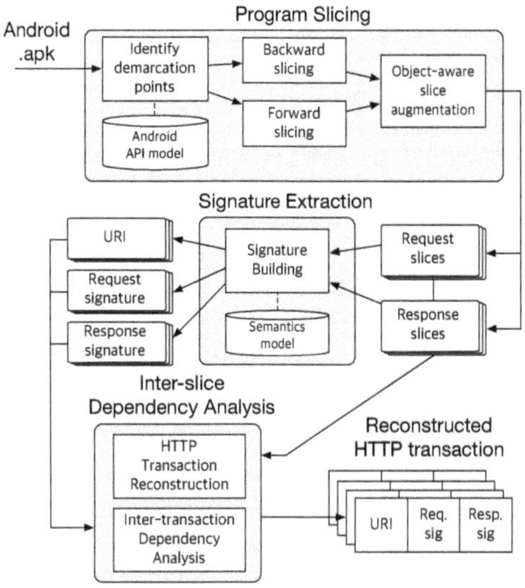

Figure 1: Design overview of Extractocol

applies a careful semantic analysis to extract message formats and signatures from the target program. In particular, it output regular expression (regex) signatures for each request (including URI, query string, request method, header, and body) and the corresponding response. It also partially reconstructs client state by tracking dependancies between messages.

In summary, this paper makes two key contributions:

- **Novel approach to Android application protocol analysis:** We present the first comprehensive protocol analysis framework for Android applications that is capable of extracting protocol behaviors, formats, and signatures, given an APK.
- **Working system prototype and its evaluation:** Our evaluation on 12 open-source demonstrates that Extractocol provides a rich and comprehensive characterization.

2. DESIGN

Figure 1 illustrates three main components of Extractocol: program slicing, signature extraction, and inter-slice dependency analysis.

Program slicing: We extend FlowDroid [2], a static taint analysis tool, to reconstruct the data dependencies arising from network I/O. We use this information to create request and response slices. A typical program contains many instructions other than protocol processing. Thus, Extractocol pre-processes the APK to extract code slices only related to protocol processing. The goal of this step is to output program slices that generate HTTP requests and process responses.

#	Request URI	Request Body
1	GET (http://www.reddit.com/api/info.json?)	-
2	GET (http://www.radioreddit.com/)(status.json)	-
3	POST (https://ssl.reddit.com/api/login)	(user=).*(&passwd=)(&api_type=json)
4	POST (http://www.reddit.com/api/)(unsave|save)	(id=).*(&uh=)(.*)
5	POST (http://www.reddit.com/api/vote)	(id=).*(&dir=).*(&uh=)(.*)
6	GET (.*)	(.*)

Dependency graph

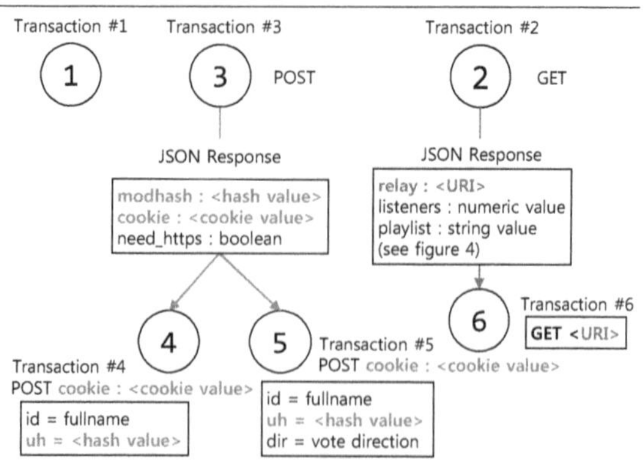

Figure 2: Reconstructed HTTP transactions and their dependency graph for Radio reddit

Signature extraction: The second phase takes the request/response slices as input and generates formats and signatures for each. To extract signatures, Extractocol performs analysis using semantic models for a set of commonly used Android and Java APIs for protocol processing, such as `java.lang.String` and `java.net`. It then outputs signatures for request URIs and request/response bodies as well as the request method and additional HTTP headers used.

Inter-slice dependency analysis: Finally, Extractocol reconstructs a complete transaction by pairing a request URI with its corresponding response. It also infers the relationship between HTTP transactions. In particular, it infers which part of request URI or body is potentially derived from prior responses. The key idea is to identify inter-slice relationships between the request and response slices. For this, Extractocol performs novel inter-slice data flow analysis and addresses a number of issues in handling subtle, but complex inter-slice dependencies that arise due to code reuse.

3. EVALUATION

We use 12 apps with network permissions from an open source app repository (F-Droid) [1]. We obtain the ground truth by carefully inspecting the **source code**. We also collect traffic traces of all HTTP(S) transactions using **manual UI-fuzzing**, which often requires manual interventions, such as signing up and logging in for services. Extractocol took 14.2 minutes to analyze all 12 apps with the optional features. Table 1 shows the ground truth number of HTTP messages by their request method and message type (e.g., request or response body) and the fraction of signatures identified by Extractocol. To demonstrate Extractocol's effectiveness in characterizing app's protocol behavior, we perform a case study on radio reddit. Radio reddit is an online music streaming client that allows users to choose radio stations and vote on or save songs using their reddit accounts. Figure 2 shows a complete analysis result with six transactions; five of them use HTTP, while login request uses HTTPS. It also shows a dependency graph identified by Extractocol. Extractocol identifies that login request (#3) includes three fields, and its response is a JSON object including "modhash" and "cookie" as keys. They use the "modhash" value in the "uh" field, and add the "cookie" value to their request headers.

4. CONCLUSION AND FUTURE WORK

This work presents Extractocol, a framework for analyzing HTTP(S)-based application protocol behaviors for Android applications. Unlike previous approaches, Extractocol only uses the application binary as input to reconstruct application-specific HTTP-based interactions using static program analysis. It combines static taint analysis and semantic analysis to provide a comprehensive characterization of application protocol behaviors. We believe Extractocol and its approach can serve as a basis for generic protocol analysis (other than HTTP) for Android applications. Finally, we plan to evaluate it on a large set of commercial applications.

App	Request			Response	#Pair
	GET	POST	Body	Body	
ADP	2 (100%)	1 (100%)	1 (100%)	1 (100%)	1 (100%)
AXV	2 (100%)	-	-	2 (100%)	2 (100%)
BLP	1 (100%)	-	-	1 (100%)	1 (100%)
DIW	1 (100%)	-	-	1 (100%)	1 (100%)
LNT	2 (100%)	-	-	1 (100%)	1 (100%)
QBT	3 (100%)	13 (100%)	13 (100%)	3 (100%)	3 (100%)
RRD	3 (100%)	3 (100%)	3 (100%)	4 (100%)	4 (100%)
RDN	3 (100%)	3 (100%)	-	6 (100%)	6 (100%)
TWT	-	11 (100%)	11 (100%)	8 (100%)	8 (100%)
TZM	2 (100%)	-	-	1 (100%)	1 (100%)
WLB	1 (100%)	-	-	1 (100%)	1 (100%)
WTN	2 (100%)	-	-	2 (100%)	2 (100%)

Table 1: Coverage: Ground truth # of request/response and % of identified signatures

5. ACKNOWLEDGMENTS

This research was supported in part by an Institute for Information communications Technology Promotion (IITP) grant funded by the Korean government (MSIP) (No. B0126-15-1078), and by Next-Generation Information Computing Development Program through the National Research Foundation of Korea (NRF) funded by the Ministry of Science, ICT & Future Planning (No. NRF-2014M3C4A7030648).

6. REFERENCES

[1] Free & open source app repository, https://f-droid.org.

[2] S. Arzt, S. Rasthofer, C. Fritz, E. Bodden, A. Bartel, J. Klein, Y. Le Traon, D. Octeau, and P. McDaniel. Flowdroid: Precise context, flow, field, object-sensitive and lifecycle-aware taint analysis for android apps. In *Proc. ACM SIGPLAN PLDI*, June 2014.

[3] S. Dai, A. Tongaonkar, X. Wang, A. Nucci, and D. Song. Networkprofiler: Towards automatic fingerprinting of android apps. In *Proc. IEEE INFOCOM*, 2013.

[4] N. K. R. M. T. M. R. G. Luis Pedrosa, Ari Fogel. Spa: A general framework for systematic protocol analysis. In *Proc. USENIX NSDI*, 2015.

[5] L. Richardson and S. Ruby. *Restful Web Services.* O'Reilly, first edition, 2007.

[6] A. Tongaonkar, R. Keralapura, and A. Nucci. Challenges in network application identification. In *Proc. USENIX LEET*, 2012.

Rule-Level Data Plane Monitoring With Monocle*

Peter Perešíni
EPFL
Lausanne, Switzerland
peter.peresini@epfl.ch

Maciej Kuźniar
EPFL
Lausanne, Switzerland
maciej.kuzniar@epfl.ch

Dejan Kostić
KTH Royal Institute of Technology
Stockholm, Sweden
dmk@kth.se

ABSTRACT

We present Monocle, a system that systematically monitors the network data plane, and verifies that it corresponds to the view that the SDN controller builds and tries to enforce in the switches. Our evaluation shows that Monocle is capable of fine-grained per-rule monitoring for the majority of rules. In addition, it can help controllers to cope with switches that exhibit transient inconsistencies between their control plane and data plane states.

CCS Concepts

•**Networks → Network reliability; Network monitoring;**

1. INTRODUCTION

Ensuring network reliability in today's networks is paramount — customers require tight service-level guarantees such as 99.99% uptime, guaranteed bandwidth, bounded latency, *etc.*. This places network operators in a difficult situation where they need to respond to problems almost immediately. To do so, the network operators constantly monitor their networks for anomalies so as to be able to pinpoint their root causes.

One of the main reasons for faulty networks is the mismatch between the high-level network policy devised by the network operators and the actual data plane configuration in switch hardware which ultimately moves the packets around. Translation between the policy and configuration takes several steps and the desynchronization can happen at any point, starting from parsing the high level network policy down to programming ASIC hardware by the switch firmware.

Ensuring that the last step of this process, *i.e.*, checking if the controller view of the network corresponds to the data plane forwarding, is becoming increasingly important with the growing number of SDN switch vendors and switch models. In particular, failures at this level may range from transient inconsistencies (*e.g.*, switch reporting a rule was updated sooner than it happens in data plane [4,6]), through systematic problems (switches incorrectly implementing the specification, *e.g.*, ignoring priority field in OpenFlow [4]), to hardware failures (*e.g.*, bit-flips, line card not responding, *etc.*) and switch software bugs [8]), neither of which can be reliably detected in the control plane only.

Unfortunately, today, the choice of data plane monitoring tools is rather limited – operators use end-to-end tools (*e.g.*, ping, traceroute, *etc.*) or periodically collect switch forwarding statistics. We argue that these methods are insufficient – while ping/traceroute can detect broken end-to-end connections, it cannot localize the problem if the ICMP traffic is handled differently from TCP flows (*e.g.*, blacklisting based on TCP ports, *etc.*). Similarly, switch statistics do not tell exactly where the problem lies, only that there is something unusual. Finally, while recent research produced a number of new tools (HSA/Netplumber, VeriFlow, ATPG [1–3, 8]), they either work only in the control plane (the first three), or, in case of ATPG, too slow to identify problems as they happen in highly-dynamic SDN networks.

2. PROBLEM STATEMENT

Our goal is to provide fine-grained, per-rule monitoring of the network data plane state, and verify that this state corresponds to its control plane view. In particular, we want to detect all aforementioned error scenarios and precisely localize the problem to a particular switch flow table and problematic rule. As such, our ultimate requirement is to periodically exercise all rules that we expect to be in the data plane. Moreover, the solution should be online (*i.e.*, quickly adapt to the always-changing global forwarding state) and non-invasive (*i.e.*, monitoring should not require big changes to the network hardware, a controller or configuration).

Monocle is our approach to solving the presented problem. To meet our goal of verifying correspondence between control and data planes, our system needs to know the control-plane view of the state. We therefore implement Monocle as a proxy between SDN controller and its switches. This allows Monocle to intercept all rule modifications issued to any switch and maintain the expected global forwarding state installed in the network as well as the (expected) contents of flow tables in each switch. After determining the expected state of a switch, Monocle can compute packet headers that exercise rules on this switch. Finally, Monocle leverages its position as a proxy to inject these generated packets to the network and observe how they are treated (*i.e.*, where they get forwarded and how they are modified). Figure 1 summa-

*Work funded by the ERC project 259110

SIGCOMM '15 August 17-21, 2015, London, United Kingdom

ACM ISBN 978-1-4503-3542-3/15/08.
DOI: http://dx.doi.org/10.1145/2785956.2790012

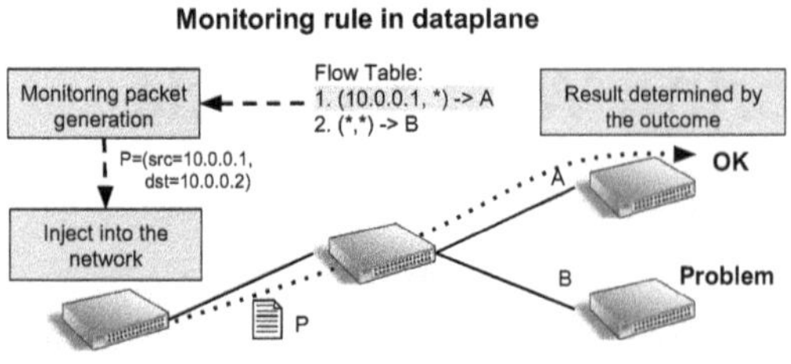

Figure 1: Overview of how data-plane monitoring works.

rizes a high level image of Monocle's operation. To detect if a rule is installed and behaves as expected, the system instructs the upstream switch to send a specially crafted monitoring packet toward the monitored switch. The downstream switch has a special catching rule that redirects the monitoring packet back to Monocle. By positioning our system as a proxy between the controller and the switches we do not require any hardware or software changes to either of them. The only modification is a small number of statically installed catching rules at each switch.

Although seemingly simple, the bulk of Monocle's complexity lies in generating the monitoring packets for arbitrary rules in switch flow tables in an online manner. Monocle leverages its knowledge of the flow tables to formulate a set of constraints that the monitoring probe has to satisfy. Without going into details, the constraints take into account: *(i)* structure of rule overlaps, including rule priorities, and *(ii)* what actions are associated with each rule (including header rewriting, packet dropping or forwarding to multiple ports).

The important part of Monocle design is the choice of converting constraints relevant for a given monitored rule into a form understood by off-the-shelf satisfiability (SMT/SAT) solvers and generating monitoring packets for each rule independently. This allows us to quickly solve the monitoring packet constraints for a single rule (less than 5 ms), in contrast to ATPG which uses header space analysis to compute monitoring packets for all rules in a single run (taking minutes to hours). The speed with which Monocle can generate monitoring packets enables new use-cases, namely monitoring rule updates as they happen in data plane as well monitoring networks undergoing frequent updates.

3. Monocle

Finally, Monocle applies a packet generation library to create real packets based on the solver's output. To collect monitoring outcomes, Monocle requires all downstream switches to recognize the monitoring packets. Since we aim to monitor all switches separately, each of them is being monitored and simultaneously collecting monitoring outcomes of all its neighbors. To prevent catching rules from interfering with monitoring, the catching rules have to differ between switches. To reduce the number of these additional rules per switch, we formulate the catching-rule selection as a well-known vertex coloring problem. As a result, our solution requires less than 10 additional rules per switch in a network containing over 10000 switches.

4. EVALUATION

There are two important questions that we need to confirm that a system like Monocle is feasible. First, can it find probes that monitor a significant fraction of rules in the network, and second, can it generate them at a rate high enough to keep up with the network reconfiguration speed? Our results show that both answers are positive. Using two real data sets: Stanford backbone router "yoza" configuration [2] and ACL rules from a large-scale campus network [7], we show that Monocle finds monitoring packets for 89% and 97% of all rules respectively and needs on average 1.44 and 4.13 ms to generate a single probe. Moreover, we verify that sending probes at a rate of 1000/s has no negative impact on rule modification rate of hardware switches.

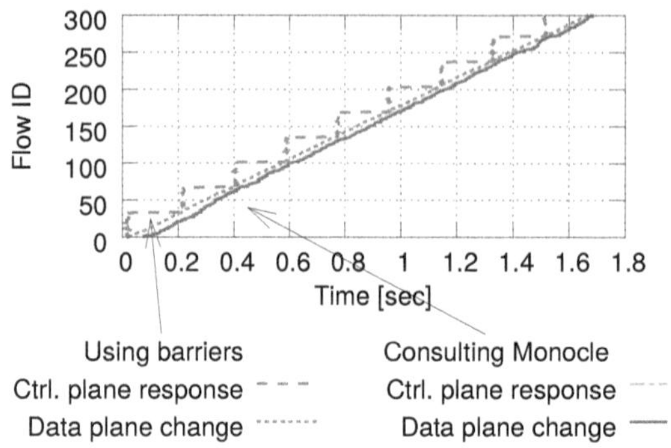

Figure 2: Finally, to demonstrate usefulness of Monocle and its online nature, we showcase how it can cooperate with the controller to provide reliable network updates. In particular, while network controllers may try to perform consistent updates of flows [5], some existing hardware switches allow a transient period during which there is inconsistency between what is reported by the control plane, and what happens in the data plane This effectively ruins the consistency guarantees as the controller might modify an upstream switch prematurely and thus send the traffic to a not-yet-ready rule (causing a temporary black hole in our experiment). By monitoring rule updates, Monocle helps the controller to reliably identify when the rules are ready in the data plane and avoids transient inconsistencies.

5. REFERENCES

[1] P. Kazemian, M. Chang, H. Zeng, G. Varghese, N. McKeown, and S. Whyte. Real Time Network Policy Checking using Header Space Analysis. In *NSDI*, 2013.

[2] P. Kazemian, G. Varghese, and N. McKeown. Header Space Analysis: Static Checking for Networks. In *NSDI*, 2012.

[3] A. Khurshid, X. Zou, W. Zhou, M. Caesar, and P. B. Godfrey. VeriFlow: Verifying Network-Wide Invariants in Real Time. In *NSDI*, 2013.

[4] M. Kuźniar, P. Perešíni, and D. Kostić. What You Need to Know About SDN Flow Tables. In *PAM*, 2015.

[5] R. Mahajan and R. Wattenhofer. On Consistent Updates in Software Defined Networks. In *HotNets*, 2013.

[6] C. Rotsos, N. Sarrar, S. Uhlig, R. Sherwood, and A. W. Moore. OFLOPS: An Open Framework for OpenFlow Switch Evaluation. In *PAM*, 2012.

[7] D. E. Taylor. Survey and Taxonomy of Packet Classification Techniques. *ACM Comput. Surv.*, 37(3):238–275, Sept. 2005.

[8] H. Zeng, P. Kazemian, G. Varghese, and N. McKeown. Automatic Test Packet Generation. In *CoNEXT*, 2012.

Santa: Faster Packet Delivery for Commonly Wished Replies

Florian Schmidt, Oliver Hohlfeld, René Glebke, Klaus Wehrle
Communication and Distributed Systems Group
RWTH Aachen University, Germany
{schmidt,hohlfeld,glebke,wehrle}@comsys.rwth-aachen.de

ABSTRACT

Increasing network speeds challenge the packet processing performance of networked systems. This can mainly be attributed to processing overhead caused by the split between the kernel-space network stack and user-space applications. To mitigate this overhead, we propose Santa, an application agnostic kernel-level cache of frequent requests. By allowing user-space applications to offload frequent requests to the kernel-space, Santa offers drastic performance improvements and unlocks the speed of kernel-space networking for legacy server software without requiring extensive changes.

CCS Concepts

•**Networks** → **Programming interfaces;**

1. THE QUEST FOR SPEED

Increasing line rates challenge the packet processing performance of current network stacks. These performance challenges can be attributed to two main overhead factors: *i)* memory allocations and copy operations, and *ii)* overheads by performing system calls and the required context switches. These costs particularly take effect at high line rates (e.g., multiple 10G interfaces) where many (small) requests need to be processed (e.g., DNS traffic). Thus, drastic increases in network line speeds significantly challenge packet processing in commodity hard- and software where CPU speeds do not scale with increasing line speeds.

One line of research addresses this problem by proposing kernel optimizations. Proposed optimizations involve to *i)* channelize processing [4], to *ii)* slim down socket buffers [2], or to *iii)* use batching to reduce overheads [5].

More radical approaches to tackle this challenge involve (partially or completely) bypassing the kernel by either *i)* offloading packet processing to specialized hardware (see e.g., [2, 7]) or by *ii)* shifting packet processing to user-land stacks (see e.g., [3, 6, 8]). The latter represents an active line of research that achieved drastic performance increases and lower CPU footprints by avoiding kernel based packet processing overheads [6]. These advances have proved to be useful for accelerating software switches [9], HTTP [3,6] and DNS servers [6].

However, the drastic performance increases of user-land stacks also come at a price. Concretely, they require specialized microstacks running in dedicated applications to show their full potential. We complement this work by proposing a middle ground. That is, we trade off some of the potential performance increases of microstacks for the ability to rely on the well-established and full-featured network stack implementation of Linux. Instead of moving all network stack logic to the application, we enable applications to move parts of their logic into the stack. In contrast to earlier approaches that implement full server-*specific* logic in kernel space (e.g., khttpd [1]), we propose Santa, an application-*agnostic* mechanism allowing user-level server applications to offload requests to common replies to a kernel-level cache.

We exemplify the benefit of Santa by using a standard DNS server and offloading frequent DNS requests to our kernel cache. In this evaluation, we achieve drastic improvements in both response time (almost 2× faster) and throughput (up to 4× higher) even with a standard stack. Thus, Santa unlocks the speed of kernel-space networking for legacy server software without requiring extensive changes or specialized implementations. By this, we aim to pave the way for new packet processing pipelines and complement the ongoing discussion on user-level network stacks.

2. SANTA ARCHITECTURE

We show the Santa architecture in Figure 1 (c) and compare it to *(a)* a traditional network stack and *(b)* netmap [8] as a well-known approach to bypass the kernel for realizing user-land protocol stacks. The Santa architecture involves realizing a kernel-level cache that is instrumented by applications to offload replies to frequent requests. This way, we achieve performance increases by avoiding costly context switches to the user-space for frequent requests.

To enable reply offloading to the kernel cache, Santa extends the Linux kernel socket interface to enable applications to control the kernel-level cache. This cache control requires application modifications and comprises ways to install, update, and remove cache entries. Each cache entry includes a filter rule applied to incoming packets. If a rule matches, the kernel replies with a pre-cached response instead of forwarding the packet to the user-level process. Otherwise, the packet is handed over to the application via the socket interface, so that the server can create and send the reply.

Since the installed filter rules do not involve application

SIGCOMM '15 August 17-21, 2015, London, United Kingdom

ACM ISBN 978-1-4503-3542-3/15/08.
DOI: http://dx.doi.org/10.1145/2785956.2790014

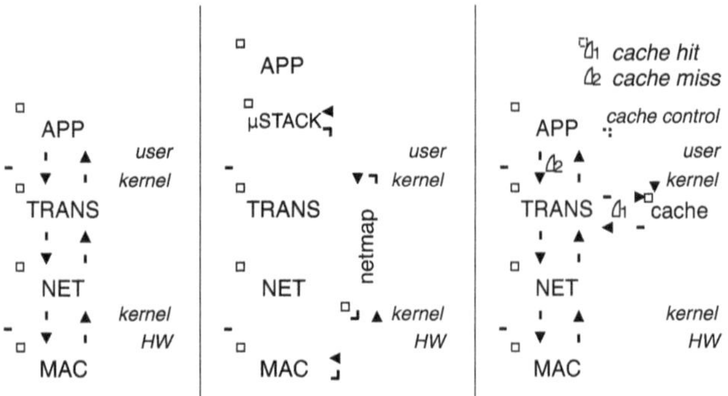

(a) Standard (b) Netmap (c) Santa

Figure 1: In a standard network stack, all packets are processed in both kernel and user space. Netmap bypasses the kernel to process packets in user space, requiring specialized microstacks. Santa provides a kernel cache to answer common requests without passing the packet to the application.

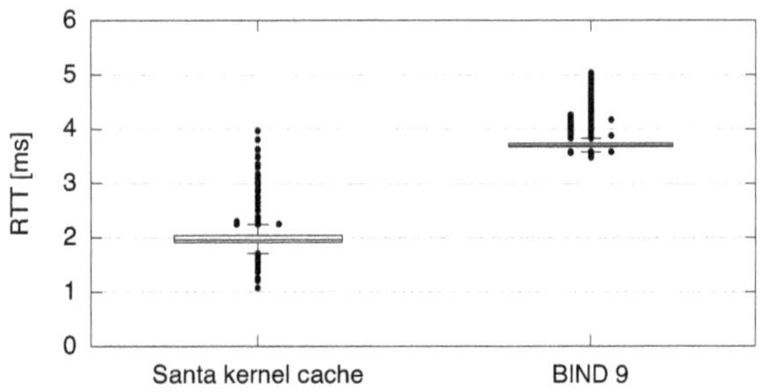

Figure 2: In a local network, the server's processing time forms a sizable part of the RTT. The Santa kernel cache provides significantly faster response times.

logic and match on packet contents, the Santa architecture is application agnostic. That is, every application can utilize the Santa API to offload packet processing to the kernel cache. In case that no cache items are installed, Santa behaves as a standard Linux kernel, i.e., all incoming packets get forwarded to the user-space process.

Santa is especially beneficial for applications that receive frequent requests that can be answered with pre-cached replies. A typical example application is DNS servers, where a small number of resource records is requested very frequently.

3. USE CASE EVALUATION: DNS SERVER

In our preliminary evaluation, we focus on accelerating BIND 9, a widely used DNS server.

Our experimental setup comprises one server (quad-core 3 GHz with 8 GB RAM) running the BIND 9 DNS server on top of our Santa kernel and four DNS clients with stock kernels generating DNS queries, connected via an Ethernet switch. Each machine is equipped with a 1 Gbit/s interface. We emulate a maximum-load scenario in which the clients send requests as fast as possible, saturating the link from the switch to the server. Figure 2 shows box plots of the round-trip time (RTT) distribution of requests, as seen by the client. Santa provides a significantly lower response time, with median values of 1.95 ms vs. 3.7 ms.

In a second set of experiments, we sent requests that hit the kernel cache with a certain probability (0%, 25%, 50%,

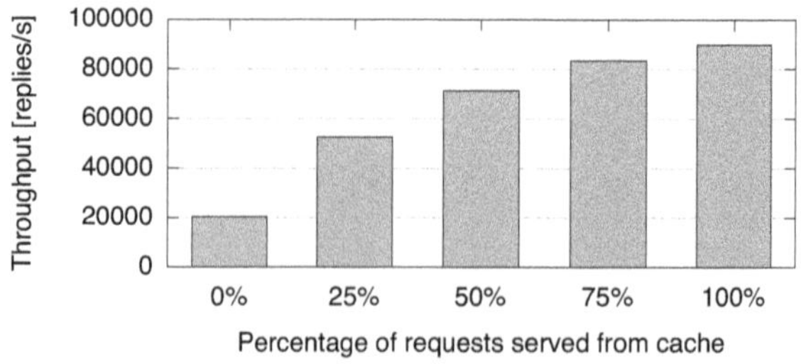

Figure 3: Serving requests with pre-cached replies drastically improves the request throughput of a server.

75%, 100%), and otherwise fell through to BIND. We then measured the number of requests that the server could process. Figure 3 shows that not only does Santa increase the throughput on our test machine by a factor of 4.4. It also shows throughput increases especially at lower cache hit rates: at 25% cache hits, throughput already increases by 258%, more than half the way to the maximum achieved increase. Thus, even in scenarios where our cache can only serve a small fraction of all requests, significant throughput improvements can be expected.

Concluding, our preliminary evaluation shows that drastic performance improvements are possible without clean-slate user-land network stack approaches.

4. FUTURE WORK

As next steps, we plan to evaluate the performance of Santa on real-world traces from major DNS servers, as well as to compare our solution with user-level network stacks. Furthermore, since Santa is currently limited to UDP, we plan to extend it to support TCP so that additional server applications can benefit from its caching.

Acknowledgments

This work has received funding from the European Union's Horizon 2020 research and innovation program 2014–2018 under grant agreement No. 644866 (SSICLOPS) and DFG CRC 1053 (MAKI). It reflects only the authors' views and the European Commission is not responsible for any use that may be made of the information it contains.

5. REFERENCES

[1] M. Bar. Kernel Korner: kHTTPd, a Kernel-Based Web Server. *Linux Journal*, 2000(76), Aug. 2000.

[2] S. Han, K. Jang, K. Park, and S. Moon. PacketShader: A GPU-accelerated software router. In *ACM SIGCOMM*, 2010.

[3] M. Honda, F. Huici, C. Raiciu, J. Araujo, and L. Rizzo. Rekindling Network Protocol Innovation with User-level Stacks. *SIGCOMM CCR*, 44(2):52–58, Apr. 2014.

[4] V. Jacobson and B. Felderman. Speeding up Networking. *linux.conf.au*, 2006.

[5] T. Marian, K. S. Lee, and H. Weatherspoon. NetSlices: Scalable Multi-Core Packet Processing in User-Space. In *ACM/IEEE ANCS*, 2012.

[6] I. Marinos, R. N. Watson, and M. Handley. Network Stack Specialization for Performance. In *ACM SIGCOMM*, 2014.

[7] I. Pratt and K. Fraser. Arsenic: A User-Accessible Gigabit Ethernet Interface. In *IEEE INFOCOM*, 2001.

[8] L. Rizzo. netmap: A Novel Framework for Fast Packet I/O. In *USENIX Security Symposium*, 2012.

[9] L. Rizzo and G. Lettieri. VALE, a Switched Ethernet for Virtual Machines. In *CoNEXT*, 2012.

Cache'n DASH: Efficient Caching for DASH

Parikshit Juluri
University of Missouri - Kansas City
pjuluri@umkc.edu

Deep Medhi
University of Missouri - Kansas City
dmedhi@umkc.edu

ABSTRACT

HTTP-based video streaming services have been dominating the global IP traffic over the last few years. Caching of video content reduces the load on the content servers. In the case of Dynamic Adaptive Streaming over HTTP (DASH), for every video the server needs to host multiple representations of the same video file. These individual representations are further broken down into smaller segments. Hence, for each video the server needs to host thousands of segments out of which, the client downloads a subset of the segments. Also, depending on the network conditions, the adaptation scheme used at the client-end might request a different set of video segments (varying in bitrate) for the same video. The caching of DASH videos presents unique challenges. In order to optimize the cache hits and minimize the misses for DASH video streaming services we propose an Adaptation Aware Cache (AAC) framework to determine the segments that are to be prefetched and retained in the cache. In the current scheme, we use bandwidth estimates at the cache server and the knowledge of the rate adaptation scheme used by the client to estimate the next segment requests, thus improving the pre-fetching at the cache.

1. INTRODUCTION

Globally, IP video traffic is dominating all consumer download traffic. Popular video streaming services e.g, Netflix and YouTube predominately use MPEG-DASH for their video delivery. With DASH, each video file is encoded into multiple different *representations*, each varying in bitrate, resolution, and format. The *representations* are divided into smaller *segments* of fixed playback duration. The individual *segments* are stored as separate files with unique URLs on the web-server. A Media Presentation Description (MPD) file is created for each video. The MPD file has a list of all *representations* and the URLs for the individual segments for the video. At the client end, the DASH video player downloads the MPD file, and retrieves the video metadata. Based on the network conditions and current video buffer occupancy, the client requests the appropriate video segment.

With the increasing popularity of video services, the network and service providers need to employ caching and prefetching strategies to reduce access latencies. Caching of web objects has been widely deployed, however, the video objects are significantly larger in size than regular web objects. Hence, aggressive prefetching of videos could be very expensive, resulting in overloading the link between the cache and the content server. In order to maximize the byte-hits using prefetching it is necessary to better predict the requests. Although the segment numbers for DASH streams is known a priori, but the main challenge is to predict the correct bitrate for the next segment.

In this paper, we propose an Adaptation Aware Cache (AAC) framework for DASH videos that uses bandwidth measurement at the cache server and the knowledge of the adaptation scheme to predict the segment requests. The main objective is to maximize the byte-hits, and minimizing the unnecessary prefetches.

2. RELATED WORK

DASH is a fairly recent technology with the first open standard for MPEG-DASH being released as recent as November, 2011. Although the use of cache servers for video streaming has been studied earlier, not many consider DASH video streaming services. Our aim is to develop a cache framework that is optimized for serving DASH video streams. We identify the areas where DASH differs from other web requests, and we propose the techniques that could be used to improve the cache performance, thus improving the QoE. Other studies have proposed modifications to the cache servers to leverage the popularity of the video streams [1]. In [1], the cache server prefetches the *segments* based on the bandwidth between the client and the cache. However, the rate adaptation in this case is driven by the cache server, which is not the case with current DASH, that uses client-end adaptation.

An integrated prefetching and caching scheme for adaptive video streaming is presented in [2]. In this study, the authors propose prefetching the next segment of the current bitrate. However, they assume a high probability of the client requesting the same bitrate. In the current framework, we use bandwidth measurements at the cache server to predict the bitrates for the next segments.

3. OVERVIEW OF THE FRAMEWORK

In this section, we describe our **Adaptation Aware Cache** (AAC) framework as shown in Fig. 1. The aim of the AAC

SIGCOMM'15, August 17–21, 2015, London, United Kingdom.

ACM ISBN 978-1-4503-3542-3/15/08..
DOI: http://dx.doi.org/10.1145/2785956.2790015

framework is to predict future requests based on the path bandwidth measurements between the cache server and the client, the expected response to the variations in the throughput by the adaptation scheme used by the client. At the highest level, the AAC framework has two modules: the DASH Request Handler and the Cache Manager.

3.1 DASH Request Handler

The DASH request handler in AAC handles all the HTTP video requests received by the cache server. For DASH streaming, the HTTP requests consists of the video MPD file followed by the individual video segment requests. The **MPD parser** module parses the DASH MPD files to retrieve the list of bitrates. A mapping for the video ID and the list of available bitrates is created and stored in a hashmap in the *Segment Request Index*. Only requests for videos that are not already in the *Segment Request Index* need to be parsed. The **Bandwidth Estimator** module measures the path bandwidth of the active HTTP sessions. The current cache servers typically run on sophisticated hardware and are equipped to collect the path bandwidth measurements [3]. The bandwidth estimator is a critical component and there is a need for a good estimator.

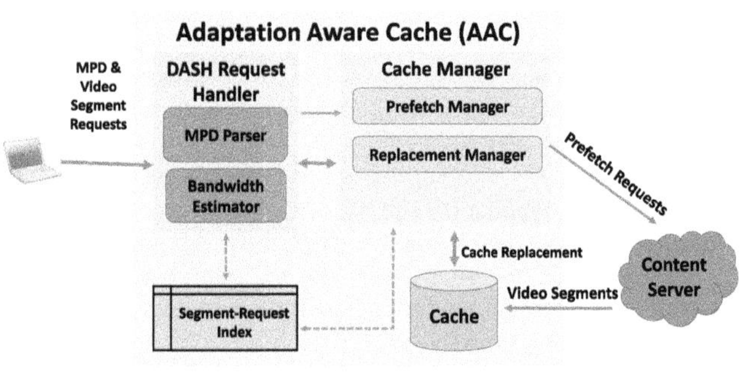

Figure 1: Adaptation Aware Cache Framework

3.2 Cache Manager Module

The cache manager module receives the video requests and the bandwidth measurement values form the *Bandwidth Estimator* module. As shown in Fig. 1, the *Cache Manager* consists of two modules: the Prefetch Manager and Replacement Manager. The cache manager interacts with the *Segment Request Index* to retrieve the video bitrate information. It also manages the requests to the cache. The cache in this case could also be a cluster of cache servers. The cache manager sends the prefetch and cache-miss requests to the content server.

Prefetch Manager: The DASH segment requests are based on a predefined order defined in the MPD file. However, the bitrate for each segment is selected by an adaptation algorithm employed by the client. Typical rate adaptation algorithms select the lowest bitrates for the initial set of segments. Later, based on the observed throughput, the algorithm ramps-up the bitrate and eventually settles at the appropriate bitrate. In Fig. 2 we plot the change in the bitrates requested by a typical rate adaptation algorithm. We found similar patterns with other adaption algorithms [4,5]. Based on these access patterns we can infer that prefetching the next segment of the current playback bitrate for the entire playback duration can result in unnecessary prefetches; especially during the ramp-up stage. Based on the bandwidth measurements collected at the cache server, the prefetch manager could predict if the client is expected to ramp-up the quality of the video. By making smart decisions on prefetches during the ramp-up phase avoids bitrate oscillations [3].

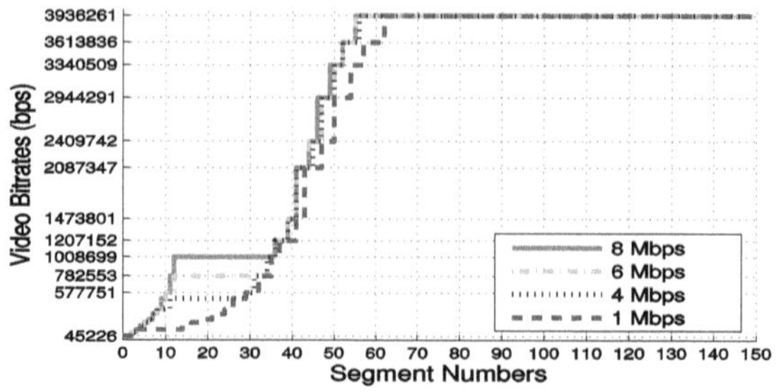

Figure 2: Bitrate Access Patterns for DASH video

Replacement Manager: The role of the replacement manager is to determine the segments that are to be replaced to accommodate new segments. The segment manager retrieves the information of the current active video streaming session from the *Segment Request Index* to determine which segments are most likely to be requested by the current video sessions and the least probable segments are replaced.

Segment Request Index stores two different hashmaps. The first hashmap is used to map the video ID with the available bitrates that are are retrieved from the DASH MPD file. The second hashmap is a mapping of the user ID with the corresponding bitrate measurements. Both these hashmaps are updated by the *Request Handler* and accessed by the *Cache Manager* modules, respectively.

4. SUMMARY AND FUTURE WORK

AAC is designed to improve the utility of the proxy cache by predicting the video segment download patterns. By using bandwidth measurements to improve the accuracy of prefetching, we can also avoid bitrate oscillations at the user end. Future work, beyond finishing the implementation and testing, focusses on optimizing the cache utility.

5. REFERENCES

[1] R. Rejaie, H. Yu, M. Handley, and D. Estrin, "Multimedia proxy caching mechanism for quality adaptive streaming applications in the internet," in *IEEE INFOCOM 2000*, vol. 2. IEEE, pp. 980–989.

[2] K. Liang, J. Hao, R. Zimmermann, and D. K. Yau, "Integrated prefetching and caching for adaptive video streaming over HTTP: an online approach," in *Proceedings of the 6th ACM MMSys*, 2015, pp. 142–152.

[3] D. H. Lee, C. Dovrolis, and A. C. Begen, "Caching in HTTP adaptive streaming: Friend or foe?" in *NOSSDAV*. ACM, 2014, p. 31.

[4] T.-Y. Huang, R. Johari, N. McKeown, M. Trunnell, and M. Watson, "A buffer-based approach to rate adaptation: Evidence from a large video streaming service," in *ACM SIGCOMM*, 2014, pp. 187–198.

[5] P. Juluri, V. Tamarapalli, and D. Medhi, "SARA: Segment Aware Rate Adaptation algorithm for Dynamic Adaptive Streaming over HTTP," in *ICC QoE-FI Workshop*, 2015.

FALE: Fine-grained Device Free Localization that can Adaptively work in Different Areas with Little Effort

Liqiong Chang, Xiaojiang Chen*, Dingyi Fang, Ju Wang,
Tianzhang Xing, Chen Liu, Zhanyong Tang
Northwest University, Xi'an, China
changliqiong@stumail.nwu.edu.cn, {xjchen,dyf,wangju,xtz,liuchen,zytang}@nwu.edu.cn

ABSTRACT

Many emerging applications and the ubiquitous wireless signals have accelerated the development of Device Free localization (DFL) techniques, which can localize objects without the need to carry any wireless devices. Most traditional DFL methods have a main drawback that as the pre-obtained Received Signal Strength (RSS) measurements (i.e., fingerprint) in one area cannot be directly applied to the new area for localization, and the calibration process of each area will result in the human effort exhausting problem.

In this paper, we propose FALE, a fine-grained transferring DFL method that can adaptively work in different areas with little human effort and low energy consumption. FALE employs a rigorously designed transferring function to transfer the fingerprint into a projected space, and reuse it across different areas, thus greatly reduce the human effort. On the other hand, FALE can reduce the data volume and energy consumption by taking advantage of the compressive sensing (CS) theory. Extensive real-word experimental results also illustrate the effectiveness of FALE.

CCS Concepts

•Human-centered computing → Ubiquitous and mobile computing design and evaluation methods;

Keywords

Device Free Localization; Received Signal Strength; Area Diversity; Transferring

1. INTRODUCTION

Recent years have witnessed a surge in the DFL [3] approaches for plenty of emerging applications. The fingerprint based DFL, which provides a fine-grained localization accuracy by using the RSS measurement (change) distorted by the object as priori knowledge, have gone mainstream.

*corresponding author.

SIGCOMM '15 August 17-21, 2015, London, United Kingdom

ACM ISBN 978-1-4503-3542-3/15/08...$15.00
DOI: http://dx.doi.org/10.1145/2785956.2790020

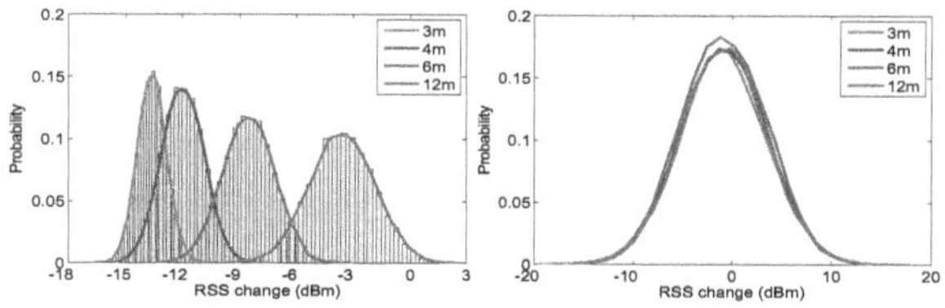

(a) before transferring (b) after transferring

Figure 1: Gaussian estimation of the RSS measurements across 4 diffeptient link lengths under the same location. (a) shows that the distributions of RSS measurements are significantly differ from each other, and after transferring by FALE, the distributions are made as close as possible in (b).

However, underlying current DFL approaches is a premise that the monitoring area is fixed, which, unfortunately, is unlikely in most practical settings. Actually, the pre-obtained fingerprint in one area is distinct from another area which has a different size. Therefore, it needs one to spend a lot of time to calibrate each location in all the areas, which is an human effort exhausting process.

To cope with this problem, this paper introduces FALE, an transferring DFL method that can adaptively works in different areas, with a fine-grained localization accuracy and without the process of exhausted retraining in each area, thus greatly reduce the human effort.

Specifically, different areas require to deploy different length of links [1], and the differences of RSS measurements are reflected in their distributions, as shown in Fig.1(a). Based on this, by utilizing the Fisher Linear Discriminant Analysis (FLDA) as subspace learning algorithm and the Bregman Divergence as a regularization term to measure the distribution distance, FALE projects the RSS measurements into a low-dimensional subspace where the distribution distance across diffrent link lengths are made as close as possible (Fig.1(b)), then the fingerprint of one area can be reused by different areas, thus greatly reduce the human effort. Moreover, we use the CS approach in [1] to perform localization accurately with a small number of RSS measurements.

2. TRANSFERRING SCHEME

In a high level, FALE goes through the following steps, and the detailed transferring is shown in Fig.2: **First**, we constructs the sensing matrix $\mathbf{x}^l$ of area $l \times a$, and collects a few of RSS measurements $\mathbf{x}^u$ for n randomly chosen locations in area $u \times b$. **Second**, based on $\mathbf{x}^l$ and $\mathbf{x}^u$, FALE solves the transferring matrix. **Third**, we transfer the sensing matrix of area $l \times a$ and the real-time RSS measurements

[1]Length of a link is the distance between the transceivers.

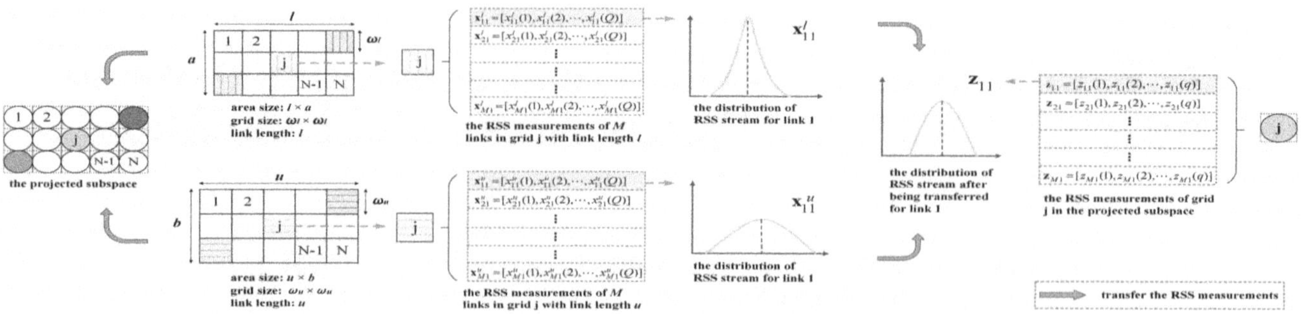

Figure 2: Transferring overview. By dividing the area into grids and deploy transceivers in the midpoint of the grid edge along two sides, the object locates in grid j will interfere some of M links, and for the same link 1, the distributions of Q continuous RSS measurements with link length l and u are distinct. By transferring the RSS streams $\mathbf{x}_{11}^l$ and $\mathbf{x}_{11}^u$ into a subspace $\mathbb{R}^q$ as $\mathbf{z}_{11}$, the distribution distance can be minimized.

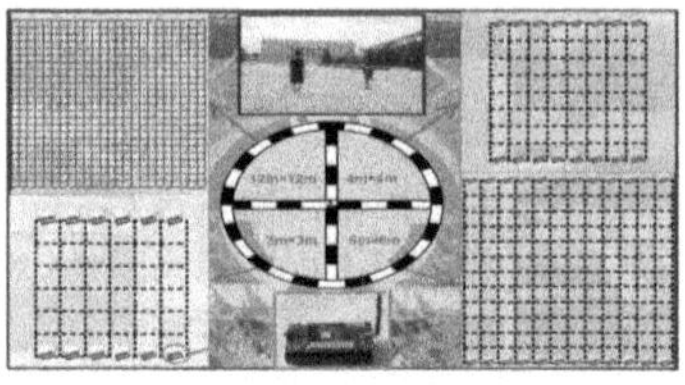

Figure 3: deployment view.

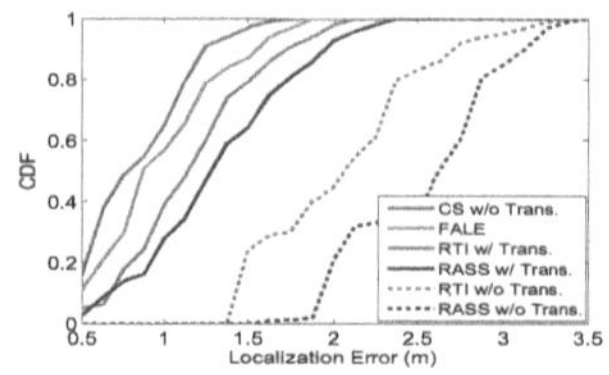

Figure 4: localization performance.

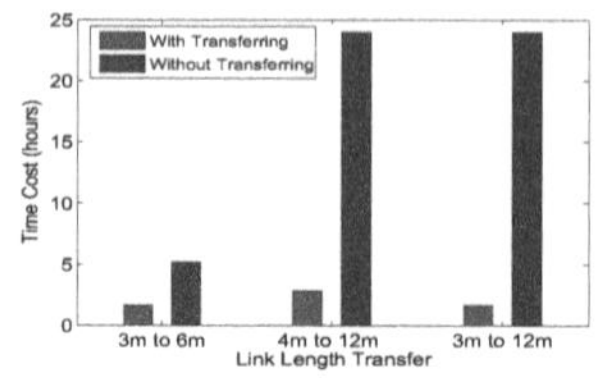

Figure 5: time cost.

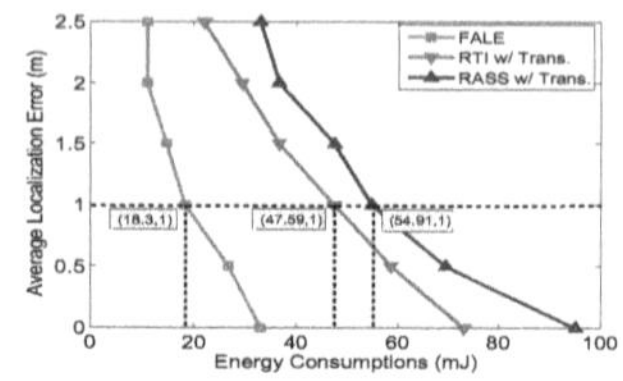

Figure 6: energy consumption.

of area $u \times b$, and estimate the locations based the CS theory.

The general framework can be presented as

$$\mathbf{z} = W^T \mathbf{x}, \tag{1}$$

$$W = \arg_{W \in \mathbb{R}^{Q \times q}} \min\{F(W) + \lambda D_W(p_l || p_u)\}, \tag{2}$$

with respect to $W^T W = I$. $F(W)$ is the FLDA which projects the RSS streams of $\mathbf{x}^l$ or $\mathbf{x}^u$ as $\mathbf{z}^l$ and $\mathbf{z}^u$. $D_W(p_l||p_u)$ is the Bregman Divergence that measures the distribution distance between $p_l(\mathbf{z})$ and $p_u(\mathbf{z})$. And the optimal W obtained by the Gradient Descent algorithm as

$$W_{k+1} = W_k - \eta(k)\left(\frac{\partial F(W)}{\partial W} + \lambda \cdot \frac{\partial D_W(p_l||p_u)}{\partial W}\right), \tag{3}$$

where $\eta_k = \eta_0 / k$ is the learning rate, and

$$\frac{\partial F(W)}{\partial W} = 2tr(W^T S_B W)^{-1} tr(S_W W)$$
$$- 2tr[(W^T S_B W)^{-1}]^2 tr(W^T S_W W) tr(S_B W), \tag{4}$$

$$\frac{\partial D_W(p_l||p_u)}{\partial W} = \sum_{i=1}^{N} \frac{\partial D_W(p_l||p_u)}{\partial \mathbf{z}_i^l} \mathbf{x}_i^l + \sum_{i=1}^{n} \frac{\partial D_W(p_l||p_u)}{\partial \mathbf{z}_i^u} \mathbf{x}_i^u, \tag{5}$$

$$\frac{\partial D_W(p_l||p_u)}{\partial \mathbf{z}_i^l} = \frac{(\sum_l)^{-1}}{N^2 \sigma_l^4} \sum_{i'=1}^{N} (\mathbf{z}_{i'}^l - \mathbf{z}_i^l) G_{2\sigma_l^2 \sum_l}(\mathbf{z}_i^l - \mathbf{z}_{i'}^l)$$
$$- \frac{2(\sigma_l^2 \sum_l + \sigma_u^2 \sum_u)^{-1}}{N n \sigma_u \sigma_l} \sum_{i'=1}^{n} (\mathbf{z}_{i'}^u - \mathbf{z}_i^l) G_{\sigma_l^2 \sum_l + \sigma_u^2 \sum_u}(\mathbf{z}_i^l - \mathbf{z}_{i'}^u),$$

$$\frac{\partial D_W(p_l||p_u)}{\partial \mathbf{z}_i^u} = \frac{(\sum_u)^{-1}}{n^2 \sigma_u^4} \sum_{i'=1}^{n} (\mathbf{z}_{i'}^u - \mathbf{z}_i^u) G_{2\sigma_u^2 \sum_u}(\mathbf{z}_i^u - \mathbf{z}_{i'}^u)$$
$$- \frac{2(\sigma_l^2 \sum_l + \sigma_u^2 \sum_u)^{-1}}{N n \sigma_u \sigma_l} \sum_{i'=1}^{N} (\mathbf{z}_i^u - \mathbf{z}_{i'}^l) G_{\sigma_l^2 \sum_l + \sigma_u^2 \sum_u}(\mathbf{z}_{i'}^l - \mathbf{z}_i^u).$$

Then in order to improve the localization accuracy in area $u \times b$, by using the RSS measurements of neighbor locations, FALE generates RSS measurements for the locations which are not represented as grids. Finally, we prove that after transferring, the transferred sensing matrix satisfies the RIP.

3. DEPLOYMENT AND RESULTS

We perform extensive experiments in an open-space depicted in Fig. 3, and we set the grid edge length as $\omega = 0.5$m when the link length is $4m$. We add our transferring scheme into two state-of-the-art algorithms RASS [4] and RTI [2], refer as RASS w/ Trans. and RTI w/ Trans. for a fair comparison. And we also compare with the traditional CS based localization method as CS w/o Trans. And we demonstrate the effectiveness of FALE as follows.

Localization Performance. Fig. 4 illustrates the performance of FALE is approximate to the CS w/o Trans., and FALE performs best with 50% and 80% error of 0.87m and 1.23m, respectively. And the performance of RTI and RASS improve 58% and 66% for 80% error respectively. **Human Effort Cost.** We use the time-cost of the pre-deployment to examine the human effort, Fig. 5 shows that the human effort decreases are 41% under transferring from 3m to 6m, 88% from 4m to 12m, 93% from 3m to 12m. **Energy Consumption.** We compare the energy consumption by increasing the number of links to reach an given localization accuracy. Fig. 6 shows that the energy consumption for FALE, RTI w/ Trans. and RASS w/ Trans. are 18.3 mJ, 47.59 mJ, and 54.91 mJ, respectively.

4. ACKNOWLEDGMENTS

This work was supported by the NSFC (61272461, 61170218). Project National Key Technology *R&D* Program 2013BAK01B02. Northwest university graduate student innovation training project YZZ14115.

5. REFERENCES

[1] J. Wang et al. LCS: Compressive sensing based device-free localization for multiple targets in sensor networks. In *IEEE INFOCOM*, pages 145–149, 2013.

[2] J. Wilson et al. See-through walls: Motion tracking using variance-based radio tomography networks. *IEEE TMC*, 10(5):612–621, 2011.

[3] M. Youssef et al. Challenges: device-free passive localization for wireless environments. In *ACM MobiCom*, pages 222–229, 2007.

[4] D. Zhang et al. Rass: A real-time, accurate, and scalable system for tracking transceiver-free objects. *IEEE TPDS*, 24(5):996–1008, 2013.

Federated End-to-End Authentication for the Constrained Internet of Things Using IBC and ECC

Tobias Markmann
HAW Hamburg
tmarkmann@acm.org

Thomas C. Schmidt
HAW Hamburg
t.schmidt@acm.org

Matthias Wählisch
Freie Universität Berlin
waehlisch@ieee.org

ABSTRACT

Authentication of smart objects is a major challenge for the Internet of Things (IoT), and has been left open in DTLS. Leveraging locally managed IPv6 addresses with identity-based cryptography (IBC), we propose an efficient end-to-end authentication that (a) assigns a robust and deployment-friendly federation scheme to gateways of IoT subnetworks, and (b) has been evaluated with a modern twisted Edwards elliptic curve cryptography (ECC). Our early results demonstrate feasibility and promise efficiency after ongoing optimisations.

Keywords

Smart objects, ID-based cryptography, end-to-end security, authentication, federation

1. INTRODUCTION

Security and privacy of critical applications in the IoT require a protection layer that provides end-to-end security over open and uncontrollable media channels. Typical deployment scenarios of highly constrained devices in low power lossy wireless networks make certificate-base public-key infrastructures (e.g, SSL) infeasible. The Internet standard DTLS introduces UDP-based encryption, but assumes authentication in place. This leaves the major challenge of authenticating huge numbers of smart objects using highly efficient algorithms, low communication overhead, and still providing a flexible, automated trust management.

End-to-end authentication is a critical requirement for many IoT scenarios as they interact with the real world in private areas, or in a security sensitive manner which needs to be protected and controlled. End-to-end security protocols do not depend on link-layer security and do not require control of all devices en route. In this work, we assume the common deployment of gateways that (a) interconnect IoT domains with the global Internet, (b) are under the same administrative control as the IoT subnet, and (c) have sufficient resources to serve as a trusted authority (TA).

SIGCOMM '15 August 17-21, 2015, London, United Kingdom

ACM ISBN 978-1-4503-3542-3/15/08.
DOI: http://dx.doi.org/10.1145/2785956.2790021

We propose identity-based cryptography (IBC) [1] for improving on the status quo—end-to-end authentication using traditional PKI with DTLS [2]. In IBC, an arbitrary bit string can be used as the public key. Keys that are addresses, for example, abandon the need for key distribution and all management overhead associated with certificates. IBC comes at the price of enhanced complexity, in particular for signature verification, and the problem of revoking identities. The size of the Internet (oT) will pose additional high scalability requirements on any IBC-type architecture.

We will address these challenges and concerns in the following approach (§ 2), and the evaluation in § 3. Here we also discuss the future steps in our ongoing work.

2. APPROACH

We consider the scenario of constrained IoT devices in subnetworks that are connected with the Internet using more powerful border gateways. Each owner of such IoT subnet is also entitled to assign the subnet-ID (IPv6 SLA) and maintains a trusted authority (TA) on the local gateway[1].

The TA is bound to IPv6 prefix (incl. subnet-ID) and assigns IP addresses to its local devices. By assigning private keys to these IPv6 addresses and distributing its public key locally, the TA enables IBC-bound authentication of the local nodes. Strictly local responsibility further assures (a) a simple, realistic management model, and (b) scalability. However, end-to-end authentication between nodes from different domains requires a federation between TAs that is protected against man-in-the-middle attacks and allows for a scalable localization of globally distributed TAs.

Our approach to a globally robust federation is based on cryptographically generated subnet-IDs. Under the common assumption of 48 bit globally routable prefix ('a /48'), we assign the subsequent (e.g., 64) bits for use as the subnet-ID, leaving a sufficient address space for assigning interface identifiers within the subnet. This subnet-ID is set to a truncated hash of the TA public key and thereby binds the responsible TA cryptographically to its subnet, while remaining resistant against accidental hash collisions. Being aware of this addressing logic and by using the full prefix with a conventional node-ID (e.g., ::001), any Internet device can request the public key from a remote TA. This allows for a scalable, fully distributed trust management, while the cryptographic binding prevents any unobserved modification along the path.

[1] A TA is comparable to a certificate authority (CA),but issues and has access to all private keys for this TA.

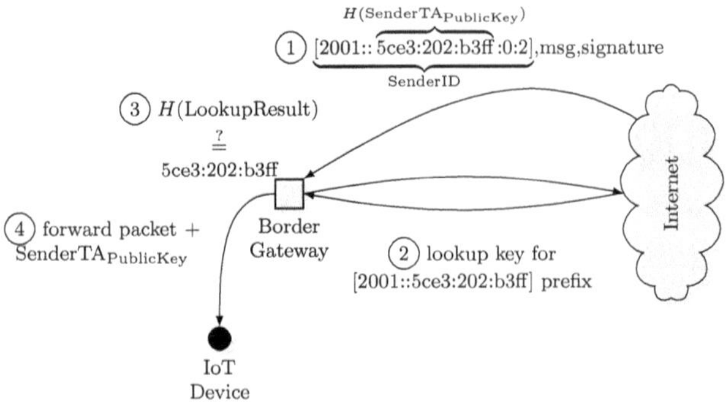

Figure 1: IBC message verification process

The detailed verification process can be seen in Figure 1. A packet that arrives at the border gateway includes the IPv6 header plus message and signature from the sender ①.

If the sender originates in the same subnet, the border gateway and a final receiver can authenticate using the same TA public key. In the case of an unknown subnet, the receiver first needs to obtain the TA public key corresponding to the sender's subnet, before it can authenticate the message in the packet ②. When verifying a signature of a device from a subnet, the subnet prefix includes a truncated hash of the corresponding TA public key. This prevents a replacement of public keys without change of the identity as part of a man-in-the-middle attack. After the verification of the received TA public key ③ the original packet and the TA public key are forwarded to the final IoT device ④.

An essential part of this *federated* end-to-end authentication is the lookup and verification of other TA public keys. There can be independent TA lookup methods that are used by more powerful devices and lookup methods that externalize the potentially complex lookup procedure from the IoT device to commonly present IoT gateways. IoT border gateways serve the connection of the IoT network to the worldwide Internet and are usually more powerful.

The border gateway can manage authentication and trust of TA key material and efficiently piggyback new and trusted TA keys to the constrained IoT device during communication, thereby avoiding additional communication load and latency. In this way verification of TA key material can be provided to highly diverse devices in the IoT.

The revocation of public keys in IBC is a non-trivial issue due to the implicit binding of public key and identity. A revocation of a public key in IBC also revokes the identity. However, identities in our approach are locally assigned IPv6 addresses, which can be renewed whenever trust to a local device requires revocation. Legitimate devices remain able to request new keys for their new identities from the TA and obtain a new IPv6 address with private identity key.

This architecture is implemented using elliptic curve cryptography based IBC to allow efficient implementation on the constrained devices of the IoT. We evaluated the use of ECC, specifically twisted Edwards curves, for constrained devices by writing an open implementation of [3] for the open-source RELIC [2] cryptographic library.

In addition, we plan to add a slight modification to the DTLS protocol, to allow two-way authentication based on IBC. This will allow end-to-end secured use of application protocols like the Constrained Application Protocol (CoAP).

[2]https://github.com/relic-toolkit/relic

3. EVALUATION AND FUTURE WORK

We now evaluate the performance of the ID-based cryptographic load by using the existing short Weierstrass ECC implementation in RELIC, as well as our twisted Edwards curve implementation using extended coordinates. A comparison between the short Weierstrass implementation and our code using Curve25519 [3] can be see in Figure 2, showing the performance of the ECC implementations under application with vBNN-IBS [4]. Using the twisted Edwards curve with extended coordinates gives a performance boost of roughly 20% on a constrained IoT platform. Without optimization, this already indicates feasibility, since the ID-based signature verification is compatible in performance to an RSA-2048 verification.

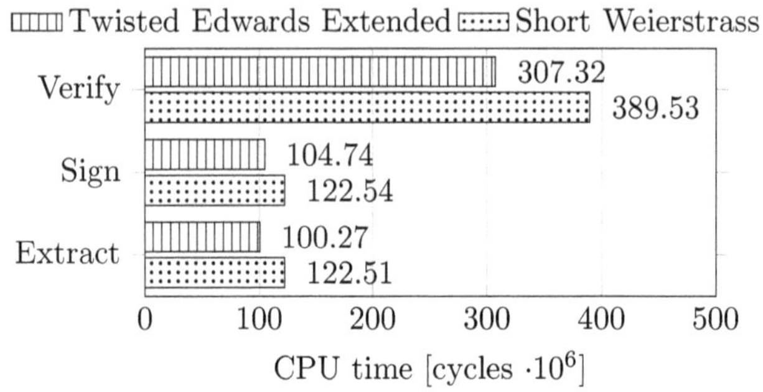

Figure 2: Performance of vBNN-IBS on a 32-bit ARM Cortex-M4 with 168 MHz clock speed.

Our next steps are further implementations of the described authentication architecture and to improve the ECC performance. There is room for a substantial performance boost that lifts the performance of RELIC in a competitive, efficient range.

We plan to evaluate the proposed system design with an open implementation using RELIC and RIOT [5], our free and open-source operating system for the IoT. Additionally, we will develop further measures to protect the local TAs.

4. REFERENCES

[1] A. Shamir, "Identity-Based Cryptosystems and Signature Schemes," in *Advances in Cryptology — CRYPTO 1984*, LNCS Springer, Aug. 1985, vol. 196, pp. 47–53.

[2] T. Kothmayr, C. Schmitt, W. Hu, M. Brünig, and G. Carle, "DTLS based security and two-way authentication for the Internet of Things," *Ad Hoc Networks*, vol. 11, no. 8, pp. 2710–2723, 2013.

[3] D. J. Bernstein, "Curve25519: New Diffie-Hellman Speed Records," in *Public Key Cryptography - PKC 2006*, LNCS Springer, 2006, vol. 3958, pp. 207–228.

[4] X. Cao, W. Kou, L. Dang, and B. Zhao, "IMBAS: Identity-based multi-user broadcast authentication in wireless sensor networks," *Comp. Comm.*, 31 (4), 2008.

[5] E. Baccelli, O. Hahm, M. Günes, M. Wählisch, and T. C. Schmidt, "RIOT OS: Towards an OS for the Internet of Things," in *Proc. of INFOCOM*, 2013.

eSDN: Rethinking Datacenter Transports Using End-Host SDN Controllers

Hasnain Ali Pirzada, Muhammad Raza Mahboob, Ihsan Ayyub Qazi
Computer Science Department
SBA School of Science and Engineering, LUMS, Pakistan
{15100061,15100140,ihsan.qazi}@lums.edu.pk

ABSTRACT

We propose eSDN; a practical approach for deploying new datacenter transports without requiring any changes to the switches. eSDN uses light-weight SDN controllers at the end-hosts for querying network state. It obviates the need for statistics collection by a centralized controller especially on short timescales. We show that eSDN can scale well and allow a range of datacenter transports to be realized.

CCS Concepts

•**Networks → Network architectures; Transport protocols; Data center networks;** *Programmable networks;*

Keywords

SDN; Datacenters; Transport Protocols

1. INTRODUCTION

Modern datacenters host a variety of popular applications such as web search, social networking, and advertising systems. These applications have very demanding performance requirements that critically depend on the underlying transport protocol. As a result, recent proposals focus on designing customized transports for datacenters (DC) to meet a variety of application goals (e.g., low latency) [1, 7]. However, many DC transports either have limited network visibility (e.g., DCTCP [1]) or require changes to switch hardware (e.g., D^3 [7]), which makes their deployment challenging.

Software-Defined Networking (SDN) can offer new opportunities for designing and implementing new DC transports. Existing SDN-based designs rely on centralized controllers for flow setup and collecting network statistics [4]. In contrast to previous approaches, we propose eSDN; a framework that augments centralized controllers with light-weight SDN controllers at the end-hosts. The role of end-host controllers is to periodically query network state (e.g., port utilization and queue length) information that is exposed by SDN/OpenFlow switches. These statistics, along with any application information, can be used to implement a range of DC transports without requiring any changes to the switch hardware. Involving end-hosts is beneficial as they have better visibility into application behavior than network devices, greater computational resources, and more flexibility to adopt new functionality. Moreover, eSDN obviates the need to go to a centralized controller for short timescale operations such as congestion control. This can be particularly beneficial for latency-sensitive short flows.

Previous approaches for obtaining data plane visibility either require custom switch hardware (e.g., Tiny Packet Programs (TPP) [5]) or are too costly at large-scale (e.g., FPGAs and network processors). In addition to being deployment friendly, eSDN offers several other advantages: (a) it can distribute load on a centralized controller to end-host controllers, (b) it enables short timescale operations, and (c) it can allow sharing of information across end-host controllers for better performance. eSDN architecture, however, raises new challenges for scalability and network efficiency. The periodic querying by end-host controllers can lead to high network overhead and requires high switch ASIC-to-controller bandwidth. We analyze the overheads and propose algorithms for reducing them. Moreover, we think that it is likely that future ASICs, designed for use in SDN switches, will provide more bandwidth for this path.

To demonstrate the feasibility of eSDN, we implement an in-network congestion control algorithm (RCP) [3] in ns2. We show how end-hosts, by periodically querying network state, can realize RCP. We would like to point out that for many in-network congestion control algorithms, port or aggregate-flow statistics suffice and more costly per-flow statistics may not be needed. Our initial results show that eSDN can enable high performance for DC transports by using rich data plane information. While eSDN impacts a broad class of network functionality (e.g., network verification), here we focus on the design and evolution of DC transports.

1.1 eSDN Design and Challenges

eSDN's primary goal is to bring low cost network visibility at the end-hosts. To achieve this, each end-host runs a light-weight OpenFlow controller that connects to switches. These controllers run in *slave* mode to ensure that they are read-only (and thus avoid conflicting flow table entries) while saving switch-controller bandwidth as asynchronous switch messages, such as `packet-in`,are not forwarded to *slave* controllers. In addition, each switch is connected to a centralized SDN controller running in master mode that can modify the switch state. The end-host controllers poll switches to collect statistics that can be used by transports.

SIGCOMM '15 August 17-21, 2015, London, United Kingdom

ACM ISBN 978-1-4503-3542-3/15/08.

DOI: http://dx.doi.org/10.1145/2785956.2790022

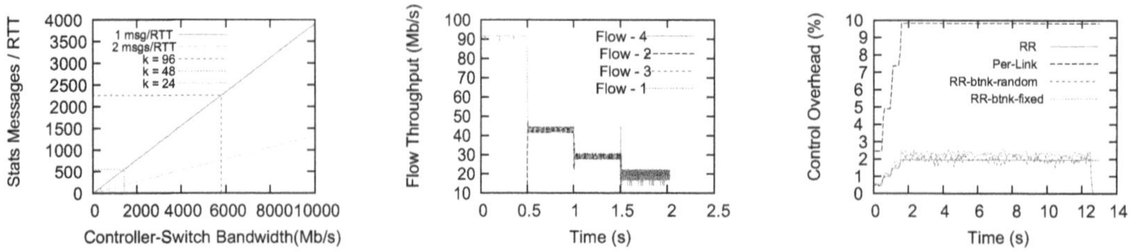

Figure 1: (a) OpenFlow statistics messages as a function of the controller-switch bandwidth. In this scenario, each of the k/2 end-hosts send one or two messages every RTT=200us in a k-ary fat-tree, (b) RCP throughput and (c) control overhead (as a fraction of link capacity=100Mbps) with RCP implementation that uses eSDN.

Switch-Controller Bandwidth: To support high frequency switch state reads, there needs to be enough bandwidth between the switch-ASIC and the controllers (which includes ASIC-CPU bandwidth and the CPU processing capability). Traditionally, switch control processors have been slow e.g., [2] report 17Mbps of switch-controller bandwidth. As ASICs are increasingly being designed for SDN switches (that require greater controller-switch interaction), this bandwidth is increasing [6]. Figure 1(a) shows the number of aggregate Read-State messages that can be handled by a switch as a function of the switch-controller bandwidth for a fat-tree of different sizes. We consider the worst-case intra-rack traffic scenario, where every host sends traffic to every other host. Assuming a polling frequency equal to RTT (=200us), ≈400 requests can be handled by the switch per RTT if the switch-controller bandwidth is 1Gbps.

Network Overhead: eSDN, that polls switches at RTT timescales, can lead to large amount of control traffic. For example, in the previous all-to-all traffic scenario, ≈77.3Mbps network capacity is required for sending 84b (with 44b request sizes and 40b for TCP/IP headers) OpenFlow aggregate-flow stats messages on every link. This amounts to ≈7.7% on a 1Gbps link. For inter-rack scenarios, probing on multiple switches will cause the host-ToR link to consume the most capacity e.g., if a flow traverses through five switches, the access link will incur $5w$ control overhead, where w is the control overhead for one stats message/RTT. This overhead can be reduced by sampling and intelligent polling.

2. CONGESTION CONTROL WITH eSDN

In-Network Transports: In-network transports, such as RCP and D^3, require explicit feedback from the switches. In case of RCP, a router maintains one fair-share rate R per link (of capacity C) which it computes periodically. When the flow count is known accurately, $R = C/N$. Otherwise, it requires knowledge of queue occupancy. With eSDN, end-host controllers can use Openflow's aggregate-flow statistics to get an estimate of the number of flows N. Port stats message can be used to obtain link utilization and queue occupancy. We have implemented eSDN and RCP in ns2. Figure 1(b) shows flow throughput over time for our end-host RCP implementation on a 4-ary fat-tree with 100Mbps links. We ran flows from every host in one pod to a particular host in another pod at different intervals through a particular core link. Thus making a single aggregate-core link the bottleneck. Observe that RCP achieves fair sharing in the face of new arrivals. The polling strategy in this scenario was to poll each link in the flow path every RTT. Due to the polling overhead, flows do not use the entire capacity.

End-host based Transports: Transports, like TCP and DCTCP use implicit (e.g., drops) or coarse-grained feedback (e.g., ECN marks) from the network, respectively. With eSDN, optimal parameters (e.g., initial window size) for these transports can be determined, thus allowing them to achieve better performance.

Algorithms for Reducing Overhead: A naive polling approach at each end-host would be to poll *every* distinct link (per RTT) that is traversed by its flows (termed as `per-link` approach). A better approach would be to poll all links in the flow path in a round-robin fashion (termed as `RR`) i.e., one switch/RTT. While this approach lowers overhead, it can reduce responsiveness. Another approach is to maintain and poll only the *bottleneck* link and re-poll all the switches either after a random or fixed time or after an implicit indication from the network (e.g., packet drops due to change in the bottleneck). Figure 1(c) compares the utilization for a core link with all these approaches for up to 16 flows, each polling for aggregate statistics only. Observe that `RR` approaches can significantly reduce overhead. In RCP, the end-hosts poll for aggregate statistics such as N. Protocols requiring both N and Q would have to fetch both aggregate and port level stats, thereby increasing overhead. An interesting future direction for overhead reduction is to design a peer-to-peer information sharing system so that only one or few controllers within a rack poll for a particular link.

3. CONCLUSION AND FUTURE WORK

We make the following contributions in this paper: (a) We presented eSDN that uses SDN controllers at the end-hosts to realize DC transports, (b) we presented a simple analysis of overhead challenges faced by eSDN and present algorithms for reducing the overhead, and (c) we implemented eSDN and RCP in ns2 and presented an initial evaluation. In the future, we plan to design new schemes for switch load distribution and network overhead reduction.

4. REFERENCES

[1] M. Alizadeh, A. Greenberg, D. Maltz, J. Padhye, P. Patel, B. Prabhakar, S. Sengupta, and M. Sridharan. Data center tcp (dctcp). In *SIGCOMM'10*.
[2] A. R. Curtis, J. C. Mogul, J. Tourrilhes, P. Yalag, P. Sharma, and S. Banerjee. Devoflow: Scaling flow management for high-performance networks. In *SIGCOMM'11*.
[3] N. Dukkipati, M. Kobayashi, R. Zhang-Shen, and N. McKeown. Processor sharing flows in the internet. In *IWQoS*, 2005.
[4] C.-Y. Hong, M. Caesar, and P. B. Godfrey. Software defined transport: Flexible and deployable flow rate control. In *ONS'14*.
[5] V. Jeyakumar, M. Alizadeh, Y. Geng, C. Kim, and D. Mazières. Millions of little minions: using packets for low latency network programming and visibility. In *SIGCOMM'14*.
[6] J. C. Mogul and P. Congdon. Hey, you darned counters! get off my asic! In *HotSDN'12*.
[7] C. Wilson, H. Ballani, T. Karagiannis, and A. Rowstron. Better never than late: Meeting deadlines in datacenter networks. In *SIGCOMM'11*.

BRB: BetteR Batch Scheduling to Reduce Tail Latencies in Cloud Data Stores

Waleed Reda
Université catholique de Louvain

Lalith Suresh*
TU Berlin

Marco Canini
Université catholique de Louvain

Sean Braithwaite
SoundCloud

ABSTRACT

A common pattern in the architectures of modern interactive web-services is that of large request *fan-outs*, where even a single end-user request (*task*) arriving at an application server triggers tens to thousands of data accesses (*sub-tasks*) to different stateful backend servers. The overall response time of each task is bottlenecked by the completion time of the slowest sub-task, making such workloads highly sensitive to the tail of latency distribution of the backend tier. The large number of decentralized application servers and skewed workload patterns exacerbate the challenge in addressing this problem.

We address these challenges through BetteR Batch (BRB). By carefully scheduling requests in a decentralized and task-aware manner, BRB enables low-latency distributed storage systems to deliver predictable performance in the presence of large request fan-outs. Our preliminary simulation results based on production workloads show that our proposed design is at the 99th percentile latency within 38% of an ideal system model while offering latency improvements over the state-of-the-art by a factor of 2.

CCS Concepts

•General and reference → Performance; •Information systems → *Distributed storage;*

1. INTRODUCTION

Recent studies [3] showed that latency distributions in Web-scale systems exhibit long-tail behaviors where the 99th percentile latency can be more than one order of magnitude higher than the median latency. To make matters worse, modern applications are highly distributed. For instance, interactive web services involve parallelization and aggregation of responses across 10s-1000s of servers, all of which need to finish for an end-user request (*e.g.*, a search query) to be considered complete.

There have been several proposals for achieving latency reduction and lowering the impact of skewed performance across backend servers. These include (*i*) duplicating or reissuing requests, predicting stragglers, or trading off completeness for latency [3], (*ii*) policy-based resource allocation and admission control (with the objective of achieving fairness or satisfying SLOs) [4], and recently (*iii*) making use of adaptive load-balancing [5]. In this work, we present BetteR Batch (BRB), which complements the above mentioned approaches using task-aware scheduling — a method of scheduling tasks across stateful backend replica servers according to expected service time of the enclosed sub-tasks.

2. BETTER BATCH OVERVIEW

In BRB, we focus on improving the performance of replicated and partitioned data stores. The system we aim to optimize consists of a set S of flexible servers and a set C of clients. Servers are flexible in that every server belongs to R replica groups and can service requests for any of the replica groups it is part of. A replica group is a collection of servers each of which contains a replica of a data partition. For simplicity, we also take R as the replication factor in the system and consider read operations where 1 out R servers is used. With the term client we mean an application server that receives user requests (*e.g.*, a request for a web page). Based on this system model, our end-goal is to provide the lowest latencies for accesses to the data store.

Our approach is based on two key observations. First, replicated data stores provide the opportunity to lower latencies via intelligent replica selection: that is, selecting one out of multiple replica servers to serve a request in a load-aware fashion, similarly to our prior work in [5]. Second, in many real-world workloads, applications have large fanouts: that is, they access several elements from the data store as a single batched request (*e.g.*, requesting all tracks in a playlist). We call the set of logically-related operations on the data store a task. Typically a task is complete only once all of its operations complete.

The nature of these workloads presents opportunities to minimize latency: in the spatial dimension, one can jointly optimize replica selection across all operations in a task; in the temporal dimension, one can optimize the schedule of operations by considering what bottleneck would affect the task completion time. Task-aware approaches have recently been applied for reducing the flow completion time in network transfers [2] but, to the best of our knowledge, no prior

*Work partly done when the author was visiting at Université catholique de Louvain and while interning at SoundCloud.

SIGCOMM '15 August 17–21, London, United Kingdom

ACM ISBN 978-1-4503-3542-3/15/08.

DOI: http://dx.doi.org/10.1145/2785956.2790023

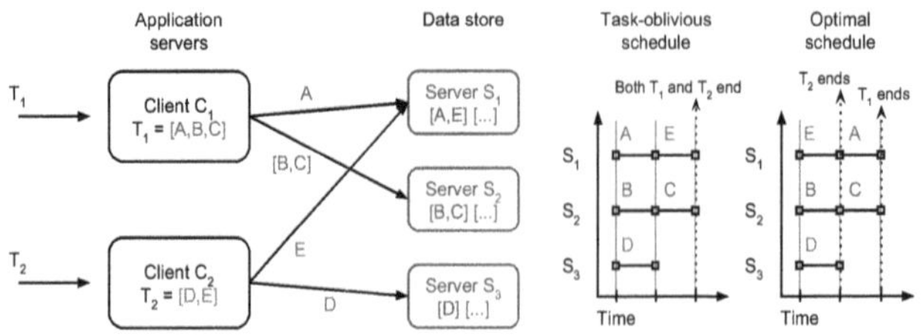

Figure 1: Intelligent replica selection and scheduling are effective techniques for reducing latencies.

work has adopted them for replicated and partitioned data stores (such as Cassandra or Riak).

Figure 1 illustrates these optimization opportunities. Assume S_1, S_2 and S_3 are the available replicas for processing tasks T_1 and T_2. Because task T_1 is complete only once all of its operations complete, it implies that there is some slack for accessing A — in particular, to cause no extra delay to T_1, the access to A can be flexibly delayed for as long as it completes within 2 time units. Crucially, if information about the deadline of a task is available, a server can choose to serve operations to meet their deadlines while minimizing the delay of other operations. In our example, S_1 can optimize the data accesses so that E is serviced before A — doing otherwise results in a suboptimal schedule where T_2 completes in 2 time units whereas in the optimal schedule the completion time of T_2 is just 1 time unit. In this simple example, it is evident that a system that makes decisions greedily for each request in a task-oblivious fashion could easily perform sub-optimally as opposed to using a task-aware approach, which is our goal in this work.

2.1 Task-Aware Scheduling Algorithms

A key insight to reduce tail latencies is that a task's response time depends on the last of its requests to complete. BRB is based on a class of algorithms for task-aware scheduling that exploit this fact. At a high-level, these algorithms run at the clients of the data store as follows. When receiving a task, clients subdivide it into a set of sub-tasks, one for each replica group; therefore, a sub-task contains all requests for a distinct replica group. Clients then determine the bottleneck sub-task based on the costliest sub-task and assign a priority to every request in the task. Then, the priority information is propagated to the servers, which based on this can decide what request to serve next. To this end, we have designed two simple yet effective priority assignment algorithms:

EqualMax: Requests are given the same priority as that of the bottleneck sub-task. The intuition is that tasks with shorter bottlenecks should be given precedence in order to minimize their makespan. This is equivalent to Shortest Job First (SJF) scheduling, however, in our case, given that task completion times are determined by the last request to finish, the bottleneck is used instead of the individual service time of requests.

UnifIncr: Requests are ranked based on the difference between the cost of the bottleneck sub-task and their individual cost. In other words, this effectively prioritizes requests according to how long they are allowed to slack behind the bottleneck. The main idea is that requests that have longer forecasted service times (based on the size of the value they are requesting) should be given a higher priority, given that they are more likely to bottleneck their respective tasks.

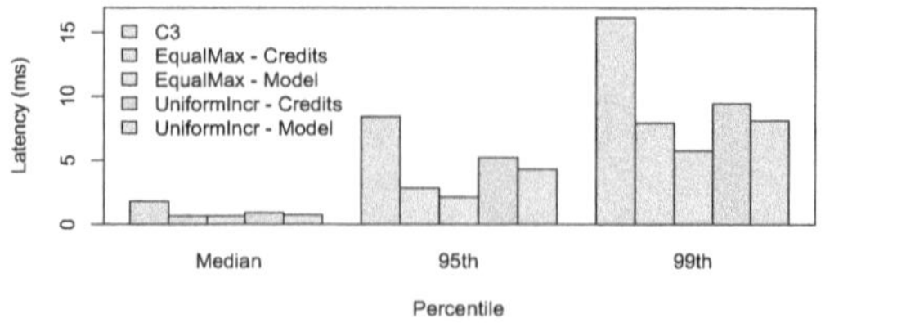

Figure 2: Task latency comparisons between BRB strategies and C3 [5].

2.2 Preliminary Evaluation

We resort to simulation to evaluate the potential benefits of our proposal. We assess BRB's latency reductions versus ideal as well as state-of-the-art approaches — in our case, C3 [5]. In an ideal case, referred to as *model*, servers utilize a work-pulling mechanism to fetch requests from a single global priority-based queue shared by all clients. However, such a model is unrealizable since it assumes perfect knowledge of global state. Hence, we develop a *credits* strategy where clients report their demands at measurement intervals and are assigned credits (*i.e.*, shares of server capacity) proportionally to demands via a logically-centralized controller; once demand exceeds server capacity, a congestion signal is sent to the controller and the credits allocations are adapted accordingly at 1s intervals. In such a realization, each server maintains a separate priority-queue.

For our evaluation, we simulate a system with 18 clients and 9 servers at a concurrency level of 4 cores, each operating at an average service rate of 3500 requests/s. We set our one-way network latency to 50 μs. The workload is gathered from SoundCloud and comprises of approximately 500,000 tasks, with an average fan-out of 8.6 requests per task. The value sizes for the requests are generated using a Pareto distribution based on a study conducted on Facebook's Memcached deployment [1]. We then generate task inter-arrival times using a Poisson process where the mean rate is set to match 70% of system capacity. The experiments are then repeated 6 times with different random seeds.

Figure 2 depicts the read latencies averaged across experiments for different percentiles. The standard deviation is not shown as it is largely negligible. As shown, the credits strategy is at most 38% of an ideal model across different simulation settings. In addition, BRB outperforms C3 across all percentiles for both EqualMax and UnifIncr and improves the latencies by up to a factor of 3 at the median and 95th percentiles and up to 2 times at the 99th percentile.

3. REFERENCES

[1] B. Atikoglu, Y. Xu, E. Frachtenberg, S. Jiang, and M. Paleczny. Workload Analysis of a Large-scale Key-value Store. In *SIGMETRICS*, 2012.

[2] M. Chowdhury, Y. Zhong, and I. Stoica. Efficient Coflow Scheduling with Varys. In *SIGCOMM*, 2014.

[3] J. Dean and L. A. Barroso. The Tail At Scale. *Communications of the ACM*, 56(2):74–80, 2013.

[4] D. Shue, M. J. Freedman, and A. Shaikh. Performance Isolation and Fairness for Multi-tenant Cloud Storage. In *OSDI*, 2012.

[5] L. Suresh, M. Canini, S. Schmid, and A. Feldmann. C3: Cutting Tail Latency in Cloud Data Stores via Adaptive Replica Selection. In *NSDI*, 2015.

Design and Implementation: the Native Web Browser and Server for Content-Centric Networking

Guoshun Nan, Xiuquan Qiao, Yukai Tu, Wei Tan[§], Lei Guo, Junliang Chen
State Key Laboratory of Networking and Switching Technology,
Beijing University of Posts and Telecommunications, 100876, Beijing, China
IBM T. J. Watson Research Center, Yorktown Heights, NY 10598, USA [§]
nanguoshun@bupt.edu.cn, qiaoxq@bupt.edu.cn, tuyukai1994@gmail.com,
wtan@us.ibm.com, guolei@upc.edu.cn, chjl@bupt.edu.cn

ABSTRACT

Content-Centric Networking (CCN) has recently emerged as a clean-slate Future Internet architecture which has a completely different communication pattern compared with exiting IP network. Since the World Wide Web has become one of the most popular and important applications on the Internet, how to effectively support the dominant browser and server based web applications is a key to the success of CCN. However, the existing web browsers and servers are mainly designed for the HTTP protocol over TCP/IP networks and cannot directly support CCN-based web applications. Existing research mainly focuses on plug-in or proxy/gateway approaches at client and server sides, and these schemes seriously impact the service performance due to multiple protocol conversions. To address above problems, we designed and implemented a CCN web browser and a CCN web server to natively support CCN protocol. To facilitate the smooth evolution from IP networks to CCN, CCNBrowser and CCNxTomcat also support the HTTP protocol besides the CCN. Experimental results show that CCNBrowser and CCNxTomcat outperform existing implementations. Finally, a real CCN-based web application is deployed on a CCN experimental testbed, which validates the applicability of CCNBrowser and CCNxTomcat.

CCS Concepts

•Information systems → Web applications; •Networks → Network experimentation;

Keywords

Content-Centric Networking, Web browser, Web server

1. INTRODUCTION

In recent years, the World Wide Web (WWW) has become one of the most fundamental Internet applications. Web browsers and servers play a key role in satisfying the needs of a large and growing community of web users. Content-Centric Networking (CCN) [1] has emerged as a clean-slate network architecture to address the problems faced by current IP networks.

Existing web browsers and servers are designed for the hypertext transfer protocol (HTTP) and IP-based Internet. Consequently, the deployment of the existing web applications on CCN is still an open issue due to the lack of interconnections tools. Current research focuses on the gateway for HTTP and CCN protocol conversion [5] or plug-in manner [4] to validate CCN under real HTTP traffic. However, a gateway is not an efficient approach given the additional cost of the protocol conversion. The lack of native support for web applications has greatly hampered the wide adoption of CCN.

To address above issues, we designed and implemented a full-fledged CCN web browser (called CCNBrowser) [2] and a server (called CCNxTomcat) [3]. CCNBrowser was developed based on the open source Webkit, and CCNxTomcat was based on Apache Tomcat. We leverage CCNx developed by PARC laboratory as the CCN prototype. Native CCN functions are integrated into implementations to support interactions among users, servers and routers in CCN. In addition, to facilitate smooth network evolution, our implementations support the content request using both 'ccnx://' and 'http://' URI schemes for HTML, CSS and JavaScript.

SIGCOMM '15 August 17-21, 2015, London, United Kingdom

ACM ISBN 978-1-4503-3542-3/15/08.

DOI: http://dx.doi.org/10.1145/2785956.2790024

2. IMPLEMENTATION

To give a clear description, architectures of CCNBrowser and CCNxTomcat are depicted in Fig. 1 and Fig. 2, respectively, where the components highlight in blue are CCN related.

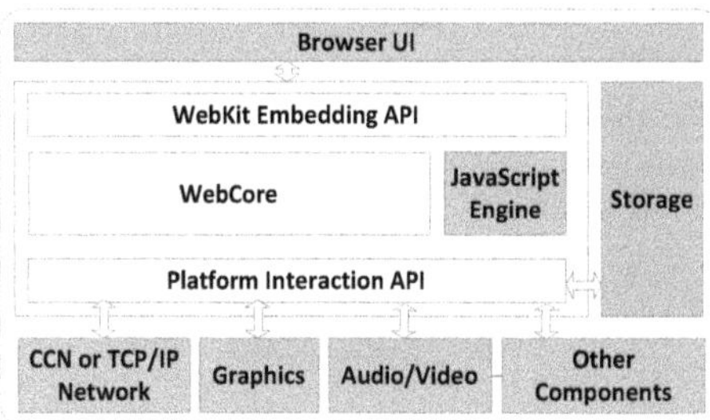

Figure 1: CCNBrowser architecture

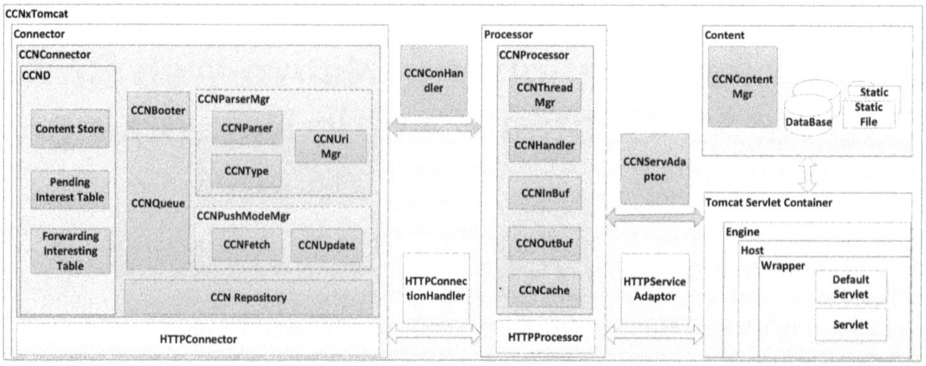

Figure 2: CCNxTomcat architecture

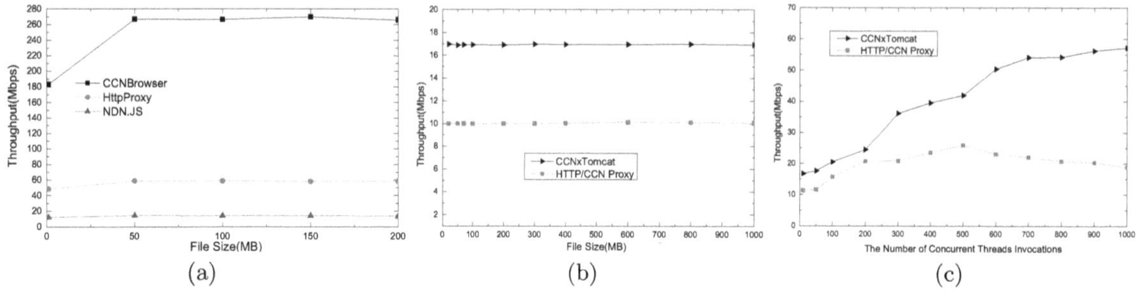

Figure 3: Test results: (a) CCNBrowser vs. NDN.JS and HTTP/CCN Proxy in terms of the single file test. (b) CCNxTomcat vs. HTTP/CCN Proxy in terms of the single file test. (c) CCNxTomcat vs. HTTP/CCN Proxy in terms of the throughput.

3. EXPERIMENT

We conduct experiments on a real testbed to compare the performance of CCNBrowser and CCNxTomcat with existing NDN.JS and HTTP/CCN proxy. The results in Fig. 3 indicate that CCNBrowser exceeds existing NDN.JS and HTTP/CCN gateway implementations by a factor of nineteen and five, in terms of the throughput, and CCNxTomcat outperforms existing HTTP/CCN implementations by 58% in a single request, and by a factor of three under 1000 concurrent requests. We also setup a real CCN-based personalized web site as shown in Fig. 4 for the practical utilization of CCNBrowser and CCNxTomcat.

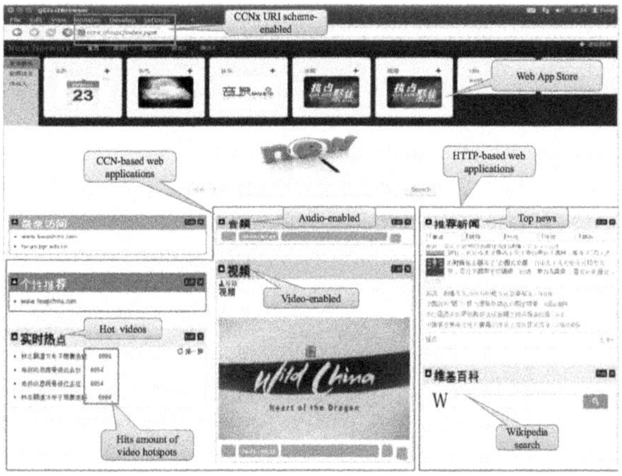

Figure 4: A real CCN-based personalized web site

4. ACKNOWLEDGMENTS

This work was supported by the National Key Basic Research Program of China (973 Program) under Grant No. 2012CB315802, the National Natural Science Foundation of China under Grants No. 61171102 and No. 61132001, the Prospective Research on Future Networks of Jiangsu Future Networks Innovation Institute under Grant No. BY2013095-4-01.

5. REFERENCES

[1] V. Jacobson, D. K. Smetters, J. D. Thornton, M. Plass, N. Briggs, and R. L. Braynard. Networking named content. CoNEXT 09. ACM, 2009.

[2] X. Qiao, G. Nan, Y. Peng, L. Guo, J. Chen, Y. Sun, and J. Chen. Ndnbrowser: An extended web browser for named data networking. *Journal of Network and Computer Applications*, 50:134–147, 2015.

[3] X. Qiao, G. Nan, W. Tan, L. Guo, J. Chen, W. Quan, and Y. Tu. Ccnxtomcat: An extended web server for content-centric networking. *Computer Networks*, 75:276–296, 2014.

[4] W. Shang, J. Thompson, M. Cherkaoui, J. Burkey, and L. Zhang. Ndn. js: a javascript client library for named data networking. In *Computer Communications Workshops (INFOCOM WKSHPS), 2013 IEEE Conference on*. IEEE, 2013.

[5] S. Wang, J. Bi, J. Wu, X. Yang, and L. Fan. On adapting http protocol to content centric networking. In *Proceedings of the 7th International Conference on Future Internet Technologies*. ACM, 2012.

Alibi Routing

Dave Levin* Youndo Lee* Luke Valenta† Zhihao Li* Victoria Lai*
Cristian Lumezanu‡ Neil Spring* Bobby Bhattacharjee*

* University of Maryland † University of Pennsylvania ‡ NEC Labs

ABSTRACT

There are several mechanisms by which users can gain insight into where their packets have gone, but no mechanisms allow users undeniable proof that their packets did *not* traverse certain parts of the world while on their way to or from another host. This paper introduces the problem of finding "proofs of avoidance": evidence that the paths taken by a packet and its response avoided a user-specified set of "forbidden" geographic regions. Proving that something did *not* happen is often intractable, but we demonstrate a low-overhead proof structure built around the idea of what we call "alibis": relays with particular timing constraints that, when upheld, would make it impossible to traverse both the relay and the forbidden regions.

We present *Alibi Routing*, a peer-to-peer overlay routing system for finding alibis securely and efficiently. One of the primary distinguishing characteristics of Alibi Routing is that it does not require knowledge of—or modifications to—the Internet's routing hardware or policies. Rather, Alibi Routing is able to derive its proofs of avoidance from user-provided GPS coordinates and speed of light propagation delays. Using a PlanetLab deployment and larger-scale simulations, we evaluate Alibi Routing to demonstrate that many source-destination pairs can avoid countries of their choosing with little latency inflation. We also identify when Alibi Routing does not work: it has difficulty avoiding regions that users are very close to (or, of course, inside of).

Categories and Subject Descriptors

C.2.2 [**Computer-Communication Networks**]: Network Protocols; C.2.0 [**Computer-Communication Networks**]: General—*Security and protection*

SIGCOMM '15, August 17–21, 2015, London, United Kingdom

 ISBN 978-1-4503-3542-3/15/08...$15.00

DOI: http://dx.doi.org/10.1145/2785956.2787509

Keywords

Alibi Routing; Provable route avoidance; Censorship avoidance; Peer-to-peer; Overlay routing

1. INTRODUCTION

Users have little control over where in the world their packets travel en route to their destinations. Some mechanisms exist to provide insight into where packets traveled, such as the record-route IP option, overlay routing systems (§7), or to a lesser extent source-routing. While these approaches expose a subset of the path the user's packets took, they do not allow a user to determine or provably influence where their packets do *not* go.

This paper introduces a new primitive we call *provable avoidance routing*. With provable avoidance routing, a user specifies arbitrary geographic regions—such as countries or UN voting blocs—to be avoided while communicating with a destination. If successful, the primitive returns *proof* that the user's packets did not traverse the forbidden regions. If it is unsuccessful, it concludes only that the packets *may have* traversed them.

The goal of provable avoidance routing is *detection*, as opposed to *prevention*. In other words, alone, it is unable to ensure a user's packets *will not* traverse a region of the world—we do not require modifications to the underlying routing protocols or hardware, and so we are subject to all of today's uncertainties as to where packets will travel. Rather, what we are able to provide is assurance that the user's packets and their respective responses took paths that *did not* traverse regions of the world. Our proofs of avoidance are provided on a per-packet basis, and are *a posteriori*: only after sending the packet and getting a reply can we ascertain whether or not the round-trip communication avoided the forbidden region.

While outright prevention would be ideal, detection can be a powerful tool, as well. For example, consider one of the greatest threats to open communication on the Internet: censorship. Beyond just dropping [34] or logging [29] users' traffic, censorship can take many forms, including *injecting* packets with false information [4]. Recent results indicate that many users may be censored not by their (or their destination's) countries, but by regimes through which their packets transit; a group of anonymous researchers demonstrated that DNS queries that merely traverse China's borders are subject to the same injection of false responses as if the queries came from one of its own citizens [4]. Incomplete deployment of authenticated protocols such as DNSSEC requires users to take other approaches, typically consisting of hiding packets' contents via encryption [10, 8], forwarding through hidden proxies [18, 46, 17], or applying steganography [11]. We offer an orthogonal approach: rather than use-and-confuse a censoring regime, we show that it is possible to simply *avoid the censor altogether.*

As another example of the usefulness of provable avoidance routing, two parties could perform Diffie-Hellman key exchange and use the proofs of avoidance to ensure that there could not have been a man-in-the-middle from user-specified forbidden regions. Subsequent communication after the initial key exchange would thus provide confidentiality even if the default route traversed the forbidden regions.

This paper makes two main technical contributions. The first is a means of proving that a packet avoided a forbidden region (§3). Our proofs of avoidance are built around the idea of using what we call "alibis": relays that are sufficiently far away from the forbidden region such that traversing both relay *and* forbidden region would result in a noticeably high delay.

The second contribution we make is the design and implementation of *Alibi Routing*, a peer-to-peer overlay routing system for finding alibis safely and efficiently (§4). Alibi Routing is secure in that, when tasked with finding alibis for a forbidden region F, it too avoids F (§5). It is efficient in that it requires a small amount of state, and takes few hops, especially when the source and destination are both reasonably far from the regions they seek to avoid. Most importantly, Alibi Routing is immediately and incrementally deployable: it requires no public key infrastructure (PKI) or modifications to existing routing protocols or switching hardware; it does not require synchronized clocks; and it does not require access to any information about the underlying routing topology of the Internet. Rather, it derives its security and proofs of avoidance from "a clock and a map": local measurements of round-trip times and a rough knowledge of one's own (and one's attacker's) GPS coordinates.

Using an implementation and deployment on PlanetLab (as well as large-scale simulations), we show that many source-destination pairs can avoid countries of their choosing with reasonably low latency inflation (§6). We also identify the instances when Alibi Routing does not work: in general, the closer a source or its destination is to a forbidden region F, the fewer potential alibis there are.

Alibi Routing is not a panacea; for instance, it is impossible for users to avoid the countries they are in—the very problem traditional censorship-resistant systems address. Our goal is not to replace such systems, but to complement them; as we will show, Alibi Routing offers an orthogonal set of properties that combine well with prior systems (§7).

2. GOALS AND NON-GOALS

In this section, we describe the goals (and non-goals) of a provable route avoidance primitive. Suppose that source s has sent a query to d and received a response, and s wishes to verify neither query nor response traversed some region of the world F. Our ultimate goal is to be able to construct a *proof* that s can check to make sure that the packet and its response *could not* have possibly traversed F.

Ideally, this primitive should be easy to deploy and use. To this end, we avoid modifications to existing routing protocols like BGP [50], or to hardware in the Internet [2, 28]. Rather, we show that users themselves can provide this service with an overlay protocol.

Provable route avoidance does *not* seek to provide two otherwise desirable properties. First, it does not seek to guarantee that an adversary would never see a *copy* of the packet. Even if the user is able to prove that the adversary was not on the packet's path, it does not stop nodes on the path from copying and later delivering the packets to the adversary. Existing approaches to anonymity (§7) can complement alibi routing to make copies less useful to a censor.

Second, alibi routing seeks to allow users to prove that a packet must have avoided F after the fact, not to guarantee that a packet will not traverse F. Higher-layer protocols must choose how to react to the absence of a proof, that is, the observation that the communication may have traversed F. Some may require that all packets avoid a part of the network: such applications should treat packets that might have traversed F as failures and retransmit. Other higher-layer protocols may permit some fraction of packets through F, for instance if they are using alibi routing for non-adversarial reasons, e.g., for performance or path diversity.

3. PROOFS OF AVOIDANCE

Here, we demonstrate how to prove that a packet and its response did not traverse a region of the world. In general, proving that some event x did *not* happen is very difficult. Our proof structure seeks to demonstrate that x did not happen because it would have been *impossible.* It consists of finding a set of events A such that:

- It can be proved that events in A *did* happen.
- A and x are mutually exclusive.

If these properties both hold, then x could not have happened: the events A serve as an *alibi* for x.

3.1 Mutually exclusive routing events

What then are the mutually exclusive events that would lead to provable route avoidance? In this setting, the event x that we wish to prove impossible is the event that a packet and its response from s to d transited forbidden region F. We need two pieces of evidence from A.

First, we must know a subset of the path that the packet took. To this end, a user forwards packets through a relay node r. r signs[1] the packet, and thus, if r can be trusted not to have shared his key, then this proves that the packet

[1]In fact, because we do not make use of digital signature's property of non-repudiation, a symmetric key MAC suffices.

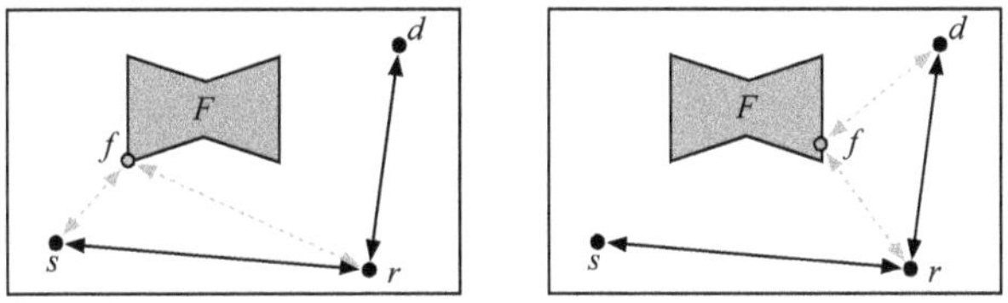

(a) $R(s,r) + R(r,d) \ll \min_f\{R(s,f) + R(f,r)\} + R(r,d)$ (b) $R(s,r) + R(r,d) \ll R(s,r) + \min_f\{R(r,f) + R(f,d)\}$

Figure 1: s and d wish to communicate without their packets traversing geographic region F. Relay r can serve as an *alibi* if packets that would traverse any possible node f in F would induce noticeably higher RTTs, as captured in Eq. (1).

must have gone through r (we define our trust assumptions in Section 4).

Second, we must know that, for any possible path that includes s, r, and d, the packets could not have also gone through F. Of course, there are many ways the packet can traverse F: r could ignore the users' wishes and forward the packet through F, or F could lie on the path between s and r or r to d. In other words, proving a *subset* of the path a packet took is feasible, but how can we prove that no node from F was anywhere on the path?

The key idea is to choose a relay that is so distant from the forbidden region that transiting both would induce noticeably high delays. Figure 1 illustrates the idea. When s routes through r to get to d, it observes the round-trip times between itself and the relay, $R(s,r)$, and the relay and the destination, $R(r,d)$. It must ensure, for every packet, that this end-to-end latency is noticeably less than *lowest possible round-trip time* for any path that also traverses F. Concretely, in order to ensure that the packet did not traverse F, we must also demonstrate that *both* of the following inequalities hold:

$$\begin{aligned} R(s,r) + R(r,d) &\ll R(s,r) + \min_{f \in F}\{R(r,f) + R(f,d)\} \\ R(s,r) &\ll \min_{f \in F}\{R(s,f) + R(f,r)\} \end{aligned} \qquad (1)$$

By "$x \ll y$", we mean "x is noticeably less than y," or more formally, that for some $\delta \geq 0$: $(1+\delta) \cdot x < y$. Thus, the first inequality states that, if a packet goes through any f in the forbidden region on the path between the relay and the destination, then the increase in latency will be noticeable. The second inequality says the same for the path between the source and the relay. Note that s can compute both inequalities locally, without synchronized clocks: the min terms are estimates (based on the speed of light, §4), and though s cannot directly measure $R(r,d)$ in the first inequality, it can measure the end-to-end RTT, $R(s,r) + R(r,d)$, and its RTT to r, $R(s,r)$.

Suppose a relay has signed a packet (proving the packet traversed that relay), and it satisfies the timing constraints in Eq. (1) for any possible $f \in F$. These events are mutually exclusive to the packet traversing F, and thus we have our proof: the packet could not have possibly traversed F.

We call relays that yield such proof *alibis*. Note that, to be an alibi, it is necessary for a relay to be far from the forbidden region: if very close, then for any x there may be an f such that $R(r,x)$ is not noticeably different than $R(r,f) + R(f,x)$. However, simply being far away is *not sufficient* for a relay to be an alibi: if F were on the path from s to r, then no matter how far r is from F, Eq. (1) will not hold. As a result, locating alibis is non-trivial; in the next section, we describe one way to do it.

3.2 Practical considerations

How to obtain proof. Equation (1) asserts that no node f in the forbidden region could unnoticeably appear on the path. It would be unrealistic to identify and enumerate all *actual* hosts in a forbidden region—particularly when it is adversarial. We demonstrate in Section 4 how to use geographic distance to estimate the lowest *possible* round-trip time between two hosts.

When to obtain proof. Our proofs of avoidance are based on local measurements of round-trip times for packets. Latencies can vary over time—e.g., due to outages, route changes, or congestion [30]—and thus a relay that is a viable alibi at one point in time may not be one later, potentially even on a per-packet basis. As a result, our proofs of avoidance must be applied to *each* packet.

The factor of δ in the above equations helps insulate provable avoidance from latency fluctuations. δ represents a trade-off between safety and efficiency; larger values of δ yield alibis who are so far away from a forbidden region that, if packets were to traverse both, there would be a very large increase in latency over a normal path through the alibi. Thus, with a large δ, one may be less likely to find a viable alibi, but that alibi is likely to work even in the face of variable round-trip times and congestion. Section 6 shows that we are successful in finding alibis for a range of δ values.

4. ALIBI ROUTING PROTOCOL

In this section, we describe Alibi Routing, a peer-to-peer overlay routing protocol for locating alibis. Once found, users forward their traffic through alibis, and apply the techniques from Section 3 to obtain proofs of avoidance. Alibi Routing is secure in that no routing messages are accepted unless they provably did not traverse the forbidden region the source node specified; we analyze its security properties in Section 5. Alibi Routing is efficient in that it finds relays quickly, without having to contact many intermediate hops; we evaluate its performance in Section 6.

4.1 Trust assumptions and attack model

Users query Alibi Routing by specifying (1) a destination with whom they wish to communicate, and (2) a geographic *forbidden region* F through which they want proof their packets do not traverse. For any peer who cannot be proved to be outside a user's specified forbidden region, we assume that it will act in a Byzantine faulty manner toward that user. The central assumption underlying Alibi Routing is that, *the user trusts all peers that are provably outside* F *to follow the protocol correctly.*[2].

The limitation is that it places the onus on users to determine where in the world their attackers are. As such, we expect Alibi Routing to be used mostly for avoiding large, very powerful adversaries [34, 37]. For example, Alibi Routing would be well-suited to avoid China's firewall, which appears to be run strictly within its borders [5, 4]. Attackers in our model can be routing-capable adversaries [37], i.e., we assume them to be capable of choosing how packets in their networks are routed, and of influencing routes to cause others' traffic to be routed through them. Fortunately, there has been significant work in identifying countries who launch such attacks, and ongoing efforts regularly identify new sources of misbehavior or malfeasance [33, 27, 7].

Even such powerful adversaries are faced with limitations, which Alibi Routing exploits. First, we make standard cryptographic assumptions; any scheme wherein an attacker cannot forge a MAC from a non-colluding peer suffices. Second, we make use of the fact that, while an attacker can lie about having greater latency to a victim, it cannot lie about having *lower* latency than it really has. This observation is commonly used in secure network coordinate systems [38, 43]. Finally, we apply the fact that information cannot travel faster than the speed of light, and that in fact most transmission media (especially fiber optic cables) peak at approximately $\frac{2}{3}c$. As we will demonstrate, these standard apparent impossibilities are sufficient for allowing many source-destination pairs to provably avoid various countries.

4.2 Query components

When a source node s wishes to find alibis, it constructs and forwards a query message, $\langle s, d, F, T \rangle$. Most of these are defined above: s and d are the source's and destination's IP addresses and ports, and F is the forbidden regions, represented by one or more ordered sets of $(\mathsf{lat}, \mathsf{lon})$ pairs. The forbidden regions are included in the query so that intermediate hops can determine which next-hop neighbors are *safe* to forward to.

The final component, T, is a set of what we call "target regions," which represent locations where alibis *might* reside. Target regions are included in queries to help guide routing towards parts of the network that make the most *progress* towards an alibi. Here, we describe how forbidden and target regions are represented; we then describe how peers forward them when routing.

4.2.1 User-specified forbidden regions

A forbidden region consists of a set of (possibly disjoint) polygons specified over a set of geographic $(\mathsf{lat}, \mathsf{lon})$ coordinates. A user wishing to avoid a particular country, for instance, can specify the country's borders. These are readily available in high precision online [13], but even an approximate circumscribing polygon can be calculated with a reasonably accurate map.

[2]This particular assumption need apply only to our protocol for finding alibis, and not to the proofs of avoidance (§3).

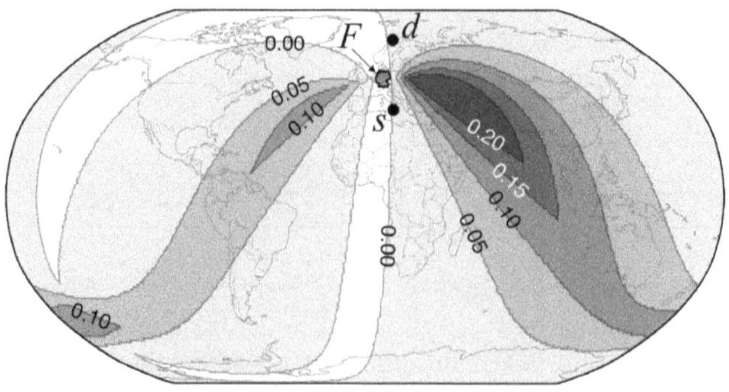

Figure 2: Example target regions, with end-hosts in Italy and Norway who seek to avoid Germany. The contours represent different values of δ in Eq. (2).

Each user can specify his or her own forbidden regions; Alibi Routing is agnostic to what these regions represent. This has the benefit that it supports a wide range of policies—users may choose to avoid cities where data logging facilities are expected to reside [29], an entire country, a UN voting bloc, and so on. Moreover, users can specify these policies without having to understand the underlying network topology: they only need to know where in the world those they do not trust reside.

4.2.2 Computed target regions

The final component of an Alibi Routing query is a set of *target regions*: geographic regions wherein alibis *may* exist. When a peer processes a query, its task is to choose next-hop neighbors who get the query closer to a target region (we describe this process in Section 4.4.2). As a result, the crucial property of a target region is that it include as many alibis as possible.

Similar to forbidden regions, target regions are represented by polygons of GPS coordinates. A node at GPS coordinate g is included in the target region if it satisfies the alibi conditions from Section 3. That is, if $D(\cdot, \cdot)$ represents the great-circle distance between two points, then g is in the target region if and only if:

$$\begin{aligned} (1+\delta)\cdot D(s,g) &< \min_{f\in F}\{D(s,f)+D(f,g)\}, \text{ and} \\ (1+\delta)\cdot D(g,d) &< \min_{f\in F}\{D(g,f)+D(f,d)\} \qquad (2) \end{aligned}$$

for some suitably large constant δ: this is the same "noticeably-larger-than" relationship as captured in Eq. (1)[3].

For an arbitrary set of forbidden regions, we do not know of a closed form solution to represent all GPS points in T. Instead, we segment the globe into a grid of points (in our implementation, we take $(\mathsf{lat}, \mathsf{lon})$ points at 2° intervals). For each such point g, we use Snell's law [12] to determine the r.h.s. of Eq. (2). If three contiguous grid points are in the target region and form a triangle, we add the entire triangle to T and take their union, forming a smaller set of polygons.

[3]The formulations of these two equations are slightly different; this is because s can accurately *estimate* the distance between relay and destination, $D(g, d)$, required in Eq. (2), but can directly *measure* only the full end-to-end RTT, $R(s, r) + R(r, d)$, required by Eq. (1).

Figure 2 illustrates the target region for a peer in Italy wishing to communicate with a peer in Norway while avoiding Germany. Note that larger values of δ result in smaller target regions; when $\delta = 0$, nearly the entire world has the potential of hosting an alibi, but when $\delta = 0.2$, alibis can only possibly be located in the Middle East, extending eastward to India.

The grid interval spacing represents a trade-off between efficiency and accuracy. With larger grids, the computation is faster and the target region's polygons can be represented with fewer points, thereby decreasing query size. However, larger grids can be inaccurate: they may miss viable relays, and, if left unchecked, could include portions of the forbidden region. To alleviate this second concern, we include each triangle in T only if it does not intersect the forbidden region. We have found grid intervals of $2°$ to be safe and efficient for all single-country forbidden regions we tested.

Target regions may (and often do) also include peers who are *not* viable relays. Consider for example a peer who has a satellite link with extremely high latencies: such a peer may never satisfy the alibi conditions, regardless of the path his or her packets take. In other words, a benevolent relay whose packets never traverse the forbidden region might never be viable simply because it has poor connectivity. With respect to safety, this is not a concern: target regions are used only to guide queries toward potential alibis, and Alibi Routing peers check the alibi conditions (Eq. (1)) to verify a relay's actions for each packet. We evaluate how likely a node is to be an alibi given that it is inside a target region in Section 6.

4.3 Neighbor maintenance

Every peer in the system maintains a constant-sized set of neighbors (32 in our implementation). Our primary requirement is that these neighbors are diverse in terms of both latency and geography, so as to increase the likelihood that peers can route queries towards a given target region (and away from the corresponding forbidden region).

To maintain as diverse a set of neighbors as possible, each peer p maintains two sets of peers: (1) a set of m *known-active* peers, whom p has heard from recently, and (2) a set of n *neighbors*, which p uses when processing queries, The known-active set is larger ($4\times$ in our implementation), and is used for populating the neighbor set as follows:

Latency diversity. Peers regularly obtain round-trip time (RTT) measurements to peers in their known-active set: they actively ping peers when they first meet (and periodically thereafter), and record the RTTs from routing messages. When a peer obtains a new RTT measurement, it updates its known-active set of peers, and decides whether or not its neighbor set should be updated. To maintain a diverse set of neighbors, the invariant we would like to maintain is that, at any point in time, a peer's relative differences in latencies to its neighbors are maximized. We approximate this with the following simple heuristic:

Periodically, each peer p determines his most redundant neighbor in terms of RTT. Suppose r_i represents neighbor i's RTT to p, and that $r_i \leq r_{i+1}$ for all i. Neighbor i's "redundancy" is captured by the inverse of its relative difference to its neighboring values: $\frac{r_i}{r_{i+1}-r_{i-1}}$ (for notational convenience, let $r_{-1} = -\infty$ and $r_{n+1} = \infty$). Peer p then removes the neighbor i with the greatest redundancy, and adds a random peer from its known-active set[4].

Geographic diversity. A geographically diverse set of neighbors is also important in Alibi Routing; it increases the likelihood that each relay has a neighbor outside of a given forbidden region. In Alibi Routing, when peers exchange entries from their known-active set with one another, they share not only a list of peers they know, but also those peers' GPS coordinates (including their own). Sharing geographic information is important for processing queries (§4.4), so we leverage them for achieving diverse neighbors, as well.

To achieve geographic diversity, we apply a similar heuristic as with latencies: Peer p computes the bearing θ_i between its GPS coordinate and q_i's, that is, $\theta_i = \tan^{-1}\left(\frac{p.\mathsf{lat}-q_i.\mathsf{lat}}{p.\mathsf{lon}-q_i.\mathsf{lon}}\right)$. p sorts these bearings (w.l.o.g., suppose $\theta_1 \leq \cdots \leq \theta_M$), and removes the "most redundant" bearing from the list. θ_i is considered the most redundant if it has the smallest average difference with its predecessor θ_{i-1} and successor θ_{i+1}.

These measures of diversity guide an Alibi Routing peer's decisions as to what neighbors to add or drop. Adding new neighbors is done as follows:

Joining. To join, n first contacts a peer p it knows, and obtains p's known-active set (this contains but is not limited to p's neighbor set). n then pings these nodes with a random nonce, asks them for their GPS coordinates, adds them to his known-active set, and uses them to construct his own neighbor set, as described above. Note that the neighbor set of a new node is likely to be different from the node that bootstrapped it (unless they are extremely close to one another). This process is trivial to bootstrap—any peer can initiate its own instance of a Alibi Routing overlay—and permits incremental deployment.

Establishing neighbors. When a peer p decides to add peer q as a neighbor, p first pings q with a random nonce, and records the RTT. All pings in Alibi Routing have such an unpredictable nonce; without it, q could under-report his RTT by constructing and sending a response before receiving p's ping[5]. The peers then exchange their GPS coordinates—precise locations would be a violation of the users' privacy, but fortunately, as Figure 2 indicates, even relatively coarse-grained GPS coordinates (city- or often even country-level) often suffice. Finally, the peers establish a shared symmetric key, which they use to compute and verify MACs on the packets they forward for one another. This same process applies when establishing a connection between a source node s and an alibi peer a: the MACs provide the proof that a indeed forwarded the packet, as described in Section 3.

[4]We considered alternative schemes such as Meridian's expanding rings [44], but, in our setting, we found their difference to be statistically insignificant in evaluation.

[5]Such an attack, which seeks to under-represent one's RTT, is similar in spirit to the TCP OptAck attack [39].

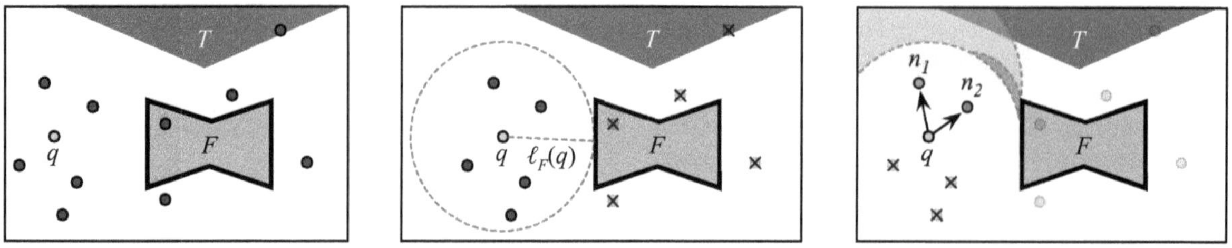

Figure 3: Choosing a set of next-hop neighbors when processing a query, with target region T and avoidance region F.

Properties. Note that our neighbor maintenance protocol does *not* explicitly invoke user trust assumptions, nor does it make use of forbidden regions. Peers can lie about the data they share—they can arbitrarily inflate latencies and completely forge GPS coordinates. However, as we will see, Alibi Routing uses the fact that attackers cannot lie about having *lower* latencies in order to filter out false information from potentially forbidden peers. We demonstrate in Section 5 that these mechanisms ensure that Alibi Routing is safe regardless of any peer's neighbor set.

4.4 Query processing

When a peer obtains a query message, its task is to determine the next-hop neighbor who has the greatest chance of locating an alibi. Because of its adversarial setting, we can think of query processing as having to satisfy two conditions: safety and progress. First, the next-hop neighbor must be *safe*, i.e., the neighbor must not reside in a forbidden region nor can communication with the neighbor traverse a forbidden region. Second, each hop must make as much *progress* as possible towards a target region. We next describe how a peer checks both of these conditions.

4.4.1 Safety: Determining trustworthy neighbors

Suppose peer q is processing a query $\langle s, d, F, T\rangle$. How does q determine with certainty that one of its neighbors, n, is not in F?

The insight is that the latency between two nodes cannot be lower than the speed of light (c) would permit. So long as peer q knows its own latitude and longitude, it can compute $d = \mathsf{ShortestDistance}(q, F)$: the great-circle distance between itself and the closest point in F. It can then use this distance to estimate what the *minimum possible RTT* is between itself and any node in the forbidden region. We denote this minimum RTT by $\ell_F(q)$. Concretely, if q's lowest measured RTT to n is $L(q, n)$, then q can be certain that n is not in the forbidden region so long as

$$L(q, n) < \ell_F(q). \tag{3}$$

A peer that satisfies this condition is certainly not in the forbidden region. However, if peer n does not satisfy the condition, it does not necessarily mean that n is in F; only that q cannot determine with certainty that n is *not* in F.

Estimating ℓ_F: the minimum possible RTT. This approach depends heavily on being able to estimate $\ell_F(q)$, the minimum possible RTT between peer q and any possible host in forbidden region F. As information cannot travel faster than the speed of light, the safest approach is to let $\ell_F(q) = \frac{2}{c} \cdot \mathsf{ShortestDistance}(q, F)$ (the factor of two captures the fact that ℓ_F represents a round-trip time).

However, assuming that all information can travel this fast may be overly conservative—real latencies are typically not so close to the speed of light, so we may be able to identify more peers as being trustworthy if we can choose a larger (but still safe) value. Agarwal and Lorch [1] observed from latency measurements on over 3.5 million gaming consoles that there is an approximately linear relationship between RTTs and the great-circle distance between two hosts on Earth. The least-squares fit they propose represents approximately a five-fold increase over the speed of light. However, their fit overestimates latencies for many node pairs. Overestimating latencies could violate correctness in our setting: it would correspond to a peer believing that one of its neighbors is not in a forbidden region when it really is.

What, then, is a mapping from distance to RTT that is *safe* (i.e., close to $2/c$) but not overly *conservative* (i.e., not much closer to $2/c$ than what current links achieve)? There are many factors that influence how close Internet communication comes to the speed of light. Most fiber-optic links achieve approximately $2/3$ the speed of light, while coaxial cables typically obtain between 66–82%, depending on the type of insulator [6]. Additionally, there are serialization delays, buffering at routers, and so on [42], but lacking a concrete understanding of how much "friction" such effects add to various regions of the Internet, we choose to err on the side of safety and assume these delays are zero.

We take the conservative approach of assuming fiber-optic links operating at $2/3$ the speed of light, and zero delays otherwise. Thus, we estimate the lowest possible RTT between q and F as follows:

$$\ell_F(q) := \frac{3}{c} \cdot \mathsf{ShortestDistance}(q, F) \tag{4}$$

We observe that all points in Agarwal and Lorch's data fall above this line. We have also verified this property with all data that we have collected in our experiments on PlanetLab.

A particularly useful property of Eqs. (3) and (4) is that they require only information that is readily accessible to the peer seeking to check the condition. Note that, to compute them, q needs to know: (1) its own geographic coordinates (we assume each user knows where he or she is, at least to some reasonably fine granularity), (2) the forbidden region (which is provided in the query), and (3) its observed RTT to n. Moreover, we argue in Section 5 that an adversarial neighbor n cannot meaningfully manipulate q's computation as to whether n meets the safety condition.

4.4.2 Progress: Efficiently finding alibis

An intermediate node q may have more than one neighbor who satisfies a query's safety condition; in the extreme, if the forbidden region were very small, all of q's neighbors might be considered safe. Forwarding to all safe neighbors would be inefficient (and could, in the extreme, lead to flooding). Instead, an intermediate Alibi Routing node returns the neighbors who are both safe and who make the most progress towards finding alibis.

Consider node q with safe neighbors $S = \{n_1, \ldots, n_{|S|}\}$. There are two broad cases to consider: (1) If q is not in a target region, it must get the query closer to one. (2) If q is in a target region, it should forward the query to a relay that reduces the latency inflation between source and destination.

Getting to a target region. If neither q nor its safe neighbors are in a target region, q must pick the neighbors who have the greatest chance of ultimately forwarding the query to someone who is. It may seem tempting to choose the safe neighbor who is the closest to some t_i, that is, the $n_i \in S$ who minimizes $\ell_T(n_i)$. This would ensure that the query makes progress at each hop, but it can also cause queries to fail. For example, neighbor n_2 in Figure 3(c) is closest to the target region, but because it is also close to the forbidden region, it is likely to have few safe neighbors to forward to.

The key insight is that neighbors with larger distances to the forbidden region will have larger values of ℓ_F, and therefore will have more neighbors who satisfy the safety condition. We balance the two goals—get closer to T while staying far from F—by having q choose neighbor n_i who minimizes $\ell_T(n_i) - \ell_F(n_i)$. In the example in Figure 3(c), the progress that q's neighbors make are represented by the shaded circles: n_i's circle is centered at n_i and has radius $\ell_F(n_i)$. A neighbor's progress is captured by how close this circle is to T. Note that n_1 maximizes progress, and is therefore the most likely to have a neighbor who is not only close to T, but possibly inside it. q would therefore choose n_1 as the next hop in this example.

4.5 Avoiding local minima

Alibi Routing is in some ways similar to prior "geographic routing" protocols, in that it uses a heuristic to measure progress towards a goal (we describe prior work in this area in Section 7). A classic problem facing greedy heuristics is that they are likely to run into *local minima*: when processing a query, peer $p \notin T$ may have the lowest value of $\ell_T - \ell_F$ out of all of its neighbors. What this means in Alibi Routing is that it may be necessary to sometimes forward queries *away* from a target region in order to find a peer who knows neighbors who can ultimately get the query to the target.

We make use of two key mechanisms to achieve this. First, each peer p maintains data about its two-hop neighbors, $\mathcal{N}^2(p)$. To do so, p periodically requests each of his one-hop neighbors $q \in \mathcal{N}^1(p)$ to send him $\mathcal{N}^1(q)$. When forwarding a query, p chooses the neighbor $q^\star \in \mathcal{N}^1(p)$ who has neighbor $n^\star$ who minimizes $\ell_T(n) - \ell_F(n)$. This helps avoid some local minima, but there may still be peers who appear to make better progress than any of their two-hop neighbors.

To this end, the second metric we make use of is *query forking*. Each peer randomly splits its neighbors into two disjoint sets, S_1 and S_2. When processing a query, the peer forwards it to peer $p_i \in S_i$ who minimizes the progress condition, $\ell_T - \ell_F$, for *both* $i = 1$ and 2. This has the possibility of introducing loops, and thus each peer maintains short-lived state of what queries they have seen; if they receive a query they have already seen, they simply drop it. Query forking also has the possibility of flooding a larger portion of the network than necessary, if left unconstrained. To address this, each query contains a TTL, and we use a simple *expanding ring* search: a source node initializes TTL to 2, and increments it until it succeeds, up to a maximum supported TTL (in our implementation, we have observed that a TTL above 7 does not yield enough marginal return to merit how many additional nodes it contacts).

Alibi Routing is unique with respect to many other overlay routing systems in that it bases its routing decisions only on a vague notion of where the destination might be (target regions can constitute a huge portion of the world). As we will demonstrate in Section 6, however, Alibi Routing is still able to achieve high success rates without contacting many nodes. Before we evaluate empirically, however, we analyze Alibi Routing's security properties.

5. SECURITY ANALYSIS

We analyze Alibi Routing's security with respect to attacks on its safety and progress, and discuss attacks that Alibi Routing does not seek to solve.

Attacks on safety. We begin our security analysis by considering attacks that seek to undetectably divert traffic through a forbidden region. First, we show that one cannot trick a trusted peer into thinking that an unsafe peer is safe:

PROPERTY 1. *If $q \in F$, then there does not exist a trustworthy peer p for which q satisfies the safety condition.*

Conceptually, this is true because q would have to fabricate a lower latency than is physically possible to appear convincingly safe to p. To see this, recall that $\ell_F(p)$ is the minimum possible latency between p and any point in F. Because $q \in F$, we have $L(p,q) \geq \ell_F(p)$, that is, there exists some $\Delta \geq 0$ such that $L(p,q) - \Delta = \ell_F(p)$. Suppose that q were indeed able to satisfy the safety condition; then $L(p,q) \ll \ell_F(p)$, that is, there would exist some $\delta > 0$ such that $L(p,q) + \delta = \ell_F(p)$. These together would imply that $\delta = -\Delta$, and thus that $\Delta < 0$, a contradiction.

We next show that the Alibi Routing protocol is not susceptible to packet manipulation by nodes within a forbidden region. Moreover, this security property ensures that any packet from an attacker in a forbidden region will be ignored altogether.

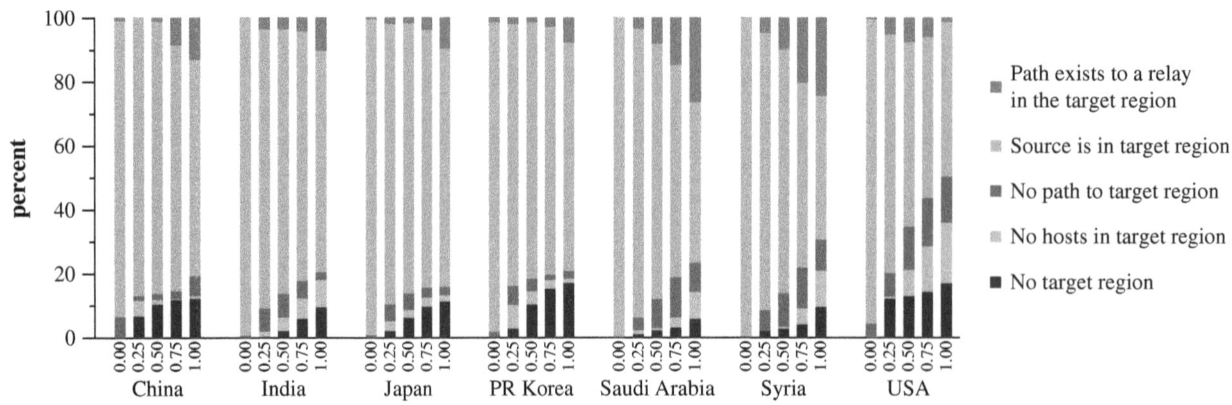

Figure 4: Feasibility of Alibi routing for different forbidden regions. (Simulated deployment on PlanetLab.)

PROPERTY 2. *All trustworthy peers ignore all packets that traverse F.*

To see this, suppose peer p is trustworthy. Suppose further that p forwarded a packet through q, but that in the process of doing so, the packet traversed F and yet p did not ignore it. Because a trustworthy peer p ignores any packet that violates Eq. (1), the supposition that p did not ignore it would mean that $R(p,q) \ll \min_{f \in F}(R(p,f) + R(f,q))$. The only way that this inequality could hold for a packet that traversed F is if q and F are colluding, and thus that $q \in F$. However, Property 1 says that, if p is trustworthy and $q \in F$, then p would not believe q to be safe, and therefore would not have forwarded a packet through q in the first place. We thus have our contradiction: a packet that traverses F must have been ignored by any trustworthy peer.

Note that establishing Properties 1 and 2 required no assumptions of the peers' neighbor sets. This leads to an interesting corollary that Alibi Routing is safe regardless of any peer's neighbor set.

Attacks on progress. An adversary could launch an eclipse attack [41] by attempting to populate a victim's neighbor set with all attackers. Note that such an attack would require an attacker to be very close to the victim. Although, as we have shown, the attacker cannot violate the victim's safety, it may be able to impact progress. Recall that next-hop peers are ranked by their progress condition: the neighbor n who minimizes $\ell_T(n) - \ell_F(n)$ makes the most progress. Peers who are most susceptible to an eclipse attack are those who are closest to $F(n)$ and thus have small values of $\ell_F(n)$ Thus, the more likely a peer n is susceptible to an eclipse attack by attackers in F, the greater the value of $\ell_T(n) - \ell_F(n)$ in general, and thus the less likely n will be chosen as a next hop in a query. Constraining progress therefore requires proximity to otherwise viable relays.

Non-attacks.

We close this section by describing some attacks on users that we do not believe need to be solved by a provable route avoidance system, as they can be solved by combining Alibi Routing with a more traditional system.

Laundering attack traffic. In any overlay routing system, relays could be used for reflecting attack traffic: s could send attack traffic to d via a relay r to make it appear that r is the one attacking. We do not believe there is any fundamental difference between such an attack in Alibi Routing and other systems, and so traditional approaches apply (e.g., white-listing sources or destinations, as in Tor [10], and rate-limiting how much a peer contributes to the system, as in BitTorrent [9]).

Sending copies of data to attackers. Any host or router on the path from s through an alibi to d could send copies of packets to the forbidden region. This does not violate Alibi Routing's goals: to establish an unadulterated path of communication between s and d. Keeping communication private is, of course, an important issue: to this end, s and d ought to employ end-to-end encryption. Further, if s and d desire sender and/or receiver anonymity, they should apply anonymous systems such as Tor [10] or $\mathcal{P}5$ [40]. Alibi Routing can be composed with such systems to provide defense in depth, for instance by using the alibi condition when constructing Tor circuits (§7).

6. EVALUATION

We present an evaluation of Alibi Routing using both simulations and an implementation deployed on PlanetLab. Our data and code are publicly available.

6.1 Who can be avoided?

The first question we seek to evaluate is: for what source, destination, forbidden region triples could alibis exist?

To answer this, we compute target regions using the method described in Section 4.2.2 with both data collected from PlanetLab and using a simulated deployment of 20,000 nodes. For forbidden regions, we used several countries identified in the 2012 Internet Enemies Report [34]—China, Syria, North Korea, and Saudi Arabia—as well as the three other countries with the most number of Internet users as of the time of this writing—USA, India, and Japan.

Who can avoid whom? Using latency data we gathered from PlanetLab, we simulated Alibi Routing with different

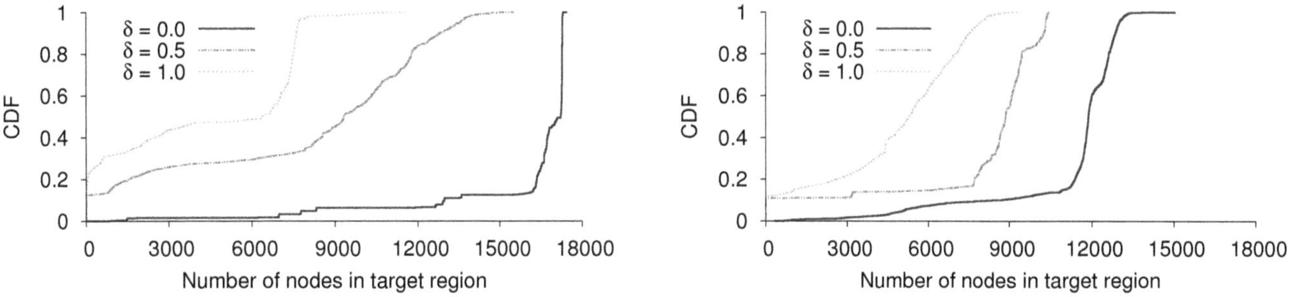

(a) USA is the forbidden region.

(b) China is the forbidden region.

Figure 5: CDF of the number of simulated nodes in the target region. (Simulated deployment of 20,000 nodes.)

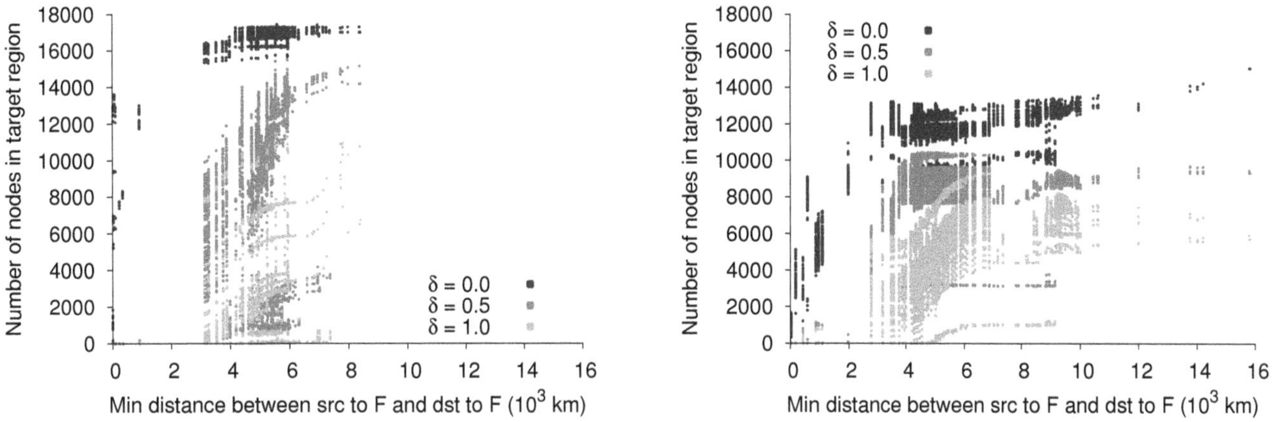

(a) USA is the forbidden region.

(b) China is the forbidden region.

Figure 6: Effect of source/destination distance on the number of nodes in the target region. The x-axis is the minimum of the distance between (source, destination) to the forbidden region. (Simulated deployment of 20,000 nodes.)

inequality values (δ from Eq. (1)). Figure 4 shows the fraction of source-destination pairs of PlanetLab nodes for which (from bottom to top):

(1) *There is no target region whatsoever.* This happens infrequently, and with greater values of δ; it reflects the instances in which the source and/or destinations are simply too close to the forbidden region to obtain proof (we do not include in our evaluation instances where s or d are *inside* F).

(2) *There are no hosts within the target region.* This would improve with a more geographically diverse deployment, yet even with our 425-node PlanetLab dataset, we find these numbers to be encouraging.

(3) *There is no safe path to the target region.* This, too would improve with a more geographically diverse deployment.

(4) *The source-destination pair does not need a relay* to be able to communicate while provably avoiding the forbidden region (i.e., the source is in the target region). This is rather common in our dataset, and corresponds to instances wherein both source and destination are far from the forbidden region (for example, two hosts on the same subnet obtaining sub-millisecond latencies would not need to use a third party relay to ensure they are avoiding someone thousands of miles away).

(5) *An alibi relay is necessary and Alibi Routing succeeds in finding one.* Finally, we see the fraction of hosts who need an alibi, and for whom Alibi Routing would be able to deliver one. This value generally increases with larger values of δ: when avoiding China, for instance, Alibi Routing would be able to locate alibis for roughly 80% of source-destination pairs when $\delta = 1.0$, but far fewer when δ is as low as 0.5. This is actually reflective of the fact that the system does not *need* alibis when δ is very low (and would have instead fallen into category (4) above). These results are also correlated with location: note that Saudi Arabia, and Syria show similar trends and are geographically proximal.

In the vast majority of cases, target regions are non-null, and in fact, Alibi Routing *can* be successful. Figure 4 only measures the case when a safe path to a node in the target region can be found: our later experiments measure the fraction of time such paths find relays that satisfy the alibi condition (Eq. (1)).

How well populated are target regions? The above results demonstrate how often an alibi is needed and, when so, how often a peer can find at least one. We next investigate *how many* alibis are available in a much larger (simulated) deployment of 20,000 nodes. We chose the location of these

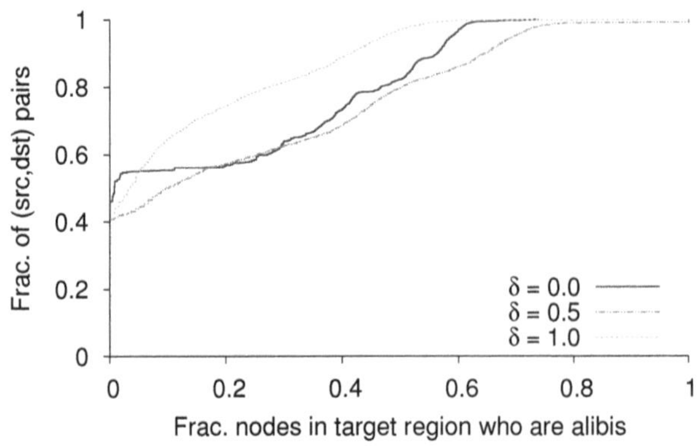

(a) USA is the forbidden region.

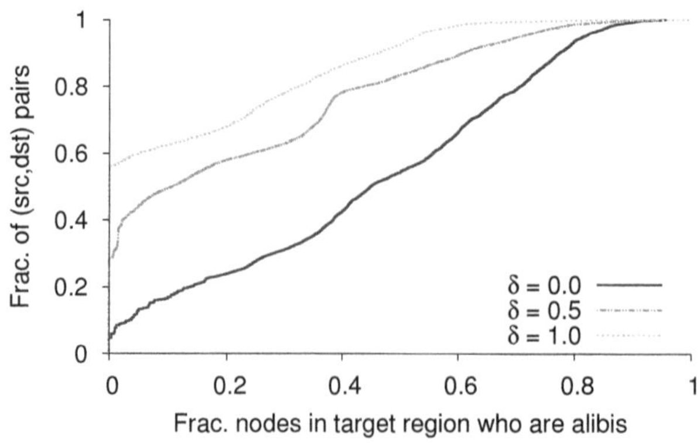

(b) China is the forbidden region.

Figure 7: Fraction of possible alibis that pass the alibi condition. (Simulated deployment of 20,000 nodes.)

nodes by subsampling the MaxMind node list [26] which provides a representative sample of global Internet deployment. For each forbidden region, and for each pair of nodes in our data set, we computed the target region (if any), and counted the number of simulated nodes contained in the target region.

Figures 5(a) and 5(b) show the CDF of number of nodes that lie in the target regions with the USA and China as forbidden regions. Each plot contains data for three different inequality factors (δ). As expected, as δ increases, constraints on the target region are stronger, which leads to smaller target regions and fewer possible relays. Figure 5(b) shows that approximately 10% of pairs are not able to provably avoid China when the inequality factor is set to 1.0; this number rises to 22% for the USA.

Intuitively, it will be more difficult to find valid alibis when the source or destination node is close to the forbidden region. Figure 6 quantifies this. Each point in this figure represents a source-destination pair, with x-value equal to the minimum distance of either the source or the destination to the forbidden region. The horizontal gaps in these plots is due to oceans: in a global deployment, distances between nodes are not uniformly distributed. The y-value corresponds to the number of possible relay nodes available to the source-destination pair for the given forbidden region.

For both the USA and China set as forbidden, Figure 6 shows the expected strong correlation between the minimum distance and the number of possible relays. In most cases, when relays cannot be found, either the source or destination is close to the forbidden region. Similarly, as the inequality factor increases, the target regions are constrained, resulting in fewer possible relays: the vertical striations in the graph captures this phenomenon.

6.2 How predictive are target regions?

Recall that target regions indicate the geographic areas wherein alibi nodes *may* exist; that is, no peers outside a target region could possibly be an alibi, but not all peers within a target region are guaranteed to have low enough latencies to be a viable alibi. We next evaluate how predictive target regions are by measuring the likelihood that a given peer within a target region can forward packets quickly enough to satisfy the alibi conditions (Eq. (1)). To assess what fraction of nodes in the target region are viable alibis, we conducted the following experiment: we periodically, once every 10 minutes, computed all-pairs pings between each pair of nodes on PlanetLab for 24 hours. During each run, each host sent five pings to all other hosts, and we recorded this data. Next, for different forbidden regions, we computed target regions, and classified whether a PlanetLab host was a possible alibi, i.e., whether or not it was in the target region.

Figure 7(a) plots, over all (source, destination, possible alibi) triples, the cumulative distribution of the fraction of times a possible alibi passes the alibi condition, i.e., the possible alibi is a viable relay. The plot shows that about half of the time, PlanetLab nodes in the target region are not able to pass the alibi condition. This is explained partly by the routing centrality of the US [19]: disproportionately many routes pass through the US, thus even if a peer is in the target region, there may not be a safe path to it. Further, delays within PlanetLab and queuing delays on the Internet ensure that only relays that are very favorably placed can pass the alibi condition. The picture is different when China is considered the forbidden region (Figure 7(b)). For low inequality values, only in about 5% of the cases can a valid alibi not be found. We acknowledge that this real-world measurement result is biased by the placement of PlanetLab nodes.

Over one day of pings, the RTTs we measured did not change enough to cause nodes to oscillate between being valid alibis and not. If a node was ever a valid alibi, it remained so (with high probability) for all our measurements. The same is true for nodes that were never a valid alibi.

We next turn to evaluating how close to these ideals our specific Alibi Routing protocol performs.

6.3 Alibi Routing success and performance

We next measure how successful Alibi Routing is at finding alibis "in the wild" by running our implementation on 370 PlanetLab hosts, and through a simulation over tens of thousands of nodes. Our findings indicate that Alibi Routing succeeds the vast majority of the time, and moreover, finds alibis quickly.

δ	Number of nodes 10,000	20,000
0	99.5	100.0
0.5	84.12	93.60
1.0	84.12	93.28

Table 1: Protocol success rate (simulation).

δ	Forbidden Region USA	China
0	100.0	97.19
0.5	99.56	100.0
1.0	100.0	97.30

Table 2: Protocol success rate (PlanetLab).

δ	Number of nodes 10,000	20,000
0.0	7.11	4.68
0.5	44.40	37.14
1.0	38.76	35.58

Table 3: Number of nodes contacted (simulation).

δ	Forbidden Region USA	China
0	1.03	1.00
0.5	1.00	1.30
1.0	1.66	1.00

Table 4: Number of nodes contacted (PlanetLab).

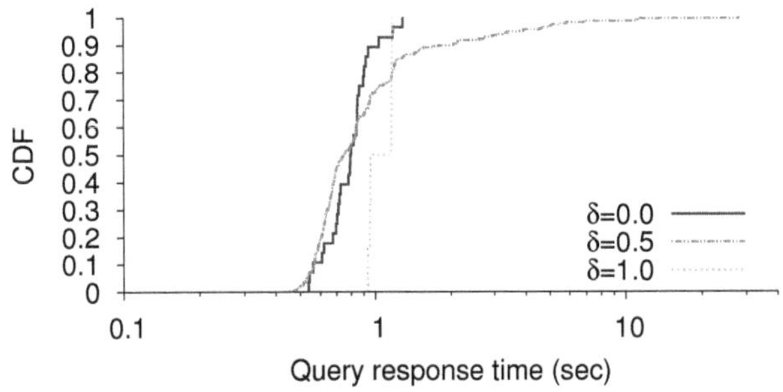

(a) USA is the forbidden region.

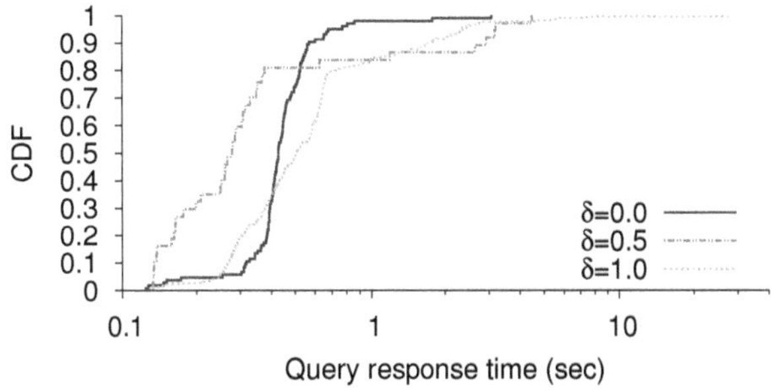

(b) China is the forbidden region.

Figure 8: Time taken to find a relay for all PlanetLab source-destination pairs. (Implementation on PlanetLab.)

Table 1 shows Alibi Routing's success rate for a simulated dataset with 10,000 and 20,000 nodes subsampled from the MaxMind node set [26]. In these results, we capped the maximum TTL to 7, and with this setting, for larger values of δ, the protocol is successful about 84% of the time for the 10,000 node deployment. Running the protocol with much larger TTLs would increase the success rate, as it would increase the chances of finding a path to a target region. However, larger TTLs impose an exponentially higher cost (in terms of messages and nodes contacted) for these queries. For our PlanetLab deployment (Table 2), our implementation (also with max TTL 7) has near 100% success rate regardless of the inequality factor.

Tables 3 and 4 show the protocol overhead in terms of average number of nodes contacted, both for simulations and the PlanetLab deployment. The average overhead is extremely low: on average, on PlanetLab, most searches terminate in two hops. In our simulations, even with 20,000 nodes, the average search cost is less than 40 nodes. The peak search cost is incurred in the 10,000 node case with inequality factor set to 0.5. This, too, is because a very low δ makes it easy to find eligible relays, and a large δ constrains the target region such that the search cannot proceed very far before all eligible nodes are exhausted.

Figures 8(a) and 8(b) show the time taken to find relays, as measured by the `gettimeofday()` call at the source for the cases when a relay is found. The plots show data for all source-destination pairs when they are trying to avoid USA or China. There are relatively few feasible pairs with a non-null target region for $\delta = 1.0$ when trying to avoid the USA, and the corresponding CDF does not have many data points. Note that the plots do *not* include the cases when a relay cannot be found: in these cases, our code waits for a maximum of 40 seconds before timing out on ongoing searches. The plots show that for successful queries, our implementation finds relays relatively quickly, the vast majority being found in less than one second. Interestingly, the time it takes to find alibis for $\delta = 0.5$ is usually higher than the time taken for $\delta = 1.0$. This is because the target regions are smaller for $\delta = 1.0$, causing more queries to fail (which is not captured in this plot but is evident in Tables 1 and 2).

Figures 9(a) and 9(b) show how Alibi Routing affects end-to-end latency. Again, the plots show the data for all pairs when they are trying to avoid either the USA or China. For many pairs, Alibi Routing *improves* latency [36, 25]. But for the vast majority, it increases latency by less than 50%. This is a surprisingly positive result, given both the geographic area covered by the USA and China, and their routing centrality. Finally, we note that when relays can be found, latency inflation is relatively insular to the inequality factor.

7. RELATED WORK

Alibi Routing is broadly related to a wide range of work towards influencing what paths users' packets take, inferring what actions were taken within a distributed system, and hiding packet contents from untrusted third parties. We discuss related work here, and observe that Alibi Routing constitutes a unique set of goals that are largely orthogonal and complementary to prior systems.

Avoidance without proof. Recently, there has been a wide array of research into systems that avoid parts of the network via explicit support from in-network routers [21, 23, 24, 49]. For example, LIFEGUARD [21] identifies routing failures and routes around them by sending BGP messages that "poison" a failure-prone area. Also, Kline and Reiher [23] propose a scheme for avoidance routing that involves explicit participation from BGP routers; the idea is to issue queries for destinations that also include requests for certain security properties, such as an AS's location.

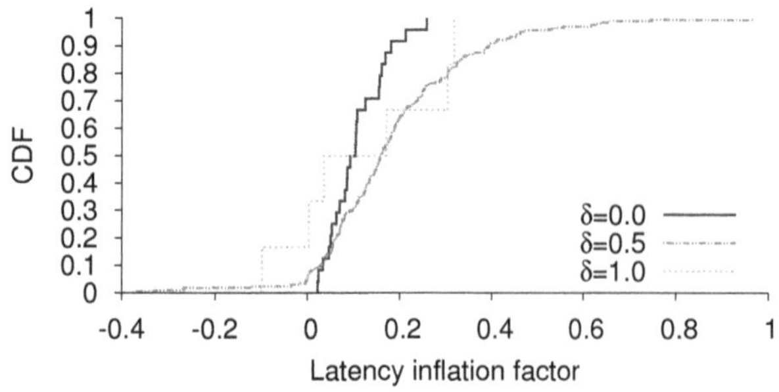

(a) USA is the forbidden region.

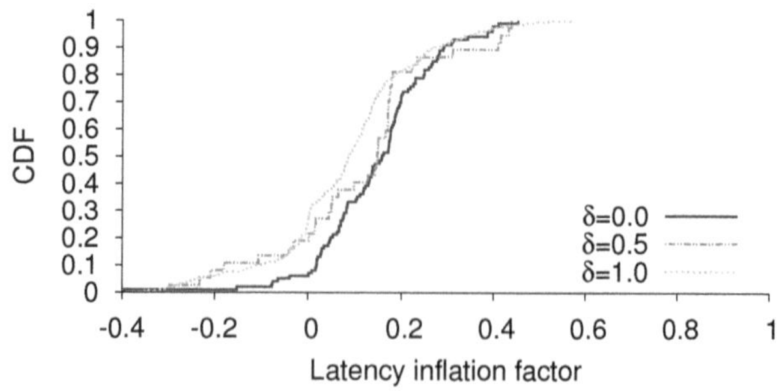

(b) China is the forbidden region.

Figure 9: Latency inflation for using Alibi Routing over the direct path. (Implementation on PlanetLab.)

However, *none of these prior systems offer* ***proof*** *of avoidance*, and are designed to operate in non-adversarial settings. Each of these prior systems trusts, to some extent, the ASes in the network to follow the protocol; for instance, to avoid an AS, LIFEGUARD relies on that AS to announce poor routes, which a routing-capable adversary [37] could easily avoid. What distinguishes our approach from these is the goal of *proving* that an area of the network was avoided, without explicit involvement of those whom users seek to avoid. Additionally, because Alibi Routing is a peer-to-peer system, it can be deployed without broad adoption by ISPs.

Policy routing. Many prior systems allow hosts to express some degree of path preference [14, 35, 47, 48], including the original IP RFC [31]. More recent systems have introduced the ability of enforcing compliance to users' desired routing policies [28, 22]; these systems in particular obtain proof that a packet traversed a sequence of locations in the network, even in an adversarial setting. However, none of these systems offer proofs of avoidance; they can ensure that a packet visits an ordered set of entities in the network, but do not detect the intermediate hops: what Kim et al. refer to as the path detour attack [22]. In this sense, Alibi Routing is orthogonal and potentially complementary; we use a much more rudimentary form of path enforcement (the relay simply signs the packet)—policy enforcement mechanisms could improve this, particularly if Alibi Routing were to be expanded to support multi-relay paths.

Obfuscating packet contents. Anonymity and censorship-resistant systems often hide packets' contents via obfuscating proxies [8, 10, 40] or steganography [11]. Whereas Alibi Routing seeks to avoid censors altogether, these approaches seek an orthogonal set of properties: to minimize what a censor can learn when it sees a user's traffic.

Several recent approaches broadly referred to as *decoy routing* [18, 46, 17], attempt to make it appear to a censor that the user is communicating with some destination d whom the censor allows. In reality, a "decoy router" on the path from the user to d intercepts these requests, and serves as a proxy to the user's true destination. As these systems also "use and confuse" forbidden regions, they too seek goals orthogonal to Alibi Routing's.

A natural question to ask is: why do we need Alibi Routing if we have systems that preserve anonymity and encrypt end-to-end? In practice, *no one approach works all the time*: anonymity systems must typically make their proxies well-known, and thus a resource-rich adversary may be able to identify and block access to them; decoy routing systems make strong trust assumptions that are not compatible with routing-capable adversaries [37]; and of course Alibi Routing itself cannot make any avoidance guarantees for users within a censored regime.

We believe, however, that Alibi Routing complements the others well. For example, consider Tor [10], in which a source chooses a set of relay nodes and constructs a virtual circuit through them. These relays are typically chosen at random, but doing so can result in two consecutive relays whose traffic transits a censoring regime. Alibi Routing can be applied to Tor's relay selection to compute which circuits provably avoid known censors. Alibi Routing also composes well with decoy routing: one could for instance use decoy routing to get out of a censored regime, and Alibi Routing to avoid others further down the path. These are but brief design sketches, but they demonstrate Alibi Routing's potential for composing with prior work.

Influencing underlay paths with overlay routes. Overlay routing protocols, such as RON [3] and SOSR [15], demonstrate that overlay paths can be used to influence and improve upon the underlay paths that packets take. A natural approach would be to use overlay routing to find a path that avoids a censor—much like how SOSR uses one-hop relays to avoid slow parts of the network. This is in essence the approach we take, but the primary challenges are in *proving* when a relay avoids a part of the network, and *finding* relays who can achieve such proof. To meet this goal, our overlay routing techniques exploit the connection between geographic distance and latencies.

Other systems incorporate latency measurements into overlay routing [25, 36, 44]. Meridian [44] is an unstructured overlay system that iteratively uses latency measurements to perform a set of queries, such as nearest-neighbor search and leader election. It may be possible to achieve some form of avoidance routing with Meridian, for instance as a sort of "nearest-but-not-too-near" neighbor search. However, Meridian is not designed to operate in an adversarial setting, and, unfortunately, it is straightforward for an attacker to appear to be "not too near" by fabricating higher

RTTs. We believe that the mechanisms we present in this paper can be generally applied in securing these systems.

Geographic routing. Geographic routing protocols incorporate the location of nodes in their routing decisions [20, 32, 23], as does Alibi Routing. The typical approach to geographic routing is to apply a greedy heuristic which attempts to move as close to the target as possible at each hop. This is similar to Alibi Routing's use of target regions, but we are not aware of any geographic routing protocol that achieves avoidance in an adversarial setting. In such a setting, applying a greedy heuristic can, in the worst case, traverse the forbidden region; even when the heuristic is safe, it may end up forwarding it to a node who is just outside the border of the forbidden country. Alibi Routing shows that progress and safety must be balanced to achieve high query success rate; we believe these lessons can apply to other geographic routing protocols, as well.

Accountability and provenance. A tempting way to prove what routers *did not* do is to exhaustively prove what actions they *did* take. There is a wealth of prior work on holding participants in a network accountable for the actions they *did* take [2, 16, 50]. For instance, PeerReview [16] assigns "witnesses" to each participant, which monitor all incoming and outgoing messages, and emulate the protocol to ensure that the participant behaved correctly. More recent findings apply counterfactual reasoning to observations about the network to achieve "negative provenance:" attributing a set of (in)actions led to the absence of an expected event [45].

Unfortunately, it is not clear how to apply these approaches to solve the problem of provable route avoidance; it would appear to require witnesses to be able to verify latency measurements (which does not seem possible in general settings, but would be an interesting area of future work).

Alibi Routing's light-weight proof structure can be performed using only local observations. We believe our "proof by alibi" can be combined with both positive and negative provenance systems to yield a broader set of inferences.

8. CONCLUSION

This paper introduces a primitive, provable avoidance routing, that, when given a destination and region to avoid, provides "proof" after the fact that a packet and its response did not traverse the forbidden region. We rely on the insight that a packet could provide an "alibi"—a place and time where it was—to prove that it must have avoided the forbidden region in transit from source to destination.

To demonstrate the feasibility of implementing this primitive, we have developed and evaluated an overlay routing protocol, Alibi Routing. Alibi Routing assumes that nodes outside the forbidden region are trustworthy in reporting their geographic locations and in vouching for neighbors that are too nearby to be in the forbidden region. It leverages this assumption to direct relay discovery queries toward a target region in which alibis might reside.

Our empirical results show that Alibi Routing is effective at finding alibis for a range of forbidden countries. However, Alibi Routing is not a panacea; primarily, it is unable to assist hosts who are very close to (or, of course, inside of) the regions they seek to avoid. But because its properties are largely orthogonal to prior work, we believe that Alibi Routing will compose well with them to strengthen their security guarantees. Moreover, we believe the techniques we have introduced can be applied to myriad other domains.

There are several possible extensions to Alibi Routing. Allowing routes through more than one relay could potentially improve Alibi Routing's success rates; discovering multi-relay paths and generating proof that they collectively avoid a forbidden region is an interesting area of future work.

Our implementation and data are publicly available at:

`https://alibi.cs.umd.edu`

Acknowledgments

We thank the anonymous reviewers and our shepherd, Xiaowei Yang, for their helpful comments. We also thank Brendan Rowan for his help in developing an earlier version of the Alibi Routing protocol, and Dave Mount for his helpful guidance on computing target regions. Finally, we thank Brandi Adams for coming up with the name "Alibi Routing." This research was supported in part by NSF grant IIS-0964541, ONR grant N00173-13-1-G001, and an Amazon Web Services in Education grant.

9. REFERENCES

[1] S. Agarwal and J. R. Lorch. Matchmaking for online games and other latency-sensitive P2P systems. In *ACM SIGCOMM*, 2009.

[2] D. G. Andersen, H. Balakrishnan, N. Feamster, T. Koponen, D. Moon, and S. Shenker. Accountable Internet Protocol (AIP). In *ACM SIGCOMM*, 2008.

[3] D. G. Andersen, H. Balakrishnan, M. F. Kaashoek, and R. Morris. Resilient overlay networks. In *ACM Symposium on Operating Systems Principles (SOSP)*, 2001.

[4] Anonymous. The collateral damage of Internet censorship by DNS injection. *ACM SIGCOMM Computer Communication Review (CCR)*, 42(3):21–27, 2012.

[5] Anonymous. Towards a comprehensive picture of the Great Firewall's DNS censorship. *USENIX Workshop on Free and Open Communications on the Internet (FOCI)*, 2014.

[6] ARRL. *The ARRL Handbook for Radio Communications*. The ARRL, 89th edition, 2012.

[7] S. Aryan, H. Aryan, and J. A. Halderman. Internet censorship in Iran: A first look. In *USENIX Workshop on Free and Open Communications on the Internet (FOCI)*, 2013.

[8] I. Clarke, O. Sandberg, B. Wiley, and T. W. Hong. Freenet: A distributed anonymous information storage and retrieval system. In *Designing Privacy Enhancing Technologies: Workshop on Design Issues in Anonymity and Unobservability*, pages 46–66, July 2000.

[9] B. Cohen. Incentives build robustness in BitTorrent. In *Workshop on Economics of Peer-to-Peer Systems (P2PEcon)*, 2003.

[10] R. Dingledine, N. Mathewson, and P. Syverson. Tor: The second-generation onion router. In *USENIX Security*, 2004.

[11] N. Feamster, M. Balazinska, G. Harfst, H. Balakrishnan, and D. Karger. Infranet: Circumventing censorship and surveillance. In *USENIX Security*, 2002.

[12] R. Feynman, R. Leighton, and M. Sands. *The Feynman Lectures on Physics Vol. 1.* (Chapter 26). Addison-Wesley, 1963.

[13] Global Administrative Areas (GADM) Database. `http://www.gadm.org`.

[14] P. B. Godfrey, I. Ganichev, S. Shenker, and I. Stoica. Pathlet Routing. In *ACM SIGCOMM*, 2009.

[15] K. Gummadi, H. Madhyastha, S. D. Gribble, H. M. Levy, and D. J. Wetherall. Improving the reliability of Internet paths with one-hop source routing. In *Symposium on Operating Systems Design and Implementation (OSDI)*, 2004.

[16] A. Haeberlen, P. Kuznetsov, and P. Druschel. PeerReview: Practical accountability for distributed systems. In *ACM Symposium on Operating Systems Principles (SOSP)*, 2007.

[17] A. Houmansadr, G. T. K. Nguyen, M. Caesar, and N. Borisov. Cirripede: Circumvention infrastructure using router redirection with plausible deniability. In *ACM Conference on Computer and Communications Security (CCS)*, 2011.

[18] J. Karlin, D. Ellard, A. W. Jackson, C. E. Jones, G. Lauer, D. P. Mankins, and W. T. Strayer. Decoy routing: Toward unblockable Internet communication. In *USENIX Workshop on Free and Open Communications on the Internet (FOCI)*, 2011.

[19] J. Karlin, S. Forrest, and J. Rexford. Nation-state routing: Censorship, wiretapping, and BGP. `http://arxiv.org/pdf/0903.3218.pdf`, Mar. 2009.

[20] B. Karp and H. T. Kung. GPSR: greedy perimeter stateless routing for wireless networks. In *ACM Conference on Mobile Computing and Networking (MobiCom)*, 2000.

[21] E. Katz-Bassett, C. Scott, D. R. Choffnes, Ítalo Cunha, V. Valancius, N. Feamster, H. V. Madhyastha, T. Anderson, and A. Krishnamurthy. LIFEGUARD: Practical repair of persistent route failures. In *ACM SIGCOMM*, 2012.

[22] T. H.-J. Kim, C. Basescu, L. Jia, S. B. Lee, Y.-C. Hu, and A. Perrig. Lightweight Source Authentication and Path Validation. In *ACM SIGCOMM*, 2014.

[23] E. Kline and P. Reiher. Securing data through avoidance routing. In *New Security Paradigms Workshop (NSPW)*, 2009.

[24] D. Levin, A. Bender, C. Lumezanu, N. Spring, and B. Bhattacharjee. Boycotting and extorting nodes in an internetwork. In *Joint Workshop on the Economics of Networked Systems and Incentive-Based Computing (NetEcon+IBC)*, 2007.

[25] C. Lumezanu, R. Baden, D. Levin, B. Bhattacharjee, and N. Spring. Symbiotic relationships in Internet routing overlays. In *USENIX Symposium on Networked Systems Design and Implementation (NSDI)*, 2009.

[26] MaxMind, Inc. `http://dev.maxmind.com/geoip/legacy/geolite/`.

[27] S. J. Murdoch and P. Zieliński. Sampled traffic analysis by Internet-exchange-level adversaries. In *Workshop on Privacy Enhancing Technologies (PET)*, 2007.

[28] J. Naous, M. Walfish, A. Nicolosi, M. Miller, and A. Seehra. Verifying and enforcing network paths with ICING. In *ACM Conference on emerging Networking EXperiments and Technologies (CoNEXT)*, 2011.

[29] J. A. Obar and A. Clement. Internet surveillance and boomerang routing: A call for Canadian network sovereignty. Online: `http://ssrn.com/abstract=2311792`, 2013.

[30] V. Paxson. End-to-End Routing Behavior in the Internet. In *ACM SIGCOMM*, 1996.

[31] J. Postel. Internet Protocol. IETF RFC-791, Sept. 1981.

[32] J. Preethi and R. Sumathi. An energy efficient on-demand routing by avoiding voids in wireless sensor network. In *Internation Conference on Information Systems Design and Intelligent Applications (INDIA)*, 2012.

[33] C. Reis, S. D. Gribble, T. Kohno, and N. C. Weaver. Detecting in-flight page changes with web tripwires. In *USENIX Symposium on Networked Systems Design and Implementation (NSDI)*, 2008.

[34] Reporters Without Borders. Enemies of the internet 2013, report. `http://surveillance.rsf.org/en/wp-content/uploads/sites/2/2013/03/enemies-of-the-internet_2013.pdf`, Mar. 2013.

[35] E. Rosen, A. Viswanathan, and R. Callon. Multiprotocol label switching. IETF RFC-3031, Jan. 2001.

[36] S. Savage, T. Anderson, A. Aggarwal, D. Becker, N. Cardwell, A. Collins, E. Hoffman, J. Snell, A. Vahdat, G. Voelker, and J. Zahorjan. Detour: Informed Internet routing and transport. *IEEE Micro*, 19(1):50–59, 1999.

[37] M. Schuchard, J. Geddes, C. Thompson, and N. Hopper. Routing around decoys. In *ACM Conference on Computer and Communications Security (CCS)*, 2012.

[38] J. Seibert, S. Becker, C. Nita-Rotaru, and R. State. Securing virtual coordinates by enforcing physical laws. In *International Conference on Distributed Computing Systems (ICDCS)*, 2012.

[39] R. Sherwood, B. Bhattacharjee, and R. Braud. Misbehaving TCP receivers can cause Internet-wide congestion collapse. In *ACM Conference on Computer and Communications Security (CCS)*, 2005.

[40] R. Sherwood, B. Bhattacharjee, and A. Srinivasan. $\mathcal{P}5$: A protocol for scalable anonymous communication. *Journal of Computer Security*, 13(6):839–876, 2005.

[41] A. Singh, M. Castro, P. Druschel, and A. Rowstron. Defending against eclipse attacks on overlay networks. In *Proc. of ACM SIGOPS European Workshop*, 2004.

[42] G. Varghese. *Network Algorithmics: An Interdisciplinary Approach to Designing Fast Networked Devices.* Morgan Kaufmann, 2004.

[43] G. Wang and T. E. Ng. Distributed algorithms for stable and secure network coordinates. In *ACM Internet Measurement Conference (IMC)*, 2008.

[44] B. Wong, A. Slivkins, and E. G. Sirer. Meridian: A lightweight network location service without virtual coordinates. In *ACM SIGCOMM*, 2005.

[45] Y. Wu, M. Zhao, A. Haeberlen, W. Zhou, and B. T. Loo. Diagnosing Missing Events in Distributed Systems with Negative Provenance. In *ACM SIGCOMM*, 2014.

[46] E. Wustrow, S. Wolchok, I. Goldberg, and J. A. Halderman. Telex: Anticensorship in the network infrastructure. In *IFIP International Information Security and Privacy Conference (SEC)*, 2011.

[47] X. Yang, D. Clark, and A. W. Berger. NIRA: A New Inter-Domain Routing Architecture. *IEEE/ACM Transactions on Networking (ToN)*, 15(4):775–788, 2007.

[48] X. Yang and D. Wetherall. Source Selectable Path Diversity via Routing Deflections. In *ACM SIGCOMM*, 2006.

[49] X. Zhang, H.-C. Hsaio, G. Hasker, H. Chan, A. Perrig, and D. G. Andersen. SCION: Scalability, Control and Isolation On Next-Generation Networks. In *IEEE Symposium on Security and Privacy*, 2011.

[50] M. Zhao, W. Zhou, A. J. T. Gurney, A. Haeberlen, M. Sherr, and B. T. Loo. Private and verifiable interdomain routing decisions. In *ACM SIGCOMM*, 2012.

ASwatch: An AS Reputation System to Expose Bulletproof Hosting ASes

Maria Konte
Georgia Tech
mkonte@cc.gatech.edu

Roberto Perdisci
University of Georgia
perdisci@cs.uga.edu

Nick Feamster
Princeton University
feamster@cs.princeton.edu

Abstract

Bulletproof hosting Autonomous Systems (ASes)—malicious ASes fully dedicated to supporting cybercrime—provide freedom and resources for a cyber-criminal to operate. Their services include hosting a wide range of illegal content, botnet C&C servers, and other malicious resources. Thousands of new ASes are registered every year, many of which are often used exclusively to facilitate cybercrime. A natural approach to squelching bulletproof hosting ASes is to develop a reputation system that can identify them for takedown by law enforcement and as input to other attack detection systems (*e.g.*, spam filters, botnet detection systems). Unfortunately, current AS reputation systems rely primarily on data-plane monitoring of malicious activity from IP addresses (and thus can only detect malicious ASes after attacks are underway), and are not able to distinguish between *malicious* and *legitimate but abused* ASes.

As a complement to these systems, in this paper, we explore a fundamentally different approach to establishing AS reputation. We present *ASwatch*, a system that identifies malicious ASes using exclusively the *control-plane* (*i.e.*, routing) behavior of ASes. *ASwatch*'s design is based on the intuition that, in an attempt to evade possible detection and remediation efforts, malicious ASes exhibit "agile" control plane behavior (*e.g.*, short-lived routes, aggressive re-wiring). We evaluate our system on known malicious ASes; our results show that *ASwatch* detects up to 93% of malicious ASes with a 5% false positive rate, which is reasonable to effectively complement existing defense systems.

CCS Concepts

• **Security and privacy** → **Network security;** • **Networks** → *Network monitoring;*

SIGCOMM '15, August 17–21, 2015, London, United Kingdom

http://dx.doi.org/10.1145/2785956.2787494

Keywords

AS Reputation; Bulletproof Hosting; Malicious Networks

1 Introduction

Today's cyber-criminals must carefully manage their network resources to evade detection and maintain profitable illicit businesses. For example, botmasters need to protect their botnet command-and-control (C&C) servers from takedowns, spammers need to rotate IP addresses to evade trivial blacklisting, and rogue online businesses need to set up proxies to mask scam hosting servers. Often, cyber-criminals accomplish these goals by hosting their services within a malicious autonomous system (AS) owned by an Internet service provider that willingly hosts and protects illicit activities. Such service providers are usually referred to as *bulletproof hosting* [7], due to their reluctance to address repeated abuse complaints regarding their customers and the illegal services they run. Notorious cases of malicious ASes include McColo [22], Intercage [19], Troyak [27], and Vline [2] (these ASes were taken down by law enforcement between 2008 and 2011). According to Hostexploit's reports [14], these types of ASes continue to appear in many regions around the world—mostly in smaller countries with lower levels of regulation, but also in the United States—to support activities ranging from hosting botnet command-and-control to phishing attacks [15]. For example, the Russian Business Network [31], one of the most notorious and still active cybercrime organizations, have decentralized their operations across multiple ASes. In most cases, nobody notices bulletproof hosting ASes until they have become hubs of illegal activities, at which point they are de-peered from their upstream providers. For example, Intercage [19] was de-peered more than ten times before it reached notoriety and was cut off from all upstream providers.

To defend against these crime-friendly ASes, the community has developed several AS reputation systems that monitor *data-plane* traffic for illicit activities. Existing AS reputation systems typically monitor network traffic from different vantage points to detect the presence of either malware-infected machines that contact their C&C servers, send spam, host phishing or scam websites, or perform other illicit activities. These systems establish AS reputation by measuring the "density" of malicious network activities hosted within an AS.

For instance, FIRE [36] tracks the number of botnet C&C and drive-by malware download servers within an AS. ASes that host a large concentration of malware-related servers are then assigned a low reputation. Similarly, Hostexploit [14] and BGP Ranking [4] compute the reputation of an AS based on data collected from sources such as DShield [11] and a variety of IP and domain name blacklists.

Unfortunately, these existing AS reputation systems have a number of limitations: (1) They cannot distinguish between *malicious* and *legitimate but abused* ASes. Legitimate ASes often unwillingly host malicious network activities (*e.g.*, C&C servers, phishing sites) simply because the machines that they host are abused. For example, AS 26496 (GoDaddy) and AS 15169 (Google) repeatedly appeared for years among the ASes with lowest reputation, as reported by Hostexploit. Although these ASes are legitimate and typically respond to abuse complaints with corrective actions, they may simply be unable to keep pace with the level of abuse within their network. On the other hand, *malicious* ASes are typically unresponsive to security complaints and subject to law-enforcement takedown. (2) Because of the inability to distinguish between *malicious* and *legitimate but abused* ASes, it is not clear how to use the existing AS rankings to defend against *malicious* ASes. (3) Existing AS reputation systems require direct observation of malicious activity from many different vantage points and for an extended period of time, thus delaying detection.

We present a fundamentally different approach to establishing AS reputation. We design a system, *ASwatch*, that aims to identify malicious ASes using exclusively *control-plane* data (*i.e.*, the BGP routing control messages exchanged between ASes using BGP). Unlike existing *data-plane* based reputation systems, *ASwatch* explicitly aims to identify *malicious* ASes, rather than assigning low reputation to legitimate ASes that have unfortunately been abused.

Our work is motivated by the practical help that an AS reputation system, which accurately identifies malicious ASes, may offer: (1) Network administrators may handle traffic appropriately from ASes that are likely operated by cyber criminals. (2) Upstream providers may use reliable AS reputation in the peering decision process (e.g. charge higher a low reputation customer, or even de-peer early). (3) Law enforcement practitioners may prioritize their investigations and start early monitoring on ASes, which will likely need remediation steps.

The main intuition behind *ASwatch* is that malicious ASes may manipulate the Internet routing system, in ways that legitimate ASes do not, in an attempt to evade current detection and remediation efforts. For example, malicious ASes "rewire" with one another, forming groups of ASes, often for a relatively short period of time [20]. Only one AS from the group connects to a legitimate upstream provider, to ensure connectivity and protection for the group. Alternatively, they may connect directly to a legitimate upstream provider, in which case they may need to change upstream providers frequently, to avoid being de-peered and isolated from the rest of the internet. Changing providers is necessary because a legitimate upstream provider typically responds (albeit often slowly) to repeated abuse complaints concerning its customer ASes. Another example is that a malicious AS may advertise and use small blocks of its IP address space, so that as soon as one small block of IP addresses is blocked or blacklisted, a new block can be advertised and used to support malicious activities. To capture this intuition, we derive a collection of *control-plane features* that is evident solely from BGP traffic observed via Routeviews [32]. We then incorporate these features into a supervised learning algorithm, that automatically distinguishes malicious ASes from legitimate ones.

We offer the following contributions:

- We present *ASwatch*, an AS reputation system that aims to identify malicious ASes by monitoring their *control plane behavior*.
- We identify three families of features that aim to capture different aspects of the "agile" control plane behavior typical of malicious ASes. (1) *AS rewiring* captures aggressive changes in AS connectivity; (2) *BGP routing dynamics* capture routing behavior that may reflect criminal illicit operations; and (3) *Fragmentation and churn of the advertised IP address space* capture the partition and rotation of the advertised IP address space.
- We evaluate *ASwatch* on real cases of malicious ASes. We collect *ground truth* information about numerous malicious and legitimate ASes, and we show that *ASwatch* can achieve high true positive rates with reasonably low false positives. We evaluate our statistical features and find that the rewiring features are the most important.
- We compare the performance of *ASwatch* with BGP Ranking, a state-of-the-art AS reputation system that relies on data-plane information. Our analysis over nearly three years shows that *ASwatch* detects about 72% of the malicious ASes that were observable over this time period, whereas BGP Ranking detects only about 34%.

The rest of the paper is organized as follows. Section 2 offers background information about bulletproof hosting ASes. Section 3 describes the features we devised and an overview of our system. Section 4 discusses the evaluation of the system. Section 5 discusses various limitations of our work, Section 6 presents related work, and Section 7 concludes.

2 Background

In this section, we describe more precisely the differences between malicious (bulletproof hosting) and legitimate ASes. We provide background information, with an emphasis on characteristics that are common across most confirmed cases of malicious ASes. We also discuss how malicious ASes tend to connect with one another, and how some ISPs (some of which are themselves malicious) provide these ASes with upstream connectivity and protection. To illustrate this behavior, we explore a case study that shows how malicious ASes may

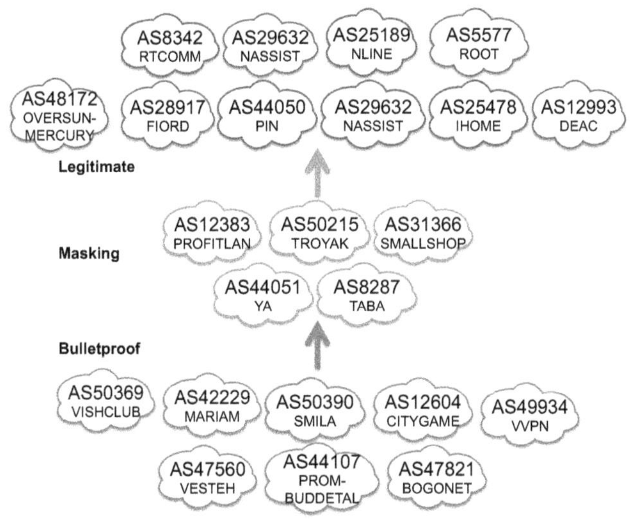

Figure 1: *The AS-TROYAK infrastructure (malicious ASes identified by* `blogs.rsa.com`*). The core of the infrastructure comprises eight bulletproof networks, which connect to legitimate ASes via a set of intermediate "masking" providers.*

be established and "rewired" in an attempt to evade current detection and takedown efforts.

Malicious vs. Legitimate ASes: We call an AS *malicious*, if it is managed and operated by cyber-criminals, and if its main purpose is to support illicit network activities (*e.g.*, phishing, malware distribution, botnets). In contrast, we refer to an AS as *legitimate*, if its main purpose is to provide legitimate Internet services. In some cases, a legitimate AS's IP address space may be abused by cyber-criminals to host malicious activities (*e.g.*, sending spam, hosting a botnet command-and-control server). Such abuse is distinct from those cases where cyber-criminals operate and manage the AS. *ASwatch* focuses on distinguishing between malicious and legitimate ASes; we aim to label *legitimate but abused* ASes as legitimate. Our approach is thus a significant departure from existing data-plane based AS reputation systems, which are limited to computing reputation by primarily focusing on data-plane abuse, rather than establishing if an AS is actually malicious.

Malicious AS Relationships: Bulletproof hosting ASes provide cyber-criminals with a safe environment to operate. Sometimes, malicious ASes form business relationships with one another to ensure upstream connectivity and protection. For example, they may connect to upstream providers that are themselves operated in part with criminal intent. In turn, these upstream ASes connect to legitimate ISPs, effectively providing cover for the bulletproof hosting ASes [2]. These "masking" upstream providers may not be actively engaged in cyber-criminal activity themselves (as observed from the data-plane). Consequently, network operators at legitimate ISPs may be unaware of the partnership among these "shady" upstream providers and bulletproof hosting ASes, making detection and remediation efforts more difficult.

Efforts to take down bulletproof hosting ASes have been ongoing since at least 2007, when upstream ISPs of the Russian Business Network (RBN) refused to route its traffic [21]. Many organizations track rogue ASes and report tens to hundreds of new rogue ASes every year [15]. Takedown efforts often result in a malicious AS moving to new upstream ISPs; for example, RBN now operates on many different ISP networks.

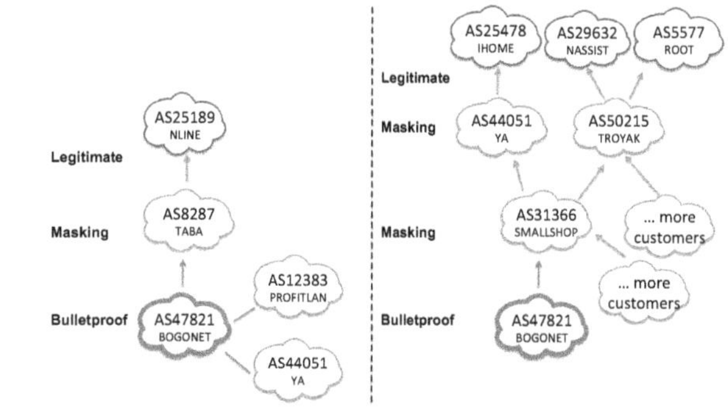

(**a**) *Bogonet (AS 47821), 2010.01.01-2010.02.01*

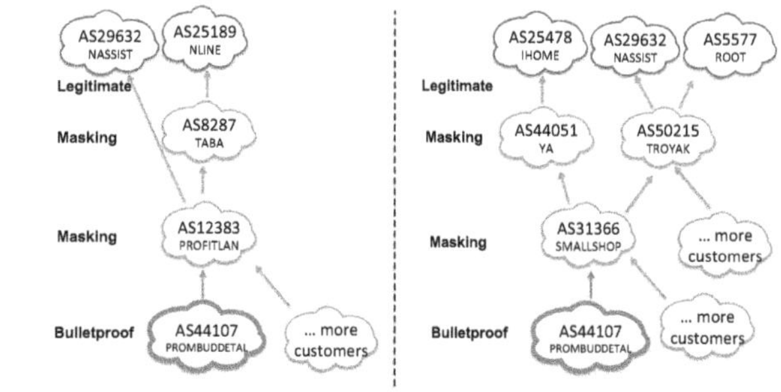

(**b**) *Prombuddetal (AS 44107), 2010.01.01-2010.02.01*

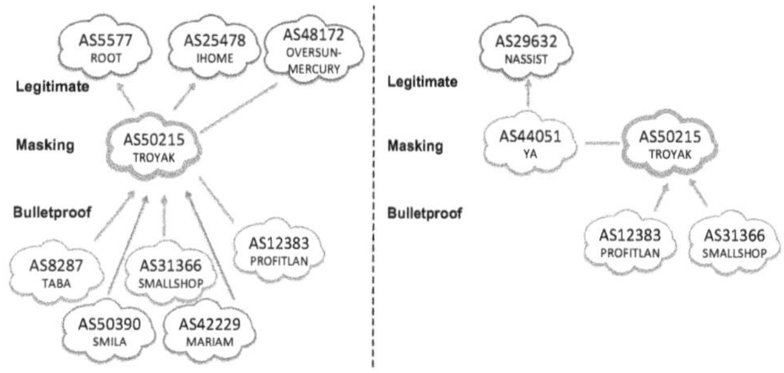

(**c**) *Troyak (AS 50215), 2010.02.01-2010.04.01*

Figure 2: *Connectivity snapshots of three cases of ASes which are operated by cyber-criminals. All connected to a "masking" upstream provider. Directed edges represent customer-provider relationships; undirected edges represent peering relationships.*

Case Study - Behavior of Malicious ASes: Figure 1 shows an example of a real network of eight bulletproof hosting ASes that connect to legitimate ASes via a set of intermediate "masking" providers. Notice that while we label the malicious ASes in this case study, based on ground truth provided by `blogs.rsa.com`, we independently derive and analyze the relationships between the ASes from routing information. At the time they were reported by `blogs.rsa.com` (March 2010), the eight bulletproof ASes hosted a range of malware, including Zeus Trojans, RockPhish JabberZeus servers, and Gozi Trojan servers. We chose this as a case study because it

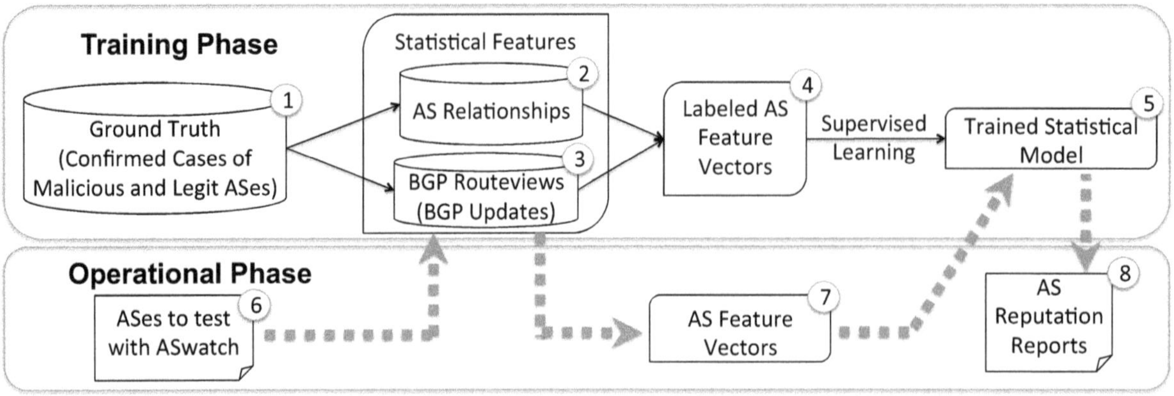

Figure 3: *ASwatch system architecture.*

represents one of the most well documented cases of known bulletproof hosting ASes, and is representative of other less well known incidents.

The bulletproof hosting ASes switched between five upstream providers, which served as intermediaries to connect to the legitimate ASes. In turn, the upstream "masking" providers were customers of nine different legitimate ISPs.

To understand how malicious ASes form business relationships and how these relationships evolve over time, we tracked the upstream and downstream connectivity of the malicious ASes, as shown in Figures 1 and 2 (the figures show an activity period from January to April 2010; the malicious ASes went offline in March 2010).

We tracked the connectivity of one "masking" AS, Troyak (AS 50215), and two bulletproof hosting ASes, Bogonet (AS 47821) and Prombuddetal (AS 44107), that belong to the Troyak infrastructure. To track their upstream and downstream connectivity, we used a publicly available dataset from CAIDA, which provides snapshots of the AS graph, annotated with business relationships [25]. Figure 2 shows snapshots of the connectivity for the reported ASes.

All of these malicious ASes connected to a "masking" upstream provider, thus avoiding direct connectivity with legitimate ISPs, and also they change their connectivity between one another. For example, before takedown, Troyak had three upstream providers: Root, Ihome, and Oversun-Mercury. After the blog report on March 2010, Troyak lost *all* of its upstream providers and relied on a peering relationship with Ya for connectivity. After April 2010, Troyak and its customers went offline. Bogonet switched from Taba to Smallshop, and Prombuddetal switched from Profitlan to Smallshop, before going offline.

3 ASwatch

ASwatch monitors globally visible BGP routing activity and AS relationships, to determine which ASes exhibit *control plane behavior* typical of malicious ASes. Because of the nature of their operations (criminal activity) and their need to fend off detection and possible take-down efforts, malicious ASes tend to exhibit control-plane behavior that is different from that of legitimate ASes. We now discuss how *ASwatch* works, including a detailed description of the features we used to differentiate between malicious and legitimate ASes, and our intuition for choosing each feature.

3.1 System Overview

Figure 3 presents an overview of *ASwatch*. The system has a training phase (Section 3.3.1) and an operational phase (Section 3.3.2). During the training phase, *ASwatch* learns the control-plane behavior of malicious and legitimate ASes. We provide the system with ① a list of known malicious and legitimate ASes (Section 4.1 describes this dataset). *ASwatch* tracks the control-plane behavior of the legitimate and malicious ASes over time using two sources of information: ② business relationships between ASes, and ③ BGP updates (from RouteViews). *ASwatch* then computes statistical features (Section 3.2 describes this process) from the previous inputs. Each AS is represented by a feature vector based on these statistical features ④. *ASwatch* uses these labeled feature vectors and a supervised learning algorithm to ⑤ train a statistical model. During the operational phase, we provide *ASwatch* with a list of new (not yet labeled) ASes ⑥ to be classified as legitimate or malicious using the same statistical features over the given time period. Then, *ASwatch* ⑦ computes the new AS feature vectors and ⑤ tests them against the previously trained statistical model. Finally, ⑧ the system assigns a reputation score to each AS.

3.2 Statistical Features

In this section, we describe the features we compute and the intuition for choosing them. Table 1 gives an overview of our feature families, and the most important group of features for each family. Given an AS, A, and time window, T, *ASwatch* monitors A's control-plane behavior and translates it into a feature vector consisting of three groups of features: rewiring activity, IP fragmentation and churn, and BGP routing dynamics.

Some of the behavioral characteristics we measure can be naturally described by a probability distribution, rather than a single numerical feature. In these cases, to capture the behavioral characteristics in a way that is more suitable for input to a statistical classifier, we translate each probability distribution into three numerical features that approximately describe the *shape* of the distribution. Specifically, we compute its 5th percentile, 95th percentile, and median. In the following, we refer to such features as *distribution characteristics.* We include these three values as features in the overall feature vector, and repeat this process for all behavioral characteristics that can be described as a probability distribution.

Notice that even though more values may more accurately summarize a distribution's shape, such a representation would significantly increase the overall size of the feature vector used to describe an AS. For this reason, we chose to only use three representative values, which we found to work well in practice.

We now explain in detail the features that *ASwatch* uses to establish AS reputation and motivate how we selected them.

3.2.1 Rewiring Activity

This group of features aims to capture the changes in A's connectivity. Our intuition is that malicious ASes have different connectivity behavior than legitimate ASes, because they tend to: (1) change providers more frequently to make detection and remediation more difficult; (2) connect with less popular providers, which may have less strict security procedures and may respond less promptly to abuse complaints, (3) have longer periods of downtime, possibly due to short-duration contracts or even de-peering from a legitimate upstream provider. In contrast, legitimate ASes tend to change their connectivity less frequently, typically due to business considerations (*e.g.*, a less expensive contract with a new provider).

To capture rewiring activity, *ASwatch* tracks changes to AS relationships (Step 2 in Figure 3). We use periodic snapshots of historic AS relationships, with one snapshot per month (Section 4.1 describes the data sets in more detail). A snapshot S_i contains the AS links annotated with the type of relationships, as observed at a given time t_i (*e.g.*, one snapshot is produced on the first day of each month).

AS presence and overall activity. Let A be the AS for which we want to compute our features. Given a sequence of N consecutive snapshots $\{S_i\}_{i=1}^{N}$, we capture the *presence* of an AS by measuring the total number of snapshots, C, and the maximum number of contiguous snapshots, M, in which A was present, the fraction C/N, and M/N (four features in total). To capture the overall activity of A, we measure the distribution (over time) of the number of customers, providers, and peers A links with for each snapshot. To summarize each of these distributions, we extract the distribution characteristics (5th percentile, 95th percentile, and median), as described earlier. This yields a total of nine features (three for each of the three types of AS relationships). We also count the total number and fraction (*i.e.*, normalized by C) of distinct customers, providers, and peers that A has linked with across all C snapshots when it was present, yielding another six features.

Feature Family	Description	Most Important Feature
Rewiring Activity	Changes in AS's connectivity (*e.g.*, frequent change of providers, customers or peers)	Link stability
IP Space Fragmentation & Churn	IP space partitioning in small prefixes & rotation of advertised prefixes	IP space fragmentation
BGP Routing Dynamics	BGP announcements patters (*e.g.*, short prefix announcements)	Prefix reachability

Table 1: *Overview of ASwatch feature families and the most important feature for each family.*

Link stability. We capture the *stability* of different types of relationships that an AS forms over time. For each of the C snapshots where A was present, we track all relationships between A and any other AS. Assuming A appeared as an upstream provider for another AS, say A^k, in v out of C snapshots, we compute the fraction $F^k = v/C$. We repeat this for all ASes where A appears as a provider at least once within C snapshots, thus obtaining a distribution of the F^k values. Finally, we summarize this distribution of the F^k values, computing the distribution characteristics as described above. We repeat this process, considering all ASes that appear as the upstream provider for A (*i.e.*, A is their customer), and for all ASes that have peering relationships with A. Overall, we compute nine features that summarize three different distributions (three features for each type of relationship).

Upstream connectivity. We attempt to capture *change* in the set of providers. Assume that from the i-th snapshot S_i we observed a total of M_i upstream providers for A, and call $\{A_i^k\}_{k=1}^{M_i}$ the set of upstream provider ASes. Then, for each pair of contiguous snapshots, S_i and S_{i+1}, we measure the Jaccard similarity coefficient $J_{i,i+1}$ between the sets $\{A_i^k\}$ and $\{A_{i+1}^k\}$. We repeat for all available $(N-1)$ pairs of consecutive snapshots, thus obtaining a distribution of Jaccard similarity coefficients. To summarize this distribution, we compute the distribution characteristics as described above, yielding three features. Figure 4 shows the CDF of the minimum Jaccard similarity, for the malicious and the legitimate ASes. Overall, the legitimate ASes tend to have higher values of the Jaccard similarity metric, which indicates fewer changes in their upstream providers.

Attachment to popular providers. We aim to capture an AS's *preference* for "popular" providers. As previous work has shown [20], malicious ASes tend to connect more often with less prominent providers, which may have less strict security procedures and may respond less promptly to abuse complaints.

We compute the popularity of each provider per snapshot and across all snapshots. To this end, we first empirically derive the distribution of the number of customers per provider. We then consider a provider to be (a) *very popular*, if it belongs to the top 1% of all providers overall; (b) *popular*, if it belongs to the top 5%; (c) *very popular with respect to a snapshot* S_i, if it belongs to the top 1% in S_i, and (d) *popular with respect to a snapshot* S_i, if it belongs to the top 5% in S_i.

We then gather all upstream providers that A has used and compute the fraction of these providers that fall into each of the four categories described above (thus yielding four features). Finally, we compute the fraction of snapshots in which A has linked to at least one provider falling into one of the above categories; we do this for each category, thus obtaining four more features.

We capture the overall rewiring behavior of an AS with a total number of thirty five features.

3.2.2 IP Space Fragmentation and Churn

Malicious ASes tend to partition their IP address space into small BGP prefixes and to advertise only some of these prefixes at any given time. One possible explanation for this behavior may be that they attempt to avoid having their entire IP address space blacklisted at once. For example, if a number of IP addresses within a given BGP prefix are detected as hosting malicious activities, a blacklist operator (*e.g.*, Spamhaus [35]) may decide to blacklist the entire prefix where the IP addresses reside. By fragmenting the IP address space and advertising only a subset of their BGP prefixes, the operators of a malicious AS may be able to quickly move malicious activities to a "fresh" space. They perform this maneuver by leveraging not-yet-blacklisted IP addresses within newly advertised prefixes. On the other hand, legitimate ASes tend to consistently advertise their available IP address space in less fragmented prefixes, as they do not need to attempt to evade blacklisting.

IP Space Fragmentation and Churn Features. We attempt to capture IP address *fragmentation* with the following features. Given a snapshot, we group the advertised BGP prefixes into contiguous IP *blocks*. For each, AS we count the number of BGP prefixes and the number of distinct `/8`, `/16`, and `/24` prefixes within each IP block. To capture the *churn* in the advertisement of the IP address space, we proceed as follows. Given a pair of adjacent snapshots for an AS, we measure the Jaccard similarity among the sets of BGP prefixes advertised by the AS in the two snapshots. Similarly, we compute the Jaccard index among the sets of `/8`, `/16`, and `/24` prefixes. We summarize the above four distributions using the *distribution characteristics* that we described earlier, thus obtaining a total of twelve features.

3.2.3 BGP Routing Dynamics

These features attempt to capture abnormal BGP announcement and withdrawal patterns. For example, to support aggressive IP address space fragmentation and churn and avoid easy blacklisting, malicious ASes may periodically announce certain prefixes for short periods of time. On the contrary, the pattern of BGP announcements and withdrawals for legitimate ASes is mainly driven by normal network operations (*e.g.*, traffic load balancing, local policy changes), and should thus exhibit BGP routing dynamics that are different to those of malicious ASes.

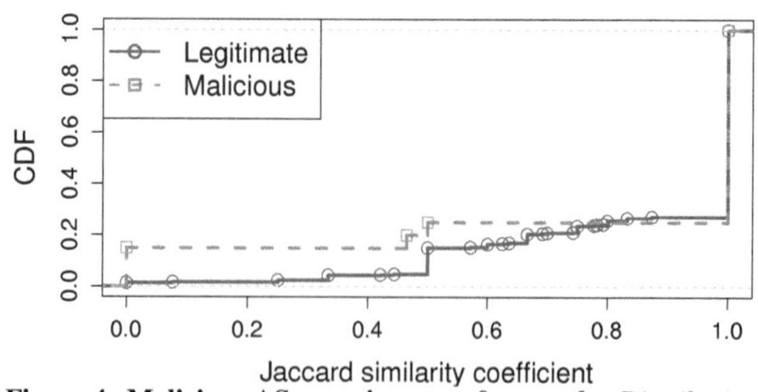

Figure 4: Malicious ASes rewire more frequently. *Distribution of the 5th percentile of the Jaccard similarity coefficient between consecutive snapshots of an AS's upstream providers. Higher values indicate fewer changes in upstream connectivity.*

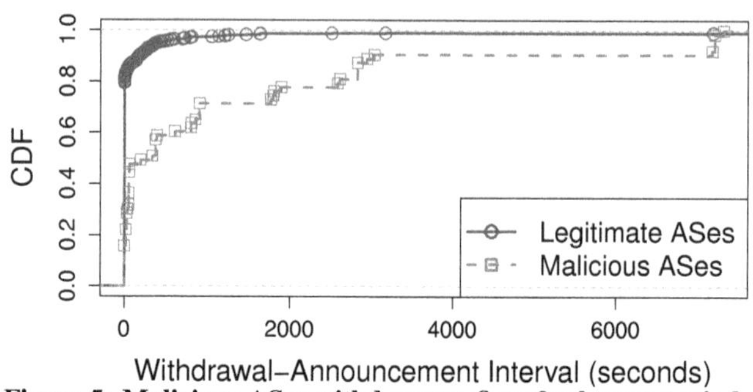

Figure 5: Malicious ASes withdraw prefixes for longer periods. *The distribution of the median interval between a prefix withdrawal and re-announcement across 15 contiguous epochs.*

Prefix reachability. We aim to capture the fraction of time that prefixes advertised by A remain reachable, which we define as *reachability*. First, we measure the time that elapses between an announcement and a withdrawal for every advertised prefix. Given the distribution of these time intervals, we extract the distribution characteristics as described above. Second, we track the time for a prefix to become reachable again after a withdrawal. Third, we measure the inter-arrival time (IAT) between withdrawals, for each of the prefixes that A announces, and compute the IAT distribution. As before, we extract the distribution characteristics for each of the three distributions, yielding a total of nine features. Figure 5 shows the CDF of the median reachability value for the malicious and the legitimate ASes over the course of one day, and over 15 days. Higher values of this feature suggest that malicious ASes tend to re-advertise their prefixes after longer delays.

Topology and policy changes. We track the *topology and policy changes*, defined as in Li *et al.* [24], that are associated with each prefix. We define a *policy change* as follows: after a path to a destination is announced, a second BGP announcement is observed with the same AS path and next-hop, yet one or more of the other attributes (such as MED or community) is different. Similarly, we define a *topology change* event as follows: after a path to a destination is announced, a second announcement follows with an alternate route (implicit withdrawal) or after a route to a destination is explicitly withdrawn, a different route (with different AS path or next-hop attributes) to the same destination is announced (explicit withdrawal).

To capture and summarize the topology and policy changes per AS, we group the prefixes per origin AS (the origin AS appears as the last AS in the AS path). We track the policy change events for each prefix, and we measure the inter-arrival time between the events per prefix. Then, we analyze the collection of inter-arrival times of the policy events for all prefixes advertised by the same AS. For each AS, we form the distribution of such intervals, and we extract the distribution characteristics as described above. We also compute the total number of events and the total number of events divided by the total prefixes advertised by the AS. We repeat this process for the topology change events. We compute a total of ten features.

3.3 System Operation

We now describe *ASwatch*'s training and operation.

3.3.1 Training Phase

To train the classifier (Steps 6 and 7 in Figure 3), we first prepare a training dataset with labeled feature vectors related to known malicious and legitimate ASes. We start with a ground truth dataset that includes confirmed cases of *malicious* ASes, and legitimate ASes (described in more details is Section 4.1).

We compute the statistical features for each labeled AS using two sources of data: BGP announcements and withdrawals from Routeviews [32], and information from a publicly available dataset [25] about the relationships between ASes. We compute the feature vectors over m contiguous epochs (in our experiments, each epoch is one day). More specifically, we maintain a sliding window of size m epochs, which advances one epoch at a time. Using this sliding window, we can compute multiple feature vectors for each AS (one per window). Then, we associate a label to each feature vector, according to the ground truth related to the AS from which a vector was computed.

Finally, to build the statistical classifier, we use the Random Forest (RF) algorithm. We experimented with different algorithms, but we chose RF because it can be trained efficiently and has been shown to perform competitively with respect to other algorithms for a variety of problems [6].

3.3.2 Operational Phase

Once the statistical classifier has been trained, *ASwatch* can assign a reputation score to new ASes (*i.e.*, ASes for which no ground truth is yet available). *ASwatch* computes a reputation score for each new AS observed in the BGP messages from Routeviews. Suppose that we want to compute the reputation of an AS, A, over some time period, T. First, we compute A's features (as explained in Section 3.2) over period T, using a sliding window procedure as in the training phase. Namely, a feature vector is computed for each window within T. Second, we classify an AS as malicious, if *ASwatch* consistently assigns it a low reputation score for several days in a row.

More specifically, let T_i be the current day of observations, f_{A,T_i} be the corresponding feature vector for A, and $s(f_{A,T_i})$ be the *bad reputation* score output by the classifier at the end of T_i. Also let $W_i = (T_i, T_{i+1}, \ldots, T_{(i+m-1)})$ be a period of m consecutive days. We report A as malicious if: (a) score $s(f_{A,T_i}) > \theta$ for 90% of the days in period W_i, where θ is a predefined threshold that can be learned during the training period; and (b) condition (a) holds for at least l consecutive periods $W_i, W_{i+1}, \ldots, W_{i+l}$.

We note that we have experimented with multiple values for m and l (see Section 4.3 for detailed discussion on parameter selection).

4 Evaluation

We now describe the data we collected and the setup for our evaluation of *ASwatch*, where we evaluate the system's accuracy. Our results show that *ASwatch* achieves a high detection rate for a reasonably low false positive rate, can detect malicious ASes before they are publicly reported by others, and can complement existing AS reputation systems that rely solely on data-plane observations. Furthermore, we find that *ASwatch* detects nearly double the fraction of confirmed cases of malicious ASes compared to BGP Ranking, a data-plane based AS reputation system.

4.1 Data

Labeling malicious ASes. Collecting reliable ground truth about malicious ASes is extremely challenging, due to the utter lack of public information available about such cases. Nonetheless, through extensive manual search and review efforts, we managed to collect a set of ASes for which there exists publicly available evidence of malicious behavior. For example, we identified a reasonable set of malicious ASes that were at some point seized by law enforcement or disconnected by other network operators.

To obtain our dataset of malicious ASes, we searched through websites that are operated by cyber-security professionals (*e.g.*, `www.abuse.ch`, `blogs.rsa.com` [1, 2, 23, 16, 13, 10]) and carefully reviewed articles about ASes known to be operated by cyber-criminals.

We observed the following common characteristics across all articles and blog reports we considered: (1) the reported ASes hosted a variety of cyber-criminal activities (*e.g.*, botnet C&C hosting, malware domains, phishing), (2) several ASes were associated with each other, either directly (*e.g.*, customer-provider relationship) or indirectly (*e.g.*, they shared the same upstream provider), (3) the operators of these ASes were uncooperative and unresponsive (*e.g.*, would not respond to abuse complaints or attempts by other AS operators to communicate with them), (4) some ASes were prosecuted by law enforcement and taken down, (5) many of these disappeared only for a relatively short time before resurfacing. From each blog report, we extracted the ASes involved and the dates

Informex, AS20564	Infium, AS40965	Vpnme, AS51354
Ecatel, AS29073	Egis, AS40989	Lyahov, AS51554
Volgahost, AS29106	K2KContel, AS43181	Taba, AS8287
RapidSwitch, AS29131	Phorm, AS48214	Retn, AS9002
Riccom, AS29550	IT-Outsource, AS48280	Vesteh, AS47560
Naukanet, AS31445	Vlaf, AS48984	Prombuddetal, AS44107
PromiraNet, AS31478	Moviement, AS49073	Citygame, AS12604
Ys-IX, AS31506	Interactive-3D, AS49544	Bogonet, AS47821
Vakushan, AS34229	Vvpn, AS49934	Troyak, AS50215
Euroaccess, AS34305	Softnet, AS50073	Vishclub, AS50369
SunNetwork, AS38197	Onlinenet, AS50722	Gaxtranz/Info, AS29371
Vline, AS39150	Digernet, AS50818	Group3, AS50033
Realhosts, AS39458	Proxiez, AS50896	Smila, AS50390
UninetMd, AS39858	Gorby, AS51303	

Figure 6: *Malicious ASes we collected from blogs.*

when they were active. Overall, we collected forty one known malicious ASes. We provide our list of ASes in Figure 6.

Labeling legitimate ASes. To collect a set of legitimate ASes, we proceeded as follows. Every day for one year, we collected the list of top one million domain names from `alexa.com`. For each of these domains, we calculated the average daily ranking; we selected the domain names that had an average ranking above 10,000. In other words, we selected only those domains that were consistently very popular. Finally, we mapped each domain name to its resolved IP addresses and mapped those IP addresses to the AS that hosted them. Overall, we collected a total of 389 ASes, which we label as *legitimate*.

Although we cannot be absolutely certain that our labeling of legitimate ASes contains no noise, we rely on two reasonable assumptions. First, we assume that websites that are consistently popular are unlikely to be offering malicious services. Intuitively, a malicious site that becomes highly popular would also have a high number of victims, and would rapidly attract attention for take-down. As a result, the site would be quickly blocked or taken down and would thus not remain consistently popular. Second, we assume that the administrators of the most popular websites are unlikely to host their services within malicious ASes. Intuitively, if they relied on malicious ASes, they would risk damaging their own reputation, not to mention extended downtimes if the hosting ASes were taken down due to abuse complaints.

Finally, to ensure that our set of legitimate ASes consists of ASes that are similar in size to the malicious ASes, we keep only those legitimate ASes that have no customers, or whose customers are all stub ASes.

AS rewiring and relationships data (CAIDA). To track how malicious ASes change their connectivity, we use a publicly available dataset that reports AS business relationships. The dataset reports one snapshot of the AS graph per month, from 1998 to 2013.

Luckie *et al.* [25] provide an AS graph built by inferring business relationships among ASes, based on AS customer cones. Although this dataset has its own limitations (see Section 5), it provides a reasonably accurate view of AS relationships, allowing us to estimate our rewiring features that we presented in Section 3.2.

BGP routing dynamics (Routeviews). To further capture the control-plane behavior of malicious and legitimate ASes, we monitored the BGP messages that originate from these ASes using the Routeviews dataset. We use this dataset to measure both the dynamics of BGP updates and the IP fragmentation and churn features.

4.2 Experiment Setup

In the following section, we describe the training and the evaluation of our system. The training period extends from January 2010 to March 2010, while the evaluation experiments extend from January 2011 to December 2013.

Computing AS feature vectors. Given a period of time (*i.e.*, m contiguous epochs) over which we want to capture the behavior of an AS, we construct the AS feature vector as follows: (1) *Rewiring activity*: We compute the rewiring features over the most recent k snapshots of the AS relationships dataset, prior to the period of interest. Our source of AS relationships provides only one snapshot per month. Given this limitation, we select a reasonable number of snapshots to capture the most recent rewiring activity of an AS. For our experiments we set $k = 4$ (see Section 4.3 on parameter selection); (2) *BGP routing activity*: To compute BGP routing dynamics features, IP address space fragmentation and churn, we collect the BGP announcements and withdrawals originating from the AS during the period of interest. We note that BGP Routeviews offers a large number of monitors. Our pilot experiments over a number of different monitors indicated that changing the monitor selection did not significantly affect the overall performance of our classifier. Therefore, to compute our routing activity features, we select one monitor and consistently use it, throughout all the experiments.

Training the AS reputation model. Because our data is derived from cases of malicious ASes publicly reported by others, we rely on the report dates for an approximate period of time when the ASes were likely to be actively used by the attackers. For example, if an AS was reported as malicious on a given day d, we assume the AS was operated by criminals for at least a few months before d (in fact, it typically takes time for security operators to detect, track, confirm, and take down a malicious AS). For the purpose of computing our labeled feature vectors and training our system, we selected a period of time with the highest concentration of active malicious ASes. This period extends from January–March 2010, during which we identified a total of 15 active malicious ASes. Even though this period may appear somewhat dated, it allows us to capture the agile behavior of several known malicious ASes within one consistent time frame, enabling a "clean" evaluation setup. Our evaluation detects a large fraction of malicious ASes that we have observed over a longer, more recent time period (2011–2013). In the future, we plan to investigate more sources of ground truth and identify additional periods of time that can be used to train our model (see Section 5 for further discussion).

Performing cross-validation tests. During the three-month training period mentioned above, we maintain a sliding window of fifteen contiguous days (epochs), sliding the window one day at a time (*i.e.*, two consecutive windows overlap by

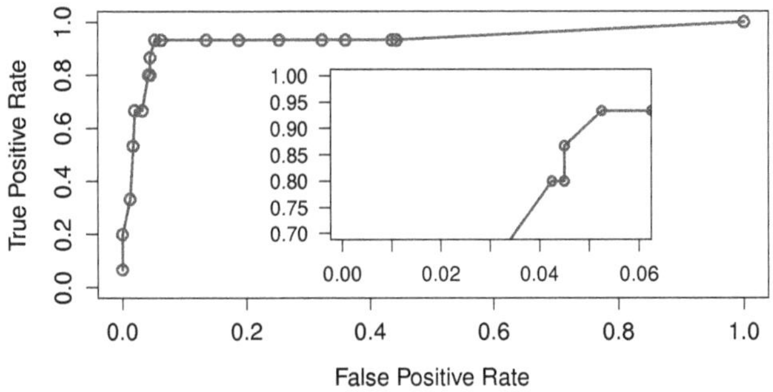

Figure 7: *The cross-validation detection and false positive rates of ASwatch.*

14 days). For each sliding window, we compute the feature vector for each AS and we perform three-fold cross-validation as follows: (1) We separate the ASes into three subsets, using two subsets to train our reputation model, and one for testing. (2) For each training subset, we balance the two classes by oversampling from the underrepresented class. After balancing, the number of feature vectors of the two classes are equal. (3) We train the model using a Random Forest classifier [6]. (4) Finally, we test all feature vectors that belong to the third fold against the model, as we described in Section 3.3. Cross-validation yields the scores from the testing phase and the true label for each AS feature vector. We plot the receiver operating characteristic (ROC), which illustrates the performance of the classifier for different values of the detection threshold. Because we perform our testing once for each sliding window, we plot a similar ROC for each sliding window. The results are reported in Section 4.3.

Evaluating ASwatch across a nearly three-year period. After the cross-validation experiments, we use our model to test new ASes whose BGP behavior was observed outside the training period over nearly three years, from 2011 to 2013. We perform this evaluation for two reasons: a) to test how well *ASwatch* performs to detect new malicious ASes (outside of the training period), and b) to compare the performance of *ASwatch* with other AS reputation systems (*e.g.*, BGP Ranking) over an extended period of time. For each (previously unseen) AS we want to test against *ASwatch*, we classify it as malicious if it has *multiple* feature vectors that are *consistently* assigned a "bad reputation" score (see Section 3.3). The results are reported in Section 4.3.

4.3 Results

How accurate is ASwatch? Evaluation with cross-validation: Figure 7 shows the detection and false positive rates for one cross-validation run. The detection rate and false positives reported on the ROC correspond to the fraction of *malicious* feature vectors that are correctly classified and *legitimate* feature vectors that are incorrectly classified, respectively. As shown by the ROC curve, *ASwatch* can achieve a detection rate of 93.33% (correctly classifying 14 out of 15 ASes as malicious), with a reasonably low false positive rate of 5.25% (20 falsely detected ASes). In practice, we believe this false positive rate is manageable, as it represents 20 falsely detected ASes over a three-month period, or one every few days. Although this false positive rate is clearly too high to automate critical decisions such as take-down efforts, *ASwatch* can still be used to significantly narrow down the set of ASes for further investigation considerably, and can thus help both law enforcement focus their investigation efforts, and network administrators make decisions on who to peer with or which abuse complaints to prioritize.

Evaluation outside the training period, over nearly three years: As described in Section 4.1, we use our model to test new ASes observed after the training period, over nearly three years, from 2011 to 2013. It is important to notice that, from a control-plane point of view, malicious ASes may not always be behaving maliciously across a three year period of time. Our ground truth information does not allow us to distinguish between the periods of activity and periods of "dormancy". Nonetheless, over time an AS operated by cyber-criminals will likely behave in a noticeably different way, compared to legitimate ASes, allowing us to detect it. Figure 10 shows the *cumulative* true positive rate of detected ASes over the testing period. At the end of this nearly three years period, *ASwatch* reached a true positive rate of 72% (21 out of 29 ASes correctly flagged as malicious).

To compute the false positives, for each month we count the number of distinct ASes that were detected as malicious. The false positives reach at most ten to fifteen ASes per month, which we believe is a manageable number, because these cases can be further reviewed by network operators and law enforcement. For instance, the upstream providers of an AS that is flagged as malicious by *ASwatch* may take a closer look at its customer's activities and time-to-response for abuse complaints. Furthermore, the output of *ASwatch* could be combined with the reputation score assigned by existing data-plane based AS reputation systems. The intuition is that if an AS behaves maliciously both at the control plane (as detected by *ASwatch*) and at the data plane (as detected by existing reputation systems), it is more likely that the AS is in fact operated by cyber-criminals.

How early can ASwatch detect malicious ASes before they are widely noticed? We want to evaluate if *ASwatch* can detect malicious ASes *before* they were reported by blog articles. For each of the 14 malicious ASes that *ASwatch* detected during the cross-validation experiments discussed earlier, we took note of the day that *ASwatch* first detected the malicious AS, and we measured the number of days between the time *ASwatch* detected the AS and the day the blog story was published. About 85% of the detected malicious ASes were detected by *ASwatch* 50 to 60 days before their story became public.

Which features are the most important? We evaluate the strength of each family of features that *ASwatch* uses. To understand which features are most important for *ASwatch*, we evaluate each family's contribution to the overall true and false positive rates. In particular, we want to study the effect of each family of features on the detection of malicious ASes,

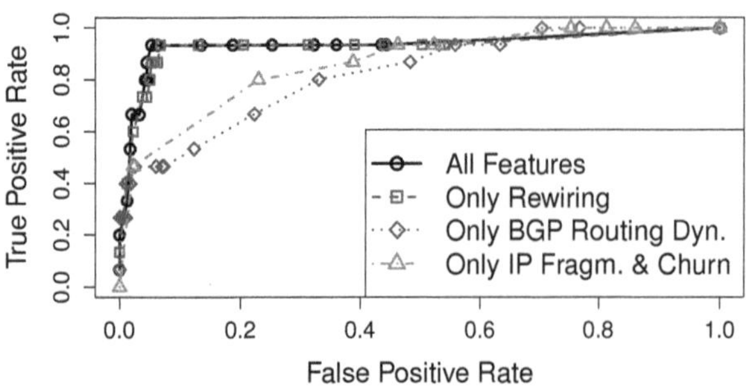

(a) *Considering each feature family separately.*

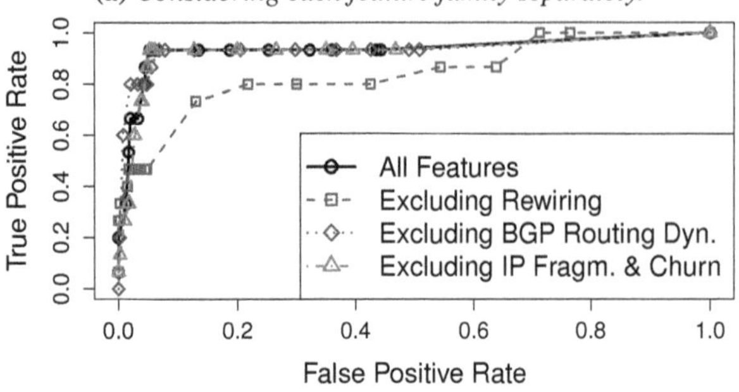

(b) *Excluding one feature family at a time.*

Figure 8: Relative importance of different types of features. *The rewiring features contribute the most to the overall detection rate; other features contribute to lower false positive rates.*

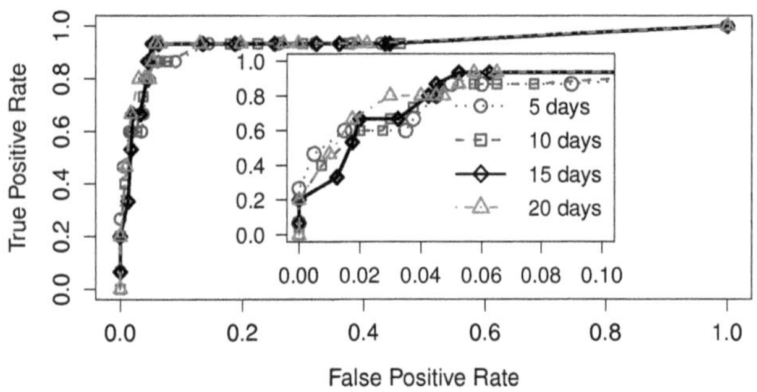

Figure 9: *The detection and false positive rates for ASwatch, if we vary the size of the sliding window. Our experiments show that the performance is not greatly affected.*

independently from the other families, and the effect of each family on the false positives when those features are excluded. To this end, we repeated the experiment described previously by excluding one family of features at a time. We repeated the experiment four times, once for each family of features, and we calculated the overall detection and false positive rates. Figure 8 shows the results of our experiments, which suggest that the rewiring features are very important, because excluding them significantly lowers the detection rate. The BGP dynamics and IP address space churn and fragmentation features help reduce the false positives slightly (the "Only Rewiring" ROC in Figure 8a is slightly shifted to the right). We followed a similar procedure to identify which features are most important for each family of features. Table 1 shows the most important features for each family.

Is ASwatch sensitive to parameter tuning? As explained in Sections 3.3.2, 4.2 we use the following parameters to classify an AS as malicious: (1) *feature vectors window size*: we compute feature vectors for an AS for a window of m consecutive days (one feature vector per day), and we repeat the feature computation over l consecutive sliding windows of size m. (2) *recent snapshots*: we compute the rewiring features for an AS over the k most recent snapshots of AS relationships.

To tune our parameters, we performed several pilot experiments, rather than an exhaustive search over the entire parameter space. Our pilot experiments showed that *ASwatch*'s performance is robust to both parameters m and l. Due to space limitations, we only show our experiments for the parameter m. Figure 9 shows the performance for window sizes of 5, 10, 15, and 20 days. Our results show that the accuracy of *ASwatch* is not overly sensitive to the choice of window size m. The ROC plots in Figure 9 show that $m = 15$ gives a higher true positive rate with a reasonable false positive rate. We therefore set $m = 15$. Using a similar approach, we set $l = 5$. We classify an AS as malicious, if it scores lower than the detection threshold over five consecutive periods of 15 days.

After we have selected parameters m and l, we proceed to set parameter k. Suppose that we want to compute the reputation of an AS A, over period T. Then, parameter k is the number of most recent AS relationship snapshots, prior to T, over which we compute the rewiring features for A (notice that our AS relationships dataset consists of one snapshot per month, as mentioned in Section 4.1). In other words, k denotes "how much" history we consider, to capture the rewiring behavior for A. Ideally, we want to accurately capture A's rewiring behavior while using a small number of snapshots. We performed experiments using different values of k (*i.e.*, 1, 2, 3, 4). We then selected $k = 4$, because further increasing its value did not produce a significant increase in classification accuracy.

4.4 Comparison to BGP Ranking

We now compare *ASwatch* with BGP Ranking. In contrast to *ASwatch*, BGP Ranking is an AS reputation system based on *data-plane* features (*e.g.*, observations of attack traffic enabled by machines hosted within an AS). Clearly, BGP Ranking is an AS reputation system that is designed differently from *ASwatch*, because it aims to report ASes that are most heavily abused by cyber-criminals, but not necessarily operated by cyber-criminals. We compare the two systems for two reasons: (1) to test how many of the malicious ASes that are operated by cyber-criminals show enough data-plane evidence of maliciousness and get detected by existing data-plane based AS reputation systems; and (2) to evaluate whether the control-plane based approach can effectively complement data-plane based AS reputation systems.

Results summary. We found that *ASwatch* detected 72% of our set of malicious ASes over a three year period, and BGP

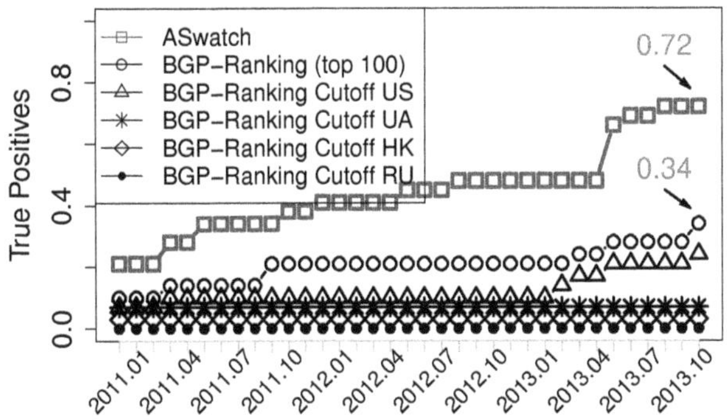

Figure 10: *True positive rates for ASwatch and BGP Ranking. Accumulation of detected ASes over nearly three years.*

Ranking detected about 34%. Both systems reported the same rate of false positives (on average 2.5% per month, which is ten to fifteen ASes per month). Combining the two systems we were able to detect only 14% of the malicious ASes, but we were able to reduce the false positives to 0.08% per month (12 ASes in total across the three year period).

BGP Ranking reports. BGP Ranking [5] has been making its AS reputation scores publicly available since 2011, along with a description of the approach used to compute the scores. BGP Ranking currently has information for a total of 14k ASes, and they announce a daily list of the worst 100 ASes by reputation score. The BGP Ranking score has a minimum value of 1 (which indicates that the AS hosts benign activity) but no maximum value (the more malicious traffic hosted by the AS, the higher the score).

Using our list of confirmed cases of malicious ASes (Section 4.1), we checked which ASes are visible from BGP Routeviews starting from 2011. We found a total of 29 ASes. We chose to check which ASes are active since January 2011, because this is the oldest date for which BGP Ranking has data available. Then, we tracked these ASes until November 2013, because the historic AS relationships dataset from CAIDA has a gap from November 2013 to August 2014. Therefore, we collected the historical scores for each active known malicious AS from BGP Ranking, from January 2011 until the end of 2013.

ASwatch setup. Using *ASwatch*, we generate the feature vectors for each AS in our list, starting from January 2011 until November 2013. To generate the feature vectors, we follow the same procedure as described in Section 3.3.2. We train *ASwatch* as previously described (on training data collected in 2010) and test the ASes observed from 2011 to 2013 against the model.

Comparing BGP Ranking with ASwatch. As mentioned earlier, BGP Ranking is not a detection system *per se*, in that it aims to report ASes that host a high concentration of malicious activities, and does not focus on distinguishing between abused ASes and ASes that are instead owned and operated by cyber-criminals. Nonetheless, for the sake of comparison it is possible to obtain a detection system by setting a threshold on the score output by BGP Ranking. BGP Ranking publishes the set of "worst" 100 ASes and their scores, which are updated daily (to obtain the historic scores for any other non-top-100 AS, one has to make explicit queries through the web portal). It also reports the average AS score per country or region, and ranks the countries that host the ASes with the lowest reputation. The four top ("worst") countries are Russia, Ukraine, Hong Kong, and the US. Using the above information we consider five distinct detection thresholds as follows: (1) average score for ASes in Russia (BGP Ranking Russia cut-off), (2) average score for ASes in Ukraine (BGP Ranking Ukraine cut-off), (3) average score for Hong Kong (BGP Ranking Hong Kong cut-off), and (4) average score for ASes in the US (BGP Ranking US cut-off). We also set a threshold based on the average score of the 100th worst AS (BGP Ranking top 100) collected from the daily reports. Figure 10 shows the detection results using these thresholds.

We then compared BGP Ranking's detection with that of *ASwatch*. Figure 10 shows the fraction of ASes that *ASwatch* and BGP Ranking detected. We show the cumulative fraction of detected ASes, from January 2011 to November 2013. At the end of the 35-month period, *ASwatch* detected about 72% of the set of ASes we tracked, while BGP Ranking detected about 34%. *We found that 72% of the malicious ASes were detected by monitoring their control-plane behavior, but only 34% of the malicious ASes showed enough data-plane activity to be detected by BGP Ranking.* BGP Ranking may have only limited visibility of malicious activities in the data plane across the entire Internet, and thus may completely miss the malicious activities of certain ASes. Naturally, it is challenging to deploy a large number of sensors dedicated to detecting malicious network communications over the entire Internet. On the other hand, *ASwatch* monitors BGP behavior, and may therefore compensate the limited visibility of data-plane based approaches.

We also compared the false positive rates of BGP Ranking and *ASwatch*. Our motivation is to see if the false positives are manageable within a reasonable period of time (*e.g.*one month). We collected the *ASwatch* scores and the BGP Ranking scores for our set of legitimate ASes (see Section 4.1). For each system, we counted the number of legitimate ASes that *ASwatch* detected per month. We found that both systems produce only ten to fifteen false positives per month on average over the total of 389 known legitimate ASes in our dataset. As we have mentioned earlier, BGP Ranking is designed differently from *ASwatch*. Although the rate we calculated does not represent the actual false positive rate for BGP ranking, it does provide an estimate of the false positive that an operator would need to deal with, if BGP Ranking were used to detect malicious ASes.

Combining control-plane with data-plane. Finally, we evaluated how the two systems would perform if we used them together. To this end, we label an AS as malicious if it was reported by both systems, with each two report dates to be at most six months apart from each other. For BGP Ranking we used the BGP Ranking top 100 threshold. We found that combining the two systems, we were able to detect 14% of our malicious ASes. This means that of 14% of the known malicious ASes exhibited both control plane and data plane malicious behavior within six months. The fraction of legitimate ASes that both systems detected as malicious is only 3% (*i.e.*, 12 ASes out of 389) for the whole three year period (which is on average 0.08% per month). Finally, five out of the 29 known malicious ASes that were active in the three year observation period were missed by both systems. For example, AS 49544 (Interactive 3D) and AS 39858 (UninetMd, now Comstar Volga Arzamas) are among the top worst ASes that both systems detected.

5 Discussion

ASwatch reputation scores in practice. *ASwatch* may help the work of network operators and security practitioners as follows: (1) *Prioritize traffic*: knowing what ASes have suspicious (low reputation) control-plane behavior may help administrators to appropriately handle traffic originating from such ASes; (2) *Peering decisions*: Upstream providers could use AS reputation scores as an additional source of information to make peering decisions, for example by charging higher costs to compensate for the risk of having a low reputation customer or even de-peer early if reputation scores drop significantly; (3) *Prioritize investigations*: law enforcement and security practitioners may prioritize their investigations and start early monitoring on low reputation ASes; (4) *Complement data-plane based systems*: *ASwatch* could be used in combination with data-plane based reputation systems, so that ASes that exhibit malicious behavior both from the control-and data-plane points of view can be prioritized first; (5) *Strengthen existing defenses*: furthermore, reputation could be used as input to other network defenses (*e.g.*, spam filters, botnet detection systems) to improve their detection accuracy.

Working with limited ground truth. We briefly summarize the challenges that we faced due to limited ground truth, and how we mitigated them. (1) *Highly unbalanced dataset*: The ratio of malicious ASes to legitimate ASes produced a highly unbalanced dataset. Before training we used well-known data mining approaches to balance the dataset, by oversampling the underrepresented class of malicious ASes (Section 4.1). (2) *Limited time period for training*: We relied on the date of the ground truth reports to estimate the period of time in which the ASes were likely to be actively used by the attackers. We were not able to obtain additional information about the activity periods (or dormancy periods) outside the report dates. Therefore, we designed AS *ASwatch* so that it does not make a final decision for an AS based on a single observation (*i.e.*, a single feature vector). Instead, we introduced parameters to ensure that we label an AS as malicious only if it is assigned consistently low scores for an extended period of time. (3) *Model update with adaptive training*: Because of the lack of information on the activity periods (or dormancy periods) outside the report dates, we were not able to periodically update our model. Therefore, we performed a one-time training on our model using a period of time (January–March 2010) for which we had "clean" data. Even though *ASwatch* uses observations of cases of malicious ASes in 2010, we believe that it effectively models fundamental characteristics of malicious ASes that are still reflected on today's cases. This belief is supported in part by the results of correlating *ASwatch*'s output with recent BGP Ranking reports (see Section 4). In our future work, we plan to investigate more sources of ground truth and identify other periods of time that could be included in our training.

Limitations of the AS relationships dataset. To measure our rewiring features, we relied on a dataset that provides snapshots of AS relationships over years (see Section 4.1). The relationship inference algorithm is based on the idea of customer cones—the set of ASes an AS can reach through its customer links. This dataset has its own set of limitations. For example, each pair of ASes is assigned only a single relationship, and visibility is limited to the monitoring points publicly available via Routeviews. It is possible that some business relationships may be missing, or that some false relationships are reported. Moreover, since the dataset is provided in snapshots (one snapshot per month), we are not able to observe rewiring activity that may be happening at a finer time scales. Nevertheless, this AS relationships dataset has the largest validated collection of AS relationships gathered to date, with about 44,000 (34.6%) of the inferences validated, and it reports the AS relationships over years, which allowed us to track our ground truth ASes over an extended period of time.

Evasion. Naturally, as for any other detection system, *ASwatch* may face the challenge of sophisticated attackers who attempt to evade it. For example, an attacker may attempt to manage her AS to mimic the BGP behavior of legitimate ASes. However, we should notice that *ASwatch* relies heavily on rewiring features, which capture how an AS connects with other ASes, including upstream providers. Mimicking legitimate behavior to evade *ASwatch* would mean that the malicious AS has to become "less agile". In turn, being less agile may expose the AS to de-peering by its upstream providers as a consequence of accumulating abuse complaints. For example, if McColo (which was taken down in 2008) had not changed ten upstream providers before it was taken down, it might have been taken down much sooner.

Future work. We plan to expand our set of features to capture other types of behavior, such as making peering arrangements for specific prefixes. We intend to expand our sources of bullet-proof hosting ASes, so that we test *ASwatch* over larger datasets and longer periods of time. We also plan to explore how we may combine our set of control plane features with data plane features.

6 Related Work

We review studies of "unclean" ASes and existing AS reputation systems, as well as applications of machine learning and signal processing to detect BGP anomalies.

Studies of "unclean" ASes. Previous studies have attempted to identify "unclean" ASes, which are ASes with a high concentration of low reputation IP addresses. In contrast, we attempt to understand the behavior of ASes that are *controlled and managed by attackers*, rather than ASes which are heavily abused. Collins [9] first introduced the term network uncleanliness as an indicator of the tendency for hosts in a network to become compromised. They gathered IP addresses from datasets of botnets, scan, phishing, and spam attacks to study spatial and temporal properties of network uncleanliness; this work found that compromised hosts tend to cluster within unclean networks. Kalafut *et al.* [18] collected data from popular blacklists, spam data, and DNS domain resolutions. They found that a small fraction of ASes have over 80% of their routable IP address space blacklisted. Konte *et al.* [20] studied ASes that are reported by Hostexploit and how they changed their upstream connectivity. Johnson *et al.* introduced metrics for measuring ISP badness [17]. Moura *et al.* studied Internet bad neighborhoods aggregation. Earlier papers have looked into IP addresses that host scam websites or part of spamming botnets are organized intro infrastructures [12, 8, 38]. Finally, Ramachandran *et al.* found that most spam originates from a relatively small number of ASes, and also quantified the extent to which spammers use short-lived BGP announcements to send spam [29, 30]. These studies suggest that it is possible to develop an AS reputation system based on analysis of control-plane features, which is the focus of our work.

AS reputation systems. The state of the art in AS reputation systems is to use features that are derived from data-plane information, such as statistics of attack traffic. Current systems correlate data from multiple sources such as spam, malware, malicious URLs, spam bots, botnet C&C servers, phishing servers, exploit servers, cyber-warfare provided by other organizations or companies. Then, then rank ASes based on the concentration of low reputations IP addresses. Organizations, such as Hostexploit [34], Sitevet [34], and BGP Ranking [4] rate each AS with an index based on the activity of the AS weighted by the size of its allocated address space. FIRE [36] examines datasets of IRC-based botnets, HTdetection-based botnets, drive-by-download and phishing hosts and scores ASes based on the longevity of the malicious services they host and the concentration of bad IP addresses that are actively involved. ASMATRA [37] attempts to detecting ASes that provide upstream connectivity for malicious ASes, without being malicious themselves.

Zhang *et al.* [39] find that there is a correlation between networks that are mismanaged and networks that are responsible for malicious activities. The authors use a mismanagement metric to indicate which ASes may be likely to exhibit malicious behaviors (e.g. spam, malware infections), which does not necessarily indicate if an AS is actually operated by cyber-criminals or not. In contrast, we focus on detecting ASes that are operated by attackers, rather than ASes that are mismanagement and likely abused. Also, [39] examined short-lived BGP announcements as an indication of BGP misconfigurations. Even though we also examine the duration of prefix announcements, this is only one of the features we use to capture control plane behavior. Our analysis shows that this feature alone is not enough to distinguish between legitimate and malicious ASes.

Roveta *et al.* [33] developed BURN, a visualization tool, that displays ASes with malicious activity, with the purpose to identify misbehaving networks. In contrast to these reputation systems that rely on data-plane observations of malicious activity from privileged vantage points, *ASwatch* establishes AS reputation using control-plane (*i.e.*, routing) features that can be observed without privileged vantage points and often before an attack.

Machine learning and signal processing approaches. These approaches detect BGP anomalies (*e.g.*, burstiness), with the goal to help system administrators diagnose problematic network behaviors, but they do not provide a connection between BGP anomalies and criminal activity. In contrast to these approaches, *ASwatch* attempts to capture suspicious control-plane behavior (*e.g.*, aggressive change of connectivity, short BGP announcements) with the goal to detect malicious ASes. Prakash *et al.* developed BGPlens, which monitors anomalies by observing statistical anomalies in BGP updates based on analysis of several features, including self-similarity, power-law, and lognormal marginals [28]. Similarly, Mai [26], Zhang [40] and Al-Rousan [3] have examined BGP update messages using tools based on self-similarity and wavelets analysis hidden Markov models to design anomaly detection mechanisms.

7 Conclusion

This paper presented *ASwatch*, the first system to derive AS reputation based on control-plane behavior. *ASwatch* is based on the intuition that malicious ASes exhibit "agile" control-plane behavior (*e.g.*, short-lived routes, aggressive rewiring). We evaluated *ASwatch* on known malicious ASes and found that it detected 93% of malicious ASes with a 5% false positive rate. When comparing to BGP Ranking, the current state-of-the-art AS reputation system, we found that *ASwatch* detected 72% of reported malicious ASes, whereas BGP ranking detected only 34%. These results suggest that *ASwatch* can better help network operators and law enforcement take swifter action against these ASes that continue to remain sources of malicious activities. Possible remediations could be assessing the risk of peering with a particular AS, prioritizing investigations, and complementing existing defenses that incorporate other datasets.

Acknowledgments

We thank our shepherd, Walter Willinger, and the anonymous reviewers for their helpful comments and guidance. This material is supported in part by National Science Foundation awards CNS-1149051, CNS-1539923, and CNS-1531281.

References

[1] abuse.ch. And Another Bulletproof Hosting AS Goes Offline, Mar. 2010. http://www.abuse.ch/?p=2496.

[2] abuse.ch. 2011: A Bad Start For Cybercriminals: 14 Rogue ISPs Disconnected. http://www.abuse.ch/?tag=vline-telecom, Jan. 2011.

[3] N. M. Al-Rousan and L. Trajkovic. Machine learning models for classification of BGP anomalies. In *High Performance Switching and Routing (HPSR)*, pages 103–108, 2012.

[4] BGP Ranking. http://bgpranking.circl.lu/.

[5] Bgp ranking reports. http://bgpranking.circl.lu/.

[6] L. Breiman. Random Forests. *Machine learning*, 45(1):5–32, 2001.

[7] Bulletproof Hosting. http://en.wikipedia.org/wiki/Bulletproof_hosting. Wikipedia.

[8] K. Chiang and L. Lloyd. A case study of the Rustock rootkit and spam bot. In *Workshop on Understanding Botnets*, 2007.

[9] M. P. Collins, T. J. Shimeall, S. Faber, J. Janies, R. Weaver, M. De Shon, and J. Kadane. Using uncleanliness to predict future botnet addresses. In *ACM SIGCOMM Internet Measurement Conference*, pages 93–104, 2007.

[10] Criminal service providers. http://cyberthreat.wordpress.com/category/criminal-service-providers/.

[11] DShield: Internet Storm Center - Internet Security. www.dshield.org/?

[12] F.Li and M. Hsieh. An empirical study of clustering behavior of spammers and group-based anti-spam strategies. In *Conference on Email and Anti-Spam (CEAS)*, 2006.

[13] Hostexploit. AS50896-PROXIEZ Overview of a crime server, May 2010. http://goo.gl/AYGKAQ.

[14] Hostexploit, June 2011. http://hostexploit.com/.

[15] Hostexploit. World Hosts Report. Technical report, Mar. 2014. http://hostexploit.com/downloads/summary/7-public-reports/52-world-hosts-report-march-2014.html.

[16] Crimeware-firendly ISPs. http://hphosts.blogspot.com/2010/02/crimeware-friendly-isps-cogent-psi.html.

[17] B. Johnson, J. Chuang, J. Grossklags, and N. Christin. Metrics for Measuring ISP Badness: The Case of Spam. In *Financial Cryptography and Data Security*, pages 89–97. Springer, 2012.

[18] A. J. Kalafut, C. A. Shue, and M. Gupta. Malicious Hubs: Detecting Abnormally Malicious Autonomous Systems. In *IEEE INFOCOM*, pages 1–5. IEEE, 2010.

[19] J. Kirk. ISP Cut Off from Internet After Security Concerns. http://www.pcworld.com/article/153734/mccolo_isp_security.html, Nov. 2008. PC World.

[20] M. Konte and N. Feamster. Re-wiring Activity of Malicious Networks. In *Passive and Active Measurement*, pages 116–125. Springer, 2012.

[21] B. Krebs. Russian Business Network: Down, But Not Out. http://goo.gl/6ITJwP, Nov. 2007. Washington Post.

[22] B. Krebs. Host of Internet Spam Groups Is Cut Off. http://goo.gl/8J5P89, Nov. 2008. Washington Post.

[23] B. Krebs. Dozens of ZeuS Botnets Knocked Offline, Mar. 2010. http://krebsonsecurity.com/2010/03/dozens-of-zeus-botnets-knocked-offline/.

[24] J. Li, M. Guidero, Z. Wu, E. Purpus, and T. Ehrenkranz. BGP Routing Dynamics Revisited. *ACM SIGCOMM Computer Communication Review*, 37(2):5–16, 2007.

[25] M. Luckie, B. Huffaker, A. Dhamdhere, V. Giotsas, et al. AS Relationships, Customer Cones, and Validation. In *Proceedings of ACM SIGCOMM Internet Measurement Conference*, pages 243–256. ACM, 2013.

[26] J. Mai, L. Yuan, and C.-N. Chuah. Detecting BGP anomalies with wavelet. In *IEEE Network Operations and Management Symposium*, pages 465–472. IEEE, 2008.

[27] R. McMillan. After Takedown, Botnet-linked ISP Troyak Resurfaces. http://goo.gl/5kOOV1, Mar. 2010. Computer World.

[28] B. A. Prakash, N. Valler, D. Andersen, M. Faloutsos, and C. Faloutsos. BGP-lens: Patterns and Anomalies in Internet Routing Updates. In *ACM SIGKDD international conference on Knowledge Discovery and Data Mining*, pages 1315–1324, 2009.

[29] A. Ramachandran and N. Feamster. Understanding the Network-Level Behavior of Spammers. In *ACM SIGCOMM*, 2006.

[30] A. Ramachandran, N. Feamster, and S. Vempala. Filtering Spam with Behavioral Blacklisting. In *ACM Conference on Computer and Communications Security (CCS)*, 2007.

[31] The Russian Business Network. http://en.wikipedia.org/wiki/Russian_Business_Network.

[32] The RouteViews Project. www.routeviews.org/.

[33] F. Roveta, G. Caviglia, L. Di Mario, S. Zanero, F. Maggi, and P. Ciuccarelli. Burn: Baring unknown rogue networks. In *International Symposium on Visualization for Cyber Security (VizSec)*, 2011.

[34] Sitevet. http://sitevet.com/.

[35] Spamhaus. www.spamhaus.org.

[36] B. Stone-Gross, C. Kruegel, K. Almeroth, A. Moser, and E. Kirda. FIRE: Finding rogue networks. In *IEEE Computer Security Applications Conference (ACSAC)*, pages 231–240. IEEE, 2009.

[37] C. Wagner, J. François, R. State, A. Dulaunoy, T. Engel, and G. Massen. ASMATRA: Ranking ASes providing transit service to malware hosters. In *IFIP/IEEE International Symposium on Integrated Network Management*, pages 260–268, 2013.

[38] Y. Xie, F. Yu, K. Achan, R. Panigrahy, and G. Hulten. Spamming Botnets: Signatures and Characteristics. In *SIGCOMM*, 2008.

[39] J. Zhang, Z. Durumeric, M. Bailey, M. Karir, and M. Liu. On the Mismanagement and Maliciousness of Networks. In *Proceedings of the 21st Annual Network & Distributed System Security Symposium (NDSS '14)*, San Diego, California, USA, February 2013.

[40] J. Zhang, J. Rexford, and J. Feigenbaum. Learning-based anomaly detection in BGP updates. In *ACM SIGCOMM Workshop on Mining Network Data (MineNet)*, pages 219–220. ACM, 2005.

Herd: A Scalable, Traffic Analysis Resistant Anonymity Network for VoIP Systems

Stevens Le Blond
MPI-SWS

David Choffnes
Northeastern University

William Caldwell
MPI-SWS

Peter Druschel
MPI-SWS

Nicholas Merritt
MPI-SWS

ABSTRACT

Effectively anonymizing Voice-over-IP (VoIP) calls requires a scalable anonymity network that is resilient to traffic analysis and has sufficiently low delay for high-quality voice calls. The popular Tor anonymity network, for instance, is not designed for the former and cannot typically achieve the latter. In this paper, we present the design, implementation, and experimental evaluation of Herd, an anonymity network where a set of dedicated, fully interconnected cloud-based proxies yield suitably low-delay circuits, while untrusted superpeers add scalability. Herd provides caller/callee anonymity among the clients within a trust zone (e.g., jurisdiction) and under a strong adversarial model. Simulations based on a trace of 370 million mobile phone calls among 10.8 million users indicate that Herd achieves anonymity among millions of clients with low bandwidth requirements, and that superpeers decrease the bandwidth and CPU requirements of the trusted infrastructure by an order of magnitude. Finally, experiments using a prototype deployment on Amazon EC2 show that Herd has a delay low enough for high-quality calls in most cases.

CCS Concepts

•**Networks** $\rightarrow$ **Network privacy and anonymity;**

Keywords

Anonymity networks; Voice-over-IP; Intersection attacks; Strong anonymity

SIGCOMM '15 August 17-21, 2015, London, United Kingdom

ACM ISBN 978-1-4503-3542-3/15/08.
DOI: http://dx.doi.org/10.1145/2785956.2787491

1. INTRODUCTION

Voice-over-IP (VoIP) systems are popular and their support for pseudonymous identities and strong encryption makes them appealing to users concerned about communication privacy. However, many nation states use Internet surveillance to monitor and repress critics [18, 14], and even western democracies conduct mass surveillance [9, 10, 8, 4]. In this environment, VoIP systems are not sufficient to ensure the anonymity of Internet users, nor the safety of political activists and whistleblowers, as illustrated, for example, by the NSA's ability to intercept Skype conversations [13].

Further, existing anonymity networks are not designed for latency sufficiently low to support VoIP, or scalability to millions of users under a strong adversarial model. For example, Tor [28] scales to large numbers of users but is vulnerable to an adversary who can eavesdrop on the ingress and egress paths of Tor circuits. Recent revelations indicate that the UK's GCHQ is pursuing this to deanonymize Tor users [1].

We demonstrate in Section 4 that a simple attack using only the start and end times would trace 98.3% of the calls of a large, real voice workload, if they had been made over Tor. (A more sophisticated attack that also considers the time series of encrypted packets would likely trace even more calls.) In addition, Tor typically incurs round trip delays between 2–4 seconds on established, sender-anonymous circuits because of random proxy selection and high-latency connections [43, 15], which is prohibitive for VoIP.

Other anonymity systems resist traffic analysis at the cost of performance or scalability [37, 47, 26, 30, 45]. For example, Dissent, the state-of-the-art Dining Cryptographers network (DC-Net), is resilient under a strong threat model but requires one *broadcast channel* per anonymity set, impacting anonymity and scalability, as well as *several round-trip times*, yielding delays significantly higher than Tor [47].

In this paper, we present the design, implementation, and evaluation of *Herd*, a scalable anonymity network that combines delays suitable for VoIP with anonymity under a strong adversarial model. *Herd* achieves these properties using a novel design tailored to the specific requirements and traffic characteristics of VoIP. In particular, (1) *Herd* leverages the multitude of jurisdictions in the Internet with a design that ensures a user's anonymity depends only on mixes located in jurisdictions that (s)he trusts, independent of her communication partners' choices; (2) it exploits the constant-rate, low-bandwidth nature of VoIP traffic to resist traffic analysis while achieving low delay; (3) it employs a novel design based on network coding to hide clients' activity patterns, which enables *Herd* to offload its trusted infrastructure with the help of untrusted peers.

At its core, *Herd* relies on a set of dedicated mixes (proxies that relay VoIP data packets) operated by independent organizations in different jurisdictions around the world. The underlying insight is that no adversary has access to mix locations everywhere in the world. *Herd* exploits this by allowing clients to choose a mix within a *trust zone*, i.e., a jurisdiction/provider that is friendly to their cause, and by guaranteeing that client anonymity depends only on this choice.

Because the set of mixes is fully connected, a *Herd* circuit involves at most three intercontinental links (usually one), which keeps delays low enough for acceptable VoIP quality. To increase scalability, *Herd* can optionally use untrusted superpeers that forward traffic between clients and a mix. Superpeers reduce the CPU and bandwidth demands on trusted infrastructure without sacrificing anonymity. Bitwise unlinkablity (i.e., decorrelating the content of packets arriving and departing a mix) and traffic-analysis resistance is achieved via encrypted connections padded using artificial traffic (*chaff*), where rate adjustments are correlated within large anonymity sets.

This paper makes the following contributions:

- We present the design of *Herd*, a scalable anonymity network with latency sufficiently low to carry VoIP calls, and anonymity under a strong adversarial model.
- A trace-based evaluation of *Herd*'s overheads and performance using a trace of 370 million mobile phone calls among 10.8 million users, and a comparison with Drac [26], an existing low-delay anonymity network.
- An open-source implementation of *Herd*.
- An experimental evaluation of *Herd*'s perceived call quality based on VoIP calls made by volunteers using a *Herd* deployment on Amazon EC2.

Our key results are as follows. First, using trace-based simulations we show that *Herd* achieves anonymity with low bandwidth requirements for millions of clients. Second, we find that superpeers decrease the bandwidth and CPU demands on trusted infrastructure by an order of magnitude, because they allow *Herd* to take advantage of resource contributions by untrusted parties without affecting anonymity. We estimate that untrusted superpeers that contribute resources for free or in exchange for free calls would reduce *Herd*'s operational costs from $10-100 to $0.10-1.14 per user/month for this workload. Third, experiments with an implementation and a prototype deployment on 4 Amazon EC2 data centers show that *Herd* incurs modest additional latency as compared to direct communication. The *Herd* source code is available under a BSD license [19].

We discuss background and related work on private voice communication in Section 2. We then present the design and implementation of *Herd* in Section 3 and compare its performance with alternative low-latency anonymity networks in Section 4. We conclude in Section 5.

2. BACKGROUND & RELATED WORK

2.1 Context

Providing anonymous communication is challenging from a technical, legal and political standpoint. Recent revelations about state-sponsored mass surveillance suggest that government agencies analyze large-scale data collected at Internet exchange points [1, 4] and request customer data from service providers [10, 9]. In this environment, achieving effective and practical anonymity is difficult.

Even in the presence of such powerful attackers, however, we posit that there exist free havens supporting private communication, even if those free havens differ depending on the communication partners and their topic.

We believe this is the case for two reasons. First, *no single adversary has access to all parts of the Internet and jurisdiction over all service providers*. This is true despite the fact that countries like the US and the UK have access to a disproportionate amount of Internet traffic today. Moreover, in the wake of the recent revelations, there is some indication that more countries may seek to establish national Cloud and Web service providers and independent Internet routes that do not needlessly cross other countries or continents [17].

Second, *for any worthy cause that a group of users pursue under the cloak of anonymity, there is likely a country that is friendly or at least indifferent to that cause*. Combined with the first point, we believe that users can find a jurisdiction that avoids legal and political challenges to anonymous communication, leaving only technical challenges.

The design of *Herd* seeks to exploit these circumstances, by allowing callers and callees to independently choose a provider within a jurisdiction they deem friendly to their cause, and through a trust model where a user's anonymity depends only on their own choice of provider. Before we describe the design of *Herd* in the next section, we review existing work in anonymous voice services.

2.2 Existing techniques

Burner phones. A simple method for anonymous voice calling is to use pre-paid SIM cards and cheap cellular phones purchased with cash and discarded after a period of use. To receive calls, a user must disseminate her current phone number to callers using an out-of-band mechanism. Using burner phones may not be appropriate in all cases due to its monetary cost, relative inconvenience, and the unavailability of unregistered, pre-paid SIM cards in some countries. Further, using a burner phone does not guarantee that calls made using the phone will not be tapped or otherwise logged.

VoIP services. In principle, VoIP services are an alternative for anonymous voice calling. While VoIP signaling protocols such as SIP and P2PSIP were not designed for anonymous call setup, it is possible, for instance, to create a Skype or Google Voice account under a pseudonym and contact the service through a VPN, which obscures the user's IP address. However, VPNs can be compelled by authorities to release the IP addresses of their customers. For instance, a UK-based VPN recently complied with a US subpoena to trace one of its users [3]. Also, it is widely assumed that Skype complies with requests for call metadata by government authorities [7], and that the NSA has the ability to intercept the contents of Skype calls [13].

Private VoIP services like RedPhone [16] and Silent Circle [12] offer end-to-end encrypted voice calls (strong encryption and at least partially open source), and advertise that no call metadata is stored. However, the services rely on rendezvous and relaying services that can be compelled by local authorities to capture and release call metadata. A subpoena against the operator of a server involved in a call may reveal the IP addresses of caller and callee.

None of the existing VoIP services are designed to resist *traffic analysis*, where a passive network observer can determine the caller and callee by matching the time series of encrypted traffic at different points in the network.

Anonymity networks. Users can improve protection against de-anonymization by accessing a VoIP service via an anonymity network like Tor [15]. Unfortunately, the typical delays incurred by Tor circuits are too high for adequate VoIP call quality. More generally, a measurement study indicates that achieving acceptable VoIP call quality using an Tor-like (onion routing) anonymity network based on volunteered resources (PlanetLab) is challenging [39].

LAP [33] is a light-weight anonymity network with near-optimal delay and low routing overhead. However, it assumes a weaker threat model than Tor and requires network support that is not deployed today.

Traffic analysis resistant anonymity. Traffic analysis consists of statistical attacks that reveal communication partners, by considering the time series of packets and user activity. Tor, like most other medium-delay anonymity networks [33, 21, 20], is not designed to withstand traffic analysis, and we empirically show the effectiveness of such attacks against Tor in Section 4.1.4.

Anonymity networks can batch messages to hide the correlation between input and output messages, as originally done in Chaumian mix-nets [24]. Batching prevents an attacker from tracing messages based on their arrival and departure times, but without chaff it requires delaying messages for substantial periods. As a result, mix-nets are suitable only for delay-tolerant communications such as e-mails [32, 40, 27].

ISDN-MIXes [44, 35] combine mixing of time-sliced channels with chaff traffic and broadcast of incoming calls on subscriber links to achieve anonymous telephony on an ISDN network. *Herd* instead provides anonymous VoIP calls over the Internet, under a threat model that considers today's powerful adversaries.

Finding the right tradeoff between delaying messages and adding chaff traffic is an open research challenge. For example, both the Java Anonymous Proxy (JAP) [21] and the Freedom Network [46] abandoned chaffing due to its high bandwidth overhead. Below, we discuss designs that combine batching with chaffing to reduce mix-net delays, as well as Dissent, a system based on DC-nets.

Aqua [37] provides k-anonymity for BitTorrent-like traffic in the presence of traffic analysis. While the designs of *Herd* and Aqua share several ideas, they support different applications and traffic types, and differ in other ways: First, *Herd* uses a hybrid architecture with trusted mixes and untrusted superpeers (SPs), where SPs improve scalability using a novel design based on network coding. Second, *Herd* leverages (a) the constant-rate nature of VoIP traffic and (b) the jurisdictional diversity of the Internet to achieve paths that require less than half the number of hops as Aqua (at most 3 versus 7 intercontinental hops) without loss of resistance against traffic analysis. Whereas Aqua requires multipath between two pairs of mixes to disperse hotspots in file-sharing traffic, constant-rate traffic does not have this constraint, enabling *Herd* to achieve latencies appropriate for VoIP calls. By organizing its infrastructure into disjoint trust zones and coupling rate adjustments both within and across them, *Herd* decouples the anonymity of users of different zones, while Aqua does not consider mixes' jurisdiction.

P^5[45] and Tarzan [30] are P2P anonymity networks that use broadcast channels and chaffing, respectively, to defend against traffic analysis. Because they use a P2P model, their security depends on forwarding traffic via a series of proxies hosted on endpoints, affecting their latency and reliability.

Dissent [47] is an infrastructure-based anonymity service with a very strong adversarial model, where a single honest proxy is sufficient to ensure anonymity, even in the face of traffic analysis attacks. The system relies on DC-nets and verifiable shuffles, and its infrastructure-based architecture scales to hundreds of clients with modest delay and bandwidth sufficient for web browsing. However, the system's capacity, scalability, and latency are subject to DC-net scaling limits with respect to the number of proxies, overhead per payload bit for cryptographic processing, and delay.

Drac [26] is a traffic-analysis resistant anonymity network for VoIP and IM that relies on a social network to provide anonymous communication among strangers and unobservable communication among friends. An important difference with *Herd* is that Drac exposes users' social network to an adversary. Drac also routes calls in a peer-to-peer fashion over the social network, which can cause impractically long latency for calls between users who are several hops apart in the social graph. Whereas *Herd* clients maintain a handful of chaffing links (e.g., 2 or 3), Drac may require substantially more (e.g., Twitter and Facebook users have on average 45 and 190 contacts, respectively [31, 29]). We provide a quantitative comparison of Drac and *Herd*, in terms of anonymity, scalability, and perceived call quality in Section 4.

2.3 Our system: Herd

Herd is designed specifically for VoIP traffic and the anonymity needs of voice callers. *Herd* takes advantage of VoIP calling patterns and traffic characteristics to provide anonymity under a strong adversarial model with reasonable overhead and delay low enough for high-quality voice calls.

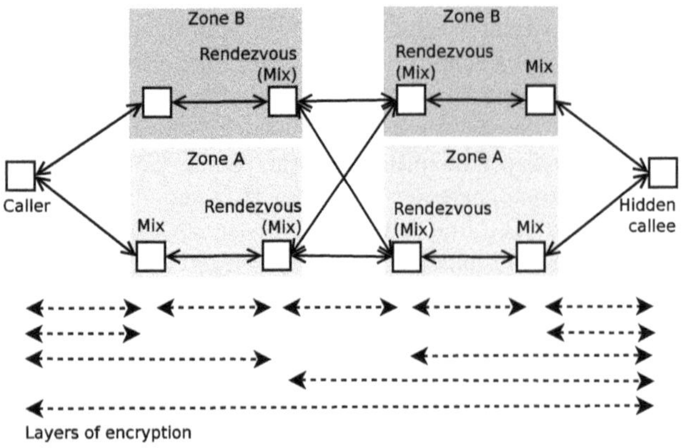

Figure 1: *Herd*'s architecture comprises clients, mixes located in trust zones, and optionally, SPs (not shown). *Herd* employs both hop-by-hop and layered encryption to hide content, routing information, and circuit IDs. Mixes can also act as rendezvous enabling clients to receive incoming VoIP calls with zone anonymity. Optionally, a caller and callee can use an additional zone (e.g., *A* and *B*) to avoid depending on the same jurisdiction.

Moreover, in *Herd*'s trust model, the anonymity of a caller or callee depends only on her own choice of a *trust zone*, i.e., a provider within a jurisdiction. Callers and callees pick a trust zone independently and do not depend on the choices made by their call partner.

3. DESIGN AND IMPLEMENTATION

System model. *Herd* comprises clients, which originate and terminate traffic; mixes, which relay traffic; and optional untrusted superpeers (SPs), which can originate, terminate, and relay traffic. We call a client initiating a call *caller* and one accepting a call *callee*. All participants are connected by links that carry encrypted and padded traffic. A client connects to at least one mix, either directly (shown in Figure 1), or via one or more SPs attached to the same mix. SPs connect to one mix. Links among the mixes form a fully connected network. *Herd* mixes are further partitioned into *trust zones*. All mixes within a trust zone are operated by a single provider under a single jurisdiction. Typically, the mixes of a trust zone are hosted in the same data center. (Because a data center can serve a large user population, small countries may have a single provider/data center, while large countries/jurisdictions would be served by multiple providers/data centers.) To bootstrap, *Herd* needs at least one zone with one mix. A new zone requires a minimum set of clients before establishing calls, which can be achieved by requiring a minimal number of initial subscribers or by splitting an existing, large zone into several partitions.

3.1 Overview

Herd adopts a hybrid of P2P and infrastructure-based architecture for performance and scalability reasons. First, a modest number of well-provisioned, dedicated mixes are connected to the core of the Internet around the world, and maintain a fully connected network of links between each other. Second, the clients and SPs served by a particular mix form a two-level, hierarchical network, with SPs as the interior nodes. SPs are highly available clients with low-latency access to the Internet and a public IP address.

All links connecting mixes, SPs and clients carry bi-directional encrypted traffic, which is padded to a uniform rate. The links connecting clients to an SP or a mix carry traffic at a small multiple of the unit rate u (the payload rate of a single voice call), irrespective of whether the client actively makes a call. All other links carry traffic at a multiple of u. The links connecting SPs to mixes within a given zone have identical rates at any given time; this rate can be changed simultaneously on all such links. Likewise, the rate on links connecting mixes within a zone, and the rate on links connecting mixes between a given pair of zones, respectively, is identical at any time and may be changed only simultaneously. Mixes periodically report their link utilization to a local, zone *directory* and rate adjustments are decided unilaterally for intrazone links, or by the two corresponding directories for interzone links.

Trust and incentive model. We assume that each zone is bound by its local laws and authorities. In particular, zone operators can be compelled by local authorities to release the information available to the mixes in their zone.

Clients and SPs trust the mix they attach to, and thus the authorities within the mix's jurisdiction, with their partial call metadata (source IP address and destination mix, duration of call). Therefore, clients and SPs should select a mix operated by a provider of their choice within a zone whose jurisdiction meets their privacy needs.

A client may select a mix in a location and jurisdiction different from her own, e.g., when she does not trust the local authorities with her partial call metadata. This presumes, however, that local authorities do not systematically block network access to such mixes. To circumvent censorship, *Herd* could rely on SPs with unpublished IP addresses (like Tor bridges) and obfuscate client traffic. Applying obfuscation mechanisms like Tor's obfsproxy [11] to *Herd* is the subject of future work. A key challenge is that appropriate cover traffic must sustain a minimum rate of one VoIP call at all times to provide obfuscation.

A client may either connect to an SP or directly to a mix. We assume there is a business model to cover the cost of operating mixes and possibly to incentivize SP operators. For instance, mixes may charge their clients a subscription fee, possibly using a digital currency such as Bitcoin [42]. Recall that clients trust their mixes, so the payment transaction need not be anonymous (which Bitcoin is not), unless the client wishes to keep her identity hidden from the mix. The mix may in turn grant the operators of SPs free calls or pay them a fee, as an incentive to relay calls from clients.

SPs learn the IP addresses of their connected clients; however, they cannot detect when a client makes a call or with whom. We assume SPs act rationally, i.e., they perform in a way that will allow them to remain in good standing as an SP for their mix. Specifically, mixes monitor and reject SPs with insufficient availability or significant packet loss/jitter.

Clients connect to *Herd* continuously (modulo power or network outages), regardless of call activity. Given the low bitrate of VoIP relative to typical flat-rate broadband capacity, chaffing at a small multiple of that rate seems reasonable. Further, VoIP users tend to remain available to receive incoming calls. For example, prior work showed that half of Skype users are available more than 80% of the time [38].

Threat model. We assume an adversary who seeks to infer the IP addresses of the caller and callee of calls made via *Herd*, their time and duration, as well as their content. The adversary is able to observe the time series of encrypted traffic on all *Herd* links as part of a *global, passive traffic analysis attack.* Within a portion of the Internet controlled by the adversary, he can additionally compromise mixes and network components, change their behavior, and modify the time series of encrypted traffic as part of a *local, active traffic analysis attack.* These assumptions are reasonable because an active subversion with global reach is harder to achieve and maintain than a passive one. An active subversion is easier to detect (and thus counteract by local authorities) and typically requires a synchronous control loop. We make the common assumption that the adversaries cannot break the cryptographic primitives or compromise the keys used by clients, SPs, or mixes they do not control.

We assume a PKI that provides a root of trust to authenticate legitimate mixes and zone directories. For instance, the root certificate can be embedded in the *Herd* client software, and a hash of the client software can be published periodically in several trusted outlets.

We assume that legitimate clients and SPs attach to mixes in a trust zone that is friendly to their cause. Clients and SPs can make their choice of a trust zone based on the zone's location, jurisdiction, history and operator.

Anonymity property. Under the threat model described above, *Herd* ensures *zone anonymity* for the caller and callee. That is, assuming a call is known to originate or terminate in a given zone, the communicating party is equally likely to be any of the users attached to the zone.

In the case of an inter-zone call (i.e., caller and callee attach to mixes in different zones), zone anonymity is independent for caller and callee. That is, even if zone anonymity is violated for one participant due to a compromised mix, it continues to hold for the other. However, in case of an intra-zone call (i.e., caller and callee attach to different mixes in the same zone), anonymity is lost for both caller and callee if the zone is compromised. If this is undesirable, users can attach to mixes in two different zones; in this case, *Herd* ensures that only inter-zone calls are established.

Roadmap. In the rest of this section, we discuss the components of *Herd*'s design. First, *layered encryption* ensures bitwise unlinkability and end-to-end confidentiality of VoIP packets. Second, *Herd* uses a *rendezvous* mechanism to establish low-delay circuits while maintaining anonymity for both caller and callee. Third, *traffic obfuscation* is used to thwart traffic analysis attacks, using appropriate mechanisms at clients, SPs, and mixes. Jointly, these components ensure that an adversary can learn only upper bounds on the volume of active calls between any given pair of zones, the volume of calls within a zone, and the maximum number of concurrently active calls among the clients attached to an SP.

Finally, *superpeers* can reduce a mix's client-side bandwidth requirements from linear in the number of online clients to linear in the number of active callers. *Herd* relies on network coding to hide from the untrusted SPs which clients are making calls.

3.2 Layered encryption

Herd uses hop-by-hop and layered encryption over a sender-receiver mutually anonymous circuit as shown in Figure 1. Mixes maintain a Datagram TLS (DTLS) link to all other mixes, SPs maintain a DTLS link to the mix they are attached to, and clients maintain either one such link to a mix, or a small number of links to SPs. All *Herd* traffic is transferred over these links.

As in Tor, mixes, SPs, and clients maintain a long-term identity key pair l used to sign DTLS certificates and their descriptors, and a short-term key pair s used to set up circuits and negotiate symmetric, ephemeral session keys e. Descriptors containing public keys l and s of the zone participants are published in their directory, where they can be queried. Mixes and users communicate via DTLS links encrypted with ephemeral key e, sealing the traffic with perfect forward secrecy. Finally, clients build circuits incrementally, negotiating a symmetric key with each mix on the circuit, one hop at the time, using s over DTLS links. We refer to the *Herd* specifications for more details [19].

Layered encryption provides bitwise unlinkability, and hides content and routing information from both individual mixes and eavesdroppers, while hop-by-hop encryption hides circuit IDs from the latter and provides perfect forward secrecy. (Circuit IDs are needed to lookup the key used to peel off a layer of encryption, so they are transmitted outside of layered encryption.) *Herd* VoIP content is encrypted end-to-end between the caller and callee using a symmetric key negotiated over two circuits concatenated at rendezvous mixes (described below). A complete circuit has five hops (up to seven if optional SPs are used), with typically at least two intra-zone (and thus intra-data center) hops, and for interzone calls, at most three intercontinental hops (at most one if clients select a zone in their respective continent).

For security, simplicity, and future interoperability *Herd* borrows most of its signaling and cryptographic protocol from Tor. This design decision enables *Herd* to build upon years of research and engineering from the Tor community.

Security. Layered and hop-by-hop encryption maintain the following security invariants: **I1:** *The encrypted content on successive links of a circuit is uncorrelated.* **I2:** *The interior mixes on a circuit know only the previous and next hop on the circuit.* **I3:** *The caller's mix knows only the caller and the next mix on the circuit; the callee's mix knows only the callee and the previous mix on the circuit.* **I4:** *A circuit includes two (not necessarily distinct) mixes in each of the caller and callee's zone. Given I2, this implies that, from the perspective of a mix in the caller's zone, the callee is equally likely to attach to any of the mixes in the callee's zone, and vice versa.*

3.3 Rendezvous

The *Herd* rendezvous mechanism connects clients anonymously, independent of their trust zones. This mechanism comprises a per-zone directory server, at least one mix for each of the caller and callee, and for each such mix, a random and not necessarily distinct rendezvous mix in the same zone. The rendezvous mix is selected and trusted by the caller (resp. callee) to initiate/accept calls on her behalf. Each zone directory server stores the rendezvous mixes of all the clients attached to that zone (client's public key and rendezvous mix IP address).

The *Herd* client software comes with a default list of zone directories and public keys used to locate and authenticate zones. Upon joining the system, a client obtains a signed certificate from a zone directory that contains a client ID and the zone's signature. We assume that users exchange certificates prior to making calls using an out-of-band mechanism. We will discuss the join protocol in detail in Section 3.5.

A call is established using the rendezvous mechanism as follows. First, a hidden callee builds a circuit comprising a mix and rendezvous mix in her trust zone and uses it to publish her rendezvous mix in the zone directory. The caller follows the same procedure to select its mix and rendezvous mix. To make a call, a caller looks up the callee's rendezvous mix in the directory of the zone contained in the callee's certificate and initiates a handshake with the hidden callee. If the call is accepted, the two clients communicate via the rendezvous mixes, hence hiding the mixes to which they attach from each other, thus maintaining zone anonymity.

As we discussed in Section 3.1 (anonymity property), zone anonymity is lost for the caller and callee if they both attach to the same, compromised zone. If they want to ensure that their anonymity does not depend on the same trust zone, they may use an alternative, pre-established circuit to a different zone to contact each other as shown in Figure 1. To do so, a caller whose certificate bears the same zone as the callee may chose a different trust zone to establish the call.

Rendezvous enables clients to receive VoIP calls while retaining zone anonymity by interposing a trusted local mix between the client's mix and an untrusted zone. This is because the interposed mix hides the actual entry mix to which a client is attached (either directly or via an SP). Although our rendezvous mechanism is similar to Tor's, *Herd* is the first system to combine it with traffic obfuscation (as we will describe below) in order to achieve zone anonymity.

Security. Rendezvous maintains security invariant **I5:** *Any mix in a client's zone is equally likely to be the client's rendez-vous mix. Thus, knowledge of a client's rendez-vous mix does not reveal any information about which mix the client attaches to.*

3.4 Traffic-analysis resistance

Despite bitwise unlinkability, an adversary can observe and correlate the time series of encrypted packets on different links. Changes in call volume, payload rate (e.g., due to congestion) or manipulation of traffic by an active adversary can cause correlated changes in the time series of encrypted packets along a flow's path. To defeat such *traffic analysis* the anonymity network must craft the time series of packets on each (per-hop) link such that the adversary is unable to infer which clients are communicating. *Herd* does this by adding chaff traffic as needed to pad flows to a constant rate.

Herd uses different padding mechanisms on the clients, SPs and mixes' links. On the clients' links, *Herd* simply maintains *constant chaffing* at a rate sufficient to carry a small number (possibly one) VoIP call(s). Chaff is then replaced with payload traffic when a call is made. On the links between SPs and mixes and among mixes, we use a dynamic chaffing strategy for traffic obfuscation, which can take advantage of temporal and spatial correlation among the payload traffic of groups of clients, in order to resist both short and long-term traffic analysis with low overhead. We describe both methods in more detail below.

3.4.1 Traffic obfuscation on client links

Each client sends and receives at a constant rate equivalent to a small number of voice calls on their SP link(s). To do so, a constant number of encrypted packets equal to the size and rate of the VoIP codec's packets is sent and received per time unit. Chaff packets, which include a sequence number, are substituted when no VoIP packets are to be sent. Both chaff and VoIP packets are encrypted with a symmetric key established between client and mix when the client joined.

Security. Consider the security properties of clients exchanging bidirectional encrypted traffic at a fixed target rate with their SP. Due to congestion and packet loss, the achieved rate on a given link may differ from the target. However, the actual link rate reflects only the capacity and congestion state of the underlying network, and reveals nothing about the payload it carries. Thus, the constant rate traffic is perfectly resistant to passive traffic analysis. Further, actively delaying or dropping traffic on a link does not leak useful information to a network observer, because the downstream node's outgoing stream rate will not be affected (it simply adds more chaff).

3.4.2 Traffic obfuscation on SP links

The links connecting SPs to their mixes carry bidirectional, encrypted and padded traffic at a rate that is a multiple of the VoIP base rate. All links between the mixes of a zone and their SPs carry traffic at the same rate at any given time, but the rate can change over time to accommodate long-term changes in call volume (e.g., based on historical call volume information). Such changes take place at time scales of hours, e.g., to accommodate diurnal load patterns, but do not reveal individual call activity. Rate changes on SP links are orchestrated by the zone directory; mixes periodically report statistics about link utilization to their directory, which then signals them to ramp up/down the rate based on a utilization metric (e.g., average link utilization).

Security. The chaffing reveals no information about individual clients' call activity. However, the sum of the rates on the mix-SP links of a zone reveals an upper bound on the maximal number of active calls originating or terminating in the zone at any given time. This is a deliberate design decision that significantly reduces the client-side bandwidth overhead of mixes, at the cost of revealing an upper bound on the per-zone call volume.

3.4.3 *Traffic obfuscation on mix links*

The mixes are fully connected by a set of encrypted and padded links. The links connecting mixes within a given zone, as well as the links connecting mixes in a given pair of zones, respectively, carry traffic at the same rate at any given time. However, the rates within a zone and between any pair of zones may change over time to accommodate changes in the aggregate call rate. As above, these rate changes take place on time scales of hours and do not reveal individual call activity. Although rate changes on links spanning a single zone are orchestrated unilaterally by their directory (as for SPs), rate changes on links crossing zones require coordination between the directories of the two zones.

Security. No information is leaked about individual call activity. However, a global observer can determine an upper bound on the volume of calls within a zone and between any given pair of zones. Again, this is a deliberate design decision that significantly reduces inter-mix bandwidth at the cost of revealing some upper bounds on aggregated call volume among large client populations, which can likely be estimated anyhow based on the number of clients and the known call volumes between different parts of the world.

Traffic obfuscation on client, SP, and mix links maintains security invariants **I6:** *The time series of encrypted packets on the links of a circuit is uncorrelated with the VoIP payload carried by the circuit* and **I7:** *Manipulating the time series of encrypted traffic on a network link does not affect the time series of encrypted traffic on downstream links.*

3.5 Join protocol

When a client wishes to join the system, it chooses a zone and is redirected by that zone's directory (hardcoded in the client software) to a mix within the zone. The client then establishes a symmetric key s with the mix, which is used for all subsequent communication with the mix, and forms the outer layer of any onion circuit subsequently established by the client. Finally, the mix either adopts the client with a direct link, or redirects the client to one or more of the superpeers (SPs) connected to the mix. Finally, the client establishes either a single padded connection to the mix, or k padded connections to the SPs, in each case encrypted with symmetric key s. In the case of a mix or superpeer failure, a client contacts another mix in the same zone and re-joins.

3.6 Superpeer architecture

Next, we describe *Herd*'s superpeer (SP) architecture. SPs are an optional component of *Herd*—the system is fully functional if all clients attach directly to mixes. However, SPs can increase *Herd*'s scalability by reducing the client-side bandwidth load of mixes by a factor of up to n/a, where a is the maximum number of active clients (i.e., those making calls) in a zone, and n is the number of online clients attached to a zone. In *Herd*, n/a is likely to be large (above 10), because clients have an incentive to remain online independent of their call activity, both to receive calls at unexpected times, and to prevent long-term intersection attacks.

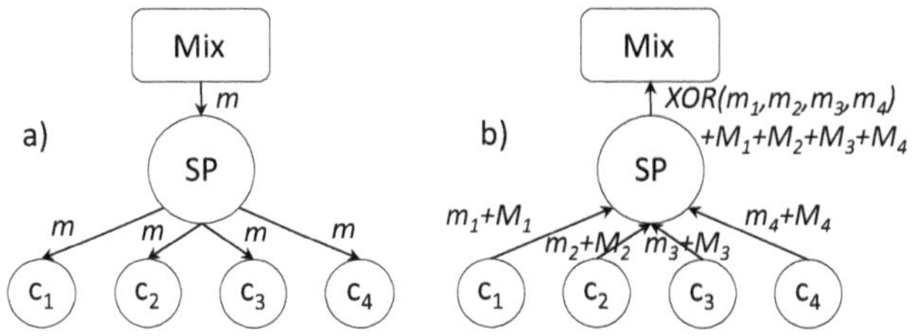

Figure 2: (a) Downstream channel operation: The SP forwards packet m received from the mix to each client. Only the active client can decrypt the packet, others discard the packet as chaff. (b) Upstream channel operation: The SP forwards to the mix the XOR of packets received from clients, concatenated with the list of packet manifests M.

SPs are well-connected, highly-available nodes with a public IP address, who invest resources to support the system altruistically or in exchange for free calls or payment. Like clients, SPs are assumed to be continuously available (modulo power/network outages). SPs are expected to perform in a way that keeps them in good standing with their mix (else they will be blacklisted), but are not otherwise trusted.

Note that an SP cannot decrypt the packets it forwards between client and mix. Moreover, it cannot distinguish chaff packets from VoIP payload packets, and thus cannot determine whether a client is active or not.

3.6.1 *Routing and network coding*

An SP with c attached clients must route information from its mix link with a rate sufficient to carry r calls to its c client links, and vice versa, where $c \geq r$. Our goal is to do this without leaking information about clients' activity to the untrusted SPs.

Downstream. Let us first consider the downstream direction. The SP receives incoming packets in rounds of r packets, where each packet contains VoIP payload for one of the r active clients. The mix must forward these packets so that each active client receives the packet destined for it. For this purpose, the clients attached to an SP are partitioned into r *channels*, and each packet in a round of r is forwarded to a different channel. Each packet includes the initialization vector (IV) used to encrypt it.

Each channel supports at most one active call. The active client can decode the packet it receives, while the remaining clients in the channel cannot—they discard the packet as chaff. To reduce the risk of call blocking when the channel to which a client attaches is occupied, clients attach to $k > 1$ channels (possibly at multiple SPs). Figure 2(a) illustrates the operation of a channel in the downstream direction.

Upstream. In the upstream direction, in each round, the SP receives a packet from each client attached to a channel. Because at most one client can be active in each channel, we can use a simple form of network coding. The SP simply forwards to the mix the XOR of the client packets received in each of the r channels, of which at most one is a VoIP packets and the rest are chaff. Because the ciphertext of the chaff packets from the idle clients is predictable to the mix (the cleartext contains a sequence number and the packets include the IVs), the mix can trivially recover the r payload packets from the r XORs it receives.

Along with each XOR packet, the client forwards the packet manifests that were attached to each client packet included in the XOR. Each of these manifests is 4 bytes long, encrypted with s, and includes the client's id within the channel, packet sequence number, and a signaling bit (described below). The information included in the manifest enables the mix to quickly decode the XOR even in the case of lost or delayed packets, at the expense of slightly more bandwidth on the mix–SP links for the manifests. Figure 2(b) illustrates the operation of a channel in the upstream direction.

Note that a malicious SP or client could deny service by sending an incorrect manifest or an unexpected chaff packet. In this case, the mix asks the SP to send the full packets (which the SP is expected to buffer for a couple of rounds) from which the packets were computed, enabling the mix to identify, drop, and blacklist the culprit's *Herd* account.

3.6.2 Signaling

Next, we describe how mix and client signal incoming and outgoing calls, in such a way that the SP does not learn when a call starts or ends, or which client is calling or being called. In the case of an incoming call, the mix simply chooses an available channel to which the callee attaches (if any), and encrypts downstream packets in the channel with the key s shared with the callee. The callee, which like every client, tries to decrypt every incoming packet on each channel, is able to decrypt the information signaling an incoming call, responds on the same channel, and once it has accepted the call, receives VoIP packets for the duration of the call.

In the case of an outgoing call, the caller sets the signaling bit in the manifest of the chaff packets it sends to the mix via the SPs. Note that the caller does not know which, if any, channel is available. The mix will respond on an available channel to which the caller attaches (if any), as in the case of an incoming call. The caller then provides signaling information for the desired outgoing call on the available channel.

3.6.3 Channel allocation

Next, we describe how the mixes allocate joining clients to channels, and incoming/outgoing calls to channels. Without loss of generality, we consider a single mix. (The set of clients and SPS attached to different mixes are disjoint.)

Each client attaches to k channels. As we will show, $k=3$ provides a good balance between blocking probability and client bandwidth overhead. The number of channels C per zone is chosen to exceed the expected number of active calls a within the zone during the busiest period, i.e., $C \geq a$.

One might consider changing C dynamically to accommodate diurnal load variations efficiently. However, such reconfigurations have significant overheads due to clients changing channels, and care must be taken not to leak information that could aid in long-term intersection attacks. Therefore, in our design, configuration changes occur infrequently and under administrator control, as necessary to accommodate changes in the client population and call volume.

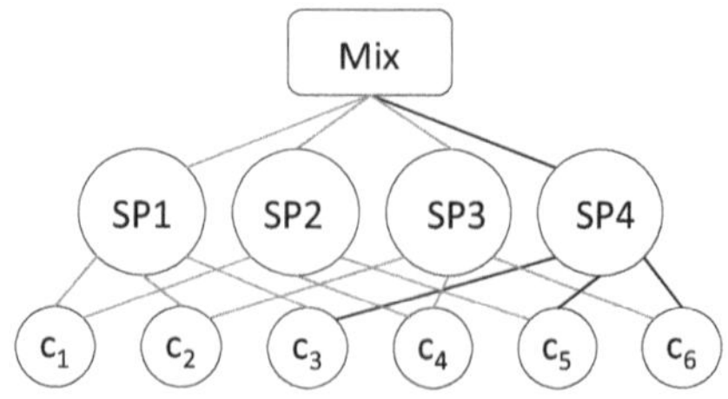

Figure 3: SP configuration with k=2, N=6, C=4, where each of the four SPs supports one channel.

The mix allocates a new client to k distinct channels. We use a greedy algorithm that picks k distinct channels randomly from the least occupied channels. Figure 3 shows an example configuration with 4 SPs, 6 clients, and $k = 2$.

An ideal configuration should enable *any* subset of C clients to make concurrent calls, thus imposing no constraints on the set of active clients. The toy configuration in Figure 3 has this property, but unfortunately, it is infeasible in large configurations for reasonable choices of k and C. In practical configurations, the maximal number of concurrent calls varies among different subsets of C clients, depending on how many channels the subset collectively attaches to.

Note that these connectivity limitation could be overcome trivially by dynamically changing the association of clients to channels, for instance by changing the "routing tables" at the SPs. Unfortunately, dynamic routing inevitably leaks information related to call activity, which could be used as part of an intersection attacks. Therefore, *Herd* uses static allocations of clients to channels. We will show experimentally in Section 4.1.6 that, despite the resulting connectivity constraints, the blocking probability remains good in practice.

Dynamic channel allocation: When an outgoing/incoming call starts, the mix must dynamically allocate to the call an available channel (if any) among the k channels to which the caller/callee attaches. This is an instance of the online bipartite matching problem. A simple, optimal algorithm exists for this problem [36]. It initially ranks all channels randomly, and then allocates the available channel with the highest rank in each step.

3.6.4 Superpeer security

With the routing and coding scheme described above, a set of colluding SPs can learn the static assignment of clients to channels. The channel assignment reveals some constraints on the possible sets of active clients. Clearly, at most C clients can be active within the zone at any one time. Due to connectivity constraints, the maximal number of active calls for a specific set of C clients may be lower than C and known to an adversary. However, without information about call activity, this information is of little use to an adversary. Call activity cannot be observed directly or indirectly either by the SPs or by an adversary with access to the network.

A compromised SP can drop or delay encrypted packets it forwards. However, mixes blacklist SPs that fail to meet a high standard of packet loss rate and jitter. Legitimate SPs that fail to meet the standard due to an unreliable network may require their clients to use error-correcting codes on their encrypted channels to the mix, thus reducing the effective loss rate to acceptable levels.

Superpeers maintain security invariant **I8:** *Superpeers do not know which of its clients are active at any time. Moreover, an SP cannot manipulate the encrypted traffic of its clients without being banned.*

3.7 Security

Next, we argue informally that *Herd*'s security invariants (summarized below) provide zone anonymity.

I1: The encrypted content on successive links of a circuit is uncorrelated.

I2: The interior mixes on a circuit know only the previous and next hop on the circuit.

I3: The caller's mix knows only the caller and the next mix on the circuit; the callee's mix knows only the callee and the previous mix on the circuit.

I4: A circuit includes two (not necessarily distinct) mixes in each of the caller and callee's zone. Given I2, this implies that, from the perspective of a mix in the caller's zone, the callee is equally likely to attach to any of the mixes in the callee's zone, and vice versa.

I5: Any mix in a client's zone is equally likely to be the client's rendez-vous mix. Thus, knowledge of a client's rendez-vous mix does not reveal any information about which mix the client attaches to.

I6: The time series of encrypted packets on successive links of a circuit is uncorrelated with the VoIP payload carried by the circuit.

I7: Manipulating the time series of encrypted traffic on a network link does not affect the time series of encrypted traffic on downstream links.

I8: Superpeers do not know which of its clients are active at any time. Moreover, an SP cannot manipulate the encrypted traffic of its clients without being banned.

I2–I5 jointly maintain zone anonymity for a caller even if the callee's zone is compromised, and vice versa. I1 and I6 maintain zone anonymity in the presence of a global, passive eavesdropper. I7 maintains zone anonymity despite an active network attacker. And invariant I8 maintains zone anonymity despite compromised SPs. A formal analysis of *Herd*'s security properties remains as future work.

Next, we discuss specific attacks within our threat model and how *Herd* defends against them.

Passive traffic analysis attack. The traffic rate on links does not depend on individual payload flows. Short-term traffic analysis is therefore unproductive. Furthermore, the overlay topology is independent of the underlying workload. Therefore, the adversary cannot tell which clients are communicating, even over long periods.

Active traffic analysis attack. Here, the adversary manipulates the flow of encrypted, chaffed *Herd* traffic by delaying, dropping, or replaying packets, or by shutting down or otherwise causing the intermittent failure of clients, SPs, or mixes. Doing so has no impact on the rate of the downstream chaffed traffic, so it does not help the adversary to trace payload flows. For that, the adversary would require access to a client's payload flow at the other end of a *Herd* circuit. However, this case is ruled out by our threat model.

Moreover, *Herd*'s design makes it hard to exploit SPs for active attacks even if the attacker has access to the payload flow on the other end, because mixes ban SPs that manifest significant jitter or packet loss.

Compromised caller/callee. The rendezvous mechanism ensures that compromised callers or callees cannot learn anything other than the zone of their communication partner from the system. However, a compromised participant could conceivably try to estimate the distance to their peer by measuring the round-trip latency on the audio channel. As part of future work, we are planning to investigate if such an attack is feasible. If so, it should be possible to add artificial delay up to the boundaries of the call's MOS quality level, as predicted by the E-Model [34].

Long-term intersection attacks. In Section 4.1.5, we will show experimentally the power of long-term intersection attacks against unanonymized voice calls. *Herd* makes such attacks unproductive, because it makes it impossible to observe when a user makes a call. Since users are online virtually all the time, an adversary cannot even observe significant periods during which a client could not make a call.

Sybil attacks. Like all open anonymous communication systems, *Herd* is susceptible to Sybil attacks, where an adversary controls a large number of clients or superpeers. SPs cannot observe which of their clients are active. Therefore, an adversary who controls SPs can learn only static, weak constraints on the possible sets of concurrently active clients, which are not useful without information about call activity.

If the adversary manages to control a large fraction of the clients attached to a zone, he is able to reduce the anonymity of the remaining legitimate clients proportionally. Since zones serve a large geographic area and user community, however, such an attack would be difficult even with large amounts of resources. Another approach for an adversary is to control all but one of the clients within an SP channel, leaving the remaining legitimate client as the only possible active user. However, such an attack would be difficult because the mix controls which SPs a client attaches to.

An adversary can also use Sybils to deny service. As described above, a misbehaving client or SP can be detected and blacklisted by the mix. To circumvent the blacklist, the adversary has to register a new account, from a new IP address and using a different payment channel, making such an attack expensive. By charging a one-time sign-up fee, the system can further increase the cost of such an attack, although it is impossible to eliminate it completely.

3.8 Herd prototype

Our prototype implementation consists of a core *Herd* module written in ClojureScript (3,289 lines) and a network module written in C (3,159 lines). The core executes on the node.js JavaScript runtime. In addition, the implementation relies on the OpenSSL and curve25519 libraries for TLS and cryptography support.

We implemented the core in a language compatible with JavaScript to enable future distribution of the *Herd* client via standard, encrypted web channels, and execution within a browser. The network component ensures consistently timed packet transmissions, despite garbage collection or other events in the managed JavaScript runtime. The mix, SP and client software currently run as standalone programs on Linux. Porting the software to MacOS or Windows is a matter of preparing appropriate installers. Finally, our *Herd* client supports the Jitsi VoIP client [6] and should support other SIP-compliant clients with minimal effort.

3.9 Summary of contributions

In summary, the key contributions of *Herd*'s design are as follows. 1) *Herd* introduces *zone anonymity*, which guarantees that a user's anonymity depends only on the their own choice of a zone provider, independent of the choice of their communication partners and other users. 2) *Herd* employs a novel hybrid architecture, which shifts resource requirements from its trusted infrastructure to untrusted superpeers without affecting anonymity. Thus, *Herd* can take advantage of untrusted peers willing to contribute resources (for free or in exchange for free calls) to increase scalability and reduce operational cost. 3) *Herd* exploits the specific workload characteristics of VoIP traffic to provide traffic-analysis resistant anonymity with low bandwidth cost.

4. EVALUATION OF HERD

To begin our evaluation, we show that when a traffic-analysis resistant anonymity network is not used, a powerful adversary could trace 98.3% of voice calls performed among millions of users in our mobile phone call trace.

We then conduct trace-driven simulations and experiments with our *Herd* implementation to compare the anonymity, scalability, and call quality of *Herd* and Drac. We find that, in the median case, *Herd* supports anonymity sets comparable to Drac and has comparable call quality, but reduces client bandwidth by up to two orders of magnitude. *Herd* requires some dedicated infrastructure. However, we show that untrusted superpeers that contribute resources for free or in exchange for free calls can reduce *Herd*'s operational costs from $10-100 to $0.1-1.14 per user and month.

4.1 Anonymity and scalability

We rely on a real trace of phone calls among millions of mobile subscribers to compare the anonymity provided by Tor, Drac, and *Herd*, and the scalability of Drac and *Herd*. Here, we use trace-driven simulations instead of testbed experiments because we are interested in comparing these systems under a large, real voice workload.

4.1.1 System models

We use simulation models of Drac, *Herd* and Tor, where the first two use a chaffing strategy as described below, and the latter uses none.

Drac. Drac maintains one chaffing connection for each link within a social network, thus hiding the call patterns within the social network. As a result, *Drac's bandwidth requirements are proportional to the degree of nodes in the social network, i.e., the size of users' contact lists.*

Herd. *Herd* relies on a small, constant number of connections at the clients (3 in our simulations), and it also employs SPs and carefully orchestrates rate changes on the links among mixes to reduce the load on its trusted infrastructure. By doing so, *Herd achieves zone anonymity while minimizing bandwidth requirements.*

Tor. *Tor does not employ chaffing and so does not offer any resistance to traffic analysis.*

4.1.2 Datasets and methodology

Mobile dataset. To determine the anonymity and scalability of the different system models, we use a month of data from August 2010, comprising 370 million calls among 10.8 million users of a large cellular provider (IRB approved). The dataset contains call times, durations, and salted hashes of caller/callee telephone numbers, and indicates which hashes are subscribers of the cell provider.

We use only the calls between subscribers of the carrier. This gives us bidirectional information for each subscriber call, and consists of subscribers who would reasonably use a single zone in *Herd*.

Social network datasets. The call partners recorded over a one month period may significantly underestimate the actual size of contact lists (which determines Drac's bandwidth overhead). Thus, we complement the mobile dataset with social network data to explore Drac's properties under a range of workloads. We use Twitter and Facebook datasets with 54 million, and 1,165 users, respectively [23, 41].

Methodology. We evaluate our system models using trace-based simulations. When evaluating anonymity for Tor (Section 4.1.4), we conduct an intersection attack using 1-second intervals for call start/end times. For the cost analysis in Section 4.1.6, we aggregate the call start and end times into one-minute bins to improve the runtime of our simulations. We determine the peak number of calls and statically provision the *Herd* topology of mixes and SPs accordingly so the network has enough capacity to handle the peak call rate.

4.1.3 Goals

Anonymity. We characterize the anonymity provided by each system as the number of clients who could be the corresponding party, given one known party in a call (anonymity set), under the threat model described in Section 3. In Drac, the size of the anonymity sets corresponds to the number of clients reachable via H hops over the social network. Al-

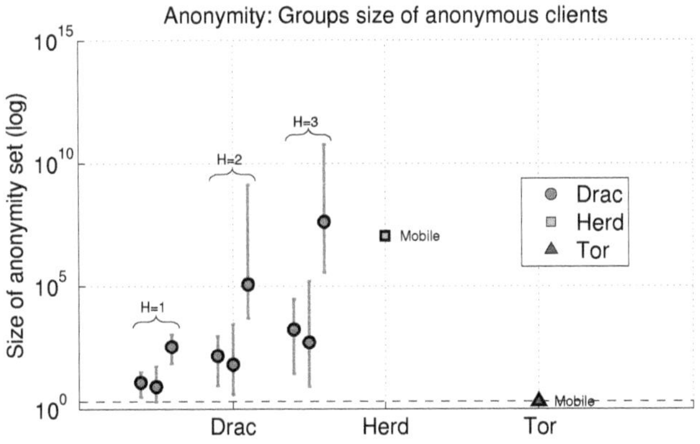

Figure 4: Size of anonymity sets for *Drac*, *Herd*, and *Tor*: median, 10th, and 90th percentiles (left to right). For Drac, we show the results for the *Mobile*, *Twitter*, and *Facebook* datasets and $H = 1, 2, 3$, and for Tor, the results for the Mobile dataset. *The size of anonymity sets in Herd is independent of the node degree and workload.*

though this size can be as large as the entire social network for a sufficiently large H, only clients relatively nearby in the social graph can expect latencies low enough for VoIP (unlike in *Herd*, all hops in Drac typically involve last-mile links). $H = 0$ means that the caller and callee communicate directly and so have an anonymity set of 1. Therefore, we show results only for $H = 1, 2, 3$. In *Herd*, the size of the anonymity set corresponds to the number of subscribers in the mobile dataset, who are assumed to be in a single zone. In Tor, the anonymity set is the set of potential communication partners identified by an intersection attack [22].

Client bandwidth requirement. The bandwidth requirement is the number of chaffing connections multiplied by the rate of a VoIP call using the G.711 codec (8KB/s). As chaff is substituted with payload during a call, the bandwidth requirement accounts for both chaff and payload traffic.

Operational Costs. We evaluate *Herd*'s operational costs in dollars per user/month using EC2 pricing [2].

4.1.4 Results: Tor's Anonymity

In the absence of chaffing, a passive attacker can correlate call start and end times to identify which partners are communicating via an intersection attack [22]. That is, the attacker sees that sets of users start and end calls simultaneously, and attempts to identify pairs of communicating clients from this set. To confirm whether a single pair of users, (u, v), is communicating, the attacker takes the intersection of the sets of users with the same call start/end times as (u, v). When the intersection set is size 2, the attacker has confirmed these communication partners.

We find that, despite the large number of subscribers in our dataset, an intersection attack is highly successful for real call patterns. In particular, after one month, an attacker can trace 98.3% of all calls when using 1-second granularity for tracking call start and end times.

Summary. Real voice communication patterns are highly susceptible to traffic analysis. Anonymity systems that do not defend against such analysis cannot provide practical anonymity. For this reason, we focus the rest of our evaluation on Drac and *Herd*.

4.1.5 Results: Anonymity/Scalability of Drac and Herd

Drac. The effective size of the anonymity sets in Drac correspond to the number of clients that can be reached within H hops in the social network, where H is the maximal number of hops that still yield latencies tolerable for VoIP. We obtain the size of the anonymity sets for $H = 1$ empirically from the different social network data sets, and estimate the sizes for $H = 2, 3$ using the median node degrees.

The median anonymity set sizes for the Mobile, Twitter, and Facebook datasets shown in Figure 4 are 12, 8, and 343 for $H = 1$, and 1728, 512, and 40 million for $H = 3$, respectively.

Drac's bandwidth demand for its clients is proportional to the median node degree. As shown in Figure 5, the median bandwidth required with the Mobile, Twitter and Facebook datasets are 96KB/s, 64KB/s, and 2.6MB/s, respectively, and the maxima are 12MB/s, 39MB/s, and 6.2GB/s.

Herd. *Herd*'s anonymity set sizes depend only on the number of clients in a zone. Consequently, the size of *Herd*'s anonymity set with the mobile workload corresponds to 10.8 millions (the number of subscribers), as we see in Figure 4. Based on our trace-based simulations, we find that 1,000 mixes is sufficient to handle the load from these users. Thus, we expect to be able to support on the order of 10M users in a large cloud provider like EC2.

Herd clients keep a small, constant number of chaffing connections k to the SPs (or only one connection if a client connects directly to a mix). As we have seen in Section 3 (and will confirm below) three connections are sufficient to achieve a very low probability for a call to block due to all its channels being busy. Even with three channels, a client's bandwidth requirement is only 24KB/s (3*8KB/s).

Summary. We showed that *Herd* has significantly lower bandwidth requirements than Drac. To achieve this, *Herd* relays VoIP traffic through a dedicated infrastructure, incurring additional costs and delays. In the rest of this section, we evaluate *Herd*'s operational costs and call quality.

4.1.6 Results: Herd's operational costs

We now evaluate the traffic volume on the *Herd* mixes with and without SPs, with interzone traffic ranging from 10-100%, and the resulting monetary cost per user. We use one week of the phone call data to drive these simulations; results for other weeks were similar.

Impact of using SPs instead of direct connections. We ran SP simulations with 100 SPs per mix and 100 clients per SP, and varied the number of clients per channel (between 5 and 50) and the number of channels each client attaches to (2 and 3). A call is blocked if there are no available channels at the caller or callee's end. In our simulations, the blocking rate for 2 channels varied between 5% and 0.1% with 50 and 5 clients per channel, respectively. We observed that the

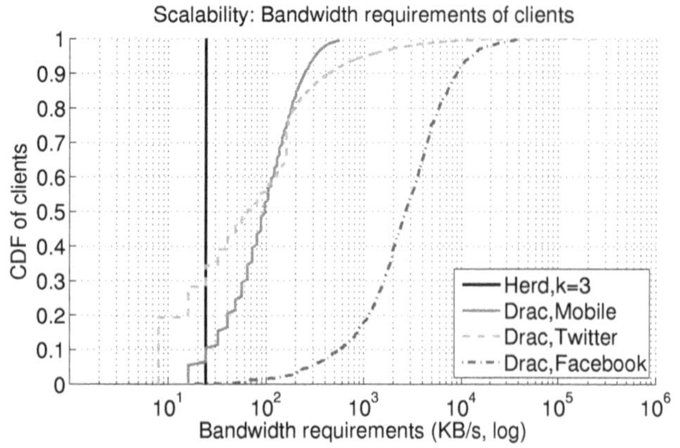

Figure 5: Bandwidth demands of Drac and Herd clients. ***Herd clients keep a small, constant number of chaffing connections, leading to uniformly low bandwidth demand.***

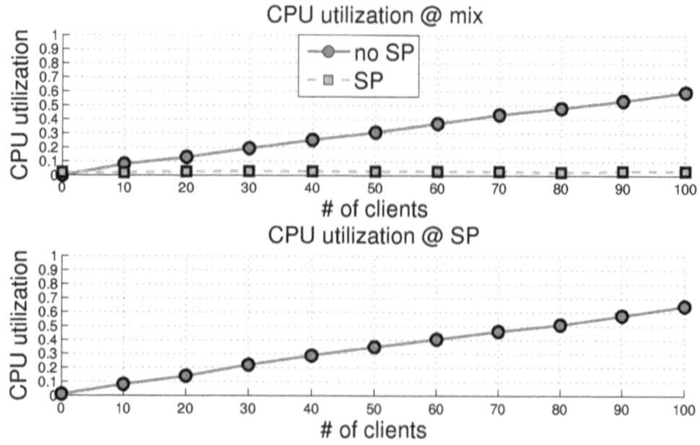

Figure 6: CPU utilization of a mix (top) and SP (bottom), as a function of the number of clients supported.

average blocking rate decreased by an order of magnitude when clients attached to 3 channels instead of 2.

SPs have the potential to greatly offload mixes. In our simulations, these savings varied between 80% and 98% with 5 and 50 clients per channel, respectively. This low blocking rate and high savings are explained by low instantaneous system utilization for voice workloads—in the day-long trace we considered, the peak duty cycle (i.e., peak fraction of users making calls simultaneously) was 1.6%.

Dollar cost per user. We now use trace-based simulation results to estimate the cost of running *Herd* for a large set of clients with Amazon EC2 mixes. We use the AWS calculator to explore the cost of several points in the design space.

The cost ranges from \$0.10 to \$1.14 per month per subscriber. The low end of the range corresponds to a call volume of 1% of users simultaneously making calls at any time and only 10% interzone calls; while the high end of range corresponds to 2% of the users making calls at any time (larger than the peak value in our traces described above) and 100% interzone calls. The reason for the relatively low cost is that intrazone traffic in EC2 (i.e., data traffic that stays within the same data center) does not incur charges, interzone traffic (i.e., between EC2 data centers) incurs low charges, and traffic to SPs and clients costs the most. Because most traffic is between mixes in the same zone, and traffic leaving the cloud is relatively small with SPs, costs are generally low. Thus, we believe that *Herd*'s design is sufficiently affordable when scaled to millions of users.

The above estimates rely on SPs that provide their services for free, and that we do not charge SPs for their use of *Herd*. As an additional incentive, we can pay SPs for their contribution to the system: in this case, the cost per paying subscriber is an additional \$0.14 per dollar we pay SPs.

Note that choosing not to include SPs in a deployment can have a significant impact on costs. Our estimates show that it will cost two orders of magnitude more per user to run *Herd* (\$10-100 per month per user).

Summary. Providing strong anonymity for VoIP in a purely infrastructure-based system is relatively expensive, but a set of well-connected, altruistic, but otherwise untrusted hosts can substantially reduce costs.

4.2 Prototype performance

Next, we present an experimental evaluation of *Herd*'s CPU, memory, and bandwidth consumption.

Goal and methodology. We evaluate the performance of the *Herd* implementation described in Section 3.8 on a mix with and without a superpeer, while varying the number of clients between 0 and 100. The mix and SP were each hosted on a Dell OptiPlex 980 (2.8Ghz Intel Core i5-760, 8GB RAM) and the clients were co-hosted on another machine of the same model (3.2GHz Intel Core i5-650, 8GB RAM). We launched three, 60-second runs for each configuration and used the Linux *time* command to measure the CPU utilization of the *Herd* network process, which performs all data-plane processing. The CPU utilization is the sum of the user and system CPU times divided by the elapsed real time.

Results. SPs reduce resource demand on the mixes. As expected, using an SP reduces the bandwidth required at the mix to support n clients by a factor of nearly n/a, where a is the number of concurrent active calls (one in our experiment). Moreover, as shown in Figure 6, without an SP, the mix's network process has a CPU utilization of 59% for 100 clients, while an SP with one chaffed connection between mix and SP reduces that utilization to only 3%. The marginal CPU utilization for supporting an additional client is .01% and .6% with and without the SP, respectively. The reason is that the network coding for an SP requires far fewer CPU cycles than maintaining a chaffed connection with multiple clients. Finally, the memory utilization on the mix is low regardless of the configuration. For example, the mix without an SP uses 3.4MB of virtual memory for 100 clients.

Summary. SPs reduce the mixes' bandwidth and CPU requirements by an order of magnitude.

4.3 Perceived call quality

We now present an experimental comparison of Drac and *Herd*'s perceived call quality.

4.3.1 Goal: Perceived call quality

We use E-Model to evaluate the quality of actual VoIP calls performed by the authors. E-Model is an analytic model of call quality defined by the International Telecommunication Union (ITU), which calculates the Rating factor (R-factor), a simple measure of voice quality [34]. The R-factor ranges from 0 to 100 and directly determines the Mean Opinion Score (MOS), which ranges from 1 (poor) to 5 (perfect). For VoIP environments, the R-factor is defined in terms of mouth-to-ear delay and packet loss. We refer to Cole et al. for more details [25].

4.3.2 Systems, deployment, and methodology

Drac. Since a Drac implementation is not available, we used *ping* to measure the direct latency between contacts ($H = 0$). *Drac calls between contacts are established directly.*
Herd. For *Herd*, we used the implementation presented in Section 3.8 in our deployment. *Herd routes traffic via sender-receiver, mutually anonymous circuits with SPs.*
Deployment. To evaluate *Herd*'s call quality in practice, we deployed a complete *Herd* system with 4 zones, and requested that volunteers make one-way calls between every zone pairs. Our deployment currently comprises of 8 mixes and rendezvous, 2 directories, and 4 SPs hosted on Amazon EC2. We used ClojureScript 0.0-2644, node.js 0.10.12, Jitsi 2.4, and EC2 small and medium instances with Core OS 522.6.0.
Methodology. For this call quality experiment, each of our 4 volunteers, who connected from university networks, called one other volunteer located in each of the 4 zones (12 calls in total), and listened to a pre-recorded voicemail hosted at the callee. Although VoIP calls are full-duplex, transmissions in each direction are logically independent and so our experiments transmit voice in only one direction. We borrowed this methodology from the industry standard ITU [5].

The *Herd* clients in this experiment conduct the following tests. First, upon receiving an incoming call, each client automatically plays a pre-recorded voicemail. (We host the voicemails at the volunteers to ensure that calls experience realistic end-to-end loss and latency.) Second, an active client periodically (i.e., every second) measures the end-to-end latency and packet loss rate between caller and callee.

4.3.3 Results: Perceived call quality

We show the perceived call quality for Drac with $H = 0$ and *Herd* in Figure 7. In the absence of packet loss, latencies between Europe, North America, and South America were of high or perfect quality, and latencies between Australia and the rest of the world were of medium quality. In our experiments, the packet loss never exceeded a few percents which, according to E-Model, would result in the loss of at most one MOS level for both systems.
Summary. *Herd* achieves modest additional latency while imposing significantly less bandwidth requirements on clients, and much larger anonymity sets for direct calls than in Drac (i.e., 10.8M vs. 1).

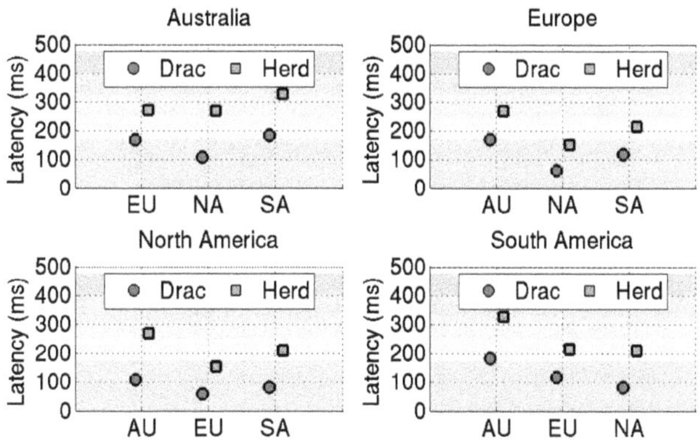

Figure 7: One-way latencies for *Drac* with $H = 0$ and *Herd*, among locations in Australia (AU), Europe (*EU*), North America (*NA*), and South America (*SA*). The colored horizontal bands from top to bottom correspond to the MOS bounds for *poor*, *low*, *medium*, *high*, and *perfect*, perceived quality. *Herd incurs a small, additional one-way latency of approximately 100ms over Drac.*

5. CONCLUSION & FUTURE WORK

Herd is a novel anonymity network for VoIP that provides strong anonymity in the face of powerful adversaries, with good call quality and modest cost. *Herd*'s architecture relies on trusted infrastructure mixes to achieve zone anonymity, where a user's anonymity among the set of clients attached to a zone depends only on that user's choice of a provider. *Herd* uses network coding in a novel way to shift resource requirements from its trusted infrastructure to untrusted superpeers, allowing it to take advantage of resource contributions by untrusted parties to increase its scalability and reduce cost. *Herd* relies on layered encryption and chaffed connections to conceal call activity from powerful adversaries with global network access, while exploiting VoIP traffic characteristics to reduce bandwidth demand. We demonstrated that *Herd* is a practical solution with good performance using an implementation deployed in Amazon EC2 and trace-based simulation with empirical call data. Currently, we are migrating mixes to diverse hosting centers in preparation for a public release. Future work includes supporting group and video calls as well as porting *Herd* to browsers and adapting it to mobile platforms.

Acknowledgements. We thank the anonymous reviewers, our shepherd Stefan Savage, and Bobby Bhattacharjee for their helpful feedback. We are grateful to Saptarshi Ghosh, Krishna Gummadi, Mainack Mondal, and Bimal Viswanath for sharing their datasets with us. Finally, we thank Zheng Leong Chua, Italo Cunha, and Vincent Gramoli for helping us test our prototype *Herd* implementation. This work was supported by the Max Planck Society, the European Research Council (ERC) under the imPACT Synergy Grant No. 610150, and the NSF under Grant No. CNS-1318396.

6. REFERENCES

[1] A potential technique to deanonymise users of the TOR network. http://www.spiegel.de/media/media-35538.pdf.

[2] Amazon Web Services Simple Monthly Calculator. http://calculator.s3.amazonaws.com/index.html.

[3] HideMyAss. http://blog.hidemyass.com/2011/09/23/lulzsec-fiasco/.

[4] Inside TAO: Documents Reveal Top NSA Hacking Unit. http://www.spiegel.de/international/world/the-nsa-uses-powerful-toolbox-in-effort-to-spy-on-global-networks-a-940969.html.

[5] International Telecommunication Union (ITU). http://www.itu.int/.

[6] Jitsi. http://www.jitsi.org.

[7] Microsoft releases 2013 Law Enforcement Requests Report. http://www.microsoft.com/about/corporatecitizenship/en-us/reporting/transparency/.

[8] NSA and GCHQ target Tor network that protects anonymity of web users. http://www.theguardian.com/world/2013/oct/04/nsa-gchq-attack-tor-network-encryption.

[9] NSA collecting phone records of millions of Verizon customers daily. http://www.theguardian.com/world/2013/jun/06/nsa-phone-records-verizon-court-order.

[10] NSA Prism program taps in to user data of Apple, Google and others. http://www.theguardian.com/world/2013/jun/06/us-tech-giants-nsa-data.

[11] obfsproxy. https://www.torproject.org/projects/obfsproxy.html.en.

[12] Silent Circle. https://silentcircle.com/.

[13] User's guide for PRISM Skype collection. http://www.spiegel.de/media/media-35530.pdf.

[14] For Syria's Rebel Movement, Skype Is a Useful and Increasingly Dangerous Tool, 2012. http://www.nytimes.com/2012/12/01/world/middleeast/syrian-rebels-turn-to-skype-for-\\communications.html.

[15] TOR Fone, 2012. http://www.torfone.org/.

[16] Creating a low-latency calling network, 2013. http://www.whispersystems.org/blog/low-latency-switching/.

[17] The future of the internet: Balkanization and borders, 2013. http://ideas.time.com/2013/10/11/the-future-of-the-internet-\\balkanization-and-borders/.

[18] Freedom on the Net 2014, 2014. https://freedomhouse.org/report/freedom-net/freedom-net-2014.

[19] Herd source code and specifications, 2015. https://aqua.mpi-sws.org.

[20] A. Back, I. Goldberg, and A. Shostack. Freedom systems 2.1 security issues and analysis. White paper, Zero Knowledge Systems, Inc., May 2001.

[21] O. Berthold, H. Federrath, and S. Köpsell. Web MIXes: A system for anonymous and unobservable Internet access. In *PET*, 2000.

[22] O. Berthold, A. Pfitzmann, and R. Standtke. The disadvantages of free MIX routes and how to overcome them. In *Workshop on Designing Privacy Enhancing Technologies*, 2001.

[23] M. Cha, H. Haddadi, F. Benevenuto, and K. P. Gummadi. Measuring user influence in twitter: The million follower fallacy. In *ICWSM*, 2010.

[24] D. Chaum. Untraceable electronic mail, return addresses, and digital pseudonyms. *CACM*, 24(2), Feb. 1981.

[25] R. G. Cole and J. H. Rosenbluth. Voice over ip performance monitoring. In *Proc. of SIGCOMM CCR*, Apr. 2001.

[26] G. Danezis, C. Diaz, C. Troncoso, and B. Laurie. Drac: An architecture for anonymous low-volume communications. In *PET*, 2010.

[27] G. Danezis, R. Dingledine, and N. Mathewson. Mixminion: Design of a Type III Anonymous Remailer Protocol. In *Proc. of IEEE S&P*, May 2003.

[28] R. Dingledine, N. Mathewson, and P. Syverson. Tor: The second-generation onion router. In *Proc. of USENIX Security Symposium*, August 2004.

[29] Facebook. Anatomy of Facebook. https://www.facebook.com/notes/facebook-data-team/anatomy-of-facebook/10150388519243859.

[30] M. J. Freedman and R. Morris. Tarzan: A peer-to-peer anonymizing network layer. In *CCS*, 2002.

[31] M. Gabielkov, A. Rao, and A. Legout. Studying Social Networks at Scale: Macroscopic Anatomy of the Twitter Social Graph. In *Proc. of SIGMETRICS*, 2014.

[32] C. Gülcü and G. Tsudik. Mixing E-mail with Babel. In *Proc. of NDSS*, 1996.

[33] H.-C. Hsiao, T. H.-J. Kim, A. Perrig, A. Yamada, S. C. Nelson, M. Gruteser, and W. Meng. LAP: Lightweight anonymity and privacy. In *IEEE Security and Privacy*, 2012.

[34] ITU-T. Recommendation G.107, the e-model, a computational model for use in transmission planning, December 1998.

[35] A. Jerichow, J. Müller, A. Pfitzmann, B. Pfitzmann, and M. Waidner. Real-Time MIXes: A Bandwidth-Efficient Anonymity Protocol. *IEEE Journal on Selected Areas in Communications*, 16(4), 1998.

[36] R. M. Karp, U. V. Vazirani, and V. V. Vazirani. An optimal algorithm for on-line bipartite matching. In *Proc. of STOC*, 1990.

[37] S. Le Blond, D. Choffnes, W. Zhou, P. Druschel, H. Ballani, and P. Francis. Towards efficient traffic-analysis resistant anonymity networks. In *SIGCOMM*, 2013.

[38] S. Le Blond, C. Zhang, A. Legout, K. Ross, and W. Dabbous. I know where you are and what you are sharing: exploiting P2P communications to invade users' privacy. In *Proc. of IMC*, November 2011.

[39] M. Liberatore, B. Gurung, B. N. Levine, and M. Wright. Empirical tests of anonymous voice over IP. *J. Netw. Comput. Appl.*, 34(1):341–350, Jan. 2011.

[40] U. Möller, L. Cottrell, P. Palfrader, and L. Sassaman. Mixmaster Protocol — Version 2. IETF Internet Draft, 2003.

[41] M. Mondal, Y. Liu, B. Viswanath, K. P. Gummadi, and A. Mislove. Understanding and Specifying Social Access Control Lists. In *Proc. of SOUPS*, 2014.

[42] S. Nakamoto. Bitcoin: A Peer-to-Peer Electronic Cash System. 2008.

[43] A. Panchenko, L. Pimenidis, and J. Renner. Performance analysis of anonymous communication channels provided by tor. In *Proc. of Availability, Reliability and Security*, 2008.

[44] A. Pfitzmann, B. Pfitzmann, and M. Waidner. ISDN-MIXes: Untraceable communication with very small bandwidth overhead. In *Proc. of the GI/ITG Conference on Communication in Distributed Systems*, 1991.

[45] R. Sherwood, B. Bhattacharjee, and A. Srinivasan. P5: A protocol for scalable anonymous communication. In *Proc. of Security and Privacy*, 2002.

[46] A. Shostack and I. Goldberg. Freedom systems 1.0 security issues and analysis. White paper, Zero Knowledge Systems, Inc., October 2001.

[47] D. I. Wolinsky, H. Corrigan-Gibbs, B. Ford, and A. Johnson. Dissent in Numbers: Making Strong Anonymity Scale. In *Proc. of OSDI*, 2012.

Statement from the SIGCOMM 2015 Program Committee: The SIGCOMM 2015 PC appreciated the technical contributions made in this paper, but found the paper controversial because some of the experiments the authors conducted raise ethical concerns. The controversy arose in large part because the networking research community does not yet have widely accepted guidelines or rules for the ethics of experiments that measure online censorship. In accordance with the published submission guidelines for SIGCOMM 2015, had the authors not engaged with their Institutional Review Boards (IRBs) or had their IRBs determined that their research was unethical, the PC would have rejected the paper without review. But the authors did engage with their IRBs, which did not flag the research as unethical. The PC hopes that discussion of the ethical concerns these experiments raise will advance the development of ethical guidelines in this area. It is the PC's view that future guidelines should include as a core principle that researchers should not engage in experiments that subject users to an appreciable risk of substantial harm absent informed consent. The PC endorses neither the use of the experimental techniques this paper describes nor the experiments the authors conducted.

Encore: Lightweight Measurement of Web Censorship with Cross-Origin Requests

Sam Burnett
School of Computer Science, Georgia Tech
sam.burnett@gatech.edu

Nick Feamster
Department of Computer Science, Princeton
feamster@cs.princeton.edu

Abstract

Despite the pervasiveness of Internet censorship, we have scant data on its extent, mechanisms, and evolution. Measuring censorship is challenging: it requires continual measurement of reachability to many target sites from diverse vantage points. Amassing suitable vantage points for longitudinal measurement is difficult; existing systems have achieved only small, short-lived deployments. We observe, however, that most Internet users access content via Web browsers, and the very nature of Web site design allows browsers to make requests to domains with different origins than the main Web page. We present Encore, a system that harnesses cross-origin requests to measure Web filtering from a diverse set of vantage points without requiring users to install custom software, enabling longitudinal measurements from many vantage points. We explain how Encore induces Web clients to perform cross-origin requests that measure Web filtering, design a distributed platform for scheduling and collecting these measurements, show the feasibility of a global-scale deployment with a pilot study and an analysis of potentially censored Web content, identify several cases of filtering in six months of measurements, and discuss ethical concerns that would arise with widespread deployment.

SIGCOMM '15, August 17–21, 2015, London, United Kingdom

ACM 978-1-4503-3542-3/15/08 ...$15.00
DOI: http://dx.doi.org/10.1145/2785956.2787485

Categories and Subject Descriptors

• **Networks → Network measurement**; *Web protocol security* • **Social and professional topics → Technology and censorship**

Keywords

Web censorship; Network measurement; Web security

1 Introduction

Internet censorship is pervasive: by some estimates, nearly 60 countries restrict Internet communication in some way [35]. As more citizens in countries with historically repressive governments gain Internet access, government controls are likely to increase. Collecting pervasive, longitudinal measurements that capture the evolving nature and extent of Internet censorship is more important than ever.

Researchers, activists, and citizens aim to understand what, where, when, and how governments and organizations implement Internet censorship. This knowledge can shed light on government censorship policies and guide the development of new circumvention techniques. Although drastic actions such as introducing country-wide outages (as has occurred in Libya, Syria, and Egypt) are eminently observable, the most common forms of Internet censorship are more subtle and challenging to measure. Censorship typically targets specific domains, URLs, keywords, or content; varies over time in response to changing social or political conditions (*e.g.*, a national election); and can be indistinguishable from application errors or poor performance (*e.g.*, high delay or packet loss). Detecting more nuanced forms of censorship requires frequent measurement from many varied vantage points.

Unfortunately, consistently and reliably gathering these types of measurements is extremely difficult. Perhaps the biggest obstacle entails obtaining access to a diverse, globally distributed set of vantage points, particularly in the regions most likely to experience censorship. Achieving widespread deployment in these locations often requires surmounting language and cultural barriers and convincing users to install measurement software. Although researchers have begun to develop custom tools to measure filtering (*e.g.*, OONI [15,38], Centinel [8]), widespread deployment remains a challenge. Instead, researchers have resorted to informal data collection (*e.g.*, user reports [23]) or collection from a small number of non-representative vantage points (*e.g.*, PlanetLab nodes [42], hosts on virtual private networks, or even one-off deployments of single vantage points) that might not observe the same filtering that typical users experience.

This paper takes an alternate approach: rather than ask each user to deploy custom censorship measurement software, we use existing features of the Web to induce unmodified browsers to measure Web censorship. Many users access the Internet with a Web browser, so inducing these browsers to perform censorship measurements will enable us to collect data from a larger, more diverse, and more representative set of vantage points than is possible with custom censorship measurement tools.

Our system, Encore, uses Web browsers on nearly every Internet-connected device as potential vantage points for collecting data about what, where, and when Web filtering occurs. Encore relies on a relatively small number of Web site operators (*webmasters*) to install a one-line embedded script that attempts to retrieve content from third-party Web sites using cross-origin requests [6,40]. The Encore script induces every visitor of these modified pages to request an object from a URL that Encore wishes to test for filtering. Although same-origin policies in browsers prohibit many kinds of requests (*e.g.*, to thwart cross-site request forgery), we demonstrate that the cross-origin requests that browsers *do* allow are sufficient to collect information and draw conclusions about Web filtering. A major contribution of our work is to show that meaningful conclusions about Web filtering can be drawn from the side channels that exist in cross-origin requests.

Encore's simplicity comes at the cost of significant limitations on the types of measurements it can collect and the conclusions we can draw from its measurements. First, Encore's measurements must operate within the constraints of the cross-origin requests that Web browsers permit. For example, the `img` HTML directive yields the most conclusive feedback about whether an object fails to load, but it can only be used to test images, not general URLs. This limitation means that while it may be useful for detecting (say) the filtering of an entire DNS domain, it cannot test the reachability of specific (non-image) URLs. Encore's design must recognize which cross-origin requests browsers permit and use combinations of these requests to draw inferences with higher confidence. Second, because Encore requires webmasters to augment their existing Web pages, Encore must be easy to install and incur minimal performance overhead on the Web sites where it is deployed. Finally, great care is required when measuring censorship because accessing sensitive sites may endanger users in repressive countries. Our research focuses on Encore's design and implementation, and is not a measurement study *per se*.

Encore can detect *whether* certain URLs are filtered, but it cannot determine *how* they are filtered. Subtle forms of filtering (*e.g.*, degrading performance by introducing latency or packet loss) are difficult to detect, and detecting content manipulation (*e.g.*, replacing a Web page with a block page, or substituting content) using Encore is nearly impossible. Thus, Encore may complement other censorship measurement systems, which can perform detailed analysis but face much higher deployment hurdles. Ultimately, neither Encore nor other censorship analysis tools can determine human motivations behind filtering, or even whether filtering was intentional; they only provide data to policy experts who make such judgments.

2 Related Work

We summarize existing censorship measurement techniques and previous studies of Internet censorship; other policy reports of Internet censorship (which can ultimately seed our measurements); and other efforts to perform measurements from clients using advertisements or embedded images. Although we broadly survey Internet censorship practices, Encore focuses on Web filtering.

Censorship measurement tools. The prevailing mode for measuring Internet censorship is to develop custom measurement software and identify users who are willing to either install the software or otherwise host a measurement device that runs the software. Existing measurement tools include OONI [15], Centinel [8], and CensMon [42]. Both OONI and Centinel can be deployed on end hosts. These tools perform much more detailed analysis of *how* censors implement blocking, but to date both have seen only limited deployment, likely because they require recruitment of users who are willing to install and maintain the measurement software. CensMon was only deployed for a brief period on PlanetLab, a global network of servers hosted in academic networks; such measurements are unlikely to be representative, as residential and mobile broadband networks can face much different censorship practices than academic and research networks [32,46]. At this point, we are not aware of any censorship measurement system that continuously collects measurements from a global set of vantage points; this is the gap that Encore aims to fill.

Censorship measurement studies. Several researchers have performed "first look" studies of censorship in various countries such as Pakistan [32], Iran [1], and China [10,11,47]. Zittrain *et al.*'s study of censorship in China [47] performed

Web requests to hundreds of thousands of sites, but did so from only a handful of dialup modems that the authors deployed. Crandall [11], Clayton [10], and Ensafi [14] exploit symmetric behavior of the Chinese firewall to measure it from clients outside China; such measurements are easier to collect than Encore, but the technique does not work in all countries. The studies of censorship in Iran and Pakistan were more limited: the Iran study apparently performed measurements from a single vantage point for only two months [1], and the Pakistan study performed measurements from only five test networks over about two months [32]. Each of these studies offers a useful snapshot into a country's filtering practices at a particular point in time, but data collection is neither widespread nor continuous. The OpenNet Initiative has conducted the only long-term study to date, but its data collection is sporadic, making it difficult to compare filtering practices across countries and time [35].

Sources of block lists. Some policy organizations publish reports concerning censorship practices around the world. For example, the Open Network Initiative routinely publishes qualitative reports based on measurements from a limited number of vantage points, with scant insight into how censorship evolves over short timescales or what exactly is being filtered [36, 37]. Other projects such as Herdict [23], GreatFire [19], and Filbaan [16] maintain lists of domains that may be blocked. Herdict compiles reports from users about domains that are blocked from a certain location; such reports lack independent verification. GreatFire monitors reachability of domains and services from a site behind China's censorship firewall; it also maintains historical measurement results. Each tool offers limited information driven by user-initiated reporting or measurements, yet these services and reports can serve as initial lists of URLs to test using Encore.

Cross-origin requests for client measurement. Bortz *et al.* use timing information from cross-site requests to infer various information, such as whether a user is logged into a particular site or whether a user has previously visited a Web page [5]. Karir *et al.* use embedded Javascript with cross-origin requests to measure IPv6 reachability and performance from large numbers of clients [29]; the use of embedded cross-origin requests to obtain large number of clients is similar to Encore's design. Other systems have used cross-origin requests to third parties to determine information such as network latency between a client and some other Internet destination [20, 33]. In particular, Casado and Freedman quantified the prevalence of clients behind NATs and proxies by delivering measurement code to clients in a manner very similar to Encore [7]. Puppetnets exploits weaknesses in browser security to coerce browsers to unwittingly participate in denial-of-service attacks [30]. These tools use similar techniques as Encore, but they primarily aim to measure network performance or past user behavior based on the timing of successful cross-origin requests. They do not infer reachability of domains, IP addresses, or URLs based on the success (or lack thereof) of cross-origin requests.

3 Background

We discuss Web filtering and threats that may interfere with attempts to measure it. We also explain cross-origin requests.

3.1 Threat Model

To implement Web filtering, smaller countries often have centralized traffic filters on a national backbone; larger countries require each ISP to implement a censorship policy; some countries, like China, do both [46]. Web filtering typically takes place when the client performs an initial DNS lookup (at which point the DNS request may result in blocking or redirection), when the client attempts to establish a TCP connection to the Web server hosting the content (at which point packets may be dropped or the connection may be reset), or in response to a specific HTTP request or response (at which point the censor may reset the TCP connection, drop HTTP requests, or redirect the client to a block page).

Our goal is to observe instances of Web filtering and report them to a central authority (*e.g.*, researchers) for analysis. We assume an adversary that can reject, block, or modify any stage of a Web connection in order to filter Web access for subsets of clients, although we assume the adversary uses a blacklist and is unwilling to filter all Web traffic, or even significant fractions of all Web traffic. This adversary influences Encore's design in three ways: (1) the main goal of Encore is to measure this adversary's Web filtering behavior; (2) the adversary may attempt to filter clients' access to Encore itself, thereby preventing them from collecting or contributing measurements; and (3) the adversary may attempt to distort Encore's filtering measurements by allowing measurement traffic but denying other access to the same site. This paper considers all three aspects of the adversary.

3.2 Cross-Origin Requests

Web browsers' *same-origin policies* restrict how a Web page from one origin can interact with resources from another; an *origin* is defined as the protocol, port, and DNS domain ("host") [40]. In general, sites can send information to another origin using links, redirects, and form submissions, but they cannot receive data from another origin; in particular, browsers restrict cross-origin reads from scripts to prevent attacks such as cross-site request forgery. However, cross-origin *embedding* is typically allowed and can leak some read access. The cornerstone of Encore's design is to use information leaked by cross-origin embedding to determine whether a client can successfully load objects from another origin.

Various mechanisms allow Web pages to embed remote resources using HTTP requests across origins; some forms of cross-origin embedding are not subject to the same types of security checks as other cross-origin reads. Examples of resources that can be embedded include simple markup of images or other media (*e.g.*, `<img>`), remote scripts (*e.g.*, `<script>`), remote stylesheets (*e.g.*, `<link rel="stylesheet" href="...">`), embedded objects and applets (*e.g.*, `<embed src="...">`),

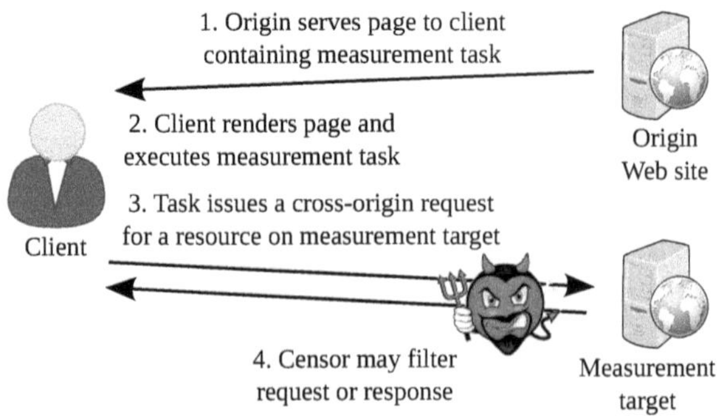

Figure 1: *Encore induces browsers to collect Web filtering measurements by bundling measurement tasks inside pages served by an origin Web site.*

and document embedded frames such as iframes (*e.g.*, `<iframe>`). Each of these remote resources has different restrictions on how the origin page can load them and hence leak different levels of information. For example, images embedded with the `img` tag trigger an `onload` event if the browser successfully retrieves and renders the image, and an `onerror` event otherwise. The ability for the origin page to see these events allows the origin page to infer whether the cross-origin request succeeded.

Although cross-origin embedding of media provides the most explicit feedback to the origin about whether the page load succeeded, other embedded references can still provide more limited information, through timing of `onload` invocation or introspection on a Web page's style. Additionally, browsers have different security policies and vulnerabilities; for example, we discovered that the Chrome browser allows an origin site to load any cross-origin object via the `script` tag, which allows us to conduct a much more liberal set of measurements from Chrome. One challenge in designing Encore is determining whether (and how) various embedded object references can help infer information about whether an object was retrieved successfully.

4 Measuring Filtering with Encore

This section explains how Encore measures Web filtering using cross-origin requests.

4.1 Overview

Figure 1 illustrates how Encore measures Web filtering. The process involves three parties: a Web client that acts as our measurement vantage point; a measurement target, which is a server that hosts a Web resource that we suspect is filtered; and an origin Web server, which serves a Web page to the Web client instructing the client how to collect measurements. In each page it serves, the origin includes a *measurement task*, which is a small measurement collection program that attempt to access potentially filtered Web resources (*e.g.*, Web pages, image files) from the target and determine whether such accesses were successful. The client runs this measurement task after downloading and rendering the page. The greatest challenge is coping with browsers' limited APIs for conducting network measurements, particularly when accessing these resources requires issuing cross-origin requests.

The scope of Web filtering varies in granularity from individual URLs (*e.g.*, a specific news article or blog post) to entire domains. Detecting Web filtering is difficult regardless of granularity. On one hand, detection becomes more difficult with increasing specificity. When specific Web resources are filtered (as opposed to, say, entire domains), there are fewer ways to detect it. Detecting filtering of entire domains is relatively straightforward because we have the flexibility to test for such filtering simply by checking accessibility of a small number of resources hosted on that domain. In contrast, detecting filtering of a single URL essentially requires an attempt to access that exact URL. Resource embedding only works with some types of resources, which further restricts the Web resources we can test and exacerbates the difficulty of detecting very specific instances of filtering.

On the other hand, inferring broad filtering is difficult because Encore can only observe the accessibility of individual Web resources, and such observations are binary (*i.e.*, whether or not the resource was reachable). Any conclusions we draw about the scope of Web filtering must be inferred from measurements of individual resources. We take a first-order glimpse at such inferences in Section 4.3 and present a filtering detection algorithm in Section 7.

4.2 Measurement tasks

Measurement tasks are small, self-contained HTML and JavaScript snippets that attempt to load a Web resource from a measurement target. Encore's measurement tasks must satisfy four requirements: First, they must be able to successfully load a cross-origin resource in locations without Web filtering. Tasks cannot use XMLHttpRequest (*i.e.*, AJAX requests), which is the most convenient way to issue cross-origin requests, because default Cross-origin Resource Sharing settings prevent such requests from loading cross-origin resources from nearly all domains. Instead, we induce cross-origin requests by embedding images, style sheets, and scripts across domains, which browsers typically allow.

Second, they must provide feedback about whether or not loading a cross-origin resource was successful. Several convenient mechanisms for loading arbitrary cross-origin requests (*e.g.*, the `iframe` tag) lack a clear way to detect when resources fail to load, and are hence unsuitable for measurement tasks.

Third, tasks must not compromise the security of the page running the task. Tasks face both client- and server-side security threats. On the client side, because Encore detects Web filtering by *embedding* content from other origins (rather than simply requesting it, as would be possible with an AJAX request), such embedding can pose a threat as the browser renders or otherwise evaluates the resource after downloading it. In some cases, rendering or evaluating the resources is always innocuous (*e.g.*, image files); in other cases (*e.g.*, JavaScripts), Encore must carefully sandbox the embedded content to prevent it from affecting other aspects of Web browsing. Requesting almost any Web object changes server state, and measurement tasks must take these possible side effects into account. In some cases, the server simply logs that the request happened, but in others, the server might insert rows into a database, mutate cookies, change a user's account settings, etc. Although it is often impossible to predict such state changes, measurement tasks should try to only test URLs without obvious server side-effects.

Finally, measurement tasks must not significantly affect perceived performance, appearance, or network usage.

Below is an example of a simple measurement task that instructs the Web client to load an image hosted by a measurement target `censored.com`:

```
<img src="//censored.com/favicon.ico"
     style="display: none"
     onload="submitSuccess()"
     onerror="submitFailure()"/>
```

This task meets the four requirements because it (1) requests an image from a remote measurement target using the `img` tag, which is allowed by browser security policy; (2) detects whether the browser successfully loaded the image by listening for the `onload` and `onerror` events; (3) trivially maintains security by not executing any code from resources served by the measurement target; and (4) preserves performance and appearance by only loading a very small icon (typically 16×16 pixels) and hiding it using the `display: none` style rule. Appendix A presents a longer example of a measurement task.

4.3 Inferring Web filtering

A measurement task provides a binary indication of whether a particular resource failed to load, thus implying filtering of that specific resource. From collections of these measurements, we can draw more general conclusions about the scope of filtering, beyond individual resources (*e.g.*, whether an entire domain is filtered, whether an entire portion of a Web site is filtered, whether certain keywords are filtered). We must do so with little additional information about the filtering mechanism. This section describes how we design sets of measurement tasks to make these inferences.

There are several ways to test accessibility of cross-origin Web resources; unfortunately, none of them work across all types of filtering, all Web browsers, and all target sites. Instead, we tailor measurement tasks to each measurement target and Web client. Detecting Web filtering gets harder as the scope of filtering becomes more specific, so we start with techniques for detecting broad-scale filtering and work toward more specific filtering schemes. Table 1 summarizes the measurement tasks we discuss in this section.

4.3.1 Filtering of entire domains

Encore performs collections of measurement tasks that help infer that a censor is filtering an entire domain. It is prohibitively expensive to check accessibility of *every* URL hosted on a given domain. Instead, we assume that if several *auxiliary* resources hosted on a domain (*e.g.*, images, style sheets) are inaccessible, then the entire domain is probably inaccessible. Our intuition is that rather than filtering many supporting resources, an adversary will more likely filter the entire domain (or at least an entire section of a site). Fortunately, detecting filtering of some auxiliary resources is straightforward because pages often embed them even across origins.

Images. Web pages commonly embed images, even across origins. Such embedding is essential for enabling Web services like online advertising and content distribution networks to serve content across many domains.

Encore attempts to load and display an image file from a remote origin by embedding it using the `<img src=...>` tag. Conveniently, all major browsers invoke an `onload` event after the browser fetches and renders the image, and invoke `onerror` if either of those steps fails; the requirement to successfully render the image means that this mechanism only works for images files and cannot decide the accessibility of non-image content. Downloading and rendering an image does not affect user-perceived performance if the image is small (*e.g.*, an icon), and measurement tasks can easily hide images from view. This technique only works if the remote origin hosts a small image that we can embed.

Style sheets. Web pages also commonly load style sheets across origins. For example, sites often load common style sheets (*e.g.*, Bootstrap [4]) from a CDN to boost performance and increase cache efficiency.

Encore attempts to load a style sheet using the `<style src=...>` tag and detects success by verifying that the browser applied the style specified by the sheet. For example, if the sheet specifies that the font color for `<p>` tags is blue, then the task creates a `<p>` tag and checks whether its color is blue using `getComputedStyle`. To prevent the sheet's style rules from colliding with those of the parent Web page, we load the sheet inside an `iframe`. Although some browsers are vulnerable to cross-site scripting attacks when loading style sheets, these issues have been fixed in all newer browsers [26]. Style sheets are generally small and load quickly, resulting in negligible performance overhead.

4.3.2 Filtering of specific Web pages

Governments sometimes filter one or two Web pages (*e.g.*, blog posts) but leave the remainder of a domain intact, including resources embedded by the filtered pages [32]. Detecting this type of filtering is more difficult because there is less flexibility in the set of resources that Encore can use for measurement tasks: it must test accessibility of the Web page in question and cannot generally determine whether the page is filtered based on the accessibility of other (possibly related) resources. Testing filtering of Web pages, as opposed to individual resources, is significantly more expensive, complicated, and prone to security vulnerabilities because such testing often involves fetching not only the page itself, but also fetching

Mechanism	Summary	Limitations
Images	Render an image. Browser fires `onload` if successful.	Only small images (*e.g.*, ≤ 1 KB).
Style sheets	Load a style sheet and test its effects.	Only non-empty style sheets.
Inline frames	Load a Web page in an iframe, then load an image embedded on that page. Cached images render quickly, implying the page was not filtered.	Only pages with cacheable images. Only small pages (*e.g.*, ≤ 100 KB). Only pages without side effects.
Scripts	Load and evaluate a resource as a script. Chrome fires `onload` iff it fetched the resource with HTTP 200 status.	Only with Chrome. Only with strict MIME type checking.

Table 1: *Measurement tasks use several mechanisms to discover whether Web resources are filtered. We empirically evaluate parameters for images and inline frames in Section 6.*

all of that page's referenced objects and rendering everything. This means we must be very careful in selecting pages to test. Many pages are simply too expensive or open too many vulnerabilities to test. Section 5 discusses the infrastructure and decision process we use to decide whether a Web page is suitable for testing.

We present two mechanisms for testing Web filtering of Web pages, and the limitations of each mechanism:

Inline frames. A Web page can include any other Web page inside itself using the `iframe` tag, even across origins. However, browsers place strict communication barriers between the inline page and the embedding page for security, and provide no explicit notification about whether an inline frame loaded successfully.

Instead, the task infers whether the resource loaded successfully by observing timing. It first attempts to load the page in an iframe; then, after that iframe finishes load,the task records how long it takes to download and render an image that was embedded on that page. If rendering this image is fast (*e.g.*, less than a few milliseconds) we assume that the image was cached from the previous fetch and therefore the Web page loaded successfully. This approach only works with pages that embed objects that will be cached by the browser and are unlikely to have been cached from a prior visit to another Web page; for example, common images like the Facebook's "thumbs up" icon appear on many pages and may be in the browser cache even if the iframe failed to load. This approach can be expensive because it requires downloading and rendering entire Web pages. Additionally, pages can detect when they are rendered in an inline frame and may block such embedding.

Scripts. Web pages often embed scripts across origins, similarly to how they embed style sheets. For example, many pages embed jQuery and other JavaScript libraries from a content distribution network or some other third-party host [28].

The Chrome browser handles script embedding in a way that lets us gauge accessibility of *non-script* resources from a remote origin. Chrome invokes an `onload` event if it can fetch the resource (*i.e.*, with an `HTTP 200 OK` response), regardless of whether the resource is valid JavaScript. In particular, Chrome respects the `X-Content-Type-Options: nosniff` header, which servers use to instruct browsers to

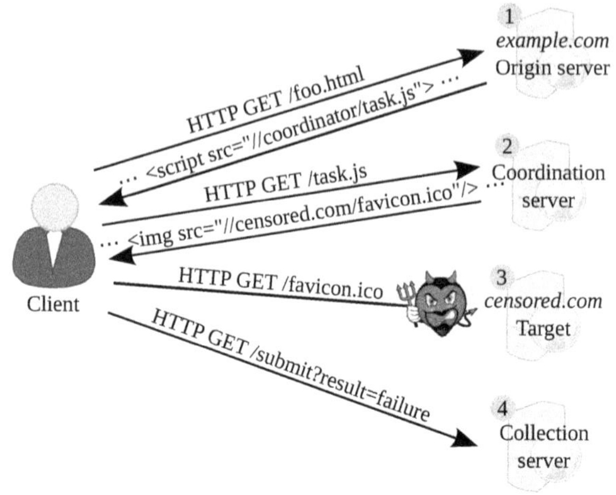

Figure 2: *An example of observing Web filtering with Encore. The origin Web page includes Encore's measurement script, which the coordinator decides should test filtering of* `censored.com` *by attempting to fetch an image. The request for this image fails so the client notifies the collection server.*

prohibit execution of scripts with an invalid MIME type [2]. Other browsers are not so forgiving, so we use this task type on Chrome only. This technique is convenient, but it raises security concerns because other browsers may attempt to execute the fetched object as JavaScript. Section 5 describes how we make this decision.

5 Encore Measurement System

This section presents Encore, a distributed platform for measuring Web filtering. Encore selects targets to test for Web filtering (§ 5.1), generates measurement tasks to measure those targets (§ 5.2), schedules tasks to run on Web clients (§ 5.3), delivers these tasks to clients for execution (§ 5.4), collects the results of each task (§ 5.5), and draws conclusions concerning filtering practices based on the collective outcomes of these tests using the inference techniques from Section 4.

Figure 2 shows an example of how Encore induces a client to collect measurements of Web filtering. The client visits a Web site `http://example.com`, whose webmaster has volunteered to host Encore. This origin page references a measurement task hosted on a coordination server; the client downloads the measurement task, which in turn instructs the client to attempt to load a resource (*e.g.*, an image) from a measurement target `censored.com`. This request is filtered, so the client informs a collection server of this filtering. The remainder of this section explains how the origin Web server, coordination server, and collection server work together to induce and collect Web filtering measurements.

5.1 Sources of measurement targets

Encore requires a set of potentially filtered Web sites and resources to test for Web filtering. This list can contain either specific URLs if Encore is testing the reachability of a specific page; or a *URL pattern* denoting sets of URLs (*e.g.*, an entire domain name or URL prefix) to test the reachability of a domain or a portion of a Web site. A small list of likely filtered targets is most useful during initial stages of deployment when clients of only a few moderately popular Web sites will likely be contributing measurements. As adoption increases, a broader set of targets can increase breadth of measurements. We explore how to obtain lists in both scenarios.

During initial deployment, Encore relies on third parties to provide lists of URLs to test for Web filtering. Several organizations maintain such lists. Some sites rely on per-country experts to curate URLs (*e.g.*, GreatFire for China [19], Filbaan for Iran [16]), while others crowdsource list creation and let anyone contribute reports of Web censorship (*e.g.*, Herdict [23]). Our evaluation in Section 6 uses a list of several hundred "high value" URLs curated by Herdict and its partners. Curating accurate and appropriate lists of potentially censored URLs is beyond the scope of this paper and an active research area.

If we deploy Encore to many geographically distributed Web clients and build a large, accurate Web index, we could instead use Encore clients to verify accessibility of the entire Web index, which would avoid the need for specialized lists of measurement targets by instead testing the entire Web. Regardless of whether Encore curates a small list of high-value measurement targets or simply extracts URLs from a large Web index, these URLs and URL patterns serve as input for Encore's next stage.

5.2 Generating measurement tasks

Measurement task generation is a three-step procedure that transforms URL patterns from the list of measurement targets into a set of measurement tasks that can determine whether the resources denoted by those URL patterns are filtered for a client. This procedure happens prior to interaction with clients (*e.g.*, once per day). Figure 3 summarizes the process. First, the *Pattern Expander* transforms each URL pattern into a set of URLs by searching for URLs on the Web that match the pattern. Second, the *Target Fetcher* collects detailed information about each URL by loading and rendering it in a real Web browser and recording its behavior in an HTTP Archive (HAR) file [22]. Finally, the *Task Generator* examines each HAR file to determine which of Encore's measurement task types, if any, can measure each resource and generates measurement tasks for that subset of resources.

The Pattern Expander searches for URLs that match each URL pattern. This step identifies a set of URLs that can all indicate reachability of a single resource; for example, all URLs with the prefix `http://foo.com/` are candidates for detecting filtering of the `foo.com` domain. Some patterns are trivial (*i.e.*, they match a single URL) and require no work. The rest require discovering URLs that match the pattern. We currently expand URL patterns to a sample of up to 50 URLs by scraping site-specific results (*i.e.*, using the *site:* search operator) from a popular search engine. In the future, Encore could use its own Web crawler to explore each pattern.

After expanding URL patterns into a larger set of URLs, the Target Fetcher renders each URL in a Web browser and records a HAR file, which documents the set of resources that a browser downloads while rendering a URL, timing information for each operation, and the HTTP headers of each request and response, among other metadata. We use the PhantomJS [39] headless browser hosted on servers at Georgia Tech. To the best of our knowledge, Georgia Tech does not filter Web requests, especially to the set of URLs we consider in this paper.

Finally, the Task Generator analyzes each HAR file to determine which subset of resources is suitable for measuring using one of the types of measurement tasks from Table 1. It examines timing and network usage of each resource to decide whether a resource is small enough to load from an origin server without significantly affecting user experience, then inspects content type and caching headers to determine whether a resource matches one of the measurement tasks. The Task Generator is particularly conservative when considering inline frames because loading full Web pages can severely impact performance and user experience (*e.g.*, by playing music or videos). Our prototype implementation excludes pages that load flash applets, videos, or any other large objects totaling more than 100 KB, and requires manual verification of pages before deployment; a future implementation could apply stricter controls. Refer back to Section 4 for more information on the requirements for each type of measurement task. Section 6.1 further explores network overhead of measurement tasks.

5.3 Scheduling measurement tasks

After generating measurement tasks, the coordination server must decide which task to schedule on each client. Task scheduling serves two purposes. First, it enables clients to run measurements that meet their restrictions. For example, we should only schedule the script task type from Table 1 on clients running Chrome. In other cases, we may wish to schedule additional tasks on clients that remain idle on an origin Web page for a long time. Second, intelligent task scheduling enables Encore to move beyond analyzing individual measurements and draw conclusions by comparing measurements between clients, countries, and ISPs. For ex-

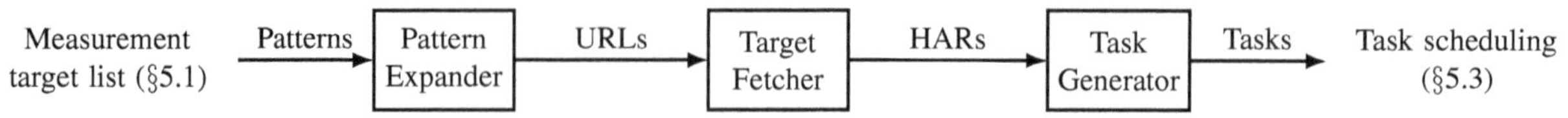

Figure 3: *Encore transforms a list of URL patterns to a set of measurement tasks in three steps. A URL pattern denotes a set of URL* (e.g., *all URLs on a domain). A HAR is an HTTP Archive [22].*

ample, a single client in Pakistan could report failure to access a URL for a variety of reasons other than Web filtering (*e.g.*, high client system load, transient DNS failure, WiFi unreliability). However, if 100 clients measure the same URL within 60 seconds of each other and the only clients that report failure are 10 clients in Pakistan, then we can draw much stronger conclusions about the presence of Web filtering.

5.4 Delivering measurement tasks

After scheduling measurement tasks for execution, Encore must deliver tasks to these clients, who subsequently run them and issue cross-origin requests for potentially filtered Web resources. To collect a significant number of useful Web filtering measurements, Encore requires a large client population that is likely to experience a diversity of Web filtering. Previous censorship measurement efforts require researchers to recruit vantage points individually and instruct them to install custom software, which presents a significant deployment barrier [15, 35]. In contrast, Encore recruits a relatively small number of webmasters and piggybacks on their sites' existing Web traffic, instantly enlisting nearly *all* of these sites' visitors as measurement collection agents.

A webmaster can enable Encore in several ways. The simplest method is to add a single `<iframe>` tag that directs clients to load an external JavaScript directly from the coordination server. The coordination server generates a measurement task specific to the client on-the-fly. This method is attractive because it requires no server-side modifications, aside from a single tag; incurs little server overhead (*i.e.*, only the extra time and space required to transmit that single line); and allows the coordination server to tailor measurement tasks to individual clients in real time. Unfortunately, this method is also easiest for censors to fingerprint and disrupt: a censor can simply block access to the coordination server, which inflicts no collateral damage. Section 8 discusses ways to make task delivery more robust to blocking, while Section 6.3 discusses incentives for webmasters to include Encore on their sites in the first place.

Rather than recruit webmasters ourselves, we have explored the possibility of purchasing online advertisements and delivering Encore measurement tasks inside them. This idea is attractive because online advertising networks already have established agreements with webmasters to display content (*i.e.*, by paying webmasters to display ads.) Ad networks even allow advertisers to target ads to specific users, which Encore could leverage to measure censorship in specific countries. Unfortunately for us, this idea works poorly in practice because most ad networks prevent advertisements from running custom JavaScript and loading resources from remote origins, with good reason; only a few niche ad networks are capable of hosting Encore. Even if more networks could serve Encore measurement tasks, they may not take kindly to perceived misuse of their service, especially if it leads to network filtering and subsequent loss of revenue in countries wishing to suppress Encore's measurements.

5.5 Collecting measurement results

After clients run a measurement task, they submit the result of the task for analysis. Clients submit the result of task (*i.e.*, whether the client could successfully load the cross-origin resource), related timing information (*i.e.*, how long it took to load the resource), and the task's measurement ID. The process of submitting results is similar to the process that clients use to obtain measurement tasks. In the absence of interference from the adversary, clients submit results by issuing an AJAX request containing the results directly to our collection server. Section 8 discusses other ways to submit results if the adversary filters access to the collection server.

6 Feasibility of Encore Deployment

We evaluate the feasibility of deploying Encore based on early experience with a prototype implementation and analysis of potential measurement targets.

6.1 Are sites amenable to Encore's tasks?

This section investigates whether real Web sites host resources that Encore's measurement tasks can use to measure filtering. We evaluate the feasibility of using Encore to measure filtering of both entire domain names and individual URLs. To measure filtering practices, we use a list of domains and URLs that are "high value" for censorship measurement according to Herdict and its partners [24]; most sites are either perceived as likely filtering targets in many countries (*e.g.*, because they are affiliated with human rights and press freedom organizations) or would cause substantial disruption if filtered (*e.g.*, social media like Twitter and YouTube). This list contains over 200 URL patterns, of which only 178 were online when we performed our feasibility analysis in February 2014.

We collect data for this set of experiments by running the first two stages of the pipeline in Figure 3, which uses the Pattern Expander to generate a list of 6,548 URLs from the 178 URL patterns in our list, then collect HAR files for each URL using the Target Fetcher. We then send these HAR files to a modified version of the Task Generator that emits statistics about sizes of accepted resources and pages.

Filtering of entire domains. We explore whether Encore can measure filtering of each of the 178 domains on the list

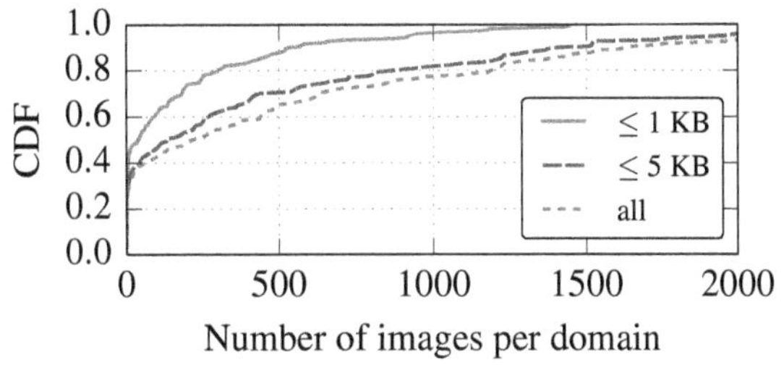

Figure 4: *Distribution of the number of images hosted by each of the 178 domains tested, for images that are at most 1 KB, at most 5 KB, and any size. Over 60% of domains host images that could be delivered to clients inside a single packet, and a third of domains have hundreds of such images to choose from.*

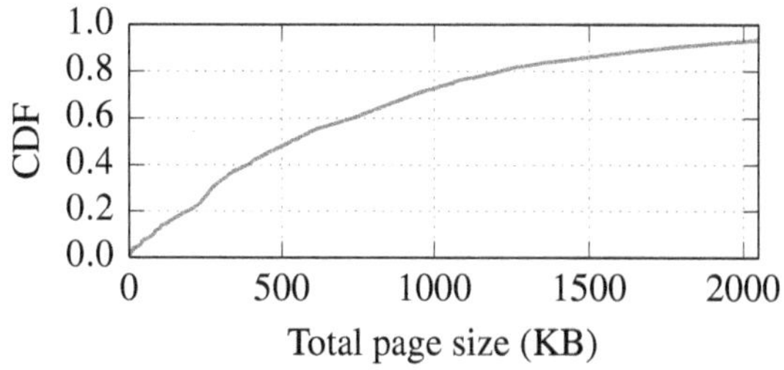

Figure 5: *Distribution of page sizes, computed as the sum of sizes of all objects loaded by a page. This indicates the network overhead each page would incur if a measurement task loaded it in a hidden iframe. Over half of pages load at least half a megabyte of objects.*

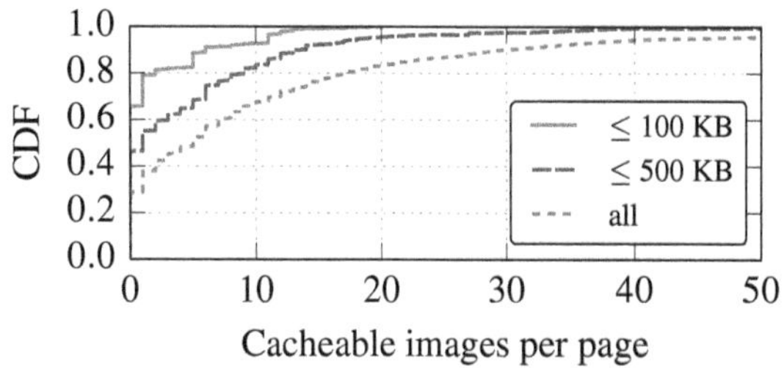

Figure 6: *Distribution of the number of cacheable images loaded by pages that require at most 100 KB of traffic to load, pages that incur at most 500 KB of traffic, and all pages. Perhaps unsurprisingly, smaller pages contain fewer (cacheable) images. Over 70% of all pages cache at least one image and half of all pages cache five or more images; these numbers drop considerably when excluding pages greater than 100 KB.*

we generated as described above. Recall from Section 4.3 that we can use either images or style sheets to observe Web filtering of an entire domain; for simplicity, this analysis only considers images, although style sheets work similarly. We can measure a domain using this technique if (1) it contains images that can be embedded by an origin site and (2) those images are small enough not to significantly affect user experience. We explore both of these requirements for the 178 domains in our list. Because our implementation expands URL patterns using the top 50 search results for that pattern, we will be analyzing a sample of at most 50 URLs per domain. Most of these domains have more than 50 pages, so our results are a lower bound of the amenability of Encore to collect censorship measurements from each domain.

Figure 4 plots the distribution of the number of images that each domain hosts. 70% of domains embed at least one image, and almost all such images are less than 5 KB. Nearly as many domains embed images that fit within a single packet, and a third of domains have hundreds of such images. Even if we conservatively restrict measurement tasks to load images less than 1 KB, Encore can measure Web filtering of over half of the domains.

Filtering of specific Web pages. We explore how often Encore can measure filtering of individual URLs by loading a Web page in an iframe and verifying that the browser cached embedded resources from that page. We can use this mechanism to measure filtering of pages that (1) do not incur too much network overhead when loading in a hidden iframe and (2) embed cacheable images.

We first study the expected network overhead from loading sites in an iframe. Figure 5 plots the distribution of page sizes for each URL, where the page size is the sum of sizes of all resources a page loads and is a rough lower bound on the network overhead that would be incurred by loading each page in a hidden iframe (protocol negotiation and inefficiencies add further overhead). Page sizes are distributed relatively evenly between 0–2 MB with a very long tail. Our prototype only permits measurement tasks to load pages smaller than 100 KB, although future implementations might tune this bound to a client's performance and preferences.

We then evaluate whether these sites embed content that can be retrieved with cross-origin requests. Figure 6 shows the distribution of the number of cacheable images per URL for pages that are at most 100 KB, at most 500 KB, and any size. Nearly 70% of pages embed at least one cacheable image and half of pages cache five or more images, but these numbers drop significantly when restricting page sizes. Only 30% of pages that are at most 100 KB embed at least one cacheable image.

Encore can measure filtering of upwards of 50% of domains depending on the sizes of images, but fewer than 10% of URLs when we limit pages to 100 KB. This finding supports our earlier observation in Section 4.3 that detecting the filtering of individual Web resources may be significantly more difficult than detecting the filtering of entire domains.

6.2 Who performs Encore measurements?

Encore requires clients to visit the Web sites that are hosting Encore scripts. The demographics of clients who perform Encore measurements is closely related those who visit a participating Web site. To evaluate whether a typical Web site will receive measurements from enough locations, we examined demographic data collected by Google Analytics for the home page of a professor in February 2014 [17].

The site saw 1,171 visits during course of the month. Most visitors were from the United States, but we saw more than 10 users from 10 other countries, and 16% of visitors reside in countries with well-known Web filtering policies (India, China, Pakistan, the UK, and South Korea), indicating that dispatching measurement tasks to sites such as academic Web pages may yield measurements from a variety of representative locations. Of these visitors, 999 attempted to run a measurement task; we confirmed nearly all of the rest to be automated traffic from our campus' security scanner. We also found that 45% of visitors remained on the page for longer than 10 seconds, which is more than sufficient time to execute at least one measurement task and report its results. The 35% of visitors who remained for longer than a minute could easily run multiple measurement tasks.

Our small pilot deployment of Encore is representative of the sites where we can expect Encore to be deployed in the short term. Although adoption of Encore by even a single high-traffic Web site would entirely eclipse measurements collected by these small university deployments, grassroots recruitment remains necessary: Encore relies on a variety of origin sites to deter an adversary from simply blocking access to all origins to suppress our measurement collection.

6.3 Will webmasters install Encore?

Encore cannot directly target specific demographics for measurement collection—the measurements that we collect arise from the set of users who happen to visit a Web site that has installed an Encore script. If the sites that host Encore are globally popular (*e.g.*, Google), then Encore can achieve an extremely widespread sampling of users; on the other hand, if the sites are only popular in particular regions, the resulting measurements will be limited to those regions.

Recruiting webmasters to include Encore's measurement scripts should be feasible. First, installing Encore on a Web site incurs little cost. Serving these scripts to clients adds minimal network overhead; our prototype adds only 100 bytes to each origin page and requires no additional requests or connections between the client and the origin server. Measurements themselves have little effect on the Web page's perceived performance because they run asynchronously after the page has loaded and rendered. However, they do incur some network overhead to clients when loading cross-origin resources, which may be undesirable to users with bandwidth caps or slow, shared network connections.

Second, we see two strong incentives for webmasters to participate in Encore. Many webmasters may support Encore simply out of greater interest in measuring Web filtering and encouraging transparency of government censorship. The grassroots success of similar online freedom projects (*e.g.*, Tor [12]) in recruiting volunteers to host relays and bridges suggests that such a population does exist. For further incentive, we could institute a reciprocity agreement for webmasters: in exchange for installing our measurement scripts, webmasters could add their own site to Encore's list of targets and receive notification about their site's availability from Encore's client population.

7 Measurements

We confirm the soundness of Encore's measurement tasks with both controlled experiments and by comparing our ability to confirm cases of Web filtering with independent reports of filtering from other research studies. We have implemented and released every component of Encore described in Section 5 and have collected seven months of measurements from May 2014 through January 2015.

To date, at least 17 volunteers have deployed Encore on their sites, although the true number is probably much higher; 3/4 of measurements come from sites that elect to strip the `Referer:` header when sending results. We recorded 141,626 measurements from 88,260 distinct IPs in 170 countries, with China, India, the United Kingdom, and Brazil reporting at least 1,000 measurements, and more than 100 measurements from Egypt, South Korea, Iran, Pakistan, Turkey, and Saudi Arabia. These countries practice some form of Web filtering. We use a standard IP geolocation database to determine client locations [31]. Clients ran a variety of Web browsers and operating systems.

7.1 Are measurement tasks sound?

To confirm the soundness of Encore's measurements, we built a Web censorship testbed, which has DNS, firewall, and Web server configurations that emulate seven varieties of DNS, IP, and HTTP filtering. For three months, we instructed approximately 30% of clients to measure resources hosted by the testbed (or unfiltered control resources) using the four task types from Table 1. For example, we verified that the *images* task type detects DNS blocking by attempting to load an image from an invalid domain and observing that the task reports filtering; we verified that the same task successfully loads an unfiltered image.

Verification is straightforward for the image, style sheet, and script task types because they give explicit binary feedback about whether a resource successfully loaded. Encore collected 8,573 measurements for these task types; after excluding erroneously contributed measurements (*e.g.*, from Web crawlers), there were no true positives and few false positives. For example, clients in India, a country with notoriously unreliable network connectivity, contributed to a 5% false positive rate for images.

Verifying soundness of the inline frame task type requires more care because it infers existence of filtering from the time taken to load resources. Figure 7 compares the time taken to load an uncached versus cached single pixel image from 1,099 globally distributed Encore clients. Cached images normally load within a few tens of milliseconds, whereas most clients take at least 50 ms longer to load the same image

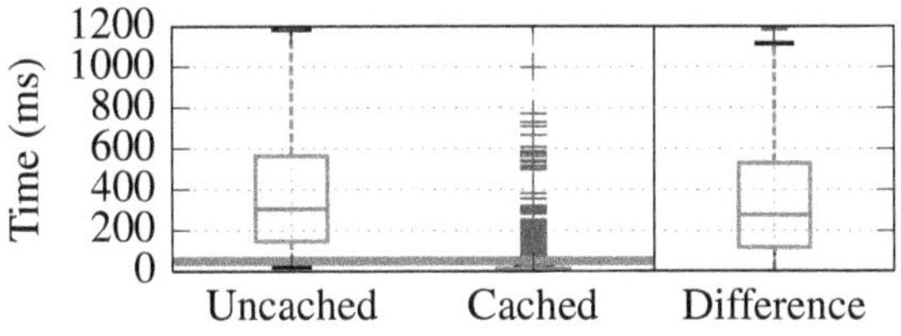

Figure 7: *Comparison between load times for cached and uncached images from 1,099 Encore clients. Cached images typically load within tens of milliseconds, whereas uncached usually take at least 50 ms longer to load, indicated by the bold red line. We use this difference to infer filtering.*

uncached. The few clients with little difference between cached and uncached load time were located on the same local network as the server. Difference in load time will be more pronounced for larger images and with greater latency between clients and content.

In both cases, false positives highlight (1) that distinguishing Web filtering from other kinds of network problems is difficult and (2) the importance of collecting many measurements before drawing strong conclusions about Web filtering. We now develop a filtering detection algorithm that addresses both concerns.

7.2 Does Encore detect Web filtering?

We instructed the remaining 70% of clients to measure resources suspected of filtering, with the goal of independently verifying Web filtering reported in prior work. Because measuring Web filtering may place some users at risk, we only measured Facebook, YouTube, and Twitter. These sites pose little additional risk to users because browsers already routinely contact them via cross-origin requests without user consent (*e.g.*, the Facebook "thumbs up" button, embedded YouTube videos and Twitter feeds). Expanding our measurements to less popular sites would require extra care, as we discuss in the next section.

We aimed to detect resources that are consistently inaccessible from one region, yet still accessible from others. For this purpose, we measure filtering of entire domains, using the image task type. This is challenging because measurement tasks may fail for reasons other than filtering: clients may experience intermittent network connectivity problems, browsers may incorrectly execute measurement tasks, sites may themselves go offline, and so on. We use a statistical hypothesis test to distinguish such sporadic or localized measurement failures from more consistent failures that might indicate Web filtering. We model each measurement success as a Bernoulli random variable with parameter $p = 0.7$; we assume that, in the absence of filtering, clients should successfully load resources at least 70% of the time. Although this assumption is conservative, it captures our desire to eliminate false positives, which can easily drown out true positives when detecting rare events like Web filtering. For each resource and region, we count both the total number of measurements n_r and the number of successful measurements x_r and run a one-sided hypothesis test for a binomial distribution; we consider a resource as filtered in region r if x_r fails this test at 0.05 significance (*i.e.*, $\Pr[\mathsf{Binomial}(n_r, p) \leq x_r] \leq 0.05$) yet does not fail the same test in other regions.

Applying this technique on preliminary measurements confirms well-known censorship of `youtube.com` in Pakistan, Iran, and China [18], and of `twitter.com` and `facebook.com` in China and Iran. Although our detection algorithm works well on preliminary data, possible enhancements include dynamically tuning model parameters to account for differing false positive rates in each country and accounting for potential confounding factors like user behavior differences between browsers and ISPs [3].

8 Ethics and Security

This section discusses barriers to Encore's widespread deployment, from the ethics of collecting measurements from unsuspecting Web users to the potential for attackers to block, disrupt, or tamper with client measurements or collection infrastructure.

Which resources are safe to measure? Encore induces clients to request URLs that might be incriminating in some countries and circumstances. In particular, the most interesting URLs to measure may be those most likely to get users into trouble for measuring them. Curating a list of target URLs requires striking a balance between ubiquitous yet uninteresting URLs (*e.g.*, online advertisers, Google Analytics, Facebook) and obscure URLs that governments are likely to censor (*e.g.*, human rights groups). Although our work does not prescribe a specific use case, we recognize that deploying a tool like Encore engenders risks that we need to better understand.

Balancing the benefit and risk of measuring filtering with Encore is difficult. This paper has made the benefit clear: Encore enables researchers to collect new data about filtering from a diversity of vantage points that was previously prohibitively expensive to obtain and coordinate. Ongoing efforts to measure Web filtering would benefit from Encore's diversity and systematic rigor [8,15,35]. The risk that Encore poses are far more nebulous: laws against accessing filtered content vary from country to country, and may be effectively unenforceable given the ease with which sites (like Encore) can request cross-origin resources without consent; there is no ground truth about the legal and safety risks posed by collecting network measurements.

Striking this balance between benefit and risk raises ethical questions that researchers in computer science rarely face and that conventional ethical standards do not address. As such, our understanding of the ethical implications of collecting measurements using Encore has evolved, and the set of measurements we collect and report on has likewise changed to reflect our understanding. Table 2 highlights a few key milestones in Encore's deployment, which has culminated

Date	Event
February 2014 and prior	Informal discussions with Georgia Tech IRB conclude that Encore (and similar work) is not human subjects research and does not merit formal IRB review.
March 13, 2014 – March 24, 2014	Encore begins collecting measurements from real users using a list of over 300 URLs. We're unsure of the exact date when collection began because of data loss.
March 18, 2014	We begin discussing Encore's ethics with a researcher at the Oxford Internet Institute.
April 2, 2014	To combat data sparsity, we configure Encore to only measure favicons [43]. The URLs we removed were a subset of those we crawled from §5.2.
May 5, 2014	Out of ethical concern, we restrict Encore to measure favicons on only a few sites.
May 7, 2014	Submission to IMC 2014, which includes results derived from our March 13 URL list.
September 17, 2014	Georgia Tech IRB officially declines to review Encore. We requested this review in response to skeptical feedback from IMC.
September 25, 2014	Submission to NSDI 2015, using our URL list on April 2.
January 30, 2015	Submission to SIGCOMM 2015, using our URL list on May 5.
February 6, 2015	Princeton IRB reaffirms that Encore is not human subjects research. We sought this review at the request of the SIGCOMM PC chairs after Nick Feamster moved to Princeton.

Table 2: *Timeline of Encore measurement collection, ethics discussions, and paper submissions. As our understanding of Encore's ethical implications evolved, we increasingly restricted the set of measurements we collect and report. See* `http://encore.noise.gatech.edu/urls.html` *for information on how the set of URLs that Encore measures has evolved over time.*

in the set of measurements we report on in this paper. The Institutional Review Boards (IRBs) at both Georgia Tech and Princeton declined to formally review Encore because it does not collect or analyze Personally Identifiable Information (PII) and is not human subjects research [9]. Yet, Encore is clearly capable of exposing its users to some level of risk. Because we do not understand the risks that a tool like Encore presents, we have focused most of our research efforts on developing the measurement technology, not on reporting results from the measurements that we gather. Other censorship measurement tools have and will continue to face similar ethical questions, and we believe that our role as researchers is to lead a responsible dialogue in the context of these emerging tools.

As part of this ongoing dialogue, we hope that the community will develop ethical norms that are grounded in theory, applicable in practice, and informed by experts. To this end, we have discussed Encore with ethics experts at the Oxford Internet Institute, the Berkman Center, and Citizen Lab, and our follow on work examines broader ethical concerns of censorship measurement [27]. We have also been working with the organizers of the SIGCOMM NS Ethics workshop [34], which we helped solicit, to ensure that its attendees will gain experience applying principled ethical frameworks to networking and systems research, a process we hope will result in more informed and grounded discussions of ethics in our community.

Schechter [41] surveyed people about the ethics of various research studies, including Encore, and found that most people felt that unconstrained use of Encore would be highly unethical. However, as the report acknowledges, the survey didn't elaborate on the inherent risks of browsing *any* Web page, the potential benefits of research like Encore, the risks of alternative means of measuring censorship, or low-risk deployment modes.

Encore underscores the need for stricter cross-origin security policy [45]. Our work exploits existing weaknesses, and if these policies could endanger users then strengthening those policies is clearly a problem worthy of further research.

Why not informed consent? The question of whether to obtain informed consent is more complicated than it might first appear. Informed consent is not always appropriate, given that in disciplines where experimental protocols for human subjects research are well-established, there are classes of experiments that can still be conducted ethically without it, such as when obtaining consent is either prohibitive or impractical and there is little appreciable risk of harm to the subject.

Researchers and engineers who have performed large-scale network measurements can appreciate that obtaining consent of any kind is typically impractical. For Encore, it would require apprising a user about nuanced technical concepts, such as cross-origin requests and how Web trackers work—and doing so across language barriers, no less. Such burdens would dramatically reduce the scale and scope of measurements, relegating us to the already extremely dangerous status quo of activists and researchers who put themselves into harm's way to study censorship. Even if we could somehow obtain consent at scale, informed consent does not *ever* decrease risk to users; it only alleviates researchers from some responsibility for that risk, and may even increase risk to users by removing any traces of plausible deniability.

We believe researchers should instead focus on reducing risk to uninformed users, as we have done with repeated iteration after consultation with ethics experts. It is generally accepted that users already have little control over or knowledge of much of the traffic that their Web browsers and devices generate (a point raised by Princeton's office of research integrity and assurance), which already gives users reasonable cover. By analogy, the prevalence of malware and third-party trackers itself lends credibility to the argument that a user cannot reasonably control the traffic that their devices send. The more widespread measurements like Encore become, the less risky they are for users.

Filtering access to Encore infrastructure. Clients can only use Encore if they can fetch a measurement task. If the domain (or URL) that hosts measurement tasks is itself blocked, clients will not be able to execute measurements. Once a client retrieves a measurement task, subsequent requests appear as ordinary cross-origin requests; as a result, the main concern is ensuring that clients can retrieve measurement tasks in the first place.

The server that dispatches tasks could be replicated across many domains to make it more difficult for a censor to block Encore by censoring a single domain. Clients could contact the coordination server indirectly via an intermediary or create mirrors of the coordination server in shared hosting environments (*e.g.*, Amazon AWS), thereby increasing the collateral damage of blocking a mirror. Going further, webmasters could contact the coordination server on behalf of clients (*e.g.*, with a WordPress plugin or Django package) by querying the coordination server and including the returned measurement task directly in the page it serves to the client; to increase scalability and decrease latency, servers could cache several tasks in advance. Similarly, collection of the results could be distributed across servers hosted in different domains, to ensure that collection is not blocked.

There are limits to Encore's ability to withstand such attacks. Because it runs entirely within a Web browser, Encore cannot leverage stronger security tools like Tor to anonymously report measurements [12,44].

Detecting and interfering with Encore measurements. Blocking Encore based on the contents of measurement tasks (*e.g.*, via deep packet inspection) should be difficult, because we can easily disguise tasks' code using JavaScript obfuscation or detection evasion techniques [13,25]. Identifying task behavior is equally difficult because it appears merely as requests to load a cross-origin object—something many Web sites do under normal operation. If a single client performs a *sequence* of cross-origin requests that appear unrelated to the content of the host site, a censor may recognize the sequence as unusual and either block the subsequent reports or otherwise attempt to distort the results. We expect such interference to be relatively difficult, however, since a censor would first have to identify a sequence of requests as a measurement attempt and interpose on subsequent requests to interfere with the reports. Although such interference is plausible, censors do not generally interfere with measurements today, so we leave this consideration to future work.

Attackers may attempt to submit poisoned measurement results to alter the conclusions that Encore draws about censorship. We could try to employ reputation systems to thwart such attacks, although it would be practically impossible to completely prevent such poisoning from untrusted clients [21].

9 Conclusion

Despite the importance of measuring the extent and nature of Internet censorship, doing so is difficult because it requires deploying a large number of geographically diverse vantage points, and recruiting volunteers for such a deployment is a significant deployment hurdle. This paper presents an alternate approach: rather than requiring users to install custom measurement software, we take advantage of the fact that users' Web browsers can perform certain types of cross-origin requests, which we can harness to induce measurements of reachability to arbitrary third-party domains. Although only a limited amount of information about the success of these requests leaks across domains, even a small amount of leakage turns out to be enough to permit inferences about the reachability of higher-level Web resources, including both entire domains and specific URLs.

Encore shifts the deployment burden from clients to webmasters. We have designed Encore so that deployment is simple (in many cases, webmasters only add one line to the main Web page source). We also point out that many webmasters are typically interested in monitoring the reachability of their sites from various client geographies and networks in any case, so deployment incentives are well-aligned.

Although the types of measurements Encore can perform may be more definitive than tools that rely on informal user reports (*e.g.*, Herdict), Encore may draw far fewer conclusions about the scope and methods of censorship than tools that measure censorship methods in detail (*e.g.*, OONI, Centinel). Ultimately, censorship measurement is a complex, moving target, and no single measurement method or tool can paint a complete picture. What is sorely missing from the existing set of measurement tools, however, is a way to characterize censorship practices in broad strokes, based on a sizeable and continuous set of client measurements. By filling this important hole in our understanding, Encore can help bridge the gap between diverse yet inconclusive user reports and detailed yet narrow or short-term fine-grained measurements.

The prospect of using Encore to collect measurements from unsuspecting users has already stirred controversy within the networking community and prompted a wider dialogue on ethics of network measurement [34]. Forthcoming guidelines for ethical measurement will hopefully help determine whether we can deploy Encore more widely. Our work is beneficial regardless: If wider deployment is appropriate, this paper has explained how Encore could yield valuable insight on Web censorship at a previously unattainable scale; if ethical concerns make further deployment infeasible, our work is evidence that attackers could use tools like Encore to place users in harm's way and that perhaps cross-origin security policy should be strengthened to prevent such attacks.

A Example of a measurement task

This is a complete example of JavaScript code that runs in a client's Web browser to measure Web filtering using cross-origin embedding of a hidden image. It uses jQuery [28]. The coordination server minifies and obfuscates the source code before sending it to a client.

See `http://goo.gl/18GU0R` for a simple demo of Encore's cross-origin request mechanism.

```
var M = Object();

// A measurement ID is a unique identifier
// linking all submissions of a measurement.
M.measurementId = ...  // a UUID.
// This function embeds an image from a remote
// origin, hides it, and sets up callbacks to
// detect success or failure to load the image.
M.measure = function() {
  var img = $('<img>');
  img.attr('src', '//target/image.png');
  img.style('display', 'none');
  img.on('load', M.sendSuccess);
  img.on('error', M.sendFailure);
  img.appendTo('html');
}
// This function submits a result using
// a cross-origin AJAX request. The server
// must allow such cross-origin submissions.
M.submitToCollector = function(state) {
  $.ajax({
    url: "//collector/submit" +
         "?cmh-id=" + this.measurementId +
         "&cmh-result=" + state,
  });
}
M.sendSuccess = function() {
  M.submitToCollector("success");
}
M.sendFailure = function() {
  M.submitToCollector("failure");
}

// Submit to the server as soon as the client
// loads the page, regardless of the
// measurement result. This indcates which
// clients attempted to run the measurement,
// even if they don't submit a final result.
M.submitToCollector("init");
// Run the measurement when the page loads.
$(M.measure);
```


Acknowledgments

This research was supported by NSF Awards CNS-1409635, CNS-1540066, and a Google Focused Research Award. We thank Joss Wright for an insightful discussion about the ethics of measuring Web censorship without informed consent. Thank you to the many webmasters who have installed Encore on their Web sites.

References

[1] S. Aryan, H. Aryan, and J. A. Halderman. Internet Censorship in Iran: A First Look. In *USENIX Workshop on Free and Open Communications on the Internet (FOCI)*, aug 2013.

[2] A. Barth, J. Caballero, and D. Song. Secure content sniffing for web browsers, or how to stop papers from reviewing themselves. In *IEEE Symposium on Security and Privacy*, pages 360–371, 2009.

[3] M. bin Tariq, M. Motiwala, N. Feamster, and M. Ammar. Detecting Network Neutrality Violations with Causal Inference. In *Proc. CoNEXT*, Dec. 2009.

[4] Bootstrap. `http://getbootstrap.com`.

[5] A. Bortz and D. Boneh. Exposing private information by timing web applications. In *International Conference on World Wide Web (WWW)*, pages 621–628, Banff, Alberta, Canada, 2007.

[6] Browser Security Handbook: Navigation and Content Inclusion Across Domains. `http://goo.gl/uMfTN5`.

[7] M. Casado and M. J. Freedman. Peering through the shroud: The effect of edge opacity on ip-based client identification. In *USENIX Conference on Networked Systems Design and Implementation (NSDI)*, Cambridge, MA, Apr. 2007.

[8] Centinel. `https://github.com/iclab/centinel`.

[9] M. Clark. IRB/Ethics Questions, Sept. 2014. `http://encore.noise.gatech.edu/irb-mail.txt`.

[10] R. Clayton, S. Murdoch, and R. Watson. Ignoring the Great Firewall of China. In *Privacy Enhancing Technologies (PET)*, pages 20–35. Springer, 2006.

[11] J. Crandall, D. Zinn, M. Byrd, E. Barr, and R. East. ConceptDoppler: A Weather Tracker for Internet Censorship. In *Proceedings of the ACM Conference on Computer and Communications Security (CCS)*, Arlington, VA, Oct. 2007.

[12] R. Dingledine, N. Mathewson, and P. Syverson. Tor: The second-generation onion router. In *Proc. 13th USENIX Security Symposium*, San Diego, CA, Aug. 2004.

[13] K. P. Dyer, S. E. Coull, T. Ristenpart, and T. Shrimpton. Protocol misidentification made easy with format-transforming encryption. In *ACM Conference on Computer & Communications Security (CCS)*, pages 61–72, 2013.

[14] R. Ensafi, J. Knockel, G. Alexander, and J. R. Crandall. Detecting intentional packet drops on the internet via tcp/ip side channels. In *Passive and Active Measurement*, pages 109–118. Springer, 2014.

[15] A. Filastò and J. Appelbaum. OONI: Open Observatory of Network Interference. In *USENIX Workshop on Free and Open Communications on the Internet (FOCI)*, Aug. 2012.

[16] Filbaan. `http://filbaan.net`.

[17] Google analytics. `https://google.com/analytics`.

[18] Google Transparency Report. `http://www.google.com/transparencyreport/`.

[19] GreatFire.org: Online Censorship in China. `http://en.greatfire.org/`.

[20] K. P. Gummadi, S. Saroiu, and S. D. Gribble. King: Estimating latency between arbitrary internet end hosts. In *Proceedings of the 2nd ACM SIGCOMM Workshop on Internet measurment*, pages 5–18. ACM, 2002.

[21] S. Hao, N. Syed, N. Feamster, A. Gray, and S. Krasser. Detecting Spammers with SNARE: Spatio-temporal Network-level Automatic Reputation Engine. In *Proc. 18th USENIX Security Symposium*, Montreal, Quebec, Canada, Aug. 2009.

[22] HAR 1.2 spec. `http://www.softwareishard.com/blog/har-12-spec/`.

[23] HerdictWeb: The Verdict of the Herd. `http://herdict.org`.

[24] Herdict: Browse Lists. `http://herdict.org/lists`. Visited 2014-02-26.

[25] F. Howard. Malware with your mocha: Obfuscation and antiemulation tricks in malicious javascript. *Sophos Technical Papers*, 2010.

[26] L.-S. Huang, Z. Weinberg, C. Evans, and C. Jackson. Protecting browsers from cross-origin CSS attacks. In *ACM Conference on Computer and Communications Security (CCS)*, pages 619–629, Chicago, IL, Oct. 2010.

[27] B. Jones, R. Ensafi, N. Feamster, V. Paxson, and N. Weaver. Ethical concerns for censorship measurement (to appear). In *Ethics in Networked Systems Research*, Aug. 2015.

[28] jQuery. `http://jquery.com`.

[29] M. Karir, G. Huston, G. Michaelson, and M. Bailey. Understanding IPv6 Populations in the Wild. In *Passive and Active Measurement (PAM)*, pages 256–259, Hong Kong, Mar. 2013.

[30] V. Lam, S. Antonatos, P. Akritidis, and K. G. Anagnostakis. Puppetnets: Misusing Web Browsers as a Distributed Attack Infrastructure. In *ACM Conference on Computer and Communications Security (CCS)*, pages 221–234, Alexandria, VA, Oct. 2006.

[31] MaxMind GeoIP Country. `http://www.maxmind.com/app/geolitecountry`. Retrieved: June 2011.

[32] Z. Nabi. The anatomy of web censorship in Pakistan. In *USENIX Workshop on Free and Open Communications on the Internet (FOCI13)*, Washington, DC, Aug. 2013.

[33] Noction: Network Intelligence. `http://www.noction.com`.

[34] Workshop on Ethics in Networked Systems Research. `http://conferences.sigcomm.org/sigcomm/2015/netethics.php`.

[35] OpenNet Initiative. `http://www.opennet.net/`.

[36] OpenNet Initiative Research Publications. `http://www.opennet.net/research/`.

[37] Report on China's Filtering Practices, 2008. Open Net Initiative. `http://opennet.net/sites/opennet.net/files/china.pdf`.

[38] Open Observatory of Network Interference (OONI). `https://ooni.torproject.org`.

[39] Phantomjs. `http://phantomjs.org`.

[40] Same Origin Policy. `https://developer.mozilla.org/en-US/docs/Web/JavaScript/Same_origin_policy_for_JavaScript`. Mozilla Developer Network.

[41] S. Schechter and C. Bravo-Lillo. Ethical-response survey report: Fall 2014. Technical Report MSR-TR-2014-140, November 2014.

[42] A. Sfakianakis, E. Athanasopoulos, and S. Ioannidis. CensMon: A Web Censorship Monitor. In *USENIX Workshop on Free and Open Communication on the Internet (FOCI)*, San Francisco, CA, Aug. 2011.

[43] How to add a favicon to your site. `http://www.w3.org/2005/10/howto-favicon`.

[44] P. Winter. Towards a Censorship Analyser for Tor. In *USENIX Workshop on Free and Open Communications on the Internet (FOCI)*, Washington, DC, Aug. 2013.

[45] Content security policy. `http://www.w3.org/TR/CSP/`, Nov. 2012.

[46] X. Xu, Z. M. Mao, and J. A. Halderman. Internet censorship in China: Where does the filtering occur? In *Passive and Active Measurement (PAM)*, pages 133–142, Atlanta, GA, 2011.

[47] J. Zittrain and B. Edelman. Internet filtering in China. *IEEE Internet Computing*, 7(2):70–77, 2003.

Author Index

www.ingramcontent.com/pod-product-compliance
Ingram Content Group UK Ltd.
Pitfield, Milton Keynes, MK11 3LW, UK
UKHW051419290926
15471UKWH00009B/1676

9 781450 340250